HOTELS
in Britain & Ireland
1994

Produced by AA Publishing
Atlas and town plans prepared by the AA's Cartographic Department
Maps © The Automobile Association 1993

Directory generated by the AA Establishment Database, Information Research and Control, Hotel and Touring Services

Cover design: The Paul Hampson Partnership, Southampton

Editor: Penny Hicks

Illustrations: Alan Roe

Advertisements
Head of Advertisement Sales: Christopher Heard Tel. 0256 20123 ext 21544
Advertisement Production: Karen Weeks Tel. 0256 20123 ext. 21545 .

Typeset, printed and bound in Great Britain by William Clowes Limited, Beccles and London

Colour origination: Sussex Litho, Chichester, Sussex

The contents of this publication are believed correct at the time of printing. Nevertheless the Publisher cannot be held responsible for any errors or omissions or for changes in the details given in this guide or for the consequences of any reliance on the information provided in the same. Although every effort has been made to ensure accuracy we always welcome any information from readers to assist in such efforts and to keep the book up to date.

Assessments of hotels and restaurants are based on the experience(s) of the AA's professional hotel and restaurant inspectors on the occasion(s) of their visit(s) and therefore the descriptions given in this guide may contain an element of subjective opinion which may not dictate a reader's experience on another occasion.

© The Automobile Association 1993

All rights reserved. No part of this publication may be reproduced, stored in a retrieval system, or transmitted in any form or by any means – electronic, mechanical, photocopying, recording, or otherwise – unless the written permission of the Publishers has been given beforehand. This book may not be lent, resold, hired out or otherwise disposed of by way of trade in any form of binding or cover other than that in which it is published, without the prior written consent of the Publisher.

A CIP catalogue record for this book is available from the British Library.

Published by AA Publishing which is a trading name of Automobile Association Developments Limited whose registered office is Fanum House, Basingstoke, Hampshire RG21 2EA, Registered number 1878435

ISBN 0-7495-0701-2

Published in the US by Hunter Publishing, Inc, 300 Raritan Center, Parkway, Edison NJ 08818

USA ISBN 1-55650-607-4

DISCOUNT SCHEME

Owners of the 1994 edition of the Hotel guide may claim a 10 per cent discount off their room bill at more than 1,100 hotels listed in the directory. The hotels which have agreed to participate in this scheme display the (£) symbol at the end of their directory entry.

In order to take advantage of the discount, you must remember to present your copy of the 1994 Hotel guide at reception when checking in. If you do not do so, the hotel may legitimately refuse to give you the discount when you check out. This is very important, because many hotel accounts are now computerised and it may cause difficulties and delays if the account has to be adjusted at the last minute.

The discount only applies to the full-tariff room rate, and does not apply if you are already benefiting from any other form of discount or a special bargain rate, including weekly terms that work out at less per night than the full tariff for a single night's stay.

The discount is off the room rate and may not be claimed for restaurant or bar meals or drinks. In the case of a joint booking for a group of individuals, the discount would only apply to the person who presents the guide on checking in, not to the entire party.

If two persons are sharing a double room, however, at the full tariff rate, the discount would apply to the double room.

Please note that the discount may only be claimed at the hotels which display the (£) symbol at the end of their directory entry, and that the bill must be settled before you leave the hotel. The discount is not applicable to company accounts.

This offer is only valid from the date of publication of this edition to 31 December 1994.

£

Contents

Bookmark: Symbols and Abbreviations in English

2 Discount Scheme : conditions of the discount scheme and how it operates

FEATURES:
5 *The Shell Guide to Food (And Fuel) Fashion*
10 *Inspectors off the Record - the Life of an AA Hotel and Restaurant Inspector*

AWARDS 1993/4
8 AA Hotel Inspectors' Selected Hotel of the Year Awards
8 'Courtesy and Care' Awards
8 Best Newcomer Awards
21 Top Hotels - Red Star Awards
24 Top Hotel Restaurants - Highest Rosette Awards

USING THE GUIDE
18 Hotel Groups
25 How We Classify Hotels
27 Sample of a Directory Entry
29 Useful Information - Britain
31 Symbols and Abbreviations in French, German, Italian and Spanish

33 DIRECTORY OF HOTELS IN BRITAIN
364 Alphabetical Index of London Hotels
366 Map of London Postal Districts
368 London Maps

679 DIRECTORY OF HOTELS IN NORTHERN IRELAND AND THE REPUBLIC OF IRELAND
 - including Useful Information
707 Company Owned Hotel Abbreviations and Central Reservation Telephone Numbers
Location Atlas

708 Best Bed & Breakfast Establishments - Selected and Premier Selected Guest Houses, Farmhouses, Inns and Private Hotels

718 Location Atlas

The Shell Guide To Food (And Fuel) Fashion

Food fashion has taken a new turn. The cult cuisine of the moment is called "Modern British" - a fantastic potpourri of tastes and traditions from all over the world, popularised by a new wave of trendy English-speaking chefs.

British chefs, yes. But English-reading menus.... you must be joking! Attempt to sample this trendy tucker and you will be confronted by menus more exotic and obscure than anything you have experienced.

But if you don't know your tempura from your tapénade, never fear. Overleaf you will find that Shell has assembled a brief dictionary of fashion-foods. So you can order with confidence.

And because fashions in fuel have become more exotic too, we have also put together a brief guide to the ingredients of today's quality petrol. Don't forget, the fuel you put in your car is as important to your engine as the food you put into your tummy is to you!

Bon appétit and good motoring

Fashion Food

AÏOLI	A garlicky mayonnaise often served with fish soup.
BRUSCHETTA	Toasted slices of bread with various toppings, usually vegetables.
CEPS	Otherwise known as porcini, these are wild mushrooms, often dried.
CONFIT	Joints of meat, usually duck, cooked very slowly with fat (and sometimes then preserved).
MILLE-FEUILLE	Generally signifies that your food will be a heap of various layers.
PESTO	A purée made with various herbs and hard cheese, most often served with pasta.
POLENTA	Italian cornmeal, usually served instead of potato. Most often grilled or fried.
ROCKET	Super-trendy salad leaf with a mustardy back-bite.
SASHIMI	Thin slices of raw fish.
TAPÉNADE	A mixture of black olives, capers and sometimes anchovies. Served as a 'dip', otherwise as an accompaniment.
TEMPURA	Japanese style batter - very light.
ZAMPONE	Stuffed pig trotter, sausage-style.

Fuel Fashion

ADDITIVE	Chemical added to a fuel to improve some aspect of its performance.
BASE FUEL	Fuel with nothing added. Very unfashionable, but widely available. Makes the inside of your engine 'dirty'.
CARBON	You don't want this. A sooty black deposit which builds up inside the engine, reducing its efficiency.
DECOKE	What you might need if you don't use fuel with detergent. Expensive.
DETERGENT	Don't fill up without it. Helps to prevent the build-up of carbon in the inlet system. Shell's detergent, compared with base fuel without detergent, is proven to improve fuel economy, reduce emissions and give you a smoother ride.
ENDORSEMENTS	More than 20 major car manufacturers now recommend the regular use of quality fuel containing detergent.
SHELL ADVANCED	Quality fuel from Shell. The connoisseur's choice.
SHELL SELECT	The name behind Shell's Service Stations. Guarantees quality fuel, quality service, cleanliness and a wide range of useful products.

AA Hotel Inspectors' Selected Hotel of the Year

ENGLAND
★★★★⚘⚘ **New Hall,** *Sutton Coldfield*

WALES
★★★⚘⚘ **Lake Hotel,** *Llangammarch Wells*

SCOTLAND
★★★⚘⚘ **Moorings Hotel,** *Fort William*

REPUBLIC OF IRELAND
★★★★⚘⚘ **Sheen Falls Lodge,** *Kenmare*

Courtesy and Care Awards

SOUTHWEST ENGLAND
★★★ **Penmere Manor,** *Falmouth*
★★ **The Oaks,** *Porlock*

SOUTHEAST ENGLAND
★★ **Holcombe,** *Deddington*
★★★ **Salterns,** *Poole*

LONDON
★★★ **Hogarth,** *SW5*
★★★★ **Halkin,** *SW1*

CENTRAL ENGLAND
★★★ **Norton Place,** *Birmingham*
★★ **Peterstow,** *Ross-on-Wye*

NORTHERN ENGLAND
★★★ **Leeming House,** *Watermillock*
★★ **Millers House,** *Middleham*

WALES
★★★★ **Llangoed Hall,** *Llyswen*
★★ **Tyddyn Llan,** *Llandrillo*

SCOTLAND
★★★ **Inver Lodge,** *Lochinver*
★★ **Kilcamb Lodge,** *Strontian*

REPUBLIC OF IRELAND
★★★ **Seaview,** *Ballylickey*

Best Newcomer Awards

SOUTHWEST ENGLAND
★★ **Woolpack Inn,** *Beckington*

SOUTHEAST ENGLAND
★★★★ **Coppid Beech,** *Bracknell*

CENTRAL ENGLAND
★★★ **Makeney Hall,** *Belper*

NORTHERN ENGLAND
★★★ **Gilpin Lodge House,** *Windermere*

SCOTLAND
★★★ **Loch Torridon,** *Torridon*

Welcome to Campanile !

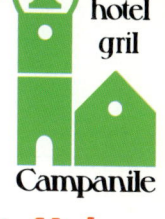

hotel gril

Campanile

14 Hotels and Restaurants in the United Kingdom

Great Value For Money !

The Campanile Restaurant offers:

- Set menus from £ **7.30*** • Daily specials from £ **4.95*** • Full English breakfast £ **4.25***
  An extensive buffet selection of hors d'oeuvres, sweets and cheeses

Special **"Campi"** children's menu

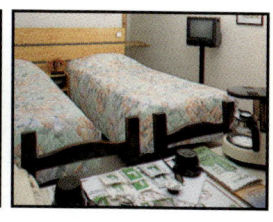

The Campanile double / twin room includes :

320 CAMPANILE HOTEL & RESTAURANTS IN EUROPE

for £ 35.75*

- Ensuite bathroom • Wake-up facilities
- Remote control colour TV • Sky channels
- Direct dial telephone • Tea & coffee making facilities

Campanile Hotels & Restaurants in Great Britain :

Basildon...............(0268) 530 810	Doncaster......(0302) 370 770
Cardiff.................(0222) 549 044	Hull...............(0482) 25530
Plymouth..............(0752) 601 087	Liverpool......(051) 709 8104
Birmingham..........(021) 622 4925	Rotherham......(0709) 700 255
Coventry North....(0203) 622 311	Runcorn.........(0928) 581 771
Coventry South....(0203) 639 922	Wakefield......(0924) 201 054
Redditch...............(0527) 510 710	Washington...(091)416 5010

For full brochure, please write to :
Campanile UK, LTD - 8 Red Lion Court -
Alexandra Road - Hounslow TW3 1JS
Quoting : AA Hotels in Britain

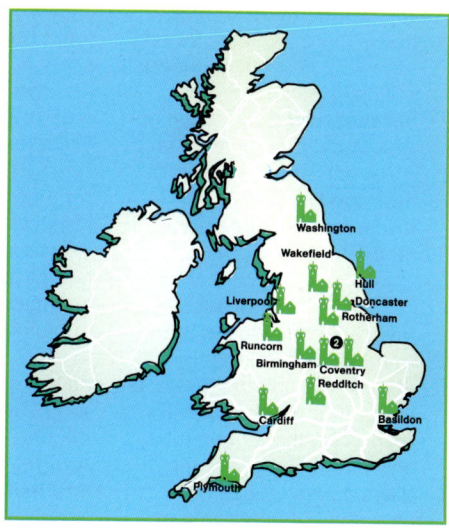

*These prices are provided as a guide only and may be changed at any time without prior notice.

Inspectors Off the Record

**What do hotel inspectors really think of their job?
To many people that job conjures up an image of one long round of being looked after at Britain's finest hotels and eating only the best of haute cuisine.
Our inspectors do, without question, enjoy their job, but they certainly have to take the rough with the smooth.**

Along with all those lovely country houses and luxury London hotels there are those which, following an inspection, are *not* appointed by the AA because they don't come up to scratch. One hotel, which is AA appointed, was described by one of our inspectors as a *'bedroom factory'*.

Even in the very best hotels, the inspectors are not there as the rest of us might be, to relax and enjoy the surroundings - they are at work from the moment they arrive to the moment they leave, taking notice of everything that is going on around them, checking every minute detail, sometimes staying up into the early hours to check on room service then grabbing a few hours sleep before finding out if the early morning call service is efficient.

The findings of the inspectors are reflected in the stars and percentage ratings given to each hotel, and in the description, but no guide book has the space to reproduce the pages and pages of check-lists and subjective reports which are filled in during each visit. And yet it is often these informal, passing comments which sum up what a hotel is really like - and what an inspector's working life is really like.

Here, for the first time, we reveal some of those comments which would never normally see the light of day in print.

Welcome to the hotel

As in most things, first impressions are very important and the inspectors take particular notice of how they are welcomed on their arrival. Hospitality is high on our list of priorities, but some reports include particularly telling comments:
'Staff do their job without extra regard to hospitality -

Inspectors Off the Record

quite typical'.

'I hardly remember a single smile from the moment I arrived' was another sad remark.

When you spend your life on the road, on a constant round of one-night stops, a smiling face and cheery greeting can mean a lot. Not only is such a welcome important to our inspectors on a personal level, it also gives a good indication of how the hotel will be perceived by other guests.

How much nicer was the report which stated:

'Mr and Mrs S are a naturally hospitable, open and hard-working couple .... If only all hotels showed the same levels of hospitality.'

But even a jolly personal approach doesn't always find favour. At a West Country establishment, there was a friendly enough welcome, but

'Mrs ..... did have the annoying habit of calling me "dear" '- with the grudging adjoinder: 'but I suppose some people like it.'

There is nothing nicer, after a long journey or a gruelling day's work, than to be fussed over on arrival at your hotel, and the offer of a nice pot of tea and, perhaps, a piece of cake to tide you over until dinner time never goes amiss. The advent of kettles, tea bags and little plastic pots of milk supplied in bedrooms has, unfortunately, done away with this nicety in many hotels. Frequently the offer *is* still made, but when it is not our inspectors will ask - with varying results.

'Tea was served after some persuasion and after making it clear that I could make my own; it then came with just a pot of tea and some milk - no cup or saucer.'

'Had to insist to get served with some tea on arrival - told that there were facilities in the bedroom. As for a sandwich, I was told that the shop next door sold them!'

'Carry your bag, sir?'

Porterage is a service which is expected in the higher star classifications, though it must be difficult for some of our heftier male inspectors to insist on help with their suitcases from some young girl at reception.

'No porter on duty to help with the luggage; with some pushing, the receptionist offered to help ...' appeared on one report.

Nevertheless, inspectors must test all services, and if porterage is offered by the hotel, it is up to the management to employ someone capable of carrying it out, whether the guest is a frail old lady or a champion weight-lifter.

At one hotel . . . 'The chef, who happened to be in reception at the same time, offered some help with my luggage; he was spontaneous and really friendly'.

And yet at another establishment . . .

'Porter watched me struggle with cases, though he did open the door'!

On one occasion our inspector had to ask for help with luggage, left the cases to be brought up to the room - and even with reminders,

Inspectors Off the Record

they did not arrive until four hours later!

At Your Service

Certain levels of service are expected at each star rating, and the requirement is not simply that certain services are available - they must also be carried out with the appropriate degree of professionalism.

'The emphasis is certainly on the relaxed approach rather than any professionalism!'

'Bar man .... was unaware of drinks, prices and their whereabouts on the shelves. When collecting glasses he took with him the plastic tray from the glass-washer and carried it around the room like a pot man!.

'There is nothing organised, supervised or professional about the service here on a Sunday night ...' stated one report for a three star hotel, where the inspector was directed to a nearby take-away pizza shop when he asked for something to eat.

And at breakfast time:

'I had to sit in a long line of people, even though half the dining room was vacant throughout service.'

The tendency towards impersonal facilities and away from good personal service in some types of hotel is often summed up not so much by what the inspectors complain about, but the services which obviously come as a pleasant surprise:

'Early call on phone was by a person!'

And:

'Tea taken in lounge; tray cleared by Mrs S, asking if I wanted anything else (not often either of these occur!)'.

A Room with a View

In the 'bedroom' section of one report form, covering an otherwise splendid hotel, was the forlorn opener:

'A typical inspector's room on the top floor, overlooking back roofs of hotel and affected by cooking smells'.

It couldn't possibly be a typical **inspector's** room, of course, because inspectors

Inspectors Off the Record

travel incognito - but obviously was *'the kind of room given to a single person staying just one night'*.

Another inspector fared better on one occasion, but *'A lovely spacious and comfortable room, which I know is the exception rather than the rule'*.

Compliments to the Chef?

So, our inspector has arrived at the hotel, duly welcomed, or not, and shown to the room - now there is dinner to look forward to. Under this heading we have found some of the most entertaining comments. Contrary to popular belief, our inspectors do not always expect a gourmet feast wherever they go, and can be just as impressed by good, plain cooking when it is in keeping with the kind of hotel they are in. It does become clear that our inspectors would prefer chefs to stick to what they know:

'Unfortunately the AA hit the hotel's Spanish week again ...... nothing as good as Murcia airport cafeteria, where I have spent some hours of my life!'

And at another establishment:

"Apple flan Normande .... as close to anything Normande as I am a giant!'

Seasonal specialities are usually worth looking out for on a menu, but you really have to watch some places. On an early spring visit our inspector noted:

'Rosettes could be worth discussion - roast grouse in March!!?'

After a particularly disappointing meal which consisted mostly of convenience food and included *'undercooked bread roll with packaging flavour, soggy vegetables with the main course and, on the dessert, odd-tasting whipped cream with an equally strange texture and colour'*, our inspector not surprisingly noted *'some room for improvement here. However, Mrs S appears quite proud of her current efforts'*.

We did have to take with a pinch of salt a report on a particular meal which complained bitterly of the lack of flavour in every single course, then concluded *'I have a terrible cold, so I couldn't taste anything anyway'*. No such luck for the inspector whose starter of chicken liver pâté and main course of chicken Daniel Defoe were both described as *'unpleasant'* or the one whose chicken dish was burnt, the sauce described as *'awful'*, the potatoes *'a cross between roast and chips, but not close to either'*.

Inspectors themselves occasionally slip up - as in this description:

'Chargrilled squid - the

13

Inspectors Off the Record

entire body stuffed with a mixture of crisp vegetables including carrot, pepper and onion. The testicles [tentacles] were separate.'

Taking it all in

Once the meal is over, the inspector can take some time to relax in the lounge and observe what is going on, the mood of the other guests and the general care and consideration with which they are treated. Hopefully not as one inspector experienced:

'The real disappointment was the lack of care and consideration to me as a guest ... eg letting the fire out in the lounge and then seating me next to a radiator that had been turned off on probably the coldest night of the year ...'

This is also the time to form an opinion of the decor and furnishings of the public areas, such as:

'I found the statues in the dining room rather OTT and felt they would be better consigned to the garden ..... The overall effect is of eccentricity rather than good taste.'

Even worse:

"A sad, lonely, soulless establishment'

Some inspectors, while following the strict guidelines for classification, will privately assess a hotel on whether or not they would spend their own money on a stay there.

'I wouldn't object to staying here again, but I certainly wouldn't consider it for a private visit.'

The summing up of this visit concluded that '...has a lot of potential but lacks any tasteful exploitation of this ... nowhere near as busy as it could be .... I overheard one lone guest making diplomatic excuses as to why he had to cancel his second night's stay.'

Sometimes, though, an inspector can seem to really take to a hotel almost in spite of himself:

'It is unusual for the AA to grant appointment to a hotel that has a complete no smoking policy, is unlicensed, does not take credit cards, does not serve meals to non residents ... and offers only a fixed price, no choice menu at a set time'.

And yet the report goes on to praise the hotel to the roof (it has red stars), though the inspector couldn't resist winding up with 'Guests are encouraged to bring their own wines, and no corkage is charged. No charge either for smoking outside in the rain!'

Personalities can't fail to come into the reckoning when subjective assessments are involved, particularly

Inspectors Off the Record

where hospitality is concerned. Personality clashes, on the other hand, do not figure anywhere other than on the occasional report - for instance, the comment about the owner of a very highly rated hotel which describes him as 'non-conformist, unconventional, eccentric even .... if these are part of the characteristics needed to succeed (in running an outstanding hotel), who are we to question them?'

Hotel guests do not come out entirely unscathed either, with more than a hint that if we were more demanding, things would improve accordingly. One report on a particularly poor hotel:

'Busy with budget commercial travellers with blindness to indifferent food, service, hospitality and poor levels of housekeeping.'

The conclusion of a hotel visit is always the meeting with the owner or manager, when a thorough inspection of the premises is made. Many inspectors feel that this is the most rewarding part of their job, when they have the opportunity to discuss, suggest, advise, congratulate and have some effect on the progress which the hotel may make in the future. Usually these meetings are amicable and useful for both parties, as at the St Tudno Hotel in Llandudno:

'Whenever the Blands are told of something needing attention, it is done.'

But there are times .....

'Quite a difficult inspection - I didn't have much chance to get views across'

and

'Mr L is an ex-policeman and a very straight talker'

Even when there is no unpleasantness involved, the meeting with the hotel owner is not always satisfactory:

'I expressed disappointment and said that either all must be improved or appointment would be withdrawn. Miss B agreed with everything I said; a real nodder and I suspect not much of a doer.'

Inspectors will always make allowances for special circumstances which affect the running of a hotel - as at the Baltasound Hotel in Unst when, on the night of our inspection, the hotel was descended upon by a plane-load of North Sea oil workers grounded by fog.

'I don't think I had a typical experience. They all ate in the bar, mobbing it, but the proprietor made special provision for me in the dining room and I must say that I was reasonably well looked after.'

We also intend to do all we can to accommodate the unfortunate hotel owner who pointed out to our inspector that for the last two years his visit has been made on a Wednesday - the Head Chef's only night off.

It should be apparent, then, that the hotel inspector's life is an interesting and challenging one, with its fair share of ups and downs. And if this all seems to have a negative bias, it is only because our inspectors tend to be more outspoken about their bad experiences than their good ones. We can assure you that an enormous number of inspection reports were read and rejected because they had only nice things to say! Be honest - would you have found them as interesting?

There is a final quote from one of our inspectors which encompasses both ends of the spectrum in one sentence:

'What a nice end to a horrible week!'

Thankyou, the Bobsleigh Inn at Bovingdon, for brightening the life of one fraught AA Inspector.

THE WOODSIDE HOTEL

HIGH STREET, ABERDOUR, FIFE KY3 0SW

For fine food in pleasant surroundings. The CLIPPER LOUNGE is one of the sights in the area. It was taken from a passenger liner. We are within walking distance of Aberdour station — Britain's prettiest station. Aberdour Castle and the picturesque harbour are nearby.

Each of our rooms is named after a clan and features the clan tartan.

Tel: (0383) 860328   Fax: (0383) 860920

GOLF COURSES IN BRITAIN AND IRELAND

The essential guide for the enthusiastic golfer on the move, whether travelling on business, on holiday, or in search of new courses to play - the AA guide to

Golf Courses in Britain and Ireland

includes useful details of over 2000 courses

About 250 new courses - including many due to open

Special Feature - Do Those Golden Fairways Always Harvest Megabucks?

£7.99

AA ★★★★ # The Raven Hotel

Impney Hotels

"A Safe Haven in the Heart of Worcestershire yet only one mile from Junction 5 of the M5"

Droitwich Spa
Worcestershire WR9 8DU
Tel: 0905 772224
Fax: 0905 772371

SPECIAL RATES

	STAND-BY RATE	NORMAL RATE
SINGLE ROOM *¹	£49.95	~~£99.95~~
DOUBLE ROOM *¹	£59.95	~~£119.95~~

*¹ AVAILABLE ONLY FOR BOOKINGS MADE LESS THAN 7 DAYS PRIOR TO ARRIVAL
*² PRICES ARE VALID AS AT TIME OF PUBLICATION. PLEASE PHONE FOR CONFIRMATION

IT'S NICE TO KNOW YOU CAN RELAX ALL OVER THE UK

Everything is possible at a Queens Moat Houses hotel.

Whether it is a traditional inn, country manor, modern airport hotel or a city centre location, every one of more than 100 Queens Moat Houses hotels throughout the UK offer the same warm friendly service, excellent cuisine, and a range of conference and leisure facilities which are second to none. Yet every hotel is as individual as you are.

Queens Moat Houses PLC

INTERNATIONAL HOTELIERS

FOR A FAST EFFICIENT SERVICE
CALL QUEENS-*LINE* UK RESERVATIONS
Tel: 0708 766677   Fax: 0708 761033   Telex: 929751
QUEENS-*LINE* UK RESERVATIONS, Queens Court, 9 - 17 Eastern Road, Romford, Essex, RM1 3NG.

Hotel Groups

In recent years many hotel companies have been developing clearly identified and identifiable 'brand' umbrellas to distinguish groups of those of their hotels that have all important characteristics and services in common.

Every brand has its own well known profile and is part of a national or international network. The brand name acts as a guarantee of certain levels of comfort and facilities whatever country or region of a country you are in.

Under the brand umbrella, each hotel shares a common philosophy and is designed to meet the needs of a particular market sector. At most of them, important facilities will be identical, though there may be some individual variation, and the trend will be for these few to offer more than the standard for its brand.

As these hotel brands in many cases correspond to, or overlap with traditional AA star-ratings, the AA is now able to recognise them by their brand alone, and to inspect them annually, in a similar way to the star-rated hotels, against a defined set of requirements and standards.

Their entries in the guide will be easy to recognise because the hotel brand symbol (eg Forte Crest, Pavilion) will appear beside their entry and they will be listed after the star-rated hotels. A full description of the style of these hotels and what they aim to offer is given below.

Most company-owned hotels prefer to convey the level of their services and facilities by remaining within the star-rating system with their own more individual identity. Where they are owned by national or international groups, or belong to a consortium, the appropriate logo appears alongside the star rating and quality assessment.

A brief brand description accompanies each of the entries in the directory, but below we summarise the philosophy behind each of the brands, and give more details about the facilities on offer.

CAMPANILE

There are 330 Campanile hotels in six European countries. They are modern and purpose built, run by a management couple. Reception is open every day from 7am to 11pm. There is parking, an adjacent bistro restaurant, which offers breakfast, lunch and dinner, licensed bar and conference room. Bedrooms have en-suite bathrooms, remote control colour TV with Sky, direct-dial telephone, alarm clock, desk area and tea and coffee making facilities. There are specially equipped rooms for disabled guests.

All rooms have the same tariff throughout the country. American Express, Visa and Access are accepted.

EDWARDIAN HOTELS

Edwardian Hotels' policy is to provide elegant hotel accommodation with high levels of service in the very heart of London's West End and near Heathrow. There is free on-site parking at Heathrow and facilities at all hotels include concierge service, 24-hour room service, separate cocktail bar or wine bar, lounge service and restaurants with international cuisine.

Luxuriously decorated bedrooms have full en-suite bathrooms, colour TV (with in-house films at selected hotels), hairdryer, trouser press and direct-dial telephone. Suites are available.

The hotels offer luxurious furnishings and restful surroundings reminiscent of a country house atmosphere, yet are ideally situated for London's shopping districts, theatres, museums and night life. They can also offer guests corporate hospitality at the top sporting occasions as well as a theatre and arts programme. Edwardian Hotels is the 'Preferred

HOTEL GROUPS

Partner' for Hertz, the 'London Hotel Partner' for British Airways and has a marketing Partnership with Radisson International Hotels.

All major credit cards are accepted.

FORTE CREST

Part of the international hotel group Forte plc, Forte Crest Hotels are mainly in the UK, with an expanding European portfolio. It is the dedicated business brand located in city centres, commercial areas and at airports.
The hotels have a range of meeting rooms, and full business support services, including secretarial service, courier and 24-hour fax/photocopying.

Bedrooms are smart and comfortable, with free satellite TV and 24-hour room service among a range of amenities. Lady Crest and no-smoking bedrooms are available. Most have parking and many have indoor leisure facilities. Service includes a lobby manager to deal with individual enquiries.

Tariff bands are the same nationwide and all major credit cards are accepted.

For central reservations tel: 0345 404040

FORTE POSTHOUSE

There are over 60 Forte Posthouse locations throughout the country. All are ideally situated for the business and leisure traveller and have free car parking.

All the comfortable bedrooms offer en-suite bathrooms, tea and coffee making facilities, colour TV, direct-dial telephone, hairdryer and trouser press. National pricing by the room means that the value for money improves with the number of occupants, making them particularly popular with families. Fifty per cent of the bedrooms are for non smokers. Many locations offer the additional comfort of executive rooms, and also have indoor swimming pools.

An informal theme is carried through from the restaurant to the bar and lounge which offer an 'Anytime' menu for light meals.

All major credit cards are accepted.

For central reservations tel: (free) 0800 404040

FORTE TRAVELODGE

There are 95 Forte Travelodges nationwide, including two in Ireland. The same quality standards are guaranteed at all Forte Travelodges, with a fixed price per room, per night, of £31.95. All rooms can comfortably sleep up to three adults, a child and a baby in a cot and come complete with en-suite bathroom and shower, tea and coffee making facilities, TV and radio, feather duvets and controllable central heating. Special facilities for disabled guests are also offered. There is ample parking at all Forte Travelodges and a family restaurant within walking distance.

Bookings are accepted up to three months in advance, and all major credit cards are accepted.

For central reservations tel: (free) 0800 850950.

GRANADA LODGES

Granada Lodges are a national network of high quality budget accommodation. There are over two dozen, located on 'A' roads or motorways. They have ample parking, 24-hour check-in and an adjacent family restaurant, open either at meal times or all day. They are attractively landscaped, red brick modern buildings, which include ground floor accommodation, and at least one room with special facilities for disabled guests, and no-smoking rooms. All bedrooms are a good size, and with en-suite bathroom and shower. Free facilities include colour TV with Sky, radio/alarm clock, controllable central heating and tea and coffee making facilities. The tariff is per room per night, for up to two adults and two children (aged up to 16).

All major credit cards are accepted.

For central reservations tel: (free) 0800 555300

HOTEL GROUPS

HILTON NATIONAL

Hilton National is a domestic chain of 23 first class, modern hotels located in key business areas on or near major motorway networks throughout Britain.
All bedrooms have private bathroom with shower and wc, remote control TV, radio, direct-dial telephone, work space, hairdryer, trouser press and tea and coffee making facilities. Bedrooms include executive, family, no-smoking and rooms specially equipped for disabled guests.

Hotels feature extensive conference and banqueting facilities, including boardrooms and training rooms, business centres, car parking and most have indoor leisure centre. There are innovative themed restaurants and bars, with room service available for light meals.

All major credit cards are accepted.

For central reservations tel: 071-734 6000

MARRIOTT HOTELS RESORTS AND SUITES

With over 250 Marriott Hotels Resorts and Suites worldwide, Marriott focus on the needs of group, business, pleasure and international travellers who desire a full line of quality services. In the United Kingdom, Marriott are represented with 14 hotels offering spacious and comfortable guest rooms, with private bathroom, remote control colour TV, direct-dial telephone, 24-hour room service and porterage; extensive meeting and banqueting facilities, restaurants and bars, and in most locations comprehensive leisure centres, an executive floor of rooms and free car parking.

All major credit cards are accepted.

For central reservations tel: (free) 0800 221222

COURTYARD BY MARRIOTT

Courtyard by Marriott hotels feature superior guest accommodation at moderate prices for both the business and pleasure traveller. There are four Courtyard hotels in the United Kingdom located at Leamington Spa, Lincoln, Northampton and Slough/Windsor, all offering well furnished guest rooms with private bathroom, remote control colour TV, direct-dial telephone, tea and coffee tray. There are informal restaurants and bars, a fitness/leisure room and small meeting facilities.

All major credit cards are accepted.

For central reservations tel: (free) 0800 221222

PAVILION LODGE

Pavilion Lodges are usually located on motorways or A-roads. They have ample parking, 24-hour check in, and an adjacent family restaurant, open either at meal times or all day. They are attractively landscaped, red-brick modern buildings, which include ground floor accommodation and at least one room with special facilities for disabled guests. All bedrooms are a good size, with double or twin beds and with en-suite bathroom, shower and wc. Facilities include colour TV with radio/alarm clock, controllable central heating, trouser press, hair dryer and tea and coffee making facilities.
The tariff is the same nationally and is per room per night. All major credit cards are accepted.

TRAVEL INN

Travel Inn is a national network of high quality budget accommodation. There are over four dozen, located on major 'A' roads and near motorways. They have ample parking, and an adjacent family restaurant and pub serving breakfast, lunch and dinner. They are attractively landscaped, modern brick buildings, which include ground floor accommodation and at least one room with special facilities for disabled guests, as well as no-smoking rooms.

All bedrooms are a very good size, and have en-suite bathroom and shower. Every room has remote control colour TV, radio/alarm clock, controllable heating and tea and coffee making facilities. The tariff is per room per night, accommodating up to two adults and two children up to 16 (at most Travel Inns). Reception is open until 11pm. Visa and Access accepted.

For further information tel: 0582 428884

Top Hotels
Red Star Awards

The award of red stars to an hotel is the most prestigious that the AA can give, indicating consistent all-round excellence. The 110 hotels listed below are those which have been judged by our inspectors to be the very best in their star classification: the best hotels in Britain.

Full details will be found in the directory.

ENGLAND

AVON

New Award
Hinton Charterhouse ★★★ **Homewood Park**

Hunstrete ★★★ **Hunstrete House**
Thornbury ★★★ **Thornbury Castle**

BUCKINGHAMSHIRE

Aylesbury ★★★★ **Hartwell House**
Taplow ★★★★★ **Cliveden**

CHESHIRE

Chester ★★★★ **The Chester Grosvenor**

CORNWALL

Liskeard ★★ **Well House**

CUMBRIA

New Award
Alston ★★ **Lovelady Shield**

Brampton ★★★ **Farlam Hall**
Grasmere ★★★ **Michael's Nook**
Grasmere ★ **White Moss House**
Howtown ★★★ **Sharrow Bay Hotel**
Keswick ★ **Swinside Lodge**

New Award
Kirkby Lonsdale ★ **Cobwebs**

Windermere ★★ **Holbeck Ghyll**
Windermere ★★ **Miller Howe**
Witherslack ★ **Old Vicarage**

DERBYSHIRE

Baslow ★★★ **Cavendish Hotel**

DEVON

Barnstaple ★ **Halmpstone Manor**
Chagford ★★★ **Gidleigh Park**
Lewdown ★★ **Lewtrenchard Manor**
South Molton ★★ **Whitechapel Manor**
Whimple ★★ **Woodhayes**

DORSET

Evershot ★★★ **Summer Lodge**
Gillingham ★★ **Stock Hill House**
Wareham ★★★ **The Priory**
Wimborne Minster ★★ **Beechleas**

EAST SUSSEX

Battle ★★★ **Netherfield Place**
Uckfield ★★ **Horsted Place**

ESSEX

Dedham ★★★ **Maison Talbooth**

GLOUCESTERSHIRE

Buckland ★★★ **Buckland Manor**

New Award
Charingworth ★★★ **Charingworth Manor**

Cheltenham ★★★ **Greenway**
Tetbury ★★★ **Calcot Manor**

HAMPSHIRE

Lymington ★★ **Gordleton Mill**
New Milton ★★★★★ **Chewton Glen**
Rotherwick ★★★★ **Tylney Hall**

TOP HOTELS

HEREFORD & WORCESTER

Broadway ★★★★ **Lygon Arms**
Leominster ★ **Marsh Country Hotel**

KENT

Ashford ★★★★ **Eastwell Manor**

LEICESTERSHIRE

Melton Mowbray ★★★ **Stapleford Park**
Oakham ★★★ **Hambleton Hall**

LONDON

SW1 ★★★★★ **Berkeley**

New Award
SW1
★★★★★ **Lanesborough**

SW1 ★★★★ **Goring**
SW1 ★ **Tophams Ebury Court**
SW3 ★★★★ **Capital**
W1 ★★★★★ **Claridges**
W1 ★★★★★ **Connaught**
W1 ★★★★★ **Dorchester**
W1 ★★★★★ **Four Seasons**
W1 ★★★★ **Athenaeum**
W1 ★★★★ **Brown's**
WC2 ★★★★★ **Savoy**

NORFOLK

New Award
Blakeney
★★ **Morston Hall**

Grimston ★★★ **Congham Hall**

NORTH YORKSHIRE

Bilbrough ★★★ **Bilbrough Manor**
York ★★★ **Grange**
York ★★★ **Middlethorpe Hall**

NORTHUMBERLAND

New Award
Powburn
★★ **Breamish House**

OXFORDSHIRE

Great Milton ★★★★ **Le Manoir aux Quat' Saisons**

SOMERSET

Dulverton ★★ **Ashwick House**
Ston Easton ★★★ **Ston Easton Park**
Taunton ★★★ **Castle**
Wiveliscombe ★★ **Langley House**

SUFFOLK

Hintlesham ★★★ **Hintlesham Hall**

SURREY

New Award
Bagshot
★★★★ **Pennyhill Park**

Gatwick Airport ★ **Langshott Manor**

WARWICKSHIRE

Leamington Spa ★★★ **Mallory Court**
Leamington Spa ★ **Lansdowne**

WEST MIDLANDS

New Award
Birmingham
★★★★ **Swallow**

WEST SUSSEX

East Grinstead ★★★ **Gravetye Manor**
Turners Hill ★★★ **Alexander House**

WEST YORKSHIRE

Wetherby ★★★ **Wood Hall**

WILTSHIRE

New Award
Castle Combe
★★★★ **Manor House**

Colerne ★★★★ **Lucknam Park**

TOP HOTELS

CHANNEL ISLANDS

JERSEY
St Saviour ★★★★ **Longueville Manor**

WALES

GWYNNED

New Award
Conwy
★ **Old Rectory**

Llandudno ★★★ **Bodysgallen Hall**
Llandudno ★★ **St Tudno**
Llangefni ★★★ **Tre-Ysgawen Hall**
Talsarnau ★★ **Maes y Neuadd**

SCOTLAND

CENTRAL

Dunblane ★★★ **Cromlix House**

DUMFRIES & GALLOWAY

Auchencairn ★★ **Collin House**
Portpatrick ★★ **Knockinaam Lodge**

FIFE

St Andrews ★★★★ **St Andrews Old Course Hotel**

GRAMPIAN

Banchory ★★★ **Banchory Lodge**

New Award
Bridge of Marnoch
★ **Old Manse of Marnoch**

New Award
Kildrummy
★★★ **Kildrummy Castle**

HIGHLAND

Arisaig ★★★ **Arisaig House**
Fort William ★★★★ **Inverlochy Castle**
Fort William ★ **Factor's House**

Inverness ★★ **Dunain Park**
Whitebridge ★★ **Knockie Lodge**

LOTHIAN

Gullane ★★★ **Greywalls**

STRATHCLYDE

Eriska ★★★ **Isle of Eriska**
Glasgow ★★★ **One Devonshire Gardens**
Maybole ★★ **Ladyburn**
Port Appin ★★★ **Airds**

New Award
Turnberry
★★★★★ **Turnberry Hotel**

TAYSIDE

Aberfeldy ★★ **Farleyer House**
Auchterarder ★★★★★ **Gleneagles**
Dunkeld ★★★ **Kinnaird**

NORTHERN IRELAND

DOWN

Annalong ★★ **Glassdrumman Lodge**

REPUBLIC OF IRELAND

GALWAY

Cashel ★★★ **Cashel House**

KERRY

Kenmare ★★★★ **Park**

WEXFORD

Gorey ★★★ **Marlfield House**
Rosslare ★★★ **Kelly's Strand**

WICKLOW

New Award
Rathnew
★★★ **Tinakilly Country House & Restaurant**

23

Top Hotel Restaurants
Rosette Awards

Our rosette scheme ranges from five rosettes for outstanding cuisine to a single rosette for enjoyable, well prepared food. Listed below are those hotel restaurants where cooking, presentation of dishes and service reach exceptionally high standards and have attained rosettes in the three highest categories. Some have been awarded rosettes for their dinner menu only - the directory gives full details.

ENGLAND

AVON
Bath ❀❀❀ Royal Crescent
Hunstrete ❀❀❀ Hunstrete House

BEDFORDSHIRE
Flitwick ❀❀❀ Flitwick Manor

BERKSHIRE
Maidenhead ❀❀❀ Fredrick's

BUCKINGHAMSHIRE
Taplow ❀❀❀ Cliveden

CHESHIRE
Chester ❀❀❀ Chester Grosvenor

CORNWALL
Liskeard ❀❀❀ Well House
Padstow ❀❀❀ Seafood Restaurant

CUMBRIA
Grasmere ❀❀❀ Michael's Nook
Howtown ❀❀❀ Sharrow Bay

DERBYSHIRE
Baslow ❀❀❀ Fischer's

DEVON
Chagford ❀❀❀ Gidleigh Park
Gulworthy ❀❀❀ Horn of Plenty
South Molton ❀❀❀ Whitechapel Manor

DORSET
Gillingham ❀❀❀ Stock Hill House

EAST SUSSEX
Uckfield ❀❀❀ Horsted Place

ESSEX
Dedham ❀❀❀ Maison Talbooth

GLOUCESTERSHIRE
Buckland ❀❀❀ Buckland Manor
Cheltenham ❀❀❀ Hotel on the Park

Lower Slaughter ❀❀❀ Lower Slaughter Manor
Stow-on-the-Wold ❀❀❀ Wyck Hill House

GREATER MANCHESTER
Bury ❀❀❀ Normandie

HAMPSHIRE
New Milton ❀❀❀ Chewton Glen

HEREFORD & WORCESTER
Ledbury ❀❀❀ Hope End

HERTFORDSHIRE
Ware ❀❀❀ Hanbury Manor

LEICESTERSHIRE
Oakham ❀❀❀ Hambleton Hall

LONDON
SW1 ❀❀❀ Lanesborough
SW3 ❀❀❀ Capital
W1 ❀❀❀ Connaught
W1 ❀❀❀ Dorchester
W1 ❀❀❀ Four Seasons
W1 ❀❀❀ Inter-Continental
W1 ❀❀❀ Le Meridien
WC2 ❀❀❀ Savoy

OXFORDSHIRE
Great Milton ❀❀❀❀❀ Le Manoir aux Quat' Saisons
Moulsford ❀❀❀ Beetle & Wedge
Stonor ❀❀❀ Stonor Arms

SOMERSET
Taunton ❀❀❀ Castle Hotel
Taunton ❀❀❀ Mount Somerset
Williton ❀❀❀ White House

SUFFOLK
Hintlesham ❀❀❀ Hintlesham Hall

SURREY
Bagshot ❀❀❀ Pennyhill Park

WARWICKSHIRE
Leamington Spa ❀❀❀ Mallory Court

Stratford-upon-Avon
❀❀❀ Billesley Manor

WEST MIDLANDS
Birmingham ❀❀❀ Swallow
Hockley Heath ❀❀❀ Nuthurst Grange

WEST SUSSEX
East Grinstead ❀❀❀ Gravetye Manor

WILTSHIRE
Bradford on Avon
❀❀❀ Woolley Grange
Colerne ❀❀❀ Lucknam Park

CHANNEL ISLANDS

JERSEY
St Saviour ❀❀❀ Longueville Manor

WALES

GWYNEDD
Pwllheli ❀❀❀ Plas Bodegroes

POWYS
Llyswen ❀❀❀ Llangoed Hall

SCOTLAND

STRATHCLYDE
Port Appin ❀❀❀ Airds

TAYSIDE
Dunkeld ❀❀❀ Kinnaird

REPUBLIC OF IRELAND

CO. CORK
Ballylickey ❀❀❀ Sea View
Mallow ❀❀❀ Longueville House

CO. DONEGAL
Donegal ❀❀❀ Harvey's Point

CO. WEXFORD
Gorey ❀❀❀ Marlfield House

Using the Guide...
How We Classify Hotels

Note: AA-inspected hotels in Northern Ireland and the Republic appear as a separate section to those in Britain - see Contents Page.

CLASSIFICATIONS

Hotels: classified with black stars, with additional quality percentage assessments.

AA Lodges: simple accommodation of fairly standard quality near main roads.

Every establishment is inspected annually and classified according to specific criteria.

THE INSPECTORS

Much of the inspectors' work consists of regular and detailed examination of premises. Inspectors either have a background in the hotel and catering industries, or training and work experience, and they also undertake regular training courses to ensure consistent nationwide standards in their assessments. A balance is therefore achieved between their specialist expertise and awareness of market trends.

HOTELS

Hotels are inspected anonymously. Having stayed a night and settled the bill in the morning, the inspector introduces herself or himself and makes a thorough inspection of the entire premises. Once granted recognition and given a rating, the hotel is inspected annually. Change of ownership means the hotel automatically loses its AA recognition and must be re-assessed under the new ownership before being re-appointed. A fee is levied for registration and appointment.

RATINGS

Black stars range from one ★ to five ★★★★★. They denote a universally accepted standard ranging from the simplest to the most luxurious hotel. In addition, all hotels are awarded percentage assessments to highlight quality differences between establishments within the same star classification.

★ Hotels generally of a small scale with good, but often simple furnishing, facilities and food. This category sometimes includes private hotels where requirements for public access and full lunch service may be relaxed. Not all bedrooms will necessarily have en suite facilities. These hotels are often managed by the proprietor and there may well be a more personal atmosphere than in larger establishments.

★★ Small to medium sized hotels offering more in the way of facilities such as telephones and televisions in bedrooms. Like one star hotels, this category can also include private hotels. At least half the bedrooms will have full en suite facilities. These can be proprietor-managed or group-owned.

★★★ Medium sized hotels offering more spacious accommodation and a greater range of facilities and services. Generally these will include a full reception service as well as more formal restaurant and bar arrangements. You can expect all rooms to provide en suite facilities, most of which will include a bath. Though often individually owned, this category encompasses a greater number of company-owned properties.

★★★★ Generally large hotels with spacious accommodation including availability of private suites. This category of hotel normally provides a full range of formal hotel services including room service, reception and porterage and may well offer more than one dining operation. En suite facilities in all rooms should include both bath and shower. High standards of comfort and food are expected at this level.

★★★★★ Large luxury hotels offering the highest international standards of accommodation, facilities, services and cuisine.

USING THE GUIDE - Hotel Classification

LODGES

Lodges offer reasonably priced accommodation catering for overnight stops and offering good, functional bedrooms with private facilities. They are usually situated adjacent to a motorway/roadside restaurant. They are of fairly standard quality and are not star rated. See also 'Hotel Groups'

MERIT AWARDS

PERCENTAGES

These are in addition to black star ratings. They indicate the difference in quality between hotels within a particular star rating, reflecting the inspectors' experiences at the time of inspection. They may alter during the currency of the guide.

PERCENTAGE ASSESSMENT

50%-59%   A sound hotel which meets all the minimum standards for AA star rating and which overall provides modest but acceptable levels of accommodation, facilities and services.

60%-69%   A particularly sound hotel which exceeds the minimum requirements for its star rating by offering higher standards in certain areas of its operation.

70%-85%   Overall a very good hotel which can be strongly recommended for providing a high level of service, food and accommodation, often with excellent standards in certain areas of the operation.

RED STARS

The AA recognises hotels which consistently provide outstanding levels of hospitality, service, food and comfort through its prestigious 'red star' award scheme. These awards are given annually to a select group of hotels considered to be the very best within their star rating. In such cases, a percentage score for quality is considered unnecessary.

In the whole of Great Britain and Ireland there are only 110 red-star hotels (see list on pages 21 - 23). They are highlighted in the A-Z directory by a pink-tinted panel containing a detailed description and a photograph.

COUNTRY HOUSE HOTELS

An AA Country House Hotel offers a relaxed and informal atmosphere and a personal welcome. Often secluded, they are not always rurally situated but are quiet.

ROSETTES

Rosettes range from one ❀ to five ❀❀❀❀❀. Hotel restaurants can be awarded rosettes to denote the quality of the food they serve, although only those establishments offering the highest international standards of cuisine will merit the AA's top awards of four and five rosettes.

❀   Enjoyable food, carefully prepared, that reflects a high level of culinary skills.

❀❀   A high standard of food that demonstrates a serious, dedicated approach to the cooking.

❀❀❀   Very fine food prepared with considerable flair, imagination and originality.

❀❀❀❀   Excellent standards of cuisine, service and wine consistently achieved.

❀❀❀❀❀   Outstanding cuisine, service and wine that reaches the highest international standards.

Using the Guide...

Sample Directory Entry

This entry is fictitious

BEESTON Derbyshire Map **15** NJ90 } **1. TOWN NAME**

★★★ 65% **Red Lion** } **2. HOTEL NAME**
The Square AB00 XY1 (GB Hotels) ☎(0685) 8276
FAX (0685) 6728
RS Nov–Mar } **3. RESTRICTED SERVICE**

Attractive old coaching inn with comfortable, pretty bedrooms.
19rm(14⇨5♠) Annexe5rm(8fb)3♨✕in 5 bedrooms CTV
in all bedrooms✕®✕ T sB&B⇨♠£16.50-£24.50 } **4. ACCOMMODATION DETAILS**
dB&B⇨♠£31-£49 ♨

Lift ⓒ CTV 100P 3🚗🚲 ⛱ ♪ nc 3yrs } **5. HOTEL FACILITIES**

♦ English & French V ✿♨✕ Lunch £3-£4.50 Tea 85p-
£1.40 High Tea £2.75-£6 Dinner £8.25-£11 &alc Last dinner } **6. MEALS**
9pm

CONF. Thtr 60 Class 20 Del from £345
Credit Cards ①②③④⑤ £ } **7. PAYMENT DETAILS**

---

1. TOWN NAME

Listed in the directory in alphabetical order. This is followed by the county or region, which is the administrative county or region and not necessarily part of the correct postal address. Towns on islands (not connected to the mainland by a bridge) are listed under the island name. Scottish regions or islands are followed by the old county name in italics. The map reference which follows denotes the map page number and grid reference. Read the first figure across, the second figure vertically, within the appropriate square.

2. HOTEL NAME

Address (including postcode), directions and telephone number with classification and percentage (see page 26 for details). Establishment names shown in italics indicate that the details have not been confirmed by the management. Within towns, hotels are listed in descending order of star rating, with red stars first, then descending order of percentage ratings. London hotels are listed under London postal districts. Company-owned hotels may have the company logo printed beside their entry, or an abbreviated name. A full list of these names is given on page 707. Some companies own hotels which conform to a brand standard, and these are now listed without a star-rating, with the brand logo. They are still inspected by the AA. See 'Hotel Groups' on page 18. The telephone exchange is that of the town heading, unless the name of the exchange is given after the ☎ symbol and before the dialling code and number. In some areas, numbers are likely to be changed during the currency of this book. In case of difficulty check with the operator. When making a reservation by telex or fax it is advisable to specify which hotel you wish to book with as some hotels (particularly those in groups) use a central telex/fax service.

3. RESTRICTED SERVICE

Some hotels, while remaining open, operate a restricted service during the less busy months. This may take the form of a reduction in meals served, accommodation or facilities available.

4. ACCOMMODATION DETAILS

The first figure shows the number of letting bedrooms. Where rooms have en suite bath or shower and WC, the number precedes the appropriate symbol.

Annexe bedrooms available in an annexe are noted only if they are at least of the same standard as those in the rest of the hotel. Facilities may not be the same as in the main building, however, and it is advisable to check the nature of the accommodation and the tariff before making a reservation. In some hotels, accommodation is available only in an annexe.

✕ number of bedrooms and/or area of the restaurant set aside for non-smokers.

fb family bedrooms.

USING THE GUIDE...

CTV/TV   means colour or black and white television in lounge or available in bedrooms. Check when making reservation.

☆   Satellite TV channels are available at no extra cost.

✖   no dogs allowed into bedrooms. Some hotels may restrict the type of dogs permitted and the rooms into which they may be taken. Hotels which do not normally accept dogs may accept guide dogs. Generally dogs are not allowed in the dining room. Check when booking the conditions under which pets are accepted.

T   automatic direct-dial telephone facilities available from bedrooms. Many hotels impose a surcharge for calls made from bedrooms, so check before making a call. A public telephone is usually available in the hotel hallway or foyer.

Prices   prices given have been provided by hoteliers in good faith and are indications rather than firm quotations. Unless otherwise stated, they include full cooked breakfast. Some hotels offer free accommodation to children provided they share the parents' room. Check current prices before booking. Prices for the Republic of Ireland are shown in Irish Punts (IR£). At the time of going to press the exchange rate is IR£1 = £1. See also page 679.

5. HOTEL FACILITIES

For key to symbols see bookmark.

⦅   All hotels employing a night porter are shown thus. Four and five star hotels all have night porters on duty.

🚌   No coaches. This information is published in good faith from information supplied by the hotels concerned. Inns, however, have well-defined legal obligations towards travellers, and it is for the customer to take up any queries with the proprietor or the local licensing authority.

♪   Live entertainment should be available at least once a week throughout the year.

Some hotels without this symbol will provide entertainment during high season or at certain other specified times only. You are advised to check this information before booking.

nc   No children. Where this abbreviation does not appear, the hotels listed will accommodate children, but may not provide any special facilities. A minimum age (eg nc4yrs – no children under four years old) may be specified. For very young children, check before booking about such provisions as cots and high chairs and any reductions made.

♧   establishments with special facilities for children, which will include baby-sitting service or baby intercom system, playroom or playground, laundry facilities, drying and ironing facilities, cots, high chairs and special meals.

CONF.   Denotes that conference facilities are available and maximum numbers theatre-style (Thtr), classroom-style (Class), Boardroom-style (Board) and the minimum overnight delegate rate (del).

Suitable for the disabled   Full details for disabled people will be found in the AA Guide for the Disabled Traveller on sale at AA shops, free to members. Intending guests with any form of disability should notify proprietors so that arrangements can be made to minimise difficulties, particularly in the event of an emergency.

6. MEALS

Details of the style of food served, last dinner orders and likely price range are given, the abbreviation '&alc' indicates that there is also an a la carte menu, which may be considerably dearer than the set menu.

V   a choice of vegetarian dishes available (but check before booking).

☕   morning coffee or afternoon tea are served to chance callers. All four and five star hotels serve morning coffee and, normally, afternoon tea to residents.

Prices   See page 30.

7. CREDIT CARDS

1   Access/Eurocard/Mastercard
2   American Express
3   Barclaycard/Visa
4   Carte Blanche
5   Diners
£   Hotel may offer a discount. See page 2.

It is advisable to check the current position regarding credit card payments when booking. Some establishments may impose a surcharge on credit card payments.

Using the Guide...
Useful Information (BRITAIN)

*I*nformation specifically relating to Northern Ireland and the Republic of Ireland precedes the Irish Directory. See Contents page.

BOOKING

Book as early as possible, particularly if accommodation is required during a holiday period (beginning of June to end of September, public holidays and, in some parts of Scotland, during the skiing season). Some hotels ask for a deposit, and some also ask for full payment in advance, especially for one-night bookings taken from chance callers. Not all hotels take advance bookings for bed and breakfast for overnight or short stays and will not accept reservations from mid-week.

CANCELLATION

Once the booking has been confirmed, notify the hotel straight away if you are in any doubt about whether you can keep to your arrangements. If the hotel cannot re-let your accommodation, you may be liable to pay about two-thirds of the price you would have paid had you stayed there (your deposit will count towards this payment).

In Britain it is accepted that a legally binding contract has been made as soon as an intending guests accepts an offer of accommodation, either in writing or on the telephone. Illness is not accepted as a release from this contract. For these reasons you are advised to effect insurance cover, eg AA Travelsure, against possible cancellation.

COMPLAINTS

Guests who wish to complain about food, services or facilities are urged to do so promptly and on the spot. This should provide an opportunity for the hotelier to correct matters. If a personal approach fails, members should inform AA Hotel Services, Fanum House, Basingstoke, Hampshire RG21 2EA.

FIRE PRECAUTIONS

As far as we can discover, every hotel in Great Britain listed in this book has applied for, and not been refused, a fire certificate. The Fire Precautions Act does not apply to the Channel Islands or the Isle of Man, which exercise their own rules regarding fire precautions for hotels.

LICENSE TO SELL ALCOHOL

All establishments in this guide are licensed unless otherwise stated. Basically, hotel residents can obtain alcoholic drinks at all times, if the owner is prepared to serve them. Non-residents eating at the hotel restaurant can obtain drinks with their meals.

The sale of alcoholic drinks is controlled by separate licensing laws in England, Wales, Scotland, Isle of Man, the Isles of Scilly and each of the islands forming the Channel Islands.

Licensing hours in public houses are generally from mid morning to early afternoon and from mid evening to an hour or two before midnight. Some will remain open throughout the afternoon.

Club Licence. Drinks can be served only to club members, but an interval of 48 hours must elapse after joining.

Children under 14 (18 in Scotland) may be excluded from bars, except areas intended for the service of food. Those under 18 are not allowed to purchase or consume alcoholic drinks.

MEALS

Unless otherwise stated, the terms quoted in the directory section of this book include full cooked breakfast.

In some parts of Britain, particularly in Scotland, high tea (ie a savoury dish followed

USEFUL INFORMATION (BRITAIN)

by bread and butter, scones, cakes etc) is sometimes served instead of dinner, which may, however, be available on request. The last time at which high tea or dinner may be ordered on weekdays is shown, but this may be varied at weekends.

On Sundays, some hotels serve the main meal at mid-day, and just a cold evening meal.

PAYMENT

Most hotels will only accept cheques in payment of accounts if notice is given and some form of identification (usually a cheque card) is produced. Travellers' cheques issued by the leading banks and agencies are accepted by many hotels but not all. If a hotel accepts leading credit or cheque cards, this is shown in the directory entry (see 'sample directory entry for details)

PRICES

The Hotel Industry Voluntary Code of Booking Practice was revised in 1986, and the AA encourages its use in appropriate establishments. Its prime object is to ensure that the customer is clear about the precise services and facilities he is buying, and what price he will have to pay, before he commits himself to a contractually binding agreement. If the price has not been previously confirmed in writing, the guest should be handed a card at the time of registration, stipulating the total obligatory charge.

The Tourism (Sleeping Accommodation Price Display) Order 1977 compels hotels, motels, guesthouses, farmhouses, inns and self-catering accommodation with four or more letting bedrooms to display in entrance halls the minimum and maximum prices charged for each category of room. This order complements the Voluntary Code of Booking Practice.

The tariffs quoted in the directory of this book may be affected by inflation, variations in the rate of VAT and many other factors. You should always ascertain the current prices before making a booking. Those given in this book have been provided by hoteliers in good faith and must be accepted as indications rather than firm quotations. Where information about 1994 prices is not given, you are requested to make enquiries direct. Prices quoted show minimum and maximum for one or two persons and include a full breakfast unless otherwise stated. Where a Continental breakfast is included in the price, this is stated in the directory. However, some prices may vary for the following reasons:

a) weekday/weekend terms offered

b) season of the year

c) if double room is used for single occupancy

d) dinner is normally charged for separately, but in some areas an inclusive dinner, bed and breakfast option may be offered at a cheaper rate.

Some hotels charge for bed, breakfast and dinner, whether dinner is taken or not. Many hotels, particularly in short-season holiday areas, accept booking only at full-board rate.

For main meals served in hotels, minimum and maximum table d'hote (set menu) prices are given. Where an a la carte menu is available, the price of a three-course dinner and lunch is shown. Where establishments offer both types of menu, table d'hote prices are the only ones shown, but the abbreviation (&alc) is used to indicate that an a la carte menu is also available.

VAT is payable, in the United Kingdom and in the Isle of Man, on both basic prices and any service. VAT does not apply in the Channel Islands. With this exception, prices quoted in this guide are inclusive of VAT and because of this will include service charge where applicable.

Symbols and Abbreviations
FRENCH AND GERMAN
(see bookmark for English)

	French		German
★	Classement des hôtels (voir p 25)	★	Hotelklassifikation (Siehe Seite 25)
⇧	Classement d'hôtels supplémentaire	⇧	Zusätzliche Hotelklassifizierung
○	Hôtels qui doivent ouvrir prochainement	○	Hotel wird während der Laufzeit dieses Führers eröffnet
⚐	Hôtel de Campagne	⚐	Landgut-Hotel
%	Pourcentage (voir p. 26)	%	Prozentsatz (Siehe Seite 26)
✿	Rosettes	✿	Rosetten

✳	prix 1993	✳	1993 Preise
☎	téléphone	☎	Telefon
⇌	salle de bain privée avec WC particulier	⇌	Privatbadezimmer mit eigenem WC
↯	Douche privée avec WC particulier	↯	Privatdusche mit eigenem WC
⊟	Lits à quatre montants	⊟	Himmelbett
®	Possibilité de faire le thé/le café dans les chambres	®	Tee/Kaffeemöglichkeiten im Zimmer
✕	Défense de garder des chiens pendant la nuit dans les chambres	✕	Hundeverbot im Zimmer während der Nacht
⊟	Ce symbole indique que l'hôtel offre des week-ends à prix réduit hors saison	⊟	Betrieb gibt Wochenendermässigung für Vor-und Nachsaison
(	Concierge de nuit	(	Nachtportier
⌸	Conditionnement d'air intégral	⌸	Klimaanlage überall
⌿	Chambres et/ou section de restaurant réservée(s) aux non-fumeurs	⌿	Zimmer bzw. Restaurantabschnitt für Nichtraucher
⛱	Satellite TV	⛱	Satellite TV
P	Stationnement à ciel ouvert pour voitures	P	Parken im Freien
🏠	Garage ou bien lieu de stationnement couvert	🏠	Garagen bzw. überdachtes Parken
⚑	Pas de stationnement sur place	⚑	Parken an Ortund Stelle
🚌	Les groupes en car ne seront pas admis	🚌	Reisebusgesellschaften nicht aufgenommen
✿	Jardin de plus de 0.20 ha	✿	Garten grösser als 0.20 ha
▣	Piscine à l'intérieur	▣	Hallenbad
⌒	Piscine à l'extérieur	⌒	Freibad
▶9▶18	Terrain de golf à 9 trous ou 18 trous	▶9▶18	Golfplatz mit 9 oder 18 Löchern
♀	Court(s) de tennis	♀	Tennisplatz (Plätze)
⌇	Pêche	⌇	Angeln
U	Ecuries d'équitation sur les lieux	U	Reitstall an Ort und Stelle
⚿	Facilités speciales pour enfants	⚿	Sonderdienstleistungen für Kinder
♫	disco, dance etc.	♫	Disco, Tanzen. usw
⚒	Categorie de cuisine. Si ce symbole ne figure pas, la cuisine est anglaise, écossaise, galloise ou l'Irlandaise, selon la région ou l'hôtel se trouve	⚒	Küche, wenn dieses Zeichen nicht aufgeführt wird, ist die Küche englisch, schottisch, walisisch oder irrisch, je nach der Gegend, wo das Hotel sich befindet
☕	Café le matin	☕	Kaffee vormittags
⚱	Thé l'après-midi	⚱	Nachmittagstee
alc	à la carte	alc	à la carte

sB&B	Chambre à un lit et petit déjeuner par personne et par nuit	sB&B	Ubernachtung in einem Einzelzimmer mit Frühstück pro Person
sB&B⇌	Chambre à un lit avec bain et WC particuliers, et petit déjeuner par personne et par nuit	sB&B⇌	Einzelzimmer mit Privatbad und WC und Frühstück pro Person pro Nacht
sB&B↯	Chambre à un lit avec douche privée et WC particulier et le petit déjeuner par personne la nuit	sB&B↯	Einzelzimmer mit Privatdusche und WC und Frühstück pro Person pro Nacht
dB&B	Chambre à deux lits (2 personnes à une chambre) avec petit déjeuner	dB&B	Doppelzimmer (2 Personen in einem Zimmer) mit Frühstück
dB&B⇌	Chambre à deux lits (2 personnes à une chambre) avec bain et WC particuliers, et petit déjeuner	dB&B⇌	Doppelzimmer (2 Personen in einem Zimmer) mit Privatbad und WC mit Frühstück
dB&B↯	Chambre à deux (deux personnes à une chambre) avec douche privée et WC particuliers et le petit déjeuner	dB&B↯	Doppelzimmer (2 Personen in einem Zimmer) mit Privatdusche und WC und Frühstück
Conf	Facilities de conférence disponibles	Conf	Tagungseinrichtungen vorhanden
CTV	TV en couleurs	CTV	Farbfernsehen
BH	Jours fériés	BH	Bankfeiertage
Etr	Pâques	Etr	Ostern
fb	Chambre de famille	fb	Familienzimmer
fr	à partir de	fr	von
Map	Repère du quadrillage de carte national	Map	Planquadratangabe
mdnt	Minuit	mdnt	Mitternacht
nc	Enfants pas admis, par ex. enfants audessous de ... ans pas admis	nc	Kinder nicht aufgenommen z.B. Kinder unter ... Jahren nicht aufgenommen
rm	Location de chambres dans le bâtiment principal	rm	Zimmeranzahl im Hauptgebäude
RS	Service limité	RS	Beschränkte Dienstleistungen
T	Téléphone dans la chambre, direct avec l'extérieur	T	Zimmertelefon mit Aussenverbindung über Telefonzentrale
TV	TV en noir et blanc	TV	Schwarzweissfernsehen
V	Menu végétarien offert	V	Vegetarische Kost vorhanden
£	Voir p. 41	£	Siehe Seite 41
xmas	Programme spécial de Noël pour les clients	xmas	Sonderweihnachtsprogramm für Gäste
→	Suite au verso	→	Fortsetzung siehe umseitig
▯	Carte de crédit	▯	Kreditkarte

Pour de plus amples renseignements sur les symboles, voir les pages 27–28

Für weitere Informationen über die Zeichen, siehe Seiten 27–28

Symbols and Abbreviations
ITALIAN AND SPANISH
(see bookmark for English)

	Italian		Spanish
★	Classificazione de gli alberghi (vedere p 25)	★	Hoteles a ser inaugurados (véase la pagina 25)
✡	Classificazione supplementare hotel AA	✡	Clasificación adicional de hoteles
O	Alberghi che saranno aperti durante il periodo di validità della guida	O	Hoteles a ser inaugur ados durante la vigencia de estaguía
⚑	Alberghi in dimore di campagne	⚑	Hoteles en casas de campo
%	Percentuale (vedere p 26)	%	Porcentaje (véase la página 26)
✿	Rosette	✿	Rosetas

✳	Prezzi dei 1993	✳	Precios de 1993
☏	Telefono	☏	Teléfono
⇋	Bagno e servizi privati	⇋	Baño y servicios en cada habitación
⌂	Doccia e servizi privati	⌂	Ducha y servicios en cada habitación
♒	Letti a quattro colonne	♒	Camas de columnas
®	Attrezzatura per fare il té o il caffé nelle camere	®	Facilidades para hacer el té o el café en las habitaciones
✗	E proibito tenere i cani nelle camere di notte	✗	Se prohibe hacer pasar la noche a los perros en las habitaciones del hotel
⌇	Questo simbolo indica che l'albergo offre fine settimana economici fuori stagione	⌇	Este simbolo indica que el hotel ofrece fines de semana económicos en l estación fuera de la temporada
(	Portiere notturno	(	Conserje nocturno
☰	Aria condizionata	☰	Aire acondicionado en todo establecimiento
⌘	Camere e/o zona di ristorante per non fumatori	⌘	Habitaciones y/o área del restaurante reservados para los no fumadores
⋈	Satellite TV	⋈	Satellite TV
P	Parcheggio macchine all'aperto	P	Aparcamiento descubierto
⚑	Garage o spazio coperto	⚑	Garaje o espacio cubierto
⚑	Vietato il pacheggio sul posto	⚑	Establecimiento sin aparcamiento
⚑	Non si accettano comitive in gita turistica	⚑	No se aceptan los grupos de viajeros en coches de linea
✿	Giardino di piú 0.20 ha	✿	Jardín de más de 0.20 ha
⌂	Piscina coperta	⌂	Piscina cubierta
⌂	Piscina scoperta	⌂	Piscina descubierta
▶9▶18	Campo da golf a 9 o 18 buche	▶9▶18	Campo de golf de 9 o 18 hoyos
♞	Campo(i) da tennis	♞	Campo(s) de tenis
J	Pesca	J	Pesca
∪	Scuola d'equitazionne sul posto	∪	Escuela hipica
⚘	Attrezzature speciali per i bambini	⚘	Facilidades especiales para los niños
♪	disco, danza etc	♪	Discoteca/baile
⚑	Tipo di cucina. Se manca questo simbolo, la cucina é inglese, scozzese, gallese o irlandese, a seconda di dove si trova l'albergo in oggetto	⚑	Tipo de cocina. Si no figura este simbolo, la cocina es inglés, escocés, galés o irlandés, según la ubicación del hotel
☕	Caffé mattutino	☕	Café de la mañana
⚑	Té pomeridiano	⚑	Té de la tarde
alc	Alla carta	alc	A la carta

sB&B	Prezzo di una camera singola con la colazione compresa (per notte)	sB&B	Precio por noche de una habitación individual con desayuno incluido
sB&B⇋	Prezzo di una camera singola con bagno e servizi e la colazione compresa (per notte)	sB&B⇋	Precio por noche de una habitación individual con bañoy servicios (desayuno incluido)
sB&B⌂	Prezzo di una camera singola con doccia e servizie colazione compresa (per notte)	sB&B⌂	Precio por noche de una habitación individual con duchay servicios (desayuno incluido)
dB&B	Prezzo di una camera doppia (2 persone per camera) con la colazione compresa	dB&B	Habitación para dos personas (compartiendo una habitación) con desayuno incluido
dB&B⇋	Prezzo di una camera doppia (2 persone per camera) con bagno e servizie colazione compresa	dB&B⇋	Habitación para dos personas (compartiendo una habitación) con bañoy servicios (desayuno incluido)
dB&B⌂	Prezzo di una camera doppia (2 persone per camera) con doccia e servizie colazione compresa	dB&B⌂	Habitación para dos personas (compartiendo una habitación) con duchay servicios (desayuno incluido)
Conf	Attrezzatura per conferenze	Conf	Facilidades para conferencias
CTV	Televisione a colori	CTV	Televisión de color
BH	Festività nazionale	BH	Dia festivo para los bancos y el comercio en general
Etr	Pasqua	Etr	Pascua de Resurrección
fb	Camera familiare	fb	Habitación familiar
fr	Da	fr	De
Map	Riferimento della cartina	Map	Referencia del mapa
mdnt	Mezzanotte	mdnt	Medianoche
nc	Proibito ai bambini. E sempio: nc sottoi .... anni	nc	Se prohibe la entrada a los niños, p.ej: nc de menos de ... años
rm	Numero di camere nell'edificio principale	rm	Número de habitaciones del edificio principal
RS	Servizio limitato	RS	Servicio limitado
T	Telefono in camera comunicante direttamente con l'esterno	T	Teléfono en la habitación, comunicando con el exterior
TV	Televisione in bianco e nero	TV	Televisión en blanco y negro
V	Si offrono pasti vegetariani	V	Se ofrecen comidas vegetarianas
£	Vedere p 41	£	Véase la página 41
xmas	Programma speciale di Natale per i clienti	xmas	Programa especial de Navidad para los huéspedes
→	La lista delle voci continua a tergo	→	La lista de simbolos continúa a la vuelta
▭	Carte di credito	▭	Tarjeta de crédito

Per ulteriori informazioni riguardanti la simbologie, vedere pp 27–28

Para más información sobe los símbolos, véase las páginas 27–28

Directory — Britain

Abberley — Aberdaron

ABBERLEY Hereford & Worcester Map **07** SO76

★★★ ✿ ♨ 78% **Elms**
WR6 6AT (on A443 between Worcester and Tenbury Wells)
☎Great Witley(0299) 896666 FAX (0299) 896804

This beautiful Queen Anne mansion is situated in acres of formal gardens. Built in 1710 by Gilbert White, a pupil of Sir Christopher Wren, it retains its original ornate plasterwork and fireplaces. Public rooms are spacious, elegant and comfortable. The Brooke Room restaurant with its ornate wooden fireplace is the setting for chef Michael Gaunt's menus. A typical meal might begin with a guinea fowl, chicken and spinach terrine with a tomato and basil coulis. Main courses could offer steak, kidney and mushroom pie, or the more delicate flavours of poached salmon scented with orange and saffron. General manager Cecilia Rydström and her team provide an excellent range of traditional services, performed with admirable warmth and professionalism.

16⇌🏠 Annexe9⇌🏠1🛏 CTV in all bedrooms T
✈ (ex guide dogs) ✱ sB&B⇌🏠£82-£105 dB&B⇌🏠£97-£150 🍴
(60P 1🅿 ✱ ♫ (hard) croquet putting *xmas*
♨ English & French V ♿ ⚏ ✱ Lunch £16-£22&alc Last dinner 9.30pm
CONF. Thtr 60 Class 28 Board 28 Del £128.50
Credit Cards [1] [2] [3] [4] [5]

★★ 65% **Manor Arms at Abberley**
WR6 6BN ☎Great Witley(0299) 896507

This 300-year-old inn is near the Norman church and the old smithy. Bedrooms, with exposed beams, are individually decorated and have a good range of modern facilities. Recently extended public areas include an attractive new restaurant, a small lounge with an inglenook fireplace and 2 popular bars.

7⇌Annexe3⇌ CTV in all bedrooms ® T ✱ sB&B⇌£30 dB&B⇌£40 🍴
40P ✱ ♫
V ♿ ⚏ ✱ Lunch £1.80-£15alc
Credit Cards [1] [3]

ABBOTSBURY Dorset Map **03** SY58

★★ 63% *Ilchester Arms*
9 Market St DT3 4JR ☎(0305) 871243

A 15th-century village centre inn of great character and charm. The atmosphere is relaxed and the 3 bars are cosy with oak beams and an open fire. In addition to the traditional dining room, there is a conservatory. The individually styled bedrooms are pretty and comfortable.

8⇌🏠 Annexe2⇌🏠(1fb)3🛏 CTV in all bedrooms ® T
40P
♨ English & Continental V ♿ ⚏ ✱ Last dinner 9pm
Credit Cards [1] [3]

ABBOT'S SALFORD Warwickshire Map **04** SP05

★★★ ✿ 75% **Salford Hall**
WR11 5UT (8m W of Stratford-upon Avon on A439) ☎Evesham(0386) 871300 FAX (0386) 871301

Closed 24 Dec-31 Dec

Parts of this beautifully preserved manor house date back to the 15th century and it provides comfortable and welcoming public areas which are nicely furnished and retain much of their character. Most of the bedrooms are in the converted coach house and styles vary considerably, but all have good quality furnishings and modern equipment. A good and varied selection of dishes is offered in the dining room on a carte and fixed price menu.

14⇌🏠 Annexe19⇌🏠8🛏 CTV in all bedrooms ® T
✈ (ex guide dogs) ✱ sB&B⇌🏠£75-£120 dB&B⇌🏠£85-£120 🍴
51P 🚗 ✱ ♫ (hard) snooker sauna solarium croquet
V ♿ ⚏ ✱ Lunch £14.95 Dinner £22.50 Last dinner 10pm
CONF. Thtr 50 Class 35 Board 30 Del from £85
Credit Cards [1] [2] [3] [5]   £

ABERDARON Gwynedd Map **06** SH12

★★ 60% *Ty Newydd*
LL53 8BE ☎(075886) 207

Closed Dec-Feb

Ty Newydd (new house) is superbly situated in this beautiful village, with direct access to the beach and a terrace with lovely sea views. Bedrooms are modest but well decorated. The busy bar provides a good selection of meals all day and there is a comfortable residents' lounge.

17rm(8⇌1🏠)(3fb) CTV in 12 bedrooms TV in 5 bedrooms ®
✈ (ex guide dogs)
CTV
♨ Mainly grills V ♿
Credit Cards [1] [3]

Remember to book early for holiday and bank holiday times.

Abberley Village, Worcestershire WR6 6BN
Telephone: (0299) 896507

Discover our delightful old beamed village inn with superior accommodation, all en suite, restaurant and bars. Nestling in the Abberley Hills within the glorious Worcestershire countryside, yet conveniently situated for Worcester, Stourport, Kidderminster, the Cotswolds, Malvern Hills, Birmingham and the NEC. For business or leisure always a warm welcome and personal service for everyone. Family owned and run.

Aberdeen - Aberdeen Airport

ABERDEEN Grampian *Aberdeenshire* Map **15** NJ90

See also **Aberdeen Airport** & **Westhill**

★★★★ 68% Ardoe House
Blairs, South Deeside Rd AB1 5YP (4m W off
B9077) ☎(0224) 867355 FAX (0224) 861283

Set in extensive parkland, this converted baronial mansion retains its splendid Victorian woodwork in the comfortable public rooms. A new wing has added 52 spacious and attractively furnished bedrooms to the older rooms.

71⇨ℕ(3fb)1⌂ℕin 15 bedrooms CTV in all bedrooms ® T
sB⇨ℕ£55-£112 dB⇨ℕ£55-£117 (room only) 🅿
Lift (200P ❉ putting petanque croquet *xmas*
♥ International V ᵛ ℒ Lunch £9.50-£20 Dinner £27&alc Last dinner 9.30pm
CONF. Thtr 200 Class 100 Board 60 Del from £95
Credit Cards [1][2][3][5]

★★★★ 64% Holiday Inn Crowne Plaza
Oldmeldrum Rd, Bucksburn AB9 2LN (3m N
A947) ☎(0224) 713911 FAX (0224) 714020

144⇨ℕ(32fb)⌘in 45 bedrooms CTV in all bedrooms ®❷ T ✱
sB⇨ℕ£79.90-£99.83 dB⇨ℕ£89.30-£111.63 (room only) 🅿
Lift (150P 45🅿 ⌭ (heated) sauna solarium gymnasium steam room *xmas*
V ᵛ ℒ ⌘ ✱ Lunch £8.95&alc Dinner £17.25&alc Last dinner 9.30pm
Credit Cards [1][2][3][5]

★★★★ 54% Skean Dhu Altens
Souter Head Rd, Altens AB1 4LF (3m S off
A956) ☎(0224) 877000 FAX (0224) 896964
RS Xmas wk

Situated beside an industrial estate, this modern purpose-built hotel caters largely for business guests. Public areas have been renovated to a good modern standard and offer a choice of restaurants. Accommodation is available in deluxe and studio rooms, which are somewhat dated in style. Staff are friendly and willing to please, but at the time of our visit service lacked polish.

221⇨ℕ(70fb)⌘in 35 bedrooms CTV in all bedrooms ® T ✱
sB⇨ℕ£83-£95 dB⇨ℕ£93-£105 (room only) 🅿
Lift (⌭ 300P ❉ ⌭ (heated) *xmas*
♥ International V ᵛ ℒ ✱ Lunch £8.35-£13.75 Dinner £13.75-£16.50 Last dinner 10.45pm
CONF. Thtr 380 Class 250 Board 100 Del from £63
Credit Cards [1][2][3][5]

★★★ 68% The Copthorne
122 Huntly St AB1 1SU (W of city centre)
☎(0224) 630404 FAX (0224) 640573

A former warehouse has been converted to create this popular hotel. Best rooms are the stylish Connoisseur rooms; Classic rooms have been cosmetically improved, but first floor rooms remain in need of refurbishment. Public areas include a bright modern foyer with a semi open-plan lounge, a bar and a restaurant.

89⇨ℕ⌘in 12 bedrooms CTV in all bedrooms ®❷ T ✱
sB⇨ℕ£99.50-£109.50 dB⇨ℕ£109.50-£119.50 (room only) 🅿
Lift (20🅿 ♪ *xmas*
♥ Scottish & French V ᵛ ℒ ✱ Lunch £15-£30alc Dinner fr£15&alc Last dinner 10pm
Credit Cards [1][2][3][4][5] £

★★★ 66% The Craighaar
Waterton Rd, Bucksburn AB2 9HS (NW near the airport)
☎(0224) 712275 FAX (0224) 716302

Within a short drive of both the airport and city centre, this efficiently run hotel is popular with business people. Comfortable public areas include a panelled bar, a conservatory lounge and formal restaurant. Less formal meals are available in the Donside Room. Bedrooms are modern in style, though they do vary in size.

53⇨ℕ(15fb) CTV in all bedrooms ®❷ T
(CTV 100P ⌭
♥ Scottish & French V ᵛ ℒ Last dinner 9.30pm
Credit Cards [1][2][3][5]

★★★ 64% Caledonian Thistle
10 Union Ter AB9 1HE (near Union Terrace
Gardens) ☎(0224) 640233 FAX (0224) 641627

In the heart of the city, this long established hotel is especially popular with business people. Lounge facilities are limited, but a Continental-style café bar serves as a meeting place and an informal alternative to the main restaurant and cocktail bar. Bedrooms are modern and well equipped.

80⇨ℕ(4fb)1⌂ℕin 12 bedrooms CTV in all bedrooms ® T ✱
sB⇨ℕ£91-£98 dB⇨ℕ£115-£127 (room only) 🅿
Lift (25P sauna ♪ *xmas*
♥ International V ᵛ ℒ ⌘ ✱ Lunch £9.95-£11.95&alc Dinner £19.50&alc Last dinner 10pm
CONF. Thtr 45 Class 15 Board 25 Del from £72
Credit Cards [1][2][3][4][5]

Travel Inn
Murcar, Bridge of Don AB2 8BP (on A92, close to Aberdeen Exhibition Centre) ☎(0224) 821217

Purpose-built accommodation offers spacious and well equipped bedrooms, all with en suite bathrooms. Meals may be taken at the nearby family restaurant and pub. For more details about Travel Inns, consult the Contents page, under Hotel Groups.

40⇨ℕ✱ B⇨ℕ£33.70 (room only)

○ **The Marcliffe at Pitfodels**
North Deeside Rd AB1 9PN ☎(0224) 861000
Due to open Nov 1993
44⇨ℕ

ABERDEEN AIRPORT Grampian *Aberdeenshire*
Map **15** NJ81

See also **Aberdeen**

★★★★ 53% Skean Dhu
Argyll Rd AB2 0DU (adjacent to main entrance 1m N of A96) ☎Aberdeen(0224) 725252 FAX (0224) 723745

We understand that refurbishment is in the pipeline for this purpose-built hotel, which should improve the rather dated, though spacious foyer lounge and bedrooms which are starting to show their age. Accommodation ranges from compact studio rooms to spacious deluxe rooms. As well as an à la carte restaurant, food is available in the bar.

148⇨ℕ(6fb)⌘in 15 bedrooms CTV in all bedrooms ® T ✱
sB⇨ℕ£83-£93 dB⇨ℕ£93-£105 (room only) 🅿
(⌭ 450P ❉ ⌭ (heated) *xmas*
♥ Scottish & French V ᵛ ℒ ⌘ ✱ Lunch £12.50-£13.50&alc Dinner £17.50-£18.50&alc Last dinner 9.45pm
CONF. Thtr 600 Class 300 Board 80 Del from £90
Credit Cards [1][2][3][5] £

Marriott
Riverview Dr, Farburn AB2 0AZ (on A947)
☎Aberdeen(0224) 770011 FAX (0224) 722347

A large and busy hotel, which is ideal for the business and leisure traveller, offering a wide range of services, a choice of eating options and indoor leisure facilities. Bedrooms are comfortable and equipped with modern facilities. For more details about Marriott hotels, consult the Contents page, under Hotel Groups.

154⇨ℕ✱ dB⇨ℕfr£110 (room only)
CONF. Thtr 400 Class 200 Board 20 Del £120

ABERDOUR Fife Map 11 NT18

★★ 67% **Woodside**
High St KY3 0SW (E of Forth Road Bridge, across rbt into town, hotel on left after garage) ☎(0383) 860328 FAX (0383) 860920
This family owned and run village-centre hotel dates from 1873 and, though it has been modernised, retains such period features as the fine stained glass and wood panelling in the Clipper Bar. Bedrooms vary in size but are all well equipped; staff are friendly.
21⇨♠3♫ CTV in all bedrooms ® T ✱ sB&B⇨♠£53 dB&B⇨♠£53-£59.50
(40P sauna *xmas*
☼ Scottish, French & Chinese V ♡ ⌑ ⌔ Lunch £10-£12&alc
High tea fr£5 Dinner fr£17.50&alc Last dinner 9.30pm
CONF. Thtr 50 Class 40 Board 25 Del from £87.70
Credit Cards [1][2][3][5]
See advertisement in colour section

ABERDOVEY Gwynedd Map 06 SN69

★★★ 67% **Trefeddian**
LL35 0SB (1m outside town beside A493) ☎(0654) 767213 FAX (0654) 767777
Closed 29 Dec-17 Mar
Set in an elevated position, this large and popular privately-owned hotel provides an extensive range of indoor and outdoor activities for adults and children, including accompanied trips in the hotel's own speedboat. Spacious lounges with sea views invite quiet relaxation. Modern bedrooms vary in size, some being very spacious, and many look across the golf course to Cardigan Bay.
46⇨♠(4fb) CTV in all bedrooms T ✱ sB&B⇨♠£27-£50 dB&B⇨♠£54-£100 (incl dinner) ⌸
Lift CTV 50P 18☂ (£2.00 per night) ⌘ ❋ ▨ (heated) ♪ (hard) snooker solarium pool table table tennis pitch & putt ⚘ *xmas*

Aberdour - Aberdovey

Westhill Hotel

AA ★★★

Ideally situated on the A944 in pleasant suburban surroundings, Westhill Hotel leads the way in conferences, business and pleasure.

Only 6 miles from central Aberdeen, it is in an excellent position for touring Royal Deeside and the North East of Scotland.

Dine in "Castles" Restaurant or enjoy a superb supper in the "Tam O'Shanter" Lounge.

Westhill Hotel — meets all your requirements.

For reservations contact
Westhill Hotel, Westhill, Aberdeen AB32 6TT
Tel: (0224) 740388 Fax: (0224) 744354

See gazetteer listing under Westhill

'You are not just a number here'

The Udny Arms Hotel
Newburgh ★ ★ ⚜

Main Street, Newburgh, Ellon
Aberdeenshire AB41 0BL

This popular award winning family run hotel which is only 15 miles from the centre of Aberdeen offers 26 en-suite bedrooms some with beautiful views over the Ythan Estuary and golf course. You can choose from three restaurants – Fine Dining, Seafood and Bistro food, and Home Cooking in the Cafe Bar. The original Sticky Toffee Pudding Place.
For more information
Telephone 03586 89244   Fax 03586 89012

★★★AA

CALEDONIAN
THISTLE HOTEL

Union Terrace, Aberdeen AB9 1HE
Tel: 0224 640233   Fax: 0224 641627

Your choice in
Aberdeen

For Reservations at over 100
Mount Charlotte Thistle Hotels
Telephone London: 071 937 8033.

THISTLE HOTELS

Aberdovey - Aberfeldy

♀ English & French V ♡ ♫ ✱ Lunch £7.50-£8.50 Dinner £15.50 Last dinner 8.45pm
Credit Cards [1][3]

★★★ 🏆 65% Plas Penhelig Country House
LL35 0NA (Welsh Rarebits) ☎(0654) 767676 FAX (0654) 767783
Closed Jan & Feb

A delightful Edwardian country house set in 14 acres of grounds and gardens, with fine views of the Dovey estuary, Plas Penhelig is personally run with friendly informality and provides comfortable accommodation and a relaxing atmosphere. Public rooms feature oak panelling, stained glass windows and log fires, while facilities include a tennis court, croquet lawn and putting green.

12⇌♤(3fb) CTV in all bedrooms ® T ✕ sB&B⇌♤£49-£60 dB&B⇌♤£76-£108 (incl dinner) 🍽
48P ⇌ ♕ ♬ (hard) croquet putting
♀ English & French V ♡ ♫ ✱ Lunch £7.50-£10 Dinner fr£16.25 Last dinner 8.45pm
CONF. Thtr 40 Class 20 Board 22 Del from £58
Credit Cards [1][3]

★★ 🏆 71% Penhelig Arms Hotel & Restaurant
LL35 0LT ☎(0654) 767215 FAX (0654) 767690
Closed 25 & 26 Dec

This delightful hotel, dating back some 200 years and offering views of the Dovey estuary, is continually being upgraded, and recent work makes better use of available space in some of the bedrooms. Public areas include an old-world bar, a quiet and comfortable sitting room, and a cottage-style dining room where the good-value fixed-price menu is changed seasonally and features local fish and seafood.

10⇌♤ CTV in all bedrooms ® T sB&B⇌♤fr£34 dB&B⇌♤£68-£82 🍽
12P ⇌
V ♡ ♫ Sunday Lunch fr£11.50&alc Dinner fr£17.50 Last dinner 9.30pm
Credit Cards [1][3]

★★ 66% Harbour
LL35 0EB (on the A493 coastal road between Dolgellau & Machynlleth) ☎(0654) 767250 & 767792 FAX (0654) 767418
RS Nov-Mar

This very friendly owner-run hotel near the harbour and overlooking the estuary has pretty bedrooms of varying size. There is a very comfortable lounge and bar, while eating options range from an all-day coffee bar, a wine bar serving bistro style dishes to the restaurant offering a choice of menus.

10⇌♤(4fb)✎in 3 bedrooms CTV in all bedrooms ® sB&B⇌♤£50-£60 dB&B⇌♤£65-£85
CTV ✎
♀ English & French V ♡ ♫ ✱ Lunch £6-£12alc High tea £3-£12alc Dinner £11-£14&alc Last dinner 9pm
Credit Cards [1][2][3][5]

★ 🏆 69% Maybank Hotel & Restaurant
4 Penhelig Rd, Penhelig LL35 0PT ☎(0654) 767500
Closed 2 Jan-10 Feb RS 2 Nov-15 Dec

This delightful small hotel run by Elizabeth Dinsdale and Paul Massey is on the edge of a beautiful village and some bedrooms have fine estuary views. At the inspection visit, Elizabeth Dinsdale's fixed price dinner began enjoyably with chicken livers fried with bacon and mushrooms, continued with an excellent poached sea bass with vermouth and cream sauce and ended with a very rich bread and butter pudding.

5rm(4⇌) CTV in all bedrooms ® sB&B♤£24.95-£29.95 dB&B♤£39.90-£49.90
CTV ✎ ⇌ ✱ xmas
♀ English, Continental & Far Eastern V ♡ Dinner £16.95-£19.95 Last dinner 8.30pm
Credit Cards [1][3]

ABERFELDY Tayside *Perthshire* Map **14** NN84

★★ 🏆 🏆 🏆
FARLEYER HOUSE
PH15 2JE (W on B846 beyond Castle Menzies)
☎(0887) 820332 FAX (0887) 829430

It is hard to believe that this delightful hotel in 70 acres of parkland started out as a simple croft in the 16th-century. Later enlarged to be the main residence of the head of the clan Menzies, it is now owned by Derek Reid, and is suitably furnished for a Highland mansion, with fine antiques, paintings and lots of fresh flowers. All the rooms are in keeping, but there are modern comforts too. Farleyer House is highly regarded for the excellent 5-course dinners served in the elegant dining room. Local game, deer and fish are often featured: starters might include salad of wood pigeon and mountain hare; and for main course perhaps Angus beef with caramelised shallots, or a ragout of turbot and west coast scallops; then a platter of Scottish cheeses and a selection of sweets such as Grand Marnier soufflé or mint and chocolate mousse. A convivial new bistro provides an alternative.

11rm(9⇌♤)(2fb)✎in 2 bedrooms CTV in all bedrooms T ✕ (ex guide dogs) sB&B⇌♤£60-£80 dB&B⇌♤£70-£100
CTV 20P ⇌ ♕ rough shooting ♬ xmas
V ♡ ♫ ✱ Lunch £10-£20alc High tea £10-£20alc Dinner £23-£29alc Last dinner 8.30pm
Credit Cards [1][2][3][5] £

★★ 63% The Weem
Weem PH15 2LD (1m NW B846) ☎(0887) 820381 FAX (0887) 820187

An historic roadside inn with a friendly informal atmosphere, offering bright functional bedrooms and a good choice of meals in the little bar or attractive dining room.

12⇌♤(4fb)✎in 4 bedrooms CTV in all bedrooms ® T ✱ sB&B⇌♤£15-£35 dB&B⇌♤£25-£60 🍽
20P ⇌ ♬ shooting loch fishing xmas
♀ European V ♡ ♫ ✱ Lunch £8-£15&alc Dinner £14-£18&alc Last dinner 8.30pm
Credit Cards [1][3]

★ 🏆 🏆 73% Guinach House
'By The Birks', Urlar Rd PH15 2ET (access off A826 Crieff rd) ☎(0887) 820251

Enthusiastically run by Bert and Marian Mackay, this delightful small hotel, in its own grounds on the edge of town, provides thoughtfully equipped bedrooms, a cosy lounge (there is no bar) and a dining room where the 4-course dinners reflect Bert's love of cooking and experience as an international master chef. The choice of dishes might include a starter of lambs kidney and local cèpes in a port wine sauce, followed by home-made soup and a main course of 'roast pavée of pork set on a garden plum and ginger jus'.

7⇌♤ CTV in all bedrooms ® ✱ sB&B⇌♤fr£35 dB&B⇌♤fr£70
12P ⇌ ♕ xmas
♀ British, French & Italian V ♡ ♫ ✱ Lunch £5-£15 Dinner £18.50 Last dinner 9.30pm
Credit Cards [1][3]

Aberfoyle - Abergavenny

ABERFOYLE Central *Perthshire* Map 11 NN50

★★**62%** Altskeith
Kinlochard FK8 3TL (4m W beside Loch Ard)
☎Kinlochard(08777) 266 FAX (08777) 223
This small family-run hotel, offering friendly and informal service, is only separated from Loch Ard by a narrow road. Bedrooms are comfortable, with quality coordinated fabrics. The fact that there are only 4 rooms now does not diminish the hotel's status, but the loss of the residents' lounge is a pity.
6⇨♠(1fb)⊁in all bedrooms CTV in all bedrooms ® T
✕ (ex guide dogs) sB&B⇨♠£29.50-£37.50 dB&B⇨♠£45-£66
🍴

20P 🚗 ❋ ♪ boats for hire shooting *xmas*
V ♡ 🍽 ⊁ ✻ Bar Lunch £3.99-£7 Dinner £12.50-£19.90&alc
Last dinner 8.30pm
Credit Cards [1][2][3] £

ABERGAVENNY Gwent Map 03 SO21

★★★❀**70%** *Llansantffraed Court*
Llanvihangel Gobion NP7 9BA (on A4598) (Welsh Rarebits) ☎Llanvihangel Gobion(0873) 840678
This impressive country house is set in open countryside, with fine views from most windows and welcoming open fires in the public rooms. Bedrooms are fitted with solid dark furniture and mini bars. There is a daily changing fixed price menu based on fresh produce, and chef Giovanni Telles is hard working and imaginative.
21⇨♠ CTV in all bedrooms

★★★**57%** *The Angel*
Cross St NP7 5EW ☎(0873) 857121 FAX (0873) 858059   FORTE Heritage

Dating from the 17th century, this friendly hotel in the town centre has a popular bar and restaurant. Bedroom refurbishment has ➡

Plas Penhelig
Country House Hotel & Restaurant

Aberdovey, Gwynedd LL35 0NA
Telephone: (0654) 767676
Fax: 0654 767783

An award winning country house situated by the sea with delightful views over the Dovey Estuary. Built in 1909, the hotel stands in seven acres of grounds including a beautiful walled kitchen garden, nine hole putting green and croquet lawn. Guests can indulge in an assortment of activities or visit the many places of interest in the vicinity. The beautiful house, with its oak-panelled entrance hall, stained glass windows and oak staircase, has been well developed by the Richardson family into a beautifully appointed hotel. An ideal venue for small wedding receptions, conferences and private parties. The fruit, vegetables and salads are provided by the hotel's gardens with local meat, game and fish all used.

Please write or call for brochure.

AA ★★★   Welsh Tourist Board Commended
             ♛♛♛♛

"THE WEEM" ★★
by Aberfeldy, Perthshire PH15 2LD
Tel: 0887 820381   Fax: 0887 820187

Nestling under the spectacular Weem Rock in glorious Breadalbane, you will find this tradtional yet fully refurbished 17th century country inn providing the ideal base for a superb holiday in the very heart of Scotland. With the widest selection of excellent golf courses, game fishing, shooting and stalking not to mention water sports, trekking, superb walking, the active will never have a dull moment! For those who prefer a more leisurely time . . . we have some of the finest scenery in the world.

Meanwhile back at "THE WEEM"
you will find comfort, excellent cuisine and a unique atmosphere. You will be pampered and guaranteed many a lighthearted moment . . . "The Weem" breeds contentment and laughter.

TREFEDDIAN HOTEL
Aberdovey, (Aberdyfi).
Wales LL35 0SB
Tel: 0654 767213. Fax: 0654 767777

Family Owned/Managed 3 Star Country Hotel. Close to sea in Snowdonia National Park. Views of Sand Dunes, Beaches, Cardigan Bay, and Aberdovey Championship Golf Links. Bedrooms en-suite, some balcony, lift. Indoor swimming pool, tennis, snooker. Children's playroom. 'A family hotel.' Ideal base for touring North/Mid-Wales. 1/2m. north of Aberdovey village.
Telephone for full colour brochure.

Abergavenny - Abersoch

provided some bright new rooms with quality furnishings while the remainder were due for upgrading to similar high standards of comfort.
29⇨ⁿ(2fb)1⌀⌀in 6 bedrooms CTV in all bedrooms ® T ✱ (room only) ₧
《 35P *xmas*
V ✿ ⌀ ⌀ Lunch £8.95-£10.95 Dinner £15.95&alc Last dinner 9.30pm
Credit Cards ①②③⑤

★★ ✹70%Llanwenarth Arms
Brecon Rd NP8 1EP (on A40 midway between Abergavenny and Crickhowell beside River Usk)
☎Crickhowell(0873) 810550 FAX (0873) 811880

D'Arcy and Angela McGregor's welcoming hotel overlooking the River Usk partly dates to the 16th century. Comfortable modern bedrooms in an adjacent wing give lovely river or mountain views and the bars and attractive restaurant both offer good-value food. Game, salmon and trout often feature, along with good home-made soups, terrines and pies. A meal here might consist of light butterfly prawns in a piquant Chinese sauce, followed by pheasant wrapped in bacon and served with a port wine sauce, then local farmhouse dairy ice cream or D'Arcy's famous waffles with maple syrup.
18⇨ⁿ CTV in all bedrooms ® T ✖ sB&B⇨ⁿ£49 dB&B⇨ⁿ£59 ₧
60P ⌀ ♩
♀ International V ✿ Lunch £9-£19alc Dinner £9-£19alc Last dinner 9.30pm
Credit Cards ①②③⑤

ABERGELEClwyd Map **06** SH97

★★ 63%Kinmel Manor
St Georges Rd LL22 9AS (at Abergele exit on A55)
☎(0745) 832014 FAX (0745) 832014

This well run residential and conference hotel stands in its own grounds. Bedrooms are spacious and well furnished, but many are now showing their age. A recently introduced bistro bar serving good-value, substantial meals has extended the range of food available. The main restaurant, with its magnificent wooden fireplace, offers traditional menus.
42⇨ⁿ(3fb) CTV in all bedrooms ® T ✱ sB&B⇨ⁿ£48 dB&B⇨ⁿ£66 ₧
120P ✿ ⌀ (heated) sauna solarium gymnasium spa bath steam room *xmas*
♀ English & French V ✿ ⌀ ⌀ Lunch £9.50&alc High tea £4.50-£6.50 Dinner £14&alc Last dinner 9.30pm
CONF. Thtr 250 Class 100 Board 70 Del £59.50
Credit Cards ①②③④⑤

ABERLADYLothian *East Lothian* Map **12** NT47

★★ 65%Kilspindie House
Main St EH32 0RE (on A198) ☎(08757) 682 due to change to (0875) 870682 FAX (08757) 504 due to change to (0875) 870504

A loyal following of golfers and business guests has been built up over 26 years by the Binnie family at their popular village hotel. A golfing theme characterises the décor of the bars; there is an attractive dining room, a cosy lounge and comfortable bedrooms.
26⇨1⌀ CTV in all bedrooms ® T sB&B⇨ⁿ£36-£45 dB&B⇨ⁿ£64-£68 ₧
CTV 30P ⌀
V ✿ ⌀ Sunday Lunch fr£9.50 High tea £6.50-£11 Dinner fr£13 Last dinner 9pm
Credit Cards ①③

Remember to book early for holiday
and bank holiday times.

ABERLOUR
See **Archiestown**

ABERPORTHDyfed Map **02** SN25

★★★ 64%Hotel Penrallt
SA43 2BS ☎(0239) 810227 FAX (0239) 811375
Closed 23-31 Dec

Set in 42 acres of pleasant parkland, this family-run hotel provides good leisure facilities. Bedrooms are spacious and comfortably furnished, and there is an attractive panelled restaurant and relaxing lounge and bars.
16⇨ⁿ(2fb) CTV in all bedrooms ® T ✱ sB&B⇨ⁿfr£48 dB&B⇨ⁿfr£75 ₧
CTV 100P ⌀ ✿ ⌀ (heated) ♃ (hard) sauna solarium gymnasium ⌀
✿ ⌀ ✱ Sunday Lunch fr£9.50 Dinner fr£15&alc Last dinner 9pm
Credit Cards ①②③⑤

★★ 68%Penbontbren Farm
Glynarthen SA44 6PE (3.5m SE off A487) (Welsh Rarebits)
☎(0239) 810248 FAX (0239) 811129
Closed 24-28 Dec

This very comfortable small hotel is run by the hospitable Humphreys family and friendly local staff. Attractive pine-furnished bedrooms are all in converted outbuildings, with a spacious lounge, restaurant and bar in the central complex.
Annexe10⇨ⁿ(6fb) CTV in all bedrooms ® T sB&B⇨ⁿ£33-£38 dB&B⇨ⁿ£58-£64 ₧
35P ⌀ ✿ ♩ *xmas*
V ✿ ⌀ ⌀ Dinner £12-£16alc Last dinner 8.15pm
CONF. Thtr 30 Class 25 Board 25 Del from £55.50
Credit Cards ①③

★★ 58%Highcliffe
SA43 2DA (off B4333) ☎(0239) 810534 FAX (0239) 810534

This family-run holiday hotel is situated above the town, a short walk from its sandy beaches. There are 2 traditional lounges for residents, and a wide choice of food is available both in the cosy bar and the restaurant. Bedrooms all have modern facilities.
9rm(6⇨1ⁿ)Annexe6⇨ⁿ(4fb) CTV in all bedrooms ® T sB&B⇨ⁿ£36 dB&B⇨ⁿ£55 ₧
CTV 18P sauna solarium gymnasium *xmas*
♀ International V ✿ ⌀ ⌀ ✱ Bar Lunch £2-£20&alc Dinner £14-£25&alc Last dinner 8.30pm
Credit Cards ①②③⑤

★ 73%Glandwr Manor
Tresaith SA43 2JH (turn off B4333 towards Tresaith, hotel in 1.25m on right) ☎(0239) 810197
Closed Nov-Feb

The Davis family offer warm hospitality at this small hotel set in pleasant grounds at Tresaith. Bedrooms are neat and cosy, and there are several lounges with log fires and an attractive restaurant offering set and à la carte menus.
7rm(2⇨3ⁿ)(2fb) ® ✖ sB&B£22-£26 sB&B⇨ⁿ£23-£27 dB&B£44-£52 dB&B⇨ⁿ£46-£54
CTV 14P ⌀ ✿
✿ ⌀ ⌀ Dinner £10-£11&alc Last dinner 8.30pm

ABERSOCHGwynedd Map **06** SH32

★★★ ⌀ 65%Porth Tocyn
Bwlch Tocyn LL53 7BU ☎(0758) 713303 FAX (0758) 713538
Closed mid Nov-wk before Etr

This delightfully situated hotel stands in 25 acres of farmland with superb views over Cardigan Bay. Owned by the same family since the 1940s it offers a relaxing informal atmosphere in the excellent

Abersoch - Aberystwyth

lounges and dining room. The cuisine has a good reputation and bedrooms are attractively furnished.
17rm(1fb) CTV in all bedrooms T sB&B⇨₤44.50-₤57 dB&B⇨₤70-₤105 ₽
CTV 50P ⚙ ❋ ⌬ (heated) ♀ (hard) windsurfing ⚓
♥ ♨ Sunday Lunch £14 High tea £3-£6 Dinner £17.50-£23 Last dinner 9.30pm
Credit Cards [1]

★★★ 64% Riverside
LL53 7HW ☎(0758) 712419 FAX (0758) 712671
Closed Dec-Feb
This family-run hotel stands beside the River Soch, its pleasant lawns providing a pleasant setting for cream teas on summer days. Bedrooms are prettily furnished, an open-plan bar overlooks the yachting harbour, and a pine-furnished restaurant serves a good value 4-course dinner.
12rm(4fb) CTV in all bedrooms ® T ✲ (ex guide dogs) ❋ sB&B⇨₤30-₤45 dB&B⇨₤60-₤80 ₽
25P ⚙ ❋ ⌬ (heated) sailing windsurfing ⚓
♥ European ♨ ♪ ♫ Bar Lunch ₤2.50-₤10 High tea ₤4.75-₤8 Dinner ₤15.95-₤21 Last dinner 9pm
Credit Cards [1][2][3][5]

★★ 63% Abersoch Harbour
LL53 7HR ☎(0758) 712406
RS Jan & Feb
This hotel with pretty lawns is in an elevated position overlooking the harbour. Bedrooms are mostly on the small side, but attractive decor more than compensate. The 4-poster room has its own balcony and lovely views. Lounges are particularly relaxing with deep sofas and armchairs. The main restaurant has its own small bar, and a bistro bar is very popular for its reasonably priced food.
9rm Annexe5rm(2fb)1⌧ CTV in all bedrooms ® T ✲ (ex guide dogs) ❋ sB&B⇨₤32-₤40 dB&B⇨₤64-₤80 ₽
50P xmas
♥ English & French V ♨ ♪ ❋ Lunch ₤10-₤15 Dinner ₤14.50-₤16.50 Last dinner 10pm
Credit Cards [1][3]

★★ 76% Neigwl
Lon Sarn Bach LL53 7DY (on A499) ☎(0758) 712363
Genuine, warm hospitality is extended to guests at a delightful little hotel pervaded by a feeling of relaxed well-being. Many of the bedrooms – with their glorious views of St Tudwal's Island and Cardigan Bay – have now been furnished with modern pine units and attractive fabrics, and there is a family suite. A small lounge for games or reading, a comfortable lounge bar and a pleasant restaurant (where good meals are served from a regularly changed menu) make up the public areas.
7rm(1⇨4⇨) Annexe2rm(2fb) CTV in all bedrooms ® ✲ (ex guide dogs) sB&Bfr₤36 sB&B⇨fr₤36 dB&Bfr₤60 dB&B⇨fr₤60 ₽
30P ⚙ ❋ ⚓ xmas
♥ ♨ Lunch fr₤10.50 Dinner fr₤16 Last dinner 8.30pm
Credit Cards [1][3][5]

★★ 70% Tudor House
Lon Sarn Bach LL53 7EB ☎(0758) 713354 FAX (0758) 713454
A warm and friendly welcome awaits guests at this small, privately owned hotel, provided by a small team of staff headed by Jennifer Jones and Jack Courtney. The bedrooms are modern and attractive, and there is a cosy lounge bar where guests can study the varied menu which includes local fish and seafood. The hotel is close to the town centre, beach and harbour.
8rm(5⇨2⇨)(1fb) CTV in all bedrooms ® sB&B⇨₤29.50-₤40 dB&B⇨₤45-₤60 ₽
CTV 14P ❋ xmas
♥ European V ♨ ♪ ❋ Lunch ₤3.50-₤9.50 High tea ₤5 Dinner ₤9.50-₤15 Last dinner 9.30pm
Credit Cards [1][3][5]

★★ 64% White House
LL53 7AG (on A449 from Pwllheli hotel is just before entering Abersoch village) ☎(0758) 713427 FAX (0758) 713512
The White House overlooks the yacht harbour and has superb views over Cardigan Bay and St Tudwals Island. It is set back off the A499 on the approach to the village and has ample car parking. Bedroom facilities are constantly being improved, and comfortable chairs and beds are standard throughout the hotel. There are 2 bars and a comfortable coffee lounge; and as well as the main restaurant, where à la carte and table d'hôte menus are available, there is a brasserie with reasonably priced meals.
10rm(1fb) CTV in all bedrooms ® T ✲ sB&B⇨₤26.50-₤36.50 dB&B⇨₤53-₤63 ₽
100P ❋
♥ ♨ ✱ Bar Lunch ₤5.50-₤16.50alc Dinner fr₤15.50&alc Last dinner 9.30pm
Credit Cards [1][3]

★★ 62% Deucoch
LL53 7LD ☎(0758) 712680
This friendly little hotel commands excellent views over Cardigan Bay from its setting just outside the village. There is a two-part lounge for residents, the bar has recently been extended by the addition of a conservatory, and bedrooms are both neat and bright. Both restaurant and bar meals attract a local clientele, and a small children's play area contributes to its popularity.
10rm(3⇨6⇨)(2fb) CTV in all bedrooms ® ✲ sB&B⇨₤22-₤26 sB&B⇨₤22-₤26 dB&B⇨₤44-₤52 dB&B⇨₤44-₤52 ₽
CTV 30P ❋ xmas
♥ ♨ ✱ Bar Lunch ₤3.50-₤7 Dinner ₤12-₤13 Last dinner 8pm
Credit Cards [1][3]

ABERYSTWYTH Dyfed Map 06 SN58

★★★ ⚘❋ 66% Conrah
Ffosrhydygaled, Chancery SY23 4DF (on A487, 3.5m S) (Welsh Rarebits) ☎(0970) 617941 FAX (0970) 624546
Closed 24-31 Dec
This elegant country mansion set in 22 acres of woodland provides a choice of comfortable lounges and a relaxing lounge bar. Consistently good food displays aspects of both the classical and nouvelle style, a typical meal perhaps including wood pigeon breasts pan-fried with garlic, grapes and baby onions, tender noisettes of Welsh lamb accompanied by a distictive tarragon mousse, and passion fruit soufflé with white chocolate ice cream. Traditional Welsh cawl (vegetable broth) is always available.
11rm Annexe9rm(1fb) CTV in all bedrooms ® T ✲ sB&B⇨fr₤56 dB&B⇨₤79-₤99 ₽
Lift 60P ⚙ ❋ ⌬ (heated) sauna table tennis croquet nc5yrs
♥ International V ♨ ♪ ❋ Lunch ₤14.75&alc Dinner fr₤22.50&alc Last dinner 9.30pm
CONF. Thtr 60 Class 30 Board 20 Del ₤92
Credit Cards [1][2][3][5]

★★ 67% Belle Vue Royal
Marine Ter SY23 2BA ☎(0970) 617558 FAX (0970) 612190
Closed 24-26 Dec
With commanding views over Cardigan Bay this friendly family-owned sea front hotel provides spacious public rooms, 2 restaurants serving good value food, small traditional bar and modern lounge. Most of the bedrooms have been upgraded with bright, fully tiled en suite facilities, quality furnishings and a pleasing decor.
37rm(32⇨)(1fb) CTV in all bedrooms ® T ✲ (ex guide dogs) sB&Bfr₤42 sB&B⇨₤45 dB&Bfr₤65 dB&B⇨₤70 ₽
(CTV 6P 9
♥ International V ♨ ♪ Lunch ₤9.95-₤10
CONF. Thtr 50 Class 20 Board 28
Credit Cards [1][2][3][5]

Aberystwyth - Accrington

★★ 63%⃝ **Four Seasons**
50-54 Portland St SY23 2DX (in town centre, car park entrance in Bath Street) ☎(0970) 612120 FAX (0970) 627458
Closed 25-28 Dec
Friendly and personally run, this hotel stands in a quiet residential road off the town centre. Most of the bedrooms have now been upgraded, with attractive wallpapers and fabrics. Public areas include a comfortable modern lounge, a small bar (shortly to undergo alterations) and two restaurants serving a range of enjoyable meals.
14rm(13⇨♠)(1fb) CTV in all bedrooms ® T
✖ (ex guide dogs) sB&B£38.50 sB&B⇨♠£44 dB&B⇨♠£68 ☒
CTV 10P
♀ English & Continental V ♂ ⚐ ✂ ✱ Sunday Lunch £11 Dinner £15-£16 Last dinner 8.30pm
Credit Cards ①②③

★★ ❀63%⃝ **Groves**
44-46 North Pde SY23 2NF (N on A487)
☎(0970) 617623 FAX (0970) 627068

Closed Xmas
A pleasant town centre hotel, run by the same family for many years, which offers a welcoming atmosphere, with well equipped bedrooms and freshly prepared food featuring many Welsh dishes. Public rooms are not spacious but are comfortably furnished. Friendly service is provided by the small team of local staff presided over by Steve Albert.
11⇨♠in 1 bedroom CTV in all bedrooms ® T
✖ (ex guide dogs) sB&B⇨♠£40-£45 dB&B⇨♠£60-£70 ☒
8P
♀ International V ♂ ✂ ✱ Sunday Lunch £6.95-£8.95 Dinner £11.90-£19alc Last dinner 8.45pm
Credit Cards ①②③⑤ £

★★ 59%⃝ **Bay**
35-37 Marine Ter SY23 2BX ☎(0970) 617356 FAX (0970) 612198
Closed 22 Dec-14 Jan
This family-run hotel is situated on the seafront and several bedrooms enjoy sea views. The hotel is conveniently located for access to most of the town's amenities.
31rm(7⇨12♠)(3fb) CTV in all bedrooms ® T sB&Bfr£18 sB&B⇨♠£24-£30 dB&B⇨♠£40-£50
20P skittle alley ♫
V ♂ ✂ Last dinner 8.30pm
CONF. Thtr 50
Credit Cards ①②③⑤ £

★★ 57%⃝ **Queensbridge**
Promenade, Victoria Ter SY23 2BX ☎(0970) 612343 & 615025 FAX (0970) 617452
Closed 1wk Xmas
Right on the seafront, this small family hotel is popular with both holidaymakers and business travellers. Bedrooms, although modestly furnished, are clean and bright. There is a comfortable lounge with an adjoining bar, and a dining room.
15⇨♠(6fb) CTV in all bedrooms ® T ✖ (ex guide dogs)
Lift CTV P
♂ ✱ Bar Lunch £5.50-£8.50alc Dinner £12.50-£14 Last dinner 8pm
Credit Cards ①②③⑤ £

ABINGDON Oxfordshire Map 04 SU49

★★★ 62%⃝ **Abingdon Lodge**
Marcham Rd OX14 1TZ ☎(0235) 553456 FAX (0235) 554117

This modern purpose built hotel is popular with business people for its spacious bedrooms and informal conservatory restaurant.

63⇨♠ ✂ in 14 bedrooms CTV in all bedrooms ® ⚡ T
✖ (ex guide dogs) sB&B⇨♠£50-£69 dB&B⇨♠£60-£79
Continental breakfast ☒
♫ 85P ♫ xmas
♀ English & French V ♂ ⚐ ✂ Lunch £7.25-£9.95 Dinner £7.95-£10.95 Last dinner 10pm
CONF. Thtr 140 Class 80 Board 48 Del from £85
Credit Cards ①②③⑤ £

★★★ 59%⃝ **Upper Reaches**
Thames St OX14 3JA ☎(0235) 522311 FAX (0235) 555182

FORTE Heritage

Situated on a man-made island in the Thames close to the ruins of Abingdon Abbey, this hotel has been converted from the abbey's old mill. Most of the modern well equipped bedrooms have recently been refurbished and public areas are comfortable, though compact, with views of the waterwheel and mill stream from the lounge and restaurant.
25⇨♠ ✂ in 10 bedrooms CTV in all bedrooms ® T ✱
sB⇨♠£78 dB⇨♠£89 (room only) ☒
80P ✿ xmas
V ♂ ⚐ ✂ ✱ Sunday Lunch £8.95-£11.95 Dinner £17.95&alc Last dinner 9.30pm
Credit Cards ①②③⑤

ABINGTON Strathclyde *Lanarkshire* Map 11 NS92
Forte Travelodge
Welcome Break Service Area, A74/M74 ML12 6RE
☎ Central Reservations (0800) 850950

FORTE Travelodge

This modern building offers a good standard of accommodation for overnight stops. Smart, spacious and well equipped bedrooms, all with en suite bathrooms, are suitable for family use, and meals may be taken at the nearby family restaurant. For more details about Travelodges, consult the Contents page, under Hotel Groups.
56⇨♠

ABOYNE Grampian *Aberdeenshire* Map 15 NO59

★★ 66%⃝ **Birse Lodge**
Charleston Rd AB34 5EL ☎(03398) 86253 & 86254
Set in its own grounds close to the River Dee, this is a popular sporting and holiday hotel. Bedrooms, with stylish soft furnishings, are bright and cheery. The lounge is quiet and relaxing, and there is a small bar with an adjoining sun lounge where the emphasis is on bar food.
12⇨♠ Annexe4⇨♠ CTV in all bedrooms ® T ✱ sB&B⇨♠£39 dB&B⇨♠£70
CTV 80P ⛳ ✿ putting green
♀ International V ♂ ⚐ ✂ Bar Lunch £3.95-£10.56alc High tea £5.25-£7.50alc Dinner £16 Last dinner 8.30pm
Credit Cards ①②③

ACCRINGTON Lancashire Map 07 SD82

★★★ 64%⃝ **Dunkenhalgh**
Blackburn Rd, Clayton le Moors BB5 5JP (adj to M65, junct 7) ☎Blackburn(0254) 398021 FAX (0254) 872230

Standing in 17 acres of parkland, this country mansion has been much extended over the years. Bedrooms vary in size and style and are located either in the main building or grouped around the courtyard. All are equipped with modern amenities, but some of the best are over the Townley Suite.
37⇨♠ Annexe42⇨♠(13fb)⚡ CTV in all bedrooms ® T ✱ sB&B⇨♠£51-£105 dB&B⇨♠£72-£130 ☒
♫ CTV 400P ✿ ☒ (heated) snooker sauna solarium gymnasium steam room ♫ xmas

Accrington - Adlington

♀ International **V** ✧ ♃ ✱ Lunch £7.50–£11.80&alc Dinner £15–£17&alc Last dinner 9.45pm
CONF. Thtr 400 Class 200 Board 100 Del from £65
Credit Cards [1] [2] [3] [5]

ACHNASHEEN Highland *Ross & Cromarty* Map **14** NH15

★★★ ❀❀ ♨ **69%** **Loch Torridon**
Torridon IV22 2EY ☎Torridon(0445) 791242 FAX (0445) 791296

Best Newcomer 1994

RS 2 Jan-Feb
Our congratulations to the Loch Torridon Hotel for scooping the AA's Best Newcomer award for Scotland this year. To so impress our inspector when at the time of his visit builders were behind schedule, staff were off sick and the hotel was unexpectedly busy is no mean achievement, and in spite of all this pressure, owners David and Geraldine Gregory maintained a relaxed and easy rapport with their guests. They have done an excellent job in restoring this former shooting lodge, which now provides supremely comfortable accommodation in wonderful surroundings. Chef Timothy Morris has had a considerable impact upon the kitchen, producing starters such as an open ravioli of scallop and prawns in a cream chive sauce, and a main course of supreme of salmon with a spaghetti of vegetables in a warm tomato and basil dressing, which demonstrate a knowledgeable skill. All in all, this is an hotel worth watching.
21⇌♠(4fb)⊬in all bedrooms CTV in all bedrooms ®⚲ T ✱ sB&B⇌♠£45–£78.50 dB&B⇌♠£70–£90 ♬
Lift 30P ⚙ ✿ *xmas*
✧ ♃ ⊬ ✱ Bar Lunch £3–£7 Dinner £25 Last dinner 8.30pm
Credit Cards [1] [3]

★★ ♨ **70%** **Ledgowan Lodge**
IV22 2EJ (0.25m on A890 to Kyle of Lochalsh)
☎(044588) 252 FAX (044588) 240
Closed Nov-Mar RS Apr & Oct
For many years enthusiastic owner George Millard has been welcoming guests to this comfortable Highland hotel – a former hunting lodge set in wooded grounds just south of the village. It has a choice of comfortable lounges, a modest bar and a pleasant dining room; there is also a new gift shop. Bedrooms are furnished in solid, traditional style. Staff throughout are friendly and willing to please.
12⇌♠ CTV in all bedrooms ®⚲ T ✖ sB&B⇌♠£39.50–£45 dB&B⇌♠£62–£98
25P ✿
♀ International ✧ ♃ Bar Lunch £2.50–£15alc High tea £3.50–£10alc Dinner £19.95–£27.50 Last dinner 8.45pm
Credit Cards [1] [2] [3] [5]

If you have booked a meal in a
hotel restaurant and cannot get there,
remember you have a contractual obligation
to cancel your booking.

ACLE Norfolk Map **05** TG41

Forte Travelodge
(junc A47 & Acle Bypass)
☎(0493) 751970 Central Res (0800) 850950
This modern building offers a good standard of accommodation for overnight stops. Smart, spacious and well equipped bedrooms, all with en suite bathrooms, are suitable for family use, and meals may be taken at the nearby family restaurant. For more details about Travelodges, consult the Contents page, under Hotel Groups.
40⇌♠ ✱ B⇌♠£31.95 (room only)

ADDERBURY Oxfordshire Map **04** SP43

★★ **65%** *Red Lion*
The Green, Oxford Rd OX17 3LU (3m S of Banbury Cross, on A423) ☎(0295) 810269 FAX (0295) 811906
This attractive 16th-century, stone-built coaching inn overlooking the village green. Bedrooms are individually furnished and decorated to a high standard. Blackboard menus are displayed in the panelled bars and guests can eat there or in the restaurant.
9rm(6⇌♠)1⚏ CTV in all bedrooms ® T ✖ (ex guide dogs) 24P
♀ English & Continental **V** ✧ ♃ ⊬ Last dinner 10pm
Credit Cards [1] [3]

ADLINGTON Lancashire Map **07** SD61

★★ **66%** **Gladmar**
Railway Rd PR6 9RG (off A6 near railway station)
☎(0257) 480398 FAX (0257) 482681
Closed 25 Dec & 1 Jan
Situated in a quiet residential area close to the railway station, this extended Victorian house with an attractive garden is carefully

➪

Aboyne, Royal Deeside AB34 5EL
Telephone: (03398) 86253

This privately owned Country House Hotel is set in its own grounds. Popular with fishers and shooters also golfing enthusiasts who have a choice of 5 Golf Courses all within a few miles of the hotel.

Adlington - Alderminster

maintained and offers a friendly, relaxing atmosphere. Well equipped bedrooms are comfortably furnished and there is a cosy lounge, small bar and attractive dining room.
20⇌↑(1fb) CTV in all bedrooms ® T ✱ (ex guide dogs) ✽ sB&B⇌↑£26-£37 dB&B⇌↑£35-£58 ₽
CTV 30P ✽
V ♡ ℒ ✽ Lunch £9.50 Dinner fr£9.50 Last dinner 8.30pm
CONF. Thtr 40 Board 18 Del £62
Credit Cards [1][2][3][5]

ALCESTER Warwickshire Map 04 SP05

★★★ 64% **Kings Court**
Kings Coughton B49 5QQ (1m N on A435)
☎(0789) 763111 FAX (0789) 400242
Closed 24-30 Dec

Kings Court is set in 4 acres of grounds around the original Tudor farmhouse. There are 4 beamed bedrooms in the farmhouse, but most rooms are in the annexe. Public areas include a large reception foyer, restaurant and a beamed bar.
4⇌↑ Annexe15⇌↑(1fb) CTV in all bedrooms ® T
sB&B⇌↑£31-£51 dB&B⇌↑£48-£62 ₽
120P ✽
V ♡ ℒ Sunday Lunch £8.50
CONF. Thtr 100 Class 40 Board 20 Del from £69
Credit Cards [1][2][3]

ALDEBURGH Suffolk Map 05 TM45

★★★ 68% **White Lion**
Market Cross Place IP15 5BJ (from A12 at Saxmundham take A1094 approx 5m on seafront) ☎(0728) 452720 FAX (0728) 452986

The White Lion is a whitewashed building located opposite the 16th-century Moot Hall. Efficient levels of service are assured in the public areas, which include a large, attractive restaurant and a smaller bar. The comfortable bedrooms are furnished in pastel colours, and some have sea views.
38⇌↑(1fb)2⌗ CTV in all bedrooms ® T ✽ sB&B⇌↑£50-£65 dB&B⇌↑£75-£100 ₽
15P ⇆ xmas
♡ English & French V ♡ ℒ Sunday Lunch £11.25 Dinner £16.95&alc Last dinner 8.45pm
CONF. Thtr 100 Class 50 Board 50 Del from £90
Credit Cards [1][2][3][5]

★★★ 67% **Wentworth**
Wentworth Rd IP15 5BD (Turn off A12 on to B1094, leave church on left and turn left at bottom of hill) ☎(0728) 452312 FAX (0728) 454343
Closed 28 Dec-10 Jan

This popular Victorian seafront hotel is comfortable and attractively furnished thoughout. Bedrooms are individually decorated and there are relaxing lounges, a small bar and an elegant dining room, with antiques and open fires. Courteous staff provide good service.
31rm(24⇌4↑) CTV in all bedrooms T sB&B⇌↑£52.50-£57.75 dB&B⇌↑£85-£105 ₽
16P ⇆ xmas
♡ English & French V ♡ ℒ ✽ Lunch £14-£15&alc Dinner £17&alc Last dinner 9pm
Credit Cards [1][2][3][5]

★★ 61% **The Brudenell**
The Parade IP15 5BU (on seafront, adjoining Fort Green car park) ☎(0728) 452071 FAX (0728) 454082

Access to this hotel is down narrow side streets, arriving at the rear of the building, but once inside, guests are greeted with courteous service by young and willing staff, and a relaxing atmosphere of the public rooms, all of which have views over the North Sea just yards

from the hotel. The majority of the bedrooms have been refurbished, with rich décor and furnishings.
47⇌↑(1fb)⇆in 11 bedrooms CTV in all bedrooms ® T ✱
sB&B⇌↑£70-£80 dB&B⇌↑£85-£95 (room only) ₽
Lift ⌇ 14P 8⇾ xmas
V ♡ ℒ ✽ Lunch £8.95-£10.95 Dinner £15.95 Last dinner 9pm
Credit Cards [1][2][3][5]

★★ 65% **Uplands**
Victoria Rd IP15 5DX (on A1094, opposite church)
☎(0728) 452420 FAX (0728) 454872
Closed 23 Dec- 3 Jan

This small family-run hotel has a lovely walled garden to the rear, with a recently renovated conservatory. The hotel has the feeling of a country home with cosy public rooms and traditional bedrooms in the main house, with period and antique furniture. There are also chalet-style garden rooms, which are more modest and practical, but are popular for their easy access.
12rm(9⇌↑) Annexe8⇌↑(2fb) CTV in all bedrooms ® T
✱ (ex guide dogs) sB&Bfr£30 sB&B⇌↑£46 dB&B⇌↑£60 ₽
CTV 22P ⇆ ✽ nc12yrs
V Dinner fr£15 Last dinner 8.30pm
Credit Cards [1][2][3][5]

ALDERLEY EDGE Cheshire Map 07 SJ87

★★★ ✪73% **Alderley Edge**
Macclesfield Rd SK9 7BJ ☎(0625) 583033 FAX (0625) 586343

This large, half-timbered hotel is in an elevated position with fine views of the surrounding area. Refurbished to a high standard, the comfortable bedrooms have firm beds and pretty coordinated décor. The open plan public areas have deep sofas and quality furnishings, and the intimate restaurant is the venue for chef Brian Joy's imaginative cooking, complemented by an extensive wine list.
32⇌↑2⌗ CTV in all bedrooms ® T ✱ sB⇌↑£87-£95
dB⇌↑£99.50-£109.50 (room only) ₽
⌇ 90P ✽ xmas
V ♡ ℒ ✽ Lunch £15.50&alc Dinner £20.50&alc Last dinner 10pm
Credit Cards [1][2][3][5]

ALDERMINSTER Warwickshire Map 04 SP24

★★★★ 75% **Ettington Park**
CV37 8BS (5m S of Stratford, off A3400)
☎Stratford-upon-Avon(0789) 450123 FAX (0789) 450472
This gothic Victorian mansion, glimpsed through the mature trees of 40 acres of parkland, now offers standards of comfort unprecedented in the many years that it has operated as a hotel. Accommodation in the modern new wing, though plainer and more uniform than the spacious, ornate and individually styled bedrooms of the main house, is equally comfortable. The restaurant enjoys a well earned reputation for good food.
48⇌1⇆in 5 bedrooms CTV in all bedrooms⇆ T
✱ (ex guide dogs) ✽ sB&B⇌fr£115 dB&B⇌fr£145 ₽
Lift ⌇ 90P ✽ ≋ (heated) ♂ (hard) ♪ ♡ sauna solarium croquet clay pigeon shooting archery xmas
♡ English & French V ♡ ℒ ✽ Lunch fr£15.75 Dinner fr£28 Last dinner 9.30pm
Credit Cards [1][2][3]
See advertisement under STRATFORD-UPON-AVON

All black star hotels are given a
percentage grading within their star bands.
See 'Using the Guide' at the front of the book
for full details.

Alderney - Alnwick

ALDERNEY
See **Channel Islands**

ALDWARK North Yorkshire Map 08 SE46

★★★♨ **70%** *Aldwark Manor*
YO6 2NF ☎(03473) 8146 FAX (03473) 8867
This impressive 19th-century manor house is set in 46 acres of parkland. Tastefully restored and furnished, it provides very spacious, comfortable bedrooms and elegant public rooms.
17⇌↑Annexe3⇌↑(2fb)2⊟⊬in 2 bedrooms CTV in 18 bedrooms ⓇT
《52P ✿ ▶ 18 ✦ coarse fishing
♥ European V ❖ ♫ Last dinner 9pm
Credit Cards ①②③⑤

ALFORD Lincolnshire Map 09 TF27

★★ **67%** *White Horse*
29 West St LN13 9DG ☎(0507) 462218
One of Lincolnshire's oldest coaching inns, with a thatched roof, low beamed ceiling and open log fires, the White Horse has been converted to retain character while offering modern conveniences. The pretty bedrooms are comfortable and cosy, if compact, and good value menus are on offer. Service is informal and friendly.
9rm(7⇌)(2fb) CTV in all bedrooms ⓇT ✻ sB&Bfr£26 sB&B⇌↑fr£30 dB&Bfr£36 dB&B⇌↑fr£40
10P 3🅿
♥ English & Continental ❖ ✻ Sunday Lunch £6.25 Dinner £7.45–£16.90 Last dinner 10pm
Credit Cards ①③

ALFRETON Derbyshire Map 08 SK45

★★★ **59%** *Granada*
Old Swanwick Colliery Rd, A38/A61 DE55 1HJ (junc A38/A61) (Granada) ☎(0773) 520040 FAX (0773) 521087
RS 25–26 Dec
Bedrooms have good range of facilities and eating arrangements are informal, 'Platters' restaurant providing all-day snacks with a grill menu at lunch and dinner.
61⇌↑(8fb)⊬in 14 bedrooms CTV in all bedrooms Ⓡ☆T ✖ (ex guide dogs) ✻ sB⇌↑£39.50–£49.50 dB⇌↑£39.50–£49.50 (room only) 🄱
《250P ✿
V ❖ ♫ ⊬ ✻ Sunday Lunch fr£6.95 Dinner fr£14&alc Last dinner 10pm
Credit Cards ①②③⑤
See advertisement under DERBY

ALFRISTON East Sussex Map 05 TQ50

★★★ **67%** *The Star*
BN26 5TA (7m off A27 at Drusillas roundabout)
☎(0323) 870495 FAX (0323) 870922
FORTE Heritage
Originally built in the 13th century, the Star was modernised in 1450 and is one of the oldest inns in the country. Much of the character and charm has been retained, from the carved wood façade to the cosy beamed lounges with inglenook fireplaces. Bedrooms, both in the main building and in the modern extension, are comfortable, and standards are high.
34⇌↑⊬in 10 bedrooms CTV in all bedrooms ⓇT
sB⇌↑£80–£85 dB⇌↑£95–£100 (room only) 🄱
《36P *xmas*
V ❖ ♫ ⊬ Sunday Lunch £14.95 Dinner £18.95–£19.95&alc Last dinner 9.30pm
CONF. Thtr 45 Class 26 Board 24 Del £110
Credit Cards ①②③⑤

ALLOA Central *Clackmannanshire* Map 11 NS89

★★★ **77%** The Gean House
Gean Park, Tullibody Rd FK10 2HS (W of town centre off B9096) ☎(0259) 219275 FAX (0259) 213827
Sandra Frost's Lutyens-style Edwardian mansion has beautifully furnished public rooms, enhanced by flamboyant floral displays and ornaments, while the individually styled bedrooms are equally impressive. Craig Samson provides front of house service while Keith Sheerer is responsible for the first class cooking.
7⇌↑ CTV in all bedrooms☆ T ✖ (ex guide dogs) ✻ sB&B⇌↑£80 dB&B⇌↑£120–£140 🄱
《30P ⊟ ✿ ℛ (hard) nc12yrs *xmas*
V ❖ ♫ ✻ Lunch £12–£16 Dinner £29–£33 Last dinner 9pm
Credit Cards ①②③⑤

ALNWICK Northumberland Map 12 NU11

★★★ **57%** White Swan
Bondgate Within NE66 1TD (CAIRN) ☎(0665) 602109 FAX (0665) 510400
This long established, traditional hotel in the centre of town offers varying standards of accommodation. While some bedrooms have been upgraded to a modern standard, others remain somewhat dated. Unfortunately, with refurbishment delayed, the public areas are also beginning to show signs of wear.
43⇌↑(4fb)⊬in 4 bedrooms CTV in all bedrooms Ⓡ T ✻ sB&B⇌↑£35–£49.50 dB&B⇌↑£50–£75 🄱
《30P *xmas*
♥ English & French V ❖ ♫ ⊬ ✻ Lunch £8.45–£13.50alc High tea £6.75–£7.50 Dinner £17&alc Last dinner 9pm
CONF. Thtr 200 Class 100 Board 50 Del from £75
Credit Cards ①②③

WENTWORTH HOTEL ★★★

Aldeburgh, Suffolk
Tel: (0728) 452312   Fax: (0728) 454343

The Hotel has the comfort and style of a Country House. Two comfortable lounges, with open fires and antique furniture, provide ample space to relax. Each individually decorated bedroom, many with sea views, is equipped with a colour television, radio, hairdryer and optional tea making facilities. The Restaurant serves a variety of fresh produce whilst a light lunch can be chosen from the Bar menu, eaten outside in the sunken terrace garden. Aldeburgh is timeless and unhurried. There are quality shops, two excellent golf courses within a short distance from the hotel, long walks and some of the best birdwatching at Minsmere Bird reserve. Music and the Arts can be heard at the Internationally famous Snape Malting Concert hall. Lastly, there are miles of beach to sit upon and watch the sea!

Alnwick - Altarnun

★★68% The Oaks
South Rd NE66 2PN (on SE outskirts) ☎(0665) 510014 FAX (0665) 603219

On the southern approach to the town centre, this is a pleasant, extended 18th-century town house. Most bedrooms are spacious, with attractive coordinated décor and all modern amenities. Public areas are more limited but include a tastefully furnished restaurant and cosy lounge bar.

9⇌🛁Annexe4⇌🛁 CTV in all bedrooms ® T
⌷ 35P
♡ English, French & Portuguese V ♂ ⌾ Last dinner 9.30pm
Credit Cards 1 2 3

★★56% Hotspur
Bondgate Without NE66 1PR ☎(0665) 510101 FAX (0665) 605033

Closed 24-26 Dec & 1 Jan

Situated in the centre of the town, this privately owned coaching inn with modern extensions offers functional and modest accommodation.

27rm(20⇌1🛁)(2fb) CTV in all bedrooms ® T
CTV 25P
V ♂ ⌾ Last dinner 9pm
Credit Cards 1 2 3 5

ALRESFORD Hampshire Map 04 SU53

★★59% Swan
11 West St SO24 9AD ☎(0962) 732302 734427 FAX (0962) 735274

Cromwell is believed to have stayed here, and the hotel still has much historic character. Some of the bedrooms are set around the car park and are particularly spacious. A buffet is available throughout the day.

23rm(10⇌)(4fb)1⌷ CTV in all bedrooms ® T sB&Bfr£20 dB&Bfr£40 dB&B⇌🛁£40-£50 🍴
CTV 75P
♡ International V ♂ ⌾ ✱ Lunch £2.50-£7.95 High tea £1.10-£3.50 Dinner £4-£15 Dinner 10pm
CONF. Thtr 80 Class 80 Board 40 Del from £45
Credit Cards 1 3

ALSAGER Cheshire Map 07 SJ75

★★★66% Manor House
Audley Rd ST7 2QQ (signposted from railway station) (Compass) ☎Crewe(0270) 884000 FAX (0270) 882483

RS 25-30 Dec

The nucleus of this modern hotel is an old farm, and the original beams are a feature of the Ostlers restaurant with its extensive and varied menu. Guests can also relax in a traditionally styled bar.

57⇌🛁(5fb)1⌷ CTV in all bedrooms ® T
(CTV 178P ✣ 🖭 (heated) snooker pool table ♪
♡ English & French V ♂ ⌾ Last dinner 9.30pm
Credit Cards 1 2 3 5

ALSTON Cumbria Map 12 NY74

★★
✽✣&♿ LOVELADY SHIELD COUNTRY HOUSE
CA9 3LF (2m E, signposted off A689) ☎(0434) 381203 FAX (0434) 381515
Closed 3 Jan-12 Feb

There is a lovely feeling of remoteness from the pressures of everyday life at this hotel.

Set among mature trees and some way back from the road, any sounds are most likely to be from sheep, cattle and wildlife, or the fast flowing River Nent which forms one of the garden's boundaries. During much of the year welcoming log fires burn in the drawing room and entrance hall sitting area. Bedrooms are warm and very comfortable, decorated in a chintzy country style, with a good combination of antiques and more modern furniture. Thoughtful extras such as bottled water and dishes of sweets are provided. The hotel has a reputation for sound British cooking though dishes such as pasta with an Italian tomato, mushroom and basil sauce may appear. A 4-course dinner is served, and breakfasts are memorable.

12⇌🛁(1fb)1⌷ CTV in all bedrooms T sB&B⇌🛁£40 dB&B⇌🛁£78-£108 🍴
20P ♂ ♫ (hard) croquet xmas
♡ English & French ♂ ⌾ ✱ Lunch £10.50-£14.50 High tea £5.50-£10.50 Dinner £23.50-£25.50 Last dinner 8.30pm
Credit Cards 1 2 3 5

★★68% Lowbyer Manor Country House
CA9 3JX ☎(0434) 381230 FAX (0434) 382937

Built from local stone this hotel was once the home of the Earl of Derwentwater and dates back to the 17th century. It stands on the edge of town and offers a warm, friendly atmosphere. The lounge is comfortable and the basement bar has lots of character. Good home cooking is provided and the choice is quite extensive.

8⇌🛁 CTV in all bedrooms ® ✱ sB&B⇌🛁£32.50 dB&B⇌🛁£59.90 🍴
14P ✣ nc8yrs xmas
V ♂ ⌾ ✱ Sunday Lunch £2-£7.95alc Dinner £14.50-£19.75alc Last dinner 9pm
Credit Cards 1 2 3 5

★★66% Nent Hall Country House
CA9 3LQ (3m E on A689) ☎(0434) 381584 FAX (0434) 382668

Nent Hall stands in open countryside and has pleasant well kept grounds. Opened only a couple of years ago, it is furnished throughout to a good standard and has a new block of attractive bedrooms. Family run, it offers friendly service and dining in either the bar or the cosy restaurant.

20rm(18⇌🛁)(2fb)2⌷ CTV in 18 bedrooms ® T sB&B⇌🛁£46-£66 dB&B⇌🛁£61-£82 🍴
CTV 48P ✣ xmas
V ♂ ⌾ ✱ Sunday Lunch £7.50-£9.50 High tea £4.50-£7.50 Dinner £17.50-£20 Last dinner 8.30pm
CONF. Thtr 50 Class 30 Board 20
Credit Cards 1 2 3

ALTARNUN Cornwall & Isles of Scilly Map 02 SX28

★★70% Penhallow Manor Country House
PL15 7SJ (in village next to the church)
☎Pipers Pool(0566) 86206 FAX (0566) 86179

Daphne du Maurier was a visitor to this Grade II listed former rectory and it appeared in Jamaica Inn as the home of the notorious Frances Davey, Vicar of Altarnun. Bedrooms are decorated with coordinating wallpapers and fabrics. Both table d'hôte and à la carte menus are offered at dinner, and afterwards, in winter, guests can relax in front of a log fire.

7⇌🛁 CTV in all bedrooms ® T
10P ✣ nc8yrs
V ♂ ⌾ ✱ Sunday Lunch £7.95 Dinner fr£14.95 Last dinner 9.30pm
Credit Cards 1 3

ALTHORPE Humberside Map 08 SE81
See also **Scunthorpe**
★★**64%** **Lansdowne House**
Main St DN17 3HJ (leave M181 at junc 1 onto A18 towards Doncaster continue over iron bridge, keep left at road fork, hotel on right) ☎Scunthorpe(0724) 783369 FAX (0724) 783369
This handsome Victorian house with attractive gardens has good-sized traditional bedrooms and spacious public rooms with ornate ceilings, including a comfortable lounge bar and restaurant.
7⇨♪Annexe3♪(5fb) CTV in all bedrooms ® T
✗ (ex guide dogs) ✻ sB&B⇨♪£42.50-£52.50 dB&B⇨♪£52.50-£62.50
CTV 40P ✿
♡ English & French V ◊ ⌴ ✻ Dinner £15.55-£28.80alc Last dinner 10pm
Credit Cards [1][2][3][5]

ALTON Hampshire Map 04 SU73
★★★**66%** **Swan**
High St GU34 1AT ☎(0420) 83777 FAX (0420) 87975

FORTE Heritage

This attractive old coaching inn in the town centre has been extensively upgraded and offers comfortable well equipped bedrooms of varying size, with room service usually available. Public rooms retain their historic character and include a restaurant, beamed bar and traditional lounge with log fires.
38⇨♪(2fb)1 ⇌ ⚹in 15 bedrooms CTV in all bedrooms ® T
(70P
V ◊ ⌴ ⚹ Last dinner 9.30pm
CONF. Thtr 70 Class 35 Board 25 Del from £60
Credit Cards [1][2][3][4][5]

★★★**62%** **Alton House**
Normandy St GU34 1DW (turn off A31, close to railway station) ☎(0420) 80033 FAX (0420) 89222
This imposing building with more modern bedroom extensions caters predominantly for commercial visitors. There is a spacious bar-lounge, and in the restaurant a choice of dishes is offered from a table d'hôte menu, with an à la carte menu available during the week. Bedrooms are comfortable.
39⇨♪ ⇌in 2 bedrooms CTV in all bedrooms ® T ⚹ sB&B⇨♪£35-£50 dB&B⇨♪£48-£60 ♬
(80P 6♿ ✿ ≋ (heated) ℘ (hard) snooker
♡ English & Continental V ◊ ⌴ ✻ Lunch fr£9.95 Dinner fr£11.95 Last dinner 9.45pm
Credit Cards [1][2][3][5]

★★**65%** **Grange**
17 London Rd, Holybourne GU34 4EG (on E outskirts) ☎(0420) 86565 FAX (0420) 541346
Further improvements are planned for this recently extended family-run hotel with attractive gardens. There is a choice of individually furnished modern bedrooms, with room service available as well as a popular restaurant with a range of menus.
26⇨♪Annexe4⇨♪(2fb) ⇌in 2 bedrooms CTV in all bedrooms ® T ⚹ sB&B⇨♪£49.50-£61 dB&B⇨♪£65-£75
CTV 48P ✿ ≋ (heated) croquet putting nc3yrs *xmas*
♡ English & French V ◊ ⌴ ⚹ ✻ Lunch £7.95-£9.95&alc Dinner £9.95-£12.25&alc Last dinner 9pm
CONF. Thtr 80 Board 30 Del from £62.50
Credit Cards [1][2][3][5]

ALTON Staffordshire Map 07 SK04
★★**62%** **Bull's Head Inn**
High St ST10 4AQ ☎Oakamoor(0538) 702307 FAX (0538) 702065
Convenient for visitors to Alton Towers, this popular village inn has a busy bar, bright modern bedrooms and a restaurant serving a wide range of food.

6rm(5♪) CTV in all bedrooms ® ✗ sB&B♪£20-£35 dB&B♪£30-£50
CTV 15P ♣
V ◊ Lunch £6.20-£12.45alc Dinner £6.20-£12.45alc Last dinner 9.15pm
Credit Cards [1][3]

ALTRINCHAM Greater Manchester Map 07 SJ78
★★★**70%** **Woodland Park**
Wellington Rd, Timperley WA15 7RG (off the A560)
☎061-928 8631 FAX 061-941 2821
This large privately owned hotel situated in a residential area of Timperley provides a high standard of friendly and attentive service. Bedrooms vary in size and style and a few have bathrooms with air spa baths. Family and ground-floor rooms are available. Public rooms offer a choice of lounges, including 2 for non smokers. The hotel has its own night club.
45⇨♪(3fb) ⇌ CTV in all bedrooms ® ⌴ T ✗ (ex guide dogs) ⚹ sB&B⇨♪£45-£70 dB&B⇨♪£60-£90
(150P 1☂ (charged)
♡ International V ◊ ⌴ ✻ Lunch £8.95&alc Dinner £14.50-£15.50&alc Last dinner 10pm
CONF. Thtr 200 Class 120 Board 50 Del from £77.50
Credit Cards [1][2][3][5]

★★★**66%** **Bowdon**
Langham Rd, Bowdon WA14 2HT (M6 leave junct 19 to airport continue until 2nd roundabout head for Bowdon/Altrincham hotel is in Langham Road) ☎061-928 7121 FAX 061-927 7560
RS 25 Dec
In a pleasant residential area convenient for the town centre, the motorway network and Manchester airport, this extended Victorian building is popular for conferences and functions. Comfortable bedrooms all have modern facilities and there is a restaurant and a lively bar.
82⇨♪(1fb) CTV in all bedrooms ® T ⚹ sB&B⇨♪£45-£58 dB&B⇨♪£52-£79 ♬
(168P ♪
♡ English & French V ◊ ⌴ ✻ Bar Lunch £2.95-£12 Dinner fr£15.95&alc Last dinner 10pm
CONF. Thtr 130 Class 60 Board 40 Del from £90
Credit Cards [1][2][3][5]
See advertisement on page 47

★★★**65%** **Cresta Court**
Church St WA14 4DP (beside A56) ☎061-927 7272 FAX 061-926 9194
The Cresta Court is a modern hotel convenient for the motorway network and Manchester Airport. The bedrooms are very well fitted though some are rather compact.
139⇨♪(5fb) CTV in all bedrooms ®⌴ T sB&B⇨♪£30-£55.50 dB&B⇨♪£56-£72 ♬
Lift (200P
♡ English & French V ◊ ⌴ ✻ Lunch £8.15-£8.95&alc High tea 80p Dinner £8.95&alc Last dinner 10.30pm
CONF. Thtr 350 Class 200 Board 60 Del from £86.50
Credit Cards [1][2][3][5]

★★★**61%** **The Swan**
WA16 6RD ☎Bucklow Hill(0565) 830295 FAX (0565) 830614
(For full entry see Bucklow Hill)

★★★**58%** **Ashley**
Ashley Rd, Hale WA15 9SF (opposite bowling green)
☎061-928 3794 FAX 061-926 9046
This modern hotel is situated above a parade of shops in Hale village, close to the railway station and convenient for Manchester city and airport. Service is friendly and bedrooms offer the expected facilities, though some rooms await upgrading. There is a small bar and restaurant.
47⇨♪ CTV in all bedrooms ® T ⚹ sB&B⇨♪£55-£60 dB&B⇨♪£65-£75 ♬

Altrincham - Amberley

Lift (CTV 100P bowling green
English & French V ☼ ⚲ ✱ Lunch £6.50-£15&alc
CONF. Thtr 200 Class 35 Board 25 Del from £65
Credit Cards 1 2 3 5

★★ 59% **Grove Park**
Park Rd, Bowden WA14 3JE (at the junct of B5160 & B5161, within easy reach of M56) ☎061-928 6191 FAX 061-941 6046
In the residential area of Bowden, this small hotel is a popular eating venue for both lunch and dinner, it offers varied and interesting menus. Bedrooms are gradually being improved, and the informal service is friendly and obliging.
14⇨✿ CTV in all bedrooms ® T ✈ ✱ sB&B⇨✿£24-£43 dB&B⇨✿£40-£55 ₧
(35P
International V ☼ ⚲ ✱ Lunch £5.95&alc Dinner £5.95-£10.95&alc Last dinner 11.30pm
CONF. Thtr 50 Class 80 Board 30 Del from £60
Credit Cards 1 3 £

★ 66% **The Unicorn**
Hale Rd, Halebarns WA15 8SS (on A538, near M56)
☎061-980 4347 FAX 061-903 9187
Providing easy access to the M56 and Manchester Airport, this popular small hotel is on the A538 in the centre of Hale Barns. The bedrooms are modern and soundly maintained, and a good range of wholesome meals is served in the busy open plan bar-restaurant, which is also a favourite venue for locals.
5⇨✿ CTV in all bedrooms ® ✈ (ex guide dogs) ✱
sB&B⇨✿£25-£35 dB&B⇨✿£35-£50
25P ⊞
V ☼ ✱ Sunday Lunch £8-£8.35alc Dinner £6.95-£12.10alc Last dinner 8.45pm
Credit Cards 1 3

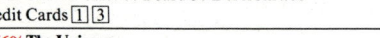

ALVESTON Avon Map 03 ST68

★★★ 73% **Alveston House**
BS12 2LJ (near A38, between juncts 14 & 16 of M5)
☎Thornbury(0454) 415050 FAX (0454) 415425
Continued good work and refurbishment at Alveston House has resulted in a pleasant combination of comfortable surroundings, a welcoming atmosphere and a good range of services. The hotel is run with enthusiasm by owner Mr Bland, manageress Julie Camm, and her equally dedicated brigade of staff. Bedrooms are decorated in soft colours with coordinated fabrics, with modern equipment.
30⇨✿(1fb) CTV in all bedrooms ® T sB&B⇨✿£60-£79.50 dB&B⇨✿£75.50-£89.50 ₧
CTV 75P ✱
English & French V ☼ ⚲ Lunch £10.75-£17&alc Dinner £14.25-£17&alc Last dinner 9.30pm
CONF. Thtr 85 Class 48 Board 50 Del from £91.50
Credit Cards 1 2 3 5 £

See advertisement under BRISTOL

Forte Posthouse
Thornbury Rd BS12 2LL (close to M4/M5 interchange) ☎Thornbury(0454) 412521 FAX (0454) 413920
Suitable for both the business and leisure traveller, this bright hotel provides modern accommodation in well equipped bedrooms with en suite bathrooms. For more details about Forte Posthouse hotels, consult the Contents page, under Hotel Groups.
74⇨✿ ✱ B⇨✿£41.50-£53.50 (room only)
CONF. Thtr 100 Class 40 Board 40 Del £89.50

Irish entries appear in a separate section that follows the main directory.

ALWALTON Cambridgeshire Map 04 TL19

★★★★ ❀63% **Swallow**
Lynchwood PE2 6GB (opposite East of England Showground)
☎Peterborough(0733) 371111 FAX (0733) 236725

Food at the Swallow is worthy of note, and chef Sydney Aldridge offers British cooking in the informal Laurels restaurant and more serious modern French food in the Emperor restaurant – both restaurants impressively decorated in Roman style. The rather stark appearance of the ultra modern bedroom fixtures has been softened by the décor and soft furnishings. All rooms are well equipped, now with Sky and free daily movie channels.
163⇨✿(10fb)⚲in 89 bedrooms CTV in all bedrooms ® T ✱ sB&B⇨✿£50-£88 dB&B⇨✿£84-£105 ₧
(CTV 200P ❀ ▢ (heated) sauna solarium gymnasium pitch & putt spa bath beauty therapist ♫ xmas
English & French V ☼ ⚲ ✱ Lunch £12.50-£15&alc Dinner £16.60-£21.50&alc Last dinner 10.30pm
CONF. Thtr 300 Class 160 Board 160 Del from £75
Credit Cards 1 2 3 4 5 £

See advertisement under PETERBOROUGH

Forte Travelodge
Great North Rd PE7 3UR (on A1, southbound)
☎Peterborough(0733) 231109 Central Res (0800) 850950

This modern building offers a good standard of accommodation for overnight stops. Smart, spacious and well equipped bedrooms, all with en suite bathrooms, are suitable for family use, and meals may be taken at the nearby family restaurant. For more details about Travelodges, consult the Contents page, under Hotel Groups.
32⇨✿ ✱ B⇨✿£31.95 (room only)

AMBERLEY Gloucestershire Map 03 SO80

★★ 65% **Amberley Inn**
GL5 5AF (on A46) ☎(0453) 872565 FAX (0453) 872738

This large, stone-built inn has views of Minchinhampton Common and the Woodchester Valley beyond. It has very congenial and popular public bars with traditional furnishings and log fires. Like the restaurant, these offer a wide range of food accompanied by a sound wine list and a selection of real ales, and friendly local staff create an informal atmosphere throughout. Bedrooms vary in size and shape, but all are equipped to meet the needs of today's traveller.
10rm(9⇨✿)Annexe4⇨✿(1fb) CTV in all bedrooms ® T 30P ✱
English & French V ☼ ⚲ ✱ Lunch £9.35-£14.50&alc Dinner £14.50-£15.50&alc Last dinner 9.30pm
CONF. Thtr 30 Class 16 Board 16 Del from £37
Credit Cards 1 2 3

AMBERLEY West Sussex Map 04 TQ01

★★★ ❀❀⊞ 77% **Amberley Castle**
BN18 9ND (SW of village)
☎Bury(0798) 831992 FAX (0798) 831998

This 12th-century castle – half ruin, half discreetly restored, and idyllically set in a tranquil fold of the Downs southwest of the village – has been transformed by the resident proprietors into an enchanting country house hotel. Some of the individually styled bedrooms contain antiques and others reproduction furniture, but all are enhanced by attractive soft furnishings, excellent bathrooms and every conceivable extra. Two lounges and a library, all warmed by log fires, invite relaxation, while the Queens Room restaurant upstairs provides an impressive setting for the enjoyment

of a range of dishes prepared in modern country house style, based on quality ingredients.
14⇌♘2☰ CTV in all bedrooms⚲ T ✱ sB&B⇌♘ £80-£195 dB&B⇌♘ £95-£225 ♫
50P ⌘ ✿ xmas
V ♡ ⚏ ⚔ ✱ Lunch £16.50-£18.50&alc Dinner fr£25.50&alc Last dinner 9.30pm
CONF. Thtr 60 Class 20 Board 30 Del from £135
Credit Cards [1][2][3][5]

AMBLESIDE Cumbria Map 07 NY30
See also **Elterwater**

★★★ ✿73% **Rothay Manor**
Rothay Bridge LA22 0EH (.25m SW on Coniston road)
☎(05394) 33605 FAX (05394) 33607
Closed 2 Jan-12 Feb
Rothay Manor is an elegant Regency-style building, which has an imposing verandah with cast iron railings. The comfortable lounges are furnished in country house style and bedrooms are individually decorated and furnished. The high standard of cuisine is predominantly British, including such items as sautéed monkfish in lime sauce as a starter, followed by rack of lamb with onion sauce. Efficient service is provided by young staff in Victorian dress.
15⇌ Annexe3⇌(6fb) CTV in all bedrooms ® T
✖ (ex guide dogs) sB&B⇌ £69-£75 dB&B⇌ £108-£152 ♫
30P ⌘ ✿ Nearby leisure centre free to guests xmas
♡ English & Continental V ♡ ⚏ Sunday Lunch fr£14.50
Dinner £21-£27 Last dinner 9pm
Credit Cards [1][2][3][5]

★★★ 65% **Regent**
Waterhead Bay LA22 0ES (1m S A591) ☎(05394) 32254 FAX (05394) 31474
Situated close to Waterhead Bay at the head of Windermere, this hotel offers well furnished and comfortable public areas. Bedrooms are either in the main house or set around the rear courtyard. Staff are keen and friendly.
21⇌♘(2fb)3☰ CTV in all bedrooms ® T sB&B⇌♘ £49.90-£89 dB&B⇌♘ £89-£109 ♫
30P ⌘ ▭ (heated) xmas
♡ English & French V ♡ ⚏ ✱ Sunday Lunch £7.95-£12.95
Dinner £16.95-£21.95 Last dinner 8.30pm
Credit Cards [1][3] £

★★★ 63% **The Salutation**
Lake Rd LA22 9BX ☎(05394) 32244 FAX (05394) 34157
Situated at the very centre of Ambleside, this hotel offers accommodation in recently upgraded bedrooms with quality fitted units and matching soft furnishings. The spacious bar lounge is about to undergo renovation, and a good range of food is available in the well furnished restaurant; service is very friendly and helpful throughout.
29⇌♘(4fb) CTV in all bedrooms ® T sB&B⇌♘ £41-£53 dB&B⇌♘ £82-£106 (incl dinner)
41P xmas
♡ English & French V ♡ ⚏ ⚔ Bar Lunch £4-£12 Dinner £14-£18&alc Last dinner 9pm
CONF. Thtr 40 Board 16 Del from £69
Credit Cards [1][3]

★★ ✿77% **Wateredge**
Borrans Rd, Waterhead LA22 0EP (on A591, at Waterhead Bay, adj Steamer Pier) ☎(05394) 32332 FAX (05394) 32332
Closed mid Dec-early Feb
Originally 2 fishermen's cottages, this is a delightfully comfortable hotel in a superb lakeside location. There are spacious lounges with lovely views and a cosy snug bar. Bedrooms are either in the main house or a rear extension. A 5-course dinner is served in the charming split-level beamed restaurant.
➥

Set in its own grounds near Lake Windermere, this elegant Regency house has been run by the Nixon family for 25 years, and is one of the country's leading Country House Hotels. It is well-known for the excellence of its cuisine and service whilst retaining a relaxed atmosphere.

**Ambleside, Cumbria LA22 0EH.
Tel: (05394) 33605**

★★★

Bowdon Hotel
Langham, Road, Bowdon,
Altrincham, Cheshire WA14 2HT
*Telephone: 061 928 7121
Fax: 061 927 7560*

★ Refurbished conference facilities
★ Parking for 150 cars
★ 10 minutes from Manchester Airport
★ 10 minutes from M6 and M56
★ 82 spacious bedrooms all with bath & shower
★ Acclaimed Number 10 Restaurant
★ Excellent real ales and good food pub

AT THE GATEWAY TO CHESHIRE

Ambleside

18⇨♙Annexe5⇨♙(1fb) CTV in all bedrooms ® T sB&B⇨♙£55-£68 dB&B⇨♙£94-£156 (incl dinner) 🍴 CTV 25P 🚗 ✻ rowing boat nc7yrs
♀ ⚲ ✂ ✱ Bar Lunch fr£6.50alc Dinner £23.90 Last dinner 8.30pm
Credit Cards [1][2][3]

★★ 72% Laurel Villa
Lake Rd LA22 0DB ☎(05394) 33290
Closed Xmas & New Year

This attractive Victorian house has recently been renovated to a very high standard. Mr and Mrs Seedhouse are attentive hosts and are always on hand to assist. Bedrooms are beautifully coordinated, and have excellent beds. There are 2 comfortable lounges, and a 5-course set dinner is provided each evening. The wine list offers mainly English wines.
7⇨♙2🚿 CTV in all bedrooms ® ✸ sB&B⇨♙£50 dB&B⇨♙£60-£80 🍴
10P 🚗
V ✤ ✂ Dinner £20-£25 Last dinner 7.30pm
Credit Cards [1][3]

★★ 72% Skelwith Bridge
Skelwith Bridge LA22 9NJ (2.5m W A593) ☎(05394) 32115 FAX (05394) 34254

On the riverside just outside Ambleside, this friendly 17th-century inn has lots of character. The spacious bar and attractive conservatory restaurant are both popular for their traditional English food and there are comfortable lounges, a cosy library bar and bedrooms equipped to good modern standards.
23⇨♙Annexe6⇨♙(3fb)2🚿 in 6 bedrooms CTV in all bedrooms ® T sB&B⇨♙£25-£50 dB&B⇨♙£45-£90 🍴
60P 🚗 ♪ ♤
♀ English & French V ✤ ⚲ ✂ Sunday Lunch £9.25-£10 Dinner £16.95-£17.50 Last dinner 9pm
CONF. Thtr 40 Class 20 Board 18 Del from £45
Credit Cards [1][3]

★★ ❀ 70% Nanny Brow Country House
Clappersgate LA22 9NF (A593) ☎(05394) 32036 FAX (05394) 32450

Dating from 1908, this delightful country house offers bedrooms which include spacious garden suites, some with lounge areas and french windows onto the garden, and standard rooms in the original house. There is a pleasant lounge and conservatory-style bar where proprietor Michael Fletcher takes orders for well cooked, enjoyable meals.
18rm(16⇨1♙)(3fb)2🚿 CTV in all bedrooms ®⚓ T
20P 🚗 ✻ solarium croquet spa bath
♀ English & French V ✤ ⚲ ✂ Lunch £10.50-£14.50 High tea £3.50-£7.75 Dinner £15-£22.50&alc Last dinner 9pm
CONF. Thtr 30 Class 30 Board 25 Del from £70
Credit Cards [1][2][3]

★★ 70% Riverside
Under Loughrigg, Nr. Rothay Bridge LA22 9LJ ☎(05394) 32395
Closed Dec-Jan

Peacefully situated in a country lane by the banks of the River Rothay, but within walking distance of the town, this comfortable small hotel has cosy lounges and bedrooms with modern facilities. Interesting dinners are provided in the pleasant dining room, with attentive service by the resident owners.
10⇨♙(2fb)2🚿 CTV in all bedrooms ® T ✸ (ex guide dogs) dB&B⇨♙£90-£100 (incl dinner)
CTV 20P 🚗 ✻ ♪ nc8yrs
♀ Continental V ✤ ⚲ ✂ Bar Lunch £3-£6alc Dinner £18&alc Last dinner 8pm
Credit Cards [1][3]

★★ ❀ 69% Borrans Park
Borrans Rd LA22 0EN (from A591 at Waterhead join A5075, hotel .50m on right, entrance opposite rugby club) ☎(05394) 33454
Closed 21-27 Dec

This charming, well furnished Georgian farmhouse surrounded by fields, is family-run and provides relaxing public rooms with books, fresh flowers and log fires. The richly furnished restaurant offers a well produced dinner, plainly cooked from the best possible produce, which may include local lamb, Scottish salmon or Lakeland trout.
12⇨♙(2fb)7🚿✂ in all bedrooms CTV in all bedrooms ® T ✸ sB&B⇨♙£27.50-£47.50 dB&B⇨♙£55-£75 🍴
20P 🚗 ✻ xmas
V ✂ ✻ Dinner £15.50 Last dinner 7pm
Credit Cards [1][3]

★★ 69% Fisherbeck
Lake Rd LA22 0DH (S on A591) ☎(05394) 33215 FAX (05394) 33600
Closed 25 Dec-10 Jan

This warm, comfortable and friendly hotel, set back from the A591 in an elevated position, has been in the same ownership for many years. Bedrooms, which vary in size, have pretty coordinated décor. A 5-course dinner is served each evening in the bright dining room, and afterwards guests can relax in the lounge or enjoy a drink in the well furnished bar.
20rm(17⇨♙)(3fb) CTV in all bedrooms ® T ✸ sB&B⇨♙£27.50-£38 dB&B⇨♙£55-£76 🍴
CTV 24P 🚗
V ✤ ⚲ ✻ Bar Lunch fr£5alc Dinner £15.95-£16.95 Last dinner 8pm
Credit Cards [1][3]

★★ 68% Kirkstone Foot Country House
Kirkstone Pass Rd LA22 9EH ☎(05394) 32232 FAX (05394) 31110
Closed 8-22 Dec & 3 Jan-early Feb

A fine 17th-century manor house, set in well cared-for grounds not far from the town centre. There is a spacious book-filled lounge and a cosy beamed restaurant where a 5-course dinner is served. Bedrooms are prettily furnished.
15⇨♙(2fb) CTV in all bedrooms ® T ✸ sB&B⇨♙£39.50-£52 dB&B⇨♙£79-£116 (incl dinner) 🍴
35P 🚗 ✻ xmas
V ✤ ⚲ Dinner £17.50-£19.25 Last dinner 8.30pm
Credit Cards [1][2][3][5]

★★ 🛏 66% Crow How
Rydal Rd LA22 9PN (0.75m N, on A591) ☎(05394) 32193
Closed Dec-Jan RS 6-29 Nov & Feb-12 Apr

This delightful Victorian country house hotel is situated along a private drive just north of Ambleside. It is surrounded by 2 acres of grounds which lead down to the river Rothay, and it is only a few minutes walk to Rydal Water. Bedrooms are bright and fresh with modern furniture, and each has a colour TV. A comfortable lounge with lots of books is available, and a well produced home-cooked dinner is provided in the charming dining room.
9rm(7⇨1♙)(2fb) CTV in all bedrooms ® sB&B£23.50-£24.50 sB&B⇨♙£28-£29 dB&B£47-£49 dB&B⇨♙£56-£58 🍴
9P 🚗 ✻ free fishing
♀ English & French V ✤ Dinner fr£11 Last dinner 7.30pm
Credit Cards [1][3]

★★ 66% Elder Grove
Lake Rd LA22 0DB (on A591 .5m S) ☎(05394) 32504
Closed mid Nov-mid Feb

This double-fronted Lakeland stone house offers bright, fresh bedrooms in modern style. An attractive dining room features exposed stone walls, the 2 lounges on the first floor are comfortable and service is warm and friendly.

For key to symbols see the Bookmark. ➡

Kirkstone Foot
Country House Hotel ★★

Next time you visit the Lake District, why not visit the Kirkstone Foot Country House Hotel delightfully situated in picturesque flower filled gardens. Inside the atmosphere is equally relaxing and friendly with a unique ambience accompanied by courteous, attentive service and widely acclaimed cuisine.
Annabel and Andrew Bedford invite you to call for full details and a colour brochure on
Ambleside (05394) 32232

Kirkstone Pass Road, Ambleside LA22 9EH
Tel: Ambleside (STD 05394) 32232

Skelwith
BRIDGE HOTEL ★★
A 17th century lakeland inn.

Situated in the heart of the Lake District National Park, our hotel provides you with an ideal base from which to explore the many mountains, fells and lakes.

All our bedrooms have their own en suite bathrooms, colour TVs, telephones and facilities for making tea and coffee. The restaurant provides excellent French and English cuisine and boasts an extensive wine cellar to complement the food.

Nr. Ambleside, Cumbria LA22 9NJ
Tel: 05394 32115 Fax: Ambleside 05394 34254

Nanny Brow ★★
Country House Hotel

An Oasis of Elegance

The Nanny Brow Country House Hotel is set in 5 acres of peaceful gardens and woodlands and enjoys spectacular views across the Brathay Valley towards the Langdale Pikes.

Grow accustomed to the comfort and contentment of gracious country house life. Relax in the comfortable drawing room, elegant lounge hall or garden room bar – there are log fires on chilly evenings. Much care has gone into creating individual pretty chintzy bedrooms, four poster suites and the luxury garden wing suites. There is a spa bath and solarium and complimentary use of the local private leisure centre. Facilities for management meetings and conferences are available. Dogs accepted by prior arrangement. Recommended by most major guides for fine wine and gourmet cuisine.

E.T.B. Four Crowns Highly Commended
Egon Ronay – Johansens – Ashley Courtenay

Nanny Brow Country House Hotel
Clappersgate, Ambleside, Cumbria LA22 9NF
Telephone: (05394) 32036 Fax: (05394) 32450

★★
Wateredge Hotel

Wateredge has developed from two 17th century fishermen's cottages and stands in a delightful position on the shores of Windermere.

Relax in our comfortable lounges overlooking the lake or on our lakeside lawn, where teas, light lunches or your evening aperitif may be served.

Dine under oak-beams and enjoy exquisitely cooked food from an imaginative menu. Log fires. Cosy bars. Private jetty. Pretty bedrooms all with ensuite facilities.

Please write or telephone for our brochure.

Waterhead, Ambleside,
Cumbria LA22 0EP
Tel: (05394) 32332

Ambleside - Andover

12⇨♠(1fb)1♯ CTV in all bedrooms ® T sB&B⇨♠£21-£26 dB&B⇨♠£42-£52 ⍾
CTV 12P ⍟
♡ English & Continental V ♥ ⚘ ✔ Bar Lunch £1.50-£4alc Dinner £15.50&alc Last dinner 8.15pm
Credit Cards [1][3]

★★ 62% *Glen Rothay*
Rydal LA22 9LR (1.25m N of Ambleside on A591)
☎(05394) 32524 FAX (05394) 31079
Closed 6 Dec-19 Dec also 6 & 25 Jan
Close to the shores of Rydal Water, this imposing 17th-century house with beams and oak panelling has much historic character. Personally run by the resident owners, it has bedrooms of varying size, a comfortable lounge and attractive dining room.
11⇨♠(2fb)4♯ CTV in all bedrooms ® T sB&B⇨♠£27-£34 dB&B⇨♠£54-£68 ⍾
35P ⍟ ❋ ♪ xmas
V ♥ ⚘ ✱ Bar Lunch £9-£16.70 Dinner £15.97-£17.95 Last dinner 8pm
Credit Cards [1][2][3][5]

★★ 61% *Waterhead*
Lake Rd LA22 0ER ☎(05394) 32566 FAX (05394) 31255

This large stone-built hotel is situated close to the lakeside. It offers spacious public rooms and bedrooms which vary in shape and quality. Staff are friendly and helpful.
26⇨♠(6fb) CTV in all bedrooms ® T
50P ❋
♡ English & French V ♥ ⚘ ✔ Last dinner 8.30pm
Credit Cards [1][2][3][5]

★★ 60% *Horseshoe*
Rothay Rd LA22 0EE ☎(05394) 32000
A pleasant, family-owned and run hotel offering good all round comforts, the Horseshoe stands close to the town's centre, overlooking a small golf course and tennis courts. Victorian-style public areas are very attractive, and a well produced dinner is served each evening. Keen staff provide very friendly service.
19rm(17⇨♠)(4fb)1♯ CTV in all bedrooms ®
CTV 19P ⍟
V ♥ ⚘ ✔ Last dinner 8.30pm
Credit Cards [1][2][3]

AMERSHAM Buckinghamshire Map **04** SU99

★★★ 63% *The Crown*
High St HP7 0DH ☎(0494) 721541 FAX (0494) 431283

The Crown has a Georgian façade, though there is Elizabethan timbering, panelling and fireplaces in many areas, including the comfortable small lounge. Most bedrooms are on the first floor of the main building, though some are in converted outbuildings. They vary in size but all are attractively decorated.
19⇨♠Annexe4⇨♠2♯ ✔ in 7 bedrooms CTV in all bedrooms ® T ❋ sB⇨♠£95 dB⇨♠£105-£135 (room only) ⍾
32P xmas
V ♥ ⚘ ✔ ❋ Lunch £13.95 Dinner £17.95&alc Last dinner 9.30pm
Credit Cards [1][2][3][5]

Some hotels within company owned groups share a uniform identity. For full details consult the Contents page, under Hotel Groups.

AMESBURY Wiltshire Map **04** SU14

Forte Travelodge
SP4 7AS (junc A345 & A303 eastbound)
☎(0980) 624966 Central Res (0800) 850950

This modern building offers a good standard of accommodation for overnight stops. Smart, spacious and well equipped bedrooms, all with en suite bathrooms, are suitable for family use, and meals may be taken at the nearby family restaurant. For more details about Travelodge, consult the Contents page, under Hotel Groups.
32⇨♠ ❋ B⇨♠£31.95 (room only)

AMLWCH

See **Anglesey, Isle of**

AMMANFORD Dyfed Map **02** SN61

★★ 67% *Mill at Glynhir*
Glyn-Hir, Llandybie SA18 2TE (3m NE off A483) ☎(0269) 850672
RS 24 Dec-4 Jan

Once a flour mill, as the name suggests, and thought to be over 250 years old, the Mill is on the side of a wooded valley with trout fishing available from the River Loughor. Bedrooms are spacious and most have comfortable armchairs; some have direct access to patios, and bathrooms have whirlpool baths. There are pretty terraced gardens, and the galleried lounge bar has an alcove overlooking the golf course (free golf for residents).
11⇨♠ CTV in all bedrooms ® T sB&B⇨♠£36 dB&B⇨♠£72 ⍾
20P ⍟ ❋ ⌺ (heated) ▶ 18 ♪ nc11yrs
♡ Welsh & French V ♥ ✔ Dinner £14.50 Last dinner 8.30pm
Credit Cards [1][3]

AMPFIELD Hampshire Map **04** SU32

★★★ 68% *Potters Heron*
SO51 9ZF (off A31) (Lansbury) ☎Southampton(0703) 266611 FAX (0703) 251359
This attractive thatched hotel has a popular galleried 'pub' with open fires, serving real ales and bar meals, and a more formal restaurant and cocktail bar overlooking the courtyard. Bedrooms, in a modern block at the rear, are spacious, comfortable and well equipped, with room service usually expected.
54⇨♠(2fb)1♯ ✔ in 20 bedrooms CTV in all bedrooms ® T ✱ (ex guide dogs) ❋ sB&B⇨♠fr£75.50 dB&B⇨♠fr£87 ⍾
Lift ⟮ 200P sauna gymnasium ⌖ xmas
♡ English & French V ♥ ⚘ ❋ Lunch fr£10.25 Dinner fr£15.50 Last dinner 10pm
CONF. Thtr 140 Class 50 Board 40 Del from £99
Credit Cards [1][2][3][5]

ANDOVER Hampshire Map **04** SU34

★★★ 61% *Ashley Court*
Micheldever Rd SP11 6LA ☎(0264) 357344 FAX (0264) 356755

Set in 4 acres, this quietly situated hotel has been skilfully extended to provide a well connected, self-contained Village Conference Suite together with 26 comfortable new bedrooms. The Rendezvous Restaurant features à la carte and table d'hôte menus, and a good range of bar meals is available.
9⇨♠Annexe26⇨♠ ✔ in 7 bedrooms CTV in all bedrooms ® T sB&B⇨♠£49-£75 dB&B⇨♠£55-£90 ⍾
⟮ CTV 120P snooker gymnasium croquet petanque xmas
♡ English & Continental V ♥ ⚘ Lunch £9.50-£14.50&alc Dinner £14.50&alc Last dinner 9.30pm
CONF. Thtr 200 Class 150 Board 50 Del from £85
Credit Cards [1][2][3]

Andover - Anglesey, Beaumaris

★★ 60% **Danebury**
High St SP10 1NX (on the A303) (Whitbread) ☎(0264) 323332 FAX (0264) 334021
The origins of this town centre hotel remain obscure, but records show a hotel on the site since 1582. With its many alterations and modernisations, the present establishment provides well furnished rooms with up-to-date amenities. There is a public bar, Henekey's restaurant and bar lounge. The rear car park, in East Street, can be difficult to find – ask for directions.
24⇨ ↑ 1 ⌘ ⌿ in 6 bedrooms CTV in all bedrooms ® ✻ T
✈ (ex guide dogs) ✱ sB&B⇨ ↑ fr£45 dB&B⇨ ↑ fr£57 ♬
⦅ 40P xmas
♡ ♢ ⌿ Last dinner 9.30pm
CONF. Thtr 80 Class 20 Board 40
Credit Cards 1 2 3 5

ANGLESEY, ISLE OF Gwynedd

AMLWCH Map 06 SH49

★★ 64% **Lastra Farm**
Penrhyd LL68 9TF ☎(0407) 830906 FAX (0407) 832522
5⇨ ↑(1fb) CTV in all bedrooms ® T sB&B⇨ ↑£25-£27 dB&B⇨ ↑£45-£48 ♬
⦅ 40P ❋
♡ Welsh & French V ♢ ⌾ ⌿ ✻ Lunch £3-£8alc Dinner £12-£18alc Last dinner 9.30pm
Credit Cards 1 3

★★ 54% **Trecastell**
Bull Bay LL68 9SA (1m N on A5025, adjacent to Golf Club) (Frederic Robinson) ☎(0407) 830651 FAX (0407) 832114
Overlooking the bay and a short walk from the local golf course, this privately run detached hotel has a small comfortable lounge plus a lounge bar offering bar meals in addition to the restaurant. Bedrooms, though now looking rather worn, all have modern facilities.
12rm(8⇨3↑)(3fb) CTV in 10 bedrooms ® T
sB&B⇨ ↑£24.50-£29.50 dB&B⇨ ↑£40-£45
CTV 60P ⇨ ❋
♡ Bar Lunch £1.50-£7 Dinner £9.25-£10.35&alc Last dinner 8.30pm
Credit Cards 1 2 3

BEAUMARIS Map 06 SH67

★★ ❀❀ 75% **Ye Olde Bulls Head Inn**
Castle St LL58 8AP (Welsh Rarebits) ☎(0248) 810329 FAX (0248) 811294
Closed 25-26 Dec
There are views across the Menai Straits to the peaks of Snowdonia from this historic 15th-century posting house with its beamed bars, elegant lounge and beautifully furnished bedrooms. In the restaurant a refreshing lack of pretention characterises the reasonably priced menu, with a stimulating range of dishes. A typical meal might consist of a salad of smoked duck breast and marinaded peppers in a Provençal dressing, followed by fillet of lamb en croute with a mild mustardy sauce and, for dessert, strawberry and passion fruit crème brûlée.
10⇨ ↑ Annexe1⇨ ↑ CTV in all bedrooms ® T
✈ (ex guide dogs) sB&B⇨ ↑ fr£42 dB&B⇨ ↑ fr£72 ♬
12P ❋
♡ English & French V ♢ ⌿ Sunday Lunch fr£14.75 Dinner fr£18.95&alc Last dinner 9.30pm
Credit Cards 1 3

★★ 66% **Bishopsgate House**
54 Castle St LL58 8BB ☎(0248) 810302 FAX (0248) 810166
Closed 22 Dec-31 Jan
This charming 19th-century house is close to the town centre and just a few yards from the seafront. Privately owned and personally run, it provides modern bedrooms which have been furnished and decorated in the style of the house, with a number of antiques. There is a cosy bar with an open fire in cold weather, and a panelled, period-style lounge. Both à la carte and table d'hôte menus are offered in the attractive restaurant.
10⇨ ↑ 1 ⌘ CTV in all bedrooms ® T ✻ sB&B⇨ ↑£28-£32 dB&B⇨ ↑£48-£54 ♬
10P ⇨ nc5yrs
♡ English & French V ♢ ⌿ ✻ Sunday Lunch £7.95 Dinner £12.95-£16.50 Last dinner 9pm
Credit Cards 1 3

★★ 63% **Bulkeley Arms**
Castle St LL58 8AW ☎(0248) 810415 FAX (0248) 810146

CONSORT HOTELS

This impressive house, built by Richard Bulkeley to honour an intended visit by the future Queen Victoria, fronts the town's main street with views of the Menai Straits from the rear. It retains much of its original character and has traditionally furnished bedrooms suitable both for commercial guests and tourists.
43rm(40⇨ ↑)(4fb) CTV in all bedrooms ® T
Lift ⦅ 30P snooker solarium
♡ International V ♢ ⌾ Last dinner 9.30pm
Credit Cards 1 2 3

★★ 63% **Henllys Hall**
LL58 8HU ☎(0248) 810412 FAX (0248) 811511
Although most of the hall was rebuilt in the 1850s following a fire, part of it dates back to 1450. It is set in 40 acres of woodland with fine views of the Menai Straits and Snowdonia. There are high ceilings in the lounge and bar and the entrance hall has an impressive wooden staircase. Popular 'Romantic' and 'Murder Mystery' breaks are run by the hotel.
22⇨ ↑(8fb)9⌘ CTV in all bedrooms ® T ✻ sB&B⇨ ↑£22-£40 dB&B⇨ ↑£40-£76 ♬

➡

Elder Grove Hotel
Lake Road, Ambleside, ★★
Cumbria LA22 0DB

A lovely Victorian, family-managed hotel, situated between the village and the lake. 12 pretty bedrooms with full facilities. Unique Lakeland Greenstone dining room with imaginative cooking. Relaxing bar and lounges. Central heating. Car park.

For colour brochure and tariff
Phone Ambleside (05394) 32504

Anglesey, Beaumaris - Trearddur Bay

Lift 100P ✻ ⌥ (heated) ♪ (hard) sauna solarium gymnasium jacuzzi table tennis pool table ⚬ *xmas*
♀ Welsh & French V ♂ ⌥ Sunday Lunch fr£7.50 Dinner £12.50-£15 Last dinner 9.30pm
CONF. Thtr 150 Class 120 Board 40 Del from £18
Credit Cards [1][2][3][5]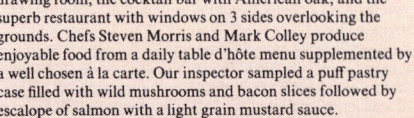

BENLLECH BAY Map 06 SH58

★★59% *Bay Court*
Beach Rd LL74 8SW ☎Tynygongl(0248) 852573
A short walk from the sandy beach, this friendly and popular hotel has a lounge bar where a good range of meals is served, and a cellar bar where locals congregate to play pool and darts. The restaurant offers fixed-price and à la carte menus, and there is a comfortable residents' lounge.
15rm(2⇨4♠)Annexe4⇨(5fb) CTV in 15 bedrooms ® sB&B£18 sB&B⇨♠£23 dB&B£36-£39 dB&B⇨♠£46 ♫ CTV 65P *xmas*
♀ English & French V ♂ ⌥ Lunch £5-£6.50&alc High tea fr£2.50 Dinner £7.50-£9&alc Last dinner 9pm
Credit Cards [1][2][3]

HOLYHEAD Map 06 SH28

★★61% *Bull*
London Rd, Valley LL65 3DP (on A5 near junct with A5025)
☎(0407) 740351 FAX (0407) 742328
The bars are very popular locally, as is the food, and good value bar and restaurant meals are available all day long.
9⇨♠Annexe5⇨♠(4fb) CTV in all bedrooms ® T ✱ (ex guide dogs) ✻ sB&B⇨♠£27.25-£28.50 dB&B⇨♠£38.50-£40 ♫
P ✻
♀ International V ♂ ⌥ ✻ Lunch £6.45 High tea £4.20-£6.30alc Dinner £8.95-£9.80&alc Last dinner 9.30pm
Credit Cards [1][3]

LLANFAIR PWLLGWYNGYLL Map 06 SH57

★★★64% *Carreg Bran Country*
Church Ln LL61 5YH (A5/A4080 junct at end of Britannia Bridge) ☎Llanfairpwll(0248) 714224 FAX (0248) 715983
This modern hotel is on the Anglesey side of the Britannia Bridge and, with its well equipped, comfortable bedrooms, good conference facilities and ease of access from the A5, is deservedly popular with business people.
29⇨♠Annexe4⇨♠(4fb) CTV in all bedrooms ® T
☾ 150P ✻
♀ Welsh & French V ♂ ⌥
Credit Cards [1][2][3][5]

LLANGEFNI Map 06 SH47

★★★

TRE-YSGAWEN HALL
Capel Coch LL77 7UR
☎(0248) 750750 FAX
(0248) 750035

Not the easiest of places to find, but worth the effort for the sense of peace at this magnificent stone mansion, which has been carefully restored to provide elegant country house accommodation. Inside there is an impressive oak staircase and the bedrooms are furnished with fine antique pieces and attractive fabrics. Public rooms include a spacious

drawing room, the cocktail bar with American oak, and the superb restaurant with windows on 3 sides overlooking the grounds. Chefs Steven Morris and Mark Colley produce enjoyable food from a daily table d'hôte menu supplemented by a well chosen à la carte. Our inspector sampled a puff pastry case filled with wild mushrooms and bacon slices followed by escalope of salmon with a light grain mustard sauce.
19⇨♠(5fb)3♫ CTV in all bedrooms T sB⇨♠£71.50-£84.50 dB⇨♠£93.50-£104.50 (room only) ♫
☾ 110P ✻ clay pigeon & game shooting *xmas*
♀ French V ♂ ⌥ Lunch fr£15 High tea £4.95-£7.95 Dinner £19.95-£22.95&alc Last dinner 9.30pm
CONF. Thtr 120 Class 110 Board 28 Del from £105
Credit Cards [1][2][3][5]

★★63% *Nant-yr-Odyn*
Llanfawr LL77 7YE (1.5m S of junction A5/A5114)
☎(0248) 723354
This friendly family-run hotel is converted from 18th-century farm buildings arranged around a courtyard. It has well equipped bedrooms with modern pine furnishings, a beamed restaurant and comfortable lounge bar.
14⇨♠ CTV in all bedrooms ® T ✱
30P ⚬
♂ ⌥
Credit Cards [1][3]

MENAI BRIDGE Map 06 SH57

★★60% *Anglesey Arms*
LL59 5EA (on left after Menai Bridge) (J W Lees)
☎(0248) 712305 FAX (0248) 712076
Set in secluded gardens at the Anglesey end of Telford's famous suspension bridge, this old coaching inn has well furnished bedrooms, many with views of the Menai Straits and Snowdonia. The popular bar serves all-day refreshments and there is a comfortable foyer lounge and a large restaurant with a dance floor.
17rm(10⇨6♠) CTV in all bedrooms ® ✻ sB&B⇨♠fr£30 dB&B⇨♠fr£45 ♫
CTV 125P ✻ *xmas*
V ♂ ⌥ ✻ Sunday Lunch fr£7.95 Dinner £6.95-£12 Last dinner 10pm
Credit Cards [1][3]

★★58% *Gazelle*
Glyn Garth LL59 5PD (2m NE A545) (Frederic Robinson)
☎(0248) 713364 FAX (0248) 713167
Situated on the edge of the Menai Straits with fine views of Snowdonia, this small hotel provides modest but well furnished bedrooms and has a popular restaurant and bars.
10rm(4⇨1♠)(1fb) CTV in all bedrooms ®♪ T ✱ (ex guide dogs) ✻ sB&B£31 sB&B⇨♠£34 dB&B£47.50 dB&B⇨♠£60
40P ✻ sailing sea fishing watersports
♂ ⌥ ✻ Lunch £7.95-£15.95alc Dinner £7.75-£15.95alc Last dinner 9pm
Credit Cards [1][3]

TREARDDUR BAY Map 06 SH27

★★★72% *Trearddur Bay*
LL68 2UN ☎(0407) 860301 FAX (0407) 861181
Friendly service is the hallmark of this hotel, a few yards from the beach. Extensive refurbishment has dramatically improved the hotel and many of the bedrooms are spacious, with attractive décor, good quality soft furnishings and fine locally crafted furniture. All have such extras as potted plants, ornaments, fruit and biscuits. There is an elegant restaurant, a choice of bars and a family room.

Anglesey, Trearddur Bay - Anstruther

31⇨ொ(7fb)1⇔⊬in 1 bedroom CTV in all bedrooms ® T ✱
sB&B⇨ொ£63-£86 dB&B⇨ொ£90-£106 ℗
《 CTV 300P ✿ 🖃 (heated) children's games room ⚬ xmas
V ⚬ ⚓ ⊬ Sunday Lunch £10.50 Dinner £16.95&alc Last
dinner 9.30pm
CONF. Thtr 120 Class 60 Board 40 Del from £90
Credit Cards ①②③④⑤

★★★ **59%** *Beach*
LL65 2YT ☎(0407) 860332 FAX (0407) 861140
Closed 24-27 Dec

Bedrooms here vary in size, many have attractive fabrics and some have canopied beds. For meals, guests can choose from table d'hôte or à la carte menus in the main restaurant, or the bistro in the London Road Bar. The first floor lounge doubles as a meeting room. The staff are friendly and helpful.

26⇨ொ(3fb) CTV in all bedrooms ® T
《 150P ✿ ♀ (hard) squash snooker sauna solarium gymnasium spa toning tables solarium 🎵 ⚬
♁ English & French V ⚬ ⚓ ⊬ Last dinner 9.30pm
Credit Cards ①②③⑤

★★ **58%** *Seacroft*
Ravenspoint Rd LL65 2YU ☎(0407) 860348

This small privately owned hotel is situated close to the beach and offers simple accommodation.

6rm(1⇨2ொ)(3fb) CTV in all bedrooms ® ✈
CTV 30P ✿
♁ French V ⚬

ANNAN Dumfries & Galloway *Dumfriesshire* Map **11** NY16

★★ **64%** Warmanbie Hotel & Restaurant
DG12 5LL (N of town off B722) ☎(0461) 204015

Set in relaxing surroundings, this family-owned and run country house stands to the north of the town. Bedrooms vary in size and style, the best being at the front, but all are equipped with thoughtful extras, and guests can relax in either the small bar or a comfortable library lounge.

7⇨ொ(1fb)2⇔ CTV in all bedrooms ® T sB&B⇨ொ£49-£54 dB&B⇨ொ£70.50-£81 ℗
25P ✿ ♪ clay pigeon shooting *xmas*
V ⚬ ⚓ ⊬ Lunch fr£8.95 Dinner £16.95 Last dinner 9.30pm
CONF. Thtr 50 Class 30 Board 22
Credit Cards ①②③

★★ **63%** Queensberry Arms
DG12 6AD (in town square, 1.5m from A75)
☎(0461) 202024 FAX (0461) 205998

Situated in the centre of town, this former coach house has been totally modernised by the current owners to provide attractive ground-floor public areas, a first-floor steakhouse with a nautical theme, a restaurant and well equipped bedrooms of varying sizes.

26⇨ொ(3fb) CTV in all bedrooms ® ⅀ T
sB&B⇨ொ£38 dB&B⇨ொ£51 ℗
《 50P ✿ 🎵 xmas
♁ International V ⚬ ⚓ ⊬ ✱ Lunch £5.10-£11.60&alc High tea £5.25-£7.25alc Dinner £5.10-£11.60&alc Last dinner 9.30pm
CONF. Thtr 150 Class 60 Board 40 Del £37.50
Credit Cards ①②③⑤

ANSTRUTHER Fife Map **12** NO50

★★ **59%** Smugglers Inn
High St KY10 3DQ ☎(0333) 310506

This historic roadside inn retains much of its original informal character. There is an attractive restaurant and first-floor lounge bar, where reception is situated. Bedrooms, though not over-large, are pleasantly furnished.

Golf Hotel ★★
Links Avenue, Powfoot,
Annan, Dumfriesshire DG12 5PN
Tel: Cummertrees (04617) 254

Situated next to an 18 hole Golf Course with fishing nearby on the River Annan, the Golf Hotel is a tempting prospect for the sportsperson. However with views over the unspoilt Powfoot Bay and with the countryside and history of South West Scotland on the doorstep, it is an excellent centre for touring. Ideal for wildfowl from September until February. Special rates for Wildfowlers. Seasonal breaks available.

Traditional Scottish food prepared where possible using local produce. All 21 bedrooms have direct dial telephone and 14 are en suite.

Les Routiers & Ashley Courtenay Recommended

WTB
♦♦♦♦

THE BULL HOTEL
AA ★ ★

LONDON ROAD, VALLEY, HOLYHEAD, ISLE OF ANGLESEY
Tel: (0407) 740351 Fax: (0407) 742328

A special welcome to the magical island of Anglesey awaits you at The Bull. Situated on the A5 only 3½ miles from the ferry to Ireland. We have fifteen well-appointed bedrooms, all with en-suite facilities and all with colour TV, internal and external telephone, coffee and tea makers and radio alarms.

Our lounge bar with its beamed ceilings and stone walls has an olde worlde character. The friendly staff serve real ale and lagers. Delicious bar food is available both at lunch-time and in the evening. Our Bull Bach dining room with its flagged floors, check tablecloths and candlelight serves a wide variety of food at very competitive prices. Children's menus are always served.

Your hosts, David and Margaret Hall will do everything possible to make your stay enjoyable.

Double/Twin £38.50; Single £27.25; Short Breaks £49.50 per person, 2 nights, bed breakfast and evening meal.

Les Routiers recommended

Anstruther - Archiestown

8⇉↑ CTV in all bedrooms ® T ✱ sB&B⇉↑£25-£27 dB&B⇉↑£50-£54
CTV 12P
♥ Scottish, French & Italian V ♦ Last dinner 9.30pm
Credit Cards 1 2 3 5

APPLEBY-IN-WESTMORLAND Cumbria Map 12 NY62

★★★ ❀♨ 70% Appleby Manor Country House
Roman Rd CA16 6JB
☎Appleby(07683) 51571 FAX (07683) 52888
Closed 24-26 Dec

An impressive mid-Victorian building with extensions housing the bedrooms and the delightful garden room lounge, Appleby Manor stands in an elevated position with impressive views. Ample lounges are provided, and bedrooms are elegantly furnished. There is a choice of 4 set price menus offering such items as fillet of lamb rolled in oatmeal, or manor house beefsteak and oyster pudding. Breads, puddings and soups are all home made.

23⇉↑ Annexe7⇉↑(8fb)2⇄ CTV in all bedrooms ® T sB&B⇉↑£57-£64 dB&B⇉↑£84-£98 ₧
40P 3🎾 (£1) ✿ 🈁 (heated) sauna solarium gymnasium croquet jacuzzi pool table steam room
V ♥ ♨ ⚡ Lunch £16.95-£17.95&alc Dinner £16.95-£19.95 Last dinner 9pm
CONF. Thtr 38 Class 25 Board 26 Del from £86.50
Credit Cards 1 2 3 5

★★★ 68% Tufton Arms
Market Square CA16 6XA
☎Appleby(07683) 51593 FAX (07683) 52761

Carefully restored by its present owners, this town centre hotel offers stylish and comfortable public areas, with a good range of food available in the bar or conservatory restaurant. Attractive bedrooms have quality furnishings and service is friendly and attentive.

19⇉↑(2fb) CTV in all bedrooms ® T sB&B⇉↑£37.50-£55 dB&B⇉↑£60-£140 ₧
CTV 15P 2🎾 ♪ shooting xmas
V ♥ ♨ ✱ Dinner £16 Last dinner 9.30pm
CONF. Thtr 130 Class 80 Board 50 Del £75
Credit Cards 1 2 3 5

★★ 63% Royal Oak Inn
Bongate CA16 6UN ☎Appleby(07683) 51463 FAX (07683) 52300
Closed 25 Dec

This friendly old coaching inn on the main street of the oldest part of the town is popular for its extensive range of food, available in the beamed and wood-panelled bars or attractive dining room. There is a small and cosy residents lounge and individually decorated bedrooms with modern facilities.

9rm(5⇉2↑)(1fb) CTV in all bedrooms ® T sB&B£25 sB&B⇉↑£38.50-£45 dB&B⇉↑£58.50-£68.50 ₧
9P
♥ International V ♥ ⚡ Last dinner 9pm
Credit Cards 1 2 3 5

★ 61% Courtfield
Bongate CA16 6UP (on Brough rd) ☎Appleby(07683) 51394

This small hotel stands in its own pleasant grounds. There is a comfortable lounge with an open fire and TV, home cooked food is provided and the atmosphere is warm and friendly. Bedrooms are simply furnished, clean and tidy, some in an adjacent modern annexe.

5rm(1⇉1↑)Annexe3rm(1⇉1↑)(1fb) CTV in 6 bedrooms ®
CTV 20P 2🎾 ❀ ✿
V ♥ ♨ ⚡ Last dinner 8pm

APPLETON-LE-MOORS North Yorkshire Map 08 SE78

★★♨ 73% Appleton Hall Country House
YO6 6TF ☎Lastingham(0751) 417227 417452 FAX (0751) 417540
Closed Jan

This large Victorian house has immaculate gardens. Décor and furnishings are of a very high standard to complement the period of the building, with its fine plasterwork and original fireplaces. Bedrooms meet every modern need; many overlook the garden, and 2 have private lounges. The very comfortable drawing room has an open fire in the winter, and the dining room provides an intimate atmosphere for the 5-course English dinners and hearty breakfasts.

12⇉↑1⇄ CTV in all bedrooms ® T ✱ sB&B⇉↑£36 dB&B⇉↑£55 ₧
Lift CTV 30P ♿ ✿ croquet nc12yrs xmas
♥ English & Continental ♥ ⚡ ✱ Sunday Lunch £9.50 Dinner £18.50-£23.50 Last dinner 8.15pm
Credit Cards 1 2 3

ARBROATH Tayside Angus Map 12 NO64

★★★ 63% Letham Grange
Colliston DD11 4RL (3m N on St Vigeans rd)
☎Gowanbank(024189) 373 FAX (024189) 414

Set in extensive parkland, this magnificent mansion not only attracts sporting enthusiasts, but also those who appreciate fine architecture. Some of the best features are in the restaurant, drawing room and cocktail bar. Bedrooms, in country mansion style, are mostly well proportioned and comfortable, and equipped for the modern traveller. Room 2 has a splendid original Victorian bathroom. The Tower Suite has steep stairs leading to a bedroom and separate dressing room, while a spiral iron staircase goes up to the penthouse lounge. Windowed all round it gives superb panoramic views.

19⇉↑ CTV in all bedrooms ® T sB&B⇉↑£73-£79 dB&B⇉↑£116-£126 ₧
《 100P ♿ ✿ ⛳ 18 ⛳ croquet putting pool tables ⚡ xmas
♥ International V ♥ ⚡ ✱ Bar Lunch £5-£8 High tea £4-£8 Dinner £18.75 Last dinner 10pm
CONF. Thtr 1000 Class 400 Board 100 Del from £95
Credit Cards 1 2 3 5 £

★★ 62% Hotel Seaforth
Dundee Rd DD11 1QF (on southern outskirts, on A92)
☎(0241) 72232 FAX (0241) 77473

This charming hotel is conveniently situated on the southern side of town, looking out to sea. Bedrooms vary in size and style, and are being re-decorated. A good range of generously portioned dishes is served in the Victorian-style restaurant, and Arbroath Smokies (grilled smoked haddock) and kippers are popular at breakfast.

20⇉↑(2fb) CTV in all bedrooms ® T sB&B⇉↑£37.50-£39.50 dB&B⇉↑£52-£56 ₧
100P ✿ 🈁 (heated) snooker solarium jacuzzi xmas
♥ Scottish & French V ♥ Lunch £7.95-£8.95 High tea fr£7.95 Dinner £14.95-£16.95&alc Last dinner 9.30pm
Credit Cards 1 2 3 5 £

ARCHIESTOWN Grampian Morayshire Map 15 NJ24

★★ ❀❀ 72% Archiestown
AB38 7QX (on B9102, 5m SW of Craigellachie)
☎Carron(03406) 218 FAX (03406) 239
Closed Dec-Feb

This 100-year-old building of mellow grey stone, enhanced by colourful window boxes, was restored by present owners, Judith and Michael Bulger. The public rooms have much charm and character, and bedrooms, particularly those on the first floor, are sizeable, some having antique furniture. Judith Bulger's scrumptious 3-course dinners are unpretentious and helpings are hearty. Starters may include salmon fishcakes or delicious home-made soup; and for main course, perhaps baked marrow stuffed with minced beef and

served with tomato sauce, or poached turbot with white butter sauce.
8rm(6⇨) CTV in all bedrooms ® T ✱ sB&Bfr£25 sB&B⇨fr£40 dB&B⇨fr£65
20P 🚗 ✿
♀ International V ♥ ⚓ ✕ ✱ Bar Lunch fr£5alc Dinner fr£20 Last dinner 8.30pm
Credit Cards [1][3]

ARCHIRONDEL
See **Jersey** under **Channel Islands**

ARDELVE Highland *Ross & Cromarty* Map 14 NG82

★🏵69% Loch Duich
IV40 8DY (beside 'Road to the Isles') ☎Dornie(059985) 213 FAX (059985) 214
Closed 4 Jan-1 Mar & 19-28 Dec RS Nov-18 Dec
(Rosette awarded for dinner only)
Beside the 'Road to the Isles', this former drovers' inn enjoys fine views over the loch to Eilean Donan Castle. It has a relaxed friendly atmosphere, with a choice of comfortable lounges and traditional bars, and offers simple bedrooms of varying size (some bathrooms are awkwardly compact). Chef Carol MacRae provides a daily changing set price dinner menu of carefully prepared traditional Scottish dishes.
18rm(5♠)(1fb) ® ✱ sB&B£18.50-£21.50 sB&B♠£21.50-£26.50 dB&B£38-£47 dB&B♠£47-£53 🍴
CTV 40P 1🚙 🚗 ✿ fishing shooting 🎵
♀ Scottish & French V ♥ ⚓ ✱ Bar Lunch £4.35-£9.50alc Dinner fr£16.25 Last dinner 9pm
Credit Cards [1][3]

HOTEL SEAFORTH
★★

Prominent seafront position in extensive grounds with ample parking. Short walk from picturesque fishing harbour, town and abbey. Rooms en suite with TV and tea/coffee. Comfortable bar and restaurant renowned for charcoal grilled steaks and seafood. Indoor swimming pool, sauna, jacuzzi. Snooker tables. Function facilities. Many fine golf courses within easy reach, together with sea and river angling.

Dundee Road, Arbroath DD11 1QF
Tel: 0241 72232   Fax: 0241 77473

★★

A lovely genuine old inn for many years, the Royal Oak Inn stands out for good food and drink and above all atmosphere.

**BONGATE
APPLEBY-IN-WESTMORLAND
CUMBRIA CA16 6UN
Tel: 07683 51463 Fax: 07683 52300**

Discussions in the Jacuzzi!

Overheard in the jacuzzi in the Appleby Manor Country House Hotel:

"... we toured the Lakes today and tomorrow we are going into the Yorkshire Dales..." "... slept like a log last night..." "... we can't keep the children out of the swimming pool..." "... I'll have to go on a diet when I get back!..." "... never seen such a view - I didn't even know Appleby had a castle..." "... Sue likes the Steam Room but I prefer the Sauna..." "... we've booked to come back in the autumn..." "... the children went pony trekking while we had a lovely round of golf..." "...Peter says he's going to sample every one of the seventy malt whiskies - some chance !..."

Join the discussion in the jacuzzi - simply phone or write for a free colour brochure:

**APPLEBY·MANOR
COUNTRY HOUSE HOTEL**
★★★ ✿ Roman Road,
Appleby - in - Westmorland,
Cumbria CA16 6JD.
Tel: Appleby (07683) 51571

Relaxing and Friendly...

Ardentinny - Arran, Lagg

ARDENTINNY Strathclyde *Argyllshire* Map 10 NS18

★★★**68%** **Ardentinny**
PA23 8TR (M8 to Gourock, ferry to Dunoon(every 30mins duration 20mins) 12m N on A880 off A815, alternative route by Erskine Bridge & Loch Lomond) ☎(036981) 209 & 275 FAX (036981) 345
Closed Nov-15 Mar

With a picturesque approach, either by the lochside or through forests, this former coaching inn is on a promontory with gardens leading down to the shore. Its bar and buttery attract non residents, and the hotel is popular with the yachting set. Bedrooms are bright and fresh, and service is friendly and attentive.

11➪♠(1fb) CTV in all bedrooms ® T sB&B➪♠£25-£39 dB&B➪♠£50-£78 ₽
30P ❊ boating
♥ Scottish, French & German V ♂ ♫ ✻ Bar Lunch £5-£15alc Dinner £21 Last dinner 9.30pm
Credit Cards [1][2][3][5]

ARDUAINE Strathclyde *Argyllshire* Map 10 NM80

★★★**70%** **Loch Melfort**
PA34 4XG (on A816) ☎Kilmelford(08522) 233 FAX (08522) 214
Closed 4 Jan-Feb

This popular tourist hotel is only 100yds or so from the seashore and has uninterrupted views of the bay, coastline and distant islands. To take advantage of the delightful location, all the bedrooms in the chalet-style Cedar Wing have either balconies or patios, and the dining room is fronted by huge picture windows. Seafood features on the menu as well as local meats, and Sunday dinner is an impressive cold buffet.

7➪♠Annexe20➪♠(2fb) CTV in all bedrooms ® T sB&B➪♠£35-£57 dB&B➪♠£60-£94 ₽
65P ❊ xmas
V ♂ ♫ ✻ Bar Lunch fr£2.50 Dinner fr£24.50 Last dinner 9pm
Credit Cards [1][3]

See advertisement under OBAN

ARDVASAR

See **Skye, Isle of**

ARISAIG Highland *Inverness-shire* Map 13 NM68

★★★❊♨ **ARISAIG HOUSE**
Beasdale PH39 4NR (3m E A830) ☎(06875) 622 FAX (06875) 626
Closed Nov-Mar

John and Ruth Smither's historic country house is set in natural woodland with formal terraced gardens and woodland walks leading to the sea shore. Many of the lovely bedrooms have sea views, and the beautifully furnished public rooms include the inner hall with an impressive oak staircase and the drawing room, with its blazing log fire and rare Italian vaulted ceiling. The panelled dining room, with polished tables and candlelight, is the setting for chef David Wilkinson's excellent dinners.

13➪ CTV in all bedrooms T ✻ (ex guide dogs) dB&B➪£136.50-£205 ₽
16P ❊ ❊ snooker croquet nc10yrs

♥ British & French V ♂ ♫ Bar Lunch £5-£15alc Dinner £29.50&alc Last dinner 8.30pm
Credit Cards [1][2][3]

★★**❊65%** **Arisaig**
PH39 4NH ☎(06875) 210 FAX (06875) 310
Closed Nov-Feb
(Rosette awarded for dinner only)

Efficiently run by the Stewart family, this popular holiday hotel beside the main road overlooks Loch Nan Ceal and has a relaxed friendly atmosphere. Bedrooms vary in size and style and there are traditional lounges and bars. In the cosy dining room, with its open fire Mrs Stewart offers enjoyable 'Taste of Scotland' dishes which regularly feature fresh local seafood.

15rm(5➪)(4fb) ® T sB£19-£23 dB£38-£46 dB➪£50-£60 (room only)
CTV 60P ♣
V ♂ ♫ ✻ Bar Lunch £10-£20alc High tea £10-£15alc Dinner £12-£22alc Last dinner 8.15pm
Credit Cards [1][3]

ARNCLIFFE North Yorkshire Map 07 SD97

★★♨**74%** **Amerdale House**
BD23 5QE ☎(0756) 770250
Closed mid Nov-mid Mar

This charming and elegant Victorian country house is in beautiful Littondale. It has a spacious chandeliered lounge, cosy bar and attractive period-style dining room. The bedrooms are equipped with modern facilities but retain their individual character. The 4-course dinner menu features local lamb, vegetables from the garden and Yorkshire cheeses.

10➪♠Annexe1➪♠(3fb)1⊞ CTV in all bedrooms ® ✻ (ex guide dogs) ❊ dB&B➪♠£49.50-£51.50 (incl dinner) ₽
30P ♣ ❊
V ♫ ✻ Dinner fr£18 Last dinner 8.30pm
Credit Cards [1][3]

ARRAN, ISLE OF Strathclyde *Bute* Map 10

BRODICK Map 10 NS03

★★★**❊75%** **Auchrannie Country House**
KA27 8BZ ☎(0770) 302234 & 302235 FAX (0770) 302812

Extensive leisure facilities together with friendly, efficient staff and good food are all part of the appeal at this sympathetically renovated Victorian mansion, which is set in 6 acres of wooded and landscaped gardens. Bedrooms, including 4-poster rooms and a suite, are tastefully decorated and comfortably furnished in the modern style. There is a choice of lounges, bars and restaurants, the more formal Garden Restaurant offering a range of tempting dishes carefully prepared from the best ingredients.

28➪♠(3fb)2⊞ CTV in all bedrooms ®♬ T ✻ (ex guide dogs) ❊ sB&B➪♠£27.50-£57 dB&B➪♠£55-£94 ₽
☾ 30P ❊ ◻ (heated) snooker sauna solarium gymnasium turkish steam room hair & beauty salon *xmas*
♥ Scottish & French V ♂ ♫ Lunch £7.50-£15.50alc Dinner £22.50&alc Last dinner 9.30pm
Credit Cards [1][3]   £

LAGG Map 10 NR92

★★**63%** **Lagg**
Kilmory KA27 8PQ ☎Sliddery(0770) 870255

Situated at the south end of the island with lovely gardens where palm trees grow alongside the Lagg Burn, this long established island inn dates back to 1791 and despite considerable alterations and extensions, much of the original character has been retained.

Efficiently run by the Stewart family, the hotel has comfortable bedrooms, a choice of lounges, cosy bar, and a large dining room in addition to the adjoining Wishing Well where all day snacks are provided.
15⇌♠(3fb)® sB&B⇌♠£40-£50 dB&B⇌♠£80-£100 (incl dinner)
CTV 40P ❋ ♪ xmas
♀ Scottish & French V ♢ ♫ ✄ Lunch £8-£15 High tea £6.50-£8 Dinner £14-£18 Last dinner 9pm

LAMLASH Map 10 NS03

★★ 68% *Glenisle*
KA27 8LS ☎(0770) 600559 & 600258
Closed Nov-15 Mar
A roadside hotel looking out across the bay to Holy Island, Glenisle has bright modern bedrooms that vary greatly in size. Good value meals are served in the dining room, and the focal point is the lounge bar, with its exposed stone walls and large woodburning stove.
13⇌♠(2fb) CTV in all bedrooms ® T
℄ 10P ⇌ ❋
♀ Scottish & French V ♢ Last dinner 9pm
Credit Cards [1][3]

ARUNDEL West Sussex Map 04 TQ00

★★★ 64% *Norfolk Arms*
High St BN18 9AD (in centre of High Street) (Forestdale)
☎(0903) 882101 FAX (0903) 884275
An original Georgian coaching inn, with an atmosphere of traditional permanence and a range of accommodation which is equipped to modern standards. The Hotel Bar offers a warm environment in addition to the lounge. The refurbished Arun Restaurant offers 2 individually priced daily menus, and bar meals are available in the Town Bar.
21⇌Annexe13⇌♠(1fb)6⇌✄ in 3 bedrooms CTV in all bedrooms ® T
℄ 15P 15⇌
♀ International V ♢ ♫ ✄ Last dinner 10pm
Credit Cards [1][2][3][4][5] £

★★♨ 62% *Burpham Country*
Old Down, Burpham BN18 9RJ (3m NE off A27)
☎(0903) 882160
A delightful small hotel, peacefully situated overlooking the South Downs, in which all of the bedrooms have been upgraded to provide good levels of comfort. A daily table d'hôte menu is offered in the dining room, and light refreshments are available throughout the day.
10⇌♠ CTV in all bedrooms ® ✈
12P ⇌ ❋ nc12yrs
V ♢ ♫ ✄ Last dinner 8pm
Credit Cards [1][3]

ASCOT Berkshire Map 04 SU96

★★★★❀❀ 71% *The Royal Berkshire*
London Rd, Sunninghill SL5 0PP (Hilton) ☎(0344) 23322 FAX (0344) 27100
A much extended, refurbished 18th-century mansion, the Royal Berkshire is a curious, though largely successful mixture of old and new. A new wing provides bedrooms of a uniformly good standard, while those in the main house come in every shape and size. There is an elegant lounge and a smart restaurant, where chef Andy Richardson produces an enjoyable style of food entirely in keeping with the surroundings. There is a short table d'hôte menu and a sensibly sized carte, which offers serious cuisine with an occasional touch of ostentation.
64⇌♠Annexe18⇌♠(2fb)2⇌ CTV in all bedrooms ® T

Arran, Lagg - Ashbourne

℄ 150P ❋ ▭ (heated) ♢ (hard) squash sauna croquet spa bath putting
♀ European V ♢ ♫ Last dinner 9.30pm
Credit Cards [1][2][3][5]

★★★★ 59% *The Berystede*
Bagshot Rd, Sunninghill SL5 9JH
☎(0344) 23311 FAX (0344) 872301

FORTE GRAND

Quietly located in 9 acres of grounds, this extended Victorian mansion has smart and comfortable public areas, furnished in keeping with the house. The best bedrooms are in the original building, where rooms are more spacious and have been refurbished to high standards. Pleasant staff provide professional service.
91⇌♠(6fb)2⇌✄ in 36 bedrooms CTV in all bedrooms ® ✈ T
❋ sB⇌♠£95 dB⇌♠£120 (room only) ₧
Lift ℄ 240P 1⇌ ❋ ≈ (heated) games room putting green croquet lawn ♫ xmas
♀ European V ♢ ♫ ✄ Lunch £13.95-£19.50 Dinner fr£20&alc Last dinner 9.45pm
Credit Cards [1][2][3][5]

★★ 66% *Highclere*
19 Kings Rd, Sunninghill SL5 9AD (opposite Sunninghill Post Office) ☎(0344) 25220 FAX (0344) 872528
Just around the corner from Sunninghill High Street, this detached Edwardian house has bright clean bedrooms with pleasantly coordinated colour schemes and modern amenities. Public areas are presently rather restricted but the owners create a friendly atmosphere in the bar and informal restaurant.
12⇌♠(2fb)✄ in 3 bedrooms CTV in 11 bedrooms ® ✈ T
✈ (ex guide dogs)
CTV 14P ⇌
♀ European V ♢ ♫ Last dinner 10pm
Credit Cards [1][2][3]

ASHBOURNE Derbyshire Map 07 SK14

★★★ 68% *Ashbourne Oaks*
Derby Rd DE6 1XH (on A52) ☎(0335) 346666 FAX (0335) 346549
Set high above the town, this modern hotel provides a good range and standard of services, with a choice of formal restaurant and all-day brasserie. Clean, well equipped bedrooms vary from spacious to quite compact, with suites and non-smokers rooms available.
50⇌♠(5fb)✄ in 11 bedrooms CTV in all bedrooms ® T
✈ (ex guide dogs) ❋ sB&B⇌♠£59 dB&B⇌♠£69 ₧
Lift ℄ 200P ❋
♀ English & French V ♢ ♫ ❋ Lunch £9.95-£12.95&alc High tea fr£4alc Dinner fr£15.95&alc Last dinner 10pm
CONF. Thtr 150 Class 60 Board 40 Del £85
Credit Cards [1][2][3][5]

★★ ❀❀♨ 75% *Callow Hall*
Mappleton Rd DE6 2AA ☎(0335) 343403 & 342412 FAX (0335) 343624
Closed 25-26 Dec & 2 wks Feb
Callow Hall is a mellow stone-built country house in a beautiful location, tucked away in 44 acres of Derbyshire countryside. Chef/patron David Spencer and his wife Dorothy provide quality accommodation and comfortable public rooms, with polite and friendly service. A new restaurant, with 2 dining rooms, essential given the popularity of David's cooking. The menus and style of cooking skilfully draw together modern English and Continental dishes. Bedrooms are charming and individually styled with a nice blend of period and antique furniture, coordinated colour schemes and bold fabrics.
15⇌♠(2fb)1⇌ CTV in all bedrooms ® T ✈ (ex guide dogs)
sB&B⇌♠£65-£80 dB&B⇌♠£90-£120 ₧
20P 1⇌ ⇌ ❋ ♪

57

Ashbourne - Ashford

English & French **V** Lunch £13.50 Dinner £28 Last dinner 9.15pm
CONF. Thtr 40 Board 20 Del £115
Credit Cards 1 2 3 5

ASHBURTON Devon Map 03 SX77

★★ 71% Holne Chase
TQ13 7NS (3m N on Two Bridges/Tavistock rd (unclass)) (Logis) ☎Poundsgate(03643) 471 FAX (03643) 453

In a lovely woodland setting, Holne Chase Hotel has been owned by the Bromage family for over 2 decades and has a comfortable, friendly atmosphere. Bedrooms are individually decorated, with attractive coordinated soft furnishings. The restaurant serves local produce cooked with care to produce honest dishes with natural flavours.

12 1 CTV in all bedrooms ® T sB&B £47.50-£62.50 dB&B £85-£115
30P croquet putting *xmas*
International **V** Lunch £14.50-£15.25 Dinner £17.50-£25 Last dinner 9pm
Credit Cards 1 2 3 5

★★ 67% Tugela House
68-70 East St TQ13 7AX ☎(0364) 652206 FAX (0364) 652206

Personally run by the Kindred family, this warm, cosy hotel is popular with both business and leisure guests. The bedrooms, including a garden suite, are well furnished and nicely decorated. Public areas are well presented and home cooked meals are served in the front facing dining room.

7 (1fb) CTV in all bedrooms ® sB&B £30-£40 dB&B £40-£50
10P 2 *xmas*
English & French **V** Lunch £12-£14alc Dinner £12-£14alc Last dinner 9pm
Credit Cards 1 3 5

★★ 62% Dartmoor Lodge
Peartree Cross TQ13 7JW (off A38) ☎(0364) 652232 FAX (0364) 653990
Closed 26 Dec-1 Jan RS Nov-May

The style of accommodation here is modern and bright while the public areas have much character and charm, with exposed beams and stone walls. Food is served all day in the Dart Inn and on Sundays and at busy times there is a carvery in addition to the à la carte menu.

30 (8fb) 2 in 2 bedrooms CTV in all bedrooms ® T sB&B £31.50-£33.50 dB&B £73-£77 (room only)
Lift CTV 50P
English & French **V** Lunch £9.60 Dinner £6.30-£15&alc Last dinner 9pm
CONF. Thtr 84 Class 48 Board 32 Del from £47.50
Credit Cards 1 2 3

ASHFORD Kent Map 05 TR04

★★★★
EASTWELL MANOR
Eastwell Park, Boughton Lees TN25 4HR (on A251, 200 yds on left from Boughton Aluph) ☎(0233) 635751 FAX (0233) 635530

When visitors to Britain finally can arrive by Eurotunnel, they will find this fine hotel within easy reach of the terminal. Set in 62 acres within the Eastwell Park estate, the house has large, elegant bedrooms named after the notables and royals associated with its past. Public rooms, with panelling, ornately plastered ceilings and open fires, include the softly lit dining room where chef Mark Clayton and his team cook in the modern style with a French influence. Our inspectors praised the breads and enjoyed starters of mushroom soup with chives and mousseline of sole with lobster and ginger, followed by a delicious main course of steamed salmon. The terrace is an ideal spot for afternoon tea in the summer.

23 CTV in all bedrooms ® T sB&B £100-£240 dB&B £120-£255
Lift 50P 10 (hard) snooker croquet pitch & putt boules *xmas*
English & French **V** Lunch fr£14.50&alc Dinner £24.50&alc Last dinner 10pm
CONF. Thtr 100 Class 40 Board 28 Del from £130
Credit Cards 1 2 3 5

★★★★ 67% Ashford International
Simone Weil Av TN24 8UX ☎(0233) 611444 FAX (0233) 627708
Closed 24-28 Dec

Built in anticipation of the Channel Tunnel, the International is uniquely designed with the foyer leading to a boulevard of shops and a central lounge. On the other side is the Continental-style Florentine Bar, the Mistral Brasserie for breakfast and informal dining, and the Alhambra Cocktail bar and à la carte restaurant. All bedrooms are furnished and equipped to a high standard and well trained, hospitable staff complement a stylish establishment.

200 (4fb) in 57 bedrooms CTV in all bedrooms ® T sB&B fr£100 dB&B fr£118
Lift 400P (heated) sauna solarium gymnasium spa bath
English & French **V** Lunch fr£11.90&alc Dinner fr£15&alc Last dinner 10.30pm
CONF. Thtr 400 Class 160 Board 200 Del from £130
Credit Cards 1 2 3 5

★★★ 59% Holiday Inn Garden Court
TN24 1AR (on A20) ☎(0233) 713333 FAX (0233) 712082

Good sized bedrooms feature Holiday Inn standards: large comfortable beds and refreshing power showers. Public areas are very limited and service is informal and amiable. There is a separate pub at the far side of the car park.

104 (9fb) in 52 bedrooms CTV in all bedrooms ® T
Lift CTV P gymnasium
V Last dinner 10pm
CONF. Thtr 30 Class 11 Board 20 Del £65
Credit Cards 1 2 3 4 5

★★★ 58% Master Spearpoint
Canterbury Rd, Kennington TN24 9QR (on A28 1m from town centre, 0.5m from junct 9 of M20) ☎(0233) 636863 FAX (0233) 610119

This extended country house is set in 5 acres of gardens. Bedrooms are equipped to modern standards, though the bathrooms are due for updating. The Parkland Restaurant offers a lunch time carvery and a choice of menus in the evening, and the comfortable bar has a good selection of beers and ales – not surprising as the owners have a small family brewery.

35 (1fb) CTV in all bedrooms ® T sB&B £40-£50 dB&B £50-£60
60P
International **V** Lunch £6-£10alc Dinner £10-£20alc Last dinner 9.45pm

Ashford - Ashton-Under-Lyne

CONF. Thtr 60 Class 40 Board 40 Del from £55
Credit Cards 1 2 3 5

Forte Posthouse
Canterbury Rd TN24 8QQ ☎ (0233) 625790 FAX (0233) 643176

Suitable for both the business and leisure traveller, this bright hotel provides modern accommodation in well equipped bedrooms with en suite bathrooms. For more details about Forte Posthouse hotels, consult the Contents page, under Hotel Groups.
60⇨♠✻ B⇨♠£41.50-£53.50 (room only)
CONF. Thtr 120 Class 70 Board 40 Del £89.50

Travel Inn
Maidstone Rd, Hothfield Common TN26 1AP (on A20, between Ashford & Charing)
☎ (0233) 712571

Purpose-built accommodation offers spacious and well equipped bedrooms, all with en suite bathrooms. Meals may be taken at the nearby family restaurant and pub. For more details about Travel Inns, consult the Contents page, under Hotel Groups.
37⇨♠✻ B⇨♠£33.50 (room only)

ASHFORD-IN-THE-WATER Derbyshire Map 07 SK17

★★★ 🎖🎖 70% **Riverside Country House**
Fennel St DE4 1QF ☎ Bakewell (0629) 814275 FAX (0629) 812873

This comfortable Georgian mansion, with its ivy-clad walls, river frontage and neatly tended gardens, is becoming increasingly popular. The public rooms are a succession of comfortable lounge areas, including a lovely new light conservatory. There is a small bar in the oak-panelled lounge, with table service to all lounges; and a separate, more formal lounge provides a peaceful retreat with pleasant views. The 2 dining rooms, each furnished with gleaming antique tables, are the setting for good food prepared by chef Jeremy Buckingham, who offers a menu of haute English cuisine in a modern style. Bedrooms are individually styled, those in the most recent wing being particularly good.
15⇨♠4🛁✻in all bedrooms CTV in all bedrooms ® T
sB&B⇨£75 dB&B⇨£85-£99 Continental breakfast 🍴
CTV 30P 🅿 ✲ croquet lawn *xmas*
♥ English & French V ✿ ♨ ✻ Lunch £13.95-£14.95&alc High tea £6.50-£9 Dinner £19.50-£29 Last dinner 9.30pm
CONF. Thtr 25 Class 16 Board 16 Del £110
Credit Cards 1 2 3

★★ 73% *Ashford*
Church St DE4 1QB ☎ Bakewell (0629) 812725
Cheerful young staff and owners help to create a friendly, relaxed atmosphere at this small inn. The bar and food operations are popular with guests and locals, and include an all day lounge and bar menu, a good restaurant choice, plus daily dishes from the blackboard. Accommodation is attractive in its rustic style, most rooms have oak beamed ceilings, and all are nicely colour coordinated and well equipped.
7⇨♠2🛁 CTV in all bedrooms ® T
CTV 50P 🅿 ✲
♥ French V ✿ ♨ ✻ Last dinner 10pm
Credit Cards 1 3

ASHINGTON West Sussex Map 04 TQ11

★★ 69% **Mill House**
Mill Ln RH20 3BZ (off A24 (northbound)) (Logis)
☎ (0903) 892426 FAX (0903) 892855
A friendly atmosphere is assured at the Mill House Hotel, where the bedrooms have a good range of equipment and useful extras. Chef Philipe Colinet offers an extensive à la carte menu and a daily fixed

price lunch menu in the candlelit restaurant and dining club. The well furnished, split-level lounge has an inglenook fireplace.
10rm(7⇨2♠)(1fb)2🛁 CTV in all bedrooms ® T
sB&Bfr£40.60 sB&B⇨♠£47 dB&B⇨♠£77.50-£87 🍴
CTV 12P 🅿 ✲ ♨
♥ English & French V ✿ ♨ ✻ Lunch £9.95-£12.95&alc High tea fr£5.50 Dinner fr£14.95&alc Last dinner 9.30pm
Credit Cards 1 2 3 4 5 £

ASHTON-UNDER-LYNE Greater Manchester Map 07 SJ99

★★ 71% **York House**
York Place, Richmond St OL6 7TT (close to junct A635/A6017)
☎ 061-330 5899 FAX 061-343 1613
Closed 26 Dec & 1 Jan RS Sun
Situated in a peaceful tree-lined cul-de-sac, this privately owned hotel has been developed from a number of Victorian properties. Bedrooms vary in shape and size, and the most comfortable are in an annexe opposite the main entrance. The Seasons Restaurant is popular, and staff provide friendly attentive service.
24⇨♠Annexe10⇨♠(2fb)🛁 CTV in all bedrooms ® T
sB&B⇨♠£50-£58.50 dB&B⇨♠£69-£75 🍴
(34P ✲
♥ English & French V ✿ ♨ ✻ Lunch £9.50&alc Dinner £12.50-£15&alc Last dinner 9.30pm
CONF. Thtr 50 Class 20 Board 26 Del from £55
Credit Cards 1 2 3 4 5 £

★ 64% **Welbeck House**
324 Katherine St OL6 7BD ☎ 061-344 0751 FAX 061-343 4278
8♠(2fb) CTV in all bedrooms ® ✻ sB&B♠£29.50-£35 dB&B♠£42-£45 🍴
(CTV 15P 🅿 games room
V ✻ Bar Lunch £7.50-£12
Credit Cards 1 2 3 5

Attractive, comfortable hotel, in a rural setting near historic Ashburton, bordering Dartmoor National Park. Ideal touring stop (midway Plymouth & Exeter). The restaurant and beamed lounge bar offer a complete range of barsnacks, beverages and full meals all day. A la carte dinner is served every evening. Bedrooms all have private bathrooms, colour TV/radio, telephone and tea making (some ground floor rooms). Two four poster rooms available, one with jacuzzi bath!
Brochure available upon request.

Ashurst - Auchencairn

ASHURST Hampshire Map 04 SU31

★★★ 66% The Woodlands Lodge
Bartley Rd SO4 2GN ☎(0703) 292257

This beautifully restored Georgian hunting lodge, set in 4 acres of grounds adjoining the forest, has a relaxed, informal atmosphere. The range of bedrooms includes some suites, and all have a king-size bed, jacuzzi and shower. Home cooked local produce is featured in the restaurant, and there is a good value wine list.

16⇌(2fb) CTV in all bedrooms ® T sB&B⇌£59-£79 dB&B⇌£89-£129

40P ❀ xmas

V ☺ ⌂ ⌖ ✱ Bar Lunch £4.95-£9.95alc High tea £4.95-£9.95alc
CONF. Thtr 32 Class 20 Board 32 Del from £95
Credit Cards 1 3

ASKRIGG North Yorkshire Map 07 SD99

★★ ❀❀ 65% King's Arms
Market Place DL8 3HQ (Logis) ☎Wensleydale(0969) 50258 FAX (0969) 50635

Dating from 1760, the King's Arms retains much of its original character, and has long been known for its hospitality and good food. These standards remain undiminished, and head chef Barry Higginbotham creates classic English dishes, served in beautifully panelled Georgian room on the first floor.

11⇌(1fb)6⇨ CTV in all bedrooms ® T ✱ sB&B⇌£40-£60 dB&B⇌£66-£90

17P nc6yrs xmas

☺ English & French V ☺ ⌂ ⌖ ✱ Lunch £12.50-£20 High tea £1.50-£10alc Dinner £25&alc Last dinner 10pm
Credit Cards 1 2 3

ASPLEY GUISE Bedfordshire Map 04 SP93

★★★ 69% Moore Place
The Square MK17 8DW ☎Milton Keynes(0908) 282000 FAX (0908) 281888

RS 26-28 Dec

This elegant Georgian mansion overlooking the village square has been skilfully extended to provide a new range of smart bedrooms with quality fabrics and modern furnishings. The conservatory restaurant, looking out onto the rock garden and cascade, offers an imaginative carte.

39⇌Annexe15⇌ CTV in all bedrooms ® T

(60P ❀

V ☺ ⌂ Last dinner 10pm
Credit Cards 1 2 3 5

ASTON CLINTON Buckinghamshire Map 04 SP81

★★★ ❀❀ 72% Bell Inn
HP22 5HP (on A41)
☎Aylesbury(0296) 630252 FAX (0296) 631250

RELAIS & CHATEAUX
Relais Gourmands

RS Sun eve & Mon

This delightful red brick former coaching house retains much of its original feel, with flagstone floors downstairs and creaking floorboards upstairs, where a few bedrooms are located. The majority of rooms are across the street, in converted malthouse and stables around the attractive cobbled courtyard of the old Bell Brewery. They are mostly spacious and comfortably furnished with fine period pieces. Several have separate lounge areas and those on the ground floor have small patios leading to walled gardens. Food and wine are at the heart of the hotel, but changes in chefs and kitchen staff over the last few years have resulted in some inconsistency. Even more regrettable is the fact that, due to the recession, standards of service in the hotel do not, for the present, merit the award of red stars.

6⇌Annexe15⇌2⇨ CTV in all bedrooms ® T ✱ sB&B⇌£92-£160 dB&B⇌£107-£189 Continental breakfast

150P ⇨ ❀ croquet xmas

☺ English & French V ☺ ⌂ ⌖ Lunch £18.50-£36 High tea £6-£8.50 Dinner £22.50-£36&alc Last dinner 9.45pm
Credit Cards 1 2 3

ATHERSTONE Warwickshire Map 04 SP39

★★ 66% Old Red Lion
Long St CV9 1BB ☎(0827) 713156 FAX (0827) 711404

The busy public areas of this partly 17th-century town-centre hostelry are full of character, with panelled walls and a stone-flagged floor in the lounge bar and exposed ceiling beams in the restaurant. There is also a cocktail bar. The modern bedrooms are well equipped.

22⇌(1fb)2⇨ CTV in all bedrooms ® ⌖ T ✖ (ex guide dogs)
(22P

☺ English & French V ☺ ⌂ ⌖ Last dinner 9.45pm
Credit Cards 1 2 3 5

★ ❀ 71% Chapel House
Friar's Gate CV9 1EY ☎(0827) 718949 FAX (0827) 717702

Closed 24-26 Dec

This delightful former dower house, dating back to 1720, has been transformed into a charming small hotel where the emphasis is on warm, friendly service and wholesome cuisine. It is tastefully furnished throughout, and extra space has been created by a conservatory extension, which overlooks the patio and pretty walled garden.

12⇌ CTV in all bedrooms ® T ✖ (ex guide dogs) ✱
sB&B⇌£37.50-£50 dB&B⇌£49.50-£60

⇨ nc12yrs

☺ English & French V ✱ Dinner £18.95-£21.95alc Last dinner 9pm
CONF. Board 20
Credit Cards 1 2 3 5

AUCHENCAIRN Dumfries & Galloway Kirkcudbright Map 11 NX75

★★★ 70% Balcary Bay
DG7 1QZ (on coast 2m from village) ☎(055664) 217 & 311 FAX (055664) 272

Closed Dec-Feb

Peacefully and most attractively situated on the seashore, this small country house, dating from the 17th century, stands in over 3 acres of grounds and has fine views of the Solway coast and Lake District mountains. Personally run by the resident proprietors, it provides pleasantly furnished and comfortable accommodation with a relaxing atmosphere. Bedrooms, the best of which have bay views, all have modern facilities, efficient heating and comfortable beds.

17⇌(1fb)1⇨ CTV in all bedrooms ® T ✱ sB&B⇌£48-£65 dB&B⇌£80-£130 (incl dinner)

50P ⇨ ❀ snooker ⌘

☺ English & French V ☺ ⌂ ✱ Lunch £14.70-£21alc Dinner £18&alc Last dinner 9pm
Credit Cards 1 3

---

*If you have booked a meal in a
hotel restaurant and cannot get there,
remember you have a contractual obligation
to cancel your booking.*

Auchencairn - Auchterhouse

 ★★

★★❀❀♨ **COLLIN HOUSE**
DG7 1QN ☎(055664) 292
Closed 6 Jan-Feb

Collin House is an impressive pink building of 1750, standing on a hillside, with superb views across the Solway Firth to the Cumbrian hills. Pam Hall and John Wood are justifiably proud of their home and welcome guests with warmth and sincerity. There is a comfortable lounge with many books and a roaring log fire. Bedrooms are generous in size, featuring antique and period pieces, and bathrooms are especially spacious. Dinner is a highlight, and John Wood produces a small menu of good, honest dishes, which might include hot kipper paté with shallot butter sauce, followed by medallions of pork with a bold stilton sauce. Hot sticky toffee pudding is a speciality. The hotel is particularly strong on helpful and attentive service.

6⇨↑ CTV in all bedrooms T sB&B⇨↑£49-£52 dB&B⇨↑£68-£74 ♫
15P 🎄 ❄ xmas
⚒ Lunch £7.50-£14.50 Dinner £26 Last dinner 8.15pm
Credit Cards [1][3]

AUCHTERARDER Tayside *Perthshire* Map 11 NN91

★★★★★
★★★★★❀❀
THE GLENEAGLES HOTEL
PH3 1NF (on A823) (Leading Hotels) ☎(0764) 662231
FAX (0764) 662134

For part of the year, this outstanding leisure hotel attracts large conferences which do not always sit comfortably with the grandeur and splendour of this most professionally run hotel, and this is most evident in the Strathearn restaurant. In some ways, this influence is a shame, since Gleneagles offers the greatest range of sporting activities of any hotel in the country. It also has a range of shops, with some well-known London stores represented, and its elegant drawing room serves an excellent afternoon tea. Bedrooms are all well equipped and tastefully furnished, though those on the top floor are awaiting refurbishment. The majority are spacious and those in the Glendevon wing have splendid views. Special mention must be made of the excellent service throughout the hotel. Courteous, pleasant and professional staff are much in evidence and contribute greatly to the success of this unique hotel.

236⇨↑ 10☐ CTV in all bedrooms ⚓ T sB&B⇨↑£150 dB&B⇨↑£210-£290 ♫
Lift (200P 🎄 ❄ 🏊 (heated) ▶ 18 ♟ (hard & grass) ⚒
squash ∪ snooker sauna solarium gymnasium croquet bowls putting shooting ♪ 🎵 xmas
⚒ International V ✂ ✳ Lunch £25&alc Dinner £38.50&alc Last dinner 10pm
CONF. Thtr 360 Class 220 Board 75 Del from £180
Credit Cards [1][2][3][4][5]

★★★❀❀♨**76%** **Auchterarder House**
PH3 1DZ (NW off B8062) ☎(0764) 663646
FAX (0764) 662939

Peacefully situated in 17 acres of pleasant grounds, this impressive baronial residence dates from 1832. Its style is still very much that of a country house where guests receive personal attention in an informal and welcoming atmosphere. The day rooms, enhanced by fresh flowers and plants, have many fine features including the marble of the restored conservatory, original wood panelling and fireplaces. Bedrooms are provided with many extras such as fruit, sherry, bathrobes and good toiletries. David Hunt is in charge of the kitchens and produces daily changing menus. The cellar is handsomely stocked and there are far more bottles than might be expected at under £15.

13⇨↑ Annexe2⇨↑ CTV in all bedrooms T sB&B⇨↑£90-£110 dB&B⇨↑£130-£195 ♫
(40P 🎄 ❄ ⚒ croquet lawn pitch & putting green nc11yrs *xmas*
♡ Scottish & French V ✂ ♨ ✂ Lunch £18.50-£30 Dinner £27.50-£50 Last dinner 10pm
CONF. Thtr 50 Class 30 Board 30 Del from £130
Credit Cards [1][2][3][4][5]

★★★❀♨**68%** **Duchally House**
PH3 1PN (2m SW off A823 Dunfermline road)
☎(0764) 663071 FAX (0764) 662464

Some of the bedrooms at this Victorian manor house are large enough to accommodate sofas as well as beds and in the public areas there are traditional open fires. Guests can choose a bistro-style meal, but the main dining room, with its crisp linen and sparkling silver, takes pride of place. A typical 3-course meal might start with consommé with Madeira, followed by fillet of beef with mushrooms served on a savoury pancake with mustard sauce, and an unusual iced chocolate and prune terrine with warm chocolate sauce.

13rm(12⇨↑)(3fb)1☐ CTV in all bedrooms ℝ T
30P ❄ snooker ⚘
V ✂ ♨ ✂ ✳ Lunch £12.50-£16.50 Dinner £16.50-£19.50&alc
Last dinner 9.30pm
CONF. Thtr 50 Class 40 Board 30 Del from £80
Credit Cards [1][2][3][5]

See advertisement on page 63

AUCHTERHOUSE Tayside *Forfarshire* Map 11 NO33

★★★♨**70%** **Old Mansion House**
DD3 0QN (take A923 from Dundee to Muirhead then B954 for 2m hotel is on left) ☎(082626) 366 FAX (082626) 400
Closed 25 Dec-3 Jan

Sympathetically converted into a hotel by owners Nigel and Eva Bell, this 16th-century baronial mansion has several interesting historical features, including original plasterwork and a Jacobean fireplace. The vaulted entrance leads up a stone staircase to a cosy library bar, and there is a separate courtyard pub which also serves food. Campbell Bruce's cooking, which has a classical influence, continues to find favour. Bedrooms retain the character of the house, but they are well equipped for the modern traveller. The Old Mansion House lies in its own grounds, which include a wooded dell with a stream.

6⇨↑ (2fb)2☐ CTV in all bedrooms ℝ T ✳ sB&B⇨↑£70-£75 dB&B⇨↑£95-£110 ♫
50P 1🚗 🎄 ❄ 🏊 (heated) ♟ (grass) squash croquet
♡ Scottish & French V ✂ ♨ ✂ Lunch £12-£15&alc Dinner £20-£28alc Last dinner 9.30pm
Credit Cards [1][2][3][5]

Hotels with red star ratings are especially high quality.

Aultbea - Aylesbury

AULTBEA Highland *Ross & Cromarty* Map 14 NG88

★★ 68% **Aultbea**
IV22 2HX (Turn off A832 at Aultbea signs, hotel will be seen at lochside after 400yds)
☎(0445) 731201 FAX (0445) 731214
RS Nov-Etr ex 24 Dec-2 Jan

Delightfully set on the shore of Loch Ewe, this small and welcoming family-run hotel has well equipped bedrooms in both modern and traditional style, some rather compact. The Waterside Bistro offers an informal alternative to the restaurant and there is a well stocked lounge bar and cosy lounge.
8⇨🛏(1fb) CTV in all bedrooms ® T sB&B⇨🛏£22-£33.50 dB&B⇨🛏£44-£78 🍴
CTV 40P ❀ pool table *xmas*
♀ International V ♿ ⌘ ✶ Sunday Lunch £7.75-£17.75alc High tea £5-£7.50alc Dinner £19-£21.50&alc Last dinner 9pm
Credit Cards [1][3]

AUST MOTORWAY SERVICE AREA (M4) Avon Map 03 ST58

Pavilion Lodge
M4 Motorway (junc 21) BS12 3BJ (junct 21)
☎Pilning (0454) 633313 FAX (0454) 633819

With a nearby family restaurant providing all meals, this modern building offers smart, spacious and well equipped bedrooms. For more details about Pavilion Lodges, consult the Contents page, under Hotel Groups.
51⇨🛏✶ sB⇨🛏£31.95 dB⇨🛏£35.95 (room only)

AUSTWICK North Yorkshire Map 07 SD76

★★ 65% **The Traddock**
LA2 8BY (4m N of Settle, off A65) ☎Clapham (05242) 51224 FAX (05242) 51224

Amidst beautiful Dales scenery, this friendly and relaxing hotel is under the personal supervision of proprietors, Frances and Richard Michaelis. Antique furniture graces the mostly spacious bedrooms, and comfortable lounges have open fires. Very good home cooking is served in the attractive beamed dining room and there is a cosy bar.
12rm(11⇨🛏)(3fb) CTV in all bedrooms ® T sB&B⇨🛏£30-£40 dB&B⇨🛏£50-£60 🍴
15P ❀ croquet putting *xmas*
♀ International V ♿ ⌘ ✶ Lunch £3.50-£12alc High tea £6-£12alc Dinner £15-£18alc Last dinner 8.30pm
CONF: Thtr 40 Class 30 Board 20 Del from £65
Credit Cards [1][3]

AVIEMORE Highland *Inverness-shire* Map 14 NH81

★★★ 54% **Red McGregor**
Main Rd PH22 1RH ☎(0479) 810256 FAX (0479) 810685

This modern hotel is situated beside the main road, just north of the centre. Public areas include a comfortable foyer lounge, coffee shop, restaurant, a choice of bars and a popular leisure centre. Bedrooms are simply decorated.
30⇨(8fb) CTV in all bedrooms ® T ✗ (ex guide dogs)
⊄ 65P 🏊 (heated) sauna solarium gymnasium beauty salon steam room
♀ English, French & Italian V ♿ ⌘ Last dinner 10pm
Credit Cards [1][2][3][5]

★★★ 52% **Aviemore Highlands**
Aviemore Centre PH22 1PJ (Principal) ☎(0479) 810771 FAX (0479) 811473

Situated in the Aviemore Centre, this modern purpose built hotel is a popular base for tour and conference groups. Although somewhat practical in appointment, planned improvements including major refurbishment along with the provision of a sports and leisure complex.
103⇨(34fb)✁in 27 bedrooms CTV in all bedrooms ® T

Lift ⊄ 140P ✶ solarium games room ♪
♀ Scottish English & French V ♿ ⌘ ✶ Last dinner 9pm
Credit Cards [1][2][3][4][5]

★★ 66% **Cairngorm**
Grampian Rd PH22 1PE (opposite railway station)
☎(0479) 810233 FAX (0479) 810791
Closed 22 Nov-5 Dec

A modern granite hotel in the centre of the village opposite the railway station, the Cairngorm offers pleasantly decorated rooms which, though mainly compact, have modern facilities. Attractively appointed public areas include a stylish restaurant, bar and coffee shop, all popular with tour groups.
32⇨🛏(4fb) CTV in all bedrooms ® ♿ T ✗ (ex guide dogs) ✶
sB&B⇨🛏£35-£45 dB&B⇨🛏£48-£59 🍴
⊄ 40P *xmas*
V ♿ ⌘ ✶ Bar Lunch £6-£12 Dinner £13.95-£14.95 Last dinner 9pm
Credit Cards [1][2][3][5] £

AXBRIDGE Somerset Map 03 ST45

★★ 63% **Oak House**
The Square BS26 2AP ☎(0934) 732444 FAX (0934) 733112

Oak House is situated within the town square overlooking the medieval St John's Hunting Lodge. Beamed public areas are pleasantly decorated and bedrooms are individually styled. The dining room is well equipped, and food is carefully prepared and cooked in the modern style.
11rm(10⇨🛏)(2fb) CTV in all bedrooms ® T ✗
♀ French V ♿ ⌘ Last dinner 10pm
Credit Cards [1][3][4][5]

AXMINSTER Map 03 SY29

See **Chardstock**

AYLESBURY Buckinghamshire Map 04 SP81

★★★★ ❀❀❀♨
HARTWELL HOUSE
Oxford Rd HP17 8NL
(signposted on A418)
☎(0296) 747444 FAX
(0296) 747450

A tree-lined drive leads to this beautifully situated stately home, built during the 16th and 18th centuries and set in over 80 acres of grounds and gardens, in which there is a ruined church and a trout-stocked lake spanned by a picturesque stone bridge. Hartwell House has both Jacobean and Georgian façades. The beauty of the interior has been enhanced by antique furnishings and tasteful décor creating an atmosphere of luxury and comfort in the spacious sitting rooms and library. The bedrooms, equipped with quality and comfort in mind, are furnished to reflect the elegance of the surroundings. Rooms in a converted stable block are more modern and less spacious, but still attain a very high standard. A new head chef has recently been appointed and we look forward to assessing Alan Maw's influence on the cuisine. The welcome from the management and staff is warm and friendly, and the standard of service is high.
31⇨🛏 Annexe16⇨🛏5♩ CTV in all bedrooms ® T
sB⇨🛏£90-£128 dB⇨🛏£135-£179 (room only) 🍴

Aylesbury - Ayr

Lift (90P 🚗 ✱ 🏊 (heated) ♪ (hard) ♦ sauna solarium gymnasium croquet nc8yrs *xmas*
V ♦ ♿ Lunch £16.50-£22.40&alc Dinner £38-£42.50alc Last dinner 9.45pm
CONF. Thtr 90 Class 36 Board 38 Del from £185
Credit Cards [1] [2] [3] [5]

Forte Posthouse
Aston Clinton Rd HP22 5AA ☎ (0296) 393391 FAX (0296) 392211

FORTE Posthouse

Suitable for both the business and leisure traveller, this bright hotel provides modern accommodation in well equipped bedrooms with en suite bathrooms. For more details about Forte Posthouse hotels, consult the Contents page, under Hotel Groups.

94⇌♦ B⇌♦£41.50-£53.50 (room only)

AYR Strathclyde *Ayrshire* Map **10** NS32
See also **Maybole**

★★★**65%** **Caledonian**
Dalblair Rd KA7 1UG (Jarvis) ☎(0292) 269331 FAX (0292) 610722
This spacious town centre hotel provides welcoming public areas incorporating lounge, brasserie bar and fashionable restaurant. Bedrooms are bright and modern, but their comfort can sometimes be impaired by an old, inflexible ducted air heating system.
114⇌♦(12fb)⚓in 22 bedrooms CTV in all bedrooms ® T ✱
Lift (70P 🏊 (heated) snooker sauna solarium gymnasium jacuzzi
V ♦ ♿✱ Lunch £9.95 High tea £6.50 Dinner £16&alc Last dinner 10pm
Credit Cards [1] [2] [3] [5] £

★★★**58%** **Savoy Park**
16 Racecourse Rd KA7 2UT ☎(0292) 266112 FAX (0292) 611488
In its own grounds on the southern side of the town, this hotel has been owned by the Henderson family for over 32 years. Bedrooms are mixed, some spacious with fine furniture, others more utilitarian, but all with the expected facilities. The dining room, with its ornate ceiling, has a pleasant outlook over the garden.
16⇌♦(4fb) CTV in all bedrooms ® T sB&B⇌♦£40-£50 dB&B⇌♦£55-£80 🍴
(CTV 80P ✱ ♪ *xmas*
♀ Scottish & French V ♦ ♿ Lunch £10-£15alc High tea £6-£9&alc Dinner £19.50-£25&alc Last dinner 9pm
CONF. Thtr 60 Class 30 Board 30 Del from £50
Credit Cards [1] [2] [3] £

★★✱♨ **LADYBURN**
KA19 7SG ☎Crosshill(06554) 585 FAX (06554) 580
(For full entry see Maybole)

★★**69%** **Carrick Lodge**
46 Carrick Rd KA7 2RE (from A77, take A79 until T-junct, then right, hotel on left) ☎(0292) 262846
Lying just south of the town centre, this well run hotel features a good range of popular bar meals in addition its restaurant food. Bedrooms are bright and cheery, some being particularly spacious.
8⇌♦(2fb) CTV in all bedrooms ® T ✖ sB&B⇌♦£38-£40 dB&B⇌♦£55-£60 🍴
(25P
V ♦ ♿ Lunch £7.95-£8.50 High tea £6.95-£9.95 Dinner £14.95-£15.50&alc Last dinner 9.45pm
Credit Cards [1] [2] [3]

★★**68%** **Pickwick**
19 Racecourse Rd KA7 2TD (Logis) ☎(0292) 260111 FAX (0292) 285348
15⇌♦(3fb)1⬜⚓in 4 bedrooms CTV in all bedrooms ®❋ T sB&B⇌♦£40-£50 dB&B⇌♦£70-£85 🍴
(100P 🚗 ✱ ♪ putting green ♧ *xmas*
♀ Scottish & French V ♦ ♿ Lunch £8.95-£10.95&alc High tea £5.95-£7.95&alc Dinner £15.95-£17.50&alc Last dinner 9.45pm
CONF. Thtr 50 Class 30 Board 20 Del from £60
Credit Cards [1] [2] [3] [5] £

★★**67%** **Burns Monument**
Alloway KA7 4PQ (2m S on B7024) ☎(0292) 442466 FAX (0292) 443174
This hotel is delightfully set in its own gardens on the banks of the River Doon, close to the Auld Brig O'Doon immortalised by Burns. The bedrooms are well equipped although they vary in size. The elegant split-level Poets restaurant and cocktail bar opens mainly at weekends or when demand justifies, but the lounge bar diner offers the same menu in addition to its own.
9⇌♦(2fb)1⬜ CTV in all bedrooms ® T sB&B⇌♦£35-£45 dB&B⇌♦£60-£75 🍴
(CTV 20P ✱ ♪ pool table ♧ *xmas*
♀ British & French V ♦ ♿ Lunch £8.95-£11.95&alc High tea £5.95-£8.95&alc Dinner £16.50-£17.75&alc Last dinner 10.30pm
CONF. Thtr 180 Class 150 Board 50 Del from £52.50
Credit Cards [1] [2] [3] [5] £

★★**66%** **Elms Court**
21 Miller Rd KA7 2AX (from A77 onto A719 continue past racecourse, left at traffic lights past railway station turn right & take town centre lane, left at 2nd traffic light)
☎(0292) 264191 & 282332 FAX (0292) 610254

Duchally House is set in 27 acres of grounds overlooking the lovely Perthshire countryside and just 2 miles off the main A9 Stirling to Perth road. Less than one hour's drive from both Glasgow and Edinburgh. This fine country house offers the best of food and wines in a relaxed and friendly atmosphere. Ten golf courses within 30 minutes drive. Open fires in public rooms and an original Victorian billiard room.

From £35 to £50 per person B&B
Special short inclusive breaks
Conference, wedding and meeting facilities available.
For further information and brochure contact
Duchally House Hotel
Near Auchterarder, Perthshire PH3 1PN
Tel: 0764 663071. Fax: 0764 662464

Ayr - Bakewell

This family-run hotel is just off the town centre. It has a comfortable lounge adjacent to the restaurant, where dinner orders are taken. Bedrooms vary in size, and the larger ones are particularly comfortable. All are well equipped, with hairdryers and trouser presses.
20⇨♠(4fb) CTV in all bedrooms ® T sB&B⇨♠£25-£35 dB&B⇨♠£50-£70 ♬
(40P xmas
♀ Scottish, French, Italian & Chinese V ♡ ♨ ✳ Lunch £4.80-£7.60alc High tea £5.60-£9.95 Dinner fr£12.50&alc Last dinner 9.30pm
CONF. Thtr 150 Class 80 Board 40 Del from £45
Credit Cards 1 2 3

★★ 64% **Annfield**
49 Maybole Rd KA7 4SF (on S outskirts on A79)
☎(0292) 441986 & 442864 FAX (0292) 442368
This purpose-built roadhouse style hotel, owned by Scots entertainer Mr Sydney Devine, is situated on the south side of the town and offers well equipped accommodation catering mainly for business guests.
8⇨♠(2fb) CTV in all bedrooms ®✕ T ✖ (ex guide dogs) ✳ sB&B⇨♠£35-£45 dB&B⇨♠£60-£70 ♬
100P ♬ xmas
♀ European V ♡ ♨ ✳ Lunch £3.50-£12
Credit Cards 1 3 5

★ 66% **The Almont Hotel**
39 Charlotte St KA7 1EA ☎(0292) 263814 FAX (0292) 263814
Close to the beach, the promenade and the town centre, this family-run hotel offers friendly service and a cosy atmosphere. Bedrooms, though compact, are brightly decorated and there is a lively bar and a small residents' lounge. The mainly home-cooked dishes can be taken in the bar or dining room.
14rm(1⇨6♠)(7fb)⅟₂in 2 bedrooms CTV in all bedrooms ®✕ ✖ sB&Bfr£25 sB&B⇨♠fr£25 dB&Bfr£50 dB&B⇨♠fr£50
CTV 12P snooker ♬
V ♡ ♨ ✳ Lunch £5.95 High tea £5.95 Dinner £5.55-£16.40alc Last dinner 9pm

★ 61% **Aftongrange**
37 Carrick Rd KA7 2RD (0.5m from rail station & city centre)
☎(0292) 265679
This friendly, family-run commercial hotel is on the south side of town but within easy walking distance of the centre. It has a good local bar trade and serves tasty food in both the bar and dining room. Bedrooms vary in size and are plainly decorated and furnished.
8rm(1⇨4♠)(2fb) CTV in all bedrooms ® T ✳ sB&B£23-£30 sB&B⇨♠£25-£30 dB&B£40-£50 dB&B⇨♠£50 ♬
30P pool table
V ♡ ♨ ✳ Lunch £7.20-£13.25 High tea £4.95-£8.70 Dinner £9.95-£11.45 Last dinner 8.30pm

BABBACOMBE
See **Torquay**

BAGSHOT Surrey Map 04 SU96

★★★★

PENNYHILL PARK
London Rd GU19 5ET (Laura Hotels) ☎(0276) 471774 FAX (0276) 473217

Surrounded by mature woodland and gardens, this hotel caters predominantly for conferences and maintains

high standards of customer care. Bedrooms are large and imaginatively decorated, some in the main house with wonderful new bathrooms and lovely views. Public areas are limited but privacy can be found. The hotel has a considerable name for good food, and with chef Karl Edmunds in charge of the kitchen this reputation is very safe. Following a starter of lobster terrine, our inspector enjoyed a trio of veal fillet, sweetbreads and liver with a superb veal stock and Cointreau sauce. The climax of the meal was a minestrone of fruit and vegetables: a brunoise (minutely diced vegetables and fruit) steeped in a syrup flavoured with lime, thyme and basil and garnished with more fruit and vanilla ice cream.
22⇨♠ Annexe54⇨♠4⊞⅟₂in 31 bedrooms CTV in all bedrooms TV in 1 bedroom T ✖ (ex guide dogs) ✳ sB⇨♠£138-£184 dB⇨♠£154-£210 (room only) ♬
(250P ❄ ☼ (heated) ▶ 9 ♀ (hard) ♪ ♁ sauna solarium clay pigeon shooting croquet xmas
♀ English & French V ♡ ♨ ✳ Lunch £18.95-£20 Dinner fr£31 Last dinner 10.30pm
CONF. Thtr 60 Class 35 Board 35 Del £225
Credit Cards 1 2 3 4 5

BAINBRIDGE North Yorkshire Map 07 SD99

★★ 65% **Rose & Crown**
Village Green DL8 3EE (on A684 in centre of village)
☎Wensleydale(0969) 50225 FAX (0969) 50735
Beamed bars, antique furniture and open fires are features of this attractive 15th-century country inn overlooking the village green. Bedrooms are compact but have most modern facilities. The restaurant offers traditional food using local produce when possible. Bar meals are also available.
12⇨♠(1fb)3⊞ CTV in all bedrooms ® sB&B⇨♠£30-£43 dB&B⇨♠£52-£70 ♬
65P ❄ ♪
V ♡ ♨ ⅟₂ ✳ Lunch fr£6.95 Dinner £16-£21.05alc Last dinner 9.30pm
Credit Cards 1 3

BAKEWELL Derbyshire Map 08 SK26

★★★ 70% **Hassop Hall**
Hassop DE45 1NS (take B6001 for approx. 2m into Hassop, hotel opposite church) ☎Great Longstone(0629) 640488 FAX (0629)640577
RS 24-26 Dec
Set in parkland amidst beautiful Peak District scenery, this historic hall retains many fine original features. High standards of service and hospitality are maintained by the Chapman family, with all breakfasts served in rooms – which vary from small and homely to huge and elegant.
13⇨♠(2fb)2⊞ CTV in all bedrooms T ✳ sB⇨♠£65-£99 dB⇨♠£75-£109 (room only) ♬
Lift 80P ❄ ♀ (hard) croquet ♬
V ✳ Lunch £8.95-£12.95 Dinner £16.50-£24.95 Last dinner 9pm
Credit Cards 1 2 3 5

★★★ ⓐ63% **Rutland Arms**
The Square DE4 1BT ☎(0629) 812812 FAX (0629) 812309

This stone-built, town centre hotel continues to improve with each year. The restaurant is an appealing room with a large marble fireplace, bold floral décor and attractive table settings. Chef Peter Saunders provides menus with a balanced mix of traditional and modern British cooking and a hint of French influence. Light meals and snacks are also served in the bar and lounge. Bedrooms vary greatly in style and size, and some have recently been upgraded.
19⇨♠ Annexe17⇨♠(2fb) CTV in all bedrooms ® T

Bakewell

(30P 2😋 🎵
♿ English & French **V** ✋ 🐕 Last dinner 9.30pm
Credit Cards 1 2 3 5

★★ ♿ 73% **Croft Country House**
Great Longstone DE45 1TF (from Bakewell follow A6 towards Buxton turn right on to A6020, turn left at sign to Great Longstone, entrance on right 0.25m into village)
☎ Great Longstone(0629) 640278
Closed 4 Jan-3 Feb

Enthusiastic proprietors and their small team ensure a friendly welcome, and comfortable public rooms and individually styled character bedrooms provide for a relaxed and peaceful stay. There is a daily changing menu with a set main course and a limited choice of starters and sweets, which offers good home cooking at a reasonable price.

9🛏 🐕 CTV in all bedrooms ® ✘ (ex guide dogs)
sB&B 🛏 🐕 £58-£63 dB&B 🛏 🐕 £85-£90 🍴
Lift CTV 40P 🐾 ❄ xmas
V ✋ 🐕 ✗ Dinner £20.50 Last dinner 7.30pm
Credit Cards 1 3

£   See advertisement on page 67

★★ 66% **Milford House**
Mill St DE45 1DA ☎(0629) 812130
Closed Jan & Feb RS Nov, Dec & Mar

This old Georgian residence is peacefully set in its own attractive gardens, some 300 yards from the town centre. The Hunt family have owned and run the hotel for many years, and offer a high level of old-fashioned hospitality, making it a favourite with regular guests.

12🛏 🐕 CTV in all bedrooms ® ⚁ ✘ sB&B 🛏 🐕 £35-£45 dB&B 🛏 🐕 £64-£75
10P 7🚗 🐾 ❄ nc10yrs
V Sunday Lunch £13.50-£15 Dinner £15.50-£18 Last dinner 7.30pm

RUTLAND ARMS HOTEL · BAKEWELL

Georgian charm in the glorious Derbyshire Peak District. Home of the famous Bakewell Pudding. Busy market each Monday. Area steeped in history. Romantic Haddon Hall and stately Chatsworth House only minutes away. Easy driving distance to Alton Towers 36 bedrooms with bath en suite, direct dial 'phones, T.V., video, tea/coffee facilities.

AA ★★★

TEL. 0629 812812

PENNYHILL PARK PLAYS HOST TO THOSE WHO TREASURE PRIVACY AND QUIET

SURROUNDED by peace and tranquillity Pennyhill Park Hotel stands in 112 acres of legendary parkland and landscaped gardens to be enjoyed whatever the season.

Seventy-six bedrooms and suites, all beautifully furnished and retaining the original charm and character of a country manor.

The Latymer Restaurant provides the elegance and quiet dignity expected from its surroundings. The food and service — known to many, is complemented by an outstanding selection of fine wines.

The Pennyhill Park Country Club's tempting pastimes are a nine-hole golf course, tennis courts, outdoor heated Roman style swimming pool, horse-riding and clay pigeon shooting.

Whatever the occasion, Pennyhill Park offers a unique setting be it business or pleasure — *slip away now and enjoy us.*

AA ★★★★

Pennyhill Park Hotel, London Road, Bagshot, Surrey GU19 5ET. Telephone: 0276 471774 Fax: 0276 473217

Bala - Ballater

BALA Gwynedd Map 06 SH93

★★★ ♨ 69% Pale Hall
Llandderfel LL23 7PS ☎Llandderfel(06783) 285

Best Newcomer 1994

Pale Hall is the very deserving winner of our Best Newcomer award for Wales this year, and our inspector was impressed by both the house and the levels of hospitality offered. The Victorian mansion stands in 16 acres of its own parkland, and has been beautifully restored. It has many magnificent features, including oak panelling in the main hall, which also has an impressive carved fireplace and a domed ceiling with leaded stained glass. Breakfast is taken in the former kitchen, complete with the original cooking range. Bedrooms are furnished to a very high standard and have good facilities – the bath in the Victoria Suite is the very one that Queen Victoria used when she visited the house shortly after the death of Prince Albert! Proprietor, Saul Nahed, is a good host and much involved with the running of his fine hotel.

17rm⇨ℳ(1fb)1🎿 CTV in all bedrooms ✈
Lift 150P 2🎾 ❀ 🎱 (heated) ♪ sauna gymnasium clay pigeon shooting
🍴 French V ♡ 🔟 ✔ Last dinner 9.30pm
Credit Cards [1][3][5]

★★ 62% Bala Lake
LL23 7YF (1m S on B4403) ☎(0678) 520344 & 520111 FAX (0678) 521193

Situated on the south eastern side of the lake this hotel is personally run by the friendly Rhiannon and Dennis Holmes. There is a foyer bar, large traditional lounge and one bedrooms has its own sitting area overlooking the golf course and swimming pool. A nominal charge is made for use of the golf course.

1⇨Annexe12ℳ(2fb) CTV in all bedrooms ® T
40P 10🎾 🚗 ⚓ (heated) ▶ 9
♡ 🔟 ✔
Credit Cards [1][3][5]

★★ 62% White Lion Royal
61 High St LL23 7AE (on A494) ☎(0678) 520314
Closed 25 Dec

Dating back to 1759, this is one of the oldest inns in Wales, with much panelling, exposed beams and open fires. Bedrooms are quite large, and there are several bars, a foyer coffee lounge and first floor quiet lounge. A good range of restaurant and bar meals is offered.

26rm(22⇨ℳ)(4fb) CTV in all bedrooms ® T sB&B⇨ℳ£36-£38 dB&B£40 dB&B⇨ℳ£64-£68 🍴
CTV 30P
V ♡ 🔟 Lunch £7.75-£8.50 Dinner £10.95-£11.50 Last dinner 8.30pm
Credit Cards [1][2][3][5] £

★★ 61% Plas Coch
High St LL23 7AB (Logis) ☎(0678) 520309 FAX (0678) 521135
Closed 25 Dec

This 18th-century, former coaching inn provides simply furnished accommodation with some rooms having been completely refurbished with good quality light stained furniture and rich fabrics.

10⇨ℳ(4fb) CTV in all bedrooms ® T sB&B⇨ℳ£35.50-£49 dB&B⇨ℳ£55.50 🍴

20P 🚗 windsurfing canoeing sailing
V ♡ 🔟 ✔ Sunday Lunch fr£6.50 Dinner fr£11&alc Last dinner 8.30pm
Credit Cards [1][2][3][5] £

BALDOCK Hertfordshire Map 04 TL23

Forte Travelodge
Great North Rd, Hinxworth SG7 5EX (on A1, southbound) ☎Hinxworth(0462) 835329 Central Res (0800) 850950

FORTE Travelodge

This modern building offers a good standard of accommodation for overnight stops. Smart, spacious and well equipped bedrooms, all with en suite bathrooms, are suitable for family use, and meals may be taken at the nearby family restaurant. For more details about Travelodges, consult the Contents page, under Hotel Groups.

40⇨ℳ ❋ B⇨ℳ£31.95 (room only)

BALLACHULISH Highland Argyllshire Map 14 NN05
See also **North Ballachulish**

★★★ 61% Ballachulish
PA39 4JY (on A828, Fort William-Oban road) ☎(08552) 606 FAX (08552) 629

Set amid beautiful loch and mountain scenery, this is a family-run holiday hotel. Public areas are spacious and comfortable, and staff are friendly and willing, though room service at the time of our visit was uncharacteristically poor. Bedrooms are well equipped and comfortably furnished in sturdy pine. The rate for single occupancy of a double or twin room varies according to demand, and at peak times may not be to everyone's liking!

30⇨ℳ(3fb)1🎿 CTV in all bedrooms ® T sB&B⇨ℳ£45.50-£55.50 dB&B⇨ℳ£68-£79 🍴
🎵 50P 4🎾 ❀ 🎱 xmas
🍴 International V ♡ 🔟 ✔ Lunch £5-£14alc High tea £4.50-£7alc Dinner £21.50&alc Last dinner 10pm
CONF. Thtr 100 Class 50 Board 40 Del from £45
Credit Cards [1][3] £
See advertisement under FORT WILLIAM

⇧The Isles of Glencoe Hotel & Leisure Centre
PA39 4HL (off A82) (Logis) ☎(08552) 602 FAX (08552) 770

This new development, standing on a peninsula jutting out into Loch Levan and surrounded by spectacular scenery, represents value of money and quality facilites. Its young owners are attempting to break the mould of traditional hotel keeping by offering guests what they want, where and (as far as possible) when they want it. Many of the spacious bedrooms have wonderful mountain views, and public areas are permeated by a relaxed and friendly atmosphere.

39⇨ℳ(6fb) CTV in all bedrooms ® T sB&B⇨ℳ£54.50 dB&B⇨ℳ£67-£89 🍴
🎵 150P ❀ 🎱 (heated) ♪ sauna turbo pool 🎱 xmas
🍴 International V ♡ 🔟 ✔ Lunch £3.50-£13alc High tea £3.50-£6alc Dinner £16.50-£18.50&alc Last dinner 10pm
CONF. Thtr 150 Class 80 Board 70 Del from £39.50
Credit Cards [1][3] £
See advertisement under FORT WILLIAM

BALLATER Grampian Aberdeenshire Map 15 NO39

★★★★ ❀❀64% Craigendarroch Hotel & Country Club
Braemar Rd AB35 5XA ☎(03397) 55858 FAX (03397) 55447

This holiday, business and conference hotel is part of a timeshare and country club complex, based on the original red sandstone mansion, overlooking the wooded Deeside hills. Attractive fabrics have been used to good effect in the bright, comfortable bedrooms.

50⇨ℳ(6fb)1🎿in 10 bedrooms CTV in all bedrooms ® T ✈ (ex guide dogs)

Ballater

Lift (100P ❀ ▨ (heated) ♆ (hard) squash snooker sauna solarium gymnasium games room beauty salon creche ♫ ⚘
♗ International V ✧ ⚏ ✗ Last dinner 10pm
Credit Cards ① ② ③ ⑤

★★★ ⊛⚑ 73% **Balgonie Country House**
Braemar Place AB35 5RQ ☎(03397) 55482 FAX (03397) 55482

Efficiently run by John and Priscilla Finnie, this lovely Edwardian house is set in 4 acres overlooking the golf course and the wooded hills beyond. Bedrooms are individually decorated, those on the first floor in traditional style, others with modern fitted units. Public areas include a comfortable sitting room, cosy bar and an attractive restaurant offering imaginative Scottish cuisine from a short, daily changing fixed price menu.

9⇨♞ CTV in all bedrooms T ✲ sB&B⇨♞£75-£85 dB&B⇨♞£130-£150 (incl dinner) ⚏
CTV 10P 2🐾 🚗 ✿ croquet *xmas*
V ✧ ⚏ ✗ ✱ Lunch £12.50-£16.50 Dinner £26-£27.50 Last dinner 9pm
Credit Cards ① ② ③ (£)

★★★ ⊛66% **Darroch Learg**
Braemar Rd AB35 5UX (on A93 at west end of town) (Logis) ☎(03397) 55443 FAX (03397) 55443
Closed Jan

From its elevated position amid 5 acres of wooded grounds, this comfortable, family-run hotel enjoys a fine outlook over the River Dee and the golf course towards Lochnagar, one of Scotland's highest peaks. There is a choice of lounges (one for non smokers) where drinks are served. An interesting and predominantly Scottish dinner menu is complemented by a carefully chosen wine list.

15⇨♞ Annexe 5⇨♞ 1⚏ ✗ in 4 bedrooms CTV in all bedrooms ® T ✲ sB&B⇨♞£34-£40 dB&B⇨♞£58-£90 ⚏
25P 🚗 ✿
✧ ⚏ ✗ Sunday Lunch £10.50 Dinner £19.75-£24.75 Last dinner 8.30pm
Credit Cards ① ③

★★ 63% **Alexandra**
12 Bridge Square AB35 5QJ ☎(03397) 55376 FAX (03397) 55466

This small, friendly hotel at the east end of town is popular with visitors to Deeside. Completely refurbished in the last few years, it offers comfortable modern bedrooms which, though compact, are nicely furnished. Public areas include an attractive restaurant and welcoming lounge bar, but there is no lounge.

7⇨♞(1fb) CTV in all bedrooms ® T ✲ sB&B⇨♞£24-£30 dB&B⇨♞£48-£56 ⚏
9P
♗ Scottish & French V Lunch £10.20-£18 Dinner £15-£22&alc Last dinner 9pm
Credit Cards ① ② ③ ④ ⑤ (£)

★★ 59% **Monaltrie**
5 Bridge Square AB35 5QJ ☎(03397) 55417 FAX (03397) 55180

This modernised Victorian hotel stands beside the River Dee and is a popular base for tour groups. It offers a choice of lounges and restaurants, one of which specializes in Thai food. Bedrooms are practical and vary in size.

23rm(18⇨3♞)(3fb)1⚏ CTV in all bedrooms ® T sB&B⇨♞£22.50-£27.50 dB&B⇨♞£45-£55
45P ✿ *xmas*
♗ Scottish & Thai V ✧ ⚏ ✗ Sunday Lunch £7.50 Dinner £16.50&alc Last dinner 9.30pm
CONF. Thtr 80 Class 40 Board 30 Del from £39.95
Credit Cards ① ② ③ ⑤

See advertisement on page 69

Red star hotels are each highlighted
by a pink tinted panel.

Alexandra Hotel

HIGHLY COMMENDED

Bridge Square, Ballater,
Royal Deeside, AB35 5QJ

AA ★★

Situated in the heart of Royal Deeside the Alexandra offers guests the hospitality of a small country hotel whilst providing luxury accommodation service and outstanding cuisine.

All seven en suite bedrooms are tastefully furnished with every facility.

Our restaurant and bar menus offer the best Scottish and French cuisine using fresh local produce complemented by fine wine from our cellar. Or sample some of the wide range of Malt Whisky available in our lounge bar.

For brochure and tariff contact:
Resident Director Alain Tabuteau
Phone: 03397 55376 Fax: 03397 55466

THE CROFT COUNTRY HOUSE HOTEL

★★ ♣♠

HIGHLY COMMENDED

Standing in three acres of secluded grounds, The Croft is located in the picturesque village of Great Longstone, three miles north of Bakewell. Conversion to a hotel in 1984 has enabled all modern facilities to be installed, whilst the decor and furnishings reflect the Victorian period from which the house dates. A spectacular feature is the Main Hall, with its lantern ceiling and galleried landing. From the latter radiate the nine en-suite bedrooms. There is a lift and two of the bedrooms are suitable for disabled guests. The Longstone Restaurant offers a table d'hôte menu changed daily. Freshly prepared food, an imaginative wine list and personal service, will all help to make your stay a memorable one.

Great Longstone, Bakewell, Derbyshire DE45 1TF
Telephone: (0629) 640278

Balloch - Bamburgh

BALLOCH Strathclyde *Dunbartonshire* Map **10** NS38

★★★★ ✿✿**71%** *Cameron House Hotel and Country Estate*
G83 8QZ (beside A86) ☎(0389) 55565 FAX (0389) 59522

A carefully restored and extended turreted mansion, with lawns sweeping down to Loch Lomond, Cameron House forms the nucleus of a fine country estate and has a very pleasant ambience. Of the two restaurants, it is the Georgian that attracted the rosette award, and offers a light 6-course Celebration Menu, the main 'carte' and a daily set-price Market Menu, which might include a terrine of rabbit and hare wrapped in leeks followed by medallions of lamb topped with basil, tomato and sweetbreads and served with a Madeira sauce. The brasserie provides a good informal alternative.
68⇌ℕ(9fb)3⊞¾in 19 bedrooms CTV in all bedrooms ®⚲T ✈ (ex guide dogs)
Lift ℂ 150P ✿ ⊡ (heated) ▶ 9 ♀ (hard) ♪ squash snooker sauna solarium gymnasium steamroom jacuzzi badminton
V ♡ ⚏ ⚓ Last dinner 10pm
Credit Cards [1][2][3][5]

BALSALL COMMON West Midlands Map **04** SP27

★★★ ✿**74%** **Nailcote Hall**
Nailcote Ln, Berkswell CV7 7DE (on B4101)
☎Berkswell(0203) 466174 FAX (0203) 470720

Originally an Elizabethan country home, this delightful hotel is set in 8 acres of mature grounds in quiet countryside on the edge of the small village, close to the Midlands motorway network and NEC. It has a high standard of accommodation and pleasant, hospitable service. The bedrooms are well proportioned and combine the charm of the old house with modern creature comforts; many of those in the new wing have terraces and patios overlooking the gardens. Chef Jonathan Twinam continues to produce well thought out seasonal menus, with dishes such as fresh scallops followed by tender noisettes of spring lamb glazed with braised leeks à la paloise.
20⇌ℕ CTV in all bedrooms ® T sB&B⇌ℕ£95-£125 dB&B⇌ℕ£115-£165 ℝ
ℂ CTV 130P ✿ ✿ ♀ (hard) croquet putting petanque ♫ *xmas*
♡ International V ♡ ⚏ ⚓ Lunch £17-£23&alc Dinner £23.50-£25&alc Last dinner 9.45pm
CONF. Thtr 100 Class 70 Board 60 Del from £130
Credit Cards [1][2][3][5] £

★★ ✿✿**68%** **Haigs**
Kenilworth Rd CV7 7EL (on A452 4m N of Kenilworth and 6m S of junct 4 of M6) ☎Berkswell(0676) 533004 FAX (0676) 534572

Closed 26 Dec-3 Jan

Owners John and Jean Cooper are welcoming hosts, and though accommodation is functional, it is well equipped and ideal for the business traveller. The dining room is not grand by any means, but it is relaxing and friendly. Chef Ian Endicott provides dishes which vary from the simple to the imaginative such as a chicken liver parfait or fresh noodles with a cheese, garlic and herb sauce, and baked fillet of cod wrapped in filo pastry with spinach and mushrooms on a tomato and red pepper sauce.
13rm(12⇌ℕ) CTV in all bedrooms ® T sB&B£25-£30 sB&B⇌ℕ£35-£51.95 dB&B⇌ℕ£42-£58.95
CTV 22P ⚛ ✿ nc4yrs
♡ French V ♡ Sunday Lunch £11.50 Dinner £15.75&alc Last dinner 9pm
Credit Cards [1][3]

See advertisement under **BIRMINGHAM (NATIONAL EXHIBITION CENTRE)**

Satellite television – look for this symbol ⚇ in the directory entries.

BAMBURGH Northumberland Map **12** NU13

★★ ✿**75%** **Waren House**
Waren Mill NE70 7EE (3m W off B1342 to Warren Mill)
☎(06684) 581 due to change to (0668) 214581 FAX (06684) 484 due to change to 0668 214484

Closed Nov-week before Etr

In 6 acres of wooded grounds overlooking Budle Bay, this fine Georgian house has been transformed into a small hotel of character by owners Peter and Anita Laverack. The dining room is particularly elegant. Bedrooms are highly individual, the one called the Nursery having masses of dolls and an old cradle. Smoking is only permitted in the library.
7⇌ℕ1⊞¾in all bedrooms CTV in all bedrooms ®⚲T ✈ (ex guide dogs) sB&B⇌ℕ£72-£87 dB&B⇌ℕ£104-£134 ▶ 20P ⚛ ✿ ♀ (hard) croquet nc14yrs
♡ European ¾ Dinner fr£22.50 Last dinner 8.30pm
Credit Cards [1][2][3][5] £

★★**69%** **Lord Crewe Arms**
Front St NE69 7BL ☎(06684) 243

Closed Nov-Etr

Situated beneath the castle walls in the centre of the town, this family-run hotel offers courteous service and sound accommodation, with neat bedrooms, two comfortable lounges and a choice of restaurants and bars that retain some of the character of the former inn.
25rm(20⇌ℕ)(1fb) CTV in all bedrooms ® sB&B£34-£35 sB&B⇌ℕ£42-£44 dB&B£46-£48 dB&B⇌ℕ£62-£65 ℝ
34P ⚛ nc5yrs
♡ English & French ♡ ¾ Bar Lunch £4.50-£12alc High tea £4.50-£12alc Dinner £17.50-£18.50 Last dinner 9pm
Credit Cards [1][3]

★★**58%** **Victoria**
Front St NE69 7BP (in centre of Bamburgh) ☎(06684) 431

This traditional family-run hotel in the centre of the village offers a mixed standard of accommodation, bedrooms varying in both size and type. The best rooms are strikingly decorated while others are much more functional. There is a comfortable residents' lounge, wood panelled dining room and attractive conservatory-style bistro.
24rm(16⇌ℕ)(5fb)⊞ CTV in all bedrooms ® T ✱ sB&B£20-£25 sB&B⇌ℕ£25-£30 dB&B£40-£50 dB&B⇌ℕ£50-£70 ℝ
7P snooker games room *xmas*
V ♡ ¾ Lunch £4-£15alc High tea £4.50-£6.50alc Dinner £17-£19&alc Last dinner 8.30pm
CONF. Thtr 50 Class 40 Del from £40
Credit Cards [1][3] £

★**63%** **The Mizen Head**
Lucker Rd NE69 7BS (turn off the A1 for Bamburgh the hotel is the first building on the left as you enter the village) ☎(0668) 214254

Situated on the edge of the village, this welcoming, family-owned hotel offers neat if slightly appointed bedrooms. Extensive public areas include a choice of bars and lounge areas including a pleasant sun lounge, while a good range of reasonably priced meals is offered in the restaurant or bar.
16rm(7⇌ℕ)(3fb) CTV in all bedrooms ® sB&B£19-£30 dB&B£31-£50 dB&B⇌ℕ£38-£65 ℝ
CTV 30P ✿ *xmas*
V ♡ Sunday Lunch £5.95&alc Dinner £11.50&alc Last dinner 8pm
Credit Cards [1][3]

★**61%** **Sunningdale**
21-23 Lucker Rd NE69 7BS ☎(06684) 334

Closed Nov-Feb

Close to the village centre, this friendly, privately owned hotel offers pleasantly decorated and comfortable public areas, including 2 lounges, a bar and games room. Bedrooms, in contrast, are simple and modestly appointed. A set 4-course dinner is served at 7pm.

19rm(6⇨)(4fb)⌿in 2 bedrooms CTV in 4 bedrooms ®
sB&B£36-£52 sB&B⇨♠£40-£54 dB&B£36-£44 dB&B⇨♠£40-£54
₽
CTV 16P games room *xmas*
V ♡ ⚓ Dinner £11.50 Last dinner 7.30pm
Credit Cards [1][3][5]

BAMFORD Derbyshire Map 08 SK28

★★68% **Yorkshire Bridge Inn**
Ashopton Rd, Yorkshire Bridge S30 2AB
☎Hope Valley(0433) 651361 FAX (0433) 651812
Good hotel accommodation has recently been added to this popular country inn, which overlooks beautiful Peak District countryside. Known locally for its cheerful atmosphere and good range of bar meals, residents can reserve tables in the conservatory dining room and have waitress service from the comprehensive bar-meal menu. Residents also have the sole use of a quieter lounge at busy times. Bedrooms are nicely furnished in a comfortable rustic style with excellent modern bathrooms.
10⇨♠(1fb) CTV in all bedrooms ®⚑ T ⋈ (ex guide dogs) ✱
sB&B⇨♠£35 dB&B⇨♠£48
CTV 12P ⚑ ✱ *xmas*
♀ English & Continental V ♡ ⚓ ⌿ Bar Lunch £2.95-£5.25alc Dinner £4.95-£8.95alc Last dinner 9.30pm
Credit Cards [1][3]

★★56% *Marquis of Granby*
Hathersage Rd S30 2BH (beside A625)
☎Hope Valley(0433) 51206
Standing in the beautiful Peak District, this friendly hotel looks out on to pleasant lawns and gardens. Panelling from the SS Olympic is much in evidence, and the bedrooms, many of which are beamed, are spacious and well equipped. There is a choice of bars and a good range of restaurant and bar meals.
7⇨♠(2fb)1⚑ CTV in all bedrooms ®
CTV 100P ✱ ♪
V ♡ ⚓
Credit Cards [1][2][3][5]

BAMPTON Devon Map 03 SS92

★★⚘72% **Bark House**
Oakford Bridge EX16 9HZ (7m N of Tiverton on the A396)
☎Oakford(03985) 236
Closed 1 Dec-28 Feb
This small country hotel, a former tannery, is set in pretty gardens in the Exe Valley, with easy road access to Exmoor and the coast. Proprietors Pauline and Douglas West are warm and welcoming hosts. Bedrooms are spotless and comfortable, the cosy lounge has a cottagey atmosphere and a small selection of carefully prepared dishes, often with a French influence, is offered in the restaurant. An inspection meal began with a creamy artichoke soup, followed by succulent fillet of roast beef with simple but interesting vegetables, and ended with a delicious treacle tart.
6rm(2⇨2♠)(1fb) CTV in 5 bedrooms T sB&B£20-£25
sB&B♠£29-£34 dB&B£40 dB&B⇨♠£46-£56 Continental breakfast
12P 2🅿 (£1 per night) ⚑ ✤ nc5yrs
♀ English, French & American ♡ ⚓ ⌿ Lunch £2-£10 Dinner £14.50 Last dinner 8.30pm
Credit Cards [1][3]

BANBURY Oxfordshire Map 04 SP44

★★★⚘70% **Wroxton House**
Wroxton OX15 6QB (follow A422 from Banbury, 2.5m to Wroxton, hotel on right on entering village) ☎(0295) 730482 & 730777 FAX (0295) 730800

Built in honey-coloured stone, this stylish hotel was created by the sensitive restoration of 3 linked 17th-century village houses. The bedrooms are individually decorated and furnished, some have original timbers, and some are housed in a new wing with a delightful clock tower. The lounges are airy and extend into a conservatory. A choice of menus is offered in the charming restaurant, with exposed beams and inglenook fireplaces. Dishes are prepared from fresh produce, and herbs from the hotel's own garden.
29⇨♠Annexe3⇨♠1⚑ CTV in all bedrooms ® T ✱
sB&B⇨♠£79-£85 dB&B⇨♠£98-£130 ₽
⟨ 40P ⚑ ✱ *xmas*
♀ English & Continental V ♡ ⚓ ✱ Lunch £17.50-£25&alc Dinner £17.50-£19.50&alc Last dinner 9.30pm
CONF. Thtr 60 Class 40 Board 30 Del from £120
Credit Cards [1][2][3][5]

See advertisement under BANBURY
See advertisement on page 71

★★★67% **Banbury Moat House**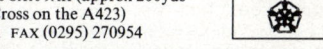
27-29 Oxford Rd OX16 9AH (approx 200yds from Banbury Cross on the A423)
☎(0295) 259361 FAX (0295) 270954
Closed 26-30 Dec
This attractive Georgian building, a short walk from the town centre, retains many moulded plaster ceilings in the well proportioned rooms. The cellar bar features monthly live jazz and the restaurant offers both table d'hôte and à la carte menus. Helpful staff create a warm, friendly atmosphere.
50⇨♠(2fb)1⚑in 10 bedrooms CTV in all bedrooms ® T ✱
sB&B⇨♠£35-£69 dB&B⇨♠£54-£79 ₽
⟨ 48P

➡

Welcome to Royal Deeside – Scotland

Glorious scenery, superb food, relaxed comfort.
Ideally situated for the Braemar Gathering, Balmoral Castle, the "Whisky Trail", Aberdeen and "Castle Country".
All rooms en-suite, with direct-dial telephones, radio/alarm, colour T.V. etc.
Fresh food from, à la carte, table d'hôte and bar menus - try our exotic "Thai Orchid" Restaurant.
Ask about our wide range of Special Events. For a memorable and pleasurable holiday please contact:

Monaltrie Hotel ★★

Bridge Square, Ballater, Aberdeenshire AB35 5QJ
Tel: 03397-55417 Fax: 03397-55180

Banbury - Banchory

♀ International **V** ❀ ⌓ ✱ Lunch £13.50&alc Dinner £14.50&alc Last dinner 9.45pm
Conf. Thtr 60 Class 30 Board 25 Del from £80
Credit Cards [1] [2] [3] [5]

★★ **63%** Whately Hall
Banbury Cross OX16 0AN ☎(0295) 263451
FAX (0295) 271736

FORTE Heritage

Set back from the main road with well kept gardens, this part 17th-century hotel has a cosy welcoming atmosphere. Bedrooms, some in a modern wing, are attractive, and have good modern facilities. Comfortable public areas with wood panelling and open fires include a restaurant offering a choice of menus.

74⇌ ⁌ ⌿ in 24 bedrooms CTV in all bedrooms ® T
Lift (60P 20⛟ ❊ croquet
V ❀ ⌓ ⌿ Last dinner 9.45pm
Credit Cards [1] [2] [3] [5]

★★ **59%** Lismore Hotel & Restaurant
61 Oxford Rd OX16 9AJ ☎(0295) 267611
Closed 24 Dec-3 Jan

This striking Victorian building has a friendly atmosphere and provides comfortable bedrooms with modern facilities, the annexe rooms being more modern but rather compact. Public areas include a cosy panelled bar and attractive dining room serving enjoyable dinners.

14rm(11⇌⁌)Annexe7⇌⁌(3fb)1⌺ CTV in all bedrooms ® T
CTV 19P
♀ English & French **V** ❀ ⌓ Last dinner 9.30pm
Credit Cards [1] [2] [3]

BANCHORY Grampian *Kincardineshire* Map **15** NO69

★★★❊⁌
BANCHORY LODGE
AB31 3HS (off A93)
☎(0330) 822625 FAX (0330) 825019
Closed 13 Dec-Jan

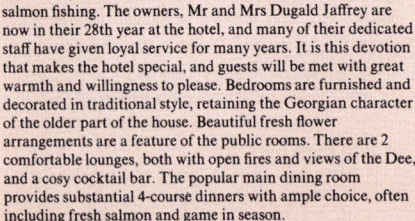

The charming country house is set on the banks of the River Dee, famed for its salmon fishing. The owners, Mr and Mrs Dugald Jaffrey are now in their 28th year at the hotel, and many of their dedicated staff have given loyal service for many years. It is this devotion that makes the hotel special, and guests will be met with great warmth and willingness to please. Bedrooms are furnished and decorated in traditional style, retaining the Georgian character of the older part of the house. Beautiful fresh flower arrangements are a feature of the public rooms. There are 2 comfortable lounges, both with open fires and views of the Dee, and a cosy cocktail bar. The popular main dining room provides substantial 4-course dinners with ample choice, often including fresh salmon and game in season.

22⇌⁌(11fb)2⌺ CTV in all bedrooms ® ✱
sB&B⇌⁌fr£63 dB&B⇌⁌£89.25-£105 ⛿
CTV 50P ⛟ ❊ ⌿ sauna pool table
♀ English & French **V** ❀ ⌓ Lunch £7.50-£13.95
Dinner £24.50 Last dinner 9.30pm
Credit Cards [1] [2] [3] [4] [5]

Remember to book early for holiday and bank holiday times.

★★★

★★★❊⁌ **INVERY HOUSE**
Bridge of Feugh AB31 3NJ
(signposted on B974)
☎(0330) 824782 FAX (0330) 824712
Closed Nov-Jan

This charming Scottish mansion is set in 47 acres of woodland, park and gardens alongside the River Feugh. Dating back to 1804, it is regarded as one of Scotland's leading country house hotels, owned and run by Stewart and Sheila Spence. Individually styled bedrooms have antique furniture and beautiful fabrics, and the many extras include a decanter of sherry, shortbreads and fresh fruit. There is an elegant and comfortable drawing room with open fire, an imposing reception lounge and a cosy bar. The sumptuous dining room is the perfect setting for the high standard of cuisine offered from the 4-course menu. Much of the produce comes from the hotel's own gardens with fish and game from local sources. Gravlax of wild salmon may feature among the starters, then a home-made soup, and perhaps medallions of venison set on a timbale of haggis. Delicious home-made sweets complete the meal.

14⇌⁌1⌺⌿ in 4 bedrooms CTV in all bedrooms ⌓ T
✈ (ex guide dogs)
(20P 2⛟ ❊ ⌿ (grass) ⌿ snooker croquet lawn putting green
♀ Scottish & French **V** ❀ ⌓ Last dinner 9.45pm
Conf. Board 24 Del from £150
Credit Cards [1] [2] [3] [5]

★★★ ❊⁌ **73%** Raemoir
AB3 4ED (Follow A980, signed Torphins, and in 2m at T-junct straight ahead for hotel drive) ☎(0330) 824884 FAX (0330) 822171
Closed 2-14 Jan

This delightful 18th-century mansion in extensive wooded grounds is run by the hospitable Sabin family, who offer a blend of old-fashioned values with modern day comforts. Bedrooms are very individual, some with tapestried walls and sturdy antique furniture. Roaring log fires and fresh flowers enhance the public areas. Chef Derek Smith's well balanced menus offer a tempting range of typically Scottish dishes, carefully prepared from the best local produce.

17⇌⁌ Annexe6⇌⁌(1fb)1⌺ CTV in all bedrooms ® T
sB&B⇌⁌£52.50-£79 dB&B⇌⁌£115-£126 ⛿
CTV 100P ⛟ ❊ ⌿ (hard) ⌿ sauna solarium gymnasium croquet pitch & put shooting stalking ⌿ *xmas*
♀ International **V** ❀ ⌓ ⌿ Sunday Lunch £14.50 High tea £10-£15alc Dinner fr£24.50&alc Last dinner 9pm
Credit Cards [1] [2] [3] [5]

★★★ **64%** Tor-na-Coille
AB31 4AB ☎(0330) 822242 FAX (0330) 824012

This Victorian mansion is set in its own wooded grounds. About half the bedrooms have been refurbished in keeping with the style of the house and public areas include an attractive restaurant and a well stocked bar. There is also a lounge, where bar meals are served. Staff are friendly and willing to please.

24⇌⁌(4fb) CTV in all bedrooms ® T sB&B⇌⁌£52.80-£81.40 dB&B⇌⁌£75-£99 ⛿
Lift 130P ❊ squash croquet lawn *xmas*

70

Banchory - Bardon Mill

 Scottish & French V ⓒ ♨ ✂ Sunday Lunch £6.05-£12.70
Dinner fr£20&alc Last dinner 10pm
CONF. Thtr 90 Class 60 Board 30 Del from £69.30
Credit Cards 1 2 3 5

★★ 62% Burnett Arms
25 High St AB31 3TD ☎(0330) 824944

This former coaching inn has a friendly atmosphere and improved public areas include a choice of bars and lounges together with a busy dining room. Refurbishment has considerably enhanced about half of the bedrooms, original rooms remaining modest and functional.
16⇌📺(1fb) CTV in all bedrooms ®⚹ T
40P
V ⓒ ♨ Last dinner 9pm
Credit Cards 1 2 3 4 5

BANFF Grampian *Banffshire* Map 15 NJ66

★★★ 57% Banff Springs
Golden Knowes Rd AB45 2JE (1st on right from main Inverness to Fraserburgh rd)
☎(0261) 812881 FAX (0261) 815546

On the western edge of the town with views of the Moray Firth, this is a purpose built commercial hotel. Bedrooms have the expected amenities, but are rather dated and functional. Public areas include a bar, foyer lounge and restaurant.
30⇌📺(4fb) CTV in all bedrooms ®⚹ T ✱ sB&B⇌📺£40.50-£45 dB&B⇌📺£58-£79 ⍾
⌘ 120P xmas
 Scottish & French V ⓒ ♨ ✱ Dinner £14-£19.50&alc Last dinner 9pm
Credit Cards 1 2 3 4 5

BANGOR Gwynedd Map 06 SH57

★★★ ✿67% Menai Court
Craig y Don Rd LL57 2BG ☎(0248) 354200 FAX (0248) 354200
Closed 27 Dec-2 Jan
The Menai Court is a well maintained hotel with a locally popular restaurant. It is signed off the Menai Bridge Road, and there are views over the Menai Straits to Anglesea from several rooms. Friendly owners Judy and Elwyn Hughes (of Black and White Minstrel fame) create an informal atmosphere. Bedrooms are modern and comfortable and there is a choices of lounges plus a conference room.
12⇌📺(2fb) CTV in all bedrooms ®⚹ T ✱ sB&B⇌📺£47 dB&B⇌📺fr£83 ⍾
22P 🚲 xmas
 British & French V ⓒ ✱ Lunch £11.95 Dinner £15&alc Last dinner 9.30pm
Credit Cards 1 2 3

★★ 64% Telford
Holyhead Rd LL57 2HX ☎(0248) 352543
Standing alongside the famous suspension bridge in 2 acres of terraced gardens leading down to the Menai Straits, this well maintained family run hotel gives splendid views from the bar, restaurant and many of the bedrooms.
10rm(4📺)(2fb)✂in 2 bedrooms CTV in 9 bedrooms TV in 1 bedroom ✂ (ex guide dogs)
⌘ ⊞ CTV 15P ✿ ♪
V ⓒ ♨ ✂ Last dinner 9pm
Credit Cards 1 3

For key to symbols see the Bookmark.

★★ 64% Ty Uchaf
Tal-y-Bont LL57 3UR ☎(0248) 352219
Closed 23 Dec-2 Jan
This small privately owned and personally run hotel offers simple but cosy accommodation, combined with friendly informal service. Prices are very competitive, which is one of the reasons why the hotel has a loyal following of regular commercial visitors, though it is equally suitable for tourists.
10⇌📺(1fb) CTV in all bedrooms ® T ✂ (ex guide dogs)
40P
V ⓒ Last dinner 8.30pm
Credit Cards 1 3

Pavilion Lodge
Bangor Services, Llandegai LL57 4BG (junc A5/A55) ☎(0248) 370345 FAX (0248) 355959

With a nearby family restaurant providing all meals, this modern building offers smart, spacious and well equipped bedrooms. For more details about Pavilion Lodges, consult the Contents page, under Hotel Groups.
34⇌📺 ✱ sB⇌📺£31.95 dB⇌📺£35.95 (room only)

BARDON MILL Northumberland Map 12 NY76

★ 68% Vallum Lodge
Military Rd, Twice Brewed NE47 7AN (on B6318)
☎Haltwhistle(0434) 344248
Closed Dec-Feb RS Nov-Mar
Close to many of the interesting sites associated with Hadrian's Wall, this small hotel offers quiet, comfortable and effectively heated accommodation. There is a cosy lounge and bar, with service provided by the friendly resident proprietors.
7rm(2⇌📺) ® sB&B£20-£24 dB&B£40-£46 dB&B⇌📺£46-£54 ⍾

Wroxton House Hotel ★★★

This deluxe Country House Hotel offers you its warm hospitality and total tranquillity with the profusion of flowers and personal touches that have traditionally graced country house life.

Built in honeyed local stone, this delightful hotel offers 32 superior bedrooms with en-suite facilities, award winning restaurant with a selection of fine wines, two private meeting/dining rooms, abundant car parking and delightful gardens.

**Wroxton St. Mary
Near Banbury, Oxfordshire
OX15 6QB
Telephone: (0295) 730777
Fax: (0295) 730800**

Bardon Mill - Barnby Moor

CTV 30P ⇨ ✿ xmas
V ⇨ ⌂ ⚐ Last dinner 8pm

BARFORD Warwickshire Map 04 SP26

★★★ **67%** The Glebe at Barford
Church St CV35 8BS ☎ Warwick(0926) 624218 FAX (0926) 624295
Built in the 1820s, The Glebe at Barford was once the rectory to the adjacent church and enjoys a tranquil village location. Guest rooms are individually styled, attractively decorated and furnished, and have a wide range of facilities. There is a well furnished conservatory restaurant and 2 bars.
41⇨♠(3fb)7⇦ CTV in all bedrooms ® ✱ T ✱ sB&B⇨♠£50-£90 dB&B⇨♠£95-£150 ⃝
Lift (56P ✿ ⬜ (heated) sauna gymnasium jacuzzi steam room croquet pool table *xmas*
⚐ English & Continental V ⇨ ⌂ ✱ Lunch £4.50-£12 High tea £7.50-£10.50 Dinner £14.95&alc Last dinner 9.45pm
Conf. Thtr 130 Class 50 Board 60 Del from £80
Credit Cards ① ② ③ ⑤

BAR HILL Cambridgeshire Map 05 TL36

★★★ **63%** Cambridgeshire Moat House
CB3 8EU (off A604) ☎ Crafts Hill(0954) 780555 FAX (0954) 780010
Closed 24-26 Dec
Refurbishment has continued over the last few years, with bright, fresh public areas, about 50 bedrooms having a new look and the compact rooms more acceptable with modern white appointments. The original bedrooms are still sound, but the bathrooms look dowdy.
100⇨♠(8fb) CTV in all bedrooms ® ✱ T sB⇨♠£53.50-£65 dB⇨♠£78 (room only) ⃝
(200P ✿ ⬜ (heated) ⏵ 18 ♀ (hard) squash sauna solarium gymnasium putting green
⚐ English & French V ⇨ ⌂ ✱ Lunch fr£15.50 Dinner £15.50&alc Last dinner 9.45pm
Conf. Thtr 180 Class 80 Board 40 Del from £98.50
Credit Cards ① ② ③ ⑤

Queens Moat Houses

BARMOUTH Gwynedd Map 06 SH61

★★ ⚜**65%** Ty'r Graig
Llanaber Rd LL42 1YN ☎(0341) 280470
FAX (0341) 280470
Closed Nov-Feb
This large Victorian house, with delightful stained glass windows and fine woodcarving, stands in its own grounds with views of the beach and Cardigan Bay. It has an elegant and comfortable lounge, an attractive dining room and a conservatory bar. Bedrooms vary in both size and style, and some enjoy sea views. As well as the carte, there is a good value fixed-price menu changes according to the season, with such dishes as leg of Welsh spring lamb baked with coriander and rosemary or perhaps a thin seafood crepe topped with cheese.
12⇨♠2⇦ ♠ in 1 bedroom CTV in all bedrooms ® ✱ T
✱ (ex guide dogs) sB&B⇨♠£36-£40 dB&B⇨♠£56-£72 ⃝
15P ⇨ ✿ windsurfing yachting sea fishing
⚐ Welsh, English & French V ⇨ ⌂ ✱ Sunday Lunch £9.25 Dinner £15.50&alc Last dinner 8.30pm
Credit Cards ① ③

★★ **63%** *Panorama*
Panorama Rd LL42 1DQ ☎(0341) 280550 FAX (0341) 280346
This stone-built hotel has superb views over the estuary. Bedrooms have pretty floral décor and matching fabrics. The hotel is family run, with Jack Flavell (ex Worcester and England cricketer) much to the fore. There is an extensive choice of food, with table d'hôte

and à la carte menus in the main restaurant, and a popular bistro open at weekends.
19rm(10⇨♠8♠)(3fb) CTV in all bedrooms ® T
CTV 40P ✿ putting green nc2yrs
⚐ English & French V ⇨ ⌂ Last dinner 9.30pm
Credit Cards ① ③

★ **69%** Llwyndu Farmhouse
Llanaber LL42 1RR (2.5m N off A496) ☎(0341) 280144
With magnificent views of the sea and surrounding hills, the 16th-century stone farmhouse has thick stone walls, large beams and stone inglenook fireplaces. The sitting room and dining room are open plan and drinks are served in the comfortable lounge. There are 4 bedrooms in a converted barn, all furnished with modern pine.
3⇨♠ Annexe4⇨♠(4fb)⚐ in all bedrooms CTV in all bedrooms ® sB&B⇨♠£35-£40 dB&B⇨♠£44-£55 ⃝
CTV 10P ⇨ ✿ *xmas*
⚐ English & French V ⇨ ⌂ Dinner £12.50-£18.50 Last dinner 7pm

★ **64%** Bryn Melyn
Panorama Rd LL42 1DQ (Logis) ☎(0341) 280556 FAX (0341) 280276
Closed Dec-Feb
This small family-run hotel with well equipped bedrooms is in an elevated position east of the town, commanding splendid views across the Mawddach Estuary to the Cader Mountains.
10rm(8♠)(1fb) CTV in 9 bedrooms ® T sB&B♠fr£32 dB&Bfr£39 dB&B♠fr£54 ⃝
10P ⇨ ✿
V ⇨ ⚐ Bar Lunch fr£3.95 Dinner fr£13 Last dinner 8.30pm
Credit Cards ① ③ ⑤

BARNARD CASTLE Co Durham Map 12 NZ01

★★ **62%** Bowes Moor
Bowes Moor DL12 9RH (4 miles W of Bowes on A66)
☎Teesdale(0833) 28331
Reputed to be England's highest hotel, the Bowes Moor stands in open moorland. Accommodation is adequate, and a good range of food is served in both bar and restaurant. There is also a cosy lounge.
10rm(8⇨♠) CTV in 9 bedrooms TV in 1 bedroom ® T sB&B⇨♠£27.50-£32.50 dB&B£35-£37.50 dB&B⇨♠£42.50-£49.50 ⃝
CTV 60P pool table darts *xmas*
V ⇨ ⌂ ⚐ Lunch £6.25&alc High tea fr£3.70 Dinner £10.50-£11.50&alc Last dinner 8.30pm
Credit Cards ① ② ③ ⑤

BARNBY MOOR Nottinghamshire Map 08 SK68

★★★ **60%** Ye Olde Bell
DN22 8QS (Principal) ☎Retford(0777) 705121 FAX (0777) 860424
This old coaching inn has retained much of its character despite modernisation. Public rooms are traditionally styled and comfortable. Though some of the bedrooms are looking dated, they are serviceable, and the remainder are modern and well decorated.
55⇨♠(4fb)1⇦⚐ in 18 bedrooms CTV in all bedrooms ® T
(250P ✿ putting green
V ⇨ ⌂ ⚐ Last dinner 9.45pm
Credit Cards ① ② ③ ⑤

The AA's star rating scheme is the market leader in hotel classification.

BARNHAM BROOM Norfolk Map 05 TG00

★★★**66%** Barnham Broom Hotel Conference & Leisure
Centre NR9 4DD ☎(060545) 393 due to change to (0603) 759393 FAX (0603) 758224

This low, sprawling red brick and pantile complex is set in 250 acres of grounds, which are home to a championship golf course and an excellent indoor leisure complex. The bedrooms are modern with simple pastel décor and quite plain soft furnishings, and facilities are good. In addition to the main restaurant, the Sports Bar serves refreshments, snacks and meals.
52⇨♺(10fb) CTV in all bedrooms ® T ✖ (ex guide dogs) sB&B⇨♺£59.50-£61 dB&B⇨♺£82-£84 ◨
〖 200P ✿ ▭ (heated) ▶ 36 ♟ (hard) squash snooker sauna solarium gymnasium hairdressing salon beautician steam room *xmas*
♀ English & Continental V ✿ ☕ ✂ ✱ Lunch £8.50-£8.95 Dinner fr£13.50&alc Last dinner 9.30pm
CONF. Thtr 150 Class 80 Board 60 Del £88.50
Credit Cards ①②③⑤

See advertisement under **NORWICH**

BARNSDALE BAR SERVICE AREA North Yorkshire Map 08 SE51

Forte Travelodge
WF8 3JB (on A1, southbound)
☎Pontefract(0977) 620711 Central Res (0800) 850950

This modern building offers a good standard of accommodation for overnight stops. Smart, spacious and well equipped bedrooms, all with en suite bathrooms, are suitable for family use, and meals may be taken at the nearby family restaurant. For more details about Travelodges, consult the Contents page, under Hotel Guides.
56⇨♺✱ B⇨♺£31.95 (room only)

BARNSLEY South Yorkshire Map 08 SE30

See also **Tankersley**
★★★**68%** Ardsley Moat House
Doncaster Rd, Ardsley S71 5EH (E off A635)
☎(0226) 289401 FAX (0226) 205374
Closed 25 Dec

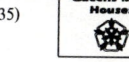

This well managed hotel converted from an 18th-century mansion is tailored to meet conference and commercial needs. Comfortable bedrooms have efficient modern bathrooms and smart public areas include an attractive restaurant, cocktail bar and separate public bar.
73⇨♺(3fb)3▦⁊in 6 bedrooms CTV in all bedrooms ® T ✱ sB⇨♺£50-£55 dB⇨♺£60-£65 (room only) ◨
〖 300P ✿ ♫
♀ English & French V ✿ ☕ ✂ Lunch fr£10&alc Dinner fr£14.75&alc Last dinner 10.30pm
CONF. Thtr 350 Class 150 Board 30 Del from £75
Credit Cards ①②③⑤

Forte Travelodge
(at Stairfoot roundabout A633/A635)
☎(0226) 298799 Central Res (0800) 850950

This modern building offers a good standard of accommodation for overnight stops. Smart, spacious and well equipped bedrooms, all with en suite bathrooms, are suitable for family use, and meals may be taken at the nearby family restaurant. For more details about Travelodges, consult the Contents page, under Hotel Groups.
32⇨♺✱ B⇨♺£31.95 (room only)

BARNSTAPLE Devon Map 02 SS53

★★★**62%** Park
Taw Vale EX32 9AE (opposite Rock park, 0.5m from town centre) (Brend) ☎(0271) 72166 FAX (0271) 78558
This modern hotel overlooks Rock Park and is a short walk from Barnstaple Bridge and the town centre. Family owned and managed, it offers a relaxed atmosphere, with smart open plan public areas and various sizes of bedrooms.
25⇨♺Annexe17⇨♺(7fb) CTV in all bedrooms ® ☂ T ✱ sB&B⇨♺£30-£47 dB&B⇨♺£45-£65 ◨
〖 80P ♫ *xmas*
♀ English & French V ✿ ☕ ✱ Lunch £8.25 Dinner £12.50&alc Last dinner 9pm
Credit Cards ①②③⑤

★★★**60%** Barnstaple Hotel
Braunton Rd EX31 1LE (on the outskirts of Barnstaple on A361) (Brend) ☎(0271) 76221 FAX (0271) 24101
This purpose built hotel is in an industrial area of the town. The public areas have been refurbished to a good standard, and by the time this guide is published the bedrooms should have received similar treatment. A la carte and table d'hôte menus are offered in the smart dining room.
57⇨♺(11fb) CTV in all bedrooms ® ☂ T ✱ sB&B⇨♺£30-£47 dB&B⇨♺£45-£65 ◨
〖 ▦ 250P ✿ ▭ (heated) snooker sauna solarium gymnasium spa bath ♫ ⚛ *xmas*
♀ English & French V ✿ ☕ ✱ Sunday Lunch £14-£20alc Dinner £12.50&alc Last dinner 9pm
Credit Cards ①②③⑤

★★**61%** Royal & Fortescue
Boutport St EX31 1HG (Brend) ☎(0271) 42289 FAX (0271) 42289
A large rambling building with bedrooms on several levels and in various shapes and sizes, this traditional hotel is in the centre of the market town. Most bedrooms have been modernised, and public areas have been smartly upgraded, with an all-day coffee shop as well as the main dining room.
52rm(47⇨♺)(5fb) CTV in all bedrooms ® ☂ T ✱ sB&B£30 sB&B⇨♺£30-£47 dB&B£45 dB&B⇨♺£45-£65 ◨
Lift 〖 CTV 20P 20 ♫ *xmas*
♀ English & French V ✿ ☕ ✱ Lunch £7.25 Dinner £12.50&alc Last dinner 9pm
Credit Cards ①②③⑤

★
★✿✿▲
HALMPSTONE MANOR
Bishop's Tawton EX32 0EA
(5m S off A377, leave A377 at Bishop's Tawton opposite BP petrol station and follow unclassified road for 2m then turn right at Halmpstone Manor sign)
☎Swimbridge(0271) 830321 FAX (0271) 830826
Closed Jan & Feb

Personally run by friendly proprietors Jane and Charles Stanbury, this charming hotel is quite special. Everything about the place speaks of quality, yet guests are made to feel so welcome and at ease. The lovely bedrooms are individually furnished and decorated and offer a high degree of comfort with many thoughtful extras. Comfortable public areas are filled with fresh flowers, and guests dine very well in the attractive panelled dining room. Jane Stanbury cooks in an accomplished manner while her husband and his team look ➡

Barnstaple - Barry

after the front of house. The set-price, 5-course menu offers some choices. On a recent stay, our inspector's meal began with a woodland salad of tender pigeon, wild rice and mushrooms, followed by a delicious fillet of roast venison in an excellent peppercorn sauce. Sweets are too good to miss – the sticky toffee pudding was scrumptious.

5rm 2fb CTV in all bedrooms ® T ✱ sB&B £65-£70 dB&B £80-£130 🅿

12P nc12yrs xmas

♥ English & French V Dinner £27.50&alc Last dinner 9pm

Credit Cards 1 2 3 5 £

⇪Cedars Lodge Inn
Bickington Rd EX31 2HP ☎(0271) 71784 FAX (0271) 25733
A recently renovated Victorian house with a comfortable bar and attractive conservatory, both serving a wide range of food. Spacious bedrooms of a good standard are in lodges set round a courtyard in the grounds.
Annexe23rm (5fb) in 3 bedrooms CTV in all bedrooms ® T ✱ sB fr£32 dB fr£43 (room only)
120P squash
V ✱ Lunch £1.45-£10.85&alc Dinner £1.45-£10.85&alc Last dinner 10pm
CONF. Thtr 100 Class 60 Board 50
Credit Cards 1 2 3

BARR, GREAT West Midlands Map 07 SP09

★★★ 58% Great Barr Hotel & Conference Centre
Pear Tree Dr, off Newton Rd B43 6HS (1m W of junc A34/A4041) ☎021-357 1141 FAX 021-357 7557
Popular with the commercial and conference trade, this hotel is located in a residential area, but has easy access to the city centre.
110rm (1fb) CTV in all bedrooms ® T ✻ (ex guide dogs) ✱ sB £40-£65 dB £50-£75 (room only) 🅿
(175P
♥ English & Continental V ✱ Lunch £10-£15&alc High tea £6-£9 Dinner £15-£20&alc Last dinner 9.45pm
CONF. Thtr 100 Class 50 Board 50 Del from £65
Credit Cards 1 2 3 4 5 £

Forte Posthouse
Chapel Ln B43 7BG (at junction M6/A34)
☎021-357 7444 FAX 021-357 7503

Suitable for both the business and leisure traveller, this bright hotel provides modern accommodation in well equipped bedrooms with en suite bathrooms. For more details about Forte Posthouse hotels, consult the Contents page, under Hotel Groups.
192rm B £41.50-£53.50 (room only)
CONF. Thtr 120 Class 80 Board 60

BARRHEAD Strathclyde Renfrewshire Map 11 NS45

★★ 62% Dalmeny Park
Lochlibo Rd G78 1LG (on A736) ☎041-881 9211 FAX 041-889 9214
Dalmeny Park is a popular commercial and function hotel set in 6 acres of grounds on the southern edge of the town. Public areas have been comfortably refurbished and plans are in hand to upgrade the well equipped bedrooms.
18rm(4 10)(2fb) in 4 bedrooms CTV in all bedrooms ® T ✱ sB&B£39.50-£63 sB&B £45-£63 dB&B£63-£87 dB&B £75-£97 🅿
(150P xmas

V ✱ Lunch £9.10-£12.45&alc High tea fr£5.95 Dinner fr£16.95 Last dinner 9.30pm
CONF. Thtr 250 Class 120 Board 86 Del from £68.95
Credit Cards 1 2 3 4 5 £

BARROW-IN-FURNESS Cumbria Map 07 SD16

★★ 65% Majestic
Duke St LA14 1HP ☎(0229) 870448
Located in the heart of the town close to indoor and outdoor markets, this recently refurbished 19th-century hotel has spacious, very well equipped bedrooms, a lively public bar and a small residents' bar next to the pleasant restaurant.
35rm (2fb)1 CTV in all bedrooms ® T
Lift (CTV 26P pool tables
V Last dinner 9.30pm
Credit Cards 1 2 3

★★ 64% Lisdoonie
307/309 Abbey Rd LA14 5LF (on A590) ☎(0229) 827312
Closed Xmas & New Year
Set in its own grounds on the main approach road to the town, this friendly owner-run hotel caters mainly to the commercial trade and has warm, comfortable lounges and bedrooms with modern furnishings. The pleasant restaurant serves a good range of food.
12rm (2fb) CTV in all bedrooms ® T sB&B £25-£41 dB&B £36-£51 🅿
CTV 30P
♥ English & French V ✱ Lunch fr£13 High tea fr£7.50 Dinner fr£16 Last dinner 7.30pm
CONF. Class 255
Credit Cards 1 2 3

BARRY South Glamorgan Map 03 ST16

★★★ 🏵 74% Egerton Grey Country House
Porthkerry CF62 3BZ (from junct 33 of M4 follow signs for airport and turn left at roundabout for Porthkerry) (Welsh Rarebits) ☎(0446) 711666 FAX (0446) 711690
Tucked away at the head of a steep wooded valley, which ends in a golf course and shingle beach, this hotel is set in 7 acres of mature gardens. The house is an elegant former rectory, richly furnished on classical lines, with ornate plasterwork, open fires, paintings and objets d'art. Bedrooms are individual and are furnished in period style; some have charming Victorian roll-top baths. Chef Joseph Lipp uses good quality local produce for his sensibly sized seasonal set menu: Welsh lamb is served with an almond and honey glaze and local salmon is used in a starter of ravioli of salmon and cheese.
10rm (4fb)2 CTV in all bedrooms ® T sB&B £50 dB&B £85-£120 🅿
30P 1 (hard) croquet xmas
V ✱ Lunch £12.50-£19.50 Dinner £19.50-£24.50 Last dinner 9.45pm
Credit Cards 1 2 3 5 £
See advertisement under CARDIFF

★★★ 56% Mount Sorrell
Porthkerry Rd CF6 8AY ☎(0446) 740069 FAX (0446) 746600

This purpose-built commercial hotel overlooking the Bristol Channel features an excellent new leisure complex and quite good function facilities. Many bedrooms have been completely modernised and upgrading is planned for all of them.
45rm (3fb) CTV in all bedrooms ® T
(17P (heated) sauna gymnasium
♥ Continental V Last dinner 10pm
Credit Cards 1 2 3 5

BARTON Lancashire Map 07 SD53

★★★ **62%** **Barton Grange**
Garstang Rd PR3 5AA (from M6 junct 32 follow A6, signed Garstang , for two and half miles) ☎Broughton(0772) 862551 FAX (0722) 861267

Barton Grange stands in its own grounds which form part of a large garden centre. It is privately owned hotel and has a friendly and welcoming atmosphere. Bedrooms vary in size and style, with some comfortable and smart executive rooms. As well as the restaurant and bar there is a coffee shop serving lighter meals between 10am and 6pm.

53⇌🐾Annexe10⇌🐾(10fb)1⊞ CTV in all bedrooms ® T
✕ (ex guide dogs) sB&B⇌🐾£68-£75 dB&B⇌🐾£78-£90 ⃞
Lift ℂ CTV 250P ❁ ▢ (heated) *xmas*
♀ English & French V ✿ ℒ ⫽ Lunch £9-£10 Dinner £17-£18&alc Last dinner 10pm
CONF. Thtr 300 Class 100 Board 80 Del from £72
Credit Cards ①②③⑤ (£)

BARTON MILLS Suffolk Map 05 TL77

Forte Travelodge
IP28 6AE (on A11)
☎(0638) 717675 Central Res (0800) 850950

FORTE Travelodge

This modern building offers a good standard of accommodation for overnight stops. Smart, spacious and well equipped bedrooms, all with en suite bathrooms, are suitable for family use, and meals may be taken at the nearby family restaurant. For more details about Travelodges, consult the Contents page, under Hotel Groups.
32⇌🐾❁ B⇌🐾£31.95 (room only)

BARTON-ON-SEA Hampshire Map 04 SZ29

★★ **72%** **The Cliff House**
Marine Dr West BH25 7QL ☎New Milton(0425) 619333 FAX (0425) 612462

There are fine sea views from this prominent cliff top position, and proprietors James and Isobel Simpson offer warm hospitality. Many popular dishes can be recommended from the timeless 'carte' of popular dishes. Bedrooms have pretty fabrics and a good range of facilities, and the hotel also has a small bar.

9⇌🐾⫽in all bedrooms CTV in all bedrooms ®✱ T
✕ (ex guide dogs) ✱ sB&B⇌🐾£35-£45 dB&B⇌🐾£60-£80 ⃞
50P ⛳ ❁ nc10yrs *xmas*
V ✿ ℒ ⫽ ✱ Lunch £10.50-£11.50&alc Dinner fr£16.50&alc Last dinner 9pm
Credit Cards ①②③

BARTON STACEY Hampshire Map 04 SU44

Forte Travelodge
SO21 3NP (on A303) ☎Andover(0264) 72260 Central Res (0800) 850950

FORTE Travelodge

This modern building offers a good standard of accommodation for overnight stops. Smart, spacious and well equipped bedrooms, all with en suite bathrooms, are suitable for family use, and meals may be taken at the nearby family restaurant. For more details about Travelodges, consult the Contents page, under Hotel Groups.
20⇌🐾❁ B⇌🐾£31.95 (room only)

All black star hotels are given a percentage grading within their star bands. See 'Using the Guide' at the front of the book for full details.

BARTON UNDER NEEDWOOD Staffordshire Map 07 SK11

Forte Travelodge (Northbound)
DE13 0ED (on A38, northbound)
☎(0283) 716343 Central Res (0800) 850950

FORTE Travelodge

This modern building offers a good standard of accommodation for overnight stops. Smart, spacious and well equipped bedrooms, all with en suite bathrooms, are suitable for family use, and meals may be taken at the nearby family restaurant. For more details about Travelodges, consult the Contents page, under Hotel Groups.
20⇌🐾❁ B⇌🐾£31.95 (room only)

Forte Travelodge (Southbound)
Rykneld St DE13 8EH (on A38, southbound)
☎(0283) 716784 Central Res (0800) 850950

FORTE Travelodge

This modern building offers a good standard of accommodation for overnight stops. Smart, spacious and well equipped bedrooms, all with en suite bathrooms, are suitable for family use, and meals may be taken at the nearby family restaurant. For more details about Travelodges, consult the Contents page, under Hotel Groups.
40⇌🐾❁ B⇌🐾£31.95 (room only)

BASILDON Essex Map 05 TQ78

★★★ **63%** **Chichester**
Old London Rd, Wickford SS11 8UE (off A129) ☎(0268) 560555 FAX (0268) 560580
This hotel, built in 1989, has been sympathetically landscaped and is in open farmland. Bedrooms are situated around an attractive garden courtyard; all have similar furnishings and comfortable seating. The Gallery restaurant is reasonably priced, there are two other bars and another restaurant.

Cedars Lodge Inn

Bickington, Nr Barnstaple, N Devon
Telephone (0271) 71784

Welcome

Conveniently located on the outskirts of Barnstaple, just half a mile off the new A361 M5 link road, Barnstaple by pass and the town centre. An elegant former country house and lodges in 3 acres of landscaped gardens, Cedars offers all the modern facilities in a traditional atmosphere. Excellent Restaurant, function and conference facilities available. Whether on business or holiday you'll discover every comfort, genuine friendly hospitality and excellent food, combining to provide superb value for money.

Basildon - Basingstoke

2⇌Annexe32⇌ CTV in all bedrooms ® T ✕ (ex guide dogs)
sB⇌£45.50-£52.50 dB⇌£54.50-£56.50 (room only)
(150P nc5yrs
♀ English & French V ✱ Lunch £8-£10.50&alc Dinner fr£13.50alc Last dinner 9.30pm
Credit Cards 1 2 3 5

Campanile
Pipps Hill, Southend Arterial Rd SS14 3AE (exit A127 at Basildon/Billericay turn off and turn left at next 2 roundabouts) ☎(0268) 530810 FAX (0268) 286710

A nearby bar and bistro restaurant provides refreshments for travellers staying at this modern accommodation building. Bedrooms are well equipped and have en suite bathrooms. For more details about Campanile, consult the Contents page, under Hotel Groups.

Annexe100⇌Ւ✱ B⇌Ւ£35.75 (room only)
CONF. Thtr 35 Class 35 Board 25 Del from £42.80

Forte Posthouse
Cranes Farm Rd SS14 3DG ☎(0268) 533955 FAX (0268) 530119

Suitable for both the business and leisure traveller, this bright hotel provides modern accommodation in well equipped bedrooms with en suite bathrooms. For more details about Forte Posthouse hotels, consult the Contents page, under Hotel Groups.

110⇌Ւ✱ B⇌Ւ£41.50-£53.50 (room only)
CONF. Thtr 300 Class 80 Board 80 Del £89.50

Travel Inn
Felmores, East Mayne SS13 1BW (take A127 towards Basildon) ☎(0268) 522227 FAX (0268) 530092

Purpose-built accomodation offers spacious and well equipped bedrooms, all with en suite bathrooms. Meals may be taken at the nearby family restaurant and pub. For more details about Travel Inns, consult the Contents page, under Hotel Groups.

Annexe32⇌Ւ✱ B⇌Ւ£33.50 (room only)

BASINGSTOKE Hampshire Map 04 SU65

See also **Odiham, Sherfield on Loddon** & **Stratfield Turgis**

★★★★ ♨ TYLNEY HALL
RG27 9AJ BASINGSTOKE ☎(0256) 764881 FAX (0256) 768141
(For full entry see Rotherwick)

★★★★ ❋70% **Audleys Wood Thistle**
Alton Rd RG25 2JT (1.5m S on A339)
☎(0256) 817555 FAX (0256) 817500

Set in wooded parkland on the southern edge of the town, this Victorian country house with much fine woodcarving and panelling has been skilfully extended to provide very comfortable, spacious bedrooms with all modern amenities. Attractively furnished public areas include a stylish restaurant offering interesting table d' hôte and carte menus and a quality wine list.

71⇌Ւ(6fb)2✱⌧in 25 bedrooms CTV in all bedrooms ® ⚡ T ✱ sB⇌Ւ£42-£85 dB⇌Ւ£84-£105 (room only) ♘
(100P ✿ croquet putting bicycles *xmas*
♀ British & French V ♎ ⚡ ✱ Lunch £13.95-£18&alc Dinner £22-£29&alc Last dinner 9.45pm
CONF. Thtr 55 Class 20 Board 26 Del from £105
Credit Cards 1 2 3 4 5

Irish entries appear in a separate section that follows the main directory.

★★★ 72% **Centrecourt**
Centre Dr, Chineham RG24 0FY ☎(0256) 816669 FAX (0256) 816727

This purpose-built complex combines a modern hotel, extensive tennis centre and leisure facilities. The variety of spacious bedrooms are particularly well furnished and equipped, and half have their own balconies. The Garden Restaurant offers a daily menu and a carte, and light snacks are also available.

50⇌Ւ(6fb)⌧in 25 bedrooms CTV in all bedrooms ® T ✱ sB⇌Ւ£80-£110 dB⇌Ւ£95-£110 ♘
Lift (CTV 120P ⌂ (heated) ♇ (hard) sauna solarium gymnasium steam room spa bath badminton *xmas*
♀ English & Continental V ♎ ⚡ ✱ Lunch fr£11.90alc Dinner £11.40-£21.50alc Last dinner 10pm
CONF. Thtr 95 Class 40 Board 40 Del from £95
Credit Cards 1 2 3 5   £

★★★ ❋68% **Basingstoke Country**
Nately Scures, Hook RG27 9JS (leave M3 exit 5 take turning on roundabout to Newnham/Basingstoke, proceed 0.5m until reaching T junct, turn left onto A30, hotel is 200yd on right) ☎(0256) 764161 FAX (0256) 768341

Once a country residence, now sympathetically extended, this popular business hotel stands back from the A30 west of Hook. Public areas include an air conditioned lounge bar and a formal restaurant, where sound and imaginative dishes are offered by chef Iain McCormack from extensive à la carte and set menus. There is an attractive courtyard, and leisure facilities housed in an eye-catching conservatory. Bedrooms are all similar, modern and of a good size.

70⇌Ւ(8fb)1✱⌧in 14 bedrooms CTV in all bedrooms ® T ✱ sB⇌Ւ£32.50-£99.50 dB⇌Ւ£65-£160 (room only) ♘
Lift (200P ✿ ⌂ (heated) sauna solarium gymnasium
V ♎ ⚡ ✱ Lunch £14.50-£19.50&alc Dinner £19.50&alc Last dinner 9.45pm
CONF. Thtr 200 Class 95 Board 80 Del from £110
Credit Cards 1 2 3 4 5   £

★★★ ❋65% **Romans**
Little London Rd RG7 2PN
☎Silchester(0734) 700421 FAX (0734) 700691
(For full entry see Silchester)

★★★ 58% **Ringway**
Popley Way, Aldermaston Roundabout, Ringway North (A339) RG24 9NV (Hilton) ☎(0256) 20212 FAX (0256) 842835

A modern building on the ring road which provides a relaxing atmosphere for the business traveller. Bedroom sizes vary, but all are similarly equipped. Public areas include an informal bar and 'Stacks Diner'.

134⇌Ւ(26fb)⌧in 34 bedrooms CTV in all bedrooms ® ⚡ T ✱ sB⇌Ւfr£49.50 dB⇌Ւfr£49.50 (room only) ♘
Lift (250P ⌂ (heated) sauna gymnasium pool ♪ *xmas*
♀ American V ♎ ⚡ ✱ Lunch £4.50-£9.50 Dinner £9.50-£15.50 Last dinner 9.45pm
Credit Cards 1 2 3 5

★★ 68% **Wheatsheaf**
RG25 2BB (Whitbread) ☎Dummer(0256) 398282 FAX (0256) 398253
(For full entry see North Waltham)

Forte Posthouse
Grove Rd RG21 3EE ☎(0256) 468181 FAX (0256) 840087

Suitable for both the business and leisure traveller, this bright hotel provides modern accommodation in well equipped bedrooms with en suite bathrooms. For more details about Forte Posthouse hotels, consult the Contents page, under Hotel Groups.

84⇌Ւ✱ B⇌Ւ£41.50-£53.50 (room only)
CONF. Thtr 180 Class 80 Board 40 Del £89.50

Basingstoke - Baslow

Forte Travelodge
Stag and Hounds, Winchester Rd RG22 6HN (off A30) ☎ (0256) 843566 Central Res (0800) 850350

This modern building offers a good standard of accommodation for overnight stops. Smart, spacious and well equipped bedrooms, all with en suite bathrooms, are suitable for family use, and meals may be taken at the nearby family restaurant. For more details about Travelodges, consult the Contents page, under Hotel Groups.
32⇌❋✶ B⇌✶ £31.95 (room only)

Hilton National Basingstoke
Old Common Rd, Black Dam RG21 3PR
☎ (0256) 460460 FAX (0256) 840441

This is a bright, modern hotel with an informal restaurant, aimed at both the business and leisure guest. All bedrooms have en-suite bathrooms and a range of modern facilities. For more details about Hilton National, see Contents page, under Hotel Groups.
140⇌❋✶ B⇌✶ £65 (room only)
CONF. Thtr 150 Class 70 Board 30 Del £110

Travel Inn
Basingstoke Leisure Park, Worting Rd RG22 6PG
☎ (0256) 811477

Purpose-built accommodation offers spacious and well equipped bedrooms, all with en suite bathrooms. Meals may be taken at the nearby family restaurant and pub. For more details about Travel Inns, consult the Contents page, under Hotel Groups.
49⇌❋✶ B⇌✶ £33.50 (room only)

BASLOW Derbyshire Map 08 SK 27

★★❀ **CAVENDISH**
DE45 1SP (on A619)
☎ (0246) 582311 FAX (0246) 582312

An inn has stood here in the village for centuries. It was rebuilt as the Cavendish in the 1970s and a new bedroom wing was added in 1984. It overlooks the Chatsworth Estate of which it is part. Individually decorated bedrooms vary in size, but all are tastefully furnished, with antiques in the older rooms. The public rooms are a delight with many beautiful pieces, some from Chatsworth House itself. Chef Nick Buckingham produces a varied and imaginative array of dishes, the presentation of which is quite superb. Menus might include a starter of monkfish sausage scented with lemon and served with a vinaigrette of lentils, and entrées such as venison with peppered poached pear and a delicate ginger sabayon. Alternatively, there is traditional roast beef and Yorkshire pudding. Children's menus and a vegetarian selection are available.
24⇌✶ 1☎ CTV in all bedrooms ®✷ T ✖ (ex guide dogs)
❋ sB⇌✶ £73-£83 dB⇌✶ £89-£99 (room only) ⛳
《 50P ⇔ ❀ ♪ putting green *xmas*
♨ European V ⇕ ⚲ ✄ ✱ Lunch £23.75 Dinner £23.75
Last dinner 11pm
Credit Cards [1][2][3][5]

★★★★ AA
AUDLEYS WOOD
A Thistle Country House Hotel

Alton Road, Basingstoke RG25 2JT
Tel: 0256 817555   Fax: 0256 817500

Your choice in Basingstoke

For Reservations at over 100
Mount Charlotte Thistle Hotels
Telephone London: 071 937 8033.

THISTLE HOTELS

★★★★

Tylney Hall

Rotherwick, Nr Hook, Hampshire RG27 9AJ
Tel: (0256) 764881   Fax: (0256) 768141

This magnificent 19th century Victorian Mansion is today one of England's most elegant country house hotels. There are 91 luxurious bedrooms and suites, spacious lounges with log fires and an oak-panelled Dining Room with gourmet cuisine. Leisure facilities include outdoor and indoor heated swimming pools, jacuzzi, sauna, gymnasium, snooker/billiards, tennis and adjacent 18 hole golf course.

Special 2 night breaks, Honeymoon Packages and Christmas Programmes are all available.

Please write or phone for further details and colour brochure.

Baslow - Bath

★★✱✱✱75% Fischer's
Baslow Hall, Calver Rd DE45 1RR (on the A623 between Baslow & Calver) ☎(0246) 583259 FAX (0256) 583818
Closed 25-26 Dec

What started out as a slightly sombre Edwardian manor house has been transformed into a stylish restaurant with individually furnished bedrooms by young owners Max and Susan Fischer. Public areas are elegantly furnished and include a choice of eating options, either the attractive main dining room or the smaller Café Max serving lighter à la carte meals. Max Fischer is a dedicated chef who cooks in an assured modern European style, keeping up to date with the latest trends. Meals may begin with good olives and dainty canapés and follow with a savoury of the day, on the occasion of one visit, a tasty piece of red snapper with sun dried tomatoes, marinated mushrooms and olive oil. At the same meal a matelote of seafood in a red wine sauce proved an enjoyable starter. Good saddle of venison followed, rather dominated by the grain mustard sauce that came with the accompanying lentils. Desserts are largely fruit based and rich, and there is an impressive cheese trolley.

6⇌🛏1🍴 CTV in all bedrooms T ✕ (ex guide dogs)
sB&B⇌🛏£70-£85 dB&B⇌🛏£95-£120 Continental breakfast 🍴
40P ♿ ✿
♬ European V ♉ ♒ ♎ Lunch £20 Dinner £34&alc Last dinner 10pm
Credit Cards [1][2][3]

BASSENTHWAITE Cumbria Map 11 NY23

★★★★✱61% Armathwaite Hall
CA12 4RE ☎Keswick(07687) 76551 FAX (07687) 76220

This magnificent 17th-century mansion house is situated in 400 acres of woodland complete with deer park. It is on the edge of Bassenthwaite Lake and offers superb views towards the lake and the surrounding hills. The hall has impressive panelled rooms with many antiques and there is an open log fires in cool weather.

42⇌🛏(4fb)1🍴 CTV in all bedrooms ® T sB&B⇌🛏£50-£117 dB&B⇌🛏£100-£184 🍴
Lift (100P ♿ ⌧ (heated) ♣ (hard) ♪ ♖ snooker sauna solarium gymnasium croquet pitch & putt beauty salon xmas
♬ English & French V ♉ ♒ ♎ ✱ Lunch £13.95 Dinner £27.95&alc Last dinner 9.30pm
CONF. Thtr 100 Class 60 Board 50 Del from £110
Credit Cards [1][2][3][5]

★★★67% Castle Inn
CA12 4RG (on A595) ☎Keswick(07687) 76401 FAX (07687) 76604

A spacious and popular hotel on the north side of Bassenthwaite Lake, the Castle Inn stands in open countryside with fine views. Considerably upgraded, it offers a good all round standard of accommodation. There are several bars and a comfortable foyer lounge. Bedrooms are modern and well equipped, and some are very spacious. The friendly service deserves special mention.

36⇌🛏(8fb)1🍴 CTV in all bedrooms ® T sB&B⇌🛏£54 dB&B⇌🛏£88 🍴
150P ✿ ⌧ (heated) ♣ (grass) snooker sauna solarium gymnasium badminton table tennis golf practice net ♪ xmas
♬ English & French V ♉ ♒ Lunch £9.50-£17.50&alc High tea £1.75-£2.95 Dinner £17.95-£19.50&alc Last dinner 9.30pm
CONF. Thtr 225 Class 75 Board 40 Del from £55
Credit Cards [1][2][3][5]
See advertisement under KESWICK

★★✱70% Overwater Hall
Ireby CA5 1HH (from Keswick on A591, turn right at Castle Inn crossroads, 2m along this road)
☎Keswick(07687) 76566

Peacefully situated amid woodland and gardens, this family-run hotel occupies one of the principal mansions of the area which dates back to 1780. The 5-course dinner menu may include stuffed tomato with tuna, chicken Roquefort and a good selection of home-made puddings. Bedrooms are mainly modern in style, and lounges are spacious and comfortable.

13⇌🛏(4fb)3🍴 CTV in all bedrooms ® sB&B⇌🛏£32.50-£56 dB&B⇌🛏£65-£102 (incl dinner) 🍴
25P ✿ xmas
♬ English & French V ♉ ♒ ♎ Lunch £10-£13 Dinner £19.95-£23.95 Last dinner 9pm
Credit Cards [1][3]

★★65% Ravenstone
CA12 4QG (4.5m N of Keswick on Carlisle road A591)
☎(07687) 76240
Mar-Oct

This delightful family-run country house, built in 1865, has lovely views towards Bassenthwaite Lake. It has a beautiful oak fireplace in its elegant lounge and a splendid oak staircase leading to the bedrooms, which mostly have modern furniture, although one has a 4-poster bed, and the newest rooms have oak furniture made by the proprietor. In addition to the lounge, there is a cosy bar and an attractive dining room.

20⇌🛏(2fb)2🍴 CTV in all bedrooms ® sB&B⇌🛏£35-£38 dB&B⇌🛏£70-£76 (incl dinner)
25P ♿ ✿ snooker
V ♉ ♎ Dinner £13.50 Last dinner 7.30pm
See advertisement under KESWICK

BATH Avon Map 03 ST76

See also Colerne & Hinton Charterhouse
★★★★★69% Bath Spa
Sydney Rd BA2 6JF ☎(0225) 444424 FAX (0225) 444006

Set in delightful gardens on a hillside overlooking the city, this fine Grecian-fronted hotel has recently been redecorated and extended. In the main restaurant, the Vellore, the new head chef Jonathan Fraser showed promise of great things to come at an inspection meal taken shortly after his arrival. Public areas are, perhaps, not as extensive as one might expect at this level, and our inspector found that staff at the leisure centre took little notice of their guests.

100⇌🛏7🍴✕ in 31 bedrooms CTV in all bedrooms ☎ T ✱
sB⇌🛏fr£125 dB⇌🛏£160-£395 (room only) 🍴
Lift (156P ✿ ⌧ (heated) ♣ (hard) sauna solarium gymnasium croquet xmas
♬ International V ♉ ♒ ♎ ✱ Lunch £17-£30alc Dinner fr£34 Last dinner 10pm
CONF. Thtr 120 Class 80 Board 55 Del from £159
Credit Cards [1][2][3][5]

★★★★✱70% The Royal Crescent
16 Royal Crescent BA1 2LS
☎(0225) 319090 FAX (0225) 339401

Following considerable refurbishment, this hotel has been restored to its former glory. The entrance is in the middle of a lovely Regency terrace, where 2 comfortable lounges and the majority of the bedrooms are housed. The restaurant, cocktail lounge and further bedrooms are in the modern Dower House, to the rear of the main building. While the bedrooms vary in size, all are attractive and many are spacious and luxurious. The smart, courteous staff are a credit to general manager Simon Coombe. In the kitchen, chef Steven Blake presides, and he offers a wide and interesting range of menus, including some vegetarian. Presentation is good, but our inspector found some dishes over-complicated. Though he did not apply this criticism to a particularly praiseworthy tortellini of scallops in a lobster and pimento dressing.

25➪♠Annexe17➪♠(8fb)4✠ CTV in all bedrooms T
✈ (ex guide dogs) ✱ sB&B➪♠fr£98 dB&B➪♠£160-£325
Continental breakfast ⊟
Lift ⟨ 12☎ ✿ croquet plunge pool *xmas*
♀ English & French V ⊕ ⚏ ✳ Lunch £14.50-£18.50 Dinner
£28&alc Last dinner 9.30pm
CONF. Thtr 70 Class 25 Board 28 Del from £130
Credit Cards [1][2][3][5]

★★★★ ❀❀67% Combe Grove Manor Hotel & Country Club
Brassknocker Hill, Monkton Combe BA2 7HS (2m SE)
☎(0225) 834644 FAX (0225) 834961

18th-century elegance is combined with modern facilities at this sympathetically restored Georgian house, perched on a hillside. Bedrooms provide all modern comforts and facilities, with king-size beds and many extra touches of luxury; garden rooms have patios and terraces commanding lovely views. Food is a major attraction: John McManus offers classical style dishes cooked with imaginative care. He has introduced some delicate terrines and fine mousselines. Recommended dishes include delicate poached fillets of sole and mussel glazed in lemon sabayon; tender breast of pheasant or rump of lamb with caramelised onions and creamed potatoes; Old English egg nog pie or iced Grand Marnier soufflé on a smooth caramel sauce with caramelised oranges.
10➪♠Annexe31➪♠(11fb)1✠⚲in 8 bedrooms CTV in all bedrooms ®⚹ T ✈ ✱ sB&B➪♠£98 dB&B➪♠£130-£195
Continental breakfast ⊟
⟨150P ♨ ✿ ▣ (heated) ⚓ (heated) ♟ (hard) squash sauna solarium gymnasium croquet spa baths steam room aerobics *xmas*
V ⊕ ⚏ ⚲ ✳ Lunch £15.50 Dinner £25&alc Last dinner 9.30pm
CONF. Thtr 100 Class 40 Board 36 Del from £145
Credit Cards [1][2][3][5]

★★★ ❀❀80% The Priory
Weston Rd BA1 2XT ☎(0225) 331922 FAX (0225) 448276

The Priory achieves a country house atmosphere in a city environment. The drawing room is furnished with deep chesterfields and rich, heavy fabrics, and overlooks the secluded garden. There is a cosy sitting room, and an elegant, mahogany furnished dining room. Bedrooms are tasteful and furnished with antiques objets d'art, with fresh fruit and flowers, and bathrooms have power showers, perfumed toiletries and bathrobes. Chef Michael Collom produces appealing dishes with honest flavours and textures.
21➪♠1✠ CTV in all bedrooms T ✈ (ex guide dogs) ✱
sB&B➪♠£85 dB&B➪♠£150-£185 (room only) ⊟
26P 1☎ ♨ ✿ ⚓ (heated) croquet *xmas*
♀ French V ⊕ ⚏ ⚲ ✳ Lunch £20.50 Dinner fr£30alc Last dinner 9.15pm
CONF. Thtr 70 Class 26 Board 30 Del from £125
Credit Cards [1][2][3][5]

★★★ ❀❀78% Queensberry
Russel St BA1 2QF ☎(0225) 447928 FAX (0225) 446065

Closed 10 days over Xmas RS Sun

Stephen and Penny Ross's delightful small Bath stone hotel continues to generate praise. The well proportioned bedrooms are stylish and very comfortable. Public rooms, leading from a central open staircase, include a sumptuous first-floor cocktail lounge and on the lower ground floor is a sophisticated modern-style bistro, making an effective contrast with the formal Olive Tree restaurant where Stephen provides honest, carefully prepared dishes from seasonal menus.
22➪♠ CTV in all bedrooms T ✈ (ex guide dogs) ✱
sB&B➪♠£84-£108 dB&B➪♠£103-£149 Continental breakfast ⊟
Lift ⟨ ♟
V ⊕ ⚏ ⚲ ✳ Lunch £10.50-£12.50&alc Dinner £17-£20&alc Last dinner 10.30pm
Credit Cards [1][2][3][4]

THE IDEAL VENUE!
CENTURION
H O T E L S

20 MINUTES FROM BATH CITY CENTRE
44 LUXURY EN SUITE BEDROOMS
RESTAURANT · CONFERENCE FACILITIES
FULL SIZE 9 HOLE GOLF COURSE
BOWLING GREEN · SQUASH COURTS
SWIMMING POOL

Please see entry under
MIDSOMER NORTON
(0761) 417711
FAX (0761) 418357
★★★
CHARLTON LANE, MIDSOMER NORTON, BATH BA3 4BD
MAJOR CREDIT CARDS ACCEPTED

THE ROYAL CRESCENT HOTEL
BATH
★★★★ ❀❀❀

Located in the central two houses of one of Europes greatest architectural masterpieces,
The Royal Crescent Hotel has 42 bedrooms and suites.
All rooms have been individually decorated, some with four posters, jacuzzi's and spa pool.

Beyond the wonderful facade lie beautiful walled gardens, secluded and peaceful for summer relaxation and open-air dining.

The Dower House Restaurant offers some of the finest food in the West Country both at lunch and dinner, special occasions or private dining.

Finally, amongst its finest attributes are the warm and friendly staff, who will care and comfort for your every need…

16 Royal Crescent, Bath,
Avon BA1 2LS
Tel: 0225 319090
Fax: 0225 339401

Bath

★★★ 66% Bath
Widcombe Basin BA2 4JP (on A36, 1m fro junct with A4)
☎(0225) 338855 FAX (0225) 428541
A modern hotel by the confluence of the River Avon and the Kennet and Avon canal, many rooms having river views. Bedrooms are brightly decorated and well furnished with a good range of modern comforts. There is an open plan conservatory restaurant and bar where smartly dressed staff provide prompt and friendly service.
96⇌♠ CTV in all bedrooms ® T sB&B⇌♠£70 dB⇌♠£70 (room only) 🍴
Lift (102P xmas
♀ English & French V ♥ ⚌ ⚄ Lunch £11-£15&alc Dinner £16&alc Last dinner 9.30pm
CONF. Thtr 80 Class 40 Board 40 Del £86
Credit Cards ① ② ③ ⑤

★★★ 64% Francis
Queen Square BA1 2HH ☎(0225) 424357 FAX (0225) 319715

FORTE Heritage

Originally 6 houses, the Francis Hotel has dominated the lower side of Queens Square for over 100 years. The smart restaurant has a charming atmosphere in the evenings when a pianist plays. Most bedrooms are spacious, particularly those in the new wing, but they lack the character of rooms in the original building, and their bathrooms are smaller. Staff are helpful and afternoon tea is a special old-fashioned treat.
93⇌♠(1fb)⚄ 30 bedrooms CTV in all bedrooms ® T sB⇌♠fr£88 dB⇌♠£108-£175 (room only) 🍴
Lift (30P xmas
V ♥ ⚌ ⚄ Lunch fr£8.95&alc Dinner fr£17.95&alc Last dinner 10pm
Credit Cards ① ② ③ ⑤

★★★ 64% Lansdown Grove
BA1 5EH ☎(0225) 315891 FAX (0225) 448092

BEST WESTERN HOTELS

A well established, family-owned hotel, the Lansdown Grove has good views across the city. Styled and run on traditional lines, it had a congenial bar and restaurant with prompt, friendly service. Bedrooms at the front are the largest and most comfortable, and they have the view, but all are nicely furnished and well equipped.
45♠(3fb)⚄ in 9 bedrooms CTV in all bedrooms ® T sB⇌♠£55-£80 dB&B⇌♠£80-£115 🍴
Lift (38P 6🅿 ❈
♀ English & French V ♥ ⚌ ⚄ ⚄ Lunch £7.50-£8.50&alc Dinner £17.50&alc Last dinner 9.30pm
CONF. Thtr 100 Class 30 Board 35 Del from £80
Credit Cards ① ② ③ ④ ⑤

★★★ 64% Compass Abbey
North Pde BA1 1LG (Compass) ☎(0225) 461603 FAX (0225) 447758
Positioned in the heart of the city, this hotel is part of a handsome Georgian terrace with good city views. It has bright, smart bedrooms which have comfortable chairs and a good range of facilities. There is an attractive and comfortable bar lounge, a coffee shop and a restaurant. Ask for advice about car parking.
54⇌♠(4fb) CTV in all bedrooms ®⚄ T ❈ sB&B⇌♠£55 dB&B⇌♠£72.50-£82.50 🍴
Lift (♪ xmas
♀ British & French V ♥ ⚌ ⚄ ❈ Lunch £5.95-£7.45 High tea £3.50 Dinner £12.95-£14.20 Last dinner 9.15pm
CONF. Thtr 36 Class 15 Board 22 Del from £59
Credit Cards ① ② ③ ⑤

★★★ 60% Pratts
South Pde BA2 4AB (Forestdale) ☎(0225) 460441 FAX (0225) 448807

Part of a fine Regency terrace, this hotel retains many original features and offers a traditional style of service. Bedrooms tend to vary in size and comfort, and though they are in the process of being upgraded all are well equipped with modern facilities.
46⇌♠(5fb)🛏⚄ in 2 bedrooms CTV in all bedrooms ® T sB&B⇌♠£39.95-£44.95 dB&B⇌♠£59.90-£71.90 🍴
Lift (♪ xmas
♀ English & French V ♥ ⚌ ❈ Bar Lunch £1.50-£4.25 Dinner £13.50-£19.50 Last dinner 9.30pm
CONF. Thtr 50 Class 12 Board 20 Del from £67.50
Credit Cards ① ② ③ ⑤

★★ 69% Duke's
Great Pulteney St BA2 4DN ☎(0225) 463512 FAX (0225) 483733
Tim and Rosalind Forester offer a hospitable welcome at their stylish small hotel, combining modern comforts and facilities with the fine original features of the Grade I listed Georgian building. Bedrooms are well proportioned, attractively decorated and well equipped. Cosy public rooms include a lounge, bar and small restaurant. There is unrestricted overnight on-street parking and a multi-storey close by.
21⇌♠(4fb) CTV in all bedrooms ® T sB&B⇌♠£45-£60 dB&B⇌♠£60-£70 🍴
1🐕 (£10 per night) 🚗 xmas
V ♥ ⚌ ❈ Dinner £11.50-£15.50 Last dinner 8.30pm
CONF. Thtr 20 Class 20 Board 20 Del from £62
Credit Cards ① ② ③ ⑤

★★ 62% Haringtons
9/10 Queen St BA1 1HE ☎(0225) 461728
On a cobbled street behind Queen Square, within walking distance of the city's many attractions, this hotel comprises four 18th-century town houses. It offers particularly good value for money, and the restaurant, which takes up the majority of the public areas, is very popular. Ask for the hotel's detailed car parking location map in advance.
12rm(8⇌♠)(4fb) CTV in all bedrooms ® T ✗ (ex guide dogs) ❈ sB&Bfr£28 sB&B⇌♠fr£32 dB&Bfr£40 dB&B⇌♠£46-£55 🍴
♪
♀ English & French Dinner £10.95&alc Last dinner 10pm
Credit Cards ① ② ③

★★ 60% Georges
2-3 South Pde BA2 4AA ☎(0225) 464923 FAX (0225) 425471
Closed 24-26 Dec
Right in the heart of the city, this friendly hotel has a good range of well equipped bedrooms. There is a popular bar and a Greek bistro restaurant.
19⇌♠(4fb)1🛏 CTV in all bedrooms ® T
(CTV ⚄ ♪
♀ English & Greek V ♥ ⚌ Last dinner Midnight
Credit Cards ① ② ③ ⑤

Hilton National Bath
Walcot St BA1 5BJ ☎(0225) 463411

This is a bright, modern hotel with an informal restaurant, aimed at both the business and leisure guest. All bedrooms have en-suite bathrooms and a range of modern facilities. For more information about Hilton National, consult the Contents page, under Hotel Groups.
150⇌♠ ❈ sB⇌♠£80 dB⇌♠£100 (room only)
CONF. Thtr 240 Class 120 Board 60 Del £115

The AA's star rating scheme is the market leader in hotel classification.

BATHGATE Lothian *West Lothian* Map 11 NS96

★★ 60% **Dreadnought**
17/19 Whitburn Rd EH48 1HE ☎(0506) 630791 FAX (0506) 630791
Established at the turn of the century, this solid stone-built commercial hotel is conveniently situated in the town centre. Bedrooms, some very compact, offer practical modern appointments and the required amenities, while public areas include a lively bar and simple foyer lounge.
19rm(18⇨)(3fb) CTV in all bedrooms ® T ✱ sB&B£30-£40 sB&B⇨£35-£45 dB&B£40-£50 dB&B⇨£45-£55
《 CTV 30P ♪
V ♥ Bar Lunch £3-£8 Dinner £9-£15 Last dinner 9pm
Credit Cards [1][2][3][5]

BATLEY *West Yorkshire* Map 08 SE22

★★ 66% **Alder House**
Towngate Rd, off Healey Ln WF17 7HR ☎(0924) 444777 FAX (0924) 442844
An impressive Georgian house in a quiet suburb of the town, which offers comfortable, attractive bedrooms; equally comfortable public areas are pervaded by a relaxing atmosphere enhanced by friendly, informal service.
22rm(21⇨)(1fb) CTV in all bedrooms ® T sB&B£35-£45 sB&B⇨£45-£55 dB&B⇨£62-£70 ᖮ
CTV 50P 2👁 ❀
♡ English & Continental V ♥ ⚑ Lunch fr£7.95 Dinner fr£12.95&alc Last dinner 9.30pm
CONF. Thtr 80 Class 40 Board 40 Del from £72
Credit Cards [1][2][3]

The WOOLPACK INN

Beckington
Near Bath BA3 6SP Tel 0373 831244

FOR FOOD & SERVICE

Dreadnought Hotel ★★

**17-19 Whitburn Road
Bathgate
West Lothian
EH48 1HE
Tel: (0506) 630791**

Recently refurbished family run hotel. Home cooked food and friendly service will always be found. Our public bar boasts a very nautical theme and our lounge has been furnished to the highest standards. A very popular disco is run every weekend.
20 bedrooms — all with colour TV, direct dial telephones, tea/coffee making, most with full private facilities.

AA ★★★   **WOOLVERTON HOUSE HOTEL**   Les Routiers

Woolverton, Bath, Somerset BA3 6QS
Telephone/fax: 0373 830415

Situated 9 miles south of Bath City centre on A36. The Hotel dates back to 1740 with much of the old charm remaining, it has been sympathetically restored to its original splendour and beauty. Set in magnificent walled gardens with authentic working water wells. Our Restaurant, breathtaking in decor, offers good old English food to match, with service, unique to our motto "Nulli Secondus" also reflecting quality and value.

See gazetteer entry under Woolverton.

Battle - Beamish

BATTLE East Sussex Map 05 TQ71

NETHERFIELD PLACE
Netherfield TN33 9PP (3m NW B2096) ☎(04246) 4455
due to change to
(0424) 774455 FAX (04246) 4024
Closed 2 wks Xmas, New Year & 2wks Jan

Michael and Helen Collier and their young team of staff provide the best of formal service in a relaxed and friendly way in this elegant 1920s Georgian-style country house. The pretty bedrooms have all the little luxuries which distinguish this kind of hotel, such as fresh fruit and quality bathrobes. The cocktail bar and lounge are beautifully proportioned rooms which combine elegance and comfort, and the splendid panelled dining room is a superb setting for Michael Collier's new menus, which show a welcome return to his no-nonsense style of cooking. Out go the wacky combinations of ingredients and intricate nouveau garnishes, in favour of such dishes as braised scallops with a flavoursome Champagne sauce, and medallions of venison in a rich port sauce.

14⇨♠(1fb)1⚏ CTV in all bedrooms T ✗ (ex guide dogs) 30P 2⚐ ⚑ ✿ ℘ (hard) croquet clay pigeon shooting archery
V ✧ ⚒ Last dinner 9.30pm
Credit Cards [1][2][3][5]
See advertisement under HASTINGS & ST LEONARDS

★★ 59% **The George**
23 High St TN33 0EA ☎(0424) 774466 FAX (0424) 774853

This traditional high street coaching inn has been refurbished in a modern style. The informal La Brasserie restaurant offers blackboard menu of mostly char-grilled dishes at competitive prices, and the small bar attracts a good local trade. An attractive spiral staircase leads to the bedrooms, many of which have pleasant coordinated décor.

22⇨♠(4fb)1⚏ CTV in all bedrooms ® T ✱ sB&B⇨♠£35-£45 dB&B⇨♠£48-£60 ♫
30P xmas
V ✧ ⚒ ✱ Lunch £6.50-£11.90&alc High tea £2.50-£4 Dinner £6.90-£11.90&alc Last dinner 9.45pm
CONF. Thtr 50 Class 25 Board 25 Del from £50
Credit Cards [1][2][3][5]

BAWTRY South Yorkshire Map 08 SK69

★★★ 66% **The Crown**
High St DN10 6JW ☎Doncaster(0302) 710341 FAX (0302) 711798

This attractive inn has a history dating back over 300 years, and sympathetic modernisation has provided up-to-date facilities without destroying its original charm. Friendly but efficient staff present a menu of British and regional dishes in the 3-tiered restaurant, and bar meals are available in the oak panelled Crown bar.

57⇨♠1⚏in 18 bedrooms CTV in all bedrooms ® T ✱ sB⇨♠£60 dB⇨♠£70-£85 (room only) ♫
☾ 60P

V ✧ ⚒ ✱ ✱ Sunday Lunch £10.95 Dinner £15.95-£16.95 Last dinner 9.30pm
CONF. Thtr 150 Class 90 Board 50 Del from £70
Credit Cards [1][2][3][5]

BEACONSFIELD Buckinghamshire Map 04 SU99

★★★ 67% **Bellhouse**
Oxford Rd HP9 2XE (2m E A40)
☎Gerrards Cross(0753) 887211 FAX (0753) 888231

Situated alongside the A40 between Beaconsfield and Gerrards Cross, this busy function and conference hotel has a Mediterranean-style frontage concealing a rather more functional bedroom block. The well equipped bedrooms are currently being refurbished with completion scheduled for March 1994. Public areas include a leisure centre, a choice of restaurants and bars, and extensive function suites.

136⇨♠(5fb)✱in 40 bedrooms CTV in all bedrooms ® T sB&B⇨♠£105-£115 dB&B⇨♠£90-£135 ♫
Lift ☾ 405P ✱ ⬜ (heated) squash snooker sauna solarium gymnasium pool table beauty therapy room xmas
♛ English & Continental V ✧ ⚒ ✱ Lunch £13.50-£16&alc High tea £5-£10 Dinner £18.50&alc Last dinner 10pm
CONF. Thtr 450 Class 250 Board 40 Del from £120
Credit Cards [1][2][3][4][5]

★★ 59% **White Hart Toby**
Aylesbury End HP9 1LW (on A40) (Toby) ☎(0494) 671211 FAX (0494) 67074

A spacious bar and Toby Restaurant form the public areas of this lively inn, which dates back to the 16th century; accommodation is for the most part in a modern annexe, though a few bedrooms in the main building have more character.

5⇨♠Annexe28⇨♠2⚏✱in 14 bedrooms CTV in all bedrooms ® T ✗ (ex guide dogs) ✱ sB&B⇨♠£29.95-£69.50 dB&B⇨♠£49.95-£79.50 ♫
☾ CTV 100P
V ✧ ✱ Last dinner 10pm
CONF. Thtr 80 Class 30 Board 30
Credit Cards [1][2][3][5]

BEAMINSTER Dorset Map 03 ST40

★★ ❀❀ 71% **Bridge House**
3 Prout Bridge DT8 3AY ☎(0308) 862200 FAX (0308) 863700

Dating back to the 13th-century, this handsome property is in a rural setting with its own walled garden. Bedrooms, in the original house, in the new wing and in the coach house vary in size, but all are well furnished. Public areas are cosy, with blazing fires in winter months. Chef Lindsay Wakeman offers a tempting menu based on fresh local produce.

9⇨♠Annexe4⇨♠ CTV in all bedrooms ® T sB&B⇨♠£31-£55 dB&B⇨♠£56-£92 ♫
22P ✱ ✿ xmas
♛ International ✧ ⚒ Lunch £10.95&alc Dinner £16.45&alc Last dinner 9pm
Credit Cards [1][2][3][5]

BEAMISH Co Durham Map 12 NZ25

★★★ ❀ 64% **Beamish Park**
Beamish Burn Rd NE16 5EG ☎Stanley(0207) 230666 FAX (0207) 281260

Standing in open countryside, this hotel is modern and comfortable, with generally spacious bedrooms. Chef Clive Imber produces a fine 3-course dinner, which might start with smoked duck salad with citrus fruits, followed, perhaps, by roast lamb filled with curry sauce

or chicken supreme with sherry sauce and wild mushrooms, with a choice of home-made puddings to finish. Service is very friendly.
47⇌↑(7fb) CTV in all bedrooms ® ⚲ T sB⇌↑£33-£46 dB⇌↑£38-£46 (room only) ⌺
《 CTV 100P ❉ xmas
♁ English & French V ✧ ⌑ ⌘ Dinner fr£15.95&alc Last dinner 9.30pm
Conf. Thtr 25 Class 10 Board 25 Del £76
Credit Cards 1 2 3 5

BEATTOCK Dumfries & Galloway *Dumfriesshire*
Map **11** NT00

See also **Moffat**

★★★ 67% *Auchen Castle*
DG10 9SH (N on A74) (SCOTLAND'S HERITAGE HOTELS)
☎(06833) 407 FAX (06833) 667
Closed 3 wks Christmas-New Year
Set in 50 acres of grounds with a trout lake and woodland walks, this fine Scottish baronial mansion, built in 1849, overlooks Upper Annandale. Owner- run, it provides friendly service, relaxing public rooms and comfortable bedrooms – large and traditionally furnished in the main house; more functional in the annexe.
15⇌↑Annexe10↑(1fb) CTV in all bedrooms ® T 35P ❉ ♪ clay shooting ⌖
V ✧ ⌑ Last dinner 9pm
Credit Cards 1 2 3 4 5

★★ 59% *Beattock House*
DG10 9QB (off A74) ☎(06833) 403 & 402
This converted Victorian mansion stands in 6 acres of grounds which incorporates a small caravan site. Family-run, it offers traditional comforts and service, with traditional style bedrooms, a small snug bar and comfortable lounge.
7rm(3↑)(2fb) CTV in 4 bedrooms TV in 1 bedroom ® ✱ sB&Bfr£30 sB&B↑fr£35 dB&Bfr£55 dB&B↑fr£55 ⌺
CTV 30P ❉ ♪ putting
V ✧ ⌑ ✱ Lunch fr£7.95 High tea fr£6.50 Dinner fr£15 Last dinner 9.30pm
Credit Cards 1 2 3 5

BEAULIEU Hampshire Map **04** SU30

★★★ ❀❀ 73% **Montagu Arms**
Palace Ln SO42 7ZL ☎(0590) 612324 FAX (0590) 612188
This creeper-clad hotel is in a picturesque location and has lovely terraced gardens. The elegant wood-panelled and beamed interior with wood- burning fires includes the candlelit restaurant, featuring chef Simon Fennell's delightful cooking. The bedrooms are individually furnished and include some suites.
24⇌↑(3fb) CTV in all bedrooms T sB&B⇌↑fr£67.90 dB&B⇌↑£95.90-£165.90 ⌺
《 80P 6⇎ ❉ xmas
♁ French V ✧ ⌑ ⌘ Lunch fr£14.95 Dinner £18.90-£23.90 Last dinner 9.30pm
Conf. Thtr 30 Class 16 Board 24 Del from £93.40
Credit Cards 1 2 3 5

★★★ 59% *Beaulieu*
Beaulieu Rd SO42 7YQ (off B3056) (Care Hotels)
☎Southampton(0703) 293344 FAX (0703) 292729
This red brick, gabled hotel shares its isolated heathland location with a railway station and the venue for well-known New Forest pony sales. The spacious ground floor has smart décor, modern leather seats and open fires. The fair sized bedrooms are nicely modernised, and 3 are in an adjacent bungalow.
18⇌↑(2fb) CTV in all bedrooms ® T sB&B⇌↑£35-£50 dB&B⇌↑£50-£80 ⌺
CTV 60P ❉ xmas

CHEQUERS INN ★★

HOTEL and RESTAURANT

Lovely 17th century coaching inn with 17 luxury bedrooms. Exceptional B.T.A. commended restaurant and delicious bar food. Ideal for exploring the Thames Valley, only 2 miles from M40 (junc 2 or 3) and 6 miles from M4 (junc 7).

*Conference Room – Weekend Breaks
Golfing Holidays – Horseracing
Weekends*

**Chequers Inn, Wooburn Common,
Nr. Beaconsfield, Bucks HP10 0JQ.
Tel: (0628) 529575 Fax: (0628) 850124**
See entry under Wooburn Common

The Montagu Arms Hotel
AT · BEAULIEU

Excellence in cuisine and service
An impressive Cellar of fine wines
Beautiful terraced gardens
Log fires and cosy lounges.

2 Red Rosettes 73%   AA ★ ★ ★
Egon Ronay

Montagu Arms Hotel, Beaulieu,
New Forest, Hampshire SO42 7ZL
Telephone: Beaulieu (0590) 612324
Fax: 0590 612188

Beaulieu - Bedale

V ⊕ ⌒ ⤴ Sunday Lunch £9.95 Dinner £13.50&alc Last dinner 8.45pm
CONF. Thtr 60 Class 40 Board 40 Del from £65
Credit Cards 1 2 3 5

BEAULY Highland *Inverness-shire* Map 14 NH54

★★★ 65% Priory
The Square IV4 7BX (signposted from A832) ☎(0463) 782309 FAX (0463) 782531

Colourful flowering baskets adorn the red sandstone walls of this popular hotel in the village square. An improvement programme has brought about a major transformation, with spacious new bedrooms, a wider range of amenities and a comfortable foyer lounge. The attractive split-level restaurant offers a varied selection of menus.

22⇌⌒(2fb) CTV in all bedrooms ® T sB&B⇌⌒£39.50-£42.50 dB&B⇌⌒£69.50-£75 ♺
Lift ♪ *xmas*
V ⊕ ⌒ ⤴ Lunch £4-£12alc High tea £4.50-£11.50alc Dinner £10-£25alc Last dinner 9pm
Credit Cards 1 2 3 5 £

★★ 66% The Lovat Arms
IV4 7BS ☎Inverness(0463) 782313 FAX (0463) 782862

A friendly atmosphere prevails at this comfortable Highland hotel near the village square. Major improvements are taking place, the bedrooms being transformed with quality furnishings, and tartan fabrics are being used to good effect. Public areas are cosy with traditional comfort.

22⇌⌒(3fb) CTV in all bedrooms ® T ✱ sB&B⇌⌒£35-£4 dB&B⇌⌒£70-£90 ♺
CTV 20P ♪ *xmas*
V ⊕ ⌒ ⤴ ✱ Lunch fr£7 High tea fr£6 Dinner fr£18.50 Last dinner 8.45pm
CONF. Thtr 60 Class 40 Board 30
Credit Cards 1 3

BEAUMARIS
See **Anglesey, Isle of**

BEAUMONT
See **Jersey** under **Channel Islands**

BEBINGTON Merseyside Map 07 SJ38

★★ 63% Bridge Inn
Bolton Rd, Port Sunlight L62 4UQ ☎051-645 8441

Designed in Edwardian times to resemble an old coaching inn, this hotel in the centre of Port Sunlight village has well equipped modern bedrooms. Food is available in both the beamed restaurant and wood-panelled lounge bar.

16⇌⌒(2fb)1⬚ CTV in all bedrooms ® ✈
50P
♀ English & Continental V ⊕ ⌒
Credit Cards 1 2 3 5

Forte Travelodge
New Chester Rd L62 9AQ (on A41, northbound off, juncnt 5 on M63)
☎051-327 2489 Central Res (0800) 850950

This modern building offers a good standard of accommodation for overnight stops. Smart, spacious and well equipped bedrooms, all with en suite bathrooms, are suitable for family use, and meals may be taken at the nearby family restaurant. For more details about Travelodges, consult the Contents page, under Hotel Groups.

31⇌⌒✱ B⇌⌒£31.95 (room only)

BECCLES Suffolk Map 05 TM49

★★ 61% Waveney House
Puddingmoor NR34 9PL ☎(0502) 712270 & 712817 FAX (0502) 712660

This hotel enjoys a riverside setting and is a popular mooring place during the season. Equally suited to the needs of leisure and commercial users, it provides well cared for, traditionally furnished accommodation and maintains a good standard of cleanliness.

13rm(7⇌4⌒)(2fb)1⬚ CTV in all bedrooms ® T
CTV 100P ✿ ♪
♀ English & French V ⊕ ⌒ ⤴ Last dinner 9.30pm
Credit Cards 1 2 3 4 5

BECKINGTON Somerset Map 03 ST85

★★ ❀73% Woolpack Inn
BA3 6SP (on A36) ☎Frome(0373) 831244 FAX (0373) 831223

Best Newcomer 1994

This is our Southwest England Best Newcomer for this year, and our congratulations go to proprietors Martin Tarr and Paul Toogood. Their combined experience in the hotel trade has certainly demonstrated itself here – the inspection visit which resulted in this award took place just two weeks after they opened for business! Our inspector was particularly taken with the natural friendliness and personality of the partners. The 16th-century coaching inn has been totally refurbished to provide individually styled bedrooms furnished in keeping with the period, but with all modern comforts. In the restaurant, chef James Dickson plans to cut down the menu choice when he has had time to assess the market, and after an enjoyable inspection meal, we have high hopes for his future.

10⇌⌒(1fb)⤴ in 4 bedrooms CTV in all bedrooms ®♉ T sB&B⇌⌒£39.50-£44.50 dB&B⇌⌒£49.50-£54.50 ♺
16P ⚑ nc5yrs *xmas*
♀ English & French V ⊕ ⌒ ⤴ ✱ Lunch £5-£25alc High tea £6.50-£9.50alc Dinner £15-£25alc Last dinner 10.30pm
Credit Cards 1 3 £

See advertisement under BATH

BEDALE North Yorkshire Map 08 SE28

★★ 62% Motel Leeming
Great North Rd DL8 1DT (1m NE junc A1/A684)
☎(0677) 422122 FAX (0677) 424507

Adjoining the Leeming service area, this motel offers compact but well equipped modern bedrooms. There is a lounge bar, meeting rooms and a restaurant plus an adjacent 24-hour café and travellers' shop.

40⇌⌒(8fb)2⬚⤴ in 12 bedrooms CTV in all bedrooms ®♉ T ✱ sB&B⇌⌒£39.50 dB&B⇌⌒£49.50-£65 ♺
(100P 14⚑ (£2 per night) ✿ ♪
♀ English & Continental V ⊕ ⌒ ⤴ Lunch £7.95-£9.95alc High tea £7.95-£9.95alc Dinner £11.95-£14.99 Last dinner 10pm
CONF. Thtr 80 Class 40 Board 30 Del £49.95
Credit Cards 1 2 3 5 £

★★ **60%** **White Rose**
DL7 9AY ☎(0677) 422707 & 424941 FAX (0677) 425123
(For full entry see Leeming Bar)

BEDDGELERT Gwynedd Map **06** SH54

★★★ **66%** **Royal Goat**
LL55 4YE (off A498) ☎(076686) 224 & 343 FAX (076686) 422
Set amidst the spectacular scenery of Snowdonia National Park, this fine 18th-century hotel welcomes sporting enthusiasts and tourists from all over the world. Generally spacious bedrooms are well equipped and there are two bars, a restaurant offering a good range of food and 4 acres of woodland walks.
32⇌♠(4fb)1♬⊁in 5 bedrooms CTV in all bedrooms ®⊠ T ✱ sB&B⇌♠£40-£45 dB&B⇌♠£68-£90 ♬
Lift ℂ 150P ✿ ♪ games room *xmas*
♡ Welsh & French V ✧ ⊻ ⊁ ✱ Lunch £9-£17&alc High tea £5-£8 Dinner fr£17&alc Last dinner 10pm
CONF. Thtr 90 Class 50 Board 60
Credit Cards ①②③⑤

★ **65%** **Sygun Fawr Country House**
LL55 4NE (off A498) ☎(076686) 258
Closed 27 Dec-mid Feb
The stone-built manor house dates back at least to the 17th century, and some parts may be even older. In a secluded location along a steep, narrow lane and surrounded by magnificent mountain scenery, it is popular with walkers. The hotel has been considerably renovated in recent times.
7⇌♠(1fb) ® sB&B⇌♠£28.50 dB&B⇌♠£48 ♬
CTV 30P ✿ sauna *xmas*
V ✧ ✱ Dinner £12-£14&alc Last dinner 8.30pm
Credit Cards ①③⑤ £

★ **58%** **Tanronen**
LL55 4YB (Frederic Robinson) ☎(076686) 347
In an area of outstanding beauty, this small hotel is popular with tourists and walkers, though bedrooms are somewhat dated. There are 2 cosy bars and a pleasant residents' lounge with an open fire. As well as the bar meals served in the coffee lounge, the restaurant serves a simple table d'hôte menu.
8rm CTV in all bedrooms ® ✈ ⊁ sB&B£20 dB&B£40 ♬
CTV 12P 3✈ *xmas*
V ✧ ✱ Lunch £8 Dinner £13.50 Last dinner 9pm
Credit Cards ①③⑤

BEDFORD Bedfordshire Map **04** TL04

★★★ **74%** **Woodlands Manor**
Green Ln, Clapham MK41 6EP (2m N A6) ☎(0234) 363281
FAX (0234) 272390
This handsome manor house, surrounded by extensive wooded grounds and gardens, offers a warm welcome and high standards of service and comfort. Bedrooms vary in size and style, newer rooms being very spacious, but all are well equipped and many have luxurious marble bathrooms. Public rooms include an elegant dining room offering a varied and imaginative menu.
22⇌♠Annexe3⇌♠ CTV in all bedrooms T
✈ (ex guide dogs)
ℂ 100P ✿ croquet nc7yrs
♡ English & French V ✧ ⊻ Last dinner 9.45pm
Credit Cards ①②③

★★★ **67%** **The Barns**
Cardington Rd MK44 3SA (on A603 1.5m E of Bedford) (Lansbury) ☎(0234) 270044 FAX (0234) 273102
A popular function and conference hotel, developed round a 17th-century manor house and medieval tithe barn, its well equipped bedrooms in a modern extension. In the restaurant overlooking the river, chef Charles College offers an interesting menu of modern and classical dishes. Our inspector enjoyed marinated pork with cajun ➥

The Famous Olde Bridge Inn Hotel ★★

Special Weekend Rates
Banqueting facilities for up to 100

Bolton Road,
Port Sunlight Village,
Bebington, Wirral,
Merseyside L62 4UQ

Telephone: 051-645 8441

BRITAINS BEST Bed and Breakfast

Whether you want to stay at an inn, enjoy a taste of the country at a traditional farmhouse, find a comfortable room for the night or book a short-break holiday, you will find all you need in

Britain's Best Bed and Breakfast

Every establishment is inspected and graded for quality. Places with a four or five 'Q' rating will appeal to those seeking luxurious accommodation while those on a budget can choose from places at £15 or under

AA

Bedford - Belper

spices and a cinnamon and apple mayonnaise, and grilled lemon sole with a rich seafood cassoulet.
49⇌♘(1fb)1🛏✂ in 11 bedrooms CTV in all bedrooms ®⚲T ✻ (ex guide dogs)✻ sB&B⇌♘fr£69.50 dB&B⇌♘fr£81 ₽
(120P ✿ ♪ sauna solarium gymnasium xmas
♀ English & Continental V ☼ ♨ ✂ Lunch fr£10.50 Dinner fr£14.50 Last dinner 9.45pm
CONF. Thtr 120 Class 50 Board 40 Del from £98
Credit Cards [1][2][3][5]

★★★ 67% **Bedford Moat House**
2 Saint Mary's St MK42 0AR (from junct 13 on M1 follow signs for town centre hotel is on right just before bridge crossing river Great Ouse) ☎(0234) 355131 FAX (0234) 340447
Closed Xmas RS Bank hols

This 1960s concrete hotel makes full use of its delightful riverside setting and the Terrace restaurant, bar and Mallards café bar (open all day in summer), as well as many bedrooms, have fine views. The bright modern bedrooms are well equipped and 24-hour room service is available.
100⇌♘(20fb)🛏 in 22 bedrooms CTV in all bedrooms ® T ✻ sB&B⇌♘fr£70 dB&B⇌♘fr£85 ₽
Lift (CTV 72P sauna jacuzzi mini-gym ♪ xmas
♀ English & Continental V ☼ ♨ ✂ Lunch fr£13.50&alc Dinner fr£15.95&alc Last dinner 9.45pm
CONF. Thtr 400 Class 120 Board 40 Del from £89
Credit Cards [1][2][3][5]

BEER Devon Map **03 SY28**

★★ 61% **Anchor Inn**
EX12 3ET ☎Seaton(0297) 20386
Closed 1 wk Xmas
This friendly inn with a cliff-top beer garden faces the village's slipway to the beach. Its bedrooms are attractive, if fairly compact, and as well as an a la carte restaurant, it offers popular meals in the bar. Daily specials often feature locally caught fish and delicious desserts are accompanied by clotted cream.
8rm(5⇌♘)(1fb) CTV in all bedrooms ® ✻ ✻ sB&B£23-£33 sB&B⇌♘£28-£42 dB&B£46-£50 dB&B⇌♘£56 ₽
CTV ✖ 🚳 nc10yrs
♀ International V ☼ Last dinner 9.30pm
Credit Cards [1][3]

BEETHAM Cumbria Map **07 SD47**

★ 62% **Wheatsheaf**
LA7 7AL (1m S of Milnthorpe, next to the church off A6) ☎Milnthorpe(05395) 62123
Closed 25 Dec
At the gateway to the Lake District, this attractive old inn provides comfortable bedrooms and an extensive range of food in the bar or dining room. It has been in the same family for many years and continues to offer friendly service.
6⇌♘ CTV in all bedrooms ® ✻ sB&B⇌♘£30 dB&B⇌♘£40 ₽
CTV 50P
V ☼ ♨ Lunch £5.35-£6.95alc Dinner £9.95-£15 Last dinner 8.15pm
Credit Cards [1][3]

BELFORD Northumberland Map **12 NU13**

★★★ 64% **Blue Bell**
Market Place NE70 7NE (centre of village on left of St Mary's church) ☎(0668) 213543 FAX (0668) 213787
Less than a mile from the A1, this Georgian village inn has been carefully modernised to offer individually designed bedrooms. There is a comfortable lounge and the restaurant offers a good range of dishes. Simpler meals are served in the buttery.

17⇌♘(1fb)1🛏✂ in 4 bedrooms CTV in all bedrooms ®⚲T ✻ sB&B⇌♘£42-£44 dB&B⇌♘£80-£92 ₽
10P ✿ xmas
♀ English/French V ☼ ♨ ✂ ✻ Sunday Lunch £8-£12&alc High tea £5-£9 Dinner £16.50-£18 Last dinner 8.45pm
CONF. Thtr 130 Class 80 Board 30 Del from £50
Credit Cards [1][2][3]

BELLINGHAM Northumberland Map **12 NY88**

★★ 66% **Riverdale Hall**
NE48 2JT ☎(0434) 220254 FAX (0434) 220457

Standing in its own grounds overlooking the North Tyne River, this extended Victorian mansion offers generally comfortable accommodation. Service is provided by a friendly team of staff, under the supervision of the resident proprietors.
20⇌♘(6fb)5🛏 CTV in all bedrooms ® T sB&B⇌♘£35-£42 dB&B⇌♘£59-£72 ₽
CTV 60P ✿ 🏊 (heated) ♪ sauna cricket field putting green croquet xmas
♀ English & Danish V ☼ ♨ ✂ Lunch £8.45 High tea fr£4 Dinner £17&alc Last dinner 9.30pm
CONF. Thtr 50 Class 40 Board 40 Del from £59
Credit Cards [1][2][3][5]

BELPER Derbyshire Map **08 SK34**

★★★ ❀❀ 73% **Makeney Hall Country House**
Makeney, Milford DE56 0RU ☎Derby(0332) 842999 FAX (0332) 842777

Best Newcomer 1994

Our Best Newcomer award winner for Central England, Makeney Hall is a large turn-of-the-century building standing in 6 acres of lovely grounds. Its generously proportioned bedrooms are decorated with a kind of reserved luxury, and all have modern amenities. Some of the bathrooms have Victorian-style tubs. From the small lounge, a bar in an ante-room leads into the dining room – part wood-panelled, part conservatory – where an elaborate menu is humorously written. There is a serious approach to the cooking, though, and chef Ronnie Wyatt-Goodwin meticulously produces fulsome traditional French dishes. Staff are smart, cheerful and attentive.
27⇌♘Annexe18⇌♘✂ in 6 bedrooms CTV in all bedrooms ®⚲T ✻ dB⇌♘£59.50-£125 (room only) ₽
Lift (150P ✿ croquet pool table bike hire ♪
V ☼ ♨ ✂ Lunch £12&alc Dinner £15.50-£17.50&alc Last dinner 9.45pm
Credit Cards [1][2][3][4][5]

See advertisement under DERBY

Red star hotels are each highlighted
by a pink tinted panel.

Belton - Betws-y-Coed

BELTON Lincolnshire Map 08 SK93

★★★★ ❀66% *Belton Woods*
NG32 2LN (2m N of Grantham on A607)
☎Grantham(0476) 593200 FAX (0476) 74547

In an attractive rural setting, this large hotel has been built in the style of a Georgian country mansion in its own 475 acres. The lofty public areas include an impressive first floor restaurant, overlooking the hotel's golf course, with its own comfortable cocktail bar. Plus Fours is less formal. The three grades of bedrooms are all spacious and some have balconies or patios to view the golf.
96⇌↑⥽in 48 bedrooms CTV in all bedrooms ®⌇T
Lift ℂ 340P ✿ ▣ (heated) ▶ 18 ♞ (hard) squash snooker sauna solarium gymnasium hair & beauty salon steamroom
♡ English & French V ✾ ♨ ⥽ Last dinner 10pm
Credit Cards ①②③⑤

BEMBRIDGE

See **Wight, Isle of**

BENLLECH BAY

See **Anglesey, Isle of**

BERKELEY Gloucestershire Map 03 ST69

★★ 63% *Old Schoolhouse*
Canonbury St GL13 9BG ☎Dursley(0453) 811711
Closed 22 Dec-7 Jan

The former village school has been converted into a small hotel that retains much of its Victorian charm. The generally spacious bedrooms have a good range of modern facilities and there is a comfortable lounge area and popular restaurant.
7⇌↑(1fb) CTV in all bedrooms ® T ✱
15P ⇗
♡ International V Last dinner 8.45pm
Credit Cards ①③

BERKELEY ROAD Gloucestershire Map 03 ST79

★★ 59% *Prince of Wales*
GL13 9HD (on A38) ☎Dursley(0453) 810474 FAX (0453) 511370
41⇌↑(1fb) CTV in all bedrooms ®⌇T ✻ sB⇌↑£35-£45 dB⇌↑£35-£45 (room only)
150P ✿
♡ English & French V ✾ ♨ ✻ Lunch £6.95-£14.95 High tea £3-£10 Dinner £8.95-£14.95 Last dinner 9pm
CONF. Thtr 200 Class 60 Board 60 Del from £50
Credit Cards ①②③⑤

BERRIEW Powys Map 07 SJ10

★★ 67% *Lion*
SY21 8PQ (centre of village, next to church) (Welsh Rarebits)
☎(0686) 640452 FAX (0686) 640844

In a village of black and white cottages, this delightful magpie-type inn dates from the 17th century and stands next to the church. There is an abundance of beams and wall timbers throughout, and the lounge bar offers a blackboard selection of good value bar meals. More formal meals are served in the attractive restaurant. Bedrooms are attractive, with pretty fabrics and canopied beds.
7⇌↑(1fb)1⍰ CTV in all bedrooms ® T ✱ ✻
sB&B⇌↑£42.50-£45 dB&B⇌↑£75-£85 ℝ
6P ♪
♡ Welsh & Continental V ✾ ✻ Sunday Lunch £8.25 Dinner £15-£18&alc Last dinner 9pm
Credit Cards ①②③   £

BERWICK-UPON-TWEED Northumberland Map 12 NT95

★★★ 61% *Turret House*
Etal Rd, Tweedmouth TD15 2EG (Logis) ☎(0289) 330808 FAX (0289) 330467

Standing in its own grounds, this extended turreted Victorian house is on the south side of the River Tweed. Bedrooms in the original house are traditional in style while those in the new wing are more functional, but all are well equipped. There is a quiet lounge bar and a small restaurant.
13⇌↑(1fb) CTV in all bedrooms ®⌇T
100P ✿
V ✾ ♨ ⥽ Last dinner 8.45pm
Credit Cards ①②③⑤

★ 60% *Queens Head*
Sandgate TD15 1EP ☎(0289) 307852

This is a simple, small, commercial town centre hotel. Bar suppers are served instead of dinner at slack times.
6⇌↑(5fb) CTV in all bedrooms ® T
CTV ⋫
V ✾ ⥽ Last dinner 8.30pm
Credit Cards ①③

BETWS-Y-COED Gwynedd Map 06 SH75

★★★ 67% *Waterloo*
LL24 0AR (close to A5, near Waterloo Bridge)
☎(0690) 710411 FAX (0690) 710666
Closed Xmas

Situated between wooded hillsides close to Waterloo Bridge, this large privately owned hotel has modern, well equipped bedrooms. The attractive Garden Restaurant offers an extensive range of food and there is a choice of bars and a good leisure complex with an all-day coffee shop.
9⇌Annexe30⇌(2fb) CTV in all bedrooms ® T ✱
sB&B⇌£45.75-£52 dB&B⇌£72.50-£79 ℝ
200P ✿ ▣ (heated) sauna solarium gymnasium jacuzzi steam room *xmas*
♡ International V ✾ ♨ ✱ Sunday Lunch £8.25-£9 Dinner £16.50-£17.25&alc Last dinner 9.30pm
Credit Cards ①②③⑤   £
See advertisement on page 89

★★★ 66% *Royal Oak*
Holyhead Rd LL24 0AY ☎(0690) 710219 FAX (0690) 710603

This stone built former coaching inn has been extended and improved to offer comfortable accommodation in mostly quite spacious bedrooms, including some suitable for family use. Guests can either eat in the pub bar, the grill room or the restaurant proper which has an extensive menu.
27⇌↑(5fb) CTV in all bedrooms T ✱ sB&B⇌↑£40-£48 dB&B⇌↑£60-£76 ℝ
ℂ 160P *xmas*
♡ English, French & Italian V ✾ ♨ Lunch fr£10 High tea £5-£7alc Dinner £14-£16&alc Last dinner 9pm
CONF. Thtr 25 Class 25 Board 25
Credit Cards ①②③⑤
See advertisement on page 89

★★★ 64% *Craig-y-Dderwen Country House*
LL24 0AS ☎(0690) 710293 FAX (0690) 710362

17⇌↑(3fb)3⍰ CTV in all bedrooms ® T ✻ sB&B⇌↑£43-£47 dB&B⇌↑£63-£115 ℝ
60P ✿ golf driving range *xmas*
♡ International V ✾ ♨ ✻ High tea fr£4.95 Dinner fr£15.95 Last dinner 8.30pm
Credit Cards ①②③

87

Betws-y-Coed - Bexhill-on-Sea

★★★♨64% **Plas Hall**
Pont-y-Pant, Dolwyddelan LL25 0PJ (3m SW A470)
☎Dolwyddelan(06906) 206 FAX (06906) 526
This family-run hotel is in peaceful surroundings on the slopes of a wooded valley, and the River Lledr (salmon and trout fishing available) runs through the grounds. Bedrooms are furnished in pine and there is a cosy residents' lounge and a bar. The restaurant offers a table d'hôte menu and a good choice 'carte', and bar meals are also available.
17⇌ℕ(4fb)2₪ CTV in all bedrooms ®✄ T ✳ sB&B⇌ℕ£25-£35 dB&B⇌ℕ£50-£60 ₽
CTV 36P ❀ ♪ games room *xmas*
♀ Welsh & French V ♂ ♡ ⅍ ✳ Lunch fr£5.95 Dinner fr£14.95 Last dinner 8.30pm
CONF. Class 30
Credit Cards [1][3] £

★★68% **Park Hill**
Llanrwst Rd LL24 0HD (N on A470) ☎(0690) 710540
Parkhill is in a pleasant setting of lawns and gardens above the Conwy valley with superb views. Bedrooms are furnished with modern fitted units and good home cooking is provided. There are 2 lounges and a cosy bar.
11rm(6⇌3ℕ)(2fb)1₪ CTV in all bedrooms ®
✘ (ex guide dogs)
CTV 14P ♣ ❀ ▭ (heated) sauna nc6yrs
♀ Welsh, English & French V ♂ ♡ ⅍ Last dinner 7.45pm
Credit Cards [1][2][3][5]

★★68% **Ty Gwyn**
LL24 0SG (at junct of A5/A470, 100yds S of Waterloo Bridge)
☎(0690) 710383 & 710787
This ancient stone-built coaching inn on the outskirts of the village, retains a wealth of charm and character. Many of its individually and tastefully styled bedrooms are furnished with antiques.
13rm(2⇌7ℕ)(1fb)4₪ CTV in 11 bedrooms ® sB&Bfr£19 sB&B⇌ℕ£26 dB&B£34 dB&B⇌ℕ£54-£78 ₽
CTV 16P *xmas*
♀ English & French V ♂ ✳ Lunch £9.95 Dinner £16.95 Last dinner 9.30pm
Credit Cards [1][3] £

★62% **Fairy Glen**
LL24 0SH (0.5m S of the A5 on the A470) ☎(0690) 710269
Closed Dec & Jan
Some 300 years ago, the Fairy Glen was built as a coaching stop on the old London to Holyhead route. Now a small, privately owned hotel, it provides comfortable accommodation with modern furnishings, and is understandably popular with tourists, many of whom have become regular visitors.
10rm(5⇌2ℕ)(3fb) CTV in all bedrooms ® sB&B£19 dB&B£38 dB&B⇌ℕ£42 ₽
♪ CTV 10P ♣ ❀
V ♂ ♡ ⅍ Bar Lunch £2.50-£5 Dinner £11 Last dinner 7.30pm
Credit Cards [1][3][5]

BEVERLEY Humberside Map **08** TA03

★★★66% **Beverley Arms**
North Bar Within HU17 8DD
☎Hull(0482) 869241 FAX (0482) 870907

FORTE Heritage

An attractive hotel with a Georgian facade, the Beverley Arms is located close to the historic town gate near St Mary's church. It is a popular meeting place for townsfolk, and has an all day lounge menu. The stone flagged area is especially attractive with its collection of antique copper. There is a choice of bars and a smart restaurant. Bedrooms are comfortably furnished in a style befitting the character of the building.
57⇌ℕ(4fb)⅍in 20 bedrooms CTV in all bedrooms ® T sB⇌ℕ£75-£80 dB⇌ℕ£90-£95 (room only) ₽
Lift ♪ 70P *xmas*

V ♂ ♡ ⅍ ✳ Lunch £9.95-£10.95&alc Dinner £15.95-£16.95&alc Last dinner 9.45pm
CONF. Thtr 65 Class 30 Board 30 Del from £90
Credit Cards [1][2][3][5]

★★★63% **Tickton Grange**
Tickton HU17 9SH (3m NE on A1035) (Logis)
☎Hornsea(0964) 543666 FAX (0964) 542556
RS 25-29 Dec
This attractive Georgian house stands in its own well tended grounds. Furnished in keeping with the period, the impressive public rooms are spacious and comfortable, and the bedrooms are individually decorated and furnished. The atmosphere is one of peace and relaxation.
16⇌ℕ(2fb)1₪ CTV in all bedrooms ® T sB⇌ℕ£33.50-£67 dB⇌ℕ£43.50-£87 (room only) ₽
65P ❀ croquet putting
V ♂ ♡ Bar Lunch £3-£7.50alc Dinner £14.95-£19.95alc Last dinner 9.30pm
Credit Cards [1][2][3][5] £

★★71% **Lairgate**
30-34 Lairgate HU17 8EP ☎Hull(0482) 882141 FAX (0482) 861067
Closed 24-27 Dec
The Lairgate Hotel is a privately owned town centre hotel with attractively furnished public areas including a particularly good lounge. The bedrooms are all quite individual, varying in size and shape, though they all have modern facilities.
23rm(9⇌10ℕ)(2fb)1₪ CTV in all bedrooms ® T
✘ (ex guide dogs) ✳ sB&B£40-£46 sB&B⇌ℕ£45-£50 dB&B£50 dB&B⇌ℕ£60 ₽
♪ CTV 18P ♫
♀ English & Continental V ♂ ♡ ⅍ Lunch fr£9 Dinner fr£15&alc Last dinner 9.30pm
Credit Cards [1][3]

BEXHILL-ON-SEA East Sussex Map **05** TQ70

★★★64% **Cooden Resort**
TN39 4TT ☎Cooden(0424) 842281 FAX (0424) 846590

RESORT HOTELS PLC

Almost on the beach, this much extended hotel offers spectacular views of Pevensey Bay. Bedrooms are modern with light wood and pastel fabrics and though bathrooms look a little more dated, they are due to be upgraded. As well as the Oceana Bar and Restaurant, there is a recently added lounge and the Sovereign public bar, which is frequented by locals.
40⇌ℕ(6fb)1₪⅍in 4 bedrooms CTV in all bedrooms ®✄ T ✳ sB⇌ℕ£65-£75 dB⇌ℕ£75-£90 (room only) ₽
♪ 60P ❀ ▭ (heated) ⌒ (heated) sauna solarium jacuzzi hair salon *xmas*
♀ English & French V ♂ ✳ Lunch £12.50-£13&alc High tea fr£1.75 Dinner £15-£17.25&alc Last dinner 9.30pm
CONF. Thtr 150 Board 30 Del from £70
Credit Cards [1][2][3][5] £

★★★60% **Granville**
Sea Rd TN40 1EE (turn off A259 coast road, hotel 50yds from main railway station) ☎Bexhill(0424) 215437 FAX (0424) 225102
Just a few minutes walk from both the town centre and seafront, the Granville is an elegant period hotel personally run by the Ramsdens. Bedrooms all provide the same modern standard with excellent beds. The traditional-style lounge bar is popular with locals, and there is a comfortable lounge and a spacious dining room with elegant chandeliers.
50⇌ℕ(1fb) CTV in all bedrooms ® T ✳ sB&B⇌ℕ£34.75-£49.75 dB&B⇌ℕ£69.50 ₽
Lift ♪ ♪ darts bar billiards *xmas*

plas hall hotel and Restaurant ★★★ AA

Pont-y-Pant, Nr. Betws-y-Coed, N. Wales
Tel: Dolwyddelan (06906) 206/306 Fax: (06906) 526
Set in own grounds on the banks of the River Lledr amidst spectacular scenery. Magnificent COUNTRY HOUSE ideally situated for over 100 attractions, plus, walking, fishing, shooting, riding, golfing etc. All rooms en suite with facilities, satellite TV. Excellent cuisine supported by superb wine list. WTB 4 crowns. Ground floor accommodation. Facilities for the disabled with 10% reduction.
  2 day Bargain Breaks from £47.50 (winter).
Write for colour brochure to Mr B. M. Williams.

Royal Oak Hotel

 ★★★ AA

Holyhead Road,
Betws y Coed, Gwynedd
Tel: 0690 710219
Fax: 0690 710603

Picturesque former coaching inn overlooking River Llugwy with 27 luxury bedrooms, all en suite. Our Grill is open daily 8am to 9pm offering varied menus, plus our excellent dining room specialising in fresh fish and meat delicacies. Our chef/manager is a member of the Chaine des Rotisseurs. Central for coast, mountains, waterfalls, fishing, golf and riding.

Short Breaks available — min 2 day stay
£39.00 per person, per night
double/twin bed & breakfast
£54.00 per person, per night
(2 day min) dinner, bed & breakfast

B

Waterloo Hotel
AND MOTEL, BETWS-Y-COED
GWYNEDD LL24 0AR

AA ★★★

The leading hotel in Snowdonia, ideally situated for touring the mountains, coastline and attractions of North Wales.

All rooms en suite with colour T.V., direct telephone, tea/coffee tray.

Beautiful Garden Room Restaurant offering table d'hote and à la carte menus along with well balanced wine list. Excellent bar meals menu.

'Now open indoor pool, gym & leisure complex'

Three well stocked bars with games room — snooker, pool, darts, real ale.
Weekend and Midweek Breaks available.
Brochure & Tariff   D.A. Nesbitt
    Tel: 0690 710 411

Bexhill-on-Sea - Bideford

V ❖ ⚇ Lunch fr£8.50 Dinner fr£13 Last dinner 9pm
CONF. Thtr 150 Class 50 Board 30 Del £65
Credit Cards 1 2 3 5

BEXLEY Greater London Map 05 TQ47

★★★★69%**Swallow**
1 Broadway DA6 7JZ (near junct 2 of M25)
☎081-298 1000 FAX 081-298 1234

Opened in early 1992, this is a stylishly designed modern hotel with intelligently designed bedrooms furnished in modern American style. The 1950s- look American Bar serves cocktails and cappuccinos all day and has a live pianist most evenings. Of the 2 restaurants the Galleria may only open at weekends, but the brasserie-style Copper Restaurant is open for all meals.
142⇨🛏(14fb)⚥in 53 bedrooms CTV in all bedrooms ® T ✱ sB&B⇨🛏£45-£84 dB&B⇨🛏£60-£94 🍴
Lift (▦ 20P 80🚗 (heated) solarium gymnasium steam room spa bath jacuzzi ♫ xmas
♀ British & European V ❖ ⚇ ⚥ ✱ Lunch £11.95&alc Dinner £18-£19.50&alc Last dinner 11pm
CONF. Thtr 200 Class 120 Board 65 Del from £90
Credit Cards 1 2 3 5

••••••••••••••••••••••••••••••••••••

Forte Posthouse
Black Prince Interchange, Southwold Rd
DA5 1ND (on junct with A2) ☎(0322) 526900
FAX (0322) 526113

Suitable for both the business and leisure traveller, this bright hotel provides modern accommodation in well equipped bedrooms with en suite bathrooms. For more details about Forte Posthouse hotels, consult the Contents page, under Hotel Groups.
102🛏✱ B⇨🛏£41.50-£53.50 (room only)
CONF. Thtr 70 Class 30 Board 30 Del £89.50

BIBURY Gloucestershire Map 04 SP10

★★★ ❀❀78%**Swan**
GL7 5NW ☎Cirencester(0285) 740695 FAX (0285) 740473

The Swan stands on the banks of the River Coln in the heart of this charming Cotswold village. The bedrooms have been individually designed, each item chosen with care, and bathrooms are stunning. Antiques, art deco and contemporary furniture mingle in the reception area, writing room and the comfortable no smoking parlour. Jankowskis Brasserie offers informal all day eating while the elegant dining room is a suitable setting for chef Alain Pochciol's à la carte and 5-course menus.
18⇨🛏(1fb)2🛁 CTV in all bedrooms T ✈ (ex guide dogs)
sB&B⇨🛏£90-£130 dB&B⇨🛏£145-£220 🍴
Lift 20P 🚗 ✱ ♫ xmas
♀ English & French V ❖ ⚇ ⚥ Lunch £18.50-£23 Dinner fr£23&alc Last dinner 9.30pm
Credit Cards 1 3

★★ 66%**Bibury Court**
GL7 5NT (beside the River Coln, behind St Marys Church) (Logis) ☎(0285) 740337 & 740324 FAX (0285) 740660
Closed 24-30 Dec
Situated on the edge of a charming Cotswold village, within walled landscaped gardens, this fine period building features flagstone floors, wood-panelled rooms and enormous minster log fires in the drawing room. Bedrooms are well proportioned, with a mixture of art deco and antique furnishings which blend surprisingly well, and there are huge Victorian style baths.
20⇨(2fb)10🛁 CTV in all bedrooms ® T ✱ sB&B⇨🛏£50-£55 dB&B⇨🛏£74-£78 Continental breakfast 🍴
CTV 100P 🚗 ✱ ♫ squash ⏱ croquet shooting
♀ English, French & Spanish V ❖ ⚇ Lunch £13.50-£15alc High tea £5-£8.50alc Dinner £20-£25alc Last dinner 9pm
Credit Cards 1 2 3 5

BICESTER Oxfordshire Map 04 SP52

★★ ❀73%**Bignell Park**
Chesterton OX6 8UE (on A4095 Witney road)
☎(0869) 241444 & 241192 FAX (0869) 241444
Situated on the edge of Chesterton, about a mile from Bicester, this Cotswold stone building has recently been extended. Bedrooms are individually designed and bathrooms have effective showers as well as baths. There is a cosy beamed bar and galleried restaurant.
5⇨🛏 CTV in all bedrooms ® T sB&B⇨🛏£50-£60 dB&B⇨🛏£60-£80 🍴
24P ✱ nc2yrs
♀ English & French V ❖ ⚥ Lunch £11.50-£12.50&alc Dinner £10-£25alc Last dinner 9.30pm
CONF. Board 20
Credit Cards 1 2 3 5

BICKLEIGH Devon Map 03 SS90

★★ 64%**Fisherman's Cot**
EX16 8RW ☎(0884) 855237 & 855289 FAX (0884) 855241
Beside the River Exe, with access from the spacious bars to the Riverside Patio, this popular thatched hotel is below the 14th-century Bickleigh Bridge which inspired the hit song, Bridge Over Troubled Water. The rooms in the main building are cottagey with exposed beams, while those in the annexe across the car park are more simple. A wide range of food is available.
23⇨🛏(5fb)1🛁⚥in 6 bedrooms CTV in all bedrooms ® T sB&B⇨🛏£46-£56 dB&B⇨🛏£56-£66 🍴
CTV 147P ✱ ♫ xmas
♀ English & French V ❖ ⚇ ⚥ ✱ Lunch £11-£18.25alc Dinner £2.65-£6.95&alc Last dinner 10pm
CONF. Thtr 30
Credit Cards 1 3

BIDEFORD Devon Map 02 SS42

See also **Landcross** & **Westward Ho!**
★★★ 67%**Royal**
Barnstaple St EX39 4AE (at eastern end of Bideford Bridge) (Brend) ☎(0237) 472005 FAX (0237) 478957
Traditional standards of hotel-keeping prevail at this hotel overlooking historic Bideford. The public areas are comfortable and attractive, and the wood-panelled Kingsley room has an ornate scrolled ceiling. Table d'hôte and à la carte menus are available in the restaurant, and staff provide a warm welcome and friendly service.
31⇨🛏(3fb) CTV in all bedrooms ® T ✱ sB&B⇨🛏£30-£47 dB&B⇨🛏£45-£65 🍴
(70P ♫ xmas
♀ English & French V ❖ ⚇ ✱ Lunch £6.50 Dinner £12.50&alc Last dinner 9pm
Credit Cards 1 2 3 5

★★ 66%**Yeoldon Country House**
Durrant Ln, Northam EX39 2RL ☎(0237) 474400 FAX (0237) 476618
At the end of a long drive, this ivy-clad country hotel is situated on the outskirts of the town with good river views. Bedrooms are being gradually upgraded and are pleasantly comfortable, and tidy public areas include an attractive combined lounge and bar. Staff are helpful and willing.
10⇨🛏(2fb)1🛁 CTV in all bedrooms ® T ✈ ✱ sB&B⇨🛏£40-£48 dB&B⇨🛏£65-£81 🍴
22P 🚗 ✱ sauna nc5yrs xmas
♀ English, French & Italian V ❖ ⚇ ⚥ ✱ Lunch £4.25-£8 Dinner £18.50&alc Last dinner 9pm
Credit Cards 1 3

90

★★ 63% **Orchard Hill Hotel & Restaurant**
Orchard Hill, Northam EX39 2QY ☎(0237) 472872
This small family-run hotel in a detached Victorian property overlooking the river and town provides bright bedrooms, all with modern facilities. There is an attractive lounge with a separate bar area and the restaurant offers a choice of dishes.
9⇌🛏 CTV in all bedrooms ® ✈ (ex guide dogs)
15P 🚗 ❋ nc8 yrs
♨ English & French V ♿ ✗
Credit Cards [1][3]

★★ 55% **Riversford**
Limers Ln EX39 2RG ☎(0237) 474239 FAX (0237) 421666
A small, family-run hotel situated down a quiet lane overlooking the River Torridge. There is a separate bar, and a lounge area within the dining room, where a choice of mainly grill dishes is available at lunch and dinner.
16⇌🛏(3fb)🛏 CTV in all bedrooms ® T sB&B⇌🛏£37.50-£47.50 dB&B⇌🛏£57-£70 🍴
《 CTV 20P 2 ❋ solarium badminton putting 🎾 xmas
♨ English & Continental V ♿ ♿ ✗ Lunch £3.85-£8&alc High tea £3.25-£6alc Dinner £12&alc Last dinner 9pm
CONF. Thtr 50 Class 30 Board 30 Del £68.30
Credit Cards [1][2][3][5]   £

BIGBURY-ON-SEA Devon Map 03 SX64

★ 69% **Henley**
TQ7 4AR (Logis) ☎(0548) 810240 FAX (0548) 810381
This cosy hotel in an elevated position has dramatic views over Bigbury Bay and a footpath (127 steps) down to a private beach. Refurbishment continues and bedrooms are exceptionally well equipped and pleasant. A well balanced table d'hôte menu is provided using fresh local produce. This is a no smoking establishment.
8⇌🛏(2fb)✗in all bedrooms CTV in all bedrooms ®✗ T
9P 🚗 ❋ 🐕
♨ English & French ♿ ♿ ✗ Last dinner 8pm
Credit Cards [1][2][3]

BIGGAR Strathclyde *Lanarkshire* Map 11 NT03

★★★ 73% **Shieldhill**
Quothquan ML12 6NA (4m NW) ☎(0899) 20035 FAX (0899) 21092
This castle-style country house, dating from 1199, is peacefully situated in rural surroundings. Individually decorated bedrooms in a variety of sizes feature Laura Ashley prints, antique furniture and large comfortable beds, some also having spa baths. There is an oak-panelled lounge with open fire and soft-cushioned sofas, as well as the elegant first-floor drawing room. A tastefully appointed dining room is the setting for enjoyable dinners prepared by Keith and Nicola Braidwood.
11⇌🛏4🛏✗in all bedrooms CTV in all bedrooms T
✈ (ex guide dogs) ❋ sB&B⇌🛏£88-£120 dB&B⇌🛏£98-£155 🍴
25P 🚗 ❋ croquet cycling nc12yrs *xmas*
♨ British & French V ♿ ♿ ✗ ❋ Sunday Lunch fr£14.50 Dinner £24.50-£28.50alc Last dinner 9pm
CONF. Thtr 25 Class 28 Board 14 Del from £89
Credit Cards [1][2][3][4][5]   £

★★★ 68% **Tinto**
Symington ML12 6PQ (SW on A723) ☎Tinto(08993) 454 FAX (08993) 520
A well run hotel popular for weddings and conferences. There are 2 restaurants, and in addition to the main lounge there is an attractive residents' lounge on the first floor. Bedrooms, including 2 suites are bright and modern.
38⇌🛏(2fb)2🛏 CTV in all bedrooms ®✗ T
➡

Bideford - Biggar

AA
★★★

A SCOTTISH COUNTRY HOUSE HOTEL

The eleven deluxe bedrooms feature luxurious ensuite bathrooms, some having four-poster beds, jacuzzis, fireplaces and all the rooms are furnished with antiques.

Located in the rolling hills of the Upper Ward of Lanarkshire, but just 27 miles for Edinburgh and 32 from Glasgow. Ideally located for touring the Borders and Strathclyde.

Awarding winning Head Chef provides both dinner and lunch which is a feast for both the eye and palate.

Personally run by the proprietors, Jack Greenwald and Christine Dunstan.

Please call or write

SHIELDHILL HOTEL, QUOTHQUAN,
BIGGAR, LANARKSHIRE ML12 6NA
Tel: (0899) 20035 Fax: (0899) 21092

The Swan Hotel, Bibury
Gloucestershire GL7 5NW
★★★

A quintessential riverside Cotswold coaching inn. The traditional accommodation, refurbished in 1991 now offers eighteen delightful bedrooms, some with four posters and "Jacuzzi" baths. Passenger lift. Elegant dining room with fine cooking to international standards. All day brasserie and summer flower filled courtyard. Houseparties & break rates.

Tel. (0285) 740695 Fax. 740473

Biggar - Birchgrove

(CTV 100P ⊞ ❋ solarium
♀ International V ✧ ⚒ Last dinner 10pm
Credit Cards [1][2][3][5]

BILBROOK Somerset Map 03 ST04

★★66% *Dragon House*
TA23 6HQ ☎Washford(0984) 40215
Dating from 1740, this pretty stone building is set in well kept gardens. The small public rooms are elegant with panelling, polished floors, antiques and pictures, and bedrooms retain their original features. The candlelit dining room provides an intimate setting for traditional English fare.
9⇨♠Annexe1⇨♠CTV in all bedrooms ® T
30P ⊞ ❋
V ✧ ⚒ ✗ Last dinner 9.30pm
Credit Cards [1][2][3]

★67% *Bilbrook Lawns*
TA24 6HE ☎Washford(0984) 40331
Closed Nov-Feb (ex Xmas)
This white painted Georgian house lies back from the road behind a well mown lawn and a flowery verandah. The spacious lounge and dining room are furnished in period style and bedrooms are neatly decorated. The Whymarks offer a pleasant and relaxed welcome.
7rm(1⇨3♠)(1fb) CTV in all bedrooms ®
8P ⊞ ❋
♀ English & French V ✧ ⚒ ✗ Last dinner 7.30pm
Credit Cards [2]

BILBROUGH North Yorkshire Map 08 SE54

★★★❀❀♨ BILBROUGH MANOR COUNTRY HOUSE
YO2 3PH
☎Tadcaster(0937) 834002
FAX (0937) 834724
Closed 25-29 Dec

Owners Colin and Susan Bell are justifiably proud of this fine turn-of-the-century property, which they have lovingly restored from a dilapidated state. It has the feel of a private house, with attentive and friendly service provided by the butler and his assistants. The spacious wood-panelled drawing room has a good selection of books, but real focal point of the hotel is the foyer lounge with its deep comfy chairs in front of the roaring log fire. Bedrooms vary in size, and are indiviually decorated. The wood-panelled dining room is the delightful setting for the French-influenced food of chef Andrew Pressley and his team. Starters such as Dublin Bay prawns and queenie scallops in a rich shellfish sauce with a light pastry case, and a main course of Gressingham duck in orange and green peppercorn sauce have pleased our inspector.
12⇨♠ CTV in all bedrooms T ✻ ❋ sB&B⇨♠fr£77 dB&B⇨♠£85-£150 ⚑
(CTV 50P ⊞ ❋ croquet nc12yrs *xmas*
♀ French V ✧ ⚒ ✗ ✻ Lunch £10.50-£14.50&alc Dinner £20-£30&alc Last dinner 9.30pm
Credit Cards [1][2][3][5]

Satellite television – look for this symbol ✶
in the directory entries.

Forte Travelodge
(A63 eastbound)
☎(0973) 531823 Central Res (0800) 850950

FORTE Travelodge

This modern building offers a good standard of accommodation for overnight stops. Smart, spacious and well equipped bedrooms, all with en suite bathrooms, are suitable for family use, and meals may be taken at the nearby family restaurant. For more details about Travelodges, consult the Contents page, under Hotel Groups.
36⇨♠✻ B⇨♠£31.95 (room only)

BILLINGHAM
See **Stockton-on-Tees**

BILLINGTON Lancashire Map 07 SD73

★★★★❀64% **Foxfields Country Hotel & Restaurant**
Whalley Rd BB6 9HY ☎Blackburn(0254) 822556 FAX (0254) 824613
Situated in the Ribble Valley, yet within easy reach of several commercial centres, this modern hotel offers spacious accommodation in comfortable suites, each with dining and lounge areas. Public rooms include an attractive restaurant and comfortable cocktail bar. Attentive service is provided by a small team of willing staff.
28⇨♠1♔ CTV in all bedrooms ® T ✻ (ex guide dogs) ❋
sB&B⇨♠£60 dB&B⇨♠£75 ⚑
(175P ❋ ♫ *xmas*
♀ English & French V ✧ ⚒ ✗ Lunch fr£8.95&alc Dinner £16.95&alc Last dinner 9.45pm
CONF. Thtr 200 Class 100 Board 50 Del from £70
Credit Cards [1][2][3][5]

BINGLEY West Yorkshire Map 07 SE13

★★★65% **Oakwood Hall**
Lady Ln BD16 4AW ☎Bradford(0274) 564123 & 563569 FAX (0274) 561477
Closed 25-28 Dec
On the northern side of town, this stone mansion dates from the early Victorian era and has an exceptional and interesting array of ornate architectural features. The bar is richly decorated in greens and reds, with striped upholstery and dark polished tables, and the attractive restaurant has a garden terrace. The bedrooms are spacious, most with solid period furniture and stylish décor.
16⇨♠(1fb)2♔ CTV in all bedrooms ® T ✻ sB&B⇨♠£50-£60 dB&B⇨♠£65-£80
(100P ❋
♀ English & French V ✧ ✻ Lunch fr£5&alc Dinner fr£15&alc Last dinner 9.30pm
Credit Cards [1][2][3][5]

BIRCHGROVE West Glamorgan Map 03 SS79

★★62% **Oak Tree Parc**
Birchgrove Rd SA7 9JR (300yds from M4 junc 44)
☎Skewen(0792) 817781 FAX (0792) 814542
Closed 25-31 Dec
This small commercial hotel, run by the friendly Tilbrook family, provides comfortable, well equipped accommodation and well cooked food.
10⇨♠(2fb) CTV in all bedrooms ® T ✻ sB&B⇨♠£41 dB&B⇨♠£57 ⚑
(40P ❋
♀ Welsh, English, French & Italian V ✧ ⚒ ✗ ✻ Lunch £8.50-£8.95&alc High tea £6.75 Dinner £10.95 Last dinner 10pm
Credit Cards [1][2][3][5] £

Birch Motorway Service Area (M62) - Birmingham

BIRCH MOTORWAY SERVICE AREA (M62) Greater Manchester Map **07 SD80**

Granada Lodge
M62 Service Area OL10 2HQ ☎061-655 3403 FAX 061-655 3358

This modern building provides smart, spacious and well equipped bedrooms, all with en suite bathrooms. Meals may be taken at a nearby family restaurant. For more details about Granada Lodges, consult the Contents page, under Hotel Groups.
37⇨✱ B⇨£34.95-£37.95 (room only)

BIRDLIP Gloucestershire Map **03 SO91**

★★★**62%** Royal George
GL4 8JH (on the B4070, off the A417) (Whitbread)
☎Gloucester(0452) 862506 FAX (0452) 862277
Standing at the edge of the attractive village and surrounded by countryside, this popular hotel has well equipped bedrooms furnished in a light modern style. Public areas include a boldly refurbished restaurant and bar.
34⇨↑Annexe2⇨↑(4fb)1🛏⚥in 6 bedrooms CTV in all bedrooms ®✷T ✻ (ex guide dogs) ✳ sB&B⇨↑fr£59.50 dB&B⇨↑fr£71 🍽
(120P ✿ sauna solarium 9 hole putting green ♣ xmas
♥ English & Continental V ❖ ♨ ⚥ ✻ Lunch fr£9.95&alc Dinner fr£14.95&alc Last dinner 9.30pm
CONF. Thtr 100 Class 50 Board 40 Del from £89
Credit Cards 1 2 3 5

BIRKENHEAD Merseyside Map **07 SJ38**

★★★**66%** Bowler Hat
2 Talbot Rd, Oxton L43 2HH (1m from junct 3 of M62)
☎051-652 4931 FAX 051-653 8127
Bedrooms are mostly in a modern extension and are very well equipped, with many thoughtful extras; furnishings are rather functional but all rooms were scheduled for refurbishment in 1993. Public areas include an attractive lounge bar and restaurant and high standards of service are maintained throughout.
32⇨↑ CTV in all bedrooms ®✷T ✻ (ex guide dogs)
sB&B⇨↑£42.50-£62.50 dB&B⇨↑£55-£85 🍽
(85P 🚗 ✿ xmas
♥ International V ❖ ♨ Lunch £9.95-£11.95&alc Dinner £16.95-£18.95&alc Last dinner 10pm
CONF. Thtr 240 Class 110 Board 60 Del from £72
Credit Cards 1 2 3 5 £

★★**62%** Riverhill
Talbot Rd, Oxton L43 2HJ (1m from M53 junct 3, along the A552 turn left onto B5151 at traffic lights hotel 0.5m on right)
☎051-653 3773 FAX 051-653 7162
A large house extended to provide hotel accommodation, the Riverhill stands in spacious gardens. Bedrooms vary in size, all have modern furnishings and equipment and some are on the ground floor.
16⇨↑(1fb)2🛏 CTV in all bedrooms ® T ✻ ✳
sB&B⇨↑£29.95-£44.95 dB&B⇨↑£43.95-£54.95
CTV 30P 🚗 ✿
♥ English, French & Italian V ✻ Lunch fr£7.95&alc Dinner £12.90-£13.75&alc Last dinner 9.30pm
Credit Cards 1 2 3 5

Some hotels within company owned groups share a uniform identity. For full details consult the Contents page, under Hotel Groups.

BIRMINGHAM West Midlands Map **07 SP08**
See also **Barr, Great, Birmingham Airport, Birmingham (National Exhibition Centre), Bromsgrove** & **Lea Marston**

B

★★★★

★★★★❀❀❀ SWALLOW
12 Hagley Rd, Five Ways
B16 8SJ ☎021-452 1144 FAX 021-456 3442

The Swallow has achieved the enviable position of being the best hotel in the city in which to stay and the best in which to eat. Very capable Jonathan Harrison, formerly the senior sous chef, has recently taken over in the kitchen – too recently, however, for us to report on his influence here. The menus are not too large, and offer a choice of 2, 3 or 4 courses. Sir Edward Elgar gives his name to the main restaurant, while Langtreys serves less expensive but specialist British regional dishes like Midlands steak and kidney pudding, boiled leg of mutton with caper sauce or West Country chicken, bacon and parsley pie.

98⇨↑2🛏⚥in 54 bedrooms CTV in all bedrooms ®✷T sB&B⇨↑fr£110 dB&B⇨↑fr£130 🍽
Lift (🏢 70P 🚗 (heated) sauna solarium gymnasium ♫ xmas
♥ English & French V ❖ ♨ Lunch £15.50-£23.50&alc Dinner £18.50-£30 Last dinner 10.30pm
Credit Cards 1 2 3 5

Billingham Arms Hotel
★★★

**The Causeway, Billingham
Cleveland TS23 2LH
Telephone: (0642) 553661 & 360880
Fax: (0642) 552104**

Renowned for its welcome and comfort, ideally situated for exploring the North Yorkshire Moors, Captain Cook's Monument & Museum, James Herriot and Catherine Cookson country. Within easy distance of the beach. A high standard of comfort will be found in all our 69 bedrooms. Berties Restaurant offers a splendid Edwardian setting to enjoy a wide and varied selection of freshly prepared dishes from the à la carte and table d'hôte menus. Ideal function and conference centre. Adjacent to the hotel is the Forum Sports Centre and there are 3 golf courses close to the hotel.

Birmingham

★★★★ **59%** **Plough & Harrow**
Hagley Rd, Edgbaston B16 8LS
☎021-454 4111 FAX 021-454 1868

FORTE Heritage

History records that there has been an inn on the site of this hotel since 1612. Today's guests are accommodated in well equipped annexe bedrooms and can eat in the restaurant, which has gained a good local reputation for its classical cuisine.
44⇌↑✗in 6 bedrooms CTV in all bedrooms ® T ✱
sB⇌↑£80 dB⇌↑£90 (room only) 🅿
Lift (80P xmas
V ⊕ ⊡ ✗ ✱ Lunch £10.25-£12.95&alc Dinner £15.95&alc Last dinner 9.30pmm
Credit Cards 1 2 3 4 5

★★★★ **58%** **The Copthorne**
Paradise Circus B3 3HJ ☎021-200 2787 FAX 021-200 1197

Copthorne Hotels

Right in the heart of the city, this bright modern business hotel has well equipped bedrooms. An attractive reception/foyer leads into an open-plan bar and restaurant, while less formal dining is available at Goldies.
212⇌↑✗in 91 bedrooms CTV in all bedrooms ®✲ T ✖ (ex guide dogs) ✱ sB⇌↑£102-£114 dB⇌↑£110-£122 (room only) 🅿
Lift (48🐕 🖵 (heated) sauna solarium gymnasium steam room whirlpool ♫ xmas
♀ International V ⊕ ⊡ ✗ ✱ Lunch £6-£16 High tea £6-£16 Dinner £6-£16 Last dinner 11pm
CONF. Thtr 200 Class 108 Board 38 Del £110.50
Credit Cards 1 2 3 5

★★★ **58%** **Holiday Inn**
Holliday St B1 1HH ☎021-631 2000 FAX 021-643 9018

This large city centre hotel is close to the new convention centre. The top floor bedrooms are the best, those on the lower floors rather lack lustre in terms of comfort décor and furnishings. The new look foyer is a great improvement and is now light and airy. The restaurant offers both a carvery and a 'carte', and the popular Terrace Bar is adjacent.
288⇌(210fb)✗in 102 bedrooms CTV in all bedrooms ®✲ T sB⇌↑fr£99 dB⇌↑fr£108 (room only) 🅿
Lift (🎱 ♫ 🖵 (heated) sauna solarium gymnasium steam room spa bath xmas
♀ International V ⊕ ⊡ ✱ Lunch fr£12.95&alc Dinner fr£15.95&alc Last dinner 11pm
CONF. Thtr 160 Class 65 Board 40 Del from £82
Credit Cards 1 2 3 4 5

★★★ **66%** *Westley Arms*
80-90 Westley Rd, Acocks Green B27 7UJ
☎021-706 4312 FAX 021-706 2824

BEST WESTERN HOTELS

This popular hotel reopened in 1989 following extensive refurbishment, and is conveniently situated close to the NEC, airport and motorway network. Accommodation is boldly decorated, with dark pine furnishings and a good range of facilities. The rooms are located in the main hotel and the adjacent town house. There is a choice of bars and a restaurant offering carvery and à la carte options.
27⇌↑Annexe10⇌↑(1fb)1⊞ CTV in all bedrooms ® T ✖ (ex guide dogs)
(CTV 100P
♀ English & French V ⊕ ⊡ ✗ Last dinner 10pm
Credit Cards 1 2 3 4 5

★★★ **63%** **Royal Angus Thistle**
St Chads, Queensway B4 6HY ☎021-236 4211
FAX 021-233 2195

THISTLE HOTELS

This modern city centre hotel has an adjoining NCP car park. Accommodation varies in size and style, and there is a continual programme of upgrading. Public rooms include the contemporary Raffles Restaurant and lounge bar overlooking St Chad's Cathedral.
133⇌↑(4fb)✗in 8 bedrooms CTV in all bedrooms ®✲ T ✱
sB⇌↑£75-£85 dB⇌↑£85-£95 (room only) 🅿
Lift (♪ xmas
♀ International V ⊕ ⊡ ✗ ✱ Lunch £10-£11.95 Dinner £16.95 Last dinner 10pm
CONF. Thtr 150 Class 80 Board 30 Del from £70
Credit Cards 1 2 3 5

★★★ **63%** **Strathallan Thistle**
225 Hagley Rd, Edgbaston B16 9RY (on A456)
☎021-455 9777 FAX 021-454 9742

THISTLE HOTELS

In this striking circular building accommodation is generally compact, outer rooms are small and wedge shaped, while those at the centre of the building can be rather dark. In contrast the public rooms are light and modern, with 2 bars and the Mange-Tout restaurant offering a range of menus.
167⇌↑(5fb)✗in 55 bedrooms CTV in all bedrooms ® T ✱
sB⇌↑fr£75 dB⇌↑fr£85 (room only) 🅿
Lift (⊞ 200P 60🐕
♀ International V ⊕ ⊡ ✗ ✱ Lunch £9.25-£12.25 Dinner £14.25-£17.25&alc Last dinner 10pm
CONF. Thtr 200 Class 90 Board 40 Del from £92
Credit Cards 1 2 3 4 5

★★★ **63%** **Westmead**
Redditch Rd, Hopwood B48 7AL (on A441, 1.5m from junct 2 of M42) (Lansbury) ☎021-445 1202 FAX 021-445 6163

Conveniently situated 1.5 miles from junction 2 of the M42, this hotel provides well equipped modern accommodation with pastel decor and light wood furnishings. The Colonial Restaurant offers à la carte and table d'hôte menus and The Cottage Pie serves joints and 'dishes of the day' in addition to light meals.
59⇌↑(2fb)2⊞✗in 6 bedrooms CTV in all bedrooms ® T ✖ (ex guide dogs) ✱ sB&B⇌↑fr£59.50 dB&B⇌↑fr£71 🅿
(250P ✿ xmas
♀ English & French V ⊕ ⊡ ✗ ✱ Lunch fr£9.95 Dinner fr£13.95 Last dinner 10pm
CONF. Thtr 300 Class 300 Board 35 Del from £85
Credit Cards 1 2 3 5

★★★ **62%** *Apollo*
243-247 Hagley Rd, Edgbaston B16 9RA (on A456) ☎021-455 0271 FAX 021-456 2394

A modern motel with easy access to the city centre. Bedrooms vary, the refurbished ones offering quality and comfort lacking in old-style rooms. A choice of carvery or restaurant is available in the central block.
126⇌↑(9fb)✗in 22 bedrooms CTV in all bedrooms ® T sB⇌↑£70-£75 dB⇌↑£75-£85 (room only) 🅿
Lift (130P
♀ English & French V ⊕ ⊡ ✗ Lunch £9.25-£21 High tea fr£5 Dinner £12.80-£23.45 Last dinner 10.30pm
CONF. Thtr 150 Class 80 Board 50 Del from £55
Credit Cards 1 2 3 5

★★★ **61%** *Grand*
Colmore Row B3 2DA ☎021-236 7951 FAX 021-233 1465
Closed 3 days Xmas

This substantial city centre hotel dates from the 19th century, and the nearest (NCP) car park is a few minutes walk away. Public areas and some bedrooms have been refurbished but the remaining

Birmingham

rooms are showing their age. Two restaurants offer both à la carte and carvery options, and there are 2 bars.
173⇌ℕ(7fb)⊁in 23 bedrooms CTV in all bedrooms ® T sB&B⇌ℕ£85 dB&B⇌ℕ£100 ⊟
Lift ((🛎 (£5-£7 per day)
♀ English & French V ✿ ⚓ ✴ Lunch £12.95&alc Dinner £12.95&alc Last dinner 9.45pm
CONF. Thtr 500 Class 250 Board 80 Del £100
Credit Cards ①②③⑤ £

★★★ 58% **Great Barr Hotel & Conference Centre**
Pear Tree Dr, off Newton Rd B43 6HS ☎021-357 1141 FAX 021-357 7557
(For full entry see Barr, Great)

★★★ 58% **Novotel**
70 Broad St B1 2HT ☎021-643 2000 FAX 021-643 9796

This busy modern hotel is close to the city centre and the International Convention Centre. Accommodation is functional with modest décor and furnishings in the typical Novotel style. Public areas include a small bar and a restaurant (open from 6am until midnight) serving a range of dishes.
148⇌ℕ(148fb)⊁in 25 bedrooms CTV in all bedrooms ® T ✴ sB⇌ℕfr£67 dBfr£77 (room only) ⊟
Lift ⊞ 65🛎 ⇌ sauna gymnasium jacuzzi
♀ International V ✿ ⚓ ⊁ ✴ Lunch £7.50-£17.50&alc Dinner £7.50-£17.50&alc Last dinner mdnt
Credit Cards ①②③⑤

★★ 67% **Copperfield House**
60 Upland Rd, Selly Park B29 7JS (off A441 at junct of Selly Park Rd and Upland Road) (Logis) ☎021-472 8344 FAX 021-472 8344
A red brick Victorian house in a pleasant residential area, offering friendly service from the owners, well equipped bedrooms, a comfortable lounge and small dining room.
17⇌ℕ(2fb) CTV in all bedrooms ® T sB&B⇌ℕ£47.50-£57.50 dB&B⇌ℕ£59-£69 ⊟
17P ✿ xmas
V ✿ ⚓ Lunch £15.95-£17.95 High tea £10-£12.50 Dinner £15.95-£17.95 Last dinner 8.30pm
Credit Cards ①②③

★★ 66% **Portland**
313 Hagley Rd, Edgbaston B16 9LQ (on A456) ☎021-455 0535 FAX 021-456 1841
Convenient for the city centre, this friendly hotel continues to be popular with business people for its well-maintained accommodation and good range of facilities.
63⇌ℕ CTV in all bedrooms ®⚓T ✖ (ex guide dogs) sB&B⇌ℕ£29.95-£39.95 dB&B⇌ℕ£45-£52.50 ⊟
Lift ((CTV 80P
♀ English & French V ⚓ Lunch £9.95-£13.95&alc Dinner £11.95-£13.95&alc Last dinner 10pm
CONF. Thtr 100 Class 60 Board 40 Del from £65
Credit Cards ①②③⑤ £

★★ 65% **Norwood**
87-89 Bunbury Rd, Northfield B31 2ET (turn left on A38 at Grosvenor shopping centre) ☎021-411 2202 FAX 021-411 2202
A popular commercial hotel to the southwest of the city, offering neat, modern accommodation with a good range of facilities. The hotel is privately owned by Mark and Julie Wall who create an informal and welcoming atmosphere.
15⇌ℕ CTV in all bedrooms ®⚓T ✴ sB&B⇌ℕ£35-£53.50 dB&B⇌ℕ£40-£59.75 ⊟
11P ✿
♀ English & French V ✿ ⚓ ✴ Bar Lunch £5-£10 Dinner £14.95 Last dinner 8.45pm
Credit Cards ①③ £

★★★AA
ROYAL ANGUS
THISTLE HOTEL

St Chad's, Queensway, Birmingham B4 6HY
Tel: 021-236 4211   Fax: 021-233 2195

Your choice in Birmingham Centre

For Reservations at over 100
Mount Charlotte Thistle Hotels
Telephone London: 071 937 8033.

THISTLE HOTELS

★★★AA
STRATHALLAN
THISTLE HOTEL

Hagley Road, Edgbaston, Birmingham B16 9RY
Tel: 021-455 9777   Fax: 021-454 9432

Your choice at Edgbaston

For Reservations at over 100
Mount Charlotte Thistle Hotels
Telephone London: 071 937 8033.

THISTLE HOTELS

Birmingham - Birmingham Airport

★★ 64% Westbourne Lodge
27/29 Fountain Rd, Edgbaston B17 8NJ (off A456)
☎021-429 1003 FAX 021-429 7436
A welcoming family-run hotel a short drive from the city centre. Bright modern bedrooms have good facilities and the extended public areas include a small bar, restaurant and quiet residents lounge.
18rm(4fb) CTV in all bedrooms ® T sB&B⇨₤30-₤39.50 dB&B⇨₤40-₤56
CTV 12P
English, French & Italian V Lunch ₤13.95 High tea ₤4 Dinner ₤13.95 Last dinner 8pm
Credit Cards 1 2 3 £

★★ 61% Edgbaston Palace
198 Hagley Rd B16 9PQ ☎021-452 1577
Closed 24-26 Dec
This predominantly commercial hotel is a short drive from the city centre and attracts a good percentage of regular guests. Recent extensions have included new bedrooms and a larger restaurant overlooking the rear garden patio area. A further wing of bedrooms should open shortly.
30rm(29⇨)(4fb)1⊞ CTV in all bedrooms ® T ✱ sB&Bfr₤30 sB&B⇨₤42.50 dB&Bfr₤40 dB&B⇨₤52.50
((CTV 50P 3
Continental V Lunch ₤5-₤10.50 High tea ₤2.50-₤3.50 Dinner ₤7.50-₤15.50 Last dinner 9.30pm
Credit Cards 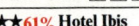 £

★★ 61% Hotel Ibis
Ladywell Walk B5 4ST ☎021-622 6010 FAX 021-622 6020

Part of the Arcadian Centre, near New Street station and within easy walking distance of the Bullring, this very modern hotel provides good value accommodation. The restaurant and lounge areas are open plan around a fountain, and there is also a piano bar. In the restaurant, daily specials supplement the set menu and the carte, providing a wide range of choices.
159⇨⌿in 40 bedrooms CTV in all bedrooms ® T ✱ sB⇨₤32-₤39.50 dB⇨₤32.50-₤39.50 (room only)
Lift
V ✱ Dinner ₤9.75-₤12.75&alc Last dinner 10.30pm
Credit Cards 1 2 3 5

★★ 60% Hagley Court
229 Hagley Rd, Edgbaston B16 9RP (on A456) ☎021-454 6514 FAX 021-456 2722
Closed Xmas
Hagley Court is a privately owned hotel with easy access to the city centre. Accommodation is very well equipped, although rooms can be compact. Willing, friendly service is provided.
27⇨(1fb) CTV in all bedrooms ® T ✖ (ex guide dogs)
(28P
English & Continental Last dinner 9.30pm
Credit Cards 1 2 3 5

★★ 56% Sheriden House
82 Handsworth Wood Rd, Handsworth Wood B20 2PL (on B4124) ☎021-554 2185 & 021-523 5960 FAX 021-551 4761
This friendly, privately owned commercial hotel is convenient for the city and the M6. Room sizes and standards vary, some are refurbished while others are more functional. Public areas are limited in size with a compact lounge, dining room and bar.
11rm(9⇨)1⊞ CTV in all bedrooms ® T ✱ sB&B₤22-₤29 sB&B⇨₤32-₤42 dB&B₤33-₤42 dB&B⇨₤44-₤55
(CTV 30P
English & French V Lunch ₤11-₤12 Dinner ₤6.50-₤12&alc Last dinner 9pm
Credit Cards 1 2 3 £

★★ 53% Beechwood
201 Bristol Rd, Edgbaston B5 7UB (on A38, 1m S of city centre) ☎021-440-2133 FAX 021-446 4549
This Edwardian house has 3 acres of gardens which include a trout lake. Service is informal and friendly and accommodation is in simply furnished bedrooms.
18rm(6⇨10⇧)(4fb) CTV in all bedrooms ® ✱ sB&B⇨⇧₤35 dB&B⇨⇧₤45
⊞ CTV 30P ✿ trout lake xmas
English & French V Lunch ₤8-₤10&alc High tea 70p-95p&alc Dinner ₤10-₤14&alc Last dinner 9.30pm
CONF. Thtr 80 Class 70 Board 70 Del from ₤65
Credit Cards 1 2 3 5

Campanile
55 Irving St B1 1DH ☎021-622 4925 FAX 021-622 4195

A nearby bar and bistro restaurant provides refreshments for travellers staying at this modern accomodation building. Bedrooms are well equipped and have en suite bathrooms. For more details about Campanile, consult the Contents page, under Hotel Groups.
Annexe50⇨⇧B⇨⇧₤35.75 (room only)
CONF. Thtr 35 Class 35 Board 25 Del from ₤42.80

Forte Crest
Smallbrook Queensway B5 4EW ☎021-643 8171 FAX 021-631 2528

A large modern hotel with a wide range of services and amenities, designed particularly for the business traveller. Bedrooms are smart, comfortable and well equipped. For more details about Forte Crest hotels, consult the Contents page, under Hotel Groups.
253⇨⇧✱ B⇨⇧₤80-₤100 (room only)
CONF. Thtr 630 Class 380 Board 50 Del from ₤80

Forte Posthouse
Chapel Ln B43 7BG ☎021-357 7444 FAX 021-357 7503
(For full entry see Barr, Great)

Travel Inn
20 Bridge St, Ladywood B1 2JH ☎021-633 4820

Purpose-built accommodation offers spacious and well equipped bedrooms, all with en suite bathrooms. Meals may be taken at the nearby family restaurant and pub. For more details about Travel Inns, consult the Contents page, under Hotel Groups.
54⇨⇧✱ B⇨⇧₤33.50 (room only)

○**The Chamberlain**
Alcester St B12 0PJ ☎021 606 9000
Due to open Nov 1993
250⇨⇧

BIRMINGHAM AIRPORT West Midlands Map 07 SP18

★★★ 61% Novotel
B26 3QL (opp main passenger terminal)
☎021-782 7000 FAX 021-782 0445
This hotel opened in 1991 offering functional, value for money accommodation in typical Novotel style. Rooms are modest in terms of décor and comfort, but all are triple glazed against aircraft noise. The hotel is linked to the airport terminal, and connected by monorail to the NEC and BR station.
195⇨⇧⌿in 130 bedrooms CTV in all bedrooms ® T ✱ sB⇨⇧₤67 dB⇨⇧₤77 (room only)
Lift (⊞

Birmingham Airport - Birmingham (National Exhibition Centre)

V ✻ ✱ Lunch £2.10-£13alc Dinner £2.10-£13alc Last dinner mdnt
Credit Cards 1 2 3 5

Forte Posthouse
Coventry Rd, Elmdon B26 3QW (A45)
☎021-782 8141 FAX 021-782 2476

FORTE Posthouse

Suitable for both the business and leisure traveller, this bright hotel provides modern accommodation in well equipped bedrooms with en suite bathrooms. For more details about Forte Posthouse hotels, consult the Contents page, under Hotel Groups.
136⇨✻ B⇨♠£41.50-£53.50 (room only)
CONF. Thtr 150 Class 80 Board 40 Del £89.50

BIRMINGHAM (NATIONAL EXHIBITION CENTRE)
West Midlands Map **07** SP18

★★★**57%** **Arden Hotel & Leisure Club**
Coventry Rd, Bickenhill B92 0EH (A45)
☎Hampton-in-Arden(0675) 443221 FAX (0675) 443225
This privately owned hotel next to the NEC offers well equipped bedrooms of adequate standard. There is a large restaurant with a lengthy menu, a bar, and the informal Trellis Room, overlooking the swimming pool, for breakfast. On our inspection visit, service left something to be desired.
146♠(4fb) CTV in all bedrooms ®☎T✻ sB⇨♠£65 dB⇨♠£72.50 (room only) ₽
Lift ℂ 300P ✻ 🗋 (heated) snooker sauna solarium gymnasium jacuzzi
♉ French V ✿ ⚄ ✗ ✻ Lunch £8.95-£13&alc Dinner £1.50-£13&alc Last dinner 10pm
CONF. Thtr 250 Class 60 Board 60
Credit Cards 1 2 3 5

★★
❀❀

**Kenilworth Road (A452), Balsall Common,
near Coventry CV7 7EL**
Tel: (0676) 533004 Fax: (0676) 534572

Within a 15 minute drive of:–
— **Junction 4 M6, Junction 6 M42**
— **National Exhibition Centre &
    Birmingham Airport**
— **Kenilworth & Warwick**
— **Coventry & Solihull**

Small, family run hotel in 1 acre where emphasis is on personal service, 13 en-suite bedrooms, award winning à la carte restaurant.

Beechwood Hotel ★★ **B**

**201 Bristol Road, Edgbaston,
Birmingham B5 7UB
Telephone: 021-440 2133 Fax: 021-446 4549**

The staff at the Beechwood Hotel extend a warm welcome to all their guests at this friendly run hotel. Although only 1 mile from the City Centre and International Convention Centre the hotel, with its beautiful 3 acres of garden offers an oasis of peace and quiet normally associated with country house hotels. Comfortable accommodation with each bedroom having colour TV, hospitality tray and telephone. A tempting à la carte menu is available. Weekends and longer stays available at discounted rates.

Beechwood Hotel is the ideal country location in the heart of the city.

Sheriden House Hotel

AA★★ *& Licensed Restaurant* ETB
**82 Handsworth Wood Road,
Handsworth Wood, Birmingham B20 2PL
Telephone: 021-554 2185 & 021-523 5960
Fax: 021-551 4761
Proprietors: G & A Harmon**

The Sheriden House Hotel is situated on the B4124. Bus Route 16 & 16a. Approximately 3½ miles north west of Birmingham City Centre and the International Convention Centre, 1½ miles from junc 7, M6 and junc 1, M5 and 20 minutes from the NEC. En suite bedrooms with telephone, TV, tea/coffee making facilities etc. Bar. Conference room. Car parking for 30 cars. Special Week-End rates.

Bishop Auckland - Blackpool

BISHOP AUCKLAND Co Durham Map 08 NZ22

★★★ **63%** *Park Head*
New Coundon DL14 8QT (1m N on A688) ☎(0388) 661727
Originally a public house dating back to 1890, the hotel has been extended to provide additional bedrooms around a rear courtyard. Rooms are well furnished and have good all-round facilities. A choice of dining is available in either the carvery or restaurant, and resident owners ensure friendly and attentive service.
8⇌↑Annexe7⇌(3fb)1⊞ CTV in all bedrooms ®
(96P ✿ ♪ ♧
♤ English, French & Italian V ♧ ⌥ ⌘ Last dinner 9.45pm
Credit Cards ①②③④⑤

★★ **61%** *The Postchaise*
36 Market Pl DL14 7NX ☎(0388) 661296 & 606312
A town-centre commercial hotel, the Postchaise has original oak beams in the public areas, but rather more functional bedrooms. A good range of food is available either in the small restaurant or the bars. Parking is available just over the road.
12⇌↑(1fb)2⊞ ✓ CTV in all bedrooms ® T ✕ sB&B⇌↑£25-£34 dB&B⇌↑£40-£45 ⛃
(✗ ⛁
✓ Lunch £4.25-£7.50 Dinner £11-£16alc Last dinner 9pm
Credit Cards ①③⑤ £

BISHOP'S STORTFORD Hertfordshire Map 05 TL42

★★★★ ❀**69%** *Down Hall Country House*
Hatfield Heath CM22 7AS (leave B183 at Hatfield Heath and turn right) ☎(0279) 731441 FAX (0279) 730416
Set in over 100 acres of parkland, this fine Victorian mansion has been skilfully extended and is elegantly furnished in keeping with the Italianate architecture. Bedrooms are spacious, very comfortable and well equipped. Public rooms include the main lounge, with a magnificent fireplace and chandeliers, cocktail bar and restaurant.
103⇌↑1⊞ CTV in all bedrooms ®✿ T ✕ sB&B⇌↑£80-£95 dB&B⇌↑£107.50-£135 (room only) ⛃
Lift (200P ✿ ⊞ (heated) ✎ (hard) snooker sauna croquet petanque lawn chess putting *xmas*
♤ International V ♧ ⌥ ✓ Lunch fr£15.50&alc High tea £7-£10.50 Dinner fr£17&alc Last dinner 9.45pm
CONF. Thtr 310 Class 154 Board 84 Del from £95
Credit Cards ①②③⑤ £

BLACKBURN Lancashire Map 07 SD62

See also **Langho**
★★★ **58%** *Blackburn Moat House*
Preston New Rd BB2 7BE (on A667/A6119 junct W of town) ☎(0254) 264441 FAX (0254) 682435

This purpose built gabled building provides well equipped if functional accommodation and extensive function and conference facilities. Regrettably, we have found service to be less than professional at times.
98⇌↑(2fb)✓ in 12 bedrooms CTV in all bedrooms ® T sB&B⇌↑fr£54.95 dB&B⇌↑fr£65.95 ⛃
Lift (CTV 350P ✿ pool table
♤ English & French V ♧ ⌥ ✕ Lunch £14.25&alc Dinner fr£14.25&alc Last dinner 10pm
CONF. Thtr 400 Class 200 Board 100 Del from £76
Credit Cards ①②③④⑤ £

★★ **76%** *Millstone*
Church Ln, Mellor BB2 7JR (3m NW off A59) (Shire) ☎Mellor(0254) 813233 FAX (0254) 812678
This delightful small hotel offers stylish and attractive, though not large, bedrooms. Thoughtful extras include towelling robes, good toiletries and chocolates in addition to more usual facilities. The cosy bars retain the character of a country inn, and the elegant wood

panelled restaurant is the setting for enjoyable meals. Friendly service is provided by uniformed staff.
21⇌↑(1fb)✓ in 4 bedrooms CTV in all bedrooms ®✿ T ✱ sB&B⇌↑£56-£66 dB&B⇌↑£74-£84 ⛃
40P *xmas*
V ♧ ⌥ ✱ Lunch £8.50-£13.50 Dinner £18&alc Last dinner 9.45pm
CONF. Thtr 25 Class 15 Board 16 Del £87
Credit Cards ①②③⑤

BLACKPOOL Lancashire Map 07 SD33

★★★ **63%** *Savoy*
Queens Promenade, North Shore FY2 9SJ ☎(0253) 352561 FAX (0253) 500735
An impressive red brick hotel overlooking the North Promenade, the Savoy provides modern, well equipped bedrooms, many of which have fine sea views. Public areas are spacious, though these can be busy as the hotel is a popular venue for functions.
147⇌↑(10fb)✓ in 18 bedrooms CTV in all bedrooms ® T ✱ sB&B⇌↑£32.50-£72.50 dB&B⇌↑£65-£105 ⛃
Lift (40P snooker *xmas*
♤ International V ♧ ⌥ ✱ Sunday Lunch £6.95-£8.50 Dinner £13.50-£14.50 Last dinner 10pm
CONF. Thtr 350 Class 250 Board 100 Del from £75
Credit Cards ①②③⑤ £

★★★ **60%** *Clifton*
Talbot Square FY1 1ND ☎(0253) 21481 FAX (0253) 27345
In the centre of the town opposite the pier, this Victorian hotel offers a modern standard of accommodation, although some of the bathrooms are more dated. Public areas include a choice of lively bars, or a quieter cocktail bar on the first floor.
77⇌↑(2fb) CTV in all bedrooms ®✿ T ✱ sB&B⇌↑fr£30 dB&B⇌↑fr£60 ⛃
Lift (CTV ✗ pool table *xmas*
♤ English, French, Italian, Indian & Mexican V ♧ ⌥ ✱ Lunch £6.50-£50 High tea fr£3.50 Dinner fr£9.95 Last dinner 10pm
CONF. Thtr 200 Class 100 Board 50 Del from £47.50
Credit Cards ①②③⑤ £

★★ **71%** *Brabyns*
Shaftesbury Av, North Shore FY2 9QQ
☎(0253) 54263 due to change to 354263 FAX (0253) 52915

Just off the Queen's Promenade, this long established, small hotel is run by proprietors Mr and Mrs Barker, who are very welcoming. Bedrooms vary in size, but all have the same modern facilities. Public rooms include a comfortable lounge bar and panelled restaurant where good value meals are served.
22⇌↑Annexe3⇌↑(10fb) CTV in all bedrooms ® T ✱ sB&B⇌↑£22.50-£35 dB&B⇌↑£45-£52 ⛃
CTV 12P *xmas*
V ♧ ⌥ ✱ Lunch £6-£6.50 Dinner £10-£11 Last dinner 7.30pm
Credit Cards ①②③⑤ £

★★ **67%** *Headlands*
611-613 South Prom FY4 1NJ (hotel at junc of promenade & Harrowside) ☎(0253) 341179 FAX (0253) 342047
Closed 2-13 Jan
This popular hotel is on the South Promenade, and regular improvements have brought about a good standard of accommodation together with friendly and attentive service. Bedrooms vary in size but are well equipped, while public areas include comfortable lounges and a wood-panelled dining room.
43⇌↑(11fb) CTV in all bedrooms ® T sB&B⇌↑£32-£45 dB&B⇌↑£64-£90 ⛃
Lift CTV 40P 8🚗 snooker solarium ♪ *xmas*
V ♧ ⌥ ✱ Lunch £7.95-£10 Dinner £13.90-£15 Last dinner 8.30pm
CONF. Thtr 70 Class 70
Credit Cards ①③ £

The Headlands Hotel has been renowned for more than sixty years for the quality of its cuisine, its atmosphere and its cleanliness. It is a family hotel situated on Blackpool's South Promenade with commanding views over the Irish Sea, and has ample parking facilities. It is one of the few hotels offering completely inclusive terms, comprising: Bedrooms (all en-suite with colour TV, Radio, direct dial telephone, tea/coffee making facilities), Full English Breakfast, 4 course Lunch (if required), Afternoon Tea and 7 course Evening Meal — Remarkable Value. The hotel is under the personal supervision of its resident proprietors, and is noted for its quiet, friendly and courteous service. The hotel has a resident organist during the season and is open for both the Christmas and New Year periods. **Theme weekends**, every weekend from November to June from £45. Also **4 day mid week specials** in March to June from £120 including half board, nightly dancing, coach trips, games and quizzes.

Lift to all floors.

Terms: B.B. & E.M. En-Suite Rooms from £32.00

Write for illustrated brochure to Mr M. Ruppert
THE HEADLANDS HOTEL 611 South Promenade, Blackpool FY4 1NJ or
Telephone (0253) 341179   Fax (0253) 342047

★ ★

★ ★ ★

Queens Promenade, Blackpool FY2 9SJ
Tel: (0253) 352561 Fax: (0253) 500735

One of Blackpool's finest and most comfortable hotels enjoying a prime seafront position on the North Shore. An ideal holiday destination for young and old alike.

★ ★ ★

Talbot Square and Promenade, Blackpool FY1 1ND
Telephone: (0253) 21481 Fax: (0253) 27345

In a prime sea front location, The Clifton Hotel offers 80 bedrooms all en suite including colour TV, radio, telephone and tea/coffee making facilities. Together with three bars and Baileys Bistro offering a wide choice of varied meals, The Clifton offers every service you could wish for.

FIRST LEISURE CORPORATION HOTELS

Blackpool - Blair Atholl

★★ 65% Ruskin
55-61 Albert Rd FY1 4PW (leaving the M55 at end, proceed N along Golden Mile, turn inland at Chapel St, bear left at the traffic lights, follow the road onto Albert Road) ☎(0253) 24063 FAX (0253) 23571

Situated in the centre of town close to the Winter Gardens and Opera House, this well managed hotel is popular with both business guests and tourists. Bedrooms, though compact, are modern in style, and public areas are comfortable and inviting. Service is provided by smartly uniformed staff.

77⇨↑(14fb)1⌀ CTV in all bedrooms ® T ✱ sB&B⇨↑fr£33 dB&B⇨↑fr£56 🍴
Lift (CTV 16☎ (£5 for 24hrs) pool table *xmas*
V ❀ ⚲ ⚱ ✱ Bar Lunch £3.50 Dinner £12-£15 Last dinner 8.30pm
Credit Cards 1 3

★★ 65% Hotel Sheraton
54-62 Queens Promenade FY2 9RP (1m N from Blackpool Tower on promenade towards Fleetwood) ☎(0253) 52723 due to change to 352723 FAX (0253) 595499

This large and friendly seafront hotel is steadily being improved, with the best bedrooms now having attractive coordinated furnishings and smart modern bathrooms. Public areas are spacious and comfortable, and a range of entertainment is provided.

119⇨↑(37fb) CTV in all bedrooms ® T ✱ sB&B⇨£20-£33 dB&B⇨↑£40-£66 🍴
Lift (20P ⊠ (heated) sauna solarium *xmas*
V ❀ ⚲ ⚱ Last dinner 7.45pm
Credit Cards 1 3

★★ 65% Warwick
603-609 New South Promenade FY4 1NG
(From M55 junct 4 take A583 for South Shore then rt on A584, Promenade South)
☎(0253) 42192 FAX (0253) 405776

[BEST WESTERN HOTELS]

This lively modern hotel is situated on the south shore overlooking the sea. Bedrooms vary in size and all have built in units. The attractive restaurant offers a good value dinner, and live entertainment is provided each evening in Rafferty's Bar. Staff are friendly and helpful.

52⇨↑(10fb) CTV in all bedrooms ® T sB&B⇨↑£38-£46 dB&B⇨↑£65-£78 🍴
(30P ⊠ (heated) solarium games room, pool table, table tennis ♫ *xmas*
☿ International V ❀ ⚲ ⚱ ✱ Bar Lunch £3-£7alc Dinner £12.95 Last dinner 8.30pm
CONF. Thtr 50 Class 24 Board 30 Del from £44
Credit Cards 1 2 3 5 £

★★ 62% Revill's
190-4 North Promenade FY1 1RJ ☎(0253) 25768 FAX (0253) 24736

Situated close to the town centre and the North Pier, this family-owned hotel, established in 1887, offers spacious and comfortable public areas including a choice of bars and lounges. Bedrooms are generally comfortable and modern in style.

47⇨↑(10fb) CTV in all bedrooms ® T ✱ sB&B⇨↑£21.50-£29 dB&B⇨↑£37-£52 🍴
Lift (CTV 23P snooker *xmas*
V ❀ ⚲ ✱ Bar Lunch £4-£7 Dinner £6.50-£8.50 Last dinner 7.30pm
Credit Cards 1 3

Remember to book early for holiday and bank holiday times.

★★ 58% Claremont
270 North Prom FY1 1SA (0.5m N of Blackpool Tower) ☎(0253) 293122 FAX (0253) 752409

This lively seafront hotel offers an extensive range of facilities, the most recent being a sauna and jacuzzi. The bedrooms are in a mixture of styles. A 5-course dinner is available each evening in the refurbished restaurant.

143⇨↑Annexe25⇨↑(51fb) CTV in all bedrooms ®⚲ T ✱ (ex guide dogs) ✱ sB&B⇨↑£30-£45 dB&B⇨↑£60-£90 🍴
Lift (60P ⊠ (heated) sauna gymnasium *xmas*
V ❀ ⚲ ⚱ ✱ Lunch £5.95-£7.50 High tea £6-£10 Dinner £11.75-£12.75 Last dinner 8.30pm
CONF. Thtr 300 Class 150 Board 150 Del from £35
Credit Cards 1 3

★★ 58% Cliffs
Queens Promenade FY2 9SG (on promenade, 1m N of Tower) ☎(0253) 595559 FAX (0253) 590394

This large hotel, with an art deco-style exterior, overlooks the seafront on the North Shore. Spacious public areas including a choice of bars, all day coffee shop and leisure facilities. Half the bedrooms have been refurbished and, although all have the same facilities, older rooms are beginning to show their age.

162⇨↑(28fb)1⌀ CTV in all bedrooms ®⚲ T ✱ (ex guide dogs) ✱ sB&B⇨↑£29.50-£70 dB&B⇨↑£59-£98 🍴
Lift (70P ⊠ (heated) squash snooker sauna solarium gymnasium jacuzzi ♫ *xmas*
☿ English & French V ❀ ⚲ ⚱ ✱ Bar Lunch £6-£10alc High tea £3-£10alc Dinner £11.50 Last dinner 9pm
Credit Cards 1 2 3

★ 63% Kimberley
New South Promenade FY4 1NQ (off the Promenade) ☎(0253) 41184 FAX (0253) 408737
Closed 3-13 Jan

Standing in a crescent off the seafront, this long established, owner run hotel offers friendly service and has comfortable lounges and simply furnished bedrooms of varying size.

54rm(36⇨↑)(8fb) CTV in all bedrooms ® ✱ sB&Bfr£26.95 sB&B⇨↑fr£30.25 dB&Bfr£47.50 dB&B⇨↑fr£53.90 🍴
Lift (CTV 26P ⨁ snooker table tennis darts *xmas*
☿ English & Continental ❀ ⚲ ✱ Lunch fr£6.25 Dinner fr£10.50 Last dinner 7.30pm
Credit Cards 1 3

BLACKWOOD Gwent Map 03 ST19

★★★ 53% Maes Manor
NP2 0AG ☎(0495) 224551 & 220011 FAX (0495) 228217

An old manor house set in several acres of woodland near the local golf course, Maes Manor is very popular locally for functions and meetings, providing spaciously comfortable bar areas, an attractive restaurant and bright, neat bedrooms.

8⇨Annexe14⇨↑(2fb)2⌀ CTV in all bedrooms ® T ✱ sB&B⇨↑£45-£50 dB&B⇨↑£57-£69 🍴
(100P ❀ ♨
☿ Welsh, English, French & Italian V ❀ ⚲ ✱ Lunch £4.75-£8.60alc Dinner £12-£20alc Last dinner 9.30pm
CONF. Thtr 200 Class 200 Board 100
Credit Cards 1 2 3 5

BLAIR ATHOLL Tayside *Perthshire* Map 14 NN86

★★ 65% Tilt
Bridge of Tilt PH18 5SU ☎(0796) 481333
Closed Jan-Etr

An hospitable hotel at the southern end of the village, with a cosy dining room, a comfortable lounge and a bar where a log fire burns in winter. Most bedrooms are tastefully furnished, and practical accommodation is also offered in good-sized chalet rooms.

28⇨↑(8fb) CTV in all bedrooms ® T

Blair Atholl – Blakeney

40P ❋ ♪ gamesroom ♫
V ❀ ⊈ Last dinner 8.30pm
Credit Cards [1] [3]

★★ **63% Atholl Arms**
PH18 5SG (off B8079) ☎(0796) 481205 FAX (0796) 81550
This spacious, long-established hotel is at the northern end of the village close to the railway station. Popular with all types of holidaymakers, tour groups and sporting enthusiasts, it has ample lounges and bars and a baronial dining hall complete with minstrels' gallery. Bedrooms vary in size.
30⇨🏠(3fb) CTV in all bedrooms ® T sB&B⇨🏠£29.50-£39.50 dB&B⇨🏠£54-£66 ♬
100P 3🏠 ❋ ♪ rough shooting *xmas*
♀ International V ❀ ⊈ ✷ Lunch £7.25-£11.50 High tea £6.25-£7.50 Dinner £10-£15.50 Last dinner 9pm
CONF. Thtr 80 Class 80 Board 30 Del from £45
Credit Cards [1] [3]

BLAIRGOWRIE Tayside *Perthshire* Map 15 NO14

★★★❀❀❀ **78% Kinloch House**
PH10 6SG (3m W on A923) ☎Essendy(0250884) 237 FAX (0250884) 333
Closed 20-29 Dec
Clad in virginia creeper, this fine country house looks out across a paddock of Highland cattle towards Loch Maree, and David and Sarah Shentall provide the best of food and hospitality. The new wing bedrooms are delightful and have refurbished bathrooms, while the original rooms retain a more traditional character. The 4-course dinners feature the best of Scottish produce. Chef Bill McNicholl combines a light modern touch with some traditional recipes, such as potted hough, boiled shin beef in jelly made from the cooking liquid. Main courses may include loin of lamb topped with spinach, Parma ham and garlic, wrapped in pastry. There is a mouth-watering dessert trolley.
21⇨🏠(1fb)6🏠 CTV in all bedrooms ® T sB&B⇨🏠£74.95 dB&B⇨🏠£144.90 (incl dinner)
CTV 40P 🏠 ❋ ♪
V ❀ ⊈ ✷ Lunch £14.50 Dinner £23.90 Last dinner 9.15pm
Credit Cards [1] [2] [3] [4] [5]

★★❀ **66% Altamount House**
Coupar Angus Rd PH10 6JN ☎(0250) 873512 & 873814 FAX (0250) 876200
Closed 6 Jan-14 Feb
This well run Georgian country house is set in 6 acres of grounds and offers friendly service. Bedrooms are thoughtfully equipped and generally spacious, while public rooms include a cosy little bar, a spacious comfortable lounge and a conservatory dining room overlooking the gardens.
7⇨🏠(2fb) CTV in all bedrooms ® T sB&B⇨🏠fr£37.50 dB&B⇨🏠fr£70
40P 3🏠 ❋
❀ ⊈ Last dinner 9pm
Credit Cards [1] [3]

★★ **62% Angus**
46 Wellmeadow PH10 6NQ ☎(0250) 872455 FAX (0250) 875615
Evidently catering for the coach-tour market, this town-centre hotel offers bright, modern accommodation and a small leisure complex. Most of the bedrooms have been attractively upgraded, and simple, keenly priced dinners are available from a modest table d'hôte menu.
86⇨🏠(4fb) CTV in all bedrooms ® ✻ T ✷ sB&B⇨🏠£25-£35 dB&B⇨🏠£50-£70 ♬
Lift 60P ⊟ (heated) squash snooker sauna solarium spa bath *xmas*
♀ British & French V ❀ ⊈ Lunch £8-£12 High tea £4-£6 Dinner fr£13.25 Last dinner 8.30pm
CONF. Thtr 200 Class 60 Board 40 Del from £49
Credit Cards [1] [2] [3]

BLAKENEY Norfolk Map 09 TG04

★★★ **69% Blakeney**
The Quay NR25 7NE ☎Cley(0263) 740797 FAX (0263) 740795
In a lovely position on the quay overlooking the tidal estuary, which is busy with pleasure craft and small boats. The hotel is traditional in style, owners and staff are polite and professional, and bedrooms, graded by size and location, are thoughtfully laid out.
50⇨🏠 Annexe10⇨🏠(4fb)4🏠 CTV in all bedrooms ® T ✷ sB&B⇨🏠£49-£59 dB&B⇨🏠£98-£134 ♬
☾ 60P 🏠 ❋ ⊟ (heated) snooker sauna gymnasium table tennis pool ๙ *xmas*
♀ English & Continental V ❀ ⊈ ✂ ✷ Lunch £11.80&alc High tea fr£4 Dinner £15-£18.50&alc Last dinner 9.30pm
CONF. Thtr 200 Class 70 Board 50 Del from £79
Credit Cards [1] [2] [3] [5]

★★
★★❀❀❀ **MORSTON HALL**
Morston NR25 7AA (1m W of Blakeney on A149 Kings Lynn/Cromer Rd)
☎Cley(0263) 741041 FAX (0263) 741041
Closed Jan-Feb

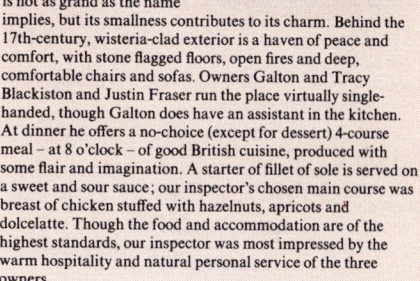

In terms of size Morston Hall is not as grand as the name implies, but its smallness contributes to its charm. Behind the 17th-century, wisteria-clad exterior is a haven of peace and comfort, with stone flagged floors, open fires and deep, comfortable chairs and sofas. Owners Galton and Tracy Blackiston and Justin Fraser run the place virtually single-handed, though Galton does have an assistant in the kitchen. At dinner he offers a no-choice (except for dessert) 4-course meal - at 8 o'clock - of good British cuisine, produced with some flair and imagination. A starter of fillet of sole is served on a sweet and sour sauce; our inspector's chosen main course was breast of chicken stuffed with hazelnuts, apricots and dolcelatte. Though the food and accommodation are of the highest standards, our inspector was most impressed by the warm hospitality and natural personal service of the three owners.
4⇨🏠 CTV in all bedrooms ® T sB&B⇨🏠£70-£80 dB&B⇨🏠£120-£130 (incl dinner) ♬
16P ❋ ๙ croquet *xmas*
V ❀ ⊈ ✂ Sunday Lunch £13 Dinner £21 Last dinner 8pm
Credit Cards [1] [2] [3]

★★ **62% Manor**
NR25 7ND (turn off A149 at St Mary's church)
☎Cley(0263) 740376 FAX (0263) 741116
Closed 7-28 Dec
The Manor House is on the edge of the village facing out over the saltings, and a short walk from the small quay. Within its flint walls you will find quite spacious public areas, the lounge being particularly comfortable, with deep, comfortable sofas and armchairs. The accommodation varies in size, but all have modern facilities.
8⇨🏠 Annexe29⇨🏠(2fb)1🏠 CTV in 36 bedrooms ® T ✷ sB&B⇨🏠£25-£33 dB&B⇨🏠£54-£78 ♬
60P ❋ bowling green nc10yrs
♀ English & Continental V ❀ ⊈ ✂ ✷ Bar Lunch £1.60-£5.40 Dinner fr£14.50&alc Last dinner 9pm

Blanchland - Blyth

BLANCHLAND Northumberland Map 12 NY95

★★ 🌹69% Lord Crewe Arms
DH8 9SP (10m S of Hexham) ☎Hexham(0434675) 251 FAX (0434675) 337
This historic inn dates back to medieval times and retains much of the charm of bygone days, with flagstone floors, original stonework and vaulted ceilings – and some badly worn carpeting! Bedrooms, half of which are in a separate house across the road, are sympathetically decorated and furnished, with many thoughtful extras. The lovely candlelit dining room is the setting for Ian Press' interesting menus, based on fresh local produce.
8⇌🚻Annexe10⇌🚻(2fb)1🛏 CTV in all bedrooms ® T sB&B⇌🚻£65-£78 dB&B⇌🚻£80-£105 🍴
🐾 ❋ xmas
V ☼ ♨ Sunday Lunch £14.50 Dinner £24-£27alc Last dinner 9.15pm
CONF. Thtr 30 Class 24 Board 18 Del from £72
Credit Cards [1][2][3][5] £

BLANDFORD FORUM Dorset Map 03 ST80

★★★ 66% Crown
8 West St DT11 7AJ ☎(0258) 456626 FAX (0258) 451084
Closed 25-28 Dec
Well managed and rather grand, the Crown stands on the edge of the town centre and provides a friendly atmosphere with courteous staff. Bedrooms are nicely furnished and practically equipped and spacious panelled public areas include a cosy bar, comfortable lounge and candlelit restaurant.
32⇌🚻(2fb)3🛏✱in 4 bedrooms CTV in all bedrooms ® ✷ T ✱
80P 4🚗 (£3) ❋ ♪ shooting
☼ English & French V ☼ ♨ ✱ Lunch £7.50-£11.50 Dinner £7.50-£11.50 Last dinner 9.15pm
Credit Cards [1][2][3][5] £

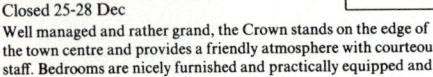

★★ 62% The Anvil Hotel & Restaurant
Salisbury Rd, Pimperne DT11 8UQ (main A354 Salisbury Rd, 2m out of Blandford on the way to Salisbury)
☎Blandford(0258) 453431 & 480182
The Anvil is a 16th-century, thatched cottage-style hotel with pretty pine furnished bedrooms. There is a cosy character restaurant, with a blazing open fire, and 2 smart modern bars. The lengthy, frequently changing menu is displayed on a blackboard, and an extensive range of bar meals is available.
9⇌🚻(1fb) CTV in all bedrooms ® T sB&B⇌🚻£40-£42.50 dB&B⇌🚻£60-£65 🍴
25P clay pigeon tuition ♫
V ☼ ♨ Lunch £10.75-£23alc Dinner £10.75-£23alc Last dinner 9.45pm
CONF. Thtr 15 Class 24 Board 12
Credit Cards [1][2][3][5] £

BLOCKLEY Gloucestershire Map 04 SP13

★★★ 64% Crown Inn
High St GL56 9EX ☎(0386) 700245 FAX (0386) 700247
This modernised 16th-century village inn retains much historic charm and offers friendly, helpful service. Bedrooms, though generally compact, are comfortable, with attractive soft furnishings and modern facilities. There are two restaurants and several cosy bar and lounge areas.
13⇌🚻Annexe8⇌🚻(2fb)2🛏 CTV in all bedrooms ® T ✱ sB&B⇌🚻fr£53 dB&B⇌🚻fr£78 🍴
50P xmas
☼ English & Continental V ☼ ♨ ✱ ✱ Sunday Lunch £13.95 Dinner £19.95 Last dinner 9.30pm
Credit Cards [1][2][3]

BLOXHAM Oxfordshire Map 04 SP43

★★ 61% Olde School
Church St OX15 4ET (3m from Banbury on A361)
☎Banbury(0295) 720369 FAX (0295) 721748
RS 1 Jan
A group of Cotswold stone buildings make up this hotel, with the restaurant, bar lounge and some bedrooms in the old school. Rooms in the other buildings are generally more spacious and are particularly well equipped. Bar meals are available in addition to the restaurant table d'hôte menu.
11⇌🚻Annexe27⇌🚻3🛏 CTV in all bedrooms ® T ✈ (ex guide dogs)
⦅ 100P squash games room
☼ English & French V ☼ ♨ ✱ Last dinner 10pm
Credit Cards [1][2][3][5]

BLUNDELLSANDS Merseyside Map 07 SJ39

★★★ 64% Blundellsands
The Serpentine L23 6TN (off the A565) (Whitbread)
☎051-924 6515 FAX 051-931 5364
This impressive Victorian hotel has a pleasant and relaxing ambience, enhanced by friendly and attentive service. Particularly noteworthy is the Mauretania Restaurant, styled after the transatlantic liner of the same name. The accommodation is modern and soundly maintained. Bedrooms vary in size but are identically furnished and equipped.
41⇌🚻(6fb)✱in 5 bedrooms CTV in all bedrooms ® ✷ T ✱ sB&B⇌🚻fr£59.50 dB&B⇌🚻fr£71 🍴
Lift ⦅ 250P
☼ English & French V ☼ ✱ ✱ Lunch fr£9.25 Dinner fr£13.45 Last dinner 9.30pm
CONF. Thtr 300 Class 120 Board 120 Del from £79
Credit Cards [1][2][3][5]

BLYTH Nottinghamshire Map 08 SK68

★★★ 64% Charnwood
Sheffield Rd S81 8HF ☎Worksop(0909) 591610 FAX (0909) 591429
A friendly welcome and polite service are appreciated by guests and locals at this hotel, set in its own established lawns and gardens. Public rooms include a small foyer lounge and a large, richly decorated lounge bar. The restaurant offers a comprehensive choice of dishes and bar snacks are available. Standard and superior bedrooms provide a mix of nicely furnished rooms with colour coordinated décor.
20⇌🚻(1fb) CTV in all bedrooms ® ✷ T ✈ (ex guide dogs)
70P ❋
☼ English & French V ☼ ♨ Last dinner 9.45pm
CONF. Thtr 80 Class 50 Board 26 Del from £69.50
Credit Cards [1][2][3][5]

Forte Travelodge
(on A1, southbound)
☎(0909) 591775 Central Res (0800) 850950

This modern building offers a good standard of accommodation for overnight stops. Smart, spacious and well equipped bedrooms, all with en suite bathrooms, are suitable for family use, and meals may be taken at the nearby family restaurant. For more details about Travelodges, consult the Contents page, under Hotel Groups.
32⇌🚻✱ B⇌🚻£31.95 (room only)

Granada Lodge
Hilltop Roundabout S81 8HG (junct. A1M/A614)
☎(0909) 591836 FAX (0909) 591831

Blyth - Bolton

This modern building provides smart, spacious and well equipped bedrooms, all with en suite bathrooms. Meals may be taken at a nearby family restaurant. For more details about Granada Lodges, consult the Contents page, under Hotel Groups.

39⇌♠※ B⇌♠£34.95-£37.25 (room only)

BOAT OF GARTEN Highland *Inverness-shire* Map 14 NH91

★★★ **64%** Boat
PH24 3BH ☎(047983) 258 FAX (047983) 414

Situated beside the Strathspey Steam Railway, this warmly welcoming family-run Highland hotel has a relaxed and friendly atmosphere, and day rooms are traditionally furnished and comfortable – the airy lounge being particularly appealing. Bedrooms vary in size and style, superior rooms having attractive coordinated soft furnishings and quality furniture.

32⇌♠(1fb) CTV in all bedrooms ®✎ T sB&B⇌♠£35-£42.50 dB&B⇌♠£70-£85 🍴
36P ❄ xmas
♀ Scottish, English & French V ♂ ♨ ✦ Lunch £10-£14 Dinner £19.50&alc Last dinner 9.30pm
CONF. Thtr 40 Class 20 Del from £55
Credit Cards 1 2 3 5

BODINNICK Cornwall & Isles of Scilly Map 02 SX15

★ ❀**69%** Old Ferry Inn
PL23 1LX ☎Polruan(0726) 870287
RS Nov-Feb

This charming inn is over 400 years old and has a cheerful and welcoming atmosphere. Many of the bedrooms have lovely views and those in the oldest part are particularly cosy, with fine old pieces of furniture. There are 2 lively bars with flagstone floors, and an elegant dining room where delicious meals are served. The menus are short and simple, but the good quality produce is local and fresh. There is a comfortable lounge with a log-burning fire, and a sun terrace.

12rm(7⇌1♠)(1fb)1🛏 CTV in 10 bedrooms ® sB&B⇌♠£27-£35 sB&B⇌♠£30-£35 dB&B£54-£64 dB&B⇌♠£64-£80 🍴
8P 2🚗 🐕
♀ English & French ♂ Bar Lunch £1.20-£5 Dinner £15-£25 Last dinner 8.15pm
Credit Cards 1 3

BODMIN Cornwall & Isles of Scilly Map 02 SX06

★★ **59%** Westberry
Rhind St PL31 2EL ☎(0208) 72772 FAX (0208) 72212
Closed 5 days Xmas/New Year

Situated near the centre of town, this modern, family-run hotel has a well furnished sun lounge and bar and a large dining room. Bedrooms are well equipped, but the ground floor annexe rooms are beginning to show their age. The à la carte menu offers a good selection of dishes including local seafood, and bar meals are popular at lunch time.

15rm(5⇌4♠)Annexe8⇌♠(3fb) CTV in 20 bedrooms ® T CTV 30P 🚗 snooker gymnasium
V ♂ ♨ Last dinner 8.45pm
Credit Cards 1 3 5

BOGNOR REGIS West Sussex Map 04 SZ99

★★★ **63%** The Inglenook
255 Pagham Rd, Nyetimber PO21 3QB
☎Pagham(0243) 262495 & 265411 FAX (0243) 262668

A 16th-century cottage hotel, skilfully extended to provide cosy public areas and particularly good bedrooms, with a wide range of facilities. In addition to the beamed bar with its log fires, there is a small lounge and a restaurant which features local seafood, fresh lobster and crab.

18⇌♠(1fb)1🛏 CTV in all bedrooms ® T sB&B⇌♠£35-£50 dB&B⇌♠£60-£80 🍴
CTV 35P ❄ xmas
V ♂ ♨ Lunch fr£9.95&alc Dinner fr£12.95&alc Last dinner 10pm
CONF. Thtr 100 Class 50 Board 50 Del from £60
Credit Cards 1 2 3 5

★ **67%** Black Mill House
Princess Av, Aldwick PO21 2QU (at rbt junct with A259/A29 take Victoria Drive, signed Aldwick. At traffic liggths turn rt into Aldwick Road) ☎(0243) 821945 & 865596
FAX (0243) 821316

This well established family-run hotel is situated in a peaceful spot on the west side of the town, but is close to the sea. Bedrooms are simply furnished, freshly decorated and offer most modern facilities. There is a choice of 2 cosy lounges, a small bar and a games room.

22rm(18⇌♠)Annexe4rm(2fb) CTV in all bedrooms ® T ❄ sB&B⇌♠£27-£31 sB&B⇌♠£32-£38.50 dB&B£46-£56 dB&B⇌♠£54-£68 🍴
Lift CTV 13P 🚗 table tennis putting ♣ xmas
♀ English & French V ♂ ♨ ❄ Lunch £7.95 High tea fr£5 Dinner £10.95 Last dinner 8pm
CONF. Thtr 55 Del from £34
Credit Cards 1 2 3 5

BOLDON Tyne & Wear Map 12 NZ36

★★★ **65%** Friendly
Witney Way, Boldon Business Park NE35 9PE (junct A19/A184) ☎091-519 1999 FAX 091-519 0655

The Friendly Hotel is a modern, low rise building on the industrial estate. Bedrooms are well equipped and similar in style, though premier plus rooms have some extra facilities. Public areas are comfortable and staff live up to the hotel's name.

84⇌♠(12fb)1🛏 ♨ in 25 bedrooms CTV in all bedrooms ®✎ T ❄ sB⇌♠£55-£67 dB⇌♠£69.50-£82 (room only) 🍴
☾ 150P 🎱 (heated) sauna solarium gymnasium jacuzzi
♀ English & French V ♂ ♨ ❄ Lunch £8.25&alc High tea £1.30-£5.95 Dinner £12.50&alc Last dinner 9.45pm
CONF. Thtr 200 Class 100 Board 75 Del from £80
Credit Cards 1 2 3 5

See advertisement on page 105

BOLTON Greater Manchester Map 07 SD70

★★★★ **59%** Georgian House
Manchester Rd, Blackrod BL6 5RU (on A6, 1m from junct 6 of M61. Follow signs for Blackrod) ☎Manchester(0942) 814598 FAX (0942) 813427
RS Xmas Day & New Years Day

Modern bedroom wings, a large leisure centre and conference facilities have been added to this attractive Georgian house with superb views of the surrounding countryside. Bedrooms are functionally modern, some in executive style. Public areas are busy, particularly the Cascades Bar with its mini waterfalls, where light snacks are available. There is also a small quiet lounge, a comfortable lounge bar and the Regency restaurant.

101⇌♠(6fb)3🛏 ♨ in 6 bedrooms CTV in all bedrooms ® T sB&B⇌♠£54-£78 dB&B⇌♠£78-£91.50 🍴
Lift ☾ CTV 250P 🚗 🎱 (heated) snooker sauna solarium gymnasium beauty therapy steam room jacuzzi ♫ ♣ xmas
♀ English & French V ♂ ♨ ❄ Lunch £9.60-£10.50&alc Dinner £15.50&alc Last dinner 10pm
CONF. Del from £72
Credit Cards 1 2 3 4 5

See advertisement on page 105

Bolton - Borehamwood

★★★ 72% Bolton Moat House
1 Higher Bridge St BL1 2EW ☎(0204) 383378
FAX (0204) 380777

This striking modern hotel, which is now a town landmark, has excellent leisure, conference and dining facilites including the attractive Cloisters restaurant, converted from a church. Bedrooms are furnished and equipped to a very high standard, with family rooms and facilities for the disabled.
128⇨♠(2fb)⌿in 32 bedrooms CTV in all bedrooms ® ⚔ T
✈ (ex guide dogs) sB&B⇨♠£65-£83 dB&B⇨♠£79-£99 ₽
Lift ℭ 30P 43🅿 ⊟ (heated) sauna solarium gymnasium jacuzzi ♪
V ♿ & ⌿ Lunch £8.76-£11.75 Dinner £14.25-£22.50&alc Last dinner 9.30pm
CONF. Thtr 370 Class 120 Board 60 Del from £80
Credit Cards [1][2][3][5] £

★★★ 65% Egerton House
Blackburn Rd, Egerton BL7 9PL (3m N A666)
☎(0204) 307171 FAX (0204) 593030

Quietly situated in 4 acres of grounds, this converted 18th-century residence retains some of its original character while providing bedrooms with modern comforts and facilities. Public areas include two cosy lounges, one with a bar, and a small restaurant overlooking the gardens.
32⇨♠(8fb)⌿in 7 bedrooms CTV in all bedrooms ® T
✈ (ex guide dogs) ✱ sB&B⇨♠£50-£74 dB&B⇨♠£70-£89 ₽
ℭ CTV 100P ❋
♿ English & French V ♿ & ✱ Lunch £9.95&alc Dinner £22-£30alc Last dinner 9.30pm
CONF. Thtr 150 Class 90 Board 64 Del from £85
Credit Cards [1][2][3][5]

★★★ 64% Last Drop
The Last Drop Village, Bromley Cross BL7 9PZ
(3m N off B6472) ☎(0204) 591131 FAX (0204) 304122

This hotel, together with a pub, bakery and other shops, is part of the popular 'living village' created from derelict old farm buildings on moorland high above the town at Bromley Cross, and now a popular tourist attraction. The well equipped bedrooms are located throughout the village, and there is a comfortable cocktail bar and attractive restaurant.
76⇨♠Annexe7⇨♠(27fb)3⌸⌿in 15 bedrooms CTV in all bedrooms ®⚔ T ✱
ℭ 400P ❋ ⊟ (heated) squash snooker sauna solarium gymnasium craft shops & galleries ♪
♿ English & French V ♿ & Last dinner 10pm
Credit Cards [1][2][3][5]

★★★ 60% Pack Horse
Bradshawgate, Nelson Square BL1 1DP ☎(0204) 27261 FAX (0204) 364152

Overlooking a small tree-lined square, this Georgian fronted town-centre hotel has well proportioned public areas including a choice of bars. Bedrooms have all the usual modern facilities but are generally rather compact, and some were in need of refurbishment at the time of our latest inspection. Guests may use an adjacent public car park free of charge during the week.
72⇨♠(4fb)⌿in 13 bedrooms CTV in all bedrooms ®⚔ T ✱
sB&B⇨♠£30-£40 dB&B⇨♠£45-£60 ₽
Lift ℭ 🅿
♿ English & Continental V ♿ & ✱ Bar Lunch £3.50-£7.50 Dinner fr£13&alc Last dinner 9.45pm
CONF. Thtr 275 Class 110 Board 60 Del from £65
Credit Cards [1][2][3][5] £

Forte Posthouse
Beaumont Rd BL3 4TA (on A58 W of town)
☎(0204) 651511 FAX (0204) 61064

Suitable for both the business and leisure traveller, this bright hotel provides modern accommodation in well equipped bedrooms with en suite bathrooms. For more details about Forte Posthouse hotels, consult the Contents page, under Hotel Groups.
96⇨♠ ✱ B⇨♠£41.50-£53.50 (room only)
CONF. Thtr 120 Class 90

BOLTON ABBEY North Yorkshire Map 07 SE05

★★★ ❀ 79% Devonshire Arms Country House
BD23 6AJ (on A59 at junct with B6160)
☎(0756) 710441 FAX (0756) 710564

This one-time coaching inn in beautiful Wharfedale has been very carefully restored and extended in recent years under the personal supervision of the Duchess of Devonshire. Bedrooms are very well furnished, and all are of a very high standard, though those in the old building have most character. The lounges are sumptuously comfortable, with lovely paintings, objets d'art and antiques. The elegant Burlington Restaurant, incorporating a Georgian-style conservatory, offers a fine standard of cuisine with a variety of classical and modern dishes
40⇨♠⚛⌿in 7 bedrooms CTV in all bedrooms ® T
sB&B⇨♠£95-£110 dB&B⇨♠£125-£140 ₽
ℭ CTV 150P ❋ ♪ clay pigeon shooting ballooning ♞ xmas
♿ English & French V ♿ & Lunch £16.95&alc Dinner £28.50&alc Last dinner 10pm
CONF. Thtr 150 Class 80 Board 40 Del from £120
Credit Cards [1][2][3][5] £

BONCHURCH
See Wight, Isle of

BONTDDU Gwynedd Map 06 SH61

★★★ ❀ 68% Bontddu Hall
LL40 2SU (on A496) ☎(034149) 661 FAX (034149) 284
Closed Nov-Etr

Standing in 14 acres of wooded grounds and beautiful landscaped gardens, this very impressive 18th-century house has superb views across the Mawddach Estuary to the Cader Idris Mountains. The bedrooms are individual in style and well equipped. Public rooms are spacious, attractive and comfortable and include two quiet and relaxing lounges.
15⇨♠Annexe4⇨♠(6fb)1⌸ CTV in all bedrooms ® T
sB&B⇨♠£52.50-£62.50 dB&B⇨♠£90-£115 ₽
50P ♿ nc3yrs
♿ British & French V ♿ & Lunch £11.75-£12.75 Dinner £23.50-£25.50 Last dinner 9.30pm
Credit Cards [1][2][3][5] £

BOREHAMWOOD Greater London Map 04 TQ19

★★★★ 65% Elstree Moat House
Barnet Bypass WD6 5PU (2m from junct 23 of M25) ☎081-953 1622 FAX 081-207 3194

This modern hotel was much extended recently, and the garden wing rooms were also refurbished, but those in the new wing are more spacious and comfortable. Public areas are elegant and stylish with warm maple wood panelling throughout the smart foyer lounge areas with marble flooring. There is a small cocktail bar adjoining the Gainsbrough restaurant, which offers a popular menu. Reels café bar is open all day and takes its theme from the local film studios.

Hotels with red star ratings are especially high quality.

A BREATH OF FRESH AIR

Escape to the Devonshire for a real change of scene and air...

An Air of Calm - relax at The Devonshire - inside and out.

Outside, there are: acres of parkland; the Dales; and a host of places to visit nearby.

Inside, there are: spacious bedrooms; stylish bars; cosy lounges; and the excellent Burlington Restaurant.

A Breath of Romance - The Devonshire's "Stay Romantic" breaks, are the perfect way to say "I love you", whatever the occasion.

A Wind of Change - Getaway breaks and our other special breaks, ranging from Golfing to Helicopter Tours are ideal ways to sample The Devonshire's very special atmosphere.

★★★

The Devonshire Arms
COUNTY HOUSE HOTEL

Bolton Abbey, Skipton, North Yorkshire. BD23 6AJ
Tel: 0756 710441. Fax: 0756 710564

BOLDON
For business or pleasure stay friendly

Friendly Hotel, Junction A19/A184, Witney Way,
Boldon, Tyne & Wear NE35 9PE.

AA ★★★

Premier Plus Rooms. Own hotel parking. Superb leisure centre. This purpose-built hotel is perfectly situated at the junction of the A19/A184 for easy access to the North-East on business or pleasure.

FOR RESERVATIONS (office hours) FREEPHONE
0800 591910
or call direct on 091-519 1999 Fax: 091-519 0655

It pays to stay Friendly

*F*OR MANY, the Georgian House Hotel is the essence of good taste — With a magnificent Georgian building dating back to the 1700s as its centrepiece the hotel has been added to with great thoughtfulness to provide 101 beautifully appointed bedrooms — As independent confirmation of its status the Georgian House Hotel has just been awarded the prestigious AA 4 star rating — Whether for private or business use the Georgian House Hotel measures its success solely in terms of its guests level of satisfaction.

AA ★★★★

WHY YOU SHOULD CHOOSE THE GEORGIAN HOUSE

- Only 1½ miles from Junction 6 on the M61 motorway ● 101 deluxe bedrooms
- Extensive conference facilities for up to 300 delegates
- Purpose built training rooms ● Luxurious leisure facilities ● Our renowned à la carte restaurant
- Competitive daily and residential conference packages

NOT JUST ANOTHER LINK IN A CHAIN
Manchester Road, Blackrod, Bolton. Telephone: 0942 814598 Facsimile: 0942 813427.

Borehamwood - Boston

130⇨🛏(5fb)✠in 14 bedrooms CTV in all bedrooms ® 🅿 T ✈ (ex guide dogs) ❋ sB&B⇨🛏£94 dB&B⇨🛏£117 🍴
Lift ℂ 250P ✿ 🅿 (heated) sauna solarium gymnasium spa bath steam room *xmas*
♨ English & French V ✿ ♨ ✠ ❋ Lunch £12&alc Dinner £17&alc Last dinner 10pm
Credit Cards [1][2][3][5]

BOROUGHBRIDGE North Yorkshire Map 08 SE36

★★★ 66% Crown
Horsefair YO5 9LB (at T junction in town centre)
☎Harrogate(0423) 322328 FAX (0423) 324512
This historic town centre hotel was one of the largest and most comfortable coaching inns on the London-Edinburgh route during the 18th and 19th centuries. Several bedrooms as well as the recently modernised public areas retain much of their original character, those in the older part of the building having some antique furnishings.
41⇨🛏(2fb) CTV in all bedrooms ® 🅿 T ❋ sB⇨🛏£49.50-£59.50 dB⇨🛏£49.50-£59.50 (room only) 🍴
Lift ℂ ⊞ CTV 60P
V ✿ ♨ ❋ Lunch £9.95 Dinner £12.95&alc Last dinner 9.15pm
CONF. Thtr 150 Class 50 Board 50 Del £75
Credit Cards [1][2][3][5] £

★★★ 64% Rose Manor
Horsefair YO5 9LL ☎Harrogate(0423) 322245 FAX (0423) 324920
Set in mature grounds and gardens, this hotel has been almost totally refurbished in recent years and provides a high standard of accommodation. The lounge is particularly elegant.
17⇨🛏(1fb) CTV in all bedrooms ® T ❋ sB⇨🛏£59 dB⇨🛏£69.50-£78 (room only) 🍴
100P ✿ *xmas*
V ✿ ♨ ❋ Lunch fr£9.50 Dinner £16.50 Last dinner 9pm
CONF. Thtr 200 Class 80 Board 80 Del £75
Credit Cards [1][2][3][5] £

BORROWDALE Cumbria Map 11 NY21
See also **Keswick** & **Rosthwaite**

★★★ ❀ 71% Borrowdale Gates Country House
CA12 5UQ (from Keswick follow Borrowdale signs on B5289, after approx 4m turn right at sign for Grange, hotel is on right approx 0.25m through village) ☎(07687) 77204 FAX (07687) 77254
This delightful country house is set in 2 acres of wooded gardens in the beautiful Borrowdale Valley. Recent upgrading has considerably enhanced the hotel and many of its individually styled bedrooms. There are several cosy lounges, some with open fires, beams and horse brasses. The semi open plan restaurant offers wide views, and Terence Parkinson's 4-course dinners provide a high standard of cooking and very good value for money.
23⇨🛏(2fb) CTV in all bedrooms ® T ✈ (ex guide dogs) ❋ sB&B⇨🛏£51-£65.50 dB&B⇨🛏£94-£124 (incl dinner) 🍴
35P ✿ 🅿 *xmas*
♨ English & French ✿ ♨ ✠ Sunday Lunch £11.75 Dinner £19.50 Last dinner 8.45pm
Credit Cards [1][3]

★★★ 67% Borrowdale
CA12 5UY (on B5289 at south end of Lake Derwentwater)
☎(07687) 77224 FAX (07687) 77338
Closed Jan
In a beautiful Lakeland setting, with pleasant gardens, this delightful former coaching inn provides modern bedrooms with good facilities. There are 2 lounges, both with log fires in wintertime. A well prepared 6-course dinner is served each evening in the traditional-style restaurant, and staff are exceedingly helpful and friendly.

34⇨🛏(8fb)6☒ CTV in all bedrooms ® T ❋ sB&B⇨🛏£41-£62 dB&B⇨🛏£72-£124 (incl dinner) 🍴
100P 🚗 ✿ *xmas*
♨ English & Continental V ✿ ♨ ❋ Lunch £1.95-£8.60alc Dinner £14.90-£17.90alc Last dinner 9.15pm
Credit Cards [1][3]

BOSCASTLE Cornwall & Isles of Scilly Map 02 SX09

★★ 64% The Wellington Hotel
The Harbour PL35 0AQ ☎(0840) 250202 FAX (0840) 250621
Closed 30 Dec-11 Feb (ex Xmas/New Year)
The 'Welly', as it is affectionately known, is steeped in history, parts dating back over 400 years. There is a choice of well equipped bedrooms, some of which are in the tower. French cuisine is accompanied by a wine list which includes several wines from the owner's vineyard (Madiran, in southwest France). Bar meals are also available. Ten acres of natural cliff and wooded hillside provide for enjoyable walks.
21rm(10⇨🛏6🛏)1☒ CTV in all bedrooms ® T sB&B£18-£22 sB&B⇨🛏£26-£31 dB&B⇨🛏£52-£61 🍴
20P ✿ games room pool ♫ nc 7yrs *xmas*
♨ French & German V ✿ ♨ ❋ Bar Lunch £1.69-£11.50alc Dinner £11.50-£15.60 Last dinner 9.30pm
Credit Cards [1][2][3][5] £

BOSHAM West Sussex Map 04 SU80

★★★ ❀ 68% The Millstream
BEST WESTERN HOTELS
Bosham Ln PO18 8HL (4m W of Chichester on A259, turn left at Bosham roundabout, 1m turn right at T junction follow signs to church & quay hotel 0.5m on right)
☎(0243) 573234 FAX (0243) 573459
In a picturesque fishing village, this house dates from 1701 and offers attractive and individually furnished bedrooms with a good range of equipment. Chef Ben Boakes' modern style of cooking is reflected in the daily fixed price seasonal menu, using good quality fresh produce and well made, classically based sauces. Service is friendly and attentive, including some room service.
29⇨🛏(2fb)1☒ CTV in all bedrooms ® T sB&B⇨🛏£59-£69 dB&B⇨🛏£89-£109 🍴
ℂ CTV 40P ✿ *xmas*
♨ English & French V ✿ ♨ ✠ Lunch £10.50-£11.50 High tea £5-£8 Dinner £16.95-£17.95 Last dinner 9.30pm
CONF. Thtr 35 Class 20 Board 23 Del from £99
Credit Cards [1][2][3][5]

BOSTON Lincolnshire Map 08 TF34

★★ 59% New England
FORTE Heritage
49 Wide Bargate PE21 6SH ☎(0205) 365255 FAX (0205) 310597
Polite and friendly staff and a relaxed informal atmosphere are the strengths of this company-owned town centre hotel.
25⇨🛏(1fb)✠in 5 bedrooms CTV in all bedrooms ® T ❋ sB&B⇨🛏fr£45 dB&B⇨🛏fr£60 🍴
ℂ 🅿 *xmas*
♨ Mainly grills V ✿ ♨ ✠ ❋ Lunch £8.50 Dinner £14.95 Last dinner 9pm
CONF. Thtr 36 Class 20 Board 20 Del £75
Credit Cards [1][2][3][5]

Rosettes range from 5 for outstanding cuisine to 1 rosette for enjoyable, well prepared food

Bothwell - Bournemouth

BOTHWELL Strathclyde *Lanarkshire* Map 11 NS75

★★★ 60% *Bothwell Bridge*
89 Main St G71 8LN ☎(0698) 852246 FAX (0698) 854686
Popular for weddings and functions, this business hotel has evolved from a Victorian mansion. Bedrooms are well equipped, the better ones in 2 extension wings where some are particularly large. When the function room is in use, bedrooms in the newest wing are reached by outside access only. Guests should be informed of this, but if in doubt enquire when booking.
76⇌🅟(5fb)1🕮✁in 10 bedrooms CTV in all bedrooms ®✎
🐾 (ex guide dogs)
Lift (110P ❀ ♫
♥ Continental V ♥ Last dinner 10.45pm
Credit Cards 1 2 3 5

★★ 62% *Silvertrees*
Silverwells Crescent G71 8DP ☎(0698) 852311
This business and function hotel has 2 annexes, a detached Victorian house and a former coach house, both in the grounds of the main building, a period mansion with an ornate foyer ceiling and fine staircase.
7⇌🅟Annexe19⇌🅟(1fb)1🕮 CTV in all bedrooms ®✎ T
100P 🚗 ❀ ⚙
V ♥ Last dinner 8.45pm
Credit Cards 1 2 3 5

BOTLEY Hampshire Map 04 SU51

★★★★ 71% *Botley Park Hotel & Country Club*
Winchester Rd, Boorley Green SO3 2UA
(Boorley Green on B3354)
☎(0489) 780888 FAX (0489) 789242

Opened 4 years ago, this modern and well designed country club hotel continues to exceed every expectation, with an excellent range of leisure facilities. There is a choice of comfortable bedrooms and suites, all with mini bars and generous bathrooms. Eating options include Plus Fours Restaurant, open all day, and the more formal Winchester Restaurant. There are good facilities for disabled guests.
100⇌🅟✁in 17 bedrooms CTV in all bedrooms ®✎ T ✱
sB&B⇌🅟£64.50-£79.50 dB&B⇌🅟£79.50-£94.50 🍴
(CTV 250P ❀ ▣ (heated) ▶ 18 ♣ (hard) squash snooker sauna solarium gymnasium croquet petanque hairdressing salon ♫ xmas
♥ English & French V ♥ ⚔ ✁ ✱ Lunch £11.95-£13.25&alc Dinner £17.95&alc Last dinner 10pm
Credit Cards 1 2 3 5 £

BOURNE Lincolnshire Map 08 TF02

★★ 56% *Angel*
Market Place PE10 9AE (in town centre) ☎(0778) 422346 FAX (0778) 393990
This busy town centre inn attracts a lively local trade to its public bar, but it also has a simply furnished restaurant and smaller, quieter bar. Accommodation is equipped to meet the needs of commercial users.
14⇌🅟(1fb)2🕮 CTV in all bedrooms ® T 🐾 (ex guide dogs)
✱ sB&B⇌🅟£22-£38.50 dB&B⇌🅟£38-£54 🍴
♫
♥ English & French V ♥ ⚔ ✱ Lunch £4.50-£10.50 Dinner £10.50&alc Last dinner 9.30pm
CONF. Thtr 100 Class 30 Board 40 Del from £48
Credit Cards 1 2 3

The AA's star rating scheme is the market leader in hotel classification.

BOURNEMOUTH Dorset Map 04 SZ09
See also **Christchurch** & **Poole**

★★★★★ ✿62% *Royal Bath*
Bath Rd BH1 2EW ☎(0202) 555555 FAX (0202) 554158

This attractive old hotel offers bedrooms in a range of sizes. The majority are spacious but a few are very compact. Occupying a fine position, high on the cliffs overlooking the sea, the hotel has much to offer, especially for families in the summer, though it must be said that the conference trade can be somewhat overbearing to the private guest. Oscar's Restaurant is an attractive place to dine. Chefs Wayne Asson and Steve Brademar offer both table d'hôte and à la carte menus, including some ambitious and elaborate nouvelle cuisine.
131⇌🅟2🕮 CTV in all bedrooms ® T 🐾 (ex guide dogs) ✱
sB&B⇌🅟£91.50-£105 dB&B⇌🅟£140-£280 🍴
Lift (120🅟 (£3.50 per day) ❀ ▣ (heated) sauna solarium gymnasium beauty salon putting green croquet xmas
♥ English & French V ♥ ⚔ ✱ Lunch £16.50
Credit Cards 1 2 3 4 5

★★★★ ✿69% *Norfolk Royale*
Richmond Hill BH2 6EN ☎(0202) 551521 FAX (0202) 299729
The holiday choice of the Duke of Norfolk during the 30s, this hotel has been well restored to its Edwardian grandeur. The bedrooms are stylish and attractive, with extras such as bathrobes, toiletries and a well stocked drinks bar. There is an open-plan foyer lounge, complete with grand piano, as well as a cosy 'club bar' and the airy conservatory-style Orangery restaurant. Service is friendly and professional, and contributes to the warm, relaxed atmosphere.

⇒→

CROWN HOTEL
Boroughbridge
★★★

A traditional English coaching inn with style and comfort

A privately owned 42 bedroomed hotel with a unique history, style and ambience. Centrally situated in the bustling North Yorkshire country town of Boroughbridge. An ideal base for touring the Dales, shopping or entertainment in York or Harrogate, a visit to one of the nearby local racecourses or the rugged east coast. Many reminders of the past including the manor house walls and fireplaces, all tastefully combined in modern style and comfort. A wide variety of meals available throughout the day. Facilities for business meetings and a large private car park are available.

**The Crown Hotel, Horsefair,
Boroughbridge, N Yorkshire YO5 9LB
Telephone: 0423 322328
Fax: 0423 324512**

107

Bournemouth

95➪ ↑ (9fb) ⊬ in 14 bedrooms CTV in all bedrooms ® ⅋ T ✻ (ex guide dogs) ✱ sB➪↑£65-£95 dB➪↑£90-£350 (room only) ➡
Lift ⓒ 85☂ ✿ ▨ (heated) sauna steamroom whirlpool ♪ xmas
♀ English & French V ♢ ⚓ ⊬ Lunch £8.50-£9.95 High tea £5.50 Dinner £18 Last dinner 10.30pm
CONF. Thtr 80 Class 40 Board 40 Del from £85
Credit Cards 1 2 3 4 5 £

★★★★ 61% **Swallow Highcliff**
St Michaels Rd, West Cliff BH2 5DU
☎(0202) 557702 FAX (0202) 292734

On the cliff top overlooking the bay, this hotel is convenient for the BIC, theatres and the town centre. The bedrooms are smart and well equipped, and the public areas are about to be refurbished. The restaurant offers both table d'hôte and à la carte menus, and the Plantation offers American food – mainly Cajun style.
107➪↑Annexe50➪↑(37fb) CTV in all bedrooms ® ⅋ T sB&B➪↑£82 dB&B➪↑£115 ➡
Lift ⓒ 130P ✿ ≋ (heated) ℘ (hard) snooker sauna solarium croquet putting ♪ ♔ xmas
♀ English & French V ♢ ⚓ ⊬ Lunch £11.75-£30&alc High tea £1.40-£5.50alc Dinner £15.95&alc Last dinner 9pm
CONF. Thtr 500 Class 250 Board 900 Del £107
Credit Cards 1 2 3 5 £

★★★ 70% **Chine**
Boscombe Spa Rd BH5 1AX ☎(0202) 396234 FAX (0202) 391737

In an enviable corner position close to Boscombe Pier, this hotel offers smart bedrooms, most of which have been refurbished. Many rooms have sea views, and public areas are traditional in style, comfortable and spacious. A daily changing table d'hôte menu is available, with dishes carefully prepared from high quality produce. Management and staff are charming and helpful.
97➪↑(20fb) CTV in all bedrooms ® ⅋ T ✻ (ex guide dogs) sB&B➪↑£45-£55 dB&B➪↑£80-£110 ➡
Lift ⓒ 50P 4☂ ✿ ▨ (heated) ≋ (heated) sauna solarium gymnasium games room ♔ xmas
♀ English & French V ♢ ⚓ Lunch £11&alc High tea £3-£10 Dinner £16&alc Last dinner 8.30pm
CONF. Thtr 150 Class 50 Board 50 Del from £75
Credit Cards 1 2 3 5 £

★★★ 70% **The Connaught**
West Hill Rd, West Cliff BH2 5PH ☎(0202) 298020 FAX (0202) 298028

This smart, privately owned hotel is convenient for the BIC, shopping areas and pier. It is well furnished and stylishly decorated throughout, and 2 of the bedrooms have water beds. In addition to the attractive lounges and bar areas, there is a dining room offering a varied menu.
60➪↑(15fb)1₦⊬in 12 bedrooms CTV in all bedrooms ® ⅋ T sB&B➪↑£40-£56 dB&B➪↑£80-£112 ➡
Lift ⓒ 45P ✿ ▨ (heated) ≋ (heated) snooker sauna solarium gymnasium pool table steam bath jacuzzi ♪ ♗ xmas
♀ English, French, Italian & Oriental V ♢ ⚓ Lunch £7.95&alc High tea £1.75-£3.25 Dinner £11.95-£18.50&alc Last dinner 10pm
CONF. Thtr 250 Class 120 Board 80 Del from £55
Credit Cards 1 2 3 5 £

★★★ 69% **East Anglia**
6 Poole Rd BH2 5OX ☎(0202) 765103 FAX (0202) 752949

Celebrating 40 years under the same family ownership in 1993, the East Anglia remains a popular hotel with both business and leisure guests. Just away from Westcliff, it is convenient for many of the town's attractions. Refurbishment continues, and in recent months some bedrooms have been upgraded and the lounge furniture has been renewed. Public areas are nicely appointed and guests are warmly welcomed and well cared for during their stay.

49➪↑Annexe24➪↑(12fb) CTV in all bedrooms ® ⅋ T ✻ (ex guide dogs) sB&B➪↑£35-£38.50 dB&B➪↑£70-£77 ➡
Lift ⓒ 73P ≋ (heated) sauna solarium gymnasium jacuzzi games room xmas
♀ English & French ♢ ⚓ ⊬ Sunday Lunch fr£8 Dinner fr£15.50 Last dinner 8.30pm
CONF. Thtr 150 Class 75 Board 60 Del from £55
Credit Cards 1 2 3 5 £

★★★ ❀69% **Langtry Manor**
26 Derby Rd, East Cliff BH1 3QB ☎(0202) 553887 FAX (0202) 290115

The Lillie Langtry and Edward VII theme runs strongly throughout this hotel: some of the suites are magnificent, including the King's Suite, a large oak panelled room with a huge 4-poster bed. Public rooms have a warm, friendly atmosphere, and in the high-ceilinged dining room guests choose from a varied table d'hôte menu or a short 'carte'. Chef Christian Lemmer's enjoyable meals are based on fresh, quality produce, and on Saturday evenings there is a 6-course Edwardian banquet.
14➪↑Annexe13➪↑(6fb)8♨⊬in 2 bedrooms CTV in all bedrooms ® T ✻ sB&B➪↑£59.50-£79.50 dB&B➪↑£79-£169 ➡
30P ✿ ♔ xmas
♀ International V ♢ ⚓ ⊬ ✱ Dinner fr£19.75 Last dinner 9pm
Credit Cards 1 2 3 5

★★★ 68% **Hotel Courtlands**
16 Boscombe Spa Rd, East Cliff BH5 1BB
☎(0202) 302442 FAX (0202) 309880

This friendly and cheerful hotel is located in a quiet residential area close to Boscombe's beaches, and is a popular choice with holidaymakers and business guests. Bedrooms are modern and nicely furnished, and a few of them have balconies. Public areas are extensive, with traditional-style lounges and a panelled dining room overlooking the garden and outdoor pool. A fine table d'hôte menu of enjoyable dishes is offered, with some à la carte choices.
60➪↑(15fb) CTV in all bedrooms ® ⅋ T sB&B➪↑£41.90-£44 dB&B➪↑£74-£78 ➡
Lift ⓒ 50P ♨ ≋ (heated) sauna solarium spa bath xmas
♀ English & French V ♢ ⚓ ⊬ ✱ Sunday Lunch £7.25-£7.50 Dinner £14.30-£14.45 Last dinner 8.30pm
Credit Cards 1 2 3 5

★★★ ❀68% **Piccadilly**
Bath Rd BH1 2NN ☎(0202) 552559 FAX (0202) 298235

Centrally located, this popular hotel provides good value for money and an enjoyable stay under the management of proprietors Mr and Mrs Cowie. Public areas are spacious, and bedrooms, though they vary in size, are smart and nicely equipped. Fountains restaurant is particularly pretty and offers a daily changing, small choice set menu, a short 'carte' and a well balanced wine list.
45➪↑(2fb)1♨ CTV in all bedrooms ® ⅋ T ✻ (ex guide dogs) sB&B➪↑£26-£42 dB&B➪↑£52-£64 ➡
Lift ⓒ 30P xmas
♀ English & French V ♢ Sunday Lunch £7.95 Dinner £14.95&alc Last dinner 9pm
CONF. Thtr 100 Class 60 Board 40 Del from £62
Credit Cards 1 2 3 5 £

★★★ 67% **Bay View Court**
35 East Overcliff Dr BH1 3AH ☎(0202) 294449 FAX (0202) 292583

The hotel stands in its own grounds close to the esplanade on the East Cliff. All the bedrooms are furnished to a good, modern standard and there is a choice of lounges and a pretty restaurant below ground-floor level with lift access. Bay View Court is personally run by the cheerful and welcoming Cox family.
64➪↑(11fb) CTV in all bedrooms ® ⅋ T ✻ sB&B➪↑£36-£43 dB&B➪↑£72-£86 (incl dinner) ➡
Lift ⓒ 58P ≋ (heated) snooker spa bath pool table ♪ xmas

Bournemouth

♥ International V ♦ ♨ ✂ Sunday Lunch £6.50 Dinner £16 Last dinner 8.30pm
CONF. Thtr 170 Class 85 Board 50 Del from £36
Credit Cards [1][2][3][5] (£)

★★★ **67%** Cadogan
8 Poole Rd BH2 5QU (Half mile from spur road and by-pass. Follow signs B.I.C. from by-pass them right at rbt into Poole Road) ☎(0202) 763006 FAX (0202) 766168
Close to the BIC and Alum Chine, this smart and friendly modern hotel has much to commend it. Bedrooms have good facilities, some front-facing rooms have balconies, and public areas are cosy and well furnished if rather limited. The pretty Opal Restaurant offers a table d'hôte menu which is varied and reasonably priced.
54⇌♠(3fb)2🚪 CTV in all bedrooms ® ⚲ T sB&B⇌♠fr£40 dB&B⇌♠fr£60 🅿
Lift (55P ✿ ♪ xmas
♥ English & French V ♦ ♨ ✂ ✱ Lunch fr£5.50 Dinner fr£13.50 Last dinner 8.45pm
CONF. Thtr 50 Class 40 Board 40 Del from £55
Credit Cards [1][2][3][5] (£)

★★★ **67%** Elstead
12-14 Knyveton Rd BH1 3QP ☎(0202) 293071 FAX (0202) 293827
Closed Oct-Mar (ex weekends)
This well managed hotel on a quiet tree-lined avenue on the East Cliff side of town has attractive bedrooms equipped with modern facilities and comfortable public areas.
51rm(39⇌11♠)(4fb)✂ in 5 bedrooms CTV in all bedrooms ® T
Lift (32P snooker ♪
V ♦ ♨ Last dinner 8.30pm
Credit Cards [1][3]

★★★ **65%** Queens
Meyrick Rd, East Cliff BH1 3DL ☎(0202) 554415 FAX (0202) 294810
Just away from the bustling promenade on the Eastcliff, this family-run hotel is popular with both business and holiday guests, particularly now that the indoor swimming pool and leisure complex is completed. Bedrooms continue to be steadily upgraded and there are now some deluxe rooms.
114⇌♠(15fb)1🚪 CTV in all bedrooms ® T
sB&B⇌♠£37.50-£47.50 dB&B⇌♠£70-£90 🅿
Lift (80P ✿ 🖾 (heated) snooker sauna solarium gymnasium beauty salon games room ♪ xmas
♥ English & French V ♦ ♨ Lunch £8-£9.50 High tea £3.95-£4.50 Dinner £16.95-£17.95 Last dinner 8.45pm
CONF. Thtr 200 Class 100 Board 50 Del from £57.50
Credit Cards [1][3]
See advertisement on page 113

★★★ **64%** Cumberland
East Overcliff Dr BH1 3AF ☎(0202) 290722 FAX (0202) 311394
This family owned hotel continues to improve. Staff are friendly and there is a warm atmosphere in the spacious and nicely furnished public areas. Bedrooms are modern and well coordinated.
102⇌♠(12fb)3🚪 CTV in all bedrooms ® T
sB&B⇌♠£19.50-£42.50 dB&B⇌♠£36-£110 🅿
Lift (65P ⌂ (heated) games room table tennis pool xmas
♥ British & Continental V ♦ ♨ ✂ Lunch £6.50-£15.50 High tea £4.95-£5.95 Dinner £13.50-£17.95 Last dinner 8.30pm
CONF. Thtr 100 Class 50 Board 45 Del from £49.50
Credit Cards [1][3] (£)
See advertisement on page 113

★★★ **64%** Hinton Firs
Manor Rd, East Cliff BH1 3HB
☎(0202) 555409 FAX (0202) 299607
In a quiet, tree-lined avenue close to the promenade, this privately owned hotel has much to commend it. The well presented bedrooms

Close to the heart of Bournemouth and a short stroll from the beach, the Elstead offers 50 comfortable en suite bedrooms with telephone, courtesy tray, television and hair dryer.

Comfortable lounges and bars, a superb restaurant, pleasant gardens and a large car park complete the picture.   ★★★

Knyveton Road, Bournemouth, BH1 3QP
Tel: 0202 293071
Fax: 0202 293827

6 POOLE ROAD, BOURNEMOUTH BH2 5QX
TEL (0202) 765163 FAX (0202) 752949

Ideally located within easy walking distance to the town centre shops, beach and BIC. Under the same family management since 1954 with a fine reputation for professional friendly service and excellent cuisine and comfort. 73 En-Suite bedrooms with satellite TV, radio, telephone, baby listening and tea/coffee making facilities. Outdoor Swimming Pool, Sauna, Jacuzzi, Solarium, Mini Gym and Games Room. Large Car Park.

Bournemouth

are comfortable and lounge areas are bright and sunny. There is a cosy bar and the well supervised dining room offers traditional and modern fare, though the tables are sometimes quite closely set.
46⇨♿ Annexe6⇨(12fb) CTV in all bedrooms ® T ✱ ✱ sB&B⇨♿£37.50-£48 dB&B⇨♿£75-£87.80 (incl dinner) 🍴
Lift (CTV 40P 🚗 ☐ (heated) ≈ (heated) sauna games room *xmas*
♿ English & French V ♿ ♿ ✱ Sunday Lunch £7.25 Dinner £11.75&alc Last dinner 8.30pm
Credit Cards [1][3]

★★★ 64% **Marsham Court**
Russell Cotes Rd BH1 3AB ☎(0202) 552111 FAX (0202) 294744
Opposite the Russell Cotes museum, this hotel is convenient for shopping, the theatre and the Promenade. Under the ownership of Mr Dixon-Box and Mrs Deavin, the hotel is steadily being improved, and the bedrooms are presently receiving attention to their décor and soft furnishings. Public areas are smart and well presented.
86⇨♿(16fb) CTV in all bedrooms ®♿ T ✱ (ex guide dogs) sB&B⇨♿£49-£69 dB&B⇨♿£78-£98 (incl dinner)
Lift (80P 20🚗 ≈ (heated) snooker *xmas*
♿ International V ♿ ♿ Lunch £9.50 High tea £5 Dinner £16-£18&alc Last dinner 9pm
CONF. Thtr 200 Class 120 Board 80 Del from £65.50
Credit Cards [1][2][3][5] £

★★★ 64% **Moat House**
Knyveton Rd BH1 3QQ ☎(0202) 293311 FAX (0202) 292221

This big hotel, boasting one of the largest function rooms in the south, is especially popular with business/conference guests, but caters equally well for holidaymakers. Refurbishment of bedrooms will have been completed during 1993. Public areas and the various lounges are comfortable and well presented.
145⇨♿(20fb) CTV in all bedrooms ® T ✱ sB&B⇨♿£63-£70 dB&B⇨♿£79-£90 🍴
Lift (100P ☐ (heated) ≈ snooker sauna gymnasium table tennis *xmas*
♿ English & French V ♿ ♿ ✱ Lunch fr£11.50&alc High tea fr£3.95alc Dinner fr£16&alc Last dinner 9.30pm
CONF. Thtr 1670 Class 811 Board 370 Del from £55
Credit Cards [1][2][3][5]

★★★ 64% **New Durley Dean**
Westcliff Rd BH2 5HE ☎(0202) 557711 FAX (0202) 292815
This popular and relaxing hotel offers a range of facilities and entertainments to suit all kinds of guest. The Green Park restaurant provides a short table d'hôte menu with one or two supplementary dishes, while breakfast is a self-serve hot/cold buffet. Bedrooms vary in size but have modern furnishings and a good range of equipment.
112⇨♿(27fb)3🛏 CTV in all bedrooms ®♿ T ✱ (ex guide dogs) sB&B⇨♿£25-£45 dB&B⇨♿£50-£90 🍴
Lift (30P ☐ (heated) snooker sauna solarium gymnasium jacuzzi table tennis steam room 🎵 *xmas*
♿ English & Continental V ♿ ♿ ✱ Lunch £4.95-£7.95 High tea £3.50-£5.25 Dinner £13.50-£18.50 Last dinner 8.30pm
CONF. Thtr 120 Class 40 Board 40 Del from £50
Credit Cards [1][2][3] £

★★★ 64% **Suncliff**
29 East Overcliff Dr BH1 3AG (Calotels) ☎(0202) 291711 FAX (0202) 293788
Located on the seafront, this large privately owned hotel offers bright, neat bedrooms of various shapes and sizes, all with modern facilities. Public rooms are spacious and a daily changing table d'hôte menu is offered in the dining room, where entertainment is provided most evenings. Staff are cheerful and polite.
95⇨♿(30fb)6🛏 CTV in all bedrooms ® T sB&B⇨♿£30-£55 dB&B⇨♿£60-£110 (incl dinner) 🍴

Lift (55P ☐ (heated) squash sauna solarium spa bath fitness room *xmas*
♿ English & French V ♿ ♿ ✱ Sunday Lunch £5.50-£12 Dinner £15-£20 Last dinner 8.30pm
CONF. Thtr 100 Class 70 Board 60 Del from £55
Credit Cards [1][2][3][5]

★★★ 64% **Trouville**
Priory Rd BH2 5DH (Close to International Centre)
☎(0202) 552262 FAX (0202) 293324
Owned by the Young family, this large, busy hotel is on the West Cliff, convenient for the BIC, pier, gardens and shopping centre. The bedrooms are fresh, attractive and comfortable and public areas have a warm, friendly atmosphere. A short, daily changing menu is offered, and lunch if required.
80⇨♿(22fb) CTV in all bedrooms ® T sB&B⇨♿£29.50-£42 dB&B⇨♿£59-£84 (incl dinner) 🍴
Lift (55P 5🚗 (£3.50 per night) sauna solarium gymnasium jacuzzi *xmas*
♿ English & French V ♿ ♿ Lunch £6.50-£8.50 High tea £2.75-£4.75 Dinner £14.19-£16.95 Last dinner 8.30pm
CONF. Thtr 50 Class 30 Board 35 Del from £52.50
Credit Cards [1][3] £

See advertisement on page 113

★★★ 64% **Wessex**
West Cliff Rd BH2 5EU (Forestdale) ☎(0202) 551911 FAX (0202) 297354
A conference-oriented hotel, the Wessex has been refurbished over the last few years and provides comfortable bedrooms, a spacious lounge and a well stocked bar. In the nicely appointed restaurant, young chef Paul Riddlough offers some well prepared dishes from a table d'hôte and an à la carte menu, though his sauces are a bit too heavy on the cream to win wholehearted commendation from our inspectors.
84rm(73⇨9♿)(15fb)✱in 3 bedrooms CTV in all bedrooms ® T ✱ sB&B⇨♿£29.95-£35.95 dB&B⇨♿£34.95-£44.95 🍴
Lift (250P ☐ (heated) ≈ (heated) snooker sauna solarium gymnasium table tennis *xmas*
♿ International V ♿ ♿ ✱ Lunch £7-£9.50 Dinner £11.95-£16.95 Last dinner 9.15pm
CONF. Thtr 400 Class 150 Board 100 Del from £59.95
Credit Cards [1][2][3][5] £

★★★ 63% **Belvedere**
Bath Rd BH1 2EU ☎(0202) 297556 FAX (0202) 294699
In an ideal central location, this hotel offers a range of spacious, comfortable public areas in addition to the Cecil restaurant, where varied table d'hôte and à la carte menus are available. Bedrooms vary in size and in the quality of furniture, but each has a good range of equipment.
62⇨♿(8fb)1🛏 CTV in all bedrooms ® T ✱ (ex guide dogs) sB&B⇨♿£30.50-£39.50 dB&B⇨♿£51-£69 🍴
Lift (50P 🎵 *xmas*
♿ English & Continental V ♿ ✱ Sunday Lunch £8.75-£9.25 Dinner £12.75-£13.25&alc Last dinner 9pm
CONF. Thtr 50 Class 16 Board 30 Del from £58
Credit Cards [1][2][3][5] £

★★★ 63% **Durlston Court**
Gervis Rd, East Cliff BH1 3DD (Quad) ☎(0202) 291488 FAX (0202) 290335
The hotel is well positioned for the shops, theatres and BIC. It is comfortably furnished, with a choice of lounge areas, and the bedrooms are modern with pretty coordinated décor. A simple table d'hôte menu is offered, with a tempting selection of desserts served from a buffet table.
54⇨♿ Annexe4⇨♿(16fb) CTV in all bedrooms ® T
Lift (50P ≈ (heated) sauna solarium gymnasium 🎵
♿ English & French V ♿ ♿ ✱ Last dinner 8.30pm
Credit Cards [1][3]

Bournemouth

★★★ 63% Pavilion
22 Bath Rd BH1 2NS ☎(0202) 291266 FAX (0202) 559264
Especially popular for conference delegates and masonic lodge weekends, this personally managed hotel also caters well for the holiday-maker, and is an ideal base for the short-stay guest. Bedrooms, which vary slightly in size, are neat, modern and well equipped. Good conference facilities are available, and public areas are comfortable with a relaxed atmosphere. A choice of table d'hôte or à la carte menu is offered.
44⇌↑(6fb)2🚭 CTV in all bedrooms ® T sB&B⇌↑£27.50-£32 dB&B⇌↑£47-£52 ♨
Lift (CTV 40P ♫ *xmas*
♀ English, French & Italian V ✡ ⚓ ✂ Lunch £7.50 High tea £4.50 Dinner £14 Last dinner 8.30pm
CONF. Thtr 100 Class 80 Board 50 Del from £50
Credit Cards [1][2][3][5]

★★★ 62% Cliffeside
East Overcliff Dr BH1 3AQ ☎(0202) 555724 FAX (0202) 555724
Its prominent position makes this hotel popular and there is a relaxed, cheery atmosphere. As with all the Young family's hotels, this one is being steadily improved and the majority of bedrooms have now been modernised and nicely decorated. Public areas are smart, and in the dining room a table d'hôte menu is offered with some supplementary dishes.
62⇌↑(10fb) CTV in all bedrooms ® T sB&B⇌↑£30-£42 dB&B⇌↑£60-£85 ♨
Lift (CTV 45P ⇌ (heated) snooker table tennis pool table *xmas*
♀ English & French V ✡ ⚓ Lunch £5.95-£8.95 Dinner £14.95-£15.95 Last dinner 8.30pm
CONF. Thtr 130 Del from £52.50
Credit Cards [1][3]

See advertisement on page 113

AA ★★★

Marsham Court Hotel

Overlooking Bournemouth Bay, in a quiet central cliff top position, Marsham Court offers the ideal venue for your summer holiday or short break.

■ 86 Bedrooms, all with private facilities, many with sea view and balcony.
■ Outdoor swimming and paddling pools, sun terraces and gardens.
■ Snooker Room   ■ Entertainment
■ Free accommodation for children.

Russell Cotes Road, Bournemouth BH1 3AB
Tel: (0202) 552711   Fax: 0202-294744

Cliff-top location close to town centre and beach.

BOURNEMOUTH

With commanding views over the whole sweep of the bay from the Purbeck Hills to the Isle of Wight, The Suncliff offers excellent food, 95 en-suite bedrooms and leisure facilities which include an indoor pool and 2 squash courts.

The purpose-built conference and meeting suites are fully equipped to meet any requirements.

★★★
The Suncliff Hotel
East Overcliff Drive, Bournemouth.
Tel: 0202 291711

Calotels

Hinton Firs
BOURNEMOUTH

INDOOR AND OUTDOOR POOLS

In the heart of the East Cliff, set amongst rhododendrons and pine trees, our friendly family hotel has 4 lounges facing sheltered gardens and sun terrace.

● 52 Rooms incl. 12 Singles, with TV, Radio, Tea-making and Direct-Dial Telephone
● Dancing • Games Room • Sauna
● Indoor and Outdoor Pools • Spa Pool
● Bar Lunches • Children's Teas
● Lift • Car Parking • Night Porter

ETB HIGHLY COMMENDED   AA ★★★   ASHLEY COURTENAY RECOMMENDED

Colour Brochure from Mr & Mrs R.A. Waters
Hinton Firs, Manor Road, East Cliff, Bournemouth BH1 3HB Tel: (0202) 555409

Bournemouth

★★★ 62% Durley Hall
Durley Chine Rd, West Cliff BH2 5JS ☎(0202) 500100 FAX (0202) 500103

A large, busy hotel on the West Cliff where refurbishment continues steadily and, while the bedrooms vary in size, most are of a good standard and some have a jacuzzi. There is an airy lounge/bar and café, and in the dining room entertainment is often provided.

69➪ƒ❀Annexe11➪ƒ❀(28fb)1⌷ CTV in all bedrooms ®⚹ T sB&B➪ƒ❀£33-£58 dB&B➪ƒ❀£66-£116 (incl dinner) ▤
Lift ℂ 150P ❅ ⌷ (heated) sauna solarium gymnasium jacuzzi steam room beauty therapist ♫ xmas
♁ English & Continental V ⚹ ♃ ✲ Sunday Lunch £7.45 High tea £5 Dinner £15.50&alc Last dinner 8.45pm
CONF. Thtr 200 Class 80 Board 35 Del from £60
Credit Cards 1 3 £

★★★ 62% Grosvenor
Bath Rd, East Cliff BH1 2EX ☎(0202) 558858 FAX (0202) 278332

Well positioned for most of the town's attractions, this hotel is steadily being improved under the guidance of Mrs Proctor. Bedrooms are modern, well equipped and nicely coordinated, and public rooms are bright and spacious.

40➪ƒ❀(10fb)2⌷ CTV in all bedrooms ® T
Lift ℂ CTV 40P ⌷ (heated) snooker sauna solarium gymnasium spa exercise area
♁ English & French V ⚹ ♃ ✙ Last dinner 8.45pm
Credit Cards 1 2 3

★★★ 61% East Cliff Court
East Overcliff Dr BH1 3NA ☎(0202) 554545 FAX (0202) 557456

Located along the East Cliff Promenade, this privately owned hotel offers very attractive public areas, and bedrooms of different shapes and sizes, the majority of which have been finished to a smart standard – some with sea facing balconies. In the restaurant a varied table d'hôte menu is offered.

70➪ƒ❀(10fb)2⌷ CTV in all bedrooms ®⚹ T sB&B➪ƒ❀£51-£55 dB&B➪ƒ❀£98-£120 (incl dinner) ▤
Lift ℂ CTV 100P ⌷ (heated) sauna solarium ♫ xmas
♁ English & French V ⚹ ♃ ✲ Lunch £4.95-£8.50 Dinner £14.25-£15 Last dinner 8.45pm
CONF. Thtr 160 Class 80 Board 40 Del from £55
Credit Cards 1 2 3 4 5 £

★★★ 60% Burley Court
Bath Rd BH1 2NP ☎(0202) 552824 & 556704 FAX (0202) 298514

Closed 30 Dec-11 Jan

Convenient for the shops, pier and seafront, this privately owned hotel has a quiet, relaxed atmosphere. Public areas are spacious and include a bar lounge, quiet lounge area and attractive dining room. While the bedrooms vary in size, refurbishment continues to upgrade them to a smart modern style.

38➪ƒ❀(8fb)1⌷ CTV in 34 bedrooms TV in 5 bedrooms ® T ✲ sB&B➪ƒ❀£29.50-£45.50 dB&B➪ƒ❀£59-£75 ▤
Lift ℂ CTV 35P ⊞ ⌷ (heated) solarium games room xmas
♁ English & French ⚹ ♃ Lunch fr£7.50 Dinner fr£12.50 Last dinner 8.30pm
Credit Cards 1 3 £

★★★ 59% Chesterwood
East Overcliff Dr BH1 3AR ☎(0202) 558057 FAX (0202) 556285

The Chesterwood enjoys a good sea front location on the Eastcliff opposite the promenade. It is steadily being upgraded, progress is rather slow but those rooms already upgraded are fairly smart and comfortable. Public areas are relaxed and cheerful, and there is a sunny terrace and popular outdoor pool.

47➪ƒ❀Annexe4➪ƒ❀(13fb) CTV in all bedrooms ® T ✈ (ex guide dogs)
Lift ℂ CTV 39P 8⊞ ❅ ⌷ (heated)
V ⚹ ♃ ✙ Last dinner 8.30pm
Credit Cards 1 2 3 5

★★★ 58% Bournemouth Heathlands
12 Grove Rd, East Cliff BH1 3AY (Quad) ☎(0202) 553336 FAX (0202) 555937

116➪ƒ❀(17fb) CTV in all bedrooms ®⚹ T
Lift ℂ 80P ❅ ⌷ (heated) sauna solarium gymnasium health club ♫
♁ English & French V ⚹ ♃ Last dinner 8.30pm
Credit Cards 1 3

★★★ 58% Embassy
Meyrick Rd, East Cliff BH1 3DW ☎(0202) 290751 FAX (0202) 557459

Convenient for the shops, railway station and the East Cliff Promenade. The majority of rooms have now attained a consistent modern standard, and redecoration and further improvements is continuing. Public areas are varied, and the dining room is particularly smart

39➪ƒ❀Annexe33➪ƒ❀(12fb)1⌷ CTV in all bedrooms ®⚹ T sB&B➪ƒ❀£25-£39.50 dB&B➪ƒ❀£50-£79 ▤
Lift ℂ CTV 75P ⌷ (heated) games room xmas
♁ British & French ⚹ ♃ ✲ Bar Lunch £1.75-£7.80 High tea £3-£5 Dinner £12.50-£17.50 Last dinner 8.30pm
CONF. Thtr 150 Class 120 Board 46 Del from £55
Credit Cards 1 2 3 5 £

★★ 68% Arlington
Exeter Park Rd BH2 5BD ☎(0202) 552879 & 553012 FAX (0202) 298317

RS Jan-Mar

In an ideal central location, this very friendly family-run hotel offers attractive neat accommodation that is good value for money. Public areas are comfortable and bedrooms, though mostly rather compact, have nicely coordinated décor and are well equipped with modern amenities.

28➪ƒ❀Annexe1ƒ❀(6fb) CTV in 28 bedrooms ®⚹ T ✈ ❅ sB&B➪ƒ❀£29-£37.50 dB&B➪ƒ❀£58-£75 (incl dinner) ▤
Lift CTV 21P ❅ nc2yrs xmas
♁ English & French V ⚹ ♃ ✲ Sunday Lunch £7 Dinner £9.75 Last dinner 8pm
Credit Cards 1 3

★★ 68% Durley Grange
6 Durley Rd, West Cliff BH2 5JL ☎(0202) 554473 & 290743 FAX (0202) 293774

Conveniently located on the West Cliff side of town, this friendly good-value hotel has been owned and managed by the charming Kirby family for many years. Accommodation is bright, modern and well equipped, though rooms vary in size and style. Public areas, refurbished in recent months, are very attractive. Enjoyable home-made fare is offered from a daily changing menu.

50➪ƒ❀(6fb) CTV in all bedrooms ® T
Lift ℂ CTV 25P ⌷ (heated) sauna solarium nc5yrs
♁ English, French & German ⚹ ✙ Last dinner 8pm
Credit Cards 1 3

★★ 67% Chinehurst
18-20 Studland Rd, Westbourne BH4 8JA ☎(0202) 764583 FAX (0202) 762854

Good value hotel with a warm and friendly atmosphere. Bedrooms vary in size but all are nicely presented and public areas are comfortable. Barbecues are held on the terrace on Friday evenings, weather permitting. There is a path down to the beach, and numerous aviaries of pretty and exotic birds.

29➪ƒ❀(4fb)2⌷✙ in 4 bedrooms CTV in all bedrooms ® T ✲ ▤
CTV 14P ❅ games room bird gardens ♫ xmas
♁ Continental V ⚹ ♃ ✙ Lunch £3.95-£10.95&alc Dinner £12.95&alc Last dinner 9pm
Credit Cards 1 2 3 5

Bournemouth

★★ 67% Mansfield
West Cliff Gardens BH2 5HL ☎(0202) 552659
Closed 2 Jan-18 Jan
This comfortable, value-for-money hotel is personally managed by the proprietor, Mr Oakley. The freshly decorated bedrooms are nicely furnished and well equipped. Public areas have a traditional feel and a friendly atmosphere. A short, daily changing menu is offered, along with a children's choice and vegetarian option – leave room for the delicious puds!
30⇨↑(7fb) CTV in all bedrooms ® T ✗ sB&B⇨↑£27-£33 dB&B⇨↑£54-£66 (incl dinner) 🍴
12P 🎄 xmas
♀ English & French V ✧ ᒲ ✄ Lunch £3-£6 Dinner £9-£10 Last dinner 8.30pm
Credit Cards 1 3

★★ 66% Durley Chine
Chine Crescent, West Cliff BH2 5LB ☎(0202) 551926 FAX (0202) 310671
This family-run hotel offers a warm, friendly atmosphere. Rooms in the Durley Suite tend to be more spacious, but all offer a good standard of décor and housekeeping. There is a comfortable lounge bar and an attractive restaurant with a daily changing menu of both English and international dishes.
22⇨↑Annexe14⇨↑(8fb)1🛏 CTV in all bedrooms ®𝒴 T 40P ✿ ≋ (heated) ♫ nc5yrs
♀ English & Continental V ✧ ᒲ ✄ Last dinner 7.30pm
Credit Cards 1 2 3

★★ 66% Hartford Court
48 Christchurch Rd BH1 3PE (on A35) ☎(0202) 551712 & 293682
Convenient for the railway station and not too far from the beaches and shops, this privately owned and personally managed hotel has a friendly atmosphere and offers good value for money. A simple set menu with a small choice is available in the evening.

34rm(27⇨↑)Annexe6⇨↑(1fb) CTV in all bedrooms ® T sB&B£16.50-£26 sB&B⇨↑£18.50-£28 dB&B£33-£52 dB&B⇨↑£37-£56 🍴
Lift CTV 40P ✿ xmas
✧ ᒲ ✄ Dinner £6-£7.50 Last dinner 7.30pm
Credit Cards 1 2 3 5

★★ 66% Whitehall
Exeter Park Rd BH2 5AX (Follow signs B.I.C. then turn into Exeter Park Road off Exeter Road) ☎(0202) 554682 FAX (0202) 554682
Closed 6 Nov-Feb
In a central location near to the BIC, shops, sea and gardens, this hotel is under the personal management of proprietors Mr and Mrs Price, who create a warm and friendly atmosphere. Bedrooms are neat and fresh, and public areas are very smart and attractively furnished.
49rm(44⇨↑)(5fb) CTV in all bedrooms ® T ✹ sB&B£20-£22 sB&B⇨↑£25-£27 dB&B£50-£54 dB&B⇨↑£50-£54 🍴
Lift ₵ 25P ✿
✧ ᒲ ✹ Bar Lunch £1.25-£3 Dinner £10 Last dinner 8pm
Credit Cards 1 2 3 5

★★ 65% Chinehead
31 Alumhurst Rd, Westbourne BH4 8EN (Between Bournemouth and Poole) ☎(0202) 752777 FAX (0202) 752778
21⇨↑(2fb)✄ in 3 bedrooms CTV in all bedrooms ® T
✗ (ex guide dogs)
20P
♀ English & Continental V ✧ ᒲ ✄
Credit Cards 1 3

For key to symbols see the Bookmark.

The Cumberland Hotel
EAST OVERCLIFF DRIVE
TEL. (0202) 290722

The Trouville Hotel
WESTCLIFFE
TEL. (0202) 552262

AA ★★★ AA
BOURNEMOUTH

These outstanding sister hotels offer real comfort and relaxation. Situated on Bournemouth's prestigious East Cliff with superb views overlooking the bay, yet near town centre and shops. Privately owned and managed by the Young family, all hotels offer Bargain Breaks, spacious accommodation, first class cuisine, recreation facilities, magnificent indoor leisure facilities, entertainment, friendly and efficient staff and ample free parking.

PHONE AND BOOK NOW

The Cliffeside Hotel
EAST OVERCLIFFE DRIVE
TEL. (0202) 555724

The Queens Hotel
MEYRICK ROAD
TEL. (0202) 554415

Bournemouth

★★ 64% Hotel Riviera
West Cliff Gardens BH2 5HL ☎(0202) 552845
Closed Dec-Mar RS 23-29 Dec
In a quiet area of West Cliff Gardens, this enthusiastically managed hotel offers a warm, friendly atmosphere. Bedrooms are freshly decorated and public areas are traditional, cosy and comfortable. A small choice table d'hôte menu is offered in the pretty dining room.
34rm(5fb) CTV in all bedrooms ® T sB&B⇌♪£24-£30 dB&B⇌♪£48-£60 ⊟
Lift (CTV 24P 🚲 ♪ ♻ xmas
V ✿ ♨ Dinner £9-£12 Last dinner 7.30pm
Credit Cards [1][3]

★★ 64% Ullswater
West Cliff Gardens BH2 5HW (on entering Bournemouth follow signs to Westcliffe, hotel just of Westcliff Road)
☎(0202) 555181 FAX (0202) 317896
The Ullswater is well managed by resident proprietors Peter and Rachael Pietruszka, who continue to improve it to a bright modern standard. Some rooms are still to be upgraded, but most are well furnished and comfortable. Public areas have a cheerful and relaxed atmosphere, and the hotel attracts a loyal clientèle.
42rm⇌♪(7fb) CTV in all bedrooms ® T ✻ sB&B⇌♪£24.50-£35 dB&B⇌♪£49-£70 (incl dinner) ⊟
Lift 10P table tennis snooker table ♪ xmas
♡ English & French ✿ ♨ Sunday Lunch £6.50 High tea £1.20-£2.50 Dinner £10.75 Last dinner 8pm
CONF. Thtr 40 Class 30 Board 24 Del from £35
Credit Cards [1][2][3]   £

★★ 63% Winterbourne
Priory Rd BH2 5DJ (From A338 follow signs B.I.C. Hotel bhind Centre) ☎(0202) 296366 FAX (0202) 780073
Closed 1-14 Jan
On the West Cliff with fine views across the bay, this popular hotel has been in the same family for over 30 years. Mr and Mrs Stebbings and their friendly team of staff promote a relaxed, cheery atmosphere. Comfortable bedrooms are varied in size, and public areas are traditional in style.
41rm⇌♪(12fb) CTV in all bedrooms ®♉ T ✻ sB&B⇌♪£31-£39 dB&B⇌♪£50-£70 ⊟
Lift 32P 🅿️ ♻ ≋ (heated) pool table, table tennis, climbing frame ♪ ♻ xmas
V ✿ ♨ Sunday Lunch fr£7 High tea fr£3.95 Dinner fr£11.50&alc Last dinner 8pm
CONF. Thtr 90 Class 50 Board 36 Del from £35
Credit Cards [1][2][3]

★★ 62% Fircroft
4 Owls Rd, Boscombe BH5 1AE (off A338 signposted Boscombe Pier, hotel is 400yds from pier close to Christchurch Road)
☎(0202) 309771 FAX (0202) 395644
Close to the shopping centre and pier, this warmly welcoming hotel is particularly popular with older guests, many of whom return here regularly. Bedrooms vary in size, some being rather compact, but all are bright and well equipped. Public areas are comfortable.
51rm⇌♪(20fb) CTV in all bedrooms ® T ✻ sB&B⇌♪£22-£26 dB&B⇌♪£44-£52 ⊟
Lift (CTV 50P sports at health club owned by hotel ♪ xmas
♡ English & French V ✿ ♥ Bar Lunch £2-£5&alc Dinner £12.50 Last dinner 8pm
CONF. Thtr 200 Class 100 Board 30 Del from £35
Credit Cards [1][2][3]   £

★★ 62% Gresham Court
4 Grove Rd, East Cliff BH1 3AX ☎(0202) 551732
The Gresham Court's main trade is group bookings and coaches, but private guests are equally welcome, and the hotel seems particularly popular with the older age group. Bedrooms are neatly decorated and furnished, and public areas are traditionally styled and comfortable. A menu with a small choice of dishes is offered at dinner and Mrs Moore's desserts should not be missed.

34rm⇌♪(12fb) CTV in all bedrooms ®
Lift CTV 35P ✿
✿ ♨ Last dinner 7.30pm
Credit Cards [1][2][3][5]

★★ 60% Riviera
Burnaby Rd, Alum Chine BH4 8JF (From 'Frizzell' rbt on A338 take The Avenue and at traffic lights left for Western Rd. At rbt into Almhurst Rd then left into Beaulie or Earl Rd) (Calotels) ☎(0202) 763653 FAX (0202) 768422
Closed 2-4 Feb
This large resort hotel caters well for families and older guests, with plenty of attractions and entertainments. Bedrooms tend to be a little compact, but each has modern facilities. The daily changing table d'hôte menu at dinner and hot or cold buffet at lunch time are popular with guests.
69rm⇌♪ Annexe9rm⇌♪(24fb) CTV in all bedrooms ® T sB&B⇌♪£30-£45 dB&B⇌♪£60-£90 (incl dinner)
Lift 79P 🅿️ (heated) ≋ (heated) snooker sauna solarium 2 games rooms, spa bath ♪ xmas
♡ English & French V ✿ ♥ Lunch £7-£8 Dinner £14.50-£16.50 Last dinner 8.30pm
Credit Cards [1][3]

★★ 60% St George
West Cliff Gardens BH2 5HL ☎(0202) 556075
Closed 27 Dec-3rd wk Mar
This hotel, with a pretty garden and lovely sea views from many rooms, remains popular with older guests who enjoy the amiable atmosphere. Bedrooms are simple with modern amenities, traditional style public areas are comfortable and a short, daily changing table d'hôte menu is offered in the dining room.
22rm(20⇌♪)(5fb) CTV in all bedrooms ®♉ T
Lift 4P pool table
♡ English, French & Italian ✿ ♥ Last dinner 7.30pm

★★ 58% County
Westover Rd BH1 2BT ☎(0202) 552385 FAX (0202) 297255
Dating back over 100 years, the County enjoys an enviable central location overlooking the sea, close to the town-centre attractions. Public areas include the ever popular Poets' Corner where music creates a lively atmosphere 7 nights a week.
51rm(37⇌9♪)(11fb) CTV in all bedrooms ® T sB£15-£25 sB⇌♪£17.50-£27.50 dB£13.50-£23.50 dB⇌♪£15-£25 (room only)
Lift (3P (£2 per day) 6🐾 (£1 per day) xmas
✿ ♥ Bar Lunch £2.50-£6.50alc Dinner £8.50 Last dinner 8pm
CONF. Thtr 25 Board 25 Del from £30
Credit Cards [1][2][3]   £

★★ 58% Russell Court
Bath Rd BH1 2EP ☎(0202) 295819 FAX (0202) 293457
In a central location, close to the shops, beaches and theatres, this hotel is popular for group bookings, particularly in the quieter months. The modern public areas include a lounge/bar where live entertainment is occasionally offered, and a simple, short daily changing menu is served in the dining room.
62rm(46⇌10♪)(6fb) CTV in all bedrooms ® T
✻ (ex guide dogs)
Lift (CTV 60P
V ✿ ♥ Last dinner 8pm
Credit Cards [1][2][3][5]

★★ 58% Sun Court
West Hill Rd, West Cliff BH2 5PH ☎(0202) 551343 FAX (0202) 316747
Convenient for the theatres, seafront and other town centre amenities, this hotel has bedrooms of varying size which are reasonably equipped. Public areas are comfortable, and in addition to the large cocktail bar/lounge there is a cosier non smoking lounge.
36rm⇌♪(4fb) CTV in all bedrooms ® T sB&B⇌♪£28.50-£38.50 dB&B⇌♪£49.50-£79 (incl dinner) ⊟

Bournemouth - Bourton-on-the-Water

Lift CTV 50P 1 (heated) solarium gymnasium *xmas*
English & Italian Sunday Lunch £5.95 Dinner £14&alc Last dinner 8.30pm
Credit Cards 1 2 3 5

★ **68%** *Lynden Court*
8 Durley Rd, West Cliff BH2 5JL ☎(0202) 553894
Closed Nov-Mar (ex Xmas & New Year)

The Reyna family are all involved in the day-to-day running of this hotel, located on the West Cliff side of town, and the atmosphere is cheerful, relaxed and friendly. Bedrooms are nicely coordinated, and the dining room is especially pretty. A good choice is offered at dinner, cooked by son Mark.

32rm(7fb) CTV in 31 bedrooms ®
Lift 20P ♫
Last dinner 7.15pm
Credit Cards 1 2 3 5

★ **64%** *Montague*
Durley Rd South BH2 5JH ☎(0202) 551074
Closed Dec-Feb

Its convenient location makes this family-run hotel an ideal choice for tourist and business guests. The bedrooms can be compact, but most are en suite and several ground floor rooms are available. There is an attractive reception foyer, a well furnished bar and dining room.

26rm(22⇌) CTV in all bedrooms ® T ✗ (ex guide dogs)
sB&B£19-£28 sB&B⇌£25-£32 dB&B£36-£54
dB&B⇌£50-£62 (incl dinner) 🍽
30P ≅ (heated) *xmas*
V ✿ ✗ Bar Lunch £5 Dinner £9.50 Last dinner 7.15pm
Credit Cards 1 2 3

★ **62%** *Taurus Park*
16 Knyveton Rd BH1 3QN ☎(0202) 557374

In a quiet residential area close to the station and East Cliff, this friendly family-run hotel is continually being improved and offers good value for money, with bright neat bedrooms, spacious public areas and simple home-cooked dinners.

46rm(8⇌25)(4fb) CTV in all bedrooms ® ✗
Lift CTV 25P games room nc3yrs
Last dinner 7.30pm

Forte Posthouse
Lansdowne BH1 2PR ☎(0202) 553262 FAX (0202) 527698

FORTE Posthouse

Suitable for both the business and leisure traveller, this bright hotel provides modern accommodation in well equipped bedrooms with en suite bathrooms. For more details about Forte Posthouse hotels, consult the Contents page, under Hotel Groups.

98⇌✳ B⇌£41.50-£53.50 (room only)
CONF. Thtr 120 Class 50 Board 40 Del £89.50

BOURTON-ON-THE-WATER Gloucestershire Map 04 SP12

★★ **70%** Dial House
The Chestnuts, High St GL54 2AN (off A429)
☎(0451) 822244 FAX (0451) 822288

Privately owned and personally run, this cosy little hotel at the heart of an attractive Costwold village dates from 1698. It has been sympathetically restored to provide small, richly furnished public rooms made inviting by open fires and many personal touches. In a candlelit dining room with inglenook fireplace and flagged floor, guests can make their selection from a short carte offering delicious country fare. Individually decorated bedrooms (some on the ground floor) vary in size but all are light and cheerful.

10⇌3 in 2 bedrooms CTV in all bedrooms ® T
✗ (ex guide dogs) sB&B⇌fr£35.75 dB&B⇌£69-£99 🍽
20P croquet lawn nc10yrs *xmas*

St. George Hotel

West Cliff Gardens, Bournemouth.

Peacefully situated on the West Cliff overlooking Bournemouth Bay, with fabulous sea views.

Eight minutes' walk to the Town and Conference Centre.

A spacious hotel, offering a high degree of comfort, personal service and an exceptionally high standard of food. Most rooms en suite with tea & coffee facilities, telephone, radio intercom and colour TV with satellite channel — lift to all floors. You will be tempted to return again and again to the relaxed atmosphere of our hotel.

Colour brochure and tariff sent on request.

Telephone: (0202) 556075

AA ★★

BOURNEMOUTH

Modern family owned hotel with extensive leisure facilities.

Overlooking wooded Alum Chine and Bournemouth Bay, The Riviera Hotel offers the ideal location for family holidays and short breaks.

Indoor and outdoor pools, spa bath, solarium and large snooker room are just some of the leisure facilities on offer.

Burnaby Road, Alum chine, Bournemouth.
Tel: 0202 763653

— **Calotels** —

Bourton-on-the-Water - Box

☆ English & French V ❀ ⚓ ✂ Lunch £6.95-£11.95&alc Dinner fr£15&alc Last dinner 9.15pm
Credit Cards 1 2 3

★★65% Old Manse
Bridge End Walk GL54 2BX (beside the River Windrush, near the War Memorial and the Motor Museum)
☎Cotswold(0451) 820082 FAX (0451) 810381

A change of ownership has bought new life and enthusiasm to this cosy Cotswold hotel, with a pretty stream at the front. Flagstone floors characterise the public areas which include a busy bar and comfortable restaurant. Bedrooms vary from the grand honeymoon suite to cosier cottage-style rooms.

12⇨♠1❀ CTV in all bedrooms ® T ✱ sB&B⇨♠£37-£72.50 dB&B⇨♠£54-£115 ₽

12P xmas
V ❀ ⚓ ✂ Lunch £5.95-£9.95 Dinner £14.50&alc Last dinner 9pm
CONF. Thtr 45 Class 20 Board 20 Del £53.75
Credit Cards 1 2 3 5

★★64% Chester House Hotel & Motel
Victoria St GL54 2BU
☎Cotswold(0451) 820286 FAX (0451) 820471
Closed mid Dec-mid Feb

This privately owned and run hotel is close to the centre of the delightful village. Bedrooms are generally spacious and comfortable with a good range of facilities. There is an attractive restaurant where an interesting selection of dishes is served.

13⇨♠Annexe10⇨♠(6fb)1❀ CTV in all bedrooms ® T ✱ sB&B⇨♠£49 dB&B⇨♠£78.50-£98 Continental breakfast ₽ 23P

☆ English & French V ❀ Lunch fr£8.50 Dinner fr£17.50 Last dinner 9.30pm
Credit Cards 1 2 3 4 5

★★64% Old New Inn
High St GL54 2AF ☎Cotswold(0451) 820467 FAX (0451) 810236
Closed 25 Dec

When the Old New Inn opened it was the only hotel in Bourton, now with lots of competition it remains popular by offering traditional hospitality and service. It has been under the management of the Morris family for over 60 years. Upgrading of the bedrooms continues, and public areas are full of character with 4 bars, a comfortable lounge and a dining room. The hotel is also home to the famous model village.

17rm(6⇨2♠)Annexe5rm1❀ CTV in 14 bedrooms ® sB&B£27-£35 sB&B⇨♠£35-£38 dB&B£54 dB&B⇨♠£70-£76 ₽

CTV 25P 6☂ (£2) ⁂ ✿
☆ English & French V ❀ Lunch £8-£14 Dinner £16-£18 Last dinner 8.30pm
Credit Cards 1 3

BOVEY TRACEY Devon Map 03 SX87

★★★67% Edgemoor
Haytor Rd TQ13 9LE (from A382 follow signs for Haytor and Widecombe) ☎(0626) 832466 FAX (0626) 834760

This charming, ivy-clad country house, built in the 1870s and peacefully set in 2-acre gardens on the edge of Dartmoor, has been sympathetically modernised. Individually decorated bedrooms are thoughtfully equipped, while public areas include a bar lounge and quiet lounge – originally the school hall – as well as an attractive dining room.

12⇨♠(1fb)2❀ CTV in all bedrooms ® T sB&B⇨♠£36.95-£45 dB&B⇨♠£70-£90 ₽

45P ⁂ ✿ petanque xmas
☆ English & French V ❀ ⚓ Lunch £9.50&alc High tea £1.75-£5.50 Dinner £17.50-£20 Last dinner 9pm
Credit Cards 1 2 3 5

★★62% **Riverside Inn**
Fore St TQ13 9AF ☎(0626) 832293 FAX (0626) 833880

This character inn is in the centre of the town, at the foot of beautiful Dartmoor, offering easy access to the south coast. There is an informal atmosphere in the busy, spacious bars, and bar snacks and an à la carte menu are available. The bedrooms are comfortable and brightly decorated, and all have a good range of modern equipment.

10⇨♠ CTV in all bedrooms ® T ✱ sB&B⇨♠fr£29.50 dB&B⇨♠fr£39.50 ₽

(100P ♪ ♫
☆ English & French V ❀ ⚓ ✂ Dinner £10 Last dinner 9pm
CONF. Thtr 80
Credit Cards 1 2 3

★★60% Coombe Cross
Coombe Cross TQ13 9EY (Logis) ☎(0626) 832476 FAX (0626) 835298

Situated in a residential area with superb views over Dartmoor, this small country house-style hotel is set in its own well tended garden. Bedrooms are bright and traditional, and there is a choice of comfortable lounges and a cosy dining room. The hotel runs its own bridge and garden holidays.

26rm(23⇨1♠)(2fb) CTV in all bedrooms ® T ✱ sB&B⇨♠£30-£35 dB&B⇨♠£50-£65 ₽

(CTV 26P ✿ ⛱ (heated) sauna solarium gymnasium
V ❀ ⚓ ✂ Bar Lunch £3-£6 High tea £2.50-£5 Dinner £14.95-£16.95 Last dinner 8pm
CONF. Thtr 60 Class 40 Board 30 Del from £50
Credit Cards 1 2 3 5

BOVINGDON Hertfordshire Map 04 TL00

★★❀74% The Bobsleigh Inn
Hempstead Rd HP3 0DS
☎Hemel Hempstead(0442) 833276 832000 FAX (0442) 832471

Closed 26 Dec-5 Jan RS Good Fri & Bank Hol Mondays

Built in 1898 as a country residence, this hotel continues to expand. Most of the bedrooms are in ground floor annexes, the most recent being spacious and comfortable with good easy chairs and en suite shower rooms. At the time of our visit a further bedroom extension, new reception and function suite were being built and are due to open at the end of 1993. In the restaurant, chef Stuart Ambury and his small team have built up a good local reputation for enjoyable cooking.

5♠Annexe18⇨♠(1fb) CTV in all bedrooms ® T ✱ sB&B⇨♠£25-£60 dB&B⇨♠£45-£70

40P 2☂ ✿ ✿
V ❀ ✱ Lunch £11.95-£13.95&alc Dinner £15.95-£17.95&alc Last dinner 9.30pm
Credit Cards 1 2 3 5

BOWMORE
See **Islay, Isle of**

BOWNESS ON WINDERMERE
See **Windermere**

BOX Wiltshire Map 03 ST86

★★❀71% Box House Hotel & Restaurant
London Rd SN14 9NR ☎Bath(0225) 744447 FAX (0225) 743971

9⇨♠(1fb) CTV in all bedrooms T ✱ sB&B⇨♠£50-£99 dB&B⇨♠£65-£99 ₽

(40P ✿ ⛱ (heated) ♪ xmas
☆ French V ❀ ⚓ ✂ ✱ Lunch fr£5.50 Dinner £18.50&alc Last dinner 10pm
Credit Cards 1 2 3

BRACKLEY Northamptonshire Map 04 SP53

★★**66%** Crown
20-22 Market Square NN13 5DP
☎(0280) 702210 FAX (0280) 601840

An inn at the centre of the market town offers bedrooms very well equipped with all modern facilities, furnished in pine and decorated in a cottagey style. Public areas include a popular bar and simply appointed restaurant.
18⇌↑(2fb) CTV in all bedrooms ® T ✱ sB&B⇌↑£24-£45 dB&B⇌↑£48-£65 ♿
CTV 6P pool *xmas*
♡ Mainly grills V ⌘ ♨ ✱ Lunch £1-£5 Dinner £4.50-£9.50
Last dinner 10pm
Credit Cards [1][2][3][5]

BRACKNELL Berkshire Map 04 SU86
See also **Wokingham**

★★★★❀**70%** Coppid Beech
John Nike Way RG12 8TF (from junct 10 on M4 take Wokingham/Bracknell option on to A329, in 2 miles at roundabout take B3408 to Binfield, hotel 200yds on the right hand side) ☎(0344) 303333 FAX 0344 301200

Best Newcomer 1994

We have pleasure in awarding the Coppid Beach our award for Best Newcomer in Southeast England this year. Owner, John Nike, is clearly committed to quality and his new hotel demonstrates excellent attention to detail. The building has an imaginative modern design of clean balconied lines, topped by steep Alpine gables. It contains a spacious marbled foyer/lounge bar, a night club, Bier Keller bar with food, and the main restaurant where chef Paul Farmer provides interesting food in both modern and traditional styles. The bedrooms are attractively decorated and comfortable and room service is particularly good. The staff, led by manager Alan Blenkinsop, are well groomed and offer good levels of service.
205⇌↑(6fb)⊁ in 138 bedrooms CTV in all bedrooms ® ⚲ T sB&B⇌↑£105 dB&B⇌↑£130 ♿
Lift (⊞ 350P ▭ (heated) sauna solarium gymnasium dry ski slope skating toboggan run ♪ ♫ *xmas*
V ⌘ ♨ ⊁ Lunch £9.50-£17.50&alc Dinner £22.50&alc Last dinner 10.30pm
CONF. Thtr 400 Class 200 Board 120 Del from £135
Credit Cards [1][2][3][5]

★★★**65%** *Stirrups Country House*
Maidens Green RG12 6LD
☎Winkfield(0344) 882284 FAX (0344) 882300

This extended inn with a Tudor gabled frontage is on the Bracknell road in the quiet village of Maidens Green. The bar is full of character with exposed beams, an open fire and a horse racing theme throughout. Bedrooms are well maintained and recently refurbished.
24⇌(6fb) CTV in all bedrooms ® T
Lift (150P ✿

The Coppid Beech welcomes its guests with a unique blend of luxury, service and style. Beautifully furnished ensuite bedrooms provide every creature comfort. Rowans Restaurant offers the finest cuisine in elegant surroundings. Our lively Bier Keller serves an exciting bistro-style menu. Apres Nightclub takes sophistication deep into the night with champagne, cocktails and dancing. And for the energetic, Waves Leisure Club provides indoor swimming, spa-bath, sauna, steam room, solaria and air conditioned gymnasium. There's even skating and dry-slope skiing!

1993 Winner of the Best New Hotel Award for South East England

Tel: (0344) 303333

John Nike Way, Bracknell, Berks RG12 8TF

Less than 3 miles from M4 Junction 10

COOMBE CROSS HOTEL AA ★★

Bovey Tracey, South Devon TQ13 9EY
Tel Bovey Tracey (0626) 832476
Fax: (0626) 835298

Ashley Courtenay Recommended
Logis of GB Hotel

A beautiful country house with spectacular views of Dartmoor. Quietly situated on the edge of town yet only 5 minutes from the A38 Exeter to Plymouth road. 23 delightful bedrooms with full facilities, **a superb new indoor pool and fitness suite.** Excellent English cuisine served in our restaurant overlooking our lovely gardens. Remarkable value 2, 3 and 7 night breaks available all year round.

Bracknell - Braemar

⚑ English & Continental **V** ⚐ Last dinner 10pm
Credit Cards [1] [2] [3] [5]

Hilton National Bracknell
Bagshot Rd RG12 3QJ ☏(0344) 424801

This is a bright, modern hotel with an informal restaurant, aimed at both the business and leisure guest. All bedrooms have ensuite bathrooms and a range of modern facilities. For more information about Hilton National, consult the Contents page, under Hotel Groups.

167⇨🛏✱ sB⇨🛏£92 dB⇨🛏£105 (room only)
CONF. Thtr 400 Class 100 Board 35 Del £145

BRADFORD West Yorkshire Map 07 SE13

★★★ 66% Tong Village
Tong Ln, Tong BD4 0RP (off A450) (Lansbury)
☏Leeds(0532) 854646 FAX (0532) 853661
The present owners have considerably improved and extended this hotel. The modern bedrooms are attractively furnished and have a good array of equipment, including trouser presses and free video films; some are on the ground floor and some are for non smokers. There is a choice of bars and an attractive restaurant with a no-smoking area.
60⇨🛏(6fb)1⚑⚐in 28 bedrooms CTV in all bedrooms ® T ✱
sB&B⇨🛏fr£69.50 dB&B⇨🛏fr£81 ₽
Lift ⟨ CTV 120P ✿ sauna solarium gymnasium
⚑ English & French **V** ⚐ ⚓ ⚒ ✱ Lunch fr£8.95&alc Dinner fr£15.50&alc Last dinner 10pm
CONF. Thtr 300 Class 150 Board 100 Del from £95
Credit Cards [1] [2] [3] [4] [5]

★★★ 57% Novotel
Merrydale Rd BD4 6SA (3m S adjacent to M606) ☏(0274) 683683 FAX (0274) 651342

This purpose built hotel on the Euroway Trading Estate offers clean, practical accommodation. Public areas have recently been attractively refurbished in a pleasing modern style.
131⇨🛏(131fb)⚐in 12 bedrooms CTV in all bedrooms ® ⚒ T
sB⇨🛏£49.50 dB⇨🛏£54.50 (room only) ₽
Lift ⟨ ⚏ 180P ✿ ⚓ (heated)
⚑ English & French **V** ⚐ ⚓ ⚒ Lunch £10-£13&alc Dinner £10-£13&alc Last dinner mdnt
CONF. Thtr 300 Class 150 Board 100 Del £83
Credit Cards [1] [2] [3] [4] [5]

★★ 66% Dubrovnik
3 Oak Av, Manningham BD8 7AQ (1.5m from city centre. Take Keighley Road, Queens Road, first left after police station, then second left and hotel on right) ☏(0274) 543511 FAX (0274) 480407
This imposing stone Victorian house has a spacious reception area, and a new bar, with modern light wood furniture and contrasting fabrics, while the dining room is high ceilinged, with floral wallpaper and a carved fireplace. The hotel is owned and run by the friendly Basic family, Yugoslavian émigrées and their choice of taped music and menu are reminders of the 'old country'. Most of the bedrooms are simply furnished, but the new bedrooms have additional facilities.
47⇨🛏(6fb)1⚑ CTV in all bedrooms ® T ✠ (ex guide dogs)
✱ sB&B⇨🛏£50-£55 dB&B⇨🛏£75-£80 ₽
⟨ CTV 60P ⚘ xmas
⚑ English & Yugoslavian **V** ⚐ ⚓ ⚒ ✱ Lunch £9-£13.50&alc Dinner £13.50-£15&alc Last dinner 9.30pm
Credit Cards [1] [2] [3] [5]

Hotels with red star ratings are especially high quality.

★★ 66% Park Drive
12 Park Dr BD9 4DR (turn off A650 Keighley rd into Emm Lane, at Lister park turn 2nd right) ☏(0274) 480194 FAX (0274) 484869
Owned and professionally run by Mr and Mrs Hilton, this hotel has lovely mature gardens. The bedrooms are somewhat plain and servicable, but each is carefully coordinated and well designed. One of the bathrooms is split level with the original 30s stained and leaded art deco windows. There is a pleasant bar/lounge and an appealing candlelit dining room with fresh flower posies on each table.
11⇨🛏(1fb) CTV in all bedrooms ® T sB&B⇨🛏£30-£46
dB&B⇨🛏£48-£56 ₽
9P ⚏
Dinner £12 Last dinner 7.30pm
Credit Cards [1] [2] [3] £

★ 69% Park Grove
Frizinghall BD9 4JY ☏(0274) 543444 FAX (0274) 495619
This large and well maintained semi-detached Victorian house stands in a quiet, tree-lined road. Now completely modernised and converted, it has comfortable and particularly well equipped bedrooms with dark furniture and bright soft furnishings. Public areas include the lounge bar and a dining room where guests can choose between a range of British dishes and an authentic Asian menu.
11⇨🛏(2fb) CTV in all bedrooms ® T ✠
CTV 8P ⚏
⚑ English & Indian **V**
Credit Cards [1] [3]

BRADFORD ON AVON Wiltshire Map 03 ST86

★★★ ❀❀❀⚑ 78% Woolley Grange
Woolley Green BA15 1TX (on B3105, 0.5m NE at Woolley Green) ☏(0225) 864705 FAX (0225) 864059

This very welcoming country hotel is set in pleasant grounds and gardens, and the informal manner in which it is run by the Chapman family makes it particularly good for families (facilities include a supervised nursery. Colin White heads the kitchen, producing interesting seasonal menus emphasising quality fresh produce. The dishes are well prepared and executed, and though they tend to over elaboration on occasions, there is a wealth of colours and textures to please the palate.
14⇨🛏Annexe6⇨🛏(6fb) CTV in all bedrooms T
sB&B⇨🛏£85-£150 dB&B⇨🛏£95-£175 ₽
CTV 40P ⚏ ✿ ⚓ (heated) ♗ (grass) badminton croquet games room ⚘ xmas
V ⚐ ⚓ ⚒ Lunch £5-£25alc Dinner fr£28&alc Last dinner 10pm
CONF. Thtr 35 Class 35 Board 22 Del £125
Credit Cards [1] [2] [3] [5]

BRAE

See **Shetland**

BRAEMAR Grampian *Aberdeenshire* Map 15 NO19

★★★ 65% Invercauld Arms
AB35 5YR (on the A93 equidistant between Perth and Aberdeen) ☏(03397) 41605 FAX (03397) 41428
This fine Victorian hotel is a popular base for tour groups, skiers and holiday-makers. Bedrooms, with bright décor and attractive fabrics, are comfortable, and there is a choice of comfortable lounges and a cocktail bar with tartan seating. The bright and airy dining room has functional stacking chairs which detract from otherwise good furnishing.
68⇨🛏(11fb)⚐in 18 bedrooms CTV in all bedrooms ® T ✱
sB&B⇨🛏£31-£60 dB&B⇨🛏£62-£85 ₽
Lift ⟨ 80P ♪ xmas

♋ International V ❍ ⌺ ✻ Lunch £6.95-£11.95 Dinner £15.50-£18&alc Last dinner 8.45pm
Conf. Thtr 60 Class 20 Board 24 Del from £60
Credit Cards ① ② ③ ⑤

★★ ❀71% *Braemar Lodge*
Glenshee Rd AB35 5YQ ☎(03397) 41627 FAX (03397) 41440
Closed Nov
Enthusiastic owners extend genuine hospitality at this delightful holiday hotel, a converted Victorian shooting lodge in its own grounds. Comfortable, traditionally furnished bedrooms have recently been redecorated, while panelled walls and log fires enhance public areas. These include a cosy, well stocked foyer bar, an attractive lounge and an elegant candlelit restaurant where excellent meals are served.
8rm(6⋔) CTV in all bedrooms ®
20P ⌬ ✿
V ⌿ Last dinner 9pm
Credit Cards ① ③

BRAINTREE Essex Map 05 TL72
★★69% *White Hart*
Bocking End CM7 6AB (in town centre) (Whitbread)
☎(0376) 321401 FAX (0376) 552268
This extended old coaching inn in the town centre has recently refurbished all its bedrooms to a similar standard of comfort. Public areas include a traditional beamed bar, an open-plan bar lounge with a small conservatory and a Beefeater restaurant with a comprehensive menu.
31⇨⋔(2fb)1⌸⌿in 9 bedrooms CTV in all bedrooms ®⋎ T
✈ (ex guide dogs) ✻ sB&B⇨⋔fr£59.30 dB&B⇨⋔fr£71 ₧
(40P sauna solarium gymnasium
♋ English & Continental V ❍ ⌺ ⌿ ✻ Lunch fr£6.24 Dinner fr£15.58 Last dinner 10.30pm
Conf. Thtr 40 Class 16 Board 24 Del from £85
Credit Cards ① ② ③ ⑤

BRAITHWAITE Cumbria Map 11 NY22
★★66% *Middle Ruddings Country Inn & Restaurant*
CA12 5RY (off A66 N of Keswick) ☎(07687) 78436 FAX (07687) 78438
RS mid Nov-Mar (ex New Year)
Set in its own grounds, this attractive family-run hotel offers caring service. The bright modern bedrooms have good facilities and the public areas are spacious and comfortable. They include a delightfully furnished conservatory and more traditional lounge. A good range of food is available.
13⇨⋔1⌸⌿in all bedrooms CTV in all bedrooms ® T
sB&B⇨⋔£36 dB&B⇨⋔£50-£70 ₧
20P 2🅿 (£20 per week) ✿ ♬ (grass) bowls nc5yrs *xmas*
♋ English & French V ❍ ⌺ ⌿
Credit Cards ① ③   £

★★ 63% *Cottage in the Wood*
Whinlatter Pass CA12 5TW ☎Keswick(07687) 78409
Closed 17 Nov-11 Mar
In woodland surroundings, this small and friendly hotel, converted from a 17th-century coaching house, has cosy bedrooms, comfortable lounges and an attractive dining room where freshly prepared 5-course dinners are served.
7⇨⋔(2fb)2⌸⌿in all bedrooms ® dB&B⇨⋔£71-£78 (incl dinner) ₧
20P ⌬ ✿ bowls
❍ ⌺ ⌿ ✻ Dinner £12-£17 Last dinner 7.30pm

For key to symbols see the Bookmark.

★★★AA
INVERCAULD ARMS
A Thistle Country House Hotel

Braemar AB35 5YR
Tel: 03397 41605   Fax: 03397 41428

Your choice at
Braemar

For Reservations at over 100
Mount Charlotte Thistle Hotels
Telephone London: 071 937 8033.

THISTLE HOTELS

OLD WHITE LION HOTEL
HAWORTH, KEIGHLEY, WEST YORKSHIRE
Tel: HAWORTH (0535) 642313 Fax: 0535 646222

This family run hotel is situated at the centre of this famous village close to the Brontë museum, church and parsonage. Catering for the discriminating businessman as well as tourists from all over the world. Fourteen comfortable bedrooms, all with en-suite facilities, colour TV, radio/direct dial telephone, tea making facilities and magnificent views. Fax facilities also available. Central heating throughout, Residents' Lounge, Cocktail and Lounge Bars. Beamed candlelit restaurant open 7 days a week — Table D'Hôte and A La Carte. Sunday lunch a speciality. Open to non-residents. Hot and cold bar snacks prepared by our chefs at all meal times. Special weekend rates available.

Bramhall - Brandon (Suffolk)

BRAMHALL Greater Manchester Map 07 SJ88

★★★ 68% **Bramhall Moat House**
Bramhall Ln South SK7 2EB (off A5102)
☎061-439 8116 FAX 061-440 8071
Closed 25-30 Dec

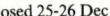

This purpose-built modern hotel close to the railway station and convenient for Manchester airport has been considerably upgraded in recent years. Bedrooms are particularly well equipped, with the spacious newer rooms offering the most comfort. Public areas include a stylish lounge and restaurant, plus the popular Shires bar which also serves food.

65⇨↑(3fb)✻in 13 bedrooms CTV in all bedrooms ® T
✻ (ex guide dogs) ✻ sB&B⇨↑£55-£75 dB&B⇨↑£65-£85 ₽
Lift ℂ 132P sauna solarium gymnasium
♡ English & French V ♢ ♨ Lunch £7.95 Dinner fr£13.50 Last dinner 9.45pm
CONF. Thtr 112 Class 42 Board 40 Del from £85
Credit Cards [1][2][3][5]

BRAMHOPE West Yorkshire Map 08 SE34

Forte Crest
Leeds Rd LS16 9JJ ☎Leeds(0532) 842911 FAX (0532) 843151

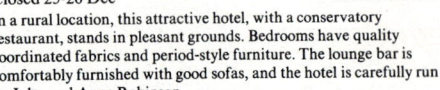

A large modern hotel with a wide range of services and amenities, designed particularly for the business traveller. Bedrooms are smart, comfortable and well equipped. For more details about Forte Crest hotels, consult the Contents page, under Hotel Groups.

126⇨↑✻ B⇨↑£89 (room only)
CONF. Thtr 160 Class 100 Board 40 Del from £115

BRAMPTON Cambridgeshire Map 04 TL27

★★ 64% **Grange**
115 High St PE18 8TG ☎Huntingdon(0480) 459516

Informal and relaxed service is offered at this small, family-run hotel, where a friendly atmosphere is encouraged by the owner Mr Fernandez. Public rooms and bedrooms are fresh and inviting and the accommodation has a good range of facilities, though the rooms tend to be compact.

9rm(1⇨7↑)(1fb) CTV in all bedrooms ® ✻ ✻ sB&Bfr£25 sB&B⇨↑£42.50-£45 dB&B⇨↑£52.50-£55
CTV 40P ✻
♡ English & Continental V ♢ Sunday Lunch £11.35-£21.80alc Dinner £11.35-£21.80alc Last dinner 10pm
Credit Cards [1][3]

BRAMPTON Cumbria Map 12 NY56

★★★✻✻❀♨ **FARLAM HALL**
Hallbankgate CA8 2NG
(from A69 take A689 to Alston, the hotel is approx 2m on the left)
☎Hallbankgate(06977) 46234 FAX (06977) 46683
Closed 26-30 Dec
(Rosettes awarded for dinner only)

Farlam Hall is a 17th-century, creeper clad Borders mansion offering an appealing blend of traditional charm and modern comfort, added to which is the Quinion and Stevenson families'

own special brand of hospitality. There is no bar, but before dinner (at 8pm) guests gather in the lounges for an aperitif and canapés while choosing from chef Barry Quinion's short but imaginative, daily, fixed-price menu. Bedrooms have attractive colour schemes, lovely antique furnishings and are supplied with many thoughtful extras. Plans are in hand to enlarge the smaller rooms.

12⇨↑Annexe1⇨↑1✻ CTV in all bedrooms ® T
sB&B⇨↑£80-£100 dB&B⇨↑£160-£200 (incl dinner) ₽
35P ✻ ❀ croquet nc5yrs
V ♢ ♨ Dinner £28.50-£29.50 Last dinner 8pm
Credit Cards [1][2][3]

★★ 64% **Kirby Moor Country House**
Longtown Rd CA8 2AB (NW off A6071)
☎(06977) 3893 FAX (06977) 41847
Closed 25-26 Dec

In a rural location, this attractive hotel, with a conservatory restaurant, stands in pleasant grounds. Bedrooms have quality coordinated fabrics and period-style furniture. The lounge bar is comfortably furnished with good sofas, and the hotel is carefully run by John and Anne Robinson.

6rm(5↑)(1fb)1✻ CTV in all bedrooms ® T sB&B£35 sB&B↑£35 dB&B£45 dB&B↑£45 ₽
40P ❀
♡ English & French V ♢ ♨ ✻ Lunch fr£11.95&alc Dinner fr£12.95&alc Last dinner 9.15pm
CONF. Thtr 30 Class 20 Board 20 Del £50
Credit Cards [1][2][3]

BRANDESBURTON Humberside Map 08 TA14

★★ 67% **Burton Lodge**
YO25 8RU (on A165, adjoining Hainsworth Park Golf Club)
☎Hornsea(0964) 542847 FAX (0964) 542847

Surrounded by 2 acres of landscaped grounds, the hotel has a comfortable lounge, a small conservatory lounge and a Victorian-style dining room where a short, set-price menu of wholesome home-cooked meals is offered. Bedrooms are furnished and equipped in modern style

8rm(7⇨)(2fb) CTV in all bedrooms ® T ✻ sB&B£28-£30 sB&B⇨↑£32-£35 dB&B⇨↑£40-£45 ₽
12P 1✻ ❀ ✻ ▶ 18 ♪ (grass)
♢ ♨ ✻ Dinner £10-£12 Last dinner 9.15pm
Credit Cards [1][3]

BRANDON Suffolk Map 05 TL78

★★★ 67% **Brandon House**
High St IP27 0AX ☎Thetford(0842) 810171
FAX (0842) 814859

An 18th-century manor house, personally run by the resident proprietors and an enthusiastic team of staff. A range of food is served in the comfortable public rooms: bar meals, daily specials and a choice of daily and seasonal dishes in the pleasant dining room. Bedrooms, though somewhat plain, are generally of a good size, thoughtfully laid out and well equipped.

15⇨↑ CTV in all bedrooms ® T ✻ sB&B⇨↑£39.50-£45 dB&B⇨↑£55 ₽
40P ✻ ❀
♡ English & French V ♢ ♨ Lunch £14.95&alc Dinner £14.95&alc Last dinner 9.15pm
Credit Cards [1][2][3][5]

Hotels with red star ratings are especially high quality.

Brandon (Warwickshire) - Brechfa

BRANDON Warwickshire Map 04 SP47

★★★ 60% Brandon Hall
Main St CV8 3FW (off A428 to Rugby)
☏Coventry(0203) 542571 FAX (0203) 544909

In a quiet village, this hotel provides comfortable accommodation with well equipped bedrooms of varying sizes and styles.
60⇌♠(4fb)✗in 20 bedrooms CTV in all bedrooms ® T ✱ sB&B⇌♠£60-£80 dB&B⇌♠£80-£90 (room only) 🚗
(CTV 250P ✿ squash pitch & putt ◊ xmas
V ◊ ♨ ✱ Lunch £9.95-£10.95&alc Dinner £16.95-£20&alc Last dinner 9.30pm
Credit Cards [1][2][3][5]

BRANDS HATCH Kent Map 05 TQ56

★★★★ 59% Brands Hatch Thistle
DA3 8PE (on A20 N of junct with M20)
☏West Kingsdown(0474) 854900 FAX (0474) 853220

Located at the entrance to the world famous Grand Prix circuit this hotel will appeal to more than just motor racing enthusiasts. Modern bedrooms have particularly good facilities and there is a Parisian-themed brasserie which is open throughout the day, a restaurant and the Bugatti Bar. Leisure amenities are available at nearby Fredericks.
140⇌♠(7fb)1🛏✗in 12 bedrooms CTV in all bedrooms ® T ✱ sB&B⇌♠£70-£80 dB&B⇌♠£80-£90 (room only) 🚗
(180P ✿ xmas
♨ English & French V ◊ ♨ Lunch £13.95-£14.95&alc High tea fr£6.25 Dinner £18.95-£19.95&alc Last dinner 10.30pm
Conf. Thtr 270 Class 120 Board 250 Del from £60
Credit Cards [1][2][3][4][5]

★★★ ❀61% Brandshatch Place
Fawkham DA3 8NQ ☏Ash Green(0474) 872239 FAX (0474) 879652

29⇌♠(3fb)4🛏✗in 4 bedrooms CTV in all bedrooms T ✱ sB&B⇌♠£75 dB&B⇌♠£90 🚗
(100P ✿ 🏊 (heated) ▶ 18 ♪ (hard) ♫ squash ◡ snooker sauna solarium gymnasium jacuzzi badminton ◊ xmas
V ◊ ♨ ✱ Lunch £17.50 High tea fr£5 Dinner £18.50 Last dinner 9.45pm
Credit Cards [1][2][3][5]

BRANKSOME

See **Poole**

BRANSTON Lincolnshire Map 08 TF06

★★★ 60% Moor Lodge
Sleaford Rd LN4 1HU (3m S of Lincoln on B1188) ☏Lincoln(0522) 791366 FAX (0522) 794389

Located at the centre of the village, this hotel has a close association with the nearby RAF bases, hence the names of the Lancaster Bar and Arnhem Room Restaurant. Accommodation is varied, and some rooms are somewhat old-fashioned, but hotel is comfortable and the carvery serves good portions of mainly fresh produce, and service is professionally efficient.
25⇌♠(4fb) CTV in all bedrooms ® T ✱ sB&B⇌♠£50-£60 dB&B⇌♠£69.50-£79.50 🚗
150P
♨ English & French V ◊ ✱ Lunch fr£9.75&alc Dinner fr£16.30&alc Last dinner 9.15pm
Conf. Thtr 200 Class 80 Board 60 Del from £60
Credit Cards [1][2][3][5]

BREADSALL Derbyshire Map 08 SK33

★★★ 72% Breadsall Priory Hotel, Golf & Country Club
Moor Rd DE7 6DL (0.5m N. Signposted off A61) ☏Derby(0332) 832235 FAX (0332) 833509

With its origins in the 13th-century, this mansion is in a lovely parkland setting on the outskirts of Derby. It offers comfortable modern accommodation in a variety of bedrooms, some in the good purpose built extension or more individually styled Priory rooms. Guests have automatic membership of the country club.
14⇌♠ Annexe77⇌♠1🛏✗in 11 bedrooms CTV in all bedrooms ® ❡ T ✈ (ex guide dogs) ✱ sB&B⇌♠£93-£108 dB&B⇌♠£108-£130 🚗
Lift (300P ✿ 🏊 (heated) ▶ 18 ♪ (hard) squash snooker sauna solarium gymnasium health/beauty salon steam room spa bath xmas
♨ French V ◊ ♨ ✗ ✱ Lunch £11.25-£12.95 High tea £4.50-£6alc Dinner £18.50&alc Last dinner 9.45pm
Conf. Thtr 100 Class 30 Board 40 Del £130
Credit Cards [1][2][3][5] £

BRECHFA Dyfed Map 02 SN53

★★ ❀72% Ty Mawr Country
SA32 7RA (off B4310 in centre of village) ☏(0267) 202332 FAX (0267) 202437

Closed Xmas week, last week Nov & last two Jan
Nothing is too much trouble for Dick and Beryl Tudhope at their delightful village hotel. Beryl, as chef, is responsible for the delicious food, and baking bread, preparing stocks and shopping for fresh produce is her delight – organic ingredients being used wherever possible. There is an elegant lounge, and stone walls, open fireplaces

➡

BRANDS HATCH
THISTLE HOTEL
❀ ★★★★ AA

Brands Hatch, Dartford DA3 8PE
Tel: 0474 854900   Fax: 0474 853220

Your choice at Brands Hatch

For Reservations at over 100
Mount Charlotte Thistle Hotels
Telephone London: 071 937 8033.

Brechfa - Brentwood

and quarry tiles feature throughout the public rooms. Bedrooms are prettily decorated.
5rm(4⇨♠)(1fb)⊛ sB&B⇨♠£44 dB&B⇨♠£68 ₽
45P ⇄ ✿
♀ International V ✿ ⚌ Lunch £9.95 Dinner £15.95-£18.75
Last dinner 9.30pm
Credit Cards 1 2 3 £

BRECHIN Tayside *Angus* Map 15 NO56

★★ 56% Northern
Clerk St DD9 6AE ☎(0356) 622156 & 625505 FAX (0356) 622714
RS 1 & 2 Jan
This traditional-style town centre hotel offers a modest standard of accommodation, the original bedrooms offering the greatest comfort and the most space. There is an attractively decorated dining room and lounge bar, both providing reasonably priced meals.
20rm(4⇨12♠) CTV in 19 bedrooms ⓇT sB&B£18 sB&B⇨♠£28 dB&B£36 dB&B⇨♠£50
CTV 20P pool table
♀ Continental V ✿ ⚌ ★ Lunch £5-£6 High tea £5.25-£7.50 Dinner £6-£18alc Last dinner 9pm
CONF. Thtr 150 Class 60 Board 20
Credit Cards 1 2 3 £

BRECON Powys Map 03 SO02

★★★ ⊛⊛⚜ 81% Peterstone Court
Llanhamlach LD3 7YB (4m from town on A40 adjacent to Llanhamlach Church) ☎(0874) 86387 FAX (0874) 86423
Our Welsh Best Newcomer award winner for 1992/3, this small luxury hotel goes from strength to strength, despite some movement of personnel in the kichen over recent times. The dedication and infectious enthusiasm of general managers Michael and Barbara Taylor has inspired the small team of staff. Most of the well proportioned bedrooms are in the original Georgian manor house. These have classical decor and stylish furnishings, while the rooms in converted stables are less opulent but have their own distinct charm. Public rooms are richly furnished, and glittering chandeliers light the restaurant where chef Maynard Harvey offers an imaginative menu gourmand and nicely balanced seasonal menus. Notable among dishes our inspectors have enjoyed are warmed salad of soya-marinated beef with bright capsicum vinaigrette, tasty roast tenderloin of local lamb with a Madeira jus, and well executed puddings.
8⇨♠Annexe4⇨♠2⇄✂in 2 bedrooms CTV in all bedrooms⚌ T sB&B⇨♠£72.50-£125 dB&B⇨♠£90-£145 ₽
Ⓒ 50P ✿ ♨ (heated) sauna solarium gymnasium spa bath ♪ xmas
♀ French V ✿ ⚌ ✂ ★ Lunch £17.95-£24.95 Dinner £14.95-£29.95 Last dinner 9.30pm
Credit Cards 1 2 3 5 £

★★ 64% Wellington
The Bulwark LD3 7AD (1m from A40/A470 junct, next to St Mary's church) ☎(0874) 625225 FAX (0874) 623223
The Wellington offers a choice of bars and an all day restaurant/coffee shop. A separate wine bar, the Bacchus, is located in the Dukes Arcade. The bedrooms are mostly spacious.
21⇨♠(3fb) CTV in all bedrooms ⓇT 🗡 (ex guide dogs) ✿ sB&B⇨♠£39 dB&B⇨♠£59 ₽
♀ xmas
♀ Welsh & French V ✿ ⚌ ✂ ★ Lunch £1.75-£8.95alc High tea £1.75-£8.95alc Dinner fr£12.50&alc Last dinner 10pm
CONF. Thtr 140 Class 30 Board 40 Del from £40
Credit Cards 1 2 3 £

★★ 63% Castle of Brecon
Castle Square LD3 9DB ☎(0874) 624611 FAX (0874) 623737

Built on the remains of the castle, this old coaching inn opened its doors in the late 18th century, and still commands a fine elevated position. Recent upgrading has improved a good proportion of the bedrooms, and there are comfortable traditional bars and lounges.
37⇨♠Annexe12♠(3fb)1⇄ CTV in all bedrooms Ⓡ⚌ T ✿ sB&B⇨♠£35-£49 dB&B⇨♠£50-£65 ₽
30P ✿
V ✿ ✿ Lunch £7.90-£14.10 Dinner £14.10&alc Last dinner 10pm
CONF. Thtr 160 Class 130 Board 80 Del £49
Credit Cards 1 2 3 5 £

★★ 62% Nant Ddu Lodge
Cwm Taf CF48 2HY BRECON
☎Merthyr Tydfil(0685) 379111 FAX (0685) 377088
(For full entry see Nant-Ddu)

★ 66% Lansdowne Hotel & Restaurant
39 The Watton LD3 7EG ☎(0874) 623321 FAX (0874) 624384
This small and welcoming family-run hotel, just outside the town centre, has modern bedrooms, a choice of lounges and an attractive restaurant serving a range of food.
10rm(3⇨5♠)(2fb) CTV in all bedrooms Ⓡ T 🗡 (ex guide dogs) ✿ sB&B£23.25-£24.50 sB&B⇨♠£26.50-£28 dB&B£39-£41 dB&B⇨♠£45.50-£47.75 ₽
CTV 4P ⇄ nc5yrs
♀ English & French V ✿ ⚌ ✂ ✿ Lunch £9.75&alc Dinner £9-£10.75&alc Last dinner 9.30pm
Credit Cards 1 2 3 5 £

BRENTWOOD Essex Map 05 TQ59

★★★★ 65% Brentwood Moat House
London Rd CM14 4NR ☎(0277) 225252 FAX (0277) 262809

This Tudor house has been sympathetically extended and most of the bedrooms are set chalet-style around the attractive garden, the few in the main house retaining their Tudor character. The lounge has heavy carved oak panelling, an ornate ceiling and stone fireplace, and the restaurant, converted from a barn, offers a lengthy 'carte' of mostly traditional dishes and flambés.
3⇨♠Annexe30⇨♠2⇄ CTV in all bedrooms Ⓡ T ✿ sB⇨♠£85-£122.50 dB⇨♠£87-£143 (room only) ₽
Ⓒ CTV 80P ⇄
♀ International V ✿ ⚌ ✿ Lunch fr£19.50alc Dinner £12-£15&alc Last dinner 10.15pm
CONF. Thtr 50 Board 25 Del from £116
Credit Cards 1 2 3 4 5

Forte Posthouse
Brook St CM14 5NF (close to M25/A12 interchange) ☎(0277) 260260 FAX (0277) 264264
Suitable for both the business and leisure traveller, this bright hotel provides modern accommodation in well equipped bedrooms with en suite bathrooms. For more details about Forte Posthouse hotels, consult the Contents page, under Hotel Groups.
111⇨✿ B⇨♠£41.50-£53.50 (room only)
CONF. Thtr 120 Class 60 Board 40 Del £89.50

Remember to book early for holiday
and bank holiday times.

For key to symbols see the Bookmark.

BRETBY Derbyshire Map 08 SK22

★★★ 65% Stanhope
Ashby Rd East DE15 0PU (on A50) (Whitbread)
☎Burton upon Trent(0283) 217954 FAX (0283) 226199
This hotel has bedrooms equipped and furnished to good modern standards. Public areas include a beamed bar and a comfortable restaurant overlooking the garden and countryside.
28⇨🛏(3fb)1⚑⚐in 5 bedrooms CTV in all bedrooms ®⚑ T
✗ (ex guide dogs) ✻ sB&B⇨🛏fr£59.30 dB&B⇨🛏fr£71 ♬
((150P ✿ sauna solarium gymnasium *xmas*
♡ Continental V ♡ ⚐ ⚑ ✻ Lunch fr£8.50&alc Dinner fr£14&alc Last dinner 10pm
CONF. Thtr 200 Board 24 Del from £85
Credit Cards [1][2][3][5]

BRIDGEND
See **Islay, Isle of**

BRIDGEND Mid Glamorgan Map 03 SS97

★★★ ❀❀72% Coed-y-Mwstwr
Coychurch CF35 6AF (leave A473 at Coychurch and turn right at petrol station. Follow signs at top of hill) (Welsh Rarebits) ☎(0656) 860621 FAX (0656) 863122
Whispering Trees is the English translation of the hotel's name, and is quite appropriate for this elegant Victorian mansion set in 17 acres of mature woodland. It is a popular conference venue, but not to the detriment of the private guest. The bedrooms are bright and modern, and there is a comfortable lounge, cocktail bar and a panelled restaurant with a vaulted ceiling. Chef Gareth Passy's seasonally changing set and à la carte menus make good use of quality produce, and his well executed dishes are only occasionally over-garnished. Our inspector enjoyed smooth terrine of smoked salmon and halibut; tender brochette of chicken marinated in honey, soy and chilli; new season's lamb stuffed with a mousse of redcurrant and asparagus, finishing with a rich pudding.
23⇨🛏(1fb) CTV in all bedrooms T ✻ ♬
Lift ((100P ✿ ≈ (heated) ♂ (hard) snooker croquet petanque table tennis ♪ *xmas*
♡ British & French V ♡ ⚐ ⚑ ✻
Credit Cards [1][2][3][5]   £

★★★ 65% Heronston
Ewenny CF35 5AW (2m S B4265) ☎(0656) 668811 FAX (0656) 767391
Closed 25-26 Dec & 1 Jan
This is a popular commercial hotel. Well furnished executive bedrooms are spaciously comfortable, and upgrading is planned for the standard rooms.
76⇨🛏(4fb) CTV in all bedrooms ®⚑ T sB&B⇨🛏£60-£85 dB&B⇨🛏£80-£105 ♬
Lift ((CTV 175P ⚑ ▭ (heated) ≈ (heated) snooker sauna solarium jacuzzi steamroom
♡ Welsh & French V ♡ ⚐ Lunch £9.50-£13.75&alc Dinner £12.75-£13.75&alc Last dinner 10pm
CONF. Thtr 180 Class 80 Board 40 Del from £80
Credit Cards [1][2][3][4][5]
See advertisement on page 125

★★★ 61% Court Colman
Pen-y-Fai CF31 4NG ☎Aberkenfig(0656) 720212 FAX (0656) 724544
This imposing house, set in 6 acres of grounds, has spacious public rooms with ornate interior architecture. Bedrooms are all well equipped but tend to differ in size. The newer rooms are of a good modern standard and while the remainder are spacious they lack the same quality.
32rm(16⇨🛏12🛏)(4fb)2⚑ CTV in 34 bedrooms ® T
✗ (ex guide dogs)
CTV 80P ✿

➔

Brentwood Moat House Hotel

AA ★★★★   INTERNATIONAL HOTELIERS

In the warm and friendly atmosphere of this genuine Tudor House, you can enjoy the traditional comfort of open log fires in oak panelled lounges.
Accommodation consists of garden suites facing onto an olde worlde garden and three luxury period rooms with four-posters and marbled spa bathrooms.
Elegant restaurant with extensive, speciality, fresh produce menu. Twenty four hour room service.
London Road, Brentwood, Essex CM14 4NR
Tel: Reception (0277) 225252, Restaurant 225656
Telex: 995182 Fax: (0277) 262809

Nant Ddu Lodge Hotel ★★

Cwm Taf, Nr Brecon, Powys CF48 2HY
Tel: (0685) 379 111 Fax: (0685) 377 088

A Hotel of Character. The Nant Ddu Lodge Hotel is an imposing old country house set in a beautiful location in the Brecon Beacons National Park. Originally Lord Tredegar's shooting lodge, the Nant Ddu is now a hotel of great character and charm. Its cosy, traditionally furnished bar sets the scene perfectly for the rest of the hotel. This is a place in which to relax and enjoy the warm, friendly atmosphere and the good food and superb surroundings. Privately run, the hotel is renowned for its genuine welcome and personal service. All fifteen bedrooms are en-suite and the restaurant serves excellent food using fresh, local produce.

Bridgend - Bridgnorth

🍴 English & French **V** ⚙ ⚖ ✳ Lunch £12-£70 Dinner £20-£30alc Last dinner 9.30pm
CONF. Thtr 200 Class 100 Board 75 Del from £70
Credit Cards 1 2 3 5

★★ **57%** *Wyndham*
Dunraven Place CF31 1JE ☎(0656) 652080 & 657421 FAX (0656) 766438
A busy town centre hotel, parts of which date back to the 17th century, the Wyndham provides neat, clean bedrooms and an additional small bar for residents and diners where a good range of food is served.
28rm(25⇨)1🛁 CTV in all bedrooms ®
《 CTV ⓟ
🍴 English & French **V** ⚙ ⚖ Last dinner 10pm
Credit Cards 1 2 3 5

Forte Travelodge
Sarn Park Motorway Services CF32 9DX
☎(0656) 659218 Central Res (0800) 850350
(For full entry see Sarn Motorway Service Area)

BRIDGE OF ALLAN Central *Stirlingshire* Map **11** NS79

★★★ ❀ **63%** *Royal*
Henderson St FK9 4HG ☎(0786) 832284
FAX (0786) 834377
Popular with residents and locals, this hotel has undergone steady improvement over the past few years. Bedrooms vary in size but all are well equipped. The cooking continues to merit an AA rosette award, with Stuart Harrow having taken over from Kevin Graham, and the table d'hôte dinner menu offers particularly good value.
32⇨🛁 🍴 in 4 bedrooms CTV in all bedrooms ® ✨ **T**
sB⇨🛁 £52.50-£55.50 dB⇨🛁 £52.50-£55.50 (room only) 🅿
Lift 《 60P *xmas*
🍴 Scottish & French **V** ⚙ ⚖ ✳ Lunch £3.50-£8.95 High tea £4.25-£8.50 Dinner £12.95-£17.50&alc Last dinner 9.30pm
CONF. Thtr 150 Class 100 Board 40 Del from £65
Credit Cards 1 2 3 5 £

See advertisement under STIRLING

BRIDGE OF CALLY Tayside *Perthshire* Map **15** NO15

★ ❀ **66%** *Bridge of Cally*
PH10 7JJ (beside bridge over River Ardle (A93))
☎(0250) 886231
Closed Nov & 1st 2 wks Dec
Set in its own gardens by the bridge over the River Ardle, this small family-run hotel has a cheerful atmosphere. Bedrooms are modest but comfortable and there is a cosy bar and attractive candlelit dining room where the 4-course dinner menu features good traditional country cooking.
9rm(3⇨3🛁) CTV in 2 bedrooms ® ✈ (ex guide dogs)
CTV 40P ⚙ ❀ ⚖
V ⚙ ⚖ Last dinner 9pm
Credit Cards 1 3 5

Rosettes range from 5 for outstanding cuisine to 1 rosette for enjoyable, well prepared food

BRIDGE OF MARNOCH Grampian *Aberdeenshire*
Map **15** NJ55

★

❀✽
OLD MANSE OF MARNOCH
AB54 5RS (on B9117 between Huntly and Banff)
☎Aberchirder(0466) 780873
Closed 2 wks Nov
(Rosette awarded for dinner only)
Receiving its Red Star award for the first time this year, the Old Manse, circa 1805, is a small and very individual privately owned country house hotel, set in 3 acres of secluded grounds and gardens. The bedrooms are spacious, comfortable and decorated in the style of the house. There are 2 lounges, one with many interesting souvenirs of owners Keren and Patrick Carter's travels around the world. The dining room has a nautical theme, and a set 4-course Taste of Scotland dinner is served at one large table, much of the produce coming from the hotel's garden. Breakfasts offer a choice of 14 hot dishes.
5⇨🛁 ® ✳ sB&B⇨🛁 £45-£60 dB&B⇨🛁 £60-£80
CTV 6P 2🚗 ⚙ ❀ nc12yrs
⚖ Lunch fr£15 Dinner £17.50-£20 Last dinner 7.30pm

BRIDGNORTH Shropshire Map **07** SO79

★★ **66%** *Croft*
Saint Mary's St WV16 4DW ☎(0746) 762816
This small and quite delightful 16th-century hotel is in the old town just off the High Street. Most bedrooms have exposed timbers, creaking floor boards and fine period furniture. There is a cosy bar for residents with a woodburning stove, the restaurant has exposed timbers and an inglenook fireplace, and there is a separate lounge.
12rm(6⇨6🛁)(3fb) CTV in all bedrooms **T**
CTV ⓟ ⚙ ⚖
V ⚙ ⚖ ✳ Dinner £9.95&alc Last dinner 9pm
Credit Cards 1 2 3

★★ **65%** *Parlors Hall*
Mill St WV15 5AL ☎(0746) 761931 FAX (0746) 767058
This small hotel in a mainly Georgian building near the riverside park in Low Town has attractive public rooms with exposed beams and oak panelling. Modernised bedrooms offer good facilities.
15⇨🛁(2fb)2🛏 CTV in all bedrooms ® **T** ✈ (ex guide dogs)
sB&B⇨🛁 £39 dB&B⇨🛁 £46
24P *xmas*
🍴 European **V** ⚙ ⚖ Lunch £7.90&alc Dinner £14.95&alc Last dinner 10pm
Credit Cards 1 3

See advertisement on page 127

★★ **60%** *Falcon*
Saint John St, Lowtown WV15 6AG ☎(0746) 763134 FAX (0746) 765401
Situated near the bridge in Lowtown, this 17th-century coaching inn has modern bedrooms. Public areas have been converted to open plan over recent years, and the bar and bistro restaurant, featuring original oak beams and open fires, are now combined. Staff are friendly and cheerful.
15rm(5⇨7🛁)(3fb) CTV in all bedrooms ® **T**
CTV 200P
🍴 English & French **V** ⚙ ⚖ Last dinner 9.30pm
Credit Cards 1 2 3

Bridge of Cally Hotel

AND RESTAURANT

★

Perthshire PH10 7JJ
Tel: Bridge of Cally
(0250) 886231

Situated on the A93 Braemar Road overlooking the River Ardle surrounded by woodland and the Perthshire hills. Fishing, golf, pony trekking, skiing all available nearby. Nine bedrooms, six with private bath, all have colour TV. Fully licensed. Restaurant noted for good food.

Brochure and tariff on application.

the HERONSTON HOTEL

★ ★ ★

Ewenny, Bridgend, Mid Glamorgan CF35 5AW

Telephone: (0656) 668811
Fax: (0656) 767391
Telex: 498232

Modern popular hotel with comfortable bedrooms, friendly service and good leisure facilities.

★ ★ ★

St. Mary's Hotel, Golf & Country Club

A luxury country hotel converted from a 17th century farmhouse, we offer elegance and comfort with first class friendly service. Set in picturesque surroundings on a privately owned 150 acre 27 hole golf complex 2 mins from M4, making it the perfect location for business or pleasure.

- 18 hole St Mary's Course
- 9 hole Sevenoaks Course
- 15 bay floodlit driving range
- Tennis court
- Equestrian centre

All rooms fitted with:
- Whirlpool baths
- Satellite TV
- Coffee & tea facilities
- Direct dial telephone

Golf, Equestrian and Weekend Breaks available.

Please call us for a FREE video and brochure and sample for yourselves "The Magic of St. Mary's".

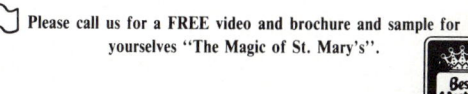

St. Mary's Golf Club Ltd. St. Mary's Hill Pencoed, South Glamorgan CF35 5EA.
Hotel Reservation: Tel: (0656) 861100 Fax: (0656) 863400

Bridgwater - Bridport

BRIDGWATER Somerset Map 03 ST33

★★★ **70%** **Walnut Tree Inn**
North Petherton TA6 6QA (3m S A38)
☎ North Petherton(0278) 662255 FAX (0278) 663946

Once a coaching inn, this busy hotel maintains good all round standards. Executive and Standard bedrooms are both individually styled and well furnished; public areas have a lively, cheerful ambience, particularly the cosy and convivial bar. The Cottage Restaurant offers a cheaper alternative to the à la carte menu of the smart Sedgemoor.

28⇌(2fb)1🍴 CTV in all bedrooms ® T 🐕 (ex guide dogs) ✱
sB&B⇌♪£25-£73 dB&B⇌♪£41-£88 ⛔

(70P solarium *xmas*
♡ V ❀ ♨ Lunch £4.30-£11.40alc Dinner fr£12&alc Last dinner 10pm
CONF. Thtr 70 Class 34 Board 46 Del from £75
Credit Cards [1][2][3][5] £

★★ **64%** **Friarn Court**
37 St Mary St TA6 3LX ☎(0278) 452859 FAX (0278) 452988

This small, town centre hotel has a small patio at the back. Public areas are rather compact, but bedrooms, reached by winding stairs and corridors, are cheerfully decorated and well equipped.

12⇌♪(2fb)1🍴 CTV in all bedrooms ® T 🐕 (ex guide dogs)
sB&B⇌♪£39.90-£69.90 dB&B⇌♪£40-£69.90 Continental breakfast ⛔

(12P
♡ International V ❀ ♨ Bar Lunch £1.50-£5 High tea £2.50-£8.50 Dinner £8.70-£15&alc Last dinner 9.30pm
CONF. Thtr 60 Class 40 Board 30 Del from £29
Credit Cards [1][2][3][5] £

BRIDLINGTON Humberside Map 08 TA16

★★★ **66%** **Expanse**
North Marine Dr YO15 2LS (follow signs North Beach P, pass under railway arch for North Marine Drive. Hotel at bottom of hill) ☎(0262) 675347 FAX (0262) 604928

To the north of the town and overlooking the expanse of bay, this privately run hotel has a friendly informal atmosphere. Attractive bedrooms have good modern facilities and there are comfortable oak-panelled lounges, a choice of bars and a restaurant with a selection of menus.

48⇌♪(4fb) CTV in all bedrooms ® T 🐕 (ex guide dogs)
sB&B⇌♪£29.50-£42.50 dB&B⇌♪£57-£68 ⛔
Lift (15P 15🚗 (£1.50) 🎵 *xmas*
♡ English & French V ❀ ♨ Lunch £6-£10 Dinner fr£13.50&alc Last dinner 9pm
CONF. Thtr 35 Class 24 Board 16 Del from £49
Credit Cards [1][2][3][5]

★★ **67%** **Monarch**
South Marine Dr YO15 3JJ (Follow sings South Beach to seafront. Hotel opposite The Spa) ☎(0262) 674447 FAX (0262) 604928

Closed Oct-9 Apr

A friendly seafront hotel, the Monarch offers stylishly decorated, comfortable bedrooms of varying size and public areas with fine views.

40rm(36⇌♪)(5fb) CTV in all bedrooms ® T
🐕 (ex guide dogs) ✱ sB&B£20 sB&B⇌♪£28-29.50 dB&B£40 dB&B⇌♪£56-£59 ⛔
Lift (CTV 10P
♡ English & French V ❀ ✱ Sunday Lunch fr£6.95 Dinner fr£12 Last dinner 8.30pm
Credit Cards [1][2][3][5] £

★★ **67%** **New Revelstoke**
1-3 Flamborough Rd YO15 2HU (take B1255 Flamborough Head rd and in half mile turn rt at mini-rbt) ☎(0262) 672362 FAX (0262) 672362

This family-owned and run hotel is convenient for both the seafront and town centre. Public areas are attractive and include a choice of bars, a small lounge and a pleasant restaurant, where a selection of popular dishes is served in generous portions. Bedrooms are modern and vary in size, some being very spacious.

26rm(17⇌4♪)(5fb) CTV in all bedrooms ® ♫ T 🐕 ✱
sB&B£27-£34 sB&B⇌♪£27-£34 dB&B£46-£54
dB&B⇌♪£46-£54 ⛔
14P 🎵
♡ English & French V ❀ ♨ ✱ Lunch £5.10-£10alc Dinner £8-£20alc Last dinner 8.30pm
CONF. Thtr 150 Class 80 Board 48 Del from £48
Credit Cards [1][2][3][5] £

BRIDPORT Dorset Map 03 SY49

★★★ **61%** **Haddon House**
West Bay DT6 4EL (From A35, half mile along B3157 , signposted to West Bay) ☎(0308) 23626 & 25323 FAX (0308)27348

This handsome Regency-style hotel, hospitably run by the Loud family for over 15 years, has spacious and comfortable public areas including a beamed dining room offering a good range of dishes. Bedrooms are quite plainly furnished but freshly decorated, of a reasonable size and well equipped.

13⇌♪(2fb) CTV in all bedrooms ® T ✱ sB&B⇌♪£39.50-£42.50 dB&B⇌♪£48-£58 ⛔
CTV 70P 4🚗 ❀ *xmas*
♡ English & French V ❀ ♨ Lunch £7.95 Dinner £14.50 Last dinner 9pm
Credit Cards [1][2][3][5]

★★ **68%** **Roundham House**
Roundham Gardens, West Bay Rd
DT6 4BD ☎(0308) 22753 & 25779 FAX (0308) 421145

Closed Nov-Jan

This handsome stone property is in an elevated position with views across West Bay. Resident proprietors Mr and Mrs Moody are an amiable couple who have continually improved and refurbished the property. Bedrooms are nicely furnished, with fresh décor and pretty fabrics. Attractive public areas include a comfortable lounge, and the dining room takes full advantage of the view. Mrs Moody's daily table d'hôte menu offers imaginative home-style cooking.

8rm(4⇌3♪)(2fb) CTV in all bedrooms ® T 🐕 (ex guide dogs) ✱ sB&B⇌♪£29.50-£35 dB&B⇌♪£47-£55 ⛔
12P 1🚗 ❀
♡ European V ❀ ♨ ✱ Lunch £8.25-£10.90 Dinner £13.25-£13.95 Last dinner 8pm
Credit Cards [1][3][5]

★ **62%** **Bridge House**
115 East St DT6 3LB (next to River Asker bridge)
☎(0308) 23371

An attractive 18th-century house on the eastern edge of the town providing friendly personal service, simply furnished bedrooms, a restaurant serving enjoyable home-cooked meals, plus a breakfast room and open-plan lounge bar.

10⇌♪(3fb) CTV in all bedrooms ® ♫ sB&B⇌♪£27.50-£30 dB&B⇌♪£41.50-£45 ⛔
12P *xmas*
V ❀ ✱ Lunch £8.50 Dinner £14.50&alc Last dinner 9pm
Credit Cards [1][2][3]

Hotels with red star ratings are especially high quality.

Bridport - Brighton & Hove

★ **58%** **Bridport Arms**
West Bay DT6 4EN (2m S off B3157 Weymouth rd)
☎(0308) 22994
Situated on the beach beside the quay at West Bay, this small thatched inn has simply furnished comfortable bedrooms, with those in the main house better equipped than those in the cottage annexe. There is a small cosy lounge, family room and choice of popular bars, plus a small restaurant.
8rm(1⇨5↑)Annexe5rm(3fb) CTV in 8 bedrooms ®
sB&B£21-£26 sB&B⇨↑£26-£29.50 dB&B£42-£46 dB&B⇨↑£49-£55 ♫
CTV 4🚗
V ♥ ✱ Sunday Lunch £1.65-£16.50alc Dinner £4.65-£16.50alc
Last dinner 8.45pm
Credit Cards [1][3]   £

BRIGG Humberside Map 08 TA00

★★ **66%** **Exchange Coach House Inn**
Bigby St DN20 8EJ ☎(0652) 657633 FAX (0652) 657636
Dating from the 1700s, this town centre coaching inn has been brought into the 1990s with great care to preserve its original character. The courtyard bedrooms have been attractively converted from stables and outbuildings. An extensive range of authentic Indian and other international dishes is available and service is friendly.
21⇨↑ CTV in all bedrooms ®✱ T ✗ (ex guide dogs)
sB⇨↑£35-£49 dB⇨↑£55-£69 (room only) ♫
24P ✱ snooker ♪
♥ English & Oriental V ♥ ♫ ✱ Lunch £1.95-£6.95&alc High tea£4.95-£7.95Dinner£2.95-£14.90&alcLastdinner11pm
Credit Cards [1][2][3]   £

BRIGHOUSE West Yorkshire Map 07 SE12

Forte Crest
Clifton Village HD6 4HW (on A644 just off junct 25 of M62) ☎(0484) 400400 FAX (0484) 400068

FORTE CREST

A large modern hotel with a wide range of services and amenities, designed particularly for the business traveller. Bedrooms are smart, comfortable and well equipped. For more details about Forte Crest hotels, consult the Contents page, under Hotel Groups.
94⇨↑✱ B⇨↑£89 (room only)
CONF. Thtr 200 Class 120 Board 60 Del £115

BRIGHTON & HOVE East Sussex Map 04 TQ30

★★★★★ **❀60%** **Grand**
Kings Rd BN1 2FW (adjacent to Conference Centre)
☎Brighton(0273) 321188 FAX (0273) 202694

DE VERE HOTELS

We are delighted to welcome this famous hotel, about which we have received many enquiries, back to the Guide following its massive refurbishment programme. Many of the sea-facing bedrooms as well as those in the new wing are of high quality, and during the next 3 years the remaining side rooms will match this standard. Chef Ivan Parnell offers English and continental food in the elegant King's Restaurant but, as the Grand is particularly popular for conferences, the individual guest can find staff in the bar and restaurant overwhelmed at times. Generally, however, the 5 star services are all in place, and afternoon tea at the weekends is especially popular.
200⇨↑(70fb)2🛏 CTV in all bedrooms ®✱ T ✱
sB&B⇨↑£60-£130 dB&B⇨↑£120-£230 ♫
Lift (65🚗 (£10 per night) 🏊 (heated) sauna solarium gymnasium hairdresser masseur spa pool steam room ♪ xmas

THE WALNUT TREE INN

North Petherton
Bridgwater, Somerset
On A38 Exit 24 M5 One Mile
Tel: (0278) 662255
Fax: (0278) 663946

AA ★★★

Set in the heart of Somerset this fully modernised 18th Century Coaching Inn makes an ideal stop over for the traveller and the businessman.

Situated on the A38 and only one mile from junction 24 on the M5.

The Walnut Tree has two Restaurants, one for casual eating and one formal à la carte Restaurant.

All rooms are quietly situated at the rear of the Hotel.

Best Western

Parlors Hall Hotel ★★

Mill Street, Bridgnorth,
Shropshire WV15 5AL
Tel: (0746) 761931 Fax: (0746) 767058

The original Parlors Hall which dates back to the 12th century became an hotel in 1929. Since then it has been carefully refurbished but keeping many of the ancient features, including the fireplaces and oak panelling. Today the hotel offers fifteen luxury en suite bedrooms, each individually decorated in keeping with the character of the building. The attractive restaurant offers an à la carte and carvery menus. Ideally located for business visitors or visiting the many tourist attractions of the area.

127

Brighton & Hove

English & French **V** ⌂ ⌖ Lunch fr£18&alc High tea fr£8 Dinner fr£24&alc Last dinner 10pm
CONF. Thtr 820 Class 380 Board 180
Credit Cards ① ② ③ ⑤ £

★★★★ **70%** Brighton Thistle
Kings Rd BN1 2GS (from Palace Pier rbt take Kings Rd for hotel in 0.5m on left)
☎Brighton(0273) 206700 FAX (0273) 820692
Right on the seafront, this is a modern and well appointed hotel with light and airy public areas including a comfortable lounge and a well stocked bar. There is a spacious carvery restaurant and a more formal restaurant where chef Colin Flood offers enjoyable dishes with well balanced flavours. Bedrooms are spacious and well appointed.
204⇌🕽⚲in 20 bedrooms CTV in all bedrooms ®✱ T ✱ sB⇌🕽£115-£139 dB⇌🕽£135-£159 (room only) 🅿
Lift (⊞ 70P ⛳ (heated) sauna solarium gymnasium ♪ xmas
English & French **V** ⌂ ⌖ ✱ Lunch £16.95&alc Dinner £16.95&alc Last dinner 10pm
Credit Cards ① ② ③ ④ ⑤

★★★ **62%** Imperial
First Av BN3 2GU ☎Brighton(0273) 777320 FAX (0273) 777310
Quietly situated close to the sea, this is a charming Victorian building. Bedrooms are in modern style with coordinated soft furnishings and smart bathrooms, and some original features have been retained. Hamiltons Brasserie offers all-day food from a varied menu, and Tates Bar is a popular meeting place. There is an elegant lounge and an Italian-style patio. Street parking is unrestricted.
76⇌🕽(2fb)4🝁⚲in 10 bedrooms CTV in all bedrooms ® T sB⇌🕽£26.25-£60 dB⇌🕽£52.50-£80 🅿
Lift (⊞ 8P xmas
French **V** ⌂ ⌖ Lunch fr£10.50&alc Dinner fr£10.50&alc Last dinner 11pm
CONF. Thtr 110 Class 50 Board 32 Del from £55
Credit Cards ① ② ③ ⑤ £

★★★ **62%** Norfolk Resort
149 Kings Rd BN1 2PP
☎Brighton(0273) 738201 FAX (0273) 821752
This attractive seafront hotel has been extensively refurbished over the last few years. Bedrooms are still being upgraded, but all are comfortable and freshly decorated. There is a choice of 2 bars, one of which offers a brasserie-style menu as an alternative to the more formal restaurant.
121⇌🕽(5fb)⚲in 7 bedrooms CTV in all bedrooms ®✱ T ✱ sB⇌🕽£55-£65 dB⇌🕽£65-£75 (room only) 🅿
Lift (10P 30🚗 (£1) 🖾 (heated) sauna solarium jacuzzi hair salon exercise equipment xmas
International **V** ⌂ ⌖ Sunday Lunch £5.95-£8.95 Dinner £11.25 Last dinner 9.45pm
Credit Cards ① ② ③ ⑤

★★★ **61%** Old Ship
King's Rd BN1 1NR (on seafront between the piers) ☎Brighton(0273) 329001 FAX (0273) 820718
Originally an inn, and one of the oldest hotels in Brighton, the Old Ship is situated on the seafront and is undergoing extensive refurbishment. Bedrooms vary in quality and size, the East Wing providing the most luxury, and many have sea views. There are smart lounges and a panelled bar. After some years adrift, this famous old vessel is apparently back on course.
152⇌🕽(19fb) CTV in all bedrooms ® T ✱ sB&B⇌🕽£60-£90 dB&B⇌🕽£75-£105 🅿
Lift (70🚗 (£6 per 24hrs) ♪ xmas
English & French **V** ⌂ ⌖ ✱ Lunch fr£13&alc Dinner fr£17.50&alc Last dinner 9.30pm
CONF. Thtr 300 Class 120 Board 60 Del from £75
Credit Cards ① ② ③ ⑤

★★★ **61%** *Sackville*
189 Kingsway BN3 4GU ☎(0273) 736292 FAX (0273) 205759
Situated in a prime position overlooking Hove Lawns, bowling greens and the sea, this distinctive Edwardian building, with its famous green exterior, has bedrooms which vary considerably in size, style and furnishings, but are all equipped to the same standard. There is an attractive oak-panelled bar lounge with Chesterfield sofas, an adjoining sun lounge and an elegant sea-facing restaurant.
45⇌🕽1🛏 CTV in all bedrooms ® T
Lift (12🚗
English & French **V** ⌂ ⌖ ⚲ Last dinner 9.30pm
Credit Cards ① ② ③ ⑤

★★ ❀❀❀ **75%** *Topps*
17 Regency Square BN1 2FG (opposite West Pier) ☎Brighton(0273) 729334 FAX (0273) 203679
RS Jan
(Rosettes awarded for dinner only)
Two Regency town houses have been converted into this high quality small hotel, owned and run by Paul and Pauline Collins. Spacious bedrooms are comfortably furnished with sofas and chairs, and many extras are provided. In the cosy restaurant Pauline's reasonably priced set menu comprises 2 courses and coffee – desserts are extra.
14⇌🕽(2fb)2🛏 CTV in all bedrooms ® T ✖ (ex guide dogs) ✱ sB&B⇌🕽£38-£64 dB&B⇌🕽£64-£99 🅿
Lift 2🚗 (£5 per night) 🚗
English & French **V** ✱ Dinner fr£21.95 Last dinner 9.30pm
Credit Cards ① ② ③ ④ ⑤

★★ **67%** Whitehaven
34 Wilbury Rd BN3 3JP ☎Brighton(0273) 778355 FAX (0273) 731177
In a quiet residential area, this attractive double fronted town house offers modern, well equipped bedrooms. There is a cosy lounge (for non smokers), a cocktail bar and the elegant Rolling Clock restaurant, named after the 17th-century clock that sits proudly on the mantelpiece. A choice of menus is offered and staff are efficient and friendly.
17⇌🕽(3fb)1🛏 CTV in all bedrooms ® T ✖ (ex guide dogs) ✱ sB&B⇌🕽£30-£52.50 dB&B⇌🕽£45-£75 🅿
⚲ nc8yrs
English & French **V** ⌂ ⌖ Lunch £13.50-£19.50 Dinner £13.50-£19.50 Last dinner 9.30pm
Credit Cards ① ② ③ ⑤ £

★★ **60%** St Catherines Lodge
Seafront, Kingsway BN3 2RZ (opposite King Alfred Leisure Centre) ☎Brighton(0273) 778181 FAX (0273) 774949
A privately owned, Regency-style hotel opposite the seafront and Hove Leisure Centre offers bedrooms varying in size and décor. Public areas, though rather in need of a facelift, comprise a cosy traditional bar, a comfortable lounge leading into the pretty breakfast room and a restaurant providing a choice of menus. Both lounge and room service are available, the latter including the luxury of early morning tea.
50rm(40⇌🕽)(4fb)2🛏 CTV in all bedrooms T sB&B£30-£36 sB&B⇌🕽£36-£45 dB&Bfr£54 dB&B⇌🕽£60-£65 🅿
Lift (CTV 5P 4🚗 (£4) games room xmas
European **V** ⌂ Lunch £5-£8.25&alc Dinner £13.50&alc Last dinner 9pm
CONF. Thtr 70 Class 40 Board 30 Del from £46
Credit Cards ① ② ③ ⑤ £

Rosettes range from 5 for outstanding cuisine to 1 rosette for enjoyable, well prepared food

Bristol

BRISTOL Avon Map **03** ST57

★★★★ ✿72% **Swallow Royal**
College Green BS1 5TA (in the city centre)
☎(0272) 255100 FAX (0272) 251515

Now finding its feet after a testing start, this prominent city-centre establishment has restored some charm and style to the Bristol hotel scene. An elegant Grade II listed building, recently extensively renovated, it has high-quality modern bedrooms and public areas, including the lofty Palm Court Ballroom and lavishly decorated restaurant are opulent. The restaurant has a reputation for its good seasonal menus and cooking of some note by chef Michael Kitts.
242⇌♠4⊞⊬in 85 bedrooms CTV in all bedrooms ®⍟T✻
sB&B⇌♠£99.50 dB&B⇌♠£125 ₧
Lift (⊞ CTV 150☎ ⊠ (heated) sauna solarium gymnasium spa bath *xmas*
♀ International V ⋄ ⚲ ⊬ Lunch £16&alc High tea £8.50 Dinner £20&alc Last dinner 10.15pm
CONF. Thtr 250 Class 160 Board 30 Del £140
Credit Cards ①②③④⑤

★★★★ 66% **Aztec**
Aztec West Business Park, Almondsbury BS12 4TS (access via M5 (junct 16) & M4) (Shire) ☎Almondsbury(0454) 201090
FAX (0454) 201593

Ideally suited for business people, this hotel is in the heart of Bristol's business park. The bright modern building has good, comfortably furnished bedrooms, styled with bold colours and fabrics. A hotel 'pub' is a relaxing setting for meals and refreshments.
88⇌♠(13fb)2⊞⊬in 12 bedrooms CTV in all bedrooms ®⍟T
✻ sB&B⇌♠£79-£89 dB&B⇌♠£98-£108 ₧
Lift (240P ✿ ⊠ (heated) squash snooker sauna solarium gymnasium spa bath steam room ♪ *xmas*
⇨

★★★★ AA

THE BRIGHTON
THISTLE HOTEL

King's Road, Brighton BN1 2GS
Tel: 0273 206700   Fax: 0273 820692

Your choice in
Brighton

For Reservations at over 100
Mount Charlotte Thistle Hotels
Telephone London: 071 937 8033.

THISTLE HOTELS

St Catherines Lodge Hotel

Visit Royal Pavilion, Lanes Antique Shops, Devils Dyke, Arundel Castle, Bluebell Railway, Goodwood House.

Kingsway, Hove, Sussex BN3 2RZ
Brighton (0273) 778181
Fax: (0273) 774949

Well established seafront hotel with fine Regency features. 50 rooms most with private bathroom all with direct dial telephone and colour TV. Four-poster beds and family rooms.
Excellent Restaurant, cocktail bar and games room.
Opposite King Alfred Leisure Centre with water slides, swimming pools and ten pin bowling.

AA★★ English Tourist Board

Bristol

♥ International V ✿ ⚜ ✂ ✱ Lunch £11.95-£13.95&alc Dinner £16-£18&alc Last dinner 9.45pm
CONF. Thtr 200 Class 120 Board 40 Del £115
Credit Cards 1 2 3 5

★★★★ 64% **Holiday Inn Crowne Plaza**
Victoria St BS1 6HY ☎(0272) 255010 FAX (0272) 255040
Closed 26-30 Dec RS 25 & 31 Dec

Close to Temple Meads station this modern hotel has spacious public rooms and, on the top floor, a hi-tec exercise area for hotel guests only. The kitchens make an honest effort to provide good food for the reasonably priced set menus.
132⇌♪(6fb)✂in 37 bedrooms CTV in all bedrooms ® ☎ T ✱
sB&B⇌♪fr£95 dB&B⇌♪fr£105 ₽
Lift (150⇔ solarium gymnasium
♥ International V ✿ ⚜ ✱ Lunch £11.50-£14.50&alc Dinner £15-£17.50&alc Last dinner 10pm
CONF. Thtr 200 Class 80 Board 50 Del from £90
Credit Cards 1 2 3 5 £

★★★ ⓑ 70% **Berkeley Square**
15 Berkeley Square, Clifton BS8 1HB ☎(0272) 254000 FAX (0272) 252970

This very friendly character hotel is set in a secluded Georgian square (as seen on the BBC's 'House of Elliot'). After considerable refurbishment, the accommodation is richly styled with deep armchairs and settees and bedrooms are well equipped. There is a Continental bar/brasserie as well as Nightingales restaurant, where chef Dermot Gale offers good seasonal menus with imaginative dishes emphasising robust flavours and textures.
43⇌♪in 9 bedrooms CTV in all bedrooms ® ☎ T
sB⇌♪£42.50-£66 dB⇌♪£56-£89 (room only) ₽
Lift (20⇔ (£2 per night)
♥ European V ✿ ⚜ Lunch £10.50-£13.50&alc Dinner £13.50&alc Last dinner 10pm
Credit Cards 1 2 3 5 £

See advertisement on page 133

★★★ ⓑ 68% **The Grange Resort**
Northwoods BS17 1RP (6m NE, 2m NW of Winterburn off B4427)
☎Winterbourne(0454) 777333 FAX (0454) 777447

Standing in 18 acres of woodland, this hotel is a popular conference venue. Bright, well proportioned bedrooms provide all modern comforts and amenities, comfortable open-plan public rooms overlook the grounds and there is a small leisure complex. Chef Richard Barker continues to produce enjoyable dishes. Smoked haddock soup, a rich terrine of guinea fowl or scallops in filo pastry are typical starters, followed by such main dishes as medallions of venison, fillet of red mullet with mussels or noisettes of lamb with lambs' kidneys.
52⇌♪✂in 19 bedrooms CTV in all bedrooms ® ☎ T
✕ (ex guide dogs) ✱ sB⇌♪£75 dB⇌♪£85 (room only) ₽
(100P ✿ ▣ (heated) sauna solarium gymnasium ballooning clay pigeon shooting *xmas*
♥ English & Continental V ✿ ✱ Lunch £11.50-£13.95&alc Dinner £16.95 Last dinner 10pm
CONF. Thtr 150 Class 72 Board 76 Del £115
Credit Cards 1 2 3 4 5

★★★ 68% **Redwood Lodge & Country Club**
Beggar Bush Ln, Failand BS8 3TG (2m W of Clifton Bridge on B3129) ☎(0275) 393901 FAX (0275) 392104

This popular hotel provides good access to the city, and there are comprehensive amenities for all the family, including a crèche. Two types of bedrooms are available, executive and standard, and plans are afoot to refurbish the latter. There are comfortable public areas.
108⇌♪(4fb)✂in 20 bedrooms CTV in all bedrooms ® ☎ T
✕ (ex guide dogs) ✱ sB&B⇌♪£60-£89 dB&B⇌♪£94-£109 ₽

(1000P ✿ ▣ (heated) ⇌ ♪ (hard) squash snooker sauna solarium gymnasium badminton cinema (wknds only) steam room *xmas*
♥ English & French V ✿ ⚜ ✂ ✱ Lunch £12 Dinner £18.50-£24.50 Last dinner 10pm
CONF. Thtr 175 Class 70 Board 40 Del from £105
Credit Cards 1 2 3 5

★★★ 64% **Avon Gorge**
Sion Hill, Clifton BS8 4LD ☎(0272) 738955 FAX (0272) 238125

This popular company-owned hotel occupies an enviable position, with scenic views of the Avon Gorge and famous Clifton suspension bridge. Bedrooms are comfortably proportioned and well equipped, those at the rear benefiting from the view. Public rooms are programmed for refurbishment.
76⇌♪(6fb)2⚜✂in 12 bedrooms CTV in all bedrooms ® ☎ T ✱
sB⇌♪£70-£75 dB⇌♪£85-£130 (room only) ₽
Lift (20P 3⇔ ✿ ♪ *xmas*
♥ English & French V ✿ ⚜ ✱ Lunch £10.75&alc Dinner £14.25&alc Last dinner 10.30pm
CONF. Thtr 100 Class 50 Board 26 Del from £55
Credit Cards 1 2 3 5

★★★ 62% **Unicorn**
Prince St BS1 4QF ☎(0272) 230333 FAX (0272) 230300

We are pleased to report continued improvements to this popular commercially orientated city-centre hotel. To date, a large percentage of the bedrooms have been upgraded to a good standard, and although some of the singles are compact they are nicely furnished and have a good range of modern facilities. Public rooms are brightly styled and include an attractive marble finished ➡

This beautiful 16th century castle, once owned by Henry VIII, stands in 15 acres of regal splendour, surrounded by its vineyard and Tudor garden and is renowned for being one of the finest country house hotels in England.

Thornbury is an ideal base from which to explore Wales and the Cotswolds. Facilities for small executive meetings and private dinner parties.

Thornbury, Avon BS12 1HH
Telephone: (0454) 281182
Fax: 0454 416188
A Pride of Britain Hotel

Redwood Lodge
Hotel & Country Club

★★★

**Beggar Bush Lane, Failand, Bristol BS8 3TG.
Tel: Bristol (0275) 393901   Fax: (0275) 392104**

108 first class bedrooms, all with private bathroom, direct-dial telephone, remote control colour television & satellite TV, tea/coffee making facilities, trouser press and hairdryer. Most rooms overlook the extensive landscaped grounds.

Situated just 3 miles from Bristol on the edge of the Ashton Park Estate, Redwood Lodge is set in beautiful wooded countryside close to the famous Clifton Suspension Bridge. Easy access from the motorway with Junction 19 of the M5 just 4 miles away.

An impressive Leisure Club is one of the most comprehensive in the UK. The Conference Centre and function suites can accommodate up to 200 for a meeting and 250 for banquets.

     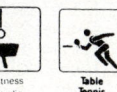

5 Tennis Courts | 8 Snooker Tables | Sauna | 6 Badminton Courts | Fitness Studio | Table Tennis | Cinema | Indoor Pool | 2 Outdoor Pools | Solarium | 12 Squash Courts

---

*C*ombine Business with Pleasure

Enjoy the welcoming, relaxed atmosphere of Alveston House Hotel, the friendly, personal service and excellent, modern facilities:

*W*ELL EQUIPPED EN SUITE BEDROOMS

*E*XCELLENT CONFERENCE FACILITIES

*W*EEKEND AND SHORT BREAKS

*S*UPERB CUISINE · FINE WINES

*B*USINESS LUNCHES

*W*EDDINGS · FUNCTIONS · SPECIAL EVENTS

*E*GON RONAY   AA ★★★

*C*LOSE TO M4 (EXIT 20) AND M5 (EXITS 14 & 16)

ALVESTON HOUSE
HOTEL

ALVESTON, THORNBURY,
BRISTOL

Telephone: (0454) 415050

Bristol

reception and a choice of restaurants. The range of services provided is exceptionally good.
245⇨♠(29fb)♦in 42 bedrooms CTV in all bedrooms ®✓T✱ sB&B⇨♠♠£62.50-£81.50 dB&B⇨♠£69.50-£81.50 ♬
Lift (♪ ♫ *xmas*
♡ International **V** ❖ ⚓ ✂ ✱ Lunch £11.95&alc Dinner fr£14.95&alc Last dinner 10.30pm
CONF. Thtr 320 Class 130 Board 40 Del from £55
Credit Cards [1][2][3][4][5] £

★★★59% Henbury Lodge
Station Rd, Henbury BS10 7QQ (4.5m NW of City centre off A4018) ☎(0272) 502615 FAX (0272) 509532
This small family run hotel is in a quiet suburb, yet convenient for both the city and motorway. Public rooms are not overly spacious but are comfortably furnished. Bedrooms in the main house are well proportioned, while rooms in the stables are cosy and bright.
11⇨♠Annexe8⇨♠(4fb)♂in 6 bedrooms CTV in all bedrooms ®✓ T sB&B⇨♠♠£29.50-£64.50 dB&B⇨♠♠£44-£74.50 ♬
24P ✪ ✿ sauna solarium gymnasium *xmas*
♡ English & Continental **V** ❖ ⚓ ✂ Lunch £16-£20alc Dinner £16-£20alc Last dinner 9pm
Credit Cards [1][2][3][4][5] £

★★★55% St Vincent Rocks
Sion Hill, Clifton BS8 4BB ☎(0272) 739251 FAX (0272) 238139

FORTE Heritage

This fine Regency building is in a prominent position overlooking Clifton Bridge and the Avon Gorge. The rather restricted public rooms, which include a restaurant and bar lounge wich scenic views, are scheduled for upgrading, to put them in line with the comfortable well equipped bedrooms.
46⇨♠1♠♦ in 10 bedrooms CTV in all bedrooms ® T ✱ sB⇨♠£85 dB⇨♠£100 (room only) ♬
(18P *xmas*
V ❖ ⚓ ✂ Lunch fr£12.95&alc High tea fr£3.25 Dinner £16.95&alc Last dinner 9.30pm
Credit Cards [1][2][3][5]

★★★69% Rodney Hotel
Rodney Place, Clifton BS8 4HY ☎(0272) 735422 FAX (0272) 467092
This attractive hotel is housed behind the stone façade of Clifton Terrace. Architectural constraints mean that the rooms are not large but they are well equipped, bright and welcoming. The main strength of the hotel is the Marguerite Restaurant, which is operated by Patrick and Sue Glennie-Smith, and offers some of the best value, flavoursome and honest food in the city. Patrick cooks with commendable skill, and fresh flavours and textures predominate.
31⇨♠♠in 2 bedrooms CTV in all bedrooms ®✓ T sB⇨♠£30.50-£52.50 dB⇨♠£45-£74 (room only) ♬
(♪
♡ English & French **V** ❖ ⚓ Dinner £13.75&alc Last dinner 10.30pm
Credit Cards [1][2][3][5] £

★★★69% Seeley's
17-27 St Paul's Rd, Clifton BS18 1LX ☎(0272) 738544 FAX (0272) 732406
Closed 24 Dec-2 Jan
Right in the heart of Clifton, this hotel is conveniently positioned for the university, business areas and shops. Recently refurbished bedrooms, both in the main building and the annexes, are attractively decorated and offer a comprehensive range of facilities. An extensive range of dishes is available in the restaurant, and staff are helpful and polite. Other facilities include a pretty terrace and a secluded city garden.
37⇨♠Annexe18⇨♠(10fb)2♯ CTV in all bedrooms ®✓ T ✱ (ex guide dogs) sB&B⇨♠£35-£55 dB&B⇨♠£44-£65 ♬
(25P 14🅿 ✿ sauna solarium gymnasium spa bath ♫ ♪

♡ International **V** ❖ Lunch £8-£12 Dinner £12&alc Last dinner 10.30pm
CONF. Thtr 90 Class 45 Board 50
Credit Cards [1][2][3] £

★★65% Parkside
470 Bath Rd, Brislington BS4 3HQ ☎(0272) 711461 FAX (0272) 715507
A neo-gothic stone building, Parkside is a popular establishment with lively Victorian-style bars, a night club and a large split-level bistro-style conservatory restaurant. The best bedrooms are in the main building, the rest are across the courtyard.
28rm(17⇨)1♯ CTV in all bedrooms ® T ✱ (ex guide dogs) (250P ✿ snooker
♡ English & French **V** ❖ ⚓ ✂ Last dinner 10.30pm
Credit Cards [1][2][3]

★★62% Glenroy
Victoria Square, Clifton BS8 4EW ☎(0272) 739058 FAX (0272) 739058
Closed 24 Dec-1 Jan
This commercial hotel, formed from 2 houses in an attractive residential area of the city, has bedrooms of varying size, all equipped with modern amenities. Public areas include a congenial bar and popular carvery restaurant.
26⇨♠Annexe24⇨♠(8fb) CTV in all bedrooms ®✓ T sB&B⇨♠£39-£47 dB&B⇨♠£48-£68
(16P
V ❖ Sunday Lunch £9.95-£10.95 Dinner £8.95-£11.95 Last dinner 9.30pm
CONF. Thtr 25 Class 16 Board 16 Del £75
Credit Cards [1][2][3] £

★★60% Clifton
St Pauls Rd, Clifton BS8 1LX ☎(0272) 736882 FAX (0272) 741082
Just off the Whiteladies Road, this popular hotel which offers friendly service, is close to the university and city centre and offers modestly priced accommodation in compact but bright and well equipped rooms. Racks Bar and Restaurant is a lively, much frequented venue.
63rm(4⇨41♠)(4fb)♂in 8 bedrooms CTV in all bedrooms ®✓ T sB&B⇨£26-£28 sB&B⇨♠£36-£47.50 dB&B⇨£37-£45.50 dB&B⇨♠£49-£64 ♬
Lift (12P ♪
♡ English & French **V** ❖ ⚓ Lunch fr£10alc Dinner fr£10alc Last dinner 11pm
Credit Cards [1][2][3][5] £

Forte Crest
Filton Rd, Hambrook BS16 1QX (6m NE off A4174) ☎(0272) 564242 FAX (0272) 569735

FORTE CREST

A large modern hotel with a range of services and amenities, designed particularly for the business traveller. Bedrooms are smart, comfortable and well equipped. For more details about Forte Crest hotels, consult the Contents page, under Hotel Groups.
200⇨♠✱ B⇨♠£89 (room only)
CONF. Thtr 500 Class 200 Board 200 Del £115

Hilton National Bristol
Redcliffe Way BS1 6NJ ☎(0272) 260041

HILTON

This is a bright, modern hotel with an informal restaurant, aimed at both business and leisure guests. All bedrooms have en-suite bathrooms and a range of modern facilities. For more information about Hilton National, consult the Contents page, under Hotel Groups.
201⇨♠✱ B⇨♠£90 (room only)
CONF. Thtr 350 Class 200 Board 40 Del £125

Bristol - Broadstairs

Marriott
Lower Castle St BS1 3AD (from M32 follow signs 'City Centre' and 'Temple Meads' – do not take underpass) ☎(0272) 294281 FAX (0272) 225838
A large and busy hotel, which is ideal for the business and leisure traveller, offering a wide range of services, a choice of eating options and indoor leisure facilities. Bedrooms are comfortable and equipped with modern facilities. For more details about Marriott hotels, consult the Contents page, under Hotel Groups.
290⇌🕻 dB⇌🕻 fr£104 (room only)
CONF. Thtr 600 Class 280 Board 30 Del £125

BRIXHAM Devon Map 03 SX95

★★★60% **Quayside**
King St TQ5 9TJ ☎(0803) 855751 FAX (0803) 882733
Closed 19 Dec-4 Jan
Formerly a row of cottages overlooking the picturesque harbour, the hotel now offers well equipped rooms. Residents on the half-board tariff can choose from the à la carte restaurant menu where fresh local fish features strongly, and service is friendly. There are two bars. Parking is restricted but the hotel has its own car park 500 yards away.
30⇌🕻(4fb)2⌘ CTV in all bedrooms ® T sB&B⇌🕻£45-£65 dB&B⇌🕻£45-£88 ♉
37P ♪
♀ English & French V ☼ ♨ ✂ Lunch £13.50-£18alc Dinner £13.50-£18alc Last dinner 9.30pm
Credit Cards 1 2 3 5

★57% **Smugglers Haunt**
Church Hill East TQ5 8HH ☎(0803) 853050 & 859416 FAX (0803) 858738
An extensive range of bar meals as well as a carte are offered in the open-plan restaurant and bar area of the Smugglers' Haunt. Friendly family ownership ensures a relaxed atmosphere, and bedrooms are well equipped, though compact and simply furnished.
14rm(4⇌)Annexe2rm(2fb) CTV in all bedrooms ® ✱ sB&B£32 sB&B⇌🕻£38 dB&B£48 dB&B⇌🕻£54
《 CTV ⚽ *xmas*
♀ English & French V ☼ ♨ ✱ Lunch £7-£14 Dinner £7-£14&alc Last dinner 10pm
Credit Cards 1 2 3 5 £

BROADSTAIRS Kent Map 05 TR36

★★❀66% **Royal Albion**
Albion St CT10 1LU ☎Thanet(0843) 868071 FAX (0843) 861509
Overlooking Viking Bay, this well established hotel offers a choice of town or sea facing bedrooms that are slowly being upgraded. The main building, with its Georgian frontage, houses the breakfast room, public bar and small lounge; all other meals are taken in Marchesi's restaurant, next door but one (room service is also an option). Chef Stephen Watson offers monthly changing set menus and a lengthy carte of interesting dishes.
19⇌🕻(3fb)⌘ CTV in all bedrooms ® ♫ T ✂ (ex guide dogs) ✱ sB⇌🕻£47.50-£50 dB⇌🕻£47.50-£55 (room only) ♉
《 CTV 20P 2🚗 *xmas*
♀ French V ☼ ♨ Lunch £8.50-£17.50&alc Dinner £13.50-£17.50&alc Last dinner 9.30pm
CONF. Thtr 60 Class 30 Board 6 Del £70
Credit Cards 1 2 3 5

★★64% **Castlemere**
Western Esplanade CT10 1TD (Logis) ☎Thanet(0843) 861566 FAX (0843) 866379
Closed 29 Dec-5 Jan
A traditional, family-run hotel, the Castlemere is in a prime situation overlooking the sea. The smart dining room offers a short ➤

CLIFTON HOTELS LTD
BRISTOL

	Tariff from
The Berkeley Square Hotel Tel: (0272) 254000	£66.00
Our delightful Flagship 3 star hotel, featuring Nightingales Restaurant	
The Rodney Hotel Tel: (0272) 735422	£52.50
Charming 2 star hotel, with two Rosette Awards for its Marguerite Restaurant	
The Clifton Hotel Tel: (0272) 736882	£28.00
An hospitable 2 star hotel, comprising the ever popular Racks Restaurant and Bar	
The Washington Hotel Tel: (0272) 733980	£27.50
A welcoming 2 Q rated hotel, close enough to allow guests to enjoy Racks' facilities	
Chesterfield Hotel Tel: (0272) 734606	£22.50
Homely, 1 Q rated hotel, small hotel offering the same high standards of hospitality, at budget prices.	

All our hotels offer special weekend rates.

Please contact the individual Hotel for reservations. For Group or Corporate business, please contact our Group Sales & Marketing Manager, Susan Evans on 0272 736882; Fax: 0272 741082

Rangeworthy Court Hotel ★★

Peaceful, relaxing, seventeenth century manor house originally built for Lord Chief Justice Sir Matthew Hale. Now a comfortable hotel: lounges with log fires, lovely gardens, outdoor heated swimming pool, popular restaurant, friendly staff. Close to M4 and M5; 20 minute drive to Bristol city centre. Ideal for combining the peace of a country house with excellent communications. Local attractions include: Berkeley Castle, Slimbridge Wildfowl Trust, the "edge" of the Cotswolds.

CHURCH LANE, WOTTON ROAD, RANGEWORTHY, NR. BRISTOL BS17 5ND
Telephone: 0454 228347 Fax: 0454 228945
See Gazetteer under Rangeworthy

Broadstairs - Brockenhurst

set menu at dinner, and the lounges, though dated, are spacious and comfortable. Bedrooms vary in size and décor, and some overlook the walled garden rather than the sea.
36rm(24⇨6♐)(3fb)2⇔ CTV in all bedrooms ® T sB&B£33.50 sB&B⇨♐£37.50 dB&B£59 dB&B⇨♐£67-72 ⏏
CTV 30P ✿ *xmas*
♀ English & French ✧ ⚏ ✻ Bar Lunch £1.85-£3 Dinner £15 Last dinner 7.45pm
CONF. Thtr 30 Class 20 Board 12 Del from £61.50
Credit Cards ①③

BROADWAY Hereford & Worcester Map **04** SP03
See also **Buckland**

★★★★❀❀
THE LYGON ARMS
High St WR12 7DU (Leading Hotels) ☎(0386) 852255 FAX (0386) 858611

Originally a 16th-century coaching inn, this famous hostelry was taken over by the Savoy Group in 1986, since when there has been a continuing programme of upgrading and development – now including a splendid indoor pool and fitness centre. The main building has a lovely Cotswold stone facade and a stone flagged, wood panelled interior. Guests particularly enjoy the 4-poster beds, the minstrels' gallery in the Great Hall dining room, the heraldic panels, cosy lounges, open fires, antiques and paintings. Two rather austere modern blocks do little to enhance the building from the outside, but they contain some of the best bedrooms. Head chef Chris Howe offers a wide range of modern British dishes from both fixed price and à la carte menus, and although there is some unevenness in the cooking, the overall result is pleasing.

61⇨♐5⇔ CTV in all bedrooms⇔T ✻ sB&B⇨♐£88-£110 dB&B⇨♐£130-£186 Continental breakfast ⏏
⦅ CTV 100P 4🚗 (£8 per night) ⇎ ✿ ▭ (heated) ♀ (hard) snooker sauna solarium gymnasium beauty treatment spa bath steam room *xmas*
♀ International V ✧ ⚏ ✻ Lunch £19.50-£20.50&alc Dinner £29.75&alc Last dinner 9.15pm
Credit Cards ①②③⑤

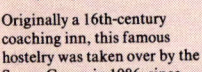

★★★❀❀70%**Dormy House**
Willersey Hill WR12 7LF (2m E off A44 in Gloucestershire) ☎(0386) 852711 FAX (0386) 858636
Closed 25 & 26 Dec

This attractive Cotswold stone hotel – originally a 17th century farmhouse – stand on Broadway's escarpment overlooking the Vale of Evesham. Transformed and sympathetically extended, it retains heavily beamed ceilings, flagstone floors and stone walls. Small lounges maintain a club-like atmosphere with mahogany furniture and rich leather chesterfields, there is a congenial bar created from an old barn, a cosy cocktail bar and a comfortable tapestry-hung conservatory restaurant offering 2 set menus and a rather more expensive carte of dishes cooked with imagination and flair. Bedrooms in adjacent former stables are pleasant and individual in style.

26⇨♐Annexe23⇨♐(3fb)2⇔ CTV in all bedrooms ® T ✻ sB&B⇨♐£55-£74 dB&B⇨♐£100-£130 ⏏
⦅ 80P ⇎ ✿ croquet putting

♀ English & French V ✧ ⚏ ✻ Lunch £14-£16&alc Dinner £25.50-£33&alc Last dinner 10pm
CONF. Thtr 200 Class 100 Board 25 Del from £135
Credit Cards ①②③⑤

★★❀♨71%**Collin House**
Collin Ln WR12 7PB (1m NW off A44) ☎(0386) 858354 & 852544
Closed 24-27 Dec

This impressive Cotswold stone house is set in several acres of mature trees, lawns and gardens. Inglenook fireplaces, exposed timbers and slab floors are features of the interior. The lounge bar, with pews and the occasional settee, serves a good range of bar meals, and there is a 2nd comfortable lounge. Bedrooms are furnished with fine period furniture. Chefs Mark Brooks and Antony Ike produce enjoyable food from a good carte, with daily specials.

7rm(5⇨1♐)2⇔ ® ✈ sB&B⇨♐£45-£47 dB&B⇨♐£86-£99 ⏏
CTV 35P ⇎ ✿ ▭ croquet
V Lunch £14.50-£15 Dinner £15-£23 Last dinner 9pm
Credit Cards ①③

BROCKENHURST Hampshire Map **04** SU30

★★★❀❀72%**Careys Manor**
SO4 7RH ☎Lymington(0590) 23551 FAX (0590) 22799

This delightful Victorian house has been sympathetically extended to provide a wide choice of comfortable bedrooms, from standard doubles to suites and romantic 4-poster rooms. The Garden Wing rooms have a terrace or balcony. Chef Kevin Dorrington has a serious approach to his cooking, using only fresh ingredients, and Le Blaireau Café Bar offers an informal alternative to the restaurant.

79⇨♐6⇔✈in 30 bedrooms CTV in all bedrooms ®⚏T ✻ sB&B⇨♐£69-£79 dB&B⇨♐£99-£149 ⏏
⦅ 180P ⇎ ▭ (heated) sauna solarium gymnasium jacuzzi steam room beauty therapist *xmas*
♀ English & French V ✧ ⚏ ✻ Lunch fr£10.95 High tea fr£7 Dinner fr£19.95&alc Last dinner 10pm
CONF. Thtr 100 Class 75 Del from £100
Credit Cards ①②③

★★★❀❀70%**Rhinefield House**
Rhinefield Rd SO42 7QB ☎Lymington(0590) 22922 FAX (0590) 22800

This fine Victorian fantasy of a country house is surrounded by formal gardens with ornamental canals. Most of the spacious and attractive bedrooms are in a modern extension, with 2 suites in the main house. Here the extensive public rooms include the impressive wood-panelled Grand Hall and a comfortable conservatory. In the Armada Restaurant, with its splendid woodcarving, chef Richard Bertinet offers a varied menu of carefully prepared dishes.

34⇨♐1⇔✈in 6 bedrooms CTV in all bedrooms ® T ✈ (ex guide dogs) ✻ ⏏
⦅ 80P ⇎ (heated) ▭ (heated) ♀ (hard) sauna solarium gymnasium jacuzzi table tennis pool table croquet *xmas*
V ✧ ⚏ ✻ Lunch fr£14&alc High tea fr£6.50 Dinner fr£19.95&alc Last dinner 10pm
CONF. Thtr 150 Board 55 Del from £125
Credit Cards ①②③⑤

★★★♨68%**New Park Manor**
Lyndhurst Rd SO42 7QH (on A337 1.5m from Lyndhurst) ☎Lymington(0590) 23467 FAX (0590) 22268

This former hunting lodge, dating from the middle ages, has been skilfully extended to provide very spacious and comfortable bedrooms. Rooms in the original building vary in size, but all are furnished to the same high standard. Public areas are rather compact, particularly the restaurant, but the welcoming atmosphere and good service more than compensates.

26⇨♐(2fb)1⇔✈in 10 bedrooms CTV in all bedrooms ®⚏T ✻ sB&B⇨♐fr£50 dB&B⇨♐£80-£120 ⏏

Brockenhurst

60P 1🛏✻🏊 (heated) ♪ (hard) ⛱ solarium croquet *xmas*
🍽 English & French **V** ♥ ⚑ ✻ Sunday Lunch £11 Dinner £19.50 Last dinner 9.30pm
Credit Cards 1 2 3 5

See advertisement on page 137

★★★63% *Balmer Lawn*
Lyndhurst Rd SO42 7ZB (In Lyndhurst follow one way system in direction of Lymington) (Hilton) ☎Lymington(0590) 23116 FAX (0590) 23864

Ideally located for the many attractions of the New Forest, this popular, long-established hotel has been extensively refurbished in recent years, and most bedrooms now provide every modern amenity. Public areas include a small bar, a well furnished foyer lounge and a restaurant.

58⇌📺(8fb)✂in 26 bedrooms CTV in all bedrooms ® T ✻
sB&B⇌📺fr£50 dB&B⇌📺fr£80 🛏
Lift (90P ✻ 🏊 (heated) 🏊 (heated) ♪ (hard) squash sauna gymnasium pool table *xmas*
V ♥ ⚑ ✂ ✻ Lunch £9.50 High tea £3.95 Dinner fr£14.50&alc Last dinner 9.30pm
CONF. Thtr 100 Class 40 Board 40 Del £97
Credit Cards 1 2 3 4 5

★★★60% *Forest Park*
Rhinefield Rd SO4 7ZG (Forestdale) ☎Lymington(0590) 22844 FAX (0590) 23948

This former vicarage in 4 acres of grounds became a hotel in 1902 and has been skilfully extended over the years. A blazing log fire greets guests in the winter months, and the young staff are friendly. Bedrooms are mostly spacious and well furnished in traditional style, and most have forest views.

38⇌📺(5fb)3🛏✂in 3 bedrooms CTV in all bedrooms ® T
(80P ✻ 🏊 (heated) ♪ (hard) ⛱ sauna pool table ♬
🍽 English & French **V** ♥ ⚑ ✂ Last dinner 10pm
Credit Cards 1 2 3 5

VOYAGER HOTELS

Rhinefield House Hotel is a stunning country house standing in 40 acres of landscaped gardens and ornamental waterways in the heart of the New Forest. With history dating back to the Roman times, this Victorian estate is now part of the Virgin Group. Rhinefield offers luxurious bedrooms, award winning cuisine, with attentive and friendly service. It is a beautiful location for weddings, dinner dances, conferences and weekend breaks.

★★★AA ✿ ✿ 70%

Rhinefield House Hotel
Rhinefield Road, Brockenhurst, Hants SO42 7QB. (0590) 22922.

CAREYS MANOR HOTEL

HIGHLY COMMENDED

In the beautiful New Forest
Wild ponies, deer, wooded glades and lovely walks in thousands of acres. London 90 minutes.

INDOOR POOL : JACUZZI : SAUNA : SOLARIUM : GYM

The hotel is proud of the personal welcome and care it extends to its visitors. The bedrooms have been comfortably and elegantly furnished to the highest standards and many have balconies or patios leading directly onto the gardens. The Restaurant offers traditional English and French cuisine professionally prepared and superbly presented. Leisure breaks.

TEL: (0590) 23551 NOW FOR A BROCHURE
BROCKENHURST   NEW FOREST   HAMPSHIRE

DORMY HOUSE HOTEL
★★★

Set high in the hills of the Cotswolds overlooking Broadway and the Vale of Evesham, the 17th century Dormy House has been meticulously converted into a delightful hotel.

Enjoy the beautifully appointed rooms, superb restaurant and high standard of service. Stay one night or pamper yourself with a Champagne Weekend or a few carefree days in the Heart of England.

For reservations:
DORMY HOUSE HOTEL,
Willersey Hill,
Broadway, Worcestershire
Telephone: (0386) 852711

DORMY HOUSE

Brockenhurst - Bromsgrove

★★ ❀❀ **74%** **Whitley Ridge Country House**
Beaulieu Rd SO4 7QL (access via B3055 towards Beaulieu) (Logis) ☎Lymington(0590) 22354 FAX (0590) 22856
This delightful country house, surrounded by forest, was built in the 18th century as a royal hunting lodge. It offers attractively coordinated bedrooms with some strikingly bold décor. The restaurant, catering mostly for residents, is nicely appointed, with both table d'hôte and à la carte menus, and the enthusiastic young chef Karen Tilt shows skill and attention to detail in her cooking.
13⇌₤🕻 CTV in all bedrooms ® T ✱ sB&B⇌🕻 £46-£52 dB&B⇌🕻 £76-£86 🄿
CTV 30P ✿ ♀ (hard) *xmas*
♬ English & French V ◊ ⚲ ⚲ ✱ Sunday Lunch £9.75-£10.50 Dinner £17.50-£18&alc Last dinner 9pm
CONF. Thtr 30 Class 30 Board 20 Del from £70
Credit Cards [1][2][3][5]   £

★★ **65%** **Cloud**
Meerut Rd SO42 7TD ☎Lymington(0590) 22165 & 22254
Closed 17 Dec-Jan
The restaurant and tearoom are both very popular at this hotel. Public rooms are particularly cosy, with a small bar lounge and several traditional lounges, and bedrooms have recently been improved. The atmosphere is relaxing, and service is attentive and friendly.
16⇌🕻(3fb)1₤ CTV in all bedrooms ® sB&B⇌🕻£36-£45 dB&B⇌🕻£72-£90 🄿
CTV 20P ⇌ ✿
V ◊ ⚲ ⚲ Lunch £5.95-£12.50 High tea £1.95-£3.95 Dinner £15-£17 Last dinner 8.30pm
Credit Cards [1][3]

★★ **61%** **Watersplash**
The Rise SO42 7ZP ☎Lymington(0590) 22344 FAX (0590) 24047
This large extended red brick Victorian house in the centre of the village has been run by the Foster family for many years. The bedrooms vary in size, outlook and location so discuss your needs on booking.
23⇌🕻(6fb)1₤ CTV in all bedrooms ® T ✱ sB&B⇌🕻£40-£48 dB&B⇌🕻£50-£80 🄿
CTV 25P 🅿 (£1.50 per night) ✿ ⌇ (heated) motor cruiser *xmas*
♬ English & Continental V ◊ ⚲ ⚲ ✱ Lunch £10-£15 High tea £2-£5 Dinner £15-£18 Last dinner 8.30pm
CONF. Thtr 90 Del from £65
Credit Cards [1][2][3]   £

BRODICK
See **Arran, Isle of**

BROMBOROUGH Merseyside Map **07** SJ38

★★★**66%** **Cromwell**
High St L62 7HZ (on A41) (Whitbread) ☎051-334 2917 FAX 051-346 1175
This friendly hotel provides comfortable bedrooms with sturdy modern furniture and a good array of equipment. The attractively furnished restaurant provides an extensive choice of international dishes. There are 2 bars, one a very large lounge bar serving a good range of bar meals.
31⇌🕻(3fb)1₤✱ in 2 bedrooms CTV in all bedrooms ®✱ T ✖ (ex guide dogs) ✱ sB&B⇌🕻£65.50 dB&B⇌🕻fr£77 🄿
(110P sauna solarium gymnasium
♬ International V ◊ ⚲ ⚲ ✱ Lunch fr£7.95&alc Dinner fr£14.95&alc Last dinner 10pm
CONF. Thtr 130 Class 30 Board 48 Del from £93
Credit Cards [1][2][3][5]

BROME Suffolk Map **05** TM17

★★★ **62%** **Oaksmere**
IP23 8AJ (from A140 take B1077 (to Eye)) ☎Eye(0379) 870326 FAX (0379) 870051
Parts of this country hotel, in its setting of well tended gardens and topiary, date back to the middle of the 16th century. Now restored and refurbished, it provides comfortable, well equipped bedrooms and a beautiful restaurant with adjoining vine-clad conservatory. The more informal bar, offering popular bar meals, is full of character, with a friendly atmosphere.
11⇌🕻(3fb)4₤ CTV in all bedrooms ® T sB&B⇌🕻fr£59.50 dB&B⇌🕻fr£74.50 🄿
90P ✿ *xmas*
♬ English & French V ◊ ⚲ Lunch fr£12.95&alc Dinner £17.50-£28alc Last dinner 9.30pm
Credit Cards [1][2][3][5]   £

★★ **66%** *Brome Grange*
IP23 8AP (on A143) ☎Eye(0379) 870456 FAX (0379) 870921
Service is warm and friendly at this inn, with well equipped motel-style accommodation provided in a block at the rear.
Annexe22⇌🕻 CTV in all bedrooms ® T
CTV 100P ✿
♬ English & French V ◊ ⚲
Credit Cards [1][2][3][5]

BROMLEY Greater London
See **LONDON SECTION, plan 1**F2
★★★**65%** **Bromley Court**
Bromley Hill BR1 4JD (N, signposted off A21. Opposite Mercedes Benz garage on Bromley Hill) ☎081-464 5011 FAX 081-460 0899

CONSORT CROWN

This grand mansion with modern extensions stands in its own grounds in a quiet residential area. Bedrooms are on several floors and wings, and they vary in size and shape, some overlooking the gardens. Public rooms include a foyer/lounge bar and a pillared cocktail bar.
120⇌🕻(5fb)✱ in 14 bedrooms CTV in all bedrooms ®✱ T ✱ sB&B⇌🕻£79-£82 dB&B⇌🕻£89-£90
Lift (100P ✿ ✱ putting green & golf driving net ♪ *xmas*
♬ English & French V ◊ ⚲ ⚲ ✱ Lunch £12.95-£15.50&alc Dinner £14.95&alc Last dinner 10pm
CONF. Thtr 180 Class 80 Board 50 Del from £99
Credit Cards [1][2][3][5]   £

BROMSGROVE Hereford & Worcester Map **07** SO97

★★★**72%** **Pine Lodge**
Kidderminster Rd B61 9AB (on A38) ☎(0527) 576600 FAX (0527) 78981
Pine Lodge is a spacious hotel with distinctive Mediterranean architecture. Bedrooms have dark wood furnishings, clean lines and comfortable seating. An impressive range of facilities is provided including the informal terrace lounge where all-day snacks and refreshments are available in addition to the Parador Restaurant and adjacent lounge bar. The hotel is well managed and has a friendly team of helpful staff.
118⇌🕻(9fb)✱ in 18 bedrooms CTV in all bedrooms ®✱ T sB&B⇌🕻£79-£100 dB&B⇌🕻£90-£110 🄿
Lift (250P ✿ ⌇ (heated) sauna solarium gymnasium threequarter size snooker table
♬ English & Continental V ◊ ⚲ ⚲ ✱ Lunch £9.50-£13.50&alc Dinner £15.50-£16.75&alc Last dinner 10pm
CONF. Thtr 200 Class 120 Board 60 Del from £105
Credit Cards [1][2][3][5]   £

See advertisement on page 139

For key to symbols see the Bookmark.

Hotels with red star ratings are especially high quality.

BROME GRANGE
EYE, SUFFOLK

A characterful 16th century hotel in a country setting in the village of Brome twixt the pretty country towns of Diss and Eye. The 22 bedrooms are chalet style within the gardens. Excellent food and great friendly hospitality.

Well appointed rooms from £39.00 B & B
(low cost all inclusive mini-break tariff also available)

Reservations: 0379 870456

BROME GRANGE ★★
Brome, Nr Eye, Suffolk

THE OAKSMERE HOTEL
BROME, NR EYE, SUFFOLK

A beautiful country house hotel with ancient origins, set in large wooded grounds with water garden. 11 individually well-appointed bedrooms with full en-suite facilities, some with 4 poster beds. Excellent food in elegant restaurant and most popular bar.

Well appointed rooms from £59.00 B & B
(all inclusive mini-break tariff also available)

Reservations: 0379 870326

THE OAKSMERE HOTEL ★★★
Brome, Nr Eye, Suffolk

★★★

NEW PARK MANOR

COMMENDED

BROCKENHURST, HAMPSHIRE SO42 7QH
Telephone: (0590) 23467   Fax: (0590) 22268

Previously a royal hunting lodge, now a country house of real character in a peaceful New Forest setting. Tastefully decorated, reflecting the high standard of accommodation, all the 26 bedrooms are individually designed with comfort in mind and have private facilities. The restaurant overlooking the park, offers discreet and efficient service, and a menu that combines good English food with French style. A friendly bar and lounge is the perfect place for relaxation or to meet fellow guests.
A self-contained Business Centre provides conference and seminar rooms. There is much to do and see locally. Activities from sailing, golf or riding, from the hotel's own stables, can be easily arranged.

Brook (Near Cadnam) - Buckden

BROOK (NEAR CADNAM) Hampshire Map 04 SU21

★★★✿65% **Bell Inn**
SO43 7HE ☎Southampton(0703) 812214 FAX (0703) 813958

Recent refurbishment has added to the facilities now provided at this golfing hotel, under the same ownership as the adjoining Bramshaw Golf Club. Bedrooms vary in size but all are well furnished. The double-sided bar and restaurant are rather spartan, but the lounge is more comfortable. Chef Malcolm Lugg is showing a lot of promise with his high standard of cooking.
22⇌(3fb) CTV in all bedrooms ® T ✱ sB&B⇌£65 dB&B⇌£100 ₽
CTV 150P ✿ ▶ 36 xmas
♀ English & French V ◊ ♨ Lunch £8-£12.50&alc Dinner £18.50&alc Last dinner 9.30pm
CONF.
Credit Cards [1][2][3][5]

BRORA Highland Sutherland Map 14 NC90

★★★68% **Royal Marine**
Golf Rd KW9 6QS (turn off A9 in village toward beach and golf course) ☎(0408) 621252 FAX (0408) 621181

Built as a private country house at the turn of the century, the Royal Marine stands in its own grounds overlooking the mouth of the River Brora. Under the ownership of Robert and Dawn Powell, refurbishment is continuing. Day rooms have a comfortable lived-in feel, with welcoming log fires. Bedrooms range from a 4-poster room with period furnishings and a roaring log fire, to smaller more modest rooms at the back of the house.
11⇌(1fb)1⊟ CTV in all bedrooms ® T ✱ sB&B⇌£50 dB&B⇌£80-£95 ₽
40P ⚙ ✿ (heated) ▶ 18 ♬ (hard) ✈ snooker sauna ice curling rink in season xmas
♀ Scottish & French V ◊ ♨ ✱ Lunch £10-£12&alc Dinner £17.50-£20&alc Last dinner 9pm
Credit Cards [1][2][3][5]

★★★58% **The Links**
Golf Rd KW9 6QS ☎(0408) 621225 FAX (0408) 621383
Closed 25 Dec-2 Jan

Under new ownership, gradual improvements are being made to this long-established holiday and sporting hotel with spectacular sea views. There is a choice of bars and lounges and the dining room and terrace have fine views. Bedrooms, which vary in size and style, are modestly furnished, but improvements are in progress. Guests may use the leisure facilities at the nearby Royal Marine Hotel.
21⇌(2fb) CTV in all bedrooms ® T
55P ✿ ▶ 18
♀ International V ◊ ♨ ✱ Last dinner 9pm
Credit Cards [1][2][3][5]

BROUGHTON IN FURNESS Cumbria Map 07 SD28

★★ 63% *Eccle Riggs*
Foxfield Rd LA20 6BN ☎(0229) 716398 & 716780

Standing in 35 acres of parkland, this Victorian stone manor house has pleasantly furnished public areas, including a lounge bar with a fine fireplace and a restaurant overlooking the gardens. Comfortable bedrooms are equipped with all modern amenities.
12⇌(6fb) CTV in all bedrooms ® T ✈ (ex guide dogs)
120P ✿ ▩ (heated) ◉ 9 sauna solarium clay pigeon shooting
♀ English & French V ◊ ♨ Last dinner 9pm
Credit Cards [1][2][3][5]

★ 60% *Old King's Head*
Station Rd LA20 6HJ ☎(0229) 716293

Dating back some 300 years, this charming inn is full of old beams and low ceilings. An extensive range of food is available in either the bar or the dining room. The comfortable bedrooms have recently been upgraded. Service is very friendly.

5rm(1⇌)(1fb) CTV in all bedrooms ®
50P ✿
◊ Last dinner 9pm

BROXTED Essex Map 05 TL52

★★★✿✿77% **Whitehall**
Church End CM6 2BZ
☎Bishops Stortford(0279) 850603 FAX (0279) 850385
Closed 26-30 Dec

Converted from a charming Elizabethan manor house, this exclusive country hotel has been considerably extended but the Keane family and their staff continue to provide good levels of service. Public areas include a small modern bar, an elegant lounge and the grand dining room with a timber vaulted ceiling. Here guests can enjoy Paul Flavell's elaborate country house cuisine; a recent meal included a terrine of confit of chicken with pickled onions and thyme, fillet of turbot with a Madeira, Champagne and truffle sauce, and a rich white chocolate and pistachio nut parfait.
25⇌ CTV in all bedrooms ✈ (ex guide dogs) ✱
sB&B⇌£75-£95 dB&B⇌£105-£155 ₽
35P ⚙ ⚙ ✿ ♬ (hard) nc5yrs
♀ French V ◊ ♨ Lunch fr£19.50 Dinner £19.50-£35 Last dinner 9.30pm
Credit Cards [1][2][3][5]

BROXTON Cheshire Map 07 SJ45

★★★62% **Broxton Hall Country House**
Whitchurch Rd CH3 9JS (on A41, at the Broxton roundabout) ☎(0829) 782321 FAX (0829) 782330
Closed Xmas Day

Broxton Hall is a beautifully preserved half timbered Tudor mansion set in 5 acres of delightful grounds. Proprietors Mr and Mrs Hadley have an international antiques business and antique and period pieces abound, along with paintings, prints and objets d'art. Welcoming log fires burn in the lounges, and an imaginative set price menu is offered by chef Jim Makin. Bedrooms vary from spacious to compact and include a 2-bedroom suite.
12⇌(1fb)1⊟ in 1 bedroom CTV in all bedrooms ® ✈ T sB&B⇌£35-£55 dB&B⇌£65-£95 ₽
30P ⚙ ♫ nc12yrs
♀ English & French V ◊ ♨ ✱ Lunch £2-£15alc Dinner £21.90 Last dinner 9.30pm
Credit Cards [1][2][3][5] £

○**The Birches Hotel Carden Park**
Carden Park, Carden CH3 9DQ ☎(0829) 731000
Due to have opened Aug 1993
83⇌

BUCKDEN North Yorkshire Map 07 SD97

★★ 65% **Buck Inn**
BD23 5JA ☎Skipton(0756) 760228 FAX (0756) 760227

This popular Georgian coaching inn is situated in the centre of a picturesque village in beautiful Upper Wharfedale. Beams, open fires and flagstone floors feature in the bars, where an extensive range of bar meals is available along with hand-pulled real ales. The residents' restaurant was converted from a courtyard where local auctions were once held. Bedrooms are modern in style, furnished mostly in pine with attractive coordinated fabrics.
15⇌(2fb) CTV in all bedrooms ® T sB&B⇌£28-£31 dB&B⇌£56-£62 ₽
36P xmas
♀ International V ◊ ♨ ✱ ✱ Lunch £12.95-£21.50alc Dinner £12.95-£21.50alc Last dinner 9.30pm
Credit Cards [1][3] £

Buckhurst Hill - Buckingham

BUCKHURST HILL Essex See London Section, plan 5 F5

★★ **59% The Roebuck**
North End IG9 5QY ☎081-505 4636 FAX 081-504 7826

Originally a small alehouse, The Roebuck is an attractive creeper-clad hotel at the edge of Epping Forest. Over half the bedrooms are of a good modern standard, the remainder being more dated. There is a popular locals bar, a small lounge and dining room which now needs a facelift.

29⇨♠⤢in 10 bedrooms CTV in all bedrooms ® T ✱
sB⇨♠fr£60 dB⇨♠fr£70 (room only) ⊟
40P ✽ xmas
V ♡ ⚏ ⤢ Lunch £8.95-£11.95 Dinner fr£15.95&alc Last dinner 10pm
CONF. Thtr 200 Class 60 Board 40 Del from £85
Credit Cards ① ② ③ ⑤

BUCKIE Grampian *Banffshire* Map 15 NJ46

★★ **61% Mill House**
Tynet AB56 2HJ (3m W on A98)
☎Clochan(05427) 233. Due to change to (0542) 850233 FAX (05427) 331 due to change to (0542) 850331

Converted and extended, this old mill is a popular base for sporting enthusiasts, tourists and business people. The old mill wheel, still in working order, can be seen in the foyer. There is a comfortable lounge and the restaurant is separate from the main bar.

15⇨♠(2fb) CTV in all bedrooms ® T sB&B⇨♠£33-£37 dB&B⇨♠£52-£57 ⊟
⟨ CTV 100P games room ♫ xmas
V ♡ ⚏ ⤢ Lunch £6-£10alc High tea £6-£6alc Dinner £8-£10.50&alc Last dinner 9pm
CONF. Thtr 100 Class 60 Board 30 Del from £345
Credit Cards ① ② ③ ⑤

BUCKINGHAM Buckinghamshire Map 04 SP63

★★★ **66% Buckingham Lodge**
Ring Rd South MK18 1RY ☎(0280) 822622
FAX (0280) 823074

Conveniently located beside the A421 close to its junction with the A413 to the south of the town, this purpose built red brick hotel offers a good standard of modern accommodation. Attractive bedrooms are comfortably furnished in contemporary style and equipped with up-to-date facilities. Executive rooms have extras such as writing desks and mini bars. There are spacious open plan public rooms.

70⇨♠(6fb)⤢in 16 bedrooms CTV in all bedrooms ®✱ T ✱
sB&B⇨♠£49-£69 dB&B⇨♠£59-£79 Continental breakfast ⊟
⟨ 120P ⊡ (heated) snooker sauna gymnasium jacuzzi ♫ xmas
♧ English & French V ♡ ⚏ ⤢ Lunch £8.75-£10.50 Dinner £9.95-£11.95&alc Last dinner 10pm
CONF. Thtr 160 Class 90 Board 50 Del from £82
Credit Cards ① ② ③ ⑤

The AA's star rating scheme is the market leader in hotel classification.

The Old Kings Head ★
Broughton in Furness, Cumbria LA20 6HJ
Telephone: (0229) 716293

Claimed to be one of the oldest inns within the district, with recorded history spanning at least 300 years. Inside is full of character, the upstairs was once the town theatre and downstairs interesting reminders of the famous Broughton family of clockmakers. A traditional country town pub with an eye for modern day comforts. All the bedrooms are well equipped with central heating throughout. The restaurant has an enviable reputation and offers a full bar menu equally highly praised. Situated in the centre just a couple of hundred yards in any direction to the edge of town and the open countryside.

★ 114 Ensuite Bedrooms
★ 2 Restaurants
★ Lounge Bar
★ Health and Leisure Club/Snooker Lounge
★ 8 Meeting Rooms
★ Banqueting Suite
★ Free Car Parking for 250 vehicles
★ Weekend Breaks – Families welcome

Set in the beautiful Worcestershire countryside, with easy access to the Midlands motorway network and only 20 minutes drive from Birmingham and the NEC, the Pine Lodge Hotel is the ideal venue for every occasion.

To make your reservation please telephone:
0527 576600

Kidderminster Road, Bromsgrove,
Worcestershire B61 9AB
Tel: 0527-576600 Fax: 0527-578981

Buckland (Near Broadway) - Bude

BUCKLAND (NEAR BROADWAY) Gloucestershire
Map **04** SP03

★★★

BUCKLAND MANOR
WR12 7LY
☎Broadway(0386) 852626
FAX (0386) 853557

Relatively new owners at Buckland Manor continue the commendable upgrading of accommodation.
Conscientious management by Savoy-trained Nigel Power permeates through to the staff, who are making this a fine hotel, their staff helped by the splendour of the building, the richly furnished lounges, and the well proportioned bedrooms. Martyn Pearn's ever changing seasonal menu provides British dishes with a hint of French influence. Recently, our inspectors have enjoyed a light pithiviers of Cornish scallops with a tasty chive and caviar sauce, and a rich galantine of quail with foie gras, pistachio and truffle, followed by Cornish lamb sautéed with basil and tomato, and a duo of Lunesdale duckling, the breast served pink with kirsch and confit of boned leg flavoured with orange.

10⇨☏(2fb)2⌺ CTV in all bedrooms T ✻
sB&B⇨☏£135-£260 dB&B⇨☏£145-£270
30P ⌺ ✻ ⌂ (heated) ♪ (hard) croquet putting green nc12yrs *xmas*
♀ International V ☙ ℒ ✂ Lunch fr£18.50&alc Dinner £26.55-£40alc Last dinner 8.45pm
Credit Cards [1][2][3]   £

BUCKLERS HARD Hampshire Map **04** SU40

★★★✿64% **Master Builders House**
SO4 7XB ☎(0590) 616253 FAX (0590) 612624

Set in the old shipbuilding village, with gardens running down to the river, this converted 18th-century house offers a choice of comfortable well furnished bedrooms, some with river views. The popular beamed bar and comfortable lounge have much historic charm and the restaurant overlooks the estuary. Menus often feature local game and home-grown produce.

6⇨☏Annexe17⇨☏(1fb)3⌺ CTV in all bedrooms ®
80P ⌺ ✻ ♪ clay pigeon shooting boating
♀ English & French V ☙ ℒ ✂ Last dinner 9.45pm
Credit Cards [1][2][3][5]

BUCKLOW HILL Cheshire Map **07** SJ78

★★★61% **The Swan**
WA16 6RD ☎(0565) 830295 FAX (0565) 830614

Originally an inn and now a busy hotel with comfortable bedrooms and a popular restaurant, the Swan is well situated for Manchester Airport and offers travellers a good value 'Before you Fly' package.

70⇨☏(11fb)3⌺✂in 14 bedrooms CTV in all bedrooms ® T 《200P ✻
♀ French & English V ☙ ℒ Last dinner 10pm
Credit Cards [1][2][3][5]

If you have booked a meal in a hotel restaurant and cannot get there, remember you have a contractual obligation to cancel your booking.

BUDE Cornwall & Isles of Scilly Map **02** SS20

★★★64% **Hartland**
Hartland Ter EX23 8JY ☎(0288) 355661 FAX (0288) 355664
Closed Dec-Feb (ex Xmas)

ExecGroup

Personally run by the Barker family for many years, this hotel has steadily been improved and accommodation includes a number of rooms with sea views. The hotel has good access to the nearby beach.

29⇨☏(2fb)3⌺ CTV in all bedrooms T sB&B⇨☏£33-£45 dB&B⇨☏£60-£72 ♪
Lift 30P ✻ ⌂ (heated) ♪ ⌬ *xmas*
♀ International ☙ ℒ Lunch £13.25 Dinner £18-£19.50 Last dinner 8.30pm

★★65% **Bude Haven**
Flexbury Av EX23 8NS ☎(0288) 352305
Closed 23 Dec-2 Jan

The Bude Haven is a well kept detached Edwardian house. Freshly cooked meals are served in the new dining room, and bedrooms are well equipped and decorated.

13⇨☏(1fb) CTV in all bedrooms ® ✻ (ex guide dogs)
sB&B⇨☏£19-£21 dB&B⇨☏£32-£36 ♪
CTV 8P ⌺
V ✂ Dinner £7.50-£8.50 Last dinner 7.30pm
Credit Cards [1][2][3]   £

★★65% **Camelot**
Downs View EX23 8RE (turn off A39 into Bude, drive through Bude cross golf course, hotel is on left overlooking golf course)
☎(0288) 352361 FAX (0288) 355470

Well kept and proprietor-run, this hotel has strong ties to the golf course across the road and offers well equipped bedrooms and a genial atmosphere.

21⇨☏(3fb) CTV in all bedrooms ® T ✻ (ex guide dogs) ✱
sB&B⇨☏£20-£25 dB&B⇨☏£40-£50 ♪
21P ⌺ solarium
V ✂ ✱ Dinner £14&alc Last dinner 8.30pm
Credit Cards [1][3]   £

★★65% **Maer Lodge**
Crooklets Beach EX23 8NG ☎(0288) 353306 FAX (0288) 353306

Set in its own garden overlooking the golf course, with easy access to beaches and the town centre, this small and welcoming hotel has been run by the Stanley family for over 30 years. It offers attentive service, clean and comfortable bedrooms, a choice of lounges and good home cooking.

19rm(15⇨☏)(3fb)✂in 19 bedrooms CTV in 19 bedrooms ®⌬
T sB&B£19-£24 sB&B⇨☏£22-£28 dB&B£34-£44 dB&B⇨☏£40-£52 ♪
CTV 20P ✻ pool table mini-golf ♪ ⌬ *xmas*
♀ English & Continental V ☙ ℒ ✱ Lunch £5-£7.50 Dinner £9-£12 Last dinner 8pm
CONF. Class 60 Board 15
Credit Cards [1][2][3][5]

★★64% **Penarvor**
Crooklets Beach EX23 8NE (on headland 50yds from Crooklets beach) ☎(0288) 352036 FAX (0288) 355027
Closed Nov-Feb

Situated overlooking the sea and the Bude and North Cornwall Golf Links, this family-run hotel provides a variety of golfing holiday packages. Public rooms comprise a popular bar and lounge, a candlelit dining room and a secure caddies' house. The modern bedrooms are well furnished, some with good sea views.

16⇨☏(3fb) CTV in all bedrooms ® T sB&B⇨☏£25-£28 dB&B⇨☏£50-£54 ♪
20P ⌺ ✻ pool table games room
♀ English & French V ☙ ℒ Last dinner 8pm
Credit Cards [1][3]   £

Bude - Bunwell

★★ 63% St Margaret's
Killerton Rd EX23 8EN ☎(0288) 352252 & 352401 FAX (0288) 355995

Quietly situated with its own immaculate garden, St Margarets has a choice of traditional or modern bedrooms, all of which have mini bars, hot drink facilities and other amenities. The attractive alcoved restaurant, bar, games room and sun lounge complete the public areas.

10⇨ᴎ(3fb) CTV in all bedrooms ® T ✱ sB&B⇨ᴎ£25-£27 dB&B⇨ᴎ£40-£44 ₧
CTV 4P ❀ ✿ games room *xmas*
♀ English & Continental V ♡ ♌ ✱ Lunch fr£6.50 Dinner fr£10&alc Last dinner 8.30pm
CONF. Class 20 Board 10 Del £40
Credit Cards [1][3]

★★ 60% Atlantic House
17-18 Summerleaze Crescent EX23 8HJ ☎(0288) 352451
Closed 10 Nov-Feb

This is a comfortable, family-run hotel, with good views over the beach and sea. It comprises a bar and lounge plus an additional sun lounge, and the dining room features a daily 5-course table d'hôte menu and a very good dessert buffet. Some bedrooms have sea views.

19rm(12⇨ᴎ)(4fb) CTV in all bedrooms ® ✈ (ex guide dogs) sB&B⇨ᴎ£30.30-£33.75 dB&B⇨ᴎ£60.60-£67.50 (incl dinner) ₧
10P games room
V ♡ ♌ Bar Lunch £1.75-£3.10 Dinner £10.50-£13.50&alc Last dinner 7.30pm
Credit Cards [1][3] £

★★ 60% Burn Court
Burn View EX23 8DB ☎(0288) 352872

Conveniently situated for the town centre and the shops, and overlooking the golf course, the Burn Court is predominantly a holiday hotel. Bedrooms are comfortable and simply coordinated and furnished. A relaxed atmosphere prevails.

32rm(5⇨16ᴎ)(1fb) CTV in 28 bedrooms TV in 4 bedrooms ® T ✱ sB&B£25-£27 sB&B⇨ᴎ£25-£27 dB&B£46 dB&B⇨ᴎ£50 ₧
10P *xmas*
V ♡ ♌ ✂ ✱ Lunch £1.50-£9.50 Dinner £10-£14.95&alc Last dinner 7.30pm
Credit Cards [1][3] £

★ 63% Meva Gwin
Upton EX23 0LY ☎(0288) 352347
Closed 8 Oct-Mar

Splendidly positioned to give sweeping views of the coastline and open countryside, this small personally run hotel offers warm hospitality, hearty food and bright, clean accommodation. Simply furnished bedrooms are well equipped and there is a popular bar, sun lounge and terrace.

11rm(4⇨6ᴎ)(4fb) CTV in all bedrooms ® ✈ sB&B£16-£20 sB&B⇨ᴎ£18-£22 dB&B⇨ᴎ£36-£44
CTV 44P ✿
♡ ♌ ✱ Lunch £8.50 Dinner £8.50 Last dinner 7.30pm

BUDOCK Cornwall & Isles of Scilly Map 02 SW73

★★ 63% Penmorvah Manor
Penjerrick TR11 5ED
☎Falmouth(0326) 250277 FAX (0326) 250509

Set in 6 acres of mature gardens and woodlands, only 2 miles from the city centre, this Victorian manor house has 20 individually styled new bedrooms (smoking discouraged) and a candlelit restaurant with a choice of fixed-price menus.

27rm(26⇨)(1fb)✂ in 20 bedrooms CTV in all bedrooms ® T ✈ (ex guide dogs) ✱ sB&B⇨ᴎ£30.75-£40 dB&B⇨ᴎ£61.50-£80 ₧

150P ✿ *xmas*
♀ English & French V ♡ ♌ ✱ Lunch fr£8.50 Dinner fr£13.50&alc Last dinner 8.30pm
CONF. Thtr 250 Class 150 Board 56 Del £51.50
Credit Cards [1][2][3] £

BUILTH WELLS Powys Map 03 SO05

★★★ ♨ 65% Caer Beris Manor
LD2 3NP (SW on A483) ☎(0982) 552601 FAX (0982) 552586

This black and white timbered manor house is set in 27 acres of parkland which includes the River Irfon and a wealth of bird life. Public rooms are comfortably appointed and include the Elizabethan panelled restaurant. Bedrooms vary in quality but all are well maintained.

22⇨ᴎ(1fb)4₪ CTV in 21 bedrooms ® ✆ T sB&B⇨ᴎ£43.50-£47.50 dB&B⇨ᴎ£67-£95 ₧
30P 2⛱ ✿ ❀ ♪ ♨ sauna gymnasium clay pigeon shooting *xmas*
♀ International V ♡ ♌ Last dinner 10pm
CONF. Thtr 120 Class 75 Board 50 Del from £49.50
Credit Cards [1][2][3][5] £

★★ 63% Pencerrig Country House
LD2 3TF (off A483) ☎(0982) 553226 FAX (0982) 552347

This friendly country house style hotel is set in pleasant gardens and has comfortable public rooms. Bedrooms vary in quality, but all have modern amenities.

20⇨ᴎ(1fb)₪ CTV in all bedrooms ® T sB&B⇨ᴎfr£43.50 ₧
(40P ✿ *xmas*
♀ Welsh & French V ♡ ♌ Lunch fr£7alc High tea fr£4alc Dinner fr£16.95alc Last dinner 9pm
CONF. Thtr 80 Class 40 Board 40 Del from £56.50
Credit Cards [1][2][3][5] £

★★ 59% Lion
2 Broad St LD2 3DT ☎(0982) 553670 FAX (0982) 553999

The Lion is a popular market town hotel near the River Wye and its bridge. Staff and owners are friendly and helpful, and the spacious public rooms include 2 bars.

20rm(12⇨2ᴎ)(4fb)1₪ CTV in all bedrooms ® T 12P
♀ English, French & Italian V ♡ ♌ Last dinner 9.30pm
Credit Cards [1][3]

BUNESSAN
See **Mull, Isle of**

BUNWELL Norfolk Map 05 TM19

★★ ♨ 63% Bunwell Manor
Bunwell St NR16 1QU ☎(0953) 788304

A delightfully, extensively renovated 18th-century building where the owners, Mr and Mrs Nylk, oversee a hospitable, well run hotel. The bar and restaurant provide wholesome cooking and the bedrooms, some with basic furnishings, have modern facilities with additional personal touches.

10⇨(2fb) CTV in all bedrooms ® T sB&B⇨ᴎ£40-£45 dB&B⇨ᴎ£60-£65 ₧
30P ✿ *xmas*
♀ English & French V ♡ Lunch £12.95&alc Dinner £12.95&alc Last dinner 9.30pm
CONF. Thtr 30 Class 20 Board 20
Credit Cards [1][2][3] £

Irish entries appear in a separate section that follows the main directory.

Burbage - Burnham

BURBAGE Wiltshire Map 04 SU26

★★ ❀67% Savernake Forest
Savernake SN8 3AY (1m NE off A346)
☎Marlborough(0672) 810206 FAX (0672) 811081
10⇨↟Annexe6⇨↟(1fb)1⌸ CTV in all bedrooms ® T ✱
sB&B⇨↟£40-£44 dB&B⇨↟£60-£66 ♉
CTV 60P ❀ ♪ ∞ xmas
♀ English & French V ✧ Last dinner 9.15pm
Credit Cards ① ② ③ ⑤
See advertisement under MARLBOROUGH

BURFORD Oxfordshire Map 04 SP21

★★★ ❀68% The Bay Tree
12-14 Sheep St OX18 4LW (off A40) ☎(099382) 2791 FAX (099382) 3008

Dating back to Tudor times, this pleasant hotel with a walled garden is just off the centre of the town. Bedrooms are individually furnished with antiques and have attractive soft furnishings. Chef Lionel McCartney offers a daily set menu and a sensible-sized carte which might include such dishes as liver parfait, grilled medallions of beef with a pepper sauce and Oxfordshire syllabub in a wafer basket.

22⇨↟3⌸ CTV in all bedrooms ® T
20P ❀ croquet
V ✧ ⚐ ✱ ✱ Lunch £10.95-£12.50 Dinner £19.50-£23.50&alc Last dinner 9pm
CONF. Thtr 40 Board 20 Del £125
Credit Cards ① ② ③ ⑤ £

★★★ 58% Inn For All Seasons
The Barringtons OX18 4TN (3m W on A40)
☎Cotswold(0451) 844324 FAX (0451) 844375

This hotel has been carefully preserved to retain the character of its coaching inn days, with open fires, exposed stone walls and period furniture. The restaurant offers a fixed-price menu and a short 'carte', and bar meals are also available.

9⇨↟(2fb) CTV in all bedrooms ®❧ T ⚐ (ex guide dogs) ✱
sB&B⇨↟£35-£45 dB&B⇨↟£60-£70 ♉
30P ❀ clay pigeon shooting nc10yrs xmas
V ✧ ✱ ✱ Sunday Lunch £9.75 Dinner £14.50&alc Last dinner 9.30pm
CONF. Board 30 Del from £75
Credit Cards ① ③ £

★★ 67% Golden Pheasant
High St OX18 4QA (Leave M40 at junct 8 and follow signs A40 Cheltenham into Burford) (Logis) ☎(099382) 3223 & 3417 FAX (099382) 2621

Dating in part from the early 1500s, this popular small hotel began life as a coaching inn. Public areas combine the charm of the original building with modern comforts; they include a lounge bar and 2 candlelit dining areas. Bedrooms in the main house have antique pieces and pretty floral fabrics. The enthusiastic staff are friendly and welcoming.

12⇨↟(2fb)2⌸ CTV in all bedrooms ® T sB&B⇨↟£50-£58 dB&B⇨↟£75-£85 ♉
10P xmas
♀ English & French V ✧ ⚐ ✱ Lunch £2.30-£11.95&alc
Credit Cards ① ② ③ £

★★ 63% Cotswold Gateway
Cheltenham Rd OX18 4HX (situated at the roundabout on the A40 Oxford/Cheltenham where the A429 enters Burford)
☎(099382) 2695 FAX (099382) 3600
Closed 25-29 Dec

This old Cotswold stone building has been attractively refurbished. Very well equipped bedrooms vary in size, and there is a cosy bar, small coffee shop and oak-panelled restaurant with a well balanced table d'hote menu.

13⇨↟Annexe4⇨↟(4fb)1⌸ ✱ in 1 bedroom CTV in all bedrooms ® T ✱ sB&B⇨↟fr£45 dB&B⇨↟fr£70 ♉
60P
♀ English & French V ✧ ⚐ ✱ Lunch £15.95 Dinner £15.95 Last dinner 9.30pm
CONF. Board 25 Del from £70
Credit Cards ① ② ③ ⑤

BURGH HEATH Surrey Map 04 TQ25

★★ 60% Heathside
Brighton Rd KT20 6BW (on S carriageway of A217)
☎(0737) 353355 FAX (0737) 370857

This extended commercial hotel provides reasonably comfortable if somewhat dated and functional bedrooms, although the 'deluxe' rooms are more modern and better equipped. Public areas include a bar and an attractive restaurant and friendly staff provide a cheerful, rather than professional service.

73⇨↟(32fb)✱ in 11 bedrooms CTV in all bedrooms ®❧ T sB&B⇨↟£50-£80 dB&B⇨↟£60-£90 ♉
(150P ❀ ▭ (heated) sauna gymnasium xmas
♀ English & French ✧ ⚐ Lunch fr£10
CONF. Del from £80
Credit Cards ① ② ③ ⑤ £

BURLEY Hampshire Map 04 SU20

★★★ 59% Burley Manor
Ringwood Rd BH24 4BS (Forestdale) ☎(0425) 403522 FAX (0425) 403227

This 19th-century manor house has an open-plan bar and lounge, and the restaurant offers interesting menus of reliably cooked dishes, along with a good wine list. Bedrooms vary in size and standard, with luxurious new rooms available in a converted stable block.

21⇨↟Annexe9⇨↟(3fb)4⌸ ✱ in 4 bedrooms CTV in all bedrooms ® T sB&B⇨↟£44.95-£49.95 dB&B⇨↟£59.90-£77.90 ♉
60P ❀ ▭ (heated) ♪ U croquet xmas
V ✧ ⚐ ✱ Lunch £5.95-£16 Dinner £14.75-£16.45&alc Last dinner 10pm
CONF. Thtr 90 Class 40 Board 40 Del £67.50
Credit Cards ① ② ③ ⑤

★★★ 59% Moorhill House
BH24 4AG (Care Hotels) ☎(0425) 403285 FAX (0425) 403715

Set back a quarter of a mile from the road east of town, this quiet hotel offers modest comfort. Rooms vary in size (check when booking) and some achieve better standards of maintenance than others. There are 2 lounges, a snug bar, a small swimming pool with a whirlpool bath, and a restaurant serving generous portions of robust food.

24⇨↟(7fb) CTV in all bedrooms ® T sB&B⇨↟£35-£50 dB&B⇨↟£50-£80 ♉
CTV 40P ⇌ ❀ ▭ (heated) sauna jacuzzi spa bath xmas
V ✧ ⚐ ✱ Dinner £13.50&alc Last dinner 8.45pm
CONF. Thtr 54 Class 48 Board 28 Del £65
Credit Cards ① ② ③ ⑤

BURNHAM Buckinghamshire Map 04 SU98

★★★ ❀64% Burnham Beeches Moat House
Grove Rd SL1 8DP (off A355 via 'Farnham Royal' roundabout) ☎(0628) 603333 FAX (0628) 603994

Some bedrooms are contained in the modern wings of this impressive Georgian country residence set in its own grounds; rooms vary in size, aspect and decorative standard, but upgrading is in progress. Public areas, in the style of the original house, include a

Burnham - Burnley

panelled restaurant where sound menus in modern style offer enjoyable dishes.
75⇌2🛏🗝in 8 bedrooms CTV in all bedrooms ®𝒫 T ✱
sB&B⇌£86-£91 dB&B⇌£98-£110 🍴
Lift ☾ 150P ✿ 🖼 (heated) ♗ (hard) sauna solarium gymnasium croquet ⚙ xmas
♒ French V ♢ ⚖ Lunch fr£16&alc Dinner fr£19&alc Last dinner 9.30pm
CONF. Thtr 180 Class 70 Board 40 Del from £100
Credit Cards [1][2][3][4][5]

BURNHAM MARKET Norfolk Map 09 TF84

★★69% Hoste Arms
The Green PE31 8HE (signposted on B1155) ☎(0328) 738257 FAX (0328) 730103
This 17th-century inn is set on the village green of an unspoilt Georgian village, associated with Lord Nelson. Owner Paul Whittome has hit on a successful formula combining a pleasant, informal atmosphere with particularly well furnished and stylish bedrooms, good value bar meals and a stoned-floored bar which is full of character. Outside is a furnished flintstone-walled garden and a patio with pergolas.
11⇌🛏(1fb)2🛏 CTV in all bedrooms ® T sB&B⇌🛏£40-£42 dB&B⇌🛏£64-£68 🍴
30P ⚙ ✿ 🖼 (heated) sauna 🎵 xmas
♒ English & French V ♢ ⚖ Lunch fr£10.50 Dinner fr£14.75alc Last dinner 9.30pm
Credit Cards [1][3]

BURNHAM-ON-SEA Somerset Map 03 ST34

★★63% Royal Clarence
31 The Esplanade TA8 1BQ ☎(0278) 783138 FAX (0278) 792965

Popular with both holidaymakers and business people, this family-run hotel on the seafront has comfortable well equipped bedrooms which are currently being upgraded. The 2 bars are popular for their wide range of beers, including three home brews, and bar meals, while table d'hôte and carte menus are offered in the Victorian-style dining room.
19rm(18⇌🛏)(2fb) CTV in all bedrooms ® T sB&B⇌🛏£32 dB&B⇌🛏£47 🍴
CTV 20P ⚙
V ♢ ⚖ Lunch £6-£6.50 Dinner £10.95-£12.95&alc Last dinner 8.30pm
Credit Cards [1][2][3][5]

BURNLEY Lancashire Map 07 SD83

★★★71% Oaks
Colne Rd, Reedley BB10 2LF (on A56 between Burnley and Nelson) (Shire) ☎(0282) 414141 FAX (0282) 33401
Standing in its own grounds, this Victorian tea merchant's mansion has been extended to provide a popular hotel with modern amenities. Features of the original house have been retained, lending elegance to the public areas which include Quills Restaurant and Authors Bar. Three types of bedroom are available, all comfortable, pleasantly furnished and well equipped.
58⇌🛏(10fb)2🛏🗝in 28 bedrooms CTV in all bedrooms ® T ✱ sB&B⇌🛏£69-£79 dB&B⇌🛏£88-£98 🍴
☾ 110P ✿ 🖼 (heated) squash snooker sauna solarium gymnasium spa pool 🎵 xmas
♒ English & French V ♢ ⚖ 🗝 ✱ Sunday Lunch £8.50 Dinner £18&alc Last dinner 9.45pm
CONF. Thtr 150 Class 50 Board 60 Del £89
Credit Cards [1][2][3][5]

★★★61% Friendly
Keirby Walk BB11 2DH ☎(0282) 427611 FAX (0282) 436370

This 1960s town centre hotel offers functional and somewhat dated accommodation. Bedrooms tend to be rather compact while public areas include a first floor restaurant and an American themed bar. Staff provide friendly service.
49⇌🛏(12fb)🗝in 12 bedrooms CTV in all bedrooms ®𝒫 T ✱
sB&B⇌🛏£52-£63 dB&B⇌🛏£59-£70.50 (room only) 🍴
Lift ☾ CTV 100P 20⚙ mini-gym
♒ English & French V ♢ ⚖ ✱ Lunch £7.50 Dinner £12.50&alc Last dinner 10pm
CONF. Thtr 300 Board 100 Del from £74
Credit Cards [1][2][3][5]

★★65% Rosehill House
Rosehill Av B11 2PW (S off A56) ☎(0282) 453931 FAX (0282) 455628
In a quiet residential area half a mile from the town centre, this Victorian residence is now a popular commercial hotel offering friendly, attentive service. Many of the original features of the house, such as ornate ceilings, have been retained, but the bedrooms offer modern amenities.
20⇌🛏(1fb)1🛏 CTV in all bedrooms ®𝒫 T
CTV 70P 1⚙ ⚙ ✿
V ♢ ⚖ ✱ Lunch £7.50-£12&alc Dinner £10.25-£12&alc Last dinner 9.30pm
Credit Cards [1][2][3][5]

★★64% Alexander
Todmorden Rd BB11 3ET (on A671) ☎(0282) 422684 FAX (0282) 424094

➡

THE HOSTE ARMS
17th Century Hotel

The Green
Burnham Market
Norfolk PE31 8HD
Tel: 0328 738257
Fax: 0328 730103

The Hoste Arms is a seventeenth century hotel set in the heart of Nelson's Norfolk, overlooking the Georgian village of Burnham Market.

Twelve beautifully furnished bedrooms all en suite and with colour TV & telephone, two rooms have four posters. Two excellent menus to dine from making use of all local fresh produce, particularly fish.

Jazz every Monday and Friday nights in the Piano Room. Rooms from £32 per person B&B.

AA★★   ❦❦❦ HIGHLY COMMENDED

143

Burnley - Burton Upon Trent

Situated in a residential area close to Towneley Hall, not far from the town centre, this large detached house offers friendly personal service, bedrooms with modern amenities and a cosy lounge bar and pleasant restaurant.
12rm(6⇨4🛉)Annexe5⇨🛉(1fb) CTV in all bedrooms ® T
sB&B£19-£23 sB&B⇨🛉£30-£35 dB&B⇨🛉£35-£45
CTV 18P
V ❖ ⚲ Sunday Lunch fr£6.95alc Dinner £7-£13alc Last dinner 9pm
Credit Cards [1][3] £

Forte Travelodge
Cavalry Barracks, Barracks Rd BB11 4AS (junc A671/A679)
☎(0282) 416039 Central Res (0800) 850950

This modern building offers a good standard of accommodation for overnight stops. Smart, spacious and well equipped bedrooms, all with en suite bathrooms, are suitable for family use, and meals may be taken at the nearby family restaurant. For more details about Travelodges, consult the Contents page, under Hotel Groups.
32⇨🛉 ✱ B⇨🛉£31.95 (room only)

BURNSALL North Yorkshire Map 07 SE06

★★**64%** *Fell*
BD23 6BT (on B660) ☎(0756) 72209
Bar meals and traditional draught ales are popular at this hotel, set in colourful gardens in an elevated position. Most of the traditionally furnished bedrooms have views of the fells, and there are 2 comfortable lounges as well as an attractive dining room which looks out towards the river.
14rm(10⇨1🛉)(4fb) ®
CTV 60P ❖ ✿
V ❖ ⚲
Credit Cards [1][2][3]

★★**56%** *Red Lion*
BD23 6BU ☎(0756) 720204
New owners have improved the facilities while retaining the historic charm of this old village inn, situated on the bank of the River Wharfe and overlooking the surrounding fells. Bedrooms are traditionally furnished, attractive public areas include a spacious lounge, and a wide range of food is available.
7⇨🛉Annexe4⇨🛉(2fb)✗ in 6 bedrooms CTV in all bedrooms ® ✗ T sB&B⇨🛉£32.50-£37 dB&B⇨🛉£59-£70 🍴
CTV 40P ♪ *xmas*
V ❖ ⚲ ✗ Lunch £9.95-£12.95 Dinner £16.50-£18 Last dinner 9.30pm
Credit Cards [1][3] £

BURNTISLAND Fife Map 11 NT28

★★**66%** *Inchview Hotel*
69 Kinghorn Rd KY3 9EB (on A921) ☎Kirkcaldy(0592) 872239
FAX (0592) 874866
Part of a Georgian terrace overlooking the Links, this small, family-run hotel provides traditionally furnished accommodation. An interesting choice of menus is offered at both lunch and dinner, served in the pleasant dining room.
12⇨🛉(3fb)1🛏 CTV in all bedrooms ® T sB&B⇨🛉£39.50-£44.50 dB&B⇨🛉£57.50-£69 🍴
15P *xmas*
♀ International V ❖ ⚲ Lunch fr£8.50&alc High tea fr£5.95 Dinner £15.95-£17.45 Last dinner 9.45pm
CONF. Thtr 80 Class 80 Board 80 Del from £60
Credit Cards [1][2][3] £

For key to symbols see the Bookmark.

BURNT YATES North Yorkshire Map 08 SE26

★★★**64%** *Bay Horse Inn & Motel*
HG3 3EJ (W on B6165 next to village church)
☎Harrogate(0423) 770230
This sympathetically extended 18th-century inn, with beamed ceilings, log fires and brasses, provides well appointed bedrooms. Bar and restaurant meals are very popular, and a wide range of menus provides a mixture of traditional and French cuisine.
6🛉Annexe10🛉(2fb) CTV in all bedrooms ® T
✗ (ex guide dogs) ✱ sB&B🛉£40 dB&B🛉£55 🍴
70P
♀ English & French V ❖ ✱ Lunch £8.95 Dinner £13.95&alc Last dinner 9.30pm
Credit Cards [1][3] £

BURRINGTON Devon Map 02 SS61

★★★❀**72%** *Northcote Manor*
EX37 9LZ (2m NW of village towards Station & A377)
☎High Bickington(0769) 60501 FAX (0769) 60770
Closed Nov-Feb

Dating from around 1760, this handsome manor house stands in 12 acres of gardens and well tended grounds in an elevated and secluded position. The proprietors, husband and wife team Glenda and Peter Brown, welcome guests into their home and take good care of them. Bedrooms are fresh and pretty and offer good facilities. Public rooms are cosy, with open fires in cooler weather. Glenda's daily menu depends on locally available produce, and the 5-course meal is a hearty affair with generous portions.
11⇨🛉1🛏 CTV in all bedrooms ® T sB&B⇨🛉£47-£51 dB&B⇨🛉£94 🍴
20P 🚗 ❖ ♪ (hard) croquet nc12yrs
♀ English & French V ❖ ⚲ ✗ Lunch £14 Dinner £18.50 Last dinner 8.30pm
Credit Cards [1][2][3][5] £

BURTON UPON TRENT Staffordshire Map 08 SK22

★★★★**69%** *Hoar Cross Hall Health Spa*
Hoar Cross DE13 8QS (follow B5017 out of Burton for 4.5m then take unclass. road to Hoar Cross) ☎Hoar Cross(028375) 671 FAX (028375) 652

This unique establishment is aptly described by proprietors Steve and Janet Joynes as a health spa resort in a stately home. The original hall retains many impressive original features, including the Long Gallery, with panelled walls, oil paintings and opulent furniture but the majority of bedrooms and almost every conceivable health, fitness and beauty facility are in a large extension. Bedrooms are modern, individually decorated and well equipped. Some of the penthouse suites have their own saunas and some rooms have four-poster water beds
22⇨🛉6🛏 CTV in all bedrooms ® T ✗ (ex guide dogs)
Lift ((180P 🚗 ❖ 📺 (heated) ▶ 9 ♪ (hard) sauna solarium gymnasium aerobic studio treatment rooms
V ✗

See advertisement under Lichfield

★★★**62%** *Riverside*
Riverside Dr, Branston DF14 3EP ☎(0283) 511234 FAX (0283) 511441
RS 24-26 & 31 Dec
Much extended and modernised, this former coaching inn stands on the bank of the River Trent at Branston. The spacious lounge bar and restaurant overlook the river and other amenities include a large banqueting suite. Bedrooms are being completely refurbished.
22⇨🛉 CTV in all bedrooms ® T sB&B⇨🛉£31-£58 dB&B⇨🛉£55-£68 🍴
((130P ❖ ♪ 🎵

Burton Upon Trent - Bury St Edmunds

♡ English & French V ✿ ⏃ ✱ Lunch £8.50-£11.75&alc Dinner £14.95&alc Last dinner 10pm
Credit Cards 1 2 3

BURTONWOOD MOTORWAY SERVICE AREA (M62)
Cheshire Map 07 SJ59

Forte Travelodge
WA5 3AX (between junc 7 & 9 M62 westbound)
☎Central Res (0800) 850950

This modern building offers a good place for overnight stops. Smart, spacious and well equipped bedrooms, all with en suite bathrooms, are suitable for family use, and meals may be taken at the nearby family restaurant. For more details about Travelodges, consult the Contents page, under Hotel Groups.

40⇌ ✱ B⇌ £31.95 (room only)

BURY Greater Manchester Map 07 SD81

★★★✿✿✿69% **Normandie**
Elbut Ln, Birtle BL9 6UT ☎061-764 3869 & 061-764 1170 FAX 061-764 4866
Closed 26 Dec-8 Jan RS Sun

An odd mix of buildings with no common architectural theme have been combined to create this hotel, set high above Bury. The establishment's reputation rests chiefly on its restaurant, where chef Pascal Pommier produces both extensive à la carte and short but well chosen table d'hôte menus. Presentation takes pride of place and sauces play an important role in a range of complex dishes which will delight those prepared to be adventurous.

20⇌ ♪ Annexe3⇌ ♪ CTV in all bedrooms ® T
✗ (ex guide dogs) sB&B⇌ ♪ £49-£69 dB&B⇌ ♪ £69-£79
Continental breakfast
Lift (60P ⏀ ✣
♡ French V ✕ Lunch £15 Dinner fr£18.95&alc Last dinner 9.30pm
Credit Cards 1 2 3 5

★★★63% **Bolholt**
Walshaw Rd BL8 1PU ☎061-764 5239 & 061-764 3888 FAX 061-763 1789

This much extended hotel is set in 50 acres of grounds and gardens. Bedrooms are modern with light pine furniture and the majority are quite spacious. Public areas include a large lounge bar and an attractive restaurant. The welcome is warm and the style of service friendly and informal – and the owners' family can communicate in no less than 7 languages between them.

47rm(43⇌ ♪)(2fb)2⎕ CTV in all bedrooms ®✣ T
✗ (ex guide dogs) sB&B£44-£48 sB&B⇌ ♪ £48
dB&B⇌ ♪ fr£53
CTV 200P ✣ ♫ (hard) ♪ sauna gymnasium bowling pool table table tennis darts ♫
♡ International V ✿ ⏃ ✱ Lunch fr£7.95 Dinner fr£13.50 Last dinner 9.30pm
Credit Cards 1 2 3 5

★58% **Woolfield House**
Wash Ln BL9 6BJ (leave M66 at Bury turn off junct 2, take first left at roundabout then right at traffic lights hotel 100yds on right) ☎061-797 9775

This privately owned and run commercial hotel provides unpretentious accommodation in generally modestly appointed bedrooms – the best being contained in a wing to the rear of the building.

16rm(3⇌7♪)1⎕ CTV in 11 bedrooms TV in 5 bedrooms ® T
✗ (ex guide dogs) ✱ sB&B£22-£23 sB&B⇌ ♪ £32-£34
dB&Bfr£39 dB&B⇌ ♪ £45-£46
40P nc3yrs
♡ ⏃ ✱ Dinner £8.50-£15alc Last dinner 8.30pm
Credit Cards 1 3

BURY ST EDMUNDS Suffolk Map 05 TL86

★★★✿76% **Angel**
Angel Hill IP33 1LT ☎(0284) 753926 FAX (0284) 750092

The Angel first became an inn in 1452 and the Vaults bistro is even older, dating back to the 11th century. There are some large bedrooms with fine period furniture, and even the smaller rooms are very attractive with coordinated décor and fabrics. The Regency restaurant has 2 menus using only fresh produce, and herbs and sauces are cleverly combined to enhance flavours.

42⇌ ♪ 4⎕ CTV in 41 bedrooms T ✱ sB&B⇌ ♪ £49.50-£65
dB&B⇌ ♪ £75-£125 ⎕
(50P 12☙
♡ English & French V ✿ ⏃ ✕ ✱ Lunch fr£10.95&alc Dinner fr£19.75&alc Last dinner 10pm
CONF. Thtr 200 Class 30 Board 40 Del from £92.50
Credit Cards 1 2 3 5 £

★★★✿70% **The Priory**
Tollgate IP32 6EH (off A1101)
☎(0284) 766181 FAX (0284) 767604

Just outside the town centre, this Georgian house with high walls enclosing its beautiful grounds has a relaxing atmosphere. Attractively decorated bedrooms, many of them in chalet-style annexes, are spacious and well equipped. The elegant restaurant offers a choice of a short set menu or more extensive carte with the emphasis on fresh ingredients.

9⇌ ♪ Annexe18⇌ ♪ (2fb)✕ in 2 bedrooms CTV in all bedrooms ® T sB&B⇌ ♪ £50-£65 dB&B⇌ ♪ £69-£80 ⎕
70P 2☙ ✣ ♤

➧

Riverside Drive, Branston, Burton on Trent, Staffordshire DE14 3EP. Tel: Burton (0283) 511234 Fax: (0283) 511441

★★★

The Riverside

Peacefully set on the banks of the River Trent, The Riverside Hotel offers all-round comfort and is very well known in the area for its food.

The 22 bedrooms, many of which have river views, are all provided with en-suite bathrooms, colour television, radio, baby listening and beverage making facilities.

Golf can be arranged at the affiliated golf course which is within a wood's drive of the hotel.

Bury St Edmunds - Buxton

❡ English & French V ❍ ❑ ✱ Lunch £16.50 High tea £5.75 Dinner £16.50&alc Last dinner 9.45pm
Credit Cards 1 2 3 5

B

★★★ ❀♨ **70% Ravenwood Hall**
Rougham IP30 9JA (3m E off A45) ☏ Beyton(0359) 70345
FAX (0359) 70788

Dating back to 1530, this elegant country house has a variety of bedrooms, including some in the mews, all furnished with fine antique pieces. There is a small bar, a comfortable lounge with a log fire, and very attractive grounds. There are several menus: our inspector sampled smoked haddock mousseline wrapped in smoked salmon with a slightly mint-flavoured tomato sauce, baked lemon sole with a crisp coconut crumb cover, and a rather heavy steamed ginger pudding with a coffee and hazlenut sauce. Quail, Scottish salmon and Aga-baked crispy duck also feature.

7➪Annexe7➪1💷 CTV in all bedrooms ® sB&B➪₣£59-£77 dB&B➪₣£77-£97 🗔
100P 3🚗 🍴 ❀ ☰ (heated) ♀ (hard) ♉ croquet shooting parties *xmas*
V ❍ ❑ Lunch fr£14.95&alc High tea £5.45-£5.95 Dinner fr£16.95&alc Last dinner 9.30pm
CONF. Thtr 150 Class 150 Board 70 Del from £99
Credit Cards 1 2 3 5

★★★ **64% Butterfly**
Symonds Rd, Moreton Hall IP32 7BW (on A45)
☏(0284) 760884 FAX (0284) 755476

CONSORT HOTELS

This modern, purpose-built hotel provides polite and friendly service in an informal atmosphere. The pine-furnished restaurant offers a carte, daily specials and a buffet-style self-service operation. Bedrooms are light and well laid out with fitted furniture giving good working space for business guests.
66➪₣(2fb) CTV in all bedrooms ® T 🐕 (ex guide dogs)
sB➪₣£39-£49 dB➪₣£39-£49 (room only) 🗔
(85P
❡ European V ❍ ❑ ✱ Lunch fr£9.50&alc Dinner fr£9.50&alc Last dinner 10pm
CONF. Thtr 40 Class 21 Board 22 Del from £75
Credit Cards 1 2 3 5

★★ **66% The Suffolk**
38 The Buttermarket IP33 1DL ☏(0284) 753995
FAX (0284) 750973

FORTE Heritage

The Suffolk is located in the centre of the busy town, and parking spaces at the rear entail a trip around the tortuous one-way system. Bedrooms are comfortable and tastefully furnished and a youthful brigade ensure a warm welcome with a good level of service, including supper trays. During the day the restaurant and bar are overshadowed by the popular coffee shop.
33➪₣(4fb)₣ in 15 bedrooms CTV in all bedrooms ® T ✱
sB➪₣fr£65 dB➪₣fr£75 (room only) 🗔
(20P 16🚗 *xmas*
V ❍ ❑ ✱ Lunch £6.50-£10.95&alc Dinner £16.95&alc Last dinner 9.30pm
CONF. Thtr 30 Class 10 Board 20 Del from £80
Credit Cards 1 2 3 5

BUTE, ISLE OF Strathclyde *Buteshire* Map **10**

ROTHESAY Map **10** NS06

★ **59% St Ebba**
37 Mountstuart Rd, Craigmore PA20 9EB ☏(0700) 502683

Overlooking the bay and Cowal peninsula to the northwest of the town, this Victorian end-of-terrace hotel has gained a sound reputation for its short à la carte menu, which features a good proportion of seafood. Intricate cornices are a feature of the public rooms, while the bedrooms are mostly bright but plainly furnished.

11➪₣(3fb) CTV in all bedrooms ® ❀ sB&B➪₣£22-£25 dB&B➪₣£44-£50
CTV 7P *xmas*
V ❍ ❑ Last dinner 9.30pm

BUTTERMERE Cumbria Map **11** NY11

★★ **67% Bridge**
CA13 9UZ ☏(07687) 70252

First licensed in 1735, this well run hotel combines old world charm with modern comforts. Bedrooms, some with 4-posters, are bright and fresh with good facilities. There is a delightful lounge, and the pub at the rear serves real ale and a good range of bar meals.
22➪₣❑2🛁 ® T
60P 🚗
❡ English & French V ❍ ❑ ✱ Last dinner 8.30pm

BUXTON Derbyshire Map **07** SK07

★★★ ❀ **69% Lee Wood**
13 Manchester Rd SK17 6TQ (NE on A5004, 200mtrs beyond the Devonshire Royal Hospital) ☏(0298) 23002 & 70421
FAX (0298) 23228

Closed 24-29 Dec

Improvements continue at this friendly, family-managed hotel. This year has seen the refurbishment of the bar, which successfully caters for both guests and locals with a wide selection of bar meals and traditional ales. New chef Shaun Ballington offers a comprehensive choice of dishes from modern British and classical French cuisine, served in the airy conservatory restaurant. Bedrooms have continued to be upgraded and provide a good level of facilities.
36➪₣(2fb)₣ in 5 bedrooms CTV in all bedrooms ® T ✱
sB➪₣£56-£68 dB&B➪₣£72-£84 🗔
Lift (CTV 50P ❀ ❁
❡ English & French V ❍ ❑ ✱ Lunch £9-£12.50 Dinner £18-£20&alc Last dinner 9.30pm
CONF. Thtr 150 Class 60 Board 40 Del from £68
Credit Cards 1 2 3 5

★★★ **62% Palace**
Palace Rd SK17 6AG ☏(0298) 22001 FAX (0298) 72131

FORTE Heritage

This impressive Victorian building overlooking the spa town provides recently upgraded bedrooms and elegant public areas.
122➪₣ in 33 bedrooms CTV in all bedrooms ® T ✱
sB➪₣£65 dB➪₣£75 (room only) 🗔
Lift (CTV 200P ❀ ☰ (heated) snooker sauna solarium gymnasium croquet & putting green *xmas*
V ❍ ❑ ✱ Sunday Lunch £9.95 Dinner £15.95 Last dinner 9pm
Credit Cards 1 2 3 5

★★ ❀ **65% Portland**
32 St John's Rd SK17 6XQ (on A53 opposite the Pavilion and Gardens) (Logis) ☏(0298) 71493 FAX (0298) 27464

Opposite the Pavilion and gardens, this large Victorian house has been hospitably run by the Millner and Gill families for over 20 years. Bedrooms vary in size and style, with newly refurbished rooms having attractive coordinated decor. Comfortable public areas include a conservatory restaurant where chef Brian Simmonds offers set-price dinners of freshly prepared dishes.
25➪₣(3fb)₣ in 1 bedroom CTV in all bedrooms ® T
sB➪₣£20-£48 dB➪₣£40-£62 🗔
18P *xmas*
❡ English & French V ❍ ❑ Lunch fr£5.50&alc High tea £4-£5 Dinner £16.50&alc Last dinner 9.15pm
Credit Cards 1 2 3 5

Buxton - Callander

★ **63% Hartington**
18 Broad Walk SK17 6JR ☎(0298) 22638
Closed 17 Dec-4 Jan RS Nov-Mar
This stone-built, Victorian house has been in the ownership of the Whibberley family for over 30 years and maintains traditional values of hospitality. Bedrooms, including 2 on the ground floor, vary in size and have pretty coordinated décor. Wholesome British food is served by friendly staff.
17rm(3⇨4♠)(3fb) CTV in all bedrooms ® ✈ (ex guide dogs)
CTV 15P
✂ Last dinner 8pm
Credit Cards ①②③

CADNAM Hampshire Map 04 SU21

★★★ **64% Bartley Lodge**
Lyndhurst Rd SO4 2NR
☎Southampton(0703) 812248 FAX (0703) 812075

Built in 1759, this red brick Georgian house was formerly a hunting lodge and is reached via a long drive through its own grounds. It has a galleried and panelled reception/lounge, and bedrooms are brightly decorated in floral fabrics and pine furniture, many with forest views.
19⇨♠(3fb)1☐ CTV in all bedrooms ® T ✻ sB&B⇨♠£35-£50 dB&B⇨♠£50-£80 ₧
CTV 50P ✿ ⊇ (heated) ♀ (hard) croquet *xmas*
V ✿ ⊑ ✂ Lunch £13.50 Dinner £13.50&alc Last dinner 8.45pm
CONF. Thtr 80 Class 62 Board 64 Del from £65
Credit Cards ①②③⑤

CAERNARFON Gwynedd Map 06 SH46

★★★ **77% Seiont Manor**
Llanrug LL55 2AQ (E on A4086) ☎(0286) 673366 FAX (0286) 672840
This high quality hotel, originally the farmstead of a Georgian manor house, stands in 150 acres of mature parkland on the edge of Snowdonia. Particularly spacious bedrooms – all comfortable and equipped with such extras as mini bars and televisions – include two family suites of inter-connecting rooms, while public areas comprise a good choice of lounges, a panelled library and a restaurant divided into four separate parts. The kitchen has a reputation for imaginative and well prepared dishes, and the daily changing fixed price menu is augmented by both a large à la carte selection and the Menu Gourmand.
28⇨♠(7fb)1☐ CTV in all bedrooms ® T ✻
sB&B⇨♠£72.50-£77 dB&B⇨♠£96.50-£124 ₧
⊙ 50P ✿ ▢ (heated) ♪ sauna solarium gymnasium *xmas*
⊙ French V ✿ ⊑ ✂ Lunch £11.50 Dinner £17.50-£19.50&alc Last dinner 10pm
CONF. Thtr 100 Class 40 Board 30 Del from £75
Credit Cards ①②③⑤

★★ **65% Stables**
LL54 5SD ☎Llanwnda(0286) 830711 & 830935 FAX (0286) 830413
(For full entry see Llanwnda)

★★ **63% Menai Bank**
North Rd LL55 1BD (on A487 towards Bangor)
☎(0286) 673297 FAX (0286) 673297
Closed Xmas
This large Victorian house, overlooking the Menai Straits, is personally run by resident proprietors Ian and Deborah Baxter, who provide friendly, informal service. Bedroom sizes and furnishings vary, from simple modern to antique. The hotel has a regular clientèle of commercial visitors, but is also suitable for, and used by, holiday-makers.

15rm(10⇨♠)(3fb) CTV in all bedrooms ® ✻ sB&B£19 sB&B⇨♠£28-£36 dB&B£29-£35 dB&B⇨♠£38-£49 ₧
CTV 10P pool table
✿ ✻ Dinner fr£13 Last dinner 7.30pm
Credit Cards ①②③

CALLANDER Central *Perthshire* Map 11 NN60

★★★ **67% Roman Camp**
FK17 8BG ☎(0877) 30003 FAX (0877) 31533
Twenty acres of grounds insulate this old manor house from the hustle and bustle of the nearby town. Public rooms have a civilised atmosphere, and though some bedrooms may have sacrificed modern comforts to period style, all have many little 'extras'. Chef Simon Burns brings a touch of flair to his Scottish ingredients. A starter of chicken mousse and strips of marinated duck wrapped in spinach leaves, a powerful hare consommé, and loin of lamb encasing a farce of morels served on a red wine sauce earned our inspector's praise.
14⇨♠(3fb)1☐ CTV in all bedrooms ® T
30P ✻ ♪ croquet
⊙ Scottish & French ✿ ⊑ ✂ Last dinner 9pm
Credit Cards ①②③⑤

★★ **69% Lubnaig**
Leny Feus FK17 8AS (off A84) ☎(0877) 30376 due to change to 330376
Closed Nov-Etr
Crawford and Sue Low's small hotel is converted from a detached Victorian property in a quiet street on the western edge of the town. Bedrooms are attractively decorated, and there are 3 lounges, but no bar. Sue Low's short daily changing menu offers honest home cooking, with such dishes as smoked goose breast with a blackcurrant coulis, and beef in Guinness with pickled walnuts.

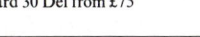

BUTTERFLY HOTELS

Situated in Bury St Edmunds, Colchester, Kings Lynn and Peterborough

All hotels are accessible, informal, comfortable and relaxing – full of style.

At each Butterfly Hotel you will find all the modern facilities today's travellers require, in a rustic traditional setting, that's welcoming and friendly. All bedrooms have private facilities.

Walt's Place – Restaurant and Bar – Where you can enjoy good food, wines and service at affordable prices.

For more information see individual sections or call Central office on (0284) 705800

Callander - Cambridge

6rm Annexe4 CTV in all bedrooms ® ✱ sB&B £25.50-£30 dB&B £51-£60 ₽
CTV 14P ⊞ ✿ nc7yrs
⌖ Dinner £17 Last dinner 8.30pm
Credit Cards [1][3]

★★ 68% Bridgend House
Bridgend FK17 8AH (on A81 to Aberfoyle) ☎(0877) 30130 due to change to 330130 FAX (0877) 31512 due to change to 331512 RS 25 Dec

Situated by the River Teith just outside the town centre, this small mock-Tudor hotel is run on friendly personal lines and the cosy accommodation includes a comfortable lounge and attractive dining room serving fresh local produce.

6rm(5⇨↑)(1fb)2⊞ CTV in all bedrooms ®✍ T sB&B £25-£29.50 sB&B⇨↑£29.50-£42.50 dB&B £29.50-£39.50 dB&B⇨↑£49-£65 ₽
CTV 30P ✿ xmas
⌖ Scottish & French V ◊ ⌖ Lunch £7-£17.50alc High tea £5.75-£7.75 Dinner £7-£21alc Last dinner 9pm
Credit Cards [1][2][3][5] £

★★ 60% Dalgair House
113-115 Main St FK17 8BQ (300 metres beyond access road to golf course on main street) ☎(0877) 30283 due to change to 330283 FAX (0877) 31114 due to change to 331114

This small, family-run hotel in the town centre has well decorated bedrooms with the expected modern facilities. Public areas, though lacking lounge space, include a choice of bars and a bright restaurant.

8⇨↑(1fb) CTV in all bedrooms ®✍ T sB&B⇨↑£40 dB&B⇨↑£52 ₽
30P xmas
V ◊ ⌖ Sunday Lunch £8-£14 High tea £5.25 Dinner £12&alc Last dinner 9pm
Credit Cards [1][2][3][5] £

★ 65% Highland House
South Church St FK17 8BN (turn off A84 in town centre and follow signs for police station) ☎(0877) 30269 due to change to 330269
Closed Dec-Feb

9rm(7⇨↑↑) in all bedrooms CTV in all bedrooms ® ✱ sB&B£19-£29 sB&B⇨↑£21-£29 dB&B£36-£42 dB&B⇨↑£42-£54 ₽
CTV ₽ ⊞
✱ Dinner £12-£15.75&alc Last dinner 7.30pm
Credit Cards [1][2][3] £

CALNE Wiltshire Map 03 ST97

★★ 63% Lansdowne Strand Hotel & Restaurant
The Strand SN11 0JR ☎(0249) 812488 FAX (0249) 815323

Built in the 16th century as a coaching inn, this historic hotel is in the centre of this attractive market town. The bedrooms are individually decorated and furnished, some with access from the courtyard. The public areas include 3 popular bars and an à la carte restaurant, where an extensive menu is available.

21⇨↑Annexe5⇨↑(3fb)1⊞ CTV in all bedrooms ® T sB&B⇨↑£46 dB&B⇨↑£55 ₽
21P xmas
⌖ English, French, German & Spanish V ◊ ⌖ ⌖ Lunch £8-£10&alc Dinner £10-£12.50&alc Last dinner 10pm
CONF. Thtr 80 Class 40 Board 40 Del from £50
Credit Cards [1][2][3][5] £

The AA's star rating scheme is the market leader in hotel classification.

CAMBERLEY Surrey Map 04 SU86

★★★ 68% Frimley Hall
Portsmouth Rd GU15 2BG ☎(0276) 28321 FAX (0276) 691253

FORTE Heritage

This rather grand Victorian manor house retains many charming features such as impressive oak panelling, ornate carving and stained glass. Bedrooms in the original building have a great deal of character, while those in the modern extension provides a uniform standard with appealing soft furnishings. In the restaurant, chef Dietmar Gvatowski prepares a daily and seasonal menu with some imaginative combinations as well as classic dishes.

66⇨↑(2fb)1⊞⌖in 16 bedrooms CTV in all bedrooms ® T ✱ sB&B⇨↑£95 dB&B⇨↑£105 (room only) ₽
⌕ 200P ✿ xmas
V ◊ ⌖ ⌖ Lunch £15.75 High tea £12 Dinner £19.75 Last dinner 10pm
CONF. Thtr 60 Class 30 Board 40 Del £120
Credit Cards [1][2][3][5]

★★★ 59% Lakeside International
Wharf Rd, Frimley Green GU16 6JR ☎Deepcut(0252) 838000 FAX (0252) 837857

This attractively situated large modern hotel is chiefly geared to conferences, and the overall complex includes a night club and a leisure centre. Bedrooms, some with balconies and lake views, are all similarly well equipped. Three-star levels of service are, however, not always available.

97⇨↑⌖in 6 bedrooms CTV in all bedrooms ® T
✚ (ex guide dogs) ✱ sB&B⇨↑£85 dB&B⇨↑£98
Lift ⌕ CTV 250P ✿ ⌖ (heated) squash snooker sauna solarium gymnasium ♪ xmas
⌖ English & French V ◊ ⌖ ⌖ Lunch £15.50&alc Dinner £15.50&alc Last dinner 10.30pm
CONF. Thtr 100 Class 60 Board 12 Del £95
Credit Cards [1][2][3][5]

CAMBORNE Cornwall & Isles of Scilly Map 02 SW64

★★★ 69% Tyacks
27 Commercial St TR14 8LD (St Austell Brewery) ☎(0209) 612424 FAX (0209) 612435

This 18th-century coaching inn has extremely smart bedrooms with excellent fabrics and impressive bathrooms. Some rooms in the older part of the hotel have low beamed ceilings. Public areas include a smart residents' lounge and bar, a popular public bar and a well appointed restaurant where a choice of good value or more extensive menus is available.

15⇨↑(2fb)⌖in 3 bedrooms CTV in all bedrooms ® T
✚ (ex guide dogs) sB&B⇨↑£37-£80 dB&B⇨↑£68-£80 ₽
42P 1⊞ (£3 per night) ♪ xmas
⌖ English & Continental V ◊ ⌖ ⌖ Lunch fr£7.50 Dinner fr£15 Last dinner 9.30pm
Credit Cards [1][2][3][5] £

CAMBRIDGE Cambridgeshire Map 05 TL45

★★★★ ❀70% Garden House
Granta Place, Mill Ln CB2 1RT ☎(0223) 63421 FAX (0223) 316605

Queens Moat Houses

This popular hotel, which is known for its consistently helpful and professional service, has now been completely refurbished. It is tucked away in an almost rural setting on the River Cam, but just a few minutes walk from the centre. A good lounge menu is served throughout the day and room service is also available.

118⇨↑(4fb)⌖in 25 bedrooms CTV in all bedrooms ®✍ T
✚ (ex guide dogs) sB&B⇨↑£90-£145 dB&B⇨↑£125-£170
Continental breakfast ₽
Lift ⌕ 180P ✿ ♪ punting xmas

Cambridge

♧ International V ❀ ⚒ Lunch £17.95-£18.95&alc Dinner £21.50-£23&alc Last dinner 9.45pm
CONF. Thtr 250 Class 100 Board 80 Del from £99.50
Credit Cards 1 2 3 5 £

★★★★ 60% **Holiday Inn**
Downing St CB2 3DT ☏(0223) 464466 FAX (0223) 464440
RS 24 Dec-4 Jan

Conveniently situated in the centre of the city, this new, purpose-built hotel has quickly become popular with guests and locals alike. The all day food service in the lounge bar is a success, though other public areas tend to be more restricted in size and comfort. Bedrooms aren't quite the usual Holiday Inn size but offer comfort and a good range of facilities. On the ground floor is a hairdressing salon.
199⇨♮in 60 bedrooms CTV in all bedrooms ® T ✶ sB⇨♮£95-£120 dB⇨♮£95-£120 (room only) 🅟
Lift (▦ 68 ⌧ (heated) *xmas*
♧ International V ❀ ⚒ ✄ ✶ Lunch fr£12.95&alc Dinner fr£18.50&alc Last dinner 10pm
CONF. Thtr 150 Class 70 Board 60 Del from £108
Credit Cards 1 2 3 5

★★★★ 57% **University Arms**
Regent St CB2 1AD ☏(0223) 351241 FAX (0223) 315256

DE VERE HOTELS

This famous city centre hotel provides bedrooms which vary greatly in size, but have charming decor of natural woods and pleasant soft furnishings. There is a comfortable central lounge, a huge restaurant with a view onto Parkers Piece, and 3 bars, all decorated and furnished to a good standard. Although in the past our inspectors have experienced some irritation with the standards of service, there has been an improvement.
115⇨♮(5fb)⚹in 14 bedrooms CTV in all bedrooms ®⚹T sB&B⇨♮£81-£86 dB&B⇨♮£110-£115 🅟
Lift (80P ♪ *xmas*
♧ English & French V ❀ ⚒ ✄ ✶ Lunch £11-£16&alc High tea £6.25 Dinner £16-£18 Last dinner 9.45pm
CONF. Thtr 200 Class 100 Board 50 Del from £113
Credit Cards 1 2 3 5

★★★ 68% **Gonville**
Gonville Place CB1 1LY ☏(0223) 66611 FAX (0223) 315470

BEST WESTERN HOTELS

A well established hotel close to the centre overlooking Parkers Piece. Major alterations have brought a completely new look to the public rooms with warm colour coordinated décor and an atrium in the bar area. Staff, always polite and efficient, are now more friendly and cheerful. Bedrooms are a little dated but of a comfortable size with more compact bathrooms.
64⇨♮(6fb) CTV in all bedrooms ® T sB&B⇨♮fr£68 dB&B⇨♮fr£85 🅟
Lift (100P *xmas*
♧ English & French V ❀ ⚒ Lunch £12-£13&alc Dinner fr£14&alc Last dinner 8.45pm
CONF. Thtr 200 Class 100 Board 50 Del £80
Credit Cards 1 2 3 4 5 £

★★★ 63% **Cambridgeshire Moat House**
CB3 8EU ☏Crafts Hill(0954) 780555 FAX (0954) 780010
(For full entry see Bar Hill)

Queens Moat Houses

★★★ 62% **Royal Cambridge**
Trumpington St CB2 1PY ☏(0223) 351631 FAX (0223) 352972
Created from a row of Georgian houses, this hotel is in a prominent position, only a short walk from colleges and shopping facilities. An extensive refurbishment programme has resulted in bright, cheerful public rooms with a Victorian theme. Bedrooms vary in size, but

décor and facilities are standard, and rooms facing the road have double glazing. Staff are very helpful and friendly.
46⇨♮(2fb) CTV in all bedrooms ® T ✶ sB&B⇨♮£69.50 dB&B⇨♮£79.50 🅟
Lift (80P *xmas*
♧ English & French V ❀ ⚒ ✶ Lunch fr£9.75&alc Dinner fr£12.50&alc Last dinner 9.30pm
Credit Cards 1 2 3 5 £

★★ 70% **Cambridge Lodge**
Huntingdon Rd CB3 0DQ (1m NW on A1307) (Qualitair) ☏(0223) 352833 FAX (0223) 355166
RS Sat
This professionally run small hotel provides quality and comfort throughout. The bedrooms are clean and equipped with a good range of facilities. An interesting daily menu and à la carte choices make this a locally popular restaurant, where attentive service by the young team is assured.
11rm(8⇨♮) CTV in all bedrooms ® T ✶ sB&B£45-£60 sB&B⇨♮£60 dB&B£50-£65 dB&B⇨♮£65 🅟
20P ⇔ ✿
♧ English & Continental V ✶ Lunch £14.95 Dinner £19.95 Last dinner 9.30pm
Credit Cards 1 2 3 5 £

★★ 69% **Centennial**
63-71 Hills Rd CB2 1PG ☏(0223) 314652 FAX (0223) 315443
Closed 23 Dec-2 Jan
Within walking distance of the city centre and railway station, this hotel provides pleasantly coordinated bedrooms. Public areas include a bar and dining room, and a comfortable lounge with leather chesterfields and richly coloured soft furnishings. Friendly service is provided by youthful, uniformed staff.
39⇨♮(1fb) CTV in all bedrooms ® T ✂ ✶ sB&B⇨♮£55-£60 dB&B⇨♮£60-£75 🅟

➡

THE GARDEN HOUSE HOTEL

Set in three acres of tranquil riverside gardens overlooking wooded fenland, yet only minutes' walk from the City Centre, *The Garden House Hotel* offers luxurious accommodation in an idyllic location.
Le Jardin restaurant, renowned for its excellent cuisine and service and the delightful Riverside Lounge both welcome non residents.

Granta Place, Mill Lane, Cambridge CB2 1RT
Telephone 0223 63421
Fax 0223 316805

AA ★★★★

Cambridge - Canterbury

(32P
♀ English & French V ↔ ⚒ ✂ Lunch £10-£15 High tea £5-£8
Dinner £13-£16.50&alc Last dinner 9.30pm
Credit Cards 1 2 3 5

★★ 68% Arundel House
53 Chesterton Rd CB4 3AN (on A1303, overlooking the River Cam) ☎(0223) 67701 FAX (0223) 67721
Closed 25-26 Dec

Situated on the edge of Jesus Green close to the city centre, this hotel has grown in both size and quality, and some bedrooms are above average for this classification. A good range of carefully prepared dishes are served in both the bar and restaurant.
82rm(76⇨♪)Annexe22⇨♪(7fb)✂in 52 bedrooms CTV in all bedrooms ® T ✗ sB&B£28-£37.50 sB&B⇨♪£38.50-£55 dB&B£39.50 dB&B⇨♪£54-£75 Continental breakfast ₽
(70P
♀ English, French & Italian V ↔ ⚒ ✂ Lunch £7.50-£9.75&alc High tea £1.95-£6.95 Dinner £13.95&alc Last dinner 9.30pm
CONF. Thtr 50 Class 34 Board 32 Del from £56.85
Credit Cards 1 2 3 5

★★ 65% Regent
41 Regent St CB2 1AB ☎(0223) 351470 FAX (0223) 356220
Closed 25 Dec-1 Jan

This family-run hotel is near the city centre on the edge of Parkers Piece. Bedrooms are well furnished with light-stained furniture and equipped with modern facilities. There is a modern bar, a separate lounge and an attractive split-level restaurant. Head chef Frank Grillet specialises in fresh fish supplied from Lowestoft. Free parking is available nearby.
25⇨♪(2fb)✂in 12 bedrooms CTV in all bedrooms ® T ✗ (ex guide dogs) sB&B⇨♪fr£55 dB&B⇨♪fr£73 ₽
Lift ℱ
♀ English & French V ↔ ⚒ ✱ Lunch £7.95-£14.95&alc Dinner £10-£16.95&alc Last dinner 10pm
Credit Cards 1 2 3 5   £

Forte Posthouse
Lakeview, Bridge Rd, Impington CB4 4PH (2.5m N, on N side of rdbt jct A45/B1049)
☎(0223) 237000 FAX (0223) 233426

FORTE Posthouse

Suitable for both the business and leisure traveller, this bright hotel provides modern accommodation in well equipped bedrooms with en suite bathrooms. For more details about Forte Posthouse hotels, consult the Contents page, under Hotel Groups.
118⇨♪ B⇨♪£41.50-£53.50 (room only)
CONF. Thtr 60 Class 30 Board 30 Del from £89.50

CAMPBELTOWN Strathclyde *Argyllshire* Map 10 NR72

★★ 63% Seafield
Kilkerran Rd PA28 6JL ☎(0586) 554385

Views over the bay are enjoyed from this small, family-run hotel. Public areas include a comfortable lounge and a snug bar decorated with old photos of the town. The extended restaurant, popular with locals as well as residents, offers an imaginative menu, with seafood and speciality steaks featuring strongly. The larger bedrooms are in the main house.
3♪Annexe6♪ CTV in all bedrooms ® T ✱ sB&B♪£32.50-£35 dB&B♪£55-£60 ₽
11P
V ↔ ✱ Lunch £10-£12.50alc High tea £10-£12.50alc Dinner £19.50-£25alc Last dinner 9pm
Credit Cards 1 3   £

★★ 62% Royal
Main St PA28 6AG ☎(0586) 552017

This popular commercial hotel occupies a corner site in the town centre close to the harbour. The first floor restaurant and lounge bar are comfortable and tastefully furnished, and there is also a coffee shop/diner on the ground floor. Bedrooms, which vary in size, are plain and practical.
16rm(8⇨4♪)(2fb) CTV in all bedrooms ® T
Lift CTV 4P ♫
♀ English & French V ↔ ⚒ ✂ Last dinner 9pm
Credit Cards 1 3

CANNICH Highland *Inverness-shire* Map 14 NH33

★★ ✿ 69% *Cozac Lodge*
Glen Cannich IV4 7LX (8m W on unclass Glen Cannich road) ☎(04565) 263

Breathtakingly rugged scenery surrounds this very civilised hotel and former hunting lodge. The delightful lounge has a roaring log fire and supply of reading matter and board games, and set 5-course dinners are served in an attractive, beamed dining room. Bedrooms are furnished in traditional style and many extra touches add to guests' comfort.
7⇨♪(1fb) CTV in all bedrooms ®
CTV 12P 🐕 ❀ ♪
♀ International
Credit Cards 1 2 3

CANNOCK Staffordshire Map 07 SJ91

★★★ 68% Roman Way
Watling St, Hatherton WS11 1SH (on A5) (Crown & Raven)
☎(0543) 572121 FAX (0543) 502749

On the old Watling Street, this hotel is appropriately designed in the style of a Roman villa. Most of the bedrooms are quite spacious. The choice of food is good, with Nero's Restaurant serving table d'hôte and à la carte dishes, and the locally popular Gilpin's Bar serving lighter meals.
56⇨♪(9fb) CTV in all bedrooms ® T ✱ sB&B⇨♪fr£59.50 dB&B⇨♪fr£59.50 ₽
(200P
♀ International V ↔ ⚒ ✂ ✱ Sunday Lunch £8.50 Dinner £12-£17 Last dinner 10pm
Credit Cards 1 2 3   £

Travel Inn
Watling St, Longford WS11 1SJ (at junct of A5/A460) ☎(0543) 572721 FAX (0543) 466130

travel inn

Purpose-built accomodation offers spacious and well equipped bedrooms, all with en suite bathrooms. Meals may be taken at the nearby family restaurant and pub. For more details about Travel Inns, consult the Contents page, under Hotel Groups.
38⇨♪ ✱ B⇨♪£33.50 (room only)

CANTERBURY Kent Map 05 TR15

★★★ 64% Falstaff
St Dunstans St CT2 8AF (opposite the Westgate of the city) (Lansbury) ☎(0227) 462138 FAX (0227) 463525

Close to the Westgate Tower, outside the city walls, this old-world hotel dates in part from the 16th century. As one expects in a building of this age, the bedrooms are all of all shapes and sizes, though they are similarly furnished and decorated. The ground floor has now been completely refurbished and, with the extended lounge, is smart and comfortable.
23⇨♪(2fb)🐕✂in 6 bedrooms CTV in all bedrooms ®✌ T ✱ sB&B⇨♪£55.50-£69.50 dB&B⇨♪fr£81 ₽
(50P *xmas*
♀ English V ↔ ⚒ ✱ Lunch £8.50-£9.95 Dinner fr£11.45&alc Last dinner 10pm
CONF. Thtr 40 Class 5 Board 20 Del from £92
Credit Cards 1 2 3 5

Canterbury - Cardiff

★★★ 60% The Chaucer
Ivy Ln CT1 1TU ☎(0227) 464427 FAX (0227) 450397

FORTE Heritage

Just a few minutes walk from the town centre and cathedral, this former Georgian residence retains a period appeal in its smartly refurbished restaurant and very comfortable lounge bar, where light meals are served all day.
42⇌♿≁in 19 bedrooms CTV in all bedrooms ® T
sB⇌♿fr£73.50 dB⇌♿fr£84 (room only) 🅿
《 45P *xmas*
V ♿ ⚓ ≁ Sunday Lunch fr£11.50 Dinner fr£18.95&alc Last dinner 9.30pm
CONF. Thtr 100 Class 45 Board 45 Del from £90
Credit Cards [1][2][3][5]

★★ 60% *Canterbury*
71 New Dover Rd CT1 3DZ ☎(0227) 450551 FAX (0227) 780145
Just a short walk away from the cathedral, this elegant 19th-century house is run as a small family hotel. The bedrooms are furnished to the same standard with pine and floral fabrics. Lounge seating is a bit limited with just a small area in the foyer/bar and a room which is often used for meetings.
27⇌♿(4fb) CTV in all bedrooms ® T
Lift CTV 40P
♿ English & French ♿ ⚓ Last dinner 10pm
Credit Cards [1][2][3][5]

CAPEL CURIG Gwynedd Map **06** SH75

★★ 64% *Cobdens*
LL24 0EE (on A5) (Logis) ☎(06904) 243 & 308 FAX (06904) 354
Set in a beautiful part of Snowdonia, Cobdens is an 18th-century hotel, which is popular with both climbers and walkers. One of the 2 bars has an exposed rock face and there is an attractive half-panelled restaurant. A good variety of simply prepared fresh food is available in the bars and restaurant.
17rm(10⇌6♿)(2fb) CTV in all bedrooms ® T ✷
sB&B⇌♿£22.50-£25 dB&B⇌♿£45-£50
60P ⛽ ✢ ⌦ ♪ *xmas*
♿ International V ✿ ✷ Lunch £5-£15alc Dinner £8-£15alc Last dinner 9pm
Credit Cards [1][2][3] £

CARBIS BAY
See **St Ives**

CARCROFT South Yorkshire Map **08** SE50

Forte Travelodge
Great North Rd (on A1)
☎(0302) 330841 Central Res (0800) 850950

FORTE Travelodge

This modern building offers a good standard of accommodation for overnight stops. Smart, spacious and well equipped bedrooms, all with en suite bathrooms, are suitable for family use, and meals may be taken at the nearby family restaurant. For more details about Travelodges, consult the Contents page, under Hotel Groups.
40⇌♿✷ B⇌♿£31.95 (room only)

CARDIFF South Glamorgan Map **03** ST17
See also **Barry**

★★★★ 64% The Copthorne
Copthorne Way, Culverhouse Cross CF5 6XJ
(exit at junct 33 of M4 and take A4232 for 2.5m in direction of Cardiff West and then A48) ☎(0222) 599100 FAX (0222) 599080

Copthorne Hotels

This comfortable modern hotel, with bright, open-plan public areas, stands in grounds which contain a small lake. Comprehensively equipped en suite bedrooms, enhanced by the use of bold coordinated fabrics, are furnished with deep armchairs, while

'Connoiseur' rooms provide extra luxury and the use of their own club lounge. Guests can dine overlooking the lake in Raglans Restaurant or more informally in Beauchamps Brasserie.
135⇌♿(10fb)≁in 29 bedrooms CTV in all bedrooms ® ✷ T ✷
sB⇌♿fr£92 dB⇌♿fr£102 (room only) 🅿
Lift 《 225P ✿ 📺 (heated) snooker sauna solarium gymnasium jacuzzi steam room
V ✿ ♿ ≁ ✷ Lunch £13.95-£17.50&alc Dinner £17.50&alc Last dinner 10pm
Credit Cards [1][2][3][5]
                                            See advertisement on page 153

★★★★ 63% Cardiff International
Mary Ann St CF1 2EQ (next to ice rink) ☎(0222) 341441 FAX (0222) 223742
Centrally positioned this comfortable modern hotel is well managed by an enthusiastic team. Bedrooms are richly decorated with deep furnishings and a worthy range of modern facilities. The open plan foyer resembles a Victorian town square complete with shops; the high-ceilinged Gazebo Restaurant is open all day and evening, and the spacious lounge and cocktail bar are richly appointed.
143⇌♿(8fb)≁in 8 bedrooms CTV in all bedrooms ® ✷ T
✷ (ex guide dogs) sB⇌♿£70 dB⇌♿£70 (room only) 🅿
Lift 《 55♿ ♪ *xmas*
♿ International V ✿ ♿ ≁ Lunch £8.95-£10.25&alc Dinner £14.50-£15.50&alc Last dinner 11pm
Credit Cards [1][2][3][5]

★★★★ 63% Cardiff Moat House
Circle Way East, Llanederyn CF3 7XF (off A48)
☎(0222) 732520 FAX (0222) 549092
Closed 23-30 Dec (ex lunch 25 Dec)

Queens Moat Houses

Refurbishment of this comfortable modern hotel is now complete, providing attractive public rooms to match the earlier upgraded bedrooms. The brightly decorated rooms have rich coordinating

THE CENTENNIAL HOTEL
63/71 HILLS ROAD, CAMBRIDGE
TEL. (0223) 314652   FAX. (0223) 315443

Set opposite the botanical gardens and only a few minutes walk from the city shopping centre, colleges and entertainment. The Centennial Hotel offers a haven of comfort and luxury. Elegantly furnished throughout, The Centennial Hotel is renowned for its friendly efficient service and its superb quality cuisine.

English Tourist Board
♛♛♛♛

AA ★★

Cardiff

fabrics, deep armchairs and plenty of facilities. The hotel operates a courtesy bus to the city centre and airport.
135⇨↑(4fb)⊁in 8 bedrooms CTV in all bedrooms ®⚐T sB&B⇨↑£84-£96 dB&B⇨↑£103-£115 ◻
Lift (300P ⊟ (heated) sauna solarium gymnasium jacuzzi baby pool ♪
⚑ Welsh & Continental V ✿ ⚒ ✱ Lunch £9.75-£13.75&alc High tea £4.95 Dinner £15.25&alc Last dinner 10pm
CONF. Thtr 290 Class 130 Board 65 Del £99
Credit Cards ①②③⑤

★★★★58% **Cardiff Park Thistle**
Park Place CF1 3UD ☎(0222) 383471 FAX (0222) 399309

This traditional hotel in the heart of the city has seen recent significant upgrading to the bedrooms. Some of the singles are rather compact but all rooms are well equipped, including those designed for lady executives. On his most recent visit, our inspector commented favourably on the standards of service but noted that refurbishment of the public rooms had not begun, due to the poor economic climate.
119⇨↑(7fb)⊁in 30 bedrooms CTV in all bedrooms ® T ✈ (ex guide dogs) ✱ sB⇨↑fr£80 dB⇨↑fr£90 (room only) ◻
Lift (80P xmas
⚑ English & French V ✿ ⚒ Lunch £10.95-£11.95 Dinner £15.95-£17.50 Last dinner 9.45pm
CONF. Thtr 300 Class 170 Board 100 Del from £79
Credit Cards ①②③④⑤

★★★70% **Manor Parc Country Hotel & Restaurant**
Thornhill Rd, Thornhill CF4 5UA (on A469) ☎(0222) 693792 FAX (0222) 614624
Closed 24-26 Dec
Popular with business guests, this hotel provides spotlessly clean, comfortable bedrooms, a few of which are compact, but all have a commendable range of facilities. Public areas are restricted but there is a congenial cocktail lounge and a restaurant with interesting Italian menus. Service, by multi-lingual Italian staff, is welcoming and prompt.
12⇨↑(2fb) CTV in all bedrooms ® T ✈ (ex guide dogs) (70P ⚑ ✿ ♪ (hard)
⚑ International V ✿ ⚒ ⊁ Last dinner 10pm
CONF. Thtr 120 Class 80 Board 60
Credit Cards ①②③

★★★63% *Celtic Bay*
Schooner Way, Atlantic Wharf CF1 5RT
☎(0222) 465888 FAX (0222) 481491

 Rank Hotels

Originally built in 1875, this impressive red brick Victorian property has undergone extensive restoration in recent times. The hotel is in a central location only 15 minutes drive from the airport. Guest rooms are attractively decorated and have specially commisioned furnishings.
64⇨↑(2fb)⊁in 15 bedrooms CTV in all bedrooms ® T
Lift (150P sauna solarium
⚑ Continental V ✿ ⚒ ⊁ Last dinner 9.45pm
Credit Cards ①②③⑤

★★★61% **Wentloog Resort**
CF3 8UQ (on A48, turn right at garden centre and takenext right turn)
☎Castleton(0633) 680591 FAX (0633) 681347

Recent work here has provided a new reception area, and the restaurant and bars have been redesigned, now all under one roof. The well equipped bedrooms tend to be compact and suited to the transient guest. There are plans to refurbish the accommodation.
55⇨↑⊁in 12 bedrooms CTV in all bedrooms ®⚐T✱ sB⇨↑£55 dB⇨↑£65 (room only) ◻
(100P ⊟ (heated) sauna solarium gymnasium jacuzzi beauty room xmas

⚑ English & French V ✿ ⚒ ⊁ ✱ Lunch £7.95-£9.95 High tea £4.50 Dinner £13.95&alc Last dinner 9.30pm
Credit Cards ①②③⑤ £

★★63% **Sandringham**
21 Saint Mary St CF1 2PL (access via junct 29 on M4, follow 'City Centre' signs) ☎(0222) 232161 FAX (0222) 383998
This city centre hotel, with concessionary local parking, provides well equipped modern bedrooms. Sandy's Bar and Restaurant next door is open all day.
28⇨↑(1fb) CTV in all bedrooms ® T ✈ (ex guide dogs) sB⇨↑£45 dB⇨↑£45 (room only) ◻
(♪ xmas
⚑ International V ✿ ⚒ ⊁ ✱ Lunch £5.35-£6 High tea £2.50 Last high tea 6pm
CONF. Thtr 100 Class 100 Board 80
Credit Cards ①②③⑤ £

★★58% *Lincoln*
118 Cathedral Rd CF1 9LQ ☎(0222) 395558 FAX (0222) 230537

Centrally situated near Sophia Gardens and the National Sports Stadium, this informal hotel in a Victorian building has bright modern bedrooms suited to business or tourist needs, a cosy bar/lounge and dining room.
18⇨↑(1fb) CTV in all bedrooms ® T ✈ (ex guide dogs) (18P
⚑ French V Last dinner 9.30pm
Credit Cards ①②③⑤

Remember to book early for holiday
and bank holiday times.

**118 Cathedral Road,
Cardiff CF1 9LQ**
Telephone: (0222) 395558
Fax: (0222) 230537

★★

A friendly welcome awaits you at this
well appointed proprietor run hotel,
situated on the edge of Bute Park
within walking distance of the
City centre.
The designer decorated rooms combine
comfort with elegance. All rooms en
suite, with colour TV, tea & coffee, hair
dryer, telephone and luggage racks.
Licensed restaurant and bar.
Secure free parking.
Owners are bilingual French speaking.
Please contact for brochure

You'll be glad you chose The Lincoln

Sandringham Hotel ★★
**21 St Mary Street, Cardiff
South Glamorgan CF1 2PL
Tel: 0222 232161   Fax: 0222 383998**

Situated in the heart of the city centre only a few minutes walk from St David's Shopping Centre, Concert Hall and Conference Centre. The hotel has earned a reputation as the "Friendly" Hotel. All 28 bedrooms have full facilities. **Stuart's Bar and Lounge** on the first floor – a quiet haven from the bustle of city life. **Sandy's Restaurant** with meals to suit all tastes open 11am-11pm. **Grosvenor Suite**, accommodation for up to 80 persons for weddings, business meetings, conferences or private functions has its own independent bar facilities, full air conditioning and is tastefully decorated.

For details on weddings, conferences or weekend breaks please contact the General Manager on **0222 232161**.

★★★★AA

THE PARK
THISTLE HOTEL

C

Park Place, Cardiff CF1 3UD
Tel: 0222 383471   Fax: 0222 399309

Your choice in Cardiff

For Reservations at over 100
Mount Charlotte Thistle Hotels
Telephone London: 071 937 8033.

THISTLE HOTELS

*Porthkerry, Near Barry, South Glamorgan
Wales CF6 9BZ*
Tel: (0446) 711666 Fax: (0446) 711690

  ★★★

Described as *"the definitive country house hotel for South Wales"* in the Egon Ronay Guide 1990, Egerton Grey is now listed by all the major independent hotel and food guides. Beautifully situated in seven acres of lush gardens, the hotel looks down a green valley facing the sea in the hamlet of Porthkerry. Ten miles from Cardiff centre and within easy driving distance of the Gower Peninsula and Brecon Beacons. Business and holiday guests will find Egerton Grey wonderfully relaxing for an overnight stay or an inexpensive two or three day break. Just telephone for a colour brochure and a tariff!

Please see our listing under Barry.

CARDIFF'S NEWEST LUXURY HOTEL!

Copthorne Hotel

**Copthorne Way
Culverhouse Cross
Cardiff CF5 6XJ
Tel: 0222 599100 Fax: 0222 599080
Telex: 498042**

Part of the Copthorne Group of hotels this new 135 bedroomed 4 star hotel is situated on the western side of the city. Adjacent to shopping complex.

Just 3 miles from junction 33 of the M4 and yet only 10 minutes from the city centre and the airport.

Extensive leisure facilities, snooker room, conference and banqueting for up to 250, informal and formal restaurants with extensive free car parking.

FS23561

Cardiff - Carlisle

★★ 57% The Phoenix
199 Fidlas Rd, Llanishen CF4 5NA ☎(0222) 764615 FAX (0222) 747812

This popular hotel in the northern suburbs of the city provides well equipped, compact bedrooms. There are good facilities, and the public areas are well maintained and comfortable.

21⇨🛏(2fb)2🚫 CTV in all bedrooms ® T ✱ sB⇨🛏£32.95 dB⇨🛏£39.95 (room only)
《CTV 30P
♀ English & French V ⊕ ⚒ ✱ Lunch £5.50-£11.95&alc Dinner £6.50-£11.95&alc Last dinner 10pm
Credit Cards [1][3][4] £

Campanile
Caxton Place, Pentwyn CF2 7HA (take Pentwyn exit from A48 and follow signs for Pentwyn Industrial Estate) ☎(0222) 549044 FAX (0222) 549900

A nearby bar and bistro restaurant provides refreshments for travellers staying at this modern accommodation building. Bedrooms are well equipped and have en suite bathrooms. For more details about Campanile, consult the Contents page, under Hotel Groups.
Annexe50⇨🛏 B⇨🛏£35.75 (room only)
CONF. Thtr 35 Class 35 Board 25 Del from £42.80

Forte Crest
Castle St CF1 2XB ☎(0222) 388681 FAX (0222) 371495

FORTE CREST

A large modern hotel with a wide range of services and amenities, designed particularly for the business traveller. Bedrooms are smart, comfortable and well equipped. For more details about Forte Crest hotels, consult the Contents page, under Hotel Groups.
155⇨🛏 ✱ B⇨🛏£75 (room only)
CONF. Thtr 150 Class 80 Board 60

Forte Posthouse
Pentwyn Rd, Pentwyn CF2 7XA ☎(0222) 731172 FAX (0222) 549147

FORTE Posthouse

Suitable for both the business and leisure traveller, this bright hotel provides modern accommodation in well equipped bedrooms with en suite bathrooms. For more details about Forte Posthouse hotels, consult the Contents page, under Hotel Groups.
142⇨🛏 ✱ B⇨🛏£41.50-£53.50 (room only)
CONF. Thtr 140 Class 70 Board 70 Del £89.50

Forte Travelodge
Circle Way East, Off A48 (M), Llanederyn CF3 7ND (4m NE of city centre, off A48(M)) ☎(0222) 549564 Central Res (0800) 850950

FORTE Travelodge

This modern building offers a good standard of accommodation for overnight stops. Smart, lounge and well equipped bedrooms, all with en suite bathrooms, are suitable for family use, and meals may be taken at the nearby family restaurant. For more details about Travelodges, consult the Contents page, under Hotel Groups.
32⇨🛏 ✱ B⇨🛏£31.95 (room only)

Marriott
Mill Ln CF1 1EZ ☎(0222) 399944 FAX (0222) 395578

Marriott
HOTELS·RESORTS·SUITES

A large and busy hotel, which is ideal for the business and leisure traveller, offering a wide range of services, a choice of eating options and indoor leisure facilities. Bedrooms are comfortable and equipped with modern facilities. For more details about Marriott hotels, consult the Contents page, under Hotel Groups.
182⇨🛏 ✱ dB⇨🛏fr£95 (room only)
CONF. Thtr 300 Class 200 Board 30 Del £105

Pavilion Lodge
Cardiff West CF7 8SB (M4, junct 33/A4232) ☎(0222) 892255 FAX (0222) 892497

PAVILION Lodge

With a nearby family restaurant providing all meals, this modern building offers smart, spacious and well equipped bedrooms. For more details about Pavilion Lodges, consult the Contents page, under Hotel Groups.
50⇨🛏 ✱ sB⇨🛏£31.95 dB⇨🛏£35.95 (room only)
CONF. Thtr 45 Board 34

Travel Inn
Newport Rd CF3 8UQ (on the old A48)
☎Castleton(0633) 680070

travel inn

Purpose-built accommodation offers spacious and well equipped bedrooms, all with en suite bathrooms. Meals may be taken at the nearby family restaurant and pub. For more details about Travel Inns, consult the Contents page, under Hotel Groups.
47⇨🛏 ✱ B⇨🛏£33.50 (room only)

CARLISLE Cumbria Map 11 NY45
See also **Crosby-on-Eden** & **Wetheral**

★★★ 66% Cumbria Park
32 Scotland Rd, Stanwix CA3 9DG (1.5m N on A47)
☎(0228) 22887 FAX (0228) 514796
Closed 25-26 Dec

With attractive gardens to the front and rear, this hotel offers 2 bedroom styles, executive and standard, and all have good furnishings. A range of food is available in either the bar or the spacious restaurant.
49⇨🛏(2fb)2🚫 ⚹ in 5 bedrooms CTV in all bedrooms ® ✱ T ✖ (ex guide dogs) ✱ sB&B⇨🛏£45-£65 dB&B⇨🛏£55-£80 ₽
Lift 《CTV 40P
♀ English & Italian V ⊕ ⚒ ⚹ ✱ Lunch fr£12.50 Dinner fr£15.95 Last dinner 9.45pm
CONF. Thtr 170 Del from £85
Credit Cards [1][2][3] £

★★★ 64% Cumbrian
Court Square CA1 1QY ☎(0228) 31951 FAX (0228) 47799

This large modern hotel, next to the railway station, offers friendly service and a warm welcome. Both bedroom and public areas have been extensive refurbished (though some annexe rooms were, at the time of our inspection, awaiting similar treatment.
70⇨🛏(5fb)1🚫⚹ in 6 bedrooms CTV in all bedrooms ® T ✱ sB&B⇨🛏£50-£79.50 dB&B⇨🛏£60-£95 ₽
Lift 《 15P 30🅿 ♪ xmas
♀ Continental V ⊕ ⚒ ⚹ Lunch £9.50&alc Dinner £14.95&alc Last dinner 10pm
CONF. Thtr 300 Class 80 Board 60 Del from £90
Credit Cards [1][2][3][5] £

★★★ 63% Central Plaza
Victoria Viaduct CA3 8AL ☎(0228) 20256 FAX (0228) 514957

CONSORT HOTELS

Situated at the heart of the city centre, this modernised Victorian hotel caters for both the tourist and commercial trade. Comfortable public areas have recently been stylishly refurbished and the varied bedrooms have all modern amenities.
84⇨🛏(2fb)2🚫 in 2 bedrooms CTV in all bedrooms ® ✱ T sB&B⇨🛏£52-£63 dB&B⇨🛏£74-£85 ₽
Lift 《12🅿 xmas
♀ English & French V ⊕ ⚒ Sunday Lunch £7.50-£9 Dinner £15.75-£17 Last dinner 9pm
CONF. Thtr 100 Class 64 Board 46 Del from £53
Credit Cards [1][2][3][5]

Carlisle - Carmarthen

★★★ **59%** **Swallow Hilltop**
London Rd CA1 2PQ (S on A6) ☎(0228) 29255
FAX (0228) 25238

A large commercial hotel with extensive, recently refurbished public areas including a good leisure club and conference facilities. Plans were in hand at the time of our visit to upgrade some of the bedrooms.
92⇌♠(10fb) CTV in all bedrooms ®⚲T ✱ sB&B⇌♠£59.50-£70 dB&B⇌♠£69.50-£80 ₽
Lift ℂ CTV 350P ✣ ▣ (heated) sauna solarium gymnasium table tennis massage games room ♪ *xmas*
♀ English & American V ❖ ⚲ ✱ Lunch £8-£20 High tea £5-£10 Dinner fr£15.95&alc Last dinner 10pm
CONF. Thtr 500 Class 250 Board 90 Del from £67
Credit Cards [1][2][3][5]

★★ **65%** **County**
9 Botchergate CA1 1QQ (opposite railway station)
☎(0228) 31316 FAX (0228) 515256
Situated in the very centre of the city, convenient for the railway station, the County has been refurbished to a good standard and facilities are modern. There is a comfortable lounge and the restaurant offers both a carvery and à la carte menu.
84⇌♠(4fb)1🚳✔in 6 bedrooms CTV in all bedrooms ®⚲T ✱ sB⇌♠£29.95-£59.95 dB⇌♠£34.95-£59.95 (room only) ₽
Lift ℂ 80P 30🅿 games room ♪ *xmas*
♀ International V ❖ ⚲ Lunch £2.95-£5.25&alc Dinner £10.95&alc Last dinner 10pm
Credit Cards [1][2][3][5]

★★ **59%** **Pinegrove**
262 London Rd CA1 2QS (on A6) ☎(0228) 24828 FAX (0228) 810941
Closed 25 & 31 Dec
Family owned and run, this is a mainly commercial hotel with modern facilities. A good range of food is available with an emphasis on steaks.
28rm(8⇌16♠)Annexe4⇌♠(8fb) CTV in all bedrooms ®⚲T sB&B£30 sB&B⇌♠£40 dB&B£40 dB&B⇌♠£50 CTV 50P ✣ pool table
V ❖ ⚲ ✔ Lunch £12-£13 High tea £4-£7.50 Dinner fr£12.50&alc Last dinner 9pm
CONF. Thtr 100 Class 100 Board 100
Credit Cards [1][3] £

★★ **57%** **Woodlands**
264/266 London Rd CA1 2QS (on A6, 2m from junct 42 of M6) ☎(0228) 45643
Closed 24 Dec-8 Jan
This owner-run, mainly commercial hotel offers friendly personal service with practical accommodation, with modestly furnished but functional bedrooms and a good choice of food served in the bar or pleasant dining room.
15rm(6⇌1♠)(1fb) CTV in all bedrooms ® T
20P 🚳
V ❖ Last dinner 9.30pm
Credit Cards [1][2][3][5]

★ **59%** **Vallum House Garden**
Burgh Rd CA2 7NB ☎(0228) 21860
Closed 25-26 Dec & 1 Jan
This small mainly commercial hotel offers good value accommodation, with well equipped bedrooms, a cosy, recently upgraded bar offering a range of food and attractive rear garden.
9rm(5⇌♠)(1fb) CTV in all bedrooms ® T ✱ sB&Bfr£30 sB&B⇌♠fr£35 dB&Bfr£45 dB&B⇌♠fr£45
CTV 30P ✣
♀ English, French & Italian V ❖ ⚲ ✔ ✱ Lunch £3.75-£7 High tea £5 Dinner £9-£11 Last dinner 9pm
Credit Cards [1][3]

Forte Posthouse
Parkhouse Rd, Kingstown CA3 0HR (junc 44/M6 take A7 into Carlisle hotel on right at first set of traffic lights) ☎(0228) 31201 FAX (0228) 43178

FORTE Posthouse

Suitable for both the business and leisure traveller, this bright hotel provides modern accommodation in well equipped bedrooms with en suite bathrooms. For more details about Forte Posthouse hotels, consult the Contents page, under Hotel Groups.
93⇌♠ ✱ B⇌♠£41.50-£53.50 (room only)
CONF. Thtr 60 Class 20 Board 25 Del £89.50

CARMARTHEN Dyfed Map 02 SN42

★★★ **63%** **The Ivy Bush Royal**
Spilman St SA31 1LG ☎(0267) 235111 FAX (0267) 234914

FORTE Heritage

This busy commercial and tourist hotel a short walk from the town centre provides helpful service and has comfortable, well maintained bedrooms. Public rooms include a popular bar and coffee lounge.
75⇌♠(4fb)✔in 21 bedrooms CTV in all bedrooms ® T sB⇌♠fr£49 dB⇌♠fr£59 (room only) ₽
Lift ℂ 75P 3🅿 sauna *xmas*
V ❖ ⚲ ✔ Sunday Lunch fr£9.50 Dinner fr£16.50&alc Last dinner 9.30pm
CONF. Thtr 200 Class 100 Board 40
Credit Cards [1][2][3][5]

★★ **62%** **Falcon**
Lammas St SA31 3AP ☎(0267) 234959 & 237152
Closed 25-26 Dec RS Sun
This friendly family-run hotel in the town centre has comfortable well furnished bedrooms and an attractive foyer and coffee lounge with an adjacent restaurant. Function facilities are also available.

**Botchergate, Carlisle CA1 1QS
Tel: Carlisle (0228) 31316. Fax: (0228) 515456**

Ideally situated at the heart of Carlisle, overlooking the massive Twin Towers of Henry VIII's Citadel — the Southern gateway to the City Centre of Carlisle, entrance to the excellent City Centre Shopping facilities.

2 miles from M6 exits, Junction 42, 43 and 44. The County is tastefully decorated, having undergone massive refurbishment in 1990. 24 hour Recorded Camera Security on Premises. Parking for 80 cars. Although retaining much of its original Georgian Grandeur, built over 200 years ago, the former "Red Lion" hotel offers today's traveller the latest "Modern Amenities" in this friendly independently owned hotel.
★ 9 miles from Gretna Green ★
★ 30 miles from the Lake District ★

Carmarthen - Cartmel

14rm(4⇨7♠)(1fb)1♯ CTV in all bedrooms ® T
30P
V ❁ ♒ Last dinner 9.30pm
Credit Cards [1][2][3][4][5]

CARNFORTH Lancashire Map 07 SD47

★★63% Royal Station
Market St LA5 9BT (opp railway station) ☎(0524) 732033 & 733636 FAX (0524) 720267

Situated opposite the railway station, this Victorian commercial hotel offers a sound standard of accommodation. Bedrooms are pleasantly furnished and equipped with all modern amenities, while public areas include a choice of bars and an attractive dining room where local staff provide informal service.

12⇨♠(1fb) CTV in all bedrooms ® T ✱ sB&B⇨♠£29-£32 dB&B⇨♠fr£46 ♬
8P 10❀
♀ English, French & Italian V ❁ ♒ Sunday Lunch fr£3.95 Dinner fr£5.95alc Last dinner 8.30pm
Credit Cards [1][2][3][5] £

CARNOUSTIE Tayside *Angus* Map 12 NO53

★★62% Carlogie House
Carlogie Rd DD7 6LD ☎(0241) 53185 FAX (0241) 56528
Closed 1-3 Jan

Set in its own grounds just north of the town, this friendly commercial and tourist hotel offers practical but well equipped bedrooms and public areas with traditional comforts.

11⇨♠(1fb) CTV in all bedrooms ® T ✈ (ex guide dogs) ✱ sB&B⇨♠fr£40 dB&B⇨♠fr£60
CTV 150P 4❀ ✿
♀ Scottish & French V ❁ ♒ ✱ Lunch fr£13.50 High tea fr£6 Dinner fr£13.50 Last dinner 9.30pm
Credit Cards [1][2][3][5]

★★62% Glencoe
Links Pde DD7 7JF ☎(0241) 53273
Closed 1 Jan

Glencoe is a golfing and commercial hotel which is literally only a pitch and putt's length from the town's championship course. Comfortable and old-fashioned in the best sense, it offers good traditional standards, the meals served in the cosy dining room representing excellent value for money.

11rm(3⇨5♠)(2fb) CTV in all bedrooms T
CTV 10P ⇢
♀ Scottish & French V ❁ ♒ Last dinner 9pm
Credit Cards [1][2][3][5]

★61% Station
DD7 6AR ☎(0241) 52447

Right next to the station, and convenient for the golf course and beaches, this family-run commercial hotel offers bright, practical accommodation and cosy bars that are full of character.

9rm(6♠)(1fb) CTV in all bedrooms ®⚲ ✱ sB&B£16 sB&B♠£20 dB&B♠£40 ♬
10P pool *xmas*
V ❁ ♒ ✱ Lunch fr£5.25 High tea fr£5.50 Dinner £11.50-£14 Last dinner 9pm
Credit Cards [1][3]

CARPERBY North Yorkshire Map 07 SE08

★★64% Wheatsheaf
DL8 4DF (from A1 take west route on A684 to Wensley, turn right signposted Castle Bolton next village is Carperby) ☎Wensleydale(0969) 663216 FAX (0969) 663019

This delightful village inn is where James Herriot spent his honeymoon in 1941. Though modernised throughout, it retains the charm and character of its earlier days. The bedrooms are attractively decorated and the lounge has a lovely stone fireplace. There is a small panelled dining room and a convivial bar.

8⇨♠(1fb)2♯ CTV in all bedrooms ® ✱ sB&B⇨♠£24-£26 dB&B⇨♠£46-£56 ♬
50P 2❀ ⇢ ✿ trout fishing can be arranged nc12yrs
V ❁ ♒ ✱ Lunch £6.50-£10 Dinner £13.50-£15&alc Last dinner 9.30pm
Credit Cards [1][2][3][5] £

CARRBRIDGE Highland *Inverness-shire* Map 14 NH92

★★70% Dalrachney Lodge
PH23 3AT ☎(047984) 252 FAX (047984) 382

Enthusiastic owners Helen and Grant Swanney continue to make improvements at this delightful Victorian hunting lodge, set in 14 acres of grounds. Welcoming log fires add to the appeal of the traditional public areas, and fresh local produce features strongly on both the carte and fixed price menu. Bedrooms are spacious and traditionally furnished.

10⇨♠(3fb)⚲in 3 bedrooms CTV in 11 bedrooms ® T sB&B⇨♠£25-£35 dB&B⇨♠£50-£70 ♬
40P ⇢ ✿ *xmas*
♀ Scottish & French V ❁ ✂ ✱ Lunch £9.50-£11&alc Dinner £18&alc Last dinner 9pm
Credit Cards [1][2][3] £

CARRUTHERSTOWN Dumfries & Galloway *Dumfriesshire* Map 11 NY17

★★★65% Hetland Hall
DG1 4JX (on A75) ☎Dumfries(0387) 84201 FAX (0387) 84211

In dramatic contrast to the elegance of the original Georgian building is the modern extension that has transformed this old mansion into an efficient business, tourist and conference hotel. Public areas are relaxing, leisure facilities good, staff are friendly and willing.

27⇨♠(3fb)⚲in 3 bedrooms CTV in all bedrooms ® T sB&B⇨♠£59-£70 dB&B⇨♠£82-£98 ♬
⟨ CTV 60P ✿ ▣ (heated) ♪ snooker sauna solarium gymnasium Indoor badminton *xmas*
♀ International V ❁ ♒ ✱ Lunch £9.50-£11.50alc Dinner £16.50-£25&alc Last dinner 9.30pm
Credit Cards [1][2][3][5] £

See advertisement under DUMFRIES

CARTMEL Cumbria Map 07 SD37

★★ ❀70% Aynsome Manor
LA11 6HH (1m N on unclass rd) ☎(05395) 36653 FAX (05395) 36016
Closed 2-24 Jan

Aynsome Manor is set in open countryside a short way from the village. There are 2 comfortable lounges with open fires in winter, and the bedrooms are prettily furnished. The carefully prepared food is a delight, and the 4-course table d'hôte menu might include pan fried mushrooms with pasta and ham in a garlic cream sauce, then roast loin of pork with Calvados sauce and lemon-sage forcemeat. The sweet trolley is laden with cream-filled puddings and is followed by assorted cheeses.

11rm(9⇨1♠)Annexe2⇨(2fb)1♯ CTV in all bedrooms ® T sB&B⇨♠£46-£55 dB&B⇨♠£77-£102 (incl dinner) ♬
20P ⇢ ✿ *xmas*
♀ English & French V ❁ ✂ Sunday Lunch £10.50 Dinner £18.50 Last dinner 8.15pm
Credit Cards [1][2][3]

Hotels with red star ratings are especially high quality.

Casterton - Castle Donington

CASTERTON Cumbria Map 07 SD67

★★66% **Pheasant Inn**
LA6 2RX ☎Kirkby Lonsdale(05242) 71230
Closed 1 wk Jan
This traditional village inn offers good comforts, including open log fires in the cosy bar and a residents' lounge with books and magazines. Bedrooms are well furnished and equipped with modern facilities. Well produced dinners, using only the best local produce, are served in the attractive restaurant.
10⇨♠(1fb)1⊞ CTV in all bedrooms ® T sB&B⇨♠£35-£40 dB&B⇨♠£52-£60
CTV 40P ✿
V ♡ ⅍ ✻ Sunday Lunch fr£10.75 Dinner £16.50&alc Last dinner 9pm
Credit Cards [1][3]

CASTLE ASHBY Northamptonshire Map 04 SP85

★★❀67% **Falcon**
NN7 1LF ☎(0604) 696200 FAX (0604) 696673

This quaint 16th-century stone-built inn is located in a quiet village surrounded by lovely countryside, on the Marquess of Northampton's estate. The accommodation is divided between the main hotel and the attractive cottage annexe; all the bedrooms are equipped with modern amenities. The cosy public areas include a dark and atmospheric cellar bar with well kept draught beers and a restaurant serving straightforward food using fresh ingredients and home-made biscuits and preserves. Proprietors Mr and Mrs Watson preside over an informal, hospitable young team, and service is attentive.
6rm(5⇨♠)Annexe8⇨♠ CTV in all bedrooms ® T ✻ sB&B⇨♠£58.50 dB&B⇨♠£73 ⬚
CTV 75P ✿
♀ English & French V ♡ ⅍ Lunch £18.50&alc Dinner £18.50&alc Last dinner 9.30pm
Credit Cards [1][2][3]

CASTLE COMBE Wiltshire Map 03 ST87

★★★★❀❀⚒
MANOR HOUSE
SN14 7HR ☎(0249) 782206 FAX (0249) 782159

Dating in parts back to the 14th and 15th centuries, this mellow stone house is in the centre of a beautiful village. Some rooms are in cottages; one, about 100yds from the main hotel, in an archway spanning the village street. General manager, Martin Clubbe has trained his staff to provide memorably good service, matched in quality by the food chef Mark Taylor produces. Soufflés have impressed our inspectors on recent visits, as did a smoked fillet of beef.
12⇨♠Annexe24⇨♠6⊞ CTV in all bedrooms T ✻ sB♠£95-£295 dB⇨♠£115-£295 (room only) ⬚
⟪ 100P ✿ ≋ (heated) ℘ (hard) ♪ croquet lawn jogging track *xmas*
♀ English & French V ♡ ⅍ ✻ Lunch £16.95&alc Dinner £32&alc Last dinner 10pm
CONF. Thtr 60 Class 36 Board 36 Del from £145
Credit Cards [1][2][3][5]

CASTLE DONINGTON Leicestershire Map 08 SK 42
See also **Shardlow**

★★★❀70% **Donington Thistle**
East Midlands Airport DE7 2SH
☎Derby(0332) 850700 FAX (0332) 850823

Very convenient for the Midlands Airport, this modern hotel has light, attractive public rooms which include a spacious foyer, the Newstead Lounge where drinks and snacks are served, and a noteworthy restaurant, where a carte and set-price menus offer a mixture of modern and traditional British dishes with a distinct French influence. Modern bedrooms are provided with a wide range of facilities and a popular room service menu.
110⇨♠(4fb)⅍in 30 bedrooms CTV in all bedrooms ® T ✻ sB⇨♠£85-£115 dB⇨♠£100-£140 (room only) ⬚
⟪ 180P ✿ ▭ (heated) sauna solarium gymnasium *xmas*
♀ International V ♡ ⅍ ✻ Lunch £13-£14&alc High tea fr£4.95 Dinner £18-£19.95&alc Last dinner 10pm
CONF. Thtr 220 Class 90 Board 30 Del from £85
Credit Cards [1][2][3][5]

★★★66% **Priest House**
Kings Mills DE74 2RR ☎Derby(0332) 810649 FAX (0332) 811141
In an attractive country setting on the banks of the River Trent, the original Priest House with its Gothic tower dates back to the Domesday book. It has been carefully extended to provide modern hotel accommodation. Comfortable public areas include a richly furnished library lounge and a traditional beamed bar with real ale and 80 malt whiskies. Individually styled bedrooms are split between the main house and cottage-style annexe, with 2 character suites in the tower.
27⇨♠Annexe18⇨♠(2fb)7⊞ CTV in all bedrooms ® T sB&B⇨♠£72-£135 dB&B⇨♠£83.50-£135 ⬚

❀ ★★★AA
THE DONINGTON
THISTLE HOTEL

Castle Donington, Derby DE7 2SH
Tel: 0332 850700   Fax: 0332 850823

Your choice at
East Midlands Airport

For Reservations at over 100
Mount Charlotte Thistle Hotels
Telephone London: 071 937 8033.

THISTLE HOTELS

Castle Donington - Chaddesley Corbett

⟨ 150P ✿ ♪ laser clay pigeon shooting *xmas*
♡ English & French **V** ⚲ ⚓ Lunch £10.95-£12.95&alc High tea £4.50-£10alc Dinner fr£17&alc Last dinner 9.30pm
CONF. Thtr 150 Class 60 Board 50 Del from £72
Credit Cards 1 2 3 4 5   £

★★★ 62% Donington Manor
High St DE7 2PP (on B6540) ☎Derby(0332) 810253 FAX (0332) 850330
Closed 27-30 Dec
Set back from the main road, this former coaching inn retains much of its Regency character. Public rooms, which can become congested, include an elegant restaurant and comfortable oak-panelled lounge. Bedrooms vary in style and size, with several of a particularly high standard, but all are attractive, with modern facilities.
35⇌Annexe3rm(1⇌)(3fb)5⊞ CTV in all bedrooms ⓡ T ✠ (ex guide dogs) sB&B⇌⎈£54-£64 dB&B⇌⎈£68-£78 ⎕
⟨ 60P
♡ English & French ⚲ ⚓ ✿ Lunch fr£8&alc Dinner fr£9.60&alc Last dinner 9.30pm
Credit Cards 1 2 3 5

★★ 63% The Lady In Grey
Wilne Ln DE7 2HA ☎Derby(0332) 792331
(For full entry see Shardlow)

CASTLE DOUGLAS Dumfries & Galloway
Kirkcudbrightshire Map **11** NX76

★★ 65% Douglas Arms
King St DG7 1DB (by town clock) ☎(0556) 2231 FAX (0556) 4000
Situated in the centre of the busy, small market town and dating from 1779, this former coaching inn is now a pleasant family-run hotel. Bedrooms vary in size, while attractive public areas include inviting lounges and a choice of bars.
22rm(15⇌)(2fb)⊞ CTV in all bedrooms ⓡ ⚑ T sB&B£17.50-£24 sB&B⇌⎈£20-£29.50 dB&B£32-£44 dB&B⇌⎈£38-£52 ⎕
6P 8⚘ *xmas*
♡ Scottish **V** ⚲ ⚓ Bar Lunch fr£3.50alc Dinner £11.50&alc Last dinner 9pm
CONF. Thtr 150 Class 30 Board 45 Del £51
Credit Cards 1 3   £

★★ Imperial
King St DG7 1AA (opposite the town library) ☎(0556) 502086 FAX (0556) 503009
RS 25-26 Dec & 1-2 Jan
This former coaching inn, situated in the main street, has a striking black and white painted exterior. The small lounge bar is often busy with locals, but there is a comfortable first-floor lounge in which to relax. Young staff provide willing service.
12⇌⎈(1fb)⚹in 6 bedrooms CTV in all bedrooms ⓡ T sB&B⇌⎈£28.50-£31.50 dB&B⇌⎈£50-£54 ⎕
20P 9⚘
V ⚲ ⚓ Lunch £6-£7.75 Dinner £7.50-£9.50&alc Last dinner 8.30pm
CONF. Class 20 Board 20 Del from £45
Credit Cards 1 3   £

CASTLETOWN
See **Man, Isle of**

CATEL (CASTEL)
See **Guernsey** under **Channel Islands**

For key to symbols see the Bookmark.

CATON Lancashire Map **07** SD56

★★ 63% Scarthwaite
Crook o Lune LA2 9HR ☎(0524) 770267

Standing in its own grounds at the western approach to the village, this former private house offers friendly informal service and a sound standard of accommodation.
9⇌⎈(2fb) CTV in all bedrooms ⓡ T ✠ (ex guide dogs) ✿ sB&B⇌⎈⎈£38 dB&B⇌⎈⎈£55 ⎕
75P ✿
V ⚲ ⚓ ✿ Lunch fr£7.95 Dinner £23&alc Last dinner 9pm
CONF. Thtr 150 Class 80 Board 40 Del from £47.50
Credit Cards 1 2 3 5   £

CATTERICK BRIDGE North Yorkshire Map **08** SE29

★★ 58% Bridge House
DL10 7PE (on bridge opp Catterick Racecourse)
☎Richmond(0748) 818331 FAX (0748) 818331
This historic coaching inn, on the banks of the River Swale and opposite the renowned race course, has a traditional atmosphere and a great deal of character in its bars and other public areas. Interesting features include the oak bedroom doors carved by 'Mousey' Thompson.
16rm(4⇌9⎈)(3fb)1⊞ CTV in all bedrooms ⓡ⚑ T ✿ sB&B£26-£36 sB&B⇌⎈£36 dB&B£42 dB&B⇌⎈£52 ⎕
CTV 70P ♪
♡ English & French **V** ⚲ ✿ Lunch £7.95-£14.45alc Dinner £12-£15alc Last dinner 10pm
Credit Cards 1 2 3 5   £

CAWSTON Norfolk Map **09** TG12

★ ✿⚘ 65% Grey Gables
Norwich Rd NR10 4EY (1m S of Cawston village at Eastgate, 1m W B1149) ☎Norwich(0603) 871259
Closed 24-26 Dec
Formerly Brandiston Rectory, this small country home offers individually designed, cottage-style rooms – lived-in rather than neat – with a good range of facilities. Public areas include a comfortable lounge and a pleasant 2-part dining room which looks lovely by candlelight. Rosalind Snaith is responsible for the cooking. The choice may be limited and guests will probably be asked to choose in advance, but this is good home cooking.
8rm(5⇌1⎈)(1fb) CTV in all bedrooms ⓡ T sB&B£19-£27 sB&B⇌⎈£40 dB&B⇌⎈£48-£58 ⎕
20P ✿ ♪ (grass)
♡English&French**V**⚹Dinner£16-£21Lastdinner8.30pm
Credit Cards 1 3   £

CHADDESLEY CORBETT Hereford & Worcester
Map **07** SO87

★★★ ✿⚘ 77% Brockencote Hall Country House
DY10 4PY (0.50 m W, off A448, opposite St Cassians Church) ☎(0562) 777876 FAX (0562) 777872
This magnificent hall stands in 70 acres of landscaped grounds which feature a gatehouse, dovecote and a lake. High-ceilinged bedrooms are carefully furnished to reflect the house's period, while elegant and very comfortable public areas with several original fireplaces include a pine and maple panelled bar. Chef Eric Bouchet superintends the preparation of a range of mainly French dishes based on fresh produce.
17⇌⎈(2fb)2⊞ CTV in all bedrooms ⓡ⚑ T ✠ sB&B⇌⎈£75 dB&B⇌⎈£90-£120 ⎕
Lift 45P ⚘ ✿ *xmas*
♡ French ⚲ ⚓ ✿ Lunch £16.50-£33.50 Dinner £21-£33.50 Last dinner 9.30pm
Credit Cards 1 2 3 5

158

Chadlington - Chagford

CHADLINGTON Oxfordshire Map 04 SP32

★★ 🍴 79% The Manor
OX7 3LX ☎(060876) 711

The Manor is a small country house hotel set in 18 acres of grounds adjacent to the village church. Bedrooms are individually furnished and all are imaginatively decorated. At dinner a fixed price 5-course menu is offered. Interesting soups such as broad bean and hazelnut are accompanied by home-made breads and well balanced main courses are served with vegetables from the kitchen garden. The wine list is extensive and includes 42 vintages of Château Latour.
7⇨ CTV in all bedrooms T ✖ (ex guide dogs) sB&B⇨£60-£80 dB&B⇨£85-£130 ₽
20P 🐾 ❄ xmas
Dinner £25.50 Last dinner 9pm
Credit Cards [1][3]

★★ 66% Chadlington House
OX7 3LZ ☎(060876) 437
Closed Jan & Feb

This attractive period property, parts of which date back to the 16th-century, enjoys glorious rural views from a quiet Cotswold village setting; the gardens at its rear are both extensive and carefully tended. Bedrooms vary in size, but all are comfortable, while well maintained public areas include a dining room offering a short table d'hôte menu of home-cooked food. Resident owners extend a genuinely warm welcome to guests.
11rm(5⇨5♪)(2fb)1🛏 CTV in all bedrooms ®
✖ (ex guide dogs)
CTV 20P 2🚗 ❄
♀ English & French V ♡ ⚡ 🍴 Last dinner 7.30pm
Credit Cards [1][3]

CHAGFORD Devon Map 03 SX78

★★★★★ 🍴 GIDLEIGH PARK
TQ13 8HH
☎(0647) 432367 & 432225
FAX (0647) 432574

A mock-Tudor country house set amid 40 acres of splendid grounds offers near-perfect surroundings. Paul and Kay Henderson's enthusiasm extends to every area of the establishment and they are assisted by two managers who engender a real warmth in the courtesy extended by their staff. Bedrooms are individually appointed in impeccable taste and furnished with antiques, while comfortable public areas have log fires and beautiful fresh flower arrangements. It is, however, the kitchen that is the heart of Gidleigh, and managing director/chef Shaun Hill stands at the forefront of the return to British country house cooking, dismissing the pretentious and elaborate in favour of the honest flavours which result from the thoughtful combination of the finest ingredients. Red mullet is served simply with a hot relish of tomato, ginger, chilli, garlic and fresh coriander, followed by a main course of succulent roast corn-fed pigeon accompanied by first-class foie gras and an excellent red wine jus; warm Bakewell tart with thick clotted cream could provide the perfect ending to the meal.
12⇨Annexe2⇨ CTV in all bedrooms T ✖ sB&B⇨£180-£310 dB&B⇨£220-£350 (incl dinner) ₽
25P 🐾 ❄ ♀ (hard) 🎾 croquet bowls

V ♡ ⚡ ✖ Lunch £35-£45 Dinner £45-£50 Last dinner 9pm
Credit Cards [1][2][3][5]

★★★ 🍴 75% Mill End
Sandy Park TQ13 8JN (2m N on A382) (Logis)
☎(0647) 432282 FAX (0647) 433106
Closed 10-20 Dec & 10-23 Jan RS Nov-12 Dec & 23 Jan-Mar

In a former flour mill, peacefully set in the Teign valley, involved proprietors offer professional yet informal attention and comfortable accommodation. A picture window in the elegant restaurant looks out onto the old water wheel. A variety of carefully prepared dishes feature on the table d'hôte menu, such as noisettes of monkfish with a saffron sauce, fillet of beef in a delicate whisky-flavoured cream sauce and a light, warm lemon pudding or a selection of unusual cheeses. Bedrooms are well equipped.
17rm(15⇨♪)(2fb) CTV in all bedrooms ® T sB&B£35-£40 sB&B⇨♪£45-£60 dB&B⇨♪£70-£90 ₽
CTV 17P 🐾 ❄ 🎾 shooting xmas
♀ English & French V ♡ ⚡ 🍴 Lunch £15-£18.50 Dinner £15-£26.50alc Last dinner 9pm
Credit Cards [1][2][3][5]   £

★★ 67% Easton Court
Easton Cross TQ13 8JL (1.5m E A382) (Logis) ☎(0647) 433469
Closed Jan

This stone-built, thatched property is set in its own walled garden. Exposed beams, stone walls and inglenook fireplaces are features of the quiet lounge, library, and bar, and a table d'hôte menu of interesting dishes is available. The colour-coordinated bedrooms are comfortable, and a warm welcome is provided by the Kidson family.
7⇨♪2🛏 CTV in all bedrooms ® T ✖ sB&B⇨♪£51-£61 dB&B⇨♪£90-£110 (incl dinner) ₽

➡

★★★ Mill End HOTEL

Sandy Park, Chagford, Devon TQ13 8JN
Tel: (0647) 432282 Fax: (0647) 433106

This old flour mill, with its wheel still turning in the peaceful courtyard, nestles in the Teign Valley on the edge of Dartmoor about one and a half hours drive from Bristol and three and a half hours from London.

The whole atmosphere is one of a rather comfortable private house, with lots of nooks and corners. Tea by the fire in Winter, drinks on the lawn in Summer – it is a most relaxing place.

The restaurant is open every day for all meals; prior booking strongly recommended.

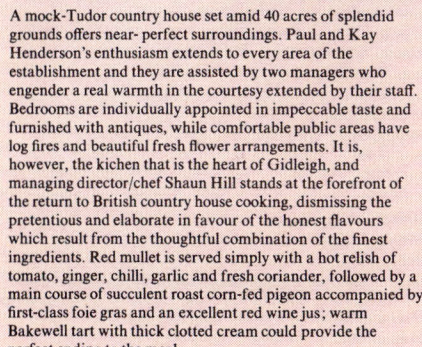

159

Chagford - Channel Islands, St Martin, Guernsey

CTV 20P ⇔ nc12yrs *xmas*
♨ English & Continental V ⊡ ✗ ✱ Dinner £22 Last dinner 8.30pm
Credit Cards [1][2][3]   £

C

CHALE
See **Wight, Isle of**

CHANNEL ISLANDS Map 16

ALDERNEY

★★★**65%** Chez André
Victoria St, St Anne GY9 ☏(0481) 822777 FAX (0481) 822962
11⇔↑(4fb)⇖in 4 bedrooms CTV in all bedrooms ® ⚐ T
sB&B⇔↑£21-£36 dB&B⇔↑£42-£72 ⌸
CTV P ⇔ *xmas*
♨ English & French V ⇖ ⊡ ✗ Lunch £7.50-£12.50&alc
Dinner fr£12.50&alc Last dinner 9.30pm
Credit Cards [1][2][3]

★★**66%** Inchalla
St Anne ☏(0481) 823220 FAX (0481) 823551
Peacefully situated in secluded grounds at the edge of St Anne, enjoying good sea views and easily accessible from both harbour and airport, this hotel offers good-sized bedrooms equipped in modern style and in most cases provided with en suite facilities. As there is no bar, each room also contains a fully stocked mini bar. A licensed restaurant serves freshly prepared, home-cooked food, guests can relax in a small residents' lounge, and the atmosphere throughout is informal and friendly under the supervision of proprietor Valerie Willis.
11rm(9⇔1↑)(2fb) CTV in all bedrooms ® ⚐ T ✶
dB&B⇔↑£64-£76 ⌸
8P ⇔ ✱ sauna solarium jacuzzi
♨ English & French V ⇖ ⊡ Sunday Lunch £8.50-£9.25 High tea £2.50-£4 Dinner £8.50-£12.50&alc Last dinner 8.30pm
Credit Cards [1][2][3]   £

GUERNSEY

CATEL (CASTEL)

★★★**65%** Cobo Bay
Cobo GY5 7HB (on coast road) ☏Guernsey(0481) 57102 FAX (0481) 54542
On the west of the island facing the sea, this hotel has comfortably furnished bedrooms in modern style, the best having double glazing, balcony and a sea view. The Chesterfield bar and lounge is furnished with leather sofas and easy chairs, and the well furnished candlelit restaurant offers both a carte and fixed price menus of enjoyable food.
36⇔↑(1fb) CTV in all bedrooms ® T ✶ (ex guide dogs) ✶
sB&B⇔↑£39-£59 dB&B⇔↑£78-£98 (incl dinner) ⌸
Lift ⟨ CTV 60P ⇔ snooker sauna solarium spa pool ♪
♨ International V ✶ Lunch £9.95-£18.95&alc Dinner £14.95-£23.95&alc Last dinner 9.45pm
CONF. Class 30 Board 30 Del from £49
Credit Cards [1][3]

★★**63%** Hotel Hougue du Pommier
Hougue Du Pommier Rd ☏Guernsey(0481) 56531 FAX (0481) 56260
This partly 18th-century farmhouse has kept much of its original character – the restaurant, for example, consists of several rooms named the Dairy, the Cider, the Tack, etc. The buffet carvery in the Tudor Bar is one of the island's most popular eating places, and there is also a formal restaurant. At the time of the inspection bedrooms were being upgraded to a very high standard.
38⇔↑(12fb) CTV in all bedrooms ® T ✶ (ex guide dogs) ✶
sB&B⇔↑£31-£43 dB&B⇔↑£62-£86 (incl dinner) ⌸

⟨ CTV 87P ✱ ⌸ (heated) ▶ 10 sauna solarium games room putting table tennis *xmas*
♨ English & Continental V ⇖ ⊡ ✶ Sunday Lunch £9.25
Dinner £11.95&alc Last dinner 9.45pm
Credit Cards [1][2][3][4][5]

FERMAIN BAY

★★★**64%** La Favorita
GY4 6SD ☏Guernsey(0481) 35666 FAX (0481) 35413
Closed 21 Dec-7 Feb RS 1-20 Dec & 8-28 Feb
This owner run, extended country house, situated in a wooded valley overlooking the bay, offers traditional services and hospitality. Some of the individually furnished, spacious bedrooms have balconies, and there is a choice of elegant drawing rooms, a café and no-smoking restaurant.
37⇔↑(6fb) CTV in all bedrooms ® T ✶ ✱ sB&B⇔↑£37-£47 dB&B⇔↑£64-£85 ⌸
Lift 40P ⇔ ✱ ⌸ (heated) sauna spa pool
♨ English & French V ⇖ ⊡ ✗ Lunch £9-£12 Dinner £12-£15
Last dinner 9pm
CONF. Thtr 70 Class 30 Board 30 Del from £35
Credit Cards [1][2][3][5]

★★★**61%** Le Chalet
☏Guernsey(0481) 35716 FAX (0481) 35718
Closed mid Oct-mid Apr   **CONSORT** HOTELS

Beautifully located in 6 acres of wooded grounds leading directly down to the bay, this is a friendly well managed hotel. Most bedrooms have been refurbished and several have balconies or terraces. The comfortable lounge, bright restaurant and popular bar command fine views.
41⇔↑(5fb) CTV in all bedrooms ® T sB&B⇔↑£38-£45
dB&B⇔↑£56-£84
35P ⇔ ✱
♨ English, Austrian & French V ⇖ ⊡ Sunday Lunch £9.50
Dinner £13&alc Last dinner 9.30pm
Credit Cards [1][2][3][4][5]

PERELLE

★★★❀❀**68%** L'Atlantique
Perelle Bay ☏Guernsey(0481) 64056 FAX (0481) 63800
This modern hotel on the coast road has well equipped bedrooms, mostly non-smoking and many with sea views. Smart public areas include a Victorian-style bar offering a range of bar meals and a restaurant with an extensive, daily changing menu of imaginative French and modern dishes often featuring locally caught seafood. Service is professional and attentive.
23⇔↑(4fb) CTV in all bedrooms ® T ✶ (ex guide dogs) ✱
sB&B⇔↑£25.50-£38 dB&B⇔↑£51-£76 ⌸
80P ⇔ ✱ ⌸ (heated) *xmas*
♨ International V ⇖ ✶ Sunday Lunch £9 Dinner £12.90&alc
Last dinner 9.30pm
Credit Cards [1][2][3][5]   £

ST MARTIN

★★★❀**68%** Idlerocks
Jerbourg Point GY4 6BJ ☏Guernsey(0481) 37711 FAX (0481) 35592
Set in 5.5 acres of gardens, this hospitable family-run hotel enjoys superb sea views from its position on the cliffs. Extensive upgrading has provided comfortable public areas and bedrooms with good facilities, including new rooms (mostly non-smoking) with large balconies. You can eat in the Raffles Bar and Terrace or the more formal restaurant.
28⇔↑(4fb)1⊞⇖in 11 bedrooms CTV in all bedrooms ® ⚐ T
sB&B⇔↑£25-£45 dB&B⇔↑£48-£170 (incl dinner) ⌸
⟨ 100P ✱ ⌸ (heated) *xmas*

Channel Islands, St Martin, Guernsey

♡ English & French **V** ✿ ⚏ Sunday Lunch £10 Dinner £13.50&alc Last dinner 10pm
Credit Cards ① ② ③ ④ ⑤

★★★68% *St Margaret's Lodge*
Forest Rd ☎Guernsey(0481) 35757 FAX (0481) 37594
This charming hotel offers a high standard of comfort in attractively decorated rooms ranging from suites and de luxe to standard and family. It is conveniently placed for the airport and for beaches and has a good restaurant where chef Kevin Buckley's modern French cuisine is served under the supervision of Manager Martin O'Mahoney.
47⇌ CTV in all bedrooms ® ⚐ T ✕
Lift (100P ⇎ ✿ ⌒ (heated) sauna solarium
♡ English & French **V** ✿ ⚏
Credit Cards ① ② ③

★★★66% *Hotel Bella Luce*
La Fosse ☎Guernsey(0481) 38764 FAX (0481) 39561
Quietly set in a peaceful lane not far from Moulin Huet Bay, this 12th-century manor house, one of the island's original Norman residences, has been thoughtfully extended and converted. Its character remains unchanged today, but pastel décor and new, coordinated soft furnishings have brought a much warmer feel to some bedrooms. In addition to the spacious beamed bar there is a very comfortably furnished lounge and an intimate restaurant within a choice of menus.
31⇌ ♠ (9fb) CTV in all bedrooms ® T sB&B⇌♠£26-£43 dB&B⇌♠£48-£82 ⊟
(50P ⇎ ✿ ⌒ (heated) sauna solarium ⚕ *xmas*
♡ English & Continental **V** ✿ ⚏ ✂ Lunch £12 High tea fr£2.75 Dinner £13&alc Last dinner 9.45pm
Credit Cards ① ② ③

Saint Margaret's Lodge Hotel ★★★ C

Forest Road, St Martin, Guernsey, CI
Tel: (0481) 35757   Fax: (0481) 37594

This elegant 47 bedroomed, 3 Star 4 Crowned Hotel set within beautiful garden surroundings and only 10 minutes drive from St Peter Port, the Harbour and Airport. All bedrooms completely refurbished to the highest possible standards. Restaurant serving wide variety of haute cuisine, gourmet, chef's celebration menus, using only the best of local products.

HOLIDAY GUERNSEY ★★★
at the
Hotel Bella Luce

La Fosse, St. Martin

The Charming and Popular 'Old World' Bella Luce is situated in one of the most beautiful parts of the island, with the nearby Cliff Walks and South Coast Bays.

The Hotel offers Traditional standards of Cuisine, Comfort and Service and has a superb à la Carte Restaurant offering Local Fresh Seafood Specialities.

Private Grounds with Heated Pool.

Fully Licensed.

Inclusive Holiday arrangements available.

TEL: 0481 38764
FAX: 0481 39561

Hotel Hougue du Pommier ★★

CÂTEL, GUERNSEY
Tel: (0481) 56531 Fax: (0481) 56260

This 1712 Farmhouse now transformed into an elegant 2 star Hotel, which stands in its own 10 acres of ground, with a solar heated swimming pool, sauna/solarium, games room, 18 hole putting green, 9 hole pitch and putt golf course offers you pleasure and relaxation. A 10 rink indoor lawn bowling centre is nearby with free membership for hotel guests. We are in close proximity to the sandy beaches of Cobo Bay and Grandes Rocques. Courtesy coach to St Peter Port Mon to Sat. Enjoy our famous Carvery luncheons in our Tudor Bar or superb Dining Room. Evening bar meals also available. An à la carte candlelit dinner in this renowned Farm House Restaurant with its extensive wine menu is a must. We are looking forward to welcoming you here to the Hougue du Pommier. Inclusive holidays available.

Channel Islands, St Martin - Vale, Guernsey

★★★ 65% Green Acres
Les Hubits (behind parish church, 2m from airport)
☎Guernsey(0481) 35711 FAX (0481) 35978
Set in attractive grounds, this well managed, friendly hotel continues to improve. It has fully equipped bedrooms, a spacious comfortable lounge, two bars and a restaurant offering a choice of menus, with local seafood a feature.
48⇨🛏(3fb) CTV in all bedrooms ® T ✻ (ex guide dogs) sB&B⇨🛏£25-£47 dB&B⇨🛏£50-£74
75P 🚗 ✳ ⛱ (heated) solarium *xmas*
♨ English & French V ♿ ♨ ✶ Bar Lunch fr£3 High tea fr£3 Dinner fr£14&alc Last dinner 8.30pm
Credit Cards [1][2][3]

ST PETER PORT

★★★★ ⚜68% St Pierre Park
Rohais ☎Guernsey(0481) 728282 FAX (0481) 712041
This modern hotel, set in 45 acres of parkland, offers a choice of eating options: the elegant and formal Victor Hugo restaurant decorated in Louis XV style, the smart but casual Cafe Renoir serving meals and snacks throughout the day, and La Fontaine (overlooking the artificial lake and fountain) for a buffet breakfast. Bedrooms have pastel décor, mahogany-look furniture and small balconies.
135⇨🛏(3fb) CTV in all bedrooms ®♉T✻ (ex guide dogs) sB&B⇨🛏£75-£95 dB&B⇨🛏£110-£135 🍴
Lift ⓛ 200P ✳ ⛱ (heated) ▶ 9 ♀ (hard) snooker sauna solarium gymnasium croquet spa bath steam room hair salon ♪ *xmas*
♨ English & French V ♿ ♨ ✶ ✻ Lunch £8.95-£12 High tea fr£5 Dinner £10.50-£25&alc Last dinner 10.30pm
CONF. Thtr 200 Class 130 Board 36 Del from £75
Credit Cards [1][2][3][5] £

★★★★ 53% Old Government House
Ann's Place ☎Guernsey(0481) 724921 FAX (0481) 724429
With fine views over the harbour, the 'OGH' has been here for a long time, with buildings added along the way. This explains the variety of the bedrooms, some of which are particularly small. The entrance hall is most attractive, but some of the public areas are looking a little tired. The food can disappoint at times, but there are three bars (one a night club in summer) and staff are friendly.
72⇨🛏(8fb) CTV in all bedrooms ♉T
Lift ⓛ 20P ⇌ (heated) solarium
♨ English, French & Italian V ♿ ♨ Last dinner 9.15pm
Credit Cards [1][2][3][5]

★★★ ⚜68% La Fregate
Les Cotils ☎Guernsey(0481) 724624 FAX (0481) 720443
Many of the rooms (all double-glazed) at this hotel overlooking the harbour have fine sea views, and some have a balcony, ideal for breakfasting. The walled, terraced gardens are a major attraction, as is the cooking of head chef, Ossie Steinsdorfer, whose timbale of shellfish with lobster sauce and rack of lamb with herbs and wine sauce was appreciated at the inspection meal. Intending guests are advised to ask for directions.
13⇨🛏 CTV in all bedrooms ® T ✻ ✶ sB&⇨🛏fr£50 dB⇨🛏£90-£95 (room only)
25P 🚗 ✳ nc14yrs
♨ Continental V Lunch £12-£13&alc Dinner fr£18&alc Last dinner 9.30pm
Credit Cards [1][2][3][4][5]

★★★ 67% Hotel de Havelet
Havelet ☎Guernsey(0481) 722199 FAX (0481) 714057

CONSORT HOTELS

Occupying one of the most prized sites in the town, with magnificent views over Castle Cornet, this extended Georgian mansion offers a range of comfortable, well equipped bedrooms. There is a traditional-style lounge, and a separate building houses the bar and restaurants – the Havelet Grill on the ground floor and the more formal Wellington Boot. Chef Hans Herrmann offers 3 menus, all making good use of local produce (particularly fish). Friendly, willing staff are very competently supervised by general manager Heinz Wegerer.
33⇨🛏(4fb) CTV in all bedrooms ®♉T✻ sB&B⇨🛏£34.50-£50 dB&B⇨🛏£61-£95 🍴
CTV 40P 🚗 ✳ ⛱ (heated) sauna jacuzzi *xmas*
♨ English, Austrian & French V ♿ ♨ Sunday Lunch £10 Dinner £13&alc Last dinner 9.30pm
Credit Cards [1][2][3][4][5]

★★★ 66% Moore's
Pollet ☎Guernsey(0481) 724452 FAX (0481) 714037

CONSORT HOTELS

Although conveniently placed in the High Street, parking here is restricted and it is best to go to nearby south shore. Bedrooms are all modern and well equipped, the best ones having a sunny aspect and good views. For dining guests can choose between a carvery and the Conservatory Restaurant, and for daytime snacks there is a Patisserie.
47⇨🛏 Annexe3⇨🛏(8fb) CTV in all bedrooms ®♉T sB&B⇨🛏£32-£62 dB&B⇨🛏£44-£80 🍴
Lift ⓛ ✗ 🚗 *xmas*
♨ English & French V ♿ ♨ Lunch £9.50&alc Dinner £12.25&alc Last dinner 9pm
Credit Cards [1][2][3][4][5] £

★★★ 62% La Collinette
St Jacques ☎Guernsey(0481) 710331 FAX (0481) 713516
This small, family run hotel, quietly situated away from the centre of town, has a secluded garden. Bedrooms in the main house are individually decorated whilst those in a rear extension are all identical, modestly furnished, but all well equipped. There is a lively public bar or a comfortable foyer lounge.
27⇨🛏 5🛏 CTV in all bedrooms ®♉T✻ (ex guide dogs) ✶ sB&B⇨🛏£20-£45 dB&B⇨🛏£40-£90 🍴
CTV 40P 🚗 ✳ ⛱ (heated) sauna solarium spa bath ⛳ *xmas*
♨ English & Continental V ♿ ♨ ✶ ✻ Lunch £6.50 Dinner fr£12.50&alc Last dinner 9pm
Credit Cards [1][2][3][5]

★★ 63% *Sunnycroft*
5 Constitution Steps ☎Guernsey(0481) 723008
Closed Nov-Mar
Uniquely situated at the top of Constitution Steps, directly above the town centre, this family owned and run hotel promotes an informal atmosphere. Bedrooms decorated in pastel shades are simply furnished, while public areas offer a choice of comfortable lounges as well as the small bar adjoining the restaurant. There is also a roof patio and a secluded terraced garden.
14⇨🛏 CTV in all bedrooms ® T ✻
CTV ✳ nc14yrs
♿ ♨ Last dinner 7.30pm
Credit Cards [1][3]

VALE

★★★ 60% Peninsula
Les Dicqs ☎Guernsey(0481) 48400 FAX (0481) 48706
Closed Jan-Feb
This modern hotel overlooking the bay, with a sandy beach nearby, is geared to family and tour group holidays. Bedrooms have functional furnishings and there is an open-plan bar and well run restaurant. Full room service is also available.
99⇨🛏(99fb) CTV in all bedrooms ®♉T sB&B⇨🛏£27.50-£46.50 dB&B⇨🛏£45-£93 🍴
Lift ⓛ 120P ✳ ⛱ (heated) ♪ ⛳ *xmas*

Channel Islands, Vale - Archirondel, Jersey

English & Continental **V** ❧ ⚏ Lunch £7-£8.75 High tea fr£3.50 Dinner £9.50 Last dinner 9.30pm
CONF. Thtr 210 Class 140 Board 105 Del from £48
Credit Cards [1][2][3][4][5]

HERM

★★ ✿74% **White House**
☎Guernsey(0481) 722159 FAX (0481) 710066
Closed 16 Oct-Mar

The only hotel on this delightful island, the White House extends a warm welcome to guests from the moment that the porter meets them from the boat. All accommodation is simple, and several rooms contained in charming cottages nearby. Public areas are full of character, with a number of cosy lounges and a carvery as well as more interesting cuisine in the dining room. The wonderful Herm oysters should not be missed, and locally caught silver hake is popular.

10⇨Annexe22⇨ ® ✈ sB&B⇨£48-£61 dB&B⇨£96-£124 (incl dinner)
♣ ✿ ❀ ⇨ (heated) ♪ (hard) ⚘
English & French **V** ❧ ⚏ Lunch £10.50-£15 High tea £4 Dinner £15.95-£17.95 Last dinner 9pm
Credit Cards [1][3]

JERSEY

ARCHIRONDEL

★★★ 67% **Les Arches**
Archirondel Bay JE3 6DR ☎Jersey(0534) 853839 FAX (0534) 856660

Standing in a sheltered bay close to the harbour town of Gorey, this well managed hotel continues to be steadily upgraded. Modern bedrooms, some with balconies, overlook the sea, pool or garden

La Collinette Hotel

Guernsey Grading
⚜ ⚜ ⚜ ⚜

AA
★★★

AND SELF-CATERING COTTAGES, GUERNSEY

BON VIVEUR — ASHLEY COURTENEY

All bedrooms with private facilities, colour TV, radio, trouser press, hair dryer, tea/coffee tray and telephone. Baby listening service.

★ Poolside bar ★ Heated swimming pool ★ Kiddies pool ★ Central heating ★ Excellent food ★ Spa ★ Solarium ★ Sauna ★ Laundry

Children under 10 years old Free All Year Round
St Peter Port - Guernsey - C.I.
Tel: (0481) 710331
Good food our speciality
ONE OF GUERNSEY'S FINEST HOTELS

La Frégate Hotel & Restaurant

3 STARS

St Peter Port, Guernsey, Channel Islands
Telephone: (0481) 724624   Fax (0481) 720443

La Frégate is a Country House Hotel tucked away in scented gardens in a quiet corner of St Peter Port with views over the harbour and islands of Herm and Sark. The French Restaurant is superb. Open all year round, 13 bedrooms, en suite, central heating, trouser press, hair dryer, TV.

Channel Islands, Archirondel - St Brelade, Jersey

and public areas include an airy restaurant, comfortable lounge and attractive bar.
54🛏🛁 CTV in all bedrooms ® ⚙ T ✱ sB&B🛏🛁£29.45-£45 dB&B🛏🛁£58-£90 ♫
(CTV 120P ♿ ✿ ♫ (heated) ♀ (hard) sauna gymnasium ⛳ xmas
♡ English & Continental V ⚙ ⚖ ✱ Lunch £10.50-£18.50 Dinner £13.50-£27 Last dinner 8.45pm
Conf. Thtr 180 Class 120 Board 120 Del from £45
Credit Cards [1] [3] [4]

BEAUMONT

★★64% Hotel L'Hermitage
JE3 7BR ☎Jersey(0534) 33314 & 58272 FAX (0534) 21207
Closed Nov-Mar

This family-run hotel is in a convenient location for St Helier and the airport. There are some bedrooms in the main house but most are set around the outdoor pool and gardens. They are traditional in style and nicely presented with some modern facilities. Public areas include an attractive lounge and bar area, as well as a large dining room where a table d'hôte menu is offered.

43🛏🛁 Annexe66🛏🛁 CTV in all bedrooms ® ✱ ✱
sB&B🛏🛁£23.50-£35.50 dB&B🛏🛁£45-£69 (incl dinner)
(100P ♿ ✿ ▣ (heated) ≋ (heated) sauna solarium spa bath ♫ nc14yrs
♡ English & French V ⚙ ⚖ ✱ Lunch £5.50 Dinner £7.50 Last dinner 8pm

GOREY

★★★63% Old Court House
JE3 9EX ☎Jersey(0534) 854444 FAX (0534) 853587
Closed Nov-Feb

Spacious public rooms and a varied choice of good size bedrooms, the best with front facing balconies, characterise this hotel. There is a well appointed bar and the large and stylish candlelit restaurant has 2 menus.

58🛏🛁(4fb) CTV in all bedrooms ⚙ T ✱ (ex guide dogs) ✱
sB&B🛏🛁£35-£54 dB&B🛏🛁£70-£108 (incl dinner)
Lift (40P ♿ ≋ (heated) sauna solarium
♡ English, French & Italian V ⚙ ⚖ ✱ Bar Lunch £3.50-£6alc Dinner £12.50&alc Last dinner 9pm
Credit Cards [1] [2] [3] [5]   £

★★67% The Moorings
Gorey Pier ☎Jersey(0534) 853633 FAX (0534) 857618

Standing by the harbour at the foot of Mont Orgueil (Gorey Castle), this small cosy hotel has glorious waterfront views from many of the rooms. Bright bedrooms with coordinated soft furnishings are all equipped with modern facilities. The attractive formal restaurant is popular for its wide choice of traditional dishes, with locally caught fish featuring daily on the menus.

16🛏🛁 CTV in all bedrooms ® T sB&B🛏🛁£35-£50 dB&B🛏🛁£70-£100 ♫
(CTV ♀ ♿ xmas
♡ English & Continental V ⚙ Lunch £10.50-£25&alc Dinner £16-£35 Last dinner 10.15pm
Credit Cards [1] [2] [3]

L'ETACQ

★★★67% Lobster Pot Hotel & Restaurant
☎Jersey(0534) 482888 FAX (0534) 481574

In an elevated position, above St Ouens Bay, this hotel has gained a good reputation, especially for the restaurant where lobster and fish are specialities. The à la carte menu is lengthy and varied, and there is a good- value menu gastronomique. Service is courteous and friendly. Bedrooms are nicely furnished and many enjoy sea views. There is a choice of bars and a quiet resident's lounge.

13🛏🛁(1fb) CTV in all bedrooms ® ⚙ T ✱ (ex guide dogs) ✱
sB&B🛏🛁£35.50-£63.50 dB&B🛏🛁£71-£107 ♫
((▦ 56P ✿ ♫ xmas
♡ English, Continental & North American V ⚙ ⚖ ✱ Lunch £9.95-£10.50 Dinner £14.50 Last dinner 10.15pm
Credit Cards [1] [2] [3] [4] [5]   £

ROZEL BAY

★★★✿✿**👍78%** Château la Chaire
Rozel Bay JE3 6AJ (Hatton) ☎Jersey(0534) 863354 FAX (0534) 865137

Situated on a terraced hillside, this hotel, built in 1843, has been beautifully furnished and retains all its original character and country house elegance, with sumptuous bedrooms and fine public rooms. The restaurant is divided into the oak panelled room and the conservatory, the latter reserved for non smokers. Chef David Tilbury goes from strength to strength with his dedicated approach Anglo-French cooking, offering a good value gastronomique menu and a carte which reflects his skill. Service is attentive and industrious, well supervised by young management and the hotel manager, Mr Alan Winch.

14🛏🛁(1fb)1▦ CTV in all bedrooms ® ⚙ T ✱ (ex guide dogs)
sB&B🛏🛁£57-£100 dB&B🛏🛁£82-£110 ♫
(30P ✿ ♫ nc7yrs xmas
♡ French V ⚙ ⚖ ✱ Lunch £13.95-£17.50&alc Dinner £22.50&alc Last dinner 10pm
Credit Cards [1] [2] [3] [5]

ST AUBIN

★★★67% Somerville
Mont du Boulevard(from village, follow harbour then take Mont du Boulevard and second right hand bend)
☎Jersey(0534) 41226 FAX (0534) 46621
Closed early Nov-mid Mar

Situated in an elevated position overlooking the bay, this handsome and very popular hotel has well equipped, attractive bedrooms, with some new de luxe rooms. Smart public areas include a spacious restaurant.

59rm(58🛏🛁)(7fb) CTV in all bedrooms ® ⚙ T ✱ ✱
sB&Bfr£27.75 sB&B🛏🛁£45.25 dB&Bfr£54.50 dB&B🛏🛁£107.50
Lift (CTV 40P ♿ ≋ (heated) games room ♫ nc4yrs
♡ English & French V ⚙ ⚖ ✱ Lunch £9.50&alc High tea £3-£3.50&alc Dinner £12-£15 Last dinner 8.30pm
Credit Cards [1] [2] [3] [4]   £

ST BRELADE

★★★★✿**71%** Hotel L'Horizon
St Brelade's Bay(Clipper) ☎Jersey(0534) 43101 FAX (0534) 46269

Set in a spectacular position on the edge of the beach at this attractive bay, this well managed hotel provides professionally efficient yet friendly service in traditional style. There is a Brasserie, the Crystal Room serving a table d'hôte menu supplemented by a limited carte, and the more formal Star Grill presenting a wide choice of dishes with local fish specialities. Bedrooms vary in both size and style, central rooms having been upgraded recently.

104🛏🛁(7fb)1▦ CTV in all bedrooms ⚙ T ✱ (ex guide dogs)
Lift (125P ♿ ▣ (heated) sauna gymnasium windsurfing/ water skiing spa yacht ⛳
♡ English, French & Italian V ⚙ ⚖
Credit Cards [1] [3]

Irish entries appear in a separate section that follows the main directory.

Channel Islands, St Brelade, Jersey

★★★★ **66%** **Atlantic**
La Moye JE3 8HE ☎Jersey(0534) 44101 FAX (0534) 44102
Closed Nov-Feb
Opposite La Moye golf course and with lovely views across the bay, this hotel continues to be steadily upgraded. During 1992/93 the public areas were refurbished with a country theme and bedrooms, while not spacious, are pretty and well furnished. The studio rooms and 2 larger suites are elegantly styled and offer extra luxury.
50⇨🛉 CTV in all bedrooms✲ T ✖ (ex guide dogs) ✹
sB&B⇨🛉£75-£100 dB&B⇨🛉£110-£275 🖃
Lift (60P 🚗 ❋ 🏊 (heated) ⚖ (heated) ♀ (hard) sauna solarium gymnasium spa pool
♀ International V ✿ ♨ ✲ Lunch fr£12&alc Dinner fr£19.50&alc Last dinner 9.15pm
CONF. Thtr 60 Class 30 Board 20 Del from £75
Credit Cards [1][2][3][5]

★★★ **67%** **St Brelade's Bay**
JE3 8EF ☎Jersey(0534) 46141 FAX (0534) 47278
Closed 12 Oct-28 Apr
Beautifully situated at one end of the pretty bay, this well managed family holiday hotel stands in some 8 acres of grounds. Comfortably furnished public areas include a choice of bars and lounges and a restaurant offering a good range of food. Attractively decorated modern bedrooms are well equipped and some have large balconies giving panoramic sea views.
72⇨🛉 (50fb) CTV in all bedrooms✲ T ✖ (ex guide dogs)
sB&B⇨🛉£58-£93 dB&B⇨🛉£58-£93 (incl dinner)
Lift (60P 🚗 ❋ 🏊 (heated) ♀ (hard) snooker sauna solarium croquet putting green petanque mini-gym ♪
♀ English & French V ✿ ⌘ Lunch fr£12 Dinner fr£18 Last dinner 9pm
Credit Cards [1][3][4]

★★★ **67%** **Silver Springs**
Route de Genets JE3 8DB ☎Jersey(0534) 46401 FAX (0534) 46823
Closed 25 Oct-23 Apr
Modern and purpose-built, this hotel stands in 7 acres of grounds. Bedrooms, several with their own balconies, are all similar in style and furnishings, and there is a choice of comfortable lounges as well as a spacious bar and a restaurant overlooking a private wooded valley. The international staff maintain traditional standards of service and hospitality. Children are both welcomed and properly catered for.
88⇨🛉(14fb) CTV in all bedrooms T ✖ sB&B⇨🛉£35-£50 dB&B⇨🛉£66-£100 (incl dinner)
(CTV 50P 🚗 ❋ 🏊 (heated) ♀ (hard) solarium putting croquet boules ♪ nc9mths
♀ English & French V Last dinner 8.30pm
Credit Cards [1][3] £

C

See advertisement on page 167

★★★ **66%** **Château Valeuse**
Rue de Valeuse, St Brelade's Bay JE3 8EE ☎Jersey(0534) 46281 FAX (0534) 47110
Closed Jan-Mar
Set back from the bay and enjoying glorious views across it, this relaxing hotel stands in well tended grounds. Bright and neat bedrooms are well equipped, the best rooms having balconies overlooking the sea. Spacious public areas include a choice of comfortable lounges, bar and popular restaurant.
33⇨🛉(1fb) CTV in all bedrooms T ✖
(50P 🚗 ❋ 🏊 (heated) nc5yrs
♀ French V ✿ ⌘ Last dinner 9.15pm
Credit Cards [1][3]

JERSEY
Far from the madding crowd

Find peace and tranquility at the
Atlantic Hotel - on the edge of La Moye golf course,
and overlooking St. Ouen's Bay.
A relaxed continental atmosphere,
cuisine extraordinaire, executive suites,
swimming pools, tennis court and a magnificent
health and leisure centre ...
The Atlantic Hotel - *par excellence*.

La Moye, St. Brelade,
Jersey, Channel Islands.
Tel (0534) 44101
Fax (0534)44102
Telex 4192405
AA ★ ★ ★ ★

THE Atlantic Hotel

★ ★ ★ ★

Channel Islands, St Brelade - St Helier, Jersey

★★ 67% Beau Rivage
St Brelades Bay JE3 8EF ☎Jersey(0534) 45983 FAX (0534) 47127
Closed Nov-mid Mar
In a prime seafront location, leading directly onto the promenade, this friendly hotel continues to gain popularity, largely due to the gregarious and cheerful manner of resident manager, Mr Riccio. There are good sun terraces and public areas include 2 lounge/bars and a comfortable lounge area tucked away for peace and quiet. Traditional table d'hôte menus are served in the pretty little dining room.
27⇌♠(9fb) CTV in all bedrooms ✈ (ex guide dogs) ✱ sB&B⇌♠£32-£57.50 dB&B⇌♠£46-£109 (incl dinner) ₽
Lift (14P sunbathing terrace video games ♪
♡ English, French & Italian V ♥ ♬ ✱ Lunch £5.50-£9&alc
High tea £2-£3.50 Dinner £13.75-£16&alc
Last dinner 7.45pm
Credit Cards [1][2][3]   £

ST HELIER

★★★★ ⑤65% The Grand
The Esplanade JE4 8WD
☎Jersey(0534) 22301 FAX (0534) 37815    DE VERE HOTELS

Totally refurbished recently, this hotel offers attractively coordinated bedrooms in a range of sizes – front-facing rooms having spectacular sea views while those to the west overlook the park. Eating options include an all-day lounge menu, the Royal Bar's range of seafood dishes, the imaginative dishes of the tastefully decorated Regency Room and the à la carte and degustation menus of Victoria's Restaurant.
115⇌♠ CTV in all bedrooms ®⌀ T sB&B⇌♠£60-£85 dB&B⇌♠£110-£160 ₽
Lift (15P 25🅿 🄳 (heated) snooker sauna solarium gymnasium spa bath hairdresser massage parlour ♪ xmas
♡ English, French & Italian V ♥ ♬ Lunch £14.75-£16.75&alc Dinner £16.50-£22.50&alc Last dinner 10pm
CONF. Thtr 200 Class 120 Board 40 Del £105
Credit Cards [1][2][3][4][5]

★★★ ⑤69% Pomme d'Or
Liberation Square JE2 3NR ☎Jersey(0534) 78644 FAX (0534) 37181
This centrally situated and largely refurbished family-run hotel is smartly presented and has much to offer. There is an informal coffee shop, an attractive harbourside restaurant with a carvery, and a new à la carte restaurant serving a tempting array of dishes. The hotel has various lounges, bars and foyer areas. Bedrooms are neat and clean and some have harbour views.
147⇌♠(3fb)⚲in 78 bedrooms CTV in all bedrooms ®⌀ T ✈ (ex guide dogs) ✱ sB&B⇌♠£57.50-£60 dB&B⇌♠£90-£120 ₽
Lift (✗ xmas
♡ International V ♥ ♬ ✱ Lunch £7.50-£12 High tea £2-£5 Dinner £15&alc Last dinner 10pm
CONF. Thtr 300 Class 130 Board 50 Del from £55
Credit Cards [1][2][3][5]   £

★★★ 68% Royal
David Place JE2 4TD ☎Jersey(0534) 26521 FAX (0534) 24035   CONSORT HOTELS

This 150-year-old central hotel has been extensively modernised to provide very smart and comfortable accommodation. All bedrooms are luxurious and several have long balconies. Elegant public areas include a quiet cocktail bar and busier public bar, comfortable lounge and stylish restaurant, with breakfast served in the conservatory.
88⇌♠(18fb)10⚲ CTV in all bedrooms ®⌀ T
sB&B⇌♠£38.75-£65.25 dB&B⇌♠£77.50-£85.50 ₽
Lift (CTV 26🅿 🄳 sauna solarium gymnasium jacuzzi pool table xmas

♡ English & French ♥ ♬ Lunch £10.50 Dinner £15 Last dinner 9pm
CONF. Thtr 270 Class 270 Board 30 Del from £49.50
Credit Cards [1][2][3][4][5]   £

★★★ 67% Beaufort
Green St JE2 4UH ☎Jersey(0534) 32471 FAX (0534) 20371
This centrally situated modern hotel has very well equipped and smartly refurbished bedrooms offering a high standard of comfort. Public areas are spacious and include a sun terrace. A good value set menu is offered in the restaurant and pleasant staff provide friendly service throughout.
54⇌♠(2fb)1⚲ CTV in all bedrooms ®⌀ T ✈ (ex guide dogs) ✱ sB&B⇌♠£55.50-£68.75 dB&B⇌♠£85-£91.50 ₽
Lift (55P 🄳 (heated) jacuzzi spa bath ♪ xmas
♡ English & French V ♥ ♬ ✱ Lunch £11 Dinner £12 Last dinner 8.45pm
Credit Cards [1][2][3][5]

★★★ 61% Apollo
St Saviours Rd JE2 4LA ☎Jersey(0534) 25441 FAX (0534) 22120
Conveniently situated in the centre of town, this popular hotel has comfortable and well equipped bedrooms which continue to be attractively refurbished to a high standard, while spacious and modern public rooms provide a choice of lounge and bar areas, a poolside bistro and a more traditional dining room.
85⇌♠(5fb) CTV in all bedrooms ®⌀ T ✈ (ex guide dogs) ✱ sB&B⇌♠£46-£61 dB&B⇌♠£76-£90 ₽
Lift (50P 🄳 (heated) sauna solarium gymnasium jacuzzi spa bath ♪ xmas
♡ English & French V ♥ ♬ ✱ Sunday Lunch fr£10.50 Dinner fr£11.50 Last dinner 8.45pm
CONF. Thtr 150 Del from £50
Credit Cards [1][2][3][5]

See advertisement on page 169

★★★ 61% Royal Yacht
The Weighbridge ☎Jersey(0534) 20511 FAX (0534) 67729
This long established Victorian hotel is in a good central location. Bedrooms are furnished in the modern style, the best and most luxurious at the front, and all have a good range of facilities. There is an elegant first-floor lounge, 3 popular bars, the London Grill and alternative Victoriana Carvery. Room service is also available.
45⇌♠ CTV in all bedrooms ®⌀ T sB&B⇌♠£35-£48 dB&B⇌♠£70-£96 ₽
Lift (CTV ✗ xmas
♡ English, French & Italian V ♥ ♬ Lunch £6.75-£18.50&alc Dinner £13.50-£30&alc Last dinner 9.30pm
CONF. Thtr 20 Class 20 Board 20 Del from £45
Credit Cards [1][2][3][4]

★★ 69% Sarum Hotel
19-21 New St John's Rd JE2 3LD ☎Jersey(0534) 58163 FAX (0534) 31340
Closed Nov-mid Mar
This hotel maintains very high standards, with a friendly and well trained staff being supervised by experienced resident managers. Bright and very well maintained bedrooms all have an intercom system and in-house video channel, the small lounge has new furniture, and both bar and dining room are spaciously comfortable.
49⇌♠(15fb) CTV in all bedrooms ✈ (ex guide dogs) ✱ sB&B⇌♠£24.50-£49 dB&B⇌♠£43-£94 (incl dinner) ₽
Lift (6P games room children's play area ♪ 🎱
♡ English & Continental V ♥ ✱ Bar Lunch £1.50-£1.75alc High tea 90p-£4.75 Dinner fr£13&alc Last dinner 7.45pm
Credit Cards [1][2][3]   £

★★ 66% Graham
60 Saint Saviours Rd JE2 4LA ☎Jersey(0534) 30126 FAX (0534) 21246
Closed Nov-mid Mar
Much work has been done to upgrade this town hotel which is only 5 minutes walk from the centre of St Helier. Bedrooms are now all

ATOL 1965 ★★★

JERSEY

The Royal has been one of Jersey's landmarks for the last 150 years. Tradition has not however prevented us from constantly upgrading our standards to meet the ever changing needs of our guests, yet we have managed to retain a relaxed and comfortable style.

Our flexible and understanding service will help to make your holiday or business plans both efficient and relaxing.

We can also help with your travel arrangements.

**David Place, St Helier,
Jersey, C.I., JE2 4TD
Tel: 0534 26521 Fax: 0534 24035**

SILVER SPRINGS
★★★ **HOTEL**
You'll be staying with friends

At Silver Springs enjoy lazy days around the pool with a game of tennis or a round of putting to give you an appetite for dinner. Seven acres of gardens and woodland in rural St Brelade where caring staff become friends as you return year after year to this family owned hotel.

**Silver Springs Hotel, St Brelade, Jersey, C.I.
Tel: 0534 46401 Fax: 0534 46823**

Beaufort Hotel

St. Helier, Jersey, JE2 4UH, Channel Islands.
Telephone: 0534 - 76500
Telex: 4192160
Fax: 0534 - 20371

Modern 3 Star Hotel well situated for shopping, business or beach in St. Helier's commercial centre. The Beaufort has been designed to offer every amenity for today's traveller. Brummels Bar for aperitifs. The Rib Room for fine cuisine. Ample car parking.

INDOOR SWIMMING POOL AND SPA

All Bedrooms are equipped with:-
- Full Bathroom and Shower.
- Hairdryer and Trouser Press.
- Tea and Coffee making facilities.
- 2 Direct Dial Telephones.
- Colour T.V. with Satellite Channels.
- Full Lounge armchairs.
- Writing Desk.
- Mini Bars.

AA ★★★ *A Huggler Hotel*

Channel Islands, St Helier, Jersey - Chardstock

furnished to the same high standard, the lounge is small and quiet, the bar modern, and the restaurant comfortable. Snacks are available throughout the day and there is a limited room service. Other facilities include a laundry room, a terrace and an outdoor swimming pool.

27⇌↑(5fb) CTV in all bedrooms ✈ (ex guide dogs) ✱ sB&B⇌↑£30-£54 dB&B⇌↑£42-£90 (incl dinner) 🄿
(11P ⇌ children's play area ♩ ⇌
♡ English & Continental V ✂ ✱ Lunch £5.25-£9&alc High tea £2-£3.50 Dinner £13-£16&alc Last dinner 7.45pm
Credit Cards 1 3   (£)

★★**62%** Mountview
New St John's Rd JE2 3LD ☎(0534) 887666 FAX (0534) 39763
Closed Nov-mid Mar
An attractive, bright holiday hotel within easy reach of the town centre. There are some self catering flats available.
35⇌↑(2fb) CTV in all bedrooms ® ✱ sB&B⇌↑£25-£43 dB&B⇌↑£40-£82 🄿
Lift (16P
♡ English & French V ✂ ⇌ ✱ Lunch £8.50-£12.50 Dinner £12.50&alc Last dinner 7.45pm
Credit Cards 1 3

ST PETER

★★★**65%** Mermaid
JE3 7BN ☎Jersey(0543) 41255 FAX (0534) 45846
Most of the bedrooms at this hotel have balconies overlooking the small lake and well kept gardens. Some also have mini bars. There is a Grill Room in addition to the restaurant, and comfortable public areas include a traditional lounge bar and popular tavern.
68⇌1☎ CTV in all bedrooms ® ⇗ T ✈ (ex guide dogs) ✱ sB&B⇌£45.25-£62.50 dB&B⇌£73.50-£94.50 🄿
(250P ❋ ⇌ (heated) ⇌ (heated) ▶ 18 ♭ (hard) sauna solarium gymnasium jacuzzi putting green croquet lawn ♩ xmas
♡ English & French V ✂ ⇌ ✂ Lunch £11 Dinner £12.50 Last dinner 9.30pm
CONF. Thtr 80 Class 60 Board 10
Credit Cards 1 2 3 5

ST SAVIOUR

LONGUEVILLE MANOR
JE2 7SA (off St Helier/Grouville Rd A3)
☎Jersey(0534) 25501 FAX (0534) 31613

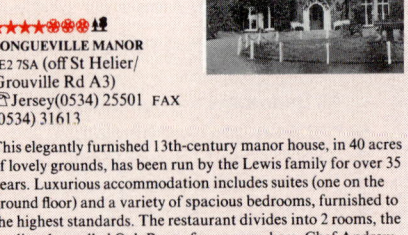

This elegantly furnished 13th-century manor house, in 40 acres of lovely grounds, has been run by the Lewis family for over 35 years. Luxurious accommodation includes suites (one on the ground floor) and a variety of spacious bedrooms, furnished to the highest standards. The restaurant divides into 2 rooms, the medieval panelled Oak Room for non smokers. Chef Andrew Baird offers a choice of menus, including a daily table d'hôte, a well balanced degustation menu, and the prestigious carte. Most of the herbs and vegetables are home grown, and local meat and seafood are used. Favourites include ravioli of Jersey crab on a shellfish cream, which can be very generous and tasty; and beautifully cooked best end of lamb topped with Provençale herby crust and served with spinach mousse and an

olive flavoured meat glacé sauce. A gratin of strawberries and rhubarb with a baked sabayon sauce completed an enjoyable meal.

32⇌↑1☎ CTV in all bedrooms T sB&B⇌↑£110-£170 dB&B⇌↑£140-£210 🄿
Lift (40P ⇌ ❋ ⇌ (heated) ♭ (hard) nc7yrs xmas
♡ English & French V ✂ ⇌ ✂ Lunch £12.50-£17.50 Dinner £28.50&alc Last dinner 9.30pm
CONF. Thtr 45 Class 30 Board 30 Del £135
Credit Cards 1 2 3 5   (£)

TRINITY

★★★**66%** Highfield Country
Route D'Ebenezer JE3 5DS ☎Jersey(0534) 862194 FAX (0534) 865342
Closed Nov-Mar
41rm(40⇌↑) CTV in all bedrooms ® T ✈ ✱ sB&B£20-£31 dB&B⇌↑£40-£72 (incl dinner) 🄿
Lift CTV 41P ⇌ ❋ ⇌ (heated) sauna solarium gymnasium ⚘ V ✂ ⇌ ✂
Credit Cards 1 3

CHAPELTOWN South Yorkshire Map 08 SK39

★★★**64%** Staindrop Lodge
Lane End S30 4UH (1m from junct 35 of M1)
☎Sheffield(0742) 846727 FAX (0742) 846783
Closed 25 & 26 Dec
This small, privately owned and personally run hotel, close to the parish church, provides spacious modern accommodation. Chef John Olerenshaw's imaginative menus have popularised the hotel restaurant.
13⇌↑(1fb) CTV in all bedrooms ® T ✈ ✱ sB&B⇌↑£55-£59 dB&B⇌↑£65-£75 🄿
(70P ❋
♡ English & French V ✂ ✱ Lunch fr£10 Dinner fr£16.50 Last dinner 9.30pm
Credit Cards 1 2 3 5

CHARDSTOCK Devon Map 03 ST30

★★★**73%** Tytherleigh Cot
EX13 7BN (take Chardstock turn off A358 and continue for 0.75m. Hotel on right)
☎South Chard(0460) 21170 FAX (0460) 21291

(Rosette awarded for dinner only)
A family-run hotel of enormous character, centred on a 14th-century cider house. The bedrooms have been converted from outbuildings and barns, and each room has been individually designed and furnished. Original beams, stonework and inglenook fireplaces enhance the character. The restaurant is in a Victorian-style conservatory, with an adjacent bar lounge. The table d'hôte menu offers dishes such as smoked salmon mousse, followed by a succulent breast of chicken filled with cheese, wrapped in puff pastry and accompanied by a cream sauce flavoured with chives. Sweets are varied and all freshly prepared under the guidance of chef proprietor Pat Grudgings who, with her husband Frank, has created a warm, friendly atmosphere.
3⇌Annexe16⇌6☎ CTV in all bedrooms ®⇗ T sB&B⇌£49-£55 dB&B⇌£98-£123 🄿
CTV 25P ❋ ⇌ (heated) sauna solarium gymnasium nc12yrs xmas
V ✂ ⇌ ✂ Lunch £8.50-£16.95 High tea £4.95-£7.50 Dinner £16.95&alc Last dinner 9.30pm
CONF. Thtr 20 Class 15 Board 12 Del from £74
Credit Cards 1 3   (£)
See advertisement under AXMINSTER

Mermaid Hotel
St. Peter, Jersey, JE3 7BN, Channel Islands.
Telephone: 0534 41255   Telex: 4192249   Fax: 0534 45826

C

Incorporating an original ancient Tavern and beautiful old Granite Grill Room dating back to 1710 The Mermaid is a modern hotel built around a small natural lake.

The Mermaid has a superb Indoor Leisure Centre including a 44ft. swimming pool, jacuzzi, solarium sun beds, saunas and gymnasium and also a 45ft. outdoor heated pool.

All bedrooms have bathrooms en suite and balconies. Deluxe rooms also available with mini bars etc.

AA ★★★ *A Huggler Hotel*   Open all year.   Ample parking.

Apollo Hotel

St. Saviour's Rd, St. Helier, Jersey, JE2 4LA, Channel Islands.
Telephone 0534 25441   Telex 4192086   Fax 0534 22120

Modern 3 Star Hotel with an Indoor Leisure Centre, built around a quiet courtyard in the middle of St. Helier.

85 rooms with bathroom en suite, colour television with satellite link, direct dial telephone, tea and coffee making facilities, hair driers and trouser press.

Indoor swimming pool, jacuzzi, saunas, sun beds, gymnasium and games room.
'The Coffee Grove' overlooking the pool,
'Le Petit Jardin' for aperitifs and fine cuisine.
'Haughty Pigeon' bar for local atmosphere.

Centrally heated throughout.
Ample car parking.
Open all year.

AA ★★★ *A Huggler Hotel*

Charingworth - Charnock Richard Motorway Service Area

CHARINGWORTH Gloucestershire Map 04 SP13

★★★
★★★★ ❀♨
CHARINGWORTH MANOR
GL55 6NS (on B4035 3m E of Chipping Campden)
☎ Paxford(0386) 78555
FAX (0386) 78353

This charming Cotswold stone manor is set in lovely gardens and grounds. Parts date back to Jacobean times, and the house has been sympathetically restored to offer comfortable accommodation and good facilities. Bedrooms in the main house have lots of character and are beautifully decorated, while the new bedrooms are nicely furnished with deep armchairs and bold fabrics. Public areas retain many original features, including open minster fireplaces, panelling and York flagstone floors. Bill Marmion has recently been appointed to head the kitchen and we have not yet had the opportunity to sample his cooking.

24⇨ ↑ 2🚻 CTV in all bedrooms ⚲ T sB&B⇨↑ £85-£155 dB&B⇨↑ £110-£180 ₧

⦅ 50P ❀ ❁ 🖃 (heated) ♀ (hard) snooker sauna solarium croquet *xmas*

♀ English & French V ☻ ⚱ Lunch £15.50 Dinner £29.50 Last dinner 9.30pm

CONF. Thtr 36 Class 16 Board 24 Del £160

Credit Cards ① ② ③ ⑤   £

CHARLBURY Oxfordshire Map 04 SP31

★★ ❀66% **The Bell**
Church St OX7 3PP (3m W of A34)
☎(0608) 810278 FAX (0608) 811447

The lounge bar at The Bell is the focal point for locals with its flagstone floor and huge inglenook fireplace, and the original character of the building has been retained throughout. Bedrooms are individually styled, annexe rooms being generally more spacious. The cosy restaurant offers a good-value table d'hôte menu and a few à la carte and vegetarian options.

10⇨↑Annexe4⇨↑(1fb) CTV in all bedrooms ® T ✱ sB&B⇨↑£50 dB&B⇨↑£75 ₧
CTV 30P ❀ clay pigeon shooting *xmas*
♀ International V ☻ ⚱ Bar Lunch £1.80-£6.50 Dinner £12.50&alc Last dinner 9.15pm
Credit Cards ① ② ③ ⑤

CHARLECOTE Warwickshire Map 04 SP25

★★★ 58% **Charlecote Pheasant Country**
CV35 9EW (Queens Moat Houses)
☎Stratford-upon-Avon(0789) 470333 FAX (0789) 470122
RS Xmas/New Year

In a quiet village setting opposite Charlecote Manor and its deer park, this hotel is converted from old farm buildings and offers modern bedrooms of varying styles and standards. The central block includes a bar and restaurant with a carvery.

Annexe67⇨↑(1fb)2🚻 in 14 bedrooms CTV in all bedrooms ®⚲ T ✕ (ex guide dogs) ✱ sB&B⇨↑£55-£69.50 dB&B⇨↑£65-£85 ₧

⦅ 120P ❀ ❁ (heated) ♀ (hard) solarium gymnasium croquet lawn steam room *xmas*
♀ English & French V ☻ ⚱ ✱ Lunch £9.95-£13&alc Dinner £13.25-£15.25&alc Last dinner 10pm
CONF. Thtr 180 Class 80 Board 40 Del from £90
Credit Cards ① ② ③ ⑤

CHARMOUTH Dorset Map 03 SY39

★★ 62% **Queen's Armes**
The Street DT6 6QF (in the centre of Charmouth village 0.5m off A35) ☎(0297) 60339
Closed end of Nov-3rd wk Feb

A hotel of great character, the hotel dates from the 15th century and its low beamed ceilings require guests to move with caution, particularly in the bedroom areas. Bedrooms are nicely furnished, clean and well equipped. Public areas include a comfortable lounge and a separate bar-lounge, together with the dining room. A small reasonably priced à la carte menu is offered.

11rm(5⇨5↑)(1fb)1🚻 in all bedrooms CTV in all bedrooms ® ✱ sB&B⇨↑£26-£28 dB&B⇨↑£52-£56 ₧
CTV 20P 🚗 ❀
♀ English V ☻ ⚱ ✱ Dinner £10-£15alc Last dinner 8pm
Credit Cards ① ③

★ 67% **Hensleigh**
Lower Sea Ln DT6 6LW ☎(0297) 60830
Closed Nov-Feb

This small, family-managed hotel is within a short walk of the sea and is popular with walkers as well as older guests. Mr and Mrs McNair and family are amiable hosts and many guests return regularly. Improvements are steadily taking place and there are plans to extend the bar and lounge areas soon. A short table d'hôte menu offers a range of home-cooked dishes.

10⇨↑(2fb) CTV in all bedrooms ® sB&B⇨↑£21.75-£24.50 dB&B⇨↑£43.50-£49 ₧
15P 🚗 nc3yrs
V ☻ ⚱ Dinner £10.50 Last dinner 7.30pm

CHARNOCK RICHARD Lancashire Map 07 SD51

★★★ 63% **Park Hall Hotel, Leisure & Conference Centre**
PR7 5LP (off A49 W of village) (Granada)
☎Eccleston(0257) 452090 FAX (0257) 451838

Adjoining Camelot Theme Park, this hotel is part of a modern village complex which includes an inn, restaurant and night club. Bedrooms, all equipped with up to date facilities, are either in the hotel itself or in the continental style village.

54⇨↑Annexe90⇨↑(55fb)2🚻 in 13 bedrooms CTV in all bedrooms ®⚲ T ✕ (ex guide dogs)
Lift ⦅ CTV 2600P ❀ 🖃 (heated) squash snooker sauna solarium gymnasium ♪
♀ English French & American V ☻ ⚱ ✱ Lunch £4.95-£10.05 High tea £4.95-£10.05 Dinner £13.50-£35 Last dinner 10pm
Credit Cards ① ② ③ ⑤   £

See advertisement under PRESTON

CHARNOCK RICHARD MOTORWAY SERVICE AREA
(M6) Lancashire Map 07 SD51

★★ 61% **Welcome Lodge**
Mill Ln PR7 5LR ☎Coppull(0257) 791746 FAX (0257) 793596

This motel-style complex by the service area has functional, well equipped bedrooms with new fabrics and recently improved bathrooms. There is a small restaurant and bar, and a foyer lounge.

100⇨↑ in 30 bedrooms CTV in all bedrooms ® T
⦅ CTV 120P
♀ Mainly grills V ☻ Last dinner 10pm
Credit Cards ① ② ③ ④ ⑤

Chatteris - Cheltenham

CHATTERIS Cambridgeshire Map 05 TL38

★65% Cross Keys
16 Market Hill PE16 6BA (at junct A141/142, opp parish church)
☎(0354) 693036 & 692644
This former coaching inn, dating back to 1540, retains much of its original character while providing accommodation with every modern comfort. Bedrooms are individually furnished and service is efficient and caring.
7rm(5♠)(1fb)1⌨⁄ in 5 bedrooms CTV in all bedrooms ® T
sB&Bfr£21 sB&B♠fr£32.50 dB&Bfr£32.50 dB&B♠fr£45 ⌗
CTV 8P
V ⊙ ⌧ ⁄ Lunch fr£7.75 High tea £2.50-£5 Dinner £12-£25alc
Last dinner 10pm
Credit Cards [1][2][3][5]

CHEDDAR
See **Axbridge**

CHELMSFORD Essex Map 05 TL70

★★★★⊙70% Pontlands Park Country
West Hanningfield Rd, Great Baddow CM2 8HR
☎(0245) 476444 FAX (0245) 478393
Closed 27 Dec-4 Jan (ex 31 Dec) RS Sat/Mon lunch & Sun dinner
The Bartella family assure a warm welcome at this converted Victorian mansion. Each of the bedrooms, old and new, are individually decorated in attractive country house style. Ground floor rooms lead on to the garden where there is a heated pool and jacuzzi in addition to Trimmers Health Centre with its own informal coffee shop. In the main dining room chef Stephen Wright offers both a set menu and carte with some ambitious dishes as well as plain grills and vegetarian meals. On Fridays and Saturdays there is a special Italian menu and a live pianist.
17⇌♠(1fb)3⌨ CTV in all bedrooms T ✠ (ex guide dogs)
sB⇌♠£75-£90 dB⇌♠£100-£110 (room only) ⌗
⊊ 100P ⌨ ✲ ⊠ (heated) ⊇ (heated) sauna solarium beauty salon jacuzzi ♫
⊙ English, French & Italian V ⊙ ⌧ ✱ Lunch £15-£20&alc
High tea fr£5 Dinner fr£20&alc Last dinner 9.45pm
CONF. Thtr 40 Class 30 Board 24 Del from £115
Credit Cards [1][2][3][5]

★★★54% South Lodge
196 New London Rd CM2 0AR (off B1007) ☎(0245) 264564
FAX (0245) 492827
Close to the town centre, this family-run hotel is popular with business people. Bedrooms are plainly decorated and furnished, those in the main building being brighter, and the chalet rooms have no direct natural light. There is a small lounge bar, and the restaurant offers a Continental-style menu.
24⇌♠ Annexe17⇌♠(3fb)⁄ in 8 bedrooms CTV in all bedrooms
® T ✱ sB&B⇌♠£37.50-£62.50 dB&B⇌♠£47.50-£77.50
Continental breakfast
⊊ 50P ⌨ games room
⊙ International V ⊙ ⌧ ⁄ ✱ Lunch £12.50&alc Dinner
£12.50&alc Last dinner 9.30pm
CONF. Thtr 45 Board 25
Credit Cards [1][2][3][5]

★★63% County
Rainsford Rd CM1 2QA (from town centre continue past railway and bus station to hotel 300yds on left beyond traffic lights)
☎(0245) 491911 FAX (0245) 492762
Closed 27-30 Dec
This friendly commercial hotel near the town centre has neat bedrooms with modern facilities, some with attractive new soft furnishings. The recently refurbished ground floor includes a traditional lounge bar and à la carte restaurant.
29rm(27⇌♠)Annexe7⇌(1fb) CTV in all bedrooms ® T
sB&Bfr£25 sB&B⇌♠£58 dB&Bfr£50 dB&B⇌♠£78 ⌗

⊊ 80P
⊙ English & French V ⊙ ⌧ ✱ Lunch £9.50-£9.95 Dinner
£11.50&alc Last dinner 9pm
CONF. Thtr 200 Class 50 Board 50 Del from £69
Credit Cards [1][2][3][5]

CHELTENHAM Gloucestershire Map 03 SO92
See also **Cleeve Hill**

★★★★60% Golden Valley Thistle
Gloucester Rd GL51 0TS (near junct 11 of M5)
☎(0242) 232691 FAX (0242) 221846 THISTLE HOTELS

This modern hotel on the outskirts of the town is geared to the conference and business market. Nearly all the well equipped bedrooms have now been refurbished and the public areas include a conservatory lounge offering refreshments and a restaurant with a choice of menus. Extensive room service is available.
124⇌♠(24fb)4⌨⁄ in 9 bedrooms CTV in all bedrooms ®✷ T
✱ sB⇌♠£80-£120 dB⇌♠£90-£160 (room only) ⌗
Lift ⊊ 275P ✲ ⊠ (heated) ♞ (hard) sauna solarium
gymnasium beauty salon *xmas*
⊙ International V ⊙ ⌧ ⁄ ✱ Lunch £13-£18.95&alc Dinner
£18.95-£30&alc Last dinner 9.45pm
CONF. Thtr 220 Class 120 Board 60 Del from £77
Credit Cards [1][2][3][4][5]
See advertisement on page 173

★★★★52% The Queen's
Promenade GL50 1NN ☎(0242) 514724 FAX
(0242) 224145 FORTE GRAND

This majestic building is prominently located at the head of Cheltenham's Promenade, and though public rooms are a little restricted, they provide an atmosphere of quiet refinement. The bedrooms are comfortable, with attractive coordinated decor.

THE·OAK·HOVSE AA★★
Axbridge
A Country House and Restaurant of Rare Distinction

13th century Hotel overlooking the Square of the ancient town of Axbridge. 10 bedrooms. All ensuite with TV and telephone. A la carte and table d'hôte menus using local fresh game, fish, vegetables and fruit. Bistro Bar has a selection of real ales and wines. Residents lounge has two inglenooks to sit beside during long cold winters. The Hotel is only 15 minutes from junctions 21 & 22 of the M5 motorway.

Special Short & Weekend Break rates available

**The Oak House
The Square, Axbridge,
Somerset BS26 2AP
Telephone: 0934- 732444 Fax: 0934-732444**

171

Cheltenham

74⇨♂(2fb)2⇔in 10 bedrooms CTV in all bedrooms ®❦T ✳ sB&B⇨♂£85 dB&B⇨♂£100 (room only) ₧
Lift ℂ 80P *xmas*
♺ French V ♢ ⚒ ✂ ✱ Lunch £16 Dinner £21 Last dinner 9.45pm
Credit Cards ①②③⑤

★★★ ❀❀❀ GREENWAY
Shurdington GL51 5UG
☎(0242) 862352 FAX (0242) 862780
Closed 3-8 Jan RS Sat & BH Mon

The house is 16th century, elegant, and ivy-clad with an open fireplace in the appealing little lobby lounge. A spacious hallway leads on to a richly decorated drawing room, and there is a cosy cocktail bar and a wood panelled restaurant with a bright conservatory overlooking the gardens. Bedrooms, either in the main house or adjacent converted coach house, are all well proportioned and furnished with antiques and reproduction pieces. Tony Elliott's professional hotel-keeping is tempered with hospitality and concern which permeates through to his equally dedicated young brigade. Just as we go to print, we have learned of a change of chef – Christopher Colmer has been appointed and we await our next inspection with interest.

11⇨♂Annexe8⇨♂ CTV in all bedrooms T ✂ ✱ sB&B⇨♂£76.50-£85 dB&B⇨♂£108-£175 ₧
50P 🅿 ❀ croquet nc7yrs *xmas*
V ✱ Lunch £15-£17 Dinner £25 Last dinner 9.30pm
Credit Cards ①②③④⑤

★★★ ❀❀❀ 75% Hotel On the Park
38 Evesham Rd GL52 2AH (opposite Pitville Park)
☎(0242) 518898 FAX (0242) 511526
RS Sun & Mon

This charming little hotel is continuing to attract praise and comment. A delightful townhouse overlooking Pittville Park, it is run with precision and style, while offering a high level of hospitality to all guests. Bedrooms combine elegance, charm and modern facilities, with crisp linen, a decanter of sherry and fresh fruit among the extras provided. Public rooms are cosy and there is a congenial lounge with a dispense bar.
Within the building is the Epicurean Restaurant, the separate, franchised business of chef Patrick McDonald, who has a fine reputation for cuisine in modern British style.
12⇨♂♂✂in 4 bedrooms CTV in all bedrooms ®❦T ✂ (ex guide dogs) sB⇨♂£70-£80 dB⇨♂£80-£100 (room only) ₧
8P 1🅱 (£10) 🅿 nc8yrs *xmas*
V ♢ ⚒ ✱ Lunch £14.50-£15&alc Dinner fr£22.50&alc Last dinner 10.30pm
CONF. Board 20 Del £115
Credit Cards ①②③⑤

★★★ 65% Carlton
Parabola Rd GL50 3AQ ☎(0242) 514453 FAX (0242) 226487
This large white Regency building stands in a wide tree-lined residential road near the town centre. An extensive upgrading programme has provided smartly modernised bedrooms, those in an adjacent building being particularly spacious.

63⇨♂ Annexe13⇨♂(3fb)3⇔ CTV in all bedrooms ® T ✱ sB&B⇨♂£35-£65 dB&B⇨♂£65-£94 ₧
Lift ℂ 80P *xmas*
V ♢ ✱ Lunch £11.50&alc Dinner £12.50&alc Last dinner 9.30pm
CONF. Thtr 240 Class 150 Board 100 Del from £65
Credit Cards ①②③⑤ £

★★★ 64% The Prestbury House Hotel & Restaurant
The Burgage, Prestbury GL52 3DN (2m NE A46)
☎(0242) 529533 FAX (0242) 227076
This elegant Georgian property is quietly situated just a mile northeast of Cheltenham, and owners Jacqueline and Stephen Whitbourn and their team provide thoughtful, friendly service. There are well proportioned bedrooms in the main house and more cottagey rooms in the coach house. Public rooms include an attractive dining room with bay windows overlooking Cleeve Hill, a cocktail bar with an open fire in winter and a panelled lounge.
9⇨♂ Annexe9⇨♂(3fb)1⇔ CTV in all bedrooms ®❦T ✂ (ex guide dogs) sB&B⇨♂£50-£65 dB&B⇨♂£60-£80 ₧
CTV 50P ❀ ☾ clay pigeon shooting croquet *xmas*
♺ English, French & Italian V ♢ ⚒ Lunch £9.95-£15&alc High tea fr£5 Dinner £16.50-£18.50&alc Last dinner 9pm
CONF. Thtr 70 Class 35 Board 30 Del from £65
Credit Cards ①②③ £

★★★ 63% White House
Gloucester Rd, Staverton GL51 0ST (3m W off B4063) ☎Gloucester(0452) 713226 FAX (0452) 857590

This hotel is in a very convenient location and has very attractive public rooms with a striking decor. The restaurant offers both a set menu and a carte, and there is a relaxing bar lounge. Guest accommodation is modern and functional, with a good range of facilities, and staff are helpful and friendly.
49⇨♂(3fb)2⇔ CTV in 50 bedrooms ®❦T ✱ sB&B⇨♂£48-£52 dB&B⇨♂£65-£70 ₧
ℂ 100P ❀ *xmas*
♺ International V ♢ ⚒ ✱ Lunch £7.25-£12&alc High tea £4.25-£7.50 Dinner fr£14&alc Last dinner 9.30pm
CONF. Thtr 170 Class 70 Board 50 Del from £75
Credit Cards ①②③⑤

★★★ 61% Hotel De La Bere
Southam GL52 3NH (3m NE on B4632)
☎(0242) 237771 FAX (0242) 236016

FORTE Heritage

This is an imposing building, dating from 1485, with many original features such as oak panelling, ornate plaster work, beams and fireplaces. Half the bedrooms are in the main house and these vary in size, shape and location (some along winding corridors or up old staircases). Room décor and soft furnishings are showing their age.
32⇨♂ Annexe25⇨♂(2fb)6⇔✂in 14 bedrooms CTV in all bedrooms ® T sB⇨♂£70 dB⇨♂£85 (room only) ₧
ℂ 150P ❀ ⌕ (heated) ℘ (hard) squash snooker sauna solarium badminton *xmas*
♺ English & French V ♢ ⚒ ✂ ✱ Sunday Lunch £11.95 Dinner fr£17.95&alc Last dinner 10pm
CONF. Thtr 100 Class 40 Board 35 Del £100
Credit Cards ①②③⑤

★★ 68% Charlton Kings
London Rd, Charlton Kings GL52 6UU (2.5m SE on A40)
☎(0242) 231061 FAX (0242) 241900
This modern purpose-built hotel is privately owned and personally run, offering good quality, well equipped accommodation.
14⇨♂(2fb)✂in 5 bedrooms CTV in all bedrooms ® T ✱ sB&B⇨♂£39-£64 dB&B⇨♂£56-£84 ₧
20P ❀ *xmas*
♺ Cosmopolitan V ♢ ⚒ ✂ ✱ Lunch £12.50-£14.95 Dinner £14.95 Last dinner 9pm
Credit Cards ①②③

Cheltenham - Chelwood

★★ 65% George Hotel
St Georges Rd GL50 3DZ ☎(0242) 235751 FAX (0242) 224359
Centrally situated 100yds from the Promenade, the George was originally a row of Georgian terraced town houses. It has attractive, well equipped bedrooms, and good quality public areas.
39⇨🛏(2fb)⊁in 2 bedrooms CTV in all bedrooms ® T
sB&B⇨🛏fr£48 dB&B⇨🛏fr£56 🍴
⟨ 30P
🍽 English & French **V** ✿ ⚏ ⊁ ✱ Lunch £7.95-£11&alc
Dinner fr£11 Last dinner 9.15pm
Credit Cards ① ② ③ ⑤   £

★★ 62% Allards
Shurdington GL51 5XA (on A46, near junct 11 of M5) ☎(0242) 862498 FAX (0242) 863017

This family owned and run hotel dates back to 1756, but has been much extended and converted to provide functional, well equipped accommodation equally suited to business or leisure guests. Public areas are attractive and include a small bar and a restaurant overlooking the large garden.
12⇨🛏(2fb) CTV in all bedrooms ® T ✖ sB&B⇨🛏£35-£37
dB&B⇨🛏£55-£60
30P 1🚗 ✿ xmas
🍽 English & French **V** ✿ ⚏ ⊁ Lunch £10.75-£13.95 Dinner £10.75-£13.95 Last dinner 9.30pm
Credit Cards ① ② ③   £

★★ 59% Cotswold Grange
Pittville Circus Rd GL52 2QH (from town centre follow signs 'Prestbury', Turn right at first roundabout, hotel 200yds on left)
☎(0242) 515119 FAX (0242) 241537
Closed 24 Dec-1 Jan
Owned and run by the friendly Weaver family, this attractive stone-built hotel is in a tree-lined avenue close to the town centre. Bedrooms vary in size and furnishings are functional in style. An à la carte menu of popular dishes is offered in the dining room.
25⇨🛏(4fb) CTV in all bedrooms ®✱ T sB&B⇨🛏£39
dB&B⇨🛏£50
CTV 20P ✿ ♤
V ✿ ⚏ ⊁ Lunch £6.50-£12.50alc Dinner £7.50-£17.50alc Last dinner 7.30pm
Credit Cards ① ② ③   £

Travel Inn
Tewkesbury Rd, Uckington GL51 9SL (on A4019)
☎Gloucester(0242) 233487

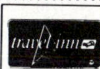

Purpose-built acccommodation offers spacious and well equipped bedrooms, all with en suite bathrooms. Meals may be taken at the nearby family restaurant and pub. For more details about Travel Inns, consult the Contents page, under Hotel Groups.
40⇨🛏 ✱ B⇨🛏£33.50 (room only)

CHELWOOD Avon Map 03 ST66

★★ ✿73% Chelwood House
BS18 4NH (on A37 200yds S of junct with A368) (Logis)
☎Mendip(0761) 490730 FAX (0761) 490730
RS 24 Dec-15 Jan
Rudi and Jill Birk's charming little hotel provides a quality, country house-style ambience in a sympathetically converted 300-year-old building. The warm, well proportioned bedrooms, are furnished with deep armchairs and settees, with such extras as home-made biscuits and magazines. Rudi cooks robust dishes with honest flavours, including some popular Bavarian dishes from his homeland, which are taken in the comfortable conservatory restaurant.
11⇨🛏(1fb)3🛏 CTV in all bedrooms ® T ✖ (ex guide dogs)
sB&B⇨🛏£49-£65 dB&B⇨🛏£69.50-£94 🍴
15P 🐾 ✿ croquet nc10yrs

➡

★★★

THE PRESTBURY HOUSE HOTEL AND RESTAURANT
The Burgage, Prestbury, Cheltenham GL52 3DN
Tel: 0242 529533 Fax: 0242 227076

300 year old family owned Georgian Country Manor House with 18 large en-suite bedrooms. Set in 4 acres of secluded grounds beneath Cleeve Hill (the Cotswold Way) and adjacent to the Racecourse. Only 1 mile from Regency Cheltenham Spa Town. Extensive menu and wine list to suit most tastes and budgets including traditional English cuisine and vegetarian dishes.

Leisure breaks, Golf, Shooting, Horse Riding, Croquet and Hill Walking.

Conference and training facilities. Private parties and weddings catered for. Brochure.

★★★★ AA

GOLDEN VALLEY
THISTLE HOTEL

Gloucester Road, Cheltenham GL51 0TS
Tel: 0242 232691   Fax: 0242 221846

Your choice in Cheltenham

For Reservations at over 100
Mount Charlotte Thistle Hotels
Telephone London: 071 937 8033.

Chelwood - Chessington

English, French & German V ⌖ ⌁ Lunch £10.50-£15.50 Dinner £14-£20alc Last dinner 9pm
Credit Cards 1 2 3 5 £

CHENIES Buckinghamshire Map 04 TQ09

★★★ 64% **Bedford Arms Thistle**
WD3 6EQ (off A404)
☎Chorleywood(0923) 283301 FAX (0923) 284825

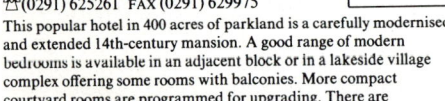

This traditional inn is in a rural village setting with its own garden. Public ares, compact but with character, comprise a small lounge, a popular public bar, a comfortable cocktail bar with an open fire and a panelled restaurant. Bedrooms are a good size and tastefully decorated. Service of early morning tea is an old fashioned treat.
10⇨↑(1fb)1⇨⌁ in 3 bedrooms CTV in all bedrooms ®⌖T✱ sB⇨↑£39-£80 dB⇨↑£78-£100 (room only) ⊟
(120P ⇶
English & French V ⌖ ⌁ ⌁ ✱ Lunch £13-16.50&alc Dinner fr£17.50&alc Last dinner 10pm
Credit Cards 1 2 3 4 5

CHEPSTOW Gwent Map 03 ST59

★★★ 69% **St Pierre Hotel, Golf & Country Club**
St Pierre Park NP6 6YA (2.5m W off A48)
☎(0291) 625261 FAX (0291) 629975

This popular hotel in 400 acres of parkland is a carefully modernised and extended 14th-century mansion. A good range of modern bedrooms is available in an adjacent block or in a lakeside village complex offering some rooms with balconies. More compact courtyard rooms are programmed for upgrading. There are comfortable lounges, a conservatory restaurant and a popular poolside grill room.
104⇨↑Annexe42⇨↑(2fb)1⇶⌁ in 25 bedrooms CTV in all bedrooms ®⌖T✻ (ex guide dogs) ✱ sB&B⇨↑£85-£115 dB&B⇨↑£100-£140 ⊟
(480P ✿ ☐ (heated) ▶ 18 ♀ (hard) squash snooker sauna solarium gymnasium beauty salon badminton steam room bowls xmas
English & French V ⌖ ⌁ ⌁ ✱ Lunch fr£12.50 Dinner fr£17.50&alc Last dinner 10pm
CONF. Thtr 220 Class 120 Board 45 Del from £85
Credit Cards 1 2 3 4 5

★★ 66% **Castle View**
16 Bridge St NP6 5EZ (opposite the castle)
☎(0291) 620349 FAX (0291) 627397

This small and friendly family-run hotel opposite the castle dates back 300 years and has comfortable public areas of some character, including a little restaurant serving a good choice of home-cooked food. Bedrooms of varying size are well equipped.
9⇨↑Annexe4⇨↑(7fb) CTV in all bedrooms ® T✱ sB&B⇨↑£39.50-£44.50 dB&B⇨↑£49.50-£59.50 ⊟
CTV ♀ ⇶ ✿ ✿
Welsh & English V ⌖ ⌁ ✱ Lunch £9.95-£15&alc Dinner £15&alc Last dinner 9pm
Credit Cards 3 £

★★ 65% **The George**
Moor St NP6 5DB (adjoining town gate)
☎(0291) 625363 FAX (0291) 627418

FORTE Heritage

This friendly inn adjoining the 16th-century town gate and medieval port wall has much historic character and the attractively refurbished bedrooms are bright and comfortable.
14⇨↑1⇶⌁ in 7 bedrooms CTV in all bedrooms ® T✱ sB⇨↑£65 dB⇨↑£75-£95 (room only) ⊟
25P ⇶ xmas

V ⌖ ⌁ ⌁ ✱ Sunday Lunch £10.95 Dinner £15.95&alc Last dinner 9.30pm
Credit Cards 1 2 3 5

★★ 61% **Beaufort**
Beaufort Square, Saint Mary St NP6 5EP ☎(0291) 622497 FAX (0291) 627389

Situated in the town centre, this 16th-century coaching inn offers friendly informal surroundings, pleasant service and functional bedrooms with a good range of modern facilities. The attractive wood-panelled dining room offers both table d'hôte and à la carte menus. A recent change of ownership has seen improvements, with a long-term refurbishment programme well in hand.
18⇨↑ CTV in all bedrooms ®⌖T✱ sB⇨↑£29.50-£36 dB⇨↑£39.50-£47 (room only) ⊟
CTV 14P
V ⌖ ⌁ ⌁ ✱ Lunch £5.95-£15&alc Dinner fr£9.95&alc Last dinner 9.15pm
Credit Cards 1 2 3 5

CHERTSEY Surrey Map 04 TQ06

★★★ 67% **The Crown**
7 London St KT16 8AP ☎(0932) 564657 FAX (0932) 570839
Annexe30⇨↑(4fb)2⇶⌁ in 13 bedrooms CTV in all bedrooms ®⌖T✱ sB&B⇨↑£80 dB&B⇨↑£90 ⊟
(50P ✿ xmas
English & French V ⌖ ⌁ ⌁ ✱ Lunch £7.95-£9.95&alc Dinner £9.95-£15.95 Last dinner 10pm
Credit Cards 1 2 3 5

CHESHUNT Hertfordshire Map 04 TL30

Marriott
Halfhide Ln, Turnford EN10 6NG (off A1170)
☎Waltham Cross(0992) 451245 FAX (0992) 440120

A large and busy hotel, which is ideal for the business and leisure traveller, offering a wide range of services, a choice of eating options and indoor leisure facilities. Bedrooms are comfortable and equipped with modern facilities. For more details about Marriott hotels, consult the Contents page, under Hotel Groups.
150⇨↑✱ B⇨↑£75-£95 (room only)
CONF. Thtr 220 Class 100 Board 90 Del from £115

CHESSINGTON Greater London

See **LONDON SECTION plan 1** B1
Travel Inn
Leatherhead Rd KT9 2NE (on A423)
☎Epsom(0372) 744060

Purpose-built accommodation offers spacious and well equipped bedrooms, all with en suite bathrooms. Meals may be taken at the nearby family restaurant and pub. For more details about Travel Inns, consult the Contents page, under Hotel Groups.
42⇨↑✱ B⇨↑£33.50 (room only)

Rosettes range from 5 for outstanding cuisine to 1 rosette for enjoyable, well prepared food

Chester

CHESTER Cheshire Map **07** SJ46
See also **Broxton & Puddington**

★★★★ ❀❀❀
THE CHESTER GROSVENOR
Eastgate St CH1 1LT
☎(0244) 324024 FAX
(0244) 313246
Closed 25-26 Dec

Extremely high levels of courtesy and professional service of the well turned out staff are the hallmarks of this splendid hotel in the heart of historic Chester. The quality of the food in the cloistered calm of the Arkle Restaurant, under the direction of chef Paul Reed, is also a major attraction. There is a monthly carte, with daily specials, and a 6-course menu gourmand: an inspection meal began with a rich fish soup, followed by a warm salad of wild duck breast. Fillet of Scottish beef was topped by a slice of foie gras, and a selection of British and French cheeses preceded the finale of poached, hollowed out pear containing a raspberry soufflé. The Parisian-style brasserie offers excellent baking and pâtisserie. Well designed bedrooms are mostly of generous, even vast proportions, all with the same high quality furniture. Residents can escape to the quiet of their own first-floor drawing room.

86⇨↑♫🛏 CTV in all bedrooms ⚲ T ✈ (ex guide dogs)
Lift (⌗ ✗ sauna solarium gymnasium ♪
♀ British & French V ♂ ⚲ ✗ ✱ Lunch £17.50-£22&alc
High tea £10-£29alc Dinner £40&alc Last dinner 11pm
CONF. Thtr 220 Class 120 Board 48 Del £150
Credit Cards [1][2][3][4][5]

★★★★ ❀71% **Moat House International**
Trinity St CH1 2BD (from City Inner Ring Road follow signs 'Wrexham & N Wales'. Leave elevated section and turn left at traffic lights, then right) ☎(0244) 322330 FAX (0244) 316118

Closed 24-27 Dec

This large modern hotel has been carefully designed to blend in with the surrounding architecture. Bedrooms vary in size and include executive rooms, suites and rooms for non smokers. The best rooms have extras such as bathrobes, fresh fruit, mineral water and chocolates. Public areas are very attractive and include a large restaurant with period-style furnishings and views over the rooftops to the distant hills of North Wales.

150⇨✗in 22 bedrooms CTV in all bedrooms ® T
sB&B⇨£60-£99.75 dB&B⇨£100-£150 🍴
Lift (70P sauna solarium gymnasium jacuzzi steam bath
♀ Continental V ♂ ⚲ Lunch £10.75-£18&alc Dinner £13.50-£18&alc Last dinner 10.30pm
CONF. Thtr 600 Class 200 Board 120 Del from £100
Credit Cards [1][2][3][4][5]
See advertisement on page 177

★★★★ ❀64% **Mollington Banastre**
Parkgate Rd CH1 6NN (A540)
☎(0244) 851471 FAX (0244) 851165

This large, privately owned hotel caters for a wide range of customers, attracted by the very impressive leisure facilities. Spacious public areas are situated around an open-plan area, where ⇨

An C18th coaching inn with the addition of 30 modern, first class bedrooms, each containing private bathroom, TV with satellite, tea/coffee making facilities, direct dial telephone, trouser press and hairdryer. Traditional English pub, serving 'Youngs' prize ales and restaurant with à la carte and carvery menus.

Children welcome, we have family bedrooms, a spacious conservatory, garden and children's menus. Specially adapted facilities for the disabled. Conference, meeting and wedding facilities available.

Special 'Weekend Break' Rates

THE CROWN HOTEL
7 LONDON ROAD, CHERTSEY KT16 8AP
TEL: 0932 564657. FAX: 0932 570839

★★★AA
BEDFORD ARMS
THISTLE HOTEL

Chenies, Rickmansworth WD3 6EQ
Tel: 0923 283301   Fax: 0923 284825

*Your choice at
Chenies*

For Reservations at over 100
Mount Charlotte Thistle Hotels
Telephone London: 071 937 8033.

Chester

the comfortable lounge bar is the focal point. There are 2 grades of modern bedrooms, 'executive' rooms being larger and slightly better equipped. The hotel stands in 7 acres of grounds and gardens.
64⇌(6fb)1⊞⌁in 5 bedrooms CTV in all bedrooms ® T ✱ sB&B⇌£77-£85 dB&B⇌£82-£105 ₽
Lift ₵300P ✿ (heated) ♀ (hard & grass)squash ∪ sauna solarium gymnasium hairdressing health & beauty salon ♫ ⚘ xmas
♀ English & French V ⚘ ℒ ✱ Lunch fr£10.50&alc Dinner fr£21&alc Last dinner 10.30pm
Conf. Thtr 300 Class 60 Board 50 Del from £97.50
Credit Cards [1][2][3][5]

★★★❀❀⚜79% **Crabwall Manor**
Parkgate Rd, Mollington CH1 6NE (NW off A540) ☎(0244) 851666 FAX (0244) 851400

Crabwall Manor, with its distinctive turrets, is set in 17 acres of mature parkland. All the bedrooms are spacious and comfortable, some with private sitting rooms. Bathrooms are particularly well equipped and most have separate showers, bidets and twin basins. There are several elegantly furnished sitting rooms. Chef Michael Truelove emphasises good quality fresh produce, with home-made bread, canapés and petits fours. Our inspector sampled a delicious ballotine of rabbit with a mild mustard sauce, followed by wild salmon served on a bed of leeks.
48⇌1⊞⌁in 2 bedrooms CTV in all bedrooms T
✕ (ex guide dogs) ✱ sB&B⇌↑fr£98.50 dB&B⇌↑fr£125 ₽
₵100P ✿ snooker croquet lawn ♫ xmas
♀ English & French V ⚘ ℒ ✱ Lunch £14.50-£35alc Dinner £14.50-£35alc Last dinner 9.45pm
Conf. Thtr 100 Class 60 Board 40 Del from £100
Credit Cards [1][2][3][5]

★★★❀72% **The Gateway To Wales**
Welsh Rd, Sealand, Deeside CH5 2HX ☎(0244) 830332 FAX (0244) 836190
39⇌↑(4fb)⌁in 8 bedrooms CTV in all bedrooms ®✱ T
✕ (ex guide dogs) ✱ sB&B⇌↑£52.88-£82.25 dB⇌↑£70.50-£82.25 (room only) ₽
Lift ₵51P ☐ (heated) sauna solarium gymnasium jacuzzi xmas
V ⚘ ℒ ✱ Lunch £6.95-£14.30&alc Dinner £14.50&alc Last dinner 9.30pm
Credit Cards [1][2][3][5]

★★★66% **Rowton Hall**
Whitchurch Road, Rowton CH3 6AD (2m SE A41) (Logis)
☎(0244) 335262 FAX (0244) 335464
Closed 25-28 Dec
Set in 8 acres of grounds and award-winning gardens, this busy conference and leisure hotel still gives the impression of a country house, retaining such original features as the Adam fireplace and carved staircase, though rooms are modern.
42⇌↑(4fb)3⊞ CTV in all bedrooms ®✱ T ✱ sB&B⇌↑£72-£86 dB&B⇌↑£68-£98 ₽
₵CTV 120P ✿ ☐ (heated) sauna solarium gymnasium ⚘
♀ English & French V ⚘ ℒ ✱ Lunch £9.95-£11.75&alc Dinner £16-£16.50&alc Last dinner 9.30pm
Conf. Thtr 180 Board 50 Del from £95
Credit Cards [1][2][3][5] £

★★★65% **Hoole Hall**
Warrington Rd, Hoole Village CH2 3PD (on A41/56 junct of ring road) (Crown & Raven) ☎(0244) 350011 FAX (0244) 320251
The original 18th-century hall has been considerably extended to provide well furnished, modern hotel accommodation. The bedrooms, some with spa baths, are attractively decorated and have a good array of equipment. The hotel provides a choice of bars, an attractive split-level restaurant and a conservatory coffee shop.
99⇌(3fb)⌁in 16 bedrooms CTV in all bedrooms ® T

Lift ₵⊞ 200P ✿ croquet ⚘
♀ European V ⚘ ℒ ✱
Credit Cards [1][2][3]

★★★63% **Grosvenor Arms**
Wrexham Rd, Pulford CH4 9DG ☎0244 570560
This former inn has been totally refurbished and extended to provide modern bedrooms, some with spiral staircases between sitting and sleeping areas. The original Edwardian building houses spacious bars and a restaurant.
42⇌↑(4fb)1⊞
₵CTV 150P
✱ Bar Lunch £3.95-£7.50 Dinner £3.75-£7.50&alc Last dinner 10pm
Conf. Thtr 80 Class 40 Board 40

★★★62% *Blossoms*
St John St CH1 1HL ☎(0244) 323186 FAX (0244) 346633

FORTE Heritage

This constantly improving traditional hotel in the heart of the city has a parking arrangement with NCP at Newgate Street. As an alternative to dining in the elegant restaurant, there is the more casual Snooty Fox 'below stairs'.
64⇌↑(2fb)1⊞⌁in 19 bedrooms CTV in all bedrooms ® T ✱ sB⇌↑£80-£95 dB⇌↑£90-£115 (room only) ₽
Lift ₵ ♪ ♫ xmas
V ⚘ ℒ ✱ Lunch £8.95-£10.95&alc Dinner £16.95&alc Last dinner 9.45pm
Credit Cards [1][2][3][5]

★★★58% *Royal Oak*
Warrington Rd, Mickle Trafford CH2 4EX (3m NE A56) (Toby)
☎(0244) 301391 FAX (0244) 301948
This extended Edwardian hotel, charmingly decorated throughout with coordinating fabrics, offers good value accommodation. Public areas include a choice of bars and a popular carvery with a good selection of roasts and daily specials. Friendly and attentive service is provided by smart, uniformed staff.
36⇌↑(10fb)⌁in 10 bedrooms CTV in all bedrooms ® T
₵150P ✿
V ⚘ ℒ Last dinner 10pm
Credit Cards [1][2][3][5]

★★★56% *Plantation Inn*
Liverpool Rd CH2 1AG ☎(0244) 374100 FAX (0244) 379240
Some 500 metres from the city's medieval centre, the Plantation Inn offers functional bedrooms including some executive rooms. The Palms Restaurant offers both table d'hôte and à la carte menus, and 2 bars are open late for dancing most evenings.
Annexe75⇌↑(4fb)⌁in 15 bedrooms CTV in all bedrooms ®✱ T ✱ sB&B⇌↑£50-£75 dB&B⇌↑£75-£95 ₽
Lift ₵900P ♫ xmas
♀ Continental V ⚘ ℒ ✱ Lunch £8.50&alc Dinner £15.25&alc Last dinner 10pm
Conf. Thtr 180 Class 70 Board 50 Del from £65
Credit Cards [1][2][3][5] £

★★70% **Green Bough**
60 Hoole Rd CH2 3NL ☎(0244) 326241 FAX (0244) 326265
Closed 22-28 Dec RS 29 Dec-10 Jan
The obvious pride of proprietors Doreen and David Castle is reflected throughout their charming hotel, in the numerous personal touches, such as ornaments and flower arrangements. The Victorian house retains many original features including ornately carved fireplaces and oak panelling. There is a comfortable lounge, a pleasant bar and an attractive dining room. Bedrooms, some with spacious than others, are individually styled and furnishings vary from simple modern to antique.
14⇌↑ Annexe5⇌↑(4fb)1⊞ CTV in all bedrooms ® T ✱ sB&B⇌↑£39.50-£44 dB&B⇌↑£48-£55 ₽

Chester

CTV 21P
V ✦ ✗ ✱ Dinner fr£11.50 Last dinner 8.30pm
Credit Cards [1] [2] [3]

★★**64%** **Brookside**
Brook Ln CH2 2AN ☎(0244) 381943 FAX
(0244) 379701

This privately owned hotel, situated just north of the city centre and offering convenient access to most amenities, complements well equipped accommodation by nicely appointed, attractive public areas.
26⇨♠(6fb) CTV in all bedrooms ® T sB&B⇨♠£30-£32 dB&B⇨♠£44-£47 ♬
13P sauna solarium gymnasium pool table *xmas*
♥French V✗Dinner£9.95-£10.95&alc Last dinner 9.30pm
Credit Cards [1] [3]

★★**63%** **Cavendish**
42-44 Hough Green CH4 8JQ (S on A549) ☎(0244) 675100 FAX (0244) 681309
This early Victorian property is now a privately owned and personally run business and holiday hotel, extensively refurbished to offer modern, well equipped bedrooms and attractive public areas. There is a pleasant garden at the rear.
18⇨♠(4fb)2♨ CTV in all bedrooms ®✗ T ✗
◊ 36P
♥ English & French V ✦ ♫ ✗ ✱
Credit Cards [1] [2] [3]

★★**62%** **Dene**
Hoole Rd CH2 3ND (on A56, 1m E city centre) ☎(0244) 321165 FAX (0244) 350277
A considerably extended house, the Dene Hotel stands in spacious gardens. It provides modern accommodation in similarly equipped bedrooms which vary in size and style. Half are on ground floor level and 8 of these are in a motel- type block. In addition to a large restaurant, there is a spacious bar and a small conservatory with a pool table.
41rm(39⇨♠)Annexe8⇨♠(4fb) CTV in all bedrooms ®✗ T sB&B£25-£27 sB&B⇨♠£38-£40 dB&B⇨♠£47-£50 ♬
CTV 55P ✿ pool table
V ✦ Bar Lunch £2-£5alc Dinner £9-£14alc Last dinner 8.30pm
Credit Cards [1] [3]
See advertisement on page 179

★★**62%** **Riverside**
22 City Walls CH1 1SB ☎(0244) 326580 FAX (0244) 311567
The frontage of this hotel looks immediately out on to the River Dee with its weir and salmon leap. There are lovely gardens, too, with a magnificent 400-year-old weeping ash. Bedrooms are currently being modernised with pine furniture and bright decor. The annexe was once the home of the Recorder of Chester. There is a bar, lounge and a modern restaurant offering a good choice of food.
12⇨♠Annexe10⇨♠(3fb)4♨✗in 10 bedrooms CTV in all bedrooms ® T ✱ sB&B⇨♠£30-£45 dB&B⇨♠£45-£60 ♬
22P ♿ ✿
V ✗ ✱ Sunday Lunch £7.95 Dinner £11.95&alc Last dinner 9pm
Credit Cards [1] [2] [3] [5]
See advertisement on page 179

★★**61%** **Eaton**
29/31 City Rd CH1 3AE ☎(0244) 320840 FAX (0244) 320850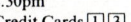

The Eaton is a cosy family hotel within easy walking distance of the city centre. The lounge bar is attractively decorated with floral wall panels and the cushioned cane furniture is covered in matching fabric. Bedrooms include several family units with intercommunicating bedrooms. Good food is available from a small fixed price menu.

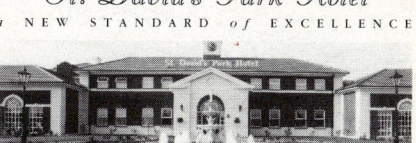

St. David's Park Hotel
a NEW STANDARD of EXCELLENCE

The location is perfect, luxury and comfort unsurpassed and facilities outstanding.

Situated at the great crossroads of North Wales, where the A55 meets the A494 and just 10 minutes from the M56 and the historic City of Chester.

AA
★★★★ ✿
♛♛♛♛♛
DE LUXE

Excellence is the keyword in everything from accommodation to cuisine, all 121 executive bedrooms contain every luxury, there are rooms especially designed for Lady Executives and for Disabled Guests. It's also the perfect Conference Venue, accommodating up to 250 delegates, with every facility.

St David's Park Hotel Leisure Club with its pool, spa bath, steam and sauna rooms, solarium, gymnasium, snooker/pool room and supervised children's area, contains something for everyone.

From May 1994, the Hotel opens Northop Country Park. Just 5 minutes from the Hotel and with free transport provided, the Country Park offers 18 hole championship golf, tennis, walks in the beautiful Welsh countryside and Superb Country Club.

 St David's Park Hotel. St David's Park, Ewloe, Nr Chester CH5 3YB.
Telephone: 0244 520800 Facsimile: 0244 520930

MOAT HOUSE INTERNATIONAL TRINITY STREET, CHESTER CHESHIRE CH1 2BD
Tel: 0244-322330. Fax: 0244-316118.

The very latest in 4 star luxury is waiting for you in the heart of the historic city of Chester. Moat House International Hotel can offer you: 150 luxury bedrooms, air conditioned bars and restaurant with spectacular views over the hills of Wales, air conditioned conference & banqueting facilities up to 400. Mini leisure facilities & car parking for 80 vehicles.

Chester - Chesterfield

19rm(14⇨♠)(4fb) CTV in all bedrooms ® T ✱ sB&Bfr£28 sB&B⇨♠fr£35 dB&Bfr£35 dB&B⇨♠fr£45 ₧
9P 1🍴 ♪
♀ English & French V ✿ ⚱ ✱ Lunch £3.95-£7.50 Dinner £8.95-£11.95 Last dinner 8pm
Credit Cards [1][2][3][5]

★ 63%Leahurst Court
74 Hoole Rd, Hoole CH2 3NL (1m from town centre on A56)
☎(0244) 327542 FAX (0244) 344889
Closed 24-31 Dec

Standing in an acre of attractive gardens, this comfortable family-run Victorian house offers bedrooms of varying size and furnishings, some in a converted coach house. There is no bar but drinks are served in the cosy lounge.

7rm(5⇨♠)Annexe5rm(3♠)(3fb) CTV in all bedrooms ® T ✈ (ex guide dogs) ✱ sB&B£18-£23 sB&B⇨♠£23-£30 dB&B£32 dB&B⇨♠£38-£42 ₧
CTV 17P 🚗 ❀
✁ ✱ Dinner fr£10.45&alc Last dinner 7pm
Credit Cards [1][3]

★ 62%The Weston
82 Hoole Rd CH2 3NT (leave M53 at junct 12, follow A56 signposted Chester to roundabout (crossed by A41) take second exit into Hoole Road) ☎(0244) 326735
Closed 24 Dec-1 Jan RS Sun

This personally run hotel in a large detached house has a friendly atmosphere and offers modest but well maintained bedrooms of varying size and style, a cosy lounge bar, small foyer lounge and simple dining room.

8rm(4⇨♠)(2fb) CTV in all bedrooms ® ✈ (ex guide dogs) ✱ sB&B£26-£30 sB&B⇨♠£33-£34 dB&B£36-£38 dB&B⇨♠£42-£44 ₧
CTV 30P 🚗
❀ ✱ Dinner £8.50-£12.50&alc Last dinner 8pm
Credit Cards [1][2][3]

Forte Posthouse
Wrexham Rd CH4 9DL (near Wrexham junct on A483, off A55) ☎(0244) 680111 FAX (0244) 674100

FORTE Posthouse

Suitable for both the business and leisure traveller, this bright hotel provides modern accommodation in well equipped bedrooms with en suite bathrooms. For more details about Forte Posthouse hotels, consult the Contents page, under Hotel Groups.

105⇨♠✱ B⇨♠£41.50-£53.50 (room only)
CONF. Thtr 100 Class 50 Board 40 Del £89.50

CHESTERFIELD Derbyshire Map 08 SK37

★★★ 62%Chesterfield
Malkin St S41 7UA (from Chesterfield town centre follow signs to railway station hotel is diagonally across from station)
☎(0246) 271141 FAX (0246) 220719

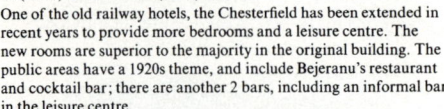

One of the old railway hotels, the Chesterfield has been extended in recent years to provide more bedrooms and a leisure centre. The new rooms are superior to the majority in the original building. The public areas have a 1920s theme, and include Bejeranu's restaurant and cocktail bar; there are another 2 bars, including an informal bar in the leisure centre.

73⇨♠(10fb) CTV in all bedrooms ® ✉ T sB&B⇨♠£62-£72 dB&B⇨♠£72-£82 ₧
Lift ⓒ 100P 🅿 (heated) snooker sauna solarium gymnasium xmas
♀ International V ✿ ✁ Lunch £8-£13.50&alc Dinner £13.50&alc Last dinner 10pm
CONF. Thtr 240 Class 150 Board 80 Del from £75
Credit Cards [1][2][3][5]

★★ 68%Sandpiper
Sheffield Rd, Sheepbridge S41 9EH ☎(0246) 450550 FAX (0246) 452805

The Sandpiper started out as a restaurant, but now provides full hotel facilities, with a modern accommodation annexe. All the bedrooms are well appointed, with a good range of amenities.

Annexe28⇨♠(3fb)1🚻✁in 4 bedrooms CTV in all bedrooms ®⚱ T ✈ (ex guide dogs) ✱ sB⇨♠£26-£46 dB⇨♠£46-£56 (room only) ₧
220P
♀ English & French V ✿ ⚱ ✱ Lunch £7.95-£8.95 Dinner £13.95-£14.95&alc Last dinner 9.45pm
CONF. Thtr 80 Class 30 Board 40 Del from £75
Credit Cards [1][2][3][5] £

★★ 65%Abbeydale
Cross St S40 4TD (from M1 or A61 follow A619 to island at end of Queens Park, turn right into Foljambe Rd, Compton St to T junct, turn right for 200yds, hotel on left)
☎(0246) 277849 FAX (0246) 558223
Closed Xmas wk

Located in a quiet residential area, the hotel is also close to the town centre and the local football ground. It is a friendly, mainly commercial establishment offering good home comforts. Public areas are modern and well maintained and a home produced evening meal is provided.

11rm(9♠) CTV in all bedrooms ® T ✈ sB&B£26 sB&B♠£37-£39.90 dB&B♠£52 ₧
CTV 15P 🚗
V ✁ Dinner £10.50-£15&alc Last dinner 8.30pm
Credit Cards [1][2][3][5]

★★ 63%Portland
West Bars S40 1AY (in town centre overlooking Market Place) ☎(0246) 234502 & 234211 FAX (0246) 550915

This predominantly commercial hotel continues to improve. Recently upgraded bedrooms are modern, with striking décor and new bath and shower rooms; the remainder are rather more modest. Bar and eating facilities are particularly popular, and value-for-money British fare is served by friendly owners and staff.

24⇨♠(3fb) CTV in all bedrooms ® T ✈ (ex guide dogs) ✱ sB&B⇨♠£35-£48 dB&B⇨♠£48-£63 ₧
⦅ CTV 30P
♀ Mainly grills V ✿ ✱ Bar Lunch £2.45-£3.15
CONF. Thtr 60 Class 50 Board 40
Credit Cards [1][2][3][5]

★★ 63%Ringwood Hall
Brimington S43 1DQ (NE on A619) ☎(0246) 280077 FAX (0246) 472241

Located on the outskirts of the town, this hotel is popular with conference and function organisers. Bedrooms have been individually renovated to a good standard, with modern facilities that include spa baths in many bathrooms.

24⇨♠(2fb)2🚻✁in 3 bedrooms CTV in all bedrooms ®⚱ T ⦅ CTV 170P ❀ bowling green
♀ English & Continental V ✿ ⚱ Last dinner 10pm
Credit Cards [1][2][3][5]

Forte Travelodge
A61 Brimmington Rd, Inner Ring Rd
☎(0246) 455411 Central Res (0800) 850950

FORTE Travelodge

This modern building offers a good standard of accommodation for overnight stops. Smart, spacious and well equipped bedrooms, all with en suite bathrooms, are suitable for family use, and meals may be taken at the nearby family restaurant. For more details about Travelodges, consult the Contents page, under Hotel Groups.

20⇨♠✱ B⇨♠£31.95 (room only)

Chesterford, Great - Chichester

CHESTERFORD, GREAT Essex Map 05 TL54

★★ ❀62% *The Crown House*
CB10 1NY ☎Saffron Walden(0799) 30515 FAX (0799) 30683
Dating back to Tudor times, this hotel is on the outskirts of the village. Bedrooms are fairly simple, but all are equipped to a good standard. There is a comfortable lounge bar leading to a small patio, a bright conservatory breakfast room and a pine-panelled restaurant, offering home-made dishes and grills from a short 'carte'.
8⇨Annexe10⇨♠4⚏ CTV in all bedrooms ® T
✘ (ex guide dogs)
CTV 30P ⚏
♀ English & French V ✧ ♨ ✁ Last dinner 9.45pm
Credit Cards ①③

CHICHESTER West Sussex Map 04 SU80

★★★ ❀67% Goodwood Park Hotel, Golf & Country Club
PO18 0QB ☎(0243) 775537 FAX (0243) 533802
(For full entry see Goodwood)

★★★ 66% Chichester Resort
Westhampnett PO19 4UL (E on A27 bypass)
☎(0243) 786351 FAX (0243) 782371

A popular and conveniently located hotel, its bedrooms all well furnished and particularly well equipped; the quietest rooms (all double glazed) overlook the courtyard. Downlands Restaurant offers a good choice of seasonal menus and friendly, well supervised service.
77⇨♠(1fb)1⚏✁in 8 bedrooms CTV in all bedrooms ®✱ T ✱
sB⇨♠£65-£75 dB⇨♠£75-£100 (room only) ♬
《 138P ☒ (heated) sauna solarium gymnasium *xmas*
♀ English & Continental V ✧ ♨ ✱ Lunch £7.95-£15.95&alc Dinner fr£13.75&alc Last dinner 9.30pm
CONF. Thtr 400 Class 120 Board 80 Del from £70
Credit Cards ①②③⑤

★★★ 62% The Dolphin & Anchor
West St PO19 1QE ☎(0243) 785121 FAX (0243) 533408

FORTE
Heritage

Originally two medieval inns, this charming town centre hotel opposite the cathedral has bedrooms of widely varying size, all equipped with good modern facilities. Public rooms include a popular all-day coffee house, plus a restaurant and comfortable bar lounge.
49⇨♠(5fb)✁in 25 bedrooms CTV in all bedrooms ® T
sB⇨♠£75-£82.50 dB⇨♠£85-£100 (room only) ♬
《 7🐾 *xmas*
V ✧ ♨ ✁ Lunch fr£10.25 Dinner £16.95 Last dinner 9.30pm
CONF. Thtr 180 Class 40 Board 40 Del from £75
Credit Cards ①②③⑤

★★ 68% Suffolk House
3 East Row PO19 1PD ☎(0243) 778899 & 778924 FAX (0243) 787282
An elegant 18th-century town house in a quiet part of the city centre has been completely modernised to provide well furnished, individually styled bedrooms equipped with many thoughtful extras. There is a small bar and comfortable dining room, and proprietors Mr and Mrs Page are very hospitable.
9⇨♠(2fb)3⚏ CTV in all bedrooms ® T ✱ sB&B⇨♠£39.50-£66.50 dB&B⇨♠£56.50-£87 ♬
3P 1🐾 ⚏
♀English&French✁✱Dinner£11&alcLastdinner9.15pm
Credit Cards ①②③⑤

Hotels with red star ratings are especially high quality.

Riverside Hotel ★★

22 City Walls off Lower Bridge Street, Chester CH1 1SB
Telephone: (0244) 326580. Fax: (0244) 311567

The Riverside Hotel and Recorder Building are situated in a peaceful location on the historic City Walls of Chester with views from most rooms overlooking the River Dee.
There is a total of 22 bedrooms all with en-suite facilities. colour television, tea/coffee facilities, direct dial telephone and hairdryer. There are a number of 4 poster bedded rooms and a deluxe room with a balcony. A large private car park is to the rear of the Hotel with access from Duke Street via Lower Bridge Street.
Edgards Restaurant provides an elegant Georgian setting where fresh food of the highest quality is served and naturally there is a licensed bar.

The Dene Hotel ★★

HOOLE ROAD (A56) CHESTER CH2 3ND
Tel: (0244) 321165 Fax: (0244) 350277

Set in its own grounds and adjacent to Alexandra Park yet only 1 mile from the City Centre, this ideally situated hotel has Residents' Bar, lounge and Elizabethan restaurant. All bedrooms have private bathrooms, colour TV, tea and coffee making facilities and direct dial telephones.

Ample Parking
Hotel and Motel Accommodation
Value Breaks Available Throughout the Year

Chichester - Chipping Campden

★★ ✱67% **Ship**
North St PO19 1NH ☎(0243) 782028 FAX (0243) 774254

Close to the shopping area, this fine Georgian-style hotel was home to Admiral Sir George Murray during the Napoleonic period. There is a choice of bedrooms (the Admiral standard are best), and well furnished public rooms. Chef Robin Castle offers a daily fixed price menu alongside a carte and lunch time bar meals. There are good home-made soups, fresh fish and delightful desserts from the chilled display.

37rm(31⇨🛁)(4fb) CTV in all bedrooms ® T ✱ sB&Bfr£36 sB&B⇨🛁£46-£60 dB&Bfr£46 dB&B⇨🛁£66-£80 🍴
Lift (35P 3🚗 (£3 per night) *xmas*
V ⊕ ⊑ ✻ Lunch £7-£9&alc High tea fr£5 Dinner £15-£17&alc Last dinner 9.30pm
Credit Cards [1][3]

★ 64% **Bedford**
Southgate PO19 1DP (from A27 (Chichester Bypass) continue N past level crossing at Chichester Station. Hotel 400yds on right) ☎(0243) 785766 FAX (0243) 533175
RS Xmas week

Dating back to 1710, this Georgian building was once 2 private residences and is now a small family-run hotel with a friendly, informal atmosphere. The bedrooms are freshly decorated and simply furnished. There is a smart, comfortable lounge to the front, a small bar and a pine panelled dining room with sliding doors to the patio.

20rm(15⇨🛁)(2fb) CTV in all bedrooms ® T sB&B£32-£37 sB&B⇨🛁£43-£48 dB&B£48.50-£52.50 dB&B⇨🛁£60-£62 🍴 CTV 8P
V ⊕ ⊑ ✻ Bar Lunch £6-£8alc Dinner £7.50-£12.50alc Last dinner 8.30pm
Credit Cards [1][2][3][5] £

CHILLINGTON Devon Map 03 SX74

★★ 69% **White House**
TQ7 2JX (on the A379)
☎Kingsbridge(0548) 580580 FAX (0548) 581124
Closed 29 Dec-Etr

This lovely Georgian house, set in attractive gardens, is run on very personal lines by Dr Michael Roberts and Mr David Alford. The bedrooms are individually styled, and each is equipped with modern facilities. Guests can relax in the Normandy Bar, and there is an elegant no smoking drawing room. At dinner a limited choice is offered, based on fresh local produce.

7⇨🛁(1fb) CTV in all bedrooms ® T dB&B⇨🛁£62-£81 🍴
CTV 8P 🚗 ✻ croquet badminton nc3yrs *xmas*
⚑ English, French & Italian ⊕ ⊑ ✼ ✻ Dinner £8-£12.95 Last dinner 8.05pm
Credit Cards [1][3]

★★ 66% **Oddicombe House**
TQ7 2JD ☎Frogmore(0548) 531234
Closed Nov-Etr

Set in 3 acres of grounds, this is a hotel of character and charm, dating in part from 1762. It is run in friendly and informal style by Bob and Monica Yapp. There is a cosy bar and comfortable TV lounge, and dinner, from a short table d'hôte menu, is cooked with some imagination by Mrs Yapp. The hotel also has 3 cats, one of which bites.

8rm(6⇨)Annexe2rm(1⇨)(3fb) ®
CTV 15P 🚗 ✻ 🏊
⚑ European ⊕ ⊑ ✻ Last dinner 8pm

The AA's star rating scheme is the market leader in hotel classification.

CHIPPERFIELD Hertfordshire Map 04 TL00

★★ 66% **The Two Brewers Inn**
The Common WD4 9BS
☎King's Langley(0923) 265266 FAX (0923) 261884

FORTE Heritage

Most of the bedrooms at this village inn have been brought up to comfortable modern standards and the friendly staff contribute to the atmosphere. The restaurant is well appointed with two menus; the lounge has papers and magazines.

20⇨🛁 in 10 bedrooms CTV in all bedrooms ® T
25P
V ⊕ ⊑ ✻ Sunday Lunch £13.95 High tea £5-£10 Dinner fr£16.95&alc Last dinner 9.30pm
CONF. Thtr 25 Class 15 Board 20 Del from £75
Credit Cards [1][2][3][5]

CHIPPING CAMPDEN Gloucestershire Map 04 SP13

★★★ ✱✱78% **Cotswold House**
The Square GL55 6AN (on B4081) ☎Evesham(0386) 840330 FAX (0386) 840310
Closed 25-27 Dec

This lovely house is elaborately decorated, with numerous trompe l'oeil features around the spiral staircase and restaurant area, as well as in the unusually designed bedrooms. Each has its own theme and offers a high level of comfort. There is an elegant dining room and lounge, and a popular all-day bistro.

15⇨🛁 1🛀 CTV in all bedrooms ⚑ T ✗ ✱ sB&B⇨🛁£60-£70 🍴
12P 🚗 ✻ croquet 🎵 nc8yrs
⚑ English & French V ⊕ ⊑ ✻ Sunday Lunch £15 Dinner £15&alc Last dinner 9.30pm
Credit Cards [1][2][3]

★★★ ✱68% **Seymour House**
High St GL55 6AH ☎(0386) 840429 FAX (0386) 804369

This small, listed Georgian property has been sympathetically restored to retain much of its original character, including an ornate staircase, beams and stonework. The modern conservatory restaurant, with a grapevine at the centre growing into a glazed cupola, blends in well. Public rooms are compact and cosy, while bedrooms are richly styled with Italian classical reproduction furnishings. The restaurant has an interesting international, but predominantly Italian menu.

11⇨🛁Annexe4⇨🛁 CTV in all bedrooms ® T
✗ (ex guide dogs) ✱ sB⇨🛁£45-£85 dB⇨🛁£55-£117.50 (room only) 🍴
28P ✻ *xmas*
⚑ English, French & Italian V ⊕ ⊑ ✻ Lunch £12.50-£15&alc High tea £3.10-£10alc Dinner fr£15.95 Last dinner 10pm
CONF. Thtr 40 Board 28 Del from £82.50
Credit Cards [1][2][3] £

★★ ✱69% **Noel Arms**
High St GL55 6AT
☎Evesham(0386) 840317 FAX (0386) 841136

BEST WESTERN HOTELS

Right in the heart of the village, this attractive Cotswold stone inn was built in the 14th century for visiting Continental wool merchants. Recent restoration work, retaining many of the original features, has provided bright and modern bedrooms around the rear courtyard; rooms in the main house have distinctive charm and are equally well equipped. There is a modern conservatory lounge, an à la carte and carvery restaurant and a cosy old bar.

26⇨🛁 2🛀 CTV in all bedrooms ® T sB&B⇨🛁£58-£62 dB&B⇨🛁£78-£82 🍴
40P *xmas*
V ⊕ ⊑ ✻ Sunday Lunch £8.95-£10.95 Dinner £12.75-£14.75&alc Last dinner 9.30pm
CONF. Thtr 60 Class 45 Board 40 Del from £70
Credit Cards [1][2][3]

Chipping Norton - Chorley

CHIPPING NORTON Oxfordshire Map **04** SP32

★★ **65%** White Hart
16 High St OX7 5AD ☎(0608) 642572 FAX (0608) 644143

The 18th-century façade of The White Hart conceals a 13th-century hostelry. La Brasserie offers mainly grill-type menus with a self-service salad bar. The majority of the bedrooms have been renovated, and the Churchill and Blenheim rooms have original 4-poster beds. The staff are smartly uniformed and friendly.
16⇌ Annexe4⇌(1fb)2⊟ CTV in all bedrooms ® ¥ T
sB&B⇌ £24-£45 dB&B⇌ £48-£60 ₧
CTV 10P 🚗 xmas
V ♡ ♨ Lunch £4.95-£8alc Dinner £1.50-£7.95alc Last dinner 10pm
CONF. Thtr 55 Class 35 Board 35 Del £55
Credit Cards 1 2 3 5

★★ **63%** The Crown & Cushion
23 High St OX7 5AD ☎(0608) 642533 & 643818 FAX (0608) 642926

This former coaching inn dates in parts back to 1497, though it found more recent renown when it was owned by Keith Moon (of 'The Who'), who hosted lavish parties here. No such revelries disturb the peace here now, and its bar, lounge and dining room have a relaxed informal atmosphere. Bedrooms are well equipped, some in the main house and some in converted cottages around the car park.
30⇌ Annexe10⇌(10fb)12⊟ CTV in all bedrooms ® T ✱
sB&B⇌ £35-£58 dB&B⇌ £45-£95 ₧
30P 🚗 ♣ (heated)
Credit Cards 1 2 3 5

CHITTLEHAMHOLT Devon Map **02** SS62

★★★⛳ **70%** Highbullen
EX37 9HD ☎(0769) 540561 FAX (0769) 540492

Highbullen is an distinctive Victorian gothic mansion, set in 60 acres. The hotel is run in a relaxed and informal style and there is a good choice of lounges with a period feel. Bedrooms, scattered between the main building and various annexes, vary in size and some have wonderful views. While some rooms are elaborate most are unfussy.
12⇌ Annexe25⇌ CTV in all bedrooms ® T
✤ (ex guide dogs) sB&B⇌ £60-£75 dB&B⇌ £95-£140
Continental breakfast (incl dinner) ₧
60P 🚗 ♣ ☒ (heated) ⛴ (heated) ▶ 9 ♙ (hard) ⚽ squash snooker sauna solarium gymnasium croquet putting indoor tennis court nc8yrs
♡ International V ♡ ♨ Bar Lunch £2.50-£7alc Dinner £17.50 Last dinner 9pm

CHOLLERFORD Northumberland Map **12** NY97

★★★ ❀**70%** George
NE46 4EW ☎Humshaugh(0434) 681611 FAX (0434) 681727

Ideally situated for Hadrian's Wall, this popular hotel stands on the banks of the North Tyne River. Bedrooms in the main building are particularly pleasant with dark pine furniture and Victorian bathroom suites, but all are comfortable and well equipped. The Riverside Restaurant is an attractive setting for Joe Hetherington's imaginative menus.
50⇌(5fb)1⊟⅛ in 19 bedrooms CTV in all bedrooms ® ¥ T
sB&B⇌ fr£78 dB&B⇌ fr£100 ₧
℄ 70P ♣ ☒ (heated) ⚽ sauna solarium putting xmas
♡ International V ♡ ♨ Lunch £3.50-£14.50&alc Dinner £19.50-£22.50&alc Last dinner 9.30pm
CONF. Thtr 60 Class 30 Board 32 Del from £90
Credit Cards 1 2 3 5

CHORLEY Lancashire Map **07** SD51

See also **Clayton-le-Woods**
★★★ **64%** Shaw Hill Hotel Golf & Country Club
Preston Rd, Whittle-le-Woods PR6 7PP (2m N A6)
☎(0257) 269221 FAX (0257) 261223

Standing in its own grounds, this fine Georgian mansion has well proportioned public areas including a choice of bars, lounges and the popular Vardon Restaurant. Bedrooms vary in size and style, the best being the executive rooms which are particularly spacious and comfortable.
22⇌(1fb)1⊟ CTV in all bedrooms ® ¥ T ✱ sB&B⇌ £35-£65.50 dB&B⇌ £59-£100 ₧
℄ CTV 200P ♣ ▶ 18 ⚽ snooker xmas
♡ International V ♡ ♨ ⅛ Lunch £10.95&alc Dinner £17.95&alc Last dinner 9.45pm
Credit Cards 1 2 3 5

★★★ **63%** Park Hall Hotel, Leisure & Conference Centre
PR7 5LP (Granada) ☎Eccleston(0257) 452090 FAX (0257) 451838
(For full entry see Charnock Richard)

★★ **66%** Hartwood Hall
Preston Rd PR6 7AX (1m N on A6, near junct 8 of M61) ☎(0257) 269966 FAX (0257) 241678
Closed 25-30 Dec

This former Victorian residence provides pleasant, if generally compact bedrooms, some in a converted coach house. Public areas include a comfortable lounge bar and restaurant with extensive lunch and dinner menus.
12rm(8⇌) Annexe10⇌(2fb)1⊟ CTV in all bedrooms ® T
sB&Bfr£32 sB&B⇌ £47 dB&Bfr£41.60 dB&B⇌ £45.61-£60 ₧
CTV 150P

➡

ESCAPE

TO THE PEACE AND TRANQUILITY OF THE COTSWOLD HOUSE - AN ELEGANT COUNTRY TOWN HOUSE IN UNCHANGING CHIPPING CAMPDEN.

JUST 15 VERY INDIVIDUAL BEDROOMS, A RESTAURANT WITH AN ENVIABLE REPUTATION AND QUIET, EFFICIENT SERVICE THAT YOU THOUGHT HAD DISAPPEARED FOR EVER. CALL TODAY FOR OUR BROCHURE.

The Cotswold House HOTEL & RESTAURANT ★★★

CHIPPING CAMPDEN · GLOUCESTERSHIRE GL55 6AN
TELEPHONE: (0386) 840330 · FAX: (0386) 840310

Chorley - Cirencester

♡ English & Continental **V** ❀ 𝒫 Last dinner 9pm
CONF. Thtr 140 Class 100 Board 60
Credit Cards 1 2 3 5   £

CHRISTCHURCH Dorset Map 04 SZ19

★★★❀74% Waterford Lodge
87 Bure Ln, Friars Cliff, Mudeford
BH23 4DN (2m E off B3059)
☎Highcliffe(0425) 272948 & 278301 FAX (0425) 279130

A favourite of one of our inspectors, this family-run hotel, near to Friars Cliff and Mudeford Quay, is particularly comfortable and well presented. Many guests return regularly, and the proprietors and staff deserve the favourable comments they attract. Manners Restaurant offers a seasonally changing carte and a chef's special menu of enjoyable dishes.
20⇨(3fb)1⌘ CTV in all bedrooms ® T sB&B⇨£66-£73 dB&B⇨£86-£93 ⅀
38P ⇔ ✻ *xmas*
♡ English & French **V** ❀ 𝒫 Lunch fr£12.95 High tea fr£4.50 Dinner fr£18.95 Last dinner 8.30pm
Credit Cards 1 2 3 5   £

★★★66% The Avonmouth
Mudeford BH23 3NT (S off A37)
☎(0202) 483434 FAX (0202) 479004

FORTE Heritage

Alongside Mudeford Quay and in attractive grounds leading down to the water, this hotel appeals particularly to the short break market. While public areas are traditional and the Harbour Restaurant benefits from good sea views, the bedrooms are modern, well decorated and nicely equipped. Staff are helpful and cheery.
27⇨↑Annexe14⇨↑(3fb)⊁in 14 bedrooms CTV in all bedrooms ® T ✻ sB⇨↑fr£75 dB⇨↑fr£85 (room only) ⅀
(100P ✻ ⇔ (heated) mini-golf croquet cricket net ♪ ⚘ *xmas*
V ❀ 𝒫 ⊁ ✻ Sunday Lunch fr£10.95 High tea fr£2.95 Dinner fr£15.95&alc Last dinner 9pm
Credit Cards 1 2 3 5   £

★★64% Fisherman's Haunt
Salisbury Rd, Winkton BH23 7AS (2.5m N on B3347)
☎(0202) 477283 & 484071 FAX (0202) 478883
Closed 25 Dec
This very busy little hotel, set amidst lovely countryside, has a wealth of cosy bars, seating areas and a popular restaurant in the main 17th-century buildings. Most of the neat and well equipped bedrooms are in more modern converted outbuildings.
5rm(1⇨2↑)Annexe15rm(13⇨)(4fb)⌘ CTV in all bedrooms ® ⚹ T ✻ sB&B£33 sB&B⇨↑£36 dB&B£54 dB&B⇨↑£59-£63 ⅀
100P ✻
V ❀ 𝒫 Lunch £7.25 Dinner £9.95&alc Last dinner 10pm
Credit Cards 1 2 3 5

Travel Inn
Somerford Rd BH23 3QG (on B3059 roundabout towards Somerford) ☎(0202) 485310

Purpose-built accommodation offers spacious and well equipped bedrooms, all with en suite bathrooms. Meals may be taken at the nearby family restaurant and pub. For more details about Travel Inns, consult the Contents page, under Hotel Groups.
38⇨↑✻ B⇨↑£33.50 (room only)

• •

Rosettes range from 5 for outstanding
cuisine to 1 rosette for enjoyable,
well prepared food

CHURCH STRETTON Shropshire Map 07 SO49

★★71% Mynd House
Little Stretton SY6 6RB (2m S B4370) (Logis) ☎(0694) 722212 FAX (0694) 724180
Closed 24 Dec-Feb & 1 wk Aug
Built in 1902, this fine house has lovely views of the Longmynd and other hills. Bedrooms include 4 standard rooms in a relatively modern block. In the main house rooms have period furnishings and include 2 full suites. A 5-course menu is available in the dining room and the hotel is well known for its 400-strong wine list which includes over 100 half-bottles. Smoking is permitted only in the lounge.
8⇨↑1⌘⊁in all bedrooms CTV in all bedrooms ® T sB&B⇨↑£36-£44 dB&B⇨↑£50-£78 ⅀
16P ⇔ ✻
♡ English, French & Italian **V** ❀ 𝒫 ⊁ Bar Lunch fr£4 Dinner £25-£36alc Last dinner 9.15pm
Credit Cards 1 2 3   £

CHURSTON FERRERS Devon Map 03 SX95

★★57% Broadsands Links
Bascombe Rd TQ5 0JT ☎Churston(0803) 842360
Quietly located with lovely views over Torbay, this hotel is set in about 2 acres of grounds with a private path to the beach. The bedrooms are simple and the spacious public areas are virtually open plan, featuring a well stocked bar with a cosy lounge. The restaurant takes full advantage of the view.
30⇨↑(3fb) CTV in all bedrooms ® ✈ (ex guide dogs) sB&B⇨↑£25-£35 dB&B⇨↑£50-£65 (incl dinner)
CTV 40P ✻ ♪ (hard) *xmas*
V ❀ 𝒫 ⊁ Lunch £5-£8 High tea £2.50 Dinner £10.50-£15 Last dinner 8pm   £

CIRCENCESTER Gloucestershire Map 04 SP00

★★★65% Fleece
Market Place GL7 2NZ ☎(0285) 658507 FAX (0285) 651017

RESORT HOTELS PLC

Many original features, such as flagstone floors and oak beams, remain in this old coaching inn. Bedrooms vary in size and style, there are 5 new rooms of a very good standard and most, not all, others have received degrees of refurbishment. Public areas have been upgraded with a new bar and cosy restaurant.
30⇨↑(3fb)⌘ CTV in all bedrooms ® T ✻ sB⇨↑£55-£65 dB⇨↑£65-£75 (room only) ⅀
(12P
♡ English & French **V** ❀ 𝒫 ✻ Lunch £4.95-£9.95 Dinner £12.95&alc Last dinner 9.30pm
CONF. Thtr 40 Board 20 Del £80
Credit Cards 1 2 3 5
                    See advertisement on page 185

★★★65% Stratton House
Gloucester Rd GL7 2LE (just outside town on A417) (Forestdale) ☎(0285) 651761 FAX (0285) 640024
This elegant hotel with walled gardens dates from Jacobean times and has a new wing of function rooms and attractively decorated bedrooms with good facilities and bright modern bathrooms. Public areas include a comfortable drawing room, attractive dining room and beamed bar serving bar meals.
41⇨↑1⌘ CTV in all bedrooms ® T
(100P ✻
♡ English & French **V** ❀ 𝒫 Last dinner 9.45pm
Credit Cards 1 2 3 5
                    See advertisement on page 185

Fisherman's Haunt Hotel

WINKTON CHRISTCHURCH DORSET
Telephone: Christchurch 477283 / 484071

Dating back to 1673 this lovely olde worlde Wisteria covered Country House offers, Lounge and Buffet Bars with Log Fires in Winter, River View Restaurant. Comfortable Bedrooms all with private facilities, also some bedrooms adapted for disabled guests. Four Poster Beds, Free House, Real Ale, Large Car Park, Children's Corner, Credit Cards taken. Fishing on the River Avon (tickets available locally).

★ ★ AA   Resident Proprietor: James Bochan.

Christchurch where time is pleasant
WATERFORD LODGE HOTEL

Stroll to the nearby Friars Cliff beach and Mudeford Harbour, drive to the wonderful New Forest or historic Christchurch with its riverside walks, shops and Priory Church

Relax in comfortable surroundings and enjoy the standards we set in hospitality, cuisine and cleanliness. 17 rooms privately owned and managed by the Badley family.

BEST WESTERN
CONNOISSEUR
Exceptionally well
appointed hotels

AA ROSETTE
Enjoyable food
carefully prepared

**87 Bure Lane, Friars Cliff, Christchurch, Dorset BH23 4DN
Telephone: (0425) 278801   Fax: (0425) 279130**

Cirencester - Clayton-le-Woods

★★★ 64% King's Head
Market Place GL7 2NR ☎(0285) 653322 FAX (0285) 655103
Closed 27-30 Dec

This former coaching inn is popular for the old fashioned standards of hospitality and service. Congenial day rooms, full of character, include both a public bar and a cocktail bar as well as the comfortable restaurant. Bedrooms vary in size, but are well equipped and an upgrading of the functional bathrooms is planned.
66⇨♠(3fb)2₤ CTV in all bedrooms ® T ✱ sB&B⇨♠£52-£65 dB&B⇨♠£67.50-£75 ₧
Lift ₢ 25P skittle alley darts table tennis pool xmas
V ♦ ♨ ¥ ✱ Lunch £8.40&alc Dinner £13.45&alc Last dinner 9pm
Credit Cards [1][2][3][5] £

★★★ 63% The Crown of Crucis
Ampney Crucis GL7 5RS (take A417 to Fairford, hotel is approx 2.5m on left hand side of road) ☎(0285) 851806 FAX (0285) 851735
Closed 24-30 Dec

Part of this privately owned hotel was a 16th-century inn and it still has a busy bar. There is also a lounge and intimate restaurant serving a wide range of value-for-money meals. Modern bedrooms, built around a courtyard, are attractively decorated and include a good range of facilities.
26⇨♠ CTV in all bedrooms ® T sB&B⇨♠£31-£49 dB&B⇨♠£48-£60 ₧
82P
V ♦ ♨ Sunday Lunch £6.85-£9.95 Dinner £13-£15&alc Last dinner 10pm
CONF. Thtr 80 Class 60 Board 35 Del from £68
Credit Cards [1][2][3][5] £

★★ 59% Corinium Court
Gloucester St GL7 2DG ☎(0285) 659711 FAX (0285) 885807

This quaint town centre hotel has an attractive rear garden, and is sited near to St Johns Hospital. The beamed restaurant has an able chef who offers a varied choice of meals, including an Italian bistro menu.
16⇨♠(1fb) CTV in all bedrooms T
40P ₡
♀ English & Italian V ♦ ♨ ¥ ✱ Lunch £4-£7.50 Dinner fr£10.50&alc Last dinner 9.30pm
Credit Cards [1][2][3][5]

CLACHAN-SEIL Strathclyde Argyllshire Map 10 NM71

★★ 66% Willowburn
PA34 4TJ (0.5m from Atlantic Bridge)
☎Balvicar(08523) 276
Closed Jan-Mar RS Nov & Dec

Looking deceptively like a modern private house, this small family managed hotel is set in gardens and lawns which run down to the sea loch. The island of Seil, on which Willowburn stands, is reached by a humpback bridge – the only one to span the Atlantic! The hotel is clean, fresh and well maintained throughout.
6⇨♠ CTV in all bedrooms ® sB&B⇨♠£40-£45 dB&B⇨♠£80-£90 (incl dinner) ₧
36P ₡ ✱ xmas
♦ ♨ ¥ Bar Lunch £6-£12 Dinner fr£17&alc Last dinner 8pm
Credit Cards [1][3]

CLACTON-ON-SEA Essex Map 05 TM11

★★ 65% Kingscliff
King's Pde, Holland on Sea CO15 5JB (1.25m from pier) ☎(0255) 812343 FAX (0255) 812271

On the coast road east of Clacton, this white-fronted hotel has a popular public bar and smaller cocktail bar adjoining the restaurant. The first-floor bedrooms are comfortably furnished and well kept.

16⇨♠(5fb)1₤ CTV in all bedrooms ® ¥ T ✱ ✱
sB&B⇨♠£49.50 dB&B⇨♠£69.50 ₧
CTV 80P 5☎ (£2 per night) ✱ xmas
♀ European V ♦ ♨ ¥ ✱ Lunch £8.75 Dinner £13.25 Last dinner 9pm
Credit Cards [1][2][3]

★ 69% Chudleigh
13 Agate Rd, Marine Pde West CO15 1RA ☎(0255, 425407 FAX (0255) 425407

This small owner-run hotel close to the seafront and town centre has a friendly atmosphere. Immaculately kept, it provides comfortably furnished bedrooms, a quiet lounge and a short menu of mostly traditional English dishes.
12rm(10⇨♠)(3fb) CTV in all bedrooms ® ✱ sB&B£25-£27.50 sB&B⇨♠£27.50-£29.50 dB&B⇨♠£45-£49.50
7P ₡
✱ Dinner £9.50-£10.50 Last dinner 6pm
Credit Cards [1][2][3][5]

CLARENCEFIELD Dumfries & Galloway Dumfriesshire Map 11 NY06

★★ ⚑ 64% Comlongen Castle
DG1 4NA (7m W of Annan on B724) ☎(038787) 283 FAX (038787) 266
Closed end Dec-mid Feb

Peacefully situated in its own grounds and approached via a long tree-lined drive, this is an unusual hotel which is part of a 15th-century castle and which retains much of its original atmosphere. Guests are invited to join candlelit tours of the medieval keep before having dinner in the Jacobean-style dining room. There is also a panelled reception hall and a lofty drawing room overlooking the garden. Generally spacious bedrooms are furnished in period style, but offer modern facilities.
9⇨♠(1fb)4₤¥in 1 bedroom CTV in all bedrooms ® T
✱ (ex guide dogs)
30P ₡ ✱ ♪ nature trail
V ♦ ♨ ¥ Last dinner 9.30pm
Credit Cards [1][3]

See advertisement under DUMFRIES

CLAWTON Devon Map 02 SX39

★★ ⚑ 70% Court Barn Country House
EX22 6PS ☎North Tamerton(040927) 219
Closed 1-7 Jan

This stone-built country house is set in its own grounds and grounds with views of the village church and open countryside beyond. Eight bedrooms have been individually decorated and comfortably furnished. There is a choice of lounges, and home-cooked dishes are offered on the table d'hôte menu in the restaurant; there is a separate breakfast room which opens onto the garden.
8rm(4⇨3♠)(3fb)1₤¥in all bedrooms CTV in all bedrooms ® T sB&B£48-£55 sB&B⇨♠£48-£55 dB&B£92-£110 dB&B⇨♠£92-£110 (incl dinner) ₧
CTV 16P 2☎ ₡ ♀ (grass) ∪ solarium croquet putting outdoor badminton ⚘ xmas
♀ English & French V ♦ ♨ ¥ Lunch £10.50-£11.50 Dinner £16.95-£19.95 Last dinner 9.15pm
Credit Cards [1][2][3][5] £

CLAYTON-LE-WOODS Lancashire Map 07 SD52

★★★ 67% Pines
PR6 7ED (1m S of M6 junc 29 on A6) ☎Preston(0772) 38551 FAX (0772) 629002
Closed 25 & 26 Dec

In its own grounds, this privately owned Victorian house has been much extended to provide a variety of bedroom styles, including some spacious suites, all equipped with a full range of amenities.

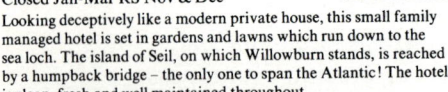

CHUDLEIGH HOTEL ★
Agate Road, Clacton-on-Sea
Essex CO15 1RA
Tel and Fax: (0255) 425407

The Hotel is central, near the Pier and Seafront gardens and within easy reach of Theatres, Cinemas, Shops. Expert attention is given to the planning of the Menus and preparation of all meals.

- 12 well appointed bedrooms, all with private bath/shower/wc
- All bedrooms with colour TV, radio/intercom Hair Dryer tea/coffee making facilities
- Residential licensed bar
- Full English breakfast menu
- Pleasant and relaxing lounge
- Parking on premises
- French & Italian spoken

**Further details from resident proprietors:
Carol & Peter Oleggini (since 1963)**

STRATTON HOUSE HOTEL
Cirencester,
Gloucestershire
GL7 2LE.
Tel: (0285) 651761
Fax: (0285) 640024
AA ★★★

An elegant Cotswold hotel standing in 2 acres of beautiful gardens. 41 en suite bedrooms all with direct dial telephone, tea and coffee making facilities, hair dryer, trouser-press and colour TV.

Excellent cuisine and fine wines served in the Dining Room which overlooks the tranquil walled gardens. Elegant drawing room and garden room. Timber beamed bar with open log fires during the winter months.

Conference/Banqueting facilities for up to 150. Three purpose built conference rooms.
Ample car parking.

A FORESTDALE HOTEL

The Kings Head Hotel
CIRENCESTER
AA ★★★ FLAG

A Comfortable Three Star Hotel in the heart of the Cotswolds, the Kings Head was formerly a historic coaching inn, retaining in its vaults the blocked up secret passage to the former abbey.

The hotel is privately owned and offers excellent food and wine. The management are proud of the reputation the hotel has gained for courteous service.

Market Place, Cirencester,
Glos GL7 2NR
Tel: 0285-653322
(Fax: 0285-655103)

THE FLEECE HOTEL
In the Market Place. ★★★
CIRENCESTER.

Finely restored Tudor Inn now with 25 superb rooms with full facilities. Renowned for excellent cuisine. Excellent location for touring the Cotswolds and Upper Thames Valley. Special weekend rates available throughout the year.

**Tel: Cirencester (0285) 658507
for reservations.**

Clayton-le-Woods - Clevedon

There is a tastefully furnished restaurant and comfortable cocktail lounge. Staff are friendly and attentive.
39⇌↑⁄ in 8 bedrooms CTV in all bedrooms ® T ✗ ✱
sB&B⇌↑£50-£60 dB&B⇌↑£55-£65 ♬
(100P ⬛ ✿ ♪
V ✿ ⚹ ✱ Lunch £9.50&alc Dinner £15.50-£18.50&alc Last dinner 9.30pm
CONF. Thtr 100 Class 150 Board 100 Del from £78
Credit Cards 1 2 3

CLEARWELL Gloucestershire Map 03 SO50

★★★ 65% **Clearwell Castle**
Church Rd GL16 8LG ☏Dean(0594) 832320 FAX (0594) 835523
Beautifully situated on the edge of a Forest of Dean village, this early 18th-century castle retains its original grandeur, with imposing, comfortable public areas, antique furnishings and spacious bedrooms that feature 4-poster and half-tester beds. The basement includes a chapel and the original servants' quarters, sometimes used for medieval banquets.
14⇌5⬛ CTV in all bedrooms ® T ✗ (ex guide dogs) ✱
sB&B⇌£57.50 dB&B⇌£80-£120
100P ✿ ♪ archery clay pigeon shooting *xmas*
♀ English & French V ✿ ⚹ ✱ Lunch £9.95 Dinner £17.50&alc Last dinner 9.30pm
CONF. Board 12 Del £89
Credit Cards 1 2 3 5

★★★ 64% **Wyndham Arms**
GL16 8JT (in centre of village on the B4231) (Logis)
☏Dean(0594) 833666 FAX (0594) 836350
This village centre inn dating back to the 13th century has been carefully modernised and extended to create a comfortable hotel of character with good modern facilities. Bedrooms in the original building are charming and comfortable, though those in the modern extension are more spacious. A good range of meals is available in both the congenial bar and popular restaurant, and smartly dressed staff are welcoming and friendly.
5⇌↑ Annexe12⇌↑(3fb) CTV in all bedrooms ® T
sB&B⇌↑£30-£50 dB&B⇌↑£60 ♬
52P 2⬛ ✿ ♪
♀ International V ✿ ⚹ Lunch £10.75&alc Dinner £15.25&alc Last dinner 9.30pm
Credit Cards 1 2 3 4 5

CLEETHORPES Humberside Map 08 TA30

★★★ 70% **Kingsway**
Kingsway DN35 0AE (junct of A1098 and seafront)
☏(0472) 601122 FAX (0472) 601381
Closed 25-26 Dec
This well established and impeccably maintained seafront hotel has been run by the Harris family for 4 generations. Bedrooms vary in size and are nicely furnished, some with sea views. In addition to the large, attractive restaurant, there is a pleasant bar and a choice of comfortable lounges.
50⇌↑ CTV in all bedrooms ® T ✗ (ex guide dogs)
sB&B⇌↑£54-£59 dB&B⇌↑£80 ♬
Lift (30P 20⬛ (£1.50) ⬛ nc5yrs
♀ English & French V ✿ ⚹ Lunch £11.50&alc Dinner £15.25&alc Last dinner 9pm
Credit Cards 1 2 3 5

CLEEVE HILL Gloucestershire Map 03 SO92

★★★ 63% **Rising Sun**
GL52 3PX (on the B4632, 4m N of Cheltenham) (Whitbread)
☏Bishops Cleeve(0242) 676281 FAX (0242) 673069
The Rising Sun enjoys a superb position with views across the Severn Valley to the Malvern Hills and beyond. Accommodation is not spacious but offers a good range of facilities, and the rooms which were more dated at the time of inspection were due for

refurbishment. Public areas include a large restaurant with striking décor, a bar and reception lounge. Staff are friendly and obliging.
24⇌↑(2fb)1⬛ in 6 bedrooms CTV in all bedrooms ® ⌃ T
sB&B⇌↑fr£59.50 dB&B⇌↑fr£71 ♬
(75P ✿ sauna *xmas*
♀ English & French V ✿ ⚹ ✱ Lunch fr£9.95 Dinner fr£14
Last dinner 10.30pm
CONF. Thtr 80 Board 30 Del from £85
Credit Cards 1 2 3 5

CLEISH Tayside *Kinross-shire* Map 11 NT09

★★★ ⊛⬛ 66% **Nivingston House**
Cleish Hills KY13 7LS (2m W of junct 5 of the M90)
☏Cleish Hills(0577) 850216 FAX (0577) 850238
Closed 1st 2 wks Jan
This 18th-century former farmhouse in 12 acres of grounds is now a relaxing country house hotel. Don't be disconcerted by the front door being shut, enter, and a bell will notify staff of your arrival. An open fire will greet you in the cosy bar and the comfortable period lounge. The bedrooms vary in size but all are well equipped, The 3-course fixed price dinner menu is augmented by a small carte which offers grills. Service throughout is attentive.
17⇌↑(1fb) CTV in all bedrooms ® T sB&B⇌↑£70-£80 dB&B⇌↑£80-£100
40P ⬛ ✿ croquet putting golf driving range *xmas*
V ✿ ⚹ ✱ Lunch £15&alc Dinner £25&alc Last dinner 9pm
CONF. Thtr 40 Class 30 Board 24 Del from £75
Credit Cards 1 2 3

CLEOBURY MORTIMER Shropshire Map 07 SO67

★★ ⊛73% **Redfern**
DY14 8AA (on A4117) ☏(0299) 270395
FAX (0299) 271011

This small but busy and constantly improving village hotel now features a new conservatory where guests can enjoy snacks prepared by Richard Redfern, while more elaborate evening meals are served in the English Kitchen Restaurant.
5⇌↑ Annexe6⇌↑(4fb)1⬛ CTV in all bedrooms ® ⌃ T
sB&B⇌↑£45-£62 dB&B⇌↑£68-£86 ♬
20P ⬛ clay pigeon shooting pheasant shooting *xmas*
♀ English & French V ✿ ⚹ ✱ Lunch £4.95-£9.25&alc Dinner fr£16.25&alc Last dinner 9.30pm
CONF. Thtr 25 Class 15 Board 12 Del £55
Credit Cards 1 2 3 5

CLEVEDON Avon Map 03 ST47

★★★ 63% **Walton Park**
Wellington Ter BS21 7BL ☏(0275) 874253 FAX (0275) 343577

On the northern outskirts of the town, this Victorian hotel is perched high up, overlooking the Bristol Channel and the expanse of coastline beyond. Bedrooms are neatly decorated and well equipped, and bright public areas include a popular bar. Prompt service is provided by a smart team of staff.
41⇌↑(4fb) CTV in all bedrooms ® T ✱ sB⇌↑fr£55
dB⇌↑fr£69.50 (room only) ♬
Lift (37P ✿ *xmas*
♀ English & French V ✿ ⚹ ✱ Lunch £8.95 Dinner £12.95&alc Last dinner 9.30pm
Credit Cards 1 2 3 5

For key to symbols see the Bookmark.

Clitheroe - Cockermouth

CLITHEROE Lancashire Map 07 SD74

★★63% Calfs Head
Worston BB7 1QA (off A59) ☎(0200) 441218 FAX (0200) 441510
Situated below Pendle Hill, this country inn is personally run by the proprietors and offers modern bedrooms. The spacious popular bar and candlelit restaurant both serve a wide range of food and there is an attractive rear garden with a stream.
6⇨ℕ(1fb) CTV in all bedrooms ® T sB&B⇨ℕ£38-£40 dB&B⇨ℕ£50 Continental breakfast 🅿
80P ✿ xmas
♨ English & French V ✿ ⚌ Lunch £8.85&alc Dinner £7.50-£15alc Last dinner 9.30pm
CONF. Thtr 70 Class 70 Board 70 Del from £65
Credit Cards [1][2][3][4][5]

CLOVELLY Devon Map 02 SS32

★62% Red Lion
The Quay EX39 5TF (Logis) ☎Bideford(0237) 431237 FAX (0237) 431044
A quaint 18th-century inn, full of character and charm overlooks the quay in this delightful village. Its bedrooms provide modern facilities without detracting from the character of the building, and most have glorious views. The bars have beamed ceilings and open fireplaces, and a selection of simple dishes is offered on the table d'hôte menu in the small dining room. Limited car parking is available, and a Land Rover 'ferry service' for those reluctant to climb Clovelly's famous steep, cobbled street.
12⇨ℕ(1fb) CTV in all bedrooms ® ✄ ✱ sB&B⇨ℕ£37.50 dB&B⇨ℕ£59 🅿
20P xmas
V ✿ ⚌ ✱ Lunch £5.50-£8.50 Dinner £14.50-£19.50 Last dinner 9pm
Credit Cards [1][3]

CLYDEBANK Strathclyde Dunbartonshire Map 11 NS56

★★★66% Patio
1 South Av, Clydebank Business Park G81 2RW ☎041-951 1133 FAX 041-952 3713
Situated in the town's business park, this bright modern hotel has open plan public areas around the focal point of an eye-catching atrium, overlooked by some well equipped, contemporary-style bedrooms. Smartly dressed staff are friendly and attentive.
80⇨ℕ✄in 16 bedrooms CTV in all bedrooms ® T sB⇨ℕ£56.50 dB⇨ℕ£66.50 (room only)
Lift ℂ 120P ✿
♨ French V ✿ ⚌ Lunch fr£11.95&alc Dinner fr£14.95&alc Last dinner 10pm
CONF. Thtr 150 Class 60 Board 30 Del £75
Credit Cards [1][2][3][5]

COALVILLE Leicestershire Map 08 SK41

★★63% Bardon Hall
Beveridge Ln, Bardon Hill LE6 5BY (1m W of junct 22 of M1, on A50) (Everards Brewery) ☎(0530) 813644 FAX (0530) 815425
Bardon Hall has comfortable purpose-built bedrooms in a motel-style operation. The main building houses the restaurant and a large bar with a conservatory extension, which is popular with families at weekends.
35⇨ℕ✄in 4 bedrooms CTV in all bedrooms ® T ✄ (ex guide dogs) ✱
150P ✿
♨ English & Continental V ✿ ⚌ ✄ ✱ Lunch fr£7.95 Dinner fr£7.95 Last dinner 10pm
CONF. Thtr 200 Class 100 Board 60 Del £70
Credit Cards [1][3]

COBHAM Surrey Map 04 TQ16

Hilton National Cobham
Seven Hills Rd South KT11 1EW
☎(0932) 864471

This is a bright, modern hotel with an informal restaurant, aimed at both the business and leisure guest. All bedrooms have en-suite bathrooms and a range of modern facilities. For more information on Hilton National, consult the Contents page, under Hotel Groups.
152⇨ℕ✱ B⇨ℕ£99 (room only)
CONF. Thtr 280 Class 170 Board 25 Del £138.50

COCKERMOUTH Cumbria Map 11 NY13

★★★63% The Trout
Crown St CA13 0EJ ☎(0900) 823591 FAX (0900) 827514
This welcoming 17th-century hotel by the River Derwent has attractive public areas with beams and stone walls. Bedrooms are prettily furnished in keeping with the style of the house and have modern facilities. A wide range of food is available in the bar and restaurant.
23⇨ℕ(2fb) CTV in all bedrooms ®✱ T sB&B⇨ℕ£30-£65 dB&B⇨ℕ£60-£75 🅿
ℂ 80P ✿ ♪ xmas
♨ English, French & Italian V ✿ ✄ Lunch £8.95-£10&alc Dinner £16.95-£19&alc Last dinner 9.30pm
CONF. Thtr 40 Class 30 Board 25 Del from £68
Credit Cards [1][3] £

Red star hotels are each highlighted by a pink tinted panel.

**35 En Suite Rooms: Close to Junction 22 M1
Conference & Meeting facilities**

All rooms with colour TV, Hair Dryer, Trouser Press, Direct Dial Telephone, Tea & Coffee making facilities.

Originally a country house, in a commanding situation overlooking the landscape. Now tastefully converted to a hotel with bars and restaurant. The hotel rooms are arranged in an attractive mews style around the main buildings.

AA ★★

Cockermouth - Colchester

★★★ 61% Broughton Craggs
Great Broughton CA13 0XW (leave A66 2m W of town, signposted Great Broughton. Over R. Derwent and up Little Brow to T-junction. Turn right.) ☎(0900) 824400 FAX (0900) 825350

This imposing stone mansion overlooks the village of Great Broughton, about 3 miles from Cockermouth. Spacious public areas include a comfortable cocktail bar, a cosy lounge with a log fire and a spacious dining room plus separate breakfast room. Bedrooms, mainly modern in style, are scheduled for upgrading during 1993.
14⇨♠(1fb)1⌂ CTV in all bedrooms ® T ✈ (ex guide dogs) sB&B⇨♠£48 dB&B⇨♠£62 ₽
CTV 60P ❈
♀ English & French V ♂ ⚓ Lunch £17.50 High tea £7.50 Dinner £17.50 Last dinner 9.30pm
Credit Cards [1][2][3] £

COGGESHALL Essex Map 05 TL82

★★★ ❀❀67% White Hart
Market End CO6 1NH ☎(0376) 561654 FAX (0376) 561789

There is plenty of historic character in this town-centre inn, with stone floors, log fires and a magnificent high beamed lounge dating back to 1420. Half of the bedrooms have been luxuriously refurbished, but the remainder are equally comfortable. The cosy bar serves informal meals, while the elegant restaurant offers an authentic Italian menu (chef Fausto Mazza makes his own pasta) supplemented by daily specials. Fresh fish dishes included delicious monkfish in a garlic and tomato sauce; vegetables are fresh and correctly cooked.
18⇨♠(1fb) CTV in all bedrooms ® T ✈ (ex guide dogs) 30P 6⚓ ⚛ ❈
♀ French & Italian V ♂ Last dinner 10pm
Credit Cards [1][2][3][5]

COLCHESTER Essex Map 05 TL92

★★★ 67% Marks Tey
London Rd, Marks Tey CO6 1DU ☎(0206) 210001 FAX (0206) 212167

Located on the A12 at its junction with the A120, this 2-storey 1960s hotel has benefited from considerable investment over the last few years. All the bedrooms have been fitted with ornate furniture and quality fabrics. The rooms have double glazing, but even with the windows open are surprisingly quiet. Staff are cheerful and additional services include porterage and 24-hour service of drinks and snacks.
110⇨♠(12fb)✂ in 16 bedrooms CTV in all bedrooms ®⚓ T ✈ (ex guide dogs) ✳ sB&B⇨♠£49.50 dB&B⇨♠£52.50 (room only) ₽
☾ 200P ❈ ♂ (hard) gymnasium xmas
♀ English & French V ♂ ⚓ Lunch £11.25-£12.95&alc Dinner fr£12.50&alc Last dinner 9.30pm
CONF. Thtr 200 Class 100 Board 60 Del £79.50
Credit Cards [1][2][3][5] £

★★★ 64% Butterfly
Old Ipswich Rd CO7 7QY (A12/A120 Crown Interchange) ☎(0206) 230900 FAX (0206) 231095

At the junction of the A12 to Ipswich and the A120, this 2-storey purpose-built hotel opened in 1992. Many of the rooms overlook the lake to the front, and the studio singles are particularly comfortable for the business guest, each having a double bed and leather easy chair. Twins and doubles are charged by the room and prices have a competitive edge. There is a rustic theme to the public areas with pine, cane, terracotta and dried flowers. Walts Restaurant caters for all tastes and breakfast is a buffet affair.
50⇨♠(2fb)✂ in 11 bedrooms CTV in all bedrooms ® T ✈ (ex guide dogs) sB&B⇨♠£39-£49 dB&B⇨♠£39-£49 (room only) ₽
☾ 85P

♀ European V ♂ ⚓ ✈ Lunch fr£9.50&alc Dinner fr£9.50&alc Last dinner 10pm
CONF. Thtr 80 Class 40 Board 40 Del from £75
Credit Cards [1][2][3][5] £
See advertisement under BURY ST EDMUNDS

★★★ 60% George
116 High St CO1 1TD (200yds beyond Town Hall) ☎(0206) 578494 FAX (0206) 761732

Rooms in the original part of this 15th-century coaching inn have oak beams, and a dozen have been upgraded in a smart modern style. It is hoped that more will have been done by the time this guide is published. There are 2 bars, one frequented by locals, the other with an adjoining carvery restaurant. The foyer lounge is popular for light lunches and snacks.
47⇨♠(3fb) CTV in all bedrooms ® T ✻ sB&B⇨♠fr£59 dB&B⇨♠fr£73 ₽
☾ 50P sauna solarium gymnasium mini-gym sauna sunbed
V ♂ ⚓ ✻ Lunch fr£10.25&alc Dinner fr£10.25&alc Last dinner 10pm
CONF. Thtr 90 Class 35 Board 40 Del £77
Credit Cards [1][2][3][5] £

★★★ 60% Red Lion
High St CO1 1DJ ☎(0206) 577986 FAX (0206) 578207

Dating back to 1470, this high street hotel has much character, its entrance hidden down an alleyway. There is a cosy residents' lounge in addition to the bar and adjoining restaurant, once the Great Hall, where original beams and fireplaces have been retained. Some of the bedrooms have old world charm, while others are furnished in modern style.
24⇨♠1⌂ CTV in all bedrooms ® T ✈ (ex guide dogs) ☾ ⚓
♀ English & French V ♂ ⚓ ✻ Lunch £14&alc Dinner £14&alc Last dinner 9.30pm
Credit Cards [1][2][3][5]

★★ 68% Kingsford Park
Layer Rd, Layer De La Haye CO2 0HS (2.5m S B1026) ☎(0206) 734301 FAX (0206) 734512

This elegant 18th-century house is set in 18 acres of gardens and woodland. Bedrooms, including a lovely honeymoon suite, are furnished to an excellent standard with quality fabrics and reproduction pieces. The small lounge bar, with a log fire and contemporary décor, leads to the modern conservatory restaurant, La Terrazza, where chef Martin Cornes specialises in Italian cooking.
10⇨♠(2fb)1⌂ CTV in all bedrooms ®⚓ T sB&B⇨♠£55-£75 dB&B⇨♠£65-£105 ₽
CTV 100P 3⚓ ❈
♀ Italian V ♂ ⚓ Lunch £15-£25alc Dinner £15-£25alc Last dinner 9.30pm
Credit Cards [1][2][3][5] £

Forte Posthouse
Abbots Ln, Eight Ash Green CO6 3QL ☎(0206) 767740 FAX (0206) 766577

FORTE Posthouse

Suitable for both the business and leisure traveller, this bright hotel provides modern accommodation in well equipped bedrooms with en suite bathrooms. For more details about Forte Posthouse hotels, consult the Contents page, under Hotel Groups.
110⇨♠ ✻ B⇨♠£41.50-£53.50 (room only)
CONF. Thtr 50 Class 18 Board 24 Del £89.50

Satellite television – look for this symbol ⚓
in the directory entries.

188

Coleford - Colonsay, Isle of

COLEFORD Gloucestershire Map 03 SO51

★★**71%** **The Speech House**
Forest of Dean GL16 7EL (on B4226 between Cinderford and Coleford)
☎Dean(0594) 822607 FAX (0594) 823658

FORTE Heritage

Full of character and deep in the heart of the Forest of Dean, this hotel has benefitted from a huge investment, resulting in very comfortable bedrooms with good modern facilities and rich, bold decor. Public rooms, including the timbered Court House restaurant and the congenial bars, recall the building's days as a royal hunting lodge.
14⇌♠4🛏⚒in 3 bedrooms CTV in all bedrooms ® T sB⇌♠£75 dB⇌♠£99 (room only)
40P ✱ xmas
♀ English & French V ♁ ⚒ Sunday Lunch fr£12.95 Dinner fr£17.95 Last dinner 9.30pm
CONF. Thtr 40 Class 25 Board 20 Del £90
Credit Cards [1][2][3][5]

COLERNE Wiltshire Map 03 ST87

★★★★

LUCKNAM PARK
SN14 8AZ ☎(0225) 742777
FAX (0225) 743536

This magnificent Georgian mansion boasts elegantly proportioned public rooms and charming bedrooms both in the main house and in garden cottages. Head chef Michael Womersley and his team use fine produce, local and regional where possible, to produce meals such as the one our inspector enjoyed – a warm terrine of Jerusalem artichokes with baby leeks, and Dover sole served with a Chardonnay sauce, followed by roast guinea fowl larded with Perigord truffles served on a bed of spinach with a Madeira sauce and to finish, a moist and delicious hot chocolate soufflé.
24⇌Annexe18⇌9🛏 CTV in all bedrooms T ✈ (ex guide dogs) sB&B⇌£95 dB&B⇌£145-£190
Continental breakfast 🍴
《 90P 🚗 ♣ 🏊 (heated) ♪ (hard) snooker sauna solarium gymnasium whirlpool croquet beauty salon xmas
♀ English & French V ♁ ⚒ ✂ Lunch £22-£25alc High tea £5.50-£11.50alc Last high tea 4.30pm
CONF. Thtr 100 Class 40 Board 40 Del from £160
Credit Cards [1][2][3][5]

COLESHILL Warwickshire Map 04 SP28

★★★**64%** **Grimstock Country House**
Gilson Rd, Gilson B46 1AJ (off A446 W of Coleshill)
☎(0675) 462369 & 462121 FAX (0675) 467646

A large privately owned hotel, Grimstock stands in spacious grounds. Bedrooms, 13 on the ground floor, are modern and equipped with the usual comforts. There is an attractive restaurant, pleasant bar and large conference suite.
44⇌♠(1fb) CTV in all bedrooms ®⚒ T ✱ sB&B⇌♠£60-£65 dB&B⇌♠£73-£75 🍴
《 80P ✱ xmas

♀ English & French V ♁ ⚒ Lunch £4-£8.95&alc Dinner fr£12.90&alc Last dinner 9.15pm
CONF. Thtr 100 Class 60 Board 50 Del from £87.90
Credit Cards [1][2][3][5]

★★**63%** **Coleshill**
152 High St B46 3BG (Whitbread) ☎(0675) 465527 FAX (0675) 464013

A popular hotel, convenient for the NEC, Coleshill provides well equipped accommodation, those rooms in the main building opposite the main building being particularly spacious. Public areas include a choice of bars as well as the popular restaurant, and staff are friendly throughout.
15⇌♠Annexe8⇌♠2🛏⚒in 8 bedrooms CTV in all bedrooms ®⚒ T ✈ (ex guide dogs) ✱ sB&B⇌♠£55.50-£62.50 dB&B⇌♠£67-£74 🍴
《 48P
♀ English & French V ♁ ⚒ ✂ Lunch fr£9.50 Dinner fr£15.50&alc Last dinner 10pm
CONF. Thtr 150 Class 40 Board 40 Del from £89
Credit Cards [1][2][3][5]

COLONSAY, ISLE OF Strathclyde *Argyllshire* Map 10

SCALASAIG Map **10** NR39

★✿**74%** **Colonsay**
PA61 7YP (400mtrs W of Ferry Pier) (Logis)
☎Colonsay(09512) 316 FAX (09512) 353
Closed 6 Nov-27 Dec & 12 Jan-Feb

Careful planning is required when visiting the beautiful island of Colonsay, as the 2.5-hour ferry crossings can be somewhat complex. The hotel is the social centre of the island, and is enthusiastically run by Kevin and Christa Byrne. It has a very comfortable lounge, ➥

★★★
✿✿
The WHITE HART HOTEL

... the ideal East Anglian location

Rich in history the White Hart Hotel is a superb, family run hotel situated in Coggeshall. This centuries old inn with parts dating back to 1420, still retains all its character and forms part of this delightful town with its abundance of antique shops. All eighteen bedrooms are en suite and well furnished. You can relax in the lounge with its beamed walls and ceiling before eating in the popular similarly beamed restaurant which is open to both residents and non residents every day.

Market End · Coggeshall Essex · CO6 1NH
Tel: (0376) 561654
Fax: (0376) 561789

Colonsay, Isle of - Colwyn Bay

and bedrooms are pleasantly furnished. A set 4-course menu is provided, ably cooked and offering good simple dishes.
10rm(1⇨7🌂)Annexe1rm(1fb) CTV in all bedrooms ®
sB&B£45-£70 dB&B⇨🌂£90-£140 (incl dinner) 🍴
32P 🚗 ❄ ✿ ▶ 18 bicycles sailing equipment
♀ European ☼ ⚖ ✂ Bar Lunch £1.50-£5 High tea £10.50 Dinner £18.75 Last dinner 7.30pm
Credit Cards ①②③⑤

COLSTERWORTH Lincolnshire Map 08 SK92

Forte Travelodge
NG33 5JJ (at roundabout of junc A1/A151)
☎(0476) 861181 Central Res (0800) 850950

This modern building offers a good standard of accommodation for overnight stops. Smart, spacious and well equipped bedrooms, all with en suite bathrooms, are suitable for family use, and meals may be taken at the nearby family restaurant. For more details about Travelodges, consult the Contents page, under Hotel Groups.
32⇨🌂※ B⇨🌂£31.95 (room only)

Granada Lodge
NG33 5JR (on A1 southbound at junct with B151/B676) ☎Grantham(0476) 860686 FAX (0476) 861078

This modern building provides smart, spacious and well equipped bedrooms, all with en suite bathrooms. Meals may be taken at a nearby family restaurant. For more details about Granada Lodges, consult the Contents page, under Hotel Groups.
38⇨🌂※ B⇨🌂£34.95-£37.95 (room only)

COLVEND Dumfries & Galloway *Kirkcudbrightshire* Map 11 NX85

★★ **65%** Clonyard House
DG5 4QW ☎Rockcliffe(055663) 372 FAX (055663) 422

In 7 acres of grounds, which provide a safe play area for children, this family-run hotel is a good base for exploring the attractive Solway coast. Bedrooms in the main house are traditional in style, while those in a ground floor wing are more modern and have their own patios. The comfortable lounge bar offers light meals at lunch time and in the evening.
15⇨🌂(2fb) CTV in all bedrooms ® T ✿ sB&B⇨🌂£35 dB&B⇨🌂£55 🍴
CTV 40P ※ ❄
♀ British & French V ☼ ✿ Sunday Lunch fr£8alc Dinner £12-£16alc Last dinner 9pm
Credit Cards ①②③ £

COLWYN BAY Clwyd Map 06 SH87

★★★ **64%** Norfolk House
Princes Dr LL29 8PF ☎(0492) 531757 FAX (0492) 533781
A large Victorian building in mature grounds just a short walk from the town centre and seafront. Very much a family run hotel, the atmosphere is friendly and relaxing. Impressive public areas include a choice of comfortable lounges with welcoming fires, the restaurant and breakfast room and a separate reading room overlooking the lawns. There is also an intimate bar.
24⇨🌂(3fb) CTV in all bedrooms ® T ✿ sB&B⇨🌂£35-£42 dB&B⇨🌂£56-£60 🍴
Lift (30P ❄
♀ English & French V ☼ ⚖ ✿ Bar Lunch £2.50-£10alc Dinner £13.75-£15 Last dinner 9pm
CONF. Thtr 35 Class 20 Board 20 Del from £60
Credit Cards ①②③⑤ £

★★★ **58%** Colwyn Bay
Penmaenhead LL29 9LD (2m E A547, follow signs 'Old Colwyn')
☎(0492) 516555 FAX (0492) 515565
Formerly called the 'Hotel 70 Degrees', this hotel is popular with business people. At the time of the inspection full-scale refurbishment was under way, including redecorating bedrooms and recarpeting the public areas.
43⇨🌂(7fb)1🚪 CTV in all bedrooms ® T sB&B⇨🌂£36.45 dB&B⇨🌂£52.95 🍴
200P xmas
♀ English & French V ☼ ⚖ Lunch £12.50-£13.80&alc Dinner £12-£19.05&alc Last dinner 9.30pm
CONF. Thtr 200 Class 100 Board 40 Del £59
Credit Cards ①②③④⑤

★★ **69%** Hopeside
Princes Dr, West End LL29 8PW (off A55) ☎(0492) 533244 FAX (0492) 532850
Conveniently situated for the town centre and seafront, this carefully maintained owner-run hotel has a warm and friendly atmosphere. Cheerful bedrooms are equipped with modern facilities and there is a small bar, comfortable foyer lounge and a restaurant offering a wide choice of dishes.
19⇨🌂✂ in 2 bedrooms CTV in all bedrooms ® T sB&B⇨🌂£25-£45 dB&B⇨🌂£40-£55 🍴
CTV 25P solarium
♀ English & French V ☼ ⚖ ✂ Lunch £5-£10&alc High tea £5-£8&alc Dinner £13-£18&alc Last dinner 9pm
CONF. Thtr 55 Class 55 Board 20
Credit Cards ①②③⑤

★★ **65%** Ashmount
College Av, Rhos-on-Sea LL28 4NT
☎(0492) 545479 & 544582 FAX (0492) 545479

The Ashmount is situated quite close to the promenade at Rhos-on-Sea. Bedrooms are furnished with good-quality dark units, and pretty coordinated fabrics are being introduced. As well as a small foyer sitting area, there is a comfortable bar and a coffee lounge adjacent to the hotel's restaurant.
17⇨🌂(4fb)✂ in 4 bedrooms CTV in all bedrooms ®❄ T sB&B⇨🌂£28.50-£35.25 dB&B⇨🌂£46-£60 🍴
10P xmas
♀ English & French V ☼ ⚖ ✿ ✂ Lunch £6.95-£20&alc Dinner £11.95-£16&alc Last dinner 8pm
Credit Cards ①②③⑤ £

★★ **64%** Lyndale
410 Abergele Rd, Old Colwyn LL29 9AB (on A547)
☎(0492) 515429 FAX (0492) 518805
This small privately owned hotel to the east of the town has bedrooms with modern furnishings and equipment. Other facilities include a lounge bar and a nicely decorated dining room with modern furniture, where a good range of popular dishes is served.
14⇨🌂(3fb)1🚪 CTV in all bedrooms ® sB&B⇨🌂£15-£32.50 dB&B⇨🌂£30-£52 🍴
CTV 20P xmas
♀ European V ☼ ⚖ ✂ Lunch £6.50-£8.50 Dinner £11-£14.50&alc Last dinner 8.30pm
Credit Cards ①②③ £

★★ **60%** Edelweiss
Lawson Rd LL29 8HD (coming from east take B5104 turn left at lights and round a right hand bend, turn left at give way on main road then 4th left into Lawson Rd) ☎(0492) 532314 FAX (0492) 534707
Close to the town centre and seafront, this friendly hotel has a games room and children's play area in the extensive lawned garden. It has modestly furnished bedrooms with modern facilities, several lounge areas, a cane-furnished bar and restaurant with a fixed price menu and carte extras.
25⇨🌂(3fb) CTV in all bedrooms ® T sB&B⇨🌂fr£23 dB&B⇨🌂fr£36 🍴

Colwyn Bay

25P ✤ solarium children's play area games room ⛳ xmas
♨ Welsh, English, French & Italian V ✿ ⌨ ✂ ✱ Bar Lunch
£1.25-£9.25alc Dinner £12.50-£18.45&alc Last dinner 8.30pm
CONF. Thtr 70 Class 50 Board 30 Del from £35
Credit Cards [1][2][3][5] (£)

★ **65% Whitehall**
Cayley Promenade, Rhos on Sea LL28 4EP ☎(0492) 547296
Closed Nov-Etr
This small and friendly, family-run holiday hotel overlooking Cayley Promenade at Rhos-on-Sea has a small patio with pretty flower borders. There is a comfortable lounge, small residents' bar and a restaurant that serves well cooked and enjoyable food. Many of the bedrooms have fine sea views.
13rm(1⇨6♠)(2fb) CTV in all bedrooms ®
CTV 5P 🚗
V ✿ ✂
Credit Cards [1][3]

★ **64% Glyndwr**
11 Marine Rd LL29 8PH (turn off A55 at Colwyn Bay sign at slip way traffic lights turn right past railway station, Marine Road is 6th on left) ☎(0492) 533254
Closed Nov-Dec
Guest are assured of a warm welcome to this friendly, family-run hotel which stands just a hundred yards from the Promenade and within easy walking distance of the shops. Neat, clean bedrooms offer comfortable beds and soft cushioned chairs, and honest home cooking is served in a dining room displaying an interesting plate collection; the cosy basement bar provides facilities for golf putting and miniature bowls.
10rm(7♠)(1fb) CTV in all bedrooms ® ✱ sB&B£16 sB&B♠£18 dB&B£28 dB&B♠£32 ⛔
CTV 10P
V ✿ ⌨ ✂ ✱ Lunch £4-£7 Dinner £7 Last dinner 7pm
Credit Cards [1][3][5] (£)

★★★ *Penmaenhead*
Old Colwyn
Colwyn Bay
Clwyd LL29 9LD
Tel: 0492 516555
Fax: 0492 515565
Previously called Hotel 70°

C

Occupying an enviable position commanding panoramic views of the Irish Sea, Colwyn Bay and the dramatic mountains of Snowdonia from all rooms.
This splendid modern Hotel offers a very high standard of comfort, service and luxury through-out. All bedrooms en suite with full facilities and sea views.
Elegant restaurant serving excellent cuisine in superb surroundings.
Ideally located for touring Snowdonia National Park and Conwy. Numerous golf courses nearby for the discerning golf enthusiast.
Excellent conference and banqueting facilities available for up to 200 persons.

Hopeside Hotel

BWRDD CROESO CYMRU
WALES TOURIST BOARD
♦♦♦♦   AA ★ ★

A quality hotel that is specifically aimed towards
The Business Traveller
All rooms are en-suite (some executive rooms)
Direct dial telephones
Colour televisions
Two conference rooms, two syndicate rooms
High quality restaurant cuisine
Solarium
Located directly off the A55
Close to the business sector of Colwyn Bay

Mid Week and Weekend Breaks available.

**WEST END, COLWYN BAY
CLWYD LL29 8PW**
Tel: 0492 533244   Fax: 0492 532850

Norfolk House Hotel ★★★

**PRINCES DRIVE, COLWYN BAY
NORTH WALES LL29 8PF
Telephone (0492) 531757
Fax (0492) 533781**

Discover old-fashioned courtesy, cordial hospitality and comfort in this family-owned hotel, with a relaxed and welcoming atmosphere. Excellent food and service. Pretty bedrooms, all en-suite, comfortable lounges and charming restaurant and bar. Situated close to beach, town and railway station. Pleasant gardens. Large Car Park. Ideal centre for touring North Wales. Short breaks a speciality.

Colwyn Bay - Coniston

★ 63% Fairways
12 Ellesmere Rd LL29 8RP ☎0492 530528 FAX 0492 534558
The Fairways is a friendly, family-run hotel a few minutes walk from the promenade, close to the town centre and railway station. The brightly decorated bedrooms vary in size but all are well equipped. There is a large lounge, small bar and separate dining room.
9⇌♠(4fb)⊁ in 1 bedroom CTV in all bedrooms ® ✱ sB&B⇌♠£18-£20 dB&B⇌♠£36-£40
CTV 4P ⊞ xmas
V ☼ ✱ Lunch £4-£6 High tea £5 Dinner £8 Last dinner 7.30pm
Credit Cards [1][3]

★ 63% Marine
West Promenade LL28 4BP ☎(0492) 530295
Closed Oct-Mar
The Marine has been run by friendly Brian and Sue Owen for over 11 years, and is situated on the promenade with good sea views from many rooms. There is a traditional lounge for residents, a small bar and restaurant serving a table d'hote menu. Bedrooms are neat and brightly decorated and all have good modern facilities.
14rm(11♠) CTV in all bedrooms ® ✱ sB&Bfr£16.50 sB&B♠£21-£22 dB&B£31-£33 dB&B♠£36-£38 🍽
CTV 11P ⊞
V ☼ ⊻ ✱ Bar Lunch £3-£7 High tea £7 Dinner fr£7 Last dinner 7pm
Credit Cards [2][5] £

COLYTON Devon Map 03 SY29

★★ 65% White Cottage
Dolphin St EX13 6NA ☎(0297) 552401 FAX (0297) 553897
A cosy, Grade II listed thatched cottage, with lots of exposed beams and stone walls, which continues to provide a warm, hospitable atmosphere. The architecture obviously imposes constraints and some rooms are small, but all are nicely decorated and well equipped with modern facilities. Honest, fresh cooking is served in the pretty little restaurant.
6⇌♠(1fb)1⊞ CTV in all bedrooms ® T ⋈ (ex guide dogs) sB&B⇌♠£31.90-£33.90 dB&B⇌♠£57.80-£59.80 🍽
16P ⊞ ✲ nc14yrs xmas
V ☼ ⊻ ✱ Lunch £6-£8.50alc High tea £4-£6alc Dinner £13.50-£19.90 Last dinner 8.45pm
Credit Cards [1][3]

COMBE MARTIN Devon Map 02 SS54

★★ 61% Rone House
King St EX34 0AD ☎(0271) 883428
Closed Nov-Feb (ex 23-27 Dec) RS Feb-Mar
This comfortable small holiday hotel is in the main street of the large village. Bedrooms vary in size, are freshly decorated and simply furnished.
11rm(4⇌4♠)(4fb) CTV in all bedrooms ® sB&B♠£16-£19 sB&B⇌♠£20-£23 dB&B£32-£38 dB&B⇌♠£36-£44 🍽
CTV 15P ⊞ ✲ ⌇ (heated) xmas
♀ International V ⊻ Bar Lunch £6-£9 Dinner £11&alc Last dinner 9.30pm
Credit Cards [1][3] £

COMRIE Tayside Perthshire Map 11 NN72

★★ 62% Comrie
Drummond St PH6 2DY (on A85) ☎(0764) 670239
RS Nov-Etr
This creeper-clad building is on the main road at the eastern end of the village. Well managed, it has a cosy atmosphere and provides good value meals and sound accommodation.
9⇌♠Annexe2⇌ CTV in all bedrooms ® T sB&B⇌♠£25-£27 dB&B⇌♠£50-£54 🍽
24P ⊞

V ☼ ⊻ Lunch £4-£6alc High tea fr£4alc Dinner £9.50-£14alc Last dinner 9pm
Credit Cards [1][3] £

★★ 60% Royal
Melville Square PH6 2DN ☎(0764) 670200
RS Oct-Mar
This traditionally run hotel is set in a small square by the main crossroads. It offers a lounge bar, a comfortable dining room and a quiet lounge upstairs. Bedrooms offer an acceptable standard of comfort.
9rm(8⇌)1⊞ CTV in all bedrooms ® T
30P 2⚘ ♪ snooker ⚙
♀ Scottish & French V ☼ Last dinner 9.30pm
Credit Cards [1][2][3]

CONGLETON Cheshire Map 07 SJ86

★★★ 64% Lion & Swan
Swan Bank CW12 1JR ☎(0260) 273115 FAX (0260) 299270
This town centre coaching inn dates back to the Tudor period and retains much of its original character with exposed beams and an ornately carved 400-year-old fireplace in the restaurant. Bedrooms vary in size and style, executive rooms are available along with 2 full suites and a honeymoon suite with a magnificent antique 4-poster bed.
21⇌♠(2fb)1⊞⊻ in 3 bedrooms CTV in all bedrooms ® T
CTV 80P 6⚘ ✲
♀ English & Continental V ☼ ⊻ Last dinner 9.30pm
Credit Cards [1][2][3][5]

CONISTON Cumbria Map 07 SD39

★★ 65% Coniston Sun
LA21 8HQ (signposted from village centre, off A593) ☎(05394) 41248
This friendly 16th-century inn standing high above the village has bright, comfortable bedrooms, an inviting lounge with books and a log fire and a cosy restaurant and bar, both offering home-cooked food.
11rm(7⇌3♠)2⊞ CTV in all bedrooms ® T ✱ sB&B⇌♠£20-£41 dB&B⇌♠£40-£70 🍽
20P ✲ xmas
V ☼ ⊻ ✱ Lunch £8.95-£15 Dinner £3.95-£11.95alc Last dinner 9pm
Credit Cards [1][3] £

★★ 64% Black Bull
Yewdale Rd LA21 8DU (in centre of village) ☎(05394) 41335 & 41668 FAX (05394) 41168
Steadily upgraded and extended over the last few years, this charming village inn dates back to the 16th century and is set in superb mountain scenery beside a rushing brook. Bedrooms are carefully decorated and an extensive range of food is available either in the bar or the pleasant restaurant.
10⇌♠Annexe5⇌♠(3fb)1⊞⊻ in 1 bedroom CTV in all bedrooms ® T ✱ sB&B⇌♠fr£30 dB&B⇌♠fr£50 🍽
CTV 12P 3⚘ ✲ pony trekking sailing wind surfing xmas
♀ English & French V ☼ ⊻ Last dinner 9pm
Credit Cards [1][3]

★★ 63% Yewdale
Yewdale Rd LA21 8LU ☎(05394) 41280
A good standard of value-for-money accommodation is provided at this delightful small hotel in the centre of the village. Bedrooms are bright, modern and freshly decorated. Part of the bar was once a bank and the bank counter is now the bar counter. A good range of food is available in both the bar and restaurant.
12rm(2⇌8♠)(4fb) CTV in all bedrooms ®
6P
V ☼ ⊻ Last dinner 8.30pm
Credit Cards [1][3]

★❀≗**73%** *Old Rectory*
Torver LA21 8AX (2.5m S of Coniston)
☎(05394) 41353 FAX (05394) 41156

This charming Victorian house stands in its own grounds and is lovingly cared for by the resident owners who provide attentive service. Bedrooms have coordinated fabrics. A well produced dinner is available from a set menu with a choice at the pudding course only. A typical meal might be haddock smokies, pork fillet Normandy, and raspberry vacherin or glazed lemon tart – home-made ice creams are also a speciality.

7⇌♠(1fb) CTV in all bedrooms ®
10P ⇌ ✿ sail boat hire
♀ English & Continental ✄

CONNEL Strathclyde *Argyllshire* Map **10** NM93

★★**65%** Falls of Lora
PA37 1PB (off A85, overlooking Loch Etive)
☎(063171) 483 FAX (063171) 694
Closed 25 Dec-Jan

This spacious roadside tourist hotel overlooks Loch Etive. It has a relaxing lounge and in addition to the restaurant there is a bar bistro with all day food and full evening meals. There are individually styled bedrooms in the original building, with more uniform style in the extension.

30⇌(4fb)1⊞ CTV in all bedrooms ® T sB&B⇌£29.50-£49.50
dB&B⇌£39-£99 ◨
CTV 40P 9⚡⇌ ✿
♀ Scottish & French V ✓ ⌸ ✄ Bar Lunch £5.75-£12.75alc
High tea £5.75-£7.75alc Dinner £17.50 Last dinner 8pm
CONF. Thtr 45 Class 20 Board 15
Credit Cards [1][2][3][5]

CONSTANTINE BAY Cornwall & Isles of Scilly
Map **02** SW87

★★★**76%** Treglos
PL28 8JH ☎Padstow(0841) 520727 FAX (0841) 521163
Closed 6 Nov-11 Mar

There is a relaxed country house atmosphere at this hotel, set in its own grounds a short walk from the beach. There are several comfortable lounges, a bridge room, open fires and indoor leisure facilities. Bedrooms are bright and clean; sizes vary, but most enjoy a view of the bay.

44⇌♠(12fb) CTV in all bedrooms T ✱ sB&B⇌♠£60-£76
dB&B⇌£111-£142 (incl dinner) ◨
Lift (CTV 50P 8⚡ (£1.50) ⇌ ✿ ▭ (heated) snooker croquet jacuzzi ♅
♀ English & French V ✓ ⌸ ✄ Lunch £11&alc High tea £7&alc Dinner £18.75&alc Last dinner 9.15pm
Credit Cards [1][3]
See advertisement under PADSTOW

CONTIN Highland *Ross & Cromarty* Map **14** NH45

★★★≗**68%** Coul House
IV14 9EY (from South by passing Inverness continue on A9 over Moray Firth bridge, after 5m take 2nd exit at roundabout on to A835 follow to Contin) ☎Strathpeffer(0997) 421487
FAX (0997) 421945

Set in 5 acres of secluded grounds, this Victorian mansion has a welcoming relaxed atmosphere. Individually furnished bedrooms vary in size but all have modern facilities, while elegant day rooms with log fires include a splendid octagonal drawing room and comfortable foyer lounge.

21⇌♠(3fb) CTV in all bedrooms ® T sB&B⇌♠£38-£54
dB&B⇌£64-£86 ◨
CTV 40P ⇌ ✿ ♪ pitch & putt ॐ xmas

➡

THE FALLS OF LORA HOTEL

AA★ ★

Oban 5 miles, only 2½-3 hours drive north-west of Glasgow or Edinburgh, overlooking Loch Etive this fine 2-star owner-run Hotel offers a warm welcome, good food, service and comfort. All rooms have central heating, private bathroom, radio/intercom, colour television and telephone. From luxury rooms (one with four-poster bed and king size round bath, another with a 7ft round bed and 'Jacuzzi' bathroom en suite) to inexpensive family rooms with bunk beds. FREE accommodation for children sharing parents' room. Relax in super cocktail bar with open log fire, there are over 100 brands of Whisky to tempt you and an extensive Bar Bistro Menu. Fishing, Gliding, Water-sports and Pony Trekking can be arranged. Out of season mini-breaks.

OPEN ALL YEAR. A FINE OWNER-RUN SCOTTISH HOTEL

Connel Ferry, By Oban, Argyll PA37 1PB
Tel: (063171) 483   Fax: (063171) 694

LION & SWAN HOTEL
Congleton, Cheshire

Maintaining a tradition of first-class food and hospitality stretching back more than 400 years, the Lion & Swan Hotel is Congleton's premier accommodation and function venue, the first and only 3-star rated establishment in this historic and bustling Cheshire market town.

With all 21 rooms recently refurbished and equipped to international standards, the Hotel offers superb modern facilities within a building of great character and charm. Noted for its exceptionally well-regarded restaurant, the Lion & Swan Hotel is operated by a talented, attentive and youthful management team who recently won an award for the quality of guest care and standard of service.

Swan Bank, Congleton, Cheshire
CW12 1JR Tel: 0260 273115
Fax: 0260 299270

Contin - Corbridge

♦ International **V** ⚜ ⚛ ✕ Lunch £10 Dinner £22.50&alc Last dinner 9pm
Credit Cards ①②⑤ £

★★ **62%Achility**
IV14 9EG ☏Strathpeffer(0997) 421355
Traditional Scottish hospitality and excellent views of the surrounding mountains are provided by this recently upgraded hotel. Bedrooms are bright and fresh, and an interesting bar features open stone walls, beams and a collection of bric a brac; a wide range of food is available both here and in the spacious restaurant.
12⇨♠ CTV in all bedrooms ® ✱ sB&B⇨♠£22.50-£27.50 dB&B⇨♠£35-£45 ₧
100P 🅿 ✿ ♪
♦ International **V** ⚜ ⚛ ✱ Lunch £8.50 Dinner £12 Last dinner 9.30pm
Credit Cards ①③

CONWY Gwynedd Map **06** SH77
See also **Rowen**

★★ **65%Sychnant Pass**
Sychnant Pass Rd LL32 8BJ (turn off A55 for Conwy, follow one way traffic, through arch and turn left on Mount Pleasant St, turn right onto Sychnant Pass, hotel 1.5m on right)
☏Aberconwy(0492) 596868 FAX (0492) 870009
This very pleasant hotel, run in informal and friendly style by Brian and Jeannie Jones, is set in 3 acres of mature grounds. Bedrooms have modern furnishings and some of the larger ones also have a sofa bed. There are two sitting rooms, a bar and the Four Seasons restaurant where local seafood frequently features on the menu.
13⇨♠(2fb) CTV in all bedrooms ® T sB&B⇨♠£30-£40 dB&B⇨♠£40-£60 ₧
CTV 30P ✿ sauna solarium jacuzzi spa bath 🅾 *xmas*
♦ British & French ⚜ ⚛ Lunch £10-£15alc High tea £3-£6alc Dinner £15-£20alc Last dinner 9.30pm
CONF. Board 20 Del from £50
Credit Cards ①②③⑤ £

★★★ **62%The Castle**
High St LL32 8DB ☏Aberconwy(0492) 592324
FAX (0492) 583351
FORTE Heritage
Established in the 15th century, this popular hotel boasts, in one of its comfortable bedrooms, a magnificent carved four-poster from Gwydr Castle, thought to date back to the same period. Other interesting features are the paintings offered and accepted from various artists over the years in return for board and lodging. The Castle Bar is very popular locally as well as with tourists.
29⇨♠(1fb)1⬚✕in 10 bedrooms CTV in all bedrooms ® T ✱ sB⇨♠£65 dB⇨♠£75 (room only) ₧
(30P *xmas*
V ⚜ ⚛ ✱ Sunday Lunch fr£10.95 Dinner fr£15.95&alc Last dinner 8.45pm
CONF. Thtr 35 Class 20 Board 20 Del from £80
Credit Cards ①②③⑤

★★ ⊛**72%Castle Bank**
Mount Pleasant LL32 8NY (follow one way system through town to BangorArchway and turn left into Mount Pleasant Road) ☏Aberconwy(0492) 593888
Closed Jan RS Dec & early-mid Feb
This impressive former school building, dating from 1850s, is in an elevated position overlooking the River Conwy estuary near the town walls. There is a comfortable bar and residents' lounge, and a pretty restaurant with stone walls and exposed beams. Here Marilyn Gilligan serves freshly cooked food from a daily changing, fixed price menu offering some fine choices.
9rm(8⇨♠)(3fb)✕in all bedrooms CTV in all bedrooms ® ✱
sB&B£25 sB&B♠£30.50 dB&B♠£53 ₧
CTV 12P 🅿

♦ International **V** Lunch fr£9 Dinner fr£13.50 Last dinner 8pm
Credit Cards ①③

★★ **57%The Park Hall**
Bangor Rd LL32 8DP (leave A55 at Conwy Morfa, 0.33m on right) ☏Aberconwy(0492) 592279
Closed 24-26 Dec
Park Hall is a small, family-run hotel. Bedrooms are modern and equipped with all the usual amenities. There are two interesting bars, one featuring a collection of old handbells and the other a display of construction helmets. Generous portions of food are served, and bar snacks are also available.
9⇨♠(2fb) CTV in all bedrooms ® T ✱ sB&B⇨♠£25-£27.50 dB&B⇨♠£45-£50
40P 🅿 ✿
♦ English, French & Italian **V** ⚜ ✕ ✱ Sunday Lunch £6.95-£7.50 Dinner £13.50-£15&alc Last dinner 9.30pm
Credit Cards ①②③⑤ £

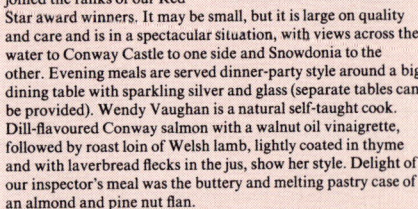

★⊛⊛⚲ THE OLD RECTORY
Llanrwst Rd LL28 5LF (0.5m from A470/A55 junct) (Welsh Rarebits)
☏Aberconwy(0492) 580611
FAX (0492) 584555
Closed 20 Dec-Jan

This year The Old Rectory has joined the ranks of our Red Star award winners. It may be small, but it is large on quality and care and is in a spectacular situation, with views across the water to Conway Castle to one side and Snowdonia to the other. Evening meals are served dinner-party style around a big dining table with sparkling silver and glass (separate tables can be provided). Wendy Vaughan is a natural self-taught cook. Dill-flavoured Conway salmon with a walnut oil vinaigrette, followed by roast loin of Welsh lamb, lightly coated in thyme and with laverbread flecks in the jus, show her style. Delight of our inspector's meal was the buttery and melting pastry case of an almond and pine nut flan.

4⇨♠Annexe2⇨♠3⬚✕in 4 bedrooms CTV in all bedrooms ® T ✱ sB&B⇨♠£53-£63 dB&B⇨♠£60-£98 (incl dinner) ₧
10P 🅿 ✿ nc5yrs
♦ British & French **V** ⚜ ✕ ✱ Dinner £26-£27.50 Last dinner 8pm
Credit Cards ①②③⑤

COPTHORNE
See **Gatwick Airport**

CORBRIDGE Northumberland Map **12** NY96

★★ **64%***Angel Inn*
Main St NE45 5LA ☏(0434) 632119
This small creeper-clad hotel in the town centre, though largely modernised, retains much historic charm. It has a comfortable wood-panelled foyer lounge, split-level restaurant and spacious lounge bar, both offering imaginative menus. Cosy bedrooms have modern amenities and staff are friendly.
5⇨♠ CTV in all bedrooms ® T ✕
5P
♦ English, French & Italian **V** ⚜ Last dinner 10pm
Credit Cards ①②③⑤

CORBY Northamptonshire Map 04 SP88

Forte Posthouse
Rockingham Rd NN17 1AE (just off A427)
☎(0536) 401348 FAX (0536) 66383

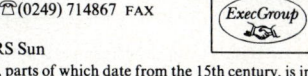

Suitable for both the business and leisure traveller, this bright hotel provides modern accommodation in well equipped bedrooms with en suite bathrooms. For more details about Forte Posthouse hotels, consult the Contents page, under Hotel Groups.
70⇌↑❋ B⇌↑£41.50-£53.50 (room only)
CONF. Thtr 400 Class 250 Board 40 Del £89.50

CORFE CASTLE Dorset Map 03 SY98

★★★ ✿64% Mortons House
East St BH20 5EE (on A351) ☎(0929) 480988 FAX (0929) 480820

This handsome manor house is steadily being improved by Mr and Mrs Langford. The bedrooms in the original house are cosy and have plenty of character, those in the modern part have pretty fabrics and fresh décor. The lounge is particularly pleasant, with a blazing open fire in cooler weather, wood panelled walls, deep sofa seating and fresh flowers. French chef Pierre Mathiot has brought a new enthusiasm to the restaurant.
14⇌↑Annexe3⇌↑(1fb)1⚁✗ in 3 bedrooms CTV in all bedrooms ® T sB&B⇌↑£55-£65 dB&B⇌↑£80-£96 ⌇
40P ❋ ✿ xmas
♨ English & French V ✧ ⚑ ✗ Lunch £12.50-£15 Dinner £22.50 Last dinner 8.30pm
CONF. Board 25 Del from £80.50
Credit Cards 1 3

CORNHILL-ON-TWEED Northumberland Map 12 NT83

★★★↯ 65% Tillmouth Park
TD12 4UU (on A698) ☎Coldstream(0890) 882255 FAX (0890) 882540

This imposing 19th-century mansion sits in its own grounds high above the River Till, close to its confluence with the Tweed. There is a cosy bar with a huge log fire, and an air of quiet relaxation prevails in the upstairs lounges and dining room. Bedrooms retain much of the style of yesteryear, quietly decorated but all with modern essentials. Staff, many long-serving, are friendly and attentive.
12⇌↑Annexe2⇌↑(1fb)1⚁ CTV in all bedrooms ® T ❋ sB&B⇌↑£58-£80 dB&B⇌↑£86-£110
50P ❋ ✿ xmas
♨ International V ✧ ⚑ ❋ Lunch £11-£15.50&alc Dinner £18.50 Last dinner 9.30pm
CONF. Thtr 40 Class 40 Board 12
Credit Cards 1 2 3 5

CORSE LAWN Hereford & Worcester Map 03 SO83

★★★ ✿71% Corse Lawn House
GL19 4LZ (on B4211 6m SW of Tewkesbury)
☎Gloucester(0452) 780479 & 780771 FAX (0452) 780840

This elegant Queen Anne building, set back from the village green, has individually styled guest rooms, many furnished with antiques, but all having good modern facilities and such thoughtful extras as home-made biscuits and fresh fruit. The restaurant is the focal point of the hotel, providing interesting menus of dishes based on the best possible ingredients. Genial hospitality and a relaxed atmosphere attract both tourists and business travellers.
19⇌↑2⚁ CTV in all bedrooms ® ✗ T sB&B⇌↑£65-£75 dB&B⇌↑£90 ⌇
50P 2☂ ❋ ✿ ≋ (heated) ♪ (hard) croquet lawn xmas

CORSHAM Wiltshire Map 03 ST86

★★★ ✿64% Rudloe Park
Leafy Ln SN13 0PA (on A4 1.5m W) ☎Bath(0225) 810555 FAX (0225) 811412

This Victorian country house is set in 4 acres of gardens and has sweeping views of the Box valley. Bedrooms are mostly spacious and offer many extras. The restaurant offers à la carte, table d'hôte and vegetarian menus. The kitchen team, led by Geoffrey Bell, carefully prepares such dishes as good home-made soups and breast of chicken chasseur, classically cooked and served with a selection of fresh vegetables. There are both sweet and cheese trollies, and an award-winning wine list.
11⇌↑(2fb)1⚁ CTV in all bedrooms ® T sB&B⇌↑£55-£65 dB&B⇌↑£60-£90 ⌇
70P ❋ ✿ croquet bowls nc10yrs xmas
♨ International V ✧ ⚑ ✗ Lunch £15-£20 Dinner £18-£23 Last dinner 10pm
CONF. Thtr 60 Class 50 Board 30 Del from £100
Credit Cards 1 2 3 4 5

★★ 65% Methuen Arms
2 High St SN13 0HB ☎(0249) 714867 FAX (0249) 712004
Closed 23-27 Dec RS Sun

This attractive hotel, parts of which date from the 15th century, is in the centre of town and is personally run by the Long family, who promote a friendly and relaxed atmosphere. Bedrooms are decorated and furnished in the style of the building, and there are popular bars, a skittle alley and a cosy restaurant with à la carte and table d'hôte menus.
19⇌↑Annexe6⇌↑(2fb) CTV in all bedrooms ® T ❋ sB&B⇌↑£41-£47 dB&B⇌↑£59-£65 ⌇
60P 3☂ (£12 per night) ✿ skittle-alley
♨ International V ✧ ❋ Lunch £14.50-£19.50&alc Dinner £14.50-£19.50&alc Last dinner 10pm
CONF. Thtr 30 Class 30 Board 18
Credit Cards 1 3

COVENTRY West Midlands Map 04 SP37

★★★★ 57% De Vere
Cathedral Square CV1 5RP ☎(0203) 633733 FAX (0203) 225299

This large hotel close to the cathedral has reserved parking in and direct access from the adjacent car park. Bedrooms are stylish, but our inspector found some less comfortably furnished than others. Bentleys Restaurant offers a carvery as well as an imaginative à la carte menu. Daimlers, the main bar, can get very busy.
190⇌↑(9fb)✗ in 20 bedrooms CTV in all bedrooms ® T ❋ sB&B⇌↑fr£75 dB&B⇌↑fr£85 ⌇
Lift ⦿ 130☂ xmas
♨ International V ✧ ⚑ ✗ ❋ Lunch £9.50-£12 High tea £3.50-£4.50 Dinner £12.95-£14.95&alc Last dinner 10.15pm
CONF. Thtr 400 Class 280 Board 40 Del from £75
Credit Cards 1 2 3 4 5

★★★ ✿69% Brooklands Grange Hotel & Restaurant
Holyhead Rd CV5 8HX (on A4114, off A45 at Allesley roundabout) ☎(0203) 601601 FAX (0203) 601277

This Jacobean farmhouse has been sympathetically converted to offer accommodation in well equipped, attractive bedrooms, those in the oldest part of the hotel having beautiful original beams. Proprietors Lesley Jackson and Charles Davis provide a personal

Coventry

service, and the staff are friendly and welcoming. The elegant restaurant offers a varied brasserie-style menu.
30⇨♠(1fb)⊁in 4 bedrooms CTV in all bedrooms ® T ✈ (ex guide dogs) sB&B⇨♠£75 dB&B⇨♠£95 ℞
《52P ✿ ♫ xmas
♀ International V ✿ ♋ ⊁ ✱ Sunday Lunch £12.50-£15.50&alc Dinner £15.50&alc Last dinner 10pm
Credit Cards 1 2 3 5

★★★ 66% **Coventry Knight**
London Rd, Ryton on Dunsmore CV8 3DY (SE on A45) (Lansbury) ☎(0203) 301585 FAX (0203) 301610
This modern, company owned hotel is convenient for the city centre. Guest rooms are spacious with fresh décor, modern furnishings and a good range of equipment. There is a large bar and an attractive restaurant.
49⇨♠(2fb)⊁in 5 bedrooms CTV in all bedrooms ®⚐T ✈ (ex guide dogs) ✱ sB&B⇨♠fr£65.50 dB&B⇨♠fr£77 ℞
《150P ♩ putting green table tennis
♀ English & Continental V ✿ ♋ ⊁ ✱ Lunch fr£8.95 Dinner fr£14.75 Last dinner 9.45pm
CONF. Thtr 300 Class 100 Board 80 Del from £95
Credit Cards 1 2 3 5

★★★ 65% **Leofric**
Broadgate CV1 1LZ ☎(0203) 221371 FAX (0203) 551352
This large city centre hotel has undergone extensive refurbishment to provide modern accommodation with a good range of facilities. Public areas include Frederic's à la carte restaurant, the Brasserie and a hair salon. It is best to ask for advice on parking when booking.
94⇨♠(5fb) CTV in all bedrooms ®⚐T ✈ (ex guide dogs)
Lift 《
♀ International V ✿ ♋ Last dinner 9.45pm
Credit Cards 1 2 3 5

★★★ 62% **Hylands**
Warwick Rd CV3 6AU (near railway station on A444) ☎(0203) 501600 FAX (0203) 501027
Closed 24-26 Dec
Accommodation consists of standard and executive rooms, all offering a wide range of facilities, some overlooking parkland opposite. The Warwick restaurant offers a carvery and à la carte menu. Friendly staff create a home- from-home atmosphere for a predominantly commercial clientèle.
55⇨♠(4fb) CTV in all bedrooms ® T sB&B⇨♠£74-£81 dB&B⇨♠£90-£100 ℞
《 CTV 60P ♫
♀ English & Continental V ✿ ♋ Last dinner 9.45pm
Credit Cards 1 2 3 5

★★★ 61% **The Chace**
London Rd, Toll Bar End CV3 4EQ (on A423) ☎(0203) 303398 FAX (0203) 301816
Convenient for the city centre, the original building dates from the 19th century and bedrooms there tend to be more spacious and of better quality than in the modern extension.
67⇨♠(2fb)⊁in 20 bedrooms CTV in all bedrooms ® T ✱ sB&B⇨♠£40-£75 dB&B⇨♠£50-£105 (room only) ℞
《80P ✿ childrens play area ♫ ✿ xmas
V ✿ ♋ ⊁ ✱ Lunch £8.50-£25 Dinner fr£15.95&alc Last dinner 9.45pm
Credit Cards 1 2 3 5

★★★ 58% **Novotel**
Wilsons Ln CV6 6HL (N, near junct 3 of M6) ☎(0203) 365000 FAX (0203) 362322
Conveniently located to the north of the city centre, this hotel offers all the standard Novotel facilities, including satellite TV in the well equipped, bedrooms. The restaurant is open from early morning

until midnight for full meals or snacks. Public areas are pleasant in a light, modern style.
100⇨♠(100fb)⊁in 26 bedrooms CTV in all bedrooms ®⚐T ✱ sB⇨♠£39.50-£53 dB⇨♠£49.50-£63 (room only) ℞
Lift 《 ⊞ CTV 160P ✿ ⚐ (heated) petanque
♀ British & French V ✿ ♋ ⊁ Lunch £3.40-£17alc Dinner £11.95-£13.95&alc Last dinner mdnt
CONF. Thtr 200 Class 100 Board 50 Del from £70
Credit Cards 1 2 3 4 5

●●●●●●●●●●●●●●●●●●●●●●●●●●●●●●●●●●
Campanile
4 Wigston Rd, Walsgrave CV2 2SD (exit 2 of M6, at 2nd roundabout turn right) ☎(0203) 622311 FAX (0203) 602362
A nearby bar and bistro restaurant provides refreshments for travellers staying at this modern accommodation building. Bedrooms are well equipped and have en suite bathrooms. For more details about Campanile, consult the Contents page, under Hotel Groups.
Annexe50⇨♠ B⇨♠£35.75 (room only)
CONF. Thtr 35 Class 35 Board 25 Del from £42.80

Campanile
Abbey Rd, Whitley CV3 4BJ (signposted from A46/A423 rdbt) ☎(0203) 639922 FAX (0203) 306898
A nearby bar and bistro restaurant provides refreshments for travellers staying at this modern accommodation building. Bedrooms are well equipped and have en suite bathrooms. For more details about Campanile, consult the Contents page, under Hotel Groups.
51⇨♠
CONF. Thtr 35 Class 35 Board 25 Del from £42.80

Forte Crest
Hinckley Rd, Walsgrave CV2 2HP
☎(0203) 613261 FAX (0203) 621736
A large modern hotel with a wide range of services and amenities, designed particularly for the business traveller. Bedrooms are smart, comfortable and well equipped. For more details about Forte Crest hotels, consult the Contents page, under Hotel Groups.
147⇨♠✱ B⇨♠£80 (room only)
CONF. Thtr 450 Class 300 Board 100 Del £115

Forte Posthouse
Rye Hill, Allesley CV5 9PH (on A45)
☎(0203) 402151 FAX (0203) 402235
Suitable for both the business and leisure traveller, this bright hotel provides modern accommodation in well equipped bedrooms with en suite bathrooms. For more details about Forte Posthouse hotels, consult the Contents page, under Hotel Groups.
184⇨♠✱ B⇨♠£41.50-£53.50 (room only)

Hilton National Coventry
Paradise Way, Walsgrave Triangle CV2 2ST
☎(0203) 603000
This is a bright, modern hotel with informal restaurant, aimed at both the business and leisure guest. All bedrooms have en-suite bathrooms and a range of modern facilities. For more information about Hilton National, consult the Contents page, under Hotel Groups.
172⇨♠✱ B⇨♠£95 (room only)
CONF. Thtr 600 Class 350 Board 30 Del £140

Remember to book early for holiday
and bank holiday times.

Craigellachie - Crathorne

COWES
See **Wight, Isle of**

CRAIGELLACHIE Grampian *Banffshire* Map **15** NJ24

★★★ ❀**74% Craigellachie**
AB38 9SR (Logis) ☎Aberlour(0340) 881204 FAX (0340) 881253
This refurbished Highland hotel combines modern facilities with Victorian charm, and is enthusiastically run. Comfortable accommodation ranges from spacious, traditional-style master rooms furnished with antiques, to modern standard rooms. There is a choice of relaxing lounges, a cosy well stocked cocktail bar and a spacious dining room, where chef John Barber offers interesting Scottish dishes cooked and presented in the modern style.
30⇌ℿ(2fb)1⊟ CTV in all bedrooms ® T sB&B⇌ℿ£54.50-£78.50 dB&B⇌ℿ£91-£113 ₧
《 70P ⊞ ❀ ♪ sauna solarium gymnasium games room *xmas*
V ✿ ♨ ✕ Bar Lunch £3-£9.75alc High tea £12.50-£15alc Dinner fr£27.50&alc Last dinner 9.30pm
CONF. Thtr 45 Class 15 Board 20 Del from £79.50
Credit Cards ①②③④⑤

CRAIL Fife Map **12** NO60

★★ **62% Balcomie Links**
Balcomie Rd KY10 3TN ☎(0333) 50237
This holiday hotel overlooking the Firth of Forth from a position just east of the picturesque village offers a sound standard of neatly maintained accommodation; public areas include a popular, spacious lounge, an attractive dining room and a games room.
11⇌ℿ(1fb) CTV in all bedrooms ® ✳ sB&B⇌ℿ£25 dB&B⇌ℿ£50
40P ⊞ games room *xmas*
V ✿ ♨ ✳ Bar Lunch £2.50-£8&alc Dinner £8-£15alc Last dinner 9.30pm

★**63% Croma**
Nethergate KY10 3TU ☎(0333) 50239
Closed Nov-Mar
Quietly situated in a residential area of the picturesque village, this privately owned hotel offers simple but clean accommodation and a friendly atmosphere.
8rm(4⇌ℿ)(2fb) CTV in all bedrooms sB&B£15-£20 sB&B⇌ℿ£20-£25 dB&B£25-£32 dB&B⇌ℿ£30-£40
10P ⊞
V ✿ ✕ Lunch £3-£5 Dinner £10 Last dinner 10pm

CRANBROOK Kent Map **05** TQ73

★★ **67% Hartley Mount Country House**
Hartley Rd TN17 3QX ☎(0580) 712230 FAX (0580) 713099
A fine Edwardian manor house, Hartley Mount has been thoughtfully furnished in keeping with the period. There are 2 comfortable lounges, with a small conservatory extension serving as a cocktail bar, and an attractive dining room offering a frequently changing set price menu. All en suite bedrooms are quite spacious, well equipped and comfortable.
6⇌ℿ(1fb)2⊟ ✕ in all bedrooms CTV in all bedrooms ® T ✕ (ex guide dogs) sB&B⇌ℿ£55-£70 dB&B⇌ℿ£70-£100 ₧ CTV 30P 2⊙ (charged) ❀ ♀ (grass) croquet pitch & putt
V ✿ ♨ ✕ Lunch fr£12.50 High tea £4-£6alc Dinner fr£15.50&alc Last dinner 9.30pm
Credit Cards ①②③

Irish entries appear in a separate section that follows the main directory.

CRANTOCK Cornwall & Isles of Scilly Map **02** SW76

★★ **67% Crantock Bay**
West Pentire TR8 5SE (off A 3075 towards West Pentire Headland) ☎(0637) 830229
FAX (0637) 831111
RS mid Nov-mid Mar
Beautifully sited on the West Pentire headland, with sandy Crantock beach below, this warm and friendly hotel gives sweeping views across the bay, particularly from its spacious lounges and attractive dining room.
35⇌ℿ(4fb) CTV in all bedrooms ® T sB&B⇌ℿ£37.50-£54.50 dB&B⇌ℿ£74-£108 (incl dinner) ₧
35P ⊞ ❀ ▦ (heated) ♀ (hard) sauna gymnasium putting croquet ⚘ *xmas*
V ✿ ♨ ✕ Sunday Lunch £8.90 Dinner £13.50 Last dinner 8pm
CONF. Thtr 50 Board 20
Credit Cards ①②③⑤

CRATHORNE North Yorkshire Map **08** NZ40

★★★★ ❀⊞**70% Crathorne Hall**
TS15 0AR (on A67, just off A19) ☎Stokesley(0642) 700398
FAX (0642) 700814
Set in 15 acres of woodland and landscaped gardens with views of the Cleveland Hills, this stately home was one of the largest to be built in the Edwardian era. It has been extensively restored retaining many original features, and the principal public rooms are all very grand and elegant. The Eden Restaurant is a worthy setting for the fine modern cooking of chef Alan Todd. Bedrooms vary from very impressive to more compact, but all are attractively furnished and decorated.
37⇌ℿ(4fb)1⊟ ✕ in 9 bedrooms CTV in all bedrooms ® T sB&B⇌ℿ£89.50-£115 dB&B⇌ℿ£110-£160 ₧
《 120P ❀ ♪ croquet jogging track ♫ *xmas*

➡

Brooklands Grange Hotel & Restaurant
Holyhead Road Coventry CV5 8HX
Telephone: (0203) 601601 Fax: (0203) 601277

Surround yourself in the comfort and charm of this beautifully restored and refurbished 16th Century Jacobean farmhouse. Offering you executive accommodation and an excellent restaurant serving you the very best in contemporary English cooking. Ideally located for easy and direct access to Birmingham International Airport, the N.E.C. and the City of Coventry.

Crathorne - Criccieth

♀ English & French V ♥ ⚲ Lunch £14.50&alc Dinner £21&alc Last dinner 10pm
CONF. Thtr 200 Class 80 Board 50 Del from £125
Credit Cards ①②③⑤

CRAWLEY
See **Gatwick Airport**

CREWE Cheshire Map 07 SJ75

★★★ 62% Hunters Lodge
Sydney Rd, Sydney CW1 1LU (1m from Crewe station, off A534)
☎(0270) 583440 & 588216 FAX (0270) 500353
Bedrooms in this modern hotel are all in red brick annexe buildings and are well appointed and comfortable. There is a choice of bars and the Tudor-style restaurant offers a good selection of food.
42⇨♚(1fb)3⚐⌁in 4 bedrooms CTV in all bedrooms ®⚑T ✗ (ex guide dogs) sB&B⇨♚£28-£50 dB&B⇨♚£44-£64 ⚑
《 CTV 240P ✿ ♪ sauna solarium gymnasium games room jacuzzi ஃ xmas
♀ International V ♥ ⚲ ✻ Lunch £7.75-£11 Dinner fr£12.50&alc Last dinner 9.30pm
CONF. Thtr 160 Class 100 Board 80 Del from £59.25
Credit Cards ①②③

★★ 68% White Lion
Weston CW2 5NA (2m S A5020) ☎(0270) 587011 & 500303 FAX (0270) 500303
Closed Xmas & New Year
This timber-framed Tudor farmhouse retains much of its original character, with lots of old beams and interesting bric-a-brac. A modern extension contains the modern, well equipped bedrooms, two with lounge areas and luxurious bathrooms, as well as the bright restaurant and pleasant cocktail bar. The carte offers a comprehensive choice of dishes, and bar meals are also available.
16⇨♚(2fb)⌁in 2 bedrooms CTV in all bedrooms ®⚑T ✻ sB&B⇨♚£47 dB&B⇨♚£57 ⚑
《 100P ✿ ♪ crown green bowling
♀ English & French V ♥ ⚲ ✻ Lunch £11.95 Dinner £14.95&alc Last dinner 9.30pm
Credit Cards ①②③④⑤

Forte Travelodge
Alasager Rd, Barthomley CW5 5PT (5m E, at junc 16 M6/A500)
☎(0270) 883157 Central Res (0800) 850950

FORTE Travelodge

This modern building offers a good standard of accommodation for overnight stops. Smart, spacious and well equipped bedrooms, all with en suite bathrooms, are suitable for family use, and meals may be taken at the nearby family restaurant. For more details about Travelodges, consult the Contents page, under Hotel Groups.
42⇨♚✻ B⇨♚£31.95 (room only)

CRIANLARICH Central Map 10 NN32

⌂ Benmore Lodge
FK20 8QS (on A85) ☎(08383) 210
RS Nov-14 Mar
This small complex lies on the eastern fringe of the village. The cosy bedrooms, in 3 pine-clad lodges with verandahs, are well laid out and cheerful in light pine. The bar and restaurant in the main building are plain and practical but offer reasonably priced meals.
Annexe8♚(2fb) CTV in all bedrooms ® dB&B♚£50-£52 ⚑
50P ✿ ♪ canoeing skiing xmas
♀ International V ♥ ⚲ Lunch £6-£12alc Dinner £13&alc Last dinner 8.45pm
Credit Cards ①③

CRICCIETH Gwynedd Map 06 SH43

★★★⚜ 67% Bron Eifion Country House
LL52 0SA (1m W on A497) ☎(0766) 522385
FAX (0766) 522003

Set just north of the town in five acres of mature grounds, this nineteenth-century country house features a unique panelled staircase and minstrels' gallery finished in pine; the hall which this overlooks is one of several relaxing lounge areas, and an attractive conservatory restaurant with views of the lovely gardens can also be used for functions. Many of the bedrooms are furnished with fine period pieces, five having four-poster beds.
19⇨♚(4fb)5⚐ CTV in all bedrooms ®⚑T ✻ sB&B⇨♚£45-£53 dB&B⇨♚£70-£94 ⚑
CTV 80P ✿ clock golf croquet outdoor chess ஃ xmas
♀ International V ♥ ⚲ ✻ Lunch £9.75-£10.95 Dinner £17.50&alc Last dinner 9.30pm
CONF. Thtr 30 Class 25 Board 25 Del from £55
Credit Cards ①②③

★★⚜ 67% Mynydd Ednyfed Country House
Caernarfon Rd LL52 0PH (0.75m N on B4411) ☎(0766) 523269
Closed 25-26 Dec
Resident proprietors continue to improve this delightful little country house hotel, which stands in 7 acres of grounds and gardens overlooking the castle and Tremadog Bay. Its attractive accommodation, equipped in modern style, will appeal equally to business people and holiday-makers.
8rm(4⇨2♚)(1fb)2⚐ CTV in all bedrooms ® T
30P ✿
♀ English & Continental V Last dinner 8.45pm
Credit Cards ①②③⑤

★★ 66% Gwyndy
Llanystumdwy LL52 0SP (turn off A497 into village of Llanystumdwy follow road for .25m, hotel is next to church) ☎(0766) 522720
Closed Nov-Feb
This friendly, personally run hotel has a cottage-style dining room, cosy lounge and old world lounge bar, with its exposed beams and inglenook fireplace, in the original 17th-century stone-built house. The spacious modern bedrooms are in 2 adjacent buildings.
Annexe10⇨♚(5fb) CTV in all bedrooms ® sB&B⇨♚£28 dB&B⇨♚£48
CTV 20P ⚐ ♪
♀ British & French ♥ ⚲ ⌁ Lunch £8.50-£10.50 Dinner £10.50-£11 Last dinner 9pm

★★ 66% Parciau Mawr
High St LL52 0RP ☎(0766) 522368
Closed Nov-Mar
Most of this large stone-built house was built at the turn of the century, but older parts date back some 300 years. It stands on the edge of town in 3 acres of ground and provides well equipped accommodation popular with holiday-makers.
6⇨♚Annexe6♚(1fb) CTV in all bedrooms ® ✻ sB&B⇨♚£27-£29 dB&B⇨♚£46-£50 ⚑
30P ⚐ ✿ nc5yrs
♀ English & French ♥ ⚲ ⌁
Credit Cards ①③

★★ 62% Plas Isa
Porthmadog Rd LL52 0HP (E on main road) ☎(0766) 522443
Closed 24-28 Dec
On the main road just east of the town centre, with views of the sea and the castle, this small personally run hotel has well equipped bedrooms with modern furnishings. Public rooms include an attractive dining room, lounge bar and small conservatory lounge.
14⇨♚(3fb) CTV in all bedrooms ®⚑T
CTV 14P
♀ Chinese, French, Indian & Italian V ♥ Last dinner 8.45pm
Credit Cards ①③⑤

Criccieth - Crickhowell

★★ 59% *Plas Gwyn*
Pentrefelin LL52 0PT (1m NE A497) ☎(0766) 522559 FAX (0766) 523200

This privately owned hotel is particularly popular with commercial guests and for local functions. It has well equipped modern bedrooms and open-plan bars, a restaurant and small entrance lounge.

14rm(6fb) CTV in all bedrooms ® T
CTV 50P
♀ English, French & Italian V ♦ ♨ Last dinner 9pm
Credit Cards [1][2][3][5]

★★ 58% Lion
Y Maes LL52 0AA (turn off A497 in the centre of Criccieth on to village green north, hotel located on green) ☎(0766) 522460 FAX (0766) 523075
RS Nov-Mar

This privately owned hotel, is centrally situated and convenient for the shops, beach and castle. It is popular with holiday-makers and coach parties.

33rm(4fb) CTV in all bedrooms ® T ✱ sB&B⇨↑£23 dB&B⇨↑£44 ◨
Lift 20P 12☟ ✿ xmas
♀ Welsh & French V ♦ ♨ ⁄ ✱ Lunch £6.75-£9.25 Dinner £12.50-£16 Last dinner 8.30pm
Credit Cards [1][2][3][5] £

★ 66% Abereistedd
West Pde LL52 0EN ☎(0766) 522710
Closed Nov-Feb

This small, friendly, privately owned and run hotel provides well maintained and comfortable accommodation. It offers uninterrupted views of Cardigan Bay and the Merioneth Mountains, and the town centre and castle are within a few minutes' walk.

12rm(8↑)(2fb) CTV in all bedrooms ® ✱ sB&B£17.50-£19.50 sB&B↑£19.50-£21.50 dB&B£35-£39 dB&B↑£39-£43 ◨
12P
♀ English & French V ♦ ♨ ⁄ ✱ Bar Lunch £2-£3.50 Dinner £9 Last dinner 7.30pm
£

★ 62% Caerwylan
LL52 0HW ☎(0766) 522547
Closed Nov-Etr

The Caerwylan is a well furnished and comfortable family-run hotel overlooking the sea.

25rm⇨ CTV in all bedrooms ® ✱ sB&B⇨↑fr£18.50 dB&B⇨↑fr£37 ◨
Lift CTV 8P 8☟ (£1.10) ✿
♦ ♨ ✱ Sunday Lunch fr£7 Dinner fr£8.95 Last dinner 7.30pm

CRICK Northamptonshire Map 04 SP57

Forte Posthouse
NN6 7XR (at junct 18 of M1) ☎(0788) 822101 FAX (0788) 823955

FORTE Posthouse

Suitable for both the business and leisure traveller, this bright hotel provides modern accommodation in well equipped bedrooms with en suite bathrooms. For more details about Forte Posthouse hotels, consult the Contents page, under Hotel Groups.

88⇨↑ ✱ B⇨↑£41.50-£53.50 (room only)
CONF. Thtr 200 Class 85 Board 60 Del £89.50

The AA's star rating scheme is the market leader in hotel classification.

CRICKHOWELL Powys Map 03 SO21

★★★ ❀❀64% Bear
NP8 1BW (Welsh Rarebits) ☎(0873) 810408 FAX (0873) 811696

A perennial favourite, this 15th-century former coaching inn now offers new bedrooms around the adjacent flower-filled courtyard, which combine modern facilities with character and charm. Rooms in the main house are not so spacious by comparison. There are congenial bars with flagstone floors and cosy little restaurants. Cooking by Shaun Ellis continues to please, with robust, honest textures and flavours.

14rm(7⇨6↑) Annexe13⇨(6fb)1☒ CTV in all bedrooms ® T sB&B⇨↑£42-£55 dB&B⇨↑£50-£70
CTV 38P
♀ English & French V ♦ Lunch £15.50-£20alc Dinner £15.50-£20alc Last dinner 9.30pm
CONF. Thtr 60 Board 40 Del from £70
Credit Cards [1][2][3]

See advertisement on page 201

★★★ 60% Manor
Brecon Rd NP8 1SE (on A40) ☎(0873) 810212 FAX (0873) 811938

In an elevated position above the town, this completely modernised hotel was the birthplace of Sir George Everest, in whose honour the mountain was named.

17rm↑(1fb) CTV in all bedrooms ® T ⚔ (ex guide dogs) ✱ sB&B⇨↑£35-£40 dB&B⇨↑£60-£85 ◨
☾ 200P ✿ ▣ (heated) sauna solarium gymnasium beauty salon spa bath steam room xmas
V ♦ ♨ ✱ Sunday Lunch £7.95
CONF. Thtr 300 Class 100 Board 150 Del from £65
Credit Cards [1][2][3]

AA ★★★   WTB ❀❀❀❀ HIGHLY COMMENDED   Ashley Courtenay
Johansens   Egon Ronay Signpost

BRON EIFION
COUNTRY HOUSE HOTEL

Criccieth, Gwynedd, North Wales LL52 0SA.
Telephone: Criccieth (0766) 522385
Fax: (0766) 522003

A magnificent Country House, with Minstrels' Gallery, vaulted ceiling and log fires. Set in the tranquillity of five acres of lovely gardens, overlooking Cardigan Bay. Relax in this super atmosphere, whilst being very close to the many tourist and sporting attractions of Snowdonia. Along with the delightful Conservatory Restaurant and fine cuisine, all rooms are en suite and fully equipped. Four posters available. Bargain breaks all year. Christmas and New Year packages.

Crickhowell - Crooklands

★★ ❀ ♨ 70% Gliffaes Country House
NP8 1RH (W, 1m from A40) ☎ Bwlch(0874) 730371 FAX (0874) 730463
Closed 6 Jan-25 Feb
Dating from the 18th century and magnificently positioned in 29 acres of garden and parkland beside the River Usk, Gliffaes is a welcoming country house hotel which has been run by the same family for over 40 years. Bedrooms, many with lovely river views, are furnished with a mixture of antiques and pine, the Lodge providing an ideal alternative for those with children or pets. There are comfortable sitting rooms and a restaurant offering table d'hôte and à la carte menus.
19⇌♠Annexe3⇌♠(3fb) CTV in all bedrooms ® T ✱
sB&B⇌♠£32.50-£41 dB&B⇌♠£65-£96 ♬
CTV 34P ✿ ♀ (hard) ♪ snooker painting croquet putting
♡ European V ♢ ℒ ⅍ Lunch £11 Dinner fr£18.50&alc Last dinner 9.15pm
Credit Cards 1 2 3 5

★★ 67% Ty Croeso
Dardy, Llangattock NP8 1PU ☎ (0873) 810573
FAX (0873) 810573

Ty Croeso means 'welcome home', and the hotel has certainly come a long way since it was the infirmary for the local workhouse! It enjoys lovely views over the valley and the Brecon and Monmouth Canal. The restaurant is popular, offering a good selection of dishes while no fewer than 30 malt whiskies are available in the comfortable lounge. Most bedrooms are furnished in modern pine.
8rm(6⇌♠)(1fb) CTV in all bedrooms ® T ✱ dB&B⇌♠£50-£65 ♬
20P ⇌ ✿ xmas
V ♢ ℒ ✱ Bar Lunch £4.95-£5.95alc Dinner £13.95&alc Last dinner 9.30pm
Credit Cards 1 2 3 ⓔ

CRIEFF Tayside *Perthshire* Map **11** NN82

★★ 68% Murray Park
Connaught Ter PH7 3DJ (off A85 to Perth)
☎ (0764) 653731 FAX (0764) 655311

Noel and Ann Scott are as enthusiastically involved as ever in their popular hotel, set in a quiet residential area. The cosy lounge bar is the focal point, while the foyer lounge and dining room extension have been built onto the original stone walls. The bedrooms are being improved, and there is an new extension containing 8 rooms.
21⇌(1fb) CTV in all bedrooms ® T ✱ sB&B⇌£42.50-£47 dB&B⇌£61-£68
50P ⇌ ✿ shooting stalking
♡ Scottish & French V ♢ ✱
CONF. Thtr 25 Class 15 Board 20 Del from £55
Credit Cards 1 2 3 5 ⓔ

★★ 59% The Drummond Arms
James Square PH7 3HX ☎ (0764) 652151 FAX (0764) 652151
Commanding a central position in the town, this traditional resort hotel, which has a popular coach tour trade, offers reasonably priced accommodation and meals.
29rm(23⇌♠)Annexe7⇌♠(3fb) CTV in all bedrooms ® T ✱
sB&Bfr£21 sB&B⇌♠fr£25.50 dB&Bfr£42 dB&B⇌♠fr£51 ♬
Lift 30P xmas
V ♢ Last dinner 8.30pm
Credit Cards 1 3 ⓔ

★ 66% Lockes Acre
7 Comrie Rd PH7 4BP ☎ (0764) 652526
Set in its own grounds on the western edge of the town overlooking the Ochil Hills, the Kennedys' small and welcoming holiday hotel offers comfortable well equipped bedrooms, though some are compact.
7rm(4♠)(2fb) CTV in all bedrooms ®

CTV 35P ⇌ ✿
♡ International V ♢ ℒ ⅍ Last dinner 8.30pm
Credit Cards 1 3

CROCKETFORD Dumfries & Galloway *Kirkcudbrightshire* Map **11** NX87

★ 56% Lochview Motel
Crocketford Rd DG2 8RF (on A75) ☎ (055669) 281
Closed 26 Dec & 1 Jan
This bungalow-style motel overlooks Loch Auchenreoch. It offers compact and modestly furnished annexe accommodation. Public areas are limited to the popular lounge bar where food is available all day.
7♠ CTV in all bedrooms ® ✖
80P ♪ ♫
♢ ℒ
Credit Cards 1 3

CROMARTY Highland *Ross & Cromarty* Map **14** NH76

★★ 66% Royal
Marine Ter IV11 8YN ☎ (03817) 217
In a waterfront setting, overlooking the small harbour and Cromarty Firth, this popular family-run holiday hotel has a relaxed atmosphere and offers a choice of inviting lounges. There is an extensive bar menu and hearty Taste of Scotland dishes are served in the spacious dining room. Smart, comfortable bedrooms are in traditional style.
10⇌♠(2fb) CTV in all bedrooms ® sB&B⇌♠£28-£30 dB&B⇌♠£50-£55 ♬
CTV 20P 3 ✿
V ♢ ℒ Lunch fr£11.50 High tea fr£6.50 Dinner £16.50-£17.50 Last dinner 8pm
Credit Cards 1 2 3

CROMER Norfolk Map **09** TG24

★★ 68% Red Lion
Brooke St NR27 9HD ☎ (0263) 514964
Closed 24-26 Dec
This small Victorian hotel is in an elevated position on the seafront. Bedrooms are generally of a comfortable size and are pleasantly furnished. The first floor residents' lounge has an unusual turret window with views over the beach and slipway. A good choice of dishes is available in the restaurant plus imaginative bar meals.
12⇌♠(1fb) CTV in all bedrooms ® ✖
CTV 8P snooker sauna solarium gymnasium
♡ English & French V ♢ ℒ Last dinner 9.30pm
Credit Cards 1 3

CROOKLANDS Cumbria Map **07** SD58

★★★ ❀ 65% Crooklands
LA7 7NW (on A65, 1.5m from junct 36 of M6) ☎ (05395) 67432 FAX (05395) 67525

(Rosette awarded for dinner only)
Set in open countryside, this attractive hotel offers 2 styles of bedroom, some in a modern extension to the rear. Bars are full of character, with roughcast walls and lots of exposed beams. The Hayloft Restaurant, also with beams, provides the perfect setting for the well produced dinner. A separate buttery restaurant is also available.
30⇌♠⅍ in 2 bedrooms CTV in all bedrooms ® T ✖ (ex guide dogs) sB&B⇌♠£45-£65 dB&B⇌♠£65-£80 ♬
150P pool table xmas
♡ French V ♢ Lunch fr£6.95&alc Dinner £17.50-£18.50&alc Last dinner 9.30pm
CONF. Thtr 100 Class 60 Board 50 Del £85
Credit Cards 1 2 3 5

CROSBY-ON-EDEN Cumbria Map 12 NY45
See also **Carlisle**

★★★ ❀ ♨ **71%** Crosby Lodge Country House
High Crosby CA6 4QZ (Leave M6 at junc 14, 3.5m from motorway on A689) ☎(0228) 573618 FAX (0228) 573428
Closed 24 Dec-mid Jan RS Sun evening
Run by Michael and Patricia Sedgwick for over 20 years, this charming country house hotel is attractively furnished throughout, with many antiques. Individually styled bedrooms have luxurious bathrooms and there are comfortable lounges and a restaurant serving home-cooked 4-course dinners of a high standard.
9⇌🛏 Annexe2⇌(3fb)2⇔ CTV in all bedrooms T ✱
sB&B⇌🛏£65-£68 dB&B⇌🛏£85-£100 🛏
40P 🚗 ✿
🍴 English & French V ✧ Lunch £15.50-£19.50&alc Dinner £25.50-£29.50&alc Last dinner 9pm
Credit Cards ①②③

CROSS HANDS Dyfed Map 02 SN51

Forte Travelodge
SA14 6NW (on A48, eastbound)
☎(0269) 845700 Central Res (0800) 850950

FORTE
Travelodge

This modern building offers a good standard of accommodation for overnight stops. Smart, spacious and well equipped bedrooms, all with en suite bathrooms, are suitable for family use, and meals may be taken at the nearby family restaurant. For more details about Travelodges, consult the Contents page, under Hotel Groups.
32⇌🛏✱ B⇌🛏£31.95 (room only)

Red Lion Hotel ★★ 68%
**Brooke Street, Cromer,
Norfolk NR27 9HD
Telephone: (0263) 514964**

RTM

A hundred years ago the Victorians discovered the best of the Norfolk Coast. Today you can rediscover the dramatic beauty of this Coastline while staying at the Red Lion Hotel, Cromer. The atmosphere reflects the unhurried life of Norfolk. Immediately overlooking Cromer Pier, Sandy Beaches and local crab boats.

All bedrooms have en suite facilities, central heating, colour television including hotel video channel, radio alarm, tea/coffee making facilities.
½ price accommodation for children under 12 years sharing parents' room.
Use of sauna, solarium and snooker room. Special rates for use of fitness gym.
Also our first class restaurant which is open 7 evenings is also open to non residents and caters for vegetarians.
3 nights bargain breaks available.

Crosby-on-Eden - Cross Hands

★★ 70%

Nestling on the edge of the picturesque sea side village of West Runton between Cromer and Sheringham in own grounds a Country House Hotel, in heart of National Trust countryside over looking sea, meadows and golf course. Excellent cuisine from table-d'hôte and à-la-carte menus. All rooms en-suite and tastefully decorated, cosy lounge with open fire, bar lounge overlooking garden and sea. Ideally situated for bird watching, walking, golfing or just relaxing. Special Winter and Spring breaks, also three day Christmas package. Lift, full central heating & large car park.

Cromer Rd., West Runton Norfolk NR27 9QA
☎ **0263 837537**

The Bear Hotel

★★★ ❀❀ 64%
*'Best Pub in Britain 1993'
Good Pub Guide*
**CRICKHOWELL, POWYS
Telephone: 0873 810408**
This lovely old historic Coaching House dates back to the 15th Century. It is very much the focal point of Crickhowell – an attractive market town in one of the most beautiful parts of Wales. It provides comfortable accommodation with luxury bedrooms, en suite bathrooms and superb honeymoon accommodation with an antique four poster bed and jacuzzi and one private suite.
Outstanding home cooking and a delightful à la carte restaurant, as well as an excellent range of bar meals served in the attractive lounge bar. Coal fires in winter, secluded garden in summer.

Crowthorne - Croydon

CROWTHORNE Berkshire Map 04 SU86

★★★ 59% Waterloo
Duke's Ride RG11 7NW ☎(0344) 777711 FAX (0344) 778913

FORTE Heritage

This nicely restored, red-brick Victorian building with modern extensions stands in a wooded location in a charming Berkshire village. The bedrooms vary in size and outlook, many are attractively decorated and all are well equipped.

58⇨🛏1🚪🛁 in 28 bedrooms CTV in all bedrooms ® T sB&B⇨🛏£39.50-£90 dB&B⇨🛏£39.50-£110 (room only) ⊟
⟪ 120P
V ✧ ⚖ ✘ Sunday Lunch £11.95 Dinner £16.50&alc Last dinner 10pm
CONF. Thtr 50 Class 30 Board 20 Del from £75
Credit Cards 1 2 3 5

CROYDE Devon Map 02 SS43

★★ 70% Croyde Bay House
Moor Ln, Croyde Bay EX33 1PA ☎(0271) 890270
Closed mid Nov-Feb

This family-run, cottage-style hotel stands on the rocks overlooking Croyde Bay, with magnificent views across to Clovelly and out to Baggy Point. Jenny and Alex Penny have now tastefully refurbished all the bedrooms, most of which have lovely views. The inviting public areas include 2 lounges, one with a bar, and a sun lounge.

7⇨🛏(2fb) CTV in all bedrooms ® ✱ sB&B⇨🛏£40.50-£59.50 dB&B⇨🛏£81-£99 (incl dinner) ⊟
8P 🅿
♕ English & French ✧ ⚖ ✘ Dinner £17.50 Last dinner 8pm
Credit Cards 1 3

★★ 69% Kittiwell House
St Mary's Rd EX33 1PG (0.5m from village in direction of Georgeham) ☎(0271) 890247 FAX (0271) 890469
Closed mid Jan-mid Feb

A charmingly thatched hotel, situated behind the village and fronted by a cobbled car park, offers accommodation in quaint, cosy bedrooms individually designed to be in keeping with the style of the building. The lounge, bar lounge and restaurant feature beams, real fires and a wealth of well chosen bric-a-brac.

12⇨🛏(2fb)3🚪🛁 in 4 bedrooms CTV in all bedrooms ® T sB&B⇨🛏£53-£58 dB&B⇨🛏£92-£102 (incl dinner) ⊟
CTV 21P 🅿 ✱ xmas
♕ English & French V ✧ ⚖ ✱ Sunday Lunch £8.95 Dinner £15.70&alc Last dinner 9.30pm
Credit Cards 1 2 3

CROYDON Greater London

See **LONDON SECTION plan 1** *D1*

★★★★ 64% Croydon Park
7 Altyre Rd CR9 5AA ☎081-680 9200 FAX 081-760 0426

BEST WESTERN HOTELS

Only 15 minutes from central London and Gatwick Airport, and only 2 minutes walk from Croydon East Station, this large modern hotel is near the town centre. All bedrooms are spacious and well equipped, some designated for non smokers. Oscar's restaurant buffet carvery offers particularly good value for money, and table service is provided in the gas lit Whistler's Bar.

214⇨🛏(40fb)🚪🛁 in 26 bedrooms CTV in all bedrooms ® T sB&B⇨🛏fr£87 dB&B⇨🛏fr£97 ⊟
Lift ⟪ ⛲ 118P 🅿 ⊠ (heated) squash sauna solarium gymnasium whirlpool bath
♕ International V ✧ ⚖ ✱ Lunch fr£13.95&alc Dinner fr£14.95&alc Last dinner 10pm
CONF. Thtr 300 Class 100 Board 100 Del £124
Credit Cards 1 2 3 4 5

★★★★ 59% Selsdon Park
Sanderstead CR2 8YA (3m SE off A2022) ☎081-657 8811 FAX 081-651 6171

Surrounded by 200 acres of parkland, this impressive mansion, an eighth of a mile long, combines a variety of architectural styles, from the tapestry-covered stone-walled foyer lounge with its ornate ceiling to the bright 70s-style Phoenix bar and brasserie. The comfortable bedrooms are equipped with all modern amenities including mini bars, south facing rooms generally being the best.

170⇨🛏(7fb)🚪🛁 in 12 bedrooms CTV in all bedrooms ® T ✱
Lift ⟪ 250P 15🅿 (£1.50) ✿ ⊠ (heated) ⌂ (heated) ⛳ 18 ♞ (hard & grass) squash snooker sauna solarium gymnasium croquet jacuzzi putting boules ♪
♕ International V ✧ ⚖ ✘ Last dinner 9.30pm
CONF. Thtr 150 Class 80 Board 30 Del from £110
Credit Cards 1 2 3 4 5

★★ 64% Central
3-5 South Park Hill Rd, South Croydon CR2 7DY
☎081-688 5644 & 081-688 0840 FAX 081-760 0861

Situated in a quiet residential area south of the town centre, this family-run commercial hotel has a friendly atmosphere and offers comfortable bedrooms with modern facilities, a bar/reception area, small lounge and attractive restaurant.

19⇨🛏(2fb)🚪 CTV in all bedrooms ® T 🐾 (ex guide dogs) sB&B⇨🛏£35-£50 dB&B⇨🛏£40-£60 ⊟
⟪ CTV 15P
V ✧ ⚖ Lunch £6-£8.50&alc Dinner £6-£8.50&alc Last dinner 8pm
Credit Cards 1 2 3 £

★★ 62% Norfolk House
587 London Rd, Thornton Heath CR7 6AY ☎081-689 8989 FAX 081-689 0335

This hotel has evolved from linking 2 houses and adding a 3-storey rear bedroom extension. There is an open-plan bar-lounge, formal reception foyer and a small restaurant. The hotel also owns the adjoining Duke of India restaurant. Room service is available and the atmosphere is friendly and informal.

78⇨🛏(3fb) CTV in all bedrooms ® T 🐾 (ex guide dogs) ✱
⟪ 150P 4🅿
V ✧ ⚖ Last dinner 10pm
Credit Cards 1 2 3 4 5

★★ 59% Briarley
8 Outram Rd CR0 6XE ☎081-654 1000 FAX 081-656 6084

This privately run and friendly commercial hotel offers an informal atmosphere throughout public areas, which include a bar/lounge with an unusual clock collection. Half the bedrooms are in the main building; those in converted neighbouring houses are larger and have been attractively refurbished.

18⇨🛏 Annexe 20⇨🛏(4fb)🚪 CTV in all bedrooms ® T ✱
sB&B⇨🛏£35-£55 dB&B⇨🛏£45-£65 ⊟
CTV 30P 🅿
♕ Mainly grills V ✘ Sunday Lunch £10.50 Dinner £10.50&alc Last dinner 10pm
Credit Cards 1 2 3 5 £

Forte Posthouse
Purley Way CR9 4LT ☎081-688 5185 FAX 081-681 6438

FORTE Posthouse

Suitable for both the business and leisure traveller, this bright hotel provides modern accommodation in well equipped bedrooms with en suite bathrooms. For more details about Forte Posthouse hotels, consult the Contents page, under Hotel Groups.

83⇨🛏🚪 B⇨🛏£41.50-£53.50 (room only)
CONF. Thtr 170 Class 80 Board 40 Del £89.50

Croydon - Cumbernauld

Hilton National Croydon
Waddon Way, Purley Way CR9 4HH
☎081-680 3000

This is a bright, modern hotel with an informal restaurant, aimed at both the business and leisure guest. All bedrooms have en-suite bathrooms and a range of modern facilities. For more information about Hilton National, consult the Contents page, under Hotel Groups.
168⇌♪✱ B⇌♪£85 (room only)
CONF. Thtr 400 Class 240 Board 80 Del £120

Travel Inn
Coombe Rd CR0 5RB (on A212) ☎081-686 2030

Purpose-built accommodation offers spacious and well equipped bedrooms, all with en suite bathrooms. Meals may be taken at the nearby family restaurant and pub. For more details about Travel Inns, consult the Contents page, under Hotel Groups.
39⇌♪✱ B⇌♪£33.50 (room only)

CRUGYBAR Dyfed Map **03** SN63

★★♨70% Glanrannell Park
SA19 8SA (Welsh Rarebits) ☎Talley(0558) 685230 FAX (0558) 685784
Closed Nov-Mar
David and Bronwen Davies have welcomed guests to Glanrannell Park for over 20 years. The hotel is fronted by a lake, where guests are invited to feed the Chinese carp after dinner, and is set in 23 acres of mature grounds. There are 2 very comfortable lounges, and the table d'hôte menu offers good honest cooking based on local produce.
8⇌(3fb) ⓡ sB&B⇌£31-£37 dB&B⇌£52-£64 ♠
CTV 30P 3🚗 (£3) ♨ ❄ ♪
♀ International ♥ ♫ ✕ Bar Lunch £5-£12.50 Dinner fr£15
Last dinner 8pm
Credit Cards ① ③

CUCKFIELD West Sussex Map **04** TQ32

★★★❀❀75% Ockenden Manor
Ockenden Ln RH17 5LD
☎Haywards Heath(0444) 416111 FAX (0444) 415549

Set in 5 acres of gardens, this fine manor house dates in part from 1520 and has elegantly furnished bedrooms, some with private staircases. There is a comfortable lounge, cosy bar and oak-panelled restaurant with a painted ceiling and stained glass windows. The Manor has a reputation for the high standard of its modern English cooking, with menus offering enterprising dishes based on fresh regional produce. Friendly and efficient staff provide attentive service, including full room service.
22⇌5🛏 CTV in all bedrooms ⓡ T ✕ ✱ sB&B⇌♪£70-£95
dB&B⇌♪£95-£165 Continental breakfast ♠
⟨ 45P ♨ ❄ xmas
V ♥ ♫ ✱ Lunch £14.95-£18.50&alc High tea £7.95 Dinner £26.50-£29.50&alc Last dinner 9.30pm
CONF. Thtr 50 Class 20 Board 30 Del from £99
Credit Cards ① ② ③ ⑤

CULLERCOATS Tyne & Wear Map **12** NZ37

★★62% Bay
Front St NE30 4QB ☎091-252 3150
This seafront hotel has lovely views over the bay. Cosy bedrooms, attractive lounges and popular, value-for-money menus are offered.
17rm(11⇌♪(2fb)3🛏 CTV in all bedrooms ⓡ T
✕ (ex guide dogs)
CTV 9P sailing sea fishing

♀ English & French ♥ ♫ Last dinner 9pm
Credit Cards ① ② ③ ⑤
See advertisement under WHITLEY BAY

CUMBERNAULD Strathclyde *Dumbartonshire* Map **11** NS77

★★★★❀❀68% Westerwood Hotel Golf & Country Club
1 St Andrews Dr, Westerwood G68 0EW ☎(0236) 457171
FAX (0236) 738478
This modern hotel sits high above the town and has fine views across its testing Ballasteros-designed golf course. The elegant main lounge leads on to the cocktail bar and the octagonal Old Masters restaurant, with a silk-draped ceiling. Our inspector enjoyed chilled roulade of monkfish, salmon and lemon sole, followed by Scottish venison with a purée of celeriac and a glazed cranberry tartlet, then a hot, bitter sweet chocolate soufflé with Calvados cream. The Clubhouse restaurant, lounge bar and courtyard brasserie provide less formal meals. Executive bedrooms offer more space and comfort than standard rooms, and have balconies.
47⇌♪✱in 4 bedrooms CTV in all bedrooms ⓡ♀T
✕ (ex guide dogs)
Lift ⟨ ☷ 200P ❄ ☐ (heated) ⌨ 18 ♪ (hard) snooker solarium gymnasium steam room bowling green driving range ♫
♀ International V ♥ ♫ Last dinner 10pm
CONF. Thtr 150 Class 80 Board 40 Del from £105
Credit Cards ① ② ③ ⑤

Some hotels within company owned groups share a uniform identity. For full details consult the Contents page, under Hotel Groups.

AA★★

CENTRAL HOTEL
3-5 SOUTH PARK HILL ROAD CROYDON CR2 7DY
Tel: (081) 688 5644
(081) 688 0840
Fax: (081) 760 0861

- Free parking
- Close to town centre
- Traditional English breakfast
- Garden theme restaurant
- 4 poster and canopied beds available
- Cable TV (Sky, Sports, CNN, MTV etc.) available
- Owner run friendly hotel
- 19 rooms all en suite, tea, TV, phone, hairdryer, trouser/skirt press

WE ARE SMALL ENOUGH TO CARE AND LOOK AFTER YOUR NEEDS, AND HOPE THAT YOU WILL JOIN OUR OTHER GUESTS FOR A FRIENDLY CHAT AT THE BAR

Cumbernauld - Darlington

Travel Inn
South Muirhead Rd G67 1AX ☎(0236) 725339

Purpose-built accommodation offers spacious and well equipped bedrooms, all with en suite bathrooms. Meals may be taken at the nearby family restaurant and pub. For more details about Travel Inns, consult the Contents page, under Hotel Groups.
37⇨🛏✱ B⇨🛏£33.50 (room only)

CUMNOCK Strathclyde *Ayrshire* Map **11** NS51
★★ **61%** *Royal*
1 Glaisnock St KA18 1BP ☎(0290) 20822 FAX (0290) 25988
This town centre commercial hotel is traditional in style, but has seen progress towards providing modern amenities. Owned by a local firm of bakers, the hotel's popular high teas are worth considering as an alternative to dinner.
11rm(2⇨3🛏)(1fb) CTV in all bedrooms ®
CTV 10P
V ☼ ⌒ Last dinner 9pm
Credit Cards ①③

DALKEITH Lothian *Midlothian* Map **11** NT36
★★ **64%** *Eskbank Motor*
29 Dalhousie Rd EH22 3AT (on B6392) ☎031-663 3234 FAX 031-660 4347
Well run by the resident owners, this popular commercial and tourist hotel has modern bedrooms in a separate building, all equipped with a wide range of amenities. Public areas in the main house include a comfortable lounge, bar and panelled restaurant.
16⇨🛏(3fb)1🛏 CTV in all bedrooms ® T sB&B⇨🛏£39-£45 dB&B⇨🛏£50-£60 🅿
(CTV 40P 6🚗 ❄
♞ International V ☼ ⌒ Lunch £7&alc High tea £7&alc Dinner £7&alc Last dinner 9pm
CONF. Class 20 Board 20 Del from £60
Credit Cards ①②③⑤ £

See advertisement under EDINBURGH

★★ **63%** *County*
High St EH22 1AY ☎031-663 3495 FAX 031-663 0208
This long-established family-run hotel in the town centre has recently been extended and refurbished. Modern décor and fabrics have been used to good effect in the comfortable bedrooms, which offer the expected facilities, and the public areas include an attractive first-floor lounge, choice of bars and an all-day restaurant.
29⇨🛏 CTV in all bedrooms ® T sB&B⇨🛏£40-£48 dB&B⇨🛏£60-£65
Lift CTV ✗ *xmas*
♞ Continental V ☼ ⌒ Lunch fr£5.20 Dinner £12-£16alc Last dinner 1pm
CONF. Thtr 120 Class 80 Board 40 Del £75
Credit Cards ①③ £

DALWHINNIE Highland *Inverness-shire* Map **14** NN68
★★ **59%** *Loch Ericht*
PH19 1AF (off A9 north of Drumochter Pass take A889 to Dalwhinnie). ☎(05282) 257 FAX (05282) 270
Closed Nov-27 Mar
The former Highland lodge has been considerably extended to create a hotel which is especially popular with tour groups. Bright, airy public rooms include, on the ground floor, a split-level bar/dining room; and a choice of lounges on the first floor. Bedrooms are modern and practical.
27⇨🛏(4fb) ® sB&B⇨🛏£22.50-£29.50 dB&B⇨🛏£39.50-£49.50 🅿
CTV 50P ❄ ♪ shooting ski-ing *xmas*

V ☼ ⌒ Lunch £3-£9.50alc Dinner £8.50-£15.50alc Last dinner 9pm
Credit Cards ①②③⑤ £

DARESBURY Cheshire Map **07** SJ58
★★★ **68%** *Lord Daresbury*
Chester Rd WA4 4BB (junc 11 of M56)
☎Warrington(0925) 267331 FAX (0925) 265615

A large, busy hotel, the Lord Daresbury is located on the A56 close to its junction with the M56 motorway on the southern outskirts of Warrington. The wide choice of modern style bedrooms includes executive, no-smoking, and rooms for lady guests. There is also a choice of restaurants, air conditioned conference and function facilities and a leisure centre.
141⇨🛏(7fb)✗in 42 bedrooms CTV in all bedrooms ® ⌒ T ✱ sB&B⇨🛏£55-£85 dB&B⇨🛏£75-£95 🅿
Lift (400P 🖃 (heated) squash snooker sauna solarium gymnasium jacuzzi steam room beautician ♞ *xmas*
♞ English & French V ☼ ⌒ ✗ Lunch £10-£12.50 High tea £2.50-£6 Dinner £15&alc Last dinner 10.30pm
CONF. Thtr 400 Class 180 Board 100 Del from £105
Credit Cards ①②③⑤

DARLINGTON Co Durham Map **08** NZ21
See also **Tees-Side Airport**
★★★ **71%** *Hallgarth Country House*
Coatham Mundeville DL1 3LU (close to A1(M) off A167) ☎Aycliffe(0325) 300400 FAX (0325) 310083

A lovely building of warm stone, dating in part from 1540, Hall Garth stands in 67 acres of garden and parkland. The extensive lounges have many antique pieces and offer great comfort. Bedrooms, either in the main house or in the nearby converted barn, are prettily decorated and well equipped.
29⇨🛏 Annexe11⇨🛏(1fb)5🛏 CTV in all bedrooms ® ⌒ T
✈ (ex guide dogs)
(150P 🚗 ❄ 🖃 (heated) ♞ (grass) sauna solarium gymnasium croquet lawn ♞
V ☼ ⌒ Last dinner 9.30pm
Credit Cards ①②③⑤

★★★ 🏵 **67%** *Headlam Hall*
Headlam, Gainford DL2 3HA (2m N of town) ☎(0325) 730238 FAX (0325) 730790
Closed 25-26 Dec
Standing in 3 acres of gardens close to the village of Headlam, this impressive Jacobean mansion has been carefully transformed into a very comfortable, family-run hotel that offers friendly professional service. Traditionally furnished bedrooms have modern facilities and spacious public areas retain their historic elegance.
17⇨🛏 Annexe9⇨🛏(3fb)12🛏 CTV in all bedrooms ®
✈ (ex guide dogs) sB&B⇨🛏£55-£75 dB&B⇨🛏£70-£90 🅿
60P ❄ 🖃 (heated) ♞ (hard) ♪ snooker sauna clay pigeon shooting croquet lawn
♞ English & French V ✱ Lunch fr£11 Dinner fr£15&alc Last dinner 9.30pm
CONF. Thtr 200 Class 40 Board 40 Del from £70
Credit Cards ①②③ £

★★★ **65%** *Swallow King's Head*
Priestgate DL1 1NW ☎(0325) 380222 FAX (0325) 382006

In the heart of town, next to the Cornmill shopping centre, this hotel has a recently built extension including a bright, comfortable lounge and several excellent bedrooms. Extensive refurbishment is due to begin in the original part of the building. Staff are very friendly and natural.

86⇨🅟(3fb)⤼in 51 bedrooms CTV in all bedrooms ®⚲ T
sB&B⇨🅟£58-£75 dB&B⇨🅟£75-£90 🄑
Lift ⦅ 24🛎 use of Dolphin Leisure Centre *xmas*
🍴 English, French & Italian **V** ✿ ⚐
CONF. Thtr 150 Class 90 Board 40 Del from £82.50
Credit Cards 1 2 3 5

★★★ **59%***White Horse*
DL1 3AD (on A167 between A1(M) and town centre)
☎(0325) 382121 FAX (0325) 355953
The White Horse is a Tudor-style public house with a modern bedroom extension to the rear. Bedrooms are equipped for the modern traveller, and there are extensive bars and a grill-type restaurant.
40⇨🅟(6fb)⤼in 20 bedrooms CTV in all bedrooms ® T
Lift ⦅ 120P
🍴 Mainly grills **V** ✿ ⚐ ⤼ Last dinner 10pm
Credit Cards 1 2 3 5

DARTMOUTH Devon Map 03 SX85
★★★ **69%***Royal Castle*
11 The Quay TQ6 9PS ☎(0803) 833033 FAX (0803) 835445
The individually styled bedrooms at this 17th-century coaching inn are all approached from galleried landings around a covered courtyard. The Adam restaurant on the first floor has two menus in which fresh local produce is used imaginatively, and there are two busy bars which are full of character and charm.
25⇨🛁6🅟 CTV in all bedrooms ® T ✱ sB&B⇨🅟 fr£48 dB&B⇨🅟£76-£104 🄑
⦅ 7🛎 (£1.50) ♫ *xmas*
🍴 English & French **V** ✿ ⚐ Lunch £8.95 Dinner £16-£23 Last dinner 9.45pm
CONF. Thtr 80 Class 30 Board 50 Del from £40
Credit Cards 1 3

★★★ **64%***Dart Marina*
Sandquay TQ6 9PH ☎(0803) 832580 FAX (0803) 835040

FORTE
Heritage

In an unrivalled position by the marina, this hotel enjoys beautiful river views. Upgraded public areas include a first-floor lounge and the River Restaurant which features seasonal table d'hôte and à la carte menus, and the long-established management team provides friendly service. Bedrooms are bright and comfortable, each one enjoying the view.
31⇨🅟Annexe4⇨🅟⤼in 10 bedrooms CTV in all bedrooms ® T
75P 🚗
V ✿ ⚐ Last dinner 9pm
Credit Cards 1 2 3 5

★★★ **59%***Stoke Lodge*
Cinders Ln, Stoke Fleming TQ6 0RA (2m S A379)
☎Stoke Fleming(0803) 770523
Surrounded by its own grounds in the village of Stoke Fleming, this friendly, family owned holiday hotel offers bright, cheerful bedrooms in a variety of sizes and a choice of lounges.
24⇨🅟 CTV in all bedrooms ® T ✱
sB&B⇨🅟£37.50-£45 dB&B⇨🅟£65-£80 🄑
50P 🚗 ✿ ▭ (heated) ⛵ (heated) 🎾 (hard) sauna solarium gymnasium jacuzzi putting table tennis croquet *xmas*
🍴 English & Continental **V** ✿ ⚐ Lunch £8.95-£9.95&alc High tea £5.25-£6.25 Dinner £16.95-£17.95&alc Last dinner 9pm
CONF. Thtr 80 Class 60 Board 30 Del from £60
Credit Cards 1 3

Hotels with red star ratings are especially high quality.

★★ **62%***New Endsleigh*
New Rd, Stoke Fleming TQ6 0NR (2m S A379)
☎Stoke Fleming(0803) 770381
This hotel is run by a friendly family team. The lively bar lounge is the ideal place to make a selection from the à la carte and blackboard menu for Bunters restaurant, and choice is varied and imaginative. Tastefully colour coordinated non-smoking bedrooms offer excellent facilities.
11rm(10⇨🅟)Annexe1🅟(1fb) CTV in all bedrooms ® ✈ (ex guide dogs)
CTV 16P 🚗 nc5yrs
🍴 English & French **V** ✿ ⚐ Last dinner 9pm
Credit Cards 1 3

DARWEN Lancashire Map 07 SD62
★★★ **62%***Whitehall*
Springbank, Whitehall BB3 2JU (off A666 S of town)
☎(0254) 701595 FAX (0254) 773426
Standing in its own grounds in a residential area, this family-run hotel offers comfortable accommodation. Practically furnished bedrooms are generally spacious and decorated with modern coordinated fabrics. The refurbished public areas include a lounge, bar and small brasserie restaurant.
15⇨🅟 CTV in all bedrooms ®⚲ T ✱ sB&B⇨🅟£42.50-£49 dB&B⇨🅟fr£62 🄑
60P ✿ ▭ (heated) snooker sauna solarium ⛳
🍴 English & French **V** ✿ ⚐ ✱ Lunch £6.50-£7.75 High tea fr£6.50 Dinner fr£10.50 Last dinner 9.30pm
CONF. Thtr 60 Class 30 Board 20 Del from £65
Credit Cards 1 2 3 5

For key to symbols see the Bookmark.

Hall Garth
Golf & Country Club
★★★ HOTEL

Coatham Mundeville
Darlington DL1 3LU
Telephone: (0325) 300400
Fax: (0325) 310083

From the style of its architecture and decor to the warmth of its hospitality, Hall Garth is English through and through.
Comprising 40 delightfully furnished fully equipped bedrooms together with full leisure facilities and a 9-hole par 74 golf course playable April 1994.
The Brafferton Suite offers unrivalled conference and banqueting facilities for any occasion.

Datchet - Deganwy

DATCHET Berkshire Map 04 SU97

★★58% The Manor
The Village Green SL3 9EA (Calotels) ☎Slough(0753) 543442 FAX (0753) 545292
An extended inn, the Manor Hotel is in the centre of the busy village. The bar is a popular venue with locals, and like other parts of the hotel is slowly undergoing improvement. Bedrooms are simply furnished but well equipped.
30⇨ ⋔(2fb)1⊞ CTV in all bedrooms ℝ T sB&B⇨⋔£35-£79 dB&B⇨⋔£70-£89
⟨ 12P *xmas*
♀ English, French, Italian & Spanish V ✧ Lunch £7.50-£15.95&alc Dinner £16-£20&alc Last dinner 9.45pm
CONF. Thtr 80 Class 60 Board 30 Del from £75
Credit Cards ①②③⑤
See advertisement under WINDSOR

DAVENTRY Northamptonshire Map 04 SP56

★★★69% Daventry Resort
Ashby Rd (A361) NN11 5SG ☎(0327) 301777 FAX (0327) 706313
Bedrooms are attractively furnished and offer a good range of modern facilities. Extensive public areas include the Waterside Restaurant and cocktail bar in addition to the less formal 'Cats Whiskers' bar.
138⇨⋔✂ in 53 bedrooms CTV in all bedrooms ℝ ♋ T ✱ sB⇨⋔£75-£85 dB⇨⋔£85-£95 (room only) ⊟
Lift ⟨ 400P ✿ ⊠ (heated) sauna solarium gymnasium *xmas*
♀ English & French V ✧ ⊻ ✱ Lunch £5.95-£13.75&alc Dinner £14-£15&alc Last dinner 10pm
Credit Cards ①②③④⑤ £

DAWLISH Devon Map 03 SX97

★★★60% Langstone Cliff
Dawlish Warren EX7 0NA (1.5m NE off A379 Exeter rd) ☎(0626) 865155 FAX (0626) 867166
Set in wooded grounds overlooking the sea and the Exe estuary, this long-established family-run hotel caters for holiday-makers in the summer season and conferences in the winter. Bedrooms of varying styles include full modern amenities and there is a choice of bars.
64⇨⋔(52fb) CTV in all bedrooms ℝ ♋ T ✱ sB&B⇨⋔£40-£45 dB&B⇨⋔£70-£100 ⊟
Lift ⟨ CTV 200P ✿ ⊠ (heated) ⌇ (heated) ℘ (hard) snooker solarium table tennis ♫ ⚙ *xmas*
V ✧ ⊻ Lunch fr£9.50 Dinner fr£14.50 Last dinner 9pm
CONF. Thtr 400 Class 200 Board 80 Del from £65
Credit Cards ①②③⑤ £

DEDDINGTON Oxfordshire Map 04 SP43

★★⊛72% Holcombe Hotel & Restaurant
High St OX15 0SL (on the A4260 between Oxford & Banbury) ☎(0869) 38274 FAX (0869) 37167

Courtesy and Care 1994

Closed 1-10 Jan
The warm, relaxed atmosphere created by the Mahfoudh family and their friendly staff has earned this charming 17th-century high street hotel an AA Courtesy and Care Award this year. The individually styled bedrooms are exceptionally well equipped. The beamed cottage bar has a cosy atmosphere with an open fire, and a range of bar meals is served. In the stone walled restaurant, chef Alan Marshall offers a fixed price menu of interesting dishes.
17⇨⋔(3fb) CTV in all bedrooms ℝ T sB&B⇨⋔£55-£69 dB&B⇨⋔£72-£85 ⊟
60P *xmas*
♀ English & French V ✧ ⊻ ✂ Lunch £14.50&alc High tea £4.50&alc Dinner £19.95&alc Last dinner 10pm
CONF. Thtr 30 Class 20 Board 18 Del from £79
Credit Cards ①②③ £

DEDHAM Essex Map 05 TM03

★★★

★★★⊛⊛⊛⁂
MAISON TALBOOTH
Stratford Rd CO7 6HN
☎Colchester(0206) 322367
FAX (0206) 322752

Maison Talbooth is an unusual hotel in that the main restaurant, Le Talbooth, is half a mile away. The main building, a pink Georgian house, is comfortable and very peaceful with attractive lawns and pretty views of Constable countryside. The stylishly designed bedrooms vary in size and some are very spacious. Particularly appealing are the excellent beds, good linen and large towels. Service is unobtrusive, and breakfast is served to the rooms.
10⇨⋔(1fb) CTV in all bedrooms T ✖ (ex guide dogs) sB&B⇨⋔£82.50-£107.50 dB&B⇨⋔£102.50-£137.50 Continental breakfast ⊟
12P 🚲 ✿ croquet
V Lunch fr£19.50&alc Dinner fr£19.50&alc Last dinner 9pm
Credit Cards ①②③

DEGANWY Gwynedd Map 06 SH78

★★66% *Bryn Cregin Garden*
Ty Mawr Rd LL31 9UR ☎(0492) 585266 FAX (0492) 596203
In an elevated position overlooking Conwy estuary and Snowdonia, this large late-Victorian house with pretty gardens has comfortable lounge areas, bars and an attractive restaurant, all of which take advantage of the view. Bedrooms vary in size and are all well equipped and attractively decorated.
17⇨⋔1⊞ CTV in all bedrooms ℝ T
30P ✿
♀ International V ✧ ⊻ ✂ Last dinner 9pm
Credit Cards ①②③⑤

For key to symbols see the Bookmark.

Derby

★★★ 69% Midland
Midland Rd DE1 2SQ ☎(0332) 45894 FAX (0332) 293522
Closed 25-26 Dec & 1 Jan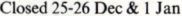

The Midland proudly claims to be the oldest purpose built railway hotel in the world, built in 1841, but it certainly hasn't remained in the past. A major alteration and expansion programme has doubled the number of bedrooms to provide de luxe accommodation. Public rooms are also to receive similar attention, though the lounge will remain unchanged, as the only room retaining its original character.
100➪↑1🛏⚲ in 3 bedrooms CTV in all bedrooms ® T
sB➪↑£68-£73 dB➪↑£77-£82 (room only) ✠
Lift (95P 25🅿 ♪
♀ English & French V ✿ ♃ ✂ ✱ Lunch £8.50-£10.50 Dinner fr£13.75 Last dinner 10pm
CONF. Thtr 150 Class 50 Board 40 Del from £85.50
Credit Cards [1][2][3][5]

★★★ 65% Hotel Ristorante La Gondola
220 Osmaston Rd DE23 8JX (on A514) ☎(0332) 32895 FAX (0332) 384512

For many years the restaurant here has been popular for its varied international cuisine and recently a wing of quality bedrooms has been built, offering warm well equipped accommodation. Close to the city on the A514, the whole complex offers friendly attentive service.
20rm(19➪↑)(7fb) CTV in all bedrooms ®⚲ T
✂ (ex guide dogs) sB➪↑£45-£56 dB➪↑£49-£56 (room only) ✠
(CTV 70P xmas
♀ Continental V ✿ ♃ Lunch fr£7.50&alc Dinner £10.50-£11.50&alc Last dinner 10pm
Credit Cards [1][2][3][4][5]

★★★ 62% International
Burton Rd (A5250) DE3 6AD ☎(0332) 369321 FAX (0332) 294430

This busy hotel has been undergoing major improvements, with 2 new annexes of generally spacious bedrooms and attractively refurbished older rooms, all very well equipped. Public areas include a smartly redecorated foyer, comfortable lounge bar and popular restaurant offering a good-value set menu.
41➪Annexe21➪(2fb) CTV in all bedrooms ®⚲ T
Lift (75P gymnasium ♪
♀ English & Continental V ✿ ♃ Last dinner 10.30pm
Credit Cards [1][2][3][5]

★★ 69% Kedleston Country House
Kedleston Rd DE22 5JD (turn off A38 onto A52 roundabout follow signs for Kedleston Hall) ☎(0332) 559202 & 556507 FAX (0332) 558822

There is a welcoming atmosphere at this hotel, with pleasant public rooms retaining much of their Georgian character. The restaurant and bar are popular with the local community, and the reasonably priced meals are based on quality fresh produce. Bedrooms are individually styled and offer modern facilities.
14➪↑🛏 CTV in all bedrooms ® T ✂ sB&B➪↑£40-£44.50 dB&B➪↑£50-£58.50 ✠
120P ♪
♀ English & French V ✿ ♃ Lunch £7.50-£10&alc Dinner £11.95-£12.95&alc Last dinner 9.15pm
Credit Cards [1][2][3][4][5]

Satellite television – look for this symbol ⚲
in the directory entries.

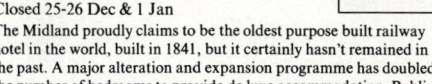

COUNTRY HOUSE HOTEL ★★★

Accommodation — traditionally furnished rooms individually decorated to the very highest standard.

Banqueting — the ideal venue for the special occasion, wedding receptions, private lunches, dinners.

Conferences — with boardrooms, conference suites and a fully self contained training centre, the ideal setting for business meetings.

Restaurant — food of the very highest calibre served in Lavinia's restaurant or the magnificent Garden Room, an experience not to be missed.

Makeney Hall Country House Hotel
Makeney, Milford, Derbyshire
Telephone: (0332) 842999
Facsimile: (0332) 842777
See gazetteer entry under Belper

A friendly hotel with a host of facilities

Set in 19 acres of wooded grounds, overlooking the sea and Exe estuary, this luxurious hotel has 64 centrally heated en suite bedrooms with colour TV, radio, intercom, baby listening and telephone. There are 3 bars, heated indoor and outdoor pools, excellent food, air conditioned restaurant, dancing and entertainment.
Cabaret weekends
It's terrific for kids and the beach is just 500 yards away. So too is an 18 hole golf course.
Free colour brochure from
Langstone Cliff Hotel, Dept AA.,
Dawlish, S. Devon, EX7 0NA
Tel: (0626) 865155
AA★★★

Derby - Dolgellau

Forte Posthouse
Pasture Hill, Littleover DE23 7BA ☎(0332) 514933 FAX (0332) 518668

Suitable for both the business and leisure traveller, this bright hotel provides modern accommodation with all equipped bedrooms with en suite bathrooms. For more details about Forte Posthouse hotels, consult the Contents page, under Hotel Groups.

62⇌❋ B⇌£41.50-£53.50 (room only)
CONF. Thtr 60 Class 40 Board 25 Del £89.50

⇧European Inn
Midland Rd DE1 2SL ☎(0332) 292000 FAX (0332) 293940
Due to have opened early Jul 1993
The European Inn is Derby's newest and most innovative hotel, close to the railway station, with ample parking within its enclosed courtyard. Bedrooms furnishings are of superior quality and have comfortable seating as well as superb bathrooms. Public areas are minimal but there is 24-hour manned reception.
88⇌↑⊬in 20 bedrooms CTV in all bedrooms ® T ❋ sB⇌↑£35 (room only)
Lift ⦅ 80P 10☂
⊬
CONF. Thtr 50 Class 30 Board 30
Credit Cards [1][2][3][5]

DERVAIG
See **Mull, Isle of**

DESBOROUGH Northamptonshire Map 04 SP88
Forte Travelodge
Harborough Rd(on A6, southbound)
☎(0536) 762034 Central Res (0800) 850950

This modern building offers a good standard of accommodation for overnight stops. Smart, spacious and well equipped bedrooms, all with en suite bathrooms, are suitable for family use, and meals may be taken at the nearby family restaurant. For more details about Travelodges, consult the Contents page, under Hotel Groups.

32⇌↑❋ B⇌↑£31.95 (room only)

DEVIL'S BRIDGE Dyfed Map 06 SN77
★★**63%** *Hafod Arms*
SY23 3JL ☎Ponterwyd(097085) 232
Closed 2-31 Jan
This creeper-clad hotel, originally built as a shooting lodge in 1787, is superbly situated overlooking the wooded gorge at this famous beauty spot. Work is well under way to modernise the hotel. There is a cocktail bar, a further public bar and an adjoining tearoom.
15rm(11⇌↑)(1fb)1⌸ CTV in all bedrooms ®
60P ✿ nc12yrs
♡ International V ⌕ ⚏ ⊬ Last dinner 9pm
Credit Cards [1]

DEVIZES Wiltshire Map 04 SU06
★★★**62%** *Bear*
Market Place SN10 1HS ☎(0380) 722444 FAX (0380) 722450
Closed 25-26 Dec
This inn of character, dating back to 1550, is centrally situated in this market town. The bedrooms vary in size but have been carefully equipped. Public areas include 2 bars and 2 eating areas offering a traditional style.
24⇌↑(5fb)3⌸ CTV in all bedrooms ® T ❋ sB&B⇌↑fr£40 dB&B⇌↑fr£60 ♬
CTV 25P (£1) ☂ (£1) solarium

V ⌕ ⚏ ⊬ Lunch fr£8.50&alc Dinner fr£14.75&alc Last dinner 9.30pm
CONF. Thtr 150 Board 50
Credit Cards [1][3]

★★★**65%** *Castle*
New Park St SN10 1DS (on A361)
☎(0380) 729300 FAX (0380) 729155
Closed 26 Dec
A former 17th-century coaching inn, the Castle Hotel is centrally situated in this attractive Wiltshire town. Public areas include a small resident's lounge, 2 lively bars where a range of bar snacks is available, and a more formal restaurant open Monday to Saturday.
18⇌↑(2fb) CTV in all bedrooms ® T sB&B⇌↑£25-£40 dB&B⇌↑£40-£55 ♬
9☂
V ⌕ ⚏ ⊬ Lunch £8&alc High tea £4.50-£12.70alc Dinner £10&alc Last dinner 8.45pm
Credit Cards [1][2][3][5]

DEWSBURY West Yorkshire Map 08 SE22
★★**68%** *Healds Hall*
Leeds Rd, Liversedge WF15 6JA ☎(0924) 409112 FAX (0924) 401895
Built in 1764 and linked with the Brontës, this family-run hotel has been carefully extended to retain the character of the building. Bedrooms are well equipped and the open plan public areas include a cosy restaurant where a well produced dinner is served.
25⇌↑(3fb) CTV in all bedrooms ®✱ T ❋ sB&B⇌↑£45-£51 dB&B⇌↑£70-£75 ♬
80P ✿
♡ International V ⌕ ⚏ ❋ Lunch £7.95-£8.95 Dinner £15.95&alc Last dinner 9pm
Credit Cards [1][2][3]

DINAS MAWDDWY Gwynedd Map 06 SH81
★★**64%** *Buckley Pines*
SY20 9LP ☎(0650) 531261
The Dovey Valley, from its views to its fishing, figures large in the life of this hotel. Bedrooms in the mid-Victorian property vary in size, but most have fairly modern furnishings. A bright and airy conservatory restaurant has views over the valley.
10rm(3⇌2↑)(1fb) CTV in all bedrooms ®
40P ⚘ ♪ pool table
♡ English & French V ⌕ ⚏ Last dinner 8.30pm
Credit Cards [1][3]

DOLGELLAU Gwynedd Map 06 SH71
★★★❀ ✿**72%** *Penmaenuchaf Hall*
Penmaenpool LL40 1YB (off A493 Tywyn road) (Welsh Rarebits) ☎(0341) 422122 FAX (0341) 422129
On the wooded slopes of the Cader Idris mountains, this Victorian stone-built mansion has excellent views over the Mawddach estuary and stands in 21 acres of mature woodland, lawns and lovely gardens. Bedrooms are in country house style, many having comfortable sofas and armchairs. Public rooms are spacious and elegant, with log fires in the colder weather. The restaurant, with its conservatory extension, offers a fixed price dinner menu often featuring local sea bass and lobster, char-grilled rabbit and local lamb.
14⇌↑1⌸ CTV in all bedrooms ® T ✕ (ex guide dogs) sB&B⇌↑£47.50-£95 dB&B⇌↑£95-£140 ♬
40P ✿ snooker ♪ xmas
V ⌕ ⚏ ⊬ ❋ Lunch £5.75-£14alc Dinner fr£19.95alc Last dinner 9.30pm
CONF. Thtr 70 Class 40 Board 18 Del from £65
Credit Cards [1][3]

Dolgellau

★★★ ♨ 70% **Dolmelynllyn Hall**
Ganllwyd LL40 2HP (3.5m N on A470)
☎Ganllwyd(034140) 273
Closed Jan-Feb RS Dec
This lovely stone house with a castellated tower and unusual black and white timbered bay windows is known affectionately as 'Dolly'. Owner Jon Barkwith is a cheerful and attentive host, greeting guests and serving drinks and food. His daughter Jo cooks with real imagination and style in a very British manner, but with modern skills.
11⇌🛏1🚿⌇in 2 bedrooms CTV in all bedrooms ®⚤T
sB&B⇌🛏£37.50-£47.50 dB&B⇌🛏£75-£95 🅿
25P 🚗 ✿ ♪ nc10yrs
V ❀ ⊡ ⌇ Bar Lunch fr£2alc
CONF. Thtr 20 Class 20 Board 20
Credit Cards

★★ ♨ 69% **Dolserau Hall**
LL40 2AG (1.5m outside town between A494 to Bala and A470 to Dinas Mawddwy)☎(0341) 422522 FAX (0341) 422400
This fine Victorian mansion with a Quaker history stands in gardens in the picturesque Wnion Valley and has a magnificent outlook from all sides. Owners Marion and Peter Kaye and their friendly staff provide a warm welcome. Chef Huw Roberts uses good local produce to create the meals served in the pretty Winter Garden Restaurant overlooking the river. The comfortable bedrooms are mostly large and there are three attractively furnished lounge areas.
14rm(13⇌🛏)(4fb) CTV in all bedrooms ®⚤T ✱ sB&B£36 sB&B⇌🛏£39 dB&B⇌🛏£72 🅿
Lift 70P 🚗 ✿ xmas
V ⌇ ✱ Dinner £17.50 Last dinner 8.30pm
Credit Cards 1 3

★★ 64% **George III**
Penmaenpool LL40 1YD (2m W on A493) ☎(0341) 422525 FAX (0341) 423565
Situated in a superb location on the Mawddach estuary, this delightful inn started life in 1650 as a pub and ships' chandlery and evidence of its past can be seen in thick walls, exposed timbers and large stone fireplaces. The bars are full of character and offer a wide range of bar meals, and there is a comfortable lounge and a pretty restaurant offering an extensive carte. Bedrooms also have exposed timbers and some are in a converted railway station a few yards away.
6⇌🛏 Annexe6⇌🛏 CTV in all bedrooms ® T
sB&B⇌🛏£37.50-£45 dB&B⇌🛏£70-£88 🅿
100P 🚗 ✿ ♪
♀ Welsh, English & French V ❀ ⊡ ⌇ ✱ Lunch fr£10.95 Dinner £15-£22alc Last dinner 9pm
Credit Cards 1 2 3

★★ 63% **Royal Ship**
Queens Square LL40 1AR (Frederic Robinson) ☎(0341) 422209
This attractive, creeper-clad inn is very much at the centre of affairs in this old market town. Bedrooms have been well modernised, there are two lounges, a coffee lounge and no fewer than 4 bars.
24rm(18⇌🛏)(4fb) CTV in all bedrooms ® 🐕 (ex guide dogs) ✱ sB&B£19 sB&B⇌🛏£32 dB&B£38 dB&B⇌🛏£64 🅿
Lift CTV 8P xmas
V ❀ ⊡ ⌇ Lunch £8.50 Dinner £13.50-£17.50&alc Last dinner 9.30pm
Credit Cards 1 3

★ ♨ 67% **Clifton House**
Smithfield Square LL40 1ES (off A470) ☎(0341) 422554
Once the county gaol, and more latterly an inn and a temperance hotel, this stone building is now a charming hotel. Bedrooms are smart and modern, and the Old County Gaol Restaurant is in the low ceilinged stone-walled cellar, furnished with cushioned chapel pews. Here Pauline Dix has gained a good reputation for her cooking. Our inspector enjoyed delicious trout fillets with a herby ➤

ROYAL SHIP HOTEL ★★
Queens Square, Dolgellau, Gwynedd.
Telephone Dolgellau 0341 422209

Family Rooms
Colour TV in Bedrooms
Ideally situated for touring North & Mid Wales
Great Little Trains of Wales
Slate Mines at Blaenau
Pony Trekking
Golf
Robinson's Traditional Draught Beer
Access and Barclaycard accepted
Colour Brochure on request

9 star accommodation.

GRANADA HOTEL ALFRETON
Old Swanwick Colliery Road, Alfreton,
Derbyshire DE55 1HJ. Tel 0773 520040.
Close to the Derbyshire Dales, just
3 miles from M1, J28.

GRANADA HOTEL SHEFFIELD
340 Prince of Wales Road, Sheffield S2 1FF.
Tel 0742 530935.
Just over 1 mile from city centre
and 3 miles from M1, J33.

GRANADA HOTEL STOKE
Newcastle Road, Talke, Stoke-on-Trent,
Staffordshire ST7 1UP. Tel 0782 777000.
Only 1½ miles from the potteries and 3
miles from M6, J16.

You'll go a long way to find such a high standard of accommodation at such competitive prices. But just off the motorway network, you don't have to go far to reach us.

Dolgellau - Dorchester-on-Thames

cream cheese wrapped in ham, followed by baked turbot, then Pauline's speciality (and our inspector's favourite) – bread pudding with a very strong brandy flavour.
7rm(4⇨🅱) CTV in all bedrooms ® ✕ sB&B£26-£30 sB&B⇨🅱£31-£35 dB&B£34-£40 dB&B⇨🅱£42-£50 🇷
3P 🚗
V ✿ ✱ Sunday Lunch fr£10.95 Dinner £13.45-£16.45alc Last dinner 9.30pm
Credit Cards 1 3 £

DOLWYDDELAN Gwynedd Map 06 SH75

★★ 63% Elen's Castle
LL25 0EJ (on A470, 5m S of Betws-y-Coed) ☎(06906) 207
This 18th-century former beer house and coaching inn is now a small, friendly, privately owned hotel with a wealth of charm and character.
9rm(7⇨🅱)(2fb)1🚪 CTV in all bedrooms ® sB&Bfr£15 dB&Bfr£23.90 dB&B⇨🅱£30-£56 🇷
CTV 40P 1🚗 ✿ ♪ sauna xmas
V ✿ 🅻 ✱ Lunch fr£7.95 High tea fr£5.50 Dinner fr£11.95&alc Last dinner 9pm
CONF. Class 20
Credit Cards 1 3 5 £

DONCASTER South Yorkshire Map 08 SE50

★★★ 67% Doncaster Moat House
Warmsworth DN4 9UX (2.5m SW on A630 at junc with A1) ☎(0302) 310331 FAX (0302) 310197
The Doncaster Moat House is a modern, purpose-built hotel in the grounds of Warmsworth Hall. A recent extension has increased the number of rooms and provided an indoor leisure complex. Meals are available in the lounge or restaurant, and the welcoming bedrooms come in a range of styles, including executive rooms and suites.
100⇨🅱(4fb)⚥ in 6 bedrooms CTV in all bedrooms ® T ✱ sB&B⇨🅱£44-£79 dB&B⇨🅱£70-£95 🇷
Lift ⊂ 200P ✿ ▨ (heated) sauna solarium gymnasium aerobic classes
⌖ French V ✿ 🅻 ⚥ ✱ Lunch fr£11.95 Dinner fr£14.50 Last dinner 10pm
CONF. Thtr 400 Class 250 Board 40 Del £89
Credit Cards 1 2 3 4 5

★★★ 64% Mount Pleasant
Great North Rd DN11 0HP ☎(0302) 868696 & 868219 FAX (0302) 865130
(For full entry see Rossington)

★★★ 62% Danum Swallow
High St DN1 1DN ☎(0302) 342261 FAX (0302) 329034

Standards continue to rise at this conference-orientated hotel, the recent refurbishment of restaurant and cocktail bar completing the upgrading of all public rooms to provide bright and comfortable areas which are well frequented by local people. Bedrooms vary in size and style, but all offer a good range of facilities.
66⇨🅱(2fb)1🚪 in 15 bedrooms CTV in all bedrooms ®⚥ T sB&B⇨🅱fr£75 dB&B⇨🅱fr£90 🇷
Lift ⊂ 60P 25🚗 xmas
V ✿ 🅻 ✱ Lunch £7.50-£8.95 High tea £5.25-£6.25 Dinner £14.95-£15.95 Last dinner 9.15pm
CONF. Thtr 300 Class 100 Board 100 Del from £84
Credit Cards 1 2 3 5

★★★ 60% Grand St Leger
Bennetthorpe DN2 6AX (off roundabout at A638/A630 junction) ☎(0302) 364111 FAX (0302) 329285
Near the racecourse and adjacent to the bloodstock sales stables, this distinctive white hotel has always had close links with the horse-racing fraternity, originally providing accommodation for

stable lads, and memorabilia, prints and pictures of famous jockeys and their mounts adorns the cosy public areas. Bedrooms are all well appointed, the newer ones being of a particularly high standard.
21⇨🅱(1fb)4🚪 CTV in all bedrooms ® T ✕ (ex guide dogs) sB&B⇨🅱£30-£66 dB&B⇨🅱£60-£80
⊂ 28P xmas
⌖ French V ✿ 🅻 Lunch £12.50-£18 High tea £1.20-£6 Dinner £15.95-£26 Last dinner 10pm
Credit Cards 1 2 3 5 £

★★ 69% Regent
Regent Square DN1 2DS (on the corner of the A630 & A638, 1m from racecourse) ☎(0302) 364180 & 364336 FAX (0302) 322331
RS Bank Hols
Located in the town centre, and adjacent to a park, this friendly family-owned hotel has a range of individually styled bars providing either a quiet or lively atmosphere and serving a popular variety of bar food and beers. Bedrooms vary in style and all are equipped with good modern facilities.
50🅱(4fb)3🚪 CTV in all bedrooms ®⚥ T sB&B⇨🅱£44-£59.50 dB&B⇨🅱£49.50-£63.50 🇷
Lift ⊂ 20P sauna
⌖ English & French V ✿ 🅻 Lunch £3.25-£15 High tea £2.50-£5 Dinner £9.99-£13.50&alc Last dinner 10pm
CONF. Thtr 50 Class 30 Board 20 Del from £75
Credit Cards 1 2 3 4 5 £

Campanile
Doncaster Leisure Park, Bawtry Rd DN4 7PD (follow signs to Dome Leisure Centre and turn left at entrance to Dome complex)
☎(0302) 370770 FAX (0302) 370813
A nearby bar and bistro restaurant provides refreshments for travellers staying at this modern accommodation building. Bedrooms are well equipped and have en suite bathrooms. For more details about Campanile, consult the Contents page, under Hotel Groups.
50⇨🅱B⇨🅱£35.75 (room only)
CONF. Thtr 35 Class 35 Board 25 Del from £42.80

DONNINGTON
See **Telford**

DORCHESTER Dorset Map 03 SY69

★★★ 67% King's Arms
DT1 1HF ☎(0305) 265353 FAX (0305) 260269

Situated in the centre of town, this 300-year-old former coaching inn has public areas of great character and charm, with fine furniture and oak beams. The attractive bedrooms include a pretty four-poster room and a couple of incredibly grand suites. An extensive choice of dishes is offered in the restaurant, and breakfast is generally served in the conservatory area.
31⇨🅱Annexe2⇨🅱(1fb)2🚪 CTV in 31 bedrooms ® T ✱ sB&B⇨🅱£25-£55.50 dB&B⇨🅱£45-£79 🇷
Lift 36P xmas
⌖ English & French V ✿ 🅻 ⚥ Last dinner 9.30pm
CONF. Thtr 100 Class 12 Board 40
Credit Cards 1 2 3 £

DORCHESTER-ON-THAMES Oxfordshire Map 04 SU59

★★★ ❀68% White Hart
High St OX10 7HN ☎Oxford(0865) 340074 FAX (0865) 341082
(Rosette awarded for dinner only)
This old coaching inn has individually styled, comfortable bedrooms, some in cottage annexes off the courtyard car park.

Public areas have lots of traditional charm and in the Friary Restaurant chef John Wills offers carefully prepared dishes which are excellent value for money. Bar meals are also available.
19rm(2fb)2🛁⊁in 2 bedrooms CTV in 20 bedrooms ® T
✗ (ex guide dogs) sB&B⇨ℕ£66.50-£80 dB&B⇨ℕ£87-£123
🅿
CTV 25P ♿

V ✿ ☑ ✱ Lunch £8-£12 Dinner £15-£20 Last dinner 9pm
CONF. Thtr 40 Board 20 Del from £100
Credit Cards 1 2 3 5

DORKING Surrey Map **04** TQ14

★★★★62% **The Burford Bridge**
Burford Bridge, Box Hill RH5 6BX (2m NE A24) ☎(0306) 884561 FAX (0306) 880386

FORTE Heritage

This popular and long established hotel with its attractive terraced gardens lies in the lee of Box Hill. The extensive lounges are most attractive and a good menu of light refreshments is served at the table. Bedrooms vary, some with elaborate beds, and the garden wing rooms with balconies.
48⇨ℕ⊁in 16 bedrooms CTV in all bedrooms ® T
sB⇨ℕfr£85 dB⇨ℕfr£85 (room only) 🅿
⊄ 100P ✲ ⇋ (heated) xmas
V ✿ ☑ ✱ Lunch fr£9.95&alc Dinner fr£20.95&alc Last dinner 10pm
CONF. Thtr 300 Class 100 Board 60 Del from £125
Credit Cards 1 2 3 5

★★★57% **The White Horse**
High St RH4 1BE ☎(0306) 881138 FAX (0306) 887241

FORTE Heritage

The old coaching inn offers limited public areas which can become rather crowded at times as they are popular with locals. Bedrooms in the main building are gradually being improved, while those in the garden annexe provide a good standard.
36⇨ℕAnnexe32⇨ℕ(2fb)1🛁⊁in 20 bedrooms CTV in all bedrooms ® T sB⇨ℕ£70 dB⇨ℕ£70-£85 (room only) 🅿
⊄ 73P xmas
V ✿ ☑ ✱ Lunch £10.25-£13.50&alc Dinner £16.95&alc Last dinner 10pm
Credit Cards 1 2 3 5

Forte Travelodge
Reigate Rd RH1 1QB (1.5m E, on A25)
☎(0306) 740361 Central Res (0800) 850950

FORTE Travelodge

This modern building offers a good standard of accommodation for overnight stops. Smart, spacious and well equipped bedrooms, all with en suite bathrooms, are suitable for family use, and meals may be taken at the nearby family restaurant. For more details about Travelodges, consult the Contents page, under Hotel Groups.
29⇨ℕ✱ B⇨ℕ£31.95 (room only)

DORNIE Highland *Ross & Cormarty* Map **14** NG82

★★64% *Castle Inn*
IV40 8DT ☎(059985) 205
RS Jan (ex New Year) & Feb

Good food and a welcoming atmosphere are just part of the appeal of this small, modernised Highland inn. There are views over Loch Long and Loch Alsh from the small lounge and attractive restaurant, where local seafood features strongly on the menu. Bedrooms provide most of the expected facilities, though several are small.
12rm(1⇨6ℕ)(1fb) CTV in all bedrooms ®

The White Hart Hotel and Restaurant
★★★
DORCHESTER ON THAMES OXFORD
Tel: Oxford (0865) 340074
Fax: Oxford (0865) 341082

17th C Coaching Inn in Thames side village offering every facility in its tastefully restored luxury suites and bedrooms.

Kings Arms Hotel

*Historic and famous, the Kings Arms is Dorchester's finest hotel, and the town's **only** genuine, officially accredited 3-star establishment. Queen Victoria stayed here; author Thomas Hardy lunched regularly in the Restaurant which now bears his name.*

With all accommodation totally refurbished to international standards, the Hotel offers a comprehensive choice from competitive business and tourist B & B rates, to incredible fantasy 'themed' suites and four-poster bedrooms, all with jacuzzi bath.

DORCHESTER, DT1 1HF.
TELEPHONE 0305 265353 FAX 0305 260269

Dornie - Draycott

20P
♀ Scottish & French **V** ✧ ⏛ Last dinner 9pm
Credit Cards [1] [3]

DORNOCH Highland *Sutherland* Map **14** NH78

★★66% **Dornoch Castle**
Castle St IV25 3SD (on A949) ☎(0862) 810216 FAX (0862) 810981
Closed Nov-Mar
Once the palace of the bishops of Caithness, parts of this building date back to the late 15th century. Two comfortable lounges overlook the sheltered formal garden; the panelled bar in the old tower reflects much of the building's original character, and the dining room offers 'Taste of Scotland' dishes. Bedrooms in the main house are in traditional style, while those in the wing have practical modern units.
4⇌↑Annexe13⇌↑(4fb) CTV in all bedrooms ℝ T sB&B⇌↑£35-£37 dB&B⇌↑£61-£78 ℞
Lift 16P ✿ ✲
♀ Scottish & Continental **V** ✧ ⏛ ✗ ✱ Lunch fr£7 Dinner fr£15.50 Last dinner 8.30pm
Credit Cards [1] [2] [3]

★★60% **Burghfield House**
IV25 3HN ☎(0862) 810212 FAX (0862) 810404
Closed Nov-Mar (ex Xmas & New Year)
This extended Victorian mansion is peacefully set in its own well tended grounds. Fine paintings and fresh flowers abound in the public rooms, which include a choice of comfortable lounges and a well stocked cocktail bar. Bedrooms vary in size, but have all the expected amenities and offer a mixture of modern and traditional styles.
14⇌↑Annexe20rm(16⇌↑)(8fb) CTV in all bedrooms ℝ T sB&B⇌↑£30-£45 dB&B⇌↑£60-£78 ℞
《 CTV 80P ✿ ✲ sauna solarium ⚬ *xmas*
♀ Scottish & French **V** ✧ ⏛ ✱ Bar Lunch fr£4.50&alc Dinner £13.75-£19.50 Last dinner 9.15pm
Credit Cards [1] [2] [3] [5]   £

DOUGLAS
See **Man, Isle of**

DOVER Kent Map **05** TR34

★★★63% **Dover Moat House**
Townwall St CT16 1SZ (on A20)
☎(0304) 203270 FAX (0304) 213230

Queens Moat Houses

This purpose-built hotel is ideally situated for the ferry ports and the town centre. More than half of the bedrooms have now been refurbished, though all rooms are spacious and have comfortable armchairs. The restaurant offers a choice of menus, and there is room service of light meals and snacks. The bar has a seafaring theme.
79⇌↑(32fb)✗ in 5 bedrooms CTV in all bedrooms ℝ T sB⇌↑£58-£76 dB⇌↑£63-£88 (room only) ℞
Lift 《 8P 🏊 (heated)
♀ English & French **V** ✧ ⏛ Lunch £10.25-£17.50&alc Dinner £15.50-£17.50&alc Last dinner 10.15pm
CONF. Thtr 80 Class 40 Board 40 Del £93
Credit Cards [1] [2] [3] [5]   £

★★★52% **White Cliffs**
Marine Pde, (Waterloo Crescent) CT17 9BW ☎(0304) 203633 FAX (0304) 216130
Closed 24-26 Dec
Upgrading continues at this functional hotel, though bedrooms are mostly spacious and its position overlooking the harbour couldn't be better. Management and staff are well intentioned, and the hotel is a useful stopover for cross-Channel traffic.

54⇌↑(6fb) CTV in all bedrooms ℝ T ✱ sB&B⇌↑£45-£55 dB&B⇌↑£72-£76 ℞
Lift 《 CTV 25 🚗 (£1 per night)
✧ ⏛ ✱ Sunday Lunch £8.95-£13.25 Dinner £8.95-£10.25&alc Last dinner 9.30pm
CONF. Thtr 25 Board 8
Credit Cards [1] [2] [3] [4] [5]   £

Forte Posthouse
Singledge Ln, Whitfield CT16 3LF (3m NW junc A2/A256) ☎(0304) 821222 FAX (0304) 825576

FORTE Posthouse

Suitable for both the business and leisure traveller, this bright hotel provides modern accommodation in well equippd bedrooms with en suite bathrooms. For more details about Forte Posthouse hotels, consult the Contents page, under Hotel Groups.
67⇌↑ ✱ B⇌↑£41.50-£53.50 (room only)
CONF. Thtr 40 Class 20 Board 20 Del £89.50

Travel Inn
Folkestone Rd CT15 7AB (on A20)
☎(0304) 213339

Purpose-built accommodation offers spacious and well equipped bedrooms, all with en suite bathrooms. Meals may be taken at the nearby family restaurant and pub. For more details about Travel Inns, consult the Contents page, under Hotel Groups.
30⇌↑ ✱ B⇌↑£33.50 (room only)

DOWNHAM MARKET Norfolk Map **05** TF60

★★64% **Castle**
High St PE38 9HF ☎(0366) 384311
Standards at the Castle Hotel continue to improve with enthusiastic proprietors gradually refreshing the public areas and bedrooms. Most of the latter are now light and cheerful with matching curtains, friezes and bedspreads. The restaurant has a predominantly French carte with tradional British dishes on the daily menus, and there is a popular range of bar meals.
12rm(9⇌↑)2₪ CTV in all bedrooms ℝ T
《 26P
♀ French **V** ✧ ⏛ ✗ Last dinner 9.30pm
Credit Cards [1] [2] [3]

DOWN THOMAS Devon Map **02** SX55

★★59% **Langdon Court**
PL9 0DY ☎Plymouth(0752) 862358 FAX (0752) 863428
This modernised Elizabethan mansion has bedrooms of varying size and quality which continue to be upgraded. The bar serves an extensive range of bar meals, with a dinner menu offered in the attractive restaurant.
15⇌↑(3fb) CTV in all bedrooms ℝ T ✱ sB&B⇌↑£28-£41.50 dB&B⇌↑£51.50-£62.50 ℞
100P ✲ nc4yrs
♀ French **V** ✧ ⏛ ✱ Sunday Lunch £8.95 Dinner £14.95&alc Last dinner 9.30pm
Credit Cards [1] [2] [3] [5]

DRAYCOTT Derbyshire Map **08** SK43

★★★56% **Tudor Court**
Gypsy Ln DE72 3PB ☎Derby(0332) 874581 FAX (0332) 873133
Standing in 8 acres of grounds, this is a modern hotel, built in traditional style.
30⇌↑(8fb)4₪ CTV in all bedrooms ℝ T sB&B⇌↑fr£48 dB&B⇌↑fr£63 ℞
《 CTV 300P ✲

♥ English & French V ❀ ⌨ ⅍ ✻ Lunch fr£6.75 Dinner fr£14.95&alc Last dinner 10pm
CONF. Thtr 200 Class 50 Board 40 Del from £70
Credit Cards [1][2][3][5]

DRIFFIELD, GREAT Humberside Map 08 TA05
★★★69% **Bell**
46 Market Place YO25 7AP
☎Driffield(0377) 46661 FAX (0377) 43228

Situated in the centre of town, this gleaming, whitewashed 250-year-old hotel has the character of a coaching inn and a friendly and deliberately informal style. Original features include oak panelling and the flagstoned Corn Exchange, once an open archway. Furnishings throughout combine solid period pieces with pretty cottage-style printed wallpaper. The restaurant is candlelit and has charming fresh flower posies.
14⇌2🛏⅍in 2 bedrooms CTV in all bedrooms ® T
✠ (ex guide dogs) sB&B⇌£65-£71 dB&B⇌£91-£96 🅿
《 50P ✿ ⌨ (heated) squash snooker sauna solarium gymnasium steam room whirlpool masseur nc12yrs
V ❀ ⌨ ⅍ Lunch fr£7.95 Dinner £12-£20alc Last dinner 10pm
CONF. Thtr 250 Class 100 Board 50
Credit Cards [1][2][3][5]   (£)

★★⎚57% **Wold House Country**
Nafferton YO25 0LD (3m E A166) ☎Driffield(0377) 254242 FAX (0377) 254242
Closed 24-27 Dec
Friendly, informal family service is provided at this distinctive country hotel which is set in spacious grounds, and enjoys panoramic views over open countryside.
9rm(7⇌✶)Annexe1 ✶(4fb) CTV in all bedrooms ®
sB&Bfr£35 sB&B⇌✶£40 dB&Bfr£55 dB&B⇌✶£65
CTV 40P ✿ ⌨ (heated) snooker putting table tennis
V ❀ Lunch £7-£9 Dinner £13-£14.50 Last dinner 8.30pm
Credit Cards [1][3]   (£)

DROITWICH Hereford & Worcester Map 03 SO86
★★★★70% **Château Impney**
WR9 0BN (on A38) (IMP) ☎(0905) 774411 FAX (0905) 772371
Closed Xmas
In the style of a French château, this beautiful and elegant hotel was built as a private house in the mid-19th century and stands in extensive landscaped parkland. Popular with a wide variety of guests, it offers good, attentive service, well equipped bedrooms and many other attributes.
67⇌✶(1fb)1🛏 CTV in all bedrooms ® T sB⇌✶£49.95-£99.95 dB⇌✶£59.95-£119.95 (room only)
Lift 《 CTV 1000P ✿ ♟ (hard) ♫
♥ English & French V ❀ ⌨ ⅍ Lunch £9.99-£10.99&alc Dinner £10.99-£15.99&alc Last dinner 9.30pm
CONF. Thtr 1000 Class 600 Board 300 Del from £93.94
Credit Cards [1][2][3][5]

★★★★57% **Raven**
WR9 8DU (IMP) ☎(0905) 772224 FAX (0905) 772371
Closed Xmas
This former coaching inn has been enlarged over the years to provide extensive conference and banqueting facilities. Public rooms have preserved a traditional character with wood-panelled walls and service is prompt and friendly. Bedrooms are in the process of upgrading.
72⇌✶(1fb)2🛏 CTV in all bedrooms ® T sB⇌✶£49.95-£99.95 dB⇌✶£59.95-£119.95 (room only)
Lift 《 CTV 250P ✿ ♫
♥ English & French V ❀ ⌨ ⅍ Lunch £9.99-£10.99&alc Dinner £10.99-£15.99&alc Last dinner 9.30pm
CONF. Thtr 150 Class 65 Board 50 Del from £99.94
Credit Cards [1][2][3][5]
See advertisement in colour section

Burghfield House Hotel
Dornoch Sutherland IV25 3HN ★★
Tel: (0862) 810212   Fax: 0862 810404

Turreted Baronial Country House Hotel run by the Currie family since 1946 and situated in 5 acres of beautiful gardens.

Extensively refurbished 1991

Superb food and wines

Golf packages on Royal Dornoch and other nearby courses

Fishing available

All rooms with private facilities and colour TV/Direct dial telephone/coffee & tea makers/hair dryer etc

3 conference rooms to accommodate 2-200

★★
CASTLE INN

8-10 FRANCIS ST. DORNIE, KYLE OF LOCHALSH ROSS-SHIRE IV50 8TD TEL 059985 205

Beautifully situated in the village of Dornie and only 2 minutes walk from Eilan Donan Castle with views over the Cullins of Skye this family run hotel is ideal for touring, walking & sea fishing.

The Hotel has been completely renovated to a high standard with 12 bedrooms — 7 en suite.

Delightful imaginative cooking

Children welcome

Only 10 minutes from ferry to Skye

Please write or telephone

Droitwich - Dulnain Bridge

Forte Travelodge
Rashwood Hill WR9 8DA (2m N, on A38 from junc 5 at M6) ☎Wychbold(052786) 545 Central Res (0800) 850950

This modern building offers a good standard of accommodation for overnight stops. Smart, spacious and well equipped bedrooms, all with en suite bathrooms, are suitable for family use, and meals may be taken at the nearby family restaurant. For more details about Travelodges, consult the Contents page, under Hotel Groups.

32⇨⇔* B⇨⇔£31.95 (room only)

DRONFIELD Derbyshire Map 08 SK37

★★**62% Chantry**
Church St S18 6QB (opp church with spire) ☎(0246) 413014 FAX (0246) 413014

This small Georgian house is tucked away in the centre of the town, set back from the road in a quiet location, with a delightful garden. Bedrooms, whilst compact, are light in appearance, well maintained and all have modern en suite facilities. Over recent years the small public rooms have been refurbished and extended, with the conservatory proving popular for morning coffee, light lunches and snacks. The philosophy of the chefs, brothers Wayne and Jamie Bosworth, is to offer modern English cooking and value for money, which is combined with a warm welcome and attentive service.

7⇨⇔ CTV in all bedrooms ✱ sB&B⇨⇔£40 dB&B⇨⇔£52-£50
28P 🚗 ❊
♀ English & French V ♢ ⚌ ✱ Lunch £3.50-£10.25alc Dinner £14.95-£20 Last dinner 10pm
Credit Cards [1] [2] [3]

DRUMBEG Highland *Sutherland* Map 14 NC13

★★**65% Drumbeg**
Assynt IV27 4NW (on B896) ☎(05713) 236 FAX (05713) 333

A complete transformation has taken place at this small Highland holiday and fishing hotel, tastefully refurbished under the caring direction of owners Jean and John Hay. Bedrooms (all no-smoking) have comfortable pine furniture and most of the expected amenities, while public areas include a choice of comfortable lounges and a well-stocked snug bar. A 4-course dinner is served in the attractive dining room.

6⇨⇔⊁in all bedrooms CTV in all bedrooms ® ⚌ ✈ sB&B⇨⇔fr£38 dB&B⇨⇔fr£66
CTV 30P ❊ nc *xmas*
V ♢ ⚌ ⊁ Sunday Lunch £10 Dinner £15&alc Last dinner 9pm
Credit Cards [1] [3]

DRYMEN Central *Stirlingshire* Map 11 NS48

★★★**66% Buchanan Highland**
G63 0BQ (Scottish Highland) ☎(0360) 60588 FAX (0360) 60943

Situated in a picturesque village, close to eastern Loch Lomondside, this former coaching inn now attracts the conference and leisure market. Bedrooms are tastefully furnished and well equipped. Public ares, in a more traditional style, include a food bar and good modern leisure facilities.

50⇨⇔(3fb)1🛏 CTV in all bedrooms ® ⚌ T sB&B⇨⇔£72-£80 dB&B⇨⇔£116-£128 🍴
(100P ❊ 🏊 (heated) squash sauna solarium gymnasium bowling green 🎵 *xmas*
♀ Scottish & French V ♢ ⚌ ⊁ ✱ Lunch £7.50-£11.75 Dinner £18.50 Last dinner 9.30pm
Conf. Thtr 180 Class 100 Board 50 Del from £75
Credit Cards [1] [2] [3] [4] [5] £

Red star hotels are each highlighted by a pink tinted panel.

DUDLEY West Midlands Map 07 SO99

See also **Himley**

★★★★**60% The Copthorne Merry Hill**
Merry Hill ☎(0384) 482882 FAX (0384) 482773

Opened in April 1993, this hotel occupies a prime position overlooking the Merry Hill Centre. Accommodation is of course modern and offers a wide range of facilities, the 4th floor is made up entirely of 'Connoisseur' rooms with a separate lounge area. Public areas include a lounge where refreshments are available, popular conference facilities and leisure amenities. Faradays Restaurant and Bar overlooks the waterfront and is open all day.

138⇨⇔*⊁in 35 bedrooms CTV in all bedrooms ®⚌ T ✱ sB⇨⇔£89.50 dB⇨⇔£99 (room only) 🍴
Lift (🎱 CTV P 🏊 (heated) sauna solarium gymnasium
♀ International V ♢ ⚌ ⊁ ✱ Lunch £3.95-£17.95alc High tea fr£6.95alc Dinner £3.95-£17.95alc Last dinner 11pm
Credit Cards [1] [2] [3] [5]

★★★**62% Ward Arms**
Birmingham Rd DY1 4RN (Crown & Raven) ☎(0384) 458070 FAX (0384) 457502

With easy access to the M5, and close to both the zoo and Black Country museum, this hotel provides well equipped modern accommodation. Mrs Simpson's Carvery is a popular local meeting place and serves 3 joints daily plus limited daily specials.

72⇨⇔*⊁in 14 bedrooms CTV in all bedrooms ® T ✱ sB&B⇨⇔£39.50-£59.50 dB&B⇨⇔£52-£59.50 🍴
(150P *xmas*
♀ English & French V ♢ ⚌ ⊁ ✱ Lunch £6.95-£9alc High tea fr£4.50 Dinner £8.45-£16.50alc Last dinner 10pm
Conf. Thtr 120 Class 50 Board 60 Del from £75
Credit Cards [1] [2] [3]

★★**60% Station**
Birmingham Rd DY1 4RA (Crown & Raven) ☎(0384) 253418 FAX (0384) 457503

This commercial hotel is situated in the heart of the black country, opposite Dudley Zoo. Accommodation has been modernised and is well equipped. Public areas have recently been refurbished, and include the 'Trindles' steak house restaurant.

38⇨⇔(7fb) CTV in all bedrooms ® T
Lift (75P
♀ English & French V ♢ ⚌ Last dinner 9pm
Conf. Thtr 250 Class 120 Board 20 Del from £65
Credit Cards [1] [2] [3]

Forte Travelodge
Dudley Rd(3m W, on A461)
☎(0384) 481579 Central Res (0800) 850950

This modern building offers a good standard of accommodation for overnight stops. Smart, spacious and well equipped bedrooms, all with en suite bathrooms, are suitable for family use. There is no restaurant adjacent to this Travelodge. For more details about Travelodges, consult the contents page, under Hotel Groups.

32⇨⇔* B⇨⇔£31.95 (room only)

DULNAIN BRIDGE Highland *Morayshire* Map 14 NH92

★★★⊛**67% Muckrach Lodge**
PH26 3LY (off A938) ☎(047985) 257 FAX (047985) 325
Closed 1-27 Nov

Ten acres of grounds provide a picturesque setting for this hunting lodge turned country-house hotel. Well equipped bedrooms are modern in style, the lounge is comfortably traditional, the cocktail bar popular for snack meals, the attractive restaurant extends to a conservatory and offers robust cooking, tending towards good local produce and rich sauces.

Dulnain Bridge - Dumfries

10⇨♠Annexe2⇨♠(3fb)1♿ CTV in all bedrooms ® T
✻ (ex guide dogs) sB&B⇨♠fr£39 dB&B⇨♠£78-£98 ♬
50P 3🛁 ⛳ ♣ ♪
♀ British & French V Lunch £10.50-£15alc Dinner £22.50&alc
Last dinner 9pm
Credit Cards 1 2 3 5

DULVERTON Somerset Map 03 SS92

★★★⭐ 71% **Carnarvon Arms**
TA22 9AE (leave A396 at Exbridge onto B3222, hotel 1m on
right) (Logis) ☎(0398) 23302 FAX (0398) 24022
This imposing Victorian railway hotel is geared to the fishing,
shooting and hunting fraternity, with its own stretch of river, gun
room and stabling. Bedrooms are of a fair size, and extensive public
areas include a series of comfortable lounges with open fires. In
addition to the main dining room, there is a buttery bar serving
snacks.
25rm(22⇨1♠)(2fb) CTV in all bedrooms T ✻ sB&B£50-£60
sB&B⇨♠£55-£75 dB&B£94-£114 dB&B⇨♠£104-£152 (incl dinner) ♬
120P ⛳ ♣ ≋ (heated) ℘ (hard) ♦ snooker clay pigeon
shooting hairdressing salon xmas
V ♀ ⚴ ⚡ ✶ Lunch fr£10.75&alc Dinner fr£19.75 Last dinner
8.30pm
CONF. Thtr 100 Class 25 Board 50 Del from £55
Credit Cards 1 3 £

★★⭐♠ **ASHWICK HOUSE**
TA22 9QD (3m NW off
B3223) ☎(0398) 23868

Built in 1901, Ashwick House
is set in a 6-acre estate on the
Exmoor hills. Its baronial hall
still displays its original
William Morris wallpaper,
there is a choice of lounges
and generously sized bedrooms some furnished with curiosities
like talking scales. Excellent personal service is provided by
proprietor Mr Sherwood, who also prepares a set 4-course
dinner which might offer a fluffy Roquefort mousse, creamy
leek and potato soup, noisettes of lamb in a simple port sauce
and delicious bread and butter pudding.

6⇨ CTV in all bedrooms T ✻ sB&B⇨£59-£73
dB&B⇨£100-£130 (incl dinner) ♬
25P 2🚗 (£2) ⛳ ♣ solarium nc8yrs xmas
♀ International ♀ ⚴ ⚡ Sunday Lunch fr£14 Dinner
fr£21 Last dinner 8.30pm £

★★ 64% **Lion**
Bank Square TA22 9BU ☎(0398) 23444
This small, popular hotel stands in the centre of the village and
locals can be found enjoying a game of snooker in the busy lounge
bar. Bedrooms are modern and well equipped. The public areas are
traditional in style with a cosy residents' lounge on the first floor.
13⇨♠(1fb)1♿ CTV in all bedrooms ®♉ T
CTV 6P clay pigeon shooting
♀ English, French & Italian V ♀ Last dinner 9pm
Credit Cards 1 3

Satellite television – look for this symbol ♉
in the directory entries.

DUMBARTON Strathclyde *Dunbartonshire* Map 10 NS37

★★ 66% *Dumbuck*
Glasgow Rd G82 1EG (on A814 on eastern outskirts)
☎(0389) 34336 FAX (0389) 34234
This popular business and function hotel lies on the eastern outskirts
of the town. Bedrooms in the original house have been upgraded,
while those in the rear extension are more functional but equally
comfortable and quieter. The restaurant, open only at lunch time,
offers a wide choice of dishes.
22⇨♠(2fb) CTV in all bedrooms ®♉ T
(200P ♣ pool table
♀ Scottish & French V ♀ ⚡ Last dinner 9.30pm
Credit Cards 1 2 3 4 5

Forte Travelodge
Milton G82 2TY (1m E, on A82 westbound)
☎(0389) 65202 Central Res (0800) 850950

*This modern building offers a good standard of accommodation
for overnight stops. Smart, spacious and well equipped
bedrooms, all with en suite bathrooms, are suitable for family
use, and meals may be taken at the nearby family restaurant. For
more details about Travelodges, consult the contents page,
under Hotel Groups.*
32⇨♠✻ B⇨♠£31.95 (room only)

DUMFRIES Dumfries & Galloway *Dumfriesshire*
Map 11 NX97

See also **Carrutherstown**
★★★ 65% **Cairndale Hotel & Leisure Club**
English St DG1 2DF ☎(0387) 54111 FAX
(0387) 50555

Centrally situated between town centre and railway station, this
privately owned hotel offers a range of bedrooms, including some
comfortable executive rooms. There is a choice of eating options.
76⇨♠(8fb)✼ in 16 bedrooms CTV in all bedrooms ®♉ T
sB&B⇨♠£69-£79 dB&B⇨♠£79-£99 ♬
Lift (CTV 70P 🅿 (heated) sauna solarium gymnasium steam
room spa bath beauty salon ♫ xmas
♀ British, French & Italian V ♀ ⚴ ⚡ ✶ Lunch £6.50-
£7.50&alc High tea fr£5 Dinner £15-£17.50&alc Last dinner
9.30pm
CONF. Thtr 120 Class 60 Board 30 Del from £75
Credit Cards 1 2 3 4 5 £

See advertisement on page 217

★★★ 63% **Station**
49 Lovers Walk DG1 1LT ☎(0387) 54316 FAX
(0387) 50388

Situated beside the station, this sandstone hotel dates from 1896 and
retains many original features, although the bedrooms are modern
in style. Lounge areas are limited but there is a spacious bar and a
choice of eating places.
32⇨♠(1fb) CTV in all bedrooms ®♉ T sB&B⇨♠£45-£70
dB&B⇨♠£55-£85 ♬
Lift (40P xmas
♀ British, Italian & French V ♀ ⚡ Bar Lunch fr£1.20&alc
High tea £5.75 Dinner £14&alc Last dinner 10pm
CONF. Thtr 60 Class 10 Board 35 Del from £60
Credit Cards 1 2 3 5 £

See advertisement on page 217

★ 61% *Skyline*
123 Irish St DG1 2NS ☎(0387) 62416
Closed 25 Dec & 1-2 Jan
Situated in a quiet side street in the town centre, this small owner-
run hotel offers friendly service and modest, well maintained
accommodation.

➤

Dumfries - Dundee

6rm(2⇌)(2fb) CTV in all bedrooms ® ✈
CTV 20P
V

DUNBAR Lothian *East Lothian* Map 12 NT67

★★65% Bayswell
Bayswell Park EH42 1AE ☎(0368) 62225 FAX (0368) 62225

From its position on the cliff top this friently family-run hotel enjoys unrestricted sea views. Bedrooms are practical and modern with a good range of facilities. On the ground floor is a well stocked snug bar, and the breakfast room (formerly the sun lounge). The residents' lounge and smart dining room are on the first floor.
13⇌(4fb) CTV in all bedrooms ® ⚥ T ✱ sB&B⇌£39.50-£42.50 dB&B⇌£59-£64 ⍰
CTV 20P putting green ♪ *xmas*
⚲ British & Italian V ✧ ⍭ ✱ Lunch fr£6.50 High tea fr£5.25 Dinner fr£12.50&alc Last dinner 9pm
Credit Cards [1][2][3][5] (£)

★★63% Redheugh
Bayswell Park EH42 1AE (Logis) ☎(0368) 62793 FAX (0368) 62793
Closed Xmas & New Year
A small and friendly private hotel in a quiet residential area on the western side of the town, with comfortable, well equipped bedrooms of varying size, suited to commercial guests. The cosy lounge has a corner bar and meals are home-cooked.
10⇌(2fb) CTV in all bedrooms ® T sB&B⇌£32-£35 dB&B⇌£50-£59 ⍰
CTV ⍟ nc8yrs
V Dinner £15.50-£16.50 Last dinner 8.30pm
Credit Cards [1][2][3][5] (£)

★❀66% *The Courtyard Hotel & Restaurant*
Wood Bush Brae EH42 1HB ☎(0368) 64169
RS 1st 3wks in Jan
Careful conversion of former fishermen's cottages has created this popular little hotel, delightfully situated by the edge of the water. Chef/patron Peter Bramley continues to offer a range of enjoyable Taste of Scotland dishes in the intimate first floor restaurant overlooking the sea. Bedrooms are compact and well kept.
6rm(1⇌) CTV in all bedrooms ®
CTV 6P
⚲ International Last dinner 9.30pm
Credit Cards [1][3]

DUNBLANE Central *Perthshire* Map 11 NN70

★★★★❀❀ ⍟
CROMLIX HOUSE
Kinbuck FK15 9JT (3 m NE B8033) ☎(0786) 822125
FAX (0786) 825450
RS Jan-Feb

This considerably extended Victorian family house was built in 1874 and stands in a 5,000-acre estate. It has a fine collection of paintings and antiques, and even has an old chapel, still used for weddings and christenings. Many of the country house-style bedrooms have their own lounges, and extensive public areas

include a large lounge, a delightful conservatory, a library, and an inviting hall with a log fire. A set 4-course dinner and a 3-course lunch is provided, with alternatives available but not encouraged. A meal might consist of loin of hare in a tart with creamed spinach, fish lasagne with langoustine sauce; breast of pigeon with blackcurrant sauce and, to finish, poached pear and layers of puff pastry in a raspberry sauce. There is an extensive wine list and many notable bins.
14⇌ CTV in all bedrooms T
50P 1⚲ ⍽ ✻ ♀ (hard) ✈ clay pigeon shooting croquet
V ✧ ⍭ Last dinner 10.30pm
Credit Cards [1][2][3][5]

★★64% Stirling Arms
Stirling Rd FK15 9EP (on B8033)
☎(0786) 822156 FAX (0786) 825300

This 17th-century hotel by the bridge in the city centre retains its historic character and provides unpretentious bedrooms, a cosy lounge bar popular with locals and a wide range of wholesome foods.
7rm(1⇌3⍯)(1fb) CTV in all bedrooms ® ⚥ T sB£35 sB&B⇌£40 dB&B£50 dB&B⇌£60
CTV 9P ⍽ ♪
⚲ International V ✧
Credit Cards [1][3]

DUNCHURCH Warwickshire Map 04 SP47

Forte Travelodge
London Rd, Thurlaston CV23 9LG (A45, westbound)
☎(0788) 521538 Central Res (0800) 850950

FORTE Travelodge

This modern building offers a good standard of accommodation for overnight stops. Smart, spacious and well equipped bedrooms, all with en suite bathrooms, are suitable for family use, and meals may be taken at the nearby family restaurant. For more details about Travelodges, consult the Contents page, under Hotel Groups.
40⇌✱ B⇌£31.95 (room only)

DUNDEE Tayside *Angus* Map 11 NO43

See also **Auchterhouse**

★★★65% Queens
160 Nethergate DD1 4DU ☎(0382) 22515 FAX (0382) 202668

CONSORT HOTELS

Substantial impovements are being made at this popular business, conference and function hotel in the city centre, with tasteful refurbishment of the cocktail bar, lounge and Brasserie Restaurant, and upgrading of many of the bedrooms.
47⇌(3fb) CTV in all bedrooms ® ⚥ T ✈ (ex guide dogs) sB&B⇌£34-£63 dB&B⇌£47-£87 ⍰
Lift ⍟ 80P
⚲ Continental V ✧ ⍭ Lunch £8.95-£9.95&alc High tea £4.85-£7.20alc Dinner £14.95-£16.95&alc Last dinner 10pm
CONF. Thtr 180 Class 60 Board 60 Del from £60
Credit Cards [1][2][3][5] (£)

See advertisement on page 219

★★★65% Swallow
Kingsway West, Invergowrie DD2 5JT (3.5m W off A972 Dundee Ring Road) ☎(0382) 641122 FAX (0382) 568340

SWALLOW HOTELS

At the western end of the bypass, this modern business hotel has evolved from extensions to a baronial mansion. Bedrooms vary in size, and there is a comfortable foyer lounge and conservatory restaurant.

Comlongon Castle Country House Hotel ★★ 64%

Clarencefield, Dumfries DG1 4NA
Tel: 038787 283   Fax: 038787 266

A medieval castle hotel set in 50 secluded acres. All rooms en suite, some with jacuzzis and 4 poster beds including 2 Honeymoon chambers.

Guests are given a pre-dinner candle light tour of the massive 15th century Keep.

Candle light dinner includes traditional Scottish Fayre.

Small wedding ceremonies can be arranged in the medieval Great Hall.

Full details and brochure on request.

AA ★★★ Country House

David and Mary Allen, your resident owners and hosts, welcome you to their country house hotel, sited in grass and parkland set back from the A75. All individually appointed bedrooms have full facilities and most have pleasant views of the surrounding countryside.

The Copper Beech Restaurant offers you an excellent cuisine, in an informal and relaxing atmosphere.

The hotel has many leisure facilities including, indoor swimming pool, fitness rooms, solarium and snooker.

The conference facilities can provide for most requests.

There are many places of interest to visit from this ideal location.

Hetland Hall Hotel
CARRUTHERSTOWN
DUMFRIES DG1 4JX
TELEPHONE: 0387 84201
FACSIMILE: 0387 84211

Doesn't this sound like a good hotel?

Free parking; friendly staff; excellent food in a stylish restaurant or continental Cafe Bar; two bars; a pleasant bedroom with tea and coffee facilities; colour TV and bath or shower en suite; an ample supply of hot water, soap, shampoo, fluffy towels; all this and a warm comfy bed.

Doesn't that sound good to you?

STATION HOTEL ★★★

Lovers Walk, Dumfries, Scotland DG1 1LT
Tel: (0387) 54316.   Fax: (0387) 50388

LEISURE BREAKS
S.T.B. ♛♛♛♛ Commended
AA ★★★

★ 14m Heated Indoor Pool ★ Sauna ★ Steam Room ★ Hot Spa Bath ★ Gymnasium ★ Sunbeds ★ Toning Tables ★ Health and Beauty Salon

76 Rooms with private facilities

Weekend Breaks from £50.00 per night

Dinner dance every Saturday with traditional Ceilidh every Sunday night during summer months

Golfing Breaks from £50.00 per person

24 hour Conference Rates £55.00 (Twin); £75.00 (Single)

Cairndale Hotel and Leisure Club
English Street,
Dumfries DG1 2DF
Tel: 0387 54111
Fax: 0387 50555

Dundee - Dunfermline

110⇌🛏2🛁🍴in 21 bedrooms CTV in all bedrooms ®☎ T ✱ sB&B⇌🛏£86 dB&B⇌🛏£100 🅿
⟨ 120P ✿ ▣ (heated) sauna solarium gymnasium mountain bike hire nature trail putting *xmas*
♀ Scottish & French V ♡ ♈ ✂ ✱ Lunch £9-£14 Dinner fr£19&alc Last dinner 9.45pm
CONF. Thtr 80 Class 30 Board 50 Del £100
Credit Cards [1][2][3][5]

★★★62% Angus Thistle
101 Marketgait DD1 1QU (500yds from railway station) ☎(0382) 26874 FAX (0382) 22564

Business guests and coach-tours are the main customers of this modern purpose-built hotel, which is also a popular for conferences and functions. It has an attractive split-level restaurant and comfortable cocktail bar.
58⇌🛏(4fb)2🍴🍴in 11 bedrooms CTV in all bedrooms ® T ✱ sB⇌🛏£72 dB⇌🛏£90 (room only) 🅿
Lift ⟨ 20P whirlpool *xmas*
♀ International V ♡ ♈ ✂ ✱ Lunch £10 Dinner £12.50&alc Last dinner 9.30pm
CONF. Thtr 500 Class 200 Board 200 Del from £70
Credit Cards [1][2][3][4][5]

★★69% The Shaftesbury
1 Hyndford St DD2 1HQ ☎(0382) 69216 FAX 0382 641598
This former jute baron's mansion has been carefully restored to create a comfortable hotel with good personal service. Bedrooms vary in size but are well equipped, and there is a honeymoon suite on the top floor. Rachel's Restaurant serves interesting food from the reasonably priced table d'hôte menu.
12⇌🛏(2fb) CTV in all bedrooms ® T sB&B⇌🛏£38-£50 dB&B⇌🛏£58-£70 🅿
CTV 2🅿 🚫
♀ Scottish & French V ♡ ♈ ✱ Lunch £5-£15 Dinner £17.50-£21 Last dinner 9.15pm
Credit Cards [1][2][3][5]   £

Travel Inn
Kingsway West, Invergowrie DD2 5JU (on A972 between Invergowrie & Dundee)
☎(0382) 561115

Purpose-built accommodation offers spacious and well equipped bedrooms, all with en suite bathrooms. Meals may be taken at the nearby family restaurant and pub. For more details about Travel Inns, consult the Contents page, under Hotel Groups.
40⇌🛏✱ B⇌🛏£33.50 (room only)

DUNDONNELL Highland *Ross & Cromarty* Map **14** NH08

★★★✪71% Dundonnell
IV23 2QS (turn off A835 at Braemore Junction on to A832)
☎(085483) 234 FAX (085483) 366
Closed 22 Nov-Feb (ex Xmas/New Year)
This welcoming Highland holiday hotel on the shore of Little Loch Broom has been run by the same proprietors for over 30 years. Bright airy bedrooms provide the expected amenities, while public areas include a well stocked cocktail bar as well as a choice of lounges; the attractive restaurant offers table d'hôte and à la carte menus which feature prime Scottish beef and the best of fresh seafood and game.
24⇌🛏 CTV in all bedrooms ® T sB&B⇌🛏£35-£49.50 dB&B⇌🛏£59-£85 🅿
60P *xmas*
V ♡ ♈ ✱ Bar Lunch £10-£20alc High tea £7.50-£8.95 Dinner £22&alc Last dinner 8.30pm
Credit Cards [1][3]

DUNFERMLINE Fife Map **11** NT08

★★★65% Pitbauchlie House
Aberdour Rd KY11 4PB (1m S of town centre on B916) ☎(0383) 722282 FAX (0383) 620738

In a residential area, south of the town centre, this privately owned hotel offers friendly, informal service and is popular with business people. Bedrooms vary in size and style, the best being the recently built executive rooms. Public areas include a choice of comfortable bars and a small restaurant.
40⇌🛏(2fb)1🍴 CTV in all bedrooms ®☎ T ✱ sB&B⇌🛏£50-£60 dB&B⇌🛏£64-£79 🅿
⟨ 70P ✿ solarium gymnasium *xmas*
♀ International V ♡ ♈ ✱ Lunch fr£7.75&alc Dinner fr£14&alc Last dinner 9pm
CONF. Thtr 150 Class 100 Board 60 Del from £72
Credit Cards [1][2][3][5]

★★★63% Keavil House
Crossford KY12 8QW (2m W A994)
☎(0383) 736258 FAX (0383) 621600

Standing in 12 acres of grounds this extended 18th-century country house caters for both business and holiday guests. Bedrooms are located in either the main house or the more modern wing overlooking the garden, and while they are generally compact and functional they have modern amenities. The hotel has a choice of restaurants at weekends.
32⇌🛏(1fb)1🍴 CTV in all bedrooms ®☎ T sB&B⇌🛏£63-£65 dB&B⇌🛏£80-£85 🅿
⟨ CTV 150P ✿ ▣ (heated) sauna solarium gymnasium jacuzzi aerobics studio steam room ♫ *xmas*
V ♡ ✂ Bar Lunch £4.50-£12.50alc Dinner £15.95-£18 Last dinner 9.30pm
CONF. Thtr 170 Class 30 Board 30 Del from £85
Credit Cards [1][2][3][5]   £

See advertisement on page 221

★★★62% King Malcolm Thistle
Queensferry Rd, Wester Pitcrenie KY11 5DS (on A823, S of town) ☎(0383) 722611 FAX (0383) 730865

Situated to the south of the town, this purpose-built, low-rise hotel offers well equipped if functional bedroom accommodation, while public areas include a pleasant restaurant and conservatory bar. The hotel is popular with tour groups.
48⇌🛏(2fb)🍴in 12 bedrooms CTV in all bedrooms ® T ✱ sB⇌🛏£65-£69 dB⇌🛏£75-£79 (room only) 🅿
⟨ 60P *xmas*
♀ Scottish & French V ♡ ♈ ✂ ✱ Lunch £4-£8.50&alc High tea fr£5.95 Dinner fr£14.95&alc Last dinner 10pm
CONF. Thtr 150 Class 50 Board 40 Del from £60
Credit Cards [1][2][3][4][5]

See advertisement on page 221

★★★56% Pitfirrane Arms
Main St, Crossford KY12 8NJ (0.5 W A994) ☎(0383) 736172 FAX (0383) 621760
This former coaching inn has been modernised and extended to provide compact, practical accommodation. Cosy public areas offer a choice of character bars, although lounge space is limited. The hotel is a popular function venue.
38⇌🛏(1fb) CTV in all bedrooms ®☎ T 🐕 (ex guide dogs) ✱ sB&B⇌🛏£25-£52 dB&B⇌🛏£36-£64 🅿
⟨ 72P sauna solarium ♫ *xmas*
♀ Scottish & French V ♡ ♈ ✂ High tea £9.50-£13.95 Dinner £9.95-£15.50&alc Last dinner 9.15pm
CONF. Thtr 40 Class 30 Board 20 Del from £45
Credit Cards [1][2][3]

Pitbauchlie House Hotel
DUNFERMLINE, FIFE

AA
★★★

Family owned and managed, a three star plus hotel set in private wooded grounds.
- 40 bedrooms, all with en-suite facilities, satellite TV and expected modern comforts.
- The Garden Restaurant, renowned locally for its unquavering excellence for lunch or dinner.
- Flexible conference facilities and ample parking.
- All facilities 7 days a week, open to non-residents.
- Only 4 miles from the Forth Road Bridge.

ABERDOUR RD, DUNFERMLINE
Tel: (0383) 722282 Fax: (0383) 620738

★★★AA

THE ANGUS
THISTLE HOTEL

Marketgait, Dundee DD1 1QU
Tel: 0382 26874   Fax: 0382 22564

Your choice in Dundee

For Reservations at over 100
Mount Charlotte Thistle Hotels
Telephone London: 071 937 8033.

THISTLE HOTELS

THE SHAFTESBURY
A Town House Hotel

AA ★★ 69%

Scottish Tourist Board HIGHLY COMMENDED

A former Jute Baron's Town House built in 1870 tastefully converted into twelve bedroom ensuite hotel. Rachel's Restaurant, during the conversions a sampler dated 1890, worked by Rachel Robertson Buist, was found, little did she know that one day a restaurant would be named after her. Our food is good, service informal. Situated near Ninewells and walking distance of the University. Dundee has much to offer the business person or tourist. Minotel corporate rates apply. Bargain breaks and special rates for all parents of all academic students of all colleges.

1Hyndford Street, Dundee DD2 1HQ
Tel: 0382 69216 Fax: 0382 641598

★★★

The Queen's
HOTEL
DUNDEE

Built in 1878 and Dundee's most prestigious privately owned City centre hotel. Locally situated for golfing, with St. Andrews and Carnoustie close by and only minutes away from Dundee shopping centres and theatre. Conference and banqueting. Facilities from "a biscuit to a banquet". Up to 180 guests.

★ 47 rooms all en suite ★ Remote control colour TV's with satellite channels ★ Radio alarm
★ Direct dial telephone ★ Tea/coffee making facilities ★ Hairdryer ★ Auto trouser press
★ Free parking for up to 80 vehicles
★ Chancellors Restaurant, Judges Lounge on first floor
★ Royal Piper Bar

For reservations contact:-
The Queen's Hotel, Nethergate, Dundee
Tel: (0382) 22515   Fax: (0382) 202668

Dunfermline - Dunoon

★★ 69% Elgin
Charlestown KY11 3EE (3m W of M90, junc 1, on loop road off A985, signposted Limekilns & Charlestown)
☎Limekilns(0383) 872257
This friendly, family-run hotel enjoys panoramic views of the Firth of Forth. Bedrooms are modern and attractive and offer a good range of facilities. Although there is a pleasant restaurant and cocktail bar, meals, other than at weekends, tend to be served in the bar area, which is also popular with non resident diners.
13⇌♠(3fb) CTV in all bedrooms ® T ⚞ (ex guide dogs) sB&B⇌♠£48-£50 dB&B⇌♠£65-£67 ⚑
70P ✻
V ◊ Bar Lunch £7-£13alc Dinner £9-£16alc Last dinner 9pm
Credit Cards ① ③

★★ 63% City
18 Bridge St KY12 8DA ☎(0383) 722538
RS 1 & 2 Jan

This lively, town centre hotel offers a sound modern standard of bedroom accommodation, a choice of bars and a coffee shop in addition to a small first floor restaurant. Lounge facilities, as such, are limited.
17⇌♠(1fb)1⚑ CTV in all bedrooms ® T
⚌ 20P
♡ French V ◊ ⚏ Last dinner 9pm
Credit Cards ① ② ③ ⑤

DUNKELD Tayside *Perthshire* Map **11** NO04

★★★✽✽✽⚏ KINNAIRD
Kinnaird Estate PH8 0LB
(4.5m N on B898)
☎Pitlochry(0796) 482440
FAX (0796) 482289
Closed Feb

Dating from 1770, this magnificent country house, which has belonged to the Ward family for over 60 years, is still lived in by Mrs Constance Ward. Resplendent with heirlooms, the elegant public rooms and discreetly luxurious bedrooms are redolent of a gracious Edwardian style. In the kitchens, Chef John Webber's touch is delicate, but the results are refreshingly distinctive. Our inspector praised a ragoût of lightly poached saltwater fish where each piece of salmon, sole, monkfish, snapper and scallop made its mark, the flavours enriched by the addition of cream, vermouth and basil to the juices. Roast breast of Gressingham duck was superbly tender, pink but with a crispy skin, and served with an interesting sauce flavoured with jasmine tea.
9⇌♠ CTV in all bedrooms T ⚞ ✻ sB&B⇌♠£135-£185 dB&B⇌♠£170-£230 ⚑
Lift 20P ⚌ ✻ ♪ (hard) ♫ snooker shooting nc12yrs *xmas*
⚏ ✻ Lunch £19.50-£24 Dinner £34-£38 Last dinner 9.30pm
Credit Cards ① ② ③

★★★ 63% Birnam
Birnam PH8 0BQ (off A9) ☎(0350) 727462 FAX (0350) 728979

This imposing period building epitomises the grand touring and coaching hotel of former days, offering spacious, comfortable public areas and soundly furnished bedrooms. Now its clientele is divided between coach parties and private tourists.
28⇌♠(1fb)1⚑ CTV in all bedrooms ® T sB&B⇌♠£45-£75 dB&B⇌♠£70-£95 ⚑
Lift 50P ✻
♡ English & French V ◊ Last dinner 8.30pm
Credit Cards ① ② ③ ⑤

DUNMOW, GREAT Essex Map **05** TL62

★★ 59% The Saracen's Head
High St CM6 1AG (take A120 towards Colchester turn left at rbt hotel 0.50m downhill) ☎(0371) 873901 FAX (0371) 875743

FORTE
Heritage

This former coaching inn dates back to 1620 though it has a Georgian façade. All but 5 bedrooms have been refurbished to the smart Heritage standard and the main building includes 3 suites with brass beds. Open plan public areas have beams and Tudor-style architecture and imminent upgrading will significantly enhance the overall appearance.
24⇌♠(3fb)⚑in 7 bedrooms CTV in all bedrooms ® T 50P
V ◊ ⚌ ⚏ ✻ Lunch £9.95 Dinner £15.95 Last dinner 9.30pm
CONF. Thtr 65 Class 30 Board 30 Del from £55
Credit Cards ① ② ③ ⑤

DUNNET Highland *Caithness* Map **15** ND27

★★ 62% Northern Sands
KW14 8DX ☎Barrock(084785) 270
A relaxed atmosphere prevails at this small, family-run hotel, close to a lovely sandy beach. The well decorated bedrooms are gradually being refurbished, and public rooms include a choice of bars, a cosy lounge and a smart restaurant offering a range of grills and pasta specialities.
9⇌♠(3fb) CTV in all bedrooms ® ⚞ (ex guide dogs) ✻ sB&B⇌♠£35.50-£40 dB&B⇌♠£57.50-£60 ⚑
CTV 50P
♡ French & Italian V ◊ ⚌ ✻ Lunch £1.95-£10.95&alc Dinner £10.95-£20alc Last dinner 8.30pm
Credit Cards ① ③

DUNOON Strathclyde *Argyllshire* Map **10** NS17

★★ 76% Enmore
Marine Pde, Kirn PA23 8HH (Logis) ☎(0369) 2230 FAX (0369) 2148
Closed 2-12 Jan RS Nov-Feb
Charmingly run by Angela and David Wilson, the Enmore is north of the town and has views over the Clyde. Some rooms have canopied or 4-poster beds, there is an elegant dining room and guests may use 2 good squash courts.
11⇌♠(2fb)3⚑ CTV in all bedrooms ® T sB&B⇌♠£28-£38 dB&B⇌♠£60-£120 ⚑
20P ⚌ ✻ squash ♁ *xmas*
♡ Scottish & French V ◊ ⚌ ⚏ Lunch £15&alc High tea fr£7.95 Dinner fr£25 Last dinner 8.30pm
CONF. Thtr 14 Class 20 Board 14 Del from £50
Credit Cards ① ③

★★ 60% Abbeyhill
Dhailing Rd PA23 8EA (on coast road, 0.75m from the pier) ☎(0369) 2204 FAX (0369) 2204
Lying between Dunoon and Kirn, this clean, fresh and well cared for resort hotel is in an elevated position with splendid views across the Firth of Clyde.
14⇌♠(3fb) CTV in all bedrooms ® T ⚞ (ex guide dogs) sB&B⇌♠£30 dB&B⇌♠£48 ⚑
40P ✻
◊ Dinner £12 Last dinner 8.30pm
Credit Cards ① ② ③

★ **69% Lyall Cliff**
141 Alexandra Pde, East Bay PA23 8AW ☎(0369) 2041
Closed 20 Dec-7 Jan
Originally a doctor's residence and surgery, this detached house overlooking the Clyde has been extended to provide comfortable, well maintained accommodation, including ground floor bedrooms. There is a lounge and a small snug bar. Food is home cooked, but be prepared to order your dinner at breakfast time; those who wait until later may find the choice more limited.
14🛏(4fb) CTV in all bedrooms ® sB&B🛏£22-£25 dB&B🛏£38-£44
12P 🚗 ✽
V ✗ Dinner £10&alc Last dinner 7.30pm
Credit Cards [1][3]

DUNSTABLE Bedfordshire Map **04** TL02
★★★ **67% Old Palace Lodge**
Church St LU5 4RT ☎(0582) 662201 FAX (0582) 696422
Closed 25-31 Dec RS Sat
This attractive ivy-clad hotel was developed around a building that may partly date back to 1100. Comfortable public areas furnished in period style include an comfortable oak-panelled lounge bar and an elegant restaurant. Bedrooms are generally spacious and include all modern comforts. A room service menu is available.
49⇨(6fb)2🛋✗in 6 bedrooms CTV in all bedrooms ® T ✽ sB⇨£43-£83.50 dB⇨£52-£83.50 (room only) 🍴
Lift ℂ 70P
♀ English & French V ☼ ♨ ✽ Lunch £16.50&alc
CONF. Thtr 45 Class 20 Board 20 Del from £85
Credit Cards [1][2][3][4][5]

For key to symbols see the Bookmark.

★★

21 Bedrooms all en-suite

PROPRIETORS: JANET & JIM INNES

RIDLEY DRIVE/HEATH ROAD, ROSYTH
Tel: (0383) 419977 Fax: (0383) 411728

The Inn is well positioned for travel to all parts of Scotland being only a few minutes from the M90. Within walking distance of Rosyth Dockyard/Naval Base.

Travelling by Motorway you should leave at Junction 1 and travel along Admiralty Road, past the Roundabout and take the first road on the left.

LIVE ENTERTAINMENT INCLUDING KARAOKE MOST EVENINGS.

★★★AA
KING MALCOLM
THISTLE HOTEL

Queensferry Road, Dunfermline KY11 5DS
Tel: 0383 722611   Fax: 0383 730865

Your choice in Dunfermline

For Reservations at over 100
Mount Charlotte Thistle Hotels
Telephone London: 071 937 8033.

THISTLE HOTELS

Spend some time in intensive care.

The recommended treatment for anyone needing to get away from it all is a relaxing stay in 3-star luxury, surrounded by twelve acres of gardens and woods, at Keavil House Hotel.

Here you'll receive a daily dosage of attentive yet unobtrusive, friendly service and be placed on a strict diet of as much superb and varied cuisine in the Keavil Restaurant as you can possibly manage.

Pamper yourself in the luxurious and extensive "Picture of Health" leisure club where help is on hand to offer intensive care, ensuring you get the most out of this special therapy.

Ideally situated for travelling all over Central Scotland, Keavil House is accustomed to offering sanctuary to those on business as well as pleasure.

KEAVIL HOUSE HOTEL
Crossford, Dunfermline
 Tel: (0383) 736258. Fax: (0383) 621600.
★★★   BEST WESTERN HOTELS

Dunstable - Durham

★★ 63% *Highwayman*
London Rd LU6 3DX ☎Luton(0582) 601122 FAX (0582) 603812
Situated south of the town, this busy commercial hotel offers smart new wing bedrooms in addition to smaller rooms in the main building, though all are equipped to the same standard. The dining room has both a set and popular à la carte menu, and there is a good range of real ales in the lounge bar.
53⇌♠(3fb) CTV in all bedrooms ® T
《 60P
♡ English & French V ♥ ⌨ Last dinner 9pm
Credit Cards ①②③⑤

Forte Travelodge
Watling St (3m N, on A5)
☎(0525) 211177 Central Res (0800) 850950

FORTE Travelodge

This modern building offers a good standard of accommodation for overnight stops. Smart, spacious and well equipped bedrooms, all with en suite bathrooms, are suitable for family use, and meals may be taken at the nearby family restaurant. For more details about Travelodges, consult the Contents page, under Hotel Groups.
28⇌♠✱ B⇌♠£31.95 (room only)

DUNSTER Somerset Map 03 SS94

★★★ 66% The Luttrell Arms
High St TA24 6SG ☎(0643) 821555 FAX (0643) 821567

FORTE Heritage

The Luttrell Arms is an interesting and historic building in a prime location opposite the famous Yarn Market. Bedrooms are of a high standard with attractive coordinating soft furnishings. The smart dining room has a gracious air and there is a hospitable feel to this well run and popular hotel.
27⇌♠4🛏⌀in 9 bedrooms CTV in all bedrooms ® T ✱
sB⇌♠fr£70 dB⇌♠fr£95 (room only) 🍴
3🐕 (£1 per night) ❋ *xmas*
V ♥ ⌨ ✱ Sunday Lunch £10.95 Dinner £16.95 Last dinner 9.30pm
Credit Cards ①②③⑤

★★ ⊛69% Exmoor House
12 West St TA24 6SN (turn off A39 Taunton/Minehead road at A396, signed Dunster, hotel 0.5m on right beyond church) ☎Minehead(0643) 821268
Closed Dec & Jan
Phil and Brendan Lally have created a 'home from home' atmosphere at their small, listed Georgian hotel, just off the busy main shopping area of Dunster. Bedrooms, all named after local villages, are attractively furnished and a ground-floor twin-bedded room is available. In the candlelit dining room Phil Lalley offers a short daily changing table d'hôte menu of wholesome dishes based on local produce.
7⇌♠⌀in all bedrooms CTV in all bedrooms ®
sB⇌♠£24.50-£35.50 dB⇌♠£49-£55 🍴
CTV ₽ ❋ nc12yrs
V ♥ ⌨ ⌀ Dinner £14.50 Last dinner 7.30pm
Credit Cards ①②③⑤

DURHAM Co Durham Map 12 NZ24
See also **Thornley**

★★★★ 68% Royal County
Old Elvet DH1 3JN (On fringe of town centre)
☎091-386 6821 FAX 091-386 0704

SWALLOW HOTELS

The Royal County is in the heart of the city, on the riverside close to the cathedral. A spacious foyer leads to an extensive range of facilities, including comfortable bars, 2 styles of dining and an extensive leisure club. Bedrooms are tastefully furnished and decorated, and many overlook the river. Staff are professional and friendly.
150⇌♠(4fb)1🛏⌀in 49 bedrooms CTV in all bedrooms ®⚡ T
sB&B⇌♠£50-£95 dB&B⇌♠£60-£115 🍴
Lift 《 120P 🏊 (heated) sauna solarium gymnasium steam room plunge pool impulse showers *xmas*
♡ International V ♥ ⌨ ⌀
Credit Cards ①②③④⑤

★★★ 70% *Ramside Hall*
Carrville DH1 1TD (3m NE A690)
☎091-386 5282 FAX 091-386 0399

CONSORT CROWN

Ramside Hall, set in beautiful, well tended grounds, has spacious public areas, including a very comfortable lounge, and 3 styles of dining in the main restaurant, the grill room or the carvery. Bedrooms are especially well furnished and spacious, some with whirlpool baths. Staff are friendly and have good professional skills.
82⇌♠(10fb)6🛏⌀in 36 bedrooms CTV in all bedrooms ®⚡ T
Lift 《 🎱 500P ❋ ♫ 🎵
V ♥ ⌨ Last dinner 10pm
Credit Cards ①②③⑤

★★★ 68% Three Tuns
New Elvet DH1 3AQ (from A1 follow A690 for city. At 1st rbt take 2nd exit then next rbt take 1st exit) ☎091-386 4326 FAX 091-386 1406

SWALLOW HOTELS

A former coaching inn dating from the 16th century, this friendly hotel in the city centre offers comfortable bedrooms with modern facilities and public areas with much historic character.
47⇌♠(1fb)⌀in 16 bedrooms CTV in all bedrooms ®⚡ T ✱
sB&B⇌♠£45-£80 dB&B⇌♠£75-£92.50 🍴
《 60P *xmas*
♡ English & French V ♥ ⌨ ⌀ ✱ Lunch £4.40-£9.25&alc Dinner £14.75&alc Last dinner 9.30pm
Credit Cards ①②③⑤

★★★ 64% Bowburn Hall
Bowburn DH6 5NH (3m SE junc A177/A1(M)) (RE)
☎091-377 0311 FAX 091-377 3459
Standing in 5 acres of grounds, this friendly hotel has well equipped bedrooms with good quality fabrics and furnishings. Food is available in the comfortable lounge bar or the restaurant with its attractive new conservatory extension.
19⇌ CTV in all bedrooms ® T ✈
CTV 100P ❋
V ♥ ⌨ Last dinner 10pm
Credit Cards ①②③⑤

★★★ ⊛63% *Hallgarth Manor*
Pittington DH6 1AB (3m E between A690 & B2183)
☎091-372 1188 FAX 091-372 1249
This attractive country house-style hotel has prettily decorated bedrooms with exposed beams and antique furniture. Public areas are spacious and interesting dinners are available in the split-level restaurant. Starters may include ham and spinach roulade, and for main course perhaps chicken in cream and mushroom sauce. Presentation is delightful and puddings are all home made.
23⇌♠ CTV in all bedrooms ® T
《 101P ❋
♡ International V ♥ ⌨ Last dinner 9.15pm
Credit Cards ①②③⑤

★★ 64% Bridge Toby
Croxdale DH1 3SP (3 miles south of city on A167) (Toby)
☎091-378 0524 FAX 091-378 9981
This modern hotel offers motel-style bedrooms with a parking space outside. An extensive range of mainly grill-type meals is available in the pleasant restaurant.
46⇌♠(4fb)⌀in 16 bedrooms CTV in all bedrooms ® T ✱
sB&B⇌♠£29.95-£49.95 dB&B⇌♠£49.95-£59.95 🍴

222

(CTV 150P ✿
🍴 Mainly grills V ⚬ 🍷 ✗ ✱ Bar Lunch £1.65-£4.25
Credit Cards 1 2 3 5

★★ **62%** *Newton Grange*
Finchale Rd, Brasside, Newton Hall DH1 5SA
☎091-386 0872

Newton Grange is family run and provides good value accommodation. An extensive range of food is offered, either in the spacious bar or beamed restaurant. There is a modern bedroom extension of well equipped rooms.
13⇌🐾(3fb)1🚭 CTV in all bedrooms ® T ✕ (ex guide dogs)
(90P 🚗 ✿ ✱ 🎵 ♿
🍴 English & French V ⚬ 🍷 Last dinner 9.45pm
Credit Cards 1 3 5

★★ **59%** *Rainton Lodge*
West Rainton DH4 6QY (4m NE on A690) ☎091-512 0540
FAX 091-584 1221

This modern-style, mainly commercial hotel provides bedrooms which vary in size, a comfortable bar and a good range of food, served in the bar or the pleasant restaurant.
27⇌🐾(1fb)1🚭 CTV in all bedrooms ® T ✕ (ex guide dogs)
✱ sB&B⇌🐾£25-£34.50 dB&B⇌🐾£35-£60 🍽
(CTV 80P ⟲ xmas
🍴 English & Italian V ⚬ 🍷 ✱ Lunch £7.95-£8.60&alc High tea £2.95-£7 Dinner £7.95-£8.60&alc Last dinner 10pm
CONF. Thtr 100 Class 60 Board 60 Del from £45.50
Credit Cards 1 3

Remember to book early for holiday
and bank holiday times.

DUROR Highland Map **14** NM95

★★ ✤✤**77%** **Stewart**
PA38 4BW ☎(063174) 268 FAX (063174) 328

Closed 16 Oct-Etr
(Rosettes awarded for dinner only)

Azaleas and rhododendrons abound in the gardens of the Lacy's extended Victorian hunting lodge. Bedrooms are all in the purpose built wing and are somewhat functional. In the kitchen is still to be found Michael Lacy's tried and tested formula for a 4-course dinner; this prepared from the best available fresh ingredients with fish and game featuring strongly. Uncomplicated modern British cooking allows natural flavours to come through well, and the wine list has something for most pockets and tastes.
20⇌🐾(2fb) CTV in all bedrooms ® T sB&B⇌🐾£40-£50 dB&B⇌🐾£80-£100 🍽
30P 🚗 ✿ ✱ clay pigeon shooting sailing
V ⚬ 🍷 ✗ Bar Lunch £5-£10 Dinner £25-£30 Last dinner 9pm
Credit Cards 1 2 3 5

DUXFORD Cambridgeshire Map **05** TL44

★★★ **62%** *Duxford Lodge*
Ickleton Rd CB2 4RU (junc 10 of M11 and A505)
☎Cambridge(0223) 836444 FAX (0223) 832271
RS Sat

This red brick Victorian house is set in neatly tended gardens in the centre of the village. With a relaxing and informal atmosphere, it has cosy public rooms used mainly by residents and diners. Bedroom styles vary, the best being in the main house, though the annexe is due for some attention.
11⇌🐾Annexe4⇌🐾 CTV in all bedrooms ® T

Durham - Duxford

Ramside Hall Hotel

Carrville
Durham DH1 1TD
DURHAM (091) 386 5282
Fax: (091) 386 0399

Location:
We're just off the A1(M)–A690 motorway interchange. Follow the dual carriageway towards Sunderland for 400 metres, turn right under the bridge and you're in our drive!

AA
★★★

Where a warm welcome awaits you . . .

82 bedrooms, all en-suite with colour TV
Trouser press • Telephones • Free in-house video
Tea and coffee making facilities

✱ *Live music seven nights a week*
✱ *The Pemberton Carvery*
✱ *Superb new Restaurant*
✱ *Steak Bar serving the finest Angus steaks*
✱ *Two Presidential Suites*
✱ *Large Ballroom*
✱ *Conference facilities*
✱ *New large car park*
✱ *Cocktail and Lounge Bars*
✱ *Sunday Luncheons*
✱ *Special weekend rates*
✱ *Wedding receptions a speciality*

Duxford - Eastbourne

34P ✤
English & French V ✤ Last dinner 9.30pm
Credit Cards 1 2 3 5

DYSERTH Clwyd Map 06 SJ27

★★★65% **Graig Park Hotel & Country Club**
LL18 6DX ☎Rhyl(0745) 571022 FAX (0745) 571024
A very modern hotel and leisure complex with just 12 bedrooms, all in an adjoining building, and each with an extra single bed available. The public areas are open plan with fine views over the sea and Rhyl. There is a bistro for informal meals, a bar and a large restaurant serving a good choice of meals.
12⇔♑(12b) in 8 bedrooms CTV in all bedrooms ® ⌿ T
sB&B⇔♑£38.50 dB&B⇔♑£52 ₽
Lift (80P ⊞ ✤ ⏹ (heated) squash sauna solarium gymnasium steamroom ⚘ xmas
English International V ✤ ⏚ ✱ Lunch £10.95&alc High tea £3.50 Dinner £10.95&alc Last dinner 9.45pm
CONF. Thtr 110 Class 80 Board 60 Del from £50
Credit Cards 1 3

EASINGTON Cleveland Map 08 NZ71

★★★✤ 🛌69% **Grinkle Park**
TS13 4UB (2m S off unclass rd linking A174/A171)
☎Guisborough(0287) 640515 FAX (0287) 641278
This impressive Victorian manor house stands in extensive grounds between the coast and the Cleveland Hills. Spacious bedrooms have good modern facilities and there are very comfortable lounges and bars with log fires. Chef Tim Backhouse offers menus of skilfully cooked dishes that make good use of local seasonal produce. A starter of chicken and prawn tartlets might be followed by guinea fowl cooked in gin and juniper berry sauce. The wine list is well chosen and service friendly and reliable.
20⇔♑2⊞ CTV in all bedrooms ® T ✱ sB&B⇔♑£65 dB&B⇔♑£80-£85 ₽
130P 2🅿 🚗 ✤ ♻ (hard) ♪ snooker croquet clay pigeon shooting xmas
English & French V ✤ ⏚ ✱ Lunch £9-£10.95alc Dinner £15.50 Last dinner 9.30pm
CONF. Thtr 60 Class 40 Board 25 Del £85.50
Credit Cards 1 2 3 5

EASINGWOLD North Yorkshire Map 08 SE56

★★62% **George**
Market Place YO6 3AD (off A19) ☎(0347) 821698 FAX (0347) 823448
Overlooking the cobbled square in the centre of the town, this is an old coaching inn with beamed bars and an attractive restaurant. Bedrooms in the main part of the hotel have more character than those in the extension at the rear, but all are shortly to be upgraded. There is an extensive range of bar and restaurant meals.
14⇔♑(2fb) CTV in all bedrooms ® T ✕ (ex guide dogs) ✱ sB&B⇔♑£20-£35 dB&B⇔♑£45-£55 ₽
8P
English & Continental V ✤ ⏚ ✱ Lunch £13.95 Dinner £13.95&alc Last dinner 9pm
Credit Cards 1 3

EAST AYTON North Yorkshire Map 08 SE98

★★66% **East Ayton Lodge**
Moor Ln, Forge Valley YO13 9EW (off A170)
☎Scarborough(0723) 864227 FAX (0723) 862080
Closed Jan-12 Feb
In 3 acres of grounds in the centre of the village, this hotel is well equipped for both business and leisure purposes. Bedrooms are of a pleasing modern standard, some in attractively converted barn

only a step from the main building. Table d'hôte and à la carte menus are available in the Victorian-style restaurant.
11⇔♑Annexe6⇔♑(1fb)2⊞ CTV in all bedrooms ® T ✱ CTV 50P ✤ xmas
English & French V ✤ ✱ Sunday Lunch £9.95-£10.95 Dinner £17.50 Last dinner 9pm
CONF. Thtr 100 Del from £60
Credit Cards 1 2 3 5

EASTBOURNE East Sussex Map 05 TV69

★★★★★✤✤62% *Grand*
King Edwards Pde BN21 4EQ
☎(0323) 412345 FAX (0323) 412233

The Grand may be looking a bit dated in parts, but the refurbishment of the bedrooms is under way. The main saving grace is General Manager, Peter Hawley, who remains as courteous and concerned as ever, and by his efforts, the staff are particularly helpful and friendly. The other chief virtue is chef Neil Wiggins' food in the Mirabelle restaurant, where fixed price and à la carte menus include such tempting seasonal dishes is jugged hare, or a supreme of maize-fed chicken filled with Boudin Blanc wrapped in Bayonne ham and savoy cabbage with a Dijon mustard sauce.
161⇔♑(12fb)1⊞⌿in 4 bedrooms CTV in all bedrooms ® ⌿ T
Lift (60P ⊞ ✤ ⏹ (heated) ⏃ (heated) snooker sauna solarium gymnasium spa bath hairdressing beauty & massage ♪ ⚘
English & French V ✤ ⏚ Last dinner 10pm
Credit Cards 1 2 3 4 5

★★★★58% **Cavendish**
Grand Pde BN21 4DH ☎(0323) 410222 FAX (0323) 410941

An imposing seafront hotel, with a loyal and well established clientèle. There is an ongoing programme of upgrading to the bedrooms, some of which are on the small side. Public rooms are decorated in pastel shades, the cocktail bar has a glitzy mirrored ceiling and the spacious dining room offers live piano entertainment most evenings.
112⇔♑ CTV in all bedrooms ® T ✱ sB&B⇔♑£50-£90 dB&B⇔♑£70-£180 ₽
Lift (50P snooker games room ♪ xmas
English & French V ✤ ⏚ ✱ Lunch fr£6.95 High tea £5-£15alc Dinner fr£17&alc Last dinner 9.30pm
CONF. Thtr 300 Class 180 Board 60 Del from £65
Credit Cards 1 2 3 4 5

★★★74% **Lansdowne**
King Edward's Pde BN21 4EE ☎(0323) 725174 FAX (0323) 39721
Closed 28 Dec-9 Jan
This professionally managed hotel in a prime seafront location has been owned by the same family since 1912. Bedrooms vary in size and style, front rooms being superior, but all are comfortable and further upgrading is underway. There are several lounges, a pleasant bar, games and snooker rooms, and two smart restaurants offering reliable, good-value English dishes.
127⇔♑(6fb) CTV in all bedrooms ® T
Lift (CTV 22🅿 (£3.25 per night) snooker darts pool table table tennis
V ✤ ⏚ ✱ Last dinner 8.30pm
Credit Cards 1 2 3 5

★★★65% **Hydro**
Mount Rd BN20 7HZ ☎(0323) 720643 FAX (0323) 641167
In a fine Victorian building with spacious and comfortable lounges and a well stocked bar, this is a well run and efficient hotel. The restaurant is quite large, and alive with the noise and bustle you would expect of a holiday hotel. The cooking does not reach any great standards, but is perfectly reasonable, and service is friendly

Eastbourne

and attentive. Many of the bedrooms have been refurbished and have all the usual facilities.
83⇌✿(1fb) CTV in all bedrooms ® T ✱ sB&B⇌✿£35-£52 dB&B⇌✿£64-£108 (incl dinner) 및
Lift ⟨ 50P ✿ ⌘ (heated) sauna solarium gymnasium croquet putting *xmas*
V ⊗ ℒ ⤫ ✱ Lunch £6.50-£9.95 Dinner fr£12.50 Last dinner 8.30pm
Credit Cards ① ③

★★★**64%** *Queens*
Marine Pde BN21 3DY ☎(0323) 722822 FAX (0323) 731056

Overlooking the pier and promenade, this hotel is positioned so that even the side rooms have sea views. Bedroom sizes vary, but all are furnished in a bright modern style. Public areas are spacious and traditionally styled, and include a pillared foyer lounge, smart cocktail bar and dining room. There is also a public bar, which is in need of a face lift.
108⇌✿(5fb) CTV in all bedrooms ® T
Lift ⟨ 90P snooker
♀ English & French V ⊗ ℒ Last dinner 9pm
Credit Cards ① ② ③ ⑤

★★★**63%** *The Wish Tower*
King Edward's Pde BN21 4EB (Principal) ☎(0323) 722676 FAX (0323) 721474
Situated on the promenade, opposite the Wish Tower and museum, this popular hotel has a spacious and comfortable bar lounge with excellent views across the Channel, and King Edward's restaurant on the lower ground floor has smart coordinated décor and fabrics. Bedrooms vary considerably, some being quite luxurious.
65rm(57⇌)⤫ in 6 bedrooms CTV in all bedrooms ® T
Lift ⟨ 3🅿 (£3 per day)
♀ English & French V ⊗ ℒ ⤫ Last dinner 8.45pm
Credit Cards ① ② ③ ④ ⑤

★★**67%** *Langham*
Royal Pde BN22 7AH ☎(0323) 731451 FAX (0323) 646623
Closed 20 Nov-11 Feb
For 4 decades the Martyr family have been running this attractive seafront hotel which was once 7 adjoining guesthouse. Bedrooms are constantly being upgraded, and many now have smart coordinated soft furnishings. The comfortable lounge bar leads to an attractive sun terrace.
87⇌✿(5fb) CTV in all bedrooms ® T ✱ sB&B⇌✿£24.95-£38.95 dB&B⇌✿£49.90-£67.90 및
Lift ⟨ 4🅿 (£4 per night) ♪
♀ European V ⊗ ℒ Lunch £5.25-£6.25 Dinner £9.50 Last dinner 9.45pm
CONF. Thtr 80 Class 40 Board 24 Del £43.50
Credit Cards ① ② ③ £

★★**67%** *West Rocks*
Grand Pde BN21 4DL ☎(0323) 725217 FAX (0323) 720421
Closed mid Nov-20 Mar
This well run, family-owned hotel is situated on the seafront and retains traditional standards of service are retained, from porterage to the luxury of early morning tea. On the ground floor there is a choice of traditionally styled lounges and a 5-course dinner is served in the elegant dining room.
52rm(42⇌✿)(4fb) CTV in all bedrooms ® T ✂ sB&B£18-£25 sB&B⇌✿£25-£40 dB&B⇌✿£36-£88 및
Lift ⟨ CTV 🅿 ⌘ nc3yrs
♀ English & French V ⊗ ℒ Bar Lunch £2.40-£8alc Dinner £8-£10 Last dinner 7.55pm
Credit Cards ① ② ③ ⑤ £

Hotels with red star ratings are especially high quality.

★★**63%** *Farrar's*
3-5 Wilmington Gardens BN21 4JN ☎(0323) 723737 FAX (0323) 732902
Closed 29 Dec-28 Jan
Farrar's is opposite the theatres and Winter Gardens, just minutes from the seafront. The bedrooms are gradually being upgraded, but several are dated in appearance though all have modern facilities. The choice of comfortably furnished lounges is noteworthy, as is the service and the friendly atmosphere.
45⇌✿(3fb) CTV in all bedrooms ® T sB&B⇌✿£29-£41 dB&B⇌✿£58-£82 및
Lift ⟨ CTV 26P *xmas*
♀ English, French & Italian V ⊗ ℒ ⤫ Bar Lunch £2.50-£8alc Dinner £12&alc Last dinner 8.30pm
CONF. Thtr 50 Class 50 Board 30 Del from £36
Credit Cards ① ② ③ £

★★**63%** *New Wilmington*
25 Compton St BN21 4DU ☎(0323) 721219
Closed Jan & Feb
This friendly family-run hotel is situated near the theatres and seafront. Bedrooms are traditional in style with comfortable seating and simple furnishings. Although lounge seating is limited, there is a smart bar where live entertainment is provided in summer. Plain home cooking is enjoyed by the many returning guests.
42⇌✿(4fb) CTV in all bedrooms ® T ✱ sB&B⇌✿£38-£44.50 dB&B⇌✿£66-£77 (incl dinner) 및
Lift ⟨ CTV 2🅿 (£3 per day) ♪ *xmas*
♀ English, French & Italian V ⊗ ℒ ⤫ ✱ Lunch £4.95-£5.95 Dinner £12.50 Last dinner 8pm
Credit Cards ① ② ③

For key to symbols see the Bookmark.

Lansdowne Hotel
King Edward's Parade ★★★
EASTBOURNE BN21 4EE
Tel: (0323) 725174 Fax: (0323) 739721
AA "COURTESY & CARE" AWARD 1992/93
Fully Licensed

Privately-owned seafront hotel close to theatres, shops and Conference Centre. 125 en-suite bedrooms all with colour TV, radio, direct dial telephone, tea/coffee making facilities. Traditional English cuisine. Spacious, elegant lounges facing sea (one for non-smokers!), 2 lifts to all floors. 23 lock-up garages, Snooker/Games/Card rooms. Summer entertainment in hotel. Light Lunches (àlc) served daily.

"Bargain Breaks" also Bridge, Gardening and Watercolour Painting Weekends Autumn/Winter/Spring. Golfing Breaks all year.

Please write or telephone for our colour brochure and tariff.

Eastbourne - East Grinstead

★ ❀ 70% Downland
37 Lewes Rd BN21 2BU (on A2021, towards town centre) ☎(0323) 732689

Closed 21 Dec-27 Jan
(Rosette awarded for dinner only)

Over the last few years considerable time, effort and expense has gone into upgrading this hotel. Bedrooms are relatively simple in style but all are attractively decorated. The menu offers some interesting and unusual flavour combinations, and though it changes with the season some popular dishes are now permanent features.

14⇨♠(3fb)1🛏 CTV in all bedrooms ® T ✕ (ex guide dogs)
sB&B⇨♠£27.50-£37.50 dB&B⇨♠£55-£75 🍴
CTV 10P 🚗
V ✧ ✱ Dinner £17.50&alc Last dinner 9pm
Credit Cards [1][2][3][5] £

★ 64% Oban
King Edward's Pde BN21 4DS ☎(0323) 731581
RS Jan & Feb

Occupying a prime sea front location close to the Wish Tower, this friendly family-run hotel provides a personal style of service. Light refreshments are now available daily in the lounge and on the sun terrace, together with light snacks in the bar, while the dining room offers a 6-course menu of wholesome cooking. Bedrooms are all en suite and well equipped, and there is a lift to all floors.

31⇨♠(3fb) CTV in all bedrooms ® T
Lift ℂ CTV ♪ ♫
V ✧ ⚲ Last dinner 7.30pm
Credit Cards [1][3]

★ 59% Lathom
4-6 Howard Square, Grand Pde BN21 4BG ☎(0323) 641986 FAX (0323) 416405

Closed Nov-Feb (ex Xmas & New Year)

Close to the theatres and seafront, this hotel is popular with coach parties and elderly guests. There is a night porter and early morning tea service. Bedrooms are plain and modestly furnished, and there is a compact dining room, and a lounge where entertainment is provided every evening.

45⇨♠(5fb) CTV in all bedrooms ® ✕ ✱
Lift ℂ 6P (£2 per day) 2🐕 (£2) xmas
V ✧ ✱
Credit Cards [1][3]

EAST DEREHAM Norfolk Map 09 TF91

★★ 63% King's Head
Norwich St NR19 1AD (on A47) ☎Dereham(0362) 693842 & 693283 FAX (0362) 693776

The King's Head is a friendly 16th-century inn a few minutes walk from the town centre, with a walled garden with a bowling green. Bedrooms have all modern facilities, both in the annexe and in the original building, which retains its historic atmosphere.

10rm(4⇨2♠)Annexe5⇨♠(1fb) CTV in all bedrooms ® T ✱
sB&Bfr£22 sB&B⇨♠£30-£36 dB&B£32-£44 dB&B⇨♠£50 🍴
30P 3🐕 ♟ (grass) bowling 🎣
♿ English, French & Italian V ✧ ⚲ ✱ Lunch £7.50-£12.05
Dinner £3-£11&alc Last dinner 9.30pm
Credit Cards [1][2][3][5] £

★ 70% George
Swaffham Rd NR19 2AZ ☎(0362) 696801

This popular and well managed hotel is situated next to the post office in the centre of town. The major feature of the rooms is their spaciousness, complemented by pine furniture and coordinating fabrics. Friendly hosts Mr and Mrs Garthwaite oversee a competent brigade in the bar and restaurant.

8⇨♠(2fb) CTV in all bedrooms ® T

40P
V ✧ ⚲
Credit Cards [1][2][3][5]

EAST GRINSTEAD West Sussex Map 05 TQ33

★★★★ ❀❀❀ ✱ Gravetye Manor
RH19 4LJ (3m SW off unclass rd joining B2110 & B2028) ☎Sharpthorne(0342) 810567 FAX (0342) 810080
RS 25 Dec

Peter Herbert, doyen of country house hoteliers, continues to run this immaculately maintained hotel with pride, unerring good taste and consistently high standards. The beautiful late 16th-century house, reached by a lovely mile long drive, is set in 30 acres in the heart of Sussex. Wood panelling, fine antique furniture and fresh flowers are all evident as one enters the lobby and the atmosphere of calm and peace is enhanced by staff trained not to intrude. Indeed one of the hallmarks of the hotel is the professionalism and courtesy of the staff, though some might wish that they be allowed to display natural warmth and personality. Cooking, under the direction of head chef Stephen Morey, is excellent, its strength lying in the superb saucing. There is a fine, mainly French wine list which, coupled with the impeccable service, ensures that dining at Gravetye is a special event.

18⇨1🛏 CTV in all bedrooms T ✕ sB⇨£85-£190 dB⇨£125-£190 (room only)
25P 🚗 ✿ 🍽 croquet nc7yrs
V ✧ ✕ Last dinner 9.30pm
Credit Cards [1][3]

★★★ 63% Felbridge Resort
London Rd RH19 2BH ☎(0342) 326992 FAX (0342) 410778

Under new ownership, this long-established and well known hotel has recently been completely refurbished and upgraded to a high standard. Whilst all improvements were not complete at the time of our visit, it is clearly going to impress, with sumptuous and very spacious Executive bedrooms as well as standard, family and 4-poster rooms. Copperfields Restaurant is to be a brasserie coffee shop, open all day for meals and light refreshments, while the Ashdown Restaurant will be more formal.

90⇨♠(7fb)✕ in 14 bedrooms CTV in all bedrooms ® ♟ T ✱
sB&B⇨♠£36-£90 dB&B⇨♠£72-£110
ℂ CTV 600P 6🐕 ✿ 🍽 (heated) ⚲ (heated) ♟ (hard) snooker sauna solarium gymnasium beauty salon steam room xmas
V ✧ ⚲ ✕ ✱ Sunday Lunch fr£10.50 Dinner fr£15 Last dinner 10pm
CONF. Thtr 300 Class 120 Board 60 Del £80
Credit Cards [1][2][3][5]

★★★ 63% Woodbury House
Lewes Rd RH19 3UD (0.5m S of town, on A22) (Logis)
☎(0342) 313657 FAX (0342) 314801
RS 26 Dec & 1 Jan

This skilfully extended, gabled house about a mile outside East Grinstead provides attractively furnished bedrooms and a welcoming atmosphere under the supervision of its owner, Mr

Dixon. For informal meals the bar/bistro is ideal and the Garden Room Restaurant offers fixed-price and full à la carte menus; whichever you choose, dishes are freshly cooked.
13⇌♠Annexe1♠1₤ CTV in all bedrooms ® T ✳
sB&B⇌♠£55-£60 dB&B⇌♠£60-£75 ₧
30P 🚗 ✿
♀ English & French V ♂ ⚲ ✳ Lunch £13.50-£17.50 Dinner £17.50 Last dinner 9.30pm
Credit Cards ①②③④⑤

EAST HORNDON Essex Map 05 TQ58

Forte Travelodge
CM13 3LL (on A127, eastbound)
☎Brentwood (0277) 810819 Central Res (0800) 850940

This modern building offers a good standard of accommodation for overnight stops. Smart, spacious and well equipped bedrooms, all with en suite bathrooms, are suitable for family use, and meals may be taken at the nearby family restaurant. For more details about Travelodges, consult the Contents page, under Hotel Groups.
22⇌♠✳ B⇌♠£31.95 (room only)

EAST HORSLEY Surrey Map 04 TQ05

★★★ ❀61% **Thatchers Resort**
Epsom Rd KT24 6TB (on A246)
☎(0483) 284291 FAX (0483) 284222

In a rural situation, just outside the village, this attractive hotel is scheduled for major development which will link the annexe to the main building and add an indoor health and leisure suite. There is a spacious lounge, and in the oak beamed restaurant head chef Paul O'Dowd produces enjoyable food from a daily set menu and seasonal 'carte'. Successful dishes sampled include pan fried pigeon breast with a Madeira and truffle dressing, and poached salmon on a tomato, olive oil and basil vinaigrette.
36⇌♠Annexe23⇌♠(4fb)2⇌♣⇌in 6 bedrooms CTV in all bedrooms ® ⚥ T ✳ sB⇌♠£75-£85 dB⇌♠£85-£95 (room only) ₧
(60P ✿ ⇌ (heated)
♀ English & French V ♂ ⚲ ✳ Lunch £12.50-£14.50&alc High tea £7.50-£10 Dinner £18.50&alc Last dinner 9.30pm
Credit Cards ①②③⑤

EAST KILBRIDE Strathclyde *Lanarkshire* Map 11 NS65

★★★★ ❀63% **Westpoint**
Stewartfield Way G74 5LA ☎(03552) 36300 FAX (03552) 33552

This modern hotel provides a full range of modern amenities and a friendly, relaxing atmosphere. A lively bar adjoins the Point Grill restaurant but it is the small, more formal Simpsons restaurant which has gained a reputation for its excellent modern-style cooking. Artistically presented dishes combine quality produce and particularly good sauces.
74⇌♠(8fb)⇌in 20 bedrooms CTV in all bedrooms ® ⚥ T ✻ (ex guide dogs) ✳ sB&B⇌♠£56-£110 dB&B⇌♠£76-£130 ₧
Lift (200P ▭ (heated) ♪ squash snooker sauna solarium gymnasium dance studio jacuzzi creche ♣ xmas
♀ Scottish & French V ♂ ⚲ ✳ Lunch £9.50-£14.95&alc Dinner £12.45-£28.95&alc Last dinner 10.30pm
Credit Cards ①②③⑤

★★★ 61% **Bruce Swallow**
Cornwall St G74 1AF ☎(03552) 29771 FAX (03552) 42216

This business hotel lies on the fringe of the shopping centre. Bedrooms have undergone a gradual upgrading over the past 2 years

and are now bright, cheery and well equipped. Hamilton's restaurant is now open only in the evening, but bar-style lunches are served in the lounge or downstairs bar.
78⇌♠⚥⇌in 10 bedrooms CTV in all bedrooms ® ⚥ T sB&B⇌♠£45-£68 dB&B⇌♠£60-£75 ₧
Lift (15P 25🚗 xmas
♀ International V ♂ ⚲ ⚥ Lunch £7.95&alc High tea £5.75-£7.75 Dinner £9.95-£15&alc Last dinner 9.45pm
CONF. Thtr 200 Class 100 Board 40 Del from £80
Credit Cards ①②③⑤

★★★ 60% **Stuart**
2 Cornwall Way G74 1JR ☎(03552) 21161 FAX (03552) 64410
Closed 25 Dec & 1 Jan
Within walking distance of the town centre, this business and function hotel provides all modern amenities and has two styles of bedrooms, both varying in size.
39⇌♠(1fb)1₤ CTV in all bedrooms ® ⚥ T ✳ sB&B⇌♠£55-£65 dB&B⇌♠£70-£90 ₧
Lift (▭ CTV ♪ xmas
♀ European V ♂ ⚲
CONF. Thtr 200 Class 90 Board 50 Del from £74.50
Credit Cards ①②③⑤

★★ 67% **Crutherland Country House**
Strathaven Rd G75 0QZ (off A725, 2m from town centre)
☎(03552) 37633
Closed 1 & 2 Jan
This renovated mansion is set in 37 acres of grounds. Most bedrooms are in a modern extension, although there are some nice spacious rooms in the original house. The lounge includes a bar and acts as reception, and there is a conservatory restaurant.
19⇌♠(1fb) CTV in all bedrooms ® T
(200P ✿ ♪
♀ Last dinner 9.30pm
Credit Cards ①②③

Travel Inn
Brunel Way, The Murray G75 0JY ☎(0355) 222809

Purpose-built accommodation offers spacious and well equipped bedrooms, all with en suite bathrooms. Meals may be taken at the nearby family restaurant and pub. For more details about Travel Inns, consult the Contents page, under hotel Groups.
40⇌♠✳ B⇌♠£33.50 (room only)

EASTLEIGH Hampshire Map 04 SU41

Forte Crest
Leigh Rd, Passfield Av SO5 5PG (off A33)
☎(0703) 619700 FAX (0703) 643945

A large modern hotel with a wide range of services and amenities designed particularly for the business traveller. Bedrooms are smart, comfortable and well equipped. For more details about Forte Crest hotels, consult the Contents page, under Hotel Groups.
120⇌♠✳ B⇌♠£75 (room only)
CONF. Thtr 250 Class 90 Board 90 Del £105

Forte Travelodge
Twyford Rd (off A335)
☎(0703) 616813 Central Res (0800) 850950

This modern building offers a good standard of accommodation for overnight stops. Smart, spacious and well equipped bedrooms, all with en suite bathrooms, are suitable for family use, and meals may be taken at the nearby family restaurant. For more details about Travelodges, consult the Contents page, under Hotel Groups.
32⇌♠✳ dB⇌♠£31.95 (room only)

East Retford - Edinburgh

EAST RETFORD Nottinghamshire Map 08 SK78

★★★ 66% West Retford
24 North Rd DN22 7XG (on A298)
☎(0777) 706333 FAX (0777) 709951

Set in mature gardens northwest of the town, this attractive 18th-century manor house has spacious, well furnished bedrooms situated in adjoining buildings. The main house contains a pretty restaurant serving a wide range of food and a bar to which improvements are currently planned.

Annexe57⇨↑(37fb)⚲in 9 bedrooms CTV in all bedrooms ®
T ✱ sB&B⇨↑£41-£72.50 dB&B⇨↑£65-£87.50 ℞
⊂130P ✿ croquet putting ♫ 🐕 xmas
♨ French V ◊ ♁ ⚲ Lunch £7.25-£10.75&alc High tea £2.50-£7.50 Dinner £17-£17.95&alc Last dinner 10pm
CONF. Thtr 150 Class 40 Board 38 Del from £75
Credit Cards ①②③⑤ £

EBCHESTER Co Durham Map 12 NZ15

★★★ 66% The Raven
Broomhill DH8 6RY (on B6309, overlooking village)
☎(0207) 560367 FAX (0207) 560262

This attractive stone building stands in an elevated position overlooking the village. The bedrooms are modern and especially pleasant. Public areas are also in a pleasant modern style, and a good range of food is available either in the bar or the restaurant.

28⇨↑(8fb)1🚭 CTV in 3 bedrooms CTV in all bedrooms ®
✱ (ex guide dogs) ✻ sB&B⇨↑£35-£60 dB&B⇨↑£60-£85 ℞
⊂100P xmas
♨ English & French V ◊ ♁ ✱ Lunch £6-£8.95&alc Dinner £10.95-£12.95&alc Last dinner 10pm
CONF. Thtr 100 Class 50 Board 30 Del from £50
Credit Cards ①②③⑤

ECCLESHALL Staffordshire Map 07 SJ82

★★ 62% St George
Castle St ST21 6DF ☎(0785) 850300 FAX (0785) 851452

This small hotel, part of which was once an undertakers, is centrally situated in the market town. It still has the original oak beamed bar where good food and company is always available, and there is an attractive restaurant for more substantial meals.

10⇨↑1🚭 CTV in all bedrooms ® T
17P
♨ English & French V ◊ ♁ ⚲ Last dinner 9.30pm
Credit Cards ①②③⑤

EDENHALL Cumbria Map 12 NY53

★★ 63% Edenhall
CA11 8SX ☏Langwathby(076881) 454

Situated in its own grounds in the picturesque village, this friendly, family-run hotel has comfortable bedrooms and a cosy lounge with a delightful old fireplace. The traditional-style dining room offers extensive menus, and a good range of bar food is also available.

21⇨↑Annexe8⇨↑(3fb) CTV in all bedrooms ® T
✱ (ex guide dogs)
🎰 CTV 80P 2🅿 ✿
♨ English, French & Italian V ◊ ♁ Last dinner 9pm
Credit Cards ①③

The AA's star rating scheme is the
market leader in hotel
classification.

EDINBURGH Lothian *Midlothian* Map 11 NT27

★★★★★ ❁68% Caledonian
Princes St EH1 2AB ☎031-225 2433 FAX 031-225 6632

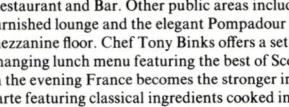

This grand old lady, affectionately known as the Caley, is 90 years old on December 21st 1993. Built as a terminus hotel of the Caledonian Railway Company, part of the original exterior has been incorporated into the recently refurbished Carriages Restaurant and Bar. Other public areas include a tastefully furnished lounge and the elegant Pompadour Restaurant on the mezzanine floor. Chef Tony Binks offers a set price monthly changing lunch menu featuring the best of Scottish produce, while in the evening France becomes the stronger influence with a stylish carte featuring classical ingredients cooked in a light, modern style.

239⇨↑(16fb)⚲in 35 bedrooms CTV in all bedrooms 🎰 T
✱ (ex guide dogs) ✻ sB⇨↑£145-£165 dB⇨↑£225-£295 (room only) ℞
Lift ⊂ 110P
♨ Scottish & French V ◊ ♁ ⚲ ✱ Lunch £13.75-£27 Dinner £35 Last dinner 10.30pm
CONF. Thtr 300 Class 150 Board 60 Del from £150
Credit Cards ①②③⑤

★★★★★ ❁59% Balmoral
Princes St EH2 2EQ ☎031-556 2414 FAX 031-557 3747

FORTE GRAND

This distinctive turn-of-the-century building, with it prominent clock tower, has an impressive part-galleried foyer with ionic pillars and marble floor. Also on the ground floor the palm court lounge and a choice of small bars, a well stocked cake and provisions shop and the bright Bridges Continental brasserie. The more serious dining takes place in the Grill Room with the modern menus of executive chef Ralph Porciani. Bedrooms are reasonably spacious, the executive rooms generally having better views.

189⇨↑2🚭⚲in 22 bedrooms CTV in all bedrooms ® 🎰 T
✱ (ex guide dogs)
Lift ⊂ ⊞ 🅿 🚭 ⛲ (heated) sauna solarium gymnasium ♫
♨ French V ◊ ♁ ⚲ Last dinner 10.30pm
Credit Cards ①②③⑤

★★★★ ❁68% Carlton Highland
North Bridge EH1 1SD (on North Bridge which links Princes St to the Royal Mile, opposite 'The Scotsman' offices) (Scottish Highland) ☎031-556 7277 FAX 031-556 2691

Conveniently placed for the city's main attractions, this modern hotel, provides a wide range of facilities. There is a comfortable lounge and bar and a choice between the carvery, serving snacks and grills all day, and elegant Quills restaurant offering a good range of Scottish and international dishes. Bedrooms, which are being redecorated, vary in size and are well equipped.

197⇨↑(20fb)⚲in 20 bedrooms CTV in all bedrooms ® 🎰 T
sB&B⇨↑£92-£116 dB&B⇨↑£148-£168 ℞
Lift ⊂ 🅿 ⛲ (heated) squash snooker sauna solarium gymnasium jacuzzi table tennis dance studio creche ♫ 🐕 xmas
♨ Scottish & French V ◊ ♁ ⚲ ✱ Lunch £14-£16&alc High tea £6.50-£17alc Dinner £16-£18.50 Last dinner 10.30pm
CONF. Thtr 300 Class 120 Board 60 Del from £118
Credit Cards ①②③④⑤ £

★★★★ ❁65% Dalmahoy Hotel, Golf & Country Club
Kirknewton EH27 8EB (7m W of Edinburgh on the A71) ☎031-333 1845 FAX 031-335 3203

Set in 1000 acres at the foot of the Pentland Hills, this impressive Georgian mansion has been considerably extended. Spacious bedrooms in the original building have fine period furnishings, while those in the wing are in the modern style. There is a choice of bars and lounges; food is available all day in the Terrace Restaurant

Edinburgh

and the more formal Pentland Restaurant provides both a carte and daily table d'hôte menu.
116⇨🐾(3fb)⊁in 19 bedrooms CTV in all bedrooms ®☒ T ✈ (ex guide dogs) ✱ sB&B⇨🐾fr£110 dB&B⇨🐾fr£125 🍴 Lift 〔 200P ▦ (heated) ▶ 18 ♫ (hard) squash snooker sauna solarium gymnasium beauty salon spa bath steam room *xmas*
♥ Scottish & French ✧ ⚌ ⊁ ✱ Lunch £12.95-£14.95 Dinner £21-£23&alc Last dinner 9.15pm
CONF. Thtr 200 Class 120 Board 24 Del from £115
Credit Cards 1 2 3 5

★★★★ ❀63% *George Inter-Continental*
19-21 George St EH2 2PB (IC) ☎031-225 1251 FAX 031-226 5644

This well run central hotel is popular with international business people and tourists. Bedrooms are comfortably furnished in traditional style, with all the expected amenities, though they vary in size. There is an impressive split-level foyer lounge with a marble floor, a club-like bar and a choice between the Carvers Grill or the elegant Chambertan restaurant, to which our rosette applies.
195⇨🐾(10fb)⊁in 32 bedrooms CTV in all bedrooms ® T Lift 〔 24P
♥ Scottish, English & French V ✧ ⚌ ⊁ Last dinner 10pm
Credit Cards 1 2 3 5

★★★ ❀❀74% Norton House
Ingliston EH28 8LX (off A8, 5m W of city centre)
☎031-333 1275 FAX 031-333 5305

This period mansion with modern extensions is peacefully situated in secluded parkland. The hotel is establishing a reputation not only for its hospitality and service but also for the quality of its food. A meal in the conservatory restaurant offers the best of Scottish meats, game and seafood cooked in the modern style. There are elegant period bedrooms in the original house and tasteful new rooms in the extension.

➡

**CASTLE STREET
ECCLESHALL
STAFFORDSHIRE
ST21 6DF**

**TEL: 0785 850300
FAX: 0785 851452**

★★

A delightful 16th century coaching inn situated midway between junction 14 and 15 of M6.
Central for all amenities.

Ten luxury bedrooms all en suite and with colour TV, dial phone and tea/coffee making facilities.

George's Bistro provides a wide and varied menu with a range of real ale also own brewery.

Weddings and private parties catered for.
Family run with a warm, friendly and relaxed atmosphere.

GREYWALLS

Muirfield, Gullane, East Lothian EH31 2EG

Built at the turn of the century this fascinating Edwardian house has been run as a hotel by the same family since the 40's. Only 30 minutes away from the centre of Edinburgh and set in a well-maintained secluded walled garden Greywalls enjoys an enviable position overlooking Muirfield golf course and within a short drive of a further 12 excellent courses.

AA ★★★ ♨ ❀❀ 79%
1992 Taste of Scotland Country House Hotel of the Year.

Tel: 0620 842144   Fax: 0620 842241
See gazetteer entry under Gullane

A delightful hotel in a rural setting, overlooking the beautiful Derwent Valley. It exudes character, attracting locals, holidaymakers and businessmen alike.

- 28 luxurious, spacious bedrooms (all en suite)
- Exquisite Conservatory Restaurant ● Tasty Bar Food
- Afternoon Teas ● Facilities for disabled guests

A real breath of fresh air, ideal for Beamish Museum, Hadrian's Wall, and other landmarks in County Durham and Northumberland ... yet only 20 minutes from Durham, Gateshead's Metro Centre and Newcastle City Centre.

The hotel is independently owned, therefore good hospitality is assured.

THE RAVEN HOTEL
Broomhill, Ebchester, Co Durham DH8 6RY

AA   Tel. (0207) 560367
★★★   Fax (0207) 560262

Edinburgh

47⇨♠(2fb)⊁ in 5 bedrooms CTV in all bedrooms ® T sB&B⇨♠£100-£115 dB&B⇨♠£120-£160 ♫
《 200P ✿ archery laser clay pigeon shooting ⌬ xmas
♀ International V ✧ ⚲ Lunch £15-£18&alc High tea £8.50 Dinner £21-£25&alc Last dinner 9.30pm
CONF. Thtr 300 Class 100 Board 40 Del from £110
Credit Cards ①②③⑤

★★★ ❋70% King James Thistle
107 Leith St EH1 3SW ☎031-556 0111 FAX 031-557 5333

Part of a shopping complex just off the east end of Princes Street, this modern hotel offers a range of bedrooms, ranging from compact Club rooms to smart modern suites. Lounge space is limited to the bright modern foyer, but there is a lively American-themed bar/diner adjacent to a smart cocktail bar and split-level brasserie which serves French and Scottish dishes.
147⇨♠(4fb)⊁ in 14 bedrooms CTV in all bedrooms ® T sB⇨♠£75-£95 dB⇨♠£95-£110 (room only) ♫
Lift 《 21P 8♦ ♪ xmas
♀ International V ✧ ⚲ ✱ Lunch £9.50-£18&alc High tea £6.50-£12&alc Dinner £10.50-£18.50&alc Last dinner 10pm
Credit Cards ①②③④⑤

★★★ 69% The Howard
Great King St EH3 6QH ☎031-557 3500 FAX 031-557 6515

An elegantly restored Georgian town house, discreetly set in a terraced row in the New Town area of the city, offers a quiet, almost club-like atmosphere. There is a relaxing drawing room and a lounge where drinks are served. Bedrooms are splendid, extremely well equipped and provided with fine bathrooms, though there are a few small singles. Services offered are impressive, though occasional low staff levels have revealed imperfections.
16⇨♠3⚲ CTV in all bedrooms T ✠ (ex guide dogs)
Lift 《 12P ⇲
V ✧ ⚲ Last dinner 10pm
Credit Cards ①②③⑤

★★★ ❋68% Channings
South Learmonth Gardens EH4 1EZ (Logis) ☎031-315 2226 FAX 031-332 9631

Quietly situated on the northwest side of the city, this conversion of 5 Edwardian town houses has a cosy atmosphere. The period flavour has been retained, with relaxing firelit lounges and a downstairs snug bar and brasserie restaurant. Menus have a Scottish flavour and cooking is in a modern style, well presented without being fussy. Bedrooms are attractively furnished, with quality fabrics. Service is well intentioned but can lack direction.
48⇨♠ CTV in all bedrooms ®⊁ T ✠ sB&B⇨♠£78-£88 dB&B⇨♠£98-£119 ♫
Lift 《 ⚥
♀ Scottish & French V ✧ ⚲ Lunch £5.95-£8 Dinner £16.50&alc Last dinner 9.30pm
CONF. Thtr 35 Class 15 Board 18 Del £98
Credit Cards ①②③⑤

★★★ 68% Roxburghe
Charlotte Square EH2 4HG ☎031-225 3921 FAX 031-220 2518

The Roxburghe is a fine example of Adam architecture, occupying a prime position in Charlotte Square. Public areas may be somewhat lacking in sparkle, but there are comfortable lounges and a well stocked cocktail bar. An informal buttery serving all-day snacks offers an alternative to the elegant restaurant's more formal menus of Scottish and international cuisine. Bedrooms range include some spacious rooms with handsome traditional furniture and fittings.
75⇨♠1⚲ CTV in all bedrooms ® T sB&B⇨♠£77.50-£95 dB&B⇨♠£94-£125 ♫
Lift 《 ✈ xmas

♀ French V ✧ ⚲ Lunch £5.50-£9.50&alc High tea £7-£10 Dinner £19&alc Last dinner 10pm
CONF. Thtr 200 Class 100 Board 100 Del from £60
Credit Cards ①②③⑤ £

★★★ 66% Bruntsfield

69/74 Bruntsfield Place EH10 4HH (on A702, S of city centre) ☎031-229 1393 FAX 031-229 5634

This well run family owned business and tourist hotel overlooks Bruntsfield Links. Public areas include a bright modern foyer, a choice of bars – one intimate, the other with a lively pub atmosphere – and an attractive restaurant/brasserie which offers varied menus. Bedrooms are in modern style with a good range of equipment, though they do vary in size, shape and standard.
50⇨♠(1fb)⚲ CTV in all bedrooms ® T sB&B⇨♠£79-£99 dB&B⇨♠£94-£130 ♫
Lift 《 25P xmas
♀ International V ✧ ⊁ ✱ Lunch £6.50-£10 Dinner £10-£19 Last dinner 10pm
CONF. Thtr 70 Class 25 Board 35 Del from £75
Credit Cards ①②③⑤ £

★★★ 65% Capital Moat House

Clermiston Rd EH12 6UG ☎031-334 3391 FAX 031-334 9712

A major transformation is taking place at this busy hotel in the west end. Improvements to the public areas include a conservatory extension and refurbishment of the Pentland Restaurant, the leisure complex and adjacent steak and pizza bar. Bedroom wings are being rebuilt to provide more spacious accommodation. The project is due to have been completed by the end of 1993.
111⇨♠(39fb)1⚲ in 6 bedrooms CTV in all bedrooms ® T ✱ sB⇨♠£78-£92 dB⇨♠£94-£125 (room only) ♫
Lift 《 150P ⚿ (heated) sauna solarium gymnasium Leisure Club steam room spa bath pool xmas
♀ Scottish & French V ✧ ⚲ ⊁ ✱ Lunch £4.95-£9.95 Dinner £14.95&alc Last dinner 10.30pm
CONF. Thtr 300 Class 150 Del from £90
Credit Cards ①②③⑤

★★★ 64% Mount Royal
53 Princes St EH2 2DG (Jarvis) ☎031-225 7161 FAX 031-220 4671

This substantially refurbished tour and business hotel overlooks the castle. Taking full advantage of this fine view, the first floor public areas are partially open plan and include a bar, popular coffee lounge and restaurant, where, in the main season, guests have the option of the carvery or 'carte'.
157rm(153⇨)(9fb)⊁ in 8 bedrooms CTV in all bedrooms ® T ✱ sB⇨fr£89 dB⇨fr£109 (room only) ♫
Lift 《 ✈ xmas
♀ Scottish & French V ✧ ⚲ ⊁ ✱ Lunch £5.90 High tea £5.75 Dinner £16&alc Last dinner 9.30pm
CONF. Thtr 50 Class 32 Board 26 Del from £90
Credit Cards ①②③④⑤ £

★★★ 63% Barnton Thistle

Queensferry Rd, Barnton EH4 6AS
☎031-339 1144 FAX 031-339 5521

On the western outskirts of the city, this business hotel has an attractive restaurant and cocktail lounge, and well equipped bedrooms.
50⇨♠(9fb)1⚥ CTV in all bedrooms ® T ✱ sB⇨♠fr£75 dB⇨♠fr£85 (room only) ♫
Lift 《 100P sauna xmas
♀ International V ✧ ⚲ ✱ Lunch £8.50-£14&alc High tea £6.50-£8 Dinner £15.95&alc Last dinner 10pm
CONF. Thtr 150 Del from £65
Credit Cards ①②③④⑤

★ ★ ★

CAPITAL MOAT HOUSE
and Leisure Club

**Clermiston Road
Edinburgh EH12 6UG**

**Telephone 031-334 3391
Fax 031-334 9712**

The Capital Moat House Hotel has recently undergone a £3½ million refurbishment programme. Available are 111 well appointed bedrooms of which 39 are family rooms. Other facilities include: The Pentlands Restaurant with breathtaking views from the Rooftop Conservatory or the informal Chatz Steak & Pizza Bar. Our superb Leisure Club is the premier club within the city offering an extensive range of facilities.

Queens Moat Houses Hotel

INTERNATIONAL HOTELIERS

Roxburghe Hotel

AA ★ ★ ★   Best Western

**Charlotte Square
Edinburgh EH2 4HG
Tel: 031-225 3921
Fax: 031-220 2518
Telex: 727054**

A tradition of fine food and service that has been its hallmark for over 150 years. The 75 elegant bedrooms all with private facilities enable guests to enjoy the atmosphere of a private house in comfort and style.
Situated in Charlotte Square, designed by Robert Adam, the Hotel is just a minute's walk from Princes Street. A la Carte Restaurant, Cocktail Bar and Buffet, all day Bistro.

E

ENJOY TRADITIONAL VALUES IN A TRADITIONAL SETTING

A place like the Bruntsfield is a real treat. An elegant townhouse style hotel, it offers high standards in facilities along with good old fashioned service and a choice of bars and a popular restaurant. The Bruntsfield is perfectly placed for exploring Edinburgh, and yet has ample free car parking.

All this is offered at prices that are surprisingly low. Find out more by calling: 031-229 1393.

THE BRUNTSFIELD HOTEL
69 Bruntsfield Place, Edinburgh EH10 4HH.
Tel: 031-229 1393. Telex: 727897. Fax: 031-229 5634.

BEST WESTERN HOTELS

★ ★ ★ AA

KING JAMES
THISTLE HOTEL

St James Centre, Edinburgh EH1 3SW
Tel: 031-556 0111   Fax: 031-557 5333

Your choice in Edinburgh Centre

For Reservations at over 100 Mount Charlotte Thistle Hotels
Telephone London: 071 937 8033.

THISTLE HOTELS

Edinburgh

★★★ 63% Ellersly House
4 Ellersly Rd EH12 6HZ (off A8 to W of city) (Jarvis)
☎031-337 6888 FAX 031-313 2543

Set in its own grounds in a west end residential area, this extended Edwardian country house has undergone major refurbishment. Public areas offer traditional comforts and the bedrooms, which vary in size, are now brighter and include up-to-date facilities.

57⇌♠(3fb)⍰⤫in 10 bedrooms CTV in all bedrooms ® T ✱
sB⇌♠£55-£79 dB⇌♠£75-£99 (room only) ♨
Lift ℂ 50P ✣ croquet *xmas*
♀ International V ♡ ⍰ ⤫ ✱ Lunch £9.95-£12.75 Dinner £33.50 Last dinner 9.30pm
CONF. Thtr 70 Class 30 Board 24 Del from £95
Credit Cards ①②③④⑤ £

★★★ 63% Swallow Royal Scot
111 Glasgow Rd EH12 8NF (on A8 on western outskirts of city) ☎031-334 9191 FAX 031-316 4507

Gradual improvements are taking place behind the unassuming façade of this modern hotel on the western fringe of the city. The best and most spacious bedrooms are in the south wing, but north wing rooms are about to undergo refurbishment. Public areas include a choice of bars and a restaurant offering both a carvery and à la carte menu.

259⇌♠(30fb)⤫in 102 bedrooms CTV in all bedrooms ® T ✱ sB&B⇌♠fr£95 dB&B⇌♠fr£120 ♨
Lift ℂ 300P ✣ ⍰ (heated) sauna solarium gymnasium steam room *xmas*
♀ International V ♡ ⍰ ⤫ ✱ Lunch fr£12.50 Dinner fr£18.75&alc Last dinner 10pm
CONF. Thtr 300 Class 140 Board 400 Del from £107
Credit Cards ①②③⑤ £

★★★ 61% Holiday Inn Garden Court
107 Queensferry Rd EH4 3HL (on the A90 approx 1m from city centre) ☎031-332 2442 FAX 031-332 3408

Bedrooms in this bright, modern hotel are well equipped and attractively priced, and the east-facing rooms have superb panoramic views of the city and the River Forth. Dinner offers both table d'hôte and à la carte menus, with an element of self service. A limited lunchtime menu is served more informally in the lounge bar.

119⇌♠(53fb)⤫in 59 bedrooms CTV in all bedrooms ®⍰ T ✱ sB⇌♠£69.50-£84.50 dB⇌♠£69.50-£84.50 (room only) ♨
Lift ℂ 80P ✣ gymnasium ♫
V ♡ ⍰ ⤫ ✱ Sunday Lunch £8.50-£9.95alc Dinner £14.95&alc Last dinner 10pm
CONF. Thtr 60 Class 30 Board 20 Del from £75
Credit Cards ①②③④⑤ £

★★★ 60% Old Waverley
Princes St EH2 2BY (in the centre of city, opposite the Scott Monument) (Scottish Highland) ☎031-556 4648 FAX 031-557 6316

The Old Waverley is conveniently situated above the shops at the east end of Princes Street and public areas – a small lounge, bar and carvery restaurant – enjoy an outlook over the gardens to the castle. Bedrooms are comfortable.

66⇌♠(6fb) CTV in all bedrooms ®⍰ T sB&B⇌♠£71-£96 dB&B⇌♠£122-£126 ♨
Lift ℂ ✣ *xmas*
♀ International V ♡ ⍰ ⤫ ✱ Lunch £4.50-£6.50 Dinner £11.75-£13.50&alc Last dinner 9.30pm
CONF. Thtr 55 Class 30 Board 32 Del from £90
Credit Cards ①②③⑤ £

★★★ 59% Braid Hills
134 Braid Rd, Braid Hills EH10 6JD (2.5m S A702)
☎031-447 8888 FAX 031-452 8477

Refurbishment has enhanced the public areas of this popular hotel south of the city centre. Bedrooms are functional but well equipped and there is a bright foyer lounge, comfortable cocktail bar and restaurant, plus a pub-like bar in an adjoining building.

68⇌♠(2fb)2⍰⤫in 8 bedrooms CTV in all bedrooms ®⍰ T ℂ 38P ✣
♀ Scottish & French V ♡ ⍰ Last dinner 9.15pm
Credit Cards ①②③⑤

★★★ 58% Donmaree
21 Mayfield Gardens EH9 2BX ☎031-667 3641 FAX 031-667 9130

In a residential area south of the city centre, this popular hotel has bedrooms of various sizes and styles, a choice of comfortable lounges and a bar and restaurant that retain their original Victorian elegance.

17⇌♠ CTV in all bedrooms ® T
ℂ 3P
♀ French V ♡ Last dinner 10pm
Credit Cards ①②③⑤

★★★ 65% Murrayfield
18 Corstorphine Rd EH12 6HN ☎031-337 1844 FAX 031-346 8159

Closed 2 days Xmas & 2 days New Year

Situated on the western approach road, this popular hotel has comfortable bedrooms, with the best rooms in the recently refurbished lodge annexe. Public areas include a lounge and a spacious bar that is about to be upgraded, plus a smart traditional restaurant.

23⇌♠ Annexe10♠ CTV in all bedrooms ® T sB&B⇌♠£52-£57 dB&B⇌♠£70-£75 ♨
ℂ 30P
♀ Scottish & European ♡ Lunch fr£9 Dinner fr£11.50alc Last dinner 9.30pm
CONF. Thtr 30 Class 12 Board 20
Credit Cards ①②③⑤ £

★★★ 63% Harp Toby
St John's Rd, Corstorphine EH12 8AX (3.5m W on A8) (Toby)
☎031-334 4750 FAX 031-334 6941

Considerable improvements have taken place at this friendly commercial hotel on the western side of the city. Bedrooms, though generally compact, have modern décor and attractive fabrics. There is no lounge but guests have a choice of comfortable bars and the Toby carvery restaurant.

24⇌♠(2fb)⤫in 9 bedrooms CTV in all bedrooms ® T ✘ (ex guide dogs) ✱ sB&B⇌♠£32-£59 dB&B⇌♠£52-£69
ℂ 50P
V ♡ ⍰ ⤫ ✱ Lunch £6-£15 Dinner £6-£15 Last dinner 10pm
CONF. Thtr 120 Class 20 Board 24 Del £79.95
Credit Cards ①②③⑤

★★ 58% Rothesay
8 Rothesay Place EH3 7SL (follow M8 into Edinburgh to the Haymarket Station, turn left at traffic lights into Palmerston Place, Rothesay place is second on right) ☎031-225 4125 FAX 031-220 4350

Part of a terrace in Edinburgh's 'New Town', this long established family-run hotel also caters for tour groups. The informal public areas include an attractive foyer lounge, a small bar, and dining room where a modest menu of mainly grills is offered. The practical bedrooms vary in size and provide all the expected facilities.

35rm(26⇌3♠)(1fb) CTV in all bedrooms ® T sB&B£23-£30 sB&B⇌♠£33-£50 dB&B£45-£55 dB&B⇌♠£50-£80
Lift ℂ CTV ♪
♀ Scottish & French V ♡ ⍰ ⤫ Dinner £8.50-£18alc Last dinner 9pm
Credit Cards ①②③④⑤

Satellite television – look for this symbol ⍰
in the directory entries.

Edinburgh

★★57% Suffolk Hall
10 Craigmillar Park EH16 5NE ☎031-668 4333 FAX 031-668 4506

Situated in a south side residential area, this popular commercial hotel is convenient for the city centre. Public areas offer practical and traditional comforts, while bedrooms, though well equipped, are somewhat dated and functional.

12rm(11⇨↑)(4fb) CTV in all bedrooms ® ⚹ T
✈ (ex guide dogs) sB&Bfr£45 sB&B⇨↑£50 dB&Bfr£60 dB&B⇨↑£65
(CTV 12P 🚗 ❀
V ✧ ♨ Last dinner 9pm
Credit Cards [1][2][3]

★62% Iona
Strathearn Place EH9 2AL ☎031-447 6264 & 031-447 5050 FAX 031-452 8574

The Iona is a popular family-run commercial hotel on the south side within easy reach of the city centre. Bedrooms are practically furnished and some are quite compact. Public areas include a busy bar, a comfortable lounge and a small dining room where the food is noted for its generous portions.

17rm(2⇨↑13↑)Annexe4rm(2fb) CTV in all bedrooms ® T ✲
sB&B£23-£25 sB&B⇨↑£45 dB&B£44 dB&B⇨↑£52
CTV 20P 🚗
V ✧ ✲ Lunch £6.20 High tea £6.50 Dinner £12-£16.30alc Last dinner 9pm
Credit Cards [1][3]

Forte Posthouse
Corstorphine Rd EH12 6UA (adjacent to Edinburgh Zoo) ☎031-334 0390 FAX 031-334 9237

Suitable for both the business and leisure traveller, this bright hotel provides modern accommodation in well equipped bedrooms with en suite bathrooms. For more details about Forte Posthouse hotels, consult the Contents page, under Hotel Groups.

200⇨↑ ✲ B⇨↑£41.50-£53.50 (room only)

Forte Travelodge
Dreghorn Link (6m S, A720 Ring Rd South)
☎031-441 4296 Central Res (0800) 850950

This modern building offers a good standard of accommodation for overnight stops. Smart, spacious and well equipped bedrooms, all with en suite bathrooms, are suitable for family use, and meals may be taken at the nearby family restaurant. For more details about Travelodges, consult the Contents page, under Hotel Groups.

40⇨↑ ✲ B⇨↑£31.95 (room only)

Hilton National Edinburgh
Bells Mills, 69 Bellford Rd EH4 3DG
☎031-332 2545 FAX 031-332 8031

This is a bright, modern hotel with an informal restaurant, aimed at both the business and leisure guest. All bedrooms have en-suite bathrooms and a range of modern facilities. For more information about Hilton National, consult the Contents page, under Hotel Groups.

144⇨↑ ✲ sB&B⇨↑£98 dB&B⇨↑£130 (room only)
CONF. Thtr 120 Class 60 Board 45 Del £132

Travel Inn
288 Willowbrae Rd EH8 7NG (2m from City east)
☎031-661 3396

Purpose-built accommodation offers spacious and well equipped bedrooms, all with en suite bathrooms. Meals may be taken at the nearby family restaurant and pub. For more details about Travel Inns, consult the Contents page, under Hotel Groups.

39⇨↑ ✲ B⇨↑£33.50 (room only)

 ★★ **66%**
Eskbank Motor Hotel
29 Dalhousie Road, Eskbank
EDINBURGH EH22 3AT
Tel: 031-663 3234 Fax No: 031-660 4347

Ideally situated for central Edinburgh and By-pass, all 16 rooms are to a high standard and all have full facilities, including direct dial telephone. Traditional warm lounge bar & restaurant. Popular 'Budget Week End Breaks' available throughout most of the year. Situated on A7 South Edinburgh. *See gazetteer under Dalkeith.*

*Access — Visa — Amex — Diners
Resident proprietors: Charles & Jane Ross

★★★AA
THE BARNTON
THISTLE HOTEL

Queensferry Road, Edinburgh EH4 6AS
Tel: 031-339 1144   Fax: 031-317 7189

Your choice in Edinburgh

For Reservations at over 100
Mount Charlotte Thistle Hotels
Telephone London: 071 937 8033.

Edzell - Elgin

EDZELL Tayside *Angus* Map **15** NO56

★★★ 60% Glenesk
High St DD9 7TF (off A94 just after Brechin Bypass)
☎(0356) 648319 FAX (0356) 647333

This family-run hotel beside the golf course is popular not only with golfers, but all types of guests. Public areas include 2 attractive lounges offering traditional comforts, and bedrooms are comfortable and well equipped.

25rm(23⇨♠)(4fb) CTV in all bedrooms ® T ✱
sB&B⇨♠£44 dB&B⇨♠fr£76 ⊟
150P 8☎ ✿ ❀ ▭ (heated) snooker sauna solarium gymnasium *xmas*
V ♡ ⌴ Lunch fr£10.50 Dinner fr£14.50 Last dinner 8.45pm
Credit Cards ①②③⑤

★★ 57% Panmure Arms
52 High St DD9 7TA ☎(0356) 648420 & 648427 FAX (0356) 648588

Popular with personnel from the nearby USAF base, the hotel offers good-value meals both in the bar and the restaurant. Bedrooms have modern furnishings.

24⇨♠(2fb) CTV in all bedrooms ® T ✱ sB&B⇨♠£31-£33 dB&B⇨♠£50-£55 ⊟
CTV 30P *xmas*
V ♡ ✱ Sunday Lunch £7.75 Dinner £14-£20&alc Last dinner 9pm
CONF. Board 115 Del from £50
Credit Cards ①②③⑤

EGHAM Surrey Map **04** TQ07

★★★★ 65% Runnymede
Windsor Rd TW20 0AG (off junc 13 of M25)
☎(0784) 436171 FAX (0784) 436340

The Runnymede is a privately owned, modern hotel, attractively situated on the River Thames. There is a bright open-plan lounge and cocktail bar with a smart conservatory extension, which leads to the terrace. The elegant River Room restaurant has a pianist playing, while Charlie Bell's cafe bar is lively and informal. Bedrooms vary in style but all offer the expected comforts, and some offer extra luxury.

171⇨♠(32fb)⌿in 31 bedrooms CTV in all bedrooms ® T ✱ sB⇨♠£105-£140 dB⇨♠£125-£140 (room only) ⊟
Lift (⊞ 300P ❀ ▭ (heated) ⌾ (hard) snooker sauna solarium gymnasium putting green croquet ♪ *xmas*
♡ International V ♡ ⌴ ✱ Lunch £16.95-£17 Dinner £19.95 Last dinner 9.45pm
CONF. Thtr 200 Class 120 Board 50 Del from £143.95
Credit Cards ①②③⑤

EGLWYSFACH Dyfed Map **06** SN69

★★★ ❀❀❀⇨ 73% Ynyshir Hall
SY20 8TA (off A487, 5.5m S of Machynlleth, signposted from the main road) ☎Glandyfi(0654) 781209 FAX (0654) 781366

This delightful Georgian house, once owned by Queen Victoria and set in 12 acres of parkland adjacent to the RSPB reserve, is the pride and joy of the enthusiastic Bob and Joan Reed. Bob's artistic influence is shown by the rooms being decorated in striking colours which complement the inherent architecture. Two bedrooms have small comfortable sitting areas and all are brightly styled, furnished with antique and period pieces, and supplied with luxurious extras. The chef, David Dressler, makes good use of quality local produce and our inspector enjoyed a tasty collection of home-made ravioli of crab with julienne of truffle, set off by a robust lobster sauce; loin of Welsh lamb on a galatte of spinach with rosemary jus and fried venison, finishing with treacle tartlet with delicious armagnac custard. Meals are served with a good selection of simply cooked al dente vegetables. Afternoon tea, with local delicacies, is served on the lawn on warmer days.

8⇨♠| ⌸⌿in 3 bedrooms CTV in all bedrooms T ✱ sB&B⇨♠£65-£85 dB&B⇨♠£90-£125 ⊟
20P ⌸ ❀ painting & drawing courses nc9yrs *xmas*
♡ Welsh, French & French V ♡ ⌴ ✱ Lunch £15-£20alc Dinner fr£25alc Last dinner 8.45pm
Credit Cards ①②③⑤ £

EGREMONT Cumbria Map **11** NY01

★★★ 56% Blackbeck Bridge Inn
CA22 2NY (Blackbeck 2.75m A595) ☎Beckermet(0946) 841661 FAX (0946) 841007

This large roadside hotel with modern extensions offers pleasant attentive service. Bedrooms are equipped with the expected modern facilities and a wide range of food is available.

22⇨♠(1fb)1⌸ CTV in all bedrooms ® T ✱ sB&B⇨♠£26-£49.50 dB&B⇨♠£38-£61.50 ⊟
60P ❀ *xmas*
♡ Mainly grills V ♡ ⌴ ✱ Sunday Lunch £5.95-£8.50 Dinner £10-£20alc Last dinner 9.30pm
Credit Cards ①②③⑤

ELGIN Grampian *Morayshire* Map **15** NJ26

★★★ ❀ 73% Mansion House
The Haugh IV30 1AW (SCOTLAND'S HERITAGE HOTELS) ☎(0343) 548811 FAX (0343) 547916
(Rosette awarded for dinner only)

Set in wooded grounds, this extended 19th-century turreted mansion is popular with all kinds of guests. Bedrooms vary in size but the majority, including twin rooms, have 4-poster beds and offer such thoughtful extras as a welcoming glass of sherry. Comfortable public areas include a choice of lounges, a small, well stocked bar and a bistro as an informal alternative to the elegant restaurant. Chef John Alexander's short but imaginative 'carte' features the best fresh ingredients.

24⇨♠(4fb)16⌸ CTV in all bedrooms ® ⌿ T ✱ sB&B⇨♠£75-£90 dB&B⇨♠£110-£150 ⊟
(30P ❀ ▭ (heated) snooker sauna solarium gymnasium jacuzzi turkish bath *xmas*
V ♡ ⌴ Lunch £12.50-£20alc Dinner £20-£30alc Last dinner 9pm
CONF. Thtr 100 Class 100 Board 100 Del from £95
Credit Cards ①②③

★★★ 68% Mansfield House
Mayne Rd IV30 1NY ☎(0343) 540883 FAX (0343) 552491

A Georgian mansion has been sympathetically restored to create this stylish hotel, efficiently run by the Murray family and providing every comfort and convenience. Public areas include an elegant little lounge, a comfortable cocktail bar and an attractive restaurant, where an imaginative à la carte menu offers fresh local seafood specialities as well as prime beef and lamb.

17⇨♠(2fb)⌿in 4 bedrooms CTV in all bedrooms ® ⌴ T ✲ (ex guide dogs) sB&B⇨♠£50-£60 dB&B⇨♠£80-£100 ⊟
Lift ⊞ 55P 2⌸ ❀ ✿ sauna gymnasium ♪ ⌾ *xmas*
V ♡ ⌴ Lunch fr£10&alc High tea fr£8 Dinner £15-£25alc Last dinner 9.30pm
CONF. Thtr 35 Class 18 Board 16 Del from £75
Credit Cards ①②③

★★ 63% Laichmoray
Station Rd IV30 1QR ☎(0343) 540045 FAX (0343) 540055

This popular, family-run hotel, in an extended Georgian building, is conveniently situated close to the railway station. Substantially refurbished public areas include a choice of bars, a smart restaurant with candlelit tables and a simple first-floor lounge. Bedrooms are practical and modern.

Elgin - Ely

34rm(33⇨⇨)(4fb) CTV in all bedrooms ® T sB&B⇨£45-£48 dB&B⇨£68-£72 ₽
CTV 60P ❋ pool table darts *xmas*
V ♦ ⚲ Lunch £8-£9.50 High tea £7-£8 Dinner £14-£25alc Last dinner 9.30pm
CONF. Thtr 200 Class 160 Board 50
Credit Cards ①②③⑤

★★ **60%** *St Leonards*
Duff Av IV30 1QS ☎(0343) 547350 FAX (0343) 550713
Efficiently run by the McAlister family, this friendly hotel caters for tourists, business people and local functions. Formerly a baronial mansion, it stands in its own grounds in easy reach of the station. Amenities include a bar, a no-smoking restaurant and a dining room for high teas.
16rm(13⇨⇨)(2fb) CTV in all bedrooms ® T
60P ❋
♢ Scottish & French V ♦ ⚲ ✂ Last dinner 8.30pm
Credit Cards ①③

ELLESMERE PORT Cheshire Map 07 SJ47
★★★ **66%** *The Woodhey*
Welsh Rd, Little Sutton L66 4PS (on A550 off junc 5 of M53)
☎051-339 5121 FAX 051-339 3214
A complete refurbishment has given new life to this hotel which now has smart well equipped bedrooms and a popular grill restaurant.
53⇨⇨ Annexe1⇨(3fb) CTV in all bedrooms ® T ❋
sB&B⇨£65 dB&B⇨£80 ₽
《 180P ▭ (heated) sauna solarium ♫ *xmas*
V ♦ ⚲ ❋ Lunch £7.95-£9alc Dinner £12.75&alc Last dinner 10pm
CONF. Thtr 250 Class 125 Board 100 Del from £76
Credit Cards ①②③⑤

ELSTREE Hertfordshire Map 04 TQ19
★★★ **67%** *Edgwarebury*
Barnet Ln WD6 3RE (on the A411 Barnet Lane, look out for concealed entrance) (Lansbury) ☎081-953 8227 FAX 081-207 3668
Set in 10 acres of grounds, this Tudor Manor house has been converted into a comfortable and peaceful hotel. Most of the well equipped bedrooms are in a modern wing, while public rooms with stone fireplaces and oak beams include a lounge bar and terrace restaurant. Service is friendly and attentive.
50⇨⇨ in 8 bedrooms CTV in all bedrooms ® ⚲ T
✈ (ex guide dogs) ❋ sB&B⇨fr£89.50 dB&B⇨fr£101 ₽
《 120P ⇔ ❋ ♀ (hard) snooker ⚔
♢ English & Continental V ♦ ⚲ ✂ ❋ Lunch fr£20.95 Dinner fr£25.95 Last dinner 10pm
CONF. Thtr 80 Class 30 Board 30 Del from £115
Credit Cards ①②③⑤

ELTERWATER Cumbria Map 07 NY30
★★★ ❀**68%** *Langdale Hotel & Country Club*
LA22 9JD ☎(05394) 37302 FAX (05394) 37694
(Rosette awarded for dinner only)
The Langdale Hotel and Country Club complex also has luxury self-catering chalets and an excellent leisure centre. Purdys is the smart, but welcoming main restaurant, where the 5-course table d'hôte menu offers good value for money with a reasonable choice. Cooking is a mixture of French and English and will satisfy every taste. Wines are mostly young, but there is a good selection of house wines and an adequate choice of half bottles.
65⇨⇨(6fb)2⊞ CTV in all bedrooms ®⚲ T ✈ (ex guide dogs)

《 100P ⚲ ▭ (heated) ♀ (hard) squash snooker sauna solarium gymnasium croquet ⚔
♢ International V ♦ ⚲ ✂ Last dinner 10pm
Credit Cards ①②③⑤

★★★ **68%** *Eltermere Country House*
LA22 9HY (On unclass rd between A593 & B5343)
☎(05394) 37207
Closed 25-26 Dec RS mid Nov-mid Feb
A relaxing stay is assured at this 250-year-old Lakeland hotel, which is quietly set in 3 acres of well tended gardens overlooking Elterwater. Public areas include a welcoming lounge, a small bar and an attractive dining room. Bedrooms, some with exposed beams, are well kept and comfortably furnished in a mixture of modern styles.
18rm(15⇨⇨)(4fb) CTV in all bedrooms ® ✈ (ex guide dogs)
25P ⇔ ❋ putting
♢ English & Continental ♦ ✂ Last dinner 8.15pm

ELY Cambridgeshire Map 05 TL58
★★ **64%** *Lamb*
2 Lynn Rd CB7 4EJ (enter Ely on A10, Hotel in centre of city near Cathedral) ☎(0353) 663574
FAX (0353) 666350
This former coaching inn, close to the cathedral, has a choice of bars and a restaurant, all popular with the locals. Bedrooms have light wood fitted furniture, pastel décor and a good range of equipment. Staff and management are polite and cheerful, encouraging a relaxed and informal atmosphere.
32⇨⇨(6fb)2⊞ CTV in all bedrooms ® T ❋ sB&B⇨£58-£62 dB&B⇨£75-£85 ₽
《 14P 1🅿 *xmas*

➤

Far from the madding crowd...

...but very close to perfection, that's the Langdale Hotel in the Lake District. Breathtaking scenery, and an amazing variety of outdoor activities. The Country Club has heated pool, exercise room, solaria, sauna, Health and Beauty Salon, also squash courts. Comfortable rooms with en-suite bathroom, direct dial telephone and satellite TV. Excellent food, served by friendly, helpful staff.

For details – including
mid-week Bargain Breaks, phone 05394 37302.

Langdale Hotel and Country Club, Great Langdale,
nr. Ambleside, Cumbria LA22 9JD. Tel: 05394 37302.

Ely - Epworth

English & French **V** ✿ ♨ ✱ Lunch £6-£11 High tea £4-£7
Dinner £13.25-£14.95 Last dinner 9.45pm
CONF. Thtr 65 Class 36 Del from £85
Credit Cards [1] [2] [3] [5]

★ 60% Nyton
7 Barton Rd CB7 4HZ ☎(0353) 662459
The Nyton is a substantial period house in lovely grounds which has been converted to provide simple accommodation and elegant public areas.
9⇨🛏 Annexe5⇨🛏(2fb) CTV in all bedrooms ®
✕ (ex guide dogs) ✱ sB&B⇨🛏£32-£35 dB&B⇨🛏£50-£54 🅿
《 25P ✿
English & French **V** ✱ Sunday Lunch fr£8 Dinner fr£15
Last dinner 8.30pm
Credit Cards [1] [2] [3] [5]

Forte Travelodge
(at roundabout A10/A142)
☎(0353) 668499 Central Res (0800) 850950

FORTE Travelodge

This modern building offers a good standard of accommodation for overnight stops. Smart, spacious and well equipped bedrooms, all with en suite bathrooms, are suitable for family use, and meals may be taken at the nearby family restaurant. For more details about Travelodges, consult the Contents page, under Hotel Groups.
39⇨🛏 ✱ B⇨🛏£31.95 (room only)

EMPINGHAM Leicestershire Map 04 SK90

★★ 66% The White Horse Inn
Main St LE15 8PR (on A606, Oakham-Stamford)
☎(078086) 221 due to change to (0780) 460221
This stone-built inn is popular locally for its food – a good choice of bar meals or table d'hôte or à la carte menus in the small restaurant. The bar dominates, and is full of character with its large fireplace and heavy beams. A comfortable lounge area and reception have been created to provide residents with a quieter option.
4⇨🛏 Annexe9⇨🛏(4fb)1▦in 1 bedroom CTV in 12 bedrooms ® T ✱ sB&B⇨🛏£30-£40 dB&B⇨🛏£40-£60 🅿
60P *xmas*
English & French **V** ✿ ♨ ✱ Lunch fr£9.95&alc High tea £5.95 Dinner £10.95&alc Last dinner 9.45pm
CONF. Thtr 60 Class 60 Board 34 Del £60
Credit Cards [1] [2] [3] [5]

EMSWORTH Hampshire Map 04 SU70

★★★ 67% Brookfield
Havant Rd PO10 7LF ☎(0243) 373363 & 376383 FAX (0243) 376342
Closed 25 Dec-1 Jan
This family-run hotel has developed from a detached period house on the former main road, with a restaurant overlooking the garden. Bedrooms in the new wing are larger but all are comfortable with good facilities.
41⇨🛏▦ CTV in all bedrooms ® T ✕ (ex guide dogs)
《 130P ⊞ ✿
English & French **V** ✿ ♨ Last dinner 9.30pm
Credit Cards [1] [2] [3] [5]

★★ 62% The Crown
8 High St PO10 7TW ☎(0243) 372806 FAX (0243) 370082
This popular and very traditional coaching inn dates back to the 16th century. Bedrooms, furnished in pine, all have a good range of equipment. The combined oak beamed bar, lounge and dining room features a farmhouse kitchen menu with steak specialities, together wih a good selection of real ales.
9rm(7⇨🛏)(1fb) CTV in all bedrooms ® T

23P ⊞
English, French & Chinese **V** ✿ ♨ Last dinner 10pm
Credit Cards [1] [2] [3] [4] [5]

ENFIELD Greater London Map 04 TQ39

★★★ 67% Enfield
52 Rowantree Rd EN2 8PW ☎081-366 3511 FAX 081-366 2432
Closed 24 Dec-1 Jan
This friendly, family-run hotel is in a quiet residential area. Public areas, though compact, are stylish and comfortable. Most bedrooms have partial wood panelling, elegant dark wood furniture and smartly tiled shower rooms. Sizes vary, so discuss your requirements on booking.
33⇨🛏🛏(1fb)1▦ CTV in all bedrooms ® T ✕ (ex guide dogs)
20P sauna gymnasium ⌘
International **V** ✿ ♨ Last dinner 10pm
Credit Cards [1] [3] [5]

★★ 59% Holtwhites
92 Chase Side EN2 0QN ☎081-363 0124 FAX 081-366 9089
This extended Victorian villa retains something of its original atmosphere in a comfortable bar/TV lounge. Bedrooms in a variety of shapes and sizes offer a range of facilities and extras, so it is important to make your needs clear. An established staff provides friendly service throughout.
30rm(28⇨🛏)(1fb) CTV in all bedrooms ® T
✕ (ex guide dogs) sBfr£31.50 sB⇨🛏fr£39.90 dB£45
dB⇨🛏£49.90 (room only) 🅿
《 30P 4⊞ ⊞ nc5yrs *xmas*
International **V** ✿ ♨ ✕ Lunch £8-£14alc Dinner £8-£14alc Last dinner 8.30pm
Credit Cards [1] [3] [5] £

EPPING Essex Map 05 TL40

Forte Posthouse
High Rd, Bell Common CM16 4DG
☎(0992) 573137 FAX (0992) 560402

FORTE Posthouse

Suitable for both the business and leisure traveller, this bright hotel provides modern accommodation in well equipped bedrooms with en suite bathrooms. For more details about Forte Posthouse hotels, consult the Contents page, under Hotel Groups.
Annexe79⇨🛏 ✱ B⇨🛏£41.50-£53.50 (room only)
CONF. Thtr 85 Class 50 Board 32 Del from £79.50

EPSOM Surrey Map 04 TQ26

★★ 60% Heathside
Brighton Rd KT20 6BW ☎Burgh Heath(0737) 353355 FAX (0737) 370857
(For full entry see Burgh Heath)

EPWORTH Humberside Map 08 SE70

★★ 64% Red Lion
Market Place DN9 1EU ☎(0427) 872208 FAX (0427) 874330
This recently renovated old coaching inn offers modern amenities while retaining much historic charm. Bedrooms, though rather compact, are cosy and attractively decorated, and the popular bars, lounge and restaurant offer a choice of good value menus.
16rm(5⇨9🛏)1▦ CTV in all bedrooms ® T ✕ (ex guide dogs)
134P sauna solarium gymnasium steam room
V ✿ ♨ Last dinner 10pm
Credit Cards [1] [2] [3] [5]

Remember to book early for holiday
and bank holiday times

Eriska - Eskdalemuir

ERISKA Strathclyde *Argyllshire* Map **10** NM94

★★★

★★★❀❀♨ **ISLE OF ERISKA**
PA37 1SD **(SCOTLAND'S HERITAGE HOTELS)**
☎Ledaig(063172) 371 FAX (063172) 531
Closed Dec-mid Mar

Set on its own beautiful island where guests are free to roam, this delightful baronial mansion is owned and run by the Buchanan-Smith family and offers a haven of peace and comfort. Bedrooms, furnished in keeping with the building, have good facilities and there are lovely lounges, a library bar and attractive dining room where the 6-course dinners make expert use of local produce; meats and fish, vegetables from the kitchen garden, Scottish cheeses. Pudding are all home made and there is a comprehensive wine list.

16⇨ℕ(1fb) CTV in all bedrooms ® T sB&Bfr£130 dB&Bfr£150-£175 ℝ
(36P ⇔ ❋ ℘ (hard) ∪ croquet watersports pitch & putt
✴ Bar Lunch £11 High tea £14 Dinner £37 Last dinner 9pm

Credit Cards [1][3]

ERMINGTON Devon Map **02** SX65

★★❀63% **Ermewood House**
Totnes Rd PL21 9NS
☎Modbury(0548) 830741

Closed 23 Dec-9 Jan

Jack and Jennifer Mellor provide a friendly and relaxed atmosphere at their country hotel overlooking the River Erme. Ever-improving facilities, and noteworthy cooking by Mr Mellor, complete the picture. Changed daily, the 6- course menu is traditional English with a few French influences, and the keynotes are fresh local produce and good strong flavours.

12⇨ℕ(1fb)≠ CTV in all bedrooms ® T sB&B⇨ℕ£43.50 dB&B⇨ℕ£60 ℝ
15P ⇔ ❋
♡ English & Continental ✂ Dinner £17.50 Last dinner 8.30pm

Credit Cards [1][3]

ERSKINE Strathclyde *Renfrewshire* Map **11** NS47

Forte Posthouse
North Barr PA8 6AN ☎041-812 0123 FAX 041-812 7642

Suitable for both the business and leisure traveller, this bright hotel provides modern accommodation in well equipped bedrooms with en suite bathrooms. For more details about Forte Posthouse hotels, consult the Contents page, under Hotel Groups.

166⇨ℕ B⇨ℕ£41.50-£53.50 (room only)
CONF. Thtr 600 Class 400 Board 40 Del £89.50

Rosettes range from 5 for outstanding cuisine to 1 rosette for enjoyable, well prepared food

---

ESCRICK North Yorkshire Map **08** SE64

★★★70% **Parsonage Country House**
Main St YO4 6LF ☎(0904) 728111 FAX (0904) 878151

This 19th-century parsonage is now a small but elegant country house-style hotel set in gardens with neat lawns, woodland and an ornate fountain. Bedrooms are individually furnished and decorated. A comfortable drawing room and attractive lounge bar overlook the gardens and the intimate dining room is a fine setting for sampling the Anglo-French cuisine.

13⇨ℕ(1fb)2≠ CTV in all bedrooms ® T ✈ (ex guide dogs)
(120P ⇔ ❋ ⚘
♡ English & French V ✩ ✂ Last dinner 9.30pm

Credit Cards [1][2][3][5]

See advertisement under YORK

ESHER Surrey

See LONDON SECTION plan 1 B1

★★63% **Haven**
Portsmouth Rd KT10 9AR (1m NE on A307) ☎081-398 0023 FAX 081-398 9463

This family run Edwardian hotel has simply decorated, comfortable and well equipped bedrooms. Public rooms are traditional in style and service is cheerfully informal.

16⇨ℕ Annexe4⇨ℕ(2fb) CTV in all bedrooms ® T
20P 1≠ ⇔
♡ International V ✩ ✂ Last dinner 8.30pm

Credit Cards [1][2][3][4][5]

ESKDALE GREEN Cumbria Map **06** NY10

★★63% **Bower House Inn**
CA19 1TD ☎Eskdale(09467) 23244 FAX (09467) 23308

This peacefully situated Lakeland pub has much historic charm and offers caring service and well furnished bedrooms. There is a comfortable lounge with a log fire and an attractive beamed restaurant where the daily changing menu offers international dishes – pork satay, tournedos Rossini, local smoked goose breast – and always includes freshly made soup and home-made desserts. An extensive range of bar food is also available.

5⇨ℕ Annexe19⇨ℕ(3fb) CTV in all bedrooms ® T ✈ ✴
sB&B⇨ℕ£38-£45 dB&B⇨ℕ£53-£58 ℝ
60P ❋ ⚘ xmas
♡ English & French V ✩ ✂ Bar Lunch £3.50-£8.50alc High tea fr£3.50alc Dinner fr£16.25alc Last dinner 8.30pm
CONF. Thtr 40 Board 30 Del £60

Credit Cards [1][3]

ESKDALEMUIR Dumfries & Galloway *Dumfriesshire*
Map **11** NY29

★★❀68% **Hart Manor**
DG13 0QQ (turn off A6 at Langholm onto B709, follow hotel signs for 12.5m) (Logis) ☎(03873) 73217 FAX (03873) 73217

Closed 25 Dec

Situated amidst unspoilt Eskdale forest and moorland, this converted 18th- century shooting lodge is run with friendly informality by the welcoming Medcalf family. Light, airy bedrooms are comfortable and the relaxing public rooms include a choice of bars. The set price menu offers a choice at each course, and the cooking style is uncomplicated with fresh and honest flavours.

7rm(5⇨ℕ)(2fb) CTV in all bedrooms ® T ✴ sB&B⇨ℕfr£26-£29 dB&B⇨ℕ£46-£52 ℝ
CTV 30P ⇔ ❋ ♪
♡ Scottish & English V ✩ ✂ ✴ Dinner fr£16.50 Last dinner 8pm

Evercreech - Evesham

EVERCREECH Somerset Map 03 ST63

★★ 58% Pecking Mill Inn & Hotel
BA4 6PG (On A371 1m W of village) ☎(0749) 830336
This well maintained 16th-century inn offers compact but well equipped bedrooms. There is a small lounge and a popular character bar.
6⇨ CTV in all bedrooms ® T
23P ⟳
♨ Mainly grills ⚜ Last dinner 10pm
Credit Cards ①②③⑤

EVERSHOT Dorset Map 03 ST50

★★★ ❀❀❀❀
SUMMER LODGE
DT2 0JR (1m W of A37 halfway between Dorchester & Yeovil)
☎(0935) 83424 FAX (0935) 83005

Resident proprietors Margaret and Nigel Corbett, along with their team of charming staff, extend a warm welcome to guests. Bedrooms are individually styled, with pretty décor, comfortable furnishings and lots of extras. Public areas are cosy, with fresh flowers, and in winter months, guests can enjoy afternoon tea by a blazing log fire. Chef Roger Jones cooks with fresh seasonal produce prepared with skill and care. Our inspector enjoyed a light, full flavoured brill and smoked salmon terrine set on a tangy tomato coulis, followed by a delicious white onion and cider soup, and then a succulent supreme of guinea fowl with glazed apples and a rich Calvados souce. The meal was nicely rounded off by a hot caramel soufflé.

11⇨Annexe6⇨(1fb) CTV in all bedrooms ® T sB&B⇨£122.50 dB&B⇨£170-£270 (incl dinner) ☐
40P ⟳ ❀ ≋ (heated) ♀ (hard & grass) croquet xmas
V ♨ ⚜ Lunch £17.50-£19.50 Dinner £25&alc Last dinner 9pm
Credit Cards ①②③

★★ 64% The Acorn Inn
28 Fore St DT2 0JW ☎(0935) 83228

ExecGroup

A warm welcome and willing service is assured at an inn of great character, which has been comfortably furnished in keeping with the building. Bedrooms vary in size and provide many modern facilities. One of the two dining rooms, where smoking is allowed, includes a bar, and the other, candlelit, is for non-smokers. An extensive menu is available in both.

8⇨(2fb)2⟳ CTV in all bedrooms ® T
℄ CTV 40P pool tables skittles
V ♨ ⚜ Last dinner 9.45pm
Credit Cards ①③

If you have booked a meal in a hotel restaurant and cannot get there, remember you have a contractual obligation to cancel your booking.

EVESHAM Hereford & Worcester Map 04 SP04

See also **Fladbury**

★★★ ❀69% The Evesham
Coopers Ln, off Waterside WR11 6DA ☎(0386) 765566 FAX (0386) 765443
Closed 25 & 26 Dec

Dating back to the early 16th-century, this very pleasant hotel near the River Avon has 2.5-acres of mature grounds. Public rooms are exceptionally comfortable, while bedrooms are equally inviting and meals are enjoyable. The owners and their loyal staff, provide friendly and hospitable service.

40⇨⨎(1fb) CTV in all bedrooms ® T sB&B⇨⨎£60-£68 dB&B⇨⨎£82-£96 ☐
50P ⟳ ❀ ≋ (heated) croquet putting
♨ International V ⚜ ♀ Lunch £10.70-£19.50alc Dinner £12.50-£19.50alc Last dinner 9.30pm
Credit Cards ①②③⑤

★★★ 59% Northwick Arms
Waterside WR11 6BT (follow A44, cross traffic lights, follow river for 0.25m hotel on right)
☎(0386) 40322 FAX (0386) 41070

The Northwick Arms is a company owned hotel just across the road from the River Avon. Five comfortable new bedrooms have been added, and while the other rooms are adequate they are looking a little tired. There is a small restaurant and hotel bar in addition to Falcons Bar, a popular meeting place across the courtyard.

30⇨⨎(4fb)1⟳ CTV in all bedrooms ® T ✱ sB&B⇨⨎£24-£45 dB&B⇨⨎£48-£60 ☐
℄ 90P ❀ ♒ xmas
♨ English & French V ⚜ ♀ Bar Lunch £1.75-£3.50alc Dinner £8-£15alc Last dinner 10pm
Credit Cards ①②③⑤ £

★★ 77% The Mill at Harvington
Anchor Ln, Harvington WR11 5NR (4.5m NE, off B439. Signposted) ☎(0386) 870688 FAX (0386) 870688
Closed 24-27 Dec

This Georgian house and converted red-brick mill on the banks of the River Avon date back to 1750. Old cast iron bakery oven doors are on view in the spacious and comfortable lounge, and there are many original wooden beams throughout the hotel. The hotel's own herb garden supplies the restaurant, where chef Jane Greenhalgh produces good quality dishes from fresh ingredients. Staff are exceptionally friendly and attentive

15⇨⨎ CTV in all bedrooms ® T ✂ (ex guide dogs)
sB&B⇨⨎£54 dB&B⇨⨎£85 ☐
50P ⟳ ❀ ≋ (heated) ♪ croquet nc10yrs
♨ English & French V ⚜ Lunch £13.95 Dinner £19.50-£27alc Last dinner 9.30pm
Credit Cards ①②③ £

★★ 77% Riverside
The Parks, Offenham Rd WR11 5JP ☎(0386) 446200 FAX (0386) 40021
RS Nov-Feb

This delightful small family-run hotel on the banks of the Avon has a happy atmosphere, and pretty accommodation. Rosemary Willmott's cooking is French and English in style, based on local ingredients wherever possible, and there is an 8-choice fixed price menu. The building is split-level, with the lounge, bar and restaurant on a lower level.

7⇨⨎ CTV in all bedrooms ® T ✂ (ex guide dogs) ✱
sB&B⇨⨎£41.50-£51 dB&B⇨⨎£50-£75 ☐
40P ❀ ♪ xmas
♨ English & French V ⚜ ♀ ✱ Lunch £15.95-£17.95 Dinner fr£19.95 Last dinner 9pm
Credit Cards ①③

Evesham - Exeter

★★ **73%Waterside**
56 Waterside WR11 6JZ (A44/B435 junc 40yds on right alongside river) ☎(0386) 442420
The owners of this family-run hotel continue to extend and make improvements. Since our last inspection, new rooms have been added and Strollers restaurant and bar, with its cheery red and white striped tablecloths and vast collection of bric-a-brac, has opened and proved popular. A range of 50 main courses is provided, including grills and Mexican dishes. Service is friendly and the welcome is warm.
14🛏🚿Annexe4🛏🚿(3fb) CTV in all bedrooms ® T sB&B🛏🚿£34-£48 dB&B🛏🚿£48-£60 🍴
30P 🎵
☐ English & American V ⊕ ⚏ ⌇ ✱ Lunch £7.85&alc Credit Cards ①②③

EWLOEClwyd Map 07 SJ36

★★★★ ❀70%**St David's Park**
St Davids Park CH5 3YB (N of A55, off A494) ☎Chester(0244) 520800 FAX (0244) 520930
RS 24-31 Dec
This high quality hotel is partly open plan, with several comfortable lounge areas and a smart bar. The attractive restaurant offers a popular carvery, a good carte and an excellent chef's gourmet menu with up to 7 courses of imaginative dishes. Staff are attentive and friendly.
121🛏🚿(13fb)2🍴⌇in 30 bedrooms CTV in all bedrooms ®💈 T ✱ sB🛏🚿£56-£79 dB🛏🚿£70-£135 (room only) 🍴
Lift ⦇ 240P ❈ ▣ (heated) snooker sauna solarium gymnasium turkish steam bath beauty therapist 🎵 ⌘ xmas
V ⊕ ⚏ ⌇ ✱ Lunch £10.95-£15.50&alc Dinner £15.50&alc Last dinner 10pm
CONF. Thtr 270 Class 150 Board 32 Del from £375
Credit Cards ①②③⑤

See advertisement under CHESTER

EXEBRIDGESomerset Map 03 SS92

★★ ❀66%**Anchor Inn**
TA22 9AZ (on B3222) ☎Dulverton(0398) 23343
Set in an acre of lawns by the banks of the River Exe, this charming old village inn featured in Blackmore's Lorna Doone and has compact, attractive bedrooms with modern facilities. There is a popular bar and quiet residents lounge adjoining the riverside restaurant, where Jane Ogbourne and David Sylvester offer an extensive choice of freshly prepared dishes that make maximum use of local fish and game.
6🛏🚿(2fb)🍴 CTV in all bedrooms ®💈 T ✱ sB&B🛏🚿fr£40 dB&B🛏🚿£66-£76 🍴
CTV 100P ❈ 🎵
V ⊕ ⚏ ✱ Sunday Lunch fr£9.95 Dinner fr£18.95 Last dinner 9pm
Credit Cards ①③

EXETERDevon Map 03 SX99
See also **Stoke Canon**

★★★71%**Royal Clarence**
Cathedral Yard EX1 1HB (facing cathedral) ☎(0392) 58464 FAX (0392) 439243
A 14th-century hotel of enormous character, the Royal Clarence occupies an enviable position on a cobbled street overlooking the cathedral. The bedrooms offer elegant styles of décor and furnishings, and some have views of the cathedral. Public areas include a busy bar and quiet residents' lounge. Chef Stephen Saunders leads a capable brigade in the kitchen.
56🛏🚿(6fb)2🍴⌇in 8 bedrooms CTV in all bedrooms ® T 🐕 (ex guide dogs) ✱ sB&B🛏🚿£75-£85 dB&B🛏🚿£98-£115 🍴

Lift ⦇ 15P xmas
☐ English & French V ⊕ ⚏ ⌇ ✱ Lunch £8-£17&alc Dinner £16-£21&alc Last dinner 9.45pm
CONF. Thtr 160 Class 60 Board 40 Del from £98
Credit Cards ①②③⑤

★★★ 67%**Rougemont**
Queen St EX4 3SP ☎(0392) 54982 FAX (0392) 420928

This impressive hotel has a grand reception hall and well equipped bedrooms with coordinated colour schemes. Opposite Exeter central station, the hotel is a few minutes from the cathedral and shops. Drake's restaurant has table d'hôte and à la carte menus and there is a choice of bars.
90🛏🚿(5fb)1🍴⌇in 13 bedrooms CTV in all bedrooms ® T ✱ sB&B🛏🚿fr£69 dB&B🛏🚿fr£79 🍴
Lift ⦇ 40P xmas
☐ English & French V ⊕ ⚏ ⌇ ✱ Lunch fr£9.50 Dinner fr£14.95 Last dinner 10pm
CONF. Thtr 300 Class 170 Board 90 Del from £84
Credit Cards ①②③⑤

★★★ ❀67%**St Olaves Court**
Mary Arches St EX4 3AZ ☎(0392) 217736 FAX (0392) 413054
Stone-built in 1827 and set in a walled garden, this personally run hotel is popular not only for its warm welcome, but also for the imaginative dishes served in the restaurant. Chef Lee Jones is the Welsh finalist in the Young Chef of the Year awards.
11🛏🚿Annexe4🛏🚿(4fb) CTV in all bedrooms ® T 🐕 (ex guide dogs) sB&B🛏🚿£40-£65 dB&B🛏🚿£55-£90 🍴
CTV 15P 🚗 ❈

➡

Chequers Inn ★★

**Chequers Lane
Fladbury, Pershore
Worcestershire WR10 2PZ
Tel: 0386 860276. Fax: 0386 860527**

14th century fully modernised Inn with eight en suite bedrooms. All with colour TV and tea/coffee facilities. Restaurants with carvery and à la carte menu. Good selection of hot & cold bar snacks. Free fishing for residents.

*Golf breaks: £225 per person
4 days Golf – 3 nights DBB
(to include green fees and VAT).*

**For information contact:
Mr. & Mrs. R. A. Corfield**

Exeter

V ♥ ⚒ Lunch £12.50-£22.50&alc Dinner £12.50-£22.50&alc Last dinner 9.30pm
Credit Cards 1 2 3 5

★★★❀64% Buckerell Lodge
Topsham Rd EX2 4SQ ☏(0392) 52451 FAX (0392) 412114

Conveniently situated for the city centre, this privately owned hotel stands in its own gardens and offers well equipped accommodation. Chef Simon Cannon produces interesting dishes for the carte and table d'hôte menu available in Raffles Restaurant.
54⇨🛏(2fb)⊬in 8 bedrooms CTV in all bedrooms ® ⚑ T sB&B⇨🛏£49-£79.50 dB&B⇨🛏£68-£87 🍴
《200P ❀ ♫ xmas
⚐ English & French V ♥ ⚒ ⊬ ✻ Lunch fr£10.50 Dinner fr£16.50&alc Last dinner 9.45pm
CONF. Thtr 60 Class 30 Board 30 Del from £69.50
Credit Cards 1 2 3 4 5 £

★★★64% White Hart
66 South St EX1 1EE ☏(0392) 79897 FAX (0392) 50159
Closed 25-26 Dec

An ancient inn retaining much of its original charm, particularly in the 15th-century wine room. Sympathetic restoration over the years has provided well equipped and attractive bedrooms, while those in a modern block are rather more functional. Public areas include several small lounges and reading rooms, and Hostlers Restaurant offering a good range of interesting old English dishes. The popular Tap Room Bar and Victorian Ale and Port House are candlelit, with mahogany furniture and sawdust-covered floors.
59⇨🛏 CTV in all bedrooms ⚑ T ✠ (ex guide dogs)
Lift 《 CTV 80P 🚗
V ♥ ⚒ Last dinner 10pm
Credit Cards 1 2 3 5

★★★61% Countess Wear Lodge
398 Topsham Rd, Exeter Bypass EX2 6HE (off A379) ☏(0392) 875441 FAX (0392) 876174

This purpose built hotel has undergone a major refurbishment programme during the last few years. The rooms are compact but tastefully decorated and equipped for the business traveller. There is a traditional à la carte restaurant with a less formal wine bar adjacent.
44⇨🛏(1fb)⊬in 4 bedrooms CTV in all bedrooms ® T sB&B⇨🛏£34-£59 dB&B⇨🛏£60-£79 🍴
《120P ❀ (hard) xmas
⚐ English & French V ♥ ⚒ ✻ Lunch £9.75-£16&alc High tea £2.95-£4.95 Dinner £10.75-£16&alc Last dinner 9.45pm
CONF. Thtr 350 Class 172 Board 168 Del from £51.50
Credit Cards 1 2 3 5 £

★★★60% Devon Motel
Exeter Bypass, Matford EX2 8XU (leave M5 at junct 30, follow signpost to Marsh Baxton Ind. Est. A379, Motel is on main A38 roundabout) (Brend) ☏(0392) 59268 FAX (0392) 413144

This busy commercial hotel has been extensively upgraded in recent years, the accommodation including executive, family, standard and generous single rooms. Public areas, comprising a restaurant, bar and carvery, are located in an adjoining Georgian manor house.
Annexe41⇨🛏(3fb) CTV in all bedrooms ® ⚑ T
《250P ❀ childrens play area ♫ 🎭
⚐ English & French V ♥ ⚒ ✻ Lunch £9 Dinner £12.50&alc Last dinner 9pm
Credit Cards 1 2 3 5 £

★★★59% Gipsy Hill
Gipsy Hill Ln, Pinhoe EX1 3RN (3m E on B3181) ☏(0392) 465252 FAX (0392) 464302

Commanding views over East Devon from its peaceful location, yet convenient for city, motorway and airport, this hotel has attractive bedrooms in the adjacent cottage annexe and further rooms in a small wing, which, though less spacious, are equally well equipped. Service is prompt and friendly throughout.
20⇨🛏 Annexe17⇨🛏 (5fb)2⚑⊬in 3 bedrooms CTV in all bedrooms ® T sB&B⇨🛏£49.50-£65 dB&B⇨🛏£60-£85 🍴
《100P ❀ ♫ xmas
⚐ English & French V ♥ ⚒ ✻ Lunch £8.50-£9.75&alc Dinner £14.50-£15.50&alc Last dinner 9.30pm
CONF. Thtr 100 Class 60 Del from £86.75
Credit Cards 1 2 3 £

★★★50% Exeter Arms Toby
Rydon Ln, Middlemoor PH7 4BP (Toby) ☏(0392) 435353 FAX (0392) 420826

This modern purpose built hotel complex is situated alongside a primary road on outskirts of city.
37⇨🛏(6fb)⊬in 10 bedrooms CTV in all bedrooms ® T ✠ (ex guide dogs) sB&B⇨🛏£29.95-£48 dB&B⇨🛏£40-£58 🍴
380P ❀
V ♥ ⚒ ⊬ Lunch £5.95-£18alc Dinner £7.25&alc Last dinner 10.30pm
CONF. Thtr 100 Class 60 Board 50 Del from £38
Credit Cards 1 2 3 5

★★★❀70% Ebford House
Exmouth Rd EX3 0QH (1m E of Topsham on A376) ☏Topsham(0392) 877658 FAX (0392) 874424

Ebford House is an attractive Georgian property, personally run by friendly proprietors Don and Samantha Horton. Bedrooms are pretty, with floral soft furnishings and subtle lighting. There is a quiet lounge and an elegant restaurant, the menu offering several imaginatively prepared dishes including plenty of local fish. Frisco's Bistro presents a wide selection of dishes from a less sophisticated blackboard menu.
17⇨🛏⚑⊬in 4 bedrooms CTV in all bedrooms ® ⚑ T ✠ (ex guide dogs) sB&B⇨🛏£50-£65 dB&B⇨🛏£55-£85 🍴
45P ❀ sauna solarium gymnasium
⚐ English & French V ♥ ⚒ ⊬ Lunch £12.95-£14.50&alc High tea £7 Dinner £15-£22&alc Last dinner 9.30pm
CONF. Thtr 20 Board 14 Del from £70
Credit Cards 1 2 3 £

★★68% St Andrews
28 Alphington Rd EX2 8HN ☏(0392) 76784 FAX (0392) 50249
Closed 25 Dec-1 Jan

This small and friendly owner-run hotel is conveniently located within walking distance of the city centre. Spotless bedrooms are well equipped for business or holiday guests and public areas include a dining room with an adjacent small bar and separate lounge.
17⇨🛏(2fb) CTV in all bedrooms ® T ✠ (ex guide dogs) sB&B⇨🛏£30-£44 dB&B⇨🛏£46-£56 🍴
20P 🚗
V ♥ ⚒ ⊬ ✻
Credit Cards 1 2 3 5 £

★★64% Fairwinds Hotel
EX6 7UD ☏(0392) 832911
(For full entry see Kennford)

★★59% Red House
2 Whipton Village Rd EX4 8AR ☏(0392) 56104 FAX (0392) 435708

This small family-run hotel on the edge of Exeter offers bedrooms which have simple décor and furnishings but all modern facilities. A range of menus is available in the popular bar with its adjacent dining area.
12⇨🛏(2fb) CTV in all bedrooms ® T
28P
⚐ English & French V ♥ ⚒ Last dinner 10pm
Credit Cards 1 3

Exeter - Exmouth

Forte Crest
Southernhay East EX1 1QF ☎(0392) 412812 FAX (0392) 413549

A large modern hotel with a wide range of services and amenities, designed particularly for the business traveller. Bedrooms are smart, comfortable and well equipped. For more details about Forte Crest hotels, consult the Contents page, under Hotel Groups.
110⇌ᴺ✱B⇌ᴺ£80 (room only)
CONF. Thtr 150 Class 50 Board 40 Del £115

Granada Lodge
Moor Ln, Sandygate EX2 4AR (M5 jnct 30)
☎(0392) 74044 FAX (0392) 410406

This modern building provides smart, spacious and well equipped bedrooms, all with en suite bathrooms. Meals may be taken at a nearby family restaurant. For more details about Granada Lodges, consult the Contents page, under Hotel Groups.
76⇌ᴺ✱B⇌ᴺ£34.95-£37.95 (room only)

EXMOUTH Devon Map **03 SY08**

★★★**62%** **Royal Beacon**
The Beacon EX8 2AF ☎(0395) 264886 FAX (0395) 268890

Overlooking pleasant gardens, the beach and Devon coastline, this Georgian hotel has relaxing public areas and a restaurant offering a choice of menus, usually including a roast of the day alongside more imaginative dishes. The bedrooms are generally spacious and comfortable, but some are now in need of modernisation.
30⇌ᴺ(2fb)2⊞½in 4 bedrooms CTV in all bedrooms ® T ✱
sB&B⇌ᴺ£34-£42 dB&B⇌ᴺ£68.00-£78 ⌧

YOUR 1st CHOICE IN EXETER

• 1km from city centre • Extensive landscaped gardens • Award Winning Raffles Restaurant • Raffles Cocktail Bar • Informal Lodge Bar • 54 well equipped en-suite bedrooms with satellite TV • free parking • Extensive Conference facilities.

THE BUCKERELL LODGE HOTEL
Topsham Road, Exeter
Tel: (0392) 52451 Fax: (0392) 412114

COMMENDED   AA★★★

Ebford House Hotel

★★ **70%**

Horton's Restaurant
Frisco's Bistro

Exmouth Road, Ebford, Exeter
Devon EX3 0QH

TEL: (0392) 877658   FAX: (0392) 874424

The charm of a Country House lives on in our delightful Hotel overlooking the River Clyst and Woodbury Common, yet convenient for Exeter and Exmouth, Westpoint, the Airport, M5 junction 30, eight Golf Clubs, walking, sailing, shooting etc.

Dine in Horton's Restaurant – the cuisine will delight the most discerning palate, or – More informally in Frisco's, our cosy Cellar Bistro.

BTA Highly Commended
Ashley Courtenay Recommended

The Barton Cross Hotel

xvii century

The only six bedroom hotel in Great Britain with AA ★★★
ETB Highly Commended Hotel

International Standard Accommodation with Superb Cuisine. Set in glorious Devon Countryside yet only four miles Exeter.

Easy access Dartmoor, Exmoor and Coast.

Relaxing Weekend and Midweek Breaks. Christmas House Party.

BARTON CROSS HOTEL & RESTAURANT
at Huxham, Exeter, EX5 4EJ
Telephone: (0392) 841245   Fax: (0392) 841942

See gazetteer under Stoke Canon

Exmouth - Falmouth

Lift CTV 15P ♂ (hard & grass)snooker *xmas*
⚑ English & French V ❦ ⚓ ⚔ Lunch £6.45-£7.95&alc Dinner £15.50-£17.50&alc Last dinner 9.30pm
CONF. Thtr 120 Class 70 Board 60 Del from £60
Credit Cards [1][2][3][4][5]

★★★61% The Imperial
The Esplanade EX8 2SW ☎(0395) 274761 FAX (0395)265161

FORTE Heritage

Probably the only hotel to have a reconstructed Grecian temple in its grounds, the Imperial is set between the town and the esplanade, and has superb views across Lyme Bay. The elegant restaurant offers both table d'hôte and à la carte menus. Bedrooms have recently been refurbished.
57⇌👤(3fb)⚔in 18 bedrooms CTV in all bedrooms ® T ✱
sB⇌👤£70 dB⇌👤£90-£105 (room only) ⚑
Lift (58P ✿ ⚘ (heated) ♂ (hard) *xmas*
V ❦ ⚓ ✱ Sunday Lunch £9.95 Dinner £16.95 Last dinner 9pm
Credit Cards [1][2][3][5]

★★66% Barn
Foxholes Hill, off Marine Dr EX8 2DF ☎(0395) 224411 FAX (0395) 224411

This is a most unusual Grade II listed building, designed by Edward Prior in a butterfly shape, not only interesting in itself, but also beautifully positioned in well tended gardens with glorious views of the Exe estuary. Inside it has been tastefully, if simply, modernised and public areas include a small reception bar and a more spacious lounge. A choice of dishes is available from the table d'hôte menu, and there is a relaxed and friendly atmosphere throughout.
11⇌👤(4fb) CTV in all bedrooms ® T ✱ sB&B⇌👤£29-£37 dB&B⇌👤£58-£64 ⚑
30P ⚘ ✿ ⚘ croquet putting green
V ❦ ⚓ ⚔ Sunday Lunch fr£7.95 Dinner £13 Last dinner 8pm
CONF. Class 40 Board 20
Credit Cards [1][3] (£)

★★58% Manor
The Beacon EX8 2AG ☎(0395) 272549 & 274477 FAX (0395) 225519

Dating back some 200 years, this family-run holiday hotel is between the town centre and the seafront in a slightly elevated position. The spacious bar lounge has recently been refurbished, and simple table d'hôte meals are served in the hotel's dining room. Bedrooms are light, airy and comfortable.
38⇌👤(3fb) CTV in all bedrooms ® T ✱ (ex guide dogs) ✱
sB&B⇌👤£20-£30 dB&B⇌👤£35-£55 ⚑
Lift (12P 3⚘ ♫ *xmas*
❦ ⚓ ✱ Bar Lunch £1-£7 Dinner £7-£9 Last dinner 8.30pm
Credit Cards [1][2][3]

★61% Aliston House
58 Salterton Rd EX8 2EW (on B3178) ☎(0395) 274119

About half a mile from the town centre and the sandy beaches, this detached property is set in its own attractive gardens. It is a relaxed and informally run hotel with bedrooms which, though not large, are comfortable and well equipped.
12rm(2⇌5👤)Annexe2👤(2fb) CTV in all bedrooms ® ✱
sB&B£20-£22 sB&B⇌👤£22-£24 dB&B£40-£44 dB&B⇌👤£44-£48 ⚑
CTV 16P *xmas*
V ❦ ⚓ Lunch £6.25-£6.50 High tea fr£4.50 Dinner fr£8.25 Last dinner 8.30pm (£)

FALMOUTH Cornwall & Isles of Scilly Map **02** SW83
See also **Mawnan Smith**
★★★⚜76% Penmere Manor
Mongleath Rd TR11 4PN ☎(0326) 211411 FAX (0326) 317588
Closed 24-26 Dec

Courtesy and Care 1994

The Pope family have owned this hotel for many years, and it is now run by the second generation. They, and their team of very friendly staff, have this year earned the AA's Courtesy and Care Award. Situated in 5 acres of wooded grounds, this Georgian manor house has sympathetic modern extensions. Bedrooms vary from spacious and elegant garden wing rooms to more compact rooms, the majority upgraded to comfortable and attractive standards. Meals are served in the Bolitho Restaurant where James Spargo offers well balanced table d'hôte menus.
39⇌👤(15fb) CTV in all bedrooms ® T sB&B⇌👤£55-£57 dB&B⇌👤£83-£112 ⚑
(50P ⚘ ✿ ▭ (heated) ⚘ (heated) sauna solarium gymnasium jacuzzi croquet table tennis ♫
V ❦ ⚓ ⚔ Bar Lunch £1.50-£10 High tea fr£6 Dinner fr£18 Last dinner 9pm
CONF. Thtr 80 Class 40 Board 30 Del £82
Credit Cards [1][2][3][5] (£)

★★★⚜73% Royal Duchy
Cliff Rd TR11 2QN (Brend) ☎(0326) 313042 FAX (0326) 319420

This fine 3-story period hotel enjoys south-facing views across the bay and is close to the beaches. It has been in the same hands for many years and offers a friendly welcome, spacious and recently upgraded lounges, and indoor leisure facilities. Bedrooms are mostly of a good size and have comfortable seating.
47⇌👤(9fb) CTV in all bedrooms ® ⚓ T ✱ sB&B⇌👤£34.50-£56 dB&B⇌👤£81-£138 ⚑
Lift (CTV 50P ✿ ▭ (heated) sauna solarium spa bath table tennis ♫ ♞ *xmas*
⚑ English & French V ❦ ⚓ ⚔ Lunch £8.50&alc Dinner £15.50&alc Last dinner 9pm
Credit Cards [1][2][3][5] (£)

★★★⚜71% Greenbank
Harbourside TR11 2SR ☎(0326) 312440 FAX (0326) 211362
Closed 23 Dec-11 Jan

The Greenbank, in a dramatic water's edge position, is said to be Falmouth's first hotel and has historical associations with the packet ships' skippers, and author Kenneth Graham. Nightingale's Restaurant (named after Florence, another famous guest) offers both table d'hôte and à la carte menus. The new River Bank wing houses some luxury bedrooms and the conference facilities. The bar on the lower ground floor is popular with locals and visitors alike.
61⇌👤(8fb)⚔in 2 bedrooms CTV in all bedrooms ® T ✱
sB&B⇌👤£56.50-£60.50 dB&B⇌👤£97-£138 ⚑
Lift (50P 24⚘ ♪ sauna solarium gymnasium hairdressing beauty salons

---

The AA's star rating scheme is the
market leader in hotel
classification.

Falmouth

⚑ English & French V ❁ ⌑ ✱ Lunch £8.50-£9.50&alc Dinner £17.50&alc Last dinner 9.45pm
CONF. Thtr 100 Class 80 Board 40 Del from £70
Credit Cards [1][2][3][5]

★★★64% Falmouth
Castle Beach TR11 4NZ ☏(0326) 312671 FAX (0326) 319533
Closed 23-31 Dec
This elegant, traditional and well managed hotel, owned by the same family for over 40 years, faces the sea from a setting in beautiful gardens. Public areas have been upgraded, and many bedrooms enjoy superb sea views (though some are a little compact). Staff are friendly, and the hotel retains an air of old-fashioned grandeur.
72⇨♠(5fb)1⌸ CTV in all bedrooms ® T
Lift ⦅ 150P ✿ ⌑ (heated) ⇨ snooker sauna solarium gymnasium croquet putting pool table ⚘
⚑ English, French & Italian V ❁ ⌑ ✂ Last dinner 9.30pm
Credit Cards [1][2][3][5]

★★★63% Green Lawns
Western Ter TR11 4QJ (on A39) ☏(0326) 312734 FAX (0326) 211427
Closed 24-30 Dec
Convenient for the town centre and beaches, this personally run hotel with colourful gardens has spacious public areas. Comfortable bedrooms are equipped with modern facilities, some with spa baths. The attractive split-level restaurant offers friendly service and an extensive choice of carefully prepared dishes.
40⇨♠(8fb)2⌸ CTV in all bedrooms ®⚑ T sB&B⇨♠£45-£65 dB&B⇨♠£56-£96 ♬
⦅ 60P 9🅿 ✿ ⌑ (heated) ⚘ (hard & grass)squash snooker sauna solarium gymnasium jacuzzi ♪
⚑ English & French V ❁ ⌑ Lunch £8.50-£9&alc High tea £2-£5 Dinner £16-£17 Last dinner 10pm
CONF. Thtr 200 Class 80 Board 100 Del from £66
Credit Cards [1][2][3][4][5]

★★★62% St Michaels of Falmouth
Gyllyngvase Beach TR11 4NB ☏(0326) 312707 FAX (0326) 211772   CONSORT HOTELS

Set in award-winning gardens adjacent to the beach, this is a popular resort hotel. Public areas are spacious, and the Benson Bar serves a variety of bar meals at lunch and dinner. Bedrooms vary in size and the majority have hairdryers, trouser presses and wall safes.
57⇨♠Annexe9⇨♠(10fb) CTV in all bedrooms ® T sB&B⇨♠£45-£70 dB&B⇨♠£89-£120 (incl dinner) ♬
⦅ 100P ✿ ⌑ (heated) sauna solarium gymnasium jacuzzi windsurfing ⚘ xmas
⚑ English & French V ❁ ⌑ ✂ Lunch £7.50-£9.50 High tea £3-£4.50 Dinner £16 Last dinner 9.30pm
CONF. Thtr 200 Class 150 Board 120 Del from £70
Credit Cards [1][2][3][5]
See advertisement on page 245

★★★60% Gyllyngdune Manor
Melvill Rd TR11 4AR ☏(0326) 312978 FAX (0326) 211881
Closed Jan
This large white Georgian manor house has fine views across the sea and is just a short walk from the beaches. Bedrooms have been upgraded in recent years, but do vary in size and outlook. Public areas include 2 lounges.
30⇨♠(3fb)3⌸ CTV in all bedrooms ® T
⦅ 25P 2🅿 (charged) ✿ ⌑ (heated) sauna solarium gymnasium table tennis ♪
⚑ English & Continental V ❁ ⌑ Last dinner 9pm
Credit Cards [1][2][3][5]
See advertisement on page 245

Falmouth's Premier Hotel

Situated in a prime location on Falmouth's sea-front, The Royal Duchy Hotel enjoys panoramic views across Falmouth's famous bay. Every bedroom is delightfully appointed, with private bathroom en-suite, colour television with satellite reception, and direct dial telephone. A lift provides easy access to all floors.

Facilities include heated indoor swimming pool complex with sauna, solarium, spa bath, snooker and table tennis room.

The Royal Duchy Hotel
AA ★★★ ❁

FOR FREE COLOUR BROCHURE AND TARIFF
PLEASE CONTACT: Mr. D. Reburn,
The Royal Duchy Hotel, Cliff Road, Falmouth,
Cornwall TR11 4NX. Tel: (0326) 313042. Fax: (0326) 319420

PENMERE MANOR HOTEL
MONGLEATH ROAD, FALMOUTH

An oasis of Comfort and Service

SOUTH WEST
COURTESY AND CARE
AWARD WINNERS 1993/1994
AA ★★★ ❁ 76%

TEL: (0326) 211411

Falmouth - Fareham

★★ 63% Broadmead
66-68 Kimberley Park Rd TR11 2DD (Turn left off A39 at traffic lights by Riders Garage, towards town centre, hotel 200 yds on left)
☎(0326) 315704 & 318036 FAX (0326) 311048
Closed 23 Dec-3 Jan

This informal family-run hotel is a large period house overlooking the attractive Kimberley Park. It has a comfortable no smoking lounge, open plan with the reception, and a smaller sun lounge at the entrance. Bedrooms vary in size and outlook and are individually decorated.

12rm(10⇨♠) CTV in all bedrooms ® T ✱ sB&Bfr£21 sB&B⇨♠fr£26 dB&B⇨♠£50-£56 ♬
CTV 8P
❀ 🏴 Bar Lunch £1.25-£5alc Dinner £11.75-£12.25&alc Last dinner 8pm
Credit Cards [1][3]   £

★★ 61% Park Grove
Kimberley Park Rd TR11 2DD ☎(0326) 313276 FAX (0326) 211926
Closed Dec & Jan

Situated opposite Kimberley Gardens, this family-owned and managed hotel offers good value accommodation and friendly service. Bedrooms vary, with some pretty coordinating fabrics, and public areas include a small lounge, bar lounge and spacious dining room with a view across the park.

17rm(15♠)(4fb) CTV in all bedrooms ® T sB&Bfr£21 sB&B♠£25 dB&Bfr£42 dB&B♠£50
25P 3🚗
❀ 🏴 Last dinner 7.30pm
Credit Cards [1][3]

★★ 60% Carthion
Cliff Rd TR11 4AP ☎(0326) 313669
Closed Nov-Feb

This fine turn-of-the-century house with a pretty garden enjoys an attractive position overlooking the sea. The bedrooms are traditionally furnished, there is a comfortable sun lounge, and Mrs Shaw and family offer informal service. There is a splendid collection of model boats to be seen throughout the hotel.

18⇨♠ CTV in all bedrooms ® ✱ sB&B⇨♠£28.50-£31.50 dB&B⇨♠£57-£87 ♬
18P ❀ ❆ nc10yrs
♀ English & French V ❀ 🏴 ✂ Bar Lunch £1.20-£4.25 Dinner £12 Last dinner 8pm
Credit Cards [1][2][3][5]   £

★★ 58% Lerryn Hotel
De Pass Rd TR11 4BJ ☎(0326) 312489

This small family-run hotel in a quiet residential area close to the seafront, offers simple, comfortable accommodation.

20⇨♠(2fb) ✱ in 10 bedrooms ® ✈ ✱ sB&B⇨♠£16.50-£22.50 dB&B⇨♠£33-£45 ♬
12P 1🚗 (£2 per day) xmas
♀ English, French & Mexican V ❀ 🏴 ✂ Lunch £9.50 High tea £5-£7 Dinner £9.50 Last dinner 8pm
CONF. Class 50 Board 30
Credit Cards [1][3]   £

FAREHAM Hampshire Map 04 SU50

★★★★ ❀❀74% Solent
Solent Business Park, Rookery Av, Whitely PO15 7AJ (5m NW, junc 9 off M27) (Shire) ☎Locks Heath(0489) 880000 FAX (0489) 880007

This tastefully designed modern hotel is in a quiet woodland setting. Its wood-panelled reception lobby is an imaginative hexagonal room, and there is a variety of comfortable seating areas. Public areas also include Nightingales cocktail bar and a smart split-level Spanish-style restaurant where chef David Fitzpatrick offers very good cooking from varied menus of modern and traditional ideas.

The bedrooms are all smartly decorated, spacious and well planned. Well groomed staff offer a professional yet unpretentious service.

88⇨♠(9fb)4🚭✂ in 12 bedrooms CTV in all bedrooms ®✱T✱ sB&B⇨♠£82-£92 dB&B⇨♠£92-£112 ♬
Lift ☾ 200P ❆ (heated) squash snooker sauna solarium gymnasium steam room spa pool ♪ xmas
♀ International V ❀ 🏴 ✂ ✱ Lunch £9.95-£12.95&alc Dinner £18&alc Last dinner 9.45pm
CONF. Thtr 250 Class 120 Board 80 Del £130
Credit Cards [1][2][3][5]

★★★ ❀67% Lysses House Hotel & Conference Centre
51 High St PO16 7BQ ☎(0329) 822622 FAX (0329) 822762
Closed 25 Dec-1 Jan RS 24 Dec

This small Georgian House has comfortable and smart public areas. Bedrooms are bright and welcoming and much of the hotel are aimed at the business traveller. Staff are friendly and efficient, and chef Clive Wright offers a wide choice of imaginative French/English dishes, with some vegetarian options.

21⇨♠ CTV in all bedrooms ® T ✈ (ex guide dogs) ✱ sB&B⇨♠£35-£53 dB&B⇨♠£54-£69
Lift ☾ 30P
♀ English & French V ❀ 🏴 ✱ Lunch £11.75-£13.75&alc Dinner £15.95-£17.95&alc Last dinner 9.45pm
CONF. Thtr 100 Class 45 Board 40 Del from £65
Credit Cards [1][2][3][5]

★★★ 63% Red Lion
East St PO16 0BP (Whitbread) ☎(0329) 822640 FAX (0329) 823579

This friendly old coaching inn close to the town centre has been skilfully extended and offers comfortable and well equipped modern bedrooms. The beamed bars serve fine ales and food is available in the lounge bar or popular restaurant.

44⇨♠(2fb)1🚭 CTV in all bedrooms ®✱T✈ (ex guide dogs) ✱ sB&B⇨♠£55.50-£65.50 dB&B⇨♠£67-£77 ♬
☾ CTV 136P 🚗
♀ English & Continental V ❀ 🏴 ✂ Lunch £9-£18 Dinner £9-£18 Last dinner 10pm
CONF. Thtr 120 Class 50 Board 60 Del from £89
Credit Cards [1][2][3][5]

★★ 67% Abshot Hotel & Country Club
Little Abshot Rd, Titchfield Common PO14 4LN
☎Locksheath(0489) 573936 & 584057 FAX (0489) 575692

The Abshot Hotel offers accommodation in a converted house dating from 1810, in a pleasant rural area. Bedrooms are mostly of a good size, attractively furnished with sturdy old pine, and well equipped. There is a small cocktail bar, with a second bar in the sports club. Mr King and his staff offer friendly and attentive service.

13rm(11⇨♠)(2fb)2🚭 CTV in all bedrooms ®✱T✱ sB£35-£45 sB⇨♠£45 dB⇨♠£45 (room only) ♬
CTV 80P ❆ (heated) ℘ (hard) squash sauna solarium gymnasium aerobics & dance studio
♀ English & French V ❀ 🏴 ✂ Sunday Lunch £6.95
CONF. Thtr 40 Class 20 Board 20
Credit Cards [1][2][3][5]

★★ 58% Maylings Manor
11A Highlands Rd PO16 7XJ ☎(0329) 286451 FAX (0329) 822584

Situated on the outskirts of town, not far from the motorway, this Edwardian house has been extended to provide modern, well equipped bedrooms. Raffles Bar is a popular feature, and a bar menu is available for lunch and evening meals as an alternative to the Fleur de Lys Restaurant.

24⇨♠(2fb)2🚭 CTV in all bedrooms ® T sB⇨♠£29.50-£40 dB⇨♠£29.50-£40 (room only) ♬
87P ❆

➡➡

THE PARK GROVE HOTEL
Kimberley Park Road, Falmouth
Telephone: (0326) 313276 ★★

A small but distinguished hotel. Centrally situated, occupying a lovely position overlooking beautiful Kimberley Park. The proprietors take a special pride in the excellent cuisine. The harbour, beaches and town are all within easy walking distance. Licensed. 17 bedrooms (15 with shower/toilet en suite). Colour TV, direct dial telephone, hair dryer, radio, intercom, child listening system, tea/coffee making facilities in all bedrooms.

The Gyllyngdune Manor Hotel
AA ★★★
Melvill Road, Falmouth, Cornwall TR11 4AR
Telephone: (0326) 312978   Fax: (0326) 211881

Old Georgian manor house, romantically situated in one acre of beautiful gardens, overlooking the Bay and Estuary. Guaranteed away from traffic, but within ten minutes' walk of the town centre and two minutes from the beach. Very large car park, covered space if required. Luxury indoor heated swimming pool, games room, Sauna and Solarium. Golf at Falmouth Golf club. All rooms en-suite with colour TV, direct dial telephone and tea/coffee making facilities. Every comfort with personal attention the primary consideration.

Broadmead Hotel ★★
Kimberley Park Road, Falmouth, Cornwall TR11 2DD
Telephone: (0326) 315704
Fax: (0326) 311048

Ideally situated overlooking beautiful Kimberley Park and a few minutes leisurely walk from the town centre and harbour. The hotel is small, select and family owned, offering a high standard of comfort and personal service. There are two comfortable lounges, one non-smoking, the other with satellite TV, and a small bar.
The restaurant enjoys a reputation for excellent cuisine. There are 12 tastefully and individually furnished bedrooms, 2 ground floor, 10 with bath or shower and toilet en suite, all have colour TV, tea/coffee making facilities, telephone, radio and central heating. Private car park.
Special Breaks available. Dogs welcome.
Please phone Chris or Jan Kempton for a brochure and tariff.

Go on... spoil yourself!

- Indoor pool, sauna, jacuzzi suite and solarium
- Watersports and gymnasium • Reduced price golf • Squash available • All rooms en-suite
- Only yards from the beach • Beautiful panoramic views • Family suites • Special offers and children's reductions • 3 acres of Award winning gardens • Excellent cuisine
- Friendly service

ST MICHAELS
OF FALMOUTH
RESORT HOTEL AND CONFERENCE CENTRE
Seafront, Falmouth, Cornwall.
Telephone 0326 312707 Fax 0326 211772
AA ★★★

Fareham - Farrington Gurney

♀ English & French V ❖ ⚜ ✳ Lunch £10.50-£15&alc Dinner £10.50-£15&alc Last dinner 9.30pm
Credit Cards [1][2][3][5]

Forte Posthouse
Cartwright Dr, Titchfield PO15 5RJ
☎(0329) 844644 FAX (0329) 844666

FORTE Posthouse

Suitable for both the business and leisure traveller, this bright hotel provides modern accommodation in well equipped bedrooms with en suite bathrooms. For more details about Forte Posthouse hotels, consult the Contents page, under Hotel Groups.
126⇨↑✳ B⇨↑£41.50-£53.50 (room only)
CONF. Thtr 140 Class 80 Board 50 Del from £89.50

FARINGDON Oxfordshire Map 04 SU29

★★★63% Sudbury House Hotel & Conference Centre
London St SN7 8AA (off A420, signposted Folly Hill) ☎(0367) 241272 FAX (0367) 242346
CONSORT HOTELS

Facilities at this purpose-built hotel are designed specifically for the conference market. Rooms are spacious, there is a bar and a very large restaurant with an ambitious menu and daily changing table d'hôte.
49⇨↑(2fb)✓in 10 bedrooms CTV in all bedrooms ® ⚜ T
✖ (ex guide dogs) ✱ sB&B⇨↑fr£58 dB&B⇨↑fr£66.50 ₽
Lift ₵ 85P ✣ croquet pitch & putt *xmas*
V ❖ ⚜ ✳ Lunch fr£9.95 Dinner fr£15.95 Last dinner 10pm
Credit Cards [1][2][3][5]

FARNBOROUGH Hampshire Map 04 SU85

★★★64% Falcon
Farnborough Rd GU14 6TH (on A325 opposite Aerospace Centre airfield) ☎(0252) 545378 FAX (0252) 522539
Closed 24 Dec-2 Jan
This hotel attracts a busy international business market, and bedrooms have been appropriately well furnished and equipped to a high standard. Public areas comprise a formal reception, bar, lounge and adequate dining room, which is open for lunch and dinner. The atmosphere is friendly and relaxed, and room service is usually available.
30⇨↑(2fb)1🛏✓in 8 bedrooms CTV in all bedrooms ® T ✖
sB&B⇨↑£45-£65 dB&B⇨↑£55-£70
₵ 30P
♀ International V ❖ ⚜ ✓ Lunch £12.50-£15.50alc Dinner £15.50-£18.50alc Last dinner 9.30pm
Credit Cards [1][2][3][5]

★58% Alexandra
144 Alexandra Rd GU14 6RP ☎(0252) 541050 FAX (0252) 371038
Well established for many years under the personal management of the friendly owners Mr and Mrs Webb, this private hotel is in a residential area. There is a cosy bar with gleaming brasses and copperware, and the spotless bedrooms are well furnished.
11⇨↑Annexe1↑(1fb) CTV in all bedrooms ® T ✖
sB&B⇨↑£45-£55 dB&B⇨↑£60-£65
CTV 11P 🚗
♀ International V ✳ Dinner £6-£12alc Last dinner 9pm
Credit Cards [1][2][3]

Forte Crest
Lynchford Rd GU14 6AZ ☎(0252) 545051 FAX (0252) 377210

FORTE CREST

A large modern hotel with a range of services and amenities, designed particularly for the business traveller. Bedrooms are smart, comfortable and well equipped. For more details about Forte Crest hotels, consult the Contents page, under Hotel Groups.
110⇨↑✳ B⇨↑£99 (room only)
CONF. Thtr 150 Class 60 Board 25 Del £125

FARNHAM Surrey Map 04 SU84

★★★61% Bush
The Borough GU9 7NN ☎(0252) 715237 FAX (0252) 733530

FORTE Heritage

This attractive ivy-clad 17th-century coaching inn is full of character, with panelled walls featuring splendid frescoes thought to date back to the 1300s. The elegant restaurant looks out on the gardens while the coffee lounge, offering informal eating, faces the cobbled courtyard. There are also 2 bars. Bedrooms are comfortable, with coordinated decor, those in the main building being the most stylish.
66⇨↑(2fb)1🛏✓in 20 bedrooms CTV in all bedrooms ® T
sB⇨↑£65 dB⇨↑£65 (room only) ₽
₵ 80P ✣ *xmas*
V ❖ ⚜ ✳ Lunch £9.95-£11.95&alc High tea £1.25-£6 Dinner fr£17.95&alc Last dinner 10pm
Credit Cards [1][2][3][5]

★★57% Trevena House
Alton Rd GU10 5ER (1m from town, off A31 Alton road)
☎(0252) 716908 FAX (0252) 722583
This interesting period house stands in its own grounds to the west of Farnham. The reception hall has a fine stone fireplace, and there is a dark panelled lounge-bar. Bedrooms are undergoing substantial upgrading to a smart modern standard.
20⇨↑ CTV in all bedrooms ® T ✖ (ex guide dogs)
sB⇨↑£20-£50 dB⇨↑£30-£60 (room only) ₽
40P ✣ ⌬ (heated) ♪ (hard) croquet putting green
♀ International V ❖ ⚜ ✓ Lunch £9.10-£15.95 High tea £1.95-£2.95 Dinner £12.95-£15.95&alc Last dinner 9.15pm
Credit Cards [1][2][3]

FARRINGTON GURNEY Avon Map 03 ST65

★★❀69% Country Ways
Marsh Ln BS18 5TT ☎(0761) 452449 FAX (0761) 453360
Closed 24-31 Dec
Owner Janet Richards provides a welcoming, informal atmosphere at this cosy little hotel, which is suited to both the business guest and tourist. The prettily decorated bedrooms are comfortable, personally styled and offer a good range of equipment and facilities. Comfortable public rooms include a small restaurant where home cooked dishes are served.
6⇨↑ CTV in all bedrooms ® T ✖ ✱ sB&B⇨↑£50-£55
dB&B⇨↑£60-£65 ₽
12P 🚗 ✣ ✓
❖ ⚜ ✓ Lunch £16.50-£22alc Dinner £16.50-£22alc Last dinner 9pm
Credit Cards [1][3][5]

See advertisement under MIDSOMER NORTON

If you have booked a meal in a hotel restaurant and cannot get there, remember you have a contractual obligation to cancel your booking.

Rosettes range from 5 for outstanding cuisine to 1 rosette for enjoyable, well prepared food

Farthing Corner Motorway Service Area - Felixstowe

**FARTHING CORNER MOTORWAY SERVICE AREA
(M2)**Kent Map **05** TQ86

Pavilion Lodge
Rainham ME8 8PQ (between juncts 4 & 5 M2)
☎Medway(0634) 377337 FAX (0634) 360848

With a nearby family restaurant providing all meals, this modern building offers smart, spacious and well equipped bedrooms. For more details about Pavilion Lodges, consult the Contents page, under Hotel Groups.
58⇨♠※ sB⇨♠£31.95 dB⇨♠£35.95 (room only)

FEARNANTayside *Perthshire* Map **11** NN74

★ **62%Tigh-an-Loan**
PH15 2PF (on A827) ☎Kenmore(0887) 830249
Closed Oct-Etr

Tigh-an-Loan is a traditional, modest but friendly village hotel with only the road between it and Loch Tay.
8rm(3⇨)(1fb) ® sB&Bfr£24 dB&Bfr£48 dB&B⇨fr£54
CTV 25P ⇨ ❋ ♪
V ♡ ⚓ ❋ Dinner fr£13 Last dinner 8pm
Credit Cards [1][3]

FELIXSTOWESuffolk Map **05** TM33

★★★ **67%Orwell Moat House**
Hamilton Rd IP11 7DX ☎(0394) 285511 FAX
(0394) 670687

This town centre hotel is ideal for the docks and beaches, and attracts both the leisure and commercial user. The style and spaciousness of public areas, and some of the services offered, are normally associated with a higher classification.
58⇨♠(10fb) CTV in all bedrooms ® T sB⇨♠£65-£75
dB⇨♠£75-£85 (room only) ⛒
Lift ℂ 150P 20⇨ ❋ ♪ xmas
♨ English & French V ♡ ⚓ ⚡ Lunch £15.50 Dinner £17.50 Last dinner 9.45pm
CONF. Thtr 220 Class 100 Board 60 Del £85
Credit Cards [1][2][3][5]

★★ **69%Waverley**
2 Wolsey Gardens IP11 7DF ☎(0394) 282811
FAX (0394) 670185

This Victorian property sits high on the cliff top overlooking the shore, but is only a short walk from the town. Public rooms are on the small side. The Wolsey Restaurant is cosy and offers table d'hôte and à la carte menus, and the lively Gladstone Bar offers a good choice of bar meals. Bedrooms are light and fresh, furnished and equipped to a comfortable modern standard.
19⇨♠(4fb)1⚐ CTV in all bedrooms ®⚡ T
sB&B⇨♠fr£46.50 dB&B⇨♠£55.95-£80 ⛒
30P ♪ xmas
♨ English & Continental V ♡ ⚓ Lunch £6-£95&alc Dinner £14-£95&alc Last dinner 10pm
CONF. Thtr 85 Class 35 Board 25 Del from £75
Credit Cards [1][2][3][5]

★★ **65%Marlborough**
Sea Front IP11 8BJ ☎(0394) 285621 FAX (0394) 670724
Situated on the seafront, the hotel offers comfortable, well equipped accommodation, a choice of menus and a popular carvery.
47⇨♠(2fb)⚐ CTV in all bedrooms ®⚡ T
Lift ℂ CTV 19P windsurfing
♨ English & French V ♡ ⚡ ❋ Lunch £5.50-£15&alc High tea £1.10-£6.45 Dinner £10.50-£12.50&alc Last dinner 9.45pm
CONF. Thtr 100 Class 60 Board 40 Del from £45
Credit Cards [1][2][3][5]

Trevena House
★★

HOTEL AND RESTAURANT
**Alton Road (A31), Farnham, Surrey GU10 5ER
Telephone: 0252 716908. Fax: 0252 722583**

A delightful country house hotel set in 5 acres of lovely Surrey countryside. Situated ¾ of a mile from Farnham's busy town centre.
Outdoor heated swimming pool and tennis court.
Our 20 superbly refurbished en suite bedrooms offer all up to date facilities, making the hotel ideal for business use and relaxing breaks.
Our à la carte menu offers a mixed and varied selection for superb value for money.
Single rooms from £33 to £45 approx
Double rooms from £38 to £50 approx
OUR RELAXED ATMOSPHERE AND FRIENDLY STAFF MAKE A HOME FROM HOME

Sudbury House
HOTEL AND CRANFIELD CENTRE FOR CONFERENCING
★★★
**56 London Street
Faringdon
Oxon SN7 8AA
Tel: 0367 241272 Fax: 0367 242346**

49 Double Bedrooms all en suite. Situated in six acres of gardens this fine old Georgian House has been sympathetically extended to form a delightful hotel. Ideally located midway between Oxford and Swindon, nestling on the edge of the Cotswolds, Sudbury House offers traditional hospitality with the best of modern English Cuisine.

***£58.00 Bed and Breakfast
Special Weekend Rates***

CONSORT HOTELS GROUP MEMBER

CCS GROUP

Fenstanton - Five Oaks

FENSTANTON Cambridgeshire Map 04 TL36

Forte Travelodge
Huntingdon Rd(6m SE of Huntingdon, on A604)
☎(0954) 30919 Central Res (0800) 850950

This modern building offers a good standard of accommodation for overnight stops. Smart, spacious and well equipped bedrooms, all with en suite bathrooms, are suitable for family use, and meals may be taken at the nearby family restaurant. For more details about Travelodges, consult the Contents page, under Hotel Groups.
40⇨ ♠ ✹ B⇨ ♠£31.95 (room only)

FERMAIN BAY
See **Guernsey** under **Channel Islands**

FERNDOWN Dorset Map 04 SU00

★★★★**65%** *Dormy*
New Rd BH22 8ES (off A347 from Bournemouth) ☎Bournemouth(0202) 872121
FAX (0202) 895388

This busy hotel caters mostly for commercial and conference guests and has excellent leisure facilities. Further upgrading is planned for 1994, but the accommodation is generally comfortable, with modern facilities. There are quiet lounges and bars and the well appointed restaurant offers a choice of menus and a well chosen wine list.
130⇨♠(8fb)2⌸✂ in 20 bedrooms CTV in all bedrooms ®❋ T Lift (CTV 220P ✿ ▦ (heated) ℘ (hard) squash snooker sauna solarium gymnasium spa bath steam room beauty salon ♪ ⚘
V ✧ ⚖ Last dinner 9.30pm
Credit Cards ①②③⑤

★★**63%** *Coach House Inn*
Tricketts Cross BH22 9NW (junc A31/A348)
☎(0202) 861222 FAX (0202) 894130

The Coach House Inn provides motel-type accommodation in 4 blocks, one of a higher quality. The bedrooms are spacious, and adequately furnished and equipped. Lounge facilities are limited, but there is a nicely appointed restaurant offering a set price and à la carte menu at lunch and dinner and snacks are available at the bar.
Annexe44⇨ CTV in all bedrooms ® T
100P 25☏ gymnasium
V ✧ English & Italian V ✧ ⚖ Last dinner 9.30pm
Credit Cards ①②③⑤

FERRYBRIDGE SERVICE AREA West Yorkshire Map 08 SE42

Granada Lodge
WF11 0AF (A1/M62 jnct 33)
☎Knottingley(0977) 670488 FAX (0977) 672945

This modern building provides smart, spacious and well equipped bedrooms, all with en suite bathrooms. Meals may be taken at a nearby family restaurant. For more details about Granada Lodges, consult the Contents page, under Hotel Groups.
35⇨♠✹ B⇨♠£34.95-£37.95 (room only)

FILEY North Yorkshire Map 08 TA18

★**65%** *Sea Brink*
The Beach YO14 9LA ☎Scarborough(0723) 513257
Small but cosy, this comfortable hotel is situated right on the seafront with magnificent views of Filey Bay. Bedrooms are attractively decorated and have modern furnishings. The residents' lounge faces the sea, as does the versatile Brink Coffee Shop, where all day snacks and refreshments are available as well as an evening

meal expertly prepared by Olga Carter, resident proprietor and cordon-bleu chef.
11⇨♠(5fb) CTV in all bedrooms ®❋ sB&B⇨♠£23-£25 dB&B⇨♠£40-£44 ⌺
CTV ℘ ⌸ xmas
V ✧ English & French V ✧ ⚖ ✂ Last dinner 10pm
Credit Cards ①②③⑤

FIR TREE Co Durham Map 12 NZ13

★★★**70%**, *Helme Park Hall Country House*
DL13 4NW (off A68) ☎Bishop Auckland(0388) 730970
Set back from the road in its own grounds, this extended former farmhouse enjoys fine views over the dales and hills to the rear. Personally run, it provides attentive service and a good and comfortable standard of accommodation.
10⇨♠(3fb)1⌸ CTV in all bedrooms ® T ✈ (ex guide dogs)
40P ✿ solarium
V ✧ English & French V ✧ ⚖ Last dinner 9.30pm
Credit Cards ①②③

★★**63%**, *Fir Tree Country*
Crook DL15 8DD ☎Bishop Auckland(0388) 762161
This modern single-storey public house has extensive bars, with food available there or in the restaurant. Motel-style bedrooms in a rear wing provide good modern facilities.
14⇨♠ in 4 bedrooms CTV in all bedrooms ®
✈ (ex guide dogs)
CTV 48P ♪
V ✧ International V ✧ ⚖ ✂ Last dinner 10pm
Credit Cards ①②③

FISHGUARD Dyfed Map 02 SM93

★★**63%**, *Cartref*
15-19 High St SA65 9AW ☎(0348) 872430 FAX (0348) 874161
A warm welcome is assured at this very friendly small hotel. Public areas include a new lounge/meeting room and a restaurant.
12rm(10⇨♠)(4fb)✂ in 4 bedrooms CTV in all bedrooms
(CTV 20P 2☏ nc7yrs
V ✧ English & Continental V ✧ ⚖ ✂ Last dinner 10pm
Credit Cards ①③

★**60%** *Abergwaun*
The Market Square SA65 9HA ☎(0348) 872077
This historic inn on the town square is a convenient touring base for Pembrokeshire or stopover for the Irish ferry. Public rooms provide good facilities and upgrading is planned for the bedrooms. Bumbles Bistro serves a good choice of snacks and meals all day.
11rm(3⇨♠)(2fb) CTV in all bedrooms ® ✹ sB&B£19.50 sB&B⇨♠£32 dB&B£32 dB&B⇨♠£45
CTV ℘
V ✧ English & French V ✧ ⚖ ✹ Lunch £6-£14alc Dinner £9.50-£17alc Last dinner 9pm
CONF. Thtr 50 Class 20 Board 24 Del from £37.50
Credit Cards ①②③⑤

FIVE OAKS West Sussex Map 04 TQ02

Forte Travelodge
RH14 9AE (on A29, northbound, 8m SW of Horsham) ☎Billingshurst (0403) 782711
Central Res (0800) 850950

This modern building offers a good standard of accomodation for overnight stops. Smart, spacious and well equipped bedrooms, all with en suite bathrooms, are suitable for family use, and meals may be taken at the nearby family restaurant. For more details about Travelodges, consult the Contents page, under Hotel Groups.
26⇨♠✹ B⇨♠£31.95 (room only)

FLADBURY Hereford & Worcester Map **03** SO94

★★**58%** **The Chequers Inn**
Chequers Ln WR10 2PZ (off A44) ☎Evesham(0386) 860276 & 860527 FAX (0386) 860527
This ancient inn at the heart of the quiet village has modernised bedrooms with good facilities. Lounge areas are limited and the focal point is the beamed bar and small restaurant with a carvery alternative Thursday to Saturday.
8⇌↑(1fb) CTV in all bedrooms ® ⚲ T sB&B⇌↑£41-£45 dB&B⇌↑£61-£65 ⋑
25P ⊞ ♪
V ♢ Lunch £12.75-£22.75&alc Dinner £12.75-£22.75alc Last dinner 9.30pm
Credit Cards [1][2][3] ⓔ
See advertisement under EVESHAM

FLAMBOROUGH Humberside Map **08** TA26

★**64%** *Flaneburg*
North Marine Rd YO15 1LF ☎Bridlington(0262) 850284
Closed Jan & Feb
This unpretentious hotel offers cosy, individually designed bedrooms. The décor is bright and cheerful, and the spacious lounge has lots of comfortable sofas and armchairs. There are good value menus in both the bar lounge and dining room, though out of season service may be restricted to bed and breakfast.
13rm(8↑)(2fb) CTV in all bedrooms ® ✈
CTV 20P ⊞
V ♢

FLEET Hampshire Map **04** SU85

★★★**60%** *Lismoyne*
Church Rd GU13 8NA ☎(0252) 628555 FAX (0252) 811761
This gabled Edwardian house, set in its own wooded grounds on the edge of the town, retains a period charm in the carved mantles and panelled staircases of its public areas. Most bedrooms are contained in a wing of their own.
42⇌↑(1fb)1⊟ CTV in all bedrooms ® T ✻ sB&B⇌↑£50-£60 dB&B⇌↑£70-£80 ⋑
⦅ 80P ✿
⊞ English & French V ♢ ⊻ ✻ Lunch fr£11.75&alc Dinner fr£12.75&alc Last dinner 9.30pm
Credit Cards [1][2][3][4][5] ⓔ
See advertisement on page 251

FLEET MOTORWAY SERVICE AREA (M3) Hampshire Map **04** SU75

Forte Travelodge
RG27 8BN (between junc 4 & 5 westbound M3)
☎(0252) 815587 Central Res (0800) 850950

FORTE Travelodge

This modern building offers a good standard of accommodation for overnight stops. Smart, spacious and well equipped bedrooms, all with en suite bathrooms, are suitable for family use, and meals may be taken at the nearby family restaurant. For more details about Travelodges, consult the Contents page, under Hotel Groups.
40⇌↑✻ B⇌↑£31.95 (room only)

FLITWICK Bedfordshire Map **04** TL03

★★★❀❀❀⚘**72%** **Flitwick Manor**
Church Rd MK45 1AE (on A5120) ☎(0525) 712242 FAX (0525) 712242
Standing in acres of lovely grounds, this hotel dates back to the 17th century. There are comfortable lounges with blazing log fires, and a sun terrace for the summer months that leads into the Brooks Dining Room. Most of the individually styled bedrooms are large, furnished with antiques and have such extras as bathrobes, a drinks
➥

Helme Park Country House Hotel ★★★

Near Fir Tree, Bishop Auckland
Co. Durham DL13 4NW. Tel: 0388 730970
Northumbria's best sited hotel.
Five acres of gardens. Highest standards of service, cuisine and appointments.
A la carte restaurant. Bar meals with approximately 75 main course choices.
Highly convenient location, tranquil setting and magnificent views for 25 miles over the hills and dales.
A perfect centre to explore Northumbria.
Thirteen en suite bedrooms.

SEA BRINK HOTEL AA★

COMMENDED

Situated literally yards from the sea, traditional hotel of character and charm. Delightful, individually decorated en suite bedrooms, many with magnificent views across Filey Bay. All have central heating, colour TV and tea/coffee making facilities. Licensed restaurant and Coffee Shop enjoying sea views and offering superb Yorkshire cooking. Guests facilities include a Jacuzzi.
French & German spoken.

Bargain Breaks

Fully inclusive, bed & breakfast & 4 course dinner
2 days – week end break – £50
5 days – mid week break – £125
Christmas Programme Available

**The Beach, Filey,
North Yorkshire YO16 9LA
Telephone: 0723 513257**

Flitwick - Forfar

tray, fresh fruit and home-made shortbread. Head chef Duncan Poyser offers an imaginative menu. Some dishes have unusual combinations that work well, such as ox tongue with a rich sauce of tarragon and orange. During this visit, enjoyable dishes included scallops served on a good onion and parsley jus with various accompaniments; flakes of cod on spinach noodles with a langoustine vinaigrette, and, the highlight of the meal, a spiced bread soufflé.

15⇌♠(2fb)5₪ CTV in all bedrooms T sB&B⇌♠£85-£155 dB&B⇌♠£105-£195 🍴
50P 🚗 ✿ ♫ (hard) ✓ croquet table tennis bicycles putting nc8yrs *xmas*
♀ English & French V ☆ ⊒ ✱ ✻ Lunch £15.50-£19.50 Dinner £29.50-£33.50 Last dinner 9.30pm
Credit Cards [1][2][3] £

FLORE Northamptonshire Map **04** SP66

★★★**64%** **Heyford Manor**
The High St NN7 4LP (on A45, between Flore and Upper Heyford) (Lansbury) ☎Weedon(0327) 349022 FAX (0327) 349017

This low brick-built hotel has comfortable, thoughtfully designed bedrooms with good facilities, including 2 adapted for disabled guests. Staff provide courteous service throughout the smart public areas.

54⇌♠(7fb)⁄ in 24 bedrooms CTV in all bedrooms ⓡ ⚲ T ✗ (ex guide dogs) ✱ sB&B⇌♠fr£65.50 dB&B⇌♠fr£77 🍴
⟨ 100P sauna gymnasium *xmas*
♀ English & Continental V ☆ ⊒ ✻ Lunch fr£10.95 Dinner fr£14.95&alc Last dinner 9.30pm
CONF. Thtr 80 Class 48 Board 48 Del from £95
Credit Cards [1][2][3][5]

FOLKESTONE Kent Map **05** TR23

★★★**62%** **Clifton**
The Leas CT20 2EB (from M20 junct 13, quarter mile west of town centre on A259) ☎(0303) 851231 FAX (0303) 851231

This Regency-style cliff top hotel retains a traditional feel along with its original features. Many bedrooms have recently been brightened with attractive soft furnishings, and dated furniture is gradually being replaced. The elegant restaurant has attractive garden views and the comfortable lounge is a popular meeting place.

80⇌♠(4fb) CTV in all bedrooms ⓡ T ✱ sB&B⇌♠£55-£67.50 dB&B⇌♠£71-£80 🍴
Lift ⟨ ✓ ✿ solarium games room ♪ *xmas*
♀ English & French V ☆ ⊒ ✻ Lunch £9.75-£10.25&alc Dinner £16-£16.50&alc Last dinner 9.15pm
Credit Cards [1][2][3][5] £

★★**66%** **Wards**
39 Earls Ave CT20 2HB ☎(0303) 245166 FAX (0303) 254480
A small family hotel, Wards is in a quiet residential area of the west end. The bedrooms, which vary in size, are all attractive with coordinating fabrics, and a couple have spa or corner baths. Public areas are not extensive, but both restaurant and bar have a tasteful 1920s theme. Service is relaxed and friendly.

10⇌♠(3fb) CTV in all bedrooms ⓡ ⚲ T ✗ (ex guide dogs) ✱ sB&B⇌♠£45-£60 dB&B⇌♠£60-£85 🍴
CTV 20P 🚗 snooker *xmas*
♀ English, French & Italian V ☆ Last dinner 9.30pm
CONF. Thtr 50 Class 40 Board 30
Credit Cards [1][2][3][5] £

The AA's star rating scheme is the market leader in hotel classification.

FONTWELL West Sussex Map **04** SU90

Forte Travelodge
BN18 0SB (on A27/A29 roundabout)
☎Eastergate(0243) 543973 Central Res (0800) 850950

FORTE Travelodge

This modern building offers a good standard of accommodation for overnight stops. Smart, spacious and well equipped bedrooms, all with en suite bathrooms, are suitable for family use, and meals may be taken at the nearby family restaurant. For more details about Travelodges, consult the Contents page, under Hotel Groups.

32⇌♠✱ B⇌♠£31.95 (room only)

FORD Wiltshire Map **03** ST87

★★**64%** *White Hart Inn*
SN14 8RP ☎Castle Combe(0249) 782213 FAX (0249) 783075

Quietly situated by a trout stream, this friendly village inn with beams and open fires dates from 1533. Bar meals are available in the very popular bars or an à la carte menu in the dining room. Comfortable bedrooms with modern facilities are mostly located in annexes across the street.

3♠Annexe8⇌♠(2fb)4₪ CTV in all bedrooms ⓡ T
80P ⚐ (heated)
V ☆ Last dinner 9.30pm
Credit Cards [1][2][3]

FORDINGBRIDGE Hampshire Map **04** SU11

★★**67%** **Ashburn Hotel & Restaurant**
Damerham Rd SP6 1JP ☎(0425) 652060

Set on a hillside overlooking the forest, this hotel offers pleasant, well maintained accommodation. In the no-smoking restaurant Chef Michael Belton offers a daily table d'hôte menu alongside an interesting carte, which changes every month or so. Cooking standards are above average and the kitchen is showing promise.

23⇌♠(3fb)1₪ CTV in all bedrooms ⓡ T ✻ sB&B⇌♠£39.50 dB&B⇌♠£69 🍴
CTV 60P ✿ ⚐ (heated)
♀ English & French V ☆ ⊒ ⁄ ✻ Sunday Lunch £8.50 Dinner £12.95&alc Last dinner 9pm
CONF. Thtr 150 Del from £55
Credit Cards [1][3] £

FOREST ROW East Sussex Map **05** TQ43

○**Ashdown Park**
Wych Cross RH18 5JR ☎(0342) 824988
Due to open Autumn 1993
96⇌♠

FORFAR Tayside *Angus* Map **15** NO45

★★★**64%** **Idvies House**
Letham DD8 2QJ (2m outside Letham village, from B9128) ☎Letham(0307) 818787 FAX (0307) 818933
Closed 24-30 Dec & 1-2 Jan

This delightful Victorian hotel has the authentic, 'lived-in', country-house atmosphere. Its bedrooms, however, successfully combine period charm with modern equipment. The bar boasts an impressive range of malts; memorable breakfasts offer of a fish course before the traditional grill; dinners feature much Scottish produce.

10⇌♠(1fb)2₪ CTV in all bedrooms ⓡ T ✻ sB&B⇌♠£38-£45 dB&B⇌♠£50-£85 🍴
60P ✿ squash croquet
♀ Scottish & French V ☆ ✻ Lunch £12-£20alc High tea £5.95-£8.45 Dinner £15.50-£23.75alc Last dinner 9.30pm
Credit Cards [1][2][3][5]

Ashburn Hotel and Restaurant

Fordingbridge, Hampshire SP6 1JP
Telephone (0425) 652060

AA ★★

COMMENDED

Licensed family-run Country Hotel on the edge of the New Forest. Superb cuisine prepared by Award-winning chefs. Candle-lit Restaurant and Bar open to non-residents daily. Bar Snacks, Cream Teas, Sunday Lunches a speciality. 20 comfortable bedrooms with en-suite facilities and country views. Beautiful landscaped garden leading to outdoor heated pool. Large free car park. Elegant Function Room for that special occasion. Conference facilities available. Bargain Breaks throughout the year.

CLIFTON HOTEL ★★★
THE LEAS, FOLKESTONE
KENT CT20 2EB
Tel and Fax: (0303) 851231

FOLKESTONE'S PREMIER HOTEL
This Regency-style, cliff-top hotel affording spectacular views of the Channel, offers the perfect venue for business conferences or a relaxing break. Ideally situated for those wishing to explore the Weald of Kent and many other places of historical interest, or a visit to France.

★ 80 well appointed bedrooms with colour television, direct-dial telephone and tea/coffee making facilities
★ Garden Restaurant and Hotel Bar
★ Banqueting, Conference facilities (8-100 covers)
★ Details of Hotel and Conference Brochure on request

THE PERFECT VENUE FOR A RELAXING BREAK

The White Hart ★★
at FORD

The old inn by the trout stream

Reputedly built in 1553 and listed as being of architectural and historical interest also one of the most attractive and interesting Inns in the West Country. Situated in the small village of Ford on the A420, just 9 miles from Bath. All bedrooms are en suite and have colour TV, radio and full central heating. Four of the bedrooms have four poster beds and two have half testers. Good food is a speciality with one of the widest selections of real beers in Wiltshire and a comprehensive wine list to complement your meal.

**FORD, NR CHIPPENHAM
WILTSHIRE SN14 8RP
TELEPHONE: (0249) 782213**

LISMOYNE Hotel

special
WEEKEND BREAKS

★ CONFERENCE FACILITIES
★ 45 ENSUITE LUXURY ROOMS ALL WITH T.V. AND REFRESHMENTS
★ ENGLISH AND FRENCH CUISINE
★ SILVER SERVICE RESTAURANT
★ HONEYMOON SUITE
★ WEDDING RECEPTIONS, CONFERENCES, FUNCTIONS
★ SATURDAY DINNER DANCES
★ SUNDAY LUNCHES

Our delightful Hotel is set in 2½ acres of parkland less than 3 miles from the M3 motorway (junction 4A). Traditional friendly service and prices will make you smile and ensure a friendly welcome.

FOR THAT SPECIAL OCCASION OR BUSINESS FUNCTION CALL TODAY.

*Lismoyne Hotel, Church Rd. Fleet, Hampshire
Tel: 0252 - 628555 Fax: 0252 - 811761*
★★★

Formby - Fort William

FORMBY Merseyside Map 07 SD30

★★ 64% Tree Tops
Southport Old Rd L37 0AB (off A565 Southport to Liverpool road) ☎(07048) 79651 FAX (07048) 79651
The former dower house to Formby Hall now houses the restaurant and bar of this hotel, and these are well furnished with leather seating, the spacious Regency-style restaurant offering an extensive dinner carte. The bedrooms are in chalet-style buildings in the pleasant grounds, and have every modern facility.
11⇨ſ(2fb) CTV in all bedrooms ® T ✶ ✱ sB&B⇨ſ£44 dB&B⇨ſ£78 ₽
100P ✿ ⇨ (heated) ♬
♀ English & French V ♂ ℒ ⇥ ✱ Lunch fr£7.95&alc High tea fr£4.50 Dinner fr£18.95&alc Last dinner 10pm
CONF. Thtr 200 Class 80 Board 40 Del from £65
Credit Cards [1][2][3][5]

See advertisement under SOUTHPORT

FORRES Grampian Morayshire Map 14 NJ05

★★ ✸68% Ramnee
Victoria Rd IV36 0BN ☎(0309) 672410 FAX (0309) 673392
Many guests return year after year to this popular hotel, set in 2 acres of gardens at the east end of the town. Well run by enthusiastic owners and their willing staff, it has comfortable public areas, including a smart cocktail bar, foyer lounge, and small restaurant where chef James Murphy offers fine Scottish and French cuisine from fixed price and à la carte menus. The 2 superior bedrooms are just that, while standard rooms vary in size and furnishings.
20⇨(3fb)1⌘ CTV in all bedrooms ® T sB&B⇨ſ£45-£50 dB&B⇨ſ£67-£80 ₽
CTV 50P ✿
♀ Scottish & French V ♂ ℒ Lunch £9.50 Dinner £16&alc Last dinner 9pm
CONF. Thtr 100 Class 30 Board 45 Del from £52.50
Credit Cards [1][2][3][5]

FORT AUGUSTUS Highland Inverness-shire Map 14 NH30

★★ 67% Lovat Arms
PH32 4DU (off A82) ☎(0320) 6206 & 6204 FAX (0320) 6677
RS winter
In a commanding position overlooking the village and close to Loch Ness, this friendly family-run hotel has comfortable bedrooms in a mix of styles, all with modern amenities. Public areas include a choice of relaxing lounges, a comfortable bar and traditional dining room.
21⇨ſ(4fb) CTV in all bedrooms ® T ✱ sB&B⇨ſ£29.50-£36.50 dB&B⇨ſ£59-£73 ₽
50P ✿ putting xmas
V ♂ ℒ Bar Lunch £10-£17.50alc Dinner £16-£18.50 Last dinner 8.45pm
Credit Cards [1][3]

★★ 67% The Brae
PH32 4DG ☎(0320) 6289
Closed Nov-7 Apr (ex wknds 5 Feb-28 Mar)

Set in its own attractive grounds, this former Victorian manse has been sympathetically converted to create a popular holiday hotel which overlooks the village and Caledonian Canal. Efficiently run by Andrew and Mari Reive, it has a relaxing atmosphere and enjoyable home cooking.
8rm(2⇨3ſ)(1fb) CTV in all bedrooms ®
CTV 12P ⇆ ✿ nc7yrs
♀ International ⇥ Last dinner 8.30pm
Credit Cards [1][3]

★★ 64% Inchnacardoch Lodge
Loch Ness PH32 4BL (N of village, off A82) ☎(0320) 6258
Closed Dec-Feb
Various alterations are under way at this Highland holiday hotel, which stands in its own grounds overlooking Loch Ness. The former bar has been converted to a comfortable no-smoking lounge, while a new lounge bar has been opened at the rear of the house. The attractive restaurant is unchanged.
15⇨ſ(6fb)⇥ in 3 bedrooms CTV in all bedrooms ® T ✶ (ex guide dogs) sB&B⇨ſ£40-£55 dB&B⇨ſ£55-£70 ₽
40P ✿ ♪
♀ International V ♂ ℒ Bar Lunch £2-£11alc Dinner £18 Last dinner 8.30pm
Credit Cards [1][2][3][5]

★ 62% Caledonian
PH32 4BQ ☎(0320) 6256
Closed Oct-Mar
This small, welcoming hotel is on the main road close to the centre of the village. Improvements here are ongoing, and traditional services and comforts are offered together with good home cooking.
11rm(7⇨ſ)(3fb) ® ✶ (ex guide dogs)
CTV 20P ✿
♀ Scottish & French V ♂ ℒ ⇥ Last dinner 9pm
Credit Cards [1][3]

FORTINGALL Tayside Perthshire Map 14 NN74

★★ 64% Fortingall
PH15 2NQ ☎Kenmore(0887) 830367 & 830368
RS Nov-Feb
This family-run hotel, which appeals to tourists and sporting people, is the focal point of the attractive conservation village. Bedrooms provide solid old-fashioned comforts and the single menu offers a good choice of dishes for both bar meals and dinners.
9rm(8⇨5ſ)(3fb) CTV in all bedrooms ® T sB&B£28-£32 sB&B⇨ſ£30-£34 dB&B£48-£52 dB&B⇨ſ£50-£54 ₽
CTV 15P 5⌂ ✿ ✱ ♪ sailing pony trekking golf ⚬
♀ French V ♂ ✱ Lunch £11-£16&alc Dinner £15-£20&alc Last dinner 8.30pm
Credit Cards [1][3]

FORTON MOTORWAY SERVICE AREA (M6) Lancashire Map 07 SD55

Pavilion Lodge
White Carr Ln, Bay Horse LA2 9DU (between juncts 32 & 33) ☎Lancaster(0524) 792227 FAX (0524) 792241
With a nearby family restaurant providing all meals, this modern building offers smart, spacious and well equipped bedrooms. For more details about Pavilion Lodges, consult the Contents page, under Hotel Groups.
41⇨ſ✶ sB⇨ſ£31.95 dB⇨ſ£35.95 (room only)

FORT WILLIAM Highland Inverness-shire Map 14 NN17

INVERLOCHY CASTLE
PH33 6SN (3m NE A82)
☎(0397) 702177 FAX (0397) 702953

Fort William

Closed Dec-1 Mar

In 1994 Grete Hobbs celebrates 25 years of owning this outstanding hotel and it is a tribute to her continued interest and commitment that one feels there is a timeless quality about this immaculate country house that restores one's faith in hotel-keeping in this country. Professional standards of the highest order continue to be consistently attained under the dedicated and watchful eye of managing directory Michael Leonard, who has been here for 17 years. Set in 500 acres in the shadow of Ben Nevis, Inverlochy Castle offers the ultimate in comfort, together with a sense of being really cossetted. Head Chef Simon Haigh is growing in stature and confidence, with skilful saucing and the use of top quality meat and fish. The highlight of a recent meal was the excellence of the wood pigeon and deliciously fresh scallops. The wine list is particularly strong on clarets.

16⇌♠ CTV in all bedrooms T ✕ ✱ sB&B⇌♠£132-£145 dB&B⇌♠£200-£250
⟨ 16P 1🏀 🏊 ✿ ♪ (hard) ♦ snooker
♀ International V ♨ ✂ Dinner £39-£43 Last dinner 9.15pm
Credit Cards 1 2 3

★★★ ❀75% **Moorings**
Banavie PH33 7LY (3m N of Fort William off A830) ☎Corpach(0397) 772797 FAX (0397) 772441

Inspectors' Choice 1994

Closed 22-26 Dec
(Rosette awarded for dinner only)

The Sinclair family have created a fine hotel which is renowned for its hospitality, service and good food and it is this year our Inspectors' Selected Hotel of the Year for Scotland. It is situated beside the Caledonian Canal almost at the head of the series of 8 locks which make up the famous Neptune's Staircase, and has fine views of both Ben Nevis and Loch Linnhe. Attractive public areas include the popular Mariners cellar bar offering as good range of bar meals and the Jacobean-themed main restaurant where a sound reputation for Scottish food, using local meat, fish and game, has been earned.

21⇌♠Annexe3♠(1fb)1🛏 CTV in all bedrooms ®✌T
✕ (ex guide dogs) ✱ sB&B⇌♠£40-£76 dB&B⇌♠£58-£90 🍴 60P ✿
V ♨ ♨ ✂ Lunch £12-£18 Dinner £23-£24&alc Last dinner 9.30pm
CONF. Thtr 120 Class 70 Board 35 Del from £65
Credit Cards 1 2 3 5

★★★ 55% **Alexandra**
The Parade PH33 6AZ (Milton) ☎(0397) 702241 FAX (0397) 705554
This traditional hotel in an extended Victorian building is popular with coach tours. Bedrooms of varying size are practical and modern, top floor rooms offering most comfort. Public areas include a foyer lounge and bar, a restaurant and an all-day coffee shop.
97⇌♠(8fb) CTV in all bedrooms ® T

Banavie, Fort William,
Inverness-shire, Scotland PH33 7LY
Tel: 0397 772 797   Fax: 0397 772 441

**The AA Hotel Inspectors'
Selected Hotel Of The Year
for Scotland**

Beautifully situated alongside the Caledonian Canal looking onto Ben Nevis.
Award-winning Taste of Scotland. Restaurant featuring the finest indigenous Scottish produce and a well stocked cellar. Popular Cellar Wine Bar for fireside meals.
Open all year.

AA ★★★ ❀❀ 75%   STB Highly Commended

★★

On the site of the original Hanoverian fort which gave this lovely village its name, close to Loch Ness, the Benedictine Monastery and the Caledonian Canal, the Lovat Arms offers 21 comfortable en-suite bedrooms with all modern facilities, a cocktail and public bar, spacious lounges and excellent food with 'Taste of Scotland' menus. Half way between Inverness and Fort William and surrounded by some of Scotland's finest scenery it is ideally situated for exploration of the Great Glen with east and west coasts easily accessible.

A warm welcome is assured throughout the year. For further details please contact the resident proprietors:

**Hector and Mary MacLean
Lovat Arms Hotel
Fort Augustus
Inverness-shire PH32 4DU
Tel: 0320 6204/6206 Fax: 0320 6677**

Fort William - Fossebridge

Lift (50P ♪
♡ Scottish & French **V** ✿ ⚲ ⚄
CONF. Thtr 140 Class 40 Board 26
Credit Cards ① ② ③ ⑤

★★ **60%** Nevis Bank
Belford Rd PH33 6BY ☏(0397) 705721 FAX (0397) 706275

Specially appealing to outdoor enthusiasts are the activity breaks offered by this privately owned commercial and holiday hotel. Situated north of town with convenient access to Glen Nevis, the hotel has a relaxed and friendly atmosphere. Bedrooms are limited in size with mixed practical facilities.
35⇌♙Annexe8⇌♙(2fb) CTV in all bedrooms ® **T** ✱
sB&B⇌♙£42-£49 dB&B⇌♙£58-£84 ♬
25P sauna solarium gymnasium *xmas*
♡ Scottish & French **V** ✿ ⚲ ✱ Bar Lunch fr£3.50alc Dinner fr£13.95 Last dinner 9pm
CONF. Thtr 40 Board 20 Del from £63.65
Credit Cards ① ② ③ ⑤ £

★★ **59%** Grand
Gordon Square PH33 6DX (on A82 at west end of High Street)
☏(0397) 702928 FAX (0397) 705060
Situated at the west end of the High Street, this long established family owned commercial hotel also caters for tour groups. Bedrooms vary in size and are functional, providing most of the expected amenities. There is a small lounge and a comfortable bar.
33⇌(4fb) CTV in all bedrooms ® **T** sB&B⇌fr£27.50 dB&B⇌fr£50 ♬
(20P
V ✿ ⚲ Lunch fr£9 Dinner fr£17 Last dinner 8.30pm
CONF. Thtr 110 Class 60 Board 20 Del from £45
Credit Cards ① ② ③ ⑤ £

★★ **59%** Imperial
Fraser's Square PH33 6DW ☏(0397) 702040 & 703921 FAX (0397) 706277
Closed 3-31 Jan
This friendly family-run commercial hotel is situated in the town centre, and is a popular base for tour groups. Public areas have been comfortably furnished in the modern style and the bedrooms are practically equipped.
34⇌♙(3fb) CTV in all bedrooms ®
CTV 20P
♡ Scottish & French ⚄ Last dinner 9pm
Credit Cards ① ③

See advertisement on page 255

★★ **59%** Milton
North Rd PH33 6TG (N of town, on A82) (Milton)
☏(0397) 702331 FAX (0397) 703695
RS Feb-mid Mar
A popular base for visiting tour groups, this purpose built holiday hotel overlooks Ben Nevis. The refurbished public rooms offer bright modern appointments, while the well equipped bedrooms have practical fitted units.
56⇌♙Annexe67⇌♙(6fb) CTV in all bedrooms ® ✱
sB⇌♙£39-£49 dB⇌♙£59-£69 (room only) ♬
(150P ♪
♡ Scottish & French ✿ ⚲ ✱ High tea £5.50-£7.50 Dinner £11-£15 Last dinner 8.30pm
CONF. Thtr 180 Class 40 Board 60 Del from £40
Credit Cards ① ② ③ ④ ⑤ £

 FACTOR'S HOUSE
Torlundy PH33 6SN (3m N on A82) ☏(0397) 705767
FAX (0397) 702953
Closed 16 Dec-15 Jan RS 16 Jan-14 Mar

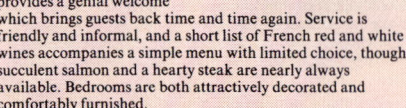

This charming little hotel in the shadow of Ben Nevis provides a genial welcome which brings guests back time and time again. Service is friendly and informal, and a short list of French red and white wines accompanies a simple menu with limited choice, though succulent salmon and a hearty steak are nearly always available. Bedrooms are both attractively decorated and comfortably furnished.
7⇌♙ CTV in all bedrooms ⚲ **T** ✖ (ex guide dogs)
sB&B⇌♙£41.25-£58.75 dB&B⇌♙£58.75-£82.25
CTV 30P ⛳ ✿ ♪ (hard) ♪ sailing nc6yrs
♡ Scottish & Continental ✱ Dinner £15-£20 Last dinner 9.30pm
Credit Cards ① ② ③ ⑤

FOSSEBRIDGE Gloucestershire Map **04** SP01

★★ **64%** *Fossebridge Inn*
GL54 3JS ☏(0285) 720721 FAX (0285) 720793
This picturesque roadside inn with landscaped gardens at the rear, is flanked by a natural lake and the River Coln. The bedrooms have been carefully upgraded to the same comfortable yet characterful standards of its public areas.

Contd. page 255 ➡

★★★

Glenspean Lodge Hotel

★ Full à la carte Restaurant with magnificent views of Glenspean
★ All rooms en suite
★ 4 poster beds and Honeymoon suite
★ In the heart of the Highlands for touring
★ 2 miles east of Roy Bridge
★ Activity holidays available
★ Live music at weekends

~ Proprietors: Neal and Isabel Smith ~

**ROY BRIDGE,
INVERNESS-SHIRE PH31 4AW
TEL: 0397 712223
FAX: 0397 712660**

The AA's star rating scheme is the market leader in hotel classification.

FREEDOM OF THE GLEN
A SPECIAL SELECTION

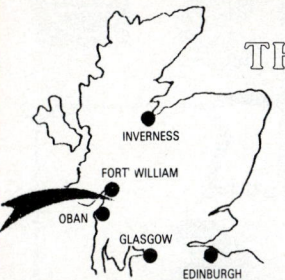

THREE RENOWNED HOTELS SET BESIDE LOCH LEVEN BELOW GLENCOE

"Astounding situation. Most remarkable Hotel"

THE LODGE ON THE LOCH

In the heart of the Highlands, where mountains and Gulf Stream meet in tranquillity.
Panoramic views from memorable bedrooms, specially furnished in a contemporary Highland style.
Renowned Restaurant serving local seafood, salmon, trout and venison with home baking as well as health foods.

ONICH nr Fort William, Inverness-shire
Tel: (08553) 237   Fax: (08553) 463
Norman & Jessie Laurence & Morag McP Young
★★★   *see gazetteer entry under ONICH*   Scottish Tourist Board HIGHLY COMMENDED

AN OLD TRADITION . . . MADE GREAT

Welcome to one of Scotland's oldest and best loved Inns. Now refurbished, this fine Baronial hotel offers stylish comfort and tempting Highland luxury. With famous mountain and lochside panoramas, renowned "Taste of Scotland" fayre and family owners to greet you — your holiday is complete.

Special Summer and Winter Packages now available.

Ballachulish, Argyll PA39 4JY
Tel: (08552) 606 Fax: (08552) 629

★★★   Scottish Tourist Board HIGHLY COMMENDED

The Isles of Glencoe
Hotel & Leisure Centre

Ballachulish, Fort William, PA39 4HL
Tel: (08552) 602 Fax: (08552) 770

Almost afloat, this exciting new hotel welcomes with:

★ Superb value tariff — from £39.95 per room!
★ The luxury of leisure — pool, sauna & steam.
★ Spectacular views to mountain, loch and glen.
★ Large, comfortable bedrooms with full services.
★ Informal, Brasserie Restaurant with mouthwatering fare.

Scottish Tourist Board COMMENDED

BRITAIN'S BEST PUBS

We have visited pubs up and down the country in search of the traditional, much loved 'local' with its friendly atmosphere and draught beers, but we have also looked for pubs that offer something exceptional such as adventurous food, facilities for children or reasonably priced accommodation.

Whatever your particular fancy, the hundreds of selected pubs in **BRITAIN'S BEST PUBS** will provide some exciting discoveries.

Produced in association with Appletise plc

10⇔♠Annexe4⇔ CTV in all bedrooms ® T
CTV 50P ✢ ♪
☉ English & French V ✿ ⌓ Last dinner 9.30pm
Credit Cards [1][2][3][5]

FOUR MARKS Hampshire Map 04 SU63

Forte Travelodge
156 Winchester Rd GU34 5HZ (on A31, northbound)
☎Alton(0420) 62659 Central Res (0800) 850950

FORTE Travelodge

This modern building offers a good standard of accommodation for overnight stops. Smart, spacious and well equipped bedrooms, all with en suite bathrooms, are suitable for family use, and meals may be taken at the nearby family restaurant. For more details about Travelodges, consult the Contents page, under Hotel Groups.
31⇔♠✱ B⇔♠£31.95 (room only)

FOWEY Cornwall & Isles of Scilly Map 02 SX15

★★⊛75% **Marina**
Esplanade PL23 1HY ☎(0726) 833315
Closed Nov-Feb
The Marina Hotel is in a commanding waterfront location with a small terrace and access down steep steps to the moorings below. Most bedrooms have superb views over the estuary and some have balconies. In the Waterside Restaurant young chef Simon Trethewey offers a daily 4-course fixed price menu alongside a weekly carte, and local seafood is a speciality. Lunchtime bar snacks are also available. Courtesy transport is provided to the town car park.
11⇔♠ CTV in all bedrooms ® T dB&B⇔♠£54-£80 ⊟
(✗ ⇌ ♪ windsurfing sailing
☉ English & French V ✿ ⌓ Bar Lunch £1.50-£5 High tea £3-£5 Dinner fr£16&alc Last dinner 8.30pm
Credit Cards [1][2][3][5]
See advertisement on page 257

FOWNHOPE Hereford & Worcester Map 03 SO53

★★65% **Green Man Inn**
HR1 4PE (on B4224) ☎(0432) 860243 FAX (0432) 860207
This village inn with its popular low-beamed bars and restaurant dates from the 15th century. Both the traditionally furnished bedrooms in the main building and the more modern annexe rooms have a very good range of facilities.
10⇔♠Annexe5⇔♠(3fb)1⚑ CTV in all bedrooms ® T ✲
sB&B⇔♠£31 dB&B⇔♠£48 ⊟
CTV 75P ✢ ♪ xmas
V ✿ ⌓ ✲ ✱ Sunday Lunch £5.25-£9.25alc
Credit Cards [1][2][3]

FRAMLINGHAM Suffolk Map 05 TM26

★★68% **The Crown**
Market Hill IP13 9AN (on A1120)
☎(0728) 723521 FAX (0728) 724274

FORTE Heritage

This delightful 16th-century inn, now a small hotel with timbered and beamed public rooms, is in the centre of the market town. The bedrooms are nearly all furnished in the comfortable Heritage style with rich colour coordination in the décor and fabrics. Staff provide cheerful, friendly service.
14⇔51⚑in 4 bedrooms CTV in all bedrooms ® T ✲
sB⇔£70-£95 dB⇔£85-£120 (room only) ⊟
30P xmas
V ✿ ⌓ ✲ ✱ Sunday Lunch £10.50 Dinner £17.50 Last dinner 9.30pm
Credit Cards [1][2][3][5]

IMPERIAL HOTEL ★★
(Fraser's Square, Fort William)
Inverness-shire PH33 6DW
Telephone: Fort William 0397 702040

Situated in the heart of Fort William, close to the shopping centre and with panoramic views of Loch Linnhe and the surrounding countryside. The Hotel offers the ideal base to explore and discover the beauty of the West Highlands by car or coach. It is one of the oldest established hotels in Fort William and has developed over the years a reputation for Highland hospitality and good food. The hotel has been substantially refurbished to provide quality accommodation at reasonable prices. All rooms with private bathroom, TV and tea and coffee facilities.

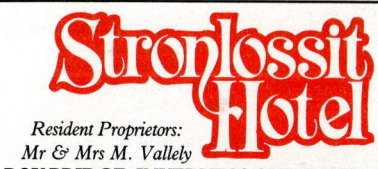

Resident Proprietors:
Mr & Mrs M. Vallely   ★★
ROY BRIDGE, INVERNESS-SHIRE PH31 4AG
Telephone: 0397 712253

Stronlossit Hotel in Roy Bridge is surrounded by some of Scotland's most delightful scenery. A dozen of the nearby mountains rise to over 3,000 ft — Ben Nevis is only a few miles away. And the first of the Great Glen's spectacular lochs is a short distance from our doorstep.

Please write or telephone to book — and for full brochure and prices.

Frankley Motorway Service Area (M5) - Gairloch

FRANKLEY MOTORWAY SERVICE AREA (M5) West Midlands Map 07 SO98

Granada Lodge
Illey Ln B32 4AR (between junc 3 and 4 of M5)
☎021-550 3261 FAX 021-501 2880

This modern building provides smart, spacious and well equipped bedrooms, all with en suite bathrooms. Meals may be taken at a nearby family restaurant. For more details about Granada Lodges, consult the Contents page, under Hotel Groups.

61⇨♠✱ B⇨♠£34.95-£37.95 (room only)

FRESHWATER
See **Wight, Isle of**

FREUCHIE Fife Map 11 NO20

★★63% **Lomond Hills**
Parliament Square KY7 7EY (in town centre)
☎Falkland(0337) 57329 & 57498 FAX (0337) 58180

This extended coaching inn at the centre of the village now offers well equipped if somewhat compact bedrooms and comfortable public areas.

25⇨♠(3fb)1⌗⌘in 3 bedrooms CTV in all bedrooms ®⚹ T ✱
sB&B⇨♠£43-£46 dB&B⇨♠£61-£66 ♫
30P ⌂ (heated) sauna solarium gymnasium skittle alley ♿
♀ Scottish & French V ♦ ♨ ✂ Lunch £11.50-£15&alc High tea £5.50-£9.50alc Dinner £13.50-£16&alc Last dinner 9pm
Credit Cards ①②③⑤

FRINTON-ON-SEA Essex Map 05 TM21

★★65% **Maplin**
Esplanade CO13 9EL (Logis) ☎(0255) 673832
Closed Jan

Built in 1911, this detached house has a lovely position overlooking the greensward and sea. Nick Turner and his wife Sue offer a warm welcome and attentive service. Bedrooms are traditional in style with a mixture of furniture and fabrics, and public areas have old-fashioned charm with original oak panelling.

12rm(9⇨1♠)(2fb) CTV in all bedrooms ® T ✱ sB&B£35 sB&B⇨♠£50-£75 dB&B⇨♠£50-£90 ♫
CTV 12P ⌗ ⌂ (heated) *xmas*
♀ English & French V ♦ ♨ ✱ Lunch £15.95&alc Dinner £19.95&alc Last dinner 9pm
Credit Cards ①②③

★67% **Rock**
The Esplanade, 1 Third Av CO13 9EQ ☎(0255) 677194 & 675173
Closed Jan

This small Victorian hotel facing the greensward on the Esplanade and personally managed by the proprietor, has a pleasant atmosphere in its convivial bar lounge and wood-panelled dining room. Bedrooms are generally spacious and comfortable, many having sea views.

6rm(5♠)(3fb)1⌗ CTV in all bedrooms ®
CTV 12P ⌗ solarium
V Last dinner 9pm
Credit Cards ①②③⑤

FRODSHAM Cheshire Map 07 SJ57

★★★64% **Forest Hill Hotel & Leisure Complex**
Bellemonte Rd, Overton Hill WA6 6HH (off B5152)
☎(0928) 735255 FAX (0928) 735517

Situated at the top of Overton Hill, famous for its panoramic views of the Mersey and the Cheshire Plain, this purpose-built complex offers modern bedrooms, with some spacious executive accommodation with quite luxurious bathrooms.

58⇨♠(4fb)⌘in 5 bedrooms CTV in all bedrooms ®⚹ T ✱
sB&B⇨♠£49-£71 dB&B⇨♠£49-£71 (room only) ♫
(CTV 350P ❋ ⌂ (heated) squash snooker sauna solarium gymnasium beauty salon jacuzzi nightclub *xmas*
♀ English & French V ♦ ✂ Lunch £9.95-£10.25 Dinner £16.50-£17.95&alc Last dinner 9.45pm
CONF. Thtr 250 Class 80 Board 48 Del from £65
Credit Cards ①②③⑤ £

FROME Somerset Map 03 ST74

★★★63% **Mendip Lodge**
Bath Rd BA11 2HP (situated on the Bath side of Frome, on the B3090, opposite Frome College) ☎(0373) 463223 FAX (0373) 463990

New owners personally supervise the friendly service in this busy hotel at the foot of the Mendips. Public areas – contained within the original Edwardian house - comprise a split-level restaurant, comfortable little lounge and bar; well equipped bedrooms are more functional in appearance, being located in motel-type blocks. Menus offer a selection of competently cooked dishes which includes a good vegetarian choice, and car parking facilities are available on site.

40⇨♠(12fb) CTV in all bedrooms ®⚹ T sB&B⇨♠£45-£60 dB&B⇨♠£60-£75 ♫
(60P 12⌗ ❋ ♿
♀ English & French V ♦ Lunch £15.50-£16.95&alc Dinner £15.50-£16.95&alc Last dinner 9.30pm
CONF. Thtr 90 Class 30 Board 40 Del from £70
Credit Cards ①②③⑤ £

★★59% **George**
4 Market Place BA11 1AF (Logis) ☎(0373) 462584 FAX (0373) 451945

A town centre former coaching inn, the George is looking rather tired in its public areas, though the bedrooms are prettily decorated, well furnished and particularly well equipped. The restaurant is cheerful with bright oil cloths, and the menu offers mainly home-made pasta dishes and pancakes, though a formal 3-course meal can be provided.

20⇨♠(3fb)1⌗ CTV in all bedrooms ®⚹ T
17⌗ solarium
♀ English & Continental V ♦ ♨ ✂ Last dinner 9.30pm
Credit Cards ①②③⑤

GAINSBOROUGH Lincolnshire Map 08 SK88

★★65% **Hickman-Hill**
Cox's Hill DN21 1HH ☎(0427) 613639

This town-centre Georgian hotel offers individually decorated bedrooms and a tranquil lounge and bar lounge. The hotel is managed by resident proprietors and service is very courteous.

8rm(3⇨3♠)(1fb) CTV in all bedrooms ® T ✱ sB&Bfr£39 dB&B⇨♠fr£57 ♫
CTV 25P ⌗ ❋ solarium *xmas*
V ♦ ♨ Lunch £6.50 Dinner £10.50&alc Last dinner 9pm
Credit Cards ①③

GAIRLOCH Highland *Ross & Cromarty* Map 14 NG87

★★★65% **Creag Mor**
Charleston IV12 2AH ☎(0445) 2068 FAX (0445) 2044

Larry and Betty Nieto's comfortable holiday hotel stands in its own extensive grounds overlooking Old Gairloch Harbour and to the Isle of Skye beyond. The bedrooms, which vary in size, have attractive decor and are equipped with the usual modern comforts. Public areas offer a choice of formal and informal restaurants and bars and in the Bothan bar there are over 100 brands of whisky to choose from.

17⇨♠ Annexe2⇨♠(1fb) CTV in 17 bedrooms ® T
sB&B⇨♠£25-£44 dB&B⇨♠£50-£84 ♫
(29P ❋ ♪ *xmas*

Gairloch - Garstang

♡ French **V** ❁ ⚑ ✗ ✱ Lunch £6-£12 Dinner £21-£24 Last dinner 9.30pm
CONF. Class 40 Del from £49
Credit Cards [1][3]

★★ 65% *Myrtle Bank*
Low Rd IV21 2BS (off B8012 Melvaig road) ☎(0445) 2004 FAX (0445) 2214
From its position beside the shore this family-run Highland hotel has fine views over Loch Gairloch and to the Isle of Skye beyond. Public areas, with comfortable modern furniture, include a well stocked bar, relaxing lounge and pleasant dining room. The well maintained bedrooms have attractive decor with matching modern units.
12⇌🛏(3fb) CTV in all bedrooms ®
🚗
V ❁ ⚑
Credit Cards [1][3]

★★ 63% *The Old Inn*
Flowerdale IV21 2BD ☎(0445) 2006 FAX (0445) 2445
A popular base for the touring holidaymaker this family-run extended coaching inn is situated south of the village and overlooks the old harbour. Bedrooms vary in size and are equipped with the usual modern amenities while public areas include a comfortable first floor lounge, choice of rustic bars serving real ale and a popular all-day bistro.
14⇌🛏(4fb) CTV in all bedrooms ® T
50P 🚗
❁ ⚑ Last dinner 9pm
Credit Cards [1][2][3]

GALASHIELS Borders *Selkirkshire* Map **12** NT43

★★★ 67% *Kingsknowes*
Selkirk Rd TD1 3HY (off A7) ☎(0896) 58375 FAX (0896) 50377
Standing in its own grounds to the south of the town, this Victorian baronial mansion has impressive public rooms with fine cornices, including a comfortable lounge, panelled cocktail bar and attractive conservatory. Bedrooms are comfortable though furnishing styles look rather dated.
11rm(10⇌🛏)(3fb) CTV in all bedrooms ® T ✱
sB&B⇌🛏£35-£50 dB&B⇌🛏£68-£80 ♫
30P ❋ ♪ (hard)
♡ English & Continental **V** ❁ Lunch £8-£12.50&alc High tea £6-£10alc Dinner £16-£18&alc Last dinner 9.30pm
Credit Cards [1][2][3][5]

★★★ 64% *Woodlands House Hotel & Restaurants*
Windyknowe Rd TD1 1RQ ☎(0896) 4722 FAX (0896) 4722
This imposing Gothic mansion stands in 2 acres of grounds just to the west of the town. Accommodation is mostly spacious and much of the house's original panelling and ornate plasterwork has been retained in the public rooms. There is a choice of restaurant styles and service is friendly.
9⇌🛏 CTV in all bedrooms ® T ✱ sB&B⇌🛏£40
dB&B⇌🛏£70 ♫
30P ❋
♡ English & French **V** ❁ ✱ Lunch £12.95 Dinner £18&alc Last dinner 9.30pm
Credit Cards [1][3]

★★ 57% *Abbotsford Arms*
63 Stirling St TD1 1BY ☎(0896) 2517 FAX (0896) 50744
Closed 24-25, 31 Dec & 1 Jan
This small and friendly traditional inn in the town centre has been modernised to provide comfortable bedrooms and a choice of bars.
14rm(10⇌🛏)(3fb) CTV in all bedrooms ®⚑ T
✈ (ex guide dogs) sB&B£26-£28 sB&B⇌🛏£32-£35 dB&B£40-£44 dB&B⇌🛏£48-£52 ♫
《 15P 🚗

V ❁ ⚑
CONF. Thtr 120 Class 120 Board 120
Credit Cards [1][3]

GARFORTH West Yorkshire Map **08** SE43
Hilton National Leeds/Garforth
Wakefield Rd, Garforth Rdbt LS25 1LH (junc A63/A642 6m E of Leeds)
☎Leeds(0532) 866556 FAX (0532) 868326
This is a bright, modern hotel with an informal restaurant, aimed at both the business and leisure guest. All bedrooms have en-suite bathrooms and a range of modern facilities. For more information on Hilton National, consult the Contents page, under Hotel Groups.
144⇌🛏✱ B⇌🛏fr£65 (room only)
CONF. Thtr 250 Class 80 Board 20 Del £110

G

GARSTANG Lancashire Map **07** SD44

★★★ 70% *Crofters*
Cabus PR3 1PH (on A6, midway between junc 32 & 33 of M6) ☎(0995) 604128
This family-owned and managed hotel offers 2 contrasting styles of bedroom: standard rooms, while spacious, are functional and modest; executive rooms are attractively decorated and have extras such as bathrobes, trouser presses and hairdryers. Comfortable public areas offer a choice of bars and places to eat.
19⇌🛏(3fb) CTV in all bedrooms ®⚑ T sB&B⇌🛏£42-£60
dB&B⇌🛏£47-£65 ♫
《 200P ♫ *xmas*
♡ English & French **V** ❁ ✱ Sunday Lunch fr£8.95 Dinner fr£13.75&alc Last dinner 10pm
CONF. Thtr 200 Class 120 Board 50 Del from £45
Credit Cards [1][2][3][5]

ESPLANADE, FOWEY, CORNWALL PL23 1HY
Telephone: 072683 3315
ASHLEY COURTENAY
WHICH HOTEL GUIDE

The Marina has a unique waterfront position overlooking the harbour. It is a charming Georgian residence with some bedrooms having balconies and the majority of bedrooms overlooking the water and harbour activities.

The restaurant also has panoramic views across the harbour and the menu provides a delicious range of local fish, meat & game.

The Hotel has its own quayside access to the water and moorings are available to guests.

Garstang - Gatwick Airport (London)

★★ 71% The Pickerings
Garstang Rd, Catterall PR3 0HD (2m S B6480) ☎(0995) 602133 FAX (0995) 602100
RS 26-28 Dec

Standing in its own grounds, this privately owned hotel is run with enthusiasm by the proprietor, assisted by a friendly team of young staff. Pleasantly furnished bedrooms are generally spacious and equipped with all modern amenities. A 5-course dinner with a good range of dishes is offered in the attractive restaurant.

14⇨🛏Annexe2rm(1fb)3🛌 CTV in all bedrooms ® T
✈ (ex guide dogs) sB&B⇨🛏£33-£53 dB&B⇨🛏£66-£86 🍴
50P ✿ xmas
♀ English & Continental V ♨ Lunch £8.50-£12.50 Dinner £12.50-£28.50 Last dinner 10pm
CONF. Thtr 30 Class 16 Board 20 Del from £60
Credit Cards £

G

GARVE Highland *Ross & Cromarty* Map **14** NH36

★★ ✿66% Inchbae Lodge
Inchbae IV23 2PH (6m W, on A835)
☎Aultguish(09975) 269
(Rosette awarded for dinner only)

This small family-run holiday hotel on the banks of the River Blackwater has a relaxed friendly atmosphere. Bedrooms of varying size and style are well decorated and there are comfortable, traditional lounges, a cosy beamed bar and a dining room where carefully prepared set-price dinners feature local game, fish and seafood.

6rm(3⇨2🛏)Annexe6🛏(2fb) ® sB&B⇨🛏£33 dB&B⇨🛏£56 🍴
30P ⚓ ✿ ✓ clay pigeon shooting xmas
❀ ♨ Bar Lunch £7.50-£14.50 High tea £7.50-£14.50alc
Dinner £21 Last dinner 8.30pm £

GATEHOUSE OF FLEET Dumfries & Galloway
Kirkcudbrightshire Map **11** NX55

★★★★ 🏨 66% Cally Palace
DG7 2DL ☎Gatehouse(0557) 814341 FAX (0557) 814522
Closed 3 Jan-Feb

Standing in over 100 acres of parkland on the outskirts of the village, this former family home of the Murrays of Gatehouse dates from 1763. Lofty public areas such as the marbled entrance hall and spacious day rooms retain much of their former elegance and are comfortably furnished in Louis XIV style. Traditionally furnished bedrooms are also generously proportioned, while those in the modern extension have small balconies. The staff are willing and friendly.

55⇨(7fb)1🛌 CTV in all bedrooms ® T
Lift ₵ 100P ⚓ ✿ ▭ (heated) ♀ (hard) ♪ sauna solarium croquet putting green ♫
V ❀ ♨ ✕ Last dinner 9.30pm
Credit Cards

★★★ 62% Murray Arms
DG7 2HY ☎Gatehouse(0557) 814207 FAX (0557) 814370
This old inn in the centre of the small country town has a friendly relaxing atmosphere. Bedrooms are traditionally furnished and there is a choice of dining areas and various cosy lounges, including one where Robert Burns wrote 'Scots Wha Hae'. A choice of eating options serve local fare.

12⇨🛏Annexe1⇨🛏(3fb) CTV in all bedrooms ® T
sB&B⇨🛏£39.50-£45 dB&B⇨🛏£60-£70 🍴
₵ CTV 50P ✿ croquet xmas
V ❀ ♨ ✕ Lunch £6.90-£18.20alc Dinner £17.50alc Last dinner 9.45pm
Credit Cards £

GATESHEAD Tyne & Wear Map **12** NZ26

★★★ 66% Swallow
High West St NE8 1PE ☎091-477 1105 FAX 091-478 7214

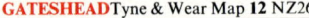

This is a modern multi-storey hotel, and though bedrooms are compact, several have recently been upgraded.
103⇨🛏(12fb)✕ in 19 bedrooms CTV in all bedrooms ® ♨ T ✱
sB&B⇨🛏fr£75 dB&B⇨🛏£88-£112 🍴
Lift ₵ 90P 100🚗 ▭ (heated) sauna solarium gymnasium spa bath steam room ♫ xmas
♀ International V ❀ ♨ ✱ Lunch £9.95-£11.25&alc Dinner £17.50&alc Last dinner 10pm
Credit Cards £

★★ ✿✿76% Eslington Villa
8 Station Rd, Low Fell NE9 6DR ☎091-487 6017 FAX 091-482 2359
Closed 25 Dec-2 Jan

This elegant Edwardian house, offering charming accommodation and renowned for its hospitality, has received many accolades for its high standard of cooking, but as we go to press we learn of a change of chef. Ian Lowrie, formerly at 21 Queen Street — a Newcastle-upon-Tyne restaurant with three rosettes — has now taken over.

12⇨🛏(2fb)2🛌 CTV in all bedrooms ® T ✱
sB&B⇨🛏£44.50-£59.50 dB&B⇨🛏£59.50-£79
₵ 15P ⚓ ✿
♀ English & French V ✕ Lunch £14.95-£17.95&alc Dinner £22.95-£25.95&alc Last dinner 10pm
Credit Cards

Forte Travelodge
Leam Ln, Wardley, Whitemare Pool NE10 8YB (at junc of A1/A194)
☎091-438 3333 Central Res (0800) 850950

This modern building offers a good standard of accommodation for overnight stops. Smart, spacious and well equipped bedrooms, all with en suite bathrooms, are suitable for family use, and meals may be taken at the nearby family restaurant. For more details about Travelodges, consult the contents page, under Hotel Groups.
41⇨🛏✱ B⇨🛏£31.95 (room only)

Marriott
Metro Centre NE11 9XF ☎091-493 2233 FAX 091-493 2030

A large and busy hotel, which is ideal for the business and leisure traveller, offering a wide range of services, a choice of eating options and indoor leisure facilities. Bedrooms are comfortable and equipped with modern facilities. For more details about Marriott hotels, consult the Contents page, under Hotel groups.
150⇨🛏 dB⇨🛏fr£98 (room only)

GATWICK AIRPORT (LONDON) West Sussex
Map **04** TQ24

See also **Burgh Heath, Dorking, East Grinstead, Reigate** and **South Godstone**

★★★★ ✿69% London Gatwick Airport Hilton
RH6 0LL ☎Gatwick(0293) 518080 FAX (0293) 28980

A covered walkway links this hotel to the South Terminal. The Garden Restaurant offers tasty, straightforward cuisine and has an adjoining bar. An escalator leads up to the main atrium, with its busy lobby area and popular American-style Amy's Diner. A good range of facilities includes a gift shop, bank, business and conference centre and leisure club. Bedrooms are smart and all have

Gatwick Airport (London)

air conditioning. The best are on the executive floor, and have exclusive use of a small lounge.
550⇨ſ CTV in all bedrooms ® T ✱ sB⇨ſfr£135 dB⇨ſfr£145 (room only)
Lift (⊞ P (charged) ☐ (heated) gymnasium
♀ International
CONF. Thtr 500 Class 225 Board 40 Del £145
Credit Cards ① ② ③ ④ ⑤

★★★★ ❊68% **Copthorne Effingham Park**
West Park Road, Copthorne RH10 3EU
☎Copthorne(0342) 714994 FAX (0342) 716039

Copthorne Hotels

Skilfully modernised and extended from a former stately home, this impressive hotel has a choice of bedrooms and suites, the best on the 3rd floor overlooking the golf course. There are 2 restaurants, the self-service Maclaren and the more formal Wellingtonia, with its own cocktail bar and extensive carte. The first-floor library lounge provides a quiet retreat, while Parkers Club Bar Lounge is more convivial. Courtesy transport is provided to and from the airport.
122⇨ſ(6fb)⊁in 27 bedrooms CTV in all bedrooms ®⚡ T ✈ (ex guide dogs) ✱ sB⇨ſ£98-£118 dB⇨ſ£108-£128 (room only) ₱
Lift (500P ❊ ☐ (heated) ► 9 sauna solarium gymnasium dance studio jacuzzi croquet bowls ♪ xmas
♀ English & French V ✧ ⚏ ⊁ ✱ Lunch £15.50&alc Dinner £25&alc Last dinner 10.30pm
CONF. Thtr 500 Class 150 Board 20 Del £135
Credit Cards ① ② ③ ⑤

★★★★ 63% **The Copthorne**
Copthorne Way RH10 3PG (on A264, 2m E of A264/B2036 rbt) ☎Copthorne(0342) 714971 FAX (0342) 717375

Copthorne Hotels

Skilful extension of a 16th-century farmhouse has resulted in an attractive hotel with bedrooms ranging from luxurious suites and 'Connoisseur' rooms to the more compact 'Classic' style. Modern comforts abound in all. There are two restaurants and two bars, the Library Lounge for teas and snacks, the White Swan more 'pubby' in style. There is courtesy transport to Gatwick.
227⇨ſ(10fb)4⊞⊁in 34 bedrooms CTV in all bedrooms ®⚡ T ✱ sB⇨ſ£98-£118 dB⇨ſ£108-£128 (room only) ₱
Lift (CTV 300P ❊ squash sauna solarium gymnasium croquet putting petanque pit pool ♪ xmas
♀ English & Continental V ✧ ⚏ ⊁ ✱ Lunch £15-£22.95&alc Dinner £15.10-£16&alc Last dinner 10.30pm
Credit Cards ① ② ③ ⑤

★★★★ 62% **Holiday Inn Gatwick**
Langley Dr RH11 7SX (4m S of airport from M23 junct 10 take A264 following Horsham signs hotel at junct with A23)
☎Crawley(0293) 529991 FAX (0293) 515913

Holiday Inn

This comfortable, modern airport hotel operates a courtesy coach to Gatwick's two terminals. As well as the Colonnade restaurant, there is an all-day brasserie. Bedrooms are small, but well equipped and extensive room service is available. The Executive Club rooms are the best.
223⇨ſ(10fb)⊁in 80 bedrooms CTV in all bedrooms ® T sB⇨ſfr£68.50 dB⇨ſfr£68.50 (room only) ₱
Lift (♪ ☐ (heated) snooker sauna solarium gymnasium jacuzzi steam rooms games room pool xmas
V ✧ ⚏ ⊁ Lunch £12.95 High tea £1.65-£4.95 Dinner £17.50 Last dinner 11pm
CONF. Thtr 200 Class 100 Board 50 Del £120
Credit Cards ① ② ③ ④ ⑤

For key to symbols see the Bookmark.

★★★★ 61% **Ramada**
Povey Cross Rd RH6 0BE
☎Horley(0293) 820169 FAX (0293) 820259

260⇨ſ(5fb)1⊞⊁in 120 bedrooms CTV in all bedrooms ® T ✱ sB⇨ſ£65-£80 dB⇨ſ£65-£80 (room only)
Lift (⊞ 250P ❊ ☐ (heated) squash sauna solarium gymnasium ♨
♀ English & French V ✧ ⚏ ⊁ ✱ Lunch £12.50-£15.50&alc High tea £2.95-£27.20alc Dinner £15.50&alc Last dinner 10pm
Credit Cards ① ② ③ ④ ⑤

★★★ 64% **Chequers Thistle**
Brighton Road, Horley RH6 8PH (on A23)
☎Horley(0293) 786992 FAX (0293) 820625

THISTLE HOTELS

This Tudor coaching inn has been considerably extended to provide a range of smart, modern bedrooms. The character of the original building has been retained in the Halfway Halt Buttery and Bar, which is open all day for informal meals, snacks and drinks. The restaurant is elegant and intimate, and room service is another option. There is a courtesy bus service to the airport.
78⇨ſ(2fb)⊁in 26 bedrooms CTV in all bedrooms ® T ✈ (ex guide dogs) ✱ sB⇨ſ£79 dB⇨ſ£89 (room only) ₱
(190P ⇨
♀ International V ✧ ⚏ ⊁ ✱ Lunch £10.95-£11.75&alc Dinner £16.95-£17&alc Last dinner 9.45pm
CONF. Thtr 60 Class 24 Board 30 Del £95
Credit Cards ① ② ③ ④ ⑤

★★★ 62% **Gatwick Concorde**
Church Rd, Lowfield Heath, Crawley RH11 0PQ (0.5m S, off A23)
☎Crawley(0293) 533441 FAX (0293) 535369

Queens Moat Houses

➤→

★★★AA
THE CHEQUERS
THISTLE HOTEL

Brighton Road, Horley, Gatwick RH6 8PH
Tel: 0293 786992 Fax: 0293 820625

Your choice at
Gatwick

For Reservations at over 100
Mount Charlotte Thistle Hotels
Telephone London: 071 937 8033.

Gatwick Airport (London) - Gifford

This popular modern hotel has been extensively upgraded in recent years. Comfortable bedrooms are well furnished and equipped, meals are available from the brasserie and adjacent bar, and service is friendly and helpful.
121⇨(7fb) CTV in all bedrooms ® T ✱ sB⇨£49.50-£75 dB⇨£49.50-£90 (room only) 🅿
Lift (⊞ 137P (Residents free)
♡ English, French & Italian V ♿ ⌕ Bar Lunch £2-£3.95 Dinner £6.50-£13.95&alc Last dinner 9.30pm
Credit Cards ①②③⑤ £

★★★ **59%** The George
High St RH10 1BS ☎Crawley(0293) 524215
FAX (0293) 548565

FORTE Heritage

The ancient gallows sign of The George spans the High Street and its original oak beamed interior dates back to the early 17th century. Bedrooms, some with half tester beds, are in the original building or a modern extension. Bar meals and a coffee lounge provide an alternative to the Shires Restaurant, which offers friendly service and daily fixed price and à la carte menus.
86⇨(3fb)🏛in 43 bedrooms CTV in all bedrooms ® T sB⇨£40-£54 dB⇨£40-£59 (room only) 🅿
(89P
V ♿ ⌕ Sunday Lunch £11.95-£13.95 Dinner £16.75-£17.95&alc Last dinner 9.30pm
Credit Cards ①②③⑤

★★★ **58%** Goffs Park
45 Goffs Park Road, Crawley RH11 8AX (Compass)
☎Crawley(0293) 535447 FAX (0293) 542050
Situated in a peaceful residential area close to Crawley town centre and convenient for the airport, this busy commercial hotel is steadily being upgraded. Comfortable modern bedrooms have a full range of facilities and there is a choice of bars, a conservatory lounge and spacious restaurant.
37⇨Annexe28⇨ CTV in all bedrooms ®⚲ T sB&B⇨fr£47.75 dB&B⇨fr£55.50
(92P xmas
♡ English & French V ♿ ⌕ Lunch fr£8.75 High tea fr£9.75 Dinner fr£13.50 Last dinner 9.30pm
CONF. Thtr 220 Class 100 Board 30 Del from £85
Credit Cards ①②③⑤ £

★ ★LANGSHOTT MANOR
Ladbroke Rd RH6 9LN
☎Crawley(0293) 786680
FAX (0293) 783905

Langshott Manor is a beautifully restored Elizabethan manor house, owned and run by Geoffrey and Patricia Noble, with the enthusiastic help of their son Christopher. The charming bedrooms are furnished with antiques, traditional pieces, attractive fabrics and the finest beds, enhanced by dried flowers, interesting books and bric-à-brac. There is an oak-panelled living rooms with roaring log fires, and a delightful dining room with a communal table (though private dining rooms are also available). Together, Patricia and Christopher prepare a short daily menu with 4 choices at each stage – all simply presented and freshly cooked. Our inspector enjoyed a smooth duck liver and pistachio paté, followed by a chunky beef entrecôte, and Marsala crème brûlée to finish. There is a short, well chosen wine list. The family and staff go out of their way to anticipate guests' needs, providing hot water bottles, morning tea, room service and trips to the airport, for example.

7⇨ CTV in all bedrooms T ✖ (ex guide dogs)
sB⇨£78-£88 dB⇨£98-£128 (room only) 🅿
18P ⛳ ❀ croquet badminton
♡ English & French ⌕ ✱ Lunch fr£20 Dinner fr£25 Last dinner 9.30pm
Credit Cards ①②③⑤ £

Forte Crest
North Terminal RH6 0PH ☎(0293) 567070 FAX (0293) 567739

A large modern hotel with a wide range of services and amenities, designed particularly for the business traveller. Bedrooms are smart, comfortable and well equipped. For more details about Forte Crest hotels, consult the Contents page, under Hotel Groups.
468⇨ ✱ B⇨£89 (room only)
CONF. Thtr 370 Class 200 Board 25 Del £115

Forte Posthouse
Povey Cross Rd RH6 0BA ☎Horley(0293) 771621
FAX (0293) 771054

FORTE Posthouse

Suitable for both the business and leisure traveller, this bright hotel provides modern accommodation in well equipped bedrooms with en suite bathrooms. For more details about Forte Posthouse hotels, consult the Contents page, under Hotel Groups.
210⇨ ✱ B⇨£41.50-£53.50 (room only)
CONF. Thtr 120 Class 70 Board 60 Del £89

GIFFNOCK Strathclyde Renfrewshire Map 11 NS55

★★★ **63%** Macdonald Thistle
Eastwood Toll G46 6RA (junc of A77 and A726)
☎041-638 2225 FAX 041-638 6231

THISTLE HOTELS

Positioned on the southernmost fringe of Glasgow's suburbs, this business and function hotel offers medium sized bedrooms, a comfortable restaurant and cocktail bar, and a popular lounge bar.
56⇨(1fb) CTV in all bedrooms ® T
(200P sauna solarium gymnasium games room
♡ International ♿ ⌕
Credit Cards ①②③④⑤

See advertisement under GLASGOW

GIFFORD Lothian East Lothian Map 12 NT56

★★ **68%** Tweeddale Arms
EH41 4QU ☎(062081) 240 FAX (062081) 488

CONSORT HOTELS

The black and white exterior of this 18th-century country inn beside the village green is enhanced by colourful window boxes and hanging baskets. Modern comforts are effectively combined with old world charm in public areas which include an inviting lounge, an attractive restaurant and a well stocked cocktail bar; bedrooms, though compact, are both comfortable and modern.
16⇨(2fb) CTV in all bedrooms ® T sB&B⇨fr£47.50 dB&B⇨fr£65 🅿
✦ snooker xmas
V ♿ ⌕ Lunch fr£12.50 High tea fr£6.50 Dinner fr£18.50 Last dinner 9pm
CONF. Thtr 60 Class 30 Board 30 Del from £70
Credit Cards ①②③ £

Hotels with red star ratings are especially high quality.

Gillan - Glasgow

GILLAN Cornwall & Isles of Scilly Map 02 SW72

★★★ **65%** *Tregildry*
TR12 6HG ☎Manaccan(032623) 378
Closed late Oct-Etr

A family-run, whitewashed hotel in a tranquil location high above Falmouth Bay, Tregildry offers good public areas which include a comfortable lounge and spacious bar. Several of the clean, bright, well kept bedrooms have lovely views. Food is honest and service cheerful and willing.

10⇌♪(2fb)✻in all bedrooms CTV in all bedrooms ®
CTV 20P ♣ ❋ boat hire windsurfing
♀ International ◊ ♫ ✗ Last dinner 8pm
Credit Cards [1][3]

GILLINGHAM Dorset Map 03 ST82

★★ ❀❀❀⛴ STOCK HILL COUNTRY HOUSE
Stock Hill SP8 5NR (3m E on B3081 off A303)
☎(0747) 823626 FAX (0747) 825628

All aspects of this hotel mark it out for excellence: the tranquillity of the grounds, always undergoing improvement; the warmth of the welcome; the high levels of service, which still include early morning tea, and Peter Hauser coming from the kitchen to carry the bags; the exemplary housekeeping; the generous, robust cuisine, which features much produce from the walled kitchen garden, and of course the comfort and style of the bedrooms and public areas. The Hausers spare no effort to ensure the comfort of their guests; equally they indulge their unique taste in decor – exhilarating and extravagant to some, outrageous to others, but never dull. Peter Hauser offers a daily changing set price menu of 4 courses. Many dishes have an Austrian touch – wise guests will look out for these – with consommé as a middle course, escalope of chicken in breadcrumbs, game dishes and some splendid rich Torten.

8⇌♪Annexe1⇌1☐ CTV in all bedrooms T ✗ ❋
sB&B⇌♪£80-£90 dB&B⇌♪£160-£210 (incl dinner) 🍴
25P ♣ ❋ ♪ (hard) croquet nc7yrs *xmas*
♀ English, Austrian & French V ✗ ❋ Lunch £18.50 Dinner £26.50 Last dinner 8.45pm
Credit Cards [1][3][5]

GILLINGHAM Kent Map 05 TQ76

Pavilion Lodge
Rainham ME8 8PQ ☎Medway(0634) 377317 FAX (0634) 360848
(For full entry see Farthing Corner Motorway Service Area (M2))

GIRVAN Strathclyde *Ayrshire* Map 10 NX19

★★ **63%** *King's Arms*
Dalrymple St KA26 9AE ☎(0465) 3322 FAX (0465) 5463

This town centre hotel attracts mainly commercial and short stay custom. It has 2 bars, a foyer lounge and a small dining room.
25⇌♪(6fb) CTV in all bedrooms ® ⚑ T ✗ (ex guide dogs)
(100P 1🎱 (£2) snooker
♀ Scottish & French V ◊ ♫
Credit Cards [1][3]

GISBURN Lancashire Map 07 SD84

★★★ ❀**63%** **Stirk House**
BB7 4LJ (W of village, on A59) ☎(0200) 445581 FAX (0200) 445744

Situated in rural surroundings, this privately owned 16th-century manor house has been enlarged and extended over the years. Bedrooms vary in size and style, but most are fairly functional if well equipped. In contrast, the public areas are cosy, and the elegant restaurant is the setting for enjoyable meals, carefully prepared by chef Keith Blackburn, using fresh local produce such as Goosnargh duck breast served with Bailey's cream sauce.

36⇌♪Annexe12⇌♪(2fb)1☐ CTV in all bedrooms ® ⚑ T
✗ (ex guide dogs) ❋ sB⇌♪£35-£45 dB⇌♪£40-£60 (room only) 🍴
(100P ♣ ▥ (heated) squash sauna solarium gymnasium
♀ English & French V ◊ ♫ ✗ Lunch £11.50-£26.50 Dinner £18&alc Last dinner 9.30pm
CONF. Thtr 250 Class 60 Board 45 Del from £60
Credit Cards [1][2][3][4][5]

GITTISHAM Devon Map 03 SY19

★★★ ❀❀⛴**68%** **Combe House**
EX14 0AD ☎Honiton(0404) 42756 & 43560 FAX (0404) 46004

RS Jan-Feb

Surrounded by rolling parkland, this impressive Elizabethan manor house has been run by the Boswell family for the last 22 years and is popular for its house party atmosphere. Bedrooms are individual and cosy, and the lounges show much artistic flair. Mark Boswell does the cooking, producing an interesting selection which may include a hearty home-made soup or twice baked cheese soufflé, followed, perhaps, by a nicely pink rack of lamb with a combination of onions, red and yellow peppers surrounded by port wine jus.

15⇌2☐ CTV in all bedrooms T sB&B⇌♪£63-£100 dB&B⇌♪£97-£135 🍴
50P 1🎱 (£3 per night) ♣ ❋ ♪ croquet ◊ *xmas*
♀ English & French V ◊ ♫ ✗ Dinner fr£20alc Last dinner 9.30pm
CONF. Thtr 34 Board 22
Credit Cards [1][2][3][5]

GLAMIS Tayside *Angus* Map 15 NO34

★★★ ❀⛴**73%** *Castleton House*
DD8 1SJ (3m W on A94) (SCOTLAND'S HERITAGE HOTELS) ☎(030784) 340 FAX (030784) 506
Closed 1 Jan

Standing in its own grounds, this Victorian country house has a relaxing atmosphere enhanced by charming young staff. Bedrooms are comfortably furnished with quality reproduction pieces. There is an elegant small dining room, but dinners are generally served in the attractive if somewhat less formal conservatory. William Little cooks in a modern style with dishes such as Cajun roasted fillet of red snapper with tomato jus and roasted red peppers.

6⇌♪ CTV in all bedrooms ® T ✗ (ex guide dogs)
15P ♣ ❋ putting green
♀ European V ◊ ♫ ✗ Last dinner 9.30pm
Credit Cards [1][2][3]

GLASGOW Strathclyde *Lanarkshire* Map 11 NS56

★★★★★ ❀**63%** *Glasgow Hilton*
1 Williams St G3 8HT ☎041-204 5555

This striking building – 20 storeys of polished granite and mirrored glass – is Glasgow's newest hotel. The focal point inside is the lofty

Glasgow

marble-floored reception lounge, which gives access to various places to eat and drink: Minsky's, the American-style deli; the Raffles bar, with an eastern colonial theme; Camerons Restaurant, the country house-style restaurant which is the showcase for chef Ferrier Richardson's modern style cooking. Bedrooms are spacious and well equipped.
319⇨ⓃCTV in all bedrooms®✱sB⇨Ⓝfr£115-£140 dB⇨ⓃΓ£115-£140 (room only) 🍴
⊞ P ⌘ (heated) sauna gymnasium
✺ International
CONF. Thtr 1100 Class 800 Board 400 Del £125
Credit Cards ①②③④⑤

★★★★✿✿70% **Moat House International**
Congress Rd G3 8QT ☎041-204 0733 FAX 041-221 2022

This impressive 18-storey mirrored glass building – one of the tallest in Scotland – has spacious open plan public areas contained behind tall sloping glass walls which look onto the River Clyde. In a central position is The Mariner Restaurant. The best of Scotland's seafood, meats and game are cooked in the modern style. A gâteau of spinach, ricotta cheese and langoustines with a tomato and basil fondue was an innovative starter. The pan roasted saddle of venison with a rich cognac and redcurrant gravy was tender and well balanced. Alternatively, the Pointhouse Restaurant offers a wide range of dishes and a first class buffet.
284⇨Ⓝ(45fb)⊁in 40 bedrooms CTV in all bedrooms®✻T Lift ⓃCTV 300P ✿ ⌘ (heated) sauna solarium gymnasium ♫
✺ International V ✿ ⌘ ✻ Last dinner 10.30pm
Credit Cards ①②③④⑤

★★★★60% **Glasgow Thistle**
36 Cambridge St G2 3HN ☎041-332 3311 FAX 041-332 4050

Right in the city centre, with its own multi-storey car park, this hotel has very spacious de luxe bedrooms and studio rooms which are not much smaller. There are 2 restaurants, the formal one having its own cocktail bar. The hotel is committed to a heavy tour trade during the summer months.
307⇨Ⓝ(66fb)⊁in 60 bedrooms CTV in all bedrooms®✻T✱ sB⇨Ⓝ£85-£95 dB⇨ⓃΓ£100-£110 (room only) 🍴
Lift Ⓝ 250🚗 xmas
✺ Scottish & American V ✿ ⌘ ✱ Lunch £14.50&alc Dinner £18.50&alc Last dinner 11.30pm
CONF. Thtr 1500 Class 800 Del from £85
Credit Cards ①②③④⑤

★★★
✿✿
ONE DEVONSHIRE GARDENS
1 Devonshire Gardens
G12 0UX ☎041-339 2001 & 041-334 9194 FAX 041-337 1663

Situated in a fashionable tree-lined Victorian terrace, 3 adjoining town houses (not internally linked) have been sympathetically restored to create one of the most distinctive and stylish hotels in the city. Enthusiastic owner Ken McCulloch firmly believes in putting people first and personal service is provided by the friendly young staff. Bedrooms are all very different, with bold, even dramatic colour schemes, fine French cherry wood furnishings and splendid Victorian-style bathrooms. Some may find the external access to the various public areas a little irksome, though the level of comfort does to a large extent compensate.

The candlelit restaurant provides an intimate setting for chef Andrew Fleming's short but imaginative 4-course set price menu. Andrew cooks in the modern style and produces some interesting and honest combinations. The wine list is comprehensive and well chosen.
27⇨Ⓝ(3fb)9🍴CTV in all bedrooms✻T
Ⓝ 12P 🚗
✺ French V ⌘ Last dinner 10pm
Credit Cards ①②③④⑤

★★★✿75% **Devonshire**
5 Devonshire Gardens G12 0UX ☎041-339 7878 FAX 041-339 3980
This fine Victorian terraced house, not to be confused with its neighbour, One Devonshire Gardens, is a delightful hotel with a country house atmosphere. Guests are given personal attention and the elegant bedrooms, some very spacious, are comfortable and have all modern amenities. Drinks are served in the relaxing lounge, there being no bar, and a 3-course dinner is available, in addition to 24-hour room service.
14⇨Ⓝ(3fb)1🍴CTV in all bedrooms✻T sB&B⇨Ⓝ£90-£120 dB&B⇨ⓃΓ£100-£150 Continental breakfast 🍴
Ⓝ P xmas
✺ Scottish & French V ✿ ⌘ Lunch £15-£20&alc Dinner £19.50-£25&alc Last dinner 9.45pm
CONF. Thtr 50 Class 50 Board 24 Del from £105
Credit Cards ①②③④⑤

★★★70% **The Copthorne**
George Square G2 1DS (take junct 15 from M8 follow signs City Centre/George Sq, travel along Cathedral St past Strathclyde University, turn left into Hanover St) ☎041-332 6711 FAX 041-332 4264

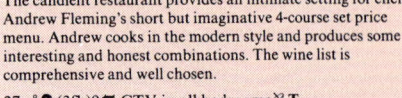

Situated right next to Queen Street Station, this hotel has been completely upgraded since its North British Hotel days, but retains some of its fine traditional features. The lofty Connoisseur bedrooms and suites have antique furnishings and elegant bathrooms. The restaurant shares a split-level, open-plan area with a popular café bar and has a conservatory area overlooking George Square. Staff are friendly and attentive throughout.
141⇨Ⓝ(1fb)1🍴⊁in 14 bedrooms CTV in all bedrooms®T ✱ (ex guide dogs) sB⇨Ⓝ£92-£104 dB⇨ⓃΓ£104-£130 (room only) 🍴
Lift Ⓝ ⌘ xmas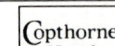
✺ International V ✿ ⌘ ✱ Lunch £12.95-£15.95&alc Dinner £12.95-£15.95&alc Last dinner 10pm
CONF. Thtr 100 Class 40 Board 40 Del from £89
Credit Cards ①②③⑤

★★★✿69% **Town House**
West George St G2 1NG ☎041-332 3320 FAX 041-332 9756
An elegant hotel, in the centre of the city, the Town House was once the Glasgow School of Music, and there are many reminders of its former use. Foremost is the ornate Music Room Restaurant, with its minstrels' gallery – a delightful setting for the cuisine provided by chef Paul McGurl and his team. Bedrooms are spacious and very comfortable.
34⇨Ⓝ(2fb)2🍴⊁in 10 bedrooms CTV in all bedrooms®T ✱ (ex guide dogs) sB⇨Ⓝ£80-£90 dB⇨ⓃΓ£90-£110 (room only) 🍴
Lift Ⓝ xmas
✺ Scottish & French V ✿ ⌘ ⊁ Lunch £12-£16 Dinner £14-£19 Last dinner 9.45pm
CONF. Thtr 120 Class 80 Board 40 Del from £110
Credit Cards ①②③⑤

Glasgow

★★★ 65% Tinto Firs Thistle
470 Kilmarnock Rd G43 2BB ☎041-637 2353
FAX 041-633 1340

Purpose-built to provide well equipped bedrooms and a comfortable cocktail lounge, this business and function hotel stands beside the A77 on the south side of the city.
28⇌ ↑(4fb)⊁in 2 bedrooms CTV in all bedrooms ® T ✱
sB&B⇌↑£70-£75 dB&B⇌↑£70-£85 ⊟
((46P ✿
♀ International V ✿ ⊑ ⊁ Lunch £7.95-£9.95&alc High tea £4.95-£6.50 Dinner fr£16.50&alc Last dinner 9.45pm
CONF. Thtr 200 Class 50 Board 50 Del from £85
Credit Cards [1][2][3][4][5] £

★★★❀63% Ewington
132 Queens Dr, Queens Park G42 8QW ☎041-423 1152
FAX 041-422 2030

Improvements are ongoing at this privately owned hotel, situated on the south side overlooking a public park. There is a comfortable lounge, restaurant and cocktail lounge. Modern fabrics have been used to good effect in the refurbished bedrooms, which vary in size.
42⇌↑(2fb)⊁in 4 bedrooms CTV in all bedrooms ® T
sB&B⇌↑£50-£65 dB&B⇌↑£70-£80 ⊟
Lift ((CTV 18P snooker *xmas*
♀ International V ✿ ⊑ Lunch £6-£8 High tea £5-£6 Dinner £12.50-£15&alc Last dinner 9pm
CONF. Thtr 40 Class 30 Board 30 Del from £60
Credit Cards [1][2][3][5] £

★★★ 62% Swallow
517 Paisley Rd West G51 1RW (off junc 23 of M8) ☎041-427 3146 FAX 041-427 4059

Built in the 70s, this business and conference hotel saw much upgrading in the late 80s, resulting in a leisure club and inviting ➡

★★★★AA
THE GLASGOW
THISTLE HOTEL

Cambridge Street, Glasgow G2 3HN
Tel: 041-332 3311   Fax: 041-332 4050

**Your choice in
Central Glasgow**

For Reservations at over 100
Mount Charlotte Thistle Hotels
Telephone London: 071 937 8033.

THISTLE HOTELS

★★★AA
TINTO FIRS
THISTLE HOTEL

Kilmarnock Road, Glasgow G43 2BB
Tel: 041-637 2353   Fax: 041-633 1340

**Your choice in
Glasgow**

For Reservations at over 100
Mount Charlotte Thistle Hotels
Telephone London: 071 937 8033.

THISTLE HOTELS

THE
EWINGTON
HOTEL
★★★ ❀

An elegant
Townhouse Hotel
situated in
Glasgow's South
Side overlooking
the beauty of
Queen's Park.

**132 QUEENS DRIVE
GLASGOW · SCOTLAND
Tel 041 423 1152
Fax 041 422 2030**

PERSONALITY HOTELS IN SCOTLAND

Glasgow

public areas, including a smart lobby, spacious bar lounge and a restaurant with the most comfortable chairs one could hope to find. Bedrooms, though well equipped, vary in size and comfort.
117⇨🏠(1fb)⊁in 34 bedrooms CTV in all bedrooms ®♎T✱ sB&B⇨🏠fr£80 dB&B⇨🏠fr£92 🅿
Lift ⓒ 150P 🖼 (heated) sauna solarium gymnasium jacuzzi steam room *xmas*
♍ Scottish & French V ♤ ⚏ ⊁ ✱ Lunch £4.50-£9.25 Dinner £15.95&alc Last dinner 9.30pm
CONF. Thtr 380 Class 200 Board 60 Del from £80
Credit Cards 1️⃣ 2️⃣ 3️⃣ 5️⃣ £

★★★ 61% Sherbrooke Castle
11 Sherbrooke Av, Pollokshields G41 4PG ☎041-427 4227 FAX 041-427 5685

This baronial mansion is in a residential area on the southwest side of the city. Family run, it offers a more informal atmosphere than most larger hotels. Bedrooms are available in bungalow and chalet buildings in the grounds as well as in the main hotel.
10⇨🏠Annexe11⇨🏠(3fb)🔒⊁in 2 bedrooms CTV in all bedrooms ®♎T✱ sB&B⇨🏠£45-£79.50 dB&B⇨🏠£50-£125 🅿
ⓒ CTV 50P ✿
♍ English & French V ♤ ⚏ ⊁ ✱ Lunch £8.50-£10.50&alc High tea £5.50&alc Dinner £16.50&alc Last dinner 9.45pm
CONF. Thtr 180 Class 140 Board 40 Del from £80
Credit Cards 1️⃣ 2️⃣ 3️⃣ 5️⃣ £

★★★ 60% Carrick
377 Argyle St G2 8LL ☎041-248 2355 FAX 041-221 1014

This modern business hotel, formerly the Glasgow Crest, has bright attractive public areas and well equipped bedrooms. It is on the western edge of the city centre, with concessionary parking in a multi-storey car park 5 minutes walk away.
121⇨🏠⊁in 79 bedrooms CTV in all bedrooms ® T ✱ (ex guide dogs) ✱ sB⇨🏠£40-£60 dB⇨🏠£40-£60 (room only) 🅿
Lift ⓒ ℘ *xmas*
♍ Continental V ♤ ⚏ ⊁ ✱ Bar Lunch £5.50-£6.50alc Dinner £11.05-£20.30alc Last dinner 9.45pm
CONF. Thtr 75 Class 40 Board 24 Del from £60
Credit Cards 1️⃣ 2️⃣ 3️⃣ 4️⃣ 5️⃣

★★★ 58% Central
99 Gordon St G1 3SF (exit 19 of M8, left into Argyle St and left into Hope St) ☎041-221 9680 FAX 041-226 3948

Popular for conferences and tour groups, this imposing Victorian railway hotel has an entrance on Central Station, with undercover access to an adjacent multi-storey car park. Several of the well equipped bedrooms overlook the station concourse and there is a carvery supplemented by a small carte.
221⇨🏠(10fb)⊁in 60 bedrooms CTV in all bedrooms ®♎T✱ sB⇨🏠£55-£67 dB⇨🏠£69.50-£82 (room only) 🅿
Lift ⓒ 🖼 (heated) sauna solarium gymnasium hair & beauty salon steamroom *xmas*
♍ European V ♤ ⊁ ✱ Lunch £9.85&alc High tea £3.50-£10alc Dinner £12.50&alc Last dinner 9.30pm
CONF. Thtr 600 Class 170 Board 120 Del from £91
Credit Cards 1️⃣ 2️⃣ 3️⃣ 5️⃣ £

★★★ 58% Jurys Pond
Great Western Rd G12 0XP (W of city, off A82) ☎041-334 8161 FAX 041-334 3846

On the northwest outskirts of the city, this purpose built hotel attracts a mixed market including tours. Bedrooms are well equipped and their rather uniform appearance is being enhanced by attractive soft furnishings, though bathrooms remain dated.

134⇨🏠(6fb)⊁in 55 bedrooms CTV in all bedrooms ® T ✱ (ex guide dogs) ✱ sB⇨🏠£62.50 dB⇨🏠£62.50 (room only) 🅿
Lift ⓒ CTV 200P ✿ 🖼 (heated) sauna solarium gymnasium whirlpool *xmas*
♍ Scottish & European V ♤ ⚏ ⊁ ✱ Lunch £8.95&alc Dinner £14.95&alc Last dinner 10pm
Credit Cards 1️⃣ 2️⃣ 3️⃣ 5️⃣ £

★★★ 57% Kelvin Park Lorne
923 Sauchiehall St G3 7TE ☎041-334 4891
FAX 041-337 1659

On the western edge of the city centre, this hotel offers a wide range of accommodation. The best are the superior and executive rooms in the Apsley wing, while the others are mostly compact. There is a spacious formal restaurant where a pianist occasionally plays.
98⇨🏠(7fb)🔒⊁in 9 bedrooms CTV in all bedrooms ®♎T sB⇨🏠£40-£95 dB⇨🏠£50-£95 (room only) 🅿
Lift ⓒ 40🛏 🎵 *xmas*
♍ Scottish & French V ♤ ⚏ ⊁ ✱ Lunch £11.95-£13.95&alc High tea £6-£10 Dinner £16.95-£18.50&alc Last dinner 10.30pm
CONF. Thtr 300 Class 150 Board 180 Del from £80
Credit Cards 1️⃣ 2️⃣ 3️⃣ 5️⃣ £

★★★ 55% The Buchanan
185 Buchanan St G1 2JY (behind Queen St railway station, take second left) ☎041-332 7284 FAX 041-333 0635

Appealing to the commercial and tour group markets, within walking distance of Central Station and right next to Buchanan Street Underground, the Buchanan has an Italian restaurant and a quiet bar. Bedrooms vary in size and comfort and several have deluxe bathrooms. Light sleepers may find the rumble of the underground irritating.
60⇨🏠⊁in 4 bedrooms CTV in all bedrooms ® T ✱ (ex guide dogs) ✱ sB&B⇨🏠£35-£55 dB&B⇨🏠£50-£70
Lift ⓒ ℘
♍ International V ♤ ✱ Lunch fr£6.15&alc Dinner fr£10.75&alc Last dinner 9pm
Credit Cards 1️⃣ 2️⃣ 3️⃣ 5️⃣

Forte Crest
Bothwell St G2 7EN ☎041-248 2656 FAX 041-221 8986

A large modern hotel with a wide range of services and amenities, designed particularly for the business traveller. Bedrooms are smart, comfortable and well equipped. For more details about Forte Crest hotels, consult the Contents page, under Hotel Groups.
251⇨🏠✱ B⇨🏠£99 (room only)
CONF. Thtr 850 Class 450 Board 70 Del £125

Marriott
500 Argyle St, Anderston G3 8RR (off junct 19 of M8) ☎041-226 5577 FAX 041-221 9202

A large and busy hotel, which is ideal for the business and leisure traveller, offering a wide range of services, a choice of eating options and indoor leisure facilities. Bedrooms are comfortable and equipped with modern facilities. For more details about Marriott hotels, consult the Contents page, under Hotel Groups.
298⇨🏠✱ dB⇨🏠fr£109 (room only)
CONF. Thtr 720 Class 450 Board 48 Del £125

Rosettes range from 5 for outstanding cuisine to 1 rosette for enjoyable, well prepared food

Glasgow Airport

GLASGOW AIRPORT Strathclyde *Renfrewshire*
Map 11 NS46

★★★**65%** **Glynhill Hotel & Leisure Club**
Paisley Rd PA4 8XB (2m E of A741, off junc 27 of M8)
☎041-886 5555 FAX 041-885 2838
Considerably extended over the years, this hotel has been in the same family ownership since it opened with only 22 bedrooms in 1970. The 50 executive rooms are particularly impressive, the larger ones having sitting areas and spa baths. Light sleepers would be well advised to ask for a room at the back of the hotel to avoid disturbance from the floodlighting, which for security reasons remains on through the night.
125⇨♠(34fb)2🏠✂in 51 bedrooms CTV in all bedrooms ®⚲
T sB&B⇨♠£69-£94 dB&B⇨♠£79-£104 ♫
(200P 30🚗 ⬛ (heated) snooker sauna solarium gymnasium spa bath steam room ♪ *xmas*
♨ International V ✿ ⚒ ✂ Lunch £9.75-£11.25&alc Dinner £14.50-£19.95&alc Last dinner 10.30pm
Credit Cards ①②③⑤ (£)

★★★**61%** **Dean Park**
91 Glasgow Road, Renfrew PA4 8YB (3m NE A8) ☎041-886 3771 FAX 041-885 0681

Queens Moat Houses

Within easy reach of the airport, this purpose built hotel is popular with tour groups as well as business people. Some of the older bedrooms are rather functional but all are well equipped. Public rooms are presently being extended and upgraded.
120⇨♠(4fb) CTV in all bedrooms ® **T** ✱ sB&B⇨♠£66 dB&B⇨♠£86
(200P ✿ solarium
♨ French V ✿ ⚒ Lunch £9.50 Dinner £13.95&alc Last dinner 9.45pm
CONF. Thtr 350 Class 150 Board 100 Del from £60
Credit Cards ①②③⑤ (£)

GLASGOW
CENTRAL HOTEL

For business or pleasure stay friendly

Central Hotel, Gordon Street, Glasgow G1 3SF.

AA ★★★

Premier Plus Rooms. Parking nearby. Leisure centre. Located in the heart of the city, with superb communication links. The ideal location for business or pleasure.

FOR RESERVATIONS (office hours) FREEPHONE
0800 591910
or call direct on 041-221 9680 Fax: 041-226 3948
It pays to stay Friendly

G

THE *Glynhill* HOTEL
AND LEISURE CLUB   AA★★★

The gateway to Scotland hotel offering businessmen and tourists alike a quality product and service. Facilities range from Diplomat Suites, American-style bedrooms, convention centre, gourmet and carverie restaurants, all complemented by a luxurious leisure centre. Private excellent value, well located hotel for the West of Scotland. Glasgow International Airport 1 mile.
THE GLYNHILL HOTEL AND LEISURE CLUB
169 Paisley Road, Renfrew PA4 8XB *(300 yds M8 J27)*
Tel: (041) 886 5555 Fax: (041) 885 0681

★★★AA
THE MACDONALD
THISTLE HOTEL

Eastwood Toll, Giffnock G46 6RA
Tel: 041-638 2225   Fax: 041-638 6231

Your choice in Giffnock/Glasgow

For Reservations at over 100
Mount Charlotte Thistle Hotels
Telephone London: 071 937 8033.

Glasgow Airport - Glenfarg

★★ 59% Rockfield
125 Renfrew Road, Paisley PA3 4EA (2m SE off A741, off junc 27 of M8) ☎041-889 6182 FAX 041-889 9526
Closed 2 days Xmas & 2 days New Year
Most of the bedrooms are in a rear extension to this comfortable commercial hotel, and although furnishings are rather dated and functional, an effort has been made by providing extras such as fresh fruit and mineral water.
20⇌♠(1fb)1⌑ CTV in all bedrooms ® T sB&B⇌♠fr£48 dB&B⇌♠fr£65 ♬
50P
☼ Scottish & European ♡ ⤴ Bar Lunch fr£6 High tea fr£6 Dinner fr£11.50&alc Last dinner 9.30pm
CONF. Thtr 50 Board 30
Credit Cards ① ② ③ ⑤

Forte Crest
Abbotsinch PA3 2TR ☎041-887 1212 FAX 041-887 3738

A large modern hotel with a wide range of services and amenities, designed particularly for the business traveller. Bedrooms are smart, comfortable and well equipped. For more details about Forte Crest hotels, consult the Contents page under Hotel Groups.
300⇌♠

Forte Posthouse
North Barr PA8 6AN ☎041-812 0123 FAX 041-812 7642

Suitable for both the business and leisure traveller, this bright hotel provides modern accommodation in well equipped bedrooms with en suite bathrooms. For more details about Forte Posthouse hotels, consult the Contents page, under Hotel Groups.
166⇌♠* B⇌♠£41.50-£53.50 (room only)
CONF. Thtr 600 Class 400 Board 40 Del £89.50

GLASTONBURY Somerset Map 03 ST53

★★ ❀❀75% No.3 Restaurant & Hotel
3 Magdalene St BA6 9EW ☎(0458) 832129
Closed Jan
This ivy covered Georgian house adjoins the abbey ruins, and owners John and Ann Tynan devote their energies into making it a rather special hotel: bedrooms are individually designed with style and flair, with such thoughtful extras as fresh fruit and flowers. There is a small cocktail bar and a comfortable residents' lounge.
3⇌Annexe3⇌♠ CTV in all bedrooms ® T ✼ (ex guide dogs)
8P ⌑ ✣
☼ English & French V ♡ ⤴ Last dinner 9pm
Credit Cards ① ③

★★ 60% George & Pilgrims
1 High St BA6 9DP ☎(0458) 831146 FAX (0458) 832152

The stone frontage and mullioned windows of this ancient hostelry overlook the busy High Street, and a municipal car park is usefully situated at the rear. Food is served in a traditional pub bar or an informal brasserie. Some bedrooms retain their old beams and confessional chambers.
14⇌♠(1fb)3⌑ CTV in all bedrooms ® T ✻ sB&B⇌♠£40-£45 dB&B⇌♠£50-£75 ♬
5P
V ♡ ⚏ ✼ Lunch £3.95-£10 Dinner £3.95-£10 Last dinner 10.30pm
Credit Cards ① ② ③ ⑤

GLENBORRODALE Highland *Argyllshire* Map 13 NM66

★★★ ❀❀⤴78% Glenborrodale Castle
PH36 4JP (on B8007, W of Glenborrodale) ☎(09724) 266 FAX (09724) 224
Closed Nov-Etr
(Rosettes awarded for dinner only)
This fine, restored baronial mansion of red sandstone stands in carefully recreated grounds amid the rugged splendour of Britain's most western peninsula. Opened as an hotel in 1993, the listed building exhibits the highest standards of decoration and furniture. Bedrooms, vary in size, but all have the expected facilities and many thoughtful extras; State Rooms feature spacious seating areas, and many of the bathrooms have claw foot/roll top baths. The intimate dining room serves a range of dishes based on local fish, meat and game, and a starter of red mullet might well precede sliced loin of lamb with a garnish of crispy sweetbreads and Madeira sauce, this perhaps being followed by a light hot apple and sultana soufflé. Friendly, attentive service and a tranquil setting make it easy to unwind here.
14⇌♠Annexe2⇌♠4⌑ CTV in all bedrooms ® T sB&B⇌♠£105-£155 dB&B⇌♠£160-£260 Continental breakfast
CTV 16P 4⇌ ⌑ ✣ ♪ (hard) ⚓ sauna solarium gymnasium croquet beauty therapist masseuse
☼ British & French V ♡ ⚏ ⤴ Lunch £19.50 High tea £8.50 Dinner £32.50 Last dinner 9pm
Credit Cards ① ② ③

GLENCOE Highland *Argyllshire* Map 14 NN15

★★ 64% Glencoe
PA39 4HW (on A82 in Glencoe village, 15m S of Fort William) ☎Ballachulish(08552) 245 & 673 FAX (08552) 492
Surrounded by loch and mountain scenery, this long established family-run hotel stands at the west end of the village. It offers a well stocked cocktail bar, comfortable foyer lounge and bright modern bedrooms of varying size.
15⇌♠(4fb) CTV in all bedrooms ® ⚏ T
30P ✣ games room
V ♡ ⚏ Last dinner 9.30pm
Credit Cards ① ② ③ ⑤

GLENEAGLES

See **Auchterarder**

GLENFARG Tayside *Perthshire* Map 11 NO11

★★ 64% Bein Inn
PH2 9PY (on B996) ☎(0577) 830216
Closed 26-28 Dec
This long-established roadside inn has a cosy lounge bar, a foyer lounge with real fires in cooler months and a characterful cellar bar open during the summer season. Most bedrooms are in a purpose-built extension, the best being 4 large studio rooms with their own front doors.
9rm(7⇌)Annexe4⇌♠(4fb) CTV in all bedrooms ® T ✼ (ex guide dogs) sB&B⇌£24-£29.50 sB&B⇌♠£39.50-£53 dB&B⇌£46-£53 dB&B⇌♠£55-£68 ♬
60P ⌑ ✣
☼ Scottish, English & French V ♡ ⚏ ⤴ Lunch £10-£14.50alc Dinner £14.50-£21alc Last dinner 9.30pm
Credit Cards ① ③
See advertisement under PERTH

★★ 61% Glenfarg
Main St PH2 9NU ☎(0577) 830241 FAX (0577) 830665
This holiday hotel is ideal for golfers, offering information on local courses and arranging rounds for guests. A good range of bar meals supplements the dinners served in the dining room, real ale is on tap, and there is a beer garden beside the small stream behind the hotel.

Glenfarg - Glossop

15⇨↑(2fb) CTV in all bedrooms ®⚹✻ sB&B⇨↑£25.50 dB&B⇨↑£51 ₧
39P ❀ ॐ xmas
V ✿ ⚲ ✗ Lunch £5.25 High tea £6.45 Dinner £12.95 Last dinner 9pm
Credit Cards £

GLENRIDDING Cumbria Map 11 NY31

★★★ 60% Ullswater
CA11 0PA ☎(07684) 82444 FAX (07684) 82303

This attractive Lakeland stone building stands in 18 acres of well kept grounds on the shore of Ullswater. The hotel provides a good standard of comfortable accommodation. There is a spacious lounge, and the attractive restaurant serves an inviting range of dishes. Service is friendly and attentive.

48⇨↑(4fb)1₧ CTV in all bedrooms ® T sB&B⇨↑fr£45 dB&B⇨↑fr£90 ₧
Lift CTV 200P ❀ ▶ 9 ♩ solarium ♫ ॐ xmas
☺ English & French V ✿ ⚲ ✗ Lunch fr£9.95 High tea fr£5.25 Dinner fr£16 Last dinner 9.30pm
CONF. Thtr 100 Class 50 Board 50 Del from £55
Credit Cards £

See advertisement under ULLSWATER

★★ 66% Glenridding
CA11 0PB ☎(07684) 82228 FAX (07684) 82555

The Glenridding Hotel is in the centre of the village with a stream leading down to the lakeside. Most of the well-equipped bedrooms have excellent views. There are 3 lounges, one with a small library, another an 8ft snooker table. The hotel continues to improve each year, and a good choice 4-course set dinner is available.

44⇨↑(6fb)1₧ CTV in all bedrooms ® T sB&B⇨↑£49-£52 dB&B⇨↑£78-£82 ₧
Lift 40P billiards library ♫ xmas
V ✿ ⚲ ✗ Bar Lunch £4.50-£5.50 Dinner £20.75-£22 Last dinner 9.30pm
Credit Cards £

GLENROTHES Fife Map 11 NO20

★★★ 69% Balgeddie House
Balgeddie Way KY6 3ET (from M90 junct 3 take A92. Enter town then over two rbts and 1st left after garage for Cedham Rd. At 2nd rbt into Fortmanthills Rd then 3rd left)
☎(0592) 742511 FAX (0592) 621702
Closed 1 & 2 Jan

This fine, small country mansion is set in 7 acres of grounds to the northwest of the town. Bedrooms vary in size and style, the most spacious on the first floor, the most stylish on the second. Public areas are more traditional in style and include a cocktail bar, comfortable lounge and candlelit dining room. Bar food is also available in a separate inn in the grounds.

18⇨↑(3fb) CTV in all bedrooms ®⚹ T ✻ (ex guide dogs) ✻ sB⇨↑£55-£65 dB⇨↑£75-£90 (room only) ₧
CTV 100P ❀ ∪ pool table
☺ Scottish & French V ✿ ⚲ ✗ Lunch £8-£16.50&alc High tea fr£4.25 Dinner £11.50-£16.50&alc Last dinner 9.30pm
Credit Cards £

★★ ❀70% Rescobie
Valley Dr, Leslie KY6 3BQ (Logis) ☎(0592) 742143 FAX (0592) 620231
RS 25 Dec

Set in 2 acres of gardens on the western edge of Leslie, this refurbished Edwardian country house offers a peaceful atmosphere. Bedrooms vary in size and style, but public areas retain much of the original character of the house and include a comfortable lounge

with a live fire, a cosy tartan themed cocktail bar and a candlelit dining room where chef Angus MacLeod offers a good choice of freshly prepared dishes featuring Scottish produce.

10⇨↑ CTV in all bedrooms ® T ✻ (ex guide dogs) ✻ sB&B⇨↑£48-£52 dB&B⇨↑£60-£70 ₧
20P ⊞ ❀ ॐ
☺ International V ✿ ⚲ Lunch £10 Dinner £16&alc Last dinner 9pm
CONF.
Credit Cards

★★ 56% Greenside
High St, Leslie KY6 3DA (2m W A911) ☎(0592) 743453
Closed 1 Jan

Situated in the main street at Leslie, this family-owned commercial hotel offers modest functional accommodation. Public areas include a choice of bars and a traditional first floor dining room.

12rm(9⇨↑) CTV in all bedrooms ® sB&B£32 sB&B⇨↑£42 dB&B£49 dB&B⇨↑£56 ₧
(CTV 50P ⊞
V ✿ Lunch £3.40-£7.50 Dinner £10.50&alc Last dinner 9pm
Credit Cards £

GLENSHEE (SPITTAL OF) Tayside *Perthshire*
Map 15 NO16

★★ 65% Dalmunzie House
PH10 7QG (off A93) ☎Glenshee(0250) 885224 FAX (0250) 885225
Closed Nov-27 Dec

An attractive, turreted house, situated in 6,000 acres of its own private glen with hills rising steeply to either side and a river running through. Very much the home of its proprietors, who welcome guests warmly, it is a great favourite with families. Many bedrooms have lovely views, and all are refreshing in their décor and furnishing.

18rm(16⇨↑) sB&B⇨↑£31-£51 dB&B⇨↑£62-£83 ₧
Lift CTV 30P ⊞ ⊞ ❀ ▶ 9 ♪ (hard) ♩ clay pigeon shooting xmas
✿ ⚲ Bar Lunch fr£1.80alc Dinner £15-£19 Last dinner 8.30pm
Credit Cards £

GLEN SHIEL (SHIEL BRIDGE) Highland *Ross & Cromarty*
Map 14 NG91

★★ 64% Kintail Lodge
IV40 8HL (on A87, at head of Loch Duich)
☎Glenshiel(059981) 275 FAX (059981) 226
Closed 24 Dec-2 Jan RS Nov-Mar

Improvements continue at this former shooting lodge, set on the shore of Loch Duich and surrounded by magnificent scenery. Bedrooms, many with fine loch views, vary in shape and size but are comfortable if modest. Light lunches and teas are served in the conservatory.

12rm(7⇨3↑)(2fb) CTV in all bedrooms ® sB&B£42-£49 sB&B⇨↑£44-£53 dB&B£84-£98 dB&B⇨↑£88-£106 (incl dinner) ₧
20P ⊞ ❀ ♫
☺ Scottish & French V ✿ ⚲ ✗ Bar Lunch £2.50-£10alc Dinner £18 Last dinner 8.30pm
Credit Cards

GLOSSOP Derbyshire Map 07 SK09

★★ 73% Wind in the Willows
Derbyshire Level, off Sheffield Rd SK13 9PT (off A57)
☎(0457) 868001 FAX (0457) 853354

Comfort, quality and a relaxed atmosphere are the hallmarks of this Victorian country house, pleasantly set in 5 acres of grounds adjacent to the local golf course. Traditional furnishings and open fires enhance the atmosphere of relaxed comfort.

Glossop - Goathland

11⇨♠(1fb)1🏥 CTV in all bedrooms ® T ✗ (ex guide dogs)
✽ sB&B⇨♠£52-£70 dB&B⇨♠£62-£90
16P 🚗 ✿ nc10yrs
❦ Dinner fr£17.50 Last dinner 7.30pm
Credit Cards 1 2 3 5

GLOUCESTER Gloucestershire Map 03 SO81

★★★ ❋76% **Hatton Court**
Upton Hill, Upton St Leonards GL4 8DE (3m SE B4073)
☎(0452) 617412 FAX (0452) 612945
A 17th-century manor house, Hatton Court enjoys spectacular views across the Severn Valley. Bedrooms are supplied with back massagers, Beatrix Potter books, plastic ducks and teddy bears. Public areas include a lounge, bar and attractive restaurant where chef Tony Warburton offers table d'hôte and à la carte menus. Attention to detail is the key here and we have received many letters of commendation from our members regarding this hotel.
17⇨♠Annexe28⇨♠2🏥 CTV in all bedrooms ® T ✗ (ex guide dogs) sB&B⇨♠£75-£85 dB&B⇨♠£90-£99 🍽
🥂 75P ✿ ☼ (heated) sauna solarium croquet *xmas*
♔ English & French V ✧ ♨ ✽ Lunch fr£14&alc Dinner fr£19.75&alc Last dinner 10pm
CONF. Thtr 50 Class 30 Board 30 Del from £99.50
Credit Cards 1 2 3 5

★★★ 69% **Bowden Hall Resort**
Bondend Ln, Upton St Leonards GL4 8ED (3m SE) ☎(0452) 614121 FAX (0452) 611885

An elegant Georgian property, extended and recently refurbished to provide modern comforts. The accommodation is attractively decorated and good use has been made of soft furnishings. Public areas include a comfortable drawing room, an adjacent bar and a restaurant.
72⇨♠(19fb)2🏥⚘in 14 bedrooms CTV in all bedrooms ®⚲ T ✽ sB⇨♠£75-£85 dB⇨♠£85-£95 (room only) 🍽
🥂 150P ✿ ☼ (heated) ♪ sauna solarium gymnasium
V ✧ ♨ ✽ Lunch £7.95-£14.95&alc High tea fr£4.25 Dinner fr£14.95&alc Last dinner 9.30pm
CONF. Thtr 80 Class 50 Board 12 Del £115
Credit Cards 1 2 3 4 5   £

★★★ 61% **Hatherley Manor**
Down Hatherley Ln GL2 9QA (on A38, off junc 11 of M5)
☎(0452) 730217 FAX (0452) 731032
A 17th-century manor with recent additions, the Manor has modern, well equipped bedrooms which are comfortable, though some are compact. There are bright open-plan public rooms and service is by a friendly team; reception is noticeably hospitable.
56⇨♠🏥 CTV in all bedrooms ® T ✽ (ex guide dogs)
🥂 350P ✿ gymnasium
♔ English & French V ✧ ♨ Last dinner 9.45pm
Credit Cards 1 2 3 4 5

★★ 61% **Twigworth Lodge**
Tewkesbury Rd, Twigworth GL2 9PG (on A38, 1m N from junc with A40) ☎(0452) 730266 FAX (0452) 730099
Twigworth Lodge, originally dating from the Regency period, is a mainly commercial hotel. Accommodation varies from functional bedrooms to more spacious rooms with pastel décor and modern furnishings. There is a large lounge area, bar and the Coach House Restaurant.
30⇨♠(3fb) CTV in all bedrooms ® T ✽ sB&B⇨♠£29-£50 dB&B⇨♠£44-£60 🍽
50P ✿ ☼ (heated)
♔ European V ✧ ♨ Sunday Lunch £5.95-£7.45 Dinner £7.45-£10&alc Last dinner 10pm
CONF. Thtr 40 Class 16 Board 22 Del from £50
Credit Cards 1 2 3 5   £

★ 64% **Rotherfield House**
5 Horton Rd GL1 3PX (adjacent to Royal Hospital)
☎(0452) 410500
A substantial Victorian building on the road to the Royal Hospital, about a mile from the city centre, has been modernised to provide neat bedrooms of varying size and style. Hospitable owners Alan and Juliet Eacott give friendly personal service.
13rm(8♠)(2fb) CTV in all bedrooms ® T ✽ sB&B£17-£19.25 sB&B♠£28.95 dB&B♠£39.50 🍽
CTV 9P 🚗
♔ English & Continental V ✧ ♨ ✂ ✽ Dinner £9.45&alc Last dinner 7.45pm
Credit Cards 1 2 3 5   £

Forte Crest
Crest Way, Barnwood GL4 7RX (on Barnwood bypass near M5) ☎(0452) 613311 FAX (0452) 371036

FORTE CREST

A large modern hotel with a wide range of services and amenities, designed particularly for the business traveller. Bedrooms are smart, comfortable and well equipped. For more details about Forte Crest hotels, consult the Contents page, under Hotel Groups.
123⇨♠ ✽ B⇨♠£89-£95 (room only)
CONF. Thtr 120 Class 70 Board 12 Del from £95

Travel Inn
Tewkesbury Rd, Longford GL2 9BE (on A38 between Longford and Gloucester)
☎(0452) 23519

Purpose-built accommodation offers spacious and well equipped bedrooms, all with en suite bathrooms. Meals may be taken at the nearby family restaurant and pub. For more details about Travel Inns, consult the Contents page, under Hotel Groups.
41⇨♠ ✽ B⇨♠£33.50 (room only)

Travel Inn
Witcombe GL3 4SS (on A417 towards Cirencester) ☎(0452) 862521

Purpose-built accommodation offers spacious and well equipped bedrooms, all with en suite bathrooms. Meals may be taken at the nearby family restaurant and pub. For more details about Travel Inns, consult the Contents page, under Hotel Groups.
39⇨♠ ✽ B⇨♠£33.50 (room only)

GLYN CEIRIOG Clwyd Map 07 SJ23

★★★ 62% *Golden Pheasant*
LL20 7BB ☎(069172) 281 FAX (069172) 479
Over 200 years old, this black and white, creeper-clad hotel is in a quiet part of the beautiful Ceiriog Valley. The Pheasant Bar still has a slab floor, and a chinoiserie-furnished cocktail bar serves the restaurant where a small fixed-price menu is offered. There is also a Victorian-style lounge. Bedrooms have pretty colour schemes and canopied beds.
18⇨♠(4fb)3🏥 CTV in all bedrooms ® T
45P ✿ ☾ game shooting during season ❦
♔ English, French & Italian V ✧ ♨ Last dinner 9pm
Credit Cards 1 2 3 5

GOATHLAND North Yorkshire Map 08 NZ80

★★ ❋71% **Mallyan Spout**
YO22 5AN ☎Whitby(0947) 86486 FAX (0947) 86427
This traditional stone built and ivy clad hotel, named after a small waterfall nearby, overlooks a wide village green where sheep roam, while from the rear are fine views of the beautiful Esk Valley. Comfortable and warm, it offers three spacious lounges, a cosy cocktail bar and a dining room serving many local dishes,

particularly seafood from nearby Whitby. Bedrooms are individually furnished and most attractively decorated.
20⇨Annexe4⇦2⌂ CTV in 20 bedrooms T sB&B⇨£45-£60 dB&B⇨£60-£120 ▯
50P ✿ xmas
♋ English & French V ♒ ⚓ ✂ ✱ Lunch fr£12.50&alc Dinner fr£18&alc Last dinner 8.30pm
CONF. Class 40 Board 30 Del £85
Credit Cards [1][3][5]

★★ 70% **Inn On The Moor**
YO22 5LZ ☎Whitby(0947) 86296 & 86410 FAX (0947) 86484
This relaxing hotel with attractive gardens overlooking the moors has comfortable public rooms and spacious bedrooms equipped with modern facilities, many of them with oak furniture made by a local craftsman.
24⇨⚌(2fb)6⌂ CTV in all bedrooms ® ℣ T sB&B⇨⚌£38.50-£50 dB&B⇨⚌£65-£72.50 ▯
CTV 30P ✿ putting hairdressing salon ⚘
V ♒ ⚓ ✱
CONF. Del from £55
Credit Cards [1][2][3]

★ 64% **Whitfield House**
Darnholm YO22 5LA (from village follow signs to Darnholm for 0.75m) *ExecGroup*
☎Whitby(0947) 86215
Closed 1 Dec-Jan
Tucked away in a corner of the tiny village, this small friendly hotel offers neat if compact accommodation.
8⇨⚌(1fb)✂in all bedrooms CTV in all bedrooms ® T sB&B⇨⚌£22-£25 dB&B⇨⚌£44-£50
10P ⚗ nc5yrs
♒ ⚓ ✂ Dinner £10-£14 Last dinner 6.30pm
Credit Cards [1][3]

GODALMING Surrey Map 04 SU94

★★ 64% **Inn on the Lake**
Ockford Rd GU7 1RH (on A2) (Logis)
☎Guildford(0483) 415575 FAX (0483) 860445
With pleasant grounds running down to a lake, this popular inn has a characterful bar and attractive restaurant. Modern extensions incorporate function rooms and individually furnished, quite spacious bedrooms, some with lake views.
20rm(17⇨⚌)1⌂ CTV in all bedrooms ® ℣ T ✱ sB&B£35-£45 dB&B⇨⚌£75-£85 ▯
100P ✿ croquet putting
♋ International V ♒ ⚓ ✱ Lunch £13.50-£16.50 High tea £6.50 Dinner £13.50-£16.50 Last dinner 10pm
Credit Cards [1][2][3][5]

GOLANT Cornwall & Isles of Scilly Map 02 SX15

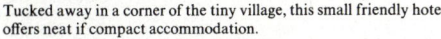
★★ ✿✿65% **Cormorant**
PL23 1LL (Logis) ☎Fowey(0726) 833426 FAX (0726) 833426
Closed first three wks Jan
Set on a steep hillside overlooking the Fowey Estuary, this personally run hotel has a friendly atmosphere. Traditional bedrooms with modern amenities all have panoramic views, as do the comfortable lounge and candlelit dining room. French chef Gilles Gaucher offers a fixed-price menu and a carte of skilfully prepared dishes, which features local seafood. Fowey scallops lightly fried in butter with fresh ginger, lime zest and sherry, and Cornish lamb in a light puff pastry case are recommended.
10⇨⚌✂in 6 bedrooms CTV in all bedrooms ® ℣ T sB&B⇨⚌£51-£61 dB&B⇨⚌£72-£84 ▯
20P ✿ ⚐ (heated) nc12yrs xmas
♋ English & French V ♒ ⚓ ✂ Bar Lunch £3-£15alc Dinner £21.50-£25&alc Last dinner 9pm
Credit Cards [1][2][3]

Inn on the Moor
GOATHLAND, NORTH YORKS MOORS
Country House Hotel in glorious scenic setting ideal for Heritage Coast.
York (only 45 minutes).
All en-suite rooms/direct dial phones.
Three bedroom family suite, seven bridal suites.
Low season rates. Summer special (7th night free).
Hairdressing salon.
Fully licensed. Open to non-residents.
'Heartbeat' country.
Proprietors: Malcolm & Judy Simpson.
Tel: 0947 86296 Fax: 0947 86484

★★ ⊛
Mallyan Spout Hotel
Goathland, Whitby
N Yorkshire
YO22 5AN
Tel: (0947) 86486
Fax: (0947) 86327

A stone-built, ivy clad building situated on the green of a beautiful Yorkshire village overlooking the wide expanses of the famous moors. The hotel takes its name from a small picturesque waterfall flowing into a wooded valley, a short walk below the hotel. Three spacious lounges command a view of the garden, moors and the beautiful Esk Valley, and in the winter you are warmed by roaring fires. Mallyan Spout is an ideal location for outdoor pursuits or peaceful pleasures of the fine food, good wines and friendly hospitality. 26 cottage style bedrooms with private bath including 4 new rooms with balconies and superb views.

Golspie - Gosport

GOLSPIE Highland *Sutherland* Map 14 NH89

★★58% **Golf Links**
KW10 6TT ☎(0408) 633408
This family-run hotel is situated beside the golf course and the sandy beach overlooking the Dornoch Firth. Bedrooms vary in size and have plain décor with a mixture of modest furnishings. There is a comfortable lounge overlooking the garden, and exposed stone walls are a feature of the neat dining room. Special golf packages are available.
9⇌ ℕ CTV in all bedrooms ® ✱ sB&B⇌ℕ£25 dB&B⇌ℕ£50 ♬
20P ✿ ❀
♀ Scottish & French V ◊ ♑ ✱ Bar Lunch £3-£9 Dinner £15.50-£19 Last dinner 8.30pm
Credit Cards [1][3]

GOMERSAL West Yorkshire Map 08 SE22

★★★66% **Gomersal Park**
Moor Ln BD19 4LT (off junc 26 of M62)
☎Bradford(0274) 869386 FAX (0274) 861042

Within its own wooded parkland, this hotel is ideally situated for access to both Leeds and Bradford. Its comfortable public areas include a well equipped leisure facility, attractive bedrooms with colour coordinated décor have been thoughtfully appointed to meet the traveller's needs, and service is particularly friendly.
52⇌ℕ(5fb) CTV in all bedrooms ®✱T ✖ (ex guide dogs) ✱ sB⇌ℕ£55-£70 dB⇌ℕ£70-£80 (room only)
(200P ✿ 🖼 (heated) sauna solarium gymnasium
V ◊ ♑ ✱ Lunch £8.95-£10.95&alc Dinner £13.95-£15.95&alc Last dinner 10pm
CONF. Thtr 120 Class 70 Board 40 Del from £79.50
Credit Cards [1][2][3][5]

GOODRICH Hereford & Worcester Map 03 SO51

★★58% **Ye Hostelrie**
HR9 6HX ☎Symonds Yat(0600) 890241
Many guests return year after year to this small family-run hotel, not far from the historic castle. It has a friendly atmosphere and the public areas provide traditional comforts, the bar being a popular meeting place for locals. Bedrooms are well decorated but modestly furnished in a mixture of modern and traditional styles.
8rm(2⇌5ℕ) CTV in all bedrooms ®
CTV 25P ✿ ❀ nc14yrs
♀ English & Continental V ◊ Last dinner 9pm
See advertisement under **ROSS-ON-WYE**

GOODRINGTON

See **Paignton**

GOODWOOD West Sussex Map 04 SU80

★★★67% **Goodwood Park Hotel, Golf & Country Club**
PO18 0QB ☎Chichester(0243) 775537 FAX (0243) 533802

This hotel, golf and country club, amid the 12,000-acre estate of Goodwood Park, is ideal for both leisure guests and conferences. The bedrooms range in style from coach house, courtyard, stable and original rooms; the Dukes Restaurant and the Circuit Bar adding a formal dimension. Chef Michael Oliver has set new standards of cooking, offering a daily fixed price and à la carte menu.
88⇌ℕ(3fb)1⊟ CTV in all bedrooms ®✱T ✖ (ex guide dogs)
✱ sB&B⇌ℕ£79-£129 dB&B⇌ℕ£94-£160 ♬
(CTV 300P ✿ 🖼 (heated) ℙ 18 ♗ (hard) squash snooker sauna solarium gymnasium beauty salon *xmas*

♀ English & French V ◊ ♑ ♒ ✱ Lunch £8.50-£29.95 High tea £1.95-£5 Dinner £18.50-£29.95 Last dinner 9.30pm
CONF. Thtr 120 Class 60 Board 60 Del from £89
Credit Cards [1][2][3][5]

GOOLE Humberside Map 08 SE72

★★61% **Clifton**
1 Clifton Gardens, Boothferry Rd DN14 6AL ☎(0405) 761336
FAX (0405) 762350
Proprietors John and Dorothy Hope, together with their staff, provide informal, attentive and friendly service. Bedrooms vary in size and have modern furnishings and equipment. Quite a lengthy list of popular dishes is provided in the cottage-style restaurant. There is also a small bar and a lounge with an open fire.
9rm(5⇌3ℕ)(1fb) CTV in all bedrooms ® T ✱ sB&B£25-£36 sB⇌ℕ£25-£36 dB&B⇌ℕ£37-£45 ♬
CTV 8P
♀ English & Continental V ◊ ♒ ✱ Lunch £7-£22.95alc Dinner £7-£22.95alc Last dinner 9pm
Credit Cards [1][2][3][5]

GORDANO MOTORWAY SERVICE AREA (M5) Avon Map 03 ST57

Forte Travelodge
BS20 9XG
☎Pill(027581) 3709 Central Res (0800) 850950

This modern building offers a good standard of accommodation for overnight stops. Smart, spacious and well equipped bedrooms, all with en suite bathrooms, are suitable for family use, and meals may be taken at the nearby family restaurant. For more details about Travelodges, consult the contents page, under Hotel Groups.
40⇌ℕ ✱ B⇌ℕ£31.95 (room only)

GOREY

See **Jersey** under **Channel Islands**

GORLESTON-ON-SEA

See **Yarmouth, Great**

GOSFORTH Cumbria Map 11 NY00

★★65% **Westlakes**
CA20 1HP (junc of A595 and B5344) ☎(09467) 25221
Set in attractive grounds outside the village, this family-run late Georgian country house offers warm personal service and has pleasantly furnished bedrooms with modern facilities, a comfortable lounge bar with open fires and a cosy 3-room restaurant offering a wide range of dishes.
6⇌ℕ(1fb) CTV in all bedrooms ® T ✱ sB&B⇌ℕ£45 dB&B⇌ℕ£48.50-£56
25P ✿ ❀
♀ English & French V ◊ ♑ ✱ Lunch £12-£19alc Dinner £12-£19alc Last dinner 8.30pm
Credit Cards [1][3]

GOSPORT Hampshire Map 04 SZ69

★★59% *Anglesey*
Crescent Rd, Alverstoke PO12 2DH ☎(0705) 582157 & 523932
FAX (0705) 502902
This friendly hotel in a Regency terrace between the seafront and town is gradually being improved under new management. Bedrooms, which vary in size, have been attractively refurbished and the popular bar lounge and restaurant are regaining a reputation for good wholesome food.
18⇌ℕ(1fb)1⊟ CTV in all bedrooms ® T

CTV 2🅦 (£1.50)
V ❦ Last dinner 9.30pm
Credit Cards [1] [2] [3]

GRANGE-OVER-SANDS Cumbria Map 07 SD47

★★★👥66% *Graythwaite Manor*
Fernhill Rd LA11 7JE ☎(05395) 32001 & 33755 FAX (05395) 35549
Closed 3-31 Jan
This beautiful old manor house is set in extensive grounds overlooking Morecambe Bay. The house is elegantly furnished, with many antiques, fresh flowers, and roaring log fires during the colder months. A 6-course dinner is provided each evening in the traditional dining room, where staff are caring and attentive. Bedrooms have good old-fashioned comforts plus modern amenities. The hotel has been in the same family since 1937.
21🛏🎔(2fb) CTV in all bedrooms ® T 🐾 (ex guide dogs)
18P 14🅦 (£1) ⚘ ♣ (hard) helicopter landing area putting
♁ English & French V ❦ ⛳ ✻ Last dinner 8.30pm
Credit Cards [1] [3]

★★★62% Grange
Station Square LA11 6EJ (opp Railway Station)
☎(05395) 33666 FAX (05395) 35064

Standing in extensive wooded grounds overlooking the town and Morecambe Bay, this large and friendly Victorian hotel has spacious, comfortable furnished public areas, including several dining rooms and lounge areas. Comfortable bedrooms of varying size are all well equipped.
41🛏🎔(6fb) CTV in all bedrooms ®☎ T ✻ sB&B🛏🎔£40-£50 dB&B🛏🎔£64-£72 🍴
《 CTV 100P ⚘ sauna solarium gymnasium 🐕 *xmas*
♁ English & French V ❦ ⛳ ✻ Bar Lunch £2-£10alc
CONF. Thtr 200 Class 100 Board 100 Del £69.50
Credit Cards [1] [2] [3] [5]

★★70% Netherwood
Lindale Rd LA11 6ET (on B5277 just before the station)
☎(05395) 32552 FAX (05395) 34121
A very impressive stone building in beautiful grounds with interesting topiary work, Netherwood has wide views over Morecambe Bay and beyond. There are extensive wood panelled lounges, and accommodation is provided in traditional rooms in the original building and executive rooms in the extension. A very good range of food is served, and the hotel is energetically run by the Fallowfield family who have been owners for many years.
29🛏🎔(5fb)🦮in 12 bedrooms CTV in all bedrooms ® T sB&B🛏🎔£41.75-£50.50 dB&B🛏🎔£83.50-£101 🍴
Lift 《 CTV 160P ⚘ 🏊 (heated) solarium gymnasium beauty salon spa bath & steam room 🐕
♁ English & French ❦ ⛳ ✻ Lunch £10.75-£13.50 High tea £8.75-£11.50 Dinner £18.25-£23 Last dinner 8.30pm
CONF. Thtr 150 Class 30 Board 40 Del from £75
Credit Cards [1] [3]

★★67% Hampsfell House
Hampsfell Rd LA11 6BG ☎(05395) 32567
Closed 25 & 26 Dec
This is an attractive family-run house, set in its own grounds and surrounded by woodland, yet close to the town centre. It provides friendly service and pleasant modern bedrooms; there is a cosy lounge and bar, and home-cooked dishes are offered in the dining room.
8🛏🎔(2fb) CTV in all bedrooms ® ✻ sB&B🛏🎔£22.50-£30 dB&B🛏🎔£39-£50 🍴
20P ⚘ ✻
❦ ⛳ ✻ Lunch £2.50-£7.50alc Dinner £13.50-£15 Last dinner 8.30pm
Credit Cards [1] [3]

★67% Clare House
Park Rd LA11 7HQ (turn off A590 onto B5277, through Lindale onto Grange, hotel 0.5m on left past Crown Hill/St Paul's Church) ☎(05395) 33026 & 34253
Closed Nov-Mar
In a lovely location overlooking Morecambe Bay, this friendly hotel has been owned and run by Mr and Mrs Read for many years. There are 2 comfortable lounges, and a well produced dinner is served each evening in the cosy restaurant. The bright, fresh bedrooms are a mixture of modern and more traditional styles.
17rm(16🛏🎔)(1fb) CTV in all bedrooms ® T
🐾 (ex guide dogs) sB&B🛏🎔£39.50-£42 dB&B🛏🎔£79-£84 (incl dinner) 🍴
18P ⚘ ♣ croquet putting nc5yrs
❦ ⛳ ✻ ✻ Lunch £5-£6 Dinner £20 Last dinner 7.15pm (£)

GRANTHAM Lincolnshire Map 08 SK93

★★★76% Swallow
Swingbridge Rd NG31 7XT (junc of A1 southbound with A607) ☎(0476) 593000 FAX (0476) 592592
Comfort and the quality of care are the outstanding features of this modern 2-storey hotel in a somewhat unprepossessing site between the A1, an industrial estate and residential blocks of flats. There is a warm, friendly atmosphere throughout, in surroundings which include open fires and rich fabrics. The restaurant has colourful wall hangings and screens, and offers a table d'hôte menu which includes a buffet and a joint of the day as well as a more sophisticated carte. Bedrooms are comfortable and pleasantly decorated.
90🛏🎔(6fb)🦮in 55 bedrooms CTV in all bedrooms ® T ✻ sB&B🛏🎔£65-£80 dB&B🛏🎔£75-£90 🍴
《 CTV 150P ⚘ 🏊 (heated) sauna solarium gymnasium steam rooms *xmas*

➡

Goodwood Park Hotel
Golf & Country Club
★★★

Goodwood, Chichester, West Sussex
PO18 0QB. Tel: (0243) 775537

Set amid the 12,000 acre Goodwood Estate, home to the Dukes of Richmond for 300 years.
• 88 bedrooms • 18 hole golf course • Extensive leisure facilities with poolside grill • 5 main meeting rooms • Wedding & Banqueting facilities
Direct reservations line (0345) 123333

Grantham - Grasmere

⚐ English & French **V** ⚑ ⚒ ✂ ✱ Lunch £8.50-£12.50&alc Dinner £17.25&alc Last dinner 10pm
CONF. Thtr 200 Class 90 Board 55 Del £105
Credit Cards [1][2][3][5]

★★★ **64%** Angel & Royal
High St NG31 6PN ☎(0476) 65816 FAX (0476) 67149

Dating back to the Knights Templar, about 750 years ago, this characteristic coaching inn has been converted to a small hotel providing polite and friendly service. Public areas are furnished in a style appropriate to its age and the restaurant, the ancient 'Chambre du Roi' with its stone walls, offers traditional British food as well as the occasional local dish. Bedrooms are decorated in pastel shades with comfortable seating in most of the larger rooms.
30⇨⚑✱in 10 bedrooms CTV in all bedrooms ® T ✱
sB⇨⚑£70-£75 dB⇨⚑£80-£85 (room only) 🍽
50P xmas
⚐ English & French **V** ⚑ ⚒ ✂ ✱ Lunch fr£9.95 Dinner fr£15.95&alc Last dinner 9pm
Credit Cards [1][2][3][5]

★★ **68%** Kings
North Pde NG31 8AU (on B1172)
☎(0476) 590800 FAX (0476) 590800

Set back from the road on the edge of the town, this extended Georgian building is personally run with friendly informality. Well furnished bedrooms of varying styles are all thoughtfully equipped and there is a restaurant plus the Orangery coffee shop, a spacious foyer lounge and smaller bar.
22rm(21⇨⚑)(1fb)⚑ CTV in all bedrooms ® T sB&B£25 sB⇨⚑£35-£45 dB⇨⚑£45-£56 🍽
(36P ✱ ♪ (hard) ♫
⚐ English & French **V** ⚑ ⚒ ✂ Lunch £9-£10.75&alc Dinner £10.75&alc Last dinner 10pm
CONF. Thtr 120 Class 60 Board 40 Del from £52.50
Credit Cards [1][2][3][5]

Forte Travelodge
Grantham Service Area NG32 2AB (4m N on A1)
☎(0476) 77500 Central Res (0800) 850950

This modern building offers a good standard of accommodation for overnight stops. Smart, spacious and well equipped bedrooms, all with en suite bathrooms, are suitable for family use, and meals may be taken at the nearby family restaurant. For more details about Travelodges, consult the contents page, under Hotel Groups.
40⇨⚑✱ B⇨⚑£31.95 (room only)

GRANTOWN-ON-SPEY Highland Morayshire Map 14 NJ02

★★★ **67%** Garth
Castle Rd PH26 3HN ☎(0479) 2836 & 2162 FAX (0479) 2116

Set in its own large garden beside the town square, this 17th-century house has been sympathetically extended and refurbished. Bedrooms are bright and well equipped, and there are cosy lounges, a well stocked cocktail bar and attractive split-level restaurant serving imaginative Taste of Scotland dishes. Willing staff provide friendly service.
17⇨⚑ CTV in all bedrooms ®⚒ T ✂ (ex guide dogs) ✱
sB&B⇨⚑£38-£47 dB&B⇨⚑£76-£84 🍽
22P ✱
⚐ French **V** ⚑ ⚒ ✂ Sunday Lunch £10 Dinner £22&alc Last dinner 8.30pm
Credit Cards [1][2][3][5]

★★ **63%** *Seafield Lodge*
Woodside Av PH26 3JN ☎(0479) 2152 FAX (0479) 2340
Closed 4 Nov-9 Dec
In a residential area near the town centre, this extended Victorian lodge is popular with tourists, sporting enthusiasts and business people alike. Some bedrooms are compact but all have modern facilities and the public rooms offer traditional comforts.
14⇨⚑ (2fb) CTV in all bedrooms ®
15P ⚒ ♪
V Last dinner 9pm
Credit Cards [1][3]

★ **73%** Tyree House
8 The Square PH26 3HF ☎(0479) 2615
This small family-run holiday and sporting hotel in the town square offers comfortable, well maintained accommodation, with compact but bright modern bedrooms, a cosy lounge and split-level bar and dining room.
9⚑(1fb) CTV in all bedrooms ® ✱ sB&B⚑fr£25 dB&B⚑fr£40
CTV 20P ⚒ ✱ xmas
V ⚑ ✱ Lunch £6-£9&alc High tea £6.60-£8alc Dinner £10-£15alc Last dinner 9pm
Credit Cards [1][3]

GRASMERE Cumbria Map 11 NY30

★★★★ **65%** Wordsworth
LA22 9SW ☎(05394) 35592 FAX (05394) 35765

This comfortable Lakeland stone hotel stands in its own grounds at the heart of the village, next to the churchyard where William Wordsworth is buried. Bedrooms are individually furnished and decorated, 2 suites offering 4-poster beds and whirlpool baths. There is a rear lounge overlooking the garden, a cosy bar with conservatory and a bright, fresh restaurant serving an extensive range of dishes. Attentive service is ably supervised.
37⇨⚑(3fb)3⚑ CTV in all bedrooms T ✂ (ex guide dogs)
sB&B⇨⚑£52-£58 dB&B⇨⚑£104-£136 🍽
Lift (60P ⚒ ✱ 🏊 (heated) sauna solarium gymnasium table tennis pool jacuzzi ♫ xmas
⚐ English & French **V** ⚑ ⚒ ✂ Lunch £18.50 Dinner £28-£29.50alc Last dinner 9pm
CONF. Thtr 100 Class 50 Board 40 Del from £78
Credit Cards [1][2][3][5]

MICHAEL'S NOOK COUNTRY HOUSE
LA22 9RP (on A591)
☎(05394) 35496 FAX (05394) 35765

A lovely country house set among the hills above Grasmere, Michael's Nook is an outstanding hotel with fine antiques and beautiful views. Staff are naturally friendly, making each guest feel personally welcome. However, as our inspector commented, owner Mr Gifford runs the hotel in idiosyncratic style and it feels more like a private home than a public hotel: you are likely to find the front door locked when you arrive, there are no pass keys to bedrooms, lunch is available only if bespoken in advance, and dinner is served at 8pm, with guests asked to order at least an hour earlier. In the kitchen, chef Kevin Mangeolles continues to gain in stature. Modern cuisine

A four-star luxury Hotel in the very heart of English Lakeland . . .

The
WORDSWORTH HOTEL
AND "PRELUDE RESTAURANT"

★★★★

GRASMERE, CUMBRIA
Tel: (05394) 35592. Fax: (05394) 35765

All bedrooms have bathrooms, colour TV, radio and telephone. There are spacious lounges and cocktail bar, indoor heated pool, jacuzzi, sauna, solarium, minigym, terrace and garden.

In the delectable "Prelude Restaurant" the finest fresh produce is skilfully presented on à la carte and table d'hôte menus. Non-residents most welcome.

Exceptional Conference and Banqueting Facilities.

Seafield Lodge Hotel
★★
Grantown-on-Spey, Moray
PH26 3JN
Tel: (0479) 2152   Fax: (0479) 2340

"VENUE FOR THE ARTHUR OGLESBY FLY FISHING COURSES"

Speyside's leading sporting and fishing hotel. Comfortable lounges and bar with log fires. Excellent "Best of Scotland" menu and bar meals. All rooms en suite with telephone etc. Two luxury suites with spa baths. Close to River Spey and golf course. Private fishing, golfing, shooting, skiing and horse riding arranged by the hotel.

G

The Square, Grantown on Spey, Morayshire
Telephone: (0479) 2615

Situated in the Square and sheltered by trees, ideal for family holidays. Only 10 minutes walk through the town for golf course, fishing, bowling green and tennis courts. Facilities for the sportsman with secure gun room and rod room. All nine bedrooms are tastefully decorated and have private facilities, TV and complimentary tea/coffee and biscuits. Comfortable residents lounge enjoys views across the square and is open at all times. Dinner can be provided in the à la carte restaurant open every evening. Ample parking. Full licence.

Proprietors: Roy & Vyvian Nelson

AA ★★★  # Garth Hotel

THE SQUARE, GRANTOWN ON SPEY
HIGHLAND PH26 3HN
Tel: 0479 2836 Fax: 0479 2116

Set amidst four acres of landscaped gardens, the Garth Hotel commands a picturesque location overlooking the historic square of Grantown on Spey in the heart of the Scottish Highlands.

This three star hotel dates back to the seventeenth century and offers olde worlde charm but with every modern comfort and convenience. Open all year round, the hotel's fourteen individually furnished bedrooms are all en suite and also offer direct dial telephone, satellite television, tea and coffee making facilities.

The hotel has an 'AA' rosette for food.

273

Grasmere

is his style and the honest, clean flavours most appealing. An impressive meal began with delicious asparagus mousse with marinated salmon, followed by delicate mushroom consommé and a main course of smoked fillet of beef with shallots and red wine sauce rounded off by a superb lemon chiffon pie.

14⇨🛏(2fb)1🚫 CTV in all bedrooms T ✝ ✳
sB&B⇨🛏fr£108 dB&B⇨🛏£152-£185 (incl dinner) 🍴
20P 🚗 ✿ croquet nc5yrs *xmas*
♀ English & French ✂ ✳
Credit Cards 1 2 3 5

★★★ 70% The Swan
LA22 9RF (on A591) ☎(05394) 35551 FAX (05394) 35741

FORTE Heritage

Over 300 years old, the Swan stands amid spectacular scenery close to the village on the A591. It has very well appointed bedrooms which include a welcoming glass of sherry, delightfully furnished lounges and an attractive restaurant. Staff are well trained, attentive and helpful.

36⇨🛏🛏in 11 bedrooms CTV in all bedrooms ® T ✳
sB⇨🛏£80-£85 dB⇨🛏£105-£120 (room only) 🍴
(40P 🚗 ✿ *xmas*
V ♂ ⚥ ✂ ✳ Lunch fr£8.50 Dinner fr£20&alc Last dinner 9pm
Credit Cards 1 2 3 5

★★★ 66% Prince of Wales
Kessick Rd LA22 9PR ☎(05394) 35666 FAX (05394) 35565

MOUNT CHARLOTTE THISTLE HOTELS

This very attractive Edwardian style building stands in a delightful position on the waters edge and has recently undergone extensive refurbishment. It now provides elegant and comfortable bedrooms with many thoughtful extras. Public areas are extensive and quite delightful, and a very good choice of dishes is available in the traditional style restaurant.

72⇨🛏(8fb)1🚫in 13 bedrooms CTV in all bedrooms ® ✳
sB&B⇨🛏£65 dB&B⇨🛏£85 🍴
(100P ✿ *xmas*
♀ International V ♂ ⚥ ✂ ✳ Bar Lunch £4.50-£6.50alc High tea £5 Dinner £16 Last dinner 8.45pm
Credit Cards 1 2 3 5

★★★ 🌹65% Gold Rill Country House

Red Bank Rd LA22 9PU (off A591) ☎(05394) 35486 FAX (05394) 35486

Closed Jan
(Rosette awarded for dinner only)

Delightfully situated in 2 acres of lawned gardens alongside the lake, this privately run hotel has a warm and friendly atmosphere. Public areas are spacious and comfortable, with open fires in winter, and attractively furnished bedrooms have views of the fells. Well prepared dinners using local produce are served in the elegant restaurant.

22⇨🛏(2fb) CTV in all bedrooms ® T ✳ sB&B⇨🛏£32-£55 dB&B⇨🛏£64-£110 (incl dinner) 🍴
35P 🚗 ✿ ⛳ (heated) putting green croquet lawn *xmas*
V ♂ ✳ Dinner £18.20 Last dinner 8.30pm
Credit Cards 1 3

★★★ 64% Red Lion
Red Lion Square LA22 9SS ☎(05394) 35456 FAX (05394) 34167

CONSORT HOTELS

This popular former coaching inn at the centre of the village offers bedrooms of a high standard. Comfortable public areas have much character and an extensive range of food is available in the bar, buttery or restaurant.

35⇨🛏(3fb) CTV in all bedrooms ® T
Lift 38P ✿

V ♂ ⚥ ✂ Last dinner 9pm
CONF. Thtr 55 Board 28 Del from £69
Credit Cards 1 2 3 5

★★ 🌹69% Oak Bank
Broadgate LA22 9TA ☎(05394) 35217

ExecGroup

Closed Xmas-Jan

This friendly family-run hotel close to the village centre has generally spacious bedrooms with comfortable furnishings, comfortable lounges and a restaurant with a bright conservatory extension. Here Mrs Savasi's well produced 4-course dinners include such dishes as eggs florentine, home-made soup, trout with rosemary, and apple and gooseberry pie.

14⇨🛏(1fb)2🚫 CTV in all bedrooms ® T ✳ sB&B⇨🛏£25-£45 dB&B⇨🛏£50-£90 🍴
CTV 14P 🚗 ✿
♀ English & Continental V ♂ ⚥ ✂ ✳ Bar Lunch £2-£6 Dinner £15-£17 Last dinner 8pm
Credit Cards 1 3

★★ 67% Grasmere
Broadgate LA22 9TA ☎(05394) 35277 FAX (05394) 35277

ExecGroup

Closed Jan-8 Feb

This personally owned and run family hotel at the village centre, surrounded by beautiful scenery, serves a well produced 4-course dinner in its very attractive rear dining room and offers good all-round standards of comfort and service.

12⇨🛏3🚫 CTV in all bedrooms ® T ✳ sB&B⇨🛏£30-£42 🍴
14P 🚗 ✿ nc7yrs *xmas*
♀ English & French V ♂ ✂ Dinner £17 Last dinner 8pm
Credit Cards 1 3

★❀❀ WHITE MOSS HOUSE
Rydal Water LA22 9SE
☎(05394) 35295
Closed mid Nov-mid Mar

Many guests return year after year to Susan and Peter Dixon's small Lakeland hotel, an 18th-century house once owned by William Wordsworth and standing in its own wooded grounds overlooking Rydal Water. Bedrooms are attractive, and there is one in a cottage in the grounds, 10 minutes walk from the hotel. Guests can take afternoon tea or a relaxing aperitif in the delightful lounge with its open fire, chintzy seating and colourful flowering plants. Peter Dixon's adventurous cooking gets better and better, and he produces a daily fixed-price menu, with choices only at the cheese and pudding stages. The wine list, with some fine vintages reflects his passion for good wine.

5⇨🛏Annexe2⇨🛏1🚫 CTV in all bedrooms ✂ T ✝
sB&B⇨🛏£39-£59 dB&B⇨🛏£78-£120 🍴
10P 🚗 ✿
✂ Dinner fr£25 Last dinner 8pm
Credit Cards 1 3

The AA's star rating scheme is the market leader in hotel classification.

Grassington - Gretna (with Gretna Green)

GRASSINGTON North Yorkshire Map **07** SE06
★**66%** *Black Horse*
Garrs Ln BD23 5AT ☎(0756) 752770
This delightful, family-run former coaching inn, now over 200 years old, is situated in one corner of the cobbled village square. Bedrooms are attractive, and a wide ranging dinner menu is offered as well as hearty bar meals.
11⇨🛏(1fb)2🛌 CTV in all bedrooms ®
CTV 2P
♀ ✿ Last dinner 9.30pm
Credit Cards 1 3

GRAVESEND Kent Map **05** TQ67
★★★**72%** *Quality Manor*
Hever Court Rd, Singlewell DA12 5UQ (A2, eastbound)
☎(0474) 353100 FAX (0474) 354978
This new, privately owned hotel has a range of smartly furnished bedrooms with plush easy chairs, quality fabrics and modern bathrooms. The tiled entrance foyer leads to a small open-plan lounge area and lounge bar, while the restaurant has a more intimate atmosphere and offers an extensive Continental 'carte' as well as a competitively priced daily menu. Room service is available 24 hours and early travellers are provided with a substantial buffet breakfast from 4am.
39⇨🛏(3fb)1🛌⊁in 12 bedrooms CTV in all bedrooms ®♺ T
✗ (ex guide dogs) ✱ sB&B⇨🛏£49.50-£125 dB&B⇨🛏£49.50-£125 (room only)
(CTV 110P ⚙ ⬚ (heated) sauna steam room *xmas*
♀ English, French & Italian V ✿ ⅍ ⊁ Bar Lunch £4.50-£12 Dinner £13-£25.80alc Last dinner 9.30pm
CONF. Thtr 210 Class 140 Board 30 Del £87.50
Credit Cards 1 2 3 5

GRAYS Essex Map **05** TQ67
★★★**67%** *Stifford Moat House*
High Rd, North Stifford RM16 1UE (from M25 junct 30/31 east on A13, signed Grays, and in 1m at rbt onto A1012 for Grays. At rbt left for hotel on right)
☎Grays Thurrock(0375) 390909 FAX (0375) 390462
Closed 27-30 Dec
Set in well maintained and quiet gardens, this extended Georgian property offers two standards of accommodation, the newer Garden wing providing higher levels of comfort and more facilities. The Regency Restaurant offers a good choice of dishes from its carte and set menus.
96⇨🛏(12fb)⊁in 16 bedrooms CTV in all bedrooms ® T
sB&B⇨🛏£47-£75 dB&B⇨🛏£65.50-£95 (room only) 🍴
Lift (130P ✱ ♪ (hard) croquet petanque ♫ *xmas*
♀ International V ✿ ⅍ ⊁ Lunch £10.95-£17.50&alc Dinner £17.50&alc Last dinner 10pm
CONF. Thtr 120 Class 48 Board 50 Del from £67.50
Credit Cards 1 2 3 4 5

GREAT Places incorporating the word 'Great' will be found under the actual place name – eg Great Yarmouth is listed under Yarmouth, Great.

GREENFORD Greater London
See LONDON plan 1 *B4*
★★★**70%** *The Bridge*
Western Av UB6 8ST (on A40) ☎081-566 6246 FAX 081-566 6140
This pub has been developed and extended into a smart and comfortable hotel. The spacious, double glazed bedrooms have been designed with an eye to detail, and the modern bathrooms include good showers. Public areas, with a choice of bars, are a relaxing blend of old and new. Staff are well turned out and cheerful.

68⇨🛏2🛌⊁in 44 bedrooms CTV in all bedrooms ®♺ T ✱
sB&B⇨🛏£50-£80 dB&B⇨🛏£55-£90
Lift (CTV 68P
♀ English & French V ✿ ⅍ ✱ Lunch fr£10.95&alc Dinner fr£14.95 Last dinner 10pm
CONF. Thtr 130 Class 60 Board 60 Del £100
Credit Cards 1 2 3 5

GREENLAW Borders *Berwickshire* Map **12** NT74
★★🍴**63%** *Purves Hall*
TD10 6UJ (4m SE off A697)
☎Leitholm(089084) 558

Peacefully situated in 10 acres of wooded parkland, this comfortable Edwardian country house gives fine views south to the Cheviot Hills. Traditionally furnished bedrooms vary in size from compact to spacious and attractive public areas include a relaxing lounge and elegant dining room.
7⇨🛏(1fb) CTV in all bedrooms ® T
20P ⚙ ✱ ⬚ (heated) ♪ (hard) croquet putting
♀ International ✿ ⅍ Last dinner 8.45pm
Credit Cards 1 2 3 5

GRETNA (WITH GRETNA GREEN) Dumfries & Galloway *Dumfriesshire* Map **11** NY36
★★**66%***Solway Lodge*
Annan Rd CA6 5DN ☎Gretna(0461) 38266
FAX (0461) 37791
Closed 25 & 26 Dec RS 10 Oct-Mar
This friendly, family-run hotel offers well kept accommodation in either attractively furnished superior rooms in the main house or in motel-style annexe rooms. There is a spacious and popular lounge

GOLF COURSES IN BRITAIN AND IRELAND

The essential guide for the enthusiastic golfer on the move, whether travelling on business, on holiday, or in search of new courses to play - the AA guide to

Golf Courses in Britain and Ireland

includes useful details of over 2000 courses

About 250 new courses - including many due to open

Special Feature - Do Those Golden Fairways Always Harvest Megabucks?

AA

Gretna (with Gretna Green) - Grindleford

bar, and a cosy residents' lounge. Reasonably priced meals are offered in both the bar and restaurant.
3⇌🌙Annexe7⇌🌙2🛏 CTV in all bedrooms ® T ✱
sB&B⇌🌙£35-£48 dB&B⇌🌙£49-£75
25P 🚗
V ♥ ♨ ⌘ Last dinner 9pm
Credit Cards 1 2 3 5

★★★**62% Garden House**
Sarkfoot Rd CA6 5EP ☎(0461) 37621 FAX (0461) 37692
21⇌🌙(2fb)4🛏 CTV in all bedrooms ® ⚥ T ✈ (ex guide dogs)
✱ sB&B⇌🌙£39 dB&B⇌🌙£80 🍴
105P ✿ xmas
♨ Continental V ♥ ♨ ⌘ Lunch £4.95-£30 High tea £20.50-£30
Credit Cards 1 2 3 4 5

★★**60% Gretna Chase**
CA6 5JB (0.25m S on B721) ☎Gretna(0461) 37517
Closed Jan
Standing on the English side of the Border beside the River Sark, the hotel's award winning gardens and proximity to the motorway make it popular with wedding groups. Bedrooms range in size and style from compact with modern fittings to spacious with brass or half-tester beds.
9rm(3⇌3🌙)1🛏 CTV in all bedrooms ® ✈ (ex guide dogs)
40P ✿
♨ English & French V ♥ Last dinner 8.30pm
Credit Cards 1 2 3 5

Forte Travelodge
CA6 5HQ (on A74, northbound) ☎Gretna(0461) 37566 Central Res (0800) 850950

This modern building offers a good standard of accommodation for overnight stops. Smart, spacious and well equipped bedrooms, all with en suite bathrooms, are suitable for family use, and meals may be taken at the nearby family restaurant. For more details about Travelodges, consult the Contents page, under Hotel Groups.
41⇌🌙✱ B⇌🌙£31.95 (room only)

GRIMSBY Humberside Map 08 TA20

★★★**59% St James**
St James' Square DN31 1EP ☎(0472) 359771
FAX (0472) 241427

This red-brick 1970s hotel in the town centre next to the main shopping areas has a convivial atmosphere created by the friendly staff. Bedrooms are well equipped with modern amenities, and food is available throughout the day.
125⇌🌙(6fb)⌘in 20 bedrooms CTV in all bedrooms ® T
sB⇌🌙£50 dB⇌🌙£50 (room only) 🍴
Lift ⓒ 100P sauna gymnasium ♫
V ♥ ♨ ⌘ Lunch £7.50-£16.50 Dinner £7.50-£16.50 Last dinner 10pm
Credit Cards 1 2 3 5

★★★**56% Yarborough**
Bethlehem St DN31 1LY (next to Grimsby Railway Station)
☎(0472) 242166 FAX (0472) 242266
Built in the classical style of the Victorian railway companies, the Yarborough is now undergoing a major refurbishment. Public areas include a choice of bars, one a very large public bar with pool tables and gambling machines. Situated next to the railway station, the hotel is convenient for most town centre amenities.
51⇌🌙(2fb)⌘in 2 bedrooms CTV in all bedrooms ® T ✱
sB&B⇌🌙£32.50-£42.50 dB&B⇌🌙£45-£55
Lift ⓒ 10P
V ♥ ♨ ✱ Bar Lunch £1.25-£6.90 Dinner £8.50-£12.50 Last dinner 9.30pm
CONF. Thtr 120 Class 60 Board 60 Del from £65
Credit Cards 1 2 3 5

Forte Posthouse
Littlecoates Rd DN34 4LX (Take A1136 and then B1444) ☎(0472) 350295 FAX (0472) 241354

Suitable for both the business and leisure traveller, this bright hotel provides modern accommodation in well equipped bedrooms with en suite bathrooms. For more details about Forte Posthouse hotels, consult the Contents page, under Hotel Groups.
52⇌🌙✱ B⇌🌙£41.50-£53.50 (room only)
CONF. Thtr 250 Class 100 Board 60 Del £89.50

GRIMSTON Norfolk Map 09 TF72

★★★⚜✿🍴 **CONGHAM HALL COUNTRY HOUSE**
Lynn Rd PE32 1AH (off A148)
☎Hillington(0485) 600250
FAX (0485) 601191

Personally run by Trevor and Christine Forecast along with a dedicated team, this delightful Georgian manor house is tucked away from a quiet village and surrounded by well tended gardens. Individually styled bedrooms vary from smaller rooms furnished in cane, rattan or pine to larger rooms, sumptuous with antique furnishings. There is a beautiful drawing room and an airy bar where aperitifs and appetisers are served before guests experience the delights of chef Murray Chapman's cooking in the Orangerie Restaurant. He offers a good value 3-course menu, a 4-course à la carte and a 7-course 'Hobson's Choice'. A typical à la carte meal could begin with lightly roasted monkfish with asparagus tips and a shallot dressing, followed by rack of lamb with a timbale of ratatouille on a sweet garlic sauce. The selection of desserts included strawberry cheesecake, blackberry and apple crumble, steamed syrup pudding and a wonderful honey ice cream.
14⇌🌙2🛏 CTV in all bedrooms T ✈ sB&B⇌🌙£65-£97 dB&B⇌🌙£97-£170 🍴
50P 🚗 ✿ ≋ (heated) ♀ (hard) croquet jacuzzi cricket nc12yrs xmas
V ♥ ⌘ Lunch £15 Dinner £19.50-£29.50&alc Last dinner 9.30pm
Credit Cards 1 2 3 5

GRINDLEFORD Derbyshire Map 08 SK27

★★★**63% Maynard Arms**
Main Rd S30 1HP ☎Hope Valley(0433) 630321 FAX (0433) 630445
In a delightful village in the heart of the Peak District National Park, yet convenient for Sheffield, the Maynard Arms has a peaceful atmosphere, even though its bar and restaurant are so popular. Bedrooms are pretty and have good facilities. There is a delightful residents' lounge, and the attractive restaurant overlooks the gardens. Well managed staff offer friendly and attentive service.
13rm(9⇌2🌙)(1fb)2🛏 CTV in all bedrooms ® T ✱
sB&Bfr£39.50 sB&B⇌🌙£49.50 dB&Bfr£49.50 dB&B⇌🌙£79.50 🍴
CTV 90P 3🛏 ✿ xmas
♨ English & French V ♥ ♨ ✱ Lunch £10.95-£12.50alc Dinner £15.50-£18.50alc Last dinner 9.30pm
CONF. Thtr 140 Class 40 Board 30 Del from £76.50
Credit Cards 1 2 3 5

GRIZEDALE Cumbria Map 07 SD39

★★ 70% Grizedale Lodge
LA22 0QL (at Hawkshead take Newby Bridge Road to right turn for Forest Park Centre.) ☎(05394) 36532
Closed Jan-mid Feb
Peacefully situated in the Grizedale forest, this hotel offers very friendly service and modern comfortable accommodation. A cosy bar lounge leads to the pleasant restaurant, serving well prepared dinners.
9⇌🌂(1fb)2🛏✕in all bedrooms CTV in all bedrooms ®
✕ (ex guide dogs) sB&B⇌🌂£45.50-£56 dB&B⇌🌂£75-£96 (incl dinner) 🍽
20P 🚗 xmas
♨ English & French ✿ ✕ Dinner £17.95 Last dinner 8pm
Credit Cards [1][3]

GROBY Leicestershire Map 04 SK50

★ 66% Brant Inn
Leicester Rd LE6 0DU (NW of Leicester, on A50)
☎Leicester(0533) 872703 FAX (0533) 875292
This lively inn offers sound but modest accommodation brightened by new soft furnishings; in eight instances a shower has been fitted within the body of the room. Ground floor public areas, considerably extended over recent years, include several bars, a wicker-furnished conservatory with a flagstone floor and a rustic-style restaurant adorned with old musical instruments.
9rm(4⇌4🌂)1🛏 CTV in all bedrooms ® T ✱ sB&B£24.50-£26.50 sB&B⇌🌂£26.50-£29.50 dB&B⇌🌂£42.50-£49.50 CTV 200P ✿
♨ English & French V ✿ 🍷 Sunday Lunch £8.95 Dinner £9.45&alc Last dinner 10pm
Credit Cards [1][3]

GUERNSEY
See **Channel Islands**

GUILDFORD Surrey Map 04 SU94

★★★ @71% The Angel Posting House and Livery
91 High St GU1 3DP ☎(0483) 64555 FAX (0483) 33770
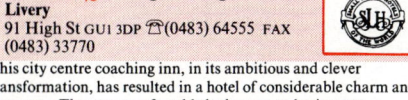
This city centre coaching inn, in its ambitious and clever transformation, has resulted in a hotel of considerable charm and character. The very comfortable bedrooms and suites are individually designed and decorated. There is much emphasis on the restaurants: the Oak Room providing good value set price menus, and The Crypt, where chef Tony O'Hare's skills are allowed to flourish.
11⇌🌂(4fb) CTV in all bedrooms T sB⇌🌂fr£110 dB⇌🌂£115-£165 (room only) 🍽
《 11P 🚗 xmas
♨ English & Continental V ✿ 🍷 ✱ Lunch fr£10.95 Dinner fr£12.50 Last dinner 10.30pm
CONF. Thtr 80 Class 40 Board 40 Del from £130
Credit Cards [1][2][3][5]

....

Forte Crest
Egerton Rd GU2 5XZ (2m SW on A3 Guildford bypass) ☎(0483) 574144 FAX (0483) 302960
FORTE CREST

A large modern hotel with a wide range of services and amenities designed particularly for the business traveller. Bedrooms are smart, comfortable and well equipped. For more details about Forte Crest hotels, consult the Contents page, under Hotel Groups.
111⇌🌂
CONF. Thtr 200 Class 154 Board 140 Del £125

Grizedale - Guildford

THE ANGEL POSTING HOUSE & LIVERY ★★★

High Street, Guildford, Surrey GU1 3DP
Tel: 0483 64555 Fax: 0483 33770

The Angel, in Guildford's High Street is one of England's oldest and most charming inns. It is a small yet luxurious hotel, with its fireplace, minstrel's gallery and original coaching clock dating from 1688 has the intimate atmosphere of a family home. The panelled Oakroom restaurant offers a wide choice of superb English and Continental cuisine together with an excellent selection of wines.

Garden House Hotel
★ ★ ★

Sarkfoot Road, Gretna, Carlisle CA65 5EP
Telephone: 0461 37621. Fax: 0461 37692

Welcome to a relaxing and enjoyable stay at the Garden House Hotel. Very centrally situated and close to romantic Gretna Green. The hotel offers a high standard of accommodation, all 21 bedrooms are en suite and individually furnished. Dining at the Garden restaurant is a pleasure, the finely prepared cultural cuisine is complemented by an extensive wine list. Should you wish to partake in any sporting activities there is a varied selection all within a few miles of the hotel. Alternatively you can relax in the extensive well maintained grounds with floodlit Japanese Water Garden.

277

Gullane - Hadley Wood

GULLANE Lothian *East Lothian* Map **12** NT48

★★★ ❀❀ ♨ **GREYWALLS**
Muirfield EH31 2EG (hotel signposted at east end of village) ☎(0620) 842144
FAX (0620) 842241
Closed Nov-Mar

Situated next to Muirfield's club house and adjacent to the 10th tee, this lovely Lutyens house is particularly popular with golfers. One of its greatest attractions, though, is the range of comfortable and appealing lounges, including a library lounge with open fire, lots of books and a piano. Open for only 7 months of the year, many of the staff have to be trained each season, and it says much for the ability and commitment of General Manager Sue Prime and her deputy that they quickly settle in to the routine, providing pleasant, unobtrusive service. Paul Baron remains as chef, and he is steadily growing in confidence and competence, offering a fixed price 4-course menu with limited choice. Saucing is a particularly strong point and there is a well-chosen wine list. Our inspector recommends the kippers at breakfast.

17⇌🛏Annexe5⇌🛏1🚪 CTV in all bedrooms T ✱
sB&B⇌🛏fr£90 dB&B⇌🛏£140-£150 🅿
(40P 🚭 🛉 ♀ (hard) croquet
♁ ⚤ ✱ Lunch £8-£25alc Dinner £33 Last dinner 9pm
Credit Cards ①②③⑤

See advertisement under EDINBURGH

GULWORTHY Devon Map **02** SX47

★★ ❀❀❀ ♨ **76%** *Horn of Plenty*
PL19 8JD ☎Tavistock(0822) 832528 FAX (0822) 832528
Closed 25-26 Dec

Basically a restaurant with rooms, this late Georgian house has spectacular views over the Tamar Valley. The heart of the establishment is the kitchen with Peter Gorton in charge. At lunchtime, good value 2-course meals are offered. Prime local ingredients are used, and simple natural unfussy styles.

1⇌🛏Annexe6⇌🛏 in 4 bedrooms CTV in all bedrooms ® T
sB&B⇌🛏£51-£70 dB&B⇌🛏£71-£90 Continental breakfast 🅿
20P 🚭 🛉 nc13yrs
♁ International V ✱ Lunch £14.50-£17.50 Dinner £25.50&alc Last dinner 9.30pm
Credit Cards ①②③

GUNTHORPE Nottinghamshire Map **08** SK64

★★ **66%** *Unicorn*
Gunthorpe Bridge NG14 7FB (MANSFIELD BREWERY PLC) ☎(0602) 663612 FAX (0602) 664801

In an attractive location beside the River Trent, this hotel has been totally re-styled, though parts still reflect its origins as a 17th-century coaching inn. The décor is richly coloured with complementary fabrics, enhanced by pictures, prints and dried flower arrangements. The Oakhouse Restaurant and Bar offers a modern grill-style menu. The atmosphere is informal and staff are neat and pleasant. Bedrooms are cheerfully chintzy and well equipped.

16⇌🛏(3fb) CTV in all bedrooms ® T ✱ (ex guide dogs)

140P ♪ water skiing boating
Credit Cards ①②③⑤

See advertisement under NOTTINGHAM

GWBERT-ON-SEA Dyfed Map **02** SN15

★★★ **56%** *Cliff*
SA43 1PP ☎Cardigan(0239) 613241 FAX (0239) 615391

This cliff top hotel has been popular with holiday-makers throughout the century. Public rooms are spacious and relaxing, and there are quite a few bars. Bedrooms are rather modest by modern standards, though a start has been made to upgrade these.

75⇌🛏(4fb)2🚪 CTV in all bedrooms ® T
(CTV 200P 🛉 (heated) ▶ 9 ♪ squash snooker sauna solarium gymnasium sea fishing pool table
♁ Welsh, English & French V ♁ ⚤ Last dinner 9pm
Credit Cards ①②③⑤

GWITHIAN Cornwall & Isles of Scilly Map **02** SW54

★ **64%** *Sandsifter*
Godrevy Towans TR27 5ED (on B3301) ☎Hayle(0736) 753314
Closed Nov-Feb

The Dryer family have offered a cheerful and personal welcome for many years at this purpose built hotel, set amid sand dunes, adjacent to the well known beaches. The bar is popular with locals and tourists, and bedrooms are on the ground floor, though some are quite compact.

7⇌🛏 CTV in all bedrooms ® ✱ ✱ sB&B⇌🛏£20-£28 dB&B⇌🛏£36-£50 🅿
(CTV 80P 🛉 nc 8yrs
♁ English & French V ♁ ⚤ Lunch £15-£25alc Dinner £8-£10&alc Last dinner 9pm

HACKNESS North Yorkshire Map **08** SE99

★★★ ♨ **65%** *Hackness Grange Country*
North Yorkshire National Park Y013 0JW (A6 to Scarborough and then A171 to Whitby/Scalby, follow signs to Hackness/Forge Valley National Park, through Hackness village on left hand side) ☎Scarborough(0723) 882345
FAX (0723) 882391

This early Victorian country house is set in extensive gardens and grounds, in the secluded and beautiful Forge Valley. Bedrooms are traditional in style but have every modern facility, some in a courtyard a little way from the hotel. There is a comfortable lounge and bar, and the restaurant, with its large open fire on colder days, overlooks the lake and grounds.

13⇌🛏Annexe15⇌🛏(7fb) CTV in all bedrooms ®♀ T
✱ (ex guide dogs) sB&B⇌🛏£59-£64 dB&B⇌🛏£118-£128 🅿
(CTV 60P 🚭 🛉 ☒ (heated) ▶ 9 ♀ (hard) ♪ croquet ⚭ xmas
V ♁ ⚤ Lunch £10.50 High tea £6.50 Dinner £17.50 Last dinner 9pm
CONF. Thtr 25 Del from £75
Credit Cards ①②③⑤ £

See advertisement under SCARBOROUGH

HADLEY WOOD Greater London Map **04** TQ29

★★★★ **61%** *West Lodge Park*
Cockfosters Rd EN4 0PY (on A111, 1m S of exit 24 on M25)
☎081-440 8311 FAX 081-449 3698

Extensive grounds, including a fine arboretum, surround this hotel which dates back to the early 19th century and retains some period features and fine pictures in its public areas. Traditionally furnished bedrooms in a variety of sizes and aspects include two in an adjacent coach house.

48⇌🛏Annexe2⇌🛏3🚪 CTV in all bedrooms ® T
✱ (ex guide dogs) ✱ sB⇌🛏£59.50-£79.50 dB⇌🛏£75-£95 (room only) 🅿
Lift (200P 🚭 🛉 putting croquet fitness trail

V ♿ ⌕ ✻ Lunch £14.85-£17.50&alc Dinner fr£14.85&alc Last dinner 9.45pm
CONF. Thtr 70 Class 45 Board 40 Del £117
Credit Cards ①②③

HAGLEY Hereford & Worcester Map 07 SO98
Travel Inn
Birmingham Rd DY9 9JS (on A456 towards Kidderminster) ☎(0562) 883120

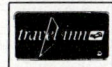

Purpose-built accommodation offers spacious and well equipped bedrooms, all with en suite bathrooms. Meals may be taken at the nearby family restaurant and pub. For more details about Travel Inns, consult the Contents page, under Hotel Groups.
40⇌♠✻ B⇌♠£33.50 (room only)

HAILSHAM East Sussex Map 05 TQ50
★★❀71% The Olde Forge
Magham Down BN27 1PN (1.5m E of Hailsham, on A271) ☎(0323) 842893
Closed 25 Dec-2 Jan
This charming 18th-century cottage hotel has cosy bedrooms which are attractively furnished. Pre-dinner drinks are served in the bar/lounge with its welcoming log fire, and the intimate beamed and candlelit restaurant offers a choice of a simple table d'hôte or traditional style à la carte menu. The standard of cooking is honest and reliable but lacks imagination. The atmosphere is informal and proprietors Edward and Ann Falconer-Wright are natural hosts.
8rm(6⇌♠)1⇌ CTV in all bedrooms ® T ✻ sB&B£30-£35 sB&B⇌♠£30-£35 dB&B£44 dB&B⇌♠£42-£50 ⊟
8P 4⊟ ⊞
♫ English & French V ✻ Dinner fr£11.50&alc Last dinner 9.15pm
Credit Cards ①②③⑤ £

Forte Travelodge
Hellingly (on A22 at Boship roundabout) ☎(0323) 844556 Central Res (0800) 850950

This modern building offers a good standard of accommodation for overnight stops. Smart, spacious and well equipped bedrooms, all with en suite bathrooms, are suitable for family use, and meals may be taken at the nearby family restaurant. For more details about Travelodges, consult the contents page, under Hotel Groups.
40⇌♠✻ B⇌♠£31.95 (room only)

HALESOWEN West Midlands Map 07 SO98
Granada Lodge
Illey Ln B32 4AR ☎021-550 3261 FAX 021-501 2580
(For full entry see Frankley Motorway Service Area (M5))

HALIFAX West Yorkshire Map 07 SE02
★★★❀73% Holdsworth House
Holmfield HX2 9TG (3m NW off A629 Keighley Road) ☎(0422) 240024 FAX (0422) 245174
Closed 25-31 Dec
This 17th-century stone Yeomans Hall is a haven of tranquility where, over the last 30 years the Pearson family have integrated 20th-century comforts and facilities with the period character of the house. The staff are unobtrusive but friendly and bedrooms are cottagey in style and include complimentary sherry. The restaurant is a heavily panelled series of rooms with leaded, mullioned windows and beamed ceilings, and the split level lounge is

particularly comfortable. The chef produces quality dishes showing English and Continental influences.
40⇌♠(1fb)5⊞⅍in 15 bedrooms CTV in all bedrooms T sB&B⇌♠£69.90-£74 dB&B⇌♠£86.50-£99.50 Continental breakfast ⊟
℄ 40P ✿
♫ English & Continental V ♿ ⌕ ⅍ Lunch £12.50&alc Dinner fr£19.50&alc Last dinner 9.30pm
CONF. Thtr 100 Class 30 Board 35 Del £95
Credit Cards ①②③⑤ £

★★★67% The Imperial Crown
42/46 Horton St HX1 1BR ☎(0422) 342342 FAX (0422) 349866
Situated in the town centre, this friendly family-run hotel is full of character. While the accommodation is not extensive, it is attractive, with a pleasant bar lounge and a striking wood-panelled restaurant. Bedrooms are equally handsome, the most comfortable being 2 new duplex suites.
42⇌♠(3fb)1⊞ CTV in all bedrooms ®⅍ T ✻ ✻ sB&B⇌♠£45-£63.50 dB&B⇌♠£56-£74.50 ⊟
℄ CTV 60P ⊞ xmas
♫ English & French V ♿ ✻ Dinner £10.50-£15.50&alc Last dinner 10pm
CONF. Thtr 150 Class 120 Board 70 Del from £60
Credit Cards ①②③⑤

★★65% Jenny Dees Motel
Canal Basin, Salterhebble Hill, Huddersfield Rd HX3 0QT ☎(0422) 347700 FAX (0422) 320793
Situated to the south of the town centre and overlooking the Calder Hebble canal, this recently built complex provides a block of comfortable well equipped bedrooms with smart bathrooms, plus a pleasant restaurant. Spacious bars are housed in a separate building.
31⇌♠(2fb)⅍in 8 bedrooms CTV in all bedrooms ® T
✈ (ex guide dogs)

West Lodge Park

The nearest country hotel to London — only 12 miles from the West End, and one mile from exit 24 on the M25, but set in 35 acres of parkland and fields. Country house atmosphere with antiques and log fires.
Individually decorated bedrooms with carefully chosen fabrics and furnishings. Some four poster bedrooms and whirlpool baths. Ask for colour brochure and details of weekend breaks.

West Lodge Park
Hadley Wood, Barnet, Herts
Tel: 081-440 8311.
Fax: 081-449 3698
AA ★ ★ ★ ★

Halifax - Hanslope

((100P ♫
V ⚹ ⚌ Last dinner 10pm
Credit Cards [1][2][3][5]

HALKIRK Highland *Caithness* Map 15 ND15
★★ 63% **Ulbster Arms**
Bridge St KY12 6XY (A9 to Latheron from Perth left on to A895)
☎(084783) 206 & 641 FAX (084783) 206
Situated beside the Thurso River, this long established Highland hotel is especially popular with sporting visitors. The atmosphere is friendly and public areas, with pine-clad walls and tartan carpets, provide traditional comforts. Bedrooms are well decorated and modestly furnished.
12rm(8⇨2🏠)Annexe16⇨ CTV in all bedrooms ® T ✱
sB&Bfr£25 sB&B⇨🏠£25-£35 dB&Bfr£50 dB&B⇨🏠£50-£70
CTV 30P 6🚗 (£2 per day) 🐾 ⚓ shooting stalking
V ⚹ ⚌ ✂ ✱ Bar Lunch £2-£7 High tea fr£8 Dinner fr£15 Last dinner 8.30pm
Credit Cards [1][3]

HALKYN Clwyd Map 07 SJ27
Forte Travelodge
CH8 8RF (on A55, westbound)
☎(0352) 780952 Central Res (0800) 850950

FORTE Travelodge

This modern building offers a good standard of accommodation for overnight stops. Smart, spacious and well equipped bedrooms, all with en suite bathrooms, are suitable for family use, and meals may be taken at the nearby family restaurant. For more details about Travelodges, consult the Contents page, under Hotel Groups.
31⇨🏠 ✱ B⇨🏠£31.95 (room only)

HALLAND East Sussex Map 05 TQ41
★★ 66% **Halland Forge**
BN8 6PW (at junct of A22/B2192)
☎(0825) 840456 FAX (0825) 840773

ExecGroup

This family-run motel offers a range of 70s-style self-contained bedrooms. All provide adequate comfort and are particularly well equipped. The main hotel provides a lounge bar, attractive restaurant, and a coffee shop which is open for light snacks and meals throughout the day.
Annexe20⇨🏠 CTV in all bedrooms ® T ✱ sB⇨🏠£32-£46 dB⇨🏠£32-£58 (room only) 🍴
70P ⚹ nc5yrs
♥ English & French V ⚹ ⚌ Lunch £10-£14.50&alc Dinner £13-£16.55&alc Last dinner 9.30pm
CONF. Thtr 26 Class 16 Board 20 Del from £60
Credit Cards [1][2][3][5] £

HAMBLETON North Yorkshire Map 08 SE53
★★ 65% **Owl**
Main Rd YO8 9JH (4m W A63) ☎Selby(0757) 228374 FAX (0757) 228125
This friendly family-run hotel is converted from an 18th-century gentleman's residence and has attractively decorated bedrooms with modern facilities. The large bar and restaurant are both popular for their food.
9⇨🏠(1fb)1 🛏 CTV in all bedrooms ® T 🚭 (ex guide dogs) ✱
sB&B⇨🏠£31.50-£35 dB&B⇨🏠£42-£47
50P 🐾 ⚹
V ⚹ ⚌ ✂ Lunch £1.40-£12alc High tea £1.40-£4alc Last high tea 6pm
Credit Cards [1][2][3][5] £

HAMILTON
See **Bothwell**

HAMILTON MOTORWAY SERVICE AREA (M74)
Strathclyde Map 11 NS75

⇧ *Roadchef Lodge*
M74 Northbound ML3 6JW ☎Hamilton(0698) 891904 FAX (0698) 891682
Closed 25 & 26 Dec
Off the northbound carriageway of the M74 between junctions 5 and 6, this lodge provides sensibly priced accommodation, with well equipped modern bedrooms and 24-hour catering available in the adjacent building, plus a conference room.
36⇨🏠(23fb)✂ in 10 bedrooms CTV in all bedrooms ® ⚐ T
🚭 (ex guide dogs)
((120P ⚹
V ✂
Credit Cards [1][2][3][5]

HAMPSON GREEN Lancashire Map 07 SD45
★★ 59% **Hampson House**
Hampson Ln LA2 0JB (off A6 at M6 junct 33)
☎Galgate(0524) 751158 FAX (0524) 751779

This 17th-century manor house stands in its own grounds. Bedrooms are modern in style and vary in size, while public areas include a comfortable lounge bar and attractive restaurant.
12⇨🏠Annexe2⇨🏠(4fb)1 🛏 CTV in all bedrooms ® ⚐ T ✱
sB&B⇨🏠£38.50 dB&B⇨🏠£49.50 🍴
45P ⚹ volleyball *xmas*
♥ English & French V ⚹ ⚌ ✱
CONF. Thtr 70 Class 30 Board 50 Del from £39.50
Credit Cards [1][2][3] £

HANDFORTH Cheshire Map 07 SJ88
★★★★ 60% **Belfry**
Stanley Rd SK9 3LD (off A34, approx 4m S of junct M63)
☎061-437 0511 FAX 061-499 0597
This modern, privately owned hotel is convenient for the city centre and is popular with business people. Bedrooms are well equipped and public areas include an attractive split-level restaurant, cocktail bar and spacious lounge.
81⇨ CTV in all bedrooms ® T ✱ sB⇨🏠£73.50-£84.50 dB⇨🏠£84.50-£94 (room only) 🍴
Lift ((150P ⚹ ♫
♥ International V ⚹ ⚌ ✱ Lunch fr£13&alc Dinner fr£16&alc Last dinner 10pm
CONF. Thtr 120 Class 70 Board 50 Del from £95
Credit Cards [1][2][3][5]
See advertisement under **WILMSLOW**

HANSLOPE Buckinghamshire Map 04 SP84
★★★ 62% **Hatton Court Resort**
Bullington End MK19 7BQ
☎Milton Keynes(0698) 510044 FAX (0908) 510945

RESORT HOTELS PLC

An elegant 19th-century country house, set in 7 acres of gardens, has been tastefully restored to provide modern comforts while retaining its historic character. Attractive bedrooms furnished with antiques provide good facilities for business or holiday guests and the conservatory restaurant offers interesting dishes.
12⇨🏠Annexe8⇨🏠(5fb)1 🛏 ✂ in 4 bedrooms CTV in all bedrooms ® ⚐ T ✱ sB⇨🏠£65-£75 dB⇨🏠£75-£85 (room only) 🍴
60P ⚹ snooker *xmas*

Hanslope - Harpenden

✿ English & French **V** ❀ ⚏ ✳ Lunch £8.95-£14.15&alc Dinner fr£16.95&alc Last dinner 9.30pm
CONF. Thtr 80 Class 35 Board 35 Del from £80
Credit Cards [1][2][3][5]

HAREWOOD West Yorkshire Map **08** SE34

★★★ 66% Harewood Arms
Harrogate Rd LS17 9LH (on A61) (Samuel Smith)
☎(0532) 886566 FAX (0532) 886064
Almost opposite the entrance to Harewood House, this popular Georgian coaching inn has an attractive restaurant open for lunch and dinner and various bar areas serving refreshments all day. Bedrooms are modern and well equipped.
24⇨♠(2fb) CTV in all bedrooms ® **T** sB&B⇨♠£47-£67 dB&B⇨♠£62-£80 ▣
(100P ✿
✿ English & French **V** ❀ ⚏ ✳ Lunch £7-£9 Dinner £14.95-£16.95&alc Last dinner 10pm
Credit Cards [1][2][3][4][5]

HARLECH Gwynedd Map **06** SH53

See also **Talsarnau**
★ 63% Noddfa
Lower Rd LL46 2UB (on A496, hotel opposite St David's Golf Club) ☎(0766) 780043 FAX (0766) 780043
The rear of this stone-built hotel is of a similar age to the castle, but the front was added in the 1850s. It enjoys fine views of the castle and the peaks of Snowdonia mountains. Gillian Davies serves honest home cooking and husband Eric looks after the guests. Eric's interest in medieval history is evident in the collection of weapons in the lounge, and as well as tours of the castle he offers tuition in archery in the hotel grounds.
6rm(4⇨♠)(1fb) CTV in all bedrooms ® ✈ (ex guide dogs) dB&B£32 dB&B⇨♠£35-£45 ▣
CTV 40P 🚲 ✿ archery nc3yrs *xmas*
✿ International **V** Dinner £14&alc Last dinner 8.30pm
Credit Cards [1][3][5]

HARLOSH

See **Skye, Isle of**

HARLOW Essex Map **05** TL41

★★★ 67% Churchgate Manor
Churchgate St, Old Harlow CM17 0JT (on B183, E of old Harlow) ☎(0279) 420246 FAX (0279) 437720
This Jacobean house has been extended and developed over the years into a popular and well run hotel, ideal for conferences and commercial guests. Bedrooms include luxurious Executive rooms with spa baths, mini bars and safes, spacious Superior rooms, and more compact and dated doubles which are due for a facelift. The elegant Manor restaurant is full of character; there is a comfortable bar lounge, and staff are professional and willing to please.
85⇨(8fb) CTV in all bedrooms ®✵ **T** sB⇨♠£53-£72 dB⇨♠£62-£92 (room only) ▣
(120P ✿ ▢ (heated) sauna solarium gymnasium *xmas*
✿ English & French **V** ❀ ⚏ ✴ Lunch £10.95-£11.95&alc Dinner fr£16.50&alc Last dinner 9.45pm
CONF. Thtr 170 Class 70 Board 40 Del £27.50
Credit Cards [1][2][3][5]

★★★ 62% Harlow Moat House
Southern Way CM18 7BA (off A414)
☎(0279) 422441 FAX (0279) 635094
Closed 24 Dec-3 Jan
Easily found on the southern approach road to Harlow, this purpose built 60s hotel is run by resident director Mr Anderson and his reliable team. Bedrooms (some no smoking) are similar in style and standard, with a good range of equipment. Some are thoughtful

designed for the female traveller. There is a popular lounge bar and a bright modern restaurant.
120⇨♠✵ in 20 bedrooms CTV in all bedrooms ® **T** ✈ (ex guide dogs) sB&B⇨♠£75 dB&B⇨♠£75 ▣
(180P pool tables
✿ English & French **V** ❀ ⚏ ✴ Lunch £16&alc Dinner £16&alc Last dinner 10pm
CONF. Thtr 150 Class 150 Board 50 Del £85
Credit Cards [1][2][3][5]

★★★ 56% Green Man
Mulberry Green, Old Harlow CM17 0ET
☎(0279) 442521 FAX (0279) 626113
This former coaching inn in the old town has a popular public bar with a log fire and a beamed lounge adjoining the cosy restaurant. Bedrooms are in a modern annexe and although all of a good size and equipped to the same standard, their furnishings and decor vary, half of them due for a facelift.
Annexe55⇨♠(1fb)✵ in 16 bedrooms CTV in all bedrooms ® **T** sB⇨♠£75 dB⇨♠£85 (room only) ▣
(75P *xmas*
V ❀ ⚏ ✴ Lunch £8.95-£10.95&alc Dinner £15.95 Last dinner 10pm
CONF. Thtr 60 Class 26 Board 35 Del £90
Credit Cards [1][2][3][5]

Travel Inn
Cambridge Rd CM20 2EP (just off A414)
☎(0279) 442545

Purpose-built accommodation offers spacious and well equipped bedrooms, all with en suite bathrooms. Meals may be taken at the nearby family restaurant and pub. For more details about Travel Inns, consult the Contents page, under Hotel Groups.
38⇨♠✳ B⇨♠£33.50 (room only)

HARLYN BAY Cornwall & Isles of Scilly Map **02** SW87

★ 67% Polmark
PL28 8SB (off B3276) ☎Padstow(0841) 520206
Remote and quietly situated facing the sea, this attractive old Cornish stone house stands within its own extensive grounds. Log fires in the winter enhance the relaxing and informal atmosphere of the wood panelled bar and well furnished lounges. The new wing has the best bedrooms, but the older rooms have more character. Service is provided by the friendly proprietors David and Anita Plume.
13rm(8⇨♠)(2fb) CTV in 8 bedrooms ®
CTV 40P ✿ ⌒ (heated)
✿ English & Continental **V** ❀ ⚏ Last dinner 7pm
Credit Cards [1][3]

HAROME

See **Helmsley**

HARPENDEN Hertfordshire Map **04** TL11

★★★ 68% Harpenden Moat House
18 Southdown Rd AL5 1PE (on A1081)
☎(0582) 764111 FAX (0582) 769758
Closed 24-30 Dec RS Bank Holidays
Overlooking the East Common on the outskirts of town, this handsome Grade 11 listed building was formerly St Dominic's Convent. A modern brick extension houses many of the bedrooms – some chalet-style reached by covered walkways. Public areas are smart but limited. The restaurant is particularly attractive, its domed ceilings adorned with cherubs, and cosy alcoves provide extra privacy.

Harpenden - Harrogate

18⇨♠Annexe35⇨♠(3fb)3⇦✂in 20 bedrooms CTV in all bedrooms ® T ✗ (ex guide dogs) ✱ sB&B⇨♠£38-£79 dB&B⇨♠£56-£95 ♬
(80P ✿ boules croquet lawn
♀ French V ◊ ⚏ ✱ Lunch £14.95 Dinner £14.95 Last dinner 10pm
CONF. Thtr 150 Class 60 Board 70 Del from £90
Credit Cards [1][2][3][5]

★★★ 65% Glen Eagle
1 Luton Rd AL5 2PX ☏(0582) 760271 FAX (0582) 460819
This converted and extended house in the centre of the town is well equipped functional bedrooms and some more spacious executive rooms with luxurious extras. The elegant restaurant overlooks the gardens; staff are friendly and 24-hour room service is available.
50⇨♠(12fb)2⇦ CTV in all bedrooms ® T ✗ ✱ sB&B⇨♠£43-£79.50 dB&B⇨♠£52-£79.50 (room only) ♬
Lift (100P ✿ xmas
♀ English & French V ◊ ⚏ ✱ Lunch £11.50-£30alc Dinner £11.50-£30alc Last dinner 10pm
CONF. Thtr 70 Class 35 Board 30 Del from £85
Credit Cards [1][2][3][4][5]

HARRIS, ISLE OF Western Isles *Inverness-shire* Map 13

TARBERT Map 13 NB10
★★ 62% Harris
PA85 3DL ☏Harris(0859) 2154 FAX (0859) 2281
Many guests return year after year to enjoy the welcoming atmosphere of this long established family-run island hotel situated close to the ferry terminal. The cosy well stocked bar and separate television lounge are augmented by two relaxing timber-clad sun lounges, and a traditional dining room serves honest home-cooked meals.
25rm(13⇨4♠)(2fb) ® ✱ sB&Bfr£28.85 sB&B⇨♠fr£32.85 dB&Bfr£55 dB&B⇨♠£62.40 ♬
CTV 30P ✿ ♣ xmas
V ◊ ⚏ ✂ ✱ Bar Lunch £2.50-£10alc Dinner £14.25-£15.50 Last dinner 8.30pm
Credit Cards [1][3]

HARROGATE North Yorkshire Map 08 SE35
See also **Burnt Yates**
★★★★⚜66% Nidd Hall
Nidd HG3 3BN (4m N off B6165) ☏(0423) 771598 FAX (0423) 770931
Set in 45 acres of landscaped grounds and gardens, this elegant Georgian manor house has an opulent entrance hall and beautiful public rooms, which include a library, drawing room, lounge bar and fine dining room, each with elaborate plasterwork, paintings and ornate fireplaces. Bedrooms are generally spacious and comfortable, furnished in a style appropriate to the period.
38⇨♠Annexe21⇨♠(3fb)4⇦ CTV in all bedrooms ®✷ T ✗ (ex guide dogs) sB&B⇨♠fr£95 dB&B⇨♠fr£120-£230 Continental breakfast ♬
Lift (90P ✿ ▦ (heated) ♞ (hard) ♪ squash snooker sauna solarium gymnasium beauty salon punting rowing croquet xmas
♀ French V ◊ ⚏ ✂ ✱ Lunch £12.95-£15.95 Dinner £20-£25 Last dinner 10pm
CONF. Thtr 250 Class 70 Board 70 Del £145
Credit Cards [1][2][3][5]

★★★★ 64% Moat House International
Kings Rd HG1 1XX ☏(0423) 500500 FAX (0423) 524435

This large modern building, with its distinctive glass façade, adjoins the International Conference Centre. Public rooms on 2 floors include the Abbey Restaurant, in which carvery and table d'hôte meals are served, and the Boulevard, a more exclusive à la carte restaurant, also offering a daily signature menu.
214⇨♠✂in 56 bedrooms CTV in all bedrooms ® T Lift (▦ 130P
♀ English & French V ◊ ⚏ Last dinner 10pm
Credit Cards [1][2][3][5]

★★★★ 60% The Majestic
Ripon Rd HG1 2HU (N of town, on A61)
☏(0423) 568972 FAX (0423) 502283

This elegant Victorian hotel is situated in an elevated position in 10 acres of grounds and gardens, overlooking the town and adjacent to the International Conference Centre. Opulent public rooms include the beautifully chandeliered dining room, the muralled main lounge and the richly panelled Regency Bar, reminiscent of a gentlemen's club. Bedrooms are mainly traditional in style; most are spacious and have every modern comfort.
156⇨♠(10fb)✂in 46 bedrooms CTV in all bedrooms ®✷ T sB⇨♠£90 dB⇨♠£110 (room only) ♬
Lift (240P ✿ ▦ (heated) ♞ (hard) squash snooker sauna solarium gymnasium health & fitness centre xmas
♀ International V ◊ ⚏ ✱ Lunch fr£14.95 High tea £7.50-£10 Dinner £21.50-£25&alc Last dinner 9.30pm
CONF. Thtr 400 Class 220 Board 65 Del £135
Credit Cards [1][2][3][5]

★★★ ❀73% Boar's Head
HG3 3AY (on the A61 Harrogate/Ripon road, the hotel is in the centre of Ripley Village) ☏(0423) 771888 FAX (0423) 771509

Part of the Ripley Castle estate, this elegant hotel offers comfortable modern accommodation and excellent food in its delightful setting overlooking the cobbled market square. Antiques and oil paintings are a feature and beautifully furnished bedrooms are situated in the main building, converted stables and another elegant house over the road. There are comfortable drawing and morning rooms and a wide choice of dishes is served in the bar. Pride of place, however, goes to the restaurant under the direction of head chef David Box, who produces excellent dishes from a 4-course fixed price menu.
19⇨♠Annexe6⇨♠(2fb) CTV in all bedrooms ® T sB&B⇨♠fr£85 dB&B⇨♠fr£105 ♬
(60P 3⇦ ✿ ♞ (hard) ♪ shooting xmas
♀ English & French V ◊ ⚏ ✱ Lunch £9.95-£15 Dinner £26.50-£28 Last dinner 9.30pm
CONF. Thtr 75 Class 28 Board 36 Del from £104
Credit Cards [1][3]

★★★ ❀69% Balmoral Hotel & Restaurant
Franklin Mount HG1 5EJ (opposite Exhibition Centre)
☏(0423) 508208 FAX (0423) 530652
(Rosette awarded for dinner only)
A peaceful country house atmosphere belies the fact that this hotel is close to the town and conference centre. Bedrooms – several with beautiful carved four-posters – are named after monarchs, and photographs and china follow the same theme. Public areas are compact but equally interesting, and include an elegant drawing room, the imaginative Oriental Bar and the adjacent Snug. Standards of cuisine are high, the restaurant's four-course menu offering such dishes as lobster timbale, salmon with coriander, fillet of lamb rosti and a range of delicious desserts.
20⇨♠(2fb)9⇦ CTV in all bedrooms ® T sB⇨♠£63-£77 dB⇨♠£78-£138 (room only) ♬
12P ✿ solarium
V ◊ ⚏ Dinner £12.50-£17.50&alc Last dinner 9pm
CONF. Thtr 30 Board 25 Del from £65
Credit Cards [1][2][3]

Harrogate

★★★ ❀67% White House
10 Park Pde HG1 5AH ☎(0423) 501388 FAX (0423) 527945

This elegant hotel, built in 1836 in the style of a Venetian villa, overlooks part of the famous Stray. 'Table d'hôte' and a 'carte' are available daily, the latter offering a good choice of dishes created by proprietress Jennie Forster. Public rooms are stylish and bedrooms are just as attractive with antique furniture and designer drapes.
13⇌ ʔ(1fb)1🚭 CTV in all bedrooms ® ✱ sB⇌ʔfr£72.50 dB⇌ʔfr£95 (room only) 🅿
CTV 10P ✿ xmas
V ♥ ⚲ ⚞ ✱ Lunch fr£12.50&alc Dinner fr£17.50&alc Last dinner 9pm
CONF. Thtr 40 Class 40 Board 30 Del from £120
Credit Cards 1 2 3 5

★★★ 65% Grants
3-13 Swan Rd HG1 2SS (off A61) ☎(0423) 560666 FAX (0423) 502550

This attractive hotel is in a Victorian terrace a few minutes walk from the town centre and conference halls. Bedrooms, although compact, are pretty and tasteful, and there is a comfortable guests' lounge as well as a roomy bar. Chimney Pots restaurant is popular for intimate evening meals.
42⇌ ʔ(2fb)3🚭 CTV in all bedrooms ® T ✱ sB&B⇌ʔ£49-£93.50 dB&B⇌ʔ£70-£137 🅿
Lift ℂ 26P xmas
♥ English & French V ♥ ⚲
Credit Cards 1 2 3 5

★★★ 65% St George Swallow
1 Ripon Rd HG1 2SY ☎(0423) 561291 FAX (0423) 530037

Restored Edwardian décor graces the elegant Swaledale Restaurant and public rooms of this centrally situated hotel, which provides every amenity for the modern traveller while retaining many of its original splendours.
93⇌ ʔ(14fb)⚞ in 29 bedrooms CTV in all bedrooms ® ♈ T ✱ sB&B⇌ʔ£85 dB&B⇌ʔ£105 🅿
Lift ℂ 60P 🖅 (heated) sauna solarium gymnasium boutique beautician masseuse whirlpool xmas
♥ English & French V ♥ ⚲ ✱ Lunch £11.50&alc Dinner £16.25&alc Last dinner 9.30pm
Credit Cards 1 2 3 5

★★★ 64% Studley
Swan Rd HG1 2SE ☎(0423) 560425 FAX (0423) 530967
Closed 25 & 26 Dec

Conveniently situated close to the town centre and Valley Gardens, this popular hotel with an attractive Georgian façade has well equipped bedrooms, a comfortable lounge and a restaurant locally reputed for its standard of cooking. Friendly staff provide efficient service.
36⇌ ʔ CTV in all bedrooms ® ♈ T ✱ sB&B⇌ʔ£64.50-£77 dB&B⇌ʔ£78-£95 🅿
Lift ℂ CTV 14P nc
♥ French ✱ Lunch £8.30-£13.15alc Dinner £14.95&alc Last dinner 10pm
Credit Cards 1 2 3 5

See advertisement on page 285

★★★ 63% The Crown
Crown Place HG1 2RZ ☎(0423) 567755 FAX (0423) 502284

Situated next to the ornate Royal Pump Room in the centre of town, this hotel features a marvellously elegant restaurant with marbled pillars, wood panelling and lush palms. Many of the bedrooms have been upgraded, and all are similarly equipped.
121⇌ ʔ(3fb)⚞ in 40 bedrooms CTV in all bedrooms ® T sB⇌ʔ£65-£80 dB⇌ʔ£90 (room only) 🅿
Lift ℂ 50P xmas

HOB GREEN
HOTEL AND RESTAURANT
★★★ ❀

For details see entry under MARKINGTON

If you are looking to relax and unwind Hob Green will not disappoint you. Set in 870 acres midway between Harrogate and Ripon the hotel enjoys magnificent views of rolling countryside.
Whilst still retaining the atmosphere of a country house Hob Green incorporates all the facilities expected of a hotel of the 1990's with attention to detail and a desire for perfection being of paramount importance.
The restaurant has an excellent reputation with the menu being changed daily.

MARKINGTON, HARROGATE HG3 3PJ.
Tel: Harrogate (0423) 770031 Fax: (0423) 771589

The Boulevard
RESTAURANT
at the
MOAT HOUSE INTERNATIONAL
★ ★ ★ ★

One of Britain's finest Restaurants where a feast of English and International dishes are freshly prepared, and served in a relaxed and friendly atmosphere.

Whether it is a business luncheon or an intimate dinner which could feature our Signature Menu.

Telephone
The Boulevard Restaurant
for reservations 0423-500000

KINGS ROAD · HARROGATE
NORTH YORKSHIRE HG1 1XX

Queens Moat Houses PLC

Harrogate

V ♿ ⚥ ✳ Lunch £8.95-£9.95 Dinner fr£16.95&alc Last dinner 9.30pm
Credit Cards ① ② ③ ⑤

★★★ 61% Harrogate Thistle
Prospect Place, West Park HG1 1LB (on A61 close to town centre) ☎(0423) 564601 FAX (0423) 507508

The inn stands back from the road on its southern approach to the town, overlooking the famous Stray. Well equipped bedrooms are a particular feature.
71⇌🛏(5fb) CTV in all bedrooms ® ⚥ T ✳ sB⇌🛏£69-£79 dB⇌🛏£79-£89 (room only) 🅿
Lift ℂ 40P xmas
♡ English & French V ♿ ⚥ ✳ Sunday Lunch £7.50 Dinner £15.50&alc Last dinner 9.30pm
CONF. Thtr 120 Class 72 Board 58 Del from £65
Credit Cards ① ② ③ ⑤

★★ 70% The Manor
3 Clarence Dr HG1 2QE ☎(0423) 503916 FAX (0423) 568709

Situated in a secluded area of the town yet within easy walking distance of all amenities, this attractive grey stone Victorian house is fronted by a colourful garden. Many bedrooms have now been upgraded to the same standard as the well furnished and decorated public rooms. These include an elegant cocktail bar, the guests' lounge and a beautifully appointed restaurant.
17⇌🛏(1fb)⚥ in 6 bedrooms CTV in all bedrooms ® T
Lift 12P 🚗
♡ English & French V ♿ ⚥ ⚥ Last dinner 8.45pm
Credit Cards ① ③

★★ 69% Albany
22-23 Harlow Moor Dr HG2 0JY ☎(0423) 565890

This late Victorian property is quietly situated overlooking the renowned Valley Gardens. It is a comfortably furnished hotel with a friendly atmosphere and the double and twin bedrooms are particularly spacious. There is a lounge bar, a comfortable guests' lounge and an attractive dining room where hearty dinners are served.
14🛏(3fb) CTV in all bedrooms ® ✈ (ex guide dogs) CTV
♡ English & Continental V ⚥ Last dinner 7.30pm
Credit Cards ① ③ ⑤

★★ 68% Ascot House
53 Kings Rd HG1 5HJ ☎(0423) 531005 FAX (0423) 503523
Closed 29 Dec-5 Jan

A Victorian residence just a short walk from the International Conference Centre and the main shopping areas, Ascot House is a family run hotel. Many of the bedrooms have recently been upgraded with attractive modern fabrics and wall coverings. English and Continental dishes are served in the elegant dining room, and there is a large and comfortable bar-lounge.
20rm(17⇌🛏)(2fb) CTV in all bedrooms ® T ✳ sB&B£39-£47.50 sB&B⇌🛏£46.50-£52 dB&B⇌🛏£62-£73 🅿
14P xmas
♡ English & Continental V ♿ ⚥ Bar Lunch £1.50-£6.50alc Dinner £12.50-£13.75&alc Last dinner 9pm
CONF. Thtr 80 Class 36 Board 36 Del from £65
Credit Cards ① ② ③ ⑤

★★ 67% Abbey Lodge
29-31 Ripon Rd HG1 2JL (on the A61 just N of Harrogate centre) ☎(0423) 569712 FAX (0423) 530570
Closed 24-26 Dec

This double-fronted Victorian house with twin gables has attractive gardens at the front. Bedrooms are furnished in both modern and traditional style, there is a comfortable guests' lounge with an adjoining bar and the attractive restaurant is now open to non-residents for dinner.

19rm(5⇌9🛏)(3fb) CTV in all bedrooms ® T ✳ sB&Bfr£25.50 sB&B⇌🛏fr£35 dB&Bfr£46 dB&B⇌🛏fr£53.50 🅿
24P
♡ English & French V ♿ Dinner fr£12.75&alc Last dinner 9pm
Credit Cards ① ③

★★ 66% Green Park
Valley Dr HG2 0JT ☎(0423) 504681 FAX (0423) 530811

This friendly, traditional hotel is on a corner overlooking Harrogate's famous Valley Gardens, some of its well furnished bedrooms having garden views. The lounges are comfortable, as is the lounge bar which leads into the spacious restaurant, where both fixed price and à la carte menus are usually available.
43⇌🛏(2fb)⚥ in 14 bedrooms CTV in all bedrooms ® T ✳ sB&B⇌🛏£49-£52 dB&B⇌🛏£70-£75 🅿
Lift ℂ 10P xmas
♡ International V ♿ ⚥ ✳ Bar Lunch £1.50-£11.55alc Dinner fr£13.25&alc Last dinner 8.30pm
Credit Cards ① ② ③ ⑤

★★ 65% Harrogate Brasserie Hotel & Bar
28-30 Cheltenham Pde HG1 1DB ☎(0423) 505041 FAX (0423) 530920

The hotel is in the centre of town, close to the conference centre. Its brasserie and bar, with French-style décor, is an attractive venue for good value meals. There is a 2-course table d'hôte menu in addition to the carte. Bedrooms are well equipped, though some single rooms are compact.
14⇌🛏(2fb) CTV in all bedrooms ®⚥ T
CTV 12P 🚗 ♫
♡ English & French V ♿ ⚥ Last dinner 10pm
Credit Cards ① ③ ⑤

Abbey Lodge & Naylor's

29-31 RIPON ROAD
HARROGATE
N. YORKSHIRE
HG1 2JL
Tel: 0423 569712
Fax: 0423 530570

AA ★★

Relax, unwind and indulge yourself at Abbey Lodge where a warm welcome awaits you.
A fine selection of food and wine is available at Naylors, from wholemeal bread to naughty but oh so nice puds, all specially prepared for you by chef proprietors Mervyn & Kate.

Call now (0423) 569712
For brochure & tariff & low season breaks

THE HARROGATE
THISTLE HOTEL
★★★ AA

Prospect Place, Harrogate HG1 1LB
Tel: 0423 564601   Fax: 0423 507508

Your choice in Harrogate

For Reservations at over 100
Mount Charlotte Thistle Hotels
Telephone London: 071 937 8033.

THISTLE HOTELS

H

THE ALBANY HOTEL

22/23 Harlow Moor Drive
Harrogate
North Yorkshire HG2 0JY
Telephone: 0423 565890

Recommended by FROMMER'S GUIDE

A warm Yorkshire welcome awaits you at the ALBANY, where your comfort comes first. Relax in a warm friendly atmosphere and enjoy our traditional Yorkshire Hospitality.

14 Bedrooms all with En-suite shower & toilet, colour T.V., radio, tea/coffee making facilities

Quietly situated directly opposite the beautiful Valley Gardens, a few minutes from the Town Centre and Conference/Exhibition Complex.
For the discerning business guest we offer quality and value, comfortable accommodation, good food and personal service.

Studley Hotel

SWAN ROAD, HARROGATE HG1 2SE
Tel: (0423) 560425 Telex: 57506
Fax: (0423) 530967

This small friendly hotel, of 36 bedrooms, all with private bathrooms, is in the ideal situation, near the Valley Gardens and within walking distance of the town centre and conference facilities. All bedrooms have direct dial telephone, colour TV with Sky TV, trouser press and tea making facilities. Bargain weekend breaks available. Car Park. Small Executive Suites available. **Le Breton French restaurant**, which serves superb French food, some of which is cooked on the genuine charcoal grill.
Small Conference Room.

Harrogate

★★ 64% Young's
15 York Rd, off Swan Rd HG1 2QL ☎(0423) 567336 & 521231 FAX (0423) 500042

Peacefully situated in the Duchy residential area yet within easy walking distance of the town centre, this small, privately owned hotel offers clean, comfortable and pleasantly appointed accommodation and a friendly, relaxed atmosphere.

16⇨⋔(2fb) CTV in all bedrooms ® T ✱ sB&B⇨⋔£35-£55 dB&B⇨⋔£55-£75 ₱
18P ✿
♀ English & French
Credit Cards ① ③

★★ 63% Valley
93-95 Valley Dr HG2 0JP ☎(0423) 504868 FAX (0423) 531940
Closed 22-31 Dec

Overlooking the renowned Valley Gardens, this hotel is part of a Victorian terrace just a short walk from the town and conference centre. Accommodation is very spacious and the food is wholesome with lots of home baking.

15⇨⋔(3fb) CTV in all bedrooms ® T ✱ sB&B⇨⋔£25-£30 dB&B⇨⋔£46-£56 ₱
Lift ⌇
♀ International V ⌇ ⌇ ✱ Dinner £9-£12alc Last dinner 9.30pm
Credit Cards ① ③

★★ 61% West Park
West Park HG1 1BJ ☎(0423) 524471

This centrally situated, friendly hotel has attractive Victorian-style public areas, including a popular grill room downstairs, and neat bedroom with modern facilities.

17⇨⋔ CTV in all bedrooms ® T
⊞ 20P
V ⌇
Credit Cards ① ② ③ ⑤

★ 72% Britannia Lodge
16 Swan Rd HG1 2SA ☎(0423) 508482 FAX (0423) 508482 ex 223

Centrally situated close to the International Conference Centre and shops, this friendly hotel, under the personal supervision of the proprietors, provides very comfortable accommodation with bedroom facilities commensurate with a higher hotel classification. Public rooms include a cosy lounge, small bar and a dining room where traditional Yorkshire home cooking is featured.

12⇨⋔(4fb) CTV in all bedrooms ®⌇ T ✠ ✱ sB&B⇨⋔£35-£45 dB&B⇨⋔£48-£62 ₱
⊞ CTV 6P 1⇨ ⌇
♀ French V ⌇ ⌇ ✱ Lunch £7.50 Dinner £12.50 Last dinner 7pm
Credit Cards ① ② ③ £

★ 70% Cavendish
3 Valley Dr HG2 0JJ ☎(0423) 509637 FAX (0423) 504429

Just a few minutes from the town centre, this gabled Victorian house overlooks Valley Gardens. Bedrooms vary in size but all are well equipped. There is an elegant lounge, a cosy bar, and evening meals in the pretty dining room are delicious.

9⇨⋔1⊞ CTV in all bedrooms ®⌇ T ✱ sB&B⇨⋔£15-£35 dB&B⇨⋔£25-£70
CTV ⌇ ⌇
V ⌇ ✱ Lunch £4-£9alc High tea £2-£5alc Dinner £5-£15alc Last dinner 9.30pm
Credit Cards ① ③ £

★ 70% Gables
2 West Grove Rd HG1 2AD ☎(0423) 505625 FAX (0423) 561312

This Victorian house is just a short walk from the International Conference Centre. Bedrooms are of a good size and all are individually decorated. There is a traditional guests' lounge, a cosy bar and an attractive dining room with blue and white linen.

9rm(8⇨⋔)(2fb) CTV in all bedrooms ® T sB&B⇨⋔£26-£31 dB&B⇨⋔£52-£62 ₱
9P
♀ Continental
Credit Cards ① ③ £

★ 69% Grafton
1-3 Franklin Mount HG1 5EJ ☎(0423) 508491 FAX (0423) 523168

17rm(15⇨⋔)(2fb) CTV in all bedrooms ® T
✠ (ex guide dogs)
CTV 2P
♀ International V ⌇ ⌇ ✱ Last dinner 9pm
Credit Cards ① ② ③ ⑤ £

★ 68% Aston
7-9 Franklin Mount HG1 5EJ (close to conference centre) ☎(0432) 564262 FAX (0423) 505542
Closed 3 Dec-1 Jan

Situated in a quiet side road convenient for the conference centre and main shops, this small, spotlessly clean hotel has comfortable public areas and prettily furnished bedrooms with modern facilities.

15⇨⋔ CTV in all bedrooms ® T sB&B⇨⋔£25-£30 dB&B⇨⋔£50-£60 ₱
CTV 10P
⌇ ⌇ Lunch £10-£15&alc Dinner £10.50-£15&alc Last dinner 7.30pm
CONF. Thtr 25 Del from £32
Credit Cards ① ③ £

★ 67% Alvera Court
76 Kings Rd HG1 5JX (opposite Harrogate Conference Centre) ☎(0423) 505735 FAX (0423) 507996

This attractive Victorian residence is opposite the International Conference Centre. It has welcoming public rooms, which include a comfortable lounge, a cosy bar and attractive dining room. Bedrooms are well equipped and varied in shape. Single rooms are compact, but most doubles are sizeable.

12⇨⋔(3fb) CTV in all bedrooms ® T ✠ (ex guide dogs) ✱ sB&B⇨⋔£23.30-£33.50 dB&B⇨⋔£47-£67 ₱
CTV 4P ⌇ xmas
V ⌇ ✱ Dinner £13.50-£16alc Last dinner 7pm
Credit Cards ① ③

★ 64% The Croft
42-46 Franklin Rd HG1 5EE (Logis) ☎(0423) 563326 FAX (0423) 530733

This friendly, family-run hotel is close to the conference centre and the town's amenities. Bedrooms are equipped to cater for business guests, conference delegates and tourists alike. There is a traditional lounge, a cosy bar, pool room and an attractive dining room where enjoyable and substantial meals are served.

13⇨⋔1⊞ CTV in all bedrooms ® T
10P pool table ⌇
♀ English & French V ⌇ ⌇ Last dinner 9.30pm
Credit Cards ① ③ £

★ 64% The Duchy
51 Valley Dr HG2 0JH ☎(0423) 565818
Closed 21 Dec-Feb

A substantial end of terrace Victorian property in an elevated position overlooking the renowned Valley Gardens. It is friendly and informal and provides a sound standard of accommodation. There is a comfortable lounge bar, a quiet lounge and a small but attractive dining room.

11⇨⋔(5fb) CTV in all bedrooms ®⌇ T ✠ ✱ sB&B⇨⋔fr£32 dB&B⇨⋔fr£50 ₱
CTV ⌇ ⌇
V ⌇ ✱ Dinner fr£10.50 Last dinner 7.30pm
Credit Cards ① ③

HARROW Greater London
See **LONDON SECTION** plan 1*B5*
★★**67%** **Cumberland**
1 St Johns Rd HA1 2EF ☎081-863 4111 FAX 081-861 5668
This hotel offers accommodation in the main building and 2 adjacent buildings around the car park. Room sizes differ but are generally good, and improvements to décor and amenities continue. Public areas are comfortable with lobby seating, a day lounge and the popular 'Parisian' bar.
30⇌↑Annexe51⇌↑(4fb)⊁in 30 bedrooms CTV in all bedrooms ®⚲T✠ (ex guide dogs) sB&B⇌↑£38-£62 dB&B⇌↑£48-£67
《55P sauna small fitness room
♀ English & French V ✿ ⚐ ⊁ Lunch £8.50-£9.95&alc Dinner £12.95-£14.50&alc Last dinner 9.30pm
CONF. Thtr 56 Class 25 Board 22 Del £94
Credit Cards [1][2][3][5]

★★**67%** **Harrow**
Roxborough Bridge, 12-22 Pinner Rd HA1 4HZ ☎081-427 3435 FAX 081-861 1370
RS Xmas
This deceptively large hotel offers accommodation on 3 floors in the main hotel and in 2 adjacent buildings. Rooms vary in size, but are well designed and generously equipped, especially for the business user. Staff are cheerful, and public areas are undergoing improvements.
76⇌↑(4fb)1⛌⊁in 3 bedrooms CTV in all bedrooms ® T ✠ (ex guide dogs) ✱ sB&B⇌↑£48-£69 dB&B⇌↑£65-£95 ⏣
《67P
♀ International V ✿ ⚐ ✱ Lunch £12.95-£16.95&alc Dinner £16.95&alc Last dinner 9.45pm
CONF. Thtr 120 Class 50 Board 40 Del £75
Credit Cards [1][2][3][5] £

★★
Harrow Hotel
12-22 Pinner Road, Harrow, Middlesex HA1 4HZ
Tel: 081-427 3435
Fax: 081-861 1370

Renowned for its friendly staff, realistic pricing and superb professionalism our 100 bedroom all en-suite Town House Hotel is the first choice for the discerning guest.

Together with its sister hotel The Park House, but a stone's throw away, we provide Harrow with the finest in room hospitality, restaurant and functions.

Try us and become another one of our regulars.

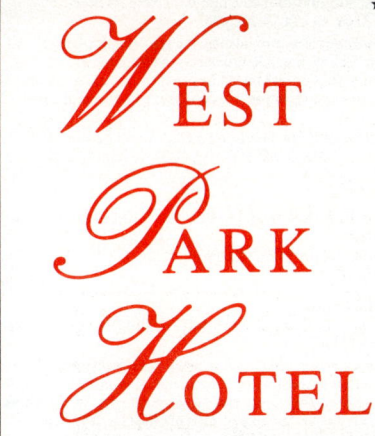

★★
WEST PARK HOTEL
West Park, Harrogate, North Yorkshire HG1 1BJ
Tel: 0423-524471 Fax: 0423-524471

YOUNG'S HOTEL
15 York Road, (Off Swan Road)
Harrogate HG1 2QL
Tel: (0423) 567336/521231
Fax: (0423) 500042

A 16 bedroom licensed hotel with all rooms having bathroom en suite, direct dial telephone, colour TV, and tea/coffee making facilities. Situated in a select residential/conservation area near to the Valley Gardens and within easy walking distance of the town centre, conference/exhibition halls. Set in ½ acre of gardens with large private car park.

**Personnally run
by Jackie &
Chris Lynch**

AA★★

Harrow - Haslemere

★★ 65% Lindal
2 Hindes Rd HA1 1SJ (off A409, opposite Tesco Superstore)
☎081-863 3164 FAX 081-427 5285

Warm, friendly service is provided by the resident proprietors of this comfortable little hotel. Bedrooms are well equipped and practical, while public areas include a panelled bar and romantic candlelit restaurant offering an à la carte menu of uncomplicated dishes.

17rm(14⇨♠)(1fb)⊁in 3 bedrooms CTV in all bedrooms ® T ✱ sB&B£30-£36 sB&B⇨♠£39.50-£44.50 dB&B£40-£44 dB&B⇨♠£45-£50 ⊟
(17P
♀ English & French V ♡ ⊒ ⊁ ✱ Dinner £10-£17.50alc Last dinner 8.30pm
CONF. Thtr 30 Board 25 Del £62.50
Credit Cards [1][3] £

★★ 54% Monksdene
2-12 Northwick Park Rd HA1 2NT (off A4006) ☎081-427 2899 FAX 081-863 2314

Situated in a residential avenue close to the town centre, the Monksdene offers reasonably priced accommodation both in the main house and annexe wing across the large car park. Some rooms are now showing wear, but upgrading is planned for 1993. On weekdays a moderately priced restaurant is open, and dinner dances are a feature at weekends.

64⇨♠ Annexe20⇨♠ (3fb) CTV in all bedrooms ®⊁ T ✖ (ex guide dogs) ✱ sB&B⇨♠£35-£59.50 dB&B⇨♠£45-£79
(CTV 65P
♀ English & French V ♡ ⊒ ⊁ Last dinner 9.45pm
Credit Cards [1][2][3][5]

HARTLEBURY Hereford & Worcester Map 07 SO87

Forte Travelodge
Shorthill Nurseries DY11 6DR (A449 southbound)
☎(0299) 250553 Central Res (0800) 850950

FORTE Travelodge

This modern building offers a good standard of accommodation for overnight stops. Smart, spacious and well equipped bedrooms, all with en suite bathrooms, are suitable for family use, and meals may be taken at the nearby family restaurant. For more details about Travelodges, consult the Contents page, under Hotel Groups.

32⇨♠ ✱ B⇨♠£31.95 (room only)

HARTLEPOOL Cleveland Map 08 NZ53

★★★ 61% The Grand
Swainson St TS24 8AA ☎(0429) 266345 FAX (0429) 265217

Much renovation work has been carried out at this splendid Victorian hotel in recent years, and though there are still one or 2 areas of faded elegance, particularly the façade, there are plans to restore it to its original grandeur. Bedrooms are particularly spacious, most have been refurbished and offer every modern convenience. A feature of the hotel is the magnificent ballroom with its unique balcony.

47⇨♠(4fb) CTV in all bedrooms ®⊁ T ✱ sB&B⇨♠£36.95-£79.95 dB&B⇨♠£63-£90 ⊟
Lift (50P
V ♡ ⊒ ✱ Lunch £3.99-£6.50 Dinner fr£8.50&alc Last dinner 9.45pm
Credit Cards [1][2][3][5] £

★★ 73% Ryedale Moor
3 Beaconsfield St, Headland TS24 0NX (access via A179) (Logis)
☎(0429) 231436 FAX (0429) 863787

In a quiet location overlooking the bay and esplanade, the Ryedale has well appointed bedrooms, and although lounge and restaurant space is limited, it is comfortable. A vegetarian dinner menu is available in addition to the good value standard menus.

13⇨♠(2fb)⊁in 5 bedrooms CTV in all bedrooms ®⊁ T ✖ ✱ sB&B⇨♠£36.50-£54 dB&B⇨♠£56.50-£60 ⊟

CTV 7P nc12yrs
♀ English, French & Indian V ♡ ⊒ ⊁ ✱ Lunch £4.90-£13&alc High tea £3.90-£6.80&alc Dinner £4.50-£13&alc Last dinner 9pm
CONF. Thtr 45 Class 35 Board 35 Del from £45
Credit Cards [1][2][3][5] £

HARTSHEAD MOOR SERVICE AREA West Yorkshire Map 07 SE12

Forte Travelodge
Clifton HD6 4RJ ☎(0274) 851706

FORTE Travelodge

This modern building offers a good standard of accommodation for overnight stops. Smart, spacious and well equipped bedrooms, all with en suite bathrooms, are suitable for family use, and meals may be taken at the nearby family restaurant. For more details about Travelodges, consult the Contents page, under Hotel Groups.

40⇨♠ ✱ B⇨♠£31.95 (room only)

HARVINGTON (NEAR EVESHAM) Hereford & Worcester Map 04 SP04

★★ ❀77% The Mill at Harvington
Anchor Ln, Harvington WR11 5NR ☎Evesham(0386) 870688 FAX (0386) 870688

(For full entry see Evesham)

HARWICH Essex Map 05 TM23

★★ ❀68% The Pier at Harwich
The Quay CO12 3HH ☎(0255) 241212 FAX (0206) 322752

This imposing quayside Victorian building is famous for its fish restaurants, but also has attractive, modern bedrooms. Fish and chips are the speciality of the Ha'penny Pier restaurant, though other popular dishes are available. Upstairs, the atmosphere is more formal, with a traditional menu, with much use of sauces to accompany the dishes. Lobster is always available, as are plainly grilled fish and meat dishes.

6⇨♠(2fb) CTV in all bedrooms ® T ✖ (ex guide dogs)
sB&B⇨♠£45-£60 dB&B⇨♠£62.50-£72.50 Continental breakfast
(10P
♀ English & French V Lunch £9-£14.25&alc Dinner £16&alc Last dinner 9.30pm
Credit Cards [1][3] £

★★ 55% Cliff
Marine Pde, Dovercourt CO12 3RE ☎(0255) 503345 & 507373 FAX (0255) 240358

Quietly situated overlooking the bay, this impressive late Victorian hotel has smartly refurbished ground-floor public rooms, making the alternative basement bar now look rather dated. Bedrooms have also recently been improved and are generally spacious and comfortable.

28⇨♠ CTV in all bedrooms ® T sB&B⇨♠£35-£48 dB&B⇨♠£45-£58 ⊟
(60P
V ♡ ⊒ Lunch £9.25&alc Dinner £10.50&alc Last dinner 9pm
CONF. Thtr 200 Class 120 Board 20 Del from £72
Credit Cards [1][2][3][4][5] £

HASLEMERE Surrey Map 04 SU93

★★★ 72% Lythe Hill
Petworth Rd GU27 3BQ (1.25m E B2131) ☎(0428) 651251 FAX (0428) 644131

Once an ancient hamlet, set in 14 acres of grounds, Lythe Hill comprises a 14th-century farmhouse and various outbuildings, converted to house stylish bedrooms which vary in size. The 2

288

Haslemere - Hastings & St Leonards

restaurants offer similar menus, though the Auberge has an ambitious French slant. Service is exceptionally good.
40⇨↑(8fb)1⊟ CTV in all bedrooms T sB⇨↑£84-£134 dB⇨↑£95-£175 (room only) ♫
(200P ✿ ♀ (hard) ♪ boules croquet games room *xmas*
♀ English & French V ✿ ♫ Lunch £17.50&alc Dinner £17.50&alc Last dinner 9.15pm
CONF. Thtr 100 Class 60 Board 40 Del from £122
Credit Cards [1][2][3]

HASTINGS & ST LEONARDS East Sussex Map 05 TQ80
★★★69% **Beauport Park**
Battle Rd TN38 8EA (3m N off A2100)
☎Hastings(0424) 851222 FAX (0424) 852345

Quietly situated north of the town, this fine Georgian house has been tastefully furnished in the country house style. The Garden Restaurant offers an extensive à la carte menu with speciality flambés and a good value table d'hôte.
23⇨↑(2fb)1⊟ CTV in all bedrooms ®⚲ T ✱ sB&B⇨↑£62 dB&B⇨↑£75 ♫
60P 4🏊 (£1.50) ✿ ⛆ (heated) ▶ 18 ♀ (hard) squash ∪ snooker putting croquet boules outdoor chess ♫ *xmas*
♀ French V ✿ ♫ ✱ Lunch £13.50&alc High tea fr£8 Dinner fr£15.50&alc Last dinner 9.30pm
CONF. Thtr 60 Class 40 Board 40 Del from £79.50
Credit Cards [1][2][3][5]

★★★67% *Cinque Ports*
Summerfields(Cinque Ports) ☎Hastings(0424) 439222 FAX (0424) 437277
This popular and conveniently situated hotel offers smart modern bedrooms and public areas which are spacious and comfortable. The bar and foyer areas have real log fires, tapestry wall hangings, stone floors and attractive oriental rugs. There is all day room service, and early morning tea is also served.
40⇨↑(4fb) CTV in all bedrooms T 🐕 (ex guide dogs)
(80P ✿
V ✿ ♫ Last dinner 10pm
Credit Cards [1][2][3][5]

★★★64% **Royal Victoria**
The Marina, St Leonards-on-Sea TN38 0BD (on western seafront) ☎Hastings(0424) 445544
FAX (0424) 721995
The Royal Victoria is an imposing building on the sea front at St Leonards. The marble pillared and mirrored grand stairway leads up to the public rooms, which include the Sea Terrace where bar snacks and teas are served. The dining room shares the channel view, and dinner dances and gourmet evenings are a regular feature here. The spacious bedrooms have separate sitting areas and nicely co-ordinated fabrics and furnishings.
50⇨↑(4fb)⊬in 2 bedrooms CTV in all bedrooms ® T sB&B⇨↑£30-£65 dB&B⇨↑£50-£90 ♫
Lift (6P *xmas*
♀ English & French V ✿ ♫ ⊬ Lunch £9.50-£11&alc High tea £5-£10 Dinner £10-£16&alc Last dinner 9.30pm
CONF. Thtr 150 Class 40 Board 25 Del from £50
Credit Cards [1][2][3][5]

★★67% **High Beech**
Battle Rd TN37 7BS (400yds from A2100)
☎Hastings(0424) 851383 FAX (0424) 854265
Situated in a residential area, this family-run hotel has benefited from extensive refurbishment. Cosy bedrooms provide every comfort, and public areas are spacious but functional. The efforts of the proprietor and management help to create a welcoming atmosphere.
17⇨↑(3fb)4⊟ CTV in all bedrooms ®⚲ T 🐕 (ex guide dogs)
➡

The Beauport Park Hotel
Hastings, Sussex TN38 8EA ★★★
Tel: 0424 851222 Fax: 0424 852345

A Georgian country house hotel set in 33 acres of parkland with its own swimming pool, tennis courts, putting green, badminton lawn, French boules, outdoor chess, croquet lawn and country walks. Candle-lit restaurant and open log fires. Adjacent to 18 hole and 9 hole golf courses, riding stables and squash courts.

Resident proprietors:
Kenneth and Helena Melsom

Special country house bargain breaks available all year. Please send for our colour brochure and tariff.

netherfield
★ ★ ★ ❁   place

This Georgian style country house hotel lies at the heart of one of the most beautiful and unspoilt areas of England.

Each of the 14 bedrooms has a private bathroom, colour TV, radio and direct dialling telephone.

Standing in 30 acres Netherfield Place is a haven for those who enjoy peace and tranquility in a grand setting; with two hard tennis courts, putting green and croquet lawn within the grounds.

Conference and Banqueting information on request.
Helen and Michael Collier
Netherfield Place, Battle, East Sussex
Tel: (0424) 774455 Fax: (0424) 774024

Hastings & St Leonards - Hawes

65P
 Continental **V** ॐ ⚓ Last dinner 9.30pm
Credit Cards [1] [2] [3] [5]

HATHERSAGE Derbyshire Map 08 SK28

★★★ 65% George
Main Rd S30 1BB (in village centre on A625) (Whitbread)
☎Hope Valley(0433) 650436 FAX (0433) 650099
Surrounded by the Peak District National Park, this 16th-century coaching inn provides the services and facilities of a good hotel yet retains the character of its past. The cosy sofas and armchairs and the log effect fire create a comfortable, welcoming atmosphere, and the Charlotte restaurant is equally comfortable. The bedrooms are pleasantly decorated and furnished.
18⇌ (3fb)1 in 6 bedrooms CTV in all bedrooms ® **T**
✕ (ex guide dogs) ✱ sB&B⇌ fr£65.50 dB&B⇌ fr£77 ₽
40P ✿ *xmas*
 International **V** ॐ ⚓ Last dinner 10pm
Credit Cards [1] [2] [3] [5]

★★ 71% Hathersage Inn
Main St S30 1BB ☎Hope Valley(0433) 650259
FAX (0433) 651199

This recently upgraded old stone inn in the town centre, equally popular with Peak District tourists and business travellers, offers attractively decorated accommodation which is furnished in period style but equipped to satisfy every modern need; executive bedrooms – four of them in a detached house next door – are larger, and family rooms are also available. Public areas include a choice of bars, a comfortable lounge and an attractively appointed split-level restaurant with stucco plaster walls.
11⇌ Annexe4rm1 CTV in all bedrooms ® **T**
20P
V ॐ ⚓ Last dinner 9.30pm
Credit Cards [1] [2] [3] [5]

HAVANT Hampshire Map 04 SU70

★★★ 57% The Bear
East St PO9 1AA (Whitbread) ☎(0705) 486501 FAX (0705) 470551
The Bear is a former coaching inn at the heart of the town which offers both a small cocktail bar and the Elizabethan public bar, the latter much improved in recent years. Bedrooms are gradually being upgraded, though all are fully equipped.
42⇌ (3fb)1 in 11 bedrooms CTV in all bedrooms ® ✻ **T**
✕ (ex guide dogs) ✱ sB&B⇌ £55.50-£65.50 dB&B⇌ £67-£77 ₽
(90P *xmas*
 European **V** ॐ ⚓ Last dinner 10pm
CONF. Thtr 120 Board 60 Del from £89
Credit Cards [1] [2] [3] [5]

HAVERFORDWEST Dyfed Map 02 SM91

★★ 67% Castle
Castle Square SA61 2AA (from the main roundabout into Haverfordwest take the town centre turn off, follow the road for approx 200yds, hotel on right hand side) ☎(0437) 769322
FAX (0437) 769493
This fine old coaching inn at the foot of the castle features a popular bar and attractive first-floor restaurant providing a wide choice of food. Bedrooms are all very pretty and comfortable, though they are all located on the 3rd and 4th floors.
9⇌ (1fb) CTV in all bedrooms ® **T** ✕ (ex guide dogs)
sB&B⇌ £32.50-£40 dB&B⇌ £47.50-£52.50
(P
 Welsh, French & Italian **V** ॐ ⚓ Lunch £2.75-£5.55
Dinner £5.45-£7.95alc Last dinner 10pm
Credit Cards [1] [3] [5]

★★ 61% Hotel Mariners
Mariners Square SA61 2DU ☎(0437) 763353
FAX (0437) 764258
Closed 26-27 Dec & 1 Jan
This family-run hotel dates back to 1625 when the town was a busy commercial centre and port. Most bedrooms have been upgraded and the bars and other public rooms are to receive the same treatment. Take care not to miss the sign to the car park – there is an extra mile round the one-way system if you do.
30⇌ (5fb) in 3 bedrooms CTV in all bedrooms ® **T**
sB&B⇌ £45-£51 dB&B⇌ £62.50-£67.50 ₽
(50P ✿ short mat bowls
 English & French **V** ॐ ⚓ Lunch £8.50 Dinner £11-£12.50&alc Last dinner 9.30pm
CONF. Thtr 50 Class 28 Board 28 Del from £60
Credit Cards [1] [2] [3] [5]

★★ 57% Pembroke House
Spring Gardens SA61 2EJ ☎(0437) 763652
This creeper-clad Georgian house a few minutes' walk from the town centre is run by the friendly Davies family. Popular with business travellers, the hotel offers well equipped bedrooms, a spacious and comfortable lounge bar and a good choice of food.
21rm(13⇌ 6)(4fb)1 CTV in all bedrooms ® **T** sB&B£33
sB&B⇌ £38 dB&B£50 dB&B⇌ £55 ₽
CTV 18P
V ॐ ⚓ ✻ Dinner £8.95-£19.95alc Last dinner 9.30pm
Credit Cards [1] [2] [3] [5]

HAWES North Yorkshire Map 07 SD88

★★ 76% Simonstone Hall
Simonstone DL8 3LY (1.5m N on road signed to Muker) (Logis)
☎Wensleydale(0969) 667255 FAX (0969) 667741
John and Sheila Jeffryes' comfortable country house has panoramic views of the dale and surrounding hills. A former home of the earls of Wharncliffe, the house was built in 1733 and features stained glass, oil paintings and old church pews in the bar. Most of the public rooms are panelled and have log fires and antique pieces.
10⇌ CTV in all bedrooms ® dB&B⇌ £110-£145 (incl dinner) ₽
24P ✿ ✿ ❀ *xmas*
 English & French **V** ॐ ⚓ Lunch £6.50-£11 Dinner £9.50-£16.50 Last dinner 8.30pm
Credit Cards [1] [3]

★★ 71% Stone House
Sedbusk DL8 3PT ☎Wensleydale(0969) 667571 FAX (0969) 667720
Closed Jan RS mid Nov-Dec & Feb
A delightful family-run Edwardian country house, this hotel is set in attractive gardens on the Upper Dale. The bedrooms on the ground floor have individual conservatories leading to the garden. Cosy lounges with log fires are a feature, and there is also a fine library and billiard room. Home-cooked Yorkshire food is served in the interesting dining room.
15rm(14⇌ 1)(1fb)2 CTV in all bedrooms ® **T** ✻
sB&Bfr£24.50 sB&B⇌ fr£24.50 dB&Bfr£49 dB&B⇌ £60-£72 ₽
15P ✿ ✿ (grass) *xmas*
V ॐ ⚓ Last dinner 8pm
Credit Cards [1] [3]

★★ 70% Rookhurst Georgian Country House
Gayle DL8 3RT (0.5m from town at Gayle, on A684) ☎Wensleydale(0969) 667454
Closed 16 Dec-Jan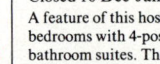
A feature of this hospitable small country house hotel is its fine bedrooms with 4-poster and half tester beds, oak beams and antique bathroom suites. The elegant dining room is beautifully furnished with antique pieces, and the relaxing lounge and bar look out

towards the surrounding hills. The atmosphere is informal, friendly and relaxing.
6rm(4⇌1♠)2⊞⤢in all bedrooms CTV in all bedrooms ®
✘ (ex guide dogs) ✻ sB&B£38-£45 dB&B⇌♠£84-£112 (incl dinner) ♫
10P ⌬ nc12yrs
✿ ⚛ ⤢ ✻ Dinner fr£20 Last dinner 7.30pm
Credit Cards [1][3]

★★ 68% **Cocketts**
Market Place DL8 3RD
☎Wensleydale(0969) 667312 FAX (0969) 667162

This ivy-clad stone-built 17th-century hotel in the centre of the town provides compact but modern accommodation in an atmosphere of old world charm and character. It is particularly hospitable, with personal service provided by the proprietors, and the standard of the food is high.
8rm(2⇌4♠)2⊞⤢in all bedrooms CTV in all bedrooms ® T
✘ (ex guide dogs) ✻ sB&B£32.50 sB&B⇌♠£37.50 dB&B£44 dB&B⇌♠£54-£64 ♫
✞ ⌬ ❋ nc10yrs xmas
♀ English & French ✿ ⚛ ⤢ Lunch fr£8.95&alc Dinner £15.95&alc Last dinner 8.30pm
Credit Cards [1][3]

★★ 61% **Fountain**
Market Place DL8 3RD ☎(0969) 667206
Closed 24-25 Dec
Situated in the market place, this 17th-century coaching inn provides modern accommodation for tourists and business people alike. There are also popular bars, a restaurant and a small guests' lounge on the first floor.
10⇌♠(2fb)⤢in 1 bedroom CTV in all bedrooms ® T
sB&B⇌♠£20-£26 dB&B⇌♠£32-£48 ♫
10P
✿ ✻ Sunday Lunch £5 Dinner £12 Last dinner 9pm
Credit Cards [1][3]

HAWICK Borders *Roxburghshire* Map **12** NT51
★★ 71% **Kirklands**
West Stewart Place TD9 8BH (.5m N from Hawick High Street, 200yds W of A7) ☎(0450) 72263 FAX (0450) 370404
This small traditional hotel offers spacious well equipped bedrooms, inviting lounges and warm friendly service. The good-value dinner menu provides a varied selection.
5⇌♠Annexe7⇌♠ CTV in all bedrooms ® T
sB&B⇌♠£48.50-£50 dB&B⇌♠£70-£75 ♫
20P ❋ snooker games room ⌬
♀ International V ✿ ⚛ ✻ Lunch £4.95-£10.95alc High tea £6.95 Dinner £17.50-£19.50&alc Last dinner 9.30pm
Credit Cards [1][2][3][5] (£)

HAWKCHURCH Devon Map **03** ST30

★★★ ⊛ ⤓ 72% **Fairwater Head**
EX13 5TX (signposted from village) ☎(0297) 678349
Closed 7 Dec-5 Mar
Set in well kept gardens and grounds amidst rolling countryside, this charming Edwardian house provides warm personal service and a peaceful atmosphere. Comfortable bedrooms are attractive, with coordinated floral soft furnishings, and there is a choice of relaxing lounges, an elegant drawing room and a dining room where 4-course dinners are based on fresh local produce.
14⇌♠Annexe7⇌♠ CTV in all bedrooms ® T ✻
sB&B⇌♠£56-£76 dB&B⇌♠£112-£144 (incl dinner) ♫
30P ⌬ ❋ croquet lawn bowls ♪ ⌬ xmas

PEMBROKE HOUSE HOTEL & RESTAURANT

Spring Gardens
Haverfordwest, Pembrokeshire
Tel: (0437) 763652

21 bedrooms, 19 en suite, all rooms with TV, tea and coffee and direct dialling. Car park, Night porter. Intimate restaurant serving à la carte and table d'hôte. Bed & Breakfast from £38.00
Bed & breakfast double from £55.00.
Visa
Access
Amex
Diners
Club

HIGH BEECH HOTEL

This delightful, privately owned Country House Hotel, situated between the two historic towns of Hastings and Battle offers good value and traditional hospitality. All rooms decorated and furnished to a very high standard. Each room en-suite (bath and shower), direct dial telephone, colour television with satellite stations, trouser press, hair dryer and beverage facilities. Some rooms with 4 poster beds, corner baths and balconies. Excellent cuisine - Mini Breaks available throughout the year. Purpose built Conference/Meeting rooms accommodating up to 200 persons, fully equipped to meet any requirements. Golf, horseriding and vineyards nearby. Ideal centre for exploring historic 1066 countryside.

HIGH BEECH HOTEL
Battle Road, St. Leonards on Sea, East Sussex TN37 7BS
Tel: 0424 851383.
AA ★★   Fax: 0424 854265

Hawkchurch - Haydock

✿ ♨ ⚥ ✱ Sunday Lunch fr£11 Dinner £18.50-£20.50 Last dinner 8.30pm
Credit Cards 1 2 3 5
See advertisement under LYME REGIS

HAWKHURST Kent Map 05 TQ73

★★★ 66% Tudor Court
Rye Rd TN18 5DA (1m S, on A268)
☎(0580) 752312 FAX (0580) 753966

This picturesque little country hotel has been skilfully extended with newer bedrooms in the Garden Wing, and while others vary in shape and size they are all well furnished. The Candelit Restaurant overlooks an extensive and beautifully kept garden, and children are well catered for. There is a traditional lounge and bar, and staff are particularly helpful.
18⇨♠(2fb)2🛏 CTV in all bedrooms ® T sB&B⇨♠£39-£49 dB&B⇨♠£79-£89 🅿
CTV 50P 1🎾 (£5 per night) 🚭 ✿ 𝒫 (hard) croquet clock golf childrens play area xmas
♀ International V ✿ ♨ ⚥ ✱ Lunch £10.50-£12.95 Dinner fr£14.95&alc Last dinner 9.15pm
CONF. Thtr 70 Class 40 Board 30 Del from £69
Credit Cards 1 2 3 4 5

HAWKSHEAD (NEAR AMBLESIDE) Cumbria
Map 07 SD39

★★🐑73% Highfield House
Hawkshead Hill LA22 0PN (on B5285)
☎Ambleside(05394) 36244
Closed 24-26 Dec

Set in woodland gardens high above the valley, this attractive stone house gives fine views from its comfortable, well furnished bedrooms. There is a very comfortable lounge and the caring owners provide friendly and atttentive service.
11⇨♠(2fb) CTV in all bedrooms ® sB&B⇨♠£32 dB&B⇨♠£59-£66 🅿
12P 🚭 ✿ 🐕
♀ English & Continental V ✿ ♨ Last dinner 8pm
Credit Cards 1 3

★★ 61% Queen's Head
Main St LA22 0NS ☎Hawkshead(05394) 36271 FAX (05394) 36722

This attractive old inn at the centre of the village, with low ceilings, oak beams and panelled walls, has modest, prettily furnished bedrooms. A wide choice of food is offered in the popular bar and cosy dining room.
10rm(1⇨7♠)Annexe4⇨♠(2fb)2🛏 CTV in all bedrooms ® T ✱ sB&B£32-£40 sB&B⇨♠£40 dB&Bfr£50.50 dB&B⇨♠£57.50-£66
10P nc8yrs xmas
♀ English & Continental V ✿ ⚥
Credit Cards 1 3

HAWNBY North Yorkshire Map 08 SE58

★★ 69% Hawnby
YO6 5QS ☎Bilsdale(04396) 202 FAX (04396) 417
Closed 25 Dec & Feb

Personal attention to guests is a hallmark of this delightful little hotel in the picturesque village of Hawnby, set amid unspoilt countryside. Attractive bedrooms, many decorated with Laura Ashley prints, have all modern comforts, and traditional English cooking is served in the dining room, with bar meals available in the cosy bar.
6⇨♠ CTV in all bedrooms ® T ✱ sB&B⇨♠£50-£64 dB&B⇨♠£70-£98 🅿

25P ✿ 𝒫 (hard) ♪ nc10yrs
V ✿ Bar Lunch £2.20-£5.25 Dinner fr£14 Last dinner 8.30pm
Credit Cards 1 3

HAWORTH West Yorkshire Map 07 SE03

★★ 66% Old White Lion
6 West Ln BD22 8DU (on A629) ☎(0535) 642313 FAX (0535) 646222

At the top of the quaint cobbled street, this stone faced inn has retained a warm and cosy character. The furnishings in the restaurant and lounge are mainly dark polished woods with tapestry upholstery. The bar is popular with locals and has a good bar food trade. The bedrooms are well equipped, but do tend to be compact. The staff are young, friendly and obliging.
15⇨♠(3fb) CTV in all bedrooms ® T ✱ (ex guide dogs) sB&B⇨♠£35 dB&B⇨♠£46 🅿
10P xmas
♀ English & French V ✿ Last dinner 9.30pm
CONF. Thtr 40 Class 40 Board 30 Del £52
Credit Cards 1 2 3 5
See advertisement under BRADFORD

★★ 64% Three Sisters
Brow Top Rd BD22 9PH ☎(0535) 643458 FAX (0535) 646842

Standing on an open hillside a short way from the village, this modern stone-built hotel provides a good all-round standard of accommodation. Public areas are spacious, and the choice of dishes offered in the restaurant, is supplemented by a range of bar meals.
9⇨♠(1fb) CTV in all bedrooms ®⚥ T ✱ (ex guide dogs) ✿ sB⇨♠£35 dB⇨♠£45 (room only) 🅿
CTV 300P ✿ xmas
♀ English & French V ✿ ♨ ⚥ ✱ Lunch £5.95-£8.95 Dinner £9.95-£15.50 Last dinner 9.45pm
Credit Cards 1 2 3

HAYDOCK Merseyside Map 07 SJ59

★★★★ 62% Haydock Thistle
Penny Ln WA11 9SG (off A599 at junc 23 of M6) ☎Ashton-in-Makerfield(0942) 272000 FAX (0942) 711092

This modern purpose built hotel with its striking neo-Georgian façade is an understandably popular meeting place, and the attractive lounge areas, furnished in country house styles, are always busy. Spacious and well furnished bedrooms offer restful décor and modern amenities.
139⇨♠(13fb)⚥ in 30 bedrooms CTV in all bedrooms ®⚥ T ✱ sB⇨♠£79 dB⇨♠£89 (room only) 🅿
☾180P ✿ 🏊 (heated) sauna solarium gymnasium pool table steam room whirlpool 🐕 xmas
♀ English & Continental V ✿ ♨ ✱ Lunch £9.75&alc Dinner £17.50&alc Last dinner 10pm
CONF. Thtr 300 Class 180 Board 90 Del from £75
Credit Cards 1 2 3 4 5

Forte Posthouse
Lodge Ln, Newton-Le-Willows WA12 0JG (adj to M6 junct 23) ☎Wigan(0942) 717878 FAX (0942) 718419

Suitable for both the business and leisure traveller, this bright hotel provides modern accommodation in well equipped bedrooms with en suite bathrooms. For more details about Forte Posthouse, consult the Contents page, under Hotel Groups.
136⇨♠ ✱ B⇨♠£41.50-£53.50 (room only)
CONF. Thtr 180 Class 100 Board 60 Del from £79.50

Forte Travelodge
Piele Rd WA11 9TL (2m W of M6, on A580 westbound)
☎(0942) 272055 Central Res (0800) 850850

This modern building offers a good standard of accommodation for overnight stops. Smart, spacious and well equipped bedrooms, all with en suite bathrooms, are suitable for family use, and meals may be taken at the nearby family restaurant. For more details about Travelodges, consult the Contents page, under Hotel Groups.
40 ⇨ ✷ B⇨ £31.95 (room only)

HAYDON BRIDGE Northumberland Map 12 NY86
★★ 60% **Anchor**
John Martin St NE47 6AB ☎(0434) 684227 FAX (0434) 684586
This riverside hotel is beside the old bridge spanning the Tyne which now provides pedestrian access from one side of the village to the other. It has a lounge adjacent to its small upstairs dining room as well as a spacious, comfortable, ground floor bar.
12rm(10)(1fb) CTV in all bedrooms ® T sB&B£37-£41 sB&B £46.50-£49.50 dB&B£49-£52 dB&B £58-£63 ₽ 25P ♪
♀ English & French V ♡ ♵ ✂ Lunch £7.50-£20&alc Dinner £17-£40alc Last dinner 9pm
Credit Cards 1 2 3 5 £

HAYES Greater London
Travel Inn
362 Uxbridge Rd UB4 0HE ☎081-573 7479

Purpose-built accommodation offers spacious and well equipped bedrooms, all with en suite bathrooms. Meals may be taken at the nearby family restaurant and pub. For more details about Travel Inns, consult the Contents page, under Hotel Groups.
40 ⇨ ✷ B⇨ £33.50 (room only)

The Three Sisters
★★ Hotel
Brow Top Road, Haworth
Nr Keighley, W.Yorkshire BD22 9PH
Tel: 0535 643458. Fax: 0535 646842

Nestled in 20 acres of rugged moorland and only minutes away from a vast choice of leisure activities, our hotel offers olde-worlde charm in a modern and lively setting.

One of Haworth's most attractive hotels, we cater for all categories of visitors with both extensive bar, food, and function facilities.

★★★★AA
THE HAYDOCK
THISTLE HOTEL

Penny Lane, Haydock WA11 9SG
Tel: 0942 272000   Fax: 0942 711092

Your choice at Haydock

For Reservations at over 100
Mount Charlotte Thistle Hotels
Telephone London: 071 937 8033.

ETB♛♛♛♛   AA★★★

Tudor Court Hotel

In the Garden of England

In the very heart of the beautiful Garden of England, at Hawkhurst, lies the Tudor Court Hotel. A country hotel, set in its own 2 acres of delightful gardens, which believes in high standards of service – and in offering traditional cuisine.
The 18 en-suite bedrooms, some with 4 poster bed, have colour television, hospitality tray and telephone. There are two bars, attractive restaurant, lounge, croquet and clock golf lawns, tennis courts, and a children's play area. Tudor Court Hotel offers tranquillity. Come and enjoy it for yourself. An excellent base to visit the many historical and other places of interest within a 15 mile radius.

For reservations please contact
Tony Climpson – Owner.

TUDOR COURT HOTEL
Rye Road, Hawkhurst,
Cranbrook, Kent TN18 5DA
Tel: 0580 752312 Fax: 0580 753966

Hayling Island - Heathrow Airport (London)

HAYLING ISLAND Hampshire Map 04 SU70

Forte Posthouse
Northney Rd PO11 0NQ ☎(0705) 465011 FAX (0705) 466468

Suitable for both the business and leisure traveller, this bright hotel provides modern accommodation in well equipped bedrooms with en suite bathrooms. For more details about Forte Posthouse hotels, consult the Contents page, under Hotel Groups.
92⇨↑ ✱ B⇨↑ £41.50-£53.50 (room only)
CONF. Thtr 180 Class 80 Board 50 Del £89.50

HAY-ON-WYE Powys Map 03 SO24

★★★❀66% The Swan
Church St HR3 5DQ ☎(0497) 821188 FAX (0497) 821424

This carefully modernised and extended Georgian hotel is right at the heart of this popular village. The bedrooms, some in a courtyard cottage, have attractive décor and coordinating fabrics. There are a number of comfortable public rooms, a terrace and a garden, and a wide range of food is served in the bar or restaurant. It has been noticed that services are covered by a minimal nucleus of staff during the winter, occasionally resulting in a more informal style.
15⇨↑ Annexe4⇨↑(1fb)1🛏 CTV in all bedrooms ®
sB&B⇨↑fr£50 dB&B⇨↑fr£60 🅿
18P ♪ xmas
V ♿ ⌴ ✔ Last dinner 9.30pm
CONF. Thtr 160 Class 160 Board 80 Del from £65
Credit Cards [1][2][3][5]

★★❀69% Old Black Lion
26 Lion St HR3 5AD ☎(0497) 820841
John and Joan Collins run this cosy hotel in a friendly, relaxed style. It dates back to the 13th century, though the main part of the building is 17th century, and it has congenial rustic bars and a small TV lounge. Bedrooms vary in size but all are pretty. Hearty breakfasts and dinner can be taken in the small, beamed restaurant where chefs Russell Sime and Nathan Mulligan produce good country cooking. You need a healthy appetite, there is no sign of nouvelle cuisine, and the food has honest flavours and textures.
6rm(5↑) Annexe4⇨↑(2fb) CTV in all bedrooms ® T
CTV 20P 🎄 ♪ nc5yrs
V ♿ ✔ Lunch £8-£15alc Dinner £10-£15alc Last dinner 9pm
Credit Cards [1][2][3]

HAYTOR Devon Map 03 SX77

★★★❀⚑77% Bel Alp House
TQ13 9XX (2.5m W of Bovey Tracey, off B3387)
☎(0364) 661217 FAX (0364) 661292
RS Dec-Feb
This Swiss chalet-style Edwardian property stands in its own beautiful gardens high up in Dartmoor National Park, with magnificent views. The family home of Roger and Sarah Curnock offers guests an extremely high standard of comfort and elegance. Spacious bedrooms, most benefiting from the view, all decorated with pretty coordinating fabrics. The lounges are peaceful and relaxing and service is warm and attentive. A set 5-course meal is carefully prepared by Sarah, and alternatives are always offered.
9⇨↑ CTV in all bedrooms ® T sB&B⇨↑£75-£87 dB&B⇨↑£126-£150
Lift 20P 🎄 ✱ snooker
♀ English & French ✔ Dinner £33-£36 Last dinner 8.30pm
Credit Cards [1][3]

★★❀70% Rock Inn
TQ13 9XP ☎(0364) 661305 & 661465 FAX (0364) 661242
This white painted inn is situated in the village below the famous Haytor Rocks. The resident proprietor is very much involved in welcoming guests who come to sample the selection of real ales, enjoy the meals prepared by chef Neil Elliot or stay in one of the comfortable bedrooms. The bars are full of character with exposed beams, inglenook fireplaces and flagstone floors, and offer a wide range of sophisticated bar meals.
9⇨↑(2fb)1🛏 in 2 bedrooms CTV in all bedrooms ® ✱ T
🐕 (ex guide dogs) ✱ sB&Bfr£27.95 sB&B⇨↑£37.95-£41.95 dB&Bfr£27.95 dB&B⇨↑£55.50-£81.50 🅿
20P 🎄 ✱ xmas
♀ English & French V ♿ ⌴ ✔ ✱ Bar Lunch £5-£20alc Dinner £19-£95&alc Last dinner 9.30pm
Credit Cards [1][2][3]

HAYWARDS HEATH West Sussex Map 04 TQ32

★★★❀60% The Birch
Lewes Rd RH17 7SF ☎(0444) 451565 FAX (0444) 440109
This comfortable hotel, converted from a late Victorian house, retains much of the original wood panelling. The Lewes bar is popular for its bar meals and real ales and there is an attractive restaurant where the new chef has introduced a daily carte. Bedrooms are well furnished in modern style, with good facilities.
53⇨↑ in 15 bedrooms CTV in all bedrooms ® T
sB&B⇨↑£25-£56.50 dB&B⇨↑£50-£70 🅿
(65P
♀ English & French V ♿ ⌴ ✔ Lunch £12.95-£13.95&alc Dinner £14.95-£15.95&alc Last dinner 9.30pm
CONF. Thtr 60 Class 30 Board 26 Del from £50
Credit Cards [1][2][3][5]

HEATHROW AIRPORT (LONDON) Greater London Map 04 TQ07

See also **Hounslow** and **Staines**

★★★★70% Holiday Inn Crowne Plaza
Stockley Rd, West Drayton UB7 9NA (2m N junc M4/A408)
☎West Drayton(0895) 445555 FAX (0895) 445122

This large modern airport hotel has recently undergone a total transformation into a Holiday Inn Crowne Plaza which has provided more luxuries and well appointed bedrooms, restaurants, public areas, conference and leisure facilities.
375⇨↑(220fb) ✔ in 187 bedrooms CTV in all bedrooms ® ⚴ T ✱
sB⇨↑£127.50-£135 dB⇨↑£142.50-£150 (room only) 🅿
Lift (🎄 400P 🎄 ✱ ⛱ (heated) ▶ 9 sauna solarium gymnasium spa steam room beauty therapy room
♀ International V ♿ ⌴ ✔ ✱ Lunch £9.75-£15.50&alc Dinner £10.75-£16.95&alc Last dinner mdnt
CONF. Thtr 200 Class 150 Board 75 Del from £125
Credit Cards [1][2][3][4][5]

★★★★66% London Heathrow Hilton
Terminal 4, Heathrow Airport TW6 3AF
☎081-759 7755

Even the roar of Concorde can hardly be heard beyond the triple glazing of this striking ultra-modern hotel, with a direct covered link with terminal 4. Beneath its vast atrium is a range of airy facilities which include a choice of eating options (Oscar's bar and grill is open 24 hours), a health and leisure club, business and conference centre, gift shop and travel desk. Bedrooms are bright and have up-to-date equipment – TV sets provide a fast check-out facility and flight information. All rooms are fully air conditioned, and the best accommodation is on the executive floor, which has its own lounge.
400⇨↑ CTV in all bedrooms ® T ✱ sB⇨↑fr£145
dB⇨↑fr£155 (room only)
Lift (🎄 P (charged) ⛱ (heated) sauna gymnasium

Heathrow Airport (London) - Hebden Bridge

♥ International
CONF. Thtr 240 Class 135 Board 50 Del £140
Credit Cards [1] [2] [3] [4] [5]

★★★★65% *The Excelsior*
Bath Rd, West Drayton UB7 0DU (adj M4 spur at junc with A4) ☎081-759 6611 FAX 081-759 3421

This very large modern hotel is only minutes from the airport. Public areas are extensive, including bars, various shops and travel offices and 3 places to eat. The hotel also provides good room service, lobby porterage and airport transfer coaches. Bedrooms are smart and well equipped and the larger Crown Club rooms have their own lounge and air conditioning.
839⇨ℳ✗in 143 bedrooms CTV in all bedrooms ®⚲T✳
sB⇨ℳ£105-£130 dB⇨ℳ£105-£130 (room only) 🍴
Lift (⊞ 540P (charged) 🏊 (heated) sauna solarium gymnasium health & fitness centre jacuzzi *xmas*
♥ English, French & Italian V ✧ ⚙ ✗ ✳ Lunch £16.50
Dinner £16.50 Last dinner midnt
Credit Cards [1] [2] [3] [5]

★★★★57% *Ramada*
Bath Rd TW6 2AQ ☎081-897 6363 FAX 081-897 1113

The Ramada is a very large hotel on the edge of Heathrow airport; its public areas include a spacious marbled lobby, a 24-hour coffee shop and the compact Flying Machine bar. Half the bedrooms have been very smartly refurbished, the rest are beginning to look dated. All are air conditioned.
636⇨ℳin 15 bedrooms CTV in all bedrooms ®⚲T
✖ (ex guide dogs)
Lift (⊞ 600P (£3.10 per day) 🏊 (heated) sauna solarium gymnasium plunge pools fitness & aerobics classes
♥ International V ✧ ⚙ ✗ Last dinner 10.30pm
Credit Cards [1] [2] [3] [5]

★★★66% *Novotel*
Junction 4 M4, Cherry Ln UB7 9HB
☎(0895) 431431 FAX (0895) 431221

Spacious and bright open-plan public areas here include a comfortable lounge and lounge bar. There is also a grill room which offers a well balanced menu of dishes cooked to order. Bedrooms are of a good size and nicely furnished. Services in some areas are limited, but staff are friendly and helpful.
178⇨ℳ(8fb)✗in 56 bedrooms CTV in all bedrooms ®⚲T✳
sB⇨ℳ£69.50 dB⇨ℳ£79.50 (room only)
Lift (170P ✿ 🏊 (heated) gymnasium
♥ International V ✧ ⚙ ✗ Lunch £10.80-£17.15&alc Dinner £10.80-£17.15&alc Last dinner mndt
Credit Cards [1] [2] [3] [5]

★★★62% *Master Robert*
Great West Rd TW5 0BD ☎081-570 6261 FAX 081-569 4016
(For full entry see Hounslow)

★★60% *Hotel Ibis*
112/114 Bath Rd UB3 5AL ☎081-759 4888 FAX 081-564 7894

Functional yet cheerful accommodation at a competitive price is the raison d'être of this modern hotel. Limited public areas include a bistro bar and provision for all day snacks and meals.
354⇨ℳ(8fb)✗in 134 bedrooms CTV in all bedrooms ®⚲T✳
sB⇨ℳ£39.50-£49.50 dB⇨ℳ£39.50-£49.50 (room only) 🍴
Lift 120P
♥ International V ✧ ⚙ ✗ ✳ Dinner £9.75&alc Last dinner 10.30pm
CONF. Thtr 120 Class 60 Board 44 Del £74
Credit Cards [1] [2] [3] [5]

The Edwardian International
Bath Rd UB3 5AW ☎081-759 6311 FAX 01-759 4559

This luxurious modern hotel offers a wide range of services and a choice of eating options for the international traveller. Bedrooms and suites are stylish and well equipped. There is a splendid indoor health club and pool. For more details about Edwardian hotels, consult the Contents page, under Hotel Groups.
459⇨ℳ sB⇨ℳ£153-£184 dB⇨ℳ£184-£434 (room only)
CONF. Thtr 500 Class 220 Board 70 Del £220

Forte Crest
Sipson Rd UB7 0JU (2m N A408) ☎081-759 2323
FAX 081-897 8659

A large modern hotel with a wide range of services and amenities, designed particularly for the business traveller. Bedrooms are smart, comfortable and well equipped. For more details about Forte Crest hotels, consult the Contents page, under Hotel Groups.
569⇨ℳ✳ B⇨ℳ£80-£99 (room only)
CONF. Thtr 200 Class 120 Board 30 Del £115

Forte Posthouse
Bath Rd UB3 5AJ (1.5m E junc A4/A437)
☎081-759 2552 FAX 081-564 9265

Suitable for both the business and leisure traveller, this bright hotel provides modern accommodation in well equipped bedrooms with en suite bathrooms. For more details about Forte Posthouse hotels, consult the Contents page, under Hotel Groups.
180⇨ℳ✳ B⇨ℳ£41.50-£53.50 (room only)
CONF. Thtr 50 Class 25 Board 30 Del £89.50

Granada Lodge
M4 Service Area, North Hyde Ln TW5 9NA
☎081-574 5875 FAX 081-574 1891
(For full entry see Heston)

Marriott
Ditton Road, Langley SL3 8PT (from junct 5 of M4/A4, follow 'Langley' signs and turn left at traffic lights into Ditton Road)
☎Slough(0753) 544244 FAX (0753) 540272

A large and busy hotel, which is ideal for the business and leisure traveller, offering a wide range of services, a choice of eating options and indoor leisure facilities. Bedrooms are comfortable and equipped with modern facilities. For more details about Marriott hotels, consult the Contents page, under Hotel Groups.
350⇨ℳ dB⇨ℳfr£118 (room only)
CONF. Thtr 300 Class 150 Board 50 Del £136

HEBDEN BRIDGE West Yorkshire Map **07** SD92

★★★70% *Carlton*
Albert St HX7 8ES ☎(0422) 844400 FAX (0422) 843117

Situated in the centre of the town, this Victorian building has been modernised and transformed into an attractive small hotel. Most of the public areas are on the first floor and include a comfortable cocktail bar and elegant restaurant, where a young team of staff provide attentive service.
18⇨ℳ CTV in all bedrooms ®⚲T sB&B⇨ℳ£45-£59
dB&B⇨ℳ£64-£79 🍴
Lift ✗ *xmas*
♥ International V ✧ ⚙ ✗ ✳ Lunch £7.50-£9.50 Dinner £12.50-£17.25&alc Last dinner 9.30pm
CONF. Thtr 150 Class 40 Board 40 Del from £62.50
Credit Cards [1] [2] [3]

Hebden Bridge - Helmsley

★★ 68% Hebden Lodge
New Rd HX7 8AD (on A646 opposite canal)
☎(0422) 845272
Closed 23-29 Dec

Hebden Lodge is a friendly and comfortable family-run hotel in the town centre, opposite the canal marina. Bedrooms and public areas are well furnished, interesting food is served in the charming restaurant and guests are given a warm welcome.

12⇨♠(1fb) CTV in all bedrooms ® T ✽ sB&B⇨♠£37.50-£47.50 dB&B⇨♠£50-65 ⊟
♪
♀ English & Continental V ♡ ⊒ ✽ Lunch £8.40-£12alc Dinner £12.50-£16.10 Last dinner 9pm
Credit Cards ①②③

HECKFIELD Hampshire Map 04 SU76

★★ 63% New Inn
RG27 0LE ☎(0734) 326374 FAX (0734) 326550
Closed 25-26 Dec

A 15th-century free house, the New Inn has been skilfully extended to provide a very well furnished choice of modern bedrooms. Plated meals are provided both in the oak beamed bars and the restaurant area.

16⇨♠1⇧ CTV in all bedrooms ® T
80P ⇧
V ♡ ⊒
Credit Cards ①②③

HEDGE END Hampshire Map 04 SU41

★★★ 63% Botleigh Grange
SO3 2GA (on A334) ☎Botley(0489) 787700 FAX (0489) 788535

Botley Grange has been skilfully extended to provide a new wing of bedrooms contrasting with the rooms in the original part of the house. Improvements are well under way and all rooms are well equipped. The new restaurant and cocktail lounge have transformed the public areas, which include the popular main lounge bar and the lounge with its decorative ceiling c1868. Limited room service is available and picnic lunches can be provided.

42⇨♠(4fb)2⇧ CTV in all bedrooms ® T sB&B⇨♠£66-£77 dB&B⇨♠£82-£93 ⊟
《 120P ✿ ♪ putting xmas
♀ English & French V ♡ ⊒ ✽ Lunch £9.50-£25 High tea £6.50 Dinner £15.45-£25 Last dinner 10pm
CONF. Thtr 200 Class 100 Board 60 Del from £49
Credit Cards ①②③⑤
See advertisement under SOUTHAMPTON

HELENSBURGH Strathclyde Dunbartonshire Map 10 NS28

★★★ 56% Commodore Toby
112 West Clyde St G84 8ER (on A814, on western outskirts) (Toby) ☎(0436) 76924 FAX (0436) 76233

This purpose built seafront hotel on the north side of town offers well equipped bedrooms, a coffee shop and a carvery restaurant.

45⇨♠(3fb)⊁in 11 bedrooms CTV in all bedrooms ® T ✽ sB&B⇨♠£29.95-£57 dB&B⇨♠£49.95-£74 ⊟
Lift 《 120P pool table xmas
V ♡ ⊒ ✽ Lunch £9.65-£14.25alc High tea fr£6.95alc Dinner £9.85-£14.25alc Last dinner 9.30pm
CONF. Thtr 250 Class 150 Board 50 Del from £62.40
Credit Cards ①②③⑤

Remember to book early for holiday
and bank holiday times.

HELLIDON Northamptonshire Map 04 SP55

★★★★ 66% Hellidon Lakes Hotel & Country Club
NN11 6LN (signposted, off A361)
☎Daventry(0327) 62550 FAX (0327) 62559

This modern brick building is set into the hillside at the centre of a testing golf course. It overlooks a series of lakes which are well stocked with fish, and home to large numbers of waterfowl. Tulipwood furniture and panelling give the hotel a light and airy look, and the bedrooms take advantage of the views. Edward Stephens has recently taken over as chef.

25⇨♠ CTV in all bedrooms ®✓ T ✖ (ex guide dogs)
sB&B⇨♠£85-£100 dB&B⇨♠£110-£125 ⊟
《 108P ⇧ ✿ ♪ 18 ♪ ∪ sauna solarium gymnasium beautician jacuzzi putting driving range xmas
♀ English & French V ♡ ⊒ ⊁ ✽ Lunch £17.50&alc Dinner £17.50&alc Last dinner 9.30pm
CONF. Thtr 50 Class 25 Board 34 Del from £100
Credit Cards ①②③⑤

HELMSLEY North Yorkshire Map 08 SE68

★★★ 78% Black Swan
Market Place YO6 5BJ (A170)
☎(0439) 70466 FAX (0439) 70174

This unique hotel comprises Elizabethan, Tudor, Georgian and modern buildings. It has been held in high esteem for many years and maintains the warmth and hospitality for which it has always been renowned. Log fires, oak beams, wooden panelling and antique pieces characterise the hotel. There is a choice of set price or seasonal dinner menus, which include some local dishes and Yorkshire cheeses. A well chosen wine list is also available.

44⇨♠(4fb)⊁ in 13 bedrooms CTV in all bedrooms ® T ✽ sB⇨♠£85 dB⇨♠£100 (room only) ⊟
《 CTV 60P ✿ croquet xmas
V ♡ ⊒ ✽ Lunch £10-£18&alc Dinner £25&alc Last dinner 9.30pm
Credit Cards ①②③⑤

★★★ 70% Feversham Arms
1 High St YO6 5AG ☎(0439) 70766 FAX (0439) 70346

This charming and friendly hotel enjoys a peaceful setting amid attractive gardens. The furnishing and décor reflect the period of the 19th-century stone building, many of the compact bedrooms having 4-poster beds and ornate bathrooms. The Goya Restaurant is renowned for its good food (especially shellfish and game in season) and for an outstanding winelist which contains many fine clarets.

18⇨♠(4fb)5⇧ CTV in all bedrooms ®✓ T sB&B⇨♠£55-£65 dB&B⇨♠£70-£80 ⊟
30P ✿ ⇧ (heated) ♀ (hard)
♀ English, French & Spanish V ♡ ⊁ Lunch fr£12&alc Dinner fr£18&alc Last dinner 9.30pm
CONF. Thtr 30 Class 30 Board 24 Del from £75
Credit Cards ①②③⑤

★★ 72% Pheasant
Harome YO6 5JG (2.5m SE, leave A170 after .25m, turn right signposted Harome for further 2m) (Logis)
☎(0439) 71241 (due to change to 771241)
Closed Jan-Feb

This delightful family-run hotel overlooks the duck pond, mill stream and nearby meadows. Formerly the village blacksmith's and 2 cottages, its oak beamed bar, comfortable drawing room and nicely furnished dining room provide a relaxed and peaceful atmosphere. Bedrooms are particularly spacious and comfortable, some with their own lounges.

Helmsley - Hemel Hempstead

12⇌Annexe2⇌ CTV in all bedrooms ® T sB&B⇌£49.95-£55 dB&B⇌£99.90-£116.40 (incl dinner) ♬
20P ♿ ✿ 🖃 (heated) nc12yrs
♡ ✗ Bar Lunch £1.50-£9alc Dinner £17.50-£21.50 Last dinner 8pm

★★67% Carlton Lodge
Bondgate YO6 5EY (on the A170 Scarborough road)
☎(0439) 70557 due to change to 770557 FAX (0439) 70623 due to change to 770623
An attractive grey stone house with a neat garden at the front, Carlton Lodge has thoughtfully furnished and tastefully decorated bedrooms, including 4 cottage-style ground floor rooms. There is a comfortable guests' lounge and a small bar, as well as the Priory Restaurant where Ryedale dinners and hearty Yorkshire breakfasts are served.
8rm(6↥)Annexe4⇌↥(1fb) CTV in all bedrooms ® sB&B⇌↥£37.50-£42 dB&B⇌↥£65-£67.50 ♬
45P *xmas*
♡ European V ♡ ✗ Lunch £18.50 Dinner £18.50 Last dinner 8.30pm
CONF. Thtr 150 Class 60 Board 50 Del from £55
Credit Cards [1] [3]
See also advertisement on page 299

★★67% Crown
Market Square YO6 5BJ ☎(0439) 70297
An attractive 16th-century inn situated in Helmsley's renowned market square. Beams, open fires and a Jacobean dining room characterise the inn's old world charm, and although the bedrooms have modern features they retain their traditional style. Country cooking is served in the dining room and a good range of bar meals are available.
14rm(12⇌↥)(1fb) CTV in all bedrooms ® T ✱
CTV 17P 3🚗 ✿
V ♡ ⌷ ✗ ✱ Lunch £9-£10 High tea £4-£7 Dinner £15-£16 Last dinner 8pm Credit Cards [1] [3]

★★59% Feathers
Market Place YO6 5BH ☎(0439) 70275 FAX (0439) 71101
Closed 23 Dec-3 Jan
Dating in part from the 15th century, this creeper-clad hotel is situated in Helmsley's renowned market place. The most appealing bedrooms are in the older part of the hotel and have much old-world character, but those in the newer wing are less distinctive. The attractive bars with local 'mouse man' furniture are very popular.
17rm(6⇌7↥)(4fb) CTV in all bedrooms ® sB&B⇌↥£16-£22 sB&B⇌↥£25-£31.50 dB&B£32-£44 dB&B⇌↥£40-£53 ♬
12P ✿
♡ English & Continental V ♡ ✱ Sunday Lunch £8.25-£14.25 High tea £3-£4.50 Dinner £12.50-£18.50 Last dinner 9pm
Credit Cards [1] [2] [3] [5]

HELSTON Cornwall & Isles of Scilly Map 02 SW62

★★🌺♨71% Nansloe Manor
Meneage Rd TR13 0SB (300yds on the left from Helston/Lizard roundabout A394/A3083) ☎(0326) 574691 FAX (0326) 564680
John and Wendy Pyatt took over this charming Georgian/Victorian hotel in early 1992. Set in 4.5 acres of wooded grounds, it has individually furnished and decorated bedrooms that are well equipped and an elegant restaurant where chef Martin Jones uses local produce to provide a good choice of dishes, such as scallops in tarragon cream sauce and lamb with rosemary sauce.
7rm(6⇌↥) CTV in all bedrooms ® T ✈ (ex guide dogs)
sB&Bfr£47 sB&B⇌↥£63 dB&B£76 dB&B⇌↥£95-£115
30P ♿ ✿ croquet nc12yrs
♡ English & Continental V ♡ ⌷ Lunch £9.50-£20alc Dinner £15-£20alc Last dinner 9pm
Credit Cards [1] [3]

★★63% The Gwealdues
Falmouth Rd TR13 8JX (on A394) ☎(0326) 572808 & 573331 FAX (0326) 561388
This friendly family-run hotel is popular for local functions, and is busy during the week with commercial guests. Bedrooms are simply furnished and well equipped with modern facilities, and the informal style of service creates a relaxed atmosphere.
17rm(5⇌8↥)(5fb) CTV in all bedrooms ® T ✱ sB&B£25-£27.50 sB&B⇌↥£30-£40 dB&B£30-£35 dB&B⇌↥£40-£50 ♬
CTV 60P ♿ ✿
V ♡ ⌷ ✗ ✱ Lunch £5.50 Dinner £10.50&alc Last dinner 9.30pm
CONF. Board 100
Credit Cards [1] [2] [3]

HEMEL HEMPSTEAD Hertfordshire Map 04 TL00

★★★58% Aubrey Park
Hemel Hempstead Rd AL3 7AF ST ALBANS
☎Redbourn(0582) 792105 FAX (0582) 792001
(For full entry see Redbourn)

Forte Posthouse
Breakspear Way HP2 4UA (exit junct 8 of M1, straight over roundabout and 1st left after BP garage) ☎(0442) 251122 FAX (0442) 211812
Suitable for both the business and leisure traveller, this bright hotel provides modern accommodation in well equipped bedrooms with en suite bathrooms. For more details about Forte Posthouse hotels, consult the Contents page, under Hotel Groups.
146⇌↥ ✱ B⇌↥£41.50-£53.50 (room only)

FORTE Posthouse

THE PHEASANT HOTEL ★★

Harome, Helmsley,
North Yorkshire YO6 5JG

Tel: Helmsley (0439) 71241 & 70416
due to change to (0439) 771241 & 770416

Former blacksmith's premises, this charming friendly hotel overlooks millstream and village pond. The hotel has 12 bedrooms all with private bathroom, colour TV and tea/coffee making facilities. Log fires. Large Garden. Heated indoor swimming pool. Bar. Car park. *Please write or telephone for brochure and tariff.*

Henley-on-Thames - Hereford

HENLEY-ON-THAMES Oxfordshire Map 04 SU78
See also **Stonor**

★★★62% Red Lion
Hart St RG9 2AR ☎(0491) 572161 FAX (0491) 410039

Attractively set beside the River Thames and the Henley road bridge, this 16th-century coaching inn has comfortable public areas which retain all the character of the old building; newly upgraded bedrooms are equally comfortable and tasteful. Restaurant menus offer an interesting range of dishes, augmented by snacks in the relaxed atmosphere of the Regatta Bar.

26rm(23⇨♠)(1fb)1⚑ CTV in all bedrooms T ✖ sB£43-£46 sB⇨♠£70-£75 dB⇨♠£83-£95 (room only) 🍴
(CTV 25P 🚗
♀ English & French V ♿ ⚲ Lunch £19.50-£20.50 Dinner £16-£28 Last dinner 10pm
CONF. Thtr 60 Class 20 Board 30 Del £108.50
Credit Cards 1 2 3

HEREFORD Hereford & Worcester Map 03 SO54
See also **Much Birch**

★★★67% Hereford Moat House
Belmont Rd HR2 7BP (1m SW on A465)
☎(0432) 354301 FAX (0432) 275114

Queens Moat Houses

A modern hotel to the southwest of the city, offering well furnished bedrooms both in the main building and in a motel-style block. Public areas include an open-plan foyer lounge with comfortable seating, an attractive restaurant with its own cocktail bar and a modern bar overlooking the pond.

28⇨♠ Annexe32⇨♠(2fb) CTV in all bedrooms ® T ✱
sB&B⇨♠£63-£73 dB&B⇨♠£73-£83 🍴
(150P ✱ ♫
♀ English & French V ♿ ⚲ ✗ ✱ Lunch £8.75 Dinner £15-£16&alc Last dinner 9.45pm
CONF. Thtr 300 Class 100 Board 50 Del £93
Credit Cards 1 2 3 5

★★★62% The Green Dragon
Broad St HR4 9BG ☎(0432) 272506 FAX (0432) 352139

FORTE Heritage

This city centre hotel close to the cathedral has undergone substantial recent refurbishment. Attractive bedrooms with quality fabrics are well equipped and public areas include an oak-panelled restaurant, a choice of bars and a comfortable lounge offering an all-day menu.

87⇨♠2⚑✱in 29 bedrooms CTV in all bedrooms ® T ✱
sB⇨♠£70-£75 dB⇨♠fr£80 (room only) 🍴
Lift (80P 80🚗 xmas
V ♿ ⚲ ✗ Lunch £6.95-£11.95 Dinner fr£16.95&alc Last dinner 9.30pm
Credit Cards 1 2 3 5

★★⊛69% Merton Hotel & Governors Restaurant
28 Commercial Rd HR1 2BD
☎(0432) 265925 FAX (0432) 354983

This friendly, mainly commercial hotel close to the city centre has well equipped, if rather compact bedrooms and comfortable public areas. The popular restaurant offers a range of interesting dishes.

19⇨♠(2fb) CTV in all bedrooms ® T sB&B⇨♠£45-£50 dB&B⇨♠£65.50-£70 🍴
25P sauna solarium gymnasium shooting & fishing by arrangement
V ♿ ⚲ ✗ Lunch £10-£28alc High tea fr£3.50 Dinner £10-£28alc Last dinner 9.45pm
Credit Cards 1 2 3 5

★★65% Dormington Court Country House
Dormington HR1 4DA (3.5m E off A438) ☎(0432) 850370 FAX (0432) 850370

This delightful small hotel, next to the medieval church and surrounded by orchards and hop fields, provides warm personal service. Partly dating from Elizabethan times, it has an attractive lounge and dining room, and comfortable, bright bedrooms.

7rm(6⇨♠)(1fb)1⚑ CTV in all bedrooms ® ✱ sB&Bfr£28 sB&B⇨♠£32-£35 dB&Bfr£50 dB&B⇨♠£54-£64 🍴
16P 🚗 ✱ nc10yrs
♀ English & French V ♿ ⚲ ✱ Sunday Lunch £9
Credit Cards 1 3

★★65% Munstone House Country
Munstone HR1 3AH (signposted off A4103, E of A49)
☎(0432) 267122

Small and very friendly, the hotel provides spacious, well equipped bedrooms, comfortable lounges and a locally popular restaurant offering a good choice of food.

6rm(3⇨2♠)(1fb) CTV in all bedrooms ®
CTV 25P 🚗 ✱
V ♿ ⚲ Last dinner 9.30pm
Credit Cards 1 3 5

★★61% Somerville
12 Bodenham Rd HR1 2TS (Logis) ☎(0432) 273991 FAX (0432) 265862
RS Xmas & New Year

Situated in a residential area, this family-run hotel has modest bedrooms but with a good range of facilities, a traditional lounge, small bright bar and a dining room with a choice of menus. Room service of meals is also available.

10rm(6⇨♠)(2fb)1⚑ CTV in all bedrooms ® T sB&B£24.50-£27 sB&B⇨♠£29.50-£33 dB&B£42-£46 dB&B⇨♠£48-£53 🍴
CTV 12P 🚗 ✱
♀ English & Continental V ♿ ⚲ Dinner £10.75-£12&alc Last dinner 9.30pm
Credit Cards 1 2 3

★★59% Castle Pool
Castle St HR1 2NR (next to Cathedral) ☎(0432) 356321

Just a short walk from the city centre, this 18th-century hotel is set in pleasant gardens that extend down to what was once the Hereford Castle moat. The bar and restaurant offer a good variety of food, and in summer barbecues are held at lunch time and in the evening. Bedrooms are bright and cosy.

26⇨♠(3fb) CTV in all bedrooms ® T sB&B⇨♠£40-£50 dB&B⇨♠£70-£82 🍴
CTV 14P ✱ xmas
♀ International V ♿ ⚲ Lunch fr£8.50 Dinner fr£16.50 Last dinner 9.30pm
CONF. Thtr 40 Class 30 Board 25 Del from £50
Credit Cards 1 2 3 5

Travel Inn
Holmer Rd, Holmer HR4 9RS (on A49 towards Leominster) ☎(0432) 274853

Purpose-built accommodation offers spacious and well equipped bedrooms, all with en suite bathrooms. Meals may be taken at the nearby family restaurant and pub. For more details about Travel Inns, consult the Contents page, under Hotel Groups.

40⇨♠ ✱ B⇨♠£33.50 (room only)

If you have booked a meal in a
hotel restaurant and cannot get there,
remember you have a contractual obligation
to cancel your booking.

Herstmonceux - Hesleden

HERM
See **Channel Islands**

HERSTMONCEUX East Sussex Map 05 TQ61

★★★ **64%** White Friars
Boreham St BN27 4SE (2m E on A271)
☎(0323) 832355 FAX (0323) 833882

This 16th-century hotel is run with relaxed charm by Mr and Mrs White. Bedrooms are in keeping with its country style, with oak furnishings, floral fabrics and comfortable armchairs. There is a choice of lounges, the beamed foyer lounge with a log fire and a peaceful residents' lounge overlooking the gardens. As well as the elegant Ashburnham restaurant, and there is a bright breakfast room and an informal cellar restaurant open during the summer.
12⇌♠Annexe8⇌♠(3fb)3✠ CTV in all bedrooms ® T
sB&B⇌♠£45-£60 dB&B⇌♠£60-£80 ⊟
((60P ✤ croquet pool table *xmas*
♥ English & French V ♥ ⌾ ✱ Lunch £9.50 Dinner fr£17.95 Last dinner 9.30pm
CONF. Thtr 40 Class 20 Board 20 Del from £60
Credit Cards [1][2][3][5]

★★ **60%** Horse Shoe Inn
Windmill Hill BN27 4RU
☎Eastbourne(0323) 833265 FAX (0323) 832001

Sympathetically designed in Tudor style, this popular village inn has 2 bars, Squires being cosier with its wood-burning stove, and the Long Bar a local's retreat. In the Baron of Beef restaurant families are welcome, and bedrooms, a little compact, are furnished with light wood furniture.
15⇌♠ CTV in all bedrooms ® T ✱ sB&B⇌♠£35-£45 dB&B⇌♠£45-£60 ⊟
100P *xmas*
V ♥ ⌾ ✱ Lunch £6.50-£12.95alc Dinner £6.50-£12.95alc Last dinner 10pm
Credit Cards [1][2][3][5]

HERTFORD Hertfordshire Map 04 TL31

★★★ **62%** White Horse
Hertingfordbury SG14 2LB (1m W on A414)
☎(0992) 586791 FAX (0992) 550809

This old coaching inn in the centre of the peaceful village has comfortable modern bedrooms, refurbished to a good standard. There is a cosy bar lounge and a conservatory restaurant overlooking the neat garden.
42⇌♠in 12 bedrooms CTV in all bedrooms ® T ✱
sB⇌♠£75 dB⇌♠£85 (room only) ⊟
((60P ✤ ♪ *xmas*
V ♥ ⌾ ✱ Lunch £10.25-£11.25 Dinner £14.95&alc Last dinner 9.30pm
Credit Cards [1][2][3][5]

HESLEDEN Durham Map 08 NZ43

★★ **69%** Hardwicke Hall Manor
TS27 4PA (NE on B1281, off A19) ☎Hartlepool(0429) 836335
FAX (0429) 837676
This impressive mansion house is a popular hotel providing a good standard of rooms with pretty soft furnishings. An extensive range of food is available at both lunch and dinner, the carvery lunch offering exceptional value.
11⇌♠(2fb)2✠ CTV in all bedrooms ® T ✱
50P ✤
♥ English & French V ♥ ⌾
CONF. Thtr 20 Class 20 Board 20
Credit Cards [1][2][3][5]

★★★

MUCH BIRCH, HEREFORD HR2 8HJ
(MIDWAY ROSS-ON-WYE AND HEREFORD ON A49)

One of the best Country House Hotels in Herefordshire – The Pilgrim
Ashley Courtenay
Recommended, 1993
● ALL BEDROOMS EN-SUITE WITH COUNTRY VIEWS
● EGON RONAY, RECOMMENDED

**GOLDEN VALLEY
(0981) 540742**

H

THE BOBSLEIGH INN
★ ★ ✪

Hempstead Road
Bovingdon, Herts HP3 0DS
Telephone: (0442) 833276
Fax: (0442) 832471

A privately owned country hotel and restaurant with a reputation for good food and service. Elegantly furnished throughout with all 23 bedrooms en suite. Easy access for M1 and M25, Luton and Heathrow airports.

Single bedrooms from £25; double bedrooms from £45 (both include VAT, service and full English breakfast).

See gazetteer entry under Bovingdon.

Heston Motorway Service Area (M4) - Hickstead

HESTON MOTORWAY SERVICE AREA (M4) Greater London

See **LONDON SECTION** plan 1*A3*
Granada Lodge
M4 Service Area, North Hyde Ln TW5 9NA
☎081-574 5875 FAX 081-574 1891

This modern building provides smart, spacious and well equipped bedrooms, all with en suite bathrooms. Meals may be taken at a nearby family restaurant. For more details about Granada Lodges, consult the Contents page, under Hotel Groups.
46⇨♠※ B⇨♠£43.95-£46.95 (room only)

HESWALL Merseyside Map 07 SJ28

Travel Inn
Chester Rd, Gayton L60 3FD ☎051-342 1982

Purpose-built accommodation offers spacious and well equipped bedrooms, all with en suite bathrooms. Meals may be taken at the nearby family restaurant and pub. For more details about Travel Inns, consult the Contents page, under Hotel Groups.
37⇨♠※ B⇨♠£33.50 (room only)

HETHERSETT Norfolk Map 05 TG10

★★★❀69% **Park Farm**
NR9 3DL (5m S of Norwich, off A11)
☎Norwich(0603) 810264 FAX (0603) 812104

Park Farm is in a secluded setting at the end of a tree-lined drive, surrounded by pasture and arable land. Individually styled bedrooms in the main house, converted outbuildings and recent extensions all offer good comfort and facilities and the extensively redeveloped public areas include an impressive health and leisure centre. The hotel staff are polite and friendly and standards of housekeeping are exemplary.
6⇨♠ Annexe32⇨♠(10fb)12⌂※in 27 bedrooms CTV in all bedrooms ® T ✖ (ex guide dogs) ✱ sB&B⇨♠£60-£90 dB&B⇨♠£90-£120 🍴
(150P 1🚗 ❁ 🏊 (heated) ♀ (hard) sauna solarium gymnasium putting croquet jacuzzi *xmas*
♡ English & French V ♂ ⚓ ✖ Lunch fr£10.25&alc High tea fr£5 Dinner fr£14&alc Last dinner 9.30pm
CONF. Thtr 150 Class 30 Board 40 Del from £95
Credit Cards [1][2][3][4][5] £

See advertisement under NORWICH

HEVERSHAM Cumbria Map 07 SD48

★★★63% **Blue Bell**
Prince's Way LA7 7EE (1m N of Milnthorpe, on A6) (Samuel Smith) ☎Milnthorpe(05395) 62018

This very popular hotel is at the gateway to the Lake District. There are 2 lounges and the bars are full of old world charm and character. Bedrooms are presently being upgraded to a very high standard.
21⇨♠(1fb) CTV in all bedrooms ® T ✱ sB&B⇨♠£35 dB&B⇨♠£70 🍴
CTV 100P ❁ *xmas*
V ♂ ⚓ ✖ Lunch £9.75&alc High tea £6.75 Dinner £14.95&alc Last dinner 9.30pm
CONF. Thtr 70 Class 24 Board 24 Del from £60
Credit Cards [1][2][3] £

Rosettes range from 5 for outstanding cuisine to 1 rosette for enjoyable, well prepared food

HEXHAM Northumberland Map 12 NY96

★★★65% **Beaumont**
Beaumont St NE46 3LT ☎(0434) 602331 FAX (0434) 602331
Closed 25-26 Dec & 1 Jan

In the centre of the town overlooking the park, this privately owned hotel has attractively decorated bedrooms which, apart from a few compact singles, have trouser presses in addition to the usual facilities. There is a choice of bars and the inviting foyer lounge, a popular venue for morning coffee, is reserved for residents in the evening.
23⇨♠(1fb)1⌂※in 15 bedrooms CTV in all bedrooms ® ♒ T ✖ sB&B⇨♠£50 dB&B⇨♠£80 🍴
Lift (6P solarium gymnasium
♡ International V ♂ ⚓ ✖ Lunch £6-£10alc Dinner £12-£18alc Last dinner 9.45pm
CONF. Thtr 100 Class 50 Board 40 Del from £65
Credit Cards [1][2][3][5]

★★64% **County**
Priestpopple NE46 1PS ☎(0434) 602030

This family-run hotel, its exterior ablaze with colourful hanging baskets and window boxes, offers traditional accommodation. Bedrooms are neatly furnished, while public areas include an attractive dining room, cosy foyer lounge and bar.
9⇨♠ CTV in all bedrooms ® T sB&B⇨♠£45 dB&B⇨♠£58 🍴
(2P
♡ International V ♂ ⚓ Lunch £3-£9alc High tea £3-£10alc Dinner £12-£22alc Last dinner 9.30pm
Credit Cards [1][2][3]

★★63% **Royal**
Priestpopple NE46 1PQ ☎(0434) 602270

This traditional town centre coaching inn dates from 1800 and offers modernised, functional bedrooms. There is a pleasant restaurant and wood panelled cocktail bar on the first floor, while the popular bistro offers more informal surroundings at lunch time.
24⇨♠(3fb) CTV in all bedrooms ® T sB&B⇨♠£32-£42 dB&B⇨♠£52-£62 🍴
CTV 24P
♡ English, Scottish & French V ♂ ⚓ Lunch £5.50-£8alc Dinner fr£12&alc Last dinner 9.30pm
CONF. Thtr 80 Class 50 Board 40
Credit Cards [1][2][3]

HEYWOOD Greater Manchester Map 07 SD81

★★60% **The Albany**
87/89 Rochdale Rd East OL10 1PX ☎(0706) 369606 FAX (0706) 627914

The Albany is a commercial hotel in two buildings. Bedrooms vary in size but have all modern amenities. There are two bars and a small attractive restaurant.
19rm(5⇨♠)(1fb)1⌂ CTV in all bedrooms ® T ✱ sB&B£20-£23.50 sB&B♠£20-£32.50 dB&B£30-£44 dB&B♠£40-£56
CTV 50P ❁ *xmas*
♡ English Spanish & Italian V ♂ ⚓ ✱ Lunch £9-£15&alc High tea £1-£5
CONF. Class 100 Board 10 Del from £60
Credit Cards [1][2][3][5]

HICKSTEAD West Sussex Map 04 TQ32

★★★64% **Hickstead Resort**
Jobs Ln, Bolney RH17 5PA (0.25m E of A23 turn off at Hickstead village towards Burgess Hill) ☎Burgess Hill(0444) 248023 FAX (0444) 245280

Quietly located in rural surroundings, this converted Victorian house has a modern wing of very comfortable bedrooms with good facilities. There is a popular restaurant offering a choice of menus.

Hickstead - Hinckley

50⇨🅟(8fb)⚹in 5 bedrooms CTV in all bedrooms ⓡ♋T sB&B⇨🅟£25-£55 dB&B⇨🅟£35-£65 (room only) 🅟
⟨ 150P ❋ 🖼 (heated) 🎵 sauna solarium gymnasium jacuzzi xmas
♀ English & Continental V ⚹ 🍴⚹ Last dinner 9.15pm
CONF. Thtr 80 Class 30 Board 30
Credit Cards ①②③⑤

HIGHBRIDGE Somerset Map 03 ST34

★★ **61%** Sundowner
74 Main Road, West Huntspill TA9 3QU (1m S on A38)
☎Burnham on Sea(0278) 784766 FAX (0278)784766
Owners Don and Fiona Fisher are very involved with the day to day running of this hotel, where bedrooms are simply furnished and reasonably equipped. The open plan bar lounge area has an information and friendly atmosphere, and bar meals are available in addition to the extensive restaurant carte.
8⇨🅟(1fb) CTV in all bedrooms ⓡ T sB&B⇨🅟£32-£36 dB&B⇨🅟£42-£48 🅟
CTV 24P ❋
♀ English & French V ⚹ Lunch £4.45-£8.75&alc Dinner £6.95-£10.45&alc Last dinner 10pm
Credit Cards ①②③

HIGHER BURWARDSLEY Cheshire Map 07 SJ35

★★ **66%** Pheasant Inn
CH3 9PQ ☎Tattenhall(0829) 70434 FAX (0829) 71097
2⇨🅟 Annexe6⇨🅟 CTV in all bedrooms ⓡ♋T ❋
sB&B⇨🅟£40 dB&B⇨🅟£60 🅟
CTV 60P 🚗
V ⚹ ❋ Sunday Lunch £9.50-£12.50alc Dinner £10-£15alc Last dinner 9.30pm
Credit Cards ①②③⑤

HIGH WYCOMBE Buckinghamshire Map 04 SU89

Forte Posthouse
Handy Cross HP11 1TL (intersection of M40 and A404) ☎(0494) 442100 FAX (0494) 439071

FORTE Posthouse

Suitable for both the business and leisure traveller, this bright hotel provides modern accommodation in well equipped bedrooms with en suite bathrooms. For more details about Forte Posthouse hotels, consult the Contents page, under Hotel Groups.
106⇨🅟❋ B⇨🅟£41.50-£53.50 (room only)
CONF. Thtr 100 Class 40 Board 40 Del £89.50

HILLINGDON Greater London

See **LONDON SECTION plan 1**A4
★★★ **62%** *Master Brewer*
Western Av UB10 9NX (Fullers) ☎Uxbridge(0895) 251199 FAX (0895) 810330
This hotel consists of a main building with an attractive foyer/lounge situated a short distance away from an annexe of spacious, well designed bedrooms with recently modernised bathrooms, most of which overlook a central garden.
106⇨🅟(22fb) CTV in all bedrooms ⓡ♋T
⟨ 200P ❋
♀ Continental V ⚹ 🍴⚹ Last dinner 11pm
Credit Cards ①②③⑤

All black star hotels are given a percentage grading within their star bands. See 'Using the Guide' at the front of the book for full details.

HILLINGTON Norfolk Map 09 TF72

★★ **62%** Ffolkes Arms
Lynn Rd PE31 6BJ (on A148 from Kings Lynn) ☎(0485) 600210 FAX (0485) 601196
This fashionably modernised flintstone inn does a busy bar meal trade in the beamed open-plan areas with deep red upholstery and dark polished tables and chairs. There is also a separate restaurant. Accommodation is in a purpose built block with an extensive range of facilities. Mr Bates, the owner, is local to the area and is a good humoured host.
Annexe20⇨🅟(1fb)1🛏 CTV in all bedrooms ⓡ T
❋ (ex guide dogs) ✱ sB&B⇨🅟£22.50-£29.75
dB&B⇨🅟£31.50-£44.50 Continental breakfast 🅟
200P ❋ snooker pool table
♀ English & French V ⚹ 🍴⚹ Lunch £5.95-£10&alc High tea £2.75-£5.50 Dinner £9.50&alc Last dinner 9.45pm
CONF. Thtr 250 Class 100 Board 50 Del from £45
Credit Cards ①②③

HILTON PARK MOTORWAY SERVICE AREA (M6) West Midlands Map 07 SJ90

Pavilion Lodge
Hilton Park Services (M6), Essington WV11 2DR (on M6 between juncts 10a & 11)
☎Cheslyn Hay(0922) 414100 FAX (0922) 418762

PAVILION *Lodge*

With a nearby family restaurant providing all meals, this modern building offers smart, spacious and well equipped bedrooms. For more details about Pavilion Lodges, consult the Contents page, under Hotel Groups.
64⇨🅟✱ sB⇨🅟£31.95 dB⇨🅟£35.95 (room only)

HIMLEY Staffordshire Map 07 SO89

★★★ **61%** *Himley Country Club & Hotel*
School Rd DY3 4LG (signposted, off A449)
☎Wombourne(0902) 896716 FAX (0902) 896668
This very modern commercial hotel is built around an old school, with carefully designed extensions. Bedrooms are fitted with good quality dark furniture, and a new conservatory has extended the restaurant. Staff are friendly and helpful, and there is choice of à la carte or good value table d'hôte menus.
76⇨🅟 CTV in all bedrooms ⓡ T ❋ (ex guide dogs)
⟨ 🍴 126P
♀ Continental V ⚹ 🍴 Last dinner 10pm
Credit Cards ①②③⑤

HINCKLEY Leicestershire Map 04 SP49

★★★ ❀**72%** Sketchley Grange
Sketchley Ln, Burbage LE10 3HU (SE of town, off A5) ☎(0455) 251133 FAX (0455) 631384

This successful commercial hotel is situated southeast of the town. Many extra bedrooms have been added over recent years and now include 12 with spa baths. A new lounge has recently been constructed and there are several bars, as well as the pretty Willow Restaurant, which overlooks the gardens. Food quality continues to improve under chef Colin Bliss, and our inspector thoroughly enjoyed his meal.
38⇨🅟(9fb)2🛏⚹in 5 bedrooms CTV in all bedrooms ⓡ♋T ❋
sB&B⇨🅟£35-£69 dB&B⇨🅟£49-£89 🅟
⟨ 200P ❋ 🎵 ♿
♀ English & French V ⚹ 🍴⚹ Lunch £7.95-£10.95&alc High tea £3.50-£5 Dinner £16.75&alc Last dinner 9.45pm
CONF. Thtr 300 Class 150 Board 50 Del from £89
Credit Cards ①②③⑤ £

See advertisement under LEICESTER

Hinckley - Hockley Heath

★★67% *Kings Hotel & Restaurant*
13/19 Mount Rd LE10 1AD (Logis) ☎(0455) 637193 FAX (0455) 636201

A husband and wife team provide personal service at this converted Victorian school house. The owner takes particular pride in the cuisine, in which traces of his Hungarian origins can be detected, and the standard is above average for this category of hotel. The décor is in 20s style, particularly in the restaurant with its dark furnishings, potted plants and low ceiling lamps.

7⇨⇧in 3 bedrooms CTV in all bedrooms ® T ✗
12P 1☙ (£5)
♀ English, French & Hungarian V ♢ ⚑ Last dinner 9.30pm
Credit Cards [1][2][3][5]

HINDON Wiltshire Map 03 ST93

★★❀68% **Lamb at Hindon**
SP3 6DP (in village centre) ☎(074789) 573 FAX (074789) 605

This attractive old village inn has recently been bought by the former general manager and his brother, who are keen to continue the hotel's tradition of warm hospitality. Bedrooms have modern amenities and attractive décor, and there is a popular bar with log fires where bar snacks are served, a quiet residents' lounge and comfortable dining room. The set-price menu offers good home-cooked dishes.

13rm(12⇨⇧)2☒ CTV in all bedrooms ® T sB&B⇨⇧£38 dB&B⇨⇧£55 ⊟
CTV 26P ❀ ❊ ♪ shooting fishing *xmas*
V ♢ ⚑ Lunch £8.25-£11.95 High tea £2 Dinner £18.95 Last dinner 9.30pm
CONF. Board 20 Del from £80
Credit Cards [1][2][3]

HINTLESHAM Suffolk Map 05 TM04

HINTLESHAM HALL
IP8 3NS (4m W of Ipswich on A1071 to Sudbury)
☎(0473) 652334 & 652268
FAX (0473) 652463
RS Sat

Hintlesham Hall stands in lovely grounds encompassing an 18-hole championship golf course. Originally Tudor, as one sees from the rear, the elegant manor house has a Georgian façade and has been carefully refurbished. There are 3 dining rooms, the 'salon' being by far the largest and most splendid. Here, chef Alan Ford presents seasonal menus of classically influenced French and international dishes from which our inspector singled out for praise a starter of braised oxtail bound by a chicken mousseline, with a rösti of walnut and celeriac soaking up the juices from the meat.

33⇨⇧(1fb)2☒⚑ in 12 bedrooms CTV in all bedrooms T ✗ sB&B⇨⇧fr£85 dB&B⇨⇧fr£97 Continental breakfast ⊟
☾ 100P ❀ ❊ ≙ (heated) ▶ 18 ♀ (hard) ♪ ☉ snooker sauna croquet clay & game shooting spa bath *xmas*
♀ English & French V ♢ ✳ Lunch fr£18.50 Dinner fr£22&alc Last dinner 10pm
Credit Cards [1][2][3][5]

HINTON CHARTERHOUSE Avon Map 03 ST75

★★★

★★★★❀❁ ☙
HOMEWOOD PARK
BA3 6BB (Between A36 & village)
☎Bath(0225) 723731 FAX (0225) 723820

A delightfully unassuming yet stylish Georgian house, set in 10 acres of mature grounds and gardens, Homewood Park is owned by the Fentum family. Day-to-day management is carried out by daughter and son-in-law Sara and Frank Gueuning, suitably backed by a small Anglo-French team of staff. Bedrooms have rich fabrics, comfortable canopied beds, deep armchairs, mahogany and antique furnishings; perfumed toiletries and deep bathrobes are provided, along with complimentary sherry. The public rooms combine classical furnishings with a comfortable lived-in feel. Tim Ford has recently taken over in the kitchen.

15⇨⇧(2fb) CTV in all bedrooms T ✗ sB&B⇨⇧£80-£110 dB&B⇨⇧£95-£135 ⊟
30P ❀ ❊ ♀ (hard) croquet *xmas*
V ♢ ⚑ Lunch fr£19.50 Dinner fr£32.50&alc Last dinner 9.30pm
Credit Cards [1][2][3][4][5]

HITCHIN Hertfordshire Map 04 TL12

★★★61% **Blakemore Thistle**
Blakemore End Rd, Little Wymondley SG4 7JJ (3m SE A602) ☎Stevenage(0438) 355821 FAX (0438) 742114

THISTLE HOTELS

Set in 6 acres of landscaped grounds, this extended country house has very well furnished modern bedrooms; the executive rooms to the rear have balconies overlooking the swimming pool. Public areas, by contrast, are dated and due for upgrading.

82⇨⇧(6fb)1☒⚑ in 23 bedrooms CTV in all bedrooms ® ✲ T ✳ sB&B⇨⇧£31-£75 dB&B⇨⇧£62-£85 (room only) ⊟
Lift ☾ 200P ❀ ≙ (heated) boule croquet ♫ *xmas*
♀ International V ♢ ⚑ ✳ Lunch £10.25-£17.25&alc Dinner £17.25&alc Last dinner 9.30pm
CONF. Thtr 200 Class 80 Board 40 Del from £80
Credit Cards [1][2][3][4][5] £
See advertisement under STEVENAGE

HOCKLEY HEATH West Midlands Map 07 SP17

★★★❀❀ ☙82% **Nuthurst Grange Country House**
Nuthurst Grange Ln B94 5NL (off A34, 2m S junction 4 M42) ☎Lapworth(0564) 783972 FAX (0564) 783919

In 7.5 acres of grounds and woodland at the end of a long drive, this beautiful country house offers spacious and luxurious bedrooms with extras such as chocolates, fruit and mineral water. The well appointed restaurant is at the heart of the hotel and chef/proprietor David Randolph's has established a well deserved reputation for excellence. Public areas are limited, but the small lounge is very comfortable and service is attentive.

15⇨⇧(2fb)1☒ CTV in all bedrooms T ✗ (ex guide dogs) ✲ sB&B⇨⇧fr£89 dB&B⇨⇧£99-£135 Continental breakfast ⊟
50P 6☙ ❀ ❊ croquet helipad
♀ English & French V ♢ ⚑ ✳ Lunch fr£14.95 Dinner fr£19.95&alc Last dinner 9.30pm
Credit Cards [1][2][3][5] £

Hockley Heath - Holywell

★★★59% Aylesbury House Resort
Aylesbury Rd, Packwood B94 6PL (Turn off A3400 left at Nags Head hotel 0.50m along on left) ☎Knowle(0564) 779207 FAX (0564) 770917
6⇌🛏Annexe28⇌🛏 CTV in all bedrooms ®⚲ T ✱
sB⇌🛏£60 dB⇌🛏£70 (room only) 🅿
(60P ✿ croquet putting green assault course
♀ English & French V ◊ ♨ ✱ Lunch fr£9.95&alc Dinner £13.50&alc Last dinner 9.30pm
CONF. Thtr 80 Class 36 Board 36 Del £80
Credit Cards [1][2][3][5]

HODDLESDEN Lancashire Map 07 SD72
★★★63% The Old Rosins Inn
Pickup Bank BB3 3QD ☎Darwen(0254) 771264 FAX (0254) 873894
This privately owned moorland inn has been extended over the years and now offers comfortable and pleasantly furnished bedrooms, with smart Victorian-style bathrooms. Public areas include a popular lounge bar, small residents' lounge and a pleasant restaurant offering a good range of menus.
15⇌🛏(3fb)1⍟ CTV in all bedrooms ®⚲ T 🐕 (ex guide dogs) ✱ sB&B⇌🛏£39.50-£49.50 dB&B⇌🛏£49.50-£69.50 🅿 200P
♀ English & French V ◊ ♨ ✱ Lunch £13.50&alc High tea £1.75-£7.25 Dinner £13.50&alc Last dinner 10pm
Credit Cards [1][2][3][5]

HODNET Shropshire Map 07 SJ62
★★64% Bear
TF9 3NH (junct of A53/A442) ☎(063084) 214 & 788 FAX (063084) 787
This 16th-century coaching inn retains its inglenook fireplaces and exposed beams. Public areas are mostly open plan, with the restaurant and bar areas attractively segregated into several sections. Bedrooms are on the small side, but all have modern facilities. The Bear is popular locally for its wide range of good value food.
6⇌🛏2⍟ CTV in all bedrooms ® T 🐕 (ex guide dogs) sB&B⇌🛏£30-£35 dB&B⇌🛏£50-£60 🅿 100P ✿
♀ International V ◊ ♨ ✱ Lunch £5-£15alc Dinner £8-£17alc Last dinner 10pm
Credit Cards [1][3]

HOLBETON Devon Map 02 SX65
★★★♨ 65% Alston Hall
Alston PL8 1HN (from Battisborough Cross, signposted on right) ☎(075530) 555 FAX (075530) 494
Built at the turn of the century, Alston Hall was the treasured home of Dame Lucille Sayers for over 50 years. Today's guests enjoy the Edwardian style of gracious living with attentive but unobtrusive service. The restaurant offers chef Malcolm Morrison's well balanced table d'hôte menus, cooked with style using fresh local ingredients, which might include duck liver parfait with toasted brioche and redcurrant sauce, and best end of lamb, served with an overpoweringly minted pear and cream rosemary sauce.
20⇌🛏(6fb) CTV in all bedrooms ® T sB&B⇌🛏£70 dB&B⇌🛏£85 🅿
100P ✿ 🏊(heated) ⇌ ♪ (hard) sauna solarium gymnasium croquet ♧ xmas
♀ English & French V ◊ ♨ ✱ Lunch £10.50-£13.50 High tea £7.50 Dinner fr£24&alc Last dinner 9.30pm
CONF. Thtr 100 Class 50 Board 36 Del £79
Credit Cards [1][2][3][4][5] £

HOLFORD Somerset Map 03 ST14
★★♨71% Combe House
TA5 1RZ (from A39 in Holford take lane between garage and Plough Inn, bear left at fork and continue for 0.25m to Holford Combe) ☎(0278) 741382
Closed Jan RS mid Nov-Dec & Feb-mid Mar
Beautifully set in 3 acres of grounds amid the Quantock Hills, this converted 17th-century tannery provides traditional country house hospitality. Bedrooms are comfortable and well equipped, there is a choice of lounges, a cosy bar with the log fire and an attractive dining room serving good home-cooked meals.
17rm(14⇌🛏2🛁)Annexe3rm(1🛁) CTV in all bedrooms ® T sB&Bfr£27 sB&B⇌🛏£32-£45 dB&B£58-£80 dB&B⇌🛏£66-£90 🅿
15P 🚗 ✿ 🏊(heated) ♪ (hard) sauna solarium ◊ ♨ ✱ Bar Lunch £2-£7.50 High tea £2.50-£4.50 Dinner £14.50-£15.50 Last dinner 8.30pm
Credit Cards [1][2][3]

HOLMES CHAPEL Cheshire Map 07 SJ76
★★★67% Old Vicarage
Knutsford Rd CW4 8EF (on the A50, 1m from junct 18 on the M6) ☎(0477) 532041 FAX (0477) 535728
Parts of this privately owned hotel date back to the 18th century, though the majority of the bedrooms are in a recently built extension. Ten of these are on ground floor level. There is a cosy bar with a low beamed ceiling and an inglenook fireplace in the original house, and an attractive brasserie restaurant.
25⇌🛏 CTV in all bedrooms ® T 🐕 (ex guide dogs) ✱ sB&B⇌🛏£31-£62 dB&B⇌🛏£48-£74 🅿
(CTV 70P
♀ English & French V ◊ ♨ ✱ Lunch £12.50-£16.90alc Dinner £12.50-£16.90alc Last dinner 10pm
CONF. Thtr 36 Class 16 Board 20 Del from £82
Credit Cards [1][2][3]

★★★64% Holly Lodge Hotel & Restaurant
68-70 London Rd CW4 7AS (A50/A54 crossroads, from junc 18 of M6) ☎(0477) 537033 FAX (0477) 535823
RS 25 Dec-31 Jan & BH Mons
A large Victorian house, Holly Lodge has a recently built mews-style annexe where some ground-floor and family rooms are available. There is a pleasant bar, and a comfortable lounge, and the spacious restaurant is attractively appointed and partioned for privacy.
33⇌🛏(2fb)1⍟♽ in 6 bedrooms CTV in all bedrooms ® T sB&B⇌🛏£41-£66 dB&B⇌🛏£56-£76 🅿
80P ✿ games room 🎵 xmas
♀ English & French V ◊ ♨ Lunch fr£8.20 Dinner £12.90 Last dinner 9.45pm
CONF. Thtr 140 Class 40 Board 50 Del from £94
Credit Cards [1][2][3][4][5] £

HOLYHEAD
See **Anglesey, Isle of**

HOLYWELL Clwyd Map 07 SJ17
See also **Nannerch**
★★64% Stamford Gate
Halkyn Rd CH8 7SJ (take Holywell turn off A55 on to A5026, hotel 1m on right) ☎(0352) 712942 & 712968 FAX (0352) 713309
Bedrooms here are furnished with modern white furniture and equipped with many extras. There is a large public bar, popular locally, and a cocktail bar for residents and diners. The restaurant has a maritime theme and a good choice of dishes. There is a further residents' lounge and a modern conservatory where breakfast is served.
12⇌🛏 CTV in all bedrooms ® T 🐕

Holywell - Hope Cove

100P
♀ English & Italian **V** ↻ Last dinner 10pm
Credit Cards [1] [3] [4]

HOLYWELL GREEN West Yorkshire Map **07** SE01

★★69% Rock Inn Hotel & Churchills Restaurant
HX4 9BS (on Halifax road, beyond Elland Golf Course)
☎Halifax(0422) 379721 FAX (0422) 379110
Ongoing improvements at this popular, friendly hotel have now provided it with comfortable, tastefully appointed public areas.
18⇌♠3🛏in 8 bedrooms CTV in all bedrooms ® ☆ **T** ✱
sB&B⇌♠£38-£59 dB&B⇌♠£50-£69 ₧
100P 2🚗 ✿ games room *xmas*
♀ English & French **V** ↻ ♨ ✱ Sunday Lunch fr£9&alc High tea £6-£10 Dinner £14&alc Last dinner 10pm
CONF. Thtr 200 Class 100 Board 100 Del £75
Credit Cards [1] [2] [3] [5]

HONILEY Warwickshire Map **04** SP27

★★★67% Honiley Court
Honiley CV8 1NP (3m W of Kenilworth on A4117) (Lansbury)
☎Haseley Knob(0926) 484234 FAX (0926) 484474
A large modern complex built onto the original Old Boot Inn offers spacious bedrooms, the majority twin or double, six of which are restricted to non smokers; fourteen are located on the ground floor, and these include two equipped for disabled guests. There are no fewer than seven conference rooms.
62⇌♠⌿in 6 bedrooms CTV in all bedrooms ® ☆ **T** ✱
sB&B⇌♠fr£65.50 dB&B⇌♠fr£77 ₧
Lift ℂ 250P ✿
♀ English & French **V** ↻ ♨ ⌿ ✱ Lunch fr£8.50 Dinner fr£13.75 Last dinner 10pm
CONF. Thtr 150 Class 50 Board 50 Del from £89
Credit Cards [1] [2] [3] [5]

HONITON Devon Map **03** ST10

See also **Yarcombe**

★★★⚜63% Deer Park
Weston EX14 0PG (2.5m W off A30) ☎(0404) 41266 FAX (0404) 46598
This Georgian mansion is set in 30 acres of parkland with 5 miles of fishing rights on the River Otter. Public areas are spacious, comfortable and traditional, and bedrooms are undergoing refurbishment. Service is friendly and quietly efficient, and the hotel's restaurant offers an extensive choice of dishes.
15⇌♠Annexe14⇌♠(2fb) CTV in all bedrooms **T**
✂ (ex guide dogs) ✱ sB&B⇌♠£35-£85 dB&B⇌♠£55-£120 ₧
ℂ CTV 40P 4🎾 ⛳ ✿ (heated) ♘ (hard) ♣ squash snooker sauna solarium croquet putting shooting ⛵ *xmas*
♀ English & French **V** ↻ ♨ Lunch £13-£16&alc High tea £5 Dinner £22.50-£25&alc Last dinner 10pm
CONF. Thtr 70 Class 40 Board 26 Del from £55
Credit Cards [1] [2] [3] [5] £

★★66% Home Farm
Wilmington EX14 9JR (3m E) ☎(0404) 831278 & 831246
This attractive, thatched former farmhouse is full of charm and character. The bedrooms are comfortable with coordinating colour schemes, some are approached from the garden and cobbled courtyard, and a good choice of dishes is served in the dining room.
7rm(3⇌)Annexe6⇌♠(3fb) CTV in all bedrooms ® **T**
sB&B£24-£28 sB&B⇌♠£28 dB&B£52-£56 dB&B⇌♠£56 ₧
CTV 25P ✿ golf practice nets *xmas*
V ♨ Sunday Lunch £8 Dinner £12&alc Last dinner 9pm
Credit Cards [1] [2] [3]

★★56% Honiton Motel
Turks Head Corner, Exeter Rd EX14 8BL (off A35)
☎(0404) 43440 & 45400 FAX (0404) 47767
This modern, flat roofed hotel is on the edge of one of Devon's oldest market towns. There is a spacious bar/lounge, popular with locals, and the Black Swan restaurant, where a grill type à la carte menu is offered, along with a simple table d'hôte menu for residents. The majority of the bedrooms are across the large car park, all at ground floor level.
Annexe15⇌♠(3fb) CTV in all bedrooms ® **T** ✱
sB&B⇌♠£28-£30 dB&B⇌♠£47-£50 ₧
50P golf practice nets
V ↻ ♨ ⌿ ✱ Lunch fr£7&alc Dinner fr£8&alc Last dinner 9pm
CONF. Thtr 150 Class 100 Board 50
Credit Cards [1] [3] £

HOOK Hampshire Map **04** SU75

★★67% Raven
Station Rd RG27 9HS (0.75m N of M3 junc 5 on B3349) (Whitbread) ☎(0256) 762541 FAX (0256) 768677
An old inn with modern extensions, the Raven Hotel is near to the station and offers well decorated bedrooms with sound bathrooms. The bar is just like a living room, with sofas, books and Victoriana.
38⇌♠(4fb)⌿in 6 bedrooms CTV in all bedrooms ® ☆ **T** ✱
sB&B⇌♠fr£69.50 dB&B⇌♠fr£81 ₧
ℂ 100P sauna *xmas*
♀ European **V** ↻ ♨ ⌿ ✱ Lunch fr£9.50 Dinner fr£10.50 Last dinner 10pm
CONF. Thtr 100 Class 60 Board 50 Del from £95
Credit Cards [1] [2] [3] [4] [5]

HOPE COVE Devon Map **03** SX64

★★66% Cottage
Inner Hope Cove TQ7 3HJ (from Kingsbridge A381 towards Salcombe, it is suggested you take 2nd right at village of Marlborough continue & turn left for Inner Hope)
☎Kingsbridge(0548) 561555
Closed 3-30 Jan
Set in 2 acres of grounds with glorious views of the coastline, the hotel has been owned and managed by the Ireland family for nearly 20 years. The deluxe bedrooms have balconies, while others are more basic. The intimate Herzogin Cecile Cabin was built from the timbers of the famous ship wrecked along the coast nearly 50 years ago. The restaurant, where an extensive choice is offered, has views over the bolt tail and the harbour.
35rm(24⇌♠)(5fb) CTV in 29 bedrooms **T** sB&B£30-£43 dB&B£60-£86 dB&B⇌♠£73.30-£110.20 (incl dinner) ₧
CTV 50P ✿ ⛵ *xmas*
♀ English & French **V** ↻ ♨ ⌿ ✱ Sunday Lunch £8.15 Dinner £16.35&alc Last dinner 8.45pm
CONF. Thtr 50 Board 24

★★64% Lantern Lodge
TQ7 3HE (turn right off A381 Kingsbridge-Salcombe road, take first right after passing Hope Cove sign then first left along Grand View Rd) ☎Kingsbridge(0548) 561280
Closed Dec-Feb
Overlooking the fishing village, with a view extending from Bolt Head to Plymouth Sound, this hotel has improved greatly during the past few years. Bedrooms are prettily decorated, with Victorian and Edwardian furniture, and public areas include several cosy sitting areas and an intimate dining room.
14⇌♠(1fb)3🛏 CTV in all bedrooms ® **T** ✂ (ex guide dogs)
✱ sB&B⇌♠£40.15-£55.55 dB&B⇌♠£73-£101 (incl dinner)
15P 1🚗 ⛳ ▢ (heated) sauna solarium putting green multi-gym nc10yrs
♀ English & French **V** ↻ ✱ Dinner £14.50 Last dinner 8.30pm
Credit Cards [1] [3]

Hope Cove - Horrabridge

★★**59%** *Sun Bay*
Inner Hope Cove TQ7 3HH ☎Kingsbridge(0548) 561371
Closed 19 Oct-27 Mar
Overlooking the unspoilt harbour of Inner Hope Bay, on the edge of the village, this family-run hotel has a relaxed, informal atmosphere. Bedrooms, whilst compact, are brightly decorated and have modern furnishings. Refreshments are served on the sun terrace in the summer.
14rm(10⇌2♠)(7fb) CTV in all bedrooms ®
CTV 12P 🚗 ✿
V ✿ ⚐ Last dinner 8.30pm

HORLEY Hotels are listed under **Gatwick Airport**

HORNBY Lancashire Map **07** SD56

★★**55%** *Castle*
Main St LA2 8JT ☎(05242) 21204
13rm(4⇌4♠)(2fb) CTV in all bedrooms ® T
50P ✿ ♪ ○
⚑ English & Continental V ✿ ⚐ Last dinner 10pm
Credit Cards [1][2][3][5]

HORNCHURCH Essex Map **05** TQ53

★★★**60%** *Palms*
Southend Arterial Rd RM11 3UJ (Hilton) ☎(0708) 346789 FAX (0708) 341719
The majority of bedrooms in this convenient roadside hotel have recently been refurbished to a smart modern standard, though they may be rather compact for double occupancy. There are, however, more spacious Plaza rooms which have lots of extras. Public areas are limited to the busy piano bar, with live music six evenings a week and the restaurant which specialises in steaks.
137⇌♠(6fb)1⊞¥in 30 bedrooms CTV in all bedrooms ® T
✱ sB⇌♠£49 dB⇌♠£49 (room only)
《 250P ✿ ♫
⚑ International V ✿ ⚐ ✱ Lunch fr£11.50&alc Dinner fr£16&alc Last dinner 10.45pm
Credit Cards [1][2][3][5]

HORNING Norfolk Map **09** TG31

★★★**64%** *Petersfield House*
Lower St NR12 8PF ☎(0692) 630741 FAX (0692) 630745
Petersfield House is a traditionally run family hotel located close to the shores of the River Bure within a few minutes walk of the village centre. The restaurant and bar overlook a large garden with a permanently erected marquee for large functions. The bedrooms are well maintained and equipped.
18⇌♠(1fb) CTV in all bedrooms ® T
70P 🚗 ✿ ♪
⚑ English & Continental V ✿ ⚐ Last dinner 9.30pm
Credit Cards [1][2][3][5]

HORRABRIDGE Devon Map **02** SX57

★★**67%** *Overcombe*
PL20 7RN (off A386)
☎Yelverton(0822) 853201

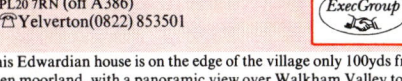

This Edwardian house is on the edge of the village only 100yds from open moorland, with a panoramic view over Walkham Valley to the high granite tors of Dartmoor. There is a comfortable lounge with an informal bar, and at dinner a short choice of dishes is offered. The hotel offers good value for money and a friendly, relaxed atmosphere.
11rm(10⇌♠)(2fb)1⊞ CTV in all bedrooms ® T ✱ sB&B£20-£25 sB&B⇌♠£25 dB&B£40-£45 dB&B⇌♠£45 ⏏
CTV 10P 🚗 croquet

The HONITON MOTEL
★★
**Turks Head Corner, Exeter Road
Honiton, Devon EX14 8BL
Tel: (0404) 43440. Fax: (0404) 47767**

A family run motel situated on the outskirts of Honiton Town. 11 miles from M5 Junction 28. Midway point between Cornwall and the North. We are an ideal venue for both business and leisure guests. Guests dine in the Black Swan restaurant from a table d'hôte menu or an extensive à la carte. 15 rooms all en-suite. Large car park.

HOME FARM
COUNTRY HOUSE HOTEL & RESTAURANT
**Wilmington, Nr Honiton,
Devon EX14 9JR** ★★

* Small but beautiful thatched farm house.
* 14 lovely rooms all with TV, coffee & tea, hair drier, clock radio alarm, telephone, baby listening.
* Far reaching views, from our 4 acres of glorious grounds.
* Draught beer, super food, log fires.
* 5 miles inland from sea.
Brochure: 0404 831278 & 0404 831286

305

Horrabridge - Hovingham

V ⌇ Dinner £11.50 Last dinner 7.15pm
Credit Cards 1 3
See advertisement under YELVERTON

HORSHAM West Sussex Map 04 TQ13
★★★★ ❀❀⚑ 74% **South Lodge**
Brighton Rd RH13 6PS HORSHAM (Laura Hotels)
☎Lower Beeding(0403) 891711 FAX (0403) 891253
(For full entry see Lower Beeding)

★★★ ❀ 68% **Random Hall**
Stane St, Slinfold RH13 7QX (on A29) ☎(0403) 790558 & 790852 FAX (0403) 791046

Dating back to the late 16th century, Random Hall retains much of its original farmhouse character, with low oak beams, flagstone floors, log burning inglenooks and the candlelit, Tudor-style restaurant. Chef Jonathan Getting's' style of British cooking is reflected in the daily fixed price and à la carte menus, and a spit roast duck is cooked daily on the lounge log fire. Bedrooms are furnished and equipped in modern style.
15⇨♠(2fb)2⚐ CTV in all bedrooms ® T ✖ (ex guide dogs)
sB&B⇨♠£65 dB⇨♠£80 (room only) 🅿
CTV 50P 🐾
V ♥ ⌇Lunch £9.50-£15.95 Dinner £15.95 Last dinner 10pm
Credit Cards 1 2 3

★★ 62% **Ye Olde King's Head**
RH12 1EG ☎(0403) 253126 FAX (0403) 242291
Situated in the centre of town, this famous medieval inn retains much of its original character. There is a wine cellar lunch-time buttery and small coffee shop, and the restaurant offers a daily menu alongside the à la carte. Bedrooms are dated in style, but most have comfortable seating.
42rm(6⇨35♠)(2fb)1⚐ CTV in all bedrooms ® T ✱
sB&B⇨♠£55-£65 dB&B⇨♠£65-£75 🅿
40P
♥ English & French V ♥ ⌇ ⌇ Lunch £5-£13.50&alc Dinner fr£13.95&alc Last dinner 9.45pm
CONF. Thtr 35 Board 45
Credit Cards 1 2 3 5

Travel Inn
57 North Rd RH12 1RB (opposite railway station)
☎(0403) 250141

Purpose-built accommodation offers spacious and well equipped bedrooms, all with en suite bathrooms. Meals may be taken at the nearby family restaurant and pub. For more details about Travel Inns, consult the Contents page, under Hotel Groups.
40⇨♠✱ B⇨♠£33.50 (room only)

HORTON-CUM-STUDLEY Oxfordshire Map 04 SP51
★★★ ❀❀⚑ 67% **Studley Priory**
OX33 1AZ (2.5m off B4027) ☎Stanton St John(0865) 351203 FAX (0865) 351613

Many periods can be traced in the building of this hotel: a 12th-century Benedictine priory, an Elizabethen manor house and a 17th century wing. It retains much of its character, with oak beams, wood panelling, mullion windows and leaded lights, enhanced by antique furniture. Bedrooms include a full suite (with a half-tester 4-poster bed dated from about 1690) and some very spacious rooms. The new chef is Duncan Basterfield.
19⇨♠2⚐ CTV in all bedrooms ® T ✖ sB&B⇨♠£88-£100 dB&B⇨♠£98-£150 🅿
100P 1🐾 ✱ ♫ (grass) croquet clay pigeon shooting *xmas*
♥ English & French V ♥ ⌇ ⌇ Lunch £19.50-£22.50&alc Dinner £19.50-£22.50&alc Last dinner 9.30pm
CONF. Thtr 50 Class 25 Board 25 Del from £110
Credit Cards 1 2 3 4 5

HORWICH Greater Manchester Map 07 SD61
★★ 65% **Swallowfield**
Chorley New Rd BL6 6HN (on A673, off junc 6 of M61)
☎(0204) 697914 FAX (0204) 68900

This much extended house is privately owned and personally run in a friendly and informal style. The bedrooms have modern furnishings and equipment, those in the newer wing tend to be more spacious, and the hotel caters mainly for commercial visitors.
31⇨♠(6fb) CTV in all bedrooms ® T
35P 🚗 ✱
♥ ⌇ Last dinner 8.30pm
Credit Cards 1 3

HOUGHTON-LE-SPRING Tyne & Wear Map 12 NZ34
★★ 59% **Chilton Lodge**
Black Boy Rd, Chilton Moor, Fencehouses ☎091-3852694
FAX 091-3852694

Situated in rural surroundings near the village of Fencehouses, about 1.5 miles southwest of Houghton Le Spring, this country pub with a modern motel-style bedroom wing has a conservatory restaurant and cosy traditional bars offering a range of food.
18⇨♠1⚐ CTV in all bedrooms ® T ✖ (ex guide dogs)
☾ 100P
♥ Last dinner 9.45pm
Credit Cards 1 3 5

HOUNSLOW Greater London
See **LONDON SECTION** plan 1 B3
★★★ 62% **Master Robert**
Great West Rd TW5 0BD (A4) ☎081-570 6261
FAX 081-569 4016

Public areas at this commercial hotel include the busy Robert Inn bar and a traditional carvery restaurant with its separate lounge bar. Spread out to the rear, in a quiet setting, are the 2 bedroom buildings and a series of chalets. The Hogarth Wing is the smartest, but all are spacious and have good facilities.
100⇨♠(8fb)⌇in 33 bedrooms CTV in all bedrooms ®♥ T ✖ (ex guide dogs) ✱ sB&B⇨♠£77 dB⇨♠£72-£87 (room only) 🅿
☾ 100P 35🚗 ✱
♥ Mainly grills V ♥ ⌇ ✱ Lunch £4.99-£12.50alc Dinner £12.50-£15.50alc Last dinner 11pm
CONF. Thtr 150 Class 80 Board 60 Del from £85
Credit Cards 1 2 3 5

HOVE
See **Brighton & Hove**

HOVINGHAM North Yorkshire Map 08 SE67
★★★ 65% **Worsley Hotel Arms**
YO6 4LA (on B1257) ☎(0653) 628234 FAX (0653) 628130
This stone-built Georgian coaching inn overlooks the village green. It was built in 1841 by Sir William Worsley, whose family still own the hotel and who live in nearby Hovingham Hall. The Cricketers' Bar in the hotel reflects the family's love of the game, with many mementos and old photographs of famous players. Bedrooms are stylish, the comfortable sitting rooms are in traditional style, and the restaurant is fast growing in reputation.
14⇨Annexe8⇨♠⌇in 4 bedrooms CTV in all bedrooms ® T sB&B⇨♠£62 dB&B⇨♠£84 🅿
CTV 50P 3🚗 ✱ ♫ (hard) squash *xmas*
♥ English & French V ♥ ⌇ ⌇ ✱ Lunch £3.50-£25alc High tea £2.50-£6 Dinner £18.50 Last dinner 9pm
Credit Cards 1 2 3

HOW CAPLE Hereford & Worcester Map 03 SO63

★★ 63% How Caple Grange
HR1 4TF (adj B4224 between Hereford & Ross-on-Wye)
☎(098986) 208 & 668 FAX (098986) 301
Part of this country mansion dates back to 1730 with a Victorian and further modern extension. The pleasant grounds include a swimming pool, and all bedrooms and public areas are comfortably furnished.
26rm(18⇨) CTV in all bedrooms ® T ✱ sB&B⇨£27.50-£42.50 dB&B⇨£50-£65 ₧
CTV 100P ❋ ≋ sauna solarium gymnasium putting *xmas*
ⓗ ⓛ Last dinner 9pm
CONF. Thtr 100 Class 50 Board 40 Del from £48

HOWTOWN (NEAR POOLEY BRIDGE) Cumbria Map 12 NY41

★★★ ❀❀❀ ♨ SHARROW BAY COUNTRY HOUSE
Sharrow Bay CA10 2LZ (at Pooley Bridge take RH fork by church to Howtown. At cross road turn R and follow Lakeside Road for 2m.)
☎Pooley Bridge(07684) 86301 & 86483 FAX (07684) 86349
Closed end Nov-early Mar

Now approaching its 46th season, this extended hotel on the edge of Ullswater has obviously acquired modern amenities over the years, but thankfully there have been no startling changes. The courtesy, care and lack of hubris shown by all its staff, from directors downwards, rank high among its attractions, and guests are made to feel at home from the time they arrive. A few of the stylishly appointed and thoughtfully equipped bedrooms are contained in the main house, but the majority are scattered around numerous lodges and cottages. Public areas consist of a string of lounges and a conservatory, all displaying treasured objets d'art, where afternoon tea has become an institution (booking recommended). Chef Juan Martin has remained oblivious of passing fads and produces a fine range of steadfastly honest dishes. Set price menus offer plenty of choice, and dinner can assume epic proportions. A tasty confit of honeyed duck might be followed by superb halibut, moistened by a bright Martini and chervil sauce, the famous cheese suissesse soufflé, a main course of best end of lamb and finally a delicious raspberry tartlet with good vanilla ice.
12rm(8⇨)Annexe16⇨ CTV in all bedrooms ® T ✱ sB&B⇨£85-£125 dB&B£75-£90 dB&B⇨£120-£150 (incl dinner)
28P 2🚗 ❋ ❋ nc13yrs
ⓗ English & French ⓗ ⓛ ✂ Lunch £25-£30 Dinner £40 Last dinner 8.30pm

HOWWOOD Strathclyde *Renfrewshire* Map 10 NS36

★★★ 62% Bowfield Country Club
Lands of Bowfield PA9 1DB (1m S off B776)
☎Kilbarchan(05057) 5225 FAX (05057) 5230
In an elevated rural position, this complex occupies what was once a bleaching mill, and much of the original character of the building remains. It is first and foremost a leisure club, with a wing of well equipped bedrooms.

12⇨(3fb) CTV in all bedrooms ® T ✱ (ex guide dogs)
sB&B⇨£55-£65 dB&B⇨£76-£90
CTV 100P ❋ ❋ ≋ (heated) ♪ squash snooker sauna solarium gymnasium jacuzzi spa & steam room
ⓗ International V ⓗ ⓛ ✂ Lunch £6.45-£14.95alc Dinner £19-£21&alc Last dinner 9.30pm
CONF. Thtr 20 Class 20 Board 20 Del from £70
Credit Cards ①②③⑤ £

HUDDERSFIELD West Yorkshire Map 07 SE11

See also **Marsden**

★★★ ❀69% Bagden Hall
Wakefield Rd, Scissett HD8 9LE ☎(0484) 865330 FAX (0484) 861001
Recently extensively refurbished, this comfortable hotel is set in 40 acres of parkland and woods, where a 9-hole golf course is about to be completed. Bedrooms are richly decorated and public areas elegantly furnished. Care is taken with the food, and chef Paul Davies produces some fine dishes.
17⇨(6fb)1⚑ CTV in all bedrooms ® T ✱ ✱ sB&B⇨£60 dB&B⇨£80-£100 ₧
《 CTV 85P ❋ ❋ ▶ 9 *xmas*
ⓗ International ⓗ ⓛ ✂ Lunch £10.75-£11.95 High tea £2.55-£5.90 Dinner £15.95&alc Last dinner 10pm
Credit Cards ①②③⑤

★★★ 66% George
St George's Square HD1 1JA (Principal) ☎(0484) 515444 FAX (0484) 435056
In the centre of town beside the railway station, this fine Victorian building has well equipped bedrooms, decorated and furnished in contemporary style. Public areas retain something of their original splendour, with smartly uniformed staff providing friendly service.
59rm(47⇨)(2fb) CTV in all bedrooms ® T

SOUTH LODGE HOTEL

Four star luxury in traditional country house set in 90 acres of beautiful Sussex parkland, with views over the South Downs.

Delicious cuisine by top chef Anthony Tobin, using local game and fish, with soft fruits and herbs from hotel's own walled garden.

Superbly appointed bedrooms and suites each individually decorated in true country house style.

Enjoy tennis, croquet, pétanque, putting, fishing, horse riding or golf at Mannings Heath Golf Club.

South Lodge is the perfect location for visiting the wealth of National Trust Gardens and Houses of Sussex.

For full details, please contact:
**South Lodge Hotel, Lower Beeding,
Near Horsham, West Sussex RH13 6PS
Telephone: 0403 891711.**

Huddersfield - Hull

Lift ℂ 24P
♀ International **V** ✿ ⚿ ✂ Last dinner 9.45pm
Credit Cards ①②③⑤

★★★**61%** Briar Court
Halifax Road, Birchencliffe HD3 3NT (on A629, 300yds S of junc 24 on M62) ☎(0484) 519902 FAX (0484) 431812
This is a purpose built hotel with an attractive local stone façade. Bedrooms are attractive in light oak and with pastel fabrics, and the location and style of the hotel make it ideal for the business user. In addition to the hotel restaurant, the adjoining Pizzeria Ristorante is popular. Staff are willing to please which, in the main, compensates for a few service errors.
47⇨🛏(3fb) CTV in all bedrooms ® T ✕ (ex guide dogs) sB&B⇨🛏£35-£65 dB&B⇨🛏£45-£85 🍽
ℂ 140P ✿
♀ English & Italian **V** ✿ ⚿ Bar Lunch £5-£30alc Dinner £10.95&alc Last dinner 11pm
CONF. Thtr 80 Class 40 Board 40 Del from £60
Credit Cards ①②③⑤

★★⚫**73%** Lodge
48 Birkby Lodge Rd, Birkby HD2 2BG (junc 24 of M62, then exit A629 for Birkby) ☎(0484) 431001 FAX (0484) 421590
Closed 26-27 Dec RS 25 Dec
This fine Victorian hotel has many of the attributes of a country house in spite of its residential location. The attractive dining room is richly decorated with William Morris fabrics, and a private dining room is also available. The food is modern English served in generous portions, and the menu is well balanced. The wine list features New World wines as well as classical European.
11⇨🛏(3fb)1🛌in all bedrooms CTV in all bedrooms ® T sB&B⇨🛏£40-£55 dB&B⇨🛏£50-£70 🍽
CTV 40P 1🚗 🚲 ✿ snooker clay pigeon shooting hot air ballooning
♀ English & French **V** ✿ ⚿ ✂ Lunch £6.95-£15alc Dinner £20.95-£22 Last dinner 9.45pm
CONF. Thtr 40 Class 24 Board 20 Del from £90
Credit Cards ①②③

★★★**67%** Huddersfield
33-47 Kirkgate HD1 1QT ☎(0484) 512111 FAX (0484) 435462
Situated in the town centre between the ring road and the parish church, this lively hotel offers a wide range of facilities including a bistro, all day brasserie, night club and small leisure suite. Bedrooms are generally compact but well equipped.
46⇨🛏(4fb)2🛌 CTV in all bedrooms ®⚿ T sB&B⇨🛏£29-£49 dB&B⇨🛏£39-£59
Lift ℂ CTV 60P sauna solarium jacuzzi pool table darts *xmas*
♀ English & French **V** ✿ ⚿ ✂ Lunch £4.95-£7.95&alc High tea £1.95-£3.95 Dinner £9.50-£14.50&alc Last dinner 11.30pm
CONF. Thtr 60 Class 40 Board 30 Del from £45
Credit Cards ①②③④⑤

★★**66%** Cote Royd Country Hotel
7 Halifax Rd, Edgerton HD3 3AN
☎(0484) 547588 FAX (0484) 547588

Set in its own grounds, this former mill owner's mansion has been refurbished to provide attractive accommodation. Bedrooms, though not spacious, are well equipped with modern facilities and the elegant public rooms include a panelled restaurant offering good value set price menus.
21⇨🛏(2fb) CTV in all bedrooms ® T ✕ ✿ sB&B⇨🛏£30-£39.50 dB&B⇨🛏£40-£50
ℂ CTV 20P ✿ sauna solarium gymnasium whirlpool bath
V ✿ ⚿ ✂ Lunch fr£9.50 Dinner fr£13.25 Last dinner 9.30pm
CONF. Thtr 60 Board 22 Del from £65
Credit Cards ①②③⑤

Hilton National Huddersfield
Ainley Top HD3 3RH ☎Elland(0422) 375431
FAX (0422) 310067

This is a bright, modern hotel with an informal restuarant, aimed at both the business and leisure guest. All bedrooms have ensuite bathrooms and a range of modern facilities. For more information on Hilton National, consult the Contents page, under Hotel Groups.
118⇨🛏 ✱ B⇨🛏£75 (room only)
CONF. Thtr 450 Class 150 Board 100 Del £125

HULL Humberside Map **08 TA02**

★★★**70%** Grange Park
Main St HU10 6EA ☎(0482) 656488 FAX (0482) 655848
(For full entry see Willerby)

★★★**70%** Willerby Manor
Well Ln HU10 6ER ☎(0482) 652616 FAX (0482) 653901
(For full entry see Willerby)

★★★**64%** Royal
Ferensway HU1 3UF ☎(0482) 25087 FAX (0482) 23172

Refurbishment has restored many of the Royal's finest features. The modern reception area leads to an elegant lounge with lofty, ornate ceilings and archways. Here an all day menu proves popular, whilst the restaurant offers a carvery and limited carte. There is a small cocktail bar which doubles as a quieter lounge area. The bedrooms (standard and premier) are comfortable and modern, and rooms are available for non smokers and disabled guests. Guests may use the small leisure centre adjacent to the hotel.
155⇨🛏(4fb)2🛌in 19 bedrooms CTV in all bedrooms ®⚿ T ✱ sB&B⇨🛏£55-£67 dB&B⇨🛏£69.50-£82 Continental breakfast 🍽
Lift ℂ CTV 60P gymnasium pool table spa pool steamroom *xmas*
♀ English & French **V** ✿ ⚿ ✂ ✱ Lunch £9&alc Dinner £12.50&alc Last dinner 10pm
CONF. Thtr 450 Class 200 Board 80 Del from £74
Credit Cards ①②③④⑤

See advertisement under SCOTCH CORNER (NEAR RICHMOND)

★★★**60%** Valiant House
11 Anlaby Rd HU1 2PJ (turn off A63 onto A1079)
☎(0482) 23299 FAX (0482) 214730
This large Victorian mansion, catering mainly for business guests, is now largely hidden behind a modern frontage. Bedrooms are mostly quite spacious and have period style reproduction furniture and a good range of equipment, including trouser presses and satellite TV.
59⇨🛏 CTV in all bedrooms ®⚿ T ✕ ✱ sB&B⇨🛏£35-£55 dB&B⇨🛏£45-£65 🍽
Lift ℂ 30P *xmas*
♀ English & French **V** ✿ ⚿ ✱ Bar Lunch £2-£10alc Dinner £12.75&alc Last dinner 9.30pm
Credit Cards ①②③⑤

★★**65%** Waterfront
Dagger Ln HU1 2LS (follow A63 into centre of Hull, turn left into Prince's Dock St and hotel is 200yds on the right hand side) ☎(0482) 227222 FAX (0482) 227222
This clever conversion of a former warehouse is in the redeveloped dock area of the old town. Many original features have been preserved, including stone- flagged floors, cast iron pillars and immense wooden beams. The large bistro on the lower ground floor has the original brick walls and arched ceiling, and there is another café/bar popular with shoppers. The attractive, well equipped bedrooms, some quite spacious, have coordinated soft furnishings.
30⇨🛏2🛌 CTV in all bedrooms ® T ✕ (ex guide dogs) sB⇨🛏£30-£45 dB⇨🛏£40-£55 (room only) 🍽

Hull

⟪ 32P
♡ English & French V ✿ ⚒ ✳ Bar Lunch £2.25-£3.95 Dinner fr£10.95&alc Last dinner 10pm
CONF. Thtr 75 Class 40 Board 40 Del from £25
Credit Cards [1][2][3]

★★ 64%Pearson Park
Pearson Park HU5 2TQ ☎(0482) 43043 FAX (0482) 447679
Closed 24 Dec-1 Jan
Converted from 4 Victorian houses, Pearson Park has been owned by the Atkinson family for more than a quarter of a century. The bedrooms mostly have modern furniture, and two ground floor rooms are available. The hotel has a small lounge bar with a real fire, a freshly decorated restaurant and a small lounge area.
32⇨ ℕ(4fb)1 ⊞ CTV in all bedrooms ® T sB&B⇨ℕ£30-£45 dB&B⇨ℕ£45-£60 ⍁
⟪ 30P
♡ English & French V ✿ ⚒ Sunday Lunch fr£7.50 Dinner fr£10.95&alc Last dinner 9pm
CONF. Thtr 50 Class 20 Board 26 Del from £60
Credit Cards [1][2][3][5]

See advertisement on page 311

....

Campanile
Beverley Rd, Freetown Way HU2 9AN (pass station and first right after crossroads)
☎(0482) 25530 FAX (0482) 587538
A nearby bar and bistro restaurant provides refreshments for travellers staying at this modern accommodation building. Bedrooms are well equipped and have en suite bathrooms. For more details about Campanile, consult the Contents page, under Hotel Groups.
Annexe50⇨ℕ B⇨ℕ£35.75 (room only)
CONF. Thtr 35 Class 35 Board 25 Del from £42.80

**Anlaby Road, Hull
North Humberside HU1 2PJ
Telephone: 0482 23299
Fax: (0482) 214730**

★★★

This modern, 57 bedroomed, extensively refurbished hotel, is ideally situated in the town centre, adjacent to the railway station. All bedrooms are en-suite and fully equipped. Free parking. English and Continental cuisine.

For details of our Conference facilities and weekend rates contact Iain Jones on 0482 23299

VALIANT HOUSE
And Conference Centre
HOTEL
The Venue for Value

The *Award Winning*
WATERFRONT HOTEL, CLUB & RESTAURANT

AA ★★

Dagger Lane, Old Town,
Kingston upon Hull, HU1 2LS
Tel: 0482 227222

The Waterfront is the result of an inspired and extensive conversion of a former Victorian dockside warehouse. Easy to find, in the heart of the Old Town, offering first class accommodation in each of our different and characterful bedrooms, excellent food in the renowned 'Sugardock Bistro' and the best Nightclub in town. Winner of national and international awards for its style and originality and perfect for weddings and functions. A thriving Cafe Bar serving tempting hot and cold food and all manner of continental beers and lagers helps to make the Waterfront the ideal location for the weekend. Indeed, all of the team here in Hull are committed to providing the highest possible standards of service and comfort throughout this varied and unique Hotel.
You can always be sure of a welcome at the Waterfront.
Why not try a 'weekend break'?

HULL
ROYAL HOTEL

For business or pleasure stay friendly

Royal Hotel, Ferensway, Hull HU1 3UF
AA ★★★

Premier Plus Rooms. Own hotel parking.
Superb leisure centre. Conveniently situated with easy access to the M62, the ideal hotel for business or pleasure.

FOR RESERVATIONS (office hours) FREEPHONE
0800 591910
or call direct on 0482-25087 Fax: 0482-23172
It pays to stay Friendly

Hull - Hunstanton

Forte Crest
Castle St HU1 2BX ☎(0482) 225221 FAX (0482) 213299

A large modern hotel with a wide range of services and amenities, designed particularly for the business traveller. Bedrooms are smart, comfortable and well equipped. For more details about Forte Crest hotels, consult the Contents page, under Hotel Groups.
99rm B £49.50-£89 (room only)
CONF. Thtr 150 Class 60 Board 50 Del from £70

Forte Posthouse
Ferriby High Rd HU14 3LG ☎(0482) 645212 FAX (0482) 643332
(For full entry see North Ferriby)

Forte Travelodge
Beacon Service Area, South Cave(A63 eastbound)
☎(0430) 424155 Central Res (0800) 850950

This modern building offers a good standard of accommodation for overnight stops. Smart, spacious and well equipped bedrooms, all with en suite bathrooms, are suitable for family use, and meals may be taken at the nearby family restaurant. For more details about Travelodges, consult the Contents page, under Hotel Groups.
40rm B £31.95 (room only)

Travel Inn
Ferriby Rd, Hessle ☎(0582) 482224

Purpose-built accommodation offers spacious and well equipped bedrooms, all with en suite bathrooms. Meals may be taken at the nearby family restaurant and pub. For more details about Travel Inns, consult the Contents page, under Hotel Groups.
40rm B £33.50 (room only)

HUMBIE Lothian *East Lothian* Map 12 NT46

★★★62% Johnstounburn House
EH36 5PL (1m S on A6137, off A68)
☎(0875) 833696 FAX (0875) 833626

This impressive baronial mansion stands in extensive grounds which ensure peace and quiet. On the first floor, lovely panelling and ornate ceilings in the dining room and lounge, reflect the charm of a bygone age, and improved seating has added to the appeal of the bar. Bedrooms are furnished in period, and a programme of improvements is under way.
11rm(10)Annexe9rm(5fb)1 CTV in all bedrooms ® T sB&B £90-£105 dB&B £125-£150
CTV 40P ✿ ♪ clay pigeon shooting all terrain vehicle *xmas*
V ❀ ⚖ ✻ Lunch £12-£15 Dinner £26 Last dinner 9pm
CONF. Thtr 60 Class 26 Board 30 Del £128
Credit Cards [1][2][3][5]

HUNGERFORD Berkshire Map 04 SU36

★★★63% The Bear
Charnham St RG17 0EL (on A4)
☎(0488) 682512 FAX (0488) 684357

This famous inn dates from 1297 and much of its character has been retained in the beamed restaurant and traditional bar with its open fire. All bedrooms are attractively decorated and well equipped, either in the main building or in one of two tastefully converted outbuildings.
13rm Annexe28rm(2fb)2 ✁ in 4 bedrooms CTV in all bedrooms ® T ✻ sB £65 dB £75 (room only)
℄ 80P *xmas*

International V ❀ ⚖ ✻ Lunch £8.75&alc Dinner £12.75&alc Last dinner 9.30pm
CONF. Thtr 100 Class 45 Board 30 Del £90
Credit Cards [1][2][3][5]

★★65% Three Swans
117 High St RG17 0DL ☎(0488) 682721 FAX (0488) 681708

This town centre coaching inn has recently undergone major refurbishment. The panelled bar is retained, and there is a comfortable lobby lounge and an all day brasserie. Bedrooms are attractively decorated and well equipped.
15rm(2fb)✁ in 6 bedrooms CTV in all bedrooms ® T ✻ sB&B £45 dB&B £60
40P 🚭
V ❀ ⚖ ✻ Lunch £7.45-£11.45alc Dinner £7.45-£11.45alc Last dinner 10pm
CONF. Thtr 60 Class 36 Board 36 Del £65
Credit Cards [1][2][3][4][5]

HUNSTANTON Norfolk Map 09 TF64

★★68% Caley Hall
Old Hunstanton Rd PE36 6HH (on A149) ☎(0485) 533486
Closed Jan-Feb RS Sun evening

This 17th-century manor house is on the edge of Old Hunstanton. The comfortable lounge bar and restaurant are housed in a clever conversion of outbuildings, and the latter serves a good-value daily set price menu. Resident proprietor Clive King and his young team of staff are friendly and helpful. Accommodation is mainly in ground floor, chalet-style bedrooms.
Annexe29rm(27)(5fb) CTV in all bedrooms ® ✁
50P
International V ❀ Last dinner 9pm
Credit Cards [1][3]

★★61% Lodge
Old Hunstanton Rd PE36 6HX (1m E) ☎(0485) 532896

This former dower house on the coast road provides accommodation in various sizes of bedroom. There is a small open-plan lounge area, and a wide range of meals are available in the bar or the dining room. Resident proprietors and staff provide willing and polite service.
16rm(3fb) CTV in all bedrooms ® T ✻ sB&B £39 dB&B £66
70P ✿ snooker games room *xmas*
English, French & Italian V ❀ ⚖ ✻ Lunch £14.95&alc Dinner £14.95&alc Last dinner 9.30pm
CONF. Class 30
Credit Cards [1][3]

★58% Wash & Tope
Le Strange Ter PE36 5AJ ☎(0485) 532250

This small inn is a short walk from the sandy beach and many of the leisure amenities of the popular resort. It has a choice of bars and a recently redecorated restaurant, and the service is informal and polite. Bedrooms vary in size and style, the front rooms (some with sea views) tend to be larger.
10rm(4 2)(1fb)1 ✁ CTV in all bedrooms ®
12P 2 🅿 pool
V ❀
Credit Cards [1][2][3]

Some hotels within company owned groups share a uniform identity. For full details consult the Contents page, under Hotel Groups.

HUNSTRETE Avon Map 03 ST66

★★★★❀❀❀⚜
HUNSTRETE HOUSE
BS18 4NS (on A368) (Clipper)
☎Compton Dando
(0761) 490490
FAX (0761) 490732

Set on the edge of the Mendip Hills, this 18th-century country house overlooks rolling fields and woodlands and has beautiful gardens. The bedrooms are individually styled and furnished to a high standard; Swallow Cottage makes an ideal honeymoon suite. The owners are keen collectors of antiques, and their collection enhances the elegant public rooms, including the hall, library, bar, drawing room and dining room. Flowers and plants create a welcoming atmosphere, along with the open fires. Chef Darren Bott produces modern Anglo-French cuisine with a pleasing mixture of imagination and tradition. A smooth crab ravioli has a piquant shellfish sauce and a topping of crisp fried strands of ginger. Many of the vegetables come from the superb walled garden. Saucing is full of flavour yet not over intense; the dishes are sometimes elaborate, but the flavours are true.

13⇨🛏Annexe11⇨🛏2🛌 CTV in all bedrooms T
✕ (ex guide dogs) sB&B⇨🛏fr£95 dB&B⇨🛏fr£150 🍽
《40P ♿ ❋ ⌒ (heated) ♬ (hard) croquet lawn nc9yrs xmas
🍴 English & French V ♥ ⚌ ✂ Lunch fr£16&alc Dinner fr£29.50&alc Last dinner 10pm
CONF. Thtr 24 Class 18 Board 16 Del from £140
Credit Cards 1 3

HUNTINGDON Cambridgeshire Map 04 TL27

★★★72% **The Old Bridge**
PE18 6TQ (off A1 at junct with A1-M1 link and A604/M11) (PH)
☎(0480) 52681 FAX (0480) 411017

This ivy-clad Georgian hotel, overlooking the River Ouse, has been carefully furnished and decorated to retain its original character. The individually styled bedrooms have quality soft furnishings and a good level of facilities. Public rooms include a panelled restaurant and an informal terrace where modern British dishes are offered. Service is polite and attentive, with lounge and room service readily available.

26⇨🛏(3fb)1🛌 CTV in all bedrooms⚌ T ✱ sB&B⇨🛏£69.50-£80 dB&B⇨🛏£95-£120 🍽
《50P ♪ private mooring for boats xmas
V ♥ ⚌ ✂ Lunch £15.95&alc Dinner £24.15-£32.15alc Last dinner 10.30pm
CONF. Thtr 60 Class 40 Board 24 Del from £127
Credit Cards 1 2 3 5

★★★61% **The George**
George St PE18 6AB ☎(0480) 432444 FAX (0480) 453130

FORTE Heritage

This former posting inn off the High Street dates back to the early 17th century and is now being sympathetically restyled. There is a relaxing lounge with comfortable seating, a smaller lounge bar offering informal meals, and a more formal restaurant with a choice of menus. Attractively refurbished and decorated bedrooms offer traditional comforts and modern amenities.

24⇨🛏(3fb)⚋in 7 bedrooms CTV in all bedrooms ® T
sB⇨🛏£75-£80 dB⇨🛏£85-£90 (room only) 🍽
71P xmas

★★★ AA
JOHNSTOUNBURN HOUSE
A Thistle Country House Hotel

Humbie, Nr Edinburgh EH36 5PL
Tel: 0875 833696   Fax: 0875 833626

Your choice in
East Lothian

For Reservations at over 100
Mount Charlotte Thistle Hotels
Telephone London: 071 937 8033.

THISTLE HOTELS

PEARSON PARK HOTEL
The Hotel in the Park   ★★
PEARSON PARK, HULL HU5 2TQ
Telephone: (0482) 43043

Proprietors: D.A. & I. Atkinson

Situated just off City Centre in a public park with rose gardens, bowling greens and conservatory, the hotel has extensive open views. All 33 rooms have telephone, radio, television, tea-making facilities and have private bathroom. The lounges and cocktail bar overlook the park. There is an excellent restaurant and a coffee shop serving light refreshments.

Huntingdon - Ilfracombe

V ♥ ♨ ⚡ ✱ Sunday Lunch fr£11.95 Dinner fr£15.95&alc Last dinner 9.30pm
CONF. Thtr 200 Class 120 Board 50 Del from £90
Credit Cards [1][2][3][5]

HUNTLY Grampian *Aberdeenshire* Map **15** NJ53

★★♨ **56%** Castle
AB54 4SH ☎(0466) 792696 FAX (0466) 792641
This sturdy 18th-century stone building is set amid extensive grounds close to the ruins of Huntly Castle. Public areas are solidly traditional in style with a lived-in feel, while bedrooms are well decorated, some spacious with fine period pieces.
21rm(20⇨♠)(4fb)3🛏 CTV in all bedrooms ® sB&B£36.50-£42 sB&B⇨♠£37.25-£43 dB&B⇨♠£54-£59 🍴
CTV 50P 3🚗 ♣ ♪ croquet putting green *xmas*
♡ Scottish & French V ♥ ♨ ⚡ ✱ Lunch £10.50 High tea £6.75-£10.50 Dinner £10.50-£14.50&alc Last dinner 9pm
Credit Cards [1][2][3]

HURLEY Berkshire Map **04** SU88

★★★ ✽**70%** Ye Olde Bell
SL6 5LX (off A423)
☎Littlewick Green(0628) 825881 FAX (0628) 825939

One of the oldest inns in England, Ye Olde Bell is set on a rural side road with its own gardens, and the small lounge and bar have original beams and a cheery open fire. Bedrooms vary in shape and size, but all are smartly furnished. The elegant oak panelled restaurant offers a fine ambience for Brendan McGee's inviting menus, which combine traditional seasonal dishes with newer ideas.
10⇨♠Annexe26⇨♠(3fb)2🛏 in 2 bedrooms CTV in all bedrooms ® T ✱ sB⇨♠£75-£85 dB⇨♠£85-£115 (room only) 🍴
(90P ♣ ♣ badminton croquet petanque *xmas*
♡ English & French V ♥ ♨ ⚡ ✱ Lunch £13.95-£17.95&alc Dinner £17.95-£18.95&alc Last dinner 9.30pm
CONF. Thtr 140 Class 60 Board 60 Del £115
Credit Cards [1][2][3][5]

HURSTBOURNE TARRANT Hampshire Map **04** SU35

★★ ♨**75%** Esseborne Manor
SP11 0ER (1.5m N 0n A343)
☎(0264) 76444 due to change to 736444
FAX (0264) 76473
A stylish, but cosy hotel, Esseborne Manor is personally run by the Yeo family. The bedrooms are individually furnished and equipped to a high standard, with extras such as bathrobes and fresh fruit. There is a pretty restaurant, elegant drawing room and snug, well stocked bar with a log-burning fire. A new chef, Andrew Norman, has recently been appointed.
6⇨♠Annexe6⇨♠1🛏 CTV in all bedrooms T ✱ (ex guide dogs) sB&B⇨♠£84 dB&B⇨♠£125 🍴
50P 🚗 ♣ ♪ (hard) croquet golf practice net nc12yrs
♡ English & French V ♥ ♨ ⚡ ✱ Lunch £14-£17.50 Dinner fr£19.50&alc Last dinner 9.30pm
Credit Cards [1][2][3][4][5]

HURST GREEN Lancashire Map **07** SD63

★★ **67%** *Shireburn Arms*
BB6 9QJ ☎Stonyhurst(025486) 518
Closed 1 Jan
Originally a farmhouse with parts dating back to 1679, this extended country inn offers both traditional-style and modern accommodation. Bedrooms vary in size but are generally comfortable and well equipped, while the spacious public rooms include various lounge areas in addition to a pleasant restaurant, which overlooks the Ribble Valley.

15⇨♠(2fb)1🛏 CTV in all bedrooms ® T
CTV 71P ♣ putting green ♪
♡ English & French V ♥ ♨
Credit Cards [1][2][3]

HYTHE Kent Map **05** TR13

★★★★ ✽**71%** The Hythe Imperial
Princes Pde CT21 6AE ☎(0303) 267441
FAX (0303) 264610

This impressive seafront hotel, built in 1880 and set in its own 52-acre estate, provides bedrooms in traditional style, some containing antique pieces and all enjoy either sea or garden views. There is an attractive restaurant, and guests have a choice of 3 bars.
100⇨♠(5fb)4🛏 CTV in all bedrooms ® T ✱ (ex guide dogs) sB&B⇨♠£80-£100 dB&B⇨♠£110-£150 🍴
Lift ⓒ 200P 2🚗 (£10 per night) ♣ ☒ (heated) ♪ 9 ♪ (hard & grass)squash snooker sauna solarium gymnasium croquet bowls putting beauty salon *xmas*
♡ English & French V ♥ ♨ ⚡ Lunch £15-£20&alc High tea £3.50-£9 Dinner £19-£22&alc Last dinner 9pm
CONF. Thtr 220 Class 100 Board 60 Del from £120
Credit Cards [1][2][3][5]

★★★ **67%** Stade Court
West Pde CT21 6DT ☎(0303) 268263 FAX (0303) 261803

This family-owned hotel has a prime sea front location, and a refurbishment programme has resulted in attractive modern rooms with coordinated colour schemes and fabrics. There are a number of unusual split-level rooms, some using the upper level as a sun lounge. There is a comfortable first-floor lounge in addition to the bar lounge and restaurant.
42⇨♠(5fb) in 7 bedrooms CTV in all bedrooms ® ⚡ T sB&B⇨♠£45-£55 dB&B⇨♠£65-£75 🍴
Lift 12P 2🚗 (£3.75 per night) ☒ (heated) ♪ 9 ♪ (hard & grass)squash snooker sauna solarium gymnasium steam room spa bath croquet putting ♣ *xmas*
♡ English & Continental V ♥ ♨ ⚡ ✱ Lunch £7.50-£10&alc Dinner £14.95&alc Last dinner 9pm
CONF. Thtr 60 Class 50 Board 30 Del £85
Credit Cards [1][2][3][5]

ILFRACOMBE Devon Map **02** SS54

★★ **67%** Elmfield
Torrs Park EX34 8AZ ☎(0271) 863777
Closed Nov-Mar (ex Xmas)
A detached Victorian house in pleasant terraced gardens, the Elmfield is a quiet hotel which provides spotlessly clean, neat bedrooms with many modern facilities. In the dining room a short menu of good home cooking is offered, but guests must order in advance. Otherwise a short à la carte of more convenience-style food is available.
12rm(11♠)Annexe2⇨♠ CTV in all bedrooms ® T ✱ ✱ sB&B⇨♠£42 dB&B⇨♠£84 (incl dinner) 🍴
14P 🚗 ♣ ☒ (heated) sauna solarium gymnasium pool table darts jacuzzi spa bath nc8yrs *xmas*
♡ English & Continental V ⚡ Bar Lunch £2.50-£8 Dinner £10&alc Last dinner 7.30pm
Credit Cards [1][3]

★★ **64%** *Tracy House*
Belmont Rd EX34 8DR ☎(0271) 863933 & 868979
RS Oct-Mar
The Watts family are the welcoming hosts at this detached Victorian house, which stands in its own grounds in an elevated residential area with views towards the sea. There is a bar and a traditionally furnished lounge. Bedrooms vary in size and aspect.

Ilfracombe - Ilkley

11rm(9⇔1♠)(2fb) CTV in all bedrooms ® T
11P 1🚗 (£2) 🚲 ❋ solarium putting
♀ English & Continental ♦ ⌐ Last dinner 8pm
Credit Cards ①②③

★★61% St Helier
Hillsborough Rd EX34 9QQ ☎Barnstaple(0271) 864906
Closed mid Oct-Apr
This family-run hotel overlooks the harbour and sea. Bedrooms are fresh and neatly furnished, and include some family suites. There is a garden, a bar open in the evenings and a small TV lounge in the reception area.
23rm(16⇔1♠)(8fb) CTV in all bedrooms ®¥ sB&B£20-£22 dB&B£38-£42 dB&B⇔♠£42-£46 🍴
CTV 20P 9🚗 🚲 ❋ pool table
♀ English & Continental V ♦ ⌐ Dinner £7.50-£8 Last dinner 7.30pm
Credit Cards ①③

★★60% Ilfracombe Carlton
Runnacleave Rd EX34 8AR ☎(0271) 862346
FAX (0271) 865379

The Ilfracombe Carlton is a popular holiday hotel with smartly dressed, friendly staff. The small bedrooms are simply furnished and very well equipped with modern facilities. Public rooms are spacious and comfortable, and a small table d'hôte menu offers traditional English fare.
48⇔♠ CTV in all bedrooms ®¥ T 🐕 (ex guide dogs) ❋ sB&B⇔♠£25-£27.50 dB&B⇔♠£45-£50 🍴
Lift ℂ 25P 🎵 xmas
♦ ⌐ ¥ ❋ Sunday Lunch £4.95-£6.95 High tea £3-£4.50 Dinner £8.50-£11.50 Last dinner 8.30pm
CONF. Thtr 50 Class 50 Board 50 Del £49
Credit Cards ①②③⑤

★★50% Arlington
Sommers Crescent EX34 9DP ☎(0271) 862002 & 862252 FAX (0271) 862803
RS Oct-Etr
A privately owned hotel in an elevated position overlooking the sea, the Arlington provides well equipped if modest accommodation and quite comfortable public areas.
32⇔♠(6fb) CTV in all bedrooms ®¥ T sB&B⇔♠£30-£40 dB&B⇔♠£60-£80 (incl dinner) 🍴
Lift 30P ⌐ (heated) sauna solarium 🎵 xmas
♦ ⌐ ¥ Bar Lunch £2-£4 Dinner £12.50 Last dinner 8pm
Credit Cards ①②③

★59% Torrs
Torrs Park EX34 8AY ☎(0271) 862334
Closed Nov-1 Mar
This extended Victorian building is in an elevated residential area, giving some fine views across the town to the sea. Bedrooms are simply furnished. The small bar and separate lounge retain some period features.
14⇔♠(5fb) CTV in all bedrooms ® sB&B⇔♠£25.50-£28 dB&B⇔♠£51-£56 (incl dinner) 🍴
14P 🚲 solarium nc5yrs
V ♦ ⌐ ¥ Lunch £4.50-£7&alc High tea £3.75 Dinner £4.50-£7&alc Last dinner 7.30pm
Credit Cards ①②③④⑤

ILKLEY West Yorkshire Map 07 SE14

★★★53% Cow & Calf
Moor Top LS29 8BT (1m off A65, signposted Cow & Calf rocks)
☎(0943) 607335 FAX (0943) 816022
Closed Xmas
High above the Victorian spa town, this hotel is situated above the Cow and Calf Rocks. It is an imposing stone building with a small bar serving both the Jardin Room and the Panorama Restaurant,

which has splendid views over the garden to the Wharfe Valley. A balustraded staircase leads to the comfortable lounge and the pretty bedrooms.
20⇔♠(1fb)1🛏¥ in 3 bedrooms CTV in all bedrooms ® T ❋ sB&B⇔♠£55-£65 dB&B⇔♠£65-£75 🍴
100P 🚲 ❋
♀ English & French V ♦ ¥ Lunch £5-£10 Dinner £13.75&alc Last dinner 9pm
CONF. Thtr 40 Class 25 Board 25 Del from £60
Credit Cards ①②③④⑤

★★❀75% Rombalds
11 West View, Wells Rd LS29 9JG ☎(0943) 603201 FAX (0943) 816586
Closed 28-30 Dec
Situated between town and moor, and part of a Georgian terrace, Ian and Jill Guthrie's lovely hotel is run by a caring team who work with enthusiasm and professionalism. There is a large, stylish lounge bar and an attractive restaurant. The accommodation varies, and those bedrooms refurbished in recent years are elegant and comfortable.
15⇔♠(5fb) CTV in all bedrooms ® T
ℂ 28P 🚲 🎵
♀ English & Continental V ♦ ⌐ ¥ Last dinner 10pm
Credit Cards ①②③⑤

★★57% Greystones
1 Ben Rhydding Rd LS29 8RJ ☎(0943) 607408
Closed 25-26 Dec & 1 Jan
This comfortably old-fashioned house stands in a quiet residential area close to the town centre. Bedrooms, though modest, are spacious and well tended, and friendly resident proprietors provide courteous service.
10⇔♠(1fb) ® T ❋ sB&B⇔♠£43 dB&B⇔♠£59 ➡

BRITAINS BEST Bed and Breakfast

Whether you want to stay at an inn, enjoy a taste of the country at a traditional farmhouse, find a comfortable room for the night or book a short-break holiday, you will find all you need in

Britain's Best Bed and Breakfast

Every establishment is inspected and graded for quality. Places with a four or five 'Q' rating will appeal to those seeking luxurious accommodation while those on a budget can choose from places at £15 or under

AA £7.99

Ilkley - Instow

CTV 17P ❋
ᛐ Last dinner 8.15pm
Credit Cards [1] [2] [3] [5]

★69% Grove
66 The Grove LS29 9PA ☎(0943) 600298
Closed 24-31 Dec
Situated to the end of a shop-lined avenue, this is a charming stone Victorian semi with an appealing entrance. The interior is in pristine condition, and Laura Ashley wallpaper accentuates the elegant period features. Proprietors Mr and Mrs Emslie run the hotel in a quiet, efficient manner.
6⇨↑(2fb) CTV in all bedrooms ® T sB&B⇨↑£40 dB&B⇨↑£52 ♬
CTV 5P ⇦ nc3yrs
✗ ❋ Bar Lunch £3-£7.50 Dinner £10-£15alc Last dinner 7.30pm
Credit Cards [1] [3]

★63% Moorview House
104 Skipton Rd LS29 9HE (on A65) ☎(0943) 600156
Large, stone-built and semi-detached, this Victorian house has a large and pleasant rear garden stretching to the bank of the River Wharfe. Bedrooms, though not luxurious, are generally spacious and comfortably furnished in traditional style. The pleasant lounge contains an abundance of objets d'art and bric-a-brac, and the atmosphere throughout is friendly and informal.
10rm(9⇨↑) CTV in all bedrooms ® ✖ (ex guide dogs) ❋ sB&B£30-£32 sB&B⇨↑£36-£42 dB&B£35-£38 dB&B⇨↑£50-£55 ♬
CTV 15P ⇦ ❋
V ᛐ ⚌ High tea £9.95-£12.95 Dinner £10.95-£14.95 Last dinner 7pm £

ILMINSTER Somerset Map 03 ST31

★★65% Shrubbery
TA19 9AR (taking the A358 towards Ilmister town centre hotel is on right hand side of hill)
☎(0460) 52108 FAX (0460) 53660

CONSORT HOTELS

This extended Victorian residence is on the western outskirts of town, overlooking its own gardens and swimming pool. Public areas have some period features and there is a choice of lounge areas. Bedrooms have been prettily redecorated in the last 2 years, the best and most spacious being those in the main building.
14⇨↑(3fb) CTV in all bedrooms ®❦ T sB&B⇨↑£55-£65 dB&B⇨↑£90-£100 ♬
CTV 100P ❋ ⇌ (heated) ♀ (grass) deep-sea fishing
V ᛐ ⚌ Lunch £10-£22.50alc High tea £3 Dinner £15-£22.50alc Last dinner 9.30pm
Credit Cards [1] [2] [3] [4] [5] £

Forte Travelodge
(on A303)
☎(0460) 53748 Central Res (0800) 850950

FORTE Travelodge

This modern building offers a good standard of accommodation for overnight stops. Smart, spacious and well equipped bedrooms, all with en suite bathrooms, are suitable for family use, and meals may be taken at the nearby family restaurant. For more details about Travelodges, consult the Contents page, under Hotel Groups.
32⇨↑❋ B⇨↑£31.95 (room only)

IMMINGHAM Humberside Map 08 TA11

★★63% Old Chapel Hotel & Restaurant
50 Station Rd DN40 3AY ☎(0469) 572377 FAX (0469) 577883
On the outskirts of the village, this small hotel caters well for the business traveller. Managed in friendly manner by the resident proprietors, it offers cosy, if compact modern bedrooms with pretty matching fabrics. There is no separate lounge, but the bar extends into a spacious conservatory. Menus offer very good value for money.
14⇨↑ CTV in all bedrooms ® T ✖ (ex guide dogs) 20P ❋
V ᛐ ⚌ Last dinner 9.30pm
Credit Cards [1] [2] [3] [5]

INCHNADAMPH Highland *Sutherland* Map 14 NC22

★★62% Inchnadamph
IV27 4HL ☎Assynt(05712) 202
Closed Nov-14 Mar
Many guests return year after year to this long-established family-run fishing and tourist hotel which stands amid spectacular mountain and loch scenery. With the emphasis on traditional service and comfort it offers good home cooking and a choice of cosy lounges.
27rm(10⇨↑)(5fb)
CTV 30P ⇦ ♪
V ᛐ ⚌ Last dinner 7.30pm
Credit Cards [1] [3] [5]

INGATESTONE Essex Map 05 TQ69

★★★64% Heybridge Moat House
Roman Rd CM4 9AB ☎(0277) 355355 FAX (0277) 353288

Queens Moat Houses

Parts of this hotel date back to the 15th century, and in the original building there is a beamed cocktail bar and restaurant, which offers a lengthy traditional carte and live music at weekends. The hotel also has one of the largest banqueting suites in Essex. The comfortable chalet-style bedrooms have recently been upgraded and have attractive soft furnishings. A bowl of fresh fruit in every room is a welcome little extra.
22⇨↑(3fb)✗in 2 bedrooms CTV in all bedrooms ®❦ T ✖ ❋ sB⇨↑£65.50-£78.50 dB⇨↑£72-£115 (room only)
⟨ CTV 200P ❋ ♪
ᛐ International V ᛐ ⚌ ❋ Lunch £13&alc Dinner £13&alc Last dinner 10.30pm
CONF. Thtr 400 Class 300 Del £114
Credit Cards [1] [2] [3] [4] [5]

INSTOW Devon Map 02 SS43

★★★68% Commodore
Marine Pde EX39 4JN ☎(0271) 860347 FAX (0271) 861453
Set in well kept gardens with attractive views over the Torridge to Appledore, this purpose built hotel has been run by the Woolaway family for over 20 years. Bedrooms are individually furnished and decorated, and those at the front have balconies. Public areas are comfortable and the spacious restaurant offers a choice of menus.
20⇨↑(4fb) CTV in all bedrooms ® T ✖ ❋ sB&B⇨↑£37.50-£70 dB&B⇨↑£75-£120 (incl dinner) ♬
⟨ 150P ⇦ ❋ xmas
ᛐ English & Continental V ᛐ ⚌ ❋ Lunch £8-£10.75&alc Dinner £19&alc Last dinner 9.15pm
CONF. Thtr 250 Board 250 Del £50
Credit Cards [1] [2] [3]

The AA's star rating scheme is the market leader in hotel classification.

For key to symbols see the Bookmark.

314

Inveraray - Inverness

INVERARAY Strathclyde *Argyllshire* Map **10** NN00

★ 66% **Fernpoint**
PA32 8UX (A83 through Inverary, hotel on Pierhead)
☎(0499) 2170 FAX (0499) 2366
Set in its own garden by the seafront, with views across Loch Fyne, this family-run hotel has bright bedrooms, reached by a spiral staircase. A wide range of bar meals is served throughout the day and evening in the popular bar, with its stone walls and lofty ceiling; there is no lounge.
7rm(5⇨♠)(4fb) CTV in all bedrooms ® ✱ sB&B⇨♠£28-£38 dB&B⇨♠£44-£64 ♬
(12P ❀ boating ♻ *xmas*
V ♡ ♨ ✱ Bar Lunch £3.95-£8.25 High tea £5.95-£6.55 Dinner £10.95-£15.95 Last dinner 9.30pm
Credit Cards [1][3]

INVERGARRY Highland *Inverness-shire* Map **14** NH30

★★▲ 64% **Glengarry Castle**
PH35 4HW ☎(08093) 254 FAX (08093) 207
Closed 19 Oct-27 Mar
The MacCallum family have been welcoming guests for almost 30 years to their efficiently run hotel, a substantial Victorian mansion set in 60 acres of secluded grounds beside the mouth of Loch Oich. Bedrooms are constantly being improved, and day rooms retain a comfortably traditional aspect. Staff are friendly and eager to please.
26rm(25⇨♠)(4fb)3⊞ CTV in all bedrooms ® T sB&B⇨♠£38-£41 dB&B⇨♠£63-£84
30P 2☎ ⊞ ❀ ♻ (hard) ♪
♀ Scottish, English & Continental V ♡ ♨ ✱ Sunday Lunch £9.50 Dinner £17-£19 Last dinner 8.30pm
Credit Cards [1][3]

INVERMORISTON Highland *Inverness-shire* Map **14** NH41

★★ 68% **Glenmoriston Arms**
IV3 6YA (at the junct of A82/A877)
☎Glenmoriston(0320) 51206 FAX (0320) 51340
This family-run old coaching inn has been sympathetically upgraded to provide modern comforts and facilities. Bedrooms of varying size and style are attractively decorated and there is a comfortable lounge, cosy bar and smart dining room serving a range of well prepared food.
8⇨♠1⊞ CTV in all bedrooms ® T sB&B⇨♠£42-£45 dB&B⇨♠£60-£64 ♬
28P ⊞ ❀ ♪ stalking shooting
♀ European V ♡ ♨ ✱ Sunday Lunch £5.80-£8.50 Dinner £16.50-£18&alc Last dinner 8.30pm
Credit Cards [1][3]

INVERNESS Highland *Inverness-shire* Map **14** NH64

See also **Kirkhill**
★★★★ 66% **Kingsmills**
Culcabock Rd IV2 3LP ☎(0463) 237166 FAX (0463) 225208

Major redevelopments are now complete at this popular business and tourist hotel. Bedrooms, mostly spacious, are tastefully furnished and 2-bedroom villas are available in a separate building. Public areas include a choice of relaxing lounges, a comfortable cocktail bar, formal restaurant and a good range of leisure facilities. Staff are friendly and willing to please.
78⇨♠Annexe6⇨♠(11fb)⊁ in 23 bedrooms CTV in all bedrooms ®☎ T ✱ sB&B⇨♠ fr£85 dB&B⇨♠£110-£130 ♬
Lift (100P ❀ ⊡ (heated) sauna solarium gymnasium putting green hair & beauty salon *xmas*
V ♡ ♨ ✱ Lunch fr£9.95 Dinner fr£19.50&alc Last dinner 9.45pm
Credit Cards [1][2][3][5]

★★★★ 63% **Culloden House**
Culloden IV1 2NZ (take A96 from town and turn right for Culloden. After 1m, turn left at White Church.) ☎(0463) 790461 FAX (0463) 792181
The McKenzie family are steadily improving the facilities at their historic, Georgian mansion which stands in 40 acres of grounds. Public areas display a wealth of chandeliers, plasterwork, marble fireplaces and antique furnishings, and the master bedrooms are all in keeping with the period. The separate garden mansion has 4 luxurious rooms for non-smokers.
20⇨♠Annexe4⇨♠(1fb)5⊞⊁ in 3 bedrooms CTV in all bedrooms T ✈ sB&B⇨♠ fr£120 dB&B⇨♠£165-£210 ♬
(50P 2☎ ⊞ ❀ ♻ (hard) snooker sauna solarium nc10yrs *xmas*
♀ Scottish & French V ♡ ♨ ✱ Lunch fr£12.95 Dinner fr£29.50 Last dinner 9pm
CONF. Thtr 30 Class 25 Board 20 Del from £99
Credit Cards [1][2][3][5]

★★★ 74% **Craigmonie**
9 Annfield Rd IV2 3HX (off A9/A96 follow signs Hilton, Culcabock pass golf course second road on right) ☎(0463) 231649 FAX (0463) 233720
Offering a wide range of modern amenities and friendly service, the Craigmonie has become a firm favourite with visitors to Inverness. Public areas include a comfortable lounge, panelled bar and a brasserie as an alternative to the formal Darnaway restaurant. Attractive bedrooms range from popular poolside suites and executive rooms to the more compact standard rooms.
35⇨♠(3fb)3⊞⊁ in all bedrooms ®☎ T ✈ (ex guide dogs) ✱ sB&B⇨♠£60-£65 dB&B⇨♠£96-£110
Lift (60P ❀ ⊡ (heated) sauna solarium gymnasium
♀ Scottish & French V ♡ ♨ ✱ Lunch £8-£10.50 Dinner £17-£30alc Last dinner 10pm
CONF. Thtr 120 Class 40 Board 40 Del from £78
Credit Cards [1][2][3][5]

★★★ ❀73% **Bunchrew House**
Bunchrew IV3 6TA (3m W off A862) ☎(0463) 234917 FAX (0463) 710620
Efficiently run by Stewart and Lesley Dykes and their friendly staff, this impressive 17th-century mansion is set in 15 acres of wooded grounds beside the Beauly Firth. Bedrooms are comfortable and attractive, the older ones gradually being improved. Relaxing public areas include a panelled drawing room, cocktail bar and spacious restaurant. The interesting, daily changing menu features quality local produce.
11⇨♠(2fb)2⊞⊁ in 2 bedrooms CTV in all bedrooms T ✈ (ex guide dogs)
40P 2☎ ⊞ ❀ ♪ clay pigeon shooting putting green ♻
♀ International V ♡ ♨ ✱ Last dinner 9pm
Credit Cards [1][2][3]

See advertisement on page 317

★★★ 63% **Loch Ness House**
Glenurquhart Rd IV3 6JL (1.5m from town centre, overlooking Tomnahurich Bridge on canal) ☎(0463) 231248 FAX (0463) 239327
Beside the golf course and the canal, this is a friendly, family-run hotel. The comfortable traditional lounge contrasts with the more lively Copper Kettle bar, and Scottish specialities feature on both the à la carte and table d'hôte menus in the attractive Cluny restaurant. Bedrooms, which vary in size, are gradually being upgraded.
22⇨♠(3fb)2⊞⊁ in 2 bedrooms CTV in all bedrooms ®☎ T sB&B⇨♠£35-£60 dB&B⇨♠£55-£85 ♬
60P ⊞ ❀ ♫ *xmas*

➡

Inverness

Scottish & French **V** ❀ ℒ ✱ Lunch £7-£12.50&alc High tea fr£4.50&alc Dinner fr£14.50&alc Last dinner 9pm
CONF. Thtr 150 Class 50 Board 24 Del from £45
Credit Cards [1][2][3] £

★★**60%** *Palace*
Ness Walk IV3 5NE (Milton) ☎(0463) 223243 FAX (0463) 236865

Situated on the banks of the river, and overlooking the castle, this solid Victorian hotel is a popular base for visiting tour groups. Public areas include an open-plan lounge and bar and the busy restaurant offers a choice of carvery or à la carte menu. Most of the bedrooms overlooking the river have been refurbished, but those at the rear remain somewhat dated in appointments. The more compact annexe rooms offer all the expected amenities.

43⇨ⁿ⟨Annexe41⇨ⁿ(12fb) CTV in all bedrooms ® **T** ✱
sB&B⇨ⁿ£59-£69 dB&B⇨ⁿ£79-£89 ℬ
Lift ℂ 40P *xmas*
Scottish & French **V** ❀ ℒ ✱ Dinner £15&alc Last dinner 9pm
Credit Cards [1][2][3][5]

★★★**59%** *Mercury*
Millburn Rd IV2 3TR (junc A9/A96)
☎(0463) 239666 FAX (0463) 711345

This high-rise modern hotel is situated at the eastern end of the town and is popular with tour groups and for local functions. Comfortably refurbished public areas include an open-plan foyer lounge, bar and restaurant with a carvery option. Bedrooms vary, the best being the refurbished executive rooms.

118⇨ⁿ(11fb)⇩in 6 bedrooms CTV in all bedrooms ® **T** ✱
sB&B⇨ⁿ£65-£75 dB&B⇨ⁿ£85-£95 ℬ
Lift ℂ 150P *xmas*
V ❀ ℒ ✱ Lunch £4.50-£8.25 Dinner £13.50&alc Last dinner 9.30pm
CONF. Thtr 230 Class 80 Board 80 Del from £55
Credit Cards [1][2][3][5] £

★★★**58%** *Caledonian*
Church St IV1 1DX (Jarvis) ☎(0463) 235181 FAX (0463) 711206
RS Xmas

A modern purpose built hotel in the centre of town overlooking the River Ness, the Caledonian caters largely for visiting tour groups and is a popular venue for functions and conferences. There are well equipped bedrooms, a range of leisure facilities and a choice of bars.

106⇨ⁿ(12fb)⇩in 6 bedrooms CTV in all bedrooms ® **T** ✱
sB⇨ⁿ£65-£80 dB⇨ⁿ£89-£109 (room only) ℬ
Lift ℂ CTV 80P ⊟ (heated) snooker sauna solarium gymnasium whirlpool spa-bath *xmas*
International **V** ❀ ℒ ✱ Lunch £8.95 High tea £6.95-£7.95 Dinner £16.95-£17.95&alc Last dinner 9.30pm
CONF. Thtr 250 Class 120 Board 90 Del from £89
Credit Cards [1][2][3][5] £

★★

★★✱ 🏨 **DUNAIN PARK**
IV3 6JN (1m from town, on A82) ☎(0463) 230512 FAX (0463) 224532
Closed 3wks Jan/Feb

In 8 years at Dunain Park Hotel Edward and Ann Nicoll have made many improvements. New wing bedrooms are very spacious and comfortable, while those in the original building have retained their traditional character and charm. The public rooms are comfortable with blazing log fires in winter. The dining room is in 3 sections, and Ann Nicoll's cooking is based on good country recipes and modern interpretations. Within the grounds there are 2 self-contained cottage bedrooms with their own lounge. Edward Nicoll is usually to the front of the house, sometimes assisted by his daughters, but we have noticed that standards can lapse if the family is not present.

12rm(10⇨ⁿ)(2fb)1⊟ CTV in all bedrooms **T**
sB&B⇨ⁿ£45-£55 dB&B⇨ⁿ£90-£140 ℬ
20P 🚗 ✱ ⊟ (heated) sauna croquet badminton *xmas*
Scottish & French **V** ❀ ℒ ✱ Dinner £12.95-£27.50alc Last dinner 9pm
Credit Cards [1][2][3][5] £

★★**66%** *Glen Mhor*
10 Ness Bank IV2 4SG ☎(0463) 234308 FAX (0463) 713170
Closed 31 Dec-2 Jan

Family-owned and run, the Glen Mohr is close to the centre and provides good standards of service and accommodation. Bedrooms are equipped to cater for the needs of today's guests. There is a cosy lounge and 2 bars and 2 restaurants, one overlooking the river, the other an informal bistro.

20⇨ⁿAnnexe10⇨ⁿ(1fb)1⊟ CTV in all bedrooms ® **T**
sB&B⇨ⁿ£55-£69 dB&B⇨ⁿ£69-£95 ℬ
ℂ 30P pool table sun terrace beautician ♪
V ❀ ℒ Bar Lunch fr£4.95&alc High tea fr£5&alc Dinner £15.75-£21&alc Last dinner 9.30pm
CONF. Thtr 50 Class 30 Board 20 Del from £54
Credit Cards [1][2][3][5] £

★★**65%** *Lochardil House*
Stratherrick Rd IV2 4LF ☎(0463) 235995 FAX (0463) 713394

Set in 5 acres of grounds this sturdy, castellated building appeals particularly to business guests. The bright modern lounge bar has an excellent reputation for its bar food, while the small tapestried formal dining room offers an imaginative 'carte'. Bedrooms have uniform modern furnishings and a wide range of amenities, though some are small.

12⇨ⁿ(2fb) CTV in all bedrooms ® ⚐ **T** 🦮 (ex guide dogs)
sB&B⇨ⁿ£55-£75 dB&B⇨ⁿ£75-£90 ℬ
120P 3🚗 ✱
Scottish & French **V** ❀ ℒ Lunch £10-£18alc High tea £5-£12alc Dinner £12-£25alc Last dinner 9pm
Credit Cards [1][2][3][5] £

★★**60%** *Beaufort*
11 Culduthel Rd IV2 4AG ☎(0463) 222897 FAX (0463) 711413

This popular business hotel is in a residential area not far from the town centre. Bedrooms, mostly in the extension, are modern and practical. Public areas include a choice of bars, with bar food much in demand, while Aberdeen Angus steaks are the speciality of the smartly refurbished dining room.

36ⁿ(6fb) CTV in all bedrooms ® **T**
⊞ 50P 🚗
V ❀ ℒ Last dinner 10pm
Credit Cards [1][2][3][5]

★★**59%** *Cummings*
Church St IV1 1EN ☎(0463) 232531 FAX (0463) 236541

This long established town centre commercial hotel is also a popular base for visiting tour groups. Public areas, though somewhat functional in appointment, have traditional comforts. Bedrooms vary in size, are simply decorated and practical.

26rm(23⇨ⁿ)(3fb) CTV in all bedrooms ® **T**
🦮 (ex guide dogs) sB&B£36-£39 sB&B⇨ⁿ£42-£45
dB&B⇨ⁿ£58-£65
Lift ℂ CTV 25P
V ❀ ℒ ✱ Lunch £5.20-£7 High tea £6-£8alc Dinner £10-£15 Last dinner 8pm £

★ 64% **Redcliffe**
1 Gorden Ter IV2 3HD (1m from junct of A9/A96)
☎(0463) 232767
This small hotel, in its own grounds close to the castle, has a friendly and informal atmosphere. Well decorated public rooms include a cosy bar, attractive dining room and a conservatory where high tea is normally served. Bedrooms, though restricted in size, are comfortable.
9rm(6⇨)(1fb) CTV in all bedrooms ® T ✱ sB&Bfr£12 sB&B⇨£26-£27.50 dB&B£33-£35 dB&B⇨£40-£45 ⊟
12P ✿
V ✿ ⚓ Sunday Lunch £5-£7alc High tea £5.50-£11alc Dinner £8-£15alc Last dinner 9pm
Credit Cards ①②③ £

INVERURIE Grampian *Aberdeenshire* Map 15 NJ72

★★★★ ❀❀67% **Thainstone House Hotel and Country Club**
AB51 5NT (on A96) ☎(0467) 621643 FAX (0467) 625084
(Rosettes awarded for dinner only)
Thainstone House has been sympathetically extended and refurbished to combine the elegance of a former age with modern facilities. The stylish Simpson's Restaurant is the setting for chef Bill Gibbs' innovative and imaginative cooking. Natural flavours shine through in dishes such as marbled terrine of smoked trout and prawn on a delicate yellow pepper sauce; or grilled duck breast with pistachio quenelles and fried celeriac on a beetroot sauce. Cammie's Grill offers an informal alternative.
48⇨⇨(3fb)2⇨ CTV in all bedrooms ® ⚓ T ✖ (ex guide dogs) ✱ sB⇨⇨£82-£92 dB⇨⇨£99-£109 (room only) ⊟
Lift ℂ 100P ✿ ▭ (heated) snooker gymnasium jacuzzi steam room *xmas*
V ✿ ⚓
CONF. Thtr 400 Class 144 Board 70 Del from £120
Credit Cards ①②③④⑤ £

★★★ 67% **Strathburn**
Burghmuir Dr AB51 4GY (at Blackhall rbt into Blackhall Rd for 100yds then into Burghmuir Drive) ☎(0467) 624422 FAX (0467) 625133
Situated in a residential area, this small, purpose built hotel is especially popular with business people. Bedrooms are comfortable and modern, though some are compact. Public areas include a popular American themed bar, foyer lounge and à la carte restaurant. Staff are friendly and willing to please.
25⇨⇨(1fb)⚡in 8 bedrooms CTV in all bedrooms ® ⚓ T ✖ (ex guide dogs) ✱ sB&B⇨⇨£40-£55 dB&B⇨⇨£58-£84 ⊟ 40P ⚘
V ✿ ⚓ ⚡ ✱ Lunch £7.50-£15.50 Dinner £17.75-£27.75&alc
Last dinner 9.30pm
Credit Cards ①②③

★★ 59% **Gordon Arms**
Market Place AB51 9SA ☎(0467) 20314 FAX (0467) 21792
This long established family-run commercial hotel is conveniently situated in the town centre close to the railway station. It has a friendly atmosphere and offers traditional services and comforts, and redecoration has brightened the bedrooms.
11rm(6⇨) CTV in all bedrooms ® ⚓ T sB&B£29.95 sB&B⇨£33 dB&B£39.50 dB&B⇨£42 ⊟
CTV 5P
♨ European V ✿ ✱ Lunch £8.50 High tea £4.50-£10.50 Dinner £9.12-£12.50 Last dinner 8pm
Credit Cards ①②③⑤

Rosettes range from 5 for outstanding
cuisine to 1 rosette for enjoyable,
well prepared food

STRATHBURN HOTEL INVERURIE

Burghmuir Drive, Inverurie,
Aberdeenshire AB5 14GY
Tel: 0467 624422 Fax: 0467 625133
AA ★★★

ALL ROOMS EN SUITE — A LA CARTE RESTAURANT

Privately owned and managed hotel bordering the town of Inverurie and overlooking Strathburn Park and play area. Excellent golf course and fishing nearby. Ideal central location for the castle trail and outdoor pursuits — hill walking, forest walks etc. On main bus route to Aberdeen and convenient for Airport.

Bunchrew House Hotel & Restaurant

INVERNESS · IV3 6TA
Telephone: 0463 234917. Fax: 0463 710620

Situated in 20 acres of beautifully landscaped gardens and woodlands on the shores of Bealy Firth a 17th century Scottish mansion steeped in history and tradition can be found. Bunchrew House has been lovingly restored to preserve its heritage whilst high standards of luxury and modern day amenities remain including warm hospitality. Traditional cuisine includes local produce and is complemented by a specially designed wine list. The eleven luxury suites are furnished to a very high standard and individually decorated to enhance its natural features. Conferences/business meetings and private parties/receptions can be accommodated. A wealth of sporting activities are well catered for with many places of interest nearby.

Ipplepen - Irvine

IPPLEPEN Devon Map 03 SX86

★★62% Old Church House Inn
Torbryan TQ12 5UR ☎(0803) 812372
6⇌ ↑ CTV in all bedrooms ® ✈ * sB&B⇌↑£30
dB&B⇌↑£90-£96
30P ♿ ⚲ xmas
V ♿ ⚳ ✂ ✱ Lunch £5-£20 Dinner £10-£20 Last dinner 9.30pm
Credit Cards [1][3]

See advertisement under TOTNES

IPSWICH Suffolk Map 05 TM14

★★★★ ⚜ HINTLESHAM HALL
IP8 3NS ☎Hintlesham(0473) 652334 & 652268
FAX (0473) 652463
(For full entry see Hintlesham)

★★★73% Belstead Brook
Belstead Rd IP2 9HB ☎(0473) 684241 FAX (0473) 681249

The Belstead Brook, in its own grounds on the edge of a residential area, is described as 'a country hotel on the edge of the town'. Enthusiastically managed, it offers good modern facilities in the charming surroundings of the 16th-century building, with original features such as Jacobean oak-panelling in the dining room. Comfortable bedrooms include 5 purpose built suites.
85⇌↑Annexe6⇌↑(2fb)1⚑ CTV in all bedrooms ®⚲ T ✱
sB&B⇌↑£49.50-£59.50 dB&B⇌↑£69.50-£85 (room only) 🍽
Lift 【 150P ✿ gymnasium
♿ English & French V ♿ ⚳ ✂ ✱ Lunch £8.50-£14&alc High tea £8.30 Dinner £8.50-£14&alc Last dinner 10pm
CONF. Thtr 60 Class 25 Board 20 Del from £80
Credit Cards [1][2][3][5]

★★★71% Suffolk Grange
The Havens, Ransomes Europark IP3 9SJ (just off A45 Ipswich By Pass towards Felixstowe take slip road to Nacton the hotel faces you) (Lansbury) ☎(0473) 272244 FAX (0473) 272484
This immaculate hotel was built in 1991 and has attractive public areas and comfortable bedrooms equipped with all the latest facilities. Staff provide helpful service throughout.
60⇌↑in 24 bedrooms CTV in all bedrooms ®⚲ T
✈ (ex guide dogs) ✱ sB&B⇌↑fr£65.50 dB&B⇌↑fr£77 🍽
Lift 【 150P sauna solarium gymnasium xmas
♿ English & French V ♿ ⚳ ✂ ✱ Lunch fr£8.75&alc Dinner fr£12.95&alc Last dinner 10pm
CONF. Thtr 180 Class 120 Board 60 Del from £98
Credit Cards [1][2][3][5]

★★★❀❀70% Marlborough
Henley Rd IP1 3SP (on A12/A1214) ☎(0473) 257677 FAX (0473) 226917

BEST WESTERN HOTELS

A family run hotel, the Marlborough has pretty gardens which are floodlit at night to provide a pleasant outlook from the restaurant. Here Simon Barker produces a good value fixed price 3- or 4-course menu using only fresh produce. The pleasant hall has deep relaxing sofas and armchairs, there is a quiet writing room. While the bedrooms are fresh and clean, they are becoming a little dated.
22⇌↑(3fb)⚲in 7 bedrooms CTV in all bedrooms ® T ✱
sB&B⇌↑£65-£70 dB&B⇌↑£75-£80 🍽
【 60P ✿ xmas
♿ English & French V ♿ ⚳ ✂ ✱ Lunch £10.50-£13.50 Dinner £17-£22 Last dinner 9.30pm
CONF. Thtr 60 Class 20 Board 34 Del from £60
Credit Cards [1][2][3][5]

★★★65% Ipswich Moat House
London Rd, Copdock IP8 3JD (just off A12 near Copdock village) ☎(0473) 730444 FAX (0473) 730801

Conferences and meetings make up much of the weekday trade at this hotel situated in pleasant countryside near Ipswich and its leisure facilities make it popular at weekends. Bedrooms are all light and modern in style. The restaurant offers a lunchtime carvery and a range of international dishes in the evening.
74⇌↑(2fb)⚑ CTV in all bedrooms ® T ✱ sB&B⇌↑fr£55
dB&B⇌↑fr£68 🍽
Lift 【 400P ✿ ⛱ (heated) sauna solarium gymnasium xmas
♿ English & Continental V ♿ ⚳ ✂ ✱ Lunch fr£7.75 Dinner fr£14.95&alc Last dinner 9.50pm
CONF. Thtr 500 Class 200 Board 50 Del from £75
Credit Cards [1][2][3][4][5]

★★★61% Novotel
Greyfriars Rd IP1 1UP (on A137)
☎(0473) 232400 FAX (0473) 232414

novotel

Food and refreshments are available from 6am until midnight in the light open-plan public areas, where service and appointments tend to be more informal in style. Bedrooms have ample work space, and each is equipped with a double bed and single studio beds so that children can stay free of charge.
101⇌↑(6fb)⚲in 45 bedrooms CTV in all bedrooms ®⚲ T ✱
sB⇌↑£57.50 dB⇌↑£62.50 (room only) 🍽
Lift 【 ⚑ 50P
♿ International V ♿ ⚳ ✂ ✱ Lunch £5.95-£14&alc Dinner £10-£14&alc Last dinner 12am
CONF. Thtr 180 Class 80 Board 50 Del from £75
Credit Cards [1][2][3][5]

★★★67% Claydon Country House
16-18 Ipswich Rd, Claydon IP6 0AR ☎(0473) 830382 FAX (0473) 832476
14⇌↑(2fb)⚑ CTV in all bedrooms ®⚲ T ✈ (ex guide dogs)
✱ sB&B⇌↑£42.50 dB&B⇌↑£49.50 🍽
60P ⚲ xmas
♿ English & French V ♿ ⚳ ✂ ✱ Lunch £11.50-£15.50 Dinner £15-£24alc Last dinner 9.30pm
Credit Cards [1][3]

Forte Posthouse
London Rd IP2 0UA (off A1214, from A12/A45)
☎(0473) 690313 FAX (0473) 680412

FORTE Posthouse

Suitable for both the business and leisure traveller, this bright hotel provides modern accommodation in well equipped bedrooms with en suite bathrooms. For more details about Forte Posthouse hotels, consult the Contents page, under Hotel Groups.
112⇌↑✱ B⇌↑£41.50-£53.50 (room only)
CONF. Thtr 120 Class 50 Board 40

IRVINE Strathclyde Ayrshire Map 10 NS33

★★★★❀52% Hospitality Inn
Annick Rd, Annickwater KA11 4LD (access via A71 to Kilmarnock)
☎(0294) 274272 FAX (0294) 277287

A programme of upgrading is planned by this large commercial/ conference hotel to maintain the high standard of its accommodation, and it is hoped that the shortfall in services for an establishment of its type may also be rectified. Bedrooms are roomy, comfortable and fully equipped, while well furnished and spacious public areas include a choice of two restaurants – the more formal Mirage, and the tropical Lagoon with its exotic plants and swimming pool.
128⇌↑(44fb)⚲in 16 bedrooms CTV in all bedrooms ® T
sB⇌↑£69 dB⇌↑£85-£90 (room only) 🍽

Irvine - Islay, Isle of Bridgend

⟪ ⌸ CTV 250P ❋ ⌺ (heated) ▶ 9 golf driving range jacuzzi
♪ xmas
⚑ Scottish & French V ✿ ⚑ Lunch £6.25&alc High tea fr£4.50
Dinner £13.95-£18.95&alc Last dinner 11pm
CONF. Thtr 320 Class 180 Board 100 Del from £50
Credit Cards ①②③④⑤

ISLAY, ISLE OF Strathclyde *Argyllshire* Map 10

BOWMORE Map 10 NR35

★★58% Lochside
19 Shore St PA43 7LB (on A846, 100yds from main village square on shore side of road) ☎(049681) 244 FAX (049681) 390
This popular, cosy little hotel fronts the High Street of one of the island's 2 main towns, but its rear patio looks right onto the seashore and the dining room and bar have a lovely view across the loch. Bedrooms are mainly small and functional, and the hotel has an exceptional range of malt whiskies.
7rm(4⇨♠) CTV in all bedrooms ® T ❋ sB&B⇨♠£30-£32 dB&B⇨♠£54-£58 ☐
♪ xmas
⚑ International V ✿ ⚑ ✂ ❋ Dinner £12-£15 Last dinner 9pm
Credit Cards ①③

BRIDGEND Map 10 NR36

★★65% *Bridgend*
PA44 7PQ ☎Bowmore(049681) 212 FAX (049681) 673
Situated at the centre of the island, this estate-owned hotel has been sympathetically renovated to retain its original Victorian character. The bedrooms, which are more modern in style, vary in size and are well equipped.

➡

THE MARLBOROUGH AT IPSWICH

This very special Hotel has a beautiful award winning Victorian restaurant overlooking lovely floodlit gardens. All the bedrooms have private bathroom and are individually designed with care and imagination. Remote control colour television, electric trouser press, direct dial telephone and hair drier. Weekend Rates: from £40.00 per person for bed & breakfast. Also many interesting weekend breaks throughout the year (from £95.00).
Perfect base for your business and pleasure needs.

Henley Road, IPSWICH, Suffolk.
Tel (0473) 257677 Fax (0473) 226927

★★★

★★67%

WE TAKE PRIDE IN OFFERING COMFORT, STYLE AND SERVICE IN A RELAXED ATMOSPHERE . . .

🖝 14 beautiful bedrooms – all en-suite and with Satellite TV
🖝 Victorian Dining Room overlooking our gardens
🖝 Cocktail Bar for Guests and Diners
🖝 Conference and Function facilities
🖝 Ample parking

. . . PROVING ELEGANCE NEED NOT MEAN EXPENSIVE . . .

Ideally situated for Ipswich, A45 and exploring Suffolk and East Anglia on a weekend break.

Ipswich Road, Claydon, Suffolk
Tel: 0473 830382 Fax: 0473 832476
Please contact us for reservations

Belstead Brook HOTEL

Set in eight acres of landscaped gardens and woodlands, comfort and luxury are guaranteed in the charm of this original 16th Century Country house.
Choose from any of our 91 rooms, including executive rooms with spa baths and garden suites with private terrace.
Our Jacobean style oak panelled restaurant is renowned for its classical English kitchen offering a wide choice of Table d'Hôte and A La Carte menus. Vegetarian, Gluten free and Diabetic dishes are also catered for, with a magnificent cellar of wines carefully chosen from producers around the world.

★★★
Belstead Brook HOTEL
Belstead Road, Ipswich, Suffolk IP2 9HB
Tel: 0473 684241   Fax: 0473 684345

Islay, Isle of, Bridgend - Kendal

10rm(5⇨4🛁)(3fb) CTV in all bedrooms ® T
30P ❋ ♪ bowls
♀ ♨ Last dinner 8pm

PORT ASKAIG Map 10 NR46

★★ 61% Port Askaig
PA46 7RD (at Ferry Terminal) ☎(049684) 245 FAX (049684) 295
This long established traditional hotel overlooks the pier and its lawns stretch down to the harbour. The focal point of this small ferry community, it also offers fine views across the Sound of Islay to the island of Jura.
9rm(2⇨2🛁)(1fb) CTV in all bedrooms ® sB&B£32-£35 sB&B⇨🛁£35-£39 dB&B£52-£56 dB&B⇨🛁£60-£68 🍴
CTV 15P 6🚗 ⇔ ❋ nc5yrs
V ♀ ♨ Lunch £8-£8.50 Dinner £16 Last dinner 9pm

ISLE OF
Places incorporating the words 'Isle of' or 'Isle' will be found under the actual name, eg Isle of Wight is listed under Wight, Isle of.

ISLE ORNSAY
See **Skye, Isle of**

JERSEY
See **Channel Islands**

JOHN O'GROATS
See **Halkirk** and **Lybster**

KEGWORTH Leicestershire Map 08 SK42

★★★ 60% Yew Lodge
33 Packington Hill DE74 2DF (off A6, close to junc 24 of M1)
☎(0509) 672518 FAX (0509) 674730
This thriving commercial hotel is near the village centre. Bedrooms are modestly furnished, but all have modern amenities. The bars and restaurant serve a good range of food, and there is a central lounge with comfortable seating.
54⇨🛁(3fb) CTV in all bedrooms ®⚲ T
Lift ⓒ 120P
♀ English & French V ♀ ♨
Credit Cards 1 2 3 5

KEIGHLEY West Yorkshire Map 07 SE04

★★ 68% Dalesgate
406 Skipton Rd, Utley BD20 6HP (2m NW A629)
☎(0535) 664930 FAX (0535) 611253
The Dalesgate is a well run and hospitable hotel with an attractive exterior and a rear parking area. It is in the village of Utley, a few minutes' drive from Keighley.
21⇨🛁(1fb) CTV in all bedrooms ® T sB&B⇨🛁£28-£44 dB&B⇨🛁£49-£54 🍴
ⓒ 30P
V Dinner £13.50-£15.50&alc Last dinner 9pm
Credit Cards 1 2 3 5 £

KELLING Norfolk Map 09 TG04

★★ 65% Pheasant
The Coast Rd NR25 7EG (on A140 mid-way between Blakeney & Sheringham) ☎Weybourne0263 70382 FAX 0263 708101
Set in 3 acres of wooded grounds, this friendly hotel has a new wing of comfortable modern bedrooms; older rooms are more modest. There is an informal value-for-money menu, with orders taken at the bar and meals served in an adjacent open-plan area or the non-smoking dining room.
30⇨🛁(1fb)✻ in 13 bedrooms CTV in all bedrooms ®⚲ T
CTV 100P
♀ English & Continental V ♀ ♨ ✻
Credit Cards 1 3

KELSO Borders *Roxburghshire* Map 12 NT73

★★★ ⌘ 75% Sunlaws House
Heiton TD5 8JZ (3m S on A698)
☎Roxburgh(0573) 450331 FAX (0573) 450611
Standing in 200 acres of grounds beside the Teviot River, this Scottish baronial house was converted into a comfortable hotel some 10 years ago by the Duke of Roxburghe. Bedrooms in the main house are generally spacious, with attractive fabrics and period furniture, while those in the courtyard annexe are modern. Log fires provide a welcome in the entrance hall and drawing room, and there is an attractive library bar. A daily changing 2 or 3-course meal features local produce cooked in a straightforward manner by chef David Bates.
22⇨🛁(2fb)2⚲ CTV in all bedrooms ® T sB&B⇨🛁£85-£90 dB&B⇨🛁£128-£160 🍴
ⓒ 50P ❋ ♀ (hard) ♪ shooting croquet *xmas*
♀ Scottish & French V ♀ ♨ Lunch £9.90-£14 High tea £5.25-£7 Dinner fr£26 Last dinner 9.30pm
CONF. Board 24 Del from £85
Credit Cards 1 2 3 5

★★★ 66% Ednam House
Bridge St TD5 7HT ☎(0573) 224168 FAX (0573) 226319
Closed 25 Dec-10 Jan
Overlooking the banks of the River Tweed, and consequently popular with fishermen, this fine Adam mansion dates from 1761, and the public rooms retain many original features. A splendid foyer leads to 3 traditionally furnished and comfortable lounges, and there are 2 bars in addition to the dining room extension. Bedrooms vary in size from modest singles to grand master rooms, but all are comfortable, pleasantly decorated and equipped with most modern amenities.
32⇨🛁(2fb) CTV in all bedrooms ® T ✻ sB&B⇨🛁fr£43 dB&B⇨🛁£63-£88 🍴
CTV 100P ⇔ ❋
V ♀ ♨ Sunday Lunch fr£11 Dinner fr£17.50 Last dinner 9pm
Credit Cards 1 3

★★★ 58% Cross Keys
36-37 The Square TD5 7HL ☎(0573) 223303
FAX (0573) 225792

A modernised old coaching inn overlooking the town square, offering neat and practical bedrooms. Public rooms are mostly on the first floor and include a popular restaurant.
24⇨🛁(4fb) CTV in all bedrooms ®⚲ T ✻ (ex guide dogs) ✻
sB&B⇨🛁£35-£45 dB&B⇨🛁£41-£58 🍴
Lift ⓒ CTV snooker sauna solarium gymnasium *xmas*
♀ Scottish & Continental V Lunch £8.90 Dinner £15.90&alc Last dinner 9.15pm
CONF. Thtr 280 Class 220 Board 70 Del from £43
Credit Cards 1 2 3 5

KENDAL Cumbria Map 07 SD59

★★★ 67% Riverside
Stramongate Bridge LA9 4BZ (Logis) ☎(0539) 724707 FAX (0539) 740274
Closed 25-26 Dec & 1 Jan
A 17th-century tannery built of grey stone, the Riverside Hotel is on the banks of the River Kent close to the centre of town. Modern and well furnished bedrooms are provided and public areas are spacious and comfortable. There are 2 bars, one to serve the upstairs restaurant and a ground floor buttery bar where bar meal are available. Staff are young and keen to please.
47⇨🛁(4fb)✻ in 4 bedrooms CTV in all bedrooms ® T ✻ (ex guide dogs)
Lift ⓒ 160P
♀ International V ♀ ♨ Last dinner 10pm
Credit Cards 1 2 3 5

Kendal - Kentallen

★★★60% **Woolpack**
Stricklandgate LA9 4ND (CAIRN) ☎(0539) 723852 FAX (0539) 728608
A large, town-centre coaching house, once the local wool auction rooms. Bedrooms, in the main building and the modern extension, are contemporary in style and offer good facilities. Stairs lead from the attractive beamed bar to a comfortable cocktail bar and a pretty restaurant. Staff are well trained and attentive.
54⇨🅽(5fb)½in 6 bedrooms CTV in all bedrooms ® T ✱
sB⇨🅽£55-£65 dB⇨🅽£70-£85 (room only) 🅿
(60P *xmas*
♀ English & French V ♡ 🖵 ✱
CONF. Thtr 200 Class 80 Board 60 Del from £70
Credit Cards ①②③

★★70% **Garden House**
Fowl-ing Ln LA9 6PH (from A685, turning at Shell Garage) ☎(0539) 731131 FAX (0539) 740064
Closed 25 Dec-12 Jan
Set in 2 acres of wooded grounds within a residential area, this attractive Regency house is personally run in friendly country house style. Pretty, individually designed bedrooms provide modern comforts and there is a comfortable bar and lounge with a log fire and a charming conservatory dining room.
10⇨🅽(2fb)1🛏½in 8 bedrooms CTV in all bedrooms ® T ✱
sB&B⇨🅽£49.50-£53 dB&B⇨🅽£64-£70 🅿
40P 🚗 ✱
♀ English & French V ♡ ½ Lunch £9.75-£10.50 Dinner £17.50-£19&alc Last dinner 9pm
CONF. Thtr 30 Class 25 Board 20 Del from £65
Credit Cards ①②③⑤ (£)

KENILWORTH Warwickshire Map **04** SP27

★★★63% *De Montfort*
The Square CV8 1ED ☎(0926) 55944 FAX (0926) 57830

DE VERE HOTELS

The comfortable accommodation provided by this group hotel near the town centre is particularly popular with business visitors to the area. Public areas include a choice of eating options.
96⇨🅽 CTV in all bedrooms ® T
Lift (85P pool table ♫
V ♡ 🖵 ½ Last dinner 9.45pm
Credit Cards ①②③⑤

★★64% **Clarendon House**
Old High St CV8 1LZ ☎(0926) 57668 FAX (0926) 50669
Situated in the centre of the Kenilworth conservation area and originally built as a tavern, this hotel dates back to 1430, and exposed beams in the lounge bar and restaurant enhance the old world ambience. The size and style of the bedrooms varies tremendously, but all have modern modern facilities. A fairly lengthy à la carte menu of popular dishes is supplemented by a blackboard selection of daily specials. The hotel is far from luxurious, but has a lot of character and provides willing service.
31⇨🅽(1fb)4🛏 CTV in all bedrooms ® T ✱
sB&B⇨🅽£49.50-£55 dB&B⇨🅽£75-£80 🅿
30P 🚗
♀ European V ♡ Sunday Lunch £8.50 Dinner £10.50-£15alc Last dinner 9.30pm
CONF. Thtr 120 Class 60 Board 40 Del from £66
Credit Cards ①③ (£)

If you have booked a meal in a hotel restaurant and cannot get there, remember you have a contractual obligation to cancel your booking.

KENNFORD Devon Map **03** SX98

★★64% **Fairwinds**
EX6 7UD (4m from Exeter, off M5) ☎Exeter(0392) 832911
Closed 10-31 Dec
This small family-owned hotel offers friendly informal service. Several of the comfortable and well equipped modern bedrooms are no-smoking, as are the bar and restaurant, where imaginative home-cooked meals are offered.
8rm(6⇨🅽)(1fb)½in 2 bedrooms CTV in all bedrooms ®⚡T ✂ sB&B£22-£25 sB&B⇨🅽£35-£38 dB&B⇨🅽£42-£48 🅿
8P 🚗
V ½ Dinner £10.75-£13.95&alc Last dinner 8pm
Credit Cards ①③

KENTALLEN Highland *Argyllshire* Map **14** NN05

★★75% **Ardsheal House**
PA38 4BX (4m S of Ballachulish Bridge on A828 between Glencoe & Appin) ☎Duror(063174) 227 FAX (063174) 342
Closed last 3 wks Jan
Well run by its enthusiastic American owners, Ardsheal is a house of much charm and character, reached by a long narrow single track road around the shore of Loch Linnhe. The individually decorated bedrooms vary in size and are comfortably furnished with antiques and sturdy traditional pieces. There is a house-party atmosphere in the public areas, which include a choice of lounges, a splendid Victorian billiard room and an attractive dining room with a conservatory extension. Chef George Kelso's daily fixed-price menus offer an alternative at each of the four stages plus a salad after the main course. Praiseworthy dishes have included delicate roulade of salmon and courgette mousse with a contrasting wild mushroom sauce; roast saddle of tender venison with onion ➡

★★

Shap Wells Hotel

CUMBRIA'S LARGEST FAMILY OWNED HOTEL

Large hotel in secluded wooded grounds mid way between **KENDAL** and **PENRITH**, only five minutes from M6 (junction 39). Ideal place from which to explore the Lakes, Dales, and Border Country. All rooms en-suite with TV, radio, etc.

Reduced rates for children and stays of two or more days.

**SHAP, PENRITH CUMBRIA CA10 3QU
Tel: Shap (0931) 716628
Fax: Shap (0931) 716377**

Kentallen - Keswick

marmalade and a delicious red wine and redcurrant sauce; and warm carrot and plum cake with ginger crème anglaise.
13⇨♠(1fb) T
CTV 20P ⊞ ❈ ♪ (hard) snooker
♀ International ✿ ⚓ ✕ Lunch £8-£17.50 High tea £10-£15 Dinner £32.50 Last dinner 8.30pm
Credit Cards [1][2][3] £

★★ **65%** *Holly Tree*
Kentallen Pier PA38 4BY ☎Duror(063174) 292 FAX (063174) 345
Closed Nov-mid Feb RS Xmas-New Year

A former railway station – with parts of its platform still in evidence – the Holly Tree stands beside the A528 on the shores of Loch Linnhe, near the old steamer pier. Though many of the building's features have been retained, most bedrooms are spacious and modern, offering fine views of the loch. Public areas include a large, comfortable lounge and an attractively appointed split-level restaurant which serves good meals based largely on local produce and seafood.

12⇨♠(3fb) CTV in all bedrooms ® T
30P ❈ ♪
♀ International ✿ ⚓ ✕ Last dinner 9.30pm
Credit Cards [1][2][3]

KENTON Greater London
See **LONDON SECTION plan 1** *B5*
Travel Inn
Kenton Rd HA3 8AT (on A4006 between Harrow and Wembley) ☎081-907 1671

Purpose-built accommodation offers spacious and well equipped bedrooms, all with en suite bathrooms. Meals may be taken at the nearby family restaurant and pub. For more details about Travel Inns, consult the Contents page, under Hotel Groups.

44⇨♠ ❈ B⇨♠£33.50 (room only)

KESWICK Cumbria Map 11 NY22

★★★ ❀**73%** *Brundholme Country House*
Brundholme Rd CA12 4NL ☎(07687) 74495 FAX (07687) 73536
Closed 20 Dec-Jan

This elegant country house dates back, in part, to the early 19th century, and is in a rural setting high above the River Greta. Once frequented by Wordsworth and Coleridge, it is now a well furnished and comfortable hotel. The bedrooms are decorated in country house style but with all modern facilities, and there is a delightful lounge with an open fire. Ian Charlton is a very capable chef/proprietor, and his 5-course dinner menu is very well prepared and presented.

12⇨♠2⊞ CTV in all bedrooms ®✕ T ❊ sB&B⇨♠£40-£65 dB&B⇨♠£60-£100 ⌼
20P ⊞ ❈ croquet bowls nc11yrs
♀ English & French V ✿ ❊ Bar Lunch £2.50-£10alc Dinner £15-£30alc Last dinner 8.45pm
Credit Cards [1][2][3] £

★★★ **63%** *Derwentwater*
Portinscale CA12 5RE (off A66)
☎(07687) 72538 FAX (07687) 71002

CONSORT HOTELS

Situated in Portinscale, this comfortable hotel has delightful grounds leading down to the shores of Derwentwater. There is a bright conservatory lounge overlooking the garden, and a carvery-style dinner with a good choice of dishes is provided in the refurbished restaurant.

52⇨♠(2fb)2⊞ CTV in all bedrooms ® T sB&B⇨♠£58.50-£60 dB&B⇨♠£92-£96 ⌼
Lift ℂ 120P ❈ ♪ putting ♫ xmas

♀ English & French V ✿ ⚓ ✕ Bar Lunch £2.25-£7.50&alc Dinner £17.95-£18.95&alc Last dinner 9.30pm
CONF. Thtr 50 Class 40 Board 30 Del from £60
Credit Cards [1][2][3][5] £

★★★ **60%** *Skiddaw*
Main St CA12 5BN (in the Market Square in heart of the town) ☎(07687) 72071 FAX (07687) 74850
Closed Xmas

Right in the town centre, the hotel is popular among residents and locals for its bar and restaurant, serving beverages, snacks and meals throughout the day and evening. There is also a quiet lounge upstairs. Bedrooms are solidly furnished and, in the main, very comfortable.

40⇨♠(7fb)1⊞ CTV in all bedrooms ®✕ T sB⇨♠£31-£32 dB⇨♠£56-£58 (room only) ⌼
Lift 12P sauna solarium
♀ English & French V ✿ ⚓ ✕ Lunch £3.85-£9.05alc Dinner £11-£15alc Last dinner 9pm
CONF. Thtr 30 Board 20 Del from £62.50
Credit Cards [1][2][3] £

★★★❀ ⛄**74%** *Dale Head Hall Lakeside*
Thirlmere CA12 4TN (off A591) ☎(07687) 72478
(Rosette awarded for dinner only)

Set in secluded gardens beside Thirlmere, this peaceful country house dates in part from the 16th century, and the dining room and some of the bedrooms have oak beams. There are comfortable lounges with log fires and the Lowe family provide warm hospitality and good home-cooking.

9⇨♠(1fb)2⊞✕in all bedrooms ® T ✠ (ex guide dogs) ❊
sB&B⇨♠£66-£75 dB&B⇨♠£102-£130 (incl dinner) ⌼

The Skiddaw Hotel

**Market Square
Keswick-on-Derwentwater
Cumbria CA12 5BN
Tel: (07687) 72071**

AA ★★★   COMMENDED

Overlooking the Market Square and famous Moot Hall, the Skiddaw Hotel is centrally situated in the Old Market Town of Keswick. The Hotel offers a high standard of comfort and cuisine to help make your stay in the Lake District a memorable one. All 40 bedrooms have private facilities, television, tea and coffee making, telephone and hairdryer. The Hotel has its own Saunas & Solarium with Golf and Squash available through the Hotel.

A full brochure is available.

ON THE LAKE SHORE!

DERWENTWATER HOTEL
(ON THE LAKE SHORE)

Portinscale, Keswick, Cumbria CA12 5RE
TEL: (07687) 72538. FAX: (07687) 71002

AA ★★★

The Derwentwater is an hotel with a difference, two country houses providing superb accommodation and self-catering apartments set in 16 acres of grounds on the shores of Lake Derwentwater. Real peace and tranquillity, yet close to all the hustle and bustle of the market town of Keswick. All rooms are en-suite with colour television, trouser press, radio and tea-making equipment. De-luxe Four Poster Suites and Family Rooms available for value for money short breaks and holidays. Deers Leap Restaurant, conservatory and conference facilities, all make the Derwentwater your ideal Lakeland Venue — whatever the occasion.

MORE THAN AN HOTEL — A HOME AWAY FROM HOME!

K

UNBEATABLE VALUE!

We would love to tell you more about our extensive leisure facilities, idyllic setting, superb food and relaxed atmosphere so please contact us for a brochure.

Please see our listing under BASSENTHWAITE

ETB ♛♛♛♛ COMMENDED   AA ★★★

CASTLE INN HOTEL
**Bassenthwaite, Nr Keswick
Cumbria CA12 4RG
TELEPHONE Bass Lake (07687) 76401**

Keswick

20P 🚗 ❋ 🐕 (grass) ♪ nc10yrs *xmas*
V ❀ 🚭 ⚿ ✱ Dinner £16.50 Last dinner 8.30pm
Credit Cards 1 3

★★ 🏆 74% Grange Country House
Manor Brow, Ambleside Rd CA12 4BA ☎(07687) 72500
Closed 2 Nov-11 Mar
Set in its own grounds close to the town centre, this delightful small hotel is caringly run by its enthusiastic proprietors. Bedrooms are bright and fresh and there are comfortable lounges and a pleasant dining room where carefully prepared home-cooked dinners are served. The menu might include coronation chicken in curry mayonnaise, freshly made soup, rack of lamb with a crust of rosemary and herbs.
10rm 2⇨ ⚿ in all bedrooms CTV in all bedrooms ® T dB&B⇨ £86-£98 (incl dinner) 🍴
12P 1🚗 🚗 ❋ nc7yrs
V ❀ 🚭 ⚿ Lunch £2.75-£6.75 Dinner £16-£17.50 Last dinner 8pm
Credit Cards 1 3

★★ 🏆 70% Lyzzick Hall Country House
Under Skiddaw CA12 4PY ☎(07687) 72277 FAX (07687) 72278
Closed 24-26 Dec & Feb
Nestling into the lower slopes of Skiddaw, this Lakeland country house enjoys fine views across the valley. Bedrooms are attractively decorated and well furnished. There are 2 lounges, both with log fires in season, and a small bar area leading to the spacious restaurant. Three dinner menus offer an interesting range of dishes.
24⇨ ⚿ Annexe1⇨ ⚿ (3fb)1🛏 CTV in all bedrooms ® T ✈ ✱
sB&B⇨ ⚿ £32-£36 dB&B⇨ ⚿ £64-£72 🍴
40P 🚗 ❋ ≋ (heated) ⚽
❀ International V ❀ ⚿ ✱ Lunch £9-£12 Dinner £18.50-£20&alc Last dinner 9.30pm
Credit Cards 1 2 3 5

★★ 68% Chaucer House
Ambleside Rd CA12 4DR (Turn right off A591 into Manor Brow, continue down hill, past Castlerigg Catholic Training Centre and sharp double bend, hotel on right) ☎(07687) 72318 & 73223 FAX (07687) 72318
Closed Dec-Feb
Chaucer House is an attractive Lakeland stone-built hotel in a quiet location close to the town centre. It has comfortable lounges and a well furnished dining room. The modern, bright bedrooms are well equipped and there is now a lift.
35rm(28⇨ ⚿)(4fb)⚿ in 6 bedrooms CTV in all bedrooms ® sB&B£22.50-£32.50 sB&B⇨ ⚿ £33.50 dB&B£36 dB&B⇨ ⚿ £54.50-£62 🍴
Lift 25P
❀ English & French V ❀ ✱ Dinner £14&alc Last dinner 9pm
Credit Cards 1 2 3 4

★★ 64% Crow Park
The Heads CA12 5ER ☎(07687) 72208 FAX (07687) 74776
Quietly situated on the south side of town, this competitively priced, family-run hotel has fine open views of the fells. Most of the bedrooms offer good views, and the dining room, cosy lounge and bar are hung with interesting prints of old Lakeland.
27rm(14⇨ 12⚿)(1fb)1🛏 ⚿ in 1 bedroom CTV in all bedrooms ® ✈ T sB&B⇨ ⚿ £19.50-£27.50 dB&B⇨ ⚿ £39-£55 🍴
CTV 27P *xmas*
❀ English & Continental V ❀ ✱ Dinner £11-£13 Last dinner 8pm
Credit Cards 1 3

★★ 64% Lairbeck
Vicarage Hill CA12 5QB ☎(07687) 73373
Tucked away in a quiet backwater yet convenient for the town, this welcoming family-run hotel has been attractively converted from a Victorian residence. Bedrooms are comfortably furnished and there is a cosy foyer lounge, bar and dining room overlooking the garden where good home-cooked dinners are served.

14⇨ ⚿ (2fb)⚿ in all bedrooms CTV in all bedrooms ® T ✈ (ex guide dogs) sB&B⇨ ⚿ £22-£29 dB&B⇨ ⚿ £44-£58 🍴
25P 🚗 ❋ croquet lawn *xmas*
❀ English & French V ⚿ Dinner £13 Last dinner 8pm
Credit Cards 1 3

★★ 🏆 63% Red House
Underskiddaw CA12 4QA (on A591) ☎(07687) 72211
An impressive Victorian country house, the hotel stands in an elevated position in 8 acres of well kept grounds with good views towards Borrowdale. Public areas are comfortable and spacious, and the hotel provides friendly, considerate service. Dogs are very welcome.
20⇨ (7fb)1🛏 CTV in all bedrooms ® sB&B⇨ £38-£53 dB&B⇨ £70-£99 (incl dinner) 🍴
CTV 25P 🚗 ❋ putting green games room ⚽ *xmas*
❀ European ❀ ⚿ Dinner £19.50 Last dinner 8.30pm
CONF. Thtr 36 Class 20 Board 20 Del from £50
Credit Cards 1 2 3

★★ 60% Queen's
Main St CA12 5JF ☎(07687) 73333 FAX (07687) 71144
Closed 24-26 Dec
Spacious and recently upgraded public areas are the main feature of this hospitable family hotel in the very centre of the town. Most of the bedrooms now have pretty décor.
37⇨ ⚿ (15fb)1🛏 CTV in all bedrooms ® ✿ T ✈ sB&B⇨ ⚿ £22-£35 dB&B⇨ ⚿ £44-£60 🍴
Lift 12🛗 (£2 per night)
❀ English & French V ❀ ⚿ ✱ Lunch £1.80-£9alc High tea £5.95 Dinner £11.50&alc Last dinner 9.30pm
CONF. Thtr 60 Class 30 Board 30
Credit Cards 1 2 3 5

★★ 55% Walpole
Station Rd CA12 4NA ☎(07687) 72072
Situated in the centre of town opposite the war memorial, this family-run hotel offers friendly service. There is a small bar and a comfortable residents' lounge with books, games and an open fire. Bedrooms are modestly furnished. An extensive menu is served in the cosy dining room.
17rm(10⇨ ⚿)(4fb) CTV in all bedrooms ® T
9P 🚗
❀ English & French V Last dinner 8pm
Credit Cards 1 3

★ ❀❀❀ SWINSIDE LODGE
Newlands CA12 5UE
☎(07687) 72948
Closed Dec-mid Feb

It is unusual for the AA to grant appointment to a hotel that imposes a total ban on smoking, is unlicensed, doesn't take credit cards and doesn't serve meals to non residents (unless the hotel isn't full) and offers only a fixed-price, no-choice menu (except for desserts) at a set time of 7.30pm. It is even more unusual for such a hotel to be granted a red star, though the justifications for doing so soon become apparent. The owner, Graham Taylor, and his staff promote a quiet, friendly atmosphere. The interior of the otherwise unexciting Victorian house is smart and modern. The bedrooms, though compact in some cases, are equally bright and attractive with a good range of facilities. Finally, Irene Dent's enjoyable British food offers excellent value for money. Guests are encouraged to bring their own wine, with no charge for corkage. No charge, either, for

smoking outside in the rain, was our inspector's valedictory remark.
9rm(8⇌♠)⊁in all bedrooms CTV in all bedrooms ®
✖ (ex guide dogs) sB&B⇌♠£60-£72 dB&B⇌♠£103-£120 (incl dinner) ᕍ
10P ⇚ ✿ nc12yrs
⊁ Dinner £20-£24 Last dinner 7.30pm

★ **73% Priorholme**
Borrowdale Rd CA12 5DD ☎(07687) 72745
Closed 5-31 Jan
This charming Georgian house has been converted to create a comfortable hotel offering modern standards. Attractively decorated bedrooms come in different sizes and shapes, and public areas include a charming dining room with a cosy bar attached and a delightful lower-ground-floor lounge.
8rm(6⇌♠) CTV in all bedrooms ® ✖ sB&Bfr£20 dB&Bfr£44 dB&B⇌♠fr£52
CTV 7P ⇚
⊁ ✻ Dinner £18 Last dinner 7.30pm
Credit Cards [1][3]

★ **72% Highfield**
The Heads CA12 5ER ☎(07687) 72508
Closed Nov-Mar
This lovely Lakeland stone building stands in an elevated position looking up the beautiful Borrowdale Valley. There are ample comfortable lounges, one with TV and the others more quiet. Bedrooms vary in size but are all brightly decorated and fitted with modern units. The hotel has been in the same family for 30 years now, and they offer warm hospitality.
19rm(15⇌♠)(3fb) CTV in 15 bedrooms ® sB&B£17 sB&B⇌♠£27.50 dB&B⇌♠£49-£55
CTV 19P ⇚ nc5yrs
V ✧ ⌴ ⊁ Dinner fr£12 Last dinner 6.30pm

★ **67% Linnett Hill**
4 Penrith Rd CA12 4HF ☎(07687) 73109
Good value accommodation is offered at this small family-run holiday hotel situated opposite a public park close to the town centre. Public areas have a friendly atmosphere and include a snug bar, relaxing lounge and an attractively decorated dining room. Bedrooms, which vary in size, have modern furnishings and equipment.
10⇌♠⊁in all bedrooms CTV in all bedrooms ®
✖ (ex guide dogs) sB&B⇌♠£23.50-£30 dB&B⇌♠£43-£43 ᕍ
12P nc5yrs *xmas*
♀ International V ✧ ⌴ ⊁ ✻ Bar Lunch fr£2 Dinner fr£11.50&alc Last dinner 7pm
Credit Cards [1][3]

KETTERING Northamptonshire Map **04 SP87**

★★★★ **67% Kettering Park**
Kettering Parkway NN15 6XT (Shire) ☎(0536) 416666 FAX (0536) 416171
88⇌♠4⇚⊁in 36 bedrooms CTV in all bedrooms ®✷ T ✻
sB&B⇌♠£90-£100 dB&B⇌♠£110-£130 ᕍ
Lift ⦇ 200P ✿ ⌧ (heated) squash snooker sauna solarium gymnasium spa pool steam rooms ♪ *xmas*
♀ International V ✧ ⌴ ✻ Lunch £9.95-£12.95&alc Dinner £20&alc Last dinner 9.30pm
CONF. Thtr 100 Class 120 Board 45 Del £30
Credit Cards [1][2][3][5]

Irish entries appear in a separate section that follows the main directory.

AA ★★

Ravenstone Hotel, Nr Keswick,
Cumbria CA12 4QG
Tel: Bassenthwaite Lake (07687) 76240

This truly lovely dower house was built in 1865 for Lady Charlotte Howard. Set in the unspoiled Northern Lakes this family run hotel stands in beautiful surroundings on the slopes of Skiddaw, looking over the valley towards the fells beyond Bassenthwaite Lake.

Elegant lounge and bar with log fires, games room with full size snooker table.

See gazetteer entry under Bassenthwaite

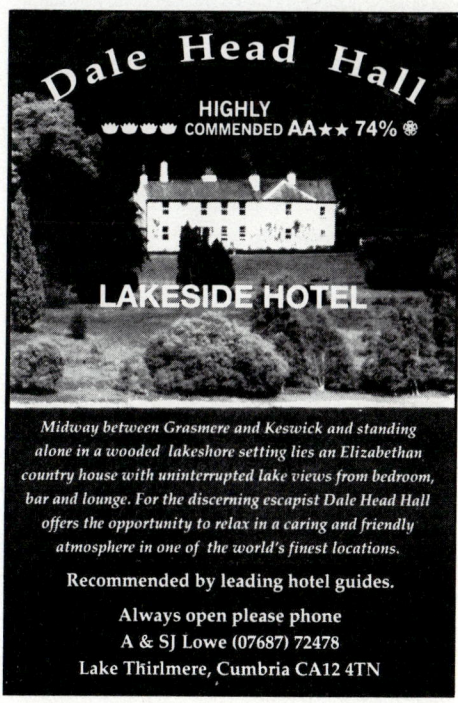

Dale Head Hall

HIGHLY COMMENDED AA ★★ 74% ✿

LAKESIDE HOTEL

Midway between Grasmere and Keswick and standing alone in a wooded lakeshore setting lies an Elizabethan country house with uninterrupted lake views from bedroom, bar and lounge. For the discerning escapist Dale Head Hall offers the opportunity to relax in a caring and friendly atmosphere in one of the world's finest locations.

Recommended by leading hotel guides.

Always open please phone
A & SJ Lowe (07687) 72478
Lake Thirlmere, Cumbria CA12 4TN

Kidderminster - Kilfinan

KIDDERMINSTER Hereford & Worcester Map 07 SO87

★★★★ 58% Stone Manor
Stone DY10 4PJ (2m SE on A448) ☎(0562) 777555 FAX (0562) 777834

In 25 acres of woodland and gardens, this fine mock Tudor country hotel is very commercial/conference orientated. The accommodation varies in standard with some well appointed bedrooms and some rather more modest, though all are well equipped. A table d'hôte and an à la carte menu is offered in the small restaurant and cooking is reasonably sound.

52⇌🏠4🛏in 6 bedrooms CTV in all bedrooms ® T ✱ sB⇌🏠£39.50-£59.50 dB⇌🏠£39.50-£59.50 (room only) 🅿
《 CTV 400P ✿ ⚲ ℛ (hard) croquet putting green
♀ International V ♥ ⚌ ✱ Lunch £10.75-£12.50&alc Dinner £16.50&alc Last dinner 10pm
Credit Cards 1 2 3 5

★★★ 59% Granary Hotel & Restaurant
Heath Ln, Shenstone DY10 4BS (3m SE, on A450)
☎(0562) 777535 FAX (0562) 777722
Closed 25-26 Dec

This small, family-run hotel offers functional, well equipped accommodation in a modern, single-storey block. Across the car park is the well established carvery restaurant, bar and guest lounge.

Annexe18⇌🏠 CTV in all bedrooms ® T ✱ sB&B⇌🏠£32.50-£39.50 dB&B⇌🏠£35-£50 Continental breakfast 🅿
《 95P ✿ ⚙
V ♥ ⚌ ✱ Lunch £5.95-£13.50 Dinner £8.95-£16.95 Last dinner 9.15pm
CONF. Thtr 80 Class 35 Board 50 Del from £55
Credit Cards 1 2 3 5 £

★★ 70% Gainsborough House
Bewdley Hill DY11 6BS ☎(0562) 820041 FAX (0562) 66179

This hotel, on the outskirts of the town, offers comfortable bedrooms with attractive furnishings and good facilities; similar standards are maintained in the public areas, making the establishment ideal for both leisure and business users. Service is professional, caring and friendly throughout.

42⇌🏠(4fb)1🛏✂in 8 bedrooms CTV in all bedrooms ® T
《 130P
♀ English & Continental V ♥ ⚌ Last dinner 10pm
Credit Cards 1 2 3 5

KILCHRENAN Strathclyde Argyllshire Map 10 NN02

★★★❀❀ 74% Ardanaiseig
PA35 1HE ☎(08663) 333 FAX (08663) 222
Closed mid Oct-Etr

For those who value peace and seclusion, this 19th-century baronial mansion is ideal – set in splendid isolation on the edge of Loch Awe, with fine woodland gardens. There is a choice of bedrooms styles, including a split level room with direct access to the garden. Friendly young staff run the hotel, and it is good to see Mark Taylor taking over the kitchens again. He cooks in modern style but prefers to let the main ingredients speak for themselves, rather than add unnecessary items. This was evident in a superb cream of spinach and pear soup which preceded the best roast lamb our inspector had tasted in a long time.

14⇌🏠 CTV in all bedrooms T ✱ sB&B⇌🏠£68-£135 dB&B⇌🏠£136-£210 (incl dinner)
20P ✿ ℛ (hard) ♪ snooker croquet boating nc10yrs
♀ ⚌ ✱ Lunch £15-£20 Dinner £30-£39.75 Last dinner 9pm
Credit Cards 1 2 3 5

★★★❀❀⚜ 67% Taychreggan
PA35 1HQ ☎(08663) 211 FAX (08663) 244

Delightfully situated on the shores of Loch Awe, surrounded by 25 acres of grounds, this one-time drovers inn has been sympathetically extended around a cobbled courtyard. Most of the bedrooms enjoy loch views, and those in the main house are the most spacious and individual. Enthusiastic new owners, Euan and Annie Paul, are busy making improvements, and their genuine hospitality makes a visit here particularly memorable. There are three comfortable lounges, a cocktail bar and a pleasant restaurant offering a daily changing set menu. A typical meal might start with an excellent ragout of wild mushrooms in a puff pastry case with Madeira sauce, a well balanced lobster bisque, then a tender fillet of beef with an intense pickled walnut sauce.

15⇌🏠1🛏 T ✱ sB&B⇌🏠£50-£55 dB&B⇌🏠£55-£70 (incl dinner)
CTV 30P ✿ ⚙ ♪ boat hire croquet windsurfing nc6yrs xmas
♀ International V ♥ ⚌ ✱ Dinner £24 Last dinner 9pm
Credit Cards 1 2 3

KILDRUMMY Grampian Aberdeenshire Map 15 NJ41

★★★❀⚜ KILDRUMMY CASTLE
AB33 8RA (off A97, Huntly-Ballater road)
☎(09755) 71288 FAX (09755) 71345
Closed 4-31 Jan

We are pleased to welcome Kildrummy Castle to our select list of Red Star award winners. It is an impressive Victorian mansion, set in several acres of gardens overlooking the 13th-century castle. Public areas are superbly comfortable, with lots of books and magazines. A carved oak staircase leads to richly furnished bedrooms, and the well produced dinner, with a choice of table d'hôte and carte, often features local game and fresh fish. Thomas and Mary Hanna are delightful hosts.

16⇌🏠(4fb)2🛏 CTV in all bedrooms ® T sB&B⇌🏠£65-£70 dB&B⇌🏠£110-£130 🅿
30P ✿ ✿ ♪ snooker shooting ⚙ xmas
♀ Scottish & French V ♥ ⚌ ✱ Lunch £13.50-£16.50&alc Dinner £25-£27&alc Last dinner 9pm
Credit Cards 1 2 3 4

KILFINAN Strathclyde Argyll Map 10 NR97

★★ 71% Kilfinan
PA21 2EP (on B8000 east coast of Loch Fyne, between Otter Ferry and Tignabruaich) ☎(070082) 201 FAX (070082) 205
Closed Feb

This former coaching inn is reached by a narrow, single track road alongside Loch Fyne. Although it is owned by the Otter Estate, managers Rolf and Lynne Mueller are very much the hosts. Lynne looks after guests while chef Rolf is in charge of the kitchen. He cooks in a modern style and presents a short but interesting set price 4-course dinner menu based on fresh local produce. The cosy lounge bar and adjoining public bar remain the hub of the hotel.

11⇌🏠(1fb) CTV in all bedrooms T 🐾 (ex guide dogs) ✱ sB&B⇌🏠£45 dB&B⇌🏠£68-£88
50P ✿ ✿ ♪ clay pigeon shooting deer stalking xmas
♀ Scottish & French V ♥ ⚌ ✂ Lunch £7.50-£12alc Dinner £22 Last dinner 9pm
Credit Cards 1 2 3

Killiecrankie - Kilwinning

KILLIECRANKIE Tayside *Perthshire* Map **14** NN96

★★❀❀73% **Killiecrankie**
PH16 5LG (turn off A9 at Killiecrankie, hotel is 3m along B8079 on right) ☎Pitlochry(0796) 473320 FAX (0796) 472451

Closed 3 Jan-Feb
(Rosettes awarded for dinner only)
Colin and Carole Anderson are genial hosts at their charming small hotel set in 40 acres of wooded gardens at the northern end of the Killiecrankie pass. There is a cosy bar and peaceful lounge, and pretty bedrooms are very comfortable. Chef Paul Booth's well balanced 4-course dinner is a highlight, and might comprise sliced ballotine of guinea fowl with chicken mousseline and sweet chestnuts, flavoursome halibut with rich lime sauce, and hot brioche and frangipan pudding filled with fruit compote.
11⇌ጮ(1fb) CTV in all bedrooms ® T ✱ sB&B⇌ጮ£39-£48 dB&B⇌ጮ£78-£92 🅿
30P ⊞ ✿ croquet putting *xmas*
V ⊘ ⊑ ✂ Bar Lunch fr£9.25alc Dinner £17.50-£25 Last dinner 8.30pm
Credit Cards [1][3]

KILLIN Central *Perthshire* Map **11** NN53

★★65% **Dall Lodge Country House**
Main St FK21 8TN ☎(0567) 820217 FAX (0567) 820726
Closed 24-27 Dec
10⇌ጮ(2fb)3🛏 CTV in all bedrooms ® T ✱ sB&B⇌ጮ£25 dB&B⇌ጮ£50-£60 🅿
CTV 8P ⊞ ✿ ⚘
❀ Scottish & French V ✂ ✱ Lunch £10-£12.50 Dinner £13.50-£15 Last dinner 9pm
Credit Cards [1][3]

★★62% **Falls of Dochart**
Main St FK21 8UW ☎(0567) 820237
Closed mid Jan-Feb
A warm, friendly atmosphere prevails at this small family-run holiday hotel, at the east end of the village. A major improvement programme has been completed and the hotel now offers bright, cheery bedrooms as well as a snug bar, cosy lounge and a spacious dining room where a reasonably priced à la carte menu is available.
9rm(1⇌5ጮ)(2fb) CTV in all bedrooms ®
CTV 20P
V Last dinner 9pm
Credit Cards [1][3]

KILMELFORD Strathclyde *Argyllshire* Map **10** NM81

★★63% **Cuilfail**
PA34 4XA ☎(08522) 274 FAX (08522) 264
This ivy-clad, roadside coaching inn is being steadily improved by new owners. The emphasis is on good quality bar food, with a fixed, no choice menu available in the dining room. There is a spacious residents' lounge and the bedrooms, which are also being upgraded, are cheerful. A 5% surcharge is levied on credit card payments.
12⇌ጮ(2fb) CTV in all bedrooms ®
CTV 20P ✿ sauna solarium gymnasium
V ⊘ ⊑ ✂ Last dinner 9.30pm Credit Cards [1][3]

KILWINNING Strathclyde *Ayrshire* Map **10** NS34

★★★❀⛳70% **Montgreenan Mansion House**
Montgreenan Estate KA13 7QZ (4m N of Irvine off A736, 3m E B785)
☎(0294) 57733 FAX (0294) 85297
Built in 1817, this splendid Scottish mansion is situated in 45 acres of secluded grounds and gardens. Family owned and managed, it

The Killiecrankie Hotel ★★

By Pitlochry, Perthshire

A charmingly appointed country hotel in lovely grounds overlooking the Pass of Killiecrankie, just three miles north of Pitlochry with its highly acclaimed Festival Theatre. The Killiecrankie Hotel combines a relaxed, friendly atmosphere with excellent standards in food and comfort. Eleven individual bedrooms with ensuite facilities, central heating, colour television and telephone. Golf, fishing, shooting, sailing, pony trekking, hill-walking and RSPB Bird Reserve in vicinity of the hotel. Lunch and Supper in the Bar until 9.30 p.m. Dinner 7.00 to 8.30 p.m.
Non-Residents, children, and dogs welcome. Special breaks available during Winter/early Spring. Closed January & February.

Resident Proprietors: Colin and Carole Anderson
Tel: (0796) 473320. Fax: (0796) 472451

KILFINAN HOTEL ★★

Discover the true flavour of the West Highlands at this 100 year old coaching Inn on the East Coast of Loch Fyne. Set amidst thousands of acres of unspoilt countryside, it is an ideal base for all outdoor activities and peaceful relaxation. Chef/Manager Rolf Mueller creates exquisite meals using seasonal produce from the adjoining estate and loch.
Luxury and comfort amidst rugged Highland scenery — and all within two hours scenic drive from Glasgow.

A warm welcome awaits you.

Kilfinan, Nr. Tighnabruaich, Argyll
Tel: 0700 82 201 Fax 0700 82 205

Kilwinning - King's Lynn

has elegant and relaxing public areas with marble fireplaces, decorative ceilings and ornate plasterwork. The main rooms have delightful views over the gardens. Bedrooms vary from compact, pine-furnished modern rooms to palatial ones, furnished with antique and reproduction items.

21➪🛏1♿ CTV in all bedrooms ® T
Lift (50P ⊞ ❀ ▶ 5 ℛ (hard) snooker clay pigeon shooting croquet
♥ Scottish & French V ✿ ♫ Last dinner 9.30pm
Credit Cards 1 2 3 5

KINCLAVEN Tayside *Perthshire* Map 11 NO13

★★★ ❀❀🛏 75% **Ballathie House**
PH1 4QN (from A9, through Stanley & signposted)
(SCOTLAND'S HERITAGE HOTELS)
☎Meikleour(0250) 883268 FAX (0250) 883396
Closed 26-27 Dec, 3-5 Jan & 17 Feb-2 Mar RS Nov-Mar
Set in 80 acres of grounds on the banks of the River Tay, this charming hotel offers a range of accommodation, from large elegant rooms to smaller cottagey ones; some overlook the river. Splendid day rooms have fine plaster ceilings, deep cushioned sofas and chairs and lots of fresh flowers. There are various lounges, a small club-style bar and a delightful dining room where a daily changing set price menu offers plenty of choice. A highlight of one inspection meal was a well balanced and full flavoured mussel and leek soup which preceded some tender loin of venison with a creamy ginger sauce.
27➪🛏(2fb)1♿ CTV in all bedrooms ® T sB&B➪🛏£60-£95 dB&B➪🛏£100-£210 🛏
50P ⊞ ❀ ℛ (hard) ♫ putting croquet clay pigeon shooting *xmas*
♥ Scottish & Continental V ✿ ♫ Lunch £10-£14alc Dinner £25&alc Last dinner 9pm
Credit Cards 1 2 3 5

KINGHAM Oxfordshire Map 04 SP22

★★★ ❀❀71% **Mill House Hotel & Restaurant**
OX7 6UH (turn off A44 at either Chipping Norton or Stow on the Wold onto B4450, hotel is on outskirts of Kingham village) ☎(0608) 658188 FAX (0608) 658492
In past years this former mill has been lovingly restored and extended to create a charming small hotel set in 7 acres of gardens. Bedrooms are individually styled and some ground floor rooms are available, though there are one or 2 steps. The comfortable lounge has french windows leading on to a sunny terrace, and there is a beamed bar where light lunches are served. Head chef Mark Robbins provides imaginative and well balanced table d'hôte menus.
21➪🛏(1fb)1♿ CTV in all bedrooms ® T ✱ (ex guide dogs) ✱ sB&B➪🛏£45-£54 dB&B➪🛏£90-£108 🛏
60P ⊞ ♫ croquet nc5yrs *xmas*
♥ English & French V ✿ ♫ ✱ Lunch £13.50-£16.50alc Hightea£5.95Dinner£18.95-£24.95alcLastdinner9.30pm
Credit Cards 1 2 3 4 5

KINGSBRIDGE Devon Map 03 SX74

★★★ ❀❀🛏 77% **Buckland-Tout-Saints**
Goveton TQ7 2DS (2.5m NE on unclass rd)
☎(0548) 853055 FAX (0548) 856321

This delightful small hotel is set in 7 acres of grounds in a sheltered rural position. The public areas are elegantly furnished and panelled, and the bar has leather chairs and sofas. Head chef Alastair Carter provides an imaginative choice in the modern British style. Bedrooms are smaller and less grand at the top of the house, but all are individually furnished.

328

12➪🛏1♿ CTV in all bedrooms T sB&B➪🛏£50-£70 dB&B➪🛏£100-£140 🛏
12P ⊞ ❀ croquet putting *xmas*
♥ English & French V ✿ ♫ ✱ Lunch £14.50 Dinner £25-£27 Last dinner 9.30pm
CONF. Thtr 40 Class 30 Board 12
Credit Cards 1 2 3

KING'S LYNN Norfolk Map 09 TF62

★★★ ❀❀🛏 **CONGHAM HALL COUNTRY HOUSE**
Lynn Rd PE32 1AH ☎Hillington(0485) 600250
FAX (0485) 601191
(For full entry see Grimston)

★★★ 68% **Knights Hill**
Knights Hill Village, South Wootton PE30 3HQ
(junct A148/A149) ☎(0553) 675566 FAX (0553) 675568
This hotel/leisure/conference complex is built around a 16th-century hunting lodge and a 17th-century farm and incorporates a country inn. Bedrooms vary in style, the courtyard rooms being plainer and more practical. There is a choice of bars and restaurants offering formal and informal dining.
39➪🛏Annexe19➪🛏2♿ ✱ in 14 bedrooms CTV in all bedrooms ® T ✱ sB&B➪🛏£62.50-£75 dB&B➪🛏£70-£85 (room only) 🛏
(350P ❀ ⛱(heated) ℛ (hard) snooker sauna solarium gymnasium jogging circuit croquet spa bath *xmas*
♥ International V ✿ ♫ ✱ Sunday Lunch £9.75
CONF. Thtr 350 Class 150 Board 30 Del from £65
Credit Cards 1 2 3 5

★★★ 65% **Butterfly**
Beveridge Way, Hardwick Narrows PE30 4NB
(junct A10/A47) ☎(0553) 771707 FAX (0553) 768027
Described as a modern coaching inn, The Butterfly offers a friendly and informal atmosphere. Bedrooms are modern, some geared specially to business users, and the open plan public areas are in cottage style. Walt's Place, the restaurant, has a tempting display of buffet hors d'oeuvres and sweets, along with a short à la carte menu and a hot buffet of freshly cooked dishes.
50➪🛏(2fb) CTV in all bedrooms ® T ✱ (ex guide dogs) sB➪🛏£39-£54.50 dB➪🛏£39-£54.50 (room only) 🛏
(70P
♥ European V ✿ ♫ ✱ Lunch fr£9.50&alc Dinner fr£9.50&alc Last dinner 10pm
CONF. Thtr 40 Class 21 Board 22 Del from £75
Credit Cards 1 2 3 5
See advertisement under BURY ST EDMUNDS

★★★ 65% **The Duke's Head**
Tuesday Market Pl PE30 1JS ☎(0553) 774996
FAX (0553) 763556
This classical Victorian hotel has been upgraded to the new Forte Heritage standards. Bedrooms are all well equipped and many are spacious; the lounge with its adjoining bar is a popular meeting place for coffee and teas. Beefy Butchers is an informal eating option while the newly refurbished restaurant has table d'hôte and à la carte menus.
71➪🛏(2fb)✱ in 33 bedrooms CTV in all bedrooms ® T ✱ sB➪🛏fr£70 dB➪🛏fr£80 (room only) 🛏
Lift (41P *xmas*
♥ English & French V ✿ ♫ ✱ Lunch £7.95-£9.95 Dinner fr£15.95&alc Last dinner 10pm
CONF. Thtr 240 Class 120 Board 60 Del from £75
Credit Cards 1 2 3 5

★★ 71% *Stuart House*
35 Goodwins Rd PE30 5QX ☎(0553) 772169
Closed Xmas & New Year

Situated in a quiet residential area, this very well maintained hotel is run with friendly informality by the Squires and offers traditional comforts with all modern facilities.

19rm(12⇨3🛁)(6fb) CTV in all bedrooms ® T ✕
CTV 25P
🍴 European V Last dinner 8.30pm
Credit Cards 1 2 3

★★ 65% *The Tudor Rose*
St Nicholas St, off Tuesday Market Place PE30 1LR
☎(0553) 762824 FAX (0553) 764894

This 15th-century inn of character and charm is just off Tuesday Market Place. The accommodation is well equipped and quite comfortable, though furnishings are modest. In addition to the popular public bar there is a second quieter bar and a lovely timbered restaurant.

14rm(11⇨🛁) CTV in all bedrooms ® T ✕ (ex guide dogs) ✱ sB&B£30 sB&B⇨🛁£38.50 dB&B⇨🛁£50 🅿
♫
🍴 French V ☱ ♨ ✔ Lunch £12.95 Dinner £12.95&alc Last dinner 9pm
Credit Cards 1 2 3 5

★★ 64% *Grange*
Willow Park, South Wootton Ln PE30 3BP ☎(0553) 673777 & 671222

The Grange Hotel is a large Edwardian property set in a quiet residential suburb of Kings Lynn. The well furnished, spacious bedrooms have unobtrusive decor and public areas include a bar and a restaurant where simply prepared food is served.

6rm(3⇨2🛁)Annexe4⇨ CTV in all bedrooms ®
15P 1🅿
♨ ✔ Last dinner 8.30pm
Credit Cards 1 2 3

KINGSTEIGNTON Devon Map 03 SX87

★★★ 71% *Passage House*
Hackney Ln TQ12 3QH (leave the A380 for the A381 and follow racecourse signs) ☎Newton Abbot(0626) 55515 FAX (0626) 63336

This modern hotel is in a delightful situation overlooking the Teign estuary and its comfortable rooms are popular with tourists and business travellers alike. In the Lighterman's Restaurant, professional staff serve food from well balanced table d'hôte and à la carte menus; a less formal alternative is the nearby Passage House Inn, dating back to 1761.

39⇨🛁(32fb)🖐in 3 bedrooms CTV in all bedrooms ® T ✱ sB&B⇨🛁£59-£69 dB&B⇨🛁£75-£85 🅿
Lift ⦅ 300P ✿ ⬚ (heated) 🎾 sauna solarium gymnasium *xmas*
V ☱ ♨ ✔ Lunch fr£9.15&alc Dinner £15.75&alc Last dinner 9.30pm
CONF. Thtr 100 Class 40 Board 40 Del from £50
Credit Cards 1 2 3 5

KINGSTON UPON THAMES Greater London
See LONDON SECTION, plan 1 *B2*
★★★ 64% Kingston Lodge
Kingston Hill KT2 7NP ☎081-541 4481 FAX 081-547 1013

Located in a pleasant suburban area, this hotel is very popular with both commercial and leisure users. An ongoing refurbishment programme to the bedrooms is producing elegant and comfortable rooms. The interesting restaurant overlooks the central garden and courtyard, and there is also a bar/lounge.

62⇨🛁1🏠🖐in 20 bedrooms CTV in all bedrooms ® T

⦅ 74P
V ♨ ✔ Last dinner 10pm
Credit Cards 1 2 3 5

KINGSWINFORD West Midlands Map 07 SO88

★★★ 58% *The Kingfisher Hotel & Country Club*
Kidderminster Rd, Wall Heath DY6 0EN (on A449, Kidderminster-Wolverhampton) ☎(0384) 273763 & 401145 FAX (0384) 277094

Situated on the edge of the Black Country, the Kingfisher is a well known cabaret nightspot which has been extended to provide modern accommodation with a good range of facilities.

23⇨🛁(2fb) CTV in all bedrooms ® ✉ T ✕ (ex guide dogs)
⦅ 200P ✿ ⬚ (heated)
V ☱ ♨ Last dinner 10.30pm
Credit Cards 1 2 3

KINGTON Hereford & Worcester Map 03 SO25

★★ 62% Burton
Mill St HR5 3BQ ☎(0544) 230323

An old coaching inn at the heart of this market town, which is near Offa's Dyke. Bedrooms are quite spacious, and public areas include 2 bars. Good food is served and the staff are friendly.

15⇨🛁(3fb)🍴 CTV in all bedrooms ® T sB&B⇨🛁fr£42 dB&B⇨🛁£55-£60 🅿
50P ✿ *xmas*
🍴 International V ☱ ♨ ✔ Lunch £11-£20.50 Dinner £11-£20.50 Last dinner 9.30pm
CONF. Thtr 150 Class 100 Board 20 Del from £37
Credit Cards 1 2 3 5

KINGUSSIE Highland *Inverness-shire* Map 14 NH70

★★ 69% Columba House
Manse Rd PH21 1JF (at N end of village just off A9)
☎(0540) 661402
Closed Nov-25 Dec

This small and relaxing family-run hotel has been converted from a 19th-century manse and stands in wooded grounds at the north end of the village. Bedrooms provide modern comforts and amenities, and there is a cosy lounge where drinks are served before Myra Shearer's good home-cooked dinners.

7⇨🛁(2fb) CTV in all bedrooms ® T sB&B⇨🛁£26-£39 dB&B⇨🛁£42-£58 🅿
12P ⛳ ✿ croquet 9-hole putting
V ☱ ♨ ✔ Lunch £5.95-£9.50 Dinner £15-£18 Last dinner 8.30pm £

★ 69% Osprey
Ruthven Rd PH21 1EN ☎(0540) 661510

Robert and Aileen Burrow run their cosy little hotel almost single-handedly and make their guests feel very much at home. There are 2 lounges, one with TV and the other with books and magazines. The pretty bedrooms vary in size and although they do not have TVs, they all have radio/alarm clocks. Aileen's good, honest home cooking is well worth savouring.

8rm(7⇨🛁) ® sB&B£38-£46 sB&B⇨🛁£43-£51 dB&B£76-£86 dB&B⇨🛁£82-£98 (incl dinner) 🅿
CTV ⛳ *xmas*
♨ ✔ Dinner £19.25-£19.75 Last dinner 7.30pm
Credit Cards 1 3

Kinlochbervie - Kirby Misperton

KINLOCHBERVIE Highland *Sutherland* Map **14** NC25

★★★ ✻**65%** *Kinlochbervie*
IV27 4RP ☎(0971) 521275 FAX (0971) 521498
RS mid Nov-Feb
Efficiently run by Rex and Kate Neame, this popular holiday hotel overlooks the harbour and many of the mostly spacious bedrooms share the view. Seafood, fresh from the harbour, features prominently on the daily changing short set menu and competent cooking is complemented by careful presentation and a well chosen wine list. Lighter meals are served in the bistro. Books, magazines and board games abound in the small sitting room and the cocktail bar has a wide range of malt whiskies.
14⇌♠(3fb) CTV in all bedrooms ® T
《 CTV 30P ✻ ♪ snooker
♀ French ♡ ♫ Last dinner 8.30pm
Credit Cards [1][2][3][5]

KINNESSWOOD Tayside *Kinross-shire* Map **11** NO10

★★ ✻**65%** **Lomond Country Inn**
KY13 7HN (on A911) (Logis) ☎(0592) 84253 FAX (0592) 84693
This small village inn has fine open views across Loch Leven. Its cosy bar is full of character with log fires and real ales. Renowned for its honest country cooking at value-for-money prices, meals can be taken in either the restaurant or the bar. Everything is home made using fresh local produce where possible.
4⇌♠ Annexe7⇌♠(1fb) CTV in all bedrooms ® T sB&B⇌♠£30-£35 dB&B⇌♠£50-£60
CTV 30P ✻ ▶ 9 ♨
V ♡ ♫
Credit Cards [1][2][3][5]

KINROSS Tayside *Kinross-shire* Map **11** NO10

★★★ **71%** **Windlestrae**
The Muirs KY13 7AS ☎(0577) 863217 FAX (0577) 864733

Extensive alterations to this family-run hotel have seen the development of an impressive leisure and conference centre and further bedrooms. A new entrance, reception and greatly extended lobby with comfortable, well spaced seating complete the picture.
45⇌♠(10fb)2⌸ CTV in all bedrooms ®≩ T sB&B⇌♠fr£65 dB&B⇌♠fr£100 ⌸
《 ⊞ 80P ✻ ▣ (heated) snooker sauna solarium gymnasium beautician steam room toning tables ⚬ *xmas*
♀ International V ♡ ♫ ✽ Lunch £11.95&alc Dinner £19.95-£25 Last dinner 9.30pm
Credit Cards [1][2][3][5] £

★★★ **67%** **Green**
2 The Muirs KY13 7AS ☎(0577) 863467 FAX (0577) 863180

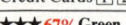

With its curling rink, 2 golf courses and leisure complex, this hotel attracts business, conference and holiday trade. Upgraded and extended in recent years, its bedrooms are tastefully furnished, well equipped and spacious. There are 4 family units comprising 2 small bedrooms.
47⇌♠(4fb)2⌸ CTV in all bedrooms ®≩ T sB&B⇌♠£65-£85 dB&B⇌♠£85-£125 ⌸
《 60P ✻ ▣ (heated) ▶ 36 ♪ squash sauna solarium gymnasium curling croquet putting ⚬ *xmas*
♀ French V ♡ ♫ Bar Lunch £7.50-£12alc High tea £6-£8 Dinner £19-£22&alc Last dinner 9.30pm
CONF. Thtr 140 Class 100 Board 60 Del from £90
Credit Cards [1][2][3][5] £

★★ **66%** *Bridgend*
High St KY13 7EN ☎(0577) 863413 FAX (0577) 864769
This attractively furnished hotel has a cosy pub bar and a cocktail lounge adjacent to the restaurant, which offers a wide range of dishes. Bedrooms, though compact, provide facilities usually associated with hotels of a higher classification.
15⇌♠(1fb)1⌸ CTV in all bedrooms ®≩ T
《 CTV 40P
♀ Scottish & French V ♡ ♫ Last dinner 10pm
Credit Cards [1][2][3][5]

★★ **60%** *Kirklands*
20 High St KY13 7AN ☎(0577) 863313
On the main street in the centre of the town, this family-run hotel offers well equipped and solidly furnished bedrooms, including an apartment comprising 2 bedrooms, a lounge and bathroom. The lounge bar offers real ales and an extensive bar menu, which is a popular alternative to the smaller set price dining room menu.
9⇌♠ CTV in all bedrooms ® T ✠ (ex guide dogs) 30P ✻
V ♡ ♫ Last dinner 9pm
Credit Cards [1][3]

Granada Lodge
Kincardine Rd KY13 7NQ (on A977, off junct 6 of M90) ☎(0577) 864646 FAX (0577) 864108

This modern building provides smart, spacious and well equipped bedrooms, all with en suite bathrooms. Meals may be taken at a nearby family restaurant. For more details about Granada Lodges, consult the Contents page, under Hotel Groups.
35⇌

KINTORE Grampian *Aberdeenshire* Map **15** NJ71

★★ **60%** *Torryburn*
School Rd AB51 0XP ☎(0467) 32269 FAX (0467) 32269
Closed 1 Jan
Considerable improvements have been made at this family-run, commercial hotel, which is set in 3.5 acres of grounds at the eastern end of the village. Bedrooms are compact with uniform modern appointments. Public areas lack lounge facilities but there is a choice of bars and a small à la carte restaurant.
9rm(8⇌♠)(1fb) CTV in all bedrooms ® T ✽ sB&B£37.50 sB&B♠£37.50 dB&B£52 dB&B♠£52
30P ♪ (hard) snooker shooting *xmas*
V ♡ ♫ ✽ Lunch £5.95-£8.95 High tea £5.95-£8.95 Dinner £10.25-£18.15alc Last dinner 9.30pm
CONF. Board 15
Credit Cards [1][3]

KIRBY MISPERTON North Yorkshire Map **08** SE77

★★ **62%** *Beansheaf Restaurant Motel*
Malton Rd YO17 0UE (S of Pickering, on A169)
☎(065386) 614 & 488 FAX (065386) 370
RS Mon
This modern roadside hotel and restaurant is renowned locally for its variety of competitively priced menus. A wine bar provides lighter meals and snacks. Bedrooms are compact but all have the necessary facilities. The atmosphere is informal and friendly.
20⇌♠(2fb)1⌸ CTV in all bedrooms ® T
CTV 60P ✻ sauna solarium
♀ English & Continental V ♡ ♫ ✠ Last dinner 10pm
Credit Cards [1][3]

See advertisement under PICKERING

Hotels with red star ratings are especially high quality.

Kirby Muxloe - Kirkby Lonsdale

KIRBY MUXLOE Leicestershire Map 04 SK50

★★ **64%** Castle Hotel & Restaurant
Main St LE9 9AP ☎Leicester(0533) 395337 FAX (0533) 387868
This well run and well maintained hotel right by the castle was originally a 16th-century farmhouse. The rooms are furnished and equipped to a high standard, although some are a bit compact. A comfortable bar, cosy lounge and a restaurant make up the ground floor and there is also a really large banqueting room. Owners and staff create a friendly atmosphere.
4⇨🛏Annexe8⇨🛏(1fb)⚡in 5 bedrooms CTV in all bedrooms ® T 🐾 (ex guide dogs) sB&B⇨🛏£30-£35 dB&B⇨🛏£40-£45
CTV 70P ✿
🍴 English & French V ✿ ♨ ⚡ Lunch £9.50&alc Dinner £16.95&alc Last dinner 9.45pm
CONF. Thtr 150 Class 100 Board 80 Del from £50
Credit Cards [1][2][3]

KIRKBURTON West Yorkshire Map 07 SE11

★★★ **71%** Springfield Park
Penistone Rd HD8 0PE (3m S, on A629, close to M1 and M62)
☎Huddersfield(0484) 607788 FAX (0484) 607961
This is a recently constructed hotel is on the site of an old mill. The smart bedrooms feature pretty floral décor, bold fabrics and attractive lighting. The comfortable foyer lounge on 2 levels provides plenty of seating and there are two separate restaurants, one a good value pizzeria and the other offering a traditional menu.
46⇨🛏(5fb)3🛋⚡in 10 bedrooms CTV in 50 bedrooms ® T 🐾 (ex guide dogs) ✱ sB&B⇨🛏£49.50 dB&B⇨🛏£62.50 🅱
(120P 🛋
🍴 English & Italian V ✿ ♨
Credit Cards [1][2][3][5]

KIRKBY FLEETHAM North Yorkshire Map 08 SE29

★★★ **73%** Kirkby Fleetham Hall
DL7 0SU ☎Northallerton(0609) 748711 FAX (0609) 748747
An impressive Georgian house in 30 acres of parkland, the hotel boasts its own lake and offers the advantages of a really peaceful atmosphere, spacious, comfortable lounges and bedrooms, charming staff and good, interesting cooking.
22⇨🛏(2fb)3🛋 CTV in all bedrooms T
40P 🛋 ✿ ♪ croquet clay pigeon shooting archery
🍴 British & French V ✿ ♨ Last dinner 9pm
Credit Cards [1][2][3][4][5]

KIRKBY LONSDALE Cumbria Map 07 SD67

★★ **69%** Whoop Hall Inn
LA6 2HP (1m E on A65) ☎Carnforth(05242) 71284 FAX (05242) 72154
This is a charming old inn offering an excellent range of food all day, either in the bar or the buttery/restaurant. Bedrooms, most of which are in a separate stone building, are of a high standard, with quality furniture and matching fabrics.
5⇨🛏Annexe11⇨🛏(3fb)2🛋⚡in 4 bedrooms CTV in all bedrooms ® T 🐾 (ex guide dogs) sB&B⇨🛏£40-£45 dB&B⇨🛏£55-£65 🅱
120P ✿ xmas
🍴 English & Italian V ✿ ♨ ⚡ Lunch £4-£8&alc High tea £4-£6.50&alc Dinner £13.50&alc Last dinner 10pm
CONF. Thtr 25 Class 12 Board 12 Del £62.50
Credit Cards [1][2][3] £

All black star hotels are given a percentage grading within their star bands. See 'Using the Guide' at the front of the book for full details.

★★✿
COBWEBS COUNTRY HOUSE
Leck, Cowan Bridge
LA6 2HZ ☎(05242) 72141
Closed Jan-Etr

We are pleased to welcome this charming little hotel to the ranks of our Red Star award winners. Guests are assured of personal care and attention by the hospitable owners, Paul Kelly and Yvonne Thompson. The bedrooms are pretty and individually styled, furnished with many antiques and have some nice personal touches. There are two cosy lounges and an attractive conservatory dining room in which to enjoy Yvonne's imaginative 6-course set dinner, based on the freshest ingredients and local produce, including game, fish and cheeses. Lighter meals are served on Sunday and Monday evenings.
5⇨🛏 CTV in all bedrooms ® T 🐾
CTV P 🛋 ✿ ♪ nc12yrs
Last dinner 7.30pm
Credit Cards [1][3]

Some hotels within company owned groups share a uniform identity. For full details consult the Contents page, under Hotel Groups.

DISCOVER THE NEW GREEN

ONCE A FAMOUS 19TH CENTURY COACHING INN, THE GREEN IS NOW ONE OF SCOTLAND'S FINE INDEPENDENTLY OWNED COUNTRY HOTELS, HAVING 47 SPACIOUS BEDROOMS ALL EQUIPPED TO THE HIGHEST STANDARD — LEISURE COMPLEX WITH INDOOR POOL, SAUNA, SOLARIUM, EXERCISE FACILITY AND SQUASH COURT — OWN TWO 18-HOLE GOLF COURSES WITH FIRST TEES A TWO MINUTE WALK FROM THE FRONT DOOR. IDEAL TOURING CENTRE — EDINBURGH, GLASGOW, STIRLING, ST. ANDREWS, PERTH, PITLOCHRY AND HIGHLAND PERTHSHIRE ARE LESS THAN AN HOUR AWAY. WRITE OR TELEPHONE FOR BROCHURE AND TARIFF QUOTING REF. AAH.

★★★

THE GREEN
HOTEL
2 The Muirs, Kinross, Scotland, KY13 7AS.
Tel: 0577 863467. Fax: 0577 863180.

Kirkbymoorside - Knaresborough

KIRKBYMOORSIDE North Yorkshire Map 08 SE68

★★66% George & Dragon
17 Market Place YO6 6AA ☎(0751) 31637
Welcoming 13th-century inn with modern bedrooms in converted stables.
14⇨♠Annexe8⇨♠(3fb) CTV in all bedrooms ® T
22P ✿
V ✿ Last dinner 9.30pm
Credit Cards [1][3]

KIRKBY STEPHEN Cumbria Map 12 NY70

★★68% The Town Head House
High St CA17 4SH (on A685) ☎(07683) 71044 FAX (07683) 72128
A charming town residence, parts of which date back to 1724, this hotel has spacious bedrooms with modern facilities, furnished in an elegant antique style. There are 2 comfortable sitting rooms on the ground floor, and a feature of the intimate dining room is a large wall safe now used as a drinks cabinet. There is a secluded garden to the rear.
6⇨♠3♠⚒in 2 bedrooms CTV in all bedrooms ® T
sB&B⇨♠£40-£47 dB&B⇨♠£61-£72 ⌑
10P 1🚗 ⚙ ✿ nc12yrs xmas
☞ English & French V ⚒ Dinner £12.50-£21alc Last dinner 8pm
Credit Cards [1][3]

KIRKCALDY Fife Map 11 NT29

★★★57% Dean Park
Chapel Level KY2 6QW (signposted from A92, Kirkcaldy West junc) ☎(0592) 261635 FAX (0592) 261371
In a new residential area northwest of the town, this old mansion is popular with business guests and for private functions. Some of the bedrooms are individual chalets in the grounds.
20⇨♠Annexe12♠(1fb) CTV in all bedrooms ®⚒T
✈ (ex guide dogs)
《 150P 🎱 snooker
☞ Scottish, French & Italian V ✿
Credit Cards [1][2][3][5]

★★64% The Belvedere
Coxstool, West Wemyss KY1 4SL ☎(0592) 654167 FAX (0592) 655279
Quietly situated in the beautifully conserved village of West Wemyss, this hotel consists of a central house with reception, bars and restaurant, and a cluster of attractive individual houses containing the majority of the bedrooms, most of which have fine sea views.
5⇨Annexe16⇨♠(2fb) CTV in all bedrooms ® T ✻
sB&B⇨♠£30-£50 dB&B⇨♠£45-£85 ⌑
50P xmas
☞ Scottish & Continental V ✿ ⚒ ✻ Lunch £11-£15 High tea £5-£9 Dinner £16-£25&alc Last dinner 9.30pm
Credit Cards [1][2][3] £

KIRKCUDBRIGHT Dumfries & Galloway Kirkcudbrightshire Map 11 NX65

★★66% Selkirk Arms
Old High St DG6 4JG ☎(0557) 30402 FAX (0557) 31639

CONSORT HOTELS

Situated in the old part of the attractive fishing town, this late 18th-century inn, where Burns reputedly wrote The Selkirk Grace, has been steadily improved by the current owners. Bedrooms are comfortably furnished and there is a popular public bar, small first-floor lounge and comfortable cocktail bar.
14⇨♠Annexe1⇨♠(2fb) CTV in all bedrooms ® T
sB&B⇨♠£42-£44 dB&B⇨♠£69 ⌑
4P 16🚗 ✿ xmas

☞ Scottish & Continental V ✿ ⚒ ✻ Dinner £17&alc Last dinner 9.30pm
Credit Cards [1][2][3][5]

KIRKHILL Highland Inverness-shire Map 14 NH54

★★66% Inchmore
IV5 7PX (at junc A862/B9164) ☎Inverness(0463) 83296
Much improved by its resident owners Inchmore is a small seaside hotel offering an informal, friendly atmosphere which will appeal to both tourists and commercial guests. Compact but comfortable bedrooms are equipped with the expected amenities, and the 'old world' lounge bar provides a popular rendezvous.
6⇨♠(1fb) CTV in all bedrooms ®⚒T
80P
V ✿ ⚒ Last dinner 8.30pm
Credit Cards [1][3]

KIRKMICHAEL Tayside Perthshire Map 15 NO06

★★61% Log Cabin
PH10 7NB (on A924)
☎Strathardle(0250) 881288 FAX (0250) 881402

ExecGroup

Closed 25-26 Dec
An ideal retreat for sporting enthusiasts of all kinds, as well as for country holidays, a large, lofty bar-lounge is the focal point of the life of this Norwegian-style pine built hotel which stands at the end of a narrow country road. There is a separate restaurant.
13⇨♠(5fb) TV available ® ✻ sB&B⇨♠£25.50-£37 dB&B⇨♠£51-£55 ⌑
CTV 50P ✿ ♪ shooting ski-ing xmas
V ✿ ⚒ ✻ Lunch fr£8.15alc Dinner £17.95 Last dinner 8.45pm
Credit Cards [1][2][3][5]

★★60% Aldchlappie
PH10 7NS ☎Strathardle(0250) 881224 FAX (0250) 881373
This small family-run hotel sits on the south side of the village overlooking the River Ardle. Service is friendly and informal and meals offer good value. A wide range of malt whiskies and real ale is stocked in the cosy bar and there is a comfortable lounge.
5⇨♠(3fb)⚒in all bedrooms CTV in all bedrooms ®
CTV 10P ⚙ ✿ ♪
V ✿ Last dinner 8.45pm
Credit Cards [1][2][3]

KIRKWALL

See **Orkney**

KIRKWHELPINGTON Northumberland Map 12 NY98

★★58% The Knowesgate
NE19 2SH (N on A696) ☎Otterburn(0830) 40261 FAX (0830) 40336
Situated to the north of the village, this family run hotel offers functional bedroom accommodation. Lounge areas are limited but there is a choice of cosy bars and a pleasant restaurant enjoying fine views of the surrounding countryside.
16⇨♠ CTV in all bedrooms ® T
100P games room
V ✿ ⚒ ⚒ Last dinner 9pm
Credit Cards [1][2][3]

KNARESBOROUGH North Yorkshire Map 08 SE35

★★★69% Dower House
Bond End HG5 9AL ☎Harrogate(0423) 863302 FAX (0423) 867665

This is an attractive, sympathetically extended Grade II listed building. Some of the double bedrooms are compact, but all are tastefully decorated and well equipped. The attractive Terrace

Knaresborough - Knutsford

Restaurant overlooks the gardens and its menus offer a wide choice. Other features are a traditional lounge and a bar lounge.
28⇨♠ Annexe4⇨♠(2fb) CTV in all bedrooms ® T ✈
sB&B⇨♠£50-£60 dB&B⇨♠£72-£83 ₽
(80P ♨ ✿ ⌂ (heated) sauna solarium gymnasium *xmas*
♡ English & French V ✤ ✂ Lunch fr£10 Dinner fr£17&alc Last dinner 9.30pm
CONF. Thtr 70
Credit Cards [1][2][3][5]

KNIGHTON Powys Map 07 SO27

★★★ 63% *Knighton*
Broad St LD7 1BL ☎(0547) 520530 FAX (0547) 520529
This hotel, set at the heart of the market town and known for many years as the Norton Arms, has been completely modernised to provide good facilities in bedrooms and public areas alike. The garlanded central staircase remains a dominant feature.
15⇨♠ CTV in all bedrooms ® T
Lift 10P snooker
♡ International V ✤ ⌕ Last dinner 9.30pm
Credit Cards [1][2][3][5]

★★ ✿72% Milebrook House
Milebrook LD7 1LT (2m E, off A4113) (Welsh Rarebits)
☎(0547) 528632 FAX (0547) 520509
RS Mon
Set in 3 acres of woodland, gardens and lawns, this 18th-century grey stone building overlooks the river. The atmosphere is welcoming and there are 2 lounges, one with a bar, and brightly decorated bedrooms. The gardens provide virtually all the vegetables for the 2 and 3-course menus. Dishes might include warm scallop and bacon salad followed by tasty local salmon with a sorrel sauce, and rich puddings such as apple pancakes with Calvados.
6⇨♠ CTV in all bedrooms ® ✈ sB&B⇨♠£43.50 dB&B⇨♠£62 ₽
20P ✿ ♪ badminton croquet nc8yrs *xmas*
♡ English & French V ✤ Lunch £8.75-£10.75 Dinner £15.95-£18.95 Last dinner 8.30pm
Credit Cards [1][3]

KNUTSFORD Cheshire Map 07 SJ77

★★★ 69% Cottons
Manchester Rd WA16 0SU (on A556) (Shire) ☎(0565) 650333
FAX (0565) 755351
This hotel with a French New Orleans theme offers good-quality accommodation and includes conference suites, a leisure club and tennis court. There is a restaurant serving well prepared meals and a comfortable conservatory lounge where snacks are available all day.
82⇨♠(6fb)3♨ in 18 bedrooms CTV in all bedrooms ®♀ T
✱ sB&B⇨♠£79-£94 dB&B⇨♠£98-£114 ₽
Lift (180P ✿ ⌂ (heated) ℘ (hard) sauna solarium gymnasium spa bath ♪ *xmas*
♡ English & French V ✤ ⌕ ✂ ✱ Lunch £11.95 Dinner £18&alc Last dinner 9.45pm
Credit Cards [1][2][3][5]

★★ ✿71% The Longview Hotel & Restaurant
Manchester Rd WA16 0LX (NW on A50)
☎(0565) 632119 FAX (0565) 652402
Closed 24 Dec-4 Jan
Pauline and Stephen West's delightful Victorian-style hotel enjoys well deserved popularity. Bedrooms are cosy, and the small lounge, bar and elegant restaurant have a Victorian theme. Head chef James Falconer-Flint changes his menu weekly, includes a vegetarian dish, and guests can opt for either 2 or 3 courses at a fixed price.
13⇨♠ Annexe10⇨♠(1fb) CTV in all bedrooms ® T ✱
sB&B⇨♠£32-£52 dB&B⇨♠£55-£70 ₽

26P ♨
♡ English & Continental V ✤ ✱ Bar Lunch £8.25 Dinner £13.25-£19 Last dinner 9pm
Credit Cards [1][2][3]

★★ ✿68% The Toft
Toft Rd WA16 9EH (1m S on A50) ☎(0565) 633470 & 63443
FAX (0565) 632603
Closed Xmas & New Year
This delightful little hotel, formerly a 16th-century farmhouse, is ideal for non-smoking vegetarians; the imaginative menus of Jean Davies earning a good reputation for the cottage-style restaurant. Bedrooms, lounge and bar are cosy.
11rm(8⇨♠)(2fb)✂ in all bedrooms CTV in all bedrooms ® T
✈ (ex guide dogs) ✱ sB&B⇨♠£40-£46 dB&B£42-£44
dB&B⇨♠£58-£62 ₽
CTV 35P ♨ nc10yrs
♡ Vegetarian V ✂ Dinner fr£18alc Last dinner 8pm
Credit Cards [1][3]

Forte Travelodge
Chester Rd, Tabley WA16 0PP (on A556, northbound)
☎(0565) 652187 Central Res (0800) 850950
FORTE Travelodge
This modern building offers a good standard of accommodation for overnight stops. Smart, spacious and well equipped bedrooms, all with en suite bathrooms, are suitable for family use, and meals may be taken at the nearby family restaurant. For more details about Travelodges, consult the Contents page, under Hotel Groups.
32⇨♠✱ B⇨♠£31.95 (room only)

For key to symbols see the Bookmark.

Longview Hotel & Restaurant
★★ ✿
Knutsford, Cheshire
"Welcome to the Historic town of Knutsford, and our friendly hotel of quality, offering. . .

• A warm welcome, comfort and good old fashioned hospitality
• Small, comfortable award winning restaurant, vegetarian food a speciality
• 23 En-suite bedrooms

"Come and enjoy our Victorian home with its many antiques and older views. We enjoy it and hope that you will too."

Pauline and Stephen West

51 & 55 Manchester Road, Knutsford, Cheshire WA16 0LX
For brochure telephone or fax:
Tel: 0565 632119
Fax: 0565 652402

Kyle of Lochalsh - Lancaster

KYLE OF LOCHALSH Highland *Ross & Cromarty*
Map **13** NG72

★★57% Kyle
Main St IV40 8AB (100 metres from the ferry crossing)
☎Kyle(0599) 4204 FAX (0599) 4932
RS Oct-Mar
Situated at the north end of the main street, this family-run hotel offers good value accommodation and is a popular base for visiting tour groups. Bedrooms are compact but modern, and public areas include a foyer with limited lounge seating, a comfortable modern bar and a small dining area.
31⇨♠in 1 bedroom CTV in all bedrooms ® T
sB&B⇨♠£25-£37 dB&B⇨♠£50-£70 ⊟
80P *xmas*
♀ French, Italian & Scottish V ◊ ⊿ ✱ Lunch £5.95-£10
Dinner £14-£16 Last dinner 9.30pm
CONF. Class 60 Board 60 Del from £30
Credit Cards [1][3]

LAGG
See **Arran, Isle of**

LAGGAN BRIDGE Highland *Inverness-shire* Map **14** NN69

★★★63% *Gaskmore House*
PH20 1BS ☎Laggan(05284) 250 FAX (05284) 207
This tastefully modernised hotel with fine views of the valley is run in country house-style, with log fires in the foyer and combined lounge and bar. Well equipped bedrooms vary in size, with 2 located in an adjacent lodge cottage.
9⇨♠Annexe2♠(3fb) CTV in all bedrooms ® T
40P ✱
V ◊ ⊿ ✱ Last dinner 9pm
Credit Cards [1][3]

LAIRG Highland *Sutherland* Map **14** NC50

★★★57% *Sutherland Arms*
IV27 4AT (Scottish Highland)(Logis) ☎(0549) 2291 FAX (0549) 2261
Closed Nov-Mar
With its lovely outlook over Loch Shin, this long-established Highland hotel has always been a favourite with anglers. It has a relaxing atmosphere and offers traditional services and comforts. Bedrooms vary in size but are well equipped with modern furnishings.
27rm(20⇨32♠)(3fb) CTV in all bedrooms ® T ✱
sB&B⇨♠£52-£69 dB&B⇨♠£92-£96 ⊟
30P ✱ ♪
◊ ⊿ ✱ Sunday Lunch £6.50-£8.50 Dinner £16-£20 Last dinner 8.30pm
Credit Cards [1][2][3][5] £

★★64% *Overscaig*
Loch Shin IV27 4NY (on A836) ☎Merkland(045983) 203
A complete transformation has taken place at this small family-run holiday and fishing hotel, by the shore of Loch Shin, 16 miles west of the village on the A838. The bright bedrooms now offer all the expected modern facilities, while public areas include a choice of bars, small quiet lounge and dining room.
9⇨♠(2fb) CTV in all bedrooms ® T ✖ (ex guide dogs)
sB&B⇨♠£20-£35 dB&B⇨♠£40-£70
CTV 30P ⇔ ✱ ♪ *xmas*
◊ ⊿ ✱ Lunch £8.50-£18alc High tea fr£2alc Dinner £11-£18alc Last dinner 9pm

Red star hotels are each highlighted by a pink tinted panel.

LAMLASH
See **Arran, Isle of**

LAMPETER Dyfed Map **02** SN54

★★★⚜67% Falcondale Country House
SA48 7RX (off A475 & A482) ☎(0570) 422910 FAX (0570) 423559
This 19th-century Italianate mansion, set in 14 acres of parkland, is situated along a private drive. Bedrooms are individually decorated with pretty wallpaper and matching fabrics, and furnished with reproduction period furniture. There is a very relaxing first-floor lounge; 2 bars and an attractive restaurant. The hotel is personally run by the Smith family, who offer warm hospitality.
19⇨♠(8fb)2🛏 CTV in all bedrooms ® T ✖ sB&B⇨♠£42-£49.50 dB&B⇨♠£60-£75 ⊟
Lift 80P ✱ ♀ (hard) ♪ 18 hole putting green *xmas*
♀ English & French V ◊ ⊿ ✱ Last dinner 9.30pm
CONF. Thtr 60 Class 20 Board 30
Credit Cards [1][3]

LAMPHEY
See **Pembroke**

LANARK
See **Biggar**

LANCASTER Lancashire Map **07** SD46
See also **Hampson Green**

★★★70% Lancaster House
Green Ln, Ellel LA1 4GJ (N on A6 towards Lancaster, pass through village called Galgate, go through traffic lights & turn right at next turning) ☎(0524) 844822 FAX (0524) 844766

Quietly situated, this modern hotel can sometimes be busy with conference delegates. Comfortable bedrooms have smart, if generally compact, bathrooms and all the expected amenities. Public areas include a pleasant foyer lounge with a log fire and an attractive split-level restaurant.
80⇨♠(10fb)✖in 21 bedrooms CTV in all bedrooms ® ✱ T sB&B⇨♠£55-£98.50 dB&B⇨♠£66-£99.50 ⊟
(100P ✱ ▭ (heated) sauna solarium gymnasium spa bath & childrens pool ♪ *xmas*
V ◊ ⊿ Lunch £9.95&alc Dinner £18.50-£19.50&alc Last dinner 9.30pm
CONF. Thtr 150 Class 50 Board 50 Del from £88
Credit Cards [1][2][3][4][5]

★★★63% Royal Kings Arms
Market St LA1 1HP (Follow 'City Centre' signs from M6, then 'Castle & Railway Station', turn off before traffic lights next to Waterstones bookshop) (Principal) ☎(0524) 32451 FAX (0524) 841698
This long-established, Victorian hotel is situated in the town centre. Bedrooms, some of which enjoy views of the castle, vary in size but are well furnished in modern style. There is a choice of bars and an attractive galleried restaurant, and the young staff are friendly.
55⇨♠(2fb) CTV in all bedrooms ® T ✱ sB⇨♠fr£49.50 dB⇨♠fr£65 (room only) ⊟
Lift (20P *xmas*
♀ English & French V ◊ ⊿ Lunch fr£7.95 Dinner £12.75-£16 Last dinner 9.30pm
CONF. Thtr 80 Class 50 Board 40 Del from £65
Credit Cards [1][2][3][5]

Hotels with red star ratings are especially high quality.

Lancaster - Langbank

Forte Posthouse
Waterside Park, Caton Rd LA1 4RA (close to junc 34 M6) ☎(0524) 65999 FAX (0524) 841265

FORTE Posthouse

Suitable for both the businesss and leisure traveller, this bright hotel provides modern accommodation in well equipped bedrooms with en suite bathrooms. For more details about Forte Posthouse hotels, consult the Contents page, under Hotel Groups.
115⇨ↂ✱ B⇨ↂ£41.50-£53.50 (room only)
CONF. Thtr 120 Class 60 Board 60 Del £89.50

LANCING West Sussex Map **04** TQ10

★★ 68% **Sussex Pad**
Old Shoreham Rd BN15 0RH (on the main A27 by Lancing College and Shoreham Airport) ☎Shoreham(0273) 454647 FAX (0273) 453010
This long-established inn has been substantially improved in recent years. Eleven new bedrooms are spacious, smart and very well equipped, though older rooms are more modest. Public areas comprise an extensive lounge-bar conservatory. The restaurant is small but plush, with a menu focusing on seafood and steaks.
19⇨ↂ2🛏 CTV in all bedrooms ® ✯ T ✱ sB&B⇨ↂ£50-£60 dB&B⇨ↂ£68-£80
60P ✱ xmas
♀ English & French V ✧ ⚏ ✂ ✱ Lunch £15-£30alc Dinner £15-£30alc Last dinner 10pm
CONF. Thtr 20 Board 20 Del from £76
Credit Cards ①②③④⑤

LANDCROSS Devon Map **02** SS42

★★ 63% **Beaconside**
EX39 5JL (1m SW on A388) ☎Bideford(02372) 77205
A warm welcome and friendly services are assured at this family-run country hotel, set in the heart of the Devonshire countryside and with its own woodland trail. Bedrooms are gradually being modernised and the bar and lounge offer a cosy atmosphere. Generous home-cooked dinners are served in the dining room.
9rm(4⇨2ↂ)(2fb) CTV in all bedrooms ✂
CTV 16P ✱ ⇨ (heated) ♂ (hard)
✧ ⚏ ✂
Credit Cards ①⑤

LAND'S END
See **Sennen**

LANGAR Nottinghamshire Map **08** SK73

★★ ◉♣ 65% **Langar Hall**
NG13 9HG (accessible via Bingham on the A52 or Cropwell Bishop from the A46, both signposted, the house adjoins the church and is hidden behind it) ☎Harby(0949) 60559 FAX (0949) 61045
Langar Hall is in a peaceful position with pleasant views over open countryside. It is the family home of Imogen Skirving who, along with a small team of staff, provides cheerful and hospitable service. Public rooms retain much of their original character with antiques and numerous paintings, and include a rather quaint study, lined with bookshelves and cased stuffed birds, and a light, comfortable drawing room. A short fixed-priced menu of English and French dishes is served in the open and airy dining room. Bedrooms are varied, all with a good range of modern facilities, and some in the courtyard stable block. There is a non smoking policy in the bedrooms.
12⇨ↂ(2fb)2🛏✂in all bedrooms CTV in all bedrooms ® T ✱ sB&B⇨ↂ£57.50-£80 dB&B⇨ↂ£80-£110 🅿
CTV 20P 🐎 ✱ croquet xmas

♀ English, French & Italian V ✧ ⚏ ✱ Lunch £15-£30alc Dinner £18-£35alc Last dinner 9.30pm
CONF. Thtr 25 Class 20 Board 20 Del from £130
Credit Cards ①②③⑤

LANGBANK Strathclyde *Renfrewshire* Map **10** NS37

★★★ ◉♣ 68% **Gleddoch House**
PA14 6YE (SCOTLAND'S HERITAGE HOTELS)
☎(047554) 711 FAX (047554) 201
Closed 26-27 Dec & 1-2 Jan
The former family home of shipping magnate Sir James Lithgow has now been sympathetically extended and converted to provide a country house hotel with good leisure facilities. Set in its own sizeable grounds, with an outlook over the River Clyde towards the Lomond hills, and complementing tastefully appointed, well equipped bedrooms by day rooms with welcoming open fires and comfortable chesterfields, this establishment has much to offer the visiting business or leisure guest alike.
33⇨ↂ(6fb)1🛏 CTV in all bedrooms ® T
(200P ✱ ▶ 18 squash ∪ sauna ♨
♀ Scottish & French V ✧ ⚏ Last dinner 9pm
Credit Cards ①②③⑤

If you have booked a meal in a hotel restaurant and cannot get there, remember you have a contractual obligation to cancel your booking.

L

FALCONDALE HOTEL
LAMPETER, DYFED
Tel: (0570) 422-910. AA★★★ Country House

Falcondale stands at the head of a forested and sheltered valley, set within 12 acres of park and woodland, 1 mile from Lampeter town centre.
The hotel has 20 bedrooms, individually designed, all rooms have bath/shower rooms, colour TV, in house film system, direct dial telephone, tea-coffee makers, central heating, radio, intercom, baby listening facilities, hair dryers.
Our restaurant has both table d'hôte and very extensive à la carte menus.
Services: 2 bars – 2 lounges; Conservatory – Log fires; Lift – Restaurant for 50; Banqueting for 140; 2 Conference – Meeting Rooms.
Sport Facilities: 10 acre lake coarse fishing; Putting green; Tennis court; With: Golf, shooting, pony trekking, salmon and sea fishing. By arrangement.
Which and
Johansen recommended.

Langdale, Great - Largs

LANGDALE, GREAT
See **Elterwater**

LANGHO Lancashire Map 07 SD73
★★★ **65%** **Mytton Fold Farm**
Whalley Rd BB6 8AB (off A59 between Langho & Whalley) ☎Blackburn(0254) 240662 FAX (0254) 248119
RS Xmas wk
This family-owned and run hotel has been created by the conversion and extention of stables to provide well equipped modern bedrooms. Public areas include an attractive bar lounge featuring an original 130-year-old cast iron fireplace. Service is friendly and the owners are always on hand.
27⇨2🛏 CTV in all bedrooms ® T ✗ (ex guide dogs) ✱ sB&B⇨£34-£43.50 dB&B⇨£54-£64.50 🍴
150P ✿ ♥ 18
V ♻ ✗ ✱ Sunday Lunch £7.95-£8.70 High tea £7.95-£8.70 Dinner £12.95&alc Last dinner 9.30pm
CONF. Thtr 300 Class 100 Board 100 Del from £55
Credit Cards [1][2][3] £

LANGHOLM Dumfries & Galloway *Dumfriesshire* Map 11 NY38
★★ **56%** **Eskdale**
Market Place DG13 0JH ☎(03873) 80357 & 81178 FAX (03873) 80357
A former coaching inn, this family-run mainly commercial hotel in the town centre has a popular public bar and quieter residents' bar and a spacious restaurant. Bedrooms vary in size and are quite practically furnished but have cheerful fabrics and modern amenities.
16rm(3⇨7♨)(2fb)✗in 3 bedrooms CTV in all bedrooms ® T ✱ sB&B£26 sB&B⇨£29 dB&B£40 dB&B⇨£46
(10P
V ♻ ✗ ✱ Bar Lunch £5-£9alc Dinner £12&alc Last dinner 8.30pm
Credit Cards [1][3] £

LANGLAND BAY West Glamorgan Map 02 SS68
See also **Mumbles** and **Swansea**
★★ ❀**67%** **Langland Court**
Langland Court Rd SA3 4TD (take B4593 towards Langland and turn left at St Peter's church) ☎Swansea(0792) 361545 FAX (0792) 362302
Family owned and managed, this Tudor-style hotel close to Langland Bay provides a welcoming ambience and thoughtfully equipped bedrooms. It has a congenial, wood-panelled restaurant where guests can enjoy the honest flavours and textures of an attractively presented range of rich terrines and pâtés, unfussy main courses and home-made puddings. The range of room services available rivals that offered by many hotels of a higher classification.
16⇨♨Annexe5⇨♨(5fb)1🛏✗in 2 bedrooms CTV in all bedrooms ® T ✗ (ex guide dogs) sB&B⇨♨£58 dB&B⇨♨£78-£80 🍴
45P 4🅿 (£5) ✿ ♨
♥ Welsh, English & Continental V ♻ Lunch £10.50-£11.50&alcDinner£16.50-£17.50&alcLastdinner9.30pm
Credit Cards [1][2][3] £

Satellite television – look for this symbol 📺 in the directory entries.

LANREATH Cornwall & Isles of Scilly Map 02 SX15
★★ **59%** **Punch Bowl Inn**
PL13 2NX ☎(0503) 220218
Dating back about 500 years, this village inn offers simple value-for-money accommodation, some bedrooms with fine 4-poster and half tester beds. The smartly refurbished Visitor's Kitchen (lounge bar) provides a contrast to the stone floored public bar. Bar meals are available and the restaurant offers table d'hôte and à la carte menus to guests.
14rm(10⇨2♨)(2fb)3🛏✗in 1 bedroom CTV in all bedrooms ® ✱ sB&B£18.50-£21.50 sB&B⇨♨£26.75-£29.75 dB&B£37-£43 dB&B⇨♨£45-£59.50 🍴
CTV 50P
V ♻ Last dinner 9pm
Credit Cards [1][3]

See advertisement under LOOE

LARGS Strathclyde *Ayrshire* Map 10 NS25
★★★ **66%** **Brisbane House**
14 Greenock Rd, Esplanade KA30 8NF (on A78) ☎(0475) 687200 FAX (0475) 676295
On the northern side of town by the Promenade, this Georgian mansion has been totally refurbished and modernised to provide tasteful public rooms, including a marble floored lobby with 2 matching sprial staircases. Bedrooms are well equipped, those at the front providing more comfort and space as well as fine views out across the Firth of Clyde.
23⇨♨(2fb) CTV in all bedrooms ® T ✗ (ex guide dogs) sB&B⇨♨£50-£65 dB&B⇨♨£80-£100 🍴
(60P ✿ *xmas*
♥ International V ♻
CONF. Thtr 100 Class 100 Board 20 Del from £70
Credit Cards [1][2][3][4][5]

★★ **68%** **Elderslie**
John St, Broomfields KA30 8DR ☎(0475) 686460 FAX (0475) 672251
Closed 25-26 Dec
On the seafront with views across to the Isle of Cumbrae and Arran in the distance, this hotel offers a good choice of lounges and a cosy little bar. Popular for its bar lunches, it also serves grills in the bar in the evening, as an alternative to dinners. With the exception of a few standard singles, bedrooms are well proportioned and nicely furnished.
25rm(9⇨4♨) CTV in all bedrooms ® T
CTV 30P ✿
♻ Last dinner 8.30pm
Credit Cards [1][2][3][5]

★★ **64%** **Willowbank**
96 Greenock Rd KA30 8PG ☎(0475) 672311 & 675435 FAX (0475) 672311
Lying on the main road on the northern edge of town, this family-run hotel is a favourite base for coach tours. Keenly priced, it also attracts business guests and tourists. Bedrooms, mostly of a good size, are comfortable and well furnished.
30⇨♨(4fb) CTV in all bedrooms ® T sB&B⇨♨£38-£48 dB&B⇨♨£60-£80 🍴
CTV 40P ✿ *xmas*
V ♻ Lunch £8.50-£12 High tea £5.50-£10 Dinner £15&alc Last dinner 9pm
Credit Cards [1][2][3][5] £

★★ **59%** **Springfield**
Greenock Rd KA30 8QL ☎(0475) 673119 & 687475 FAX (0475) 673119
Large seafront hotel catering mainly for the holiday and coach tour trade, with fine views out to the Isle of Cumbrae. The accommodation is bright and practical and a good range of food is provided in the recently extended dining room.

58⇨🏠(4fb) CTV in all bedrooms ® T sB&B⇨🏠£42.50 dB&B⇨🏠£58.50 ♨
Lift CTV 80P ✿ putting green ♪ xmas
♉ Scottish, French & Italian V ♥ ♏ ≠ Lunch £6–£10 High tea £5–£10alc Dinner £15.50&alc Last dinner 8.30pm
Credit Cards [1] [2] [3] [5]

LARKFIELD Kent Map 05 TQ65

★★★63% **Larkfield Priory**
London Rd ME20 6HJ (on A20)
☎West Malling(0732) 846858 FAX (0732) 846786

FORTE Heritage

A Victorian house set in its own grounds has been considerably extended to provide a range of well furnished modern bedrooms. The Club House lounge and bar are spacious and comfortable and there is a split-level restaurant with an attractive conservatory extension.
52⇨🏠1☐⁄₂ in 24 bedrooms CTV in all bedrooms ® T ✱
sB⇨🏠£39.50-£55 dB⇨🏠£39.50-£55 (room only) ♨
(80P ✿ xmas
V ♥ ♏ ≠ ✱ Lunch £10.95 High tea £3–£5 Dinner £15.95&alc Last dinner 9.30pm
Credit Cards [1] [2] [3] [5]

LASTINGHAM North Yorkshire Map 08 SE79

★★★⚑66% *Lastingham Grange*
YO6 6TH ☎(07515) 345
Closed mid Dec–Feb

This charming 17th-century farmhouse, is set in secluded gardens on the edge of the North Yorkshire moors. It has been owned and run by the same family since the mid 1950s, and is renowned for its traditional service and hospitality. Bedrooms are comfortable and pretty, with all modern amenities. The comfortable lounge has an open fire and direct access to the garden. Splendid 5-course dinners are served in the attractive dining room by courteous waitresses.
12⇨🏠 CTV in all bedrooms ®
30P 2🚗 🚲 ✿ ♂
V ♥ ♏ ≠
Credit Cards [2] [5]

LAUNCESTON

See **Lifton**

LAVENHAM Suffolk Map 05 TL94

★★★⚑70% *The Swan*
High St CO10 9QA ☎(0787) 247477 FAX (0787) 248286

FORTE Heritage

This lovely 14th-century hotel stands proudly in the unspoilt High Street of the Tudor village. There are 5 comfortable lounge areas with log fires in winter and a busy afternoon tea trade. The heavily beamed restaurant with its minstrels' gallery is the setting for an interesting selection of British dishes, varying with the seasons. Service is polite and cheerful, though a little rushed. Accommodation varies between feature rooms, 4-poster suites and Heritage standard rooms, which are generally comfortable and nicely furnished. However, housekeeping on our last few visits have let the side down with its general lack of attention to detail.
47⇨🏠2☐⁄₂ in 13 bedrooms CTV in all bedrooms ® T
sB⇨🏠£85-£90 dB⇨🏠£110-£145 (room only) ♨
(60P ✿ croquet ♪ xmas
♉ English & French V ♥ ♏ ≠ Lunch £16.95–£17.95 High tea £6.50–£7.50 Dinner £19.95–£20.95&alc Last dinner 9.30pm
CONF. Thtr 60 Class 35 Board 25 Del from £95
Credit Cards [1] [2] [3] [5]

ELDERSLIE HOTEL LARGS ★★AA

Situated on the sea front at Largs 'Elderslie' commands breathtaking views over the Firth of Clyde. Fully licensed with central heating throughout.
Extensive lounges ★ Private car park
Wide choice of menus ★ A warm welcome guaranteed
All bedrooms are equipped with television, wash basin, radio, telephone and tea making facilities. Many have private bathroom or shower.
Send now for colour brochure and tariff.

**ELDERSLIE HOTEL
BROOMFIELDS, LARGS, AYRSHIRE KA30 8DR
Tel: Largs (0475) 686460**

★★ The Eskdale Hotel

**Langholm, Dumfriesshire DG13 0JH
Telephone: Langholm (03873) 80357**

The Eskdale Hotel is a former coaching inn in the centre of Langholm on the Scottish border. The hotel offers a high degree of comfort, facilities and good quality home cooking. There are tea/coffee making facilities, colour TV, radio and full central heating in all rooms, $^2/_3$ of rooms have en suite facilities. Lively atmosphere with two bars, games room and à la carte restaurant. Ample parking is available in the hotel which is a good base for touring the Border region. Fishing, shooting and golf are all available in the area. Fishing permits available from Hotel.

Lavenham - Leamington Spa (Royal)

★ 73% Angel
Market Place CO10 9QZ (Logis) ☎Sudbury(0787) 247388 FAX (0787) 247057

This 14th-century inn, which overlooks the market place of the historic and picturesque town, combines the qualities of a cheerfully busy 'local' with those of a popular restaurant. Informal service is both friendly and helpful, and barbecues are held in the quiet garden during the summer months. Well equipped bedrooms are furnished in keeping with the character of the building.

7⇨🏠(1fb) CTV in all bedrooms ® T ✱ sB&B⇨🏠£40-£50 dB&B⇨🏠£50-£60 🍴
CTV 5P ✿ ♫
V ✿ ⚡ ✱ Lunch £6-£16alc Dinner £8-£18alc Last dinner 9.30pm
Credit Cards [1][3]

LEA MARSTON Warwickshire Map 07 SP29

★★★ 64% Lea Marston Hotel & Leisure Complex
Haunch Ln B76 0BY (off A4097, close to junc 9 of M42) ☎Curdworth(0675) 470468 FAX (0675) 470871

Part of an extensive leisure complex, this modern hotel provides accommodation in spacious bedrooms.

22⇨🏠 CTV in all bedrooms ®⚡ T ✱ (ex guide dogs) ✱ sB&B⇨🏠fr£45 dB&B⇨🏠£50-£155 🍴
(CTV 165P ✿ ▶ 9 ♪ (hard) sauna solarium gymnasium crown green bowls indoor bowls
♀ English & French V ✿ ⚡ ✱ ✱ Lunch £9.55-£13.95 Dinner £11.95-£13.95&alc Last dinner 10pm
CONF. Thtr 140 Class 80 Board 50 Del from £90
Credit Cards [1][2][3]

LEAMINGTON SPA (ROYAL) Warwickshire Map 04 SP36

★★★✿✿✿⚓
MALLORY COURT
Harbury Ln, Bishop's Tachbrook CV33 9QB (2m S off B4087 towards Harbury)
☎Leamington Spa(0926) 330214 FAX (0926) 451714

Built at the turn of the century, Mallory Court is the quintessential English country house, resplendent among smooth manicured lawns. Hotels of this ilk and undisputed quality are generally the showcases of the interior designer, all effect and very little character, but this isn't the case here. The elegant oak panelled dining room has stone mullioned windows with lovely views. The food is good and excels in the lighter mousse and soufflé compositions. Mousseline of salmon and scallop was very light and moist, hollowed to reveal fresh white crab meat and a pungent, deep coral coloured sauce. A main course of rack of lamb sliced into thick wedges with a herb breadcrumbed crust was pink, tender and true in flavour, set on a tomato based jus. The highlight was a caramel soufflé, of nigh on perfect execution, accompanied by a tuille/almond basket of vanilla ice cream. An expansive (and expensive) wine list has a limited selection of halves and none from the New World.

10⇨🏠(1fb)1🛏 CTV in all bedrooms T ✱
sB&B⇨🏠£100-£140 dB&B⇨🏠£145-£210 Continental breakfast 🍴
50P 2🅿 (£6 per night) 🚗 ✿ ⚡ ♪ (hard) squash croquet nc9yrs xmas

★★ 73% Regent
77 The Parade CV32 4AX ☎(0926) 427231 FAX (0926) 450728

Many famous people, including Queen Victoria, have visited this delightful hotel, where a high level of personal service is provided. Individually styled bedrooms have benefited from recent refurbishment and public areas include a choice of bars and a spacious lounge. The impressive Chandos Restaurant tends to be used mainly for breakfasts and banquets, while the cellar Vaults Restaurant provides an intimate setting for the fixed price and à la carte menus.

80⇨🏠(7fb)1🛏 CTV in all bedrooms ® T
Lift (CTV 70P 30🚗 table tennis pool table
♀ English, French & Italian V ✿ ⚡ Last dinner 10.45pm
Credit Cards [1][2][3][5]

★★★ 62% Falstaff
16-20 Warwick New Rd CV32 5JQ (on A4099) ☎(0926) 312044 FAX (0926) 450574

Formed from 3 Regency buildings on the western outskirts of the town, this smartly refurbished hotel has bedrooms of varying size and style, all well equipped with good quality furnishings. Comfortable public areas include an attractive restaurant.

63⇨🏠(2fb) CTV in all bedrooms ® T ✱ (ex guide dogs) ✱
sB&B⇨🏠£25-£59 dB&B⇨🏠£50-£69 🍴
(CTV 80P xmas
♀ English & French V ✿ ⚡ ✱ Lunch £5.50-£7.95 Dinner £14&alc Last dinner 9.15pm
Credit Cards [1][2][3][4][5]

★★★ 61% Angel
143 Regent St CV32 4NZ ☎Leamington Spa(0926) 881296 FAX (0926) 881296

A Regency coaching inn, the Angel is conveniently situated for access to the town centre. New owners in 1992 have begun to make extensive improvements. These include equipping the bedrooms to a high modern standard, as well as creating a larger restaurant, a new lounge and conference facilities. The new, more sensibly balanced menu should also give good results in the dining room.

36rm(35⇨🏠)(3fb)2🛏 CTV in all bedrooms ®⚡ T ✱
sB&B⇨🏠£25.50-£49.50 dB&B⇨🏠£39-£59 🍴
Lift (30P xmas
♀ English & French V ✿ ⚡ ✱ Lunch £5-£7.95 Dinner £12.50 Last dinner 9.30pm
CONF. Thtr 100 Class 80 Board 50 Del £60
Credit Cards [1][2][3]

★★★ 59% Manor House
Avenue Rd CV31 3NJ ☎(0926) 423251 FAX (0926) 425933

This 18th-century manor house, close to the town centre, offers varying standards of accommodation, some nicely renovated, some awaiting attention and some, in the Saddle Wing, more compact and basic. Public areas include a light, airy restaurant where table d'hôte and seasonal menus are served, and a comfortable open-plan lounge/bar and foyer.

53⇨🏠(2fb)✱ in 21 bedrooms CTV in all bedrooms ® T ✱
sB⇨🏠fr£68 dB⇨🏠fr£83 (room only) 🍴
Lift (130P ✿ xmas
V ✿ ⚡ ✱ Lunch £10.95 Dinner £15.95 Last dinner 10pm
CONF. Thtr 100 Class 50 Board 35 Del from £65
Credit Cards [1][2][3][4][5]

Leamington Spa (Royal) - Ledbury

★★ 68% Adams
22 Avenue Rd CV31 3PQ ☎(0926) 450742 & 422758 FAX (0926) 313110
This impeccably maintained Georgian house a few minutes walk from the town centre is personally run and has been tastefully converted to provide comfortable accommodation with modern amenities and quality furnishings in period style. Dinner service is restricted at weekends.
14rm CTV in all bedrooms T ✱ sB&B£38.95-£49.75 dB&B£49.50-£59.75 ₽
14P ✿ ✻
V ☉ ☷ Lunch £16.50-£22.50&alc Dinner £16.50-£18.75&alc Last dinner 8pm
Credit Cards 1 2 3 5 £

★★ 63% Beech Lodge
Warwick New Rd CV32 5JJ (off A445, opposite Mid-Warwickshire College) ☎Leamington Spa(0926) 422227
Closed 24 Dec-3 Jan
Personal service from the proprietors ensures a comfortable stay at this privately owned and run hotel. Simply furnished bedrooms, though compact, offer a good range of modern facilities, the cosy public areas are welcoming and an attractive restaurant serves generous portions of home-cooked food.
13rm(11⇌↑) CTV in all bedrooms ® T sB&B£21-£32 sB&B⇌↑£32-£43 dB&B⇌↑£45-£60 ₽
CTV 16P ✿
♀ English & French V ✻ Sunday Lunch £8-£10 Dinner £10.75-£18 Last dinner 8pm
Credit Cards 1 2 3 £

★★ 57% Abbacourt
40 Kenilworth Rd CV32 6JF ☎Leamington Spa(0926) 451755 FAX (0926) 450330
Immediately recognisable by its white exterior with turquoise-painted woodwork, this predominantly commercial hotel is within easy reach of the town centre. Bedrooms exhibit a mixture of styles and furnishings, a pleasant restaurant serves a range of Spanish and French dishes, and the bar overlooks the garden patio.
24⇌↑(4fb) CTV in all bedrooms ® T
30P
♀ Continental V ☉ ☷ Last dinner 10pm
Credit Cards 1 2 3 4 5

★ ✿ LANSDOWNE
87 Clarendon St CV32 4PF
☎Leamington Spa
(0926) 450505
FAX (0926) 421313
RS 24 Dec-7 Jan

This delightful Georgian hotel is conveniently situated close to the town centre, and guests enjoy a high level of personal service and hospitality provided in an informal and friendly style by David and Gillian Allen and their loyal staff. The individually decorated bedrooms vary in size but all are well equipped and furnished in sturdy pine. Public areas include an intimate dining room, small pleasant bar and a comfortable lounge with period furnishings. Gillian is assisted in the kitchen by Lucinda Button and they produce a varied but not overly ambitious table d'hôte menu. A typical starter might be home-made cream of cauliflower soup, with toasted pine kernels, followed by Scotch salmon and monkfish, in a cream and fennel sauce, wrapped in a filo parcel. Dessert selections include baked hot dishes as well as a good choice of cheeses.

15rm(12⇌↑)(1fb) CTV in 12 bedrooms ® T
✱ (ex guide dogs) sB&B£29.95 sB&B⇌↑£37.95-£48.95 dB&B£39.90 dB&B⇌↑£49.90-£59.90 ₽
CTV 11P ✿ nc5yrs
♀ English, French & Italian V ☉ ☷ Dinner £10.95-£17.95&alc Last dinner 8.30pm
Credit Cards 1 3 £

★ 65% Milverton House
1 Milverton Ter CV32 5BE
☎Leamington(0926) 428335

This substantial Victorian property is now a pleasant family-run hotel, located near the fire station in a mainly residential area, within 5 minutes' walk of the town centre. Bedrooms are attractive and comfortable. A small but good-value menu is offered in the dining room, which has an impressive fireplace and large brass chandelier.
10rm(7⇌↑)(1fb) CTV in all bedrooms ® T ✻ sB&B£20-£22 sB&B⇌↑£30-£34 dB&B£30-£34 dB&B⇌↑£40-£46 ₽
CTV 6P ✿
V ☉ ☷ Lunch £5-£8.50 High tea £1.50-£2.50 Dinner £7.50-£8.50 Last dinner 7.30pm
Credit Cards 1 3

Courtyard by Marriott
Olympus Av, Tachbrook Park CV34 6RJ
☎(0926) 425522 FAX (0926) 881322

Well furnished guest bedrooms have en suite bathrooms, remote control CTV and direct-dial telephone at this modern hotel, and there is an informal restaurant and bar. For more details about Courtyard by Marriott, consult the Contents page, under Hotel Groups.
94⇌↑ dB⇌↑fr£62 (room only)

LEDBURY Hereford & Worcester Map 03 SO73
★★★ 55% Feathers
High St HR8 1DS ☎(0531) 635266 FAX (0531) 632001
The traditional black and white frontage of this historic coaching inn (dating from 1546) is a landmark at the heart of the busy little town, and its bar and restaurant areas are very popular locally. Beams, exposed timbers and open fires are much in evidence throughout, and cosy bedrooms are quaint in style.
11⇌↑(2fb)1✿ CTV in all bedrooms ® T sB&B⇌↑£65 dB&B⇌↑£85 ₽
(10P 6✿ squash *xmas*
♀ English & French V ☉ ☷ Sunday Lunch £13.95 High tea £3 Dinner £20&alc Last dinner 9.30pm
CONF. Thtr 100 Class 100 Board 80 Del £99.50
Credit Cards 1 2 3 5

★★ ✿✿✿ ♨ 70% Hope End Country House
Hope End HR8 1JQ (2.5m NE unclass rd) ☎(0531) 633613 FAX (0531) 636366
Closed mid Dec-mid Feb
Approaching this hotel, down an unmade track to an assortment of buildings in a small valley, is like travelling back in time. Forty acres of natural parkland, a walled garden and two courtyards do little to dispel this feeling, which is confirmed on entering the fine Georgian house. Owners John and Patricial Hegarty make a deliberate attempt to lessen the effect of modern-day living in favour of the natural and fundamental attractions of the past. The bedrooms, while lacking TV and radio, do not overlook the comforts and needs of the 20th century. The heart of the hotel is in the kitchen, where Patricia Hegarty uses fresh, organic produce from John's walled garden in what can only be described as old-

Ledbury - Leeds

fashioned English cooking. Peace and tranquility are assured at this delightful refuge.
7⇨Annexe2⇨1⊞ CTV in 1 bedroom ® T ✖ ✱ sB&B⇨£87-£131 dB&B⇨£99-£143 ♫
10P ⇔ ✿ nc12yrs
V ⥊ ✱ Dinner £30 Last dinner 8.30pm
Credit Cards ① ③

★★**62%** **The Verzons Country House**
Trumpet HR8 2PZ (3m W A438) ☎Trumpet(0531) 670381
Closed 25-26 Dec
Set in 4 acres of grounds with views over the Malvern Hills, this 18th-century country house is run on friendly personal lines by the Coomber family. Large bedrooms include 2 family rooms and there is a cheerful bar with its own small restaurant, plus the main restaurant, both popular for their wide choice of dishes.
9⇨♪(2fb)1⊞ CTV in all bedrooms ® sB&B⇨♪£45-£50 dB&B⇨♪£60-£75 ♫
50P ✿ clay pigeon shooting
♀ English & French V ♡ ⊻ Sunday Lunch £9.95-£10.50
Credit Cards ① ③

LEEDS West Yorkshire Map 08 SE33

★★★★**69%** *Holiday Inn*
Wellington St LS1 4DL ☎(0532) 442200 FAX (0532) 440460

This modern city centre hotel is well managed and prides itself on the quality of its staff and levels of service provided. Public areas include a choice of bars and a restaurant. The attractive bedrooms are air-conditioned, comfortably furnished and offer a range of extras such as slippers, bathrobes and fruit.
125⇨♪2⊞⥊ in 25 bedrooms CTV in all bedrooms ® ⌀ T ✖ (ex guide dogs)
Lift ⊄ ⊞ 25P 100⊛ ⏏ (heated) snooker sauna solarium gymnasium whirlpool spa beauty studio steam room
♀ English & French V ♡ ⊻ ⥊ Last dinner 10pm
Credit Cards ① ② ③ ④ ⑤

★★★★**66%** **The Queen's**
City Square LS1 1PL ☎(0532) 431323 FAX (0532) 425154

FORTE GRAND

A grand 1930s hotel retaining many original fixtures and fittings, Queen's has been revitalised in recent years to suit modern requirements. Its city-centre location makes its Palm Court lounge a popular meeting place and there is a carvery and cocktail bar as well as the formal Harewood Restaurant. There is a handy valet parking service.
190rm(188⇨♪)⥊ in 62 bedrooms CTV in all bedrooms ® ⌀ T ✱ sB⇨♪£90 dB⇨♪£100 (room only) ♫
Lift ⊄ 60⊛ *xmas*
♀ International V ♡ ⊻ ✱ Lunch £9.50-£13.95&alc Dinner £13.95-£17&alc Last dinner 10pm
Credit Cards ① ② ③ ⑤

★★★⊛⊛**79%** **Haley's Hotel & Restaurant**
Shire Oak Rd, Headingley LS6 2DE (2m N of Leeds city centre off A660 Otley Road) ☎(0532) 784446 FAX (0532) 753142
Staff are a credit to owner J T Appleyard and general manager Stephen Beaumont, who aim to keep this the best hotel in Leeds. There are 2 lounges, one with a cocktail dispense bar, and both have comfortable settees and armchairs. Bedrooms vary in size but are identically equipped. Chef Chris Baxter produces a sensible à la carte of 5 or 6 dishes to a course, starting perhaps with spicy fish soup without pastry, or terrine of chicken with orange, redcurrant and peppercorn sauce.
22⇨ CTV in all bedrooms ® ⌀ T ✖ (ex guide dogs) sB&B⇨♪£95 dB&B⇨♪£112 ♫
⊄ 18P ⇔ *xmas*

V ♡ ⊻ Lunch £13.95-£16.95&alc Dinner £18.95-£23.95&alc Last dinner 9.45pm
CONF. Thtr 30 Class 20 Board 25 Del from £110
Credit Cards ① ② ③ ⑤ £

★★★**66%** **Merrion Thistle**
Merrion Centre LS2 8NH ☎(0532) 439191 FAX (0532) 423527

THISTLE HOTELS

This city centre hotel has recently been totally refurbished and improved. Bedrooms, while not large, are now attractively appointed in contemporary style and fully equipped with modern facilities. Extensive use of marble and wood has created stylish public areas, most of which are on the first floor.
109⇨♪⥊ in 76 bedrooms CTV in all bedrooms ® ⌀ T ✱ sB⇨♪£75-£85 dB⇨♪£85-£95 (room only) ♫
Lift ⊄ *P xmas*
♀ English & French V ♡ ⊻ ✱ Sunday Lunch £14.75&alc High tea fr£5.85 Dinner £14.75&alc Last dinner 10.30pm
CONF. Thtr 80 Class 25 Board 25 Del from £95
Credit Cards ① ② ③ ⑤

★**63%** **Aragon**
250 Stainbeck Ln LS7 2PS (off A61 2m from city centre) ☎(0532) 759306 FAX (0532) 757166
Closed 24 Dec-2 Jan
A Victorian mill-owner's house in a residential area 2 miles north of the city centre has been converted into a small hotel with practically furnished bedrooms, a comfortable lounge and cosy bar. The atmosphere is informal and friendly and home-cooked dinners and bar meals are available.
14rm(8⇨2♪)(1fb) CTV in all bedrooms ® T sB&B£25.08 sB&B⇨♪£39.40 dB&B£38.10 dB&B⇨♪£49
24P ⇔ ✿
V ♡ ⊻ Bar Lunch £1.50-£10.50alc High tea £1.50-£5alc Dinner £10.50 Last dinner 6.30pm
CONF. Thtr 20 Board 14
Credit Cards ① ② ③ ⑤ £

Forte Posthouse
LS25 5LF ☎South Milford (0977) 682711 FAX (0977) 685462
(For full entry see Lumby)

Hilton National Leeds City
Neville St LS1 4BX ☎(0532) 442000 FAX (0532) 433577

HILTON

This is a bright, modern hotel with an informal restaurant, aimed at both the business and leisure guest. All bedrooms have en-suite bathrooms and a range of modern facilities. For more information about Hilton National, consult the Contents page, under Hotel Groups.
206⇨♪✱ B⇨♪£89 (room only)
CONF. Thtr 400 Class 180 Board 80 Del £125

Marriott
☎(0532) 366366 FAX (0532) 366367

A large and busy hotel, which is ideal for the business and leisure traveller, offering a wide range of services, a choice of eating options and indoor leisure facilities. Bedrooms are comfortable and equipped with modern facilities. For more details about Marriott hotels, consult the Contents page, under Hotel Groups.
244⇨♪ dB⇨♪fr£120 (room only)

Remember to book early for holiday
and bank holiday times.

LEEK Staffordshire Map 07 SJ95

★★ 65% Bank End Farm Motel
Leek Old Rd ST9 9QJ (2m SW off A53) ☎(0538) 383638
10rm(9⇌♐)(2fb)⚹in 1 bedroom CTV in all bedrooms ® T
sB&Bfr£25 sB&B⇌♐£30 dB&B⇌♐£42
25P ⇌ ✿ ⊡ (heated) ♪ ⚘
V Dinner £10-£16.50 Last dinner 8.30pm

LEEMING BAR North Yorkshire Map 08 SE28

★★ 62% Motel Leeming
Great North Rd DL8 1DT ☎Bedale(0677) 422122 FAX (0677) 424507
(For full entry see Bedale)

★★ 60% White Rose
DL7 9AY (on A684, E of A1 junc) ☎Bedale(0677) 422707 & 424941 FAX (0677) 425123
This mainly commercial hotel provides bedrooms equipped with every modern facility (making some rooms rather crowded). There is a large bar-lounge and restaurant.
18⇌♐(2fb) CTV in all bedrooms ® ⚹ T ✱ sB&B⇌♐fr£29.50 dB&B⇌♐fr£43
50P
V ✿ ⚏ ✱ Lunch £7.75 High tea £7.50 Dinner £11.95&alc Last dinner 9.45pm
Credit Cards [1][2][3][5]

LEE-ON-THE-SOLENT Hampshire Map 04 SU50

★★★ 64% Belle Vue
39 Marine Pde East PO13 9BW ☎(0705) 550258 FAX (0705) 552624
Closed 25 & 26 Dec
This seafront hotel with views across the Solent to the Isle of Wight offers accommodation in well decorated and equipped bedrooms. The bar is popular with locals, and arriving guests are cheerfully welcomed at reception.
24⇌♐Annexe3⇌♐(4fb) CTV in all bedrooms ® T sB⇌♐£35-£55 dB⇌♐£35-£55 (room only) ♬
《 CTV 55P ♪
V ✿ ⚹ ✱ Lunch £7-£20alc Dinner £9.50-£20alc Last dinner 9.45pm
Credit Cards [1][2][3]

LEICESTER Leicestershire Map 04 SK50

★★★★ 60% Holiday Inn
St Nicholas Circle LE1 5LX (from junct 21 off M1/M69 take A46 to city centre for approx 3.5m) ☎(0533) 531161 FAX (0533) 513169
Gradual refurbishment work continues here, including a comfortable new foyer lounge. The bedrooms offer a mixture of styles: executive rooms fresh and modern, standard rooms more dated and modest; all are quite spacious. There is an informal, rustic-style restaurant providing all-day service, while Carey's bar is a comfortable retreat with table service and cocktails.
188⇌♐(99fb)⚹in 79 bedrooms CTV in all bedrooms ® T sB⇌♐£84-£94 dB⇌♐£94-£104 (room only) ♬
Lift 《 ⊞ ♇ ⊡ (heated) sauna solarium gymnasium whirlpool health bar steam room
♈ International V ✿ ⚏ ⚹ Lunch £11-£17.50&alc High tea £5-£12 Dinner £16-£22&alc Last dinner 10.15pm
CONF. Thtr 300 Class 140 Board 40 Del from £80.30
Credit Cards [1][2][3][4][5]

★★★ ❀70% Belmont House
De Montfort St LE1 7GR ☎(0533) 544773 FAX (0533) 470804

BEST WESTERN HOTELS

Closed 25-28 Dec

Leek - Leicester

★★★ AA
THE MERRION
THISTLE HOTEL

Wade Lane, Leeds LS1 4AE
Tel: 0532 436454   Fax: 0532 429327

Your choice in Leeds

For Reservations at over 100 Mount Charlotte Thistle Hotels
Telephone London: 071 937 8033.

THISTLE HOTELS

★★★
HALEY'S
HOTEL & RESTAURANT

★ An elegant Victorian town-house hotel just 2 miles from Leeds City Centre in quiet conservation area.

★ 22 luxurious bedrooms furnished with antiques and rich fabrics.

★ Excellent meeting & private dining facilities.

★ Ample free car parking.

★ The best Restaurant in Leeds (2 AA Rosettes).

Shire Oak Road, Headingley, LEEDS LS6 2DE. Tel: 0532 784446.

AA BEST NEW HOTEL NORTH OF ENGLAND 1991/92

Leicester

Belmont House, built in the early 1860s, is now within a conservation area of that era. The generous proportions of the building make for comfortable public rooms, which include a choice of lounges, an open-plan lounge bar providing all-day light meals, and the Cherry restaurant. Here chef Mark Crockett and his small team offer a daily table d'hôte and an à la carte menu of what is best described as modern British and French cuisine. Bedroom styles vary but all the rooms have light, fresh décor.

44⇨♠Annexe21⇨♠(7fb)⤴in 9 bedrooms CTV in all bedrooms⊕⚏T sB&B⇨♠£72-£85 dB&B⇨♠£84-£95 ⛔
Lift (60P
♉ English & French V ⚘ ⚏ ✻ Lunch £10.95-£11.95&alc Dinner fr£16.50&alc Last dinner 10pm
CONF. Thtr 150 Class 60 Board 60 Del from £84
Credit Cards ①②③⑤

★★★ 67% Leicestershire Moat House

Wigston Rd, Oadby LE2 5QE (3m SE A6, on B582 opposite St Peter's Church)
☎(0533) 719441 FAX (0533) 720559
Following extensive refurbishment, this former gentleman's residence is now a comfortable hotel with good conference facilities. Bedrooms have quality fabrics and light wood furniture. There is an open plan bar and lounge area, plus a smaller bar leading into Czar's Restaurant where a wide range of dishes is served.

57⇨♠(4fb)⤴in 14 bedrooms CTV in all bedrooms⊕ T sB&B⇨♠£66-£74 dB&B⇨♠£77-£93 (room only) ⛔
Lift (CTV 160P ✿
♉ English & French V ⚘ ⚏ ⤴ Lunch £11.25&alc High tea £4.20-£7.85 Dinner £14.65&alc Last dinner 9.45pm
CONF. Thtr 250 Class 65 Board 60 Del from £54
Credit Cards ①②③⑤ £

★★★ 63% Stage

299 Leicester Rd, Wigston Fields LE18 1JW (S on A50) ☎(0533) 886161 FAX (0533) 811874

This popular hotel is to the south of the town. Bedrooms have fitted furniture and pretty coordinated fabrics. There are plenty of options for meals in the bar or restaurant; the bar features a collection of photographs of celebrities who have appeared in Leicester over the years.

79⇨♠(8fb)⤴in 6 bedrooms CTV in all bedrooms⊕ T ✈ (ex guide dogs) sB&B⇨♠£39-£69 dB&B⇨♠£45-£79 ⛔
(200P ⛱ (heated) sauna solarium gymnasium spa bath steam room ♫ xmas
♉ International V ⚘ ⚏ ⤴ Lunch fr£7.95&alc Dinner £8.95-£10.95&alc Last dinner 10pm
CONF. Thtr 300 Class 150 Board 100 Del from £75
Credit Cards ①②③④⑤ £

★★★ 61% Leicester Forest Moat House

Hinckley Rd, Leicester Forest East LE3 3GH (on A47) ☎(0533) 394661 FAX (0533) 394952
RS 25-27 Dec

The Sportsmans Bar has been upgraded over recent years and has proved popular locally for its bar food and atmosphere. For diners there is a cosy cocktail bar adjacent to the restaurant, which serves a full range of more formal meals. Limited seating is available in the foyer.

34⇨♠⤴in 3 bedrooms CTV in all bedrooms⊕ T sB⇨♠£45-£52 dB⇨♠£55-£62 (room only) ⛔
(200P ✿ putting
♉ English & French V ⚘ ⚏ ⤴ Lunch fr£8.65 Dinner fr£12.30&alc Last dinner 9.45pm
CONF. Thtr 85 Class 70 Board 60 Del from £65
Credit Cards ①②③⑤

★★★ 58% Saint James

Abbey St LE1 3TE ☎(0533) 510666 FAX (0533) 515183
The hotel occupies the top tiers of a circular car park near St Margaret's bus station, inside the inner ring road. Accommodation is modern in style and the highest floor is taken up by the restaurant which has views over the city skyline.

72⇨♠(3fb) CTV in all bedrooms⊕ T
Lift (✱
♉ English & French V ⚘ ⚏ Last dinner 10pm
Credit Cards ①②③⑤

★★ 69% Red Cow

Hinckley Rd, Leicester Forest East LE3 3PG (4m W on A47) (Everards Brewery) ☎(0533) 387878 FAX (0533) 387878
This thatched inn has a busy local trade, attracted by the good range of meals and snacks on offer in the cottagey restaurant, lounge bar and conservatory. Its pleasantly decorated bedrooms, in a modern building close to the inn, are also popular, since they represent very good value for money.

31⇨♠(27fb)⤴in 4 bedrooms CTV in all bedrooms⊕ T ✈ (ex guide dogs)
120P
♉ French V ⚘ ⚏ ⤴ ✻ Lunch fr£7.95 Dinner fr£7.95 Last dinner 10pm
Credit Cards ①③

★★ 64% Old Tudor Rectory

Main St, Glenfield LE3 8DG ☎(0533) 320220 FAX (0533) 876002
This former rectory, with parts dating back to Tudor times, sits in an acre of grounds. Privately owned, it offers a friendly relaxed atmosphere in its small public rooms. There is a comfortable lounge dining room with polished wooden tables and cheerful decor. Bedroom styles vary considerably, from the Tudor 4-poster rooms to more modern accommodation.

15⇨♠Annexe1⇨♠(2fb)2⚏ CTV in all bedrooms⊕ T sB&B⇨♠£34.07-£41.13 dB&B⇨♠£52.88-£58.75 ⛔
37P ✿ solarium gymnasium beauty salon
V ⚘ ⚏ Last dinner 9.30pm
Credit Cards ①②③

★★ 56% Gables

368 London Rd LE2 2PN (on A6) ☎(0533) 706969
The Gables is a busy commercial hotel with a friendly environment. The snug bar acts as a lounge, and the restaurant provides an above-average choice of meals in generous portions.

31⇨♠(9fb) CTV in all bedrooms⊕ T ✈ (ex guide dogs)
29P ⇔
♉ English & French V ⚘ Last dinner 9.30pm
Credit Cards ①②③⑤

Forte Posthouse

Braunstone Ln East LE3 2FW (on A46 approach from junc 21 of M1/M69) ☎(0533) 630500 FAX (0533) 823623

Suitable for both the business and leisure traveller, this bright hotel provides modern accommodation in well equipped bedrooms with en suite bathrooms. For more details about Forte Posthouse hotels, consult the Contents page, under Hotel Groups.

172⇨♠✻ B⇨♠£41.50-£53.50 (room only)
CONF. Thtr 100 Class 54 Board 45 Del from £79.50

Rosettes range from 5 for outstanding cuisine to 1 rosette for enjoyable, well prepared food

For key to symbols see the Bookmark.

English Tourist Board

The Old Tudor Rectory

★★

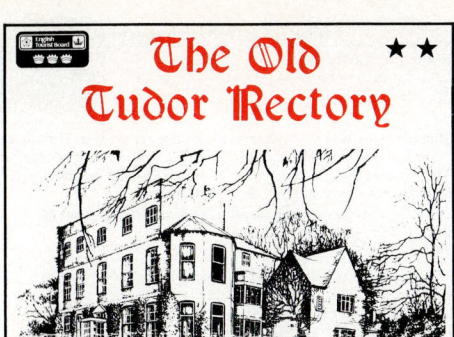

Fifteenth Century House in Garden Setting.

Original Staircases and Wealth of Old Timbers.

Four Poster Beds. Rooms Ensuite.

A la Carte Restaurant.

Ten minutes from M1 and City Centre.

Glenfield, Leicester. Tel. (0533) 320220

THE RED COW

—HOTEL, RESTAURANT & BARS—

Hinckley Road, Leicester Forest East, Leicester.
Tel: 0533 387878 Fax: 0533 387878

31 En Suite Rooms:
Close to M1 and Leicester City

All rooms with Colour TV, Hair Dryer, Trouser Press, Direct Dial Telephone, Tea & Coffee making facilities.

A famous and very popular historic thatched Inn which has been carefully refurbished. Well fitted Hotel Rooms housed in a detached modern annexe adjacent to the main building.

AA★★

EVERARDS
AN ORIGINAL INN

NOTTINGHAM
BURTON UPON-TRENT
LOUGHBOROUGH
MELTON MOWBRAY
A444
A453
A50
A6
A46
A607
TAMWORTH
B4109
A47
LEICESTER
SKETCHLEY GRANGE
Sketchley Lane
A5
M69
Sketchley Business Park
HINCKLEY
M42
M1
M6
NATIONAL EXHIBITION CENTRE
COVENTRY
RUGBY
A45
M45
LEAMINGTON SPA
WARWICK
NATIONAL AGRICULTURAL CENTRE
A46
STRATFORD UPON-AVON
PLACES OF INTEREST
1. Warwick Castle
2. Bosworth Battle Centre
3. Stratford-on-Avon
4. Twycross Zoo
5. Drayton Manor Park
6. Coventry Cathedral
7. N.E.C.
8. Mallory Park
9. National Agricultural Centre
10. Donnington Park
11. Belvoir Castle
12. Stamford Hall
13. Shackerstone Steam Railway
14. Foxton Locks
15. Stoney Cove
16. Hinckley Golf Course

Sketchley Grange

AA★★★

Country House Hotel and Conference Centre

SKETCHLEY LANE · BURBAGE · HINCKLEY · LEICESTERSHIRE LE10 3HU · ENGLAND
Telephone: 0455 251133 Fax: 0455 631384

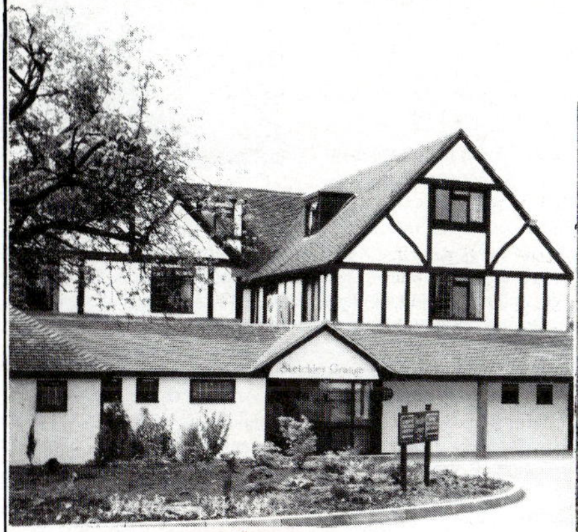

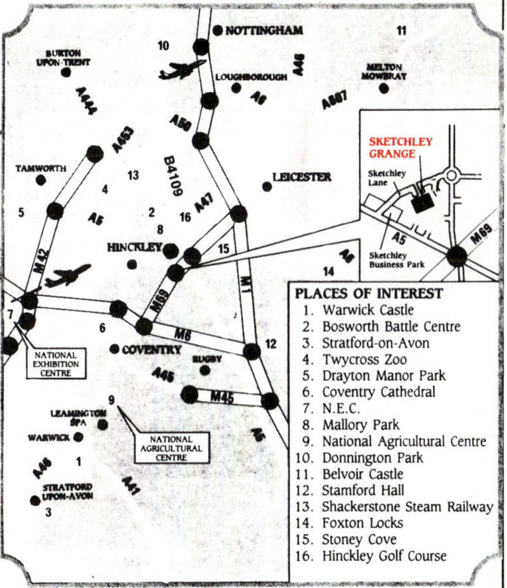

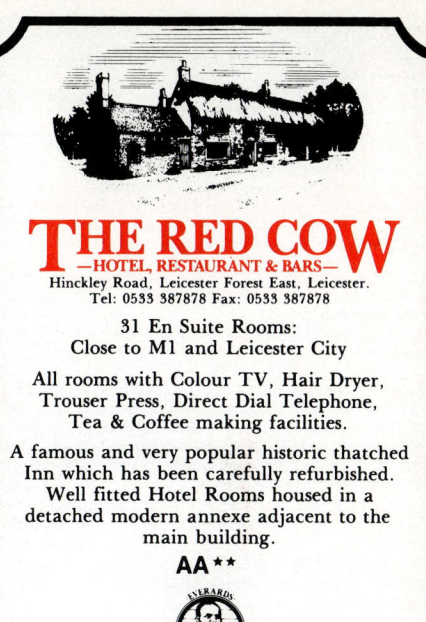

Leigh Delamere Motorway Service Area (M4) - Leominster

LEIGH DELAMERE MOTORWAY SERVICE AREA (M4)
Wiltshire Map **03** ST87

Granada Lodge
M4 Service Area SN14 6LB
☎Chippenham(0666) 837097 FAX (0666) 837112

This modern building provides smart, spacious and well equipped bedrooms, all with en suite bathrooms. Meals may be taken at a nearby family restaurant. For more details about Granada Lodges, consult the Contents page, under Hotel Groups.

34⇨♠ ✱ B⇨♠ £34.95-£37.95 (room only)

LEIGHTON BUZZARD Bedfordshire Map **04** SP92

★★★ **60%** Swan
High St LU7 7EA ☎(0525) 372148 FAX (0525) 370444

The Swan is a town-centre Georgian coaching inn. Bedrooms are individually decorated and furnished; some are beginning to look tired but are scheduled to be refreshed during 1993. There is a traditional feel to the oak carved Hunter's Bar, and the restaurant is elegantly appointed, with a small conservatory extension overlooking the cobbled courtyard.

38⇨♠(1fb)1🛏in 13 bedrooms CTV in all bedrooms ® T ✱ sB&B⇨♠£28-£62.50 dB&B⇨♠£56-£80 🍴
(10P ♫
♿ European V ♥ ♨ ✂ ✱ Lunch £6.95-£11.15&alc Dinner £10.95-£13.50&alc Last dinner 9.30pm
CONF. Thtr 50 Class 25 Board 25 Del from £60
Credit Cards [1][2][3][5]

LEISTON Suffolk Map **05** TM46

★ **64%** White Horse
Station Rd IP16 4HD (on B1119, signposted Leiston, 4m onto hotel) ☎(0728) 830694 FAX (0728) 833105

On the edge of the town centre, this personally run hotel with a busy bar trade offers warm hospitality and simple but comfortable accommodation and is popular with commercial guests.

10rm(1⇨7♠)Annexe3♠(1fb) CTV in all bedrooms ® T ✱ sB&B£27.50-£32.50 sB&B⇨♠£33.50-£35 dB&B£45 dB&B⇨♠£52 🍴
CTV 14P 3🚗 ✿ ♿ xmas
♿ English & French V ♥ ♨ ✂ ✱ Lunch £6.95&alc Dinner £10-£17.50alc Last dinner 9.30pm
Credit Cards [1][3][5] £

LENHAM Kent Map **05** TQ85

★★ **62%** Dog & Bear
The Square ME17 2PG (1m from Lenham station) (Shepherd) ☎Maidstone(0622) 858219 FAX (0622) 859415

This renovated coaching inn in the attractive village square dates back to 1602 &has a popular bar with an open fire, pool table and darts, and a beamed restaurant offering pies, grills and deep-fried dishes. Bedrooms, many in the converted stables are all comfortably furnished to a good modern standard.

25⇨♠(3fb)1🛏 CTV in all bedrooms ® T sB&B⇨♠£35-£45 dB&B⇨♠£45-£55 🍴
40P xmas
V ♥ ♨ Lunch £5.95-£8.95&alc Dinner £8.50-£14.50alc Last dinner 10pm
CONF. Thtr 40 Class 25 Board 20 Del from £62.50
Credit Cards [1][3]

Irish entries appear in a separate section that follows the main directory.

LEOMINSTER Hereford & Worcester Map **03** SO45

★★★ **57%** Talbot
West St HR6 8EP ☎(0568) 616347 FAX (0568) 614880

Situated at the Iron Cross in this ancient market town, the Talbot is a combination of buildings dating from the 15th to the 20th century. There is a wealth of exposed timbers and welcoming log fires, and a start has been made on upgrading the bedrooms.

20⇨♠(3fb) CTV in all bedrooms ® T sB&B⇨♠£38-£44 dB&B⇨♠£64-£72 🍴
20P xmas
♿ English & French V ♥ ♨ ✱ Lunch £10-£10.50 Dinner £15.50-£16&alc Last dinner 9.30pm
CONF. Thtr 130 Class 60 Board 40 Del from £65
Credit Cards [1][2][3][5] £

★★ **56%** Royal Oak
South St HR6 8JA (junct A44/A49)
☎(0568) 612610 FAX (0568) 612710

Near the town centre, this old coaching inn dating back to 1723 offers traditional services and a good choice of food. Bedrooms are modestly appointed, and ground floor areas are scheduled for refurbishment.

17⇨♠Annexe1⇨♠(2fb)1🛏 CTV in all bedrooms ® ✱ sB&B⇨♠£29.50-£31.50 dB&B⇨♠£45-£48 🍴
CTV 24P 1🚗
V ♥ ♨ Lunch £6.50-£10.25&alc Dinner £6.50-£10.25&alc Last dinner 9pm
CONF. Thtr 250 Class 120 Board 50 Del £49.50
Credit Cards [1][2][3][5]

★ ★✿✿ MARSH COUNTRY
Eyton HR6 0AG (leave B4361 signposted Eyton & Lucton, continue along lane until the common, hotel on the right) ☎(0568) 613952

Situated in a delightful rural location, with a pretty garden, this small hotel comprises 3 buildings in one, the oldest part a 14th-century timbered house. The friendly owners, Jacqueline and Martin Gilleland, run the place almost entirely on their own, Jacqueline concentrating on the kitchen and Martin on the front of house. Most bedrooms are quite compact, but they are tastefully decorated and have all modern facilities. Downstairs, a barn with a flagstone floor and a high beamed ceiling has been converted into a spacious and comfortable lounge, and next door is the equally comfortable lounge bar. The L-shaped dining room is the lovely setting for the choice of fixed price menus featuring honest and enjoyable British food. Smoking is only allowed in the lounges.

5⇨♠✂in all bedrooms CTV in all bedrooms T
✘ (ex guide dogs) sB&B⇨♠£74 dB&B⇨♠£100-£110 🍴
15P 🚗 ✿ xmas
✂✱Lunch£17.50-£18.50Dinner£27.50Lastdinner9pm
Credit Cards [1][2][3] £

LERWICK
See **Shetland**

L'ETACQ
See **Jersey** under **Channel Islands**

LETHAM Fife Map 11 NO31
★★★ 58% Fernie Castle
KY7 7RU ☎(0337) 810381 FAX (0337) 810422

Fernie Castle lies in its own wooded grounds complete with a small lake. A real castle, it has evolved over the centuries, and the vaulted Keep Bar and the tower have the most historic associations. Popular with tourists, golfers and business guests, the bedrooms are generally of contemporary design.

15rm(2fb)1⇩ CTV in all bedrooms ® T ✱ sB&B⇩£37-£43 dB&B⇩£58-£98 ⇩
80P ⇩ ✻ xmas
V ⇩ ⇩ ✻ ✱ Lunch £9-£15.50 Dinner £16.50-£19.50&alc Last dinner 9.30pm
CONF. Thtr 140 Class 50 Board 20 Del from £70
Credit Cards [1][2][3][4]

LETTERFINLAY Highland *Inverness-shire* Map 14 NN29
★★ 64% Letterfinlay Lodge
PH34 4DZ (7m N of Spean Bridge, on A82)
☎Spean Bridge(0397) 712622
Closed Nov-Feb

This popular family-run holiday hotel enjoys a spectacular outlook over Loch Lochy. The public rooms include a well stocked snug bar, a cosy television room and an attractive sun lounge. Bedrooms vary in size and style, and are for the most part simply appointed.
13rm(11⇩)(5fb) CTV in all bedrooms ® ✻ sB&Bfr£20 sB&B⇩£20-£39.50 dB&Bfr£40 dB&B⇩£40-£79 ⇩
⊞ CTV 100P ⇩ ✻ ♪
V ⇩ ✻ Bar Lunch £2.50-£20alc Dinner £17.50 Last dinner 8.30pm
Credit Cards [1][2][3][4][5] £

LEVEN Fife Map 11 NO30
★★★ 56% New Caledonian
81 High St KY8 4NG ☎(0333) 424101 FAX (0333) 421241

This privately owned commercial hotel in the town centre offers functional accommodation which is beginning to show its age. Public areas include a split-level lounge and bar, small dining room and separate bistro, with informal service provided by local staff.
17⇩(1fb) CTV in all bedrooms ® ☆ T ✻ sB&B⇩£45-£50 dB&B⇩£60-£70 ⇩
(⊞ CTV 50P *xmas*
⇩ English & French V ⇩ ⇩ ✻ ✱ Lunch £6.95-£8.95&alc High tea £5.95-£8.95&alc Dinner £13.95-£16.95&alc Last dinner 9.30pm
CONF. Thtr 200 Del from £60
Credit Cards [1][2][3][5] £

LEWDOWN Devon Map 02 SX48

★★
★★ ❀❀❀ ⇩
LEWTRENCHARD MANOR
EX20 4PN ☎(056683) 256 & 222 FAX (056683) 332

Set in gardens in a quiet wooded valley, this 17th-century manor house is run by James and Sue Murray and their small team of staff as a haven of comfort, good food and hospitality. There are 2 restaurants, and head chef Patrick Salvadori creates a daily table d'hôte menu in addition to a short à la carte. Our inspector served

a duck and mushroom galantine with an orange and rosemary yoghurt sauce, followed by roast grouse with bacon and chick peas and a gamey red wine sauce.
8rm(7⇩)2⇩ CTV in all bedrooms T
50P ⇩ ✻ ♪ croquet clay pigeon shooting nc8yrs
⇩ English & French V ⇩ ⇩ ✻ ✱ Lunch £16 Dinner £24.50&alc Last dinner 9.30pm
CONF. Thtr 60 Class 60 Board 60
Credit Cards [1][2][3][5]

LEWES East Sussex Map 05 TQ41
★★★ 54% Shelleys
High St BN7 1XS ☎(0273) 472361 FAX (0273) 483152

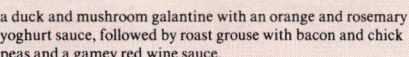

This former inn, dating from 1526, was converted into a manor house and became the home of the Shelley family in 1663. Now providing comfortable accommodation and modern facilities, the hotel also has a pretty restaurant offering a choice of menus.
21⇩ ✻ 2⇩ CTV in all bedrooms T ✻ sB⇩£65-£75 dB⇩£99-£130 (room only) ⇩
(25P 3⇩ ✻ *xmas*
⇩ European V ⇩ ⇩ ✻ Lunch £13.50&alc Dinner £18&alc Last dinner 9.15pm
CONF. Thtr 50 Class 20 Board 28 Del from £120
Credit Cards [1][2][3][5]

See advertisement on page 347

Hotels with red star ratings are especially high quality.

12 miles south of Tay Bridge on A914 in the heart of Historic Kingdom of Fife, Home of Golf, Fernie Castle is a privately owned Country Hotel in 25 acres of mature grounds with its own small loch.

15 comfortable en suite bedrooms with all facilities. Only fresh local produce is used in our creative Traditional Scottish menus. Stylish public rooms, candlelit dungeon bar, and Balfour function suite with unique circular ballroom. Ideal for weddings, functions, conferences or a break from the bustle of life.

AA ★ ★ ★
STB ⇩⇩⇩ Commended   Taste of Scotland

Letham · Nr. Cupar · Fife KY7 7RU
Tel: (033 781) 381 · Fax: (033 781) 422

Lewes - Lifton

★★ 63% *White Hart*
55 High St BN7 1XE ☎(0273) 474676 & 476694
FAX (0273) 476695

Dating from the 16th century, this former coaching inn retains much of its original character, while being slowly upgraded. In addition to the original beamed bedrooms, a bedroom extension has recently been added, and there are new conference and banqueting suites. Other facilities include a coffee shop lounge, carvery, Conservatory Restaurant, beamed bar, roof garden and foyer lounge. Room service is available as well as a night porter, and an indoor leisure centre is under construction.
19rm(14⇨↑)Annexe21⇨↑(4fb)2⊞ CTV in all bedrooms ®T
⟨ 50P
♀ English & French V ✓ ⎓ ✗ Last dinner 10pm
Credit Cards [1][2][3][5]

LEWIS, ISLE OF Western Isles *Ross & Cromarty* Map **13**

STORNOWAY Map **13** NB43

★★★ 67% *Caberfeidh*
PA87 2EU ☎(0851) 702604 FAX (0851) 705572

Situated on the edge of town, this modern purpose-built holiday and business hotel also caters for the conference and function markets. Upgraded public areas include a choice of bars, a comfortable foyer lounge and an attractive split-level restaurant. Bedrooms, apart from a few singles, are spacious, offering comfortable modern appointments and a wide range of amenities.
46⇨↑(36fb) CTV in all bedrooms ®T
Lift ⟨ ⊞ CTV 100P ✿
♀ French V ✓ ⎓ Last dinner 9.30pm
Credit Cards [1][2][3][4][5]

LEYBURN North Yorkshire Map **07** SE19

★ 58% *Golden Lion*
Market Place DL8 5AS ☎Wensleydale(0969) 22161 FAX (0969) 23836
Closed 25 & 26 Dec

This popular hotel was built in 1765 and overlooks Leyburn's well known market square. The bedrooms are mostly furnished in stripped pine with plain décor, and are equipped with modern amenities. The bars and eating areas are often busy, especially on market days.
14rm(10⇨1↑)(5fb) CTV in all bedrooms ®T sB&B£20-£23 sB&B⇨↑£21-£24 dB&B£40-£46 dB&B⇨↑£44-£48 ⊟
Lift 130P ⇔
♀ English & Continental V ✓ ⎓ Lunch £7-£10 Dinner £12.50&alc Last dinner 9pm
Credit Cards [1][3][4] £

LEYLAND Lancashire Map **07** SD52

★★★ 56% *Leyland Resort*
Leyland Way PR5 2JX (from junct 28 of M6 turn left at end of slip road)
☎Preston(0772) 422922 FAX (0772) 622284

This purpose built modern hotel offers practical accommodation which, while offering modern facilities, is beginning to show its age.
93⇨↑(6fb)✗in 10 bedrooms CTV in all bedrooms ®✗T✴ sB⇨↑£55-£60 dB⇨↑£65-£70 (room only) ⊟
⟨ CTV 150P ⌧ (heated) snooker sauna solarium *xmas*
♀ English & French V ✓ ⎓ ✗ Lunch £9-£10&alc Dinner £14-£15&alc Last dinner 9pm
Credit Cards [1][2][3][5] £

LICHFIELD Staffordshire Map **07** SK10

★★★ 63% *Little Barrow*
Beacon St WS13 7AR (on A5206) ☎(0543) 414500 FAX (0543) 415734

This privately run hotel close to the city centre and cathedral has a friendly informal atmosphere and offers spacious modern bedrooms, a comfortable lounge bar and attractive restaurant with a choice of menus.
24⇨↑ CTV in all bedrooms ®T✗ (ex guide dogs) ✴ sB&B⇨↑£55 dB&B⇨↑£65 ⊟
⟨ ⊞ CTV 70P
♀ French V ✓ Lunch £8.50&alc Dinner £11.50&alc Last dinner 9.30pm
Credit Cards [1][2][3][5]

★★ 65% *Fradley Arms*
Rykneld St, Fradley WS13 8RD (on A38, 3m NE)
☎Burton-on-Trent(0283) 790186 & 790977 FAX (0283) 791464
This old coaching inn, now a family-run hotel, stands in a large garden just north of Lichfield. Bedrooms have been modernised to provide comfortable accommodation, and meals can be taken either in the cottage-style restaurant or in the attractive, beamed lounge bar where the blackboard menu offers a good daily choice.
6rm(1⇨1↑)(1fb) CTV in all bedrooms ®T
CTV 200P ✿ childrens play area
♀ English & French V ✓ ⎓ Last dinner 9.30pm
Credit Cards [1][2][3][5]

★★ 64% *The Olde Corner House*
Walsall Rd, Muckley Corner WS14 0BG (at junct of A5/A461)
☎(0543) 372182 FAX (0543) 372211
Brian and Pamela Higgins have extensively renovated this old inn, parts of which date back to 1683. There is a choice of bars and 2 restaurants, which between them offer an extensive range of dishes.
11⇨↑✗ in all bedrooms CTV in all bedrooms ®T✗ ✴ sB&B⇨↑£25-£37 dB&B⇨↑£45-£65 ⊟
65P ✿ *xmas*
♀ International V ✓ ⎓ ✗ ✴ Lunch £6-£10&alc Dinner £6-£10&alc Last dinner 10pm
Credit Cards [1][3]

★★ 61% *Angel Croft*
Beacon St WS13 7AA ☎(0543) 258737 FAX (0543) 415605
Closed 25 & 26 Dec RS Sun evenings
This privately owned and personally run hotel is close to both cathedral and city centre. Bedrooms, some in the adjacent Georgian town house having views of the cathedral, are traditionally furnished and have a period feel.
11rm(3⇨6↑)Annexe8⇨↑(2fb)1⊞ CTV in all bedrooms ®T ✗ (ex guide dogs)
60P ✿
♀ ⎓ Last dinner 9pm
Credit Cards [1][3][5]

LIFTON Devon Map **02** SX38

★★★ ✿✿71% *Arundell Arms*
PL16 0AA ☎(0566) 784666 FAX (0566) 784494

Closed 2 days Xmas

This hospitable old coaching inn on the edge of Dartmoor, with 20 miles of fishing waters, is popular for sporting holidays, though its comfortable bedrooms with modern amenities are equally suited to business guests. The attractive lounge and bar have flagstone floors and log fires, while the elegant restaurant offers a choice of carefully considered menus. Imaginative dishes, prepared by chef Philip Burgess, include local fish and game.
24⇨↑Annexe5⇨↑ CTV in all bedrooms ®T
sB&B⇨↑£39-£57 dB&B⇨↑£78-£92 ⊟
80P ⇔ ✿ ♪ skittle alley games room

Lifton

♡ English & French V ♢ ⌐ ⊁ Lunch £15&alc Dinner £23&alc Last dinner 9.30pm
CONF. Thtr 100 Class 36 Board 46 Del from £65
Credit Cards [1][2][3][5]

See advertisement on page 349

★★ 60% **Lifton Cottage**
PL16 0DR (off A30) ☎(0566) 784289
This family-run hotel offers a relaxed and informal atmosphere, and easy access to all parts of Devon and Cornwall. Public rooms include a comfortable lounge, a separate character bar, and a small restaurant offering an à la carte menu of steak house type dishes.
13rm(10⇨)(3fb) CTV in all bedrooms ® T ✱ sB&Bfr£25 sB&B⇨♠£29.95 dB&B⇨♠£49.95 ♬
CTV 25P ✿
V ♢ ⌐ ⊁ ✱ Lunch £6.50-£6.95 Dinner £11.95&alc Last dinner 9pm
Credit Cards [1][2][3][5]

★ ⊛70% **Thatched Cottage**
Sprytown PL16 0AY (100yds from Sprytown Cross x-roads)
☎(0566) 784224 FAX (0566) 784334
A friendly, hospitable atmosphere pervades this pretty, 16th-century thatched cottage set in 2.5 acres of well tended, flower-filled grounds. Charming public areas in the main building retain original features such as beams and inglenook fireplaces, and an attractive restaurant provides imaginative à la carte menus and a good, balanced wine list. Freshly decorated bedrooms with smart modern facilities are in a converted stable block across the garden.
Annexe5⇨♠ CTV in all bedrooms ® ✖ sB&B⇨♠£35-£49.50 dB&B⇨♠£70-£90 ♬
CTV 12P ⊞ ✿ nc8yrs
♡ International V ♢ ⌐ Last dinner 9.30pm
Credit Cards [1][2][3][5]

We take care of YOU at

HOAR CROSS HALL

THE HEALTH SPA RESORT IN A STATELY HOME

**Hoar Cross Hall,
Hoar Cross, Near Yoxall
Staffordshire DE13 8QS
Tel: (028375) 671   Fax: (028375) 652**

Superb amenities complete relaxation in elegant luxury ★★★★ standard.

L

Beacon Street, Lichfield, Staffordshire
Telephone: (0543) 414500

A modern and popular hotel offering old world charm combined with every comfort you would expect of a first class hotel. Situated in Beacon Street, the hotel is in the perfect position for the business man or the tourist. There is a large car park to the rear and most of the city's business, tourist and shopping areas are within walking distance.

★★★AA

Shelleys Hotel
A Thistle Country House Hotel

High Street, Lewes BN7 1XS
Tel: 0273 472361   Fax: 0273 483152

Your choice in Lewes

For Reservations at over 100
Mount Charlotte Thistle Hotels
Telephone London: 071 937 8033.

Limpley Stoke - Lincoln

LIMPLEY STOKE (NEAR BATH) Wiltshire Map 03 ST76

★★★ 69% Cliffe
Crowe Hill BA3 6HY ☎(0225) 723226 FAX (0225) 723871

An elegant Bath stone property, th hotel stands in an elevated position overlooking the Avon valley. New proprietors Barbara and Richard Okill are working hard to restore the lovely gardens and are gradually redecorating the interior of the house. The spacious bedrooms are equipped with every modern facility, and a comfortable guests' lounge and small bar are provided. Chef Peter Spittals is responsible for the interesting dishes offered from varied menus.

11⇌ ♠(3fb)1♛ CTV in all bedrooms ® T sB&B⇌ ♠£66.50-£77 dB&B⇌ ♠£77-£105 ♬
40P ♨ ❋ ⌇ (heated) xmas
♡ English & French V ♢ ♉ ⚒ Lunch £14-£25 Dinner £15&alc Last dinner 9.30pm
Credit Cards ① ② ③

LINCOLN Lincolnshire Map 08 SK97

★★★★ 63% The White Hart
Bailgate LN1 3AR ☎(0522) 526222 FAX (0522) 531798

FORTE Heritage

This 15th-century inn, associated with Richard II (whose emblem was a white hart), is between the minster and castle walls and approached along cobbled lanes. Public areas include a charming lounge with a decorative fireplace and furnished – like the bedrooms – with antiques and reproduction pieces, a small panelled bar and an elegant restaurant. More informal meals are served in the Orangery.

48⇌ ♠(4fb)¥ in 18 bedrooms CTV in all bedrooms ® T ✱ sB⇌ ♠£75-£80 dB⇌ ♠£95-£180 (room only) ♬
Lift 《 60P 35♨ ⌇ ♪ xmas
♡ English & Continental V ♢ ♉ ⚒ ¥ Lunch £7.95-£10.95&alc Dinner fr£17.95 Last dinner 10pm
Credit Cards ① ② ③ ⑤

★★★★ 64% Washingborough Hall Country House
Church Hill, Washingborough LN4 1BE (3m E B1190) ☎(0522) 790340 FAX (0522) 792936

Washingborough Hall is a stone-built Georgian house set in 3 acres of gardens. The emphasis is on old-fashioned comfort and friendly service from the resident proprietors and their local staff. The bedrooms, some rather compact, are furnished in keeping with the house, including some period pieces and a relaxing atmosphere prevails in the bar, lounge and dining room.

14⇌ ♠♛¥ in 2 bedrooms CTV in all bedrooms ® T sB&B⇌ ♠£49-£59 dB&B⇌ ♠£69-£85 ♬
50P ♨ ❋ ⌇ (heated)
♡ International V ♢ ♉ ⚒ Sunday Lunch £7.50-£12.50 Dinner £14.50-£21.50alc Last dinner 8.30pm
Credit Cards ① ② ③ ⑤ £

★★★ 60% Moor Lodge
Sleaford Rd LN4 1HU ☎(0522) 791366 FAX (0522) 794389
(For full entry see Branston)

CONSORT HOTELS

★★ 69% Hillcrest
15 Lindum Ter LN2 5RT ☎(0522) 510182 FAX (0522) 510182
Closed 20 Dec-3 Jan

ExecGroup

Situated close to the city centre, overlooking parkland to the rear, this converted Victorian rectory is elegantly decorated and furnished throughout. A peaceful atmosphere prevails from the comfortable bar lounge with its adjoining conservatory to the bright, individually designed modern bedrooms.

17⇌ ♠(4fb)¥ in 6 bedrooms CTV in all bedrooms ® T sB&B⇌ ♠£34-£45 dB&B⇌ ♠£56-£62.50 ♬
8P
♡ International V ♢ ♉ ⚒ ✱ Bar Lunch £7.45-£9.50alc Dinner £11.70-£15.25alc Last dinner 8.45pm
Credit Cards ① ② ③ £

★★ 64% Castle
Westgate LN1 3AS (opp castle) ☎(0522) 538801 FAX (0522) 510291

Situated close to the cathedral and the shopping area. Though modestly furnished, the bedrooms are quite spacious and comfortable. The open plan lounge bar and restaurant are attractive and the hotel's great strength is in the warm welcome and friendly, attentive service.

15⇌ ♠Annexe4♠(2fb) CTV in all bedrooms ® T sB&B⇌ ♠£38-£48 dB&B⇌ ♠£48-£60 ♬
21P xmas
♡ Continental V ♢ ♉ Lunch £5.95-£6.70 High tea £5.95 Dinner £7.50-£14.50alc Last dinner 9.30pm
Credit Cards ① ③ ⑤ £

★★ 64% Loudor
37 Newark Rd, North Hykeham LN6 8RB (3m SW A1434) ☎(0522) 680333 & 500474 FAX (0522) 680403

This small and friendly owner-run hotel provides very well maintained accommodation, popular with commercial guests.

9⇌ ♠Annexe1♠(1fb) CTV in all bedrooms ® T ✈ ✱ sB&B⇌ ♠£28-£32 dB&B⇌ ♠£36-£40
12P ♨
♡ English & French ♢ ✱ Dinner £8.95-£12.95 Last dinner 8.15pm
Credit Cards ① ② ③ ⑤

Courtyard by Marriott
Brayford Side North LN1 1YW
☎(0522) 544244 FAX (0522) 560805

COURTYARD Marriott

Well furnished guest bedrooms have en suite bathrooms, remote control CTV and direct-dial telephone at this modern hotel, and there is an informal restaurant and bar. For more details about Courtyard by Marriott, consult the Contents page, under Hotel Groups.

95♠ dB⇌ ♠fr£58 (room only)

Forte Posthouse
Eastgate LN2 1PN ☎(0522) 520341 FAX (0522) 510780

FORTE Posthouse

Suitable for both the business and leisure traveller, this bright hotel provides modern accommodation in well equipped bedrooms with en suite bathrooms. For more details about Forte Posthouse hotels, consult the Contents page, under Hotel Groups.

70⇌ ♠ ✱ B⇌ ♠£41.50-£53.50 (room only)
CONF. Thtr 90 Class 50 Board 40 Del £89.50

Travel Inn
Lincoln Rd, Cantwick Hill LN4 2RF (on the junc of B1188 to Branston and B1131/A607 to Bracebridge Heath) ☎(0522) 525216

Purpose-built accommodation offers spacious and well equipped bedrooms, all with en suite bathrooms. Meals may be taken at the nearby family restaurant and pub. For more details about Travel Inns, consult the Contents page, under Hotel Groups.

40⇌ ♠ ✱ B⇌ ♠£33.50 (room only)

Red star hotels are each highlighted by a pink tinted panel.

LISKEARD Cornwall & Isles of Scilly Map 02 SX26

★★

★★✿✿✿⚜ **WELL HOUSE**
St Keyne PL14 4RN
☎(0579) 342001

This lovely house enjoys an idyllic setting, surrounded by naturally cultivated grounds and gardens. Bright, airy public rooms include a comfortable lounge and a cosy little bar, while the spacious bedrooms are individually designed and stylishly appointed. Renowned for its hospitality, the hotel is also popular for the quality meals produced by chef David Woolfall and his small team. The daily menu, sensibly sized and well balanced, is based as far as possible on local ingredients and features honest, unfussy dishes chosen to represent the best of each season. A spring meal, for example, could include a hot mousseline of crab and lobster served with a creamy shellfish sauce, then nicely cooked medallions of lamb accompanied by a little aubergine moussaka and a rosemary jus; an excellent crème brûlée with chopped pears preceding the finale of coffee and good petits fours.

7🛏🛁(1fb) CTV in all bedrooms T sB&B🛏🛁£60 dB&B🛏🛁£67.50-£105 Continental breakfast ♬
30P 🚗 ✿ ⚲ (heated) ♫ (hard) croquet
V ❀ ℒ ✱ Lunch £21 Dinner £19.95-£29.70 Last dinner 9pm
Credit Cards [1][3]

★★ 60% **Country Castle**
Station Rd PL14 4EB ☎(0579) 342694
Closed Jan RS Feb

A friendly, easy going establishment, run by charming resident proprietor Mrs Rosemary Wilmott, the hotel is set in 2.5 acres of well tended gardens with views out across Looe Valley. Bedrooms are individually decorated, public areas are bright and nicely presented, and the evening meal is wholesome and home-cooked.
10🛏🛁(1fb) CTV in all bedrooms ® T ✱ sB&B🛏🛁£42 dB&B🛏🛁£59-£72 ♬
50P ✿ ⚲ croquet boules
❀ English & French V ❀ ℒ ✱ Lunch fr£12 Dinner fr£16.50&alc Last dinner 7.45pm
Credit Cards [1][3] £

★★ 57% **Lord Eliot**
Castle St PL14 3AQ (take A38 from Plymouth into Liskeard, hotel first left past St Martins Church) ☎(0579) 342717 FAX (0579) 347593

Conveniently close to major routes and just away from the centre of town, this commercial hotel is best suited to short-stay clientèle. Bedrooms are compact and modestly furnished but reasonably equipped. Public areas are more traditional in style.
15rm(4🛏🛁10🛁)(3fb)✻ in 2 bedrooms CTV in all bedrooms ® T ✱ sB&Bfr£27 sB&B🛏🛁fr£27 dB&B🛏🛁fr£54 ♬
《 CTV 60P xmas
❀ English & French V ❀ ℒ ✱ Lunch £7-£20&alc High tea £2-£5 Dinner £11.50-£25&alc Last dinner 9.30pm
CONF. Thtr 250 Class 100 Board 80 Del from £50
Credit Cards [1][2][3][5] £

For key to symbols see the Bookmark.

LITTLEBOURNE Kent Map 05 TR25

★★ 59% *The Bow Window Inn*
High St CT3 1ST ☎Canterbury(0227) 721264

This 300-year-old cottage hotel and restaurant has been thoughtfully modernised and well furnished throughout. There is a beamed bar and in the restaurant the atmosphere is relaxed and informal.
8🛏🛁🛁(2fb)2♬ CTV in all bedrooms ® ✈ (ex guide dogs) 20P
❀ English & French V ❀ ℒ Last dinner 9.30pm
Credit Cards [1][2][3][5]

LITTLE HALLINGBURY
See **Bishop's Stortford**

LITTLE LANGDALE Cumbria Map 07 NY30

★★ 64% *Three Shires Inn*
LA22 9NZ ☎Langdale(05394) 37215
Closed Xmas-Jan RS mid Nov-mid Feb

Built in 1872 from local slate, this family-run inn, 5 miles west of Ambleside, is an ideal base for the touring holiday-maker. Bedrooms are bright and airy, though they aren't large and lack amenities such as TVs and telephones. Public areas include a choice of lounges, one with colour TV; a character bar with ceiling beams and a flagstone floor, and a small dining room.
11rm(7🛏🛁)(1fb) ® ✈
CTV 20P 2♬ 🚗
❀ British & Continental ❀ ℒ ✱ Last dinner 8pm

Satellite television – look for this symbol
in the directory entries.

THE ARUNDELL ARMS HOTEL
Lifton, Devon. PL16 0AA
★★★ 71% ✿✿
Tel: 0566 784666 Fax: 0566 784494

A 250-year-old former coaching inn near Dartmoor, now a famous sporting hotel with 20 miles of our own salmon and trout rivers, pheasant and snipe shoots, riding and golf. Log-fire comfort with superb food and wines; winter gourmet evenings by our French-trained chef. Splendid centre for exploring Devon and Cornwall. Excellent conference facilities.

Details: Anne Voss-Bark.
One third of a mile off A30, 38 miles from M5 motorway at Exeter.

Little Weighton - Livingston

LITTLE WEIGHTON Humberside Map 08 SE93

★★★ ♨ 65% Rowley Manor
Rowley Rd HU20 3XR ☎Hull(0482) 848348 FAX (0482) 849900
A Georgian house, set in 34 acres of parkland, lawns and rose gardens, which offers a quiet relaxing environment, where the resident owners and staff provide genuinely friendly service. The individually styled bedrooms are generally of a comfortable size with the majority graced by period furniture. The spacious public rooms have a tasteful mix of traditional furnishings which enhance the character of the house.
16⇨♙2⽥ CTV in all bedrooms T ✱ sB&B⇨♙£55-£60 dB&B⇨♙£70-£85 ♬
(80P ✿ solarium croquet *xmas*
♡ International V ♡ ⚲ ✱ Bar Lunch £2.95-£10.75
Credit Cards ①②③⑤

LIVERPOOL Merseyside Map 07 SJ39
See also **Blundellsands**

★★★★59% Liverpool Moat House
Paradise St L1 8JD ☎051-709 0181 FAX 051-709 2706

This modern 9-storey hotel near the Albert Dock continues to be upgraded. The majority of bedrooms feature 2 large beds and modern facilities, and the most recently decorated have smart, if compact, bathrooms. Public areas offer a choice of eating and drinking options, the informal Terrace Restaurant and Bar providing all day service in bistro-style surroundings.
251⇨♙(202fb)⚲in 110 bedrooms CTV in all bedrooms ® T ✱ sB&B⇨♙£90 dB&B⇨♙£116 ♬
Lift (⽥ ♪ ▣ (heated) sauna solarium gymnasium whirlpool *xmas*
♡ English & French V ♡ ⚲ Lunch £10-£12&alc High tea fr£8.70 Dinner £14.25&alc Last dinner 10.30pm
CONF. Thtr 450 Class 210 Board 152 Del £145
Credit Cards ①②③④⑤ £

★★★★51% Atlantic Tower Thistle
Chapel St L3 9RE ☎051-227 4444 FAX 051-236 3973

Close to the Liver Building, this modern and unusual concrete tower hotel is currently undergoing renovation. Apart from the corner bedrooms and the attractive top-floor suites, rooms and bathrooms are compact, those on the lower floors currently providing the best standards. Public areas offer a choice of restaurants and bars.
226⇨♙(6fb)⚲in 24 bedrooms CTV in all bedrooms ® T ✱ sB&B⇨♙£79-£89 dB&B⇨♙£89-£99 ♬
Lift (⽥ 60P *xmas*
♡ European V ♡ ⚲ ✱ Lunch fr£12.95&alc Dinner fr£18.25&alc Last dinner 10.15pm
CONF. Thtr 120 Class 70 Board 30 Del from £80
Credit Cards ①②③④⑤

★★★52% St George's
St John's Precinct, Lime St L1 1NQ (opp Lime Street railway station) ☎051-709 7090 FAX 051-709 0137

Part of a shopping centre built opposite Lime Street station in the early seventies, this city centre hotel provides functional accommodation which is now showing signs of age.
155⇨♙⚲in 80 bedrooms CTV in all bedrooms ® T ✱ sB⇨♙£49.50 dB⇨♙£49.50 (room only) ♬
Lift (⽥ 15P 20🚗 *xmas*
V ♡ ⚲ ✱ Lunch £7.95 Dinner £12.95 Last dinner 9pm
CONF. Thtr 250 Class 280 Board 80 Del £80
Credit Cards ①②③⑤

★★ 63% *Grange*
Holmfield Rd, Aigburth L19 3PG ☎051-427 2950 FAX 051-427 9055
Set in a quiet residential area of Aigburth, this extended Victorian gabled house offers rather mixed standards of bedrooms, varying in size and style, but the inviting public areas are comfortably furnished with leather armchairs. Smart staff provide friendly and helpful service, particularly in the professionally run restaurant where interesting and enjoyable meals are served.
25⇨♙(1fb)4⽥ CTV in all bedrooms ® T ✕ (ex guide dogs) CTV 50P ✿
♡ French V ♡ ⚲ ⚲ Last dinner 9pm
Credit Cards ①②③⑤

★★ 57% Green Park
4/6 Greenbank Dr L17 1AN ☎051-733 3382
Two large semi-detached houses have been converted into a private hotel. The bedrooms, some on the ground floor are all quite spacious and many have benefited from recent refurbishment. The modestly furnished public areas include a lounge bar, which is popular with locals, and a simple lounge.
23rm(21⇨♙)(3fb) CTV in all bedrooms ® T sB&B⇨♙£24-£32 dB&B⇨♙£32-£42
(⽥ CTV 25P ✿
V ♡ ⚲ Lunch £5.25-£8.27 Dinner £5.25-£13.95&alc Last dinner 9.30pm
CONF. Thtr 60 Class 40 Board 20 Del from £30
Credit Cards ①②③⑤ £

Campanile
Chaloner St, Queens Dock ☎051-709 8104 FAX 051-709 8725

A nearby bar and bistro restaurant provides refreshments for travellers staying at this modern accommodation building. Bedrooms are well equipped and have en suite bathrooms. For more details about Campanile, consult the Contents page, under Hotel Groups.
78⇨♙ B⇨♙£35.75 (room only)
CONF. Thtr 35 Class 35 Board 25 Del from £42.80

Travel Inn
Queensdrive, West Derby L13 0DL (on A5058)
☎051-228 4724

Purpose-built accommodation offers spacious and well equipped bedrooms, all with en suite bathrooms. Meals may be taken at the nearby family restaurant and pub. For more details about Travel Inns, consult the Contents page, under Hotel Groups.
40⇨♙ ✱ B⇨♙£33.50 (room only)

LIVINGSTON Lothian Map 11 NT06

Hilton National Livingston
Almondvale East EH54 6QB ☎(0506) 31222 FAX (0506) 34666

This is a bright, modern hotel with an informal restaurant, aimed at both the business and leisure guest. All bedrooms have en-suite bathrooms and a range of modern facilities. For more information about Hilton National, consult the Contents page, under Hotel Groups.
120⇨♙✱ B⇨♙£60 (room only)
CONF. Thtr 120 Class 60 Board 40 Del £105

Red star hotels are each highlighted
by a pink tinted panel.

LIZARD, THE Cornwall & Isles of Scilly Map 02 SW71

★★ 69% Housel Bay
Housel Cove TR12 7PG ☎The Lizard(0326) 290417 FAX (0326) 290359
Closed Jan-10 Feb

This solid stone house in an isolated cliff top setting has a wonderful view across the sea and Lizard promontory from its comfortable lounge and popular bar as well as from many bedrooms. Guests are offered a friendly and attentive welcome by proprietors of many years' standing.

23⇨⇧♠(1fb)2🛏⊁in 2 bedrooms CTV in all bedrooms ®✌T✱ sB&B⇨⇧♠£25-£30 dB&B⇨⇧♠£50-£90 ❒
Lift CTV 25P 4🎾 (£3 per night) ✿ xmas
♡ International V ✿ ♫ ⊁ Sunday Lunch fr£7.50 Dinner fr£16&alc Last dinner 9pm
Credit Cards 1 3

LLANARMON DYFFRYN CEIRIOG Clwyd Map 07 SJ13

★★ 69% West Arms
LL20 7LD (Welsh Rarebits) ☎(069176) 665 FAX (069176) 622

This 16th-century farmhouse is in the centre of the village deep in Ceiriog Valley. Low ceilings, exposed beams, timbers and log fires characterise the building. There is a separate TV lounge and 2 bars, one with an ornately carved confessional box. The front bedrooms have fine period furniture while the back rooms are furnished in a more modern style. The menu offers just 3 choices, but the food is fresh and enjoyable.

14⇨⇧♠(1fb)⊁in 5 bedrooms CTV in 2 bedrooms
CTV 30P 2🎾 ♣ ✿ ♪
♡ English & Continental V ✿ ♫ ⊁ Last dinner 9pm
Credit Cards 1 2 3 5

LLANBEDR Gwynedd Map 06 SH52

★★ 61% Ty Mawr
LL45 2NH ☎(034123) 440
Closed 24-26 Dec

Once a farmhouse, this small, family-run hotel lies in its own pretty grounds opposite the River Artro. The stone-floored bar has a cheerful wood-burning stove and attractive cane furnishings, the lounge is modern and comfortable with an open fire, and there is a cosy pine furnished restaurant. Bedrooms are mostly compact.

10⇨⇧♠(2fb) CTV in all bedrooms ® ✱ sB&B⇨⇧♠£20-£27 dB&B⇨⇧♠£40-£54 ❒
CTV 30P ♣ ✿ ♪ ⚙
♡ Welsh English & French V ✿ ♫ ⊁ ✱ Lunch £1.60-£8 Dinner fr£6&alc Last dinner 8.30pm

★★ 🏛 60% Cae Nest Hall
LL45 2NL ☎(034123) 349
Closed Jan (ex New Year)

This 15th-century manor house enjoys a peaceful location on the outskirts of the village, within 3 acres of grounds. Owners Anita and Robert Mann offer friendly and informal service, and in the evenings, Robert, a talented pianist and organist, regularly entertains guests in the lounge.

10⇨⇧♠(2fb)1🛏 CTV in all bedrooms ® sB&B⇨⇧♠£18-£26.50 dB&B⇨⇧♠£40-£53 ❒
12P ♣ ✿ xmas
♡ British & Continental V ⊁ Dinner £12&alc Last dinner 7.30pm

LLANBERIS Gwynedd Map 06 SH56

★★ 63% Padarn Lake
High St LL55 4SU (opp church)
☎(0286) 870260 FAX (0286) 870007

ExecGroup

Padarn Lake is a privately owned and personally run hotel in the town centre. Bedrooms are bright and modern, and some are quite

TŶ MAWR HOTEL
LLANBEDR, GWYNEDD 034123 440

★★

Ty Mawr is a fully licensed country house, set in a lovely garden, situated in Snowdonia National Park, near the sea and mountains. We have ten tastefully furnished bedrooms, all en-suite with central heating, tea-coffee making facilities, colour TV. Excellent food is served in the Dining Room, with Real Ale, Bar Meals, and Log fires to ensure a warm and friendly stay. Open all year.

★★★★ AA

ATLANTIC TOWER
THISTLE HOTEL

Chapel Street, Liverpool L3 9RE
Tel: 051-227 4444   Fax: 051-236 3973

Your choice in Liverpool

For Reservations at over 100
Mount Charlotte Thistle Hotels
Telephone London: 071 937 8033.

Llanberis - Llandrindod Wells

spacious. Public areas include a choice of bars and a traditionally furnished dining room where popular dishes, including locally caught fish, are served.
18⇨ℕ(4fb) CTV in all bedrooms ® T ✱ sB&B⇨ℕfr£29 dB&B⇨ℕfr£49 ₽
15P ✿ ✱ ♫ *xmas*
V ✿ ✱ Bar Lunch £1.20-£6.50 Dinner fr£10.95&alc Last dinner 9.30pm
Credit Cards 1 2 3 5

★**61%** *Gallt-y-Glyn*
Caernarfon Rd LL55 4EL (W on A4086) ☎(0286) 870370
Closed 25 Dec
Resident proprietors Helen and Peter Rayment provide informal, friendly and personal service at this small hotel. The bedrooms are quite compact but soundly maintained and the majority have fairly modern, albeit simple, furnishings. Public rooms include a cosy lounge with a welcoming real fire.
9rm(5ℕ)(1fb)⊁in 1 bedroom CTV in 1 bedroom ®
✈ (ex guide dogs) ✱ sB&B£18.50-£20 sB&Bℕfr£25 dB&B£35 dB&Bℕ£40 ₽
CTV 12P ⇔ ✿
V ⊁ ✱ Bar Lunch £3-£8 Dinner £10-£15 Last dinner 8pm
Credit Cards 1 3

LLANDDEINIOLEN Gwynedd Map **06** SH56
★★**71%** *Ty'n Rhos Country House*
Llanddeiniolen LL55 3AE (situated in the hamlet of Seion between B4366 and B4547) ☎Port Diorwic(0248) 670489 FAX (0248) 670079
Closed 2wks in Nov & 20 Dec-15 Jan
11⇨ℕ(1fb) CTV in all bedrooms ® T ✈ (ex guide dogs) sB&B⇨ℕ£30-£35 dB&B⇨ℕ£50-£70 ₽
14P ⇔ ✿ nc6yrs
V Dinner £16.50-£18.50 Last dinner 7pm
Credit Cards 1 3

LLANDEILO Dyfed Map **02** SN62
★★★**60%** *Cawdor Arms*
SA19 6EN ☎(0558) 823500
This Georgian building is at the heart of the market town. The elegant lounges and some of the bedrooms have changed little for many years, with rich colour schemes that some might consider somewhat overpowering. They are comfortable, though, and some bedrooms have recently been redecorated with lighter schemes. The restaurant offers a good range of food.
17⇨ℕ♪✱ CTV in all bedrooms
7P
♀ English & French ✿ ⚲
Credit Cards 1 2 3 5

If you have booked a meal in a hotel restaurant and cannot get there, remember you have a contractual obligation to cancel your booking.

LLANDRILLO Clwyd Map **06** SJ03

★★❀❀♨**76%** Tyddyn Llan Country House Hotel & Restaurant
LL21 0ST (on B4401, Corwen-Bala road) (Welsh Rarebits)
☎(049084) 264

Courtesy and Care 1994

Peter and Bridget Kindred promote an informal atmosphere, and the local staff are friendly and attentive, earning for Tyddyn Llan an AA Courtesy and Care Award this year. The hotel is set in its own attractive grounds in the beautiful Vale of Edeyrnion and has 3 elegant lounges where guests can relax. The individually styled bedrooms are furnished with antique and other period furniture. Dominic Gilbert has taken over as chef and our inspector enjoyed delicious quenelles of salmon mousse topped with hollandaise sauce, cream of leek and watercress soup followed by appetising Welsh lamb cutlets. Local produce is used when available and vegetarians are well catered for.
10⇨ℕ(2fb) T sB&B⇨ℕ£56.50-£60.50 dB&B⇨ℕ£88-£96 ₽
CTV 30P ⇔ ✿ ♪ croquet lawn *xmas*
V ✿ ⚲✱ Lunch £12 Dinner £21.50-£25 Last dinner 9.30pm
Credit Cards 1 3

LLANDRINDOD WELLS Powys Map **03** SO06
See also **Penybont**
★★★**62%** Hotel Metropole
Temple St LD1 5DY (off A483) ☎(0597) 823700 FAX (0597) 824828

A family-run, traditional hotel in the heart of this famous spa town, the Metropole boasts a popular leisure complex and beauty salon. Some bedrooms had recently been refurbished to a very good standard at the time of the inspector's visit, and all were due to have been upgraded by 1994.
121⇨ℕ(2fb)⊁in 10 bedrooms CTV in all bedrooms ® T sB&B⇨ℕ£57-£77 dB&B⇨ℕ£77-£97 ₽
Lift (150P ✿ ▣ (heated) sauna solarium steamroom whirlpool beauty salon *xmas*
♀ English & Continental V ✿ ⚲ Lunch £8.15-£9.75 High tea fr£4.75 Dinner fr£16.50 Last dinner 9pm
CONF. Thtr 300 Class 200 Board 140 Del from £65
Credit Cards 1 2 3 4 5

★★**68%** The Bell Country Inn
Llanyre LD1 6DY (1.5m NW on Rhayader Road)
☎(0597) 823959 FAX (0597) 825899
In the village of Llanyre, this busy country inn provides bright, well furnished bedrooms. There is a popular bar serving food and also a choice of 2 restaurants.
9⇨ℕ(2fb)⊁in 1 bedroom CTV in all bedrooms ® ⚲ T sB&B⇨ℕ£32.50-£40 dB&B⇨ℕ£57.50-£65 ₽
20P ♪ *xmas*
♀ English & French V ✿ ⚲⊁ Lunch £7.50-£10&alc High tea fr£5.50 Dinner fr£14.95&alc Last dinner 10pm
Credit Cards 1 3

352

Llandrindod Wells - Llandudno

★★ 59% **Hotel Commodore**
Spa Rd LD1 5ER (in centre of town off A483 to left if travelling from south, right if travelling from north) ☎(0597) 822288 FAX (0597) 824828

A busy commercial and holiday hotel at the centre of this mid-Wales town, the Commodore offers bedrooms with, for the most part, dark fitted furniture. The lounge is spacious and there is a cosy bar. Guests have the use of the leisure centre at a nearby sister hotel, the Metropole.

32⇌Annexe22⇌(6fb) CTV in all bedrooms ® T ✱
sB&B⇌£46.50-£62 dB&B⇌£62 ♫
Lift (CTV 100P ✿ ⌧ (heated) squash *xmas*
♡ English & Continental V ♡ ⌧ Lunch fr£5.95 Dinner fr£14&alc Last dinner 9.15pm
Credit Cards [1][2][3]

LLANDUDNO Gwynedd Map **06** SH78

★★★
★★★❀❀⚜
BODYSGALLEN HALL
LL30 1RS (on A470 Llandudno link road)
☎Aberconwy(0492) 584466
FAX (0492) 582519

Synonymous with gracious living, this beautifully restored 17th-century house is set in some 200 acres of mature parkland, a mile from the popular resort with fine views of Conwy Castle and Snowdonia. Three comfortable sitting rooms are available with table service of drinks. Bedrooms are furnished in a style appropriate to the building, and include several cottage suites in the grounds. Mair Lewis has now established herself in the kitchen. The daily changing bill of fare offers a fixed price 3 or 4-course menu of country house cooking using local produce wherever possible, much from the kitchen garden. The poached brill enjoyed by our inspector had delicious flavour and texture, competing with Welsh lamb, honey roast duck and guinea fowl.

19⇌ ↑ Annexe9⇌ ↑ (3fb)1☐ CTV in all bedrooms ® T
sB⇌ ↑ fr£82 dB⇌ ↑ fr£135 (room only) ♫
(70P 1🎾 ✈ ✿ ♪ (hard) croquet nc8yrs *xmas*
V ♡ ⌧ ✂ Sunday Lunch £11-£15.90 Dinner fr£27 Last dinner 9.45pm
CONF. Thtr 45 Class 35 Board 26 Del from £125
Credit Cards [1][2][3][5]

★★★ 75% **Empire**
Church Walks LL30 2HE ☎(0492) 860555 FAX (0492) 860791
Closed 18-30 Dec
(Rosette awarded for dinner only)
The Maddocks family have run this popular hotel for more than 50 years, constantly investing in its improvement. Bedrooms are lavishly equipped with all manner of little luxuries – from sherry to video recorders. For meals, guests choose between the coffee shop overlooking the swimming pool or the restaurant where there is a daily table d'hôte 4 course dinner.
50⇌ ↑ Annexe8⇌ ↑ (7fb) CTV in all bedrooms ® ✤ T
✂ (ex guide dogs) sB&B⇌ ↑ £45-£55 dB&B⇌ ↑ £65-£85 ♫
Lift (40P 5🎾 (£5 per night) ⇌ ⌧ (heated) ⇌ (heated) sauna indoor/outdoor heated whirlpools ♪

♡ French V ♡ ⌧ ✂ Sunday Lunch £10.50 Dinner £16.85 Last dinner 9.30pm
CONF. Thtr 30 Class 20 Board 25 Del from £55
Credit Cards [1][2][3][5] £

★★★ 66% *Imperial*
The Promenade LL30 1AP ☎(0492) 877466
FAX (0492) 878043

This large and impressive Victorian hotel on the sea front offers a wide range of facilities for business and leisure guests. Well equipped bedrooms vary in size and style, most of them having good quality modern furniture. Lounge and bar areas are spacious and comfortable and the restaurant offers a good choice of dishes.
100⇌ ↑ (10fb) CTV in all bedrooms ® T
Lift (40P ⌧ (heated) snooker sauna solarium gymnasium steam room beauty therapist hairdressing ♪
V ♡ ⌧ ✂ Last dinner 9.30pm
Credit Cards [1][2][3][5]

See advertisement on page 355

★★★ 64% **Gogarth Abbey**
West Shore LL30 2QY ☎(0492) 876211 FAX (0492) 879881
Standing on the west shore with magnificent views of the Conwy Estuary, Anglesey and Snowdonia, Gogarth Abbey was built in 1862 by the Rev H G Liddell, whose daughter Alice was the inspiration for Lewis Carroll's Alice in Wonderland. Now a privately owned hotel, it provides spacious public areas and well equipped bedrooms.
40⇌ ↑ (4fb) CTV in all bedrooms ® T ✂ (ex guide dogs)
sB&B⇌ ↑ £30-£38 dB&B⇌ ↑ £60-£76 ♫
(40P ✿ ⌧ (heated) sauna solarium table tennis boules croquet putting *xmas*

Church Walks, Llandudno LL30 2HE
Tel: (0492) 860555
Fax: (0492) 860791

Long standing family run hotel. Luxury accommodation, antiques and fine painting throughout. All bedrooms with Italian marble jacuzzi bathrooms, satellite television/video (free video library). All modern amenities. Attractive restaurant, traditional cooking using finest local ingredients. AA rosette awarded. Coffee shop, Cocktail Bar, Indoor and Outdoor Heated Pools, Sauna, Steam Room, Beauty Therapist. Roof Patios. Dancing Saturdays. Car parks. Mini breaks all year.

Llandudno

♋ English & French V ♦ ♫ ⚹ Lunch £8-£7.50 High tea £5 Dinner £10-£17.50 Last dinner 8.45pm
CONF. Thtr 40 Class 50 Board 30 Del from £40
Credit Cards [1][2][3][5] £

★★★ 61% Chatsworth House
Central Promenade LL30 2XS ☎(0492) 860788
Closed 28 Dec-12 Jan
A large and privately owned hotel contained within an elegant Victorian terrace on the Promenade offers fine sea views from many of its rooms. Well equipped modern bedrooms are complemented by spacious public areas which include a choice of lounges and a charming Victorian-style coffee shop.
58⇨♟(13fb)1⊞ CTV in all bedrooms ® T
Lift ℂ 9P ⌂ (heated) sauna solarium jacuzzi ♫
V ♦ ♫ ⚹ Last dinner 8.30pm
Credit Cards [1][3]

★★★ 61% St George's
The Promenade LL30 2LG ☎(0492) 877544 FAX (0492) 877788
One of the first major hotels to be built in Llandudno, in 1854, St George's is in the central promenade and features original ornate ceilings. Bedrooms vary from seafront suites to smaller rear rooms. All are similarly equipped and the décor is bright. Part of the restaurant also has good sea views. Here, a fixed price menu is on offer.
87⇨♟(4fb)1⊞ CTV in all bedrooms ® ⚿ T
Lift ℂ 36P sauna solarium gymnasium hairdressing health & beauty salon
♋ English & French V ♦ ♫ Last dinner 9.30pm
Credit Cards [1][2][3][5]

★★★ 59% Risboro
Clement Av LL30 2ED ☎(0492) 876343 FAX (0492) 879881
Situated at the foot of the Great Orme, the Risboro is only a short walk from the sea front and town centre. Conference facilities are extensive and the restaurant overlooks a large swimming pool.
65⇨♟(7fb)1⊞ CTV in all bedrooms ® ⚿ T sB&B⇨♟£25-£35 dB&B⇨♟£50-£70 ♫
Lift ℂ 40P ⌂ (heated) squash ∪ snooker sauna solarium gymnasium ♫ xmas
♋ English & French V ♦ ♫ Lunch £7.50-£10 High tea fr£5 Dinner £16-£17.50 Last dinner 8.45pm
CONF. Thtr 150 Class 80 Board 80 Del from £45
Credit Cards [1][2][3][5] £

★★❀❀ ST TUDNO
Promenade LL30 2LP (Welsh Rarebits) ☎(0492) 874411 FAX (0492) 860407
Set among a number of promenade hotels, the St Tudno stands out, not only for its colourful cosiness but also for the hospitality of its enthusiastic owners, Martin and Janette Bland. Services by the small team of keen staff are professional, but with a friendly, personal touch. The bedrooms, while compact, are individually styled and combine elegance with comfort and some personal touches. Those at the front are larger and offer fine sea views. In the Garden Room Restaurant chef David Harding makes good use of quality fresh produce in the nicely balanced seasonal à la carte and set menus. Taste of Wales specialities are often featured and fish is also prominent. The well chosen wine list includes a selection of New World wines, and there is a good range of Welsh cheeses. The restaurant is said to be one of the prettiest in Wales, with its green and white décor, trellis work and pot plants.

21⇨♟(4fb)1⊞ CTV in all bedrooms ® ⚿ T
Lift 4P 5⌂ (charged) ⛔ ⌂ (heated)
V ♦ ♫ ⚹ Last dinner 9.30pm
Credit Cards [1][2][3]

★★ 72% Dunoon
Gloddaeth St LL30 2DW (Logis) ☎(0492) 860787 FAX (0492) 860031
Closed Nov-mid Mar
The Dunoon offers guests all modern comforts whilst retaining something of the elegant ambience of times gone by, especially in its panelled public rooms. There are two lounges for simply sitting and chatting or reading, and a third with a pool table and television as well as a bar. For guests who want to be independent, the Chadderton family also let out a holiday flatlet nearby.
56⇨♟ Annexe14⇨♟(22fb) CTV in all bedrooms ® ⚿ T sB&B⇨♟£30-£36 dB&B⇨♟£46-£72
Lift CTV 24P solarium
V ♦ ♫ Lunch £8-£9 Dinner £11.50-£15.50 Last dinner 8pm
Credit Cards [1][3]

★★ 70% Belle Vue
26 North Pde LL30 2LP ☎(0492) 879547
Closed Dec-Feb RS Nov & Mar
The friendliness and hospitality of this impeccable hotel have understandably earned it a loyal following. In an elevated position close to the Pier, it commands excellent views of the bay and Promenade from the front terrace and lounge as well as several of the bedrooms – the latter all furnished in modern style with thoughtful extras such as videos and hair dryers.
17⇨♟(2fb) CTV in all bedrooms ® T sB&B⇨♟£22.50-£27.50 dB&B⇨♟£45-£59 ♫
Lift 12P ⛔ table tennis
♋ French & Italian V ♦ Bar Lunch £4 Dinner £9&alc Last dinner 8pm
Credit Cards [1][2][3][5] £

★★ 69% Tan-Lan
Great Orme's Rd, West Shore LL30 2AR ☎(0492) 860221
Closed Nov-19 Mar
The Tan-Lan is a family-run hotel in peaceful surroundings under the Orme and near the West Shore. The bright, airy bedrooms all have modern en suite bath or shower facilities and comfortable furnishings. There is a residents' lounge, separate bar, and a good value fixed price 6-course menu which also caters for vegetarians.
18⇨♟(4fb) CTV in all bedrooms ® sB&B⇨♟£22-£26 dB&B⇨♟£44-£50 ♫
CTV 15P ⛔
♋ English, French & Italian V ♦ ♫ Lunch £7 High tea £5 Dinner £11.50 Last dinner 8pm
Credit Cards [1][3]

★★ 67% Merrion
Promenade, South Pde LL30 2LN ☎(0492) 860022 FAX (0492) 860378
Closed Feb
The Merrion is a friendly family-run hotel in a prime position on the Promenade at the Great Orme end of the town. The comfortable public rooms include a lounge bar, a quiet lounge and an attractive dining room. Guests can also dine at the renowned La Mouette Restaurant at the end of the Victorian terrace which is under the same family ownership.
67⇨♟(7fb) CTV in all bedrooms ® T
Lift ℂ CTV 16P 25⌂
♋ English & French V ♦ ♫ Last dinner 8.30pm
Credit Cards [1][2][3]

Llandudno

★★ 67% Sandringham
West Pde LL30 2BD ☎(0492) 876513 & 876447
RS 25 & 26 Dec

Run by the experienced Kavanagh family, this continually improving hotel is situated on the West Shore. The fairly new restaurant looks out over the Conwy estuary on one side and the Great Orme on the other, and there are similar views from many other rooms. Bedrooms are bright and modern. There is a comfortable lounge for residents and a buttery bar where a wide range of à la carte and bar meals is available. The main restaurant serves a fixed price table d'hôte menu.

18⇨♠(4fb)⊁in 3 bedrooms CTV in all bedrooms ®¥ T ✈
6P
V ☼ ⊁ ✱ Sunday Lunch £8.95 Dinner £11.95&alc Last dinner 8pm
Credit Cards ①③⑤

★★ 66% Sunnymede
West Pde LL30 2BD ☎(0492) 877130
Closed mid Nov-Feb

Sunnymede is an impressive black and white painted, double fronted building on the west shore. Many bedrooms and the public rooms have lovely views across the Conwy estuary to Snowdonia. Public areas are particularly comfortable; bedrooms, too, are mostly spacious, with easy chairs.

18rm(14⇨3♠)(3fb)1₩ CTV in all bedrooms ®¥ ✱ sB&Bfr£28.50 sB&B⇨♠£33.95 dB&Bfr£30 dB&B⇨♠£33.95 (incl dinner) 🖃
18P *xmas*
V ☼ ⊉ Last dinner 7pm
Credit Cards ①③

★★ 66% Tynedale
Central Promenade LL30 2XS ☎(0492) 877426 FAX (0492) 871213
52⇨♠Annexe2rm(4fb) CTV in all bedrooms ®
✈ (ex guide dogs)
Lift ℂ 30P ♪
♀ English & French V ☼ ⊉ ⊁
Credit Cards ①③

★★ 65% Bedford
Promenade LL30 1BN ☎(0492) 876647 FAX (0492) 860185
This privately owned hotel, standing on the Promenade towards the eastern end of the town, offers a choice of bars, a Trattoria restaurant serving predominantly Italian dishes, and modern bedrooms – the majority with attractive Italian furniture and some also enjoying sea views.

27⇨♠(2fb) CTV in all bedrooms ® T ✱ sB&B⇨♠£15-£23 dB&B⇨♠£30-£46 🖃
Lift ℂ CTV 20P *xmas*
♀ English, French & Italian V ☼ ⊉ ✱ Lunch £5.50-£7.50&alc Dinner £7.50-£11&alc Last dinner 10.30pm
Credit Cards ①③

★★ 65% Bromwell Court
Promenade LL30 1BG ☎(0492) 878416 FAX (0492) 874142
Guests can enjoy lovely views from the lounge and front bedrooms of the Ireland family's impeccably maintained and friendly hotel which stands on the promenade at Craig-y-Don between the Great and Little Ormes.

11⇨♠(2fb) CTV in all bedrooms ® T ✈ (ex guide dogs) ✱ sB&B⇨♠£21.50-£25.50 dB&B⇨♠£40-£47 🖃
₽ ₼
V⊁ BarLunch£1.50-£5 Dinner£10.50 Last dinner 7.30pm
Credit Cards ①③

★★ 65% Bryn-y-Bia Lodge
Craigside LL30 3AS ☎(0492) 549264 & 540459
Closed 23 Dec-2 Jan

Dating from the mid 19th century, and situated at the Little Orme end of the promenade, this pleasant little hotel is set in its own walled gardens with lovely views over the bay and town. Lounge areas are comfortably furnished, and bedrooms have pretty floral décor. The fixed price 4-course table d'hôte menu of enjoyable food changes every day.

13⇨♠(2fb)1₩ CTV in all bedrooms ® T sB&B⇨♠£25-£33.50 dB&B⇨♠£48-£63 🖃
20P 🚗 ❋ ⌀
♀ English & Continental V ☼ ⊁ ✱ Lunch £10-£12alc Dinner £17&alc Last dinner 8.30pm
Credit Cards ①②③⑤ £

★★ 64% Headlands
Hill Ter LL30 2LS ☎(0492) 877485
Closed Jan-Feb

This privately owned and run hotel commands spectacular views of sea, Snowdonia and the Conwy estuary from its position at the foot of the Great Orme. Bedrooms vary in size, and their styles and furnishings range from traditional to modern, but all are similarly equipped. Public areas include a choice of lounges and a small bar.

17rm(15⇨♠)(4fb)2₩ CTV in all bedrooms ® T ✱ sB&B£26 dB&Bfr£60 dB&B⇨♠£72 🖃
CTV 7P 🚗 nc5yrs *xmas*
☼ ⊁ Bar Lunch £1.50-£2.50alc Dinner £15.50 Last dinner 8pm

Credit Cards ①②③⑤ £

★★ 63% Royal
Church Walks LL30 2HW ☎(0492) 876476 FAX (0492) 870210
The Royal is one of the oldest established hotels and is pleasantly set in secluded gardens in the shelter of the Great Orme. Staff are friendly and helpful, in the summer entertainment is provided in the lounge and bedrooms are all brightly and freshly decorated.

35rm(33⇨♠)(6fb) CTV in all bedrooms ®¥ T
✈ (ex guide dogs)

One of Llandudno's largest hotels, set proudly on the promenade with 100 en-suite bedrooms, 3 bars and a health & fitness centre

The Promenade, Llandudno, Gwynedd,
North Wales, LL30 1AP
Telephone: (0492) 877466/9
Facsimile: (0492) 878043

Llandudno

Lift 30P ❀ putting green pool table ⚲
♨ European V ✧ ⚏ ✂ Last dinner 8pm
Credit Cards [1] [3]

★★63% *Sherwood*
Promenade LL30 1BG ☎(0492) 875313
Closed Xmas & New Year RS Nov-Feb

On the promenade at Craig-y-Don, this family-run hotel offers modern bedrooms of varying size, including family rooms. The brightly decorated dining room has sea views, as does the lounge bar, and there is a cosy and comfortable lounge.
15⇨♘(5fb) CTV in all bedrooms ®✻✱ sB&B⇨♘£22–£25 dB&B⇨♘£40–£48 ⊟
15P games room pool table
V ✧ ✂ ✱ Dinner fr£7.50 Last dinner 8pm
Credit Cards [1] [3]   £

★★62% *Branksome*
Lloyd St LL30 2YP ☎(0492) 875989
Closed Jan-Mar

Centrally situated between the West Shore and the Promenade, this large, privately owned and personally run hotel also offers convenient access to the town centre. All bedrooms have modern furnishings and equipment, and some are located on the ground floor. Public areas include a large lounge bar with dance area and a games room with darts board and pool table.
48rm(7⇨10♘)Annexe5rm(10fb)
CTV 12P sauna solarium gymnasium ♬
♨ English, French & Italian V ✧ ⚏

★★61% *Kensington*
Central Promenade LL30 1AT ☎(0492) 876784 FAX (0492) 876784
Closed 2 Jan-Feb

This privately owned hotel is centrally situated on the Promenade, and the dining room, both lounges and several bedrooms enjoy sea views. All the bedrooms have modern furnishings and equipment. Live entertainment is often provided in the lounge bar and the hotel is particularly popular with senior citizens' coach parties.
36⇨♘(6fb) CTV in all bedrooms ® ✖ (ex guide dogs) sB&B⇨♘£32 dB&B⇨♘£54 (incl dinner) ⊟
Lift CTV 36P *xmas*
CONF. Class 50 Board 30 Del £31
Credit Cards [1] [3]   £

★★61% *Southcliffe*
Hill Ter LL30 2LS ☎(0492) 876277
Closed Nov-15 Dec & 5 Jan-Mar

From its elevated position on the side of the Great Orme, a privately owned hotel catering for coach tour parties and particularly popular with elderly holiday-makers enjoys superb views of beach, Promenade, and town.
30rm(19⇨♘)(7fb) CTV in all bedrooms ®
✖ ♬ nc7yrs
✧ ⚏ ✂ Last dinner 8.30pm

★★61% *Wavecrest*
St Georges Crescent, Central Promenade LL30 2LF
☎(0492) 860615 FAX (0492) 876340
Closed Nov-Mar

This popular hotel is on the Central Promenade and offers nicely decorated, well equipped bedrooms and a choice of comfortable lounges.
41⇨♘(7fb) CTV in all bedrooms ® ✻ sB&B⇨♘£26–£34 dB&B⇨♘£52–£68 (incl dinner)
Lift 12P ♬
V ✧ ✂ Bar Lunch £1.20–£4 Dinner £12&alc Last dinner 7.30pm
Credit Cards [1] [3]

★★60% *Castle*
Vaughan St LL30 1AG ☎(0492) 877694 & 876868
Closed Jan

Large and privately owned, this hotel at the centre of the town has recently refurbished bedrooms, and caters for a wide range of customers, including coach parties and delegates attending local conferences.
56rm(51⇨3♘)(19fb) CTV in all bedrooms ®
Lift ⊙ 30P ♬
V ✧ ⚏ ✂ Last dinner 7.30pm
Credit Cards [1] [3]

★★60% *Ormescliffe*
Promenade LL30 1BE ☎(0492) 877191 FAX (0492) 860311

A large hotel situated on the Promenade, within easy reach of the town centre and other amenities, catering mainly for coach party business, and particularly suitable for senior citizens. Improvements currently under way have ensured good modern standards of comfort.
60⇨♘(11fb) CTV in all bedrooms ® ✖ (ex guide dogs)
Lift ⊙ CTV 12P pool table tennis ⚲
♨ International ✧ ⚏ Last dinner 8pm
Credit Cards [1] [3]

★★60% *Somerset*
St Georges Crescent, Promenade LL30 2LF ☎(0492) 876540
FAX (0492) 876540
Closed Nov-Feb

This large privately owned hotel is centrally situated on the promenade and the bedrooms at the front overlook the sea.
37⇨♘(4fb) CTV in all bedrooms ® ✻ sB&B⇨♘£32–£36 dB&B⇨♘£64–£72 (incl dinner)
Lift 20P pool table darts games room ♬ *xmas*
V ✧ ✂ Bar Lunch £1.50–£5.50 Dinner £15&alc Last dinner 7.30pm
Credit Cards [1] [3]

★★58% *Esplanade*
Glan-y-Mor Pde, Promenade LL30 2LL (turn off A55 at Llandudno junct & proceed on A470) ☎(0492) 860300 FAX (0492) 860418

Under the same ownership for over 50 years, this is a popular seafront hotel. Plans are now in hand to upgrade bedrooms and bathrooms where the décor is becoming a little tired. The bar is in 3 parts and the Buttery serves snacks from mid-morning until late afternoon. A table d'hôte menu is served in the pretty restaurant.
59⇨♘(15fb) CTV in all bedrooms ® T sB&B⇨♘£24–£41 dB&B⇨♘£48–£70 ⊟
Lift ⊙ 30P pool table table tennis *xmas*
♨ English & French V ✧ ⚏ ✂ Bar Lunch £2–£5alc Dinner £10–£13alc Last dinner 8pm
CONF. Thtr 120 Class 60 Board 50
Credit Cards [1] [2] [3] [5]   £

★★58% *Four Oaks*
Promenade LL30 1AY ☎(0492) 876506
RS Nov-Feb

This large, privately owned hotel is situated on the Promenade, within easy reach of the town centre. Many of its bedrooms enjoy sea views, and it is particularly popular with coach tour parties.
57rm(19⇨8♘)(25fb) CTV in all bedrooms ®
Lift ⊙ CTV ✂ ♬ ⚲
V ✧ ⚏ Last dinner 7.30pm

★75% *Epperstone*
15 Abbey Rd LL30 2EE ☎(0492) 878746 FAX (0492) 871223
Closed Jan-Feb RS Nov-Dec

Situated in a quiet residential area close to the shops and seafront, this delightful 19th-century corner house with many original features has prettily decorated bedrooms with modern facilities and 2 comfortable lounges. Good value 5-course dinners include a vegetarian choice.

356

Llandudno

8⇨🛏(5fb)⚹in 1 bedroom CTV in all bedrooms ® T
sB&B⇨🛏£20-£23 dB&B⇨🛏£40-£46 🍽
8P ⛔ ✤ xmas
♿ ♨ ⚹ Dinner £10 Last dinner 7.30pm
Credit Cards [1][3]

★68% Banham House
2 St Davids Rd LL30 2UL ☎(0492) 875680 FAX (0492) 875680
Closed 31 Dec-2 Jan
Situated in a quiet residential area, Patricia and Tony Sharpe's small family hotel is in easy walking distance of the town centre and seafront. It has a comfortable residents' lounge and the newly decorated restaurant also has a bar. Bedrooms are bright and fresh.
6⇨🛏⚹in 2 bedrooms CTV in all bedrooms ® ✈
sB&B⇨🛏£20-£25 dB&B⇨🛏£40
CTV 5P ⛔ nc12yrs xmas
V ♿ Lunch £7 Dinner £7.50 Last dinner 9.30pm

★68% Clontarf
1 Great Ormes Rd, West Shore LL30 2AR ☎(0492) 877621
Closed 30 Dec-Feb
This cheerful, family-run hotel is just a stone's throw from the resort's West Shore. Residents have the use of a small bar and a comfortable modern lounge. The pretty restaurant is the setting for Pam Tunstall's honest home cooking – don't miss the rhubarb crumble if it's on!
10rm(1⇨3🛏)(2fb) ® ✈
CTV 10P ⛔ ✤ nc3yrs
V ♿ ♨ ⚹ Last dinner 7.30pm

★67% Gwesty Leamore
40 Lloyd St LL30 2YG ☎(0492) 875552
Closed Dec
This delightful small hotel is a distinctive white, pebble-dash building near to the town centre and promenade. Owners Fred and Beryl Owen offer genuine Welsh hospitality and Welsh specialities such as Bara Brith, Welsh choral singing as background music, and even a surprisingly pleasant Welsh white wine. Bedrooms are neat, bright and well equipped, and there are a cosy residents' bar and lounge.
12rm(1⇨6🛏)(4fb) CTV in all bedrooms ®✱ ✈ sB&B£19
sB&B⇨🛏£21 dB&B£35 dB&B⇨🛏£49 🍽
CTV 4P ⛔
V ⚹ ✱ Bar Lunch £2.50-£5 Dinner £7-£9 Last dinner 7.30pm

★67% White Lodge
9 Neville Crescent, Central Promenade LL30 1AT
☎(0492) 877713
Closed Nov-Apr
This small family-run hotel is situated in an excellent position in the quiet part of the Central Promenade. Bedrooms are modern, there is a comfortable residents' lounge, and a restaurant and bar on the lower ground floor.
12⇨🛏(4fb) CTV in all bedrooms ®✱ ✱ sB&B⇨🛏fr£24.50
dB&B⇨🛏fr£39 🍽
CTV 12P ⛔ nc5yrs
♿ ♨ ⚹
Credit Cards [2]

★66% Ravenhurst
West Pde LL30 2BB (on West Shore, opposite boating pool)
☎(0492) 875525
Closed Dec-Feb
Run by the experienced and friendly Carrington family, this hotel has a superb site on the west shore, with lovely views across the estuary to Snowdonia from the restaurant. Table d'hôte and à la carte menus give plenty of choice and special diets can be accommodated. There are 2 lounges, a residents' bar and a quiet card room. Bedrooms are modern and the decor first class.
25⇨🛏 Annexe1⇨🛏(4fb) CTV in all bedrooms ®
sB&B⇨🛏£34-£37 dB&B⇨🛏£68-£74 (incl dinner) 🍽
15P ♪

THE Ormescliffe HOTEL
Promenade, Llandudno
Tel: (0492) 877191 Fax: (0492) 860311
★★ WTB 👑👑👑

This large and privately owned Hotel occupies a premier position on Sea Front. Recently refurbished bedrooms are equipped with en suite facilities, tel, TV, tea/coffee. Lift to all floors, 24hr Porterage. Caters for Private Tours specialising in Ballroom Dance Parties throughout year with extensive Christmas/ New Year programme.

BRANKSOME HOTEL ★★
Lloyd Street, Llandudno, Gwynedd LL30 2YP
Telephone: 0492 875989

The hotel occupies a unique position in a quiet area completely on the level, minutes from both Shores, main shops and the Oval Sports Centre with tennis, bowls, cricket, etc. There are also 3 championship golf courses on the doorstep. The Branksome offers first class catering, comfort and personal service. Open all year with special Christmas programme. Reduced terms for children. Special 3 days breaks – Mini Weekends. Conferences most welcome.

Llandudno

V ♿ ⌴ ✻ Lunch fr£5&alc Dinner £9-£10&alc Last dinner 7pm
Credit Cards 1 2 3 5 £

★ **65% Oak Alyn**
Deganwy Av LL30 2YB ☎(0492) 860320
Closed Dec-mid Feb RS Feb
Privately owned and personally run, the Oak Alyn is centrally situated and convenient for the shops and other amenities. It has its own car park and provides quite well equipped accommodation.
13rm⇔♚(1fb) CTV in all bedrooms ®
CTV 16P
♀ British & Continental ♿ ⌴
Credit Cards 1 3

★ **65% Tan-y-Marian**
87 Abbey Rd, West Shore LL30 2AS ☎(0492) 877427
Closed mid Oct-mid Mar
The friendly Owen family are justly proud of their small hotel, which is situated on the resort's west shore. Further en suite shower rooms have recently been added and the use of coordinating fabrics and wall paper has made the bedrooms very attractive. The hotel faces the Great Orme and the lounge and several of the bedrooms have pleasant views. There is a residents' lounge and a small foyer bar, and good home cooking is available.
8rm(4♚)(2fb)⌴ in 1 bedroom ® sB&B£18-£20 dB&B£32-£36 dB&B♚£36-£40
CTV 5P ♿ nc2yrs
V ⌴ Last dinner 7pm

★ **64% Stratford**
8 Craig-y-Don Pde, Promenade LL30 1BG (from A55 take A470 to Llandudno at 3rd roundabout take Craig-y-don sign to Promenade) ☎(0492) 877962
This traditional Victorian resort hotel, set on the seafront at Craig-y-Don, offers sweeping views of the bay from several of its attractively furnished and coordinated modern bedrooms. A comfortable lounge is available for residents' use, and there is a cosy bar and a restaurant which serves good home-cooked meals.
10rm(3⇔6♚)(5fb) CTV in all bedrooms ®✲ ✻ dB&B£17 dB&B⇔♚£18.50-£23 ᛟ
CTV ℙ ♿
V ⌴ ✻ Dinner £8.50 Last dinner 7pm
Credit Cards 1 3 £

★ **63% Brigstock**
1 St David's Place LL30 2UG ☎(0492) 876416
Closed Dec-Jan
Very much the friendly resort hotel, run almost entirely by Pauline and Ray Southon, it stands in a quiet residential area just a few minutes' walk from the shops and seafront. The bedrooms are brightly decorated and modern, and guests have the use of a very comfortable sitting room and small bar.
10rm(3⇔2♚)(2fb)⌴ in all bedrooms CTV in all bedrooms ® ✻ sB&B£17-£19 dB&B£34-£36 dB&B⇔♚£36-£38
CTV 5P ♿ nc3yrs
V ⌴ Last dinner 6pm £

★ **63% Crickleigh**
Lloyd St LL30 2YG ☎(0492) 875926
This cheerful family-run hotel just a short walk from the seafront and shops provides good value accommodation. Bedrooms are brightly decorated and there is a comfortable modern lounge, a small cosy bar and a large and airy restaurant.
15rm(7♚)(4fb) ® ✖ (ex guide dogs)
CTV 12P
♀ International V ♿ ⌴ Last dinner 7pm
Credit Cards 1 3

★ **62% Concord**
35 Abbey Rd LL30 2EH ☎(0492) 875504
Closed mid Oct-mid Mar
This large privately owned and personally run small hotel, is situated close to the Great Orme and the West Shore. The accommodation, while not luxurious, is soundly maintained, and the bedrooms are furnished in modern style. There is a small bar area in the dining room and the comfortable lounge has a colour TV.
11⇔♚(7fb) ® ✖ (ex guide dogs) dB&B⇔♚fr£36
CTV 11P ♿ nc5yrs
♿ ⌴ Last dinner 7pm

★ **62% Quinton**
36 Church Walks LL30 2HN (150yds from St George's church) ☎(0492) 876879 & 875086
This large Victorian house is situated between the 2 beaches and is close to the town centre, pier and other amenities. Privately owned and personally run in an informal and friendly manner, it provides simple but sound accommodation, catering mainly for holidaymakers.
15rm(4⇔5♚)(8fb) CTV in all bedrooms ®✲ T ✻ sB&B£16-£18 sB&B⇔♚£18-£20 dB&B£32-£36 dB&B⇔♚£36-£40 ᛟ
12P ♪ xmas
♿ ⌴ ✻
Credit Cards 1

★ **61% Bryn-y-Mor**
North Pde LL30 1LP ☎(0492) 876790 FAX (0492) 860825
Situated on the Promenade near the pier, this friendly hotel gives fine sea views from many of the bright, warm bedrooms and public areas, which include a very comfortable lounge, small bar and restaurant.
18rm(7⇔♚)(5fb) CTV in all bedrooms ® ✖ (ex guide dogs)
CTV 1P
V ⌴ Last dinner 7pm
Credit Cards 1 2 3 5

★ **61% Hilbre Court**
Great Ormes Rd, West Shore LL30 2AR ☎(0492) 876632
Closed Nov-Feb (ex Xmas)
Well maintained bedrooms are provided at this family-run hotel near the West Shore, which is convenient for the town centre and other amenities.
9rm(4⇔3♚)(1fb)⌴ in 2 bedrooms CTV in all bedrooms ® ✻ sB&B£15-£18 sB&B⇔♚£16-£20 dB&B£30-£36 dB&B⇔♚£32-£40 ᛟ
CTV 6P ♿ xmas
V ♿ ⌴ ✻ Sunday Lunch £8.50 Dinner £8.50 Last dinner 8pm

★ **60% Heath House**
Central Promenade LL30 1AT ☎(0492) 876538 FAX (0492) 860307
This friendly family-run hotel in a Victorian terrace on the Central Promenade provides simply furnished bedrooms. Honest home cooking is served in the restaurant, with an adjacent small bar and dance floor.
22rm(12⇔)(14fb) CTV in all bedrooms ® T ✖ (ex guide dogs)
CTV ℙ
♿ ⌴ ⌴ Last dinner 7.30pm

★ **60% Min-y-Don**
North Pde LL30 2LP ☎(0492) 876511
Closed Dec-Jan
A happy holiday hotel, the Min-y-Don is situated on the promenade opposite the pier. It has a small car park and street parking is also available. All bedrooms have TVs and tea trays, and most have sea views. There are two comfortable lounges, one for non smokers, a bar and a small ballroom where regular entertainment is provided for guests.

Llandudno - Llangurig

28rm(2⇌17↑)(12fb) CTV in all bedrooms ® ✈
sB&Bfr£21.75 sB&B⇌↑fr£23.75 dB&Bfr£37 dB&B⇌↑fr£39 ⧈
⊞ CTV 7P *xmas*
V ❖ ⚲ ✗ Lunch fr£3.95 High tea fr£1 Dinner fr£5.95 Last dinner 7.30pm
Credit Cards [1][3]

LLANELLI Dyfed Map 02 SN50

★ **65%** Miramar
158 Station Rd SA15 1YU ☎(0554) 754726 & 773607 FAX (0554) 772454
Family owned the run, this small, friendly hotel is conveniently positioned right next to the station. Bright, comfortable en suite bedrooms are comprehensively equipped to meet modern requirements, the congenial bar serves a wide range of meals and a well appointed first floor restaurant offers the extensive hours of service normally associated with larger establishments.
10rm(8↑) CTV in all bedrooms ®⚲ ✈ (ex guide dogs) ✱
sB&B£16 sB&B↑£20-£22 dB&B£30 dB&B↑£36-£40 6P
♀ International ✱ Lunch £5.25-£9.75&alc
CONF.
Credit Cards [1][2][3][5] £

LLANFAIR PWLLGWYNGYLL
See **Anglesey, Isle of**

LLANFYLLIN Powys Map 06 SJ11

★★⚐ **72%** Bodfach Hall
SY22 5HS (0.5m W) ☎(0691) 648272 FAX (0691) 648272
Closed 19 Dec-4 Mar
Set back from the main road just north of the town, this elegant 17th-century country house with ornate ceilings and wood-panelled walls nestles amid trees and lawns. Bedrooms and public areas are comfortable and well equipped, food is good, and the hotel is personally run by its friendly owners.
9⇌↑(2fb) CTV in all bedrooms ®⚲ sB&B⇌↑fr£32.50 dB&B⇌↑fr£65 ⧈
20P ⚗ ✱ ⚲ putting green
V ❖ Sunday Lunch £9.50 Dinner £15 Last dinner 8.45pm
Credit Cards [1][2][3][5]

LLANGAMMARCH WELLS Powys Map 03 SN94

★★★ ❀❀⚐ **77%** Lake
LD4 4BS (from Builth Wells head W on A483 to Garth (6m approx) turn left for Llangammarch Wells follow signs for hotel) (Welsh Rarebits) ☎(05912) 202 & 374 FAX (05912) 457

Inspectors Choice 1994

Over the years the owners have transformed this hotel into a very welcoming, comfortable and congenial retreat, and this year it is the winner of our Inspectors' Selected Hotel of the Year Award for Wales. In a beautiful setting overlooking lake and river, it offers excellent accommodation in richly decorated bedrooms which provide a high level of creature comforts. The high-ceilinged dining room offers dishes such as fillet of Welsh venison marinaded in port and served with juniper and caramelised shallots on a sweet bread of braised red cabbage with chestnuts.
19⇌↑(1fb)3⚑⁕ in 6 bedrooms CTV in all bedrooms T ✱
sB&B⇌↑£75 dB&B⇌↑£98-£120 ⧈
⟪ 70P 2⇎ ⚗ ✱ ♀ (hard) ⚲ snooker clay pigeon shooting nc7yrs *xmas*
♀ English & French ❖ ⚲ ✗ ✱ Lunch £15.50 High tea £3.50-£9 Dinner £24.50 Last dinner 8.45pm
CONF. Thtr 80 Class 30 Board 25 Del from £85
Credit Cards [1][2][3] £

LLANGEFNI
See **Anglesey, Isle of**

LLANGOLLEN Clwyd Map 07 SJ24

★★★ ❀❀ **63%** Bryn Howel
LL20 7UW (2m E on A539) ☎(0978) 860331 FAX (0978) 860119
Closed 25 Dec
Set in immaculately kept grounds in the beautiful Vale of Llangollen, this extended late Victorian mansion offers warm hospitality. Refurbishment of the well equipped but rather dated bedrooms has begun, there are comfortable lounges, a small cocktail bar or large panelled bar and a restaurant featuring local meat, fish and game on its good value menu.
38⇌↑(1fb) CTV in all bedrooms ® T ✱ sB&B⇌↑£36-£65 dB&B⇌↑£72-£105 ⧈
Lift CTV 200P ✱ ⚲ sauna solarium
V ❖ ⚲ Lunch £12.90 Dinner fr£19.90 Last dinner 9pm
CONF. Thtr 300 Class 60 Board 40 Del £89.90
Credit Cards [1][2][3] £

★★★ **57%** The Royal
Bridge St LL20 8PG ☎(0978) 860202 FAX (0978) 861824

FORTE Heritage

Perched above the bank of the River Dee by the old stone bridge, this early 19th-century coaching inn where Queen Victoria once stayed has a friendly relaxing atmosphere. Both the restaurant and traditional lounge with a log fire overlook the river and comfortable bedrooms have attractive coordinated fabrics.
33⇌↑(3fb)✗ in 8 bedrooms CTV in all bedrooms ® T ✱
sB⇌↑£65-£75 dB⇌↑£75-£80 (room only) ⧈
⟪ 20P ⚲ *xmas*
V ❖ ⚲ ✗ Sunday Lunch £10.95 High tea £1.20 Dinner £14.95-£16.95&alc Last dinner 9pm
Credit Cards [1][2][3][5]

LLANGURIG Powys Map 06 SN98

★★ **69%** Glansevern Arms
Pant Mawr SY18 6SY (4m W on A44) ☎(05515) 240
Guests are assured of a warm welcome at this very pleasant small hotel in the Upper Wye Valley. Bedrooms are well decorated and cosy, there is a comfortable lounge and bar with log fires and the 6-course fixed price menu is good value.
7⇌↑ CTV in all bedrooms ®
40P ⚗
❖ Last dinner 8pm

All black star hotels are given a
percentage grading within their star bands.
See 'Using the Guide' at the front of the book
for full details.

Llangybi - Llanwrtyd Wells

LLANGYBI Gwent Map 03 ST39

★★★★ 59% Cwrt Bleddyn Hotel & Country Club
NP5 1PG ☎Tredunnock(0633) 49521 FAX (0633) 49220
This country mansion with modern extensions is set in attractive parkland between Caerleon and Usk. Accommodation, ranging from that contained in the modern annexe to 3 period rooms, includes several luxurious suites, while public areas are relaxing and comfortable.
29⇌ ↑ Annexe7⇌ ↑ (5fb) ⊞ CTV in all bedrooms ® T
(⊞ 100P ✿ ⊠ (heated) ℘ (hard) squash snooker sauna solarium gymnasium croquet boules clay pigeon shooting ஃ
♡ Welsh & French V ✧ ℥ Last dinner 10pm
Credit Cards [1][2][3][5]

LLANRWST Gwynedd Map 06 SH76

★★★ 64% Plas Maenan Country House
Conway Valley LL26 0YR (3m N) ☎Dolgarrog(0492) 660232 FAX (0492) 660551
Plas Maenan, very much a family concern, stands in 12 acres of grounds in an elevated position with superb views of the Conwy Valley and Snowdonia. Recently added conservatories have proved a popular venue for the wide range of bar food served, and bedrooms have also been improved.
15⇌ ↑ (2fb)1 ⊞ CTV in all bedrooms ® T
100P ✿
♡ Welsh, English & French V ✧ ℥ Last dinner 9pm
Credit Cards [1][3]

★★★ 61% The Priory
Maenan LL26 0UL (3m N on A470) ☎(0492) 660247 FAX (0492) 660734
With its magnificent galleried staircase this impressive Victorian house, set in 11 acres of woodland and neat gardens, offers well equipped bedrooms, first floor lounge and 2 bars – one of which serves a selection of bar meals. The residents' bar is ideal for a relaxing pre-dinner drink and the restaurant, with its adjacent coffee lounge, provides a table d'hôte menu of popular dishes.
12⇌ ↑ (2fb)2 ⊞ CTV in all bedrooms ® T ✱ sB&B⇌ ↑ fr£39 dB&B⇌ ↑ fr£49 ℞
60P ✿ ♪ clay pigeon shooting ♫ ஃ xmas
♡ Welsh, English & French V ✧ ℥ ✗ ✱ Lunch fr£8.95&alc Dinner fr£14.50&alc Last dinner 9.30pm
Conf. Class 40 Board 15 Del £55
Credit Cards [1][2][3][5]

★★ 63% Eagles
LL26 0LG ☎(0492) 640454 FAX (0690) 710777
Dating from 1785, the Eagle is very much the hub of life in the town. There are 2 bars and a pleasant restaurant. Many of the bedrooms have lovely views over the gardens and the River Conwy. Taste of Wales dishes are prominently featured on the menu, and the hotel is well known for its extensive range of open sandwiches – over 200 at the last count.
12⇌ ↑ (5fb) CTV in all bedrooms ® T
CTV 50P ♪ sauna solarium gymnasium pool ஃ
♡ Welsh, English & French V ✧ ✗ Last dinner 9pm
Credit Cards [1][3]

LLANTWIT MAJOR South Glamorgan Map 03 SS96

★★ 66% West House Country Hotel & Restaurant
West St CF61 1SP ☎(0446) 792406 & 793726 FAX (0446) 796147
The modern conversion of this 18th-century farmhouse has created a cosy little hotel and restaurant with bright, well equipped bedrooms. There is a comfortable new conservatory lounge with an adjacent bar leading on to the small restaurant. The atmosphere is relaxed and friendly.
21⇌ ↑ 1⊞ CTV in all bedrooms ® T ✱ sB&B⇌ ↑ £45-£55 dB&B⇌ ↑ £58-£68 ℞
(CTV 60P ✿ ஃ xmas
♡ English & French V ✧ ℥ ✗ Lunch £6.50-£9.95&alc High tea £2.95-£6.50 Dinner £13.50&alc Last dinner 9.30pm
Conf. Thtr 70 Class 40 Board 20 Del from £60
Credit Cards [1][2][3] £

LLANWDDYN Powys Map 06 SJ01

★★★ ❀ 71% Lake Vyrnwy
Lake Vyrnwy SY10 0LY (on A495, 200yds past dam)
☎(069173) 692 FAX (069173) 259
This Victorian grey stone building overlooks the lake from its setting in extensive woodland at the foot of the Berwyn mountains. Public rooms are impressive: the drawing room, with its grand piano, deep sofas and armchairs, has good lake views, as does the bar and restaurant. Bedrooms have period and antique furnishings. Our inspector was pleased to report that the food continues to improve under Andrew Wood's influence, the busy kitchen producing its own bread, marmalade, preserves, petits fours and sweets.
38⇌ ↑ (4fb)2 ⊞ CTV in all bedrooms T ✕ ✱
sB&B⇌ ↑ fr£55.50 dB&B⇌ ↑ fr£69.50-£118.50 ℞
70P ✿ ℘ (hard) ♪ game shooting sailing cycling archery xmas
♡ International V ✧ ℥ ✱ Lunch fr£10.45 High tea fr£3.50 Dinner fr£21.50 Last dinner 9.30pm
Conf. Thtr 50 Class 100 Board 50 Del from £75
Credit Cards [1][2][3][4][5]

LLANWNDA Gwynedd Map 06 SH45

★★ 65% Stables
LL54 5SD (S of Caernarfon, on A499) ☎(0286) 830711 & 830935 FAX (0286) 830413
This hotel has 15 acres of land on which the owners keep Shetland ponies. Converted Victorian stables house a restaurant and bar, popular with locals. Well equipped bedrooms are in a modern motel-style block which overlooks an outdoor swimming pool and includes a small foyer lounge and breakfast room.
Annexe14⇌ ↑ (2fb)1 ⊞ CTV in all bedrooms ® T
40P ⇌ ✿ ⊠
♡ International V Last dinner 9.30pm
Credit Cards [1][2][3]

LLANWRTYD WELLS Powys Map 03 SN84

★ ❀ 68% Carlton House
Dolycoed Rd LD5 4SN ☎(05913) 248
(Rosettes awarded for dinner only)
A small family-run hotel at the centre of the picturesque village offers good food and a warm welcome from very experienced proprietors. Bedrooms are both attractive and comfortable, a log fire burns in the lounge, and there is a small bar.
6rm(1⇌1 ↑)(1fb) CTV in all bedrooms ® sB&B£20 dB&B£34 dB&B⇌ ↑ £40 ℞
℘ ⇌ pony trekking mountain biking
V ✧ ℥ ✗ Dinner £12&alc Last dinner 8.30pm
Credit Cards [1][3] £

Some hotels within company owned groups share a uniform identity. For full details consult the Contents page, under Hotel Groups.

LLYSWEN Powys Map 03 SO13

★★★★ ❀❀❀ 75% **Llangoed Hall**
LD3 0YP (access from A470)
☎Brecon(0874) 754525 FAX (0874) 754545

Courtesy and Care 1994

Allegedly the home of the Welsh parliament, which stood on this site, the present hall was completed in 1918 after the original Jacobean mansion was restructured by Sir Clough William Ellis. Thanks to the efforts of Sir Bernard Ashley, the house has been painstakingly restored and transformed into a luxury hotel. The well proportioned bedrooms have a good collection of antiques and art deco furnishings with, of course, Laura Ashley fabrics. Sir Bernard's impressive collection of paintings is displayed, and another strength of the hotel is the commendable cooking of chef Mark Salter.
23rm(5fb)❀ CTV in all bedrooms T ✖ (ex guide dogs) sB&B⇨£95-£175 dB&B⇨£145-£285 ₧
《 80P 5❀ ⇌ ❋ ♃ (hard) ♪ croquet nc8yrs *xmas*
V ♥ ♎ ⌇ Lunch £16 High tea £7.50 Dinner £35.50-£39.50&alc Last dinner 9.30pm
CONF. Thtr 26 Board 26 Del from £145
Credit Cards [1][2][3][5]

★★ 64% **Griffin Inn**
LD3 0UR (on A470) ☎(0874) 754241 FAX (0874) 754592
This delightful family owned and personally run inn has congenial log-fired bars serving a wide range of food, as well as the cosy little à la carte restaurant. Bedrooms are simply styled, and there are 2 comfortably furnished residents' lounges on the first floor.
8rm(7⇨)® T sB&Bfr£26 sB&B⇨fr£30 dB&Bfr£55 dB&B⇨fr£55 ₧
CTV 14P ⇌ ♃ ♕
V ♥ ⌇ Sunday Lunch fr£12alc Dinner £12-£20alc Last dinner 9pm
Credit Cards [1][2][3][5]

LOCHCARRON Highland Map 14 NG83

★★ 63% **Lochcarron**
IV54 8YS (E end of village on Lochcarron) ☎(05202) 226
Improvements are steadily being made to this small family-run hotel overlooking the loch at the edge of the village. Modest but comfortable bedrooms are being upgraded and traditionally cosy public areas include a bar and restaurant both featuring fresh local seafood on the menus.
10rm(9⇨)(1fb) CTV in all bedrooms ® T sB&Bfr£32.50 sB&B⇨£35 dB&B⇨£52-£65
30P ⇌ boat hire
V ♥ ⌇ Lunch fr£6.90&alc High tea fr£7alc Dinner fr£15.50&alc Last dinner 8.30pm
Credit Cards [1][3]

LOCHEARNHEAD Central *Perthshire* Map 11 NN52

★ 68% **Mansewood Country House**
FK19 8NS (on the A84 Stirling/Crianlarich rd on left as you enter village) ☎(0567) 830213

Set in its own gardens on the southern outskirts of the village, this former toll house is personally run and provides meticulously maintained, comfortable accommodation, with bright, compact bedrooms, a comfortable lounge and an attractive dining room serving set dinners.
8rm(5⇨1♙)® ✹ sB&B£20 sB&B⇨♙£23 dB&B£40 dB&B⇨♙£46
CTV 16P ⇌ ❋ surfing sailing canoeing water-skiing
V ♥ ⌇
Credit Cards [1][3]   £

★ 62% **Lochearnhead**
Lochside FK19 8PU ☎(0567) 830229 FAX (0567) 830364
Closed mid Nov-end Mar
This friendly family-run hotel with fine views over the loch shore provides bright modest accommodation. A good range of dishes is offered in the attractive restaurant and bar.
14rm(1⇨3♙) CTV in all bedrooms ®⌇ sB&B£24.20-£31.60 sB&B⇨♙£31.60 dB&B⇨♙£43-£53 ₧
CTV 80P ❋ ♪ squash water skiing windsurfing sailing
⚑ Scottish & French V ♥ ⌇ Bar Lunch £2-£16 High tea £6.50-£7.50 Dinner £17.50 Last dinner 9pm
Credit Cards [1][2][3][5]

LOCHGILPHEAD Strathclyde Map 10 NR88

★★ 66% **The Stag**
Argyll St PA31 8NE ☎(0546) 602496 FAX (0546) 603549
This popular tourist and commercial hotel in the town centre offers practical, fully equipped bedrooms, a bright modern dining room with adjacent lounge and a busy lounge bar which features live music on 2 evenings a week.
17⇨♙ CTV in all bedrooms ®⌇ T ✹ sB&B⇨♙£30-£35 dB&B⇨♙£55-£60 ₧

The Priory

Maenan, Llanrwst, Gwynedd LL26 0UL
Tel: 0492 660247 Fax: 0492 660734

The Priory, a Victorian house built on the site of the Cistercian Maenan Abbey, is a country hotel in attractive gardens set back from the A470 in the beautiful Conwy Valley and convenient for the A55 Expressway.

A warm welcome awaits you, freshly prepared food is served in the cosy Bars and Restaurant of repute and there are 12 fully equipped en-suite bedrooms available.

The hotel is the perfect setting for conferences and functions as well as the ideal base from which to discover Snowdonia and North Wales.

Lochgilphead - Lolworth

⚓ sauna solarium ♪ xmas
V ❖ ℒ ✻ Bar Lunch £5-£10&alc Dinner £12.50-£15&alc Last dinner 8.30pm
CONF. Thtr 50 Class 25 Board 25 Del from £50
Credit Cards ①③

LOCHINVER Highland *Sutherland* Map **14** NC02

★★★ 78% **Inver Lodge**
IV27 4LU (A835 to Lochinver continue through village and turn left after village hall, follow private road for .50m) ☎(05714) 496 FAX (05714) 395
Closed 17 Oct-25 Apr

Courtesy and Care 1994

Nicholas Gorton is the affable manager of this hotel, and much credit is due to him and his eager young staff for maintaining the standards of service and hospitality which have earned this hotel an AA Courtesy and Care Award this year. Our inspector noted that guests were constantly seen to thank staff for their efforts. Set high above the village, this modern hotel was built in 1988 and all its spacious, thoughtfully equipped bedrooms have fine views over Inver Bay. There are 2 large, comfortable lounges plus an attractive cocktail lounge leading to the dining room, where locally caught fish is always on the varied menu.
20⇌(2fb) CTV in all bedrooms ® T sB&B⇌£56-£66 dB&B⇌£100-£112 ♻
30P 🅿 ❀ ♪ snooker sauna solarium *xmas*
♕ Scottish & French V ❖ ℒ ✼ ✻ Sunday Lunch £14 Dinner £27&alc Last dinner 9pm
Credit Cards ①②③⑤

LOCKERBIE Dumfries & Galloway *Dumfriesshire*
Map **11** NY18

★★★ 66% **Dryfesdale**
DG11 2SF (from A74 take 'Lockerbie North' junction) ☎(0576) 202427 FAX (0576) 204187
Standing in its own grounds to the north of the town this 18th-century former manse, personally run by members of the Smith family, offers comfortable accommodation. The most spacious bedrooms are in a small ground floor extension, and public areas include an attractive restaurant and cosy bar.
15⇌ℕ(1fb) CTV in all bedrooms ® T ✻ sB&B⇌ℕ£46-£50 dB&B⇌ℕ£72-£74 ♻
50P ❀ *xmas*
♕ English & French V ❖ ℒ ✻ Lunch £11.50&alc Dinner £16.50&alc Last dinner 9.30pm
Credit Cards ①②③

★★ 68% **Somerton House**
Carlisle Rd DG11 2DR (off A74) ☎(0576) 202583 FAX (0576) 202384
Closed 25 Dec
This late Victorian mansion retains many of its fine original features, notably some exceptional timber panelling and ornate cornices, but still offers all modern facilities in comfortably appointed bedrooms and tastefully decorated public areas. The menus offer good value, freshly prepared and enjoyable dishes.
7⇌ℕ(2fb) CTV in all bedrooms ® T
100P ❀
♕ International V ❖ ℒ ✼ Last dinner 9.30pm
Credit Cards ①②③

★ 64% **Ravenshill House**
12 Dumfries Rd DG11 2EF (on A709, 400yds from A74 slip road) ☎(0576) 202882 FAX (0576) 202882
A small redstone villa situated in a residential area to the west of the town, the hotel provides a friendly atmosphere and comfortable accommodation in simply furnished bedrooms. Public areas are limited to a cosy bar and pleasantly appointed restaurant.
7rm(6⇌ℕ)(1fb)1🛏 CTV in all bedrooms ® T sB&B⇌ℕfr£32 dB&B⇌ℕfr£49.50
35P ❀
♕ Scottish, French & Italian V ✼ Sunday Lunch £8.75-£10.50alc Dinner £7.50-£18alc Last dinner 9pm
Credit Cards ①②③ £

LOLWORTH Cambridgeshire Map **05** TL36

Forte Travelodge
Huntingdon Rd CB3 8DR (on A604) ☎Crafts Hill (0954) 781335 Central Res (0800) 850950

This modern building offers a good standard of accommodation for overnight stops. Smart, spacious and well equipped bedrooms, all with en suite bathrooms, are suitable for family use, and meals may be taken at the nearby family restaurant. For more details about Travelodges, consult the Contents page, under Hotel Groups.
20⇌ℕ✻ B⇌ℕ£31.95 (room only)

AA

Best Restaurants
In Britain

The Abbey Well Guide to
AA Recommended Restaurants

THIS NEW EDITION ONCE AGAIN FEATURES ONLY THE VERY BEST RESTAURANTS, ASSESSED BY THE AA'S HIGHLY PROFESSIONAL HOTEL AND RESTAURANT INSPECTORS.

OUR ROSETTE AWARD SYSTEM RECOGNISES FLAIR, IMAGINATION AND ORIGINALITY IN FOOD AND PRESENTATION. WITH MORE THAN 1000 ENTRIES, CHOOSING THE PLACE FOR THAT SPECIAL MEAL HAS NEVER BEEN SIMPLER.

AVAILABLE FROM AA SHOPS AND GOOD BOOKSELLERS AT £11.99

Index of London Hotels

Page No.	Hotel	No. shown on plan	Plan Reference
394	Academy (WC1)	1	Plan 4 B6
387	Athenaeum (W1)	1	Plan 3 E4
378	Bardon Lodge (SE3)		Plan 1 E3
382	Basil Street (SW3)	2	Plan 3 D3
379	The Berkeley (SW1)	3	Plan 3 D4
390	The Berkshire (W1)	2	Plan 4 A5
394	Bonnington (WC1)	3	Plan 4 C6
387	Britannia Inter-Continental (W1)	4	Plan 3 E5
387	Browns (W1)	4	Plan 4 A4
382	Capital (SW3)	5	Plan 3 D3
384	Cannizaro (SW19)		Plan 1 C2
391	Carnarvon (W5)		Plan 1 B4
391	Central Park (W2)	6	Plan 3 A5
378	Charles Bernard (NW3)		Plan 1 D4
388	Chesterfield (W1)	7	Plan 3 E5
387	Churchill Inter-Continental (W1)	8	Plan 3 D6
378	Clarendon (SE3)		Plan 1 E3
384	Claridge's (W1)	9	Plan 3 E6
388	Clifton-Ford (W1)	10	Plan 3 E6
378	The Clive Hotel (NW3)		Plan 1 D4
391	Coburg (W2)	11	Plan 3 A5
385	Connaught (W1)	12	Plan 3 E5
392	The Copthorne Tara (W8)	13	Plan 3 A3
388	The Cumberland (W1)	14	Plan 3 D6
385	The Dorchester (W1)	15	Plan 3 E5
395	Drury Lane Moat House (WC2)	1	Plan 2 D5
381	Duke's (SW1)	2	Plan 2 A1
382	Forte Crest (SW1)	3	Plan 2 A2
390	Forte Crest (W1)	5	Plan 4 A6
394	Forte Crest (WC1)	6	Plan 4 C6
378	Forte Posthouse (NW3)		Plan 1 D4
384	Forum (SW7)	16	Plan 3 A2
385	Four Seasons (formerly Inn on the Park) (W1)	25	Plan 3 E4
384	Gloucester (SW7)	17	Plan 3 A2
380	Goring (SW1)	7	Plan 4 A2
390	The Grafton (W1)	8	Plan 4 A6
386	Grosvenor House (W1)	18	Plan 3 E5
381	Grosvenor Thistle (SW1)	9	Plan 4 A1
381	Halkin (SW1)	19	Plan 3 E3
395	The Hampshire (WC2)	10	Plan 4 C4
636	Hilton National (Wembley)		Plan 1 B4
393	Hilton National (W14)		Plan 1 C3
383	Hogarth (SW5)	20	Plan 3 A2
378	Holiday Inn Garden Court (NW2)		Plan 1 C4
384	Holiday Inn Kensington (SW7)	21	Plan 3 A2
393	Holiday Inn Kings Cross (WC1)	11	Plan 4 D6
388	Holiday Inn Mayfair (W1)	12	Plan 4 A4
391	Hospitality Inn Bayswater (W2)	22	Plan 3 A5
380	Hyatt Carlton Tower (SW1)	23	Plan 3 D3
380	The Hyde Park (SW1)	23	Plan 3 D3
378	Ibis (NW1)		Plan 1 D4
379	Ibis Greenwich (SE10)		Plan 1 E3
385	Inn on the Park (now Four Seasons) (W1)	25	Plan 3 E4
386	Hotel Inter-Continental (W1)	26	Plan 3 E4
394	The Kenilworth (WC1)	13	Plan 4 C5
377	Kennedy (NW1)		Plan 1 D4
392	Kensington Close (W8)	27	Plan 3 A3
393	Kensington Hilton (W11)		Plan 1 C3
392	Kensington Palace Thistle (W8)	28	Plan 3 A3
392	Kensington Park Thistle (W8)	29	Plan 3 A3
380	Lanesborough (SW1)	30	Plan 3 E4
386	Langham Hilton (W1)	14	Plan 4 A5
392	Hotel Lexham (W8)	31	Plan 3 A2

364

INDEX OF LONDON HOTELS

Page No.		No. shown on plan	Plan Reference
387	**London Hilton** (W1)	32	Plan 3 E4
394	**London Ryan** (WC1)		(not on plan)
381	**The Lowndes** (SW1)	33	Plan 3 D3
394	**The Marlborough** (WC1)	4	Plan 2 C5
389	**Mandeville** (W1)	34	Plan 3 E6
378	**Mariott** (NW3)		Plan 1 D4
390	**Marriott** (Grosvenor Sq) (W1)	35	Plan 3 E6
390	**Marriott** (George St) (W1)	36	Plan 3 C6
386	**May Fair Inter-Continental** (W1)	15	Plan 4 A4
386	**Le Meridien London** (W1)	5	Plan 2 A2
387	**Montcalm** (W1)	37	Plan 3 D6
389	**Mostyn** (W1)	38	Plan 3 D6
395	**The Mountbatten** (WC2)	16	Plan 4 C5
389	**Mount Royal** (W1)	39	Plan 3 D6
392	**Novotel** (W6)		Plan 1 C3
391	**Park Court** (W2)	40	Plan 3 A5
388	**Park Lane** (W1)	41	Plan 3 E4
391	**Plaza on Hyde Park** (W2)	42	Plan 3 B5
377	**Raglan Hall** (N10)		Plan 1 D5
390	**Regent Palace** (W1)	6	Plan 2 B3
378	**Regents Park Hilton** (NW1)		Plan 1 D4
384	**Rembrandt** (SW7)	43	Plan 3 C3
377	**Ridgeway** (E4)		Plan 1 E5
386	**Ritz** (W1)	17	Plan 4 A3
392	**Royal Garden** (W8)	44	Plan 3 A4
382	**Royal Horseguards Thistle** (SW1)	7	Plan 2 D1
390	**Royal Lancaster** (W2)	45	Plan 3 B5
395	**Royal Trafalgar Thistle** (WC2)	8	Plan 2 C2
381	**Royal Westminster Thistle** (SW1)	18	Plan 4 A1
381	**Rubens** (SW1)	19	Plan 4 A2
393	**Hotel Russell** (WC1)	20	Plan 4 C6
388	**St George's** (W1)	21	Plan 4 A5
394	**The Savoy** (WC2)	9	Plan 2 E3
390	**The Savoy Court** (W1)	46	Plan 3 D6
388	**Selfridge** (W1)	47	Plan 3 E6
389	**Sherlock Holmes** (W1)	48	Plan 3 E6
381	**Stafford** (SW1)	10	Plan 2 A1
395	**Strand Palace** (WC2)	11	Plan 2 E3
382	**Swallow International** (SW5)	49	Plan 3 A2
382	**Tophams Ebury Court** (SW1)	50	Plan 3 E3
377	**Tower Thistle** (E1)	1	Plan 5 C3
384	**The Vanderbilt** (SW7)	51	Plan 3 B2
395	**The Waldorf** (WC2)	12	Plan 2 E4
388	**The Westbury** (W1)	22	Plan 4 A4
390	**White's** (W2)	52	Plan 3 B5

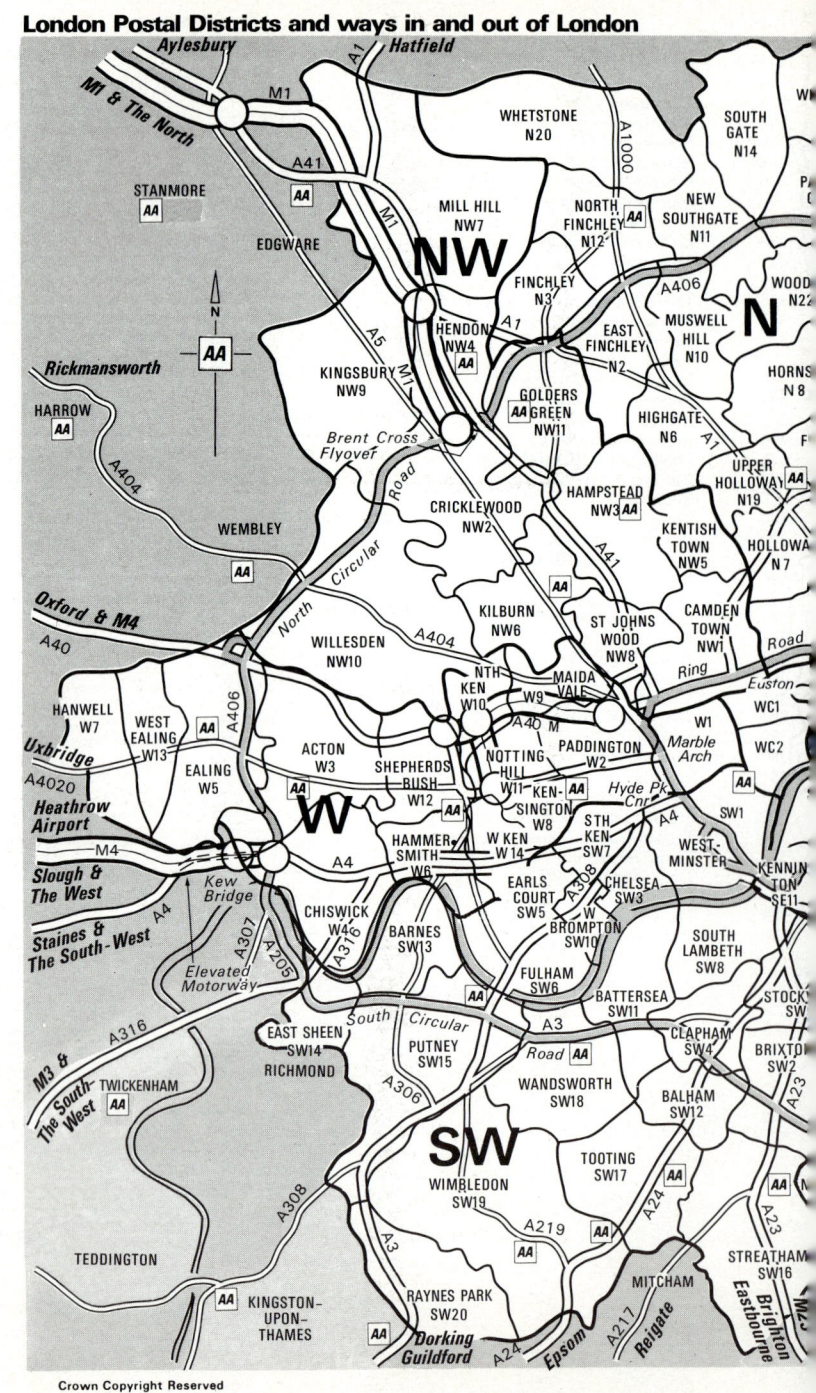

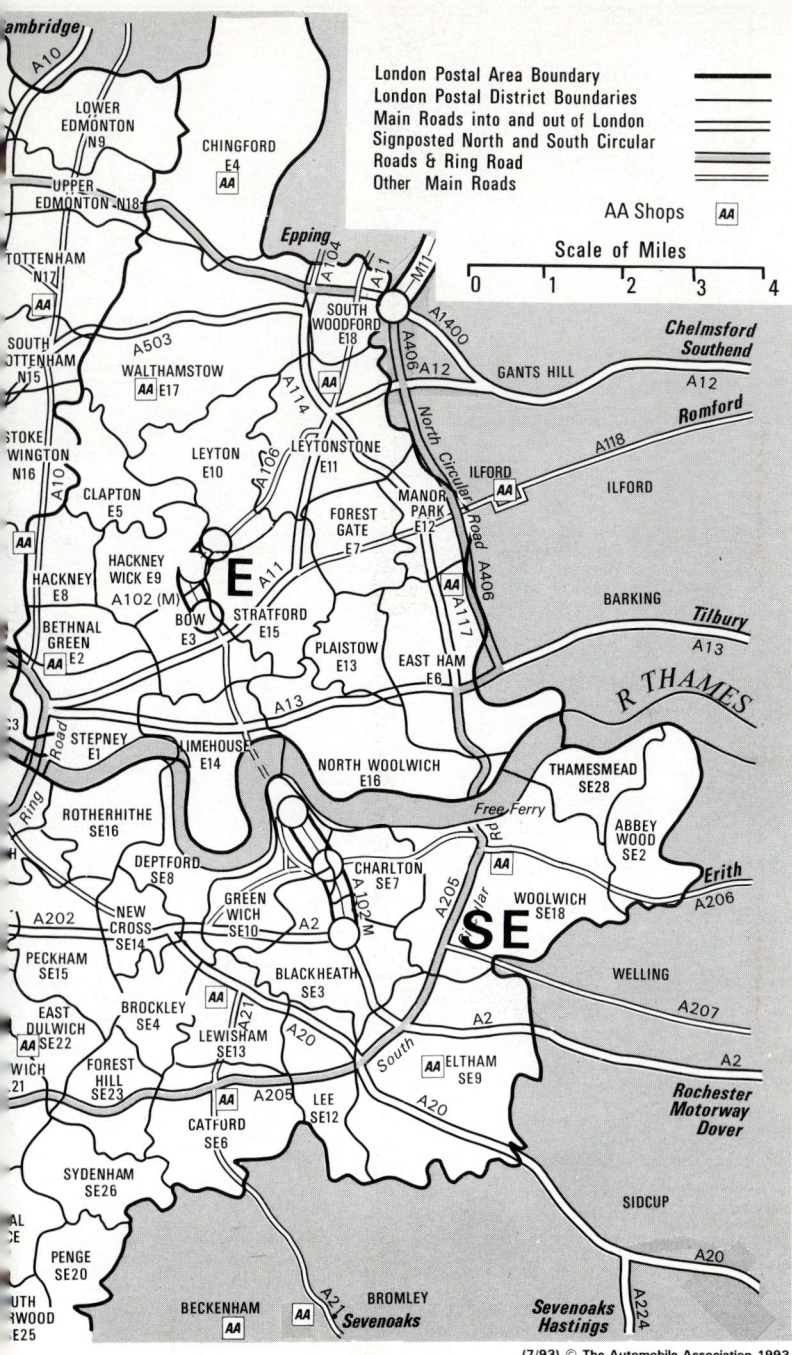

London Plan 1

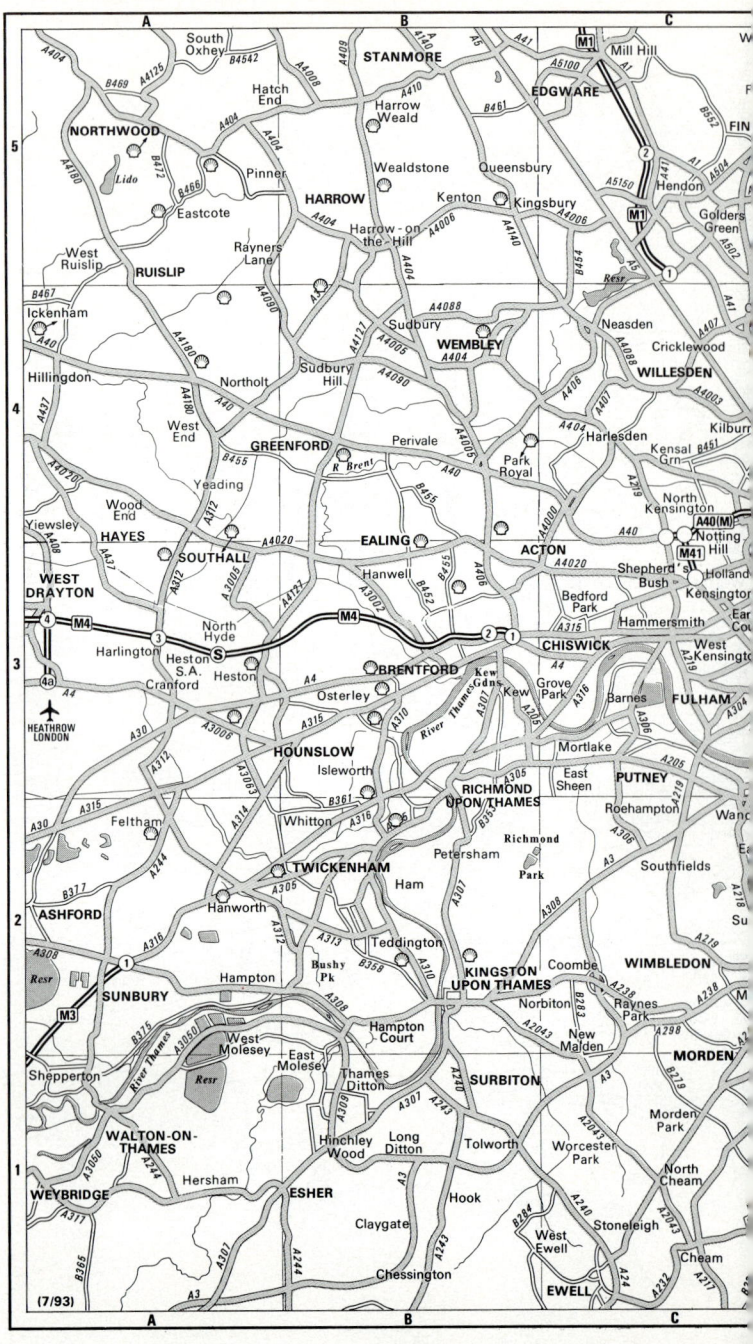

London Plan 1

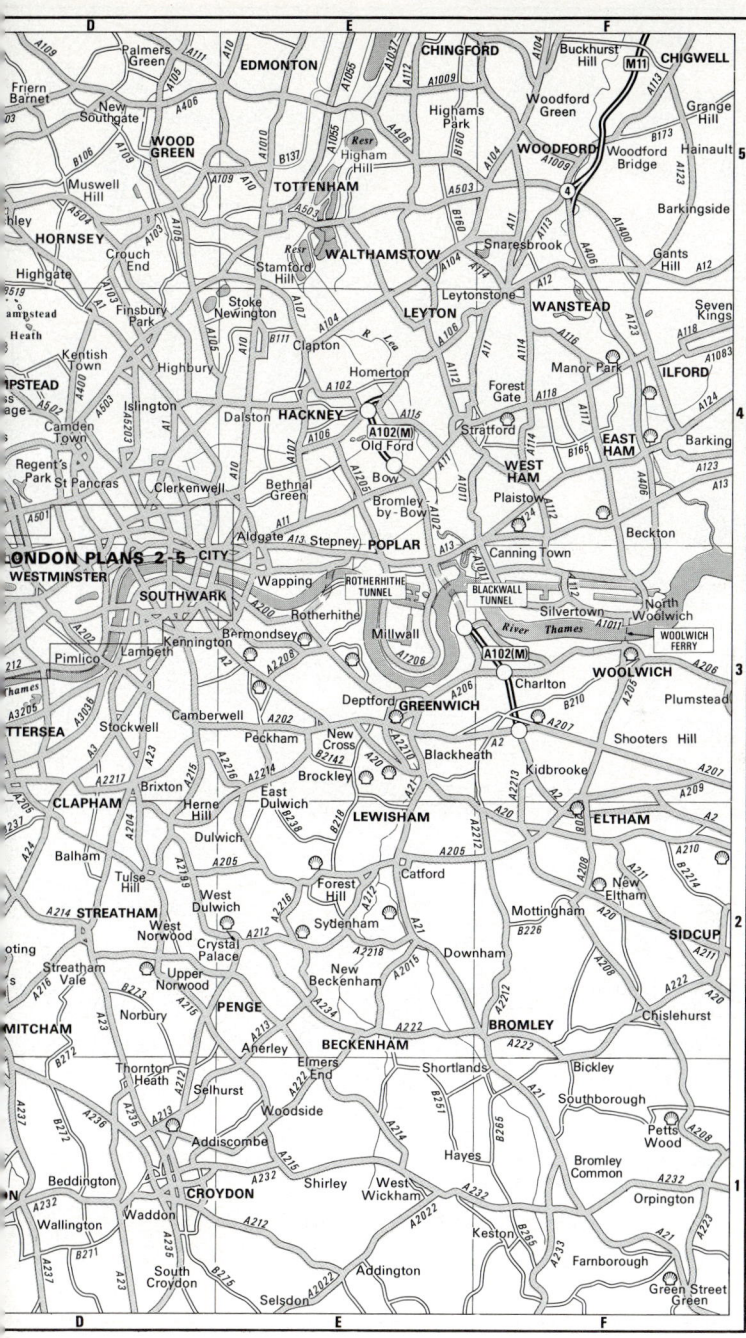

© The Automobile Association 1993

London Plan 2

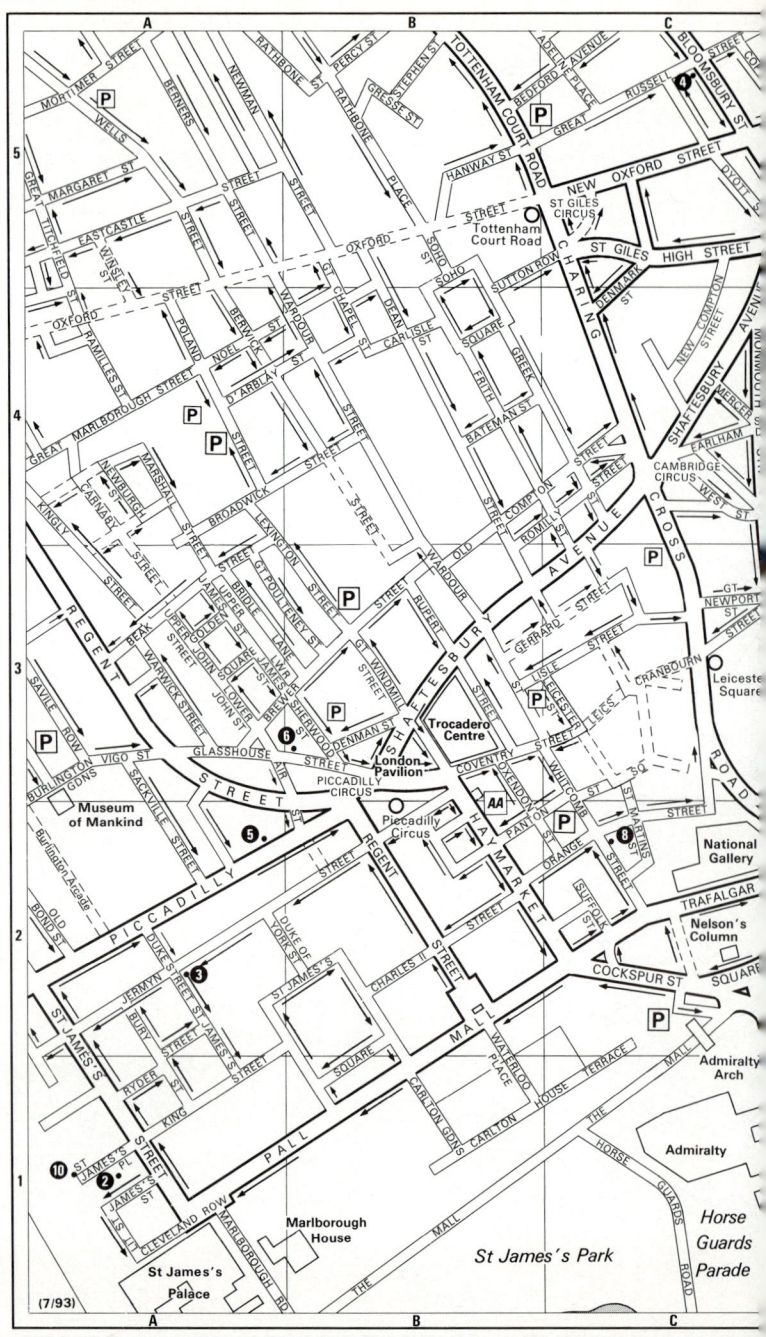

London Plan 2

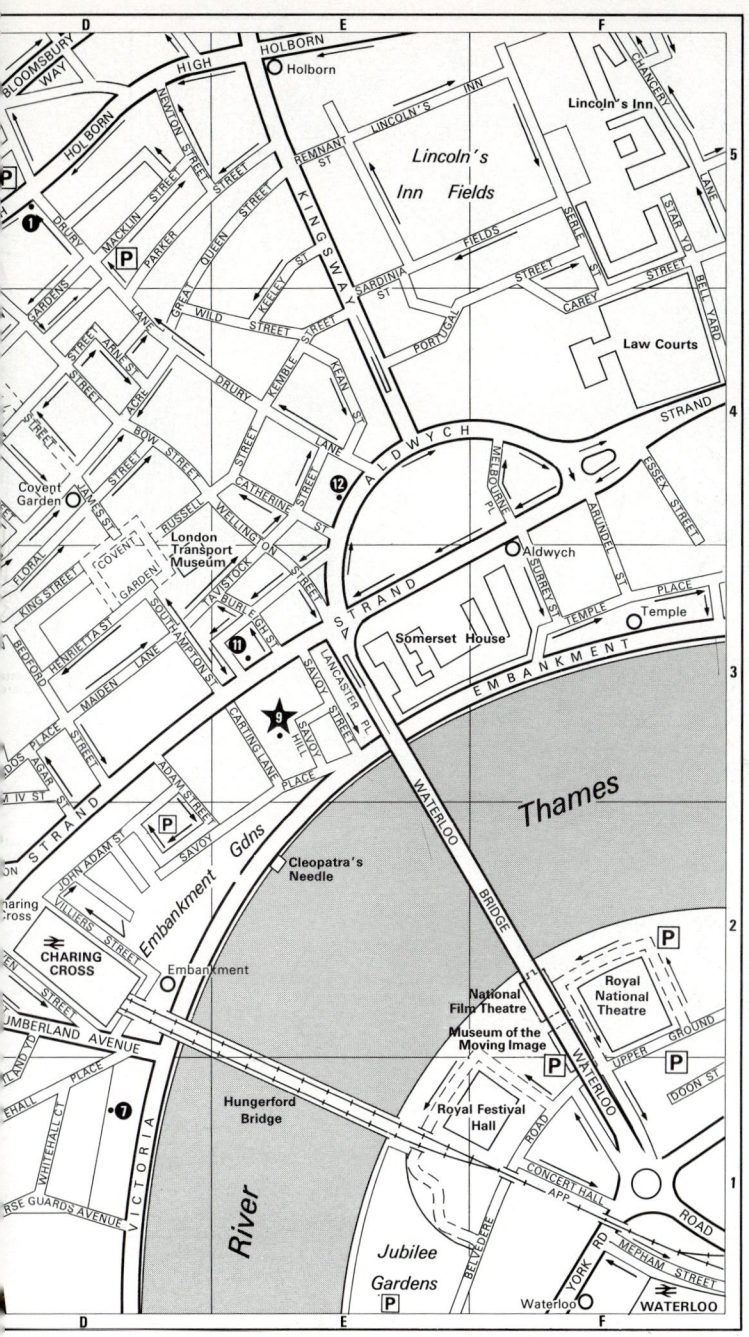

London Plan 3

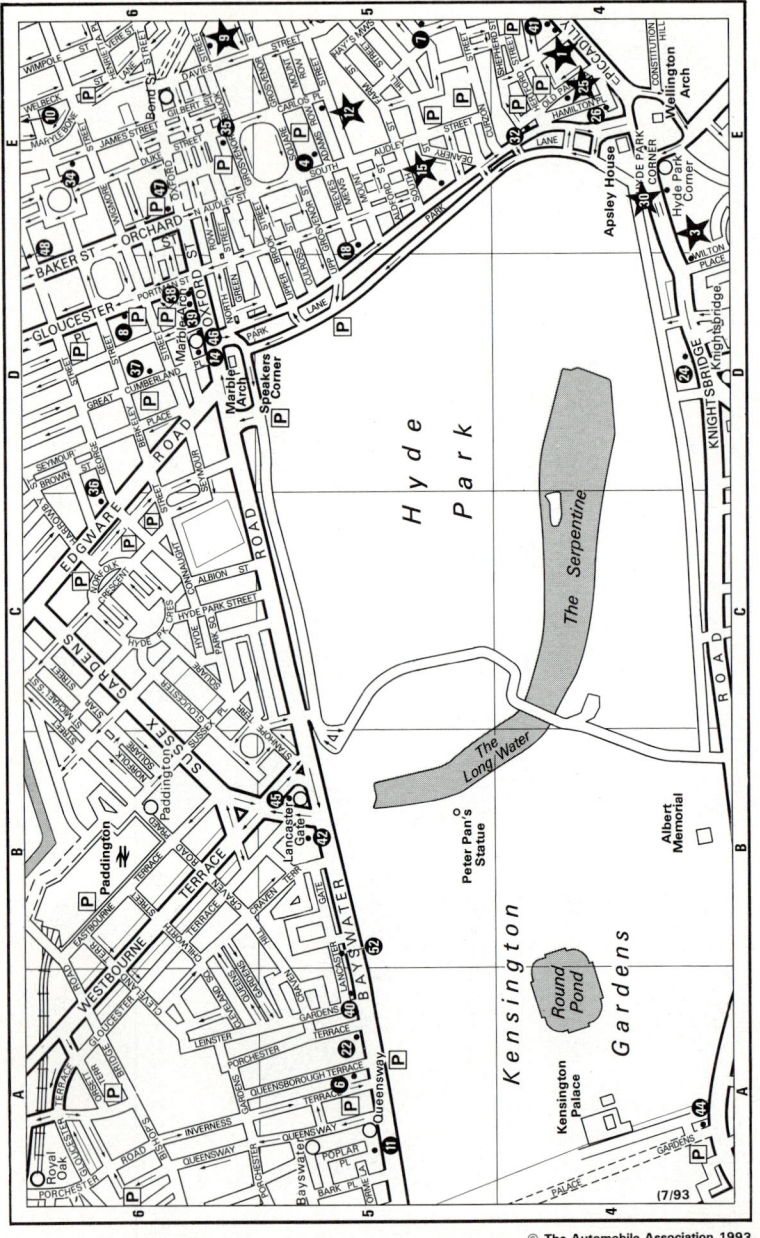

London Plan 3

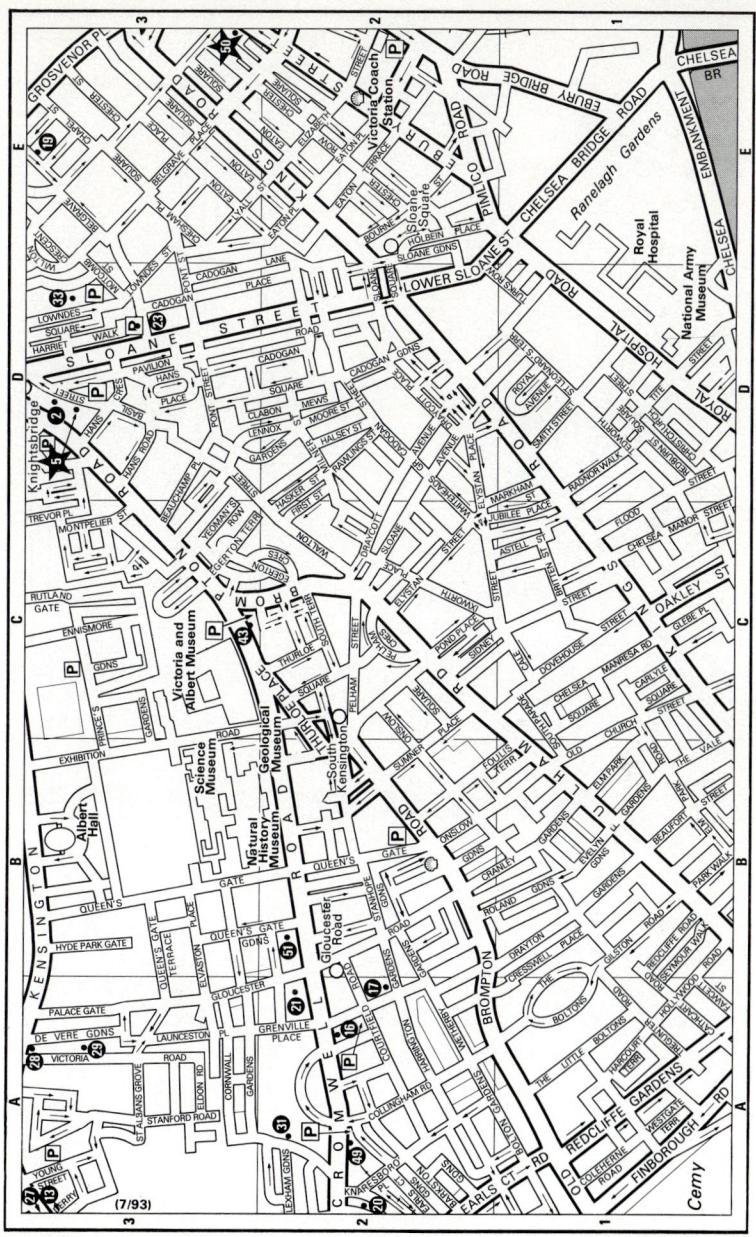

London Plan 4

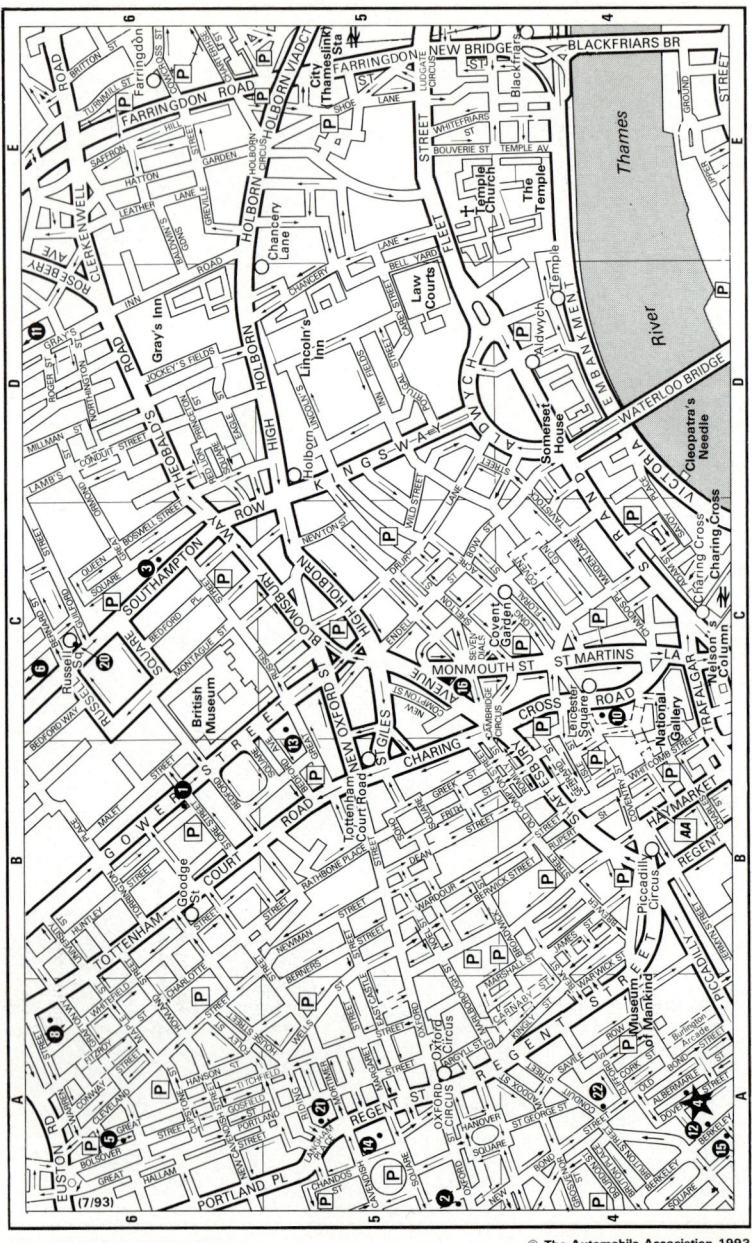

London Plan 4

London Plan 5

London E1 Stepney - NW1 Regents Park

LONDON Greater London Plans 1–5, pages 366–376. (Small scale maps 4 & 5 at back of book.) A map of the London postal area appears on pages 366–367. Hotels are listed below in postal district order. Detailed plans 2–5 show the locations of AA-appointed hotels within the Central London postal districts which are indicated by a number, followed by a grid reference e.g. A5 to help you find the location. Plan 1 shows the districts covered within the outer area keyed by a grid reference e.g. A1. Other places within the county of London are listed under their respective place names and are also keyed to this plan or the main map section.

E1 STEPNEY AND EAST OF THE TOWER OF LONDON

★★★★64% **Tower Thistle**
St Katharine's Way E1 9LD ☎071-481 2575
FAX 071-488 4106

THISTLE HOTELS

Overlooking Tower Bridge from its spectacular location on the banks of the Thames, this is a large modern and busy hotel. Smart public areas offer a range of eating options, one of which doubles as a nightclub after dark. The rather functional bedrooms were scheduled for upgrading at our last visit, and some of them offer splendid views. Service in most areas reflects a genuine desire to please.
808⇌♠(24fb)⊁in 320 bedrooms CTV in all bedrooms ® T ✱
✻ sB&♠£115–£145 dB⇌♠£135–£165 (room only) 🍴
Lift ⦅ ▦ 136P (£1.50 per hour) 116🛎 (£1.50 per hour) ♪ *xmas*
♡ International V ♢ ⚏ ⊁ ✱ Lunch £14.95–£23.50 High tea fr£5.50 Dinner £14.95–£15.20 Last dinner 10.30pm
CONF. Thtr 250 Class 150 Board 28 Del £15
Credit Cards [1][2][3][4][5]

E4 CHINGFORD

See LONDON plan 1 *F5*
★★64% **Ridgeway**
115/117 The Ridgeway, North Chingford E4 6QU (on B169, leave M25 at junc25/ M11 at junc 4) ☎081-529 1964 FAX 081-524 9130
This family-run hotel in a residential area has been refurbished throughout to provide modern, comfortable accommodation. Public areas are limited to a small lounge bar and a bright dining room, which offers a set price menu and a carte.
20⇌♠(4fb)🎛 CTV in all bedrooms ® T ✱ (ex guide dogs)
✻ sB&B⇌♠£25–£40 dB&B⇌♠£40–£50 🍴
⦅ CTV 9P ⊞ ✿ *xmas*
♡ English & Continental
Credit Cards [1][2][3]

N10 MUSWELL HILL

See LONDON plan 1*D5*
★★★62% **Raglan Hall**
8-12 Queens Ave, Muswell Hill N10 3NR ☎081-883 9836 FAX 081-883 5002
46⇌♠(7fb)2🎛⊁in 6 bedrooms CTV in all bedrooms ® T ✱ (ex guide dogs) ✻ sB&B⇌♠£42.50–£69 dB&B⇌♠£65–£79 🍴
⦅ 7P ✿
V ♢ ⚏ ⊁ ✱ Lunch £8.95 Dinner £14.95&alc Last dinner 10pm
Credit Cards [1][2][3][5]

NW1 REGENT'S PARK

See LONDON plan 1*D4*
★★★63% **Kennedy**
Cardington St NW1 2LP ☎071-387 4400 FAX 071-387 5122

MOUNT CHARLOTTE THISTLE HOTELS

This modern hotel is in a side street close to Euston station and partly overlooks a quiet park. Public areas are spacious, comfortable ➭

AA ★★ **Ridgeway Hotel** ★★ AA

This welcoming family run hotel has a comfortable Bar and Lounge area plus a beautiful Regency Style restaurant offering fresh cuisine daily. The twenty luxurious bedrooms are all appointed with en-suite facilities. Located just 5 minutes from the M25 and the North Circular Road, there is also ample car parking available.

**115-117 THE RIDGEWAY
NORTH CHINGFORD
LONDON E4 6QU
TEL: 081-529 1964   FAX: 081-524 9130**

★★★★AA

THE TOWER
THISTLE HOTEL

St Katharine's Way, London E1 9LD
Tel: 071-481 2575   Fax: 071-488 4106

*Your choice in
the City*

For Reservations at over 100
Mount Charlotte Thistle Hotels
Telephone London: 071 937 8033.

THISTLE HOTELS

London

NW1 Regent's Park - SE3 Blackheath

and well staffed. Bedrooms, all of a similar size, are well equipped and air conditioned, the executive rooms being more attractive.
360⇨♠(25fb)⚲in 18 bedrooms CTV in all bedrooms ® T ✗ (ex guide dogs) ✱ sB⇨♠£75-£90 dB⇨♠£85-£105 (room only) 旦
Lift ⓒ 24☎ (£5 per night)
♀ English & French V ❀ ⚱ ⚲ ✱ Lunch £12.50&alc Dinner £12.50&alc Last dinner 10.30pm
CONF. Thtr 100 Class 45 Board 48 Del £105
Credit Cards [1][2][3][5]

★★58% Hotel Ibis Euston
3 Cardington St NW1 2LW ☎071-388 7777
FAX 071-388 0001

300⇨♠✱in 65 bedrooms CTV in all bedrooms ®⚱ T sB⇨♠£39.50-£49.50 dB⇨♠£39.50-£49.50 (room only)
Lift ☎ (charged)
♀ English & French V ❀ ⚱ ⚲ ✱ Lunch £8.50-£10.50&alc Dinner £8.50-£10.50&alc Last dinner 10.30pm
CONF. Thtr 200 Class 70 Board 60 Del from £79
Credit Cards [1][2][3][5]

NW2 BRENT CROSS

See LONDON plan 1*C4*
○**Holiday Inn Garden Court**
Tilling Rd, Brent Cross NW2 3DS
☎081-208 1818 081-452 5001 FAX 081-208 2265
Due to open Autumn 1993
153⇨♠

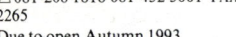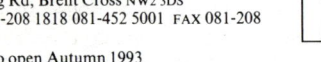

NW3 HAMPSTEAD AND SWISS COTTAGE

See LONDON plan 1*D4*
★★★60% The Clive
Primrose Hill NW3 3NA (Hilton) ☎071-586 2233 FAX 071-586 2233
96⇨♠ CTV in all bedrooms ® T sB&B⇨♠£52.50-£55 dB&B⇨♠£61.74-£66 旦
Lift ⓒ CTV 20P V ❀ ⚱ Lunch £9.95-£17.50&alc Dinner £13.50-£17.50&alc Last dinner 10pm
Credit Cards [1][2][3][4][5]

★★★55% Charles Bernard
5-7 Frognal, Hampstead NW3 6AL ☎071-794 0101 FAX 071-794 0100

Situated just off Finchley Road, this hotel benefits from free car parking. Compact bedrooms have bright modern decor; there is an open-plan lounge bar with 24-hour reception; breakfast, in the small dining room, is self-service.

57⇨♠ CTV in all bedrooms ®⚱ T ✗ sB&B⇨♠£45-£59.50 dB&B⇨♠£55-£69 旦
Lift ⓒ CTV 15P
♀ English & French ❀ ⚱ Lunch £10.50-£17alc High tea £3.75-£5.75alc Dinner fr£9.50&alc Last dinner 9.15pm
Credit Cards [1][2][3][5]

Forte Posthouse
Haverstock Hill NW3 4RB ☎071-794 8121 FAX 071-435 5586

Suitable for both the business and leisure traveller, this bright hotel provides modern accommodation in well equipped bedrooms with en suite bathrooms. For more details about Forte Posthouse hotels, consult the Contents page, under Hotel Groups.
140⇨♠✱ B⇨♠£41.50-£53.50 (room only)
CONF. Thtr 30 Board 12 Del from £79.50

Marriott
128 King Henry's Rd NW3 3ST (near Swiss Cottage Underground Station) ☎071-722 7711
FAX 071-586 5822

A large and busy hotel, which is ideal for the business and leisure traveller, offering a wide range of services and a choice of eating options. Bedrooms are comfortable and equipped with modern facilities. For more details about Marriott hotels, consult the Contents page, under Hotel Groups.
303⇨♠✱ dB⇨♠fr£155 (room only)
CONF. Thtr 400 Class 220 Board 35 Del £155

NW8 REGENT'S PARK

See LONDON plan 1*D4*
★★★★61% London Regents Park Hilton
18 Lodge Rd NW8 7JT ☎071-722 7722

This modern hotel overlooks Lords Cricket Ground. Busy public areas revolve around an open plan lobby and bar/lounge and an informal American brasserie. Bedrooms are well equipped with up-to-date facilities, including air conditioning and minibars. Japanese guests have their own restaurant, and room service dishes. Services include parking and fast checkout.
377⇨♠ CTV in all bedrooms ® T ✱ sB⇨♠£99-£125 dB⇨♠£125-£135 (room only)
囲 P
♀ International
CONF. Thtr 150 Class 75 Board 60 Del £125
Credit Cards [1][2][3][4][5]

SE3 BLACKHEATH

See LONDON plan 1 *E3*
★★65% Bardon Lodge
Stratheden Rd SE3 7TH ☎081-853 4051 FAX 081-858 7387
Under new ownership, this friendly and well run hotel is currently being refurbished and upgraded. In the Lamplight Restaurant chef Marcel Obery offers an interesting and varied menu of reliable and consistent dishes cooked in modern style. There is a comfortable bar and a small lounge, and service is friendly and helpful.
37rm(5⇨23♠)(3fb)2☒ CTV in all bedrooms ® T ✗ (ex guide dogs) ✱ sB&B£40-£45 sB&B⇨♠£45-£55 dB&B⇨♠£49-£90 旦
ⓒ CTV 16P ✻ *xmas*
V ❀ ⚱ ⚲ ✱ Lunch £11.15-£13.65alc Dinner fr£9.95&alc Last dinner 9.30pm
CONF. Thtr 35 Class 20 Board 20 Del from £73.50
Credit Cards [1][2][3][5]

★★58% Clarendon
8-16 Montpelier Row, Blackheath SE3 0RW ☎081-318 4321
FAX 081-318 4378
The Clarendon is part of an impressive Georgian building with views over the common of Blackheath to the walled edges of Greenwich Park. Though still very traditional in appearance, improvements are ongoing and the smart Chart Bar and residents' lounge have been completed to a good standard. Bedrooms tend to be dated, particularly those at the front.
197rm(151⇨)(37fb)2☒ CTV in all bedrooms ® T sB&B£45.50 sB&B⇨£49.50 dB&B£73.50 dB&B⇨£84 旦
Lift ⓒ CTV 80P ✻ hairdressing salon
♀ English French & Italian V ❀ ⚱ ⚲ ✱ Lunch £8.50-£9.25 Dinner £8-£9&alc Last dinner 9.45pm
CONF. Thtr 150 Class 50 Board 120 Del £75
Credit Cards [1][2][3][4][5]

For full, independent restaurant reviews,
see the AA Abbey Well *Restaurant Guide*

SE10 GREENWICH

See LONDON plan 1*E3*
★★ 54% **Hotel Ibis**
30 Stockwell St SE10 9JN ☎081-305 1177 FAX 081-858 7139

In the heart of Greenwich, this modern hotel offers budget accommodation in bedrooms which are functional and somewhat stark, but have bright bathrooms. Public areas are open plan, and both the bar and restaurant are open all day. Breakfast is entirely self-service, to the extent of having to collect your own place setting. 82⇨⇧ CTV in all bedrooms ® T
Lift 40P
♀ English & French V ✿ ⚲ ⚡ ✳ Bar Lunch £2.50-£7 High tea fr£3.95 Dinner fr£9.75&alc Last dinner 10.15pm
Credit Cards ①②③④⑤

SW1 WESTMINSTER

★★★★★❀❀
THE BERKELEY
Wilton Place,
Knightsbridge SW1X 7RL
(Leading Hotels)
☎071-235 6000 FAX 071-235 4330

Discreet luxury abounds at the Berkeley, attracting a regular and stylish clientèle. While retaining old-fashioned standards of hotel-keeping, it has advanced technologically to satisfy the ➪

Charles Bernard Hotel Ltd
5 Frognal, Hampstead, London NW3
Telephone: 071-794 0101
Fax: 071-794 0100   ★★★   Telex: 23560
The Charles Bernard Hotel is purpose built, privately owned, and situated near to Hampstead Heath.
Completely refurbished in 1989, all 57 rooms have private facilities, colour TV plus satellite, telephone, tea and coffee facilities, trouser press and hair dryer. Pleasant efficient staff ensure that your stay is comfortable and enjoyable.

A home from home.

It has to be the Clarendon....

At the end of a hard day on the road, what better way to relax than with a drink at the Chart Room bar in The Clarendon Hotel.

Perhaps a quiet read in our relaxing lounge, arrange for a trim in our unisex hairdresser or settle down to watch television; put your feet up and call the family on the direct line telephone in your room.

The Clarendon Hotel ... we like to think you will always feel at home with us.

Montpelier Row, Blackheath, London SE3 ORW
Tel: 081 318 4321   Telex No. 896367 CLALDN G   Fax: 081 318 4378
SMALL ENOUGH TO CARE - BIG ENOUGH TO COPE

VIP ROOM
BRIDAL SUITE
WEDDING
RECEPTIONS.
WEEKEND
BREAKS
BAR
&
RESTAURANT.

AA
★★★

the Clarendon Hotel

SW1 Westminster

demands of the international traveller. Bedrooms still have bells for summoning the valet, maid or floor waiter, but a fax machine is just as easily available. The panelling, marble flooring and pillars of the lobby are unspoilt by the usual modern reception desk, which is hidden to the rear, and the foyer leads into an agreeable lounge, and from there into the main restaurant. Chef Schmidl's cuisine is traditionally conservative, of the old school of classical training. Unfashionable, perhaps, but it is nonetheless enjoyable to see a menu of considerable length, not over ambitious, and using good quality ingredients. Under the guidance of Mr Sebastiani, service is very refined and attentive, and room service is a particular strength.

160⇌♠ CTV in all bedrooms🛏 T ✈ ✱ sB⇌♠£188-£235 dB⇌♠£258.50-£293.75 (room only) 🍴
Lift ⟨ 🏛 50🚗 (£20 per 24hrs) ⇌ 🏊 (heated) sauna solarium gymnasium cinema ♫ xmas
♀ International V ♂ ♃ ✱ Lunch £19.50&alc Dinner £21&alc Last dinner 10.45pm
CONF. Thtr 200 Class 70 Board 50
Credit Cards 1 2 3 5

★★★★★

★★★★★✿✿✿✿ **LANESBOROUGH**
Hyde Park Corner SW1X 7TA
☎071-259 5599 FAX 071-259 5606

Remodelled at enormous expense from the old St George's Hospital, the Lanesborough is not only the most technologically advanced hotel, it also has the highest staff/guest ratio in London, and each guest is assigned a personal butler. The public rooms exude quality: a lovely mahogany panelled cocktail bar, an elegant – though not particularly comfortable – lounge and a marbled foyer (it is said that an entire hillside was excavated to ensure the same strain and quality of marble was used throughout the hotel!) Executive Chef Paul Gaylor has steered the cuisine towards an eclectic style, with some eastern influences and food that is refreshingly straightforward and highly enjoyable: saute of red mullet with a pungent sardine tapenade; scallops in batter with a remoulade sauce; medallions of venison with a beautifully balanced elderberry sauce and a pear poached in red wine with a cinnamon mousse and iced caramel parfait.

95⇌♠✱in 24 bedrooms CTV in all bedrooms🛏 T ✱ sB⇌♠£194-£223 dB⇌♠£258.50-£324 (room only)
Lift ⟨ 🏛 38🚗 (£20 per night) ⇌
♀ International V ♂ ♃ ✱ Lunch £20.50-£24&alc Dinner fr£26.50&alc Last dinner mdnt
CONF. Thtr 75 Class 40 Board 40
Credit Cards 1 2 3 4 5

★★★★★✿✿**75%** **The Hyde Park**
Knightsbridge SW1Y 7LA ☎071-235 2000
FAX 071-235 4552

EXCLUSIVE HOTELS of the World

One of the Forte Group flagships, the Hyde Park with all its Edwardian splendour sits conveniently in the heart of Knightsbridge. A new car valet parking service has been introduced, complementing the excellent luggage handling service. Refurbishment continues in the substantial bedrooms, many featuring antique furniture and marbled bathrooms. There are 2 restaurants: The Cavalry Grill and Bar and the Park Room. Chef Fabrizio Cadei invites you to experience La Cucina Mediterranea, in which traditional Italian dishes have been influenced by his modern approach. Our inspector sampled rosettes of salmon and turbot with an excellent basil coulis, followed by fillet of beef gratinated with wild mushrooms and garnished with polenta.

185⇌♠2🛏✱in 19 bedrooms CTV in all bedrooms🛏 T ✈ (ex guide dogs) ✱ sB⇌♠£229-£252 dB⇌♠£252-£323 (room only) 🍴
Lift ⟨ 🏛 ♪ ⇌ ♫ xmas
♀ English, French & Italian V ♂ ♃ ✱ Lunch £21.50&alc Dinner £29.50&alc Last dinner 10.30pm
CONF. Thtr 250 Class 140 Board 65 Del £230
Credit Cards 1 2 3 4 5

★★★★★✿✿**73%** **Hyatt Carlton Tower**
Cadogan Place SW1X 9PY ☎071-235 5411 FAX 071-235 9129

This tall Knightsbridge hotel is popular with a mainly international clientele, and the stylish public areas are bustling with people. The two restaurants offer a contrast of styles: the Rib Room, with its hearty cuts of beef and the more demure Chelsea Room where chef Bernard Gaume offers polished French cuisine from a menu encompassing fish specialities (inspectors have enjoyed some delicious lobster and turbot fricassee), grills, vegetarian meals, some classics (succulent duck terrine studded with foie gras) and some splendid desserts.

224⇌♠✱in 23 bedrooms CTV in all bedrooms🛏 T ✈ (ex guide dogs) ✱ sB⇌♠fr£199.75 dB⇌♠£246.75-£282 (room only) 🍴
Lift ⟨ 🏛 40🚗 (£1.80 per hour) ⇌ ✿ ♪ (hard) sauna solarium gymnasium beauty treatment hair salon health club ♫
♀ International V ♂ ♃ ✱ Lunch fr£21.50&alc Dinner fr£29.50&alc Last dinner 11.15pm
CONF. Thtr 207 Class 220 Board 16 Del from £252.25
Credit Cards 1 2 3 4 5

★★★★

★★★★✿✿ **GORING**
Beeston Place, Grosvenor Gardens SW1W 0JW (behind Buckingham Palace, right off Lower Grsvenor Place, just prior to the Royal Mews on the left) ☎071-396 9000 FAX 071-834 4393

This fine hotel was the first in the world to have both private bathrooms and central heating in every bedroom when it was opened by O R Goring in 1910, and technological advances have kept pace with modern expectations under the direction of the same family ever since. Its real strength, however, is the continuing commitment to a traditional style of hotel keeping, with willing and courteous service from a team of experienced staff. Individually designed and elegant bedrooms combine quality with comfort and are refreshingly free of gimmickry. Discreet public areas include a comfortable lounge leading to a small bar, and a pretty dining room. Chef John Elliot's straightforward cuisine includes such dishes as grilled calves' liver and bacon with mashed potatoes and Cumberland sausages with onion gravy, though a more elaborate meal might include a tasty appetiser of beef carpaccio and mozzarella, mousseline of sole with crab sauce, roast Gressingham duck and an enjoyable Devon apple tart served with a Calvados ice cream.

SW1 Westminster

80⇌↑ CTV in all bedrooms♪ T ✗ sB⇌↑£135-£141 dB⇌↑£170-£180 (room only) ₧
Lift ℂ 4P (£10.00) 4⚐ (£10.00) ⇎ ♫ xmas
♡ English & French V ✿ ℒ Lunch £19.50-£25 Dinner £25-£29 Last dinner 10pm
CONF. Thtr 60 Class 30 Board 30
Credit Cards [1][2][3][5]

★★★★ ❀❀77% **Halkin**
Halkin St, Belgravia SW1X 7DJ
☏071-333 1000 FAX 071-333 1100

Courtesy and Care 1994

The AA Courtesy and Care Award has this year been given to The Halkin, for its particularly high levels of discreet, professional and friendly service. It is an ulta-modern hotel, unique in both concept and design. A strong Italian influence is evident from its close links with the Armani fashion house. Although the public areas are limited in terms of comfort and space, intelligent use of lighting and mirrors creates an airy atmosphere in the marbled foyer area, and a small cocktail bar has recently been added. Fixed price menus are offered in the restaurant, with a strong emphasis on plain food using top quality produce. Most of the bedrooms are spacious and though a little stark to some, all are smart and feature modern technology at an advanced level.
41⇌↑⚓in 9 bedrooms CTV in all bedrooms♪ T
✗ (ex guide dogs) dB⇌↑£235-£288 (room only) ₧
Lift ℂ ⊞ ⚐ (£15 per day) ⇎ ♫
♡ Italian V ✿ ℒ Lunch £19-£25 Dinner £35-£45alc Last dinner 10.30pm
CONF. Thtr 42 Class 29 Board 26
Credit Cards [1][2][3][4][5]

★★★★ ❀❀❀76% **Duke's**
35 St James's Place SW1A 1NY
☏071-491 4840 FAX 071-493 1264

This deluxe hotel, offering personal service and a discreet but friendly welcome, is tucked away in a flowery courtyard in St James's. There is a very small lounge and bar where afternoon tea may be taken, or apéritifs while studying Steve Robinson's à la carte and daily menus. Cooking is in modern style, with a hint of the Mediterranean: beef consommé; lobster and roquette with mango dressing; tender pink venison with a pungent juniper sauce and crisp endive. Plain grills are also available. Bedrooms, half of them suites, are decorated with much style and are well supported by room and valet service.
66⇌↑(4fb)1⚓ CTV in all bedrooms♪ T ✗ (ex guide dogs)
sB⇌↑£185-£215 dB⇌↑£215-£275 (room only) ₧
Lift ℂ ♪ ⇎ nc5yrs xmas
♡ English & French V ✿ ℒ Lunch £19.95&alc Dinner £28.50&alc Last dinner 10pm
CONF. Thtr 55 Board 28 Del from £235
Credit Cards [1][2][3][5]

*For full, independent restaurant reviews,
see the AA Abbey Well Restaurant Guide*

★★★★ 75% *Stafford*
16-18 St James's Place SW1A 1NJ
☏071-493 0111 FAX 071-493 7121

Quietly tucked away in the heart of St James', this charming small hotel is the very model of discreet elegance. It dates from the 17th-century and retains much of the atmosphere of its former incarnation as a private residence and club. The individually furnished bedrooms do vary in size but are all stylishly decorated, and rooms in the converted former stables are extremely popular. The elegant restaurant serves enjoyable classic Continental dishes as well as a fine selection of wines, and there is a comfortable drawing room, complete with resident cat. In the lively American bar Charles the barman has been serving drinks for over 30 years. In fact it is the highly personalised, courteous and friendly service that makes this such a special hotel.
74⇌↑4⚓ CTV in all bedrooms♪ T ✗
Lift ℂ ♪ ⇎
♡ French V ✿ ℒ Last dinner 10pm
Credit Cards [1][2][3][4][5]

★★★★ ❀67% **The Lowndes**
21 Lowndes St SW1X 9ES ☏071-823 1234 FAX 071-235 1154
78⇌↑⚓in 31 bedrooms CTV in all bedrooms♪ T
✗ (ex guide dogs) ✱ dB⇌↑£135.12-£211.50 (room only)
Lift ℂ ⊞ ♪ ⇎ xmas
♡ European V ✿ ℒ ✱ Lunch fr£17.50 High tea fr£9.75alc Dinner fr£21.50 Last dinner 11.15pm
Credit Cards [1][2][3][5]

★★★★ 65% *Royal Westminster Thistle*
49 Buckingham Palace Rd SW1W 0QT
☏071-834 1821 FAX 071-931 7542   THISTLE HOTELS

An ideal location for business and holiday guests, this modern hotel is close to Victoria Station and Buckingham Palace. Bedrooms are generally spacious and offer an excellent range of facilities including mini bars, safes and air conditioning. Snacks are served all day in the foyer lounge and there is a choice of restaurants, the Parisian-style café or more formal Brasserie Saint Germain. An extensive 24-hour room service menu is also available.
134⇌↑(69fb)⚓in 67 bedrooms CTV in all bedrooms T
✗ (ex guide dogs)
Lift ℂ ⊞ ♪
♡ English & French V ✿ ℒ ✱ Last dinner 11pm
Credit Cards [1][2][3][5]

See advertisement on page 383

★★★★ 60% **Grosvenor Thistle**
Buckingham Palace Rd, Victoria SW1W 0SJ
(adjacent to Victoria railway station)   THISTLE HOTELS
☏071-834 9494 FAX 071-630 1978

An impressive Victorian building houses this elegant and spacious hotel which is scheduled for a complete refurbishment in late 1993/early 1994. The pillared lobby has a fine marble staircase leading up to the well appointed bedrooms. There is a spacious restaurant offering a carte as well as the carvery, and light snacks are available all day in the pleasant lounge. There is also a club-style lounge bar.
366⇌↑(36fb)1⚓⚓in 37 bedrooms CTV in all bedrooms ® T
✱ sB⇌↑£98 dB⇌↑£120 (room only) ₧
Lift ℂ CTV xmas
V ✿ ℒ ⚓ ✱ Lunch £13.25-£16.35&alc Dinner £13.25-£16.35&alc Last dinner 10pm
CONF. Thtr 200 Class 80 Board 80 Del £139
Credit Cards [1][2][3][5]

See advertisement on page 383

★★★ 66% **Rubens**
Buckingham Palace Rd SW1W 0PS (opp Royal Mews) (Sarova)
☏071-834 6600 FAX 071-828 5401
An attractive property directly opposite the Royal Mews and within easy walking distance of Victoria Station, the hotel continues to attract an international clientèle. Bedrooms are well furnished and

SW1 Westminster - SW5 Earl's Court

equipped, executive rooms are largest, and 24-hour room service is provided. Public areas include a gallery lounge where a range of snacks is available, a library lounge and comfortable lounge bar adjacent to the Old Master's Restaurant, where a carvery and à la carte menu are offered.

188⇨🛏(10b)1🚻⊁in 44 bedrooms CTV in all bedrooms ®⚋ T 🐕 (ex guide dogs) ✱ sB⇨🛏£97-£115 dB⇨🛏£123-£138 (room only) 🍴
Lift ⦅ 🎵 xmas
♨ International V ⚛ ⚌ ⊁ Lunch £13.50-£14.95 ✱ Dinner £13.50-£14.95&alc Last dinner 10pm
Credit Cards [1][2][3][5]

★★★ 62% Royal Horseguards Thistle
Whitehall Court SW1A 2EJ ☎071-839 3400
FAX 071-925 2263

THISTLE HOTELS

This substantial period hotel lies in a quiet side street near Whitehall. The public areas have the style and space of a grander hotel with a marbled lobby, coffee shop, restaurant and panelled cocktail bar. Bedrooms are very varied in quality and size, and some have views of the river. There is good porterage and 24-hour room service. A refurbishment programme is planned for 1993-4.

376⇨🛏(98b)⊁in 95 bedrooms CTV in all bedrooms ®⚋ T 🐕
Lift ⦅ 🎵
♨ International ⚛ ⚌ ⊁ Last dinner 10.30pm
Credit Cards [1][2][3][4][5]

**TOPHAMS EBURY COURT
28 Ebury St SW1 0LU
☎071-730 8147 FAX 071-823 5966
Closed 21 Dec-4 Jan

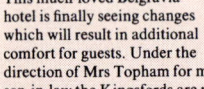

This much-loved Belgravia hotel is finally seeing changes which will result in additional comfort for guests. Under the direction of Mrs Topham for many years, her daughter and son-in-law the Kingsfords are now in charge and the lovely old-fashioned manner of service is one tradition that is upheld. Bedrooms are still smallish but en suite bathrooms are being added. A new chef promises good things for the dining room.

46rm(22⇨🛏)(3fb)4🚻 CTV in all bedrooms ®⚋ T
Lift ⦅ 🎵 🚗
V ⚛ ⚌ Last dinner 10.30pm
Credit Cards [1][2][3][5]

••

Forte Crest
81 Jermyn St SW1Y 6JF ☎071-930 2111 FAX 071-839 2125

FORTE CREST

A large modern hotel with a wide range of services and amenities, designed particularly for the business traveller. Bedrooms are smart, comfortable and well equipped. For more details about Forte Crest hotels, consult the Contents page, under Hotel Groups.

256⇨🛏✱ B⇨🛏£99 (room only)
CONF. Thtr 80 Class 35 Board 50 Del £145

Rosettes range from 5 for outstanding
cuisine to 1 rosette for enjoyable,
well prepared food

SW3 CHELSEA, BROMPTON

RELAIS & CHATEAUX
Relais Gourmands

★★★★

★★★★❀❀❀ CAPITAL
Basil St, Knightsbridge
SW3 1AT ☎071-589 5171
FAX 071-225 0011

First impressions of this modern hotel can be disappointing – public areas are all limited in space, and a few bedrooms and bathrooms are distinctly compact – but on further acquaintance the appeal quickly surfaces, as the charm, atmosphere and quality emerge. The many virtues include the friendly, welcoming and thoroughly competent staff, led by owner David Levin and manager Jonathan Orr-Ewing. Head chef Philip Britten, operates with creative skill from a tiny kitchen which some diners can view from their tables, and offers a wide range of dishes. His experiments do not always work, but his inventiveness is commendable – and the restaurant is always full. Some regular dishes remain, such as delicate ravioli filled with crab meat on a scallop mousse enhanced with ginger. The wine list deserves a special mention for its modest prices (by London standards).

48⇨🛏 CTV in all bedrooms T sB⇨🛏£185-£220 dB⇨🛏£220-£315 (room only)
Lift ⦅ 🚻 3P (charged) 12🚗 (£15) 🚗
♨ French V ⚛ ⚌ ✱ Lunch £20-£25&alc Dinner £25&alc Last dinner 11.15pm
CONF. Thtr 20
Credit Cards [1][2][3][5]

★★★ ❀74% Basil Street
Basil St, Knightsbridge SW3 1AH ☎071-581 3311 FAX 071-581 3693

It is hard to believe that the hustle and bustle of Knightsbridge are just around the corner from this Edwardian hotel, which is dedicated to gracious living. Privately owned and under the same management for 30 years, it provides a haven of old fashioned charm and elegance in one of the most sought after areas of London. The ground floor is also home to the Parrot Club, a private ladies club offering free access to lady residents. Head chef James Peake is responsible for the à la carte menu, and our inspector enjoyed a succulent chicken breast served on a rich and flavoursome wild mushroom and Madeira sauce.

94rm(85⇨🛏) CTV in all bedrooms ✱ sBfr£59 sB⇨🛏fr£110.50 dBfr£90.30 dB⇨🛏fr£156.50 (room only) 🍴
Lift ⦅ 🎵 🚗 xmas
♨ International V ⚛ ⚌ Lunch fr£14.95&alc Dinner fr£20&alc Last dinner 10pm
CONF. Thtr 80 Class 32 Board 32 Del from £149
Credit Cards [1][2][3][4][5]

SW5 EARL'S COURT

★★★ 69% Swallow International
Cromwell Rd SW5 0TH ☎071-973 1000 FAX 071-244 8194
Closed 24-26 Dec

SWALLOW HOTELS

Swallow Hotels' London 'flagship', this large, modern, purpose built and particularly well managed hotel offers a choice of accommodation styles varying from recently renovated Executive standard to the older-style, rather modest, twin-bedded rooms in the Knaresborough Building. The Fountain Brasserie provides all-day

SW5 Earl's Court

meals and snacks, the more formal Blayneys Restaurant only opening for dinner. Twenty-four-hour room service is available, and guests are assured of both a warm welcome and good luggage handling on arrival. Leisure club facilities and on site parking are two further facets of an ever increasing range of amenities.
417⇨♠(36fb)1⊟⊁in 40 bedrooms CTV in all bedrooms ®⚣
T✳ sB⇨♠£95-£105 dB⇨♠£110-£120 (room only) ❘
Lift ₵ 60P (£15.50 per day) 20🚗 (£15.50 per day) ⊠ (heated) sauna solarium gymnasium whirlpool spa turkish steamroom ♪
♨ International V ✿ ⚑ ⚒ ✻ Lunch £10-£15alc High tea £6.50-£10alc Dinner £15-£17.25&alc Last dinner mdnt
CONF. Thtr 220 Class 90 Board 50 Del from £115
Credit Cards 1 2 3 5

★★★ **67%** Hogarth
33 Hogarth Rd, Kensington SW5 0QQ
☎071-370 6831 FAX 071-373 6179

Courtesy and Care 1994

Genuinely friendly young staff make a stay at this hotel a particular pleasure, and for that reason The Hogarth is this year a recipient of ⇒→

★★★★ AA
ROYAL WESTMINSTER
THISTLE HOTEL

Buckingham Palace Road, London SW1W 0QT
Tel: 071-834 1821 Fax: 071-931 7542

Your choice near Buckingham Palace

For Reservations at over 100
Mount Charlotte Thistle Hotels
Telephone London: 071 937 8033.

THISTLE HOTELS

★★★ AA
ROYAL HORSEGUARDS
THISTLE HOTEL

Whitehall Court, London SW1A 2EJ
Tel: 071-839 3400 Fax: 071-925 2263

Your choice in Whitehall

For Reservations at over 100
Mount Charlotte Thistle Hotels
Telephone London: 071 937 8033.

THISTLE HOTELS

★★★★ AA
THE GROSVENOR
THISTLE HOTEL

Buckingham Palace Road, London SW1W 0SJ
Tel: 071-834 9494 Fax: 071-630 1978

Your choice in Victoria

For Reservations at over 100
Mount Charlotte Thistle Hotels
Telephone London: 071 937 8033.

THISTLE HOTELS

SW5 Earl's Court - W1 West End

the AA Courtesy and Care Award. Situated off the Earls Court Road, convenient for the tube and exhibition centre, this purpose-built hotel has recently been refurbished. While bedrooms vary in size, all are now furnished to an agreeable modern standard, though bathrooms remain modest. Public areas are attractive and include a pleasant small bar and restaurant serving enjoyable meals at both lunch and dinner.

85➪↑(12fb)⌇in 2 bedrooms CTV in all bedrooms ®⚐T✻ sB&B➪↑£74-£82 dB&B➪↑£89-£105 🍴
Lift (20🛎 (£10 per night)
🍷 English & French V ✧ ⚐ ✻ Lunch £12.50&alc High tea 50p-£2.95alc Dinner £13.50&alc Last dinner 9.30pm
CONF. Thtr 50 Class 20 Board 24 Del £110
Credit Cards ①②③⑤

SW7 SOUTH KENSINGTON

★★★★ 65% **Gloucester**
4-18 Harrington Gardens SW7 4LH ☎071-373 6030 FAX 071-373 0409

This early 70s hotel is in a peaceful residential quarter next to Gloucester Road tube station. Bedrooms include some luxurious club rooms with extra facilities and services. The remaining rooms are less glamorous but perfectly comfortable. Leading from the spacious pillared lobby there is a lounge bar, an à la carte restaurant, the informal Appleyard Café and a small shop.

548➪↑(2fb)⌇in 90 bedrooms CTV in all bedrooms ®⚐T
Lift (⊞ 100🛎 (fr £10) ♫
🍷 English & Continental V ✧ ⚐ ✻ Last dinner 10.30pm
Credit Cards ①②③④⑤

★★★★ 62% **Holiday Inn Kensington**
100 Cromwell Rd SW7 4ER (close to Gloucester Rd tube station) ☎071-373 2222 FAX 071-373 0559

This is a new purpose-built hotel behind a period façade. Bedrooms vary from duplex suites with spiral staircases to executive and standard rooms, all well equipped, air conditioned, triple glazed and quiet. The lively Precinct Café/Bar and the compact Serenity Health and Leisure Club are located in the basement with Olivers Bar and Restaurant on the ground floor providing self- service breakfast, lunch and dinner.

162➪↑(96fb)⌇in 60 bedrooms CTV in all bedrooms ®⚐T ✈ (ex guide dogs) ✻
Lift (⊞ CTV 4P (£12.50) ✿ sauna gymnasium whirlpool steam room ♫
🍷 English & French V ✧ ⚐ ✻ Lunch fr£9.95&alc High tea fr£7.25 Dinner £9.96-£15&alc Last dinner 10.30pm
CONF. Thtr 150 Class 60 Board 54 Del from £145
Credit Cards ①②③④⑤

★★★ 69% **Forum**
97 Cromwell Rd SW7 4DN ☎071-370 5757 FAX 071-373 1448
910➪↑↑⌇in 12 bedrooms CTV in all bedrooms ®⚐T✻ sB➪↑£102.20-£115.25 dB➪↑£123.37-£136.30 (room only) 🍴
Lift (70🛎 (charged) ✿ gymnasium ♫ xmas
🍷 International V ✧ ⚐ ✻ ⌇ Lunch £3-£10.50 Dinner £3-£14.70&alc Last dinner 10.30pm
Credit Cards ①②③⑤

★★★ 69% **Rembrandt**
11 Thurloe Place SW7 2RS (opp Victoria & Albert Museum) (Sarova) ☎071-589 8100 FAX 071-225 3363

The Rembrandt was commissioned at the beginning of the century as luxury suites for Harrods and is just a short stroll from the great store, opposite the Victoria and Albert Museum. A third of the bedrooms are excellent executive rooms, with king size beds and luxurious marbled bathrooms with jacuzzi baths and power showers. The remainder are less glamorous but equally comfortable. Light meals and drinks are available all day in the lounge bar and adjoining conservatory. The more formal Masters restaurant offers a

choice of à la carte or traditional carvery menus, and a full room service menu is provided.

195➪⛌(25fb)⌇in 28 bedrooms CTV in all bedrooms ®⚐T✻ ✱ sB➪↑£105-£125 dB➪↑£125-£140 (room only) 🍴
Lift (𝄞 ▭ (heated) sauna solarium gymnasium health & fitness centre xmas
🍷 International V ✧ ⚐ ✻ Lunch £9.95-£12.50&alc High tea £3.50 Dinner £13.75-£15.95&alc Last dinner 10pm
Credit Cards ①②③④⑤ £

The Vanderbilt
68/86 Cromwell Rd SW7 9HD ☎071-589 2424
FAX 071-225 2293

This stylish period hotel offers a wide range of services and a choice of eating options for the international traveller. Bedrooms are smart and individually furnished, and are fully equipped with modern facilities. For more details about Edwardian hotels, consult the Contents page, under Hotel Groups.

223➪↑✻ sB➪↑£92-£100 dB➪↑£120-£135 (room only)
CONF. Thtr 120 Class 36 Board 40 Del £149

SW19 WIMBLEDON

See LONDON plan 1C2

★★★★ ❀67% **Cannizaro House**
West Side, Wimbledon Common
SW19 4UF ☎081-879 1464 FAX 081-879 7338

Cannizaro House has been converted into a hotel of real quality. Public areas retain original features, such as a fine staircase and moulded cornices, and overlook the gardens and common. Chef Nigel Couzens, produces imaginative dishes like fresh ravioli with lobster and crab served with a red onion and malibu cream sauce, followed by noisettes of lamb with a raspberry and shallot mousse, served with honey and thyme sauce. The table d'hôte menu is also well thought out and offers good value.

46➪4🚽 CTV in all bedrooms ® T ✻ sB➪↑£102-£118 dB➪↑£118-£290 (room only) 🍴
Lift (60P ✿
🍷 International V ✧ ⚐ ✻ ⌇ Lunch £21.55&alc Dinner £21.55-£25.75&alc Last dinner 10.30pm
CONF. Thtr 45 Class 16 Board 22 Del from £120
Credit Cards ①②③④⑤

W1 WEST END

★★★★★

★★★★★❀❀ **CLARIDGE'S**
Brook St W1A 2JQ (Leading Hotels) ☎071-629 8860
FAX 071-499 2210

This quintessentially English hotel has long been a 'pied à terre' for visiting royalty, heads of state and the British aristocracy, but business people and tourists will also be made to feel at home by the many faithful members of staff under the management of Michael Bentley and director Ronald Jones. Discreetly formal service is of the essence here; room service is the best that can be provided, with meals waiter-served course by course from well laid trolleys. Bedrooms are all spacious, elegant and comfortable, and bathrooms lack nothing in luxury. Public rooms retain their traditional splendour, from the impressive marble-floored entrance hall and foyer lounge to the art deco style main restaurant. Food is flown in from around the world to cater for the whims of the clientele, though quality British produce features in the cooking under chef Marjan Lesnik.

189⇨↑ CTV in all bedrooms ✱ T ✱ (ex guide dogs) ✻ sB⇨↑£211.50-£252.62 dB⇨↑£270.26-£329 (room only) ▯

Lift (♪ ✱ ♫ xmas

♡ International V ◊ ♙ ✻ Lunch £28-£34&alc Dinner £28-£34&alc Last dinner 11.15pm

CONF. Thtr 250 Board 64

Credit Cards [1][2][3][5]

almost the entire dessert selection is brought to the table on trays to help the diner make a decision.

252⇨↑ 31 ☐ ✻ in 17 bedrooms CTV in all bedrooms ✱ T ✱ (ex guide dogs) ✻ sB⇨↑£211.50-£252.63 dB⇨↑£252.63-£282 (room only) ▯

Lift (☐ 9P (£20 per 24hrs) 16🅿 (£20 per 24hrs) ⓢ sauna solarium gymnasium health club ♫ xmas

♡ English, French & Cantonese V ◊ ♙ ✻ Lunch £20-£25&alc Dinner £20-£40&alc Last dinner 11.30pm

CONF. Thtr 550 Class 300 Board 42

Credit Cards [1][2][3][5]

★★★★★❀❀❀
CONNAUGHT
Carlos Place W1Y 6AL
(Leading Hotels)
☏ 071-499 7070 FAX 071-495 3262

Undoubtedly one of the great hotels of the world and certainly the most select in London, this unique establishment started life in 1897 and while it has not stood still it has a timeless quality. For nearly 20 years managing director Paolo Zago has rigorously maintained the highest standard of hotel keeping. The kitchens have long been the domain of Maitre Cuisinier de France, Michel Bourdin, who oversees the production of an impressive array of French and English classical dishes. Game in season can be excellent, but vegetables can be under par. Sauces retain their classical character but have a pleasing modern lightness. Puddings, like the petits fours, can be very good, or a selection of savouries can round off the meal. Stylish service is provided by an army of formally dressed and highly professional waiters, courteous and attentive as are all the staff throughout the hotel.

90⇨↑ CTV in all bedrooms T ✱

Lift (3🅿 (£18 per night) ⓢ

♡ English & French ♙ ✻ Lunch fr£25&alc Dinner fr£35&alc Last dinner 10.30pm

Credit Cards [1][2][3]

★★★★★❀❀❀
FOUR SEASONS
Hamilton Place, Park Ln
W1A 1AZ (Leading Hotels)
☏ 071-499 0888 FAX 071-493 6629

This fine hotel (formerly the Inn on the Park, but renamed the Four Seasons in early 1993) provides friendly and efficient service, under the general management of Ramon Pajares, who recognises that it takes more than quality appointments to make a hotel great – and the Four Seasons is richly appointed with marble, wood panelling and a sweeping central staircase. The principal public areas are on the first floor, including the popular Lanes Restaurant, which offers a choice of fully inclusive menus, and the more formal Four Seasons Restaurant. Chef Bruno Loubet's style is ➭

❀ ★★★★ AA
CANNIZARO HOUSE
A Thistle Country House Hotel

Wimbledon Common, London SW19 4UF
Tel: 081-879 1464   Fax: 081-879 7338

Your choice in
Wimbledon

For Reservations at over 100
Mount Charlotte Thistle Hotels
Telephone London: 071 937 8033.

★★★★★❀❀❀
THE DORCHESTER
Park Ln W1A 2HJ (Leading Hotels) ☏ 071-629 8888
FAX 071-409 0114

Following its massive and hugely expensive refurbishment, the Dorchester is undoubtedly the most glamorous hotel in London, with its ballroom, newly opened health spa and the most magnificent suites. The richly furnished Promenade Lounge dominates the public areas, with all 3 restaurants, the Terrace Room, the Oriental and the Grill Room, leading off. Executive chef, Willi Elsener, seems to have set the Terrace back on the tracks of culinary excellence after a short period when it seemed to have lost some of its verve. An early summer meal started with a freshly flavoured salmon and prawn tartare, followed by a stunningly presented chilled three-pepper mousse, served with a row of tiger prawns coated in a good sweet and sour sauce. The main course was roast duckling with peaches, accompanied by a jus of the highest order. Then

W1 West End

creative, retaining natural flavours with intensive sauces. Our inspector enjoyed lovely steamed scallops with ginger and coriander; boned saddle of rabbit wrapped in parma ham; and an orange flavoured crème brûlée with madeleine and ice cream. Bedrooms are all very spacious, and there are some interesting mini suites with a conservatory-type extension onto a communal roof garden.

227⇨♠(227fb)✕in 84 bedrooms CTV in all bedrooms✱ T ✖ sB⇨♠£200-£220 dB⇨♠fr£245 (room only) 🅟
Lift (⊞ 65⚬ (fr £3.60 1hr) ♿ gymnasium ♫ *xmas*
♀ International V ☆ ⚐ ✕ ✱ Lunch £24.75 Dinner £19.50-£35.50alc Last dinner mdnt
Credit Cards ①②③④⑤

★★★★★ ❀❀❀73% **Le Meridien London**
21 Piccadilly W1V 0BH ☎071-734 8000 FAX 071-437 3574
There are so many attractions inside this city-centre hotel that some visitors may forget to venture out. Bedrooms are double-glazed and offer a fair degree of luxury in their furnishings. A lounge area which is a perfect setting for afternoon teas, leads to the award-winning Oak Room Restaurant beyond, where chef David Chambers continues to attract the most discerning lovers of good food; he finely hones the menu by regular exchange visits with one of France's top chefs, Michel Lorain. The Terrace Garden offers breakfast or light meals throughout the day, and if you prefer exercise to eating, next door is Champneys health club. Staff are a great strength: there is a friendliness and spontaneity of response that promotes a very pleasant atmosphere.

263⇨♠1⌂ CTV in all bedrooms ® T ✖ (ex guide dogs) ✱
sB⇨♠£190-£210 dB⇨♠£210-£230 (room only) 🅟
Lift (⊞ 🅿 ♿ 🅟 (heated) squash snooker sauna solarium gymnasium health & leisure club ♫
♀ International V ☆ ⚐ ✕ ✱ Lunch fr£18.50 Dinner fr£18.50 Last dinner 11.30pm
CONF. Thtr 250 Class 160 Board 80
Credit Cards ①②③④⑤

★★★★★ ❀❀❀73% **Ritz**
Piccadilly W1V 9DG ☎071-493 8181 FAX 071-493 2687

Still one of the most fashionable addresses in London, the Ritz epitomises luxury; queues are as long as ever for the famous afternoon tea served in the Palm Court, and the splendid restaurant's glittering ornamentation continues to attract both celebrities and those out for a night of a lifetime. Though the recession has brought about a drop in staffing levels, a programme of bedroom upgrading continues, and there is talk of extending the lounge facilities to provide guests with yet more comfort and seclusion. New executive chef David Nicholls has created not only a relatively straightforward carte based on luxury ingredients (and priced accordingly), but also an intricate 4-course set menu that defies the modern trend towards simplicity. A millefeuille of salmon with lime and coriander, for example, might be followed by a mousseline of foie gras accompanied by a sweetish jus and a main course of good lamb cooked in a pancake of thinly sliced potato with ratatouille and a flamboyant crispy basket of asparagus, the meal ending with a vey enjoyable bread and butter pudding.

129⇨♠ CTV in all bedrooms✱ T ✖ (ex guide dogs) ✱
sB⇨♠£190-£220 dB⇨♠£220-£265 (room only) 🅟
Lift (⊞ 🅿 ♿ ♫ *xmas*
♀ International V ☆ ⚐ ✕ ✱ Lunch fr£26&alc Dinner £39.50-£43.50&alc Last dinner 11.15pm
CONF. Thtr 50 Class 50 Board 30
Credit Cards ①②③④⑤

For full, independent restaurant reviews,
see the AA Abbey Well *Restaurant Guide*

★★★★★ ❀❀❀71% *Hotel* **Inter-Continental**
1 Hamilton Pl, Hyde Park Corner W1V 0QY (IC)
☎071-409 3131 FAX 071-493 3476
Popular with international travellers, this modern hotel has excellent services for a business clientele, and a popular health club. The Soufflé Restaurant reveals its speciality in its name, and the lengthy menu offers plenty of choice. A recent visit began enjoyably with asparagus soufflé on an artichoke heart base, with pine kernels, cheeks of anglerfish, tomato and balsamic sauce. The main course of French lamb served with coriander-scented jus was most flavoursome.

467⇨♠✕in 58 bedrooms CTV in all bedrooms T
✖ (ex guide dogs)
Lift (⊞ 100⚬ (£21.50 24 hrs) ♿ sauna gymnasium health centre ♫
♀ English, French, Italian & Oriental V ☆ ⚐ ✕ Last dinner 11.30pm
Credit Cards ①②③④⑤

★★★★★ ❀❀❀70% **Grosvenor House**
Park Ln W1A 3AA ☎071-499 6363 FAX 071-493 3341

The spacious marble-floored reception at the Grosvenor House Hotel is approached from the gated entrance drive to the rear. Afternoon tea here is a real treat. The recently refurbished Pavilion Restaurant serves traditional English food, Pasta Vino serves Italian specialities; Nico's at Ninety has its own entrance, and 86 Park Lane is the hotel's reception and business centre. Bedrooms include recently refurbished rooms on the 5th and 6th floors and Crown Club rooms. Service is very professional and staff are willing and helpful.

454⇨♠✕in 70 bedrooms CTV in all bedrooms✱ T
✖ (ex guide dogs) sB⇨♠£211-£252 dB⇨♠£230-£282 (room only) 🅟
Lift (⊞ 20P 100⚬ (charged) 🅟 (heated) sauna solarium gymnasium health & fitness centre *xmas*
♀ English, French & Italian V ☆ ⚐ ✕ ✱ Lunch fr£13.50
CONF. Thtr 1500 Class 500 Board 150 Del £220
Credit Cards ①②③⑤

★★★★★ ❀68% **The Langham Hilton, London**
Langham Place W1N 3AA ☎071-636 1000

The Langham reopened its doors to guests again in 1991, the first time it had done so since this distinguished building was bombed during World War II. The refurbishment has been sympathetically carried out, and in the public rooms there is a sense of grand luxury and occasion. Well furnished bedrooms are spacious and have all the modern amenities expected of a top hotel.

386⇨♠ CTV in all bedrooms ® T ✖ sB⇨♠£165-£240 dB⇨♠£185-£255 (room only)
⊞ sauna solarium gymnasium
♀ International
CONF. Thtr 320 Class 190 Board 80 Del £222
Credit Cards ①②③④⑤

★★★★★ ❀63% **May Fair Inter-Continental**
Stratton St W1A 2AN (IC) ☎071-629 7777 FAX 071-629 1459
Considerable changes have taken place here recently, designed to make the hotel less 'stuffy' whilst still meeting the expectations of its 5-star rating. General Manager and 1992 Hotelier of the Year, Dagmar Woodward places customer care very high on her list of priorities, together with an environmentally aware attitude towards energy consumption and recycling. The majority of the bedrooms are both spacious and beautifully furnished. The Foyer Lounge and Le Chateau Restaurant have both been renovated, the latter now offering less formal menus and services; lighter meals and snacks are served in the Café, while a late night supper can be enjoyed in the Chateau Bar.

W1 West End

287⇨↑(14fb)⊁in 37 bedrooms CTV in all bedrooms✹T
✕ (ex guide dogs) ✱ sB⇨↑£199.75-£211.80 dB⇨↑£188-£270.25 (room only)
Lift (⊞ ♪ ⇶ ☐ (heated) sauna solarium gymnasium *xmas*
♡ English & French V ⇌ ⚲ ⊁ Lunch £22&alc Dinner £26.50&alc Last dinner 11pm
CONF. Thtr 292 Class 108 Board 70 Del from £165
Credit Cards ① ② ③ ⑤

★★★★★ 61% **The London Hilton on Park Lane**
22 Park Ln W1A 2HH ☎071-493 8000 FAX 071-493 4957

This eye-catching modern landmark, with a popular and bustling atmosphere, overlooks Hyde Park. The views are enjoyed by many of the well-equipped bedrooms, some of which have recently undergone refurbishment, and also the top floor Windows on the World bar and restaurant. Guests also have the choice of two other eating options, shops and executive suites.
448⇨↑ CTV in all bedrooms T sB⇨↑£229-£329 dB⇨↑£229-£329 (room only)
Lift (⊞ P (charged)
♡ International V ⇌ ⚲ ⊁
CONF. Thtr 1000 Class 850 Board 150 Del from £140
Credit Cards ① ② ③ ④ ⑤

★★★★★ ❀60% *Churchill Inter-Continental*
30 Portman Square W1A 4ZX (IC) ☎071-486 5800 FAX 071-486 1255
It's all change at the Churchill, with new ownership and, as we go to print, the beginning of a massive refurbishment programme, starting with the bedrooms and bathrooms. A new chef, too – Idris Caldaro – and it is anticipated that, once he has settled in, cuisine will improve considerably.
452⇨↑⊁in 66 bedrooms CTV in all bedrooms✹T
Lift (⊞ ⇶ ❄ ♀ (hard) free membership to David Lloyd club
♡ International V ⇌ ⚲ ⊁ Last dinner 11pm
Credit Cards ① ② ③ ④ ⑤

★★★★ ❀❀ **ATHENAEUM**
116 Piccadilly W1V 0BJ (overlooking Green Park)
☎071-499 3464 FAX 071-493 1860

During a period of some change, with new ownership and management, it is remarkable that the standards of service and courtesy for which the Athenaeum is renowned have been maintained totally. The new owners have embarked on a multi-million pound programme of improvements that will encompass every bedroom before moving on the public areas and finally providing leisure facilities – the minimising of disruption to guests during this process being an absolute priority. It is likely that food and beverage operations will see further changes as a result of improvements, but at present chef David Marshall's sensibly sized carte and good value set price menus provide an interesting choice of inventive dishes, a typical meal perhaps comprising a well made mousseline of scallops and scampi, followed by roast best end of lamb with tasty kidneys in an intense sauce, and a good iced orange soufflé.
112⇨↑⊁in 27 bedrooms CTV in all bedrooms✹T
sB⇨↑£180-£195 dB⇨↑£205-£225 (room only) 🍴
Lift (⊞ 300 🚗 (£25.50 per day) ⇶
♡ International V ⇌ ⚲ ⊁ ✱ Lunch fr£19.50&alc Dinner £19.50&alc Last dinner 10pm

CONF. Thtr 55 Class 30 Board 36 Del from £195
Credit Cards ① ② ③ ④ ⑤   £

★★★★ ❀ **BROWN'S**
Albemarle St, Dover St
W1A 4SW ☎071-493 6020
FAX 071-493 9381

This famous Georgian hotel
just a short walk from Piccadilly exudes a reassuring air of permanence with its wood panelling, stained glass and corniced ceilings. Afternoon tea here is a London institution, and restaurant meals also have a staunchly English feel, with dishes such as braised oxtail, grilled Dover sole, liver and bacon, 2 roasts at lunchtime and always a fruit crumble. The bedrooms on the Albemarle Street side are the best and most recently redecorated. Staff are attentive; regular guests are known and cosseted, and it is no surprise that they consider Browns their London home.
120⇨↑(14fb)⊁in 40 bedrooms CTV in all bedrooms✹
✕ (ex guide dogs) gentlemans hairdresser
Lift (♪ ⇶
V ⇌ ⚲ ⊁ Last dinner 10pm
Credit Cards ① ② ③ ⑤

★★★★ 73% **Montcalm**
Great Cumberland Place W1A 2LF ☎071-402 4288 FAX 071-724 9180
Tucked away in a quiet tree-lined Georgian crescent near Marble Arch, the Montcalm is a luxurious hotel. A major bedroom refurbishment is presently underway and those rooms already completed are furnished to the highest of standards. Guests can also choose from duplex suites and studios. Public areas are somewhat limited, but this is more than compensated for by the truly professional service provided by a loyal team of international staff.
116⇨↑⊁in 5 bedrooms CTV in all bedrooms✹T
✕ (ex guide dogs) ✱ sB⇨↑£176.25-£199.75 dB⇨↑£199.75-£223.25 (room only) 🍴
Lift (⊞ ♪ ⇶ ♫
♡ French V ⇌ ⚲ ⊁ ✱ Lunch £16.50-£18.50&alc Dinner £22.50&alc Last dinner 10pm
CONF. Thtr 80 Class 36 Board 36
Credit Cards ① ② ③ ④ ⑤   £

★★★★ ❀71% **Britannia Inter-Continental**
Grosvenor Square W1A 3AN (IC) ☎071-629 9400 FAX 071-629 7736
This modern, purpose built hotel has a discreet entrance off Grosvenor Square, while its main entrance is in a quiet back street. A varied choice of food is available at most times: Adams Restaurant for formal dining and self-service breakfast, and the Shogun Japanese restaurant for dinner only. Bedrooms vary in size and style, from standard to superior deluxe. A number of suites are also available. Bathrooms are strikingly furnished in marble, though are fairly restricted in size.
317⇨⊁in 40 bedrooms CTV in all bedrooms✹T
✕ (ex guide dogs) ✱ sB⇨£125-£210 dB⇨£160-£210 (room only) 🍴
Lift (⊞ 15P gents & ladies hairdresser *xmas*

London

W1 West End

English, American, French, Italian & Japanese V ✿ ⚒ ⚔
✱ Lunch fr£24 Dinner fr£24 Last dinner 10.30pm
CONF. Thtr 100 Class 54 Board 55
Credit Cards 1 2 3 4 5

★★★★✱70% **Park Lane**
Piccadilly W1Y 8BX ☎ 071-499 6321 FAX 071-499 1965
This long established hotel facing Hyde Park is still privately owned and makes much virtue of traditional service. For greatest effect enter from Piccadilly and cross the marbled lobby to find the grand Palm Court lounge. The luxurious Bracewells Restaurant offers some elaborate cuisine alongside plain grills, and the sweet trolley brooks no refusal. There is also an informal brasserie. Bedrooms, currently being upgraded, vary a lot in size and the décor is refreshingly unfussy.
310⇌✎(32fb)⚔ in 44 bedrooms CTV in all bedrooms T ✱
sB⇌✎£150-£175 dB⇌✎£175-£215 (room only) ⌂
Lift (180☎ (charged) solarium gymnasium ♫
⚑ International V ✿ ⚒ ⚔ ✱ Lunch fr£18.50&alc Dinner fr£23&alc Last dinner 10.30pm
CONF. Thtr 500 Class 300 Board 50 Del from £190
Credit Cards 1 2 3 5

★★★★✱68% **The Selfridge**
Orchard St W1H 0JS ☎ 071-408 2080 FAX 071-409 2295

In a central location well positioned for Oxford Street, this popular hotel benefits from the use of Selfridge's shop car park. Bedrooms are rather compact but have received some refurbishment during 1993. Spacious public areas include the reception/foyer with business centre and shop, a lounge, rustic bar and a choice of restaurants. Chef Mark Page has enthusiasm and commitment, his cooking shows great care and the results are pleasing.
296⇌✎in 110 bedrooms CTV in all bedrooms T ✈ ✱
sB⇌✎£135-£155 dB⇌✎£160-£180 (room only) ⌂
Lift (☒ ♪ xmas
⚑ International V ✿ ⚒ ⚔ ✱ Lunch £13.90-£16.50&alc High tea £9.95&alc Dinner £27&alc Last dinner 11pm
CONF. Thtr 260 Class 140 Board 24
Credit Cards 1 2 3 4 5

★★★★✱67% **The Westbury**
Bond St, Conduit St W1A 4UH ☎ 071-629 7755
FAX 071-495 1163

This popular hotel in London's Mayfair has an attractive marbled foyer and reception leading into the cosy Polo Bar, and the gracious panelled lounge which is open 24 hours for refreshments. The Polo Restaurant offers well balanced menus. Refurbishment has softened the bedrooms with quality décor and coordinating fabrics. Rooms are individually styled and offer a high standard of facilities, though en suites tend to be compact. Conscientious management is a strength here, with good front of house, valet and room services.
244⇌✎in 38 bedrooms CTV in all bedrooms ®✱ T ✱
sB⇌✎£155-£165 dB⇌✎£180-£200 (room only) ⌂
Lift (20P
⚑ International V ✿ ⚒ ⚔ ✱ Lunch £19.75-£22.25 Dinner £19.75-£22.25 Last dinner 11pm
Credit Cards 1 2 3 4 5

★★★★✱65% **Holiday Inn Mayfair**
3 Berkeley St W1X 6NE ☎ 071-493 8282
FAX 071-629 2827

185⇌✎(67fb)17⌂⚔in 56 bedrooms CTV in all bedrooms ®
T ✈ (ex guide dogs) dB⇌✎£140-£155 (room only) ⌂
Lift (☒ ♪ ⌂ ♫
⚑ International V ✿ ⚒ ⚔ Lunch fr£15.75 High tea fr£6.95 Dinner £9.95-£19.50&alc Last dinner 11pm
CONF. Thtr 70 Class 36 Board 38 Del £116
Credit Cards 1 2 3 5

★★★★✱60% **The Cumberland**
Marble Arch W1A 4RF ☎ 071-262 1234 FAX 071-724 4621

This grand old hotel caters successfully for both the leisure and corporate markets. Some bedrooms have been refurbished to a very good standard; others have received cosmetic attention, though 2 floors remain quite basic by comparison. There is a good range of food, including the original carvery and a Japanese restaurant, as well as a choice of bars. Queues soon form at breakfast time, so room service is a sensible option.
894⇌✎(38fb)⚔in 238 bedrooms CTV in all bedrooms ®✱ T
✈ (ex guide dogs) ✱ sB⇌✎fr£105 dB⇌✎fr£120 (room only) ⌂
Lift (♪ ⚔ xmas
⚑ English Japanese & Chinese V ✿ ⚒ ⚔ ✱ Lunch fr£14.95 Dinner fr£15.95 Last dinner 10pm
Credit Cards 1 2 3 5

★★★★✱52% **St George's**
Langham Place W1N 8QS ☎ 071-580 0111 FAX 071-436 7997

Centrally situated above the BBC offices in Henry Wood House, this modern high rise hotel offers one of the most spectacular views of London's skyline. Recently upgraded open plan public areas at the top of the building include a cocktail bar lounge and split-level restaurant. Bedrooms are comfortable but now look rather tired. Extensive services are available and staff are willing but can lack direction.
86⇌✎(8fb)⚔in 11 bedrooms CTV in all bedrooms ®✱ T ✱
sB⇌✎£105-£175 dB⇌✎£125-£210 (room only) ⌂
Lift (2P ♪ xmas
⚑ International V ✿ ⚒ ⚔ ✱ Lunch fr£16&alc High tea fr£16 Dinner fr£17&alc Last dinner 10pm
CONF. Thtr 35 Class 20 Board 24 Del from £135
Credit Cards 1 2 3 5

★★★✱75% **Clifton-Ford**
47 Welbeck St W1M 8DN ☎ 071-486 6600 FAX 071-486 7492

This modern hotel is quietly concealed in the neighbourhood of Marylebone, yet is only a few minutes from Oxford Street. Bedrooms have striking colour schemes and stylish furnishings. The spacious lounges are light and airy while the dark bar has a clubby ambience. Doyles Restaurant has the look of a smart brasserie and bar, and the menu created by Mark Dancer is in the eclectic modern vein.
200⇌✎(4fb) CTV in all bedrooms ®✱ T
Lift (20☎ (£16.50) ♪
⚑ International V ✿ ⚒ Lunch £18-£30alc Dinner £18-£30alc Last dinner 11pm
CONF. Thtr 180 Class 80 Board 40
Credit Cards 1 2 3 5

★★★✱71% **Chesterfield**
35 Charles St W1X 8LX ☎ 071-491 2622 FAX 071-491 4793

Situated in the heart of Mayfair, this privately owned hotel has an intimate and exclusive ambience. There is a charming oak-panelled library lounge for afternoon tea, and the clubby bar and adjoining terrace serves light meals and snacks throughout the day. Butlers Restaurant is professionally run and chef David Needes' short 'carte' features some imaginative and classic dishes, such as home-made fettucine in a ceps and white truffle sauce, and tip top brill with a crab crust, caramelised onions and ginger. Bedrooms have smart modern bathrooms, stylish furnishings and many extras. Twenty-four hour room service is available. Management and staff are committed to making this one of the best hotels in London and further improvements are planned.
110⇌✎(4fb)⚔in 10 bedrooms CTV in all bedrooms ✱ T
✈ (ex guide dogs) ✱ sB⇌✎£115-£120 dB⇌✎£140-£170 (room only) ⌂
Lift (♪ ⚔ ♫

W1 West End

V ✿ ⚏ Lunch £16.50-£19.95&alc Dinner £19.50-£25&alc Last dinner 10pm
CONF. Thtr 100 Class 60 Board 60 Del from £150
Credit Cards 1 2 3 5 £

★★★ 65% **Mostyn**
4 Bryanston St W1H 0DE ☎071-935 2361 FAX 071-487 2759
This is one of the best hotels for shopping in Oxford Street. All bedrooms are furnished to the same standard, but vary considerably in shape and size. There are superior bedrooms, and some quiet ones that overlook the courtyard and Bryanston Street. Twenty-four-hour room service is provided and also a full lounge service: the Tea Planter colonial-style restaurant has an international 'anytime' menu, and although breakfast is self service, it integrates well with the friendly and attentive service from all the staff and helpful management.
122⇌✿(24fb)✂in 27 bedrooms CTV in all bedrooms T
✈ (ex guide dogs) ✱ sB&B⇌✿fr£98 dB&B⇌✿fr£124
Lift ℂ
♥ International V ✿ ⚏ ✂ ✱
Credit Cards 1 2 3 5 £

★★★ 64% **Sherlock Holmes**
108 Baker St W1M 1LB (Hilton) ☎071-486 6161 FAX 071-486 0884
Full of memorabilia of the famous sleuth, this hotel is just a few minutes' walk from Baker Street underground station. The range of bedrooms includes suites, no-smoking and spacious Plaza rooms. Dr Watson's bar and restaurant is open throughout the day for light refreshments, full meals and Mrs Hudson's Afternoon Teas; 24-hour room service is also available.
125⇌✿✂in 14 bedrooms CTV in all bedrooms ® T
✈ (ex guide dogs) ✱ sB&B⇌✿£90 dB&B⇌✿£110 (room only)
Lift ℂ ♪
V ✿ ⚏ ✂ ✱ Lunch £16.50&alc Dinner £16.50&alc Last dinner 10pm
Credit Cards 1 2 3 5

★★★ 62% **Mandeville**
Mandeville Place W1M 6BE ☎071-935 5599 FAX 071-935 9588
The Mandeville is tucked away behind Wigmore Street, just a few minutes walk from Oxford Street. Bedrooms are similarly furnished and decorated, though they do vary in size. The restaurant is open all day and serves anything from a light snack to a full à la carte meal. Boswells Bar is very much a traditional pub, while the Studio Bar is open late. Though service is generally sound, a full house may result in delays at breakfast.
165⇌✿ CTV in all bedrooms T ✈ (ex guide dogs) ✱
sB&B⇌✿£99 dB&B⇌✿£122 Continental breakfast ♬
Lift ℂ ♪
♥ International V ✿ ✱ Lunch £12-£18alc Dinner £12-£18alc Last dinner 10.30pm
Credit Cards 1 2 3 5 £

★★★ 57% **Mount Royal**
Bryanston St, Marble Arch W1A 4UR
☎071-629 8040 FAX 071-499 7792

This 30s building has undergone extensive refurbishment to provide smart modern public areas. Beyond the reception is a light, brasserie-style restaurant and the elegant Glenn Miller Bar. Bedrooms are spacious with separate dressing areas but very compact bathrooms, and while over half have been refurbished, standard rooms remain tired and dated.
691⇌✿(20fb)✂in 20 bedrooms CTV in all bedrooms ®⚏ T
✈ (ex guide dogs) sB&B⇌✿£85-£95 dB&B⇌✿£105-£115
Continental breakfast
Lift ℂ ♪
♥ English, French & Italian V ✿ ⚏ ✂ ✱ Lunch fr£12.95
High tea fr£4.95 Dinner fr£12.95 Last dinner 10.30pm
CONF. Thtr 400 Class 250 Board 75 Del from £118
Credit Cards 1 2 3 4 5

MANDEVILLE HOTEL
Mandeville Place, London W1M 6BE
Telephone: 071 935 5599
Telex: 269487 ★ ★ ★ Fax: 071 935 9588

Inviting Hotel catering mainly for corporate and individual business. Near Oxford Street, convenient for shopping and theatres.

Well equipped rooms with bathroom and shower, direct-dial telephone, radio, colour television, in-house movies, hair dryer and trouser press. Restaurant, Coffee Shop, Residents Lounge Bar and Pub. Services include telex, fax translation and secretarial services. Refurbished in 1980.

❋ ★★★★ AA
THE SELFRIDGE

Orchard Street, London W1H 0JS
Tel: 071-408 2080   Fax: 071-409 2295

Your choice in
Mayfair

For Reservations at over 100
Mount Charlotte Thistle Hotels
Telephone London: 071 937 8033.

W1 West End - W2 Bayswater, Paddington

★★ 52% Regent Palace
Glasshouse St, Piccadilly W1A 4BZ
☎ 071-734 7000 FAX 071-734 6435

Because of its central location and reasonable tariff, the Regent Palace is one of the most popular hotels in London, despite a lack of en suite bathrooms. However, most of the bedrooms are of a decent size and adequately equipped. Lounge facilities are limited, but other amenities include a carvery, a new brasserie and a games room, plus a number of shops.

887rm(12fb)⌘ in 336 bedrooms CTV in all bedrooms ® T
sBfr£39 dBfr£55 (room only) ⋈
Lift (♪ games room *xmas*
V ✧ ⌘ ⌘ Lunch £14.95 Dinner £14.95 Last dinner 9pm
CONF. Thtr 160 Class 100 Board 40 Del from £75
Credit Cards [1][2][3][5]

The Berkshire
Oxford St W1N 0BY (opposite Bond Street Underground Station) ☎ 071-629 7474 FAX 071-629 8156

This stylish period hotel offers a wide range of services and a choice of eating options for the international traveller. Bedrooms are smart and individually furnished, and are fully equipped with modern facilities. For more details about Edwardian hotels, consult the Contents page, under Hotel Groups.

147⇨⌘ sB⇨⌘£158-£169 dB⇨⌘£204-£434 (room only)
CONF. Thtr 45 Class 20 Board 20 Del £179

Forte Crest
Carburton St, Regents Park W1P 8EE
☎ 071-388 2300 FAX 071-387 2806

A large modern hotel with a wide range of services and amenities, designed particularly for the business traveller. Bedrooms are smart, comfortable and well equipped. For more details about Forte Crest hotels, consult the Contents page, under Hotel Groups.

320⇨⌘ B⇨⌘£99 (room only)
CONF. Thtr 650 Class 300 Board 50 Del £125

The Grafton
130 Tottenham Court Rd W1P 9HP
☎ 071-388 4131 FAX 071-387 7394

This stylish period hotel offers a wide range of services and a choice of eating options for the international traveller. Bedrooms are smart and individually furnished, and are fully equipped with modern facilities. For more details about Edwardian hotels, consult the Contents page, under Hotel Groups.

324⇨⌘ sB⇨⌘£111-£135 dB⇨⌘£140-£255 (room only)
CONF. Thtr 130 Class 45 Board 40 Del £175

Marriott
134 George St W1H 6DN ☎ 071-723 1277 FAX 071-402 0666

A large and busy hotel, which is ideal for the business and leisure traveller, offering a wide range of services and a choice of eating options. Bedrooms are comfortable and equipped with modern facilities. For more details about Marriott hotels, consult the Contents page, under Hotel Groups.

239⇨⌘ ✱ dB⇨⌘fr£188 (room only)
CONF. Thtr 120 Class 72 Board 40 Del £115

Marriott
Grosvenor Square W1A 4AW ☎ 071-493 1232 FAX 071-491 3201

A large and busy hotel, which is ideal for the business and leisure traveller, offering a wide range of services and a choice of eating options. Bedrooms are comfortable and equipped with modern facilities. For more details about Marriott hotels, consult the Contents page, under Hotel Groups.

223⇨⌘ ✱ B⇨⌘£123-£198 (room only)

The Savoy Court
Granville Place W1H 0EH ☎ 071-408 0130 FAX 071-493 2070

This stylish period hotel offers a wide range of services and a choice of eating options for the international traveller. Bedrooms are smart and individually equipped with modern facilities. For more details about Edwardian hotels, consult the Contents page, under Hotel Groups.

95⇨⌘ sB⇨⌘£81 dB⇨⌘£118 (room only)

W2 BAYSWATER, PADDINGTON

★★★★ 70% White's
Lancaster Gate W2 3NR ☎ 071-262 2711 FAX 071-262 2147

This elegant Victorian building overlooks Hyde Park. The bedrooms are all comfortably spacious and attractive, with carefully coordinated soft furnishings. They have good quality furniture and ornate fittings, including chandeliers; deluxe rooms are larger and have sofas; some rooms have private balconies and those on the 3rd floor are for non smokers. The suites have spa baths and bidets in their bathrooms. Public areas include an attractive dining room with an ornate ceiling, chandeliers and oil paintings and an adjacent cocktail bar with leather chairs and a terrace. In addition to the foyer lounge there is a second quiet lounge. Willing and enthusiastic service is provided by an efficient team of staff who are refreshingly unpretentious.

54⇨⌘ in 10 bedrooms CTV in all bedrooms ✱ T
✈ (ex guide dogs) ✱ sB⇨⌘£135 dB⇨⌘£170-£225 (room only) ⋈
Lift (25P ♯ ✱ *xmas*
♀ English & French V ✧ ⌘ ⌘ ✱ Lunch fr£16&alc Dinner fr£19.50&alc Last dinner 10.30pm
CONF. Thtr 25 Class 20 Board 20 Del from £160
Credit Cards [1][2][3][4][5]

★★★★ 67% Royal Lancaster
Lancaster Ter W2 2TY (directly above Lancaster Gate Underground Station)
☎ 071-262 6737 FAX 071-724 3191

This 18-storey hotel has splendid views of Kensington Gardens as well as the City from its higher floors. Accommodation, in view of the general calibre of the establishment, is rather mediocre in some cases; Reserve Club rooms are most spacious and comfortable. Impressive public areas comprise a relaxing Italianate lounge with adjoining bar and the graceful La Rosette restaurant which, in addition to its carte, features an excellent value set-price dinner which includes half a bottle of wine. A recommended meal included terrine of chicken and duck, layered with spinach and accompanied by a good Cumberland sauce, poached salmon with a first-class hollandaise, and an attractively presented wild berry cheesecake.

418⇨⌘ (4fb)⌘ in 28 bedrooms CTV in all bedrooms ✱ T
✈ (ex guide dogs) ✱ sB⇨⌘£125-£153 dB⇨⌘£140-£170 (room only) ⋈
Lift (50P (£15 per day) 50☎ (£15 per day) ♯ ♪ *xmas*
♀ International V ✧ ⌘ ⌘ ✱ Lunch £19.50-£22.50&alc Dinner £21-£25.75&alc Last dinner 10.45pm
CONF. Thtr 1400 Class 650 Board 130 Del from £120
Credit Cards [1][2][3][4][5]

For full, independent restaurant reviews, see the
AA Abbey Well *Restaurant Guide*.

Remember to book early for holiday and bank holiday times.

W2 Bayswater, Paddington – W5 Ealing

★★★ 63% **Central Park**
Queensborough Ter W2 3SS ☎071-229 2424 FAX 071-229 2904
This modern hotel is close to the underground station, offering easy access to central London. It offers spaciously comfortable, air-conditioned public areas, and bedrooms which vary in size – most with very compact bathroom/shower facilities. Twenty-four hour room service and underground car parking are available.
251rm(210⇨31👁)(10fb) CTV in all bedrooms ® T ✱
sB&B⇨👁£87 dB&B⇨👁£98-£115 Continental breakfast
Lift (10P (£1.50) 20🚗 (£1.50) sauna solarium gymnasium xmas
☐ International V ♥ ⚲ ⚔ ✱ Lunch fr£14.75 Dinner fr£14.75 Last dinner 10pm
CONF. Thtr 200 Class 150 Board 50 Del from £88.50
Credit Cards [1][2][3][5] £

★★★ 💐62% **Coburg Resort**
129 Bayswater Rd W2 4RJ ☎071-221 2217
FAX 071-229 0557

The Coburg is a domed Edwardian hotel overlooking Kensington Gardens. Bedrooms vary in size and outlook, but are all richly decorated and those at the top have splendid views. Public areas are a little limited but do include The Spice Merchant restaurant, where imaginative and carefully cooked Indian cuisine is available. Spices are freshly ground to give dishes distinct and vibrant flavours and there are succulent tandoori specialities.
132⇨👁 in 25 bedrooms CTV in all bedrooms ®⚲ T ✱
sB⇨👁£95 dB⇨👁£105 (room only) 🛏
Lift (🅿
☐ International V ♥ ⚲ ⚔ ✱ Lunch £6.50-£20&alc Dinner £12.95-£15.95&alc Last dinner 11.30pm
CONF. Thtr 80 Class 40 Board 40 Del from £95
Credit Cards [1][2][3][5] £

★★★ 59% **Hospitality Inn**
104/105 Bayswater Rd W2 3HL ☎071-262 4461
FAX 071-706 4560

With splendid views over Hyde Park, this hotel is a popular tourist venue. Bedrooms on the 2nd, 3rd, 8th and 9th floors have been totally refurbished, and the remainder look rather tired in comparison. Public areas are on the first floor, the Hartford Restaurant benefitting from the views. The hotel offers free car parking to hotel residents – a unique feature in central London.
175⇨👁 in 44 bedrooms CTV in all bedrooms ® T
sB⇨👁£75-£85 dB⇨👁£85-£105 (room only) 🛏
Lift (▦ 20P 40🚗
☐ International V ♥ ⚲ ✱ Bar Lunch £2.25-£5.95alc Dinner £10.50-£16alc Last dinner 10.30pm
CONF. Thtr 40 Class 25 Board 22
Credit Cards [1][2][3][4][5]

★★★ 58% **Plaza on Hyde Park**
Lancaster Gate W2 3NA (Hilton) ☎071-262 5022 FAX 071-724 8666
Opposite Hyde Park and just a few minutes' walk from Marble Arch, this busy and well run hotel provides modern accommodation in a variety of bedrooms, including suites, no-smoking and sumptuous Plaza rooms. There is a spacious reception foyer, and the bar/lounge offers light refreshments throughout the day as an alternative to the Hyde Restaurant.
402⇨👁(8fb) CTV in all bedrooms ® T ✱ sB⇨👁£69-£88 dB⇨👁£79-£108 (room only) 🛏
Lift (♯ ♫
☐ International V ♥ ⚲ ⚔ ✱ Lunch fr£9.95&alc Dinner fr£14.75&alc Last dinner 11pm
Credit Cards [1][2][3][5]

Hotels with red star ratings are especially high quality.

★★★ 53% **Park Court**
75 Lancaster Gate, Hyde Park W2 3NN
☎071-402 4272 FAX 071-706 4156

This very large and busy hotel faces across the Bayswater Road to Hyde Park. Bedrooms are slowly being upgraded, the best being the executive rooms. There is an open plan lobby bar-lounge and a brasserie where self service breakfast is provided.
398⇨👁(11fb)⚔ in 201 bedrooms CTV in all bedrooms ®⚲ T
Lift (🅿 ❋
V ♥ ⚲ ⚔ Last dinner 11pm
Credit Cards [1][2][3][4][5]

W5 EALING
See LONDON plan 1 B4

★★★ 67% **Carnarvon**
Ealing Common W5 3HN (at the junction of North Circular A406 with Uxbridge Road A4020) ☎081-992 5399 FAX 081-992 7082

A modern hotel in a useful location, the Carnarvon has open plan public areas incorporating a comfortable lobby and lounge bar. Bedrooms are modern and well equipped, double rooms offering a little more space. The restaurant menus include home-made soups and desserts, interesting fresh vegetables and carefully cooked traditional dishes.
145⇨👁 in 30 bedrooms CTV in all bedrooms ®⚲ T
🐕 (ex guide dogs) sB⇨👁£87-£97 dB⇨👁£110-£120 (room only) 🛏
Lift (150P
☐ European V ♥ ⚲ ⚔ ✱ Lunch £14-£20alc Dinner £15.95-£17.95&alc Last dinner 9.30pm
CONF. Del from £110
Credit Cards [1][2][3][5] £

★★★★ AA
Whites Hotel
A Thistle Country House Hotel

Hyde Park, Lancaster Gate, London W2 3NR
Tel: 071-262 2711 Fax: 071-262 2147

Your choice at
Lancaster Gate

For Reservations at over 100
Mount Charlotte Thistle Hotels
Telephone London: 071 937 8033.

W6 Hammersmith - W8 Kensington

W6 HAMMERSMITH

See LONDON plan 1*C3*

★★★ **61%** Novotel
1 Shortlands W6 8DR ☎081-741 1555 FAX 081-741 2120

This large and very busy hotel attracts a considerable international trade and tour business. Large groups have their own separate check in and dining arrangements. Public areas, including a choice of bars occupy a vast open plan concourse. Bedrooms are a good size, with a wide range of facilities and extended room service.

635rm in 231 bedrooms CTV in all bedrooms ® T ✱ sB £79 dB £89 (room only) 🍴
Lift CTV 230P (£7.50)
♿ English & French V ✧ ♨ ✱ Lunch £6.95&alc Dinner fr£6.95&alc Last dinner mdnt
Credit Cards 1 2 3 5

W8 KENSINGTON

See LONDON plan 1*C3*

★★★ ★★❀❀**61%** Royal Garden
Kensington High St W8 4PT
☎071-937 8000 FAX 071-938 4532

 Rank Hotels

This modern hotel on the southwest corner of Hyde Park, has bright, comfortably furnished public rooms, with a choice of bars and restaurants. Hospitality is a strong point and staff provide attentive service under the general manager Brian Murphy. Bedrooms, many with views over the park, are well equipped; they vary in size (some are quite compact) and refurbishment is continuing. The ground floor Garden Café is open all day; the 10th floor Royal Roof Restaurant, with stunning views, has a reputation for its French cuisine. The arrival of new chef Mr Zimmerman, means that we have not yet been able to assess the new cooking standards.

398rm 7🐕 in 12 bedrooms CTV in all bedrooms ♨ T
✱ (ex guide dogs) ✱ sB £150-£186 dB £170-£199 (room only)
Lift 160P (£16 per 24hrs) *xmas*
♿ International V ✧ ♨ ✱ Lunch £14.50-£18.50&alc High tea £6.50 Dinner £19.50&alc Last dinner 11pm
CONF. Thtr 750 Class 420 Board 50 Del from £99
Credit Cards 1 2 3 4 5

★★★★ ❀**65%** *The Copthorne Tara*
Scarsdale Place, off Wrights Ln W8 5SR
☎071-937 7211 FAX 071-937 7100

Copthorne Hotels

Well placed for shoppers, sightseers and commercial travellers, this large hotel offers a high standard of housekeeping in bedrooms which tend to be compact – though there is a slightly more spacious 'Connoisseur' grade. The usual modern facilities are supplemented by foreign language TV channels, reflecting the international mix of clients. There are several choices for a meal or a drink, including the intimate Jerome K Jerome Restaurant which serves competently prepared French cuisine.

825rm in 115 bedrooms CTV in all bedrooms ® T
✱ (ex guide dogs)
Lift 30P 80P (£10 per 24hrs) ♫
♿ French V ✧ ♨ Last dinner 1am
Credit Cards 1 2 3 4 5

★★★★ **60%** Kensington Park Thistle
16-32 De Vere Gardens, Kensington W8 5AG
☎071-937 8080 FAX 071-937 7616

THISTLE HOTELS

This large hotel is just off busy Kensington High Street. Bright and spacious public areas are comfortable and well designed, with much use of polished stone, and include an elegant wood-panelled grill restaurant with an ambitious menu and an airy glass-domed brasserie open all day. Bedrooms, including a few luxury suites and some rather compact rooms, are fully equipped with modern amenities and very well maintained; 24-hour room service is available.

332rm (14fb) in 90 bedrooms CTV in all bedrooms ® ♨ T
✱ (ex guide dogs) ✱ sB £105-£125 dB £128-£145 (room only) 🍴
Lift ♨ *xmas*
♿ English & French V ✧ ♨ ✱ Lunch fr£13.95&alc Dinner fr£13.95&alc Last dinner 11pm
CONF. Thtr 125 Class 75 Board 40 Del from £110
Credit Cards 1 2 3 5

★★★★ **55%** Kensington Palace Thistle
De Vere Gardens W8 5AF ☎071-937 8121 FAX 071-937 2816

 THISTLE HOTELS

This popular large hotel close to the Albert Hall offers a range of bedrooms, from very spacious executive rooms to smaller standard rooms, all with modern facilities. Air-conditioned public areas include an all-day café and restaurant, a cocktail lounge bar and a pub-style bar. Services are traditional and include 24-hour room service.

298rm (27fb) in 112 bedrooms CTV in all bedrooms ® T
✱ (ex guide dogs) ✱ sB £85-£115 dB £95-£135 (room only) 🍴
Lift ♨ ♫
♿ International V ✧ ♨ ✱ Lunch £10.50&alc Dinner £10.50&alc Last dinner 11.30pm
CONF. Thtr 200 Class 110 Board 70 Del from £93
Credit Cards 1 2 3 4 5

★★★ **65%** Kensington Close
Wright's Ln, Kensington W8 5SP
☎071-937 8170 FAX 071-937 8289

FORTE HOTELS

This extensive modern property is a short walk from Kensington High Street. Three floors of bedrooms have been refurbished to offer bright coordinating furnishings, while the lower floors are still in need of upgrading. There are 2 dining areas, one carvery and an Italian bistro adjacent to the bar lounge.

530rm in 150 bedrooms CTV in all bedrooms ® ♨ T
✱ (ex guide dogs) ✱ sB £99-£120 dB £99-£120 (room only) 🍴
Lift 100P (£16 per 24hrs) ❄ ▢ (heated) squash sauna solarium gymnasium health & fitness centre with beauty room *xmas*
♿ English & Italian V ✧ ♨ ✱ Lunch £14.95-£25 Dinner £14.95-£25 Last dinner 11.25pm
Credit Cards 1 2 3 5

★★ **57%** Hotel Lexham
32-38 Lexham Gardens W8 5JU (off A4 (Cromwell Road) just past Cromwell Hospital) ☎071-373 6471 FAX 071-244 7827
Closed 23 Dec-2 Jan

A long established, family-run hotel, the Lexham is quietly situated and conveniently placed for good access to central London. Resident proprietors Mr and Mrs Wilson, together with a team of loyal staff, provide helpful service. Bedrooms are simply furnished and a continuous programme of improvements is maintained.

66rm(48)(13fb) CTV in all bedrooms ✱ (ex guide dogs) ✱ sB&B£31.50-£34.50 sB&B £44-£48.50 dB&B£39.50-£45.50 dB&B £49.50-£69.50 🍴
Lift CTV P ♿ ❄
♿ English & Continental V ✧ ♨ Lunch fr£5.50&alc Dinner £8.75 Last dinner 8pm
Credit Cards 1 2 3   £

For key to symbols see the Bookmark.

W11 Holland Park, Notting Hill - WC1 Bloomsbury, Holborn

W11 HOLLAND PARK, NOTTING HILL
See LONDON plan 1C3
★★★★62% **London Kensington Hilton**
Holland Park Av W11 4UL ☎071-603 3355
FAX 071-602 9397

Standing adjacent to Holland Park, close to the West End and fashionable Kensington, this hotel provides accommodation in exceptionally well appointed and equipped bedrooms which feature mini bars, air conditioning and electronic security locks; two restaurants – the Market and the Hiroko Japanese – plus the Crescent Lounge offer a good range of eating options, pleasant service being given by well-turned-out staff.
603⇌⋔ CTV in all bedrooms ®⅋ T ✱ sB⇌⋔fr£110 dB⇌⋔fr£125 (room only)
Lift ⦅ ⊞ P (charged)
♀ International
Conf. Thtr 250 Class 150 Board 60 Del £125
Credit Cards ①②③④⑤

W14 WEST KENSINGTON
See LONDON plan 1C3
Hilton National London, Olympia
380 Kensington High St W14 8NL
☎071-603 3333

This is a bright, modern hotel with an informal restaurant, aimed at both the business and leisure guest. All bedrooms have en-suite bathrooms and a range of modern facilities. For more information about Hilton National, consult the Contents page, under Hotel Groups.
406⇌⋔✱ sB⇌⋔£110 dB⇌⋔£125 (room only)
Conf. Thtr 90 Class 35 Board 35 Del £115

WC1 BLOOMSBURY, HOLBORN
★★★★65% **Holiday Inn**
1 Kings Cross Rd WC1X 9HX (0.50m from Kings Cross station on the corner of King Cross Rd and Calthorpe St) ☎071-833 3900
FAX 071-917 6163

Within easy reach of Kings Cross station and the city, this striking modern hotel has smart public areas which include a good lounge. Attractive bedrooms are spacious and comfortable, all with either one or two double beds.
405⇌⋔(163fb)⊁in 160 bedrooms CTV in all bedrooms ®⅋ T ✱ sB⇌⋔£105 dB⇌⋔£115 (room only) 月
Lift ⦅ ⊞ 14⊛ ▭ (heated) squash sauna solarium gymnasium steam room whirlpool hair & beauty salon *xmas*
♀ International V ✧ ⌨ ⊁ ✱ Lunch £8.50-£14.50 Dinner £14.50&alc
Conf. Thtr 240 Class 110 Del £135
Credit Cards ①②③④⑤

★★★★59% **Hotel Russell**
Russell Square WC1B 5BE ☎071-837 6710 FAX 071-837 2857

This hotel retains many splendid architectural features, including its original marbled foyer and staircase. The bedrooms range in size and comfort: the best are on the executive 7th floor and the spacious front rooms. There is a good value carvery restaurant and the very efficient and popular King Bar Lounge, open throughout the day. Virginia Woolf's offers a pub-style environment, and the new Library Lounge is a quiet place to relax, though it is sometimes used for private meetings.
328⇌⋔(1fb)⊁in 23 bedrooms CTV in all bedrooms ®⅋ T ✱ sB⇌⋔£95-£120 dB⇌⋔£120-£140 (room only) 月
Lift ⦅ ♟ *xmas*

➡→

★★★★AA

KENSINGTON PALACE
THISTLE HOTEL

De Vere Gardens, London W8 5AF
Tel: 071-937 8121   Fax: 071-937 2816

A superb location opposite Kensington Gardens

For Reservations at over 100
Mount Charlotte Thistle Hotels
Telephone London: 071 937 8033.

THISTLE HOTELS

★★★★AA

KENSINGTON PARK THISTLE HOTEL

De Vere Gardens, London W8 5AG
Tel: 071-937 8080   Fax: 071-937 7616

A tranquil oasis in Kensington

For Reservations at over 100
Mount Charlotte Thistle Hotels
Telephone London: 071 937 8033.

WC1 Bloomsbury, Holborn - WC2 Soho, Strand

V ❊ ⌂ ✂ ✱ Lunch £12.95-£14.50 Dinner £16.50-£17.50 Last dinner 10pm
CONF. Thtr 450 Class 200 Board 35 Del £135
Credit Cards ①②③⑤

★★★ 64% **Bonnington**
92 Southampton Row WC1B 4BH ☎071-242 2828 FAX 071-831 9170

Centrally situated for the West End theatres, this well established family owned hotel provides traditional standards in modern surroundings. Bedrooms are simply decorated and furnished, but are well equipped. Waterfalls Restaurant offers a choice of value-for-money dishes from à la carte and table d'hôte menus. Lighter meals are also available in the bar.

215⇌(16fb) in 54 bedrooms CTV in all bedrooms ®❊ T sB&B⇌£50-£85 dB&B⇌£90-£108 ♬
Lift ℂ
♿ English & French V ❊ ⌂ Lunch fr£9&alc Dinner fr£15.95&alc Last dinner 10.30pm
CONF. Thtr 250 Class 70 Board 40 Del from £88.75
Credit Cards ①②③⑤

★★★ 64% **London Ryan**
Gwynne Place, Kings Cross Rd WC1X 9QN
☎071-278 2480 FAX 071-837 3776

A popular and well managed modern hotel, the London Ryan has been completely upgraded in recent years. The range of well furnished bedrooms includes executive, standard and others ideal for families. The Casablanca Restaurant and Bar offers an attractively priced daily menu and a grill selection.

211⇌ ♠ (73fb) ✂ in 20 bedrooms CTV in all bedrooms ® T
✈ (ex guide dogs)
Lift ℂ 28P 8⬚
♿ English & Continental V ❊ ⌂
Credit Cards ①②③⑤

★★ ❊❊❊ 65% *Academy*
17-21 Gower St WC1E 6HG ☎071-631 4115

Three Georgian town houses have been combined to produce this small hotel and club of considerable character. Bedrooms range from compact standard rooms without private facilities to more spacious studio suites, but all are attractively furnished with rich fabrics and good beds, although some rooms can be noisy. Public rooms include a small library lounge and pleasant patio garden. Residents are automatically given membership to the club, with access to the GHQ restaurant and bar. Chef John O'Riordan offers a short, good value set menu for lunch and dinner and although dishes may be simple in composition and presentation, they are capably handled and always tasty. At a recent meal a flavoursome fish broth with decent chunks of excellent fish was particularly enjoyed, though a crème brûlée was less successful. Main courses might include escalopes of veal with mushrooms and Calvados or wild boar sausages with onion sauce and creamed potatoes.

33rm(26⇌♠)(2fb) CTV in all bedrooms ® T
✈ (ex guide dogs)
Lift ♪ ⊜
♿ English & French V ❊
Credit Cards ①②③⑤

⋯⋯⋯⋯⋯⋯⋯⋯⋯⋯⋯⋯⋯⋯⋯⋯⋯⋯⋯

For full, independent restaurant reviews, see the
AA Abbey Well *Restaurant Guide*.

Forte Crest
Coram St WC1N 1HT ☎071-837 1200 FAX 071-837 5374

A large modern hotel with a wide range of services and amenities, designed particularly for the business traveller. Bedrooms are smart, comfortable and well equipped. For more details about Forte Crest hotels, consult the Contents page, under Hotel Groups.

284⇌♠ ✱ B⇌♠ £99 (room only)
CONF. Thtr 750 Class 300 Del £125

The Kenilworth
Great Russell St WC1B 3LB ☎071-637 3477 FAX 01-631 3133

This stylish period hotel offers a wide range of services and a choice of eating options for the international traveller. Bedrooms are smart and individually furnished, and are fully equipped with modern facilities. For more details about Edwardian hotels, consult the Contents page, under Hotel Groups.
192⇌♠ sB⇌♠£111-£130 dB⇌♠£152-£255 (room only)
CONF. Thtr 200 Class 120 Board 60 Del £134

The Marlborough
Bloomsbury St WC1B 3QD ☎071-636 5601 FAX 071-636 0532

This stylish period hotel offers a wide range of services and a choice of eating options for the international traveller. Bedrooms are smart and individually furnished, and are fully equipped with modern facilities. For more details about Edwardian hotels, consult the Contents page, under Hotel Groups.
169⇌♠ sB⇌♠£143 dB⇌♠£167-£312 (room only)
CONF. Thtr 200 Class 120 Board 60 Del £134

WC2 SOHO, STRAND

★★★★★ ❊❊❊ **THE SAVOY**
Strand WC2R 0EU (Leading Hotels) ☎071-836 4343
FAX 071-240 6040

(Rosettes awarded for Savoy Restaurant)

In these days of staff cutbacks and declining service, it is somehow reassuring that the Savoy disdains such short-term measures. Floor service, housekeeping, valet service and the provision of afternoon tea in the stylish River Lounge are second to none in terms of professionalism. Some bedrooms are compact, but the attention to detail more than compensates – comfortable beds, linen sheets, generous bathrobes, deep baths and the famous 'thunderstorm' showers, plus the push button service for the valet, floor waiter or maid. The Riverside Restaurant is splendidly and satisfyingly traditional and though the popularity of the large room creates a good atmosphere, it also makes booking advisable. The menu – in French – has a sound basis of classic dishes, but chef Anton Edelman brings innovative touches. The carte might offer gulls' eggs, consommé royale, tournedos rossini and grilled fish, while the set menu includes such dishes as asparagus and goats' cheese tart, tagliatelle with seafood and pesto, and daube of beef. Desserts include classic French and traditional English puddings. The Savoy Grill is equally popular. More creative touches have been introduced to the traditional means for which the Grill is famous.

WC2 Soho, Strand

200↰M⚹in 30 bedrooms CTV in all bedrooms T ✻ (ex guide dogs) ✱ sB↰M fr£199.75 dB↰M fr£229.13 (room only) 🍴
Lift 🛗 58🛏 (£21 per 24hrs) 🅿 🏊 (heated) sauna solarium gymnasium ♪ xmas
🍽 English & French V ✿ ♨ ✱ Lunch fr£25 Dinner fr£35 Last dinner 11.30pm
Credit Cards 1 2 3 5

★★★★ 71% The Waldorf
Aldwych WC2B 4DD ☏071-836 2400 FAX 071-836 7244

After a multimillion pound refurbishment this famous hotel in the heart of theatreland reopened in 1993, its 85th year of operation. All the bedrooms have been totally refurbished in handsome styles, with bold wall coverings and quality fabrics, fine reproduction furniture and spacious gleaming bathrooms. The restored polished marble flooring extends from the entrance and foyer to the Palm Court lounge, the hotel's focal point.

292↰M 1🛏⚹in 109 bedrooms CTV in all bedrooms ®✱ T ✻ (ex guide dogs) sB↰M£150 dB↰M£180-£210 (room only) 🍴
Lift 🛗 🎲 𝒫 hairdressing salon ♪
🍽 International V ✿ ♨ ✱ Lunch £21-£25 Dinner £21-£25 Last dinner 11pm
Credit Cards 1 2 3 5

★★★★ ❋61% Drury Lane Moat House
10 Drury Ln WC2B 5RE ☏071-836 6666 FAX 071-831 1548

Conveniently positioned for theatre land, Covent Garden and the City, this hotel is ideal for business or leisure. Bedrooms range from standard to executive and suites are available. The air-conditioned Maundie's Bar and Restaurant is a popular rendezvous and chef Charles Cooper offers a choice of daily fixed price and vegetarian menus, a pre-theatre menu and an interesting carte.

153↰M (15fb)⚹in 40 bedrooms CTV in all bedrooms ® T ✻ sB↰M£80-£99 dB↰M£100-£148 (room only) 🍴
Lift 🛗 🎲 30🛏 (£10 per 24hrs) xmas
🍽 French V ✿ ♨ ✱
CONF. Thtr 100 Class 40 Board 40 Del from £99
Credit Cards 1 2 3 4 5

★★★ 61% Strand Palace
Strand WC2R 0JJ ☏071-836 8080 FAX 071-836 2077

This popular hotel was built in 1909 and is one of the largest in the city. There is no shortage of eating options with 3 restaurants and an all-day café. All are open for breakfast, but there can be delays at weekends. There are also 2 bars, a gift shop, theatre kiosk and a newly fitted currency machine. Bedrooms are modern, but some doubles are compact. Many of the rooms face the 6 wells and although they have no view they are quiet.

777↰M (24fb)⚹in 224 bedrooms CTV in all bedrooms ®✱ T ✻ sB↰M£99 dB↰M£105 (room only) 🍴
Lift 🛗 𝒫 xmas
🍽 International V ✿ ♨ ⚹ ✱ Lunch £14.95 Dinner £15.95 Last dinner 11.30pm
Credit Cards 1 2 3 5

★★★ 60% Royal Trafalgar Thistle
Whitcomb St WC2H 7HG ☏071-930 4477 FAX 071-925 2149

Standing next to the National Gallery, off Trafalgar Square, this friendly, well managed modern hotel offers generally compact accommodation which is ideal both for business clients and weekend visitors; the best rooms are sited on the sixth floor. The traditional Battle of Trafalgar pub offers lunchtime bar snacks as an alternative to the French cuisine of Hamiltons Brasserie, where a wide range of meals and snacks is served throughout the day.

108↰M⚹in 36 bedrooms CTV in all bedrooms ® T ✻ sB↰M£99-£110 dB↰M£115-£125 (room only) 🍴
Lift 🛗 𝒫
🍽 English & French V ✿ ♨ ⚹ Last dinner 11.30pm
Credit Cards 1 2 3 4 5

....

The Hampshire
Leicester Square WC2 7LH ☏071-839 9399 FAX 071-960 8122

This stylish period hotel offers a wide range of services and a choice of eating options for the international traveller. Bedrooms are smart and individually furnished, and are fully equipped with modern facilities. For more details about Edwardian hotels, consult the Contents page, under Hotel Groups.

124↰M sB↰M£184 dB↰M£220-£730 (room only)
CONF. Thtr 100 Class 60 Board 28 Del £260

The Mountbatten
Monmouth St, Seven Dials, Covent Garden WC2H 9HD ☏071-836 4300 FAX 071-240 3540

This stylish period hotel offers a wide range of services and a choice of eating options for the international traveller. Bedrooms are smart and individually furnished, and are fully equipped with modern facilities. For more details about Edwardian hotels, consult the Contents page, under Hotel Groups.

127↰M sB↰M£153-£165 dB↰M£181-£393 (room only)
CONF. Thtr 75 Class 40 Board 32

★★★ AA
ROYAL TRAFALGAR THISTLE HOTEL

Whitcomb Street, London WC2H 7HG
Tel: 071-930 4477   Fax: 071-925 2149

Your choice at Trafalgar Square

For Reservations at over 100 Mount Charlotte Thistle Hotels Telephone London: 071 937 8033.

THISTLE HOTELS

London Airports - Looe

LONDON AIRPORTS
See under **Gatwick** & **Heathrow**

LONG EATON Derbyshire Map 08 SK43
See also **Sandiacre**

★★★ 62% Novotel
Bostock Ln NG10 4EP (S of M1 junc 25)
☎(0602) 720106 FAX (0602) 465900

Recent work on the main public areas of this Novotel has resulted in a lighter look with colour coordination throughout. In the evening the French-based restaurant serves meals until midnight. The style is uncomplicated with daily choices and an à la carte menu available. Bedrooms are clean and quite spacious, but are modest in style and comfort.

110⇌(110fb) 30 bedrooms CTV in all bedrooms ® T
✱ sB⇌♠£49.50-£52.50 dB⇌♠£54.50-£57.50 (room only) ⊟
Lift 180P ❋ ⌇ (heated) xmas
♥ English & French V ◊ ⚏ ✱ Lunch £6-£10&alc Dinner £8-£12&alc Last dinner mdnt
CONF. Thtr 220 Class 150 Board 100 Del from £70
Credit Cards [1][2][3][5]

★★ 67% Sleep Inn
Bostock Ln NG10 5NL (0.25m from junc 25 M1)
☎Nottingham(0602) 460000 FAX (0602) 460726

The hotel comprises an accommodation block and adjacent bar/restaurant complex. Bedrooms are well designed with the commercial guest in mind; the décor and furnishings follow clean, simple lines and facilities include video and data access points. Branaghans is an all-day American-style diner with friendly, theatrical service. Overall, the hotel offers excellent value.

101⇌(20fb) 30 bedrooms CTV in all bedrooms ® T
sB⇌♠£29.95-£39.50 dB⇌♠£34.95-£39.50 (room only)
(160P
V ◊ ⚒ ✱ Lunch £2.95-£5.95 Dinner £6-£9.50 Last dinner 9pm
Credit Cards [1][2][3][5]

★★ 60% Europa
20 Derby Rd NG10 1LW (on A6005) ☎(0602) 728481 FAX (0602) 728481
RS 23 Dec-2 Jan

This small and modest town-centre hotel is popular with business people and locals. Modestly furnished bedrooms are clean and light, and home-cooked meals are served in the pleasant dining room, with daytime refreshments offered in the small conservatory.

15⇌(2fb) CTV in all bedrooms ® T ✈ (ex guide dogs) ✱
sB&B⇌♠£25-£40 dB&B⇌♠£40-£48
(CTV 27P
V ◊ ⚏ ✱ Lunch £7.50 Dinner £9-£14 Last dinner 8.30pm
Credit Cards [1][2][3]

LONGHORSLEY Northumberland Map 12 NZ19

★★★★ ❀ 75% Linden Hall
NE65 8XF (0.5m N off A697) ☎Morpeth(0670) 516611 FAX (0670) 188544

This splendid Georgian country house stands in 450 acres of park and woodland. The porticoed entrance leads to a grand inner hall, but the public rooms, including a drawing room and restaurant are fairly restrained in style. For a livelier atmosphere, the old stables have been converted into an attractive pub and restaurant. Bedrooms, all attractively decorated, come in a variety of sizes and styles, the best being the newer rooms. Chef Keith Marshall's cooking is modern in style with adventurous combinations of flavours.

52⇌♠(4fb)5⊕ CTV in all bedrooms ® ⚒ T sB&B⇌♠£84.50-£114.50 dB&B⇌♠£114.50-£144.50 ⊟
Lift (260P ❋ ▦ (heated) ♬ (hard) ♪ snooker sauna solarium gymnasium croquet hairdressing putting spa bath xmas

---

V ◊ ⚏ ✱ Lunch £16.50-£19.50&alc Dinner £18.50-£21.50&alc Last dinner 10pm
CONF. Thtr 325 Class 150 Board 40 Del from £115
Credit Cards [1][2][3][5]

LONG MELFORD Suffolk Map 05 TL84

★★★ 64% The Bull
Hall St CO10 9JG ☎Sudbury(0787) 378494 FAX (0787) 880307

FORTE Heritage

An inn since the 16th century with origins in the 15th century, the Bull's timbers and carvings have been unusually well preserved and are enhanced by sympathetic décor and furnishings. The lounges provide the focal point, and recent refurbishment in all areas has improved the overall quality.

25⇌♠(3fb) in 11 bedrooms CTV in all bedrooms ® T
sB⇌♠£75-£90 dB⇌♠£85-£110 (room only) ⊟
20P ♫ xmas
V ◊ ⚏ Sunday Lunch fr£14.95 Dinner fr£18.95&alc Last dinner 9.30pm
CONF. Thtr 60 Class 30 Board 35 Del from £80
Credit Cards [1][2][3][5]

★★ ❀ 73% Countrymen Restaurant At The Black Lion Hotel
The Green CO10 9DN (at junct of A134/A1092)
☎Sudbury(0787) 312356 FAX (0787) 374557
Closed 23 Dec-3 Jan RS Sun eve & Mon

The Black Lion is a family run 17th-century coaching inn with a relaxed, informal atmosphere. Bedrooms are individually styled and well equipped. Public rooms include a comfortable lounge, an informal bar and a popular restaurant which offers monthly changing set price menus along with a good range of wines.

9⇌♠(5fb)3⊕ CTV in all bedrooms ® T ✱ sB&B⇌♠£45-£55 dB&B⇌♠£65-£75 ⊟
8P 1☐ ⚒
♥ International V ◊ ✱ Lunch £11.25-£18 Dinner £15-£26 Last dinner 9.30pm
Credit Cards [1][3]

LONG SUTTON Lincolnshire Map 09 TF42

Forte Travelodge
(on junc A17/B1359)
☎(0406) 362230 Central Res (0800) 850950

FORTE Travelodge

This modern building offers a good standard of accommodation for overnight stops. Smart, spacious and well equipped bedrooms, all with en suite bathrooms, are suitable for family use, and meals may be taken at the nearby family restaurant. For more details about Travelodges, consult the Contents page, under Hotel Groups.

40⇌♠✱ B⇌♠£31.95 (room only)

LOOE Cornwall & Isles of Scilly Map 02 SX25

★★★ 58% Hannafore Point
Marine Dr, Hannafore PL13 2DG
☎(05036) 3273 FAX (05036) 3272

Commanding far-reaching sea vistas from its position overlooking the headland and Looe Bay, this superbly located hotel has floor-to-ceiling windows in its public areas, to make the most of the magnificent views. Practically equipped, reasonably modern and well presented bedrooms are popular with both business and leisure guests.

37⇌♠(10fb) CTV in all bedrooms ® T
Lift (35P ▦ (heated) squash sauna solarium gymnasium
♥ English, French & Italian V ◊ ⚏ ✱ Last dinner 9.30pm
Credit Cards [1][2][3][5]

★★ **70% Fieldhead**
Portuan Rd PL13 2DR ☎(0503) 262689 FAX (0503) 264114
Closed Jan
This peaceful family-run hotel, built at the turn of the century, overlooks the bay and many of its attractive well equipped bedrooms have sea views. The recently extended, first-floor public areas include a candlelit restaurant featuring local seafood and there is a terraced garden.
14⇌ ƒ (2fb)2⊞ CTV in all bedrooms ® T ⋈ (ex guide dogs)
sB&B⇌ ƒ £27-£35 dB&B⇌ ƒ £52-£68 ₪
14P ✿ ≊ (heated) nc5yrs xmas
V ♂ ⚏ Sunday Lunch £7.50 Dinner £13.95 Last dinner 8.30pm
Credit Cards ①②③

★★ **68% Commonwood Manor**
St Martin's Rd PL13 1LP (on B3253) ☎(0503) 262929
Closed Xmas
Set in 3 acres of grounds in an elevated position overlooking the East Looe River with panoramic woodland and town views, this hotel offers tastefully furnished accommodation. Public rooms comprise a dining room and bar and a separate traditional lounge. There is also an attractive terraced garden.
10⇌ ƒ (2fb) CTV in all bedrooms ® T sB&B⇌ ƒ £27-£37 dB&B⇌ ƒ £49-£66 ₪
CTV 20P ⊞ ✿ ≊ (heated) nc8yrs
♀ English & Continental V ♂ ⚏ ⊁ Bar Lunch £2.50-£7 Dinner £10.50-£13.50 Last dinner 8pm
Credit Cards ①②③

LOSTWITHIEL Cornwall & Isles of Scilly Map **02** SX15

★★★ **63% Restormel Lodge**
Hillside Gardens PL22 0DD (on A390)
☎Bodmin(0208) 872223 FAX (0208) 873568 **CONSORT** HOTELS

A combination of modern comfort and traditional hospitality at this hotel is personally supervised by the proprietor Mr Hanson. The bedrooms, including some suitable for families, are very well equipped. The restaurant offers an interesting choice of dishes and tasty bar meals are available at lunch-time.
21⇌ ƒ Annexe12⇌ ƒ (3fb) CTV in all bedrooms ®⚷ T
sB&B⇌ ƒ £39-£40 dB&B⇌ ƒ £49-£50 (room only) ₪
40P ✿ ≊ (heated) ⚽ xmas
V ♂ ⚏ ⊁ Bar Lunch £2-£14alc Dinner £15-£16.50&alc Last dinner 9.30pm
CONF. Thtr 100 Class 80 Board 40 Del from £55
Credit Cards ①②③⑤

See advertisement on page 399

★★ **66% Lostwithiel Golf & Country Club**
Lower Polscoe PL22 0HQ (off A390) ☎(0208) 873550 FAX (0208) 873479
Set in wooded hills on the edge of the town, this new development has skilfully converted the original stone barns to provide comfortable modern bedrooms with all the expected facilities. There is a spacious restaurant and first-floor bar lounge offering bar snacks.
18⇌ ƒ CTV in all bedrooms ® T ✳ sB&B⇌ ƒ £41-£46 dB&B⇌ ƒ £62-£72 ₪
CTV 120P ⊞ ▣ (heated) ▶ 18 ♟ (hard) ♪ snooker undercover floodlit driving range
V ♂ ⚏ ⊁ ✳ Dinner fr£14.95 Last dinner 9.30pm
CONF. Thtr 75 Board 25 Del £65.50
Credit Cards ①③

Looe - Lostwithiel

PUNCH BOWL INN
LANREATH BY LOOE, CORNWALL

Ancient hostelry 6 miles from Looe, situated in a delightful old-world village. Excellent accommodation, some four-poster beds, most rooms have private bathroom. The bars and Stable Restaurant have the traditional atmosphere of days long ago, when the Inn was a Court House, coaching Point and Smugglers' distribution centre.
Tel: Lanreath (0503) 220218. *Recommended by Les Routiers, Ashley Courtenay, Egon Ronay, Logis of Gt. Britain*
See gazetteer entry under Lanreath

FIELDHEAD HOTEL ★★
in a beautiful garden overlooking the sea
**Portuan Road, Hannafore
West Looe, Cornwall PL13 2DR**

Built around the turn of the century, our hotel is traditionally appointed, warm and friendly and offers a high standard of comfort and service. Afternoon tea can be enjoyed in the seclusion of our lovely garden or take a dip in our heated swimming pool and enjoy the panoramic views of the Bay and St George's Island. Most bedrooms have sea view but all have en suite facilities, colour TV, tea/coffee making facilities and direct dial telephone. The Fieldhead is the perfect spot for total relaxation with short breaks available throughout the year.

Loughborough - Ludlow

LOUGHBOROUGH

LOUTH Lincolnshire Map 08 TF38

★★★ 62% **Beaumont**
Victoria Rd LN1 0BX ☎(0507) 605005 FAX (0507) 607768
Situated in a quiet residential district on the outskirts of the town, this hotel offers good facilities which will appeal to both the tourist and the business guest. Service is both friendly and attentive, well furnished bedrooms include 3 very spacious suites, and there are comfortable, tastefully decorated public areas.
17⇨✶(1fb) CTV in all bedrooms ®⚁T✱ sB⇨✶£45 dB⇨✶£55 (room only) 🅿
Lift 70P *xmas*
♀ English & French V ♿ ⚇ ✱ Lunch £4.95-£20 Dinner £12.95&alc Last dinner 10pm
CONF. Thtr 112 Class 34 Board 46 Del £72.50
Credit Cards ①②③

LOWER BEEDING West Sussex Map 04 TQ22

★★★★ ✿✿♨74% **South Lodge**
Brighton Rd RH13 6PS (off A281) (Laura Hotels)
☎(0403) 891711 FAX (0403) 891253
In an elevated and secluded position overlooking the rolling South Downs, this Victorian country house has one of the best rhododendron collections in the country. It has lots of charm and character in its fine wood panelled lounge and the separate library bar. In the dining room, chef Anthony Tobin shows his skills with his signature and à la carte menus. Standards of service and hospitality are commendable, due in large part to general manager David French's attention to detail.
39⇨2🛏 CTV in all bedrooms T ✗ (ex guide dogs) sB⇨£90-£255 dB⇨✶£110-£255 (room only) 🅿
⦅ 80P ⛳ ✿ ♀ (hard) ♪ golf-driving net croquet shooting ♫ *xmas*
♀ English & French V ♿ ⚇ ✱ Lunch £17.50-£20 Dinner £25-£32&alc Last dinner 10.30pm
CONF. Thtr 85 Class 40 Board 30 Del from £130
Credit Cards ①②③⑤ ⓔ
See advertisement under HORSHAM

LOWER SLAUGHTER Gloucestershire Map 04 SP12

★★★ ✿✿✿76% **Lower Slaughter Manor**
GL54 2HP ☎Cotswold(0451) 820456 FAX (0451) 822150

Courtesy and Care 1994

Closed 2 weeks Jan
This is a grand 17th-century house in the heart of the pretty Cotswold village, and stands in mature grounds and gardens. It is not too grand, however, to offer the kind of friendly and attentive service which has earned the hotel an AA Courtesy and Care Award this year. Richly styled public rooms are furnished with deep comfortable seating, antiques and objets d'art setting off the ornate interior architecture. Bedrooms in the main house are well proportioned and tasteful, many with glorious garden views. The coach house rooms are not quite so opulent, though they are bright and well equipped. The elegant dining room is well supervised by a

pleasing Anglo/French team, and new chef Julian Ehlers has just taken over in the kitchen.
10⇨✶ Annexe5⇨✶2🛏 CTV in all bedrooms T
✗ (ex guide dogs) sB&B⇨✶£145-£195 dB&B⇨✶£185-£275 (incl dinner) 🅿
35P ⛳ ✿ ⚇ (heated) ♀ (hard) sauna croquet putting nc10yrs *xmas*
♀ English & French V ♿ ⚇ ✱
CONF. Thtr 30 Board 14 Del from £140
Credit Cards ①②③

★★★ 64% **Washbourne Court**
GL54 2HS ☎(0451) 822143 FAX (0451) 821045
Right at the heart of a charming Cotswold village, beside the pretty trout stream, this cosy hotel has a welcoming air. The character of the building retained in stone walls, flagstone floors and beamed ceilings has been combined successfully with up-to-date facilities and modern comforts, and as well as the tastefully furnished bedrooms of the main house there are quality cottage suites for extra comfort and independence. The restaurant provides a pleasant setting in which to enjoy the well cooked dishes based on excellent local produce.
5⇨✶ Annexe10⇨✶(4fb) CTV in all bedrooms ® T sB&B⇨✶£65-£75 dB&B⇨✶£85-£125 🅿
67P ⛳ ✿ ♀ (hard) *xmas*
V ♿ ⚇ ✱ Lunch £12.10-£14.10alc Dinner £20.95&alc Last dinner 9.15pm
CONF. Thtr 20 Board 18 Del from £110
Credit Cards ①②③ ⓔ

LOWESTOFT Suffolk Map 05 TM59

★★ 63% **Broadlands**
Bridge Rd, Oulton Broad NR32 3LN
☎(0502) 516031 FAX (0502) 501454

CONSORT HOTELS

Built around a small shopping precinct, this busy hotel offers comfortable bedrooms with modern amenities. Public rooms include a large restaurant and bar, a cabaret bar and a small lounge, largely occupied by a games area.
52⇨✶(2fb)🛏 in 15 bedrooms CTV in all bedrooms ®⚁T
⦅ CTV 120P ⊟ (heated) snooker sauna solarium gymnasium
♀ English & Italian V ♿ ⚇
Credit Cards ①②③⑤

LOWESWATER Cumbria Map 11 NY12

★ 66% **Grange Country House**
CA13 0SU ☎Lamplugh(0946) 861211 & 861570
Closed 20-30 Dec RS 1-19 Dec & 5 Jan-Feb
In the same family for 50 years, this peacefully positioned hotel provides a good old fashioned style of service. The house was built in 1658 close to Loweswater amid superb mountain scenery, and now provides comfortable public areas including a lounge with lake views and a bar with an open log fire. A choice of dishes is offered at dinner in the cosy dining room.
7⇨Annexe5⇨(1fb)2🛏 CTV in all bedrooms ® ✱ sB&B£30-£32 sB&B⇨✶£32-£35 dB&B£58-£60 dB&B⇨✶£64-£68
CTV 20P 2⚍ (charged) ⛳ ✿
V ♿ ⚇ ✱ Lunch £6.50-£9.50 High tea £7.50-£9 Dinner £12-£14.50 Last dinner 8pm

LUDLOW Shropshire Map 07 SO57

★★★ 69% **Overton Grange**
SY8 4AD (on B4361) ☎(0584) 873500 FAX (0584) 873524

This pleasant country hotel, built as a private residence at the turn of the century, is in 4 acres of lawns and parkland. Public areas include a half- panelled hall and restaurant, a modern bar with an open fire and a separate lounge. Bedrooms vary, many being quite

large and some have attractive canopied beds. A wide choice of food is available from fixed price menus and a carte.
16rm(13⇨)(2fb) CTV in 15 bedrooms ® T
✈ (ex guide dogs) ✱ sB&B£31-£35 sB&B⇨£54-£58 dB&B£56-£60 dB&B⇨£78-£90 ♬
80P ✿ croquet *xmas*
♡ English, French & Italian V ♡ ♢ Lunch £10.95-£12.95 Dinner £15.50-£19.50 Last dinner 9.30pm
Credit Cards [1] [2] [3] [5]

★★★ 🏵68% **Dinham Hall**
SY8 1EJ ☎(0584) 876464 FAX (0584) 876019

Superbly situated opposite the castle, Dinham Hall dates from 1792 and is a country house-style hotel in town. The bedrooms vary in size, though most are spacious. All have good quality furniture and many have lovely views. The comfortable lounge has an interesting carved wooden fireplace, and the Merchant Suite has several 14th-century timbers. The main restaurant offers 2 fixed price menus, and lighter meals are served in de Ludlows Brasserie.
13⇨(1fb)2🎗 CTV in all bedrooms ® T sB&B⇨£64-£70 dB&B⇨£89-£94 ♬
24P ✿ sauna gymnasium *xmas*
♡ International V ♡ ♢ ✗ Sunday Lunch fr£10.50 Dinner £15.95-£19.95 Last dinner 9.30pm
CONF. Board 25 Del £95
Credit Cards [1] [2] [3] £

★★★ 68% **The Feathers at Ludlow**
Bull Ring SY8 1AA (in the town centre) ☎(0584) 875261 FAX (0584) 876030

One of England's most famous inns, its façade including impressive motifs, carved timberwork and arches, and its interior full of panelled walls, original fireplaces, beams and ornate carvings. There is a wide range of public rooms. Bedrooms are furnished with solid ➡

Ludlow

★★★★

You'll find the comfortable atmosphere of this award winning hotel is designed to impress, but not to overwhelm. You'll have as much personal care and attention — and as much time to yourself — as you need. Particular emphasis is given to the enjoyment of food, with the Orangery and the Shires Restaurants offering two distinctive atmospheres.

**QUORN/QUORNDON
LOUGHBOROUGH
LEICS LE12 8BB**
Telephone: 0509-415050
Fax No: 0509-415557

L

BROADLANDS HOTEL
OULTON BROAD, NR LOWESTOFT

A modern hotel with 52 bedrooms, all with full en-suite facilities. Indoor leisure facilities including swimming pool, spa, solarium, etc. Snooker room. Carvery Restaurant with á la carte selection.

Well appointed rooms from £49.00 B & B
(low cost all inclusive mini-break packages also available)

Reservations: 0502 516031
BROADLANDS HOTEL ★★
Oulton Broad, Lowestoft, Suffolk

A CORNISH HAVEN

Conveniently situated in the small and ancient town of Lostwithiel, which nestles in the beautiful Fowey Valley, with numerous National Trust properties and lovely coastal walks nearby. This highly recommended hotel offers warm, spacious en-suite bedrooms with colour TV, telephone and teamaker. Delicious food and imaginative menus using local sea and farm produce. Heated swimming pool. Friendly efficient service.
Midweek/Weekend Breaks & Weekly Tariff available.
For a Colour Brochure please write to or phone:

AA ★★★   **Restormel Lodge HOTEL**   AA ★★★
LOSTWITHIEL, CORNWALL, PL22 0DD

(0208) 872223

Ludlow - Luton

furniture in keeping with the hotel's character, including 4-poster and canopied beds, and fabrics are used to good effect. The beamed and timbered restaurant provides a good range of food and bar meals are also available.

40⇌🛁(3fb)8🌿in 5 bedrooms CTV in all bedrooms ® T
sB&B⇌🛁£65-£115 dB&B⇌🛁£104-£124 🍴
Lift (37P snooker *xmas*
V ॐ 🍴 Lunch £11-£13&alc Dinner £19.50&alc Last dinner 9pm
CONF. Thtr 100 Class 30 Board 50 Del from £85
Credit Cards ① ② ③ ④ ⑤ £

★★ 63% Dinham Weir
Dinham Bridge SY8 1EH ☎(0584) 874431
This hotel by the side of the weir has a pretty garden where one may enjoy the peaceful surroundings. Chef Mrs Moseley cooks enjoyable meals with a choice from a fixed price or à la carte menu. Modern bedrooms are well equipped, and some restaurant tables overlook the river.
8⇌🛁1🌿in 2 bedrooms CTV in all bedrooms ® T ✱
sB&B⇌🛁£50-£55 dB&B⇌🛁£65-£70 🍴
10P nc5yrs *xmas*
V ॐ 🍴 Lunch £12.50&alc Dinner £12.50&alc Last dinner 9pm
Credit Cards ① ② ③ ⑤ £

★★ 59% Cliffe
Dinham SY8 2JE ☎(0584) 872063
The Cliffe is a small, personally run hotel at the foot of Ludlow town with good views of the castle. The public areas have recently been refurbished and have provided the hotel a new lease of life, and attractive well laid out grounds surround the building.
10rm(3⇌4🛁)(1fb) CTV in all bedrooms ® ✱ sB&B£20-£25 sB&B⇌🛁£25 dB&Bfr£40 dB&B⇌🛁fr£45 🍴
50P 🐕 ✿
V ॐ ✱ Lunch fr£6.95 Dinner £8.95-£10.95 Last dinner 8.30pm
Credit Cards ① ② ③

Forte Travelodge
Woofferton(on A49 at junct A456/B4362)
☎(0584) 711695 Central Res (0800) 850950

This modern building offers a good standard of accommodation for overnight stops. Smart, spacious and well equipped bedrooms, all with en suite bathrooms, are suitable for family use, and meals may be taken at the nearby family restaurant. For more details about Travelodges, consult the Contents page, under Hotel Groups.
32⇌🛁✱ B⇌🛁£31.95 (room only)

LUDWELL Wiltshire Map **03** ST92

★★ 68% Grove House
SP7 9ND (2m E of Shaftesbury on A30)
☎Donhead(0747) 828365 FAX (0747) 828365
Once the residence of the wealthy Grove family, the hotel offers a very warm and friendly atmosphere. The majority of rooms are peacefully situated at the rear with views of the pretty garden. Public areas are cosy and comfortable, and the home cooking is enjoyable. Many guests return regularly, but the most loyal are the badgers who come each evening to feed.
9rm(4⇌4🛁) CTV in all bedrooms ® ✱ sB&B⇌🛁£27.50-£32.50 dB&B⇌🛁£55 🍴
12P 🐕 ✿ nc5yrs *xmas*
♥ English & Continental V ॐ 🍱 ✱ Bar Lunch £4.75-£9.50 Dinner £17 Last dinner 9pm
Credit Cards ① ③

Hotels with red star ratings are especially high quality.

LULWORTH COVE
See **West Lulworth**

LUMBY North Yorkshire Map **08** SE43

Forte Posthouse
LS25 5LF (southern junc A1/A63)
☎South Milford(0977) 682711 FAX (0977) 685462

Suitable for both the business and leisure traveller, this bright hotel provides modern accommodation in well equipped bedrooms with en suite bathrooms. For more details about Forte Posthouse hotels, consult the Contents page, under Hotel Guides.
105⇌🛁✱ B⇌🛁£41.50-£53.50 (room only)
CONF. Thtr 120 Class 48 Board 48 Del from £79.50

LUNDIN LINKS Fife Map **12** NO40

★★★ 66% Old Manor
Leven Rd KY8 6AJ (off A912) ☎(0333) 320368 FAX (0333) 320911
New owners continue to improve this hotel, a traditional mansion house with fine views over the Lundin Links golf course and the Firth of Forth. Bedroom furnishings are all modern. The elegant restaurant produces an imaginative menu, while the Coachman's Grill in the grounds offers an informal alternative with grills, seafood and real ale.
19⇌🛁(3fb) CTV in all bedrooms ® T sB&B⇌🛁£60 dB&B⇌🛁£79.50 🍴
(80P ✿ ▶ 18
♥ Scottish & Continental V ॐ 🍱 Lunch £11.50-£12.50&alc High tea £6-£7.50 Dinner £19.50-£23&alc Last dinner 9.30pm
CONF. Thtr 120 Class 60 Board 40 Del from £65
Credit Cards ① ② ③ £

LUTON Bedfordshire Map **04** TL02

★★★ 69% Strathmore Thistle
Arndale Centre LU1 2TR ☎(0582) 34199 FAX (0582) 402528

THISTLE HOTELS

A modern hotel within the Arndale shopping centre, with free car parking in the adjoining multi storey car park (tokens issued at reception). Bedrooms are all similar, although executive rooms have lots of extras. Off the spacious and comfortable lobby is a small cocktail bar and the elegant Angeline's restaurant with a choice of menus. Informal dining and all day snacks can be enjoyed in Balzac's café bar, and Mr Bumble's public bar is popular with locals.
150⇌🛁(7fb)🌿in 55 bedrooms CTV in all bedrooms ®🎧 T ✱
sB⇌🛁£75-£89 dB⇌🛁£89-£130 (room only) 🍴
Lift (44P *xmas*
♥ International V ॐ 🍱 ✱ Lunch £8.50-£11&alc Dinner £17.25&alc Last dinner 10pm
CONF. Thtr 200 Class 120 Board 60 Del from £85
Credit Cards ① ② ③ ④ ⑤

★★★ 64% The Chiltern
Waller Av, Dunstable Rd LU4 9RU (turn off A505 at Lex Vauxhall Garage)
☎(0582) 575911 FAX (0582) 581859

This modern hotel is geared towards the business guest. Bedrooms on the first and 2nd floors have recently been upgraded, while those on the 3rd floor are dull and dated (and generally let last). Room service is available 24 hours, a lounge menu is on display throughout the day, and the restaurant caters for all tastes and most diets.
91⇌🛁🌿in 27 bedrooms CTV in all bedrooms ®🎧 T ✱
sB⇌🛁£45-£72 dB⇌🛁£45-£72 (room only) 🍴
Lift (150P *xmas*
♥ European V ॐ 🍱 ✱ Lunch £13-£21.50&alc Dinner £13-£21.50&alc Last dinner 10pm
Credit Cards ① ② ③ ④ ⑤

★★ 67% Red Lion
Castle St LU1 3AA (Whitbread) ☎(0582) 413881 FAX (0582) 23864

Check for directions or, ideally, request a map to find your way round the one way system to this traditional coaching inn. Bedrooms are smart and public areas are attractive. In the coffee shop, breakfast and lunch are served in informal surroundings, and the Market Tavern public bar is a popular meeting place for young locals.

24⇨ℕ Annexe15⇨ℕ(4fb)1⬚⌇in 6 bedrooms CTV in all bedrooms ® T ℋ (ex guide dogs) ✱ sB&B⇨ℕ£59.50-£69.50 dB&B⇨ℕfr£81
☾ 50P
♀ English & Continental V ✿ ⚙ ⌇ ✱ Lunch fr£7.95&alc Dinner fr£12.50&alc Last dinner 10pm
CONF. Thtr 50 Board 25 Del from £89
Credit Cards

★★ 56% Hotel Ibis
Luton Airport, Spittlesea Rd LU2 9NZ
☎(0582) 424488 FAX (0582) 455511

Part of a budget European chain, this modern purpose built hotel is the only hotel within an airport complex. Every bedroom is identically decorated and furnished in a modest, no frills style. All have good en suites with a bath as well as a shower. The bar and restaurant are open all day and breakfast, not included in the competitive room charge, is an entirely self-service affair.

98⇨ℕ(6fb)⌇in 30 bedrooms CTV in all bedrooms ®⚙ T ✱ dB⇨ℕ£32-£39.50 (room only)
Lift ☾ ⎕ 150P xmas
♀ English & French V ✿ ⚙ ⌇ ✱ Lunch £1.95-£9.75 Dinner £9.75 Last dinner 10.30pm
Credit Cards

Forte Posthouse
Dunstable Rd LU4 8RQ ☎(0582) 575955 FAX (0582) 490065

Suitable for both the business and leisure traveller, this bright hotel provides modern accommodation in well equipped bedrooms with en suite bathrooms. For more details about Forte Posthouse hotels, consult the Contents page, under Hotel Groups.

117⇨ℕ ✱ B⇨ℕ£41.50-£53.50 (room only)

LUTTERWORTH Leicestershire Map 04 SP58

★★★ 65% Denbigh Arms
High St LE17 4AD ☎(0455) 553537 FAX (0455) 556627

This converted Georgian coaching inn is located at the southern end of town, a short drive from junction 20 of the M1 motorway. Bedrooms are mostly spacious, comprehensively equipped, and well furnished with natural pine and floral fabrics. Public areas include the quiet foyer lounge and the comfortable Players Bar across the courtyard: a good-sized attractively appointed lounge bar, Lamberts Restaurant, offers a fixed-price daily menu together with a carte. There is a meeting room and facilities for larger conferences.

31⇨ℕ(4fb)⌇in 2 bedrooms CTV in all bedrooms ® T ✱ sB&B⇨ℕ£37.50-£55 dB&B⇨ℕ£56-£65 ♺
☾ 30P pool table xmas
♀ English & French V ✿ ⚙ ✱ Sunday Lunch £7.30-£8.30 Dinner £1.50-£7.95alc Last dinner 9.30pm
CONF. Thtr 60 Class 25 Board 25 Del from £65
Credit Cards

Red star hotels are each highlighted by a pink tinted panel.

★★★AA
STRATHMORE
THISTLE HOTEL

Arndale Centre, Luton LU1 2TR
Tel: 0582 34199   Fax: 0582 402528

Your choice in
Luton

For Reservations at over 100
Mount Charlotte Thistle Hotels
Telephone London: 071 937 8033.

THISTLE HOTELS

STB ✿✿✿✿ COMMENDED   ★★★

The Old Manor Hotel

Leven Road, Lundin Links, Fife KY8 6AJ.
Telephone: 0333-320368
Fax: 0333-320911

Country House hotel, near St. Andrews, one mile East of Leven on A915, with impressive views over Largo Bay and Lundin Links Golf course. Restaurant renowned for fresh local seafood. Table d'hôte and à la Carte menus complemented by a well balanced wine list. For alternative eating experience our unique Coachman's Grill and Alehouse, offers chargrilled steaks, seafood, and a range of real ales. 20 rooms, all en suite.

Lutterworth - Lyme Regis

★★★62% Fernie Lodge Restaurant & Hotel
Berridges Ln, Husbands Bosworth LE17 6LE
☎Market Harborough(0858) 880551 FAX (0858) 880014
18⇌♠(3fb) CTV in all bedrooms ®✌ T ✱ sB&B⇌♠£55-£59 dB&B⇌♠£67-£74 🄿
50P ♪ xmas
V ♦ ♨ ⚹ ✱ Lunch £11.25
Credit Cards [1][2][3]

LYBSTER Highland *Caithness* Map **15** ND23

★★63% Portland Arms
KW3 6BS ☎(05932) 208
Popular commercial, tourist and fishing hotel, conveniently positioned beside the A9. Public areas include an inviting lounge, a panelled snug bar, a foyer lounge, a bright dining room and a separate bar food dining area. Bedrooms are smartly decorated and offer a good range of amenities.
19⇌♠(3fb)2🛏 CTV in all bedrooms ® T
(CTV 50P ▶ 9 ♩
♀ Scottish & French V ♦ ♨ Last dinner 9.30pm
Credit Cards [1][3]

LYDDINGTON Leicestershire Map **04** SP89

★★55% Marquess of Exeter
Main Rd LE15 9LT (Logis) ☎Uppingham(0572) 822477 FAX (0572) 821343
This 16-century coaching inn with ample car parking facilities behind it stands at the centre of an attractive historic village surrounded by fields. Large, well equipped bedrooms are gradually being redecorated and there are three bar areas; competently prepared bar snacks provide an alternative to the well cooked meals served in the restaurant.
Annexe17⇌♠ CTV in all bedrooms ® T ✈
70P 🚳 ✿
♀ English & French V ♦ ♨ Last dinner 9.45pm
Credit Cards [1][2][3][5]

LYDFORD Devon Map **02** SX58

★★♿67% Lydford House
EX20 4AU (turn off A386 halfway between Okehampton and Tavistock, signpost Lydford, 500yds on right hand side)
☎(082282) 347 FAX (082282) 442
Tucked away in 8 acres of mature gardens and pasture, this cosy, relaxed and friendly family-run hotel was once the home of Victorian artist William Widgery, whose scenes of Dartmoor still hang in the comfortable lounge. Public rooms are welcoming, bedrooms are pleasant and comfortable, and meals are home-cooked. The hotel also has a riding school, run by the owner's daughter.
13rm(11⇌♠)(2fb)1🛏in 1 bedroom CTV in all bedrooms ® T sB&B⇌♠£32.25 dB&B⇌♠£64.50 🄿
30P 🚳 ✿ ʊ nc5yrs
V ♦ ♨ ⚹ ✱ Sunday Lunch £7.25 Dinner fr£14 Last dinner 8pm
Credit Cards [1][2][3]

LYDNEY Gloucestershire Map **03** SO60

★★59% Feathers
High St GL15 5DN ☎Dean(0594) 842815 & 842386
There is a friendly atmosphere in this popular town centre hotel, which offers a choice of à la carte dining room or carvery, and there are also good bar menus available.
14⇌♠(3fb)1🛏in 2 bedrooms CTV in all bedrooms ® T
50P
V ♦ ♨ Last dinner 9pm
Credit Cards [1][2][3]

LYME REGIS Dorset Map **03** SY39
See also **Rousdon**

★★★70% Alexandra
Pound St DT7 3HZ ☎(0297) 442010 FAX (0297) 443229
Closed 23 Dec-6 Feb
Built in 1735, this hotel has views over Lyme Bay, and a path through its attractive gardens leads to Langmoor Gardens and The Cobb. All the attractive bedrooms have pretty soft furnishings, and public areas retain the charm and character of the original building; a light, airy dining room offers both table d'hôte and à la carte menus, while morning coffees, light lunches and afternoon teas are served in the sun lounge. Service is efficient and friendly.
26rm(23⇌♠)(6fb) CTV in all bedrooms ® T sB&B⇌♠£50-£55 sB&B⇌♠£50-£55 dB&B⇌♠£90-£100 dB&B⇌♠£114-£124 (incl dinner) 🄿
(24P 1🚗 🚳 ✿ ⚘
♀ English & French V ♦ ♨ ⚹ ✱ Lunch £10-£12.50&alc High tea fr£4.50 Dinner fr£17.50 Last dinner 8.30pm
Credit Cards [1][2][3][5] £

★★68% Buena Vista
Pound St DT7 3HZ ☎(0297) 442494
Closed Dec
The Buena Vista is a well maintained and comfortable hotel on the fringe of the town centre. Bedrooms vary in size but are nicely furnished and well equipped. There is a relaxing atmosphere in the public areas, and in the dining room a daily changing dinner menu is offered.
17⇌♠(1fb) CTV in all bedrooms ® T
20P 🚳 ✿
V ♦ ♨ ⚹ Last dinner 8.30pm
Credit Cards [1][2][3][5]

★★❀68% Kersbrook
Pound Rd DT7 3HX ☎(0297) 442596
Closed 2 Dec-Jan
In a quiet position high above the town, this fine 18th-century building has glorious views across the surrounding area. Bedrooms, though quite small, are all very pretty and have lots of individual style. The comfortable public areas have a traditional feel and are filled with the scent of fresh flowers. Chef Norman Arnold's accomplished cooking is appreciated by the guests who can choose between lengthy table d'hôte and à la carte menus.
10⇌♠✱in all bedrooms CTV in all bedrooms ® ✱
sB&B⇌♠£45-£55 dB&B⇌♠£60-£70 🄿
14P 🚳 ✿
♀ English, French & Italian V ♦ ♨ ⚹ Sunday Lunch £3.50-£8.95 Dinner fr£16.50&alc Last dinner 9pm
Credit Cards [1][2][3] £

★★66% Dorset
Silver St DT7 3HX ☎(0297) 442482
Closed Nov-Mar
A privately owned and personally run hotel, the Dorset has a friendly atmosphere and provides efficient and attentive service. Bedrooms are bright, clean and well equipped, and other facilities include a bar and comfortable lounge. In the dining room, the dinner menu offers a good choice daily changing menu of mainly English cooking. This is accompanied by a short, reasonably priced wine list.
14rm(12⇌♠)(1fb) CTV in all bedrooms ® T sB&B⇌♠£34.50-£38 sB&B⇌♠£34.50-£38 dB&B⇌♠£69-£76 dB&B⇌♠£69-£76 (incl dinner) 🄿
13P
V ♦ ♨ Dinner fr£14 Last dinner 8pm
Credit Cards [1][3]

For key to symbols see the Bookmark.

Lyme Regis - Lymington

★★ 64% **Royal Lion**
Broad St DT7 3QF ☎(0297) 445622 FAX (0297) 445859
Closed 3 days Xmas

In the centre of the bustling seaside town, this personally managed hotel is filled with character and charm. The original building dates from 1601, and it is here that the cosy bars are located. Some bedrooms are in the old part, while those in the modern wing are more spacious, some with balconies and views over the town and sea. There is a choice of lounges and a traditional dining room offering table d'hôte and à la carte menus.
30⇨♠(4fb)1∰ CTV in all bedrooms ® T ✱ sB&B⇨♠£33-£35 dB&B⇨♠£66-£70 (incl dinner) ♬
36P ♯☐ (heated) snooker gymnasium games room steam room jacuzzi
♢ ⚏ ✱ Bar Lunch £1.55-£5.50 Dinner £14.75 Last dinner 9pm
Credit Cards [1][2][3][5]

★★ 62% **Bay**
Marine Pde DT7 3JQ ☎(0297) 442059
Closed Dec-Feb

The only hotel to enjoy such a position directly on the promenade, the Bay is a popular choice with both frequently returning and new guests. The lounge and sunny balcony have glorious views out across the Cobb, and there is a busy dining room and convivial bar. Bedrooms are simply decorated and neatly presented, many offering en suite facilities.
21rm(12⇨♠)(3fb) CTV in 20 bedrooms ® sB&B£28-£35 sB&B⇨♠£29-£36 dB&B⇨♠£60-£72 ♬
20🚗 🞉 snooker sauna solarium gymnasium
♢ English & French ♢ ⚏ High tea £4-£50 Dinner £17-£50
Last dinner 8.30pm
Credit Cards [1][3]

★ 56% **Tudor House**
Church St DT7 3BU ☎(0297) 442472
Closed Nov-mid Mar

An hotel of charm and character, dating back over 400 years and conveniently positioned in the town centre, Tudor House offers accommodation in bedrooms which are simply decorated, furnished and equipped. Cosy public areas include both quiet and television lounges as well as a beamed, flagstone-floored bar in the basement which has its own spring. Friendly resident proprietors offer a warm welcome and genuine hospitality.
17rm(4⇨♠)(10fb) ®
CTV 12P
♢ Last dinner 7.30pm
Credit Cards [1][3]

LYMINGTON Hampshire Map **04** SZ39

★★★🍴 73% **Passford House**
Mount Pleasant Ln SO41 8LS (from A337 over mini rbt then 1st left onto Sway Road and in 0.75m right into Mount Pleasant Lane) ☎(0590) 682398 FAX (0590) 683494

This long established hotel is in a peaceful location, surrounded by extensive grounds which include attractive gardens and sports facilities. The public areas offer the old-fashioned virtues of several comfortable lounges (including no smoking), attentive uniformed staff and simple decoration. Bedrooms are either standard or superior, most of a good size.
54⇨♠ Annexe2⇨♠(2fb)1∰ CTV in all bedrooms ® T sB&B⇨♠£75-£100 dB&B⇨♠£112-£130 ♬
《 100P 4🚗 (£4) ✱ (heated) ⇌ (hard) sauna solarium gymnasium croquet putting table tennis pool table ♤ xmas
♢ English & French V ♢ ⚏ Lunch fr£11.50 High tea fr£6.50 Dinner fr£21 Last dinner 9pm
CONF. Thtr 60 Class 30 Board 30 Del from £96
Credit Cards [1][2][3]

See advertisement on page 405

Hotel Buena Vista
Pound St. ● Lyme Regis
Ashley Courtenay   AA★★

Situated in an unrivalled position with spectacular sea views, only minutes walk from the town and beaches. The Regency style house, set in its own attractive garden, has a country house ambience which coupled with good food and old fashioned hospitality offers guests a relaxed, peaceful stay.
All rooms en-suite, with colour TV/radio, direct dial telephone and tea/coffee making facilities and most have sea/coastal views, some of which have balconies. AMPLE PARKING.
Telephone: (0297) 442494

NEAR LYME REGIS & AXMINSTER

Peaceful country house in glorious countryside. Award winning gardens, 21 immaculate en suite bedrooms, comfortable lounges, billiards room, safe parking.
Where guests return year after year.

FAIRWATER HEAD
Country House Hotel
Hawkchurch, Devon EX13 5TX
Telephone: (0297) 678349
AA★★★ (72%) ❀
See gazetteer entry under Hawkchurch

Lymington - Lyndhurst

★★★ ❀69% Stanwell House
High St SO41 9AA (A337 to town centre) (Clipper)
☎(0590) 677123 FAX (0590) 677756
This attractive town centre hotel provides a choice of individually furnished bedrooms and elegant public areas, including a small drawing room, library lounge and cocktail bar. Railing's Restaurant, with its delightful paved garden, is a sophisticated venue for head chef Mark Hewitt's interesting daily recipe and ambitious carte. Telephone for directions as car arrivals can be difficult at busy times.
35⇨1✿ CTV in all bedrooms ® T ✖ (ex guide dogs) sB&B⇨fr£72.50 dB&B⇨£98-£108 ₽
(✱ ✤ ❀ ⌒ xmas
♀ English & French V ✧ ⏉ Lunch fr£12&alc Dinner fr£20&alc Last dinner 9.30pm
CONF. Thtr 15 Class 14 Board 16 Del from £90
Credit Cards 1 3

★★❀❀ GORDLETON MILL
Silver St, Hordle SO41 6DJ
(2m NW on Hordle road)
☎(0590) 682219 FAX (0590) 683073
Closed 1-3 Jan RS Sun & Tue

This delightful creeper-clad, converted mill house re-opened in 1991 after its owner, William Stone, had completed major renovation work. The restaurant is the mainstay of the hotel's operation, and meals are served most professionally in the attractive Provence Restaurant. The new chef is Didier Heyl, formerly at Hartwell House in Aylesbury, with experience in various top French restaurants, and first impressions are encouraging. His skill and flair are evident already, and he is keen to introduce his own ideas to the menu at the earliest opportunity.
7⇨✿✖ in 4 bedrooms CTV in all bedrooms ✖
60P ✤ ❀ nc7yrs
♀ French V ✧ ⏉ ✖ Last dinner 10pm
Credit Cards 1 2 3 5

★★75% String of Horses
Mead End Rd, Sway SO41 6EH ☎(0590) 682631
This delightful small hotel is set in 4 acres of mature grounds on the edge of the New Forest. The modern bedrooms, 2 with balconies, have been tastefully furnished and most have spa baths with showers. No smoking public areas include the Carriages Restaurant, the small Tandem Bar and a traditional lounge. The chef's carte is particularly recommended for dishes such as chef's pâté; fresh salmon with dill and white sauce, and the choice of home-made puddings.
8⇨✿3✿ CTV in all bedrooms ® T ✖ (ex guide dogs) 20P ✤ ❀ ⌒ (heated) nc16yrs
♀ English & French V ✧ ⏉ ✖ Sunday Lunch £10.95 Dinner £16.50-£17.50&alc Last dinner 9pm
Credit Cards 1 2 3

If you have booked a meal in a hotel restaurant and cannot get there, remember you have a contractual obligation to cancel your booking.

LYMM Cheshire Map 07 SJ68
★★★ 59% Lymm
Whitbarrow Rd WA13 9AQ ☎(092575) 2233 FAX (092575) 6035
RS New Year
The Lymm is a fully extended hotel in a quiet residential area with a popular lounge bar and restaurant. Many of the bedrooms are in the rear extension, as is the main reception. Competitive rates are available at weekends and when flying from Manchester Airport.
22⇨✿Annexe47⇨✿(1fb) CTV in all bedrooms ®
sB&B⇨✿£40-£70 dB&B⇨✿£70-£85 ₽
(120P
♀ English & French V ✧ ⏉ ✱ Lunch fr£14.50 Dinner £14.50-£16.50 Last dinner 10pm
CONF. Thtr 120 Class 60 Board 40 Del from £90
Credit Cards 1 2 3 5

DE VERE HOTELS

LYMPSHAM Avon Map 03 ST35
★★★❀ 64% Batch Farm Country
BS24 0EX ☎Weston-super-Mare(0934) 750371 FAX (0934) 750371
Closed Xmas
This long, white building, in the grounds of a working farm, is a friendly, relaxing small hotel in a peaceful rural location. There is a good choice of comfortable lounges where Mr Brown is a most genial host. Mrs Brown runs the kitchen, and the fresh vegetables and dessert trolley are noteworthy.
8⇨✿(4fb)✖ in 2 bedrooms CTV in all bedrooms ® ✖
sB&B⇨✿£33-£35 dB&B⇨✿£54-£58 ₽
CTV 50P ✤ ❀ ♪ snooker croquet
♀ English & Continental V ✧ ⏉ ✖ Bar Lunch £5-£6 Dinner £11-£13&alc Last dinner 8.45pm
CONF. Thtr 70 Class 60 Board 40
Credit Cards 1 2 3 5   £

See advertisement under WESTON-SUPER-MARE

LYNDHURST Hampshire Map 04 SU30
★★★ ❀❀✤ 74% Parkhill
Beaulieu Rd SO43 7FZ (off B3056 to Beaulieu)
☎(0703) 282944 FAX (0703) 283268
Reached by a long winding drive, this fine 18th-century manor house overlooks heathland. Improvements continue to the well equipped bedrooms, with some very comfortable large rooms in a converted coach house and cottage. Public areas retain their period elegance. In the restaurant chef Richard Turner offers a seasonal carte of skilfully prepared dishes in modern English style. An inspection meal began with home-smoked breast of duck on a bed of fresh egg noodles in bacon and garlic cream, followed by baby brill on lemon grass moistened with hazelnut oil and served with a saffron sauce; the chocolate soufflé proved a delicious finish.
15⇨✿Annexe5⇨✿(2fb)2✿ CTV in all bedrooms ® T ✱
sB&B⇨✿£39-£69 dB&B⇨✿£78-£118 ₽
75P 2✤ ❀ ⌒ (heated) ♪ croquet outdoor chess putting xmas
♀ English & French V ✧ ⏉ ✖ ✖ Lunch £15&alc Dinner £23.50&alc Last dinner 9.30pm
CONF. Thtr 65 Class 40 Board 35 Del £85
Credit Cards 1 2 3 4 5

★★★ ❀70% Crown
High St SO43 7NF (in the centre of the village, opposite the church)
☎(0703) 282922 FAX (0703) 282751

There has been an inn on this site since the 1600s and the present building dates from 1897. The accommodation retains a traditional style with real fires, comfortable lounges, wood panelled bar and well appointed, candlelit restaurant, Bedrooms have been refurbished to a good standard. Chef Stephen Greenhalgh offers a daily fixed price menu and an à la carte selection.

40⇨♠(6fb)1⊞ CTV in all bedrooms ® T ✱ sB&B⇨♠£57-£63 dB&B⇨♠£88-£99 ♬
Lift 60P *xmas*
♡ European V ✧ ⚏ ⚹ Lunch £10.50-£14.50&alc Dinner £14.50&alc Last dinner 9.30pm
Credit Cards [1][2][3][5]

See advertisement under SOUTHAMPTON

★★★ 62% **Lyndhurst Park**
High St SO43 7NL (Forestdale) ☎(0703) 283923 FAX (0703) 283019

This extended Georgian mansion on the east of the main New Forest town is set in extensive grounds and has popular leisure and conference facilities. Bedrooms vary in size, many overlooking the lawns, but all are well equipped with modern comforts.
59⇨♠(3fb)3⊞⚹in 3 bedrooms CTV in all bedrooms ® T ✱ sB&B⇨♠£39.95-£44.95 dB&B⇨♠£59.90-£69.90 ♬
Lift ℂ 100P ✽ ≋ (heated) ℘ (hard) snooker sauna table tennis *xmas*
♡ English & Continental V ✧ ⚏ ✱ Lunch £9.25-£16.95 High tea fr£4.95 Last high tea 6.30pm
CONF. Thtr 300 Class 120 Board 80 Del from £65
Credit Cards [1][2][3][4][5]

★★★ 57% **Forest Lodge**
Pikes Hill, Romsey Rd SO43 7AS (Care Hotels) ☎(0703) 283677 FAX (0703) 283719

This attractive shuttered white Georgian building is set in its own grounds on the edge of Lyndhurst. Rooms are soundly furnished, but do vary in size and outlook. Public areas are comfortable.
23⇨♠(1fb)1⊞⚹in 5 bedrooms CTV in all bedrooms ® T sB&B⇨♠£35-£50 dB&B⇨♠£50-£80 ♬
CTV 50P ✽ ≋ (heated) pool table *xmas*
V ✧ ⚏ ⚹ ✱ Sunday Lunch £9.95 Dinner £13.10&alc Last dinner 8.45pm
Credit Cards [1][2][3][5]

South Lawn Hotel & Restaurant ★★★ ❋

Milford-on-Sea, Lymington, Hampshire SO41 0RF
Tel: Lymington (0590) 643911 Fax: (0590) 644820

Delightful Country House Hotel in peaceful surroundings where comfort and good food predominate. Owner/Chef Ernst Barten supervises excellent cuisine. Specially imported wines from Germany.

All rooms en-suite, colour TV, phone and trouser press. Facilities nearby include windsurfing and sailing from Keyhaven, Golf at Brockenhurst and Barton-on-Sea, the Beach at Milford and walking or riding in the beautiful New Forest.

AN OASIS OF PEACE AND TRANQUILITY IN THE HEART OF THE NEW FOREST

★ ★ ★ AA ❋ ❋

PARKHILL HOTEL AND RESTAURANT

A delightful 20 bedroom Georgian Country House Hotel nestling in 12 acres of glorious pasture and parkland offering the highest standards of hospitality and service together with award winning cuisine in a relaxed and comfortable atmosphere.

Outdoor facilities include Giant Chess, Putting Green, Croquet Lawn and Outdoor Pool, heated in season.

BEAULIEU ROAD, LYNDHURST, HAMPSHIRE
Tel: (0703) 282944   Fax: (0703) 283 268

★ ★ ★
73%
'The Hotel on the edge of the New Forest'

PASSFORD HOUSE HOTEL

This very special Country Hotel
Delightfully situated in ten acres of its own grounds. Four miles from the sea. Regency style restaurant. 50 bedrooms, all with colour TV and private bathroom. Sauna, Tennis Court, Putting and Croquet Lawn, Heated Swimming Pool, Games Room. Riding stables and yachting facilities nearby. Indoor Leisure Complex.

Mount Pleasant, Near Lymington, Hampshire SO41 8LS
Telephone: (0590) 682398 Fax: (0590) 683494
Proprietors: Mr & Mrs Patrick Heritage

Lyndhurst - Lynton

★ **70% Knightwood Lodge**
Southampton Rd SO43 7BU (on A35)
☎Southampton(0703) 282502 FAX (0703) 283730
Closed 25 Dec

Personally managed by the amiable proprietors, Mr and Mrs Sanderson, this small, friendly hotel continues to improve and offers good, comfortable accommodation. Bedrooms are pretty and well equipped. There is a sunny dining room, a small bar and a well furnished lounge with books and magazines.
15⇌↑(3fb)1🛌 CTV in all bedrooms ® ⚡ T ✗ (ex guide dogs) sB&B⇌↑£25-£36 dB&B⇌↑fr£44.50 ₽
15P 🚗 ▢ (heated) sauna solarium jacuzzi steam room
V ✂ Bar Lunch £1.95-£5.95 Dinner fr£7.75&alc Last dinner 8pm
Credit Cards [1][2][3][5]

LYNMOUTH Devon Map **03** SS74
See also **Lynton**

★★★ **60% Tors**
EX35 6NA ☎Lynton(0598) 53236
Closed 4 Jan-mid Feb RS Feb

This large Victorian building clings to the hillside above Lynmouth, commanding splendid views over the village and bay. The open-plan public areas are both stylish and comfortable, in smart pastel colours and fabrics. Bedrooms vary in size, décor and outlook, and are slowly being upgraded.
35rm(33⇌↑)(5fb) CTV in all bedrooms ® T sB&B⇌↑£37-£77 dB&B⇌↑£64-£94 ₽
Lift 40P ✿ ▢ (heated) table tennis pool table *xmas*
♀ English & French V ♂ ✂ Lunch £20-£35alc Dinner £17-£19&alc Last dinner 8.45pm
CONF. Thtr 60 Class 40 Board 40 Del from £55
Credit Cards [1][2][3][5] £

★★ **❀70% Rising Sun**
Harbourside EX35 6EQ ☎Lynton(0598) 53223 FAX (0598) 53480

This 14th-century thatched smugglers inn, on the attractive harbourside, has narrow staircases, uneven floors, beams and timbers. The bar is popular, and residents have a smart lounge on the first floor. The panelled, candlelit restaurant offers a daily set-price manu and a longer carte – delicious fish dishes are a highlight. Bedrooms are compact but attractive and many have sea views. There is a secluded cottage at the end of the sloping sunny garden.
11⇌🎐 Annexe5⇌↑(2fb)2🛌 ✂ in 6 bedrooms CTV in all bedrooms ® T sB&B⇌↑£39.50-£45 dB&B⇌↑£79-£90 ₽ CTV 🅿 🚗 ✿ ♪ nc5yrs *xmas*
♀ English & French V ♂ ✂ ✳ Lunch fr£14.50&alc Dinner fr£21.50&alc Last dinner 9pm
Credit Cards [1][2][3][5] £

★★ **67% Bath**
Sea Front EX35 6EL ☎Lynton(0598) 52238
Closed Nov-Feb RS Mar

This friendly traditional hotel, full of character, is in the village centre, near the harbour. Bedrooms vary in size and view, and there is a cheerful cocktail bar, a small sun lounge and a separate public bar. The restaurant has a daily changing menu, featuring an imaginative choice of vegetables and home-made desserts.
24⇌↑(9fb) CTV in all bedrooms ® T sB&B⇌↑£26-£35 dB&B⇌↑£52-£70 ₽
11P 4🚗 (£1.75 per night)
♀ English & French V ♂ ✂ ✳ Lunch fr£7.75 Dinner fr£14 Last dinner 8.30pm
Credit Cards [1][2][3][5] £

★ **70% Rock House**
EX35 6EN ☎Lynton(0598) 53508 FAX (0598) 52432

This small, part-Georgian hotel has an unrivalled position, perched on the water's edge overlooking the harbour. The public rooms are full of character, and include a spacious lounge, a cosy panelled bar and a candlelit dining room. Bedrooms differ in size, furnishings and views, but all have modern facilities.
6rm(1⇌3🎐)(2fb)1🛌 CTV in all bedrooms ® sB&B£27-£35 sB&B⇌↑fr£35 dB&Bfr£54 dB&B⇌↑fr£70 ₽
CTV 7P 🚗
♀ English & French V ♂ ✂ Bar Lunch £6.50-£9 High tea £4-£6 Dinner fr£14&alc Last dinner 9pm
Credit Cards [1][2][3][5]

LYNTON Devon Map **03** SS74
See also **Lynmouth**

★★★ **❀70% Lynton Cottage**
North Walk EX35 6ED (Take turning next to St Mary's church and first right.) ☎(0598) 52342 FAX (0598) 52597
Closed Jan RS Dec & Feb

Set in an elevated position overlooking Lynmouth Bay and the wooded valley, this hotel provides comfortable, tranquil surroundings which are enhanced by charming service from the resident owners. Bedrooms are very inviting – those at the front have delightful views – and attractive public areas include the restaurant where a regularly changed fixed price menu features a range of interesting choices freshly and imaginatively prepared by the proprietor; the wine list boasts a good selection at reasonable prices.
17⇌🎐1🛌 CTV in all bedrooms ® T ✳ sB&B⇌↑£57-£72 dB&B⇌↑£111-£138 (incl dinner) ₽
26P 🚗 ✿ nc10yrs
♀ French ♂ ✂ ✳ Lunch £10-£20alc Dinner £21.50-£27alc Last dinner 8.45pm
Credit Cards [1][2][3][5]

★★ **❀⛊ 72% Hewitts**
The Hoe, North Walk EX35 6HJ ☎(0598) 52293 FAX (0598) 52489
Closed Jan

Standing within its own grounds in a delightful location overlooking the sea, this very attractive house offers a tranquil, relaxing atmosphere. Bedrooms have recently been upgraded, while the tastefully appointed lounge, bar and dining room display a wealth of interesting antiques.
9rm(7⇌🎐)(1fb) ✂ in 2 bedrooms CTV in all bedrooms ® T
12P 🚗 ☼ jacuzzi
♀ European V ♂ ✂ ✂ Last dinner 9pm
Credit Cards [1][3]

★★ **❀66% Neubia House**
Lydiate Ln EX35 6AH ☎(0598) 52309 & 53644

Closed 30 Nov-10 Feb

Mr and Mrs Murphy create a warm and friendly atmosphere in this small, well established hotel in the centre of the village. Bedrooms and bathrooms tend to be compact but are bright and fresh with pretty wallpaper and pine furniture. The small bar is crowded and convivial before dinner; a short set price menu offers adventurous dishes, and there are delicious home-made puddings.
12⇌🎐(2fb) 🛌 CTV in all bedrooms ® T ✳ sB&B⇌↑£28-£30 dB&B⇌↑£56-£60 ₽
14P 🚗
V ✂ ✳ Dinner £12.75-£14.75 Last dinner 8pm
Credit Cards [1][3]

For full, independent restaurant reviews, see the AA Abbey Well *Restaurant Guide*

Hotels with red star ratings are especially high quality.

Lynton

★★ **61%** **Sandrock**
Longmead EX35 6DH ☎(0598) 53307
Closed Dec-Jan
This friendly holiday hotel, on the road to the Valley of Rocks, has been run by the Harrisons for many years. Bedrooms are bright and comfortable, with several smart modernised bathrooms. There is a first floor lounge and a popular bar with a separate pool and darts rooms.
9rm(5⇨2↑)(3fb) CTV in all bedrooms ® T sB&B£19.50-£22.50 dB&B⇨↑£39-£47 ⧇
9P ⚑ pool table
♥ ♐ ✱ Bar Lunch £2.50-£10 Dinner £10.50-£12.90 Last dinner 7.45pm
Credit Cards 1 2 3 £

★ ⊕♨ **72%** **Combe Park**
Hillsford Bridge EX35 6LE (0.25 from junct of A39/B3223 at Hillsford Bridge) ☎(0598) 52356
Closed Nov-mid Mar (ex Xmas) RS Xmas
This former hunting lodge is in a picturesque location of wooded countryside, with Hoar Oak Water tumbling by at the end of the lawn. There are 2 comfortable lounges and a small bar. Dinner offers a choice of starters and desserts around a set main course, all prepared with great care by Shirley Barnes. Bedrooms are simply and restfully furnished in traditional style. Dogs are welcome.
9rm(6⇨2↑) ® sB&B⇨↑£63 dB&B⇨↑£88 (incl dinner)
CTV 11P ⚑ ✿ bird watching nc12yrs *xmas*
⫛ Dinner £19 Last dinner 7.15pm

★ **69%** **Seawood**
North Walk EX35 6HT ☎(0598) 52272
Closed Dec-Feb
The Peacock family have been welcoming guests for many years now to this lovely Victorian house nestling on the wooded cliffs overlooking Lynmouth Bay. Bedrooms are attractive, and the lounge and bar are comfortable. The menu offers enjoyable home ⇨

The Rising Sun Hotel

Proprietor: H.F. St H. Jeune ★★ ⊕

Lynmouth, Devon, EX35 6EQ
FULLY LICENSED

Tel: LYNTON (0598) 53223

14th-Century thatched Smugglers Inn overlooking Lynmouth Bay, and small picturesque harbour. 16 very comfortable rooms all with en suite facilities. A most attractive bar and oak panelled dining room specialising in local game and seafood. Situated within Exmoor National Park with its wonderful coastline and scenery. Riding and fishing close by.

Hewitt's

...a perfect
Agatha Christie set...

an apt description of this lovely 1860's country house with its galleried main hall, cosy log fires, stained glass windows and private 150 foot sun terrace. Tranquil, elegant and relaxing, the hotel has panoramic sea views and all the expected modern conveniences. The Hoe Restaurant is widely acclaimed for its fresh and imaginative cuisine.
Open to non-residents.

HEWITT'S, LYNTON, DEVON EX35 6HJ
Telephone: (0598) 52293 Fax: (0598) 52489

      AA★★ *(72%)* Ashley Courtenay
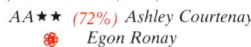   ⊕   Egon Ronay

KNIGHTWOOD LODGE HOTEL ★ 70%

Southampton Road, Lyndhurst
Hampshire SO43 7BU
Tel: (0703) 282502 Fax: (0703) 283730

Overlooking open forest and within easy walking distance of the 'capital' village of the New Forest.

Well equipped en suite bedrooms. Indoor leisure centre with heated swimming pool and spa. Cosy bar. Parking.

Special Breaks available all year.

For brochure and tariff phone resident proprietors Paul and Jackie Sanderson.

Lynton - Lytham St Annes

cooking with an especially appetising trolley of desserts – try pear and almond flan or hot chocolate pudding.
12⇌♠(1fb)4🛏 CTV in all bedrooms ® ✱ sB&B⇌♠£27-£30 dB&B⇌♠£50-£55 🍴
12P 🚗 ❋
♚ English & Continental V ✌ Last dinner 7.30pm £

★ **68%** **Chough's Nest**
North Walk EX35 6HJ ☎(0598) 53315
Closed mid Oct-Mar
The Harrops have run this friendly hotel for over 20 years. It is an attractive stone building on the wooded hillside overlooking the bay and most bedrooms enjoy the view. There is a pleasant lounge and home cooked dinners are served in a pleasant dining room. Breakfast orders are taken the night before. The hotel is now a no smoking establishment.
11⇌♠(2fb)2🛏 CTV in all bedrooms ® ✱ sB&B⇌♠£24-£26 dB&B⇌♠£50
10P 🚗 ❋ nc2yrs
V ❋ ✌ Dinner £12 Last dinner 7.30pm £

★ **68%** **Rockvale**
off Lee Rd EX35 6HW (A39 Lynton to Lynmouth road, entrance left hand side of Lynton Town Hall) ☎(0598) 52279 & 53343
RS 16 Nov-14 Feb
Peacefully set in an elevated position with views across the town and hills to Exmoor and Countisbury, this small hotel is very hospitably run by Mrs Spiers and her son Peter, and offers a friendly relaxed atmosphere. Bedrooms are well equipped and public rooms include a well stocked bar and a lounge with plenty of books and games.
8rm(5⇌1♠)(2fb)1🛏 CTV in all bedrooms ® T sB&B£18-£20 sB&B⇌♠£18-£25 dB&B£36-£45 dB&B⇌♠£38-£48 🍴
9P 🚗 ❋ nc4yrs
♚ European ❋ ✌ Bar Lunch £2.50-£6 Dinner £10-£12 Last dinner 7.30pm
Credit Cards [1][3] £

★ **66%** **North Cliff**
North Walk EX35 6HJ ☎(0598) 52357
Closed Dec-Jan
With glorious views over the bay, this small family-run hotel offers cheerful public rooms and bright bedrooms. For many years the Irlams have been offering warm hospitality and continue to make small improvements for guests' comfort.
15rm(11⇌2♠)(2fb) CTV in 13 bedrooms ® sB&B£34-£35 sB&B⇌♠£36.50-£37.50 dB&B£68-£70 dB&B⇌♠£73-£75 (incl dinner) 🍴
CTV 15P 🚗 table tennis pool table
❋ ✌ Dinner £10 Last dinner 6pm

★ **60%** **Fairholme**
North Walk EX35 6ED ☎(0598) 52263
Closed Oct-Apr
Superb views over Lynmouth and friendly service from resident proprietors feature among the attractions of a hotel offering neat, well tended bedrooms, a comfortable lounge and dining room and a separate tea shop.
12rm(7⇌)(2fb) CTV in all bedrooms ✖ ✱ dB&B⇌£42
CTV 12P 🚗 ❋ 🖼 (heated) sauna nc10yrs
❋ ✌

LYTHAM ST ANNES Lancashire Map **07** SD32

★★★★ **54%** **Clifton Arms**
West Beach, Lytham FY8 5QJ (on the A584 along the seafront) (Whitbread) ☎(0253) 739898 FAX (0253) 730657
This friendly, traditional hotel overlooks Lytham's seafront. It offers bedrooms in contemporary style, equipped with modern amenities but varying in comfort. The best are spacious front facing rooms

enjoying views of the Ribble estuary. Gradually improving public areas include a small foyer lounge and cocktail bar.
41⇌♠1🛏✌in 4 bedrooms CTV in all bedrooms ®✌T ✱ sB&B⇌♠fr£75.50 dB&B⇌♠fr£87 🍴
Lift ℂ 50P sauna solarium *xmas*
♚ English & French V ❋ ✌ ✱ Lunch £8.70-£17.70 Dinner £13.15-£23.40alc Last dinner 9.45pm
CONF. Thtr 230 Class 160 Board 100 Del from £95
Credit Cards [1][2][3][5]

★★★ **66%** **Chadwick**
South Promenade FY8 1NP ☎(0253) 720061 FAX (0253) 714455
On a corner site overlooking the seafront, this long-established hotel provides friendly attentive service from smartly dressed staff. Bedrooms are generally spacious, well maintained and equipped with modern amenities. There is a large restaurant and ample lounges with modern picture windows facing the sea.
72⇌♠(24fb)3🛏 CTV in all bedrooms ®✌T
✖ (ex guide dogs) sB&B⇌♠£32-£36 dB&B⇌♠£44-£48 🍴
Lift ℂ 40P 🖼 (heated) sauna solarium turkish bath jacuzzi games room 🎵 🛝 *xmas*
♚ English & French V ❋ ✌ ✱ Lunch £6.50-£7 Dinner £13.50-£14.50 Last dinner 8.30pm
CONF. Thtr 70 Class 24 Board 28 Del from £47.50
Credit Cards [1][2][3][5]

★★★ **64%** **Bedford**
307-311 Clifton Dr South FY8 1HN
☎(0253) 724636 FAX (0253) 729244

Situated close to the shopping centre and the Promenade, this small family-run hotel has been steadily improving over the years. Bedrooms, though generally compact, are attractively decorated and equipped with modern amenities, while public rooms include a comfortable lounge bar, restaurant and coffee shop.
36⇌♠(6fb)1🛏 CTV in all bedrooms ®✌T ✱ sB&B⇌♠£32-£45 dB&B⇌♠£59-£72 🍴
Lift ℂ CTV 20P sauna solarium gymnasium jacuzzi steam room *xmas*
♚ English & Continental V ❋ ✌ Lunch £7.50 High tea £5-£7alc Dinner £13&alc Last dinner 8.30pm
CONF. Thtr 150 Class 100 Board 56 Del from £45
Credit Cards [1][2][3][5]

★★ **66%** **New Glendower**
North Promenade FY8 2NQ ☎(0253) 723241
FAX (0253) 723241

This large Victorian hotel overlooks the seafront, close to the pier and near to the shopping centre. The accommodation is suitable both for families and business people; bedrooms vary from compact rear rooms to spacious rooms on the front, but all are equipped with modern facilities. The attractive restaurant overlooks the sea.
60⇌♠(17fb) CTV in all bedrooms ®✌T ✱ sB&B⇌♠£36-£45 dB&B⇌♠£72-£89 🍴
ℂ CTV 45P 🖼 (heated) sauna solarium badminton pool table 🎵 *xmas*
V ❋ ✱ Bar Lunch £2-£4.50 High tea £3.95-£3.95 Dinner £14.25 Last dinner 8pm
CONF. Thtr 150 Class 120 Board 40 Del from £58
Credit Cards [1][2][3][5]

★★ **66%** **St Ives**
7-9 South Promenade FY8 1LS ☎(0253) 720011 FAX (0253) 724447
Closed 24-26 Dec
This friendly hotel is situated on the seafront close to the pier, with several bedrooms overlooking the sea, some with their own balconies. The rooms vary in size and shape, and those recently upgraded are bright and modern. Public areas include a spacious dining room, foyer lounge, bar and ballroom.

Lytham St Annes - Macduff

70rm(60⇌3♠)(44fb) CTV in all bedrooms ® T sB&B£17.50 sB&B⇌♠£37 dB&B£50 dB&B⇌♠£71 (incl dinner) ⊟
⦅ ⊞ CTV 100P ⊠ (heated) snooker sauna solarium ♪ ⚭ xmas
♀ English & French V ❀ 𝒥 Dinner £11.50 Last dinner 8.30pm
CONF. Thtr 100 Class 100 Board 50 Del from £35
Credit Cards ①③

★★**58%** *Admirals*
320-326 Clifton Dr North FY8 2PB ☎(0253) 728657 FAX (0253) 729517
Situated close to the town centre and to the sea, this adequately furnished, family-run hotel offers good value for money, and friendly, helpful service from the staff.
40rm(22⇌14♠)(8fb)1⌸ CTV in all bedrooms ® T CTV 24P ♪
❀ 𝒥
Credit Cards ①③

★**69%** Lindum
63-67 South Promenade FY8 1LZ (opposite the putting green) ☎(0253) 721534 & 722516 FAX (0253) 721364
This popular owner-run hotel on the seafront provides cheerful service. Well equipped modern bedrooms vary in size and extensive public areas include comfortable lounges and a spacious semi-basement restaurant.
80⇌♠(25fb) CTV in all bedrooms ®⚹ T sB&B⇌♠£27-£30 dB&B⇌♠£45-£50 ⊟
Lift ⦅ CTV 20P sauna solarium jacuzzi xmas
V ❀ 𝒥 Sunday Lunch £8 High tea £6 Dinner £10.50 Last dinner 7pm
CONF. Thtr 80 Class 20 Board 30 Del from £35
Credit Cards ①②③ £

★**64%** Ennes Court
107 South Prom FY8 1NP ☎(0253) 723731
This family-run hotel is situated on the seafront close to various leisure amenities and the pier. The bedrooms, are simply decorated and furnished, and several have sea views. There is a choice of lounges, a lounge bar and a recently enlarged dining room.
10⇌♠(2fb) CTV in all bedrooms ® ⚹ (ex guide dogs) CTV 9P 🚲 nc3yrs

MACCLESFIELD Cheshire Map 07 SJ97
See also **Pott Shrigley**
★★★**61%** *Lukic-Belgrade*
Jackson Ln, Kerridge, Bollington SK10 5BG
☎Bollington(0625) 573246 FAX (0625) 574791
Set in extensive grounds, this carefully extended Victorian Gothic building has a rear wing of modern bedrooms with good facilities. Comfortable public areas retain many fine original features and are adorned with many pictures and ornaments that reveal the owner's Eastern European origins.
54⇌♠(2fb) CTV in all bedrooms ® T ⚹ (ex guide dogs) sB&B⇌♠£47.50-£58 dB&B⇌♠£66-£72 ⊟
⦅ CTV 200P ❋ xmas
♀ English & French V ❀ 𝒥 ⚹ Lunch £9.75 Dinner fr£13.95&alc Last dinner 10pm
CONF. Thtr 80 Class 50 Board 50 Del £75
Credit Cards ①②③⑤ £

★★**66%** Park Villa
Park Ln SK11 8AE ☎(0625) 511428 & 614173 FAX (0625) 614637
This large, impeccably maintained house with a pleasant rear garden was built in 1880 and is close to the town centre. The bedrooms have modern furnishings and equipment, and in addition to the spacious lounge, there is a cosy bar and an attractive dining room with period furniture. Friendly, attentive service is provided by the owners.
7⇌♠(2fb)⚹in 2 bedrooms CTV in all bedrooms ® T sB&B⇌♠£35-£47.50 dB&B⇌♠£51-£67 ⊟

Lift ⦅ CTV 14P 🚲 bridge courses xmas
V ❀ 𝒥 ⚹ Lunch fr£6.50 High tea £4.50-£6 Dinner £8.50-£11 Last dinner 8.45pm
Credit Cards ①②③⑤ £

★**65%** Crofton
22 Crompton Rd SK11 8DS (A537 from Knutsford, taking 2nd right after Regency Hill roundabout) ☎(0625) 434113 FAX (0625) 613539
This small hotel – close to the town centre and popular with business guests – is privately owned and personally run in a friendly and informal style. Bedrooms vary in size, but all are furnished and equipped to modern standards.
8⇌♠(2fb) CTV in all bedrooms ® ⚹ sB⇌♠£31.95-£36.95 dB⇌♠£42.95-£47.95 (room only)
9P 🚲
V Dinner £7.95-£10.95&alc Last dinner 8.45pm
Credit Cards ①②③⑤ £

★**60%** Moorhayes House
27 Manchester Rd, Tytherington SK10 2JJ ☎(0625) 433228
9rm(5♠) CTV in all bedrooms ® ❋ sB&B£23-£26 sB&B♠£32 dB&B£36 dB&B♠£39.95
14P 🚲
❋ Dinner £9.50 Last dinner 7pm

MACDUFF Grampian *Banffshire* Map 15 NJ76
★★**60%** The Highland Haven
Shore St AB44 1UB ☎(0261) 32408 FAX (0261) 33652

Situated on the harbour front, this family run hotel has a pleasant restaurant and bar on the first floor and adequately equipped bedrooms. The lounge at the rear of the building has no windows. ➡

M

The Chadwick Hotel
★★★
South Promenade, Lytham St Annes FY8 1NP
Telephone: (0253) 720061

Modern family run hotel and leisure complex. Renowned for good food, personal service, comfortable en suite bedrooms and spacious lounges. The Health complex is designed on a Grecian theme with indoor swimming pool, sauna, Turkish bath and solarium. Daily dinner, room and breakfast terms from £33.50 per person.

409

Macduff - Maidstone

20⇌🅟(2fb) CTV in all bedrooms ®🅟 T ✱ sB&B⇌🅟£26.95-£34.95 dB&B⇌🅟£48-£56 🅿
CTV 6P snooker sauna solarium gymnasium turkish steamroom whirlpool spa *xmas*
V ⌂ 🅛 ✻ Lunch £6-£12 High tea £7-£13 Dinner £15.95&alc Last dinner 9pm
CONF. Thtr 40 Class 40 Del from £52
Credit Cards [1][3][4]

MACHYNLLETH Powys Map 06 SH70

See also **Eglwysfach**

★★ 64% **Wynnstay Arms**
Maengwyn St SY20 8AE (at junct of A487/A470) ☎(0654) 702941 FAX (0654) 703884

The Wynnstay, near the famous town clock, is very much the centre of activities in this old mid-Wales market town. Bathrooms are gradually being refurbished to excellent standards with marble floors and Italian tiling. There is a choice of lounges, and the restaurant has fixed price and à la carte menus and a carvery. A good range of bar meals is also available.
20⇌🅟(3fb) in 7 bedrooms CTV in all bedrooms ® T sB&B⇌🅟£37.50-£42.50 dB&B⇌🅟£52.50-£57.50 🅿
CTV 30P *xmas*
⌂ International V ⌂ 🅛 ✱ Sunday Lunch £6.50-£9.50 Dinner fr£12.50&alc Last dinner 9pm
CONF. Thtr 40 Class 20 Board 16 Del from £50
Credit Cards [1][2][3][5]

MADELEY Staffordshire Map 07 SJ74

★★ 65% **Crewe Arms**
Wharf St, Madeley Heath CW3 9LP (Off A525, near junct with A531) ☎Stoke-on-Trent(0782) 750392
The Crewe Arms is a pleasant, family-run hotel. There are 2 busy bars, an attractive restaurant and a small breakfast room. Bedrooms are large and comfortable and there is a relaxing residents' lounge.
10⇌(2fb) CTV in all bedrooms ® T ✱ (ex guide dogs)
CTV 50P pool table
V ⌂ 🅛
Credit Cards [1][3]

MAIDENCOMBE

See **Torquay**

MAIDENHEAD Berkshire Map 04 SU88

★★★★ ❀❀❀73% **Fredrick's**
Shoppenhangers Rd SL6 2PZ ☎(0628) 35934 FAX (0628) 771054
Closed 24-30 Dec

Fredrick's is a fine hotel with manicured grounds hidden in the leafy residential outskirts of the town. A turn of the century red brick house, its discreet exterior gives no hint of the splendours within: the reception lobby has bold, shining chandeliers, mirrors and a waterfall. There is a winter garden overlooking the terrace, a stylish cocktail bar and a comfortable, well run restaurant offering good traditional cuisine. The bedrooms are spacious and comfortable, many with garden views. Standards of service are very high, a happy blend of formality and willing hospitality.
37⇌🅟 CTV in all bedrooms 🅟 T ✱ ✱ sB&B⇌🅟£120-£130 dB&B⇌🅟£155-£165
⦅ 90P 🚲 ✱ croquet
⌂ English & French V ⌂ ✱ Lunch £19.50&alc Dinner £28.50&alc Last dinner 9.45pm
CONF. Thtr 120 Class 80 Board 60 Del from £190
Credit Cards [1][2][3][5]

★★★★ 57% **Holiday Inn Maidenhead/Windsor**
Manor Ln SL6 2RA (once in Shoppenhanger Road go straight across two mini-roundabouts, hotel on right behind Esso Garage) ☎(0628) 23444 FAX (0628) 770035

On the outskirts of the town, this modern hotel is popular with business people during the week. Most of the bedrooms are compact, but have all the expected facilities, including 24-hour room service. There is a pleasant restaurant on two levels.
189⇌🅟(20fb)⚥in 40 bedrooms CTV in all bedrooms ®🅟 T ✱ (ex guide dogs) sB⇌🅟fr£105 dB⇌🅟fr£125 (room only) 🅿
Lift ⦅ CTV 400P 🅟 (heated) squash snooker sauna solarium gymnasium
⌂ International V ⌂ 🅛 ✱ ✱ Lunch £12.65-£15.65&alc Dinner £14.20-£17.20&alc Last dinner 10.30pm
CONF. Thtr 400 Class 200 Board 120 Del £138
Credit Cards [1][2][3][5]

★★★ 63% **Thames Riviera**
At the Bridge SL6 8DW ☎(0628) 74057 FAX (0628) 776586
Closed 26-30 Dec RS 25 Dec

This substantial Victorian hotel is near the bridge where the A4 crosses the Thames to the east of the town. Bedrooms are in the main building or the attractive Waterside Lodge across the car park. Rooms are well equipped but do vary in size. Special features and services include 24-hour room service and a small daytime coffee shop in addition to the split-level restaurant.
34⇌🅟Annexe18⇌🅟(1fb)1🅐 CTV in all bedrooms ® T ⦅ 50P 10🚲 ✱ ♪ ♫
⌂ English & French V ⌂ 🅛 Last dinner 9.45pm
Credit Cards [1][2][3][4][5]

MAIDSTONE Kent Map 05 TQ75

★★★★ 61% **Tudor Park Hotel, Golf & Country Club**
Ashford Rd, Bearstead ME14 4NQ (2m E, heading towards Ashford) ☎(0622) 734334 FAX (0622) 735360

Built in the late 1980s the hotel is a low-rise building in its own grounds. All the bedrooms are fitted to the same standard, each being spacious and practical for the business person. There is a piano bar and an adjoining cocktail bar for pre-dinner drinks. The Garden Restaurant is a bit pricey, but less formal dining is available in the Waterside Grill, open from morning till late evening.
119⇌🅟(6fb)⚥in 29 bedrooms CTV in all bedrooms ®🅟 T ✱ sB&B⇌🅟fr£93 dB&B⇌🅟fr£108 🅿
⦅ CTV 260P ✱ 🅟 (heated) ▶ 18 ♪ (hard) squash snooker sauna solarium gymnasium table tennis health & beauty salon ♫ 🏓 *xmas*
⌂ English & Continental V ⌂ 🅛 ✱ ✱ Lunch £12.50&alc High tea £5.10 Dinner £16.50&alc Last dinner 10pm
CONF. Thtr 300 Class 160 Board 50 Del £115
Credit Cards [1][2][3][5]

★★★ 63% **Larkfield Priory**
London Rd ME20 6HJ
☎West Malling(0732) 846858 FAX (0732) 846786
(For full entry see Larkfield)

★★ 64% **Grange Moor**
St Michael's Rd ME16 8BS (off A26) ☎(0622) 677623 FAX (0622) 678246

Grange Moor hotel is run in a friendly, informal manner by the Salt family. Annexe bedrooms across the road in the refurbished house of Grange Park have better décor and furnishings, though they lack telephones. There is a pub-type bar, and a mock-Tudor restaurant with a choice of à la carte or bar snack menus.
47rm(1⇌42🅟)(3fb)3🅐 CTV in all bedrooms ® T ✱ sB&B£20-£46 sB&B⇌🅟£30-£46 dB&B£42-£52 dB&B⇌🅟£42-£52 🅿

✆ 60P
♉ English & French V ✿ ⚲ Lunch £12 Dinner £10-£15alc
Last dinner 10pm
CONF. Thtr 100 Class 50 Board 50
Credit Cards [1] [3]

★★ **55%Boxley House**
Boxley Rd, Boxley ME14 3DZ (3m N between
A249 & A229, follow signs to Boxley hotel
next to church) ☎(0622) 692269 FAX (0622)
683536
A 17th-century house in 20 acres of parkland, with modest,
traditional-style bedrooms. There is a bar lounge to the front of the
house and 2 rooms which interchange between restaurant and
function room. There is also a small lounge and a simple breakfast
room which has attractive views of the grounds.
11⇨♠Annexe7⇨♠(2fb)2🛏✂in 2 bedrooms CTV in all
bedrooms ® T ✱ sB&B⇨♠£35-£41 dB&B⇨♠£55-£68 (room only)
CTV 150P ✿ ⚲ (heated)
♉ English & French V ✿ ⚲ ✂ ✱ Lunch £12.50-£16.95 Dinner
£16.95-£19.95 Last dinner 9.15pm
CONF. Thtr 120 Class 36 Board 34 Del from £68.90
Credit Cards [1] [2] [3] [5]

MALDONEssex Map **05** TL80
★★ **64%The Blue Boar**
Silver St CM9 7QE (just off the High Street)
☎(0621) 852681 FAX (0621) 856202

FORTE
Heritage

This 14th-century coaching inn has an appealing black and white
façade. Three cosy bars with beams, oak panelled walls and log fires
greet guests. Most bedrooms have been attractively refurbished with
mahogany furniture and attractive coordinating fabrics. A few
rooms are reached from the courtyard. Staff are friendly and young.
21⇨♠Annexe8⇨♠(1fb)✂in 12 bedrooms CTV in all
bedrooms ® T ✱ sB&B⇨♠fr£70 dB&B⇨♠fr£80 (room only) 🍽
✆ 43P *xmas*
V ✿ ⚲ ✂ ✱ Sunday Lunch fr£10.95 Dinner fr£15.95 Last
dinner 9.30pm
Credit Cards [1] [2] [3] [5]

MALLAIGHighland *Inverness-shire* Map **13** NM69
★★ **61%Marine**
PH41 4PY (adjoining railway station) ☎(0687) 2217 FAX (0687)
2821
Closed Xmas & New Year RS mid Nov-Mar
This family-run commercial and tourist hotel offers comfortable
accommodation with modern appointments, rooms in the rear wing
tending to be more compact; the well stocked refurbished bar on the
first floor has a small but comfortable lounge area at the top end, and
fresh seafood features daily on the dinner menu.
21rm(16⇨♠)(2fb) CTV in all bedrooms ® sB&Bfr£22
sB&B⇨♠fr£30 dB&Bfr£40 dB&B⇨♠fr£50 🍽
CTV 6P
V ✿ ⚲ ✂ Bar Lunch fr£7.95alc Dinner fr£15.75alc Last
dinner 9pm
Credit Cards [1] [3]

★★ **58%West Highland**
PH41 4QZ ☎(0687) 2210 FAX (0687) 2130
Closed 15 Nov-15 Mar
This family-run Highland hotel is perched on a hillside above the
town enjoying fine views over the Inner Minch to Skye and the small
isles. Bedrooms vary in size and are practically furnished, and
public rooms offer traditional comforts.
34⇨♠(6fb) CTV in all bedrooms ® sB&B⇨♠£25-£33
dB&B⇨♠£50-£66 🍽
40P ✿ ♪
V ✿ ⚲ ✱ Lunch £6-£9alc Dinner £17 Last dinner 8.30pm
Credit Cards [1] [3] [4]

MALLWYDGwynedd Map **06** SH81
★ **61%Brigand's Inn**
SY20 9HJ (on A470/A458 junct)
☎Dinas Mawddwy(0650) 531208
Closed Feb
This 15th-century former coaching inn is popular for its private
fishing and shooting rights. It has neat modest bedrooms and cosy
beamed public areas where bar and restaurant meals are available.
14rm(4⇨1♠)(2fb) ® ✱ sB&Bfr£21 sB&B⇨♠fr£24
dB&Bfr£40 dB&B⇨♠fr£46 🍽
CTV 40P ♪ *xmas*
V ✿ ⚲ ✂ ✱ Lunch £4.50-£4.95 Dinner £13.50-£15 Last dinner
9.15pm
Credit Cards [1] [3]

MALMESBURYWiltshire Map **03** ST98
★★★ **74%Whatley Manor**
Easton Grey SN16 0RB (3m W on B4040) ☎(0666) 822888 FAX
(0666) 826120
This attractive stone-built manor house, set in acres of grounds and
gardens, has generally spacious bedrooms, either in the main house
or the adjacent Tudor and Terrace wings. There is a range of elegant
lounges, one with a small bar, the most impressive being the oak
panelled drawing room with an open fire. An interesting table
d'hôte menu is offered in the dining room.
18⇨Annexe11⇨(3fb)🛏 CTV in all bedrooms ® T ✱
sB&B⇨£85-£96 dB&B⇨£112-£136 🍽
✆ 60P ✪ ✿ ⚲ (heated) ♟ (hard) ♪ sauna solarium croquet
table tennis jacuzzi *xmas*
♉ English & Continental V ✿ ⚲ ✱ Lunch fr£14.50 High tea
fr£7.50 Dinner fr£28 Last dinner 9pm
Credit Cards [1] [2] [3] [5]

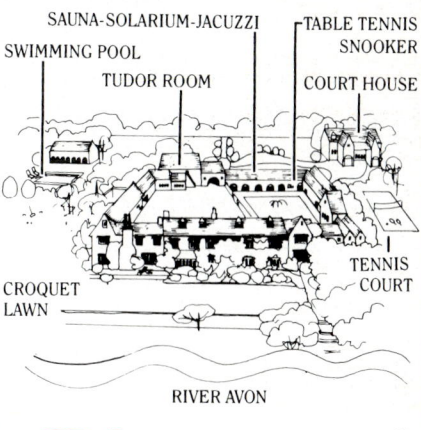

Malmesbury - Malvern

★★★ 63% Old Bell
Abbey Row SN16 0BW (on A429) (Clipper) ☎(0666) 822344 FAX (0666) 825145

Beside the abbey of this attractive town on the edge of the Cotswolds, this hotel, said to be England's oldest, offers individually decorated bedrooms (some housed in a former stable block). One of the comfortable rooms features an impressive 700-year-old fireplace, and a spacious restaurant offers both a carte and a set price menu.

37⇌🛏 Annexe1⇌1🛏 CTV in all bedrooms ® T ✈ (ex guide dogs) sB&B⇌🛏fr£72.50 dB&B⇌🛏£98-£108 🍽
(30P ✽ xmas
♀ English & French V ♀ ♀ Lunch fr£12&alc Dinner fr£20&alc Last dinner 9.30pm
CONF. Thtr 24 Class 14 Board 16 Del from £95
Credit Cards ①③

★★ 66% Mayfield House
SN16 9EW (on A429) ☎(0666) 577409 & 577198 FAX (0666) 577977

Proprietors Max Strelling and Chris Marston put guests at ease with a relaxed and friendly atmosphere. Bedrooms, including ground floor rooms, vary in size and shape, and are comfortably though simply furnished. Pettifers Bar offers a range of bar meals while the intimate restaurant provides a well balanced 'table d'hôte' menu.

20⇌🛏(1fb) CTV in all bedrooms ® T sB&B⇌🛏£35-£40 dB&B⇌🛏£58 🍽
CTV 50P ✽ xmas
♀ English & French V ♀ ♀ ✱ Sunday Lunch £9.95 Dinner £13.95-£16&alc Last dinner 9.30pm
CONF. Thtr 40 Class 30 Board 25 Del from £69
Credit Cards ①②③ £

MALTON North Yorkshire Map 08 SE77

★★★ ❀ 🛎 70% Burythorpe House
Burythorpe YO17 9LB (4m S) ☎Burythorpe(065385) 200 FAX (065385) 204
Closed 25-26 Dec

Race horses are trained in the grounds of this delightful Georgian country house where accommodation comprises spacious and individually styled bedrooms, an elegant drawing room with a small bar, and a beautiful oak-panelled dining room. Cooking by owner Sheila Austin, assisted by her husband, is very accomplished and a wide variety of dishes is offered from the à la carte menu.

10⇌🛏(2fb)2🛏 CTV in all bedrooms ® T ✈ (ex guide dogs) sB&B⇌🛏£40-£50 dB&B⇌🛏£60-£110 🍽
50P ✽ ✱ ▫ (heated) ♀ (hard) snooker sauna solarium gymnasium
♀ International V ♀ Lunch £10.75 Dinner £15.50&alc Last dinner 9.30pm
Credit Cards ①③

★★ 59% Talbot
Yorkersgate YO13 0PB (Logis) ☎(0653) 694031 FAX (0653) 693355

Dating from the 18th century, this hotel retains much of its original atmosphere with antique furnishings, log fires, deep armchairs and settees. The dining room has fine views over the Derwent Valley. Some of the bedrooms have been upgraded in recent years, and it is advisable to ask specifically for one of these.

29⇌🛏(3fb)1🛏 CTV in all bedrooms ® T
(30P 6🚗 (£3 per night) ✽
V ♀ ♀ Last dinner 9pm
Credit Cards ①②③④⑤

★ 62% Wentworth Arms
Town St, Old Malton YO17 0HD (on A169, close to its junct with A64) ☎(0653) 692618
Closed 25 Dec

An 18th-century coaching inn, the Wentworth Arms is a friendly hotel with traditional bars, comfortable bedrooms, and hearty, value-for-money meals served in the attractive stone walled dining room.

5rm(4🛏) CTV in all bedrooms ® ✈ sB&B£21-£22 sB&B🛏£21-£22 dB&B£42-£44 dB&B🛏£42-£44
30P ✽ nc6yrs
♀ ♀ Lunch £3.25-£9.50alc
Credit Cards ①③

MALVERN Hereford & Worcester Map 03 SO74

★★★ ❀ 🛎 67% Cottage in the Wood
Holywell Rd, Malvern Wells WR14 4LG (3m S A449) ☎(0684) 573487 FAX (0684) 560692

Set in 7 acres of wooded grounds and commanding stunning views across the Severn valley, this delightful, personally run hotel is made up of a Georgian dower house with a nearby cottage and coach house containing attractive bedrooms with modern facilities. The elegant dining room offers a 'carte' of interesting, freshly prepared dishes. An enjoyable inspection meal began with celery, apple and walnut croquettes with apple and mint sauce, followed by turkey with avocado and peppercorns.

8⇌🛏 Annexe12⇌🛏2🛏 CTV in all bedrooms ® T ✱ sB&B⇌🛏£58-£74 dB&B⇌🛏£95-£130 🍽
50P ✽ ✱ xmas
V ♀ ♀ Lunch £12.95-£23.25&alc Dinner £21-£25alc Last dinner 9pm
Credit Cards ①②③ £

★★★ 64% Colwall Park
Colwall WR13 6QG (3m SW B4218) ☎(0684) 40206 FAX (0684) 40847

Situated in the centre of the village, this hospitable hotel is set in pleasant gardens. Bedrooms are well equipped, with dark wood or pine furnishings, and there is a cosy lounge bar, traditional lounge and panelled restaurant.

20⇌🛏(fb) CTV in all bedrooms ® T sB&B£47.50-£57.50 sB&B🛏£53.50-£63.50 dB&B⇌🛏£76.50-£86.50 🍽
50P ✽ croquet xmas
V ♀ ♀ Lunch £3.50-£15 Dinner £17.50-£19.50 Last dinner 9pm
CONF. Thtr 100 Class 40 Board 40 Del from £82.50
Credit Cards ①②③

★★★ 63% Abbey
Abbey Rd WR14 3ET ☎(0684) 892332 FAX (0684) 892662

This traditional hotel is in a splendid situation adjoining the fine Benedictine priory. Rooms are modern, with light wood furnishings and every convenience. Table d'hôte and à la carte menus are served in the attractive restaurant, which has large windows overlooking the priory.

105⇌🛏(4fb)1🛏 CTV in all bedrooms ® T
Lift (120P ✽
V ♀ ♀ Last dinner 8.30pm
Credit Cards ①②③⑤

★★★ 58% Foley Arms
Worcester Rd WR14 4QS (M5 exit 7 north or 8 south, M50 exit 11, proceed to Great Malvern on A449) ☎(0684) 573397 FAX (0684) 569665

Built in 1810, the Foley Arms is Malvern's oldest hotel and enjoys a central, elevated position with some superb views across the Severn Valley. Accommodation standards vary in terms of size and décor, some rooms are rather dated, as are the bathrooms, but a refurbishment programme is planned. Public areas include an intimate restaurant, a popular bar and several comfortable lounge areas including one for non smokers.

Malvern

26⇨♠Annexe2⇨♠(2fb)2☐½in 1 bedroom CTV in all bedrooms® ✓ T sB&B⇨♠£55-£62 dB&B⇨♠£78-£88 ♫
(45P 4☂ ❋ ♪ xmas
☐ English & French V ♡ ♑ ½ ✱ Sunday Lunch £8.95-£10.25 Dinner £15.50-£17&alc Last dinner 9.30pm
CONF. Thtr 125 Class 60 Board 45 Del from £72
Credit Cards [1][2][3][5] ⓔ

★★ ❀✿ 73% **Holdfast Cottage**
Little Malvern WR13 6NA (4m SE) (Logis)
☎Hanley Swan(0684) 310288

Set in 2 acres of grounds, this charming family-run hotel just outside Malvern has pretty bedrooms with a range of modern facilities and small but comfortable public areas which include a small bar, traditional lounge and a dining room overlooking the gardens.
8⇨♠(1fb)½in all bedrooms CTV in all bedrooms ® T ✱ sB&B⇨♠£35-£44 dB&B⇨♠£66-£72 ♫
15P ⊞ ❋ croquet xmas
♡ ♑ ½ ✱ Lunch £14-£17.50 Dinner £16-£17.50 Last dinner 9pm
Credit Cards [1][3]

★★ 64% **Broomhill**
West Malvern Rd, West Malvern WR14 4AY (2m W B4232)
☎(0684) 564367
9rm(2⇨3♠) CTV in all bedrooms ® ✱ sB&B⇨♠£20-£22.95 dB&B⇨♠£40-£45.90 ♫
CTV 9P ⊞ xmas
V ♡ ½ ✱ Bar Lunch £2.50-£5 Dinner £10-£12.50 Last dinner 8.15pm
Credit Cards [1][3] ⓔ

For key to symbols see the Bookmark.

The TALBOT
HOTEL and RESTAURANT

AA ★★   Yorkersgate, Malton
North Yorkshire YO17 0AA
Telephone: 0653 694031 Fax: 0653 693355

Situated at the heart of the bustling market town of Malton, in private gardens with ample free car parking. This vine covered Georgian coaching inn has been fully transformed to cater for your comforts. Traditional lounges with welcoming log fires, and an excellent restaurant serving appetising Yorkshire fare. 27 charming, individual en suite bedrooms, including suites. Meeting facilities for up to 50 delegates. Ideal and tranquil location for visiting York, the Yorkshire Moors and Castle Howard.

An English Rose Hotel.

Holywell Road, Malvern Wells, Worcs.
Tel: (0684) 573487 Fax: (0684) 560662

THE COTTAGE IN THE WOOD
★★★ ❀

A delightful country house hotel and restaurant set high on the Malvern Hills with 30 mile views, giving 'The best view in England' - Daily Mail. Our seven acres open directly onto the Hills.

Fabulous walks. Fine touring base.

Proprietor owned and run.

Bargain break rates all year from £48pp/pn.

Open daily for lunch and dinner.

Mayfield House
HOTEL & RESTAURANT

CRUDWELL, MALMESBURY, WILTSHIRE SN16 9EW

Delightful Country House Hotel set in 1½ acres of walled gardens. Elegant restaurant serving freshly prepared food. The hotel is ideally situated for touring the Cotswolds and Bath, and has easy access from the M4 (Junction 17).

Telephone: (0666) 577409

AA ★★   ASHLEY COURTENAY   E.T.B. ⚌⚌⚌

Malvern - Man, Isle of, Douglas

★★ 64%Great Malvern
Graham Rd WR14 2HN ☎(0684) 563411 FAX (0684) 560514
Closed 25 Dec

This 18th-century hotel in the town centre, formerly the Royal, offers generally spacious and comfortable bedrooms with a mix of furnishings. Meals are available in the popular bar and the new owners plan to extend the restaurant opening hours (at present breakfast only).
14rm(13⇌🛁) CTV in all bedrooms ® T ✖ (ex guide dogs)
sB&Bfr£32 sB&B⇌🛁£42-£50 dB&Bfr£42 dB&B⇌🛁£52-£66 ⊟
Lift 9P
V ⊘ ⍑ Sunday Lunch £10.50 Dinner £5.75-£19alc Last dinner 9pm
CONF. Thtr 60 Class 20 Board 30 Del from £35
Credit Cards 1 3 5 £

★★ 63%Essington
Holywell Rd, Malvern Wells WR14 4LQ (3m S A449)
☎(0684) 561177
This secluded hotel has been under the same ownership for over 20 years. Dating from 1817, it is set in 2 acres of landscaped gardens and mature trees. A 5-course fixed price dinner menu is on offer in the attractive restaurant, which also has a lounge area, and there is a cosy bar complete with cheery log fire.
9⇌🛁(1fb)1⌺ CTV in all bedrooms ®
30P 🚗 ✿
⍑ ⍊ Last dinner 8.15pm
Credit Cards 1 3

★★ 62%Mount Pleasant
Belle Vue Ter WR14 4PZ (on A445, 0.5m from Great Malvern station) ☎(0684) 561837 FAX (0684) 569968
Closed 25 & 26 Dec
This privately owned hotel near the town's priory church dates from 1830 and retains attractive original features. Bedrooms are mostly spacious and traditionally furnished, and there is a popular restaurant offering daytime refreshments and an extensive evening menu.
15rm(11⇌3🛁) CTV in all bedrooms ® T ✖ (ex guide dogs)
20P ✿
⚥ English & Spanish V ⊘ ⍑ ⍊ Lunch £7.50-£12.50 Dinner £14.95-£16.95&alc Last dinner 9.30pm
CONF. Thtr 80 Class 40 Board 45 Del from £55
Credit Cards 1 2 3 5 £

★★ 60%Cotford
51 Graham Rd WR14 2HU ☎(0684) 572427
Closed 25 Dec-11 Jan
Originally built for the Bishop of Worcester in 1851, this welcoming small hotel is set back from the road in pleasant grounds a short walk from the town centre. Bedrooms vary in style and standard and there is a comfortable traditional lounge, small bar and dining room.
16⇌🛁(4fb) CTV in all bedrooms ® T sB&B⇌🛁fr£33 dB&B⇌🛁fr£58 ⊟
15P 🚗 ✿
V ⍊ ✱ Dinner fr£15 Last dinner 8pm
Credit Cards 1 3

★★ 58%Montrose
23 Graham Rd WR14 2HU ☎(0684) 572335
Closed 1 wk Xmas RS 12 Dec-2 Feb
This friendly family-run hotel in a Grade II listed building is set in mature gardens within easy walking distance of the town centre, and provides simple, comfortable bedrooms with bright, fresh décor, a spacious lounge and cosy bar. Restaurant dinner service is not usually available in the winter months.
14rm(5⇌6🛁)(3fb) CTV in all bedrooms ®
CTV 18P ✿
V ⍑ Last dinner 7pm
Credit Cards 1 2 3

★★ 57%*Malvern Hills*
Wynds Point WR13 6DW (4m S, at junct of A449 with B4232)
☎Colwall(0684) 40237 & 40690 FAX (0684) 40327
This hotel is conveniently situated for touring the area. Bedrooms are pretty and there is a small lounge for residents.
16⇌🛁(1fb)1⌺ CTV in all bedrooms ® T
CTV 35P 🚗 ✿ solarium
⚥ English & French V ⍊ Last dinner 9.45pm
Credit Cards 1 3

★ 63%Bredon House
34 Worcester Rd WR14 4AA (on A449) ☎(0684) 566990
This very friendly small hotel is a listed Regency house. There are pleasant gardens and lawns with picturesque views of the area. Bedrooms are cosy and modern, good food is served and the lounge has an honesty bar.
9⇌🛁(4fb)⍊in 1 bedroom CTV in all bedrooms ® T ✱
sB&B⇌🛁£25-£32 dB&B⇌🛁£36-£45 ⊟
10P 🚗 xmas
V ✱ Dinner £12.95 Last dinner 7.30pm
Credit Cards 1 2 3

MAN, ISLE OF Map 06

CASTLETOWN Map 06 SC26

★★★ 66%*Castletown Golf Links*
Fort Island ☎(0624) 822201 FAX (0624) 824633

Forming part of the challenging Castletown Golf Course, and understandably popular with golfers, this hotel has the sea on 3 sides. Individually decorated bedrooms vary from comfortably furnished suites and executive rooms to more compact standard singles, but all are equipped with modern facilities. L'Orangerie is the à la carte restaurant and there is also a lively bistro in the leisure centre.
58⇌🛁(3fb)1⌺ CTV in all bedrooms ®⍊ T
《 CTV 100P ✿ ▭ (heated) ► 18 snooker sauna solarium croquet ♪
⚥ English & French V ⊘ ⍑ ⍊ Last dinner 10pm
Credit Cards 1 2 3 5

DOUGLAS Map 06 SC37

★★★ 71%Empress
Central Promenade IM2 4RA ☎(0624) 661155 FAX (0624) 673554
Overlooking Douglas Bay, this seafront hotel has been totally refurbished to provide a very good standard of modern accommodation. Mirrored pillars and marble give a light, elegant feel to the spacious foyer lounge, bar and conservatory. The French-style brasserie is open all day until 10.45pm and provides an extensive menu and friendly service. Bedrooms vary in size but all are attractively furnished.
102⇌🛁(20fb) CTV in all bedrooms ® T ✖ (ex guide dogs)
sB⇌🛁£65-£75 dB⇌🛁£70-£80 (room only) ⊟
Lift 《 ▦ ⌨ ▭ (heated) sauna solarium gymnasium steam room jacuzzi beautician ♪ xmas
⚥ International V ⊘ ⍑
CONF. Thtr 180 Class 100 Del from £85
Credit Cards 1 2 3 4

★★★ 65%Sefton
Harris Promenade ☎(0624) 626011 FAX (0624) 676004
Situated next to the Gaiety Theatre and convenient for the centre of town, this Victorian seafront hotel with its distinctive pink and white exterior continues to be improved. Many bedrooms have recently been refurbished with attractive modern fabrics, and the extensive and comfortably furnished public areas offer a variety of places to eat and drink. It has a warm, friendly atmosphere.

80🛏🛁(5fb) CTV in all bedrooms ® 🍽 T 🐕 (ex guide dogs)
sB&B🛏🛁£28-£51 dB&B🛏🛁£56-£69.50 🍳
Lift (52P 🅿 (heated) sauna solarium gymnasium steam rooms
beauty therapy service
V ♿ ⏳ Lunch £5.75-£8 Dinner £9-£14&alc Last dinner 9.30pm
CONF. Thtr 90 Class 40 Board 30
Credit Cards [1][2][3][5]

★★★ 63% **Palace Hotel & Casino**
Central Promenade ☎(0624) 662662 FAX
(0624) 625535

Situated right on the seafront and enjoying fine views over the bay,
this purpose built hotel offers a wide range of facilities including a
casino, nightclub, cinema and an attractive fully equipped leisure
centre. Bedrooms aren't large, but they are practically furnished in
contemporary style and equipped with all modern amenities. Public
areas, which are beginning to show their age, include a choice of
spacious bars and a small à la carte restaurant where formally
dressed staff provide attentive service.
135🛏🛁in 18 bedrooms CTV in all bedrooms ® 🍽 T ✳
sB&B🛏🛁£60-£90 dB&B🛏🛁£90-£120 🍳
Lift (180P 🅿 (heated) snooker sauna solarium gymnasium
beauty therapy cinema casino *xmas*
🍷 European V ♿ ⏳ Sunday Lunch £13-£15 Dinner £18-
£23&alc Last dinner 10pm
CONF. Thtr 320 Class 150 Board 50 Del from £75
Credit Cards [1][2][3][5] £

PORT ERIN Map 06 SC16

★★★ 62% *Cherry Orchard*
Bridson St ☎(0624) 833811 FAX (0624) 833583
Part of a small time-share development, the hotel is in the centre of
town and provides functional acommodation. Bedrooms are
equipped with modern amenities and guests have the use of the
leisure facilities.
31🛏🛁(12fb)1🛏 CTV in all bedrooms ® T 🐕 (ex guide dogs)
Lift (80P 🅿 (heated) sauna solarium gymnasium games room
♿
🍷 English & French V ♿ ⏳ Last dinner 9.30pm
Credit Cards [1][2][3][5]

RAMSEY Map 06 SC49

★★★ 68% *Grand Island*
Bride Rd ☎(0624) 812455 FAX (0624) 815291
Peacefully situated to the north of the town, this distinctive
whitewashed building enjoys delightful sea and mountain views.
Individually styled bedrooms vary in size from comfortable suites to
compact singles, while public areas, furnished with antiques,
provide a choice of restaurants and a small leisure centre. The hotel
is home to the island's croquet association and boasts no less than 5
lawns. Friendly, courteous service is provided by a loyal team of
staff.
54🛏🛁(4fb)1🛏 in 2 bedrooms CTV in all bedrooms ® T
🐕 (ex guide dogs)
Lift (150P 🅿 ✳ 🅿 (heated) ♀ (hard) ⛳ snooker sauna
solarium gymnasium shooting steam room croquet putting
🍷 International V ♿ ⏳ Last dinner 10pm
Credit Cards [1][2][3][5]

MANCHESTER Greater Manchester Map 07 SJ89
See also *Salford*

★★★★ 67% **Holiday Inn Crowne Plaza**
Peter St M60 2DS (close to G-Mex Centre)
☎061-236 3333 FAX 061-228 2241

In the heart of the city this grand Edwardian hotel, where Mr Rolls
and Mr Royce first became partners, has been restored to its former
glory. A lofty, spacious reception foyer with white pillars, hanging

greenery and glass roof adjoins the raised Terrace Lounge, and there
is a choice of bars and restaurants. Bedrooms vary in size, but all
have large beds and smart modern bathrooms, and those
overlooking the vast internal wells are particularly quiet. Services
(including car parking) are provided by friendly, smart staff.
303🛏🛁(63fb)1🛏🍽 in 120 bedrooms CTV in all bedrooms ®
T 🐕 (ex guide dogs) sB🛏🛁£99-£105 dB🛏🛁£111-£116 (room
only) 🍳
Lift (🏢 CTV 🚗 (£4.50) 🅿 (heated) squash sauna solarium
gymnasium jacuzzi *xmas*
🍷 English & French V ♿ ⏳ ✳ Lunch £17.95&alc High tea
£12-£20alc Dinner £14.50-£25alc Last dinner 10.30pm
Credit Cards [1][2][3][5] £

★★★★ ✿67% **Victoria & Albert**
Water St M60 9EA ☎061-832 1188 FAX 061-834 2484
This newly opened luxury hotel is converted from an early Victorian
warehouse on the bank of the River Irwell, oppposite Granada TV
studios. Original oak beams, iron pillars and exposed brickwork
give much character to both the public rooms and bedrooms, all of
which are individually and subtly styled according to famous
Granada programmes. Bedrooms have all the latest facilities, with
room services shown on the TV screen. Off the elegant foyer is the
Café Maigret and the comfortable and spacious Watsons Bar
adjoining the Sherlock Holmes restaurant, offering modern British
cooking.
132🛏🛁(2fb)⏳ in 24 bedrooms CTV in all bedrooms ® 🍽 T
🐕 (ex guide dogs) ✳ sB🛏🛁£115-£145 dB🛏🛁£115-£145
(room only) 🍳
Lift (17P 80🚗 sauna gymnasium sunbed
V ♿ ⏳ ✳ Lunch £9.95-£20 High tea fr£6.95 Dinner £9.95-
£14.50alc Last dinner 10.30pm
Credit Cards [1][2][3][5] £

See advertisement on page 417

*Experience friendly hospitality and
relaxation at the*

Mount Pleasant Hotel

**Great Malvern, Worcs
Telephone: (0684) 561837**

Set in attractive gardens this early Georgian hotel is
close to the town centre with splendid views
overlooking the Priory Church and Severn Valley. It
is ideally situated close to the theatre, shops and the
Winter Gardens with its leisure pool and yet has
direct access to the Malvern Hills through the 99
steps. The Hotel is owned and run by the proprietors
in an efficient and friendly manner for both tourists
and travelling business people with an emphasis on
personal attention, comfort and good food.

**Special Breaks on offer all year
Fully licensed with private car park
Conference and function facilities**

Manchester

★★★★ 63% Ramada
Blackfriars St M3 2EQ ☏061-835 2555 FAX 061-835 3077

Centrally situated, this modern hotel provides spacious bedrooms, decorated in restful pastel shades. The Deansgate Terrace is a lively bar with an all-day menu; the mezzanine floor lounge quieter and more comfortable, but it is necessary to telephone for service. Staff compensate for any lapses in service by their friendly and helpful attitude, and an efficient car parking service is provided.

200⇨♠(150fb)⊁in 75 bedrooms CTV in all bedrooms ®⚡T sB⇨♠£107 dB⇨♠£107 (room only) 🅿
Lift ⟨ 80⛱ ♫ xmas
♨ International V ♡ ♨ ⊁ Last dinner 10.30pm
Credit Cards [1][2][3][4][5] £

★★★★ 60% The Copthorne
Clippers Quay, Salford Quays M5 3DL (close to M602) ☏061-873 7321 FAX 061-873 7318

Copthorne Hotels

This large, modern, purpose-built hotel is at the transformed Salford Quays. Many bedrooms have waterfront views, as does one of the two restaurants which provide a wide range of eating options including a carvery. Lounge capacity is at present rather limited, comprising only a lounge bar and aperitif bar, but this should be increased in the very near future.

166⇨♠ CTV in all bedrooms ®⚡T sB⇨♠£97-£102 dB⇨♠£107-£112 (room only) 🅿
Lift ⟨ 120P ⛭ (heated) ⛱ sauna solarium gymnasium sun beds jacuzzi
♨ English & French V ♡ ♨ ✻ Lunch £11.95-£14.95&alc Dinner £14.95&alc Last dinner 10pm
CONF. Thtr 150 Class 75 Board 70 Del from £75
Credit Cards [1][2][3][5]

★★★★ 50% Portland Thistle
3/5 Portland St, Piccadilly Gdns M1 6DP (in city centre, overlooking Piccadilly Gardens) ☏061-228 3400 FAX 061-228 6347

Centrally situated overlooking Piccadilly Gardens, this is a modern hotel with an attractive Victorian façade which has a small basement leisure centre as well as a choice of bars and eating options. Bedrooms (most of them small) await upgrading.

205⇨♠(6fb)2⊞⊁in 51 bedrooms CTV in all bedrooms ®T
Lift ⟨ ⊞ 25P ⛭ (heated) sauna solarium gymnasium whirlpool
♨ International V ♡ ♨ ⊁ Last dinner 10pm
Credit Cards [1][2][3][5]

★★★ 58% Willow Bank
340-342 Wilmslow Rd, Fallowfield M14 6AF (on B5093) ☏061-224 0461 FAX 061-257 2561

Willow Bank is a converted Victorian house with large modern extension offering functional accommodation and 24-hour room service. Long-serving, mainly Italian staff provide traditional service in a reasonably priced restaurant.

116⇨♠(2fb) CTV in all bedrooms ®T ✠ (ex guide dogs) sB⇨♠£30-£48 dB⇨♠£49.50-£65 (room only) 🅿
⟨ CTV 70P 30⛱ ♫
♨ English & Continental V ♡ ♨ ⊁ ✻ Lunch fr£7&alc High tea fr£5&alc Dinner fr£9.50&alc Last dinner 10.15pm
CONF. Thtr 50 Class 30 Board 25 Del from £45
Credit Cards [1][2][3][5] £

★★★ 57% Novotel
Worsley Brow M28 4YA ☏061-799 3535 FAX 061-703 8207
(For full entry see Worsley)

★★ 67% Crescent Gate
Park Crescent, Victoria Park, Rusholme M14 5RE (off B5091) ☏061-224 0672 FAX 061-257 2822
Closed Xmas

This much extended house is within easy reach of the university and the Royal Infirmary. The bedrooms, most of which are singles, have modern furnishings and a good range of equipment. Family owned and run, it provides informal, friendly and willing service. A good value set price menu offers a short selection of simple but wholesome dishes.

15rm(2⇨5♠)Annexe11⇨♠(1fb) CTV in all bedrooms ®⚡T sB&B£27.50 sB&B⇨♠£35 dB&B⇨♠£48
CTV 18P ⟲
V ♡ ♨ Bar Lunch £2-£8alc Dinner £10 Last dinner 8pm
Credit Cards [1][2][3][5] £

See advertisement on page 419

★★ 62% Mitre
Cathedral Gates M3 1SW (next to Cathedral) ☏061-834 4128 FAX 061-839 1646

This impressive building, next to the cathedral in the oldest part of the city, was built in 1815 and originally named the Old Church Tavern. In addition to the separate public bar on the ground floor, the hotel has a cosy residents'/diners' bar on the first floor. Bedrooms are simple but sound and have fairly modern furnishings and equipment.

28rm(20⇨♠) CTV in all bedrooms ® T ✠ (ex guide dogs) sB⇨♠£41 sB⇨♠£48-£55 dB£49-£56 dB⇨♠£52-£59 (room only) 🅿
⟨ CTV ♪
♨ English & French V ♡ ♨ ⊁ ✻ Lunch £6&alc Dinner £9.95-£10.50&alc Last dinner 9.30pm
CONF. Thtr 90 Class 60 Board 35 Del from £65
Credit Cards [1][2][3][5] £

The Old Mill Hotel ★★★

Springwood Street, Ramsbottom,
Lancashire BL0 9DS
Telephone: 0706 822991
Fax: 0706 822291

Delightful Tudor style building. The Hotel offers two restaurants, French and Italian, serving à la carte and table d'hôte menus. All 36 bedrooms are en suite with self dial telephone, radio, colour television, trouser press, hair dryer, tea/coffee making facilities, fruit and biscuits. The Leisure centre is equipped with pool, whirlpool, sauna, solarium and gym. Conferences are catered for.

   Les Routiers   Ashley Courtenay

Satellite television – look for this symbol 📺 in the directory entries.

★★★★ AA
THE PORTLAND
THISTLE HOTEL

Piccadilly Gardens, Manchester M1 6DP
Tel: 061-228 3400   Fax: 061-228 6347

Your choice in Manchester

For Reservations at over 100
Mount Charlotte Thistle Hotels
Telephone London: 071 937 8033.

THISTLE HOTELS

★★★★ AA
THE PINEWOOD
THISTLE HOTEL

Wilmslow Road, Handforth, Manchester SK9 3LG
Tel: 0625 529211   Fax: 0625 536812

Situated south of the city this hotel is conveniently located for Manchester Airport. There is also nearby access to the motorway network.

Each of the 64 bedrooms is refurbished to the highest standards and there is an excellent restaurant and adjoining bar.

The hotel has various meeting rooms and ample car parking is available for hotel users.

Courtesy transportation to and from the airport is available for hotel residents.

Your choice close to Manchester Airport

For Reservations at over 100
Mount Charlotte Thistle Hotels
Telephone London: 071 937 8033.

THISTLE HOTELS

VOTED THE WORLD'S BEST NEW HOTEL IN 1993.

Executive Travel readers voted the
four-star Victoria & Albert Hotel 'the world's best new hotel, 1993'.
So don't just stay in the best new
hotel in Manchester, stay in the best new hotel anywhere!

VICTORIA & ALBERT HOTEL
★ ★ ★ ★ ❋

Water Street, Manchester M60 9EA   Tel 061 832 1188

Manchester - Marazion

★★ 60% Montana
59 Palatine Rd, Withington M20 9LJ ☎061-445 6427 FAX 061-448 9458
22rm(19⇨↑)(4fb)⌿in 3 bedrooms CTV in 19 bedrooms TV in 3 bedrooms ® ♉ T ✱ sB&Bfr£20 sB&B⇨↑fr£28 dB&Bfr£36 dB&B⇨↑£40-£43 ⊟
CTV 40P
✿ ⌿ ✱ Dinner £5-£8alc
Credit Cards [1][3]

Forte Posthouse
Palatine Rd, Northenden M22 4FH (beside B5167)
☎061-998 7090 FAX 061-946 0139

Suitable for both the business and leisure traveller, this bright hotel provides modern accommodation in well equipped bedrooms with en suite bathrooms. For more details about Forte Posthouse hotels, consult the Contents page, under Hotel Groups.

198⇨↑ ✱ B⇨↑£41.50-£53.50 (room only)
CONF. Thtr 150 Class 80 Board 80 Del £89.50

MANCHESTER AIRPORT Greater Manchester
Map **07** SJ88

★★★★ 64% Manchester Airport Hilton
Outwood Ln, Ringway M22 5WP
☎061-436 4404 FAX 061-436 1521

This large well maintained modern hotel has a busy lively atmosphere and features attractively designed open-plan public areas complete with a small stream. Eating options include the popular Fountains Bar and more intimate Portico Restaurant. Sound-proofed bedrooms are all well equipped, with the Plaza and Executive rooms offering an extra degree of comfort. A small leisure complex and good conference facilities are also available.
222⇨↑ CTV in all bedrooms ® T ✱ sB&B⇨↑fr£107 dB&B⇨↑fr£138 (room only)
Lift (⊞ P 🏊 (heated) sauna
♀ International
CONF. Thtr 200 Class 90 Board 60 Del £145
Credit Cards [1][2][3][4][5]

★★★★ 61% Pinewood Thistle
180 Wilmslow Rd, Handforth, Wilmslow (on A34 3m from junct 10 of M63)
☎(0625) 529211 FAX (0625) 536812

This modern hotel close to the airport was undergoing major refurbishment as this guide went to print. Bedrooms are smart, with quality fitted furniture and fittings and rich fabrics, and many have good work surfaces to suit business guests. The new restaurant and cocktail bar, overlooking the garden, have been beautifully equipped.
58⇨↑ ⌿in 20 bedrooms CTV in all bedrooms ® T ✱ (ex guide dogs) ✱ sB⇨↑£64-£70 dB⇨↑£75-£80 (room only) ⊟
Lift (200P ✱ xmas
♀ International V ✿ ⌫ ⌿ ✱ Lunch £9.50-£11.50&alc Dinner fr£16 Last dinner 10pm
CONF. Thtr 150 Class 80 Board 20 Del from £95
Credit Cards [1][2][3][4][5]

See advertisement under MANCHESTER

★★★ 67% Wilmslow Moat House
Altrincham Rd SK9 4LR (leave M56 at junc 6, take A538 towards Wilmslow, hotel on left after tunnel) ☎Wilmslow(0625) 529201 FAX (0625) 531876

Built in the style of a Swiss chalet, this hotel is in an attractive valley besides the River Bollin, just 5 minutes drive from the Airport. Bedrooms are very well equipped and modern, the largest being in the new wing. There is a comfortable reception lounge-bar adjoining the popular restaurant.

125⇨↑ 2 ⌿in 4 bedrooms CTV in all bedrooms ® T ✱ sB⇨↑£76-£80 dB⇨↑£85-£90 (room only) ⊟
Lift (400P ✱ 🏊 (heated) squash snooker sauna solarium gymnasium jacuzzi steam room beauty therapy
♀ International V ✿ ⌫ ⌿ Lunch £14-£35alc Dinner fr£14.95&alc Last dinner 10.30pm
CONF. Thtr 300 Class 150 Board 100 Del from £97.50
Credit Cards [1][2][3][5] £

Forte Crest
Ringway Rd, Wythenshawe M22 5NS
☎061-437 5811 FAX 061-436 2340

A large modern hotel with a wide range of services and amenities, designed particularly for the business traveller. Bedrooms are smart, comfortable and well equipped. For more details about Forte Crest hotels, consult the Contents page, under Hotel Groups.
290⇨↑
CONF. Thtr 200 Class 100 Board 60 Del £115

Travel Inn
Finney Ln, Heald Green SK8 2QH ☎061-499 1944

Purpose-built accommodation offers spacious and well epuipped bedrooms, all with en suite bathrooms. Meals may be taken at the nearby family restaurant and pub. For more details about Travel Inns, consult the Contents page, under Hotel Groups.
41⇨↑ ✱ B⇨↑£33.50 (room only)

MANORBIER Dyfed Map **02** SS09

★★ 62% Castle Mead
SA70 7TA (follow signs for beach and castle) ☎(0834) 871358
Closed Nov-Etr
5⇨Annexe3⇨(2fb)⌿in 2 bedrooms CTV in all bedrooms ® ✱ sB&B⇨£25-£27.50 dB&B⇨£50-£55 ⊟
20P ⌂ ✱
V ✿ ⌫ ✱ Lunch £8.95 Dinner £10 Last dinner 8.30pm
Credit Cards [1][3]

MANSFIELD Nottinghamshire Map **08** SK56

★★ 64% Pine Lodge
281-283 Nottingham Rd NG18 4SE (off A617) ☎(0623) 22308 FAX (0623) 656819
Pine Lodge is a family-run hotel on the edge of town. The bedrooms have most of the amenities required by the traveller, and there is a small, well maintained garden to the rear.
20rm(19⇨↑)(2fb) CTV in all bedrooms ® ♉ T ✽
sB&Bfr£38.50 sB&B⇨↑£46.50-£59.50 dB&B⇨↑£68-£70 ⊟
40P ⌂ sauna solarium
♀ English & Italian V ✿ ⌫ Dinner £15.95&alc Last dinner 9pm
CONF. Thtr 50 Class 35 Board 30
Credit Cards [1][2][3][5]

MARAZION Cornwall & Isles of Scilly Map **02** SW53

★★ ❀68% Mount Haven
Turnpike Rd TR17 0DQ
☎Penzance(0736) 710249 FAX (0736) 711658

Closed 24-27 Dec RS Nov-Mar
John and Delyth James are the friendly and dedicated owners of this hotel, which is set in its own grounds and has superb views over Mounts Bay and St Michael's Mount. Bedrooms vary in size, shape and style, but most have good views. The split-level restaurant offers table d'hôte and à la carte menus.

Marazion - Market Harborough

17⇨🛏(5fb)1🛁 CTV in all bedrooms ® T sB&B⇨🛏£30-£38 dB&B⇨🛏£50-£64 🍽
30P 🚗
🍴 English & French V ☆ ♨ ⚒ Sunday Lunch fr£8 Dinner fr£14.25&alc Last dinner 9pm
Credit Cards [1][2][3]

See advertisement under **PENZANCE**

MARCH Cambridgeshire Map **05** TL49

★ **67%** *Olde Griffin*
High St PE15 9EJ ☎(0354) 52517 FAX (0354) 50086
Now with a refurbished bar and lounge area, this town centre, 16th-century inn continues to be extended and improved by Dee and David Reeve. Bedrooms all have en suite bathrooms but, unlike the newly created 4-poster bedroom, some are still modest.
20rm(16⇨3🛏)(2fb) CTV in all bedrooms ® T ✈
50P
🍴 English & Continental V ☆ Last dinner 9.30pm
Credit Cards [1][3]

MARCHWIEL Clwyd Map **07** SJ34

★★ **※65%** *Cross Lanes Hotel & Restaurant*
Cross Lanes, Bangor Rd LL13 0TF (3m SE of Wrexham, on A525)
☎Bangor-on-Dee(0978) 780555 FAX (0978) 780568

CONSORT HOTELS

Closed 25 Dec (night) & 26 Dec
This impressive Victorian country house is set in several acres of mature grounds. The hall has old oak panelling and there is a modern lounge, a choice of bars and bedrooms which are mostly compact. Food, offered from fixed price and à la carte menus, is most enjoyable.
18⇨🛏(1fb)1🛁 CTV in all bedrooms ® T sB&B⇨🛏£49.95-£62 dB&B⇨🛏£66-£94 Continental breakfast 🍽
80P ✿ 🏊 (heated) sauna croquet putting
🍴 International V ☆ ♨ ⚒ Lunch £9.95-£12.95&alc Dinner fr£16.95&alc Last dinner 9.30pm
CONF. Thtr 100 Class 60 Board 40 Del from £69
Credit Cards [1][2][3][5]

MARKET DRAYTON Shropshire Map **07** SJ63

★★★ **※⚒70%** *Goldstone Hall*
Goldstone TF9 2NA (4m S, signposted from A529)
☎Cheswardine(063086) 202 & 487 FAX (063086) 585

ExecGroup

Once the seat of Shropshire squires, this creeper-clad, red brick house, dating from the early 17th century, is set in 5 acres of mature grounds. A log fire in the entrance hall greets guests in cold weather, and there are several more in the wide choice of sitting rooms, with their exposed beams and panelled walls. Bedrooms are furnished with appropriate period furniture. Young chef Nigel Huxley, prepares a daily changing 6-course menu.
8⇨🛏1🛁 CTV in all bedrooms ® T ✈ (ex guide dogs) ✱
sB&B⇨🛏£58.65 dB&B⇨🛏£74.50 🍽
60P ✿ 🎱 snooker
V ☆ ♨ Lunch £14.90&alc Dinner £22.40-£28.50alc Last dinner 10.30pm
Credit Cards [1][2][3]

★★ **62%** *Rosehill Manor*
Rosehill TF9 2JF (SW, on A41) ☎Tern Hill(0630) 638532
Run by the friendly Shuttleworth family, this small country hotel is set in 1.5 acres of mature grounds. The oak beamed bar opens out onto the patio and lawns, or has an open fire in colder weather. Bedrooms have private bathrooms, though not all are en suite. The

popular restaurant offers a simple table d'hôte menu and a large carte.
6rm(4⇨🛏)(1fb)1🛁 CTV in all bedrooms ® ✈ (ex guide dogs)
20P 🚗 ✿
V Last dinner 8.30pm
Credit Cards [1][3]

MARKET HARBOROUGH Leicestershire Map **04** SP78

★★★ **※64%** *Three Swans*
21 High St LE16 7NJ ☎(0858) 466644 FAX (0858) 433101

This former coaching inn dating back over 500 years has been expanded and improved in keeping with its original style. Guests have a choice of 3 bars, one with two open fires and ornate carved pillars. A well appointed cocktail bar adjoins the delightful air-conditioned Swans Restaurant where professional staff offer varied and interesting menus of dishes in English style, prepared by chef Richard Payne. Light meals and snacks are available all day in the conservatory lounge.
20⇨🛏 Annexe16⇨🛏(3fb)2🛁 ⚒ in 4 bedrooms CTV in all bedrooms ® T ✈ (ex guide dogs) sB&B⇨🛏£52-£75 dB&B⇨🛏£72-£85 🍽
🕯40P 8🚗
🍴 International V ☆ ♨ ✱ Lunch fr£9.95 Dinner fr£17.95 Last dinner 9.45pm
CONF. Thtr 100 Class 75 Board 50 Del from £75
Credit Cards [1][2][3][4][5]

Remember to book early for holiday and bank holiday times.

Park Crescent, Victoria Park, Rusholme, Manchester M14 5RE
Tel: 061-224 0672   Fax: 061-257 2822

A 26 bedroom hotel ideally situated in a tree-lined crescent only 2 miles from the city centre. Most rooms with en-suite bathroom. All have colour TV, direct dial telephone, tea maker. Private car park.

ONE OF MANCHESTER'S MOST POPULAR INDEPENDENT HOTELS

COMMENDED, LES ROUTIERS

Please write or telephone for further details and brochure

Markfield - Marlow

MARKFIELD Leicestershire Map 08 SK41

★★★71% Field Head
Markfield Ln LE67 9PS (access via B5327, off roundabout junct with the A50, 1m from junct 22 of the M1) (Whitbread) ☎(0530) 245454 FAX (0530) 243740

Originally a farmhouse dating back to 1672, the property has been considerably extended in recent years. The restaurant, in the old building, comprises 4 rooms with thick walls, exposed timbers and fireplaces. A central courtyard is surrounded by bars and comfortable lounge areas. The attractive bedrooms have rich floral décor with matching fabrics and good quality furniture.

28⇌♠(2fb)1⌑ in 6 bedrooms CTV in all bedrooms ®⚡T ✈(ex guide dogs) ✱ sB&B⇌♠fr£59.50 dB&B⇌♠fr£71 ☐ (70P
♀ English & French V ♡ ⚑ ✗ ✱ Lunch fr£8.50&alc Dinner fr£13.95&alc Last dinner 10pm
CONF. Thtr 70 Board 30 Del from £89
Credit Cards [1][2][3][5]

Granada Lodge
Little Shaw Ln LE6 0PP (on A50 junct with M1 motorway) ☎(0530) 244237 FAX (0530) 244580

This modern building provides smart, spacious and well equipped bedrooms, all with en suite bathrooms. Meals may be taken at a nearby family restaurant. For more details about Granada Lodges, consult the Contents page, under Hotel Groups.
39⇌✱ B⇌£34.95-£37.95 (room only)

MARKHAM MOOR Nottinghamshire Map 08 SK77

Forte Travelodge
DN22 0QU (on A1 northbound) ☎Retford (0777) 838091 Central Res (0800) 850950

This modern building offers a good standard of accommodation for overnight stops. Smart, spacious and well equipped bedrooms, all with en suite bathrooms, are suitable for family use, and meals may be taken at the nearby family restaurant. For more details about Travelodges, consult the Contents page, under Hotel Groups.
40⇌♠✱ B⇌♠£31.95 (room only)

MARKINCH Fife Map 11 NO20

★★★★❀⚑73% Balbirnie House
Balbirnie Park KY7 6NE
☎Glenrothes(0592) 610066 FAX (0592) 610529

This classical mansion house is set in over 400 acres of parkland. The attractively decorated bedrooms range from sumptuous suites to modest singles. Public rooms include a vaulted long gallery, relaxing drawing room and a book-lined library bar. There are 2 dining rooms, where chef Ian MacDonald presents an interesting menu based largely on fresh Scottish produce. The Game Keeper's Inn and Bistro offers an alternative at lunch time.

30⇌♠(9fb)1⌑ CTV in all bedrooms ®⚡T sB&B⇌♠£85-£95 dB&B⇌♠£125-£180 ☐
(120P ❀ ▶ 18 xmas
♀ International V ♡ ⚑ ✗ Dinner £22.50 Last dinner 9.30pm
CONF. Thtr 150 Class 70 Board 50 Del £135
Credit Cards [1][2][3][5]

MARKINGTON North Yorkshire Map 08 SE26

★★★❀⚑76% Hob Green
HG3 3PJ (exit A61 4m after Harrogate and turn right at Wormald Green)
☎Harrogate(0423) 770031 FAX (0423) 771589

This charming country house is situated in over 800 acres of farm and woodland, surrounded by magnificent Yorkshire countryside. The elegant public rooms comprise a beautifully furnished hall, a drawing room with a log fire and antique furniture and a sun lounge opening onto the front lawn. Bedrooms are tastefully furnished and decorated, with modern fabrics, period furnishings, and every modern comfort. The attactive dining room is the setting for excellent food provided from a small but varied carte, many of the vegetables from the hotel's own kitchen garden.

12⇌♠1⌑ CTV in all bedrooms ®⚡T sB&B⇌♠£59-£70 dB&B⇌♠£80-£90 ☐
40P ⇌ ❀ croquet
♀ English & French V ♡ ⚑ ✗ Sunday Lunch £11.95-£12.95 Dinner £18.50-£25alc Last dinner 9.30pm
Credit Cards [1][2][3][5]

See advertisement under HARROGATE

MARLBOROUGH Wiltshire Map 04 SU16

★★★❀72% Ivy House Hotel & Garden Restaurant
High St SN8 1HJ ☎(0672) 515333 FAX (0672) 515338

Overlooking the famous high street, this ivy-clad Grade II Georgian residence started life in 1707 as the Marlborough Academy for Boys. There is a comfortable guest lounge, a garden room bistro and an elegant and spacious restaurant. Here two menus show the skills of a team of creative young chefs, styles varying from traditional to progressive. Bedrooms are in the hotel and 2 other nearby buildings. Staff are friendly and professional.

12⇌♠ Annexe16⇌♠(2fb) CTV in all bedrooms ®⚡T sB&B⇌♠£50-£69.50 dB&B⇌♠£70-£89 ☐
30P xmas
♀ English & French V ♡ ⚑ ✗ ✱ Lunch fr£10.95&alc Dinner fr£16.50&alc Last dinner 9.30pm
CONF. Thtr 50 Class 35 Board 30 Del from £85
Credit Cards [1][3]

★★★60% The Castle & Ball
High St SN8 1LZ ☎(0672) 515201 FAX (0672) 515895

This centrally situated inn dating from the 17th century extends a warm welcome to guests. Character public areas include an open-plan lounge/bar as well as a restaurant serving table d'hôte meals which provide a choice of dishes. Bedrooms are all equipped to meet the needs of both business and holiday guests.

34⇌♠ Annexe2⇌♠(1fb)1⌑ in 13 bedrooms CTV in all bedrooms ®⚡T ✱ sB⇌♠£80 dB⇌♠£95-£108 (room only) ☐
48P xmas
V ♡ ⚑ ✗ Lunch £13.95 High tea £12.95-£13.95alc Dinner £16.95 Last dinner 9.30pm
Credit Cards [1][2][3][5]

MARLOW Buckinghamshire Map 04 SU88

★★★★❀70% The Compleat Angler
Marlow Bridge SL7 1RG (by Marlow Bridge) ☎(0628) 484444 FAX (0628) 486388

(Rosette awarded for dinner only)

This well known hotel on a curve of the River Thames near the town centre is a successful synthesis of country house style and international luxury. Outside there are lawns and a waterside terrace; inside an elegant panelled bar, a small lounge and a conservatory for light snacks and afternoon teas. The Valaison restaurant offers a 'carte' and set price menus of dishes based on fine French cuisine, often presented in elaborate style. Bedrooms are generally stylish and comfortable, many with river views, some with balconies. Sizes vary – the new wing rooms are most spacious, and their bathrooms the most luxurious.

62⇌♠5⌑ ✗ in 16 bedrooms CTV in all bedrooms ®⚡T sB⇌♠£125-£160 dB⇌♠£145-£180 (room only) ☐

420

Lift (100P ♿ ✤ ♪ (hard) ♪ xmas
V ☺ ⚒ ✂ Lunch £17.50-£29.50&alc Dinner fr£29.50&alc Last dinner 10pm
Credit Cards [1][2][3][5]

MARPLE Greater Manchester Map 07 SJ98
★ **74% Springfield**
Station Rd SK6 6PA (beside A626) ☎061-449 0721
There is a friendly atmosphere at this charming small hotel, decorated in Victorian country house style. A well produced dinner is served in the pretty dining room/conservatory, and there is a cosy bar lounge. The attractive bedrooms offer a good range of facilities.
6⇌♠ CTV in all bedrooms ® T ✱ sB&B⇌♠£30-£40 dB&B⇌♠£40-£50 ⌂
CTV 10P ♿ ✤
☺ ⚒ Dinner £15 Last dinner 8.30pm
Credit Cards [1][2][3][5]

MARSDEN West Yorkshire Map 07 SE01
★★★ **63% Hey Green**
Waters Rd HD7 6NG (off A62) ☎Huddersfield(0484) 844235
FAX (0484) 847605
Standing in 7 acres of woodland, this quietly run hotel, popular as a wedding venue, offers well appointed accommodation, with attractively furnished and well equipped bedrooms.
10⇌♠(2fb)1⌂ CTV in all bedrooms ® T ✱ sB&B⇌♠£55-£60 dB&B⇌♠£75-£80 ⌂
70P ♿ ♪ orienteering course
V ☺ ⚒ ✱ Lunch £9.50-£23.50 Dinner £18.50-£23.50 Last dinner 9pm
Credit Cards [1][2][3][5]   £

MARSTON MORETAINE Bedfordshire Map 04 SP94
Forte Travelodge
Beancroft Rd Junction MK43 0PZ (on A421, northbound) ☎Bedford(0234) 766755
Central Res (0800) 850950

FORTE Travelodge

This modern building offers a good standard of accommodation for overnight stops. Smart, spacious and well equipped bedrooms, all with en suite bathrooms, are suitable for family use, and meals may be taken at the nearby family restaurant. For more details about Travelodges, consult the Contents page, under Hotel Groups.
32⇌♠✱ B⇌♠£31.95 (room only)

MARSTON TRUSSELL Northamptonshire Map 04 SP68
★★ **63% The Sun Inn**
LE16 9TY ☎Market Harborough(0858) 65531
An inn enjoying a peaceful location in a small village just outside Market Harborough providing well equipped modern bedrooms. Public areas are popular with locals and residents alike, both bar and restaurant serving extensive menus.
10⇌ CTV in all bedrooms ®
CTV 35P 2🚗 ✤ ⚹
☺ English & Continental V ☺ Last dinner 9.30pm
Credit Cards [1][2][3]

MARTINHOE Devon Map 02 SS64
★★ 🍴 **71% Old Rectory**
EX31 4QT ☎Parracombe(05983) 368 FAX (05983) 567
Closed 21 Dec-1 Jan RS Nov-20 Dec & Jan-Etr
The Bradbury family, previously of Kilcamb Lodge in Scotland, have recently bought this former rectory and have done much to improve the hotel giving it a cosy but stylish feel with good-quality furnishings and fabrics. The proprietors' son Daniel is a talented furniture maker and many of the pieces are credited to him. Suzanne Bradbury cooks wholesome fare from good fresh produce,

★★ ❀ **67%**

There's **"really excellent"**
(Harpers & Queen Magazine)
food and wine
in our beautiful, tranquil
Victorian hotel in glorious countryside.

The perfect centre for touring the gardens, great houses and historic sites of the West Country, only 1¼ hours from London.

**Bargain weekend and mid-week breaks.
Mountain bikes for hire.**

Brochure on request.

THE SAVERNAKE FOREST HOTEL & RESTAURANT
Burbage, nr Marlborough, Wilts SN8 3AY
Telephone 0672-810206. Fax 0672-811081

THE IVY HOUSE HOTEL
and Garden Restaurant ★★★
High Street, Marlborough, Wiltshire SN8 1HJ
Telephone: (0672) 515333

This Grade II Georgian Residence, overlooking the famous high street, has been completely transformed by resident owners David Ball and Josephine Scott into a 3 star luxury hotel which offers the best in comfort, facilities and service. Their aim is to provide first class hospitality and service in a friendly country house hotel atmosphere. They offer quality accommodation, excellent food and wine and relaxing lounges and bars. A team of dedicated and professional staff ensure that guests to the Ivy House enjoy efficient and courteous service.

Martinhoe - Matlock

and the home-made puddings should not be missed. There are also two luxurious self-catering cottages.
8⇨🛏(1fb) CTV in all bedrooms ® ✈ (ex guide dogs) ✽ sB&B⇨🛏£50-£55 dB&B⇨🛏£100-£110 (incl dinner) 🍴
14P 🚗 ✿
V ⚲ ⚑ ✂ ✽ Dinner £21 Last dinner 6.30pm

MARTOCK Somerset Map 03 ST41

★★★ 68% The Hollies
Bower Hinton TA12 6LG (just off A303) ☎(0935) 822232 FAX (0935) 822249
The main building of this attractive stone-built farmhouse houses the bar and dining areas, while the comfortable bedrooms are in a modern annexe and look onto a central, grassy courtyard.
Annexe15⇨🛏(2fb)in 4 bedrooms CTV in all bedrooms ®⚲ T ✽ sB&B⇨🛏£42.50-£49.50 dB&B⇨🛏£45-£59.50 🍴
CTV 50P ✿ ♋
V ✂ ✽ Lunch £8.95&alc Dinner £7.95-£19alc Last dinner 9pm
CONF. Thtr 60 Class 40 Board 40 Del from £55
Credit Cards [1][2][3][5] £

MARYPORT Cumbria Map 11 NY03

★★ 62% Ellenbank
Birkby CA15 6RE (2m NE A596) ☎(0900) 815233
Standing on a small hill to the north of the town, this impressive stone building with attractive grounds has a new rear extension of modern bedrooms plus a large conference room. A wide range of food is available in the cosy bar or traditional restaurant.
26⇨🛏(3fb) CTV in all bedrooms ® T
CTV 40P ✿
♡ English & Continental V ⚲ ⚑ Last dinner 9.30pm
Credit Cards [1][3]

★ 58% Waverley
Curzon St CA15 6LW ☎(0900) 812115 FAX (0900) 817734
Offering good value for money, this friendly town centre hotel caters mainly for a commercial clientele. Bedrooms are simply furnished but all have colour TV. An extensive range of food is available either in the bar or the dining room.
20rm(2⇨2🛏)(2fb) CTV in all bedrooms ® ✽ sB&Bfr£18 sB&B⇨🛏fr£28 dB&Bfr£33 dB&B⇨🛏fr£42 🍴
CTV ℘ pool table
♡ English & Continental V ⚲ ⚑ ✂ ✽ Lunch fr£7.50 High tea fr£5.50 Dinner fr£9 Last dinner 9.30pm
Credit Cards [1][3]

MASHAM North Yorkshire Map 08 SE28

★★ ❀ 74% Jervaulx Hall
HG4 4PH (on A6108 midway between Masham & Middleham adjacent to Jervaulx Abbey)
☎Bedale(0677) 60235 FAX (0677) 60263
Closed end Nov-mid Mar
The Sharp's unpretentious home epitomises the English country house hotel at its best. Bedrooms are well proportioned and traditionally furnished, and have fresh fruit and magazines instead of telephones and televisions. There are 2 lounges and an honesty bar at the foot of the stairs. While the 4-course menu may be short it offers the best of country cooking.
10⇨🛏 ® T ✽ sB&B⇨🛏£75 dB&B⇨🛏£120-£136 (incl dinner) 🍴
CTV 15P 🚗 ✿ croquet
✂ ✽ Dinner fr£20 Last dinner 8pm £

For full, independent restaurant reviews,
see the AA Abbey Well *Restaurant Guide*

MATLOCK Derbyshire Map 08 SK36

★★★ ❀ 73% Riber Hall
DE4 5JU (1m off A615 at Tansley)
☎(0629) 582795 FAX (0629) 580475

This beautifully restored Elizabethan manor house high above Matlock retains much of its original character. There is an impressive carved fireplace in the lounge, and bedrooms combine antiques with every modern facility. In the kitchen good local produce, particularly game in season, (and with the herb garden always in evidence) is used to create imaginative dishes which are coupled to a predominantly French wine list.
Annexe11⇨🛏9🍴 CTV in all bedrooms ®⚲ T
✈ (ex guide dogs) ✽ sB&B⇨🛏£78-£92 dB&B⇨🛏£92-£137 Continental breakfast 🍴
50P 🚗 ✿ ℘ (hard) nc10yrs
♡ English & French V ⚲ ⚑ ✽ Lunch fr£14.50 Dinner £21.50-£30alc Last dinner 9.30pm
Credit Cards [1][2][3][4][5]

★★★ 70% The New Bath
New Bath Rd DE4 3PX (2m S off A6)
☎(0629) 583275 FAX (0629) 580268

This rambling hotel is set in extensive grounds. Continued improvements have created attractive public areas and comfortable, well equipped bedrooms of varying sizes, colour coordinated in deep rich colours, many with beautiful views. An all day menu is available in the relaxing lounge.
55⇨🛏✂in 11 bedrooms CTV in all bedrooms ® T ✽ sB⇨🛏£70 dB⇨🛏£90 (room only) 🍴
(200P ✿ ⟿ ℘ (hard) sauna solarium thermal plunge pool ⚭ xmas
V ⚲ ⚑ ✂ ✽ Lunch £8.95-£12.95&alc High tea £3.80 Dinner £17.95&alc Last dinner 9.30pm
CONF. Thtr 130 Class 60 Board 46 Del £95
Credit Cards [1][2][3][5]

★★★ ❀ 72% Red House
Old Rd, Darley Dale DE4 2ER (just off A6 2.5m north of Matlock) ☎(0629) 734854
Improvements continue at this comfortable small hotel. Family run, it provides warm hospitality and relaxing public rooms, with fine views of the surrounding countryside and attractive rear garden. A set price menu of mainly British dishes changes daily.
7⇨🛏Annexe2⇨🛏3🍴 CTV in all bedrooms ® T
sB&B⇨🛏£50-£55 dB&B⇨🛏£70-£75 🍴
16P 🚗 ✿
♡ English & French V ✂ Lunch £10.95-£13.95 Dinner £17.50-£18.95 Last dinner 9pm
Credit Cards [1][2][3][5]

★★ 67% Temple
Temple Walk, Matlock Bath DE4 3PG ☎(0629) 583911 FAX (0629) 580851
The Temple is a well run family hotel with panoramic views over Matlock Bath from its position on a steep wooded hillside. It provides good quality accommodation with modern facilities. Chef/patron Siegfried Essl is well known locally for his varied menus with seasonal specials, particularly game.
14⇨🛏(1fb) CTV in all bedrooms ®⚲ T ✈
(CTV 40P ✿
♡ English, French & Austrian V ⚲ ⚑ ✂ Last dinner 9.45pm
Credit Cards [1][2][3][5]

★★ 62% Gullivers Woodland Lodge
Temple Walk, Matlock Bath DE4 3PG ☎(0629) 580540 FAX (0629) 57710
This pleasant hotel adjoins the Gulliver's Kingdom Theme Park. Lodge-style bedrooms are situated in the grounds and offer sound comforts and facilities. Public areas include a comfortable

conservatory, a bar and an attractive restaurant. Staff are friendly and helpful, and a good range of food is available.
Annexe14⇨(6fb) CTV in all bedrooms ® T ✗ (ex guide dogs)
30P 🚗
♀ English & French V ♦ ⚲
Credit Cards ① ③

MAWDESLEY Lancashire Map 07 SD41

★★ 72% **Mawdesley Eating House and Hotel**
Hall Ln L40 2QZ ☎Rufford(0704) 822552 & 821874 FAX (0704) 822096
This one time basket works has been developed into an attractive complex including a separate block of modern, well equipped bedrooms. The restaurant offers good value menus at both lunch and dinner. Cheerful, courteous staff help to create a relaxed and friendly atmosphere.
25⇨(5fb)1🛏 CTV in all bedrooms ®⚤ T ✗ (ex guide dogs)
100P ⚲ (heated) sauna solarium gymnasium
V ♦ ✻ Lunch £8.50 Dinner £7.50-£12.75alc Last dinner 10pm
CONF. Thtr 50 Class 30 Board 30 Del £65
Credit Cards ① ② ③ £

MAWGAN PORTH Cornwall & Isles of Scilly Map 02 SW86

★★ 66% **Tredragon**
TR8 4DQ (Logis) ☎St Mawgan(0637) 860213 FAX (0637) 860269
In a glorious position overlooking the cove and bay, the hotel has direct access to the sandy beaches. Bedrooms come in a variety of shapes and sizes, all fresh and bright.
27⇨(12fb) CTV in all bedrooms ® T ✻ sB&B⇨£38-£50 dB&B⇨£60-£96 (incl dinner) 🅿
CTV 30P ❋ ⚲ (heated) sauna solarium ⚬ xmas
♀ English & French V ♦ ⚲ ✻ Sunday Lunch £7-£12 Dinner £12.50-£13.50 Last dinner 8pm
CONF. Thtr 50 Class 30 Board 30 Del from £35
Credit Cards ① ③ £

MAWNAN SMITH Cornwall & Isles of Scilly Map 02 SW72

★★★ 73% **Meudon**
TR11 5HT ☎Falmouth(0326) 250541 FAX (0326) 250543
Closed Dec-Feb
In a tranquil setting, surrounded by National Trust land, this late Victorian mansion with a modern wing has been in the same family for over 20 years and offers high standards of service and hospitality. Bedrooms are of a good size, well furnished and, like the smart public areas, have views across the wonderful sub-tropical gardens that run down a sheltered valley to the sea.
32⇨(1fb) CTV in all bedrooms T
(50P 2☎ (£5 per night) 🚗 ❋ ♪ ⚬ nc5yrs
♀ English & French V ♦ ⚲ Last dinner 9pm
Credit Cards ① ③ ⑤

★★★ 72% **Budock Vean**
TR11 5LG ☎Falmouth(0326) 250288 FAX (0326) 250892
Closed Jan & Feb
Set in beautiful countryside, with 65 acres of mature grounds stretching down to the Helford river, this is an attractive, continually improving hotel. Bedrooms, which are being upgraded, are practical and comfortable, and most enjoy valley or golf course views. Lounges are large, and a high standard of friendly service includes room service, helpful porterage and professional restaurant and bar staff.
58⇨(6fb)1🛏 CTV in all bedrooms T
Lift (100P 🚗 ❋ ⚲ (heated) ▶ 9 ♟ (hard) ♪ snooker ♫
♀ English & French V ♦ ⚲ Last dinner 9pm
Credit Cards ① ② ③ ⑤

Matlock - Maybole

★★★ 64% *Trelawne*
TR11 5HS ☎Falmouth(0326) 250226 & 250417 FAX (0326) 250909
Closed 29 Dec-5 Mar
Situated between the Fal and the Helford, in an area of unspoilt coastline, the Trelawne Hotel has been owned and managed by the Gibbons family for many years. Improvements are constantly being made to the bedrooms. A varied table d'hôte menu is served nightly, with imaginative salads, robust home-made soups and a well balanced choice of main courses.
14⇨(2fb) CTV in all bedrooms ® T
20P 🚗 ❋ ⚲ (heated)
♦ ⚲ ✗ Last dinner 8.30pm
Credit Cards ① ② ③ ⑤

See advertisement on page 425

MAYBOLE Strathclyde *Ayrshire* Map 10 NS20

★★

★★⚲ **LADYBURN**
KA19 7SG
☎Crosshill(06554) 585 FAX (06554) 580
Closed 31 Dec & 1 Jan
(Rosette awarded for dinner only)

Jane and David Hepburn and their friendly staff welcome guests to their delightfully peaceful home. A former dower house, set in carefully tended gardens surrounded by beautiful wooded countryside, it opened in 1990 as a country house hotel ➡

LUXURY CORNISH COUNTRY HOUSE HOTEL

Idyllically situated in 65 acres, on the banks of the Helford River with private Golf Course, spectacular indoor pool and championship tennis courts – all free to guests.

Comfortable and stylish accommodation, superb cuisine with an excellent selection of wines.

Enjoy the unique atmosphere of this fine hotel.

Associated hotel Treglos Hotel, Padstow.

BUDOCK VEAN
GOLF AND COUNTRY HOUSE HOTEL ★★★
FALMOUTH · CORNWALL · TR11 5LG TEL: 0326 250288 FAX: 0326 250892

Maybole - Melrose

and has quickly made its mark. There are 2 comfortable lounges, one with an extensive selection of books while the drawing room has an inviting open fire. Bedrooms are prettily decorated and have lots of thoughtful extras including fresh fruit, fresh milk and books. Meals are light in style and include such dishes as roast beef, fish pie, bread and butter pudding and rhubarb crumble, and an adequate wine list is available. Hospitality is the keynote here and Ladyburn justly deserves our Red Star award.

8rm(4⇨3♠)(2fb)⌿ in all bedrooms CTV in all bedrooms ® T ✕ (ex guide dogs) ✻ ♬
12P ⚘ ✿ croquet nc12yrs
V ✧ ⚑ ⌿
Credit Cards [1][2][3]

MELKSHAM Wiltshire Map 03 ST96

★★★❀❀♨74% Beechfield House
Beanacre SN12 7PU (1m N A350) ☎(0225) 703700 FAX (0225) 790118

This elegant Victorian Bath stone hotel has 8 acres of beautifully kept gardens where a lot of the fruit and vegetables for the kitchen are grown. Lounges are tastefully decorated, fresh flowers adding a welcome touch, and log fires blaze on cool evenings. Bedrooms are all are spacious and fully equipped. A new head chef, Ray Langley, has recently been appointed.

20⇨1♠ in 8 bedrooms CTV in all bedrooms T ✕ (ex guide dogs)
40P ⚘ ✿ ⌂ (heated) ♪ (grass) croquet
V ✧ ⚑ ⌿ Last dinner 9.30pm
Credit Cards [1][2][3][5]

★★66% Shaw Country
Bath Rd, Shaw SN12 8EF (2m NW A365) ☎(0225) 702836 & 790321 FAX (0225) 790275

This attractive stone-built, creeper clad property, thought to date from the late 16th century, stands in its own gardens on the edge of the town. It retains some original features, combined with the comforts of 20th-century living. There is a choice of lounges, one with a bar. Some bathrooms have circular baths. Both table d'hôte and à la carte menus are available in the dining room, which has exposed stone walls and ornate arches.

13⇨♠(2fb)3🚫 CTV in all bedrooms ® T ✻ sB&B⇨♠£40-£45 dB&B⇨♠£59-£78 ♬
30P ⚘ ✿
♀ English & French V ✧ ⚑ ✻ Lunch fr£9.95&alc Dinner fr£14&alc Last dinner 9pm
Credit Cards [1][2][3]

★★63% Conigre Farm
Semington Rd SN12 6BZ ☎(0225) 702229
Closed 26 Dec-1 Jan

This 17th-century Cotswold stone farmhouse has comfortable, simply decorated and well equipped bedrooms, some of them in a converted stable block a few yards from the main hotel. Public areas include a spacious conservatory lounge and a restaurant serving traditional English dishes.

4rm(1⇨)Annexe5⇨♠1🚫 CTV in all bedrooms ® T ✕ (ex guide dogs) ✻ sB&Bfr£29 sB&B⇨♠fr£36 dB&B£40 dB&B⇨♠fr£50 ♬
(12P 2⚘ ⚘ ✿
V ✧ ⚑ ✻ Lunch £7.50-£14.95&alc Dinner fr£14.95&alc Last dinner 10pm
CONF. Class 40 Board 40
Credit Cards [1][3]

★★62% Kings Arms
Market Place SN12 6EX (in town centre opposite LLoyds Bank) ☎(0225) 707272 FAX (0225) 702085

This character coaching inn on the edge of the town has a delightful cobbled courtyard. There is a comfortable pub, a bright lounge and a spacious restaurant with a popular carte. Bedrooms are prettily decorated and well equipped, and the jolly proprietors lead a small team of pleasant staff.

14rm(10⇨♠) CTV in all bedrooms ® T ✻ sB&Bfr£35 sB&B⇨♠fr£49 dB&B⇨♠fr£59 ♬
40P
V ✧ ⚑ ✻ Lunch £7-£11.50&alc Dinner fr£11.50&alc Last dinner 9pm
Credit Cards [1][2][3][5]

MELLING Lancashire Map 07 SD57

★★58% Melling Hall
LA6 2RA (on A683, at northern edge of village) ☎Hornby(05242) 21298

With views over the Lune Valley, this mainly commercial hotel is converted from a 17th-century manor house. Bedrooms are generally spacious and public areas include a choice of bars and a traditional dining room.

14rm(7⇨3♠)(1fb) CTV in all bedrooms ® ♋ T ✻ sB&B£26-£35 sB&B⇨♠£35-£40 dB&B£40-£45 dB&B⇨♠£50-£55 ♬
40P ✿ xmas
♀ English & French ✧ ✻ Sunday Lunch £6.95 Dinner £11.95&alc Last dinner 9.30pm
Credit Cards [1][2][3]

MELROSE Borders Roxburghshire Map 12 NT53

★★★59% Burt's
The Square TD6 9PN ☎(089252) 2285 FAX (089252) 2870

This old-established coaching inn dates back to the 18th century and overlooks the market square of an historic town. Rooms of varying sizes are all very well equipped, there is a quiet residents' lounge as well as a traditional bar and pleasant restaurant.

21⇨♠ CTV in all bedrooms ® T ✻ sB&B⇨♠£40-£44 dB&B⇨♠£68-£72 ♬
40P ⚘ ✿ snooker shooting game
♀ English & French V ✧ Lunch £13.50-£16 Dinner £19.50-£25&alc Last dinner 9.30pm
Credit Cards [1][2][3][5]

★★67% Bon Accord
Market Square TD6 9PQ ☎(089252) 2645 FAX (089252) 3474

This friendly family-run hotel in the town centre has attractively redecorated public areas which, though lacking lounge space, include a choice of bars and a split-level dining room. Refurbished bedrooms are bright and comfortable, with modern furnishings and facilities.

10⇨♠(1fb)1🚫 CTV in all bedrooms ® T ✕ (ex guide dogs) ✻ sB&B⇨♠£38.50 dB&B⇨♠£65 ♬
♪ xmas
V ✧ ⚑ ✻ Bar Lunch £6.80-£14.45alc Dinner fr£14.50&alc Last dinner 9pm
Credit Cards [1][2][3]

★★62% George & Abbotsford
TD6 9PD ☎(089252) 2308 FAX (089252) 3363

This large 18th-century coaching inn in the town centre has been modernised to provide comfortable bedrooms. An extensive range of meals is served in both the lounge bar and restaurant.

30⇨♠(3fb)1🚫 CTV in all bedrooms ® ♋ T sB&B⇨♠£35-£42 dB&B⇨♠£55-£70 ♬
150P ✿ ⚙ xmas

For key to symbols see the Bookmark.

424

Melrose - Melton Mowbray

🍴 British & French **V** ⚭ Bar Lunch £3.50-£10 Dinner £17.50&alc Last dinner 9.30pm
CONF. Thtr 120 Class 50 Board 30 Del from £60
Credit Cards [1] [2] [3] [5]

MELTON MOWBRAY Leicestershire Map **08** SK71

STAPLEFORD PARK
Stapleford LE14 2EF (off B676 towards Colsterworth)
☏ Wymondham
(057284) 522 FAX (057284) 651

A truly splendid country house, Stapleford Park is set in a 500-acre estate complete with its own lake, stables and church. Relaxation and country pursuits are the order of the day, though Stapleford is becoming increasingly popular as a venue for select conferences and promotions. The magnificent public rooms are furnished in great style, with the emphasis on comfort and quality. Bedrooms are unique, individually designed by as many as 20 different companies and designers, with discreet modern facilities. The cuisine is predominantly American-style and includes interpretations of the cuisine of many continents, all based on good fresh produce. Proprietors Bob and Wendy Payton have cultivated a dedicated and genuinely hospitable staff who provide most attentive service.

Shaw Country Hotel
★★ & Restaurant

SHAW, NR MELKSHAM, WILTS SN12 8EF
Telephone: Melksham (0225) 702836/790321
Fax: 790275

Proprietors Mr & Mrs Lewis

This 400 year old farmhouse is now an elegant Country Hotel with a glowing reputation for fine food. 13 Bedrooms all with en-suite facilities, colour TV, radio, direct line telephone, beverage facilities and fresh fruit. (3 rooms with four poster bed, one with jacuzzi bath.) Table d'hôte and à la carte menus available in the large licensed restaurant. Ample Car Parking. Ideal centre for touring Bath, Lacock, Longleat etc.

M

BURTS HOTEL

MELROSE
ROXBURGHSHIRE

Distinguished family-run town house Hotel built in 1722. Tastefully furnished with 21 en suite bedrooms all with modern facilities including colour television, direct-dial telephone, Tea/Coffee facilities, etc.

Elegant restaurant offering both á la carte and table d'hôte menus together with extensive wine list. Lounge bar serving light lunches and suppers daily, billiards room, two lounges, private car park and extensive gardens.

Burts Hotel is the ideal centre for touring the beautiful Border country and enjoying traditional Scottish hospitality. Several golf courses are within easy reach, salmon and trout fishing can be arranged. Game shooting on local estates also available with prior notice.

For brochure write to: Graham and Anne Henderson, Proprietors. Phone: (089682) 2285 Fax: (089682) 2870

AA★★★ ❀❀❀❀ Commended, Egon Ronay, Johansens, Les Routiers and Taste of Scotland recommended.

Slip away any day. Spring, Autumn & Winter breaks

Trelawne Hotel
★ ★ ★ ❀
MAWNAN SMITH, FALMOUTH TR11 5HS
TEL: (0326) 250226

A fine country house hotel, three miles south of Falmouth, quietly situated in 2 acres of gardens overlooking Falmouth Bay and within easy reach of Falmouth, beaches and coastal walks. All tastefully furnished rooms, most with en suite facilities, have telephone, TV, tea and coffee making facilities. Indoor heated swimming pool and games room.

Melton Mowbray - Merthyr Tydfil

35⇨🛁1🚲 CTV in all bedrooms ⚹ T dB&B⇨🛁£125-£285 Continental breakfast 🍴
Lift (120P 🚗 ✱ ♪ (hard) ♪ ∪ mini golf croquet basketball shooting ♫ *xmas*
☺ American/European V ✿ ⚓ ⚹ ✱ Lunch £4.50-£42.50alc Dinner £4.50-£42.50alc Last dinner 10.30pm
Credit Cards ① ② ③ ④ ⑤

★★ 64% Sysonby Knoll
Asfordby Rd LE13 0HP (0.5m from town centre beside A6006) (Logis) ☎(0664) 63563 FAX (0664) 410364
Closed Xmas
This friendly, family-run hotel is a red brick building, extended around a central courtyard with 2 acres of secluded grounds running down to the River Eye. Bedrooms vary in size, some singles being quite compact, but they have recently been improved with new decor and soft furnishings. Wholesome food is served in either the bar or restaurant.
23⇨🛁Annexe1⇨🛁(2fb)2🚲 CTV in all bedrooms ® T ✱ sB&B⇨🛁£34-£39.50 dB&B⇨🛁£45-£49 🍴
CTV 30P ✱ ⇌ ⚓
☺ English & French V ✿ ✱ Bar Lunch £3.65-£6alc Dinner £9.50&alc Last dinner 9pm
Credit Cards ① ② ③

MELVICH Highland *Caithness* Map **14** NC86
★★ 64% Melvich
KW14 7YJ (on A836, Thurso-Bettyhill) (Logis) ☎(06413) 206 FAX (06413) 347
Closed 25 Dec & 1-2 Jan
At the west end of the village, this friendly, family-run holiday hotel enjoys a fine outlook over the Pentland Firth to the Orkneys beyond. Bedrooms are in a modern wing, and public areas offer traditional comforts. The cosy bar has a good range of malts in stock.
14🛁 CTV in all bedrooms ® ✱ sB&B🛁£25.50-£30 dB&B🛁£47-£52.50 🍴
10P 🚗 ✱ ♪ snooker ⚓
☺ Scottish, English, French & Italian V ✿ ⚓ ✱ Sunday Lunch £8-£10alc High tea £4.75-£9alc Dinner £15-£20alc Last dinner 8pm
CONF. Board 20 Del from £48.50
Credit Cards ① ② ③

MENAI BRIDGE
See **Anglesey, Isle of**

MENDHAM Suffolk Map **05** TM28
★ 64% Sir Alfred Munnings Country Hotel
Studio Corner IP20 0NH ☎Harleston(0379) 852358
Painted in typical Suffolk pink, this 16th-century building is situated in a peaceful hamlet. Most of the rooms have recently been redecorated in individual colour schemes. There is a comfortable lounge, a bar and restaurant offering standard fare and a large 'cabaret' room.
9rm(6🛁) ® ✻
CTV 60P ♪ wind surfing
V ✿ ⚓ Last dinner 2pm
Credit Cards ① ③ ④ ⑤

MERE Wiltshire Map **03** ST83
★ 62% The Talbot
The Square BA12 6DR ☎(0747) 860427
7⇨🛁(3fb) CTV in all bedrooms ® ✱ sB&B⇨🛁£32.50 dB&B⇨🛁£53 🍴
25P

V ✿ ⚹ ✱ Lunch £3.95-£12.95alc Dinner £3.95-£12.95alc Last dinner 9pm
Credit Cards ① ② ③

MERIDEN West Midlands Map **04** SP28

★★★★ ❀66% Forest of Arden Hotel, Golf & Country Club
Maxstoke Ln CV7 7HR (off A45)
☎(0676) 22335 FAX (0676) 23711

Set amid lovely countryside, surrounded by woods, lakes and 2 golf courses, the emphasis at this hotel is undoubtedly on sport, leisure and conferences. The attractive split-level restaurant is proving popular, and there is the Poolside Grill for a totally informal atmosphere. Standard and 'executive' bedrooms with better working facilities are offered; both styles are spacious.
152⇨🛁(4fb)⚹in 29 bedrooms CTV in all bedrooms ® ⚹ T ✻ (ex guide dogs) ✱ sB&B⇨🛁£110 dB&B⇨🛁£125 🍴
Lift (400P ▣ (heated) ▶ 18 ♪ (hard) ♪ squash snooker sauna solarium gymnasium dance studio steam room beauty salon *xmas*
☺ International V ✿ ⚓ ⚹ ✱ Lunch £18.50 Dinner £18.50 Last dinner 9.45pm
CONF. Thtr 150 Class 120 Board 35 Del £142
Credit Cards ① ② ③ ⑤

★★★ 68% Manor
Main Rd CV7 7NH ☎(0676) 22735 FAX (0676) 22186

Conveniently situated in the centre of the village, this attractive Georgian property has been much extended to create a comfortable modern hotel. Rooms are well planned and attractive with pastel décor and light wood furnishings. There are 2 bars and the popular Regency Restaurant.
74⇨🛁 in 11 bedrooms CTV in all bedrooms ® ⚹ T sB&B⇨🛁£75-£85 dB&B⇨🛁£85-£95 🍴
(250P ✱
☺ English & French V ✿ ⚓ Lunch £11.95-£15.95&alc Dinner £11.95-£15.95&alc Last dinner 10pm
CONF. Thtr 275 Class 120 Board 44 Del from £102.50
Credit Cards ① ② ③ ⑤

MERTHYR TYDFIL Mid Glamorgan Map **03** SO00
See also **Nant-Ddu**
★★★ 60% Baverstock
The Heads Of Valley Rd CF44 0LX (approx 3m from Merthyr Tydfil on the A465 westbound) ☎(0685) 386221 FAX (0685) 723670
Bright open-plan public rooms and extensive function and meeting rooms are available at this busy commercial hotel on the Heads of the Valley road. Bedrooms are small but well equipped.
53⇨🛁(3fb) CTV in all bedrooms ® ⚹ T ✻ (ex guide dogs) ✱ sB&B⇨🛁£22-£39.50 dB&B⇨🛁£44-£55 🍴
(300P ✱ pool table snooker table *xmas*
☺ European V ✿ ⚓ ⚹ ✱ Lunch £7.25 Dinner £12.95&alc Last dinner 10pm
CONF. Thtr 400 Class 200 Board 40 Del £62.50
Credit Cards ① ② ③ ⑤

★★ 68% Tregenna
Park Ter CF47 8RF ☎(0685) 723627 & 382055 FAX (0685) 721951
Tregenna is a deservedly popular, family-run hotel, a short walk from the town centre. Bedrooms around the car park are large, and though some in the main house are compact, all have excellent facilities. There is a modern bar where bar meals are served. The main restaurant offers a lengthy carte with additional specials.
14🛁Annexe7⇨🛁(6fb)1🚲 CTV in all bedrooms ® T sB&B⇨🛁fr£39 dB&B⇨🛁fr£49 🍴
(CTV 60P *xmas*

426

♀ English, Indian, Italian & Philippino V ♂ ⚥ ⚲ Lunch fr£8&alc Dinner fr£8&alc Last dinner 10pm
CONF. Thtr 50 Board 12
Credit Cards [1][2][3]

⇧**Little Diner/L'European**
Dowlais Top CF48 2YE (NE of town, directly at junct of A470/A465) ☎(0685) 723362 FAX (0685) 376540
This small American-style diner, open from 7.30am to 9.50pm, serves a good range of budget-conscious family food. Bright, spotlessly clean and comfortable bedrooms are designed for both family and business guests and are best suited for a short stay.
6⇨♠(1fb) CTV in all bedrooms ® T ✻ sB⇨♠fr£28.50 dB⇨♠fr£30.50 (room only)
⊞ CTV 32P ♿
♂ ♌ ⚥
Credit Cards [1][2][3][5]

MEVAGISSEYCornwall & Isles of Scilly Map **02** SX04
★ **69%** *Sharksfin*
The Quay PL26 6QU ☎(0726) 843241
Closed Nov-Etr RS Oct-Nov
An unrivalled quayside location provides excellent views, particularly from the comfortable first-floor lounge. Bedrooms vary in size, but all have modern facilities including mini bars. The Quay-Hole is open all day for snacks, and there is a bar and attractive restaurant. Car parking can be difficult, though the Quay Wall car park is available at £1 a day. There are also 2 self-catering flats.
11rm(4♠)(2fb) CTV in all bedrooms ® T ✖
⚥ ♿
V ♂ ♌ Last dinner 9.50pm
Credit Cards [1][2][3][5]

MEYHighland *Caithness* Map **15** ND27
★★ **62%** **Castle Arms**
KW14 8XH (on A836) ☎(084755) 244 FAX (084755) 244
RS Nov-Mar
This small 19th-century roadside inn has recently been modernised to provide all the expected comforts. Some bedrooms are in the original building, but most are in converted stables overlooking a central courtyard. An attractive modern dining room offers a full à la carte menu, and a tempting range of dishes is also available in the popular lounge bar.
3⇨♠Annexe5⇨♠(1fb) CTV in all bedrooms ®
sB&B⇨♠£39 dB&B⇨♠£58
30P ❋ ♪ ♎
V ♂ ♌ Lunch £7.50 High tea £6.45 Dinner £16 Last dinner 9pm
Credit Cards [1][3] (£)

MICKLETONGloucestershire Map **04** SP14
★★★ **61%**Three Ways
GL55 6SB (Logis) ☎(0386) 438429 FAX (0386) 438118
The Three Ways has become famous for its Pudding Club, which meets once a fortnight to enjoy a range of classic English puddings. The restaurant serves a table d'hote menu and bar meals are also available. Privately owned and run by the Turner family, the hotel offers traditional levels of hospitality, and service is provided by friendly, willing staff. Bedrooms vary in size and can be rather dated but are warm and well equipped.
40⇨♠(5fb) CTV in all bedrooms ® T sB&B⇨♠fr£46 dB&B⇨♠fr£72 ♫
♪ 37P ❋ ♪ *xmas*
♀ English & Continental V ♂ ♌ Sunday Lunch fr£13 Dinner fr£17.50 Last dinner 9.30pm
CONF. Thtr 130 Class 40 Board 35 Del from £80
Credit Cards [1][2][3][5]

MIDDLEHAMNorth Yorkshire Map **07** SE18
★★ ❀**73%** **Millers House**
DL8 4NR ☎Wensleydale(0969) 22690 FAX (0969) 23570

Courtesy and Care 1994

Closed Jan
A delightful Georgian country house in a corner of the cobbled market square, this hospitable hotel is run under the personal supervision of owners Judith and Crossley Sunderland. They and their friendly staff have this year earned the AA's Courtesy and Care Award for their high standard of service and the warmth of their welcome. There has been extensive refurbishment in recent years, and the bedrooms are individually designed to retain character but provide every modern convenience. A fixed price menu with a good choice at each course is provided in the elegant dining room.
7rm(6⇨♠)1♫ CTV in all bedrooms ® T ✖ (ex guide dogs) ✻
sB&B£33.50-£41 dB&B⇨♠£67-£76 ♫
8P ♿ nc10yrs *xmas*

SYSONBY KNOLL
COMMENDED
HOTEL ★★

A privately owned and run hotel standing in its own grounds. All bedrooms have bathrooms en suite, TV and tea/coffee making facilities. Some ground floor bedrooms, also four poster bedrooms. Pleasant dining room overlooking swimming pool and gardens. Cosy bar and two lounges. Bar snacks, table d'hôte and à la carte menus available.

Reduced rates for weekends and bargain breaks available.

**Asfordby Road, MELTON MOWBRAY, Leics.
Tel: (0664) 63563.**

Middleham - Midhurst

♀ English & French **V** ♡ ✂ ✴ Dinner £17-£19.50 Last dinner 8.30pm
Credit Cards 1 3

MIDDLESBROUGH Cleveland Map 08 NZ42

★★★ 56% Marton Way Toby
Marton Rd TS4 3BS (S, off A172) (Toby) ☏(0642) 817651 FAX (0642) 829409
RS 24-25 Dec
This modern hotel has functional bedrooms set around a courtyard car park, and a popular carvery restaurant. Attractive flower tubs flank the main entrance.
53⇌♕(4fb)⊁in 18 bedrooms CTV in all bedrooms ® T ✴
sB&B⇌♕£25-£37.50 dB&B⇌♕£40-£47.50 ₧
(500P
♀ British & Continental **V** ♡ ♨ ✂ ✴ Lunch £5.99-£10.50
Dinner £5.99-£10.50 Last dinner 9.30pm
CONF. Thtr 85 Class 50 Board 40 Del from £55
Credit Cards 1 2 3 5

★ 63% The Grey House
79 Cambridge Rd, Linthorpe TS5 5NL
☏Middlesborough(0642) 817485
Set within its own rose gardens, this handsome Victorian house offers comfortable traditional bedrooms and a most inviting spacious lounge. Service from the resident proprietors is friendly and informal.
9⇌♕(1fb) CTV in all bedrooms ® sB&B⇌♕£32-£37 dB&B⇌♕£44-£49
10P ⊞
Credit Cards 1

MIDDLETON-IN-TEESDALE Co Durham Map 12 NY92

★★ 62% Teesdale
Market Place DL12 0QG ☏Teesdale(0833) 40264
This attractive stone-built hotel offers prettily furnished bedrooms with matching fabrics and wallpaper. There is a pleasant lounge on the first floor, and a well produced dinner is served in the restaurant each evening. The hotel is family owned and run and provides a good level of service.
13rm(7⇌3♕)(1fb)1⊞ CTV in all bedrooms T
sB&B⇌♕£38.50-£42.50 dB&Bfr£49.50 dB&B⇌♕£60.50-£85 ₧
14P ⊞ xmas
♀ English, French, German & Italian **V** ♡ ♨ ✴ Lunch £9.95
Dinner fr£16.95 Last dinner 8.30pm
Credit Cards 1 3 £

MIDDLETON STONEY Oxfordshire Map 04 SP52

★★ 67% Jersey Arms
OX6 8SE (on the B430 10m N of Oxford, between junct 9 & 10 of M40)
☏(086989) 234 & 505 FAX (086989) 565

This 17th-century coaching inn has old beams, granite lintels and log fires to create a traditional and relaxing atmosphere. Bedrooms vary from spacious courtyard rooms and suites to more compact rooms in the main building. Chef Alan Jefferson-Mackney has recently taken over in the kitchen.
6⇌Annexe10⇌(3fb)1⊞ CTV in all bedrooms T
✈ (ex guide dogs) sB&B⇌£59.50-£70 dB&B⇌£72-£105 ₧
55P ⊞ xmas
♀ English & French **V** ♡ ♨ Lunch £19.50-£25alc Dinner £19.50-£25alc Last dinner 9.30pm
Credit Cards 1 2 3 5

Hotels with red star ratings are especially high quality.

MIDDLE WALLOP Hampshire Map 04 SU23

★★ ❀❀71% Fifehead Manor
SO20 8EG ☏Andover(0264) 781565 FAX (0264) 781400
Closed 2wks Xmas
This country manor, parts of which date from the 11th century, has spacious bedrooms, an elegant drawing room, bar, reception foyer and attractive restaurant. The latter has a fine beamed ceiling, mullioned windows and stone fireplaces. Chef Mark Robertson has an uncomplicated modern style of cooking and he is assisted by an equally able patissière.
10⇌ CTV in all bedrooms T sB&B⇌£50 dB&B⇌£85-£95 ₧
50P ⊞ ✿ croquet
♀ English & French **V** ♡ ♨ Lunch £17.50&alc High tea £10-£12&alc Dinner £24&alc Last dinner 9.30pm
CONF. Thtr 40 Class 40 Board 20 Del £100
Credit Cards 1 2 3 5

MIDHURST West Sussex Map 04 SU82

★★★ ❀❀75% Angel
North St GU29 9DN ☏(0730) 812421 FAX (0730) 815928
This handsome old coaching inn with a walled garden has a popular public bar and the varied bedrooms are imaginatively furnished. There is an elegant small lounge, informal brasserie and a smart restaurant where chef/proprietor Peter Crawford-Rolt offers a daily changing carte offering a mix of traditional and modern dishes, unpretentiously and skilfully cooked. Our inspector enjoyed some delicious saddle of venison with a rich port sauce and an excellent crisp and piquant orange tart.
17⇌♕(2fb)1⊞⊁in 2 bedrooms CTV in all bedrooms T
✈ (ex guide dogs) ✴ sB&B⇌♕£55-£95 dB&B⇌♕£55-£95 ₧
40P ✿ xmas
♀ English & French **V** ♡ ♨ Lunch £3.50-£11.85alc Dinner £3.50-£11.85alc Last dinner 10pm
CONF. Thtr 80 Class 80 Board 80 Del from £105
Credit Cards 1 2 3 5 £

★★★ ❀68% Southdowns
Trotton GU31 5JN (on A272, after town turn left at Keepers Arms)
☏Rogate(0730) 821521 FAX (0730) 821790

This well managed hotel has a choice of individually furnished bedrooms with a good range of equipment. The Tudor Bar offers an alternative to the Country Restaurant, which has a dispense bar lounge, and there is now a new conservatory.
22⇌(3fb)1⊞⊁in 4 bedrooms CTV in all bedrooms ® T ✈
sB&B⇌£45-£60 dB&B⇌£70-£100 ₧
CTV 70P ✴ ⊟ (heated) ♁ (hard) ♪ sauna solarium croquet exercise equipment xmas
V ♡ ♨ ✴ Lunch £9.50-£20&alc High tea £5-£10 Dinner £12.50-£25alc Last dinner 10pm
CONF. Thtr 120 Class 30 Board 30 Del from £85
Credit Cards 1 2 3 5 £

★★★ ❀68% Spread Eagle
South St GU29 9NH ☏(0730) 816911 FAX (0730) 815668
This former coaching inn, dating back to 1430, retains many of its old beams and wood-panelled walls. Log fires burn throughout the hotel in the colder months and friendly professional staff provide good levels of service. Bedroom styles vary between rooms in the new and old wings or in a converted Elizabethan house opposite, but all are comfortable, well equipped and attractively furnished with antiques or reproduction pieces.
37⇌♕Annexe4♕5⊞ CTV in all bedrooms T sB&B⇌♕£59-£85 dB&B⇌♕£78-£130 Continental breakfast ₧
(80P ⊞ ✿ xmas

Midhurst - Milford on Sea

♧ English & French V ♤ ♧ ✂ ✱ Lunch £12.95-£16 Dinner £25.75 Last dinner 9.30pm
CONF. Thtr 70 Class 40 Board 35 Del £94
Credit Cards [1][2][3][5]

MIDSOMER NORTON Somerset Map 03 ST65

★★★**68%** Centurion
Charlton Ln BA3 4BD ☎(0761) 417711 FAX (0761) 418357
This pleasant family-run hotel incorporates the adjacent Fosseway Country Club with its golf course and other leisure amenities. Recently extended and upgraded, it has an attractive lounge and spacious, comfortable bedrooms furnished to a high standard with rich colour coordinated fabrics, the new rooms being particularly sumptuous.
44⇌♠(4fb) CTV in all bedrooms ® T ✈ (ex guide dogs) ⊄ 100P ✣ ⌷(heated) ▶ 9 squash snooker bowling green sports field
♧ English & Continental V ♤ ♧ Lunch £8.90&alc High tea £2.50-£5 Dinner £15.50&alc Last dinner 10pm
CONF. Thtr 180 Class 120 Board 50 Del £80
Credit Cards [1][2][3][5]

See advertisement under BATH

MILDENHALL Suffolk Map 05 TL77

★★★**64%** Smoke House Inn
Beck Row IP28 8DH (beside A1101)
☎(0638) 713223 FAX (0638) 712202 **CONSORT HOTELS**

The original part of this hotel dates from around 1600, with later additions in compatible style. All bedrooms offer modern amenities, the majority also containing good light furniture, though some annexe rooms are a little dated. Public areas include a choice of timbered bars with open fires and a 2-part restaurant.
105⇌♠Annexe10⇌♠(20fb) CTV in all bedrooms ®✸ T ✈ (ex guide dogs) sB&B⇌♠£66-£70 dB&B⇌♠£77-£85 ♬
⊄ CTV 200P ✣ ♗ (hard) snooker ♪ ♒ xmas
V ♤ ♧ ✂ Lunch £7.50-£12.50&alc High tea £6.50-£8.50 Dinner £16.50-£18.50&alc Last dinner 10pm
CONF. Thtr 120 Class 80 Board 40 Del from £90
Credit Cards [1][2][3][5]

★★★✿**63%** Riverside
Mill St IP28 7DP (taking A1101 into town, left at mini roundabout along High St, hotel is last building on left before bridge)
☎(0638) 717274 FAX (0638) 715997 **BEST WESTERN HOTELS**

This privately owned hotel, dating from 1720, lies on the banks of the River Lark. The bedrooms are attractively furnished with Laura Ashley fabrics and bathrooms are being modernised. There are 2 bars and a comfortable and attractive restaurant – the main feature of the hotel – overlooking the lawns and river and offering table d'hôte and à la carte menus.
21⇌♠(4fb)1⍰ CTV in all bedrooms ® T sB&B⇌♠fr£50 dB&B⇌♠£78-£90 ♬
Lift 50P ✣ ♪ private boats croquet xmas
♧ International V ♤ ♧ ✂ Sunday Lunch fr£11.50 High tea fr£5 Dinner fr£15&alc Last dinner 9pm
CONF. Thtr 50 Class 30 Board 26 Del from £83
Credit Cards [1][2][3][5]

MILFORD HAVEN Dyfed Map 02 SM90

★★**63%** Lord Nelson
Hamilton Ter SA73 3AL (follow signs for railway station and docks) ☎(0646) 695341 FAX (0646) 694026
Originally The New Inn, this harbour-front hotel dating from 1795 changed its name after a visit by the famous admiral. Bedrooms equipped with dark fitted furniture include a 4-poster suite with separate lounge, and guests can choose between the Trafalgar

Restaurant's à la carte menu and wide range of light meals served in the Hamilton Bar.
32⇌♠(1fb)1⍰✂in 2 bedrooms CTV in all bedrooms ® T ✈ (ex guide dogs) ✱ sB&B⇌♠£28-£42 dB&B⇌♠£44-£65 ♬
⊄ 26P ✣
♧ English, French & Italian V ♤ ✱ Lunch £10.95&alc Dinner £10.95&alc Last dinner 9.30pm
Credit Cards [1][2][3][5]

See advertisement on page 431

MILFORD ON SEA Hampshire Map 04 SZ29

★★★✿**72%** South Lawn
Lymington Rd SO41 0RF ☎Lymington(0590) 643911 FAX (0590) 644820
Closed 20 Dec-12 Jan
Ernst and Jennifer Barten maintain high standards of comfort at this quietly situated and well run hotel. Bedrooms, already well equipped, are being upgraded, and there is a spacious bar and lounge. Chef David Gates has an intelligent approach to cooking, and fresh local fish is particularly recommended, as are the home-made soups, home-smoked pork pâté and excellent crème caramel.
24⇌♠(2fb) CTV in all bedrooms T ✈ ✱ sB&B⇌♠£47.50-£54 dB&B⇌♠£84 ♬
50P ✣ nc7yrs
♧ International V ♤ ♧ ✂ Sunday Lunch fr£10 Dinner fr£15 Last dinner 8.30pm
Credit Cards [1][3]

See advertisement under LYMINGTON

For key to symbols see the Bookmark.

★★ ✿
Country Ways

**Marsh Lane, Farrington Gurney, Bristol.
Telephone: Temple Cloud (0761) 452449**

Spend some time relaxing in the warm, informal atmosphere of our country hotel situated halfway between Bath and Wells.
Enjoy a drink in front of the fire in winter or on the terrace when the sun shines, followed by good food and wine served with a smile.
Six delightful bedrooms all with bathrooms, telephone, colour television, radio and welcome tray.
See gazetteer entry under Farrington Gurney.

Milford on Sea - Milton Keynes

★★★ **60%** *Westover Hall*
Park Ln SO41 0PT ☎Lymington(0590) 643044 FAX (0590) 644490
On the western edge of the village overlooking Christchurch Bay, this late Victorian building has a galleried hall and wood-panelled public rooms, including a comfortable bar and restaurant offering a good standard of cooking. Bedrooms vary and provide old-fashioned comfort.
13⇌ CTV in all bedrooms ® T
50P 🚗 ❄
♀ English & French **V** ◊ ⊥ Last dinner 10pm
Credit Cards [1][2][3][5]

MILNGAVIE Strathclyde *Dunbartonshire* Map **11** NS57

★★★ **65%** Black Bull Thistle
Main St G62 6BH ☎041-956 2291 FAX 041-956 1896

THISTLE HOTELS

Once the village inn but now extended to cater for business guests and functions, the Black Bull has kept its period character. Bedrooms are all well equipped and there is a comfortable cocktail lounge adjoining the restaurant.
27⇌♠(2fb) CTV in all bedrooms ® T ✳ sB⇌♠£62-£75 dB⇌♠£75-£85 (room only) 🍴
(60P
♀ International **V** ◊ ⊥ ✳ Lunch £9.50 Dinner fr£15.75&alc Last dinner 9.30pm
Credit Cards [1][2][3][4][5]

MILTON Dyfed Map **02** SN00

★★ **62%** Milton Manor
SA70 8PG (3m E of Pembroke, off A477)
☎Carew(0646) 651398 FAX (0646) 651897

ExecGroup

Set in 6 acres of woodland, this Georgian manor house has modern, quite modest but well equipped bedrooms, several of them on the ground floor. There is a choice of lounges, a cosy bar and a restaurant offering a variety of dishes.
19⇌♠(1fb) CTV in all bedrooms ® T sB&B⇌♠£36 dB&B⇌♠£48 🍴
40P 3🅿 ❄ putting *xmas*
♀ International **V** ◊ ⊥ Lunch £2-£5.75 Dinner £12.75-£16.50 Last dinner 9pm
Credit Cards [1][3]

MILTON COMMON Oxfordshire Map **04** SP60

★★★ **68%** Belfry
Brimpton Grange OX9 2JW (on A40)
☎Great Milton(0844) 279381 FAX (0844) 279624
Closed 25-30 Dec RS Sat
This well managed hotel offers a variety of accommodation: suites, carefully designed new rooms and those of more modest standing. Formal meals are served in the attractive restaurant by smart and attentive staff, and the Tudor bar provides a relaxing atmosphere.
77⇌♠ CTV in all bedrooms ® T sB&B⇌♠fr£72.50 dB&B⇌♠fr£92.50 🍴
(200P ❄ ⬜ (heated) sauna solarium gymnasium
♀ English & Continental **V** ◊ ⊥ ✳ Lunch fr£15.50&alc Dinner fr£18.50&alc Last dinner 9.30pm
CONF. Thtr 250 Class 100 Board 60 Del £107.50
Credit Cards [1][2][3][5]
See advertisement under OXFORD

Irish entries appear in a separate section that follows the main directory.

MILTON, GREAT Oxfordshire Map **04** SP60

RELAIS & CHATEAUX. *Relais Gourmands*

★★★★
★★★★★❀❀❀❀🏅
LE MANOIR AUX QUAT' SAISONS
OX44 7PD ☎Great Milton (0844) 278881
FAX (0844) 278847

Raymond Blanc and his wonderful hotel and restaurant are most highly esteemed, and rightly so. Country house style prevails in a beautiful Cotswold stone manor house; the two lounges are models of comfort and good taste and bedrooms are delightful, mostly very spacious and with interesting antique furniture. Those in the stable wing have private patios and some also have whirlpool baths and steam showers. The kitchen has an idealistic dedication to the quality of ingredients, the integrity of flavours and the lightness of texture without sacrificing any vitality or imagination, and while the menus may comprise some of the most expensive dishes in the country, they are certainly among the best. Diners with a robust palate should try the foie gras layered with crispy galettes of potato and turnip, with a profound sherry sauce. Main courses might include oxtail with hermitage sauce or suckling pig with marjoram. And to round off the meal, a pistachio soufflé is light and full flavoured, with a hidden richness of chocolate ice cream within. The wine list is extensive and extravagant with plenty of bottle age and excellence of production.
19⇌♠4🛏 CTV in all bedrooms ⚜ T ✕ (ex guide dogs) dB⇌♠£165-£375 (room only) 🍴
(60P ❄ ⬜ (heated) ♪ (hard) ⚽ croquet *xmas*
♀ French **V** ◊ ⊥ ⚡ Lunch £29.50-£59.50&alc Dinner £59.50&alc Last dinner 10.30pm
CONF. Thtr 36 Board 32 Del from £190
Credit Cards [1][2][3][4][5]

MILTON KEYNES Buckinghamshire Map **04** SP83
See also **Hanslope** & **Woburn**

★★★★ ❀**70%** Milton Keynes Hotel & Conference Centre
Timbold Dr, Kents Hill MK7 6HL
☎(0908) 694433 FAX (0908) 695533

CONSORT CROWN

Comfortable and imaginative Spanish style public areas include an open-plan bar, separate residents' lounge and choice of restaurants – the more formal, Cellini's, offering carefully cooked traditional and modern French dishes. The spacious, comfortable bedrooms contained in a separate wing are all stylishly modern and provided with up-to-date amenities.
145⇌♠✕in 32 bedrooms CTV in all bedrooms ® T ✕ (ex guide dogs) sB&B⇌♠£55-£89.50 dB&B⇌♠£65-£99.50 Lift (220P ❄ ⬜ (heated) sauna spa bath steam room
♀ International **V** ◊ ⊥ ✳ Lunch fr£12.50 Dinner fr£16.50&alc Last dinner 10pm
CONF. Thtr 300 Class 120 Board 30 Del from £120
Credit Cards [1][2][3][4][5]

★★★ **67%** Coach House
London Rd, Moulsoe, Newport Pagnell MK16 0JA (1m from junct 14 of M1 on the A509) (Lansbury)
☎Newport Pagnell(0908) 613688 FAX (0908) 617335

Milton Keynes

An extended Georgian building enclosing a pretty courtyard and overlooking farmland to its rear. Bedrooms of a good size are very well equipped and attractive, with light oak furniture and modern fabrics, while public areas are both spacious and comfortable.
49⇌🚭(2fb)1🚭✄in 6 bedrooms CTV in all bedrooms ®⚡T ✗ (ex guide dogs) ✱ sB&B⇌🚭fr£79.50 dB&B⇌🚭fr£91 🍴
⟨ 162P sauna solarium gymnasium
♡ English & Continental V ⟡ ✄ ✻ Lunch £8.50-£10.50 Dinner fr£15.75 Last dinner 9.45pm
CONF. Thtr 200 Class 100 Board 50 Del from £110
Credit Cards [1] [2] [3] [5]

★★★ 61%Friendly
Monks Way, Two Mile Ash MK8 8LY (junct A5/A422) ☎(0908) 561666 FAX (0908) 568303

This modern hotel has bright and open plan public areas, which are a little limited in comfort, and breakfast is mainly self service. On the other hand, bedrooms are spacious and attractively furnished, and the hotel has a cheerful and informal atmosphere.
88⇌(20fb)2🚭✄in 20 bedrooms CTV in all bedrooms ®⚡T✻ sB⇌🚭£55-£67 dB⇌🚭£69.50-£82 (room only) 🍴
⟨ CTV 125P ✿ ▨ (heated) sauna solarium gymnasium jacuzzi
♡ English & French V ⟡ ⚲ ✄ ✻ Lunch £9.95&alc Dinner £12.50&alc Last dinner 9.45
CONF. Thtr 130 Class 60 Board 45 Del from £91
Credit Cards [1] [2] [3] [5]

★★ 62%Swan Revived
High St, Newport Pagnell MK16 8AR
☎Newport Pagnell(0908) 610565 FAX (0908) 210995
This extended and modernised coaching inn stands in the high street. Bedrooms vary in size and are contained on 3 floors, but all are smart, while public areas include a dark panelled reception lounge and a choice of bars.

MILTON KEYNES
For business or pleasure stay friendly

Friendly Hotel, A5/A422 Junction 14(M1), Monks Way, Two Mile Ash, Milton Keynes MK8 8LY.

AA ★★★

Premier Plus Rooms and Suites.
Own hotel parking. Fully equipped leisure centre. Situated in one of Europes rapidly expanding commercial centres, with easy access to the M1.

FOR RESERVATIONS (office hours) FREEPHONE
0800 591910
or call direct on 0908 561666 Fax: 0908 568303

It pays to stay Friendly

★★★AA
BLACK BULL
THISTLE HOTEL

Main Street, Glasgow G62 6BH
Tel: 041-956 2291 Fax: 041-956 1896

Your choice in
Milngavie

For Reservations at over 100
Mount Charlotte Thistle Hotels
Telephone London: 071 937 8033.

THISTLE HOTELS

LORD NELSON HOTEL
Hamilton Terrace, Milford Haven,
Dyfed SA73 2AL
Telephone: (0646) 695341
Fax: 0646 694026

AA ★★
WALES TOURIST BOARD ♛♛♛♛

Overlooking the Milford Waterway, the Lord Nelson Hotel is a comfortable modernised hotel that has not lost the personal touch.

Nearby attractions include the Pembrokeshire National Park, Pembroke Castle, also several sandy beaches.

Please telephone for brochure and special rates.

Milton Keynes - Moffat

42rm(40⇨♠)(2fb)1🛏 CTV in 40 bedrooms ®T
sB&B⇨♠£30-£58 dB&B⇨♠£55-£70 🍴
Lift (15P 3🚗
♀ English & Continental V ✿ ⌘ ✱ Lunch £8.50-£17.50alc
Dinner £8.50-£17.50alc Last dinner 10pm
Conf. Thtr 70 Class 30 Board 28 Del from £85
Credit Cards [1][2][3][5] £

• •

Forte Crest
500 Saxon Gate West MK9 2HQ ☎(0908) 667722
FAX (0908) 674714

A large modern hotel with a wide range of services and amenities, designed particularly for the business traveller. Bedrooms are smart, comfortable and well equipped. For more details about Forte Crest hotels, consult the Contents page, under Hotel Groups.

163⇨✱ B⇨£89 (room only)
Conf. Thtr 150 Class 60 Board 50 Del £115

Travel Inn
Secklow Gate West MK9 3BZ (follow H6 route)
☎(0908) 663388

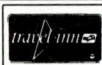

Purpose-built accommodation offers spacious and well equipped bedrooms, all with en suite bathrooms. Meals may be taken at the nearby family restaurant and pub. For more details about Travel Inns, consult the Contents page, under Hotel Groups.

38⇨♠ ✱ B⇨♠£33.50 (room only)

MINEHEAD Somerset Map **03** SS94

★★★**70%** Benares
Northfield Rd TA24 5PT (along sea front 75yds before harbour turn left into Blenheim Rd then right into Northfield Rd)
☎(0643) 704911 FAX (0643) 706373
Closed 6 Nov-21 Mar (ex Xmas)

This extended Edwardian house stands in a quiet residential road only a short walk from the town centre. Bedrooms are brightly decorated, and some enjoy views across the bay. Public areas are spacious and comfortable, with deep chintzy armchairs, a fine Italian fireplace and several coloured-glass windows.

19⇨♠(3fb) CTV in all bedrooms ®T sB&B⇨♠£36.50-£42.50 dB&B⇨♠£68-£79 🍴
20P 2🚌 (£1.75) 🎾 ✿ 🐕 *xmas*
♀ English, French & Italian V ✿ ⌘ ✱ Dinner £17 Last dinner 8.30pm
Credit Cards [1][2][3][5]

★★★**67%** Northfield
Northfield Rd TA24 5PU ☎(0643) 705155 FAX (0643) 707715

The hotel is set in beautiful gardens in an elevated position a short distance from the seafront. Bedrooms are generally of a reasonable size, simply furnished in traditional style, but many have good views. Public areas, also decorated in an older style, are spacious and comfortable. A table d'hôte menu is offered in 2 part wood panelled dining rooms.

24⇨♠(7fb) CTV in all bedrooms ®T sB&B⇨♠£43-£52 dB&B⇨♠£84-£94 🍴
Lift 44P 🎾 ✿ 🅿 (heated) solarium gymnasium putting green steam room spa bath *xmas*
V ✿ ⌘ ✱ Sunday Lunch fr£5alc Dinner fr£15 Last dinner 8.30pm
Credit Cards [1][2][3][5] £

Hotels with red star ratings are especially high quality.

★★🌸🌸♨**74%** Periton Park
Middlecombe TA24 8SW (Logis) ☎(0643) 706885 FAX (0643) 706885

This tranquil, well run hotel which dates back to 1875 still retains the ambience of a gentleman's country residence. Thoughtful service is provided by the proprietors, and chef Angela Hunt has recently been appointed to head the kitchen team. Elegantly stylish bedrooms equipped with modern facilities enjoy attractive views across the countryside, while public areas include a comfortable, book-filled drawing room.

8⇨♠(1fb)✂in 2 bedrooms CTV in all bedrooms ®T✱ sB&B⇨♠£59-£64 dB&B⇨♠£78-£88 🍴
12P 🎾 ✿ ♀ croquet nc12yrs *xmas*
♀ English & French V ✂ ✱ Dinner £19 Last dinner 9pm
Conf. Thtr 24 Board 14 Del £85
Credit Cards [1][2][3]

★★★**64%** Beaconwood
Church Rd, North Hill TA24 5SB ☎(0643) 702032
Closed Nov-Feb (ex Xmas)

This fine Edwardian country house hotel, personally run by its charming young owners, is set in 2 acres of well tended terraced gardens. Spacious and very comfortable public areas, filled with fresh flowers, provide a welcoming atmosphere in which to relax, while bedrooms, some with balconies, are steadily being improved. The restaurant's 4-course table d'hôte menu offers imaginative dishes prepared with flair.

16rm(13⇨♠)(3fb) CTV in all bedrooms ®T sB&B£28-£33 sB&B⇨♠£33-£38 dB&B£40-£45 dB&B⇨♠£50-£55 🍴
(25P ✿ ⌒ (heated) ♀ (grass) 🐕
V ✿ ⌘ ✱ Bar Lunch £1.50 High tea £6.50 Dinner £13 Last dinner 8pm
Credit Cards [1][3] £

MISKIN Mid Glamorgan Map **03** ST08

★★★**69%** Miskin Manor
CF7 8ND ☎Llantrisant(0443) 224204 FAX (0443) 237606

This elegant house is set back in 20 acres of woodland and gardens on the banks of Ely River. There are high-ceilinged, richly furnished public rooms of charm and character, including wood-panelled lounges, a cocktail bar and a comfortable restaurant. Bedrooms are very well proportioned with decent armchairs and a nice combination of antique and reproduction furniture.

35⇨♠2🛏✂in 12 bedrooms CTV in all bedrooms ®T
✈ (ex guide dogs)
(150P 🎾 ✿ ⌒ (heated) squash snooker sauna solarium gymnasium steam room badminton clay pigeon shoot
V ✿ ⌘ ✱ Last dinner 9.45pm
Credit Cards [1][2][3][5]

MOFFAT Dumfries & Galloway *Dumfriesshire* Map **11** NT00
See also **Beattock**
★★★**65%** Moffat House
High St DG10 9HL ☎(0683) 20039 FAX (0683) 21888

This family-run Georgian mansion house in the town centre has bright, mostly modern bedrooms, those in the former coach house being particularly spacious. A conservatory lounge overlooks the rear gardens and the spacious lounge bar is popular for its extensive bar menu.

16⇨♠ Annexe4⇨♠(3fb)1🛏 CTV in all bedrooms ®T sB&B⇨♠£35-£49 dB&B⇨♠£50-£75 🍴
40P 2🚌 ✿ 🐕
♀ Scottish & French V ✿ ⌘ ✱ Bar Lunch £4-£10alc Dinner £14.50-£17.50&alc Last dinner 8.45pm
Conf. Thtr 80 Class 20 Board 20 Del from £70
Credit Cards [1][2][3][5]

★★ ❀72% Beechwood Country House
Harthope Place DG10 9RS ☎(0683) 20210 FAX (0683) 20889
Closed 3 Jan-14 Feb

A school for young ladies in Victorian times, this friendly, family-run hotel has relaxing public areas and bedrooms which are individually decorated and equipped with a wide range of thoughtful extras. Chef Carl Shaw offers an imaginative fixed price menu, carefully prepared from the best fresh Scottish ingredients. Meals are efficiently served at candlelit tables in the neat dining room.

7⇌🅟(1fb) CTV in all bedrooms ® T
15P ₥ ✿
♀ English & French V ◊ ♨ ✂ Last dinner 9pm
Credit Cards ①②③

★★ 63% Annandale
High St DG10 9HF ☎(0683) 20013 FAX (0683) 21395

Family owned and run, this 18th-century coaching inn at the centre of the town offers friendly, willing service. Bedrooms range from the modestly appointed to more attractive rooms with smart modern bathrooms, while public areas include both a popular lounge bar and a stylish litle restaurant serving enjoyable meals.

(1fb)
40P
V ◊ ♨ Last dinner 9pm
Credit Cards ①③

★ ❀❀77% Well View
Ballplay Rd DG10 9JU (on A708 from Moffat, pass fire station and first left.) (Guestaccom) ☎(0683) 20184
Closed wk Jan & wk Nov

In an elevated position, this detached Victorian villa is run with care and enthusiasm by John and Janet Schuckardt. Bedrooms vary in size and style, but most have such extras as bathrobes and sherry decanters. There are 2 cosy lounges, and a small dining room is the setting for the 5-course dinners carefully prepared by Janet. Although her repertoire is not large, scallops, filo pastry and creamy sauces being favourites, everything from the tasty canapés to the petits fours is home made, and while some dishes are more successful than others, you are unlikely to be disappointed.

6⇌🅟1 ₥ ✂ in 2 bedrooms CTV in all bedrooms ®
sB&B⇌🅟£30-£40 dB&B⇌🅟£46-£76 🅁
8P ₥ ✿ xmas
♀ Scottish & French ◊ ♨ ✂ Lunch £9-£10 Dinner £20-£22
Last dinner 8.30pm
Credit Cards ①③ £

MOLD Clwyd Map 07 SJ26
See also **Nannerch** & **Northop Hall**

★★ 64% Bryn Awel
Denbigh Rd CH7 1BL (NW edge of town, on A541)
☎(0352) 758622 FAX (0352) 758625

Resident proprietors Terry and Heather Lally continue to improve this small, personally run hotel. The bedrooms are bright and modern, and there is a choice of eating options, with an à la carte restaurant and a good range of bar meals, which can be served in the bar or the pine furnished buttery.

7⇌🅟Annexe10⇌🅟1 ₥ ✂ in 5 bedrooms CTV in all bedrooms ® T ✱ sB&B⇌🅟£35-£38 dB&B⇌🅟£48-£50 🅁
40P 4₥ ✿
♀ English & Continental V ◊ ♨ Lunch £9.95&alc Dinner £9.95&alc Last dinner 9.30pm
Credit Cards ①②③⑤ £

For key to symbols see the Bookmark.

★★★
Moffat House Hotel
HIGH STREET, MOFFAT
DUMFRIESSHIRE DG10 9HL
Tel: (0683) 20039 Fax: (0683) 21288

Moffat House is a gracious 18th-c Adam mansion, centrally situated in 2½ acres of our own gardens. The charming village of Moffat is just off the A74 and provides an ideal stop-over for breaking your journey north/south. The hotel is fully licensed and we provide a wide range of bar lunches/suppers together with an extensive dinner menu. All our rooms have bath/shower with WC, central heating, telephone, colour TV, radio, tea/coffee tray and hairdryer.

We offer a 3 day D, B&B break throughout the season (any three days) for only £144.00 per person (until end March £132.00). Please send for brochure quoting MHH4 to 'the Reid family'.

BENARES HOTEL
★★★ 70%
Northfield Road, Minehead,
Somerset TA24 5PT.
Telephone (0643) 704911
Resident Proprietors: Peter Maskrey and Ray Thomas

Nestling at the foot of North Hill, 150 yards from the sea-front and set in one and a half acres of beautifully kept gardens, Benares Hotel is ideally situated for touring Exmoor, The Quantock Hills and the outstanding scenery of the Somerset and North Devon Coastline. To cope with large appetites after a day out on the moors, we serve a five course dinner with a number of choices for each course. All our bedrooms have bathrooms en suite and many have views over the bay, all have colour television, telephone and tea and coffee making facilities. *Car parking is available in the grounds.*

Moniaive - Morar

MONIAIVE Dumfries & Galloway *Dumfriesshire* Map **11** NX79

★★**64%** Woodlea
DG3 4EN (1.5m SW, beside A702) ☎(08482) 209
Closed Nov-mid Feb

Woodlea, a hotel geared to providing family holidays, is run in a relaxed, informal manner by its enthusiastic owners and their young staff. Guests are encouraged to make full use of all the facilities on offer and, as many of the activities provided are suitable for children of all ages, families return year after year to this unspoilt corner of Scotland.

12rm(10⇨)(7fb) CTV in all bedrooms ® T ✱ sB&B⇨£22-£42 dB&B⇨£44-£84 (incl dinner) 🍴
CTV 20P ✿ 🖾 (heated) ℘ (hard) sauna solarium pony riding croquet putting games room ⚒
V ✓ 🖳 ✱ Bar Lunch fr£2 High tea fr£3 Dinner fr£14 Last dinner 8.30pm

---

MONK FRYSTON North Yorkshire Map **08** SE52

★★★🏨**68%** Monk Fryston Hall
LS25 5DU (off A63) ☎South Milford(0977) 682369 FAX (0977) 683544

The Hall dates, in part, from the Middle Ages, and its grey stone walls, mullioned windows and wood panelling are characteristic of its age. Blazing log fires in the public rooms are a welcome sight on chilly days, and bedrooms are comfortable and have every modern facility. The restaurant, which features good British cooking, looks out on to the terrace and park.

28⇨(2fb)1🛏 CTV in all bedrooms ® T sB&B⇨£64-£82 dB&B⇨£98-£110 🍴
(60P ✿ ✱ xmas
✓ 🖳 ✱ Lunch £12.50-£14.50&alc Dinner £20-£24&alc Last dinner 9.30pm
CONF. Thtr 50 Class 40 Board 30 Del from £110
Credit Cards [1][2][3]

MONMOUTH Gwent Map **03** SO51

★★★**58%** Kings Head
Agincourt Square NP5 3DY ☎(0600) 712177 FAX (0600) 713545

There has been an improvement in the operation of this hotel with the fairly recent change of ownership. It has popular bars, full of character, and a choice of restaurants with friendly service provided by a young team of staff. A programme of upgrading has been embarked upon.

29rm(27⇨♠)(2fb)1🛏 CTV in all bedrooms ® T sB&B£25-£40 sB&B⇨♠£30-£44 dB&B£40-£50 dB&B⇨♠£50-£65 🍴
(35P 🅿 xmas
V ✓ 🖳 ✱ Lunch £5-£20&alc High tea £5-£20&alc Dinner £10-£50&alc Last dinner 9.45pm
CONF. Thtr 200 Class 120 Board 50 Del from £70
Credit Cards [1][2][3][5] £

★★**70%** Riverside
Cinderhill St NP5 3EY ☎(0600) 715577 & 713236

Situated close to the River Monnow, this popular, bustling little hotel makes a good business or holiday base and offers a sound standard of comfort. Proprietors Rodney and Judith Dodd promote a friendly, welcoming atmosphere.

17⇨♠(2fb)⊬ in 2 bedrooms CTV in all bedrooms ®✱ T sB&B⇨♠£35-£48 dB&B⇨♠£50-£68 🍴
30P xmas
✓ European V ✓ 🖳 ⊬ Sunday Lunch £7.95&alc Dinner £13&alc Last dinner 9.30pm
CONF. Thtr 200 Class 80 Board 80 Del from £37
Credit Cards [1][2][3] £

MONTACUTE Somerset Map **03** ST41

★★❀**67%** Kings Arms Inn
TA15 6UU ☎Martock(0935) 822513 FAX (0935) 826549
Closed 25-26 Dec

This small, creeper-clad inn is next to the church. Bedrooms are equipped with mini bars and many other thoughtful extras. The bar and lounge are cosy, and an interesting à la carte menu is available in the candlelit restaurant. Bread rolls are home made, and our inspector particularly enjoyed beautifully tender noisettes of lamb served with a red wine and shallot sauce.

11⇨♠1🛏 CTV in all bedrooms ® T ✖ (ex guide dogs) ✱ sB&B⇨♠£46-£59 dB&B⇨♠£64-£79 🍴
15P 🚲 ✿
✓ English & French V ✓ 🖳 ⊬ ✱ Dinner £14-£17alc Last dinner 9pm
Credit Cards [1][2][3][5]

MONTGOMERY Powys Map **07** SO29

★★**65%** Dragon SY15 6AA (behind the Town Hall)
☎(0686) 668359 & 668287 FAX (0686) 668359

Situated below the castle ruins, this former coaching inn dates back to the 17th century and some of its beams are said to have come from the castle. The former coach entrance has been converted into an enclosed patio lounge, the bar areas are comfortable and a good choice of food is available. The bedrooms are modern.

14⇨♠(5fb)⊬ in 2 bedrooms CTV in all bedrooms ® T sB&B⇨♠£41 dB&B⇨♠£67 🍴
21P 🖾 (heated) xmas
✓ Welsh & French V ✓ 🖳 ⊬ ✱ Lunch £9.75-£15.50&alc Dinner £15.50&alc Last dinner 9pm
Credit Cards [1][2][3]

MONTROSE Tayside *Angus* Map **15** NO75

★★★**61%** Park
61 John St DD10 8RJ ☎(0674) 73415 FAX (0674) 77091

Catering mainly for a business clientele, many of whom come from the Offshore Fire Training School, this hotel has been extended to offer practical, modern bedrooms which, at the time of the inspection, were being extended.

59rm(48⇨5♠)(4fb) CTV in all bedrooms ®✿ T sB&B⇨♠£45-£75 dB&B⇨♠£55-£85 🍴
(CTV 50P ✱ xmas
V ✓ 🖳 ✱ Lunch £6.50-£9&alc Dinner £16.50&alc Last dinner 9.30pm
CONF. Thtr 250 Class 80 Board 50 Del from £51.50
Credit Cards [1][2][3][5]

MORAR Highland *Inverness-shire* Map **13** NM69

★★**61%** Morar
PH40 4PA ☎Mallaig(0687) 2346 FAX (0687) 2130
Closed 22 Oct-Mar

This family-run Highland hotel, beside the railway station and overlooking the famous silver sands, is a popular base for tour groups. It offers good value, practical accommodation together with traditional services and comforts.

27⇨(3fb) CTV in all bedrooms ® ✱
CTV 50P ♪
✓ French V ✓ 🖳 ✱ Bar Lunch £2-£5alc Dinner £16-£20 Last dinner 8.30pm

---

All black star hotels are given a percentage grading within their star bands. See 'Using the Guide' at the front of the book for full details.

MORCOTT Leicestershire Map 04 SK90

Forte Travelodge
Uppingham (on A47, eastbound)
☎(0572) 87719 Central Res (0800) 850911

This modern building offers a good standard of accommodation for overnight stops. Smart, spacious and well equipped bedrooms, all with en suite bathrooms, are suitable for family use, and meals may be taken at the nearby family restaurant. For more details about Travelodges, consult the Contents page, under Hotel Groups.
40⇌♠✷ B⇌♠£31.95 (room only)

MORDEN Greater London

See **LONDON SECTION plan 1**C1
Forte Travelodge
Epsom Rd (on A24)
☎081-640 8227 Central Res (0800) 850950

This modern building offers a good standard of accommodation for overnight stops. Smart, spacious and well equipped bedrooms, all with en suite bathrooms, are suitable for family use, and meals may be taken at the nearby family restaurant. For more details about Travelodges, consult the Contents page, under Hotel Groups.
32⇌♠✷ B⇌♠£31.95 (room only)

MORECAMBE Lancashire Map 07 SD46

★★★**66%** Strathmore
East Promenade LA5 5AP ☎(0524) 421234
FAX (0524) 414242

Situated on the seafront with fine views over the bay, this well managed, very clean hotel has a friendly atmosphere. Bedrooms are generally compact but are thoughtfully designed and have all modern amenities. Attractive modern public areas include a comfortable lounge bar and popular restaurant.
51⇌♠(6fb) CTV in all bedrooms ®⚓T✱ (ex guide dogs)
Lift (30P 12☎ ♫
♢ French V ✿ ♨ ✣ Last dinner 10pm
CONF. Thtr 200 Class 100 Board 70 Del £74
Credit Cards ①②③⑤ £

★★★**64%** Elms
Bare Village LA4 6DD ☎(0524) 411501 FAX (0524) 831979

Standing in its own grounds just off the seafront at Bare, this well managed hotel continues to be improved. Individually decorated bedrooms are equipped with modern facilities and friendly staff provide attentive service in the traditional-style public areas.
40⇌♠(3fb)3⚑ CTV in all bedrooms ® T✱ sB&B⇌♠£50-£55 dB&B⇌♠£72 ☒
Lift (CTV 80P ✣ ⚑ xmas
♢ English & French V ✿ ♨ ✱ Lunch £9.75-£9.95&alc High tea fr£5.95 Dinner fr£14.95&alc Last dinner 9.30pm
CONF. Thtr 200 Class 72 Board 60 Del £54
Credit Cards ①②③⑤ £

★★★**59%** Headway
Marine Rd East LA4 5AW ☎(0524) 412525 FAX (0524) 832630
RS Nov-Apr

Located on the Eastern Promenade, this friendly seafront hotel is popular with coach tours and offers generally compact, plainly furnished bedrooms. Public areas include a spacious lounge bar and a large, garden-level restaurant.
51⇌♠(4fb)1⚑ CTV in all bedrooms ® T✱ (ex guide dogs)
✷ sB&B⇌♠£35-£42.50 dB&B⇌♠£60-£69
Lift (20P xmas

V ✿ ♨ ✷ Bar Lunch £1.50-£5alc Dinner £12&alc Last dinner 8pm
CONF. Thtr 200 Class 50 Board 100 Del from £25
Credit Cards ①②③⑤

★★**60%** Clarendon
Promenade, West End LA4 4EP ☎(0524) 410180 FAX (0524) 421616
Closed Xmas wk
This sound seafront hotel popular with both tourists and business guests, offers neat bedrooms, a popular bar and a quieter residents' lounge on the first floor.
31rm(28⇌♠)(5fb) CTV in all bedrooms ® T✱ sB&B£25-£29 sB&B⇌♠£25-£29 dB&B£40-£45 dB&B⇌♠£40-£45 ☒
Lift (CTV ⚑ games room
V ✿ ♨ Sunday Lunch £6.25 Dinner £6.20-£13.40 Last dinner 9pm
CONF. Thtr 40 Board 20 Del from £36
Credit Cards ①②③⑤ £

MORETONHAMPSTEAD Devon Map 03 SX78

★★**70%** The White Hart
The Square TQ13 8NF (at junct of A382/B3212)
☎(0647) 40406 FAX (0647) 40565
Closed 25-26 Dec

This white-painted Georgian posting house is popular with visitors to the moor who will find a warm welcome, comfortable accommodation, good ale and hearty meals. The bedrooms incorporate present day comforts while retaining their original charm. An extensive choice of dishes is available from the table d'hôte with à la carte menus in the traditional dining room.
20⇌♠(3fb)✣ in 2 bedrooms CTV in all bedrooms ®⚓T✱ sB&B⇌♠£43 dB&B⇌♠£63 ☒
12P nc10yrs *xmas*

Moretonhampstead - Mousehole

English & French V Sunday Lunch £6.25-£9.25
Dinner £15.95-£17.50&alc Last dinner 8.30pm
CONF. Thtr 80 Class 50 Board 40 Del from £48
Credit Cards 1 2 3 5 £

MORETON-IN-MARSH Gloucestershire Map 04 SP23

★★★ ❀69% **Manor House**
High St GL56 0LJ ☎(0608) 50501 FAX (0608) 51381

Dating from the 16th century, this hotel is undergoing a complete refurbishment which will retain many original features such as beams and flagstone floors. Chef Luc Gabard offers inviting table d'hôte and à la carte menus. A typical meal may begin with a wild mushroom risotto, followed by chicken thighs with a leek mousse on a watercress sauce, finishing with banana parfait with a rich dark chocolate sauce.
38rm 4 CTV in all bedrooms ® T ✱ sB&B £63.50-£72 dB&B £83-£98
Lift 25P (heated) sauna spa bath xmas
English & French V Lunch fr£12.95&alc Dinner fr£19.50&alc Last dinner 9.30pm
CONF. Thtr 80 Class 55 Board 50 Del £110
Credit Cards 1 2 3 5

★★ 61% **The White Hart Royal**
High St GL56 0BA (on Fosse Way (A429))
☎(0608) 650731 FAX (0608) 650880

Bedrooms are in the process of being upgraded at this Cotswold inn with its flagstone and cobbled floors. The bar is congenial and justifiably popular, the restaurant pleasant and there is a cosy residents' lounge.
20rm (4fb) 1 CTV in all bedrooms ® T sB&Bfr£50 sB&B £50-£60 dB&B £65-£85
CTV 7P xmas
V Sunday Lunch £8.95-£12.95 High tea £2.50-£6
Dinner £13.95-£16.95&alc Last dinner 9.30pm
CONF. Thtr 60 Class 20 Board 20 Del from £65
Credit Cards 1 2 3 4 5 £

MORFA NEFYN Gwynedd Map 06 SH24

★★ 58% **Linksway**
LL53 6BG ☎Nefyn(0758) 720258 FAX (0758) 720895

This small holiday hotel, close to both the beach and golf course, provides friendly informal service. Bedrooms are neat and compact and the open-plan public areas are comfortable.
26rm(11⇨10)(1fb) CTV in all bedrooms ®
(ex guide dogs) sB&B £25-£40 dB&B £35-£50
CTV 60P xmas
V Bar Lunch £1.15-£7.70 Dinner £11.50&alc Last dinner 9pm
Credit Cards 1 3 £

MORPETH Northumberland Map 12 NZ28

★★★★ ❀75% **Linden Hall**
NE65 8XF ☎(0670) 516611 FAX (0670) 188544
(For full entry see Longhorsley)

If you have booked a meal in a hotel restaurant and cannot get there, remember you have a contractual obligation to cancel your booking.

MORTEHOE

See **Woolacombe**

MOTHERWELL Strathclyde *Lanarkshire* Map 11 NS75

Travel Inn
Glasgow Rd, Newhouse ML1 5SY (leave M74 junc5 onto A725 then follow A8 until M8 roundabout. Turn right onto A73 then first left)
☎Cleland (0698) 860277

Purpose-built accommodation offers spacious and well equipped bedrooms, all with en suite bathrooms. Meals may be taken at the nearby family restaurant and pub. For more details about Travel Inns, consult the Contents page, under Hotel Groups.
40⇨ ✱ B £33.50 (room only)

MOULSFORD Oxfordshire Map 04 SU58

★★ ❀❀❀74% **Beetle & Wedge**
Ferry Ln OX10 9JF ☎Cholsey(0491) 651381 FAX (0491) 651376
Closed 25 Dec

In pretty gardens on the banks of the Thames is Richard and Kate Smith's Beetle & Wedge. The majority of bedrooms have river views, and bathrooms are mostly Victorian in style, spacious and indulgent. The large lounge has a coal fire, and in the dining room Richard Smith's daily carte is offered. A recent test meal consisted of a delicately flavoured hot spinach soufflé with a shrimp sauce. A supreme of Aylesbury duck with apples and Somerset brandy sauce followed and the final course was an individual raspberry and apple crumble with rather grainy home-made vanilla ice cream. Across the car park is the old beamed boathouse, which has been established as an informal bar restaurant with an open char-grill.
6rm Annexe4⇨ 1 in 6 bedrooms CTV in all bedrooms ® T ✱ sB&B £65-£100 dB&B £75-£125
34P
V
CONF. Thtr 50 Class 30 Board 25
Credit Cards 1 2 3 5

MOUNT HAWKE Cornwall & Isles of Scilly Map 02 SW74

★ ❀75% **Tregarthen Country Cottage**
Banns Rd TR4 8BW (from the A30 turn off at Three Burrows roundabout onto the B3277 St Agnes road, take first left and follow signs to Mount Hawke approx 2m)
☎Porthtowan(0209) 890399 FAX (0209) 891041

This charming little hotel on the edge of the village provides guests with a warm welcome. The comfortable, prettily decorated bedrooms have many thoughtful extras, there is a cosy lounge and bar area, and a set menu of traditional home-cooked dishes.
6⇨ in all bedrooms (ex guide dogs) sB&B £35 dB&B £70 (incl dinner)
CTV 12P
✱ Dinner £10-£12 Last dinner 8pm

MOUSEHOLE Cornwall & Isles of Scilly Map 02 SW42

★★ 67% **Lobster Pot**
South Cliff TR19 6QX ☎Penzance(0736) 731251 FAX (0736) 731140
Closed last 3 wks Jan RS Feb-mid Mar

This delightful harbourside hotel and restaurant offers a range of services normally associated with hotels of a higher classification. Literally hanging over the harbour, the cottagey bedrooms lack space because of architectural constraints, but are pleasantly furnished and decorated. The restaurant serves a good range of fresh dishes with fish predominating.
13⇨ Annexe12rm(9⇨)(5fb) CTV in all bedrooms ® T (ex guide dogs)

Mousehole - Mull, Isle of, Bunessan

CTV ♪
English & French V ⌀ ⚲ ✂ Last dinner 9.45pm
Credit Cards [1][3]

★★ 59% **Carn Du**
Raginnis Hill TR19 6SS ☎Penzance(0736) 731233
The Carn Du is a friendly hotel, modestly appointed, serving worthy home-cooked food with the emphasis on fish. The elevated position offers unrestricted views over the southwest peninsula and out to sea. Bedrooms are a little small but soundly furnished.
7⇨↑ CTV in all bedrooms ® ✖ sB&B⇨↑£25-£30 dB&B⇨↑£50-£60 ⎕
12P 🚗 ❄
English & German V ⌀ ✂ Bar Lunch £3.95-£5.95 Dinner £14.95 Last dinner 8pm
Credit Cards [1][2][3]

MUCH BIRCH Hereford & Worcester Map 03 SO53

★★★ 60% **Pilgrim**
Ross Rd HR2 8HJ (on A49, between Hereford & Ross on Wye)
☎Golden Valley(0981) 540742 FAX (0981) 540620
Set in 4 acres of grounds, this family-run modernised rectory has a cosy lounge, good bar and restaurant. Upgrading of the modern bedrooms, many with country views, should shortly be completed.
20⇨↑(3fb)2🚭 CTV in all bedrooms ® ✖ sB&B⇨↑£39.50-£69.50 dB&B⇨↑£45-£90 ⎕
40P 🚗 ❄ croquet putting pitch & putt badminton *xmas*
English & French V ⌀ ⚲ ✖ Bar Lunch £2.75-£5.95alc Dinner £19.50&alc Last dinner 9.45pm
Credit Cards [1][2][3][5] (£)

See advertisement under HEREFORD

MUCH WENLOCK Shropshire Map 07 SO69

★★ 69% **Raven**
30 Barrow St TF13 6EN ☎(0952) 727251 FAX (0952) 728416
Situated in the heart of this historic Shropshire town, the Raven dates from 1700, when it was a coaching inn. Complete refurbishment was underway when this guide went to print, and the bedrooms so far completed offer an excellent standard of accommodation. The bar is very comfortable and there is a small, pretty restaurant (a larger one is planned for 1994); food is offered on a small carte and a wide range of bar meals.
8⇨↑ CTV in all bedrooms ®🐾 T ✖ (ex guide dogs) ✱
sB&B⇨↑fr£45 dB&B⇨↑fr£58 Continental breakfast ⎕
30P 🚗 ♫
International V ✂ ✱ Sunday Lunch £8-£10alc Dinner £12-£16.50alc Last dinner 9.30pm
Credit Cards [1][2][3]

★★ 66% **Wheatland Fox**
TF13 6AD ☎(0952) 727292
This small personally run hotel in the centre of the medieval town dates in part from 1669 and has bedrooms with all modern facilities, those in the main house having beams and uneven floors. Both the pretty restaurant and cheerful bar offer good-value food.
3⇨↑Annexe2⇨↑ CTV in all bedrooms ® ✖ sB&B⇨↑£35-£45 dB&B⇨↑£50-£60 ⎕
12P 🚗
English & French V ⌀ ⚲ ✂ ✱ Sunday Lunch £6.95-£8.95alc Dinner £8.95-£15alc Last dinner 9pm
Credit Cards [1][2][3][5] (£)

★★ 59% **Gaskell Arms**
Bourton Rd TF13 6AQ (on A458) ☎(0952) 727212 FAX (0952) 727736
This creeper-clad inn has traditional, beamed bars with polished tables and open log fires, which are popular for their convivial atmosphere and good bar food. In summer, guests can sit in the beautifully kept garden, and there is also a separate restaurant. Bedrooms are neat and well decorated.

11rm(6⇨↑)(2fb) CTV in all bedrooms ® T ✖ sB&B£20-£28 sB&B⇨↑£36 dB&B£44-£46 dB&B⇨↑£50-£56 ⎕
30P 1🚗 ❄ ♪
V ⌀ ✂ Lunch £8.95-£10.95&alc Dinner £10.95&alc Last dinner 9.30pm
CONF. Del from £40
Credit Cards [1][2][3] (£)

MUDEFORD
See **Christchurch**

MULL, ISLE OF Strathclyde *Argyllshire* Map **10**

BUNESSAN Map **10** NM32

★🔴 66% **Assapol Country House**
PA67 6DW (turn off A849 just after Bunessan School and follow signpost for 1m on minor road) ☎Fionnphort(06817) 258 FAX (06817) 445
Closed Nov-Mar
This former manse with grounds leading down to the lochside has been converted into a cosy hotel by Harry and Mary Kay, who provide warm hospitality and good home-cooked dinners. Bedrooms give fine views and there is a comfortable lounge where drinks are served.
7⇨↑(1fb)✂in all bedrooms ® ✖ (ex guide dogs)
sB&B⇨↑£24-£28 dB&B⇨↑£48-£56
CTV 12P 🚗 ❄ ♪ nc12yrs
✂ Dinner £14 Last dinner 7pm
Credit Cards [1][3]

Hotels with red star ratings are especially high quality.

Mousehole, Cornwall
Tel: (0736) 731251 Fax: (0736) 731140

This 25 bedroomed Hotel & Restaurant, perched on the harbour's edge in Mousehole, offers a comfort and cuisine out of the ordinary. Seafood is a speciality and can be found daily on both the Table d'hôte and A la Carte Menus.

We offer bargain Mid-Week and Week-End Breaks, including dinner throughout the year.

Family rooms are available with special rates for Children.

Open to Non-Residents

Mull, Isle of, Dervaig - Musselburgh

DERVAIG Map 13 NM45

★ 🍴 79% **Druimard Country House**
PA75 6QW ☎(06884) 345
RS Nov-Feb

This delightful small hotel overlooks the glen and the River Bellart and its new owners, Mr and Mrs Hubbard, though new to the hotel business, show a natural flair and offer warm hospitality. Bedrooms are plain, but well equipped and public areas include a very cosy lounge, a bright conservatory bar and a dining room where well presented and carefully cooked dishes are served.

7rm(3⇨)(1fb) CTV in all bedrooms ® T ✱ sB£49.50 dBfr£66 dB⇨£77 (room only) 🅿
20P 🚭 ❀
V ✄
Credit Cards 1 3

PENNYGHAEL Map 10 NM52

★★ 66% **Pennyghael**
PA70 6HB (Logis) ☎(06814) 288 & 205
Closed Nov-Feb

This former byre has been through various stages of development and is now a charming little holiday hotel, by the shore of Loch Scridain on the road to the Iona ferry. Cottage-style bedrooms are well equipped and the atmosphere is informal and relaxed.

6⇨ CTV in all bedrooms ® T sB&B⇨£45-£65 dB&B⇨£90-£110 (incl dinner)
30P 🚭 ❀
❀ ✄ Last dinner 8.30pm
Credit Cards 1 3

TOBERMORY Map 13 NM55

★★★ 68% **Western Isles**
PA75 6PR ☎(0688) 2012 FAX (0688) 2297
Closed 1st week Feb

Dramatically situated, with spectacular views across the picturesque village and the Sound of Mull, this traditional hotel is constantly being improved. All bedrooms have been individually decorated and attractively furnished; the best, named after whisky distilleries, are particularly relaxing. Interesting paintings and prints enhance public areas.

27⇨(2fb)1🛁 CTV in all bedrooms ® T sB&B⇨£34.50-£70 dB&B⇨£68-£140 🅿
20P ❀ ♭ 9 xmas
☕ French V ❀ ✄ ✱ Bar Lunch £4-£9 Dinner fr£21.50 Last dinner 8.30pm
Credit Cards 1 3

★ 63% **Ulva House**
PA75 6PR ☎(0688) 2044
Closed Nov-Feb

This family-run Victorian house sits high above the town, with splendid views of the bay. David Woodhouse, a talented artist and authority on the island's wildlife, organises wildlife expeditions, with the possibility of spotting otters, badgers and many other kinds of animals and birds. Joy Woodhouse's hearty cordon bleu dinners provide the perfect conclusion to the day.

6rm(1⇨2🛁)(3fb) ® sB&B£25.95-£40.95 sB&B⇨🛁£40.95 dB&B£51.95 dB&B⇨🛁£68.90
CTV 8P 🚭 ❀
☕ International V ❀ ✱ Lunch £14.50 Dinner £14.50 Last dinner 8pm

★ 60% **Mishnish**
Main St PA75 6NU ☎(0688) 2009 FAX (0688) 2462

This harbour-front hotel is popular with the sailing fraternity, but is not for those seeking a quiet and restful atmosphere as the bars are always busy and offer live entertainment most evenings.

12rm(7⇨2🛁)(2fb) CTV in all bedrooms ®
🅿 ✄ ♪
V ❀ ✄ Last dinner 9pm

MULLION Cornwall & Isles of Scilly Map 02 SW61

★★★ 🍴74% *Polurrian*
TR12 7EN ☎(0326) 240421 FAX (0326) 240083
Closed Nov-Mar

This whitewashed Edwardian hotel stands on the cliff top above Polurrian Cove. It is professionally run by the welcoming Francis family, with cheerful staff and high standards of service. Public rooms are smart and comfortably furnished, and bedrooms are attractively decorated, many with sea views.

40rm(38⇨🛁)(22fb)5🛏 CTV in all bedrooms T
☾ 80P ❀ 🏊 (heated) ⛱ (heated) ♞ (hard) squash snooker sauna solarium gymnasium cricket net whirlpool putting croquet 🛷
☕ English & French V ❀ ✄ Last dinner 8.45pm
Credit Cards 1 2 3 5

MUMBLES (NEAR SWANSEA) West Glamorgan Map 02 SS68

See also **Langland Bay** and **Swansea**
★ 63% **St Anne's**
Western Ln SA3 4EY ☎Swansea(0792) 369147 FAX (0792) 360537

Many rooms in this popular holiday and commercial hotel overlooking Swansea Bay have fine views. Bedrooms are currently being improved and there is a comfortable residents' lounge.

24rm(15⇨🛁)Annexe4rm(2🛁)(1fb) CTV in all bedrooms ® T sB&B£29 sB&B⇨🛁£33 dB&B£47 dB&B⇨🛁£54.50 🅿
CTV 50P ❀ snooker gymnasium 🛷
V ❀ ✄
Credit Cards 1 3

MUNGRISDALE Cumbria Map 11 NY33

★ 🍴 **The Mill**
CA11 0XR ☎Threlkeld(07687) 79659

Closed Dec & Jan

This charming little hotel standing on a gentle hillside beside a trout stream is run by hospitable owners Richard and Eleanor Quinlan. There are cosy bedrooms and comfortable lounges. Eleanor's 5-course dinners are highly enjoyable. Breads, soups and puddings are all home-made and the daily changing menu relies on fresh local produce, with lamb a regular speciality.

7rm(5⇨🛁) CTV in all bedrooms ® sB&B£25-£30 sB&B⇨🛁£30-£35 dB&B£50-£60 dB&B⇨🛁£60-£70
CTV 15P 🚭 ❀ ♪ games room
☕ English & French V ❀ ✄ ✱ Dinner £18.50-£19.50 Last dinner 8pm

MUSSELBURGH Lothian *Midlothian* Map 11 NT37

Granada Lodge
A1 Old Craighall EH21 8RE (off A1, 2m from eastern outskirts Edinburgh) ☎031-653 2427 FAX 031-653 6106

This modern building provides smart, spacious and well equipped bedrooms, all with en suite bathrooms. Meals may be taken at a nearby family restaurant. For more details about Granada Lodges, consult the Contents page, under Hotel Groups.

44⇨🛁 ✱ B⇨🛁£34.95-£37.95 (room only)

Nairn - Nantwich

NAIRN Highland *Nairnshire* Map **14** NH85

★★★★60% Golf View
Seabank Rd IV12 4HG ☎(0667) 52301 FAX (0667) 55267
Pleasantly situated in a quiet residential area and directly overlooking the Moray Firth, this well established resort hotel is once again in private ownership. A programme of refurbishment has begun and some of the public areas have already been improved; work on the bedrooms is to continue through 1994.
47⇌♠(3fb)1⌑ CTV in all bedrooms ®≩ T ✱
sB&B⇌♠£49.50-£75 dB&B⇌♠£88-£128 (incl dinner) 🅿
Lift (❀ ⌆ (heated) ♪ (hard) sauna ♫ xmas
♡ ⌆ ✱ Lunch £7.60-£12alc Dinner £17.95-£21&alc Last dinner 9.15pm
Credit Cards ①②③⑤

★★63% Claymore House
45 Seabank Rd IV12 4EY ☎(0667) 53731 FAX (0667) 55290
This extended Victorian house, in a quiet residential area, is a popular base for business guests and holiday-makers. Tastefully appointed public areas include an attractive restaurant and comfortable lounge bar. Bedrooms are modern, and though they vary in size they provide a good range of amenities.
12⇌♠(1fb) CTV in all bedrooms ®≩ T
35P ❀ ♫
♡ International V ♡ ⌆ Last dinner 9.30pm
Credit Cards ①②③

★★59% Alton Burn
Alton Burn Rd IV12 5ND ☎(0667) 52051
RS Oct-Mar
This popular family-run golfing and holiday hotel on the western fringe of the town enjoys views across the golf course to the Moray Firth. It offers traditional services and practical, rather dated bedrooms to which improvements are planned.
19rm(14⇌3♠)Annexe7⇌♠(6fb) CTV in 25 bedrooms ®
CTV 30P ❀ ⌆ (heated) ♪ (hard) ⌂ putting green games room ⌑
♡ International V ♡ Last dinner 9pm
Credit Cards ①③

★★59% Carnach House
Delnies IV12 5NT (2m W A96) ☎(0667) 52094
Set in 8 acres of wooded grounds overlooking the Moray Firth, this attractive Edwardian house is personally run and has generally spacious bedrooms with amenities suited to business or tourist guests. Public rooms include a well stocked bar and comfortable lounge.
14rm(13⇌♠)(1fb)1⌑ CTV in all bedrooms ® T
15P ⛟ ❀ ☉
♡ European V ♡ ⌁ Last dinner 9pm
Credit Cards ①②③

NANNERCH Clwyd Map **07** SJ16

★★68% The Old Mill
Melin-Y-Wern, Denbigh Rd CH7 5RH
☎Mold(0352) 741542 FAX (0352) 741542
Closed 24-26 Dec
Set in 1.5 acres of grounds and flanked by a mill stream and the River Wheeler, this delightful small hotel with a strict no-smoking rule forms part of a complex including an art gallery showing the works of resident artist Alex Campbell. A fixed price evening menu offers a good choice with some Indian and vegetarian dishes.
7⇌♠(3fb)⌁ in all bedrooms CTV in all bedrooms ® T
sB&B⇌♠£32.50-£36 dB&B⇌♠£46.50-£49.50 🅿
12P ⛟ ❀
V ⌁ ✱ Dinner £14-£19.75 Last dinner 7.30pm
Credit Cards ①②③⑤

NANT-DDU (NEAR MERTHYR TYDFIL) Powys
Map **03** SO01

★★62% Nant Ddu Lodge
Cwm Taf CF48 2HY (5m N of Merthyr Tydfil on A470 near Brecon)
☎Merthyr Tydfil(0685) 379111 FAX (0685) 377088
Originally a shooting lodge, this hotel at the heart of the Brecon Beacons stands among tall pine trees. Most bedrooms are fitted with dark reproduction furniture, one with a private sitting room. The cheerful bar, warmed by a wood-burning stove, offers a wide range of bar food as an alternative to the restaurant's more substantial meals.
14⇌♠(1fb)2⌑ CTV in all bedrooms ®≩ T ✱
sB&B⇌♠£37.50-£45 dB&B⇌♠£49.50-£60 🅿
30P ❀
V ♡ ⌁ ✱ Lunch £7.95-£11.95alc Dinner £9.95-£16.95alc
Last dinner 9pm
CONF. Thtr 30 Class 20 Board 20 Del from £45
Credit Cards ①②③   £
See advertisement under BRECON

NANTWICH Cheshire Map **07** SJ65

★★★★⌂70% Rookery Hall
Worleston CW5 6DQ (2m N B5074) ☎(0270) 610016 FAX (0270) 626027
Built in 1816 and surrounded by 200 acres of grounds, this Regency country mansion has recently been extended to provide extra accommodation. Public areas include 2 delightful lounges, an elegant dining room, and a morning room where breakfast is served. Chef David Alton produces an imaginative set price menu. Attentive personal service is provided by manager Philip Parker and his professional team.

THE WESTERN ISLES HOTEL
★★★

TOBERMORY, ISLE OF MULL
Tel: 0688 2012 Fax: 0688 2297

Superbly situated overlooking Tobermory Bay and the Sound of Mull. The hotel offers peace and tranquillity with well-appointed rooms. The hotel, under the ownership of Sue & Michael Fink has undergone complete redecoration and refurbishment.

We offer a high standard of cuisine using local produce served in a non-smoking dining room. Light lunches, afternoon tea and coffee served in the Conservatory overlooking the Harbour and Calve Island.

Telephone or write for details. We also offer special 3 and 7 day breaks.

Nantwich - Nether Stowey

30⇨♠Annexe15⇨♠1⌸⊬in 4 bedrooms CTV in all bedrooms ® T ✗ (ex guide dogs) ✱ sB&B⇨♠£95-£195 dB&B⇨♠£115-£215 ⊟
Lift (CTV 150P 1🚗 ⇔ ❄ ♀ (hard) ♪ clay pigeon shooting putting croquet *xmas*
♡ English & French V ♥ ⊻ ⊬ ✱ Lunch £16.50-£18.50&alc Dinner £25&alc Last dinner 9.30pm
CONF. Thtr 90 Class 40 Board 30 Del £125
Credit Cards ①②③⑤

★★ **64%** Crown
High St CW5 5AS ☎(0270) 625283 FAX (0270) 628047

This small, privately owned hotel dates back to the late 16th century and has a wealth of old world character. The bedrooms have modern furnishings and equipment, though sizes and styles vary. The first floor dining room is furnished in period style and a section of wattle and daub walling has been retained as a feature. There are 2 busy lounge bars and a small bistro.
18⇨(2fb) CTV in all bedrooms ®⚲ T ✱ sB&B⇨£49-£55 dB&B⇨£54-£69 ⊟
(60P
♡ English & Continental V ♥ ⊻ ⊬ ✱ Lunch fr£5.95 Dinner £13.95&alc Last dinner 11pm
CONF. Thtr 200 Class 150 Board 70 Del from £65
Credit Cards ①②③⑤ £

★★ **58%** Cedars Hotel & Restaurant
136 Crewe Rd CW5 6NB (on A534, towards outskirts of town) ☎(0270) 626455 FAX (0270) 626336
This friendly family-run hotel, converted from a Victorian hunting lodge on the eastern side of town, is popular with business guests during the week. Bedrooms are simply furnished and there is an informal restaurant and a lounge.
24rm(21⇨♠)Annexe3⇨♠(4fb) CTV in all bedrooms ® T ✱ sB&B⇨£25-£39.50 sB&B⇨♠£25-£39.50 dB&B⇨£36-£47.50 dB&B⇨♠£36-£47.50 ⊟
(80P ❄ ♫ *xmas*
♡ English & French V ♥ ⊻ ⊬ ✱ Lunch £8&alc Dinner £9-£12.50&alc Last dinner 9.30pm
CONF. Thtr 60 Class 40 Board 30 Del from £60
Credit Cards ①③ £

NARBERTH Dyfed Map 02 SN11

★★ **61%** *Plas-Hyfryd*
Moorfield Rd SA67 7AB (Guestaccom) ☎(0834) 860653
Plas Hyfryd, run by the friendly Grimwood family, is set in pretty grounds with lawns and mature trees. There is a lounge bar, furnished with comfortable cane and cottage-style seating, where drinks and bar meals are served. The bedrooms are simply furnished but all have modern comforts.
12⇨♠(1fb) CTV in all bedrooms ® T
CTV 30P ❄ ⌂ (heated)
♡ British, French & Spanish V ♥ ⊻ Last dinner 9.30pm
Credit Cards ①③

NARBOROUGH Leicestershire Map 04 SP59

★★ **63%** *Charnwood*
48 Leicester Rd LE9 5DF (off A46 2m S of M1, junc 21) ☎Leicester(0533) 862218 FAX (0533) 750119
Closed 1 wk from 25 Dec RS Sun
Tucked away in a residential area of the village, the Charnwood provides polite service in a relaxed and informal environment. The restaurant is light and cheerful, with views of the garden. The lounge bar with open fire is cosy, and is also popular for bar meals. Bedrooms offer light décor and a good range of facilities.
20⇨♠ CTV in all bedrooms ® T

50P ⇔ ❄
♡ English & French V ♥ ⊻ Last dinner 9.30pm
Credit Cards ①②③

NEASHAM Co Durham Map 08 NZ31

★★★ *Newbus Arms*
Hurworth Rd DL2 1PE
☎Darlington(0325) 721071 FAX (0325) 721770
Closed 24-28 Dec
This small country house-style hotel is in open countryside. Bedrooms are comfortably furnished and staff provide friendly and attentive service. Two types of dining are offered, a formal restaurant and a bistro, both with a good choice of dishes.
15⇨♠3⌸ CTV in all bedrooms ® T
80P 2🚗 (£5 per night) ⇔ ❄ squash
♡ European V ♥ ⊻ Last dinner 9.30pm
Credit Cards ①②③⑤

NEATH West Glamorgan Map 03 SS79

★★ **64%** Castle Hotel
The Parade SA11 1RB (in town centre) (Whitbread) ☎(0639) 641119 & 643581 FAX (0639) 641624
This friendly coaching inn in the heart of the town, reputedly frequented by Nelson and the place where the Welsh Rugby Union was founded, is popular for its bars and restaurant.
28⇨♠(3fb)1⌸⊬in 4 bedrooms CTV in all bedrooms ® T ✱ sB&B⇨♠fr£49.50 dB&B⇨♠fr£61 ⊟
(20P 6🚗 sauna solarium *xmas*
♡ English & Continental V ♥ ⊻ ⊬ ✱ Lunch fr£6.50 Dinner £9.95-£14.50&alc Last dinner 10pm
CONF. Thtr 160 Class 75 Board 46 Del from £75
Credit Cards ①②③⑤

NEFYN Gwynedd Map 06 SH34

★ **60%** *Caeau Capel*
Rhodfar Mor LL53 6EB ☎(0758) 720240
Closed Nov-Etr
This family-run holiday hotel is set in pleasant lawns and gardens in a quiet residential area, yet within easy reach of beaches and golf courses. Most of the bright, cheerful bedrooms have views over the gardens to the sea. There are two lounges, a residents' bar and a games room. The attractive restaurant overlooks the gardens and offers a fixed-price menu.
13rm(12♠)Annexe5⇨♠(6fb) ® ✱ sB&B⇨♠£24.50 dB&B⇨♠£49 ⊟
CTV 20P ❄ ♀ (grass) putting pool
V ♥ ⊻ ✱BarLunchfr£2Dinnerfr£12.50Lastdinner7.30pm
Credit Cards ①③

NETHER STOWEY Somerset Map 03 ST13

★★ **61%** Apple Tree Inn
Keenthorne TA5 1HZ (on A39) ☎(0278) 733238 FAX (0278) 732693
This small roadside hotel offers warm hospitality and a variety of bedrooms. The newest and best are situated in the garden, and though the rooms in the main building tend to be smaller, they are well furnished. Public areas include a cosy library, a beamed dining room and a sunny conservatory.
15⇨♠(1fb)⊬in 3 bedrooms CTV in all bedrooms ® T ✗ (ex guide dogs)
60P ❄
♡ English & European V ♥
Credit Cards ①②③

NETHER WASDALE Cumbria Map 11 NY10
★★62% **Low Wood Hall**
CA20 1ET ☎Wasdale(09467) 26289 FAX (09467) 26289
Closed 24 Dec-13 Jan
Set in attractive grounds, this Victorian country house is hospitably run by its enthusiastic owners and has well equipped bedrooms either in the main house or a converted barn. Public areas, which include a library, have a Victorian atmosphere, with gas chandeliers and marble fireplaces.
13⇨♠(4fb) CTV in all bedrooms ®⚲ T ✱ sB&B⇨♠fr£35 dB&B⇨♠fr£57
CTV 24P ⬚ ❋ pool table
♀ European V ⌘ Last dinner 8.45pm
Credit Cards [1][3]   (£)

NEVERN Dyfed Map 02 SN03
★★63% **Trewern Arms**
SA42 0NB (off A487 coast road) ☎Newport(0239) 820395
This charming extended 18th-century inn is set in a secluded valley. Bedrooms are spacious and modern and there are quite extensive comfortable public rooms.
9⇨♠(3fb) CTV in all bedrooms ® ✱ ❋ sB&B⇨♠fr£28 dB&B⇨♠fr£45
CTV 100P ❋ ♪ ☉ solarium gymnasium pool table *xmas*
V ♢ ✱
Credit Cards [1][3]

NEWARK-ON-TRENT Nottinghamshire Map 08 SK75
★★69% **Grange**
73 London Rd NG24 1RZ (outskirts of town off A1)
☎Newark(0636) 703399 FAX (0636) 702328
Closed 24 Dec-2 Jan
This cheerful, well run hotel, situated on the outskirts of town on the A1 offers English-style cooking with daily specials featured in the lounge bar.
10⇨♠Annexe5⇨♠(2fb)1⇎⌘in 2 bedrooms CTV in all bedrooms ® T ✱ sB&B⇨♠£39.50-£45 dB&B⇨♠£52.50-£65 ♬
CTV 19P ⬚
V ⌘ ✱ Dinner £11.95&alc Last dinner 9pm
CONF. Thtr 20 Class 20 Board 20
Credit Cards [1][2][3]

★★62% **South Parade**
117-119 Baldertongate NG24 1RY ☎Newark(0636) 703008 FAX (0522) 510182
Closed 21 Dec-2 Jan
This listed Gerogian building is situated in Balderton Road, with the entrance in William Street and car parking at the rear. Bedrooms vary in size and style, from older rooms to pleasantly decorated, modern, ground-floor rooms. Guests have the use of a small bar and restaurant, where bar snacks and a grill menu are available.
16rm(10⇨♠)(2fb) CTV in all bedrooms ® T sB&B£30-£34 sB&B⇨♠£35-£42 dB&B£48-£52 dB&B⇨♠£50-£56 ♬
《10P
♀ English & French V ♢ ⌘ ✱ Dinner £11.50 Last dinner 8.30pm
Credit Cards [1][2][3]   (£)

★★55% **Midland**
Muskham Rd NG24 1BL ☎(0636) 73788
This family-run budget style hotel lies adjacent to the cattle market near a railway line on the edge of town.
10rm(2⇨♠)(2fb) CTV in all bedrooms ® ✱
CTV 20P
V ♢ Last dinner 8.30pm
Credit Cards [1][2][5]

Forte Travelodge
North Muskham NG23 6HT (3m N, on A1 southbound) ☎Newark(0636) 703635
Central Res (0800) 850950
This modern building offers a good standard of accommodation for overnight stops. Smart, spacious and well equipped bedrooms, all with en suite bathrooms, are suitable for family use, and meals may be taken at the nearby family restaurant. For more details about Travelodges, consult the Contents page, under Hotel Groups.
30⇨♠ ✱ B⇨♠£31.95 (room only)

FORTE
Travelodge

NEWBURGH Grampian *Aberdeenshire* Map 15 NJ92
★★❀62% **Udny Arms**
Main St AB41 0BL (in village centre) ☎(03586) 89444 FAX (03586) 89012
Now under the ownership of the Craig family, this long established business and sporting hotel is in the centre of the village with views over the Ythan estuary. Public areas have a relaxed, informal atmosphere, include an elegant Victorian dining room where a short but imaginative carte reflects excellent use of fresh produce. A split-level bistro offers an informal alternative.
26⇨♠(1fb) CTV in all bedrooms ® T ✱ sB&B⇨♠£25-£49.50 dB&B⇨♠£45-£54 (room only) ♬
50P ▶ 9 ♪ petanque
♀ Scottish & French V ♢ ⌘ ✱ Lunch £15-£30&alc Dinner £15-£20&alc Last dinner 9.30pm
CONF. Thtr 100 Class 20 Board 60 Del from £49.50
Credit Cards [1][3]   (£)
See advertisement under ABERDEEN

Plas-Hyfryd ★★
HOTEL and RESTAURANT
A magnificent 18th century mansion, situated on the edge of the town of Narberth is set in large attractively lawned gardens with mature trees which complement the elegance of the house. The hotel had been carefully restored to include all the bedrooms with their own private bathrooms. The dining room offers a varied cuisine using local fresh fish, meat and vegetables where practicable. A large heated pool (May-September) with childrens paddling pool is equipped with waterslide and spring diving board or you can sit by the edge and soak up the atmosphere. An ideal hotel to explore the many beaches, historic towns and places of interest in this corner of Wales. Open all year.

Narberth, Pembrokeshire, Dyfed SA67 7AB
Telephone: (0834) 860653

Newbury

NEWBURY Berkshire Map **04** SU46

See also **Thatcham**

★★★★ 69% Donnington Valley
Old Oxford Rd, Donnington RG14 9AG ☎(0635) 551199 FAX (0635) 551123

Take the Oxford road out of Donnington to find this quietly placed hotel with golf course. Its modern exterior gives no hint of the splendid and imaginatively designed public areas which include a high-ceilinged, split-level bar and lounge. Bedrooms, lavishly decorated, enjoy rural views.

58⇌♞(11fb)⌀in 12 bedrooms CTV in all bedrooms ® ♘ T ✻ sB⇌♞£55-£129 dB⇌♞£40-£136 (room only) ᖴ
Lift (⌗ CTV 140P ✻ ▶ 18 ♪ xmas
♡ English & French V ♢ ⌁ ✻ Lunch £10.50-£12.50&alc Dinner £12.50-£14.50&alc Last dinner 10pm
CONF. Thtr 140 Class 80 Board 50 Del £136.50
Credit Cards 1 2 3 5 £

★★★ 66% Foley Lodge
Stockcross RG14 8JU ☎(0635) 528770 FAX (0635) 528398

This attractive Victorian hunting lodge, set in its own landscaped grounds, has a fine indoor pool with a high pagoda ceiling. Public areas include a comfortable lobby/lounge, 2 conservatories (one with a bar), and a brasserie.

69⇌♞(3fb)⌀in 16 bedrooms CTV in all bedrooms ® ♘ T ✻ (ex guide dogs) ✻ sB⇌♞£90 dB⇌♞£110 (room only) ᖴ
Lift (140P ✻ ⌁ (heated) snooker croquet short tennis ⚐
♡ English & French V ♢ ⌁ ✻ Lunch £12-£20&alc Dinner £20-£40alc Last dinner 10pm
CONF. Thtr 220 Class 90 Board 30 Del from £99
Credit Cards 1 2 3 5 £

★★★ ❀63% Regency Park
Bowling Green Rd RG13 3RP NEWBURY
☎Thatcham(0635) 871555 FAX (0635) 871571
(For full entry see Thatcham)

★★★ ❀❀⌁76% Hollington House
Woolton Hill RG15 9XR ☎(0635) 255100 FAX (0635) 255075

This magnificent Edwardian manor house, with its succession of elegant sitting rooms and sumptuous restaurant, was bought in 1992 by John and Penny Guy, fresh from the experience of running one of Australia's top hotels. Spacious bedrooms have truly splendid bathrooms, some with spa baths and deluge showers. Chef Richard Lovett has recently been appointed to head the kitchen team.

20⇌♞(1fb)⌀in 2 bedrooms CTV in all bedrooms ® T ✻ (ex guide dogs) sB&B⇌♞£80-£110 dB&B⇌♞£90-£250 ᖴ
Lift (39P ⚐ ✻ ⌁ (heated) ♃ (hard) xmas
♡ English & French V ♢ ⌁ ✻ Lunch £12.50-£15.50 High tea £2.50-£6.50 Last high tea 5pm
CONF. Thtr 38 Class 30 Board 25 Del from £165
Credit Cards 1 2 3 £

★★★ ❀74% Elcot Park Resort
RG16 8NJ (6m W, 1m N of A4 Newbury-Hungerford road)
☎Kintbury(0488) 58100 FAX (0488) 58288

Set in 16 acres of grounds amidst wooded countryside and farmland, this Georgian country house has been extensively developed. Bedrooms, in the original house, a new wing or in converted stables nearby are all spacious and furnished to a very high standard. Public areas include a conservatory lounge and elegant restaurant offering an interesting range of modern and traditional dishes.

56⇌♞Annexe19⇌♞(4fb)⌀in 8 bedrooms CTV in all bedrooms ® ♘ T ✻ sB⇌♞£75-£100 dB⇌♞£85-£100 (room only) ᖴ
(138P ✻ ⌁ (heated) ♃ (hard) sauna solarium gymnasium hot air ballooning clay pigeon shooting xmas

---

♡ English & Continental V ♢ ⌁ ✻ Lunch £12.95-£16.95&alc Dinner £15-£16.95&alc Last dinner 9.30pm
CONF. Thtr 110 Class 60 Board 50 Del from £70
Credit Cards 1 2 3 5 £

★★★ 65% Millwaters
London Rd RG14 2BY ☎(0635) 528838 FAX (0635) 523406

A Georgian house extended in a modern but sympathetic style, Millwaters lies in 8 acres on the eastern outskirts of Newbury, with the rivers Kennet and Lambourn flowing through the grounds. The individually decorated bedrooms have smart modern furnishings, and most have a sofa. Public areas are restricted to an attractive lobby lounge and a high ceilinged bar/restaurant.

30⇌♞(2fb)3⌀ CTV in all bedrooms ® T ✻ sB&B⇌♞£55-£75 dB&B⇌♞£70-£90 ᖴ
50P ✻ ♪ croquet boules xmas
♡ English & French V ♢ ⌁ ✻ Lunch fr£13.95 Dinner fr£13.95 Last dinner 9.30pm
Credit Cards 1 2 3 5

★★★ 60% The Chequers
Oxford St RG13 1JB ☎(0635) 38000 FAX (0635) 37170
RS Sat

This long-established, town-centre hotel stands at the end of the main shopping street and has a small garden. Public areas include comfortable lounge seating and a popular bar. Bedrooms vary widely in size, outlook and location, and some are in an extension around the car park, but all are equipped with modern comforts.

45⇌♞Annexe11⇌♞(3fb)⌀in 19 bedrooms CTV in all bedrooms ® T sB⇌♞£80 dB⇌♞£95 (room only) ᖴ
(60P ✻ xmas
V ♢ ⌁ ✻ Lunch £7.95-£9.95&alc Dinner £15.95&alc Last dinner 10pm
Credit Cards 1 2 3 5

NEWBURY • BERKSHIRE

- Set in Berkshire countryside
- Surrounded by an 18 hole golf course
- 58 luxury executive bedrooms
- Private dining suites
- Purpose-built conference facilities
- Superb restaurant
- M4/A34 2 miles

Tel: (0635) 551199 • Fax: (0635) 551123
Old Oxford Road, Donnington, Newbury, Berks.

Regency Park Hotel
- where service comes naturally.

Location
The Regency Park Hotel near Newbury sits comfortably in 5 acres of beautiful countryside. A peaceful haven in Royal Berkshire, yet only 7 minutes from Junction 13 on the M4 and 45 minutes from Heathrow.

Accommodation
50 luxurious bedrooms, all en-suite, are generously sized and provide every convenience: satellite TV, mini bar, trouser press, etc. Many have private balconies. **Children under 12 (sharing parents' room) stay FREE.**

Dining
Terraces Restaurant opens for lunch and dinner and offers a fine à la carte menu. Both Terraces Restaurant and Fountains Bar are fully air-conditioned for your comfort. We offer 24 hour room service.

Functions
The Parkside Room is ideal for weddings and private functions and boasts its own dance floor and sound/lighting system. The Regency Park has on-site parking for 120 cars.

Business
The purpose designed Business Centre, with a range of meeting rooms, will suit the Conference Organiser. It is linked to the hotel providing seclusion and privacy. A bespoke team is on hand to provide administrative back-up services, as required.

Reservations
Simply call: (0635) 871555 or
Fax: (0635) 871571

Regency Park Hotel
Bowling Green Road, Thatcham,
Newbury, Berks RG13 3RP

Call us now for a brochure and details of our special events.

Newbury - Newcastle upon Tyne

Hilton National Newbury
Pinchington Ln RG14 7HL ☎(0635) 529000

This is a bright, modern hotel with an informal restaurant, aimed at both the business and leisure guest. All bedrooms have en-suite bathrooms and a range of modern facilities. For more information about Hilton National, consult the Contents page, under Hotel Groups.
109⇌✶ B⇌ℕ£85 (room only)
CONF. Thtr 200 Class 100 Board 80 Del £130

NEWBY BRIDGE Cumbria Map 07 SD38

★★★❀71% Lakeside
LA12 8AT ☎(05395) 31207 FAX (05395) 31699

Closed 3-13 Jan
This constantly improving hotel is beautifully positioned on the very edge of Lake Windermere. Most of the spacious bedrooms have lake views, and there is a comfortable conservatory. A high standard of cooking is served in the elegant panelled restaurant. Dishes mentioned by our inspectors include a casserole of avocado and sweet pepper served in a puff pastry willow, and strips of pan-fried beef with a rum and green peppercorn sauce.
69⇌ℕ(8fb)2🚭⊁in 6 bedrooms CTV in all bedrooms ®✻T
Lift (CTV 100P ✿ launching for boats private jetty ♫
♥ English & French V ❀ ♫ ⊁ ✻
CONF. Thtr 100 Class 50 Board 40 Del from £66
Credit Cards [1][2][3][5] £

★★★69% Whitewater
The Lakeland Village LA12 8PX
☎(05395) 31133 FAX (05395) 31881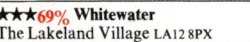

This centuries-old stone and slate building was originally a mill, and alteration has been carefully carried out to avoid destroying its atmosphere. Several of the modern and spacious bedrooms overlook the fast-flowing River Leven, as does the restaurant, which serves a good selection of dishes.
35⇌ℕ(10fb)1🚭 CTV in all bedrooms ®✻T sB&B⇌ℕ£64 dB&B⇌ℕ£96 🍴
Lift (50P 🏊 (heated) ♪ (hard) squash sauna solarium gymnasium health spa putting green xmas
V ❀ ♫ ⊁ ✻ Sunday Lunch £5.50-£14.65alc Dinner £7.25-£25alc Last dinner 9pm
CONF. Thtr 70 Class 32 Board 40 Del £90
Credit Cards [1][2][3][5]
See advertisement under WINDERMERE

★★★66% The Swan
LA12 8NB ☎(05395) 31681 FAX (05395) 31917
Closed 3-13 Jan

The Swan is an attractive, white-painted riverside hotel to the southern end of Windermere. There are extensive public areas which include a restaurant with exposed stone walls next to a comfortable cocktail lounge bar. Bedrooms are modern in style and have good facilities. Staff are extremely friendly and helpful.
36⇌ℕ(6fb) CTV in all bedrooms ®✻T 🐕 (ex guide dogs)
CTV 100P 🚭 🎿 ✿ ♪ croquet table tennis ♫ 🎯
♥ English & French V ❀ ♫ Last dinner 9.30pm
Credit Cards [1][2][3][5]

The AA's star rating scheme is the market leader in hotel classification.

NEWCASTLE-UNDER-LYME Staffordshire Map 07 SJ84

★★60% Borough Arms
King St ST5 1HX (on A53) ☎(0782) 629421
FAX (0782) 712388

Converted from an old pottery and Victorian coaching inn, this commercial hotel has a popular restaurant offering a wide range of dishes. Better bedrooms are in the main building and though some tend to be compact, all are equipped with modern amenities.
30⇌ℕ Annexe15⇌ℕ CTV in all bedrooms ® T 🐕 (ex guide dogs) ✻ sB&B⇌ℕ£29.50-£46 dB&B⇌ℕ£45-£60.25
(40P
♥ International V ❀ ♫ ✻ Lunch £9-£13.25&alc Dinner £10.70&alc Last dinner 10pm
CONF. Thtr 90 Class 45 Board 35 Del £56.50
Credit Cards [1][2][3][5] £

Forte Posthouse
Clayton Rd ST5 4DL (on A519 at junct 15 of M6)
☎(0782) 717171 FAX (0782) 717138

Suitable for both the business and leisure traveller, this bright hotel provides modern accommodation in well equipped bedrooms with en suite bathrooms. For more details about Forte Posthouse hotels, consult the Contents page, under Hotel Groups.
119⇌ℕ✶ B⇌ℕ£41.50-£53.50 (room only)
CONF. Thtr 70 Class 40 Board 34 Del £89.50

NEWCASTLE UPON TYNE Tyne & Wear Map 12 NZ26
See also **Seaton Burn** & **Whickham**

★★★★❀67% The Copthorne
The Close, Quayside NE1 3RT
☎091-222 0333 FAX 091-230 1111

The light sandstone façade of this hotel was designed to blend in with its environment, and a notable feature is its location on the banks of the Tyne, close to the city centre, with all bedrooms facing the river. The hotel offers many facilities, including 2 restaurants, a leisure centre, conference and banqueting rooms, a business centre and an extensive car park.
156⇌ℕ(15fb)🚭⊁in 28 bedrooms CTV in all bedrooms ® T ✻ sB⇌ℕ£99-£114 dB⇌ℕ£110-£125 (room only) 🍴
Lift (🎱 CTV 180P 🏊 (heated) sauna solarium gymnasium whirlpool steam room xmas
♥ International V ❀ ♫ ⊁ ✻ Lunch £11.95-£12.50&alc Dinner £15.25&alc Last dinner 10.15pm
CONF. Thtr 250 Class 150 Board 80 Del from £107.50
Credit Cards [1][2][3][5] £

★★★★67% Swallow Gosforth Park
High Gosforth Park, Gosforth NE3 5HN (off A1 Western Bypass at A1056 junct)
☎091-236 4111 FAX 091-236 8192

This purpose built hotel is in 12 acres of parkland close to 2 golf courses and the racecourse. Public areas, which include 2 restaurants, have high standards of quality and comfort. Well turned out staff provides efficiently attentive service.
178⇌ℕ(14fb)3🚭⊁in 24 bedrooms CTV in all bedrooms ®✻ T sB&B⇌ℕ£98-£103 dB&B⇌ℕ£120-£130 🍴
Lift (CTV 300P ✿ 🏊 (heated) ♪ (hard) squash sauna solarium gymnasium spa pool steam room ♫ xmas
♥ English & French V ❀ ♫ ✻ Lunch £14.50-£15.50&alc High tea £6-£8&alc Dinner £15-£19.50&alc Last dinner 10.30pm
Credit Cards [1][2][3][5]

Newcastle upon Tyne

★★★★ **54%** **Holiday Inn**
Great North Rd NE13 6BP ☎091-236 5432
FAX 091-236 8091
(For full entry see Seaton Burn)

★★★ **67%** **County Thistle**
Neville St NE99 1AH (opposite Central Station)
☎091-232 2471 FAX 091-232 1285

Tastefully appointed public areas include the elegant, wood-panelled Café Mozart Restaurant and comfortable cocktail bar; guests preferring a livelier atmosphere choose the American-style Boston Bean Company Bar and Diner. Attractively furnished bedrooms are equipped to good modern standards, and service is provided by friendly, smartly uniformed staff.
115⇨↑(4fb)✂in 32 bedrooms CTV in all bedrooms ® T
sB⇨↑£72-£85 dB⇨↑£80-£120 (room only) ☐
Lift (25P
☐ International ☐ ☐ ✂ ✱ Lunch £10.50-£17 Dinner £15.25-£19.75&alc Last dinner 9.45pm
CONF. Thtr 130 Class 80 Board 60 Del from £84
Credit Cards ① ② ③ ④ ⑤

★★★ **66%** **Swallow Hotel-Gateshead**
High West St NE8 1PE ☎091-477 1105 FAX 091-478 7214
(For full entry see Gateshead)

★★★ **65%** **New Kent Hotel**
Osborne Rd NE2 2TB (beside B1600)
☎091-281 1083 FAX 091-281 3369

Situated in a mainly residential area within easy reach of the city centre, this quietly run, small family hotel offers friendly service. The generally compact bedrooms are pleasantly decorated and have smart modern bathrooms.

★★★ AA

THE COUNTY
THISTLE HOTEL

Neville Street, Newcastle upon Tyne NE99 1AH
Tel: 091-232 2471   Fax: 091-232 1285

Your choice in Newcastle

For Reservations at over 100
Mount Charlotte Thistle Hotels
Telephone London: 071 937 8033.

NEW KENT HOTEL
Osborne Road, Jesmond
Newcastle upon Tyne NE2 2TB
Tel: 091 281 1083. Fax: 091 281 3369

★★★   **65%**

THE CITY'S HIGHEST RATED PRIVATELY OWNED HOTEL

A privately owned, personally operated family hotel established for over twenty years. Ideally situated in a quiet suburban location just minutes away from the City centre. The restaurant is a regular venue for residents and non residents alike. Serving the best of modern and classical cuisine and renowned for professional but friendly service. All bedrooms are en suite and tastefully furnished and decorated. A comfortable base for business and tourist alike.

LAKESIDE HOTEL

Newby Bridge, Cumbria LA12 8AT
Telephone (05395) 31207
Telex 65149 Fax (05395) 31699
★ ★ ★ ✿

Unique tanquil setting: superb lake frontage with private jetties and gardens to lake shore. Most of the bedrooms including the Restaurant enjoy superb lake views.

Completely refurbished with a beautiful conservatory also overlooking the lake, while maintaing the character of a traditional Lakeland hotel.
All room en-suite.

15 minutes from M6 exit 36.

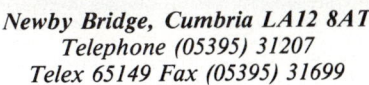

Newcastle upon Tyne - Newcastle upon Tyne Airport

32⇌🛏(4fb) CTV in all bedrooms ® T 🐕 (ex guide dogs) ✳
sB&B⇌🛏£30-£65 dB&B⇌🛏£50-£80 🍴
《 38P 🚗
♀ International V ✂ ✳ Bar Lunch £4-£8alc Dinner £7-£15alc Last dinner 10pm
Credit Cards ① ② ③ ④ ⑤ £

See advertisement on page 447

★★★ **65%** Washington Moat House
Stone Cellar Rd, District 12, High Usworth
NE37 1PH ☎091-417 2626 FAX 091-415 1166
(For full entry see Washington)

★★★ **64%** Novotel
Ponteland Rd, Kenton NE3 3HZ (off A1 (M) NW of city) ☎091-214 0303 FAX 091-214 0633

Belonging to the French-owned Novotel Group, this hotel is north-west of the city centre, convenient for the airport. Bedrooms are spacious though without 'frills', and a large working surface is provided. Open plan-lounges are comfortable.
126⇌🛏(126fb)✂ in 51 bedrooms CTV in all bedrooms ® T ✳
sB⇌🛏£60.50 dB⇌🛏£65.50 (room only) 🍴
Lift 260P 🏊 (heated) sauna exercise equipment
♀ English & French V ☆ ♨ ✳ Lunch £7.85-£17.10alc Dinner £9.70-£17.10alc Last dinner mdnt
Credit Cards ① ② ③ ⑤

★★★ **62%** Swallow
Newgate Arcade NE1 5SX ☎091-232 5025 FAX 091-232 8428

A large modern hotel in the city centre. Bedrooms are compact and rather dated but contain all expected facilities and in the 6th-floor restaurant diners can enjoy a good standard of food as well as panoramic views of the city.
93⇌🛏✂ in 41 bedrooms CTV in all bedrooms ® T
sB&B⇌🛏£77-£79 dB&B⇌🛏£90-£93 🍴
Lift 《 120P *xmas*
♀ English & French V ☆ ♨ ✳ Lunch £8.75-£10.25alc Dinner £15-£16.75alc Last dinner 10pm
Credit Cards ① ② ③ ⑤

★★★ **60%** Newcastle Moat House
Coast Rd NE28 9HP ☎091-262 8989 & 091-262 7044 FAX 091-263 4172
(For full entry see Wallsend)

★★★ **59%** Imperial Swallow
Jesmond Rd NE2 1PR (on A1058)
☎091-281 5511 FAX 091-281 8472

A busy commercial hotel at Jesmond near the city centre, the Imperial is just completing a modernisation programme to upgrade the bedrooms. There are good leisure facilities, a choice of restaurants and ample parking.
125⇌🛏(4fb)✂ in 53 bedrooms CTV in all bedrooms ® T ✳
sB&B⇌🛏£35-£75 dB&B⇌🛏£70-£88 🍴
Lift 《 🎱 110 🏊 (heated) sauna solarium gymnasium steam room spa bath *xmas*
V ☆ ♨ ✳ Lunch £5.95-£8.25&alc Dinner fr£14.95&alc Last dinner 9.45pm
Credit Cards ① ② ③ ⑤ £

★★★ **57%** Hospitality Inn
64 Osborne Rd, Jesmond NE2 2AT (off A1058)
☎091-281 7881 FAX 091-281 6261

Bedrooms at this mainly commercial hotel are beginning to show their age, though the suites are of a very high standard. Public rooms are compact, the foyer lounge and lounge bar are comfortable. Eating here, in the all-day Coffee House, is informal, but the Northumbria – a sister hotel across the road – has a more formal restaurant.

89⇌🛏(6fb)1🚿✂ in 10 bedrooms CTV in all bedrooms ® T ✳
sB&B⇌🛏fr£69 dB&B⇌🛏fr£79 🍴
Lift 《 70P 🚗 (£2.50 per night) *xmas*
♀ English & French V ☆ ♨ ✳ Lunch fr£8.75&alc Dinner fr£15.75&alc Last dinner 9.30pm
CONF. Thtr 120 Class 60 Board 50 Del from £79
Credit Cards ① ② ③ ⑤

★★ ❀❀❀**76%** Eslington Villa
8 Station Rd, Low Fell NE9 6DR ☎091-487 6017 FAX 091-482 2359
(For full entry see Gateshead)

★★ **60%** Cairn
97/103 Osborne Road, Jesmond NE2 2TJ ☎091-281 1358 FAX 091-281 9031

This mainly commercial hotel is in a residential area of Jesmond, about a mile from the city. The well equipped bedrooms are geared very much to the business guest. Staff are friendly and helpful.
50⇌🛏(6fb)2🚿 CTV in all bedrooms ®✂ T sB&B⇌🛏£45-£49.90 dB&B⇌🛏£49.90-£65 🍴
《 20P *xmas*
V ☆ ♨ Dinner £11.50-£13.50&alc Last dinner 9.15pm
CONF. Thtr 150 Class 120 Board 100 Del from £56
Credit Cards ① ② ③ ⑤ £

★★ **59%** Whites
38-40 Osborne Road, Jesmond NE2 2AL (1m N) ☎091-281 5126
A friendly and popular family-run commercial hotel in a Victorian terrace about a mile from the centre, Whites is gradually being improved. There is a spacious restaurant, pleasant bar and cosy residents' lounge.
25rm(15⇌7🛏)(1fb) CTV in all bedrooms ® 🐕
《 CTV 30P
V ☆ ♨ Last dinner 9.30pm
Credit Cards ① ② ③ ⑤

★ **64%** Osborne
Osborne Road, Jesmond NE2 2AE (1.5m N) ☎091-281 3385
This friendly, unpretentious hotel is currently updating its somewhat plain bedrooms; improvements are also planned to public rooms which comprise a comfortable residents' lounge, a lounge bar and a neat dining room.
25rm(1⇌9🛏) CTV in all bedrooms ® T
CTV 6P 1☂
V ☆ ♨ Last dinner 8.30pm
Credit Cards ① ② ③ ⑤

••

Forte Crest
New Bridge St NE1 8BS ☎091-232 6191 FAX 091-261 8529

A large modern hotel with a wide range of services and amenities, designed particularly for the business traveller. Bedrooms are smart, comfortable and well equipped. For more details about Forte Crest hotels, consult the Contents page, under Hotel Groups.
166⇌🛏 ✳ B⇌🛏£75 (room only)
CONF. Thtr 500 Class 300 Board 12 Del from £90

Forte Posthouse
Emerson District 5 NE37 1LB ☎091-416 2264 FAX 091-415 3371
(For full entry see Washington)

••

NEWCASTLE UPON TYNE AIRPORT Tyne & Wear
Map 12 NZ17

★★★ **64%** Airport Moat House
Woolsington NE13 8DJ
☎Ponteland(0661) 824911 FAX (0661) 860157

This purpose built hotel offers spacious and comfortable public areas. Bedrooms are currently undergoing refurbishment to bring

them in line with the expectations of the 90s' traveller. Staff provide friendly and professional service.
100⇨♠⊁in 12 bedrooms CTV in all bedrooms ® ✷ T ✱ sB&B⇨♠£40-£69 dB&B⇨♠£50-£79 ☐
Lift ⓒ 200P *xmas*
♡ English & French V ♢ ⚏ ⊁ ✱ Lunch £8.25-£10.95&alc Dinner £13.50&alc Last dinner 9.45pm
Credit Cards [1][2][3][5]

NEWMARKET Suffolk Map 05 TL66
★★★ 68% **Bedford Lodge**
Bury Rd CB8 7BX ☎(0638) 663175 FAX (0638) 667391

This recently much enlarged hotel, centring on a Georgian former hunting lodge and set in lawned grounds, has retained its relaxing country house atmosphere under manageress Belinda Drummond and her friendly staff. Public areas include 2 comfortable lounges and an attractively redecorated bar and restaurant. Bedrooms, now including an ultra-modern wing, are spacious and beautifully decorated, with good facilities.
56⇨♠(7fb) CTV in all bedrooms ® T sB&B⇨♠£65-£75 dB&B⇨♠£85-£95 ☐
Lift ⓒ CTV 90P ✿ *xmas*
♡ English & French V ♢ ⚏ Lunch £14.95&alc Dinner £14.95&alc Last dinner 9.30pm
CONF. Thtr 200 Class 80 Board 60 Del from £90
Credit Cards [1][2][3][5]

Newcastle upon Tyne Airport - Newmarket

Cairn Hotel ★★
97/103 Osborne Road
Newcastle upon Tyne NE2 2TJ
Tel: 091-2811358

Superbly situated in the select area of Jesmond, just minutes from a metro station. The city centre is approx ½ mile away. The restaurant and newly refurbished Oswald's Bar is open every night

---

AA ★★★

BEDFORD LODGE HOTEL

Bury Road, Newmarket
Suffolk CB8 7BX
Telephone: (0638) 663175
Fax: (0638) 667391

An exceptional combination of Georgian hunting lodge and sympathetically designed, modern hotel complex in secluded gardens. 49 executive style bedrooms, 7 luxury suites (all with private bathrooms); restaurant; comfortable bar; relaxing atmosphere. Purpose designed Conference complex. Ideally located for horse racing or exploring the region. Suitable for private or business functions.

New for 1994 – Leisure facilities
check at time of booking

Prices include full English breakfast & VAT.

Host: Belinda Drummond

Access: A45 east to A142 left at clocktower, A45 west to A1304 over at clocktower. On left. Stansted Airport 20 miles. Station 1 mile.

WHITES HOTEL ★★ AA

38-42 Osborne Road, Newcastle Upon Tyne, Tyne & Wear
Telephone 091-281 5126

Modern, comfortable hotel behind impressive Victorian Facade where friendly proprietors create a welcoming atmosphere.
40 Bedrooms, of which 36 have en suite facilities and direct dial telephone. Large car park. Night porter.

Newmarket - Newport (Gwent)

★★★ ❀ 65% Newmarket Moat House
Moulton Rd CB8 8DY ☎(0638) 667171
FAX (0638) 666533

Situated close to the town centre on the edge of the Heath, this red-brick modern hotel is well run by friendly staff and has comfortable, sensibly designed bedrooms. The restaurant offers a broad range of dishes from a 4-course set menu or an extensive à la carte. All are freshly cooked, making use of quality produce to provide good flavours.

47⇌♟(2fb) CTV in all bedrooms ® T sB&B⇌♟£35-£60 dB&B⇌♟£70-£95 ♬
Lift (CTV 60P 10⊞ xmas
♀ English & French V ♂ ♬ Lunch £12.95-£15.95&alc Dinner £15.95-£17.95&alc Last dinner 9.45pm
CONF. Thtr 80 Class 35 Board 40 Del from £65
Credit Cards 1 2 3 5

£

★★ 68% Rosery Country House
15 Church St, Exning CB8 7EH (2m NW B1103)
☎Exning(0638) 577312

The hotel is owned by the gregarious and competent Guy and Hazel Pidsley, who offer a warm welcome and a cheerful atmosphere, and provide a level of service which draws both commercial and leisure users. Bedrooms are varied in size and comfort but equipped to the same standard.

11rm(7⇌1♟)1⊞ CTV in all bedrooms ® T ✕ (ex guide dogs) 20P ♎ ❀ croquet ♘
♀ English & French V ♂ ♬ Last dinner 9.30pm
Credit Cards 1 2 3 5

NEW MILTON Hampshire Map 04 SZ29

★★★★★ ❀❀❀❀ 🏅
CHEWTON GLEN
Christchurch Rd BH25 6QS
☎Highcliffe(0425) 275341
FAX (0425) 272310

There is a continuous drive for improvement at this world famous hotel. A new bedroom wing has resulted in the sumptuous and imaginative extension of the public areas. Chef Pierre Chevillard offers a menu which aims to accommodate various diets, so vegetarian and low calorie choices are no problem, but most guests will be allured by the seasonally changing specialities. The hotel lies between the forest and the sea, so both game and fish feature strongly as in ravioli of langoustine with Savoy cabbage and coriander and orange sauce, or noisettes of roe deer with red-wine sauce. A recent inspection meal began with a flavoursome consommé of ceps and shiitake mushrooms, followed by calves' liver in Madeira sauce, and rounded off by hot pistachio soufflé. Service by the professional bi-lingual team is exemplary, and the wine department has a reputation second to none; the list is excellent and the sommelier has a special dedication and a natural approach.

58⇌♟1⊞ CTV in all bedrooms ♂ T ✕ (ex guide dogs) ❊ sB⇌♟£178-£345 dB⇌♟£178-£345 (room only) ♬
(100P ❀ ▢ (heated) ⇌ ▶ 9 ♝ (hard) snooker sauna solarium gymnasium steam room treatment rooms hairdresser nc7yrs xmas

♀ French V ♂ ♬ ✕ Lunch fr£22.50alc Dinner £25-£39&alc Last dinner 9.30pm
Credit Cards 1 2 3 4 5

NEWPORT Gwent Map 03 ST38

★★★★ ❀ 63% Celtic Manor
Coldra Woods NP6 2YA (near junct 24 of M4)
☎(0633) 413000 FAX (0633) 412910

Perched high above the M4, this stylish manor house has been considerably enlarged and a golf course is due to open in late 1994. Of the two restaurants, Hedleys best displays the range of chef Trefor Jones's cooking. Our inspector praised a starter of crab and avocado ravioli, on a bright, buttery crab sauce. Delicious Lunesdale duck was presented with a delicate filo pastry parcel of candied onions. Puddings had not quite the same finesse but were none the less enjoyable.

73⇌♟(1fb)2⊞ CTV in all bedrooms ®♂ T ✕ (ex guide dogs)
Lift (⊞ 150P 1⊞ ❀ ▢ (heated) sauna solarium gymnasium
♀ French V ♂ ♬ Last dinner 10.30pm
Credit Cards 1 2 3 5

★★★ 67% Kings
High St NP1 1QU (from town centre, take left hand road (not flyover) right hand lane to next roundabout, 3rd exit off across front of hotel then left for carpark) ☎(0633) 842020 FAX (0633) 244667
Closed 25-30 Dec

Good all-round facilities are provided by this popular and well run hotel near the city centre. Bedrooms are well appointed, spaciously comfortable public areas include a popular carvery restaurant featuring an à la carte menu.

47⇌♟(10fb)✕ in 2 bedrooms CTV in all bedrooms ®♂ T ✕ (ex guide dogs) ❊ sB⇌♟fr£39 dB⇌♟fr£49 (room only)
Lift (20P 10⊞
♀ International V ♂ ♬ ❊ Sunday Lunch £7.50-£9.95 Dinner £7.50-£11.95 Last dinner 9.30pm
CONF. Thtr 200 Class 100 Board 50 Del £75
Credit Cards 1 2 3 5

★★★ 63% Newport Lodge
Bryn Bevan NP9 5QN ☎(0633) 821818 FAX (0633) 856360

Situated in a residential area high on Bryn Bevan hill, this is a small, personally run modern hotel overlooking the motorway and the countryside beyond. Public rooms are rather restricted but bedrooms tend to compensate: all are richly furnished, comfortable and have a good range of modern facilities.

27⇌♟(20fb) CTV in all bedrooms ® T
(63P
♀ British French & Italian V Last dinner 9.30pm
Credit Cards 1 2 3 5

★★★ 61% Westgate
Commercial St NP1 1TT (Principal) ☎(0633) 244444 FAX (0633) 246616

Situated just at the edge of the pedestrian area of the town at the foot of Stow Hill, this historic hotel with strong 18th-century connections and popular bars has recently been refurbished. Bedroom upgrading is in its final stages with only a minority of rooms left to do.

69⇌♟(11fb) CTV in all bedrooms ®♂ T
Lift (CTV 14P ♘
♀ French & Italian V ♂ ♬ ✕ Last dinner 10pm
Credit Cards 1 2 3 5

●●●●●●●●●●●●●●●●●●●●●●●●●●●●●●●●●●●●●●

For full, independent restaurant reviews,
see the AA Abbey Well *Restaurant Guide*

Newport (Gwent) - Newport (Shropshire)

Granada Lodge
Magor Service Area (M4 junct 2, 3) NP6 3YL
☎ Magor 0633 880111

This modern building provides smart, spacious and well equipped bedrooms, all with en suite bathrooms. Meals may be taken at a nearby family restaurant. For more details about Granada Lodges, consult the Contents page, under Hotel Groups.
43⇌♘❋ B⇌♘ £34.95-£37.95 (room only)

Hilton National Newport
The Coldra NP6 2YG ☎(0633) 412777 FAX (0633) 413087

This is a bright, modern hotel with an informal restaurant, aimed at both the business and leisure guest. All bedrooms have en-suite bathrooms and a range of modern facilities. For more information about Hilton National, consult the Contents page, under Hotel Groups.
119⇌♘❋ sB⇌♘ £75 dB⇌♘ £85 (room only)
CONF. Thtr 500 Class 250 Board 50 Del £85

NEWPORT Shropshire Map 07 SJ71

★★ **64%** *Royal Victoria*
St Mary's St TF10 7AB (Crown & Raven) ☎(0952) 820331 FAX (0952) 820209
Named following a luncheon visit by the young Princess Victoria in 1832, this now fully modernised hotel lies in the centre of the pretty market town. The bedrooms are well furnished, there are 2 popular bars, and good value food is served in the pretty restaurant. Victorian decor is the theme throughout the hotel, with some interesting pictures and old photographs.
24rm(16⇌7♘)(1fb) CTV in all bedrooms ® T

THE
Celtic Manor
HOTEL

★★★★

**Coldra Woods, Newport, Gwent
(M4 — Junction 24)
Tel: Newport (0633) 413000**

★ 73 elegant comfortable rooms, all with bath, colour TV, satellite TV, radio, 24 hour room service.
★ Special weekend-break rates.
★ Two luxurious restaurants and two intimate bars.
★ Heated indoor pool, sauna, solarium, multi gym.
★ Welsh Chef of the Year and Restaurant of the Year (Gwent).
★ Impeccable service in this beautifully restored Manor House.
★ Conference & Banqueting up to 300.

★★★

♛ Ideal location in the town centre, opposite the train station and minutes from exit 26 of the M4.
♛ 47 luxurious ensuite bedrooms with colour and satellite TV, radio and direct dial telephone, tea and coffee making facilities, hair drier, iron and board. Special weekend rates available on request.
♛ Elegant Lounge Bar and a superb Restaurant with Hot Carvery, Grills menu and extensive A La Carte menu.
♛ A range of five function suites suitable for conferences, weddings and banquets to hold 2-300 people.
♛ Free Car Parking.
♛ **A genuine warm & friendly welcome awaits you.**

**High St., Newport, Gwent NP9 1QU
Tel: (0633) 842020 Fax: (0633) 244667**

★★(68%)

A genuine welcome awaits at the Rosery, in the village of Exning (2 miles from Newmarket) an 11 bedroom family run hotel is the ideal place to relax & unwind. We admit a little self indulgent pride in the good reputation we have for our restaurant which overlooks the garden.

**15 Church Street, Exning, Newmarket, Suffolk CB8 7EH
Telephone: Exning (0638) 577312**

N

449

Newport (Shropshire) - Newquay

(100P
♥ English & French V ⚭ ⚌ Last dinner 10pm
Credit Cards 1 2 3

NEWQUAY Cornwall & Isles of Scilly Map 02 SW86

★★★ 65% Hotel Bristol
Narrowcliff TR7 2PQ ☎(0637) 875181 FAX (0637) 879347
In a prime location overlooking the sea, this long established family run hotel has been constantly improved over recent years, without sacrificing its traditional values of comfort and hospitality. It has comfortable lounges, a cocktail bar and a restaurant offering a choice of menus, served by skilled, attentive staff. Bedrooms vary in standard, including some suites.
76⇌↑(23fb) CTV in all bedrooms T ✱ sB&B⇌↑£48-£50 dB&B⇌↑£72-£80 ♬
Lift (CTV 100P 5♿ (£5 per day) ◻ (heated) snooker sauna solarium pool table *xmas*
V ⚭ ⚌ Lunch fr£9.95&alc Dinner fr£16&alc Last dinner 8.45pm
CONF. Thtr 180 Class 80 Board 10 Del from £60
Credit Cards 1 2 3 5

★★★ 64% Headland
Fistral Bay TR7 1EW (above Fistral Beach) ☎(0637) 872211 FAX (0637) 872212
Closed early Nov-late Dec & early Jan-mid Mar
Splendidly situated on Towan Head peninsula, overlooking the sea on three sides and a golf course on the other, this impressive hotel prides itself on its friendly efficient service supervised by owners John and Carolyn Armstrong. Public areas are spacious and comfortable.
104⇌↑(56fb)1⚏ CTV in all bedrooms ® T sB&B⇌↑£30-£49 dB&B⇌↑£50-£90 Continental breakfast ♬
Lift (CTV 400P ✿ ◻ (heated) ⚌ (heated) ▶ 9 ♿ (hard) snooker sauna solarium putting table tennis croquet playroom ♫ ✿
♥ English & French V ⚭ ⚌ Bar Lunch £7.50-£12.50 Dinner £15.95-£17.95&alc Last dinner 9pm
CONF. Thtr 250 Class 120 Board 50 Del from £55
Credit Cards 1 2 3

★★★ 64% Trebarwith
Island Estate TR7 1BZ ☎(0637) 872288
Closed Jan-Mar & 30 Oct-Dec
In a wonderful cliff top location with private steps to the beach, this hotel is popular with many loyal, returning guests and continues to improve under the leadership of owner Mr Tarrant. Public areas, which include a small cinema, all enjoy glorious views, as do some of the bedrooms.
41⇌↑(8fb)4⚏ CTV in all bedrooms ® T ✘ (ex guide dogs) sB&B⇌↑£23-£45 dB&B⇌↑£46-£90 (incl dinner) ♬
(CTV 40P ✿ ◻ (heated) ♪ snooker sauna solarium spa bath video theatre games room ♫ ✿
V ⚭ ⚌ Bar Lunch £1-£5 Dinner £13 Last dinner 8.30pm
Credit Cards 1 3

★★★ 60% Kilbirnie
Narrowcliff TR7 2RS ☎(0637) 875155 FAX (0637) 850769
Close to the seafront and convenient for the centre of town, this long established hotel is a popular choice for both holiday and business guests, and is constantly improving. The well equipped bedrooms include a video recorder. Spacious public areas comprise a large ballroom, cosy cocktail bar and an attractive dining room.
74⇌(17fb) CTV in all bedrooms ®⚹ T sB&B⇌£30-£40 dB&B⇌£60-£80 ♬
Lift (⚏ 60P 8♿ ◻ (heated) ⚌ (heated) snooker sauna solarium table tennis *xmas*
⚭ ⚌ Bar Lunch £1.40-£3.75alc Dinner £10.50-£12.50 Last dinner 8.30pm
Credit Cards 1 3

★★ 57% Barrowfield
Hilgrove Rd TR7 2QY ☎(0637) 878878 FAX (0637) 879490
This popular holiday hotel offers friendly and efficient service, with light meals available throughout the day. Bedrooms are in the process of being upgraded.
81⇌↑(18fb)11⚏ CTV in all bedrooms ®⚹ T ✱ sB&B⇌↑£36 dB&B⇌↑£72 ♬
Lift (CTV 54P 16♿ ◻ (heated) ⚌ (heated) snooker sauna solarium gymnasium games room *xmas*
♥ French V ⚭ ⚌ Bar Lunch £1.25-£3 Dinner £12&alc Last dinner 9pm
CONF. Thtr 150 Class 50 Board 50 Del £52
Credit Cards 1 3

★★ 70% Whipsiderry
Trevelgue Road, Porth TR7 3LY ☎(0637) 874777
Closed Nov-Etr (ex Xmas)
Run by the Drackford family for over 20 years, this friendly, good value hotel has built up a loyal following of returning guests. Bedrooms vary in size but all are freshly decorated. There is a choice of lounges, a cosy bar and a traditional dining room. Guests are often enthralled by the family of badgers who visit the hotel to be fed.
24rm(5⇌14↑)(5fb) CTV in all bedrooms ®
sB&B⇌↑£19.50-£30.50 dB&B⇌↑£39-£78 ♬
CTV 30P ✿ ⚌ (heated) sauna putting green pool table ✿ *xmas*
♥ English & Continental V ⚭ ⚌ Bar Lunch £1.75-£6.50alc Dinner £10.50-£14.50 Last dinner 8pm
Credit Cards 1 3

★★ 64% Corisande Manor
Riverside Av, Pentire TR7 1PL (from A392 Newquay road follow signs for Pentire) ☎(0637) 872042
Closed 9 Oct-14 May
A beautifully situated property – built in 1900 by an Austrian Count – features a dining room with a ceiling made from the keel beams of a Spanish schooner wrecked in the bay 300 years ago, and other public areas are similarly steeped in history. Bedrooms are comfortable, though simply decorated, and most of them have good views.
19rm(5⇌11↑)(3fb) CTV in all bedrooms ® sB&B£18-£24 sB&B⇌↑£20-£26 dB&B£36-£48 dB&B⇌↑£40-£52 ♬
19P ♿ ✿ solarium croquet putting green outdoor chess nc3yrs
♥ English, French & Italian ⚭ ⚌ ✘ Bar Lunch £5-£6.75 Dinner £12-£12.50 Last dinner 8pm
Credit Cards 1 3

★★ 62% Philema
1 Esplanade Rd, Pentire TR7 1PY ☎(0637) 872571 FAX (0637) 873188
Closed Nov-Feb
With panoramic views across Fistral Bay, this friendly family holiday hotel offers good value for money. Comfortably furnished modern bedrooms are well equipped and pleasant public areas overlook the sea. A simple table d'hôte menu is offered in the dining room, where a glass wall gives guests a view into the indoor pool.
37rm(32⇌↑)(24fb)1⚏ CTV in all bedrooms ®⚹ T sB&B£17-£30 sB&B⇌↑£18-£32 dB&B£34-£60 dB&B⇌↑£36-£64 ♬
37P ⚏ ◻ (heated) snooker sauna solarium table tennis pool table jacuzzi ♫
♥ English & Continental V ⚭ ⚌ ✱ Bar Lunch £1.20-£2.95 High tea £2-£3 Dinner £7.50-£14&alc Last dinner 7.30pm
Credit Cards 1 3

★★ 61% Porth Veor Manor Hotel & Restaurant
Porth Way TR7 3LW (off A392, on Padstow road)
☎(0637) 873274 FAX (0637) 851690
16⇌↑(3fb) CTV in all bedrooms ® sB&B⇌↑£30-£40 dB&B⇌↑£60-£80 (incl dinner) ♬
CTV 40P ✿ croquet putting *xmas*

Philema Hotel ★★

PENTIRE · NEWQUAY · CORNWALL
Tel: (0637) 872571   Fax: (0637) 873188
Resident Proprietor: Jim Nettleton

A family Hotel gloriously situated in its own grounds, 150 yards from Fistral beach, 31 bedrooms and 8 apartments enjoying superb views of beach and golf course and all with excellent facilities.

* Indoor heated pool * Sauna * Solarium * Spa Bath * Full Central Heating * Laundry Room * Snooker Room * Excellent food and wines * Ideal for short breaks.

Whipsiderry Hotel   AA ★★ 🌟 70%

**TREVELGUE ROAD, PORTH,
NEWQUAY, CORNWALL, TR7 3LY**
Telephone: (0637) 874777

Overlooking Porth beach and standing in its own grounds (approx 2½ acres) this hotel has breathtaking views of both sea and country. A very attractive lounge bar and a heated swimming pool set in the most beautiful surroundings. We serve a 6 course dinner with choice of menu. Bar snacks available.

★ Heated swimming pool ★ Sauna ★ Full central heating ★ Detached launderette ★ Licensed for residents ★ Excellent and varied cuisine   ★ All rooms en suite with tea making facilities ★ Putting green. Detached American Pool Room ★ Colour TV, radio and intercom all rooms ★ Entertainments.

Plus nightwatch of the badgers.

Ashley Courtenay highly recommended.

Kilbirnie Hotel
AA ★★★
Newquay · Cornwall

The Kilbirnie Hotel has been one of the leading hotels in Newquay for over 30 years. During it's long history it has had the opportunity of arranging and catering for many Golfing and Bowling organisations. Mr and Mrs Cobley enjoy taking a personal interest in making your holiday a memorable one. Breakfast and evening dinner will be served in our elegant Dining Room where all our catering staff take pride in their attention to detail. Our head chef Mr Phillip Ryder who has been with this establishment for over 16 years, has always during his career made sure that all the produce brought into the hotel is of the highest standard and quality. The hotel has a heated indoor and outdoor swimming pool, sauna, solarium, spa bath, snooker, pool and table tennis.

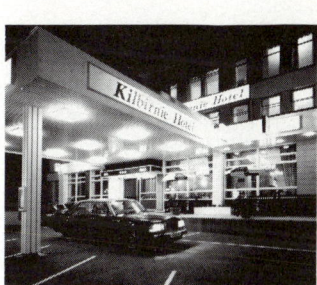

Special Golfing Holidays
7 nights, 5 rounds from £275.00 inc VAT or 5 nights, 5 rounds from £240.00 inc VAT — Golf Courses to include Carlyon Bay, Trevose, Tehidy, Newquay and Bowood.

**For details and reservations
Tel: (0637) 875155 Fax: (0637) 850769**

Newquay - Newtonmore

♀ International V ♦ ⌂ ✂ Sunday Lunch £5.95-£8.95 Dinner £8.95-£11.95&alc Last dinner 8.45pm
Credit Cards 1 3 £

★★60% *Cedars*
Mount Wise TR7 2BA ☎(0637) 874225
Closed Dec-Mar (ex Xmas)
The choice of bedrooms at the Cedars ranges from superior rooms with a sitting area and balcony to reasonably furnished standard rooms. Further improvements are planned for basic bedrooms and the lodge annexe has ground floor rooms and family accommodation. Public rooms are spacious and comfortable, and a simple style of cooking is available with friendly and efficient dining room service and a coffee shop counter.
36rm(15⇨16♠)(8fb) CTV in all bedrooms ® T
CTV 40P 2♣ ❋ ⌂ (heated) sauna solarium gymnasium ♦ ⌂ ✂

★★59% *Beachcroft*
Cliff Rd TR7 1SW ☎(0637) 873022
Closed mid Oct-early Apr
This long established and very popular family-run hotel enjoys a good location with private access to the beach below. Bedrooms are traditionally furnished, and several have very good sea views. Generous public rooms are comfortably furnished and include a small coffee shop and well run dining room.
69rm(29⇨25♠)(12fb) CTV in 59 bedrooms ® T
Lift (CTV 80P ❋ ⌂ (heated) ⌂ (heated) ♪ (hard) sauna solarium games room putting ♣
V ♦ ⌂
Credit Cards 1 3

★★58% *Tremont*
Pentire Av TR7 1PB ☎(0637) 872984 FAX (0637) 851984
This privately owned holiday hotel offers a varied choice of functional, though well equipped bedrooms which are steadily being upgraded. Public areas are spacious and live entertainment is often provided. Wholesome fare is served by a team of helpful staff in the dining room.
57rm(54⇨♠)Annexe7⇨♠(26fb) CTV in all bedrooms ® T
sB&B£20-£30.85 sB&B⇨♠£22.30-£34 dB&B⇨♠£44.60-£68 (incl dinner) ♬
Lift 60P ❋ ⌂ (heated) ♪ (hard) squash sauna solarium gymnasium putting table tennis ♪ ♣ *xmas*
♀ English & French ♦ ⌂ Bar Lunch fr£1.70alc Dinner £8.50-£11.50 Last dinner 7.30pm
Credit Cards 1 3 £

★64% *Trevone*
Mount Wise TR7 2BP ☎(0637) 873039 FAX (0637) 851334
Closed 16 Oct-16 Apr
This well established hotel has been run by the Chegwin family since 1924 and is now in the capable hands of Pam Chegwin. Bedrooms are generally compact, but some have fine sea views. There is a comfortable lounge, a dining room with crisp linen cloths and a bar. There is also a lovely enclosed garden at the rear.
32rm(27⇨♠)(3fb) ❋ ✈ (ex guide dogs) sB&B£12-£24 sB&B⇨♠£13-£25 dB&B£24-£48 dB&B⇨♠£26-£50 ♬
CTV 20P ❋ games room
♀ English, French, Indian & Italian ♦ ✂ Dinner £10.50 Last dinner 7.30pm

NEW QUAY Dyfed Map 02 SN35

★★62% *Black Lion*
SA45 9PT ☎(0545) 560209 FAX (0545) 560585
Closed Jan-Feb
Dating from the early 18th century, this small family-run holiday hotel overlooks Cardigan Bay. It has character bars, good lounge facilities and bedrooms which have been upgraded. A good range of food is served.
7rm(4⇨2♠)(3fb) CTV in all bedrooms ® ❋ sB&B£22.50-£32.50 sB&B⇨♠£27.50-£35 dB&B£35-£40 dB&B⇨♠£40-£50

CTV 40P ♿
♀ British & Continental V ♦ ❋ Bar Lunch £2.75-£9 Dinner £6-£11 Last dinner 9.30pm
Credit Cards 1 2 3 £

NEWTON ABBOT Devon Map 03 SX87

★★59% *Queens*
Queen St TQ12 2EZ ☎(0626) 63133 & 54106
FAX (0626) 64922

CONSORT HOTELS

This friendly traditional hotel is in a central position near the station. It offers a wide range of dishes from 2 fixed price menus served in the Regency Restaurant. Informal meals are available in the Queen's Pantry adjacent to the popular bar. Bedrooms are all equipped to the same standard.
24rm(20⇨♠)(1fb) CTV in all bedrooms TV in 1 bedroom ® T
sB&B£35 sB&B⇨♠£45 dB&B£50 dB&B⇨♠£62 ♬
8P ♪
♀ English & French V ♦ ⌂ Lunch £6.95-£12.25 Dinner £12.25&alc Last dinner 8.45pm
Credit Cards 1 2 3 £

★65% *Hazelwood*
33A Torquay Rd TQ12 2LW ☎(0626) 66130 & 65021
Conveniently positioned for the town centre, this small, privately owned hotel is personally run by Mr and Mrs Newnham. An attractive bar lounge with colour TV is provided, and the restaurant offers a varied choice from a fixed-price menu. Bedrooms are individually furnished and decorated.
7rm(5⇨♠) CTV in all bedrooms ® T ❋ sB&B£25-£29.50 sB&B⇨♠£30-£35 dB&B£35-£41 dB&B⇨♠£44-£49 ♬
CTV 10P ♿ solarium body toning studio beauty therapy
V ♦ ❋ Bar Lunch £2.50-£7.50 Dinner £8.50-£11.95 Last dinner 8pm
Credit Cards 1 3 £

NEWTON-LE-WILLOWS Merseyside Map 07 SJ59

★★63% *Kirkfield*
2/4 Church St WA12 9SU ☎(0925) 228196 FAX (0925) 228196
Parts of this privately owned hotel date back 200 years, and there are old beams in the bar and restaurant. Under the supervision of resident managers Mr and Mrs Hirst, it provides informal and friendly service. Recent improvements to the ground floor have enhanced the spacious lounge bar and the cottage-style restaurant. Bedrooms, most with simple modern furniture, are well equipped.
17⇨♠(1fb)1♬ CTV in all bedrooms ® ✈ (ex guide dogs)
(CTV 50P
♦ ⌂ Last dinner 9pm
Credit Cards 1

★★59% *The Pied Bull*
58 High St WA12 9SH (on A49) ☎Warrington(0925) 224549 FAX (0925) 291929
Situated in the centre of town, this pub and commercial hotel offers a sound standard of practical accommodation. Some of the best bedrooms are in a neighbouring cottage. Public areas are limited to a spacious bar, a colourful restaurant and a small residents' lounge.
11rm(2⇨5♠)Annexe7⇨ CTV in all bedrooms ® T
✈ (ex guide dogs) ❋ sB&Bfr£22 sB&B⇨♠fr£29.50 dB&Bfr£32 dB&B⇨♠fr£38 Continental breakfast ♬
CTV 45P
V ♦ ⌂ ❋ Lunch £3.95-£6.75 Dinner £3.95-£6.75 Last dinner 10pm
CONF. Board 40
Credit Cards 1 3 £

NEWTONMORE Highland *Inverness-shire* Map 14 NN79

★★★63% *Gaskmore House*
PH20 1BS ☎Laggan(05284) 250 FAX (05284) 207
(For full entry see Laggan Bridge)

Newton Stewart - Northallerton

NEWTON STEWART Dumfries & Galloway *Wigtownshire* Map **10** NX46

★★★ ❀♨ 72% *Kirroughtree*
Minnigaff DG8 6AN ☎(0671) 2141 FAX (0671) 2141
Closed 26 Jan-4 Mar

Eight acres of attractive landscaped gardens surround this 18th-century mansion, now a family owned and personally managed hotel with exemplary standards of service and hospitality. Thoughtfully equipped bedrooms range from standard to spacious deluxe. Public areas include the main lounge, a cocktail bar and two elegant dining rooms. The dinner menu is short but carefully chosen – a recent inspection meal consisted of chicken liver and foie gras parfait, escalope of salmon with leeks and a Champagne sauce, and a delicious caramelised lemon tart with honey Anglaise and Armagnac caramel.

19⇨ℳ Annexe2⇨ℳ(2fb) CTV in all bedrooms ® T
⟨ 50P ❀ ♀ (grass) croquet pitch and putt ♫ nc12yrs
♀ French ✿ ♨ ✿ Last dinner 9.30pm
Credit Cards [1][3]

★★★ 57% *Bruce*
88 Queen St DG8 6JL (on A75) ☎(0671) 2294 FAX (0671) 2294
Closed Dec & Jan

This privately owned hotel, close to the town centre, is informally run and offers a modest but improving standard of accommodation. Public areas include a cosy lounge bar and first floor lounge.

18⇨ℳ(2fb)1🛏 CTV in all bedrooms ® T sB&B⇨ℳ£40-£42 dB&B⇨ℳ£62-£64 🎀
20P 🚗 solarium gymnasium ♨
♀ English & French V ✿ ♨ ✿ Bar Lunch £4-£16.25alc Dinner £14-£17.50alc Last dinner 8.30pm
Credit Cards [1][2][3][5]

★★ 66% *Creebridge House*
DG8 6NP (off A75) ☎(0671) 2121 FAX (0671) 3258

CONSORT HOTELS

Formerly the shooting lodge of the Earls of Galloway, this pleasantly sited hotel is just across the River Cree from the town centre. The bedrooms overlooking the gardens offer the most comfort, though all are similarly equipped. The public areas include a restful lounge, an attractive dining room and a lovely bar popular with locals. Fresh produce is a feature of the varied menus both in the bar and dining room.

20⇨ℳ(2fb) CTV in all bedrooms ® T ✿ sB&B⇨ℳ£30-£40 dB&B⇨ℳ£50-£70 🎀
CTV 50P ❀ ♫ xmas
♀ Scottish & French V ✿ ♨ ✿ ✿ Sunday Lunch £7.50-£9.50 Dinner £16.95-£17.50&alc Last dinner 8.30pm
CONF. Thtr 70 Class 20 Board 30 Del from £39.50
Credit Cards [1][3]

★★ 60% *Crown*
101 Queen St DG8 6JW (off A75) ☎(0671) 2727

Close to the market and within easy reach of the town centre, this traditional Galloway listed building provides unpretentious accommodation and friendly service under the personal direction of the owners. There is a choice of pleasant bars which are well patronised by locals and visitors alike, and for fishermen the hotel has 2 private rods on the River Cree.

11rm(5⇨4ℳ)(1fb) CTV in all bedrooms ® T
✵ (ex guide dogs) ✿ sB&B£23 sB&B⇨ℳ£28.50 dB&B£46 dB&B⇨ℳ£51
CTV 20P ♫
V ✿ ♨ Lunch £6-£12 Dinner fr£13.50&alc Last dinner 8.30pm
Credit Cards [1][3]

For key to symbols see the Bookmark.

NEWTOWN Powys Map **06** SO19

★★ 63% *Elephant & Castle*
Broad St SY16 2BQ ☎(0686) 626271 FAX (0686) 622123
RS 24-26 Dec

A busy hotel located beside the River Severn in the town centre, the Elephant and Castle offers a variety of bedrooms, those in the new annexe being particularly well equipped. A small but comfortable residents' lounge augments its good range of bars, and a wide choice of food is available.

25⇨ℳ Annexe11⇨ℳ(3fb) CTV in all bedrooms ®♀ T ✵
sB&B⇨ℳ£38.50 dB&B⇨ℳ£55
⟨ 🎀 CTV 60P ♫
V ✿ ♨ ✵ Lunch £7.70 Dinner £8-£13alc Last dinner 9.30pm
Credit Cards [1][2][3][5]

NEWTOWN LINFORD Leicestershire Map **04** SK50

★★ 61% *Johnscliffe Hotel & Restaurant*
73 Main St LE6 OAF ☎Markfield(0530) 242228 & 243281 FAX (0533) 312767
Closed 24 Dec-4 Jan

This hotel and restaurant are set in a very pretty village. Seven bedrooms are in the old part of the house, the rest are in a modern extension. There are attractive lawns and gardens, overlooked by the restaurant and open plan conservatory lounge.

15⇨ℳ(1fb)4🛏 CTV in all bedrooms ® T
CTV 50P ❀ ♨
♀ English & French V ✿ ♨ Last dinner 9.45pm
Credit Cards [1][2][3]

NORMAN CROSS Cambridgeshire Map **04** TL19

Forte Posthouse
Great North Rd PE7 3TB (on southbound A1 at junct with A15) ☎Peterborough(0733) 240209
FAX (0733) 244455

FORTE Posthouse

Suitable for both the business and leisure traveller, this bright hotel provides modern accommodation in well equipped bedrooms with en suite bathrooms. For more details about Forte Posthouse hotels, consult the Contents page, under Hotel Groups.

93⇨ℳ ✵ B⇨ℳ£41.50-£53.50 (room only)
CONF. Thtr 50 Class 20 Board 20 Del from £79.50

NORMANTON Leicestershire Map **04** SK90

★★★ ❀68% *Normanton Park*
LE15 8RP (1m E unclass road) ☎Stamford(0780) 720315
FAX (0780) 721086

By following the signs to Normanton and Rutland Water – South Shore – you will find this elegant Georgian building with its grounds descending to the water's edge. Rooms vary in size, those to the side of the building being the largest. The bar provides a full range of snacks while the restaurant offers a more comprehensive choice of dishes.

6⇨ℳ Annexe8⇨ℳ(5fb) CTV in all bedrooms ®♀ T
⟨ 60P ❀ sailing canoeing windsurfing cycle hire
♀ English & French V ✿ ♨ Last dinner 9.50pm
Credit Cards [1][2][3]

NORTHALLERTON North Yorkshire Map **08** SE39

★★★ ❀69% *Solberge Hall*
Newby Wiske DL7 9ER (3.25m S off A167)
☎(0609) 779191 FAX (0609) 780472

BEST WESTERN HOTELS

This charming and relaxing Victorian country house hotel is set in extensive gardens and woodland. Public rooms reflect the elegance of the building with panelled walls and period fireplaces and many of the bedrooms retain much original character, particularly the

Northallerton - Northampton

master rooms at the front. The Garden Room restaurant provides a high standard of cuisine from a choice of menus, and the set 4-course evening meal is particularly good value.
25⇨🛏(2fb)🖵 CTV in all bedrooms ® T
100P ❋ snooker croquet clay pigeon shooting
♀ English & French V ◊ 🖵 Last dinner 9.30pm
Credit Cards ①②③⑤

★★★ 66% *Sundial*
Darlington Rd DL6 2XF (N on A167) ☎(0609) 780525 FAX (0609) 780491

This modern hotel is on an open site just north of the town centre. Bedrooms are well proportioned and have many modern features, and Winston's restaurant provides a pleasant ambience for lunch and dinner.
28⇨🛏(8fb)⚲in 22 bedrooms CTV in all bedrooms ®⚲ T ℂ 100P ❋ ♫
V ◊ 🖵 ⚲ Last dinner 9.30pm
Credit Cards ①②③⑤

★★ 69% *The Golden Lion*
Market Place DL7 8PP ☎(0609) 777411 FAX (0609) 773250

FORTE
Heritage

This Georgian coaching inn is in the centre of the town, and many of the bedrooms have recently been upgraded to an excellent modern standard, while retaining the ambience of the historic inn which once served travellers on the old Great North Road.
26rm(21⇨🛏)⚲in 12 bedrooms CTV in all bedrooms ® T
sB⇨🛏£70-£75 dB⇨🛏£80-£85 (room only) 🍴
CTV 100P *xmas*
V ◊ 🖵 ⚲ Sunday Lunch £10.95-£12.95&alc Dinner £15.75-£16.75&alc Last dinner 9.30pm
Credit Cards ①②③⑤

NORTHAMPTON Northamptonshire Map 04 SP76

★★★★ 60% *Swallow*
Eagle Dr NN4 0HW (off A45, between A428 & A508) ☎(0604) 768700 FAX (0604) 769011

SWALLOW
HOTELS

Polite staff provide a range of services throughout the public rooms, including a flexible range of food. Light snacks are available in the lounge, there is the informal Springs restaurant and the more serious Spires restaurant offering international dishes from its à la carte menu. Rooms service is available. Bedrooms, like the public areas, are fitted out in ultra modern style.
122⇨🛏⚲in 38 bedrooms CTV in all bedrooms ®⚲ T ✱
sB&Bfr£35 sB&B⇨🛏£90 dB&B⇨🛏£70-£99 🍴
ℂ 166P (heated) sauna solarium gymnasium jacuzzi steam room *xmas*
♀ English, French & Italian V ◊ 🖵 ⚲ Lunch fr£12.50 Dinner £15-£17.50&alc Last dinner 10.30pm
CONF. Thtr 225 Class 100 Board 202 Del from £75
Credit Cards ①②③⑤

★★★ 66% *Northampton Moat House*
Silver Street, Town Centre NN1 2TA
☎(0604) 22441 FAX (0604) 230614
Closed 24-26 Dec

Queens Moat Houses

This modern multi-storey hotel in the town centre has generally spacious bedrooms which are attractively furnished and fully equipped with modern facilities. There is a choice of bars and eating options, with an all-day menu available.
142⇨🛏(4fb)⚲in 21 bedrooms CTV in all bedrooms ® T ✱
sB&B⇨🛏£66.60-£74 dB&B⇨🛏£83.70-£93 🍴
Lift ℂ 200P sauna solarium jacuzzi hairdresser
♀ English & French V ◊ 🖵 ⚲ ✱ Lunch £12.25&alc Dinner £13.50&alc Last dinner 10.30pm
Credit Cards ①②③④⑤

★★★ 63% *Westone Moat House*
Ashley Way, Weston Favell NN3 3EA (off A4500 in Weston Favell) ☎(0604) 406262
FAX (0604) 415023
Closed Xmas-1 Jan

Queens Moat Houses

This hotel enjoys a secluded setting in a convenient position. The main part of the house dates from 1914, but rooms have now been refurbished to provide a good range of modern facilities, and the building has been substantially extended to create annexe accommodation.
31⇨🛏Annexe35⇨🛏(3fb)⚲in 15 bedrooms CTV in all bedrooms ®⚲ T sB&B⇨🛏£69 dB&B⇨🛏£79 🍴
Lift ℂ CTV 100P 2🚗 (charged) ❋ sauna solarium gymnasium croquet putting
♀ International V ◊ 🖵 ✱ Lunch £10.75
CONF. Thtr 150 Class 70 Board 50 Del £92
Credit Cards ①②③⑤ £

★★ 69% *Lime Trees*
8 Langham Place, Barrack Rd NN2 6AA (from city centre follow sign A508 Leicester) ☎(0604) 32188 FAX (0604) 233012
RS 27 Dec-New Year

A predominantly commercial hotel with enthusiastic and hospitable owners who are continually investing in the future. The most recent addition is a small pool room and bar on the lower ground floor. The attractive restaurant, adorned with original dance paintings, is fully air conditioned and bedrooms, though simply decorated, are generally of a good size.
21rm(19⇨🛏)(2fb)1🖵 CTV in all bedrooms ® T ✱
CTV 20P 1🚗 🚲
V ◊ 🖵 Last dinner 9pm
Credit Cards ①②③⑤

★★ 65% *Thorplands Toby*
Talavera Way, Round Spinney NN3 4RN (Toby)
☎(0604) 494241 FAX (0604) 790532
Closed 25, 26 Dec & 1 Jan

A modern accommodation block provides bedrooms with a good range of modern facilities, while a popular Toby restaurant and bars are situated across the car park. Both staff and management are cheerful and eager to please.
31⇨🛏⚲in 8 bedrooms CTV in all bedrooms ® T ✱
ℂ 100P ❋ pool table ♫
V ◊ 🖵 ⚲ Last dinner 10.30pm
Credit Cards ①②③⑤

★★ 60% *Grand*
Gold St NN1 1RE ☎(0604) 250511 FAX (0604) 234534

CONSORT
HOTELS

This large traditional hotel is situated in the heart of the town. Public areas are rather dated, but bedrooms have been upgraded over recent years and, while modest, offer modern facilities at a reasonable price.
62⇨🛏(2fb) CTV in all bedrooms ® T ✱ sB&B⇨🛏fr£37.50 dB&B⇨🛏fr£45 🍴
Lift ℂ 70P 2🚗
V ◊ 🖵 ✱ Bar Lunch £2.50-£5&alc Dinner £10-£14alc Last dinner 9.30pm
CONF. Thtr 130 Class 45 Board 40 Del from £50
Credit Cards ①②③⑤ £

Courtyard by Marriott
Bedford Rd NN4 0YF ☎(0604) 22777 FAX (0604) 35454

Well furnished guest bedrooms have en suite bathrooms, remote control CTV and direct-dial telephone at this modern hotel, and there is an informal restaurant and bar. For more details about Courtyard by Marriott, consult the Contents page, under Hotel Groups.
104⇨🛏 dB⇨🛏fr£62.50 (room only)

454

Northampton - Northleach

Forte Travelodge
Upton Way NN5 6EG (A45, towards M1 junct 16)
☎(0604) 758395 Central Res (0800) 850950

This modern building offers a good standard of accommodation for overnight stops. Smart, spacious and well equipped bedrooms, all with en suite bathrooms, are suitable for family use, and meals may be taken at the nearby family restaurant. For more details about Travelodges, consult the Contents page, under Hotel Groups.
40⇌♠✱ B⇌♠£31.95 (room only)

Travel Inn
Harpole Turn, Weedon Rd, Harpole NN7 4DD (on A45) ☎(0604) 832340

Purpose-built bedrooms accommodation offers spacious and well equipped bedrooms, all with en suite bathrooms. Meals may be taken at the nearby family restaurant and pub. For more details about Travel Inns, consult the Contents page, under Hotel Groups.
51⇌♠✱ B⇌♠£33.50 (room only)

NORTH BALLACHULISH Highland *Inverness-shire*
Map **14** NN06

★★ **60%** **Loch Leven**
Onich PH33 6SA (off A82) ☎Onich(08553) 236 & 459
By the northern shore of the loch, this 17th-century coaching inn enjoys spectacular views. Family-run, it has a friendly atmosphere, with homely public areas and refurbished bedrooms equipped with modern comforts.
10⇌♠(1fb) CTV in all bedrooms ® T sB&B⇌♠£22-£32 dB&B⇌♠£44-£64
CTV 60P ✱
♀ Scottish & Continental V ♂ ⌂ ✂ Bar Lunch £3.50-£10alc Dinner £16.50-£18alc Last dinner 8.30pm
Credit Cards [1] [3]

NORTH BERWICK Lothian *East Lothian* Map **12** NT58

★★★ **65%** **The Marine**
Cromwell Rd EH39 4LZ ☎(0620) 2406 FAX (0620) 4480

Situated in a quiet residential area overlooking the golf course to the Firth of Forth, this turreted Victorian hotel appeals to tourists and golf enthusiasts alike. Spacious public areas include a comfortable foyer lounge, a golfing theme bar and an attractive restaurant. Bedrooms are generally well proportioned and suites are available.
83⇌♠✂in 20 bedrooms CTV in all bedrooms ® T ✱ sB⇌♠£50-£75 dB⇌♠£75-£110 (room only) ⊟
Lift ℂ 200P 2⊟ ✱ ⊡ (heated) ♂ (hard) squash snooker sauna solarium putting childrens playground ♂ *xmas*
♀ International V ♂ ⌂ Lunch £7.95-£10.95 Dinner £17.95-£19.95&alc Last dinner 9.30pm
Credit Cards [1] [2] [3] [5]

★★ **63%** **Point Garry**
West Bay Rd EH39 4AW ☎(0620) 2380 FAX (0620) 2848
Closed Nov-Mar
This sturdy Victorian house in a quiet residential area is particularly popular with visiting golfers, enjoying a fine outlook over the west golf course to the sea. Efficiently run by resident owners, it provides a friendly and relaxing atmosphere in its comfortable cocktail bar and cosy panelled lounge. Bedroom standards vary.
16rm(12⇌♠)(6fb) CTV in all bedrooms ® T
14P ✂ snooker
♀ International V ♂ ⌂ Last dinner 9pm
Credit Cards [1] [3]

★★ **62%***Nether Abbey*
20 Dirleton Av EH39 4BQ ☎(0620) 2802 FAX (0620) 5298
Improvements continue at this family-run golfing, commercial and holiday hotel, which is situated in the west end a few minutes walk from central amenities. Bedrooms offer a variety of styles and standards, some having been upgraded to a modern standard. Public areas include a bright foyer with a comfortable lounge, a smartly refurbished bar and an attractive dining room.
16rm(4⇌6♠)(5fb) CTV in all bedrooms ® T
40P ✱
V ♂ Last dinner 8.30pm
Credit Cards [1] [3]

NORTH FERRIBY Humberside Map **08** SE92
Forte Posthouse
Ferriby High Rd HU14 3LG (on A63, W of Hull)
☎Hull(0482) 645212 FAX (0482) 643332

Suitable for both the business and leisure traveller, this bright hotel provides modern accommodation in well equipped bedrooms with en suite bathrooms. For more details about Forte Posthouse hotels, consult the Contents page, under Hotel Groups.
95⇌♠✱ B⇌♠£41.50-£53.50 (room only)
CONF. Thtr 100 Class 40 Board 40 Del from £79.50

NORTHLEACHGloucestershire Map **04** SP11
★★ **64%***Wheatsheaf*
GL54 3EZ ☎Cotswold(0451) 60244
In the heart of the village, this attractive ivy-clad inn offers bright individually styled bedrooms with a good range of facilities, many of the rooms overlooking the garden at the rear. There are congenial bars and a pretty little restaurant with crisp linen and nice table settings.

Sundial Hotel

★★★

**Darlington Road, Northallerton
N Yorkshire DL6 2XF
Telephone: (0609) 780525
Fax: (0609) 780491**

This attractive, recently built hotel is quietly situated in its own grounds with a large secure car park.

The Restaurant specialises in Thai cuisine.

The hotel can cater for conferences, banquets and weddings.

All the 28 bedrooms are en suite and have full facilities expected of a three star hotel.

Centrally situated to enjoy the Dales and Yorkshire Moors.

Northleach - Norton

8⇌🛏 CTV in all bedrooms ® T
15P 3🚗 🚙 ✿
V ♥ Last dinner 9.30pm
Credit Cards 1 3

NORTHOP HALL Clwyd Map 07 SJ26

★★★ 64% *New Chequers Country House Hotel*
Chester Rd CH7 6HJ ☎Deeside(0244) 816181
FAX (0244) 814661

Standing in fine woodlands and gardens, this large Victorian house is just 10 minutes drive from Chester. Bedrooms are named after castles, British prime ministers and American presidents. Rooms in the extension have modern furniture and those in the main house have a more period feel. Interesting features include ornate oak carving in the panelled cocktail bar.

27⇌🛏(2fb)1 🚙⌘in 2 bedrooms CTV in all bedrooms ®⚡ T
CTV 100P 2🚗 ✿
♀ International V ♥ ⚡ ✽ Lunch fr£15.50 Dinner fr£15.50 Last dinner 9.30pm
CONF. Thtr 120 Board 35 Del from £55
Credit Cards 1 2 3

★★ 60% *Autolodge*
Gateway Services, Westbound A55 CH5 6HB
☎Chester(0244) 550011 FAX (0244) 550763

This modern, functional hotel offers good-value accommodation with up-to-date facilities. Bedrooms provide a bed settee as well as a double bed. Public areas are limited to a foyer lounge area and an open-plan bar with a conservatory extension. Friendly staff create an informal atmosphere, and an à la carte menu supplements the daily table d'hôte.

38⇌🛏(38fb) CTV in all bedrooms ® T ✖ (ex guide dogs)
⌖ 45P ✿
♀ English French & Italian V ♥ ⚡ ⌘ ✽ Dinner £12&alc Last dinner 9.30pm
Credit Cards 1 2 3

....
Forte Travelodge
(on A55, eastbound)
☎(0244) 816473 Central Res (0800) 850950

FORTE Travelodge

This modern building offers a good standard of accommodation for overnight stops. Smart, spacious and well equipped bedrooms, all with en suite bathrooms, are suitable for family use, and meals may be taken at the nearby family restaurant. For more details about Travelodges, consult the Contents page, under Hotel Groups.

40⇌🛏✖ B⇌🛏£31.95 (room only)

NORTH QUEENSFERRY Fife Map 11 NT18

★★★ 70% *Queensferry Lodge*
St Margaret's Head KY11 1HP ☎Inverkeithing(0383) 410000
FAX (0383) 419708

Enjoying a spectacular position overlooking the Firth of Forth and the famous rail and road bridges, this privately owned, purpose-built hotel has spacious, comfortably furnished bedrooms equipped with all modern amenities. Public areas offer a choice of bars and restaurants plus a craft shop, heritage centre and tourist information centre.

32⇌🛏 CTV in all bedrooms ® T
Lift ⌖ 130P ✿
♀ Scottish & French V ♥ ⚡ ⌘ Last dinner 10pm
Credit Cards 1 2 3

Satellite television – look for this symbol ⚡
in the directory entries.

NORTH WALTHAM Hampshire Map 04 SU54

★★ 68% **Wheatsheaf**
RG25 2BB (on A30) (Whitbread) ☎Dummer(0256) 398282 FAX (0256) 398253

This is a former coaching inn with modern extensions. Public areas are open plan and vary in levels of comfort and styles of eating. Bedrooms are comfortable, with modern amenities and attractive furnishings.

28⇌🛏(1fb)1🚙⌘in 5 bedrooms CTV in all bedrooms ® T ✱
sB&B⇌🛏fr£45 dB&B⇌🛏fr£56.50 🛏
⌖ 70P *xmas*
♀ Continental V ♥ ⚡ ⌘ ✽ Lunch £8.25-£9.25 Dinner £12-£13.50 Last dinner 10pm
CONF. Thtr 80 Class 25 Board 30 Del from £95
Credit Cards 1 2 3 4 5

NORTHWICH Cheshire Map 07 SJ67

★★★ 64% *Hartford Hall*
School Ln, Hartford CW8 1PW (2m SW off bypass A556)
☎Hartford(0606) 75711 FAX (0606) 782285

Set in extensive grounds in the quiet village of Hartford, this period mansion has comfortable public rooms furnished in character with the house. Bedrooms are in a separate modern wing and have modern facilities.

20⇌🛏(2fb) CTV in all bedrooms ®⚡
⌖ CTV 50P ✿
V ♥
Credit Cards 1 2 3 5

★★ 62% *Wincham Hall*
Hall Ln, Wincham CW9 6DG (on A559) ☎(0606) 43453 FAX (0606) 40128

This early medieval hall has been much altered over the years. Bedrooms are bright and modern, with coordinated soft furnishings, and public areas include a pleasant restaurant with panelled walls, a comfortable lounge and large lounge bar.

10rm(9⇌🛏🛏)(1fb) CTV in 9 bedrooms ® T
CTV 200P ✿
V ♥ ⚡ Last dinner 9.45pm
Credit Cards 1 3

NORTH WOOTTON Somerset Map 03 ST54

★★ 60% *Crossways Inn Restaurant & Hotel*
BA4 4EU ☎Pilton(074989) 237 & 476

In a rural situation, this hotel has a busy bar and restaurant. The bedrooms are well equipped, adequately furnished and comfortable for short stays. The large beamed dining room does a brisk trade in inexpensive roasts and grills with a blackboard of special dishes.

17⇌🛏(3fb) CTV in all bedrooms ® T ✖ (ex guide dogs)
CTV 150P 🚙 ✿
V ♥ ⌘
Credit Cards 1 3

See advertisement under WELLS

NORTON Shropshire Map 07 SJ70

★★ 73% **Hundred House**
Bridgnorth Rd TF11 9EE (on A442 6m N of Bridgnorth) ☎(095271) 353 FAX (095271) 355

This Georgian inn on the outskirts of the town has welcoming public rooms with oak panelling and log fires. Individually decorated bedrooms include all modern amenities and the popular restaurant makes good use of fresh herbs from the large herb garden.

10⇌🛏(5fb)3🚙 CTV in all bedrooms ® T sB&B⇌🛏£59-£69 dB&B⇌🛏£69-£88 🛏
40P ✿

♡ English & French V ✧ ⌁ ✳ Lunch £15-£28alc Dinner £15-£28alc Last dinner 10pm
Credit Cards [1][3]

NORWICH Norfolk Map 05 TG20

★★★★ 68% Sprowston Manor
Wroxham Road, Sprowston NR7 8RP (2m NE A1151) ☎(0603) 410871 FAX (0603) 423911

An impressive manor house, this popular hotel has recently been developed to provide modern, well equipped accommodation including rooms and junior suites. A few older rooms in the main house of a lower standard are rarely let. Public areas are extensive and the attractive restaurant is divided into 3 intimate areas. A lounge menu is available all day, and service is good natured.
97⇨♠(12fb)8🅱 CTV in all bedrooms ®♋T
✗ (ex guide dogs) sB⇨♠fr£75 dB⇨♠fr£85 (room only) ♻
Lift (120P ✿ ⌇ (heated) ▶ 18 sauna solarium gymnasium croquet beauty salon *xmas*
♡ English & French V ✧ ⌁ ✂ Lunch £15-£16&alc High tea £10.50-£16.75 Dinner £16.75-£18.75&alc Last dinner 10pm
CONF. Thtr 50 Class 50 Board 90 Del from £95
Credit Cards [1][2][3][5]   £

★★★ 66% Hotel Nelson
Prince of Wales Rd NR1 1DX ☎(0603) 760260 FAX (0603) 620008

The riverside location and accessibility to the city centre make this a very popular venue for both the commercial and leisure user. Under excellent management and with a caring professional team of staff, guests' comfort is the prime consideration.
120⇨♠3🅱 CTV in all bedrooms ® T ✗ (ex guide dogs) sB&B⇨♠£71-£76 dB&B⇨♠£82.50-£97 ♻
Lift (151P 30🅿 ✿ *xmas*
➪

PARK·FARM·HOTEL
— and Restaurant —
Hethersett, Norwich NR9 3DL
Tel: Norwich (0603) 810264 Fax: (0603) 812104
An exclusive Country House Hotel, set in delightful landscaped gardens, just off the A11, five miles south of Norwich.
The original Georgian farmhouse has been carefully and tastefully extended to include a superb leisure complex, with large heated swimming pool, sauna, steam room, solarium, spa-bath, gymnasium and an aerobics studio.
38 individually designed en-suite bedrooms. The executive rooms have four poster beds and whirlpool baths.
The Georgian restaurant and adjacent conference facilities provide the perfect setting and ambiance for a private dinner, business meeting, or a larger celebration.
Hard Tennis court, croquet and putting on front lawns. Light aircraft landing strip and helipad on grounds. Special weekend rates available. Open all year.
Egon Ronay,   AA★★★ 🏵🏵🏵🏵🏵 HIGHLY COMMENDED Tourist Board

★★
WINCHAM HALL HOTEL
Hall Lane, Wincham, Northwich
Cheshire CW9 6DG
Tel: (0606) 43453. Fax: (0606) 40128
Under the personal supervision of Jane and Richard Clemetson, Wicham Hall can provide the perfect setting for any occasion.
In the 17th century surroundings and with 5 acres of beautiful grounds we can cater for up to 150 guests. Visit our restaurant and enjoy superbly cooked food in select surroundings. We also have accommodation available if you would like to stay.
Private Functions, Conferences, etc. also catered for.
Open Monday to Saturday. Lunches on Sunday.
Bar meals also available. Fully Residential.

★★
THE WHEATSHEAF HOTEL
West End, Northleach, Gloucestershire GL54 3EZ
Telephone: (0451) 860244. Fax: (0451) 861037

The Wheatsheaf provides the perfect setting and accommodation for those who enjoy excellent home cooked imaginative food, welcoming bars with logs fires and attractive individually furnished bedrooms. This lovely period coaching inn has all these plus being situated in this ancient small town in the heart of the Cotswolds. There are many fascinating walks with many places of interest to visit.

Norwich

♨ European V ❖ ⚏ ✱ Lunch £9.75&alc Dinner fr£12.50 Last dinner 9.45pm
CONF. Thtr 90 Board 44 Del £103
Credit Cards [1][2][3][5]

★★★ 66% Hotel Norwich
121-131 Boundary Rd NR3 2BA (1.5m NW, between A1067 & A140 intersections)
☎(0603) 787260 FAX (0603) 400466

This is a modern hotel on the ring road. Gates Bar and the Rouen Restaurant reflect durability rather than style, though the lounge area is light and inviting. Bedrooms are thoughtfully laid out and the last phase of redecorating older rooms was due to be completed by the time this guide was published.

108⇌ƒ(15fb)⚞in 30 bedrooms CTV in all bedrooms ®✱ T ✖ (ex guide dogs) ✱ sB&B⇌ƒ£56.50-£66.50 dB&B⇌ƒ£61.50-£71.50 ₽
(225P ⌂ (heated) sauna solarium gymnasium steam room spa bath *xmas*
♨ International V ❖ ⚏ ✼ ✱ Lunch £5.75-£15 Dinner £12.50-£13.50 Last dinner 10pm
Credit Cards [1][2][3][5]

★★★ 65% Friendly
2 Barnard Rd, Bowthorpe NR5 9JB (1st roundabout on A1074 from Swaffham)
☎(0603) 741161 FAX (0603) 741500

This hotel has open-plan public areas with the same pleasing colour scheme and furnishings linking the foyer lounge, 2 bars and restaurant. The latter provides an à la carte menu and a carvery with daily specials. Most bedrooms have now been upgraded to the group's Premier status.

80⇌ƒ(14fb)2⚞in 11 bedrooms CTV in all bedrooms ®✱ T ✱ sB⇌ƒ£55-67 dB⇌ƒ£69.50-£82 (room only) ₽
(100P ⌂ (heated) sauna solarium gymnasium jacuzzi *xmas*
♨ English & French V ❖ ⚏ ✱ Lunch £9.90 Dinner £12.50&alc Last dinner 9.45pm
CONF. Thtr 200 Class 75 Board 40 Del from £74
Credit Cards [1][2][3][5] £

★★★ 62% Norwich Sport Village & Hotel in Broadland
Drayton High Rd, Hellesdon NR6 5DU
☎(0603) 788898 FAX (0603) 406845

This functional modern hotel forms part of an impressively equipped sports and leisure complex which includes an aqua-park, and is ideal for business use. Public areas do tend to mingle with sports facilities but not inconveniently so, and the bedroom accommodation is separate and secure.

56⇌ƒ(2fb) CTV in all bedrooms ®✱ T ✱ (ex guide dogs)
Lift (CTV 800P ✼ ⌂ (heated) ♪ (hard) squash snooker sauna solarium gymnasium jacuzzi badminton table tennis
♨ International V ❖ ⚏ Last dinner 9.30pm
Credit Cards [1][2][3][5]

★★★ 61% Maids Head
Tombland NR3 1LB ☎(0603) 761111 FAX (0603) 613688

This old coaching inn is slightly old-fashioned and looking a little tired in places, though the refurbished bedrooms in the older wing are attractive, and considerably better than the 'new' wing of bedrooms (scheduled for demolition and replacement). Public areas are spread out, with a comfortable split-level lounge, and staff are smart and friendly.

81⇌ƒ(2fb)2⚞ CTV in all bedrooms ® T ✱ sB&B⇌ƒ£39-£79 dB&B⇌ƒ£76-£92 ₽
Lift (80P 20⚞ *xmas*
♨ English & French V ❖ ⚏ ✱ Lunch £2.60-£13.75alc High tea £4.90 Dinner £14.95&alc Last dinner 9.45pm
CONF. Thtr 210 Class 100 Board 400 Del from £60
Credit Cards [1][2][3][5] £

★★ 71% Annesley House
6 Newmarket Rd NR2 2LA (on A11) ☎(0603) 624553 FAX (0603) 624553
RS Xmas

Located a short distance south of the town centre on the A11, the Annesley is a collection of well maintained Georgian buildings. Over the years the proprietors have improved the accommodation to a high standard, enhanced by meticulous housekeeping. A friendly young team provide good service in the cosy bar and restaurant, making this a popular choice for both business and leisure travellers.

17⇌ƒAnnexe7⇌ƒ(3fb) CTV in all bedrooms ®✱ T ✖ (ex guide dogs) sB&B⇌ƒ£39.50-£54.50 dB&B⇌ƒ£49.50-£64.50 ₽
25P ⇌ ✼
♨ English & French V ❖ ⚏ Lunch £12.95 Dinner £12.95&alc Last dinner 9pm
Credit Cards [1][2][3][5]

★★ 66% Cumberland
212-216 Thorpe Rd NR1 1TJ (on A1247, 1m from railway station) ☎(0603) 34550 & 34560 FAX (0603) 33355
Closed 23 Dec-4 Jan

A refurbishment programme is underway at this commercial hotel. Public areas have already been upgraded and both the bar and restaurant offer good value food.

23⇌ƒAnnexe4⇌ƒ(2fb) CTV in all bedrooms ® T ✖ (ex guide dogs) ✱ sB⇌ƒ£29.95 dB⇌ƒ£33-£50 (room only) ₽
(CTV 60P 3⊘ (charged) ✼
V ❖ ⚏ ✼ ✱ Lunch £6.50-£12.50&alc Dinner £11.50-£12.25&alc Last dinner 9.30pm
Credit Cards [1][2][3][5] £

★★ 66% Oaklands
89 Yarmouth Rd, Thorpe St Andrew NR7 0HH
☎(0603) 34471 FAX (0603) 700318

Beyond reception there is a bar straddling 2 public areas: a private members' club with gaming machines and the residents' lounge. This arrangement may sometimes restrict access to the garden lounge. The restaurant's imaginative menus and popular carvery reflect good efforts in the kitchen.

39rm(38⇌ƒ)(4fb)⚞in 11 bedrooms CTV in all bedrooms ®✱ T
(CTV 90P ✼
V ❖ ⚏ ✼ Last dinner 9.30pm
Credit Cards [1][2][3][5]

★★ 62% Arlington
10 Arlington Ln, Newmarket Rd NR2 2DA (off A11)
☎(0603) 617841 FAX (0603) 663708

The Arlington provides well equipped accommodation, some recently refurbished rooms being particularly attractive and comfortable; public areas are limited but adequate to the needs of a mainly commercial clientèle. The dining room offers a choice of à la carte or carvery menus, and a competent team of pleasantly mannered staff.

44⇌(3fb)⚞in 9 bedrooms CTV in all bedrooms ®✱ T sB&B⇌ƒ£43.50-£65.50 dB&B⇌ƒ£54.50-£76.50 ₽
(60P solarium ♪ *xmas*
♨ English & French V ❖ ⚏ ✱ Lunch £8-£19alc High tea fr£2.75 Dinner £15.95-£19.95 Last dinner 10pm
CONF. Thtr 60 Class 40 Board 20 Del from £60
Credit Cards [1][2][3][5] £

See advertisement on page 461

★★ 62% Beeches Hotel & Victorian Gardens
4-6 Earlham Rd NR2 3DB (on B1108) ☎(0603) 621167 FAX (0603) 620151

A private hotel which occupies 2 impressive 18th-century houses, the Beeches is next to the Plantation Garden, which is being restored to its former glory. Bedrooms vary in size and style. There

OAKLANDS HOTEL
NORWICH, NORFOLK

Great hospitality awaits you at the Oaklands. A friendly hotel set in landscaped grounds overlooking picturesque river valley on the outskirts of Norwich within easy access of the Norfolk Broads. Excellent food in the **Garden Restaurant**. Privileged membership of the nearby Oasis Leisure Club with swimming pool, gym, etc.

Well appointed rooms from £52.00 B & B
(low cost all inclusive mini-break tariff also available)

Reservations: 0603 34471
OAKLANDS HOTEL ★★
Thorpe Road, Norwich, Norfolk

NORWICH
For business or pleasure stay friendly

Friendly Hotel, 2 Barnard Road, Bowthorpe, Norwich NR5 9JB
AA ★★★
Premier Plus Rooms. Own hotel parking. Superb leisure centre. Located on the A47, west of the ancient city, the hotel offers the ideal stop-over point for visiting Norfolk and East Anglia on business or pleasure.

FOR RESERVATIONS (office hours) FREEPHONE
0800 591910
or call direct on 0603 741161 Fax: 0603 741500

It pays to stay Friendly

Friendly HOTELS

The Sporting Businessmans No1 Choice in Norfolk

For business or pleasure you will find it hard to beat the excellent value offered within the well-equipped hotel and sports complex at The Norwich Sport Village.

This unique complex houses the most up to date sport & leisure facilities within East Anglia, combined with a friendly atmosphere, superb restaurants and bars, and a team of dedicated professionals on hand to ensure your stay is the best ever.

★★★

The Package
Rates include full English breakfast, VAT and service.
Special rates for weekend 2 night breaks.
All residents (subject to availability) enjoy free use of, Gymnasium, Sauna Snooker and Aerobics and entry to Broadland Aquapark, East Anglia's most spectacular swimming paradise.

NORWICH SPORT VILLAGE & HOTEL
in Broadland

The Location
Easy access from all directions, close proximity to Norwich Airport and main British Rail station.

To make a reservation please call
Norwich Sport Village and Hotel in Broadland
Drayton High Road Hellesdon Norwich NR6 5DU
Telephone: (0603) 789469

AA ★★★

BARNHAM BROOM HOTEL

GOLF, CONFERENCE AND LEISURE
Barnham Broom, Norwich NR9 4DD
Tel: (0603) 759393 Fax: (0603) 758224

In a beautiful valley, this modern hotel and leisure complex has 52 bedrooms all with private bathrooms; a spacious lounge with open log fire; two bars; and a host of leisure facilities including two 18 hole championship golf courses (one par 71, one par 72), practice holes and putting green areas.

Inside the leisure centre are a heated indoor swimming pool; sauna; solarium; steam room; a beauty and hairdressing salon and a fully equipped gymnasium. Other sports facilities include four squash courts, 3 all-weather tennis courts and full size snooker table.

The complex also contains a spacious and comprehensively equipped conference centre.

Prices include full English breakfast.
Children charged for meals as taken.
Host: Richard Bond

Access: From London and the South via A11; from Midlands and the North via A47. 10 miles west of Norwich. Norwich Airport 10 miles.

Norwich - Nottingham

is a bistro-style dining room with a limited fixed-price menu, but the hotel was unlicensed when inspected.
28⇌🏠(2fb)✠in 24 bedrooms CTV in all bedrooms ® ❇ T ✖ (ex guide dogs) sB&B⇌🏠£36-£47.50 dB&B⇌🏠£49.50-£65 🅿
24P ✿
♡ English & Italian V ✧ ⚏ ✠ Dinner £8-£9.50&alc Last dinner 8pm
Conf. Thtr 30 Class 20 Del £58.50
Credit Cards 1 2 3

Forte Posthouse
Ipswich Rd NR4 6EP (on A40, just south of outer ring road) ☎(0603) 56431 FAX (0603) 506400

FORTE Posthouse

Suitable for both the business and leisure traveller, this bright hotel provides modern accommodation in well equipped bedrooms with en suite bathrooms. For more details about Forte Posthouse hotels, consult the Contents page, under Hotel Groups.
116⇌🏠✠ B⇌🏠£41.50-£53.50 (room only)
Conf. Thtr 100 Class 45 Board 30 Del from £79.50

NOTTINGHAM Nottinghamshire Map **08** SK 54

★★★★ **64%** Royal Moat House International
Wollaton St NG1 5RH ☎(0602) 414444 FAX (0602) 475667
Closed 25-26 Dec

Queens Moat Houses

Popular for the varied food and bars available, this hotel has 4 restaurants providing a range of styles from steaks and grills through to well presented French cuisine in the Restaurant l'Avenue. All but the Penthouse bar are located in an 'avenue' planted with tropical trees and plants; the Penthouse offers panoramic views over the city. Free parking for residents is available in the adjacent multi-storey.
201⇌🏠✠in 68 bedrooms CTV in all bedrooms ® T ✖ (ex guide dogs)
Lift ⌇ ⌸ 600P squash solarium gymnasium
♡ English, French & American V ✧ ⚏ ✠ Last dinner 11pm
Credit Cards 1 2 3 5

★★★ **70%** Nottingham Gateway
Cinderhill NG8 6AZ (take A610 from junct 26 of M1) ☎(0602) 794949 FAX (0602) 794744
The 2 wings of this modern purpose built hotel are connected by a smoked glass atrium giving a conservatory effect to the marble floored reception and lounge areas on each level. There is a lounge bar and dining area comprising carvery, coffee shop and brasserie, the latter offering a Thai menu on weekdays, and to each there is a self-service element. Twenty-four-hour room service is also provided. All bedrooms are similarly furnished with coordinated décor. A very willing uniformed team operate efficiently and with ready smiles.
108⇌(8fb)✠in 54 bedrooms CTV in all bedrooms ® T ✖ (ex guide dogs) sB⇌£23.50-£48.50 dB⇌£32.70-£65 (room only) 🅿
Lift ⌇ ⌸ 250P
♡ English, French & Thai V ✧ ⚏ ✠ Lunch £4.95-£8.50&alc High tea £3.50 Dinner £10.95-£14.35&alc Last dinner 10pm
Conf. Thtr 300 Class 150 Board 50 Del from £55
Credit Cards 1 2 3 5

★★★ **70%** Nottingham Moat House
Mansfield Rd NG5 2BT ☎(0602) 602612 FAX (0602) 691506
Closed 24-29 Dec

Queens Moat Houses

Located about a mile north of the city this purpose-built hotel offers a choice of restaurants and fare ranging from informal light meals to a selection of international dishes. These value-for-money meals are very popular and booking is advisable for all restaurants. Bedrooms are in 2 styles, the more spacious in the newer wing, but all have full

---

modern facilities. Guests are assured of polite, smiling service from the neatly dressed staff.
172⇌🏠✠in 66 bedrooms CTV in all bedrooms ® T sB⇌🏠£57.50-£60 dB⇌🏠£77.50-£80 (room only) 🅿
Lift ⌇ 250P 90🚗
♡ International V ✧ ⚏ ✠ ✻ Lunch £7.95 Dinner fr£10.95&alc Last dinner 11pm
Conf. Thtr 180 Class 80 Board 60 Del from £70
Credit Cards 1 2 3 5

★★★ **66%** Rutland Square
St James St NG1 6FJ ☎(0602) 411114 FAX (0602) 410014
104⇌🏠(3fb)1⌘✠in 38 bedrooms CTV in all bedrooms ® ❇ T ✻ sB⇌🏠£52.50 dB⇌🏠£58.50 (room only)
Lift ⌇ ♪
♡ English & French V ✧ ⚏ ✠ Lunch £3-£12alc Dinner £12.50-£16.50 Last dinner 11pm
Credit Cards 1 2 3 5

★★★ **64%** Swans Hotel & Restaurant
84-90 Radcliffe Rd, West Bridgford NG2 5HH (on A6011) ☎(0602) 814042 FAX (0602) 455745
Situated near to Trent Bridge cricket ground, this completely refurbished hotel has public areas full of floral displays, smart and well equipped bedrooms, and a restaurant offering skilfully prepared meals chosen from either a daily set menu or the carte.
31⇌🏠(3fb)1⌘ CTV in all bedrooms ® ❇ T ✖ (ex guide dogs) ✻ sB&B⇌🏠£29.50-£49.50 dB&B⇌🏠£49.50-£59.50 🅿
Lift ⌇ 25P ♪ xmas
♡ English & French V ✧ ⚏ ✠ ✻ Lunch £13.95&alc Dinner £13.95&alc Last dinner 10pm
Conf. Thtr 50 Class 30 Board 35 Del £64
Credit Cards 1 2 3 5

★★★ **63%** Westminster Hotel
310-318 Mansfield Rd, Carrington NG5 2EF (on A60 1.5m N of town centre) ☎(0602) 623023 FAX (0602) 691156
Closed 26 Dec-30 Dec RS Xmas & New Year
This busy commercial hotel about a mile from the city centre has well equipped bedrooms with good quality furnishings. There is a comfortable bar and restaurant offering a good value table d'hôte menu.
58⇌🏠 CTV in all bedrooms ® ❇ T ✖ (ex guide dogs) ✻ sB⇌🏠fr£44 dB⇌🏠fr£54 (room only) 🅿
Lift ⌇ 38P
♡ English & Continental V ✧ ⚏ ✻ Bar Lunch £7-£12 Dinner £9-£16 Last dinner 9.15pm
Conf. Thtr 60 Class 28 Board 30 Del £75
Credit Cards 1 3

★★★ **61%** Strathdon Thistle
Derby Rd NG1 5FT ☎(0602) 418501 FAX (0602) 483725

THISTLE HOTELS

This purpose-built city centre hotel is popular with business users. Parking is limited, but discounts are available at a nearby multi-storey. Light, attractive public areas include a comfortable reception foyer, and a lively American-themed bar, a more sedate first-floor Cocktail Bar and an airy conservatory lounge. In Bobbins Restaurant French cuisine predominates. Bedrooms are nicely decorated and have a good range of facilities, but are on the small side.
69⇌🏠(8fb)✠in 8 bedrooms CTV in all bedrooms ® ❇ T ✻ sB⇌🏠£64-£72 dB⇌🏠£84-£92 (room only) 🅿
Lift ⌇ 10P 5🚗
♡ International V ✧ ⚏ ✠ Lunch £8.90-£12.95&alc Dinner £13.50-£14.70&alc Last dinner 10.30pm
Conf. Thtr 900 Class 200 Board 100 Del from £60
Credit Cards 1 2 3 4 5

Nottingham

★★★ **60%** Holiday Inn Garden Court
Castle Marina Park NG7 1GX (on A453 to Castle Marina) ☎(0602) 500600 FAX (0602) 500433

This modern purpose built hotel, conveniently situated in the Castle Marina business and retail park, offers value for money in its smart bedrooms, with their good range of equipment and tiled bathrooms. Public areas are limited to a small bar and bright compact restaurant and the range of services available is restricted. Staff however, are pleasant and helpful throughout.
100⇨♠⤓in 50 bedrooms CTV in all bedrooms ® T ✱
sB⇨♠£44.50-£64.50 dB⇨♠£49.50-£69.50 (room only) ⊟
Lift (100P
V ✿ ♨ ✱ Bar Lunch £2.50-£7 Dinner £12.50&alc Last dinner 10pm
Credit Cards 1 2 3 5

★★★ **58%** *The Stage*
Gregory Boulevard NG7 6LB ☎(0602) 603261 FAX (0602) 691040
Formerly known as the Sherwood, this hotel has been extensively extended and refurbished to provide good value accommodation. Bedrooms, standard or executive, are very well equipped, the latter having quality fitted furniture and attractive coordinating fabrics. Public areas are limited to a lounge bar and a foyer lounge.
58⇨♠ CTV in all bedrooms ® T

★★ **70%** Hotel Windsor Lodge
116 Radcliffe Rd, West Bridgford NG2 5HG (A6011 & A52 Grantham, 0.5m Trent Bridge Cricket Ground)
☎(0602) 813773 FAX (0602) 819405
Closed 25-26 Dec
This family-run hotel offers good quality accommodation and a simple but enjoyable English menu in the restaurant, freshly prepared to order.

➤

THE STAGE HOTEL

GREGORY BOULEVARD, NOTTINGHAM NG7 6LB
Phone: (0602) 603261
Fax: (0602) 691040

- ★ 52 modern en-suite bedrooms with 16 de-luxe rooms.
- ★ Ground floor bedroom adapted for disabled use.
- ★ Very competitive rates. Further reduction for weekend and group bookings.
- ★ Three conference suites provide modern facilities and natural daylight for 2-100.
- ★ Easy access from M1 off Junction 26.
- ★ Free parking at rear of hotel.
- ★ 10 minutes from City centre.
- ★ Sherwood bar and restaurant offers romantic surroundings with an excellent à la carte and table d'hôte menu.

 AA
★★★

 COMMENDED

★★★ AA
THE STRATHDON
THISTLE HOTEL

Derby Road, Nottingham NG1 5FT
Tel: 0602 418501   Fax: 0602 483725

Your choice in Nottingham

For Reservations at over 100 Mount Charlotte Thistle Hotels Telephone London: 071 937 8033.

THISTLE HOTELS

ARLINGTON HOTEL
NORWICH, NORFOLK

Intimate hotel in leafy setting just a short stroll from the centre of beautiful Norwich. Great food and hospitality in elegant restaurants and bustling bar. Privileged membership of the Oasis Leisure Club with swimming pool etc. *(10 minute drive)*

Well appointed rooms from £39.00 B & B
(low cost all inclusive mini-break tariff also available)

Reservations: 0603 617841
ARLINGTON HOTEL ★★
Newmarket Road, Norwich, Norfolk

Nottingham - Nuneaton

49⇨🛏(15fb) CTV in all bedrooms ® ⚷ T ✱ sB&B⇨🛏£22.50-£40 dB&B⇨🛏£40-£50
CTV 50P ♿ snooker
✱ Bar Lunch £6 Dinner £11.75 Last dinner 8.30pm
Credit Cards [1][2][3][5]

★★ 67% Priory
Derby Rd, Wollaton Vale NG8 2NR (3m W, on A52) (Toby)
☎(0602) 221691 FAX (0602) 256224
This fairly large complex is fronted by the popular Toby restaurant and bars, with adjoining bedrooms at the rear. Rooms are spacious, well furnished and equipped with many extras. The restaurant, in several parts, serves mainly grills, and the lounge bar, on a lower level, offers a selection of bar meals at lunch time.
31⇨🛏(4fb)⚹in 12 bedrooms CTV in all bedrooms ® T
🐕 (ex guide dogs) ✱ sB&B⇨🛏£24-£62 dB&B⇨🛏£48-£73 🅿
(200P ♫
🏛 Mainly grills V ◊ 🎬 ⚹ ✱ Lunch £5-£15alc Dinner £5-£20alc Last dinner 10pm
Credit Cards [1][2][3][5] £

★★ 65% Rufford
53 Melton Road, West Bridgford NG2 7NE (on A606, near junct A60 Loughborough Road) ☎(0602) 814202 FAX (0602) 455801
Closed Xmas
This popular establishment provides well equipped accommodation and pleasant public rooms.
35🛏 CTV in all bedrooms ® ⚷ T 🐕 (ex guide dogs) ✱
sB&B🛏£30.55-£35.25 dB&B🛏£45-£47
(CTV 35P
◊ 🎬 ⚹ ✱ Dinner £11.75-£14.10 Last dinner 8pm
Credit Cards [1][2][3][5]

★★ 62% Balmoral
55-57 Loughborough Rd, West Bridgford NG2 7LA (beside A60 Loughborough Road) ☎(0602) 455020 & 818588 FAX (0602) 455683
A popular family-run hotel on the outskirts of the city, the Balmoral provides good standards of accommodation throughout. Predominantly good value grill menus are served in a friendly and informal manner.
31🛏 CTV in all bedrooms ® T 🐕 (ex guide dogs) ✱
sB&B⇨🛏£22.50-£35 dB&B⇨🛏£42-£48
CTV 33P
V ◊ 🎬 Last dinner 8pm
Credit Cards [1][3]

Forte Crest
Saint James's St NG1 6BN ☎(0602) 470131 FAX (0602) 484366

FORTE CREST

A large modern hotel with a wide range of services and amenities, designed particularly for the business traveller. Bedrooms are smart, comfortable and well equipped. For more details about Forte Crest hotels, consult the Contents page, under Hotel Groups.
130⇨🛏✱
CONF. Thtr 600 Class 350 Board 120 Del £105

Hilton National Nottingham
Derby Rd, Lockington DE7 2RH
☎(0509) 674000

HILTON

This is a bright, modern hotel with an informal restaurant, aimed at both the business and leisure guest. All bedrooms have en-suite bathrooms and a range of modern facilities. For more information about Hilton National, consult the Contents page, under Hotel Groups.
152⇨🛏✱ B⇨🛏£89 (room only)
CONF. Thtr 260 Class 115 Board 45 Del £140

NUNEATON Warwickshire Map **04** SP39

★★ 63% Longshoot Toby
Watling St CV11 6JH (on A5/A47 junct) (Toby) ☎(0203) 329711 FAX (0203) 344570
Closed 24 Dec-4 Jan
Similar to other establishments in this well known chain, this particular hotel is situated at the junction of major roads – in this case the A5 and A47 – to the north of Nuneaton. The modern bedrooms, all twins or doubles, are located in a separate purpose-built motel block, adjacent to the restaurant and half are at ground floor level. There is a choice of bars, one of which offers bar meals as an alternative to the grill and carvery restaurant, which also has a bar.
Annexe47⇨🛏 CTV in all bedrooms ® 🐕
(120P
V ◊ ⚹ Last dinner 10pm
Credit Cards [1][2][3][5]

Forte Travelodge
Bedworth CV12 0BN (2m S, on A444)
☎(0203) 382541 Central Res (0800) 850950

FORTE Travelodge

This modern building offers a good standard of accommodation for overnight stops. Smart, spacious and well equipped bedrooms, all with en suite bathrooms, are suitable for family use. There is no restaurant adjacent to this Travelodge. For more details about Travelodges, consult the Contents page, under Hotel Groups.
40⇨🛏✱ B⇨🛏£31.95 (room only)

Remember to book early for holiday
and bank holiday times.

Traditional values in a perfect setting

THE UNICORN - *Gunthorpe Bridge*
- *Fabulous River location*
- *Ideal for business or pleasure*
- *16 Bedrooms (all modern Amenities)*
- *Superb Restaurant*
- *Prices from £37.50 per night*

GUNTHORPE BRIDGE, GUNTHORPE, NOTTS Tel: 0602 663612

HOTEL

Windsor Lodge

116 Radcliffe Road
West Bridgford
Nottingham NG2 5HG
Telephone: (0602) 813773 & 811229
Fax: (0602) 819405

54 BEDROOMS

A well deserved reputation for good quality bedrooms, all en suite, all facilities
•
Good quality cuisine in attractive dining room
•
Conference facilities
•
Large private car park

Rufford Hotel ★★

53 Melton Road, West Bridgford, Nottingham NG2 7NE
Telephone: Nottingham (0602) 814202 & 811233
Fax No. (0602) 455801

Welcome to Nottingham

A regular visitor or just passing through, why not enjoy a stay in one of Nottingham's premier locations. Ideally situated just 1½ miles from the City Centre and close to the International Water Sports Centre at Holme Pierrepont, two Football Grounds and the famous Trent Bridge Cricket Ground make this quality hotel the ideal choice.

Family owned and managed for the last 22 years, the Rufford boasts 35 bedrooms all with private facilities, colour television and telephone. A comprehensively stocked bar complete with friendly efficient staff to make your visit that touch more enjoyable.

Top of the list for Nottingham in a leading American Tourist Guide.
Small Wedding Receptions a speciality.

Nuneaton - Oban

Travel Inn
Coventry Rd CV10 7PJ (S of town near A444/
B413 junct) ☎(0203) 343584 FAX (0203) 327156

Purpose-built accommodation offers spacious and well equipped bedrooms, all with en suite bathrooms. Meals may be taken at the nearby family restaurant and pub. For more details about Travel Inns, consult the Contents page, under Hotel Groups.
48⇨ ❋ B⇨₤33.50 (room only)

NUTFIELD Surrey Map 04 TQ35

★★★ ❀❀ 74% Nutfield Priory
RH1 4EN ☎Redhill(0737) 822066 FAX (0737) 823321

This magnificent and extravagant Victorian folly stands high on Nutfield Ridge and enjoys outstanding views. The comfortable cloistered restaurant is a fine setting for chef Stewart Dunkley's imaginative dishes in the modern vein: game terrine with elderberry vinaigrette; millefeuille of crab; halibut with a cinnamon nage; lamb with a risotto of sun dried tomato; hot ginger pudding, and iced nougat parfait. Bedrooms are spacious and stylish.
52⇨ 2🛏 ≠ in 12 bedrooms CTV in all bedrooms T ✈ (ex guide dogs) sB&B⇨£95-£105 dB&B⇨£115-£205 Continental breakfast 🍴
Lift ℂ 130P 🅿 ❋ 🏊 (heated) squash snooker sauna solarium gymnasium badminton steam room beauty treatment *xmas*
V ❀ ℒ ❋ Lunch £12-£17&alc Dinner £20-£25&alc Last dinner 9.45pm
CONF. Thtr 85 Class 45 Board 35 Del from £155
Credit Cards ①②③⑤ £

OAKHAM Leicestershire Map 04 SK80

★★★ ❀❀❀ 🍴 HAMBLETON HALL
Hambleton LE15 8TH (3m E off A606) ☎(0572) 756991
FAX (0572) 724721

Set in a peaceful little village which is surrounded on 3 sides by Rutland Water, this is a fine Victorian manor house. Quality of service is the hallmark of the establishment, with friendly and hospitable staff combining professionalism with a more individualistic and personalised approach. Chef Aaron Patterson concentrates on predominantly British cuisine in modern style, influenced by his experience with Anton Mosimann and Raymond Blanc. A recent inspection meal featured excellent roast lamb stuffed with spring cabbage and apricot served with a light jus flavoured with lemon grass. Fricassé of wild mushrooms and sweetbreads in a pastry cup with foie gras is among several starters praised by our inspectors. A wide variety of desserts completes the meal, and a long, varied and interesting wine list includes some fine clarets.
15⇨ 1🛏 CTV in all bedrooms T sB&B⇨£100-£120 dB&B⇨£100-£265 Continental breakfast 🍴
Lift 40P ❋ ≋ (heated) ♪ (hard) *xmas*
V ❀ Lunch fr£27.50&alc Dinner fr£27.50&alc Last dinner 9.30pm
Credit Cards ①②③

★★★ ❀ 71% Barnsdale Lodge
The Avenue, Rutland Water LE15 8AH (3m E on A606)
☎(0572) 724678 FAX (0572) 724961

This farmhouse hotel, built of local stone, sits high above Oakham and Rutland Water. Attention to detail is the priority of proprietor Mr Reid, who is actively involved in the daily running of the hotel. The public rooms tend to be dominated by the service of food, both in the lounge bar and in the 3 separate dining rooms. Bedrooms are fresh and nicely appointed.
17⇨ (2fb) 🛏 CTV in all bedrooms ® T ❋ sB&B⇨£49.50 dB&B⇨£69.50-£79.50 🍴
ℂ 150P ❋ 🐕 *xmas*
V ❀ ℒ ❋ ❋ Lunch £13.95-£24alc Dinner £18-£24alc Last dinner 9.30pm
CONF. Thtr 50 Class 15 Board 30 Del £75
Credit Cards ①②③⑤ £

★★★ ❀ 68% Normanton Park
LE15 8RP ☎Stamford(0780) 720315 FAX (0780) 721086
(For full entry see Normanton)

★★★ ❀ 68% Whipper-in Hotel
Market Place LE15 6DT ☎(0572) 756971 FAX (0572) 757759

This sympathetically restored inn has been furnished throughout with antique and period furniture, old prints and rich fabrics, and bedrooms are pleasantly colour coordinated. The restaurant is smart and comfortable, and chef Carl Bontoft presents interesting menus of modern British cuisine and some fine wines.
21⇨ Annexe3⇨ 2🛏 CTV in all bedrooms ® T
ℂ
V ❀ ℒ Last dinner 9.30pm
Credit Cards ①②③⑤

★★ 65% The Boultons Country House
4 Catmose St LE15 6HW ☎(0572) 722844 FAX (0572) 724473

CONSORT HOTELS

The Boultons comprises a listed building, a stone cottage and a modern extension, which includes improved reception facilities and a new wing of bedrooms. These newer bedrooms are comfortable, with pine furniture and Laura Ashley fabrics; the original rooms are more dated in comparison. Service is effective and friendly, and room service is available during restaurant service hours.
25⇨ (2fb)1🛏 CTV in all bedrooms ® T sB&B⇨£45-£60 dB&B⇨£55-£70 🍴
15P *xmas*
🍴 French V ❀ ℒ Lunch £5-£8.50&alc Dinner fr£14&alc Last dinner 9.30pm
CONF. Thtr 60 Class 40 Board 30 Del from £70
Credit Cards ①②③⑤ £

OBAN Strathclyde *Argyllshire* Map 10 NM83

★★★ 58% *Alexandra*
Corran Esplanade PA34 5AA ☎(0631) 62381 FAX (0631) 64497
Closed Nov-Mar

In a commanding position on the esplanade, with a lovely outlook over the bay to the islands of Kerrera and Mull, this renovated Victorian resort hotel is a popular base for tour groups and holiday-makers. Public areas are comfortable and modern, with bright, airy lounges, a bar and dining room. Bedrooms vary in size but have bright colour schemes and light wood furniture.
55⇨ (1fb) CTV in all bedrooms ® T
Lift ℂ 80P pool table ♪
🍴 International V ❀ ℒ Last dinner 9pm
Credit Cards ①②③⑤

Oban

★★★ 56% Caledonian
Station Square PA34 5RT (Milton) ☎(0631) 63133 FAX (0631) 62998
Catering mainly for tourists, this town centre hotel is close to the ferry terminal and looks out over Oban Bay to the islands of Kerrera and Mull. Bedrooms have been steadily upgraded, and as well as the main dining room the hotel has a popular all day restaurant. Parking can be difficult.
70⇌(10P) CTV in all bedrooms ® T sB&B⇌£39-£59 dB&B⇌£59-£89 ₽
Lift (6P ♯ ♪ xmas
♀ Scottish & French V ♥ ♨ ✗ Lunch £5-£10 High tea £5-£6 Dinner £9-£15 Last dinner 11pm
CONF. Thtr 100 Class 80 Board 60 Del from £45
Credit Cards 1 2 3 5

★★ ❀76% Manor House
Gallanach Rd PA34 4LS (SCOTLAND'S HERITAGE HOTELS) ☎(0631) 62087 FAX (0631) 63053
Closed 25 Dec-31 Jan
With grounds leading down to the shore, this small hotel looks out across Oban Bay. Its Georgian character is most evident in the cosy lounges and the low ceilinged, half-panelled restaurant, where the original range is a feature. Seafood figures strongly, and in addition to the 5-course, ostensibly Scottish dinner menu there is a longer, mainly seafood carte. Bedrooms they have many thoughtful extras.
11⇌♠ CTV in all bedrooms ® T sB&B⇌♠£64-£112 dB&B⇌♠£84-£132 (incl dinner) ₽
20P ♯ ❀ nc10yrs
♀ Scottish, French & German V ♥ ♨ ✗ Lunch £15-£25alc Dinner £20-£25&alc Last dinner 9pm
Credit Cards 1 3

★★ 64% Argyll
Corran Esplanade PA34 5PZ ☎(0631) 62353 FAX (0631) 65472
CONSORT HOTELS
Overlooking the pier, this friendly family-run hotel has well equipped modern bedrooms and an attractive restaurant serving a wide range of dishes.
27⇌♠(5fb)2♯ CTV in all bedrooms ®♯ T
(CTV 6P
♀ European V ♥ ♨
Credit Cards 1 2 3 5

See advertisement on page 467

★★ 58% Lancaster
Corran Esplanade PA34 5AD (on seafront near St Columba's Cathedral) ☎(0631) 62587
This family-run holiday hotel overlooks the esplanade and West Bay. Public areas have a 60s feel and include a small bar, choice of lounges and dining room, all with impressive sea views. Bedrooms are generally compact with a mix of practical furnishings.
27rm(3⇌21♠)(3fb) CTV in all bedrooms ®♯ ✱
sB&Bfr£22.50 sB&B⇌♠fr£27.75 dB&B⇌♠fr£49
20P ♯ ▭ (heated) sauna solarium jacuzzi
V ♥ ♨ ✱ Lunch fr£6.25&alc Dinner fr£9.25&alc Last dinner 8pm
Credit Cards 1 3

★ ⚑ 67% Foxholes
Cologin, Lerags PA34 4SE (3m S, off A816) ☎(0631) 64982
Closed Nov-14 Mar
Looking much like a private residence, this modern house enjoys a peaceful rural setting. Family-run with friendly, informal service, there is a relaxing lounge with French windows leading onto a patio overlooking the gardens. The home cooking is enjoyable, but be prepared to choose your main course for dinner at breakfast time.
7⇌♠ CTV in all bedrooms ® ✱ ✱ dB&B⇌♠£70-£94 (incl dinner)
8P ♯ nc7yrs

Loch Melfort Hotel ★★★ ❀

The finest location on the West Coast of Scotland Right Beside Arduaine Gardens

The perfect place for a relaxing holiday or short break.

Comfortable accommodation with full ensuite facilities and spectacular views.

Superb cuisine with seafood a speciality. Non-residents welcome for all meals.

Spring, Autumn and Winter Breaks available together with special Christmas and New Year Holidays.

AA Hotel Inspectors Selected Hotel of the Year Scotland

**Arduaine, by Oban, Argyll PA34 4XG
Tel 08522 233 Fax 08522 214**

THE WHIPPER-IN HOTEL ★★★ ❀

**Market Place, Oakham, Leicester LE15 6DT
Tel: 0572 756971. Fax: 0572 757759**

Situated in the centre of Oakham, the capital of the ancient country of Rutland. The Whipper-In offers unrivalled comfort. All 25 bedrooms are individually decorated to reflect local rural themes. The Restaurant and bar are recognised as being among the best in the area. Close to Rutland Water, the hotel is ideal for touring the heart of England.

Ockley - Oldham

OCKLEY Surrey Map 04 TQ13

★★ 65% Gatton Manor Hotel Golf & Country Club
Standon Ln RH5 5PQ (off A29) ☏Oakwood Hill(0306) 627555 FAX (0306) 627713

Gatton Manor is an extended 18th-century manor house, in a rural setting of some 200 acres. The open plan bar lounge doubles as the golf club. The good size bedrooms have been tastefully furnished, and many bathrooms have large oval baths.

10⇌ CTV in all bedrooms ® T ✖ (ex guide dogs) sB&B⇌£45 dB&B⇌£70 🍴
CTV 150P ⇌ ✢ ▶ 18 ♪ (grass) ♪ bowling green *xmas*
♥ English & French ⇌ ⚲ ✱ Lunch £1.75-£9.75 High tea £2.50-£4.95 Dinner fr£15&alc Last dinner 9.45pm
CONF. Thtr 70 Board 40
Credit Cards [1][3]

ODIHAM Hampshire Map 04 SU75

★★ 66% George
High St RG25 1LP ☏(0256) 702081 FAX (0256) 704213

This historic 15th-century inn was refronted in the Georgian period. Behind this façade many original features remain including the beautiful oak panelling and flag stones in the dining room. Bedrooms range from character rooms in the main house to more spacious and modern annexe rooms. The bars are popular with non residents, and an extensive selection of dishes is offered.

9⇌ Annexe9⇌🍴(1fb)2⇌ in 5 bedrooms CTV in all bedrooms ®⚲ T sB&B⇌🍴£40-£62 dB&B⇌🍴£62-£85 🍴
20P ⇌ ✢
♥ English & French V ⇌ ⚲ ✱ Sunday Lunch £13.75 Dinner £9.76-£18.50alc Last dinner 10pm
Credit Cards [1][2][3][5]

OKEHAMPTON Devon Map 02 SX59

Forte Travelodge
Sourton Cross EX20 4LY (4m W, on A30)
☏(0837) 52124 Central Res (0800) 850950

This modern building offers a good standard of accommodation for overnight stops. Smart, spacious and well equipped bedrooms, all with en suite bathrooms, are suitable for family use, and meals may be taken at the nearby family restaurant. For more details about Travelodges, consult the Contents page, under Hotel Groups.
32⇌ ✱ B⇌🍴£31.95 (room only)

OLDBURY West Midlands Map 07 SO98

★★★ ❀74% Jonathans'
16-24 Wolverhampton Rd B68 0LH (junct with A456/ A4123, 1m from junct 2 or 3 off M5) ☏021-429 3757 FAX 021-434 3107

The façade and location of this hotel do not prepare guests for what amounts to a trip back in time. The building is a maze of rooms, passages and narrow corridors, every corner crammed with Victoriana. Rooms are individually styled with antique furnishings and interesting bric-a-brac alongside modern facilities. Eating options include Littlejohn's Bistro, the Fish Market, specialising in fish and vegetarian dishes, and The Original Restaurant, which concentrates on traditional old English cooking such as game paté, prawned trout rolls, and Jonathan's renowned trifle.

29⇌2⇌ in 2 bedrooms CTV in all bedrooms ® T ✖ (ex guide dogs) sB&B⇌£69-£75 dB&B⇌£80-£89 🍴
(12P ⇌ *xmas*
♥ English & Continental V ⇌ ⚲ ✱ Lunch £5-£25 High tea £2-£6 Dinner £12-£30 Last dinner 10.30pm
CONF. Thtr 50 Class 50 Board 36 Del £98
Credit Cards [1][2][3][5]

Forte Travelodge
Wolverhampton Rd B69 2BH (on A4123, northbound)
☏021-552 2967 Central Res (0800) 850950

This modern building offers a good standard of accommodation for overnight stops. Smart, spacious and well equipped bedrooms, all with en suite bathrooms, are suitable for family use, and meals may be taken at the nearby family restaurant. For more details about Travelodges, consult the Contents page, under Hotel Groups.
33⇌ ✱ B⇌🍴£31.95 (room only)

OLDHAM Greater Manchester Map 07 SD90

★★★ 70% Hotel Smokies Park
Ashton Rd, Bardsley OL8 3HX (on A627)
☏061-624 3405 FAX 061-627 5262

This modern hotel is a friendly establishment with a number of particularly well equipped and comfortable executive rooms. The main restaurant offers an interesting choice from its carte and daily table d'hôte menu and a good value buffet lunch.
47⇌ CTV in all bedrooms ® T ✖ (ex guide dogs) ✱ sB&B⇌🍴£25-£70 dB&B⇌🍴£50-£80 🍴
(120P sauna solarium gymnasium steam room
♥ English & French V ⇌ ⚲ ✱ Lunch £3.95&alc Dinner £12.50-£14.50 Last dinner 10.30pm
CONF. Thtr 300 Class 125 Board 50 Del from £75
Credit Cards [1][2][3][5]

★★★ 66% Avant
Windsor Rd, Manchester St OL8 4AS (W on A62) ☏061-627 5500 FAX 061-627 5896

Bedrooms are well equipped at this modern hotel, and public rooms include a choice of bars and a large restaurant.
103⇌🍴(2fb)⇌ in 16 bedrooms CTV in all bedrooms ® ⚲ T Lift (120P
♥ English & French V ⇌ ⚲ ✱ Last dinner 10pm
Credit Cards [1][2][3][5]

★★★ 62% The Bower
Hollinwood Av, Chadderton OL9 8DE (2.25m SW A6104) ☏061-682 7254 FAX 061-683 4605
RS 25-31 Dec

Once a large family house, this mainly commercial hotel with a modern bedroom wing stands in its own grounds. The lounge and bar, with reproduction, period- style furniture, give an impression of the character of the old house, the old and new blending well together.
66⇌🍴(1fb)1⇌ CTV in all bedrooms ® T
(140P ✢
♥ Continental V ⇌ ⚲ Last dinner 9.30pm
Credit Cards [1][2][3][5]

★★ 65% High Point
Napier St East OL8 1TR (SW of town, near A62)
☏061-624 4130 FAX 061-627 2757

This white-fronted Victorian building stands in a residential area southwest of the town centre where extensive redevelopments are in progress at the time of our visit. Popular with commercial guests, it offers particularly warm and helpful service, well equipped bedrooms furnished to a good modern standard and a recently extended busy restaurant.
19rm(17⇌🍴)(2fb)1⇌ CTV in all bedrooms ® T sB&B£35 sB&B⇌🍴£40-£55 dB&B£45 dB&B⇌🍴£55-£70 🍴
(42P 2⇌ ♪
♥ English & French V ⇌ ⚲ ✱ Lunch £7-£7.70 Dinner £9.95-£10.95&alc Last dinner 9.45pm
CONF. Thtr 30 Class 25 Board 20
Credit Cards [1][2][3][5]

Old Meldrum - Ollerton

OLD MELDRUM Grampian *Aberdeenshire* Map 15 NJ82
★ 65% **Meldrum Arms**
The Square AB51 0DS ☎(0651) 872238
Conveniently situated in the town centre, this family-run commercial hotel also caters for the touring holiday-maker. Bedrooms are compact and practically furnished. The well stocked bar is comfortable, and the range of meals available includes high teas and bar suppers as well as à la carte dinners. The friendly local staff are willing to please.
7🛏 CTV in all bedrooms ® T ✖ (ex guide dogs) ✱
sB&B🛏fr£33 dB&B🛏fr£45
25P
V ⊙ ⎵ ✱ Lunch £5.35-£8.10alc High tea £4.75-£9.75alc
Dinner £8.85-£16.60alc Last dinner 9.30pm
Credit Cards [1] [2] [3]

OLD RAYNE Grampian *Aberdeenshire* Map 15 NJ62
★★ 61% **Lodge**
AB52 6RY (just off A96) ☎(04645) 205
Closed 25 Dec & 1 Jan
This is a friendly, family-run commercial and tourist hotel. Two main house bedrooms were recently refurbished, and the timber walled annexe rooms offer practical modern furnishings. The hotel has no lounge, but there is a comfortable bar and smart dining room.
2rmAnnexe4⇌🛏(1fb) CTV in all bedrooms ® T sB&B£30-£35 sB&B⇌🛏£35-£40 dB&B£43-£48 dB&B⇌🛏£48-£53
20P
⊙ ⎵
Credit Cards [1] [2] [3]

OLD SODBURY Avon Map 03 ST78
★★ 66% **Cross Hands**
BS17 6RJ (on A46/B4040 crossroads 2m N of M4)
☎Chipping Sodbury(0454) 313000 FAX (0454) 324409
RS Xmas Night
This former posting house provides for the needs of modern travellers. Bedrooms vary in size and are generally compact, but offer a good range of modern facilities. The busy bars have some character and charm, and the formal restaurant is open for both lunch and dinner.
24rm(3⇌17🛏)1⚑ CTV in all bedrooms ® T ✱
sB&B⇌🛏£55.50 dB&B⇌🛏£39.50-£81.50 Continental breakfast 🍴
(I CTV 200P ✿ *xmas*
🍽 International V ⊙ ✱ Lunch £12.50-£25.50alc Dinner £12.50-£25.50alc Last dinner 10.30pm
Credit Cards [1] [2] [3] [5] £

OLLERTON Nottinghamshire Map 08 SK66
★★ 64% **Hop Pole**
Main St NG22 9AD (Samuel Smith)
☎Mansfield(0623) 822573 & 822305
This village-centre hotel dates back to the 1750's, its name coming from the local hop industry. Bedrooms are all smart and modern, with light fitted furniture. There is a small residents' lounge and extensive bars, where a good range of meals is served. The Carvery Restaurant is very popular locally.
11rm(10⇌🛏)(1fb) CTV in all bedrooms ® T
✖ (ex guide dogs) sB&B⇌🛏fr£32 dB&B⇌🛏fr£45 🍴
CTV 30P ✿ darts pool table
V ⊙ ⎵ Lunch £7.65-£8.50 Dinner £9.25-£12.50 Last dinner 9.45pm
Credit Cards [1] [2] [3]
See advertisement on page 469

STB commended AA ★★

Polfearn Hotel

The Polfearn Hotel is situated on the shores of Loch Etive where the River Awe passes the hotel in an unspoilt country location. Savour local seafood specialities in our restaurant or a bar meal in the bar and enjoy the magnificent views as you eat. An excellent base to explore the Highlands and Islands. The resident proprietors will ensure a warm welcome and a memorable stay.

**Polfearn Hotel, Taynuilt, Argyll PA35 1JQ
Telephone (08662) 251**

The Argyll Hotel
★★

Corran Esplanade · Oban
Telephone: 0631 62353 · Fax: 0631 65472

Situated on the seafront with spectacular views across the sheltered Oban Bay to the magnificent mountains of Mull. The Argyll Hotel is family owned and run priding themselves in doing the utmost to make your stay as comfortable and relaxing as possible. All the bedrooms have been recently refurbished to include en suite facilities. The comfortable restaurant offers a high standard of cuisine using a wide choice of local produce tastefully prepared with a selection of fine wines, malt whiskies and liqueurs to complement your meal. Entertainment can be enjoyed in the lounge bar, provided by local artists. Limited car parking available but there is a large public car park adjacent to the hotel.

Onich - Osterley

ONICH Highland *Inverness-shire* Map **14** NN06

★★★63% Lodge on the Loch
Creag Dhu PH33 6RY (beside A82) ☎(08553) 237 FAX (08553) 463

Closed Nov-Jan (ex Xmas-New Year)

Efficiently run by the Young family, this popular holiday hotel is set in its own grounds and has beautiful loch and mountain views. Modern bedrooms vary in size but all are comfortable and well equipped. Public areas include relaxing lounges, a snug bar and attractive restaurant.

20rm(18⇨↑)(2fb) CTV in all bedrooms ® T sB&B£31-£43.50 sB&B⇨↑£56-£68.50 dB&B£62-£87 dB&B⇨↑£112-£137 (incl dinner) 🅿

25P 🚗 ✿ 🎵 ॐ *xmas*

♀ International **V** ✿ ♨ ⚑ Lunch £5.50-£14.50alc Dinner £21.50-£22.50&alc Last dinner 9.30pm

CONF. Thtr 50 Class 30 Board 30 Del from £55
Credit Cards ①③ £

See advertisement under FORT WILLIAM

★★❀73% Allt-Nan-Ros
PH33 6RY (1.5m N of Ballachulish Bridge on A82)
☎(08553) 210 & 250 FAX (08553) 462

Closed late Nov-19 Dec

This friendly family-run holiday hotel, converted from a Victorian shooting lodge, is set in well tended gardens overlooking Loch Linnhe and the surrounding mountains. Many of the comfortable bedrooms have views of the loch and the public rooms are bright and airy. A fixed price menu offers modern adaptations of traditional Scottish dishes.

21⇨↑(2fb)1🛏 CTV in all bedrooms ® T sB&B⇨↑£37.50-£47.50 dB&B⇨↑£75-£95 (incl dinner) 🅿

50P 🚗 ✿

♀ Scottish & French ✿ ♨ ⚑ Lunch £6-£14alc Dinner £19.50-£22.50 Last dinner 8.30pm
Credit Cards ①②③⑤ £

★★65% Onich
PH33 6RY (beside A82, 2m N of Ballachulish Bridge) ☎(08553) 214 & 266 FAX (08553) 484
RS Nov-Mar

Enjoying fine views across Loch Linnhe to Glencoe, this popular family-run holiday hotel has gardens running down to the lochside. Comfortable bedrooms of varying size provide modern amenities and the smartly refurbished public areas include an attractive restaurant, comfortable lounge and choice of bars.

27⇨↑(6fb) CTV in all bedrooms ® T sB&B⇨↑£27.50-£43.50 dB&B⇨↑£45-£77 🅿

50P 🚗 ✿ solarium gymnasium jacuzzi games room water sports ski hire ॐ

♀ International **V** ✿ ♨ ⚑ Bar Lunch £10-£16alc Dinner £17.50-£19 Last dinner 9.00pm
Credit Cards ①②③⑤ £

★★58% Creag Mhor
PH33 6RY (beside A82) ☎(08553) 379

Closed Nov-Mar

14rm(9⇨↑)(3fb) CTV in all bedrooms ®
20P ✿ ♪

V ✿ ⚑ Last dinner 8.30pm
Credit Cards ①③

ONNELEY Staffordshire Map **07** SJ74

★★69% *Wheatsheaf Inn at Onneley*
Barhill Rd CW3 9QF (beside A525)
☎Stoke-On-Trent(0782) 751581 FAX (0782) 751399

Dating back to 1769, this family run hotel has been considerably extended over the years and has 2 comfortable bars. There is a popular blackboard selection of bar meals, and the restaurant has a

Spanish theme. Bedrooms are spacious and attractively furnished with coordinated fabrics and canopied beds.

5↑ CTV in all bedrooms ®⚐ T
150P ▶ 9 🎵

♀ English & Spanish **V** ✿ ⚑ Last dinner 9.30pm
Credit Cards ①②③

ORFORD (NEAR WOODBRIDGE) Suffolk Map **05** TM44

★★64% The Crown & Castle
IP12 2LJ (turn right from B1084 on entering village)
☎Orford(0394) 450205 FAX (0394) 450176

This hotel, with its black and white timbered façade, is close to the castle on the edge of the quiet coastal village. New owners have continued to improve main house bedrooms, though the Garden Studio Rooms are more spacious and easily accessible. The staff are polite and helpful, and in the dining room a simple choice, table d'hôte menu is available.

10rm(1⇨5↑)Annexe10⇨↑(10fb)1🛏 CTV in all bedrooms ® T sB&B£32.50 sB&B⇨↑£37.50 dB&B£55 dB&B⇨↑£60 🅿

20P *xmas*

V ✿ ♨ ⚑ Sunday Lunch fr£9.95 High tea fr£2.50 Dinner fr£12.95 Last dinner 8.45pm
Credit Cards ①②③⑤

ORKNEY Map **16**

KIRKWALL Map **16** HY41

★★65% Ayre
Ayre Rd KW15 1QX ☎(0856) 873001 FAX (0856) 876289

Oriented towards the business traveller, this hotel has two standard types of bedroom; both are comfortable, spacious and well equipped. Public areas are limited, but there is an attractive dining room with views of the harbour offering quite simple but well prepared dishes. A warmly hospitable atmosphere prevails.

34rm(30⇨↑)(3fb) CTV in all bedrooms ® T
25P trout & sea fishing

♀ International **V** ✿ ⚑ Last dinner 9pm
Credit Cards ①③

ORMSKIRK Lancashire Map **07** SD40

★★★67% Beaufort
High Ln, Burscough L40 7SN (1m N, on A59)
☎Burscough(0704) 892655 FAX (0704) 895135

This modern purpose-built hotel has comfortable bedrooms with Italian furnishings and all modern amenities. Public areas include two pleasant bars and a beamed restaurant offering a choice of menus. Service is professional and attentive.

21⇨↑ CTV in all bedrooms ®⚐ T ✳ sB&B⇨↑£27-£56 dB&B⇨↑£69 🅿

☾ 126P 🚗

♀ International **V** ✿ ♨ ✳ Lunch £4.95-£10.50&alc Dinner fr£16.95&alc Last dinner 10pm
Credit Cards ①②③⑤ £

OSTERLEY Greater London

See **LONDON SECTION** plan 1*B3*

★★57% Osterley
764 Great West Rd TW7 5NA ☎081-568 9981
FAX 081-569 7819

Once a Tudor-style pub, this hotel has extended its public areas into a conservatory. Useful accommodation is provided in a motel annexe, in the main building or over the bar.

57⇨👤Annexe5rm(9fb) CTV in all bedrooms ® T
sB&B⇨👤£49-£69 dB&B⇨👤£59-£79 Continental breakfast
🍴
(140P 3🏊
V ⚙ 🐕 ✗ Lunch £9.95-£13 Dinner £6.95-£13&alc Last dinner
10pm
CONF. Thtr 250 Class 126 Board 80 Del from £98
Credit Cards [1][2][3][5]

OSWESTRY Shropshire Map **07** SJ22

See also **Whittington**
★★★**67%** **Wynnstay**
Church St SY11 2SZ ☎(0691) 655261 FAX (0691) 670606
Completely transformed, this hotel now offers very comfortable
bedrooms and a ground floor area which consists of an elegant
library, lounge bar, the Camellia restaurant and a conservatory.
27⇨👤(4fb)2🛏✗ in 12 bedrooms CTV in all bedrooms ® T ✱
sB⇨👤£39.95-£75 dB⇨👤£39.95-£85 (room only) 🍴
70P ✿ crown green bowling xmas
♿ French V ⚙ 🐕 ✱ Lunch £5-£17.50alc High tea £3.50-£7.50
Dinner £14.95-£17.50&alc Last dinner 9.30pm
CONF. Thtr 200 Class 120 Board 60 Del from £64
Credit Cards [1][2][3][4][5]

★★**67%** **Pen-y-Dyffryn Hall Country Hotel**
Rhydycroesau SY10 7DT (from A5 into
Oswestry town centre, follow signs to
Llansilin on B4580, hotel is 3m W of Oswestry
just before Rhydycroesau village)
☎0691 653700
Situated just inside the English border, this fine stone-built house
faces the Welsh hills. Open-plan public areas include a cosy bar and
lounge with an adjacent restaurant. Bedrooms are pretty with floral
decor and matching fabrics.
7⇨👤(1fb)1🛏 CTV in all bedrooms ® sB&B⇨👤£36-£43
dB&B⇨👤£57-£64 🍴
30P ✿ 🎵 ♿
V✗BarLunch£5-£10Dinner£13.50&alcLastdinner8.30pm
Credit Cards [1][2][3]
....

Forte Travelodge
Mile End Service Area SY11 4JA (junct A5/A483)
☎(0691) 658178 Central Res (0800) 850910
This modern building offers a good standard of accommodation
for overnight stops. Smart, spacious and well equipped
bedrooms, all with en suite bathrooms, are suitable for family
use, and meals may be taken at the nearby family restaurant. For
more details about Travelodges, consult the Contents page,
under Hotel Groups.
40⇨👤✱ B⇨👤£31.95 (room only)

OTLEY West Yorkshire Map **08** SE24

★★★**63%** **Chevin Lodge Country Park**
Yorkgate LS21 3NU (signed from A658
Bradford to Harrogate road) ☎(0943) 467818
FAX (0943) 850335
This unique wooden structure is set in 50 acres of wooded parkland
with a lake that can be viewed from the balconied restaurant, where
well prepared meals are served.
18⇨👤 Annexe34⇨👤(5fb) CTV in all bedrooms ® T ✱
sB&B⇨👤£55-£86.50 dB&B⇨👤£74.50-£96.50 🍴
(⊞ 100P ✿ 🎣 (hard) 🎵 sauna solarium cycling games room
xmas
♿ English & French V ⚙ 🐕 ✱ Lunch £10.50-£11.50&alc
Dinner £16.75&alc Last dinner 9.30pm
CONF. Thtr 120 Class 90 Board 40 Del from £78
Credit Cards [1][2][3]

Onich Hotel — Onich ★★
NEAR FORT WILLIAM
INVERNESS-SHIRE PH33 6RY
Tel: Onich (08553) 214, Visitors 266
Fax: (08553) 484

Occupying one of the finest situations in the Scottish Highlands this hotel is the only one in the area with gardens extending to the lochside. The views over Loch Linnhe to Glencoe & Morvern are absolutely breathtaking. This family run hotel has a very real reputation for excellent food and a warm welcoming atmosphere. The new Deerstalker Lounge is open all day for meals and drinks and offers a large selection of malt whisky & real ale on draught. This is an ideal base for climbing, hillwalking, windsurfing, skiing, touring or just relaxing. All 27 rooms have Bath/Shower, TV/Radio, Phone and Tea/Coffee maker. In-house facilities includes Solarium, Jacuzzi, Exercise Equipment, Games Room.

★★
THE HOP POLE HOTEL
**Ollerton Village
Nottinghamshire
NG22 9AD
Tel: 0623 822573**

Set in the heart of Robin Hood country. Eleven bedrooms with private bath/shower room, colour TV, direct dial telephone and tea and coffee tray.

Carvery restaurant every evening. Bar meals every lunchtime and evening. Car parking and large beer garden with childrens play equipment.

Ottershaw - Oxford

OTTERSHAW Surrey Map 04 TQ06

○ **Foxhills**
KT16 0EL ☎(0932) 872050
open
16⇌🏠

OTTERY ST MARY Devon Map 03 SY19

★★ 68% **Tumbling Weir Hotel & Restaurant**
EX11 1AO ☎(0404) 812752 FAX (0404) 812752
This is a lovely renovated 17th-century thatched cottage between the River Otter and its millstream. Care has been taken to retain the period character of the property with its original beams and fireplaces. Bedrooms are comfortable and gently colour coordinated, with excellent facilities. In the candlelit restaurant an interesting table d'hôte menu is offered along with a short carte.
12⇌🏠 CTV in all bedrooms ®✱ sB&B⇌🏠£25-£33.25 dB&B⇌🏠£45-£50.25 🍴
CTV P ✿ ♪ xmas
🍽 French Hungarian & Italian V ♦ ⊉ ⊁ ✱ Lunch £3.50-£8.50
Credit Cards 1 2 3 £

OUNDLE Northamptonshire Map 04 TL08

★★★ 62% **The Talbot**
New St PE8 4EA ☎(0832) 273621 FAX (0832) 274545

FORTE Heritage

An imposing building in the centre of town, the Talbot was built from the stone of Fotheringay Castle back in 1626, and still has exposed beams and transomed windows. There is a choice of bars and a restaurant serving traditional British fare. Accommodation has more recently been refurbished, with rich colour coordinated fabrics, dark wood furniture and modern facilities.
40⇌🏠(4fb)⊁in 15 bedrooms CTV in all bedrooms ® T sB⇌🏠£70-£80 dB⇌🏠£90-£105 (room only) 🍴
《 60P xmas
V ♦ ⊉ ⊁ ✱ Sunday Lunch £11.95 Dinner £17.95 Last dinner 9.30pm
CONF. Thtr 120 Class 60 Board 60 Del £90
Credit Cards 1 2 3 5

OUTLANE West Yorkshire Map 07 SE01

★★★ 67% **Old Golf House Hotel**
New Hey Rd HD3 3YP (on the A640 to Rochdale) (Lansbury)
☎Elland(0422) 379311 FAX (0422) 372694
Originally part of the Golf Club, this comfortable hotel stands within three acres of landscaped gardens. Its spacious and attractively decorated bedrooms provide all the facilities expected of a modern hotel, while lounges, bar and restaurant are all very inviting and service is friendly.
50⇌🏠(4fb)⊁in 5 bedrooms CTV in all bedrooms ®✱ T 🐕 (ex guide dogs) ✱ sB&B⇌🏠£65.50-£75.50 dB&B⇌🏠£77-£87 🍴
《 70P ✿ sauna solarium gymnasium pitch & putt xmas
🍽 English & Continental V ♦ ⊁ ✱ Lunch fr£9.50 Dinner fr£13.50&alc Last dinner 10pm
CONF. Thtr 100 Class 40 Board 30 Del from £95
Credit Cards 1 2 3 5

OXFORD Oxfordshire Map 04 SP50

See also **Milton Common**

★★★ ❀❀❀❀🍷
LE MANOIR AUX QUAT' SAISON
OX44 7PD ☎Great Milton(0844) 278881
FAX (0844) 278847

RELAIS & CHATEAUX Relais Gourmands

(For full entry see Milton, Great)

★★★★ 60% **The Randolph**
Beaumont St OX1 2LN ☎(0865) 247481 FAX (0865) 791678

FORTE GRAND

The Randolph is an old city centre hotel of enormous character. The refurbishment programme is under way in the bedrooms, and is completed in the public areas which have been restored to their former elegance and comfort.
109⇌🏠⊁in 50 bedrooms CTV in all bedrooms ®✱ T sB⇌🏠🏠fr£115 dB⇌🏠🏠fr£150 (room only) 🍴
Lift 《 60🚗 ♪ xmas
🍽 International V ♦ ⊉ ⊁ ✱ Lunch £15.50-£17.50&alc Dinner fr£25&alc Last dinner 10pm
CONF. Thtr 300 Class 120 Board 35 Del £145
Credit Cards 1 2 3 5

★★★ ❀ 69% **Hawkwell House**
Church Way, Iffley OX4 4DZ ☎(0865) 749988 FAX (0865) 749988

Quietly set in 2 acres of grounds, this hotel has recently undergone major refurbishment and extension. In the stylish Orangery Restaurant, professional staff serve a fixed price menu of modern British cuisine. Our inspector enjoyed char-grilled escallops of turkey with a Calvados sauce. Most of the bedrooms are decorated and furnished in similar style, except the 2nd floor honeymoon room which features a Grecian-style double jacuzzi.
21⇌🏠(2fb) CTV in all bedrooms ® T sB&B⇌🏠£70-£85 dB&B⇌🏠£80-£125 🍴
《 80P ✿ snooker xmas
V ♦ ⊉ ⊁ Lunch £13.50&alc Dinner £21.25&alc Last dinner 10pm
CONF. Thtr 150 Class 80 Board 50 Del from £99
Credit Cards 1 2 3 5   £

★★★ ❀❀🍷 67% **Studley Priory**
OX33 1AZ ☎Stanton St John(0865) 351203 FAX (0865) 351613
(For full entry see Horton-cum-Studley)

★★★ 65% **Eastgate**
The High, Merton St OX1 4BE ☎(0865) 248244 FAX (0865) 791681

FORTE Heritage

The Eastgate is a city-centre hotel surrounded by imposing college buildings. The majority of the bedrooms have been upgraded over the last few years using attractive fabrics and quality furniture. The Shires Restaurant serves traditional English cooking from a table d'hôte and short à la carte menu. Snacks and beverages are available all day in the panelled Eastgate Bar.
43⇌🏠(18fb)🏠⊁in 7 bedrooms CTV in all bedrooms ® T ✱ sB⇌🏠£69-£93 dB⇌🏠£110 (room only) 🍴
Lift 《 27P xmas
V ♦ ⊉ ⊁ ✱ Lunch £11.95 High tea £3.95-£12.15alc Dinner £16.95&alc Last dinner 9.30pm
Credit Cards 1 2 3 4 5

★★★ 64% **Cotswold Lodge**
66A Banbury Rd OX2 6JP ☎(0865) 512121 FAX (0865) 512490
Closed 25-30 Dec

This family-run hotel, with friendly, courteous staff, is situated a short distance from the city centre and is popular with business people. Interesting menus are offered in the refurbished restaurant, and bedrooms, which vary in size and style, are well appointed.
52⇌🏠(2fb) CTV in all bedrooms ® T 🐕 (ex guide dogs)
《 60P
🍽 English & French V ♦ ⊉ Last dinner 10.30pm
Credit Cards 1 2 3 5

★★★ 63% **Oxford Moat House**
Godstow Rd, Wolvercote Rbt OX2 8AL
(adjacent to A34/A40, 2m from city centre)
☎(0865) 59933 FAX (0865) 310250
Closed 27 Dec-1 Jan

Queens Moat Houses

Oxford

The hotel offers comfortable accommodation for the business and conference market. Imaginative table d'hôte and buffet-style menus are available in the smart first floor restaurant and there is a brasserie in the Beaumont Leisure Club. A friendly young team of staff provide helpful service.
155⇌(17fb)⊁in 31 bedrooms CTV in all bedrooms ® ⁂ T ✻ sB&B⇌fr£87 dB&B⇌fr£105 ♖
⦅ 250P ▨ (heated) squash snooker sauna solarium gymnasium whirlpool pitch & putt
♁ English & French V ✿ ♨ ✻ Lunch £10.50-£12.50 Dinner fr£15.50 Last dinner 9.45pm
Conf. Thtr 150 Class 60 Board 50 Del from £70
Credit Cards ① ② ③ ⑤

★★★ **61% Linton Lodge**
Linton Rd OX2 6UJ (Hilton) ☎(0865) 53461 FAX (0865) 310365
In a quiet residential area off the Banbury road, this hotel is converted from several houses with various modern extensions. The Library Restaurant offers a buffet-style breakfast, a carvery lunch, and a fully served dinner menu. Bedrooms have been recently refurbished.
71⇌♠(2fb)1♿in 6 bedrooms CTV in all bedrooms ® T
sB⇌♠£85 dB⇌♠£115 (room only) ♖
Lift ⦅ 40P ✿ croquet lawn
♁ English & French V ✿ ♨ Lunch £10.25 Dinner £18.50&alc Last dinner 9.30pm
Conf. Thtr 120 Class 60 Board 40 Del £115
Credit Cards ① ② ③ ⑤

★★ **67% The Tree Hotel**
Church Way, Iffley OX4 4EY (3m SE off A4158)
☎(0865) 775974 & 778190 FAX (0865) 747554
Quietly situated in the pretty village of Iffley, this refurbished Victorian pub is now a personally run hotel, with a friendly atmosphere, comfortable public areas and cheerful, spotlessly clean bedrooms equipped for the needs of business or leisure travellers.
7⇌♠(1fb)1♿ CTV in all bedrooms ® T ✖ (ex guide dogs)
20P 3🐾 (£1 per night)
V ✿ ♨ ⊁
Credit Cards ① ② ③

★★ **62% Welcome Lodge**
Peartree Roundabout OX2 8JZ (junc A34/A343)
☎(0865) 54301 FAX (0865) 513474

FORTE HOTELS

This lodge offers comfortable modern bedrooms, many of them annexe rooms with their own front doors. There is a bright carvery-style restaurant with a small bar and a separate small TV lounge: all excellent value for money.
100⇌(41fb) CTV in all bedrooms ®
CTV 120P ✿
♁ Mainly grills V ✿ ♨ ⊁ Last dinner 9.30pm
Credit Cards ① ② ③ ④ ⑤

★★ **59% Victoria**
180 Abingdon Rd OX1 4RA ☎(0865) 724536 FAX (0865) 794909
Closed 20 Dec-20 Jan
Popular with both business people and tourists, this small family-run hotel is just south of the city centre and offers a friendly atmosphere and simply furnished comfortable bedrooms. A wide range of home-cooked meals are served in the dining room.
23rm(13⇌♠)(2fb)1♿ CTV in all bedrooms ® T ✻
sB&B£35.50-£37.50 sB&B⇌♠£48.50-£52.50 dB&B£48.50-£55.50 dB&B⇌♠£52-£65.50 ♖
CTV 17P
♁ Italian & Yugoslav V ✿ ♨ ⊁ ✻ Lunch £10.50-£18.50 Dinner £10.50-£18.50&alc Last dinner 9pm
Credit Cards ① ③

The Belfry Hotel
Milton Common, Oxford OX9 2JW ★★★
Telephone: 0844 279381
Fax: 0844 279624

80 bedrooms all with private facilities, colour TV, radio, telephone, tea/coffee facilities. LEISURE COMPLEX including indoor pool, sauna, solarium and mini gym. Parking 200 cars. Extensive conference facilities.
40 minutes Heathrow. Situated on A40 near junctions 7 and 8 of M40. Week-end breaks.

OXFORD
Hawkwell House ★★★
HOTEL
Orangery
RESTAURANT

Set in its own gardens in an elevated position overlooking the famous dreaming spires of Oxford. Hawkwell House offers the relaxed, luxurious atmosphere of a country house, and with the convenience and attractions of the historic city of Oxford only 2 miles away.

The hotel provides the perfect setting for conferences, wedding receptions and private dining for up to 160 guests.

You are assured of a comfortable stay and warm welcome from friendly, professional staff whose attention to detail is of paramount importance.

**Hawkwell House
Iffley Village
Oxford OX4 4DZ
Telephone: 0865 749988 Fax: 0865 748525**

Oxford - Padworth

★ 60% Palace
250 Iffley Rd OX4 1SE (on A4128) ☎(0865) 727627 FAX (0865) 200478
Closed 15 Dec-15 Jan
Attractively presented bedrooms with modern facilities, together with limited public areas, are provided by this hotel, conveniently close to the city centre and personally run by its proprietors. A choice of simply cooked and presented dishes is available at dinner, and, though the establishment is unlicensed at present, a residents' bar is planned for the near future.
8⇨♠(2fb) CTV in all bedrooms ® ✱ ✱ sB&B⇨♠£35-£40 dB&B⇨♠£50-£60
CTV 6P ✱
V ✿ ✱ Dinner £7.50-£12.50 Last dinner 8pm
Credit Cards [1][3][5]

★ 60% River
17 Botley Rd OX2 0AA (1m along Botley Road from ring road west exit, beside Osney Bridge) ☎(0865) 243475 FAX (0865) 724306
Closed 21 Dec-4 Jan RS wknds
The River Hotel overlooks the Thames at Osney Bridge, and is within walking distance of the city centre. Bedrooms are simply furnished and well equipped, some in an annexe across the road. The restaurant, where smoking is not encouraged, has river views.
16rm(5⇨7♠)Annexe8rm(3⇨3♠)(2fb) CTV in all bedrooms ® T ✱ (ex guide dogs) ✱ sB&B£39 sB&B⇨♠£52-£57 dB&B⇨♠£64-£70
CTV 25P ✱ ✿ ♪
V ✿ ✱ Bar Lunch fr£3 Dinner £6.50-£10 Last dinner 7.30pm
CONF. Thtr 50 Class 25 Board 25
Credit Cards [1][3]

Forte Travelodge
London Rd, Wheatley (off A40)
☎(0867) 75705 Central Res (0800) 850950
This modern building offers a good standard of accommodation for overnight stops. Smart, spacious and well equipped bedrooms, all with en suite bathrooms, are suitable for family use, and meals may be taken at the nearby family restaurant. For more details about Travelodges, consult the Contents page, under Hotel Groups.
24⇨♠ ✱ B⇨♠£31.95 (room only)

OXWICH West Glamorgan Map 02 SS48

★★ 64% Oxwich Bay
Oxwich Bay SA3 1LS (Turn left at x-rds in Oxwich village hotel at end of road) ☎Swansea(0792) 390329 FAX (0792) 391254
Closed 25 Dec
This family-run hotel is superbly located fronting Oxwich Bay, one of the beauty spots of the Gower Peninsula. Guest rooms are modern with attractive coordinating décor and soft furnishings. The hotel's lounge bar, which can get very busy in summer, serves popular bar snacks, and table d'hôte and à la carte menus are available in the restaurant.
13⇨♠(11fb) CTV in all bedrooms ®✳ ✱ (ex guide dogs) sB&B⇨♠£25-£50 dB&B⇨♠£40-£77 ♬
350P ✿
V ✿ ✱ Lunch £5.95-£6.95&alc Dinner £12&alc Last dinner 8.30pm
Credit Cards [1][3]

PADSTOW Cornwall & Isles of Scilly Map 02 SW97
See also **Constantine Bay**

★★★ 64% Old Custom House Inn
South Quay PL28 8ED (St Austell Brewery) ☎(0841) 532359
The Old Custom House is an attractive period property overlooking the busy harbour. Cream teas are served in the conservatory, and the interesting bar is busy in season. The restaurant is well appointed and professionally run, extensive menus are available which make full use of local fish. Bedrooms are attractively coordinated and well equipped – the honeymoon suite has a 4-poster bed and a double whirlpool bath.
27⇨♠1♠ CTV in all bedrooms ® T
CTV ✱
V ✿ ✱ English & French V ✿ ✱ Last dinner 9.30pm
Credit Cards [1][2][3][5]

★★★ 58% The Metropole
Station Rd PL28 8DB ☎(0841) 532486 FAX (0841) 532867
FORTE Heritage
Offering excellent views of the Camel estuary, this traditional hotel has been a firm favourite for many years. The bedrooms in several styles are being upgraded. The public areas include the Verandah Bar and Lounge, and Harbour Restaurant, offering a reliable standard of cooking. Service is friendly, helpful and well managed.
44⇨♠(5fb)♠in 19 bedrooms CTV in all bedrooms ® T ✱ sB&B⇨♠£58-£65.50 dB&B⇨♠£116-£140 (incl dinner)
Lift 38P ✿ ⌒ (heated) ♪ xmas
V ✿ ✱ ✱ Sunday Lunch £9.95 High tea £1.95-£6.50 Dinner £16.95 Last dinner 9pm
CONF. Thtr 50 Class 20 Board 20 Del from £60
Credit Cards [1][2][3][4][5]

★★ ✱✱✱72% Seafood Restaurant
Riverside PL28 8BY ☎(0841) 532485 FAX (0841) 533344
Closed Jan RS Res closed May 1st & Sundays
10⇨♠ CTV in all bedrooms ® T sB&B⇨♠£34-£86 dB&B⇨♠£56-£107 ♬
12P
V ✿ English, French, Italian & Oriental Lunch £20.25&alc Dinner £28&alc Last dinner 9.30pm
Credit Cards [1][2][3]

★ 62% St Petroc's House
4 New St PL28 8EA (50 metres from the Central Square in Padstow, on one way system out of town on the right hand side) ☎(0841) 532700
Closed Jan-Feb
A 17th-century Grade II listed town house in the centre of Padstow, the hotel has an unusual lounge with a barrel ceiling. An à la carte menu is available in the dining room, with several grilled dishes and other specialities. Bedrooms are well equipped and furnished in character, and the bar has a nautical theme.
11rm(8⇨♠)(3fb) CTV in all bedrooms ® T ✱ sB&B£19-£29 sB&B⇨♠£24-£34 dB&B£30-£58 dB&B⇨♠£48-£78 ♬ ✱
V ✿ Mediterranean V ✿ ✱ ✱ Dinner £10-£15alc Last dinner 10pm
Credit Cards [1][3]

PADWORTH Berkshire Map 04 SU66

★★★ 70% Padworth Court
Bath Rd RG7 5HT (leave the M4 at junct 12 and follow A4 towards Newbury, hotel is 3.5m on left) (Lansbury)
☎Reading(0734) 714411 FAX (0734) 714442
Padworth Court is a purpose-built hotel which offers tastefully styled, comprehensively equipped and air-conditioned bedrooms with the emphasis on comfort. Reception areas include a galleried lounge as well as the Courtyard Restaurant with its table d'hôte à la carte menus; bar snacks are available all day in the adjacent Brightwell Arms.
50⇨♠♠in 26 bedrooms CTV in all bedrooms ® T ✱ (ex guide dogs) ✱ sB&B⇨♠fr£69.50 dB&B⇨♠fr£81

Irish entries appear in a separate section that follows the main directory.

Padworth - Paignton

《 ⌂ 140P sauna solarium gymnasium *xmas*
♀ English & Continental V ✧ ♃ ✄ ✱ Lunch fr£10.95 Dinner fr£14.50 Last dinner 10pm
CONF. Thtr 200 Class 50 Board 60 Del from £98
Credit Cards [1] [2] [3] [5]

PAIGNTON Devon Map 03 SX86
★★★65% Redcliffe
Marine Dr TQ3 2NL ☎(0803) 526287 FAX (0803) 528030
This unusual castellated building is superbly situated in 5 acres of grounds adjoining Paignton's sandy beach, with direct access to the beach through a tunnel. Bedrooms have recently been renovated. Loyal, friendly staff provide good service.
59⇌♠(8fb) CTV in all bedrooms ® T ✄ (ex guide dogs) sB&B⇌♠£38-£48 dB&B⇌♠£76-£94 ℞
Lift 《 CTV 80P ✱ ▱ (heated) ⌂ (heated) ♪ sauna solarium gymnasium putting green table tennis ♫ ⌂ *xmas*
♀ English & French V ✧ ♃ Sunday Lunch £8.75-£9.75 Dinner £13.75-£14.75&alc Last dinner 8.30pm
CONF. Thtr 160 Class 50 Board 50 Del from £50
Credit Cards [1] [3]

★★★60% The Palace
Esplanade Rd TQ4 6BJ (opp Paignton pier)
☎(0803) 555121 FAX (0803) 527974

FORTE
Heritage

Prominently situated near the seafront, the Palace Hotel is set in a well tended garden. The bedrooms vary in standard from the attractive, recently refurbished west wing rooms to some that are rather dated. Public areas are spacious and in the Paris Restaurant, simple dishes are offered on the fixed- price menu, with some à la carte choices.
52⇌♠(1fb)⊁in 14 bedrooms CTV in all bedrooms ® T ✱
sB⇌♠fr£73.50 dB⇌♠fr£89.25 (room only) ℞

The Redcliffe Hotel

AA ★ ★ ★
Marine Drive, Paignton
S. Devon TQ3 2NL
Tel: (0803) 526397

Superbly situated in 4 acres of grounds directly adjoining Paignton's sandy beach. All rooms have private bathroom, radio, telephone, colour TV and tea making facilities, the majority with fine sea and coastal views.
* Heated Outdoor Pool
* Putting Green
* Hairdressing Salon
* Ample parking
* Ballroom with regular dancing during the season
* Excellent cuisine and service.

76% ★★★

Treglos Hotel

Constantine Bay, Nr Padstow, Cornwall PL28 8JH
Telephone: (0841) 520727 Fax: (0841) 521163

Guests return year after year to enjoy the personal attention, high standard of service, the superb restaurant and luxurious comfort. Specializing in local seafood, vegetables from the hotel garden and home made desserts with cornish cream. Six course table d'hôte and extensive à la carte menu.
Write to owner managers Ted and Barbara Barlow for colour Brochure.
See gazetteer under Constantine Bay
Associate hotel – Budock Vean, Mawnan Smith

Excellent accommodation and traditional English fayre.

WANTAGE

Close to the university city of Oxford and ideally suited for an overnight stay. The Bear Hotel offers the traveller superb standards of comfort and cuisine.

This charming Georgian coaching inn is equally suitable for business accommodation or weekend breaks.

Market Place, Wantage.
Tel: 02357 66366

Paignton - Parbold

Lift (60P ❋ ⇱ (heated) ♂ (hard) sauna solarium gymnasium games room *xmas*
V ⌂ ⚏ ⚒
Credit Cards ①②③⑤

★★**64%** Sunhill
Alta Vista Rd TQ4 6DN ☎(0803) 557532 FAX (0803) 663850
Situated in a quiet area of Paignton, the hotel has good views over the public gardens to Goodrington Sands and distant Brixham. Some of its airy bedrooms have balconies. The informal restaurant offers a set menu with choice of dishes including a vegetarian one.
28⇌**↾**(3fb) CTV in all bedrooms ®♉ T
Lift 31P snooker sauna solarium nc4yrs
♄ English & French ❅ ⚏ ⚒ Last dinner 7.30pm
Credit Cards ①②③

★★**63%** Preston Sands
10/12 Marine Pde TQ3 2NU ☎(0803) 558718
A large, safe and sandy beach is just across Marine Parade – which carries no through traffic – and guests can enjoy the outlook from a peaceful front terrace. Comfortable and attractive bedrooms have satellite TV and hairdryers as well as the more usual facilities. There is a residents' bar and a dining room serving a carefully balanced choice of dishes, and involved proprietors create a friendly, relaxed atmosphere.
31rm(29⇌**↾**)(3fb) CTV in all bedrooms ®♉ T
CTV 24P nc10yrs
V ⌂ ⚏ Last dinner 7.30pm
Credit Cards ①②③

★★**63%** Torbay Holiday Motel
Totnes Rd TQ4 7PP (on A385 Totnes/Paignton road, 2.5m from Paignton) ☎(0803) 558226 FAX (0803) 663375
Closed 24-31 Dec
This modern motel complex provides spacious bedrooms with good facilities, and they are kept very warm in winter. An extensive choice of dishes is available on table d'hôte, à la carte and bar snack menus.
16⇌**↾** CTV in all bedrooms ®♉ T sB&B⇌**↾**£28.50-£30.50 dB&B⇌**↾**£45-£49
CTV 150P ❖ ❋ ▣ (heated) ⇱ (heated) sauna solarium gymnasium crazy golf adventure playground ⚽
♄ English & French V ❅ ❋ Bar Lunch £4.55-£10.55alc Dinner £8.95&alc Last dinner 9pm
Credit Cards ①③

★★**62%** Dainton
95 Dartmouth Rd, Three Beaches, Goodrington TQ4 6NA ☎(0803) 550067 & 525901 FAX (0803) 666339
During the summer months this attractive Tudor-style property is ablaze with colour from hanging baskets and tubs. The popular beamed restaurant serves a residents' menu at 6.30pm, in addition to the à la carte selection and range of bar meals. The bedrooms are simply furnished. The hotel is a pleasant 2 minute walk from the beach and leisure park.
11⇌**↾**(3fb) CTV in all bedrooms ® T ❋ sB&B⇌**↾**fr£25 dB&B⇌**↾**fr£44 ⊟
(CTV 20P ⚬ solarium *xmas*
♄ English & Continental V ⌂ ⚏ ❋ Lunch fr£7.25&alc Dinner fr£13alc Last dinner 9.30pm
Credit Cards ①③

★**59%** South Sands
Alta Vista Rd TQ4 6BZ ☎(0803) 557231 & 529347
South Sands Hotel is central, but quietly situated overlooking Goodrington Sands and the Bay. Tony and Cecile Cahill and their family enjoy looking after their guests, and a good choice of home-cooked meals is served at dinner. Bedrooms are simply furnished.
19⇌**↾**(14fb) CTV in all bedrooms ® T sB&B⇌**↾**£25-£33 dB&B⇌**↾**£50-£66 (incl dinner) ⊟
CTV 17P pool table *xmas*

♄ International V ⌂ ⚏ ❋ Bar Lunch £1.50-£5&alc Dinner £5-£10&alc Last dinner 7.30pm
Credit Cards ③

PAINSWICK Gloucestershire Map **03** SO80

★★★ ❀❀**71%** Painswick
Kemps Ln GL6 6YB (off A46, in centre of village, 2nd road behind church off Tibbiwell) ☎(0452) 812160 FAX (0452) 814059
This elegant 18th-century rectory, behind the parish church, has been attractively refurbished by its enthusiastic owners. Comfortable bedrooms in rich coordinating colours have modern facilities plus many thoughtful extras, such as fresh flowers, fruit and magazines, and public rooms with antiques and open fires include 2 drawing rooms, a library lounge and cosy little cocktail lounge. The wood-panelled restaurant is comfortably elegant and a new chef, Robert Maughan, has recently been appointed.
19⇌**↾**(4fb)2⚑ CTV in all bedrooms ® T ❋ sB&B⇌**↾**fr£65 dB&B⇌**↾**£85-£135 ⊟
25P ⚬ ❋ croquet *xmas*
V ⌂ Lunch £15.50-£29.50 Dinner £19.50-£29.50 Last dinner 9.30pm
CONF. Thtr 38 Class 30 Board 16 Del £110
Credit Cards ①②③

PAISLEY Hotels are listed under Glasgow Airport.

PANGBOURNE Berkshire Map **04** SU67

★★★**61%** The Copper Inn
Church Rd RG8 7AR ☎Reading(0734) 842244 FAX (0734) 845542
RESORT HOTELS PLC
This 19th-century coaching inn is in the busy village centre. Public areas include a comfortable reception lounge, public bar, and sitting room. Bedrooms in the main building have been more recently refurbished than those in an adjacent building, and several overlook the garden.
22⇌**↾**(1fb)1⚑ CTV in all bedrooms ® T ❋ sB⇌**↾**£65 dB⇌**↾**£75 (room only) ⊟
20P ⚬ ❋
♄ English & French V ⌂ ⚏ ❋ Lunch £10.95&alc Dinner £13.95&alc Last dinner 9.30pm
CONF. Thtr 60 Class 24 Board 30 Del from £65
Credit Cards ①②③⑤

PAPWORTH EVERARD Cambridgeshire Map **04** TL26

★★**60%** Papworth
Ermine St South CB3 8PB ☎(0954) 718851 718852 FAX (0954) 718853
20⇌**↾**(1fb) CTV in all bedrooms ® T ❋ sB&B⇌**↾**£25-£35 dB&B⇌**↾**£35-£50 ⊟
CTV 35P ♫ *xmas*
♄ French & Greek V ⌂ ⚏ ❋ Sunday Lunch £8.95 Dinner £7-£15&alc Last dinner 10pm
Credit Cards ①②③⑤

PARBOLD Lancashire Map **07** SD41

★★**63%** Lindley
Lancaster Ln WN8 7AB ☎(0257) 462804
A Victorian residence set in its own grounds near the village has now been converted into a popular hotel and restaurant – the latter serving mostly grill type meals. Good extras are provided in bedrooms which, like the public areas, are furnished in modern style, with co-ordinated fabrics. Service is friendly and attentive throughout.
8⇌**↾**(1fb) CTV in all bedrooms ® T ✖ (ex guide dogs) ❋ sB&B⇌**↾**£33 dB&B⇌**↾**£42-£47

60P
English & French V Lunch £7.90-£8.45
Credit Cards 1 2 3

PARKGATE Cheshire Map 07 SJ27

★★ 64% The Ship
The Parade L64 6SA ☎051-336 3931 FAX 051-393 0051
RS 25-28 Dec

FORTE
Heritage

Parts of this pleasant hotel, overlooking the Dee estuary, date back to the early 19th century. The bedrooms are not large but have modern furnishings and equipment. Public areas include an attractive restaurant, a lounge bar and a cosy and comfortable residents' lounge. Willing and attentive service is provided by the general manager and his team of staff.
26➪2 in 2 bedrooms CTV in all bedrooms ® T
sB➪£40 dB➪£50 (room only)
100P
English & French V Sunday Lunch £7.95 Dinner £15.95 Last dinner 9.30pm
Credit Cards 1 2 3 5

★★ 61% Parkgate
Boathouse Ln L64 6RD (on the B5135) (Whitbread)
☎051-336 5001 FAX 051-336 8504
This extended country house is a popular venue for wedding receptions and conferences. Public areas include an attractive split-level restaurant and a large bar. At the time of our last inspection the bedrooms, although well equipped were in need of refurbishment, which will hopefully be completed by 1994.
27➪(3fb)1 in 7 bedrooms CTV in all bedrooms ® T
(ex guide dogs) sB&B➪£49.50-£59.50 dB&B➪fr£71
150P xmas
English & French V Lunch fr£8.75 Dinner fr£13.95 Last dinner 9.45pm
CONF. Thtr 110 Board 40 Del from £75
Credit Cards 1 2 3 5

PARKHAM Devon Map 02 SS32

★★★ 69% Penhaven Country House
EX39 5PL (turn off A39 at Horns Cross and follow signs to Parkham, turn left after church)
☎Horns Cross(0237) 451388 & 451711 FAX (0237) 451878
Penhaven Country House is a former rectory dating from the 18th century, and stands in 11 acres of gardens and woodland on the edge of the village, surrounded by beautiful countryside. The spacious bedrooms have been decorated and furnished in quiet colours, and all have modern facilities. There are 2 comfortable lounges, one with a bar, and a choice of dishes is offered from the table d'hôte menu, which usually included in the price of accommodation for residents.
12➪1 CTV in all bedrooms ® T sB&B➪£54.95 dB&B➪£104-£122 (incl dinner)
50P 9 acre nature trail nc10yrs xmas
English & French V Sunday Lunch fr£9 Dinner fr£13.50&alc Last dinner 9pm
Credit Cards 1 2 3 5 £

PATELEY BRIDGE North Yorkshire Map 07 SE16

★★ 65% Grassfields Country House
Wath Rd HG3 5HL ☎Harrogate(0423) 711412
Closed Dec-28 Feb
This attractive Georgian country house peacefully stands in its own grounds has a delightful drawing room overlooking the gardens, with a marble fireplace, large floral armchairs and settees. A small bar is provided for guests and a well produced home-cooked dinner is served in the cosy dining room. Bedrooms, several with fine antiques, are pretty and well equipped.

Dainton Hotel and Licensed Restaurant ★★

95 Dartmouth Road, Three Beaches, Goodrington, Paignton, Devon TQ4 6NA
Telephone: (0803) 550067

Attractive hotel and licensed restaurant combining charm, warmth and character with modern facilities. Delightful olde worlde restaurant serving table d'hote, a la carte and bar meals. Wedding receptions and celebration meals also catered for. Well appointed bedrooms all ensuite and all with tea & coffee making facilities and colour TV plus views of Torbay. Beach 250 yards, Torquay 4 miles, Brixham 3 miles. Golf nearby. Bargain Breaks available. Ample parking.

TORBAY HOLIDAY MOTEL ★★

THE IDEAL CENTRE FOR TOURING SOUTH DEVON

Open all year

All rooms en suite with colour TV (inc 'SKY'), radio, telephone & tea/coffee facilities.

★ Indoor & outdoor pools ★ Solarium ★ Sauna ★ Mini-Gym ★ Launderette ★ Crazy golf ★ Restaurant ★ Bar ★ Shop ★ Ample parking ★ 35-acre picnic area ★

Also studio apartments & luxury suites available.

Brochure from: Dept AA, Torbay Holiday Motel, Totnes Road, Paignton, Devon TQ4 7PP.
Telephone: 0803 558226.

Pateley Bridge - Peebles

9⇨♠(3fb) CTV in all bedrooms ® ✱ sB&B⇨♠£30 dB&B⇨♠£50-£55 ⊟
CTV 15P ⇌ ✱
V ◐ ⚘ ⚲ Dinner £12 Last dinner 7.30pm

PATTERDALE Cumbria Map 11 NY31

★★ 58% Patterdale
CA11 0NN ☎Glenridding(07684) 82231 FAX (07684) 82440
Closed Jan-Feb

Patterdale is a 200-year-old Lakeland stone hotel which has been in the hands of the same family for 3 generations and has now been extensively modernised. Real ale is served in the bar, and there are 3 lounges.

57⇨♠(4fb) CTV in all bedrooms ® T sB&B⇨♠£25-£27.50 dB&B⇨♠£50-£55 ⊟
CTV 30P 1☎ ✱ ♪ ♫ xmas
V ◐ Lunch £7.50 Dinner £15 Last dinner 8pm
Credit Cards ① ③

PATTINGHAM Staffordshire Map 07 SO89

★★★ 61% Patshull Park Hotel Golf & Country Club
Patshull WV6 7JD (1.5m W of Pattingham) ☎(0902) 700100 FAX (0902) 700874

This is very much a sports and leisure hotel, standing in 280 acres of beautiful parkland alongside 80 acres of fishing lakes. It has two styles of bedroom, the older rooms being smaller, with older furniture, but decor and fabrics have all been renewed. As well as the formal Lakeside restaurant, there is a coffee shop serving all day meals and snacks.

48⇨♠ CTV in all bedrooms ® T ✱ sB&B⇨♠£42.50-£62.50 dB&B⇨♠£55-£85 ⊟
(CTV 200P ✱ ▭ (heated) ▶ 18 snooker sauna solarium gymnasium xmas
V ◐ ⚘ ⚲ Lunch fr£9.75 Dinner fr£12.75&alc Last dinner 9.30pm
Credit Cards ① ② ③ ⑤

PEASMARSH East Sussex Map 05 TQ82

★★★ ⊛68% Flackley Ash
TN31 6YH (3m from Rye, beside A268)
☎(0797) 230651 FAX (0797) 230510

A welcoming and informal atmosphere prevails at this Georgian manor house in 5 acres of attractive grounds. A new wing offers accommodation of a generally uniform standard, though executive rooms are more spacious and better equipped; bedrooms are also available in the original building. A restaurant and bar overlook the well kept gardens, and there is a comfortable lounge.

32⇨♠(3fb)3⊞ CTV in all bedrooms ® T sB&B⇨♠£69-£83 dB&B⇨♠£98-£112 ⊟
70P ✱ ▭ (heated) sauna solarium gymnasium spa bath croquet beautician hairdresser xmas
⚘ English & French V ◐ ⚲ Lunch £12.95-£16.15 High tea £1.95-£6 Dinner £19.15-£24.15 Last dinner 9.30pm
CONF. Thtr 100 Class 50 Board 40 Del from £96
Credit Cards ① ② ③ ⑤ £
See advertisement under RYE

PEEBLES Borders Peeblesshire Map 11 NT24

★★★ 67% Peebles Hydro
EH45 8LX ☎(0721) 720602 FAX (0721) 722999

Standing in extensive grounds a short walk from the town centre, this large holiday and conference hotel provides well equipped bedrooms of varying size which are being upgraded. The public rooms are spacious and service is friendly and well managed.

137⇨♠(25fb) CTV in all bedrooms ® T ✖ (ex guide dogs) sB&B⇨♠£64-£71.50 dB&B⇨♠£101-£154 (incl dinner) ⊟

Lift (200P ✱ ▭ (heated) ♪ (hard) squash ∪ snooker sauna solarium gymnasium pitch & putt badminton beautician ♫ ⊛ xmas
V ◐ ⚘ ⚲ Lunch fr£12 Dinner fr£17 Last dinner 9pm
CONF. Thtr 450 Del from £95.25
Credit Cards ① ② ③ ⑤

★★★ 65% Park
Innerleithen Rd EH45 8BA ☎(0721) 720451 FAX (0721) 723510

Overlooking the River Tweed from a setting in its own grounds, this hotel offers a variety of bedroom styles, a comfortable lounge bar and an attractive wood-panelled restaurant. Friendly, smartly dressed staff provide willing service, and guests can make use of leisure facilities at the Peebles Hydro – a sister hotel half a mile away.

24⇨♠1⊞ CTV in all bedrooms ® T ✱ sB&B⇨♠£42.15-£50.65 dB&B⇨♠£57.50-£114.25 ⊟
(50P ✱ putting xmas
V ◐ Lunch £6.80-£12 High tea £6.30-£6.75 Dinner £16-£17 Last dinner 9.30pm
CONF. Thtr 40 Class 20 Board 25 Del from £43
Credit Cards ① ② ③ ⑤

★★ ⊛ 77% Cringletie House
EH45 8PL (Logis) ☎Eddleston(0721) 730233 FAX (07213) 244

Closed 2 Jan-12 Mar

Set in 28 acres of wooded grounds, this imposing baronial mansion is personally run by the Maguires and has a peaceful unassuming atmosphere. Individually decorated bedrooms have good modern bathrooms and enjoy fine views, as do the first-floor public rooms, including an impressive panelled drawing room. Cooking, under the direction of Mrs Maguire, is unpretentious and honest, the carefully executed dishes making maximum use of fresh local ingredients.

13⇨♠(2fb) CTV in all bedrooms T
Lift 40P ⇌ ✱ ♪ (hard) putting croquet
⚘ International V ◐ ⚘ ⚲ Last dinner 8.30pm
Credit Cards ① ③

★★ ⊛ 67% Venlaw Castle
Edinburgh Rd EH45 8QG ☎(0721) 720384

Closed Nov-Mar

A family-owned Scottish baronial mansion set in 6-acres of quiet wooded gardens, offering home-cooked meals in its neat, traditionally furnished dining room. Characterful public rooms include an invitingly relaxing lounge and an unusual library cocktail bar, and bedrooms – though simple by contrast – are generally spacious, comfortable and equipped with modern amenities.

12rm(5⇨5♠)(4fb) CTV in all bedrooms ® T
20P ✱ ✱
⚘ English & French V ◐ Last dinner 8pm
Credit Cards ① ② ③ ④ ⑤

★★ 66% Kingsmuir
Springhill Rd EH45 9EP ☎(0721) 720151 FAX (0721) 721795
RS 25-26 Dec & 1-2 Jan

Situated in a residential area to the south of the town centre, this friendly family-run hotel has bedrooms of varying size but all equipped and furnished to a similar standard. Public areas include a comfortable residents lounge and popular bar and restaurant.

10⇨♠(2fb) CTV in all bedrooms ® T ✱ sB&B⇨♠£33-£40 dB&B⇨♠£58-£68 ⊟
27P ✱ ✱ ⚘
⚘ Scottish & French V ◐ ⚘ ⚲ ✱ Lunch £9.50&alc Dinner £13.50&alc Last dinner 9pm
Credit Cards ① ② ③ £

For full, independent restaurant reviews, see the
AA Abbey Well *Restaurant Guide*.

PELYNT Cornwall & Isles of Scilly Map 02 SX25

★★ 63% *Jubilee Inn*
PL13 2JZ ☎Lanreath(0503) 220312 FAX (0503) 220920
This character 16th-century inn stands in the centre of the pretty village. Bedrooms are traditional in style in the main building, modern in the extension, and there are 3 very smart rooms in the lodge just across the garden. There are 3 very popular and busy bars, where bar meals are available, and a more formal dining room offering an a la carte menu. The staff are friendly and the atmosphere is relaxed.
12⇌↟(3fb)1⊞ CTV in all bedrooms ® T
CTV 80P 6🚗 ✿
♀ English & Continental V ♦ ⚏ Last dinner 10pm
Credit Cards [1][3]

PEMBROKE Dyfed Map 02 SM90

★★★ ✿⊞ 69% *Court*
Lamphey SA71 5NT
☎Lamphey(0646) 672273 FAX (0646) 672480

BEST WESTERN HOTELS

Among the improvements Mr and Mrs Lain have recently made to their popular hotel are a conservatory and some studio bedrooms in an adjacent coach house. This stately Georgian mansion has excellent leisure facilities and stands in extensive grounds. High quality local fish and seafood are frequently on the menu, cooking skills are good and portions generous.
22⇌↟ Annexe8⇌↟(15fb) CTV in all bedrooms ®✡ T ✱
sB&B⇌↟£59.50-£68 dB&B⇌↟£79-£99 🄑
⊞ 50P ✿ ▭ (heated) ♀ (hard) sauna solarium gymnasium *xmas*
♀ English & French V ♦ ⚏ ⚌ Lunch £15.95&alc High tea £2.50-£7.50 Dinner £15.95&alc Last dinner 9pm
CONF. Thtr 100 Class 60 Board 60 Del from £69.50
Credit Cards [1][2][3][5]

★★ 60% *Coach House Inn*
116 Main St SA71 4HN ☎(0646) 684602 FAX (0646) 687456
Closed 24-26 Dec
A busy town centre hotel, this was once a coaching inn. The old courtyard is now a pleasant bar with a small gallery lounge above, and the bedrooms are all pine furnished. A good range of food is available in the bar and in the à la carte restaurant.
14⇌↟(3fb) CTV in all bedrooms ® T ✱ sB&B⇌↟£35-£37.50 dB&B⇌↟£54-£57 🄑
10P ✿ solarium
♀ Welsh V ♦ ⚏ ✱ Lunch £12.95-£18.25alc Dinner £15&alc Last dinner 9pm
Credit Cards [1][2][3][5]

See advertisement on page 479

★★ 58% *Old Kings Arms*
Main St SA71 4JS ☎(0646) 683711
Closed 25-26 Dec & 1 Jan
Under the same family ownership for over 30 years, this old coaching inn in the town centre has compact bedrooms fitted with modern facilities and a large traditional-style residents' lounge. Food is available in the popular bars and attractive slab-floored restaurant with log fire.
21⇌↟ CTV in all bedrooms ® T ✱ sB&B⇌↟£30-£37 dB&B⇌↟£45-£47
21P
V ♦ Lunch fr£10.50alc Dinner fr£12.50alc Last dinner 10pm
Credit Cards [1][2][3]

Irish entries appear in a separate section that follows the main directory.

Venlaw Castle Hotel ★★
Peebles EH45 8QG
Telephone: 0721 720384

Venlaw Castle Hotel offers all the comforts of a modern hotel, with excellent cuisine, while retaining the atmosphere of gracious living of a bygone age.
The castle was built in 1782, in the Scottish Baronial style of architecture, on the site of the old Scottish keep of Smithfield Castle, and commands a magnificent view of the surrounding coutryside.

Peebles HOTEL HYDRO ★★★

Set in the heart of the beautiful Scottish Borders, the Peebles Hydro offers comfort, service, and a complete range of indoor and outdoor facilities.

Just 700 yards away, our sister hotel — the Park — enjoys a reputation for peace and quiet, together with a fine restaurant.

For full details please contact:
The Peebles Hotel Hydro,
Peebles EH45 8LX
Tel: (0721) 720602 Telex: 72568

Peebles HOTEL HYDRO
Peebles EH45 8LX Scotland
COMFORT, SERVICE, LEISURE AND HEALTH FACILITIES

Pembroke Dock - Penrhyndeudraeth

PEMBROKE DOCK Dyfed Map 02 SM90

★★★ 63% Cleddau Bridge
Essex Rd SA72 6UT ☎Pembroke(0646) 685961 FAX (0646) 685746

This busy commercial hotel is on the banks of the River Cleddau next to the toll bridge. The spacious bar and restaurant look out over Pembroke Haven to Neyland on the opposite shore, and there is a small but comfortable sitting area in the foyer. Bedrooms are all on the ground floor and surround the outdoor swimming pool. There is a choice of table d'hôte and à la carte menus.

24🛏️🛎️ CTV in all bedrooms ® T
(150P ❀ 🏊 (heated) 🏊 (heated)
♀ British & French V ❀ ♨ ✗ Last dinner 9.30pm
Credit Cards 1 2 3 5

PENARTH South Glamorgan Map 03 ST17

★ 65% Walton House
37 Victoria Rd CF6 2HY ☎(0222) 707707 FAX (0222) 711012
RS Sun

Walton House is a small family-run hotel in a quiet residential part of town, which is both friendly and well managed. Very popular with business travellers, it has an attractive restaurant also much used by locals.

13rm(11🛏️🛎️) CTV in all bedrooms ® T ✗ (ex guide dogs) ❀ sB&B£23.50 sB&B🛏️🛎️£28.50-£32 dB&B£39 dB&B🛏️🛎️£42-£45
16P 🚗 ❀
♀ English, French, Italian & Spanish V ✳ Lunch £12&alc Dinner £12&alc Last dinner 9pm
Credit Cards 1 3

PENCOED Mid Glamorgan Map 03 SS98

★★★ 70% St Mary's Hotel & Country Club
St Marys Golf Club CF35 5EA (just off junct 35 of M4) ☎Bridgend(0656) 861100 FAX (0656) 863400

BEST WESTERN HOTELS

This new hotel and golf complex is an attractive combination of 16th-century country house and modern hotel standards. Bedrooms are very good and many have whirlpool baths. There is a good choice of bars and eating options. Professional service is provided by smart staff, and the atmosphere is welcoming and hospitable.

24🛏️🛎️(18fb)1⌘ CTV in all bedrooms ®☼ T
✗ (ex guide dogs) sB&B🛏️🛎️£60 dB&B🛏️🛎️£85 🍴
(140P ❀ ▶ 27 ♀ (hard) ♪ ∪ floodlit driving range *xmas*
♀ International V ❀ ♨ ✗ ✳ Lunch fr£14.50&alc Dinner £14.50 Last dinner 9.45pm
CONF. Board 30 Del £80
Credit Cards 1 2 3 5
See advertisement under BRIDGEND

Forte Travelodge
Old Mill, Felindre Rd CF3 5HU (on A473)
☎(0656) 864404 Central Res (0800) 850950

FORTE Travelodge

This modern building offers a good standard of accommodation for overnight stops. Smart, spacious and well equipped bedrooms, all with en suite bathrooms, are suitable for family use, and meals may be taken at the nearby family restaurant. For more details about Travelodges, consult the Contents page, under Hotel Groups.

40🛏️❀ B🛏️🛎️£31.95 (room only)

Rosettes range from 5 for outstanding cuisine to 1 rosette for enjoyable, well prepared food

PENCRAIG Hereford & Worcester Map 03 SO52

★★🐕 62% Pencraig Court
HR9 6HR (off A40, 4m S of Ross-on-Wye)
☎Ross-on-Wye(0989) 770306
Closed Nov-Feb

A Grade II listed Georgian manor house retaining many original fireplaces where logs burn during the colder weather. It offers accommodation in generally spacious bedrooms, many provided with easy chairs. Drinks are served in two sitting rooms, both of which are comfortable, and the restaurant, overlooking 3-acres of attractive grounds, serves a fixed price 4-course dinner.

11🛏️🛎️(2fb)1⌘ ✗ in 1 bedroom CTV in all bedrooms ® T
✗ (ex guide dogs) sB&B🛏️🛎️£40-£44 dB&B🛏️🛎️£58-£66 🍴
25P 🚗 ❀ ∪
♀ English & French V ❀ ♨ ✗ ✳ Sunday Lunch £9.50 Dinner £13.50 Last dinner 9pm
Credit Cards 1 2 3 5
See advertisement under ROSS-ON-WYE

PENMAEN West Glamorgan Map 02 SS58

★★ 65% Nicholaston House
Nicholaston SA3 2HL ☎Swansea(0792) 371317

Run by the friendly Peter and Pat Lewis, this hotel, built in the 1880s, enjoys an excellent position looking out over Oxwich Bay. Accommodation, with sea or country views, has modern furnishings. The restaurant, bar and small lounge overlook the bay and there is a separate breakfast room.

11🛏️🛎️(4fb)1⌘ CTV in all bedrooms ® ✗ (ex guide dogs)
CTV 35P ❀ snooker 9 hole putting green
V ❀ ✗ Last dinner 9pm
Credit Cards 1 3

PENNAL Gwynedd Map 06 SH60

★★ 61% Llugwy Hall Country House
SY20 9JX (1m E on A493) ☎(0654) 791228 FAX (0654) 791231
Closed 24 Dec-2 Jan

With 40 acres of gardens and grounds along the River Dovey, this 17th-century former country house offers bedrooms which vary in size and quality; many are quite simply furnished but have modern equipment.

15🛏️🛎️(4fb) CTV in all bedrooms ® T
40P ❀ croquet clay pigeon shooting
V ❀ ♨ Last dinner 9pm
Credit Cards 1 2 3 5

PENNYGHAEL
See **Mull, Isle of**

PENRHYNDEUDRAETH Gwynedd Map 06 SH63

★★★ ❀76% The Hotel Portmeirion
Portmeirion LL48 6ET (2m W, Portmeirion village is S off A487) ☎Porthmadog(0766) 770228 FAX (0766) 771331
Closed 10 Jan-4 Feb

In the heart of this unique Italianate village, the Hotel Portmeirion is superbly situated on the estuary banks. Bedrooms, in the main hotel or scattered throughout the village, are individually furnished with fine antiques, period pieces and striking fabrics. The hotel has several impressive lounges, while rooms in the village have separate sitting rooms. The food has improved since the arrival of young chef Craig Hindley, who has introduced a good range of imaginative dishes to the daily fixed-price menu.

14🛏️🛎️ Annexe20🛏️🛎️(4fb)2⌘ CTV in all bedrooms ®☼ T ✗
✳ sB🛏️🛎️£57-£102 dB🛏️🛎️£67-£146 (room only) 🍴
(40P 🚗 ❀ 🏊 (heated) ♀ (hard) *xmas*

♨ French V ✂ ✱ Lunch fr£13.50 Dinner fr£25 Last dinner 9.30pm
CONF. Del from £120
Credit Cards 1 2 3 5

PENRITH Cumbria Map **12** NY53

See also **Edenhall, Shap** & **Temple Sowerby**
★★★ **73%** **North Lakes**
Ullswater Rd CA11 8QT (Shire) ☎(0768) 68111 FAX (0768) 68291
This spacious and comfortable hotel has impressive public areas, with huge beamed ceilings and a large stone fireplace. Bedrooms are comfortable, very well equipped and have matching soft furnishings.
85⇌🅱(6fb)4🛏✂in 12 bedrooms CTV in all bedrooms ® ♈ T ✱ sB&B⇌🅱£89-£99 dB&B⇌🅱£108-£118 🍴
Lift ⸨ 150P 🅿 (heated) squash snooker sauna solarium gymnasium spa pool ♬ xmas
♨ English & French V ✂ ♿ ✱ Lunch £11.95&alc Dinner £16-£18&alc Last dinner 9.45pm
CONF. Thtr 200 Class 140 Board 34 Del £112
Credit Cards 1 2 3 5

★★ **65%** **George**
Devonshire St CA11 7SU (Logis) ☎(0768) 62696 FAX (0768) 68223
Closed 25-26 Dec & 1 Jan
This coaching house in traditional style, owned by the same family for over 15 years, stands at the centre of the market town. Most of the bedrooms have matching fabrics; dinner is served each evening in the cosy restaurant, and the spaciously comfortable lounge foyer offers a good range of snacks.
31⇌🅱(1fb) CTV in all rooms ® T sB&B⇌🅱fr£41 dB&B⇌🅱fr£55 🍴
⸨ 30P
♨ English & French ✂ ♿ Lunch fr£8 Dinner fr£13 Last dinner 9pm
Credit Cards 1 3   £

★★ **62%** *Clifton Hill*
Clifton CA10 2EJ (2.75m S A6) ☎(0768) 62717
This large, family owned and run hotel stands in an elevated position in its own grounds. There are spacious public areas which include 3 dining rooms, a function room, bar and sunny conservatory. Bedrooms vary in size and style but all have modern fittings. Clifton Hill specialises in coach tours which the hotel organises itself.
57⇌🅱(2fb) CTV in all bedrooms
CTV 200P 25🅿 ✱
V ✂ ♿ ✂

★★ **61%** **Roundthorn Country**
Beacon Edge CA11 8SJ ☎(0768) 63952
Closed Nov-Mar RS Oct
Set in an elevated position, with very pleasant views across the valley, this attractive stone built hotel is family owned and run. Attractively decorated and furnished bedrooms offer all modern facilities, the comfortable restaurant serves a good range of food, and there is a cosy lounge bar.
7⇌🅱(1fb)2🛏 CTV in all bedrooms ® ✱ sB&B⇌🅱£25-£30 dB&B⇌🅱£40-£50 🍴
40P 2🅿 ✱ nc5yrs
✂ ✱ Dinner £11-£12.50&alc Last dinner 9pm
Credit Cards 1 3   £

★ **58%** *Glen Cottage*
Corney Square CA11 7PX ☎(0768) 62221
Closed 25-26 Dec & 1 Jan
This small, friendly, family-run hotel at the centre of the town provides fairly simple but very good value accommodation.

➥

Penrhyndeudraeth - Penrith

★★

Clifton, Penrith Cumbria CA10 2EJ Tel: Penrith (0768) 62717

A traditional hotel set back from the A6, 3 miles south of Penrith. Ideally situated for touring the Lake District or for a stop on the way to Scotland. The Ullswater Restaurant overlooks the beautiful gardens with good views of the Pennines.

★★   BWRDD CROESO CYMRU / WALES TOURIST BOARD

116 MAIN STREET · PEMBROKE · DYFED · SA71 4HN
Telephone: (0646) 684602
Fax: (0646) 687456

- Modern, comfortable bedrooms, all en suite and with colour TV, coffee/tea making facilities and direct dial telephone.
- Cottage style restaurant which boasts excellent cuisine using seafood and an abundance of fresh local produce.
- Attractively designed bar and gallery lounge.
- Excellent base for exploring the beautiful Pembrokeshire countryside and coastline plus many attractions.

Telephone now for our colour brochure.

P

479

Penrith - Penzance

Bedrooms are cosy and well equipped, while public areas include a compact lounge with separate bar and a wood-panelled dining room offering a short fixed price menu at a very reasonable price.
7rm(4⇨🏠)(3fb) CTV in all bedrooms ®
3🐕 (60p per night)
✿ Last dinner 9pm
Credit Cards 1 3

Forte Travelodge
Redhills CA11 0DT (on A66)
☎(0768) 66958 Central Res (0800) 850950

FORTE Travelodge

This modern building offers a good accommodation for overnight stops. Smart, spacious and well equipped bedrooms, all with en suite bathrooms, are suitable for family use, and meals may be taken at the nearby family restaurant. For more details about Travelodges, consult the contents page, under Hotel Groups.

32⇨🏠✱ B⇨🏠£31.95 (room only)

PENYBONT Powys Map 03 SO16

★★**63%** **Severn Arms**
LD1 5UA (on A44/A488 junct) ☎(0597) 851224 & 851344 FAX (0597) 851693
Closed Xmas wk

Run by involved resident proprietors, this 19th-century coaching inn offers friendly and relaxed service – and six miles of free fishing on the River Ithon. A good choice of meals is served in the two bars and restaurant, all with attractive beams, while bedrooms combine traditional style with modern facilities.

10⇨🏠(6fb) CTV in all bedrooms ® T sB&B⇨🏠£28 ♻
CTV 20P 2🐕 ✱ ♪
V ✿ Sunday Lunch £7 Dinner fr£12&alc Last dinner 9pm
Credit Cards 1 2 3 5

PENZANCE Cornwall & Isles of Scilly Map 02 SW43

★★**61%** **Higher Faugan**
Newlyn TR18 5NS (off B3115 0.75m from Newlyn crossroads)
☎(0736) 62076 FAX (0736) 51648
RS Nov-Mar

Built in 1904 for the artist Stanhope Forbes RA, Higher Faugan is set in 10 acres of lawns and gardens with commanding rural and coastal views. It is the small family business of Michael and Christine Churchman who oversee the relaxed and informal service. Bedrooms are individually furnished and decorated while public areas include a cosy bar and a comfortable lounge. There is a short table d'hôte dinner menu.

11⇨🏠(2fb)🚭 CTV in all bedrooms ® T sB&B⇨🏠£40-£45 dB&B⇨🏠£80-£98 ♻
20P ✱ ⛱ (heated) ♪ (hard) snooker solarium gymnasium putting green
V ✿ English, French & Italian ✿ ♻ ✂ Bar Lunch £2-£5alc High tea fr£5 Dinner fr£14.50 Last dinner 8.30pm
Credit Cards 1 2 3 5 £

★★★**57%** **Mount Prospect**
Britons Hill TR18 3AE (approaching on the A30 pass the heliport straight on to the next roundabout take third turning on the right hotel is on right hand side) ☎(0736) 63117 FAX (0736) 50970

Two semidetached Victorian villas were joined together to create this friendly family-run hotel, which offers panoramic views across Penzance to Mounts Bay. The rooms vary in outlook, some are no smoking and a gradual upgrading programme is in progress.

24⇨🏠(2fb)✓ in 9 bedrooms CTV in all bedrooms ®✓ T ✱ sB&B⇨🏠£39-£45 dB&B⇨🏠£58-£68 ♻
⦗ CTV 14P ✱ ⛱ (heated)

✿ English & Continental ✿ ♻ ✂ Bar Lunch £6.80-£12.50alc Dinner £10.50-£14&alc Last dinner 9pm
Credit Cards 1 2 3 5

★★★**52%** **Queen's**
The Promenade TR18 4HG ☎(0736) 62371 FAX (0736) 50033

This traditional town resort hotel overlooks the busy promenade and seafront. Features of the public areas include a wide foyer with a fine staircase and an extensive collection of pictures, many painted by one of the directors. Bedrooms vary in size and outlook, and are slowly being upgraded.

71⇨🏠(9fb)3🚭 CTV in all bedrooms ®✓ T sB&B⇨🏠£33-£50 dB&B⇨🏠£54-£90 ♻
Lift ⦗ CTV 50P snooker sauna solarium gymnasium ⛱ xmas
✿ English & French V ✿ ♻ ✂ Lunch £7.50 Dinner £16 Last dinner 8.45pm
CONF. Thtr 150 Class 70 Board 70 Del £56.80
Credit Cards 1 2 3 5

★★**60%** **Sea & Horses**
6 Alexandra Ter TR18 4NX (enter town on A30, stay on seafront follow signs Newlyn/Mousehole for approx 1m, hotel set back off main road) ☎(0736) 61961
Closed mid Nov-mid Feb

Set back from the promenade, this small hotel is part of a terrace overlooking Mounts Bay. The Mansfields have been here many years and offer a warm welcome to guests. There is a comfortable lounge with an adjacent small bar area, and the bedrooms are clean and simply furnished.

11rm(2⇨🏠6🏠)(4fb) CTV in all bedrooms ® T ✱ ✱ sB&B£22 sB&B⇨🏠£24 dB&B£40 dB&B⇨🏠£44-£48
8P 1🐕 (£1) 🚭
V ✿ ♻ Bar Lunch £1.20-£3.50 Dinner £9.85 Last dinner 7.30pm
Credit Cards 1 3

★**⊛72%** **Tarbert**
11-12 Clarence St TR18 2NU (take Land's End turning at town approach. At 2nd roundabout turn left) ☎(0736) 63758 FAX (0736) 331336

Closed 22 Dec-25 Jan

Friendly hospitality is provided at this terraced Georgian house, with a whitewashed exterior and striped awnings. The entrance hall and stairways are rather narrow, but bedrooms are pretty and the lounge bar is very spacious. Food is freshly prepared and cooked with care.

12⇨🏠 CTV in all bedrooms ® T ✂ sB&B⇨🏠£25-£27.50 dB&B⇨🏠£45-£55 ♻
CTV 5P 🚭 nc 4yrs
✿ English & French V ✿ ♻ Bar Lunch £2.50-£3.75 Dinner £10.95-£13&alc Last dinner 8.30pm
Credit Cards 1 2 3 5 £

★**70%** **Estoril**
46 Morrab Rd TR18 4EX ☎(0736) 62468 & 67471
Closed Dec-Jan

This small hotel, run by the Marshment and Regan families, is conveniently situated for the town centre and sea front. Bedrooms are well presented and equipped and one ground floor room is available. There is a high standard of housekeeping is evident throughout the hotel.

10⇨🏠(2fb) CTV in all bedrooms ® T ✂ sB&B⇨🏠£24-£26 dB&B⇨🏠£48-£52 ♻
4P 🚭
V ✂ Dinner £11 Last dinner 7.30pm
Credit Cards 1 3

Hotels with red star ratings are especially high quality.

PERELLE
See **Guernsey** under **Channel Islands**

PERRANPORTH Cornwall & Isles of Scilly Map 02 SW75
★65% **Beach Dunes**
Ramoth Way, Reen Sands TR6 0BY ☎Truro(0872) 572263 FAX (0872) 573824
Closed Nov & Dec RS Jan & Feb
Set high above the beach, this small family-run hotel gives fine views and has a friendly atmosphere. It offers neat well equipped bedrooms, some of them in an annexe, cosy public areas with sunny patios, and wholesome home-cooking.
6rm(5⇨ฅ)Annexe3⇨ฅ(2fb) CTV in all bedrooms ® T
15P ⊞ ✿ ▭ (heated) ▶ 18 squash nc3yrs
V ✿ ⚏ ✗ Bar Lunch £2.50-£7.50alc Dinner £12.50 Last dinner 7.30pm
Credit Cards [1][3]

PERRANUTHNOE Cornwall & Isles of Scilly Map 02 SW52
★63% *Ednovean House*
Ednovean Ln TR20 9LZ (on A394 5m E of Penzance)
☎Penzance(0736) 711071
This period house is in a peaceful location with superb views across fields to the bay and St Michael's Mount. The bedrooms are bright though compact, and most enjoy the view. There is a comfortable lounge and a separate bar. The atmosphere is informal, and Val Compton uses good local ingredients for her home cooking and vegetarian menus.
9rm(6ฅ)(1fb) ®
CTV 16P ⊞ ✿ putting green croquet
V ✿ ⚏ ✗
Credit Cards [1][2][3]

SEA & HORSES HOTEL

AA ★★
6 ALEXANDRA TERRACE, PENZANCE, CORNWALL TR18 4NX.
Tel: (0736) 61961

A small hotel on the sea front with a reputation for cleanliness, friendliness, and good food. Most rooms are fully en suite with all having shower or bath. All rooms have tea/coffee making facilities, colour TV, radio and telephone. Spacious lounge with uninterrupted views over Mounts Bay, fully licensed. Free private parking.

Estoril Hotel

46 Morrab Road, Penzance, Cornwall
Telephone:
(0736) 62468/67471

You will find this small comfortable hotel ideally situated between the promenade and the town centre.
A warm welcome awaits guests at all times. Highly recommended. All rooms are en suite and have colour TV, telephone and tea and coffee facilities.
Access   Visa

MOUNT HAVEN HOTEL

AA ★★ 68% ♛♛♛♛ COMMENDED

Turnpike Rd., Marazion, Nr. Penzance
Cornwall TR17 0DQ
Tel: 0736 710249

Comfortable, family-run hotel with own grounds in quiet coastal village. All rooms *en suite*, colour TV, central heating, tea/coffee facilities, etc. Most rooms have stunning views overlooking St. Michael's Mount and the sea, some with balconies. Unique galleried restaurant with excellent à la carte menu. Large private car park. Ideal base for touring the Land's End Peninsula.

See gazetteer under Marazion.

Perth

PERTH Tayside *Perthshire* Map **11** NO12

★★★ ♨ 78% **Murrayshall Country House Hotel & Golf Course**
New Scone PH2 7PH (4m N of Perth) ☎(0738) 51171 FAX (0738) 52595

This pink sandstone mansion, set in 300 acres of parkland, has a fine golf course and views of the Grampians. While most bedrooms are attractive, with thoughtful extras like fruit and good toiletries, several are surprisingly functional. Public areas are boldly decorated with quality materials. In the restaurant a choice of 3 menus covers the best of Scottish produce from West Coast scallops to local Roe deer and a subtler, less flamboyant style developed in the kitchens brings praise from our inspector. Less formal eating is available in the attractive Club House restaurant. Service is very good.

19⇨ ♠(3fb) CTV in all bedrooms ⚲ T ✱ sB&B⇨ ♠£60-£75 dB&B⇨ ♠£105-£125 🄟

(50P ❀ ▶ 18 ♪ (hard) bowling green croquet driving range *xmas*

V ❀ ⚲ Lunch £4-£11alc Dinner £17.50&alc Last dinner 9.30pm

CONF. Thtr 780 Class 30 Board 30 Del from £85

Credit Cards 1 2 3 5

★★★ ❋72% **Parklands**
St Leonards Bank PH2 8EB ☎(0738) 22451 FAX (0738) 22046

(Rosette awarded for lunch only)

This elegant hotel is near the railway station and town centre. Bedrooms of varying sizes all have modern décor and quality fabrics. Both the restaurant and bar lounge have conservatory areas and there is also a cosy lounge. The kitchen has adopted a simpler cooking style, though the food is enjoyable, though menu descriptions can be careless.

14⇨ ♠ CTV in all bedrooms ® ⚲ T ✱ sB&B⇨ ♠£75-£110 dB&B⇨ ♠£90-£140

40P ⇎ ❀

♀ International V ❀ ⚲ ✱ Lunch £17&alc Dinner £26&alc Last dinner 9pm

Credit Cards 1 2 3

★★★ ❋67% **Huntingtower**
Crieff Rd, Almondbank PH1 3JT (3m W off A85) ☎(0738) 83771 FAX (0738) 83777

A popular business hotel and an ideal venue for weddings, this country house with a mock Tudor façade is less than 10 minutes drive from the town centre. Bedrooms range from the spacious master rooms to rather smaller examples, but all are nicely furnished, and there are 7 modern log cabins in the grounds. Public room have some fine wood panelling, particularly in the restaurant. Bar and restaurant meals attract local custom, and seafood is invariably featured.

35⇨ ♠(2fb) ⚹in 5 bedrooms CTV in all bedrooms ® T ✱ sB&B⇨ ♠£39.50-£62.50 dB&B⇨ ♠£79-£96 🄟

(CTV 100P ❀ sauna solarium gymnasium putting turkish bath *xmas*

♀ Scottish & Continental V ❀ ⚲ ⚹ ✱ Lunch £9.50-£11.50&alc Dinner £13.50-£18.35&alc Last dinner 9.30pm

CONF. Thtr 300 Class 160 Board 50 Del £56

Credit Cards 1 2 3 5

★★★ ❋64% **Newton House**
Glencarse PH2 7LX (off A85, 4m E of Perth) ☎Glencarse(073886) 250 FAX (073886) 717

ExecGroup

(Rosette awarded for dinner only)

This former dower house in the village of Glencarse, 4 miles east of Perth, is run in country house style by Geoffrey and Carol Tallis and their cheery staff. Bedrooms vary in size and are attractive. There is a traditional residents' lounge and a bar with meals available at lunchtime and through the evening. The daily changing 4-course dinner menu in the restaurant features Scottish food.

10⇨ ♠(2fb) CTV in all bedrooms ® T sB&B⇨ ♠£46-£50 dB&B⇨ ♠£68-£75 🄟

50P ❀ ⚱ *xmas*

♀ Scottish & French V ❀ ⚲ ⚹ Lunch £10-£12&alc High tea £8&alc Dinner £15-£17&alc Last dinner 9pm

CONF. Thtr 60 Class 40 Board 30 Del from £65

Credit Cards 1 2 3 5

£

★★★ 60% **Lovat**
90 Glasgow Rd PH2 0LT ☎(0738) 36555 FAX (0738) 43123

This modern business and tour hotel has a comfortable lounge serving popular bar meals, a small restaurant and well equipped bedrooms.

30⇨ ♠(1fb) CTV in all bedrooms ® T ✱ (ex guide dogs) ❋ sB&B⇨ ♠£46-£51 dB&B⇨ ♠£64-£74 🄟

(60P *xmas*

V ❀ ⚲ Lunch £7.50-£8.25 High tea £6.45-£6.75 Dinner £10.75-£11.75 Last dinner 9.30pm

CONF. Thtr 250 Class 120 Board 70 Del from £60

Credit Cards 1 2 3 5

£

★★★ 60% **Queens Hotel**
Leonard St PH2 8HB ☎(0738) 25471 FAX (0738) 38496

Located close to both railway and bus stations, this hotel caters for a mixed market, including tours. It has well equipped, if functional, bedrooms.

50rm(40⇨9♠)(7fb)1🄐 CTV in all bedrooms ®⚲ T ✱ (ex guide dogs) sB&B⇨ ♠£49.50-£59.50 dB&B⇨ ♠£65-£77 🄟

Lift (30P 🞖 (heated) sauna solarium gymnasium *xmas*

V ❀ ⚲ Lunch £7.95-£8.95 Dinner £12.95-£13.95&alc Last dinner 9.30pm

CONF. Thtr 300 Class 80 Board 80 Del from £72.50

Credit Cards 1 2 3 5

£

★★★ 60% **The Royal George**
Tay St PH1 5LD ☎(0738) 24455 FAX (0738) 30345

FORTE Heritage

A traditional old country town hotel, the Royal George overlooks the River Tay and backs onto the town centre shopping area. Its lounges provide a popular venue, and the restaurant, open only in the evening, offers good value menus in attractive surroundings. Bedrooms are being upgraded.

42⇨ ♠⚹in 14 bedrooms CTV in all bedrooms ® T ✱ sB⇨ ♠£70 dB⇨ ♠£85 (room only) 🄟

(18P *xmas*

V ❀ ⚲ ✱ Sunday Lunch £9.95 Dinner fr£15.95&alc Last dinner 9.30pm

Credit Cards 1 2 3 5

★★★ 54% *Isle of Skye Toby*
Queen's Bridge, Dundee Rd PH2 7AB (Toby) ☎(0738) 24471

This business and conference hotel is conveniently located on the north side of the River Tay. Its attractive, period-style carvery restaurant and bar contrasts with the more functional nature of the other public areas. The modern north wing bedrooms offer the greatest comfort, but the older wing is scheduled for upgrading.

56⇨ ♠(2fb)⚹in 14 bedrooms CTV in all bedrooms ® ✱ (ex guide dogs)

Lift (70P

❀ ⚲ ⚹ Last dinner 9pm

Credit Cards 1 2 3 5

⌂ Beaumont
15 St Johns Place PH1 5SZ ☎(0738) 441770 FAX (0738) 441870

Lodge-style town-centre hotel with modern practical bedrooms. There is 24- hour reception and breakfast and light meals are available in the coffee shop. Parking is restricted during the day.

36⇨ ♠(9fb)⚹in 6 bedrooms CTV in all bedrooms ® T

Lift (4P

Credit Cards 1 2 3 5

Peterborough

PETERBOROUGH Cambridgeshire Map **04** TL19
See also *Alwalton*
★★★★ ❀63% Swallow
Lynchwood PE2 6GB PETERBOROUGH
☎(0733) 371111 FAX (0733) 236725
(For full entry see Alwalton)

★★★ **70%** Orton Hall
Orton Longueville PE2 7DN ☎(0733) 391111
FAX (0733) 231912

The history of Orton Hall goes back many centuries, much of the building being Tudor with 19th-century enrichment. It stands in 20 acres of parkland, and the original stables have been converted into the Ramblewood Inn offering bar meals and real ales, while the main hall contains the elegant drawing room, conservatory and oak panelled dining room. Here classical and international dishes are featured on the carte and fixed price menu. Bedrooms, in a sympathetic extension, are spacious and have every modern facility. 49⇨♪(2fb)5⇨⊁ in 17 bedrooms CTV in all bedrooms ® T ✱ sB⇨♪£69-£112 dB⇨♪£96-£130 (room only) ₽
⟮ 200P ✿ *xmas*
V ♡ ⚏ ⊁ ✱ Lunch fr£13.95 Dinner £27 Last dinner 9.30pm
CONF. Thtr 120 Class 48 Board 42 Del from £95
Credit Plan ① ② ③ ⑤   £

★★★ **68%** Peterborough Moat House
Thorpe Wood PE3 6SG (on A1260, overlooking the golf course) ☎(0733) 260000 FAX (0733) 262737

This Moat House is adjacent to Thorpe Wood Golf Course and 500 acres of parkland. An informal alternative to the main restaurant is a small dining area in the Chase Bar. Bedrooms are furnished in light woods with coordinated décor, good amenities and modern bathrooms.

➡

NEWTON HOUSE HOTEL ★★★ AA

This former Dower House, circa 1840, is only 4 miles from Perth, 13 from Dundee and an ideal base to explore the dramatic countryside and numerous places of interest such as Glamis Castle, Scone Palace and World famous golf courses. All the 10 en suite bedrooms overlook the gardens whilst the Country House Restaurant features fresh local produce with a Scottish/French flavour. Also bar meals and snacks.

Your hosts: Christopher & Carol Tallis

Glencarse, Nr Perth, Perthshire PH2 7LX
Telephone: (073 886) 250.
Fax: (073 886) 717.

Scottish Tourist Board HIGHLY COMMENDED

The Bein Inn ★★
Glenfarg
Perthshire PH2 9PY Telephone (0577) 830216

Nestling in beautiful Glenfarg, eight miles south of Perth just off the M90, is where you will find the Bein Inn.

The public rooms are in the traditional style, comfortable and full of atmosphere. The bedrooms all with private bath and TV, are spacious, bright and modern.

Edinburgh, Perth, Dundee and St. Andrews, are all within easy motoring distance.

A golfers' paradise with St. Andrews, Gleneagles, Carnoustie and many more within easy reach.

Special Bargain-Break prices available for Spring/Autumn.
Send for brochure and terms.
**Personally supervised by
Mike and Elsa Thompson**

HUNTINGTOWER HOTEL ★★★

A magnificent Country House Hotel ~ the finest in PERTH for business or pleasure.

CRIEFF ROAD · PERTH
S C O T L A N D
Tel   0738 · 83771
Fax   0738 · 83777

Peterborough - Pickering

125⇨♠♣in 45 bedrooms CTV in all bedrooms ® T ✱
sB⇨♠£77 dB⇨♠£77 (room only) ₽
Lift ⦅230P ❋ ▭ (heated) sauna solarium gymnasium jacuzzi spa pool ♫
♡ International V ♧ ⚒ ✂ Lunch £11.50-£15.75&alc Dinner £15.75&alc Last dinner 9.45pm
CONF. Thtr 400 Del from £71
Credit Cards 1 2 3 5

★★★65% **Butterfly**
Thorpe Meadows, Off Longthorpe Parkway
PE3 6GA (off A1170) ☎(0733) 64240 FAX (0733) 65538

Adjacent to the rowing course in Thorpe Meadows, this waterside hotel has access to nearby parkland, lakes and river walks. There is a relaxed atmosphere throughout the public areas, particularly the informal restaurant, which has an element of self-service if you make a choice from the hors d'oeuvres buffet or dessert selection. The main course is chosen from the carte or daily roast on a carvery. Bedrooms are light, warm and modern, and studio rooms are particularly suitable for business guests.
70⇨♠(2fb) CTV in all bedrooms ® T ✂ (ex guide dogs)
sB⇨♠£39-£57.50 dB⇨♠£39-£57.50 (room only) ₽
⦅85P
♡ European V ♧ ⚒ ✂ Lunch fr£9.50&alc Dinner fr£9.50&alc Last dinner 10pm
CONF. Thtr 80 Class 50 Board 50 Del from £75
Credit Cards 1 2 3 5

See advertisement under BURY ST EDMUNDS

★★★60% **Bull**
Westgate PE1 1RB ☎(0733) 61364 FAX (0733) 557304
This characterful former coaching inn in the town centre provides efficient friendly service and a good range of commercial facilities. Bedrooms vary and have attractive soft furnishings.
103⇨(3fb) CTV in all bedrooms ® T ✱ sB&B⇨£68.50 dB&B⇨£79 ₽
⦅100P
♡ English & French V ♧ ⚒ ✱ Lunch £9.95-£12.50&alc Dinner fr£12.50&alc Last dinner 10.30pm
CONF. Thtr 200 Class 80 Board 60 Del £87.50
Credit Cards 1 2 3 5

Forte Posthouse
Great North Rd PE7 3TB ☎(0733) 240209 FAX (0733) 244455
(For full entry see Norman Cross)

Forte Travelodge
Great North Rd PE7 3UR
☎(0733) 231109 Central Res (0800) 850950
(For full entry see Alwalton)

Travel Inn
Ham Ln, Orton Meadows (take A605 & follow signs to Nene Park) ☎(0733) 235794

Purpose-built accommodation offers spacious and well equipped bedrooms, all with en suite bathrooms. Meals may be taken at the nearby family restaurant and pub. For more details about Travel Inns, consult the Contents page, under Hotel Groups.
40⇨♠✱ B⇨♠£33.50 (room only)

PETERHEAD Grampian *Aberdeenshire* Map 15 NK14

★★★67% **Waterside Inn**
Fraserburgh Rd AB42 7BN (A952 to roundabout on outskirts of Peterhead and turn left for Fraserburgh) ☎(0779) 71121 FAX (0779) 70670

This modern hotel is especially popular with business guests. Lounge facilities are limited, but there is a choice of formal and informal bars and restaurants. Cosmetic improvements are underway in the main house bedrooms, which are generally spacious and comfortable. Studio rooms in the annexe are more modern and lack some of the amenities of the main house rooms.
70⇨♠Annexe40⇨♠(70fb)✂in 14 bedrooms CTV in all bedrooms ® T ✱ sB&B⇨♠£50-£82.50 dB&B⇨♠£61-£89.50 ₽
⦅250P ❋ ▭ (heated) snooker sauna solarium gymnasium steam room spa bath ♫ *xmas*
♡ Scottish & French V ♧ ⚒ ✂ Lunch £6.95-£15&alc Dinner £16.95-£20.95&alc Last dinner 10pm
CONF. Thtr 250 Class 100 Board 50 Del from £78
Credit Cards 1 2 3 5

PETTY FRANCE Avon Map 03 ST78

★★★★69% **Petty France**
GL9 1AF (on A46 S of junct with A433)
☎Chipping Sodbury(0454) 238361 FAX (0454) 238768

Set in attractive gardens this former dower house offers a hospitable atmosphere and comfortable surroundings, with open fired lounges, fresh flowers and country house-style furnishings. Bedrooms in the main house are on traditional lines; those in the converted stables are modern yet cottagey. Good efforts are made in the kitchen using fresh produce for well executed dishes showing a degree of flair.
8⇨♠Annexe12⇨♠(1fb)1⊟ CTV in all bedrooms ® T
sB⇨♠£65-£89 dB⇨♠£85-£110 (room only) ₽
50P ⇞ ❋ croquet *xmas*
♡ International V ♧ ⚒ ✂ Lunch £19-£30alc Dinner £19&alc Last dinner 9.30pm
CONF. Thtr 25 Class 20 Board 20 Del from £98
Credit Cards 1 2 3 5

PEVENSEY East Sussex Map 05 TQ60

★★58% *Priory Court*
Castle Rd BN24 5LG ☎Eastbourne(0323) 763150
Dating back to the 15th century, this former vicarage with a pleasant garden stands directly opposite Pevensey Castle in 2 acres of gardens. Bedrooms are furnished in a traditional style. Meals are served in the small restaurant or the beamed bar with its cosy log fire, and service is informal.
9rm(6⇨1♠)(1fb)1⊟ CTV in all bedrooms ®
CTV 60P ⇞ ❋
♡ Mainly grills V ♧ ⚒ Last dinner 9.30pm
Credit Cards 1 3

PICKERING North Yorkshire Map 08 SE78

See also advertisement for the Beansheaf on page 487

★★❀70% **Forest & Vale**
Malton Rd YO18 7DL ☎(0751) 72722 FAX (0751) 72972

A delightfully traditional hotel, parts of which date back to the 18th century, set in its own gardens at Pickering's Eastgate. Bedrooms are modern in style; master bedrooms are enormous, others are smaller and some are in an adjacent cottage. The main dining room overlooks the walled garden, there is a comfortable lounge bar and a small first-floor lounge.
16⇨♠Annexe5⇨♠(3fb) CTV in all bedrooms ® T ✱
sB&B⇨♠£39-£59 dB&B⇨♠£58-£86 ₽
70P ❋
♡ English & French V ♧ ⚒ ✱ Lunch £6.95-£9.25&alc Dinner £16.70&alc Last dinner 9.30pm
Credit Cards 1 2 3 5

Pickering - Pickhill

★★ ⊛69% Fox & Hounds Country Inn
Main St, Sinnington YO6 6SQ (3m west of town, off A170)
☎(0751) 31577
This charmingly restored traditional country inn, situated in a delightfully unspoilt village, offers pine-furnished, oak-beamed bedrooms with much character and charm, one featuring a Victorian brass bedstead. Public areas include a comfortable guests' lounge, beamed bars serving popular bar meals and a dining room, renowned for its standards, which offers a variety of British and international dishes from a moderately priced carte.
8⇌♠(1fb) CTV in all bedrooms ® ✻ T ✱ sB&B⇌♠£25-£30 dB&B⇌♠£47-£50 ♫
40P *xmas*
♛ British & International V ♢ ♨ ✱ Lunch £8-£12alc Dinner £11-£19alc Last dinner 9pm
Credit Cards [1] [3] £

★★ 64% Cottage Leas Hotel
Nova Ln, Middleton YO18 8PN (2m E, take A170 towards Thirsk, in Middleton turn right between pub & church, hotel 1.50m along single track lane) ☎(0751) 72129
This 18th-century farmhouse is on the edge of the moors overlooking the Vale of Pickering. Freshly prepared food is served in the attractive dining room and the modest but comfortable accommodation includes a lounge and cosy bar.
11⇌♠(2fb)1☲ CTV in all bedrooms ® T sB&B⇌♠£38-£40 dB&B⇌♠£70-£75 ♫
60P ✿ ♪ (hard) croquet badminton *xmas*
♛ English & French V ♢ ♨ ✱ Lunch £7.95-£9.95 High tea £5-£7 Dinner £12-£16&alc Last dinner 9.30pm
Credit Cards [1] [3] £

★★ 64% White Swan
Market Place YO18 7AA ☎(0751) 72288 due to change to 472288
This charming old coaching inn, situated in the town centre, features well appointed bedrooms with attractive fabrics and modern furniture. There is a cosy bar with a blazing log fire in winter. Bar meals are available at lunchtime, as an alternative to the attractive restaurant, and there is a comfortable guests' lounge is with antique furniture, easy chairs and a selection of magazines.
13⇌♠(1fb)✂in 2 bedrooms CTV in all bedrooms ® T sB&B⇌♠£55-£71.50 dB&B⇌♠£77-£110 (incl dinner) ♫
35P ☜ ✿ *xmas*
♛ English & French V ♢ Lunch fr£10.50 Dinner fr£19.50 Last dinner 9pm
Credit Cards [1] [3] £

PICKHILL North Yorkshire Map **08 SE38**

★★ 64% Nags Head Country Inn
YO7 4JG (6m SE of Leeming Bar) ☎Thirsk(0845) 567391 & 567570 FAX (0845) 567212
This delightful country inn is owned by brothers Raymond and Edward Boynton, who have carefully upgraded the hotel to a modern standard while retaining much of its historic character, especially in the beamed bars with their open fires and a vast display of neck ties. The inn is renowned for its food and its traditional ales. Bedrooms are functional and tidy.
8⇌♠Annexe7⇌♠ CTV in all bedrooms ® T ✱ sB&B⇌♠£32 dB&B⇌♠£45
50P
♛ International V ♢ ♨ ✱ Lunch £9.75-£10.95 Dinner £12-£17.50alc Last dinner 9.30pm
CONF. Thtr 36 Class 25 Board 25 Del from £40
Credit Cards [1] [3]

Red star hotels are each highlighted
by a pink tinted panel.

Priory Court Hotel
Pevensey, East Sussex BN24 5LG ★★
Telephone (0323) 763150

17th century hotel situated in 2½ acres, opposite Pevensey Castle. Offers 9 well equipped bedrooms and 2 oak beamed à la carte restaurants, serving excellent cuisine. Four-poster bedroom. Large free car park. Hotel includes free house pub, serving inexpensive bar snacks. Children's play area.

Open all year including Christmas bargain breaks. Midweek bookings.

Entertain in Style
AT THE SWALLOW

163 luxury Bedrooms with large double beds, free in-house movie channels, mini-bars, tea & coffee facilities with "fresh" milk and Iron & Ironing board in every room. Large Leisure Complex with adult and children's pool, steam room, sauna, spa and gym. Resident Beauty Therapist (by appointment).

Conference & Banqueting facilities in our Sir Henry Royce Suite (300) plus 11 Board rooms and Syndicate rooms all with Audio Visual equipment built in.

All Public Areas, Bars, Restaurants & Conference rooms are fully air conditioned.

THE EMPEROR RESTAURANT
The Award Winning Emperor Restaurant features the culinary skills of Executive Chef, Sydney Aldridge. His experience gained in 1st class establishments such as 'The Ritz' and 'Inigo Jones', together with the service supervision of our Restaurant Manager, guarantees a gourmet's delight.
Large A la Carte, supplemented by the Chef's Speciality Menu including two course Business Lunch, for those in a hurry.

THE LAURELS BRASSERIE RESTAURANT
Bright modern and cheerful, the Laurels Brasserie Restaurant provides a range of meals and refreshments from tea, coffee to full carvery lunches and dinners, as well as a new a la carte menu. Come and help yourself from our buffet or enjoy friendly table service.

SWALLOW HOTEL PETERBOROUGH
★★★★ AA
(Opposite East of England Showground),
Lynch Wood, Peterborough Business Park,
Peterborough PE2 0GB.
Tel: (0733) 371111, Fax: (0733) 236725

Piddletrenthide - Pitlochry

PIDDLETRENTHIDE Dorset Map 03 SY79

★★ 63% Old Bakehouse
DT2 7QR (turn off A35 E of Dorchester onto B3143, for hotel in 6m) ☎(03004) 305
Closed 25-26 Dec & Jan RS Nov-Feb
In peaceful rural surroundings, this modest country hotel has a cosy lounge and bar, while the dining room, on two levels, is richly appointed. A reasonable choice of dishes is offered and the wine list is above average for this type of hotel. Bedrooms are comfortable, those in the main building being the most spacious.
3rm Annexe7rm(6fb) 3☎ CTV in all bedrooms ® ✱
sB&B→⌐£27.50 dB&B→⌐£48-£55 ⌐
16P ❋ ❋ ⌐ (heated) nc12yrs
♀ English & Continental V ✱ Dinner £9.50-£17.20alc Last dinner 9pm
Credit Cards ①③

PIERCEBRIDGE Co Durham Map 08 NZ21

★★ 64% The George
DL2 3SW ☎Darlington(0325) 374576 FAX (0325) 374577
This delightful old whitewashed coaching inn stands on the River Tees. It offers spacious modern bedrooms, each with hairdryer and good comfortable seating. Bars are full of character with open coal fires, oak beams and many antique pieces. An extensive menu is provided in the restaurant which overlooks the river.
22rm Annexe8rm(6fb) 1☎ CTV in all bedrooms ® T ✖ (ex guide dogs) ✱ sB&B→⌐£45-£55 dB&B→⌐£55-£65 ⌐
130P ❋ ✱ xmas
♀ International V ❋ ⌐ Lunch £9.50-£15.50alc High tea £9.50-£15alc Dinner £12-£17alc Last dinner 9.45pm
Credit Cards ①②③ £

PITLOCHRY Tayside Perthshire Map 14 NN95

★★★ 71% Pine Trees
Strathview Ter PH16 5QR ☎(0796) 472121 FAX (0796) 472460
Built in 1892, this fine country mansion has some splendid period features. The panelled lobby leads, by way of a marble staircase with an iron and brass bannister, to an elegant drawing room with an ornate plasterwork ceiling and 2 marble fireplaces. There is a comfortable cocktail lounge and a delightful dining room. A featureless 1970s extension has recently been skilfully transformed to better blend in with the period of the main house. Bedrooms are steadily being enhanced and improved; most are tastefully modern but with traditional fixtures and fittings.
20rm(19→⌐) CTV in all bedrooms ® T ✖ (ex guide dogs) sB&B→⌐£45-£65 dB&B→⌐£114-£126 ⌐
40P ❋ ❋ putting xmas
♀ Scottish & French V ❋ ⌐ ✱ Lunch fr£12 Dinner fr£20 Last dinner 8.30pm
Credit Cards ①③ £

★★★ 65% Pitlochry Hydro
Knockard Rd PH16 5JH (Scottish Highland) ☎(0796) 472666 FAX (0796) 472238
Closed Jan
From its position high above the town, this large resort hotel commands splendid views across the valley. The spacious and comfortable lounge areas are complemented by nicely furnished and well equipped bedrooms which vary in size.
64rm(6fb) CTV in all bedrooms ®☎ T ✖ (ex guide dogs) sB&B→⌐£53-£62 dB&B→⌐£98-£102 ⌐
Lift (CTV 100P ❋ ⌐ (heated) snooker sauna solarium gymnasium putting green croquet lawn xmas
♀ Scottish, English & French V ♀ Bar Lunch £3.50-£8 Dinner £16&alc Last dinner 9pm
CONF. Thtr 130 Class 36 Board 45 Del from £78
Credit Cards ①②③ £

★★★ 60% Green Park
Clunie Bridge Rd PH16 5JY (Logis) ☎(0796) 473248 FAX (0796) 473520
Closed 2 Nov-26 Mar
Set in its own grounds on the picturesque shores of Loch Faskally, this friendly family-run hotel has a relaxed atmosphere and offers comfortable lounges and neatly decorated, well equipped bedrooms. Sunday dinner features a cold buffet, with the carte as an alternative.
37rm→⌐(10fb) CTV in all bedrooms ® T ✖ sB&B→⌐£38-£43 dB&B→⌐£76-£86 ⌐
50P 4☎ (£1.50) ❋ ❋ ✱ putting table tennis bar billiards
♀ Scottish & French V ❋ ⌐ ✱ Lunch fr£9 Dinner fr£17.50&alc Last dinner 8.30pm
CONF. Thtr 90 Class 60 Board 45
Credit Cards ①③

★★★ 60% Scotland's
40 Bonnethill Rd PH16 5BT ☎(0796) 472292 FAX (0796) 473284

This friendly, family-run hotel in the town centre is gradually being improved. Bedrooms, while offering modern amenities, do vary in size and style, the best having Laura Ashley décor and fabrics, but many only offer en suite showers. Public areas are a mix of traditional and contemporary styles.
60rm→⌐(14fb) CTV in all bedrooms ®☎ T sB&B→⌐£45-£60 dB&B→⌐£78-£100 ⌐
Lift (CTV 80P ❋ ⌐ (heated) sauna solarium gymnasium pool table beauty salon jacuzzi xmas
V ❋ ⌐ Lunch £12 High tea fr£8 Dinner fr£17 Last dinner 8.30pm
CONF. Thtr 200 Class 100 Board 50 Del from £58
Credit Cards ①②③ £

★★ 70% Acarsaid
8 Atholl Rd PH16 5BX ☎(0796) 472389
Closed 3 Jan-12 Mar
Attractive, comfortable lounges, a spacious dining room and thoughtfully equipped bedrooms are offered by this well maintained hotel, set well back from the road in its own gardens on the south side of the town.
18rm→⌐(1fb) CTV in all bedrooms ® T ✖ sB&B→⌐£25-£36 dB&B→⌐£50-£72
20P ❋ putting xmas
♀ International V ❋ ⌐ ✱ Lunch £2.50-£10alc Dinner £15-£17.50 Last dinner 8pm
Credit Cards ①③

★★ ❀70% Knockendarroch House
Higher Oakfield PH16 5HT ☎(0796) 473473 FAX (0796) 474068
Closed 15 Nov-Mar
This delightful 19th-century house is perched on a hillside overlooking the town and has its own pleasant gardens. John and Mary McMenemie run the hotel enthusiastically, and like to take time to chat to guests. There is a spacious country house-style lounge with deep settees and a grand piano, and drinks are served here as there is no bar. Bedrooms are carefully furnished and generally spacious, and two have their own balcony. A well produced 3-course dinner is quite likely to include local salmon and home made soups.
12rm→⌐(1fb)2☎ ⌐ in all bedrooms CTV in all bedrooms ® dB&B→⌐£47.50-£66 ⌐
(12P ❋ ❋ xmas
♀ Scottish & French V ⌐ Dinner £14-£18 Last dinner 7.45pm
Credit Cards ①②③

Hotels with red star ratings are especially high quality.

Pitlochry

★★ 69% Birchwood
2 East Moulin Rd PH16 5DW (Logis) ☎(0796) 472477 FAX (0796) 473951
Closed Nov-Feb
Birchwood is a detached period house secluded in 4 acres of gardens at the southern end of the town, and it is run with commitment by the Harmon family. Bedrooms are nicely decorated and have little extras such as fresh fruit, and those in a modern bungalow in the grounds and are equally popular. While there is no bar as such, drinks are served in the comfortable lounge.
12⇨♠Annexe5♠(4fb) CTV in all bedrooms ® T sB&B⇨♠£30-£36 dB&B⇨♠£50-£62 ₽
25P ❀
V ♡ ☑ ⚒ Lunch £7.25-£14.75alc Dinner £17&alc Last dinner 8.15pm
Credit Cards ① ③

★★ 69% Dundarach
Perth Rd PH16 5DJ (S of town centre)
☎(0796) 472862 FAX (0796) 473024
Closed Feb RS 14 Nov-Jan

Popular with coach tours, this fine mansion set in its own grounds at the southern end of the town offers a high level of service from the Smaile family and their staff. Lounge areas are spacious and comfortable, and the well furnished bedrooms have good facilities.
23⇨♠Annexe3⇨(2fb) CTV in all bedrooms ® T sB&B⇨♠£27.50-£44 dB&B⇨♠£55-£74 ₽
30P ❀
♁ International V ♡ ⚒ ✱ Dinner £14-£17.35 Last dinner 8pm
CONF. Thtr 26 Class 26 Board 26 Del from £58
Credit Cards ①②③   £

★★ 69% Westlands of Pitlochry
160 Atholl Rd PH16 5AR ☎(0796) 472266 FAX (0796) 473994
Lawns lead up to this attractive stone building standing a few hundred yards from the town centre. Public areas – welcoming reception, cosy bar offering good snacks, quiet lounge and spacious dining room – create a pleasing impression on arrival. Bedrooms offer good, comfortable accommodation.
15⇨♠(2fb) CTV in all bedrooms ® T sB&B⇨♠£23.50-£47.25 dB&B⇨♠£47-£74.50 ₽
28P ❀ ♪ xmas
V ♡ ⚒ Bar Lunch £8.70-£15alc Dinner £16-£18.50 Last dinner 9pm
CONF. Thtr 40 Class 20 Board 24 Del from £60
Credit Cards ① ③

★★ 67% Castlebeigh
10 Knockard Rd PH16 5HJ ☎(0796) 472925
FAX (0796) 474068
Closed 1-23 Dec & 3-31 Jan
This sturdy stonebuilt Victorian house stands in 3 acres overlooking tree studded hills. Efficiently run by the resident proprietors, it has a peaceful atmosphere and offers a choice of comfortable lounges, one of which has a bar. Bedrooms are spacious and comfortable.
21rm(20⇨♠)(2fb)1⌸ CTV in all bedrooms ® sB&B£30-£47.50 sB&B⇨♠£30-£47.50 dB&B£60-£95 dB&B⇨♠£60-£95 (incl dinner) ₽
36P ⇌ ❀ putting xmas
♁ Scottish English & French V ⚒ ✱ Dinner £12-£17 Last dinner 8pm
Credit Cards ① ③   £

★★ 66% Balrobin
Higher Oakfield PH16 5HT ☎(0796) 472901 FAX (0796) 474200
Closed Nov-Feb
This friendly hotel, enthusiastically run by resident proprietors, has fine views of the surrounding hills. Recent extensions have added a new lounge bar and additional bedrooms and though some rooms are compact, all are neatly maintained and well cared for. Simple, modestly priced meals are served, including pre-theatre dinners.

15⇨♠(2fb) CTV in all bedrooms ® sB&B£20-£25 sB&B⇨♠£25-£35 dB&B⇨♠£40-£70 ₽
15P ⇌ ❀ nc10yrs
⚒ Dinner £12-£15 Last dinner 7.30pm
Credit Cards ① ③   £

★★ 66% Claymore
162 Atholl Rd PH16 5AR ☎(0796) 472888 FAX (0796) 474037
Closed 3 Jan-14 Feb
Situated just west of the town centre, this small family-run hotel stands in its own well tended grounds and is a popular base for the touring holiday-maker. It is efficiently run by enthusiastic owners Joyce and Harold Beaton, and offers neatly appointed public rooms, together with comfortable and well equipped bedrooms.
7⇨♠Annexe4rm(2♠)(1fb)⚒in 1 bedroom CTV in all bedrooms ® T sB&B£22-£35 dB&B⇨♠£44-£70 ₽
25P ⇌ ❀ xmas
♁ European V ♡ ⚒ ✱ Bar Lunch £6.50-£16.50alc Dinner £16.95&alc Last dinner 9pm
Credit Cards ① ③

★★ 62% Craigvrack
West Moulin Rd PH16 5EQ (from town centre take road signposted 'Kirkmichael and Braemar' at Pitlochry Knitwear Shop. Hotel 500yds on right) ☎(0796) 472399 FAX (0796) 473990

This family-run hotel, converted from a traditional stone-built house, is fronted by a patio and terraced lawns. Public rooms are bright and comfortable, and bar meals prove a popular alternative to the formal restaurant. Bedrooms are rather compact in size.
18rm(10⇨5♠)(2fb) CTV in all bedrooms ® T ✱ sB&B£21-£24 sB&B⇨♠£29-£36 dB&B£42-£48 dB&B⇨♠£50-£56 ₽
22P xmas

RESTAURANT & HOTEL
Bean Sheaf

(Proprietors: M. & E. Sardone)

KIRBY MISPERTON   Telephone:
MALTON,   Kirby Misperton 614
N. YORKS.   or 488

Situated in the Vale of Pickering. Ideally placed as a centre for touring North Yorkshire Moors and East coast. 20 en suite rooms with central heating, colour TV, telephone, radio alarms and hair dryer. Sauna. Pleasantly appointed, friendly atmosphere, renown for excellent English and Continental cuisine. Extensive choice of menus and value.
Recently received Heartbeat Healthy Eating Award.

Most guests have said: 'Never had so much, so good, for so little.'

Pitlochry - Plymouth

♕ International V ✧ ✕ ✱ Bar Lunch £3.50-£11.75alc High tea £5.80-£11.75alc Dinner £14.50&alc Last dinner 8.30pm
Credit Cards [1][2][3] £

★♿65% **Fasganeoin**
Perth Rd PH16 5DJ (situated on the main approach to Pitlochry from the A9, directly opposite Bell's Distillery)
☎(0796) 472387 FAX (0796) 472387
Closed mid Oct-early Apr
A late Victorian residence in secluded gardens on the southern approach to the town, the Fasganeoin is a friendly, family-run hotel with lots of character and charm. There is fine period furniture throughout and bedrooms are spacious and comfortable. Formal dinner is not served, but a substantial high tea is available; the hotel is also proud of its traditional afternoon teas.
9rm(5⇨🎔)(3fb) ✈ (ex guide dogs) sB&B£19-£22 dB&B£38-£42 dB&B⇨🎔£49-£56
CTV 12P ✿
✧ ⚲ ✕ Lunch £2.50-£9.50 High tea £7.95-£11 Last high tea 7.15pm
Credit Cards [1][3][4]

★61% **Craig Urrard**
10 Atholl Rd PH16 5BX ☎(0796) 472346
Situated at the east end of town, this small, friendly, family-run tourist hotel is well maintained and offers good value accommodation.
10rm(7🎔)Annexe2🎔(2fb) CTV in all bedrooms ® ✈
CTV 12P ♿ ✿
✕ Last dinner 8pm
Credit Cards [1][2][3]

PLOCKTON Highland *Ross & Cromarty* Map **14** NG83

★★77% **Haven**
IV52 8TW (turn off A82 just before Kyle of Loclalsh, after Balmacara there is a signpost to Plockton, hotel on main road just before lochside) ☎(059984) 223 & 334
Closed 18 Dec-9 Feb RS 10 Feb-1 Apr & Nov-17 Dec
Guest return year after year to this charming little hotel on the main street of the beautiful lochside village, attracted by the attentive service and comfortable accommodation provided by the enthusiastic owners Marjorie Nichols and John Graham, with their staff. Bedrooms are equipped with a wide range of modern amenities and there are two cosy lounges, a snug bar and attractive restaurant.
13⇨🎔 CTV in all bedrooms ® T sB&B⇨🎔£32-£35 dB&B⇨🎔£64-£70 🍽
7P ♿ nc7yrs
V ✧ ⚲ ✕ Lunch £5-£15alc Dinner £19-£20 Last dinner 8.30pm
Credit Cards [1][3]

PLYMOUTH Devon Map **02** SX45

See also **Down Thomas**
★★★★65% **The Copthorne**
Armada Way PL1 1AR (from town centre follow signs for railway station and ferryport)
☎(0752) 224161 FAX (0752) 670688

Copthorne Hotels

The somewhat austere exterior of this prominent hotel belies an interior which is bright and modern. Bedrooms are well insulated and have a movie channel in addition to the usual facilities expected of its classification. The Burlington Restaurant serves an à la carte menu while the brasserie-style Bentleys offers an informal alternative.
135⇨🎔(29fb)✕ in 18 bedrooms CTV in all bedrooms ® T sB⇨🎔£55-£85 dB⇨🎔£65-£98 (room only) 🍽
Lift (10P 40⌂ 🎱 (heated) sauna solarium gymnasium pool table

♕ International V ✧ ⚲ ✕ Lunch £9.95 Dinner £15.50 Last dinner 10.30pm
CONF. Thtr 70 Class 30 Board 30 Del £87
Credit Cards [1][2][3][5] £

★★★★60% **Plymouth Moat House**
Armada Way PL1 2HJ (A374 city centre then follow signs for Barbican & Hoe B3240)
☎(0752) 662866 FAX (0752) 673816

Queens Moat Houses

Between the city centre, Barbican and The Hoe, this large purpose-built hotel has been undergoing an extensive improvement programme. Work is complete on the 11th-floor Blue Riband Restaurant and its adjoining terrace bar, which have stunning views, and offer imaginative dishes on table d'hôte and à la carte menus. At the time of our visit, about half of the bedrooms had been refurbished and a new grill-style restaurant was due to open on the ground floor.
212⇨🎔(102fb)✕ in 16 bedrooms CTV in all bedrooms ® ♿ T ✱ sB⇨🎔£74-£89 dB⇨🎔£84-£99 (room only) 🍽
Lift (30P 150⌂ 🎱 (heated) sauna solarium gymnasium steam room table tennis pool & *xmas*
♕ International V ✧ ⚲ ✱ ✕ Lunch £8-£14.50 Dinner £17.50&alc Last dinner 10.30pm
CONF. Thtr 425 Class 150 Board 50 Del from £65
Credit Cards [1][2][3][5] £

★★★69% **Boringdon Hall**
Colebrook, Plympton PL7 4DP (A38 at Marsh Mills rdbt follow signs for Plympton along dual carriageway to small island turn left over bridge and follow tourist signs) ☎(0752) 344455 FAX (0752) 346578
Boringdon Hall has royal connections and dates back many centuries. It was carefully restored and transformed into a hotel in 1985, and a new courtyard of bedrooms was opened in 1991, built to complement the original Grade I Elizabethan mansion. The gallery restaurant overlooks the great hall bar, and the Admiral's Carvery offers a dining alternative.
41⇨🎔(5fb)4⚲ CTV in all bedrooms ® ♿ T sB&B⇨🎔£55-£65 dB&B⇨🎔£65-£75 🍽
(CTV 150P 🎱 (heated) ▶ 9 ♿ (hard) sauna gymnasium
♕ English & French V ✧ ⚲ Lunch £14.94-£21alc Dinner £16.95-£23alc Last dinner 10pm
CONF. Thtr 140 Class 60 Board 50 Del from £85
Credit Cards [1][2][3][5] £

★★★67% **Duke of Cornwall**
Millbay Rd PL1 3LG ☎(0752) 266256 FAX (0752) 600062

BEST WESTERN HOTELS

The Duke of Cornwall is an impressive listed Victorian building, centrally situated with easy access to the city centre, Barbican and continental ferry ports. All the bedrooms have their own special character, and some of the suites and master rooms have original four-poster beds. Public areas are spacious, and carefully prepared British and Continental cuisine is featured in the Devonshire Restaurant.
70⇨🎔(6fb)2⚲✕ in 20 bedrooms CTV in all bedrooms ® T sB&B⇨🎔£54.50-£69.50 dB&B⇨🎔£64.50-£85 🍽
Lift (50P games room *xmas*
♕ English & French V ✧ ⚲ ✱ Lunch £10.50-£16.95alc Dinner £16.95-£21.95alc Last dinner 10pm
CONF. Thtr 300 Class 125 Board 84 Del from £50
Credit Cards [1][2][3][5] £

★★★66% **Elfordleigh**
Colebrook, Plympton PL7 5EB ☎(0752) 336428 FAX (0752) 344581
Situated in the Plympton Valley, the hotel provides excellent sporting facilities. For formal dining there is Churchill's restaurant, while the Country Pantry offers a more relaxed style of service. Bedrooms are attractively coordinated, comfortable and well equipped.

Plymouth

18⇌🛏(3fb)1🏨 CTV in all bedrooms ®⚲ T ⚔ ✱
sB&B⇌🛏fr£57 dB&B⇌🛏fr£75 🍴
CTV 250P 🚗 ✿ 🏊(heated) ≋ (heated) ▶ 9 ♀ (hard) ♪
squash snooker sauna solarium gymnasium jacuzzi beauty
therapy croquet *xmas*
♨ European V ✿ ♋ ✱ Sunday Lunch £8.95 Dinner
£17.50&alc Last dinner 9.30pm
Credit Cards 1 2 3 5

★★★64% New Continental
Millbay Rd PL1 3LD (from the city centre follow signs for the
Pavilions which are adjacent to hotel) ☏(0752) 220782 FAX
(0752) 227013
Closed 24 Dec-2 Jan
Bedrooms here are attractively coordinated and include 15
executive rooms. The Executive restaurant serves both table d'hôte
and à la carte menus, bar food and room service meals are available.
99⇌🛏(20fb)2🏨 CTV in all bedrooms ®⚲ T sB&B⇌🛏£45-
£65 dB&B⇌🛏£55-£100 🍴
Lift ℂ 100P 🏊(heated) sauna solarium gymnasium
♨ English, French & Greek V ✿ ♋ ✂ ✱ Lunch £8.50&alc
Dinner £13.50&alc Last dinner 10pm
CONF. Thtr 375 Class 100 Board 60 Del from £80
Credit Cards 1 2 3

★★★60% Strathmore
Elliot St, The Hoe PL1 2PR ☏(0752) 662101
FAX (0752) 223690

Situated near Plymouth's famous Hoe and convenient for the city
centre, the hotel forms part of a well maintained Victorian terrace.
Bedrooms vary in size though all are furnished to the same standard.
The popular heraldic theme restaurant serves both table d'hô te and
à la carte menus, and in addition to the simply furnished circular
bar there is a night spot open until late.
➡

★★★
ELFORDLEIGH
HOTEL & COUNTRY CLUB

A Special Welcome to a Very Special Place

Inviting you to discover Elfordleigh, where you will relieve all
work and worry symptoms in one of the most beautiful places
in the whole of Devon.
Situated in 65 acres, the luxury hotel enjoys magnificent views
overlooking Plym Valley, surrounded by its own Golf Course.

● CONFERENCE FACILITIES ●
● SOCIETY GOLF, BUSINESS OR PLEASURE ●
● SPORT AND LEISURE CLUB,
INCORPORATING ELABORATE ROMAN STYLE
INDOOR SWIMMING POOL ●
● ELEGANT A LA CARTE RESTAURANT AS WELL
AS COUNTRY CLUB BARS AND RESTAURANTS FOR
LIGHTER REFRESHMENTS ●
● BUSINESS LUNCHES AND DINNERS AVAILABLE ●
● WEDDING SPECIALISTS ●

For details contact: Elfordleigh Hotel, Country Club,
Colebrook, Plympton, Plymouth, Devon — we will be
delighted to help Tel: (0752) 336428. Fax: (0752) 344581

Plymouth's only Four Star Hotel overlooking the Historic Hoe and Plymouth Sound

★ 212 Four Star International Air Conditioned Bedrooms ★
★ Magnificent Panoramic Penthouse Restaurant and Bar ★
★ Metropolitan Leisure Club and Indoor Swimming Pool ★

Telephone: (0752) 662866

Plymouth Moat House

PLYMOUTH HOE
★ ★ ★ ★

Armada Way, Plymouth, Devon PL1 2HJ

THE SOUTH WEST'S SHINING LIGHT OF QUALITY.

for business ....
.... or pleasure

Perfect city centre location, yet
convenient for the quick get away to
beaches, moors or countryside.

Two superb restaurants, leisure club,
shop and top class accommodation
add to the attractions of ....

The
Copthorne
★★★★
Plymouth

Simply the brightest light in Plymouth.

Armada Way, Plymouth, Devon, PL1 1AR
Tel (0752) 224161 Fax (0752) 670688

Plymouth - Pocklington

54⇌♠(6fb) CTV in all bedrooms ®⚡✱ sB&B⇌♠£35-£50 dB&B⇌♠£45-£60 ₧
Lift ⓒ ♂ xmas
♀ English & Continental V ✿ ✱ Lunch £7.50 Dinner £12.50 Last dinner 10pm
Conf. Thtr 60 Class 40 Board 20 Del from £50
Credit Cards [1][2][3][5] £

★★★ 58% Novotel
Marsh Mills Roundabout, 270 Plymouth Rd PL6 8NH (beside A38) ☎(0752) 221422 FAX (0752) 221422

Bedrooms here are ideal for short stay guests, being well equipped though rather functional. There is a small restaurant with a French theme, bar facilities are readily available, but lounge areas are limited.
100⇌♠⊬in 19 bedrooms CTV in all bedrooms ®⚡ T ✱ sB⇌♠£39.50 dB⇌♠£44.50 (room only) ₧
Lift ⓒ 140P ✿ ⌬ (heated)
♀ French V ✿ ♬ ✱ Lunch £12.95-£14.40&alc Dinner £12.95-£14.40&alc Last dinner mdnt
Conf. Thtr 250 Class 150 Board 100 Del £70
Credit Cards [1][2][3][5]

★★ 65% Camelot
5 Elliot St, The Hoe PL1 2PP
☎(0752) 221255 & 669667 FAX (0752) 603660

Near the famous Hoe and Barbican, and within easy walking distance of the city centre, the Camelot offers comfortable, well equipped accommodation. A Camelot theme runs through the lounge and bar, and the Round Table Restaurant which serves an excellent value table d'hôte menu and a more extensive carte.
17⇌♠(4fb) CTV in all bedrooms ® T ✱ (ex guide dogs) sB&B⇌♠fr£38 dB&B⇌♠fr£50 ₧
CTV ⇎
♀ English & French V ✿ ♬ ⊬ Lunch fr£12&alc Dinner fr£12&alc Last dinner 9pm
Conf. Thtr 60 Class 50 Board 40 Del from £54
Credit Cards [1][2][3][5] £

★★ 65% Invicta
11-12 Osborne Place, Lockyer Street, The Hoe PL1 2PU
☎(0752) 664997 FAX (0752) 664994
Closed 25 Dec-5 Jan

This friendly, family-run hotel is opposite the famous bowling green and within easy reach of the city centre and the Barbican. Bedrooms are attractively coordinated and well equipped. Table d'hôte and à la carte menus are served in the ground floor dining room.
23rm(20⇌♠)(4fb) CTV in all bedrooms ® T ✱ (ex guide dogs) sB&B⇌£26-£28 sB&B⇌♠£38-£40 dB&B⇌£38-£40 dB&B⇌♠£49-£52 ₧
ⓒ CTV 10P
♀ Mainly grills ✿ Dinner £8.50-£9&alc Last dinner 9pm
Conf. Thtr 65 Class 80 Board 65 Del from £42
Credit Cards [1][2][3]

★ 68% Victoria Court
62/64 North Rd East PL4 6AL ☎(0752) 668133
Closed 22 Dec-1 Jan

Mr and Mrs Robinson have tastefully converted two terraced Victorian houses to form this hotel, retaining much of its character. Bedrooms are comfortable and nicely decorated and public areas include a comfortable lounge, a cosy bar and an elegant dining room offering a choice of popular dishes.
14rm(7♠)(4fb) CTV in all bedrooms ® T ✱ sB&Bfr£23 sB&B♠fr£35 dB&Bfr£35 dB&B♠fr£49 ₧
CTV 6P ⇎
♀ European V ✿ ♬ ✱ Dinner fr£12.50 Last dinner 8pm
Credit Cards [1][2][3][5] £

★ 66% Imperial
Lockyer Street, The Hoe PL1 2QD ☎(0752) 227311 FAX (0752) 674986
Closed 25-31 Dec

Resident proprietors Alan and Pru Jones provide a friendly welcome at their Grade II listed hotel, situated conveniently for the city centre and the Hoe. The spacious log fired lounge adjoins the cosy panelled Worcester Bar, and a good value fixed price menu offers a wide choice. Bedrooms vary in size and standard, but there is a programme of upgrading.
22rm(4⇌12♠)(4fb) CTV in all bedrooms ® T ✱ sB&B£28-£29.75 sB&B⇌♠£38-£39.75 dB&B£42-£45 dB&B⇌♠£48-£49.75 ₧
CTV 16P
V ✿ ♬ Bar Lunch £2.40-£3.50 Dinner £12.95 Last dinner 8.15pm
Conf. Thtr 25 Class 25 Board 18 Del from £49
Credit Cards [1][2][3][5] £

★ 62% Drake
1 & 2 Windsor Villas, Lockyer Street, The Hoe PL1 2QD (Logis)
☎(0752) 229730 FAX (0752) 255092
Closed Xmas

Two Victorian town houses have been linked to form this hotel close to the Hoe. Bedrooms vary in standard, but upgrading is on-going and all will be completed by 1995. There is a comfortable, well-stocked bar and the dining room offers a good value set menu as well as a carte with a range of popular dishes. Service is friendly and attentive.
36rm(27⇌♠)(3fb) CTV in all bedrooms ® T ✱ (ex guide dogs) ✱ sB&B£25-£28 sB&B⇌♠£35-£40 dB&B£40-£42 dB&B⇌♠£44-£50 ₧
25P ⇎
♀ Mainly grills V ✿ ⊬ Lunch £11&alc Dinner £11&alc Last dinner 9pm
Credit Cards [1][2][3][5]

Campanile
Marsh Mills, Longbridge Rd PL6 8LD (off A38)
☎(0752) 601087 FAX (0752) 223213

A nearby bar and bistro restaurant provides refreshments for travellers staying at this modern accommodation building. Bedrooms are well equipped and have en suite bathrooms. For more details about Campanile, consult the Contents page, under Hotel Groups.
50⇌♠✱ B⇌♠£35.75 (room only)
Conf. Thtr 35 Class 35 Board 25 Del from £42.80

Forte Posthouse
Cliff Rd, The Hoe PL1 3DL ☎(0752) 662828 FAX (0752) 660974

FORTE Posthouse

Suitable for both the business and leisure traveller, this bright hotel provides modern accommodation in well equipped bedrooms with en suite bathrooms. For more details about Forte Posthouse hotels, consult tje Contents page, under Hotel Guides.
106⇌♠✱ B⇌♠£41.50-£53.50 (room only)
Conf. Thtr 80 Class 50 Board 40 Del £69.50

POCKLINGTON Humberside Map 08 SE84

★★ 69% Barmby Moor Country
Hull Rd, Barmby Moor YO4 5EZ
☎(0759) 302700 FAX (0759) 306459
RS last 2 wks Jan

This friendly 18th-century coaching inn has been sympathetically converted to provide modern comforts, its bedrooms, in traditional or modern style, having the same comprehensive facilities. A comfortable lounge leads to the bar lounge and restaurant, both overlooking the courtyard, swimming pool and gardens.
10⇌♠(1fb) CTV in all bedrooms ® T ✱ (ex guide dogs) sB⇌♠£36-£38 dB⇌♠£46-£48 (room only) ₧

Pocklington - Pontypridd

30P 🚗 ❀ ⌁ (heated)
V ❖ ✗ Lunch £8-£9 High tea £5-£14alc Dinner £5-£14alc Last dinner 8pm
Credit Cards [1][2][3]

★★ 64% **Feathers**
Market Square YO4 2AH ☎(0759) 303155
This old town centre inn has been considerably modernised to provide busy open plan public areas off a central lounge bar. In the pleasant restaurant, with a conservatory extension, a good range of popular meals is served. Bedrooms are mostly spacious, and equipped with such items as hairdryers and trouser presses. Those in the main building are traditional in style, while those in a single storey annexe are modern.
6⇨♠Annexe6⇨♠(1fb)1🛏 CTV in all bedrooms ® T
✗ (ex guide dogs)
CTV 60P 6🚗
V ❖ Last dinner 9.30pm
Credit Cards [1][2][3][5]

★ 67% **Yorkway Motel**
South Moor, Hull Rd YO4 2NX (between Beverley & York on the A1079 with the junc of B1247) ☎(0759) 303071 304852
Closed 25 Dec-1 Jan
10rm(9♠)(1fb) CTV in all bedrooms ® T ✗ (ex guide dogs) ✳
sB&B♠£35-£38 dB&B♠£40-£46
CTV 30P 🚗 ❀
❖ ♨ ✳ Lunch £6.50-£11alc High tea £6.50-£11alc Dinner £9-£14.50alc Last dinner 8.30pm
Credit Cards [1][2][3][5]

PODIMORE Somerset Map 03 ST52

Forte Travelodge
BA22 8JG (on A303, S of junct with A37)
☎Yeovil(0935) 840074
Central Res (0800) 850950

This modern building offers a good standard of accommodation for overnight stops. Smart, well equipped and spacious bedrooms, all with en suite bathrooms, are suitable for family use, and meals may be taken at the nearby family restaurant. For more details about Travelodges, consult the Contents page, under Hotel Groups.
31⇨♠✗ B⇨♠£31.95 (room only)

POLMONT Central *Stirlingshire* Map 11 NS97

★★★ 68% **Inchyra Grange**
Grange Rd FK2 0YB (just beyond B P social club) ☎(0324) 711911 FAX (0324) 716134

Once a country mansion, and still set in its own grounds, this hotel has been modernised and extended to provide well appointed bedrooms ranging from compact singles to comfortable junior suites. Public areas include an attractive foyer lounge.
43⇨♠(5fb)✗in 8 bedrooms CTV in all bedrooms ® T
sB⇨♠£80-£88 dB⇨♠£100-£110 (room only) 🍴
(150P ❀ 🏊 (heated) snooker sauna solarium gymnasium spa bath steam room beauty therapy room *xmas*
♀ Scottish & French V ❖ ♨ Lunch £9.50-£10.50&alc High tea £7.10-£11.50 Dinner fr£19.95&alc Last dinner 9.30pm
CONF. Thtr 220 Class 100 Board 60 Del from £95
Credit Cards [1][2][3][5]

POLPERRO Cornwall & Isles of Scilly Map 02 SX25

★ ❀68% **Claremont**
Fore St PL13 2RG (Logis) ☎(0503) 72241 FAX (0503) 72241
RS 10 Oct-1 Apr
On the flower filled terrace of this small hotel guests can enjoy lunch or afternoon tea and watch the world go by. Young French proprietors create a relaxed atmosphere and guests appreciate their caring attitude. In the restaurant both à la carte and fixed price menus are offered, and our inspector enjoyed crab bisque, 'retour de la peche' – a mixture of local sole, monkfish and salmon on a light cream and wine sauce, and hazelnut meringue. Bedrooms are simply appointed and well equipped.
10⇨♠(3fb) CTV in all bedrooms ® T sB&B⇨♠£18-£27 dB&B⇨♠£36-£50 🍴
CTV 16P 🚗 *xmas*
♀ French ❖ ♨ ✗ Bar Lunch £2-£6alc Dinner £9-£16&alc Last dinner 8.30pm
Credit Cards [1][2][3]

POLZEATH Cornwall & Isles of Scilly Map 02 SW97

★★ ❀70% **Pentire Rocks**
PL27 6US (off B3314) ☎Trebetherick(0208) 862213 FAX (0208) 862259
Closed 3 Jan-5 Feb
On the road leading down to Sandy Bay, this friendly well run hotel has bright, well furnished bedrooms including some easy-access rooms in the garden wing. There is a restaurant, a bar/sun lounge and a TV lounge. A good value, fixed-price daily table d'hôte menu with supplementary specialities is featured, and chef Graham Holder shows a serious approach to his cooking, with good quality ingredients, home-made breads and a lovely selection of desserts.
16rm(1⇨14♠)(2fb)1🛏 CTV in all bedrooms ® T
sB&B⇨♠£35 dB&B⇨♠£70 🍴
CTV 20P 🚗 ❀ ⌁ (heated) *xmas*
♀ English & French V ❖ ♨ ✗ Dinner £22.50&alc Last dinner 9pm
Credit Cards [1][2][3] £

PONTERWYD Dyfed Map 06 SN78

★★ 60% **Dyffryn Castell**
SY23 3LB (beside A44, 2m E) ☎(097085) 237
Over 400 years old and once a coaching inn, this hotel now offers bright, cheerful bedrooms and public areas which include an attractive restaurant, cosy bars and a games room.
9rm(3⇨3♠)(6fb)✗in 2 bedrooms CTV in 6 bedrooms ®
sB&Bfr£20 sB&B⇨♠£22.50 dB&Bfr£39 dB&B⇨♠£41 🍴
CTV 75P games room
V ✳ Bar Lunch fr£1 Dinner £6.50-£8.50 Last dinner 6pm
Credit Cards [1][3]

PONTYPRIDD Mid Glamorgan Map 03 ST08

★★★ 66% **Heritage Park**
Coed Cae Rd, Trehafod CF37 2NP (off A4058, next to the Rhondda Heritage Park) ☎Trehafod(0443) 687057 FAX (0443) 687060
This is a modern red brick building with bright, comfortable bedrooms, richly styled with bold fabrics, quality furnishings and deep tub chairs. There is a welcoming open plan bar leading to a loft restaurant – a galleried bistro with highly polished floors and pine furniture. A variety of value-for-money dishes is offered from the daily blackboard as well as the carte, and service is friendly.
50⇨♠(4fb)✗in 20 bedrooms CTV in all bedrooms ® T ✳
sB&B⇨♠£37-£52 dB&B⇨♠£51-£65 🍴
(CTV 146P small health & fitness centre *xmas*
♀ English & French V ❖ ♨ ✳ Lunch £6.95-£8.95 Dinner £11-£18 Last dinner 10pm
CONF. Thtr 200 Class 160 Board 80 Del £69
Credit Cards [1][3] £

★★★ 62% **Llechwen Hall**
Llanfabon CF37 4HP (1m off A470) ☎Abercynon(0443) 742050 FAX (0443) 742189
This one-time farmhouse and Victorian gentleman's residence stands in 6 acres of grounds overlooking 4 surrounding valleys. It has been transformed into a small quality hotel of character, run on formal lines with prompt services provided by well turned out staff.

Pontypridd - Poole

Bedrooms are tastefully decorated with bold fabrics, with Victorian-style bathrooms. There is a choice of 2 restaurants, one with a carte for more intimate and formal dining.
11⇨♠(1fb)4🛏 CTV in all bedrooms ® T sB&B⇨♠£35-£48.50 dB&B⇨♠£45-£90 ₧
CTV 100P ✿
V ✿ ⚘ Lunch £9.95&alc Dinner £9.95&alc Last dinner 9.45pm
Credit Cards ①②③⑤ £

POOLE Dorset Map 04 SZ09
See also **Bournemouth**

★★★★ ❀❀68% Haven
Banks Rd, Sandbanks BH13 7QL (From junct 1 of M27 follow sings Ringwood, then Poole. Hotel next to the Swanage Ferry departure point) ☎(0202) 707333 FAX (0202) 708796

On top of the Sandbanks peninsula with wide views over Poole harbour to the Isle of Wight, this comfortable hotel offers spacious and well furnished public areas. Bedrooms are attractive and of a good size, particularly those at the rear. The standard of cuisine is high, and a varied table d'hôte menu with supplementary dishes caters for all tastes. Fine, fresh ingredients and are prepared with skill by a team led by executive chef Heinz Karl Nagler, who has gained many accolades
94⇨♠(6fb) CTV in all bedrooms ®✔ T ✈ (ex guide dogs) ✱ sB&B⇨♠£65-£75 dB&B⇨♠£105-£130 ₧
Lift (150P 🛏 ▣ (heated) ⚘ (heated) ✍ (hard) squash sauna solarium gymnasium steam room spa pool ♫ xmas
♡ English & French V ✿ ⚘ ✕ ✱ Lunch f 13.50 Dinner £10-£20&alc Last dinner 9.30pm
Credit Cards ①②③⑤ £

★★★★ 58% Quay Thistle
The Quay BH15 1HD ☎(0202) 666800 FAX (0202) 684170

THISTLE HOTELS

68⇨♠(4fb)⚥ in 22 bedrooms CTV in all bedrooms ® T sB&B⇨♠£75-£79 dB&B⇨♠£85-£89 ₧
Lift (150P ♫ xmas
♡ French V ✿ ⚘ Lunch £10.50-£17.95&alc High tea £3.50 Dinner £17.95-£18.95&alc Last dinner 10pm
CONF. Thtr 65 Class 20 Board 25 Del from £60
Credit Cards ①②③④⑤

★★★★ ❀❀79% Salterns
38 Salterns Way, Lilliput BH14 8JR (From Poole follow B3369 Sandbanks rd. In one mile at Lilliput shops turn into Salterns Way) ☎(0202) 707321 FAX (0202) 707488

BEST WESTERN HOTELS

Courtesy and Care 1994

In an enviable position alongside the marina overlooking Brownsea Island and Poole Harbour, Salterns Hotel is in Lilliput, midway between Poole and Sandbanks. There is a warm and friendly atmosphere throughout, and the proprietors and their professional team of staff work hard to ensure guests' comfort. The hotel is continually improving, and a worthy winner of the AA Courtesy and Care Award. The restaurant has a fine reputation, and chef

Duncan Englefield and his small brigade prepare imaginative dishes with care and skill.
16⇨♠ CTV in all bedrooms ® T sB⇨£66 dB⇨£86 (room only) ₧
(150P 🛏 ✿ ♪ squash snooker xmas
♡ English & French ✿ Lunch £15.50 Dinner £22.50 Last dinner 9.45pm
Credit Cards ①②③⑤ £

★★★ ❀❀75% Mansion House
Thames St BH15 1JN ☎(0202) 685666 FAX (0202) 665709

This handsome, carefully restored hotel dates in parts from the late 1700s, and its bedrooms are pretty and well furnished. Public areas are smart and relaxing. Head Chef Tony Parsons and Executive Chef, Gerry Godden, produce good English dishes without pretentions, such as wild mushrooms in a pastry case, with a cream and herb sauce, and tender, pink calves' liver with creamed potatoes and delicious onion gravy. Tempting desserts might include bread and butter pudding, jam roly-poly and treacle tart. The hotel has a popular dining club.
28⇨♠(2fb) CTV in all bedrooms T sB&B⇨♠£67.50-£75 dB&B⇨♠£70-£110 ₧
(40P 🛏 xmas
♡ English & French V ✿ ⚘ ✕ Lunch £13-£16 High tea £7.50-£10.50alc Dinner £15-£17&alc Last dinner 9.30pm
CONF. Thtr 40 Class 18 Board 20 Del from £89
Credit Cards ①②③⑤ £

★★★ ❀71% Sandbanks
Banks Rd, Sandbanks BH13 7PS (Logis) ☎(0202) 707377 FAX (0202) 708885

In a marvellous position on Sandbanks beach, with glorious views across the harbour and bay, this hotel is popular with families but also caters well for business people. The mostly spacious bedrooms have been refurbished to a good overall standard and many have balconies. Public areas, especially the lounges, have been upgraded in recent months and there are plans to improve the restaurant.
105⇨♠(27fb) CTV in all bedrooms ®✔ T ✈ (ex guide dogs)
Lift (200P ✿ ▣ (heated) sauna solarium gymnasium steam room ⚘
♡ International V ✿ ⚘ Last dinner 8.30pm
Credit Cards ①②③⑤

★★★ ❀68% Harbour Heights
73 Haven Rd, Sandbanks BH13 7LW ☎(0202) 707272 FAX (0202) 708594

This hotel is in a superb elevated position with wonderful views across Poole harbour and Brownsea Island. Most of the larger bedrooms have balconies and lovely views; the smaller rear and side rooms are equally well furnished. Bar food here is very popular, while the Harbour View Restaurant is more formal in style and appearance. The menus are interesting and varied, with a wide choice from the table d'hôte and à la carte menus. The staff are efficient and helpful throughout the hotel, but are particularly charming in the restaurant.
49⇨♠(5fb) CTV in all bedrooms ®✔ T sB&B⇨♠£43-£45 dB&B⇨♠£70-£75 ₧
Lift (84P ✿ ⚘
♡ English French & Italian V ✿ ⚘ Sunday Lunch £10.95-£11.50 High tea £3 Dinner £16-£16.50&alc Last dinner 9.30pm
Credit Cards ①②③⑤

★★ 68% Arndale Court
62/66 Wimborne Rd BY15 2BY ☎(0202) 683746 FAX (0202) 668838

This refurbished hotel is popular with business people on weekdays, but is less busy at weekends, making it the ideal base for a short break. Bedrooms vary in size but all are very smart with extras such as mini bars, irons and trouser presses. Public areas are relaxed and friendly, and in additional to restaurant meals an extensive bar menu is available.
32⇨♠(7fb) CTV in all bedrooms ®✔ T sB&B⇨♠£52 dB&B⇨♠£62

Poole - Porlock

(32P
English & French **V** Sunday Lunch fr£11&alc High tea fr£4.50 Dinner fr£12.50&alc Last dinner 9pm
CONF. Thtr 50 Class 35 Board 35 Del from £65
Credit Cards 1 2 3 5   £

★★ 63% **Norfolk Lodge**
1 Flaghead Rd, Canford Cliffs BH14 7JL ☎(0202) 708614 & 708661 FAX (0202) 708614
A handsome Victorian property, close to a footpath leading down to Sandbanks, the hotel is in a corner plot with well kept grounds and an array of exotic birds in aviaries. Bedrooms are nicely presented and public areas are cosy and comfortable.
19rm(17⇨♠)(4fb) CTV in all bedrooms ® T *
sB&B⇨♠£34-£38 dB&B⇨♠£54
16P ✿ xmas
Lunch £7.50-£9.50 Dinner £10 Last dinner 8pm
Credit Cards 1 2 3

★ 63% **Fairlight**
1 Golf Links Rd, Broadstone BH18 8BE (3m NW B3074)
☎(0202) 694316 & 605349
This small, personally managed hotel is in a residential area of Broadstone, close to the golf course. Bedrooms are neat and fresh, and there is a comfortable lounge and a cosy bar. The dining room, recently redecorated, is very pretty and sunny. Mrs Middlehurst provides a set meal but will cater for special diets or dislikes, preferably with advance notice.
9rm(7⇨♠)(1fb) CTV in all bedrooms ® sB&B£20-£22 sB&B⇨♠£25-£30 dB&B£30-£36 dB&B⇨♠£40-£46
CTV 10P ✿
Dinner £6-£10 Last dinner 7.30pm
Credit Cards 1 3

••
Travel Inn
Ringwood Rd, Tricketts Cross, Ferndown
BH22 9BB (off A348) ☎(0202) 874210

Purpose-built accommodation offers spacious and well equipped bedrooms, all with en suite bathrooms. Meals may be taken at the nearby family restaurant and pub. For more details about Travel Inns, consult the Contents page, under Hotel Groups.
32⇨♠ * B⇨♠£33.50 (room only)

POOLEY BRIDGE Cumbria Map 12 NY42
★★ 60% **Swiss Chalet Inn**
CA10 2NN ☎(07684) 86215
Closed 3-18 Jan
This Swiss-style building is in the centre of the village, not far from the lake. Staff are young and friendly, and a good range of food is available in the bar or the Swiss-style restaurant. Bedrooms are furnished with pine units and have good facilities.
9rm(8⇨♠)(1fb)⌧ CTV in all bedrooms ® * sB&B£27-£32 sB&B⇨♠£27-£32 dB&B⇨♠£44-£52
40P ✿ xmas
English, Italian & Swiss **V** Bar Lunch £3.25-£6.95alc Dinner £7.30-£15.25alc Last dinner 9.30pm
Credit Cards 1 3   £
See advertisement under ULLSWATER

PORLOCK Somerset Map 03 SS84
★★★ 63% **Anchor & Ship**
Porlock Harbour TA24 8PB ☎(0643) 862636 FAX (0643) 862843
RS Jan
Overlooking the harbour, this long established family hotel offers traditional accommodation which has recently been upgraded and improved to a good standard. There is a comfortable drawing room and the candle-lit Harbour Restaurant features both a fixed price

***
SALTERNS
·HOTEL·

The setting of this charming hotel never ceases to appeal, located on the waters edge with superb views across the lovely harbour of Poole.

Salterns Hotel with its south facing position sits in fourteen acres of marina, with its own waterside patio, lawns and pretty borders of carefully kept shrubs.

It would be difficult to imagine that this stunning location could be bettered for here you have found the perfect choice.

Salterns Hotel, 38 Salterns Way, Lilliput,
Poole Dorset. BH14 8JR
Tel: (0202) 707321. Fax: (0202) 707488.

★★★★ AA
THE QUAY
THISTLE HOTEL

The Quay, Poole BH15 1HJ
Tel: 0202 666800   Fax: 0202 684470

This modern hotel overlooks Poole harbour. There are 68 en suite bedrooms offering stylish accommodation. In addition to the excellent à la carte restaurant there is a choice of bars in which to relax and unwind.

Ample car parking is available for resident use.

Your choice in Poole

For Reservations at over 100
Mount Charlotte Thistle Hotels
Telephone London: 071 937 8033.

P

menu and a carte; local seafood is particularly recommended. Extensive bar meals are also available in the Ship Inn.
20⇨♠(3fb)1🛏 CTV in all bedrooms ® T
25P ❋
♀ English & French V ❦ ℒ Last dinner 9pm
Credit Cards 1 2 3

★★❀77% **The Oaks**
Doverhay TA24 8ES ☏(0643) 862265 FAX (0643) 862265

Courtesy and Care 1994

Exceptionally high standards of friendly and attentive service has earned The Oaks the AA's Courtesy and Care Award this year. It is an attractive Edwardian house at the edge of the village with fine views towards the sea. There is a cosy bar, a smart lounge and a dining room where most tables catch the view. The set price 4-course menu offers short choices at each stage. A fillet of moist Scottish salmon many be served with a cream sauce; guinea fowl comes with apple and cider, and the wine list has interesting bottles at fair prices. Bedrooms are mostly pretty and fully equipped.
10⇨♠(2fb) CTV in all bedrooms ® T sB&B⇨♠fr£47.50 dB&B⇨♠fr£75 🛏
12P 🅿 ❋ xmas
♀ English & French ❦ ✗ Dinner £19 Last dinner 8.30pm
Credit Cards 1 2 3   (£)

PORT APPIN Strathclyde *Argyllshire* Map **14** NM94

★★★❀❀❀ **AIRDS**
PA38 4DF
☏Appin(063173) 236 & 211 FAX (063173) 535
Closed 7 Jan-9 Mar

Magnificently situated on the banks of Loch Linnhe, Airds Hotel was originally a ferry inn for travellers to the island of Lismore. Today it is a small luxury establishment owned by Eric and Betty Allen; Mrs Allen and son Graeme look after the kitchen while Mr Allen, handsomely kilted, attends to the front of house assisted by courteous young staff. Bedrooms are tastefully furnished and decorated, several with loch and hill views, and one with its own sitting room. There are 2 cosy lounges with log fires and fresh flowers, and dinner is served in the attractive restaurant overlooking the loch. The 4-course fixed price menu offers ample choice, which could include warm mousse of mussels with a muscadet sauce, poached fillet of wild salmon with hollandaise and roast rack of lamb with sweetbreads. The wine list is outstanding.
12⇨♠ CTV in all bedrooms ✗ (ex guide dogs)

30P 🅿 ❋ nc5yrs
❦ ℒ ✗ Last dinner 8.30pm

PORT ASKAIG
See **Islay, Isle of**

PORT ERIN
See **Man, Isle of**

PORT GAVERNE Cornwall & Isles of Scilly Map **02** SX08

★★❀69% **Port Gaverne**
PL29 3SQ (signposted from B3314) ☏Bodmin(0208) 880244 FAX (0208) 880151
Closed 8 Jan-19 Feb
Built around 1608, this medieval inn retains much of its original character and old world charm and has been personally run by Frederick and Marjorie Ross for many years. Head chef Ian Brodey is assisted by Eden Osabufu and Earnest Platt, and this partnership produces a very reliable standard of cooking. Bar meals are available, and there is an à la carte menu in the candlelit restaurant which features local produce and seafood, as well as daily specials and flambé dishes cooked at your table.
16⇨♠ Annexe3⇨♠(5fb) CTV in 18 bedrooms ® T sB&B⇨♠£41-£47 dB&B⇨♠£82-£94 🛏
CTV 30P 🅿 xmas
♀ International V ❦ ✽ Lunch £4.75-£13.85alc Dinner £14.25-£21.65alc Last dinner 9.30pm
Credit Cards 1 2 3 5

★★66% **Headlands**
PL29 3SH ☏Bodmin(0208) 880260 FAX (0208) 880885
This cliff top hotel with sweeping views of the coast provides personal service. Individually styled bedrooms are furnished to modern standards and there is a traditional lounge, small bar and restaurant featuring fresh local produce.
11⇨♠(1fb) CTV in all bedrooms ®
35P 🅿 ❋ sauna
♀ European V ❦ ℒ Last dinner 9.30pm
Credit Cards 1 2 3 5

PORTHCAWL Mid Glamorgan Map **03** SS87

★★★60% **Seabank**
The Promenade CF36 3LU (Whitbread) ☏(0656) 782261 FAX (0656) 785363
This well established hotel, in a prominent position on the promenade, has comfortable public rooms and well equipped bedrooms. At the time of our last visit the hotel had embarked upon a major refurbishment programme to the exterior and the bedrooms. Completion is anticipated by the publication of this edition.
61⇨♠(1fb)✗in 6 bedrooms CTV in all bedrooms ® ✈ T ✽ sB&B⇨♠fr£59.50 dB&B⇨♠fr£71 🛏
Lift ℂ 150P ❋ sauna solarium gymnasium jacuzzi xmas
♀ English & French V ❦ ℒ ✗ ✽ Lunch fr£8 Dinner fr£14.95 Last dinner 9.45pm
CONF. Thtr 200 Class 130 Board 70 Del from £85
Credit Cards 1 2 3 5

★★61% **Glenaub**
50 Mary St CF36 3YA ☏(0656) 788242
This busy little family-run hotel is just a short walk from the seafront. It has well equipped modern bedrooms with satellite TV, and a cosy bar lounge. The hotel is popular with business guests as well as tourists, and the restaurant offers long hours of service for a small establishment.
18⇨ CTV in all bedrooms ® ✈
CTV 12P 🅿
♀ International V ❦ ℒ Last dinner 10pm
Credit Cards 1 2 3 4 5

PORTHLEVEN Cornwall & Isles of Scilly Map 02 SW62

★★**62%** *Harbour*
Commercial Rd TR13 9JD (St Austell Brewery)
☎Helston(0326) 573876
RS 25 Dec
Situated on the east side of the village adjacent to the harbour and only a 250yd level walk to the beach, the hotel has a spacious public bar and a good size family-style restaurant offering a wide range of meals. Bedrooms are comfortable and well equipped.
10rm(8⇨)(1fb) CTV in all bedrooms ® T ✕ (ex guide dogs)
CTV 10P 🚲 pool table ♪
V ♂ ✕ Last dinner 9.30pm
Credit Cards [1][2][3]

PORT ISAAC Cornwall & Isles of Scilly Map 02 SW98

See also **Port Gaverne**
★★**64%** Castle Rock
4 New Rd PL29 3SB ☎Bodmin(0208) 880300 FAX (0208) 880219
Described as 'the hotel with the view', the Castle Rock overlooks the sea and the coastline. There is a varied choice of bedrooms, many have sea views and some are on the ground floor. The standard of cooking is very reliable and particularly well organised, and both Major and Mrs Wells provide cordial hospitality.
17rm(12⇨3♠)(3fb) CTV in 16 bedrooms ® T sB&B£25-£2
sB&B⇨♠£28-£30 dB&B£50-£52 dB&B⇨♠£56-£60 🍽
CTV 20P ❋ *xmas*
V ♂ ⚌ ✕ Sunday Lunch fr£6.95 Dinner £12-£15&alc Last dinner 8.30pm
CONF. Class 24 Board 18 Del from £36
Credit Cards [1][3]   (£)
See advertisement on page 497

PORT GAVERNE HOTEL
Near Port Isaac, Cornwall PL29 3SQ
Telephone: Bodmin (0208) 880244
FULLY LICENSED – FREE HOUSE
★★

Gently comfortably restored 17thC Coastal Inn -
● Internationally recognized dining
● All bedrooms en suite with colour TV, tea & coffee making facilities and direct dial telephone
● Central heating and log fires
● A staff who know how to care

ALSO 7 self-catering character cottages.
Write or telephone for a free brochure
Mrs. Marjorie Ross
Resident Proprietor (25 years)

AA
★★

HEADLANDS
PORT GAVERNE
PORT ISAAC
CORNWALL

Beautiful cliff-top location with magnificent sea views from all rooms. Comfort, hospitality and delicious international cuisine. Special breaks available all year.

Write for colour brochure and tariff or telephone (0208) 880 260

The ANCHOR HOTEL & ★★
──── SHIP INN ────
EXMOOR NATIONAL PARK

Just 5 yards from the water's edge of a small picturesque harbour amidst Exmoor's magnificent scenery and dramatic coastline. This is old rural England with wildlife and memorable walks and is ideal for relaxing and unwinding. Very comfortable and quiet, part 15th century hotel.

Bargain Break terms.
Please phone 0643 862636

THE ANCHOR HOTEL and THE SHIP INN
PORLOCK HARBOUR · SOMERSET TA24 8PB

Portland - Portscatho

PORTLAND Dorset Map 03 SY67

★★★ 63% Portland Heights
Yeates Corner DT5 2EN ☎(0305) 821361 FAX (0305) 860081
This friendly and well managed modern hotel is set high above the village, overlooking Chesil Beach and Portland Bay. Public areas include a first-floor bar and restaurant with fabulous views as far as Lyme Regis on a clear day. Bedrooms are in functional modern style, softened by coordinated fabrics.
66⇌♠(8fb) CTV in all bedrooms ® T sB&B⇌♠£39.90-£42 dB&B⇌♠£49.90-£62 ♬
《 160P ⇨ (heated) squash sauna solarium gymnasium steam room *xmas*
♀ International V ❀ ☑ ✕ ✱ Lunch £10-£12&alc High tea £1-£3.50 Dinner £17&alc Last dinner 9.30pm
CONF. Thtr 200 Class 120 Board 80 Del from £79
Credit Cards ① ② ③ ⑤ £

PORT OF MENTEITH Central *Perthshire* Map 11 NN50

★★ 73% Lake
FK8 3RA (SCOTLAND'S HERITAGE HOTELS)
☎(08775) 258 FAX (08775) 671
This well established hotel on the lake shore has been refurbished in 1930s style but with modern facilities and many thoughtful extras. Bedrooms vary in size, with the best offering lake views. The conservatory restaurant overlooks the lake, with more informal meals available in the popular bar or bistro.
13⇌♠ CTV in all bedrooms ® T sB&B⇌♠fr£64 dB&B⇌♠fr£84 (incl dinner) ♬
35P ✎ nc9yrs *xmas*
♀ Scottish & French V ❀ ☑ ✕ Sunday Lunch £21 Dinner £21&alc Last dinner 9pm
Credit Cards ① ③

PORTPATRICK Dumfries & Galloway *Wigtownshire* Map 10 NX05

★★★ 66% Fernhill
DG9 8TD ☎(077681) 220 due to change to (0776) 810220 FAX (077681) 596 due to change to (0776) 810596
Closed Xmas

Enjoying fine views over the fishing village and sea, this family-run hotel is set in attractive grounds by Dunksey golf course. Improvements continue and public areas include a stylish foyer lounge and pleasant conservatory restaurant. Bedrooms vary, though all are well equipped, the best being in a small new extension, all overlooking the sea.
15rm(14⇌♠)Annexe6⇌♠(1fb) CTV in all bedrooms ® T ✱ sB&B£30-£35 sB&B⇌♠£50-£65 dB&B⇌♠£70-£90 ♬
50P ✤ ✎ *xmas*
♀ Scottish & French V ❀ ☑ ✕ ✱ Sunday Lunch £6.50-£7.50 High tea fr£6 Dinner fr£16.50&alc Last dinner 10pm
Credit Cards ① ② ③ ⑤ £

KNOCKINAAM LODGE
DG9 9AD (2m S on unclass rd) ☎(077681) 471 due to change to (0776) 810471
FAX (077681) 435 due to change to (0776) 810435
Closed 5 Jan-14 Mar

First sight of this fine hotel is dramatic, as the long drive gives suddenly onto a spectacular view of the Irish Sea. The 2-storey house stands in complete isolation, bordered on 3 sides by cliffs, on the other by lawns that lead down to the bay. The second impression, on entering the hotel is of the warmth of the welcome and the friendliness of the staff, led by the dedicated and hospitable owners, Marcel and Corinna Frichot. There are two comfortable lounges and a cosy bar, and though bedrooms are mostly compact, they are bright and tastefully decorated. Only a few overlook the bay. Stuart Muir has taken over as head chef and the format remains as before, with a fixed-price, limited choice menu with a strong French influence. A highlight of a recent inspection meal was the Bordelaise sauce that accompanied a fillet of Galloway beef. Fish remains a strength and dining at Knockinaam is a formal, unhurried and enjoyable occasion.
10⇌1⚐ CTV in all bedrooms T ✱ sB&B⇌fr£68 dB&B⇌£100-£136 ♬
25P ✎ ✤ croquet
♀ French V ❀ ☑ ✕ ✱ Lunch £22.50 High tea £8 Dinner £30 Last dinner 9pm
Credit Cards ① ② ③ ⑤

★★ 63% Portpatrick
DG9 8TQ ☎(077681) 333 due to change to (0776) 810333 FAX (077681) 457 due to change to (0776) 810457
Closed Dec-early Mar (ex Xmas/New Year)

Perched on the cliff top, with fine views over the town and harbour as well as out to sea, this former resort hotel now attracts mainly tour and golfing groups. Though bedrooms vary in size they are generally comfortable, with good beds, and the dining room offers a limited but adequate choice of dishes.
57⇌♠(5fb)1⚐✕in 12 bedrooms CTV in all bedrooms ® ✱ sB&B⇌♠£45 dB&B⇌♠£70 ♬
Lift 《 60P ✤ ⇨ (heated) ➤ 9 ♠ (grass) snooker games room *xmas*
♀ English & French V ❀ ☑ ✱ Bar Lunch £3.50-£7.50alc High tea £6.50 Dinner £13.50 Last dinner 9pm
CONF. Thtr 60 Class 30 Board 24 Del from £45
Credit Cards ① ② ③ ⑤

★ 65% Mount Stewart
South Crescent DG9 8LE ☎(077681) 291 due to change to (0776) 810291
In an elevated situation overlooking the harbour and sea, this traditional hotel provides modest but reasonably priced bedrooms and very friendly informal service. Menus at both lunch and dinner, in the bar or restaurant, offer interesting, freshly prepared dishes and represent very good value.
8rm(4♠)(3fb) CTV in all bedrooms ® sB&B£18-£20 sB&B♠£26-£36 dB&B£36-£46 dB&B♠£42-£46 ♬
15P ✎
♀ International V Lunch £3-£10&alc High tea £4-£6&alc Dinner £10-£18&alc Last dinner 10pm
Credit Cards ① ③

PORTREE
See **Skye, Isle of**

PORTSCATHO Cornwall & Isles of Scilly Map 02 SW83

★★★ 63% Rosevine
Porthcurnick Beach TR2 5EW ☎(0872) 580206 & 580230
Closed Nov-Etr

Set in 3.5 acres of gardens with a path leading to the beach, this privately run, former Georgian manor house has a relaxed and friendly atmosphere. Attractive and well equipped bedrooms, some with balconies, are continually being upgraded and the traditional

Portscatho - Portsmouth & Southsea

public areas include a sun lounge and large dining room where enjoyable meals feature locally caught fresh fish.
14⇨👤Annexe1⇨👤(2fb) CTV in all bedrooms ® T
sB&B⇨👤£39-£60 dB&B⇨👤£78-£140 (incl dinner) 🍴
((CTV 40P 🚗 ❄
♀ International V ♿ ♨ ✂ Bar Lunch £4-£9alc Dinner £16-£19.75 Last dinner 8.30pm
Credit Cards [1][3]

★★❀71% **Gerrans Bay**
Gerrans TR2 5ED (turn off A3078 at Trewithian follow signs for Gerrans Hotel past church on road to St Anthony Head) ☏(0872) 580338
Closed Nov-Mar (ex Xmas)
Personally run by caring owners, this hotel provides simple bedrooms which are steadily being upgraded. The choice of lounges includes one with television and a cosy bar area. New arrivals are welcomed with a pot of tea and home-cooked fare is served in generous portions at mealtimes.
14rm(12⇨👤)(2fb) ® sB&B£31.50-£44 dB&B⇨👤£63-£88 (incl dinner)
CTV 16P 🚗 xmas
♿ ♨ ✂ Sunday Lunch £8.75 Dinner £16.25-£18.25 Last dinner 8pm
Credit Cards [1][2][3]

★★❀♨67% *Roseland House*
Rosevine TR2 5EW (Logis) ☏(0872) 580644
Closed Dec-Feb
In an enviable cliff-top position, this hotel has 6 acres of gently sloping terraced gardens with a wooded path leading down to a safe and secluded sandy beach, with magnificent views of the Roseland coastline. There is a well furnished bar, a comfortable lounge and well appointed dining room where Carolyn Hindley's daily 6-course table d'hôte dinner is served. Bedroom upgrading continues.
19⇨👤(5fb)2🍴 ✈ (ex guide dogs)
CTV 25P 3🏠 🚗 ❄ ♪ private beach nc5yrs
V ♿ ♨ ✂ Last dinner 8pm

PORTSMOUTH & SOUTHSEA Hampshire Map **04** SZ69

★★★60% *Hospitality Inn*
St Helens Pde PO4 0RN
☏Portsmouth(0705) 731281 FAX (0705) 817572
This large seafront hotel faces Southsea pier. The smart foyer is open plan with the lounge bar and is gradually being upgraded. Bedrooms come in two standards and vary in size, many having sea views.
115⇨👤(6fb)✂in 13 bedrooms CTV in all bedrooms ® T
Lift ((50P
♀ English & French V ♿ ✂ Last dinner 9.45pm
Credit Cards [1][2][3][5]

MOUNT CHARLOTTE THISTLE HOTELS

★★67% *The Beaufort*
71 Festing Rd PO4 0NQ
☏Portsmouth(0705) 823707

ExecGroup

Quietly situated close to the seafront and local attractions, this small and smart hotel is personally run and offers warm hospitality. Bedrooms have been furnished to a high standard and there is a comfortable lounge and attractive dining room and bar.
19⇨👤(3fb)✂in 4 bedrooms CTV in all bedrooms ® ♻ T ✈
CTV 10P
V ✂ Last dinner 8.30pm
Credit Cards [1][3]

See advertisement on page 499

Hotels with red star ratings are especially high quality.

Gerrans Bay HOTEL

GERRANS,
PORTSCATHO,
TRURO,
TR2 5ED.

AA ★★❀

ETB - 3 Crowns Commended.
Ashley Courtenay Recommended.

Our family run, 14 bedroom hotel is situated in the heart of the countryside on the Roseland Peninsula, yet only minutes from sandy beaches and picturesque fishing ports.

Ideally situated for touring, walking, birdwatching, fishing and visiting National Trust Gardens.

Peaceful, quiet and a relaxed atmosphere.
Excellent home cooking. Personal service.

FOR COLOUR BROCHURE
ANN AND BRIAN GREAVES

(0872) 580338

★ **The** ★
Castle Rock Hotel
"The hotel with the view"
Port Isaac,
North Cornwall PL29 3SB
Tel: 0208 880300 Fax: 0208 880219

Superbly situated overlooking the Atlantic and Port Isaac Bay, with magnificent panoramic views of the North Cornish Heritage Coast.
17 en-suite bedrooms, fully licensed, sea view restaurant, cocktail bar and sun lounge.
Budget Break-a-Ways available in the Spring and Autumn and also a popular Christmas and New Year package.
Open all year.
★ ★ ★ ★
Brochure with pleasure!

Portsmouth & Southsea - Port Talbot

★★ 62% Seacrest
12 South Pde PO5 2JB (junc.12 off M27, onto M275, follow signs for Southsea seafront)
☎Portsmouth(0705) 733192 FAX (0705) 832523

Antoinette Stretton has renovated her fine Victorian seafront hotel to provide good facilities for both leisure and business guests. Public areas have real leather sofas and armchairs, and the dining room was being completely renovated during 1993. Bedrooms, already comfortably furnished and well equipped, will be receiving attention during 1994.

26⇌↑(2fb) CTV in all bedrooms ® ⚓ T sB&B⇌↑ £28-£40 dB&B⇌↑ £38-£60 ⊟
Lift 7P xmas
✧ ⚓ ✗ Dinner £10.95-£12.95&alc Last dinner 7.30pm
Credit Cards [1][2][3] (£)

★★ 62% Westfield Hall
65 Festing Rd PO4 0NQ ☎Portsmouth(0705) 826971 FAX (0705) 870200

In a wide, leafy road close to the boating lake, this imposing Edwardian building has been carefully improved over the years by proprietors Margaret and John Daniels. Bedrooms are comfortable and have pretty coordinating colour schemes. Public areas include a very comfortable lounge, a garden lounge with terrace and an intimate restaurant/bar offering a choice of menus. Service is friendly and attentive.

17rm(14⇌↑)(4fb) CTV in all bedrooms ® ⚓ T ✗ ✱ sB&B£23-£25 sB&B⇌↑ £28-£38 dB&B⇌↑ £48-£56 ⊟
CTV 18P xmas
V ✗ Dinner £10.95-£12.50&alc Last dinner 8pm
Credit Cards [1][2][3]

★★ 61% Hotel Ibis
Winston Churchill Av PO1 2DG
☎Portsmouth(0705) 640000 FAX (0705) 641000

This bright, modern hotel is right in the heart of the city. Bedrooms are of a uniform style and standard and public areas are open plan, with all-day bar snacks as well as restaurant meals.

144↑ CTV in all bedrooms ® ⚓ T sB↑ £32-£39.50 dB↑ £32-£39.50 (room only)
Lift 𝄞 50P
♀ English & French V ✧ ⚓ ✗ ✱ Bar Lunch £1.95-£4.50alc Dinner £9.95&alc Last dinner 10.30pm
Credit Cards [1][2][3][5]

★★ 60% Keppels Head
PO1 3DT (opp Harbour Railway Station)
☎Portsmouth(0705) 833231 FAX (0705) 838688

FORTE Heritage

Located just 200yds from the historic dockyard, this traditional hotel has comfortable modern bedrooms with good facilities. There is an attractive carvery-style restaurant and a bar lounge. Service, under the management of Mr D Schlieben, is friendly and helpful.

27⇌↑(6fb) ✗ in 8 bedrooms CTV in all bedrooms ® T ✱ sB⇌↑ fr£45 dB⇌↑ £55-£65 (room only) ⊟
Lift 𝄞 18P
V ✧ ⚓ ✗ ✱ Lunch £4.95-£10.95 Dinner £14.95-£17.50 Last dinner 9pm
CONF. Thtr 60 Class 30 Board 24 Del from £81
Credit Cards [1][2][3][5]

★★ 60% Sandringham
Osborne Rd, Clarence Pde PO5 3LR (facing Southsea Common)
☎Portsmouth(0705) 822914 & 826969 FAX (0705) 822330

This extensively refurbished, popular hotel on the seafront has a range of modern bedrooms all with good facilities. There is a wine bar in addition to the hotel bar, restaurant and comfortable lounge with large-screen television.

45⇌↑(7fb)2⊞ CTV in all bedrooms ® T ✗ (ex guide dogs) sB&B⇌↑ £25-£35 dB&B⇌↑ £38-£50 ⊟
Lift CTV bingo dancing lessons ♪ ⚓ xmas

♀ English & French V ✧ ⚓ ✗ Lunch £6-£12 High tea £3.50-£4.50 Dinner £10-£15&alc Last dinner 9pm
CONF. Thtr 100 Class 80 Board 110 Del from £48
Credit Cards [1][2][3][5] (£)

Forte Posthouse
Pembroke Rd PO1 2TA
☎Portsmouth(0705) 827651 FAX (0705) 756715

FORTE Posthouse

Suitable for both the business and leisure traveller, this bright hotel provides modern accommodation in well equipped bedrooms with en suite bathrooms. For more details about Forte Posthouse hotels, consult the Contents page, under Hotel Groups.

163⇌↑✱ B⇌↑ £41.50-£53.50 (room only)
CONF. Thtr 220 Class 80 Board 80

Hilton National Portsmouth
Eastern Rd, Farlington PO6 1UN
☎Portsmouth(0705) 219111

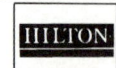

This is a bright, modern hotel with an informal restaurant, aimed at both the business and leisure guest. All bedrooms have en-suite bathrooms and a range of modern facilities. For more details about Hilton National, consult the Contents page, under Hotel Groups.

122⇌↑✱ B⇌↑ £75 (room only)
CONF. Thtr 300 Class 100 Board 100 Del £99

Marriott
North Harbour PO6 4SH (at the junct of A27/A3)
☎Portsmouth(0705) 383151 FAX (0705) 388701

A large and busy hotel, which is ideal for the business and leisure traveller, offering a wide range of services, a choice of eating options and indoor leisure facilities. Bedrooms are comfortable and equipped with modern facilities. For more details about Marriott hotels, consult the Contents page, under Hotel Groups.

170⇌↑✱ dB⇌↑ fr£97 (room only)
CONF. Thtr 280 Class 180 Board 36 Del £117

PORT TALBOT West Glamorgan Map 03 SS79

★★★ 60% Aberavan Beach
SA12 6QP (follow signs for Aberavon Beach)
☎(0639) 884949 FAX (0639) 897885

CONSORT HOTELS

A bright new indoor swimming pool complex and a comfortable restaurant have recently been added to this purpose-built hotel overlooking Aberavon beach. The open plan public rooms are spacious, and bedrooms are undergoing upgrading.

52⇌↑(6fb) CTV in all bedrooms ® T sB&B⇌↑ £43-£53 dB&B⇌↑ £50-£57 ⊟
Lift 𝄞 150P ⊞ (heated) sauna all weather leisure centre ♪ xmas
♀ Welsh, English & French V ✧ ⚓ Lunch fr£8.50 Dinner fr£12&alc Last dinner 10.15pm
CONF. Thtr 350 Class 200 Board 80 Del from £47.25
Credit Cards [1][2][3][5] (£)

Travel Inn
Baglan Rd SA12 8ES (on roundabout junc 42 M4)
☎(0639) 813017

Purpose-built accommodation offers spacious and well equipped bedrooms, all with en suite bathrooms. Meals may be taken at the nearby family restaurant and pub. For more details about Travel Inns, consult the Contents page, under Hotel Groups.

40⇌↑✱ B⇌↑ £33.50 (room only)

Port William - Pott Shrigley

PORT WILLIAM Dumfries & Galloway *Wigtownshire*
Map 10 NX34

★★★♨ 63% **Corsemalzie House**
DG8 9RL (on B7005, turn off A714 at Bladnoch) (Logis)
☎Mochrum(098886) 254 FAX (098886) 213
Closed 21 Jan-5 Mar

Set in 40 acres of wooded grounds, this friendly and informal 19th-century mansion is popular with anglers and sportsmen as well as with tourists seeking a quiet retreat. Attractively decorated bedrooms have practical modern amenities and there is a cosy bar serving bar meals and a restaurant with a short Taste of Scotland menu.
14⇌ⁿ(1fb) CTV in all bedrooms ® T sB&B⇌ⁿ£39.50-£51 dB&B⇌ⁿ£58-£82 ₽
30P ⇌ ✿ ♩ croquet game shooting putting ₰ *xmas*
♀ Scottish & French V ♡ ⚌ Lunch £11.50-£15.25&alc Dinner £17.50-£20.50&alc Last dinner 9.15pm
Credit Cards

POTT SHRIGLEY Cheshire Map 07 SJ97

★★★★ 61% **Shrigley Hall Golf & Country Club**
Shrigley Park SK10 5SB ☎Bollington(0625) 575757 FAX (0625) 573323

This comfortable hotel offers a wide range of leisure activities including a championship golf course.
156⇌ⁿ⌷ CTV in all bedrooms ®♀ T
Lift 《 600P ⇌ ✿ ▭ (heated) ▶ 18 ♀ (hard) ♩ squash snooker sauna solarium gymnasium jacuzzi beauty salon steam spa ♫ ₰
♀ International V ♡ ⚌ ⌶ Last dinner 9.45pm
Credit Cards

**12 South Parade, Southsea,
Portsmouth, Hants PO5 2JB
Tel: 0705 733192 & 875666 Fax: 0705 832523**

A 2 star Hotel enjoying a premier position on Southsea Seafront, commanding fine panoramic views of the Solent with its ever changing panorama of naval shipping, fishing vessels and small craft.

★ 26 well appointed bedrooms, all with private facilities, CTV, tea-making and direct-dial telephones.

★ Passenger lift, car park and licensed bar.

★ Off-season bargain-breaks and special businessmen rates available.

MINOTEL MEMBER (another great little Hotel)

★★
AA
ETB COMMENDED

Westfield Hall Hotel
'Your pleasure is our business'

Set in our own private grounds with the unique facility of parking for all guests. Located near the Sea Front, also within easy reach of the City Centre, the M27 and the Continental Ferry Port.

All our 17 prestigious en-suite bedrooms are designed and furnished with your comfort in mind. Our licensed Restaurant offers both A La Carte and Table D'hôte meals (which are changed daily).

65 Festing Road
Southsea
Portsmouth
Hants PO4 0NQ

Telephone 0705 826971
Fax No 0705 870200

Special Business Personnel rates available — Winter and Weekend Breaks

---

AA ★★ Member of **ExecHotels** Group ETB COMMENDED

THE BEAUFORT HOTEL
SOUTHSEA

**71 Festing Road, Southsea PO4 0NQ
Tel: 0705 823707 Fax: 0705 870270**

Welcome to the heart of Southsea to an exclusive but warm and friendly hotel. Ideally situated for both businessmen and tourists. The proprietors, manager and staff pride themselves in the quality of service offered to their guests. All 19 superbly appointed bedrooms are en suite and have satellite TV, direct dial telephone, hair dryer, trouser press and beverage facilities. Some rooms offer sea views or views of the garden. The chef takes pride in using local and fresh produce for the à la carte or table d'hôte menus.
The promenade is two minutes walk from the hotel and close by are the historical ships and the cross channel ferryport.

Poulton-le-Fylde - Preston

POULTON-LE-FYLDE Lancashire Map 07 SD33

★★ 🏵67% Mains Hall Country House
Mains Ln, Little Singleton FY6 7LE ☎(0253) 885130 FAX (0253) 894132

Reached via a long drive from the A585, and standing in 4 acres of grounds, this Grade II listed house dates from the 16th century and has some fine oak panelling in the entrance hall. Other public areas include a small library lounge, cocktail bar and intimate restaurant, where chef Simon Dobson presents an interesting menu of fresh food in the modern style. Bedrooms are individually furnished and well equipped, some with 4-poster beds.

9rm(7⇨)1⊞½in all bedrooms CTV in all bedrooms ® T ✱ sB&Bfr£50 sB&B⇨♠fr£75 dB&Bfr£75 dB&B⇨♠fr£100 🅿 12P 🚗 ❀ ⚭ xmas

♡ ⚲ ½ ✱ Lunch £12.50 Dinner £18.95-£22.50&alc Last dinner 8.30pm
Credit Cards [1][2][3]

POWBURN Northumberland Map 12 NU01

★★ 🏵🏵🏵⚜
BREAMISH HOUSE
NE66 4LL ☎(066578) 266 & 544 FAX (066578) 500
Closed Jan

Doreen and Allan Johnson's fine hotel provides all one would expect of a country retreat, with two comfortably furnished, elegant lounges and individually designed bedrooms. Fresh flowers and interesting objets d'art abound and a peaceful, relaxing stay is assured. The dining room, in two sections, is softly decorated and furnished with chairs from the SS Bermuda. Doreen Johnson presides over the kitchen, her simple style allowing natural flavours to be enhanced by honest cooking. Terrines and pates are particularly good and our inspector praised a main course of fillet of cod baked with a parsley crust and served with a sharp, creamy vermouth sauce.

10rm(9⇨♠)Annexe1⇨♠ CTV in all bedrooms ® T ✱ sB&B⇨♠£68 dB&B⇨♠£108-£137 (incl dinner) 🅿 30P 2🚗 🏟 ❀ nc12yrs xmas

♡ ⚲ ½ ✱ Sunday Lunch £12.95 Dinner £19.95 Last dinner 8pm
Credit Cards [1][3] £

POWFOOT Dumfries & Galloway *Dumfriesshire* Map 11 NY16

★★64% Golf
Links Av DG12 5PN (turn off A74 at Gretna onto A75 round Annan bypass, hotel sign 2m on turn left follow sign to Powfoot village) ☎Cummertrees(04617) 254

Attractively situated beside the golf course and overlooking the Solway Firth to the Lake District mountains, this family owned hotel offers comfortable public areas and friendly service. Bedrooms continue to be improved, the best now having modern facilities.

19rm(14⇨♠)(2fb)½in 2 bedrooms CTV in 15 bedrooms ® T ✱ (ex guide dogs) ✱ sB&B£33-£44 sB&B⇨♠fr£44 dB&Bfr£44 dB&B⇨♠fr£56 🅿
⊞ CTV 100P 10🚗 ▶ 18 ♪ pool table darts bridge xmas
 ♡ ⚲ ½ ✱ Lunch fr£6 High tea fr£6 Dinner fr£12 Last dinner 8.30pm
CONF. Thtr 100 Class 50 Board 40
Credit Cards [1][3] £

See advertisement under ANNAN

PRAA SANDS Cornwall & Isles of Scilly Map 02 SW52

★★56% Prah Sands
Chy An Dour Rd TR20 9SY ☎Penzance(0736) 762438

Just 300 yards from the beach, with no main roads to cross and an unrestricted view of the coastline, this family-run hotel provides friendly service and good meals. Public rooms achieve a nice balance of comfort and charm, while bedrooms are compact, with simple furnishings and appointments.

21rm(10⇨♠)(4fb) CTV in all bedrooms ® ✈ ✱ sB&B£27-£33 dB&B£54-£70 dB&B⇨♠£60-£80 (incl dinner) 🅿
CTV 12P 🚗 ❀ ⚭ (heated) ♪ (hard) snooker keep fit classes ♫
♡ ⚲ ✱ Bar Lunch fr£3.95 Dinner fr£12 Last dinner 8pm
Credit Cards [1][3]

PRESTATYN
See **Dyserth**

PRESTBURY Cheshire Map 07 SJ97

★★★62% Bridge
The Village SK10 4DQ (off A538 through village, hotel next to church) ☎(0625) 829326 FAX (0625) 827557

This unusual hotel is in the centre of this lovely village. The bedrooms are attractively decorated and many overlook the River Bollin. The traditionally styled restaurant offers extensive choices at lunch and dinner.

23⇨♠(4fb) CTV in all bedrooms ® T ✱ (ex guide dogs) ✱ sB⇨♠£69-£74 dB⇨♠£69-£79 (room only) 🅿
(CTV 52P ❀ ♫
V ♡ ⚲ ✱ Lunch £8.20-£9.20 Dinner £10.50-£11.50 Last dinner 9.45pm
CONF. Del £95
Credit Cards [1][2][3][5]

PRESTEIGNE Powys Map 03 SO36

★★68% Radnorshire Arms
High St LD8 2BE ☎(0544) 267406 FAX (0544) 260418

A perfect example of Elizabethan 'Magpie' architecture, this elegant coaching house is in the centre of the town. It has a log-fired bar, panelled lounges and other public rooms which simply exude history. Bedrooms, in the process of refurbishment, are all well equipped and comfortable.

8⇨Annexe8⇨♠(10fb)½in 8 bedrooms CTV in all bedrooms ® T ✱ sB⇨♠£65-£80 dB⇨♠£75-£90 (room only) 🅿
50P 5🚗 ❀ xmas
V ♡ ⚲ ½ ✱ Lunch £8.95-£10.95 Dinner £15.95 Last dinner 9pm
Credit Cards [1][2][3][5]

PRESTON Lancashire Map 07 SD52
See also **Barton**

★★★ 🏵69% Broughton Park Hotel & Country Club
Garstang Rd, Broughton PR3 5JB (3m N on A6) ☎(0772) 864087 FAX (0772) 861728

Standing in its own grounds, this extended red brick Victorian manor is a popular conference and function venue. Bedrooms are modern in style, though some bathrooms are a little dated, and all are well equipped. Executive rooms offer the most space and extras. Chef Neil McKevitt produces some interesting and enjoyable dishes on a seasonally changing carte, such as a fresh tasting terrine of guinea fowl with basil mayonnaise or delicious noisettes of lamb set on a potato and garlic pancake, accompanied by a red wine and rosemary essence.

500

Preston

98⇌♠(6fb)3⇛⚹in 11 bedrooms CTV in all bedrooms ®♋T
✘ (ex guide dogs) ✱ sB&B⇌♠£47.50-£82 dB&B⇌♠£75-
£112 ▯
Lift (220P ✱ ▭ (heated) squash snooker sauna solarium
gymnasium spa bath steam room beauty salon *xmas*
♀ English & French V ♢ ♧ Last dinner 10pm
CONF. Thtr 180 Class 80 Board 80 Del from £95
Credit cards ① ② ③ ⑤

★★★65% Tickled Trout
Preston New Rd, Samlesbury PR5 0UJ (close to
M6 junct 31) ☎(0772) 877671 FAX (0772)
877463

Overlooking the River Ribble, this hotel offers generally
comfortable if somewhat functional bedrooms, all with modern
amenities. Uniformed staff provide friendly service in the beamed
restaurant and cocktail lounge.
72⇌♠(56fb)2⇛⚹in 10 bedrooms CTV in all bedrooms ® T
sB&B⇌♠£84.50-£99 dB&B⇌♠£98.50-£115 ▯
(150P 6🛌 ♪ sauna solarium gymnasium wave pool steam
room ♫ *xmas*
♀ International V ♢ ♧ ⚹ Lunch £12.95-£13.50&alc Dinner
£14.95-£15.50&alc Last dinner 9.45pm
CONF. Thtr 100 Class 45 Board 40 Del from £80
Credit cards ① ② ③ ⑤

★★★62% Swallow Trafalgar
Preston New Rd, Samlesbury PR5 0UL (1m
from M6, on A59/A677 junct)
☎(0772) 877351 FAX (0772) 877424

This much extended hotel offers pleasant and well equipped
bedrooms. Single rooms are the most comfortable, although they
have showers rather than baths. Public areas include a choice of
bars.
78⇌♠⚹in 16 bedrooms CTV in all bedrooms ®♋T
sB&B⇌♠£75 dB&B⇌♠£85 ▯
Lift (300P ▭ (heated) squash sauna solarium gymnasium
steam room spa pool *xmas*
♀ International V ♢ ♧ ⚹ Lunch fr£8.95&alc Dinner
fr£14.55&alc Last dinner 9.30pm
CONF. Thtr 250 Class 100 Board 80 Del £90
Credit cards ① ② ③ ⑤

★★★57% Novotel
Reedfield Place, Walton Summit PR5 6AB (on
junct 29 of M6/junct 9 of M61)
☎(0772) 313331 FAX (0772) 627868

novotel

This purpose-built hotel offers spacious modern bedrooms and
attractively refurbished public areas.
98⇌♠(98fb)⚹in 35 bedrooms CTV in all bedrooms ®♋T ✱
sB⇌♠£49.50 dB⇌♠£53.50 (room only) ▯
Lift (120P ✱ ⌂ (heated)
♀ Continental V ♢ ♧ ✱ Lunch fr£4.95&alc Dinner £10.50-
£13.50&alc Last dinner midnt
CONF. Thtr 180 Class 60 Board 40 Del from £65
Credit cards ① ② ③ ⑤

★★★56% Leyland Resort
Leyland Way PR5 2JX ☎(0772) 422922 FAX
(0772) 622282
(For full entry see Leyland)

RESORT HOTELS PLC

★★69% Vineyard
Cinnamon Hill, Chorley Rd, Walton-Le-Dale PR5 4JN (2m S
A49) ☎(0772) 54646
Closed 25 Dec night & 1 Jan night
Continental in appearance, the Vineyard offers comfortable and
stylish bedrooms equipped with all modern facilities. Public areas
include a spacious lounge bar and popular split-level restaurant,
serving a good range of menus at both lunch and dinner. Friendly
service is provided by uniformed staff.
16⇌♠(1fb) CTV in all bedrooms ®♋T

➡

PARK ALL.

Modern 3 star quality hotel • Camelot Theme Park
adjacent (phone for opening dates and times) • indoor
lagoon swimming pool, sauna, spa pool • health &
squash clubs • night club • antiques fair every Sunday
• extensive conference and banqueting facilities.

Park Hall offers more facilities
for business and leisure than any other hotel in the
North West.

PARK HALL HOTEL
LEISURE & CONFERENCE CENTRE
★ ★ ★
Charnock Richard, Chorley, Preston PR7 5LP
Tel (0257) 452090. Fax (0257) 451838

Breamish Country House Hotel
Powburn, Alnwick,   ★★
Northumberland NE66 4LL
Telephone: Powburn (066 578) 266
Fax: (066 578) 500

Set in 5 acres of its own grounds, beautifully
located at the foot of the Cheviot Hills, an
area many people consider to be the most
beautiful and unspoiled in the country.

The Hotel prides itself on the quality of the
rooms, restaurant and service, offering the
very best of English cuisine with our kitchen
garden supplying most of the hotel's needs.

Restaurant open to non-residents.

Preston - Pulborough

(200P
♥ French **V** ✿ ⚲ Last dinner 10pm
Credit Cards ①②③⑤

★★68% *Dean Court*
Brownedge Ln, Bamber Bridge PR5 6TB ☎(0772) 35114 FAX (0772) 628703
This unpretentious, family-run hotel is 3 miles south of the town centre at Bamber Bridge, convenient for junction 29 of the M6. The best bedrooms to the rear of the property, feature 4-poster beds, though the more modestly appointed rooms have similar facilities. Public areas include a small lounge, a choice of bars and a popular restaurant offering a wide range of substantial dishes.
9⇨⋔5⌸ CTV in all bedrooms ® T ✗
CTV 35P nc10yrs
♥ English & Continental **V** ✿ ⚲ Last dinner 10pm
Credit Cards ①③

★★67% *Claremont*
516 Blackpool Rd, Ashton-on-Ribble PR2 1HY (on A538) ☎(0772) 729738 FAX (0772) 726274
Situated to the northwest of the town centre, this friendly, privately owned hotel is well looked after. Bedrooms vary in size but all are equipped with modern facilities, and public areas include a cosy lounge bar and a neatly furnished restaurant.
14rm(12⇨⋔)1⌸ CTV in all bedrooms ® T ✗ (ex guide dogs)
sB&Bfr£30 sB&B⇨⋔£36 dB&B⇨⋔£49-£65
25P ❀ ✿
V ✿ ⚲ Lunch fr£8.75 Dinner £8.75-£12.95 Last dinner 8.30pm
Credit Cards ①②③⑤

Forte Posthouse
The Ringway PR1 3AU ☎(0772) 59411 FAX (0772) 201923

Suitable for both the business and leisure traveller, this bright hotel provides modern accommodation in well equipped bedrooms with en suite bathrooms. For more details about Forte Posthouse hotels, consult the Contents page, under Hotel Groups.
126⇨⋔❀ B⇨⋔£41.50-£53.50 (room only)
CONF. Thtr 120 Class 50 Board 40 Del from £79.50

Travel Inn
Blackpool Rd, Lea PR4 0XL (off A583) ☎(0772) 720476

Purpose-built accommodation offers spacious and well equipped bedrooms, all with en suite bathrooms. Meals may be taken at the nearby family restaurant and pub. For more details about Travel Inns, consult the Contents page, under Hotel Groups.
38⇨⋔❀ B⇨⋔£33.50 (room only)

PRESTWICK Strathclyde *Ayrshire* Map **10** NS32
★★★60% **Carlton Toby**
187 Ayr Rd KA9 1TP (on A79 2m from airport) (Toby) ☎(0292) 76811 FAX (0292) 74845
This purpose-built business hotel has a split-level Toby Carvery Restaurant with a conservatory area and its own bar, in addition to the popular lounge bar. Staff are cheery and obliging.
37⇨⋔(2fb)¥ in 9 bedrooms CTV in all bedrooms ® T ✻
sB&B⇨⋔£29-£49.50 dB&B⇨⋔£48-£65 ⌸
(100P ✿ ♪ *xmas*
♥ European **V** ✿ ⚲ ✁ Lunch £7.98-£12.45 High tea £3-£6 Dinner £11.15-£12.45 Last dinner 10pm
Credit Cards ①②③⑤

★★62% *Parkstone*
Esplanade KA9 1QN ☎(0292) 77286
On the seafront, in a quiet residential area close to the golf course, this former resort hotel now concentrates on business and function custom. The bedrooms are sensibly furnished and some have comfortable seating.
15⇨⋔(1fb) CTV in all bedrooms ® ✁ T ✗ sB&B⇨⋔£38-£40 dB&B⇨⋔£48-£52 ⌸
(30P 4✿
V ✿ Lunch £7.50-£8.50 Dinner £13.50-£14.50 Last dinner 9pm
CONF. Thtr 100
Credit Cards ①②③

★★62% *St Nicholas*
41 Ayr Rd KA9 1SY ☎(0292) 79568
Situated on the main road, this commercial and tourist hotel offers good value dinners, high teas and bar meals. Bedrooms vary in size from very large to very small and are in general attractively decorated and well equipped.
17rm(13⇨⋔)(7fb) CTV in all bedrooms ® T
✗ (ex guide dogs)
CTV 50P
V ✿ Last dinner 9.30pm
Credit Cards ①②③⑤

PUDDINGTON Cheshire Map **07** SJ37
★★★❀❀⌸68% *Craxton Wood*
Parkgate Rd L66 9PB ☎051-339 4717 FAX 051-339 1740
Closed Sun, BH, last 2 wks Aug & 1st wk Jan
Craxton Wood hotel and restaurant, well run by the Petranca family for over 25 years, is set in 35 acres of parkland, lawns and gardens. The restaurant has long featured in our guidebooks because of the quality of the food, which is decidedly French, reflecting the background of the proprietor, but cooked by Scotsman James Minnis. Various fixed price menus are offered supplemented by extras. Our inspector began his meal with quenelles of salmon with pieces of lobster and a rather thin cream sauce, followed by delicious collops of veal, pink and topped with glazed foie gras and finished with rich onion sauce. A sweet of chocolate mousse and bavarois completed this enjoyable meal.
14⇨⋔ CTV in all bedrooms T ✗ (ex guide dogs) ✻
sB&B⇨⋔£49.50-£74 dB&B⇨⋔£94.50-£98.50 ⌸
P ❀ ✿
♥ French **V** ✻ Lunch £19.85&alc Dinner £19.85&alc Last dinner 10pm
Credit Cards ①②③⑤

PULBOROUGH West Sussex Map **04** TQ01
★★70% *Chequers*
Church Place RH20 1AD (off A29, opposite the church) ☎(0798) 872486 FAX (0798) 872715

Overlooking the Pulborough Wild Brooks and the Sussex Downs, this comfortable hotel has continually been improved by Mr and Mrs Searancke over their 30-year ownership. Bedrooms are individually furnished and have good facilities. The Conservatory Coffee Shop is open all day for light meals, snacks and delicious home-made cakes and teas. The restaurant offers a daily fixed price menu and fine wine list.
11⇨⋔(3fb)1⌸ CTV in all bedrooms ® T sB&B⇨⋔£44.50-£49.50 dB&B⇨⋔£69-£79 ⌸
20P ❀ ✿ ♪ *xmas*
V ✿ ⚲ Lunch £5-£8.50 High tea £3.50-£5.50 Dinner fr£15.95 Last dinner 8.30pm
CONF. Thtr 20 Class 20 Board 20 Del £57.50
Credit Cards ①②③⑤ £

For key to symbols see the Bookmark.

For full, independent restaurant reviews, see the
AA Abbey Well *Restaurant Guide.*

Pulborough - Raglan

★★ **65%** **Arun Cosmopolitan**
87 Lower St RH20 2BP ☎(0798) 872162 FAX (0798) 872935
This small, friendly, family-run hotel is situated in the heart of Pulborough with panoramic views over the River Arun, Wild Brooks and the South Downs. Bedrooms are attractively coordinated. Blakes Bar offers a warm welcome with its open fire, and a selection of bar meals is provided. A table d'hôte menu is served in the candlelit restaurant, and a cosy lounge is also available.
6⇌♠ CTV in all bedrooms ® T sB&B⇌♠£38-£45 dB&B⇌♠£60-£70 🍴
CTV 5P 10💤 🐕 xmas
V ♥ ℒ ✂ Sunday Lunch £8.95-£10.95 Dinner £12.95-£16.95&alc Last dinner 9pm
Credit Cards 1 2 3 5

PURTON Wiltshire Map **04** SU08

★★★ ❀**74%** **The Pear Tree at Purton**
Church End SN5 9ED (from junct 16 of M4 follow signs to Purton, at Spar grocers turn right hotel is 0.25m on left) ☎Swindon(0793) 772100 FAX (0793) 772369
This delightful stone-built former vicarage, standing in 7.5 acres of grounds with a landscaped Victorian garden, has recently been sympathetically extended. It has a light, airy split-level lounge with small bar and a restaurant with an attractive conservatory; fixed price menus make good use of local beef, lamb and pork and fish delivered regularly from Devon. Bedrooms are comfortable and individually designed, several with balconies and all having fresh flowers, bottled water and a large decanter of sherry. The resident proprietors and their friendly staff are welcoming and friendly.
18⇌♠(2fb)3🛏 CTV in all bedrooms💤 T sB&B⇌♠£50-£102 dB&B⇌♠£70-£133 🍴
60P 🚗 ✿ croquet
V ♥ ℒ Lunch £17.50 Dinner £27.50 Last dinner 9.30pm
CONF. Thtr 70 Class 30 Board 30 Del £133
Credit Cards 1 2 3 5

PWLLHELI Gwynedd Map **06** SH33

★★ ❀❀❀🍴**76%** **Plas Bodegroes Restaurant**
LL53 5TH (1.5m W on Nefyd rd) (Welsh Rarebits) ☎(0758) 612363 FAX (0758) 701247
Closed Nov-Feb & Mon ex BH's
Plas Bodegroes is a small Georgian hotel set in an enchanting and peaceful location. Menus and apéritifs are offered in a small, attractively decorated lounge, but if the restaurant is busy, be prepared to be seated in the adjoining corridor bar. The menu features exciting modern British cuisine – 5 courses with 4 or 5 choices at each – and the cooking is assured. The wine list offers over 200 wines with a well chosen house selection. Service is efficient and formal.
8⇌♠2🛏 CTV in all bedrooms T
25P 🚗 ✿ croquet
✂ Last dinner 9.30pm
Credit Cards 1 3

★ **65%** **The Seahaven**
West End Pde LL53 5PN ☎(0758) 612572
Situated on the seafront overlooking Cardigan Bay, this small hotel provides warm personal service and has simply furnished bedrooms, a small bar, bright dining room and a lounge with karaoke equipment.
10rm(5♠)(3fb) CTV in all bedrooms ® ✳ sB&Bfr£21 sB&B♠fr£27 dB&Bfr£32 dB&B♠fr£37 🍴
CTV 🚗 nc3yrs
♥ ℒ Last dinner 7.15pm

QUORN Leicestershire Map **08** SK51

★★★★ **67%** **Quorn Country**
Charwood House, Leicester Rd LE12 8BB (on A6 in village centre) ☎(0509) 415050 FAX (0509) 415557
RS 26 Dec & New Year
Smaller than the usual 4-star establishment, this village-centre hotel provides courteous and friendly service. Two restaurants provide different styles of dining, the intimate Shires Restaurant offering a carte, with lighter meals in the open, cheerful Orangery. Bedroom refurbishment continues, all are comfortable and suites are available.
19⇌♠(1fb)1🛏✂ in 3 bedrooms CTV in all bedrooms ® T sB⇌♠£59.50-£79.50 dB⇌♠£72-£92 (room only) 🍴
(🎱 CTV 100P ✿ 🎾
♥ English & Continental V ♥ ℒ ✳ Lunch fr£11.45 Dinner fr£18.45 Last dinner 10pm
CONF. Thtr 100 Class 48 Board 36 Del from £104.95
Credit Cards 1 2 3 5
See advertisement under LOUGHBOROUGH

★★★ ❀**69%** **Quorn Grange**
88 Wood Ln LE12 8DB ☎(0509) 412167 FAX (0509)415621
Set in 10 acres of landscaped gardens and mature trees, this 19th-century creeper-clad manor house is predominantly a restaurant, though it does have excellent bedrooms. Those in the new wing are quite spacious, and all are well equipped. The restaurant deservedly has a large local following, and chef Gordon Lang offers a constantly changing menu featuring such dishes as rack of lamb, salmon, lemon sole, and mushroom and asparagus casserole, as well as seasonal specials
17⇌♠ Annexe2⇌♠ CTV in all bedrooms ® T ✳ sB&B⇌♠£50-£69 dB&B⇌♠£67-£82 Continental breakfast 🍴
(🎱 119P ✿ solarium
♥ English & French V ♥ ℒ ✳ Lunch £9.85-£15.95&alc High tea £5.50 Dinner fr£15.95&alc Last dinner 9.45pm
Credit Cards 1 2 3 4 5

RAASAY, ISLE OF Highland *Inverness-shire* Map **13** NG53

★★ **64%** *Isle Of Raasay*
IV40 8PB ☎Isle of Raasay(0478) 660 222 226
Closed Oct-Mar
A Victorian mansion house has been renovated and extended to create this comfortable island hotel, which looks out over the Narrows of Raasay to Skye. It has a relaxed, friendly atmosphere and offers a choice of lounges, while the bar is popular with locals. Bedrooms are practical, with most of the usual facilities. Drivers, please note that petrol is not available on the island.
12⇌♠ CTV in all bedrooms ®
CTV 12P 🚗 ✿
♥ Scottish, French, Indian & Italian V ♥ ℒ ✂ Last dinner 7.30pm

---

RAGLAN Gwent Map **03** SO40

★★ **63%** **Beaufort Arms**
High St NP5 2DY ☎(0291) 690412 FAX (0291) 690412
This friendly owner-run inn in the village dates back to the 15th century and its busy bars and restaurant have much historic charm. Extensions house comfortable modern bedrooms which are equipped for today's traveller.
10⇌♠ Annexe5⇌♠(2fb) CTV in all bedrooms ® T ✖ (ex guide dogs) ✳ sB&B⇌♠£35 dB&B⇌♠£45 🍴
CTV 80P xmas
♥ English, French & Italian V ♥ ℒ ✳ Lunch £7.95 Dinner £7.95-£18&alc Last dinner 9.30pm
CONF. Thtr 200 Board 50 Del from £50
Credit Cards 1 2 3 5

Rainhill - Ravenstonedale

RAINHILL Merseyside Map 07 SJ49

★ **56%** **Rockland**
View Rd L35 0LG (leave M62 junc 7, take A57 towards Rainhill, after 1m turn left into View Rd, hotel .25m on left)
☎051-426 4603 FAX 051-426 0107
This small, personally run village-centre hotel has been in the same family for some 50 years. The accommodation is modest and, overall, the hotel is rather dated and used mainly by business visitors, though family accommodation is available.
10rm(9⇨♋)(2fb) CTV in all bedrooms ® sB&B£22-£28.50 sB&B⇨♋£25-£33.50 dB&B£30-£38.50 dB&B⇨♋£35-£44 ♬
30P ❋
V ♡ ♨ Lunch £5-£6.50&alc Dinner £9.95&alc Last dinner 8.15pm
Credit Cards ①③

RAMSBOTTOM Greater Manchester Map 07 SD71

★★★ **62%** **Old Mill**
Springwood BL0 9DS ☎(0706) 822991 FAX (0706) 822291
This black and white building is close to the town centre and has a new leisure centre. There are 2 restaurants, one offering fixed price and à la carte menus, and the trattoria serving budget price Italian dishes. Bedrooms have good facilities but the original rooms are more compact in size. Staff are friendly and helpful.
36⇨(3fb)♋ CTV in all bedrooms ® T ✖
《 CTV 85P ♣ ♫ ☐ (heated) sauna solarium gymnasium
♡ French & Italian V ♡ ♨ Last dinner 10.30pm
Credit Cards ①②③④⑤
See advertisement under MANCHESTER

RAMSEY
See **Man, Isle of**

RAMSGATE Kent Map 05 TR36

★★ **62%** **Marina Resort**
Harbour Pde CT11 8LJ ☎(0843) 588276 FAX (0843) 586866

This modern hotel overlooks the harbour, with some bedrooms having a view and those without the view compensated by being less compact. Admirals restaurant offers a choice of popular, keenly priced menus. The small bar is modestly furnished and there is no lounge facility. Room service is available 24 hours.
59⇨♋(7fb)♋ in 6 bedrooms CTV in all bedrooms ®❣T ✱ sB⇨♋fr£55 dB⇨♋fr£65 (room only) ♬
Lift 《 ♫ ☐ (heated) sauna solarium exercise equipment jacuzzi xmas
♡ English & Continental V ♡ ♨ ✄ ✱ Lunch £9.95&alc High tea 95p-£5 Dinner £5.25-£12.95&alc Last dinner 10pm
CONF. Thtr 120 Class 70 Board 50 Del £80
Credit Cards ①②③⑤

RAMSGILL North Yorkshire Map 07 SE17

★★ **◉72%** **Yorke Arms**
HG3 5RL (turn off A61 at Ripley onto B6165 to Pateley Bridge. Turn right at Nidderdale Motors)
☎Harrogate(0423) 755243 FAX (0423) 755243
Closed first week Feb
This creeper-clad, mellow stone hotel is in beautiful Upper Nidderdale and has accommodation of a particularly high modern standard. There is a comfortable guests' lounge, a beamed bar with a flagstone floor and a restaurant with beams, a tapestry and fine display of pewter. Fresh flowers add to the charming atmosphere. Dinner is particularly recommended, since chef Nick Robinson has successfully combined quality with quantity. Local game and fish feature as well as a variety of international dishes.

13⇨♋(2fb) CTV in all bedrooms ® T ✖ sB&B⇨♋£47-£55 dB&B⇨♋£69-£85 ♬
20P ♣ ❋ nc5yrs xmas
V ♡ ♨ Lunch £12.95-£15.95 Dinner fr£16.95&alc Last dinner 9pm
Credit Cards ①③

RANGEWORTHY Avon Map 03 ST68

★★ **68%** **Rangeworthy Court**
Church Ln, Wotton Rd BS17 5ND (signposted off B4058) ☎(0454) 228347 FAX (0454) 228945
This imposing manor house is set in attractive grounds, and owners Mr and Mrs Gillett provide warm hospitality and a good range of services. Comfortable bedrooms are well equipped with modern facilities and public areas include cosy lounges with log fires.
16⇨♋(2fb)2♋ CTV in all bedrooms ® T sB&B⇨♋£48-£53 dB&B⇨♋£58-£76 ♬
50P ♣ ❋ ☐ (heated) xmas
V ♡ Lunch £9.95-£15&alc Dinner £14.95-£16.50&alc Last dinner 9pm
Credit Cards ①②③⑤
See advertisement under BRISTOL

RAVENSCAR North Yorkshire Map 08 NZ90

★★★ **60%** **Raven Hall**
YO13 0ET ☎Scarborough(0723) 870353 FAX (0723) 870072
An old established, family owned hotel – part of which was once the royal retreat of King George III Raven Hall commands dramatic views of Robin Hood's Bay from its setting 600 feet above sea level. Standing in 100 acres of grounds and gardens, it offers some bedrooms which have been upgraded to a good modern standard, while others are more dated. Service is friendly and attentive.
53⇨♋(14fb)✂ in 3 bedrooms CTV in all bedrooms ® T ✖ (ex guide dogs) ❋ sB&B⇨♋£58-£82 dB&B⇨♋£102-£146 (incl dinner) ♬
《 200P 3♣ (charged) ❋ ☐ ♞ ♪ ♫ (hard) snooker sauna crown green bowls croquet giant chess ♫ ♧ xmas
V ♡ ♨ ✂ ✱ Lunch £3.50-£9.75 High tea £2.75-£6 Dinner £17.50 Last dinner 9pm
Credit Cards ①②③⑤
See advertisement under SCARBOROUGH

RAVENSTONEDALE Cumbria Map 07 NY70

★★ **70%** **Black Swan**
CA17 4NG ☎Newbiggin-on-Lune(05396) 23204
The Black Swan is a charming stone-built country hotel, close to a meandering beck. Public areas are welcoming, with open fires in the cosy bars, and a spacious lounge is provided upstairs. Bedrooms have pretty floral décor and many thoughtful extras including electric blankets. A well produced 4-course dinner is served in one of the 2 charming dining rooms. A typical starter might be sliced dessert pears, oven baked with fresh cream and stilton followed by a fine home-made soup. The game pie cooked in Hartleys beer would test anyone's appetite, but do leave room for one of the delicious home-made puddings.
14rm(11⇨♋)Annexe4⇨♋(1fb) CTV in all bedrooms ® T sB&B⇨♋£41 dB&B⇨♋£60 ♬
CTV 30P ♣ ❋ ♪ (hard) ✈ ♧ xmas
V ♡ ♨ ✂ Lunch £8.50 & alc Dinner £20 & alc Last dinner 9pm
Credit Cards ①②③⑤

★★ **65%** **The Fat Lamb**
Crossbank CA17 4LL (midway between Lakes and Dales on A683)
☎Newbiggin-on-Lune(05396) 23242
Amidst rolling hills and dales, this attractive family-run inn, converted from a 17th-century stone-built farmhouse, has spacious

bar and lounge areas. Comfortably furnished bedrooms include some ground floor rooms.
12⇨♠(4fb)⊁in all bedrooms CTV in all bedrooms ®
sB&B⇨♠£34.50-£35.50 dB&B⇨♠£54-£56 ♬
CTV 60P ✿ ♪ private 5 acre nature reserve *xmas*
☺ International V ❊ ⚑ ⊁ Lunch £11.50-£12 Dinner £16-£17 Last dinner 9pm

(£)

READING Berkshire Map 04 SU77

See also **Wokingham**

★★★★61% **Holiday Inn**
Caversham Bridge, Richfield Av RG1 8BD (M4 junct 10/A329M to Reading. Join A4 follow signs to Caversham) ☎(0734) 391818 FAX (0734) 391665

This modern hotel by Caversham Bridge gives views of the Thames from many of its rooms. A high canopied ceiling emphasises the spaciousness of the open-plan lobby, restaurant and bar, and there is a separate pub-bar. Well equipped bedrooms are all in practical modern style.
112⇨♠1🛏⊁in 15 bedrooms CTV in all bedrooms ® ℣ T
sB⇨♠£102 dB⇨♠£102 (room only) ♬
Lift ⓒ 200P 🅿 (heated) sauna solarium gymnasium
V ❊ ⚑ ⊁ Lunch £14.50 High tea £3.50-£6.95 Dinner £18.95&alc Last dinner 10pm
CONF. Thtr 250 Class 150 Board 50 Del from £120
Credit Cards [1][2][3][5]

(£)

★★★★60% **Ramada**
Oxford Rd RG1 7RH ☎(0734) 586222 FAX (0734) 597842

This modern hotel with parking available at a nearby multi-storey car park, has well equipped bedrooms with double or king-sized beds and individual air-conditioning; bathrooms are compact but have good showers. Open-plan public areas include the Pavilion Bar with piano music, Froggie's bar-café offering all-day snacks and the formal Caversham restaurant.
196⇨♠(91fb)⊁in 51 bedrooms CTV in all bedrooms ® ℣ T
✗ (ex guide dogs) sB⇨♠£90-£99 dB⇨♠£90-£99 (room only) ♬
Lift ⊞ 75☂ 🅿 (heated) sauna solarium gymnasium turkish bath jacuzzi beauty salon ♪
☺ International V ❊ ⚑ ⊁ Lunch £12.50-£16 Dinner £7.50-£12.50&alc Last dinner 10pm
CONF. Thtr 220 Class 130 Board 30 Del from £84.50
Credit Cards [1][2][3][4][5]

★★★68% **Kirtons Resort Hotel & Country Club**
Pingewood RG3 3UN ☎(0734) 500885 FAX (0734) 391996

In a rural setting a few miles south of the town, this large modern hotel has outstanding indoor and outdoor leisure facilities, especially water sports. Bedrooms are all spacious and well equipped, with balconies overlooking the lake. Public ares, which are rather spread out, include 3 eating options: the country club itself, the Lakeside Brasserie and small formal Pavilion Restaurant.
81⇨♠(10fb)⊁in 15 bedrooms CTV in all bedrooms ® ℣ T
sB⇨♠£80-£125 dB⇨♠£90-£125 (room only) ♬
Lift ⓒ CTV 200P ✿ 🅿 (heated) ♀ (hard) ♪ squash snooker sauna solarium gymnasium jetskiing waterskiing quad bikes *xmas*
☺ English & French V ❊ ⚑ Sunday Lunch £9.95 Dinner £16.95&alc Last dinner 10.30pm
CONF. Thtr 120 Class 45 Board 54 Del from £71.50
Credit Cards [1][2][3][5]

(£)

Ravenstonedale - Reading

★★ ❀59% **Upcross**
68 Berkeley Av RG1 6HY ☎(0734) 590796 FAX (0734)576517
Closed 27 Dec-1 Jan
A red brick Victorian building in its own grounds, yet centrally situated in the town, Upcross Hotel is personally run along country house lines and provides a welcoming atmosphere. Bedrooms are split between the main house and another house in the grounds. Public areas include a comfortable lounge, conservatory bar and an attractive dining room, where interesting dishes are offered from table d'hôte and à la carte menus.
16⇨♠Annexe4⇨♠(1fb) CTV in all bedrooms ® T ✱
sB&B⇨♠£59 dB&B⇨♠£65 ♬
40P ✿ ❊ ♪
☺ French ❊ ⚑ ✱ Lunch £14.95&alc Dinner £14.95&alc Last dinner 10pm
Credit Cards [1][2][3][4]

See advertisement on page 507

Forte Posthouse
Basingstoke Rd RG2 0SL ☎(0734) 875485 FAX (0734) 311958

Suitable for both the business and leisure traveller, this bright hotel provides modern accommodation in well equipped bedrooms with en suite bathrooms. For more details about Forte Posthouse hotels, consult the Contents page, under Hotel Groups.
138⇨♠✱ B⇨♠£41.50-£53.50 (room only)
CONF. Thtr 100 Class 50 Board 50 Del £89.50

Hotels with red star ratings are especially high quality.

AT RAVENSTONEDALE
Kirkby Stephen, Cumbria CA17 4NG
Tel: (05396) 23204

Built of Lakeland stone at the turn of the century and situated in the foothills of the Eden Valley. The hotel has fourteen en suite bedrooms and three rooms available for disabled guests all tastefully furnished. The resident owner's belief that a hotel should emulate "home from home" whenever possible, and every effort is made to ensure warm hospitality, great comfort and fine food. Private fishing available. Combine all this with the surrounding countryside, and we feel sure you will enjoy your stay and wish to return. Ravenstonedale is less than ten minutes from junction 38 of the M6.
Midweek and weekend breaks available. OPEN ALL YEAR.

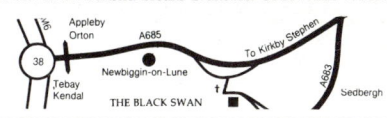

Reading - Redruth

Forte Travelodge
387 Basingstoke Rd RG2 0JE (on A33, southbound)
☎(0734) 750618 Central Res (0800) 850950

This modern building offers a good standard of accommodation for overnight stops. Smart, spacious and well equipped bedrooms, all with en suite bathrooms, are suitable for family use, and meals may be taken at the nearby family restaurant. For more details about Travelodges, consult the Contents page, under Hotel Groups.
36⇌♠✻ B⇌♠£31.95 (room only)

REDBOURN Hertfordshire Map 04 TL11

★★★58% Aubrey Park
Hemel Hempstead Rd AL3 7AF ☎(0582) 792105 FAX (0582) 792001
Within 6 acres of gardens, this hotel provides all the expected amenities in smart modern bedrooms, de luxe rooms also having whirlpool baths. There is a comfortable lounge bar and a choice of restaurants, the beamed Ostlers Room being more informal; a room service menu is also available.
119⇌♠(2fb) CTV in all bedrooms ®⚋ T ✻ sB&B⇌♠£40-£65 dB&B⇌♠£50-£75 ♬
(160P ✻ ⌕ (heated) pitch & putt games room jogging trail ♪
♀ English & French V ♡ ⚌ ✻ Lunch fr£13.50 Dinner fr£16.50&alc Last dinner 10pm
Credit Cards [1][2][3][5] £

See advertisement under ST ALBANS

REDBROOK Clwyd Map 07 SJ54

★★59% Redbrook Hunting Lodge
Wrexham Rd SY13 3ET ☎Redbrook Maelor(094873) 204 & 533 FAX (094873) 533
(For full entry see Whitchurch (Shropshire))

REDDITCH Hereford & Worcester Map 07 SP06

★★★60% Southcrest
Pool Bank, Southcrest B97 4JG ☎(0527) 541511 FAX (0527) 402600
Closed 24 Dec-2 Jan & BH's RS Sun evenings
This privately owned business hotel is in a quiet situation close to the town centre. The majority of the bedrooms are functional, warm and well equipped, while those in the oldest part of the hotel are of a superior standard. There is a cosy cocktail bar and a restaurant overlooking the gardens and woodland.
58⇌♠(2fb)2⊟ CTV in all bedrooms ®⚋ T
(100P ✻
♀ French V ♡ Last dinner 9.15pm
Credit Cards [1][2][3][5]

Campanile
Far Moor Ln, Winyates Green B98 0SD (A435 towards Redditch) ☎(0527) 510710 FAX (0527) 517269

A nearby bar and bistro restaurant provides refreshments for travellers staying at this modern accommodation building. Bedrooms are well equipped and have en suite bathrooms. For more details about Campanile, consult the Contents page, under Hotel Groups.
Annexe50⇌♠ B⇌♠£35.75 (room only)
CONF. Thtr 35 Class 35 Board 25 Del from £42.80

Some hotels within company owned groups share a uniform identity. For full details consult the Contents page, under Hotel Groups.

REDHILL
See **Nutfield**

REDRUTH Cornwall & Isles of Scilly Map 02 SW64

★★★65% Penventon
TR15 1TE ☎(0209) 214141 FAX (0209) 219164
A Georgian manor house standing in its own extensive grounds, Penventon has been owned by the friendly Pascoe family for the past 24 years. The ornate public areas have been beautifully restored, and while bedrooms are rather more functional, they are steadily being upgraded. A varied menu and a well balanced wine list prove popular with residents and locals alike.
50⇌♠(3fb)1⊟ CTV in all bedrooms ®⚋ T sB&B⇌♠£25-£49 dB&B⇌♠£39-£79 ♬
(100P ✻ ⌕ (heated) snooker sauna solarium gymnasium leisure spa jacuzzi masseuse steam bath ♪ ⚘ xmas
♀ English French & Italian V ♡ ⚌ Lunch £9.50&alc Dinner £12.95-£13.95&alc Last dinner 9.30pm
CONF. Thtr 200 Class 150 Board 60 Del from £35
Credit Cards [1][2][3] £

★★⚘69% Aviary Court
Mary's Well, Illogan TR16 4QZ (off A3047) (Logis)
☎Portreath(0209) 842256
The Studley family have continued to improve this charming 300-year-old Cornish country house set in well tended grounds on the edge of Illogan Woods between Redruth and Portreath. The small welcoming hotel now has more spacious bedrooms, individually and attractively decorated, with modern facilities and many little extras. Cosy comfortable public rooms include a new lounge and Mrs Studley makes good use of quality Cornish produce in the generous meals served in the attractive restaurant.
6⇌♠(1fb) CTV in all bedrooms ® T ✗ sB&B⇌♠£38-£42 dB&B⇌♠£54-£58
25P ❀ nc3yrs
♀ English & French Sunday Lunch £8.50 Dinner £11.50&alc Last dinner 8.45pm
CONF. Thtr 20 Class 20 Board 20
Credit Cards [1][2][3][5]

★★68% Crossroads
Scorrier TR16 5BP (2m E off A30) ☎(0209) 820551 FAX (0209) 820392
Conveniently located, this hotel provides a variety of accommodation – executive bedroo s being larger, more comfortable and of a generally higher quality, though all are well equipped with modern facilities. There is also a choice of restaurants, and the à la carte menu features a wide selection of interesting dishes. Popular bars provide friendly, informal attention and there is good room service.
35⇌♠(4fb)✗in 2 bedrooms CTV in all bedrooms ® T sB&B⇌♠£28.50-£44.50 dB&B⇌♠£38.50-£56 ♬
Lift 140P
♀ English & French V ♡ ⚌ Lunch £8.50-£9.50 Dinner £10.75-£12.75&alc Last dinner 9.30pm
CONF. Thtr 120 Class 30 Board 30 Del from £60
Credit Cards [1][2][3][5]

See advertisement under TRURO

★★67% Inn for All Seasons
Treleigh TR16 4AP (leave A30 Redruth/Portreath junct, follow signs Cardrow Industrial Estate, 0.5m from junct on the right)
☎(0209) 219511 FAX (0209) 219751
This popular tourist and business hotel has a rather dull modern facade that belies its imaginative interior. Comfortable bedrooms with every modern convenience are decorated with attractive stencilwork. A well furnished bar decorated in rich colours offers a varied bar menu plus as well as a carvery, and the restaurant is usually open at weekends.
12⇌♠ CTV in all bedrooms ® T sB&B⇌♠£27.50 dB&B⇌♠£55 ♬

100P nc10yrs
♦ International V ♦ ❋ Sunday Lunch £8.95 Dinner £8.95&alc
Last dinner 9.30pm
Credit Cards [1][3]   £

REDWORTH Co Durham Map 08 NZ22

★★★★ ❀71% **Redworth Hall Hotel & Country Club**
DL5 6NL (off A6072) ☎Bishop Auckland(0388) 772442
FAX (0388) 775112

The splendid Jacobean frontage of this country mansion house cunningly conceals the modern extensions to the rear, housing spacious bedrooms, some with separate sitting areas and some overlooking the inner courtyard and part of the leisure complex. There are 2 restaurants, the Blue Room providing chef Scott Macrae's more adventurous carte of modern-style classically influenced cuisine. Staff throughout the hotel are cheerful, competent and helpful.
100⇨↾(10fb)3♯⊁in 31 bedrooms CTV in all bedrooms ® T ❋ sB&B⇨↾£89-£99 dB&B⇨↾£105-£135 ₽
Lift (⊞ 200P ✿ ⊠ (heated) ♬ (hard) squash snooker sauna solarium gymnasium croquet spa pool ♪ xmas
♦ English & Continental V ♦ ⚏ ❋ Lunch £11.50&alc High tea £1.95-£7.25 Dinner £16.95&alc Last dinner 10pm
CONF. Thtr 300 Class 150 Board 35 Del from £94
Credit Cards [1][2][3][5]

REIGATE Surrey Map 04 TQ25

★★★65% **Reigate Manor Hotel**
Reigate Hill RH2 9PF ☎(0737) 240125 FAX (0737) 223883

This Georgian manor house has been converted and extended to become a popular commercial hotel. Bedrooms in the new wing are of a comfortable uniform standard, while those in the main building vary in size and style – some being rather small. There is a small, smartly furnished foyer lounge, as well as a bar and restaurant.
51⇨↾(1fb)1♯ CTV in all bedrooms ® T ✻ (ex guide dogs)
sB&B⇨↾£40-£75 dB&B⇨↾£78-£85 ₽
(130P sauna solarium gymnasium
♦ English & French V ♦ ⚏ Lunch £14.50-£15.50&alc Dinner £17.50-£18.50&alc Last dinner 10pm
CONF. Thtr 180 Class 80 Board 50 Del from £85
Credit Cards [1][2][3][5]   £

★★★60% **Bridge House**
Reigate Hill RH2 9RP (on A217) (Logis) ☎(0737) 246801 & 244821 FAX (0737) 223756

Built in the 60s, this hillside hotel has excellent views of Reigate Valley. Motel-style bedrooms, many with their own balconies, are spacious but functional, and are beginning to look dated. Lounge facilities are limited, but there is a large trattoria-style Continental restaurant with a resident band on 5 evenings a week.
40⇨↾(3fb) CTV in all bedrooms ® T ✻ ♦ sB&B⇨↾£40-£50 dB&B⇨↾£50-£75 (room only) ₽
(110P ♪ xmas
♦ English & French V ♦ ❋ Lunch £12.75-£15.75&alc Dinner £14.75-£24&alc Last dinner 10pm
CONF. Thtr 40 Class 18 Board 24 Del from £78
Credit Cards [1][2][3][5]   £

RENFREW For hotels see **Glasgow Airport**

RENISHAW Derbyshire Map 08 SK47

★★59% **Sitwell Arms Toby**
S31 9WE (Toby) ☎Eckington(0246) 435226 FAX (0246) 433915

This extended old coaching inn, set in 6 acres of grounds, has a popular public bar, with the rest of the hotel in quieter surroundings to the rear. Bedrooms, except for 5 very small singles on the top floor, are generally spacious, though beginning to look rather tired. There is a carvery restaurant and comfortable open-plan lounge bar.
30⇨↾✻in 10 bedrooms CTV in all bedrooms ® T
(150P ✿ darts pool table
V ♦ ⚏ ⊁ Last dinner 10.30pm
CONF. Thtr 150 Class 60 Board 80
Credit Cards [1][2][3][5]

REYNOLDSTON West Glamorgan Map 02 SS48

★★ ♨70% *Fairyhill Country House*
SA3 1BS (Welsh Rarebits) ☎Gower(0792) 390139 FAX (0792) 391358
Closed Dec-Jan

A carefully restored 18th-century mansion at the heart of the Gower, set in 24 acres of woodland with its own trout stream, provides a warmly hospitable atmosphere, smart, well equipped bedrooms and elegant lounges with woodburning stoves.
11⇨↾Annexe2⇨↾ CTV in all bedrooms ® T
50P ⇔ ✿ ♪
♦ English & French V ♦ Last dinner 9pm
Credit Cards [1][3]

RHAYADER Powys Map 06 SN96

★★60% **Elan Valley Hotel**
LD6 5HN (2.5m W of Rhayader, on B4518) ☎(0597) 810448
FAX (0597) 810448
RS Nov-Mar

Situated amid lovely scenery, this peaceful small hotel has modern bedrooms, 2 bars and a comfortable lounge with a full-size snooker table.
10rm(9⇨↾)(1fb) CTV in 8 bedrooms ® ❋ sB&B£30
sB&B⇨↾£30 dB&B£42.50-£50 dB&B⇨↾£42.50-£50 ₽

UPCROSS
Restaurant and Hotel
★★ 59% ❀

Set in beautiful gardens, this privately owned hotel is an oasis of charm and tranquillity. A high standard of French cuisine is provided at affordable prices — table d'hôte menu from £9.95 for two courses. The à la carte menu is changed monthly.
A minute's drive from the town centre with easy access to the M4 — ample free car parking.
Telephone: 0734 590796
Fax: 0734 576517
68 Berkeley Avenue, Reading RG1 6HY

Rhayader - Ripon

CTV 50P 2🅿(£2) ✿ ♪ snooker
V ✿ ♀ ⨯ ✱ Bar Lunch £1.50-£11alc Dinner £10-£15alc Last dinner 8pm
Credit Cards 1 3

RHU Strathclyde *Dunbartonshire* Map **10** NS28

★★★❀❀62% **Rosslea Hall**
G84 8NF (on A 814, past post office)
☎(0436) 820684 FAX (0436) 820897

Rosslea Hall is an extended Victorian mansion in secluded grounds overlooking the Gareloch. Predominantly a business hotel, it has a bright and cheerful lounge with an eating area, the substantial range of dishes served here providing an alternative to the more classical table d'hôte and à la carte menus of the main restaurant. There is also a cocktail bar and a comfortable lounge. Bedrooms are solidly furnished, those in the older part of the house being more spacious but having somewhat dated bathrooms.
30⇨ ⋔ (2fb) CTV in all bedrooms ® ⨯ T sB&B⇨ ⋔ £63-£68 dB&B⇨ ⋔ £77-£80 🅿
(🎱 80P ✿ *xmas*
♀ Scottish & French V ✿ ♀ ✱ Lunch £12.50-£17.50 High tea £6.50-£10.50 Dinner £17.50-£21.50&alc Last dinner 9.30pm
CONF. Thtr 150 Class 40 Board 40 Del from £80
Credit Cards 1 2 3 5

RHYL Clwyd Map **06** SJ08

★★61% **Marina**
Marine Dr LL18 3AU ☎(0745) 342172 FAX (0745) 342172
A proprietor-run hotel manned by cheerful local staff stands on the East Promenade only a short walk from the Sun Centre. Bedrooms, though modest, are equipped with modern facilities, and each of the 2 restaurants has an adjoining bar.
26rm(20⇨2 ⋔)(6fb)2🎱 CTV in all bedrooms ®
✈ (ex guide dogs) sB&B£22.50-£27.50 sB&B⇨ ⋔ £22.50-£55 dB&B⇨ ⋔ £45-£55 🅿
Lift (75P *xmas*
V ✿ ♀ Lunch £4.90-£7.50
CONF. Class 300
Credit Cards 1 2

RICHMOND North Yorkshire Map **07** NZ10

★★67% **King's Head**
Market Place DL10 4HS ☎(0748) 850220 FAX (0748) 850635

The King's Head is a historic building with an elegant Georgian façade overlooking the cobbled market square, and the first floor dining room particularly benefits from this view. The spacious lounges retain much of the character of the period with an abundance of antiques. Many of the bedrooms also have antique furniture, others are adequately but more modestly furnished.
24⇨ ⋔ Annexe4⇨ ⋔ (1fb)3🎱 ⨯ in 11 bedrooms CTV in all bedrooms ® T ✱ sB&B⇨ ⋔ £53-£57 dB&B⇨ ⋔ £76-£90 🅿
(25P *xmas*
♀ International V ✿ ♀ ✱ ⨯ Sunday Lunch £6.95-£9.95 Dinner fr£15.95&alc Last dinner 9.15pm
Credit Cards 1 2 3 5 £

★★59% **Frenchgate**
59-61 Frenchgate DL10 7AE (Turn left at mini-roundabout by Methodist Church, take next left into Frenchgate)
☎(0748) 822087 & 823596
Closed Dec-Feb

Originally a Georgian town house, the hotel is set in a quiet cobbled street in one of the attractive original gates to the old walled town. Bedrooms are simply furnished but well equipped, there are several cosy lounge areas and the proprietors offer friendly, efficient service.

13rm(3⇨4 ⋔) CTV in all bedrooms ® T ✱ sB&B£27 sB&B⇨ ⋔ £36 dB&B£51 dB&B⇨ ⋔ £58 🅿
6P 🚗 nc7yrs
V ✱ Dinner £11.50&alc Last dinner 8.30pm
Credit Cards 1 2 3 5

RICHMOND UPON THAMES Greater London
See **LONDON SECTION plan 1** *B3*

★★★64% **Richmond Hill**
146-150 Richmond Hill TW10 6RW
☎081-940 2247 & 081-940 5466 FAX 081-940 5424

This Georgian hotel is just by Richmond Park, with views over the Thames. Bedrooms vary in size and style and are currently being upgraded; all are equipped with modern amenities. The wood-panelled restaurant offers a choice of menus; as an alternative there is room service, afternoon tea and lounge service.
124⇨ ⋔ (9fb)1🎱 ⨯ in 31 bedrooms CTV in 123 bedrooms ® T sB&B⇨ ⋔ £88-£98 dB&B⇨ ⋔ £98-£108 🅿
Lift (150P squash *xmas*
♀ English & French V ✿ ♀ ✱ Lunch fr£13.50 Dinner fr£18.50 Last dinner 9pm
CONF. Thtr 180 Class 100 Board 50 Del £110
Credit Cards 1 2 3 5

RINGWOOD Hampshire Map **04** SU10

★★★66% **Tyrrells Ford Country House**
Avon BH23 7BH (4m S on B3347) ☎Bransgore(0425) 672646 FAX (0425) 672262

This period country house stands in its own grassy wooded grounds. Most of the bedrooms have a lovely view and many have brass beds; executive rooms are larger and better equipped. Public areas include the popular freehouse bar and an attractive galleried residents' lounge with a fine hunting tapestry.
16⇨ ⋔ CTV in all bedrooms ® T ✈ (ex guide dogs) sB&B⇨ ⋔ £45-£60 dB&B⇨ ⋔ £70-£85 🅿
100P ✿ *xmas*
♀ English & French V ✱ Lunch £10.95-£12.95 Dinner £16.95&alc Last dinner 10pm
Credit Cards 1 3

★★❀❀70% **Moortown Lodge Hotel**
244, Christchurch Rd BH24 3AS (1.5m S on B3347) (Logis)
☎(0425) 471404
Closed 24 Dec-14 Jan

Resident owners Jilly and Bob Burrows-Jones provide a friendly and relaxed style of personal service, with Jilly in charge of the cooking. The individually furnished bedrooms vary in size and all come with a good range of equipment. The standard of cooking is one of the hotel's strengths, and the fixed price menu is excellent value. Recommendations this year are floating cheese island and the tempting home-made puddings. Most of the produce is local, including game in season.
6rm(1⇨4 ⋔)(1fb)1🎱 ⨯ in 1 bedroom CTV in all bedrooms ® T ✈ sB&B£30-£32 sB&B⇨ ⋔ £38-£42 dB&B⇨ ⋔ £52-£80 🅿
8P 🚗
♀ British & French V ✱ Dinner £14.95-£16.95&alc Last dinner 8.30pm
Credit Cards 1 3

RIPON North Yorkshire Map **08** SE37

★★★66% **Ripon Spa**
Park St HG4 2BU (on B6265 Pately Bridge road) ☎(0765) 602172 FAX (0765) 690770

This traditional Edwardian hotel is set in 7 acres of grounds. Recent extension of the lounge bar and the main lounge, which overlook the gardens, has increased their versatility. The elegant main restaurant has similar views, but is not always used in quieter times. The Turf

Ripon - Rochford

Tavern serves popular bar meals, and with its open fire is particularly cosy in winter. Bedrooms are individually styled and most are spacious.
40⇌🛏(5fb)2⚃ CTV in all bedrooms ® T ✻ sB&B⇌🛏£51-£56 dB&B⇌🛏£69.60-£90 🍴
Lift (80P ❀ croquet lawn *xmas*
V ✿ ⚓ ✶ Lunch £9.50-£12&alc Dinner £14.75-£15.50&alc Last dinner 9pm
CONF. Thtr 180 Class 100 Board 80 Del from £80
Credit Cards ①②③⑤

★★✱75% *Bridge*
16-18 Magdalen Rd HG4 1HX ☎(0765) 603687
Only a short walk from the cathedral and shopping area, this hotel forms part of a Victorian terrace overlooking the River Ure at the northern end of the city. Decor and furnishings, along with fine antiques and curios, reflect the Victorian era, and there is a warm, comfortable atmosphere. The stylish dining room, with a modern conservatory extension overlooking the garden, features a popular four-course menu offering a choice at each course.
15⇌🛏(7fb)1⚃⤴in 4 bedrooms CTV in all bedrooms ® T 15P 🚲
✿ English, French & Italian V ✿ ⚓ ⚐ Last dinner 9pm
Credit Cards ①②③⑤

★★56% *Unicorn*
Market Place HG4 1BP (on south east corner of Market Place) ☎(0765) 602202 FAX (0765) 600321
RS 24-27 Dec

Situated close to the cathedral in Ripon's medieval market square, this historic hotel provides friendly service and a relaxing atmosphere. Neatly furnished bedrooms include modern facilities and there is a traditional bar decorated with murals of town scenes.
33⇌🛏(4fb) CTV in all bedrooms ® T sB&B⇌🛏£35-£37.50 dB&B⇌🛏£42-£49 🍴
(15P 🚗
✿ English & French V ✿ ✶ Sunday Lunch £4.75-£5.75alc Dinner £13-£15&alc Last dinner 9pm
CONF. Thtr 60 Class 16 Board 26 Del from £75
Credit Cards ①②③⑤

ROBIN HOOD'S BAY North Yorkshire Map **08** NZ90

★63% *Grosvenor*
Station Rd YO22 4RA ☎Whitby(0947) 880329
Built in 1906, this hotel is in the higher part of Robin Hood's Bay. Comfortable and cosy public areas include an attractive dining room. Bedrooms are more functional but have modern facilities.
13rm(3⇌🛏2🛏)(2fb) CTV in 6 bedrooms ® T ✱ (ex guide dogs) CTV
✿ Last dinner 9pm
Credit Cards ①③

ROCHDALE Greater Manchester Map **07** SD81

★★★68% *Norton Grange*
Manchester Rd, Castleton OL11 2XZ (beside A664) ☎(0706) 30788 FAX (0706) 49313

Surrounded by 9 acres of grounds, this Victorian mansion has been extended to create a wing of particularly comfortable and attractively appointed bedrooms. Public areas include a choice of bars, and smartly dressed staff provide friendly service throughout.
50⇌🛏(28fb)1⚃⤴in 5 bedrooms CTV in all bedrooms ® T sB&B⇌🛏fr£74.50 dB&B⇌🛏fr£89.50 🍴
Lift (150P ❀ *xmas*
✿ International V ✿ ⚓ Lunch £3.75-£6 Dinner £14.50&alc Last dinner 9.45pm
Credit Cards ①②③④⑤

★★61% *Midway*
Manchester Rd, Castleton OL11 2XX (alongside A664)
☎(0706) 32881 FAX (0706) 53522
This much extended, privately owned hotel provides friendly, informal service. Four bedrooms have recently been refurbished to a high standard, but the remainder are mostly modest and in need of improvement, though all have an adequate range of equipment. One room is in fact a spacious suite with a separate lounge.
24⇌🛏1⚃ CTV in all bedrooms ® T ✱ (ex guide dogs)
(100P
✿ English & French V ✿ ⚓ Last dinner 9.45pm
Credit Cards ①②③⑤

ROCHESTER Kent Map **05** TQ76

★★★★68% *Bridgewood Manor Hotel*
Bridgewood Roundabout, Maidstone Rd
ME5 9AX (adjacent to roundabout on A229)
☎Medway(0634) 201333 FAX (0634) 201330

Ideally placed for the M20 and M2, this low-rise, modern hotel was designed as a high-quality conference centre. The prime consideration of the small family company which owns it is looking after its guests, and this creates a warm atmosphere. Bedrooms include some de luxe rooms and suites.
100⇌🛏(12fb)⤴in 25 bedrooms CTV in all bedrooms ® ✈ T sB&B⇌🛏£85-£95 dB&B⇌🛏£105-£120 🍴
Lift (178P ❀ 🏊 (heated) ♪ (hard) snooker sauna solarium gymnasium spa bath putting green hairdressing 🎵 🐕 *xmas*
✿ English & French V ✿ ✶ Lunch fr£12 Dinner fr£19.50&alc Last dinner 10pm
Credit Cards ①②③⑤

★★63% *Royal Victoria & Bull Hotel*
16-18 High St ME1 1PX (off A2) ☎(0634) 846266 FAX (0634) 832312
This 16th-century coaching inn is easily found at the top end of the High Street. Bedrooms are traditional in style with floral décor and candlewick bedspreads. The cocktail bar and smart restaurant are found across the courtyard and there is a popular public bar which has recently been upgraded.
28rm(21⇌🛏)(2fb)2⚃ CTV in all bedrooms ® T sB&B£38 sB&B⇌🛏£45 dB&B£45 dB&B⇌🛏£55 🍴
(CTV 25P 🎵
✿ International V ✿ ⚓ ⚐ Lunch £7.95&alc Dinner £10-£15alc Last dinner 11pm
CONF. Thtr 100 Class 60 Board 60 Del £59.50
Credit Cards ①②③⑤

•••••••••••••••••••••••••••••
Forte Posthouse
Maidstone Rd ME5 9SF (on A229 1m N of M2 jnct 3) ☎Medway(0634) 687111 FAX (0634) 684512

Suitable for both the business and leisure traveller, this bright hotel provides modern accommodation in well equipped bedrooms with en suite bathrooms. For more details about Forte Posthouse hotels, consult the Contents page, under Hotel Groups.
135⇌🛏✱ B⇌🛏£41.50-£53.50 (room only)
CONF. Thtr 120 Class 70 Board 70 Del £89.50

ROCHFORD Essex Map **05** TQ89

★★★✱66% *Hotel Renouf*
Bradley Way SS4 1BU (turn off A127 onto B1013 to Rochford, at 3rd mini roundabout turn right & keep right)
☎Southend-on-Sea(0702) 541334 FAX (0702) 549563
Closed 26-30 Dec
This purpose-built town-centre hotel provides smart modern accommodation, with a range of well equipped bedrooms. In the stylish restaurant chef/owner Derek Renouf offers an extensive carte of skilfully prepared dishes, with pressed duck a house

509

Rochford - Rosedale Abbey

speciality. Our inspector enjoyed a rich and creamy shellfish soup and sliced fillet of beef with oyster mushrooms.
24⇨📞(2fb) CTV in all bedrooms ®⚓ T ✱ sB&B⇨📞£47-£68 dB&B⇨📞£68-£97.50
(25P 🚗 ✿ xmas
♨ French V ✱ Lunch £20-£40alc Dinner £20-£40alc Last dinner 9.45pm
Conf. Thtr 70 Class 70 Board 70 Del from £76
Credit Cards ①②③⑤

See advertisement under SOUTHEND-ON-SEA

ROCK (NEAR ST MINVER) Cornwall & Isles of Scilly Map 02 SW97

★★ 67% **St Enodoc**
PL27 6LA ☎Trebetherick(020886) 3394
Enjoying splendid views over the Camel estuary, this friendly hotel has varied bedrooms which are continually being upgraded. A short table d'hôte menu is offered in the candlelit restaurant, and bar meals are also available.
13⇨📞(2fb) CTV in all bedrooms T
CTV 33P 🚗 ✿ ≋ (heated) squash snooker sauna solarium gymnasium water-skiing windsurfing pony-trekking
♨ English & Continental V ✿ ⌾ Last dinner 9.30pm
Credit Cards ①②③

ROMALDKIRK Durham Map 12 NY92

★★ ❀❀71% **Rose & Crown**
DL12 9EB (6m W from Barnard Castle on B6277)
☎Teesdale(0833) 50213 FAX (0833) 50828
Closed 25 & 26 Dec
This charming old inn at the centre of the village retains much of its historic character while providing good modern facilities. There is a cosy bar with a log fire, a separate bar serving food and an attractive wood-panelled dining room where chef/patron Chris Davy offers interesting dishes that make good use of fresh local produce, for example sautéed chicken livers with green peppercorns served with fresh gnocchi, local roast lamb or breast of guinea fowl. Friendly service is provided by the Davys and their young staff.
7⇨📞Annexe5⇨📞(1fb)🚻 CTV in all bedrooms ® T ✱ sB&B⇨📞£52 dB&B⇨📞£74 ₧
40P
♨ English & French ✿ ⌾ ✱ Sunday Lunch £10.75-£12.75 Dinner £22-£24.95 Last dinner 9pm
Credit Cards ①③

ROMSEY Hampshire Map 04 SU32

★★★ 68% **Potters Heron Hotel**
SO51 9ZF (Lansbury) ☎Southampton(0703) 266611 FAX (0703) 251359
(For full entry see Ampfield)

★★★ 63% **The White Horse**
Market Place SO51 8ZJ ☎(0794) 512431 FAX (0794) 517485

FORTE Heritage

Behind its Georgian façade, the White Horse dates back to Elizabethan times. The lounge retains some of the original character, and bedrooms are traditionally styled, though furnished and equipped to a modern standard. Bar meals are popular, and the elegant Lucilla Dixon Restaurant has a good atmosphere, attentive service and a choice of daily fixed price and à la carte menus.
33⇨📞(7fb)✄ in 11 bedrooms CTV in all bedrooms ® T ✱ sB⇨📞£80 dB⇨📞£90 (room only) ₧
(60P xmas
V ✿ ⌾ ✱ Sunday Lunch fr£11.95 Dinner fr£15.95&alc Last dinner 9.30pm
Conf. Thtr 40 Class 20 Board 20 Del £90
Credit Cards ①②③④⑤

★★★ 62% **New Forest Heathlands**
Romsey Rd, Ower SO51 6ZJ
☎Southampton(0703) 814333 FAX (0703) 812123
RS Sat

CONSORT HOTELS

The hotel, on the edge of the New Forest at Ower, comprises an attractive pub bar, The Vine Inn, and soundly equipped modern bedroom accommodation in purpose built wings.
52⇨📞(2fb) CTV in all bedrooms ®⚓ T sB&B⇨📞£40-£77 dB&B⇨📞£77-£92 ₧
(150P ✿ sauna solarium gymnasium mini-golf jacuzzis croquet
♨ International V ✿ ⌾ ✱ Lunch £7.50-£8.50 High tea £1.50-£3.50 Dinner £14.75-£16.75&alc Last dinner 9.15pm
Conf. Thtr 200 Class 100 Board 70 Del from £60
Credit Cards ①②③⑤

ROSEBANK Strathclyde Lanarkshire Map 11 NS84

★★★ 63% **Popinjay**
Lanark Rd ML8 50B (on A72 between Hamilton & Lanark)
☎Crossford(055586) 441 due to change to (0555) 860441 FAX (055586) 204 due to change to (0555) 860204

CONSORT HOTELS

The Popinjay, with its mock Tudor façade, has an attractive riverside setting and is the focal point of the small Clyde Valley village. It has a reputation for its good value meals. The modern bedrooms are very well equipped which compensates for some being rather compact.
38⇨📞Annexe5⇨📞(2fb)2🚻 CTV in all bedrooms ®⚓ T ✱ sB&B⇨📞£46-£55 dB&B⇨📞£55-£125 ₧
(100P ✿ ♪ 🎵 xmas
♨ International V ✿ ⌾ ✱ Lunch fr£7.45 High tea fr£6.25 Dinner fr£13.50 Last dinner 10pm
Conf. Thtr 220 Class 150 Board 50
Credit Cards ①②③⑤

ROSEDALE ABBEY North Yorkshire Map 08 SE79

★★★ ❀68% **Blacksmiths Arms**
Hartoft End YO18 8EN ☎Lastingham(07515) 331
A charming, restored and extended 16th-century farmhouse retaining a great deal of character with beams, open fires, period furniture and stonework. Bedrooms are pretty and most have fine views. In the elegant restaurant many local dishes can be sampled from the good value 4-course 'table d'hôte' menu, and bar meals are also popular.
14⇨📞 CTV in all bedrooms ® T
80P 🚗 ✿ ♪
♨ English & French V ✿ ⌾ ✄ Last dinner 8.45pm
Credit Cards ①②③⑤

★★ ❀70% **Milburn Arms**
YO18 8RA (7m N of A170) (Logis)
☎Lastingham(07515) 312 & 313
RS 24 & 25 Dec
This attractive Yorkshire stone building is in the heart of the Moors, in a picturesque village. Guests can relax in the friendly atmosphere here, either in the comfortable lounge or in the character bar. Bedrooms are spacious and pretty, with thoughtful facilities. A well produced 3-course dinner is served in the split-level restaurant, and dishes might include Greenland prawns with curried mayonnaise, loin of pork and mustard sauce and apple pie and cream.
3⇨📞Annexe8⇨📞(2fb)🚻 CTV in all bedrooms ® T sB&B⇨📞£36-£42.50 dB&B⇨📞£57-£70 ₧
35P 🚗 ✿ pool table xmas
♨ English & French V ✿ ⌾ ✄ ✱ Sunday Lunch £8.50-£10 Dinner £17.50-£22&alc Last dinner 9pm
Credit Cards ①③⑤

★★ 63% White Horse Farm
YO18 8SE ☎Lastingham(07515) 239 due to change to (0751) 417781 FAX (07515) 7781 due to change to (0751) 417781
Closed 25 Dec

In an elevated position overlooking the dale and village, this charming hotel has had a licence since 1702, and its beamed bars, old prints, photographs and farm implements reflect its long history. Bedrooms are attractive; 2 have small sitting rooms and those at the front have fine views over the dale. Local game, fish, meats and poultry feature on the restaurant menu, and there is a good selection of bar meals.

11⇨🐾 Annexe4⇨🐾(2fb) CTV in all bedrooms ® T ✱
sB&B⇨🐾£32-£35 dB&B⇨🐾£54-£60 ♬
50P ⇔ ✱ xmas
♡ English & Continental V ✱ Sunday Lunch £7.50 High tea 70p-£2.50alc Dinner £15-£16 Last dinner 8.45pm
CONF. Thtr 25 Class 25 Board 25 Del from £37
Credit Cards [1][2][3][5]

ROSEHALL Highland *Sutherland* Map 14 NC40

★★ 61% Achness
IV27 4BD (just off A837 Bonar Bridge to Lochinver Road)
☎(054984) 239 FAX (054984) 324
Closed Oct-Feb

Improvements are steadily taking place at this privately run Highland hotel which is popular with anglers and holidaymakers. It offers a choice of comfortable lounges and a well stocked, snug bar. At dinner, guests help themselves from a hot buffet set out in the attractive dining room. Bedrooms, at present somewhat modestly furnished, are being refurbished.

5rmAnnexe7⇨🐾 TV available ® ✱ sB&Bfr£25
sB&B⇨🐾fr£30 dB&Bfr£50 dB&B⇨🐾£60-£73
CTV 40P ⇔ ✱ ♪

The Blacksmith's Arms Hotel ★★★ ❀

Deep in the heart of Ryedale yet easily accessible for touring the Yorkshire Dales and surrounding glorious countryside. A charming 16th century farmhouse that has been carefully restored and extended but still retains its atmosphere and old world charm. Dine in the elegant restaurant or relax with an aperitif in the beamed cocktail bar. Unwind in the comfortable beds, gracious furnishings and en suite facilities. All the bedrooms are harmoniously designed. Weddings, Family Celebrations and Corporate Hospitality are all well catered for. Short Breaks available.

**Hartoft End, Rosedale Abbey
Pickering, N Yorks YO18 8EN
Telephone: (07515) 331**

The ROSE & CROWN HOTEL

Christopher & Alison Davy

invite you to discover glorious Teesdale and relax at their
18th Century coaching inn
set on the middle green in one of England's prettiest villages.

13 en-suite rooms,
first class English cooking
and good old fashioned hospitality.

Egon Ronay Pub of the Year '93.

★★ 71% ❀❀

Romaldkirk, Barnard Castle
Co Durham DL12 9EB
Telephone Teesdale (0833) 50213

St. Enodoc Hotel
ROCK, NR. WADEBRIDGE,
★★ CORNWALL

**Telephone:
Trebetherick
(020 886) 3394
for brochure and tariff**

Spectacular views of the Camel Estuary. Private bathrooms, full central heating, colour TV and telephone in all bedrooms. Attractive restaurant serving fresh food with quality wines. Leisure complex provides heated swimming pool, squash, sauna, jacuzzi, solarium, snooker and gymnasium. Golf packages year round. Golf on adjoining St Enodoc Golf Course. Surfing, sailing, fishing, water-skiing and riding locally.

Rosehall - Ross-on-Wye

V ❀ ⚒ ✻ Bar Lunch £1.10-£8.50 Dinner £18.50 Last dinner 8pm
Credit Cards [1][3]

ROSSETT Clwyd Map 07 SJ35

★★★❀⚑**72%** Llyndir Hall
LL12 0AY (5m S of Chester follow signs for Pulford on B5445 on entering Rossett hotel is set back off road)
☎Chester(0244) 571648 FAX (0244) 571258

This imposing country house with modern extensions is set in several acres of mature parkland. Bedrooms in the new extension are large and comfortable. Public rooms include an elegant cocktail bar and sitting room, and the leisure centre has its own bar serving light meals. Restaurant food has much improved, with a fine selection offered from 3 menus.
38⇨↑✓in 12 bedrooms CTV in all bedrooms ®✻ T
✖ (ex guide dogs) ✻ sB⇨↑fr£74 dB⇨↑fr£110 (room only) 🅿
《 80P ✿ 🏊 (heated) solarium gymnasium croquet spa bath steam room *xmas*
🍷 English & French V ❀ ⚒ ✂ ✻ Lunch £11.50-£14.50 Dinner fr£17.50&alc Last dinner 10pm
CONF. Thtr 150 Class 50 Board 35 Del from £98
Credit Cards [1][2][3][5] £

★★★**70%** Rossett Hall
Chester Rd LL12 0DE (in centre of village on B5445) ☎Chester(0244) 571000 FAX (0244) 571505

Parts of this sound, well run hotel date back to 1750 and the original part is attractively creeper clad. There have been modern extensions in recent years and a range of bedrooms is now offered, including some with bathrooms suitable for disabled guests. There is a comfortable lounge with deep, relaxing sofas and armchairs, a lounge bar and a dining room where the daily changing set menu is supplemented by a good carte.
30⇨↑(2fb)✓in 5 bedrooms CTV in all bedrooms ®✻ T ✖
sB⇨↑£54.50-£68 dB⇨↑£62.50-£90 🅿
《 90P ✿ *xmas*
🍷 International V ❀ ⚒ ✂ ✻ Lunch £7.50-£12&alc Dinner £12.50-£15.50&alc Last dinner 10pm
CONF. Thtr 200 Class 100 Board 100 Del from £60
Credit Cards [1][2][3][5] £

ROSSINGTON South Yorkshire Map 08 SK69

★★★**64%** Mount Pleasant
Great North Rd DN11 0HP (On A638 Great North Rd 1.5m E of village)
☎Doncaster(0302) 868696 & 868219 FAX (0302) 865130
Closed 25 Dec

Formerly the estate house to Rossington Hall, and dating back to the 18th century, the hotel provides a wide variety of accommodation and plenty of cosy lounge areas. It stands in spacious grounds.
32⇨↑(4fb)4🛏 CTV in all bedrooms ®✻ T ✖ (ex guide dogs)
sB⇨↑£42-£52 dB⇨↑£52-£62 🅿
《 100P ✿ solarium gymnasium
🍷 English & French V ❀ ⚒ ✻ Lunch £7.95-£19.95 Dinner £11.95-£19.95 Last dinner 9.30pm
CONF. Thtr 60 Class 40 Board 40 Del from £75
Credit Cards [1][2][3][5] £

Remember to book early for holiday
and bank holiday times.

ROSS-ON-WYE Hereford & Worcester Map 03 SO62

See also **Goodrich, Pencraig** and **Symonds Yat**

★★★❀⚑**69%** Pengethley Manor
HR9 6LL (4m N on A49 Hereford rd)
☎Harewood End(098987) 211 FAX (098987) 238

Situated in its own 15 acres of gounrds, with an original Tudor oak panelled entrance hall, Pengethley Manor offers a variety of bedrooms. Public areas include a comfortable library with an open fire and a dining area overlooking the grounds. Chef Ferdinand Van Der Knaap presents à la carte and table d'hôte menus which offer a good balance of dishes showing imagination and skill.
11⇨↑Annexe13⇨↑(3fb)4🛏 CTV in all bedrooms ® T ✻
sB&B⇨↑£70-£115 dB&B⇨↑£100-£160 🅿
70P ✿ 🏊 (heated) ♪ snooker 9 hole mini golf croquet *xmas*
🍷 English & French V ❀ ⚒ ✻ Lunch £16 Dinner £24&alc Last dinner 9.30pm
Credit Cards [1][2][3][5] £

★★★**66%** Chase
Gloucester Rd HR9 5LH (E side of town, on A40)
☎(0989) 763161 FAX (0989) 768330

This former country house is set in several acres of attractive parkland, yet is just a few minutes from the town centre. It has just undergone a complete renovation programme and provides all the facilities expected of a modern commercial hotel.
39⇨↑(1fb)2🛏 CTV in all bedrooms ® T ✖ (ex guide dogs)
✻ sB&B⇨↑£50 dB&B⇨↑£60 🅿
《 200P ✿ *xmas*
V ❀ ⚒ ✻ Lunch £12.50&alc Dinner £19.95&alc Last dinner 9.45pm
Credit Cards [1][2][3][5]

★★★**65%** Royal
Palace Pound HR9 5HZ ☎(0989) 65105 FAX (0989) 768058

Built in 1837, the Royal is a traditional hotel, overlooking the horseshoe bend of the River Wye, and is equally suited to business or leisure guests. Most bedrooms have been refurbished, with attractive décor and soft furnishings. There is a comfortable guests' lounge where afternoon tea is served, a small bar popular with locals and residents alike, and a dining room overlooking the garden.
40⇨↑(4fb)✓in 11 bedrooms CTV in all bedrooms ® T ✻
sB⇨↑£75 dB⇨↑£95 (room only) 🅿
70P ✿ ♪ *xmas*
V ❀ ⚒ ✻ Sunday Lunch £9.95 Dinner £15.95&alc Last dinner 9.30pm
CONF. Thtr 80 Class 35 Board 25 Del from £80
Credit Cards [1][2][3][5]

★★❀⚑**74%** Peterstow Country House
Peterstow HR9 6LB (3m NE, off A49 next to St Peter's Church) (Logis) ☎(0989) 62826 FAX (0989) 67264

Courtesy and Care 1994

A very warm welcome awaits guests at this delightful Georgian rectory, standing in 25 acres of woodlands and pastures, and this, together with its high standards of service, has earned Peterstow an AA Courtesy and Care Award this year. The rooms are individually styled, some grand, some cottagey, with bold soft furnishings. The spacious flagstoned entrance hall is impressive, there is a cosy bar to one side, and a spacious drawing room to the other. The restaurant is the heart of the house, a civilised environment in which to enjoy chef Andrew Thomas' imaginative menus.

9⇨𝄞(3fb) CTV in all bedrooms ® T ✖ (ex guide dogs) ✱
sB&B⇨𝄞£38.50-£69 dB&B⇨𝄞£50-£90 🎵
60P 🐕 ❋ ♪ clay pigeon shooting nc8yrs *xmas*
♘ English & French V ♤ ⚌ Lunch £12.50 Dinner £19.50-£22.50 Last dinner 9pm
Credit Cards 1 2 3 5 £

★★ 71% *Glewstone Court*
Glewstone HR9 6AW ☎Llangarron(0989) 770367 FAX (0989) 770282
Closed 25-27 Dec
Set in 3 acres of mature trees and lawns overlooking orchards, this relaxing hotel is personally run by Christine and William Reeve-Tucker and has been thoughtfully furnished and decorated throughout. The comfortable, individually styled bedrooms are mostly very large, and there is an elegant drawing room with deep sofas and a roaring log fire.

7⇨𝄞1♨ CTV in all bedrooms ® T
20P 🐕 ❋ ♪ croquet lawn hot air ballooning
♘ English & French V ♤ Last dinner 9.30pm
Credit Cards 1 3

★★ 66% **Hunsdon Manor**
Gloucester Rd, Weston-Under-Penyard HR9 7PE (2m E A40)
☎(0989) 62748 & 63376 FAX (0989) 768318
Set in 2.5 acres of grounds, this personally run hotel retains traces of its origins as an Elizabethan manor house. Bedrooms, located in the main house and courtyard annexe, vary in size and style but all are ➧

The Chase Hotel
AT ROSS-ON-WYE

After complete refurbishment, the Hotel has become the premier Hotel in the area.

All bedrooms have en-suite facilities, together with colour T.V., Radio, Tea & Coffee making facilities, and Hairdryer.

The Restaurant enjoys a good reputation using fresh local produce.

Special rates available for weekends.
For a Brochure please contact:
**The Chase Hotel,
Gloucester Road,
Ross-on-Wye
Herefordshire HR9 5LH
Tel: (0989) 763161. Fax: 0989 768330**
AA ★ ★ ★   ETB ♛♛♛♛

Peterstow Country House
★ ★ C/H
❀❀

**PETERSTOW COUNTRY HOUSE
PETERSTOW, ROSS-ON-WYE,
HEREFORDSHIRE HR9 6LB
Tel: 0989 62826 Fax: 0989 67264**
*Award Winning Restaurant and Hotel
Country House Status*

Beautifully restored by its present owners Mike and Jeanne Denne, this magnificent Georgian rectory next to the village Church of St Peter is surrounded by 28 acres of pastures and woodlands. Well known for the hotel's warmth of hospitality Peterstow's centrepiece is its award winning restaurant, where modern English and French cuisine are served, the chefs consistently aiming to create new flavour combinations incorporating seasonal vegetables, fruit and organic produce from their adjoining farm. Dinner and light lunches served 7 days a week, also three course Traditional Sunday Lunch, morning coffee and afternoon teas.
Table D'Hôte Dinner £22.50 Three course lunches £12.50

Pengethley Manor

GEORGIAN COUNTRY HOTEL & RESTAURANT
Nr. Ross-on-Wye, Herefordshire HR9 6LL
Tel: Harewood End (098 987) 211
Fax: (098 987) 238

This delightful hotel and restaurant is quietly situated in 15 acres of gardens and grounds, has its own vineyard, with lovely views of the Herefordshire countryside.

The attractive, elegant restaurant features fresh local produce such as Wye Salmon, Herefordshire Beef and Welsh Lamb, and fresh herbs come from the hotel's own gardens.
A la Carte and Table D'hôte menus are available.

A separate Conference Centre provides everything you need for meetings 'away from it all'.

To help you relax, we have a heated outdoor swimming pool, 9 hole golf improvement course, designer walks, trout pond, croquet and snooker.

AA★★★ ❀
Egon Ronay
BTA Commended Country House Hotel
Derek Johansen Recommended Hotels,
British Relais Routier,
Arthur Eperon's British Selection

Ross-on-Wye - Rotherham

well equipped with modern amenities. Meals are available in both the bar and restaurant and friendly staff provide thoughtful services.
13🛏️🛁Annexe12🛏️🛁(3fb)2🛌 CTV in all bedrooms ® T ✱ sB&B🛏️🛁£38-£45 dB&B🛏️🛁£50-£70 🍴
55P 🎾 ❄️ sauna solarium *xmas*
V ♿ ❄️ ✱ Sunday Lunch £8.50-£12.50&alc Dinner £12.50-£14.50&alc Last dinner 9.30pm
CONF. Thtr 60 Class 42 Board 24 Del from £57.50
Credit Cards 1 2 3 5 £

★★**65%** **Bridge House**
Wilton HR9 6AA (adjacent A40/A49 junc beside the River Wye) ☎(0989) 62655
This small family-run hotel is situated between the town and the bypass in the village of Wilton. The food choice is quite good, the bar and lounge are both cosy and comfortable, and the bedrooms have modern facilities.
8🛏️🛁1🛌 CTV in all bedrooms ® T ✱ sB&B🛏️🛁£31.50-£33 dB&B🛏️🛁£54-£58 🍴
CTV 14P 🎾 ❄️ nc10yrs *xmas*
♿ English & French V Dinner £12.50-£13.50&alc Last dinner 9pm
Credit Cards 1 3

★★**63%** **King's Head**
8 High St HR9 5HL ☎(0989) 763174
Closed 24-26 Dec
Right in the centre of the picturesque town, this historic inn dates back to 1380. Old beams abound throughout the hotel and much local flavour is to be found in the bar and coffee lounge. Bedrooms are quite comfortable and good food is always available.
16🛏️🛁Annexe10🛏️🛁(6fb) CTV in all bedrooms ® T sB&B🛏️🛁fr£43 dB&B🛏️🛁fr£70 🍴
20P 🎾
V ♿ ❄️
Credit Cards 1 3 £

★★**63%** **Orles Barn**
Wilton HR9 6AE (off A40) ☎(0989) 62155 FAX (0989) 768470
Closed Nov
This family-run former farmhouse stands in attractive grounds. Most of the neat well maintained bedrooms have modern bathrooms and there is a cosy lounge bar leading to the restaurant, both offering a range of food.
9rm(8🛏️🛁)(1fb) CTV in all bedrooms ® sB&B🛏️🛁£30-£45 dB&B🛏️🛁£50-£65 🍴
𝅘𝅥 20P ❄️ ⌘ (heated) ⛳
♿ English, French & Spanish V ♿ ❄️ ✱ Lunch £8.50-£12.50&alc Dinner £10.75-£12.75&alc Last dinner 9pm
Credit Cards 1 2 3

★★**59%** **Chasedale**
Walford Rd HR9 5PQ (from Ross-on-Wye town centre head south on B4234, hotel 0.5m on left) ☎(0989) 62423
This family-run hotel is set in pleasant grounds which include mature trees and a kitchen garden. A start has been made to modernise the spacious bedrooms and a pine furnished suite has been completed. There is a pleasant lounge and bar, and a restaurant on 2 levels where a good choice of food is available.
10rm(9🛏️🛁)(3fb)✱in 1 bedroom CTV in all bedrooms ® T sB&Bfr£28 sB&B🛏️🛁£28-£29 dB&B£40-£42 dB&B🛏️🛁£56-£58 🍴
14P 🎾 *xmas*
♿ English & French V ♿ ❄️ ✱ Lunch £7.25-£7.50 Dinner £11.50-£11.75&alc Last dinner 9pm
Credit Cards 1 3 4 5 £

The AA's star rating scheme is the market leader in hotel classification.

ROSTHWAITE Cumbria Map **11** NY21
See also **Borrowdale**
★★★**61%** **Scafell**
CA12 5XB (on B5289) ☎Keswick(07687) 77208 FAX (07687) 77280
Closed 2 Jan-9 Feb
This popular family-run hotel is in beautiful surroundings alongside a fast flowing river. It provides modern bedrooms, comfortable lounges and a large bar where a good range of bar meals is served. A well produced dinner is served in the spacious, traditionally styled dining room by young attentive staff.
24🛏️🛁(3fb) CTV in all bedrooms ® T ✱ sB&B🛏️🛁£40-£51.50 dB&B🛏️🛁£80-£103 (incl dinner) 🍴
50P 🎾 *xmas*
♿ International V ♿ ❄️ Bar Lunch £7.75-£12.50alc
Credit Cards 1 3

ROSYTH Fife Map **11** NT18
★★**59%** **Gladyer Inn**
Heath Rd, off Ridley Dr KY11 2BT
☎Inverkeithing(0383) 419977 FAX (0383) 411728
Live entertainment is a regular feature at this purpose-built commercial and function hotel on the east side of town. Bedrooms are compact and functional, and public areas include a choice of lively bars, a foyer lounge and small restaurant.
21🛏️🛁(3fb) CTV in all bedrooms ® T sB&B🛏️🛁£30-£35 dB&B🛏️🛁£50-£55 🍴
𝄞 CTV 81P *xmas*
V ♿ Lunch £6-£12 High tea £5-£6 Dinner £13.50-£15&alc Last dinner 9.30pm
CONF. Class 80 Board 20 Del from £45
Credit Cards 1 2 3 £

See advertisement under **DUNFERMLINE**

ROTHERHAM South Yorkshire Map **08** SK49
★★★**70%** **Swallow**
West Bawtry Rd S60 4NA ☎(0709) 830630 FAX (0709) 830630
100🛏️🛁(2fb)✱in 44 bedrooms CTV in all bedrooms ®✱ T ✱ sB&B🛏️🛁£78 dB&B🛏️🛁£96 🍴
Lift 𝄞 222P 🅿️ (heated) gymnasium spa bath steam room sunbeds *xmas*
V ♿ ❄️ ✱ Lunch £8.95-£11.95&alc Dinner £15&alc Last dinner 10pm
CONF. Thtr 300 Class 120 Board 75 Del £100
Credit Cards 1 2 3 5

★★★**66%** **Rotherham Moat House**
Moorgate Rd S60 2BG (on A618)
☎(0709) 364902 FAX (0709) 368960
Over the last few years a third floor of bedrooms has been added to this hotel. These are modern and well furnished in comparison to the remaining rooms which are rather dated – the compact bathrooms are currently being redecorated. The leisure club is also undergoing extensive refurbishment.
80🛏️🛁(6fb)✱in 22 bedrooms CTV in all bedrooms ®✱ T
Lift 𝄞 CTV 95P sauna solarium gymnasium jacuzzi 🎵
♿ English & French V ♿ ❄️ ✱ Last dinner 9.45pm
Credit Cards 1 2 3 5

★★★**65%** **Consort**
Brampton Rd, Thurcroft S66 9JA
☎(0709) 530022 FAX (0709) 531529

Modern accommodation which is both well equipped and comfortable is provided by this hotel. The friendly proprietor and staff provide cheerful service in the newly refurbished restaurant and bar, and the comfortable airy lounge.

SCAFELL *Hotel*

ROSTHWAITE, BORROWDALE, CUMBRIA CA12 5XB
Tel: Borrowdale (07687) 77208. Fax: (07687) 77280

Situated in the heart of Borrowdale Valley, just off the main road which goes on to Honister Pass and Buttermere, the Scafell Hotel was formerly a Coaching Inn frequented by travellers making the journey over Honister Pass from Keswick to Cockermouth. Tastefully modernised it still retains its old world charm and character. 24 bedrooms all en-suite, our dining room/restaurant (open to non-residents) is renowned for its fine food and wines. 5 course table d'hôte, or late supper menu available. Fully licensed with cocktail and public (riverside) bar selling real ale, both well noted for bar lunches.

PENCRAIG COURT HOTEL & RESTAURANT

Nr. ROSS-ON-WYE
HEREFORDSHIRE
HR9 6HR
Tel: 0989-770306

Resident Proprietor:
Duncan Sykes

Georgian Country House Hotel with lovely gardens high on the banks of the River Wye between Ross and Monmouth. Very fine views across the Herefordshire countryside. The hotel has been in the same ownership since 1973 and offers a quiet, comfortable, relaxing atmosphere. All meals are freshly prepared to order. Quality but inexpensive wines from our cellar.

Open March to October
AA ★ ★

Price guide about £40 for 4-course dinner, bedroom with bath and English breakfast
Free colour brochure

YE HOSTELRIE HOTEL
GOODRICH, ROSS-ON-WYE,
HEREFORDSHIRE, HR9 6HX
SYMONDS YAT (0600) 890 241

Enjoy seclusion, comfort, and good food at this fully centrally heated 17th Century Inn. Sited in a beautiful part of the Wye Valley it affords easy access to the Forest of Dean and Rural Herefordshire. The Hotel has a reputation for quality food at a reasonable price. We offer salmon straight from the Wye, and use fresh vegetables whenever possible.
See directory under Goodrich   ★ ★

Hunsdon Manor Hotel ★★

Weston Under Penyard
Ross-on-Wye, Hereford & Worcester
Tel: (0989) 62748 and 63376

A 16th century Manor House given to Baron Hunsdon by Queen Elizabeth I. Fully licensed hotel and restaurant standing in 2 acres of gardens on the A40, 2 miles from Ross-on-Wye, 14 miles Gloucester. Ideally situated for exploring the beautiful Wye Valley, Royal Forest of Dean and the Welsh Borders. Colour TV, tea and coffee making facilities and direct dial telephone in all rooms. Ground floor rooms available overlooking garden. The Restaurant offers a wide choice of dishes.
Leisure facilities comprise Finnish sauna.

Personal attention from resident owner and Manager.

Conference facilities.

Rotherham - Rothley

18⇨♠(1fb) CTV in all bedrooms ® T ✗ (ex guide dogs)
sB&B⇨♠£25-£57 dB&B⇨♠£40-£67 ₽
₵ 90P
V ✪ ⌘ ✗ ✱ Lunch £13.95&alc Dinner £13.95&alc Last dinner 9.30pm
CONF. Thtr 300 Class 150 Board 40 Del £77
Credit Cards [1][2][3] £

★★★ 65% **Elton**
Main St, Bramley S66 0SF (3m E A631)
☎(0709) 545681 FAX (0709) 549100

Recent extensive alterations and renovation work have totally transformed this privately owned hotel. There is a new block of 16 spacious bedrooms, the original bedrooms have been upgraded and the restaurant has been enlarged.

13⇨♠Annexe16⇨♠(4fb)♠in 5 bedrooms CTV in all bedrooms ® T sB&B⇨♠£50-£60 dB&B⇨♠£70-£74 ₽
₵ 44P
♀ English & French V ✪ ⌘ ✗ Lunch £8.95-£10.50&alc Dinner £16.95&alc Last dinner 9.30pm
Credit Cards [1][2][3][5] £

★★ 66% **Brentwood**
Moorgate Rd S60 2TY ☎(0709) 382772 FAX (0709) 820289
Closed 26 & 27 Dec RS BH's

With gardens which were winners of the Rotherham in Bloom competition, this extended stone-built Victorian house is a pleasant place to stay. Many original features have been retained, such as stained glass and the moulded cornices. The a la carte restaurant is popular with locals and the bedrooms, in a purpose-built extension are well equipped.

33⇨♠Annexe10⇨♠(4fb)2♠ CTV in all bedrooms ® T
sB&B⇨♠£35-£48 dB&B⇨♠£40-£65 ₽
₵ 60P ✪ ♪ (grass)
♀ English & Continental V ✪ Lunch fr£11.50&alc Dinner £12.80-£16.50&alc Last dinner 9.30pm
Credit Cards [1][2][3][5] £

Campanile
Hellaby Industrial Estate, Lowton Way, Off Denby Way S66 8RY (junct 1 of M18. Follow directions to Maltby off roundabout. At traffic lights turn left and take 2nd road on left)
☎(0709) 700255 FAX (0709) 545169

A nearby bar and bistro restaurant provides refreshments for travellers staying at this modern accommodation building. Bedrooms are well equipped and have en suite bathrooms. For more details about Campanile, consult the Contents page, under Hotel Groups.

51⇨♠B⇨♠£35.75 (room only)
CONF. Thtr 35 Class 35 Board 25 Del from £42.80

Travel Inn
Bawtry Rd S65 3JB (on A631 towards Wickersley) ☎(0709) 543216

Purpose-built accommodation offers spacious and well equipped bedrooms, all with en suite bathrooms. Meals may be taken at the nearby family restaurant and pub. For more details about Travel Inns, consult the Contents Page, under Hotel Groups.

37⇨♠✱ B⇨♠£33.50 (room only)

The AA's star rating scheme is the market leader in hotel classification.

ROTHERWICK Hampshire Map 04 SU75

★★★★

★★★★♀♣ **TYLNEY HALL**
RG27 9AJ ☎(0256) 764881
FAX (0256) 768141

This impressive Grade II listed building with its tree-lined drive stands in 66 acres of parkland and gardens originally designed by Gertrude Jekyll to feature lakes and woodland and now being extensively restored. Public areas combine great comfort with the architectural splendour of Italianate ceilings, carved balustrades and a panelled library. A la carte and set daily menus in modern Anglo-French style, include such dishes as loin of pork with sage and onion stuffing or venison with a celeriac galette and Calvados sauce. Bedrooms in both the main house and sympathetically extended courtyard buildings are of good size, tastefully decorated and equipped with thoughtful extras. Many have fine views, and suites are available.

35⇨♠Annexe56⇨♠(1fb)3♠ CTV in all bedrooms ® T ✗ (ex guide dogs)
Lift ₵ 120P ⇔ ✪ ⊠ (heated) ⇨ (heated) ♪ (hard) snooker sauna gymnasium croquet ♫
♀ English & French V ✪ ⌘ ✗ Last dinner 9.30pm
Credit Cards [1][2][3][5]

See advertisement under BASINGSTOKE

ROTHES Grampian *Morayshire* Map 15 NJ24

★★★♣ 61% **Rothes Glen**
AB38 7AH (6m S of Elgin, on A941) ☎(03403) 254 & 255 FAX (03403) 566
Closed Jan-Feb

Designed by the architect of Balmoral Castle, this impressive baronial mansion is set in extensive grounds at the head of the Glen of Rothes. Day rooms are comfortable and relaxed, and bedrooms range from the compact and practical to large rooms furnished with antiques.

16⇨♠(4fb) CTV in all bedrooms ® T ✱ sB&B⇨♠£70-£75 dB&B⇨♠£110-£120 ₽
CTV 40P ⇔ ✪
✪ ⌘ ✗ Lunch £12.50 Dinner £25&alc Last dinner 9pm
Credit Cards [1][2][3][5]

ROTHESAY
See **Bute, Isle of**

ROTHLEY Leicestershire Map 08 SK51

★★★ 70% **Rothley Court**
Westfield Ln LE7 7LG (on B5328)
☎Leicester(0533) 374141 FAX (0533) 374483

In a rural location on the edge of Rothley village this lovely old manor house is set in 6 acres of grounds. The original 11th-century tenants constructed the Knights Templar chapel which adjoins the main house and is open to guests. Public rooms retain much of their original character, with fine fireplaces, oak panelling and stained glass windows. The comfortable lounge bar is softly lit and furnished with leather armchairs. Babington's restaurant offers some unusual choices of British cooking. Accommodation can be in traditionally furnished main house bedrooms, or in the annexe.

15⇨🛏Annexe21⇨🛏(3fb)2⚿⌇in 8 bedrooms CTV in all bedrooms ® T ✻ sB⇨🛏fr£75 dB⇨🛏fr£85 (room only) ℝ ⟨ 100P ✿ croquet putting green xmas
V ✿ Lunch £9.25-£12.25 High tea fr£6.50 Dinner £19.95&alc Last dinner 9.30pm
CONF. Thtr 100 Class 40 Board 35 Del from £70
Credit Cards [1][2][3][5]

★★ **70%** **The Limes**
35 Mountsorrel Ln LE7 7PS ☎Leicester0533 302301
Closed 23 Dec-2 Jan
An unassuming, ivy-clad turn-of-the-century building, The Limes is a popular hotel, its success due in large measure to the natural hospitality of the owners, Mr and Mrs Soper. Although some of the bedrooms may be on the small side, they are particularly well equipped with modern amenities.
11⇨🛏 CTV in all bedrooms ®⚿ T 🕱 (ex guide dogs) ✻ sB&B⇨🛏£39.50-£45 dB&B⇨🛏£45-£60
15P ⇔ nc
V ✻ Dinner £11.95-£13 Last dinner 9pm
Credit Cards [1][2][3]

ROTHWELL West Yorkshire Map **08** SE32
★★★★ **75%** **Oulton Hall**
Rothwell Ln LS26 8HN ☎(0532) 821000 FAX (0532) 828066

Set in lovely grounds and surrounded by acres of parkland, this is a superb conversion and restoration of an elegant hall. Enthusiastic management and smartly uniformed staff are particularly cheerful and helpful, successfully combining professional service with a friendly, caring manner. Stylish and comfortable public rooms have been faithfully restored, with ornate plasterwork, hand finished timbers and antique furniture. Bedrooms are attractive and comfortable, with good modern facilities; a high proportion are no-smoking rooms.
152⇨🛏(4fb)⌇in 128 bedrooms CTV in all bedrooms ®⚿ T ✻ sB&B⇨🛏£85 dB&B⇨🛏£95 ℝ
Lift ⟨ 260P ✿ ▤ (heated) ▶ 18 squash snooker sauna solarium gymnasium xmas
♨ English & French V ✿ ⚘ ⌇ ✻ Lunch £11 Dinner £10&alc Last dinner 10pm
CONF. Thtr 338 Class 200 Board 34 Del £145
Credit Cards [1][2][3][5]

ROUSDON Devon Map **03** SY29
★★ **64%** **Orchard Country**
DT7 3XW (off A3052 between Lyme Regis & Seaton)
☎Lyme Regis(0297) 442972
Closed Nov-Mar
The Orchard Country is a peaceful little hotel in immaculate gardens. There is a comfortable lounge with dispense bar, and a well maintained dining room, together with useful modern bedrooms providing essential facilities. High standards are maintained under the careful direction of the resident owners. Daily changing menus offer a straightforward choice.
12⇨🛏⌇in 2 bedrooms CTV in all bedrooms ® sB&B⇨🛏£38 dB&B⇨🛏£64 ℝ
CTV 30P ✿ nc8yrs
V ✿ ⚘ ⌇ ✻ Bar Lunch £5 Dinner £15 Last dinner 8pm
Credit Cards [1][3]   £

ROWARDENNAN Central Stirlingshire Map **10** NS39
★ **58%** **Rowardennan Hotel Loch Lomond**
G63 0AR (access via B837) ☎Balmaha(036087) 273 FAX (036087) 251
Closed Nov RS Oct-Mar
On the eastern shore of Loch Lomond surrounded by beautifully rugged scenery, this hotel offers modest, but comfortable and warm

accommodation. It is particularly popular with walkers travelling the West Highland Way, which passes the hotel. A good range of bar meals is available all day in season.
11rm(1⇨)(2fb) CTV in all bedrooms ® sB&B£22-£25 dB&B£36-£45 dB&B⇨🛏fr£45 Continental breakfast
CTV 50P ⇔ water-skiing boating
V ✿ Bar Lunch £3.50-£10 Dinner fr£13.50
Last dinner 8.45pm   £

ROWEN Gwynedd Map **06** SH77
★★ 🛌 **63%** **Tir-y-Coed Country House**
LL32 8TP (turn off B5106 into unclassified road signposted Rowen, hotel is on fringe of village) ☎Tynygroes(0492) 650219
Closed Xmas & New Year RS Nov-Feb
This large, well maintained house is set in spacious mature gardens and is situated on the edge of a small village in the picturesque Conwy Valley.
7⇨🛏Annexe1🛏(1fb) CTV in all bedrooms ®
sB&B⇨🛏£21.25-£25.25 dB&B⇨🛏£40-£45.90 ℝ
8P ⇔ ✿ ♨
✿ ⚘ ⌇ Bar Lunch £2.50-£7.50alc Dinner £10.45 Last dinner 7.30pm   £

ROWSLEY Derbyshire Map **08** SK26
★★★ 🛌 **64%** **East Lodge Country House**
DE4 2EF ☎Matlock(0629) 734474 FAX (0629) 733949
This country house is set in 10 acres of well kept gardens and grounds, which include a magnificent seasonal display of rhododendrons and an ornamental pool. Relaxed, informal service is provided by the resident proprietors and their staff. Public rooms are comfortable and bedrooms are individually styled, and a set price menu provides freshly prepared dishes.
14⇨🛏(1fb) CTV in all bedrooms ® T 🕱 ✻ sB&B⇨🛏£48-£55 dB&B⇨🛏£70-£95
30P ⇔ ✿ croquet lawn xmas
♨ International ✿ ⚘ ⌇ Lunch £11.50-£13.50&alc Dinner £18.50-£20 Last dinner 8.30pm
Credit Cards [1][2][3][5]   £

ROY BRIDGE Highland Inverness-shire Map **14** NN28
★★★ **62%** **Glenspean Lodge**
PH31 4AW (2m E) ☎Spean Bridge(0397) 712223 FAX (0397) 712660
Improvements continue at this family-run holiday and sporting hotel, in well tended grounds. Public rooms have been substantially refurbished over the past few years and offer comfortable appointments. Bedrooms are tastefully decorated and have smart modern bathrooms.
12rm(9⇨🛏)(2fb) CTV in all bedrooms ® T
CTV 30P 1 (£5 per night) ✿ 🎣 clay pigeon & rough shooting stalking
♨ Scottish & French V ✿ ⚘ ⌇ Last dinner 9.30pm
Credit Cards [1][3]
See advertisement under FORT WILLIAM

★★ **60%** **Stronlossit**
PH31 4AG ☎Speanbridge(0397) 712253
Closed 10 Nov-10 Dec & Jan
This family-run tourist hotel at the east end of the village offers a blend of the old and new. Public areas provide traditional comfort while bedrooms are bright and equipped with modern amenities.
9⇨🛏(2fb) CTV in all bedrooms ®
30P ✿
V ✿ ⚘ Last dinner 9.30pm
Credit Cards [1][2][3][5]
See advertisement under FORT WILLIAM

Ruabon - Runcorn

ROZEL BAY
See **Jersey** under **Channel Islands**

RUABON Clwyd Map 07 SJ34

★★ 56% Wynnstay Arms
High St LL14 6BL (off A483) (Frederic Robinson)
☎(0978) 822187
This former coaching inn in the village centre provides modest but comfortable accommodation and has a small grill restaurant. Friendly staff provide hospitable service.
9rm(3⇨🛁)(1fb) CTV in all bedrooms ® sB&Bfr£28 sB&B⇨🛁fr£33 dB&Bfr£38 dB&B⇨🛁fr£43
80P 2🚗
♀ English & French V ♂ Lunch fr£7.50&alc Dinner fr£9.50&alc Last dinner 9.45pm
CONF. Thtr 100 Board 50
Credit Cards 1 2 3 4 5 £

RUAN HIGH LANES Cornwall & Isles of Scilly
Map 02 SW93

★★ 71% Hundred House
TR2 5JR (from A390, 4m W of St Austell turn left onto B3287 to Tregony/St Mawes, turn left onto A3078 to St Mawes, hotel 4m along on right) ☎Truro(0872) 501336
Closed Nov-28 Feb
This delightful country house style hotel is personally run in a relaxed and friendly style by Mike and Kitty Eccles. Bedrooms continue to be upgraded and each is prettily decorated in an individual style. The comfortable lounge, quiet library and convivial bar are filled with ornaments, books and fresh flowers, and Kitty Eccles provides a simple home-cooked dinner.
10⇨🛁 CTV in all bedrooms ® T sB&B⇨🛁£42-£50 dB&B⇨🛁£84-£100 (incl dinner) 🍴
15P 🚲 ✿ croquet nc6yrs
♂ 🍷 High tea £3 Dinner £18.50 Last dinner 6pm
Credit Cards 1 3

★★ 69% Pendower
Gerrans Bay TR2 5LW (at Pendower Beach)
☎Truro(0872) 501257
Closed Dec-Feb
Along a quiet country lane towards Pendower beach, this hotel offers magnificent views far out across the peninsula. Bedrooms are bright and fresh and are equipped with modern conveniences. Public areas are well presented, and the TV lounge has sea views. Tranquility is carefully guarded by the friendly proprietors.
14⇨🛁(2fb) CTV in all bedrooms ® T ✳ sB&B⇨🛁£40-£50 dB&B⇨🛁£72-£100 (incl dinner)
30P 2🚗 (£1 per day) 🚲 ✿ 🏊 nc12yrs
V ♂ 🍷 ⚡ ✳ Lunch £9.50&alc Dinner £6-£15alc Last dinner 9pm
Credit Cards 1 3 £

RUGBY Warwickshire Map 04 SP57

★★★ 60% Grosvenor
Clifton Rd CV21 3QQ ☎(0788) 535686 FAX (0788) 541297
This privately owned and run hotel near the town centre offers good though somewhat compact bedrooms and public areas which include a popular restaurant and small bar.
21⇨🛁 CTV in all bedrooms ® T 🐾 (ex guide dogs)
((40P 🚲 📺 (heated) sauna solarium gymnasium jacuzzi 🎵
V ♂ 🍷 Last dinner 10pm
CONF. Thtr 35 Class 14 Board 24 Del from £99
Credit Cards 1 2 3 5

★★ 64% Hillmorton Manor
78 High St, Hillmorton CV21 4EE (2m SE off A428)
☎(0788) 565533 & 572403 FAX (0788) 540027
This personally run hotel in a Victorian manor house in the eastern suburbs of Rugby has attractively decorated bedrooms with modern furnishings and facilities. Public rooms include an elegant restaurant, relaxing lounge bar and small lounge area with open fires.
11⇨🛁(1fb) CTV in all bedrooms ® T 🐾 (ex guide dogs) ✳
sB&B⇨🛁£35-£45 dB&B⇨🛁£45-£58
40P
♀ English & French V ♂ ✳ Lunch £9-£10.50 Dinner £14.50 Last dinner 10pm
Credit Cards 1 2 3 4

Forte Posthouse
NN6 7XR ☎Crick (0788) 822101 FAX (0788) 823595
(For full entry see Crick)

FORTE Posthouse

RUGELEY Staffordshire Map 07 SK01

★★ 59% Cedar Tree
Main Road, Brereton WS15 1DY (on A51, between Rugeley & Lichfield) (Logis) ☎(0889) 584241
Closed 3 days Xmas RS Sun evenings
The Cedar Tree is a busy, modest business hotel. The restaurant and bar have a traditional style of décor and offer a range of menus to suit all tastes.
14rm(7⇨🛁)Annexe14⇨🛁(1fb) CTV in 25 bedrooms ® T 🐾 CTV 200P squash solarium pool table
♀ English & French V ♂ Lunch £7-£10.50&alc Dinner fr£10.50&alc Last dinner 9.30pm
Credit Cards 1 2 3 5 £

Forte Travelodge
Western Springs Rd WS15 2AS (on A51/B5013)
☎(0889) 570096 Central Res (0800) 850950

FORTE Travelodge

This modern building offers a good standard of accommodation for overnight stops. Smart, sapcious and well equipped bedrooms, all with en suite bathrooms, are suitable for family use, and meals may be taken at the nearby family restaurant. For more details about Travelodges, consult the Contents page, under Hotel Groups.
32⇨🛁 ✳ B⇨🛁£31.95 (room only)

RUNCORN Cheshire Map 07 SJ58

Campanile
Lowlands Rd WA7 5TP (signposted from junct 12 of M56) ☎(0928) 581771 FAX (0928) 581730

A nearby bar and bistro restaurant provides refreshments for travellers staying at this modern accommodation building. Bedrooms are well equipped and have en suite bathrooms. For more details about Campanile, consult the Contents page, under Hotel Groups.
53⇨🛁 B⇨🛁£35.75 (room only)
CONF. Thtr 35 Class 35 Board 25 Del from £42.80

Forte Posthouse
Wood Ln, Beechwood WA7 3HA ☎(0928) 714000 FAX (0928) 714611

FORTE Posthouse

Suitable for both the business and leisure traveller, this bright hotel provides modern accommodation in well equipped bedrooms with en suite bathrooms. For more details about Forte Posthouse hotels, consult the Contents page, under Hotel Groups.
135⇨🛁 B⇨🛁£41.50-£53.50 (room only)
CONF. Thtr 500 Class 200 Board 12 Del £89.50

For key to symbols see the Bookmark.

Rushden - Rye

RUSHDEN Northamptonshire Map 04 SP96

Forte Travelodge
Saunders Lodge (on A45)
☎(0933) 57008 Central Res (0800) 850950

This modern building offers a good standard of accommodation for overnight stops. Smart, spacious and well equipped bedrooms, all with en suite bathrooms, are suitable for family use, and meals may be taken at the nearby family restaurant. For more details about Travelodges, consult the Contents page, under Hotel Groups.
40⇨♠✱ B⇨♠£31.95 (room only)

RUSHYFORD Co Durham Map 08 NZ22

★★★**60%** **Eden Arms Swallow**
DL17 0LL (on A167)
☎Bishop Auckland(0388) 720541 FAX (0388) 721871

This attractive old coaching inn has been considerably extended and modernised and offers a good all round standard of accommodation with well furnished bedrooms and extensive public areas.
46rm(45⇨♠)(4fb)1⊞ ⊬in 20 bedrooms CTV in all bedrooms ® sB&B⇨♠£45-£75 dB&B⇨♠£60-£90 ⊟
《 200P ✿ ⊠ (heated) sauna solarium gymnasium jacuzzi steam room impulse shower *xmas*
♀ English & French V ♂ ⊻ ✱ Lunch £4.95-£7.95&alc
CONF. Thtr 100 Class 40 Board 50 Del from £70
Credit Cards 1 2 3 5

RUSPER West Sussex Map 04 TQ23

★★★**65%** **Ghyll Manor**
RH12 4PX ☎(0293) 871571 FAX (0293) 871419

Set in 40 acres of grounds and landscaped gardens, this historic manor house has been sympathetically converted, furnished in period style and includes a small oak-panelled library with open log fire and an elegant restaurant. Bedrooms, many in the stable mews or modern annexes, are all equipped with good facilities and include very spacious suites.
7⇨♠Annexe18⇨♠(2fb)5⊞ ⊬in 7 bedrooms CTV in all bedrooms ® T ✖ sB⇨♠£75-£90 dB⇨♠£75-£90 (room only) ⊟
《 CTV 150P ✿ ♪ (hard) croquet lawn *xmas*
V ♂ ⊻ ✱ Lunch £13.95 Dinner £16.95&alc Last dinner 9.15pm
Credit Cards 1 2 3 5

RUTHIN Clwyd Map 06 SJ15

★★★**63%** **Ruthin Castle**
LL15 2NU ☎(0824) 702664 FAX (0824) 705978

This hotel is in an authentic castle. The ruins and dungeons of the original 13th-century castle can still be seen, but happily the hotel accommodation is far more inviting. Traditionally furnished bedrooms are all spacious and some are very large indeed. Public rooms are also large and medieval banquets are a popular event. Set in 30 acres of parkland, the hotel is understandably popular with tourists, but also caters for business people.
58⇨♠(6fb)1⊞ CTV in all bedrooms ® T ✖ (ex guide dogs) sB&B⇨♠£59-£65 dB&B⇨♠£79-£85 ⊟
Lift 《 CTV 200P ✿ ♪ snooker *xmas*
♀ International V ♂ ⊻ Sunday Lunch £5.95-£8.95 Dinner £12-£21 Last dinner 9.30pm
CONF. Thtr 150 Class 60 Board 60 Del from £66
Credit Cards 1 2 3 5

★**66%** **Ye Olde Anchor Inn**
Rhos St LL15 1DX ☎(0824) 702813 FAX (0824) 703050
9⇨♠ CTV in all bedrooms ®⊻ ✱ sB&B⇨♠£25 dB&B⇨♠£42 ⊟
CTV 20P ♪ *xmas*
♀ English & French V ♂ ⊻ ⊬ ✱ Lunch £6.95 High tea £4.50 Dinner £9.50-£16.50alc Last dinner 9.30pm
Credit Cards 1 3

RYDE

See **Wight, Isle of**

RYE East Sussex Map 05 TQ92

★★★**⬢64%** *Mermaid Inn*
Mermaid St TN31 7EU (Cinque Ports) ☎(0797) 223065 FAX (0797) 226995

The ancient Mermaid Inn was rebuilt in 1420, and is one of the oldest inns in England, full of period charm, with oak panelling, beams, wall paintings and the inevitable creaking floorboards. The intimate restaurant overlooks the courtyard and fountain and Chef Steven Call offers a daily changing menu as well as a traditional-style carte. No two bedrooms are the same and they vary from the grand (Dr Syn's Bedchamber) to more compact doubles.
28rm(21⇨♠5♠)3⊞ CTV in all bedrooms T ✖ (ex guide dogs)
《 CTV 25P nc8yrs
V ♂ Last dinner 9.15pm
Credit Cards 1 2 3 4 5

★★**69%** *Broomhill Lodge*
Rye Foreign TN31 7UN (1.5m N on A268) ☎Iden(0797) 280421 FAX (0797) 280402

This delightful 19th-century Jacobean house with its friendly, informal atmosphere enjoys lovely views over rolling farmland. It has been the subject of major improvements, the elegant drawing

Pendower Hotel

Gerrans Bay, Ruan High Lanes ★★
Nr. Truro, Cornwall. Tel: (0872) 501257

Superbly situated above Gerrans Bay and surrounded by National Trust land, this 14 bedroom, family run hotel offers a warm welcome. All rooms are centrally heated, fully en-suite with colour TV, D/D telephone and tea/coffee making facilities. The hotel prides itself for its cuisine — special diets catered for if advised. Children over 12 and dogs welcome.

Rye - St Albans

room now restored to its former glory. The rear extension contains a modern dining room and a small bar which leads onto the patio and two acres of well kept gardens. Bedrooms are individual, all pleasantly coordinated and with modern facilities.
12⇌🏠2🛏 CTV in all bedrooms ® T 🐾 (ex guide dogs) CTV 20P ❋ snooker sauna
♀ English & French V ✿ ⚲ Last dinner 9.30pm
Credit Cards [1][2]

★★**69%** **The George**
High St TN31 7JP ☎(0797) 222114 FAX (0797) 224065

FORTE Heritage

This welcoming 16th-century coaching inn offers a good standard of accommodation in bedrooms with attractive soft furnishings and modern facilities. Renovated public areas include a traditional bar and a choice of lounges, one warmed by its original log-burning fire, the other more spacious and elegant. The restaurant is popular for light lunches, and provides for relaxed dining.
22⇌🏠(2fb)⚥ 6 bedrooms CTV in all bedrooms ® T ✱ sB⇌🏠£70 dB⇌🏠£80-£100 (room only) 🍴
9P 9🚗 xmas
V ✿ ⚲ ✱ Sunday Lunch £10.95 Dinner £15.95&alc Last dinner 9pm
Credit Cards [1][2][3][5]

SAFFRON WALDEN Essex Map 05 TL53

★★**65%** *Saffron*
10-18 High St CB10 1AY ☎(0799) 522676 FAX (0799) 513979

This friendly 16th-century inn at the centre of the attractive market town has recently been upgraded and extended to provide a new reception, smart lounge and elegant conservatory restaurant with a choice of interesting menus. Improvements are now planned for the bedrooms, which vary in size and style.
21rm(8⇌8🏠)(2fb)3🛏 CTV in all bedrooms ® T
10P
♀ English & French V ✿ Last dinner 9.30pm
Credit Cards [1][2][3][5]

ST AGNES Cornwall & Isles of Scilly Map 02 SW75

★★♨**66%** **Rose in Vale Country House**
Rose in Vale, Mithian TR5 0QD ☎Truro(0872) 552202 FAX (0872) 552700

Set in 11 acres of gardens and grounds with a swimming pool and sun terrace, this attractive Georgian country house is continually being improved. Many of the bedrooms have been very smartly refurbished, with good facilities; remaining rooms in the main house are smaller and cosier. There are comfortable lounges, now also being upgraded, and an increased choice of food and wines.
17⇌🏠1🛏 CTV in all bedrooms ® T ✱ sB&B⇌🏠£44-£45 dB&B⇌🏠£78-£90 (incl dinner) 🍴
CTV 40P ❋ ⚲ (heated) solarium croquet badminton table tennis billiards ⛳ xmas
♀ English & Continental V ✿ ⚲ ⚥ ✱ Lunch £7.95 Dinner £15.50&alc Last dinner 8.30pm
Credit Cards [1][2][3]

★★**66%** **Rosemundy House**
Rosemundy TR5 0UF (turn off A30 to St Agnes continue for approx 3m, on entering village take turning on the right signposted Rosemundy, hotel is at foot of the hill)
☎(0872) 552101
Closed 3 Oct-5 Apr

Competently and family owned, this hotel stands in lovely, well tended gardens with a sun terrace. Constant upgrading has provided a choice of comfortable lounges, a convivial bar area and neat, attractively presented bedrooms, and there is a warm, friendly atmosphere throughout.

44⇌🏠(16fb) CTV in all bedrooms ® sB&B⇌🏠£25-£39 dB&B⇌🏠£50-£78 (incl dinner)
CTV 50P ❋ ⚲ (heated) badminton games room croquet putting
✿ ⚲ ⚥ Bar Lunch £1.50-£5 Dinner £12 Last dinner 8pm
Credit Cards [1][3]

★★♨**62%** **Beach**
Porthtowan TR4 8AE (on the beach road)
☎Porthtowan(0209) 890228
Closed Jan & last 2 wks Nov

There are steep steps down from the car park to this cliff side hotel, but the climbing is repaid by magnificent views across Porthtowan beach from almost every one of its bright cosy rooms. Home-cooked evening meals are offered from an interesting table d'hôte and small a la carte menu.
11🏠 CTV in all bedrooms ® T ✱ sB&B🏠£28-£60 dB&B🏠£56-£120 (incl dinner) 🍴
13P ⚛ ❋ xmas
♀ English & French ✿ ⚲ High tea £3 Dinner £8-£16&alc Last dinner 8pm
Credit Cards [1][2][3][5]

★**67%** **Sunholme**
Goonvrea Rd TR5 0NW (on B3277, leisure park on right, museum on left. Turn left after 150 yds.) ☎(0872) 552318 & 552154
Closed Jan

A friendly holiday hotel commanding spectacular views of surrounding countryside, offers simply furnished bedrooms which are tastefully decorated with coordinating colour schemes. The comfortable lounge and bar promote a relaxed, easy going atmosphere, and the restaurant's table d'hôte menu provides a limited choice of home-cooked dishes.
10🏠(4fb) CTV in all bedrooms ® T ✱ sB&B🏠£25-£28 dB&B🏠£50-£56 🍴
CTV 12P ⚛ ❋ xmas
✿ ⚲ ⚥ ✱ Lunch £10-£12 Dinner £11-£12.50 Last dinner 5pm
Credit Cards [1][2][3]

ST ALBANS Hertfordshire Map 04 TL10

★★★★♨**72%** **Sopwell House Hotel & Country Club**
Cottonmill Ln, Sopwell AL1 2HQ (follow St Albans sign to M10 rbt then take A414, first left and follow Sopwell signs)
☎(0727) 864477 FAX (0727) 844741/845636

Once the country home of Lord Mountbatten, this delightful Georgian house in 11 acres of gardens has been considerably extended over the years. Bedrooms, in the original house and the new wings, are all furnished to the highest standard, with elegant drapes and marble bathrooms. Bejerano's Brasserie is the informal option for meals, with many calorie counted dishes. More intimate is the Magnolia conservatory restaurant where chef Andrew Bennet presents traditional English lunch menus and an imaginative seasonal carte. Presentation is refreshingly simple and the emphasis is on flavours. Mille-feuilles of duck: tasty duck confit layered between crispy potato cakes and set on a blackcurrant vinegar sauce is particularly popular.
92⇌🏠(6fb)22🛏 CTV in all bedrooms ®⚡ T sB⇌🏠£67.50-£99.50 dB⇌🏠£84.75-£111.50 (room only) 🍴
Lift (200P ❋ ▭ (heated) snooker sauna solarium gymnasium health & beauty spa steam room whirlpool xmas
V ✿ ⚲ ✱ Lunch £14.95-£18.50&alc Dinner fr£19.50&alc Last dinner 10pm
Credit Cards [1][2][3][5]

For full, independent restaurant reviews, see the
AA Abbey Well *Restaurant Guide*.

HIDDEN TREASURES . . . ?

This 16th Century Building has been extensively refurbished over the last two years and now boasts a charming conservatory restaurant and a relaxing residents lounge. All our rooms are individually decorated and furnished. Three of these are exceptional, having four poster beds and luxury bathrooms.

The food in our à la carte restaurant (with a daily changing Table d'hôte menu) is prepared to the highest standards, and you can be assured of a friendly welcome.

The SAFFRON Hotel ★★
The High Street
Saffron Walden, Essex CB10 2AY
Telephone 0799 522676 Fax 0799 513979

NEAR RYE
FLACKLEY ASH HOTEL
Peasmarsh, near Rye,
East Sussex ★★★
Telephone 0797 230651
Fax 0797 230510

A Georgian Country House Hotel set in five acres of beautiful grounds in a quiet village four miles northwest of Rye. Speciality candlelit restaurant serves fresh local fish, fresh vegetables and Scotch steaks. Four poster bed deluxe rooms and suites available. Indoor swimming pool, saunas, whirlpool spa, mini-gym, and solarium. Explore Rye and the historic castles and gardens of Sussex and Kent.

2 NIGHT BREAKS FROM £114 PER PERSON Clive and Jeanie Bennett

Sopwell House
Hotel
and
Country Club

. . . for business, pleasure and leisure

An elegant Georgian country house set in 12 acres of grounds in unspoiled countryside, yet only minutes off the M1, M10 and M25 and half an hour from London.

The well appointed 92 bedrooms with every amenity assure a high degree of comfort — all furnished in true country style, including many four posters and two suites.

Dine in the award winning Magnolia Conservatory Restaurant with resident pianist on Friday and Saturday evenings, or for light, healthy eating, sample a dish in the Club Brasserie. Indulge in a traditional English tea in the library or on the terrace.

The lavish function rooms, with magnificent St Albans ballroom overlooking the gardens, are eminently suited for small numbers to many hundreds.

Relax in an oasis of luxury and tranquillity in the Country Club and Spa with indoor pool, spa bath, steam and sauna, fitness centre and hairdressing salon. Pamper yourself from a wide range of treatments in the health and beauty spa.

Whatever the occasion, we extend our reputation for hospitality and service and offer the perfect venue.

Special break programmes include Health and Fitness, Easter and Christmas.

★★★★   Cottonmill Lane, Sopwell, St. Albans, Hertfordshire AL1 2HQ   COMMENDED
Telephone: (0727) 864477   Fax: (0727) 844741/845636

St Albans - St Andrews

★★★ ❀73% Noke Thistle
Watford Rd AL2 3DS (2.75m S at junct A405/B4630) ☎(0727) 854252 FAX (0727) 841906

This well managed hotel is built around an attractive country house. Executive bedrooms in the new wing are elegantly decorated and furnished, with many extras; the less luxurious club rooms are being upgraded. A cocktail bar lounge leads to the intimate restaurant where chef Derek Abbot offers imaginative, sometimes ambitious dishes. Less formal food is served in the American-themed bar.

111⇌♠(4fb)⌁in 21 bedrooms CTV in all bedrooms ® T ✱ sB⇌♠£79-£85 dB⇌♠£89-£95 (room only) ☒
(150P ✿
♀ International V ♢ ⚖ ⌁ ✱ Lunch £14-£17.50&alc Dinner £17.50-£21&alc Last dinner 10pm
CONF. Thtr 50 Class 22 Board 24 Del from £105
Credit Cards ① ② ③ ④ ⑤

★★★ 65% St Michael's Manor
Fishpool St AL3 4RY ☎(0727) 864444 FAX (0727) 848909
Closed 27-30 Dec

Warm hospitality and good old-fashioned services are the keynotes at this charming old manor house, which is set in 5 acres of beautiful gardens with a lake and ducks. Although some bedrooms remain dated, improvements are steadily being made, several rooms have been completely refurbished. Traditional public areas include a restaurant and lounge with views over the grounds.

22⇌4⌑ CTV in all bedrooms T ✱ sB&B⇌♠£50-£80 dB&B⇌♠£80-£100
(CTV 80P ⇔ ✿
♀ English & French V Lunch £16.50 Dinner £19 Last dinner 9pm
Credit Cards ① ② ③ ⑤

★★★ 64% Hertfordshire Moat House
London Rd, Markyate AL3 8HH (Exit M1 junct 9 north towards Dunstable/Whipsnade hotel is 1m from motorway on right)
☎(0582) 840840 FAX (0582) 842282

Well furnished and nicely appointed bedrooms are offered at this purpose-built hotel. The restaurant is pleasant and offers some good dishes from the carte and the set menu.

89⇌♠(16fb)⌁in 16 bedrooms CTV in all bedrooms ® ⍁ T ✱ sB⇌♠£50-£79 dB⇌♠£60-£89 (room only) ☒
(350P solarium gymnasium
♀ International V ♢ ⚖ ⌁ ✱ Lunch £13.95-£16.95&alc Dinner £13.95-£16.95&alc Last dinner 10pm
CONF. Thtr 350 Class 120 Board 60 Del from £85
Credit Cards ① ② ③ ⑤

★★ 59% Avalon
260 London Rd AL1 1TJ ☎(0727) 856757 FAX (0727) 856757

This extended detached house is set back from the A1081. Bedrooms are all of a good standard, with attractive coordinated décor and fabrics and modern facilities. At the time of our visit public areas were restricted to a small TV lounge and compact dining room offering a simple, limited choice dinner, but the addition of a lounge bar was imminent.

9⇌♠(3fb) CTV in all bedrooms ® T ⚔
CTV 12P
♀ English, Italian & Oriental ♢
Credit Cards ① ③

ST ANDREWS Fife Map 12 NO51

★★★★
★★★★❀❀ ST ANDREWS OLD COURSE HOTEL
Old Station Rd KY16 9SP ☎(0334) 74371 FAX (0334) 77668

Overlooking the 17th hole of the famous Old Course, the hotel's starkly modern exterior belies its elegance. An intimate library lounge leads off the spacious foyer, and there is an attractive conservatory for light meals during the summer as well as a cocktail bar and grill restaurant. Luxurious bedrooms include marble bathrooms, and suites have stunning views of the Old Course. Chef Billy Campbell produces straightforward and frequently changing menus. Typical of his repertoire are dishes such as terrine of wild mushrooms with pickled walnut dressing, breast of guinea fowl with roasted shallots and garlic, or darne of salmon with sorrel sauce.

125⇌♠ CTV in all bedrooms T ✱ sB&B⇌♠£150-£205 dB&B⇌♠£200-£235 ☒
Lift (150P ✿ ▭ (heated) sauna solarium gymnasium health spa jacuzzi
♀ Scottish & French V ♢ ⚖ ✱ Lunch £2.25-£12.50alc Dinner fr£32.50 Last dinner 10pm
Credit Cards ① ② ③ ⑤

★★★★ 59% Rusacks
Pilmour Links KY16 9JQ ☎(0334) 74321 FAX (0334) 77896

FORTE GRAND

Golf enthusiasts at this traditional Victorian hotel can enjoy a view of the 1st tee and 18th fairway of the Old Course. Bedrooms are traditionally furnished and, when the inspection visit took place, some offered scope for refurbishment. The foyer and sun lounges are attractive.

50⇌♠⌁in 5 bedrooms CTV in all bedrooms ® T ✱ sB⇌♠£90-£95 dB⇌♠£130-£145 (room only) ☒
Lift (21P ⇔ sauna solarium xmas
♀ European V ♢ ⚖ ✱ Lunch £7-£10.50 Dinner £24.95&alc Last dinner 10pm
Credit Cards ① ② ③ ⑤

★★★ ❀71% Rufflets Country House
Strathkinness Low Rd KY16 9TX (1.5m W on B939) (SCOTLAND'S HERITAGE HOTELS) ☎(0334) 72594 FAX (0334) 78703
RS Nov-Apr

This hotel stands in 10 acres of award-winning gardens and is built around a striking private house which has an informal and friendly atmosphere. Bedrooms are individually decorated with attractive fabrics and have modern facilities. With lovely views of the gardens and open fires in winter, public rooms are relaxing. The Garden restaurant specialises in Scottish dishes using home-grown produce where possible.

23⇌♠ Annexe3⇌♠(10fb)1⌁in 8 bedrooms CTV in all bedrooms ® T ⚔ (ex guide dogs) sB&B⇌♠£65-£75 dB&B⇌♠£130-£150 ☒
(50P 2⛟ ✿ putting xmas
V ♢ ⚖ ⌁ Lunch £14.50 Dinner £23.50&alc Last dinner 9.30pm
CONF. Thtr 60 Class 40 Board 30 Del £82
Credit Cards ① ② ③ ⑤

Rosettes range from 5 for outstanding cuisine to 1 rosette for enjoyable, well prepared food

St Andrews

★★★ ❀70% **St Andrews Golf**
40 The Scores KY16 9AS (follow signs 'Golf Course' into Golf Place and in 200yds right into The Scores)
☎(0334) 72611 FAX (0334) 72188

Overlooking the seafront near the Old Course, this friendly family-run hotel has a good deal of charm and character. Bedrooms vary in size, some of the more spacious enjoying views of St Andrews Bay, but all are thoughtfully equipped with such extras as fruit, towelling robes and dried flower arrangements. Public areas are also attractive, and the oak panelled restaurant is the setting for chef Adam Harrow's interesting menus.

23⇌♠(10fb)1⌗ CTV in all bedrooms ®≨ T sB&B⇌♠£66-£76 dB&B⇌♠£105-£139 ₽
Lift ⓒ 6P sauna solarium *xmas*
♺ Scottish & French V ♢ ⊻ ⨝ ✱ Lunch £6-£13alc High tea £13 Dinner £21.50-£23.50&alc Last dinner 9.30pm
CONF. Thtr 200 Class 50 Board 30 Del from £77.50
Credit Cards [1][2][3][4][5] £

★★★ 64% *Scores*
76 The Scores KY16 9BB ☎(0334) 72451 FAX (0334) 73947
Closed 24-27 Dec

BEST WESTERN HOTELS

This well managed hotel is convenient for the Old Course and enjoys commanding sea views. Most bedrooms are furnished in the modern style, despite the 19th-century origins of the house, and public rooms include a choice of bars, a coffee shop and the small, formal Alexanders Restaurant.
30⇌♠(1fb) CTV in all bedrooms ® T ✕ (ex guide dogs)
Lift ⓒ 10P ⇌ ✿
♺ British & French V ♢ Last dinner 9.30pm
Credit Cards [1][2][3][4][5]

★★★
THE AUBREY PARK HOTEL

Set in six acres of landscaped gardens. 119 deluxe rooms with all modern comforts including spa baths. There is a choice of restaurants and a comfortable lounge bar. Outdoor heated pool, games room and ample car parking. Excellent conference facilities are also available.

**Aubrey Park, Hemel Hempstead Road
Redbourn, St. Albans AL3 7AF
Tel: (0582) 792105
Fax: (0582) 792001**

YOU DON'T HAVE TO BE A GOLFER TO ENJOY ST. ANDREWS.

With magnificent panoramic views over St Andrews Bay, this traditional 30 bedroomed hotel is literally only yards from the 1st tee of "The Old Course", and a few minutes walk from the historic town centre.
The hotel, which is independently owned, has a patio garden, car parking, two lounge bars, an all day coffee shop and a respected a la carte restaurant. All bedrooms are en suite.
Short breaks are offered throughout the year, and we will be delighted to send details.

**The Scores Hotel
St. Andrews, Fife, KY16 9BB
Scotland
Tel: (0334) 72451 Fax: (0334) 73947**

❀★★★AA
THE NOKE
THISTLE HOTEL

Watford Road, St Albans AL2 3DS
Tel: 0727 854252   Fax: 0727 841906

*Your choice in
St Albans*

For Reservations at over 100
Mount Charlotte Thistle Hotels
Telephone London: 071 937 8033.

THISTLE HOTELS

St Andrews - St Aubin

★★ 67% Russell Hotel
26 The Scores KY16 9AS ☎(0334) 73447 FAX (0334) 78279
Closed 25 Dec-mid Jan

Pleasantly situated overlooking St Andrews Bay and convenient for the town centre, this small family-run hotel has a welcoming atmosphere. Attractively decorated bedrooms vary in size and though lacking a separate lounge, there is a popular Victorian bar serving real ales and malt whiskies and a cosy supper room offering imaginative dinners.

10rm(8⇌🛁)(1fb) CTV in all bedrooms ®⚲ T
✖ (ex guide dogs)
CTV ⌿ ⇌
♀ Scottish & French V ☼ ⌿ ⚲ Last dinner 9.30pm
Credit Cards [1][2][3]

★★ ✻64% Parklands Hotel & Restaurant
Kinburn Castle, Double Dykes Rd KY16 9DS (Logis)
☎(0334) 73620

The cooking of chef/proprietor Brian Maclennan has made this small mansion hotel, opposite Kinburn Park, popular with the local university. Dishes on the reasonably priced menus enjoyed by inspectors include bouillabaisse, halibut with grapes and a white wine and cream sauce and best end of lamb with apricots and a chestnut cream sauce.

15rm(8⇌1🛁)(2fb) CTV in all bedrooms ® T
✖ (ex guide dogs) ✻ sB&B£26 sB&B⇌🛁£38.50 dB&B£47.50 dB&B⇌🛁£64 ♫
15P
♀ French ☼ ⌿ ✻ Lunch £10 High tea £5.50
Credit Cards [1][3]

★★ 62% Ardgowan
2 Playfair Ter KY16 9HX ☎(0334) 72970 FAX (0334)78380
Closed 25 Dec-15 Jan RS Nov-24 Dec & 16 Jan-Apr

A sound standard of accommodation will be found at this family owned town centre hotel. Bedrooms vary in size, mostly modern in furnishing with good showers. Reasonably priced meals are served by friendly, smartly dressed staff in the restaurant or bar.

13rm(11⇌🛁)(2fb) CTV in all bedrooms ®
CTV
♀ Scottish & French V Last dinner 9.30pm
Credit Cards [1][3]

ST ANNES
See **Lytham St Annes**

ST ASAPH Clwyd Map 06 SJ07

★★★ 65% Talardy Park
The Roe LL17 0HY (at A525's junct with A55 coastal expressway) ☎(0745) 584957 FAX (0745) 584385

Set in 4.5 acres of lovely grounds and gardens, this modern hotel has generally spacious bedrooms with good quality furnishings. Extensive alterations were being made to the public areas at the time of our latest visit.

11⇌🛁(1fb)1⌑ CTV in all bedrooms ® T ✖ (ex guide dogs)
⟨ CTV 120P ⇌ ✻ ⌬
V ☼ ⌿ ⌘ Last dinner 10pm
Credit Cards [1][2][3][5]

See advertisement under **LLANDUDNO**

★★★ 61% Oriel House
Upper Denbigh Rd LL17 0LW (1m S on A525) ☎(0745) 582716 FAX (0745) 582716

A family-run hotel, set in 3 acres of pleasant grounds, this is a popular venue for conferences, weddings and other private functions. Bars and lounges are comfortable, the restaurant offers a good choice of dishes.

19⇌🛁(1fb)1⌑ CTV in all bedrooms ®⚲ T ✻ sB&B⇌🛁£40-£47 dB&B⇌🛁£66-£77 ♫
200P ✻ ♪ snooker

♀ English & French V ☼ ⌿ ✻ Lunch £10 Dinner £15.95&alc Last dinner 9.45pm
CONF. Thtr 250 Class 150 Board 40 Del £70
Credit Cards [1][2][3][5] £

★★ 66% Plas Elwy Hotel & Restaurant

The Roe LL17 0LT (close to A55 at junct with A525) ☎(0745) 582263 & 582089 FAX (0745) 583864
Closed 26-31 Dec

This very friendly hotel has been much improved and extended by owners Phillip and Caroline Woolley. The rooms in the annexe, where there is also a small lounge, are larger than those in the main building, but all are furnished and equipped to a high standard.

7⇌🛁Annexe6⇌🛁(2fb)1⌑ CTV in all bedrooms ® T
✖ (ex guide dogs) ✻ sB&B⇌🛁£39-£45 dB&B⇌🛁£52-£60 ♫
CTV 28P ⇌
V ☼ ⌿ ✻ Sunday Lunch £6.95 Dinner £12.95&alc Last dinner 10pm
Credit Cards [1][2][3][5] £

ST AUBIN
See **Jersey** under **Channel Islands**

ST AUSTELL Cornwall & Isles of Scilly Map 02 SX05

★★★★ 61% Carlyon Bay
Sea Rd, Carlyon Bay PL25 3RD (Brend) ☎(0726) 812304 FAX (0726) 814938

Popular with business guests, family parties and tourists alike, the hotel is set in 250 acres of mature grounds and garden. Traditionally styled public areas offer a choice of lounges which, like the restaurant, command unspoiled sea views, and though bedrooms vary in size (those at the front being more spacious) they have recently been refurbished and have a good range of facilities.

73⇌🛁(14fb) CTV in all bedrooms ®⚲ T ✖ (ex guide dogs) ✻ sB&B⇌🛁£61-£74 dB&B⇌🛁£116-£164 ♫
Lift ⟨ CTV 100P 1⌂ (£8 per day) ⇌ ✻ ⌬ (heated) ⌿
(heated) ▶ 18 ♀ (hard) snooker sauna solarium spa bath table tennis putting ♪ ♘ xmas
♀ English & French V ☼ ⌿ ✻ Lunch £10.50&alc Dinner £18.50&alc Last dinner 9pm
Credit Cards [1][2][3][5] £

★★★ 63% Cliff Head
Sea Rd, Carlyon Bay PL25 3RB (2m E off A390) ☎(0726) 812345 FAX (0726) 815511

Set in 2 acres of mature grounds, the Cliff Head has been extensively refurbished over the years, and more bedrooms are gradually being upgraded to a higher standard. Run by John and Rita Kneale, the atmosphere is relaxed and informal. Public areas are bright and spacious, comprising a traditional lounge, bar and attractive dining room.

47rm(44⇌🛁)(10fb)1⌑ CTV in all bedrooms ® T
⟨ CTV 60P 8⌂ ✻ ⌿ (heated) sauna solarium gymnasium pool table
V ☼ ⌿ ⌘ Last dinner 9.30pm
Credit Cards [1][2][3][5]

★★★ 63% Porth Avallen
Sea Rd, Carlyon Bay PL25 3SG ☎Par(0726) 812802 & 812183 FAX (0726) 817097
Closed Xmas & New Year

This long established traditional hotel, set in its own grounds overlooking Carlyon Bay, offers bedrooms in a range of styles, all equipped with modern facilities and undergoing refurbishment. There is a comfortable oak-panelled lounge with a terrace, a bar and dining room.

23rm(22⇌🛁)(2fb)2⌑ CTV in all bedrooms ® T
✖ (ex guide dogs)

(CTV 50P ✿
♀ English & French V ♱ ♨ Last dinner 9pm
Credit Cards 1 2 3

★★❀♨78% Boscundle Manor
Tregrehan PL25 3RL (2m E off A390) ☎(0726) 813557 FAX (0726) 814997
Closed end Oct-Mar
This delightful 18th-century manor house, set in secluded grounds, is personally run by Mary and Andrew Flint. Individually styled bedrooms include 2 cottages and several suites, tastefully furnished with antiques, and many bathrooms have a spa bath or jacuzzi and power shower. Mary has gained a good reputation for her eclectic, self-taught style of cooking, and Andrew looks after services and an excellent wine cellar of over 150 fine vintages.
7⇌♠Annexe3⇌♠ CTV in all bedrooms ® T sB&B⇌♠£50-£70 dB&B⇌♠£80-£120
15P ☞ ✿ ⇌ (heated) ► gymnasium croquet practice golf course
♀ International ✗ Dinner £22.50 Last dinner 9pm
Credit Cards 1 3

★★64% Pier House
Harbour Front, Charlestown PL25 3NJ ☎(0726) 67955 FAX (0726) 69246
Dating back to 1793 and set on the harbour side in Charlestown, Pier House has recently undergone considerable improvement, both public areas and bedrooms now being bright, attractively decorated and well equipped. As well as a cosy lounge and dining room with superb harbour and sea views, there is an intimate public bar, and friendly staff create a warm, relaxed atmosphere.
12⇌♠(4fb)1✥ CTV in all bedrooms ® T ✖ (ex guide dogs)
CTV 1P 7☞
V ♱ ♨ Last dinner 10pm
Credit Cards 1 3

★★60% White Hart
Church St PL25 4AT (St Austell Brewery) ☎(0726) 72100 FAX (0726) 74705
Closed 25 & 26 Dec
This popular commercial town centre pub hotel has been tastefully upgraded and well furnished throughout. Public areas comprise 2 bars, a foyer lounge and small dining room. Service is available throughout the day, including cream teas and bar lunches and daily specials. The bedrooms are well equipped.
18⇌♠ CTV in all bedrooms ® T ✖ (ex guide dogs) ✱
sB&B⇌♠fr£40 dB&B⇌♠fr£63.50 ♬
V ♱ ♨ ✱ Lunch £6.95-£7.95 High tea £2.90-£8.95 Dinner £11-£12 Last dinner 9pm
CONF. Thtr 50 Board 20 Del from £40
Credit Cards 1 2 3 5

★65% Selwood House
60 Alexandra Rd PL25 4QN ☎(0726) 65707 FAX (0726) 68951
A business hotel on the edge of the town centre with a friendly atmosphere and neatly decorated rooms.
11⇌♠(2fb) CTV in all bedrooms ® sB&B⇌♠fr£34 dB&B⇌♠fr£65
CTV 12P nc12yrs
V ♱ ♨ ✗ Dinner £10 Last dinner 7pm
Credit Cards 1 2 3 5 £

ST BOSWELLS Borders *Roxburghshire* Map **12** NT53

★★★♨74% Dryburgh Abbey
TD6 0RQ (off B6356) ☎(0835) 22261 FAX (0835) 23945
New owners have totally refurbished this red sandstone building which overlooks the ruins of Dryburgh Abbey and the River Tweed. Bedrooms, named after fishing flies, are attractively and comfortably furnished; public rooms include 2 lounges and an elegant restaurant.
➥

CLIFF HEAD HOTEL ★★★
Carlyon Bay, Nr. St. Austell, Cornwall PL25 3RB
Telephone: Reception (072) 681 2125/2345

The Hotel faces south and stands in its own extensive grounds of over two acres, of delightful multi-coloured hydrangeas in the centre of the Cornish Riviera, ideally situated for touring Cornwall. Privately owned, it is the aim of both proprietors and staff to ensure that your stay is a pleasant one. Thirty-five en suite bedrooms with colour TV, intercom and direct dial telephone system. Business travellers catered for.

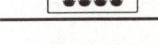

ON THE COAST

In the lap of luxury

... the perfect ingredients for a luxury family holiday. The highest standards of comfort, cuisine and personal service are assured. All bedrooms are en-suite with satellite TV, radio and direct dial phone, most providing superb sea views. Facilities include large indoor and outdoor heated pools, sauna, solarium, spa bath, snooker, tennis and outdoor children's adventure play area.
FREE GOLF ON OUR CHAMPIONSHIP 18 HOLE COURSE and 9 hole approach course all within 250 acres of magnificent grounds.

The Carlyon Bay Hotel
AA ★★★★
FOR FREE COLOUR BROCHURE, BREAK TARIFFS AND CHILD REDUCTIONS PLEASE CONTACT:
Mr. P. Brennan, Manager,
The Carlyon Bay Hotel, Nr St. Austell, Cornwall PL25 8RD.
Tel: (0726) 812704. Fax: (0726) 814938.

St Boswells - St Helens

25⇌♠Annexe1⇌♠(3fb)1🛁 CTV in all bedrooms ® T ✻
sB&B⇌♠£45-£110 dB&B⇌♠£90-£200 ♬
Lift 《 50P 3🚗 ✿ ♪ xmas
♀ Scottish English & French V ♡ ⚲ ⚡ ✻ Lunch £3.50-£15alc
Dinner £15-£21.50&alc Last dinner 9.15pm
CONF. Thtr 150 Class 80 Board 60 Del from £65
Credit Cards [1][3]

★★**69%** Buccleuch Arms
The Green TD6 0EW (on A68) ☎(0835) 22243 FAX (0835) 23965
Opposite the village green, this friendly inn dating back to the 1700s
has cosy well equipped bedrooms, a comfortable lounge and a
popular wood-panelled lounge bar and restaurant, both offering an
extensive choice of food.
19rm(17⇌♠)(1fb) CTV in all bedrooms ® T sB&B⇌♠£38-£40 dB&B£50-£55 dB&B⇌♠£68-£70 ♬
50P 2🚗 ✿ xmas
♀ International V ♡ ⚲ ⚡ ✻ Lunch £14.25 High tea £5.75
Dinner £16.95&alc Last dinner 10pm
CONF. Thtr 100 Class 50 Board 50 Del from £50
Credit Cards [1][2][3][5] £

ST BRELADE
See **Jersey** under **Channel Islands**

ST CLEARS Dyfed Map 02 SN21

★★**66%** Forge Restaurant & Motel
SA33 4NA (1m E, beside A40) ☎(0994) 230300 FAX (0994) 230300
Closed 25 & 26 Dec
This friendly motel-style operation offers well equipped rooms in
annexes set well back from the road. A busy restaurant/diner
provides meals all day and evening.
Annexe18⇌♠(4fb) CTV in all bedrooms ® T ✻
sB&B⇌♠£35 dB&B⇌♠£55
80P ⛳ ✿ (heated) sauna gymnasium
♀ Mainly grills V ♡ ⚲ ⚡ Lunch £6-£16alc Dinner £6-£16alc
Last dinner 9.30pm
Credit Cards [1][3] £

ST COMBS Grampian *Aberdeenshire* Map 15 NK06

★★**64%** Tufted Duck
AB4 5YS ☎Inverallochy(0346) 582481 & 582482/3 FAX (0346)582475
The Tufted Duck is a friendly family-run hotel with commanding
sea views. Public rooms are comfortably appointed in the modern
style, and the extensive à la carte menu in the bright restaurant
offers a varied choice. Bedrooms have sturdy fitted units and are
well equipped.
18⇌♠(5fb) CTV in all bedrooms ®⚡ T ✻ sB&B⇌♠£25-£51.50 dB&B⇌♠£45-£61.50 ♬
CTV 50P ✿ ♪
♀ Scottish, French & Italian V ♡ ⚲ ⚡ ✻ Lunch £9.95-£25&alc High tea fr£5.95 Dinner £9.95-£15&alc Last dinner 9.30pm
Credit Cards [1][3] £

ST DAVID'S Dyfed Map 02 SM72

★★★**64%** Warpool Court
SA62 6BN ☎(0437) 720300 FAX (0437) 720676
Closed Jan
There are beautiful views over St Brides Bay from this imposing
hotel, built as a cathedral choir school in the 1860s. It has an
interesting collection of some 3,000 hand-painted wall tiles,
displayed throughout the hotel. Lounges, sitting rooms and the
spacious restaurant overlook the Italian garden. Chef Mark
Strangward uses local produce, with Welsh lamb and beef, locally
caught sewin, crab and sea bass and farm cheeses always available.

25⇌♠(4fb) CTV in all bedrooms ®⚡ T ✻ sB&B⇌♠£45.50-£61.50 dB&B⇌♠£69-£143 ♬
100P ✿ (heated) ℘ (hard) sauna gymnasium croquet pool
table childrens play area xmas
♀ English & French V ♡ ⚡ Lunch £13.95-£20 Dinner £19.50-£25.50 Last dinner 9.15pm
CONF. Thtr 40 Class 25 Board 25
Credit Cards [1][2][3][5]

★★**62%** Old Cross
Cross Square SA62 6SP ☎(0437) 720387 & 720394
Closed Nov-Feb
A stone's throw from the cathedral, this creeper-clad hotel has
friendly staff and a good range of comfortable public rooms. A wide
choice of bar meals is available in addition to the restaurant.
Bedrooms are now being upgraded and those already completed are
to a good standard.
16⇌♠(1fb)⚡ 6 bedrooms CTV in all bedrooms ® T
✕ (ex guide dogs) sB&B⇌♠£32-£36 dB&B⇌♠£60-£65 ♬
18P ⛳
♀ European & Oriental V ♡ ✻ Dinner £14&alc Last dinner 8.30pm
Credit Cards [1][3] £

ST FILLANS Tayside *Perthshire* Map 11 NN62

★★★**66%** The Four Seasons Hotel
PH6 2NF (on A85) ☎(0764) 685333 FAX (0764) 685333
Closed Jan-Feb
(Rosette awarded for dinner only)
Situated amid spectacular scenery with stunning views down Loch
Earn, this charming hotel is owned and run by the friendly and
welcoming Scott family. The accommodation may be simple, but
bedrooms are generally spacious, efficiently heated and have
comfortable beds, deep baths and glorious views. There are various
sitting areas, including a cosy library off the half landing and a plain
dining room, where chef Andrew Scott provides a daily changing
menu featuring fresh Scottish produce in season.
12⇌♠(2fb) CTV in all bedrooms ® T sB&B⇌♠£38-£50
dB&B⇌♠£62-£80
25P ⛳ ♪
♀ International V ♡ ⚲ ⚡ Lunch £13 Dinner £20-£22 Last
dinner 9.30pm
Credit Cards [1][2][3] £

★★**69%** Achray House
PH6 2NF (on A85) ☎(0764) 685231 FAX (0764) 685320
Closed Nov-Feb
Tony and Jane Ross's small tourist hotel is set well back from the
road and has fine views across Loch Earn to the mountains on the
far side. Chef Bernard Steinka produces carefully prepared dishes
from fresh local produce, and Jane Ross offers a tantalising choice
of home-made hot and cold desserts. The excellent bar menu is
popular with non-residents, too.
10rm(7⇌♠)(1fb) CTV in all bedrooms ® T ✕ (ex guide dogs)
dB&B£44 dB&B⇌♠£56-£58 ♬
CTV 20P ⛳
♀ Scottish & French V ⚡ Sunday Lunch £6-£12 Dinner £14-£18alc Last dinner 9.30pm
Credit Cards [1][3]

ST HELENS Merseyside Map 07 SJ59

★★★★**64%** Chalon Court
Chalon Way, Linkway West WA10 1NG
☎Waiding(0744) 453444 FAX (0744) 454655

84⇌♠(16fb)⚡ in 44 bedrooms CTV in all bedrooms ®⚡ T
sB⇌♠£52-£79.50 dB⇌♠£52-£79.50 (room only)
Lift 《 ⛿ 140P (heated) sauna solarium gymnasium spa bath
♪

St Helens - St Ives (Cornwall)

V ❖ ⚘ Lunch £3.50-£9.95alc Dinner £16.95-£17.95&alc Last dinner 10pm
CONF. Thtr 220 Class 120 Board 60 Del from £70
Credit Cards [1][2][3][5] £

Forte Posthouse
Lodge Ln, Newton-Le-Willows WA12 OJG
☎Wigan(0942) 717878 FAX (0942) 718419
(For full entry see Haydock)

ST HELIER
See *Jersey* under *Channel Islands*

ST IVES Cambridgeshire Map 04 TL37

★★★ 65% Olivers Lodge
Needingworth Rd PE17 4JP ☎Huntingdon(0480) 463252 FAX (0480) 461150
Just off the ring road, this small friendly hotel has recently been extended and refurbished. Bedrooms are well equipped with modern furniture and there are good public areas.
11🛏🍴Annexe5🛏🍴(4fb) CTV in all bedrooms ® T ✱
sB&B🛏🍴£45-£52 dB&B🛏🍴£50-£58 ₽
30P *xmas*
☺ International **V** ❖ ⚘ ✱ Lunch £8.50-£15alc Dinner £8.50-£15alc Last dinner 9.30pm
CONF. Thtr 80 Class 65 Board 30 Del from £65
Credit Cards [1][3] £

★★★ 65% Slepe Hall
Ramsey Rd PE17 4RB ☎(0480) 463122 FAX (0480) 300706
Closed 25-26 Dec
There is a cordial atmosphere at this small, well established hotel. The small public rooms make for a cosy and relaxed environment, and there is a good choice of food from the bar menu or the à la carte restaurant. The older bedrooms are decorated in fresh floral styles, while those in the newer wing are light and modern.
16rm(15🛏🍴)(1fb)1🛁 CTV in all bedrooms ® T ✱
sB&B🛏🍴fr£49.50 dB&B🛏🍴£59.50-£65 ₽
70P 🚗
V ❖ ⚘ ✂ ✱ Lunch £9.95-£12.95&alc Dinner £9.95-£12.95&alc Last dinner 9pm
Credit Cards [1][2][3][5] £

★★★ 64% Dolphin
Bridge Foot, London Rd PE17 4EP ☎(0480) 466966 FAX (0480) 495597
Closed 27-31 Dec
This modern hotel occupies a pleasant riverside setting beside the town bridge over the Great Ouse. Its recently completed extension programme has both increased the number of attractive, well equipped bedrooms and greatly improved the lounge, which has a pleasant outlook over the river. The restaurant, with similar views, offers a good choice of dishes which represent good value-for-money.
31🛏🍴Annexe16🛏🍴(2fb) CTV in all bedrooms ® T
(300P ✿ ♪
V ❖ ⚘ Last dinner 9.30pm
Credit Cards [1][2][3][5]

ST IVES Cornwall & Isles of Scilly Map 02 SW54

★★★ 68% Porthminster
The Terrace TR26 2BN (on A3074)
☎Penzance(0736) 795221 FAX (0736) 797043

Overlooking the town, harbour and bay, with easy access to the beach, this hotel has a warm and friendly atmosphere. Though some bedrooms have been upgraded to more modern standards, others are in need of attention. Spacious and elegant public areas include a comfortable lounge, lounge bar and ballroom. A choice of menus is available in the ground floor restaurant.

➡

The Dolphin Hotel

**Bridge Foot, London Road, St Ives,
Huntingdon, Cambs PE17 4EP
Tel: 0480 466966 Fax: 0480 495597**

A small friendly hotel situated on the banks of the Great Ouse in the picturesque town of St Ives. The Waterside Restaurant is elegantly and imaginatively designed with a superb view across the meadows and up the river to the old bridge.

Warpool Court Hotel

*Relax amidst 3000 hand painted antique tiles at this famous Country house hotel dating back to 1860. Good food, interesting wines. Sea fish and local crab a chef's speciality. Situated on the outskirts of St Davids in its own grounds, overlooking the coast with beautiful sea views. Indoor heated swimming pool (Easter to October), sauna and exercise room, tennis court, croquet. Free golf at St Davids Golf Club.
Special breaks available throughout the year.
Christmas and New Year packages.*

**St Davids, Pembrokeshire
Tel: 0437 720300
Fax: 0437 720676**

St Ives (Cornwall)

48⇨♠(10fb) CTV in all bedrooms ®♀T sB&B⇨♠£46-£54 dB&B⇨♠£92-£108 ♬
Lift ((CTV 40P 3☎ ❀ ▣ (heated) ⇔ (heated) sauna solarium gymnasium ♣ xmas
♀ English & French V ♀ Lunch £16.50-£28.50alc Dinner £17&alc Last dinner 8.30pm
CONF. Thtr 80 Board 25
Credit Cards 1 2 3 4 5 £

★★★ ✪66% **Garrack**
Higher Ayr TR26 3AA
☎Penzance(0736) 796199 FAX (0736) 798955

This peaceful family-run hotel stands in 2 acres of grounds overlooking Porthmeor beach and provides a welcoming country house atmosphere. Well equipped bedrooms vary, with large, more functional rooms in the modern wing. Public areas are limited but comfortable and in Olivers restaurant chef Graham Jones offers attractively presented dishes based on fresh quality produce, including home-grown vegetables. Seafood, including lobster, features daily along with meat and poultry.
16⇨♠Annexe2rm(3fb)2♨ CTV in all bedrooms T ✱ sB&B⇨♠£36-£55.50 dB&B⇨♠£72-£111 ♬
CTV 30P ♨ ❀ ▣ (heated) sauna solarium gymnasium xmas
♀ English & French V ♀ ♀ ✱ Sunday Lunch £7 High tea £6 Dinner £16.50 Last dinner 8.30pm
Credit Cards 1 2 3 4 5 £

★★★ 59% **Carbis Bay**
Carbis Bay TR26 2NP ☎Penzance(0736) 795311 FAX (0736) 797677
Closed Jan-Etr
This long-established, family-run hotel, popular with coach tours, actually owns Carbis Bay beach and clearly benefits from its fine seaside location. The hotel is gradually being upgraded and has modern bedrooms, 2 lounges (one non smoking), a restaurant and bar. Service is particularly helpful and friendly, supervised by the proprietor's family.
30⇨♠(9fb)2♨ ♀in 5 bedrooms CTV in all bedrooms ® T ✱ dB&B⇨♠£50-£70 ♬
CTV 200P 6☎ ❀ ▣ (heated) ♪ snooker private beach ♫ ♣ xmas
♀ English & Continental V ♀ ♀ ♀ ✱ Bar Lunch £1.50-£7.95 High tea £2.50 Dinner £18&alc Last dinner 8.30pm
CONF. Del from £60
Credit Cards 1 2 3 5

★★ 66% **Boskerris**
Boskerris Rd, Carbis Bay TR26 2NQ (upon entering Carbis Bay take 3rd turning right after garage) ☎Penzance(0736) 795295 FAX (0736) 798632
Closed Nov-Xmas & 29 Dec-Etr RS Xmas
This attractive and personally run hotel offers access to the beach by a footpath through the gardens. Upgraded public areas have been tastefully decorated and furnished, most of them, along with the very comfortable bedrooms, enjoying distant views across the bay. A choice of home-cooked dishes is available from the informal dining room's set menu.
13rm(11⇨♠)Annexe5⇨♠(4fb) CTV in all bedrooms ® T sB&B£40-£49.95 sB&B⇨♠£49-£52 dB&B⇨♠£89.60-£99.90 (incl dinner) ♬
CTV 20P ❀ ⇔ (heated) putting games room xmas
♀ English & French V ♀ ♀ ✱ Bar Lunch 75p-£3.50 Dinner £16 Last dinner 8.30pm
Credit Cards 1 3 5 £

★★ 65% **Pedn-Olva**
The Warren TR26 2EA ☎Penzance(0736) 796222 FAX (0736) 797710
This charming, privately owned holiday hotel stands at the waters' edge, at the end of a labyrinth of narrow, winding streets. Many of the neat bedrooms have glorious views across the bay, and the public area also take full advantage of the location with their vast picture windows. Staff are friendly and helpful, and among many loyal guests are some who have been visiting for nearly 30 years.
28⇨♠Annexe7rm(4⇨♠)(5fb) CTV in all bedrooms ® T ((21P (£2.51 per day) ⇔ (heated)
♀ English & French V ♀ ♀ Last dinner 9.15pm
Credit Cards 1 3

★★ ✪65% **Skidden House**
Skidden Hill TR26 2DU (Logis) ☎Penzance(0736) 796899 FAX (0736) 798619
RS Jan-Feb
This 16th-century hotel is tucked away in a narrow street close to the beach. Bedrooms are cosy, pretty and well equipped. Public areas are also comfortable, and in the intimate dining room tempting dishes are served from both carte and speciality menus. The cooking has a French flavour, everything carefully prepared from fresh local produce where possible. While access can be tricky and parking is limited, the warmth of the welcome and the caring service more than compensate.
7♠ CTV in all bedrooms ® T sB&B♠£30-£35 dB&B♠£60-£75 ♬
CTV 7P ♨ xmas
♀ English & French V ♀ ♀ Bar Lunch £5.25-£10alc Dinner £14.50-£19.50&alc Last dinner 9pm
Credit Cards 1 2 3 5 £

★★ 63% **Chy-an-Dour**
Trelyon Av TR26 2AD (turn off A30 onto A3074, hotel on the right just past garage) ☎Penzance(0736) 796436 FAX (0736) 795772
This welcoming personally run hotel stands in a pretty garden on the edge of the town with superb views across the bay. Comfortable public rooms include an attractive dining room offering good home cooking. Though some of the bedrooms are rather compact, they are are bright and well equipped.
23⇨♠(2fb) CTV in all bedrooms ® T ✘ (ex guide dogs) sB&B⇨♠£29-£34 dB&B⇨♠£50-£58 ♬
Lift CTV 23P ❀
♀ English & Continental V ♀ ♀ Bar Lunch fr£2 Dinner £13-£16.50 Last dinner 8pm
Credit Cards 1 3 £

See advertisement on page 531

★★ 63% **Chy-an-Drea**
The Terrace TR26 2BP
☎Penzance(0736) 795076
Closed Dec-12 Mar

With superb views over St Ives Bay, this hotel has been run by the Boss family for many years and has a friendly and relaxed atmosphere. The public areas are bright and comfortably furnished, and the pretty dining room offers a daily changing table d'hôte menu of traditional cuisine. Bedrooms vary in size, and the front-facing singles are compact, though they do have superb views and small balconies.
33⇨♠(4fb) CTV in all bedrooms ® T
5P 20☎ ♨ jacuzzi fitness equipment nc5yrs
♀ English & French ♀ Last dinner 8.30pm
Credit Cards 1 2 3 5

★★ 60% **Chy-an-Albany**
Albany Ter TR26 2BS ☎Penzance(0736) 796759
This family-run holiday hotel offers a relaxed and friendly atmosphere. Almost all bedrooms have been refurbished to a bright modern standard, with the few remaining due for the same treatment, and some have splendid views across the town and the bay. There is a choice of lounge areas.
34rm(9⇨18♠)(14fb) CTV in all bedrooms ®
✘ (ex guide dogs) sB&B£33-£40 sB&B⇨♠£38-£45 dB&B£66-£80 dB&B⇨♠£76-£90 (incl dinner) ♬
37P xmas

The Garrack Hotel

★★★ 🌑 66%
ST IVES, CORNWALL

Owned and managed by the Kilby family for 27 years this small hotel of character stands in 2 acres of grounds 10 minutes from old St Ives and overlooking 30 miles of coastal scenery. Adjacent to the coastal footpath, some bedrooms with four-posters or personal spa baths, together with a small leisure centre with indoor pool and a reputation for good food. Combine to provide an ideal holiday base for both grown-ups and children.

Tel: (0736) 796199. Fax: (0736) 798955

Stay awhile and enjoy our style !

In or out of season you can enjoy our full comfort, superb cuisine and exceptional location. We offer sub-tropical gardens, direct access to the beach and horizon clear sea views, 50 en-suite bedrooms, passenger lift, indoor leisure pool complex, outdoor heated pool (June – Sept), direct dial telephones, 4 channel TV with video and a level of service that is second to none. Short breaks are available out of season.

PORTHMINSTER HOTEL
St. Ives, Cornwall
Tel: (0736) 795221

AA ★★★ June 1994 to May 1995 CENTENARY YEAR

THE CARBIS BAY HOTEL

★★★

CARBIS BAY, ST IVES, CORNWALL TR26 2NP
Telephone 0736-795311 Fax 0736-797677

Ideally situated by our own beach. Beautiful views across St Ives Bay. 28 en suite rooms all with direct dial telephone, colour television, radio, intercom and baby listening service, hairdryer.
Holiday flats also available.
Excellent English and French cuisine.
Renowned for our superb selection of wines – definitely the hotel for lovers of good food and fine wine. Heated swimming pool, sheltered sunbathing area.
Good centre for walking, riding, surfing and sight seeing.
One mile from West Cornwall Golf Club.
Open Easter to January.
Special terms for early and late season bookings.
Please write or phone for our colour brochure.
Resident Proprietor Mr M W Baker.

COMMENDED

St Ives (Cornwall) - St Mawes

⚑ English & Continental V ✧ ⚖ ✂ Bar Lunch £1.75-£5
Dinner £15 Last dinner 8pm
CONF. Class 30 Board 20
Credit Cards [1][2][3] £

★★ **57%** *St Uny*
Carbis Bay TR26 2NQ ☏Penzance(0736) 795011
Closed early Oct-mid Apr
This castle-style family hotel is set in 2 acres of grounds and gardens close to the beach with commanding views over Carbis Bay. Public rooms include a spacious open-plan lounge, a cosy television lounge, a congenial bar and a pleasant dining room where wholesome cooking is served. Bedrooms tend to be a little functional although the views compensate to a degree.
30rm(14⇨5♠)(4fb)1⌘ ✈
CTV 28P 4🚗 ❋ snooker table tennis 9 hole putting green nc5yrs
V ✧ ⚖ ✂ Last dinner 8pm
Credit Cards [1][3]

★ **65%** *Hotel Rotorua*
Trencrom Ln, Carbis Bay TR26 2TD ☏Penzance(0736) 795419
Closed Nov-Etr
In a leafy lane a short distance from Carbis Bay, this purpose built hotel stands in well tended gardens. Bedrooms are of a good size and have modern furniture and pretty fabrics. Public areas are spacious and include a comfortable lounge, a separate bar lounge and a pine-furnished dining room. Friendly and attentive service is provided by the owners and their staff.
13⇨♠(10fb)2⌘✂in 40 bedrooms CTV in all bedrooms ® ✱
sB&B⇨♠£18-£23 dB&B⇨♠£36-£46
CTV 10P 🚗 ⚐ (heated) ⛳

★ **55%** *Dunmar*
Pednolver Ter TR26 2EL ☏Penzance(0736) 796117
A small, informal family-run holiday hotel, the Dunmar is close to the town centre and beaches, in an elevated position with views over St Ives bay. Compact bedrooms are modestly furnished, but many have modern facilities and the cosy dining room offers traditional dishes from a set menu.
17rm(4⇨7♠)(7fb) CTV in all bedrooms ®
CTV 20P
✧ ⚖ ✂
Credit Cards [1][3]

ST LAWRENCE
See **Wight, Isle of**

ST LEONARDS Dorset Map **04** SU10

★★★ **67%** *St Leonards Hotel*
BH24 2NP (1.5m from Ringwood on the A31 between Ferndown and Ashley Heath) (Whitbread) ☏(0425) 471220 FAX (0425) 480274
This popular modern hotel is well managed and staffed by a friendly, helpful team. Public areas are quite compact, but attractive and bedrooms are of a good size, well furnished and equipped with modern facilities. A cosy public house next to the hotel provides an informal alternative to dining in the restaurant.
33⇨♠(4fb)1⌘✂in 8 bedrooms CTV in all bedrooms ®⚑ T
✈ ✱ sB&B⇨♠fr£45 dB&B⇨♠fr£56.50 🍴
☾ 250P ❋ sauna gymnasium
⚑ European V ✧ ⚖ ✂ Lunch fr£8.95&alc Dinner fr£13.50 Last dinner 9.45pm
CONF. Thtr 100 Class 50 Board 40 Del from £85
Credit Cards [1][2][3][5]

ST LEONARDS-ON-SEA
See **Hastings& St Leonards**

ST MARTIN
See **Guernsey** under **Channel Islands**

ST MARY CHURCH
See **Torquay**

ST MARY'S
See **Scilly, Isles of**

ST MAWES Cornwall & Isles of Scilly Map **02** SW83

★★★ ❀❀**68%** *Idle Rocks*
Tredenham Rd TR2 5AN ☏(0326) 270771 FAX (0326) 270062
Superbly situated on the water's edge overlooking the sheltered harbour, this fine hotel continues to improve with individual style and thoughtful attention to detail. Accommodation varies from rooms with a view to larger rooms in the Bohella Annexe. There is a new bar and the Water's Edge Restaurant where chef Alan Vickops offers a fixed price daily menu as well as a carte in summer. Our inspector has recently enjoyed mulligatawny soup, textured with toasted coconut and marinated cucumber and dill; and rosettes of beef fillet with Stilton and tarragon sauce which were generously flavoured and tender.
17rm(3♠)Annexe7rm(1♠)(6fb) CTV in all bedrooms ® T
sB&B♠£37-£73 dB&B♠£64-£136 🍴
✗ xmas
⚑ English & Continental V ✧ ⚖ ✂ ✱ Lunch £12-£19&alc Dinner £15-£19&alc Last dinner 9.30pm
Credit Cards [1][3] £

★★ ❀**68%** *Rising Sun*
TR2 5DJ (from A39 take A3078 signposted St Mawes, hotel is in centre of village) (St Austell Brewery) ☏(0326) 270233
In a quaint fishing village, this bustling and friendly inn of character and charm has lovely views over the harbour and Fal estuary. Well presented bedrooms provide modern facilities and such thoughtful extras as fresh fruit and flowers. There is a small residents' lounge and 2 bars, one offering an extensive range of bar meals. There is also a pretty dining room where chef Paul Groves presents a tempting menu featuring locally-caught fish.
12rm(9⇨♠) in all bedrooms CTV in all bedrooms ®⚑ ✱
sB&B£17.50-£45 sB&B⇨£17.50-£45 dB&B£35-£90
dB&B⇨£35-£90 🍴
6P 🚗 squash
⚑ English, French & Italian ✧ ⚖ ✱ Sunday Lunch £7.95 High tea fr£2.95alc Dinner £14.95-£16.95&alc Last dinner 9.30pm
Credit Cards [1][2][3] £

★★ ❀**61%** *St Mawes*
The Seafront TR2 5DW ☏(0326) 270266
Closed Dec & Jan
Steeped in history, this 17th-century house stands on the seafront and is personally run by resident owners Juliet and Clifford Burrows. The best rooms, some with a balcony, enjoy harbour views. Public rooms comprise a bar-lounge, restaurant and small writing room. The fixed-price, 3-course menu changes daily and includes some popular grills. Orders for dinner are usually taken early (6.15pm), enabling the kitchen to provide freshly prepared dishes.
7rm(5⇨♠) CTV in all bedrooms ® T sB&B⇨♠£55-£72
dB&B£68 dB&B⇨♠£76-£100 (incl dinner) 🍴
✗ 🚗 nc5yrs
⚑ English & French V ✧ Lunch £11.50 Dinner £16-£24 Last dinner 8.15pm
Credit Cards [1][3]

Rosettes range from 5 for outstanding cuisine to 1 rosette for enjoyable, well prepared food

St Mawgan - Salcombe

ST MAWGAN Cornwall & Isles of Scilly Map 02 SW86

★★ 59% *Dalswinton*
TR8 4EZ ☎(0637) 860385
Peacefully situated in its own grounds, yet quite close to the airport, this handsome stone-built Victorian property is now a personally run hotel. The accommodation is gradually being upgraded to a fresh, comfortable standard, and public areas have a cosy, traditional feel. A simple table d'hôte menu is offered, cooked by Mrs Read, while her husband is the host.
9⇌↑(4fb) CTV in all bedrooms ®
CTV 15P ♿ ✱ ⌣ (heated) ⌒
♉ English & Continental ✿ ♒ ⌘ Last dinner 9pm
Credit Cards [1][3]

ST MELLION Cornwall & Isles of Scilly Map 02 SX36

★★★ 65% St Mellion
St Mellion Golf & County Club PL12 6SD (St Mellion is on the A388 approx 4m N of Saltash) ☎Liskeard(0579) 50101 FAX (0579) 50116
Closed 24-27 Dec
Forming part of the St Mellion International complex, with its lodges, suites, conference and banqueting rooms, sports and leisure club, this is primarily a golf and country club. The 19th hole is the new Garden Room coffee bar and restaurant serving breakfast, light meals and refreshments, while the main restaurant opens daily for dinner. Bedrooms, all well equipped, are located in an annexe, and other facilities include a spacious bar-lounge and members' bar.
Annexe24⇌↑⌘in 12 bedrooms CTV in all bedrooms ®⛧ T
✈ sB&B⇌↑£39.50-£69.50 dB&B⇌↑£59.50-£100 ₽
《 CTV 500P ♿ ✱ ⌂ (heated) ► 36 ♙ (hard) squash snooker sauna solarium gymnasium badminton table tennis keep fit jacuzzi *xmas*
♉ English & Continental V ✿ ♒ ⌘ Sunday Lunch £9.50&alc
CONF. Thtr 200 Class 80 Board 50 Del from £64
Credit Cards [1][2][3][5]

ST NEOTS Cambridgeshire Map 04 TL16

★★ 64% *Abbotsley Golf*
Eynesbury Hardwicke PE19 4XN ☎Huntingdon(0480) 474000 FAX (0480) 403280
This is a new hotel, converted from farm buildings, within the golf course to the southeast of town. Bedrooms are neat and modern, and there is a comfortable galleried lounge bar overlooking the restaurant, which provides a range of good quality food.
15⇌↑⌘in 4 bedrooms CTV in all bedrooms ® T
CTV 150P ♿ ✱ ► 18 squash snooker sauna solarium driving range putting green
V ✿ ♒ ⌘ Last dinner 9.30pm
Credit Cards [1][3]

ST PETER
See **Jersey** under **Channel Islands**

ST PETER PORT
See **Guernsey** under **Channel Islands**

ST SAVIOUR
See **Jersey** under **Channel Islands**

SALCOMBE Devon Map 03 SX73

★★★ ✿79% *Tides Reach*
South Sands TQ8 8LJ ☎(0548) 843466 FAX (0548) 843954
Closed Dec-Feb
Sheltered by a wooded valley, delightfully positioned alongside South Sands beach and surrounded by gardens which contain a large duck pond, the hotel is personally run by proprietors of 25 years' standing. Spaciously comfortable public areas make good use ➥

THE IDLE ROCKS HOTEL
ST MAWES, CORNWALL ★★★

Experience luxury, style and exceptional value at the finest Hotel in St Mawes.
Situated on the harbourside in this sub-tropical village, The Idle Rocks enjoys a reputation for providing every comfort and first class cuisine in our Water's Edge Restaurant, recently awarded 2 AA Rosettes.
Most of our bedrooms have superb sea views and all have been designed to meet international standards. Open all year round, the Idle Rocks is the answer for a main holiday or a short break. Ideal for walking, fishing or sailing enthusiasts or as a base for touring Cornwall's magnificent gardens.
Our staff will be delighted to help you plan your stay.

Telephone 0326 270 771   Fax 0326 270 062
Phone free 0800 243020

CHY·AN·DOUR HOTEL ★★
OPEN THROUGHOUT THE YEAR
Trelyon Avenue, St Ives, Cornwall TR26 2AD
Tel: (0736) 796436   Fax: (0736) 795772

View from Hotel garden

A comfortable and pleasant hotel situated on the seaward side, affording an uninterrupted panoramic view of St Ives, the harbour and coast. Porthminster Beach is a short stroll away. All rooms are en-suite, the majority with superb sea views, and all have full facilities. Family rooms and ground floor bedrooms available. Lift to all floors. Dining room, bar and lounge with sea views. Extensive table d'hôte menu (six courses). Short break and weekly terms available.
Please write or telephone to:
Mr & Mrs David Watson (Chef Proprietor)

Salcombe - Salisbury

of quality soft furnishings to create a relaxed atmosphere. The Garden Room Restaurant offers a carte and a table d'hôte menu, head chef Finn Ibsen producing a range of dishes in modern British style
39⇨♠(5fb) CTV in all bedrooms ® T ✶ sB&B⇨♠£58-£87 dB&B⇨♠£96-£192 (incl dinner) ⌶
Lift (100P ✿ ✽ ▭ (heated) squash snooker sauna solarium gymnasium windsurfing nc8yrs
♀ English & Continental V ♂ ⚏ ✶ Bar Lunch £2.50-£7.50 Dinner £23.75&alc Last dinner 9.30pm
Credit Cards 1 2 3 5

★★★ ✿73% **Soar Mill Cove**
Soar Mill Cove, Malborough TQ7 3DS (3m W of town off A381 at Malborough. Follow signs 'Soar')
☎Kingsbridge(0548) 561566 FAX (0548) 561223
Closed Nov-11 Feb
This hotel overlooks what is often described as the most beautiful cove in Britain. It is a single storey building with well kept grounds, owned and attentively managed by Keith and Norma Makepeace. Each bedroom opens onto a private patio, and public areas are mostly open-plan with quality modern furniture. Chef Christian Miquel continues to win praise for his well balanced, imaginative menus.
16⇨(2fb) CTV in all bedrooms ® T sB&B⇨£58-£74 dB&B⇨£116-£146 (incl dinner) ⌶
30P ✿ ✽ ▭ (heated) ≈ ♪ (grass) table tennis ⚂
♀ International ♂ ⚏ ✂ Lunch £15-£30alc Dinner £29-£37 Last dinner 9pm
Credit Cards 1 3

★★★ 72% **Bolt Head**
TQ8 8LL ☎(0548) 843751 FAX (0548) 843060
Closed mid Nov-mid Mar

BEST WESTERN HOTELS

Magnificently situated overlooking the Salcombe estuary, this Norwegian-designed wooden building dates from 1901. Privately owned, it has an efficient management team and smartly uniformed staff. The spacious, light and airy lounge enjoys the view, as does the split-level restaurant, where a 4-course dinner is offered with a vegetarian choice. Bedrooms are furnished in pine with simple Laura Ashley décor.
28⇨♠(6fb) CTV in all bedrooms ®? T sB&B⇨♠£59-£79 dB&B⇨♠£118-£178 (incl dinner) ⌶
30P ⇔ ✿ ≈ (heated) boule court
♀ English & French V ♂ ⚏ ✶ Bar Lunch £7.25-£12 Dinner £21-£35 Last dinner 9pm
Credit Cards 1 2 3 5

★★★ 65% **South Sands**
South Sands TQ8 8LL ☎(0548) 843741 FAX (0548) 842112
Closed Dec-Feb
With direct access to safe sands, and just a mile from the ferry to Salcombe, this hotel offers comfortable accommodation in well equipped bedrooms. Public areas are on two levels and include a spacious reception lounge with a well stocked bar and a separate public bar. The bright, modern restaurant overlooks the sea.
30⇨♠ CTV in all bedrooms ®? T ✶ sB&B⇨♠£40-£68 dB&B⇨♠£80-£136 (incl dinner) ⌶
50P ⇔ ▭ (heated) sauna solarium ⚂
♀ English & Continental V ♂ ⚏ ✶ Lunch £8.75 Dinner £17.50&alc Last dinner 9pm
Credit Cards 1 3

★★ 68% **Grafton Towers**
Moult Rd, South Sands TQ8 8LG ☎(0548) 842882
Closed mid Oct-Mar
Superbly placed for spectacular coastal walks and panoramic views of the estuary, this Victorian mansion is peacefully set in well kept lawns. The unhurried atmosphere and warm welcome is very relaxing, and recently upgraded, tastefully decorated public areas include a restaurant with a fixed price menu and an interesting

choice of home-cooked dishes. Bedrooms have bright coordinating colour schemes and are well equipped.
13rm(9⇨3♠) CTV in all bedrooms ® ✶ sB&B⇨♠£34-£38 dB&B⇨♠£68-£72 ⌶
12P ⇔ ✿
♀ English and French V ✶ Dinner £14 Last dinner 8pm
Credit Cards 1 3

★ 69% **Woodgrange Hotel**
Devon Rd TQ8 8HJ (on A381) ☎(0548) 842439 FAX (0548) 842006
Closed Nov-Etr
This small hotel faces due south overlooking the estuary, and resident proprietors Mary and Peter Fleig extend a warm welcome to guests. The bedrooms are comfortable and very well equipped, and the cosy lounge has a beautiful view. There is a well stocked bar and home-cooked fare is featured on the table d'hôte menu.
7⇨♠(1fb) CTV in all bedrooms ® T ✶ sB&B⇨♠£23-£28 dB&B⇨♠£46-£56 ⌶
12P ⇔
♀ ⚏ ✂ ✶ Bar Lunch £2-£5 Dinner £13-£15 Last dinner 7pm
Credit Cards 1 2 3 5

★ 66% **Sunny Cliff**
Cliff Rd TQ8 8JX ☎(0548) 842207
RS Nov-Mar
Enjoying a glorious position overlooking the estuary right on the water's edge, this small hotel has a friendly, relaxed atmosphere. Bedrooms are compact, but brightly furnished and decorated. All public rooms enjoy the views, and in the attractive dining room well balanced short table d'hôte menus are offered.
14rm(9⇨♠)Annexe4⇨♠(3fb) CTV in all bedrooms ® ✶ sB&B£25-£31.80 sB&B⇨♠£28-£35 dB&B£50-£62 dB&B⇨♠£56-£70.30 ⌶
16P 2⇔ ✿ ≈ (heated) ♪ moorings and landing stage
♀ English & French ♂ ⚏ ✂ Bar Lunch £1.50-£4.50 Dinner £12 Last dinner 8pm
Credit Cards 1 3

SALFORD Greater Manchester Map 07 SJ89
See also **Manchester**
★ 63% **Beaucliffe**
254 Eccles Old Rd, Pendleton M6 8ES (beside A576)
☎061-789 5092 FAX 061-787 7739
Closed 25 Dec
This large Victorian house is privately owned and personally run, providing willing and informal service. Public areas include a cosy bar, a comfortable lounge and a cottage-type dining room, all enhanced by bric-à-brac, pictures and antiques. The majority of the bedrooms are modestly furnished, although all have modern equipment.
21rm(2⇨15♠)(2fb) CTV in all bedrooms ® ✈ sB&B£25-£32 sB&B⇨♠£28-£39 dB&B£36-£42 dB&B⇨♠£40-£52 ⌶
CTV 25P ⇔
♀ European V ♂ ⚏ Lunch fr£7 Dinner £7-£8.95&alc Last dinner 8.45pm
Credit Cards 1 2 3 5

SALISBURY Wiltshire Map 04 SU12
★★★ 70% **Rose & Crown**
Harnham Rd, Harnham SP2 8JQ
☎(0722) 327908 FAX (0722) 339816

Queens Most Houses

This extended 14th-century hotel occupies an enviable position beside the River Avon, with rural views across to the cathedral. Bedrooms in the main building have original features such as exposed beams and stonework. Public areas include 2 popular bars and an attractive conservatory restaurant beside the river, where an extensive selection of dishes is offered.

Salisbury

28🛏🛁(6fb)1⊞ CTV in all bedrooms ®☎ T ✱ sB&B🛏🛁£80–£90 dB&B🛏🛁£115–£150 ₽
(40P ❀ *xmas*
♀ English & French V ❀ ⚒ ✂ ✱ Lunch £10–£15&alc Dinner £15–£17.50&alc Last dinner 10pm
Credit Cards 1 2 3 5

★★★ **63%** The White Hart
Saint John St SP1 2SD ☎(0722) 327476 FAX (0722) 412761

FORTE Heritage

The White Hart is a popular hotel, close to the cathedral. Older style bedrooms are being redecorated and all are well equipped. There is a comfortable reception lounge, and interesting dishes are offered on 2 set price menus in the spacious Shires Restaurant, overlooking the attractive inner courtyard.
68🛏🛁(3fb)2⊞✂in 20 bedrooms CTV in all bedrooms ® T ✱ sB🛏🛁fr£80 dB🛏🛁fr£95 (room only) ₽
(90P *xmas*
V ❀ ⚒ ✂ ✱ Lunch £8.95–£13.95&alc High tea £1.20–£6 Dinner £16.95&alc Last dinner 9.30pm
CONF. Thtr 80 Class 40 Board 40 Del from £85
Credit Cards 1 2 3 5

★★★ **61%** Red Lion
Milford St SP1 2AN ☎(0722) 323334 FAX (0722) 325756

BEST WESTERN HOTELS

A centrally located, creeper-clad hotel, the Red Lion is said to have been built in the 13th century to provide lodgings for the draughtsmen who designed the cathedral. Owned and managed by the Maidment family for over 75 years, the hotel has a warm and friendly atmosphere. Bedrooms vary in style, some are still due to be refurbished, but all offer modern facilities and thoughtful extras. Public areas include a lounge, a cosy bar and a beamed restaurant.

➥

The Rose & Crown Hotel ★★★

This 28 bedroom hotel dates back to the 13th Century and is set in a beautiful rose garden beside the River Avon, overlooking Salisbury Cathedral and the surrounding water meadows.

There are individual oak beamed bedrooms or attractive modern rooms with views across to the Cathedral.

The hotel is ideal for small conferences up to 60 delegates and has a conservatory Restaurant which offers an extensive menu and wine list.

Special Weekend rates are available upon request.

**Harnham Road, Harnham
Salisbury, Wiltshire SP2 8JQ
Tel: 0722 327908. Fax: 0722 339816**

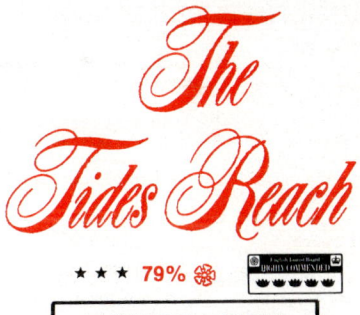

The Tides Reach
★★★ 79% ❀

LUXURY HOTEL AND RESTAURANT

South Sands, Salcombe, Devon. Tel: (0548) 843466

Outstanding location in a tree-fringed sandy cove. This elegant hotel is in a commanding position overlooking the Estuary and is ideally situated for swimming, fishing and sailing. Luxury indoor heated swimming pool, spa bath, sauna, solarium, health & beauty spa and sun decks. Squash and Recreation area including snooker, gym & games room. Mediterranean atmosphere and superb cuisine and service. 40 rooms including family suites. And some with balconies. Ample parking for cars and mooring for boats with Boat House on the Beach. Special Bargain Breaks spring and autumn.

New Brochure on Request. Resident Proprietor Roy Edwards F.H.C.I.

Salisbury - Sandiway

56⇌♠(4fb)3☎ CTV in all bedrooms ® T ✖ (ex guide dogs) sB&B⇌♠£60-£70 dB&B⇌♠£80-£110 ₽
Lift ℂ 8P 10☜ *xmas*
♀ English & French V ❀ ℒ ✂ ✱ Lunch £11-£13&alc Dinner £15-£16&alc Last dinner 9pm
CONF. Thtr 100 Class 50 Board 40 Del from £69.50
Credit Cards ①②③⑤

★★ 61% The Trafalgar
33 Milford St SP1 2AP (1m from A36)
☎(0722) 338686 FAX (0722) 414496

Conveniently situated for the city centre, this hotel offers simply furnished but comfortable bedrooms; all are well equipped, though a few singles are rather compact. Public areas include a spacious bar lounge and the popular Brasserie Restaurant offering grills, vegetarian options and daily specials.
18⇌♠1☎ CTV in all bedrooms ® T sB&B⇌♠£24-£45 dB&B⇌♠£48-£60 ₽
🅿 ⛪
♀ International V ❀ ℒ Lunch £3.95-£7.95alc
CONF. Thtr 40 Class 25 Board 25 Del £65
Credit Cards ①②③⑤

★★ 60% King's Arms
9-11 Saint John's St SP1 2SB ☎(0722) 327629 FAX (0722) 414296

Dating back to the 13th century and situated at the edge of the city centre, this inn is full of character, with sloping floors and old beams in its well equipped, nicely decorated bedrooms. The panelled restaurant features a popular carte, and Tavern Fayre meals are served in the public bar; guests can also relax in a cosy snug bar.
12⇌♠Annexe3⇌♠(1fb)2☎ CTV in all bedrooms ® T sB&B⇌♠£45-£55 dB&B⇌♠£58-£78 ₽
♀ English & French V ❀ ℒ Lunch £7.95-£9.95 Dinner £6.95-£12.75alc Last dinner 9.30pm
Credit Cards ①②③⑤ £

SALTASH Cornwall & Isles of Scilly Map 02 SX45
Granada Lodge
Callington Rd, Carkeel PL12 6LF (on A38 Saltash By-Pass)☎Plymouth(0752) 848408 FAX (0752) 848346

This modern building provides smart, spacious and well equipped bedrooms, all with en suite bathrooms. Meals may be taken at a nearby family restaurant. For more details about Granada Lodges, consul the Contents page, under Hotel Groups.
32⇌✱ B♠£34.95-£37.95 (room only)

SAMPFORD PEVERELL Devon Map 03 ST01

★★ ⊛70% Parkway House
EX16 7BJ ☎Tiverton(0884) 820255 FAX (0884) 820780
Set in its own grounds on the edge of the village, this relaxing and informal hotel has been run by the friendly Susan and John Radford. Bedrooms have been refurbished to a good standard, and public areas include a bar lounge and a conservatory restaurant. Here chef Damon Shoreland offers dishes which combine hearty portions with good flavours, catering for the popular market as well as those seeking finer cuisine.
10⇌♠(2fb) CTV in all bedrooms ® T ✱ sB&B⇌♠£32 dB&B⇌♠£45 ₽
100P ✿ ♨
V ❀ ℒ ✂ Lunch £9.95&alc Dinner £9.95&alc Last dinner 9.30pm
Credit Cards ①③ £

Hotels with red star ratings are especially high quality.

Forte Travelodge
Sampford Peverell Service Area EX16 7HD (junc 27, M5) ☎Tiverton(0884) 821087
Central Res (0800) 850950

This modern building offers a good standard of accommodation for overnight stops. Smart, spacious and well equipped bedrooms, all with en suite bathrooms, are suitable for family use, and meals may be taken at the nearby family restaurant. For more details about Travelodges, consult the Contents page, under Hotel Groups.
40⇌♠✱ B⇌♠£31.95 (room only)

SANDBACH Cheshire Map 07 SJ76

★★★ 65% Chimney House
Congleton Rd CW11 0ST (on A534, 1m from M6 junct 17 heading for Congleton) (Lansbury) ☎Crewe(0270) 764141 FAX (0270) 768916
Chimney House is a busy hotel, with a Tudor-style entrance and an eye-catching garden forecourt. The rooms are attractively designed and well equipped for business or leisure guests.
48⇌♠(3fb)✂ in 6 bedrooms CTV in all bedrooms ®❀ T ✖ (ex guide dogs) ✱ sB&B⇌♠fr£69.50 dB&B⇌♠fr£81 ₽
ℂ 110P ✿ sauna solarium putting green *xmas*
♀ English & French V ❀ ℒ ✂ ✱ Lunch fr£11 Dinner fr£17&alc Last dinner 10pm
CONF. Thtr 120 Class 60 Board 50 Del from £95
Credit Cards ①②③⑤

★★★ 63% Saxon Cross
Holmes Chapel Rd CW11 9SE (on A5022 towards Holmes Chapel) ☎Crewe(0270) 763281 FAX (0270) 768723
This hotel is popular for conferences, wedding receptions and private parties. All the spacious modern bedrooms are contained in 3 single-storey motel style blocks, each room having an exterior door with parking space adjacent.
52⇌♠(13fb)✂ in 5 bedrooms CTV in all bedrooms ®❀ T ✱ sB&B⇌♠£33-£54 dB&B⇌♠£45-£68 ₽
ℂ 200P ✿
♀ English & French V ❀ ℒ ✱ Lunch fr£8.20 High tea fr£1.50 Dinner fr£14.50&alc Last dinner 9.30pm
CONF. Thtr 80 Class 40 Board 45 Del from £72
Credit Cards ①②③⑤ £

SANDBANKS
See **Poole**

SANDIACRE Derbyshire Map 08 SK43
See also **Long Eaton**
Forte Posthouse
Bostocks Ln NG10 5NJ (N of M1 junc 25)
☎(0602) 397800 FAX (0602) 490469

Suitable for both the business and leisure traveller, this bright hotel provides modern accommodation in well equipped bedrooms with en suite bathrooms. For more details about Forte Posthouse hotels, consult the Contents page, under Hotel Groups
91⇌♠ B⇌♠£41.50-£53.50 (room only)
CONF. Thtr 60 Class 30 Board 30 Del from £79.50

SANDIWAY Cheshire Map 07 SJ67

★★★ ⊛⊛⚜ 81% Nunsmere Hall Country House
Tarporley Rd CW8 2ES (on A49)
☎Northwich(0606) 889100 FAX (0606) 889055
Nunsmere Hall is surrounded by mature woodland and gardens, bordered on 3 sides by a lake teeming with wildlife. Malcolm and Julie McHardy have transformed this elegant house into the most comfortable country hotel, with fine antiques, quality fabrics, fresh fruit and sweets in the bedrooms. Public rooms, with beautiful

Sandiway - Saundersfoot

wooden floors with oriental rugs, include a cosy bar and a restaurant where the elaborately presented dishes of chef Paul Kitching are offered.
32⇌♠4⛔⊁in 8 bedrooms CTV in all bedrooms ®⚲ T
✠ (ex guide dogs) ✱ sB&B⇌♠£95-£115 dB&B⇌♠£120-£220
Continental breakfast ℞
Lift ℂ 80P ⛔ ✿ snooker archery golf nets clay pigeon shooting ♪ xmas
♀ French V ✿ ☒ ⊁ ✱ Lunch £15.50-£17.35 Dinner £22.50-£28.50 Last dinner 10pm
CONF. Thtr 48 Class 22 Board 28 Del from £145
Credit Cards ① ② ③ ⑤

SANDOWN
See **Wight, Isle of**

SANQUHAR Dumfries & Galloway *Dumfriesshire*
Map **11** NS70

★★ 65% Blackaddie House
Blackaddie Rd DG4 6JJ ☎(0659) 50270
Dating from 1540, this sympathetically converted country house stands in its own grounds beside the River Nith. Some bedrooms are fairly compact but attractively furnished, and public areas include a relaxing lounge and a cosy snug bar with a real fire. Service is friendly and informal.
10⇌♠(2fb) CTV in all bedrooms ® ✠ (ex guide dogs) ✱
sB&B⇌♠£32-£35 dB&B⇌♠£50-£60 ℞
20P ⛔ ✿ ♣ 9 ♪ ⛳ game shooting *xmas*
♀ Scottish & French V ✿ ⊁ Last dinner 9pm
Credit Cards ① ③ (£)

★★ 60% Mennockfoot Lodge
Mennock DG4 6HS (off A76) ☎(0659) 50382 & 50477
In an attractive location beside the River Nith, this small family-run hotel is understandably popular with anglers. Bedrooms, most of which are in a wooden chalet-style annexe, are generally compact and simply furnished, while public areas include a comfortable lounge, small bar and a dining room overlooking a pleasant garden.
1⇌Annexe8⇌♠(1fb) CTV in all bedrooms ® T
sB&B⇌♠£30-£35 dB&B⇌♠£48-£54
CTV 25P ⛔ ✿
♀ British & Continental V ✿ ⊁ ✱ Lunch £8-£12alc Dinner £12-£22alc Last dinner 8.30pm
Credit Cards ① ③ (£)

SARN PARK MOTORWAY SERVICE AREA (M4) Mid Glamorgan Map **03** SS98

Forte Travelodge
Sarn Park Motorway Services CF32 9RW
(junction 36, M4) ☎ Bridgend(0656) 659218
Central Res (0800) 850950
This modern building offers a good standard of accommodation for overnight stops. Smart, spacious and well equipped bedrooms, all with en suite bathrooms, are suitable for family use, and meals may be taken at the nearby family restaurant. For more details about Travelodges, consult the Contents page, under Hotel Groups.
40⇌♠ ✱ B⇌♠£31.95 (room only)

SARRE Kent Map **05** TR26

★★ 65% Crown Inn
Ramsgate Rd CT7 0LF (on A28) (Shepherd) ☎(0843) 47808 due to change to 847808 FAX (0843) 47914 due to change to 847914
This small coaching inn, dating from 1500, has attractive colour-coordinated bedrooms and a series of small bars, with bar snacks available in addition to the carte. The hotel is better known as the famous cherry brandy house, after the Huguenots who arrived here in 1650 and made the liqueur. The same recipe is still used and

guests receive a glass on arrival. Dickens is said to have written Pickwick Papers here and Rudyard Kipling was also a guest.
12⇌♠(1fb)1⛔ CTV in all bedrooms ® T ✱ sB&B⇌♠£35-£45 dB&B⇌♠£45-£55 ℞
CTV 25P *xmas*
V ✿ ☒ Sunday Lunch £5.95-£10.50alc Dinner £7.50-£15.50alc
Last dinner 9.30pm
Credit Cards ① ③

SAUNDERSFOOT Dyfed Map **02** SN10

★★★ 66% St Brides
St Brides Hill SA69 9NH (on Tenby road, overlooking the harbour) (Logis) ☎(0834) 812304 FAX (0834) 813303
Closed 1-19 Jan
Excellent views are available from many of the rooms at this modern hotel overlooking the harbour and beach. Professionally run by the same family for almost 25 years, it offers a variety of well equipped bedrooms, some with small lounge areas. Public rooms are spaciously comfortable, and friendly staff provide helpful service.
45⇌♠(4fb)1⛔⊁in 4 bedrooms CTV in all bedrooms ®⚲ T
sB&B⇌♠£56-£80 dB&B⇌♠£88-£130 ℞
ℂ 70P ✿ ≋ (heated) ♪ *xmas*
♀ English & French V ✿ ☒ Lunch £11.50-£16&alc Dinner £17.50-£22.50&alc Last dinner 9.15pm
CONF. Thtr 150 Class 80 Board 60 Del from £60
Credit Cards ① ② ③ ⑤

★★ 64% Rhodewood House
St Brides Hill SA69 9NU ☎(0834) 812200 FAX (0834) 811863
This popular family-run resort hotel is set in attractive gardens just above the town. The comfortable Taffy's Bar features an interesting collection of old picture postcards. Bedrooms are well equipped, 2 lounges are available and the Upstairs Downstairs Restaurant serves a good choice of food.

Milford Street, Salisbury, Wiltshire SP1 2AN
Tel: (0722) 323334   Fax: (0722) 325756

Salisbury's leading independent hotel, situated in the heart of the city within walking distance of the Cathedral and all local attractions.

Ideal for touring to Stonehenge, Longleat, Wilton House, the New Forest and the coast.

Special short-break prices available.

An ideal conference and meetings venue.

For further information about
The Red Lion and Salisbury,
telephone 0722 323334.

Saundersfoot - Scarborough

34⇨♠(6fb)⊬in 6 bedrooms CTV in all bedrooms ® ⚐ T
sB&B⇨♠£23-£37 dB&B⇨♠£36-£64 ⚑
70P ✿ snooker solarium games room ♫ ◎ xmas
V ♡ ⚐ ⚐ Sunday Lunch £4.95-£6.95 Dinner £7-£9.25&alc
Last dinner 9.30pm
Credit Cards [1][2][3][5] £

★★ 63% *Merlewood*
St Brides Hill SA69 9NP ☎(0834) 812421 & 813295
Closed Nov-Etr
This busy, family-run, seasonal hotel, which commands panoramic views of the coastline from its situation just off St Brides Hill, offers modern accommodation and spacious grounds in which to relax.
34rm(17⇨13♠)(8fb) CTV in all bedrooms ®
✈ (ex guide dogs)
34P ✿ ✧ ≋ (heated) ◎
V ⚐ Last dinner 8pm
Credit Cards [1][3]

SAUNDERTON Buckinghamshire Map 04 SP70

★★ 62% *Rose & Crown*
Wycombe Rd HP27 9NP (on A4010)
☎Princes Risborough(0844) 345299 FAX (0844) 343140
Closed 25-31 Dec

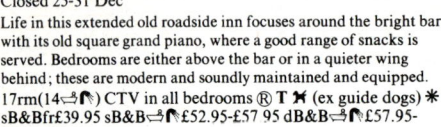

Life in this extended old roadside inn focuses around the bright bar with its old square grand piano, where a good range of snacks is served. Bedrooms are either above the bar or in a quieter wing behind; these are modern and soundly maintained and equipped.
17rm(14⇨♠) CTV in all bedrooms ® T ✈ (ex guide dogs) ✱
sB&B⇨♠£52.95-£57 95 dB&B⇨♠£57.95-£62.95 ⚑
50P ⇎ ✿ nc5yrs
♡ English & French ♡ ⚐ ✱ Lunch £10.70-£23alc Dinner £17.15-£23alc Last dinner 9.30pm
Credit Cards [1][2][3][5]

SAUNTON Devon Map 02 SS43

★★★★ 63% *Saunton Sands*
EX33 1LQ (turn off A361 at Braunton, signposted Croyde B3231 hotel 2m on left hand side) (Brend) ☎Croyde(0271) 890212 FAX (0271) 890145
Saunton Sands is an imposing modern hotel in an enviable position commanding wonderful sea views and with direct access to 5 miles of sandy beach, famous for its surfing. A full range of traditional services is offered with the emphasis on a friendly, caring style. The location combined with extensive leisure facilities makes it ideal for family holidays, and many of the bedrooms have separate but integral children's accommodation.
92⇨♠(39fb) CTV in all bedrooms ® ⚐ T ✈ (ex guide dogs) ✱
sB&B⇨♠£59-£72 dB&B⇨♠£114-£156 ⚑
Lift ⦗ CTV 140P 2⚙ ⇎ ✿ ≋ (heated) ♫ (hard) squash snooker sauna solarium putting table tennis spa bath ♫ ◎ xmas
♡ English & French V ♡ ⚐ ✱ Lunch £11&alc Dinner £18.50&alc Last dinner 9pm
Credit Cards [1][2][3][5] £

★★ 64% *Preston House*
EX33 1LG ☎Croyde(0271) 890472 FAX (0271) 890555
RS Dec-Feb
Delightfully set in an elevated position which commands views along the beach, this hotel has cosy bedrooms, a large comfortable lounge and attractive restaurant, all very well maintained.
15⇨♠2⚐ CTV in all bedrooms ® T ✈ ✱ sB&B⇨♠fr£30 dB&B⇨♠£60-£85 ⚑
CTV 20P ⇎ ✿ ≋ (heated) ♫ (hard) sauna solarium clay pigeon shooting nc12yrs
♡ English & Continental V ♡ ⚐ Last dinner 8.30pm
Credit Cards [1][3]

SAWLEY Lancashire Map 07 SD74

★★ 63% *Spread Eagle*
BB7 4NH (off A59) ☎Clitheroe(0200) 441202 FAX (0200) 441973
Improvements are on-going at this old inn, beautifully situated beside the River Ribble. Bedrooms, in an adjacent converted stone barn, have solid fitted furniture, coordinated fabrics and all modern amenities. Cheerful staff provide friendly service in the beamed lounge bar and recently refurbished restaurant, serving a wide range of food.
10⇨♠(2fb)1⚐ CTV in all bedrooms ® T ✈ sB&B⇨♠£42-£48 dB&B⇨♠£54-£59 ⚑
100P
V ♡ ✱ Lunch £9.95-£15alc Dinner £16.95&alc Last dinner 9pm
CONF. Thtr 90 Del from £80
Credit Cards [1][2][3][5] £

SAXMUNDHAM Suffolk Map 05 TM36

★★ 69% *Satis House*
Yoxford IP17 3EX ☎(072877) 418 & 640
Located on the eastern edge of the village of Yoxford just off the A12, this 18th-century country house has an informal, friendly atmosphere. The restaurant specialises in Chinese-influenced Malaysian cuisine, though an Anglo-French menu is also available. Many of the attractive bedrooms have antique furniture.
7⇨♠2⚐ CTV in all bedrooms ® T ✈ ✱ sB&B⇨♠£47.50-£55 dB&B⇨♠£59-£74.50 ⚑
20P ⇎ ✿ ♫ (hard) sauna solarium whirlpool spa nc12yrs
♡ English, French & Malaysian V ⊬ ✱ Lunch £12.75-£16.75alc Dinner £15.75-£20alc Last dinner 9.30pm
Credit Cards [1][2][3][5]

★ 63% *Bell*
High St IP17 1AF (off A12) ☎(0728) 602331 FAX (0728) 833105
King George II is said to have stayed here once, and the Bell has certainly served travellers well for the past 300 years. Behind its attractive Georgian façade, it offers spacious, well furnished bedrooms, a comfortable lounge and a public bar, popular for its bar meals. The restaurant is in keeping with the period of the building and service, though unpolished, is very attentive and friendly.
14rm(8⇨♠)(2fb) CTV in all bedrooms ® T ✱ sB&Bfr£25 sB&B⇨♠£33.50 dB&B⇨♠£45 dB&B⇨♠£52 ⚑
30P xmas
♡ English & Italian V ♡ ⚐ ✱ Lunch £3.50-£5.95
CONF. Board 35 Del from £33.50
Credit Cards [1][3][5] £

SCALASAIG

See **Colonsay, Isle of**

SCARBOROUGH North Yorkshire Map 08 TA08

★★★ 63% *Esplanade*
Belmont Rd YO11 2AA ☎(0723) 360382 FAX (0723) 376137
This Victorian hotel has fine views over the South Bay and harbour from its elevated position on the south cliff. It is a traditional hotel, retaining the style of the period, particularly in the lounge and bar, but many of the bedrooms have been tastefully modernised. The Landau Restaurant is a recent addition, with an oriole window overlooking the castle and harbour.
73⇨♠(9fb) CTV in all bedrooms ® T ✱ sB&B⇨♠£38 dB&B⇨♠£68.50-£76.50 ⚑
Lift ⦗ CTV 24P ✿ darts table tennis pool xmas
♡ English & French V ♡ ⚐ ✱ Bar Lunch £5-£10alc Dinner £14.25&alc Last dinner 9pm
CONF. Thtr 150 Class 80 Board 50 Del from £52
Credit Cards [1][2][3][5]

Scarborough

★★★62% Palm Court
Nicholas Cliff YO11 2ES ☎(0723) 368161 FAX (0723) 371547
Centrally situated between beach and shops, this is a friendly hotel popular with business and pleasure users alike, offering accommodation in both traditional and modern bedrooms.
47⇨ℕ(7fb) CTV in all bedrooms ® T ✈ (ex guide dogs) sB&B⇨ℕ£36 dB&B⇨ℕ£64-£74 ₽
Lift ℂ CTV 6P 80⭓ ▱ (heated) sauna table tennis ♫ ℘ xmas
♀ English & French V ✧ ⚏ ⨉ Sunday Lunch fr£8.75 Dinner fr£12&alc Last dinner 9pm
CONF. Thtr 200 Class 100 Board 50 Del from £41
Credit Cards [1][2][3][5]

★★★♨61% Wrea Head Country
Scalby YO13 0PB (3m NW off A171) (Logis) ☎(0723) 378211 FAX (0723) 371780
This peaceful Victorian country house is set in landscaped grounds which offer a fine open outlook. Public areas are adorned with paintings and prints, and a log fire burns in the hall in season. As with most country houses, the bedrooms vary greatly in size.
21⇨ℕ(2fb) CTV in all bedrooms T
ℂ 50P 4⭓ (£3 per night) ⚘ ❀ putting green croquet
♀ English & French V ✧ ⚏ Last dinner 9.15pm
Credit Cards [1][2][3][5]

★★★60% Hotel St Nicholas
St Nicholas Cliff YO11 2EU (Principal) ☎(0723) 364101 FAX (0723) 500538
Occupying a central position on St Nicholas Cliff overlooking South Bay, this hotel caters mainly for business people, providing mostly modern, recently refurbished accommodation. Spacious, comfortable public areas, including open-plan lounges, are attractively furnished in modern style.
141⇨ℕ(18fb)4⚐ CTV in all bedrooms ® T

➡

NORTH DEVON'S FINEST HOTEL

Commanding spectacular views of Devon's coastline with direct access to five miles of unspoilt beach and dunes, The Saunton Sands provides a wealth of facilities including large indoor heated pool, squash and tennis courts, spa bath, sauna, solarium, snooker, nursery and hair-dressing salon etc. Every bedroom has private bathroom en suite, satellite TV, radio and telephone, most enjoying panoramic sea views. Open throughout the year with luxury self contained apartment suites also available.

The Saunton Sands Hotel
AA ★★★★
FOR FREE COLOUR BROCHURE, BREAKS TARIFF AND CHILD REDUCTIONS PLEASE CONTACT:
Mr. J. Belchamber, Manager,
The Saunton Sands Hotel, Braunton, North Devon, EX33 1LQ.
Tel: (0271) 890212. Fax: (0271) 890145

Wrea Head ★★★ Country Hotel

Beautiful Victorian Country House set in acres of glorious gardens and parklands. Oak panelled lounges with log fires. Renowned English food with fresh home grown produce in Flint Restaurant. Twenty two charming, individual en suite bedrooms with panoramic views over the gardens. Ample free car parking. Just two miles from the centre of Scarborough. Conference facilities for boardroom meetings.

An English Rose Hotel.

**Scalby, Scarborough YO13 0PB.
Tel: 0723 378211. Fax: 0723 371780**

MERLEWOOD HOTEL ★★
COMMENDED
**ST BRIDES HILL, SAUNDERSFOOT
DYFED SA69 9NP · TEL: (0834) 812421**

Set in peaceful surroundings in its own grounds with superb views over the beach and village. All rooms except for the singles are en suite and have TV, teamaker, radio and baby listening. Family suites with adjoining room for children are also available. The hotel has an outdoor heated swimming pool with a sun terrace, play area, mini golf and launderette. In the main season there is entertainment 3 nights a week. Just 5 minutes from the beach and village. Ample parking. Sorry no pets.

Scarborough - Scilly, Isles of, Tresco

Lift ℂ 15🛗 (£3) 🖼 (heated) sauna solarium children's games room
V ♻ ⚲ Last dinner 9pm ♫
Credit Cards ①②③⑤

★★ 70% Gridley's Crescent
The Crescent YO11 2PP (on entering Scarborough travel towards railway station then follow signs to Brunswick Pavilion, at traffic lights turn into Crescent) ☎(0723) 360929 FAX (0723) 354126

This friendly family-run hotel is centrally situated and convenient for the town centre, beach, spa and other amenities. All bedrooms are modern and exceedingly well equipped. Public areas are comfortable and well designed, and there is a downstairs bar and carvery.
20🛏(1🛗)⚲in 5 bedrooms CTV in all bedrooms ® T
✻ (ex guide dogs) sB&B🛏♺£36.50-£40 dB&B🛏♺£73-£80 🍴
Lift ℂ ♟ 🛗 nc6yrs
V ♻ ⚲ Sunday Lunch fr£9 Dinner fr£14.50&alc Last dinner 10pm
CONF. Thtr 40 Board 15 Del from £67.50
Credit Cards ①③

★★ 68% The Mount
Cliff Bridge Ter, Saint Nicholas Cliff YO11 2HA
☎(0723) 360961 FAX (0723) 360961
Closed Jan-mid Mar

An elegant Regency building in a commanding position overlooking the South Bay coastline, The Mount is tastefully furnished throughout and retains a quiet luxury not always encountered in resort hotels. A new meeting or small conference room has been opened, confirming the hotel's suitability for both business and leisure purposes
50🛏♺(5fb)⚲in 2 bedrooms CTV in all bedrooms ® T
Lift ℂ
V ♻ ⚲
Credit Cards ①③

★★ 64% Red Lea
Prince of Wales Ter YO11 2AJ ☎(0723) 362431 FAX (0723) 371230

This popular hotel, converted from 6 Victorian terraced houses, overlooks the seafront from its prominent position on South Cliff. Comfortable bedrooms have modern facilities and there is a choice of lounges and a restaurant serving good value 5-course dinners.
67🛏(7fb) CTV in all bedrooms ® T ✻ (ex guide dogs) ✳ sB&B🛏♺£28.50-£30.50 dB&B🛏♺£57-£61
Lift ℂ CTV ♟ 🖼 (heated) sauna solarium gymnasium *xmas*
♋ International ♻ ⚲ ✳ Lunch fr£7.50 Dinner fr£10.50 Last dinner 8.30pm
Credit Cards ①③ £

★★ 62% The Pickwick Inn
Huntriss Row YO11 2ED ☎(0723) 375787 FAX (0723) 374284

Comfortably furnished and well equipped bedrooms are a feature of the Pickwick Inn, suited to both business and leisure users. The shower rooms are modern and particularly well styled. The hotel is in the centre of Scarborough, within easy reach of all amenities, and has spacious public bars and a first floor dining room.
11🛏♺1🛗 CTV in all bedrooms ® T ✻ (ex guide dogs) sB&B🛏♺£27-£32 dB&B🛏♺£44-£55 🍴
Lift 🛗 *xmas*
V ♻ Sunday Lunch £5.25-£7.75&alc Dinner £5.25-£7.75&alc Last dinner 9pm
Credit Cards ①②③⑤ £

★★ 61% Southlands
15 West St, South Cliff YO11 2QW ☎(0723) 361461 FAX (0723) 376035

This comfortable, privately owned hotel is just 4 minutes' walk from the South Cliff and convenient for the town centre. Bedrooms are conventionally furnished and decorated, and all have modern amenities.

58🛏♺(8fb) CTV in all bedrooms ® ✲ T sB&B🛏♺£20-£38 dB&B🛏♺£40-£66 🍴
Lift ℂ CTV 45P ♫
V ♻ ⚲ ✻ Bar Lunch £1.50-£4alc Dinner fr£13 Last dinner 8.30pm
CONF. Thtr 100 Class 30 Board 30 Del from £45
Credit Cards ①②③⑤ £

★★ 58% Brooklands
Esplanade Gardens, South Cliff YO11 2AW ☎(0723) 376576 & 361608 FAX (0723) 376576

Brooklands is a friendly, unpretentious hotel less than a minute's walk to the Esplanade and the cliff tramway. Most bedrooms have en suite facilities and there are comfortable lounges together with a traditional dining room.
61rm(52🛏4♺)(9fb) CTV in all bedrooms ® T
✻ (ex guide dogs) sB&B🛏♺£28.50-£30 dB&B£53-£58 dB&B🛏♺£60-£65 🍴
Lift 1🛗 (£1 per night) pool table ♫ *xmas*
V ♻ ⚲ Lunch £5 High tea £2-£3 Dinner £9 Last dinner 8pm
CONF. Thtr 60 Class 40 Board 20 Del from £25
Credit Cards ①③

★★ 51% Central
1-3 The Crescent YO11 2PW ☎(0723) 365766 FAX (0723) 360448

This friendly, but modestly furnished and decorated hotel, is situated a short distance from both the town and the beach. Bar meals are a feature, and the restaurant offers both table d'hôte and à la carte menus.
36rm(13🛏12♺)(4fb) CTV in all bedrooms ® T ✳
Lift 18P
♋ English & Continental V ♻ Last dinner 10.30pm
Credit Cards ①②③⑤

SCILLY, ISLES OF (No map)

ST MARY'S

★★ 71% Tregarthens
Hugh Town TR21 0PP (100yds from the quay)
☎Scillonia(0720) 22540 FAX (0720) 22089
Closed late Oct-mid Mar

BEST WESTERN HOTELS

Just above the quay, with fine views across the water, this popular holiday hotel offers a nice mix of modern comfort and local charm. Refurbishment continues, thanks to dedicated management, and though bedrooms vary in size, access and outlook, all are well furnished. The smart public areas take full advantage of the view, and there is a small terrace and garden.
28🛏Annexe1🛏(5fb) CTV in all bedrooms ® T ✻
sB&B🛏♺£54-£70 dB&B🛏♺£96-£140 (incl dinner) 🍴
♋ English & French V ♻ ⚲ Bar Lunch £5.45-£8.15alc High tea £4-£7alc Dinner fr£19.50 Last dinner 8pm
Credit Cards ①②③⑤

TRESCO

★★★ ❀❀ 78% The Island
TR24 0PU ☎Scillonia(0720) 22883 FAX (0720) 23008
Closed Nov-Feb

Whether you land by helicopter or by boat, transport will be arranged to take you across the beautiful island to this hotel in sub-tropical gardens with wonderful sea views. It offers the ultimate in peace and tranquility, together with a high standard of accommodation and very good food. Chef Christopher Wyburn Risdale offers imaginative dishes, cooked with style and flair and presented in the modern way.
40🛏♺(19fb) CTV in all bedrooms ® T ✻ (ex guide dogs) sB&B🛏♺£60-£95 dB&B🛏♺£120-£250 (incl dinner) 🍴
♟ 🛗 ✻ ≋ (heated) ♀ (hard) ♪ croquet boating table tennis *xmas*

➡

Tregarthen's Hotel ★★

**ST MARY'S
ISLES OF SCILLY
Tel: 0720 22 540**

A quiet, peaceful and well established hotel, ideally situated within 2 minutes walk of the quay where you can catch boats to the off-islands or saunter through the small "capital" of the island – Hugh Town.

The hotel's comfortable lounge and restaurant look out over panoramic views. You can enjoy our excellent cuisine and service before retiring to one of our 33 well furnished bedrooms, all of which have colour TV, radio, telephone and Tea and Coffee making facilities.

The Mount Hotel

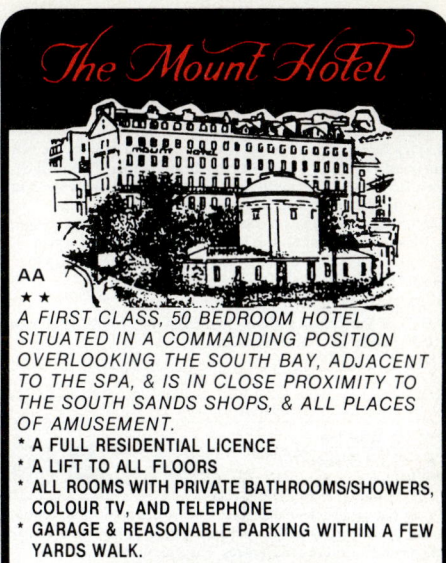

AA
★★
A FIRST CLASS, 50 BEDROOM HOTEL SITUATED IN A COMMANDING POSITION OVERLOOKING THE SOUTH BAY, ADJACENT TO THE SPA, & IS IN CLOSE PROXIMITY TO THE SOUTH SANDS SHOPS, & ALL PLACES OF AMUSEMENT.
* A FULL RESIDENTIAL LICENCE
* A LIFT TO ALL FLOORS
* ALL ROOMS WITH PRIVATE BATHROOMS/SHOWERS, COLOUR TV, AND TELEPHONE
* GARAGE & REASONABLE PARKING WITHIN A FEW YARDS WALK.

**SCARBOROUGH
(0723) 360961**
CLIFF BRIDGE TERRACE, ST. NICHOLAS CLIFF, SCARBOROUGH

BROOKLANDS
**Esplanade Gardens,
Scarborough YO11 2AW ★★**

**Telephone:
(0723) 376576/890314**

- New Conference Suite
- Seating up to 200 Delegates
- Specialised Conference Equipment Available according to requirements
- A few minutes from the Spa

Old established Hotel with every modern convenience. Situated in the most desirable part of the South Cliff, with level approach to Gardens, lift to Spa and beach, central heating, lifts to all floors. The majority of rooms have bathroom en suite all have colour television, radio, tea and coffee-making facilities, BT telephones in all bedrooms. Residential and restaurant licence.

Raven Hall
★★★
COUNTRY HOUSE HOTEL & GOLF COURSE

Half way between Scarborough and Whitby, this historic country house hotel is situated in 100 acres of award winning gardens and battlements.
★ 53 en-suite bedrooms ★ Private cliff top golf course ★ Tennis ★ Croquet ★ Putting ★ Crown Bowls ★ Swimming Pool ★ Snooker ★ Hair & Beauty Salon ★ Sauna ★ Conference facilities ★ Children welcome ★ Parking for 200 cars
. . . and an enviable reputation for good food & warm hospitality.

**Tel: (0723) 870353   Fax: (0723) 870072
Ravenscar, North Yorkshire YO13 0ET**

Scilly, Isles of, Tresco - Scunthorpe

♀ English & Continental V ✿ ⎵ ✱ Lunch £1.50-£15 Dinner £14.50-£24.50&alc Last dinner 9.30pm
Credit Cards 1 2 3

★★ 66% New Inn
TR24 0QQ ☎Scillonia(0720) 22844

Graham and Sue Shone took over this small inn in early 1993, after working here for several years. The only pub on the island, the New Inn is just a short walk from the New Grimsby Quay. The public bar offers popular light meals, while in the low ceilinged restaurant Graham Shone offers a daily changing menu which features excellent local fish. There is a small residents' lounge and a lounge bar. Bedrooms are simply furnished and vary in size and aspect.
12rm(10⇨) CTV in all bedrooms ® T ✈ (ex guide dogs) ✱ sB&B£35-£56 dB&B⇨£70-£112 (incl dinner) ⍰
♣ ⊞ ≘ (heated) sea fishing xmas
V ✿ ⎵ ✱ Bar Lunch £1.85-£15alc High tea £1.40-£7alc Dinner £10.50-£18.50 Last dinner 8.30pm
Credit Cards 1 3

SCOLE Norfolk Map 05 TM17

★★ 62% Scole Inn
IP21 4DR ☎Diss(0379) 740481 FAX (0379) 740762

BEST WESTERN HOTELS

Choose between ancient and modern bedrooms at this 17th-century listed inn. The listing walls in the main building's bedrooms contain solid period furniture and chintzes. The annexe rooms are away from the road and more functional. The quite elegant restaurant has pink and white candlelit tables and sponge-painted walls.
12⇨⋔Annexe11⇨⋔(2fb)3⌺⥋in 3 bedrooms CTV in all bedrooms ® T ✱ sB&B⇨⋔£45-£75 dB&B⇨⋔£65-£90 ⍰ CTV 60P xmas
♀ English & French V ✿ ⎵ Last dinner 10pm
Credit Cards 1 2 3 5

SCOTCH CORNER (NEAR RICHMOND) North Yorkshire Map 08 NZ20

★★★ 62% Scotch Corner
DL10 6NR (at A1/A66 junct)
☎Richmond(0748) 850900 FAX (0748) 825417

Friendly HOTELS PLC

This long established, ivy-clad hotel occupies a position where for centuries travellers have turned in their journeys between England and Scotland. Recent refurbishment has enhanced the hotel, which has particularly spacious public rooms. Bedrooms have every modern facility; some are located in the older part of the house, others are in the new wing at the rear.
90⇨⋔(5fb)1⌺⥋in 30 bedrooms CTV in all bedrooms ®✈ T ✈ (ex guide dogs) ✱ sB⇨⋔£52-£63 dB⇨⋔£59-£70 (room only) ⍰
Lift (150P 5≘ gymnasium xmas
♀ English & French V ✿ ⎵ ✱ Lunch £8.30&alc High tea £1.30-£5.95 Dinner £12.50&alc Last dinner 9.45pm
CONF: Thtr 280 Class 110 Board 90 Del from £74
Credit Cards 1 2 3 5

Forte Travelodge
Skeeby DL10 5EQ (0.5m S on A1)
☎Richmond(0748) 3768
Central Res (0800) 850920

FORTE Travelodge

This modern building offers a good standard of accommodation for overnight stops. Smart, spacious and well equipped bedrooms, all with en suite bathrooms, are suitable for family use, and meals may be taken at the nearby family restaurant. For more details about Travelodges, consult the Contents page, under Hotel Groups.
40⇨⋔✱ B⇨⋔£31.95 (room only)

Pavilion Lodge
A1/A66, Middleton Tyas Ln DL10 6PQ
☎Darlington(0325) 377177 FAX (0325) 377890

PAVILION Lodge

With a nearby family restaurant providing all meals, this modern building offers smart, spacious and well equipped bedrooms. For more details about Pavilion Lodges, consult the Contents page, under Hotel Groups.
50⇨⋔✱ sB⇨£31.95 dB⇨£35.95 (room only)

SCOURIE Highland Sutherland Map 14 NC14

★★ 68% Eddrachilles
Badcall Bay IV27 4TH (2m S on A894) ☎(0971) 502080 FAX (0971) 502477
Closed Nov-Feb

Sympathetically refurbished, this former manse in 320 acres has magnificent views over Badcall Bay, particularly from the delightful sun lounge. The dining room has natural stone walls and floor. Bedrooms are comfortable with mixed modern appointments and wide amenities.
11⇨⋔(1fb) CTV in all bedrooms ® T ✈ (ex guide dogs) sB&B⇨⋔£36-£52 dB&B⇨⋔£62-£72 ⍰
25P ⊞ ✿ ✈ boats for hire nc3yrs
V ✿ Bar Lunch fr£3.50alc Dinner fr£10.50&alc Last dinner 8pm
Credit Cards 1 3

★★ 65% Scourie
IV27 4SX ☎(0971) 502396 FAX (0971) 502423
Closed Nov-mid Mar RS mid Mar-mid May

ExecGroup

With extensive fishing rights on a 25,000 acre estate, this long established family hotel is an angler's paradise. It offers a choice of lounges, each comfortably traditional with welcoming log fires and a well stocked cocktail bar. Spotless bedrooms have individual décor and mixed modern appointments.
18rm(16⇨)Annexe2⇨(2fb) ® T ✱ sB&Bfr£29 sB&B⇨fr£39 dB&Bfr£52 dB&B⇨fr£68 ⍰
30P ⊞ ✈
♀ British & French ✿ ✱ Bar Lunch £3.60-£9.15 Dinner fr£12.50 Last dinner 8.30pm
Credit Cards 1 2 3 5

SCUNTHORPE Humberside Map 08 SE81

★★★ 67% Briggate Lodge Inn
Ermine St, Broughton DN20 0NQ (200yds from junct 4 on the M180, on the Brigg-Scunthorpe roundabout)
☎Brigg(0652) 650770 FAX (0652) 650495

Set in wooded grounds, this modern purpose-built hotel is privately run. Popular with both business and holiday guests, it has attractive bedrooms with quality furnishings and facilities, and comfortable, spacious public areas which include a choice of bars and eating options.
50rm(21⇨⋔)2⌺ CTV in all bedrooms ®✈ T ✈ (ex guide dogs) ✱ sB&B⇨⋔£67-£74 dB&B⇨⋔£76-£82 ⍰
Lift (250P ✿ ♪ xmas
♀ International V ✿ ⎵ ⥋ Last dinner 10pm
CONF: Thtr 100 Class 60 Board 50 Del from £96
Credit Cards 1 2 3

★★★ 65% Wortley House
Rowland Rd DN16 1SU ☎(0724) 842223 FAX (0724) 280646

This popular commercial hotel, close to the railway station, provides a sound standard of accommodation. Public areas include a pleasant lounge serving light refreshments all day, a spacious cocktail lounge and a small restaurant open at lunch and dinner.
38⇨⋔(2fb)3⌺ CTV in all bedrooms ®✈ T sB&B⇨⋔£60-£65 dB&B⇨⋔£70-£75 ⍰
(100P xmas

🍴 English & French V ♿ 🚭 Lunch £12.75-£15 High tea £4.50-£6 Dinner £12.75-£15&alc Last dinner 9.30pm
CONF. Thtr 300 Class 200 Board 100 Del from £80
Credit Cards 1 2 3 4 5 £

★★**64%** **Royal**
Doncaster Rd DN15 7DE ☎(0724) 282233 FAX (0724)281826

FORTE Heritage

This friendly, traditionally styled hotel is sited on a busy road into the town. The bedrooms are warm and comfortably furnished with modern amenities.
33⇨🐕(1fb)1🛁🚭in 6 bedrooms CTV in all bedrooms ® ✱ sB⇨🐕£60-£70 dB⇨🐕£70-£80 (room only) 🍴
(33P *xmas*
V ♿ 🚭 ✱ Lunch £7-£8.95 Dinner £14.95 Last dinner 8.45pm
Credit Cards 1 2 3 5

SEAHOUSES Northumberland Map 12 NU23

★★**72%** **Beach House**
Sea Front NE68 7SR ☎(0665) 720337 FAX (0665) 720921
Closed Nov-Mar

This quiet, personally run hotel on the seafront offers friendly service and has rather compact but comfortably furnished bedrooms with many modern amenities, two comfortable lounges and a restaurant serving home-cooked 5-course dinners.
14⇨🐕(3fb)🚭 CTV in all bedrooms ® T sB&B⇨🐕£30-£39 dB&B⇨🐕£60-£72 🍴
CTV 16P 🎾 ♣ spa bath games table
V ♿ 🚭 Dinner £18.75-£19.50 Last dinner 8pm
Credit Cards 1 3 £

★★**70%** **Olde Ship**
NE68 7RD ☎(0665) 720200 FAX (0665) 721383
Closed Dec-Jan

This long-established family-run hotel close to the harbour exudes friendly charm. Bedrooms, though mostly compact, are thoughtfully equipped and there is a comfortable lounge, two popular bars and a small dining room serving reasonably priced meals.
12⇨🐕 Annexe3⇨🐕2🛁 CTV in all bedrooms ®🚭 T ✱ sB&B⇨🐕£31-£33 dB&B⇨🐕£62-£66 🍴
CTV 14P 2🚗 🎾 putting green nc10yrs
V ♿ ✱ Bar Lunch fr£6 Dinner £12.50-£13 Last dinner 8.30pm
Credit Cards 1 3

★★**69%** **Bamburgh Castle**
NE68 7SQ ☎Alnwick(0665) 720283

Enthusiastic young owners and staff are transforming this tourist hotel overlooking the harbour. Although some bedrooms are small, all are attractive and comfortably furnished and ground-floor rooms have direct access to the car park.
21⇨🐕(2fb)1🛁🚭in 3 bedrooms CTV in all bedrooms ® T
CTV 30P ♣ putting small exercise room
V ♿ 🚭 Last dinner 8.30pm

SEATON BURN Tyne & Wear Map 12 NZ27

★★★★**54%** **Holiday Inn**
Great North Rd NE13 6BP (3m W of Tyne Tunnel towards Morpeth) ☎091-236 5432 FAX 091-236 8091

Improvements are gradually being made to this modern, purpose built hotel. Bedrooms, though somewhat functional, are generally spacious and all have double beds. There is a carvery restaurant and lounge, and uniformed staff provide friendly, cheerful service.
150⇨🐕(77fb)🚭in 74 bedrooms CTV in all bedrooms ® T ✱ sB⇨🐕£100 dB⇨🐕£110 (room only) 🍴
(🍽 300P ♣ 🏊 (heated) sauna solarium gymnasium childrens playroom assault course 🎵 *xmas*

For business or pleasure stay friendly

Scotch Corner Hotel, Junction A1/A66,
Nr. Darlington, North Yorkshire DL10 6NR

AA ★★★

Premier Plus Rooms and Suites.
Own hotel parking. Situated in the heart of England, with easy access to the A1. Its convenient location makes Scotch Corner Hotel ideal for business or pleasure.

FOR RESERVATIONS (office hours) FREEPHONE
0800 591910
or call direct on 0748 850900 Fax: 0748 825417

It pays to stay Friendly

Friendly HOTELS

THE SCOLE INN
DISS, NORFOLK

The Scole Inn is an exceptionally beautiful 17th century Coaching Inn which has retained all of its ancient charm. The hospitality is excellent with great food and most friendly service. It has a very popular bar with log fires in winter. There are 24 individually appointed bedrooms, all with full en-suite facilities.

Well appointed rooms from £49.00 B & B
(low cost all inclusive mini-break tariff also available)

Reservations: 0379 740481

THE SCOLE INN ★★
Scole, Nr Diss, Norfolk

Seaton Burn - Sennen

⚑ International **V** ✧ ⌂ ⚹ ✱ Lunch fr£15.95 Dinner fr£16.95&alc Last dinner 10.30pm
CONF. Thtr 400 Class 150 Board 40 Del £128
Credit Cards [1][2][3][4][5]

SEAVIEW
See **Wight, Isle of**

SEDBERGH Cumbria Map 07 SD69

★★ 66% *Oakdene Country House*
Garsdale Rd LA10 5JN (1m E on A684 Hawes road)
☎(05396) 20280
Closed Jan & Feb

Oakdene is a very pleasant Victorian house about a mile from Sedbergh. Its comfortable lounge has a log fire and the attractive dining room overlooks green fields. Dinners, cooked to order, offer a good choice of dishes.

6⇨⌂(1fb) CTV in all bedrooms ® ✈
15P ⇔ ✿ nc8yrs
⚑ English, French & Italian
Credit Cards [1][3]

SEDGEFIELD Co Durham Map 08 NZ32

★★★ 67% *Hardwick Hall*
TS21 2EH (RE) ☎(0740) 20253 FAX (0740) 22771

This pleasant country house is set in extensive grounds and gardens. The spacious, well furnished restaurant has an attractive ceiling, and there are good public areas enhanced by fresh flowers. Bedrooms are richly furnished and decorated using quality fabrics and wallcoverings.

17⇨⌂(2fb) CTV in all bedrooms ® T ✈ (ex guide dogs)
200P ✿ ⇔
⚑ English & French **V** ✧ ⌂ Last dinner 9.30pm
Credit Cards [1][2][3][5]

★★ 66% *Crosshill*
1 The Square TS21 2AB (access via A689) ☎(0740) 20153 FAX (0740) 21206

Close to the old church in the centre of the village, this comfortable hotel has a warm and friendly atmosphere. Bedrooms are well equipped and the cosy bar and restaurant offer a wide range of food.

8⇨⌂(2fb) CTV in all bedrooms ® T sB&B⇨⌂£40-£48 dB&B⇨⌂£50-£58 ₽
⚓ 9P xmas
⚑ English & Continental **V** ✧ ⌂ Sunday Lunch £7.50-£9alc High tea £1.75-£8 Dinner £1.75-£8.80&alc Last dinner 9.30pm
CONF. Thtr 20 Class 30 Board 40 Del from £60
Credit Cards [1][2][3] £

SEDGEMOOR MOTORWAY SERVICE AREA (M5)
Somerset Map 03 ST35

Forte Travelodge
BS24 0JL (junc 22 M5 northbound)
☎Weston-Super-Mare(0934) 750831
Central Res (0800) 850950

FORTE Travelodge

This modern building offers a good standard of accommodation for overnight stops. Smart, spacious and well equipped bedrooms, all with en suite bathrooms, are suitable for family use, and meals may be taken at the nearby family restaurant. For more details about Travelodges, consult the Contents page, under Hotel Groups.

40⇨⌂ ✿ B⇨⌂£31.95 (room only)

The AA's star rating scheme is the market leader in hotel classification.

SEDLESCOMBE East Sussex Map 05 TQ71

★★ 70% *Brickwall*
The Green TN33 0QA (off A229) ☎(0424) 870253 FAX (08424) 870785

Built in 1597 for the local ironmaster, this extended mansion with pretty gardens overlooks the village green. Bedrooms in the original building have more character than the spacious new wing rooms, and there is a comfortable residents' lounge in addition to the large lounge bar that adjoins the beamed restaurant. The young staff, under the direction of the owner, Mr Pollio, are professional and caring.

23⇨⌂(2fb)4⇔ CTV in all bedrooms ® T ✱ sB&B⇨⌂£40-£52 dB&B⇨⌂£58-£90 ₽
25P ⇔ ✿ ⌂ (heated) xmas
⚑ English, French & Italian **V** ✧ ✱ Lunch £10-£12.50 Dinner £14.50-£16 Last dinner 9pm
Credit Cards [1][2][3][5]

SELBY North Yorkshire Map 08 SE63

★★ 65% *Owl*
Main Rd YO8 9JH ☎(0757) 228374 FAX (0757) 228125
(For full entry see Hambleton (4m W A63))

★★ 62% *Park View*
20 Main St, Riccall YO4 6PX (Follow road through village on left) ☎(0757) 248458

This former farmhouse stands in its own grounds in the village of Riccall. It offers well equipped bedrooms, an attractive restaurant and bar, and hospitable service provided by the owners.

7⇨⌂ Annexe2⇨⌂(3fb) CTV in all bedrooms ® T ✱ sB&B⇨⌂fr£38 dB&B⇨⌂fr£48 ₽
CTV ✿ snooker
V ✧ ⌂ ⚹ ✱ Lunch £5.95-£12.95alc Dinner £3.75-£8.25&alc
CONF. Board 24
Credit Cards [1][3]

SELKIRK Borders *Selkirkshire* Map 12 NT42

★★ 61% *Heatherlie House*
Heatherlie Park TD7 5AL ☎(0750) 21200
Closed 25-26 Dec & 1 Jan

This privately owned Victorian residence in its own grounds offers sound accommodation. Bedrooms vary in size and are generally simply furnished and decorated. Reasonably priced menus offer a range of home-cooked dishes.

7rm(6⌂)(2fb) CTV in all bedrooms ® ✈ ✱ sB&B£20 sB&B⌂£26 dB&B⌂£46 ₽
12P ⇔ ✿
⚑ European **V** ✱ High tea £6.25-£9.35 Dinner £10.50&alc Last dinner 8pm
Credit Cards [1][3] £

SENNEN Cornwall & Isles of Scilly Map 02 SW32

★★ 64% *The State House*
TR19 7AA ☎Penzance(0736) 871844 FAX (0736) 871599

CONSORT HOTELS

The State House is right on the cliff top at Lands End with views of the Long Ships lighthouse and the Scillies beyond. The Observatory Restaurant, where table d'hôte and gourmet menus are served, makes full use of its position. Bedrooms are attractive with coordinating soft furnishings, though some rooms are compact.

34⇨⌂(1fb)3⇔ ✈ in 5 bedrooms CTV in all bedrooms ® ✈ T ✈ (ex guide dogs)
⚓ 50P ♫ ⇔
⚑ English & French **V** ✧ ⌂ ⚹ Last dinner 9.30pm
Credit Cards [1][2][3]

Sennen - Shaftesbury

★★ 66% Old Success Inn
Sennen Cove TR19 7DG (off A 30, signposted) ☎(0736) 871232 FAX (0736) 788354
With the dramatic backdrop of Sennen cove, this little beachside inn is full of character, particularly the bar and small, bright restaurant offering carefully prepared, home-cooked meals. Bedrooms are cosy and comfortable, and the majority have excellent sea views. Attractively furnished, they have a good range of equipment.
12rm(10⇨)(1fb)2⊞ CTV in all bedrooms ®⚡ ✱ sB&B£20-£25 sB&B⇨£25-£30 dB&B£35-£40 dB&B⇨£40-£60 ⊟
CTV 14P xmas
V ✿ Lunch £5.95-£8.95 Dinner £9.50-£12.50&alc Last dinner 9.30pm
Credit Cards [1][3]

SETTLE North Yorkshire Map **07** SD86

★★★ 63% Falcon Manor
Skipton Rd BD24 9BD (turn off A65 on roundabout at southern end of Settle by-pass, continue for 0.50m) ☎(0729) 823814 FAX (0729) 822087
Situated on the southern edge of the town with beautiful views of the surrounding hills, this early Victorian manor house retains many original features. Individually styled bedrooms are all very well equipped and there are 2 bars, a comfortable lounge and elegant restaurant.
15⇨ᐅAnnexe5⇨ᐅ(3fb)4⊞ CTV in all bedrooms ® T sB&B⇨ᐅ£49-£60 dB&B⇨ᐅ£66-£88 ⊟
85P ✿ bowling green croquet lawn xmas
✿ English & Continental V ✿ ⚡ ✱ Sunday Lunch fr£9.50 Dinner fr£17.50&alc Last dinner 9.30pm
Credit Cards [1][3][5]

★★ ❀68% Royal Oak
Market Place BD24 9ED (turn off A65 by-pass at roundabout follow road into town, hotel situated on left hand side of market square) ☎(0729) 822561 & 823102
Closed Xmas day night
Situated in the town centre, and overlooking the market square, this friendly family-run hotel dates back to 1686. An excellent a la carte dinner, with a wide choice of dishes prepared by head chef Philip Longrigg – son of the owners – is served in the oak-panelled dining room. Public areas include spacious bars, where bar meals are popular at both lunchtime and in the evening, and a comfortable residents' lounge.
6⇨ᐅ CTV in all bedrooms ® T ✱ (ex guide dogs) sB&B⇨ᐅ£29.95 dB&B⇨ᐅ£49.95
20P 2🅿
✿ English & French V ✿ ⚡ ✱ Sunday Lunch £10.80 High tea £4.95-£7.95 Dinner £14.85-£23.95alc Last dinner 10pm

---

SEVENOAKS Kent Map **05** TQ55

★★★ ❀67% Royal Oak
Upper High St TN13 1HY (on A225, opp Sevenoaks School) ☎(0732) 451109 FAX (0732) 740187
The bedrooms at this attractive 17th-century hotel, at the quieter end of the High Street, have benefitted from the skilful eye of an interior designer. A small conservatory lounge adjoins the bar, with its interesting bar menu and in the smart restaurant, chef James Butterfill offers a daily changing set menu and imaginative carte, from which our inspector enjoyed a warm potato and skate salad, potted confit of duck wrapped in leeks, canon of lamb with tomato and basil jus, and a rich casserole of seafoods with home-made noodles.
21⇨ᐅAnnexe16⇨ᐅ1⊞ CTV in all bedrooms ® T ✱ sB⇨ᐅ£55-£65 dB⇨ᐅ£75-£85 (room only) ⊟
𝄞 50P ♪ (hard) xmas

✿ English & French V ✿ ⚡ ✱ Lunch £11.50-£15.50&alc High tea £6.95 Dinner £18.50&alc Last dinner 10pm
Credit Cards [1][2][3][5]

★★ 59% Sevenoaks Park
Seal Hollow Rd TN13 3SH (at N of town, leave A225 and fork right into B2019) ☎(0732) 454245 FAX (0732) 457468
This extended family-run private house stands in 3 acres of well tended Elizabethan gardens. Bedroom standards vary considerably from the smart, modern and spacious garden rooms, to the more compact rooms in the main house.
16rm(3⇨3ᐅ)Annexe10⇨ᐅ(3fb) CTV in all bedrooms ® T ✱ (ex guide dogs) sB&B£30-£50 sB&B⇨ᐅ£40-£50 dB&Bfr£40 dB&B⇨ᐅ£50-£65 ⊟
CTV 33P ❉ ♒ (heated) ♪ (hard)
✿ English & French V ✿ ⚡ ✱ Sunday Lunch £6-£11 High tea fr£3.50 Dinner £6-£11 Last dinner 9pm
CONF. Thtr 40 Class 40 Board 20 Del from £55
Credit Cards [1][2][3][5]

SHAFTESBURY Dorset Map **03** ST82

See also **Ludwell**

★★★ ❀67% Royal Chase
Royal Chase Roundabout SP7 8DB
☎(0747) 53355 due to change to 853355
FAX (0747) 51969 due to change to 851969
Originally a Georgian monastery, this is a comfortable hotel with a team of helpful staff and professional management. Bedrooms vary from pretty and cosy in the orginal building, to spacious modern rooms in the newer wings. Public areas are smart, with a choice of restaurants.
35⇨ᐅ(15fb) CTV in all bedrooms ® T ✱ sB&B⇨ᐅ£66-£77 dB&B⇨ᐅ£81-£116 ⊟

➥

THE ROYAL OAK HOTEL ★★★
High Street, Sevenoaks, Kent TN14 5PG
Tel: 0732 451109. Fax: 0732 740187
Close to the M25, M20, M26 and located in the centre of this ancient market town, the Royal Oak Hotel has been providing hospitality for over 200 years. The hotel has 40 stunning, individually decorated bedrooms all feature a wealth of fine paintings and antiques. The elegant Restaurant is among the best locally. The snug bistro and sunny conservatory provides welcome spots for a snack or afternoon tea.

Shaftesbury - Sheffield

CTV 100P ✿ ⌧ (heated) solarium croquet putting turkish steam bath ⚭ xmas
♀ English & Continental V ♁ ⚒ ✱ Lunch £11–£25&alc High tea £4.45–£11.25alc Dinner £20.50–£25&alc Last dinner 9.45pm
Credit Cards [1][2][3][5]

★★★58% The Grosvenor
The Commons SP7 8JA ☎(0747) 852282 FAX (0747) 854755

FORTE Heritage

This former coaching inn, in the heart of the market town, continues to be upgraded. While the bedrooms are of variable size, they are nicely presented and comfortable. There is a busy bar area, frequented by locals, and a first floor lounge with a magnificent Chevy Chase antique carved sideboard.
35⇌🛏(4fb)2⌸⚒in 14 bedrooms CTV in all bedrooms ® T sB⇌🛏fr£65 dB⇌🛏fr£80 (room only) 🅿
✗ xmas
V ♁ ⚒ ⚒ Sunday Lunch £11.95 High tea £7.50 Dinner £17.95&alc Last dinner 9.30pm
CONF. Thtr 150 Del £75
Credit Cards [1][2][3][5]

SHALDON
See **Teignmouth**

SHANKLIN
See **Wight, Isle of**

SHAP Cumbria Map 12 NY51

★★66% Shap Wells
CA10 4QU (situated 3m SW of Shap Village off A6)
☎(0931) 716628 FAX (0931) 716377
Closed 2 Jan–14 Feb
This large family owned hotel, set in open fell land, is popular for conferences and tour groups. Bedrooms continue to be improved and the best are comfortable and well furnished in contemporary style. Spacious day rooms offer various lounge and bar areas and a games room.
88⇌🛏(11fb) CTV in all bedrooms ® ⚗ T sB&B⇌🛏£38–£45 dB&B⇌🛏£59–£65 🅿
CTV 200P ✿ ♪ (hard) snooker games room ♫
♀ English & French V ♁ Lunch £6.50–£7.50 Dinner £13–£15 Last dinner 8.30pm
CONF. Thtr 400 Class 200 Board 100 Del from £60
Credit Cards [1][2][3][5]

See advertisement under KENDAL

SHARDLOW Derbyshire Map 08 SK43

★★63% The Lady In Grey
Wilne Ln DE7 2HA (7m SE of Derby, off A6)
☎Derby(0332) 792331
This attractive white-painted house is set in its own grounds, with a rear gate leading down to the canal side. Bedrooms are mainly modern in style and an extensive range of food is available in the spacious restaurant.
9⇌🛏(2fb)2⌸ CTV in all bedrooms ® T ⚒ ✱
sB&B⇌🛏£32.50–£39.50 dB&B⇌🛏£38–£49.50
30P ⚗ ✿
♀ International V ✱ Sunday Lunch fr£8.50&alc Dinner fr£11.50&alc Last dinner 9.45pm
Credit Cards [1][2][3][5]

Rosettes range from 5 for outstanding cuisine to 1 rosette for enjoyable, well prepared food

SHEDFIELD Hampshire Map 04 SU51

★★★66% Meon Valley Hotel Golf & Country Club
Sandy Ln SO3 2HQ ☎Wickham(0329) 833455
FAX (0329) 834411

This modern hotel in a rural location caters well for both conference and leisure guests. The all-day informal grill with bar provides a less formal alternative to the main restaurant and lounge bar, and well equipped modern accommodation includes some spacious executive rooms.
83⇌🛏(2fb)⚒ in 16 bedrooms CTV in all bedrooms ® ⚗ T ✗ (ex guide dogs) ✱ sB&B⇌🛏£60–£79 dB&B⇌🛏£75–£94 🅿
(CTV 300P ✿ ⌧ (heated) ▶ 18 ♪ (hard) squash snooker sauna solarium gymnasium health & beauty salon dance studio xmas
♀ English & French V ♁ ⚒ ✱ Lunch fr£9.50&alc Dinner fr£20&alc Last dinner 10pm
CONF. Thtr 100 Class 60 Board 60 Del from £95
Credit Cards [1][2][3][5]

SHEFFIELD South Yorkshire Map 08 SK38

★★★❀❀71% Charnwood
10 Sharrow Ln S11 8AA (on A621) ☎(0742) 589411 FAX (0742) 555107
Recent extensions to this Georgian house have provided light, inviting bedrooms, quiet lounge areas and a choice of eating options – the brasserie's all-day food operation and blackboard list of 'specials' offering a quality alternative to a more formal restaurant's excellent shorter menu of classical European dishes with a detectable oriental influence – an unusual but surprising delicious starter of chicken and shellfish roll on a cream of onion sauce, for example, perhaps preceding a Scotch fillet with slivers of foie gras and a concentrated Madeira sauce.
22⇌🛏(1fb) CTV in all bedrooms ® T ✗ (ex guide dogs) sB&B⇌🛏£65–£75 dB&B⇌🛏£80–£90 🅿
(22P ⚗ ♫
V ♁ ⚒ Lunch £11–£22.75&alc High tea £11–£22.75 Dinner £11–£22.75&alc Last dinner 11pm
CONF. Thtr 100 Class 45 Board 40 Del from £65
Credit Cards [1][2][3][5]

★★★71% Sheffield Moat House
Chesterfield Rd South S8 8BW (on A61)
☎(0742) 375376 FAX (0742) 378140
RS 25-26 Dec & 1 Jan

This new hotel is deservedly popular. Clean and well maintained, it provides efficient friendly service, extensive conference and banqueting facilities and a well equipped indoor leisure centre. Modern bedrooms are comfortable with good facilities.
95⇌🛏(9fb)⚒in 40 bedrooms CTV in all bedrooms ® T sB⇌🛏£40–£71 dB⇌🛏£50–£84 (room only) 🅿
Lift (260P ✿ ⌧ (heated) sauna solarium gymnasium health & beauty treatment room
♀ English & French V ♁ ⚒ ⚒ ✱ Lunch fr£10.50 Dinner fr£15.50&alc Last dinner 9.45pm
CONF. Thtr 500 Class 300 Board 95 Del from £85
Credit Cards [1][2][3][5]

★★★69% Harley
334 Glossop Rd S10 2HW (situated west of the city centre on the inner ring road close to its junction with the A57)
☎(0742) 752288 FAX (0742) 722783
RS Sun
This red brick Victorian building has been totally refurbished to provide quality bedrooms. Public areas include an intimate bar and elegant restaurant decorated in soft shades with good china, silver cutlery and crisp linen. Though there is no car park, the adjacent free street parking is scanned by security cameras.
22⇌🛏in 11 bedrooms CTV in all bedrooms ® ⚗ T ✗ (ex guide dogs)

Sheffield

(♪ ♫ ♬ nc12yrs
♥ English & French V ♦ ♘ ✂ Last dinner 9.45pm
Credit Cards [1][2][3][5]

★★★ 68% Beauchief
161 Abbeydale Rd South S7 2QW (on A621, 3m SW) (Lansbury)
☎(0742) 620500 FAX (0742) 350197

This modern hotel, with well furnished bedrooms, provides a choice of bars and restaurants, and is popular with guests and locals alike. A trout stream runs through the spacious grounds.

41⇨♠2🛏in 21 bedrooms CTV in all bedrooms ®✻ T
✕ (ex guide dogs) ✱ sB&B⇨♠fr£72.50 dB&B⇨♠fr£84 ₽
(200P ✿ sauna solarium gymnasium jacuzzi
♥ English & Continental V ♦ ♘ ✂ Last dinner 9.30pm
CONF. Thtr 100 Class 50 Board 20 Del from £98
Credit Cards [1][2][3][5]

★★★ 66% Whitley Hall
Elliott Ln, Grenoside S30 3NR ☎(0742) 454344 FAX (0742) 455414
RS BH

Whitley Hall is a charming old house near Whitley village and stands in extensive grounds with delightful formal gardens. Dating in parts from 1584, it preserves its panelled walls, impressive staircase, flagstone floored entrance hall and the exposed beams of a bar that also has a priesthole. Bedrooms vary in size, but all are tastefully decorated and well equipped.

15⇨♠1🛏 CTV in all bedrooms ® T sB&B⇨♠£40-£58
dB&B⇨♠£50-£90 ₽
(100P ⛳ ✿ putting green ♫
♥ English & French V ♦ ♘ Lunch fr£11.50&alc Dinner fr£18&alc Last dinner 9.30pm
Credit Cards [1][2][3][5]

★★★ 65% Mosborough Hall
High St, Mosborough S19 5AE (7m SE A616)
☎(0742) 484353 FAX (0742) 477042

CONSORT HOTELS

This 16th-century manor house has been carefully restored to provide character bars and an inviting restaurant. There are bedrooms of varying sizes in the original building, some very spacious with Tudor oak panelling, while the modern bedrooms offer well equipped rooms and an attractive conservatory breakfast room.

23⇨♠(1fb)3🛏 CTV in all bedrooms ® T sB&B⇨♠£37-£67
dB&B⇨♠£52-£87 ₽
(CTV 100P ✿ ♫
♥ English & French V ♦ ♘ Lunch £7.50-£12 Dinner £15.95-£18&alc Last dinner 9.30pm
CONF. Thtr 55 Class 35 Board 40 Del from £75
Credit Cards [1][2][3] £

★★★ 65% Novotel
50 Arundel Gate S1 2PR ☎(0742) 781781 FAX (0742) 787744

novotel

A newly built hotel in the heart of the city, the Novotel benefits from some underground car parking. Public areas are much in the style of the brand, but have spacious open-plan areas where guests can take light snacks or full meals throughout the day. Each of the bedrooms can sleep three and has a generous writing area.

144⇨♠(20fb)✂in 108 bedrooms CTV in all bedrooms ®✻ T
✱ sB⇨♠£55 dB⇨♠£60 (room only) ₽
Lift (⊞ 15P 35🚌 ▥ (heated) xmas
♥ International V ♦ ♘ ✂ ✱ Lunch £2.60-£20&alc Dinner £2.60-£20&alc Last dinner mdnt
Credit Cards [1][2][3][4][5]

★★★ 64% Staindrop Lodge
Ln End S30 4UH ☎(0742) 846727 FAX (0742) 846783
(For full entry see Chapeltown)

★★★ 64% Swallow
Kenwood Rd S7 1NQ ☎(0742) 583811 FAX (0742) 500138

SWALLOW HOTELS

Situated in 11 acres of grounds, this large modern hotel has bedrooms ranging from small studios to executive suites, all well equipped for business or leisure guests. Attractive open-plan public areas include intimate bars and a carte restaurant.

141⇨♠ CTV in all bedrooms ® T sB&B⇨♠fr£82
dB&B⇨♠fr£96 ₽
Lift (200P ✿ ▥ (heated) ♪ sauna solarium gymnasium spa bath mini gym steam room xmas
♥ English & French V ♦ ♘ ✱ Lunch fr£13.25&alc Dinner fr£17&alc Last dinner 10pm
CONF. Thtr 200 Class 100 Board 80 Del from £90
Credit Cards [1][2][3][5]

★★★ 60% Granada
340 Prince of Wales Rd S2 1FF (at A6102/A57/A630 junct) (Granada) ☎(0742) 530935 FAX (0742) 642731
RS 25-26 Dec

This modern motor hotel is adjacent to a service station, but differs from the usual lodge in that it offers a licensed restaurant with a range of popular dishes. It also has a selection of standard and family bedrooms with satellite TV and good working surfaces for the business guest.

61⇨♠(10fb)✂in 10 bedrooms CTV in all bedrooms ®✻ T
✕ (ex guide dogs) ✱ sB⇨♠£39.50-£49.50 dB⇨♠£39.50-£49.50 (room only) ₽
(93P
♥ English & French V ♦ ♘ Sunday Lunch fr£8.95 Dinner fr£14&alc Last dinner 10pm
Credit Cards [1][2][3][5]   £

9 star accommodation.

GRANADA HOTEL SHEFFIELD
340 Prince of Wales Road, Sheffield S2 1 FF.
Tel 0742 530935.
Just over 1 mile from city centre
and 3 miles from M1, J33.

GRANADA HOTEL ALFRETON
Old Swanwick Colliery Road, Alfreton,
Derbyshire DE55 1HJ. Tel 0773 520040.
Close to the Derbyshire Dales, just
3 miles from M1, J28.

GRANADA HOTEL STOKE
Newcastle Road, Talke, Stoke-on-Trent,
Staffordshire ST7 1UP. Tel 0782 777000.
Only 1½ miles from the potteries and 3
miles from M6, J16.

You'll go a long way to find such a high standard of accommodation at such competitive prices. But just off the motorway network, you don't have to go far to reach us.

Sheffield - Sherborne

★★ 69% **Andrews Park**
48 Kenwood Rd S7 1NQ ☎(0742) 500111 & 553454 FAX (0742) 555423
In a quiet residential area 2 miles from the city centre, this small immaculately kept hotel has been run for many years by the hospitable Morris family. Some bedrooms are compact but all are well equipped for business or leisure.
11rm(2⇨5🛏)Annexe2⇨🛏(2fb) CTV in all bedrooms ® T
sB&B⇨£37 sB&B⇨🛏£30-£42 dB&B£40-£48
dB&B⇨🛏£48-£56
⫛ CTV 15P
♀ English & French V ✿ ♨ ✂ Lunch £3.50-£9.50 High tea £2.50-£5.50 Dinner £8.50-£12.95 Last dinner 10pm
CONF. Thtr 50 Class 40 Board 30 Del from £50
Credit Cards [1][2][3] £

★★ 69% **Rutland**
452 Glossop Rd, Broomhill S10 2PY (on A57, located next to the Royal Hallamshire Hospital) ☎(0742) 664311 FAX (0742) 670348
The Rutland Hotel, in a leafy suburb, is owned by the Pickworth family who are assisted by a smart brigade of professional staff. It consists of 7 Victorian houses, now linked and extended by a conservatory restaurant and bar. Bedrooms are attractive, and though some are quite small they are well designed, and all have coordinating décor.
73rm(68⇨1🛏)Annexe17⇨🛏(9fb) CTV in all bedrooms ® T
sB&B£33 sB&B⇨🛏£35.50-£49 dB&B⇨🛏£60-£70 ₽
Lift ⫛ CTV 80P *xmas*
♀ English & French V ✿ ♨ Last dinner 9.30pm
CONF. Thtr 100 Class 40 Board 40 Del from £42
Credit Cards [1][2][3][5]

★★ 65% **Roslyn Court**
178-180 Psalter Ln, Brincliffe S11 8US ☎(0742) 666188 FAX (0742) 684279
Roslyn Court is a popular hotel in a residential area on the city outskirts, offering modern, generally compact accommodation. A busy function trade restricts service at weekends.
31⇨🛏(2fb) CTV in all bedrooms ® ✱ sB&B⇨🛏fr£29
dB&B⇨🛏fr£38
⫛ 25P
♀ English & French V ✿ ♨ ✱ Sunday Lunch fr£6.75 Dinner fr£10.50 Last dinner 8.45pm
Credit Cards [1][2][3][5]

⏠**Comfort Inn**
George St S1 2PF (city centre adjacent to Crucible Theatre)
☎(0742) 739939 FAX (0742) 768332
Closed 24 Dec-3 Jan
This modern lodge in the city centre offers good-value bedroom accommodation with friendly concierge service. Lunches and dinners are available in the Chinese restaurant.
50⇨🛏(2fb)✂in 7 bedrooms CTV in all bedrooms ® T
sB⇨🛏£34.95-£39.95 dB⇨🛏£39.95-£44.95 (room only) ₽
Lift ⫛ ⫛ ✐
♀ Chinese V ✿
Credit Cards [1][2][3][5]

Forte Crest
Manchester Rd, Broomhill S10 5DX
☎(0742) 670067 FAX (0742) 682620

FORTE CREST

A large modern hotel with a wide range of services and amenities, designed particularly for the business traveller. Bedrooms are smart, comfortable and well equipped. For more details about Forte Crest hotels, consult the Contents page, under Hotel Guides.
135⇨🛏✱ B⇨🛏£75 (room only)
CONF. Thtr 300 Class 120 Board 80 Del £105

SHEPPERTON Surrey
See LONDON SECTION plan 1A1
★★★ 59% **Shepperton Moat House**
Felix Ln TW17 8NP
☎Walton-on-Thames(0932) 241404 FAX (0932) 245231

Queens Moat Houses

This purpose-built modern hotel is popular with commercial guest and for conferences. Smart and spacious public areas include a lounge bar where piano or jazz music is played on most evenings. Bedrooms, which are all very similar, are soundly equipped.
156⇨🛏(5fb)✂in 17 bedrooms CTV in all bedrooms ® T
sB&B⇨🛏£45-£86.50 dB&B⇨🛏£62.50-£108 ₽
Lift ⫛ 225P ✱ snooker sauna solarium gymnasium 9 hole putting ♪ *xmas*
♀ English & French V ✿ ♨ ✂ Lunch £12-£16.50 Dinner £16-£18.50&alc Last dinner 10pm
CONF. Thtr 450 Class 300 Board 100 Del from £114
Credit Cards [1][2][3][5] £

SHEPTON MALLET Somerset Map 03 ST64
★★ 70% *Thatched Cottage Inn*
63-67 Charlton Rd BA4 5QF ☎(0749) 342058 FAX (0749) 343265
This 300-year-old thatched inn has old beams and original fireplaces. The first-floor bedrooms are of a generous size and attractively furnished in old pine and ash, with smart modern bathrooms. Downstairs there is an extended open-plan bar area which offers a good choice of snacks as an alternative to the restaurant.
8⇨🛏 CTV in all bedrooms ® T ✂ (ex guide dogs)
⫛ 40P nc5yrs
♀ French V ✿ ♨ ✂ Last dinner 9.30pm
Credit Cards [1][3]

SHERBORNE Dorset Map 03 ST61

★★★ ❀70% **Eastbury**
Long St DT9 3BY (on A352) (Clipper) ☎(0935) 813131 FAX (0935) 817296
Located in a quiet area of Sherborne, this handsome Georgian town house hotel is well managed and staffed by a friendly team. Bedrooms are comfortable and very pretty with coordinating Laura Ashley prints. There is a comfortable drawing room as well as a quieter library, and the bar is cosy. The restaurant has a bright conservatory extension and there is an attractive rear garden.
15⇨(1fb)1🛏 CTV in all bedrooms ® T ✂ (ex guide dogs)
sB&B⇨fr£72.50 dB&B⇨🛏£98-£108 ₽
24P ⛳ croquet ⚘ *xmas*
♀ English & French V ✿ ♨ Lunch fr£12&alc Dinner fr£20&alc Last dinner 9.30pm
CONF. Thtr 60 Class 40 Board 28 Del from £85
Credit Cards [1][3]

★★★ 64% **Antelope**
Greenhill DT9 4EP (on A30) ☎Yeovil(0935) 812077 FAX (0935) 816473
Full of character, with a warm and friendly atmosphere, this 17th-century hotel stands on the edge of the town centre. Bedrooms are quaint, with nooks and crannies and beamed ceilings, but each is equipped in a modern style. Public areas are cosy and in addition to the popular public bar and 2-roomed restaurant, there is a small first floor residents' lounge.
19⇨🛏(1fb)2🛏 in 1 bedroom CTV in all bedrooms ® T ✱
sB&B⇨🛏£35-£50 dB&B⇨🛏£45-£60 ₽
⫛ 22P *xmas*
♀ English & Continental V ✿ ♨ ✱ Lunch £3.50-£10alc Dinner £4.95-£12alc Last dinner 10.30pm
Credit Cards [1][2][3][5]

Sherborne - Shetland, Lerwick

Forte Posthouse
Horsecastles Ln DT9 6BB ☎(0935) 813191 FAX (0935) 816493

FORTE Posthouse

Suitable for both the business and leisure traveller, this bright hotel provides modern accommodation in well equipped bedrooms with en suite bathrooms. For more details about Forte Posthouse hotels, consult the Contents page, under Hotel Groups.
59⇨↾ ✻ B⇨↾ £41.50-£53.50 (room only)
CONF. Thtr 80 Class 35 Board 30 Del £89.50

SHERFIELD ON LODDON Hampshire Map **04** SU65

★★ 67% *Wessex House*
Reading Rd RG27 0EX ☎ Basingstoke(0256) 882243 FAX (0256) 881131
Closed 25 Dec-1 Jan
Wessex House has been skilfully extended to provide comfortable modern bedrooms. Public areas include the Regency Restaurant, together with a small bar lounge and formal reception. Chef Jo Lado has introduced an aspiring à la carte menu alongside the daily table d'hôte.
17⇨↾ CTV in all bedrooms ® T ✠ (ex guide dogs) 《 49P
V Last dinner 9.30pm
Credit Cards [1][2][3][5]

SHERINGHAM Norfolk Map **09** TG14

★★ 65% *Beaumaris*
South St NR26 8LL ☎(0263) 822370
Closed 19 Dec-7 Feb
In a quiet, mainly residential road within walking distance of the town and seafront, this hotel offers a warm welcome. Proprietors are enthusiastic and helpful, as are the staff. The hotel is traditional in many respects, and some facilities are now a little dated, yet quite serviceable and comfortable.
24rm(17⇨5↾)(5fb) CTV in all bedrooms ® T
CTV 25P
V ✿ ♫ ⚹ Last dinner 8.30pm
Credit Cards [1][2][3][5]

★★ 63% *Southlands*
South St NR26 8LL ☎(0263) 822679
Closed Oct-Etr
Located in a quiet residential area, but within easy reach of the town, Southlands has a cheerful and friendly atmosphere. A large, comfortable lounge is the principal feature of the public areas, with a small residents' lounge at one end and the dining room at the other. Bedrooms are traditional in style and are generally well lit and of reasonable size.
18rm(13⇨1↾)(1fb) CTV in all bedrooms ® ✻ sB&B£30-£40 sB&B⇨↾£30-£40 dB&B£60-£80 dB&B⇨↾£60-£80
15P
⚹ ✻ Dinner £13.50 Last dinner 7.45pm
Credit Cards [1][3]

SHETLAND Map **16**

BRAE Map **16** HU36

★★★☖ 67% *Busta House*
ZE2 9QN (After Brae follow road north, bearing left around Busta Voe, within 1m hotel signposted with Muckle Roe)
☎(080622) 506 FAX (080622) 588
Closed 23 Dec-2 Jan
Dating in part from 1714, this house is beautifully located on the shore of Busta Voe with its own small harbour and garden sloping down to the water's edge. There are 2 excellent lounges with books and magazines, and the bar boasts over 120 single malt whiskies.

Bedrooms are well equipped though some tend to be strictly practical.
20⇨↾(2fb) ⌘ CTV in all bedrooms ® T sB&B⇨↾£60 dB&B⇨↾£80-£105 ᖆ
35P ⇎ ✿ sea fishing water sports
♡ International V ✿ ♫ ⚹ ✻ Bar Lunch £7.60-£16.50 Dinner fr£21.50 Last dinner 9pm
Credit Cards [1][2][3][5]

See advertisement on page 549

LERWICK Map **16** HU44

★★★ 66% *Shetland*
Holmsgarth Rd ZE1 0PW ☎(0595) 5515 FAX (0595) 5828
Modern and spacious, the Shetland Hotel is situated opposite the ferry terminal and is popular with both tourists and business people. It provides well equipped bedrooms with functional fittings and comfortable public rooms. A leisure club is available for guests' use.
65⇨↾(4fb)⚹ in 5 bedrooms CTV in all bedrooms ®⚷ T ✻ sB&B⇨↾ fr£64.95 dB&B⇨↾ fr£73.86 ᖆ
Lift ⓵ 150P ✿ ▭ (heated) sauna solarium gymnasium
V ✿ ♫ ✻ Lunch £7.50 Dinner £15.50&alc Last dinner 9.30pm
Credit Cards [1][2][3][4][5]

★★★ 64% *Kveldsro House*
ZE1 0AN ☎(0595) 2195 FAX (0595) 6595
Standing in a quiet area of the town, this small business hotel offers functional but thoughtfully equipped bedrooms, sound menus which combine quality with quantity, and limited lounge facilities.
14rm(9⇨) CTV in all bedrooms ® T ✠ (ex guide dogs)
28P ⇎
V ✿ ♫ Last dinner 9pm
Credit Cards [1][2][3][4][5]

SNAKE PASS INN ★★

Snake Pass, Bamford, Sheffield S30 2BJ
Telephone: (0433) 51480

Built by the Duke of Devonshire as a coaching house in the 18th century, and set in the beautiful Ashopton Woodlands of the Peak District on the A57 Snake Pass Road. All 7 bedrooms are en suite and have satellite TV, tea and coffee making facilities, and radio alarm clock. Ample car parking and ideal as a centre for the Peak District.

Shetland, Lerwick - Shrawley

★★★**58%** **Lerwick**
15 South Rd ZE1 0RB (signposted from main road)
☎(0595) 2166 FAX (0595) 4419
A modern hotel with excellent views over the bay, the Lerwick caters for both the business and tourist trade alike. Bedrooms are practical and well equipped, and an extensive range of food is available in the bar and restaurant. Extensive refurbishment is underway.
35⇌ℕ(2fb)1⌥ CTV in all bedrooms ® T ✻ (ex guide dogs) sB&B⇌ℕfr£58.50 dB&B⇌ℕfr£75 ⍾
《 30P
♡ International V ✧ ⌤ ✱ Lunch £4.95-£11.95 Dinner £15.95&alc Last dinner 9pm
CONF. Thtr 80 Class 50 Board 25
Credit Cards [1][2][3]

UNST Map **16** HU60

★★**58%** **The Baltasound**
ZE2 9DS ☎Baltasound(095781) 334
10rm(3⇌ℕ)Annexe17⇌ℕ(17fb) CTV in all bedrooms ® T ✻ (ex guide dogs) sB&B⇌Bfr£36 sB&B⇌ℕfr£39.50 dB&Bfr£50 dB&B⇌ℕfr£54
CTV 20P ✿ ♪ pool table
V ✧ ⌤ ✱ Bar Lunch fr£7.20 Dinner fr£13.50 Last dinner 8pm

SHIELDAIG Highland *Ross & Cromarty* Map **14** NG85

★★❀**67%** **Tigh an Eilean**
IV54 8XN ☎(05205) 251 FAX (05205) 321
Closed Nov-Etr
This small family-run Highland holiday hotel is in a picture postcard setting on the waterfront overlooking the loch. Bedrooms, though compact, are fresh and cheery. There are 3 pretty lounges, one with an honesty bar. In the smart modern dining room chef/patron Callum Stewart offers a daily changing short table d'hôte menu of honest, refreshingly unpretentious dishes, prepared from the best available local produce.
11⇌(1fb) ® ✻ sB&B⇌fr£35.70 dB&B⇌fr£79.40
CTV 15P ✿ ♪
♡ Scottish & French ✧ ✱ Dinner fr£17.75 Last dinner 8.30pm
Credit Cards [1][3]

SHIFNAL Shropshire Map **07** SJ70

★★★★**62%** **Park House**
Silvermere Park, Park St TF11 9BA
☎Telford(0952) 460128 FAX (0952) 461658

Two Georgian country houses and their grounds have been combined to create this hotel complex with extensive conference and leisure facilities. Bedrooms are comfortable and equipped to a high standard, there is a choice of grill room or French-style restaurant and the welcoming staff provide attentive service.
38⇌ℕ Annexe16⇌ℕ(2fb)≠in 10 bedrooms CTV in all bedrooms ®✻ T ✱ sB&B⇌ℕ£45-£79.50 dB&B⇌ℕ£65-£94.50 ⍾
Lift 《 160P ✿ ⌥ (heated) sauna solarium jacuzzi *xmas*
♡ English & French V ✧ ⌤ ✱ Lunch £9.50-£11&alc High tea fr£7.50 Dinner £16&alc Last dinner 10.30pm
Credit Cards [1][2][3][5]

SHIPHAM Somerset Map **03** ST45

★★★❀❀**69%** **Daneswood House**
Cuck Hill BS25 1RD (signposted from A38 Bristol/Bridgwater road) (Logis) ☎Winscombe(0934) 843145 & 843945 FAX (0934) 843824
RS 24 Dec-6 Jan
This relaxing Edwardian country house stands in well tended gardens with breathtaking views. Over the years David and Elise

Hodges have made many improvements, all in keeping with the gracious style of the building. Individually decorated bedrooms include garden suites with separate lounges. In the subtly lit dining room chef John Dawson provides imaginative and carefully prepared dishes.
9⇌ℕAnnexe3⇌ℕ(3fb) CTV in all bedrooms ®❀ T ✻ (ex guide dogs) sB&B⇌ℕ£57.50-£69.50 dB&B⇌ℕ£79.50-£112.50 ⍾
《 25P 2⇎ ⇔ ❀
♡ English & Continental V ✧ ⌤ ≠ ✱ Lunch fr£19.95 Dinner £19.95-£21.50 Last dinner 9.30pm
Credit Cards [1][2][3][5]

SHIPLEY West Yorkshire Map **07** SE13

★★★**69%** **Hollings Hall**
Hollins Hall, Baildon BD17 7QW (3m N of Shipley on A6083 Otley road) (Lansbury) ☎Bradford(0274) 530053 FAX (0274) 530187
A converted manor house with sympathetic extensions, Hollings Hall is in an elevated position in attractive grounds. The bedrooms are delightfully furnished and decorated, with good facilities, and public areas retain a country house style. Friendly staff provide willing service.
59⇌ℕ(2fb)≠in 22 bedrooms CTV in all bedrooms ®❀ T ✻ (ex guide dogs) ✱ sB&B⇌ℕfr£79.50 dB&B⇌ℕfr£91 ⍾
Lift 《 130P ✿ sauna solarium gymnasium
♡ English & French V ✧ ⌤ ≠ ✱ Lunch fr£9.95 Dinner fr£17.50 Last dinner 10pm
CONF. Thtr 200 Class 60 Board 60 Del from £99
Credit Cards [1][2][3][5]

SHIPSTON ON STOUR Warwickshire Map **04** SP24

★★**63%** **The Red Lion**
Main St, Long Compton CV36 5JS
☎Long Compton(060884) 221
5⇌ℕ(1fb) CTV in all bedrooms ® ✻ sB&B⇌ℕ£29.50 dB&B⇌ℕ£45
60P ✿
♡ English & French V ✧ ✱ Lunch £8.50-£12.50alc Dinner £12-£16alc Last dinner 9pm
Credit Cards [1][3]

SHIPTON-UNDER-WYCHWOOD Oxfordshire Map **04** SP21

★★**64%** **Shaven Crown**
OX7 6BA (on A361, halfway between Burford and Chipping Norton opposite village green and church) ☎(0993) 830330
Dating from the 14th century, this former hospice to Bruern Abbey is in the centre of the village set around an attractive courtyard. The reception lounge has an unusual double collar braced roof, and the cosy bar at the rear serves an interesting selection of bar meals. The Brookes family have created a warm, relaxed atmosphere, and the hotel is an ideal base for touring the Cotswolds.
9rm(5⇌3ℕ)(1fb)1⌥ CTV in all bedrooms ®
✻ (ex guide dogs) sB&B⇌ℕ£33 dB&B⇌ℕ£68-£82 ⍾
15P ✿ bowling green *xmas*
♡ Continental V ✧ ⌤ ≠ Sunday Lunch £14.50 Dinner £18.50 Last dinner 9.30pm
Credit Cards [1][3]

SHRAWLEY Hereford & Worcester Map **07** SO86

★★★**60%** **Lenchford**
WR6 6TB (beside B4196, N of its junct with A443)
☎Worcester(0905) 620229 FAX (0905) 621125
RS 25 Dec-2 Jan
Superbly set on the banks of the River Severn, with excellent views from many bedrooms, this hotel's accommodation is in the process of upgrading.

16rm(14⇨1♠)(1fb) CTV in all bedrooms ® T ✱ ✱ sB&B£25-£32.50 sB&B⇨♠£25-£39.50 dB&B⇨♠£45-£49.50 ♪
50P ✿ ⇨ (heated) ♩ pool table
♀ English & French V ❖ ✱ Sunday Lunch £10.95 Dinner £8.95-£18.95alc Last dinner 9.30pm
Credit Cards 1 2 3 5

SHREWSBURY Shropshire Map 07 SJ41

★★★★ 56% Albrighton Hall
Albrighton SY4 3AG (2.5m N on A528)
☎Bomere Heath(0939) 291000 FAX (0939) 291123
Superbly situated in 14 acres of lake and parkland, this restored country mansion is a popular venue for weddings and other functions. The bedrooms are all modern, though some are reached by 6 flights of stairs. Plans are in hand to refurbish the public rooms.
29⇨♠Annexe10⇨♠(2fb)6♬ CTV in all bedrooms ® T ✱
(120P ✿ ▭ (heated) squash snooker sauna solarium gymnasium health & leisure club racquet ball ♫
♀ International V ❖ ⚏ ✱ Lunch £5.95-£11.95&alc Dinner £15.95&alc Last dinner 9.30pm
CONF. Thtr 300 Class 60 Board 50 Del from £70
Credit Cards 1 2 3 5

★★★ ❀❀ 76% Albright Hussey
Ellesmere Rd SY4 3AF (2m N, off A528)
☎Bomere Heath(0939) 290571 & 290523 FAX (0939) 291143
The walls of Albright Hussey are crammed with history. The timber frame section of the moated manor dates back to 1524, and the brick and stone wing was built in 1600. It stands in 4 acres of landscaped gardens. Bedrooms and bathrooms are elegantly furnished with antiques, 4-posters, and French silk covered beds. Most have spa baths. There is an impressive panelled restaurant with an à la carte menu. Franco Subbiani, the proprietor, is constantly on hand to greet guests.
5⇨♠1♬ CTV in all bedrooms ® T sB&B⇨£65-£85 dB&B⇨£85-£110 ♪
(50P 2🚗 (£10) ✿ nc3yrs xmas
♀ English, French & Italian V ✂ Lunch £10-£12&alc Dinner £16-£17.50&alc Last dinner 10pm
CONF. Thtr 50 Class 30 Board 28 Del £95
Credit Cards 1 2 3 4 5

★★★ 67% Prince Rupert
Butcher Row SY1 1UQ ☎(0743) 236000 FAX (0743) 357306

Beams and sloping floors abound in the old part of this historic hotel in the town centre where the panelled lounge once served as Prince Rupert's headquarters. Refurbishment has provided bedrooms with good modern facilities, comfortable bar and lounge areas, and a smart modern restaurant in addition to a trattoria across from the main building.
65⇨♠(4fb)2♬ CTV in all bedrooms ® T ✱ sB&B⇨£70-£73.50 dB&B⇨£85-£89.25 ♪
Lift (60P games room
♀ English, French & Italian V ❖ ⚏ Lunch £11.75-£12.50&alc Dinner £17-£17.85&alc Last dinner 10.15pm
CONF. Thtr 120 Class 70 Board 50 Del from £75
Credit Cards 1 2 3 5

★★★ 62% The Lion
Wyle Cop SY1 1UY ☎(0743) 353107 FAX (0743) 352744

Dating back to 1618 the latest, this historic inn still has a wealth of original beams, timbers and ornate carvings. Many bedrooms have exposed timbers, including the Dickens' Suite with its half tester bed. The grand ballroom, built in the 18th century in the

Robert Adam style, is still used for local functions. Staff are particularly friendly and helpful.
59⇨♠(3fb)1♬✂in 24 bedrooms CTV in all bedrooms ® T sB⇨♠fr£75 dB⇨♠fr£85 (room only) ♪
Lift (35P 35🚗 xmas
V ❖ ⚏ ✂ Sunday Lunch £5.50-£11.50 Dinner fr£17.50 Last dinner 9.30pm
CONF. Thtr 200 Class 80 Board 80 Del from £95
Credit Cards 1 2 3 5

★★ 64% Shelton Hall
Shelton SY3 8BH (2m NW A5) ☎(0743) 343982 FAX (0743) 241515
Closed Xmas
This small family-run hotel with attractive gardens has a friendly country house atmosphere and offers warm, well-equipped bedrooms and good food in its popular restaurant.
10rm(9⇨♠)(2fb) CTV in all bedrooms ® T ✱ sB&B£31 sB&B⇨♠£49.50 dB&B⇨♠£64 ♪
CTV 50P 🚗 ✿
♀ English & Continental V ❖ Sunday Lunch £10.50 Dinner £15.50 Last dinner 8.30pm
Credit Cards 1 3

See advertisement on page 551

★★ 64% The Shrewsbury
Bridge Place, Old Welsh Bridge SY1 1TU
☎(0743) 231246 FAX (0743) 240093

This long established hotel lies near the River Severn. Bedrooms are well furnished and comfortable and there is a choice of bars serving a good range of meals. The restaurant is in several parts with a separate sitting area, and there are lounge areas on the landings of the first and second floors. Staff are very friendly.
24⇨♠(6fb) CTV in all bedrooms ®✂ T

Busta, Brae, Shetland.
Tel. Brae (080622) 506 Fax: (080622) 588

This former home of the Lairds of Busta dating from 1588 combines old world charm with modern comfort. Family owned and run. Good food, fine wines, real fires and a warm welcome await you at Busta House.

Telephone for details of our Holidays plus Travel and Car Hire

Shrewsbury - Sidmouth

⟨ CTV 34P
V ✋ Last dinner 9pm
Credit Cards [1][2][3][5]

★★ 61% Lion & Pheasant
49-50 Wyle Cop SY1 1XJ (town centre, by
English Bridge, 2m from M54 motorway link)
☎(0743) 236188 FAX (0743) 343740

Originally a coaching house on the main London to Holyhead route,
the building is 16th-century at the latest and is situated near the
English Bridge. There are timbers, sloping floors and original
fireplaces – the one in the bar is a large inglenook where logs blaze
in winter. There is a comfortable foyer lounge and a first-floor
timbered restaurant. Bedrooms vary, but most have solid furniture.
20rm(17⇨♪)(1fb) CTV in all bedrooms ® T
✖ (ex guide dogs) sB&B£23.50-£28.75 sB&B⇨♪£25.50-
£39.50 dB&B£45-£50 dB&B⇨♪£50-£56.20 ♬
CTV 20P *xmas*
♀ English & Spanish V ✋ ♫ ✱ Lunch fr£10.95&alc High tea
fr£4.95&alc Dinner fr£10.95&alc Last dinner 9.30pm
Conf. Thtr 30 Class 25 Board 20 Del from £60
Credit Cards [1][2][3][5]

SIBSON Leicestershire Map **04 SK 30**

★★ 62% Millers Hotel & Restaurant
Main Rd CV13 6LB (6m N of Nuneaton on A444 road to Burton)
☎Tamworth(0827) 880223 FAX (0827) 880223 ext222
This one-time bakery and watermill, now a popular small hotel,
retains many features of its past including the working waterwheel.
It provides well equipped bedrooms with modern facilities and a bar
and restaurant much frequented by locals.
40⇨♪(1fb)2🛏 CTV in all bedrooms ® ❋ T sB⇨♪£18-£41
dB⇨♪£18-£51 (room only) ♬
⟨ CTV 100P 2🅿 (£5 per night) games room 🎱 *xmas*
♀ English & Continental V ✋ ♫ Lunch £10.95&alc Dinner
£13.95&alc Last dinner 9.45pm
Conf. Thtr 50 Class 20 Board 24 Del from £54.95
Credit Cards [1][2][3][5] £

SIDMOUTH Devon Map **03 SY18**

★★★★ 67% Belmont
The Esplanade EX10 8RX (Brend) ☎(0395) 512555 FAX (0395)
579101
Built as a private residence in the 18th century, this hotel still retains
the elegance of the period. It is well set back from the esplanade and
has spacious lounges, one a quiet lounge for non smokers, and the
restaurant, though compact, offers à la carte and table d'hôte menus.
Some of the bedrooms have good sea views, and service is formal,
but with natural friendliness.
54⇨♪(10fb) CTV in all bedrooms ® ❋ T ✖ (ex guide dogs) ✱
sB&B⇨♪£64-£78 dB&B⇨♪£98-£156 ♬
Lift ⟨ 45P ✿ putting green ♫ 🎱 *xmas*
♀ English & French V ✋ ♫ ✱ Lunch £10.25 Dinner £17&alc
Last dinner 9pm
Credit Cards [1][2][3][5] £

★★★★ 65% Victoria
Esplanade EX10 8RY (Brend) ☎(0395) 512651 FAX (0395)
579154
The atmosphere of Victorian permanence here is coupled with
friendly but efficiently professional standards of service – room
service is particularly good. Bedrooms are bright and well furnished,
and there are extensive and comfortable lounge facilities.
61⇨♪(18fb) CTV in all bedrooms ® ❋ T ✖ (ex guide dogs) ✱
sB&B⇨♪£57-£70 dB&B⇨♪£115-£170 ♬
Lift ⟨ 100P 4🅿 (£4 per day) ✿ 🏊 (heated) ⇨ (heated) ℘
(hard) snooker sauna solarium spa bath putting green ♫ 🎱
xmas

♀ English & French V ✋ ♫ ✱ Lunch £10.25 Dinner £16.50-
£20.50&alc Last dinner 9pm
Credit Cards [1][2][3][5] £

★★★ 78% Riviera
The Esplanade EX10 8AY ☎(0395) 515201 FAX (0395) 577775
In a prime seafront position overlooking Lyme Bay, this Regency
hotel has been run by the hospitable Wharton family for over 20
years and offers old-fashioned attentive service and a quiet relaxing
atmosphere. Many of the pleasant and well equipped bedrooms
have been refurbished, and further improvements are underway.
The elegant lounge and bar are comfortable and the busy restaurant
offers an extensive choice of home-cooked dishes.
29⇨♪(6fb) CTV in all bedrooms ❋ T sB&B⇨♪£58-£78
dB&B⇨♪£106-£146 (incl dinner) ♬
Lift ⟨ 14P 9 (£2.50 per 24hrs) ✿ ✱ *xmas*
♀ English & French V ✋ ♫ ✱ Lunch £11.50&alc Dinner
£18.50&alc Last dinner 9pm
Conf. Thtr 85 Class 60 Board 30 Del from £61.25
Credit Cards [1][2][3][5]
See advertisement on page 553

★★★ 72% Westcliff
Manor Rd EX10 8RU ☎(0395) 513252 FAX (0395) 578203
Closed 21 Dec-1 Feb RS Nov-20 Dec & 2 Feb-6 Apr
With splendid views over the town and sea, this hotel stands in
award-winning gardens. Bedrooms have been tastefully decorated,
several with sea views and balconies, and public areas are
comfortable. A selection of dishes is offered from a set menu or the
carte, and a warm, friendly atmosphere is created by the attentive
staff.
40⇨♪(15fb) CTV in all bedrooms ® ❋ T ✖ sB&B⇨♪£40-
£64.35 dB&B⇨♪£80-£141.50 (incl dinner) ♬
Lift CTV 40P ✿ ✱ ⇨ (heated) solarium gymnasium croquet
putting jacuzzi pool table
♀ English & Continental V ✋ ♫ ✱ Sunday Lunch £9.50
Dinner £17&alc Last dinner 8.45pm
Credit Cards [1][3]

★★★ 66% Salcombe Hill House
Beatlands Rd EX10 8JQ ☎(0395) 514697 & 514398
Closed Nov-Feb
Set in its own gardens, this Georgian hotel about half a mile from
the seafront has a friendly country house atmosphere. Bedrooms of
varying size are well equipped and there is a choice of lounges, one
with a small bar, and a dining room offering table d'hôte and à la
carte menus.
30⇨♪(5fb) CTV in all bedrooms ® T ✱ sB&B⇨♪£34-£54
dB&B⇨♪£68-£108 (incl dinner) ♬
Lift ⟨ 35P 4 (£3.60 daily) ✿ ✱ ⇨ (heated) ℘ (grass) putting
games room pool nc3yrs
V ✋ ♫ ✱ Sunday Lunch £7-£8&alc Dinner £12-£14&alc
Last dinner 8.30pm
Credit Cards [1][3][5]

★★★ 61% Fortfield
Station Rd EX10 8NU ☎(0395) 512403 FAX (0395) 512403
A short walk from the seafront, this comfortable hotel has well
managed, competent staff. The atmosphere is convivial and the
property is continually improving. There is limed oak panelling in
the public rooms and deep armchairs in the lounges. A 4-course
menu of largely home-made fresh food, including local fish.
Bedrooms are simply furnished but are freshly decorated.
52⇨♪ Annexe3⇨♪(7fb) CTV in all bedrooms ® T
sB&B⇨♪£25-£55.50 dB&B⇨♪£50-£111 ♬
Lift ⟨ CTV 60P ✱ 🏊 (heated) sauna solarium health & beauty
salon games room 🎱 *xmas*
V ✋ ♫ ✱ Sunday Lunch £8.50 Dinner £12 Last dinner 8.30pm
Conf. Thtr 130 Class 70 Board 40 Del from £50
Credit Cards [1][2][3][5] £

ONE OF ENGLAND'S FINEST HOTELS

The Victoria offers a unique combination of sports and leisure facilities with unrivalled standards of comfort and cuisine.

Located at the western tip of Sidmouth's Esplanade, the town's Regency centre is just a short level walk away. Every bedroom offers a private bathroom en-suite, colour television with satellite reception, direct dial telephone and twenty four hour room service.

Facilities include heated indoor and outdoor swimming pools, tennis, sauna, solarium, spa bath, full size snooker table, hair-dressing salon, games rooms and gift shop.

AA ★★★★

FOR FREE COLOUR BROCHURE AND TARIFF PLEASE
CONTACT: Mr. M. Raistrick,
The Victoria Hotel, Sidmouth, Devon EX10 8RY.
Tel: (0395) 512651. Fax: (0395) 579154.

AA ★★

Lion & Pheasant Hotel

49-50 Wyle Cop, Shrewsbury, SY1 1XJ
Telephone: 0743 236288 Fax: 0743 343740

OPEN ALL YEAR

Popular with visitors, this old coaching inn is situated close to the river just minutes from the main shopping area. The olde worlde split level restaurant offers extensive à la carte and table d'hôte dinners and a comprehensive bar snack lunchtime menu.

19 rooms   13 shower   4 bath

All rooms have colour television, hot and cold running water, telephone, tea and coffee making facilities.

1992 tariff — B&B single room from £25.00-£44.50
All charges per B&B twin room from £44.00-£56.20
room per night. B&B double room from £44.00-£56.20

Lunch from £3.50, dinner from £10.95 & à la carte. Last orders 9.30 pm.

Credit cards accepted — Access, Mastercard, Visa, American Express, Diners, Consort Cards.

Luxury, Elegance & Style

Situated just a short level walk from Sidmouth town centre and the famous Esplanade, The Belmont Hotel provides modern luxury in a singularly elegant style.

Bedrooms are luxuriously appointed. All feature colour TV and private bathroom, many have the most dramatic sea views.

Excellent cuisine, with table d'hote and à la carte menus, is complemented by the Belmont's distinctly personal style of service. Indoor and outdoor pools and fine leisure facilities are freely available just yards away at The Victoria, The Belmont's sister hotel.

The Belmont Hotel

AA ★★★★

FOR FREE COLOUR BROCHURE AND TARIFF
PLEASE CONTACT: Mr. A. Dennis,
The Belmont Hotel, The Esplanade, Sidmouth, Devon.
Tel: (0395) 512555. Fax (0395) 579101.

Shelton Hall Hotel
Country House   AA ★★

Shelton, Shrewsbury, SY3 8BH

Set amidst Shropshire countryside, yet only 1½ miles from the centre of the medieval town of Shrewsbury. We are a friendly family-run licensed hotel in 3½ acres of lovely gardens. We are situated 1 mile from the main A5 London to Holyhead route with easy access to Wales and the Marches.

Open all year.

Telephone: Shrewsbury (0743) 343982
Fax: (0743) 241515

Sidmouth

★★★ 60% Royal Glen
Glen Rd EX10 8RW ☎(0395) 513221 & 578124
Once the summer residence of the Duke and Duchess of Kent and their daughter, the future Queen Victoria, this characterful hotel in a quiet location close to the seafront is furnished in keeping with the Victorian style. Bedrooms, some quite compact, are comfortable and there is a delightful drawing room.
34rm(32⇌ℕ)(4fb) CTV in all bedrooms ® T sB&B£22.50-£34.50 sB&B⇌ℕ£26-£40 dB&B£52-£80 ₽
CTV 16P 8🐾 (£1 per night) ⇔ ▱ (heated) nc8yrs *xmas*
♀ English & French ✿ ♨ ✴ Lunch £6.50 Dinner fr£11.50 Last dinner 8.30pm
Credit Cards [1][2][3] ⓔ

★★⯁ 70% Brownlands
Sid Rd EX10 9AG (turn off A3052 at Sidford, at Fortescue/Sidford sign, hotel 1m on left) ☎(0395) 513053
Closed Jan RS Dec
On the wooded slopes of Salcombe Hill, with views over Sidmouth and Lyme Bay, this Victorian country house has been converted into an attractive relaxing hotel, family run in informal style. Light and airy bedrooms of varying size are well equipped, and public rooms include an oak-panelled dining room and a conservatory overlooking the gardens.
14⇌ℕ(1fb) CTV in all bedrooms ® T sB&B⇌ℕ£40-£44 dB&B⇌ℕ£80-£99.70 (incl dinner) ₽
CTV 25P ⇔ ✿ ♎ (hard) putting nc8yrs *xmas*
♀ International V ✿ ♨ ✴ Sunday Lunch £9.75 Dinner £17.95 Last dinner 8pm

★★ 70% Mount Pleasant
Salcombe Rd EX12 8JA ☎(0395) 514694
Closed Oct-Etr
This attractive early Georgian residence with well kept gardens is convenient for the seafront and town centre. Bedrooms are of a high standard, comfortable and tastefully decorated. There is a bar lounge and a lounge for non-smokers, and in the intimate dining room a limited choice of traditional home-cooked fare is offered from a table d'hôte menu.
16⇌ℕ(1fb) ⇔ CTV in all bedrooms ® ✴ sB&B⇌ℕ£28-£31 dB&B⇌ℕ£58-£62 ₽
22P 1🐾 ⇔ ✿ ✿ 9 nc8yrs
✿ ♨

★★ 68% Abbeydale
Manor Rd EX10 8RP ☎(0395) 512060
Closed 2 Nov-28 Mar
Close to the Esplanade and set in an attractive garden, this long established family-run hotel has well equipped bedrooms and a spacious comfortable lounge. A short table d'hôte menu is served in the no-smoking dining room, with bar meals available at lunch time in the bar lounge.
17⇌ℕ(2fb) CTV in all bedrooms ® T 🍴 sB&B⇌ℕ£25-£37 dB&B⇌ℕ£50-£74 ₽
Lift 24P ⇔ ✿ nc4yrs
♀ English & French ✿ ♨ ✴ Bar Lunch fr£1.30alc Dinner fr£14 Last dinner 8pm

★★ 66% Kingswood
Esplanade EX10 8AX ☎(0395) 516367 FAX (0395) 51385
Closed mid Nov-mid Mar
This popular, friendly, family-run hotel enjoys glorious views from its central position on the sea front. All its tastefully decorated and well furnished bedrooms are equipped to meet the needs of either commercial visitors or holiday-makers, a spacious lounge combines comfort with quality, and the informal dining room offers a table d'hôte menu.
26⇌ℕ(7fb)1⇔ CTV in all bedrooms ® T ✴ sB&B⇌ℕ£21-£25 dB&B⇌ℕ£44-£50 ₽
Lift CTV 7P 2🐾 (£17.50 per wk)

♀ English & French ✿ ♨ ✴ Bar Lunch £2-£5 Dinner £12-£14 Last dinner 7.30pm

★★ 65% Littlecourt
Seafield Rd EX10 8HF ☎(0395) 515279
Closed 2 Nov-21 Dec & 29 Dec-10 Mar RS 22-28 Dec
This friendly Regency hotel close to the seafront and town centre has attractively decorated bedrooms and comfortable public areas, including a spacious drawing room and a no-smoking TV lounge. In the dining room, a short table d'hôte menu is offered.
21rm(12⇌7ℕ)(3fb) CTV in all bedrooms ® ✴ sB&B£26.75-£37.25 sB&B⇌ℕ£32-£46.20 dB&B⇌ℕ£64-£96 (incl dinner) ₽
CTV 17P ✿ ⇔ (heated) *xmas*
♀ English & French V ✿ ♨ ✴
Credit Cards [1][2][3]

★★ 65% Royal York & Faulkner
Esplanade EX10 8AZ ☎(0395) 513043 Freephone 0800 22071 FAX (0395) 577472
Closed 3 Jan-4 Feb
Personally run by the Hook family for 50 years, this attractive Regency hotel at the centre of the Esplanade provides comfortable well-equipped bedrooms and a newly refurbished bar lounge.
68⇌ℕ(8fb) CTV in all bedrooms ® T ✴ sB&B⇌ℕ£26.25-£50 dB&B⇌ℕ£52.50-£100 (incl dinner) ₽
Lift CTV 7P snooker sauna solarium gymnasium jacuzzi spa pool indoor bowls ♪ *xmas*
♀ English & French V ✿ ♨ ✴ Bar Lunch £5.50-£10alc Dinner £13 Last dinner 8.30pm
Credit Cards [1][3] ⓔ

★★ 65% The Salty Monk
Church St, Sidford EX10 9QP (2m N A3052) ☎(0395) 513174
Originally a staging post for monks and their donkeys carrying salt from Lyme Regis to Exeter, this small hotel in the village centre has much historic character. It offers friendly service, simple but comfortable bedrooms with modern facilities and freshly prepared meals, served in the cosy lounge bar or restaurant.
8rm(3⇌1ℕ)⯎ in all bedrooms CTV in all bedrooms ® ✴ sB&Bfr£20 sB&B⇌ℕfr£23 dB&Bfr£36 dB&B⇌ℕfr£40
12P ⇔ ✿ *xmas*
♀ English & French V ✿ ♨ ✴ Lunch £4.50-£6.50&alc Dinner £9.50-£15alc Last dinner 9pm
Credit Cards [1][3]

★★ 56% Woodlands
Station Rd EX10 8HG ☎(0395) 513120
This traditional, old-fashioned hotel, a short walk from the seafront, is in country cottage style with a pleasant garden. There are several lounges and a grandfather clock ticks audibly in the front hall. The short dinner menu provides traditional British dishes, and what bedrooms lack in modern facilities they make up for in old-world charm and comfort.
30rm(14⇌4ℕ)(1fb) CTV in 4 bedrooms ®
CTV 22P ⇔ ✿ putting nc3yrs
✿ ♨ Last dinner 8pm
Credit Cards [1][3]

★★ 54% Westbourne
Manor Rd EX10 8RR ☎(0395) 513774
Closed Nov-Feb
Close to the beaches and well kept gardens of the pretty seaside town, this traditional family-run hotel is especially popular with older guests. Bedrooms are rather dated in style, but there are plans to upgrade some of these in the coming months. Cosy public areas include a bright sun lounge and an attractive dining room.
14rm(8⇌1ℕ)(2fb) CTV in all bedrooms ®
16P ⇔
V ✿ ♨ ✴ Last dinner 7.30pm
Credit Cards [1][3]

Woodlands Hotel
SIDMOUTH – DEVON
★★

Situated in a superb award winning garden near the sea, bounded by fine trees, a gentle babbling stream with ponds and fountains. Spacious Regency rooms retain their elegance and comfort. Well maintained with modern facilities, the hotel takes pride in personal service and courteous attention. Excellent cuisine using Devon meat and dairy produce with West Country specialities included. Relax in the lounge or large garden room which overlooks the stream and peaceful garden.

Woodlands offers all this and more!

**COTMATON CROSS, SIDMOUTH EX10 8HG
Telephone: 0395 513120**

THE KINGSWOOD HOTEL

★★

The Esplanade, Sidmouth, Devon EX10 8AX
Telephone: (0395) 516367
Fax: (0395) 513185

Come and enter into a piece of history, the hotel is incorporated into a building built in 1891 that was originally a social club for local gentlemen of standing. Then in 1895 considerable alterations took place and the Sidmouth Bath Company was formed providing spa facilities with curative and therapeutic benefits. But in 1938 the property was sold and the Kingswood Hotel emerged. Whilst retaining the spacious charm and elegance of the last century the hotel has been fully modernised throughout. Situated in the middle of the Esplanade just a minute across to the beach and not many more minutes' stroll into the old world charm of the town.

> *The hotel has a long tradition of hospitality and is perfect for unforgettable holidays, long weekends, unwinding breaks and all the spirit of the glorious Festive Season ... you will be treated to the kind of friendly, personal attention that can only be found in a privately-owned hotel of this quality.*

AA ★★★ 78%
Courtesy and Care Award 1992/1993

HOTEL RIVIERA
THE ESPLANADE SIDMOUTH DEVON
TEL: 0395 515201 FAX: 0395 577575

The choice for the discerning in search of relaxation and quieter pleasures.

Silchester - Skelmorlie

SILCHESTER Hampshire Map 04 SU66

★★★ ❀65% **Romans**
Little London Rd RG7 2PN
☎(0734) 700421 FAX (0734) 700691

Closed Xmas & New Year

Built as a private residence in 1901, the main house retains much of its character with fine panelling, a small dining room, a well furnished bar lounge with a log fire, and spacious bedrooms. Chef Shelley May has cooked here for over 15 years and his daily hand-written, fixed price menu of freshly prepared dishes is recommended.

11🛏Annexe13🛏🕻(1fb)1🚭 CTV in all bedrooms ® T sB&B🛏🕻£55-£70 dB&B🛏🕻£75-£85 🍴
(40P 🚗 ✿ ⌇ (heated)
♨ European ✄ Lunch £13-£17 Dinner £16-£20 Last dinner 9pm
CONF. Thtr 60 Class 24 Board 20 Del from £80
Credit Cards [1][2][3][5] £

SILLOTH Cumbria Map 11 NY15

★★★ 70% **The Skinburness Hotel**
CA5 4QY (2m NE on coast road) ☎(06973) 32332 FAX (06973) 32549

Situated in the hamlet of Skinburness to the north of Silloth, close to a fine golf course and coastal walks, this recently renovated and very well furnished hotel has comfortable modern bedrooms with good facilities. There is an attractive lounge, bar and split-level restaurant offering well prepared food.

25🛏🕻 CTV in all bedrooms ® T sB&B🛏🕻frf45 dB&B🛏🕻frf60 🍴
70P ✿ snooker sauna solarium gymnasium 🎵 🎱 xmas
♨ English & French V ✄ ✻ Lunch £9.50 High tea £2.75 Dinner £12.50-£16.50 Last dinner 9pm
CONF. Thtr 120 Class 100 Board 60 Del from £55.50
Credit Cards [1][2][3][5] £

★★ 62% **Golf**
Criffel St CA5 4AB ☎(06973) 31438 FAX (06973) 32582
Closed 25 Dec

Popular with locals and close to the seafront, this town centre hotel offers good bar food, and the intimate restaurant has an Italian feel. Bedrooms are modern with varying styles of décor.

22🛏🕻(4fb)1🚭 CTV in all bedrooms ®
🎱
♨ English & Continental ✄ ✿ Last dinner 9.15pm
Credit Cards [1][2][3][5]

SIMONSBATH Somerset Map 03 SS73

★★ ❀♨ 74% **Simonsbath House**
TA24 7SH (situated on the B3223) ☎Exford(064383) 259
Closed Dec-Jan

A delightful 17th-century property, Simonsbath House has charming bedrooms with modern facilities and thoughtful extras. There is a panelled lounge and library lounge bar, with log fires on cool evenings, and in the dining room Mrs Burns provides imaginative dishes cooked from fresh local ingredients. There are 3 self-catering cottages and an informal restaurant in converted buildings in the grounds.

7🛏🕻3🚭 CTV in all bedrooms T ✖ sB&B🛏🕻£44-£60 dB&B🛏🕻£78-£90 🍴
40P 🚗 ✿ nc10yrs
✄ Dinner £18 Last dinner 8.30pm
Credit Cards [1][2][3][5]

SIX MILE BOTTOM Cambridgeshire Map 05 TL55

★★★ 72% **Swynford Paddocks**
CB8 0UE (6m SW of Newmarket, on A1304) (Qualitair)
☎(063870) 234 FAX (063870) 283
Closed 3-5 days over Xmas & New Year RS Sat lunch-closed

A former country mansion with gabled roof and attractive greenery stands in well maintained gardens southwest of Newmarket. The house retains many original features; panelled rooms are furnished in keeping with its period, and the balustraded and galleried hallway leads to a range of quality bedrooms with luxurious bathrooms.

15🛏2🚭 CTV in all bedrooms ® T sB&B🛏🕻£70-£85 dB&B🛏🕻£107-£150 🍴
120P 🚗 ✿ ⌇ (hard) croquet putting outdoor chess 🎵

♨ English & Continental V ✄ ✻ Lunch £14.95-£16.95&alc Dinner £19.95-£21.95&alc Last dinner 9.30pm
CONF. Thtr 30 Board 22 Del from £108
Credit Cards [1][2][3][5]

SKEABOST BRIDGE

See **Skye, Isle of**

SKEGNESS Lincolnshire Map 09 TF56

★★★ 58% **Crown**
Drummond Rd, Seacroft PE25 3AB ☎(0754) 610760 FAX (0754) 610847

An attractive, rambling property within its own walled car park, the Crown is a traditional resort hotel. The spacious bar lounge provides plenty of comfortable seating which compensates for the limited seating in the foyer lounge. Bedrooms are compact and similar in style, with modern furnishings and pastel décor.

27🛏🕻(7fb) ® T ✖ (ex guide dogs)
Lift (CTV 90P ⌇ (heated)
♨ English & French V ✄ ✻ Lunch £11.95&alc High tea £2.75-£3.95 Dinner £11.95&alc Last dinner 9.30pm
CONF. Thtr 120 Class 130 Board 120
Credit Cards [1][2][3][5]

★★ 62% **North Shore**
North Shore Rd PE25 1DN ☎(0754) 763298 FAX (0754) 761902

This seaside golf hotel has direct access to the beach and is close to all amenities. Bedrooms vary in shape and size, some are rather compact, but all feature modern furnishings, matching fabrics and bright décor. The lounge has superb views, and the buzz of golfing talk is evident in the popular bar, where substantial bar meals are served.

30🛏Annexe3🛏🕻(4fb) CTV in all bedrooms ® T ✖ (ex guide dogs) ✻ sB&B🛏🕻£25-£50 dB&B🛏🕻£50-£100 (incl dinner) 🍴
(CTV 120P ✿ ♠ 18 🎱 (hard) snooker xmas
V ✄ ✻ Lunch £7.50-£10&alc Dinner £14&alc Last dinner 9pm
CONF. Thtr 120 Class 120
Credit Cards [1][3] £

SKELMORLIE Strathclyde Ayrshire Map 10 NS16

★★★♨ 61% **Manor Park**
PA17 5HE (off A78, 2m from Largs) (SCOTLAND'S HERITAGE HOTELS) ☎Wemyss Bay(0475) 520832 FAX (0475) 520832

Set in delightful gardens and grounds where peacocks strut, with fine views across the Firth of Clyde, this personally run country mansion offers a relaxed atmosphere and old-style comforts. The main house includes traditionally furnished, spacious bedrooms

---

For full, independent restaurant reviews, see the
AA Abbey Well *Restaurant Guide*.

while the stables have been converted into small suites and studio rooms, some with their own kitchen.
10⇨↑ Annexe13⇨↑ CTV in all bedrooms ® T sB&B⇨↑£45-£70 dB&B⇨↑£65-£100 ♫
150P ❋ putting green *xmas*
♡ British & Continental V ✧ ⚏ ✂ Lunch fr£12.50&alc High tea £7.50-£12.50alc Dinner £19.50-£21&alc Last dinner 9.30pm
CONF. Thtr 160 Class 100 Board 80 Del from £75
Credit Cards [1][2][3][5] (£)

SKIPTON North Yorkshire Map 07 SD95

★★★ ❀66% **Randell's**
Keighley Rd, Snaygill BD23 2TA (on A629, 1m from town)
☎(0756) 700100 FAX (0756) 700107
(Rosette awarded for dinner only)

The back of this large modern hotel overlooks the Leeds and Liverpool Canal, and guests eating in the elegant Waterside Restaurant can enjoy the view whilst sampling an expertly prepared and imaginative range of mainly British dishes. As well as the roomy lounges and bars, there is a supervised nursery.
60⇨↑1☐ CTV in all bedrooms ® ☼ T ✶ sB&B⇨↑£35-£67.50 dB&B⇨↑£55-£77.50 ♫
Lift ☾ 200P ▣ (heated) squash sauna solarium gymnasium pool, table whirlpool spa steam room ⚘ *xmas*
V ✧ ⚏ ✂ ✻ Lunch fr£8.75 High tea fr£5 Dinner fr£15.95 Last dinner 9.30pm
Credit Cards [1][2][3][5]

See advertisement on page 557

For key to symbols see the Bookmark.

CROWN HOTEL
★★★
**Drummond Road, Skegness,
Lincolnshire PE25 3AB
Tel: (0754) 610760 Fax: (0754) 610847**

Completely refurbished family owned hotel situated in a quiet area of Seacroft, a few minutes from the town centre and beach. All 27 bedrooms are en suite and have all amenities. The superb Sovereign Restaurant and tastefully decorated lounge bar with an air of sophistication guaranteed to enhance the existing character. The indoor swimming pool and garden are ideal to relax in. For Golfing enthusiasts there are several professional golf courses nearby. Conferences and business guests are well catered. Winter/summer breaks available. Open all year.

The Skinburness Hotel
★ ★ ★

**Silloth on Solway, Carlisle,
Cumbria CA5 4QY
Tel: (06973) 32332 Fax: (06973) 32549**

Delightful Victorian Hotel set 200 yards from the shores of the Solway Firth. Twenty-five en suite bedrooms, friendly and welcoming staff, superb restaurant and comfortable bar. Tempting table d'hôte dinners and delicious bar meals served daily. Leisure facilities include gymnasium, sauna and sun-bed. Forty minutes from borders and lakes.

Westbourne Hotel
**MANOR ROAD, SIDMOUTH, DEVON EX10 8RR
TELEPHONE: (0395) 513774**
★★ *Personal courteous service and
attention at all times*

We are specially noted for excellent cuisine and our cocktail bar has a wide selection of wine and spirits. Our gracious Victorian drawing room and relaxing sun lounge overlook the prize winning gardens. Situated only 200 yards from the Connaught Garden and Jacob's Ladder bathing beach, the town centre and sea front being only a short easy stroll away, so your car may be left in our own private car park. All bedrooms are en suite and decorated in keeping with its own individual character and charm.
**Bargain breaks out of season including Easter.
Please write for a colour brochure.**

Skipton - Skye, Isle of, Portree

★★63% Herriots
Broughton Rd BD23 1RT (off A59, opposite station)
☎(0756) 792781 FAX (0756) 792781

A Victorian railway hotel, opposite the station, Herriots has recently been upgraded in a fashionable style which has yet retained much original grandeur. Hearty bar meals offer an alternative to the open-plan restaurant.

11⇨🐾(2fb) CTV in all bedrooms ® T ✻ sB&B⇨🐾£35-£45 dB&B⇨🐾£45-£49.50 🍽
25P
♿ International V ✱ ✻ Sunday Lunch £5.95 Dinner £8-£14alc Last dinner 9.45pm
CONF. Thtr 35 Class 15 Board 20 Del from £56
Credit Cards [1] [3] £

Forte Travelodge
Gargrave Rd BD23 1UD (A65/A59 roundabout)
☎(0756) 798091 Central Res (0800) 850950

This modern building offers a good standard of accommodation for overnight stops. Smart, spacious and well equipped bedrooms, all with en suite bathrooms, are suitable for family use, and meals may be taken at the nearby family restaurant. For more details about Travelodges, consult the Contents page, under Hotel Groups.

32⇨🐾✻ B⇨🐾£31.95 (room only)

SKYE, ISLE OF Highland *Inverness-shire* Map 13

ARDVASAR Map 13 NG60

★★❀69% Ardvasar
IV45 8RS ☎(04714) 223
Closed 24-25 Dec & 1-3 Jan RS Nov-Mar
(Rosette awarded for dinner only)

In a convenient situation for the Armadale-Mallaig ferry, this delightful holiday hotel is a popular base for visitors to Skye. Smart pine furnishings are gradually being introduced to the cheery bedrooms, where to ensure peace there is no TV between 11pm and 8am. Public areas include a choice of cosy lounges and bars, and the dining room offers a variety of fresh produce carefully prepared by proprietor Bill Fowler.

10⇨🐾(3fb) CTV in all bedrooms ® ✈ (ex guide dogs) sB&B⇨🐾£35 dB&B⇨🐾£60-£65
30P ❀
♿ Scottish & French V ✿ ✱ Bar Lunch £1.70-£10alc Dinner £10-£25alc Last dinner 8.30pm
Credit Cards [1] [3]

HARLOSH Map 13 NG24

★❀76% Harlosh House
IV55 8ZG (A863 between Roag & Caroy, follow sign for Harlosh) ☎Dunvegan(047022) 367 FAX (047022) 413
Closed mid Oct-Etr

Efficiently run by Peter and Lindsey Elford, this delightful small holiday hotel is peacefully situated on a peninsula with spectacular views over Loch Caroy to the majestic Cuillins beyond. There is a welcoming atmosphere in the cosy bar lounge and small, intimate restaurant, where Peter's imaginative modern cooking is sure to please. His interesting carte is prepared from the best available ingredients; fish and shellfish are the speciality, but prime Scottish beef, lamb and game also feature.

6rm(5⇨🐾)(3fb)✱ in all bedrooms TV available ®
✈ (ex guide dogs) sB&B⇨🐾£66 dB&B⇨🐾£86 dB&B⇨🐾£86
10P ❀ ✿
♿ Scottish & French ✿ ✱ Dinner £20-£25alc Last dinner 8.30pm
Credit Cards [1] [3]

ISLE ORNSAY Map 13 NG61

★★❀68% Kinloch Lodge
IV43 8QY ☎(04713) 214 & 333 FAX (04713) 277
Closed Dec-14 Mar

You will find Lord and Lady Macdonald's sturdy, white-painted Edwardian lodge at the end of a long bumpy drive. The position is secluded, but the view across Loch Na Dal to the rugged mainland hills beyond is quite spectacular. Complete tranquillity prevails throughout the house. The elegant dining room, with its family portraits, is the setting for Lady Macdonald's daily changing limited choice fixed price menu. Dishes are prepared from the best available fresh Scottish produce, including local seafood. The small, modest bedrooms are comfortable but have few of the usual amenities.

10rm(8⇨)✱ in all bedrooms ® sB&B£40-£85 sB&B⇨£40-£85 dB&B£80-£170 dB&B⇨£80-£170
18P ⏰ ❀ ✱ stalking
♿ ✱ Dinner £25-£35 Last dinner 8pm
Credit Cards [1] [3]

★★64% Duisdale
IV43 8QW (on A851 Armadale to Broadford road, just north of the village of Isle Ornsay) ☎(04713) 202 FAX (04713) 363
Closed 5 Jan-Etr

Delightfully situated in its own garden on the Sleat peninsula, this friendly, family-run hotel is popular with tour groups. Public areas are traditional in style, while bedrooms, which vary in size, have a mixture of practical modern furnishings.

19rm(14⇨🐾)(4fb)1🛏 ® sB&B£26.50 sB&B⇨🐾£36.75-£42 dB&B£53 dB&B⇨🐾£63-£86 🍽
CTV 20P ❀ croquet putting *xmas*
V ✿ ✱ Dinner £18.50 Last dinner 8.30pm
Credit Cards [1] [2] [3] £

★68% Hotel Eilean Iarmain
IV43 8QR ☎(04713) 332 FAX (04713) 260

Since Effie Kennedy took over the daily running of this island inn there have been considerable improvements. Beautifully situated beside a natural harbour overlooking the Sound of Sleat, the hotel offers modern facilities while retaining its original character. Public areas include a comfortable lounge and a public bar, and enjoyable home cooking is served in the small dining room. The traditionally furnished bedrooms are divided between the main house and the garden annexe opposite.

6rm(4⇨🐾)Annexe6⇨🐾(2fb)1🛏 ® T
TV 30P ❀ ✱
V ✿ ✱ Last dinner 8.30pm
Credit Cards [1] [3]

PORTREE Map 13 NG44

★★★70% Rosedale
IV51 9DB ☎(0478) 613131 FAX (0478) 612531
Closed Oct-mid May

Three adjoining 19th-century harbourfront buildings have been converted to create this popular holiday hotel. Bedrooms are pretty and comfortable, though some are rather compact. A bewildering range of corridors and stairs link the buildings, which offer a choice of traditional lounges, a cocktail bar and a small dining room with a harbour view.

20⇨🐾 Annexe3⇨🐾(1fb) CTV in all bedrooms ® T
sB&B⇨🐾£33-£37 dB&B⇨🐾£66-£74 🍽
18P ⏰
Dinner £21 Last dinner 8.30pm
Credit Cards [1] [3]

Hotels with red star ratings are especially high quality.

Skye, Isle of, Portree - Uig

★★ 62% **Royal**
IV51 9BU (turn off A850 on to A855, hotel is on corner overlooking the harbour) ☎(0478) 612525 FAX (0478) 613198
A long established business hotel, the Royal enjoys views of the harbour and is a popular base for tour groups. The practically furnished bedrooms vary in size, and the public areas include a choice of bars, a refurbished lounge, the main dining room and the less formal bistro.
25⇌ ᴎ(6fb)⊁in 5 bedrooms CTV in all bedrooms ® ✱
sB&B⇌ᴎ£35-£41 dB&B⇌ᴎ£55-£59 ♬
14P ⇔
V ✧ ℒ ⊁ Lunch £4.50-£12&alc Dinner £14.50-£19.50&alc Last dinner 9pm
CONF. Thtr 130 Board 16 Del from £48
Credit Cards [1][3] £

★ 62% **Isles**
Somerled Square IV51 9EH ☎(0478) 612129
Closed Nov-Mar
Conveniently situated beside the main square, this small, family-run hotel is popular with holiday-makers. It has a relaxed and friendly atmosphere and offers traditional service and comforts together with bright, airy bedroom accommodation.
10rm(5ᴎ) CTV in all bedrooms ®
CTV ₧ ✻ clay pigeon shooting
Last dinner 8.30pm

SKEABOST BRIDGE Map 13 NG44
★★★⊞ 66% **Skeabost House**
IV51 9NR ☎(047032) 202 FAX (047032) 454
Closed 25 Oct-Mar
A peacefully located family-run hotel in well kept grounds surrounded by 12 acres of woods. Public rooms are extensive, and bedrooms vary in size and colour schemes, with some in the garden house. In August and September the hotel's fishing boat sails from the private jetty.
21⇌ᴎAnnexe5⇌ᴎ(3fb)1♬ CTV in all bedrooms ® T
sB&B⇌ᴎ£36-£44 dB&B⇌ᴎ£78-£100
《 CTV 40P ✻ ▶ 9 ♪ snooker
✩ Scottish & French V ✧ ℒ ⊁ ✱ Bar Lunch £5-£8.50 Dinner £18-£22.50 Last dinner 8.30pm
Credit Cards [1][3]

TEANGUE Map 13 NG60
★★ 66% **Toravaig House**
IV44 8RJ (on A851) ☎Isle Ornsay(04713) 231
Closed Nov-Etr
Situated in the Sleat peninsula, this friendly family-run hotel stands in 8 acres of wooded grounds and is an ideal base from which to explore the island. Public areas include a relaxing lounge, well stocked bar and a neat dining room, where good home cooked food is served. Bedrooms are comfortable with modern appointments.
9⇌ᴎ CTV in all bedrooms ® sB&B⇌ᴎ£35-£40
dB&B⇌ᴎ£50-£60 ♬
CTV 20P ⇔ ✻
✧ ℒ ⊁ Lunch £9-£12 Dinner £16.50 Last dinner 8pm
Credit Cards [1][3]

UIG Map 13 NG36
★★ 66% **Uig**
IV51 9YE (Logis) ☎(047042) 205 FAX (047042) 308
Closed 8 Oct-mid Apr
This hotel stands in a delightful elevated position overlooking Uig Bay. Public rooms are comfortable and include a reading room, and the family offer friendly and helpful service. Bedrooms have coordinated fabrics and modern furniture.
11⇌ᴎAnnexe6⇌ᴎ(1fb) CTV in all bedrooms ® T ➡

ISLE ORNSAY HOTEL ★
(Tigh osda Eilean Iarmain)

A small hotel situated in Sleat "the Garden of Skye", offers a friendly, relaxed Gaelic atmosphere beside the sea with its own private pier and oysters. The hotel is 100 years old. Traditional furniture and each room has its own character, private bathrooms throughout. Our food is exclusive. Open all year. Two restored function rooms. Art exhibitions held frequently.

**For details write to
Effie Kennedy, Manager,
Sleat, Isle of Skye IV43 8QR
Telephone: 04713 332 Fax: 04713 275**

A traditional Gaelic Inn

★★★
Randell's ❀
HOTEL, CONFERENCE
AND LEISURE CENTRE
KEIGHLEY ROAD
SNAYGILL, SKIPTON,
NORTH YORKSHIRE

Our pool's relaxing, our spa invigorating and our gymnasium exhausting . . . our food's mouthwatering, our surroundings charming and our countryside exhilarating . . . join us for the weekend and we'll throw in a 3rd night free, phone for brochure

NESTLING IN THE FOOTHILLS OF THE YORKSHIRE DALES

Tel: 0756 700100

Skye, Isle of, Uig - Solihull

20P ⇆ ❈ ↻ nc12yrs
V ☉ ⌶ ⌁ Last dinner 8pm
Credit Cards ① ② ③ ④ ⑤

★ 71% **Ferry Inn**
IV51 9XP (on main road) ☎(047042) 242
Closed 25 Dec & 1-2 Jan RS Nov-Etr

Major improvements have been made at this small, family-run Highland inn, convenient for the Outer Isles ferry terminal. Immaculate bedrooms have been tastefully refurbished and offer the expected comforts and amenities, though some are compact. Public areas include a choice of bars, a relaxing lounge and an attractive dining room, where enjoyable home cooking is served.

6⇌♟ CTV in all bedrooms ® sB&B⇌♟£25-£30 dB&B⇌♟£50-£55
CTV 12P ⇆
V ☉ ⌶ ❋ Bar Lunch £2.50-£5&alc Dinner £15-£20alc Last dinner 9pm
Credit Cards ① ③

SLEAFORD Lincolnshire Map 08 TF04

Forte Travelodge
Holdingham(1m N, at roundabout A17/A15)
☎(0529) 414752 Central Res (0800) 850950

This modern building offers a good standard of accommodation for overnight stops. Smart, spacious and well equipped bedrooms, all with en suite bathrooms, are suitable for family use, and meals may be taken at the nearby family restaurant. For more details about Travelodges, consult the Contents page, under Hotel Groups.

40⇌♟❋ B⇌♟£31.95 (room only)

SLOUGH Berkshire Map 04 SU97

★★★★ ❀65% **The Copthorne**
400 Cippenham Ln SL1 2YE (at junct of A355/A4) ☎(0753) 516222 FAX (0753) 516237

Convenient for the M4, this tall modern hotel has a welcoming and stylish open-plan lobby lounge with comfortable sofas and armchairs. All the bedrooms have good-sized beds and all modern amenities, with power showers in the en suites. The main restaurant, Reflections, offers capable modern French cooking, while the Verandah is more informal.

219⇌♟(19fb)⌁in 39 bedrooms CTV in all bedrooms ® T ✈ (ex guide dogs) ❋ sB⇌♟£110 dB⇌♟£120 (room only) ℞
Lift ⓘ ⊞ 320P ▣ (heated) snooker sauna solarium gymnasium Turkish & spa bath *xmas*
♍ International V ☉ ⌶ ❋ Lunch £15.50-£18.50 Dinner £26-£28alc Last dinner 10pm
CONF. Thtr 250 Class 160 Board 80 Del from £107
Credit Cards ① ② ③ ④ ⑤

Courtyard by Marriott
Church St, Chalvey SL1 2NH ☎(0753) 551551
FAX (0753) 553333

Well furnished guest bedrooms have en suite bathrooms, remote control CTV and direct-dial telephone at this modern hotel, and there is an informal restaurant and bar. For more details about Courtyard by Marriott, consult the Contents page, under Hotel Groups.

150⇌♟ dB⇌♟fr£68 (room only)

The AA's star rating scheme is the market leader in hotel classification.

SMALLWAYS North Yorkshire Map 12 NZ11

★ 56% **A66 Motel**
DL11 7QW ☎Teesdale(0833) 27734

Converted from a 19th-century farmhouse, this small motel has beamed bars and compact modest bedrooms, with redecoration scheduled for some single rooms.

6rm(3♟) CTV in all bedrooms ® ❋ sB&B£23 sB&B♟£26.50 dB&B♟£45
30P ❈
V ☉ ❋ Lunch fr£8 Dinner fr£15 Last dinner 10.30pm
Credit Cards ① ③ ⑤

SNAKE PASS Derbyshire Map 07 SK19

★★ 59% *Snake Pass Inn*
S30 2BJ (on A57 Sheffield to Glossop road)
☎Hope Valley(0433) 51480

This roadside inn is in open country and woodland. Bedrooms are prettily decorated with coordinated fabrics. An extensive range of food is available, either in the bar or the dining room. The location, in the heart of the Peak District National Park, is ideal for walkers.

7⇌♟(1fb)1⊞ CTV in all bedrooms ®⌶ ✈ (ex guide dogs)
40P ❈
V ☉ ⌶ ⌁
Credit Cards ① ② ③

See advertisement under SHEFFIELD

SOLIHULL West Midlands Map 07 SP17

★★★★ ❀64% **Solihull Moat House**
61 Homer Rd B91 3QD ☎021-711 4700
FAX 021-711 2696

This relative newcomer is proving popular for its well equipped modern bedrooms with attractive décor, and for the choice of eating options – Jaspers Brasserie or the more formal Brookes restaurant, overlooking the lake. Both à la carte and table d'hôte menus are offered, and the dishes show flair and imagination. A typical meal might start with a spinach soup with cheese straws, followed by chicken with Dijon mustard sauce, and to finish a creamy prune and Armagnac parfait.

115⇌♟(5fb)⌁in 42 bedrooms CTV in all bedrooms ®⌶ T ❋ sB⇌♟£85-£97 dB⇌♟£100-£112 (room only) ℞
Lift ⓘ 164P ❈ ▣ (heated) sauna solarium gymnasium ♪
♍ International V ☉ ⌶ ⌁ ❋ Lunch £10.75-£12.50&alc Dinner £14.85-£16.50&alc Last dinner 10.30pm
CONF. Thtr 220 Class 120 Board 90 Del from £58
Credit Cards ① ② ③ ④ ⑤

★★★ 67% *Regency*
Stratford Rd, Shirley B90 4EB (beside A34, 0.5m from junct 4 of M42) (Crown & Raven) ☎021-745 6119 FAX 021-733 3801

This popular hotel has been extended in recent years and provides a mix of spacious older bedrooms and more compact newer rooms, all well furnished and equipped. Public areas include a new leisure centre, restaurant and choice of bars.

112⇌♟(10fb)⌁in 59 bedrooms CTV in all bedrooms ® T ❋ sB⇌♟£45-£89.50 dB⇌♟£57-£89.50 ℞
Lift ⓘ 300P ▣ (heated) sauna solarium gymnasium jacuzzi *xmas*
♍ English & French V ☉ ⌶ ⌁ ❋ Lunch £11.25&alc Dinner £15.30&alc Last dinner 10pm
Credit Cards ① ② ③

★★★ 63% **St John's Swallow**
651 Warwick Rd B91 1AT ☎021-711 3000 FAX 021-705 6629

Refurbishment of guest rooms continues, and those which have been completed now offer a good standard of accommodation. Staff are friendly and professional.

177🛏🅿🍴in 40 bedrooms CTV in all bedrooms ® ♉ T ✱
sB&B🛏🍴£82-£88 dB&B🛏🍴£97-£105 🚭
Lift ᶜ CTV 380P ✿ 🏊 (heated) sauna solarium gymnasium ♫
xmas
♕ English & French V ♥ ⌂ ✂ ✳ Lunch £12.50&alc Dinner
£19&alc Last dinner 9.45pm
Credit Cards 1 2 3 4 5   (£)

★★ **57%** **Flemings**
141 Warwick Rd, Olton B92 7HW ☎021-706 0371 FAX 021-706 4494

Closed 4 days Xmas

Flemings is a privately owned commercial hotel on a busy road. Rooms sizes and standards vary, some are compact and dated while others have been enlarged and redecorated. A well integrated team of staff create a home-from-home atmosphere.

84🛏🍴(4fb) CTV in all bedrooms ® T sB&B🛏🍴£24.50-£45 dB&B🛏🍴£40-£56 🚭
ᶜ CTV 85P ✿ snooker
♕ Asian & European V ♥ ⌂ Lunch £6.50-£10.50 Dinner £11.50 Last dinner 9.30pm
CONF. Del from £60
Credit Cards 1 2 3 5

• •

Travel Inn
Stratford Rd, Shirley B90 4PT (on A23)
☎021-744 2942

Purpose-built accommodation offers spacious and well equipped bedrooms, all with en suite bathrooms. Meals may be taken at the nearby family restaurant and pub. For more details about Travel Inns, consult the Contents page, under Hotel Groups.

51🛏🍴✱ B🛏🍴£33.50 (room only)

SOURTON Devon Map **02** SX59
★★ **77%** **Collaven Manor**
EX20 4HH (on A386) ☎Bridestowe(083786) 217 & 522 FAX (083786) 570

This small 15th-century manor house, of creeper-covered mellow stone, stands in 5 acres of well kept gardens on the northwest edge of Dartmoor. The comfortably furnished bedrooms have many thoughtful extras such as decanters of sherry and fresh fruit; each has its own style and a view of the garden. There is a charming heavily beamed lounge with an inglenook fireplace and exposed stone walls and a bar with an ambience of warmth and elegance. The table d'hôte menu offers a choice of interesting dishes.

9🛏🍴1⚭ CTV in all bedrooms ® T ✱ sB&B🛏🍴£51-£75 dB&B🛏🍴£79-£95 🚭
20P ⚭ ✿ croquet pitch & putt *xmas*
♕ English & French V ♥ ⌂ ✂ ✳ Lunch £10.95-£11.95 Dinner £16.50-£21 Last dinner 9pm
Credit Cards 1 3   (£)

SOUTHAMPTON Hampshire Map **04** SU41
See also **Shedfield**
★★★ **63%** **Southampton Park**
Cumberland Place SO9 4NY (Forestdale) ☎(0703) 223467 FAX (0703) 332538
Closed 25 & 26 Dec nights

This centrally situated hotel overlooking West Park has well designed bedrooms with modern facilities. Both the formal restaurant and bistro-style cellar restaurant offer imaginative menus.

72🛏🍴⚭ CTV in all bedrooms ® T ✱ sB🛏🍴£42.50-£45 dB🛏🍴£42.50-£55 (room only) 🚭
Lift ᶜ 🅿 🏊 (heated) sauna solarium gymnasium massage jet stream jacuzzi   ➡

Solihull - Southampton

Hedge End, Southampton SO3 2GA
Tel: (0489) 787700 Fax: (0489) 788535

Five miles from Southampton. Four miles from Hamble. Five miles from Eastleigh Airport. ¼ mile M27 (Junction 7). 2 miles to Railway Station.

Magnificent 17th-Century Hotel where Oliver Cromwell once stayed.

★ All bedrooms with Colour TV, Radio and Direct Dial Telephone
★ Comfortable country house atmosphere
★ Extensive parkland and lakes
★ Conference facilities
★ 10 minutes from Southampton Airport
★ 15 minutes from New Forest
★ Excellent new cocktail lounge and restaurant, with an extensive choice of traditional dishes using the best of fresh produce. Good value business luncheon menu
★ Specialists in Wedding Receptions
★ Honeymoon and Romantic Breaks
★ Weekend Breaks
★ Four poster rooms overlooking lakes & garden

For SOUTHAMPTON, try LYNDHURST

A mere 10 miles away from the centre of Southampton but a world away in atmosphere and style.

Elegant, traditional, independent, individual. 40 sparklingly clean, pretty, ensuite rooms: colour TV, trouser press, tea/coffee tray, minibar, direct dial telephone & hair dryer. Spacious lounges; restaurant and bar meals. Meeting rooms. Lift. **Large car park.**

The Crown Hotel
★★★
High Street, Lyndhurst, New Forest,
Hants SO43 7NF
Telephone: (0703) 282922
Telex: 9312110733CHG
Fax: (0703) 282751

Southampton

♨ English & French V ♿ ⚐ ✻ Bar Lunch £1.50-£3.75alc
High tea £3.50-£6.50alc Dinner £12.50-£15.50&alc Last dinner 11pm
CONF. Thtr 200 Class 120 Board 50 Del from £69
Credit Cards 1 2 3 5

★★★ 61% Novotel
1 West Quay Rd SO1 0RA ☎(0703) 330550
FAX (0703) 222158

Bedrooms at this hotel are simply furnished and effectively double glazed. Le Grill restaurant offers food throughout the day, and full room service is also available. Service is by a young team of staff, some of them French.
121⇨♠♿in 42 bedrooms CTV in all bedrooms ®⚌T✻
sB⇨♠£52-£59.50 dB⇨♠£62-£69.50 (room only) ♬
Lift (⊞ 300P ☒ (heated) sauna gymnasium ♻
♨ International V ♿ ⚐ ✻ Lunch £2.50-£20alc Dinner £2.50-£14 Last dinner mdnt
CONF. Thtr 450 Class 200 Board 100 Del £80
Credit Cards 1 2 3 5

★★★ 60% The Dolphin
High St SO9 2DS ☎(0703) 339955 FAX (0703) 333650

FORTE Heritage

This city centre hotel in traditional style has an elegant first-floor restaurant serving 2 fixed-price menus and an attractive bar. The bedrooms have recently been completely refurbished.
73⇨♠(2fb)1⚏✻in 14 bedrooms CTV in all bedrooms ® T ✻
sB⇨♠fr£60 dB⇨♠fr£70 (room only) ♬
Lift (⊞ 90P xmas
♨ English & Continental V ♿ ⚐ ✻ Sunday Lunch fr£9.95 Dinner fr£15.95 Last dinner 9.30pm
CONF. Thtr 90 Class 30 Board 45 Del from £60
Credit Cards 1 2 3 5

★★★ 60% The Polygon
Cumberland Place SO9 4GD (follow signs for docks and railway station) ☎(0703) 330055
FAX (0703) 332435

FORTE HOTELS

The Polygon is the grande dame of Southampton hotels, set in a residential area but close to the city centre. Rooms vary in shape and size, and there are lifts to the 5 floors. Public areas can be busy, and an improvement programme started with the lobby and lounge.
119⇨♠(1fb)✻in 30 bedrooms CTV in all bedrooms ® T ✻
sB⇨♠fr£39.50 dB⇨♠fr£39.50 (room only) ♬
Lift (120P xmas
♨ International V ♿ ⚐ ✻ Lunch fr£10.95alc Dinner fr£12.50alc Last dinner 10pm
Credit Cards 1 2 3 5

★★★ 60% Southampton Moat House
Highfield Ln, Portswood SO9 1YQ
☎(0703) 559555 FAX (0703) 583910

Queens Moat Houses

There is a choice of well furnished modern bedrooms here, all with a good range of equipment. Hamiltons Restaurant features daily fixed price and popular à la carte menus, and the City Side pub-style bar offers an alternative with good value lunch time meals and snacks.
66⇨♠(6fb)✻in 3 bedrooms CTV in all bedrooms ® T ✻
sB&B⇨♠fr£53.50 dB&B⇨♠fr£63.50 ♬
(100P sauna gymnasium xmas
♨ International V ♿ ⚐ ✻ Lunch fr£14/alc High tea fr£2.50 Dinner fr£14alc Last dinner 10pm
CONF. Thtr 250 Class 100 Board 60 Del from £70
Credit Cards 1 2 3 4 5 £

★★ 65% Busketts Lawn
174 Woodlands Rd, Woodlands SO4 2GL (A35 W of city through Ashurst, over railway bridge, sharp right into Woodlands Road) ☎Ashurst(0703) 292272 & 292077 FAX (0703) 292487

Dating from 1875, this well run and friendly hotel is celebrating its 25th anniversary under the personal ownership of Mr and Mrs Hayes. Individually furnished bedrooms are well equipped and room service is available 7am-11pm.
14⇨♠(3fb)1⚏ CTV in all bedrooms ® T ✻ sB&B⇨♠£35-£48 dB&B⇨♠£50-£68 ♬
CTV 50P ✿ ≈ (heated) putting croquet football xmas
♨ English & Continental V ♿ ⚐ ✻ Lunch £10.50-£12.50&alc
High tea £5-£8.50 Dinner £15.50 Last dinner 8.30pm
Credit Cards 1 2 3 5

★★ 64% Elizabeth House
43-44 The Avenue SO1 2SX (on the A33, left hand side travelling towards city centre) ☎(0703) 224327 FAX (0703) 224327
Elizabeth House is set back off The Avenue not far from the city centre and with easy access to the airport, docks, university and Cherbourg ferry. Rooms are bright and well equipped and service friendly. Guests can eat informally in the Cellar Bar or have full meal service in the dining room.
24rm(20⇨♠) CTV in all bedrooms ® T sB&Bfr£25
sB&B⇨♠fr£30 dB&B⇨♠fr£40 ♬
CTV 20P ⚙
V ♿ Lunch fr£8.80alc Dinner fr£8.80alc
Last dinner 9.15pm
Credit Cards 1 2 3 5 £

★★ 63% Star
High St SO9 4ZA ☎(0703) 339939 FAX (0703) 335291
Closed 24-26 Dec
This old coaching inn retains much of its original character, while the accommodation is slowly being upgraded to a good standard. Service is particularly friendly and well managed, with room service available throughout the day. Victoria's Restaurant and Carvery supplemented by good value bar meals.
45rm(38⇨♠)✻in 7 bedrooms CTV in all bedrooms ® T ✻
sB&B⇨£22-£32 sB&B⇨♠£32-£47 dB&B£48-£57
dB&B⇨♠£53-£63 ♬
Lift (20P 10⚙
♨ English & French V ♿ Lunch £7.95&alc Dinner £9.75-£17alc Last dinner 9.30pm
CONF. Thtr 70 Class 40 Board 20 Del from £30
Credit Cards 1 2 3 5

★★ 57% Hotel Ibis
West Quay Rd, Western Esplanade SO1 0RA (opposite Central Railway Station)
☎(0703) 634463 FAX (0703) 223273

93⇨♠(8fb)✻in 27 bedrooms CTV in all bedrooms ®⚌ T
sB⇨♠£32-£39.50 dB⇨♠£32-£39.50 (room only)
Lift (280P
♨ English & French V ♿ ⚐ ✻ Bar Lunch £2.50-£4.50alc
Dinner £6-£12&alc Last dinner 10.30pm
CONF. Thtr 80 Class 44 Board 30 Del £65
Credit Cards 1 2 3 4 5

Forte Posthouse
Herbert Walker Av SO1 0HJ ☎(0703) 330777 FAX (0703) 332510

FORTE Posthouse

Suitable for both the business and leisure traveller, this bright hotel provides modern accommodation in well equipped bedrooms with en suite bathrooms. For more details about Forte Posthouse hotels, consult the Contents page, under Hotel Groups.
128⇨♠✻ B⇨♠£41.50-£53.50 (room only)
CONF. Thtr 200 Class 80 Board 40 Del £89.50

Irish entries appear in a separate section that follows the main directory.

Southampton - Southend-on-Sea

Hilton National Southampton
Bracken Place, Chilworth SO2 3UB
☎(0703) 702700

This is a bright, modern hotel with an informal restaurant, aimed at both the business and leisure guest. All bedrooms have en-suite bathrooms and a range of modern facilities. For more information about Hilton National, consult the Contents page, under Hotel Groups.
135⇌✿✱ B⇌✿£75 (room only)
CONF. Thtr 200 Class 90 Board 24 Del £110

Travel Inn
Romsey Rd, Nursling SO1 9XJ (off A3057)
☎(0703) 732262

Purpose-built accommodation offers spacious and well equipped bedrooms, all with en suite facilities. Meals may be taken at the nearby family restaurant and pub. For more details about Travel Inns, consult the Contents page, under Hotel Groups.
32⇌✿✱ B⇌✿£33.50 (room only)

SOUTH BRENT Devon Map 03 SX66

★★❀♨74% *Glazebrook House Hotel & Restaurant*
TQ10 9SE ☎(0364) 73322 FAX (0364) 72350
Laurence and Sue Cowley have continued to upgrade this delightful mid- Victorian house, which stnds in 4 acres of beautiful gardens within the Dartmoor National Park. Rooms vary in size but all are individually decorated, and have full facilities. There is an intimate residents' dining room, a larger dining room for functions and a comfortable bar lounge. Chef David Merriman produces interesting dishes, such as a puff pastry case filled with salmon mousse, with a cucumber flavoured butter-based sauce, pan fried fillets of beef with a tangy grain mustard sauce and marzipan pancake with a raspberry coulis.
11⇌✿3⚑⚑in 1 bedroom CTV in all bedrooms ® T ✗
CTV 50P ⚑ ✿ ♨
♨ English & French V ❀ ⚑ ⚑ Last dinner 9pm
Credit Cards 1 3

SOUTH CAVE Humberside Map 08 SE93

★★65% Fox & Coney Inn
Market Place HU15 2AT (0.50m off A63, main Market Weighton to York road, A1034) ☎Howden(0430) 422275 FAX (0430) 421552
8⇌✿(1fb) CTV in all bedrooms ®✗ T ✗ (ex guide dogs) ✱
sB⇌✿ fr£35 dB⇌✿ fr£45 (room only) ⚑
28P ⚑ ✿
♨ English & French V ❀ ⚑ ✱ Bar Lunch fr£2.95&alc
Credit Cards 1 2 3

SOUTHEND-ON-SEA Essex Map 05 TQ88

★★65% *Camelia*
178 Eastern Esplanade, Thorpe Bay SS1 3AA ☎(0702) 587917 FAX (0702) 585704
On the seafront at Thorpe Bay, this small hotel has been completely refurbished to a very high standard. Bedrooms are attractive, with coordinating pastel décor and fabrics. There is a small cocktail bar, and the restaurant is popular locally. Staff are friendly and genuinely interested.
16⇌✿(1fb)1⚑ CTV in all bedrooms ®✗ T ✗ (ex guide dogs)
✱ sB&B⇌✿£38.50-£65 dB&B⇌✿£45-£80 ⚑
CTV 100P ♪ *xmas*
♨ English & French V ✱ Lunch fr£9.75 Dinner fr£12.95&alc Last dinner 10.30pm
Credit Cards 1 3

FREE HOUSE

Fox & Coney Inn

EN SUITE ACCOMMODATION
OPEN 7 DAYS
Situated 12 miles from Hull and 9 miles from Beverley
Ideal for business or tourists
★ Single ★ Double ★ Twin ★ Family rooms ★
Disabled facilities on ground floor
All with easy access to main building and private parking through the archway
All rooms en-suite with colour TV, satellite, telephone, coffee making facilities, hair dryer and trouser press
EXCELLENT FOOD SERVED FROM THE VARIED BAR MENU. SPECIALS OF THE DAY. A LA CARTE RESTAURANT SERVING A TEMPTING CHOICE OF INDIVIDUALLY PREPARED DISHES (EVENINGS ONLY)

TEL (0430) 422275 FAX (0430) 421552
52 MARKET PLACE, SOUTH CAVE, BROUGH

AA ★★

Busketts Lawn Hotel

Woodlands, Nr. Southampton
Hampshire SO4 2GL
Tel: (0703) 292272/292077 Fax: (0703) 292487
Delightful family run Country House Hotel in quiet New Forest setting, yet only 15 minutes to Southampton and 5 minutes M27.

★ First class accommodation – all rooms en suite, colour TV, direct dial telephone, trouser press, hair dryer and hospitality tray.
★ Excellent cuisine, service and comfort.
★ Two luxurious function suites for seminars, conferences, wedding receptions, and dinner dances.
★ Seasonal heated swimming pool. Football-pitch. Putting, croquet. 2 acre garden.

AA ★ ★   ESTABLISHED
                     1968

Southend-on-Sea - South Normanton

★★ ❀64% Schulers Hotel & Restaurant
161 Eastern Esplanade SS1 2YB (from A127 change to A1159 continue to roundabout, turn right into Hamstel Rd and drive straight on into Lifstan Way, at seafront turn right) ☎Southend(0702) 610172 FAX (0702) 466835

Closed 24 Dec-2 Jan RS Sun pm & Mon lunch

Swiss chef/owner Manfred Schuler has a loyal local following for his continental cuisine with the emphasis on seafood. Fresh lobster soup and salmon strudel with coriander, ginger and sour cream were much enjoyed. There is a comfortable lounge and plain modern bedrooms designed to suit business guests.

9rm(5⇨↑)(1fb) CTV in all bedrooms ® T ✖ (ex guide dogs) ✻ sBfr£20.75 sB⇨↑£20.75-£43.50 dB£28.95-£43.50 dB⇨↑£31-£43.50 (room only)

14P

♫ International V ✻ Lunch £11.50&alc Dinner £11.50&alc Last dinner 9.45pm

Credit Cards ① ② ③ ⑤

★ 69% Balmoral
34 Valkyrie Rd, Westcliffe-on-Sea SS0 8BU (off A13)
☎(0702) 342947 FAX (0702) 337828

This small hotel close to Westcliffe seafront, has been run efficiently for many years by Peggy and Jimmy Anderson. Bedrooms are all well equipped and the public areas enlivened by photos of the proprietors in amateur operatic roles.

22⇨↑(4fb) CTV in all bedrooms ® T sB&B⇨↑£35-£38 dB&B⇨↑£48-£55 ♫

CTV 19P 🅿 ♿

♫ English & French V ♿ ⚐ Last dinner 7.30pm

CONF. Board 25

Credit Cards ① ③

SOUTH MIMMS Hertfordshire Map 04 TL20

Forte Posthouse
Bignells Corner EN6 3NH (junc A1/A6)
☎Potters Bar(0707) 643311 FAX (0707) 646728

FORTE Posthouse

Suitable for both the business and leisure traveller, this bright hotel provides modern accommodation in well equipped bedrooms with en suite bathrooms. For more details about Forte Posthouse hotels, consult the Contents page, under Hotel Groups.

120⇨↑ ✻ B⇨↑£41.50-£53.50 (room only)

CONF. Thtr 170 Class 85 Board 60 Del from £79.50

Forte Travelodge
Bignells Corner EN6 3QQ (junc 23, M25)
☎(0707) 665440 Central Res (0800) 850950

FORTE Travelodge

This modern building offers a good standard of accommodation for overnight stops. Smart, spacious and well equipped bedrooms, all with en suite bathrooms, are suitable for family use, and meals may be taken at the nearby family restaurant. For more details about Travelodges, consult the Contents page, under Hotel Groups.

52⇨↑ ✻ B⇨↑£31.95 (room only)

Rosettes range from 5 for outstanding cuisine to 1 rosette for enjoyable, well prepared food

SOUTH MOLTON Devon Map 03 SS72

★★★❀❀❀❀⚐ WHITECHAPEL MANOR
EX36 3EG ☎(0769) 573377
FAX (0769) 573797

A delightful Elizabethan manor house, this hotel is set in terraced gardens on the edge of Exmoor. On arrival, guests can enjoy tea and home-made cake or biscuits in the Great Hall and admire its Jacobean carved oak screen, William and Mary plasterwork, panelling and Knole sofas. In the dining room, Chef Thierry Leprêtre-Granet presents 2 set price menus. His cooking is relatively simple, but displays finesse and imagination in the handling of ingredients. Typical dishes might be turbot in excellent seaweed butter sauce, seared foie gras of duck with asparagus and walnut oil dressing, tenderloin of local wild deer in a balsamic vinegar sauce, and roasted calf's sweetbreads with an intense cep jus on a bed of puy lentils. Hot apple tart with caramel ice cream is, by popular vote, permanently on the menu.

10⇨↑(1fb)1⚐ CTV in all bedrooms T ✖ (ex guide dogs) sB&B⇨↑£65-£145 dB&B⇨↑£98-£160 ♫

40P ❀ croquet xmas

♫ French ♿ ⚐ Lunch £26-£37&alc Dinner £26-£37&alc Last dinner 8.45pm

CONF. Class 26 Board 22 Del from £98

Credit Cards ① ② ③ ⑤

★★ ❀71% Marsh Hall
EX36 3HQ (1.25m N towards North Molton off A361)
☎(0769) 572666 FAX (0769) 574230

Said to have been built by the local squire for his mistress, this 17th-century house stands in beautifully kept grounds not too far from the north Devon link road. Accommodation is furnished in keeping with the house and offers excellent standards of comfort. The peaceful lounge is well supplied with reading material, there is a separate bar lounge and good, home-cooked food is served in enjoyable surroundings.

7⇨↑1⚐ CTV in all bedrooms ® T sB&B⇨↑£38-£51 dB&B⇨↑£65 ♫

20P 🅿 ❀ nc12yrs xmas

♫ English & Continental V ♿ Bar Lunch £7.50 Dinner £18.50 Last dinner 8.30pm

Credit Cards ① ② ③

SOUTH NORMANTON Derbyshire Map 08 SK45

★★★★ 62% Swallow
Carter Ln East DE55 2EH (junct 28 of M1)
☎Ripley(0773) 812000 FAX (0733) 580032

Recent improvements to this hotel have added a further wing of high quality bedrooms, and the earlier bedrooms have been made more comfortable. Apart from the extensive all-day snack menu in the lounge/bar, there are 2 restaurants: the formal Pavilion and the Lacemaker where grills and lighter dishes are served.

161⇨↑(6fb)⚐ in 100 bedrooms CTV in all bedrooms ®✉ T ✻ sB&B⇨↑£86 dB&B⇨↑£99 ♫

(200P ❀ ⚐ (heated) sauna solarium gymnasium whirlpool spa bath steam room xmas

♀ International V ❊ ⚏ ✂ ✱ Lunch £10.50-£12.50&alc High tea £15.25-£24.75alc Dinner £13.50-£18.50&alc Last dinner 10.30pm
CONF. Thtr 220 Class 100 Board 50 Del £105
Credit Cards 1 2 3 5

SOUTHPORT Merseyside Map 07 SD31
See also **Formby**
★★★ **65%** **Scarisbrick**
Lord St PR8 1NZ ☎(0704) 543000 FAX (0704) 533335
Situated in fashionable Lord Street, this busy Victorian hotel offers modernised and well equipped bedrooms. There are a number of lively bars and a disco, but for quieter surroundings a pleasant restaurant and cocktail bar are to be found on the first floor.
65⇨♠(5fb)6🛏 CTV in all bedrooms ® ⚲ T sB&B⇨♠£60-£70 dB&B⇨♠£70-£120 🍴
Lift (48P 12🅿 ♫ *xmas*
♀ English & French V ❊ ⚏ ✂ Lunch £7.75-£8.75&alc High tea £4.95-£7.50 Dinner £13-£15.50&alc Last dinner 9.30pm
CONF. Thtr 200 Class 100 Board 80 Del from £65
Credit Cards 1 2 3 5

★★★ **64%** **Royal Clifton**
Promenade PR8 1RB ☎(0704) 533771 FAX (0704) 500657

BEST WESTERN HOTELS

The Royal Clifton is a large hotel on the promenade and conveniently placed for the town centre. The bedrooms, including some on the ground floor, are generally very spacious, well furnished and equipped. Ironing boards are supplied in those designated specifically for women. Extensive public areas include several bars and restaurants, a disco club, and a leisure centre.
107⇨♠(2fb)2🛏✂in 2 bedrooms CTV in all bedrooms ® T ✖ (ex guide dogs)
Lift (40P 🅟 (heated) sauna solarium gymnasium sunbed jacuzzi ♫
♀ English & French V ❊ ⚏ ✂ Last dinner 9.45pm
Credit Cards 1 2 3 5

★★ **68%** **Balmoral Lodge**
41 Queens Rd PR9 9EX ☎(0704) 544298 & 530731 FAX (0704) 501224
Closed 24-26 Dec & 31 Dec
Privately owned by the McLachlan family, this detached Edwardian house, with a pleasant garden, is run in a friendly and informal style. The accommodation is not luxurious but is soundly maintained, and the bedrooms have a good range of equipment. Ground floor are mostly quite spacious with patio doors leading out to the garden. The hotel has a cottage-style bar, a comfortable lounge and a traditionally furnished restaurant.
15⇨♠(1fb)1🛏 CTV in all bedrooms ® T ✖
CTV 10P 🚗 sauna
Last dinner 8.30pm
Credit Cards 1 2 3 5

★★ **68%** **Stutelea Hotel & Leisure Club**
Alexandra Rd PR9 0NB (off the promenade near town & Hesketh Park) ☎(0704) 544220 FAX (0704) 500232
This popular family-run hotel in a quiet side road close to the town centre has been continually improved and provides bright and comfortable modern bedrooms with good facilities.
20⇨♠(3fb)2🛏 CTV in all bedrooms ® ⚲ T ✖ (ex guide dogs) sB&B⇨♠£45 dB&B⇨♠£60-£65 🍴
Lift CTV 18P 🚗 ✱ 🅟 (heated) sauna solarium gymnasium games room jacuzzi keep fit classes
V ❊ ⚏ ✱ Bar Lunch £3-£5 Dinner £8-£15alc
Last dinner 9pm
Credit Cards 1 2 3 5

South Normanton - Southport

STUTELEA HOTEL
& *Leisure Club* AA ★★
ALEXANDRA ROAD, SOUTHPORT PR9 0NB
TEL: (0704) 544220
English Tourist Board COMMENDED ♛♛♛♛
FAX: 0704 500232

20 deluxe bedrooms (single to family suites) all with private bathroom, some with balconies overlooking gardens.
8 apartments (studio to 2 bedroom) all with private bathroom and fitted kitchen.
All accommodation has colour TV, radio, direct dial telephone, hair dryer, trouser press and tea/coffee making facilities.
Heated indoor swimming pool, jacuzzi, Scandinavian sauna, steam room, 2 solaria, gymnasium, games room. Gardens and car park. 2 Licensed bars, restaurant, lounge with library, lift.

★★★

Hotel Renouf

BRADLEY WAY · ROCHFORD
NR. SOUTHEND-ON-SEA · ESSEX SS4 1BU
TEL: 0702 541334 · FAX: 0702 549563

A family owned 24 bedroom hotel situated in the old market town of Rochford, 3 miles from Southend.

All rooms en suite, with colour TV, Sky TV, tea/coffee making facilities, direct dial telephone and hair dryer. 4 deluxe rooms with jacuzzi, bath robes, mini bar and trouser press.

For the complete service

★ Specialists in wedding planning
★ Conference suites provided
★ Ideal for business professionals
★ Quality accommodation

A la carte and table d'hôte —
for the person who enjoys that little extra luxury

Listed by all major food guides

Renoufs Restaurant
is situated within the Hotel
Telephone: 0702 544393 for reservations.

Southport - Southwell

★★ **65%** *Bold*
Lord St PR9 0BE ☎(0704) 532578 FAX (0704) 532528
At the northern end of Lord Street, the entrance to this modernised Victorian hotel opens directly onto the lively lounge bar. Reception is on the first floor, where refurbished bedrooms have attractive coordinated fabrics. An extensive menu provides an eclectic selection, and a young staff provide cheerful and willing service.
23rm(15⇌7♘)(4fb) CTV in all bedrooms ® T
✈ (ex guide dogs)
《 8P ♫
♡ English, French & Italian V ♡ ⚏ Last dinner 9.45pm
Credit Cards ①②③④⑤

★★ **63%** Metropole
Portland St PR8 1LL ☎(0704) 536810 FAX (0704) 549041

Improvements continue at this centrally located family-owned hotel where freshly decorated public rooms include a small bar. Bedrooms, though modestly appointed, offer modern facilities.
24rm(11⇌10♘)(3fb) CTV in all bedrooms ® T ✱ sB&B⇌♘£29-£33.50 dB&B⇌♘£50-£56.50 ◻
CTV 12P ⌥ snooker *xmas*
♡ English & French V ♡ ✱ Lunch £5-£10alc Dinner £10-£12&alc Last dinner 8.30pm
Credit Cards ①②③ £

★★ **61%** *Lockerbie House*
11 Trafalgar Rd, Birkdale PR8 2EA ☎(0704) 565298
This large Victorian house is situated close to Birkdale Station. Privately owned, it provides accommodation which, while not luxurious, is soundly maintained. The bedrooms vary in size, some being very spacious. Facilities include a spacious lounge and a small bar.
14⇌♘(3fb) CTV in all bedrooms ®
CTV 14P 2🅿 ❄ snooker
V ♡ ⚏ Last dinner 8pm
Credit Cards ①②③⑤

★★ **59%** *Shelbourne*
1 Lord St PR8 2BH (Lord St signposted from Motorway) ☎(0704) 541252 & 530278 FAX (0704) 501293
Situated at the southern end of Lord Street, this family-run commercial hotel offers modest but improving standards of accommodation. Bedrooms vary in size and style, while public areas include a comfortable lounge bar and restaurant. Service, supervised by the proprietor, is relaxed and informal.
18⇌♘(2fb)⚲in 3 bedrooms CTV in all bedrooms ® T ✱ sB&B⇌♘£28-£36 dB&B⇌♘£35-£48
18P ⌥ Games room nc8yrs
V ♡ ⚏ ⚲ Lunch £6.95-£7.95 High tea £4.75-£6.75 Dinner £6.95-£8.95&alc Last dinner 9pm
CONF. Class 40 Board 40 Del from £30
Credit Cards ①②③

SOUTH QUEENSFERRY Lothian *West Lothian*
Map 11 NT17

★★★ **60%** Forth Bridges Moat House
Forth Bridge EH30 9SF ☎031-331 1199 FAX 031-319 1733

Situated on the south side of the river, overlooking the famous bridges, this purpose-built tourist and business hotel has modern style foyer lounge, bar and first-floor restaurant, offering a carvery and à la carte menu. Generally spacious bedrooms furnished with fitted units provide the expected amenities.
108⇌♘(30fb)⚲in 5 bedrooms CTV in all bedrooms ® T sB⇌♘£72-£76 dB⇌♘£97-£102 (room only) ◻
Lift 《 200P ❄ 🅾 (heated) squash snooker sauna solarium gymnasium dance studio *xmas*

♡ Scottish & French V ♡ ⚏ ✱ Lunch fr£12.50&alc Dinner fr£14.75&alc Last dinner 9.45pm
CONF. Thtr 200 Class 80 Board 40 Del from £108
Credit Cards ①②③⑤

SOUTHSEA
See **Portsmouth** & **Southsea**

SOUTH SHIELDS Tyne & Wear Map 12 NZ36

★★★ **60%** Sea
Sea Rd NE33 2LD (on A183) ☎091-427 0999 FAX 091-454 0500
Closed 25-27 Dec
On the seafront near the amusement park, this functional hotel offers friendly service and very good value menus.
33⇌♘(2fb)1⚓ CTV in all bedrooms ® T ✱ sB&B⇌♘£58-£62 dB&B⇌♘£63-£75 ◻
《 70P
♡ English, French & Italian V ♡ ⚏ ✱ Lunch £6.50-£7.50&alc Dinner £9.50-£10.50&alc Last dinner 9.30pm
CONF. Thtr 150 Class 70 Board 30 Del from £55
Credit Cards ①②③⑤ £

SOUTHWAITE MOTORWAY SERVICE AREA (M6)
Cumbria Map 12 NY44

Granada Lodge
Broadfield Site CA4 0NT (on M6)
☎Southwaite(06974) 73131 FAX (06974) 73669

This modern building provides smart, spacious and well equipped bedrooms, all with en suite bathrooms. Meals may be taken at a nearby family restaurant. For more details about Granada Lodges, consult the Contents page, under Hotel Groups.
39⇌♘✱ B⇌♘£34.95-£37.95 (room only)

SOUTH WALSHAM Norfolk Map 09 TG31

★★★ ⚜ **65%** South Walsham Hall
The Street NR13 6DQ (E of Norwich on B1140 towards Acle)
☎(060549) 378 & 591 FAX (060549) 519
Closed 1-15 Jan
Located on the fringes of the village, this country house is surrounded by expansive grounds with a swimming pool, tennis courts and fitness centre, and from which the Fairhaven Trust gardens are readily accessible. Bedrooms vary in style, but are comfortable. Staff are professional, committed and enthusiastic.
10⇌♘Annexe7⇌♘(2fb) CTV in all bedrooms ® T ✱ sB&B⇌♘£40-£80 dB&B⇌♘£60-£120 ◻
50P ⌥ ❄ 🅾 (heated) ♬ (hard) ♪ squash ∪ sauna solarium gymnasium water gardens *xmas*
♡ English & French V ♡ ⚏ Lunch £11.25-£17.50&alc Dinner £12.50-£17.50&alc Last dinner 9.45pm
CONF. Thtr 30 Class 20 Board 15 Del £70
Credit Cards ①②③⑤ £

SOUTHWELL Nottinghamshire Map 08 SK75

★★★ **64%** Saracen's Head
Market Place NG25 0HE ☎(0636) 812701 FAX (0636) 815408

Just a stroll from the 12th-century minster, this well preserved, half-timbered inn has been a feature of the town centre for well over 3 centuries. A happy mix of bedrooms provides modern rooms in the extension at the rear of the hotel and traditional rooms in the older part. Bar snacks are available in addition to the daily table d'hôte and à la carte menus, with some interesting regional British dishes, on offer in the restaurant.
27⇌♘1⚓⚲in 12 bedrooms CTV in all bedrooms ® T ✱ sB⇌♘£70-£95 dB⇌♘£80-£130 (room only) ◻

564

((80P *xmas*
V ⚙ 🍽 ✱ Lunch £8.95-£11.95 Dinner £11.50-£25alc Last dinner 10.15pm
CONF. Thtr 120 Class 40 Board 50 Del £90
Credit Cards [1][2][3][5]

SOUTH WITHAM Lincolnshire Map 08 SK91

Forte Travelodge
New Fox LE15 8AU (on A1, northbound)
☎Thistleton(057283) 586
Central Res (0800) 850950

FORTE Travelodge

This modern building offers a good standard of accommodation for overnight stops. Smart, spacious and well equipped bedrooms, all with en suite bathrooms, are suitable for family use, and meals may be taken at the nearby family restaurant. For more details about Travelodges, consult the Contents page, under Hotel Groups.
32⇨🍴✱ B⇨🍴£31.95 (room only)

SOUTHWOLD Suffolk Map 05 TM57

★★★ ❀69% *Swan*
Market Place IP18 6EG ☎(0502) 722186 FAX (0502) 724800
RS 3 Jan-wk before Etr
This restored 17th-century inn provides attentive service and comfortable bedrooms furnished to a good standard. The attractive drawing room has open fires, and the elegant restaurant, with huge bay windows overlooking the street, serves mainly English dishes. The wine list, from the award-winning wine merchant, Adnams, provides a good range.
27⇨🍴Annexe18⇨(2fb) CTV in all bedrooms ⚔ T
Lift ((50P 🚗
V ⚙ 🍽 🍴 Last dinner 9.30pm
Credit Cards [1][2][3]

★★ ❀66% Crown at Southwold
90 High St IP18 6DP ☎(0502) 722275 FAX (0502) 724805
Closed 1st & 2nd wk Jan
This 17th-century inn is well worth a visit for the food and wine. It is certainly popular with the locals: it is invariably busy, with polite staff providing attentive service. Chef Andrew Mulliss presents a short daily set price menu of modern British cooking. Fresh fish figures strongly, as does game in season. Public rooms are light and cheerful; some of the tasteful bedrooms, with period and antique furniture, are compact.
12rm(8⇨1🍴)(1fb) CTV in all bedrooms ✈ (ex guide dogs) ✱
sB&B⇨🍴£37-£47 dB&B⇨🍴£57 Continental breakfast
15P 8🚗 🚙 *xmas*
⚙ 🍴 ✱ Lunch £12.75-£14.75 Dinner £17.25-£19.25 Last dinner 9.45pm
Credit Cards [1][2][3]

SOUTH ZEAL Devon Map 03 SX69

★★ 62% Oxenham Arms
EX20 2JT ☎Okehampton(0837) 840244 & 840577 FAX (0837) 840791
This village inn, dating back to the 12th century, is full of character and interesting architectural detail in exposed beams, arched doors, original granite pillars and open fireplaces. Simply decorated bedrooms are furnished with heavy antique pieces. Bars are popular locally, as are the table d'hôte and bar snack menus available in the intimate dining room.
8rm(7⇨🍴)1🛏 CTV in all bedrooms ® T sB&B£35
sB&B⇨🍴£45 dB&B£40 dB&B⇨🍴£50
CTV 8P 🚗 ❀ *xmas*
♀ International V ⚙ 🍽 🍺 Bar Lunch £3.95-£5.50alc Dinner £15
Last dinner 9pm
Credit Cards [1][2][3][5]

Southport Old Road, Formby, Nr Southport, Merseyside L37 0AB

Unique in the area a Country House Restaurant beautifully furnished and renowned for its cuisine with a Motel nestling amidst five acres of delightful grounds with swimming pool and patio area. All accommodation is en suite with every comfort for our guests. Relax and enjoy peace and tranquillity yet be close to all amenities including five championship golf courses.

Phone us now on (07048) 79651

The Bold Hotel
AA ★★
Lord Street, Southport, Merseyside PR9 0BE
Telephone Southport (0704) 532578

A centre piece of the beautiful Lord Street Conservation Area the Bold Hotel has extensive modern facilities, whilst retaining the traditional service and atmosphere of its Victorian origins.
A convenient centre for all the business and leisure facilities of the North West, the Bold is surrounded by some of the greatest Golf Courses in Britain.
Public Bar & Restaurant recently refurbished to a very high standard. Now including Raphaels bar/cafe. Continental Cafe Bar informal but comfortable bar/restaurant.

Sowerby Bridge - Stamford

SOWERBY BRIDGE West Yorkshire Map 07 SE02

★★ 70% The Hobbit
Hob Ln, Norland HX6 3QL ☎Halifax(0422) 832202 FAX (0422) 835381

Situated up a steep road, this attractive stone inn gives fine views of the Pennine countryside from many of its comfortable bedrooms. Staff are very friendly and the restaurant and bars are popular with locals for the extensive range of food available.

17⇨🛏Annexe5⇨🛏(2fb)1🛌 CTV in all bedrooms ® ⚓ T ✈ (ex guide dogs) sB&B⇨🛏£30-£56 dB&B⇨🛏£43-£72 🍴
CTV 100P ♫ xmas
♨ English, French & Italian V ♿ ⚐ ✗
Credit Cards [1][2][3] £

SPEAN BRIDGE Highland *Inverness-shire* Map 14 NN28
See also **Letterfinlay** and **Roy Bridge**
★★ 59% Spean Bridge
PH34 4ES (beside A82) ☎(0397) 712250
Closed 23 Dec-3 Jan

This friendly, family-run Highland hotel is in the centre of the village. Public areas, which include a choice of lounges have a friendly atmosphere and provide traditional comforts. Bedrooms, including the annexe chalets, vary in size and are simply furnished.

22⇨🛏Annexe10⇨🛏(4fb) CTV in all bedrooms ®
sB&B⇨🛏£29-£43 dB&B⇨🛏£50-£66 🍴
CTV 50P ▶ 9 ♪ snooker
V ♿ ⚐ ✱ Bar Lunch £2-£11alc Dinner £2-£11alc Last dinner 9pm
Credit Cards [1][3][5]

STAFFORD Staffordshire Map 07 SJ92

★★★ 64% Tillington Hall
Eccleshall Rd ST16 1JJ (off A5013, W of town) ☎(0785) 53531 FAX (0785) 59223
RS Xmas & New Year

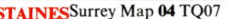

A popular commercial hotel, Tillington Hall offers accommodation in bedrooms which are gradually being refurbished and improved. Public rooms are particularly comfortable with a spacious foyer lounge, bars and restaurant.

90⇨🛏(3fb)1🛌✗in 16 bedrooms CTV in all bedrooms ®⚓ T ✱ sB&B⇨🛏£70-£105 dB&B⇨🛏£85-£110 🍴
Lift (150P 🏊 (heated) ♪ (hard) snooker sauna solarium gymnasium jacuzzi beauty salon ♫ xmas
♨ English, French & German V ♿ ⚐ ✗ ✱ Lunch £7-£8.95&alc Dinner £12.95-£14.75&alc Last dinner 9.45pm
CONF. Thtr 200 Class 80 Board 40 Del from £60
Credit Cards [1][2][3][5]

★★ 65% Garth
Wolverhampton Rd, Moss Pit ST17 9JR (Crown & Raven) ☎(0785) 56124 FAX (0785) 55152
RS 25-26 Dec

Set in attractive lawns and mature trees, this modern hotel's public areas have now been completely refurbished. A stylish foyer with marble tiled floor leads to the open plan lounge, cocktail bar and restaurant. The lounge bar is on 2 levels with a good range of bar meals. Most bedrooms have recently been upgraded to a good modern standard but a few still remain to be done.

60⇨🛏(3fb)✗in 20 bedrooms CTV in all bedrooms ® T ✱
sB&B⇨🛏£59.50 dB&B⇨🛏£66-£59.50 🍴
(175P ✿
♨ English & French V ♿ ⚐ Last dinner 10pm
CONF. Thtr 120 Class 30 Board 48 Del from £79.50
Credit Cards [1][2][3]

For key to symbols see the Bookmark.

★★ 59% *Vine*
Salter St ST16 2JU (Crown & Raven) ☎(0785) 51071 & 44112 FAX (0785) 46612

This 17th-century inn is close to the main shopping area. The bedrooms have pretty décor and attractive pine furniture, along with modern facilities and equipment. A good selection of simple, wholesome dishes is offered from a mainly grill-type menu, available in the no-smoking dining area or the bar.

27⇨🛏(1fb) CTV in all bedrooms ® T
30P
♨ English & French V ♿ ⚐
Credit Cards [1][2][3]

★★ 57% *Abbey*
65-68 Lichfield Rd ST17 4LW ☎(0785) 58531
Closed 23 Dec-7 Jan

This busy, personally run hotel south of the town centre caters mainly for commercial guests. Bedrooms are simple, the more modest rooms being in an adjoining property with access to the lounge bar and restaurant via an interconnecting conservatory.

20rm(5⇨🛏6🛏)(1fb) CTV in all bedrooms ® ✈ ✱ sB&B£19-£21 sB&B⇨🛏£28.50-£32 dB&B£28-£34 dB&B⇨🛏£39-£50 🍴
CTV 21P 5🚗 (£3 per night) 🐕
♨ English & French V ♿ Bar Lunch £2.60-£5alc Dinner £6-£8&alc Last dinner 8.30pm
Credit Cards [1][3] £

STAINES Surrey Map 04 TQ07
★★★ 58% *The Thames Lodge*
Thames St TW18 4SF ☎(0784) 464433 FAX (0784) 454858

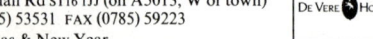
FORTE Heritage

This extended Victorian hotel has a delightful riverside setting, a short walk from the town centre, and both the restaurant and terraced bar are popular with locals. Half the bedrooms have now been smartly refurbished; most have a river view and some a balcony.

44⇨🛏✗in 14 bedrooms CTV in all bedrooms ® T
(60P
V ♿ ⚐ ✗ Last dinner 10pm
Credit Cards [1][2][3][5]

STALLINGBOROUGH Humberside Map 08 TA11
★★ 62% *Stallingborough Grange*
Riby Rd DN37 8BU ☎Roxton(0469) 61302 FAX (0469) 61302

This attractive thatched house has been extended to provide the facilities expected by modern travellers while retaining a homely atmosphere. Neat unpretentious bedrooms have good quality soft furnishings and there are comfortable bar lounges.

17⇨🛏(2fb) CTV in all bedrooms ® T ✈ (ex guide dogs) 70P ✿
♨ English & French V ♿ Last dinner 10pm
Credit Cards [1][3]

STAMFORD Lincolnshire Map 04 TF00

★★★ ❀75% *George of Stamford*
St Martins PE9 2LB (turn off A1 onto B1081, 1m on left) (PH) ☎(0780) 55171 FAX (0780) 57070

This delightful town centre coaching inn has earned a good reputation for both comfort and food. Good taste is evident throughout, from the comfortable lounge overlooking the cobbled patio garden to the inviting bar lounge and impressive wood panelled restaurant, and many original features have been retained. The bedrooms are quite luxurious, with period furnishings and many extras. The menus, for light snacks, bar meals and the restaurant, offer well produced and imaginative fare served by attentive staff.

47⇨🛏(2fb)4🛌 CTV in all bedrooms⚓ T ✱ sB&B⇨🛏£66-£81 dB&B⇨🛏£100-£154 🍴

Stamford - Steeple Aston

◖ 120P ✿ croquet *xmas*
♡ English, French & Italian V ⊙ ⊒ ✱ Lunch £15.50-£18.50&alc Dinner £18.40-£35.75alc Last dinner 10.30pm
CONF. Thtr 50 Class 24 Board 25
Credit Cards ①②③⑤

★★★65% Garden House
St Martin's PE9 2LP ☎(0780) 63359 FAX (0780) 63339
Resident proprietors have created a country house atmosphere in the town in their small hotel. The cosy lounge opens onto a conservatory with a rambling walled garden to the rear, and the restaurant is pretty. Unpretentious bedrooms vary in shape and size, but all are carefully furnished to maximise space. Service throughout is courteous, warm and friendly.
20⇌ ℕ(1fb)1⚏ CTV in all bedrooms ® T sB&B⇌ ℕfr£58.50 dB&B⇌ ℕfr£76.50 ₽
25P 5☂ ✿ ⚲
♡ English & French V ⊙ ⊒ Lunch fr£17.55alc Dinner fr£17.55alc Last dinner 9.30pm
CONF. Thtr 40 Board 14 Del from £85
Credit Cards ①②③

★★61% Crown
All Saints Place PE9 2AG (behind the church in the main square) ☎(0780) 63136 FAX (0780) 56111
Closed 25 Dec
This 16th-century stone inn by the church in the town centre has a convivial atmosphere and provides clean, well furnished, comfortable accommodation. The Coffee Room is popular for lunches.
17rm(15⇌ ℕ)(2fb)1⚏ CTV in 18 bedrooms ® T ✱ sB&B£42 sB&B⇌ ℕ£42 dB&B£48 dB&B⇌ ℕ£55
40P
♡ European V ⊙ ⊒ ⚝ ✱ Lunch £7.25-£15 Dinner fr£10.95&alc Last dinner 9.30pm
CONF. Thtr 40 Class 40 Board 30 Del from £65
Credit Cards ①②③⑤

★★61% Lady Anne's
37-38 High Street, St Martins PE9 2LJ ☎(0780) 481184 FAX (0780) 65422
Closed 27-30 Dec
The hotel is set in its own pleasant grounds, making it a popular venue for weddings and conferences. Inside, there is a small bar, an attractive restaurant and a series of well furnished lounge areas, though these double as meeting rooms so are not always available to guests. The bedrooms vary in size and style.
29rm(17⇌10ℕ)(6fb)2⚏ CTV in all bedrooms ® T
CTV 150P ✿ ♗ (hard)
V ⊙ ⊒ Last dinner 9.30pm
Credit Cards ①②③④⑤

STANDISH Greater Manchester Map **07** SD51

★★★64% Almond Brook Moat House
Almond Brook Rd WN6 0SR (200yds from junct 27 of M6, on A5209) ☎(0257) 425588 FAX (0257) 427327
Closed 25-30 Dec

122⇌ ℕ(33fb)⚝ in 5 bedrooms CTV in all bedrooms ® T sB&B⇌ ℕ£45-£75 dB&B⇌ ℕ£60-£90 ₽
Lift ◖ ⊞ 400P ▱ (heated) sauna solarium gymnasium jacuzzi
♡ English & French V ⊙ ⊒ ⚝ Lunch £5.95-£9.50&alc Dinner £12.50-£13.25&alc Last dinner 10pm
CONF. Thtr 150 Class 40 Board 50 Del from £75
Credit Cards ①②③④⑤

Red star hotels are each highlighted by a pink tinted panel.

STANLEY Co Durham Map **12** NZ15

★★64% *South Causey Hotel & Equestrian Centre*
Beamish Burn Rd DH9 0LS (N off A6076) ☎(0207) 235555 FAX (0207) 230137
Created from a collection of stone farm buildings in an equestrian centre, this hotel has been pleasantly furnished throughout. Bedrooms are modern in style and have good facilities, and there is a large restaurant and an equally spacious lounge bar.
16⇌ ℕ CTV in all bedrooms ® T
◖ ⊞ CTV 100P ✿ ∪ ♪ ⚲
V ⊙ ⊒ Last dinner 9.30pm
Credit Cards ①②③

STANLEY Tayside Map **11** NO13

★★⊛59% The Tayside
Mill St PH1 4NL (6m N of Perth) ☎(0738) 828249 FAX (0738) 33449
Popular with fishing, shooting and golfing enthusiasts, this hotel has traditional, practical bedrooms and Victorian-style public rooms. Good-value, honest country cooking is offered in the dining room, where a short daily changing menu of generous home-made dishes is augmented by a longer carte.
17rm(2⇌11ℕ)(2fb) CTV in all bedrooms ® sB&Bfr£19.50 sB&B⇌ ℕfr£32.50 dB&Bfr£39 dB&B⇌ ℕfr£45 ₽
50P 4☂ ♪ *xmas*
♡ Scottish, English & French V ⊙ ⊒ Lunch £5-£12.50alc Dinner £14.50-£22.50 Last dinner 8.30pm
CONF. Thtr 100 Class 75 Del from £40
Credit Cards ①③

STANSTED AIRPORT Essex Map **05** TL52

Hilton National Stansted
Round Coppice Rd CM24 8SE
☎Bishop Stortford(0279) 680800 FAX (0279) 680890
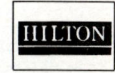
This is a bright, modern hotel with an informal restaurant, aimed at both the business and leisure guest. All bedrooms have en-suite bathrooms and a range of modern facilities. For more information on Hilton National, consult the Contents page, under Hotel Groups.
238⇌ ℕ ✱ B⇌ ℕ£75 (room only)

STAVERTON Devon Map **03** SX76

★67% *Sea Trout Inn*
TQ9 6PA ☎(0803) 762274 FAX (0803) 762506
This 15th-century inn with popular bars is tastefully decorated, comfortably furnished and well equipped for holiday and commercial visitors. An extensive choice of dishes is offered from the range of menus and a small restaurant area forms part of the busy lounge bar, an arrangement which can be quite limited on a Sunday.
10⇌ ℕ(2fb)1⚏ CTV in all bedrooms ®⚝ T
70P ⇔ ✿
♡ English & French V ⊙ Last dinner 9.45pm
Credit Cards ①②③

STEEPLE ASTON Oxfordshire Map **04** SP42

★★★58% Hopcrofts Holt
OX6 3QQ (junct of B4030/A4260)
☎(0869) 40259 FAX (0869) 40865

This much extended old coaching inn between Oxford and Banbury offers a range of well equipped bedrooms, from smaller rooms in the original building to larger modern rooms. Set and carte menus are available in the informal restaurant and there is a busy public bar and popular conference and function facilities.

Steeple Aston - Stilton

88rm(86⇨ᐥ)(2fb) CTV in all bedrooms ® T ✱
sB&B⇨ᐥ£35-£65 dB&B⇨ᐥ£55-£80 🍴
《 CTV 200P ❀ putting green ♪ xmas
♨ English & French V ❖ ♨ ✱ Lunch £7.50-£10.95 High tea fr£2.75 Dinner fr£16.95&alc Last dinner 9.45pm
Credit Cards ①②③⑤ £

STEPPS Strathclyde *Lanarkshire* Map **11** NS66

★★★**65%** Garfield House
Cumbernauld Rd G33 6HW (off A80) ☏041-779 2111 FAX 041-779 2111

This popular commercial hotel continues to improve; a recent extension has provided bedrooms that are both modern and well appointed, while public areas now include a new residents' lounge as well as the busy lounge bar, and a split-level restaurant where pleasant tartan-skirted staff provide cheerful, relaxed service.

27⇨ᐥAnnexe19⇨ᐥ(2fb)⇨ᐥin 4 bedrooms CTV in all bedrooms ® T ✱ sB&B⇨ᐥfr£60 dB&B⇨ᐥ£75-£95 🍴
《 100P ♪ xmas
♨ British, Indian & Italian V ❖ ♨ ✱ Lunch £5.50-£7.50 Dinner £10-£16&alc Last dinner 9.15pm
CONF. Thtr 24 Class 35 Board 7 Del from £75
Credit Cards ①②③⑤ £

STEVENAGE Hertfordshire Map **04** TL22

★★★**68%** Stevenage Moat House
High St, Old Town SG1 3AZ ☏(0438) 359111 FAX (0438) 742169

Refurbished from top to toe, this Grade II listed former farmhouse looks very smart indeed. Bedrooms have been restructured to provide more spacious rooms, and though the decor and fabrics are similar, the furniture varies from mahogany to limed oak. There is a cosy panelled cocktail bar and candlelit restaurant in addition to the less formal Oliver's Country Kitchen.

56⇨ᐥ(4fb)3⇨ᐥin 8 bedrooms CTV in all bedrooms ® ⚲ T sB&B⇨ᐥ£45-£80 dB&B⇨ᐥ£55-£85 🍴
《 100P ❀
♨ English & French V ❖ ♨ ✱ Lunch £12.75&alc Dinner £12.75&alc Last dinner 9.45pm
CONF. Thtr 200 Class 60 Board 60 Del from £77.50
Credit Cards ①②③④⑤ £

★★★**61%** Blakemore Thistle
Blakemore End Rd, Little Wymondley SG4 7JJ STEVENAGE ☏(0438) 355821 FAX (0438) 742114

(For full entry see Hitchin)

★★★**61%** Hertfordpark
Danestrete SG1 1EJ (in town centre adjacent to Westgate Car Park) ☏(0438) 350661 FAX (0438) 741880

This tall modern building, at the heart of the new shopping centre, has on its first floor the Village Restaurant and the lounge bar. Bedrooms on the second floor have been refurbished with attractive décor and coordinating soft furnishings; other are older in style, but all are equipped to up-to-date standards. Free parking is available in an adjacent multi-story car park.

100⇨ᐥin 28 bedrooms CTV in all bedrooms ® T ✱ sB&B⇨ᐥ£22.50-£59 dB&B⇨ᐥ£45-£69 🍴
Lift 《 ♪ ♫
♨ International V ❖ ♨ ✱ Lunch fr£12&alc Dinner £12-£16.95&alc Last dinner 9.45pm
CONF. Thtr 150 Class 70 Board 40 Del £85
Credit Cards ①②③⑤ £

★★★**59%** Novotel
Knebworth Park SG1 2AX (at junct A1/A602) ☏(0438) 742299 FAX (0438) 723872

This modern hotel offers plain, identically furnished bedrooms, suited mainly to business guests. Bright open-plan public areas include an all-day bar and grill restaurant.

100⇨ᐥ(100fb)⇨ᐥin 13 bedrooms CTV in all bedrooms ® ⚲ T ✱ sB⇨ᐥ£59.50 dB⇨ᐥ£64.50 (room only)
Lift 《 120P ❀ ≅ (heated)
♨ International V ❖ ♨ ✱ Lunch fr£7.25&alc Dinner fr£13.50&alc Last dinner mdnt
Credit Cards ①②③⑤

Forte Posthouse
Old London Rd, Broadwater SG2 8DS ☏(0508) 365444 FAX (0508) 741308

Suitable for both the business and leisure traveller, this bright hotel provides modern accommodation in well equipped bedrooms with en suite bathrooms. For more details about Forte Posthouse hotels, consult the Contents page, under Hotel Groups.

54⇨ᐥ✱ B⇨ᐥ£41.50-£53.50 (room only)
CONF. Thtr 60 Class 30 Board 35 Del £89.50

STEWARTON Strathclyde *Ayrshire* Map **10** NS44

★★★★⊛**75%** Chapeltoun House
KA3 3ED (off B796, 2m from SW of town) ☏(0560) 482696 FAX (0560) 485100

Peacefully situated in 20-acre grounds, this former private residence dating from the turn of the century has well proportioned rooms and fine wood panelling. Welcoming log fires burn in the comfortable, relaxing public areas on even the hottest days, and traditionally furnished bedrooms offer a wealth of thoughtful extras. Involved proprietors are always on hand to ensure that guests receive every attention, and a set-price menu features fresh Scottish produce.

8⇨ᐥ CTV in all bedrooms T sB&B⇨ᐥ£65-£89 dB&B⇨ᐥ£90-£134 🍴
50P 🚗 ❀ ♪ nc12yrs
♨ French V ❖ ♨ ✱ Lunch £15.50 Dinner £26.80 Last dinner 9pm
Credit Cards ①②③ £

STEYNING West Sussex Map **04** TQ11

★★★**65%** The Old Tollgate
The Street BN44 3WE ☏(0903) 879494 FAX (0903) 813399

Built on the site of the old toll house, this hotel has very well designed bedrooms fully equipped with modern amenities. Public areas focus on the popular carvery restaurant, but there is a small lounge.

11⇨ᐥAnnexe20⇨ᐥ(5fb)2🍴 CTV in all bedrooms ® ⚲ T ✘ (ex guide dogs) ✱ dB⇨ᐥ£52-£72 (room only) 🍴
Lift 《 60P ❀ xmas
V ♨ Lunch £11.95-£13.95alc
CONF. Thtr 50 Board 26 Del from £70
Credit Cards ①②③⑤ £

STILTON Cambridgeshire Map **04** TL18

★★★**67%** Bell Inn
Great North Rd PE7 3RA ☏Peterborough(0733) 241066 FAX (0733) 245173

Closed 24-25 Dec

The Bell Inn, in the centre of the quiet village, is built around an old courtyard with good integration of new and old stone buildings. Much of the character is retained in the public rooms, with exposed stone walls, beams and open log fires in the galleried restaurant and

the popular public bar. Several small lounge areas provide peace and quiet for guests. Bedrooms come in 3 styles, deluxe rooms having whirlpool baths.
19⇌🏠(1fb)2⬜⊁in 4 bedrooms CTV in all bedrooms ®✌ T
✝ (ex guide dogs) ✻ sB&B⇌🏠£50-£72 dB&B⇌🏠£62-£82 🚰
(30P ♫ ⚙
♡ English & French V ✿ ⚇ ✻ Lunch £9.50-£14.50 Dinner £14.50-£21.50&alc Last dinner 9.30pm
Credit Cards 1 2 3 5   £

STIRLING Central *Stirlingshire* Map **11** NS79
See also **Bridge of Allan**

★★★★ ✿✿65% **Stirling Highland**
Spittal St FK8 1DU (Scottish Highland) ☏(0786) 475444
FAX (0786) 462929

Retaining many of the original features of the old High School, from which it was imaginatively converted, this unique hotel, close to Stirling Castle, has panoramic views. Set around a quadrangle, the stylish public areas feature vaulted ceilings and wood panelling. All the well equipped bedrooms are in a new wing. Rizzio's is a cheery trattoria on 2 levels with its own bar, while the main restaurant, Scholars offers a high standard of cooking in modern style, with a French influence.
76⇌🏠(21fb)⊁in 22 bedrooms CTV in all bedrooms ®✌ T
sB&B⇌🏠£96-£134 dB&B⇌🏠£128-£134 🚰
Lift (96P 🅿 (heated) squash snooker sauna solarium gymnasium spa bath steam room *xmas*
♡ Scottish & Italian V ✿ ⚇ Lunch £10.50-£12.50&alc Dinner £19.75&alc Last dinner 10.30pm
CONF. Thtr 170 Class 70 Board 50 Del from £97
Credit Cards 1 2 3 5   £

★★ 65% **Terraces**
4 Melville Ter FK8 2ND (off A728)
☏(0786) 472268 FAX (0786) 450314

CONSORT HOTELS

Situated in a tree-lined terrace within walking distance of the town, this family-run commercial hotel is popular for functions and business meetings and for its honest good value cooking and reasonable priced wine list. Bedrooms, though mostly compact, are well equipped with such extras as hairdryers.
18⇌🏠(4fb) CTV in all bedrooms ® T ✻ sB&B⇌🏠fr£52.50 dB&B⇌🏠fr£67 🚰
(25P ♫ *xmas*
♡ International V ✿ ⊁ ✻ Lunch £3.95-£12.50alc Dinner £3.95-£12.50alc Last dinner 9pm
CONF. Thtr 150 Class 45 Board 30 Del from £67.50
Credit Cards 1 2 3

★★ 57% **King Robert**
Glasgow Rd, Bannockburn FK7 0LT
☏Bannockburn(0786) 811666 FAX (0786) 811507

This functional, purpose built hotel beside the Bannockburn Heritage Centre is gradually being improved. Although all the rooms are equipped to the same good standard, the most comfortable are in a new bedroom wing.
53⇌🏠(3fb)⊁in 3 bedrooms CTV in all bedrooms ® T
✝ (ex guide dogs)
(CTV 100P ✿
V ✿ ⚇
Credit Cards 1 2 3 5

If you have booked a meal in a
hotel restaurant and cannot get there,
remember you have a contractual obligation
to cancel your booking.

Stilton - Stirling

Located in the centre of Stirling – the Gateway to the Highlands – the 4 star Stirling Highland Hotel is one of the finest Hotels in the area.

- **76 STYLISH, WELL EQUIPPED, BEDROOMS** • **SCHOLARS A LA CARTE RESTAURANT** • **RIZZIO'S ITALIAN RESTAURANT**
- **MAGNIFICENT LEISURE CLUB WITH HEATED POOL, SAUNAS, STEAM ROOMS, SQUASH COURTS, GYMNASIUM, SNOOKER ROOM**
- **ONLY FORTY MINUTES FROM GLASGOW AND EDINBURGH**

For brochure and reservations contact:

Stirling Highland Hotel, Spittal Street, Stirling FK8 1DU. Tel: 0786 475444

★★★AA
THE BLAKEMORE
THISTLE HOTEL

Little Wymondley, Hitchin, Stevenage SG4 7JJ
Tel: 0438 355821   Fax: 0438 742114

Your choice in
Stevenage

For Reservations at over 100
Mount Charlotte Thistle Hotels
Telephone London: 071 937 8033.

Stirling - Stockton-on-Tees

Granada Lodge
Pirnhall Roundabout, Snabhead FK7 8EU (junct M9/M80) ☎(0786) 815033 FAX (0786) 815900

This modern building provides smart, spacious and well equipped bedrooms, all with en suite bathrooms. Meals may be taken at a nearby family restaurant. For more details about Granada Lodges, consult the Contents page, under Hotel Groups.

37⇨✱ B⇨£34.95-£37.95 (room only)

STOCKBRIDGE Hampshire Map 04 SU33

★★★ 61% Grosvenor
High St SO20 6EU (on the A30 in village centre) (Whitbread) ☎Andover(0264) 810606 FAX (0264) 810747

This traditional hotel with many Georgian features stands in the broad village high street. The bar, where snacks are served, is popular with locals and has an open fire in winter. Bedrooms are either in the newer wing at the back overlooking the garden, or in the main building looking over the street.

25⇨♖1🛏⊬in 3 bedrooms CTV in all bedrooms ®✷ T ✱ (ex guide dogs) ✱ sB&B⇨♖fr£65.50 dB&B⇨♖fr£77 ♬
(60P ✿ snooker sauna
♀ Continental V ♀ ♴ ⊬ Last dinner 9.45pmm
CONF. Thtr 70 Class 20 Board 30 Del from £89
Credit Cards 1 2 3 5

STOCKPORT Greater Manchester Map 07 SJ88

★★★ 68% Bramhall Moat House
Bramhall Ln South SK7 2EB ☎061-439 8146
FAX 061-440 8071
(For full entry see Bramhall)

★★ 70% Red Lion Inn
112 Buxton Rd, High Ln SK6 8ED (beside A6, 1m from Lyme Country Park) ☎Disley(0663) 765287 FAX (0663) 762170

This popular inn offers tasteful accommodation. Bedrooms are not large but they are equipped with all modern amenities and thoughtful extras, and have attractive fabrics, period furniture and smart, well lit bathrooms. Public areas are limited to a very busy brasserie/café bar which offers all-day meals and refreshments.

6⇨♖(1fb) CTV in all bedrooms ® T ✱ (ex guide dogs) ✱ sB&B⇨♖£25.50-£46.50 dB&B⇨♖£44-£58.50
100P ⇌
V ♀ ♴ ⊬ Lunch fr£5.95 Dinner £10.25 Last dinner 10pm
Credit Cards 1 2 3 5

★★ 66% Saxonholme
230 Wellington Rd SK4 2QN (N, beside A6) ☎061-432 2335
FAX 061-431 8076

This privately owned hotel offers modern accommodation, mostly in a new bedroom wing to the rear of the building. By contrast, public areas have a more traditional atmosphere, although there are plans to add a large conservatory. Friendly staff provide helpful service and 24-hour room service is available.

30⇨♖(4fb)⊬in 12 bedrooms CTV in all bedrooms ®✷ T ✱ sB&B⇨♖£25-£42 dB&B⇨♖£32-£52
Lift (CTV 36P
♀ English & French V ♀ ♴ ⊬ Last dinner 9.15pm
CONF. Thtr 80 Board 20
Credit Cards 1 2 3

★★ 63% Wycliffe
74 Edgeley Rd, Edgeley SK3 9NQ (on right after passing Alexandra Park) ☎061-477 5395 FAX 061-476 3219
RS BH's

This friendly family-run hotel is situated in a pleasant residential area close to Alexandra Park. Recently extended and modernised, it has comfortable bedrooms of varying size. There is a comfortable lounge bar and a restaurant featuring Italian dishes.

20⇨♖ CTV in all bedrooms ® T ✱ ✱ sB&B⇨♖£33-£43 dB&B⇨♖£39-£51
(CTV 48P ⇌
♀ English, French & Italian V ♀ ♴ ✱ Lunch £7-£14&alc Dinner £10.50&alc Last dinner 9.30pm
Credit Cards 1 2 3 5

★★ 58% Rudyard Toby
271 Wellington Rd North, Heaton Chapel SK4 5BP (1.5m N off A6) (Toby) ☎061-432 2753 FAX 061-431 0260

This popular, modernised Victorian hotel offers a carvery restaurant and a choice of bars. Bedrooms are well equipped, but planned improvements have had to be delayed.

21⇨♖(2fb)⊬in 8 bedrooms CTV in all bedrooms ® T ✱ sB&B⇨♖£22-£49 dB&B⇨♖£44-£56 ♬
(82P
V ♀ ♴ ⊬ ✱ Lunch fr£5.99 Dinner fr£5.99 Last dinner 10pm
CONF. Thtr 150 Class 30 Board 40 Del from £65
Credit Cards 1 2 3 4 5 £

Forte Travelodge
London Rd South SK12 4NA (on A523)
☎(0625) 875292 Central Res (0800) 850950

This modern building offers a good standard of accommodation for overnight stops. Smart, spacious and well equipped bedrooms, all with en suite bathrooms, are suitable for family use, and meals may be taken at the nearby family restaurant. For more details about Travelodges, consult the Contents page, under Hotel Groups.

32⇨♖✱ B⇨♖£31.95 (room only)

STOCKTON-ON-TEES Cleveland Map 08 NZ41

★★★★ 58% Swallow
10 John Walker Square TS18 1AQ
☎(0642) 679721 FAX (0642) 601714

This large modern hotel in the town centre offers free parking in the adjoining multi-storey car park. There is a choice of restaurant or brasserie and the bedrooms are generally spacious and well equipped, though some rooms require updating to match the improvements in others.

125⇨♖(12fb)⊬in 51 bedrooms CTV in all bedrooms ®✷ ✱ sB&B⇨♖£80 dB&B⇨♖£92 ♬
Lift (400⇌ ⊠ (heated) sauna solarium gymnasium jacuzzi steam room *xmas*
♀ English & French V ♀ ♴ ✱ Lunch £12.25&alc Dinner £17.75&alc Last dinner 10.30pm
CONF. Thtr 300 Class 220 Board 40 Del from £80
Credit Cards 1 2 3 4 5 £

★★★ ❀70% Parkmore
636 Yarm Rd, Eaglescliffe TS16 0DH (3m S A19) ☎(0642) 786815 FAX (0642) 790485

The Parkmore is a former Victorian residence which has been modernised and extended and now incorporates an excellent leisure centre as well as the facilities of a modern hotel. The Carlton restaurant offers table d'hote and a la carte menus and the staff throughout this family-run hotel are friendly and helpful.

55⇨♖(3fb)6🛏⊬in 4 bedrooms CTV in all bedrooms ®✷ T ✱ sB&B⇨♖£40-£60 dB&B⇨♖£50-£80 ♬
(CTV 120P ✿ ⊠ (heated) snooker sauna solarium gymnasium jacuzzi steam room beauty salon
♀ English & French V ♀ ♴ ✱ Lunch £11.50-£13.50&alc Dinner £15-£25alc Last dinner 9.30pm
CONF. Thtr 150 Class 40 Board 40 Del from £70
Credit Cards 1 2 3 5

Stockton-on-Tees - Stoke-on-Trent

★★★**57%** **Billingham Arms**
The Causeway, Billingham TS23 2HD (3m NE A19)
☎(0642) 553661 & 360880 FAX (0642) 552104
On the edge of the town's shopping precinct, this busy commercial hotel has a number of spacious public bars, one with carved cedar panelling designed for SS Britannica (sunk by a mine in 1916). There is an Edwardian theme in Bertie's Restaurant, with its adjoining cocktail bar, and the Langtry Buttery. Bedrooms are modern in style with some small singles.
69⇨ ♔(6fb)2🛏½in 4 bedrooms CTV in all bedrooms ® ⚲ T ✱
sB⇨ ♔£37-£49 dB⇨ ♔£57-£64 (room only) 🍴
Lift (🎱 150P 2🏊 solarium pool table xmas
♨ International V ☯ ⚖ ✱ Lunch £7.50&alc Dinner £12.95&alc Last dinner 11pm
Credit Cards ① ② ③ ④ ⑤

★★**62%** **Claireville**
519 Yarm Rd, Eaglescliffe TS16 9BQ (3m S A135, adjacent to Eaglescliffe Golf Course) ☎(0642) 780378 FAX (0642) 784109
RS Xmas & New Year
This detached Victorian house is situated in its own grounds and gardens. It is a friendly, family-run hotel with facilities to suit the business or leisure traveller.
19rm(16⇨ ♔)(2fb) CTV in all bedrooms ® ⚲ T ✱
sB&B£21.50-£28.50 sB&B⇨ ♔£33-£40 dB&B⇨ ♔£44-£54 CTV 20P ✱
♨ English & French V ☯ ⚖ ✱ Lunch £8.95 Dinner £12.95&alc Last dinner 8.30pm
Credit Cards ① ③ ⑤

Forte Posthouse
Low Ln, Thornaby-on-Tees TS17 9LW (SE on A144) ☎Middlesbrough(0642) 591213 FAX (0642) 594989

Suitable for both the business and leisure traveller, this bright hotel provides modern accommodation in well equipped bedrooms with en suite bathrooms. For more details about Forte Posthouse hotels, consult the Contents page, under Hotel Groups.
135⇨ ✱ B⇨ ♔£41.50-£53.50 (room only)

STOKE CANON Devon Map 03 SX99

★★★🌺**70%** **Barton Cross Hotel & Restaurant**
Huxham EX5 4EJ (0.5m off A396 at Stoke Canon)
☎Exeter(0392) 841245 & 841584 FAX (0392) 841942
This small, family-run 17th-century thatched hotel is in a rural situation. Public areas are cosy and full of character with exposed beams and inglenook fireplaces, and include the popular galleried restaurant. Chef Stuart Fowles' table d'hôte menu includes some interesting dishes making use of local meat and fish.
6⇨ ♔ CTV in all bedrooms ® ⚲ T ✱ sB&B⇨ ♔fr£63.50 dB&B⇨ ♔fr£85 🍴
25P windsurfing instruction xmas
♨ English & French V ☯ ⚖ ✱ Lunch £24 Dinner £24 Last dinner 9.30pm
Credit Cards ① ② ③ ⑤

See advertisement under EXETER

STOKE D'ABERNON Surrey Map 04 TQ15

★★★🌺**68%** **Woodlands Park**
Woodlands Ln KT11 3QB (on A245 between Cobham & Leatherhead) ☎Oxshott(0372) 843933 FAX (0372) 842704
Retaining much of its Victorian splendour, this delightful mansion has an elegant Grand Hall lounge with stained glass, an ornate ceiling, an elaborate carved balcony and a log-burning fire. Bedrooms are comfortably and tastefully furnished and have smart modern bathrooms. In the Oak Room restaurant, chef Nigel Beckett offers a short seasonal carte, with weekly changing specialities, cooked in light modern style.

58⇨ ♔2🛏 CTV in all bedrooms ® T ✱ (ex guide dogs)
sB⇨ ♔fr£100 dB⇨ ♔fr£130 (room only) 🍴
Lift (150P ✱ ♣ (hard) croquet putting xmas
♨ English & French V ☯ ⚖ ✱ Lunch £12.50 Dinner £15.75 Last dinner 10pm
CONF. Thtr 300 Class 150 Board 60 Del £147
Credit Cards ① ② ③ ⑤

STOKE GABRIEL Devon Map 03 SX85

★★★⚜**71%** **Gabriel Court**
TQ9 6SF (off A385) ☎(0803) 782206 FAX (0803) 782333
The Beacom family offer warm hospitality at this hotel which dates, in parts, back to 1487 and is set in beautifully kept Elizabethan style terraced gardens. Bedrooms are individually furnished and decorated, and in the cooler months log fires blaze in the lounges. The dinner menu features mainly traditional British dishes, with fresh vegetables from the hotel garden.
20⇨ ♔ CTV in all bedrooms ® T sB&B⇨ ♔£45-£52 dB&B⇨ ♔fr£76
CTV 13P 7🅿 🚲 ✱ ⚲ (heated) croquet ⚽ xmas
☯ ⚖ ✱ Sunday Lunch fr£11 Dinner fr£22 Last dinner 8.30pm
Credit Cards ① ② ③ ⑤

STOKE-ON-TRENT Staffordshire Map 07 SJ84

See also **Newcastle-under-Lyme**

★★★**62%** **Stoke-on-Trent Moat House**
Etruria Hall, Festival Way, Etruria ST1 5BQ (situated on the Festival Park)
☎(0782) 219000 FAX (0782) 284500
Etruria Hall, the family home of Josiah Wedgwood, is incorporated into this new hotel, and the juxtaposition of new and old has been carefully designed, enhanced by many of the original decorative features. The public areas are on 2 floors with a large roof garden adjacent to reception. The bedrooms have been designed with commercial clients in mind, though leisure guests will not find them disappointing.
143⇨ ♔(10fb)½in 42 bedrooms CTV in all bedrooms ® ⚲ T ✱ (ex guide dogs) ✱ sB&B⇨ ♔£82 dB&B⇨ ♔£99 🍴
Lift (🎱 350P ✱ 🏊 (heated) sauna solarium gymnasium leisure club xmas
♨ International V ☯ ⚖ ½ Last dinner 10.30pm
CONF. Thtr 550 Class 320 Board 124 Del £120
Credit Cards ① ② ③ ⑤

★★★**62%** **George**
Swan Square, Burslem ST6 2AE ☎(0782) 577544 FAX (0782) 837496
Built in 1929, The George has been completely refurbished over the last year or so. Bedrooms all have attractive wood furniture and many extra facilities. A small but comfortable and impressive residents' lounge is situated on the first floor and the restaurant offers a choice of menus.
30⇨ ♔(5fb) CTV in all bedrooms ® ⚲ T ✱ (ex guide dogs) ✱ sB&B⇨ ♔£35-£40 dB&B⇨ ♔£50-£60 🍴
Lift (13P 10🚗 xmas
♨ English & Continental V ☯ ⚖ ✱ Lunch £10.95&alc Dinner £15.95&alc Last dinner 9pm
Credit Cards ① ② ③

★★★**62%** **Haydon House**
1-13 Haydon St, Basford ST4 6JD (off A53 near junct with A500)
☎(0782) 711311 FAX (0782) 717470
Completely modernised, this family-run hotel has comfortable, Victorian-themed public areas, with a collection of around 80 clocks; some of the bedrooms are luxurious, others are more standard.
18⇨ ♔Annexe14⇨ ♔(4fb)1🛏 CTV in all bedrooms ® T ✱ sB⇨ ♔£40-£62 dB⇨ ♔£40-£62 (room only) 🍴
52P xmas

♥ English & French **V** ✧ ☞ ✱ Lunch £10.50&alc Dinner £12.90&alc Last dinner 9.45pm
Credit Cards 1 2 3 5

★★ **55%** *Crown*
Times Square, Longton ST3 1HD ☎(0782) 599343 FAX (0782) 598062

This modernised business hotel stands close to Longton town centre.
40⇨🐾 CTV in all bedrooms ® T ✖ (ex guide dogs)
CTV 38P
♥ International **V** ✧ ☞ Last dinner 10pm
Credit Cards 1 2 3 5

STONE Staffordshire Map **07** SJ93

★★★ **67%** *Stone House*
ST15 0BQ (beside A34) (Lansbury) ☎(0785) 815531 FAX (0785) 814764

A one-time country house set in pleasant gardens has been converted and extended to create a good, well run hotel offering comfortable modern bedrooms. The attractive Garden Restaurant provides a good choice of food, and guests can relax in a small cocktail bar or one of the 2 comfortable lounges.
47⇨🐾(2fb)2✱½ in 10 bedrooms CTV in all bedrooms ® 𝒴 T ✖ (ex guide dogs) ✱ sB&B⇨🐾fr£69.50 dB&B⇨🐾fr£81 🍴
Lift (⊞ CTV 100P ✿ 🖼 (heated) ♪ (hard) sauna solarium gymnasium pitch and putt ✦ *xmas*
♥ International **V** ✧ ☞ ½ ✱ Lunch fr£9.75&alc Dinner fr£15.50&alc Last dinner 10pm
CONF. Thtr 200 Class 200 Board 60 Del from £95
Credit Cards 1 2 3 5

STON EASTON Somerset Map **03** ST65

STON EASTON PARK
BA3 4DF
☎Mendip(0761) 241631
FAX (0761) 241377

This lovely Palladian mansion is set in parkland with the River Norr running through mature gardens. Guests can glimpse the 'upstairs, downstairs' world of the 18th century in the early kitchens, linen room, servants hall, game room and wine cellars. Public rooms are beautifully decorated and furnished, and each bedroom has a unique appeal. Head chef Mark Harrington offers a fixed-price menu using garden produce, local game and best quality fish. Our inspector enjoyed a well constructed galantine of maize-fed chicken studded with pistachio and chopped ham and tongue; a roundel of Scotch beef with a sautée of foie gras and confit of shallots; and finished with a hot pudding of poached pear filled with chocolate.
19⇨🐾Annexe2⇨🐾6🛏 CTV in all bedrooms ® T ✖ (ex guide dogs) sB&B⇨🐾£85-£165 dB&B⇨🐾£135-£340 Continental breakfast 🍴
CTV 100P ✿ ♪ (hard) snooker croquet hot air ballooning nc7yrs *xmas*
♥ English & French **V** ✧ ☞ ½ Lunch fr£26 Dinner fr£38 Last dinner 9.30pm
CONF. Thtr 30 Class 15 Board 24 Del from £140
Credit Cards 1 2 3 5

STONEHAVEN Grampian *Kincardineshire* Map **15** NO88

★★ **59%** *County*
Arduthie Rd AB3 2EH ☎(0569) 64786

This friendly, family-run hotel is gradually being upgraded by the enthusiastic owners. Though there is no lounge, there is a choice of bars, where the emphasis is on popular bar food, and hearty portions from the carte are served in the attractive dining room. Bedrooms vary in size and appointments.
14⇨🐾(2fb) CTV in all bedrooms ® T ✖ (ex guide dogs)
40P 🚗 ✿ squash sauna solarium gymnasium
♥ Scottish, English & French **V** ✧ Last dinner 9pm
Credit Cards 1 3

STONEHOUSE Gloucestershire Map **03** SO80

★★★ **67%** *Stonehouse Court*
Bristol Rd GL10 3RA (on A419) (Clipper) ☎(0453) 825155 FAX (0453) 824611

Standing in 6.5 acres of grounds, this delightful Grade II listed house has comfortable wood-panelled public areas and a range of bedrooms, those in the main house being the more spacious. Chef Alan Postill offers a short table d'hôte menu in addition to a seasonal carte. Inventive starters such as wild mushroom galette and scampi and scallop samosas might be followed by guinea fowl with a Marsala sauce. Desserts could include a platter of chocolates or an iced chestnut parfait.
37⇨🐾1🛏 CTV in all bedrooms ® T ✖ (ex guide dogs) sB&B⇨🐾£72.50-£85 dB&B⇨🐾£98-£120 🍴
(150P ✿ croquet bowls ✦ *xmas*
♥ English & French **V** ✧ ☞ Lunch fr£12.50&alc Dinner fr£20&alc Last dinner 9.30pm
CONF. Thtr 120 Class 70 Board 60 Del from £100
Credit Cards 1 3

STONOR Oxfordshire Map **04** SU78

★★★ **77%** *Stonor Arms*
RG9 6HE ☎Turville Heath(0491) 638345 FAX (0491) 638863

Originally the village pub, dating from the 18th century, this privately owned hotel and restaurant enjoys an enviable location in the Thames Valley, adjoining the Stonor Park estate. Accommodation is of the highest standard, with spacious, comfortable bedrooms furnished with antiques. Serious food is served in the Stonor Restaurant, surrounded by a splendid collection of paintings. Ratatouille roulade with all the flavour of the Mediterranean would delight vegetarians and meat eaters alike, followed by a mixed lamb platter including cutlets, kidneys, tongue and sweetbreads in a rich tomato and tarragon gravy. Blades Brasserie in the conservatory is so popular booking is essential; here one can sample pork rillettes, fillet of smoked haddock with cous-cous or char-grilled leg steak of lamb. Chef-proprietor Stephen Frost has such an efficient kitchen brigade that he is able to appear as host rather than chef, and service by a team of young staff is natural and attentive.
9⇨🐾 CTV in all bedrooms ® T ✖ (ex guide dogs)
sB&B⇨🐾£82.50-£127.50 dB&B⇨🐾£92.50-£137.50 🍴
27P 🚗 ✿
Bar Lunch £15-£25alc Dinner £27.50-£32alc Last dinner 9.30pm
Credit Cards 1 2 3

For full, independent restaurant reviews, see the
AA Abbey Well *Restaurant Guide*.

Stourbridge - Stow-on-the-Wold

STORNOWAY
See **Lewis, Isle of**

STOURBRIDGE West Midlands Map **07** SO88
★★**64%** Talbot
High St DY8 1DW (Crown & Raven) ☎(0384) 394350 FAX (0384) 371318
This former coaching inn dating back to the 16th century retains much historic character with its exposed beams and sloping floors. Modernised bedrooms are attractively decorated (though some single rooms are compact) and as well as the restaurant, there are popular bars serving all-day refreshments.
25⇌⋔(4fb)1⍁ CTV in all bedrooms ® T ✻ sB&B⇌⋔fr£49.50 dB&B⇌⋔fr£49.50 ₧
(25P
♀ English & French V ⌀ ⚑ ✻ Lunch £1.75-£9.75alc High tea £1.75-£9.75alc Dinner £1.75-£9.76alc Last dinner 10pm
CONF. Thtr 150 Class 80 Board 60 Del from £73
Credit Cards [1][2][3]

STOURPORT-ON-SEVERN Hereford & Worcester Map **07** SO87
★★★**67%** Stourport Moat House
35 Hartlebury Rd DY13 9LT (E, off B4193)
☎(0299) 827733 FAX (0299) 878520

Queens Moat Houses

This former home of Stanley Baldwin has been significantly extended and developed to provide a comfortable, modern hotel. Accommodation is attractive with pastel decor, light wood furniture, soft fabrics and the well equipped bedrooms have in-room movies. The public areas are extensive and include a bar with lounge seating, and the Cottage restaurant.
68⇌⋔(8fb)⚑in 6 bedrooms CTV in all bedrooms ® T sB&B⇌⋔£45-£57.50 dB&B⇌⋔£50-£65 ₧
(400P ✿ ⌲ ℘ (hard) squash snooker sauna gymnasium clay pigeon shooting golf driving range
♀ English & French V ⌀ ⚑ ⚑ Lunch £10-£12.50&alc Dinner fr£13.50&alc Last dinner 10pm
CONF. Thtr 400 Class 150 Board 50 Del from £75
Credit Cards [1][2][3][5]

STOWMARKET Suffolk Map **05** TM05
★★**59%** Cedars
Needham Rd IP14 2AJ (A1308 1m outside Stowmarket on road to Needham Market)
☎(0449) 612668 FAX (0449) 674704
Closed Xmas-New Year

Located on the ring road to the south of the town, the hotel has been extended to provide additional bedrooms and a purpose built conference/banqueting suite, though there are still a few rooms in the original farmhouse. The bar and restaurant provide simply prepared food in a friendly setting. Bedrooms vary in size and are furnished in a cosy but simple fashion.
24⇌⋔(2fb) CTV in all bedrooms ®⚑ T sB&B⇌⋔£38-£42 dB&B⇌⋔£45-£48 ₧
75P ✿
♀ English & French V ⌀ ⚑ ⚑ Lunch £5.50-£18alc Dinner £5.50-£18alc Last dinner 9pm
CONF. Thtr 150 Class 100 Board 80 Del from £60
Credit Cards [1][2][3][5]

Some hotels within company owned groups share a uniform identity. For full details consult the Contents page, under Hotel Groups.

Forte Travelodge
IP14 3PY (on A45)
☎(0449) 615347 Central Res (0800) 850950

FORTE Travelodge

This modern building offers a good standard of accommodation for overnight stops. Smart, spacious and well equipped bedrooms, all with en suite bathrooms, are suitable for family use, and meals may be taken at the nearby family restaurant. For more details about Travelodges, consult the Contents page, under Hotel Groups.
40⇌⋔✻ B⇌⋔£31.95 (room only)

STOW-ON-THE-WOLD Gloucestershire Map **04** SP12

★★★★❀❀❀**71%** Wyck Hill House
Burford Rd GL54 1HY (1.5m SE on A424)
☎Cotswold(0451) 831936 FAX (0451) 832243

Under the personal and dedicated management of the ebullient Peter Robinson, this hotel goes from strength to strength. It is fronted by beautifully manicured lawns and flower beds, with glorious views over Bourton-on-the-Water. Elegant public rooms are on classical lines, but there is a comfortable warmth in the library, foyer lounge and clubby cocktail bar. Bedrooms vary, but all are well proportioned and furnished with antiques and bold fabrics. The Courtyard and Orangery bedrooms are not quite so opulent, but equally comfortable, some with patio doors to the gardens. The ornate restaurant is the ideal setting for chef Ian Smith to demonstrate his talents with imaginative dishes, rich in flavours.
16⇌⋔ Annexe14⇌⋔1⍁ CTV in all bedrooms ® T sB&B⇌⋔£65-£100 dB&B⇌⋔£95-£180 ₧
Lift (100P ✿ archery croquet clay pigeon shooting *xmas*

Hotels with red star ratings are especially high quality.

9 star accommodation.

GRANADA HOTEL STOKE
Newcastle Road, Talke, Stoke-on-Trent, Staffordshire ST7 1UP. Tel 0782 777000.
Only 1½ miles from the potteries and 3 miles from M6, J16.

GRANADA HOTEL ALFRETON
Old Swanwick Colliery Road, Alfreton, Derbyshire DE55 1HJ. Tel 0773 520040.
Close to the Derbyshire Dales, just 3 miles from M1, J28.

GRANADA HOTEL SHEFFIELD
340 Prince of Wales Road, Sheffield S2 1FF.
Tel 0742 530935.
Just over 1 mile from city centre and 3 miles from M1, J33.

You'll go a long way to find such a high standard of accommodation at such competitive prices. But just off the motorway network, you don't have to go far to reach us.

GRANADA HOTELS

Stow-on-the-Wold - Stranraer

♀ British & French **V** ✧ ⚏ ✕ Lunch £7-£16.50 Dinner £18-£34alc Last dinner 9.30pm
CONF. Thtr 50 Class 16 Board 22 Del £120
Credit Cards [1][2][3][5]   (£)

★★★ 62% **The Unicorn**
Sheep St GL54 1HQ (situated at the crossroads on the A429 & A436)
☎(0451) 830257 FAX (0451) 831090

FORTE
Heritage

This popular hotel dates from the 17th century and has much historic character with beams, sloping floors and log fires. Public areas include a convivial bar, restaurant and comfortable residents' lounge. Many bedrooms have been refurbished to a good modern standard and have quality furnishings; the remaining rooms are scheduled for similar treatment.
20⇨🛏2🚭in 2 bedrooms CTV in all bedrooms ® T ✱
sB⇨🛏fr£68 dB⇨🛏fr£83 (room only) 🅿
CTV 45P *xmas*
V ✧ ⚏ ✕ Lunch £7.95-£10.95&alc Dinner £16.95&alc Last dinner 9.30pm
Credit Cards [1][2][3][5]

★★ ❀77% **Grapevine**
Sheep St GL54 1AU (on A436 towards Chipping Norton. 150 yds on right, facing green) ☎Cotswold(0451) 830344 FAX (0451) 832278

BEST
WESTERN
HOTELS

Closed 24 Dec-10 Jan
This Cotswold hotel has received much acclaim from all quarters and rightly so. The hallmark of the hotel is the warmth, hospitality and infectious enthusiasm of proprietor Sandra Elliot, manager Brian Bradshaw and their staff. Bedrooms are a mixture of shapes and sizes, those in the main building are cosy and full of character. There is a conservatory-style restaurant (with a grapevine), where chef Matt Rolinson provides appealing table d'hôte menus and bar meals.
12rm(11⇨🛏)Annexe10🛏(2fb)1🚭✕in 4 bedrooms CTV in 23 bedrooms ® T ✖ sB&B⇨🛏£67-£109 dB&B⇨🛏£88-£178 (incl dinner) 🅿
23P 🚭
♀ English, French & Italian **V** ✧ ⚏ ✕ Lunch £6.95-£11.75 Dinner £15.95-£23.95 Last dinner 9.30pm
Credit Cards [1][2][3][5]   (£)

★★ 72% **Fosse Manor**
GL54 1JX (1m S on A429, 300yds past junction with A424) ☎Cotswold(0451) 830354 FAX (0451) 832486

CONSORT
HOTELS

Closed 22-29 Dec
This charming owner-run hotel provides warm personal service and comfortable accommodation. Individually styled bedrooms are thoughtfully equipped and delightful public areas include an intimate restaurant, very comfortable lounge serving refreshments and a popular bar offering varied bar meals.
14⇨🛏Annexe6rm(4⇨🛏)(6fb)1🚭✕ CTV in all bedrooms ® T ✱
sB&B⇨🛏£47.50-£55 dB&B£50-£95 dB&B⇨🛏£95-£130 🅿
CTV 40P ✿ solarium croquet beautician *xmas*
♀ English & Continental **V** ✧ ⚏ ✕ Lunch fr£12.95&alc Dinner fr£15.95&alc Last dinner 9.30pm
CONF. Thtr 40 Class 20 Board 22 Del from £80
Credit Cards [1][2][3][5]

★★ 70% **Stow Lodge**
The Square GL54 1AB (in town centre)
☎Cotswold(0451) 830485
Closed 20 Dec-mid/late Jan
In a central location, set in its own pretty grounds and gardens, this family-run hotel offers comfortable accommodation and prompt, hospitable service. The bedrooms are bright and well furnished with a good range of modern facilities, some in the adjacent converted coach house. There are comfortable lounges and a congenial bar with a good range of home-cooked food, and a pleasant restaurant.

12rm(10⇨🛏)Annexe10⇨🛏(2fb)1🚭✕in 1 bedroom CTV in all bedrooms ® ✖ ✱ sB&B⇨🛏£37-£55 dB&B⇨🛏£56-£86 🅿
(30P 🚭 ✿ nc5yrs
V ✧ ⚏ ✕ Bar Lunch £3-£12alc Dinner £12.75-£13.25&alc Last dinner 9pm
Credit Cards [2][5]

★★ 66% **Old Stocks**
The Square GL54 1AF ☎Cotswold(0451) 830666 FAX (0451) 870014
Closed 21-29 Dec
Next to the green in this Cotswold market town, the Old Stocks is a personally run hotel formed from three 16th and 17th-century buildings, and its cosy lounge, bar and restaurant retain much of their original character. Bedrooms are all well proportioned, comfortable and equipped with modern facilities.
16⇨🛏Annexe3⇨🛏(1fb) CTV in all bedrooms ® T
sB&B⇨🛏£33-£38 dB&B⇨🛏£66-£76 🅿
CTV 14P ✿ *xmas*
V ✧ ⚏ ✕ Sunday Lunch £9.95 Dinner £12.75 Last dinner 9.30pm
Credit Cards [1][2][3]   (£)

★★ 64% **Old Farmhouse**
Lower Swell GL54 1LF (1m W on B2052)
☎Cotswold(0451) 830232 FAX (0451) 870962
Closed 4-20 Jan
Situated in a pretty village a mile west of Stow, this character converted farmhouse has a cosy bar, restaurant and bedrooms in the main house, and additional, bright and well equipped rooms in a former stable block. There is also an attractive self-contained flat. Friendly, informal service is conducted by a willing team of local staff.
7rm(4⇨🛏)Annexe7⇨🛏(1fb)2🚭✕in 6 bedrooms CTV in all bedrooms ® T ✱ sB&B£18.50-£35.50 sB&B⇨🛏£28.50-£54 dB&B£37-£68 dB&B⇨🛏£60-£111 🅿
25P 🚭 ✿ *xmas*
V ✧ ⚏ ✕ Lunch £2-£7.25 Dinner £14.50 Last dinner 9pm
Credit Cards [1][3]

STRACHUR Strathclyde *Argyllshire* Map **10** NN00

★★★ 60% **Creggans Inn**
PA27 8BX ☎(036986) 279 FAX (036986) 637
Standing on the north side of the village overlooking Loch Fyne, this friendly and well managed roadside hotel has simple cottage-style bedrooms and includes a tea room and gift shop as well as a popular bar and comfortable upstairs lounge. The short, interesting dinner menu features Scottish seafood and meat dishes – our inspector enjoyed the Ayreshire duckling with honey and pineapple sauce – and is known for its good pâtés and terrines and its desserts.
21rm(17⇨🛏) CTV in all bedrooms T ✱ sB&B⇨🛏£30-£49 dB&B⇨🛏£60-£98 🅿
CTV 80P ✿ ♪ *xmas*
♀ Scottish & French **V** ✧ ⚏ ✕ Lunch £8-£25 High tea £5.50-£12 Dinner £8-£25 Last dinner 9.30pm
CONF. Thtr 80 Class 80 Board 80
Credit Cards [1][2][3][5]

STRANRAER Dumfries & Galloway *Wigtownshire* Map **10** NX06

★★★★ 68% **North West Castle**
DG9 8EH (on seafront) ☎(0776) 4413 FAX (0776) 2646

ExecGroup

Conveniently situated for the ferry terminal, this former home of Arctic explorer Sir John Ross was converted and extended by the McMillan family who continue to make improvements. Today it offers comfortable, well equipped bedrooms and a number of suites, while the spacious public rooms retain much of their original elegance. However, it is the warmth of the welcome and the

Old Farmhouse Hotel ★★

Lower Swell, Stow-on-the-Wold,
Glos GL54 1LF
Tel: Cotswold (0451) 830232 Fax: (0451) 870962

Well placed for touring, exploring and sound sleeping, a 16th-Century traditional Cotswold farmhouse in a peaceful hamlet 1 mile west of Stow, sympathetically converted to a warm and comfortable small hotel of 14 bedrooms, all different, mostly en suite. The hotel has the relaxed and friendly air of its farmhouse origins and a varied cuisine, including traditional. There are log fires, a walled garden and ample private parking.

★★ FOSSE·MANOR

Fosse Way
Stow on the Wold
Gloucestershire GL54 1JX
Tel: (0451) 830354 Fax: (0451) 832486

Standing in sixteen acres of beautiful gardens 1 mile south of Stow-on-the-Wold on the A429. Ideally situated for Cotswolds, Stratford, Oxford, Cheltenham and Worcester. Tastefully decorated with a warm family welcome. Excellent food and efficient staff.

Stow Lodge Hotel ★★

The Square, Stow-on-the-Wold,
Cheltenham, Glos. GL54 1AB
Tel: (0451) 830485

Set back in its own grounds far enough from the Market Square to allow guests complete peace and relaxation. 20 bedrooms, all with private bath and toilet, television, radio, tea and coffee-making facilities. Full central heating. Open log fires in both the Bar and Lounge. The restaurant which is non smoking seats 30 persons and offers a varied table d'hôte menu and à la carte with traditional English fare at its very best. Fully licensed Bar offering a selection of light lunches daily to the traveller not wishing to linger. Private Car park for approx 30 cars.
A perfect centre for touring the Cotswolds and Shakespeare country.

WYCK HILL HOUSE ★★★★ 71% ❀❀❀

Country Hotel and Restaurant
Stow-on-the-Wold Gloucestershire GL54 1HY

This lovely 18th Century Manor House is set in almost 100 acres of grounds overlooking the Windrush Valley in the heart of the Cotswolds.

30 luxuriously appointed bedrooms and the elegant lounges and restaurant provide a delightful atmosphere in which to relax and enjoy Ian Smith's fine classical cuisine.

Telephone: 0451 831936 Fax: 0451 832243
2 miles south of Stow, on the Burford Road (A424)

Stranraer - Stratford-upon-Avon

attentive attitude of the staff that make a visit to this hotel so enjoyable.
71⇌☏(22fb)1⌷ CTV in all bedrooms ® T ✖ (ex guide dogs) sB&B⇌☏£56-£76 dB&B⇌☏£72-£92 ⌸
Lift ⌇ 100P ⛳ ▣ (heated) snooker sauna solarium gymnasium curling (Oct-Apr) games room ♪ xmas
♨ Scottish & French V ☯ ⚚ ❋ Bar Lunch £8-£16alc Dinner fr£20&alc Last dinner 9pm
CONF. Thtr 150 Class 60 Board 40 Del from £51

STRATFIELD TURGIS Hampshire Map 04 SU65

★★67% **Wellington Arms**
RG27 0AS (by A33) (Badger Inns) ☎Basingstoke(0256) 882214 FAX (0256) 882934
This former coaching inn with a white Georgian façade has a new wing of smart, spacious bedrooms, contrasting with the large rooms in the main house, some with impressive antiques reputedly from adjacent Stratfield Saye, home of the Duke of Wellington. There is a comfortable, elegantly furnished lounge bar serving meals in addition to the restaurant.
35⇌☏(2fb)1⌷⚚in 3 bedrooms CTV in all bedrooms ® T 150P ❄
V ☯ ⚚ Last dinner 10pm
Credit Cards [1][2][3][5]

STRATFORD-UPON-AVON Warwickshire Map 04 SP25

★★★★❀❀❀⚚73% **Billesley Manor**
Billesley B49 6NF (off A46 towards Alcester) ☎(0789) 400888 FAX (0789) 764145
Set in 11 acres, this historic manor is richly furnished, with oak panelling and ornately carved fireplaces. A range of bedrooms is available, some large and comfortable with deep armchairs, bold fabrics and sumptuous bathrooms. All have excellent facilities, fresh fruit and magazines. The restaurant is ably managed by Christophe Gallot and the short daily menu and seasonal carte reflect the considerable skills of chef Mark Naylor. Starters may include chicken mousse stuffed with Cornish crab, or classic fish soup with aïoli and Gruyere, followed by a remarkably robust roast Gressingham duckling with fresh ginger and onion confit. A fine wine list with knowledgable service is always to hand.
41⇌☏(6fb)3⌷ CTV in all bedrooms T ✖ ✱ sB&B⇌☏£99 dB&B⇌☏£135-£160 ⌸
⌇100P ❄ ▣ (heated) ♇ (hard) croquet pitch & putt xmas
♨ English & French V ☯ ⚚ ❋ Lunch £17&alc Dinner £26&alc Last dinner 9.30pm
CONF. Thtr 100 Class 60 Board 40 Del £150
Credit Cards [1][2][3][5] £

★★★★64% **Welcombe**
Warwick Rd CV37 0NR (1.5m NE on A439) ☎(0789) 295252 FAX (0789) 414666
Closed 28 Dec-3 Jan
Standing on the outskirts of Stratford in a parkland estate, this Jacobean mansion features truly traditional service rendered by a charming and efficient staff. Public rooms are comfortable, and a major refurbishment programme is upgrading most bedrooms and suites to a luxurious standard, though the older, garden wing accommodation remains simple.
76⇌☏(2fb)⌷ CTV in all bedrooms T sB&B⇌☏£95-£105 dB&B⇌☏£120-£145 ⌸
⌇200P 6♋ ❄ ▶ 18 ♇ (hard) ♪ snooker putting xmas
♨ English & French V ☯ ⚚ Lunch £16.50-£18&alc Dinner fr£27.50&alc Last dinner 9.30pm
CONF. Thtr 100 Class 55 Board 30 Del £145
Credit Cards [1][2][3][5] £

★★★★62% **Moat House International**
Bridgefoot CV37 6YR (adjoining Stratford Leisure Centre) ☎(0789) 414711 FAX (0789) 298589
This large hotel overlooking the river and close to the centre offers modern, well equipped bedrooms and a wide range of facilities including a choice of grill or carvery restaurant, shops and night club.
247⇌☏(20fb)⚚in 64 bedrooms CTV in all bedrooms ® T sB&B⇌☏£50-£95 dB&B⇌☏£100-£125 ⌸
Lift ⌇⛌ CTV 350P ❄ ▣ (heated) ♪ snooker sauna solarium gymnasium steam room beautician hair stylist ♫
♨ British & French V ☯ ⚚ ❋ Lunch £10.50-£18.95 High tea £5-£10 Dinner £14.25&alc Last dinner 11pm
Credit Cards [1][2][3][5]

★★★★61% **Arden Thistle**
Waterside CV37 6BA (Follow town centre signs turn left into High St from Bridge St then 2nd left into Chapel Ln) ☎(0789) 294949 FAX (0789) 415874
Situated in the heart of Stratford, opposite the Royal Shakespeare and Swan Theatres, this hotel has recently been extensively refurbished to greatly enhance the quality and comfort of the entire building. Bedrooms have attractive period-style furniture and quality soft furnishings and there is a choice of room types, including no-smoking rooms. There is a quiet and comfortable first-floor lounge, an elegant restaurant with an adjacent terrace and a pleasant lounge bar.
63⇌☏(2fb)2⌷in 25 bedrooms CTV in all bedrooms ® T ✖ (ex guide dogs) sB&B⇌☏£69-£79 dB&B⇌☏£89-£99 ⌸
⌇ CTV 70P ❄ ♒ xmas
♨ English & Continental V ☯ ⚚ ❋ Lunch £7.50-£9.50&alc Dinner £15&alc Last dinner 9.30pm
Credit Cards [1][2][3][4][5]

★★★★ AA
THE ARDEN THISTLE HOTEL

Waterside, Stratford upon Avon CV37 6BA
Tel: 0789 292929   Fax: 0789 415874

Your choice in Stratford

For Reservations at over 100
Mount Charlotte Thistle Hotels
Telephone London: 071 937 8033.

★★★★ 73% ♨♣

Billesley Manor
STRATFORD · UPON · AVON

Set in 11 acres of gardens and parkland, Billesley Manor is a 16th century house, steeped in history.

There are 41 well-appointed rooms, including four-posters and suites, many overlooking our famous Topiary Garden.

As well as the attractive, large indoor swimming pool there are two tennis courts, croquet and pitch and putt.

Many visitors stay at Billesley simply for the pleasure of dining in the award-winning restaurant.

**BILLESLEY MANOR, BILLESLEY
Nr. STRATFORD-UPON-AVON
WARWICKSHIRE B49 6NF
TEL: (0789) 400888**

Ettington Park is a superb country house near Stratford upon Avon with 48 bedrooms, including 9 suites, each individually furnished, offering magnificent views across the surrounding countryside.

It boasts its own stables, tennis courts, indoor swimming pool, sauna, solarium, fishing, clay pigeon shooting and archery as well as being highly acclaimed for its award winning restaurant and fine wine list.

★★★★
ETTINGTON PARK HOTEL
Alderminster, Stratford upon Avon,
Warwickshire CV37 8BS
Telephone: 0789-450123

See gazetteer under Alderminster

WELCOMBE HOTEL AND GOLF COURSE
Stratford-upon-Avon
★★★★

Magnificent Jacobean style mansion, set in its own parkland estate with extensive formal gardens and own 18 hole, par 70 golf course.

Unrivalled views from the renowned restaurant, where French and regional cuisine is complemented by a fine wine cellar.

Traditional afternoon teas and light snacks are served in the superb oak panelled lounge, where warming fires are lit during the winter months.

76 bedrooms include imposing period suites, many with antiques and four poster beds.

FOR BROCHURE, PLEASE CALL (0789) 295252.   FAX (0789) 414666

Stratford-upon-Avon

★★★★ 61% The Shakespeare
Chapel St CV37 6ER (adjoining town hall)
☎(0789) 294771 FAX (0789) 415411

Magnificently situated in the heart of Stratford, the Shakespeare dates back to 1637, and its 9-gabled and timbered façade is a splendid example of the era. Recent refurbishment to most of the public rooms has been sympathetic, using period styles and colours. Exposed beams, open fires, antique furnishings and traditional prints feature in the lounge areas and restaurant. Bedrooms have also been tastefully renovated and altered.

63⇨🛏3🚪⚓in 20 bedrooms CTV in all bedrooms ® T ✱ sB⇨🛏£85 dB⇨🛏£110-£150 (room only) ♫
Lift (45P ♪ xmas
V ♿ ⚲ ✱ Lunch £9.25-£12.50&alc High tea £2-£4.95alc Dinner £19.95&alc Last dinner 10pm
Credit Cards [1][2][3][5]

★★★ ❋75% Salford Hall
WR11 5UT ☎Evesham(0386) 871300 FAX (0386) 871301
(For full entry see Abbot's Salford)

★★★ 74% Windmill Park Hotel & Leisure Club
Warwick Rd CV37 0PY (2.5m on A439)
☎(0789) 731173 FAX (0789) 731131

The exterior of this modern hotel is painted with scenes depicting the 4 seasons. Bedrooms are simply decorated, with contemporary dark furniture, comfortable seating and a good range of modern facilities. Public areas include a large, split-level restaurant and extensive bar. A team of willing staff promotes a happy atmosphere.

100⇨🛏(4fb)8⚓ CTV in all bedrooms ®⚹ T ✱ sB&B⇨🛏£82.50 dB&B⇨🛏£98 ♫
Lift (220P ❋ ⛲ (heated) ♞ (hard) sauna solarium gymnasium steam room games room ⚐ xmas
♿ English & Continental V ♿ ⚲ Lunch £11.50-£20&alc Dinner £14.50-£25&alc Last dinner 9.45pm
CONF. Thtr 360 Class 160 Board 50 Del from £102.50
Credit Cards [1][2][3][5]

★★★ 67% Grosvenor House
Warwick Rd CV37 6YT (on A439 Warwick road) ☎(0789) 269213 FAX (0789) 266087

This large privately owned hotel is situated on the Warwick road close to the town centre. Bedrooms are modern and well equipped. Public areas include an attractive restaurant with an unusual mural and a choice of lounges including a conservatory.

40⇨🛏(1fb) CTV in all bedrooms ® T ✱ sB&B⇨🛏£68-£72 dB&B⇨🛏£91-£95 ♫
(40P xmas
♿ English & Continental V ♿ ⚲ Lunch £9.50-£10.50&alc Dinner £11.50&alc Last dinner 9.30pm
CONF. Thtr 100 Class 50 Board 40 Del from £75
Credit Cards [1][2][3][5]

★★★ 63% Alveston Manor
Clopton Bridge CV37 7HP (first roundabout before Clopton Bridge) ☎(0789) 204581 FAX (0789) 414095

Recent refurbishment has greatly enhanced the public areas and many of the bedrooms at this considerably extended old house in 7 acres of grounds close to the Royal Shakespeare Theatre. There is now a wide variety of bedrooms, including suites. The ambience of the public rooms is greatly enhanced by the oak panelled walls, beamed ceilings and welcoming fires.

108⇨🛏(6fb)2⚓in 30 bedrooms CTV in all bedrooms ®⚹ T
(200P ❋ pitch & putt
♿ International V ♿ ⚲ Last dinner 9.30pm
CONF. Thtr 180 Class 70 Board 60 Del from £120
Credit Cards [1][2][3][5]

★★★ 62% Dukes
Payton St CV37 6UA (Logis) ☎(0789) 269300 FAX (0789) 414700
Closed Xmas & New Year

Converted from a pair of Georgian town houses, much of the original character of the building have been retained, and is enhanced by the antique and period furnishings in the lounge and dining room. There is also a cosy bar. Bedroom sizes vary, but all have modern equipment.

22⇨🛏2⚓ CTV in all bedrooms ®⚹ T ✱ sB&B⇨🛏£50-£55 dB&B⇨🛏£69.50-£85 ♫
30P ❋ ⚐ nc12yrs
♿ European V ♿ ✱ Lunch £18-£22alc Dinner £18-£22alc Last dinner 9.45pm
Credit Cards [1][2][3][5]

★★★ 60% Falcon
Chapel St CV37 6HA (town centre-opposite Guidl Chapel and Nash House)
☎(0789) 205777 FAX (0789) 414260

Dating from 1640, this ancient town-centre inn retains much of its original character with exposed beams, oak panelling, stone-flagged floors and open fires in the public areas. Several of the older bedrooms are also beamed and have period-style furniture, but all have modern equipment. The hotel offers a choice of bars and lounge areas, including a conservatory, and good conference and function rooms.

73⇨🛏(13fb)1⚓✱in 27 bedrooms CTV in all bedrooms ® T sB&B⇨🛏£60-£85 dB&B⇨🛏£70-£99 ♫
Lift (100P 24⚓ ❋ xmas
♿ French & Italian V ♿ ⚲ Lunch £13-£18.50&alc Dinner £18.50&alc Last dinner 9pm
CONF. Thtr 200 Class 110 Board 40 Del from £94
Credit Cards [1][2][3][4][5]

★★★ 58% Charlecote Pheasant Country
CV35 9EW ☎(0789) 470333 FAX (0789) 470222
(For full entry see Charlecote)

★★★ 58% The White Swan
Rother St CV37 6NH ☎(0789) 297022 FAX (0789) 268773

In a convenient location, close to the town centre and Shakespeare's birthplace, the White Swan is a half timbered building retaining many original features. Accommodation varies in size and shape, but all rooms offer modern facilities.

37⇨🛏(3fb)1⚓✱in 12 bedrooms CTV in all bedrooms ® T ✱ sB⇨🛏£80 dB⇨🛏£95-£110 (room only) ♫
(9P ♪ xmas
V ♿ ⚲ ✱ Sunday Lunch fr£10.95 High tea £5-£15 Dinner fr£16.95 Last dinner 9pm
Credit Cards [1][2][3][5]

★★ 71% Stratford House
Sheep St CV37 6EF (100yds from the Royal Shakespeare Theatre) ☎(0789) 268288 FAX (0789) 295580
Closed Xmas RS 4 days from Xmas day

This small and privately owned Georgian hotel decked with hanging baskets is close to the shops and the theatre. Some bedrooms are compact, but all provide a good range of facilities. The lounge, with its open fire and comfortable sofas, is personalised by antiques, china and pictures, while the Shepherds Garden Restaurant offers interesting menus of well prepared dishes which have earned it a good local reputation.

11rm(7⇨3🛏)(1fb) CTV in all bedrooms ® T
✱ (ex guide dogs) ✱ sB&B⇨🛏£50-£60 dB&B⇨🛏£55-£82 ♫
(♟ ⚓ nc2yrs
♿ English & French V Last dinner 9.15pm
Credit Cards [1][2][3][5]

Stratford-upon-Avon - Strathaven

★★ 68% **Stratford Court**
Avenue Rd CV37 6UX ☎(0789) 297799 FAX (0789) 262449
Experienced hoteliers Alex and June Giles purchased this hotel in late 1992 and have carried out an extensive and tasteful refurbishment programme, taking great care to preserve the Edwardian character of the building. Surrounded by extensive gardens and with rural view, the hotel has all the qualities and ambience of a country house, and yet is only a few minutes' walk from the town centre. The bedrooms are of a good size with period furniture and modern equipment. In addition to the comfortable lounge and attractive restaurant, there is a cosy bar.
11⇨♠2♨ CTV in all bedrooms ® ✱ sB&B⇨♠£30-£50 dB&B⇨♠£65-£105
CTV 15P ♨ ✻ xmas
♕ English & French V ✿ ♨ ✼ ✱ Lunch £13.50 Dinner £13.50 Last dinner 8.30pm
Credit Cards 1 3

★★ 65% **The Coach House Hotel**
16-17 Warwick Rd CV37 6YW (in town centre) (Logis)
☎(0789) 204109 & 299468 FAX (0789) 415916
Standing at the edge of the town centre, this personally run hotel is formed from adjacent Georgian and Victorian houses and has bedrooms of varying sizes, all equipped with modern facilities, and a lower-level bar and restaurant with a good choice of dishes.
10⇨♠ Annexe13rm(8⇨♠)(3fb)1 ♨✼in 3 bedrooms CTV in all bedrooms ® T ✖ (ex guide dogs) ✱ sB&Bfr£26 sB&B⇨♠£48-£55 dB&Bfr£42 dB&B⇨♠£65-£95 ₽
30P xmas
♕ English & French V ✿ ♨ ✼ ✱ Lunch fr£7.50 Dinner fr£12.50 Last dinner 10pm
CONF. Thtr 24 Class 24 Board 16 Del from £71.90
Credit Cards 1 2 3

★★ 61% **Swan House**
The Green CV37 9XJ ☎(0789) 267030 FAX (0789) 204875
(For full entry see Wilmcote)

●●

Forte Posthouse
Bridgefoot CV37 7LT ☎(0789) 266761 FAX (0789) 414547

FORTE Posthouse

Suitable for both the business and leisure traveller, this bright hotel provides modern accommodation in well equipped bedrooms with en suite bathrooms. For more details about Forte Posthouse hotels, consult the Contents page, under Hotel Groups.
60⇨♠ ✱ B⇨♠£41.50-£53.50 (room only)
CONF. Thtr 120 Class 80 Board 40 Del £89.50

STRATHAVEN Strathclyde Map 11 NS74

★★★ 64% **Strathaven**
Hamilton Rd ML10 6SZ (off A723 Hamilton road) ☎(0357) 21778 FAX (0357) 20789

CONSORT HOTELS

This Robert Adam designed house is popular with business people, it also has a reputation for its bar meals which it is hoping to extend into the restaurant, where both table d'hôte and à la carte menus are offered. Bedrooms, though modern and well equipped, vary in size and comfort and our inspectors have reported some problems with soundproofing. There is a bar and a spacious lounge, either of which may be taken over for wedding receptions.
10⇨♠ CTV in all bedrooms ® ✷ T ✱ sB&B⇨♠£30-£45 dB&B⇨♠£50-£71 ₽
⊄80P ✻
♕ Scottish & French V ✿ ♨ ✱ Lunch fr£8.95&alc Dinner £11.95-£14.95&alc Last dinner 10pm
Credit Cards 1 2 3

★★
COACH HOUSE HOTEL
& Cellar Restaurant
**16/17 Warwick Road
Stratford-Upon-Avon
Warwickshire CV37 6YW
Tel: 0789 204109 Fax: 0789 415916**

Situated only a few minutes walk from the town centre and Royal Shakespeare Theatre. Only 25 minutes drive to NEC, Birmingham airport and Stoneleigh.

We provide excellent accommodation with 22 bedrooms mostly with private bath. 4 Poster and Victorian Suite available.

Nearby are Sports Centre and 18 Hole Golf Course.

Restaurant and Bar — ample parking.

Ideal for Business or Independent Travel.

★★
Stratford House
Hotel and
Shepherd's Restaurant

A quality small privately owned hotel, in an agreeable Georgian house, a fashionable street, one hundred yards from The Royal Shakespeare Theatre and River Avon. Eleven well furnished spotless bedrooms with en suite bathroom, television and telephone. A distinctive restaurant, internationally recommended, listed in Egon Ronay's and other major Hotel and Restaurant guides. ETB Four Crown commended. AA rating 71%.

Theatre tickets and private car tours can be arranged on request. Small wedding receptions catered for.

A small intimate bar with log fire leads into a stylish, modern restaurant with the unusual feature of a conservatory opening out to a walled garden, where diners can enjoy eating 'al fresco' on warmer days. The cooking is based entirely on the best quality fresh ingredients used imaginatively on a short regularly changing menu. There is also a very interesting wine list offering excellent value.

**Sheep Street, Stratford-upon-Avon, Warwickshire CV37 6EF
Telephone: (0789) 268288 Fax: (0789) 295580**

Strathblane - Stretton

STRATHBLANE Central *Stirlingshire* Map 11 NS57

★★★ 62% Kirkhouse Inn
G63 9AA ☎Blanefield(0360) 70621 due to change to 770621 FAX (0360) 70896 due to change to 770896

Set at the foot of the Campsie Fells, this extended coaching inn provides friendly service and pleasant accommodation. Attractively decorated bedrooms have all modern amenities, with 24-hour room service available, and there is a popular lounge bar and restaurant.

15⇨╣(2fb)1⌺ CTV in all bedrooms ® T ✱
sB&B⇨╣fr£55.25 dB&B⇨╣fr£72 ⊟
(350P beauty therapy room ♫ xmas
♡ Scottish & French V ❀ ♨ ✱ Lunch £11.50&alc High tea £2.50-£5 Dinner £17.50&alc Last dinner 9.30pm
CONF. Thtr 45 Class 20 Board 20 Del from £50
Credit Cards [1][2][3][5]   (£)

STRATHPEFFER Highland *Ross & Cromarty* Map 14 NH45

★★ 65% Brunstane Lodge
Golf Rd IV14 9AT ☎(0997) 421261
Closed 1 & 2 Jan RS mid Oct-Apr

A warm, friendly atmosphere prevails at this small, efficiently run holiday hotel. Set in its own well tended gardens in a quiet residential area, it offers comfortable bedrooms which, though variable in size, have tasteful modern furnishings. There is no lounge, but there is a cosy bar lounge, and enjoyable home cooking is served in the neat dining room.

7rm(6⇨╣)(2fb) CTV in all bedrooms ® ✈ ⠀ sB&B£25-£32 dB&B⇨╣£50-£70 ⊟
20P ❀ ⠀
V ♨ Bar Lunch £3.50-£6 Dinner £13-£15 Last dinner 8.30pm
Credit Cards [1][3]

★★ 64% *Holly Lodge*
IV14 9AR ☎(0997) 21254

This attractive stone-built hotel stands in its own grounds overlooking the town. It offers warm hospitality and good food influenced by a hint of the orient. The public rooms – in particular the charming residents' lounge area and the comfortable bedrooms – also have an oriental feel about them.

7rm(3⇨3╣) CTV in all bedrooms ®
CTV 15P 2⊟ ⇚ ❀ shooting ♫
♡ Scottish & Oriental ❀ ♨ Last dinner 9pm

STREATLEY Berkshire Map 04 SU58

★★★★ ❀❀68% Swan Diplomat
High St RG8 9HR ☎Goring-on-Thames(0491) 873737 FAX (0491) 872554

Beautifully situated alongside the Thames, with its own moorings and barge, this is an elegant and well equipped hotel. The Riverside Restaurant head chef Christopher Cleveland offers a daily table d'hôte menu and a seasonally changing 'carte' of classic dishes. Our inspector recently enjoyed the ravioli of woodland mushrooms and French corn-fed pigeon on a bed of Le Puy lentils, garnished with mushrooms, bacon and grapes and served with a port sauce. Service is friendly and efficient.

46⇨╣1⌺ in 2 bedrooms CTV in all bedrooms ®✉ T
sB⇨╣£86.50-£99.50 dB⇨╣£115-£126.50 (room only) ⊟
(CTV 135P ❀ ▦ (heated) sauna solarium gymnasium croquet boat hire badminton pool table *xmas*
♡ French V ❀ ♨ Lunch £19.25-£21&alc Dinner £24-£26&alc Last dinner 9.30pm
CONF. Thtr 100 Class 50 Board 40 Del from £164
Credit Cards [1][2][3][5]   (£)

STREET Somerset Map 03 ST43

★★★ 68% Bear
53 High St BA16 0EF ☎(0458) 42021 FAX (0458) 840007

This small town centre hotel remains popular and well run. Substantially furnished bedrooms are being softened by the addition of pretty fabrics and room service menu provides food throughout the night. Cobblers bar is busy at lunch time serving bar snacks, and the restaurant offers formal menus of English food at dinner.

10⇨╣Annexe5⇨╣(3fb) CTV in all bedrooms ® T ✈ (ex guide dogs)
(36P ❀
♡ English & French V ❀ ♨ ♃ Last dinner 9.30pm
Credit Cards [1][2][3]

STRETTON Cheshire Map 07 SJ68

★★★★ 68% Park Royal International
Stretton Rd WA4 4NS
☎Warrington(0925) 730706 FAX (0925) 730740

CONSORT HOTELS

The early Victorian house that was once the Old Vicarage Hotel has now been completely overwhelmed by a recently completed large modern complex, renamed the Park Royal International. The comfortable modern bedrooms include 2 luxurious suites and several ground floor rooms, one designed for disabled guests. Public areas are attractively decorated, and there is a large self contained conference and banqueting suite. A leisure centre should be completed during the currency of this guide.

74⇨╣(4fb) CTV in all bedrooms ®✉ T ✱ sB⇨╣fr£69.50 dB⇨╣fr£79.50 (room only) ⊟
Lift (400P ❀
♡ English & French V ❀ ♨ ♃ ✱ Lunch £6.25-£7.45&alc Dinner fr£14.85&alc Last dinner 10pm
Credit Cards [1][2][3][5]

See advertisement under **WARRINGTON**

STRETTON Leicestershire Map 08 SK91

★★ ❀68% Ram Jam Inn
Great North Rd LE15 7QX (on northbound carriageway of A1) ☎Stamford(0780) 410776 FAX (0780) 410361
Closed 25 Dec

This unusual development of an old inn remains popular with travellers. Inside the main entrance there is an American-style coffee bar, with a high counter and fixed bar stool seating. Hotel guests take breakfast here, with a good choice of superior fast food available the rest of the day. Waiter service of home-made traditional English dishes is available in the open-plan bar on a lower level, and there is a slightly more formal restaurant. Bedrooms are generally quite spacious and comfortable.

Annexe7⇨╣(1fb) CTV in all bedrooms ® T sB⇨╣£39 dB⇨╣£49 (room only)
100P ❀
♡ English & Continental V ❀ ♨ Bar Lunch £3.55-£5.95alc
CONF. Thtr 40 Class 40 Board 25 Del £69.50
Credit Cards [1][2][3][5]

The AA's star rating scheme is the market leader in hotel classification.

For key to symbols see the Bookmark.

STRONTIAN Highland *Argyllshire* Map **14** NM86

★★★❀♨**70% Kilcamb Lodge**
PH36 4HY (off A861) ☏(0967) 2257 FAX (0967) 2041

Courtesy and Care 1994

Closed Nov-Mar
(Rosette awarded for dinner only)
The owners and staff provide warm hospitality and high levels of service at this delightful small hotel, earning it an AA Courtesy and Care Award this year. An 18th-century former hunting lodge, it is set in wooded grounds beside the shore of Loch Sunart and provides modest, but comfortable bedrooms (smoking discouraged) and relaxing public areas which include a choice of cosy lounges and a small bar with a good range of malts. A short daily changing dinner menu offers dishes carefully prepared from fresh local produce.
9rm(2⇨6♠)(1fb) ® ✱ sB&B⇨♠£64 dB&B⇨♠£64 (incl dinner) ⊟
CTV 20P 🚲 ✿ boat hire mountain bike hire
♀ Scottish & French V ⊘ ⌺ ⌇ Dinner £24 Last dinner 7pm
Credit Cards ①③

★★**55%** *Strontian*
PH36 4HZ ☏(0967) 2029
Substantial improvements have been made to this old Highland inn overlooking Loch Sunart. Modernised bedrooms, though mostly small, are pretty, with pine furnishings, and smartly upgraded public areas include a bright dining room and two timber-clad bars with external access.
7rm(5⇨♠)(1fb) CTV in all bedrooms ® T
30P 🚲 ✿
♀ ⌺ Last dinner 9pm
Credit Cards ①③

STROUD Gloucestershire Map **03** SO80
See also **Amberley**
★★★♨**65% Burleigh Court**
Minchinhampton GL5 2PF (0.75m off A419 E of Stroud)
☏Brimscombe(0453) 883804 FAX (0453) 886870
Closed 25 Dec-4 Jan RS Sun
Set in 6 acres of grounds and with beautiful countryside views, this delightful 18th-century manor house is run with friendly informality by the Benson family. Comfortable bedrooms of varying size are individually decorated, with cottage-style rooms in the adjacent converted stable block. Welcoming public rooms with open fires include a wood-panelled bar.
11⇨♠Annexe6⇨♠(1fb) CTV in all bedrooms ® T
✻ (ex guide dogs) ✱ sB&B⇨♠£59-£64 dB&B⇨♠£76-£96 ⊟
40P 1🏠 🚲 ✿ ⌲ (heated) putting green
♀ English & French V ⊘ ⌺ ⌇ ✱ Lunch £11.65-£13.95 High tea £5-£10alc Dinner £13-£25alc Last dinner 8.45pm
Credit Cards ①②③⑤

Satellite television – look for this symbol 📡
in the directory entries.

★★★**62%** The Bear of Rodborough
Rodborough Common GL5 5DE (1m S on A46, turn left to Rodborough Common)
☏(0453) 878522 FAX (0453) 872523

FORTE
Heritage

This historical inn has been modernised, yet maintains its original features, although there is a modern bedroom extension to the rear of the main building. Many of the rooms have breathtaking views of the Woodchester Valley.
47⇨♠(1fb)1🏠⌇in 15 bedrooms CTV in all bedrooms ® T ✱
sB⇨♠£68 dB⇨♠£78 (room only) ⊟
200P ✿ croquet *xmas*
V ⊘ ⌺ ⌇ Sunday Lunch £11.95-£12.95 Dinner £16.95-£17.95&alc Last dinner 9.30pm
CONF. Thtr 60 Class 30 Board 30 Del from £75
Credit Cards ①②③⑤

★★**65%** *London*
30-31 London Rd GL5 2AJ (E, on A419) ☏(0453) 759912 FAX (0453) 753363
Catering for a predominantly commercial clientèle, this hotel has fresh, well equipped rooms, though some are compact. Cosy public areas include a small bar and adjacent restaurant, where a good range of meals is served. Friendly services are provided by owners Mr and Mrs Portal and their staff.
12rm(2⇨6♠) CTV in all bedrooms ® T ✻ sB&B£26 sB&B⇨♠£39-£45 dB&B£39 dB&B⇨♠£49-£59 ⊟
10P 🚲 nc2yrs
♀ Continental V ⊘ ⌺ Lunch £5.60-£10.65alc Dinner £12.95&alc Last dinner 9.30pm
Credit Cards ①②③④⑤ £

For key to symbols see the Bookmark.

★ ★ ★ ★ ★ ❀❀

The Swan Diplomat, situated on the banks of The River Thames in one of Berkshire's prettiest villages, offers traditional English hospitality combined with classic French cuisine.

The hotel has 46 bedrooms, a superb leisure complex and meeting suites for up to 100 guests.

Oxford, Windsor, London and Heathrow Airport are all within one hour's drive of this peaceful and tranquil hotel.

Berkshire, England RG8 9HR
Telephone Goring on Thames
(0491) 873737 Fax (0491) 872554

Stroud - Sunderland

★★63% The Bell
Wallbridge GL5 3JA ☎(0453) 763556

The Bell is a family-run, pub-style hotel offering friendly and informal services. Bedrooms have good facilities and are bright, fresh and well maintained. Public areas are limited in size but include a convivial bar, an attractive restaurant and adjacent wine bar. An extensive range of meals is served from à la carte, table d'hôte and bar menus.

12rm(10⇨♠)(1fb)1⊞ CTV in all bedrooms ® ⚓ T ✱ sB&Bfr£25 sB&B⇨♠£30-£62 dB&Bfr£32 dB&B⇨♠£38-£87 ⛑

CTV 20P ✿ ♪ xmas
♀ Continental V ✿ ✱ Lunch £13.25&alc Dinner £13.25 Last dinner 9.30pm
CONF. Thtr 28 Class 20 Board 26 Del from £48
Credit Cards [1][3]

STUDLAND Dorset Map 04 SZ08

★★★65% Knoll House
Ferry Rd BH19 3AH (0.5m from Studland village on B3351)
☎(092944) 251 FAX (092944) 423
Closed Nov-Mar

Beautifully set in a National Trust reserve with views over the sea, this welcoming and very comfortable hotel caters for family holidays, with good leisure amenities and many special facilities for children. Well kept bedrooms, many with sea views, vary in size.

57rm(42⇨♠)Annexe22rm(15⇨♠)(30fb) T ✱ sB&B£54-£70 sB&B⇨♠£68-£83 dB&B£108-£140 dB&B⇨♠£128-£168 (incl dinner)
《 CTV 100P ❀ ✿ ≏ (heated) ▶ 9 ♞ (hard) sauna solarium gymnasium boutique jacuzzi leisure centre ⚽
✿ ⚖ ✱ Lunch fr£14 Dinner fr£16 Last dinner 8.30pm

★★❀♨64% Manor House
BH19 3AU ☎(092944) 288
Closed 19 Dec-Jan

This historic hotel with well tended gardens is in an enviable position with lovely views across the bay. Bedrooms include large oak panelled rooms with 4-poster beds and rather cosier rooms, which still have lots of character. Public areas include a conservatory extension to the dining room. Chef David Rolfe's menus usually contain plenty of fish dishes.

20⇨♠(9fb)4⊞ CTV in all bedrooms ® T sB&B⇨♠£47-£62 dB&B⇨♠£94-£124 (incl dinner) ⛑
40P ✿ ♞ (hard) nc5yrs
♀ English & French V ✿ ⚖ ✂ Sunday Lunch £5.95-£6.95 High tea fr£3.50 Dinner £19.50-£23 Last dinner 8.30pm
CONF. Class 25
Credit Cards [1][3]

STURMINSTER NEWTON Dorset Map 03 ST71

★★★❀❀68% Plumber Manor
Hazelbury Bryan Rd DT10 2AF
☎(0258) 472507 FAX (0258) 473370

Closed Feb

This lovely Jacobean manor in well tended grounds has been owned by the Prideaux-Brune family for centuries. There are traditional style bedrooms in the main house and de luxe rooms in 2 converted barns. Undoubtedly, the heart of the establishment is the restaurant, where Brian Prideaux-Brune cooks with care and unpretentious skill. His delicious sauces enhance rather than mask the dishes, as in a starter of fluffy smoked haddock mousse with slithers of smoked salmon on a cheesy sauce, flavoured with purée of sun-dried tomatoes. A fillet of lamb, cooked pink with a herb crust and piquant sauce was equally excellent. The hot, wickedly good sticky ginger pudding should not be missed.

6rm(5⇨♠)Annexe10⇨♠ CTV in all bedrooms ® T ✈ (ex guide dogs) sB&B⇨♠£60-£75 dB&B⇨♠£85-£120 ⛑
30P ❀ ✿ ♞ (hard) croquet nc12yrs
♀ English & French V Sunday Lunch fr£17.50 Dinner £20-£27 Last dinner 9.30pm
CONF. Thtr 20 Board 14 Del from £100
Credit Cards [1][2][3][5]

SUDBURY Derbyshire Map 07 SK13

★★★66% The Boars Head
Lichfield Rd DE6 5GX ☎Burton-on-Trent(0283) 820344 FAX (0283) 820075

This recently extended inn is popular with locals for its choice of bars, manned by helpful and courteous staff, and for the range of meals. The good standard of accommodation has proved successful with business users and tourists alike. Bedrooms are generally of a good size, with modern facilities.

22⇨♠ CTV in all bedrooms ® ⚓ T ✈ (ex guide dogs)
《 85P solarium
♀ International V ✿ ⚖ Last dinner 9.30pm
Credit Cards [1][2][3][5]

SUDBURY Suffolk Map 05 TL84

★★★69% Mill
Walnut Tree Ln CO10 6BD (on A120)
☎(0787) 375544 FAX (0787) 373027

Peacefully standing, as it has done for 300 years, on the Stour watermeadows on the outskirts of Sudbury, the Mill has been attractively refurbished. The working wheel, glass encased, divides the public areas. The wing rooms are particularly attractive with fashionable blue and yellow fabrics and tulip wood fittings. The service is both competent and solicitous.

52⇨♠(2fb)1⊞ CTV in all bedrooms ® ⚓ T ✱ sB⇨♠£50-£60 dB⇨♠£78-£98 (room only) ⛑
《 60P ♪ xmas
♀ English & French V ✿ ⚖ Lunch £8.75-£12.50 Dinner £17.50&alc Last dinner 9.30pm
Credit Cards [1][2][3][5]

SUNDERLAND Tyne & Wear Map 12 NZ35

★★★71% Swallow
Queen's Pde, Seaburn SR6 8DB ☎091-529 2041 FAX 091-529 4227

This seafront hotel provides accommodation of a high standard. Attractively furnished bedrooms equipped with all facilities include some smaller rooms and several luxury rooms with their own lounge areas. Comfortable public areas include a log-fired foyer lounge, an elegant restaurant featuring a wrought-iron bandstand and the Mariner cocktail bar. Friendly staff provide a wide range of services.

66⇨♠(3fb)⚋in 25 bedrooms CTV in all bedrooms ® ⚓ T ✱ sB&B⇨♠£85-£95 dB&B⇨♠£95-£120 ⛑
Lift 《 CTV 110P 4🅿 ⛱ (heated) sauna solarium gymnasium xmas
♀ English & French V ✿ ⚖ ✱ Lunch £12.50-£14.50 Dinner £19.50-£20.50 Last dinner 9.30pm
CONF. Thtr 350 Class 150 Board 100 Del from £105
Credit Cards [1][2][3][5]

• •

*If you have booked a meal in a
hotel restaurant and cannot get there,
remember you have a contractual obligation
to cancel your booking.*

Sunderland - Sutton Coldfield

Travel Inn
Wessington Way (A1231 at junc of A19)
☏ (0582) 482224

Purpose-built accommodation offers spacious and well equipped bedrooms, all with en suite bathrooms. Meals may be taken at the nearby family restaurant and pub. For more details about Travel Inns, consult the Contents page, under Hotel Groups.
41⇨♠✱ B⇨♠£33.50 (room only)

SUTTON Greater London
See **LONDON SECTION plan 1**C*1*
★★★★ 62%**Holiday Inn**
Gibson Rd SM1 2RF (from M25 junct 8 follow A217 then B2230 to hotel entrance)
☏081-770 1311 FAX 081-770 1539

This striking modern hotel has well designed public areas including a smart bar, a spacious restaurant, and a small lounge where refreshments are available all day. Bedrooms are sensibly laid out, the best being the 'executive' category. On a test visit, our inspectors were particularly impressed by the warmth of the welcome and the general attitude of the staff.
116⇨♠✱in 45 bedrooms CTV in all bedrooms ® T sB⇨♠£99.50-£115 dB⇨♠£110-£125 (room only) ⊟
Lift (🎵 80P 40🚗 ⊠ (heated) snooker sauna solarium gymnasium jacuzzi steam room beauty room *xmas*
♡ International V ✿ ⚐ ✱ Lunch £10.95-£13.95&alc Dinner £16.95-£17.75&alc Last dinner 9.45pm
CONF. Thtr 200 Class 118 Board 60 Del from £99
Credit Cards 1 2 3 4 5

SUTTON COLDFIELD West Midlands Map 07 SP19

★★★★ ❀❀75%**New Hall**
Walmley Rd B76 8QX (off B4148)
☏021-378 2442 FAX 021-378 4637

Inspectors Choice 1994

This splendid hotel is our Inspectors' Hotel of the Year for England this year and we offer our congratulations. We found many aspects of New Hall which warranted high praise, but it was the wonderful hospitality which most impressed our inspector – staff appear 'as if by magic' whenever you want something. Reputedly the oldest moated manor house in England, New Hall, set in 26 acres, retains many fine architectural features. Bedrooms in the main house are furnished with antiques and beautiful fabrics. New-wing rooms are smaller but still of a high standard. Chef Glenn Purcell's imaginative menus might start with crab tortellini with a warm shellfish vinaigrette, followed perhaps by wonderfully flavoured Gressingham duck sliced on a Bramley apple compôte. Hot praline soufflé with Baileys ice cream might complete the meal.
62⇨♠3⊟ CTV in all bedrooms ® T ✖ (ex guide dogs) ✱
sB⇨♠£93-£110 dB⇨♠£110-£265 (room only) ⊟
(80P ✿ ✔ archery croquet golf driving net putting nc8yrs *xmas*

♡ International V ✿ ⚐ ✱ ✱ Lunch £16.50-£18.85&alc Dinner £24.95-£27.30&alc Last dinner 10pm
CONF. Thtr 50 Class 30 Board 30 Del from £135
Credit Cards 1 2 3 4 5 £

See advertisement on page 585

★★★ 67%**Marston Farm**
Bodymoor Heath B76 9JD (take A4091 in direction of Tamworth and turn right for Bodymoor Heath. Turn right after humpback bridge) ☏Tamworth(0827) 872133 FAX (0827) 875043

This hotel enjoys a charming rural location in 9 acres of meadowland bordered by the Birmingham/Fazeley Canal. Bedrooms in a new extension are spacious and comfortable, and those in the original 17th-century farmhouse offer the same modern facilities. The beamed Bracebridge Room Restaurant provides an intimate setting for the enjoyment of both table d'hôte and à la carte meals, and friendly staff provide attentive service.
37⇨♠1⊟✱in 5 bedrooms CTV in all bedrooms ® ✱ T
sB&B⇨♠£25-£65 dB&B⇨♠£50-£85 ⊟
(150P ✿ ♪ (hard) ✔ croquet boules 🎵 *xmas*
♡ English & French V ✿ ⚐ ✱ ✱ Lunch £9.50-£15.50&alc Dinner £12.50-£15.50&alc Last dinner 9.30pm
CONF. Thtr 50 Class 40 Board 25 Del from £60
Credit Cards 1 2 3 5 £

See advertisement on page 585

★★★ 67%**Moor Hall**
Moor Hall Dr, Four Oaks B75 6LN
☏021-308 3751 FAX 021-308 8974

A popular privately owned hotel in a quiet residential area, Moor Hall can be a little tricky to find so ask for directions. Rooms vary in size and style, those in the new wing being very spacious and comfortable. The hotel has a choice of restaurants, the French

---

★★★
THE KNOLL HOUSE
A COUNTRY HOUSE HOTEL

- Within a National Trust reserve – overlooking three miles of golden beach and native heath.
- An independent country-house hotel under the third generation of personal owner management. A civilised and relaxing holiday for all ages.
- Six fine lounges and restaurant; tennis courts, nine acre golf course and outdoor heated pool. Jacuzzi, sauna, Turkish room, plunge-pool and gym.
- Family suites, two games rooms, separate young children's restaurant, playroom and fabulous SAFE adventure playground.
- The many ground-floor and single rooms are a popular all-age asset, rare in most hotels.
- Daily full board terms:
  £53–£78 incl. VAT and service.
  Children's terms according to age.
  Dogs welcome.

Open Easter – end of Oct 1994.

STUDLAND BAY DORSET
BH19 3AA
092 944 251

Sutton Coldfield - Swaffham

restaurant with its table d'hôte menu or the less formal Country Kitchen.
75⇨♠(3fb)3⚏⊁in 5 bedrooms CTV in all bedrooms ®T sB&B⇨♠£80-£99 dB&B⇨♠£94-£106 ⛌
Lift ℭ 180P ❉ 🖃 (heated) sauna solarium gymnasium *xmas*
♡ International V ⚘ ♨ Lunch £7.50-£12.50 Dinner £19-£21 Last dinner 10.30pm
CONF. Thtr 300 Class 120 Board 60
Credit Cards [1][2][3][5] £

★★★ 59% **Sutton Court**
60-66 Lichfield Rd B74 2NA ☎021-355 6071 FAX 021-355 0083
A privately owned commercial hotel, Sutton Court is in the town centre. Room sizes and standards vary, but all are well equipped. The restaurant has recently changed to offer a simple steakhouse-style menu in informal surroundings.
56⇨♠Annexe8⇨♠(9fb)⚏⊁in 13 bedrooms CTV in all bedrooms ®⚹T sB⇨♠£30-£65 dB⇨♠£39.50-£74 (room only) ⛌
ℭ 90P *xmas*
♡ English & French V ⚘ ♨ Lunch £8.95-£9.50 High tea £3.50-£6.50 Dinner £15.95&alc Last dinner 10pm
CONF. Thtr 90 Class 70 Board 50 Del from £50
Credit Cards [1][2][3][4][5] £

★★ 59% **The Lady Windsor**
17 Anchorage Rd B74 2PJ ☎021-354 5181 FAX 021-355 0095

This privately owned commercial hotel in a residential area close to the railway station has embarked upon a programme of refurbishment. The garden restaurant, in a conservatory extension, offers a wide range of dishes from à la carte, table d'hôte and daily special menus. Service is friendly and welcoming.
21⇨♠(2fb) CTV in all bedrooms ®T ✱ (ex guide dogs) sB&B⇨♠£43 dB&B⇨♠£53 ⛌
ℭ CTV 46P ⚏ ❉ *xmas*
♡ British & Continental V ⚘ ♨ ✻ Sunday Lunch £9.95 Dinner £11.95 Last dinner 9.30pm
Credit Cards [1][2][3] £

Forte Travelodge
Boldmere Rd B73 5UP (2m S, on B4142)
☎021-355 0017 Central Res (0800) 850950

This modern building offers a good standard of accommodation for overnight stops. Smart, spacious and well equipped bedrooms, all with en suite bathrooms, are suitable for family use, and meals may be taken at the nearby family restaurant. For more details about Travelodges, consult the Contents page, under Hotel Groups.
32⇨♠

SUTTON IN THE ELMS Leicestershire Map **04** SP59

★★ 63% **Mill On The Soar**
Coventry Rd LE9 6QD (SE of Leicester, on B4114) (Everards Brewery) ☎Hinckley(0455) 282419 FAX (0455) 285937
A busy country inn with its public bar built around an old mill – the wheel and gushing water can be seen from inside the bar. The beamed restaurant on the first floor offers a predominantly grill-style menu. Accommodation is in an adjacent 2 storey annexe of freshly decorated, comfortable rooms.
20⇨♠(10fb) CTV in all bedrooms ®T ✱ (ex guide dogs)
200P ❉ ♪
V ⚘ ♨ ⊁ Lunch fr£7.95 Dinner fr£7.95 Last dinner 10pm
CONF. Thtr 50 Class 20 Board 15 Del £80
Credit Cards [1][2][3][5]

SUTTON ON SEA Lincolnshire Map **09** TF58

★★ 69% **Grange & Links**
Sea Ln, Sandilands LN12 2RA (A1111 to Sutton-on-Sea, follow signs to Sandilands) ☎(0507) 441334 FAX (0507) 443033
Conveniently situated for access to the beach, this well established hotel provides comfortable bedrooms which are currently undergoing refurbishment. There is a range of comfortable lounges, a lounge bar offering a popular bar menu, and a restaurant where interesting dishes are cooked to order. Fresh fish is a speciality, and the home-made puddings are mouthwatering.
23⇨♠(10fb)1⚏ CTV in all bedrooms ®T sB&B⇨♠fr£50 dB&B⇨♠fr£65 ⛌
ℭ CTV 60P ❉ ⚑ 18 ♞ (hard) snooker croquet bowls putting *xmas*
♡ French V ⚘ Sunday Lunch fr£11.50&alc Dinner fr£15alc Last dinner 8.30pm
CONF. Thtr 100 Board 100 Del from £75
Credit Cards [1][2][3][5]

SUTTON SCOTNEY Hampshire Map **04** SU43

Forte Travelodge (North)
SO21 3JY (on A34 northside)
☎Winchester(0962) 761016
Central Res (0800) 850950

FORTE Travelodge

This modern building offers a good standard of accommodation for overnight stops. Smart, spacious and well equipped bedrooms, all with en suite bathrooms, are suitable for family use, and meals may be taken at the nearby family restaurant. For more details about Travelodges, consult the Contents page, under Hotel Groups.
31⇨♠

Forte Travelodge (South)
SO21 3JY (on A34 southside)
☎Winchester(0962) 760779
Central Res (0800) 850950

FORTE Travelodge

This modern building offers a good standard of accommodation for overnight stops. Smart, spacious and well equipped bedrooms, all with en suite bathrooms, are suitable for family use, and meals may be taken at the nearby family restaurant. For more details about Travelodges, consult the Contents page, under Hotel Groups.
40⇨♠

SUTTON UPON DERWENT Humberside Map **08** SE74

★★ 64% *Old Rectory*
YO4 5BX ☎York(0904) 608748
This former rectory, owned and run by Mr and Mrs Ward, is in a quiet village location. Its simplicity is valued by many returning guests.
6rm(2♠)(2fb) CTV in all bedrooms ®
50P ⚏ ❉
⚘
Credit Cards [1]

SWAFFHAM Norfolk Map **05** TF80

★★★ 60% **George**
Station Rd PE37 7LJ ☎(0760) 721238 FAX (0760) 725333

Situated in the corner of the market place, the George is owned and managed by the Collins family. Public areas comprise a pleasant bar where locals meet and bar meals are served; and comfortable lounges have rich coordinated decor. There are 2 bedroom styles, of which the modern rooms are uniformly fitted with dark laminates and hard wearing fabrics.
27rm(24⇨1♠)(1fb)⚏ CTV in all bedrooms ®T ✻ sB&Bfr£40 sB&B⇨♠£40-£45 dB&B⇨♠£59 ⛌

THE MILL
ON THE SOAR
— HOTEL, RESTAURANT & BARS —
Coventry Road, (B4114)
Sutton in the Elms, Near Broughton Astley,
Leicestershire Tel: 0455 282419

20 En Suite Rooms: Close to M1 & M69
NEC 30 Minutes Drive

All rooms with Colour TV, Hair Dryer,
Trouser Press, Direct Dial Telephone,
Tea & Coffee making facilities.

A delightful country hotel built around a
historic mill set in extensive grounds which
include a fishing lake and falconry centre.

AA★★

AN ORIGINAL INN

MARSTON FARM
HOTEL

Marston Farm Hotel, a converted 17th Century
Farmhouse, is ideally situated in 9 acres of Warwickshire
Countryside, yet just 3 miles from Junction 9 of the M42
and 10 minutes from Birmingham's National Exhibition
Centre and International Airport.

38 En-suite Bedrooms, a highly acclaimed Restaurant,
Inglenook fireplaces and cosy snugs all combine to create
a very welcoming atmosphere.

**MARSTON FARM HOTEL, BODYMOOR HEATH,
SUTTON COLDFIELD B76 9JD
TEL: 0827 872133 FAX: 0827 875043**

★★★ AA

SUTTON COURT HOTEL
60-66 Lichfield Road, Sutton Coldfield,
West Midlands B74 2NA
Tel: 021 355 6071 Telex: 334175 Sutton G
Fax: 021 355 0083
Proprietor Peter Bennett

8 GOLF COURSES WITHIN 15 MINUTES OF THE HOTEL
The hotel is situated within easy travelling distance of the NEC,
M6/M5, M42 and A38. Nearby are a choice of 8 golf courses
including the Brabazon, home of the Ryder Cup played here
September 1989. The new Courtyard Restaurant enjoys an
excellent reputation and is in keeping with the fine Victorian
building combining a chic atmosphere with elegant furnishings
reminiscent of a bygone era. The Chef de cuisine and his
brigade of chefs prepare a variety of imaginative dishes from
the finest of fresh produce personally selected. The spacious
individually designed bedrooms include private bathroom,
colour TV, in-house movies, direct dial telephone, trouser press,
hair dryer and refreshment tray. 24 hour room service. Contact
Reservations for weekend rates. 24 hour and day conference
rates available.
ASHLEY COURTENAY RECOMMENDED.

❀❀★★★★ AA

A Thistle Country House Hotel

Walmley Road, Sutton Coldfield B76 8QX
Tel: 021-378 2442   Fax: 021-378 4637

Your choice in
Sutton Coldfield

For Reservations at over 100
Mount Charlotte Thistle Hotels
Telephone London: 071 937 8033.

Swaffham - Swansea

100P *xmas*
English & French V Lunch £7.95-£14.50&alc Dinner £14.50&alc Last dinner 9.30pm
CONF. Thtr 150 Board 70 Del from £60
Credit Cards 1 2 3 4 5

SWALLOWFIELD Berkshire Map 04 SU76

★★ 67% The New Mill House
Old Basingstoke Rd RG7 1PY Reading(0734) 883124 FAX (0734) 885550

This fine Georgian building, once part of the Duke of Wellington's estate, has an attractive walled garden. Bedrooms are mixed in size, prettily decorated and well equipped. Downstairs is an open-plan reception, bar and lounge with a high ceiling and comfortable seating.

10 1 in 2 bedrooms CTV in all bedrooms ® T
(ex guide dogs) sB&B £48 dB&B £58
25P croquet
English, French and Italian V Lunch £10-£15alc Dinner £10-£20alc Last dinner 10.30pm
Credit Cards 1 2 3 5

SWANAGE Dorset Map 04 SZ07

★★★ 66% Grand
Burlington Rd BH19 1LU (on cliff top above town) (0929) 423353 FAX (0929) 427068

BEST WESTERN HOTELS

In its cliff-top position, with spectacular views out across the bay, this hotel is especially popular for short breaks and holidays. The refurbished bedrooms are stylish, and small public rooms include a leisure area. The views from the Renaissance Restaurant are splendid and the food is imaginative and nicely presented.

30 (5fb) CTV in all bedrooms ® T sB&B £45-£50 dB&B £90-£100
Lift 15P (heated) sauna solarium gymnasium spa bath table tennis *xmas*
English & French V Lunch £7.50-£21.35alc Dinner £14.50-£15.50&alc Last dinner 9.30pm
Credit Cards 1 2 3 5

★★★ 64% The Pines
Burlington Rd BH19 1LT (0929) 425211 FAX (0929) 422075

In a superb location overlooking the sea and Ballard Down, this good value hotel has been in the ownership of the Puddepha family for more than 25 years. The newly refurbished lounge area is most attractive and comfortable. The restaurant and bar areas have also been smartly redecorated. Neat bedrooms, some with balconies, have comfortable armchairs. A varied and lengthy table d'hôte menu is available.

51rm(49)(26fb) CTV in all bedrooms ® T sB&B £32-£40 sB&B £32-£40 dB&B £64-£80 dB&B £64-£80
Lift 60P *xmas*
Continental V Lunch £9-£11 Dinner £11-£18.50 Last dinner 9pm
CONF. Thtr 60 Class 40 Board 30 Del from £58.50
Credit Cards 1 3

SWANICK

See **Alfreton**

SWANSEA West Glamorgan Map 03 SS67

See also **Langland Bay, Mumbles** and **Oxwich**

★★★ 63% Fforest
Pontardulais Rd, Fforestfach SA5 4BA (on A483 1.5m S of M4 junc 47) (Whitbread) (0792) 588711 FAX (0792) 586219

This popular commercial hotel has bedrooms which are well equipped, and an upgrading programme is planned for the bars. Our inspectors have felt that food standards could sometimes be higher.

34 1 in 4 bedrooms CTV in all bedrooms ® T
(ex guide dogs) sB&B fr£59.50 dB&B fr£71
CTV 150P sauna solarium
English & French V Lunch fr£7&alc Dinner fr£13.95 Last dinner 10pm
CONF. Thtr 200 Class 100 Board 40 Del from £85
Credit Cards 1 2 3 5

★★★ 58% Dolphin
Whitewalls SA1 3AB (opposite Littlewoods Department Store) (0792) 650011 FAX (0792) 642871

This town centre hotel with popular bars is still in the process of refurbishment, with about 70 per cent of the accommodation meeting modern standards. It is hoped that the final phase will soon be undertaken. Parking is provided by arrangement with a nearby multi-storey.

66 (5fb) CTV in all bedrooms ® T sB&B £30-£50 dB&B £40-£65 (room only)
Lift
English & Continental V Lunch £10-£15&alc High tea £6-£9 Dinner £15-£20&alc Last dinner 9.30pm
CONF. Thtr 400 Class 250 Board 90 Del from £55
Credit Cards 1 2 3 5

★★ 72% Beaumont
72 Walter Rd SA1 4QA (on A4118) (0792) 643956 FAX (0792) 643044

A little gem of hospitality, comfort and good food, the Beaumont is still being improved by owners Wynne Jones and John Colenso. The bedrooms have quality furnishings and modern facilities. Crisp linen and quality appointments in the conservatory restaurant mark the beginning of chef Brian Evans' domaine. Imaginative use of fresh ingredients reflect his international experience, demonstrated by a rich mushroom soufflé and a bold ragout of beef bourguignonne.

17 1 in 1 bedroom CTV in all bedrooms ® T sB&B £47.50-£58 dB&B £59.50-£80
10P
Welsh, French & Italian V Lunch fr£14.50 High tea fr£9.50 Dinner fr£18.75&alc Last dinner 9.30pm
Credit Cards 1 2 3 5

See advertisement on page 589

★★ 65% Nicholaston House
Nicholaston SA3 2HL (0792) 371317
(For full entry see Penmaen)

★★ 62% Oak Tree Parc
Birchgrove Rd SA7 9JR Skewen(0792) 817781 FAX (0792) 814542
(For full entry see Birchgrove)

★ 71% Windsor Lodge
Mount Pleasant SA1 6EG (Logis) (0792) 642158 & 652744 FAX (0792) 648996
Closed 25-26 Dec

This delightful Georgian house, personally run by Ron and Pam Rumble, is neatly tucked away close to the town centre, and has a firm following of both tourist and business guests. Architectural constraints tend to dictate here: the bedrooms are compact, but they are nonetheless comfortable and facilities are superior to the classification. Ron cooks with some depth, and daily set menus promote sound cooking with true flavours and textures.

18rm(12 4) CTV in all bedrooms ® T sB&B £35-£40 sB&B £43-£50 dB&B £40-£50 dB&B £45-£60
25P (£2) sauna
English, French & Welsh V Bar Lunch £3-£10 High tea £4-£9 Dinner £13-£22 Last dinner 9.30pm
CONF. Thtr 20 Class 20 Board 20 Del from £50
Credit Cards 1 2 3 5

See advertisement on page 589

THE DOLPHIN
And Conference Centre
HOTEL
IN THE HEART OF THE CITY

AA ★★★

The Dolphin Hotel is ideal for business and holiday visitors, easily accessible by road or train and within easy reach of all major routes via the M4 motorway. All 66 bedrooms have en suite facilities, colour television, in house movies, tea/coffee making facilities and direct dial telephone. Enjoy a bar lunch in our Cocktail Bar and Restaurant or experience an evening meal in Flipper's Bistro. The popular 'Strudles' coffee shop is a well known rendezvous in Swansea.
Extensive Conference and Banqueting facilities for up to 400 guests.
Weekend Breaks available.
Car park for residents.

**Whitewalls, Swansea SA1 3AB
Telephone: 0792 650011
Telex: 48128 Fax: 0792 642871**

The Pines Hotel
★★★ BURLINGTON ROAD, SWANAGE, DORSET BH19 1LT
Tel: 0929 425211 Fax: 0929 422075

This 50-bedroomed family run Hotel occupies the most envied position in Swanage, situated at the secluded end of the bay.

Every bedroom is equipped with en suite bathroom, colour TV, radio, telephone and tea-making facilities.

Ease of access is assured by a lift to all floors.

Children of all ages are welcome and specially catered for.

Our reputation is founded on cuisine and service.

THE
GRAND
HOTEL
★★★

Set in a superb clifftop position on Dorset's Heritage Coast, steps from the lawn lead down to the secluded sandy beach.

The spacious lounge, sun lounge, bars and restaurant combine the best traditions of hospitality, comfort, excellent cuisine and entertainment; all have breathtaking views.

The 30 en suite bedrooms have colour TV, in house video, clock radio, direct dial telephone, tea/coffee making facility and hair dryer. A lift serves all floors.

The Burlington Club, within the Hotel, offers its full facilities to residents — plunge pool, spa bath, steam room, sauna, solarium, and gymnasium/fitness centre.

The Hotel, 7 miles from Bournemouth via the ferry, is an ideal centre for water sports, golf, walking and bird watching, or simply relaxing!

**Swanage, Dorset BH19 1LU
Telephone: Swanage (0929) 423353
Fax: (0929) 427068**

Swansea - Swindon

★65% Parkway
253 Gower Rd, Sketty SA2 9JL ☎(0792) 201632 FAX (0792) 201839
Closed 25 Dec-1 Jan
This friendly and popular hotel, personally owned and run by Mr and Mrs Wearing, is an extended house, recently upgraded, with modern, well equipped bedrooms and comfortable open-plan public rooms. The hotel is set back in its own small garden.
15🛏 CTV in all bedrooms ® T ✱ sB&B🛏£37.50 dB&B🛏£49 🍴
CTV 16P 🚭 ≏ games room
✱ Dinner fr£8.50 Last dinner 8pm
Credit Cards [1][2][3][5] £

Forte Crest
The Kingsway Circle SA1 5LS ☎(0792) 651074 FAX (0792) 456044

A large modern hotel with a wide range of services and amenities, designed particularly for the business traveller. Bedrooms are smart, comfortable and well equipped. For more details about Forte Crest hotels, consult the Contents page, under Hotel Groups.
99🛏🍴 B🛏£49.50-£75 (room only)
CONF. Thtr 200 Class 100 Board 20 Del £100

Hilton National Swansea
Phoenix Way, Swansea Enterprise Park SA7 9EG (1m S M4, jct 44 & 45, SW of Llansamlet) ☎(0792) 310330 FAX (0792) 797535

This is a bright, modern hotel with an informal restaurant, aimed at both the business and leisure guest. All bedrooms have en-suite bathrooms and a range of modern facilities. For more information on Hilton National, consult the Contents page, under Hotel Groups.
118🛏🍴 ✱ B🛏🍴£60 (room only)
CONF. Thtr 180 Class 90 Board 60 Del £85

Marriott
The Maritime Quarter SA1 3SS ☎(0792) 642020 FAX (0792) 650345

A large and busy hotel, which is ideal for the business and leisure traveller, offering a wide range of services, a choice of eating options and indoor leisure facilities. Bedrooms are comfortable and equipped with modern facilities. For more details about Marriott hotels, consult the Contents page, under Hotel Groups.
118🛏🍴 dB🛏🍴fr£92 (room only)

Pavilion Lodge
(M4 junct 47/A483) ☎(0792) 894894

With a nearby family restaurant providing all meals, this modern building offers smart, spacious and well equipped bedrooms. For more details about Pavilion Lodges, consult the Contents page, under Hotel Groups.
50🛏🍴 ✱ B🛏🍴 (room only)

SWAVESEY Cambridgeshire Map 04 TL36

Forte Travelodge
A604 Cambridge Rd
☎(0954) 789113 Central Res (0800) 850850

This modern building offers a good standard of accommodation for overnight stops. Smart, spacious and well equipped bedrooms, all with en suite bathrooms, are suitable for family use, and meals may be taken at the nearby family restaurant. For more details about Travelodges, consult the Contents page, under Hotel Groups.
40🛏🍴 ✱ B🛏🍴£31.95 (room only)

SWAY Hampshire Map 04 SZ29

★★60% White Rose
Station Rd SO41 6BA (off B3055)
☎Lymington(0590) 682754

This long established family-run hotel in 5 acres of grounds is in the centre of the village. Accommodation is slowly being upgraded and bedrooms are being refurbished to a good and comfortable standard with new bathrooms. The lounge bar is a popular local rendezvous, and lunch time bar meals are available in addition to the à la carte and table d'hôte menu choices.
11rm(10🛏)(2fb) CTV in all bedrooms ® T sB&B🛏£39-£45 dB&B🛏£58-£70 🍴
Lift 50P 🚭 ✱ ≏ xmas
V 🍷 ⌃ ✱ Lunch £9-£12&alc Dinner £9-£12&alc Last dinner 9pm
Credit Cards [1][2][3] £

SWINDON Wiltshire Map 04 SU18
See also **Inglesham**

★★★★73% De Vere
Shaw Ridge Leisure Park, Whitehill Way SN5 7DW ☎(0793) 878785 FAX (0793) 877822

Set in the business area of the town, this modern hotel offers spacious, comfortable bedrooms and a pleasant lounge, library and bar lounge, with attractive colour schemes throughout. The Seasons Restaurant provides a good choice of imaginative dishes on à la carte and table d'hôte dinner menus. Management and staff extend a friendly welcome, and service is attentive throughout.
154🛏🍴(12fb)✱in 77 bedrooms CTV in all bedrooms ®⛳ T sB&B🛏🍴£90-£94.50 dB&B🛏🍴£100-£105 🍴
Lift (CTV 170P ✱ 🏊 (heated) snooker sauna solarium gymnasium jacuzzi beauty therapist Turkish bath 🎵 xmas
V 🍷 ⌃ ✱ Lunch fr£13.50 Dinner fr£17.50&alc Last dinner 10pm
Credit Cards [1][2][3][5] £

★★★★70% Blunsdon House Hotel & Leisure Club
Blunsdon SN2 4AD (3m N off A419)
☎(0793) 721701 FAX (0793) 721056

With its extensive range of leisure facilities, this hotel appeals to a range of markets, and has recently won an award for the welcome extended to children. Bedrooms are brightly decorated; those in the Concord wing being more practical, while the rest are generally more spacious and comfortable. There are 2 restaurants, Carrie's Carvery and the more formal Ridge Restaurant.
88🛏🍴(13fb)5❄✱in 16 bedrooms CTV in all bedrooms ®⛳ T 🐕 (ex guide dogs) ✱ sB&B🛏🍴£72.50-£79.50 dB&B🛏🍴£92.50-£100 🍴
Lift (CTV 300P ✱ 🏊 (heated) ▶ 9 ♞ (hard) squash snooker sauna solarium gymnasium spa pool skittles beauty therapy 🚲 xmas
V 🍷 ⌃ ✱ Lunch £10.75&alc Dinner £11.75-£17.50&alc Last dinner 10pm
CONF. Thtr 300 Class 200 Board 40 Del from £97.50
Credit Cards [1][2][3][5] £

★★★✿✿73% Chiseldon House
New Rd, Chiseldon SN4 0NE (on B4006) ☎(0793) 741010 FAX (0793) 741059

Chiseldon house, a charming Regency property, has been sympathetically extended to provide spacious and attractively furnished bedrooms. Public areas, small enough to retain an intimate atmosphere, include meeting rooms, a quiet drawing room and a split-level bar area open plan with the Orangery Restaurant. Chef Christopher Fisher takes a great pride in the standard of the food, and his menu is designed to offer a set of plainly cooked dishes contrasting with a more imaginative section. Our inspector chose a delicately flavoured warm mousse of Tay salmon, topped with a filo

➡

Blunsdon House Hotel

AND LEISURE CLUB

*Blunsdon, Swindon
Wiltshire SN2 4AD*

Tel: (0793) 721701. Fax: (0793) 721056

Blunsdon House Hotel is peacefully set in 30 acres of magnificent grounds, overlooking the Vale of Cricklade.

Our superb facilities which cater for both business and pleasure are second to none and include a leisure club, 9 hole golf course, 2 restaurants, 3 bars and conference rooms.

Privately owned and managed by the Clifford family for thirty years.

Why not call in and let us look after you?

★★★★

THE WINDSOR LODGE
HOTEL

Windsor Lodge is a grade II listed Georgian building. It was changed into a hotel in 1970 by the present owners. During that time the hotel has earned a reputation for its food and sympathetic adaptation of a Georgian building for modern use. In 1994 all rooms will be en-suite and have telephones, T.V. and tea making facilities. The hotel has a country house atmosphere while very close to the city centre and possessing its own car park.

In 1991 Windsor Lodge was included in the AA's top twenty one star hotels of Great Britain.

**Mount Pleasant, Swansea SA1 6EG
Telephone: 0792 642158/648996
Fax: 0792 648996**

Parkway Hotel ★
At the Gateway to the Gower.

15 bedrooms all with en-suite shower/wc, tea/coffee trays, TV, radio, telephone. Licensed bar, coffee lounge, TV room. Private car parking.

Proprietors Bruce & Heather Wearing.

PARKWAY HOTEL
253, Gower Road, Sketty,
Swansea SA2 9JL
Tel: Swansea (0792) 201632
Fax No: (0792) 201839

OPEN ALL YEAR

AA★★

The Beaumont Hotel and Restaurant

72-73 Walter Road, Swansea, West Glamorgan
Tel: (0792) 643956 Fax: (0792) 643044

A smart seventeen bedroomed hotel situated near the city centre with a country house atmosphere refurbished recently in the Victorian style with an award winning restaurant of great charm. The hotel is a haven for businessmen and ideal for a wonderful holiday break. The kitchen staff produce excellent food under the direction of the chef and first class produce is sympathetically cooked to bring out the full flavour – the cooking being firmly rooted in the classical style. There are comfortable areas to sit and enjoy an apéritif with canopés or a digestif with good petit fours, safe in the knowledge that your car can be locked away in the car park.

Swindon - Talland Bay

pastry case, his enjoyment slightly diminished by an over salted butter sauce. A main course of breast of chicken was nicely cooked and succulent, though again the garlic butter sauce could be criticised as being too strongly flavoured. The lemon tart was filled with a delicious cream and served with a lemon flavoured custard.
20⇨2🛏 CTV in all bedrooms ® 💈 ✈ (ex guide dogs) sB&B⇨♠£55-£80 dB&B⇨♠£70-£110 🍴
《 35P ⇔ ❀ ≌ (heated)
V ♡ ♨ ⚲ Lunch £9.50-£14.95 Dinner fr£21.50 Last dinner 9.30pm
Credit Cards [1][2][3][5] £

★★★ **64%** Wiltshire
Fleming Way SN1 1TN ☎(0793) 528282 FAX (0793) 541283

Conveniently situated for the town centre, this modern hotel has easy parking in the adjacent multi-storey car park. There are bedrooms on 8 floors, with pleasant coordinated furnishings contributing to comfortable surroundings. Some rooms have only skylight windows, and some overlook the car park. There is a bar in the reception area of the dining room, where à la carte and table d'hôte menus are offered.
93⇨♠⚲in 13 bedrooms CTV in all bedrooms ® T sB⇨♠£75-£85 dB⇨♠£85-£95 (room only) 🍴
Lift 《 ♪ xmas
♀ English & French V ♡ ♨ ✻ Lunch £10.50-£12.75&alc Dinner £14.50-£16.50&alc Last dinner 10pm
CONF. Thtr 250 Class 40 Board 60 Del from £85
Credit Cards [1][2][3][5]

★★ **57%** Hotel Ibis Swindon
Delta Business Park, Great Western Way SN5 7XG (2m from M4 junct 16 & 1m W of town centre) ☎(0793) 514777 FAX (0793) 514570

120⇨♠(6fb)⚲in 42 bedrooms CTV in all bedrooms ® 💈 T sB⇨♠£32-£39.50 dB⇨♠£32-£39.50 (room only)
Lift 《 120P ❀
V ♡ ♨ ⚲
CONF. Thtr 90 Class 40 Board 40 Del £65
Credit Cards [1][2][3][5]

Forte Crest
Oxford Rd, Stratton St Margaret SN3 4TL (3m NE A420) ☎(0793) 831333 FAX (0793) 831401

A large modern hotel with a wide range of services and amenities, designed particularly for the business traveller. Bedrooms are smart, comfortable and well equipped. For more details about Forte Crest hotels, consult the Contents page, under Hotel Groups.
91⇨♠
CONF. Thtr 80 Class 40 Board 44 Del from £90

Forte Posthouse
Marlborough Rd SN3 6AQ ☎(0793) 524601 FAX (0793) 512887

Suitable for both the business and leisure traveller, this bright hotel provides modern accommodation in well equipped bedrooms with en suite bathrooms. For more details about Forte Posthouse hotels, consult the Contents page, under Hotel Groups.
98⇨♠✻ B⇨♠£41.50-£53.50 (room only)
CONF. Thtr 80 Class 50 Board 28 Del £89.50

Marriott
Pipers Way SN3 1SH (from junct 15 of M4 follow A419, then A4259 to Coate roundabout and B4006 signed 'Old Town') ☎(0793) 512121 FAX (0793) 513114

A large and busy hotel, which is ideal for the business and leisure traveller, offering a wide range of services, a choice of eating options and indoor leisure facilities. Bedrooms are comfortable and equipped with modern facilities. For more details about Marriott hotels, consult the Contents page, under Hotel Groups.
153⇨♠✻ dB⇨♠fr£102 (room only)
CONF. Thtr 280 Class 150 Board 50 Del £125

SYMONDS YAT (EAST) Hereford & Worcester Map **03** SO51

★★ **62%** Royal
HR9 6JL (off A40 onto B4229 after 0.50m turn right on B4432) ☎Symonds Yat(0600) 890238 FAX (0600) 890238
Closed 2-16 Jan
Superbly situated on the bank of the river Wye, this peaceful, family-run hotel is ideal for tourists, walkers and anglers. Modern facilities are on offer but there are no televisions because of reception difficulties.
20⇨4🛏 ® T ✈ (ex guide dogs) sB&B⇨♠£22.50 dB&B⇨♠£47-£67 🍴
80P ⇔ ❀ ⚲ sauna solarium abseiling canoeing clay pigeon shooting nc12yrs *xmas*
♀ British & French V ♡ ♨ Bar Lunch £3-£12 Dinner £16.50&alc Last dinner 8.30pm
Credit Cards [1][2][3]

TAIN Highland *Ross & Cromarty* Map **14** NH78

★★★ **63%** Morangie House
Morangie Rd IV19 1PY ☎(0862) 892281 FAX (0862) 892872
Carefully modernised to provide all the comforts and facilities expected today, yet retaining such original features as stained glass windows, this Victorian mansion offers good views over the Dornich Firth to the mountains beyond. Family owned and run, it provides friendly service, bedrooms which are both attractive and thoughtfully equipped, and well prepared meals in an elegant restaurant.
13⇨♠(1fb)1🛏 CTV in all bedrooms ® T sB&B⇨♠£45-£50 dB&B⇨♠£65-£75 🍴
30P ❀
♀ Scottish & Continental V ♡ ♨ Lunch £6-£8&alc Dinner £16.50-£18&alc Last dinner 10pm
Credit Cards [1][2][3][5] £

TALKE Staffordshire Map **07** SJ85

★★★ **64%** Granada
Newcastle Rd ST7 1UP (at junct of A34/A500) (Granada) ☎(0782) 777148 & 777000 FAX (0782) 777162
RS 25-26 Dec
Particularly well equipped bedrooms are provided here, as well as a small but very comfortable first-floor residents' lounge. A wide choice of food is served in either the Silver Platter Restaurant or adjoining Corner Kitchen which is open all day for reasonably priced snacks and teas.
62⇨♠(20fb)⚲in 14 bedrooms CTV in all bedrooms ® 💈 T ✈ (ex guide dogs) ✻ sB⇨♠£39.50-£49.50 dB⇨♠£62.50 (room only) 🍴
《 100P ❀
♡ ♨ ✻ Sunday Lunch fr£8.95 Dinner fr£13.50&alc Last dinner 10pm
CONF. Thtr 50 Class 25 Board 32 Del £62.50
Credit Cards [1][2][3][5] £
See advertisement under **STOKE-ON-TRENT**

TALLAND BAY Cornwall & Isles of Scilly Map **02** SX25

★★★🎖 **72%** Talland Bay
PL13 2JB (signposted from crossroads on A387 Looe/Polperro road) ☎Polperro(0503) 72667 FAX (0503) 72940
Closed 2 Jan-10 Feb

Talland Bay - Tal-y-Llyn

This charming old Cornish country house is set in beautiful gardens with panoramic views and provides a wonderfully relaxing retreat. Well coordinated bedrooms successfully blend traditional comfort and modern facilities, while stylish public areas filled with the scent of fresh flowers include a quiet (no smoking) sitting room, an elegant lounge and a cosy bar. The restaurant offers a choice of menus, the enjoyable food being accompanied by a good wine list.

20⇨♠Annexe4⇨♠(2fb)2⚑ CTV in all bedrooms ® T sB&B⇨♠£54-£80 dB&B⇨♠£108-£180 (incl dinner) ♨ 25P ⇦ ❊ ⌇ (heated) sauna solarium croquet games room putting *xmas*

⚐ English & French **V** ⚑ ⚒ ✂ ✱ Sunday Lunch £9.75 High tea £6-£7 Dinner £24&alc Last dinner 9pm
CONF. Thtr 30 Board 30 Del from £70
Credit Cards ① ② ③ ⑤

★ ❀ **68%** **Allhays Country House**
PL13 2JB ☎ Polperro(0503) 72434 FAX (0503) 72929
Closed 24 Dec-7 Jan

A few minutes walk uphill from the sea, this friendly family-run hotel offers a choice of bedrooms, the best having en suite facilities and sea views. Lynda Spring's award-winning West Country Fayre includes home grown produce, local seafood, and home-made bread, all cooked in a traditional Aga. A set dinner is usually served at 7pm, but guests are asked to select dishes some time in advance.

6rm(3⇨1♠)Annexe1⇨(1fb)1⚑⚒ in 1 bedroom CTV in all bedrooms ® T ✱ sB&B£28 dB&B£56 sB&B⇨♠£64-£72 ♨
12P ⇦ ❊ croquet putting nc10yrs
V ⚑ ⚒ ✂ Dinner £13 Last dinner 7pm
Credit Cards ① ② ③ £

TALSARNAU Gwynedd Map **06** SH63

★★ ❀ ❦ **MAES Y NEUADD**
LL47 6YA (2m SE on unclass rd off B4573)
☎ Harlech(0766) 780200
FAX (0766) 780211

A charming 14th-century country house built of granite and slate, the hotel is perched between the Snowdonia National Park and the estuary, and has spectacular views. Each of the rooms is individually styled with pretty decor and good quality furniture and those facing front have a magnificent outlook. In the elegant dining room chef Peter Jackson offers a 3, 4 or 5-course dinner. A typical menu may begin with a filo parcel of creamed mushrooms on a bed of leeks, followed by a soup of the day and a fish course. Main courses such as pork with an apricot and herb crust and a Dijon mustard essence are served with good fresh vegetables. The hotel is owned and run by the Slatter and Horsfall families, with a very obliging young team providing old-fashioned hospitality at its best.

12⇨♠Annexe4⇨♠1⚑ CTV in all bedrooms T sB&B⇨♠£69-£110 dB&B⇨♠£153-£194 (incl dinner) ♨
50P ⇦ ❊ croquet lawn *xmas*
⚐ International **V** ⚑ ⚒ ✂ ✱ Lunch £11.25-£14 Dinner £20.50-£20.50 Last dinner 9pm
CONF. Thtr 20 Class 20 Board 16 Del from £85
Credit Cards ① ② ③ ⑤ £

★★ **65%** **Tregwylan**
LL47 6YG (0.5m N) ☎ Penrhyndeudraeth(0766) 770424

This large Edwardian house commanding fine views over Cardigan Bay has been run by the present owners for more than 20 years. It is a small and welcoming hotel with comfortable bedrooms which are equally suitable for holiday-makers and business people.

10⇨♠ (3fb) CTV in all bedrooms ® ✈ (ex guide dogs)
sB&B⇨♠£26-£28 dB&B⇨♠£45-£48 ♨
CTV 20P ⇦ ❊
V ⚑ ⚒ ✂ Lunch £6.95-£8.50 Dinner £11.50-£13.50 Last dinner 8.30pm
Credit Cards ① ③

TAL-Y-BONT (NEAR CONWY) Gwynedd Map **06** SH76

★★ **65%** **Lodge**
LL32 8YX (on B5106, hotel on right hand side of the road when entering village) ☎ Aberconwy(0492) 660766 FAX (0492) 660534
RS Nov

Standing in well kept lawns and gardens, the Lodge is a small and friendly hotel in the Conwy Valley. All its bedrooms have good quality furnishings and are in an annexe at the back. In the main building are a comfortable bar and lounge and a restaurant offering a large choice of dishes, with local fish and seafood prominently featured.

Annexe10⇨ CTV in all bedrooms ® T ✱ sB&B⇨£33.95-£37 dB&B⇨£50-£55 ♨
50P ❊ *xmas*
⚐ British & French **V** ⚑ ⚒ ✂ ✱ Lunch £5.50-£6.50 Dinner £14.95-£15.50&alc Last dinner 9pm
Credit Cards ① ② ③ £

TAL-Y-LLYN Gwynedd Map **06** SH70

★★ **66%** **Tyn-y-Cornel**
LL36 9AJ (1.5m from junct B4405/A487, on shore of lake) (Welsh Rarebits) ☎ Abergynolwyn(0654) 782282 & 782223 FAX (0654) 782679

Delightfully situated on the lake shore amid mountain scenery, this comfortable 19th-century hotel is popular with fishermen as well as business and holiday guests. It has well equipped modern bedrooms and attractive public areas.

7rm(4⇨2♠)Annexe9⇨♠(2fb) CTV in 15 bedrooms ® T sB&B⇨♠fr£60 dB&B⇨♠fr£120 (incl dinner)
60P 1⚐ ⇦ ❊ ⌇ (heated) ♪ sauna solarium mountain bikes & helmets for hire
⚐ Welsh & Continental **V** ⚑ ⚒ ✂ ✱ Lunch £10-£12.50&alc Dinner £16.50-£20&alc Last dinner 9.30pm
CONF. Thtr 30 Class 30 Board 20 Del from £65
Credit Cards ① ② ③ ⑤

★ ❀ **75%** **Minffordd**
Minffordd LL36 9AJ (at junct of A487/B4405) (Welsh Rarebits) ☎ Corris(0654) 761665 FAX (0654) 761517
Closed Jan-Feb RS Nov-Dec & Mar

Originally a 17th-century drovers' inn, this hotel enjoys a spectacular location at the foot of Cader Idris. Bedrooms are well equipped, and the cottage atmosphere is enhanced by low beams, exposed stone, slate, and log fires in winter. The welcoming public areas include a pleasant bar, parlour and sun room, with the heart of the hotel firmly in the dining room. A short menu is available offering the best local produce, carefully prepared.

6⇨♠ in all bedrooms ® T ✈ sB&B⇨♠fr59 dB&B⇨♠fr£84 (incl dinner) ♨
12P ⇦ ❊ nc3yrs
⚐ French ⚑ ✂ Dinner £17 Last dinner 8.30pm
Credit Cards ① ③ ⑤

Tamworth - Tarbert Loch Fyne

TAMWORTH Staffordshire Map **07** SK20

★★ 64% **Globe Inn**
Lower Gungate B79 7AW (follow road traffic system to town centre. Hotel next to public car park) ☎(0827) 60455 FAX (0827) 63575

Empty and derelict for several years, The Globe has been extensively renovated and modernised to provide attractive modern accommodation. Facilities include a spacious Victorian-style lounge bar, an adjacent dining area serving a range of mainly grill-style meals, and a cosy residents' lounge.

18⇌♠(2fb)1⊭½in 2 bedrooms CTV in all bedrooms ®¥ T ✘ (ex guide dogs) sB&Bfr£32 sB&B⇌♠£32-£40 dB&B⇌♠£52-£60 ♬
CTV
V ♺½✱ Lunch £5.50-£10.50 Dinner £5.50-£10.50 Last dinner 9pm
Credit Cards [1][3]

Granada Lodge
(A5/M42 junct 10) ☎(0827) 260123 FAX (0827) 260145

This modern building provides smart, spacious and well equipped bedrooms, all with en suite bathrooms. Meals may be taken at a nearby family restaurant. For more details about Granada Lodges, consult the Contents page, under Hotel Groups.

63⇌♠✱ B⇌♠£34.95-£37.95 (room only)

Travel Inn
Bitterscote, Bonehill Rd B78 3HQ (follow A4091 towards Tamworth) ☎(0827) 54314

Purpose-built accommodation offers spacious and well equipped bedrooms, all with en suite bathrooms. Meals may be taken at the nearby family restaurant and pub. For more details about Travel Inns, consult the Contents page, under Hotel Groups.

40⇌♠✱ B⇌♠£33.50 (room only)

TANKERSLEY South Yorkshire Map **08** SK39

★★★ 67% **Tankersley Manor**
Church Ln S75 3DQ ☎Barnsley(0226) 744370 FAX (0226) 745405

Grade II listed, this 17th-century former farmhouse and outbuildings has been tastefully restored and converted into a quality hotel. Much of the original character is retained in the exposed beams, stone walls and open fires, but the comfortable bedrooms are equipped to meet modern expectations. The large lounge bar serves popular bar food, and there is an attractive, split-level restaurant with adjoining cocktail bar.

20⇌♠in 10 bedrooms CTV in all bedrooms ®¥ T ✘ (ex guide dogs) ✱ sB&B⇌♠£47.50-£59.50 dB&B⇌♠£60-£69.50
☾120P 🚗
♀ English & French V ♺♨✱ Lunch £9.50-£12&alc Dinner £17.45-£25.90alc Last dinner 9.45pm
CONF. Thtr 160 Class 80 Board 100 Del £75
Credit Cards [1][2][3][5]

TAPLOW Buckinghamshire Map **04** SU98

★★★★★
★★★★★●●●●♨
CLIVEDEN
SL6 0JF ☎Maidenhead (0628) 668561 FAX (0628) 661837

Guests cannot fail to be impressed with this magnificent stately home – one of England's greatest houses on cliffs 200 feet above the Thames. In addition to the usual services, guests' cars are parked (and will be washed before they leave) and a maid will offer to unpack. Eminently comfortable, the bedrooms are furnished and equipped to the highest standards. One-time home to a Prince of Wales, 3 dukes and the Astors, the house contains a superb art collection and suitably grand public rooms, the finest being the sumptuous Terrace dining room, with stunning views. Here the cooking is accomplished and the menu offers a blend of modern and traditional English and French dishes. The club-like Waldo's represents chef Ron Maxfield's personal approach to modern cookery: adventurous in style and artistic in presentation. Flavours are, perhaps, not always perfectly balanced, but there was no mistaking the aroma of ceps in a red wine sauce which accompanied a vertically arranged dish of English partridge, perched on delicious red cabbage, spinach and a potato galette.

25⇌♠Annexe6⇌♠2⊭½in 1 bedroom CTV in all bedrooms T
Lift ☾30P 3🚗 🐎 ✽ ▦ (heated) ≈ (heated) ♀ (hard) ♪ squash ∪ snooker sauna solarium gymnasium indoor tennis Turkish bath massage
V ½✱ Lunch fr£31&alc Dinner fr£41.50&alc Last dinner 9.30pm
CONF. Thtr 40 Board 24 Del from £198
Credit Cards [1][2][3][4][5]

TARBERT
See **Harris, Isle of**

TARBERT LOCH FYNE Strathclyde *Argyllshire*
Map **10** NR86

★★★ 61% **Stonefield Castle**
PA29 6YJ (off A83, 2m N) ☎Tarbert(0880) 820836 FAX (0880) 820929

Breathtaking views, particularly from the restaurant, are a feature of this fine period mansion which lies in 60 acres of wooded grounds on the shores of Loch Fyne. Public areas are spacious, and bedrooms are situated in either the original building or the purpose built wing.

33⇌♠(4fb) CTV in all bedrooms ® T sB&B⇌♠£45-£75 dB&B⇌♠£90-£150 (incl dinner) ♬
Lift CTV 50P ✽ ≈ (heated) ♪ snooker sauna solarium *xmas*
♺ ♨ ½✱ Lunch £7.50-£17.50alc Dinner £19.50-£22.50&alc Last dinner 10pm
CONF. Thtr 80 Class 50 Board 30 Del from £50
Credit Cards [1][2][3][5]

Rosettes range from 5 for outstanding cuisine to 1 rosette for enjoyable, well prepared food

Remember to book early for holiday and bank holiday times.

Tarporley - Taunton

TARPORLEY Cheshire Map **07** SJ56

★★★ **69%** **The Wild Boar**
Whitchurch Rd, Beeston CW6 9NW (2.5m S off A49) ☎Bunbury(0829) 260309 FAX (0829) 261081

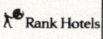 Rank Hotels

This city hotel has a dramatic half timbered façade. A modern extension houses spacious bedrooms and function rooms, while the old house has a popular beamed restaurant and comfortable lounge areas.
37⇨♠(19fb)⊬in 12 bedrooms CTV in all bedrooms ® T ✳ sB&B⇨♠£39.50-£62.50 dB&B⇨♠£54.50-£77.50 ⛟
(70P ✣ xmas
♥ English & French V ♂ ⚒ ✳ Lunch £12.50-£14.50&alc Dinner £17.25&alc Last dinner 10pm
CONF. Thtr 60 Class 30 Board 38 Del from £85
Credit Cards [1][2][3][5]   £

★★★ ♨ **62%** *The Willington Hall*
Willington CW6 0NB (3m NW off unclass rd linking A51 & A54)
☎Kelsall(0829) 52321 FAX (0829) 52596
Closed 25 Dec
This Elizabethan-style house is set in 17 acres of parkland and gardens surrounded by pastureland, views of which may be enjoyed from the dining room. Bar snacks are also available at lunch and at dinner.
10⇨♠(1fb) CTV in all bedrooms ® T
60P ♨ ✣ ♪ (hard) ♂
V Last dinner 9.30pm
Credit Cards [1][3][5]

TAUNTON Somerset Map **03** ST22

★★★

★★★♨♨♨ **CASTLE**
Castle Green TA1 1NF
☎(0823) 272671 FAX (0823) 336066

A spacious hall with a magnificent tapestry-hung staircase is the first introduction to this imposing hotel, but it is also a place to relax, with a warm atmosphere in its comfortable lounges. The bedrooms are immaculate, well furnished and have been individually designed. Taking its name from the Norman castle which once occupied the site, the Castle Hotel has been owned by the Chapman family for over 40 years. Kit Chapman now maintains its high standards, particularly its reputation for excellent food and wines and the quality of service in the restaurant. Phil Vickery is the talented and skilful chef, offering a choice of menus of British cooking with some classical touches. A delicious inspection meal began with a crab tart, followed by Tournedos Rossini with a well balanced sauce and a generous piece of foie gras.
33⇨♠1⛟ CTV in all bedrooms T Continental breakfast Lift (30P 10☂ (£10 per person) ✣ ♫
V Lunch £14.50-£29.90 Dinner £18.90-£29.90 Last dinner 9pm
CONF. Thtr 100 Class 45 Board 40 Del from £95
Credit Cards [1][2][3][5]

★★★♨♨♨ **81%** *The Mount Somerset Country House*
Lower Henlade TA3 5NB ☎(0823) 442500 FAX (0823) 442900
This Regency house of classic elegance overlooks some of Somerset's most beautiful countryside from its setting on the slopes of the Blackdown Hills and offers a pleasing balance of natural friendly hospitality and professional service. In recent years it has been lovingly fashioned into a country house hotel of great comfort and charm, all of the main rooms retaining their period features. Bedrooms offer the perfect combination of quality, practical use and comfort, along with every modern facility: most have double baths. Chef Richard Smith delighted our inspector with pan-fried sea bass served with a beaurre blanc and fresh asparagus, followed by rump of lamb, set on a puree of aubergines and minced lamb and a confit of red onions, timbale of wild mushrooms and dauphinois potato arranged around it. A delicious caramelised lemon tart rounded off the meal.
11⇨♠1⛟ CTV in all bedrooms ❀ T ✶ sB&B⇨♠£90 dB&B⇨♠£110-£200 ⛟
Lift 54P ♨ ✣ ♪ (hard) nc12yrs *xmas*
♥ ⊬ Lunch £6-£16 Dinner £25&alc Last dinner 9pm
Credit Cards [1][2][3][5]

★★★ **67%** **Rumwell Manor**
Rumwell TA4 1EL (2m S, on A38 Wellington road) ☎(0823) 461902 FAX (0823) 254861

Set in well kept grounds with views to the Blackdown Hills, this personally run Georgian country house provides guests with a warm welcome and attentive service. Bedrooms of varying size and style are comfortably furnished and there is a cosy lounge, adjacent bar and candlelit dining room.
10⇨♠Annexe10⇨♠(3fb)3⛟⊬in 2 bedrooms CTV in all bedrooms ® T sB&B⇨♠£40-£48 dB&B⇨♠£60-£85 ⛟
40P ♨ ✣ ♂ *xmas*
♥ English & French V ♂ ⚒ ⊬ Lunch £8-£11.95 High tea £4-£7 Dinner £15.95&alc Last dinner 8.30pm
CONF. Thtr 40 Class 30 Board 20 Del £69.50
Credit Cards [1][2][3]   £

Stonefield Castle Hotel
A very special place

Stonefield Castle sits in 60 acres of wooded gardens overlooking Loch Fyne. Comfortable, well-appointed bedrooms retain the character of this charming baronial home. Dining room (Egon Ronay recommended), cocktail bar, comfortable lounges, library and snooker room. Sauna, solarium, open-air heated swimming pool. Golf, riding and pony trekking nearby.
At Stonefield Castle Hotel you are assured of a memorable holiday — a pleasure to anticipate and a delight to look back upon.

OPEN ALL YEAR

A A ★★★   S.T.B. 4 Crown Commended Hotel
Tarbert, Loch Fyne, Argyll PA29 6YJ
Tel. (0880) 820836. Fax No. (0880) 820829.

593

Taunton - Taynuilt

★★★ 59% The County
East St TA1 3LT ☎(0823) 337651 FAX (0823) 334517

The County is a large, period hotel in the town centre, with a spacious lounge and various styles and sizes of bedrooms.
66⇌ ᴺ(2fb)⊬in 30 bedrooms CTV in all bedrooms ® T
sB⇌ᴺ£55-£65 dB⇌ᴺ£70-£80 (room only) 🅿
Lift (110P xmas
V ✿ ☑ ⊬ ✷ Sunday Lunch £9.95-£10.95 Dinner £16.95-£18.95 Last dinner 9.15pm
Credit Cards [1][2][3][5]

★★ 65% Falcon
Henlade TA3 5DH (3m E A358)
☎(0823) 442502 FAX (0823) 442670

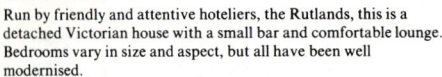

Closed 25 Dec
Run by friendly and attentive hoteliers, the Rutlands, this is a detached Victorian house with a small bar and comfortable lounge. Bedrooms vary in size and aspect, but all have been well modernised.
11⇌ᴺ(2fb)1🛏⊬in 3 bedrooms CTV in all bedrooms ®✱ T
sB&B⇌ᴺ£35-£45 dB&B⇌ᴺ£45-£65 🅿
25P ✿ ♿
♀ International V ✿ ☑ ⊬ ✷ Lunch £6.50 High tea £4.50 Dinner £13.50&alc Last dinner 9pm
CONF. Thtr 50 Class 36 Board 30 Del from £47.50
Credit Cards [1][2][3][5]

Forte Posthouse
Deane Gate Av TA1 2UA ☎(0823) 332222 FAX (0823) 332266

Suitable for both the business and leisure traveller, this bright hotel provides modern accommodation in well equipped bedrooms with en suite bathrooms. For more details about Forte Posthouse hotels, consult the Contents page, under Hotel Groups.
97⇌ᴺ✷ B⇌ᴺ£41.50-£53.50 (room only)
CONF. Thtr 280 Class 110 Board 105 Del £89.50

Travel Inn
81 Bridgwater Rd TA1 2DU (leave M5 junc 25 towards Taunton then head for Corfe Racecourse) ☎(0823) 321112

Purpose-built accommodation offers spacious and well equipped bedrooms, all with en suite bathrooms. Meals may be taken at the nearby family restaurant and pub. For more details about Travel Inns, consult the Contents page, under Hotel Groups.
40⇌ᴺ✷ B⇌ᴺ£33.50 (room only)

TAUNTON DEANE MOTORWAY SERVICE AREA (M5)
Somerset Map 03 ST12

⇧ Roadchef Lodge
Trull TA1 4BA (between junct 25 & 26 of M5)
☎Taunton(0823) 332228 FAX (0823) 338131
Closed 24-26 Dec
Particularly well presented and equipped accommodation, spotlessly clean and with a wealth of modern facilities, is provided by this good-value lodge. Continental breakfast can be served in rooms, other meals being taken at one of the eating options offered by the large motorway service area.
39⇌ᴺ(24fb)⊬in 20 bedrooms CTV in all bedrooms ® T
✖ (ex guide dogs)
(39P ✿
V ✿ ☑ ⊬
Credit Cards [1][2][3][4][5]

TAVISTOCK Devon Map 02 SX47
See also **Mary Tavy**

★★★ 62% The Bedford
Plymouth Rd PL19 8BB ☎(0822) 613211 FAX (0822)618034

An impressive castellated stone building, the Bedford is situated near the town centre. The majority of the well equipped bedrooms have been refurbished to a high standard. Traditional table d'hôte and a short à la carte menu are served in the Woburn Restaurant. Public areas are spacious and open plan.
31rm(30⇌ᴺ)(1fb)⊬in 11 bedrooms CTV in all bedrooms ® T
sB⇌ᴺfr£70 dB⇌ᴺfr£80 (room only) 🅿
45P 3🚗 xmas
V ✿ ☑ ⊬ Sunday Lunch fr£10.95 Dinner fr£16.95&alc Last dinner 9pm
Credit Cards [1][2][3][5]

★★ 💤 62% Moorland Hall
Brentnor Rd, Mary Tavy PL19 9PY (4m N, signposted from A386 in Mary Tavy) (Logis) ☎Mary Tavy(0822) 810466
Run on very relaxed and informal lines by Gillian and Andrew Farr, this cosy hotel was converted from a farmhouse and stands in 4 acres of secluded gardens. Character public rooms overlook the garden, and home cooking by Gillian Farr is served in the comfortable dining room. Bedrooms are bright, combining modern facilities with period character.
8⇌ᴺ(1fb)2🛏 CTV in all bedrooms ® sB&B⇌ᴺ£33 dB&B⇌ᴺ£50-£56
20P 🚲 ✿ bar billiards croquet lawn xmas
♀ English & French V ⊬ ✷ Dinner £13.50 Last dinner 8pm
Credit Cards [1][3]

TAYNUILT Strathclyde Argyllshire Map 10 NN03

★★ 67% Brander Lodge
Bridge of Awe PA35 1HT (2m E, off A85)
☎(08662) 243 & 225 FAX (08662) 273

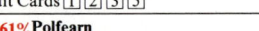

Set in its own grounds, this hotel has evolved from the original farmhouse, although bedrooms are contained in a plain purpose built extension. The hotel is family run with the help of friendly, well turned out staff.
20⇌ᴺ(2fb) CTV in all bedrooms ®✱ T ✷ sB&B⇌ᴺ£32-£34 dB&B⇌ᴺ£64-£68 🅿
100P ✿ pool table xmas
♀ International V ✿ ☑ ⊬ ✷ Lunch £2-£15 High tea £2-£15 Dinner £16&alc Last dinner 8.30pm
Credit Cards [1][2][3][5]

★★ 61% Polfearn
PA35 1JQ (turn N off A85, continue 1.5m through village down to Loch Shaw) ☎(08662) 251
Situated a mile north of the village close to Loch Etive pier, this family- run hotel looks out onto fine loch and mountain scenery, with the river Awe to one side. It offers modest bedrooms, attentive service and interesting bar and dinner menus that attract residents and non-residents.
16rm(2⇌12ᴺ)(2fb) CTV in all bedrooms ® sB&B£17-£27 sB&B⇌ᴺ£25-£31 dB&B£36-£56 dB&B⇌ᴺ£36-£56 🅿
CTV 20P xmas
V ✿ ☑ ⊬ ✷ Bar Lunch £5-£15&alc High tea £5-£15 Dinner £13-£16&alc Last dinner 9pm
CONF. Del from £30
Credit Cards [1][3]

See advertisement under OBAN

Irish entries appear in a separate section that follows the main directory.

Tees-side Airport - Telford

TEANGUE
See **Skye, Isle of**

TEES-SIDE AIRPORT Co Durham Map **08** NZ31
★★★ 64% **St George**
Middleton St George DL2 1RH
☎Darlington(0325) 332631 FAX (0325) 333851

This modern hotel is right on the doorstep of the airport, very convenient for Darlington, Stockton and Middlesborough, yet it is set in delightful Cleveland countryside. The bedrooms meet all the expectations of modern travellers and a good range of food is served either in the elegant restaurant or the bar.
59⇨🛏(2fb)1🛏✗in 8 bedrooms CTV in all bedrooms ® T ✷ sB&B⇨🛏£45-£69 dB&B⇨🛏£50-£79
(200P 20🚗 (£2.50 per day) ✻ squash sauna solarium *xmas*
♥ English & French V ⊙ ⊇ ✷ Lunch £7.50-£8.25&alc Dinner £13.50&alc Last dinner 9.45pm
CONF. Thtr 150 Class 60 Board 50 Del from £70
Credit Cards 1 2 3 5

TEIGNMOUTH Devon Map **03** SX97
★★ 65% **Ness House**
Marine Dr, Shaldon TQ14 0HP ☎Shaldon(0626) 873480 FAX (0626) 873486
This elegant Georgian property is on the outskirts of Shaldon, overlooking the estuary and just 200yds from the Smugglers Tunnel to Ness Beach. Annexe bedrooms are charming, and rooms in the original building are soon to be renovated. The Sea Terrace Restaurant serves an à la carte menu, and there is an extensive range of good value bar meals.
7⇨🛏Annexe5rm(2fb)1🛏 CTV in all bedrooms ® ⚲ T ✖ (ex guide dogs) sB&B⇨🛏£35-£48 dB&B⇨🛏£60-£78 ₽ 20P 🚗 ✻ ♤ *xmas*
♥ English & French V ⊙ ⊇ Lunch £6.50-£11.50&alc Dinner fr£11.50&alc Last dinner 10.15pm
Credit Cards 1 2 3 £

★ 63% **Belvedere**
Barnpark Rd TQ14 8PJ ☎(0626) 774561
The Belvedere is a white Victorian villa overlooking the town's rooftops to the sea and hills beyond, and many of the traditionally furnished bedrooms enjoy this view. Public areas include a comfortable lounge, with a coal fire for chilly evenings, a small bar and a well tended garden and patio.
13rm(12⇨🛏)(4fb) CTV in all bedrooms ® ✖
CTV 10P 1🅿 ✻
V ⊙ ⊇
Credit Cards 1 3

★ 63% **Glenside**
Ringmoor Rd, Shaldon TQ14 0EP (1m S on B3195) ☎Shaldon(0626) 872448
Closed Nov & 3-4 wks during Feb or Mar

A stone's throw from the southern bank of the Teign Estuary, this is an attractive, cottagey hotel set in colourful gardens. The accommodation is simple and comfortable, and the table d'hôte menu offers a limited choice.
10rm(1⇨🛏6🛏)(1fb) CTV in all bedrooms ® ✷ sB&B£17.50-£21.15 sB&B⇨🛏£19-£23.50 dB&B£35-£42 dB&B⇨🛏£38-£47 ₽
10P 🚗 *xmas*
V ✷ Bar Lunch £3.50 Dinner £10-£11 Last dinner 6.30pm

For full, independent restaurant reviews, see the
AA Abbey Well *Restaurant Guide.*

TELFORD Shropshire Map **07** SJ60

★★★ ✻72% **Madeley Court**
TF7 5DW ☎(0952) 680068 FAX (0952) 684275
Originating in medieval times, this house has now been restored in Elizabethan style, retaining such features as open fires, panelled walls and a unique spiral oak staircase. A new accommodation wing supplements older, character bedrooms, and there are 2 restaurants. Modern cooking marries imaginative sauces with good quality fish, meat and game.
16⇨🛏Annexe31⇨🛏(1fb)2🛏✗in 2 bedrooms CTV in all bedrooms ® T ✖ (ex guide dogs) ✻ sB&B⇨🛏£63-£85 dB&B⇨🛏£73-£95 ₽
(180P ✻ ♪ *xmas*
V ⊙ ⊇ ✗ ✷ Sunday Lunch £9.50-£12.50 High tea £6.50-£10.50 Dinner £14-£35alc Last dinner 10pm
CONF. Thtr 220 Class 150 Board 50 Del from £90
Credit Cards 1 2 3 5

★★★ ✻69% **Holiday Inn**
St Quentin Gate TF3 4EH (just off junct 4 of M4) ☎(0952) 292500 FAX (0952) 291949

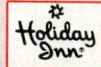

This popular modern hotel is close to the shopping centre. The accommodation is modern, with up-to-date facilities such as a TV video channel. Public areas are located around a raised central bar lounge. Courts Restaurant offers a wide range of meals with some Japanese dishes. Staff are welcoming and obliging.
100⇨🛏✗in 35 bedrooms CTV in all bedrooms ® T ✷ sB⇨🛏£91-£110 dB⇨🛏£91-£130 (room only) ₽
Lift (120P 🏊 (heated) ♀ (hard) squash snooker sauna solarium gymnasium steam room whirlpool spa
♥ English, French & Japanese V ⊙ ⊇ ✗ ✷ Lunch £9.95-£10.50 Dinner £16-£17&alc Last dinner 10pm
Credit Cards 1 2 3 4 5

★★ **THE FALCON HOTEL**

Henlade, Taunton, Somerset TA3 5DH

Family owned and run Country House Style Hotel standing in landscaped gardens only one mile East off M5 (Junction 25).

Relaxed informal atmosphere.

All bedrooms en-suite and equipped to a very high standard.

Comfortable lounge with log fires.

Table D'Hôte and A la Carte Menus.

Comprehensively Stocked Bar.

Conference Facilities for up to 50 delegates.

Ample car parking in grounds.

Ashley Courtenay Recommended.

English Tourist Board ✦✦✦✦

Tony & Glenis Rutland
THE FALCON HOTEL
Taunton
Tel: 0823 442502   Fax: 0823 442670

Telford

★★★69% Telford Moat House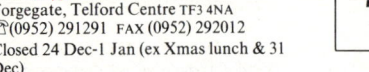
Forgegate, Telford Centre TF3 4NA
☎(0952) 291291 FAX (0952) 292012
Closed 24 Dec-1 Jan (ex Xmas lunch & 31 Dec)

The Moat House is a popular commercial hotel close to the shopping centre. The light modern-style bedrooms are equipped with a good range of facilities, including in-house videos. Public areas include Ashgrove Restaurant which has its own bar and serves a wide range of meals. Service is efficient and thoughtful.

148⇨🛌(8fb)⊁in 3 bedrooms CTV in all bedrooms ®T sB&B⇨🛌£79.95-£86.50 dB&B⇨🛌£95-£105 🍽
Lift ℂ CTV 300P 🔲 (heated) sauna solarium gymnasium games room jacuzzi pool table ♪
♀ English & French V ✿ ♨ ✱ Lunch £14.25&alc Dinner £14.25&alc Last dinner 9.45pm
CONF. Thtr 500 Class 250 Board 12 Del £105
Credit Cards [1][2][3][4][5]

★★★68% Telford Hotel Golf & Country Club
Great Hay Dr, Sutton Hill TF7 4DT (off A442 on Bridgenorth side of town) ☎(0952) 585642 FAX (0952) 586602

This large multi-purpose hotel overlooks the beautiful Ironbridge Gorge. Bedrooms are furnished to a good standard. In addition to the general restaurant, a Japanese restaurant has recently been opened.

86⇨🛌(10fb)⊁in 9 bedrooms CTV in all bedrooms ®T sB&B⇨🛌£84-£90 dB&B⇨🛌£94-£100 🍽
ℂ CTV 200P ❋ 🔲 (heated) ▶ 9 squash snooker sauna solarium gymnasium steam room masseur spa pool ⛳ xmas
♀ International V ✿ ♨ ✱ Lunch £4.50-£14&alc High tea fr£4.25 Dinner £15.75-£19.75&alc Last dinner 9.45pm
CONF. Thtr 240 Class 140 Board 60 Del from £120
Credit Cards [1][2][3][4][5]

★★★67% Buckatree Hall
The Wrekin, Wellington TF6 5AL (exit 7 of M54, turn left and left again for 1m)
☎(0952) 641821 FAX (0952) 247540

Set in impressive wood and parkland, this privately owned hotel is south of junction 7 of the M54. About half of the bedrooms are in the garden wing, including several with 4-poster and water beds; suites are also available. Public areas are modern and the pretty restaurant offers a table d'hôte menu supplemented by a good range of special dishes.

64⇨🛌(4fb)4🛏🛌in 10 bedrooms CTV in all bedrooms ®📺T ✱ sB&B⇨🛌fr£72 dB&B⇨🛌fr£79 🍽
Lift ℂ 120P ❋ xmas
♀ International V ✿ ♨ ⊁ ✱ Lunch fr£10.95 Dinner fr£16.50 Last dinner 10pm
CONF. Thtr 166 Class 66 Board 40 Del from £89
Credit Cards [1][2][3][5]

T ★★★59% Valley
TF8 7DW ☎(0952) 432247 FAX (0952) 432308

This attractive hotel situated in secluded grounds is personally run by the Casson family. The property was once the home of a 19th-century tile manufacturer, and is has been sympathetically restored and extended and many of his designs are on display. Young chef, Andy Careless produces interesting and varied menus.

34⇨🛌2🛏 CTV in all bedrooms ®📺T ✱ (ex guide dogs) ✱ sB&B⇨🛌£49-£62 dB&B⇨🛌£60-£72 🍽
ℂ 100P ❋
♀ International V ✿ ♨ ⊁ ✱ Lunch £10-£14.50 High tea £3.50-£6.50 Dinner £10-£20alc Last dinner 9.30pm
CONF. Thtr 250 Class 100 Board 50 Del £65
Credit Cards [1][2][3]

★★64% White House
Wellington Rd, Muxton TF2 8NG (off A518 Telford-Stafford road) ☎(0952) 604276 FAX (0952) 670336

Set in 2 acres of pleasant grounds, this popular hotel has been run by the same family for nearly 30 years. Public rooms are modern, bright and cheerful with 2 bars, a restaurant and a small first floor lounge for residents. The staff are friendly, and a wide choice of good value food is available.

30⇨🛌(4fb) CTV in all bedrooms ® T sB&B⇨🛌fr£49.50 dB&B⇨🛌fr£59.50 🍽
CTV 100P ❋
♀ English & French V ✿ ♨ ⊁ Last dinner 9.30pm
Credit Cards [1][2][3]

★★61% Oaks Hotel & Restaurant
Redhill, St Georges TF2 9NZ (2.5m E on A5) ☎(0952) 620126 FAX (0952) 620257

This small, family-run hotel has modest and functional bedrooms, and meals are available in the cosy bar or St Georges restaurant. Friendly proprietors play an active role in providing a personal service.

12⇨🛌(4fb) CTV in all bedrooms ® T ✱ (ex guide dogs) sB&B⇨🛌£25-£38 dB&B⇨🛌£35-£46 🍽
36P ❋ ✿
♀ English & French V ✿ ✱ Lunch fr£8.95&alc Dinner fr£8.95&alc Last dinner 9.30pm
Credit Cards [1][2][3][5]

★★58% Falcon
Holyhead Road, Wellington TF1 2DD (on Holyhead rd, west of Wellington) ☎(0952) 255011
Closed Xmas RS Sun

Bedrooms at this old coaching inn are simply furnished with comfortable beds and good armchairs. A small lounge is available, and the bar has an interesting collection of copper utensils. Bar meals are a popular feature and the restaurant serves à la carte meals.

13rm(7⇨🛌)(1fb) CTV in all bedrooms ® ✱ ✿ sB&B£28-£32 sB&B⇨🛌£30-£40 dB&B£35-£40 dB&B⇨🛌£40-£50 🍽
CTV 30P 🚭 nc2yrs
♀ English & Continental V ✿ ✱ Dinner £9.50-£20alc Last dinner 9pm
Credit Cards [1][3]

★66% Arleston Inn
Arleston Ln, Wellington TF1 2LA ☎(0952) 501881 FAX (0952) 506429

This small, privately owned inn is convenient for Telford and the M54. Accommodation is modern and well equipped, although some rooms are rather compact. Bar areas are cosy and a simply appointed restaurant serves popular meals.

7🛌 CTV in all bedrooms ® T ✱ (ex guide dogs) ✱ sB&B🛌£26-£36 dB&B🛌£36-£46 🍽
CTV 40P ✿
V ✱ Sunday Lunch £3.95-£6.45 Dinner £8-£15alc Last dinner 10pm
Credit Cards [1][3] £

Forte Travelodge
New Whitchurch Rd (1m NW, on A5223)
☎(0952) 251244 Central Res (0800) 850950

FORTE Travelodge

This modern building offers a good standard of accommodation for overnight stops. Smart, spacious and well equipped bedrooms, all with en suite bathrooms, are suitable for family use, and meals may be taken at the nearby family restaurant. For more details about Travelodges, consult the Contents page, under Hotel Groups.

40⇨🛌✱ B⇨🛌£31.95 (room only)

For key to symbols see the Bookmark.

Temple Sowerby - Tenby

TEMPLE SOWERBY Cumbria Map 12 NY62

★★ ❀74% Temple Sowerby House
CA10 1RZ ☎Kirkby Thore(07683) 61578 FAX (07683) 61958

This elegantly furnished hotel stands in 2 acres of walled gardens. The bedrooms are individually styled and furnished with quality fabrics. Public areas are richly decorated and have antiques, fresh flowers and open fires. A well produced 5-course dinner is provided – our inspector enjoyed robust chicken livers in a pastry case with red wine cream; lightly poached fillets of trout with a dill cream sauce, and rich chocolate mousse in a brandy snap basket.
8⇨Annexe4⇨(2fb)2🚭 CTV in all bedrooms ® T
sB&B⇨fr£46 dB&B⇨fr£62 🅿
30P 🚭 ❀ croquet badminton boules *xmas*
♿ International V ✿ ⚤ ✕ Lunch fr£11.95 High tea fr£7
Dinner fr£21 Last dinner 9pm
Credit Cards [1][2][3][5]

TENBURY WELLS Hereford & Worcester Map 07 SO56

★★61% Cadmore Lodge
Berrington Green WR15 8TQ ☎(0584) 810044 FAX (0584) 810044

Set by a lake in 50 acres of grounds, this popular family-run hotel provides simply decorated bedrooms, all no smoking, with a good range of modern facilities.
8⇨🛏(1fb)⚤in all bedrooms CTV in all bedrooms ® T 🍴 ❋
sB&B⇨🛏£25-£34.50 dB&B⇨🛏£57.50-£60 🅿
CTV 80P ❀ 🏊 9 ⛳ (hard) 🎵 bowling green
♿ International V ✿ ⚤ ❋ Lunch £5-£10&alc High tea £2.50-£5 Dinner £15&alc Last dinner 9.30pm
Credit Cards [1][3]

CADMORE LODGE HOTEL
★★

AND COUNTRY CLUB

*Dining Room open daily for lunches and dinners
Table d'Hote, A la Carte and Bar Menu available
Private 9 hole golf course
Club nights Tuesday and Wednesday.
Professional Tuition for new members
Day tickets available
Tennis and Bowls — Trout Fly Fishing
Purpose built function room, overlooking lake, complete with dance floor and sound system
Ideal for Weddings, private parties or conferences
8 en-suite accommodation*

For bookings or further details contact Elizabeth Weston
**CADMORE LODGE, TENBURY WELLS
Tel: 0584 810044**

TENBY Dyfed Map 02 SN10

★★★67% Atlantic
Esplanade SA70 7DU ☎(0834) 842881 & 844176 FAX (0834) 842881 ex 256

This popular hotel has lovely sea views to Caldey Island and beyond, and an Italianate garden separates the hotel from the beach. Bedrooms are bright, well equipped and pleasantly decorated; those at the front are particularly comfortable and have glorious views. There is a comfortable country house- style lounge, cocktail bar and bright restaurant. A great attraction here is the hospitality of the owners and their willing and friendly staff.
40⇨🛏(9fb)1🚭⚤in 2 bedrooms CTV in all bedrooms ® T
sB&B⇨🛏£45-£51 dB&B⇨🛏£70-£80 🅿
30P ❀ 🏊 (heated) solarium spa bath
♿ Welsh & French V ✿ ⚤ ⚤ Sunday Lunch fr£8.50 High tea fr£3.99 Dinner £10-£16 Last dinner 8.30pm
CONF. Thtr 40 Class 26 Board 26 Del from £65
Credit Cards [1][2][3]

★★ ❀80% Penally Abbey Country House
Penally SA70 7PY (on A4139) (Welsh Rarebits)
☎(0834) 843033 FAX (0834) 844714

Superbly situated in 5 acres of woodland and gardens including Caldey Island, Penally Abbey features its own Flemish chimney, ruined chapel and wishing well. Bedrooms are individually decorated and furnished with antiques and period furniture. Candlelit dinners are served in the attractive restaurant, where vegetarian dishes are available in addition to the fixed price menu. The influence of chef Ellen Warren's time in a French château is noticeable, and dishes have natural flavours and mild sauces.
8⇨🛏Annexe4⇨(5fb)7🚭 CTV in all bedrooms ® T 🍴
sB&B⇨🛏£78 dB&B⇨🛏£136 (incl dinner) 🅿
14P 🚭 ❀ 🏊 (heated) snooker croquet *xmas*
♿ British & French ✿ ⚤ ⚤ Bar Lunch £6-£8 Dinner £22.50 Last dinner 9pm
Credit Cards [1][3]

Buckatree Hall Hotel ★★★

The Wrekin, Wellington, Telford, Shropshire TF6 5AL
Tel: (0952) 641821   Fax: (0952) 247540
1 MILE FROM EXIT 7 AT THE END OF M54
Near Ironbridge Gorge

Escape to the delightfully rolling Shropshire countryside to Buckatree Hall with its own lake, waterfall and gardens, nestling in woodlands at the foot of famous Wrekin Hill.

Most bedrooms have balconies overlooking gardens or lake. Some hi-tech water beds. Satellite television, teasmaid and garment press. Penthouse Suite with whirlpool. Dine by candlelight in our Terrace Restaurant overlooking the gardens and patio.

WEEKEND BREAK on any 2 nights of the weekend, Dinner, Bed & Traditional English Breakfast.

Tenby - Tetbury

★★ 68% Fourcroft
The Croft SA70 8AP ☎(0834) 842886 FAX (0834) 842888
Closed Jan & Feb
This friendly family-run hotel is in an enviable position overlooking the town's north beach and harbour. Bedrooms and lounge areas are well maintained and offer good facilities and comfort.
43⇌♙(8fb) CTV in all bedrooms ® T ✱ sB&B⇌♙£36-£44 dB&B⇌♙£66-£82 ₽
Lift ₵ 5P (£1.50 per night) ❋ ⌇ (heated) sauna gymnasium games room spa pool xmas
♨ International V ◊ ⌇ ✱ Bar Lunch £1-£8alc High tea £2-£6alc Dinner £13.50-£15&alc Last dinner 8.30pm
CONF. Thtr 80 Class 60 Board 80 Del from £35
Credit Cards 1 3

★★ 65% Esplanade
The Esplanade SA70 7DU ☎(0834) 843333
This modern family-run hotel on the promenade overlooking the sandy south beach is popular with business travellers and holiday-makers alike. Bedrooms are well furnished and equipped. There is a comfortable first-floor residents' lounge, and the open-plan bar/restaurant serves a full choice of food.
15⇌♙Annexe3⇌♙(5fb) CTV in all bedrooms ® T
♯ ⌘
♨ French ◊ ⌇ Last dinner 9.30pm
Credit Cards 1 2 3 5

★★ 64% Harbour Heights
11 The Croft SA70 8AP ☎(0834) 842132
Overlooking the sands of the North Beach, this small, family-run hotel is comfortable and well equipped. Fresh produce is used in the kitchens and the food is good, although the choice of dishes is necessarily fairly small.
8⇌♙(4fb) CTV in all bedrooms ® ✈
♯ ⌘ nc8yrs
♨ English & Continental Last dinner 9.30pm
Credit Cards 1 2 3 5

★★ 62% Buckingham
Esplanade SA70 7DU ☎(0834) 842622
Closed Nov-Feb RS Mar & Oct
Situated directly opposite the sandy South Beach, the Buckingham is run by Veronica and Tom Rooke who take a pride in welcoming their guests. The hotel has a small but cosy residents' bar, and the open plan lounge and restaurant looks out over the sea. Bedrooms are neat and modern with laminated fittings.
8⇌♙(1fb)♙in 4 bedrooms CTV in all bedrooms ® sB&B⇌♙£20-£28 dB&B⇌♙£35-£45 ₽
♯ ⌘ nc4yrs
V ◊ ⌇ Dinner £12.50 Last dinner 7.45pm
Credit Cards 1 3

★★ 59% Albany
The Norton SA70 8AB (follow signs for North Beach)
☎(0834) 842698
The Albany is a very pleasant resort hotel near the north shore and harbour, and just a short walk from the town centre. Bedrooms are bright and well maintained, there are 3 bars, and a swimming pool outside for good weather. Staff are friendly and helpful, and a good choice of food is available.
24⇌♙(2fb) CTV in all bedrooms ® sB&B⇌♙£25-£29 dB&B⇌♙£44-£52 ₽
CTV ♯ xmas
♨ French V ◊ ⌇ Lunch £9.95 Dinner £12.95&alc Last dinner 9.30pm
Credit Cards 1 2 3 £

★★ 50% Royal Lion
High St SA70 7EX ☎(0834) 842127 FAX (0834) 842441
Closed mid Oct-May
This Victorian hotel occupies a fine seafront position with views over the harbour; the comfortable bedrooms are well equipped, and service is friendly.

31rm(19⇌♙1♙)(8fb) CTV in all bedrooms ® T ✱ sB&B⇌♙fr£25 dB&B⇌♙fr£40 ₽
Lift CTV 30P
◊ ⌇ ✱ Lunch fr£7.95 Dinner fr£12.50 Last dinner 8.30pm
Credit Cards 1 3 5

TENTERDEN Kent Map 05 TQ83

★★★ 56% White Lion
High St TN30 6BD ☎(in town centre) ☎(0580) 765077 FAX (0580)764157

This traditional 16th-century coaching inn is in the heart of the town. Bedrooms are of a good standard and include spacious 4-poster and family rooms with sofa beds; all are particularly well equipped. Public areas are limited to the double sided public bar and the beamed restaurant, which offers a short set menu and a popular á la carte.
15⇌♙(2fb)2♙⇌in 2 bedrooms CTV in all bedrooms ® T ✱ sB&B⇌♙£45 dB&B⇌♙£60 ₽
20P
V ◊ ⌇ ✱ Lunch £3.95-£10.50 Dinner £10.50-£13&alc Last dinner 9.30pm
Credit Cards 1 2 3 5 £

TETBURY Gloucestershire Map 03 ST89

CALCOT MANOR
Calcot GL8 8YJ (4m W at junc A4135/A46)
☎(0666) 890391 FAX (0666) 890394

Brian and Barbara Ball, so long the guiding lights of this excellent hotel, have recently sold up, but new owners have kept son Richard Ball on as manager, a move which is likely to ensure continuity and maintain the standards for which Calcot Manor is known. At first sight these Cotswold stone buildings look more like a farm than an hotel, a tribute to the skill with which these outbuildings were transformed to provide the cottage-style bedrooms. One of the joys of Calcot is that it has remained faithful to good old country house values. In the elegant restaurant, chef Ben Davies has introduced a robust style of cooking influenced by experience in Provence.
7⇌♙Annexe8⇌♙1♙ CTV in all bedrooms T ✈ (ex guide dogs) sB&B⇌♙£75-£100 dB&B⇌♙£87-£135 Continental breakfast ₽
40P 3➤ ⌘ ❋ ⌇ (heated) croquet lawn clay pigeon shooting xmas
♨ English & French ◊ ⌇ Lunch £15-£17alc Dinner £18-£26alc Last dinner 9.30pm
CONF. Thtr 20 Class 25 Board 20 Del £115
Credit Cards 1 2 3 5

★★★ 79% Close
8 Long St GL8 8AQ ☎(0666) 502272 FAX (0666) 504401
The Close is a real retreat in the heart of the town, with a lovely walled garden to the rear. Built 400 years ago as the home of a wealthy wool merchant, it has been carefully restored to provide a charming hotel. As we go to press we have heard that the hotel has new owners.

Tetbury - Tewkesbury

15⇨↑3🛁 CTV in all bedrooms T ✕ (ex guide dogs) ✱
sB&B⇨↑£65-£120 dB&B⇨↑£75-£135 🍴
20P 1🅿 🐕 xmas
V ♿ ⚲ ✕ ✱ Lunch £15-£19 Dinner £19-£24&alc Last dinner 10pm
CONF. Thtr 30 Class 20 Board 22 Del from £135
Credit Cards [1][2][3][5] £

★★★ 64% **Hare & Hounds**
Westonbirt GL8 8QL (2m SW on A433)
☎(0666) 880233 FAX (0666) 880241

This traditional hotel of Cotswold stone is set in its own attractive grounds and gardens. Bedrooms, in the main hotel, converted stables and cottages, vary in size and style but all are well equipped. Public areas include 3 cosy bars, 2 comfortable lounges and a character dining room.
22⇨↑Annexe8⇨↑(3fb)5🛁 CTV in all bedrooms ® T ✱
sB&B⇨↑£55-£65 dB&B⇨↑£75-£85 🍴
80P 2🅿 ✱ 🎾 (hard) squash croquet table tennis xmas
♿ English & French V ♿ ⚲ ✱ Lunch £12.75-£25 Dinner £16.75-£25 Last dinner 9pm
CONF. Thtr 150 Class 75 Board 50 Del from £90
Credit Cards [1][2][3] £

★★★ 62% **Priory Inn**
London Rd GL8 8JJ (on A433) ☎(0666) 502351
FAX (0666) 503534

Carefully modernised and extended, the Priory Inn features a slab-floored, stone-walled bar which attracts a good local following; during the summer months the front patio is also very much in use. Restaurant and bar provide a complete range of meals, and well equipped bedrooms are all similarly furnished in dark wood with fitted wardrobes.
16⇨↑✕in 7 bedrooms CTV in all bedrooms ® ⚲ T
sB&B⇨↑£50 dB&B⇨↑£75 🍴
CTV 44P xmas
V ♿ ⚲ Dinner £14.50&alc Last dinner 10pm
CONF. Thtr 30 Board 30 Del from £75
Credit Cards [1][2][3] £

★★ 64% **Hunters Hall Inn**
Kingscote GL8 8X2 (on A4135) (Logis) ☎Dursley(0453) 860393
FAX (0453) 860707
This friendly old inn on the rural outskirts of Kingscote village has cosy bars and bright modern bedrooms housed separately in converted stables. The intimate restaurant offers a dinner menu of good home-cooked dishes.
Annexe12⇨↑(1fb) CTV in all bedrooms ® T
✕ (ex guide dogs) sB&B⇨↑£44 dB&B⇨↑£58 🍴
120P ✱ xmas
V ♿ ⚲ Lunch £16 Dinner £20&alc Last dinner 9.30pm
CONF. Thtr 40 Class 30 Board 20 Del from £60
Credit Cards [1][2][3][5] £

TEWKESBURY Gloucestershire Map 03 SO83

★★★ ✿ 74% **Puckrup Hall**
Puckrup GL20 6EL (2m N A38) ☎(0684) 296200 FAX (0684) 850788
This fine Regency mansion in 114 acres of grounds has been sympathetically restored and converted into a hotel that meets modern demands while retaining much of the original character. The bedrooms are individually styled and comfortable, and there are nice extras such as fresh fruit and flowers. There is a richly furnished drawing room, a club-style bar and a bright orangery. Cooking by Geoffrey Balharrie continues to receive praise, and his Anglo-French menus, while classically based, display flair and imagination.
84⇨↑(7fb)2🛁✕in 34 bedrooms CTV in all bedrooms ® ⚲ T
sB&B⇨↑£69.50-£95 dB&B⇨↑£79.50-£125 (room only) 🍴

Lift ⚫ 200P 🅿 🐕 ✱ 🖼 (heated) ▸ 18 ⛳ snooker sauna solarium gymnasium croquet putting shooting aerobics xmas
♿ English & French V ♿ ⚲ ✕ Lunch fr£15.25&alc Dinner £8-£25alc Last dinner 10.30pm
Credit Cards [1][2][3][5] £

★★★ 66% **Tewkesbury Park Golf & Country Club**
Lincoln Green Ln GL20 7DN (S on A38)
☎(0684) 295405 FAX (0684) 292386
RS No Sat lunch (Garden Restaurant)

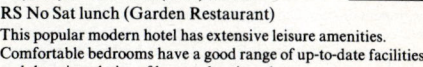

This popular modern hotel has extensive leisure amenities. Comfortable bedrooms have a good range of up-to-date facilities and there is a choice of bars and eating places.
78⇨↑(10fb)✕in 4 bedrooms CTV in all bedrooms ® ⚲ T
✕ (ex guide dogs) ✱ sB&B⇨↑£80-£85 dB&B⇨↑£96-£100 🍴
⚫ 250P ✱ 🖼 (heated) ▸ 18 🎾 (hard) squash snooker sauna solarium gymnasium health & beauty salon putting green xmas
♿ English & French V ♿ ⚲ ✱ Lunch £12&alc High tea £2.50-£3.50 Dinner £19&alc Last dinner 10pm
CONF. Thtr 150 Class 100 Board 25 Del £115
Credit Cards [1][2][3][4][5] £

★★★ 61% **Royal Hop Pole**
Church St GL20 5RT ☎(0684) 293236 FAX (0684) 296580

FORTE Heritage

This former coaching inn in the town centre dates from the 14th century though it was largely rebuilt in Georgian times and retains much historic charm, with sloping floors and exposed beams. Some bedrooms await refurbishment but all have good modern facilities and there is a comfortable lounge, popular bar and restaurant.
24⇨↑Annexe5⇨↑(1fb)1🛁✕in 14 bedrooms CTV in all bedrooms ® T sB⇨↑fr£75 dB⇨↑fr£93 (room only) 🍴
⚫ 50P ✱ xmas

TENBY

THE ALBANY HOTEL

Tel: (0834) 842698

Ashley Courtenay highly recommended

Small and very friendly 'home from home'.
Wonderful chef, romantic restaurant.
Comfortable en-suite rooms.
Beautiful Pembrokeshire.

LATE BOOKING BARGAIN BREAKS

Available throughout the year
Full details from:–

**Claire Summers (Resident Director)
Albany Hotel, Norton, Tenby,
Dyfed SA70 8AB**

Tewkesbury - Thaxted

V ❀ ⚘ ✱ Lunch fr£8.95&alc Dinner fr£16.95&alc Last dinner 9.30pm
Credit Cards ①②③⑤

★★★ 60% **Bell**
Church St GL20 5SA (on A38 opposite Abbey)
☎(0684) 293293 FAX (0684) 295318
RS 27 Dec-5 Jan

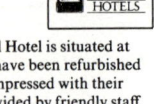

A half timbered former coaching inn, the Bell Hotel is situated at the heart of the town. Most of the bedrooms have been refurbished by the present owners. Our inspectors were impressed with their hospitable approach, with caring service provided by friendly staff and management. Public rooms include a convivial bar, a spacious restaurant with a lounge area and a terrace area for popular bar snacks.
25⇨(1fb)3⌹ CTV in all bedrooms ® T ✱ sB&B⇨£58-£68 dB&B⇨£75-£90 ₧
(55P xmas
♀ English & French V ❀ ⚘ ✻ ✱ Lunch £9.95-£15 Dinner £15.95-£20.95 Last dinner 9.30pm
CONF. Thtr 50 Class 20 Board 20 Del from £80
Credit Cards ①②③⑤ £

★★ 64% **Tudor House**
High St GL20 5BH ☎(0684) 297755 FAX (0684) 290306

This former inn, founded by the Pilgrim Fathers in 1540, now offers comfortable bedrooms equipped for the modern traveller. The new wing of bedrooms at the rear overlooks the river. Other improvements include the introduction of a Brasserie bistro for informal good value dining. Service is provided by a smart and friendly brigade, and room service is also available.
21⇨(2fb)1⌹ CTV in all bedrooms ® T sB&B⇨£fr£45 dB&B⇨£fr£60 ₧
30P ❋
♀ English & French V ❀ ⚘ Lunch £1.50-£6.50&alc Dinner £1.50-£6.50 Last dinner 10.15pm
CONF. Thtr 40 Class 30 Board 16 Del £60
Credit Cards ①②③④⑤ £

THAKEHAM (NEAR STORRINGTON) West Sussex Map 04 TQ11

★★★ ❀❀ ❀ 74% **Abingworth Hall**
Storrington Rd RH20 3EF (2m N of Storrington on B2139)
☎West Chiltington(0798) 813636 FAX (0798) 813914

There has been a house on this site for over 700 years, though the present house dates from 1914. The accommodation has been completely refurbished to provide every comfort, with individually furnished bedrooms. There is an oak panelled library in addition to the main drawing room which extends into the conservatory overlooking the lake. The restaurant, though rather lacking in atmosphere, is a major part of the hotel's success. Recent recommendations from chef Peter Cannon's carte and fixed price menus include smooth duck paté with excellent Cumberland sauce and hot brioche; and shredded tarragon and sorrel under roast best end of lamb with a garlic and herb crust.
20⇨ CTV in all bedrooms T ✱ sB&B⇨£70 dB&B⇨£80 ₧
50P ❋ ❀ ♫ (hard) ♪ croquet lawn nc10yrs xmas
♀ English & French V ❀ ✱ Lunch fr£12.50 Dinner fr£19.50&alc Last dinner 9pm
CONF. Thtr 50 Class 20 Board 25 Del from £100
Credit Cards ①③④ £

For full, independent restaurant reviews, see the
AA Abbey Well *Restaurant Guide*.

THAME Oxfordshire Map 04 SP70

★★★ ❀ 72% **Spread Eagle**
Cornmarket OX9 2BW (on A418) ☎(0844) 213661 FAX (0844) 261380
Closed 28-30 Dec
The classic Georgian façade of the Spread Eagle fronts Thame High Street. Bedrooms range from those in the Tudor wing to the Georgian rooms, and the recently constructed Brideshead Wing. All rooms are restfully coordinated and comfortable. Fothergills Restaurant offers a selection of fixed price menus, offering such dishes as crab tart and lobster sauce and fillet of lamb with a herb and garlic crust on a sweet redcurrant sauce.
33⇨(1fb)⌹ CTV in all bedrooms T ✈ (ex guide dogs) ✱ sB&B⇨£67.50-£77.50 dB&B⇨£73.50-£88.50 Continental breakfast ₧
(80P xmas
♀ English & French V ❀ ✱ Lunch £16.75-£17.75&alc Dinner £18.30-£18.95&alc Last dinner 9pm
CONF. Thtr 250 Class 100 Board 50 Del from £100
Credit Cards ①②③⑤ £

THATCHAM Berkshire Map 04 SU56

★★★★ ❀ 63% **Regency Park**
Bowling Green Rd RG13 3RP ☎(0635) 871555 FAX (0635) 871571

This turn of the century house with modern extensions stands in its own grounds on the northerly outskirts of Thatcham. Bedrooms have attractive limed oak furniture; public areas are rather limited in space, but do include a business centre and Terraces Restaurant. Here, chef Michael Carney offers dishes of some richness and complexity.
50⇨(12fb) CTV in all bedrooms ®⚘ T ✱ sB&B⇨£75-£80 dB&B⇨£85-£90 (room only) ₧
Lift (120P ❋ ❀ ♫ xmas
♀ English & Continental V ❀ ⚘ ✻ ✱ Lunch £10.95-£13.95&alc High tea fr£5.95 Dinner £18.50-£19.95&alc Last dinner 10.30pm
CONF. Thtr 70 Class 40 Board 30 Del from £100
Credit Cards ①②③⑤ £

See advertisement under NEWBURY

THAXTED Essex Map 05 TL63

★★ 64% **Four Seasons**
Walden Rd CM6 2RE (0.5m N of Thaxted on the B184 at the junction with the B1051 Gt Sampford/Haverhill road)
☎(0371) 830129 FAX (0371) 830835
Set in 2 acres of grounds on the outskirts of the town, this modernised old inn has a friendly relaxing atmosphere. Simply furnished bedrooms are equipped with modern amenities and there is a traditional bar serving bar meals as well as a cosy restaurant (no smoking) with a short carte, plus a small lounge upstairs.
9rm(8⇨)✈in all bedrooms CTV in all bedrooms ® T ✈ ✱ sB&B⇨£50-£55 dB&B⇨£65-£70 ₧
CTV 100P ❀ ❋ nc12yrs
♀ English & French V ❀ ✻ ✱ Lunch £15.50-£23alc Dinner £15.50-£23alc Last dinner 9.30pm
Credit Cards ①②③

★★ 61% **The Swan**
Bullring, Watling St CM6 2PL ☎(0371) 830321 FAX (0371) 831186
This popular village inn opposite the parish church has a beamed bar serving real ales and hearty snacks, and a cosy restaurant for more formal eating. Bedrooms, in the main building or more peaceful rear annexe, are all well equipped, with quality pine furnishings and floral fabrics.
13⇨ Annexe7⇨(2fb) CTV in all bedrooms ® T ✱ sB&B⇨£25-£65 dB&B⇨£50-£80 ₧

(24P ♪ *xmas*
V ♿ ⚲ ✱ Lunch £9.95 Dinner £9.95-£16.95 Last dinner 10pm
CONF. Thtr 50 Class 30 Board 20 Del from £65
Credit Cards [1] [2] [3]

THETFORD Norfolk Map 05 TL88

See also **Brandon (Suffolk)**
★★ 62% **The Bell**
King St IP24 2AZ (off A134) ☏(0842) 754335
FAX (0842) 755552

FORTE Heritage

Tucked away in the town centre on the banks of the River Ouse, the Bell retains much of its 15th-century character. Uniformed staff provide polite service throughout the public rooms, which include a choice of bars and a traditional quiet lounge. The accommodation is gradually being refurbished with comfortable armchairs and rich coordinated décor and soft furnishings.
47⇨⇧(1fb)1⌧⌦in 11 bedrooms CTV in all bedrooms ® T ✱
sB&B⇨⇧£70 dB&B⇨⇧£85-£105 (room only) 🍴
(82P *xmas*
V ♿ ⚲ ✱ Lunch £6.95-£10.95&alc Dinner £15.95&alc Last dinner 9.45pm
CONF. Thtr 50 Class 40 Board 50 Del £85
Credit Cards [1] [2] [3] [5]

★★ 65% **Historical Thomas Paine**
White Hart St IP24 1AA ☏(0842) 755631 FAX (0842) 766505

BEST WESTERN HOTELS

Named after the great campaigning writer and local boy, this small hotel is run by a friendly couple and their helpful staff. Bedrooms vary in size and provide the comforts required by business and leisure guests alike. There is a large bar, popular at lunchtime, and a cosy restaurant where simple, well prepared dishes are served.

13⇨⇧(1fb)1⌧ CTV in all bedrooms ® T ✱
sB&B⇨⇧£46.50-£50 dB&B⇨⇧£58-£62 🍴
30P
V ♿ ⚲ ✱ Lunch £9.50-£14.50&alc High tea £5-£6 Dinner £14.50-£15.50&alc Last dinner 9.30pm
Credit Cards [1] [2] [3] [5]

★ 67% **Wereham House**
24 White Hart St IP24 1AD ☏(0842) 761956

Within close walking distance of the centre of town, this family-run hotel provides a hospitable welcome and well modernised bedrooms. A cosy bar and large restaurant round off the amenities nicely.
8⇧(1fb) CTV in all bedrooms ® T ✈ (ex guide dogs)
sB&B⇧£30-£39.50 dB&B⇧£40-£47 🍴
25P ♣ ✱
V ♿ ⚲ ✱ Sunday Lunch £8.95 Dinner £9.50&alc Last dinner 9.30pm
Credit Cards [1] [3]

THIRSK North Yorkshire Map 08 SE48

★★ 73% **Sheppard's**
Church Farm, Front St, Sowerby YO7 1JF (take A61 Ripon road from Market Sq, at mini roundabout turn left towards Sowerby, hotel on right .25m along Sowerby road) ☏(0845) 523655 FAX (0845) 524720

ExecGroup

Much of this charming hotel has been converted from stables and the granary of a former farm, and the rustic theme prevails in the flagstone floors, beams, hay mangers, horse brasses and tack, particularly in the Bistro and Sheppard's Table Restaurant. Food is very much a feature, helpings are huge and both the cooking and

Come & be spoilt ....by us!

AA ★★★ 72%

HOSPITALITY IS OUR SPECIALITY

The Spread Eagle Hotel

THAME   OXFORDSHIRE   OX9   2BW

TELEPHONE *(0844)* 213661

Thirsk - Thornthwaite

presentation are of a high standard. Bedrooms are mostly furnished in antique pine.
8⇌ⓝ(1fb)1⌸⁄in 2 bedrooms CTV in all bedrooms ® T ✘ ✱ sB&B⇌ⓝ£50-£55 dB&B⇌ⓝ£64-£84 ₪
30P nc10yrs
♥ International V ❀ ✱ Lunch £10.75-£17.75alc Dinner £18.75-£27.75alc Last dinner 10pm
Credit Cards [1] [3]

★★61% **Three Tuns Hotel**
Market Place YO7 1LH ☎(0845) 523124 FAX (0845) 526126
Originally a Georgian dower house, and later a coaching inn on the Leeds/Edinburgh run, this hotel stands in the town's cobbled square. Most of the bright, cheerful bedrooms have been upgraded recently, the cocktail bar adjoining the foyer has also been attractively redecorated, and there is a comfortable and relaxing lounge. Bar meals are served, and the first-floor restaurant is more formal.
11⇌ⓝ(3fb)1⌸ CTV in 10 bedrooms ® T sB&B⇌ⓝ£30-£38 dB&B⇌ⓝ£45-£65 ₪
50P 2🛎 xmas
V ❀ ⚏ ⁄ Lunch fr£8.50&alc
Credit Cards [1] [2] [3] [5]

★56% **Old Red House**
Station Rd YO7 4LT (1m W) ☎(0845) 524383 FAX (0845) 525902
The Old Red House is a family-run pub, its bar recently redecorated, about a mile west of the town, opposite the railway station. Some bedrooms are in a bungalow-style annexe, including one for disabled guests; other more traditional rooms are above the pub.
6⇌ⓝAnnexe6⇌ⓝ(5fb)1⌸⁄in 1 bedroom CTV in all bedrooms ® T ✱ sB&B⇌ⓝ£18-£25 dB&B⇌ⓝ£30-£32 ₪
30P xmas
V ❀ ⚏ ✱ Lunch £6-£12&alc Dinner £6-£12&alc Last dinner 9.30pm
CONF. Del from £37
Credit Cards [1] [3] [5]

THORNBURY Avon Map 03 ST69

THORNBURY CASTLE
BS12 1HH ☎(0454) 281182
FAX (0454) 416188
Closed 2 days Jan

One of the oldest authentic castles left in Britain, with a Tudor walled garden and vineyard, this unique building has been lovingly restored by the present owner, Maurice Taylor. Public areas are baronial in style with panelled walls, heraldic shields, tapestries, suits of armour and beautiful antique furniture. The main apartments provide bed chambers furnished in Tudor style, but with every modern convenience, and some have fine oriel windows. Head chef Peter Brazill has compiled an interesting menu suitably supported by an extensive wine list. Our inspector chose a plait of Dover sole (a little chewy but tasty) accompanied by a cream-based sauce flavoured with lobster and brandy. This was followed by rack of lamb, which could have been more pink, topped with a crumb of mint and almond served with a Madeira sauce. A delicious butterscotch pudding completed the meal, served with butterscotch sauce and fresh vanilla custard.

18⇌ⓝ8⌸ CTV in all bedrooms T ✘ ✱ sB&B⇌ⓝ£75-£85 dB&B⇌ⓝ£95-£200 Continental breakfast ₪
(40P ⇔ ✱ croquet hot air ballooning archery nc12yrs xmas
♥ English & French V ⚏ ✁ ✱ Lunch £17.75 Dinner £31 Last dinner 9.30pm
CONF. Thtr 14 Board 24
Credit Cards [1] [2] [3] [5]
See advertisement under BRISTOL

THORNE South Yorkshire Map 08 SE61

★★68% **Belmont**
Horsefair Green DN8 5EE (Logis) ☎(0405) 812320 FAX (0405) 740598
This extended Victorian building in the town centre has been attractively refurbished and offers comfortable bedrooms with modern facilities and open-plan public areas which include a popular restaurant and 3 bars.
23⇌ⓝ(3fb)1⌸ CTV in all bedrooms ® T sB&B⇌ⓝ£46.95-£54.50 dB&B⇌ⓝ£60-£80 ₪
(30P ♫ xmas
♥ English & French V ❀ ⚏ Lunch £6.95-£11.95&alc Dinner £9.95-£11.95&alc Last dinner 9.30pm
CONF. Thtr 60 Class 35 Board 25 Del from £61.50
Credit Cards [1] [2] [3] [5]

THORNHILL Dumfries & Galloway Dumfriesshire Map 11 NX89

★★72% **Trigony House**
Closeburn DG3 5EZ (2m S off A76)
☎(0848) 31211

Once a hunting lodge, this hotel has been tastefully refurbished by the family who own and run it. Though bedrooms vary in size and shape all are charmingly decorated, while the pleasant public areas include an inviting comfortable small lounge, a cosy bar and a neat dining room where guests can enjoy home-cooked meals based on local produce. Service is informal but attentive.
9⇌ⓝ CTV in all bedrooms ® T ✘ (ex guide dogs) sB&B⇌ⓝ£33.50-£40.50 dB&B⇌ⓝ£57-£64 ₪
30P ⇔ ✱ nc10yrs
V Bar Lunch £7-£11.50alc Dinner £16-£18.50 Last dinner 8.30pm
Credit Cards [1] [3]

THORNLEY Durham Map 08 NZ33

★★63% **Crossways**
Dunelm Rd DH6 3HT (5m SE of Durham City, on A181)
☎(0429) 821248 FAX (0429) 820034
This is a well furnished, mainly commercial hotel. Bedrooms are modern and equipped with items such as hairdryers and trouser presses. There is also an extensive range of food served either in the bar or the cosy restaurant.
23⇌ⓝ(9fb)1⌸ CTV in all bedrooms ®⚏ T
CTV 150P ✱ sauna solarium fitness room
♥ English & French V ❀ ⚏ ⁄ Last dinner 9.45pm
Credit Cards [1] [2] [3] [5]

THORNTHWAITE Cumbria Map 11 NY22

★★⁂69% **Thwaite Howe**
CA12 5SA (signposted from centre of village)
☎Braithwaite(07687) 78281
Closed Nov-Feb

An attractive country house, standing in 2.5 acres of grounds in an elevated position with fine Lakeland views, Thwaite Howe is a

Thornthwaite - Three Cocks

friendly and well run hotel offering good all round comforts and service. Bedrooms meet all modern needs, and well prepared home cooking is served in the cosy dining room. Public rooms are non smoking.
8rm CTV in all bedrooms ® T dB&B £70-£78 (incl dinner)
12P ⇌ ❀ nc12yrs
♀ English & French ✂ ✲ Dinner £12.50-£15 Last dinner 7pm

★★ 60% Ladstock Country House
CA12 5RZ ☎Braithwaite(07687) 78210 & 78349
Closed Jan
Ladstock is a fine rambling old oak-panelled house on a hillside overlooking Bassenthwaite and Skiddaw with the welcoming Sandham family as hosts. The hotel has ample lounges and individually furnished bedrooms. Mainly English cooking served in a restaurant with fine views adds to the picture of this peaceful hotel.
22rm(11⇌7↑)(2fb)3☐ CTV in all bedrooms ® T
✈ (ex guide dogs)
CTV 50P ❀
V ♿ ♄ Last dinner 8.30pm
Credit Cards [1][3]

★★ 60% Swan
CA12 5SQ (turn off A66 at Braithwaite following signs for Thornthwaite village, hotel just beyond village on the right)
☎Braithwaite(07687) 78256
Closed Dec-Mar
With a bright restaurant that overlooks the valley and fells beyond, this former coaching inn is in a quiet, by-passed village. Owned and run by the same family for almost 30 years, it has warm and modern bedrooms, spacious lounges and home produced dinners.
13rm(3⇌6↑) CTV in all bedrooms ✲ sB&B£23.70-£27.25 dB&B£47.40-£54.50 dB&B⇌↑£56.50-£64 (incl dinner) 🅿
CTV 60P 3🅿 (£1.75) ⇌ ❀
♀ English & Continental V ♿ ♄ ✂ Bar Lunch £1.50-£8.75alc Dinner £17.50 Last dinner 8.30pm
Credit Cards [1][2][3]   £

THORNTON HOUGH Merseyside Map 07 SJ38

★★★ 67% Thornton Hall
Neston Rd L63 1JF (access with B5136) ☎051-336 3938 FAX 051-336 7864
Set in 7 acres of grounds, this comfortable privately owned hotel was the former country residence of a major shipping family and public areas retain magnificent wood carving and panelling. Spacious bedrooms equipped to a high standard are mainly located in a separate, modern wing, with executive rooms including jacuzzis in the main house.
5⇌↑Annexe58⇌↑1☐ CTV in all bedrooms ® ✂ T
✈ (ex guide dogs)
(250P ❀
♀ English, French & Italian V ♿ ♄ Last dinner 9.30pm
CONF. Thtr 250 Class 200 Board 100 Del £84
Credit Cards [1][2][3][4][5]   £

THORNTON WATLASS North Yorkshire Map 08 SE28

★ 66% Buck Inn
HG4 4AH (opposite cricket green) ☎Bedale(0677) 422461
This charming and hospitable country inn is on the edge of the green in a picturesque village, overlooking the cricket pitch. Home cooking is very much a feature, both in the cosy bar and dining room. Bedrooms are attractive, all with exceptionally good facilities. There is a small guests' lounge with TV and a garden at the rear with play equipment for children.
6rm(5⇌↑)(1fb) ♁ sB&B⇌↑£27-£30 dB&B⇌↑£45-£55 🅿
CTV 10P ❀ ♪ quoits pool table childrens play area ♫

V ♿ ♄ Sunday Lunch fr£8 Dinner £10-£15alc Last dinner 9.30pm
Credit Cards [1][2][3]

THORPE (DOVEDALE) Derbyshire Map 07 SK15

★★★ 67% Peveril of the Peak
DE6 2AW ☎Thorpe Cloud(033529) 333 FAX (033529) 507

FORTE Heritage

Popular for its superb location at the foot of Thorpe Cloud in lovely Peak District countryside, this hotel has a cosy bar and a light, freshly decorated restaurant; all are well served by the polite and cheerful staff. The majority of the comfortable bedrooms have been refurbished and most have views over the 11 acres of grounds and gardens.
47⇌↑(11fb)✂ in 20 bedrooms CTV in all bedrooms ® T ✲
sB&B⇌↑£70-£75 dB&B⇌↑£85-£100 (room only) 🅿
(60P ❀ ♄ (hard) xmas
V ♿ ♄ ✂ ✲ Lunch fr£11.95 Dinner fr£16.95&alc Last dinner 9pm
Credit Cards [1][2][3][5]

★★★ 61% Izaak Walton
DE6 2AY (1m W on Ilam rd) ☎Thorpe Cloud(033529) 555 FAX (033529) 539
This much extended former farmhouse, dating from the 17th century, has impressive views of Dovedale and Thorpe Cloud. The bright restaurant and adjoining lounge have quality fabrics and panoramic views of the surrounding countryside. The bar has a pleasant mixture of easy chairs, with prints and paintings, brasses and flower arrangements. Bedrooms offer a range of modern facilities and most have good views.
34⇌↑(2fb)3☐ CTV in all bedrooms ® T ✲
sB&B⇌↑£77.50 dB&B⇌↑£99-£120 🅿
(80P ❀ ♪ xmas
♀ English & French V ♿ ♄ ✂ Sunday Lunch fr£14.25 Dinner fr£12&alc Last dinner 9pm
CONF. Thtr 100 Class 40 Board 30 Del from £95
Credit Cards [1][2][3][5]   £

THRAPSTON Northamptonshire Map 04 SP97

Forte Travelodge
Thrapston Bypass(on A14 link road A1/M1)
☎(0801) 25199 Central Res (0800) 850950

FORTE Travelodge

This modern building offers a good standard of accommodation for overnight stops. Smart, spacious and well equipped bedrooms, all with en suite bathrooms, are suitable for family use, and meals may be taken at the nearby family restaurant. For more details about Travelodges, consult the Contents page, under Hotel Groups.
40⇌↑✲ B⇌↑£31.95 (room only)

THREE COCKS Powys Map 03 SO13

★★ ❀❀ 72% Three Cocks
LD3 0SL (on A438, between Brecon & Hereford, next to BP petrol station) (Logis) ☎Glasbury(0497) 847215
Closed Dec & Jan RS Sun lunch & Tue
This small, ivy-clad hotel is in the Brecon Beacons National Park, and parts of it date back to the 15th century. The heavy stone walled and beamed interior is spotlessly bright and clean, and there is a welcoming ambience created by owners Marie-Jeanne and Michael Winstone. The bedrooms are warm and richly furnished in heavy dark oak. There is a choice of comfortable lounges, and the style of food is modern.
7rm(5⇌1↑)(2fb) ✈ ✲ sB&B⇌↑£35-£60 dB&Bfr£60 dB&B⇌↑£60 🅿

Three Cocks - Tintern

CTV 40P 🚗 ✤
♿ Continental V ❀ ✱ Lunch £24 Dinner £24
Last dinner 9pm
Credit Cards [1][3]   £

THRUSSINGTON Leicestershire Map 08 SK61

Forte Travelodge
Green Acres Filling Station LE7 8TE (on A46, southbound) ☎Rearsby(0664) 424525
Central Res (0800) 850950

FORTE Travelodge

This modern building offers a good standard of accommodation for overnight stops. Smart, spacious and well equipped bedrooms, all with en suite bathrooms, are suitable for family use, and meals may be taken at the nearby family restaurant. For more details about Travelodges, consult the Contents page, under Hotel Groups.

32⇨♠✱ B⇨♠£31.95 (room only)

THURLESTONE Devon Map 03 SX64

★★★★**65%** Thurlestone
TQ7 3NN (signposted off A379) ☎Kingsbridge(0548) 560382 FAX (0548) 561069

In a fine location overlooking the gardens and the coast, this long-established hotel offers superb leisure facilities. Public rooms are smart and comfortable while the bedrooms vary in size, the best being designated 'de luxe'. The experience of our inspector on his most recent visit suggested that cooking was not in the same class as the rest of the hotel, though there was a good wine list and staff were friendly and attentive.

68⇨♠(16fb) CTV in all bedrooms T ✱ sB&B⇨♠£53-£81 dB&B⇨♠£106-£162 ♨
Lift ℂ 100P 19🚗 🚗 ✤ 🖼 (heated) ⇨ (heated) ▶ 9 ♪ (hard) squash snooker sauna solarium gymnasium games room badminton spa bath 🌿 xmas
♿ English V ❀ ♨ ⛾ ✱ Lunch £12-£14.85alc High tea £6.50 Dinner £15-£29.50 Last dinner 9pm
CONF. Thtr 120 Class 90 Board 38 Del from £85
Credit Cards [1][3]

THURSO Highland *Caithness* Map 15 ND16

★★**62%** Pentland
Princes St KW14 7AA ☎(0847) 63202 FAX (0847) 62761

This family-run, town centre commercial hotel also caters for tourists. The bar, restaurant and coffee lounge are furnished in modern style, while the first floor lounges provide more traditional comforts.

53rm(28⇨11♠)(4fb) CTV in all bedrooms T sB&Bfr£20 sB&B⇨♠fr£25 dB&Bfr£40 dB&B⇨♠fr£50
ℂ ✎
V ❀ ♨ Lunch fr£6.10alc High tea fr£5.85alc Dinner fr£11alc Last dinner 8.30pm
Credit Cards [1][3]

TICEHURST East Sussex Map 05 TQ63

★★★★✤✤**70%** Dale Hill Hotel & Golf Club
TN5 7DQ ☎(0580) 200112 FAX (0580) 201249

This attractive modern hotel sits alongside the golf course in a peaceful setting. The bedrooms are large and impressive, and there is a comfortable open plan bar lounge on the ground floor and a restaurant upstairs. At the time of going to press, a new chef was about to be appointed.

25⇨♠(6fb) CTV in all bedrooms ⛾ T sB&B⇨♠fr£70 dB&B⇨♠£114-£132 ♨
Lift ℂ 220P 🚗 ✤ 🖼 (heated) ▶ 18 snooker sauna solarium gymnasium xmas
♿ English & French V ❀ ♨ ⛾ ✂ Lunch £14.95-£18.50&alc Dinner fr£21.95&alc Last dinner 10pm
CONF. Thtr 32 Class 22 Board 28 Del from £100
Credit Cards [1][2][3][5]   £

TINTAGEL Cornwall & Isles of Scilly Map 02 SX08

★★★**71%** The Wootons Country Hotel
Fore St PL34 0DD ☎Camelford(0840) 770170 FAX (0840) 770978

This town centre hotel, close to the sea and surrounded by open country, has been rebuilt and renovated to a high standard. Attractive, comfortable bedrooms with modern facilities have thoughtful extras and the spacious, modern public areas include all-day bars offering a range of dishes and a small restaurant serving evening meals.

11⇨♠1♨ CTV in all bedrooms ® T 🐾 (ex guide dogs) sB&B⇨♠fr£25 dB&B⇨♠fr£50 ♨
CTV 35P snooker xmas
V ❀ ♨ Lunch fr£7.50 High tea fr£1.95 Dinner fr£9&alc Last dinner 9.30pm
Credit Cards [1]   £

★★**62%** Bossiney House
PL34 0AX (from A39 take B3266 into Tintagel, then Boscastle road for 0.75m to hotel on left) ☎Camelford(0840) 770240 FAX (0840) 770501

Closed Jan-Mar RS Nov-Dec

Although the bedrooms at Bossiney House lack telephones and colour TVs, the latter can be hired, and several bedrooms have recently been upgraded with good quality furnishings. Public rooms comprise a cosy lounge (with TV) and a modern dining room. The hotel stands in 2.5 acres.

17⇨♠Annexe1⇨(1fb) ® ✱ sB&B⇨♠£33-£37 dB&B⇨♠£60-£64 ♨
CTV 30P ✤ 🖼 (heated) sauna solarium gymnasium putting green
♿ English, French & Portuguese V ❀ ♨ ✱ Bar Lunch £3-£5 Dinner £12-£14 Last dinner 8pm
Credit Cards [1][2][3][5]   £

★★**55%** Atlantic View
Treknow PL34 0EJ ☎Camelford(0840) 770221

Closed 23 Dec-2 Jan

Quietly located with sea and rural coastal views, the hotel comprises a comfortable lounge, small bar, dining room and additional sun lounge. A daily menu is provided and freshly prepared dishes are usually ordered in advance after breakfast. Service is friendly and mostly provided by the proprietor Mrs Beverley Taylor and her family.

9⇨♠(2fb)4♨ CTV in all bedrooms ®⛾ ✱ sB&B⇨♠£17.50-£24 dB&B⇨♠£35-£48 ♨
CTV 20P 🚗 ✤ 🖼 (heated) solarium pool table nc2yrs
♿ European V ❀ ♨ ⛾ ✱ Lunch £5-£7.50 Dinner £10-£14 Last dinner 9pm
Credit Cards [1][3]   £

TINTERN Gwent Map 03 SO50

★★**64%** Parva Farmhouse Hotel & Restaurant
NP6 6SQ (N of village, on A466) (Logis) ☎(0291) 689411 & 689511 FAX (0291) 689757

This cosy 17th-century Wye Valley farmhouse has been converted into an appealing small modern hotel, a personal atmosphere being promoted by its welcoming owners Mr and Mrs Stubbs. Bedrooms are well equipped, and there is a comfortable lounge complete with honesty bar. Enjoyable home cooking is prepared using local produce.

9rm(7⇨♠)(3fb)2♨ CTV in all bedrooms ® T sB&B£32-£39 sB&B⇨♠£39 dB&B£48 dB&B⇨♠£58-£68 ♨
10P
♿ European V Dinner £16.50&alc Last dinner 8.30pm
Credit Cards [1][3]   £

Hotels with red star ratings are especially high quality.

Tintern - Todmorden

★★ **64%** **Royal George**
NP6 6SF (on A466) ☎(0291) 689205 FAX (0291) 689448

In an attractive setting close to the abbey, this hospitable 17th-century hotel has cosy public rooms of some character, with a choice of bars, conservatory lounge and spacious restaurant. Most bedrooms in annexes are set around the gardens and are spacious and well equipped, some with balconies.
5rm(2⇨↑)Annexe14⇨↑(15fb)1📺 CTV in all bedrooms ® T sB&B⇨↑£50 dB&B⇨↑£71.50 🍴
50P ✿ xmas
♨ English & French V ♥ ♨ ✂ Lunch £8.95-£11.95 High tea £5 Dinner £16.95 Last dinner 9.30pm
CONF. Thtr 100 Class 50 Board 30 Del £65
Credit Cards [1][2][3][5] £

TITCHWELL Norfolk Map **09** TF74

★★ ❀**70%** **Titchwell Manor**
PE31 8BB (on A149) ☎Brancaster(0485) 210221 FAX (0485) 210104

This delightful family-run hotel is in an unspoilt location overlooking salt marshes and sea. It has comfortable and attractive guest rooms which are sensibly planned and practical, but the hotel's main asset is the relaxing, friendly atmosphere created by Margaret and Ian Snaith and their team. The garden restaurant is an attractive setting for the menu which makes good use of local fish, and some unusual soups; bar meals are also available.
11rm(7⇨↑)Annexe4⇨↑(2fb) CTV in all bedrooms ® T sB&B£35-£49 sB&B⇨↑£35-£49 dB&B£70-£78 dB&B⇨↑£70-£78 🍴
50P 🚗 ✿ xmas
♨ European V ♥ ♨ Lunch £10-£20 High tea £3-£10 Dinner £17.50&alc Last dinner 9.30pm
Credit Cards [1][2][3][5] £

TIVERTON Devon Map **03** SS91

★★★**61%** **Tiverton**
Blundells Rd EX16 4DB ☎(0884) 256120 FAX (0884) 258101
This modern, purpose built hotel close to the town centre has an open-plan lounge bar, restaurant and reception area. Spacious bedrooms in the newer extensions are bright and modern in style, those in the original building are simpler.
75⇨↑(75fb) CTV in all bedrooms ® T sB&B⇨↑£33-£51 dB&B⇨↑£66-£78 🍴
(130P ✿ xmas
♨ English, French & Italian V ♥ ♨ ✂ ✱ Lunch £7.50-£8.50&alc Dinner £10.50&alc Last dinner 9.15pm
CONF. Thtr 250 Class 120 Board 60 Del from £362
Credit Cards [1][2][3][5]

★★**58%** **Hartnoll**
Bolham EX16 7RA (1.5m N on A396) ☎(0884) 252777 FAX (0884) 259195
This attractive property is set in its own well kept gardens running down to a stream. The bedrooms are brightly decorated and some are in a cottage annexe across the car park. Public areas include an airy conservatory lounge with access to the garden and a spacious bar lounge. A range of menus is on offer in the intimate dining room.
11⇨↑Annexe5↑(3fb)1📺 CTV in all bedrooms ® T ✱ sB&B⇨↑£35 dB&B⇨↑£50 🍴
100P ✿ 🎱
♨ English & Continental V ♥ ♨ ✱ Lunch £5.65-£12&alc Dinner £10-£12&alc Last dinner 9.15pm
CONF. Thtr 150 Class 80 Board 30 Del from £50
Credit Cards [1][3] £

TOBERMORY
See **Mull, Isle of**

TODDINGTON MOTORWAY SERVICE AREA (M1)
Bedfordshire Map **04** TL02

Granada Lodge
M1 Motorway LU5 6HR (between junct 11 & 12)
☎(05255) 5150 FAX (05255) 5945

This modern building provides smart, spacious and well equipped bedrooms, all with en suite bathrooms. Meals may be taken at a nearby family restaurant. For more details about Granada Lodges, consult the Contents page, under Hotel Groups.
43⇨❋ B⇨£34.95-£37.95 (room only)

TODMORDEN Lancashire Map **07** SD92

★★★ **64%** *Scaitcliffe Hall*
Burnley Rd OL14 7DQ ☎(0706) 818888 FAX (0706) 818825
This beautifully restored house stands in manicured grounds on the Burnley road. The conference and function facilities in the adjacent coach house, and the pizza pub do not detract from the peaceful country house style hotel.
13⇨↑(2fb)1📺 CTV in all bedrooms ® ⚲ T
(200P ✿ 🎱
V ♥ ♨ Last dinner 10pm
Credit Cards [1][2][3][5]

Rosettes range from 5 for outstanding
cuisine to 1 rosette for enjoyable,
well prepared food

THE ULTIMATE VENUE...

Scaitcliffe Hall

COUNTRY HOUSE HOTEL

Located on the outskirts of Todmorden off the main Burnley Road within easy access of Rochdale, Burnley and Halifax. Ideal for exploring the Dales, Lake District and Bronte Country. The main hall was built in 1666 and nestles in 16½ acres of beautiful gardens and woodlands, offering unrivalled views of the Pennine landscape with the tranquillity one expects of a country hall hotel. Traditional English bedrooms. The best classical and innovative cuisine. Extensive wine cellar. The Croslegh Banqueting and Conference Centre. This idyllic setting together with our many years of experience, will ensure a successful and memorable occasion.

Burnley Road, Todmorden, Lancs OL14 7DQ
Tel: 0706 818888 Fax: 0706 818825

605

Todwick - Torpoint

TODWICK South Yorkshire Map 08 SK48

★★★ 68% Red Lion
Worksop Rd S31 0DJ (on A57) (Whitbread)
☎Worksop(0909) 771654 FAX (0909) 773704
Located a mile east of junction 31 of the M1 on the A57, this former coaching inn provides attractive modern accommodation in well furnished bedrooms. Comfortable public rooms include an attractive restaurant, cocktail and public bar, plus a range of conference and meeting rooms.
29⇨ℕ(1fb)1🛏in 9 bedrooms CTV in all bedrooms ®⚲T ✕ (ex guide dogs) ✱ sB&B⇨ℕfr£65.50 dB&B⇨ℕfr£77 ₧
(90P xmas
♀ English & French V ♂ ♀ ✱ Lunch fr£8.95&alc Dinner fr£12.50&alc Last dinner 9.45pm
CONF. Thtr 80 Class 30 Board 24 Del from £89
Credit Cards 1 2 3 5

TONBRIDGE Kent Map 05 TQ54

★★★ 61% The Rose & Crown
High St TN9 1DD ☎(0732) 357966 FAX (0732)357194

FORTE Heritage

This old coaching inn, parts of which date back to the 15th century, has been sympathetically extended to provide a new wing of comfortable bedrooms with coordinated furnishings. Original rooms, though retaining much of their historic character, are also equipped with modern furniture and amenities. The restaurant offers interesting menus which include at least one local dish.
50rm(49⇨ℕ)(2fb)1🛏in 20 bedrooms CTV in all bedrooms ®T ✱ sB⇨ℕ£55-£65 dBfr£70 dB⇨ℕ£65-£75 (room only) ₧
(62P xmas
V ♂ ♀ ✱ Sunday Lunch fr£10.95 Dinner fr£15.95&alc Last dinner 9pm
Credit Cards 1 2 3 5

⇧Chimneys Motor Inn
Pembury Rd TN11 0NA (S off A21) ☎(0732) 773111 FAX (0732) 771534
This new lodge, with a first floor lounge area, offers a range of smart bedrooms at a very competitive price, and the equipment provided includes satellite TV. All meals are taken in the adjacent Chimneys restaurant and bar, which specialises in steaks and grills, though more informal meals can be enjoyed in the bar.
39⇨ℕ(5fb)✕in 10 bedrooms CTV in all bedrooms ®⚲ ✕ (ex guide dogs) ✱ sB⇨ℕ£36 dB⇨ℕ£36 (room only)
120P
V ♂ ✱ Lunch £4.95-£11.50alc Dinner £4&alc Last dinner 9.45pm
Credit Cards 1 3 £

TONGUE Highland Sutherland Map 14 NC55

★★ 68% Ben Loyal
IV27 4XE (Tongue lies at the intersection of the A838/A836, hotel is in the centre of village) (Logis) ☎(084755) 216
Closed Jan-10 Feb
A phased improvement programme is nearing completion at this small, friendly, family-run hotel. It stands on the edge of the village overlooking the Kyle of Tongue. More en suite bathrooms have been added to the refurbished bedrooms which have pretty coordinated soft furnishings and modern pine units. The comfortable quiet lounge has a welcoming log fire, the bar a good range of malts.
12rm(9⇨ℕ)1🛏 CTV in all bedrooms ® sB&B£22.50-£25 sB&B⇨ℕ£28.80-£47 dB&B£45-£50 dB&B⇨ℕ£52.20-£64 ₧
19P ✱ ♪ ♫
♀ Scottish & French V ♂ ♀ ✱ Lunch £12.95-£18.50 Dinner £18.50&alc Last dinner 8.30pm
Credit Cards 1 3

TOPCLIFFE North Yorkshire Map 08 SE47

★★ 66% The Angel Inn
Long St YO7 3RW ☎Thirsk(0845) 577237 FAX (0845) 578000
The Angel is an attractive village inn with a rear garden, old world bars, cosy guests' lounge and pleasant restaurant. Bedrooms are in a well designed modern wing.
15⇨ℕ(1fb) CTV in all bedrooms ®⚲T ✕ (ex guide dogs) sB&B⇨ℕ£35-£40 dB&B⇨ℕ£50-£60 ₧
150P ✱ ♪
♀ English & Continental V ♂ ♀ ✱ Lunch £7.95-£10.95alc High tea £4.95-£5.95alc Dinner £12.95-£14.95alc Last dinner 9.30pm
Credit Cards 1 3 £

TORBAY
See under **Brixham, Paignton** & **Torquay**

TORCROSS Devon Map 03 SX84

★ 66% Grey Homes
TQ7 2TH ☎Kingsbridge(0548) 580220
Closed Nov-Mar
This small, comfortable hotel overlooks the freshwater lake beside the sea and the little fishing village of Torcross. Built in the 1920s by the grandfather of the present proprietor, it has comfortable bedrooms which all share the same beautiful views. There is a cosy lounge, a separate bar and a dining room offering a limited menu of home-cooked dishes, and guests are assured of a warm welcome.
7⇨(1fb) CTV in all bedrooms ® sB&B⇨£30-£32 dB&B⇨£50-£54 ₧
15P ♿ ✱ ♪ (hard) nc2yrs
♂ ♀ ✱ Dinner £11 Last dinner 7.30pm
Credit Cards 1 3

TORMARTON Avon Map 03 ST77

★★ 67% Compass Inn
GL9 1JB (0.5m from junct 18, M4)
☎Chipping Sodbury(0454) 218242 & 218577
FAX (0454) 218741
Closed Xmas

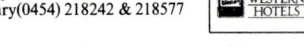
BEST WESTERN HOTELS

This family-run former coaching inn has characterful bars serving real ales and vintage cider and offers a range of food in the restaurant or bar. Most bedrooms are in a modern extension and come in 2 standards, but all are well equipped with modern amenities.
31⇨ℕ(7fb)1🛏 CTV in all bedrooms ®⚲T
160P ✱
V ♂ ♀ Last dinner 9.30pm
CONF. Thtr 80 Class 30 Board 34 Del £92.50
Credit Cards 1 2 3 5

TORPOINT Cornwall & Isles of Scilly Map 02 SX45

★★ 64% Whitsand Bay Hotel Golf & Country Club
Portwrinkle PL11 3BU (5m W, off B3247)
☎St Germans(0503) 30276 FAX (0503) 30329
Closed Jan-mid Mar RS Nov-24 Dec
Standing in 6 acres of grounds in a secluded fishing hamlet, this unique Tudor-Gothic hotel was rebuilt in 1911. The wood panelled interior has an interesting architectural style with excellent stained glass windows, and the accommodation has recently been upgraded.
34rm(32⇨ℕ)(10fb) CTV in 32 bedrooms ® sB&B£18.80-£21.15 sB&B⇨ℕ£22.50-£28.78 dB&B£35-£40 dB&B⇨ℕ£43-£57.50 ₧
CTV 60P ✱ ▭ (heated) ▶ 18 sauna solarium gymnasium beauty salon steam room hairdressers ♂ xmas
♀ English & Continental V ♂ ♀ Sunday Lunch £7.50 Dinner £13.50&alc Last dinner 8.30pm
CONF. Class 40 Board 40 Del from £50 £

Torquay

TORQUAY Devon Map 03 SX96

★★★★★ 60% **The Imperial**
Park Hill Rd TQ1 2DG ☏(0803) 294301 FAX (0803) 298293

Recent and continuing investment is slowly bringing this hotel back to its former standard, and as we go to print major changes are taking place to the entrance, reception hall, lounge, ballroom and bar. There is still only one restaurant, newly renovated and very attractive, and one bar, but the improved lounge should provide more comfortable seating and continue the tradition of music, dancing and excellent afternoon teas. Improvements continue to the bedrooms, many of which have balconies with spectacular views.
167⇌🛏(7fb)⌇in 67 bedrooms CTV in all bedrooms ® T ✻ sB&B⇌🛏£80–£107.50 dB&B⇌🛏£140–£175 ⊟
Lift ℂ 150P 30🚗 (£5 per day) ✤ ▣ (heated) ⇌ (heated) ℘ (hard) squash snooker sauna solarium gymnasium health fitness centre croquet *xmas*
V ✿ ⌇ ⌇ ✻ Lunch fr£16&alc Dinner fr£29&alc Last dinner 9.30pm
CONF. Thtr 400 Class 200 Board 12 Del £135
Credit Cards ① ② ③ ⑤

★★★★ 60% **Grand**
Sea Front TQ2 6NT ☏(0803) 296677 FAX (0803) 213462
Agatha Christie is said to have spent her honeymoon at this imposing Victorian hotel on the seafront. Accommodation includes some suites, and the buffet meals served in Boaters bar lounge offer an alternative to the à la carte and table d'hôte menus of the Gainsborough.
112⇌🛏(30fb)⌇in 30 bedrooms CTV in all bedrooms ® T ✻ sB&B⇌🛏£63–£75 dB&B⇌🛏£98–£133 ⊟
Lift ℂ 35🚗 ✤ ▣ (heated) ⇌ (heated) ℘ (hard) snooker sauna solarium gymnasium jacuzzi hairdressers ♫ *xmas*

♀ English & French V ✿ ⌇ Lunch £13.50&alc High tea £6.50 Dinner £18.50&alc Last dinner 9.30pm
CONF. Thtr 300 Class 100 Board 45 Del from £65
Credit Cards ① ③

See advertisement on page 609

★★★★ 56% **Palace**
Babbacombe Rd TQ1 3TG ☏(0803) 200200 FAX (0803) 299899

This extensive and rather grand resort hotel has spent some time in the doldrums, but we are pleased to report that significant upgrading is under way, designed to transform the spacious public areas and to bring all the remaining bedrooms up to the standard of those already refurbished. Staff make an effort to please and the food in the vast dining room is straightforward.
141⇌🛏(10fb) CTV in all bedrooms ® T ✻ (ex guide dogs) sB&B⇌🛏fr£45 dB&B⇌🛏fr£90 ⊟
Lift ℂ CTV 100P 40🚗 (£5 per night) ✤ ▣ (heated) ⇌ (heated) ▶ 9 ℘ (hard) squash snooker sauna croquet putting table tennis ♫ 🚴 *xmas*
♀ English & French V ✿ ⌇ Lunch £12.50 Dinner £18.50 Last dinner 9pm
CONF. Thtr 300 Class 150 Board 60 Del £92
Credit Cards ① ③ ⑤

See advertisement on page 608

★★★ 🌼🌼🌼 72% **Orestone Manor**
Rockhouse Ln, Maidencombe TQ1 4SX (off B3199 coast road, Torquay-Teignmouth) ☏(0803) 328098 & 328099 FAX (0803) 328336
Closed Jan
Built in the early 19th century, Orestone Manor has 2 acres of mature gardens and delightful country views. It has been restored to its former glory by Mike and Gill Staples who, together with their ➢→

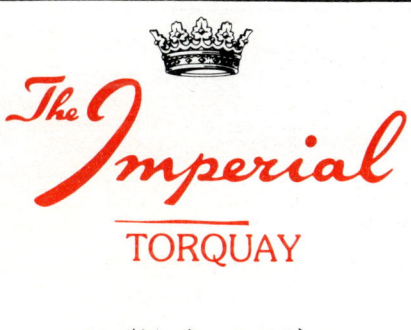

The Imperial, the only 5 star hotel in the South West, has been England's foremost exclusive resort hotel ever since it was opened in 1866. Situated on a clifftop with a perfect panoramic view over the whole of Torbay, surrounded by 5 acres of beautiful gardens, it commands a unique position.

The hotel has 150 luxurious bedrooms and 17 superbly appointed suites, most of which have sea views and private balconies. Guests have the use of the fully equipped Health and Leisure Club.

The Imperial is world famous for its special events; Gastronomic, Art & Antique, Gardening, Murder & Mystery, Music at Leisure. The superb Banqueting and Conference facilities can cater for up to 350 people.

★★★★★

The Imperial, Torquay, England
[0803] 294301

Torquay

son Paul, provide a warm welcome. Chef, Ashley Carkeet, provides innovative and imaginative menus which are changed daily. Bedrooms vary in size and style, and there is a choice of lounges.
18⇨📞(2fb) CTV in all bedrooms ® T sB&B⇨📞£38-£90 dB&B⇨📞£76-£120 ₽
CTV 30P ⇔ ✻ ⇔ (heated) nc10yrs *xmas*
🍴 English & French V ☯ ⚖ ✻ Lunch £9.50-£22.50 High tea £4-£10alc Dinner £25-£30&alc Last dinner 8.45pm
Credit Cards [1][2][3][5]
See advertisement on page 611 £

★★★**70%** **Corbyn Head**
Torquay Rd, Sea Front, Livermead TQ2 6RH ☎(0803) 213611 FAX (0803) 296152
This modern, well maintained seafront hotel has sea views from many of the bedrooms and all the public areas. There are 2 restaurants, a lounge-bar and a further lounge with a dance floor. The bedrooms vary in size but all are well equipped and have been pleasantly decorated with coordinating colour schemes.
51⇨📞(1fb) CTV in all bedrooms ® T sB&B⇨📞£40-£60 dB&B⇨📞£80-£120 ₽
《 50P ⇔ (heated) *xmas*
V ☯ ⚖ ✻ ✻ Bar Lunch £3.50-£15alc High tea £3.50-£8.50alc Dinner £18.50-£21.50&alc Last dinner 9pm
Credit Cards [1][2][3][5] £

★★★**69%** **Abbey Lawn Hotel**
Scarborough Rd TQ2 5UQ ☎(0803) 299199 FAX (0803) 291460
Set in a secluded yet central location overlooking private tennis courts and the bay beyond, this spacious Georgian hotel has been refurbished throughout to a good standard. Public areas are richly furnished in leather; there is a new conservatory lounge, and the hotel offers traditional services.
56⇨📞 CTV in all bedrooms ® T ✻ sB&B⇨📞fr£38 dB&B⇨📞fr£76 ₽
Lift 《 50P ✻ 🖃 (heated) ⇔ (heated) ₽ (hard & grass)sauna solarium gymnasium 🎵 nc 4yrs *xmas*
🍴 English & French V ☯ ⚖ ✻ Lunch fr£9alc Dinner fr£15.50&alc Last dinner 8.30pm
Credit Cards [1][2][3][5] £
See advertisement on page 611

★★★**68%** **Livermead Cliff**
Torbay Rd TQ2 6RQ (on seafront, follow signs 'Livermead, Paignton') ☎(0803) 299666 & 292881 FAX (0803) 294496
One of the few hotels literally on the water's edge, this family-owned establishment is also within easy reach of the town centre. Bedrooms vary in size, and all are due to be refurbished over the next 3 years. A well balanced fixed price menu is offered in the restaurant, and Marilyn Pope's home-made desserts continue to please guests.
64⇨📞(21fb)1🛏 CTV in all bedrooms ® T sB&B⇨📞£32-£56 dB&B⇨📞£60-£108 ₽
Lift 《 CTV 60P 12⇔ ✻ ⇔ (heated) ♪ solarium sun terrace ⚜ *xmas*
🍴 English & Continental V ☯ ⚖ Lunch £7.65&alc Dinner £16&alc Last dinner 8.30pm
CONF. Thtr 70 Class 30 Board 24 Del from £46
Credit Cards [1][2][3][5]

★★★**67%** **Homers**
Warren Rd TQ2 5TN ☎(0803) 213456 FAX (0803) 213458
This detached Victorian house is in an elevated position with spectacular views over Torbay. The furnishings and décor reflect its luxurious past. Bedrooms vary in size and some are quite dramatic in style. Les Ambassadeur Restaurant offers a 3-course table d'hôte menu and an imaginative carte. Proprietors, Pamela and Derek Oatley are totally involved in the running of the hotel.
14rm(13⇨📞)(1fb)1🛏 CTV in all bedrooms T ✻ sB&B£30-£36 sB&B⇨📞£42-£48 dB&B⇨📞£60-£98 ₽
CTV 5P ⇔ ✻ nc7yrs *xmas*

➡

Seafront · Torquay · Devon
Torquay (0803) 213611

Situated directly on the seafront with unequalled views across Torbay. The Corbyn Head Hotel offers superb food in two restaurants. All 52 bedrooms have recently been refurbished to the highest standards. All have private bathroom, colour TV and tea making facilities.

Special breaks are available all year round.

★★★★
The Palace Hotel Torquay
"Once you get here its all free"

We have 25 acres of colourful gardens and woodland leading down to the sea, with the following sports facilities included in the price of this famous 4-star hotel, 6 tennis courts (2 indoor), 9 hole, par 3 golf course, indoor and outdoor heated swimming pool, saunas, 2 squash courts, billiards room. Children are well looked after with our resident nanny, all rooms en-suite with colour TV including 6 luxury suites.

The Palace Hotel
Babbacombe Road, Torquay TQ1 3TG
Telephone 0803 200200
Fax: 0803 299899

TORQUAY

Set in its own grounds with panoramic views over Torbay, The Grand Hotel has reigned supreme as "Queen of the English Riviera" for over 100 years.

With our award winning cuisine, sumptuous surroundings, the best indoor and outdoor swimming pools in the bay, complemented by our friendly and attentive staff, The Grand offers the best value for money in the South West for a short break or holiday — winter through to summer.

The Grand Hotel, Sea Front, Torquay, Devon TQ2 6NT.
0803 296677

TORQUAY'S ONLY ★ ★ ★ ★ SEAVIEW HOTEL

Torquay

European **V** ✩ ♨ ✂ ✱ Lunch £10.50-£16 Dinner £15.85-£23 Last dinner 9pm
Credit Cards 1 2 3 5

★★★ 63% Belgrave
Seafront TQ2 5HE (adjacent to Torre Abbey Gardens)
☎(0803) 296666 FAX (0803) 211308

A major attraction of this well maintained hotel is its location, separated from the beach only by its lawn and the main road. Some of the bedrooms have wonderful sea views, all have good facilities and are steadily being upgraded. There is a popular lounge bar, an outside terrace, and a large dining room where a simple table d'hôte menu is offered.

68⇨➥(16fb) CTV in all bedrooms ® T sB&B⇨➥£38-£49 dB&B⇨➥£76-£98 ♨
Lift (80P 6🚗 (£2 per day) ⊞ ✱ ≃ (heated) *xmas*
English & French **V** ✩ ♨ ✂ Bar Lunch fr£3 Dinner fr£10 Last dinner 8.30pm
CONF. Thtr 150 Class 66 Board 50 Del from £49
Credit Cards 1 3 5

See advertisement on page 613

★★★ 63% Toorak
Chestnut Av TQ2 5JS (opposite Riviera Conference Centre)
☎(0803) 291444 FAX (0803) 291666

Visitors to this pleasant resort hotel can enjoy impressive leisure facilities shared with its adjoining sister properties. Well designed bedrooms are mostly of the same modern style and are more than adequately equipped. Snacks are served at lunchtime, and at dinner there is a short table d'hôte menu with a few à la carte supplements.

91⇨➥(29fb) CTV in all bedrooms ® T sB&B⇨➥£30-£48 dB&B⇨➥£60-£96 ♨
Lift (90P ✱ 🖃 (heated) ≃ (heated) ℘ (hard) snooker croquet lawn ♫ *xmas*
English & French **V** ✩ ♨ ✱ Bar Lunch fr£2.50 High tea fr£5.50 Dinner fr£14 Last dinner 8.30pm
CONF. Thtr 200 Class 150 Board 40 Del from £45
Credit Cards 1 3

★★★ 60% Kistor
Belgrave Rd TQ2 5HF ☎(0803) 212632 FAX (0803) 293219

This large, friendly holiday hotel is conveniently positioned for the sea front and town centre. Public areas are spacious and comfortable, and a games room is available beneath the main lounge. Table d'hôte menus are served in the dining room, and crazy golf and putting are provided outside, together with a small play area for children.

56⇨➥(18fb)1⊞ ✂ in 2 bedrooms CTV in all bedrooms ®♻ T
Lift (50P 🖃 (heated) sauna solarium gymnasium games room putting table tennis ♫
English & French **V** ✩ ♨ ✂ Last dinner 8.30pm
Credit Cards 1 2 3

★★★ 58% Lincombe Hall
Meadfoot Rd TQ1 2JX ☎(0803) 213361 FAX (0803) 211485

Set in an elevated position in a neat garden with mature trees, this hotel comprises 2 elegant houses joined by a covered walkway. Newly renovated rooms are smartly colour-coordinated, with modern furniture, while the remaining rooms are more traditional in style.

42⇨➥(8fb) CTV in all bedrooms ® T
(40P ✱ ≃ (heated) ℘ (hard) sauna solarium putting spa bath croquet
V ✩ ♨ ✂ Last dinner 8.30pm
Credit Cards 1 2 3 5

★★★ 58% Livermead House
Torbay Rd TQ2 6QJ (from seafront follow A379 towards Paignton and Livermead) ☎(0803) 294361 FAX (0803) 200758

Conveniently situated for the town centre and the beaches, with lovely views of Torbay, this hotel is professionally managed by the Rew family. Traditional table d'hôte menus are served in the

restaurant, and bedrooms are undergoing an extensive refurbishment programme.

64⇨➥(6fb) CTV in all bedrooms ® T sB&B⇨➥£30-£50 dB&B⇨➥£60-£100 ♨
Lift (90P ✱ ≃ (heated) ℘ (hard) squash snooker sauna solarium gymnasium ♫ *xmas*
English & French **V** ✩ ♨ ✂ Lunch £7.95-£9&alc Dinner £17.50-£19&alc Last dinner 8.30pm
CONF. Thtr 100 Class 30 Board 40 Del from £45
Credit Cards 1 2 3 5

★★★ 56% Devonshire
Parkhill Rd TQ1 2DY (from harbour clock tower, turn right up hill) ☎(0803) 291123 FAX (0803) 291710

A long-established, family-owned hotel in a quiet area in walking distance of the harbour and town centre. Bedrooms are being renovated and the best rooms have recently been completely refurbished and double-glazed. The lodge annexe is modern, with some ground-floor bedrooms. Live entertainment is provide on some evenings and there are two lounges, a popular bar and a spacious restaurant.

59⇨➥ Annexe12⇨➥(9fb) CTV in all bedrooms ® T sB&B⇨➥£26-£36 dB&B⇨➥£52-£72 ♨
(CTV 50P ✱ ≃ (heated) snooker *xmas*
English & French **V** ✩ ♨
CONF. Del from £52
Credit Cards 1 3 4 5

★★ 68% Coppice
Barrington Rd TQ1 2QJ ☎(0803) 297786
Closed Oct-Mar

A personally managed hotel set in its own well tended gardens, just off the Babbacombe road, offering good value for money. Bedrooms are fresh and bright; public areas are comfortable and entertainment is provided on some evenings. A floodlit water display from the swimming pool provides a nice backdrop for a relaxing 5-course evening meal. Staff are friendly and helpful.

40rm(33⇨➥6➥)(10fb) CTV in all bedrooms ® T
(CTV 30P ✱ ≃ (heated) solarium
✩ Last dinner 8pm

★★ 67% Frognel Hall
Higher Woodfield Rd TQ1 2LD ☎(0803) 298339 FAX (0803) 298339
Closed end Dec-Feb RS Xmas & New Year

Frognel Hall is in a quiet position, but is just a few minutes from the town centre and harbour. It is a Victorian villa, carefully and sympathetically restored by proprietors Lynne and Michael Hookings. Bedrooms are simply furnished and decorated, and a continual programme of upgrading is under way. Traditional English food is featured on the table d'hôte menu.

27rm(25⇨➥)(4fb) CTV in all bedrooms ® sB&B⇨➥£17.50-£29.50 dB&B⇨➥£35-£59 ♨
Lift CTV 25P ✱ sauna solarium croquet games room exercise equipment ♫ *xmas*
English & French **V** ✩ ♨ ✂ Bar Lunch £2.50-£5.50 Dinner £12.95-£16.95 Last dinner 7.30pm
CONF. Thtr 60 Class 40 Board 20
Credit Cards 1 3

★★ 66% Burlington
462-466 Babbacombe Rd TQ1 1HN ☎(0803) 294374 FAX (0803) 200189

A friendly tourist hotel about a quarter of a mile from the harbour and town centre, offering value for money accommodation. The split-level restaurant serves generous portions of wholesome food. Bedrooms are currently undergoing refurbishment.

55⇨➥(7fb)1⊞ CTV in all bedrooms ® T sB&B⇨➥£28-£37 dB&B⇨➥£48-£66 ♨
(CTV 20P 🖃 (heated) sauna solarium pool table spa bath ♫ *xmas*

The Devonshire Hotel

Parkhill Road, Torquay, Devon TQ1 2DY.
Tel: (0803) 291123. Fax: (0803) 291710

AA ★★★  English Tourist Board COMMENDED

- Tranquil Garden Setting
- Licensed Lounge Bar
- Full Size Snooker Table
- Direct Dial Phones
- Free Car Park
- Heated Outdoor Pool
- Night Porter
- Tea/Coffee making facilities

Whether it be a short break or a longer holiday you can be assured of a warm welcome at the Abbey Lawn Hotel.
Simply laze on the terrace or enjoy a swim in our outdoor pool or leisure centre.
For business meetings or conferences, one phone call to us and we can organise everything you need.
Telephone or fax for your brochure.

★★★
ABBEY LAWN HOTEL

Scarborough Road, Torquay TQ2 5UQ
Tel: (0803) 299199
Fax: (0803) 291460

AA COUNTRY HOUSE AWARD ★★★   B.T.A. COMMENDED
COUNTRY HOUSE HOTEL & RESTAURANT

72%   **Orestone Manor**

ROCKHOUSE LANE, MAIDENCOMBE, TORQUAY TQ1 4SX

FOR THE THIRD CONSECUTIVE YEAR – TORQUAY'S HIGHEST RATED HOTEL
NOW WITH **TWO ROSETTES** *FOR OUR SUPERB ANGLO-FRENCH CUISINE*
The only **official** AA Country House Hotel in Torquay, Orestone Manor, situated on the Teignmouth Road (B3199), is only 3 miles from the Harbour side. We offer peace and tranquillity. Our lovely sheltered garden, with heated swimming pool (summer only), gives extensive views over Lyme Bay. 18 en suite rooms with direct dial phone, colour TV, radio etc. Spring, Autumn and Winter breaks available.
Telephone (0803) 328098 Fax: 0803 328336

Torquay

⚑ English, French & Italian V ✦ ⚑ ✂ ✱ Sunday Lunch
£3.50-£6 Dinner £5-£8&alc Last dinner 8pm
Credit Cards [1][3]

★★ 66% Chelston Tower
Rawlyn Rd TQ2 6PQ ☎(0803) 607351
Closed Jan
This fine Victorian former family home set in 2 acres of secluded woodland still retains much of its original charm and is in walking distance of both the sea and town centre. Personally run, the hotel has traditionally furnished but well equipped bedrooms, some overlooking the gardens, some on the ground floor. There is a comfortable lounge and bar, and the dining room can be used for private parties. The varied set-price menu changes daily. Service is friendly.
23rm(9⇨4⚐)(12fb) T
CTV 30P ❋ ⚐ (heated) games room
V ✦ ⚑ Dinner £15.50 Last dinner 7.30pm
Credit Cards [1][3]

★★ 66% Red House
Rousdown Rd, Chelston TQ2 6PB ☎(0803) 607811 FAX (0803) 200592
Quietly located yet within easy reach of the town and beaches, this hotel offers bright, comfortable bedrooms. The coffee shop, situated around the excellent leisure facilities, provides all day service for meals and light snacks. A simple table d'hôte menu is served to residents.
10⇨⚐(3fb) CTV in all bedrooms ® sB&B⇨⚐£27.50-£50 dB&B⇨⚐£55-£70 (incl dinner) ⚑
10P ❋ ❋ ▣ (heated) ⚐ sauna solarium gymnasium games room spa pool *xmas*
⚑ English & French V ✦ ⚑ ✂ Lunch £2.95-£7.95alc High tea £1.90-£3.60alc Dinner £10.50-£12&alc Last dinner 8pm
Credit Cards [1][3]

★★ 65% Albaston House
27 St Marychurch Rd TQ1 3JF ☎(0803) 296758
Closed Dec
Situated at the top of the town, this welcoming and relaxing hotel is within easy reach of many of Torquay's beaches. The cosy bar is the ideal venue for a quiet apéritif, and a varied table d'hôte menu is served in the dining room, featuring home-made bread rolls, soups and puddings. Bedrooms are comfortable and attractively coordinated.
13⇨⚐(4fb) CTV in all bedrooms ® T
CTV 12☎ ❋
⚑ English & French V ✦ ⚑
Credit Cards [1][3]

★★ 65% Ansteys Lea
Babbacombe Rd, Wellswood TQ1 2QJ (from Torquay harbour take Torwood Street which runs into Babbacombe Road, Hotel is just past St Matthias Church on the left hand side)
☎(0803) 294843 FAX (0803) 294843
Closed Jan-Feb RS Dec & early Mar
This friendly, family-run holiday hotel near Babbacombe Beach and Kent's Cavern is converted from a large Victorian villa and has an attractive garden. Bedrooms are presently being refurbished.
24⇨⚐(2fb) CTV in all bedrooms ® T ✂ (ex guide dogs) ✱
sB&B⇨⚐£26-£33 dB&B⇨⚐£52-£66 (incl dinner) ⚑
CTV 18P ❋ ⚐ (heated) *xmas*
⚑ English & French V ✦ ⚑ ✂ ✱ Bar Lunch £1.75-£5 Dinner £6-£7.95 Last dinner 7.30pm
Credit Cards [1][3] £

★★ 65% Dunstone
Lower Warberry Rd TQ1 1QS ☎(0803) 293185
Closed Nov-Feb
An imposing hotel, peacefully set in its own gardens with beautiful views over the bay. Bedrooms have been redecorated, with cheerful decor and modern furnishings. The lounge and conservatory bar retain more of the building's original elegance and the proprietor,

Mr Dennys, a professional musician, often entertains guests at the grand piano. A table d'hôte menu offers a choice of home-cooked fare in the congenial dining room.
14rm(13⇨⚐)(3fb) CTV in all bedrooms ® T ✂
CTV 18P ❋ ❋ ⚐ (heated) pool table table tennis badminton nc5yrs
V ✦ ⚑ ✂ Last dinner 7.30pm
Credit Cards [1][3]

★★ 65% Gresham Court
Babbacombe Rd TQ1 1HG (0.25m from harbourside)
☎(0803) 293007 & 293658 FAX (0803) 215951
Closed Dec-Feb
Close to the harbour and town centre, this long established family-run hotel offers friendly service, modestly furnished but clean and comfortable bedrooms and modern-style public areas which include a restaurant with a choice of menus.
30⇨⚐(6fb) CTV in all bedrooms ® sB&B⇨⚐£21-£28 dB&B⇨⚐£42-£56
Lift CTV 4P
V ✱ Bar Lunch £1.25-£3.50 Dinner £7 Last dinner 8pm
Credit Cards [1][3]

★★ 65% Hunsdon Lea
Hunsdon Rd TQ1 1QB ☎(0803) 296538
Closed Nov-Etr
Set in its own gardens in a quiet street away from, but convenient for the town centre, this hotel offers friendly and well equipped bedrooms, comfortable public areas and a warm welcome. Dishes on both à la carte and table d'hôte menus are home-cooked from the best of fresh produce.
12rm(7⇨2⚐)(3fb) CTV in all bedrooms ® T ✂
CTV 12P ❋ ⚐ (heated) solarium pool table table tennis
V ✦ ⚑ ✂ Last dinner 8pm

★★ 65% Oscar's Hotel & Restaurant
56 Belgrave Rd TQ2 5HY ☎(0803) 293563
Closed 12 Nov-17 Dec
This handsome Victorian property stands in a corner position, enjoying a good location close to both the sea front and town centre. The Cellar restaurant and bar offers a fixed-price menu for residents, as well as a short à la carte menu and daily specials featuring good Cajun and Caribbean dishes. Staff are helpful and pleasant.
12rm(1⇨8⚐)(2fb) CTV in all bedrooms ® T
✂ (ex guide dogs)
CTV 8P ❋
⚑ International V ✦ Last dinner 8pm
Credit Cards [1][3][4]

★★ 64% Seascape
8-10 Tor Church Rd TQ2 5UT ☎(0803) 292617 FAX (0803) 292617
Closed 3 Jan-Feb
Not far from the centre, this hotel has been completely refurbished and offers good value for money. Public areas are comfortable and bright, with a lively, cheery atmosphere and include a bar and lounge, complete with dance floor. The dining room serving simple menus, overlooks the garden. Bedrooms are well presented and there is a lift to all floors.
63rm(56⇨⚐)(14fb) CTV in all bedrooms ® ✱ T
✂ (ex guide dogs) ✱ sB&B£20-£31 sB&B⇨⚐£22-£33 dB&B£40-£56 dB&B⇨⚐£42-£58 (incl dinner) ⚑
Lift CTV 15P 15☎ ❋ sauna solarium gymnasium table tennis pool table ♪ *xmas*
V ⚑ ✂ ✱ High tea fr£1.20alc Dinner fr£7.50alc Last dinner 7.30pm
Credit Cards [1][3] £

For key to symbols see the Bookmark.

Torquay

★★ 63% **Bute Court**
Belgrave Rd TQ2 5HQ ☎(0803) 293771 FAX (0803) 213429
Bute Court has been in the same family since the early 1940s. It is centrally situated with easy access to the beach, English Riviera Centre and the shops. Ample public areas are provided, and the short 5-course table d'hôte menu offers variety and value for money.
48rm(44⇨♠)(10fb) CTV in all bedrooms ® T sB&B£15-£27.50 sB&B⇨♠£20-£32.50 dB&B£30-£55 dB&B⇨♠£40-£65 ♩
Lift ℭ CTV 37P ✿ ⌒ (heated) snooker table tennis darts *xmas*
♡ English & Continental ✧ ⚑ Bar Lunch £2-£5alc High tea £1.50-£5alc Dinner £7.50-£9.50 Last dinner 8pm
Credit Cards [1][2][3][5]

★★ 61% *Carlton*
Falkland Rd TQ2 5JJ ☎(0803) 291555 FAX 0803 291666
The Carlton Hotel is situated close to the seafront and the Riviera Leisure Centre. The public areas and bedrooms are undergoing complete refurbishment, following the hotel's purchase in 1992 by the Torquay Leisure Hotels Group. A short table d'hôte menu is served in the dining room.
32⇨♠(18fb) CTV in all bedrooms ® T ✕ (ex guide dogs)
Lift ℭ 18P ⌒ (heated) snooker ♪
V ✧ ⚑ Last dinner 8.15pm
Credit Cards [1][3]

★★ 61% *Roseland*
Warren Rd TQ2 5TT ☎(0803) 213829 FAX (0803) 291266
Originally the home of Lord Lytton, Viceroy of India, the hotel has spectacular views over Torbay to Paignton. Simple, well balanced table d'hôte meals are served.
34⇨♠Annexe1♠(5fb)3☐ CTV in all bedrooms ® T
Lift ℭ CTV ✿ sauna solarium pool table games room jacuzzi
V ✧ ⚑ ✂
Credit Cards [1][3]

★★ 61% **Hotel Sydore**
Meadfoot Rd TQ1 2JP ☎(0803) 294758 FAX (0803) 294489
This detached Georgian villa with a covered veranda and its own attractive gardens is located within easy reach of the harbour and town centre. Bedrooms are well equipped, although without telephones. The lounge and bar have individual style and charm, and in the evening a well balanced table d'hôte menu is offered.
13⇨♠(5fb)1☐ CTV in all bedrooms ® sB&B⇨♠£18.50-£30.50 dB&B⇨♠£37-£61 ♩
CTV 17P ✿ games room croquet *xmas*
♡ English & Continental V ✧ ⚑ ✂ Lunch £7.50&alc High tea £1.50 Dinner £7.50&alc Last dinner 8.45pm
CONF. Thtr 20 Class 20 Board 20
Credit Cards [1][3]

★★ 60% **Hotel Balmoral**
Meadfoot Sea Rd TQ1 2LQ ☎(0803) 293381 & 299224 FAX (0803) 299224
Hotel Balmoral is set in a large, peaceful garden with glimpses through the trees to Meadfoot Beach. The refurbished restaurant and lounge are light and airy, and the bedrooms are in the process of being upgraded. The Heather Bar reflects the Scottish theme, and offers a fine choice of about 60 whiskies.
24⇨♠(7fb) CTV in all bedrooms ® T ✱ sB&B⇨♠£22-£30.50 dB&B⇨♠£39-£61 ♩
18P ✿ *xmas*
♡ English & French ✧ ⚑ ✂ Lunch £7.50 Dinner £10.50 Last dinner 8.30pm
Credit Cards [1][2][3]

★★ 59% **Norcliffe**
7 Babbacombe Downs Rd, Babbacombe TQ1 3LF
☎(0803) 328456 & 328023

★ Superb Seafront location. Easy level walk to theatre, harbour and main shopping areas.
★ Seventy bedrooms with private bathroom, colour television, radio, telephone, tea and coffee making facilities.
★ Spacious, modern, restaurant, bars, sun lounge and heated outdoor swimming pool. Large car park and lock-up garages.
Open all year. "Torquay Weekend Away" special terms from October to April.
Residential conference facilities.

Sea Front Torquay TQ2 5HE   Telephone: 0803 296666   Fax: 0803 211308

Torquay - Totnes

This family-run holiday hotel overlooks the gardens of Babbacombe Downs and has spectacular views of the bay. The dining room, where simple, varied menus are served, has been extended to accommodate extra residents and various functions.
28⇨♠(2fb)1⊞ CTV in all bedrooms ® T sB&B⇨♠£28.50-£35.70 dB&B⇨♠£57-£71.40 (incl dinner)
Lift 22P 🅿 (heated) sauna gymnasium *xmas*
♥ ♨ ✳ Sunday Lunch £6.50-£8.50 Dinner £8.50-£12.50 Last dinner 7.30pm
Credit Cards ①③ £

★★ 56% Bancourt
Avenue Rd TQ2 5LG ☎(0803) 295077 FAX (0803) 201114
The Proctor and Timms families have recently taken over at the Bancourt, a popular coaching and commercial hotel. Simply furnished bedrooms are on 2 floors, the dining room serves a table d'hôte menu at dinner, and there is evening entertainment at times in the ballroom. Guests may relax in the gardens at the rear of the hotel.
40⇨♠(11fb) CTV in all bedrooms ® T sB&B⇨♠£18-£30 dB&B⇨♠£36-£60 🅿
《 CTV 50P ❉ 🅿 (heated) snooker games room ♫ *xmas*
♥ English & French ♥ ♨ ✳ Dinner £10.50 Last dinner 7.30pm
Conf. Thtr 30 Class 40 Board 20
Credit Cards ①③⑤ £

★ 71% Fairmount House
Herbert Road, Chelston TQ2 6RW
☎(0803) 605446 FAX (0803) 605446
Closed Nov-Feb
ExecGroup
A friendly welcome is assured at this attractive little hotel, which offers bright bedrooms, a small bar in a conservatory off the dining room, and wholesome home cooked food freshly prepared by proprietor Maggie Tolkien. The hotel is personally run by Maggie and husband Noel, and their dedication to customer care is reflected in careful attention to detail and friendly, helpful service.
8⇨♠(3fb) CTV in all bedrooms ®⚹ sB&B⇨♠£24.50-£27.50 dB&B⇨♠£49-£55 🅿
CTV 9P ❉
♥ English & Continental V ♥ ♨ ✳ Sunday Lunch £11 Dinner £11 Last dinner 7.30pm
Credit Cards ①②③ £

★ 66% Shelley Court
Croft Rd TQ2 5UD ☎(0803) 295642 FAX (0803) 2157963
Offering southerly views over the town, and access by private path to the seafront 250 yards away, this hotel is managed by caring and attentive resident proprietors. Bedrooms are attractively decorated, though some are compact. The dining room offers a simple set price menu, and the lounge bar features entertainment some evenings.
28rm(7⇨19♠)(3fb) CTV in all bedrooms ® ✗
CTV 20P ❉ ♫
♥ ✳ Last dinner 7.30pm
Credit Cards ①③

★ 66% Westwood
111 Abbey Rd TQ2 5NP ☎(0803) 293818
This friendly, informal hotel is convenient for the town centre and not far from the sea front. Bedrooms are bright and equipped with modern amenities, and there is a first-floor lounge area. Downstairs there is a nicely appointed bar/lounge where entertainment is often provided. Home-cooked dishes are served in the evening in the pretty, no-smoking dining room.
26⇨♠(4fb) CTV in all bedrooms ® ✗ (ex guide dogs) ✳ sB&B⇨♠£16-£20 dB&B⇨♠£32-£40 🅿
CTV 12P ❉ *xmas*
V ✳ Dinner £5-£6 Last dinner 7.30pm
Credit Cards ①③

★ 64% Ashley Rise
18 Babbacombe Rd, Babbacombe TQ1 3SJ ☎(0803) 327282
Closed Dec-Mar (ex Xmas & New Year)
A popular family-run holiday hotel located near Babbacombe Downs. Personally run by the proprietors for many years, the hotel has been continually improved, and bedrooms now offer more facilities including modern en suite shower rooms. Pleasant public areas include a dining room where a small choice of home-cooked dishes are offered from a table d'hôte menu.
25⇨♠(8fb) CTV in all bedrooms ® sB&B⇨♠£16-£23 dB&B⇨♠£32-£46
CTV 14P solarium ♫ *xmas*
♥ ✳ Last dinner 7pm £

★ 62% Hotel Fluela
15-17 Hatfield Rd TQ1 3BW ☎(0803) 297512 FAX (0803) 296261
This large Victorian house is a few minutes walk from the town centre and within easy reach of the seafront. The garden porter bar has a friendly and informal atmosphere, and in the dining room a choice of menus is offered. Bedrooms are very well equipped and each room has its own character.
13⇨♠(3fb) CTV in all bedrooms ® T ✗ (ex guide dogs) dB&B⇨♠£32-£45
CTV 20P 🚲 *xmas*
V ✳
Credit Cards ①②③

★ 62% Sunleigh
Livermead Hill TQ2 6QY ☎(0803) 607137
Closed Dec-Etr
This Victorian property is set in its own garden overlooking Torbay. The attractive bar opens onto the dining area, where simple table d'hôte menus are served. Bedrooms are simply furnished and decorated. Guests receive a warm, friendly greeting from the hotel's resident proprietors.
20♠(4fb) CTV in all bedrooms ® ✳ sB&B♠£24-£30 dB&B♠£48-£60 (incl dinner) 🅿
CTV 18P *xmas*
✳ ✳ Dinner fr£10.50 Last dinner 7pm
Credit Cards ①②③ £

★ 61% Sunray
Aveland Rd, Babbacombe TQ1 3PT (opposite Torquay United FC) ☎(0803) 328285 FAX (0803) 328285
RS Dec-Mar
Established by proprietor Derek Day's father in 1945, this small family-run hotel is in a peaceful residential area close to Cary Parks. Bedrooms are fresh and bright, open-plan public areas have been upgraded in recent years, and there is a fully stocked bar and entertainment during the summer.
22rm(21⇨♠)(3fb) CTV in all bedrooms ® sB&B⇨♠£20-£26 dB&B⇨♠£40-£52 (incl dinner) 🅿
CTV 15P 1🅿 *xmas*
♥ English, French & Italian V ♥ ✳ Dinner £7.50 Last dinner 8pm
Conf. Class 40 Board 40 Del from £25
Credit Cards ①③

TOTLAND BAY
See **Wight, Isle of**

TOTNES Devon Map **03** SX86
See also **Staverton**
★★ 61% Royal Seven Stars
The Plains TQ9 5DD ☎(0803) 862125 & 863341 FAX (0803) 867925
Positioned at the foot of this ancient and historic town's main street, this hotel dating back to 1660 offers accommodation in well equipped bedrooms. The Carriage room buffet bar serves snacks throughout the day, while the Brutus Room restaurant provides a

18rm(12⇨♠)(2fb)2⊟ CTV in all bedrooms ® T sB&B£40-£46 sB&B⇨♠£50-£56 dB&B£50-£56 dB&B⇨♠£54-£70 ♬
CTV 20P *xmas*
♋ English & Continental V ✧ ✂ Lunch fr£7.50 Dinner fr£14.50 Last dinner 9.30pm
CONF. Thtr 60 Class 40 Board 30
Credit Cards [1][3][5]

TOWCESTER Northamptonshire Map **04** SP64

★★★ 64% *Saracens Head*
219 Watling St NN12 7BX ☎(0327) 50414 FAX (0327) 359879
This ancient inn which is said to have inspired Dickens' Pickwick Papers has been extensively refurbished. The pine-furnished bedrooms have the latest amenities and the comfortable lounge with open fireplace and leaded windows is separated from the bar and restaurant by the original coach entrance. Cheerful staff provide willing service.
21⇨♠(3fb)2⊟ CTV in all bedrooms ® T ✗ (ex guide dogs) ℂ 48P
♋ International V ✧ ✂ ✂
Credit Cards [1][2][3][5]

Forte Travelodge
NN12 0DD (A43 East Towcester by-pass)
☎(0327) 359105 Central Res (0800) 850950

FORTE Travelodge

This modern building offers a good standard of accommodation for overnight stops. Smart, spacious and well equipped bedrooms, all with en suite bathrooms, are suitable for family use, and meals may be taken at the nearby family restaurant. For more details of Travelodges, consult the Contents page, under Hotel Groups.
33⇨♠✱ B⇨♠£31.95 (room only)

TREARDDUR BAY
See **Anglesey, Isle of**

TREFRIW Gwynedd Map **06** SH76

★★ ❀73% **Hafod House**
LL27 0RQ (on B5106) ☎Llanrwst(0492) 640029 FAX (0492) 641351
This small, friendly hotel is in the lovely Conwy valley. The bedrooms are pretty, with coordinated fabrics and colour schemes. The restaurant is full of character with a stone fireplace and collection of brass and bric-à-brac, and there is a comfortable bar and lounge. Well prepared table d'hôte and à la carte menus are on offer, using local fish and other produce. Our inspector particularly enjoyed a rich bread and butter pudding.
7⇨♠1⊟ CTV in all bedrooms ® T ✗ (ex guide dogs) sB&B⇨♠£25-£35 dB&B⇨♠£50-£70 ♬
20P ✿ nc11yrs *xmas*
♋ English & French V ✧ ✂ ✂ Lunch £5.95-£9.95 Dinner £14.95-£17.95 Last dinner 9.30pm
Credit Cards [1][2][3][5]

TRESCO
See **Scilly, Isles of**

TREYARNON BAY Cornwall & Isles of Scilly Map **02** SW87

★★ ❀67% **Waterbeach**
PL28 8JW ☎Padstow(0841) 520292 FAX (0841) 521102
Closed Nov-Feb
Located on the rugged, beautiful North Cornish coast, the Waterbeach is personally run by Tony and Vicky Etherington and has a friendly, relaxed atmosphere. Bedrooms are clean and bright, and those without en suite facilities have bathrooms close. Vicky's ➤

AA ★★

The Old Church House Inn
[A.D. 1400]
Torbryan, Ipplepen, Nr. Totnes South Devon TQ12 5UR Tel: (0803) 812372

A comfortable family run Listed 13thC coaching inn of immense character. An olde worlde charm of inglenook fireplaces with log fires and stone walls with oak beamed ceilings. Situated between Dartmoor and the coastal towns of Torquay (6 miles) and Totnes (5 miles). An ancient Saxon town. All rooms have en-suite. Double room comforts. Excellent food in restaurant and bars.
Proprietors: E.G. & C.I. Pimm

Bancourt Hotel
AA ★★
On the English Riviera

Avenue Road, Torquay, Devon TQ2 5LG Telephone: 0803 295077 Fax: 0803 201114

Centrally situated and just a short level walk to most of Torquay's major attractions. A family run hotel providing personal service and a homely atmosphere. The exquisite cuisine and spacious comfort of the elegant Restaurant and Lounges contribute to a memorable stay. Relax in the landscaped gardens, an ideal setting to enjoy sheltered sun bathing, lunch, cream teas or just a refreshing drink. For the energetic the heated indoor pool is a major attraction. Entertainment is provided during the season. Wedding receptions, functions and conferences are a speciality. Short Breaks are available throughout the year, information on request.

Treyarnon Bay - Troon

enjoyable, unfussy home-cooked food is based on fresh local produce, prepared with flair. The 6-course table d'hôte menu is well planned.
20rm(7⇌2⋔)(2fb) CTV in all bedrooms ® T ✂ sB&B£31-£38 dB&B£62-£76 dB&B⇌⋔£68-£80 (incl dinner) CTV 20P ⚙ ✻ ℓ (hard) putting
V ⬡ ⚲ ✻ Dinner £12.50 Last dinner 8.15pm
Credit Cards [1][2][3]

TRING Hertfordshire Map 04 SP91

★★★★ 59% *Pendley Manor*
Cow Ln HP23 5QY ☎(0442) 891891 FAX (0442) 890687
An attractive late Victorian country house set in 35 acres of wooded parkland, Pendley Manor was a private residence until 1987, when it was considerably extended. An impressive galleried staircase leads to the bedrooms in the original house which have more character, though all are furnished to the same standard. The original library is now the dining room, there is an elegant drawing room and a modern conservatory-style bar.
71⇌⋔(4fb) CTV in all bedrooms T
Lift (100P ✻ ℓ (hard)
♀ English & French V ⬡ ⚲ ✂ Last dinner 9.30pm
Credit Cards [1][2][3][5]

★★ 68% Rose & Crown
High St HP23 5AH (Whitbread) ☎(0442) 824071 FAX (0442) 890735
This is a striking Tudor-style hotel in the centre of the town. Bedrooms in the original building tend to be larger but all are similarly well furnished and equipped in bright modern style. There is a popular lounge bar and attractive split-level restaurant with a conservatory extension. A new chef, Greg Barnes, has recently been appointed.
27⇌⋔(2fb)2⚙✂ in 5 bedrooms CTV in all bedrooms ®⚲ T ✂ (ex guide dogs) ✻ sB&B⇌⋔£59.50-£69.50 dB&B⇌⋔fr£71 ⌂
(70P *xmas*
♀ English & Continental V ⬡ ⚲ ✂ ✻ Lunch fr£9.95 Dinner fr£14.95 Last dinner 10pm
CONF. Thtr 80 Class 24 Board 30 Del from £92
Credit Cards [1][2][3][5]

Travel Inn
Tring Hill HP23 4LD (on A41 towards Aylesbury) ☎(0442) 824819

Purpose-built accommodation offers spacious and well equipped bedrooms, all with en suite bathrooms. Meals may be taken at the nearby family restaurant and pub. For more details about Travel Inns, consult the Contents page, under Hotel Groups.
30⇌⋔✻ B⇌⋔£33.50 (room only)

TRINITY

See *Jersey* under *Channel Islands*

TROON Strathclyde *Ayrshire* Map 10 NS33

★★★★ 63% *Marine Highland*
KA10 6HE (Scottish Highland) ☎(0292) 314444 FAX (0292) 316922
Commanding fine views across the Firth of Clyde to the island of Arran, this long-established hotel is popular with tourists, business people and the conference trade but is known primarily as a golfing hotel – it overlooks the 18th fairway of Troon's championship golf course. Bedrooms vary in size and comfort, with more luxury provided in the Ambassador rooms. Public rooms include relaxing lounges, the attractive, split-level Fairways Restaurant and stylish Crosbie's Brasserie.
72⇌⋔(7fb)1⚙✂ in 6 bedrooms CTV in all bedrooms ®⚲ T sB&B⇌⋔£82-£108 dB&B⇌⋔£138-£188 ⌂

Lift (CTV 200P ✻ ▣ (heated) squash snooker sauna solarium gymnasium beautician jacuzzi steam room ♪ ⚙ *xmas*
♀ International V ⬡ ⚲ ✂ Lunch £9.95-£13.50&alc Dinner £19.95-£21&alc Last dinner 10.30pm
CONF. Thtr 220 Class 170 Del from £105
Credit Cards [1][2][3][5] £

★★★ ❀❀❀ 74% *Lochgreen House*
Monktenhill Road, Southwood KA10 7EN (off Ayr-Prestwick rd) ☎(0292) 313343 FAX (0292) 318661
Set in 15 acres of lawns and wooded grounds, this fine turn-of-the-century mansion has spacious bedrooms, individually styled with attractive fabrics, antiques and superior bathrooms. Fresh flowers and welcoming open fires add to the appeal of the splendid day rooms. The new owner/chef Bill Costley has retained the services of Jim Allison to work with him in the kitchen.
7⇌⋔ CTV in all bedrooms ® T
(P ✻ ℓ (hard)
V ⬡ ⚲ ✂
Credit Cards [1][2][3]

★★★ ❀❀ 69% *Highgrove House*
Old Loans Rd KA10 7HL ☎(0292) 312511 FAX (0292) 318228
This small family-run hotel enjoys sweeping views of the coast. Bedrooms are attractively decorated and thoughtfully equipped. There is a cosy bar and a split-level restaurant. Bar-style meals are also served at lunchtime (booking advisable).
9⇌⋔(2fb) CTV in all bedrooms ® T ✂ (ex guide dogs)
(50P ⚙ ✻
♀ French V ⬡
Credit Cards [1][2][3]

★★★ 66% *Piersland House*
Craigend Rd KA10 6HD ☎(0292) 314747 FAX (0292) 315613
A very popular 19th-century mock-Tudor hotel, Piersland House retains many of the features of a private house. It has a splendid, partially wood panelled reception lounge bar which does a good trade in bar meals, as well as an elegant restaurant. Cottage annexe bedrooms, though less spacious than those in the main building, have small lounge areas.
15⇌⋔Annexe4⇌⋔(2fb)1⚙ CTV in all bedrooms ® T ✻ sB&B⇌⋔£56-£82 dB&B⇌⋔£89.50-£115 ⌂
(150P ✻ croquet putting ⚙ *xmas*
♀ British & Continental V ⬡ ✻ Lunch fr£10.95&alc High tea £5.95-£12.95alc Dinner fr£16.50&alc Last dinner 9.30pm
CONF. Thtr 100 Class 60 Board 40 Del from £66
Credit Cards [1][2][3][5] £

★★ 62% *Craiglea*
South Beach KA10 6EG ☎(0292) 311366 FAX (0292) 311366
Looking out across the south links to the sea, this long established hotel, although somewhat old-fashioned, is warm and comfortable and offers traditional values and attentive service provided by the Calderwood family and their staff.
20rm(10⇌⋔)(2fb) CTV in all bedrooms ® T sB&B£25-£35 sB&B⇌⋔£30-£45 dB&B£45-£55 dB&B⇌⋔£50-£65 ⌂
CTV 14P *xmas*
V ⬡ Lunch £6.50-£7.50&alc Dinner £7.50-£12.50&alc Last dinner 8.45pm
Credit Cards [1][2][3][5]

★★ 59% *Ardneil*
51 Saint Meddans St KA10 6NU ☎(0292) 311611
Accommodation in practical, mainly compact bedrooms is provided by this friendly commercial hotel. Bar and dining areas are popular for their sensibly priced meals, while the restaurant and cocktail bar are also used for functions.
9rm(3⇌4⋔)(2fb) CTV in all bedrooms ®⚲
100P ✻ snooker
V ⬡ ⚲ ✂ Last dinner 9pm
Credit Cards [1][2][3]

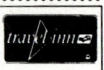

TROUTBECK (NEAR WINDERMERE) Cumbria
Map 07 NY40

★★72% **Mortal Man**
LA23 1PL (2.5m N from junct of A591/A592, 1st turning left after Jesus church) ☎Ambleside(05394) 33193 FAX (05394) 31261
Closed mid Nov-mid Feb
This historic hotel stands in an open, rural location with one of the best views in Lakeland, especially from the restaurant where a well produced dinner is served each evening. The bedrooms have a good range of facilities, and pretty coordinated fabrics add charm. The bars are full of character and a cosy lounge is also provided. Staff are genuinely caring.
12⇌⋔ CTV in all bedrooms ® T sB&B⇌⋔£50-£55 dB&B⇌⋔£110 (incl dinner) 🖃
20P ⇌ ✿ nc5yrs
V ✿ ⴲ ✻ Sunday Lunch £12 Dinner £18.50
Last dinner 8pm

TROWBRIDGE Wiltshire Map 03 ST85

★★60% **Polebarn**
Polebarn Rd BA14 7EW (off A361 in town centre, follow signs 'Police Station' ☎(0225) 777006 FAX (0225) 754164
This late Georgian Grade II listed building has an impressive façade and entrance hall, with an intimate bar and restaurant. Bedrooms vary in size but all are simply decorated and equipped with modern facilities. The husband and wife managers and friendly staff provide helpful service.
13rm(4⇌3⋔)(1fb) CTV in all bedrooms ® T ✻ sB&B⇌⋔£39.50 dB&B⇌⋔£50
CTV 10P 2🚗
♀ French ✻ Lunch fr£8.95 Dinner fr£11.95 Last dinner 8.45pm
Credit Cards 1 2 3

★65% **Hilbury Court**
Hilperton Rd BA14 7JW (0.5m from town centre on A361)
☎(0225) 752949 FAX (0225) 777990
Closed 24-31 Dec
An attractive Georgian property, Hilbury Court is set in its own beautiful gardens on the outskirts of town. Bedrooms are comfortable, and a spacious lounge and separate bar-lounge are provided. Dinner is a set meal served at a set time.
13rm(4⇌3⋔)(2fb) CTV in all bedrooms ® T ✻ (ex guide dogs) sB&B£32-£36 sB&B⇌⋔£39 dB&B£44 dB&B⇌⋔£52
CTV 14P ⇌ ✿
V ✿ ⴲ ✻ Bar Lunch £2-£4.50 Dinner £8-£10.50 Last dinner 7.30pm
Credit Cards 1 3

TRURO Cornwall & Isles of Scilly Map 02 SW84

★★★✦71% **Alverton Manor**
Tregolls Rd TR1 1XQ (on A390 towards St Austell)
☎(0872) 76633 FAX (0872) 222989
Built about 200 years ago and set in 6 acres of grounds, the main house and east wing of Alverton Manor have been beautifully restored to provide spacious and well furnished bedrooms. Public areas include a library, bar, lounge and candlelit restaurant. Chef Mike Smith provides enthusiastic standards of cooking in the modern English style.
25⇌⋔ CTV in all bedrooms T ✻ (ex guide dogs) ✻ sB&B⇌⋔£45-£59 dB&B⇌⋔£55-£69 🖃
Lift (60P ✿ snooker ⴲ xmas
♀ English & French V ✿ ⴲ ✻ ✻ Lunch £12.20-£15.55 Dinner fr£16.50&alc Last dinner 9.30pm
CONF. Thtr 200 Class 200 Board 200 Del £75
Credit Cards 1 2 3 5
See advertisement on page 619

Troutbeck - Truro

PIERSLAND
HOUSE HOTEL
★★★

A unique and historic Country House Hotel famed throughout Ayrshire for its hospitality.

TROON · AYRSHIRE
SCOTLAND
Tel 0292 · 314747
Fax 0292 · 315613

ARISTO
PERSONALITY HOTELS IN SCOTLAND

MARINE
HIGHLAND
HOTEL

This magnificent 4-star hotel overlooks the 18th Fairway of Royal Troon Championship Golf Course, with breathtaking views across the Firth of Clyde to the Isle of Arran, and is the perfect base for the business man and holidaymaker.

For the golfer, it's paradise! There are 22 other courses in the area, including such well known ones as Prestwick, Turnberry, Gailes, Barassie and many more.

All bedrooms are equipped to the highest standards and feature a number of superb Suites.
The award winning Marine Leisure and Sports Club offers a 50' × 27' heated swimming pool, jacuzzi, solaria, squash courts, saunas, gymnasium, beauty room, snooker room. Fairways Restaurant and Crosbie's Brasserie propose superlative choices for food and wines. The Conference and Banqueting centre accommodates up to 200 guests in a variety of first class suites.

★★★★

Marine Highland Hotel, Troon, Ayrshire KA10 6HE
Tel: 0292 314444. Fax: 0292 316922

Truro - Turnberry

★★★ 65% Brookdale
Tregolls Rd TR1 1JZ (on main A390) ☎(0872) 73513 & 79305 FAX (0872) 72400
Closed Xmas wk
Owners Ludi and Janet Marciano are totally involved in the professional management of this small hotel only 5 minutes walk from the city centre. The well equipped bedrooms are continually being upgraded and high standards of housekeeping are maintained.
22⇨(1fb) CTV in all bedrooms ® T ✻ (ex guide dogs) sB&B⇨↑fr£55 dB&B⇨↑fr£65 🍴
50P 10🚗
♥ English, French & Italian Dinner £16 Last dinner 8.45pm
Credit Cards ①②③⑤

★★ 59% Carlton
Falmouth Rd TR1 2HL ☎(0872) 72450 FAX (0872) 223938
Closed 21 Dec-5 Jan
This Victorian hotel is in an elevated position within walking distance of the city centre. Bedrooms are comfortable though simply furnished, and a busy bar is available to guests.
30rm(5⇨22↑)(4fb) CTV in all bedrooms ® T ✻ sB&B£29 sB&B⇨↑£33.50-£38.50 dB&B£40.30 dB&B⇨↑£47.75 🍴
32P 🚗 sauna solarium gymnasium spa bath
♥ ♫ ✻ Dinner £8.15&alc Last dinner 8pm
Credit Cards ①②③ £

○ Royal
Lemon St TR1 2QB ☎(0872) 70345 FAX (0872) 42453
Open
34⇨↑

TUNBRIDGE WELLS (ROYAL) Kent Map 05 TQ53

★★★ ⊛72% Spa
Mount Ephraim TN4 8XJ (follow signposts in Tunbridge Wells to A264 East Grinstead, hotel is on right hand side on leaving Tunbridge Wells)
☎Tunbridge Wells(0892) 520331 FAX (0892) 510575

For 3 generations the Goring family have harmonised traditional standards of hotel keeping with modern and progressive standards of management at the Spa Hotel, which was built around 1766. Set in its own landscaped parkland with 2 lakes, the hotel retains much of its original architectural grace. Services under the personal direction of the general manager Andrew Salter are extensive and attentive. Chef James Donaldson offers a daily set price lunch and dinner menu, together with an interesting international carte.
76⇨↑(10fb)1🛏⚿in 13 bedrooms CTV in all bedrooms ®⚷T ✻ (ex guide dogs) sB⇨↑£69-£90 dB⇨↑£84-£120 (room only) 🍴
Lift ℂ 120P ❋ 🏊 (heated) ℘ (hard) sauna solarium gymnasium croquet dance studio jacuzzi putting 🎱 xmas
♥ English, French & Japanese V ♫ ♪ ✻ Lunch £5-£15 Dinner £16-£25 Last dinner 9.30pm
CONF. Thtr 300 Class 150 Board 60 Del from £80
Credit Cards ①②③④⑤

★★★ 68% Pembury Resort
8 Tonbridge Rd, Pembury TN2 4QL (Pembury signed off A21) ☎(0892) 823567 FAX (0892) 823931

The nucleus of this new building in 1900s style is an oast house reception area. The bar and attractive lounge are furnished in a contemporary style and the Mallows Restaurant was named after the designer of the original dower house built at the time of the Arts and Crafts movement. All standard bedrooms have a double and single bed, and there are executive rooms and suites.
80⇨↑(8fb)⚿in 20 bedrooms CTV in all bedrooms ®⚷T ✻ sB⇨↑£65-£75 dB⇨↑£75-£85 (room only) 🍴
ℂ 150P 🏊 (heated) sauna solarium spa bath xmas

♥ English & French V ♫ ♪ ✻ Lunch £10-£19.95alc Dinner £16.50-£30alc Last dinner 10pm
Credit Cards ①②③⑤ £

★★ 67% Swan
The Pantiles TN2 5TD ☎(0892) 541450 & 527590 FAX (0892) 541465
On the Pantiles, the oldest part of the town, this fine family-run hotel has been completely redesigned and upgraded, and offers a choice of beautifully furnished modern bedrooms in various shapes and sizes. Chef Clive Standbridge produces a seasonally changing à la carte menu of dishes freshly prepared to order. The Pantiles Bar serves good lunch time bar food. Room service is provided.
17⇨↑(1fb)2🛏 CTV in all bedrooms ®⚷T ✻ ✻ sB&B⇨↑£40-£60 dB&B⇨↑£80-£110 🍴
ℂ CTV 12P 6🚗 xmas
V ♫ ♪ ✻ Lunch fr£11&alc Dinner fr£16&alc Last dinner 9.30pm
CONF. Thtr 60 Class 30 Board 30 Del from £80
Credit Cards ①②③⑤ £

★★ ⊛66% Royal Wells Inn
Mount Ephraim TN4 8BE
☎Tunbridge Wells(0892) 511188 FAX (0892) 511908

Closed 25-26 Dec RS 1 Jan & BH Mons
Built in Victorian times, this impressive family-run hotel overlooks the common and is well placed for the town centre and attractions. Bedrooms are of good standard, many with brass beds and period furniture. Guests have a choice of eating in the formal dining room, the first floor conservatory with its set or fish menu, or in the brasserie. Our inspector enjoyed Atlantic fish broth; sirloin with a red wine and shallot sauce, and a warm orange tart.
25rm(22⇨↑)2🛏 CTV in all bedrooms ® T
Lift 28P 4🚗 🚗
♥ English & French V ♫ Last dinner 10pm
Credit Cards ①②③⑤

★★ 64% Russell
80 London Rd TN1 1DZ (at junct A26/A264 uphill onto A26, hotel on right)
☎Tunbridge Wells(0892) 544833 FAX (0892) 515846

Formed from 3 Victorian houses near the town centre, this informal family-run hotel offers well equipped bedrooms, modern and spacious in the main house, and studio suites with luxurious bathrooms in the annexe. There is a cosy cocktail bar and a restaurant with a choice of menus.
21⇨↑ Annexe5⇨↑(3fb)⚿in 10 bedrooms CTV in all bedrooms ®⚷T ✻ (ex guide dogs) ✻ sB&B⇨↑£68-£80 dB&B⇨↑£82-£90 🍴
ℂ 20P xmas
♥ English & French V ♫ ♪ ✻ Lunch £9.50-£17.95&alc Dinner £9.50-£17.50&alc Last dinner 9.30pm
Credit Cards ①②③⑤ £

See advertisement on page 621

TURNBERRY Strathclyde Ayrshire Map 10 NS20

★★★★★⊛⊛
TURNBERRY HOTEL, GOLF COURSES & SPA
KA26 9LT (Leading Hotels)
☎(0655) 31000 FAX (0655) 31706

The Turnberry Hotel is a newcomer to our Red Star awards, and we know it

➡➡

618

THE SWAN HOTEL ★★

The Pantiles, Royal Tunbridge Wells, Kent TN2 5TD
Telephone: (0892) 541450/27590
Fax: (0892) 541465

The Swan Hotel is situated in the very heart of the Pantiles, the original part of the old spa town of Royal Tunbridge Wells. Dating from the late 1600's the Swan has been sympathetically restored and refurbished to provide stylish and comfortable accommodation in a prime location. The restaurant enjoys an excellent reputation, alternatively enjoy a light meal in the Pantiles Bar.

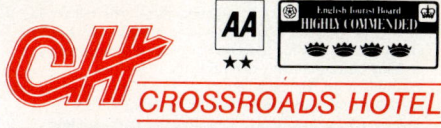

CROSSROADS HOTEL

SCORRIER · REDRUTH · CORNWALL TR16 5BP
TEL: (0209) 820551   FAX: (0209) 820392

SITUATED AT THE SCORRIER EXIT OF THE A30

This purpose built hotel offers high standard accommodation with all rooms en suite, central heating, tea/coffee, colour TV.
Ideal central location for visiting all parts of Cornwall. Excellent reputation for good food at reasonable prices with a choice of three menus.

CONFERENCE FACILITIES AND LARGE CAR PARK.

The Carlton Hotel
Falmouth Road, Truro, Cornwall
Tel: 0872 72450   ★★
Fax: 0872 223938

We are a family run hotel with all home cooking, table d'hôte and à la carte menus. 32 bedrooms, most with private bathroom and Colour TV, tea & coffee making facilities. Central heating throughout the Hotel. 3 residents' lounges. Large dining room. Sauna, gym & spa bath.

**Resident proprietors
Roy and Sheila Palmer.**

AA ★★★    Les Routiers

Alverton Manor HOTEL

Cornwall's Premier Country House Hotel set in 6 acres of wooded gardens, a short walk from the Cathedral City of Truro.

Explore the beautiful coastline of Cornwall, absorbing its history of King Arthur, smuggling and tin mining.

Truro is the ideal centre, Alverton Manor, with its grace and elegance the perfect base.

Leisure Breaks from £45 per person per night dinner accommodation and breakfast.

**For an occasion to savour and memory to treasure:
Tregolls Road, Truro
Reservations Tel: (0872) 76633**

Turnberry - Two Bridges

wholeheartedly. A fine Edwardian building, with two world-famous golf courses, it has been a good hotel for many years and has now made the transition to a very fine one which can look forward confidently to hosting the 1994 Open Championship. The most recent addition is the impressive spa and leisure complex – its swimming pool even has an underwater sound system! – including the appealing Bay Restaurant serving health-conscious cuisine. The hotel's main restaurant has a magnificent outlook taking in the golf course and the sea. Its sensibly sized à la carte menu tends towards the classical, and the supporting daily menu allows the kitchens to fulfil their more imaginative ideas. Bedrooms vary in size, but all are suitably appointed; Ocean View rooms have the best views. Public areas are extensive, elegant and comfortable and the hotel's management ethos encourages the highest levels of hospitality and unobtrusively efficient service from the smartly uniformed staff.

132⇨♨2🛏 CTV in all bedrooms ® T sB&B⇨♠£130-£195 dB&B⇨£145-£230 🅿
Lift (200P ❀ ❋ 🅰 (heated) ▶ 18 ♟ (hard) squash ↻ snooker sauna solarium gymnasium Spa & Leisure Centre 🎵 🐕 xmas
♀ Scottish & French V ♡ ♨ ✗ Lunch £18.75&alc Dinner £35&alc Last dinner 10pm
Conf. Thtr 160 Class 115 Board 50 Del from £158
Credit Cards 1 2 3 5

★★★ 69% **Malin Court**
KA26 9PB ☎(0655) 31457 FAX (0655) 31072
As well as being a hotel, this modern 2-storey building is also a residential home for the elderly. There is nothing at all institutional about its atmosphere or appearance, though – the décor is tasteful and attractive: there is a comfortable foyer lounge with a welcoming open fire; the well furnished restaurant has a strikingly draped ceiling. Bedrooms are not large but sensibly furnished and well equipped.
17⇨♠(2fb) CTV in all bedrooms ® T sB&B⇨♠£55-£85 dB&B⇨♠£90-£140 🅿
Lift (CTV 110P xmas
V ♡ ♨ Lunch £11.95&alc High tea £6-£8 Dinner £18.95&alc Last dinner 9.30pm
Conf. Thtr 200 Class 100 Board 40 Del from £45
Credit Cards 1 2 3 4 5

TURNERS HILL West Sussex Map **04** TQ33

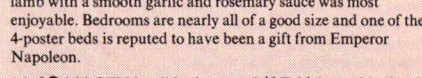

ALEXANDER HOUSE
East St RH10 4QD (on B2110 between Turners Hill and East Grinstead, 6m from junct 10 on M23)
☎Copthorne(0342) 714914 & 716333 FAX (0342) 717328
This magnificent country house is in a quiet rural setting yet not far from Gatwick Airport. If the entrance lobby seems a little small, the public rooms soon compensate – the south drawing room, the oak panelled library with its open log fire and the smaller western drawing room – all with fine furnishings and some superb paintings, creating an elegant and relaxing atmosphere. Chef Alan Pierce offers excellent cuisine. Fish is notably fresh, perhaps sea bass with scallops, or nage of red mullet and lobster. Soufflées are often available, and a succulent rack of

lamb with a smooth garlic and rosemary sauce was most enjoyable. Bedrooms are nearly all of a good size and one of the 4-poster beds is reputed to have been a gift from Emperor Napoleon.
16⇨♨♠2🛏 CTV in all bedrooms ® T ✗ (ex guide dogs) ✶ sB&B⇨♠fr£125 dB&B⇨♠fr£185 🅿
Lift (CTV 50P ❀ ❋ 🅰 (hard) ♟ snooker croquet clay pigeon shooting archery 🎵 nc7yrs xmas
♀ English & French V ♡ ♨ ✗ Lunch £18.50-£23&alc Dinner fr£35&alc Last dinner 9.30pm
Credit Cards 1 2 3 5

TURVEY Bedfordshire Map **04** SP95
★★ 59% **Laws**
High St MK43 8DB ☎(0234) 881213 & 881655 FAX (0234) 888864
This attractive stone house in the centre of the village has spacious comfortable bedrooms in the main building, with more compact rooms in a modern extension; all have modern facilities. The restaurant overlooks the attractive garden and there is a small lounge bar.
23rm(20⇨♠)(2fb)1🛏 CTV in 19 bedrooms ® T ✶ sB&B£25-£42 sB&B⇨♠£25-£42 dB&B⇨♠£44-£55 🅿
(35P ❀ ❋ gymnasium 🐕 xmas
♀ Continental V ♡ ♨ Last dinner 9.30pm
Conf. Thtr 50 Class 20 Board 18
Credit Cards 1 2 3

TUTBURY Staffordshire Map **08** SK22
★★★ 62% **Ye Olde Dog & Partridge**
High St DE13 9LS ☎Burton-on-Trent(0283) 813030 FAX (0283) 813178
Closed 25-26 Dec & 1 Jan
In the centre of the village, this 15th-century inn has a very busy self-service carvery restaurant – reservations are a necessity. Most of the bedrooms are in adjacent Georgian houses and are tastefully decorated with most amenities provided.
3⇨Annexe14⇨♠(1fb)3🛏 CTV in all bedrooms ® T ✶ sB&B⇨♠£55-£65 dB&B⇨♠£72.50-£80 🅿
(120P ❋ ❀
♀ English & French V ♡ ♨ ✗ Lunch £9.25-£15.75 Dinner £9.25-£15.75 Last dinner 10pm
Credit Cards 1 2 3

TWO BRIDGES Devon Map **02** SX67

★★ ❀♨ 74% **Prince Hall**
PL20 6SA (on B3357) (Logis) ☎Princetown(0822) 890403 FAX (0822) 890676
phone for details
Prince Hall, a former gentleman's residence set deep in the Dartmoor National Park, has fast gained a reputation for comfort and quality food. Bedrooms are spacious and elegantly furnished, and there is a choice of lounges. The intimate dining room has a distinctly French style, and the dishes prepared by chef/patron Jean-Claude Denat might include a delicate starter of terrine of fish accompanied by a tart cold lemon sauce. Game often features as a main course, and fresh fish dishes such as fricassée of sole, salmon, scallops and prawns with ginger and spring onions. Tessa Denat is a natural hostess.
8⇨♠(1fb)2🛏 CTV in all bedrooms ® T sB&B⇨♠£42.50-£60.50 dB&B⇨♠£85-£105 (incl dinner) 🅿
15P ❀ ❋ clay pigeon shooting
♀ English & French ✗ Dinner £19.95 Last dinner 8.30pm
Credit Cards 1 2 3 5

Tynemouth - Uckfield

TYNEMOUTH Tyne & Wear Map 12 NZ36
★★★ 58% *Park*
Grand Pde NE30 4JQ ☎091-257 1406 FAX 091-257 1716
RS Xmas & New Year
This friendly hotel occupies a prime position overlooking the coastline and sea, with easy access to major roads and the Tyne Tunnel. Bedroom standards vary, new rooms providing good modern facilities while others are rather dated and tired. Public areas are sound, though some stairways and corridors are in need of the attention which is scheduled. The staff throughout are friendly and helpful.
49rm(43⇨♠)(4fb) CTV in all bedrooms ® T
(400P sauna solarium gymnasium ♫
♀ English & French V ♥ ✗ Last dinner 9.30pm
Credit Cards 1 2 3 5

TYWYN Gwynedd Map 06 SH50
★★ 59% *Corbett Arms*
LL36 9DG (near cinema) ☎(0654) 710264 FAX (0654) 711775

This 18th-century hotel, popular with coach parties, is set in pretty lawns and gardens, and many bedrooms have lovely views of the surrounding mountains. Bedrooms are modestly furnished but have modern facilities. There is a choice of bars and the restaurant serves daily table d'hôte meals. There is a panelled residents' lounge as well as a foyer sitting area.
40⇨♠(2fb) CTV in all bedrooms ® T
60P 8🐾 ❊ croquet ♫
♀ English & French V ♥ ⌾ Last dinner 8.30pm
Credit Cards 1 2 3

★ 58% *Greenfield*
High St LL36 9AD (on A493, opposite leisure centre)
☎(0654) 710354
Closed Dec RS Jan-Mar
This small family-run hotel is in the High Street a short walk from the seafront. As well as the residents' dining room, which offers a fixed price menu, there is a separate restaurant open to the public in season serving a good range of light meals. There is a cosy bar and a small 2nd floor residents' lounge. Bedrooms are modestly furnished.
8rm(5⇨♠)(2fb) CTV in all bedrooms ® ✈ (ex guide dogs)
sB&B£17 sB&B⇨♠£19.50 dB&B£34 dB&B⇨♠£39
💃 🚭
V ♥ Lunch £4.75-£6.95 Dinner £6.95&alc Last dinner 9pm

UCKFIELD East Sussex Map 05 TQ42

★★★

★★★🌸🌸🌸⛳
HORSTED PLACE
Little Horsted TN22 5TS (2m S on A26 towards Lewes)
☎Isfield(0825) 750581 FAX (0825) 750459
This majestic hotel now forms part of the East National Golf Club estate. An obvious choice for golfers and those attending the European Golf Championship, the hotel retains its mansion house character. Accommodation is elegantly furnished and offers considerable luxury. Staff are courteous, formal and discreet, yet keen to please. The attractive, no smoking dining room is in 2 sections, and here chef Allan Garth offers a carte and a fixed price menu which changes every month. His ➡

Ye Olde Dog and Partridge ★★★
HIGH STREET, TUTBURY, STAFFS.
Telephone: 0283 813030

This mid 15th-century Inn famed for its association with Bull Running, and Mary Queen of Scots offers luxury accommodation. All rooms have private bath, colour television, radio alarm, tea and coffee-making facilities and a bar fridge.

Renowned carvery/rotisserie open seven days a week. Music on the grand piano nightly.

BTA commended.

COMFORT AND CONVENIENCE IN ROYAL TUNBRIDGE WELLS

A warm welcome awaits you in the family run Russell Hotel. You'll find it in a delightful location overlooking the Common, a few minutes walk from the town centre.

All 26 bedrooms are equipped to the very highest standards, including five studio suites for those who appreciate that extra touch of luxury.

All this plus a lounge bar, a restaurant serving freshly prepared specialities, full conference facilities and free parking make the Russell Hotel the perfect place to stay whether your visit to Tunbridge Wells is for business or pleasure.

THE *Russell* HOTEL
80 London Road, Tunbridge Wells, Kent TN1 1DZ
Tel: 0892 544833. Fax: 0892 515846. Telex: 95177G

Uckfield - Upper Slaughter

eclectic style of cooking offers a wide range of dishes, with starters such as 'ballotine de foie gras', pressed duck liver with a Sauternes jelly, and main courses like poached fillets of sole with slices of succulent lobster served in a fine butter and fish-stock sauce with wholemeal tagliatelli. Special praise is deserved for the variety and originality of the dessert menu, and for the well balanced wine list.

17🏠 CTV in all bedrooms T 🍽 (ex guide dogs) ✱
dB&B🍽£115-£245 Continental breakfast 🍴
Lift 30P 6🏊 ✿ 🅲 (heated) ▶ 18 ♫ (hard) ♪ croquet shooting *xmas*
♀ English & French V ✿ 🍷 ✂ ✱ Lunch £14.95-£18.50&alc Dinner £28.50&alc Last dinner 9.30pm
CONF. Thtr 45 Class 50 Board 28 Del from £130
Credit Cards 1 2 3 5

UDDINGSTON Strathclyde *Lanarkshire* Map **11** NS66

★★**64%** Redstones
8-10 Glasgow Rd G71 7AS (1m along A721) ☎(0698) 813774 & 814843 FAX (0698) 815319
Closed 24-25 Dec & 1-2 Jan
Two red sandstone villas have been linked to create this popular and friendly family-run business hotel. Recent improvements have enhanced the public areas, which include a comfortable, well stocked bar, a small foyer lounge and an attractive restaurant where table d'hôte and à la carte menus are available. Bedrooms are well equipped and practical.
18rm(16🛁🍽)2🏠 CTV in all bedrooms ®♫ T
🍽 (ex guide dogs) sB&B£38 sB&B🍽£55-£62 dB&B🍽£69-£78 🍴
🍸 CTV 33P 🎵 ✿
♀ Scottish, French & Italian V ✿ ✱
CONF. Thtr 20 Class 16 Board 14
Credit Cards 1 2 3 5

UIG

See **Skye, Isle of**

UIST (SOUTH), ISLE OF

See **South Uist, Isle of**

ULLAPOOL Highland *Ross & Cromarty* Map **14** NH19

★★**66%** Ceilidh Place
West Argyle St IV26 2TY ☎(0854) 612103 FAX (0854) 612886
Closed 2wks in Jan
Music, drama and art exhibitions are regular features at Robert and Jean Urquhart's delightful Highland hotel. The well maintained bedrooms are furnished in cottage style and the public areas – with their white stone walls, beamed ceilings and stone floors – include a coffee shop/bar, pleasant dining room and well stocked bookshop. There is a comfortable first floor lounge and refreshments, sometimes on a self-help basis, are available in the adjoining pantry.
13rm(10🍽) T sB&B£35 sB&B🍽£49.50 dB&B£70 dB&B🍽£99 🍴
30P ✿ *xmas*
♀ International V ✿ 🍷 ✂ Bar Lunch £7-£10alc High tea £8 Dinner £24 Last dinner 9pm
Credit Cards 1 2 3 5

ULLSWATER

See **Glenridding, Patterdale, Pooley Bridge** & **Watermillock**

Hotels with red star ratings are especially high quality.

ULVERSTON Cumbria Map **07** SD27

★★◉**65%** Virginia House
Queen St LA12 7AF (on B5281) ☎(0229) 584844
Chef/owner Alastair Sturgis and his Colombian wife Patricia are the excellent hosts at this small, town centre hotel. The bedrooms are modern in style and have good facilities. There is a modern bar/lounge, and a good dinner is served each evening in the attractive restaurant. Pâtés, soups, breads and puddings are all home made, and interesting main courses include many Colombian dishes.
7🏠(1fb) CTV in all bedrooms ® T 🍽 ✱ sB&B🍽£32-£37 dB&B🍽£44-£49 🍴
♪ 🎵 ✿
♀ International V ✿ 🍷 ✱ Dinner £13.95&alc Last dinner 8.45pm
Credit Cards 1 2 3 5

UNST

See **Shetland**

UPHALL Lothian *West Lothian* Map **11** NT07

★★★◉**65%** Houstoun House
EH52 6JS ☎Broxburn(0506) 853831 FAX (0506) 854220
Within easy reach of Edinburgh, this extended white gabled tower house stands in 20 acres of formal gardens and mature trees. Bedrooms in the original house are spacious traditional in style, while the more compact wing rooms are furnished in pine. There is a comfortable foyer and a vaulted bar with welcoming open fire and fine range of malts. A stone staircase leads up to the 3 dining areas, where chef Robert Taylor offers interesting Scottish dishes.
28🛁🍽Annexe2🛁🍽10🏠 CTV in all bedrooms ® T
sB&B🍽£89-£99 dB&B🍽£110-£140 (room only) 🍴
🍸 100P ✿ ▶ 18 *xmas*
V ✿ 🍷 ✂ ✱ Lunch £9.50-£15.50 Dinner fr£27.50&alc Last dinner 9.30pm
CONF. Thtr 65 Class 24 Board 30 Del from £97.50
Credit Cards 1 2 3 4 5

UPHOLLAND Lancashire Map **07** SD50

★★★**62%** Holland Hall
6 Lafford Ln WN8 0QZ (off A577) ☎(0695) 624426 FAX (0695) 622533
RS 25 Dec & 2 Jan
In a rural location overlooking a golf course this extended 17th-century country house has attractive bedrooms equipped with modern amenities, though some single rooms are rather compact. Public areas include a small comfortable lounge, elegant restaurant and lively pizza bar.
28🛁🍽Annexe6🛁🍽(1fb)1🏠 CTV in all bedrooms ® T 🍽 ✱
sB&B🍽£40-£49 dB&B🍽£46-£60 🍴
🍸 200P ✿
♀ English & American V ✿ 🍷 ✱ Sunday Lunch £7.95 Dinner £13.95 Last dinner 10pm
CONF. Thtr 200 Class 100 Board 80 Del from £69.50
Credit Cards 1 2 3 5

UPPER SLAUGHTER Gloucestershire Map **04** SP12

★★★◉◉♨**79%** Lords of the Manor
GL54 2JD (2m W of A429)
☎Cotswold(0451) 820243 FAX (0451) 820696
On the edge of an unspoiled village in 8 acres of gardens and parkland that include a trout lake, Lords of the Manor is a Cotswold stone house dating back to the 1650s which has benefited from numerous additions. The latest is a traditional-style courtyard, partly enclosed by new bedrooms, with period furniture and with

such thoughtful extras as bathrobes, quality soaps, fresh flowers and lovely Victorian watercolours. Public areas, with antiques and chintz, are peaceful and comfortable. Chef Clive Dixon has recently been appointed to head the kitchen.
29⇨🛏3🚻 CTV in all bedrooms T 🐕 (ex guide dogs) ✱
sB&B⇨🛁£80 dB&B⇨🛁£97.50-£185 🅿
(40P ✿ ♪ croquet *xmas*
V ⚭ ⚤ ✂ ✱ Lunch £14.40-£21.80alc Dinner £24.50&alc Last dinner 9.30pm
Credit Cards 1 2 3 5

UPPINGHAM Leicestershire Map 04 SP89

★★★61% Falcon
High St East LE15 9PY ☎(0572) 823535 FAX (0572) 821620
The Falcon is a hotel with lots of character in the middle of the town opposite the market place. The bright lobby area is popular for morning coffee and afternoon tea, and snacks are offered in the 2 bars. The restaurant provides favourite dishes prepared to a high standard. Bedrooms are adequately furnished and mostly spacious.
26⇨🛁(2fb)1🚻 CTV in all bedrooms ® T ✱ sB⇨🛁£40-£65 dB⇨🛁£50-£75 (room only) 🅿
(25P 3🎮 *xmas*
♥ English & French V ⚭ ⚤ ✱ Lunch £10.25&alc Dinner fr£14.25&alc Last dinner 10pm
CONF. Thtr 55 Class 30 Board 30 Del from £65
Credit Cards 1 2 3 5

★★🎖69% Lake Isle
High St East LE15 9PZ ☎(0572) 822951 FAX (0572) 822951
From the outside, the Lake Isle gives the impression of being a restaurant, which is a good indication of the importance attached to the meals here. The emphasis in the kitchen is on fresh, high quality ingredients, matched with honest seasoning to produce uncomplicated and well prepared meals from a short, daily changing menu and lunch-time carte. As in many European hotels, the attractive bedrooms are above the dining room and small bar; most are spacious, there are two full suites in a neighbouring cottage and great emphasis is laid on personal touches.
10⇨🛁Annexe2rm(1fb) CTV in all bedrooms ® T
sB&B⇨🛁£45-£55 dB&B⇨🛁£66-£76 🅿
6P 1🚗 🚭 *xmas*
♥ English & French V Lunch £9.75-£14&alc Dinner £20.50-£24.50 Last dinner 10pm
Credit Cards 1 2 3 5

★68% Crown
High St East LE15 9PY ☎Oakham(0572) 822302 & 821809 FAX (0572) 822942
RS Sun
A 17th-century inn, the Crown is located in the centre of town and offers spacious neatly furnished bedrooms with modern amenities. Public areas comprise a bar and dining room where meals are served. Staff are friendly and efficient.
7⇨🛁 CTV in all bedrooms ® T ✱ sB&B⇨🛁£33-£35 dB&B⇨🛁£44-£48
15P 🚭
V ⚭ ⚤ ✱ Lunch £3.95-£7.95alc Dinner £3.95-£7.95alc Last dinner 10pm
Credit Cards 1 2 3

UPTON UPON SEVERN Hereford & Worcester
Map 03 SO84

★★★59% White Lion
High St WR8 0HJ
☎Upton on Severn(0684) 592551 FAX (0684) 592251
Closed 25-26 Dec
Situated centrally in the town, this privately owned hotel dates from Tudor times, despite the Georgian facade. Bedrooms are generally compact, those in the original building having exposed timbers and

THE SWISS CHALET INN

Pooley Bridge, Lake Ullswater,
Cumbria CA10 2NN
Telephone & Fax: (07684) 86215

★ Popular family owned Inn, with accommodation en suite, colour TV etc
★ Close to shores of beautiful Lake Ullswater, in unspoilt countryside
★ A la carte menu of Swiss, Continental and English fayre cuisine
★ Only 5 miles from J40 of M6

Please write or telephone for brochure

Ullswater Hotel ★★★

Glenridding,
Cumbria CA11 0PA
Tel: (07684) 82444 Fax: (07684) 82303

An impressive hotel of lakeland slate, set in 20 acres on the shores of Lake Ullswater. 48 en suite bedrooms with special Honeymoon and four poster accommodation. Fine wines and first class food and accommodation. An ideal base for a walking holiday or exploring the Lakes by car. Free launching facilities. Helipad.
Relax and enjoy a holiday or break away from cares of everyday life.

Upton upon Severn - Wadebridge

stylish décor. Meals are available in the popular bar, with adjacent lounge area, and in the beamed restaurant which serves both à la carte and table d'hôte menus.
10⇌📞1🛏 CTV in all bedrooms ® T ✱ sB&B⇌📞fr£54.50 dB&B⇌📞£74.50-£82.50 🍴
18P 1🐾
♀ English & French V ♥ ♨ Lunch fr£14.95&alc Dinner fr£14.95&alc Last dinner 9.15pm
CONF. Thtr 30 Class 10 Board 20 Del from £70
Credit Cards 1 2 3 5

★★ **59%** Star
High St WR8 0HQ ☎(0684) 592300 FAX (0684) 592929

This converted 17th-century inn standing on the river bank at the heart of the town has a relaxed friendly atmosphere. Bedrooms vary in size and have a good range of facilities and there is an attractive beamed lounge bar and wood-panelled restaurant.
17⇌📞(2fb) CTV in all bedrooms ®☆ T ✱ sB&B⇌📞£30-£45 dB&B⇌📞£40-£60 🍴
8P 2🐾 ♨
V ♥ ♨ ✂ Lunch £8.50 High tea £1.75-£11.50 Dinner £11.50 Last dinner 9.30pm
CONF. Thtr 80 Class 50 Board 50 Del £65
Credit Cards 1 2 3 5

USK Gwent Map **03** SO30
★★ **73%** Glen-yr-Afon House
Pontypool Rd NP5 1SY (just outside town, on Pontypool road)
☎(0291) 672302 & 673202 FAX (0291) 672597
Surrounded by 3 acres of pleasant woods and grassland, this very well run hotel boasts an impressive circular library which is used for dinner parties and small meetings; the bar and lounge are very comfortable, while bedrooms are modern and well equipped. A good range of food is served, and staff are friendly and helpful.
27rm(26⇌📞)(2fb)⚹in 12 bedrooms CTV in all bedrooms ® T sB&Bfr£48.18 sB&B⇌📞£51.70 dB&Bfr£59.93 dB&B⇌📞£63.45 🍴
Lift 《 CTV 100P 1🐾 ✱ croquet ⛳ xmas
V ♥ ♨ ✂ Lunch £12-£16&alc High tea £4.50-£6.50 Dinner fr£14.75&alc Last dinner 9pm
CONF. Thtr 150 Class 120 Board 50 Del £71
Credit Cards 1 2 3

UTTOXETER Staffordshire Map **07** SK03
★★ **65%** Bank House
Church St ST14 8AG (opp St Mary the Virgin church)
☎(0889) 566922 FAX (0889) 567565
Once a bank, this property was built in 1777 and is close to the town centre and market. The attractively decorated bedrooms are furnished in keeping with the Georgian character of the building, but with modern facilities and equipment. The dining room is also in period style, and there is a pleasant lounge bar and residents' lounge.
16⇌📞(2fb)1🛏⚹in 2 bedrooms CTV in all bedrooms ® T ✱ sB&B⇌📞£37.50-£49.50 dB&B⇌📞£49.50-£69.50 🍴
CTV 16P xmas
♀ European V ♥ ♨ ✱ Sunday Lunch fr£7.95 Dinner fr£5.95alc Last dinner 9.45pm
Credit Cards 1 2 3 5

•••
Forte Travelodge
Ashbourne Rd ST14 5AA (on A50/A5030)
☎(0889) 562043 Central Res (0800) 850990

FORTE Travelodge

This modern building offers a good standard of accommodation for overnight stops. Smart, spacious and well equipped

bedrooms, all with en suite bathrooms, are suitable for family use, and meals may be taken at the nearby family restaurant. For more details about Travelodges, consult the Contents page, under Hotel Groups.
32⇌📞✱ dB⇌📞£31.95 (room only)

UXBRIDGE Greater London Map **04** TQ08
★★★ **62%** Master Brewer
Western Av UB10 9NX (Fullers) ☎(0895) 251199 FAX (0895) 810330
(For full entry see Hillingdon)

VALE
See **Guernsey** under **Channel Islands**

VENTNOR
See **Wight, Isle of**

VERYAN Cornwall & Isles of Scilly Map **02** SW93

★★★★ ❀**70%** Nare
Carne Beach TR2 5PF (from Tregony follow A3078 for approx 1.5m turn left at signpost Veryan, drive straight through village towards sea and hotel)
☎Truro(0872) 501279 FAX (0872) 501856
Closed 5 Jan-17 Feb
The Nare Hotel stands in extensive grounds surrounded by National Trust land and enjoys some of the best uninterrupted sea views in Cornwall. The accommodation has undergone major improvements in recent years and larger deluxe rooms have their own balcony or patio. Elegant public rooms, with log fires and fresh flowers in season, are furnished with antiques. Chef Malcolm Sparks offers professional cooking with particularly good home-made patisserie, vegetables, poultry and shellfish.
33⇌📞(4fb) CTV in all bedrooms ® T sB&B⇌📞£45-£104 dB&B⇌📞£90-£178
80P 🚗 ✱ ⇌ (heated) ♪ (hard) snooker sauna solarium gymnasium boating windsurfing ⛳ xmas
♀ English & French V ♥ ♨ Sunday Lunch £10&alc Dinner £25&alc Last dinner 9.30pm
Credit Cards 1 3

★★ **63%** Elerkey House
TR2 5QA ☎Truro(0872) 501261
This welcoming owner-run hotel in the pretty village provides neat and well equipped bedrooms with modern facilities (all no-smoking). The cosy traditionally furnished public areas have a pleasant atmosphere and the dining room offers a carte of home-cooked dishes.
7⇌📞⚹in all bedrooms CTV in all bedrooms ® T ✂
CTV 10P 🚗 ✱ nc10 yrs
♥ ♨ ✂ Last dinner 8pm
Credit Cards 1 3

WADEBRIDGE Cornwall & Isles of Scilly Map **02** SW97
★★ **58%** Molesworth Arms
Molesworth St PL27 7DP ☎(0208) 812055 FAX (0208) 814254
This 16th-century inn still has its original cobbled courtyard and archway entrance. A programme of renovation and improvement has been under way and bedrooms, which retain much of their original character, are now furnished with antiques and have good facilities. The panelled lounge bar provides a wide range of bar meals in a relaxed and informal atmosphere.
14rm(9⇌3📞)(2fb)1🛏 CTV in all bedrooms ® T
CTV 14P ⛳
V ♥ ♨ Last dinner 9.30pm
Credit Cards 1 3

WADHURST East Sussex Map 05 TQ63

★★ ❀❀❀ 68%Spindlewood Country House Hotel & Restaurant
Wallcrouch TN5 7JG (2.25m SE of Wadhurst on B2099)
☎Ticehurst(0580) 200430 FAX (0580) 201132
Closed 4 days Xmas RS Bank Hols
Run by the Fitzsimmons family, this late Victorian country house, set in 5 acres of gardens and woodland, has spacious bedrooms in period style. Chef Harvey Lee Aram offers a set menu, with daily fish and game specials. Starters may include a coarse rabbit and pigeon terrine or a firm sausage of seafood with a light fennel seed sauce. A main course of marinated venison is particularly tender and and there is always a hot pudding, and savouries such as Welsh rarebit and Scotch woodcock. The wine list features European and New World wines as well as local English wines.
9⇨↑(1fb) CTV in all bedrooms ® T ✱ (ex guide dogs)
sB&B⇨↑£47.50-£52 dB&B⇨↑£62.50-£85 ➡
60P ❀ ✿
♀ English & French V ◊ Lunch £14.95-£15.50&alc Dinner £23.20-£25alc Last dinner 9pm
CONF. Thtr 25 Class 16 Board 16 Del from £95
Credit Cards ⏍⑶

WAKEFIELD West Yorkshire Map 08 SE32

★★★ 71%St Pierre
Barnsley Rd, Newmillerdam WF2 6QG (3m S on A61)
☎(0924) 255596 FAX (0924) 252746
Ultra-modern and purpose-built, this hotel at the edge of the village has comfortable, well decorated bedrooms; one is suitable for disabled guests, there are 2 suites, and rooms for non-smokers. Public areas include a pleasant lounge bar, a bright lounge with an extensive all-day menu and an attractive bistro-style restaurant offering a wide range of dishes. Service is attentive and friendly.
44⇨↑⇋in 17 bedrooms CTV in all bedrooms ® ♀ T
sB&B⇨↑£49.50-£74.50 dB⇨↑£49.50-£74.50 (room only)
Lift ⦅ 80P pool table
♀ English & Continental V ◊ ⚏ ✱ Lunch £7.50-£7.95&alc Dinner £9.95-£12.95&alc Last dinner 10.30pm
Credit Cards ⏍②③④⑤

★★★ 70%Waterton Park
Walton Hall, The Balk, Walton WF2 6PW (3m SE off B6378) ☎(0924) 257911 FAX (0924) 240082   CONSORT HOTELS
This beautiful manor house enjoys a unique setting on an island in the middle of a wildfowl lake. Its dignified public rooms are spacious and comfortable, and the bedrooms have recently been attractively redecorated.
31⇨↑(1fb)3⇋ CTV in all bedrooms ® T ✱ ❉
sB&B⇨↑£68-£73 dB&B⇨↑£80-£98 ➡
⦅ 100P ❀ ⌺ (heated) ✦ squash snooker sauna solarium gymnasium boating jacuzzi beautician masseur *xmas*
♀ English & French V ◊ ⚏ ✱ Lunch fr£11 Dinner fr£17.95&alc Last dinner 9.30pm
Credit Cards ⏍②③⑤

★★★ 66%Cedar Court
Denby Dale Road, Calder Grove WF4 3QZ (adjacent to junct 39 on M1) ☎(0924) 276310 FAX (0924) 280221
This large modern hotel is conveniently placed, and offers spacious, inviting bedrooms, pleasant bar and lounge areas, and two restaurants, both serving imaginative food. Service is courteous.
151⇨↑⇋in 59 bedrooms CTV in all bedrooms ® ♀ T
sB⇨↑£48.50-£75 dB⇨↑£48.50-£85 (room only) ➡
Lift ⦅ ⏛ 350P ❀
♀ English, French & Italian V ◊ ⚏ ✱ Lunch £9.25-£12.50&alc Dinner £13.95-£14.50&alc Last dinner 10pm
CONF. Thtr 400 Class 200 Board 150 Del from £80
Credit Cards ⏍②③⑤

The Nare Hotel

Carne Beach, Veryan, Truro
Cornwall TR2 5PF
Telephone: (0872) 501279
★ ★ ★ ★ AA ❀

Open throughout the year to enjoy the desirable climate and outstanding beauty of the coast and countryside. The hotel stands in extensive grounds with uninterrupted views of the sea and coastline. All bedrooms are well appointed and comfortable, many with sea views and patios. Excellent cuisine – specialities are local seafood – extensive and varied wine list. Heated swimming pool with sun terraces overlooking the beach. Hotel boat, concessionary golf, tennis court.

Glen-yr-Afon House Hotel ★★

Pontypool Road, Usk, Gwent NP5 1SY
Tel: (0291) 672302 or 673202 Fax: (0291) 672597

An elegant country house, providing gracious service and fine home-cooked food in a warm, friendly atmosphere. Situated in mature, secluded grounds, five minutes walk from the historic village of Usk. It has tastefully decorated rooms all with private bath or shower, three comfortable lounges (one with colour TV, the other containing a fully stocked bar). Under the personal supervision of the proprietors.

American Express, Visa and Access accepted

Wakefield - Wallingford

★★★ 61% Swallow
Queens St WF1 1JV ☎(0924) 372111 FAX (0924) 383648

A modern multi-storey hotel beside the Ridings Shopping Centre. The smart first floor restaurant and cocktail bar have dark wood panelling and blue/green décor. Bedrooms on the upper floors belong to a previous decade with solid teak fittings, and are generally in need of refreshing, but are roomy and comfortable. Staff are very friendly and helpful.

64⇨↑(4fb)⊬in 17 bedrooms CTV in all bedrooms ®✻ T ✱ sB&B⇨↑fr£72 dB&B⇨↑fr£86 ⊟
Lift ⦅ 40P xmas
♀ English & French V ◊ ⊒ ⊬ ✱ Lunch fr£8 Dinner fr£13.50 Last dinner 9.45pm
CONF. Thtr 200 Class 90 Board 40 Del £92
Credit Cards ①②③⑤

Campanile
Monckton Rd WF2 7AL ☎(0924) 201054 FAX (0924) 201055

A nearby bar and bistro restaurant provides refreshments for travellers staying at this modern accommodation building. Bedrooms are well equipped and have en suite bathrooms. For more details about Campanile, consult the Contents page, under Hotel Groups.

Annexe77⇨↑ B⇨↑£35.75 (room only)

Forte Posthouse
Queen's Dr, Ossett WF5 9BE ☎(0924) 276388 FAX (0924) 276437

Suitable for both the business and leisure traveller, this bright hotel provides modern accommodation in well equipped bedrooms with en suite bathrooms. For more details about Forte Posthouse hotels, consult the Contents page, under Hotel Groups.

99⇨↑✱ B⇨↑£41.50-£53.50 (room only)
CONF. Thtr 140 Class 100 Board 100

Granada Lodge
M1 Service Area, West Bretton WF4 4LQ
☎(0924) 830569 FAX (0924) 830609
(For full entry see Woolley Edge)

WALKERBURN Borders Peeblesshire Map 11 NT33

★★★⛷ 57% Tweed Valley Hotel & Restaurant
Galashiels Rd EH43 6AA (on A72 overlooking the River Tweed) (Logis) ☎(089687) 636 FAX (089687) 639
Closed 25 & 26 Dec

Standing in its own grounds and enjoying lovely views over the valley, this friendly, family-run hotel offers a relaxed and informal atmosphere. The public areas feature oak panelling and ornate ceilings, while bedrooms are more functional. Rooms in the rear wing are more compact.

16⇨↑(2fb)1⊞ CTV in all bedrooms ® T sB&B⇨↑£40-£52 dB&B⇨↑£80-£92 ⊟
35P ✿ ♪ sauna solarium gymnasium shooting stalking ⚘ xmas
♀ Scottish, English & French V ◊ ⊒ ⊬ Lunch £8.50-£10.50 High tea £5.50-£12alc Dinner £23&alc Last dinner 9.30pm
CONF. Thtr 65 Class 30 Board 50 Del from £58.50
Credit Cards ①③

The AA's star rating scheme is the market leader in hotel classification.

WALLASEY Merseyside Map 07 SJ29

★★ 68% Grove House
Grove Rd L45 3HF ☎051-639 3947 & 051-630 4558 FAX 051-630 0028
RS no restaurant BH's

This small personally run hotel is located in a quiet residential area close to the underground station for trains to Liverpool. Service is friendly and attentive and the attractive modern bedrooms include many thoughtful extras. There is a comfortable bar and pleasant panelled restaurant, plus a rear garden.

14⇨↑(1fb)1⊞ CTV in all bedrooms ®✻ T ✱ sB⇨↑£29.50-£45 dB⇨↑£29.50-£45.50 (room only)
⦅ 20P ⇌ ✿
♀ English & French V Last dinner 10pm
CONF. Thtr 50 Class 35 Board 20 Del £69
Credit Cards ①③

WALLINGFORD Oxfordshire Map 04 SU68

★★★ ✪ 74% Springs
Wallingford Rd, North Stoke OX10 6BE (on the B4009)
☎(0491) 836687 FAX (0491) 836877

This mock Tudor style hotel, dating from 1874, stands in 30 acres of gardens and grounds overlooking the spring fed lake from which it gets its name. The bedrooms are tastefully decorated and furnished, and many have balconies. The lounge bar and restaurant are in the original building and are full of character, with wood panelling and open fireplaces. A regularly changing carte and table d'hôte menu are available; soups are popular and seafood is generally featured.

36⇨↑(4fb) CTV in all bedrooms T ✱ sB&B⇨↑£75-£85 dB&B⇨↑£100-£115 ⊟
⦅ 130P ✿ ⇌ (heated) ♪ (hard) sauna croquet putting xmas
♀ English & French V ◊ ⊒ ✱ Lunch £12.50-£18&alc Dinner £19.50-£21&alc Last dinner 9.45pm
CONF. Thtr 50 Class 16 Board 28 Del from £125
Credit Cards ①②③④⑤

★★★ 66% George
High St OX10 0BS ☎(0491) 836665 FAX (0491) 825359

This friendly hotel in the town centre dates to Tudor times and has a choice of beamed bars and a restaurant offering imaginative dishes. Bedrooms are comfortable and well equipped, with characterful rooms in the main building and attractive modern rooms in the extension.

39⇨↑(1fb)⊬in 9 bedrooms CTV in all bedrooms ® T ✱ sB⇨↑£59-£69 dB⇨↑£79-£89 (room only) ⊟
⦅ 60P xmas
♀ English & French V ◊ ⊒ ⊬ ✱ Lunch £9.95-£12.95&alc High tea £4.75-£6.75 Dinner £16.95&alc Last dinner 10.30pm
CONF. Thtr 120 Class 60 Board 40 Del from £75
Credit Cards ①②③⑤

★★★ 65% Shillingford Bridge
Shillingford OX10 8LZ (2m N A329) (Forestdale)
☎Warborough(086732) 8567. Due to change to (0865) 858567 FAX (086732) 8636 due to change to (0865) 858636

The Shillingford Bridge is in a delightful Thameside location with gardens down to the river and its own moorings. The majority of the bedrooms have been refurbished since 1990, with 11 new rooms added in 1993. Public areas are spacious and have been upgraded to provide colour coordinated comfort.

34⇨↑ Annexe8⇨↑(6fb)2⊞⊬in 4 bedrooms CTV in all bedrooms ® T sB&B⇨↑£44.95 dB&B⇨↑£59.90-£79.90 ⊟
100P ✿ ⇌ (heated) ♪ squash ♫ xmas
♀ International V ◊ ⊒ ✱ Lunch £11.95-£17.95&alc Dinner £14.75-£17.95&alc Last dinner 10pm
Credit Cards ①②③⑤

WALLSEND Tyne & Wear Map 12 NZ26

★★★ 60% **Newcastle Moat House**
Coast Rd NE28 9HP (on junct of A19/A1058, just N of Tyne tunnel) ☎091-262 8989 & 091-262 7044 FAX 091-263 4172

Recent refurbishment of public areas and the provision of a health and leisure complex, together with the upgrading of some bedrooms, has considerably enhanced this hotel; the majority of bedrooms are now somewhat dated, though improvements are planned.

147⇌♠(4fb)⚹in 10 bedrooms CTV in all bedrooms ® T ✱ sB&B⇌♠fr£58 dB&B⇌♠fr£68 ◪
Lift ⓒ 500P sauna solarium gymnasium steam room plunge pool jacuzzi *xmas*
♀ English & Continental V ♢ ♨ ✱ Lunch £10-£11.95&alc Dinner £13.80-£14.25&alc Last dinner 9.45pm
CONF. Thtr 500 Class 250 Board 150 Del from £78
Credit Cards [1][2][3][5]

WALSALL West Midlands Map 07 SP09

See also **Barr, Great**

★★★ ❀66% **Fairlawns**
178 Little Aston Road, Aldridge WS9 0NU
(3m NE off A454)
☎Aldridge(0922) 55122 FAX (0922) 743210
RS 24 Dec-2 Jan

This privately owned hotel offers modern accommodation with a good range of facilities. The hotel is justifiably proud of its restaurant, where chef Stefan Wilkinson offers table d'hôte and à la carte menus supplemented by daily fish specialities.

35⇌♠(5fb) CTV in all bedrooms ® T ✱ sB&B⇌♠£39.50-£69.50 dB&B⇌♠£50-£79.50 ◪
ⓒ 80P ❀
♀ English & French V ♢ ♨ ⚹ ✱ Lunch £2.20-£26.50alc Dinner £19.95&alc Last dinner 10pm
CONF. Thtr 80 Class 40 Board 36 Del from £49.50
Credit Cards [1][2][3][4][5]

★★★ 66% **Friendly Hotel**
20 Wolverhampton Rd West, Bentley WS2 0BS
(junct 10, M6) ☎(0922) 724444 FAX (0922) 723148

This conveniently located modern hotel provides spacious and well equipped bedrooms and open-plan public areas with plenty of comfortable seating. There is a carvery restaurant and a range of leisure facilities.

155⇌♠(20fb)2⌸⚹in 60 bedrooms CTV in all bedrooms ®⚹ T ✱ sB⇌♠£55-£67 dB⇌♠£69.50-£82 (room only) ◪
ⓒ 200P ❀ ▭ (heated) sauna solarium gymnasium jacuzzi
♀ English & French V ♢ ♨ ⚹ ✱ Lunch fr£8.50&alc Dinner fr£12.50&alc Last dinner 9.45pm
CONF. Thtr 180 Class 80 Board 70 Del from £80
Credit Cards [1][2][3][5]

★★★ 60% **Beverley**
58 Lichfield Rd WS4 2DJ (1m on A461) ☎(0922) 614967 & 22999 FAX (0922) 724187

This privately owned hotel has continued to expand from its origins as a late 19th-century family home. The well equipped bedrooms vary in size and have dark furnishings. There is a bar with a conservatory extension and a restaurant serving a popular menu. Staff are pleasant and welcoming, creating a home-from-home atmosphere for a predominantly commercial clientèle.

30⇌♠(2fb)⚹in 2 bedrooms CTV in all bedrooms ® T ✘ (ex guide dogs) ✱ sB&B⇌♠£35-£40 dB&B⇌♠£35-£49.50 ◪
ⓒ CTV 60P 8⛟ sauna solarium gymnasium games room
♀ English & French V ♢ ♨ ⚹ ✱ Lunch fr£6.95&alc Dinner £12.95&alc Last dinner 9.30pm
Credit Cards [1][2][3]

WALSALL
For business or pleasure stay friendly

Friendly Hotel, Junction 10-M6, 20 Wolverhampton Road West, Bentley, Walsall, West Midlands WS2 0BS.

AA ★★★

Premier Plus Rooms and Suites. Own hotel parking. Superb leisure centre. Conveniently situated off junction 10 of the M6, guarantees you an ideal base for the West Midlands and the NEC.

FOR RESERVATIONS (office hours) FREEPHONE
0800 591910
or call direct on 0922 724444 Fax: 0922 723148

It pays to stay Friendly

A "GROVE HOUSE" HOTEL AND RESTAURANT
GROVE ROAD, WALLASEY

AA ★★

GREAT VALUE LUXURY BEDROOMS

• ALL WITH EN SUITE • 4 POSTER BRIDAL SUITE • TV & SATELLITE TV • SPECIAL WEEKEND RATES • A LA CARTE & TABLE D'HOTE RESTAURANT
OPEN 7 DAYS
• FUNCTION SUITE – UP TO 110 FOR WEDDINGS & SPECIAL CELEBRATIONS

5 MINS FROM M53 & WALLASEY TUNNEL
051 630 4558
GROVE ROAD, WALLASEY, MERSEYSIDE L45 3HF

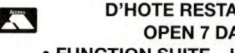

Walsall - Ware

★★★ 58% Barons Court
Walsall Rd, Walsall Wood WS9 9AH (3m NE A461) (Fine English) ☎Brownhills(0543) 452020 FAX (0543) 361276
This popular mock-Tudor hotel has ornate public areas with lots of brass, copper and Cotswold stone. Plainly decorated bedrooms, many with 4-poster beds, are well equipped and the hotel has a health hydro with a heart-shaped swimming pool.
100⇨(5fb)23⊞⧫in 6 bedrooms CTV in all bedrooms ®⚁T sB&B⇨£50-£60 dB&B⇨£60-£70 ₽
Lift ℂ 180P ⊡ (heated) sauna solarium gymnasium health hydro whirlpool ♫
♀ English & French V ♡ ⚒ ⧫ Lunch £6.50-£14.95 Dinner £14.95&alc Last dinner 9.45pm
CONF. Thtr 110 Class 60 Board 50 Del from £69.50
Credit Cards 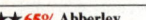 £

★★ 65% Abberley
Bescot Rd WS2 9AD (junct 9 of M6 and A461) ☎(0922) 27413 FAX (0922) 720933
This family-run hotel in a large Victorian building offers comfortably furnished well decorated accommodation, with facilities geared to the commercial user.
28⇨ℕ(4fb)⊞ℕ in 4 bedrooms CTV in all bedrooms ®⚁T sB&B⇨ℕ£39.90-£42 dB&B⇨ℕ£45-£52.90 ₽
ℂ 29P practice golf net xmas
♀ English & French V ♡ ⚒ ⧫ Sunday Lunch £8.50-£10.25 High tea £5.50 Dinner £9.75-£10.20&alc Last dinner 8.30pm
CONF. Thtr 40 Class 30 Board 25 Del from £58
Credit Cards ① ② ③ £

★★ 54% Bescot
Bescot Rd WS2 9DG (junct 9, M6, off A317) ☎(0922) 22447 FAX (0922) 30256
This privately run hotel with a largely commercial clientèle provides a convivial atmosphere and has a tiny, popular bar and modest bedrooms with modern facilities.
13rm(12⇨ℕ)Annexe11⇨ℕ(1fb) CTV in all bedrooms ®⚁T ✠ (ex guide dogs) ✱ sB&B⇨ℕ£29.50 dB&B⇨ℕ£55 ₽
ℂ 40P
♀ International V ♡ ⚒ ✱ Lunch £7.25 Dinner £9.50 Last dinner 9.30pm
Credit Cards ① ② ③ ⑤

Forte Posthouse
Birmingham Rd WS5 3AB ☎(0922) 33555 FAX (0922) 612034

FORTE Posthouse

Suitable for the business and leisure traveller, this bright hotel provides modern accommodation in well equipped bedrooms with en suite bathrooms. For more details about Forte Posthouse hotels, consult the Contents page, under Hotel Groups.
98⇨ℕ ✱ B⇨ℕ£41.50-£53.50 (room only)
CONF. Thtr 45 Class 20 Board 20 Del £89.50

WALTHAM ABBEY Essex Map 05 TL30

★★★★ 63% Swallow
Old Shire Ln EN9 3LX (off junct 26 of M25) ☎Lea Valley(0992) 717170 FAX (0992) 711891

SWALLOW HOTELS

Its convenient position makes this modern hotel popular for business meetings and conferences. Spacious bedrooms have been designed with guests' comfort in mind with such thoughtful extras as fresh milk and soft drinks in the fridges and an ironing board. The foyer cocktail bar is being redesigned and every evening a pianist plays. The 2 restaurants, an informal brasserie and the Glade à la carte, are contemporary in style with modern prints, furnishings and a high domed ceiling.
163⇨ℕ(10fb)4⊞⧫in 60 bedrooms CTV in all bedrooms ®⚁ T sB&B⇨ℕ£60-£95 dB&B⇨ℕ£70-£115 ₽
ℂ ⊞ 240P ⊡ (heated) sauna solarium gymnasium steam room ♫ xmas

♀ English & Continental V ♡ ⚒ Lunch £9.50-£14.75&alc High tea £9-£11 Dinner £16.50-£21&alc Last dinner 11pm
CONF. Thtr 250 Class 100 Board 80 Del from £98
Credit Cards ① ② ③ ⑤ £

WALTON UPON THAMES
See **Shepperton** & **Weybridge**

WANSFORD Cambridgeshire Map 04 TL09

★★★ 66% The Haycock Hotel
PE8 6JA (at junct of A47/A1) (PH) ☎Stamford(0780) 782223 FAX (0780) 783031
A 17th-century coaching inn, with substantial grounds and gardens, in a peaceful village location. Above average accommodation is provided, each bedroom individually styled with good soft furnishings. There is a choice of buttery or restaurant, and services, including early morning tea and shoe cleaning, are provided by a courteous youthful team.
51⇨ℕ(4fb)4⊞ CTV in all bedrooms⚁ T ✱ sB&B⇨ℕ£69-£85 dB&B⇨ℕ£89-£130 ₽
ℂ 300P ✿ ♪ petanque outdoor chess xmas
♀ V ♡ ⚒ ⧫ ✱ Lunch £14.95&alc Dinner £23-£27alc Last dinner 10.15pm
CONF. Thtr 250 Class 60 Board 60 Del from £99
Credit Cards ① ② ③ ⑤

WANTAGE Oxfordshire Map 04 SU48

★★ 62% Bear
Market Place OX12 8AB (10m from junct 14 of M4, follow A338 to Wantage) (Calotels) ☎(0235) 766366 FAX (0235) 768826
This historic hotel at the centre of the town has an attractive beamed restaurant on the first-floor, offering a wide range of dishes on its table d'hôte and carte menus. Bedrooms vary in size and style but all are well equipped and there is a comfortable lounge and a bar serving bar meals.
34⇨ℕ(2fb) CTV in all bedrooms ® T sB&B⇨ℕ£29-£55 dB&B⇨ℕ£58-£65
Lift ℂ ⚒ xmas
♀ French V ♡ Lunch £8.25-£10 Dinner £14.50-£20&alc Last dinner 9.30pm
CONF. Thtr 80 Class 25 Board 30 Del from £70
Credit Cards ① ② ③ ⑤
See advertisement under OXFORD

WARE Hertfordshire Map 05 TL31

★★★★★ ❀❀❀ 78% Hanbury Manor
SG12 0SD (on A10) ☎(0920) 487722 FAX (0920) 487692

Set in extensive parkland, of which the main feature is the golf course designed by Jack Nicklaus II, this luxurious hotel dates from the Jacobean area. From its early and rather hesitant beginnings, the hotel has grown in stature, much of the success being due to the general manager Jean Jacques Pergant and his well trained staff. Of the three restaurants, The Zodiac Room, with its choices of imaginative menus, shows off the skills of executive chef Rory Kennedy and his team to best advantage. His style is a clever combination of modern trends, well tried classics and occasional innovation. The soufflé suissesse Gavroche is a permanent feature, wonderfully light in texture and set in a rich cheese sauce. Inspectors have praised the tip-top quality of the shellfish here, and on a recent visit found the lamb wrapped in caul succulent and full of flavour. Other enjoyable dishes have been oysters alenoise with watercress purée, confidently cooked breast of duck with olives and délice de Gascogne, a confection including chocolate, prunes and armagnac that revealed a new level of expertise in the pastry section. Wine service has disappointed our inspectors, who have found that the staff lacked sufficient knowledge and were apt to serve incorrect vintages.

Ware - Wareham

69⇨↾ Annexe27⇨↾4🛏↳in 10 bedrooms CTV in all bedrooms ®✡T sB&B⇨↾£98-£340 dB&B⇨↾£108-£350 ♨ Lift ✆200P ❋ 🖳(heated) ▶ 18 ♬ (hard) squash sauna solarium gymnasium whirlpool beauty studio hair salon xmas
♡ English & French V ♡ ⚏ ↳ ✱ Lunch £18.75-£26&alc Dinner £25&alc Last dinner 10.30pm
CONF. Thtr 140 Class 54 Board 50 Del from £150
Credit Cards

⭐⭐⭐ **64%** **Ware Moat House**
Baldock St SG12 9DR (on A1170, on left behind fire station) ☎(0920) 465011 FAX (0920) 468016

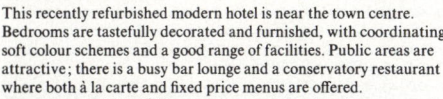
Queens Moat Houses

Closed 24 Dec-4 Jan
This recently refurbished modern hotel is near the town centre. Bedrooms are tastefully decorated and furnished, with coordinating soft colour schemes and a good range of facilities. Public areas are attractive; there is a busy bar lounge and a conservatory restaurant where both à la carte and fixed price menus are offered.
50rm(43⇨6↾)(1fb)↳in 16 bedrooms CTV in all bedrooms ® T ✱ sB&B⇨↾fr£69.50 dB&B⇨↾fr£80 ♨
Lift ✆100P
♡ English & Continental V ♡ ⚏ ↳ ✱ Lunch £10-£16.50&alc Dinner £16.50-£18&alc Last dinner 9.30pm
Credit Cards 1 2 3 4 5

WAREHAM Dorset Map 03 SY98

⭐⭐⭐

⭐⭐⭐❋❋ **PRIORY**
Church Green BH20 4ND
☎(0929) 552772 & 551666
FAX (0929) 554519

An early 16th-century priory has been sympathetically converted to create this hotel of considerable character and charm with 4 acres of magnificent gardens stretching down to the banks of the River Frome. Bedrooms are individually furnished with family pieces and many thoughtful extras. There is a drawing room and a garden terrace, ideal for afternoon tea. Breakfast and lunch are served in the Greenwood Dining Room and dinner in the vaulted Abbots Cellar Restaurant. Chef Michael Rust offers monthly changing, fixed-price and à la carte menus. All dishes are freshly prepared and cooked with dedicated care by the reliable kitchen. The hospitality and levels of service provided under the supervision of the proprietor, John Turner, make the Priory Hotel one of Britain's best.
15⇨↾Annexe4⇨↾2🛏 CTV in all bedrooms T ✈ (ex guide dogs)
✆25P ❋ ❋ ♪ croquet sailing ♫
V ♡ ⚏ Last dinner 10pm
Credit Cards 1 2 3 5

⭐⭐⭐ ❋**71%** **Springfield Country**
Grange Road, Stoborough BH20 5AL (From Wareham take Stoborough road then first right in village to join by-pass. Take first turn immediately on right for hotel)
☎(0929) 552177 FAX (0929) 551862

A smart, mainly commercial and conference hotel, the Springfield offers a high standard of accommodation with well equipped and comfortable bedrooms, good lounge facilities and a lounge bar. A superb leisure centre was nearing completion at the time of our visit. In the main restaurant, chef Andy Cannon offers an interesting, set-price menu with a good choice of French classic dishes.

32⇨↾(7fb) CTV in all bedrooms ®✡T sB&B⇨↾£55-£65 dB&B⇨↾£90-£110 ♨
Lift ✆100P ❋ ❋ 🖳(heated) ⌕ (heated) ♬ (hard) squash snooker sauna solarium gymnasium table tennis pool table nc2yrs 🐕
♡ English & Continental V ♡ ⚏ ✱ Sunday Lunch £8.95-£10.95 High tea £4-£8alc Dinner fr£16.95&alc Last dinner 9pm
Credit Cards 1 2 3

⭐⭐ ❋**67%** *Kemps Country House*
East Stoke BH20 6AL ☎Bindon Abbey(0929) 462563 FAX (0929) 405287
Closed 26-31 Dec
This former Victorian rectory is personally managed by the charming Mr and Mrs Warren who are always on hand to ensure that guests enjoy their stay. Bedrooms range from standard to superior, with new wing rooms being particularly luxurious. Public areas include a convivial bar and lounge plus a small, quiet study. The restaurant has a conservatory extension, and both daily changing and à la carte menus are available.
5rm(1⇨3↾)Annexe10⇨↾(4fb)1🛏 CTV in all bedrooms ® T ✈
50P ❋ ❋
♡ English & French V ♡ ↳ Last dinner 9.30pm
Credit Cards 1 2 3 4 5

⭐⭐ **63%** *Worgret Manor*
BH20 6AB ☎(0929) 552957
This fine Georgian building is to the west of the town. The hotel continues to improve and offers comfortable, well equipped bedrooms and a small, modern-style lounge. The attractive restaurant offers an interesting carte of carefully prepared dishes, while light hot and cold snacks are available in the popular bar.
10rm(5↾)(3fb) CTV in all bedrooms ® T ✱ sB&B£32-£36 sB&B↾£36 dB&B£44 dB&B↾£50-£56 ♨ ➤

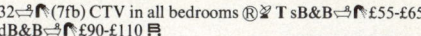

The BESCOT Hotel
⭐⭐

Privately owned hotel
Close to junction 9, M6
34 luxury en suite bedrooms
Relaxed and friendly atmosphere
Ample parking

Bescot Road, Walsall
West Midlands WS2 9DG

Telephone:
(0922) 22447
Fax: (0922) 30256

Wareham - Warrington

CTV 40P ✿
♿ English & French V ✿
Credit Cards [1][3]

WARMINSTER Wiltshire Map 03 ST84

★★★★ ●●♨♣ 68% **Bishopstrow House Hotel**
BA12 9HH (off A36) ☎(0985) 212312 FAX (0985) 216769

This charming creeper-clad Georgian country house, set in its own grounds and gardens, has comfortable and elegant public areas which include a choice of lounges where drinks and snacks are served throughout the day. Bedrooms are tastefully decorated and some have spa baths and private sitting rooms; courtyard rooms are more modern in style. An attractive restaurant offers set-price menus from which guests can such dishes as terrine of baby leeks with walnut mayonnaise, brill with a sauce of creamed fennel and saffron, and rich treacle tart.

32⇨🐾(3fb)1🛏✄in 1 bedroom CTV in all bedrooms T sB&B⇨🐾fr£98 dB&B⇨🐾£98-£175 🍴
《60P ✿ 🅿 (heated) ⚓ (heated) ♟ (hard) ♪ sauna solarium clay pigeon shooting archery *xmas*
♿ English & French V ✿ ⚓ Lunch fr£10.50&alc High tea fr£5 Dinner fr£31&alc Last dinner 9pm
Credit Cards [1][2][3][5] £

Granada Lodge
A36 Bath Rd BA12 7RU ☎(0985) 219319 FAX (0985) 214380

This modern building provides smart, spacious and well equipped bedrooms, all with en suite bathrooms. Meals may be taken at a nearby family restaurant. For more details about Granada Lodges, consult the Contents page, under Hotel Groups.
31⇨✳ B⇨£34.95-£37.95 (room only)

WARRINGTON Cheshire Map 07 SJ68

★★★★ 68% **Park Royal International**
Stretton Rd WA4 4NS WARRINGTON
☎(0925) 730706 FAX (0925) 730740
(For full entry see Stretton (Cheshire))

★★★ 68% **Lord Daresbury**
Chester Rd WA4 4BB ☎(0925) 267331 FAX (0925) 265615
(For full entry see Daresbury)

★★★ 64% **Fir Grove**
Knutsford Old Rd WA4 2LD ☎(0925) 267471 FAX (0925) 601092

Situated close to the Manchester Ship Canal swing bridge, this modern hotel has a good range of extras including satellite TV and good working surfaces for the business guest. There is a new foyer, with comfortable occasional seating and a refurbished restaurant which now offers a good carvery at lunch time.
40⇨🐾 CTV in all bedrooms ®♥ T ✱ sB&B⇨🐾£25-£55 dB&B⇨🐾£36-£66
《100P ✿ *xmas*
♿ English & French V ✿ ⚓ ✱ Lunch £12&alc Dinner £12&alc Last dinner 10pm
CONF. Thtr 200 Class 100 Board 50 Del from £83
Credit Cards [1][2][3][5]

★★★ 59% **Holiday Inn Garden Court**
Woolston Grange Av, Woolston WA1 4PX (off junct 21 of M6) ☎(0925) 831158 & 838779 FAX (0925) 838859

This bright modern hotel was the first of a fast growing branded chain which provides a high standard of bedroom accommodation at an attractive price. The open plan public areas are pleasant but

---

on a small scale, and the range of food and services is deliberately limited.
100⇨🐾(41fb)✄in 50 bedrooms CTV in all bedrooms ® T sB⇨🐾£62-£65 dB⇨🐾£62-£65 (room only) 🍴
Lift 《108P ✿
V ✄ ✱ Dinner £11.95-£21alc Last dinner 9.45pm
Credit Cards [1][2][3][4][5]

★★ 70% *Rockfield*
Alexandra Rd, Grappenhall WA4 2EL (1.75m SE off A50)
☎(0925) 262898 FAX (0925) 263343
Closed 25-26 Dec RS restricted menu

This large, detached Edwardian house with delightful gardens is situated in a quiet residential. Proprietors Ron and Pam Jackman have made many improvements, combining modern facilities with tasteful period-style elegance. The bedrooms are equipped to a modern standard, some in an adjacent house. The attractive restaurant serves a good selection of popular dishes, and there is a cosy lounge and a pleasant bar area.
6⇨🐾Annexe6⇨🐾 CTV in all bedrooms ® T ✱
sB&B⇨🐾£30-£45 dB&B⇨🐾£40-£55 🍴
CTV 25P ✿
♿ English, French & Italian V ✿ ⚓ ✱ Lunch £10-£12 High tea £8 Dinner £14&alc Last dinner 9pm
Credit Cards [1][3][5]

★★ 56% *Paddington House*
514 Old Manchester Rd WA1 3TZ (junct 21, M6, off A57) ☎(0925) 816767

This rather dated, privately owned hotel caters mainly for commercial visitors and provides simple bedrooms with modern equipment. At the time of our last inspection some redecoration work had commenced, hopefully this will continue.
37⇨🐾(1fb)1🛏 CTV in all bedrooms ® T
《100P 2🚗 (£5) ✿
♿ English & French V ✿ ⚓ Last dinner 9pm
Credit Cards [1][3]

★ 68% *Kenilworth*
2 Victoria Rd, Grappenhall WA4 2EN (1.5m E off A50)
☎(0925) 262323 & 268320

This extended red-brick Edwardian house has been extensively upgraded by the Strickland family to provide bedrooms which, though they vary greatly in size, are all well equipped with good furnishings and attractive colour schemes. Public areas include a comfortable lounge with a Challon baby grand piano, and a cottagey dining room where guests can enjoy generous servings of fresh, well cooked food.
17rm(16🐾)(1fb) CTV in all bedrooms ® T
CTV 18P
♿ Cosmopolitan V
Credit Cards [1][3]

★ 55% *Ribblesdale*
Balmoral Rd, Grappenhall WA4 2EB (off A50) ☎(0925) 601197 FAX (0925) 262135
A Victorian house in a quiet residential area offers friendly service and simple accommodation popular with commercial guests. There is a small lounge bar and dining room.
14rm(12⇨) CTV in all bedrooms ® T
20P 🚗 ✿
♿ French V ✿ ⚓ Last dinner 9pm
Credit Cards [1][2][3]

•••

For full, independent restaurant reviews, see the
AA Abbey Well *Restaurant Guide*.

Travel Inn
Winwick Rd (just off junc 9 of M62 towards
Warrington) ☎(0925) 414417

Purpose-built accommodation offers spacious and well equipped bedrooms, all with en suite bathrooms. Meals may be taken at the nearby family resaurant and pub. For more details about Travel Inns, consult the Contents page, under Hotel Groups.
40⇨♠✻ B⇨♠£33.50 (room only)

WARWICK Warwickshire Map **04** SP26
See also **Barford** and **Leamington Spa (Royal)**
★★**64%** **Lord Leycester**
Jury St CV34 4EJ (Calotels) ☎(0926) 491481 FAX (0926) 491561
This is a commercial style hotel, on the main street through Warwick. It has a busy coach party trade among visitors to Shakespeare country.
52⇨♠(3fb)1🛏 CTV in all bedrooms ® T sB&B⇨♠£28-£58 dB&B⇨♠£56-£70
Lift (40P *xmas*
♀ English & French V ✿ ⚖ Lunch £9-£15 Dinner £15-£17.50
Last dinner 9pm
CONF. Thtr 250 Class 100 Board 60 Del from £60
Credit Cards ① ② ③ ⑤

★★**58%** **Warwick Arms**
High St CV34 4AJ ☎(0926) 492759 FAX (0926) 410587

This privately owned hotel dates back to the 18th century and is situated close to Warwick Castle. Famous visitors have included, at various times in the past, Lord Nelson, Ivor Novello and ⇨

WARWICK

A premier hotel on ancient Jury Street.

This superb Georgian hotel is ideally situated for the executive with business in the Midland's commercial centre, or for weekend breaks in England's historic heartland.

All who visit the Lord Leycester will enjoy the excellent food, high standard of service and comfortable accommodation.

LORD LEYCESTER HOTEL ★★

Jury Street, Warwick.
Tel: 0926 491481

Calotels

The Park Royal
International Hotel

★★★★
68%

Stretton Road, Stretton, Warrington, Cheshire WA4 4NS
Telephone: 0925 730706 Fax: 0925 730740

A Hotel which offers a Standard of Service and Excellence which is Unrivalled

- Brand new, fully air conditioned Conference & Banqueting Suite.
- The Royal Suite for up to 400 guests.
- The Garden Suite for up to 150 guests.
- Plus a selection of smaller suites.
- Extensive free car parking.
- 100 deluxe bedrooms.

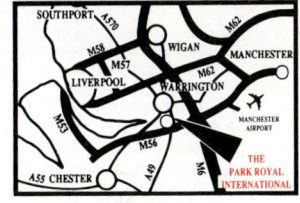

Location 1 min from M56 junction 10. 3 mins from M6 junction 20 – Manchester Airport 15 mins – Manchester 25 mins – Liverpool 25 mins – Chester 20 mins.

Warwick - Wateringbury

Frank Sinatra. There is a simple lounge bar, a comfortable foyer lounge and a small coffee shop.
35⇨♠(4fb)1⌂ CTV in all bedrooms ® T sB&B⇨♠£39-£45 dB&B⇨♠£55-£65 ♬
((21P
♀ English & French V ♦ ♫ Sunday Lunch £7.50-£8.50 Dinner £12-£15 Last dinner 9.30pm
CONF. Thtr 110 Class 50 Board 50 Del from £50
Credit Cards [1][2][3][5]

★63% **Penderrick**
36 Coten End CV34 4NP (opp Millwright Arms public arms)
☎(0926) 499399 & 497252
This small hotel, situated on the Leamington Spa road, is run by the friendly Blackband family. The rooms are a mixture of sizes and styles, and all offer a good range of facilities, though some have rather cramped en suites which may lack privacy. There is a cosy lounge with a residential bar, and the dining room offers a simple fixed price menu.
7rm(4♠)(2fb)1⌂ CTV in all bedrooms ® T ✱ sB&B£26.50-£29.50 dB&B£38-£40 dB&B♠£44-£50 ♬
CTV 9P 2🅿
V ♦ ♥ ✱ Dinner £14.50 Last dinner 7pm
Credit Cards [1][2][3][5]

Hilton National Warwick/Stratford
A46, Stratford Rd CV34 6RE (junc A41/A46/A429) ☎(0926) 499555 FAX (0926) 410020

This is a bright, modern hotel with an informal restaurant, aimed at both the business and leisure guest. All bedrooms have en-suite bathrooms and a range of modern facilities. For more information about Hilton National, consult the Contents page, under Hotel Groups.
181⇨♠ B⇨♠£85 (room only)
CONF. Thtr 500 Class 260 Board 100 Del £125

WASDALE HEAD Cumbria Map 11 NY10

★★67% **Wasdale Head Inn**
CA20 1EX (turn off the A595 at Gosforth and follow signs to Wasdale Head (approx 9m) the inn is at the head of the valley)
☎Wasdale(09467) 26229 FAX (09467) 26334
Closed mid Nov-28 Dec & mid Jan-mid Mar
Surrounded by mountains and fells, this famous old inn stands in a unique location at the head of Wasdale. An extensive range of food is available in either the busy bar or the wood-panelled dining room, and there is a comfortable residents' lounge. Bedrooms have no TVs as the reception is poor in this area. Staff are very friendly and helpful.
6⇨(2fb)® T ✱ sB&B⇨£25 dB&B⇨£50
50P 🅿 ♣
V ♦ ♥ ✱ Bar Lunch £7.65-£12.25alc Dinner £11.05-£16.20alc Last dinner 9pm
Credit Cards [1][3]

WASHINGTON Tyne & Wear Map 12 NZ35

★★★65% **Washington Moat House**
Stone Cellar Rd, District 12, High Usworth
NE37 1PH ☎091-417 2626 FAX 091-415 1166

Extensive leisure facilities make this modern hotel popular. Bedrooms are currently being refurbished and plans are in hand to extend and improve the public areas.
105⇨♠(9fb)3⌂♥ in 35 bedrooms CTV in all bedrooms ® T ✱ sB⇨♠£30-£67 dB⇨♠£60-£77 (room only) ♬
((CTV 200P ❋ ▨ (heated) ▷ 18 squash snooker sauna solarium gymnasium golf driving range *xmas*
♀ English & French V ♦ ♫ Lunch £7.25-£8.25alc
High tea fr£14.50 Dinner fr£13.75&alc Last dinner 10pm

CONF. Thtr 200 Class 100 Board 80 Del from £64.50
Credit Cards [1][2][3][5]

Campanile
Emerson Rd NE37 1LE ☎091-416 5010 FAX 091-416 5023

A nearby bar and bistro restaurant provides refreshments for travellers staying at this modern accommodation building. Bedrooms are well equipped and have en suite bathrooms. For more details about Campanile, consult the Contents page, under Hotel Groups.
Annexe77⇨♠ B⇨♠£29.50-£35.75 (room only)
CONF. Thtr 35 Class 35 Board 25 Del from £42.80

Forte Posthouse
Emerson District 5 NE37 1LB (off A1 (M))
☎091-416 2264 FAX 091-415 3371

Suitable for both the business and leisure traveller, this bright hotel provides modern accommodation in well equipped bedrooms with en suite bathrooms. For more details about Forte Posthouse hotels, consult the Contents page, under Hotel Groups.
138⇨♠ ✱ B⇨♠£41.50-£53.50 (room only)
CONF. Thtr 100 Class 40 Board 50 Del £89.50

WASHINGTON SERVICE AREA Tyne & Wear Map 12 NZ25

Granada Lodge
A1M, Portobello DH3 2SJ ☎091-410 0076 FAX 091-410 0057

This modern building provides smart, spacious and well equipped bedrooms, all with en suite bathrooms. Meals may be taken at a nearby family restaurant. For more details about Granada Lodges, consult the Contents page, under Hotel Groups.
35⇨♠ ✱ B⇨♠£34.95-£37.95 (room only)

WATERGATE BAY Cornwall & Isles of Scilly Map 02 SW86

★★★59% **Tregurrian**
TR8 4AB (on B3276 3m from Newquay)
☎St Mawgan(0637) 860280
Closed Nov-Feb
A family-run hotel on the edge of the bay, though simply furnished, offers good facilities and live entertainment during the high season.
27rm(2⇨20♠)(8fb)2⌂ CTV in all bedrooms ®♥ sB&B£17-£23 sB&B⇨♠£19-£27 dB&B£34-£48 dB&B⇨♠£38-£54 ♬
CTV 26P ❋ ▷ (heated) sauna solarium jacuzzi spa pool games room ♣
♀ English & Continental ♦ ♫ Dinner £8.50 Last dinner 7.30pm
Credit Cards [1][3]

WATERINGBURY Kent Map 05 TQ65

★★★67% **Wateringbury**
Tonbridge Rd ME18 5NS (on the A26 between Maidstone and Tonbridge) (Whitbread) ☎Maidstone(0622) 812632 FAX (0622) 812720
Originally a village inn, this pleasant hotel has been sympathetically extended to blend in with its surroundings. Bedrooms are modern; some have been recently refurbished with attractive matching fabrics and décor, and there are plans to upgrade the others. The conservatory lounge leads to a garden terrace, and the country-style restaurant offers an imaginative menu.
37⇨♠(1fb)1⌂♥ in 12 bedrooms CTV in all bedrooms ®♥ T ✖ (ex guide dogs) ✱ sB&B⇨♠£45-£55.50 dB&B⇨♠£56.50-£67 ♬
((CTV 60P ❋ sauna

Wateringbury - Watford

♿ European V ❦ ⚑ ✂ Last dinner 9.30pm
CONF. Thtr 80 Class 40 Board 30 Del from £85
Credit Cards 1 2 3 5

WATERMILLOCK Cumbria Map **12** NY42

★★★ ❀❀ 78% **Leeming House**
CA11 0JJ (on A592)
☎Pooley Bridge(07684) 86622 FAX
(07684) 86443

FORTE GRAND

Courtesy and Care 1994

Friendly, considerate staff contribute much to the quality of a stay at this lovely hotel, and this has earned for Leeming House an AA Courtesy and Care Award this year. Set in 20 acres of landscaped gardens and woodland on the shores of Lake Ullswater, the hotel has beautiful views of the fells beyond. Many of the bedrooms are luxurious, several with private balconies, and a new wing has been added. Public rooms are very comfortable, with open fires, and the elegant mirrored dining room is a perfect setting for the excellent 3- or 6-course dinners. There is a well chosen wine list with all major areas represented.
40⇨♘✂in 9 bedrooms CTV in all bedrooms ®✷T✳
sB⇨♘£95-£110 dB⇨♘£130-£155 (room only) 🅿
⟨ 50P ⊞ ✿ ♪ *xmas*
V ❦ ⚑ ✂✳ Lunch £14-£21alc Dinner £27.50-£34.50 Last dinner 8.45pm
Credit Cards 1 2 3 5

★★★ ❀❀ **Rampsbeck Country House**
CA11 0LP ☎Pooley Bridge(07684) 86442 & 86688 FAX (07684) 86688
Closed 6 Jan-early Feb
(Rosettes awarded for dinner only)
This charming 18th-century country house is beautifully situated in 18 acres of parkland and formal gardens overlooking Lake Ullswater and spectacular fell and mountain scenery. Owners Tom and Marion Gibb provide most courteous service and excellent food. Many bedrooms have lake views, some have balconies, and a spacious ground floor room has a separate sitting room. There is an elegant dining room, a traditional bar, and a candlelit dining room where chef Andrew McGeorge's exquisite dinners are served. Notable dishes have included baked pithivier of quail with a Madeira flavoured natural jus, garnished with woodland mushrooms and deep fried celeriac; roast fillet of Dornoch beef served with a red wine sauce and a tartlet of braised oxtail; and Baileys Irish Cream soufflé.
20⇨♘1🛏✂in 2 bedrooms CTV in all bedrooms T
sB&B⇨♘£48-£70 dB&B⇨♘£72-£140 🅿
30P ⊞ ✿ ♪ croquet lawn nc5yrs *xmas*
♿ English & French V ❦ ⚑ ✂ Lunch £22.95-£35 Dinner £25-£35 Last dinner 8.30pm
Credit Cards 1 3

Rosettes range from 5 for outstanding cuisine to 1 rosette for enjoyable, well prepared food

WATFORD Hertfordshire Map **04** TQ19

★★★ 59% **Dean Park**
30-40 St Albans Rd WD1 1RN ☎(0923) 229212
FAX (0923) 254638

Queens Moat Houses

Conveniently situated for the motorway network and close to the station and town centre, this purpose-built hotel has compact modern bedrooms designed for the business person. Refurbishment is planned for the now dated public areas. Staff are helpful and 24-hour room service is available.
90⇨♘(2fb)✂in 18 bedrooms CTV in all bedrooms ® T
✈ (ex guide dogs) ✳ sB&B⇨♘£39.50-£69 dB&B⇨♘£49.50-£79 🅿
Lift ⟨ CTV 12P
♿ French V ❦ ⚑ ✂ ✳ Lunch £5-£14.50 Dinner fr£14.50&alc Last dinner 10pm
CONF. Thtr 250 Class 100 Board 80 Del from £78.50
Credit Cards 1 2 3 5

★★ 61% **The White House**
Upton Rd WD1 2EL ☎(0923) 237316 FAX (0923) 233109
This informally run hotel in the town centre offers a choice of newly refurbished modern bedrooms in the main building or more modestly furnished rooms in the annexe opposite. Open-plan public areas include a restaurant and comfortable lounge with a lounge menu.
62⇨♘Annexe26⇨♘(1fb)✂in 5 bedrooms CTV in all bedrooms ® T ✳ sB&B⇨♘£60-£69 dB&B⇨♘£70-£79 🅿
Lift ⟨ CTV 40P
♿ English & French V ❦ ⚑ ✳ Lunch £8.95 Dinner £15.95&alc Last dinner 9.45pm

➦

＊Washington Moat House＊
★ ★ ★

The Washington Moat House extends a stylish welcome with a warmth that's special to the North-East and offers a combination of first class business and leisure facilities for both the energetic and the pampered which are second to none.

Facilities include:
★ Leisure Club ★ 18 Hole Championship Golf Course ★
9 Hole Par 3 Golf Course ★ Floodlit Driving Range
★ Squash Courts ★ Indoor Heated Swimming Pool ★ Spa Bath and Sauna ★ Solarium ★ Multi-Gym ★ Lincolns Restaurant ★ Abrahams Bar ★ Bunkers Bar ★
Extensive parking

For business or pleasure, the

WASHINGTON MOAT HOUSE
provides your every need.
STONE CELLAR ROAD,
HIGH USWORTH DISTRICT 12,
WASHINGTON, TYNE & WEAR NE37 1PH.
Tel: 091-417 2626

Watford - Wells

CONF. Thtr 150 Class 65 Board 60 Del £95
Credit Cards 1 2 3 5

Hilton National Watford
Elton Way, Watford Bypass WD2 8HA
☎(0923) 35881 FAX (0923) 220836

This is a bright, modern hotel with an informal restaurant, aimed at both business and leisure guests. All bedrooms have en-suite bathrooms and a range of modern facilities. For more information about Hilton National, consult the Contents page, under Hotel Groups.
195⇌♠★ B⇌♠£90 (room only)
CONF. Thtr 350 Class 350 Board 30 Del £115

WEEDON Northamptonshire Map **04** SP65
★★66% **Heart Of England**
Daventry Rd NN7 4QD (beside A45) ☎(0327) 40335
Rooms are attractive and well equipped at this hotel which dates back to the 18th century. Good levels of hospitality and service are maintained by a particularly friendly staff, and a selection of grill meals is available in the Gables Restaurant.
12rm(1⇌1♠)1⌕ CTV in all bedrooms ® ✈ (ex guide dogs)
70P ⊞ ❀
V ✧ ⚑ Last dinner 10pm
Credit Cards 1 2 3 5

★★61% **Globe**
High St NN7 4QD (at crossroads of A5/A45) ☎(0327) 40336
FAX (0327) 349058
The Globe is a privately owned country inn. Accommodation is well equipped, though a couple of the single rooms are compact, and equally suitable for business guests or tourists. Improvements continue, and the restaurant and bar have recently been upgraded.
17⇌♠(3fb) CTV in all bedrooms ®⚡ T ✱ sB&B⇌♠£28.50-£42 dB&B⇌♠£38-£49.50 ⚑
40P ♫
♥ International V ✧ ⚑ Lunch £8.45-£14.50alc Dinner £11.50-£14.50alc Last dinner 10pm
CONF. Board 20 Del from £40
Credit Cards 1 2 3 5

WELLINGBOROUGH Northamptonshire Map **04** SP86
★★★63% **Hind**
Sheep St NN8 1BY ☎(0933) 222827 FAX (0933) 441921

The Hind Hotel is a 16th-century property in the centre of town. Bedrooms are decorated to a high standard and include a bridal suite with a 4-poster bed and reproduction furniture. Public areas include 2 bars, a lounge and restaurant.
34⇌♠(2fb)1⌕ CTV in all bedrooms ® T sB&B⇌♠£35-£75 dB&B⇌♠£60-£90 ⚑
《 13P 3⇪
♥ English & Continental V ✧ ⚑ ✱ Lunch fr£10.45&alc Dinner fr£12.45&alc Last dinner 10pm
CONF. Thtr 100 Class 50 Board 40 Del from £85
Credit Cards 1 2 3 4 5

★★63% **Columbia**
19 Northampton Rd NN8 3HG (access from town centre via Oxford Street)
☎(0933) 229333 FAX (0933) 440418
Closed 24-27 Dec

This personally run hotel is situated conveniently close to the town centre. Bedrooms fall short of the high standard of décor in the reception and lobby area, though they are of a good size and have good modern facilities. Reasonably priced bar lunches are available, and an extensive menu is available in the elegantly furnished restaurant.

29⇌♠(1fb) CTV in all bedrooms ®⚡ T ✈ (ex guide dogs) ✱ sB&B⇌♠£32-£49.50 dB&B⇌♠£48-£62 ⚑
CTV 18P
♥ English & French V ✧ ⚑ ✱ Lunch £8.75-£16&alc Dinner £11.95-£16&alc Last dinner 9.30pm
CONF. Thtr 24 Class 12 Board 16 Del from £32
Credit Cards 1 2 3

★★61% **High View**
156 Midland Rd NN8 1NG ☎(0789) 278733 FAX (0789) 225948
Conveniently close to the railway station and a short distance from the town centre, this hotel has simply decorated bedrooms. Owners Mr and Mrs Hunter ensure personal service by sharing duties on reception, serving in the bar and overseeing the limited restaurant operation.
14⇌♠Annexe3rm(2fb) CTV in all bedrooms ® T sB&B£15-£24 sB&B⇌♠£27-£44 dB&B£30-£34 dB&B⇌♠£37-£50 ⚑
CTV 8P 1⇪ ❀
V ✧ ⚑ Lunch fr£6.60&alc Dinner fr£6.60&alc Last dinner 8.30pm
Credit Cards 1 2 3 5

WELLINGTON
See **Telford**

WELLINGTON Somerset Map **03** ST12
★★55% **Beambridge**
Sampford Arundel TA21 0HB (1.5m W on A38)
☎Greenham(0823) 672223 FAX (0823) 67100
Recommended bedroom accommodation is on the 1st floor of this hotel; on the ground floor are a lounge bar and popular function rooms.
10rm(9⇌1♠)Annexe8rm1⌕ CTV in 10 bedrooms ® T ✈ (ex guide dogs) sB&B£35 sB&B⇌♠£31.50-£35 dB&B⇌♠£43-£49
100P ♫
V ✧ ⚑ Lunch £7-£11alc Dinner £7-£11alc Last dinner 9pm
CONF. Class 120 Board 120 Del from £55
Credit Cards 1 3

WELLS Somerset Map **03** ST54
★★★66% **Swan**
Sadler St BA5 2RX (opp cathedral)
☎(0749) 678877 FAX (0749) 677647

Situated close to the Market Square with views of the cathedral, the Swan retains traditional values with friendly and obliging staff. Bedrooms are individually furnished and decorated, and many have original 4-poster beds. In the narrow panelled restaurant a varied table d'hôte menu is offered with the roast joint of the day served from a trolley. Public areas are full of character with log fires in the chilly months.
38⇌♠(2fb)9⌕ CTV in all bedrooms ® T sB&B⇌♠£65-£70 dB&B⇌♠£86-£95 ⚑
《 30P squash *xmas*
V ✧ ⚑ Lunch £11.50-£12.50 Dinner £15.50-£17.50 Last dinner 9.30pm
CONF. Thtr 120 Class 30 Board 40 Del from £75
Credit Cards 1 2 3 5

★★59% **The Star**
18 High St BA5 2SQ ☎(0749) 673055 & 670500
FAX (0749) 672654

Bedrooms here are attractively decorated in soft shades, substantially furnished and equipped with a host of modern facilities. The Tudor Bar is popular and La Brasserie restaurant has a short menu of char-grilled dishes. The young staff are friendly and the atmosphere is informal.

12⇨🏠(3fb) CTV in all bedrooms ® T ✱ sB&B⇨🏠£34-£45 dB&B⇨🏠£48-£60 🍴
✗ xmas
⚑ English & Cosmopolitan V ♥ ⚒ ⚔ ✱ Lunch £6.95-£13.85
High tea £4 Dinner £6.95-£13.85 Last dinner 10pm
Credit Cards [1][2][3][5]

★⊛65% **Ancient Gate House**
Sadler St BA5 2RR ☎(0749) 672290
Closed 24-26 Dec
This ancient hotel has an unrivalled position within the cathedral close, and some rooms have uninterrupted views across the green to the floodlit face of the cathedral. The interior is characterised by beams, panelling and steep stone spiral staircases. Two bedrooms are in the gatehouse, itself designated an Ancient Monument. The Rugatino Restaurant provides both table d'hôte and á la carte menus of traditional Italian dishes. Most of the food is home made, and respresents very good value for money.
9rm(2⇨5🏠)(1fb)6🛁 CTV in all bedrooms ® T
sB&B⇨🏠£40-£45 dB&B£45-£50 dB&B⇨🏠£55-£60 🍴
✗
⚑ English & Italian V ♥ ✱ Lunch £4.95-£6.90&alc Dinner £12.75-£14.75&alc Last dinner 10.30pm
Credit Cards [1][2][3][5]

WELLS-NEXT-THE-SEA Norfolk Map 09 TF94
★★56% **Crown**
The Buttlands NR23 1EX (Logis) ☎Fakenham(0328) 710209 FAX (0328) 711432
This attractive inn with a Georgian façade is set on the village green. The public areas offer a nicely furnished restaurant and a cheerful but very busy bar. The bedrooms are simply furnished, and the small team of staff are friendly and helpful.
15rm(5⇨5🏠)(3fb) CTV in all bedrooms ® T ✱ sB&B£34-£45 sB&B⇨🏠£45-£55 dB&B£58-£60 dB&B⇨🏠£65-£70 🍴
CTV 10P 🚲 xmas
⚑ English & Continental V ♥ ⚒ ✱ Lunch £10.50-£16.50&alc Dinner fr£16.50&alc Last dinner 9.30pm
Credit Cards [1][2][3][5]

★70% **Scarborough House**
Clubbs Ln NR23 1DP ☎Fakenham(0328) 710309 & 711661
Closed 24-25 Dec
A friendly welcome awaits guests at this small, family-run hotel whose comfortable public rooms retain many Victorian features. At the time of our visit a large conservatory was being added to the small bar which serves the adjacent beamed restaurant. A good range of wholesome British dishes is offered, and the Saturday night carvery is particularly popular.
6⇨🏠Annexe8⇨🏠(1fb)3🛁 CTV in all bedrooms ®
sB&B⇨🏠£29-£34 dB&B⇨🏠£48-£55 🍴
14P
⚑ English & French V Dinner £10.95-£15 Last dinner 9pm
Credit Cards [1][2][3][5]

WELSHPOOL Powys Map 07 SJ20
★★♨72% **Golfa Hall**
Llanfair Rd SY21 9AF (1.5m W off A458) (Guestaccom)
☎(0938) 553399 FAX (0938) 554777
Overlooking the hills adjoining Powys Castle, this delightful small hotel with 10 bedrooms is west of the town. There are pretty fabrics in the bedrooms which are well equipped. The dining room is sub-divided for extra privacy; public rooms are comfortable.
12⇨🏠(3fb) CTV in all bedrooms ® T sB&B⇨🏠£39-£45 dB&B⇨🏠£59-£69 🍴
50P 🚲 ✿ xmas
⚑ English & Continental V ♥ ⚒ ⚔ Bar Lunch £1.75-£6.75
High tea £3-£6 Last high tea 6pm
Credit Cards [1][2][3][5]

Crossways Inn ★★
North Wootton, Shepton Mallet,
Somerset BA4 4EU
Telephone: (0749) 890237
Fax: (0749) 890476

The Crossways Inn is situated in an ideal position, overlooking the historic Vale of Avalon and within sight of the famous Tor. Well suited for a touring holiday or a restful break away from the hustle and bustle of life today. The accommodation is of a high standard, all 17 bedrooms are en suite and have full facilities. The buffet bar serves a variety of hot meals, home cooked cold meats and salads whilst a larger menu is available in the Restaurant.

WILDTREE HOTELS

White House Hotel
★★
Upton Road, Watford, Herts WD1 2EL
Tel: 0923 237316 Fax: 0923 233109

Watford's first luxurious town house hotel with 50 newly built bedrooms with en suite facilities providing the highest standard of personal service. Located in the heart of Watford on the ring road with free parking for cars and coaches. The main motorways nearby are M1 and M25.
The hotel has air conditioned function rooms for conferences, seminars and social events, serving good food and wine with friendly professional staff serving in a homely atmosphere and catering to the clients' needs.

Welshpool - West Chiltington

★★ 65% *Royal Oak*
SY21 7DG ☎(0938) 552217 FAX (0938) 552217
For a long time the heart of this mid-Wales market town, this hotel has 2 comfortable lounges and a choice of bars, where bar meals offer an alternative to the table d'hôte and à la carte choices offered in the timbered restaurant. Fairly modern bedrooms make effective use of matching fabrics.
24⇌ ʀ(3fb)1 ♿ CTV in all bedrooms ® T ✈ (ex guide dogs) CTV 60P
♨ English, French & Italian V ♿ ⚤ Last dinner 9pm
Credit Cards [1][2][3][5]

WELWYN GARDEN CITY Hertfordshire Map **04** TL21

★★★ 57% The Homestead Court
Homestead Ln AL7 4LX (on A1000)
☎(0707) 324336 FAX (0707) 326447

Situated in the middle of the residential district of Woodhall, this popular commercial hotel has functional bedrooms with full modern facilities. Room service is available and staff are cheerful and helpful.
58⇌ ʀ ⚥ in 25 bedrooms CTV in all bedrooms ® T ✱
sB⇌ʀ£40-£60 dB⇌ʀ£40-£60 (room only) ♖
Lift ℂ 80P ✿ *xmas*
♨ English & Continental V ♿ ⚤ ⚥ ✱ Sunday Lunch £9.95
Dinner £14.95&alc Last dinner 9.45pm
CONF. Thtr 80 Class 45 Board 40 Del from £60
Credit Cards [1][2][3][5]

WEMBLEY Greater London

See LONDON SECTION plan 1*B4*
Hilton National Wembley
Empire Way HA9 8DS ☎081-902 8839

This is a bright, modern hotel with an informal restaurant, aimed at both the business and leisure guest. All bedrooms have en-suite bathrooms and a range of modern facilities. For more information on Hilton National, consult the Contents page, under Hotel Groups.
306⇌ ʀ ✱ sB⇌ʀ£99 dB⇌ʀ£109 (room only)
CONF. Thtr 250 Class 160 Board 56 Del £110

WENTBRIDGE (NEAR PONTEFRACT) West Yorkshire Map **08** SE41

★★★ ⚔ **65%** Wentbridge House
WF8 3JJ (off A1) ☎Pontefract(0977) 620444 FAX (0977) 620148
Closed Xmas night
This is a fine old village house, with 15 acres of landscaped gardens and grounds, has lots of wood panelling and other attractive features. The hotel has a good reputation locally for its food and extensive wine list, so it is necessary to reserve a table in the intimate Fleur De Lys restaurant.
12⇌ ʀ 1 ♿ CTV in all bedrooms ® T ✈ (ex guide dogs) 100P ⛟ ✿
♨ English & French V ♿ ✱ Lunch £13.75-£20.75&alc Dinner fr£19.75&alc Last dinner 9.30pm
CONF. Thtr 120 Class 100 Board 60 Del £120
Credit Cards [1][2][3][5]

WEST BAY
See **Bridport**

WEST BEXINGTON Dorset Map **03** SY58

★★ ❀67% Manor
Beach Rd DT6 9DF (Logis)
☎Burton Bradstock(0308) 897616 FAX (0308) 897035
In peaceful rural surroundings with glorious views across Chesil Beach, this handsome old stone house has cottage-style bedrooms with antique furnishings and many thoughtful extras. There are two comfortable lounges plus a conservatory lounge serving bar meals and a cellar bar. The restaurant menus take advantage of locally caught fish and shellfish, and offers a wide choice of carefully prepared dishes such as escalope of rabbit with wild mushrooms and a creamy sorrel-scented sauce.
13⇌ʀ(1fb) CTV in all bedrooms ® T ✈ ✱ sB&B⇌ʀ£43-£44 dB&B⇌ʀ£72-£74 ♖
28P ✿
V ♿ ⚤ Last dinner 10pm
Credit Cards [1][2][3][5]

WEST BROMWICH West Midlands Map **07** SP09

See also **Barr, Great**
★★★ 61% West Bromwich Moat House
Birmingham Rd B70 6RS ☎021-553 6111 FAX 021-525 7403
Closed 24 Dec-30 Dec RS 31 Dec

This Moat House is a popular meeting place and conference venue. Accommodation varies in size and style, some rooms look rather dated, but all offer a good range of facilities. The restaurant has a carvery as well as its à la carte menu.
180⇌ ʀ(115fb) ⚥ in 17 bedrooms CTV in all bedrooms ® T ✱
sB⇌ ʀ£35-£69.50 dB⇌ ʀ£35-£79.50 (room only) ♖
Lift ℂ 200P
♨ English & French V ♿ ⚤ ✱ Lunch £12.50&alc Dinner £14.50&alc Last dinner 10pm
CONF. Thtr 180 Class 80 Board 60 Del from £80
Credit Cards [1][2][3][5]

★★★ 58% Great Barr Hotel & Conference Centre
Pear Tree Dr, off Newton Rd B43 6HS ☎021-357 1141 FAX 021-357 7557
(For full entry see Barr, Great)

WEST CHILTINGTON West Sussex Map **04** TQ01

★★★ 64% Roundabout
Monkmead Ln RH20 2PF (1.75m S via A283)
☎(0798) 813838 FAX (0798) 812962

This Tudor-style hotel is quietly situated with its own mature grounds and gardens. Bedrooms are furnished in mock Tudor style, with wall tapestries, oak furniture and very comfortable armchairs, and bathrooms have recently been upgraded. Public areas include a log fired bar, adjoining lounge and candlelit restaurant. Service is friendly and well managed by general manager Leon Maile.
23⇌ ʀ(4fb)4 ♿ CTV in all bedrooms ® T sB&B⇌ ʀ£59.75-£62.75 dB&B⇌ ʀ£77.75-£85.75 ♖
46P ✿ nc3yrs *xmas*
♨ English & French V ♿ ⚤ ⚥ Lunch £5.75-£11.75&alc Dinner £16.75-£17.75&alc Last dinner 9pm
CONF. Thtr 55 Class 25 Board 30 Del £89.75
Credit Cards [1][2][3][4][5]

Rosettes range from 5 for outstanding cuisine to 1 rosette for enjoyable, well prepared food

The AA's star rating scheme is the market leader in hotel classification.

WESTCLIFF-ON-SEA
See **Southend-on-Sea**

WESTERHAM Kent Map 05 TQ45

★★★ ✿65% *Kings Arms*
Market Square TN16 1AN ☎(0959) 562990 FAX (0959) 561240

An attractive Georgian coaching inn in the centre of town with public areas furnished in country house style. Chef Paul Webster offers interesting menus, a monthly changing set menu and a seasonally changing carte. Simpler, traditional English fare is served in the recently opened Town Jail bistro. Good management and a smart team of staff provide attentive service.
16⇌ ↑(2fb)1 ⊞ ⥅ in 3 bedrooms CTV in all bedrooms ® T
✕ (ex guide dogs)
70P 4⛟ ❈ ⦿
V ⦿ ⦿ Last dinner 10pm
Credit Cards ① ② ③ ⑤

WESTGATE ON SEA Kent Map 05 TR37

★★ 55% *Ivyside*
25 Sea Rd CT8 8SB ☎Thanet(0843) 831082 FAX (0843) 831082

Overlooking the sands of St Mildreds Bay, this popular, privately owned hotel is a combination of several houses and offers a range of simply furnished bedrooms. Those with interconnecting bunk rooms are ideal for families. Public rooms are spacious, if a little dated.
67rm(65⇌↑)(58fb) CTV in all bedrooms ® T
✕ (ex guide dogs) ✱ sB&B⇌↑£29-£33 dB&B⇌↑£58-£66
(CTV 30P ❈ ▢ (heated) ⤒ (heated) squash snooker sauna solarium gymnasium spa pool steam room table tennis ♬ *xmas*
♡ English & French V ⦿ ⦿ ✱ Lunch fr£8.50 High tea fr£4.50 Dinner fr£10.50 Last dinner 8.30pm
CONF. Thtr 200 Class 100 Board 80 Del from £42
Credit Cards ① ② ③

See advertisement on page 639

WESTHILL Grampian *Aberdeenshire* Map 15 NJ80

★★★ 61% **Westhill**
AB32 6TT (on A944) ☎Aberdeen(0224) 740388 FAX (0224) 744354

CONSORT HOTELS

This purpose built commercial hotel also caters for local functions. Public areas include a smart split-level restaurant and a more functional lounge bar with a lively atmosphere. Seven bedrooms have been completely upgraded to a tasteful executive standard; the others, though well equipped, remain plain and practical.
37⇌Annexe14⇌↑(2fb) CTV in all bedrooms ® T
sB&B⇌↑£52.50-£70 dB&B⇌↑£66-£85 ⌶
Lift (350P solarium ♬ *xmas*
♡ International V ⦿ ⦿ Lunch £6.50-£11.95&alc Dinner £13.75-£20.25&alc Last dinner 9.30pm
CONF. Thtr 300 Class 200 Board 200 Del £70
Credit Cards ① ② ③ ⑤

£

See advertisement under ABERDEEN

WESTLETON Suffolk Map 05 TM46

★★ 72% *The Crown at Westleton*
IP17 3AD ☎(072873) 777 FAX (072873) 239
Closed 25-26 Dec

This delightful village inn, constantly being improved, offers varied but for the most part well furnished and comprehensively equipped accommodation. The public bar – simply styled to retain its rustic charm – is supplemented by a comfortable lounge, and the bar and restaurant meals are popular.
10⇌Annexe9⇌↑(3fb)⊞ CTV in all bedrooms ® T

➡

THE KINGS ARMS HOTEL
Westerham
★ ★ ★ ✿

Ideally situated, the hotel is close to Chartwell, Hever Castle, Gatwick, and M25. Our 16 ensuite bedrooms, including Henry VIII four-poster room, have combined tradition with the comforts of home.

The Restaurant and Conservatory, which has recently been awarded an AA rosette for culinary standards, leads onto the terrace and garden, and offers fine English cuisine. Alternatively, our Cellar Bistro Bar has a relaxed atmosphere and exciting menu.

The Bar and Lounge allows you to enjoy a drink or afternoon tea in comfort.

The Kings Arms also caters for all conference and banqueting requirements, including weddings.

**The Kings Arms Hotel, Westerham, Kent TN16 1AN
Tel: (0959) 562990 Fax: (0959) 561240**

Roundabout Hotel

**Monkmead Lane,
West Chiltington,
Nr Pulborough,
West Sussex
Telephone:
West Chiltington (0798) 813838**

★★★

Best Western

Tucked away in beautiful countryside close to the Sussex South Down Way, our peaceful Tudor style hotel is nowhere near a roundabout. All 23 bedrooms are individually styled with private facilities, antique oak furniture, tapestries, TV, radio, telephone and tea/coffee making facilities. Candlelit restaurant and Winter log fire, four poster and executive rooms, also 6 ground floor rooms available.

Special 2 day breaks all year round. 30 minutes drive to Brighton and 15 to Worthing. Many country walks and historic houses near by.

Westleton - Weston-super-Mare

⟨ 30P ✿
V ♥ ⚹ Last dinner 9.30pm
Credit Cards 1 2 3 5

WEST LULWORTH Dorset Map 03 SY88

★★ 67% **Gatton House**
BH20 5RU (Logis) ☎(092941) 252 FAX (092941) 252
Closed 2 Jan-Feb
Gatton House is an attractive hotel in an elevated position with superb views across rolling Dorset countryside, just a short walk from the beautiful cove. Bedrooms, all en suite, are cosy and nicely furnished. Public areas have a traditional feel, and a home cooked evening meal is offered. In summer guests can relax and enjoy a cream tea in the well tended garden.
8⇌🛉(2fb) CTV in all bedrooms ® sB&B⇌🛉£29.50-£37 dB&B⇌🛉£41-£56 🏳
12P 🐕
♘ English & French V ♥ ⚑ ⚹ Dinner £14.50-£15.50 Last dinner 7.30pm
Credit Cards 1 3

★★ 63% **Cromwell House**
Lulworth Cove BH20 5RJ ☎(092941) 253 & 332 FAX (092941) 566
In a lovely setting with splendid views across Lulworth Cove, this hotel offers a choice of bedrooms ranging from those with pretty 4-poster beds to more compact and functional rooms, though each is comfortable. Cosy public areas have a cheerful atmosphere, and the proprietors, Mr and Mrs Miller, are making many improvements since taking over in 1992.
14⇌🛉(2fb) 🛏 CTV in all bedrooms ® T sB&B⇌🛉£28.50-£39.50 dB&B⇌🛉£55-£70 (incl dinner) 🏳
CTV 14P 1🚗 ✿ ≋ ≎ (heated) solarium
V ♥ ⚑ ✱ High tea £3-£5 Dinner fr£10&alc Last dinner 8.15pm
Credit Cards 1 2 3

★ 69% **Shirley**
Main Rd BH20 5RL ☎(092941) 358 FAX (092941) 358
Closed Dec-Jan
Owners for 20 years or so, Jesse and Tony Williams continue to make improvements to their hotel, the latest being the enclosure of the pool and the addition of a jacuzzi bath. The bedrooms are freshly decorated and comfortable, and in addition to the pool area there is a lounge and a pretty dining room with an open plan bar at one end. A coin-operated laundry is also available.
18⇌🛉(3fb) CTV in all bedrooms ® T ✱ sB&B⇌🛉£24.50-£26.50 dB&B⇌🛉£49-£53 🏳
20P 🐕 ▢ (heated) giant chess pool table spa pool
V ♥ ⚑ ✱ Dinner £11&alc Last dinner 8pm
Credit Cards 1 2 3 5

WESTON-ON-THE-GREEN Oxfordshire Map 04 SP51

★★★ ❀68% **Weston Manor**
OX6 8QL ☎Bletchington(0869) 50621 FAX (0869) 50901
This splendid manor house, dating in part back to the 11th century, is set in 13 acres of beautiful gardens. The bedrooms are tastefully decorated and furnished with antiques, some are in separate garden cottages, others in the coach house, but all are equipped with modern facilities. There is an elegant lounge bar, reception lounge and an impressive wood-panelled dining room with minstrels' gallery.
17⇌🛉Annexe20⇌🛉(3fb)2🛏 CTV in all bedrooms ® T ✖ (ex guide dogs) ✱ sB&B⇌🛉fr£85 dB&B⇌🛉fr£105 🏳
⟨ 150P ✿ ≎ (heated) squash croquet xmas

♘ English & French V ♥ ⚑ ✱ Lunch £15.50 Dinner £24.50 Last dinner 9.30pm
CONF. Thtr 40 Class 20 Board 26 Del from £105
Credit Cards 1 2 3 5 £

WESTON-SUPER-MARE Avon Map 03 ST36

★★★ ❀64% **Commodore**
Beach Rd, Sand Bay, Kewstoke BS22 9UZ
(1.5m NW of town centre)
☎(0934) 415778 FAX (0934) 636483
Overlooking the sands at Kewstoke, this modern hotel has bright, open-plan day rooms which include a popular public bar, a small cocktail bar/lounge and a comfortable restaurant, where generous portions of attractively presented modern dishes are served. Most of the main house bedrooms have sea views and, though not spacious, are bright and well maintained. Those in the annexe are more functional, but there are plans to upgrade.
12⇌🛉Annexe6⇌🛉(4fb) CTV in all bedrooms ® T ✖ (ex guide dogs) sB&B⇌🛉£40-£50 dB&B⇌🛉£52-£65 🏳
85P ✿ adventure play park putting ♪ 🎱
♘ English & French V ♥ ⚑ ⚹ Lunch £10.25 Dinner £12-£14.25alc Last dinner 9.30pm
CONF. Thtr 120 Class 80 Board 72 Del from £63.50
Credit Cards 1 2 3 5 £

★★★ 63% **The Grand Atlantic**
Beach Rd BS23 1BA ☎(0934) 626543 FAX (0934) 415048
After a major upgrading programme, the bedrooms at this attractive Victorian seafront hotel now match the comfortable public rooms in the quality of décor and furnishings. Friendly staff provide traditional services, though food standards have occasionally been disappointing.
76⇌🛉(5fb)⚹in 22 bedrooms CTV in all bedrooms ® T ✱
sB⇌🛉fr£68 dB⇌🛉fr£78-£98 (room only) 🏳
Lift ⟨ 100P ✿ ≎ (heated) ♬ (hard) xmas
V ♥ ⚑ ✱ Sunday Lunch £10.95 Dinner £16.95&alc Last dinner 9.30pm
Credit Cards 1 2 3 5

★★★ 56% **Royal Pier**
Birnbeck Rd BS23 2EJ ☎(0934) 626644 FAX (0934) 624169
A well positioned traditional style of hotel with comfortable public areas and popular bars, enjoying commanding views across Weston Bay.
40⇌🛉(4fb) CTV in all bedrooms ® T ✖ ✱ sB&B⇌🛉£45-£49.50 dB&B⇌🛉£65-£75 🏳
Lift ⟨ CTV 70P pool table xmas
♘ European V ♥ ⚑ ✱ Lunch fr£9.50 Dinner fr£12.95 Last dinner 9.15pm
CONF. Thtr 65 Class 30 Board 30 Del from £55
Credit Cards 1 2 3 5 £

★★ 64% **Beachlands**
17 Uphill Rd North BS23 4NG ☎(0934) 621401 FAX (0934) 621966
This small family-owned hotel is in a residential area close to the beach and overlooking the golf course. Spacious public areas include a congenial bar, comfortable lounges and dining room, and though some bedrooms are small, all are well equipped. Friendly efficient staff provide a range of services more usually associated with larger hotels.
18⇌🛉(5fb) CTV in all bedrooms ® T ✱ sB&B⇌🛉fr£31 dB&B⇌🛉fr£62 🏳
CTV 18P 3🚗 🐕

Weston-super-Mare - Westward Ho!

English & French V ✿ ⚥ ✘ ✱ Lunch £9.95 High tea fr£6.50 Dinner fr£12 Last dinner 8.30pm
CONF. Thtr 80 Class 25 Board 35 Del £49.50
Credit Cards 1 2 3 5

★★ **61%** Rozel
Madeira Cove BS23 2BU ☎(0934) 415268 FAX (0934) 415268
This long established resort hotel, owned by the same family for over 70 years, overlooks the North Shore. The popular lounge bar is open plan with a comfortable coffee lounge at the lower end. Bedrooms vary, some are currently being refurbished and showers are being added to the bathrooms. A simple fixed price menu is offered.
46⇨♠(15fb) CTV in all bedrooms ® T ✱ sB&B⇨♠£35-£45 dB&B⇨♠£64-£95 ♫
Lift (30P 50🚗 ❋ ⇨ (heated) xmas
English & French V ✿ ⚥ ✱ Bar Lunch fr£1 Dinner £12.50 Last dinner 8.30pm
CONF. Thtr 140 Class 60 Board 60 Del from £40
Credit Cards 1 3 5

★★ **59%** *Old Manor Inn*
Queensway, Worle BS22 9LP (off A370) ☎(0934) 515143 FAX (0934) 521738
This popular inn has busy bars and friendly, informal service. A good range of bar food is available in addition to restaurant meals, and the skittle bar is a lively rendezvous for locals. Bedrooms in the adjacent block are a little functional but are well equipped with modern facilities and are programmed for some upgrading.
Annexe21⇨♠(4fb) CTV in all bedrooms ® T ✘
75P ❋ sauna solarium gymnasium skittle alley games room
V ✿ ⚥ Last dinner 10pm
Credit Cards 1 2 3 5

WEST RUNTON Norfolk Map 09 TG14

★★ **70%** **Dormy House**
Cromer Rd NR27 9QA (E on A149) ☎(0263) 837537
On the A149 to the east of the village and surrounded by National Trust land, this friendly owner-run hotel provides comfortable modern accommodation, with a lift serving most of the bedrooms. A good choice of dishes is offered on the reasonably priced set dinner menu, with a carte menu also available.
16⇨♠(1fb) CTV in all bedrooms ® T ✘ sB&B£25-£40 sB&B⇨♠£30-£45 dB&B⇨♠£36-£52 ♫
Lift 60P 🚗 ❋ nc7yrs xmas
V ✿ ⚥ Sunday Lunch £8.50-£10.50 Dinner £14.50-£16&alc Last dinner 9pm
Credit Cards 1 2 3 5

See advertisement under CROMER

WEST THURROCK Essex Map 05 TQ57

Granada Lodge
RM16 3BG (off A1306 Arterial Rd)
☎(0708) 891111 Central Res (0800) 555340 FAX (0708) 860971
This modern building provides smart, spacious and well equipped bedrooms, all with en suite bathrooms. Meals may be taken at a nearby family restaurant. For more details about Granada Lodges, consult the Contents page, under Hotel Groups.
44⇨♠✱ B⇨♠£43.95-£46.95 (room only)

WESTWARD HO! Devon Map 02 SS42

★★ **62%** **Culloden House**
Fosketh Hill EX39 1JA ☎Bideford(0237) 479421
Closed Nov-Feb
Run by the hospitable Shaw family, this solid Victorian house is in an elevated position with sea views across to Lundy and the National Trust's Kipling Tor. It is essentially a golfers' hotel

---

BATCH FARM COUNTRY HOTEL
AA ★★
LYMPSHAM, Nr WESTON-SUPER-MARE SOMERSET (0934) 750371
Proprietors: Mr & Mrs D. J. Brown

A family run hotel with a long reputation for friendly atmosphere and excellent traditional English food, à la carte menus also available. Delightfully situated in own grounds, panoramic views from all rooms. 5 miles Weston-super-Mare. 5 miles Burnham-on-Sea. Fishing in river. Fully licensed lounge bar. All bedrooms are en suite and have colour TV and tea making facilities. Ample parking. Short Breaks available.
Egon Ronay/Ashley Courtenay recommended.

---

ivyside Hotel

AA ★★ Seafront, Westgate-on-Sea, Kent.

70 BEDROOMS
With bath/WC and Telephones, Satellite.

FOR FAMILIES
Interconnecting Family Suites, Baby Sitting, Mothers' Room. Playroom

TARIFF
Dinner, B&B from £32 pp CHILD FREE.

HOTEL FACILITIES
Indoor Swimming pool and spa.
Outdoor Heated pool. Sauna & Steam Room.
2 Squash Courts, Solarium, Sun Bed.
Masseuse. Full-size Snooker Table and Games room, Night Porter.

RESERVATIONS (0843) 831082
Seen on "Wish You Were Here"

Westward Ho! - Wetherby

specialising in golfing breaks. Fairly simple bedrooms are provided along with comfortable public rooms.
9rm(2⇨5🏠)(2fb) CTV in all bedrooms ® sB&B⇨🏠£25-£35 dB&B£40-£50 dB&B⇨🏠£45-£55
CTV 9P ⊞ ❀
V ⊁ Last dinner 8.45pm
Credit Cards [1][2][3][5] £

WEST WITTON North Yorkshire Map 07 SE08

★★68% **Wensleydale Heifer Inn**
DL8 4LS (on A684 Leyburn to Hawes road)
☎Wensleydale(0969) 22322 FAX (0969) 24183

Amid beautiful countryside, this charming 17th-century coaching inn with beams and open fires has a comfortable lounge, cosy bar and a popular restaurant, serving 5-course dinners, plus a more informal bistro. Bedrooms, some of them in nearby buildings, are all equally well equipped.
9⇨🏠Annexe10⇨🏠(1fb)3⊞ CTV in all bedrooms ® T sB&B⇨🏠£40-£45 dB&B⇨🏠£60-£70 ❚
25P xmas
V ⓥ ⚑ Sunday Lunch fr£11.50 Dinner fr£22.50 Last dinner 9.30pm
Credit Cards [1][2][3][5] £

WETHERAL Cumbria Map 12 NY45

★★★★65% *Hayton Hall*
CA4 8QD (on A69) ☎Carlisle(0228) 70651 FAX (0228) 70010
This secluded country estate hotel is set in many acres of park and woodland with ornamental lakes and rose gardens. Renovation has resulted in a very high standard of individually styled, very comfortable bedrooms, with sumptuous drapes and rich wall coverings. The spacious drawing room has lots of books and fresh flowers. Well produced meals are provided in the elegant dining room. Staff are friendly and considerate.
17⇨🏠(4fb)2⊞⊁in 2 bedrooms CTV in all bedrooms ® T
(150P ❀ ♪
V ⓥ ⚑ ⊁ Last dinner 9pm
Credit Cards [1][2][3][5]

★★★67% **Crown**
CA4 8ES (Shire) ☎(0228) 561888 FAX (0228) 561637
Tucked away in the charming village of Wetheral, only 2 miles from the M6, this Grade II listed building has comfortable public areas, including an attractive conservatory restaurant overlooking the gardens. Bedrooms are well equipped, with spacious modern rooms in a recent extension and more traditional rooms in the main house.
49⇨(3fb)1⊞⊁in 10 bedrooms CTV in all bedrooms ®⚐ T ✻ sB&B⇨£68-£88 dB&B⇨£108-£118 ❚
(80P ❀ ⊠ (heated) squash snooker sauna solarium gymnasium spa pool xmas
♀ English & French V ⓥ ⚑ ⊁ ✻ Lunch £9.95-£11.95 Dinner £16-£18&alc Last dinner 9.30pm
CONF. Thtr 175 Class 90 Board 50 Del £105
Credit Cards [1][2][3][5]

If you have booked a meal in a hotel restaurant and cannot get there, remember you have a contractual obligation to cancel your booking.

WETHERBY West Yorkshire Map 08 SE44

★★★  **WOOD HALL**
Trip Ln, Linton LS22 4JA
(take Harrogate road N from market place and turn left to Linton)
☎(0937) 587271 FAX (0937) 584353

A Georgian mansion, delightfully situated in open parkland overlooking the wooded valley of the River Wharf, Wood Hall is reached by a private estate road which runs from the village of Linton. Recent sympathetic extensions have added more bedrooms and a leisure club. The bedrooms, original and new, are individually furnished and divided into several categories according to comfort and view; most are generously proportioned. Public rooms are of cosier dimensions, cheerfully furnished in chintz, the bar being the exception with its heavy oak panelling. Chef Simon Ward presents an interesting à la carte menu of modern and traditional British dishes based on high-quality local produce where possible, with every item of the meal made on the premises.
37⇨🏠Annexe6⇨🏠1⊞ CTV in all bedrooms ®⚐ T ✻ sB&B⇨🏠£84-£130 dB&B⇨🏠£94-£135 ❚
Lift (120P ❀ ⊠ (heated) ♪ snooker sauna solarium gymnasium Treatment room for massage and facials xmas
♀ British & French ⓥ ⚑ ⊁ Lunch £12.95-£15.50 Dinner £25-£32alc Last dinner 9.30pm
CONF. Thtr 100 Class 60 Board 30 Del from £99
Credit Cards [1][2][3][5]

★★★76% *Linton Spring Country House*
Sickling Hall Rd LS22 4AF ☎(0937) 585353 FAX (0937) 67579
Closed 1-8 Jan
This former shooting lodge, a solid stone-built house, is set in attractive park and woodland. The helpful staff are a great asset, and the softly lit, open plan reception, lounge and cocktail bar are very welcoming. Bedrooms are large, all with oak panelling and every modern facility. The restaurant menu features some traditional, country dishes and there is always a roast rib of Aberdeen Angus beef.
12rm(10⇨🏠)2⊞ CTV in all bedrooms T ✈ (ex guide dogs)
(55P ⊞ ❀ nc5yrs
V ⓥ Last dinner 9.30pm
Credit Cards [1][2][3][5]

★★★60% **Wetherby Resort**
Leeds Rd LS22 5HE (junc A1/A58)
☎(0937) 583881 FAX (0937) 580062

A modern-style, mainly commercial hotel, the Wetherby Resort has open-plan public areas which are comfortable in design and include a foyer lounge, restaurant and spacious bar. Bedrooms, although fairly compact, have all modern facilities.
72⇨🏠(2fb)⊁in 12 bedrooms CTV in all bedrooms ®⚐ T ✻ sB⇨🏠£55 dB⇨🏠£65 (room only) ❚
(150P ❀ xmas
V ⓥ ⚑ ⊁ Lunch £3.95-£12 Dinner £12-£14&alc Last dinner 9.45pm
CONF. Thtr 160 Class 50 Board 55
Credit Cards [1][2][3][5] £

Weybridge - Weymouth

WEYBRIDGE Surrey
See **LONDON SECTION** plan 1*A1*

★★★ ❀75% Oatlands Park
146 Oatland Dr KT13 9HB ☎(0932) 847242
FAX (0932) 842152

Closed 25-30 Dec

Built as a country house in 1794, on a site where Henry VIII once had a hunting lodge, this hotel is surrounded by 10 acres of grounds overlooking Broadwater Lake. The accommodation has been upgraded in recent years to provide a choice of bedroom styles, all equally well equipped. The galleried atrium foyer lounge is is neo-classical style, while the restaurant is traditional Edwardian. Here chef John Hayes cooks in French classical style and dishes usually arrive with lots of garnish. Recommendations include duck and venison terrine with lime jelly, and medallions of venison with wild mushrooms. Service is professional, friendly and attentive.

117⇨ ♠(3fb)1 ⊞ ⅍ in 12 bedrooms CTV in all bedrooms ® ⚓ T ✻ sB&B⇨ ♠£108 dB&B⇨ ♠£143 🏵
Lift (99P 3⊜ (£5 per night) ✿ croquet lawn jogging course
♫ International V ✧ ℒ Lunch £15-£16&alc Dinner £16-£18&alc Last dinner 10pm
Credit Cards [1][2][3][5]

★★★ 63% Ship Thistle
Monument Green KT13 8BQ ☎(0932) 848364
FAX (0932) 857153

Popular with business people, this small, town centre hotel offers bedrooms in a comfortable modern style. Cosy public areas include an appealing lounge bar and the adjoining L'Escales restaurant – both with a nautical theme. The popular public bar is due for complete refurbishment. Staff have a lighthearted and friendly attitude.

39⇨ ♠⅍ in 10 bedrooms CTV in all bedrooms ® T
✻ (ex guide dogs) ✻ sB⇨ ♠£89-£99 dB⇨ ♠£99-£115 (room only) 🏵
(55P 20⊜ ♪
♫ International V ✧ ℒ ⅍ ✻ Lunch fr£13.50&alc Dinner fr£15.75&alc Last dinner 9.45pm
CONF. Thtr 140 Class 70 Board 60 Del from £59
Credit Cards [1][2][3][4][5]

WEYMOUTH Dorset Map 03 SY67

★★ 64% Crown
51-52 St Thomas St DT4 8EQ ☎(0305) 760800 FAX (0305) 760300
Closed 25-26 Dec

In a central location with views of the harbour and quay, this friendly hotel is particularly popular for group holidays. The Victorian frontage hides a converted banana warehouse which includes a ballroom and the popular Vaults bar and restaurant. Bedrooms are neat and practical, with comfortable beds.

77⇨ ♠(10fb) CTV in all bedrooms ®⚓ ✻ (ex guide dogs) sB&B⇨ ♠£29-£33 dB&B⇨ ♠£54-£57 🏵
Lift (8⊜
V ✧ Lunch £5.25-£6.25&alc Dinner £5.50-£8.25 Last dinner 8pm
Credit Cards [1][2][3][5]   £

★★ 64% Hotel Rex
29 The Esplanade DT4 8DN (On seafront opposite Alexandra Gardens) ☎(0305) 760400 781024 FAX (0305) 760500
Closed Xmas

In a good central location along the Esplanade, the Hotel Rex offers smart public areas including a lounge, cellar restaurant and reception area. The bedrooms have recently been attractively redecorated. In the restaurant interesting dishes are offered from a short table d'hôte menu and a lengthy à la carte.

31⇨ ♠(5fb)1 ⊞ CTV in all bedrooms ® T ✻ sB&B⇨ ♠£40-£47 dB&B⇨ ♠£64-£80 🏵
Lift (CTV 6⊜ (£1.50 night)
♫ International V ✧ ℒ Dinner £12.50&alc Last dinner 10.00pm
CONF. Thtr 40 Class 30 Board 25 Del from £65
Credit Cards [1][2][3][5]   £

★★ 63% Glenburn
42 Preston Rd DT3 6PZ (3m NE A353) ☎Preston(0305) 832353
Closed 25 Dec-1 Jan

This popular small hotel has a warm and homely atmosphere created by the amiable and energetic owners, Mr and Mrs Cotton. Bedrooms, though simply furnished, are comfortable, neat and clean. The dining room, where dinner dances are held, offers an extensive choice of dishes including fresh, locally caught fish.

13rm(12⇨ ♠)(1fb) CTV in all bedrooms ® ✻ sB&B⇨ ♠£30-£33 dB&B⇨ ♠£50-£57.50 🏵
30P ⚿ ✿ nc3yrs
♫ English & French V ✧ ℒ ⅍ ✻ Lunch fr£4.95 High tea fr£5 Dinner fr£12 Last dinner 8.30pm
Credit Cards [1][3]   £

★★ 61% Streamside
29 Preston Rd DT3 6PX (Logis) ☎Preston(0305) 833121 FAX (0305) 832043

This attractive, friendly hotel has simply furnished bedrooms which, though rather compact, are freshly painted and well equipped. There is a comfortable lounge, smart bar and choice of intimate restaurant or larger dining room.

15rm(8⇨1 ♠)(4fb) CTV in all bedrooms ® T ✻ sB&B£32-£35 sB&B⇨ ♠£32-£44 dB&B£35-£50 dB&B⇨ ♠£50-£68 🏵
35P ✿ games room
♫ English & French V ✧ ✻ Lunch fr£9.95&alc Dinner fr£9.95&alc Last dinner 9pm
Credit Cards [1][2][3][5]   £

★★★AA

THE SHIP
THISTLE HOTEL

Monument Green, Weybridge KT13 8BQ
Tel: 0932 848364   Fax: 0932 857153

Your choice in Weybridge

For Reservations at over 100
Mount Charlotte Thistle Hotels
Telephone London: 071 937 8033.

Weymouth - Whitby

★ 60% Alexandra
27/28 The Esplanade DT4 8DN ☎(0305) 785767 FAX (0305) 773336

Originally two properties, this attractive Georgian building is close to the centre of town on the Esplanade. The hotel offers comfortable public areas including a well stocked bar, traditional lounge and a front-facing dining room where a home-cooked evening meal is served. Most of the bedrooms are bright and nicely furnished, but those on the top floor have still to be modernised.

20rm(5⇨9♠)(4fb) CTV in 14 bedrooms ® ✱ sB&B£15-£20 sB&B⇨♠£27-£50 dB&B£30-£40 dB&B⇨♠£42-£60 ₽
7P
V ♥ ☑ Last dinner 7pm
Credit Cards ① ③

WHATTON Nottinghamshire Map 08 SK73

★★ 63% The Haven
Grantham Rd NG13 9EU (on A52) ☎(0949) 50800 FAX (0949) 51454

Set in 5 acres of gardens, this family-run hotel has extensive public areas including several bars serving a wide range of food. Bedrooms are well equipped with modern facilities and most have pine furnishings.

33⇨♠(5fb)3⚐ CTV in all bedrooms ®❦ T
70P ⊞ ✿
V ♥ ☑ Last dinner 9.45pm
Credit Cards ① ② ③ ⑤

WHEDDON CROSS Somerset Map 03 SS93

★★⚐ 71% Raleigh Manor
TA24 7BB ☎Timberscombe(0643) 841484
Closed end Oct-mid Mar

The comfortable family home of the resident proprietors stands in over an acre of grounds and gardens overlooking Snowdrop Valley. Bedrooms with coordinating fabrics and antique furnishings offer comfortable and spotlessly clean accommodation. There is a choice of lounges with log fires, and interesting home-cooked dishes are available on the table d'hôte menu served in the dining room.

7⇨♠(1fb)1⚐ CTV in all bedrooms ® ✱ sB&B⇨♠£39-£42 dB&B⇨♠£78-£96 (incl dinner) ₽
10P ⊞ ✿
V ♥ ☑ ✂ ✱ Dinner £15 Last dinner 8pm
Credit Cards ① ③

WHICKHAM Tyne & Wear Map 12 NZ26
See also **Newcastle upon Tyne**

★★★ 70% Gibside Arms
Front St NE16 4JG ☎091-488 9292 FAX 091-488 8000

This comfortable family-owned hotel in the village centre offers friendly service. Modern bedrooms with attractive coordinated furnishings contain the latest facilities and there is an elegant restaurant and Eqyptian-styled bar with a comprehensive bar menu.

45⇨♠(2fb) CTV in all bedrooms ®❦ T ✠ (ex guide dogs) sB&B⇨♠£45-£59 dB&B⇨♠£60-£78 ₽
Lift ⓛ 18P 10☂ xmas
♦ English & French V ♥ ☑ ✂ Bar Lunch fr£5.70
Credit Cards ① ② ③ ⑤

If you have booked a meal in a
hotel restaurant and cannot get there,
remember you have a contractual obligation
to cancel your booking.

WHIMPLE Devon Map 03 SY09

★★❀⚐ WOODHAYES
EX5 2TD (under 1m from A30, Exeter rd)
☎(0404) 822237

There is a friendly, family atmosphere at Woodhayes. Frank Rendle, quiet, unassuming and helpful, usually greets guests, carries their cases and shows them to their room, and his unobtrusive style puts them at their ease. Peace and privacy are assured, especially in the 2 comfortable lounges and the attractive flagstoned bar. The bedrooms are well furnished, and many are particularly spacious. Katherine Rendle is a natural hostess and puts guests at their ease. She prepares the 6-course dinners, and discusses the menu with guests to find out any pet dislikes. A meal may start with smoked salmon, followed by a delicious soup, then fish – for example, red mullet – and a main course of duck with port and orange sauce. Desserts round off the meal and should not be missed.

6rm(5⇨) CTV in all bedrooms ⚐ T ✠ ✱ sB&B⇨fr£65 dB&B⇨fr£85 ₽
20P 2☂ ⊞ ✿ ℘ (grass) croquet nc12yrs xmas
♦ English & French V Lunch £15 Dinner £25 Last dinner 9.30pm
Credit Cards ① ② ③ ⑤

WHITBURN Lothian West Lothian Map 11 NS96

★★★ 60% The Hilcroft
East Main St EH47 0JU (Turn off M8 junct 4 follow signs for Whitburn hotel 0.5m on left from junct) ☎(0501) 740818 FAX (0501) 744013
Closed 1-2 Jan

Many improvements have recently been carried out at this purpose built and family run hotel. A popular venue for local functions, it offers a choice of bars – one of them semi open plan with the split level restaurant where both table d'hôte and à la carte meals are served. The new wing's attractive bedrooms are comfortably furnished in modern style, while those in the main house are more compact and traditional.

30⇨♠(5fb) CTV in all bedrooms ® T ✠ (ex guide dogs) sB&B⇨♠£35-£45 dB&B⇨♠£35-£45
ⓛ 90P ✿ xmas
♦ French & Italian V ♥ ☑ ✱ Lunch £7.95&alc High tea £5.95-£6.95 Dinner £11.95&alc Last dinner 9.30pm
Credit Cards ① ② ③

WHITBY North Yorkshire Map 08 NZ81

★★ 72% Kimberley
7 Havelock Place YO21 3ER ☎(0947) 604125 & 606147 FAX (0947) 606147
RS Sun & Mon evening Nov-Jun

Quietly situated just off the seafront, this delightful privately owned hotel offers comfortable bedrooms and inviting lounges. The popular restaurant has a strong Italian influence and features some pasta dishes as well as imaginative meat and fish dishes.

7rm(6♠)(1fb) CTV in all bedrooms ® T
℘ ⊞ nc5yrs
♦ Italian V ♥ ✂
Credit Cards ① ③

★★ 70% Saxonville
Ladysmith Av, (Off Argyle Road) YO21 3HX ☎(0947) 602631 FAX (0947) 820523
Closed mid Oct-mid May
An immaculately maintained family-run hotel in a quiet road behind the North Promenade, offering modern facilities and traditional food, hospitality and comforts.
24⇨♠(2fb) CTV in all bedrooms ® T ✱ (ex guide dogs) 20P
V ✿ Last dinner 8.30pm
CONF. Thtr 100 Class 50 Del from £43.50
Credit Cards [1][3]

★★ 65% Larpool Hall Country House
Larpool Ln YO22 4ND (Logis) ☎(0947) 602737 FAX (0947) 602737
This elegant, stone-built Georgian mansion stands in extensive gardens overlooking the Esk Valley. Public rooms include an attractive restaurant, a comfortable lounge bar, a guests' lounge and a library. Spacious bedrooms, some with antique furniture, all have modern facilities.
14⇨♠(3fb)1⚁ CTV in all bedrooms ® T ✱ (ex guide dogs) ✱ sB&B⇨♠£39.50 dB&B⇨♠£35-£45 🍴
CTV 20P ✿ snooker table *xmas*
♨ International V ✿ ⚏ ⚒ ✱ Lunch £9.95-£14.95alc High tea £4.95-£6.50 Dinner £14.95-£17 Last dinner 9pm
Credit Cards [1][3][5]

★★ 65% White House
Upgang Lane, West Cliff YO21 3JJ (on A174 beside the golf course) ☎(0947) 600469 FAX (0947) 821600
Situated at the northern end of the town overlooking Sandsend Bay and next to the golf course, this friendly family-run hotel has attractively decorated bedrooms and is popular for its food, available in the dining room, lounge or bar.
12rm(7⇨4♠)(3fb) CTV in all bedrooms ® T ✱ sB&B£18.50-£20.50 sB&B⇨♠£20.50-£24.50 dB&B£41-£45 dB&B⇨♠£46-£55 🍴
CTV 50P ✿ *xmas*
♨ English & French V ✿ ✱ Lunch £6.95-£8.55 Dinner £10.95-£11.95 Last dinner 9.30pm
Credit Cards [1][3]

★★ 64% Old West Cliff
42 Crescent Av YO21 3EQ ☎(0947) 603292
Closed Feb
This friendly family-run hotel in a Victorian terrace close to the sea and Crescent Gardens has well equipped bedrooms with modern bathrooms, a comfortable lounge and attractive bar, and a cosy restaurant serving generous meals.
12⇨♠(6fb) CTV in all bedrooms ® ✱ sB&B⇨♠£25 dB&B⇨♠£40
CTV ✗ 🚲
V ✿ ⚏ ⚒ ✱ Dinner fr£8.75 Last dinner 8pm
Credit Cards [1][2][3][5]

★★ 64% Stakesby Manor
Manor Close, High Stakesby YO21 1HL (at roundabout junct of A171/B1416 take road for West Cliff. Third turning on right) ☎(0947) 602773 FAX (0947) 602140
Closed 25-30 Dec
This Georgian manor house stands in its own grounds in a quiet area about a mile from the sea and town. It is a family-run, friendly and relaxing hotel, featuring a panelled restaurant as well as a comfortable bar and lounge.
8⇨♠ CTV in all bedrooms ® T ✱ (ex guide dogs) sB&B⇨♠£38-£48 dB&B⇨♠£54-£60 🍴
40P 🚲 ✿ ⚛
♨ International V Dinner £12.95&alc Last dinner 9.30pm
Credit Cards [1][2][3]

WHITCHURCH Shropshire Map 07 SJ54

★★★ 63% Terrick Hall Country
Hill Valley SY13 4JZ (off A49 NE of town centre)
☎(0948) 663031
With fine views of the Hill Valley Golf Course a few yards away, this traditional hotel is set in 4 acres of mature grounds with tennis courts and small lakes. Most of the bedrooms are in the main house and are furnished with period pieces, and there are 7 rooms in converted stables with lovely views and peaceful surroundings. The Oak Room is used as both a lounge and meeting room and features a carved wooden ceiling. Golfing breaks are popular, and the hotel's guests have guaranteed starting times each morning.
10⇨♠Annexe7⇨♠(7fb) CTV in all bedrooms ® T
CTV 50P ✿ ▶ 36 ✐ (hard) squash snooker sauna
♨ International V ✿ ⚏ Last dinner 9pm
Credit Cards [1][2][3][5]

★★★ 55% Dodington Lodge
Dodington SY13 1EN (at A41/A49 junct) ☎(0948) 662539
With an attractive raised dining area off the bar, this family-run commercial hotel has a regular following. The restaurant offers a full carte. There are 10 bedrooms, all fully equipped with modern facilities.
10rm(9⇨♠)(2fb)1⚁ CTV in all bedrooms ® T
sB&B⇨♠£42.50-£45 dB&B⇨♠£52.50-£57.50 🍴
70P ✿ *xmas*
V ✿ ⚏ ✱ Lunch £6.50-£9.50&alc High tea fr£4.50 Dinner fr£9.50 Last dinner 10pm
Credit Cards [1][3]

See advertisement on page 645

Satellite television – look for this symbol ⛱ in the directory entries.

Saxonville Hotel

Ladysmith Avenue, Whitby, North Yorkshire YO21 3HX

As featured in ITV's Wish you were here!

Telephone: Whitby (0947) 602631

AA ★ ★

Close to seafront, 24 bedrooms all with private facilities, radio, colour T.V., courtesy tray and direct dial telephone. Well appointed dining room and excellent choice of food. Attractive lounge, bar, car park. Family owned and run.

Whitchurch - Whitley Bay

★★ **59%** **Redbrook Hunting Lodge**
Wrexham Rd SY13 3ET (2.5m W, at A495/A525 junct)
☎Redbrook Maelor(094873) 204 & 533 FAX (094873) 533
This family-run hotel has 2.5 acres of lawns and gardens. Popular locally, it has a modern bar with an open fire, and there has been a recent extension to the dining areas. The large open plan foyer is comfortably furnished with modern sofas and armchairs, and bedrooms are being improved.
13⇨🏠(3fb)2🛏 CTV in all bedrooms ® T 🐕 (ex guide dogs) sB&B⇨🏠£45-£50 dB&B⇨🏠£60-£65 ♨
100P ✿
☐ English & French V ☺ ♨ Lunch £8-£11&alc Dinner £11&alc Last dinner 9pm
Credit Cards [1][2][3]   £

WHITEBRIDGE Highland *Inverness-shire* Map **14** NH41

★★❀❀☘ **KNOCKIE LODGE**
IV1 2UP
☎Gorthleck(0456) 486276
FAX (0456) 486389
Closed 30 Oct-29 Apr

Knockie Lodge must rank as one of Britain's most peacefully located hotels, set amid mountains and forests with a loch on its doorstep, and superb views of Loch Ness are just a short walk away. Ian and Brenda Milward, here since the early 80s, have created a naturally warm atmosphere. Bedrooms, all with fine views, are furnished with antiques. There is a lovely drawing room with open log fires, books and fresh flowers, and a sun lounge facing the loch. Dinner is a highlight, and chef Chris Freeman's set 5-course menu might offer mushroom timbale followed by home-made soup, then, perhaps, quail in filo pastry with a vermouth sauce. There is a choice of 2 puddings and cheeses from around the world. Service is provided by attentive young staff.
10⇨🏠 T sB&B⇨🏠fr£75 dB&B⇨🏠£125-£190 (incl dinner)
20P 🚗 ✿ ♪ snooker sailing nc10yrs
Dinner £28 Last dinner 8pm
Credit Cards [1][2][3][5]

★★ **63%** **Whitebridge**
IV1 2UN ☎Gorthleck(0456) 486226 & 486272 FAX (0456) 486413
Closed 21 Dec-Feb
Good value accommodation is offered at this long established family-run holiday and sporting hotel. Public areas include a small bar for residents as well as a timbered public bar, a comfortable lounge with an open fire and a pleasant dining room serving good home cooking.
12rm(10⇨🏠)(3fb) CTV in all bedrooms ® sB&B£22-£25 sB&B⇨🏠£27-£30 dB&B£40-£46 dB&B⇨🏠£44-£50
30P 2☂ (50p) 🚗 ✿ ♪
♨ Bar Lunch £3-£15alc Dinner £13-£15 Last dinner 9pm
Credit Cards [1][2][3][5]   £

Remember to book early for holiday
and bank holiday times.

WHITEBROOK Gwent Map **03** SO50

★★ ❀❀**71%** **Crown at Whitebrook**
NP5 4TX (turn W off A466, 50yds S of Bigsweir Bridge)
☎Monmouth(0600) 860254 FAX (0600) 860607

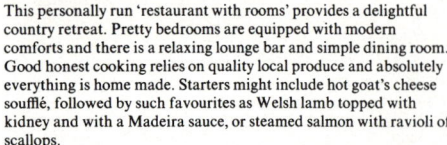

Closed 2 wks Jan
This personally run 'restaurant with rooms' provides a delightful country retreat. Pretty bedrooms are equipped with modern comforts and there is a relaxing lounge bar and simple dining room. Good honest cooking relies on quality local produce and absolutely everything is home made. Starters might include hot goat's cheese soufflé, followed by such favourites as Welsh lamb topped with kidney and with a Madeira sauce, or steamed salmon with ravioli of scallops.
12⇨🏠1🛏 CTV in all bedrooms ® T ✱ sB&B⇨🏠£70-£77 dB&B⇨🏠£120-£134 (incl dinner) ♨
40P 🚗 ✿
☐ French V ✂ Lunch £14.50&alc Dinner £24.50 Last dinner 9.30pm
Credit Cards [1][2][3][4][5]   £

WHITEHAVEN Cumbria Map **11** NX91

★★ **60%** **The Chase**
Inkerman Ter CA28 8AA ☎(0946) 693656 & 693714 FAX (0946) 590807
Set in its own grounds close to the town centre this family-run hotel offers bedrooms with good facilities. A wide range of food is available in the bar or dining room.
11rm(8⇨🏠)(1fb)1🛏 CTV in all bedrooms ®✓ T ✱ sB&B£26.50-£39 sB&B⇨🏠£26.50-£39 dB&B⇨🏠£49.50-£54.50
50P ✿ ♒
☐ English & French V ✱ Dinner £5-£15alc Last dinner 9pm
Credit Cards [1][3]

WHITLEY BAY Tyne & Wear Map **12** NZ37

★★ **68%** **High Point**
The Promenade NE26 2NJ ☎091-251 7782 FAX 091-251 6318
Overlooking the bay, this mainly commercial hotel has been partly rebuilt and totally refurbished. Bedrooms are comfortable and well equipped and there are spacious public areas with a nautical theme.
14⇨🏠(3fb) CTV in all bedrooms ® T 🐕 (ex guide dogs) ✱ sB&B⇨🏠£40-£48 dB&B⇨🏠£48-£55
(20P *xmas*
V ☺ ♨ ✱ Lunch £7.95 Dinner £3-£7&alc Last dinner 9.30pm
Credit Cards [1][2][3][5]

★★ **67%** **Windsor**
South Pde NE26 2RF ☎091-251 8888 FAX 091-297 0272
RS 25 Dec
This privately owned hotel, close to the town centre and the seafront, continues to be improved. Bedrooms are all now furnished to a good contemporary standard, with coordinated décor and modern amenities. Public areas are spacious and comfortable, and friendly staff provide helpful service.
64⇨🏠(24fb) CTV in all bedrooms ®✓ T sB&B⇨🏠£35-£55 dB&B⇨🏠£45-£60 ♨
Lift (CTV 30P 2☂ *xmas*
☐ European V ☺ ♨ Dinner £12&alc Last dinner 9.30pm
Credit Cards [1][2][3][5]   £

★★ **60%** **Park Lodge Hotel**
160-164 Park Av NE26 1AU ☎091-253 0288 & 091-252 6879 FAX 091-297 1006
Closed 24-26 Dec
Enthusiastically run by the resident proprietress, this commercial hotel is on the one-way system close to the sea front. Bedrooms vary in size and have recently been attractively re-decorated.

Whitley Bay - Wickham

16rm(12⇌🌂)(1fb) CTV in all bedrooms ® ✠ T
🐕 (ex guide dogs)
CTV 8P ⌘ solarium gymnasium nc
✿ ⚓ ✠ Last dinner 9.30pm
Credit Cards [1][2][3][5]

★★59% **Holmedale**
106 Park Av NE26 1DN ☎091-251 3903 &
091-253 1162 FAX 091-253 0053
Closed evening 24-evening 26 Dec

Situated between the town and the seafront, this small commercial and family hotel is quietly run. Bedrooms are generally compact but most have smart modern bathrooms. There is a comfortable combined bar and lounge.

18⇌🌂(3fb)1⚓ CTV in all bedrooms ® T 🐕 (ex guide dogs)
✱ sB&B⇌🌂 £20-£38 dB&B⇌🌂£40-£51.30 🍴
CTV 10P darts pool table
♀ English & Continental V ✱ Bar Lunch fr£2alc Dinner
£9.75&alc Last dinner 8pm
CONF. Thtr 80 Class 50 Board 40 Del from £45
Credit Cards [1][2][3][5]

★57% **Cavendish**
51 Esplanade NE26 2AS ☎091-253 3010

This seaside hotel, managed by the resident proprietors, offers friendly informal service, neat and simple accommodation and good value menus.

11rm(5⇌1🌂)(2fb) CTV in all bedrooms ® ✱ sB&Bfr£20
sB&B⇌🌂£30 dB&B⇌🌂£45
CTV 12P
V ✱ Sunday Lunch £6.95 Dinner £9.75 Last dinner 9.30pm
Credit Cards [1][3]

WHITTINGTON Shropshire Map 07 SJ33

★60% **Ye Olde Boot Inn**
SY11 4DG (Frederic Robinson) ☎Oswestry(0691) 662250

An old coaching inn with a wealth of exposed timbers in its bar and restaurant, opposite the castle and moat. Very popular with locals – not least for its good-value, generously served meals and friendly service – it also offers accommodation in brightly decorated bedrooms.

6⇌🌂(2fb) CTV in all bedrooms ® ✱ sB&B⇌🌂£23
dB&B⇌🌂£38
100P
V ✿ ⚓ Last dinner 10pm
Credit Cards [1][3]

WICK Highland *Caithness* Map 15 ND35

★★58% **Mackay's**
Union St KW1 5ED ☎(0955) 2323 FAX (0955) 5930
Closed 1-2 Jan

This long established family-run commercial hotel is on the south bank of the River Wick close to the town centre. It offers a choice of refurbished bars and also has 2 lounges. Bedrooms, though functional and plain, have all the expected amenities.

26rm(23⇌1🌂)(4fb) CTV in all bedrooms ® T
Lift ℂ CTV 12P ⌘
V ✿ ✠
Credit Cards [1][3]

WICKHAM Hampshire Map 04 SU51

★★❀❀73% **Old House**
The Square PO17 5JG (at the junction of the B2177 and the A32) ☎(0329) 833049 FAX (0329) 833672
Closed 10 days Xmas, 3 days Etr & 2 wks Jul/Aug RS Mon-Sat

Built around 1715, this elegantly furnished house has retained much of its original character. Bedrooms are furnished with antiques, and all have a good range of modern equipment; room 5 has a sunken ➥

Seafront, Cullercoats
Telephone:
Whitley Bay (091) 2523150

Occupying one of the best positions on Cullercoats' beautiful sea front and only steps away from the lovely safe sandy beach. Within walking distance the coastline changes from rocky outcrops to secluded coves, from cliffs to sand dunes. The 22 bedrooms are all tastefully decorated and well furnished. Most rooms are en suite and many overlook the beautiful bay. You will find peace or excitement, rest or entertainment, an active or lazy life.

Cullercoats Bay — about 10 miles east of Newcastle upon Tyne.

THE DODINGTON
LODGE HOTEL AA ★★★
Whitchurch, Shropshire SY13 1EN
Telephone: (0948) 662539

A friendly family run Georgian Hotel situated just minutes walk from the centre of this historic market town. The comfortable bedrooms are all en suite and have radio, colour television and direct dial telephone along with a hospitality tray. With good food and a choice of real ales, look no further than the Dodington for your stay in North Shropshire. An ideal base for visiting Chester and Shrewsbury both 20 minutes, with Ironbridge, North Wales and the Potteries all within easy reach. The wonderful scenery of Shropshire is all around you in an area of Britain still unspoilt. Or, play golf at one of the many first class courses within easy 'driving' distance. We would be delighted to organise tee times for you. Brochure available, details of rates and short breaks on request.

Wickham - Wight, Isle of, Freshwater

bath. There are 2 lounges, a breakfast room, and a provincial French-style bar. Chef Nick Harman offers an imaginative French carte which changes weekly. The highlight of our inspector's meal was a very good ox tongue with Madeira sauce.
9⇨🛏 Annexe3⇨🛏(1fb) CTV in all bedrooms ® T ✈
sB&B⇨🛏fr£75 dB&B⇨🛏fr£85 🍴
12P 🚗
♀ French V Lunch fr£25 Dinner fr£25 Last dinner 9.30pm
Credit Cards 1 2 3 5

WIDNES Cheshire Map 07 SJ58

★★66% **Hill Crest**
75 Cronton Ln WA8 9AR (on A5080 NW) ☎051-424 1616 FAX 051-495 1348
Bedrooms vary in style and quality at this large privately owned hotel on the outskirts of Widnes, but at the time of our last inspection work was about to start to replace a block of old rooms with newly constructed ones. Facilities include a large restaurant, a choice of bars and 2 function/conference rooms.
57⇨🛏(1fb)3🛌 CTV in all bedrooms ® T sB&B⇨🛏£35-£65 dB&B⇨🛏£50-£90
Lift (200P 🎵 *xmas*
♀ Continental V ♥ ♨ Lunch £7.50-£12.75&alc Dinner £12.75&alc Last dinner 10pm
CONF. Thtr 120 Class 40 Board 40 Del from £76
Credit Cards 1 2 3 5

WIGAN Greater Manchester Map 07 SD50

★★★64% **Almond Brook Moat House**
Almond Brook Rd WN6 0SR
☎Standish(0257) 425588 FAX (0257) 427327
(For full entry see Standish)

★★64% **Bel-Air**
236 Wigan Ln WN1 2NU (1m N on A49) ☎(0942) 41410 FAX (0942) 43967
This friendly, privately owned hotel provides modern, well equipped accommodation. There is a comfortable lounge bar and a recently redecorated restaurant, where a wide range of British and international dishes, including vegetarian, is served.
12⇨🛏(3fb)1🛌 CTV in all bedrooms ® T ✳ sB&B⇨🛏£30-£39.50 dB&B⇨🛏£40-£49.50 🍴
CTV 12P
♀ English & Continental V ♥ ♨ ✂ ✳ Lunch £7.30-£10.50alc Dinner £7.30-£10.50alc Last dinner 9pm
Credit Cards 1 3

★★61% **Brocket Arms**
Mesnes Rd WN1 2DD ☎(0942) 46283
This privately owned hotel caters mainly for commercial guests and provides sound but rather dated accommodation. At the time of our last visit, work was about to commence on refurbishing the lounge bar and the restaurant was temporarily closed, though meals were readily available in the bar.
27⇨🛏 CTV in all bedrooms ® ✈
(60P
V ♥ Last dinner 9.30pm
Credit Cards 1 2 3 5

WIGHT, ISLE OF Map 04

BEMBRIDGE Map 04 SZ68

★★57% **Birdham**
1 Steyne Rd PO35 5UH (signpost to Lifeboat Station, on B3395) ☎Isle of Wight(0983) 872875
This popular hotel has a very cordial, bar-orientated style. The proprietor, Mrs Linda Kaz, generates a warm atmosphere and the friendly staff work well together. Public rooms comprise the main bar, the public bar, a small dining room leading off the lounge, and a

separate breakfast room. Bar meals are available throughout the day, along with an à la carte menu for the restaurant. The hotel has a large rear garden.
14rm(12⇨)(5fb)⚲ in 4 bedrooms CTV in all bedrooms ®
sB&B£15 sB&B⇨£25 dB&B£30 dB&B⇨£45
(CTV 100P ✿ pool table petanque darts 🚲
♀ English & Continental V ♥ ✂ ✳ Lunch £7.70-£10&alc Dinner £7.70-£10&alc Last dinner 9.30pm

BONCHURCH See *Ventnor*

CHALE Map 04 SZ47

★★63% **Clarendon Hotel & Wight Mouse Inn**
PO38 2HA (on B3399) (Logis) ☎Isle of Wight(0983) 730431 FAX (0983) 730431
The Clarendon Hotel provides an exciting and lively atmosphere for guests. The dining area within the hotel has been extended and improvements have been made throughout. Bedrooms are individually furnished with style and taste and the service is relaxed and friendly. Wholesome food is on offer from a table d'hôte and extensive à la carte menu. Children are catered for extremely well here.
14rm(4⇨6🛏)(9fb) CTV in all bedrooms ® sB&B£20-£37.50 sB&B⇨🛏£20-£42 dB&B£40-£59 dB&B⇨🛏£4000-£65.80 🍴
200P ✿ petanque 🎵 🚲 *xmas*
V ♥ ♨ Lunch £6-£12&alc High tea £5-£6&alc Dinner £10-£15&alc Last dinner 10pm
Credit Cards 1 3

COWES Map 04 SZ49

★★★67% **New Holmwood**
Queens Rd, Egypt Point PO31 8BW (from Cowes Parade turn right by Royal Yacht Squadron) ☎Isle of Wight(0983) 292508 FAX (0983) 295020
New Holmwood hotel is in an excellent location facing the sea at Egypt point, providing unrivalled views of the Solent. Bedrooms range from a full suite to deluxe and standard rooms, all with a good range of modern equipment. The restaurant features a popular carvery at weekends. Room service is available throughout the day.
25⇨🛏 CTV in all bedrooms ® T ✳ sB&B⇨🛏£65-£100 dB&B⇨🛏£80-£110 🍴
17P ⛱ (heated) *xmas*
♀ French V ♥ ♨ Lunch £10.50&alc Dinner £16&alc Last dinner 9.30pm
Credit Cards 1 2 3 5

★★62% **Fountain**
High St PO31 7AN (Whitbread) ☎Isle of Wight(0983) 292397 FAX (0983) 299554
A long established, centrally located hotel, the Fountain is especially popular with commercial and business guests. Accommodation is fresh and modern with pretty décor. The bar is popular with both residents and locals, and snacks are available here in addition to the more formal Patio Restaurant.
20⇨🛏 CTV in all bedrooms ®⚲ T ✈ (ex guide dogs) ✳
sB&B⇨🛏fr£52 dB&B⇨🛏fr£64 🍴
♫ 🚗
♀ European V ♥ ♨ Last dinner 10.30pm
Credit Cards 1 2 3 4 5

FRESHWATER Map 04 SZ38

★★★59% **Albion**
PO40 9RA ☎Isle of Wight(0983) 753631 FAX (0983) 755295
This large hotel enjoys a very prominent position on the seashore and promenade, overlooking the bay. The public areas are spacious, comfortable and smart, and take advantage of the views. Bedrooms have been undergoing refurbishment, which continues steadily, but

646

they are generally bright with sunny balconies. Staff are courteous and helpful.
42⇌☏(28fb) CTV in all bedrooms ® T sB&B⇌☏£39-£42 dB&B⇌☏£75-£79 ⏣
《 CTV 75P beauty clinic putting *xmas*
♡ International V ✧ ⚏ ✳ Sunday Lunch £9.50 Dinner £17.50&alc Last dinner 9pm
CONF. Thtr 100 Class 75 Board 90 Del from £40
Credit Cards 1 2 3 5

RYDE Map 04 SZ59

★★**65%** **Biskra House Beach**
17 Saint Thomas's St PO33 2DL ☏Isle of Wight(0983) 567913 FAX (0983) 616976
Guiseppe's Cellar Restaurant offers very reliable and authentic Italian cuisine, earning chef/patron Guiseppe Cretella a good local reputation. A small breakfast room augments the larger lounge bar, and meals are served on the Beach Terrace when weather permits. Individually furnished bedrooms offer many extras, including mini bars. Service is particularly friendly.
9⇌☏ CTV in all bedrooms ® T ✳ sB&B⇌☏£25-£31.50 dB&B⇌☏£40-£57.50 ⏣
14P ⌬
♡ English & Italian V ✧ Bar Lunch £4-£9.50 Dinner £13.95&alc Last dinner 10pm
Credit Cards 1 3

See advertisement on page 649

★★**61%** **Yelf's**
Union St PO33 2LG ☏Isle of Wight(0983) 564062 FAX (0983) 563937
Centrally located in one of the main shopping streets, this is a popular hotel with a pretty flower-filled terrace. Public areas are smartly furnished, and the restaurant is again open for business ➡

Wight, Isle of, Freshwater - Ryde

Leeson Road, Bonchuch, Ventnor, Isle of Wight PO38 1PU Telephone: (0983) 852800

★★

We extend to you a warm invitation to visit our attractive country house hotel which stands amid glorious gardens overlooking the sea in one of the prettiest corners of the Isle of Wight. The hotel is tastefully and attractively furnished and the ideal place to relax, enjoy good food prepared by our chef using only the finest ingredients.
Prices: Daily rate B/B from £19, ED, B/B from £29.50
Weekly ED, B/B from £215; B/B from £136.50
Resident proprietors: Dennis & Thelma Flaherty

NEW HOLMWOOD HOTEL
Queens Road, Egypt Point, Cowes, I.O.W. PO31 8BW.
Phone: (0983) 292508 Facsimile: (0983) 295020

A Magnificent Location
The New Holmwood Hotel not only offers the highest standards on the Island in terms of decor, comfort and food but also its unique position on the water's edge at Egypt Point, Cowes provides unrivalled panoramic views of the Solent.
All rooms en suite, luxurious restaurant, swimming pool and spa bath.
Purpose built Conference facilities.
Courtesy car from Red Funnel terminal. Deep water moorings
TELEPHONE: (0983) 292508
FOR FURTHER DETAILS

Wight, Isle of, Ryde - Shanklin

after refurbishment, with two new chefs installed. Bedrooms are steadily being redecorated and improved.
21⇨🛏(2fb) CTV in all bedrooms ® T
🍴 🚗
V ☆ ♿ ⚠ Last dinner 9pm
Credit Cards ① ② ③ ⑤

ST LAWRENCE Map 04 SZ57

★★ 64% Rocklands
PO38 1XH ☎Ventnor(0983) 852964
Closed Nov-Apr
Built in 1842, this quietly situated hotel stands in its own well kept grounds. Traditional in style, Rocklands is gradually being upgraded, and public rooms are spacious and comfortably appointed. Amiable manager, Brenda Robertson-Walker, is a charming hostess, attuned to guests' needs.
14⇨🛏Annexe5rm(4⇨🛏)(9fb)1🛌 CTV in all bedrooms ®
🍴 (ex guide dogs) sB&B⇨🛏£50.53-£52.88
dB&B⇨🛏£101.06-£105.76 (incl dinner)
CTV 18P ❋ ≋ (heated) snooker sauna solarium croquet ♪ ⛳
♿ English & Continental V ☆ ♿ Bar Lunch £2.50-£10alc
High tea £1.50-£5alc Dinner £10-£12alc Last dinner 8.15pm

SANDOWN Map 04 SZ58

★★★ 57% Melville Hall
Melville St PO36 9DH ☎Isle of Wight(0983) 406526 FAX (0983) 407093
Quietly situated in well kept gardens not far from the seafront, this long established family-run hotel offers a choice of bedrooms with modern facilities. Public rooms include a large restaurant and a bar providing daytime meals, with service from friendly young staff.
33⇨🛏(11fb) CTV in all bedrooms ® T 🍴 (ex guide dogs)
《 30P ❋ ≋ (heated) 9 hole putting ♪
♿ English & Continental V ☆ ♿ Last dinner 9.30pm
Credit Cards ① ② ③ ⑤

SEAVIEW Map 04 SZ69

★★ ❋❋ 75% Seaview
High St PO34 5EX (Logis) ☎Isle of Wight(0983) 612711
FAX (0983) 613709
Set in the heart of this seaside resort and harbour village, the hotel has a refreshing charm and honesty. The restaurant is the focal point, where Charles Bartlett makes good use of locally landed fish. He runs the kitchen with little assistance and provides bar meals as well as maintaining commendable standards in the restaurant. The public bar is full of character, and cosy bedrooms are pretty and well equipped; there are 2 comfortable sitting rooms.
16⇨🛏(2fb) CTV in all bedrooms T ✱ sB&B⇨🛏£40-£65
dB&B⇨🛏£60-£80 🍴
12P 🚗 xmas
♿ English & French V ☆ ♿ ⚠ ✱ Lunch fr£17.85alc Dinner fr£17.85alc Last dinner 9.30pm
Credit Cards ① ② ③ ⑤

SHANKLIN Map 04 SZ58

★★★ 62% Holliers
Church Rd, Old Village PO37 6NU
☎Isle of Wight(0983) 862764 FAX (0983) 867134
This 18th-century coaching inn is located in the Old Village amid several pretty thatched cottages. It is a comfortable hotel with fresh accommodation and plenty of facilities. Guests may choose from a number of eating areas, including the restaurant, wine bar, or the Village Inn adjacent to the hotel.
35⇨🛏(8fb)3🛌 CTV in all bedrooms ®🍽 T 🍴 (ex guide dogs)
sB&B⇨🛏£39 dB&B⇨🛏£60-£78 🍴
40P ❋ ≋ (heated) ≋ (heated) sauna solarium multigym xmas

V ☆ ♿ Bar Lunch fr£2.50&alc Dinner fr£16.25 Last dinner 8.30pm
Credit Cards ① ② ③ £

★★★ 59% Cliff Tops
Park Rd PO37 6BB ☎Isle of Wight(0983) 863262 FAX (0983) 867139
This hotel enjoys a prominent position facing the sea, and the best of its well equipped bedrooms have balconies. The range of meals served in the Carvery is augmented by the Asquith Restaurant's carte, and guests can relax over a drink in either the Promenade Bar Lounge or the lively Beacon Bar.
88⇨🛏(8fb) CTV in all bedrooms ® T
Lift 《 30P ❋ ≋ (heated) snooker sauna solarium gymnasium steam room beautician hairdresser ♪
♿ English & French V ☆ ♿ Last dinner 10pm
Credit Cards ① ② ③ ⑤

★★ 69% Fernbank
Highfield Rd PO37 6PP ☎(0983) 862790 FAX (0983) 864412
Closed Xmas
Opposite Big Mead and the lovely Manor Walk, this detached hotel stands in well tended grounds. It has been caringly improved by the Sladden family to provide modern amenities without losing the character and charm of the building. Bedrooms are very well equipped and prettily decorated, while public areas are spacious and comfortable.
19⇨🛏Annexe5⇨🛏(fb)1🛌 CTV in all bedrooms ® T ✱
sB&B⇨🛏£25.50-£36.25 dB&B⇨🛏£51-£72.50 (incl dinner) 🍴
22P ❋ ≋ (heated) sauna solarium pool table whirlpool bath nc7yrs
♿ English, French & Italian V ☆ ♿ ⚠ ✱ Lunch £5-£8.50
Dinner £10-£13.50&alc Last dinner 10.30pm
Credit Cards ① ③ ⑤ £

★★ 68% Keats Green
3 Queens Rd PO37 6AN ☎Isle of Wight(0983) 862742 FAX (0983) 868868
Closed mid Oct-Etr
In a commanding position overlooking the bay, and just a hundred yards from the beach lift, this hotel has been greatly improved by the resident owners in recent years. Bedrooms are comfortable and pretty and public areas are spacious, including a large bar lounge and a separate no-smoking lounge, both with fine sea views. The elegant dining room offers a choice of menus.
34rm(23⇨🛏10🛏)(3fb) CTV in all bedrooms ® T ✱
sB&B⇨🛏£25-£30 dB&B⇨🛏£46-£58 🍴
34P ❋ ≋ (heated)
V ☆ ✱ Dinner £7.50-£9 Last dinner 7.45pm
Credit Cards ① ③

★★ 66% Luccombe Hall
Luccombe Rd PO37 6RL ☎Isle of Wight(0983) 862719 FAX (0983) 863082
Mature grounds and a well kept garden surround this hotel overlooking the sea. Accommodation is slowly being upgraded and the more spacious bedrooms in the new wing are all well equipped. An efficiently managed restaurant provides attentive silver service and a six-course daily table d'hôte menu. Involved proprietors create a relaxed, informal atmosphere throughout.
29⇨🛏(14fb)2🛌 CTV in all bedrooms ® T sB&B⇨🛏£40-£49.50 dB&B⇨🛏£80-£99 (incl dinner) 🍴
CTV 30P ❋ ≋ (heated) ≋ (heated) ♫ (grass) squash sauna solarium gymnasium games room xmas
♿ English & Continental ☆ ♿ ⚠ Lunch £10-£15 Dinner £16 Last dinner 8.30pm
Credit Cards ① ③ ⑤

Hotels with red star ratings are especially high quality.

Wight, Isle of, Shanklin - Ventnor

★★ **61%** **Melbourne Ardenlea**
Queen's Rd PO37 6AP ☎Isle of Wight(0983) 862283 FAX (0983) 862865
Closed mid Dec-mid Feb RS Nov-mid Dec & mid Feb-Mar
Close to the old village, this Victorian property has been steadily improved by the proprietors over the last 20 years. It has bedrooms of various sizes, but all are well equipped with modern facilities. Public areas are spacious and traditionally furnished, and include a foyer lounge where entertainment is provided most nights of the week. Staff are friendly and helpful.
51⇨🛏(9fb) CTV in all bedrooms ® T ✱ sB&B⇨🛏£29-£42 dB&B⇨🛏£58-£84 (incl dinner) 🍴
Lift CTV 28P ✿ 🍽 (heated) sauna solarium games room spa bath
♀ English & French V Bar Lunch £1.50-£5 Dinner £9-£12&alc Last dinner 8pm
Credit Cards [1][2][3]

★★ **59%** **Malton House**
8 Park Rd PO37 6AY ☎Isle of Wight(0983) 865007
This Victorian villa is handy for the town and the lift to the beach. The hotel is family run in a relaxed, informal manner and the bedrooms are all of a similar standard. The simple table d'hôte menu at dinner, which represents good value for money, offers a choice of 4 main courses and sweets.
15⇨🛏(3fb) CTV in all bedrooms ® ⚔ ✱ sB&B⇨🛏£20-£24 dB&B⇨🛏£36-£44
CTV 12P 🚗 nc3yrs xmas
♀English&ContinentalV✱Dinner£7-£9Lastdinner8pm
Credit Cards [1][3]

TOTLAND BAY Map **04** SZ38
★★ **67%** *Sentry Mead*
Madeira Rd PO39 0BJ ☎Isle of Wight(0983) 753212
This handsome Victorian property with mature gardens is in a quiet and picturesque setting. It is owned and run by the Hodgson family in a friendly and relaxed manner. Bedrooms are attractive and public areas are traditionally styled and comfortable. Home cooked fare is prepared by Mrs Hodgson and overall the hotel offers good value for money.
14⇨🛏(4fb) CTV in all bedrooms ®
CTV 12P 🚗 ✿ putting
♀ European ✿ ⚔ ✂ Last dinner 8pm
Credit Cards [1][2][3]

VENTNOR Map **04** SZ57
★★★ **62%** **Ventnor Towers**
Madeira Rd PO38 1QT (first left after Trinity church, follow road for .25m)
☎Isle of Wight(0983) 852277 FAX (0983) 855536

CONSORT HOTELS

Ventnor Towers enjoys a good cliff-top position and is personally run by the Janzen family, who provide a friendly, family atmosphere in traditional surroundings, which are steadily being improved. A choice of table d'hôte and à la carte menus is offered and on some evenings there are dinner dances or musical entertainment, often provided by Mr Janzen himself.
27⇨🛏(4fb)1🛁 CTV in all bedrooms ® T ✱ sB&B⇨🛏£42-£52 dB&B⇨🛏£76 🍴
CTV 40P 1🅿 ✿ ✂ (heated) ▶ 9 ♦ (hard) croquet games room ♫ xmas
♀ English & French V ✿ ⚔ ✱ Lunch fr£7.50 Dinner fr£12.95&alc Last dinner 8.30pm
CONF. Thtr 40 Class 20 Board 16 Del from £39
Credit Cards [1][2][3][5]

For key to symbols see the Bookmark.

★★ 🏨 **71%** **Madeira Hall Country House**
Trinity Rd, Bonchurch PO38 1NS ☎Isle of Wight(0983) 852624 FAX (0983) 854906
Quietly set in its own grounds, this lovely Victorian manor house has been sympathetically restored and upgraded. Bedrooms vary in size and the best have lovely garden views. Proprietors Cindy and Peter Witheridge are personally involved and create an informal atmosphere. There is a small lounge, a small bar and 'Miss Haversham's' dining room, offering a carte to suit all tastes. Smoking is only permitted in the bar and garden.
8⇨🛏(2fb)3🛁✂in all bedrooms CTV in all bedrooms ® T ✘ (ex guide dogs) sB&B⇨🛏£30-£35 dB&B⇨🛏£60-£70
20P ✿ ✂ (heated) putting green bowls green nc7yrs
♀ English & Continental V ✿ ⚔ ✂ Last dinner 7.30pm
Credit Cards [1][3][4]

★★ **68%** **Burlington**
Bellevue Rd PO38 1DB ☎Isle of Wight(0983) 852113
Closed Nov-Feb
This family owned hotel is set high above the town, with good views. Bedrooms are nicely furnished and brightly decorated and some have balconies with sea views. There is a cosy bar and traditional lounge, and the dining room offers a table d'hôte style menu and a carte of enjoyable food. The McToldridge family assure a warm welcome and excellent value for money.
23⇨🛏(8fb)1🛁 CTV in all bedrooms ® T ✘
sB&B⇨🛏£26.50-£32.50 dB&B⇨🛏£53-£65 🍴
20P 🚗 ✿ ✂ (heated) nc3yrs
✿ ⚔ ✂ Bar Lunch £1-£5 Dinner £12.50 Last dinner 8.30pm
Credit Cards [1][3]

Irish entries appear in a separate section that follows the main directory.

Biskra House Beach Hotel
AA ★★

A privately owned small select hotel, fronting the sea. Beautiful gardens. Large tasteful bar. Bedrooms equipped to a very high standard. Romantic Italian Cellar Restaurant.

**17 St Thomas's Street, Ryde, Isle of Wight
Telephone (0983) 567913**

W

Wight, Isle of, Ventnor - Williton

★★ 63% Eversley
Park Av PO38 1LB ☎ Isle of Wight(0983) 852244 & 852462 FAX (0983) 853948
Closed Nov-22 Dec & 28 Dec-15 Mar

Under the personal management of Mr and Mrs Stritton, this hotel is next to Ventnor Park and close to the centre of town and the seafront. Bedrooms are fresh, bright and neatly furnished and all have modern facilities. The day rooms are comfortable, with a cheery atmosphere, and the grounds include sheltered gardens and a children's play area. Varied menus in the dining room might include local lobster.

32⇌♠(14fb) CTV in all bedrooms ® T ✻ sB&B⇌♠£19-£25 dB&B⇌♠£36-£50
CTV 23P ✿ ≏ (heated) solarium ♪ ⚬♂ xmas
☼ English & Continental V ✿ ♡ ✻ Bar Lunch £2.50-£5 Dinner £8-£10.50 Last dinner 8.30pm
CONF. Class 50
Credit Cards ①③ £

★★ 63% Highfield
Leeson Rd, Bonchurch PO38 1PU
☎ Isle of Wight(0983) 852800 & 854611
Closed Nov-Feb

In a superb situation overlooking the sea, this extended Victorian house is run by the Flaherty family, who have steadily improved standards and facilities over the years. Pretty bedrooms are of a good size and public areas include a bar lounge, a comfortable sitting room with a verandah and a spacious dining room. Service is friendly.

12⇌(1fb)2⚏ CTV in all bedrooms ® T
12P ⚑ ✿ nc5yrs
☼ English & French V ✿ ♡ ✼
Credit Cards ①③

See advertisement on page 647

WIGTON Cumbria Map 11 NY24

★★ 59% Wheyrigg Hall
Wheyrigg CA7 0DH (4m NW on B5302)
☎ Abbeytown(06973) 61242 FAX (06973) 61020

Situated in open countryside, this family-run converted farmhouse has a warm, friendly atmosphere and offers well equipped bedrooms, cosy bars and a range of hearty food.

10⇌♠(2fb) CTV in all bedrooms ® T ✖ (ex guide dogs) ✻ sB&B⇌♠£32 dB&B⇌♠£46 ℞
CTV 60P ✿ ♪ xmas
☼ English. Italian & French V ✿ ♡ ✻ Lunch fr£7.40&alc High tea fr£3.50&alc Dinner £10-£20&alc Last dinner 9pm
CONF. Thtr 100 Board 50 Del from £40
Credit Cards ①②③ £

★★ 56% Greenhill Lodge
Red Dial CA7 8LS (2m S off A595) ☎ (06973) 43304

This impressive 18th-century sandstone mansion is set in several acres of parkland. It is a mainly commercial-style hotel, run by the resident owners. A fine Georgian staircase leads to the adequately furnished bedrooms, and a good range of food is available in the popular bar or in the restaurant.

7⇌♠2⚏ CTV in all bedrooms ® T ✻ sB&B⇌♠fr£31 dB&B⇌♠fr£45 ℞
100P ✿ ▶ 7 nc xmas
☼ International V ✿ ✻ Lunch £7.50-£15 Dinner £15&alc Last dinner 9pm
Credit Cards ①③ £

WILLERBY Humberside Map 08 TA03

★★★ 70% Grange Park
Main St HU10 6EA (off A164)
☎ Hull(0482) 656488 FAX (0482) 655348

This splendid red brick manor house has been carefully extended in a modern style which is in sympathy with the original building.

Public rooms and accommodation are bright and inviting and the bedrooms, with light oak furniture, co-ordinated decor and soft furnishings are well equipped with the usual modern comforts. There are 2 restaurants, lounge service of snacks and refreshments all day, plus a good 24-hour room service menu.

104⇌♠4⚏⅟ in 4 bedrooms CTV in all bedrooms ® ✌ T ✻ sB⇌♠£68.50 dB⇌♠£78 (room only) ℞
Lift ⟨ ⚏ 600P ✿ ▭ (heated) sauna solarium gymnasium hairdressing beauty clinic ♪ xmas
☼ English, French & Italian V ✿ ♡ ✼ ✻ Lunch fr£14alc Dinner fr£13.95&alc Last dinner 10pm
CONF. Thtr 650 Class 250 Board 80 Del from £70
Credit Cards ①②③⑤ £

★★★ 70% Willerby Manor
Well Ln HU10 6ER ☎ Hull(0482) 652616 FAX (0482) 653901

An elegant manor house, set within a village on the outskirts of Hull, which offers guests professional service and a hospitable atmosphere. Bedrooms vary in size and style and the contemporary decor in the public rooms accentuates the Victorian features. A formal, tastefully appointed restaurant provides an interesting variety of dishes whilst the lounge bar serves a range of light meals and snacks at lunch time and in the evening.

36⇌♠(3fb)2⚏ CTV in all bedrooms ® T ✖ (ex guide dogs) ✻ sB⇌♠£59-£65 dB⇌♠£74.50-£82 (room only) ℞
⟨ 250P ✿ ♪ xmas
☼ French V ✿ ♡ ✻ Lunch fr£10.50 Dinner fr£14&alc Last dinner 9.45pm
CONF. Thtr 500 Class 200 Board 100 Del from £68
Credit Cards ①②③

WILLINGTON Co Durham Map 12 NZ13

★★ 64% Kensington Hall
Kensington Ter DL15 0PJ (off A690)
☎ Bishop Auckland(0388) 745071 FAX (0388) 745800

A further bedroom extension is under construction at this family-run hotel, and the existing bedrooms have good modern facilities. There is a comfortable lounge bar and another cosy bar attached to the dining room. Extensive menus offer good value for money.

10⇌♠(1fb)1⚏ CTV in all bedrooms ® T ✖ (ex guide dogs) sB&B⇌♠£30-£35 dB&B⇌♠£45-£48 ℞
40P
V ⅟ Lunch £3.95-£5.50&alc Dinner £9.95-£10.95&alc Last dinner 9.45pm
CONF. Class 150 Del from £38.95
Credit Cards ①②③⑤ £

WILLITON Somerset Map 03 ST04

★★ ❀❀❀ 72% White House
Long St TA4 4QW (Logis) ☎ (0984) 632306 & 632777
Closed 3 Nov-19 May

In the centre of the village, this attractive all-white Georgian house draws visitors back year after year to sample the cooking of Kay and Dick Smith. Fixed-price menus offer a choice of dishes which are uncomplicated in style and honest in flavour, showing British cuisine at its best. An excellent wine list includes a particularly good choice of half bottles. Pretty bedrooms contain some antique furniture and offer good facilities. Involved owners provide low-key, informal service throughout.

8rm(5⇌♠)Annexe4⇌(1fb) CTV in all bedrooms T ✻ sB&B£32 sB&B⇌♠£39-£45 dB&B£56 dB&B⇌♠£68-£78 ℞
15P ⚑
☼ English & French ⅟ ✻ Dinner £25 Last dinner 8.30pm

Hotels with red star ratings are especially high quality.

Williton - Winchester

★ ❀75% **Curdon Mill**
Yellow TA4 4LS (2m SE off A358)
☎Stogumber(0984) 56522 FAX (0984) 56197
6⇌♠6⇌♠in 12 bedrooms CTV in all bedrooms ®
✈ (ex guide dogs)
100P ♪ ☾ nc8yrs

WILMCOTE Warwickshire Map **04** SP15

★★ 61% **Swan House**
The Green CV37 9XJ (off A3400)
☎Stratford-upon-Avon(0789) 267030 FAX (0789) 204875
Closed 24-28 Dec
This privately owned and personally run inn, dating from the 18th century, is in the village centre close to Mary Arden's house. Bedrooms are simply but soundly furnished and have modern equipment. The lounge bar reflects the building's period and has great character, with exposed beams and log fires.
8⇌♠(1fb)1🛏 CTV in all bedrooms ® ✈ (ex guide dogs)
sB&B⇌♠£36-£40 dB&B⇌♠£56-£66 🍴
40P ✿
♡ English & French V ♡ 🍷 Sunday Lunch fr£9.95
Credit Cards ① ② ③

WILMSLOW Cheshire Map **07** SJ88

See also **Manchester Airport**
★★★★ 63% **Mottram Hall**
Wilmslow Rd, Prestbury SK10 4QT
☎Prestbury(0625) 828135 FAX (0625) 829284

Set in 270 acres of parkland which include a golf course, this hotel has been considerably extended from the original Georgian mansion. The original hall includes an elegant restaurant and cocktail bar, while the most recent developments are a new golf centre with its own bar/restaurant and a wing of good-quality modern bedrooms.
133⇌♠(7fb)8🛏✱in 6 bedrooms CTV in all bedrooms ® ✲ T
Lift (250P 🅿 ☐ (heated) ⬧ 18 ♫ (hard & grass) ♪ squash snooker sauna solarium gymnasium croquet putting ♫
♡ English & French V ♡ 🍷 ✱ Last dinner 9.45pm
Credit Cards ① ② ③ ⑤

★★★ ❀70% **Stanneylands**
Stanneylands Rd SK9 4EY (leave M56 at junct 5 follow signs to Styal follow B5166 and then B5358, hotel signposted on right hand side) ☎(0625) 525225 FAX (0625) 537282
RS 1 Jan & Good Fri
This delightful country house promotes a restful atmosphere. Stylishly furnished throughout, the hotel features a comfortable lounge bar with an open fire, and a gleaming oak-panelled restaurant. Very informative menus list a range of innovative and decorative dishes which are carefully produced, though sauces are sometimes over-flavoured and acidic. Service is above average, and includes morning tea with newspapers.
33⇌♠🛏 CTV in all bedrooms T ✈ ✱ sB⇌♠£79-£95
dB⇌♠£87-£95 (room only) 🍴
(80P 🅿
V ♡ 🍷 ✱ Lunch £9.50-£12.50&alc Dinner fr£25&alc Last dinner 10pm
CONF. Thtr 100 Class 50 Board 40 Del £100
Credit Cards ① ② ③ ⑤

See advertisement on page 653

WIMBORNE MINSTER Dorset Map **04** SZ09

★★★ 61% **The King's Head**
The Square BH21 1JA ☎(0202) 880101 FAX (0202) 881667

Located in the square of this attractive country town, the hotel is staffed by a friendly team who contribute to the warm atmosphere. Bedrooms are pretty and smart, and while public areas are, perhaps, in need of some redecoration, they are cosy. A table d'hôte and small carte are offered in the formal restaurant, and bar meals are served in the rustic bar.
27⇌♠(1fb)🛏✱in 8 bedrooms CTV in all bedrooms ® T
sB⇌♠£70-£77.50 dB⇌♠£80-£95 (room only) 🍴
Lift 25P *xmas*
V ♡ 🍷 ✱ ✱ Sunday Lunch fr£11.95 High tea £1.20-£2.95 Dinner £15.95&alc Last dinner 9pm
Credit Cards ① ② ③ ⑤

★★ ❀ **BEECHLEAS**
17 Poole Rd BH21 1QA (on A349)
☎Wimborne(0202) 841684
Closed 25 Dec-Jan

Good housekeeping is exemplified at this Georgian town-house hotel. Bedrooms, both in the main building and the coach house, are spotlessly clean and many personal extras are provided. Blazing log fires are lit in the restaurant and lounge, and a daily changing menu of freshly prepared food is offered. Staff are unfailingly helpful, even bringing guests a hot drink in the morning.
5⇌♠ Annexe4⇌♠✱in all bedrooms CTV in all bedrooms T ✈ (ex guide dogs) sB⇌♠£53-£73 dB⇌♠£63-£83 (room only) 🍴
9P 📷
✱
Credit Cards ① ② ③

★★ 63% **Coach House Inn**
Tricketts Cross BH22 9NW
☎Ferndown(0202) 861222 FAX (0202) 894130
(For full entry see Ferndown)

WINCANTON Somerset Map **03** ST72

★★🍴 59% **Holbrook House**
Holbrook BA9 8BS (from A303 at Wincanton, turn left on A371 towards Castle Cary and Shepton Mallet) ☎(0963) 32377
Closed 31 Dec
This charming, if somewhat old fashioned, country house set in pretty grounds with mature trees and clipped box hedges. Mr and Mrs Taylor provide warm hospitality and are untiring hosts. The comfortable lounges have log fires and deep armchairs, while the candlelit dining room offers a short carte of popular dishes.
20rm(8⇌🛏)(2fb) ® T ✈ (ex guide dogs) sB&B£30
sB&B⇌♠£39.50-£47.50 dB&Bfr£60 dB&B⇌♠£72 🍴
CTV 30P 4🚗 ✿ ☐ (heated) ♫ (hard & grass)squash croquet table tennis
V ♡ 🍷 Lunch £8-£20alc Dinner £10-£21alc Last dinner 8.30pm
Credit Cards ① ② ③

WINCHESTER Hampshire Map **04** SU42

★★★★ ❀❀🍴 74% **Lainston House**
Sparsholt SO21 2LT (3m NW off A272) (Laura Hotels)
☎(0962) 863588 FAX (0962) 776672
Set in 70 acres of mature grounds, with its own stretch of the River Test, this fine William and Mary country mansion has been skilfully converted to provide excellent accommodation. Elegant public rooms include a wood-panelled bar, relaxing drawing room and the

651

Winchester - Windermere

panelled restaurant. Chef Friedrich Litty's interesting, well balanced menu of British dishes, using fresh produce and including fish and vegetarian choices, is complemented by a fine wine list.
38rm(37⇌🅽)(1fb)2🛁 CTV in all bedrooms🐕 T sB⇌🅽fr£95 dB⇌🅽fr£125 (room only) 🅿
⟨ 150P 🏊 ❋ ♪ archery croquet clay pigeon shooting *xmas*
♀ English & French 🍴 ❦ ⌷ ✻ Lunch fr£15.50 High tea fr£16.95 Dinner fr£32.50 Last dinner 10pm
Credit Cards [1][2][3][4][5]

★★★**68%** **Winchester Moat House**
Worthy Ln SO23 7AB (on A3090)
☎(0962) 868102 FAX (0962) 840862

This modern hotel is quietly located away from the town centre, and features an attractive tropical atrium housing leisure facilities. Bedrooms are spacious, and the comfortable bar/lounge adjoins L'Escale Restaurant where both table d'hôte and à la carte menus are offered.
72⇌🅽(6fb) CTV in all bedrooms ® T sB&B⇌🅽£45-£86 dB&B⇌🅽£74-£98 🅿
⟨ 72P 🏊 (heated) sauna solarium gymnasium steam room jacuzzi *xmas*
♀ English & French V 🍴 ❦ ⌷ ⅄ ✻ Lunch fr£13.50&alc Dinner £17.50-£19.50&alc Last dinner 9.45pm
CONF. Thtr 250 Class 100 Board 70 Del from £105
Credit Cards [1][2][3][5]

★★★**66%** **Marwell Resort**
Colden Common, Marwell SO21 1JY (on B2177) ☎Owslebury(0962) 777681 FAX (0962) 777625

Four pavilions – Leopard, Jaguar, Panda and Gazelle – interconnect with the colonial-style main building to provide well designed acommodation at this hotel in mature woodland in the grounds of Marwell Zoological Park. Public areas include La Bambouseraie Restaurant, a modern foyer reception, bar and lounge, the Forest Glade Conference Centre and Palm Springs indoor health and leisure centre.
68⇌🅽(10fb)⅄ in 6 bedrooms CTV in all bedrooms ®🐕 T ✻ sB⇌🅽fr£65 dB⇌🅽fr£75 (room only) 🅿
⟨ 150P 🏊 (heated) sauna solarium beautician *xmas*
♀ English & Continental V 🍴 ❦ ⌷ ⅄ ✻ Sunday Lunch £9.95 Dinner £16&alc Last dinner 10pm
Credit Cards [1][2][3][5] £

★★★**65%** **Royal**
Saint Peter St SO23 8BS ☎(0962) 840840 FAX (0962) 841582
A former convent, this well managed and popular hotel has been extensively upgraded over the years and has a modern wing extension of spacious bedrooms as well as the equally well furnished rooms in the main house. Public areas are restricted, the candlelit restaurant is rather small, but there is a very comfortable lounge. Service is efficient and 24-hour room service is provided. Chef Paul Wilson has a serious approach to his cooking, and there are plans to develop and extend the restaurant, bar and lounge.
75⇌🅽(1fb)1🛁⅄ in 6 bedrooms CTV in all bedrooms ®🐕 T sB&B⇌🅽£75-£95 dB&B⇌🅽£85-£105 🅿
⟨ 59P ❋ *xmas*
♀ English & French V 🍴 ❦ ⌷ ⅄ ✻ Lunch £7.50-£9.75 Dinner £18-£25alc Last dinner 9.30pm
Credit Cards [1][2][3][5] £

★★**59%** **Chantry Mead**
Bereweeke Rd SO22 6AJ ☎(0962) 844166 FAX (0962) 852767
The Northern outskirts of the city are served by this informal hotel with a residential and restaurant licence. The best of the bedrooms have been recently upgraded to a high standard and all have a good range of facilities.
16rm(14⇌🅽)(2fb)⅄ in 3 bedrooms CTV in all bedrooms ® T CTV 20P ❋ 🐾

V ❦ ⌷ Last dinner 9.30pm
Credit Cards [1][3]

• •

Forte Crest
Paternoster Row SO23 9LQ ☎(0962) 861611 FAX (0962) 841503

FORTE CREST

A large modern hotel with a wide range of services and amenities, designed particularly for the business traveller. Bedrooms are smart, comfortable and well equipped. For more details about Forte Crest hotels, consult the Contents page, under Hotel Groups.
94⇌🅽✻ B⇌🅽£98 (room only)
CONF. Thtr 100 Class 30 Board 40 Del £115

WINDERMERE Cumbria Map **07** SD49

★★★★**58%** **The Old England**
Church St, Bowness LA23 3DF (on A592, behind St Martins church) ☎(05394) 42444 FAX (05394) 43432

FORTE Heritage

A well established hotel in an enviable position, offering bedrooms in a variety of styles, the most attractive in the west wing. Accommodation in the modern extension, though utilitarian, has good views. There is a comfortable main lounge, a rather small split-level cocktail bar and a restaurant providing uncomplicated table d'hôte menus. Staff are friendly and efficient, and car parking service is provided.
79⇌🅽(8fb)⅄ in 24 bedrooms CTV in all bedrooms ® T ✻ sB⇌🅽£85-£100 dB⇌🅽£105-£130 (room only) 🅿
Lift ⟨ 82P ❋ 🏊 (heated) snooker sauna solarium golf driving net *xmas*
V ❦ ⌷ ⅄ ✻ Lunch £10.95-£12.50 Dinner £17.95-£19.95&alc Last dinner 9.15pm
Credit Cards [1][2][3][5]

AA ★★★

ROYAL HOTEL

St. Peter Street,
Winchester, Hampshire SO23 8BS
Tel: (0962) 840840 Telex: 477071 Royal G
Fax: (0962) 841582

Quietly situated in the centre of England's ancient capital. This former convent became an Hotel in the last century.
Only two minutes' walk from the Cathedral and Winchester's historic attraction.
Dine in our conservatory restaurant overlooking the award winning walled garden.

LAINSTON HOUSE HOTEL ★★★★ ❦❦

where English Tradition remains our hallmark

Set in sixty three acres of tranquil Hampshire downland, just 2½ miles from the Historic Cathedral City of Winchester. Lainston House is an elegant William and Mary House with thirty eight individually designed bedrooms and suites. The charm of the reception rooms is enhanced by the peace and serenity of this period house. Our highly praised restaurant offers gourmet food freshly prepared with local ingredients and the superb service is complemented by breathtaking views over the tranquil parkland. Lainston House offers the discerning guest the delights of Traditional English Gracious Living with memories that linger on.

(Open seven days a week to non-residents for lunch and dinner).

Lainston House Hotel & Restaurant, Sparsholt, Winchester, Hampshire SO21 2LT
Telephone: (0962) 863588 Fax: (0962) 776672.
Situated on the A272 Stockbridge Road out of Winchester

Two distinctive hotels. Quite different, yet closer to each other than you might first think.

STANNEYLANDS ★★★ A handsome country house set in beautiful gardens. Classically furnished. Quietly luxurious. It has a dignified, rural character all of its own.

BELFRY ★★★★ Urban, sophisticated, stylish. Imbued with quiet, unobtrusive efficiency. Yet for all their differences, it is what Stanneylands and the Belfry share that sets them apart from other hotels. Both hotels are run by the Beech family — truly experienced hoteliers, totally involved with their hotels and their guests.

Gastronomically both are magnificent. In addition to the AA Restaurant Rosette, Stanneylands holds many national and international awards for excellence. Private dining and conference facilities available for 8-130 people.

The Stanneylands Hotel
Stanneylands Road · Wilmslow · Cheshire
Tel: 0625 525225.

The Belfry Hotel
Handforth · Wilmslow · Cheshire
Tel: 061-437 0511.
Fax: 061-499 0597

Windermere

★★★ ❀ ♨ 74% Linthwaite
Crook Rd, Bowness LA23 3JA (on B5284) ☎(05394) 88600 FAX (05394) 88601
(Rosette awarded for dinner only)
Set high above Windermere in 14 acres of gardens and woodland, this delightful hotel enjoys superb Lakeland views. Individually styled bedrooms are very well equipped, and there are comfortable lounges, a conservatory and an attractive dining room serving excellent 4-course dinners. Our inspector enjoyed warm blue cheese beignets with onion sauce, followed by courgette and cucumber soup and a main course of chicken breast on a chicken liver croute with port wine sauce. Desserts included spotted dick as well as cold choices.
18⇨♠3🛏✕in 12 bedrooms CTV in all bedrooms ®♿T
✖ (ex guide dogs) ❋ sB&B⇨♠£50-£75 dB&B⇨♠£90-£140
30P 🚗 ❋ ♪ croquet putting green *xmas*
V ♦ ♿ ✕ Sunday Lunch fr£10.95 Dinner fr£25 Last dinner 9pm
Credit Cards 1 2 3 5   £

★★★ ❀❀ 72% Gilpin Lodge Country House Hotel & Restaurant
Crook Rd LA23 3NE (on B5284) ☎(05394) 88818 FAX 05394 88058

Best Newcomer 1994

A lovely Lakeland house with 20 acres of woodland and gardens, Gilpin Lodge is our Best Newcomer for the North of England. It has superb day rooms with deep sofas, fresh flowers, log fires and lots of books and magazines. The bedrooms are furnished in country style with some beautiful four-poster and brass beds, and big bathrooms are a feature. Chef Christopher Davies, who trained at the Connaught and gained experience in France, offers an interesting range of dishes on a set price 5-course menu. Starters may include baked field mushrooms filled with a fricassée of button mushrooms, smoked bacon and shallots on a roast garlic and red wine fumet. Main courses include beef, lamb, duck and fish with carefully constructed sauces.
9⇨♠(1fb)3🛏 CTV in all bedrooms ®♿T ✖ (ex guide dogs) sB&B⇨♠£40-£65 dB&B⇨♠£60-£120 🍴
30P 🚗 ❋ croquet nc9yrs *xmas*
V ♦ ♿ ✕ ❋ Sunday Lunch £12.75 Dinner £24 Last dinner 8.45pm
Credit Cards 1 2 3 5   £

★★★ 70% Wild Boar
Crook LA23 3NF (2.5m S of Windermere on B5284 Crook road) ☎(05394) 45325 FAX (05394) 42498

Peacefully situated in the Winster valley 2.5 miles south of the town, this delightful hotel provides caring attentive service and has relaxing lounges with beamed ceilings and log fires. A spacious restaurant offers varied menus, and comfortable bedrooms have attractive coordinated décor and good facilities.
36⇨♠(3fb)4🛏✕in 6 bedrooms CTV in all bedrooms ®♿T sB&B⇨♠£52-£80 dB&B⇨♠£104-£128 🍴
60P 🚗 ❋ free boat launching facilities *xmas*

★★★ ❀ 68% Burn How Garden House Hotel
Back Belsfield Rd, Bowness LA23 3HH ☎(05394) 46226 FAX (05394) 47000

(Rosette awarded for dinner only)
This family-run hotel, which offers excellent value of money, stands in its own secluded gardens. Food, under the personal supervision of Margaret Johnson, is very good and the daily changing table d'hôte menu includes such delights as salmon with white grapes, and pork with Madeira sauce. There is always a delicious home-made soup and mouth-watering puddings. Bedrooms include chalets in the gardens, traditional rooms and more modern ones. Some have sun balconies.
Annexe26⇨♠(10fb)4🛏 CTV in all bedrooms ®♿T
✖ (ex guide dogs) ❋ sB&B⇨♠£46-£50 dB&B⇨♠£72-£87 🍴
30P 🚗 ❋ sauna solarium gymnasium water sports *xmas*
♦ English & French V ♦ ♿ ✕ Bar Lunch £1.75-£8alc Dinner £17.50&alc Last dinner 9pm
Credit Cards 1 2 3

★★★ ♨ 67% Langdale Chase
LA23 1LW (3m N of Windermere) ☎(05394) 32201 FAX (05394) 32604
Landscaped grounds stretch right down to the lakeshore and guests can enjoy superb views over the water from this beautifully sited and gracious hotel, with its extensive comfortable lounges, lovely restaurant and elegantly furnished bedrooms. Well trained staff provide caring service.
24⇨♠Annexe7⇨♠(1fb)2🛏 CTV in all bedrooms ®♿T ❋ sB&B⇨♠£40-£45 dB&B⇨♠£80-£140 🍴
🎱 36P 🚗 ❋ ♪ (grass) croquet rowing boats putting *xmas*
♦ English & French V ♦ ♿ ✕ ❋ Lunch £13 Dinner £21&alc Last dinner 8.45pm
Credit Cards 1 2 3 5

★★★ 66% Craig Manor
Lake Rd LA23 3AR ☎(05394) 88877
16⇨♠4🛏

★★★ 65% Burnside
Kendal Road, Bowness LA23 3EP ☎(05394) 42211 FAX (05394) 43824
A Victorian house with extensions, this large hotel stands in its own grounds overlooking the lake. Bedrooms are spacious and modern with good facilities, and there are several comfortable lounges, 2 restaurants and an extensive leisure club.
44⇨♠(11fb)4🛏 CTV in all bedrooms ®♿T sB&B⇨♠£35-£61 dB&B⇨♠£70-£120 🍴
Lift 80P ❋ ▨ (heated) squash snooker sauna solarium gymnasium watersports steam room badminton ♪ *xmas*
V ♦ ♿ ✕ ❋ Sunday Lunch £9.50-£12 High tea £6-£8 Dinner fr£17&alc Last dinner 9.45pm
CONF. Thtr 80 Class 40 Board 30 Del from £53
Credit Cards 1 2 3 5   £

★★★ ♨ 65% Merewood Country House
Ecclerigg LA23 1LH (3m N, on A591 just beyond the National Park Visitor Centre) ☎(05394) 46484 FAX (05394) 42128
The lake is visible above the tree tops from several front facing rooms of this elegant late 19th-century country house, situated in 20 acres of woodland and gardens. The opulent public rooms include a splendid hall, a comfortable drawing room and an adjoining library with a log fire, and a distinctive Edwardian-style bar. There are 2 dining rooms, one in Victorian style with a lovely carved fireplace, the other new and beautifully decorated.
20⇨♠(3fb)2🛏✕in 2 bedrooms CTV in all bedrooms ®♿T
✖ (ex guide dogs) ❋ sB&B⇨♠£75.50-£86 dB&B⇨♠£109-£130 (incl dinner) 🍴

Windermere

CTV 60P 🚭 ✿ croquet 🎵 xmas
V ✿ ⚲ ✲ ✱ Lunch £9.95-£17.75 High tea £5.95 Dinner £17.95 Last dinner 8.45pm
CONF. Thtr 150 Class 75 Board 60 Del from £95
Credit Cards 1 2 3

★★★ 64% Low Wood
LA23 1LP (3m N A591)
☎Ambleside(05394) 33338 FAX (05394) 34072

Only the Windermere to Ambleside road separates this large hotel from the shore of Windermere. Public areas are spacious and comfortably furnished and include a choice of restaurants plus a wine bar. Bedrooms vary in size and style but all have good facilities.
99➪♠(10fb)3🚭 CTV in all bedrooms ®⚲ T sB&B➪♠£59-£69 dB&B➪♠£118-£148 🄿
Lift ⓒ 200P ✿ 🏊 (heated) 🎾 squash snooker sauna solarium gymnasium water skiing sub aqua diving windsurfing 🎵 🎠 xmas
🍴 International V ✿ ⚲ ✲ ✱ Lunch £8.50-£21alc Dinner fr£17.50&alc Last dinner 10pm
CONF. Thtr 350 Class 180 Board 70 Del from £89
Credit Cards 1 2 3 5

★★★ 63% The Belsfield
Kendal Rd, Bowness LA23 3EL
☎(05394) 42448 FAX (05394) 46397

A large and impressive Victorian hotel overlooking the lake offers spacious, comfortable public areas, with lounge services provided by friendly, attentive staff. Bedrooms have all modern amenities and include some suites and several recently upgraded rooms with fine-quality fabrics and furnishings.
64➪♠(6fb)2🚭✲in 6 bedrooms CTV in all bedrooms ® T sB➪♠£75 dB➪♠£95-£133 (room only) 🄿
Lift ⓒ 100P ✿ 🏊 (heated) 🅿 (grass) snooker sauna solarium mini golf putting green xmas
V ✿ ⚲ ✲ ✱ Bar Lunch £1.20-£6 Dinner £15.95&alc Last dinner 9.30pm
CONF. Thtr 130 Class 60 Board 50 Del from £80
Credit Cards 1 2 3 5

★★★ 58% Hydro
Helm Rd, Bowness LA23 3BA ☎(05394) 44355
FAX (05394) 88000

A large hotel in an elevated position just off the town centre, with views over lake and fells, the Hydro offers individually furnished, well appointed bedrooms and friendly service.
96➪♠(9fb)1🚭 CTV in all bedrooms ® ✱ sB&B➪♠£38-£53 dB&B➪♠£76-£96 🄿
Lift ⓒ 140P pool table xmas
V ✿ Bar Lunch £1.95-£10alc High tea £4.50-£7.50 Dinner £12-£15.50 Last dinner 9pm
CONF. Thtr 220 Class 100 Board 100 Del from £45
Credit Cards 1 2 3 5

★★
★★★ ❀ 🏃 HOLBECK GHYLL COUNTRY HOUSE
Holbeck Ln LA23 1LU (2m N off A591, signposted 'Troutbeck')
☎(05394) 32375 FAX (05394) 34743

The essence of any top hotel is quality, both in service and in cooking, and David and Patricia Nicholson's charming hotel lives up to these virtues. On our visit the set dinner consisted of seafood risotto with a light but zesty lemon butter sauce; red lentil soup with crème fraîche and chives; 2 cuts of Hardwick lamb – rack filled with duxelle and leaf spinach held by a lattice of pastry, and roast loin served on a croûton with lamb jus – and for pudding, excellent home-made brandy snaps with caramel cream.
14➪♠(1fb)1🚭 CTV in all bedrooms T sB&B➪♠£65-£110 dB&B➪♠£110-£180 (incl dinner) 🄿
20P 🚭 ✿ putting green xmas
🍴 English & French V ✿ ⚲ ✲ ✱ Dinner £27-£32 Last dinner 8.45pm
Credit Cards 1 2 3

★★
★★★ ❀❀ MILLER HOWE
Rayrigg Rd LA23 1EY (on A592 between Bowness & Windermere)
☎(05394) 42536 FAX (05394) 45664
Closed early Dec-early Mar (ex Xmas)

Much has been written about this internationally renowned hotel, but for all the accolades showered upon it and its proprietor John Tovey, Miller Howe retains the relaxed, informal atmosphere of an unpretentious ➡

AA★★★ ❀   ETB 👑👑👑👑

🌸 Garden House Hotel · Motel & Restaurant 🌸
Bowness-on-Windermere, Cumbria
Tel. Windermere. (05394) 46226

Enjoy the unique Burn How experience: elegance, comfort and superb service in a secluded garden setting in the heart of Bowness.
Relax in elegant four poster beds, beautiful en-suite bedrooms or spacious family chalets, and dine in our highly recommended restaurant.

We look forward to welcoming you.

Windermere

Edwardian house. Many of the bedrooms enjoy spectacular views, and all are comfortable and crammed with extras. Like the bedrooms, public areas are adorned with objets d'art, and fine paintings adorn the walls. There are a number of lounges, and a conservatory extension offers unrivalled views of Lake Windermere and the Langdale Fells. Dinner has always been the raison d'être for Miller Howe, and while the theatricality, lack of choice and regimented style of service (8 for 8.30pm) may not be to everyone's taste, there is no denying that it has a strong following. There has been a conscious effort to move away from rich ingredients such as eggs, butter and cream, though alcohol continues to play an important part.

13⇨↑1⇗ CTV in all bedrooms T ✳ sB&B⇨£75-£120 dB&B⇨£150-£240 (incl dinner) ⌂
40P ⇎ ✲ nc12yrs *xmas*
V ♡ ⚲ ✔ ✳ Dinner fr£32 Last dinner 8.30pm
Credit Cards [1][2][3][5]

★★ ❀74% Lindeth Fell
Upper Storrs Park Rd, Bowness LA23 3JP (1m S on A5074)
☎(05394) 43286 & 44287
Closed mid Nov-mid Mar

Splendidly set in beautiful grounds high above the lake, this Edwardian country house is owned and run by the hospitable Pat and Diana Kennedy. Most of the comfortable bedrooms have fine views and there are relaxing lounges with books and log fires. Good English country cooking is offered in the attractive dining room, where a typical dinner might consist of baked mushrooms with Stilton, home-made soup, honey-glazed ham with Cumberland sauce or halibut with shrimp and parsley sauce, and a choice of traditional puddings, followed by good cheeses.

14⇨↑(2fb) CTV in all bedrooms ® T ✳
sB&B⇨↑fr£49.50 dB&B⇨↑£93-£110 (incl dinner)
20P ⇎ ✲ ♪ (grass) ♩ croquet putting nc7yrs
♡ ⚲ ✔ Lunch fr£10
Credit Cards [1][3]

★★ ❀72% Cedar Manor Hotel & Restaurant
Ambleside Rd LA23 1AX (by St Marys Church) ☎(05394) 43192 FAX (05394) 459707

This attractive Lakeland stone house in delightful grounds is well furnished throughout, and great care has gone into the overall design. An excellent dinner is served each evening in the bright restaurant. Lynn Hadley is the cook, who learnt her skills from her mother and has a natural flair which is evident her imaginative dishes. Mr and Mrs Hadley are charming hosts and care greatly for their guests' comfort.

10⇨↑Annexe2⇨↑(4fb)1⇎ CTV in all bedrooms ® T
sB&B⇨↑£39-£55 dB&B⇨↑£78-£90 (incl dinner) ⌂
15P ⇎ *xmas*
♡ English, French & Italian V ♡ ⚲ ✔ Dinner £16.50-£19.50 Last dinner 8.30pm
Credit Cards [1][3]

★★ 70% Glenburn
New Rd LA23 2EE ☎(05934) 42649 FAX (05394) 88998

This very friendly and comfortable small hotel, situated between Windermere and Bowness, has been completely refurbished by its present owners. Attractive bedrooms with good facilities include non-smoking rooms, and there is a comfortable lounge and elegant restaurant.

16⇨↑(4fb)2⇎✔ in 8 bedrooms CTV in all bedrooms ® T
✖ (ex guide dogs) ✳ sB&B⇨↑£28-£38 dB&B⇨↑£44-£64 ⌂
CTV 17P ⇎ solarium nc5yrs *xmas*
V ♡ ⚲ ✔ Dinner £14.20 Last dinner 8pm
Credit Cards [1][3]

★★ 70% Hillthwaite House
Thornbarrow Rd LA23 2DF ☎(05394) 43636 & 46691

This atttractive hotel, standing in well kept grounds in a peaceful backwater of Windermere, has been run by the same family for over 20 years and offers very friendly service and home comforts. Modern bedrooms have good facilities and there are peaceful lounges.

25⇨↑(2fb)8⇎ CTV in all bedrooms ®
26P ⇎ ✲ ▭ (heated) sauna solarium
♡ English & French V ♡ ⚲ Last dinner 9pm
Credit Cards [1][2][3]

★★ 69% Crag Brow Cottage
Helm Rd LA23 3BU ☎(05394) 44080 FAX (05394) 46003

This attractive white-painted house stands in an elevated position in its own well tended grounds. Family owned and run with pride, it has attractive, well equipped bedrooms. There are 2 comfortable lounges, and an extensive range of well prepared food is available in the elegant restaurant.

11⇨↑(3fb) CTV in all bedrooms ®✎ T ✖ (ex guide dogs) ✳
sB&B⇨↑£35-£45 dB&B⇨↑£55-£75 ⌂
30P ✲ free membership to leisure club *xmas*
♡ English, French & Italian V ♡ ⚲ ✔ ✳ Sunday Lunch fr£9.95 Dinner fr£18.95 Last dinner 9.30pm
Credit Cards [1][3]

★★ ❀69% Quarry Garth Country House Hotel & Restaurant
Troutbeck Bridge LA23 1LF (on A591) (Logis)
☎(05394) 88282 FAX (05394) 46584

A lovely old country house set in well kept gardens offers peace, warm hospitality and home comforts. Bedrooms are attractively furnished and there are two very comfortable lounges and an elegant restaurant where chef George Jardine offers well prepared interesting dishes.

10⇨↑(2fb) CTV in all bedrooms ® T ✳ sB&B⇨↑£45-£65 dB&B⇨↑£90-£130 (incl dinner) ⌂
35P ⇎ ✲ ♩ *xmas*
♡ English & Continental V ♡ ⚲ Dinner £19.50 Last dinner 9pm
Credit Cards [1][2][3][5]   £

★★ 68% Bordriggs Country House
Longtail Hill, Bowness LA23 3LD ☎(05394) 43567 FAX (05394) 46949

Friendly and attentive service is provided by Mr and Mrs Stones at this comfortable hotel set in its own grounds close to Bowness. Bedrooms are bright and fresh. The cosy lounge has lots of books and magazines, and a well produced dinner is served in the dining room.

9⇨↑Annexe2⇨↑(2fb)1⇎✔in all bedrooms CTV in all bedrooms T ✖ (ex guide dogs)
20P ⇎ ✲ ▭ (heated) croquet badminton nc10yrs
♡ English & Continental V ✔ Last dinner 7.30pm

★★ 66% Hideaway
Phoenix Way LA23 1DB ☎(05394) 43070
Closed Jan after New Year

Situated in a quiet backwater of the town, yet very convenient for the centre, this friendly owner-run hotel has recently been refurbished and offers comfortable public areas and attractively furnished bedrooms.

10⇨↑Annexe5⇨↑(3fb)4⇎ CTV in all bedrooms ® T
sB&B⇨↑£36-£48 dB&B⇨↑£72-£96 (incl dinner) ⌂
16P ⇎ ♩ *xmas*
♡ English & Continental V ♡ ⚲ ✔

Red star hotels are each highlighted by a pink tinted panel.

Windermere

★★ 66% **Ravensworth**
Ambleside Rd LA23 1BA ☎(05394) 43747 FAX (05394) 43670
A friendly, personally run hotel set in pleasant grounds close to the village. Attractive bedrooms have very good facilities and there is a cosy lounge and conservatory restaurant.
12⇨↑ Annexe2⇨↑(1fb)4🛏 CTV in all bedrooms ® ⚲ T ✱
sB&B⇨↑ £27-£49 dB&B⇨↑ £49-£75 ☐
17P 🚭 *xmas*
⚘ English & French **V** ◊ ⚹ ✱ Dinner £10.45-£15.45alc Last dinner 8.30pm
Credit Cards 1 3 £

★★ 62% **Cranleigh**
Kendal Rd, Bownes LA23 3EW (turn left off Lake Road, opposite St Martin's church) ☎(05394) 43293
This family-run Victorian house, only 2 minutes walk from Bownes and the lake, has a friendly atmosphere and comfortable bedrooms, either in the main house or a similar property next door. There is a choice of lounges and an attractive dining room serving 4-course dinners.
9⇨↑ Annexe6⇨↑(2fb) CTV in all bedrooms ®
✈ (ex guide dogs) sB&B⇨↑ £20-£30 dB&B⇨↑ £38-£60 ☐
CTV 15P 🚭
V ◊ ⚇ ⚹ ✱ Lunch £7-£20alc High tea £7-£20alc Dinner £7-£20alc Last dinner 9pm
Credit Cards 1 3 £

★★ 61% **Royal**
Queens Square, Bowness-on-Windermere LA23 3DB
☎(05394) 43045 FAX (05394) 44990
Closed 25-26 Dec
The Royal, in the centre of Bowness village just a short walk from the lake, is reputed to be the oldest established hotel in the Lake District and has a long history of royal patronage. Bedrooms vary in size, shape and quality but have all modern comforts.
29⇨↑(4fb)1🛏 CTV in all bedrooms ® T ✱ sB&B⇨↑£22.50 dB⇨↑£39-£49 (room only)
16P 5🚗 🚭 ♨ pool table
⚘ English & French **V** ✱ Lunch £7.15-£13.65alc
Credit Cards 1 2 3 5

★★ 60% **Knoll**
Lake Rd, Bownes LA23 2JF ☎(05394) 43756
Closed Dec-Feb
This large Victorian house stands in its own well kept grounds yet is convenient for the village centre. It retains many original features, including a panelled hall, stained glass windows and a galleried staircase, and there is a comfortable lounge with a log fire. In the same ownership for many years, the hotel provides good, traditional service.
12rm(9⇨↑)(4fb) CTV in all bedrooms ® T ✈ sB&B£32.50-£40 sB&B⇨↑£37.50-£40 dB&B⇨↑£75-£80 (incl dinner) ☐
CTV 20P ✿ nc3yrs
V ◊ ⚹ Dinner £12.50-£15 Last dinner 7.30pm
Credit Cards 1 3

★ 64% **Willowsmere**
Ambleside Rd LA23 1ES (stay on A591, just past St Marys Church) ☎(05394) 43575
Closed Dec-beginning Jan
This friendly, family-run hotel is close to Windermere village centre. It provides good all round standards of comfort, with bedrooms of varying shape and size, a cosy lounge and a separate bar. A set 5-course dinner is served in the pretty dining room each evening.
13⇨↑(7fb) ® sB&B⇨↑£22-£24 dB&B⇨↑£44-£48 ☐
CTV 20P 🚭
⚘ English & Austrian ◊ ⚇ ⚹ Dinner £12-£14 Last dinner 7pm
CONF. Del from £38
Credit Cards 1 2 3 5

Hideaway Hotel ★★
Windermere

This 15 bedroom privately-owned hotel is rather special. All the pretty bedrooms have private facilities, colour TV, radio/direct dial telephone and tea-making facilities. There are open fires in the cosy bar and beautiful lounge and well trained chefs prepare super table d'hôte dinners for you (BTA award for cuisine held for seven years). A central and yet quiet location makes this one of the most sought after hotels in the area.   **Please ring
Windermere (05394) 43070**

GLENBURN HOTEL ★★

New Road, Windermere, Cumbria LA23 2EE
Tel: 05394 42649 Fax: 05394 88998

Please telephone for Brochure and Reservations

*Licensed Bar * Large private car park
OPEN ALL YEAR

David and Evelyne Limbrey would like to welcome you to the Glenburn hotel. We have recently extended and redesigned Glenburn for your utmost comfort and enjoyment. 16 large delightful en-suite bedrooms all with colour TV, radio and telephone. Charming dining room. Wide choice menu. Leisure facilities including indoor swimming pool available exclusively to our guests at the nearby Windermere Marina Village.

We are ideally positioned between Windermere and the Lake.

Special 3 and 5 night breaks.

Windsor - Wishaw

WINDSOR Berkshire Map 04 SU97
See also **Datchet**

★★★★ ❀❀71% Oakley Court
Windsor Road, Water Oakley SL4 5UR
(2m W A308)
☎Maidenhead(0628) 74141 FAX (0628) 37011

This hotel beside the Thames, in the style of a French château, was a location for Dracula and the St Trinian films. Fear not for horrors though, as the house has been lovingly restored and extended. Public areas retain many original features and offer a choice of comfortable lounges. The intimate Oakleaf Restaurant is the setting for master chef Murdo MacSween's fine cuisine. A choice of menus is available, offering such dishes as lobster and crab bisque with quenelles of sole, or a main course of best end of spring lamb with foie gras and parma ham, served with a Sauternes and carrot jus.
65⇌♪ Annexe27⇌♪ 5⬚4⊁ in 6 bedrooms CTV in all bedrooms ® ⚲ T ✕ (ex guide dogs) ✳ sB⇌♪£125-£245 dB⇌♪£145-£375 (room only) 🏱
(120P ❀ ➤ 9 ♪ snooker croquet boating *xmas*
♺ English & French V ♢ ✳ Lunch £14.50-£23.50&alc Dinner fr£29&alc Last dinner 10pm
CONF. Thtr 160 Class 100 Board 48 Del from £166
Credit Cards [1][2][3][5] £

★★★ 67% The Castle
High St SL4 1LJ ☎(0753) 851011 FAX (0753) 830244

Centrally situated almost opposite the castle, this impressive Georgian hotel has attractive public rooms including an elegant restaurant, a conservatory bar and a bright all day brasserie. Fully equipped contemporary-style bedrooms are located in the original building and the tasteful modern wing, and comprehensive room service is available.
104⇌(40fb)4⬚4⊁in 41 bedrooms CTV in all bedrooms ® ⚲ T ✳ sB⇌£95 dB⇌♪£125-£145 (room only) 🏱
Lift (116P 40⬚ *xmas*
V ♢ ✳ ⊁ ✳ Lunch £15-£25alc
Credit Cards [1][2][3][5]

★★ ❀71% Aurora Garden
14 Bolton Av SL4 3JF ☎(0753) 868686 FAX (0753) 831394
In a quiet residential road, this extended detached villa has an agreeable atmosphere, with friendly staff providing helpful and attentive service. Pine-furnished bedrooms are comfortable and day rooms include inviting lounge areas and a conservatory-style restaurant overlooking the terrace and water garden. Chef Janice Timothy provides a good range of interesting menus, include a vegetarian menu.
15⇌♪ CTV in all bedrooms ® T sB&B⇌♪£60-£65 dB&B⇌♪£72-£78 🏱
(25P ❀
♺ English & French V ♢ ✳ Lunch £12-£13.95&alc Dinner £13.95-£16.50&alc Last dinner 9pm
CONF. Thtr 90 Class 30 Board 25 Del from £90
Credit Cards [1][2][3][5] £

WINSFORD Somerset Map 03 SS93

★★ ❀74% Royal Oak Inn
Exmoor National Park TA24 7JE
☎(064385) 455 FAX (064385) 388

This picturesque thatched inn, dating from the 12th century, is in the centre of this Exmoor village. Bedrooms in the main building retain original features, and there are prettily furnished rooms of an equally high standard in the cottage-style annexe. There are 3 very comfortable, well furnished lounges, with fresh flowers, books and magazines. In the restaurant a table d'hôte menu offers a reasonable array of dishes and bar meals are available.

8⇌♪Annexe6⇌♪(1fb) CTV in all bedrooms ® T ✳ sB&B⇌£67-£80 dB&B⇌♪£104-£130 (incl dinner) 🏱
CTV 20P 3⬚ ♪ hunting shooting *xmas*
V ♢ ♪ Lunch £12.50-£15 Dinner £22.50-£25 Last dinner 9.30pm
Credit Cards [1][2][3][5] £

WISBECH Cambridgeshire Map 05 TF40

★★ 65% Crown Lodge
Downham Rd, Outwell PE14 8SE (5m SE, on A1122 close to junct with A1101) ☎(0945) 773391 & 772206 FAX (0945) 773391
This unusual small hotel with good leisure facilities is a clever conversion from a car showroom and garage. More recently a quiet lounge area has been introduced and also an expansion of the snooker room. The modern accommodation has also been extended to provide additional bedrooms, all with good bathrooms.
10⇌♪ CTV in all bedrooms ® T ✕ (ex guide dogs) ✳ sB&B⇌♪£33.75 dB&B⇌♪£45
65P ⬚ squash snooker solarium
♺ International V ♢ ✳ Lunch £3.50-£10.50alc Dinner £7.50-£20alc Last dinner 10pm
CONF. Thtr 100 Class 60 Board 40 Del from £47.75
Credit Cards [1][2][3][5] £

★★ 63% Queens
South Brink PE13 1JJ ☎(0945) 583933 FAX (0945) 474250
Located next to the River Nene, the Queens Hotel is in a splendid row of Georgian buildings. The owners are actively involved in the daily running of the hotel, and Mr Wilson will often chat with guests in the cosy lounge bar, where a roaring log fire is a welcome sight in the winter months. High standards are maintained throughout the hotel.
12⇌♪Annexe6⇌♪(3fb)2⬚ CTV in all bedrooms ® ⚲ T 40P ❀
♺ English & French V ♢ ✳ Last dinner 10pm
Credit Cards [1][2][3][5]

WISHAW West Midlands Map 07 SP19

★★★★ 68% The Belfry
Lichfield Rd B76 9PR (A446)
☎Curdworth(0675) 470301 FAX (0675) 470178

This impressive hotel, golf and leisure complex, set in 370 acres of parkland, was largely refurbished for the 1993 Ryder Cup. Smart public areas include 2 restaurants, and there is a popular night-club in the grounds. A serious approach to food has been introduced by chef Eric Bruce and maître d'hôtel Pepe Massari, especially in the French restaurant, which offers good value, set-price menus. A meal may begin with parma ham, baby avocado and a fruit coulis, or a good mousseline of wild mushrooms served with a rich port wine sauce, followed by a delightful cream of crab soup poured over a plump scallop, garnished with chives. Our inspector's 'chartreuse' of lamb fillet served with a rosemary sauce and an interesting range of vegetables was nicely cooked but the meat was of disappointing quality. The wine list takes no risks and consequently lacks much interest.
219⇌♪(34fb)2⬚⊁ in 64 bedrooms CTV in all bedrooms ® ⚲ T ✕ (ex guide dogs) ✳ sB&B⇌♪£95-£230 dB&B⇌♪£130-£230 🏱
Lift (1500P ❀ ⬚ (heated) ➤ 18 ♪ (hard) squash snooker sauna solarium gymnasium archery clay pigeon shooting ⬚ *xmas*
♺ French V ♢ ✳ Lunch £14.95 Dinner £19.50-£24.95&alc Last dinner 10pm
CONF. Thtr 350 Class 200 Board 600 Del from £85
Credit Cards [1][2][3][5] £

★★★ **58%** *Moxhull Hall*
Holly Ln B76 9PD ☎021-329 2056

This Victorian mansion, in extensive wooded grounds, has retained a traditional style in its public rooms, which feature a magnificent oak staircase, 400 years old, originally from nearby Kenilworth Castle and fine wood panelling in the restaurant. The bedrooms (some in a separate building) are, by contrast, light and modern in decor.
21⇨ ♠ (2fb)1₩ CTV in all bedrooms ® T
60P ✿ croquet
♀ English & French V ♡ Last dinner 10pm
Credit Cards [1][2][3][5]

WITHAM Essex Map 05 TL81

★★★ **64%** *Rivenhall Resort*
Rivenhall End CM8 3BH (off A12 between Chelmsford & Colchester) ☎(0376) 516969
FAX (0376) 513674

RESORT HOTELS PLC

Conveniently accessed from the A12, this roadside hotel offers a range of modern bedrooms, most of which are located around the main building and reached by covered walkways so that guests have the convenience of parking directly outside their room. A converted barn houses a good health and leisure club.
7⇨♠Annexe48⇨♠(3fb)⊁in 14 bedrooms CTV in all bedrooms ® ✱ T ✱ sB⇨♠£55 dB⇨♠£65 (room only) ₽
《 200P ✿ ▢ (heated) squash sauna solarium gymnasium beautician massage spa bath
♀ English & French V ♡ ♿ ✱ Lunch £7.95-£11.50&alc Dinner fr£15.50&alc Last dinner 9.30pm
CONF. Thtr 185 Class 65 Board 60 Del £80
Credit Cards [1][2][3][5]

WITHERSLACK Cumbria Map 07 SD48

★ ✪♨ **OLD VICARAGE COUNTRY HOUSE**
LA11 6RS ☎(05395) 52381
FAX (05395) 52373

Situated in 5 acres of informal gardens and woodland, this delightful country house dates back to 1803. Now a lovely small hotel, run by two families, it has the authentic atmosphere of a family country house. Bedrooms are full of character, but those in the bungalow in the grounds are the most sought-after. The set 5-course dinner our inspector enjoyed began with a delicious haddock roulade, followed by artichoke soup. Chateaubriand steak with both Béarnaise and Bordelaise sauces was the main feature, and two contrasting desserts completed the meal. There is a fine selection of British cheeses, with emphasis on northern specialities. The wine list is extensive and service is friendly and attentive.
9⇨♠Annexe5⇨♠1₩ CTV in all bedrooms ® T ✱
sB&B⇨♠£59-£79 dB&B⇨♠£98-£138 ₽
25P ⇔ ✿ ♃ (hard) *xmas*
♡ ♿ ⊁ ✱ Lunch £15-£18 Dinner £19.50-£27.50 Last dinner 8pm
Credit Cards [1][3]

Wishaw - Withypool

WITHYPOOL Somerset Map 03 SS83

★★ ✪**71%** *Royal Oak Inn*
TA24 7QP (Logis) ☎Exford(064383) 506 FAX (064383) 659
Closed 25 & 26 Dec

This typical village inn combines charm and character with standards that more than satisfy the expectations of the discerning guest. Cosy, well furnished bedrooms are equipped in modern style, and there are two bars with inglenook fireplaces – one of them quiet, the other very popular with locals – where a good selection of beers and wines is always available. An extensive range of commendable bar and restaurant meals makes good use of quality fresh ingredients, featuring such local produce as fresh Exmoor venison accompanied by generous portions of simply cooked vegetables, and rich home-made puddings are a speciality.
8rm(5⇨♠1♠)(1fb)₩ CTV in all bedrooms ® T sB&B£32-£34 sB&B⇨♠£45-£48 dB&B£64-£66 dB&B⇨♠£68-£72 ₽
20P ⇔ ♩ clay pigeon shooting nc10yrs
♀ English & French V ♡ ♿ Sunday Lunch £10.50 Dinner £20-£24&alc Last dinner 9pm
Credit Cards [1][2][3][5]

★★ ✪♨**70%** *Westerclose Country House*
TA24 7QR ☎Exford(064383) 302
Closed 31 Dec-Feb

An attractive former hunting lodge, this hotel stands in a tranquil location overlooking Exmoor. There are 2 comfortable lounges, one with a log-burning stove, and a cheerful conservatory bar. Delicious food is prepared using local produce, and herbs and vegetables from the kitchen garden; dishes include plain grilled fish, vegetarian

A tranquil setting close to London's Heathrow.

WINDSOR

This fine and very comfortable hotel overlooking Datchet Village Green is only minutes from the M4/M25 interchange and very conveniently placed for the airport.

The Manor Hotel offers superb cuisine, easy access to London and is ideally suited to the the needs of todays business executive.

The **Manor** Hotel ★★
Village Green, Datchet.
Tel: 0753 543442

Calotels

Withypool - Wolverhampton

options and perhaps lamb with Madeira sauce; puddings reflect the seasons, with gooseberry roulade and poached plums as summer examples. Bedrooms include 2 spacious first-floor rooms, and more cottagey rooms on the 2nd floor.
10⇨✕(1fb)1⌀ CTV in all bedrooms ® ✱ sB&B⇨✕£28-£30 dB&B⇨✕£58-£65 ⌿
CTV 15P ⇎ ✿ ♣ ♪ ∪ xmas
V ⊖ ⚑ ⊁ ✱ Lunch £12-£19&alc High tea £3-£8alc Dinner £19-£21&alc Last dinner 9.15pm
Credit Cards

WITNEY Oxfordshire Map 04 SP30

★★★67% Witney Lodge
Ducklington Ln OX8 7TS (off A415, Witney-Abingdon) ☎(0993) 779777 FAX (0993) 703467

Situated on the edge of the town, this modern hotel, purpose-built in Cotswold style, has popular conference and leisure facilities. Neat bedrooms are well equipped and the fairly informal Buttercross Restaurant offers a varied choice of dishes.
74⇨✕(10fb)⊁ in 16 bedrooms CTV in all bedrooms ®❷ T ✖ (ex guide dogs) sB&B⇨✕£49-£69 dB&B⇨✕£59-£79 Continental breakfast ⌿
(⊞ 170P ⊡ (heated) snooker sauna solarium gymnasium whirlpool spa ♫ ⋇ xmas
V ⊖ ⚑ ⊁ Lunch £7.25-£11 Dinner £9.95-£11.50 Last dinner 10pm
CONF. Thtr 160 Class 80 Board 46 Del from £85
Credit Cards

★★66% The Marlborough
28 Market Square OX8 7BB (in town centre overlooking Market Square) ☎(0993) 776353 FAX (0993) 702152
RS 24 Dec-2 Jan

The Marlborough is a renovated coaching inn with well furnished bedrooms, especially those in the cottage across the car park; all have the usual modern facilities. A cosy bar has comfortable old settees and armchairs, beams and an open fire, while the attractive panelled dining room offers a varied carte of freshly prepared dishes.
14⇨✕Annexe6⇨✕(1fb)⊁ in 6 bedrooms CTV in all bedrooms ® T sB&B⇨✕£45-£52.50 dB&B⇨✕£50-£60 ⌿
18P
⊖ ⚑ ✱ Lunch £13.35-£23alc High tea £5.25-£7.25alc Dinner £13.35-£23alc Last dinner 9pm
CONF. Thtr 70 Class 30 Board 20 Del £69
Credit Cards

WIVELISCOMBE Somerset Map 03 ST02

★★✿✿⚑ LANGLEY HOUSE
Langley Marsh TA4 2UF (1m N on unclass rd)
☎(0984) 23318 FAX (0984) 24573

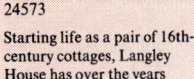

Starting life as a pair of 16th-century cottages, Langley House has over the years acquired an elegant Georgian appearance. A profusion of flowers gives a warm and welcoming feel, especially to the drawing room. For dinner, there is a set menu starting, on the inspection visit, with a sliced dessert pear with creamy blue cheese and walnut dressing. Next came a nicely risen, flavoursome smoked salmon soufflé, followed by tender mignons of beef rather let down by sauce of questionable consistency. For dessert there is always a choice.

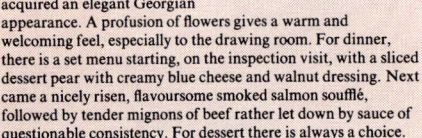

8⇨✕(1fb)1⌀ CTV in all bedrooms T ✱ sB&B⇨✕£58-£68.50 dB&B⇨✕£79-£104.50 ⌿
16P 4⇎ (£3.50) ⇎ ✿ croquet xmas
⊖ ⚑ ⊁ ✱ Dinner £22.50-£28.50 Last dinner 8.30pm
Credit Cards

WOBURN Bedfordshire Map 04 SP93

★★✪69% The Bell Inn
34 Bedford St MK17 9QE (at the northern end of Woburn Main St) ☎(0525) 290280 FAX (0525) 290017

Closed 25-30 Dec

The Bell Inn comprises 2 separate buildings on either side of the main street of this attractive village. The majority of the rooms are in the converted Georgian house, all similarly styled with coordinated fabrics and decor. There is also a residents' bar and lounge. The original inn is full of character with oak beams, and the restaurant, thought to be the oldest building in Woburn, dates back to Elizabethan times.
21⇨✕Annexe6rm(3⇨1✕)(2fb) CTV in all bedrooms ® T ✖ (ex guide dogs) sB&B£40 sB&B⇨✕£58-£66 dB&B£63 dB&B⇨✕£72-£80 ⌿
(50P ⇎
⚐ English & French V ⊖ ✱ Lunch £14.50-£16.95 Dinner £14.50-£16.95 Last dinner 9.30pm
CONF. Thtr 36 Class 36 Board 25 Del £90
Credit Cards

WOKINGHAM Berkshire Map 04 SU86

★★★66% Reading Moat House
Mill Ln, Sindlesham RG11 5DF
☎Reading(0734) 351035 FAX (0734) 666530

This substantially extended 19th-century mill house offers a good range of public facilities; a carvery and more formal restaurant, cocktail bar with table service, a separate pub and night club. Bedrooms are smart, modern and well equipped.
96⇨✕(10fb) CTV in all bedrooms ® T ✱ sB⇨✕fr£93 dB⇨✕fr£103 (room only) ⌿
Lift (350P ⇎ ♪ sauna gymnasium jacuzzi steam room ♫ xmas
⚐ International V ⊖ ⚑ ⊁ ✱ Lunch £14.25 Dinner £14.50-£16.50&alc Last dinner 10.30pm
Credit Cards

WOLVERHAMPTON West Midlands Map 07 SO99

See also **Himley**
★★★64% Novotel
Union St WV1 3JN ☎(0902) 871100 FAX (0902) 870054

This large and fairly new red brick hotel provides well equipped accommodation in spacious bedrooms. Public areas are open plan and staff are bright and cheerful, promoting a friendly atmosphere throughout the hotel.
132⇨✕⊁ in 32 bedrooms CTV in all bedrooms ®❷ T ✱ sB⇨✕£55 dB⇨✕£65 (room only) ⌿
Lift (120P ⇌ (heated)
⚐ International V ⊖ ⊁ ✱ Lunch £3-£15alc Dinner £3-£15alc Last dinner mdnt
Credit Cards

For key to symbols see the Bookmark.

Wolverhampton - Woodbridge

★★★ 60% **Goldthorn**
Penn Rd WV3 0ER (on A449 Kidderminster route)
☎(0902) 29216 FAX (0902) 710419
This is a popular, predominantly commercial hotel. Guest rooms vary from compact singles to the spacious rooms of the business centre, and continued refurbishment is planned. Public areas are ornate, particularly the wood panelled bar with its painted ceiling.
66⇨ⁿ Annexe27⇨ⁿ (1fb)⚭ ½ in 22 bedrooms CTV in all bedrooms ® ⚲ T ✱ sB&B⇨ⁿ £35-£55 dB&B⇨ⁿ £50-£65 ⊟
(120P ✿ *xmas*
♨ English & French V ♦ ⚿ ✱ Lunch £9.45-£9.95&alc Dinner £14.50&alc Last dinner 9.30pm
Credit Cards 1 2 3 5

★★★ 60% *Park Hall*
Park Drive, Goldthorn Park WV4 5AJ (2m S off A459)
☎(0902) 331121 FAX (0902) 344760
An 18th-century house, much extended, now offers bedrooms with a good range of modern facilities and a restaurant whose carvery operation and friendly staff make it popular with non-residents as well as residents.
57⇨ⁿ (20fb) ½ in 4 bedrooms CTV in all bedrooms ® T
(408P ✿
♨ English & French V ♦ ⚿ Last dinner 9.45pm
Credit Cards 1 2 3 4 5

★★ 68% **Ely House**
53 Tettenhall Rd WV3 9NB (on A41)
☎(0902) 311311 FAX (0902) 21098
Until recent years a private girls' school, Ely House has been converted into a modern hotel with well equipped bedrooms and a comfortable lounge bar. The friendly Tarry family, together with their staff, ensure a warm welcome, and the pretty restaurant serves a wide choice of food a carte supplementing the daily table d'hôte menu.
18⇨ⁿ CTV in all bedrooms ® T sB&B⇨ⁿ £39-£48 dB&B⇨ⁿ £48-£68 ⊟
CTV 20P ⚛ nc7yrs
♨ English & Continental V ♦ Lunch £8.90-£11.95&alc Dinner £12.95&alc Last dinner 8.45pm
Credit Cards 1 2 3 5

WOOBURN COMMON Buckinghamshire Map 04 SU98

★★ ✿67% **Chequers Inn**
Kiln Ln HP10 0JQ (1m W unclass towards Bourne End)
☎Bourne End(0628) 529575 FAX (0628) 850124
The original part of this characterful village inn dates back to the 17th century, the popular bar retaining its beams and flagstoned floor. A restaurant decorated with palm trees and period advertisements offers à la carte and set-price menus which incorporate both traditional and more modern dishes. Bedrooms are contained in their own wing, prettily decorated in a cottagey style and very well equipped with modern facilities.
17⇨ⁿ 1⚭ CTV in all bedrooms ® T ✠ (ex guide dogs)
60P ✿
♨ English & French V ♦ Last dinner 9pm
CONF. Thtr 50 Class 30 Board 24 Del from £70
Credit Cards 1 2 3
See advertisement under BEACONSFIELD

The AA's star rating scheme is the market leader in hotel classification.

WOODBRIDGE Suffolk Map 05 TM24

★★★★⚭ 73% **Seckford Hall**
IP13 6NU (signposted on A12 (Woodbridge bypass). Do not follow signs for town centre) ☎(0394) 385678 FAX (0394) 380610
Closed 25 Dec
Set in formal gardens and woodlands, this peaceful Elizabethan manor house has many impressive architectural features around which modern facilities have been sympathetically incorporated. Guests receive a warm welcome, and service in the lounges and restaurant is professional. Bedrooms are very well furnished, with some smart modern suites in the converted Tudor tithe barn.
23⇨ⁿ Annexe10⇨ⁿ (4fb)5⚭ CTV in 34 bedrooms ® T sB&B⇨ⁿ £79-£99 dB&B⇨ⁿ £99-£135 ⊟
(200P ✿ ▣ (heated) ▶ 18 ♪ solarium gymnasium spa bath
♨ International V ♦ ⚿ ✱ Lunch £11.50-£13.50&alc High tea £3.50-£6.50 Dinner £22-£36alc Last dinner 9.30pm
CONF. Thtr 100 Class 50 Board 30 Del £110
Credit Cards 1 2 3 5

★★★ 68% **Ufford Park Hotel Golf & Leisure**
Yarmouth Rd, Ufford IP12 1QW (N on B1438)
☎(0394) 383555 FAX (0394) 383582

In 120 acres of parkland, this purpose-built hotel has open-plan public areas and a good level of services, the latter provided by friendly yet professional staff; bar and lounge offer an all-day menu while carvery and à la carte choices are available in the restaurant. Identically furnished modern bedrooms are made attractive by the use of coordinated colour schemes and quality soft fabrics. ➩

The Bell Inn Woburn
★★ 69%

21 Bedford Street, Woburn, Beds MK17 9QD
Telephone: 0525 290280 Fax: 0525 290017

This friendly family owned Inn is a mixture of Tudor, Georgian and Victorian architecture. The beamed Elizabethan restaurant serves excellent food and wine or try real ale and bar food with the locals in our pub. Bedrooms are individual with tasteful fabrics and furnishings. Woburn Abbey with its beautiful park is close by, as is Woburn Golf Club, home to the Dunhill Masters.

Best Western Hotel   *Egon Ronay listed*

Woodbridge - Woolacombe

25⇨♠(2fb)⌖in 4 bedrooms CTV in all bedrooms ℝ T
✈ (ex guide dogs) sB&B⇨♠£34.50-£54.50 dB&B⇨♠£54.50-£74.50
⦅160P ✿ ▭ (heated) ▶ 18 sauna solarium gymnasium beautician dance studio spa bath *xmas*
♡ ⦿ ⏒ ⌖ Lunch £13.50-£14.50&alc
Conf. Thtr 180 Class 60 Board 80 Del from £79
Credit Cards 1 2 3

★★60% **The Crown**
2 Thoro'fare IP12 1AD ☏(0394) 384242 FAX (0394) 387192

Located in the centre of Woodbridge this converted 16th-century coaching inn is run by a friendly and cheerful team. Bedrooms provide good levels of comfort. The cosy bar and the restaurant, with its short table d'hôte menu, provide a balanced range of food.
10⇨♠Annexe10⇨♠ CTV in all bedrooms ℝ T ✱
sB⇨♠fr£70 dB⇨♠fr£80 (room only) 🅿
35P *xmas*
♡ English & French V ✿ ⏒ ⌖ Sunday Lunch £11.25 Dinner £15.95 Last dinner 9pm
Credit Cards 1 2 3 5

WOODFORD GREEN Greater London See **LONDON SECTION** plan 1 *F5*

★★★68% **Woodford Moat House**
Oak Hill IG8 9NY ☏081-505 4511 FAX 081-506 0941

Situated in a residential area close to the North Circular, this modern business hotel offers good value, well equipped accommodation together with a range of up-to-date conference facilities. General manager Mr Stohr presides over a very efficient team, including a skilled restaurant staff, though warmth can be lacking on occasion.
99⇨♠ CTV in all bedrooms ℝ T ✈ (ex guide dogs) sB&B⇨♠£58-£62 dB&B⇨♠£67-£70 🅿
Lift ⦅ CTV 150P
♡ English & French V ✿ ⏒ Lunch £14.80-£16&alc Dinner £14.80-£16&alc Last dinner 10.15pm
Conf. Thtr 160 Class 90 Board 48
Credit Cards 1 2 3 5

WOODHALL SPA Lincolnshire Map **08** TF16

★★★68% **Petwood House**
Stixwould Rd LN10 6QF ☏(0526) 352411 FAX (0526) 353473
This impressive, rambling house, built at the turn of the century, has been sympathetically converted to provide modern day comforts while retaining character. Mellow wood abounds in the public areas, and there is a magnificently ornate wooden staircase. Bedrooms are most inviting with coordinating fabrics and fittings, and the restaurant offers an interesting, regularly changing menu.
46⇨♠(5fb)3⌖in 8 bedrooms CTV in all bedrooms ℝ T
✈ (ex guide dogs) * sB&B⇨♠£69.70 dB&B⇨♠£81 🅿
Lift ⦅ 80P ✿ snooker croquet bowls putting green *xmas*
♡ English & European V ✿ ⏒ ⌖ Lunch £6.95-£9.85
Conf. Del £79.95
Credit Cards 1 2 3 5

WOODSTOCK Oxfordshire Map **04** SP41

★★★63% **Bear**
Park St OX20 1SZ (opp town hall)
☏(0993) 811511 FAX (0993) 813580

For 4 centuries a creeper-clad coaching inn has stood in the centre of this historic village on the edge of the Cotswolds, within walking distance of Blenheim Palace. It provides comfortable bedrooms recently upgraded to modern standards. Public areas, with an old

world atmosphere and many original features, include a small guests' lounge upstairs and a bar lounge where afternoon teas are also served. Interesting à la carte and fixed price menus.
33⇨♠Annexe12⇨♠(1fb)7⌖in 14 bedrooms CTV in all bedrooms ℝ T sB⇨♠£95-£100 dB⇨♠£115-£170 (room only) 🅿
⦅30P *xmas*
♡ ⦿ ⏒ ⌖ Lunch £5.95-£19.50&alc Dinner £21.50-£23.50&alc Last dinner 9.30pm
Credit Cards 1 2 3 5

★★★✿✿77% **Feathers**
Market St OX20 1SX ☏(0993) 812291 FAX (0993) 813158
General manager Tom Lewis and his team clearly enjoy caring for guests. Bedrooms are comfortable and individually decorated, but some of the stairways to them are narrow and steep. Elegant public areas have log fires in winter, and the Whinchat Bar has doors onto the delightful courtyard garden. In the restaurant head chef David Lewis offers innovative menus in modern British style. A recent test meal included a delicious light smoked haddock soufflé with wild rice and lime, followed by a pot roasted breast of pheasant with a mellow red wine sauce.
17⇨♠ CTV in all bedrooms T ✱ sB&B⇨♠£75-£95 dB&B£98-£138 dB&B⇨♠£170 Continental breakfast 🅿
✎ 🚴 mountain bikes ♫ *xmas*
♡ ⦿ ⏒ ✱ Lunch £15.50-£18.50&alc Dinner £19.50-£24.50&alc Last dinner 9.45pm
Credit Cards 1 2 3 5

WOODY BAY Devon Map **03** SS64

★★70% **Woody Bay**
EX31 4QX ☏Parracombe(05983) 264
Closed early Jan-mid Feb RS mid Feb-mid Mar & Nov-Dec
Peacefully set high above a wooded valley and with fine sea views, this hotel has a comfortable lounge with open fire and a convivial real ale bar. Bedrooms are freshly decorated and have modern fitted furniture, though there are few facilities. The dining room provides a short, fresh table d'hôte menu and a rather longer carte; cooking is good and portions generous.
14rm(13⇨♠)(1fb)2⌖ ℝ
15P ✿ ✱ ♫ nc8yrs
♡ English & French V ✿ ⏒ Last dinner 8.30pm
Credit Cards 1 3

WOOKEY HOLE Somerset Map **03** ST54

★★⦿68% **Glencot House**
Glencot Ln BA5 1BH ☏(0749) 677160 FAX (0749) 670210
Quietly situated overlooking a curve in the river, this Grade II Victorian mansion has been restored to its former glory. The individually furnished and decorated bedrooms include spacious honeymoon rooms. Public areas are spacious, with lots of wood panelling, and in the restaurant, chef Danny Cannon provides short fixed price menus, cooked and presented with modern influences.
12⇨♠(2fb)4⌖ CTV in all bedrooms ℝ T ✱ sB&B⇨♠£45-£48 dB&B⇨♠£58-£75 🅿
CTV 21P ✿ ▭ (heated) ♪ snooker sauna solarium table tennis pool *xmas*
♡ ⏒ ✱ Dinner £17.50-£22.50 Last dinner 8.30pm
Conf. Thtr 35 Class 24 Board 20 Del from £68
Credit Cards 1 3

WOOLACOMBE Devon Map **02** SS44

★★★✿73% **Watersmeet**
Mortehoe EX34 7EB ☏(0271) 870333 FAX (0271) 870890
Closed Dec-mid Feb
(Rosette awarded for dinner only)
This fine hotel stands on the cliff edge at Mortehoe, with glorious sea views and steps from the grounds down to the rocky cove; most of ➔

Watersmeet Hotel

🏵 73% ★★★

COUNTRY HOUSE
STYLE AND ELEGANCE BY THE SEA

Award winning restaurant, comfort and hospitality

Lawn tennis and outdoor heated pool

Bridge and painting holidays

Spring and Autumn Breaks

**Watersmeet Hotel, Mortehoe,
Woolacombe, North Devon EX34 7EB
Tel: (0271) 870333   Fax: (0271) 870890**

TEL: (0526) 352411   FAX: (0526) 353473

Petwood
H·O·U·S·E ★★★

THE FAMOUS DAMBUSTERS HOTEL

Unique Country House hotel set in 30 acres of secluded gardens and woodland, ideally situated for quiet breaks
★ 46 luxurious bedrooms, including 4-posters
★ Tennysons Restaurant, renowned for its superb cuisine ★ Snooker Room ★ Putting Green ★ Croquet
★ Golf Practice Area

For further information contact
PETWOOD HOUSE, WOODHALL SPA, LINCS

Woodford Moat House ★★★

INTERNATIONAL HOTELIERS

**Oak Hill, Woodford Green, Essex IG8 9NY
Telephone: 081-505 4511 Telex: 264428 Fax: 081-506 0941**

The Woodford Moat House is a modern three star hotel providing comprehensive facilities for both business and pleasure. Here you can enjoy peace and quiet in comfortable surroundings, designed to make your stay as pleasant and as enjoyable as possible.
All 99 rooms have private shower or bath en suite, hair dryer, trouser press, colour TV, radio, telephone, and tea, coffee making facilities.
The Churchill Restaurant with its beautiful wood panelling enjoys a high reputation for serving fresh produce, a comprehensive wine list and friendly and attentive staff. An ideal venue for conferences, exhibitions, training courses, meetings, business interviews also specialists in banquets, dinner dances, wedding receptions and private parties.

W

Woolacombe - Woolverton

the attractive bedrooms also enjoy the view. There is a cocktail bar, a lounge and a terrace bar for lunchtime snacks and drinks. The very good cooking combines traditional English dishes with imaginatively sauced ones. Owners, management and staff are charming, friendly and efficient.

23⇨♠(3fb)1🛏 CTV in all bedrooms T 🏃 (ex guide dogs) ✳ sB&B⇨♠£55-£78 dB&B⇨♠£94-£178 (incl dinner) 🅿
20P 18🅿 🚲 ✿ ⌒ (heated) ♀ (grass)
♀ English & French V ♢ ♃ ✄ ✳ Dinner £24.50&alc Last dinner 8.30pm
CONF. Class 20 Board 20 Del from £70
Credit Cards [1][2][3][5]

★★★ 66% Woolacombe Bay
South St EX34 7BN ☎(0271) 870388 FAX (0271) 870613
Closed Jan & 2wks Feb

Significantly improved over recent years, this hotel now features bedrooms which are both bright and comfortable – many of them also boasting glorious sea and coastline views; public areas have been similarly upgraded. An extensive range of sporting and recreational activities (both indoor and out) together with six-acre grounds adjacent to the sands make it ideal for families, and a range of self-catering apartments is available. Within the hotel, Maxwell's Bistro provides an alternative to the more formal restaurant.

59⇨♠(26fb)1🛏 CTV in all bedrooms ® ♂ T 🏃 ✳ sB&B⇨♠£35-£100 dB&B⇨♠£70-£200 (incl dinner)
Lift (100P ✿ ⌒ (heated) ⌒ (heated) ▶ 9 ♀ (hard) squash snooker sauna solarium gymnasium spa bath masseur steam room table tennis ♫ 🎵 xmas
♀ English & French V ♢ ♃ ✄ ✳ Lunch £5-£8 High tea £7 Dinner £17 Last dinner 9.45pm
CONF. Thtr 200 Class 150 Board 100 Del from £65
Credit Cards [1][2][3][5] £

★★ ❀70% Little Beach
The Esplanade EX34 7DJ (junct 27 of M5 take A361 through Barnstaple towards Ilfracombe, Woolacombe is signposted at Mullacott Cross roundabout)
☎Barnstaple(0271) 870298
Closed Nov-Feb

Amiable proprietors Nola and Brian Welling provide a warm welcome at this sea front Edwardian hotel. The individually decorated bedrooms are pretty and bright and some front-facing rooms have balconies. The cosy public rooms are more traditionally furnished and both the bar and dining room have excellent views. A short choice 5-course menu of wholesome cooking is offered, with delicious home-made sweets.

10rm(4⇨4♠) CTV in all bedrooms ® T sB&Bfr£28 sB&B⇨♠£28-£31 dB&B⇨♠£48-£73 🅿
8P 🚲 nc7yrs
♀ English & Continental V ✄
Credit Cards [1][3]

★★ 61% Devon Beach
The Esplanade EX34 7DJ ☎(0271) 870449
Closed mid Oct-Etr

The Devon Beach is right on the seafront with a sun-trap terrace offering fine views. Bedrooms have modern furniture and facilities, suites are available and some rooms have balconies. Public areas include a small smoking lounge and a disco dance floor. A 6-course dinner menu is served by cheerful staff.

33rm(26⇨)(20fb) CTV in all bedrooms ® ✳ sB&B£32-£38 sB&B⇨£39-£46 dB&B⇨♠£66-£90 (incl dinner)
28P 3🅿 (£5 per day) 📺 (heated) solarium
♀ English, French & Italian V ♢ ♃ ✳ Dinner £9.50-£10.50 Last dinner 8.15pm
Credit Cards [1][3]

★★ 60% Atlantic
Sunnyside Rd EX34 7DG ☎(0271) 870469 FAX (0271) 870223
Closed Nov-Feb

This small, informal holiday hotel enjoys fine sea views from its elevated position. It is ideal for families with its unfussy bedrooms and spacious games room. The TV lounge has a personal feel with ornaments and dried flowers; and the bar, like many of the rooms, takes a share of the view.

16rm(9⇨3♠)(10fb)✄ in 4 bedrooms CTV in all bedrooms ® CTV 16P ✿ table tennis pool table
♀ English & Continental V ♢ ♃ ✄ Last dinner 7.30pm

★ 70% Crossways
The Esplanade EX34 7DJ (M5 junct 27 then A361 to Barnstaple, follow signs for Ilfracombe and then Woolacombe)
☎(0271) 870395
Closed last Sat in Oct-1st Sat in Mar

This small hotel is in an elevated position above Combesgate Beach, with direct access to National Trust moorland at the rear. Warm, friendly hospitality comes from the owners Dave and Chris Ellis – and from chirpy zebra finches in the comfortable lounge. The bar has an interesting collection of model cars. The attractive bedrooms are generally a good size, most with a sea view.

9rm(5♠)(5fb) CTV in all bedrooms ® sB&B£18-£24.50 sB&B⇨♠£20.50-£24.50 dB&B♠£36-£49 dB&B♠£41-£49 🅿
9P 🚲
V ✄ Bar Lunch £1-£3alc

WOOLER Northumberland Map 12 NT92

★★ 56% Tankerville Arms
Cottage Rd NE71 6AD (on A697)
☎(0668) 81581 FAX (0668) 81787
Closed 22-28 Dec

A 17th-century coaching inn on the northern edge of the town offers friendly service, a range of meals in the bars or restaurant and some recently refurbished bedrooms with modern amenities.

17⇨♠(1fb) CTV in all bedrooms ® T ✳ sB&B⇨♠fr£36.50 dB&B⇨♠fr£59 🅿
100P ✿
V ♢ ✄ ✳ Sunday Lunch fr£7.50alc Dinner fr£12.95alc Last dinner 9pm
CONF. Thtr 80 Class 50 Board 40 Del from £49.50
Credit Cards [1][3]

WOOLLEY EDGE MOTORWAY SERVICE AREA (M1)
West Yorkshire Map 08 SE31

Granada Lodge
M1 Service Area, West Bretton WF4 4LQ (between junct 38/39, adj to service area)
☎Wakefield(0924) 830569 FAX (0924) 830609

This modern building provides smart, spacious and well equipped bedrooms, all with en suite bathrooms. Meals may be taken at a nearby family restaurant. For more details about Granada Lodges, consult the Contents page, under Hotel Groups.

31⇨♠ B⇨♠£34.95-£37.95 (room only)

WOOLVERTON Somerset Map 03 ST75

★★★ 63% Woolverton House
BA3 6QS ☎Frome(0373) 830415 FAX (0373) 830415

This attractive late-Georgian house is set well back from the road in gardens that are being recultivated. Comfortable bedrooms vary in size, with large and standard rooms. There is a relaxing conservatory bar and an attractive restaurant serving well prepared straightforward meals.

11⇨♠ Annexe4⇨♠(1fb)🛏✄ in 4 bedrooms CTV in all bedrooms ® T ✳ sB&B⇨♠£44 dB&B⇨♠£59 🅿
(50P 2🅿 🚲 ✿ archery
V ♢ ✄ ✳ Lunch £7-£18alc Dinner £7-£18alc Last dinner 9pm

CONF. Thtr 50 Class 8 Board 12 Del from £59
Credit Cards ①②③
See advertisement under BATH

WOOTTON BASSETT Wiltshire Map 04 SU08

★★★ 66% **Marsh Farm**
Coped Hall SN4 8ER (on B4041, Hook-Purton)
☎Swindon(0793) 848044 FAX (0793) 851528
Marsh Farm is a personally run hotel in the countryside near Swindon. A modern extension provides well equipped bedrooms and in the original house there are lounges, one with a bar, and an attractive restaurant.
4⇌𝄞Annexe24⇌𝄞(1fb)1⌀ CTV in all bedrooms ® T ✱ (ex guide dogs) sB&B⇌𝄞£25 dB&B⇌𝄞£50-£85 ₧
100P ⚓ ✻
V ⊙ ⏀ ⚤ ✱ Lunch £9.50-£12.50&alc Dinner £9.50-£12.50&alc Last dinner 9pm
Credit Cards ①②③

WORCESTER Hereford & Worcester Map 03 SO85

★★★ 👁👁 69% **Fownes Resort**
City Walls Rd WR1 2AP (beside A38 Inner Ring Road, 100 yds from Cathedral)
☎(0905) 613151 FAX (0905) 23742

This Victorian glove factory by the inner ring road has been converted into a successful modern hotel with nicely furnished bedrooms and pleasant public areas including a library, cocktail bar and the elegant Kings Restaurant where a typical meal might begin with salmon terrine, followed by strips of pork Chinese style with sesame and ginger, finishing with chocolate truffle cake.
61⇌𝄞(4fb) CTV in all bedrooms ®⚤ T ✱ sB⇌𝄞fr£75 dB⇌𝄞fr£85 (room only) ₧
Lift ⌇ 94P sauna gymnasium *xmas*
V ⊙ ⏀ ✱ Lunch fr£8.95&alc Dinner fr£14.95&alc Last dinner 9.45pm
Credit Cards ①②③⑤ £

★★★ 61% **Star**
Foregate St WR1 1EA (Crown & Raven) ☎(0905) 24308 FAX (0905) 23440
The Star is a popular city-centre hotel on a busy one-way street. Bedrooms vary in size, some singles are quite compact, but all are attractive with mainly pine furniture and a good range of facilities. Public areas include 2 bars, a restaurant and an all-day coffee shop.
46⇌𝄞(2fb) CTV in all bedrooms ® T ✱ sB&B⇌𝄞£45-£55.50 ₧
Lift ⌇ 55P *xmas*
♬ English & French V ⊙ ⏀ ✱ Sunday Lunch £5.45-£7.95 Dinner £10&alc Last dinner 9.45pm
Credit Cards ①②③

★★★ 58% **The Giffard**
High St WR1 2QR (opp Worcester Cathedral)
☎(0905) 726262 FAX (0905) 723458

The bar, restaurant and lounges of this large commercial hotel are on the first floor and there is a cheerful coffee shop at street level. Bedrooms are a little dated but are soon to be upgraded. Double and twin rooms are quite roomy but single rooms are rather small. Staff are friendly and attentive.
103⇌𝄞(2fb)⚤ in 25 bedrooms CTV in all bedrooms ® T ✱ sB⇌𝄞fr£42.50 dB⇌𝄞fr£49.50 (room only) ₧
Lift ⌇ snooker *xmas*
♬ English & International V ⊙ ⏀ ⚤ ✱ Sunday Lunch fr£8.95 Dinner fr£12.95 Last dinner 10pm
Credit Cards ①②③⑤

★★ 65% **Loch Ryan Hotel**
119 Sidbury Rd WR5 2DH (on A44 London road) ☎(0905) 351143 FAX (0905) 764407

This very well run hotel is a short walk from the cathedral and town centre. There is a comfortable residents' sitting room and a small foyer bar, and the bedrooms are spotlessly clean and well furnished.
10⇌𝄞(1fb) CTV in all bedrooms ® ✱ sB&B⇌𝄞£37.50-£45 dB&B⇌𝄞£45-£60 ₧
CTV ♪ ✻
V ⊙ ⏀ ⚤ ✱ Dinner £11.50-£13.50alc Last dinner 8pm
Credit Cards ①②③⑤

★★ 62% **Ye Olde Talbot**
Friar St WR1 2NA (in city centre opposite Cathedral) (Whitbread) ☎(0905) 23573 FAX (0905) 612760
This former coaching inn in the city centre partly dates to the 13th-century and offers comfortable accommodation, well equipped with modern facilities to meet the needs of business travellers. The cosy dining room offers a simple grill-style menu.
29⇌𝄞(6fb)1⌀ ⚤ in 2 bedrooms CTV in all bedrooms ®⚤ T ✱ (ex guide dogs) ✻ sB&B⇌𝄞fr£49.50 dB&B⇌𝄞fr£61 ₧
⌇ CTV 8⚓
♬ English & Continental V ⊙ ⏀ ⚤ ✱ Lunch fr£7.20&alc Dinner fr£12.95&alc Last dinner 9.45pm
Credit Cards ①②③⑤

★ 59% **Park House**
12 Droitwich Rd WR3 7LJ ☎(0905) 21816 FAX (0905) 612178

The friendly Smith family are enthusiastic hoteliers and offer warm hospitality to their guests. Bedrooms have been much improved recently and there is a comfortable traditional lounge for residents. The hotel has a small garden at the rear.
7rm(4⇌𝄞)(1fb)⚤ in 4 bedrooms CTV in all bedrooms ®⚤ sB&B£20-£30 sB&B𝄞£24-£34 dB&B£30-£36 dB&B𝄞£36-£42
CTV 10P ⚓
V ⊙ ⏀ ⚤ ✱ Dinner £6-£9&alc Last dinner 7.30pm

WORFIELD Shropshire Map 07 SO79

★★★ 👁👁⌀ 74% **Old Vicarage**
WV15 5JZ (off A454 between Bridgnorth & Wolverhampton) (Logis) ☎(07464) 497 FAX (07464) 552
Christine and Peter Iles are continually improving this fine Edwardian parsonage, set in 2 acres of lawns and gardens. The coach house has been converted to provide 4 excellent bedrooms with French oak furniture and jacuzzi bathrooms. Main house rooms are also good but rather smaller. Public areas have fine paintings, antiques and quality rugs and carpets. John Williams presides over food operations; our inspector sampled a starter of wild pigeon supreme, slightly pink and moist, followed by excellent baked red mullet.
10⇌𝄞Annexe4⇌𝄞(1fb)1⌀ ⚤ in 6 bedrooms CTV in all bedrooms ® T ✱ sB&B⇌𝄞£63.50-£74.50 dB&B⇌𝄞£85-£100 ₧
30P ⚓ ✻ ⚓
V ⊙ ⏀ ⚤ Lunch £14.50-£19.50 Dinner £19.50-£27.50 Last dinner 9pm
Credit Cards ①②③⑤

WORKINGTON Cumbria Map 11 NX92

★★★ 68% **Washington Central**
Washington St CA14 3AW ☎(0900) 65772 FAX (0900) 68770
This modern hotel in the town centre has adequate nearby parking. It caters for both business and tourist guests and offers a good standard of hospitality. Bedrooms are prettily coordinated, warm and well equipped. Extensive menus are provided in the Carlton Restaurant on the first floor, and there is a buttery at street level.
40⇌𝄞(4fb) CTV in all bedrooms ®⚤ T ✱ (ex guide dogs) ✻ sB&B⇌𝄞£52.50-£68 dB&B⇌𝄞£74-£88 ₧
Lift ⌇ 50P ⌁ (heated) sauna solarium gymnasium

Workington - Worthing

♥ English & French V ✿ ⚓ ✕ Lunch £9.50&alc High tea £6.50-£8.50 Dinner £15.95-£17.25&alc Last dinner 9.30pm
CONF. Thtr 200 Class 120 Board 40
Credit Cards [1][2][3][5]

★★ 57% Crossbarrow Motel
Little Clifton CA14 1XS (3m E on A595) ☎(0900) 61443 FAX (0900) 61443

This motel-style operation stands in open countryside with views towards the Cumbrian fells. Public areas in a converted farmhouse include a bar lounge and dining room. Bedrooms, in a separate building to the rear, are modern and functional.

Annexe26⇨♠(1fb) CTV in all bedrooms ® T ✱
sB&B⇨♠£36 dB&B⇨♠£52 ♫
50P ✿ xmas
V ✿ ⚓ ✕ Lunch £3.65-£7.95 Dinner £6.95-£10.50alc Last dinner 8.30pm
CONF. Thtr 40 Board 20
Credit Cards [1][2][3]

WORKSOP Nottinghamshire Map 08 SK57

★★★ 69% Clumber Park
Clumber Park S80 3PA (on A614, 5m NE) (Lansbury) ☎Mansfield(0623) 835333 FAX (0623) 835525

Standing on the A614 opposite Clumber Park, this relatively new hotel has quickly become popular for its comfortable and well appointed accommodation. Public rooms offer a good range of facilities, with the choice of bars and eating areas. Light snacks and meals are served all day in the Dukeries Tavern, or a more interesting choice of menus is offered in the more formal Lime Trees Restaurant. The young staff and enthusiastic management provide friendly, helpful service throughout.

48⇨♠(4fb)♥in 23 bedrooms CTV in all bedrooms ®✗T ✱ ✕ (ex guide dogs) ✱ sB&B⇨♠fr£65.50 dB&B⇨♠fr£77 ♫
℄ 208P sauna solarium gymnasium pool table ⚽ xmas
♥ English & French V ✿ ⚓ ✕ ✱ Lunch £8.50-£11 Dinner fr£15 Last dinner 10pm
CONF. Thtr 250 Class 120 Board 72 Del from £89
Credit Cards [1][2][3][5]

★★ 72% Lion
112 Bridge St S80 1HT ☎(0909) 477925 FAX (0909) 479038

A redeveloped and extended coaching inn dating back to the sixteenth century stands at the centre of the town, close to the market place. Modern, well equipped bedrooms are generally spacious, and room service of meals is available; non-smoking accommodation, a room with a half-tester bed and the recently added bridal suites are all particularly popular.

30⇨♠(3fb)1⊞ CTV in all bedrooms ®✗T ✱ sB&B⇨♠£45-£55 dB&B⇨♠£55-£65 ♫
℄ ⊞ 50P sauna solarium gymnasium
♥ French V ✿ ⚓ ✱ Lunch £12.50 Dinner £12.50-£15.45 Last dinner 10pm
CONF. Thtr 70 Class 70 Board 70 Del from £70
Credit Cards [1][2][3]

★★ 64% Regency
Carlton Rd S80 1PS (adjacent to railway station) ☎(0909) 474108 FAX (0909) 479398

This busy, family-run commercial hotel aims to provide value for money and has certainly succeeded - bar, food and accommodation are all very popular. The public areas have been re-styled with a modern colour coordinated look. The lounge bar has a large dark wood bar and many pictures, plates and brasses. There is also a small quiet lounge for residents.

13rm(7♠)(1fb) CTV in all bedrooms ® T ✱ sB&B£27-£32 sB&B♠£32 dB&B£39-£49 dB&B♠£49
CTV 25P 5⚫ ♣ sauna solarium gymnasium

V ✱ Lunch £3.50&alc Dinner £6.90-£7.90&alc Last dinner 8pm
Credit Cards [1][2][3][5]

Forte Travelodge
Dunkeries Mill(on roundabout junct of A60/A57) ☎(0909) 501528 Central Res (0800) 850950

FORTE Travelodge

This modern building offers a good standard of accommodation for overnight stops. Smart, spacious and well equipped bedrooms, all with en suite bathrooms, are suitable for family use, and meals may be taken at the nearby family restaurant. For more details about Travelodges, consult the Contents page, under Hotel Groups.

40⇨♠✱ B⇨♠£31.95 (room only)

WORSLEY Greater Manchester Map 07 SD70

★★★ 57% Novotel
Worsley Brow M28 4YA (adjacent to M62 junc 13) ☎061-799 3535 FAX 061-703 8207

novotel

Purpose built and modern, this hotel provides clean if slightly functional accommodation. It is a popular venue for business meetings, and the restaurant – part of a spacious open-plan area – is open from 6am until midnight.

119⇨♠(119fb)♥in 20 bedrooms CTV in all bedrooms ®✗T ✱ sB⇨♠£59.50 dB⇨♠£64.50 (room only) ♫
Lift 133P ✿ ⚊ (heated)
♥ English & French V ✿ ⚓ ✕ ✱ Lunch £12-£17alc Dinner £15-£20alc Last dinner mdnt
Credit Cards [1][2][3][5]

WORTHING West Sussex Map 04 TQ10

★★★ 66% Beach
Marine Pde BN11 3QJ ☎(0903) 234001 FAX (0903) 234567

The Beach Hotel faces the sea within walking distance of the shops. Extensive traditional services are maintained, and the spacious lounge has made the hotel a popular rendezvous. Most of the good size, comfortable bedrooms have sea views and some have balconies. A cocktail bar augments the lounge and large no-smoking restaurant.

80⇨♠(8fb) CTV in all bedrooms ®✗T ✕ sB&B⇨♠£51-£59.25 dB&B⇨♠£76.50-£86.50 ♫
Lift ℄ 55P ⊞ xmas
V ✿ ⚓ ✱ Lunch £2.50-£11&alc Dinner fr£15.50&alc Last dinner 8.45pm
Credit Cards [1][2][3][4][5]

★★★ 63% Windsor House
14/20 Windsor Rd BN11 2LX ☎(0903) 239655 FAX (0903) 210763

Closed Xmas

Close to the seafront, this family-run hotel has gone from strength to strength over the last few years. Refurbished to a good standard, it offers well appointed bedrooms, a bright conservatory-style entrance and a comfortable lounge bar. The attractive restaurant offers a choice of menus, including a very good carvery. Staff are very friendly and helpful, under the personal supervision of the proprietor.

30⇨♠(4fb)1⊞♥in 2 bedrooms CTV in all bedrooms ®✗T ✕ (ex guide dogs) sB&B⇨♠£36.50-£52.50 dB&B⇨♠£65-£79 ♫
CTV 18P ♪
♥ English & French V ✿ ⚓ Lunch £6.50-£12.95 Dinner fr£13.50&alc Last dinner 9pm
CONF. Thtr 120 Del from £65
Credit Cards [1][3]

666

Worthing - Wrightington

★★★ 58% **Chatsworth**
Steyne BN11 3DU (just beyond the pier) ☎(0903) 236103 FAX (0903) 823726
Built in the early 19th century, the Chatsworth has an attractive Georgian façade and is pleasantly situated overlooking Steyne Gardens and the sea. Bedrooms are dated in style and furnishings, but all are well equipped. The ground floor has been completely redecorated, including the spacious restaurant and bar/lounge.
107⇌↑(5fb) CTV in all bedrooms ® T sB&B⇌↑£45-£59.90 dB&B⇌↑£77-£81 ⏏
Lift ⦅ 150P ✿ snooker games room *xmas*
♀ English & Continental V ✧ ⚤ ⚹ ✴ Lunch £9.85&alc High tea fr£6.50 Dinner fr£14.95 Last dinner 8.30pm
CONF. Thtr 150 Class 80 Board 46 Del from £49.50
Credit Cards [1][2][3][5] £

★★★ 58% **Kingsway**
Marine Pde BN11 3QQ ☎(0903) 237542 FAX (0903) 204173
This small seafront hotel has been ably run by the Howlett family for more than 20 years. The majority of the bedrooms have now been upgraded with modern fitted furniture, and all are comfortable. The 2 cosy lounges overlook the sea, as does the buttery bar which offers a popular and extensive menu. Alternatively, the restaurant provides a carvery and an à la carte menu.
28⇌↑(1fb) CTV in all bedrooms ® ⚤ T sB&B⇌↑£37.50-£55 dB&B⇌↑£50-£85 ⏏
Lift ⦅ 12P ≢ *xmas*
♀ English & French V ✧ ⚤ ✴ Lunch £8.90-£12.95&alc Dinner fr£14.95&alc Last dinner 9pm
CONF. Thtr 50 Class 20 Board 30
Credit Cards [1][2][3][5]

★★ 65% **Ardington**
Steyne Gardens BN11 3DZ ☎(0903) 230451 FAX (0903) 230451
Closed Xmas
Close to the sea and shops, and overlooking gardens, this hotel continues to improve, with recently upgraded bedrooms in soft pastel shades. Refreshments are available in the bar lounge, while the restaurant offers both a carte and set menus.
47⇌↑(4fb)⚥in 10 bedrooms CTV in all bedrooms ® ⚤ T sB&B⇌↑£47-£58 dB&B⇌↑£73-£80 ⏏
⦅ 25P
♀ International V ✧ ⚤ Lunch £12-£18alc Dinner fr£13.50&alc Last dinner 8.30pm
CONF. Thtr 120 Class 60 Board 50 Del from £50
Credit Cards [1][2][3][5]

★★ 65% **Cavendish**
115/116 Marine Pde BN11 3QG
☎(0903) 236767 FAX (0903) 823840

This small Victorian end of terrace hotel is personally run by proprietors Mr and Mrs Higgins and is perfectly positioned on the seafront. Bedrooms have attactive soft furnishings and many have sea views. The smart restaurant offers a monthly menu in addition to the good-value set menu. Guests can enjoy drinks in the informal atmosphere of the combined bar/lounge.
15rm(13⇌↑)(1fb) CTV in all bedrooms ® T ✖ (ex guide dogs) ✴ sB&Bfr£25 sB&B⇌↑fr£42.50 dB&B⇌↑fr£69 ⏏
⦅ CTV 4P ≢
♀ English & Continental V ✧ Lunch fr£8.95 Dinner fr£11.95 Last dinner 9pm
CONF. Class 30 Board 16
Credit Cards [1][2][3][5] £

WREXHAM Clwyd Map **07** SJ34
See also **Marchwiel**

★★★↟ 64% **Llwyn Onn Hall**
Cefn Rd LL13 0NY (Welsh Rarebits) ☎(0978) 261225 FAX (0978) 261225
Built around 1700 as a manor house, the hotel is set in several acres of parkland in a completely rural location, although it is just a short distance from the industrial estate. Bedrooms have period furniture with one 4-poster and several brass beds. Public rooms comprise a bar and entrance hall with open fires, an elegant sitting room and a restaurant in several parts where a good range of food is available.
13⇌↑(2fb)1≢ CTV in all bedrooms ® T ✖ (ex guide dogs) ✴ sB&B⇌↑£46-£52 dB&B⇌↑£66-£80 ⏏
40P ✿
V ✧ ⚤ ⚹ ✴ Lunch £9.95&alc Dinner £13.95&alc Last dinner 9.30pm
Credit Cards [1][2][3][5]

★★★ 64% **Wynnstay Arms**
High Street/Yorke St LL13 8LP ☎(0978) 291010 FAX (0978) 362138
This centrally positioned Georgian hotel, with its comfortable lounges and open kitchen servery in the restaurant, is a popular centre for local activities. The fresh, bright bedrooms are well equipped and contain thoughtful extras.
76⇌↑(8fb)⚥in 4 bedrooms CTV in all bedrooms ® T
Lift ⦅ CTV 50P 20⚲
♀ British, French, Mexican & Italian V ✧ ⚤ ⚹ Last dinner 9.45pm
Credit Cards [1][2][3][5]

Forte Travelodge
Wrexham By Pass, Rhostyllen LL14 4EJ (4m S, A483/A5152 roundabout) ☎(0978) 365705
Central Res (0800) 850950
This modern building offers a good standard of accommodation for overnight stops. Smart, spacious and well equipped bedrooms, all with en suite bathrooms, are suitable for family use, and meals may be taken at the nearby family restaurant. For more details about Travelodges, consult the Contents page, under Hotel Groups.
32⇌↑ ✴ B⇌↑£31.95 (room only) FORTE Travelodge

WRIGHTINGTON Lancashire Map **07** SD51

★★★ 65% **Wrightington Hotel & Restaurant**
Moss Ln WN6 9PB (off junct 27, M6) ☎Standish(0257) 425803 FAX (0257) 425830
In a rural situation, yet convenient for the M6, this modern, purpose-built hotel offers spacious accommodation in well equipped bedrooms. In addition to a fully equipped leisure centre, public areas include a comfortable lounge and a beamed restaurant where staff provide attentive service.
47⇌↑(4fb) CTV in all bedrooms ® ⚤ T ✴ sB&B⇌↑fr£53 dB&B⇌↑fr£64 ⏏
⦅ 80P ☐ (heated) squash sauna solarium gymnasium
♀ International V ✧ ⚤ Last dinner 10pm
CONF. Thtr 60 Class 20 Board 40 Del £82
Credit Cards [1][2][3][5]

All black star hotels are given a percentage grading within their star bands. See 'Using the Guide' at the front of the book for full details.

Satellite television – look for this symbol ⚤ in the directory entries.

Wrotham - Yarmouth, Great

WROTHAM Kent Map 05 TQ65

Forte Posthouse
London Rd, Wrotham Heath TN15 7RS
☎Borough Green(0732) 883311 FAX (0732) 885850

Suitable for both the business and leisure traveller, this bright hotel provides modern accommodation in well equipped bedrooms with en suite bathrooms. For more details about Forte Posthouse hotels, consult the Contents page, under Hotel Groups.
106⇌⋔* B⇌⋔£41.50-£53.50 (room only)
CONF. Thtr 60 Class 30 Board 30 Del £89.50

Travel Inn
London Rd, Wrotham Heath TN15 7RX (follow A20 Wrotham & West Malling road)
☎Borough Green(0732) 884214

Purpose-built accommodation offers spacious and well equipped bedrooms, all with en suite bathrooms. Meals may be taken at the nearby family restaurant and pub. For more details about Travel Inns, consult the Contents page, under Hotel Groups.
40⇌⋔* B⇌⋔£33.50 (room only)

WROXHAM Norfolk Map 09 TG21

★★★ 59% *Broads*
Station Rd NR12 8UR ☎(0603) 782869 FAX (0603) 784066
Situated at the heart of the Broads, beside the river at Hoveton, this well kept family owned and run hotel offers good-value accommodation equally suited to the needs of commercial and leisure users.
21⇌⋔Annexe7⇌⋔(1fb) CTV in all bedrooms ® T
40P ♪
♀ English & French V ♡ ⚏ Last dinner 9.30pm
Credit Cards [1][2][3][5]

WYKEHAM (NEAR SCARBOROUGH) North Yorkshire Map 08 SE98

★★ 65% *Downe Arms*
YO13 9QB (on the main A170 Scarborough to Pickering road approx 6m from Scarborough) ☎Scarborough(0723) 862471 FAX (0723) 864329
The Downe Arms is a restored coaching inn between Pickering and Scarborough. The bedrooms have all been modernised, and the bars comfortably refurbished – bar meals being a popular feature.
10⇌⋔(2fb) CTV in all bedrooms ® T ✻ sB&B⇌⋔fr£25 dB&B⇌⋔fr£35 Continental breakfast ♬
CTV 150P 2🚗 ❀ shooting *xmas*
♀ English & French V ♡ ⚏ ✻ Sunday Lunch fr£8.45
Credit Cards [1][2][3][5]

WYMONDHAM Norfolk Map 05 TG10

★★ 65% *Sinclair*
28 Market St NR18 0BB ☎(0953) 606721 FAX (0953) 601361
Closed Xmas
Popular with commercial and leisure guests, this friendly family-run hotel is in a central position and offers well maintained bedrooms, with the restaurant and bar providing a simple choice of food and drink.
20⇌⋔(2fb)1🎌in 12 bedrooms CTV in all bedrooms ® T ✗ ✻ sB&B⇌⋔£35-£40 dB&B⇌⋔£45-£50 ♬
8P ❀ sauna
V ♡ ⚏ ✻ Lunch £5-£15 Dinner £12.50-£15&alc Last dinner 9.30pm
Credit Cards [1][2][3]

★★ 63% Abbey
Church St NR18 0PH ☎(0953) 602148 FAX (0953) 606247

The Abbey Hotel is a red brick building in a leafy street close to the 12th-century abbey. The accommodation varies in size and levels of comfort, and there is a small lounge, a bar, and an efficiently run restaurant providing simple meals.
25⇌⋔Annexe1⇌⋔(3fb) CTV in all bedrooms ® T
sB⇌⋔£35-£40 dB⇌⋔£45-£50 (room only) ♬
Lift ⓒ 3P *xmas*
V ♡ ⚏ Lunch £5-£10 Dinner £13-£20 Last dinner 9.30pm
CONF. Thtr 40 Class 15 Board 20 Del from £58
Credit Cards [1][2][3][5]   £

YARCOMBE Devon Map 03 ST20

★★ 69% *The Belfry Country Hotel*
EX14 9BD (on A30) ☎Upottery(040486) 234 & 588 FAX (040486) 579

This flint and stone building, formerly the village school, is now a small hotel of some character, with warm and welcoming resident owners. The bedrooms are attractive and equipped with modern facilities. There is a cosy lounge and wood-panelled dining room with a well stocked bar and a set menu of home- cooked dishes.
6⇌⋔(1fb)⚑in 2 bedrooms CTV in all bedrooms ® T ✻ sB&B⇌⋔£40-£44 dB&B⇌⋔£60-£64 ♬
10P ✗ nc12yrs *xmas*
♀ English, French & Italian V ♡ ⚏ ⚑ Dinner £12.75-£16.95 Last dinner 8.45pm
Credit Cards [1][3][4]   £

YARMOUTH, GREAT Norfolk Map 05 TG50

★★★ 69% *Cliff*
Gorleston NR31 6DH (2m S A12)
☎Great Yarmouth(0493) 662179 FAX (0493) 653617

Overlooking the harbour, this privately owned hotel has friendly, helpful staff. There is a lounge bar, and a smaller cocktail bar adjacent to the lofty Chandelier Restaurant, offering a choice of 2 fixed price menus and a large carte. Bedrooms have good quality dark furniture and rich fabrics; new rooms include the Versailles Suite, furnished in early 1800s French style. The proprietor also owns a small brewery, producing 3 choices of beer.
39⇌⋔(5fb)1🎌⚑in 2 bedrooms CTV in all bedrooms ® T
ⓒ 70P ❀
V ♡ ⚏ ⚑ Last dinner 9.30pm
Credit Cards [1][2][3][5]

★★★ 66% Carlton
Marine Pde NR30 3JE (opp Wellington Pier)
☎Great Yarmouth(0493) 855234 FAX (0493) 852220
The Carlton offers comfortable public rooms, and modern accommodation that is particularly well equipped. A good range of services – a blend of the formal and informal – are readily provided in a polite and efficient manner, suitable for both the holiday-maker and business guest.
95⇌⋔(10fb)3🎌⚑in 7 bedrooms CTV in all bedrooms ® ✗ T ✻ sB&B⇌⋔£56-£78.50 dB&B⇌⋔£78.50-£150 ♬
Lift ⓒ 22P (£2-£3) 30🚗 (£3) hairdressing salon *xmas*
V ♡ ⚏ ⚑ ✻ Lunch £3.95-£8.95 Dinner £13.95&alc Last dinner 10pm
CONF. Thtr 150 Class 140 Board 85 Del £60
Credit Cards [1][2][3][4][5]

★★★ 62% Imperial
North Dr NR30 1EQ ☎Great Yarmouth(0493) 851113 FAX (0493) 852229

This family owned and run Victorian hotel overlooks the sea on North Beach, the quieter side of the resort. There are comfortable

and tastefully decorated lounge areas, and the Rambouillet restaurant continues to provide reliable food at affordable prices, the fresh fish particularly noteworthy.
39⇌↑(4fb) CTV in all bedrooms ®⚥ T ✱ sB&B⇌↑£52.50 dB&B⇌↑£65 ⊟
Lift ☾ CTV 50P *xmas*
♀ English & French **V** ✿ ⚏ Lunch £11.50&alc Dinner £14.50&alc Last dinner 10pm
Credit Cards ① ② ③ ④ ⑤

★★★ 60% *Dolphin*
Albert Square NR30 3JH ☎Great Yarmouth(0493) 855070 FAX (0493) 853798
Situated to the south of the town, set back from the beach and its pleasure attractions, this is a well kept hotel where a simple style of service is provided by a team of friendly local youngsters. The bedrooms are quite attractively furnished though a few are a little compact.
49⇌↑(3fb) CTV in all bedrooms ® T
☾ CTV 12P 12🛥 ❋ ⚊ (heated) sauna gymnasium whirlpool
♀ English & French **V** ✿ ⚏ Last dinner 9.30pm
Credit Cards ① ② ③ ⑤

★★ 64% *Burlington*
11 North Dr NR30 1EG (Logis)
☎Great Yarmouth(0493) 844568 & 842095 FAX (0493) 331848
Closed Jan-Feb RS Dec
This well established family-run hotel faces the sea at the quieter end of the resort. Public rooms offer traditional comforts and bedrooms are continually undergoing refurbishment; the newer rooms are light and pleasant with coordinated fittings and furnishings.
28rm(26⇌↑)(9fb)⚥in 5 bedrooms CTV in all bedrooms ® T
✻ (ex guide dogs) ❋ sB&B£25-£30 sB&B⇌↑£39-£45 dB&B£40-£50 dB&B⇌↑£50-£60 ⊟

Yarmouth, Great

THE CARLTON HOTEL
GREAT YARMOUTH, NORFOLK

One of East Anglia's premier resort hotels. All bedrooms have full en-suite facilities, many with sea views. Simpsons Restaurant offers the highest standards of food. Privileged access to Marina Leisure Centre.

Well appointed rooms from £56.00 B & B
(low cost all inclusive mini-break tariff also available)

Reservations: 0493 855234

THE CARLTON HOTEL ★★★
Marine Parade, Great Yarmouth, Norfolk

Regency DOLPHIN HOTEL
Enjoyment begins with the right choice

Location
The Dolphin Hotel is situated just off the sea front. Our peaceful location remains within walking distance of Great Yarmouth's many attractions. On-site parking is available.

Accommodation
50 well appointed bedrooms, all en-suite, provide every comfort with colour TV, satellite, radio, direct dial telephones, tea and coffee making facilities. **Children under 12 (sharing parents' room) stay FREE.**

Facilities
Our Restaurant is open for lunch and dinner, along with the lounge bar. The Garden Room can accommodate up to 120 persons and is available for conferences and private functions.

Leisure & Health Club
Includes gym, sauna and whirlpool bath. Heated outdoor pool & patio area (open in Summer).

For Reservations
Call: (0493) 855070 or Fax: (0493) 853798

Regency DOLPHIN HOTEL
Albert Square
Great Yarmouth NR30 3JH

Yarmouth, Great - York

Lift CTV 40P ⌂ (heated) sauna solarium gymnasium jacuzzi turkish steam room *xmas*
☗ English & French V ✧ ⚘ ⊁ ✳ Lunch fr£7.50 Dinner fr£12.50 Last dinner 8pm
Credit Cards [1] [2] [3] [5]

★★ 64% Regency
5 North Dr NR30 1ED ☏Great Yarmouth(0493) 843759 FAX (0493) 330411

Overlooking the seafront and tennis courts at the quieter end of the resort, this friendly family-run hotel offers warm hospitality and is popular with both business and leisure guests. Modestly furnished compact bedrooms are very well maintained and have modern facilities.
13⇨♠(1fb) CTV in all bedrooms ® T ✖ ✳ sB&B⇨♠fr£25 dB&B⇨♠£50-£56 ⛃
CTV 10P ⚘ nc 7yrs *xmas*
V ⊁ ✳ Lunch £10.50 Dinner £10.50 Last dinner 8.30pm £
Credit Cards [1] [2] [3] [5]

YATTENDON Berkshire Map 04 SU57

★★ ❀❀❀73% Royal Oak
The Square RG16 0UF ☏Hermitage(0635) 201325 FAX (0635) 201926
Closed 25 Dec

The epitome of the English country inn, this 17th-century wisteria clad hostelry offers accommodation of character matched by relaxed and attentive service under the direction of owner Julie Huff. Bedrooms are due to be refurbished and should be completed by publication of this guide. Food is very much at the heart of the hotel, and meals are taken in the tiny restaurant or in the livelier bar. Talented new chef Paul Collins is providing meals of an increasingly high standard and an agreeable lightness. Our inspector enjoyed plump roasted scallops on a bed of provencale vegetables, followed by tender best end of lamb with a delicate garlic sauce, accompanied by good noodles and crisp vegetables.
5rm(3⇨) CTV in all bedrooms T
40P ⚘ ❀
☗ English & French V ✧ ⚘ Last dinner 10pm
Credit Cards [1] [2] [3] [4] [5]

YELVERTON Devon Map 02 SX56

★★★ 69% Moorland Links
PL20 6DA (on A386) (Forestdale) ☏(0822) 852245 FAX (0822) 855004
Closed 24 Dec-1 Jan

Set in 9 acres of well tended gardens with far-reaching views over the Tamar Valley, this 1930s hotel is just a short drive from the centre of Plymouth. Bedrooms are stylish and include equipment such as trouser presses and hairdryers. In the restaurant imaginative choices are offered on table d'hôte and à la carte menus.
30⇨♠ in 6 bedrooms CTV in all bedrooms ® T sB&B⇨♠£59.95 dB&B⇨♠£65.90-£79.90 ⛃
《 120P ❀ ♪ (hard)
☗ English & French V ✧ ⚘ ⊁ ✳ Lunch £10.75-£16.75&alc Dinner fr£16.75&alc Last dinner 10pm
CONF. Thtr 170 Class 80 Board 40 Del from £65
Credit Cards [1] [2] [3] [5] £

YEOVIL Somerset Map 03 ST51
See also **Martock**

★★★67% Yeovil Court
West Coker Rd BA20 2NE (2.5m W on A30)
☏(0935) 863746 FAX (0935) 863990

There is a relaxed and cheerful atmosphere at this smart modern hotel on the western fringes of the town. Bedrooms are attractively decorated and furnished, and there are 4 larger rooms with whirlpool baths. Public areas are bright and comfortable, and the

restaurant features some very capable cooking from chef Howard Mosely.
15⇨♠Annexe3⇨♠(4fb) CTV in all bedrooms ® T ✳ sB&B⇨♠£49-£59 dB&B⇨♠£59-£69 ⛃
75P ❀ *xmas*
☗ English & French V ✧ ⚘ ✳ Lunch £4.95-£22alc Dinner £11-£22alc Last dinner 10pm
Credit Cards [1] [2] [3] [5]

★★★ 64% The Manor
Hendford BA20 1TG ☏(0935) 23116 FAX (0935) 706607

A town-centre hotel, parts of which date back to the 17th century. The Eliot Restaurant supplements imaginative table d'hôte menus with a short carte, bedrooms in a variety of styles and sizes are all well equipped, and staff are friendly and obliging.
20⇨♠Annexe21⇨♠(2fb)1 ♿ ⊁ in 12 bedrooms CTV in all bedrooms ® T ✳ sB&B⇨♠£70 dB&B⇨♠£80-£95 (room only) ⛃
《 41P *xmas*
V ✧ ⚘ ✳ Lunch £9.95 Dinner £16.95 Last dinner 10pm
Credit Cards [1] [2] [3] [5]

★ ❀❀80% Little Barwick House
Barwick Village BA22 9TD (2m S) (Logis) ☏(0935) 23902 FAX (0935) 20908
Closed 4-24 Jan

This listed Georgian property, in pretty gardens and with lovely country views, is a haven of peace and relaxation. Christopher Colley looks after guests front of house, while his wife Veronica is the talented chef, producing an appealing menu with a long list of supplementary dishes, with extensive use of local produce. Our inspector's meal began with locally caught trout in a delicious marinade, quickly grilled and served with a refreshing cucumber and creamy yoghurt sauce. West Bay sole, stuffed with leeks and tarragon on a creamy Noilly Prat sauce, was excellent.
6⇨♠ CTV in all bedrooms ® T ✳ sB&B⇨♠£46 dB&B⇨♠£72 ⛃
P ⚘ ❀
☗ English & French V ⊁ ✳ Dinner £20.90-£22.90 Last dinner 9pm
Credit Cards [1] [2] [3] £

★ 61% Preston
64 Preston Rd BA20 2DL ☏(0935) 74400 FAX (0935) 410142

This small, informally run hotel has a warm, friendly atmosphere much appreciated by the regular business guests. Bedrooms vary from spacious modern annexe rooms to smaller, cosier rooms in the main house. A bistro-style dining room serves simple grill dishes.
7rm(2⇨3♠)Annexe8⇨♠(2fb) CTV in all bedrooms ® T 19P
☗ English & French V ✧ ⚘ ⊁ Last dinner 9pm
Credit Cards [1] [2] [3] [5]

YORK North Yorkshire Map 08 SE65
See also **Escrick** & **Pocklington**

★★★★ 64% Swallow
Tadcaster Rd YO2 2QQ (W on A1036)
☏(0904) 701000 FAX (0904) 702308

Once known as the Chase Hotel and identified by a large saddle, mounted, at the front, this spacious hotel overlooks the famous race course. It has 2 dining rooms, a well proportioned leisure club, conference and banqueting rooms and a self contained, purpose built management training centre. Bedrooms are mostly spacious and comfortable and several have views over the race course.
113⇨♠(14fb)⊁in 40 bedrooms CTV in all bedrooms ® ⚯ T ✳ sB&B⇨♠£85 dB&B⇨♠£105 ⛃
Lift 《 200P ❀ ⌂ (heated) sauna solarium gymnasium putting green golf practise net croquet *xmas*

♡ English & French V ⊕ ⌂ ⊁ ✳ Lunch £11-£12.75&alc High tea £2.75-£9alc Dinner £17.95&alc Last dinner 10pm
CONF. Thtr 200 Class 150 Board 400 Del from £85
Credit Cards [1] [2] [3] [5]   (£)

★★★★ 59% *Royal York*
Station Rd YO2 2AA (Principal) ☎(0904) 653681 FAX (0904) 623503
This grand old hotel, still known locally as the Station Hotel, has good views across the rose gardens towards the minster. Bedrooms are mostly spacious with bold colour schemes and rich fabrics. The sweeping staircase is a focal point of the main bar and lounge area, and a traditional restaurant provides friendly service and sound Yorkshire fare. Staff are friendly and courteous.
123⇌ ⋔(4fb) CTV in all bedrooms ® ⚥ T
Lift ⦅ 150P 🎱 ✿ snooker ♫ ♒
V ⊕ ⌂ ⊁ Last dinner 9.45pm
Credit Cards [1] [2] [3] [4] [5]

All black star hotels are given a percentage grading within their star bands. See 'Using the Guide' at the front of the book for full details.

THE
ROYAL YORK
HOTEL
YORK
★★★★
Station Road, York, YO2 2AA
Tel: 0904 653681 Fax: 0904 623503

Reminiscent of an age of past elegance, this magnificent recently refurbished Victorian Hotel with a unique atmosphere of romantic splendour is set within its own delightful private grounds overlooking the City walls.

Bygone Breakaways - Enjoy a luxury break inclusive of dinner, bed and full English breakfast and free admission to many of York's historic attractions. From £48.00 per person per night.

Conferences and Meetings - Superb range of period conference rooms available. A Guest Liaison Manager is on hand to assist conference organisers.

There is a large car park within the hotel grounds and the main line railway station is close by.

YEOVIL *Court*
H·O·T·E·L
& Restaurant

★★★ ⊛

West Coker Road, Yeovil, Somerset BA20 2NE
Telephone: (093586) 3746
Fax: (093586) 3990

18 rooms, 4 luxury suites.
All rooms superbly furnished.
En suite, colour remote TV, direct dial telephone, tea/coffee facilities.
Ample car parking.

The restaurant is featured in "Which" Good Food Guide

Try our West Country Weekend Breaks.
Situated 2½ miles west of Yeovil.

Overcombe Hotel
HORRABRIDGE Nr. YELVERTON

Visiting, walking, touring? – Your holiday centre. A small country hotel on the edge of Dartmoor, between Plymouth and Tavistock. Licensed. Downstairs rooms, 1 suitable for wheelchairs available. Dogs welcome. Special walking weekends in Spring and Autumn.

Ashley Courtenay recommended.   **AA★★**
Tel: Yelverton (0822) 853501

York

★★★★ 55% **Viking**
North St YO1 1JF ☎(0904) 659822 FAX (0904) 641793

This modern high rise hotel is situated on the banks of the River Ouse, just a short walk from the city centre. Bedrooms are of various sizes and shapes, the best overlooking the river. This is a popular conference venue, and the hotel is also popular with coach parties.
188⇌↑(7fb)⊁in 114 bedrooms CTV in all bedrooms ® ⚏ T ✻ (ex guide dogs) sB&B⇌↑£92.50-£106 dB&B⇌↑£112.50-£126 ♬
Lift (15P 70🚗 (£5 per night) sauna solarium gymnasium spa bath golf driving range ♪ xmas
♡ International V ♡ ♨ ⅍ Lunch £9.50-£10.50 Dinner £14-£15&alc Last dinner 9.45pm
CONF. Thtr 300 Class 150 Board 60 Del from £110
Credit Cards 1 2 3 5 £

★★★ ✿✿✿ BILBROUGH MANOR COUNTRY HOUSE
YO2 3PH ☎Tadcaster(0937) 834002 FAX (0937) 834724
(For full entry see Bilbrough)

★★★ ✿ **THE GRANGE**
Clifton YO3 6AA (on A19)
☎(0904) 644744 FAX (0904) 612453

Within a few minutes walk of the minster, the Grange is a Regency-style house which opened as a hotel in 1990. Careful restoration and the choice of fabrics and furnishings has produced a delightful hotel supported by a dedicated team of staff. The tastefully decorated bedrooms are comfortable and well equipped with mini bars, hairdryers and books. There is a sumptuous lounge with a log fire and guests can dine in the elegant restaurant with its superb collection of racehourse and birds of prey prictures, or the basement brasserie with its arched brick ceiling. Food in the restaurant is notable, from both à la carte and table d'hôte menus.
29⇌↑2⚏ CTV in all bedrooms⊁ T sB&B⇌↑£85 dB&B⇌↑£98-£135 ♬
(26P ♪ xmas
♡ English & French V ♡ ♨ ⅍ ✻ Lunch £12.50-£15 Dinner £19&alc Last dinner 10pm
CONF. Thtr 45 Class 20 Board 25 Del £120
Credit Cards 1 2 3 5 £

★★★ ✿✿
MIDDLETHORPE HALL
Bishopthorpe Rd YO2 1QB
(1.5m SW) ☎(0904) 641241
FAX (0904) 620176

This magnificent William III country house, in beautiful parkland, has been carefully restored to become a comfortable hotel. Guests can really relax in the sumptuous drawing room with its deep armchairs and settees, living fire and beautiful oil paintings. Bedrooms vary in size, some being vary spacious. but all have quality décor and several antique pieces. The panelled dining rooms, looking out onto the gardens, are the perfect setting for the imaginative and well produced food at both lunch and dinner. Table d'hôte as well as a carte are available, including such delights as steamed mussels served with herb risotto; roast breast of guinea fowl with a light citrus sauce, or saddle or rabbit on a port wine sauce with mulled pears. Puddings are quite exquisite, and there is an extensive wine list.
30⇌↑1⚏ CTV in all bedrooms® T ✻ ✻ sB⇌↑£83-£99 dB⇌↑£115-£189 (room only) ♬
Lift (70P ✿ croquet nc8yrs xmas
V ♡ ♨ ⅍ ✻ Lunch £14.90-£16.90 Dinner £26.95-£29.95&alc Last dinner 9.45pm
CONF. Thtr 68 Class 30 Board 30 Del from £125
Credit Cards 1 2 3 5

★★★ 70% **Dean Court**
Duncombe Place YO1 2EF ☎(0904) 625082 FAX (0904) 620305

This comfortable hotel almost opposite the Minster was converted from houses built for the clergy in 1850. It has recently been totally refurbished, providing modern bedrooms with all the latest facilities while retaining its Victorian character. Considerate staff provide willing service, including valet parking.
40⇌↑(2fb) CTV in all bedrooms ® T ✻ sB&B⇌↑£65-£75 dB&B⇌↑£100-£120 ♬
Lift (25P xmas
♡ English & French V ♡ ♨ ✻ Lunch £8.95-£11.20 Dinner £16.25-£18 Last dinner 9.30pm
CONF. Thtr 40 Class 25 Board 30 Del from £80
Credit Cards 1 2 3 4 5 £

★★★ ✿70% **Mount Royale**
The Mount YO2 2DA (S on A1036, towards racecourse)
☎(0904) 628856 FAX (0904) 611171
Closed 24-31 Dec
Richard and Christine Oxtoby established this hotel, converted from 2 Georgian houses, in 1965, and their collection of paintings, antiques and objets d'art gives it character. Most bedrooms are spacious, particularly the Garden Rooms which open on to the English garden, and many have their own dressing rooms. In the restaurant chef Karen Brotherson's cooking is mostly British, with a fixed price menu and daily specialities at a supplement.
23⇌↑(2fb)3⚏ CTV in all bedrooms ® ⚏ T ✻ sB&B⇌↑£65-£90 dB&B⇌↑£75-£110 ♬
(CTV 18P ✿ ☂ (heated) snooker sauna solarium gymnasium ♪
♡ International V ♡ Dinner £25-£95 Last dinner 9.30pm
Credit Cards 1 2 3 5

★★★ ✿68% **Ambassador**
125 The Mount YO2 2DA ☎(0904) 641316 FAX (0904) 640259

This small but elegant hotel, with a beautiful garden, was built in the early 19th century as a merchant's residence, and much of its original character has been preserved. Bedrooms are furnished in both modern and antique styles. The cuisine for the short, good value table d'hôte menu in the Washington Restaurant is of a high standard.
24⇌↑(2fb) CTV in all bedrooms ® ⚏ T ✻ (ex guide dogs) sB&B⇌↑£79-£89 dB&B⇌↑£95-£105 ♬
Lift ▦ 35P 🚗 ♪ xmas

York

V ♥ ♨ ⚥ ✷ Lunch £12.50-£14.50 Dinner £15-£17.50&alc Last dinner 10pm
CONF. Thtr 60 Class 30 Board 30 Del from £75
Credit Cards [1][3] £

★★★ ●68% York Pavilion
45 Main St, Fulford YO1 4PJ (on A19, opposite garage on Fulford main st)
☎(0904) 622099 FAX (0904) 626939

This elegant Georgian house with a warm and relaxing atmosphere, is set in walled grounds and gardens. It is not large, but has the style of a country house, with its deep armchairs and open fire. Bedrooms in the main house are traditional in style, many with antique furniture, while those in the converted stable block are more modern. A varied choice of dishes in the restaurant might include delicious braised pheasant or beautifully poached salmon in white wine and chervil butter sauce.
11⇌♠Annexe10⇌♠(3fb)1⚐ CTV in all bedrooms ® T ✷ sB&B⇌♠£55-£75 dB&B⇌♠£95-£117 ₽
(55P
V ♥ ♨ ⚥ ✷ Lunch £8.95-£10.95&alc Dinner £9.95-£16.95&alc Last dinner 9.30pm
CONF. Thtr 150 Class 70 Board 50 Del £95
Credit Cards [1][2][3][5] £

★★★ 64% Kexby Bridge
Hull Rd, Kexby YO4 5LD ☎Pocklington(0759) 388223 & 388154 FAX (0759) 388822

This modern hotel is set in 8 acres of grounds and gardens with a nature reserve to the rear. Bedrooms are similarly designed with much use of attractive white rattan-style furniture, also evident in the public areas.
32⇌♠⚥in 8 bedrooms CTV in all bedrooms ® T ✖ (ex guide dogs) ✷ sB&B⇌♠£50 dB&B⇌♠£75 ₽
CTV 60P ✿ ♪ ♫ xmas
♡ English & French V ♥ ♨ ⚥ ✷ Lunch £4.95-£17 Dinner £17 Last dinner 9.30pm
Credit Cards [1][3]

★★★ 63% Novotel
Fishergate YO1 4AD (S off A19)
☎(0904) 611660 FAX (0904) 610925   **novotel**

This impressive modern building is on the banks of the River Foss close to where it merges with the River Ouse. Bedrooms are practical and include communicating family rooms and 4 rooms for the disabled. The restaurant has recently been extended, and is spacious, light and airy and looks out onto a large sun terrace.
124⇌♠(124fb)⚥in 31 bedrooms CTV in all bedrooms ® ❦ T sB⇌♠fr£57.50 dB⇌♠fr£69.50 (room only) ₽
Lift (150P ▣ (heated) ⚭ xmas
♡ English & French V ♥ ♨ ⚥ Lunch £6-£15alc Dinner £7-£15alc Last dinner mdnt
CONF. Thtr 200 Class 150 Board 100 Del from £84
Credit Cards [1][2][3][5] £

★★★ 62% Monkbar
Monkbar YO3 7PF ☎(0904) 638086 FAX (0904) 629195   **CONSORT HOTELS**

Modern, well furnished bedrooms are a feature of this hotel, which is just outside Monk Bar and a short walk from the famous Shambles. Public areas are compact but functional, and the hotel's own 'Monk Bar' and Cloisters Restaurant are popular.
47⇌♠(3fb)4⚐ CTV in all bedrooms ® T ✷ sB&B⇌♠£65-£75 dB&B⇌♠£85-£95 ₽
Lift (50P xmas
V ♥ ♨ ⚥ ✷ Lunch £15-£22alc Dinner £14.95 Last dinner 10pm
Credit Cards [1][2][3][5] £

The Parsonage Country House Hotel
Escrick, York YO4 6LF
Tel: 0904 728111 Fax: 0904 728151

A delightful country house hotel set in six acres of grounds just 5 miles from the centre of York. The hotel provides an oasis of comfort and tranquillity with the opportunity to be transported back to the days of elegance, tradition and lavish hospitality. An ideal base for touring the Yorkshire Dales and coastline. Enjoy the excellent Anglo French cuisine and fine wines from our extensive wine cellar in the candlelit restaurant also open to non residents. The superb banqueting suite for up to 150 guests is ideal for conferences, private functions, dinner dances and weddings. To save the trauma of parking in the city the hotel operates a courtesy car.

Dean Court Hotel

Superbly situated in the shadow of the magnificent York Minster, the Dean Court Hotel has an unrivalled position in the heart of York. We pride ourselves on our high standard of service and you will be assured of a very warm Yorkshire welcome. Dine in our elegant restaurant which has a reputation for its excellent cuisine and comprehensive wine list. Secure car park.

YORK

Duncombe Place, York YO1 2EF
Tel (0904) 625082   Fax (0904) 620305
AA ★★★

York

★★★ 58% Abbey Park Resort
The Mount YO2 2BN ☎(0904) 658301 FAX (0904) 621224

Recent refurbishment of public rooms has enhanced this tourist and business hotel, just a short walk from Micklegate. Bedrooms are modern and well equipped, but some are still to be refurbished.
85rm(5fb) in 11 bedrooms CTV in all bedrooms ® ✲ T ✱ sB&B £36-£65 dB&B £72-£75 🅿
Lift (30P *xmas*
V ☉ ☑ ✱ Bar Lunch £1.60-£4.80alc Dinner £12.50&alc Last dinner 9.30pm
Credit Cards [1][2][3][5]

★★ 73% Kilima
129 Holgate Rd YO2 4DE (on A59, on W outskirts) ☎(0904) 658844 & 625787 FAX (0904) 612083

This one-time Victorian parsonage offers very comfortable accommodation, and all bedrooms have every modern convenience. Two rooms on the ground floor are equipped for disabled guests. This is a very friendly and hospitable hotel, tastefully decorated throughout in sympathy with its Victorian architecture. There is a delightful candlelit restaurant, extending from a charming vaulted cellar bar. Excellent à la carte and fixed price menus are offered; there is an extensive wine list.
15rm(1fb)3🛏 CTV in all bedrooms ® T ✱ sB&B fr£45 dB&B £71-£81 🅿
20P *xmas*
☉ English & French V ☉ ☑ ✲ ✱ Lunch £9.25-£11.50&alc Dinner fr£17.95&alc Last dinner 9.30pm
Credit Cards [1][2][3][5] £

★★ 70% Heworth Court
76-78 Heworth Green YO3 7TQ ☎(0904) 425156 FAX (0904) 415290

Near the eastern city walls, this friendly family-run hotel has well equipped bedrooms that are either in the main house or two annexes, several of them overlooking an attractive courtyard. Public areas include a cosy lounge and popular restaurant, plus some small meeting rooms.
15rm Annexe10rm(7fb) in 1 bedroom CTV in all bedrooms ® T ✱ sB&B £35.27-£41.50 dB&B £36-£72 🅿
CTV 27P 1🏠 *xmas*
☉ English & Continental V ☉ ☑ ✲ Lunch £8.50-£16&alc High tea £1.10 Dinner £9.50-£16&alc Last dinner 9.30pm
CONF. Board 16 Del from £70
Credit Cards [1][2][3][5] £

★★ 69% Beechwood Close
19 Shipton Rd, Clifton YO3 6RE ☎(0904) 658378 FAX (0904) 647124
Closed 25 Dec

This family-run hotel has extremely well furnished bedrooms. The spacious dining room, offering a wide ranging menu, overlooks a secluded garden at the rear, and there is a comfortable cocktail bar.
14rm(2fb) CTV in all bedrooms ® T ✱ sB&B £39.50-£45 dB&B £62.50-£65 🅿
CTV 36P
V ☉ Lunch £7-£7.70 High tea £6-£7.50 Dinner £13.50-£14.50 Last dinner 9pm
Credit Cards [1][2][3][5] £

★★ 66% Disraelis
140 Acomb Rd YO2 4HA ☎(0904) 781181 FAX (0904) 788044
Closed 25 Dec-1 Jan

This friendly, privately owned hotel stands in its own grounds within easy reach of the city centre and northern bypass. It provides a good standard of accommodation for both business and leisure guests. The elegant restaurant offers both à la carte and table d'hôte menus, and in the evening guests can also eat in the comfortable bar lounge.
12rm(8rm)(4fb) CTV in all bedrooms ® T ✱ (ex guide dogs)

CTV 40P ✲ ✲ 🛎
☉ Cosmopolitan V ☉ ☑ Last dinner 9.30pm
Credit Cards [1][2][3]

★★ 65% Hudsons
60 Bootham YO3 7BZ (situated on the A19 which runs from the north of the city into city centre, just after Bootham Park and before city walls) ☎(0904) 621267 FAX (0904) 654719

Only a few minutes walk from the Minster, this friendly hotel is converted from 2 Victorian houses with a modern rear extension containing comfortable, thoughtfully designed bedrooms; rooms in the main house are lofty and spacious, many with antique furnishings. Meals are available in the elegant Victorian restaurant or the bistro and bar.
30rm(3fb)1🛏 CTV in all bedrooms ® ✲ T ✱ (ex guide dogs) ✲ sB&B £45-£55 dB&B £69-£79 🅿
Lift 34P *xmas*
☉ English & French V ☉ ☑ ✱ Bar Lunch fr£2 Dinner £10-£16 Last dinner 9.30pm
CONF. Thtr 80 Class 40 Board 30 Del from £69.95
Credit Cards [1][2][3][5]

★★ 65% Knavesmire Manor
302 Tadcaster Rd YO2 2HE (follow signs for York (West) A1036) (Logis) ☎(0904) 702941 FAX (0904) 709274

This personally run hotel, converted from a late Georgian house overlooking the racecourse, has attractive public rooms, including an oak-panelled bar, elegant restaurant and comfortable lounge. Bedrooms vary from the compact to the spacious, with some motel-style rooms in the garden.
12rm Annexe9rm(2fb)1🛏 CTV in all bedrooms ® ✲ T sB&B £39.50-£55 dB&B £59-£75 🅿
Lift 26P 1🏠 ⛱ (heated) sauna *xmas*
☉ English & Continental V ☉ ☑ Dinner £13.75-£16&alc Last dinner 9pm
CONF. Thtr 40 Class 50 Board 30 Del from £49
Credit Cards [1][2][3][5] £

★★ 65% Town House
98-104 Holgate Rd YO2 4BB (on A59) ☎(0904) 636171 FAX (0904) 623044

Closed 24-31 Dec

Being a discreet conversion of several terraced houses, with car park and reception to the rear, the size of this hotel is not immediately obvious. There is a cosy bar and elegant lounge as well as a dining room, where an interesting range of dishes is served. The city centre is within walking distance.
23rm(21rm)(3fb) CTV in all bedrooms ® T ✱
25P 🛎
☉ European V ☉ ☑ ✱ Bar Lunch £2.50-£5alc High tea £2.50-£6alc Dinner £12&alc Last dinner 9.15pm
CONF. Class 25 Del from £55
Credit Cards [1][3]

★★ 64% Cottage
3 Clifton Green YO3 6LH (N off A19) ☎(0904) 643711 FAX (0904) 611630
Closed 24-26 Dec

Charming public areas with old beams and exposed brickwork are a feature of this compact, family-run hotel, with a bar lounge which is only open to residents and diners. In contrast the bedrooms are bright and modern, varying greatly in size, the larger rooms being in a rear extension with separate access.
16rm Annexe4rm(3fb) CTV in all bedrooms ® ✲ T ✲ (ex guide dogs) ✱ sB&B £25-£40 dB&B £45-£60 🅿 12P
V ☉ Last dinner 8.30pm
Credit Cards [1][2][3][5]

Hotels with red star ratings are especially high quality.

ETB ✿ ★★ 👑👑👑👑

The place to stay in town. An attractively refurbished Victorian Hotel close to York City Centre and Racecourse, ideally situated for business or leisure.

- Renowned restaurant 'The Grapevine'.
- Relaxing bar, lounge and conservatory.
- Large private car park.

**The Town House Hotel, Holgate Road,
YORK YO2 4BB.**
*Reservations Tel 0904 636171
Fax 0904 623044*

★★ HEWORTH COURT HOTEL

Lamp Light RESTAURANT

**76 HEWORTH GREEN
YORK YO3 7TQ
Telephone: 0904 425156 or 425157**

Excellent family run hotel with easy access, guaranteed private car parking and friendly staff. Short walk from York Minster.

4 crown commended, cosy lounge bar and restaurant with excellent menus and an extensive wine list featuring some superb wines. All bedrooms are en-suite with colour T.V., direct telephone & tea/coffee makers

"Pink Elephant Breaks" for stays of two days or longer, Christmas & New Year breaks, and special low-season rates of UP TO 50% OFF!

Telephone for a free brochure and reservations.

Cottage Hotel ★★

**3 Clifton Green, York YO3 6LH.
Tel: (0904) 643711   Fax: (0904) 611230**

Overlooking the Village Green of Clifton, a 10 minute walk will take you to the historic core of this vibrant city. Careful attention has been taken to cater for individual needs, and the comfortable but stylish bedrooms boast en-suite facilities.

Hudson's HOTEL

★★

**60 BOOTHAM YORK YO3 7BZ
Tel: (0904) 621267 Fax: (0904) 654719**

Only two minutes from
York Minster.
Victorian styled Restaurant and Bar
Car Park.
Credit cards & cheques welcome.
"LET'S GO" Winter rates
available.

York

★★ 63% Clifton Bridge
Water End, Clifton YO3 6LL (NW side of city between A19 & A59) ☎(0904) 610510 FAX (0904) 640208
Closed 24-31 Dec

Standing opposite Homestead Park in a residential area on the north side of the city, this is a neat, compact hotel. Modern bedrooms with fitted furniture have every facility, while public areas include a cosy, oak-panelled residents' lounge with adjoining bar and a well appointed dining room.

14⇨♠(1fb) CTV in all bedrooms ® T ✱ sB&B⇨♠£35-£43 dB&B⇨♠£45-£60 🅿
12P 2🚗 ⚡

♀ English & French V ♀ ♨ ✂ ✱ Dinner £7.50-£9.50&alc
Last dinner 8pm
Credit Cards 1 2 3 £

★★ 63% Savages
15 St Peters Grove YO3 6AQ (off A19 at Clifton) ☎(0904) 610818 FAX (0904) 627123
Closed 25 Dec

This Victorian house is situated in a cul-de-sac of similar properties, within walking distance of the city centre. Bedrooms have every modern facility, and though variable in shape and size, are tastefully furnished and decorated. The lounge bar is particularly comfortable with deep sofas and armchairs, and the dining room, where English cuisine is served, has an intimate atmosphere.

20rm(19⇨♠)(3fb)1🛏 CTV in all bedrooms ® T ✂ (ex guide dogs) sB&B£20-£26 sB&B⇨♠£30-£40 dB&B⇨♠£50-£68 🅿
CTV 16P

V ♀ ♨ ✂ Dinner £11.50-£13 Last dinner 9pm
CONF. Thtr 30 Board 25 Del from £49
Credit Cards 1 2 3 5 £

★★ 62% Ashcroft
294 Bishopthorpe Rd YO2 1LH (turn off A64 on to A1036 and follow signs to Bishopthorpe, turn left in village and take road to York, hotel is 1.5m on right) ☎(0904) 659286 FAX (0904) 640107
Closed Xmas & New Year

Originally a Victorian residence, this hotel stand in 2.5 acres of grounds close to the racecourse. Personally supervised by the manager, it offers particularly well equipped accommodation, several rooms also enjoying views across the gardens towards the River Ouse.

11⇨♠Annexe4⇨♠(3fb) CTV in all bedrooms ® T ✱ sB&B⇨♠fr£40.50 dB&B⇨♠fr£68 🅿
CTV 40P ✿

V ♀ ✂ Dinner fr£11&alc Last dinner 8pm
CONF. Thtr 60 Class 25 Board 30 Del from £56
Credit Cards 1 2 3 5 £

★★ 62% Elliotts
Sycamore Place, Bootham YO3 7DW ☎(0904) 623333
Closed 25 Dec-9 Jan

Elliotts Hotel comprises 2 converted Victorian houses, decorated in a heavy Victorian style, and is in the popular Bootham area, within walking distance of the city. The spacious dining room offers a wide variety of dishes from table d'hôte and à la carte menus.

18⇨♠(1fb)1🛏 CTV in all bedrooms ® T
10P
V ♀ ♨ Last dinner 9.30pm
Credit Cards 1 3 4 5

★★ 62% Fairmount
230 Tadcaster Rd, Mount Vale YO2 2ES (overlooking golf course) ☎(0904) 638298 FAX (0904) 627626

This elegant Victorian villa is a friendly, privately owned hotel with good sized bedrooms on the ground and first floors, and slightly smaller rooms on the 2nd floor; all have modern facilities. There is a traditional lounge, a cosy bar and an attractive restaurant overlooking the racecourse.

12rm(10⇨♠)(4fb) CTV in all bedrooms ®
10P
♀ International V ♀ ♨ ✂ Last dinner 9pm
Credit Cards 1 3

★★ 62% Holgate Bridge
106-108 Holgate Rd YO2 4BB (on A59 Harrogate road) ☎(0904) 635971 FAX (0904) 670049
Closed 24-26 Dec

This conversion of 2 terraced town houses retains the appearance of private residences, the main entrance and reception being at the rear off the car park. Catering solely for residents, it has a cosy bar and dining room serving good value meals. Bedrooms vary in size, but all are well equipped. Staff are attentive and smart.

14rm(11⇨♠)(4fb)1🛏 CTV in all bedrooms ® T sB&Bfr£22 sB&B⇨♠£36 dB&Bfr£35 dB&B⇨♠£55 🅿
14P
V Bar Lunch £3-£10alc Dinner fr£10.75&alc
Last dinner 9pm
Credit Cards 1 2 3 £

★★ 62% Lady Anne Middletons Hotel
Skeldergate YO1 1DS ☎(0904) 632257 & 630456 FAX (0904) 613043
Closed 24-27 Dec

This charming hotel close to the south bank of the River Ouse is formed from several historic houses which have been linked, extended and modernised to provide spacious conservatory lounges and dining areas. Bedrooms vary in size but all have modern facilities.

40⇨♠Annexe15⇨♠(3fb)3🛏 CTV in all bedrooms ® T ✂ (ex guide dogs) ✱ sB&B⇨♠£58 dB&B⇨♠£70 🅿
(CTV 56P ✿ 🏊 (heated) sauna solarium gymnasium health & fitness centre
V ♀ ♨ ✂ Lunch fr£5 High tea fr£5 Dinner fr£13.95 Last dinner 9pm
CONF. Thtr 60 Class 20 Board 30 Del £100
Credit Cards 1 2 3

★★ 61% Alhambra Court
31 St Mary's, Bootham YO3 7DD (off Bootham A19) ☎(0904) 628474

Comfortable lounges are a feature of this late Georgian building, and its bedrooms all have modern facilities.

25⇨♠(5fb)1🛏 CTV in all bedrooms ® T ✱ sB&B⇨♠£31.50-£36.50 dB&B⇨♠£49.50-£56 🅿
Lift CTV 25P xmas
♀ English & French Dinner fr£10.50 Last dinner 9pm
Credit Cards 1 3

★★ 60% Newington
147 Mount Vale YO2 2DJ (W on A1036) ☎(0904) 625173 FAX (0904) 679631

The Newington stands at the end of the famous race course, which is also visible from some of the bedrooms. These are modern and well fitted but tend to be small. Public areas include a recently refurbished lounge, there is also a cosy cocktail bar and a sizeable restaurant.

25⇨♠Annexe15⇨♠(3fb)2🛏 CTV in all bedrooms ® T ✂ ✱ sB&B⇨♠£36-£42 dB&B⇨♠£50-£56 🅿
Lift 40P 🏊 (heated) sauna solarium xmas
V ♀ ✱ Sunday Lunch £7.50-£8.95 Dinner £13.25-£15.75 Last dinner 9pm
Credit Cards 1 2 3 £

★★ 59% Abbots' Mews
6 Marygate Ln, Bootham YO3 7DE ☎(0904) 634866 FAX (0904) 612848

In a quiet location just a few minutes' walk from the city centre, this is a former Victorian coachman's cottage. Bedrooms are either in the main building or in cottages and houses adjacent, but all are

676

similarly equipped. There is a small garden, floodlit at night, in the centre of the hotel.
12↑Annexe41⇨↑(9fb) CTV in all bedrooms ® T ✕ ✱
sB&B⇨↑£30-£35 dB&B⇨↑£50-£60 ₽
30P xmas
♀ International V ✿ ⚏ ✱ Lunch £7.95-£10.50 Dinner fr£14.50&alc Last dinner 9.30pm
CONF. Thtr 50 Class 40 Board 35 Del from £68
Credit Cards [1][2][3][5]

See advertisement on page 678

Forte Posthouse
Tadcaster Rd YO2 2QF (W on A1036)
☎(0904) 707921 FAX (0904) 702804

FORTE Posthouse

Suitable for both the business and leisure traveller, this bright hotel provides modern accommodation in well equipped bedrooms with en suite bathrooms. For more details about Forte Posthouse hotels, consult the Contents page, under Hotel Groups.
139⇨↑✱ B⇨↑£41.50-£53.50 (room only)
CONF. Thtr 40 Class 30 Board 40 Del from £79.50

HOLGATE BRIDGE HOTEL

Friendly family run hotel close to the city centre offering single, double and family accommodation.
All rooms have colour T.V., teamaker, radio & telephone. Most en-suite. Full English breakfast and excellent evening meals are offered. Special Breaks always available. Private car park.
Residential licence.
Write or phone for brochure
HOLGATE BRIDGE HOTEL
106-108 Holgate Road · York · Telephone (0904) 635971
Guests (0904) 647288   Fax: (0904) 670049

AA
★★

The Alhambra Court Hotel ★★

31 St. Mary's, York YO3 7DD
Telephone: York (0904) 628474
Proprietors: Mr & Mrs L. S. Secchi

Situated in one of the most popular locations. A Georgian town residence in a quiet cul-de-sac near the city centre. 25 bedrooms all with en suite bathroom, colour TV, tea/coffee making tray, direct dial telephone, radio and baby listening. One with four poster bed. Lift. Bar & restaurant. Private car park. Winter & summer breaks available. Open to non residents.

YORK AA ★★
THE HOTEL FAIRMOUNT

The Hotel Fairmount,
230 Tadcaster Road,
York YO2 2ES.
Tel: York (0904) 638298.

A warm welcome awaits you at the Hotel Fairmount. In an unrivalled position overlooking York racecourse we provide an ideal base for you to discover the historical splendours of ancient York. Imaginative and tempting four course dinner menu, with an affordable selection of wines. A varied choice of breakfasts for everyone's taste. Most rooms have en-suite facilities with colour TV. And for guests in need of a night cap you'll find refreshments on hand in our licensed cocktail bar. We combine good food, comfortable accommodation and excellent company to make your stay a memorable one. Send for full details and tariff Ground Floor facilities for the disabled now available.

Member of the Yorkshire and Humberside Tourist Board registered with the English Tourist Board.

·Y·O·R·K·
CITY CENTRE

* Close to Minster   * Luxury hotel in gardens
* Elegant Restaurant   * Special Breaks
* Self-catering holiday flats   * Car parking
* Conference facilities

★★
Abbots Mews Hotel Ltd.

Marygate Lane, Bootham, York YO3 7DE
Tel. (0904) 634866/622395   Fax. (0904) 612848

Northern Ireland and the Republic of Ireland
Useful Information

In most instances, the details for establishments in the Irish section are outlined in the 'Using the Guide' section on page 25, including 'How we Classify Hotels', 'Sample Directory Entry' and 'Useful Information'.

PRICES

In the Republic of Ireland prices are quoted in Punts, indicated by the symbol IR£. The rates of exchange between pounds sterling and Punts is liable to fluctuate.

In the Republic of Ireland, as part of the registration scheme operated by Bord Failte, establishments must disply tariffs; these are usually shown in bedrooms or reception. The application of VAT and service charges varies, but all prices quoted must be inclusive of VAT.

TELEPHONE NUMBERS

The area codes shown against the numbers in the Republic of Ireland are applicable within the Republic only. Similarly, the area codes shown for entries in Great Britain and Northern Ireland cannot be used directly from the Republic of Ireland. Check your telephone directory for details.

FIRE PRECAUTIONS

Northern Ireland: The Fire Precautions Act 1971 does not apply here. The Fire Services (NI) Order 1984 covers hotels and boarding houses providing sleeping accommodation for more than six persons, which must have a fire certificate issued by the Northern Ireland Fire Authority. Properties that accommodate fewer than six persons must satisfy the Authority that they have adequate exits.

Republic of Ireland: AA officials inspect emergency notices, fire-fighting equipment and fire exits, although fire safety regulations are a matter for local authority fire services. You are strongly urged to read and understand emergency notices for your own and other people's safety.

LICENSING REGULATIONS

Northern Ireland: public houses open 11.30-23.00 Monday to Saturday, 12.30-14.30 and 19.00-22.00 Sunday. Also Christmas Day 12.30-22.00. Hotels can serve residents seven days a week without restriction. On Sundays non-residents may be served 12.00-14.30 and 19.00-22.00, and on Christmas Day 12.30-22.00.

Children under 18 are not allowed in the bar area of licensed premises, neither can they buy or consume liquor in hotels.

Republic of Ireland: general licensing hours under present legislation are 10.30-23.00 Monday to Saturday in winter and 10.30-23.30 in summer. On Sundays and St Patrick's Day (17 March) 12.30-14.00 and 16.00-23.00. No service on Christmas Day and Good Friday.

Directory — Northern Ireland and Republic of Ireland

ABBEYFEALE Co Limerick Map 01 B2

★ **54%** *Leen's*
☎Listowel(068) 31121
Closed 24-31 Dec
This small family-run commercial hotel has been in the Leen family for over 100 years. It is situated on the main street en route to Limerick/Killarney.
13rm(3⇌3🛏)(1fb) 🐾 (ex guide dogs)
CTV 🅿 ♫
V ✧ 🍽 Last high tea 8.30pm
Credit Cards [1][3]

ADARE Co Limerick Map 01 B3

★★★★ ❀❀ **76%** Adare Manor
☎(061) 396566 FAX (061) 396124

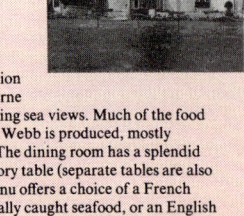

This magnificent manor house, for centuries the home of the Earls of Dunraven, is situated in 840 acres of formal gardens, park and woodland on the broad River Maigue. Recently converted, the house reflects all the grandeur of its past combined with the facilities of a modern luxury hotel.
28⇌🛏 Annexe36⇌🛏 CTV in all bedrooms 🍽 T
🐾 (ex guide dogs) ❋ sB⇌🛏IR£112-IR£270 dB⇌🛏IR£112-IR£270 (room only) 🍴
Lift 🛗 CTV 70P ❋ 🏊 (heated) ♟ (hard) ♪ ♿ snooker sauna gymnasium clay pigeon shooting *xmas*
🍷 Irish, English & French V ✧ 🍽 Lunch IR£15 Dinner IR£28 Last dinner 10pm
CONF. Thtr 90 Class 46 Board 36 Del from IR£118
Credit Cards [1][2][3][4][5]

★★★ ❀❀ **73%** Dunraven Arms
☎(061) 396209 FAX (061) 396541
This lovely old-style country inn has been in operation since 1792, and is situated in the midst of thatched cottages in Ireland's prettiest village. An ideal touring base, the hotel provides modern facilities as well as an old world atmosphere, and it has a beautiful garden.
45⇌🛏(1fb)1⛨ CTV in all bedrooms 🍽 T sB⇌🛏IR£44-IR£66 dB⇌🛏IR£66-IR£94.50 (room only) 🍴
🛗 CTV 300P ❋ *xmas*
🍷 Irish & French V ✧ 🍽 Lunch IR£7-IR£15 High tea IR£5-IR£15 Dinner IR£20-IR£25&alc Last dinner 9.30pm
CONF. Thtr 300 Class 200 Board 20 Del from IR£50
Credit Cards [1][2][3][4][5]

AHERLOW Co Tipperary Map 01 B3

★★★ **61%** Aherlow House
☎Tipperary(062) 56147 FAX (062) 56212
RS 11 Jan-12 Mar & 1 Nov-16 Dec
A warm welcome is assured at this very attractive Tudor-style house, situated in a coniferous forest with panoramic views of the Galtee mountains.
10⇌🛏(2fb) CTV in all bedrooms 🍽 T 🐾 (ex guide dogs)
sB⇌🛏IR£29-IR£30 dB⇌🛏IR£44-IR£45 (room only) 🍴
🛗 CTV 200P 3⛟ ❋
🍷 English & French V ✧ 🍽 ✶ Lunch IR£9.50-IR£9.75 Dinner IR£17.50 Last dinner 9.30pm
CONF. Thtr 300 Class 150
Credit Cards [1][2][3][5]

ANNALONG Co Down Map 01 D4

★★

❀❀❀ **GLASSDRUMMAN LODGE**
85 Mill Rd BT34 4RH
☎(03967) 68451

Glassdrumman Lodge, converted from a farm building, is a lovely, quiet retreat in a dramatic location in the foothills of the Mourne mountains, with far reaching sea views. Much of the food prepared by chef Stephen Webb is produced, mostly organically, by the farm. The dining room has a lovely polished pitch pine refectory table (separate tables are also available). The dinner menu offers a choice of a French cooking, using mainly locally caught seafood, or an English menu. The drawing room has a stone fireplace with a peat burning fire, and drinks are served here by the very attentive butler. The furnishings and objets d'art throughout contribute towards the feeling of staying in a private house, and proprietor Joan Hall is a most charming hostess.
9⇌🛏 CTV in all bedrooms ® T

ARDMORE Co Waterford Map 01 C2

★ **59%** *Cliff House*
☎Youghal(024) 94106 FAX (024) 94496
Closed Oct-Apr
Situated overlooking the bay, this quiet family-run hotel caters mainly for tourists.
21rm(2⇌11🛏)(2fb) ® 🐾 (ex guide dogs)
CTV 30P 🚲 ❋ ♫
V ✧ 🍽 Last dinner 9pm
Credit Cards [1][2][3][5]

ASHFORD Co Wicklow Map 01 D3

★ **52%** *Cullenmore*
(N on N11) ☎Wicklow(0404) 40422 & 40187 FAX (0404) 47744
This streetside hotel with a small side garden is a family-run establishment with a good meals service.
14⇌🛏(4fb) CTV in all bedrooms ® T 🐾 (ex guide dogs)
CTV 200P ❋
🍷 Irish & French V ✧ 🍽 ✶ Last dinner 10pm
Credit Cards [1][2][3][5]

ATHLONE Co Westmeath Map 01 C4

★★★ **63%** *Hodson Bay*
2/3 Garden Vale ☎(0902) 92446 FAX (0902) 92688
On the County Roscommon side of the River Shannon and right on the shore of Lough Ree, this historic hotel has recently been reconstructed and extended to provide comfortable accommodation. With a golf course to the rear and a marina to the front, most of the rooms have excellent views.
46⇌🛏(10fb) CTV in all bedrooms ® 🍽 T 🐾 (ex guide dogs) ❋
sB&B⇌🛏frIR£50 dB&B⇌🛏frIR£70 🍴
Lift 🛗 300P ❋ 🏊 (heated) ♣ 18 ♟ (hard) ♪ sauna solarium gymnasium steam room ♫ *xmas*

V ❖ ⚒ ✹ ✳ Lunch IR£9-IR£10.50&alc Dinner IR£18&alc Last dinner 9.45pm
Credit Cards 1 2 3 5

★★★ ❀58% **Prince Of Wales**
☎(0902) 72626 FAX (0902) 75658
Closed 25-29 Dec
This modern town centre hotel has a large comfortable restaurant and pleasant, friendly staff.
72⇨🐾(2fb)⚒ in 4 bedrooms CTV in all bedrooms ®⚡ T ✳ (ex guide dogs) sB&B⇨🐾IR£30-IR£45 dB&B⇨🐾IR£50-IR£75 ₽
《 CTV 35P
🍴 French V ❖ ⚒ Lunch IR£8.50-IR£12.50 Dinner IR£13-IR£16.95&alc Last dinner 9.15pm
CONF. Thtr 300 Class 250 Board 235 Del from IR£40
Credit Cards 1 2 3 4 5

★★ 68% **Royal Hoey**
Mardyke St ☎(0902) 72924 & 75395 FAX (902) 75194
Closed Xmas
Upholding a tradition of warm hospitality is the priority at this family-run hotel in the centre of town. Bedrooms are well appointed, and snacks are available all day in the coffee shop.
38⇨🐾(8fb) in 10 bedrooms CTV in all bedrooms ⚡ T ✳ (ex guide dogs) ✱ sB&B⇨🐾IR£24-IR£29 dB&B⇨🐾IR£52-IR£56 ₽
Lift 《 ▦ CTV 50P ✿
🍴 Irish, English & Italian V ❖ ⚒ ✳ ✹ Lunch IR£9&alc High tea IR£6-IR£11alc Dinner IR£14-IR£16 Last dinner 9.30pm
CONF. Thtr 150 Class 100 Board 100 Del from IR£50
Credit Cards 1 2 3 4 5

BALLINA Co Mayo Map **01 B4**

★★★ 61% **Downhill**
☎(096) 21033 FAX (096) 21338
Closed 23-25 Dec
This family owned and managed hotel is set in beautiful grounds; the atmosphere is peaceful and facilities include a health and leisure centre, with salmon fishing and nearby golf available. Variety is the keynote in the restaurant where good value, well prepared dishes are served, and entertainment is provided in 'Frogs' piano bar.
50⇨🐾(13fb) CTV in all bedrooms ®⚡ T ✳ (ex guide dogs)
《 CTV 300P ✿ 🗔 (heated) ♟ (hard) squash snooker sauna solarium gymnasium sunbed jacuzzi ♪ ⚜
🍴 Irish & French V ❖ ⚒ Last dinner 9pm
CONF. Thtr 500 Class 25 Board 100 Del from IR£72
Credit Cards 1 2 3 4 5

BALLINASLOE Co Galway Map **01 B4**

★★★ 62% **Hayden's**
(located on the main Dublin/Galway road N6) ☎(0905) 42347 FAX (0905) 42895
RS 24 & 26 Dec
This hotel has been family owned and managed for 4 generations. It is renowned for hospitality and good food, either in the Coffee Shop, serving tasty home-made snacks throughout the day, or the Garbally Restaurant with its extensive à la carte menu – both overlooking a garden.
50⇨🐾(7fb) CTV in all bedrooms ®⚡ T ✳ sB⇨🐾IR£25-IR£27 dB⇨🐾IR£42-IR£46 (room only) ₽
Lift 《 CTV 100P ♪
🍴 International V ❖ ⚒ ✳ Lunch IR£9.25-IR£11.50 High tea IR£10-IR£17alc Dinner IR£15-IR£17.50 Last dinner 9.15pm
CONF. Thtr 300 Class 160 Board 50 Del from IR£48
Credit Cards 1 2 3 5

BALLYBOFEY Co Donegal Map **01 C5**

★★★ 59% **Kee's**
Stranolar(1m NE on N15) ☎Letterkenny(074) 31018 FAX (074) 31917
This tastefully restored old posting house has been run by the Kee family for 5 generations. It is cosy and intimate, with a hospitable atmosphere. There are 10 new bedrooms and some recently refurbished rooms – be sure to request one of these. Fresh produce is used in the carefully prepared food.
35⇨🐾(5fb) CTV in all bedrooms ®⚡ T sB&B⇨🐾IR£31-IR£35 dB&B⇨🐾IR£52-IR£60 ₽
《 90P 🗔 (heated) sauna solarium gymnasium mountain bikes for hire ♪ *xmas*
V ❖ ⚒ ✹ Sunday Lunch IR£8.50-IR£9.50 Dinner IR£15.50-IR£16.50 Last dinner 9.15pm
CONF. Thtr 250 Class 100 Board 30 Del from IR£50
Credit Cards 1 2 3 5

BALLYCOTTON Co Cork Map **01 B2**

★★★ 62% **Bay View**
☎(021) 646746 FAX (021) 646824
Closed Nov-Apr
This hotel has been re-built to very high standards, reflecting the owner's wish to retain the character of the original building while providing modern comforts and facilities. It has an attractive gabled exterior and inside the public areas are spacious. Bedrooms are comfortable, some with superb views over Ballycotton Bay. Staff are friendly and efficient.
35⇨🐾 CTV in all bedrooms ⚡ T sB&B⇨🐾frIR£50 dB&B⇨🐾frIR£80
Lift 《 ▦ 40P ✿ cruiser for hire
V ❖ ⚒ ✳ Lunch frIR£12 Dinner frIR£22 Last dinner 9pm
Credit Cards 1 2 3

BALLYGALLY Co Antrim Map **01 D5**

★★★ 55% **Ballygally Castle**
274 Coast Rd BT40 2QR (HG) ☎Larne(0574) 583212 FAX (0574) 583681
Situated to the north of Larne overlooking a sandy beach and enjoying fine coastal views, this extended hotel incorporates parts of the original castle dating from 1625, such as the character dungeon bar. Bedrooms, while offering modern amenities, are generally very compact and somewhat dated in style, and it is hoped that these will be refurbished before too long.
30⇨🐾(1fb) CTV in all bedrooms ®⚡ T ✳ sB&B⇨🐾fr£45 dB&B⇨🐾fr£66 ₽
《 100P ✿ ♟ (hard) ♪ ♪ ⚜ *xmas*
🍴 French V ❖ ⚒ ✳ Lunch fr£8.50 High tea fr£6alc Dinner fr£16 Last dinner 9.30pm
CONF. Thtr 150 Class 70 Board 25 Del from £65
Credit Cards 1 2 3 5

If you have booked a meal in a
hotel restaurant and cannot get there,
remember you have a contractual obligation
to cancel your booking.

Ballylickey - Ballyvaughan

BALLYLICKEY Co Cork Map 01 A2

★★★ ✿✿✿ 👤 69% **Sea View**
(on N71 6m on the Glengarriff side of Bantry)
☎Bantry(027) 50073 & 50462 FAX (027) 51555

Courtesy and Care 1994

Closed mid Nov-mid Mar
Irish hospitality is legendary, and there is nowhere better to sample it than at this delightful country house overlooking Bantry Bay, the only hotel in Ireland to receive an AA Courtesy and Care Award this year. Set in well tended gardens back from the main Bantry/Cork road, it has cosy lounges with turf fires and comfortable, pleasantly redecorated bedrooms. The hotel caters for the fishing and golfing enthusiast and is also a good touring base for West Cork and Kerry.
17⇌𝕋 Annexe5rm(4fb) T sB&B⇌𝕋IR£43-IR£50 dB&B⇌𝕋IR£66-IR£100 🍴
CTV 30P 🚲 ✿
V ❁ ⚲ ✱ Lunch IR£11 Dinner IR£20 Last dinner 9.30pm
Credit Cards ① ② ③ ⑤

BALLYLIFFEN Co Donegal Map 01 C6

★★ 63% **Strand**
☎(077) 76107 FAX (077) 76486
Closed 24-25 Dec
Intimate and family run, this small hotel looks out on the North Atlantic and caters mainly for tourists and family holidays. It offers attractively furnished accommodation in the modern style.
12⇌𝕋(4fb) CTV in all bedrooms ®✉T ✂ (ex guide dogs)
sB&B⇌𝕋IR£25-IR£30 dB&B⇌𝕋IR£38-IR£45 🍴
CTV 30P 🚲 ✿ ▶ 18 🎵
♿ English V ❁ ⚲ Lunch IR£8.50 Dinner IR£16.95 Last dinner 9.30pm
Credit Cards ① ③

BALLYMENA Co Antrim Map 01 D5

★★★ 62% **Adair Arms**
Ballymoney Rd BT43 5 (HG) ☎(0266) 653674 FAX (0266) 40436
Closed 25 Dec
Conveniently situated in the town centre, this traditionally styled Victorian hotel, with more modern extensions to the rear, offers comfortable and attractive public areas. Bedrooms, while generally roomy and well equipped, are beginning to show their age, though they are expected to be refurbished during 1994. The hotel is well managed and smartly uniformed staff provide friendly service.
39⇌𝕋 CTV in all bedrooms ®✉T ✂ (ex guide dogs)
sB&B⇌𝕋£51-£55 dB&B⇌𝕋£70-£75 🍴
(50P
♿ English & French V ❁ ⚲ Last dinner 9.30pm
CONF. Thtr 250 Class 150 Board 80 Del from £65
Credit Cards ① ② ③ ⑤

BALLYNAHINCH Co Galway Map 01 D5

★★★ 👤 67% **Ballynahinch Castle**
(take Roundstone turn off from N59, 3m after Recess)
☎(095) 31006 & 31086 FAX (095) 31085
Closed 1-17 Feb
Situated at the base of Ben Lettery, this hotel overlooks the Owenmore River. It has spacious bedrooms, ample lounge accommodation and cheerful open fires; the restaurant offers excellent food.
28⇌𝕋 6🛏 CTV in 8 bedrooms T ✂ (ex guide dogs)
sB&B⇌𝕋IR£55-IR£77 dB&B⇌𝕋IR£80-IR£120 🍴
CTV 45P ✿ 🎣 (hard) 🎵 🎵 *xmas*
♿ Irish & French V ❁ ⚲ ✱ Bar Lunch IR£12.50 Dinner IR£23 Last dinner 8.30pm
CONF. Thtr 70 Board 28 Del from IR£76
Credit Cards ① ② ③ ⑤

BALLYSHANNON Co Donegal Map 01 B5

★★ 67% **Dorrians Imperial**
☎(072) 51147 FAX (072) 51001
Closed 24-31 Dec RS Good Fri & 25 Dec
Extensive renovations were being carried out to this attractive hotel at the time of our most recent visit, when already completed work had provided a richly decorated and inviting lobby, with comfortable sofas and chairs, and a new restaurant. The remainder of the work, to the bedrooms and fitness centre, should be completed by the time this guide is published.
26⇌𝕋(6fb) CTV in all bedrooms T ✂ (ex guide dogs)
CTV 30P gymnasium steam room jacuzzi
V ⚲ Last dinner 8.30pm
Credit Cards ① ③

BALLYVAUGHAN Co Clare Map 01 B3

★★★ ✿✿✿ 👤 75% **Gregans Castle**
(3.5m S on N67) ☎(065) 77005 FAX (065) 77111
Closed Nov-Feb
Situated at the foot of Corkscrew Hill with dramatic views over Galway Bay, the hotel is situated in an area which is rich in archaeological, geological and botanical interest. Hosts Peter and Moira Haden are warm and welcoming, and are a mine of information about the area. A high level of personal service and hospitality have earned them special commendations in recent years, and the emphasis here is on good food using fresh local produce.
22⇌𝕋 3🛏 T ✂ sB&B⇌𝕋IR£45-IR£85 dB&B⇌𝕋IR£67.50-IR£112 🍴
CTV 22P ✿ croquet lawn
♿ Irish & French V ❁ ⚲ ✂ Bar Lunch IR£10-IR£33alc Dinner IR£31&alc Last dinner 8.30pm
Credit Cards ① ③

★★ 66% **Hyland's**
☎(065) 77037 & 77015 FAX (065) 77131
Closed Dec-Jan

Good food is served in the bar and restaurant of this hotel, where sometimes the Seanchai, or storyteller, drops in in the evening to regale those present in the bars with stories in the old Irish tradition.
20⇌𝕋(3fb) CTV in 19 bedrooms ®✉T ✂ ✱
sB&B⇌𝕋IR£38-IR£44 dB&B⇌𝕋IR£50-IR£66 🍴
CTV P ✿ croquet lawn
♿ French & Irish V ❁ ⚲ ✱ Bar Lunch IR£5.50-IR£15.50alc Dinner IR£14.50-IR£18.50&alc Last dinner 9.30pm
Credit Cards ① ③

For key to symbols see the Bookmark. | Hotels with red star ratings are especially high quality.

Bantry - Blessington

BANTRY Co Cork Map 01 A2

★★★ 57% Westlodge
☎(027) 50360 FAX (027) 50438
This modern hotel is set in its own grounds on the outskirts of town overlooking the bay.
90⇌🛏(20fb) CTV in all bedrooms T 🐕 (ex guide dogs) sB&B⇌🛏IR£40-IR£50 dB&B⇌🛏IR£65-IR£80 🍴
(▦ CTV 400P ✿ 🏊 (heated) ℘ (hard) squash snooker sauna solarium gymnasium jacuzzi ♫
V ✧ ♨ ⚠ ✱ Lunch IR£8.50-IR£10.50 Dinner IR£18-IR£21 Last dinner 9pm
CONF. Thtr 400 Class 200 Board 24 Del from IR£40
Credit Cards 1 2 3 4 5

BELFAST Map 01 D5

★★★ 69% Stormont
587 Upper Newtonards Rd BT4 3LP (4m E) (HG)
☎(0232) 658621 FAX (0232) 480240
Closed 25 Dec
This modern hotel, overlooking the grounds of Stormont Castle, is a favourite function and meeting venue and is consequently very busy. Expansive public areas include a choice of restaurants, one an all-day brasserie, and various lounge areas, but only one bar which can get very crowded. The hotel was recently extended to provide executive bedrooms with big, comfortable beds; standard rooms remain rather more dated in style.
106⇌🛏 in 23 bedrooms CTV in all bedrooms ® ♨ T 🐕 (ex guide dogs)
Lift (600P ♫
♧ French ✧ ♨ ✱ Lunch £11.50-£15.50 Dinner £7-£21.50&alc Last dinner 10pm
CONF. Thtr 400 Class 120 Board 60 Del from £69
Credit Cards 1 2 3 5

★★★ 61% Dukes
65 University St BT7 1HL ☎(0232) 236666 FAX (0232) 237177
A Victorian gentleman's residence close to the University and Botanic Gardens has been transformed into a bright modern hotel. Generally spacious bedrooms are equipped with modern amenities, and comprehensive room service is available 24 hours. Lounge space is rather limited but there is a pleasant restaurant and lively bar.
21⇌🛏(2fb)⚠ in 5 bedrooms CTV in all bedrooms ® ♨ T 🐕 (ex guide dogs) sB⇌🛏£35-£69 dB⇌🛏£45-£79 (room only) 🍴
Lift (℘ 🚲 ✿ sauna gymnasium
♧ International V ✧ ♨ ⚠ ✱ Lunch fr£8.50&alc
CONF. Thtr 150 Class 60 Board 30 Del from £60
Credit Cards 1 2 3 5

★★★ 60% Novotel
Belfast International Airport BT29 4AB
☎(081)563 01 00

Within yards of the airport terminal building, this strikingly modern hotel offers a uniform standard of accommodation. Le Grill restaurant is open from 6am to midnight, and staff are generally friendly and helpful.

★★★ 50% Plaza
15 Brunswick St BT2 7GE ☎(0232) 333555 FAX (0232) 232999
A purpose-built hotel close to the city hall and opera house, offering generally compact but comfortable, well equipped bedrooms. Public areas include a conservatory restaurant and a public bar with live entertainment at weekends.
72⇌🛏(3fb)⚠ in 14 bedrooms CTV in all bedrooms ® ♨ T 🐕 (ex guide dogs) sB&B⇌🛏£35-£59 dB&B⇌🛏£45-£69 Continental breakfast 🍴
Lift (CTV 10P *xmas*

♧ International V ✧ ♨ ⚠ ✱ Lunch £9.50 High tea £5.75-£9.95 Dinner £8.95&alc Last dinner 12.30am
CONF. Thtr 80 Class 40 Board 40
Credit Cards 1 2 3 5

★★ 58% Renshaws
75 University St BT7 1HL ☎(0232) 333366 FAX (0232) 333399
Conveniently situated for the university, this recently established hotel is a popular drinking venue for locals and students, and the wooden-floored public areas, which include an Indian restaurant, can get very crowded. Bedrooms are contemporary in style, although not always as well arranged as they might be.
20⇌🛏(2fb)⚠ in 6 bedrooms CTV in all bedrooms ®♨ T 🐕 sB&B⇌🛏£55.95-£57.95 dB&B⇌🛏£67.95-£68.95 Continental breakfast
Lift (CTV ℘
♧ European & Indian V ✧ ♨ ✱ Lunch £5.05-£11.35alc High tea £5.05-£11.35alc Dinner £9.95-£16.95&alc Last dinner 11pm
CONF. Thtr 80 Class 60 Board 40 Del from £45.95
Credit Cards 1 2 3 5

Forte Crest
Kingsway, Dunmurry BT17 9ES
☎Dunmurry(0232) 612101 FAX (0232) 626546

A large modern hotel with a wide range of services and amenities, designed particularly for the business traveller. Bedrooms are smart, comfortable and well equipped. For more details about Forte Crest hotels, consult the Contents page, under Hotel Groups.
82⇌🛏✱ B⇌🛏£80 (room only)
CONF. Thtr 450 Class 230 Board 80 Del £105

BIRR Co Offaly Map 01 C3

★★ 62% County Arms
☎(0509) 20791 & 20193 FAX (0509) 21234

This fine Georgian house, built in 1810, has outstanding and well preserved interior features. The hotel offers a warm, cosy atmosphere and its garden and glasshouses provide fresh produce for the restaurant.
18⇌🛏(4fb) CTV in all bedrooms ® T 🐕 (ex guide dogs)
(CTV 150P ✿ squash sauna ♫ ⚲
♧ Irish & French V ✧ ♨ ⚠ Last dinner 9pm
Credit Cards 1 2 3 4 5

BLARNEY Co Cork Map 01 B2

★★★ ✿68% Blarney Park
☎(021) 385281 FAX (021) 381506
Situated in 10 acres of gardens and lawns beneath the woods of Blarney Castle, this hotel provides bright airy bedrooms and friendly efficient service. The hotel's excellent leisure facilities include a 40-metre water slide.
76⇌🛏(20fb)🐕 in 2 bedrooms CTV in all bedrooms ♨ T 🐕 (ex guide dogs)
(100P ✿ 🏊 (heated) ℘ (hard) sauna gymnasium steam room childrens pool ♫ ⚲
V ✧ ♨ ⚠ Last dinner 9.30pm
Credit Cards 1 2 3 5

BLESSINGTON Co Wicklow Map 01 C3

★★★ 56% Downshire House
(on N81) ☎Naas(045) 65199 FAX (0454) 65335
Closed 31 Dec-6 Jan
This small Georgian house with modern extensions is situated on the main street and caters for both tourist and commerical guests.
14⇌🛏 Annexe11⇌🛏 CTV in all bedrooms ® T 🐕 (ex guide dogs) sB⇌🛏IR£30 dB⇌🛏IR£47 (room only)

Blessington - Carrickfergus

C

(CTV 30P ✿ ♟ (hard) table tennis croquet
V ✧ ⚲ ✂ Lunch IR£8-IR£12 High tea IR£8.30-IR£17.50alc Dinner IR£15-IR£19 Last dinner 9.30pm
Credit Cards [1] [3]

BORRIS-IN-OSSORY Co Laois Map 01 C3

★★**68%** Leix County
☏(0505) 41213
Recently modernised, the Leix County Hotel offers a high standard of bedroom accommodation, spacious lounges and pleasant, helpful staff.
19⇌(2fb) CTV in all bedrooms ✈ (ex guide dogs)
⊞ CTV ♫
✧ ⚲
Credit Cards [1] [2] [3]

BOYLE Co Roscommon Map 01 B4

★★**61%** Royal
☏(079) 62016
Closed Xmas

A family-run, town-centre hotel with pleasant, friendly staff. The comfortable bedrooms overlook the Boyle river at close quarters.
16⇌♞(5fb) CTV in all bedrooms ® T
(CTV 120P ▶ 9
♀ Irish, French & Italian V ✧ ⚲ ✂ Last dinner 9pm
Credit Cards [1] [2] [3] [4] [5]

BRAY Co Wicklow Map 01 D3

★★**64%** Royal
Main St ☏(01) 2862935 FAX (01) 2867373
This streetside hotel in a seaside town provides modernised bedrooms of a good standard.
73rm(72⇌♞)(5fb)1⊞ CTV in all bedrooms ® ⚱ T
✈ (ex guide dogs) sB&B⇌♞IR£42-IR£45 dB&B⇌♞IR£72-IR£78 ℞
Lift (⊞ CTV 110P ♫ xmas
♀ European V ✧ ⚲ ✂ Lunch frIR£9.25 Dinner frIR£14&alc Last dinner 11pm
CONF. Thtr 400 Class 350 Board 300 Del from IR£50
Credit Cards [1] [2] [3] [5]

BUNRATTY Co Clare Map 01 B3

★★★**63%** Fitzpatrick Bunratty Shamrock
☏Shannon(061) 361177 FAX (061) 471252
RS 25 Dec
Situated in the picturesque village of Bunratty, famous for its medieval castle, this modern ranch-style building is surrounded by lawns and flower beds. Bedrooms and public rooms are timbered, and there is a helipad in the grounds.
115⇌♞(6fb)✂in 2 bedrooms CTV in all bedrooms⚱ T
✈ (ex guide dogs) ✱ sB⇌♞IR£63.39-IR£80.70
dB⇌♞IR£80.70-IR£111.80 (room only) ℞
(CTV 150P ✿ ⌷ (heated) sauna steam room ♫
♀ European V ✧ ⚲ ✂ ✱ Lunch frIR£9.95 High tea frIR£6 Dinner frIR£17.50&alc Last dinner 9.30pm
CONF. Thtr 200 Class 140 Board 80 Del from IR£85
Credit Cards [1] [2] [3] [4] [5]

CAHERDANIEL Co Kerry Map 01 A2

★★**64%** Derrynane
☏(0667) 5136 FAX (0667) 5160
Closed Nov-14 Mar

This company-owned hotel on the Ring of Kerry caters mainly for holidaymakers and some coach parties.

75⇌(30fb) T ✱ sB&B⇌♞IR£32-IR£37 dB&B⇌♞IR£55-IR£66 ℞
(CTV 60P ✿ ⌷ (heated) ♟ (hard) ♪ snooker ♫ ♣
♀ International V ✧ ⚲ Last dinner 9.30pm
Credit Cards [1] [2] [3] [4] [5]

CAHIR Co Tipperary Map 01 C2

★★**62%** Kilcoran Lodge
(5m W on N8 Dublin/Cork road) ☏(052) 41288 & 41465 FAX (052) 41994
Comfortable old-style bedrooms and spacious lounges are offered at this former shooting lodge set in its own grounds with good views of the Galtee Mountains.
18⇌Annexe5rm(5fb) CTV in all bedrooms ® ⚱ T
sB&B⇌IR£35-IR£45 dB&B⇌♞IR£60-IR£90 ℞
(100P ✿ ⌷ (heated) sauna solarium gymnasium jacuzzi ✿ xmas
♀ Irish & French V ✧ ⚲ Lunch IR£5.25-IR£9.50 Dinner IR£12.50-IR£14.50&alc Last dinner 9.15pm
CONF. Thtr 250 Class 150 Board 80 Del from IR£54
Credit Cards [1] [2] [3] [5]

CARLOW Co Carlow Map 01 C3

★★❋**52%** Royal
☏(0503) 31621 FAX (0503) 31621
Closed 25 Dec
Located in the heart of Carlow with a private garden, the Royal Hotel was established in 1800 as a coaching inn. It offers a warm welcome and personal attention, and there is an excellent choice of well presented food.
34⇌♞(3fb)1⊞ CTV in all bedrooms ® ⚱ T ✈ (ex guide dogs)
✱ sB&B⇌♞IR£29-IR£32 dB&B⇌♞IR£55 ℞
(CTV 50P ♫ ♣
♀ Continental V ✧ ⚲ ✂ ✱ Lunch IR£8.95&alc Dinner IR£11.95-IR£13.95&alc Last dinner 10pm
CONF. Thtr 275 Class 100 Board 40 Del from IR£45
Credit Cards [1] [2] [3] [5]

CARNLOUGH Co Antrim Map 01 D5

★★**69%** Londonderry Arms
BT44 0EU (14m N from Larne on the Coast road)
☏(0574) 885255 FAX (0574) 885263
In the centre of a conservation village on the Antrim Coast Road, close to the Glens of Antrim, this Georgian coaching inn is a well established family-run hotel of great character. Public areas offer traditional comforts, while bedrooms vary in size, the more spacious furnished with period pieces. All have attractive fabrics. There is a garden running down to the water's edge.
21⇌♞(5fb) CTV in all bedrooms T ✈ sB&B⇌♞£45 dB&B⇌♞£65 ℞
⊞ CTV 26P ✿ ♫ xmas
V ✧ ⚲ Lunch £5-£10&alc High tea £6-£10alc Dinner £15 Last dinner 9pm
CONF. Thtr 100 Class 80 Board 40 Del £55
Credit Cards [1] [2] [3] [5]   (£)

CARRICKFERGUS Co Antrim Map 01 D5

★**59%** Dobbins Inn
6-8 High St BT38 7AP ☏(0960) 351905 FAX (0960) 351905
Closed 25 & 26 Dec RS Good Friday
Dating from the 16th century, this friendly, family-run commercial hotel in the centre of the town is gradually being improved. Bedrooms are modest, but equipped with modern amenities, and the public areas are full of character. The popular bar has a nautical flavour, there is a beamed restaurant and a coffee lounge offering home baking throughout the day.

13✧♠(2fb) CTV in all bedrooms ® T sB&B✧♠£30-£39 dB&B✧♠£50-£60 🍴
《 🐾 ♫
♆ English & French V ✧ ⚲ ✱ Sunday Lunch £5.30-£8 Hightea£7.80-£10Dinner£15.25-£20alcLastdinner9.15pm
Credit Cards 1 2 3 5

CASHEL Co Galway Map 01 A4

★★★❀♨ **CASHEL HOUSE**
☎Clifden(095) 31001 FAX (095) 31077

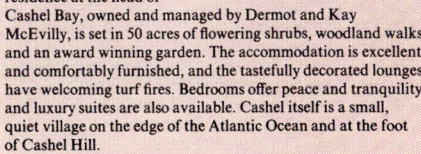

This converted country residence at the head of Cashel Bay, owned and managed by Dermot and Kay McEvilly, is set in 50 acres of flowering shrubs, woodland walks and an award winning garden. The accommodation is excellent and comfortably furnished, and the tastefully decorated lounges have welcoming turf fires. Bedrooms offer peace and tranquility and luxury suites are also available. Cashel itself is a small, quiet village on the edge of the Atlantic Ocean and at the foot of Cashel Hill.
32✧♠(4fb)1🛏 CTV in all bedrooms✱ T ✱
sB&B✧♠IR£51.75-IR£100 dB&B✧♠IR£103.50-IR£121.50 🍴
CTV 40P 🚗 ❋ ≋ ♜ (hard) ♪ ∪ nc5yrs xmas
♆ Irish & French V ✧ ⚲ ✱ Bar Lunch IR£12.50-IR£20alc Dinner IR£29.25-IR£31.50&alc Last dinner 9pm
Credit Cards 1 2 3 4

★★★❀72% **Zetland House**
☎(095) 31111 FAX (095) 31117
Closed 2 Nov-14 Apr
Set in attractive gardens overlooking Cashel Bay, the hotel is owned and managed by John and Mona Prendergast who invite guests to enjoy gracious living with warm hospitality, good food and service to match. There is a private fishery, and shooting parties are arranged in season for snipe and woodcock.
19✧♠(2fb) T
CTV 20P 🚗 ❋ ♜ (hard) ♪ snooker
♆ International V ✧ ⚲
Credit Cards 1 2 3 5

CASHEL Co Tipperary Map 01 C3

★★★★❀♨70% **Cashel Palace**
(on N8) ☎Tipperary(062) 61411 FAX (062) 61521
RS 25-26 Dec
This elegant Palladian mansion was once a bishop's palace and is now a luxury hotel with elegant rooms and all the good services associated with a hotel of this calibre. It has lovely gardens with a private walk to the famous Rock of Cashel.
20✧2🛏 CTV in all bedrooms✱ T ✱ (ex guide dogs) ✱
sB✧IR£85-IR£125 dB✧IR£105-IR£225 (room only) 🍴
《 100P ❋ ♪
♆ Irish & French V ✧ ⚲ ✱ Bar Lunch IR£12.50-IR£22.50alc Dinner IR£22-IR£28 Last dinner 10pm
Credit Cards 1 2 3 5

CASTLEBALDWIN Co Sligo Map 01 B4

★★★❀♨75% **Cromleach Lodge Country House**
Ballindoon(signposted from Castlebaldwin on the N4 north of Boyle) ☎Sligo(071) 65155 FAX (071) 65455
Closed 25-26 Dec & 7-31 Jan
A feeling of welcome and homeliness fills this hotel, in the hills overlooking Lough Arrow. Luxuriously furnished, it is not only a haven of peace and comfort but also justly renowned for its fine cuisine. Moira and Christy Tighe and their staff ensure that your stay will be a memorable experience.
10✧♠✂in 5 bedrooms CTV in all bedrooms ® T ✱
sB&B✧♠IR£55-IR£78 dB&B✧♠IR£90-IR£135 🍴
25P 🚗 ❋ ♪
♆ French V ✧ ⚲ ✱ Lunch frIR£14.95 Dinner frIR£27 Last dinner 9pm
Credit Cards 1 2 3 5

CASTLEBAR Co Mayo Map 01 B4

★★★62% **Breaffy House**
☎(094) 22033
Closed 23-26 Dec

This converted mansion with modern extensions is set in about 60 acres of parkland estate. It caters for the holiday and commercial trade and is an ideal touring base.
40✧♠(3fb) CTV in all bedrooms ® T
Lift 《 CTV 100P ❋ pool table croquet crazy golf
♆ Irish & French V ✧ ⚲ ✱ Last dinner 9pm
Credit Cards 1 2 3 5

KILCORAN LODGE HOTEL
CAHIR, CO. TIPPERARY

 An intimate and most welcoming hotel set in beautiful spacious grounds with wonderful views. 24 well-appointed bedrooms, leisure club with swimming pool, gym, spa, sauna and solarium.

Bed and breakfast from £39.00
(low cost fully inclusive flexi-break tariff also available)

Reservations: 052 41288

KILCORAN LODGE HOTEL ★★
Cahir, Co. Tipperary

Castlebar - Cork

★★❀70% Welcome Inn
☎(094) 22288 & 22054 FAX (094) 21766
Closed 23-25 Dec
This family-run hotel has recently been refurbished to a high standard. It offers excellent accommodation, good food and friendly, helpful staff.
43⇨♠(5fb)2☎ CTV in all bedrooms T ✕ (ex guide dogs)
《 CTV 100P ♫
♀ Irish & French V ♦ ♫ ✕ Last dinner 9.15pm
Credit Cards ①②③

CASTLECONNELL Co Limerick Map 01 B3

★★★60% Castle Oaks House
☎Limerick(061) 377666 FAX (061) 377717
Closed 25 Dec
This Georgian mansion is set in 25 acres of mature grounds bounded on 3 sides by the River Shannon.
11⇨♠(6fb) CTV in all bedrooms ♫ T ✕ (ex guide dogs) ❋ sB&B⇨♠IR£42-IR£60 dB&B⇨♠IR£54-IR£80 ♬
《 200P 200☎ ❋ ▭ ♀ (hard) ♪ sauna gymnasium angling centre ♫ xmas
♀ French V ♦ ♫ ✕ ❋ Lunch IR£9.25 Dinner IR£14.50-IR£17&alc Last dinner 9.30pm
CONF. Thtr 250 Class 100 Board 50 Del from IR£60
Credit Cards ①②③④⑤

CLIFDEN Co Galway Map 01 A4

★★★★❀♨70% Rock Glen
☎(095) 21035 & 21393 FAX (095) 21737
Closed 29 Oct-14 Mar
John and Evangeline Roche run this converted 18th-century shooting lodge set in its own grounds. The emphasis is on traditional hospitality, with award-winning cuisine under the personal supervision of John. There are comfortable lounges with turf fires, and a cosy convivial cocktail bar. A leisurely feeling of well being pervades the hotel.
29⇨♠(5fb) CTV in all bedrooms ® ♫ T ✕ (ex guide dogs) sB&B⇨♠IR£50-IR£56 dB&B⇨♠IR£78-IR£90 ♬
CTV 50P ❋ ♀ (hard) snooker croquet putting ♫
♀ Irish & French V ♦ ♫ ✕ Lunch frIR£15 Dinner IR£23-IR£25 Last dinner 9pm
Credit Cards ①②③④⑤

★★★65% Ardagh
Ballyconneely Rd(N59 Galway to Clifden, signposted for Ballyconneely) ☎(095) 21384 FAX (095) 21314
Closed Nov-Mar
This modern family-run hotel is situated on the rocky edge of Ardnear Bay, just over a mile from Clifden. The restaurant, overlooking the bay, specialises in local seafood.
21⇨♠(2fb) CTV in all bedrooms ® T ✕ sB&B⇨♠IR£41.50-IR£49.50 dB&B⇨♠IR£63-IR£79 ♬
35P ☎
♦ ♫ ✕ Dinner IR£16.50-IR£22 Last dinner 9.30pm
Credit Cards ①②③⑤

★★★54% Abbeyglen Castle
Sky Rd(0.5m W) ☎(095) 21201 FAX (095) 21797
Closed 11 Jan-2 Feb
Set in its own grounds with panoramic views over Clifden Bay, this friendly family-run hotel gives high priority to hospitality and good food. Musical evenings are a regular occurence, creating a good atmosphere in the cosy bar with its turf fires. Extensive grounds include a helipad.
40⇨♠✕in 10 bedrooms CTV in all bedrooms ♫ T sB&B⇨♠IR£37-IR£59 dB&B⇨♠IR£70-IR£99 (incl dinner) ♬

CTV 40P ☎ ❋ ▭ (heated) ▶ 9 ♀ (hard) snooker sauna solarium ♫ xmas
♀ International V ♦ ♫ ✕ Lunch IR£5-IR£11alc Dinner IR£16.50-IR£19.50 Last dinner 10pm
CONF. Thtr 100 Class 50 Board 40 Del from IR£37
Credit Cards ①②③④⑤

CLONMEL Co Tipperary Map 01 C2

★★★70% Minella
☎(052) 22388 & 22717 FAX (052) 24381
This mansion stands in 9 acres of grounds on the banks of the River Suir. The public rooms are in the main building, while the east wing extension houses comfortable, well equipped bedrooms, some with jacuzzis. All rooms have good views. The hotel is owned and managed by the Nallen family.
45⇨♠(28fb)✕in 6 bedrooms CTV in all bedrooms ® ♫ T
《 CTV 200P ❋ ⚘
♀ European V ♦ ♫ Last dinner 9.30pm
Credit Cards ①②③

★★★63% Clonmel Arms
Sarsfield Rd(in town centre) ☎(052) 21233 FAX (052) 21526
In the town centre, backing onto the River Suir, this friendly hotel is owner managed. Refurbishment of the bedrooms is now under way and a number have been completed, combining richly coloured fabrics with cherry wood furniture. The popular buttery serves food all day, while the restaurant offers more formal dining.
31⇨♠(4fb) CTV in all bedrooms ® ♫ sBIR£30 sB⇨♠IR£31-IR£42 dB⇨♠IR£60-IR£70 (room only) ♬
Lift 《 CTV ♀
♀ Irish & French V ♦ ♫ Lunch IR£8.75-IR£9 Dinner IR£12.50 Last dinner 10pm
CONF. Thtr 600 Class 400 Board 100 Del IR£68
Credit Cards ①②④⑤

CORK Co Cork Map 01 B2

★★★★68% Jurys
Western Rd(close to city centre, on main Killarney road as you exit Cork) ☎(021) 276622 FAX (021) 274477
Closed Xmas
Refurbishment continues at this popular hotel which is a central meeting point for leisure and business guests. It is within walking distance of the city centre and has comfortable bedrooms.
185⇨♠(36fb)✕in 2 bedrooms CTV in all bedrooms ® ♫ T ✕ (ex guide dogs) ❋ sB⇨♠IR£85 dB⇨♠IR£99 (room only) ♬
Lift 《 400P ▭ (heated) ▭ (heated) ♀ (hard) squash sauna gymnasium jacuzzi ♫ ⚘
♀ French V ♦ ♫ ✕ Lunch IR£8.50-IR£13.50&alc High tea IR£1.50-IR£8 Dinner IR£16.50-IR£23&alc Last dinner 11pm
CONF. Thtr 700 Class 400 Board 150 Del IR£87
Credit Cards ①②③④⑤

★★★★62% Fitzpatrick Silver Springs
Tivoli ☎(021) 507533 FAX (021) 507641
Closed 25 Dec
This modern hotel is situated on high ground overlooking the River Lee and the harbour. It has open plan public rooms, bright airy bedrooms and superb conference and leisure facilities.
109⇨♠(50fb)✕in 4 bedrooms CTV in all bedrooms ® ♫ T ✕ (ex guide dogs) ❋ sB⇨♠IR£65-IR£75 dB⇨♠IR£75-IR£92 (room only) ♬
Lift 《 450P ❋ ▭ (heated) ▶ 9 ♀ (hard) squash snooker sauna solarium gymnasium creche indoor tennis ♫
♀ International V ♦ ♫ ✕ ❋ Lunch IR£10-IR£13 High tea IR£6-IR£20alc Dinner IR£18-IR£20&alc Last dinner 9.30pm
CONF. Thtr 800 Class 500 Board 40 Del from IR£89
Credit Cards ①②③⑤

Cork - Donegal

★★ 61% Vienna Woods
Glanmire (off R639) ☎(021) 821146 FAX (021) 821120
This 18th-century house is situated in 20 acres of garden and woodlands overlooking Cork Harbour.
20⇨♠(2fb) CTV in all bedrooms ®♨ T sB&B⇨♠IR£34 dB&B⇨♠IR£50
CTV 150P ❈
♀ English & French V ⊕ ⌴ ✔ Sunday Lunch IR£8-IR£10&alc Dinner IR£12-IR£16alc Last dinner 9.30pm
CONF. Thtr 200 Class 100 Board 40 Del IR£40
Credit Cards ①②③⑤

Forte Travelodge
Blackash ☎Dublin (01) 800 709709   FORTE Travelodge
This modern building offers a good standard of accommodation for overnight stops. Smart, spacious and well equipped bedrooms, all with en suite bathrooms, are suitable for family use, and meals may be taken at the nearby family restaurant. For more details about Travelodges, consult the Contents page under Hotel Groups.
40⇨♠❈ B⇨♠IR£31.95 (room only)

COURTMACSHERRY Co Cork Map **01 B2**

★★ ❀60% Courtmacsherry
☎Bandon(023) 46198 FAX (023) 46137
Closed Oct-Mar
This Georgian house is set in attractive grounds near the beach in a pretty village. The friendly, hospitable owners ensure that guests enjoy their stay here, and owner Terry Adams supervises the cooking in his award-winning restaurant where fresh local produce is a feature.
15rm(9⇨)(1fb) CTV in all bedrooms♨ T sB&BIR£22.50-IR£27.50 sB&B⇨IR£30-IR£35 dB&BIR£45-IR£55 dB&B⇨IR£50-IR£65 ♬
CTV 60P ❈ ♪ (hard & grass)⌴
♀ International V ⊕ ⌴ ✔ Sunday Lunch IR£10-IR£11 Dinner IR£18-IR£19 Last dinner 9pm
Credit Cards ①③

COURTOWN HARBOUR Co Wexford Map **01 D3**

★★ 69% Courtown
☎Gorey(055) 25210 & 25108 FAX (055) 25304
Closed 8 Nov-1 Apr

Situated in a picturesque seaside resort, this long-established family-run hotel is noted for good food and the friendly atmosphere of its lounge bars. Summer entertainment takes the form of dinner theatre shows.
21⇨♠(4fb) CTV in all bedrooms T ✈ (ex guide dogs) sB&B⇨♠IR£38.54-IR£45 dB&B⇨♠IR£70-IR£80 ♬
《 CTV 5P ❈ 🄳 (heated) ▶ 18 ♪ (hard & grass)♫ squash ⌴ sauna gymnasium jacuzzi steam room
♀ Irish, English & French V ⊕ ⌴ ✱ Lunch IR£10.50-IR£11.50&alc Dinner IR£17.90-IR£18.90&alc Last dinner 9.30pm
Credit Cards ①②③⑤

★★ 65% Bay View
☎(055) 25307 FAX (055) 25576
Closed Nov-14 Mar
17⇨♠(12fb) CTV in all bedrooms ® T ✈ (ex guide dogs)
CTV 30P ♪ (hard) squash
⊕ ⌴ ✔ Last dinner 9pm
Credit Cards ①②③

CRAWFORDSBURN Co Down Map **01 D5**

★★★ 63% Old Inn
15 Main St BT19 1JH (on B20) ☎Helens Bay(0247) 853255 FAX 852775
Closed 25-26 Dec
One of Ireland's oldest hostelries, with records dating back to 1614, this character inn with pleasant gardens is in a pretty village setting. Individually decorated and furnished bedrooms vary in size and style, with good use being made of contemporary fabrics in the recently refurbished rooms. Public areas are warm and inviting and include an elegant restaurant, informal bistro and spacious cocktail lounge in addition to the popular bar.
32⇨♠ 3🛏 CTV in all bedrooms ® T ✈ ✱ sB&B⇨♠£39-£65 dB&B⇨♠£59-£85 ♬
《 CTV 65P ❈ ♫
V ⊕ ✱ Lunch £12 High tea £7 Dinner £16&alc Last dinner 9.30pm
CONF. Thtr 100 Class 50 Board 30 Del £74
Credit Cards ①②③⑤

CUSHENDALL Co Antrim Map **01 D6**

★★ 56% Thornlea
6 Coast Rd BT44 0RU ☎Cushendal(02667) 71223 FAX (02667) 71362
This privately owned hotel continues to offer a warm welcome and a friendly atmosphere. However, standards of accommodation remain rather modest.
13rm(1⇨11♠)(3fb) CTV in all bedrooms ®
CTV 25P ❈ pool table darts ♫
V ⊕ ⌴ Lunch £6.95 High tea £7.50 Last high tea 7.30pm
CONF. Thtr 20 Class 20 Board 20
Credit Cards ①②③⑤

DINGLE Co Kerry Map **01 A2**

★★★ ❀❀70% Skellig
☎(066) 51144 FAX (066) 51501
Closed mid Nov-mid Mar
On the outskirts of town overlooking the bay, this modern hotel has bright airy bedrooms and pleasant public areas.
115⇨♠ TV available♨ T ✈ (ex guide dogs)
《 CTV ❈ 🄳 (heated) ♪ (hard) snooker sauna solarium ⚕
♀ French V ⊕ ⌴
Credit Cards ①②③

★★★ 53% Benner's
Main St ☎(066) 51638 FAX (066) 51412
Friendly staff ensure a warm welcome at this beautifully restored town centre coaching inn.
25⇨♠(2fb)2🛏 ✔ in 4 bedrooms CTV in all bedrooms T ✈ (ex guide dogs)
《 20P ❈ ♪ (hard) ♫
V ⊕ ⌴ ✔ Last dinner 9.30pm
Credit Cards ①②③⑤

DONEGAL Co Donegal Map **01 B5**

★★★ ❀❀67% Harvey's Point Country
Lough Eske ☎(073) 22208 FAX (073) 22352
This modern hotel is in a superb lakeside location on Lough Eske, and was built with guests' peace and comfort in mind. There are spacious public rooms, excellent cuisine and a wide range of facilities.
20⇨♠ Annexe12♠ 4🛏 CTV in all bedrooms ® T

➡

Donegal - Dublin

☾ 200P ❀ ♃ (hard) ♒ bicycles rowing boats canoes available ♪
⚑ Irish, French & Swiss V ✧ ⚖ ✄
Credit Cards [1] [2] [3] [5]

★★★**63%** *Abbey*
The Diamond ☏(073) 21014 FAX (073) 21014
Mainly commercial but with some tourist trade in season, this owner-managed hotel is situated in the centre of town.
49⇨♠(7fb) CTV in all bedrooms ❅ T ✱ sB&B⇨♠IR£25-IR£30 dB&B⇨♠IR£55-IR£70 ⊟
Lift ☾ ⊞ CTV 70P ❀ ♃ (hard & grass) ♒ squash ⊎ snooker
⚑ Irish, French & Swiss V ✧ ⚖ ✄ ✱ Lunch frIR£9 High tea frIR£5 Dinner frIR£10 Last dinner 9.30pm
CONF. Thtr 1200 Class 600 Board 600 Del from IR£35
Credit Cards [1] [2] [3] [4] [5]

★★★**61%** *The Hyland Central*
The Diamond ☏Donegal Town(073) 21027
FAX (073) 22195
Closed 25-27 Dec

BEST WESTERN HOTELS

This family-run hotel is located in picturesque Donegal town square, with a garden view overlooking Donegal Bay. It has an excellent leisure centre and a pleasant, lively atmosphere.
70⇨♠(2fb) CTV in all bedrooms ®❅ T ✱ (ex guide dogs) sB&B⇨♠IR£38-IR£55 dB&B⇨♠IR£66-IR£88 ⊟
Lift ☾ 18P ⊠ (heated) ▶ 18 ♃ (hard) squash ⊎ sauna solarium gymnasium ♪
V ✧ ⚖ Lunch IR£11-IR£12 High tea IR£12-IR£20alc Dinner IR£20-IR£22 Last dinner 9.30pm
CONF. Thtr 350 Class 300 Board 100 Del from IR£60
Credit Cards [1] [2] [3]

DOOLIN Co Clare Map **01** B3

★★**68%** *Aran View House*
Coast Rd ☏(065) 74061
Closed Nov-28 Feb
Situated in 100 acres of rolling farmland and commanding panoramic views of the Aran islands, this hotel offers attractive and comfortably furnished accommodation. Owner managed by John and Teresa Linnane, the atmosphere is convivial and there is traditional music and song in the bar 3 times a week.
11⇨♠Annexe6⇨♠(1fb) CTV in all bedrooms T
CTV P ⚙ ❀ pool table table tennis
V ✧ ⚖ ✄ Last dinner 9.30pm
Credit Cards [1] [2]

DROGHEDA Co Louth Map **01** D4

★★★**62%** *Boyne Valley*
☏(041) 37737 FAX (041) 39188
This 18th-century mansion stands in 16 acres of gardens and woodlands on the outskirts of Drogheda. Under new ownership it has been undergoing refurbishment and 18 new bedrooms have been built. The Cellar Restaurant serves good food in the evening; there is also a grill room and a conservatory bar where snacks are available.
35⇨♠(4fb) CTV in all bedrooms ® T
☾ CTV 200P ❀ ▶ 18
⚑ Continental V ✧ ⚖ ✄ Last dinner 10pm
Credit Cards [1] [2] [3] [5]

DUBLIN Co Dublin Map **01** D4

★★★★✿✿**72%** *Conrad*
Earlsfort Ter ☏(01) 6765555 FAX (01) 6765424
This modern hotel has a friendly atmosphere and luxuriously furnished bedrooms and public areas. It is situated just off St Stephens Green and opposite the National Concert Hall, and is only a short walk from the business, shopping and cultural centre of the city.
191⇨♠✄in 31 bedrooms CTV in all bedrooms❅ T
✱ (ex guide dogs) sB⇨♠IR£145 dB⇨♠IR£170 (room only) ⊟
Lift ☾ ⊞ 80☛ *xmas*
⚑ Irish & Continental V ✧ ⚖ ✄ ✱ Lunch IR£16.95 High tea IR£6 Dinner IR£26.50&alc Last dinner 10.45pm
CONF. Thtr 400 Class 220 Del from IR£165
Credit Cards [1] [2] [3] [5]

★★★★**64%** *Burlington*
Leeson St ☏(01) 605222 FAX (01) 608496
Situated on the outskirts of the city, this hotel has attractive public rooms and is ideally located for both the leisure and business guest. It is a popular place to eat, offering 2 restaurants and food in the recently refurbished main bar.
500⇨♠ CTV in all bedrooms❅ T ✱ (ex guide dogs)
Lift ☾ 450P
⚑ Irish & French V ✧ ⚖ ✄ Last dinner 11.45pm
Credit Cards [1] [2] [3] [4] [5]

★★★★✿✿**64%** *Jurys*
Pembroke Rd, Ballsbridge ☏(01) 6605000 FAX (01) 6605540
Business and leisure travellers alike will find something that appeals in this popular hotel to the south of the city centre. A wide range of accommodation is available, including luxury rooms in the 'Tower at Jurys'. There are 2 restaurants, a coffee shop and excellent facilities for the disabled.
284⇨♠Annexe100⇨♠✄in 59 bedrooms CTV in all bedrooms T ✱ (ex guide dogs) ✱ sB⇨♠IR£115-IR£164.08 dB⇨♠IR£135.26-IR£198.46 (room only) ⊟
Lift ☾ 280P ⊠ (heated) ⌂ (heated) whirlpool ♪ *xmas*
⚑ International V ✧ ⚖ ✄ ✱ Lunch IR£13-IR£15.50&alc Dinner IR£17.50-IR£19.95&alc Last dinner 10.15pm
CONF. Thtr 850 Class 450 Board 100 Del IR£90
Credit Cards [1] [2] [3] [5]

★★★**68%** *Doyle Montrose*
Stillorgan Rd(adjoining University College) ☏(01) 2693311
FAX (01) 2691164
Smartly decorated, attractive, comfortable bedrooms have resulted from the refurbishment of this hotel which overlooks the campus of University College. The public areas include good lounge space, a carvery bar and a more formal restaurant. The hotel is in a quiet suburb a short distance from the city.
180⇨♠(6fb) CTV in all bedrooms ®❅ T ✱ (ex guide dogs)
Lift ☾ 150P sauna
V ✧ ⚖ ✄ Lunch IR£10-IR£13&alc Dinner IR£11-IR£14&alc Last dinner 10.30pm
Credit Cards [1] [2] [3] [4] [5]

★★★**67%** *Stephen's Hall*
14/17 Lower Leeson St(off Leeson St) ☏(01) 610585 FAX (01) 610606
37⇨♠(9fb) CTV in all bedrooms ®❅ T ✱ (ex guide dogs) ✱ sB⇨♠IR£75-IR£90 dB⇨♠IR£90-IR£130 (room only) ⊟
Lift ☾ 40P ☛
⚑ European V ✧ ⚖ ✄ Lunch IR£7.50-IR£9.50 Dinner IR£10-IR£18&alc Last dinner 10pm
Credit Cards [1] [2] [3] [5]

★★★**63%** *Central*
1-5 Exchequer St ☏(01) 6797302 FAX (01) 6797303
Closed 23-26 Dec
This city centre hotel has recently been completely refurbished, and now offers modernised bedrooms and smart public rooms off a chequered marble lobby.
70⇨♠(8fb)⚐✄in 9 bedrooms CTV in all bedrooms ®❅ T
✱ (ex guide dogs) sB⇨♠IR£63-IR£84 dB⇨♠IR£84-IR£116 (room only) ⊟

Lift (
♨ International V ❆ ⚑ ✘ Lunch IR£10-IR£11 Dinner IR£18.50-IR£19.50 Last dinner 10pm
CONF. Thtr 80 Class 60 Board 30 Del from IR£62
Credit Cards 1 2 3 5

★★★ 61% **Doyle Skylon**
Drumcondra Rd ☎(01) 379121 FAX (01) 372778
This modern hotel, situated on the main road to the airport, caters mainly for commercial guests.
92⇨♠(4fb) CTV in all bedrooms ® T ✘ (ex guide dogs) ✳ sB⇨♠frIR£61.50 dB⇨♠frIR£82 (room only) ⊟
Lift (100P *xmas*
V ❆ ⚑ Last dinner 10.30pm
Credit Cards 1 2 3 4 5

★★★ ✿✿61% **Marine**
Sutton Cross ☎(01) 322613 FAX (01) 390442
Closed 24-26 Dec
On the north shore of Dublin Bay with attractive gardens and seashore walks, the Marine Hotel is convenient for Dublin Airport and the car ferry, and caters for tourists and the business sector.
27⇨♠ CTV in all bedrooms❆ T ✘ ✳ sB&B⇨♠IR£58-IR£65.50 dB&B⇨♠IR£95-IR£110 ⊟
(150P ✿ ▭ (heated) sauna
♨ International V ❆ ⚑ ✘ Lunch IR£10-IR£12 Dinner IR£16.50-IR£19&alc Last dinner 10.15pm
CONF. Class 200 Board 30 Del from IR£60
Credit Cards 1 2 3 5

★★★ 58% *Doyle Tara Tower*
Merrion Rd ☎(01) 2694666 FAX (01) 2691027
This modern company hotel is situated overlooking Dublin Bay.
100⇨♠(1fb) CTV in all bedrooms ® T ✘ (ex guide dogs)
Lift (CTV 300P
♨ European V ❆ ⚑ ✘ Last dinner 9.30pm
Credit Cards 1 2 3 4 5

★★★ 56% *Doyle Green Isle*
Clondalkin(on N7) ☎(01) 593406 FAX (01) 592178
Situated outside the city, this modern hotel offers a friendly atmosphere and an all-day food service. Family suites and chalets are available.
48⇨♠Annexe35⇨♠ CTV in all bedrooms T ✘ (ex guide dogs)
(400P ✿ ▶ 18 ♪ (hard) ♩ squash ∪ snooker sauna solarium gymnasium ♫ ♾
V ❆ ⚑ Lunch IR£8.80-IR£11.55&alc Dinner IR£14.50-IR£18&alc Last dinner 10.30pm
Credit Cards 1 2 3 5

★★ ✿✿73% **Longfield's**
Fitzwilliam St ☎(01) 6761367 FAX (01) 6761542
This intimate townhouse hotel is situated close to the city centre. Particular emphasis is placed on personalised service, good food and a relaxed atmosphere.
28⇨♠ CTV in all bedrooms❆ T ✘ (ex guide dogs)
sB&B⇨♠IR£55-IR£89.95 dB&B⇨♠IR£80-IR£104 ⊟
Lift (✐
♨ Irish & French V ❆ ⚑ Lunch IR£1.95-IR£18&alc Dinner IR£17.50-IR£19.95 Last dinner 10pm
Credit Cards 1 2 3 5

★★ 68% *Georgian House*
20 Baggot St Lower ☎(01) 6618832 FAX (01) 6618834
Just 5 minutes' walk from St Stephen's Green, this charming hotel has been refurbished throughout to provide every comfort. Furnishings, some in period style, are very attractive and a number of new bedrooms in smart contemporary style have recently been added. The popular restaurant has an emphasis on seafood and there is also Maguires Pub.

➠

ARAN VIEW HOUSE HOTEL★★ and Restaurant

Doolin, Co Clare
Tel: (065) 74061. Fax: (065) 74540

Situated amidst 100 acres of rolling farmland, Aran View House offers fine views of the sea and the surrounding countryside.
Built around 1736 this Georgian house has been in the same family for generations.
Today comfortable accommodation and an à la carte restaurant specialising in seafood, provide its guests with that touch of fine living. Special facilities for disabled guests.
Closed 1st November – 1st March.

HARVEY'S POINT COUNTRY HOTEL
Superb Swiss Accommodation
★★★ ✿✿✿
Exquisite French and Swiss Gourmet Cuisine in our award winning Restaurant. Fabulous Facilities, privacy and peace.

Lough Eske, Donegal Town
Co. Donegal
Tel. Eire 073 22208
Tel. UK + NI 010 353 73 22208
Fax 010 353 73 22352

Dublin - Dun Laoghaire

17⇨♦Annexe16⇨♦(27fb) CTV in 34 bedrooms ✗ (ex guide dogs) sB&B⇨♦IR£45-IR£65 dB&B⇨♦IR£66-IR£92
18P
Credit Cards [1][2][3]

Forte Crest
Cloghran ☎(01) 379211 FAX (01) 425874

A large modern hotel with a wide range of services and amenities, designed particularly for the business traveller. Bedrooms are smart, comfortable and well equipped. For more details about Forte Crest hotels, consult the Contents page, under Hotel Groups.
188⇨♦❋ sB⇨♦IR£106.89 dB⇨♦IR£124.14
CONF. Thtr 150 Class 70 Board 40 Del IR£85

Forte Travelodge
Swords By Pass ☎(01) 800 709 709

This modern building offers a good standard of accommodation for overnight stops. Smart, spacious and well equipped bedrooms, all with en suite bathrooms, are suitable for family use, and meals may be taken at the nearby family restaurant. For more details about Travelodges, consult the Contents page, under Hotel Groups.
40⇨♦❋ B⇨♦IR£31.95 (room only)

○**Hibernian**
Eastmoreland Place, Ballsbridge ☎(01) 6687666
Open
30⇨♦

○**Jurys Christchurch Inn**
Christchurch Place ☎(01) 4750111
Open
182⇨♦

○**Temple Bar**
Temple Bar ☎(01) 6773255
Open
108⇨♦

DUNDALK Co Louth Map 01 D4

★★★65% **Ballymascanlon House**
☎(042) 71124 FAX (042) 71598
Closed 24-26 Dec

Standing in its own grounds, this large converted mansion with modern extensions caters for both leisure and commercial guests.
36⇨♦(11fb) CTV in all bedrooms ®✎ T
《 CTV 250P ❋ ▭ (heated) ▶ 9 ♀ (hard) squash snooker sauna solarium gymnasium ♪
♀ Irish & French ❋ ♨ ✂ Last dinner 9.30pm
Credit Cards [1][2][3][4][5]

★★56% **Imperial**
☎(042) 32241 FAX (042) 37909
Closed 25 Dec

This large modern streetside hotel caters for commercial trade and functions.
47⇨♦(47fb) CTV in 31 bedrooms T ❋ sB&B⇨IR£38-IR£40 dB&B⇨IR£52-IR£56
Lift 《 CTV 100P
V ❋ ♨ ✂ Lunch IR£7.50-IR£10.75 High tea IR£3.70-IR£7 Dinner IR£12.50-IR£14 Last dinner 9.30pm
CONF. Thtr 400 Class 125 Board 50
Credit Cards [1][2][3][4][5]

DUNDRUM Co Tipperary Map 01 B3

★★♨66% **Rectory House**
☎Tipperary(062) 71266 FAX (062) 71115
Closed Dec-Feb

This fine old country house in secluded surroundings is now a small family-run hotel offering peace, quiet and good food.
10⇨♦ CTV in all bedrooms T ✗ (ex guide dogs)
CTV 300P ❋ ♨
♀ French V ❋ ♨ ✂ Last dinner 9.30pm
Credit Cards [1][2][3]

DUNFANAGHY Co Donegal Map 01 B6

★★69% **Carrig Rua**
(on N56) ☎(074) 36133 & 36469 FAX (074) 36277
Closed Nov-Etr

This old former coaching inn, now a modern family-run hotel, offers a high standard of comfort and personal attention. Most of the bedrooms have views of the sea and Horn Head, and the hotel is situated near a safe sandy beach.
22⇨♦(6fb) CTV in all bedrooms T ✗ (ex guide dogs) ❋ sB&B⇨♦IR£23-IR£28 dB&B⇨♦IR£46-IR£56 ♩
20P
♀ English & French V ❋ ♨ ❋ Bar Lunch IR£3-IR£9alc High tea IR£9-IR£13alc Dinner IR£18&alc Last dinner 8.15pm
Credit Cards [1][2][3]

★★68% **Arnold's**
☎Letterkenny(074) 36208 & 36142 FAX (074) 36352
Closed Nov-Mar

This family owned and managed hotel has been going for 3 generations. It offers good food and friendly, efficient service. The hotel has well cultivated mature gardens and splendid views over Sheephaven Bay and Horn Head.
34⇨♦(10fb) CTV in all bedrooms ® T ✗ (ex guide dogs)
sB&B⇨♦IR£35-IR£42 dB&B⇨♦IR£50-IR£64 ♩
《 CTV 60P ❋ ♀ (hard) ♪ croquet 9 hole pitch 'n' putt
V ❋ ♨ ✂ Last dinner 9pm
Credit Cards [1][2][3][5]

DUNGARVAN Co Waterford Map 01 C2

★★★59% **Lawlors**
☎(058) 41122 & 41056 FAX (058) 41000

An ideal touring centre, this family-run, streetside hotel caters for both leisure and business guests.
89⇨♦(8fb) CTV in all bedrooms T
Lift 《 CTV P ♪
V ❋ ♨ Last dinner 10pm
Credit Cards [1][2][3]

DUN LAOGHAIRE Co Dublin Map 01 D4

★★★59% **Hotel Victor**
Rochestown Av ☎(01) 2853555 & 2853102
FAX (01) 2853914

This modern suburban hotel caters for both tourists and commercial guests.
64⇨♦(8fb) CTV in all bedrooms T ✗ (ex guide dogs) ❋ sB&B⇨♦IR£30-IR£40 dB&B⇨♦IR£50-IR£75 ♩
Lift 《 ⊞ CTV P ❋ ♨
♀ Irish & French V ❋ ♨ Last dinner 9.30pm
Credit Cards [1][2][3][4][5]

★★61% **Pierre**
Victoria Ter, Seafront ☎(01) 2800291 FAX (01) 2843332
RS 24-25 Dec

Dun Laoghaire - Ennis

Friendliness is the keynote at this prominent seaside hotel overlooking the car ferry. Bedrooms, which are steadily being improved, are well equipped and comfortable.
40⇌♠(5fb)⊬in 4 bedrooms CTV in all bedrooms T ✘ (ex guide dogs) sB&B⇌♠IR£29-IR£35 dB&B⇌♠IR£55-IR£65 ₽
⟪ CTV 20P ♫ xmas
V ♡ ♎ ✱ High tea frIR£7.95alc Dinner IR£7.95-IR£10.95alc Last dinner 9.30pm
CONF. Thtr 100 Class 40 Board 30 Del from IR£30
Credit Cards [1][2][3]

DUNMORE EAST Co Waterford Map 01 C2

★★**57%** *Haven*
☎Waterford(051) 83150 & 83540 FAX (051) 83488
Closed Nov-Feb
Situated in its own grounds with views of the sea and cliffs, the Haven Hotel offers large airy public rooms and bedrooms.
14⇌♠(3fb) CTV in all bedrooms⊬ T ✘ (ex guide dogs) CTV 40P ✿ sauna solarium
V ♡ ⊬
Credit Cards [1][3]

★**59%** *Candlelight Inn*
☎Waterford(051) 83215 & 83239 FAX (051) 83289
This friendly family-run hotel overlooks the river estuary. In addition to the restaurant, there is a bistro open May to September, serving seafood, pasta and grills.
11⇌♠(3fb) CTV in all bedrooms T ✘ (ex guide dogs) CTV 9P ⇰ ✿ ⌒ (heated) ♫
V ♡
Credit Cards [1][3]

EMO Co Laois Map 01 C3

★★★**56%** *Hotel Montague*
Portlaoise ☎Portlaoise(0502) 26154 FAX (0502) 26229

This modern roadside establishment, recently remodelled and extended, caters for holiday and commercial trade.
75⇌♠(2fb) CTV in all bedrooms T
⟪ CTV P ✿
🍴 European V ♡ ♎ ⊬ Last dinner 9.30pm
Credit Cards [1][2][3][5]

ENNIS Co Clare Map 01 B3

★★★**67%** *Old Ground*
O'Connell St ☎(065) 28127 FAX (065) 28112

FORTE Heritage

58⇌♠(12fb)⊬in 8 bedrooms CTV in all bedrooms ®⊻ T ✱ sB&B⇌♠IR£50-IR£80 dB&B⇌♠IR£70-IR£99 ₽
⟪ 100P ✿ All facilities above are situated nearby ♫
V ♡ ♎ ⊬ ✱ Sunday Lunch IR£9.50-IR£12.50 Dinner IR£18.50-IR£21.50 Last dinner 9.30pm
CONF. Thtr 250 Class 100 Board 60 Del from IR£80
Credit Cards [1][2][3][5]

★★★**65%** *Auburn Lodge*
Galway Rd(Galway Rd on the outskirts of Ennis N18)
☎Limerick(065) 21247 FAX (065) 21202
There is a friendly atmosphere and bright, comfortable rooms at this modern hotel on the outskirts of town.
100⇌♠(70fb)⊬in 15 bedrooms CTV in all bedrooms ®⊻ T ✘ (ex guide dogs) ✱ sB&B⇌♠IR£25-IR£42 dB&B⇌♠IR£45-IR£65 ₽
⟪ CTV 200P ✿ ♪ (hard) xmas

➡→

EMO, PORTLAOISE,
CO. LAOIS, IRELAND.
Telephone: (0502) 26154
Fax: (0502) 26229
Telex: 60036

The Montague Hotel ★★★

E

This attractive modern hotel situated on the N7 route, is the perfect touring base to explore many parts of Ireland. Each of our 75 bedrooms are en suite with direct dial telephone, TV, and radio. Enjoy our Carvery for snacks & lunches, Maple Restaurant for dinner, our bar with its relaxed atmosphere is ideal for a quiet drink. A warm friendly welcome awaits you at the Montague Hotel.

Finnstown Country House Hotel & Golf Course ★★★

Newcastle Road, Lucan, Co Dublin
Tel: 6280644 Fax: 6281088
Finnstown Country House is only eight miles from Dublin city centre. Situated off the main road and on 50 acres of mature woodlands, guests may relax and enjoy the friendly atmosphere and service of a small grade A country house hotel together with the amenities of today and a fine Restaurant. The hotel has its own wooded walks, 9 hole golf course, hard tennis courts, outdoor pool, gymnasium, saunas and Turkish bath.
A beautiful place in a great location.

Ennis - Galway

♨ Irish & Continental V ✧ ⚥ ⚲ ✻ Lunch IR£6-IR£8.50 High tea IR£5-IR£8&alc Dinner IR£13-IR£17&alc Last dinner 10pm
CONF. Thtr 500 Class 200 Del from IR£45
Credit Cards 1 2 3 5

★★★ 58% West County Inn
Clare Rd(10mins walk from Ennis Town, next to St Flannans College) ☎(065) 28421 FAX (065) 28801

This modern, company-run hotel caters for both tourist and commercial trade.
110⇌🛏 CTV in all bedrooms⚥ T ✈ (ex guide dogs) ✻
sB&B⇌🛏IR£35-IR£45 dB&B⇌🛏IR£66-IR£75 (room only) ⌧
Lift ⟪ CTV 300P ✿ snooker sauna gymnasium
♨ Irish & French V ✧ ⚥ ⚲ ✻ Lunch IR£8-IR£15 High tea IR£6-IR£18 Dinner IR£15-IR£20 Last dinner 9.30pm
CONF. Thtr 1000 Class 500 Board 40 Del from IR£65
Credit Cards 1 2 3 4 5

★★ 69% Queen's
Abbey St(in the centre of town adjacent to ruins of Franciscan Friary) ☎(065) 28963 FAX (065) 28128

Recently modernised, this family-run, town centre hotel is convenient for Shannon Airport and Bunratty Castle.
52⇌🛏(20fb)⚲in 5 bedrooms CTV in all bedrooms ®⚥ T ✈ (ex guide dogs) ✻ sB&B⇌🛏IR£25-IR£38 dB&B⇌🛏IR£45-IR£65 ⌧
Lift ⟪ CTV P ♪ xmas
♨ Irish & Continental V ✧ ⚥ ⚲ ✻ Lunch IR£6-IR£8.50 High tea IR£5-IR£8&alc Dinner IR£13-IR£16&alc Last dinner 10pm
Credit Cards 1 2 3 5

ENNISCORTHY Co Wexford Map 01 C3

★★ 58% Murphy-Flood's
Market Square ☎(054) 33413
Closed 25 Dec
A family-run hotel in the centre of a lively market town, Murphy-Flood's has a comfortable bar where carvery lunches, grills and snacks are served throughout the day. The hotel is currently undergoing refurbishment.
21rm(5⇌13🛏)(2fb) CTV in all bedrooms ®⚥ T ✈ (ex guide dogs)
⟪ CTV P ♪
V ✧ ⚥ ⚲ Last dinner 9.30pm
Credit Cards 1 2 3 4 5

ENNISKERRY Co Wicklow Map 01 D3

★★ 65% Enniscree Lodge Hotel & Restaurant
Glencree Valley(off N11) ☎2863542 FAX 2866037
RS 6 Jan-3 Mar
This cosy owner-managed lodge is set in the Glencree Valley and has uninterrupted views of the Wicklow mountains. Bedrooms are comfortable, there is an intimate bar and good food is served in the attractive restaurant, which has panoramic mountain views.
10⇌🛏(1fb) CTV in 5 bedrooms ® T ✈ (ex guide dogs) sB&B⇌🛏frIR£55 dB&B⇌🛏frIR£75
CTV 20P ⇄ ✿ xmas
V ✧ ⚥ ⚲ Sunday Lunch IR£12.50-IR£15alc Dinner IR£15-IR£25alc Last dinner 9.30pm
Credit Cards 1 2 3 5

Rosettes range from 5 for outstanding cuisine to 1 rosette for enjoyable, well prepared food

ENNISKILLEN Co Fermanagh Map 01 C5

★★★ 58% Killyhevlin
BT74 4AU (2m S, off A4) ☎(0365) 323481 FAX 324726
Beautifully situated on the shores of Lough Erne to the southeast of the town, this distinctive white-painted hotel enjoys fine views from several of its balconied bedrooms, and also from the popular lounge bar, where snacks are available throughout the day and evening. Staff provide friendly service.
22⇌🛏 Annexe26rm(17fb) CTV in 22 bedrooms ® T ✈ (ex guide dogs) sB&B⇌🛏£42.50-£60 dB&B⇌🛏£62.50-£90 ⌧
⟪ CTV 500P ✿ ♪
♨ International V ✧ ⚥ ⚲ ✻ Lunch £4.50-£9.50&alc High tea fr£10alc Dinner £14-£18&alc Last dinner 9.15pm
CONF. Board 100 Del £65
Credit Cards 1 2 3 5 £

★ 66% Railway
☎(0365) 22084
Closed 25 Dec
This friendly commercial hotel close to the town centre continues to improve. Bedrooms, though generally compact, have modern decor and amenities, and pleasantly refurbished public areas include a restaurant serving well prepared meals.
18⇌🛏(4fb) CTV in 14 bedrooms ®
⟪ CTV ▶ ♪ ⚘
V ✧ ⚥ Last dinner 9.15pm
Credit Cards 1 3

FURBO Co Galway Map 01 B3

★★★★ 62% Connemara Coast
(between Barna and Spiddal) ☎Galway(091) 92108 FAX (091) 92065
Situated overlooking Galway Bay, this recently extended and modernised hotel has superb accommodation, including an executive suite. The atmosphere is one of quality, style and comfort.
112⇌🛏(30fb) CTV in all rooms⚥ T ✈ (ex guide dogs) sB&B⇌🛏IR£45-IR£77.50 dB&B⇌🛏IR£85-IR£117.50 ⌧
⟪ CTV 100P ✿ ⊡ (heated) ℘ (hard) sauna solarium gymnasium steam bath ♪ ⚘ xmas
♨ Irish & French V ✧ ⚥ ⚲ Lunch IR£12-IR£16 Dinner IR£19.75-IR£22.50&alc Last dinner 9.30pm
CONF. Thtr 500 Class 450 Board 150
Credit Cards 1 2 3 4 5

GALWAY Co Galway Map 01 B4

★★★★ 67% Great Southern
Eyre Square(next to railway and bus stations) ☎(091) 64041 FAX (091) 66704
The Great Southern Hotel is an imposing granite building on Eyre Square, with large, elegant public rooms including a restaurant, and a rooftop swimming pool.
114⇌🛏(12fb)1🚹⚲in 10 bedrooms CTV in all rooms ®⚥ T ✈ (ex guide dogs) ✻ sB&B⇌🛏IR£68.25-IR£74.30 dB&B⇌🛏IR£102-IR£114.20 ⌧
Lift ⟪ CTV ℘ ⊡ (heated) sauna ♪ xmas
♨ French V ✧ ⚥ ⚲ ✻ Lunch frIR£9&alc Dinner frIR£18&alc Last dinner 9.30pm
CONF. Thtr 400 Class 200 Board 200 Del from IR£50
Credit Cards 1 2 3 4 5

★★★★ 64% Glenlo Abbey
Bushypark ☎(091) 26666 FAX (091) 27800
This restored old Abbey building with added bedroom wing is in extensive wooded grounds reaching to the nearby river and lakeshore. Facilities and service are excellent.
42⇌🛏2⚥⚲in 6 bedrooms CTV in all bedrooms⚥ T ✈ (ex guide dogs) sB&B⇌🛏IR£65-IR£80 dB&B⇌🛏IR£96-IR£115 ⌧

Galway - Glendalough

Lift (CTV 100P ✿ ▶ 9 ♀ (hard) ♪ gymnasium
V ✿ ♨ ♀ Lunch IR£9.75-IR£12 Dinner IR£22-IR£25&alc
Last dinner 10pm
CONF. Thtr 40 Class 30 Board 20
Credit Cards 1 2 3 5

★★★★**59%** **Corrib Great Southern**
Dublin Rd ☎(091) 55281 due to change to 755281 FAX (091) 51390
Closed 25-26 Dec
Situated on the outskirts of Galway, this hotel has recently been extensively refurbished, and the new 'executive' bedrooms have won high praise from our inspectors. The décor is attractive, with comfortable easy chairs and a second desk telephone among the modern facilities provided.
180⇌♠(10fb)⌿in 20 bedrooms CTV in all bedrooms ® ♀ T ✹ (ex guide dogs) ✱ sB⇌♠IR£63.78-IR£69.46 dB⇌♠IR£91.12-IR£102.37 (room only) ⍰
Lift (350P ✿ ▭ (heated) ♀ snooker table tennis jacuzzi steam room ♪
♀ Irish & French V ✿ ♨ ♀ ✱ Lunch IR£10 Dinner IR£17&alc Last dinner 8.50pm
CONF. Thtr 850 Class 400 Del from IR£70
Credit Cards 1 2 3 4 5

★★★**71%** **Ardilaun House**
Taylor's Hill ☎(091) 21433 FAX (091) 21546
Closed 23-29 Dec
The comfortable public rooms at this hotel include large lounges, and the bedrooms are also spacious and well furnished. Warmly inviting, the hotel successfully marries traditional standards of service with tasteful furnishings and modern facilities.
92⇌♠(19fb) CTV in all bedrooms ® ♀ T
Lift (CTV 200P ✿ snooker sauna gymnasium ♪
V ✿ ♨ ♀ Lunch IR£7.50-IR£9.75&alc Dinner IR£15.50-IR£19.50&alc Last dinner 9.30pm
Credit Cards 1 2 3 5

★★★**63%** **Galway Ryan**
Dublin Rd(1m from city centre, on main Dublin/Galway Road N6) ☎(091) 53181 FAX (091) 53187
This modern, company-owned hotel is situated on the eastern edge of the city and caters for both tourists and commercial guests.
96⇌♠(96fb) CTV in all bedrooms T ✹ ✱ sB⇌♠IR£60-IR£85 dB⇌♠IR£80-IR£110 (room only) ⍰
Lift (100P ✿ xmas
♀ French V ✿ ♨ ✱ Lunch IR£8-IR£12 Dinner IR£14-IR£18&alc Last dinner 9pm
CONF. Thtr 80 Class 45 Board 30 Del from IR£75
Credit Cards 1 2 3 5

★★**64%** **Anno Santo**
Threadneedle Rd, Salthill ☎(091) 23011
Closed 21-31 Dec
Situated off the seafront in Salthill, this family-run hotel offers comfortable, well furnished bedrooms.
14⇌♠ CTV in all bedrooms ® T ✹
CTV 12P
✿ ♨ ♀ Last dinner 9pm
Credit Cards 1 2 3 5

★★**61%** **Lochlurgain**
22 Monksfield, Upper Salthill(on R286) ☎(091) 22122 FAX (091) 22399
Closed 2 Nov-13 Mar
This family-run hotel is situated close to the promenade and beach.
13⇌♠(3fb) CTV in all bedrooms ♀ T ✹ (ex guide dogs) sB&B⇌♠IR£19-IR£44.95 dB&B⇌♠IR£35.90-IR£69.90 ⍰
CTV 8P
♀ English & French ✿ ♨ ✱ Lunch IR£9.50 Dinner IR£16.95 Last dinner 8pm
Credit Cards 1 3

★**53%** **Atlanta**
Dominick St ☎(091) 62241 FAX (091) 63895
RS Sun
The Atlanta is situated in the centre of the city. Some of the bedrooms have been refurbished and have attractive décor and en suite showers; the others remain modest.
18rm(11♠)(2fb)⌿in 7 bedrooms CTV in 10 bedrooms ® ✹ ✱ sB&B♠IR£40 dB&B♠IR£60
CTV 35P ⚲
♀
Credit Cards 1 3

○ **Brennans Yard**
Lower Merchants Rd ☎(091) 68344
24⇌♠

○ **Jurys Galway Inn**
Quay St ☎(091) 666444
Open
129⇌♠

GARRETTSTOWN Co Cork Map **01** B2

★★**58%** **Coakley's Atlantic**
☎Cork(021) 778215 FAX (021) 778215
RS Jan-16 Mar
Catering mainly for tourists, this modern family-run hotel overlooks the bay.
22⇌♠(2fb) ✹ (ex guide dogs)
(CTV 60P ✿
V ✿ ♀ Last dinner 8.45pm
Credit Cards 1 2 3 5

GARRYVOE Co Cork Map **01** C2

★★**63%** **Garryvoe**
☎Castlemartyr(021) 646718 FAX (021) 646824
Closed 25 Dec
A comfortable, family-run hotel with caring staff, the Garryvoe has recently been refurbished. It is in a delightful position facing a sandy beach, and the first floor residents' lounge overlooks the sea. There is a hotel bar, and a public bar where locals meet and chat.
20⇌♠(3fb) CTV in all bedrooms T ✹ (ex guide dogs) ✱ sB&B⇌♠IR£30 dB&B⇌♠IR£50 ⍰
CTV 20P ✿ ▶ 18 ♀ (hard)
V ✿ ♨ ✱ Lunch IR£9-IR£14.50 Dinner IR£18.50&alc Last dinner 8.45pm
Credit Cards 1 2 3 5

GLENDALOUGH Co Wicklow Map **01** D3

★★★**60%** **The Glendalough**
☎Wicklow(0404) 5135 FAX (0404) 5142
Closed Nov-15 Mar
Situated beside the famous monastic site and bordered by woodland, this long established hotel is run by the Casey family. The charming restaurant overlooks river and forest, and bar food is also available. The hotel has been completely refurbished to a high standard, combining traditional atmosphere with attractive modern furnishing.
17⇌♠ T ✹ (ex guide dogs) sB&B⇌♠IR£35-IR£37 dB&B⇌♠IR£57-IR£62 ⍰
Lift CTV 100P ♪ ⚲
♀ French V ✿ ♨ ♀ Last dinner 8.45pm
Credit Cards 1 2 3 4 5

For key to symbols see the Bookmark.

Glounthaune - Irvinestown

GLOUNTHAUNE Co Cork Map 01 B2

★★ **68%** *Ashbourne House*
☎Cork(021) 353319 & 353310 FAX (021) 354338
This owner-managed hotel set in beautiful gardens attracts mostly tourist business with some commercial trade.
26⇌♠(3fb) CTV in all bedrooms ® ⚲ T
CTV 100P ❋ ⌤ (heated) ℘ (hard) sauna
♀ French V ✧ ⌶ Last dinner 10pm
Credit Cards ①②③④⑤

GOREY Co Wexford Map 01 D3

★★★❀❀❀♣
MARLFIELD HOUSE
☎(055) 21124 FAX (055) 21572
Closed 10-31 Jan

This lovely old Regency house stands in 35 acres of grounds, allowing ample room for guests to stroll about and enjoy the wooded walks. Once the Dower House on the estate of the Earls of Courtown, it has been tastefully decorated and furnished in a style befitting its grand origins. An extension has been added to make a semi-circular marble entrance hall and bedrooms have been beautifully furnished with period pieces and fireplaces.
19⇌♠(5fb)6❄✂in all bedrooms CTV in all bedrooms T ✈
♣ ❋ ℘ (grass) sauna
♀ Irish & French V ✧ ⌶ Last dinner 9pm
Credit Cards ①②③⑤

GOUGANE BARRA Co Cork Map 01 B2

★★ **60%** *Gougane Barra*
☎(026) 47069 & 47223 FAX (026) 47226
15 Apr-7 Oct
Right on the lake shore, this hotel has been in the Lucey family for generations. Recent refurbishments have improved the restaurant, bedrooms and bathrooms, all of which have lovely views. Guests can be met from their train, boat or plane by prior arrangement.
25rm(24⇌)CTV in 24 bedrooms T ✈ (ex guide dogs)
CTV 25P ♣ ♪ nc5yrs
♀ Irish & French V ✧ ⌶ ✂ Last dinner 8.30pm
Credit Cards ①②③⑤

HOLYWOOD Co Down Map 01 D5

★★★★ ❀**70%** *Culloden*
BT18 0EX (HG) ☎(0232) 425223 FAX (0232) 426777
Closed 24 & 25 Dec
Standing in its own attractive grounds, with views over Belfast Lough and the Antrim coastline, this 19th-century baronial mansion has been sympathetically extended to provide a comfortable, well managed hotel which is widely regarded as the finest in the Province. Many original features have been retained, including fine plasterwork and stained glass, while a modern wing of spacious bedrooms provides all the facilities expected by today's travellers. Paul McKnight offers a traditional menu of dishes which have a bias towards fish and grills, with a variety of sauces. Meals are also available in the less formal bar.
91⇌♠4❄✂in 4 bedrooms CTV in all bedrooms ® ⚲ T

Lift ℓ 500P ❋ ⌤ (heated) ℘ (hard) squash snooker sauna solarium gymnasium putting croquet ⚘
♀ French V ✧ ⌶ ✂ Last dinner 9.45pm
Credit Cards ①②③⑤

HOWTH Co Dublin Map 01 D4

★★★ **60%** *Howth Lodge*
☎Dublin(01) 321010 FAX (01) 322268
Closed 24-27 Dec

This modernised hotel is situated in its own grounds in a seaside location on the edge of the small, northside suburban resort.
46⇌♠(5fb) CTV in all bedrooms ® T ✈ (ex guide dogs)
sB&B⇌♠IR£50-IR£55 dB&B⇌♠IR£70-IR£80 ♬
Lift ℓ 200P ❋ ⌤ (heated) sauna solarium gymnasium plunge pool in Leisure Club
♀ Irish & French V ✧ ⌶ Sunday Lunch IR£10-IR£15 Dinner IR£17-IR£22&alc Last dinner 9.30pm
CONF. Thtr 200 Class 80 Board 60 Del from IR£75
Credit Cards ①②③④⑤

INCHIGEELAGH Co Cork Map 01 B2

★ **52%** *Creedon's*
☎(026) 49012
This small, family-run hotel caters mainly for tourists.
16rm(8⇌♠) ✈
CTV 4P
Credit Cards ③

INISHANNON Co Cork Map 01 B2

★★ **63%** *Inishannon House*
(off N71 at eastern end of village) ☎Innishannon(021) 775121 FAX (021) 775609
Conal and Vera O'Sullivan took over this charming country house in 1989 and have been restoring it since then. The River Bandon flows by the house, and there are attractive walks and gardens. Good food is prepared from the freshest ingredients, with seafood a speciality.
13⇌♠(2fb)2❄ CTV in all bedrooms T ❋ sB&B⇌♠IR£40-IR£90 dB&B⇌♠IR£75-IR£125 ♬
100P ❋ ♪ ⚘ xmas
♀ Irish & French V ✧ ⌶ ✂ ❋ Lunch IR£9.75-IR£12.50&alc High tea IR£7.50-IR£10.50alc Dinner IR£18.50-IR£21.50&alc Last dinner 9.30pm
CONF. Thtr 250 Class 60 Board 40 Del from IR£70
Credit Cards ①②③④⑤

IRVINESTOWN Co Fermanagh Map 01 C5

★★ **64%** *Mahons*
BT74 1GS (on B32 midway between Enniskillen and Omagh)
☎(03656) 21656 FAX (03656) 28344
Closed 25 Dec
This long established family-run hotel in the town centre, offers friendly service and the public areas have displays of personal momentoes and bric-á-brac. Bedrooms vary in size and style but all are thoughtfully equipped.
18⇌♠(4fb)2❄ CTV in all bedrooms⚲ T sB&B⇌♠£29.50 dB&B⇌♠£56 ♬
CTV 30P 10⚘ solarium ♫
V ✧ ⌶ Lunch £7.50 Dinner fr£12.50alc Last dinner 9pm
CONF. Thtr 500 Class 200 Board 150 Del from £80
Credit Cards ①③

Remember to book early for holiday
and bank holiday times.

Kells - Kilkenny

KELLS Co Meath Map **01** D5

★★**60%** *Headfort Arms*
Ceanannus ☎(046) 40063 & 40121 FAX (046) 40587
Closed Good Fri & 25 Dec
18⇌♠(4fb) CTV in all bedrooms ®⚲T
《 CTV 6P ✱
♀ Irish & Continental V ♥ ☑ ✂
Credit Cards ①②③

KENMARE Co Kerry Map **01** A2

★★★★❀❀♨ PARK
(on R569)
☎Killarney(064) 41200
FAX (064) 41402
Closed 2 Jan-3 Apr & Nov-23 Dec

The Park Hotel is synonymous with all the expectations of a luxurious country house hotel. On the famous Ring of Kerry, it stands above terraced gardens which overlook the estuary of the Kenmare River, with a glorious backdrop of mountains. Splendid antique furnishings, warm hospitality and sheer professionalism combine to draw guests back here time after time, and the restaurant offers very good food and fine wines.

50⇌♠(2fb) CTV in all bedrooms ⚲T ✈ (ex guide dogs)
sB&B⇌♠IR£110-IR£128 dB&B⇌♠IR£184-IR£264
Lift 《 CTV 60P ✱ ▶ 18 ℘ (hard) snooker *xmas*
V ♥ ☑ Lunch IR£18&alc Dinner IR£25.95-IR£36&alc Last dinner 9pm
CONF. Thtr 60 Class 40 Board 30 Del from IR£125
Credit Cards ①②③④⑤

★★★★❀❀♨**82%** Sheen Falls Lodge
(from Kenmare take N71 to Glengarriff over the suspension bridge, take the first turn left)
☎Killarney(064) 41600 FAX (064) 41386

Inspectors Choice 1994

Closed beginning Jan-beginning Feb
Young, friendly and courteous staff maintain country house traditions in the contemporary elegance of this fine hotel, superbly situated beside the Sheen River in 300 acres of woodland. Excellent public rooms include a cosy cocktail bar, well-stocked library, a choice of lounges and the restaurant. Bedrooms are spacious, some overlooking the beautiful gardens and waterfalls which are floodlit at night. We are very pleased to announce that Sheen Falls Lodge is

the winner of our Inspectors' Selected Hotel of the Year for Ireland this year.
40⇌♠(11fb) CTV in all bedrooms⚲T ✈ (ex guide dogs)
sB&B⇌♠IR£155-IR£175 dB&B⇌♠IR£190-IR£350 ⓟ
Lift 《 CTV 75P ✱ ℘ (hard) ♪ ♨ snooker sauna solarium gymnasium jacuzzi croquet table tennis steamroom ♫ ⚀ *xmas*
V ♥ ☑ ✱ Sunday Lunch IR£17.50 High tea IR£16.25-IR£27alc Dinner IR£35&alc Last dinner 9.30pm
CONF. Thtr 120 Class 70 Board 35
Credit Cards ①②③④⑤

★★**66%** *Lansdowne Arms*
☎(064) 41368 FAX (064) 41114
Kenmare's first hotel, dating back to the 1760's, is in a streetside location of the popular tourist town on the Ring of Kerry.
25⇌♠ CTV in all bedrooms ® T ✈
《 CTV
V ♥ ☑

KILKEE Co Clare Map **01** A3

★★**59%** Halpin's
Erin St ☎(065) 56032 FAX (065) 56317
Closed 3 Jan-15 Mar
The finest tradition of personal service is offered at this family-run hotel which has a commanding view over the old Victorian town. The attractive bedrooms have recently been refurbished.
12⇌♠(6fb)✂in 4 bedrooms CTV in all bedrooms ®⚲T ✈
sB&B⇌♠IR£24-IR£34 dB&B⇌♠IR£40-IR£55 ⓟ
《⊞ CTV ▶ 18 ℘ (hard) *xmas*
V ♥ ☑ ✂ ✱ Lunch IR£4.50-IR£8.50alc High tea IR£10-IR£16alc Dinner IR£10-IR£18alc Last dinner 9pm
CONF. Thtr 60 Board 30 Del from IR£45
Credit Cards ①②③④⑤

KILKENNY Co Kilkenny Map **01** C3

★★★**65%** Hotel Kilkenny
College Rd ☎(056) 62000 FAX (056) 65984
This modern hotel and leisure complex is built around the home of the noted architect Sir William Robertson. It combines old world charm with high standards and efficiency, and public areas include a conservatory and sun lounge.
60⇌♠(20fb) CTV in all bedrooms⚲T sB&B⇌♠IR£45-IR£50 dB&B⇌♠IR£80-IR£90 ⓟ
《 250P ✱ ⌧ (heated) ℘ (hard) sauna solarium gymnasium turbo jacuzzi *xmas*
♀ French V ♥ ☑ ✱ Lunch frIR£9&alc High tea IR£7-IR£9 Dinner IR£15.95&alc Last dinner 9.30pm
CONF. Thtr 500 Class 300 Board 40 Del from IR£50
Credit Cards ①②③

★★★**65%** *Newpark*
☎(056) 22122 FAX (056) 61111
This converted country house with modern extensions is situated in 50 acres of parkland on the outskirts of town. It caters mainly for commercial trade and functions.
60⇌♠(18fb) CTV in all bedrooms ®⚲T ✈ (ex guide dogs)
《 CTV 350P ✱ ⌧ (heated) ℘ (hard) sauna solarium gymnasium jacuzzi plunge pool
V ♥ ☑ Last dinner 10.15pm
Credit Cards ①②③④⑤

★★**55%** Club House
☎(056) 21994 FAX (056) 21994

An old world atmosphere prevails at this fine hotel, run under the personal supervision of the proprietor/manager.
27rm(22⇌♠) CTV in all bedrooms ®⚲T ✱ sB&BIR£26.50-IR£37.50 sB&B⇌♠IR£32.50-IR£44 dB&BIR£53.75-IR£65 dB&B⇌♠IR£55-IR£85 ⓟ

Kilkenny - Killarney

((CTV 80P squash sauna solarium gymnasium
♀ Irish & French V ✿ 🐾 ✂ Last dinner 9.30pm
CONF. Thtr 120 Class 80 Board 50
Credit Cards 1 2 3 4 5

KILLARNEY Co Kerry Map 01 A2

★★★★✿✿75% Aghadoe Heights
☎(064) 31766 FAX (064) 31345

Situated in a commanding position overlooking the lakes of Killarney and the surrounding countryside, the Aghadoe Heights offers excellent accommodation.

60⇨♠(5fb) CTV in all bedrooms♂ T ✈ (ex guide dogs) ✱
sB&B⇨♠IR£72-IR£100 dB&B⇨♠IR£105-IR£145 🅿
((180P ✿ ⛱ (heated) ► 18 ♪ (hard) ♫ sauna solarium gymnasium jaccuzzi ♫ xmas
♀ French V ✿ 🐾 ✂ ✱ Lunch IR£17.50&alc Dinner IR£29.50&alc Last dinner 9.30pm
Credit Cards 1 2 3 5

★★★★71% Killarney Park
Kenmare Place ☎(064) 35555 FAX (064) 35266

Located on the edge of town, this charming purpose built hotel combines elegance with comfort. The entrance lobby with blazing fire gives the first hint of the warmth of atmosphere created by both the innovative décor, rich in colours and fabrics and the friendly efficient staff. Public rooms and bedrooms are very comfortable.

46⇨♠(4fb) CTV in all bedrooms ® ♂ T ✈ (ex guide dogs) ✱
sB&B⇨♠IR£40-IR£75 dB&B⇨♠IR£70-IR£110 🅿
Lift ((🏛 CTV 70P ✿ (heated) gymnasium steam room ♫ xmas
V ✿ 🐾 ✂ ✱ Lunch IR£11-IR£13 Dinner IR£18.50-IR£20&alc Last dinner 10.15pm
CONF. Thtr 150 Class 100 Board 40 Del from IR£65
Credit Cards 1 2 3

★★★★66% Great Southern
☎(064) 31262 FAX (064) 31642
Closed 6 Jan-20 Feb

Standing in 35 acres of wooded gardens, this gracious hotel has benefited considerably from recent refurbishment to public areas. The elegant entrance hall and comfortable lounges, reading room and new conservatory and bar all combine to give guests space and comfort in which to relax. It is an ideal touring centre.

180⇨♠(35fb) CTV in all bedrooms ♂ T sB&B⇨♠IR£65-IR£72 dB&B⇨♠IR£96-IR£110 🅿
Lift ((200P ✿ ⛱ (heated) ♪ (hard) sauna gymnasium jacuzzi plunge pool steam room xmas
♀ International V ✿ 🐾 ✂ Bar Lunch IR£2.50-IR£12 Dinner frIR£16.50 Last dinner 9.30pm
CONF. Thtr 1000 Class 700 Board 40 Del from IR£40
Credit Cards 1 2 3 5

★★★64% Castlerosse
☎(064) 31144 FAX (064) 31031
Closed Nov-Mar

Set in 6,000 acres of lakeland overlooking Lough Leane, this beautifully situated hotel adjoins a 36-hole championship golf course. The hotel offers warm hospitality and good food as well as special facilities to the golf course. Boating and fishing trips are available on the nearby lakes.

67⇨♠(2fb) CTV in all bedrooms T ✱ sB&B⇨♠IR£49-IR£66 dB&B⇨♠IR£64-IR£98 🅿
((100P ✿ snooker sauna gymnasium putting green
V ✿ 🐾 ✂ Last dinner 8.45pm
Credit Cards 1 2 3 5

★★★61% Killarney Ryan
Cork Rd(on N22 route) ☎(064) 31555 FAX (064) 32438
Closed Dec-Feb

This hotel is conveniently located on the outskirts of Killarney. Excellent leisure facilities have recently been added, and a crèche is provided in summer with 'Friendly Fellows' to supervise. Guests will also enjoy the hotel grounds.

168⇨♠(168fb) CTV in all bedrooms♂ T ✈ ✱ sB⇨♠IR£60-IR£80 dB⇨♠IR£80-IR£115 (room only) 🅿
Lift ((150P ✿ ⛱ (heated) ♪ (hard) sauna pitch & putt steamroom jacuzzi ♫
♀ French V ✿ 🐾 ✂ ✱ Dinner IR£14-IR£18&alc Last dinner 9pm
CONF. Thtr 50 Class 30 Board 20 Del from IR£60
Credit Cards 1 2 3 5

★★★60% Lake
Muckross Rd ☎(064) 31035 FAX (064) 31902
Closed Dec-Feb

Originally a mansion, converted in 1850, this hotel offers spectacular views of Killarney's lakes and mountains. It has old world charm with open log fires, spacious lounges and comfortable bedrooms.

65⇨♠(10fb) CTV in all bedrooms♂ T ✈ (ex guide dogs)
sB&B⇨♠IR£29-IR£54 dB&B⇨♠IR£46-IR£78 🅿
((🏛 CTV 120P 2⛽ ✿ ♪ (hard) ♫ ♫
♀ Irish, French & Italian V ✿ 🐾 ✱ Lunch IR£7.50-IR£9 High tea IR£4-IR£19alc Dinner IR£13-IR£17 Last dinner 9pm
CONF. Thtr 100 Class 50 Board 30 Del from IR£49
Credit Cards 1 3

★★★59% International
Kenmare Pl ☎(064) 31816 FAX (064) 31837
Closed Nov-Feb

Situated in the centre of town, this large, recently modernised hotel offers good food and service for both the tourist and commercial trade.

87⇨♠(14fb) CTV in all bedrooms ® ♂ T sB⇨♠IR£35-IR£42 dB⇨♠IR£46-IR£60 (room only) 🅿
Lift ((CTV ♪
V ✿ Lunch IR£8.50-IR£10.50 Dinner IR£11-IR£15.50 Last dinner 10pm
CONF. Thtr 150 Class 100 Board 40
Credit Cards 1 2 3 5

★★★58% Torc Great Southern
☎(064) 31611
Closed 11 Oct-14 Mar

This company-owned, comfortable modern hotel is situated in its own spacious grounds with splendid views of the Kerry mountains, and is just 5 minutes' walk from the town centre.

96⇨♠(15fb) CTV in all bedrooms T
((100P ✿ ⛱ (heated) ♪ (hard) sauna ♫
Credit Cards 1 2 3 5

★★★56% Gleneagle
☎(064) 31870 FAX (064) 32646

This family-run hotel on the outskirts of town specialises in evening entertainment. It has a superb swimming pool and good all-round leisure facilities.

177⇨♠(6fb) CTV in all bedrooms T ✈ (ex guide dogs)
Lift ((CTV 500P ✿ ⛱ (heated) ► 36 ♪ (hard) ♫ squash snooker sauna gymnasium table tennis steam room
V ✿ 🐾 Last dinner 8.30pm
Credit Cards 1 2 3 5

The AA's star rating scheme is the market leader in hotel classification.

Hotels with red star ratings are especially high quality.

KILLINEY Co Dublin Map 01 D3

★★★ 71% Fitzpatrick Castle
☎Dublin(01) 2840700 FAX (01) 2850207
This converted castle with modern extensions is set in its own attractive gardens and grounds with views over Dublin Bay. There is a helipad, and a courtesy coach is available for transfers to and from the airport.
90⇨ʼn(6fb)12☐ CTV in all bedrooms ® T ✖ ✱
sB⇨ʼnIR£66.60-IR£83 dB⇨ʼnIR£87.10-IR£114.80 (room only) ⌂
Lift (300P ✿ ☐ (heated) ♀ (hard) squash sauna solarium gymnasium beauty salon hairdressing salon ♫ xmas
♀ International V ♦ ♱ ✘ Lunch IR£9.95 Dinner IR£18.50&alc Last dinner 10.30pm
CONF. Thtr 560 Class 270 Board 180 Del IR£94
Credit Cards [1][2][3][4][5]

★★★ 59% Court
☎Dublin(01) 2851622 FAX (01) 2852085
Closed 25-26 Dec
This converted Victorian mansion with tasteful modern extensions is set in its own spacious grounds overlooking Dublin Bay. It offers extensive conference facilities, bright airy rooms and efficient service, catering for both tourist and conference business.
86⇨ʼn(29fb)✘in 8 bedrooms CTV in all bedrooms ® T ✖ (ex guide dogs) sB&B⇨ʼnIR£34-IR£49 dB&B⇨ʼnIR£44-IR£68 ⌂
Lift (200P ✿ snooker
♀ International V ♦ ♱ ✘ Lunch IR£10.75&alc Dinner IR£18.95&alc Last dinner 11.15pm
CONF. Thtr 300 Class 180 Board 60 Del from IR£89
Credit Cards [1][2][3][5]

KINSALE Co Cork Map 01 B2

★★★ ❀70% Trident
Worlds End ☎Cork(021) 772301 FAX (021) 774173
Charmingly situated at the water's edge, overlooking the harbour, this hotel has been completely refurbished to a very high standard. Bedrooms and public rooms alike have delightful views, and guests relaxing in the first-floor lounge or on the patio can watch the world sail by. Seafood is a speciality of the restaurant, pleasant staff provide helpful service.
58⇨ʼn CTV in all bedrooms ♱ T ✖ (ex guide dogs) ✱
sB&B⇨ʼnIR£45-IR£60 dB&B⇨ʼnIR£66-IR£98 ⌂
Lift (CTV 60P sauna gymnasium jacuzzi steam room
♀ Irish & European V ♦ ♱ ✘ ✱ Sunday Lunch IR£9 Dinner IR£15-IR£17&alc Last dinner 10.00pm
CONF. Thtr 200 Class 100 Board 10 Del from IR£60
Credit Cards [1][2][3][5]

★★★ 69% Acton's
Pier Rd ☎Cork(021) 772135 FAX (021) 772231

FORTE Heritage

57⇨ʼn(15fb) CTV in all bedrooms ® ♱ T sB&B⇨ʼnIR£55-IR£80 dB&B⇨ʼnIR£70-IR£110 ⌂
Lift (60P ✿ ☐ (heated) sauna solarium gymnasium ♫ xmas
♀ Irish & French V ♦ ♱ ✘ Lunch IR£9.50-IR£12alc Dinner IR£18-IR£22.50 Last dinner 9.30pm
CONF. Thtr 350 Class 200 Board 100 Del from IR£80
Credit Cards [1][2][3][4][5]

If you have booked a meal in a hotel restaurant and cannot get there, remember you have a contractual obligation to cancel your booking.

LETTERKENNY Co Donegal Map 01 C5

★★ 67% Clanree
(on N13 Derry road) ☎(074) 24369 FAX (074) 25389
This red-brick building has been extended and totally refurbished and is on the outskirts of the town, an ideal location from which to tour north Donegal. Attractively decorated public rooms are both warm and inviting and bedrooms are well appointed.
21⇨ʼn

LIMERICK Co Limerick Map 01 B3

★★★★ 68% Castletroy Park
Dublin Rd(off N7) ☎(061) 335566 FAX (061) 331177
Situated in parkland grounds and lovely gardens within Plassey Park Technological Centre, this hotel has excellent facilities for both the corporate sector and the leisure market. It has a warmth of atmosphere that you might not expect to find behind such a modern exterior, and guests can enjoy a drink in the Merry Pedlar Bar or relax in the conservatory lounge.
107⇨ʼn✘in 41 bedrooms CTV in all bedrooms ® ♱ T ✖ (ex guide dogs) sB⇨ʼnIR£91.30-IR£159.50 dB⇨ʼnIR£118.80-IR£206.80 (room only) ⌂
Lift (160P ✿ ☐ (heated) sauna gymnasium steam room all weather running track jacuzzi
♀ International V ♦ ♱ ✘ Lunch frIR£15.95 High tea frIR£6 Dinner frIR£21.45 Last dinner 9.30pm
CONF. Thtr 450 Class 270 Board 100 Del from IR£109
Credit Cards [1][2][3][5]

★★★ ❀69% Jurys
Ennis Rd ☎(061) 327777 FAX (061) 326400
Professional standards of service are the norm at this comfortable hotel, in 4 acres of grounds and landscaped gardens beside the River Shannon, yet just a short stroll from the city centre. The award-winning Copper Room restaurant is a favourite with our inspectors;

➡

★★★
Gleneagle Hotel
KILLARNEY, CO. KERRY
TEL. 064-31870. FAX. 064-32646

Located in 25 acres of landscaped parkland, on the banks of the river Flesk, adjacent to the 25,000 acre National Park – the Gleneagle is ideally situated for a wide range of leisure holidays and general and special activities.

With 3 bars, 3 restaurants, 3 conference rooms, it is the ideal choice for meetings, seminars with a full business and social programme. Swimming pool, sauna, gym, jacuzzi, steam room, pitch and putt, tennis, squash, children's playground, creche – all on site. Lake cruises, coach tours, fishing, golf, pony trekking, cycle hire etc. are all arranged by the hotel.

Free colour brochure available.

IRELAND'S LEADING LEISURE HOTEL

Limerick - Lucan

it offers a wide range of food, including vegetarian, and flambée dishes are a speciality.
95⇨🛏(32fb) CTV in all bedrooms⚲ T 🐕 (ex guide dogs) ✱ sB⇨🛏IR£75.90 dB⇨🛏IR£95.70 (room only) 🍽
(180P ✱ 🏊 (heated) ℘ (hard) sauna gymnasium steam room
xmas
♀ International V ❁ ⚑ ✂ ✱ Lunch IR£9.50&alc Dinner IR£10.90-IR£19.50&alc Last dinner 10.30pm
CONF. Thtr 200 Class 100 Board 45 Del IR£66
Credit Cards [1][2][3][5]

★★★ ❀66% Limerick Inn
Ennis Rd(on N18) ☎(061) 326666 FAX (061) 326281
Closed 25 Dec
The Limerick Inn is a modern hotel with spacious, well furnished bedrooms, drawing rooms and lounges.
153⇨ CTV in all bedrooms ®⚲ T 🐕 (ex guide dogs)
sB⇨IR£78-IR£85 dB⇨IR£92-IR£103 (room only) 🍽
Lift (CTV 1000P ✱ 🏊 (heated) ℘ (hard) sauna solarium gymnasium jacuzzis steam room hair & beauty salon ♫
♀ International V ❁ ✂ ✱ Lunch IR£11&alc Dinner IR£22.50&alc Last dinner 8.45pm
Credit Cards [1][2][3][4][5]

★★★ 66% Limerick Ryan
Ennis Rd(on N22, Ennis road) ☎(061) 453922 FAX (061) 326333
Conveniently situated close to the city, the Limerick Ryan, with an original main wing dating from 1780, has attractive public areas with beautiful original plasterwork on ceilings. Comfortable lounges, the conservatory and the patio gardens all contribute to a delightful, relaxed atmosphere.
181⇨🛏(181fb) CTV in all bedrooms⚲ T 🐕 ✱ sB⇨🛏IR£60-IR£75 dB⇨🛏IR£80-IR£90 (room only) 🍽
Lift (180P ✱ *xmas*
V ❁ ⚑ ✱ Lunch IR£6-IR£10 Dinner IR£14.50&alc Last dinner 10pm
Credit Cards [1][2][3][5]

★★★ ❀❀62% Green Hills
Caherdavin ☎(061) 453033 FAX (061) 453307
Set in 3.5 acres of lovely landscaped gardens, this hotel has recently been refurbished and extended, adding some large, comfortable and well appointed bedrooms. It has superb conference and leisure facilities.
59⇨(3fb) CTV in all bedrooms ®⚲ T 🐕
(CTV 150P ✱ 🏊 ℘ (hard) sauna solarium gymnasium
V ❁ ⚑ ✂ Last dinner 10pm
Credit Cards [1][2][3][4][5]

★★★ 60% Two Mile Inn
Ennis Rd(on N22, near Bunratty Castle & airport) ☎(061) 453122 FAX (061) 453783

Situated on the outskirts of Limerick city near Bunratty Castle and Shannon Airport, the Two Mile Inn has new and comfortable bedrooms built to a very high standard with attractive furnishings. The restaurant is very good value.
123⇨(3fb) CTV in all bedrooms ® T 🐕 (ex guide dogs)
(CTV 300P ✱
♀ International V ❁ ⚑ ✂ Last dinner 9.30pm
Credit Cards [1][2][3][5]

★★ ❀66% The George
O'Connell St ☎(061) 414566 FAX (061) 317171
Closed 25 Dec
This busy city centre hotel caters for both tourist and commercial trade.
54⇨🛏(7fb) CTV in all bedrooms⚲ T 🐕 (ex guide dogs)
Lift (50 🚗 (charged) ♫
♀ International V ❁ ⚑ ✂ Last dinner 10pm
Credit Cards [1][2][3][5]

LISDOONVARNA Co Clare Map 01 B3

★★ 70% Sheedy's Spa View Hotel & Orchid Restaurant
☎Ennis(065) 74026 FAX (065) 74555
Closed Oct-14 Mar
This well run family hotel provides warm hospitality, comfort, and good food from its award-winning restaurant. It is situated beside the spa complex in well tended gardens in an area which abounds in interest.
11⇨🛏 T 🐕 ✱ sB&B⇨🛏frIR£35 dB&B⇨🛏frIR£55
CTV 40P 2🚗 🛗 ℘ (hard)
♀ Irish, English & French ❁ ⚑ ✱ Dinner IR£17.50-IR£23.50 Last dinner 8.30pm
Credit Cards [1][2][3][5]

LISMORE Co Waterford Map 01 C2

★★ ⛳ 53% Ballyrafter House
☎Dungarvan(058) 54002
Closed Oct-Mar
At the foot of the Knockmealdown mountains and looking across the Blackwater River to the spectacular Lismore Castle, the hotel is set in a richly wooded demesne – a prime salmon fishing area. Mrs Willoughby and her family provide a tranquil atmosphere, and home cooking of fresh produce is a speciality.
12rm(4⇨) ® 🐕 (ex guide dogs)
CTV 40P 2🚗 🛗 ✱ 🎠
♀ Irish & Italian V ❁ ⚑ Last dinner 8.30pm
Credit Cards [1][3][5]

LONDONDERRY Co Londonderry Map 01 C5

★★★ 66% Everglades
Prehen Rd BT47 2PA (1m from city centre) ☎(0504) 46722 FAX (0504) 49200
Closed 25 Dec
Situated by the banks of the River Foyle, this purpose built hotel offers particularly comfortable and well equipped bedrooms, decorated in pastel shades. Public areas are less impressive, but major refurbishment is scheduled, to be completed by the end of 1994. Meanwhile, smartly uniformed staff continue to provide attentive service.
52⇨🛏(1fb)3🛋 CTV in all bedrooms ® T 🐕 (ex guide dogs) ✱ sB&B⇨🛏£60-£70 dB&B⇨🛏£76-£86 🍽
Lift (CTV 250P ✱ *xmas*
♀ International V ❁ ⚑ ✱ Lunch £8.50-£12alc High tea £8.50-£10alc Dinner £12-£17.50alc Last dinner 9.45pm
Credit Cards [1][2][3][5] £

LUCAN Co Dublin Map 01 D4

★★★ 57% Finnstown Country House Hotel & Golf Course
Newcastle Rd(on B200) ☎(01) 6280644 FAX (01) 6281088
An impressive range of leisure facilities is offered at this 18th-century house set in 22 acres of woodland.
25⇨🛏(10fb) CTV in all bedrooms ®⚲ T sB⇨🛏IR£69 dB&B⇨🛏IR£100 🍽
(CTV 90P ✱ 🏊 (heated) ▶ 9 ℘ (hard) sauna solarium gymnasium turkish bath table tennis croquet lawn ♫ *xmas*
♀ International V ❁ ⚑ ✂ Lunch IR£14.95&alc Dinner IR£22&alc Last dinner 9.30pm
CONF. Thtr 60 Class 45 Board 32 Del IR£100
Credit Cards [1][2][3][5]
See advertisement under DUBLIN

★★★ 54% Lucan Spa
☎Dublin(01) 6280494 FAX (01) 6280841
This long established, modernised hotel is equipped for business conferences and meetings.
50⇨🛏(15fb)1🛋 CTV in all bedrooms ®⚲ T ✱
sB&B⇨🛏IR£42.50 dB&B⇨🛏IR£70 🍽
(🍴 CTV 90P ✱ ▶ 18

V ❄ ⌘ ✻ Lunch IR£9-IR£9.75 Dinner IR£15.50-IR£16.50 Last dinner 9.30pm
Credit Cards 1 2 3 4 5

MACROOM Co Cork Map 01 B2

★★66% Castle
Main St(on N22) ☎(026) 41074 FAX (026) 41505
Closed 25-27 Dec

Situated in the Square of the town centre, this old hotel has begun a programme of refurbishment and some of the bedrooms have already been upgraded to provide attractive and comfortably appointed accommodation. Bar food is served all day.
26rm(5fb) CTV in all bedrooms ®⌛T ✻ sB&B⇨↑IR£25-IR£35 dB&B⇨↑IR£45-IR£60 ₽
(⊞ CTV 6P squash gymnasium ♪
V ❄ ⌘ ⌘ Lunch IR£9-IR£12&alc High tea IR£8-IR£12&alc Dinner IR£12.50-IR£19.50&alc Last dinner 9pm
CONF. Thtr 50 Class 30 Board 20 Del from IR£50
Credit Cards 1 2 3 4 5

★★61% Victoria
(on N22) ☎(026) 41082 & 42143 FAX (026) 42148
Closed 25-29 Dec

Situated in the town centre square, this hotel caters for tourists and commercial guests.
16rm(10fb) CTV in all bedrooms ®⌛T ✻ sB&B⇨↑IR£25-IR£30 dB&B⇨↑IR£46-IR£50 ₽
CTV 4P
♀ Irish, French, Italian & American V ❄ ⌘ ⌘ ✻ Lunch IR£8-IR£9 Dinner IR£14-IR£15&alc Last dinner 9.30pm
Credit Cards 1 2 3 5

MALAHIDE Co Dublin Map 01 D4

★★★63% Grand
☎(01) 8450000 FAX (01) 8450987
Closed 25-26 Dec

This fine old hotel has an imposing pillared entrance and lobby, and a smart modern extension houses comfortable rooms, many with good sea views.
100rm(20fb)⌖in 3 bedrooms CTV in all bedrooms T ✻ (ex guide dogs) sB&B⇨↑IR£58.50-IR£65.35 dB&B⇨↑IR£94.50-IR£103.50 ₽
Lift (CTV 600P ✽
♀ European V ❄ ⌘ ⌘ Lunch frIR£9.15 High tea frIR£9 Dinner frIR£16.60&alc Last dinner 10.15pm
Credit Cards 1 2 3 5

MALIN Co Donegal Map 01 C6

★58% Malin
☎(077) 70606 & 70645

Overlooking the village green in the most northerly village in Ireland, the hotel has a friendly, welcoming atmosphere and is an ideal centre for exploring the rugged coastline and sandy beaches. Bar snacks are available all day.
12rm(2⇨) CTV in all bedrooms T ✻
CTV 100P ♪ ⚲
♀ English V ❄ ⌘ Last dinner 9.30pm
Credit Cards 1 3 5

MALLOW Co Cork Map 01 B2

★★★❀❀❀70% Longueville House
☎(022) 47156 & 47306 FAX (022) 47459

Closed 23 Dec-Feb

This 18th-century Georgian mansion, with large, stylish bedrooms and public rooms, is set in the centre of a 500-acre wooded estate in the valley of the River Blackwater. The O'Callaghans make guests feel at home, and the award-winning President's Dining Room offers excellent fresh produce from their own fishery, farm and kitchen garden.
17rm⇨↑3⊞ CTV in all bedrooms T ✻
CTV 50P 3⛳ ⚸ ✽ ⚲ snooker nc8yrs
♀ Irish & French V ❄ ⌘ Last dinner 9.30pm
Credit Cards 1 2 3 4

MIDLETON Co Cork Map 01 B2

★★★❀❀71% Midleton Park
☎(021) 631767 FAX (021) 631605

This new luxury hotel, set in attractive surroundings, is richly furnished and offers first class comfort. The bedrooms are fully equipped and the food is excellent.
40rm⇨↑(10fb) CTV in all bedrooms T ✻ (ex guide dogs) ✻ sB&B⇨↑IR£35-IR£55 dB&B⇨↑IR£30-IR£80 ₽
(300P ✽ ♪
♀ Irish & French V ❄ ⌘ ⌘ Lunch frIR£8.50 High tea frIR£4.50 Dinner frIR£15.50 Last dinner 9.30pm
CONF. Thtr 350 Class 200 Board 60 Del from IR£65
Credit Cards 1 2 3 5

MOVILLE Co Donegal Map 01 C6

★★56% McNamara's
Foyle St ☎(077) 82010 FAX (077) 82564

Situated in the picturesque village of Moville on the shores of Lough Foyle and well positioned for touring Donegal, McNamara's offers a warm friendly atmosphere.
18rm(8⇨↑)(1fb) ✻ (ex guide dogs)

★★★

SPA HOTEL
LUCAN on N4
CO. DUBLIN
Telephone (01) 6280494
Fax (01) 6280841

This 100 year old, 53 bedroomed hotel is an ideal venue for conferences, functions and weddings, with modern comforts.

Special Bed and Breakfast rates.

Carvery lunch served Monday to Sunday.

Evening special table d'hôte and à la carte menu served in our Honora d' Restaurant.

ENTERTAINMENT
FRIDAY/SATURDAY/SUNDAY

Moville - Oughterard

⟮ CTV 60P ⇌ ▶ 18 ♪ ⚬ᵇ
V ✿ ⚷ ✂ Last dinner 10pm
Credit Cards ①②③④⑤

NEWCASTLE Co Down Map **01** D5

★★★ **60%** *Slieve Donard*
BT33 0AH (HG) ☎(03967) 23681 FAX (03967) 24830
Splendidly situated at the foot of the Mourne Mountains, this impressive late Victorian former railway hotel has a private beach. Bedrooms, many of them very spacious, are all equipped to a good modern standard and extensive public areas include a choice of restaurants and bars.
120⇨(20fb) CTV in all bedrooms ®❣ T
Lift ⟮ ⊞ CTV 500P ✻ ⊠ (heated) ▶ 18 ♪ (hard) solarium gymnasium turkish baths jacuzzi beauty salon
♀ English & French V ✿ ⚷ Last dinner 9.30pm
Credit Cards ①②③⑤

★★ **64%** *Enniskeen*
98 Bryansfold Rd BT33 0LF ☎(03967) 22392 FAX (03967) 24084
Closed 12 Nov-22 Mar
Set in its own grounds in a quiet residential area north of the town centre, this friendly family-run hotel offers unpretentious, traditional style accommodation, with many rooms enjoying fine mountain and sea views.
12⇨♠(1fb)✂in 2 bedrooms CTV in all bedrooms ® T ✠
CTV 45P ✻ ♪ (grass) ⚬ᵇ
V ✿ ⚷ Last dinner 80.30pm
Credit Cards ①③

NEWMARKET-ON-FERGUS Co Clare Map **01** B3

★★★ **63%** Clare Inn
☎(061) 368161 FAX (061) 368622
The Clare Inn is set in open countryside in the centre of an 18-hole golf course just 10 minutes from Shannon Airport. It is a comfortable hotel with excellent leisure facilities and friendly staff to ensure an enjoyable stay.
121⇨♠(20fb)✂in 4 bedrooms CTV in all bedrooms❣ T ✱
sB&B⇨♠IR£50-IR£60 dB⇨♠IR£65-IR£90 (room only) 🍴
⟮ CTV 150P ✻ ⊠ (heated) ▶ 18 ♪ (hard) ✿ sauna solarium gymnasium cruiser for hire ♫ ⚬ᵇ xmas
♀ Irish & Continental V ✿ ⚷ ✱ Lunch IR£8-IR£15 High tea IR£6-IR£8.50 Dinner IR£18-IR£22 Last dinner 10pm
Credit Cards ①②③④⑤

NEWPORT Co Mayo Map **01** A4

★★★ ✿✰♨ **74%** *Newport House*
☎(098) 41222 & 41154 FAX (098) 41613

Closed Oct-18 Mar
Good food and comfortable accommodation are the hallmarks of this beautiful old country mansion on edge of Newport village, coupled with old fashioned service at its best – a warm welcome and complimentary afternoon tea await new arrivals. The hotel has extensive fishing rights on surrounding lakes and rivers. Much of the food is from the fishery, garden or farm and is carefully cooked and presented in elegant surroundings.
13⇨♠Annexe7⇨♠(2fb)2❣ T
⟮ ⊞ 50P ✻ ♪ billiards ⚬ᵇ
♀ Irish & French V ✿ ⚷ Last dinner 9.30pm
Credit Cards ①②③

Irish entries appear in a separate section that follows the main directory.

NEWTOWNABBEY Co Antrim Map **01** D5

★★★ **54%** *Chimney Corner*
630 Antrim Rd BT36 8RH (beside A6) ☎Belfast(0232) 844925 & 844851 FAX (0232) 844352
Closed 24-26 Dec
Situated midway between Belfast and the Airport, this busy commercial hotel has grown from a 19th century inn. It offers compact but well equipped modern bedrooms, extensive function facilities and a choice of eating venues.
63⇨♠in 10 bedrooms CTV in all bedrooms ® T
✠ (ex guide dogs)
⟮ CTV 300P ♪ (hard) sauna bicycles
♀ British & French V ✿ ⚷ Last dinner 9.30pm
Credit Cards ①②③④⑤

OMAGH Co Tyrone Map **01** C5

★★ **65%** Royal Arms
51 High St BT78 1BA ☎(0662) 243262 FAX 245011
Closed 25 Dec
This long established family-run hotel in the town centre dates back to 1787 and attractive public areas with historic character include a beamed restaurant, bistro bar and daytime coffee shop cum evening lounge bar. Refurbished bedrooms have modern facilities.
21⇨♠1❖ CTV in all bedrooms ®❣ T sB&B⇨♠fr£34.50 dB&B⇨♠fr£64 🍴
⟮ CTV 200P ▶ 18 ♪ ∪ snooker ♫
V ✿ ⚷ ✱ Lunch fr£6.95 High tea fr£7.50 Dinner fr£9.75 Last dinner 9.30pm
CONF. Thtr 400 Class 400 Board 30 Del from £50
Credit Cards ①③

OUGHTERARD Co Galway Map **01** B4

★★★ **63%** Connemara Gateway
(on N59) ☎Galway(091) 82328 FAX (091) 82332
Closed 1-28 Dec & 3-31 Jan
Located on the main route through Connemara, this hotel is set in its own well maintained gardens. An open turf fire greets guests in the pine panelled lobby/reception area, and the bedrooms and public areas are modern and well furnished.
62⇨♠(24fb) CTV in all bedrooms ®❣ T ✠ (ex guide dogs) ✱
sB&B⇨♠IR£45-IR£75 dB&B⇨♠IR£85-IR£105 🍴
CTV 80P ✻ ⊠ (heated) ♪ (hard) sauna solarium croquet table tennis ♫ ⚬ᵇ
♀ Irish & French V ✿ ⚷ ✂ ✱ Lunch IR£11.50-IR£15.50 High tea IR£6.75-IR£9.75 Dinner IR£18.50-IR£22.50&alc Last dinner 9.15pm
CONF. Thtr 320 Class 270 Board 80
Credit Cards ①③④⑤

★★ **69%** *Corrib*
☎(091) 82204 FAX (091) 82522
Closed Jan-Feb

This family-run hotel is set in the picturesque village of Oughterard, and provides good food and courteous personal attention. Bedrooms and public rooms are comfortable and tastefully decorated.
18⇨♠Annexe8⇨♠ CTV in all bedrooms ® T
✠ (ex guide dogs) ✱ sB&B⇨♠IR£25-IR£27.50
dB&B⇨♠IR£50-IR£55 🍴
CTV 30P ✻ ♪
✿ ⚷ ✱ Lunch IR£4.50-IR£10.50alc Dinner IR£14.95-IR£24.95alc Last dinner 9pm
Credit Cards ①②③④

Red star hotels are each highlighted by a pink tinted panel.

PARKNASILLA Co Kerry Map **01** A2

★★★★73% Great Southern
☎(064) 45122 FAX (064) 45323
Closed 2 Jan-12 Mar
The Great Southern is superbly located on Kenmare Bay with fine sea views from many of its bedrooms. There are spacious, comfortable lounges, the excellent Pygmalion Retaurant and an impressive range of leisure facilities.
25⇨Annexe59⇨(6fb) CTV in all bedrooms T (ex guide dogs) sB&B⇨IR£89-IR£99 dB&B⇨IR£133-IR£155
Lift 60P (heated) 9 (hard) snooker sauna jacuzzi bicycle hire windsurfing ♫ *xmas*
International **V** Bar Lunch IR£4-IR£14 Dinner IR£25 Last dinner 8.45pm
CONF. Thtr 80 Class 50 Board 20
Credit Cards 1 2 3 5

PORTBALLINTRAE Co Antrim Map **01** C6

★★60% Beach House
The Sea Front BT57 8RT ☎(02657) 31214 FAX (02657) 31664
Conveniently situated for the beach, this resort hotel offers generally spacious if rather functional accommodation. Bedrooms are equipped with modern facilities and many enjoy sea views.
32⇨(17fb) CTV in all bedrooms ® **T** (ex guide dogs) sB&B⇨£38-£42 dB&B⇨£60-£68
CTV 40P table tennis pool table ♫ *xmas*
French **V** Lunch £7-£9 High tea £5-£9alc Dinner £14-£16 Last dinner 9pm
CONF. Thtr 150 Class 50 Board 20 Del from £38
Credit Cards 1 3

PORTLAOISE Co Laois Map **01** C3

★★60% *Killeshin*
Dublin Rd ☎(0502) 21663 FAX (0502) 21976
This bustling hotel on the main Dublin road caters for commercial and conference business.
44⇨ CTV in all bedrooms ® **T**
100P ♫
V Last dinner 9.30pm
Credit Cards 1 2 3 5

PORTRUSH Co Antrim Map **01** C6

★★★58% Causeway Coast
36 Ballyreagh Rd BT56 8LR (on A2 between Portrush & Portstewart) ☎(0265) 822435 FAX (0265) 824495
In a commanding position between Portrush and Portstewart, with fine coastal views, this modern hotel is part of an apartment and conference centre. Bedrooms are functional, but well equipped, and public areas include a popular wine bar and grill room, although the latter is not always open.
21⇨(1fb) CTV in all bedrooms ® **T** (ex guide dogs) ✱ sB&B⇨fr£45 dB&B⇨fr£60
180P snooker ♫ *xmas*
British & French **V** ✱ Sunday Lunch fr£9 Dinner fr£12.50 Last dinner 9.30pm
CONF. Thtr 500 Class 170 Board 108 Del from £49
Credit Cards 1 2 3

PROSPEROUS Co Kildare Map **01** C4

★★56% Curryhills House
(5m from N7 and N4) ☎(045) 68150 FAX (045) 68805
Closed 23-30 Dec
This 19th-century house with a modern bedroom extension stands in 100 acres of gardens and parklands.
10⇨(10fb) CTV in 5 bedrooms ® **T** ✱ sB&B⇨IR£27.50-IR£37 dB&B⇨IR£45-IR£60
CTV 50P clay pigeon shooting ♫
✱ Dinner frIR£16.50&alc Last dinner 10.30pm
Credit Cards 1 3

RATHMULLAN Co Donegal Map **01** C6

★★★62% Fort Royal
Fort Royal(take L77 from Letterkenny, through Rathmullen village, hotel is signposted) ☎Letterkenny(074) 58100 FAX (074) 58103
Closed Oct-Etr
Situated on the shores of Lough Swilly, this charming converted country residence has mature gardens and wooded grounds reaching down to a secluded beach. The hotel offers cosy lounges with open fires, and is personally supervised by Robin and Ann Fletcher.
11⇨Annexe4⇨(3fb) CTV in 8 bedrooms **T** ✱ sB&B⇨IR£32.50-IR£60 dB&B⇨IR£65-IR£80
CTV 40P 9 (hard) squash
Irish & French **V** ✱ Sunday Lunch IR£13.50 Dinner IR£17-IR£20 Last dinner 9pm
Credit Cards 1 2 3 5

★56% *Pier*
☎(074) 58178
Closed 2 Mar-Sep
A friendly, family-run hotel in a seaside village, this is an angler's paradise and there is boating and a safe beach in front of the hotel. Free rough shooting is available.
16rm(11⇨)

RATHNEW Co Wicklow Map **01** D3

★★★

★★★
TINAKILLY COUNTRY HOUSE & RESTAURANT
☎(0404) 69274 FAX (0404) 67806
We are pleased to welcome Tinakilly Country House to the ranks of our Red Star award winners. Built in 1870, it is an elegant house is set in 7 acres of 19th-century gardens with breathtaking views of the sea. It offers the highest standards of accommodation and hospitality, its bedrooms tastefully decorated with period furnishings and some 4-poster beds. Country house cuisine is served, including fresh fish, game and home-grown vegetables.
29⇨5 CTV in all bedrooms ® **T** (ex guide dogs) sB&B⇨IR£75-IR£110 dB&B⇨IR£100-IR£170
60P (hard) croquet putting ♫ *xmas*
Lunch IR£16.50 Dinner frIR£27.50&alc Last dinner 9pm
CONF. Thtr 150 Class 60 Board 40 Del from IR£92
Credit Cards 1 2 3 4 5

★★70% Hunter's
☎(0404) 40106 FAX (0404) 40338
RS 25 Dec
In the same family for generations, this 200-year-old hotel has real old world charm and hospitality. It is also noted for its beautiful gardens.
18rm(10⇨) **T** (ex guide dogs) ✱ sB&B⇨frIR£37.50 dB&B⇨frIR£75
CTV 50P

→

Rathnew - Rosslare Harbour

♥ Irish & French ✿ ☞ ✱ Lunch frIR£12.50 Dinner frIR£18
Last dinner 9pm
Credit Cards 1 2 3 5

RECESS Co Galway Map 01 A4

★★★✿✿♨73% Lough Inagh Lodge
Inagh Valley ☎Clifden(095) 34706 & 34694 FAX (095) 34708
Closed 25 Oct-1 Apr
This 19th-century shooting lodge has been skilfully restored and upgraded into a luxurious hotel. It is in a superb location, fronted by a good fishing lake and with lovely mountain views. Large lounges with blazing fires and a cosy oak-lined bar offer great warmth and comfort. The spacious, high- ceilinged bedrooms are beautifully furnished. Food and presentation are excellent, and overall a friendly informal atmosphere prevails.
12⇨♠2🛏 CTV in all bedrooms T ✈ (ex guide dogs) ✱
sB&B⇨♠IR£53-IR£77 dB&B⇨♠IR£80-IR£120 🅿
⊞ 16P 🚗 ✿ ♪
♥ Irish & French V ✿ ☞ ✱ Bar Lunch IR£2-IR£10 Dinner IR£23 Last dinner 9pm
Credit Cards 1 2 3 5

RENVYLE Co Galway Map 01 A4

★★★68% Renvyle House
☎(095) 43511 FAX (095) 43515
Closed 7 Jan-14 Mar
Once the home of Oliver St John Gogarty, this historic country house is set on the shore of the Atlantic ocean, in the wild splendour of Connemara. The hotel is warmly inviting with log fires and comfortable public rooms.
65⇨♠ CTV in all bedrooms ✈ T
(CTV 100P ✿ ≋ (heated) ▶ 9 ♀ (hard) ♪ ♾ snooker croquet boating lawn bowls bicycle hire ♫ 🎱
♥ International V ✿ ☞ ✱ Lunch IR£11 Dinner IR£22 Last dinner 9pm
Credit Cards 1 2 3 5

ROSCOMMON Co Roscommon Map 01 B4

★★★63% Abbey
Galway Rd ☎(0903) 26240 & 26505 FAX (0903) 26021
RS 25 Dec
This family-run hotel is a converted 19th-century manor house set in its own attractive grounds. It caters for tourist and commercial trade, offering a good standard of public rooms and bedrooms.
20⇨♠ CTV in all bedrooms ® ✈ T ✈ ✱ sB&B⇨♠IR£44-IR£50 dB&B⇨♠IR£55-IR£60
(⊞ CTV 45P ✿
♥ Irish & French V ✿ ☞ ✱ Lunch IR£9-IR£12 High tea IR£7.75-IR£10 Dinner IR£17-IR£19.50&alc Last dinner 9.30pm
CONF. Thtr 300 Class 200 Board 30 Del from IR£50
Credit Cards 1 2 3 5

ROSSCAHILL Co Galway Map 01 B4

★★★63% Ross Lake House
☎(091) 80109 & 80154 FAX (091) 80184
Closed Apr-Oct

This modern Georgian house is situated at the end of a winding country road in a panoramic garden setting. It is family run and offers well furnished accommodation and a comfortable, relaxed atmosphere.
13⇨♠ T ✈ (ex guide dogs) sB&B⇨♠IR£43-IR£48.50 dB&B⇨♠IR£66-IR£77 🅿

CTV 100P ✿ ♀ (hard)
V ✿ ☞ Dinner IR£19 Last dinner 9pm
Credit Cards 1 2 3 4 5

ROSSLARE Co Wexford Map 01 D2

★★★

★★★ KELLY'S STRAND
☎(053) 32114 FAX (053) 32222
Closed mid Dec-late Feb
Since 1895 successive generations of the Kelly family have extended and improved the original building to create this truly fine hotel, with an emphasis on all-year-round family holidays. There is plenty to do, or guests can relax in one of the many comfortable lounges, and entertainment is provided nightly in the hotel's own ballroom. A lasting impression of a stay at the hotel is the effort made by the Kellys to cater in every possible way for their guests. Menus are varied and generous, reflecting careful preparation, and fresh local fish and shellfish are very popular.
Annexe99⇨♠(15fb) CTV in all bedrooms ✈ T ✈
sB&B⇨♠IR£45-IR£50 dB&B⇨♠IR£80-IR£98 🅿
Lift (CTV 99P 🚗 ✿ 🎬 (heated) ♀ (hard) squash snooker sauna solarium gymnasium bowls croquet jacuzzi plunge pool ♫ 🎱
♥ English & French V ✿ ☞ ✱ Lunch IR£11-IR£15 Dinner IR£20-IR£23 Last dinner 9pm
Credit Cards 1 2 3

★★★63% Cedars
☎(053) 32124 FAX (053) 32243
Closed 11 Oct-10 Mar
Situated 5 minutes' drive from Rosslare Ferryport and close to the 'blue flag' beach, this hotel has pleasant public areas and spacious bedrooms. It has recently undergone extensive refurbishment, and there are pleasant public areas and spacious bedrooms. There are 2 restaurants and 2 bars, the Casket Lounge and the Casablanca.
34⇨♠(34fb) CTV in all bedrooms ® T ✈ (ex guide dogs)
(⊞ CTV 150P ✿ sauna solarium gymnasium ♫ 🎱
♥ French V ✿ ☞ ✱ Last dinner 9.45pm
Credit Cards 1 3 4

ROSSLARE HARBOUR Co Wexford Map 01 D2

★★★64% Great Southern
☎Wexford(053) 33233 FAX (053) 33543
Closed 4 Jan-9 Mar
This very comfortable hotel beside the ferryport has well furnished bedrooms and excellent lounges with attractive decor. Entertainment is provided during the summer season, and there is a new patio garden overlooking the harbour.
99⇨♠(28fb) CTV in all bedrooms T
(CTV 100P 🎬 (heated) ♀ (hard) snooker sauna gymnasium steam room 🎱
V ✿ ☞ ✱ Last dinner 9pm
Credit Cards 1 2 3 5

★★★56% Hotel Rosslare
☎(053) 33110 & 33312 FAX (053) 33386
Closed 25 Dec
Ideally situated for the car ferryport, this hotel overlooks the harbour and is a short distance from sandy 'blue flag' beaches. A friendly atmosphere and good food are the priorities, and there is an

interesting old bar full of seafaring lore and local history, with a pleasant beer garden outside.
25rm(22⇨🛁)(7fb) CTV in all bedrooms **T**
⦅ ⊞ 50P squash snooker sauna
♀ International **V** ✧ ⚿ ✁ Last dinner 8.45pm
Credit Cards ①②③⑤

ROSSNOWLAGH Co Donegal Map **01** B5

★★★✿✿**72%** Sand House
☎Sligo(072) 51777 FAX (072) 52100
Closed early Oct–Etr
Set in a crescent of golden sands 5 miles north of Ballyshannon, this owner-managed hotel is well known for its hospitality, good cuisine and personal service. Many rooms have sea views, and a conservatory lounge overlooking Donegal Bay provides a relaxing retreat. The beach at Rossnowlagh is ideal for safe bathing and surfing.
42⇨🛁(6fb)3⊞ **T** sB&B⇨🛁 IR£35-IR£50 dB&B⇨🛁 IR£60-IR£90 🅿
CTV 40P 2🛋 ✿ ♪ (hard) croquet miniature golf surfing ♫
♀ Irish & French **V** ✧ ⚿ ✁ Lunch IR£9.50-IR£12.50 Dinner IR£15-IR£20 Last dinner 9pm
CONF. Thtr 60 Class 40 Board 30 Del from IR£50
Credit Cards ①②③⑤

SALTHILL
See **Galway**

SHANNON Co Clare Map **01** B3

★★★★**59%** The Great Southern
Shannon Airport(opp main terminal building) ☎(061) 471122 FAX (061) 471982
Closed 25-26 Dec
This warmly inviting hotel, right opposite the main airport terminal, has been handsomely refurbished and is an ideal location for passengers, tourists and corporate guests. Rooms are available on a convenient 'day-let' basis; there is a restaurant open all day, and a porter service to and from the airport.
115⇨🛁(7fb)✁in 14 bedrooms CTV in all bedrooms ®✿ **T** ✱ sB⇨🛁 frIR£60 dB⇨🛁 frIR£82 (room only) 🅿
Lift ⦅ CTV 150P ✿ ♫
♀ European **V** ✧ ⚿ ✁ ✱ Lunch frIR£8 Dinner frIR£16.50&alc Last dinner 9.30pm
Credit Cards ①②③④⑤

SLANE Co Meath Map **01** C4

★★**57%** Conyngham Arms
☎Drogheda(041) 24155 FAX (041) 24205
Closed Good Fri & Xmas
Situated in the picturesque village near the famous prehistoric tombs of New Grange, the hotel has very comfortable public rooms including the unique Estate Agent's Restaurant. Five new bedrooms have recently been added and are equipped with excellent bathrooms. There are attractive gardens to the rear, and this is an ideal location from which to explore the historic area which includes Tara and the Boyne Valley. Fishing, horse riding and tennis are available locally.
16rm(15⇨🛁)(4fb)1⊞ CTV in all bedrooms **T**
✱ (ex guide dogs)
12P 12🛋 ✿
♀ Irish & French **V** ✧ ⚿ ✁ Last dinner 9.45pm
Credit Cards ①②③⑤

Satellite television – look for this symbol ✍
in the directory entries.

SLIGO Co Sligo Map **01** B5

★★★**69%** Sligo Park
Pearse Rd ☎(071) 60291 FAX (071) 69556
Situated on the outskirts of town among tranquil fields, this hotel prides itself on its friendly and welcoming atmosphere. It caters for tourists and business guests, offering excellent leisure facilities and executive rooms.
89⇨🛁 CTV in all bedrooms **T**
⦅ ⊞ CTV P ✿ 🖾 (heated) ♪ (hard) snooker sauna gymnasium jacuzzi steamroom plunge pool
♀ Irish & French **V** ✧ ⚿ ✁ Last dinner 9.15pm
Credit Cards ①②③⑤

★★★**58%** Ballincar House
Rosses Point Rd ☎(071) 45361 FAX (071) 44198
Closed 23-28 Dec
A friendly, relaxed atmosphere is one of the characteristics of this converted country house, set in 6 acres of mature gardens midway between Sligo and Rosses Point. The attractively redecorated restaurant overlooks gardens where good food in comfortable surroundings makes dining an enjoyable experience. Parking is provided and the hotel is suitable for both tourists and business guests.
26⇨🛁 CTV in all bedrooms **T** ✱ (ex guide dogs)
⦅ CTV 60P ✿ ♪ (hard) snooker sauna
♀ French **V** ✧ ⚿ ✁ Last dinner 9.30pm
Credit Cards ①②③⑤

★★**60%** Silver Swan
☎(071) 43231 FAX 42232
Closed 25 & 26 Dec
Family owned, this hotel is situated on the banks of the Garavogue River in the heart of Sligo and attracts both business guests and tourists. Recently redecorated bedrooms are well furnished and comfortable with good bathrooms, some with aero-spa baths. The ➔

★★★ Cedars Hotel

Rosslare
Co Wexford

Telephone
053 5332124

Rosslare Harbour - Sligo

Sligo - Tralee

Horseshoe Bar is a popular spot for snacks and drinks and there is a car park to the rear.
27⇆↑ CTV in all bedrooms ® T ✈ (ex guide dogs) (40P
V ✿ ⚡ ⚐
Credit Cards 1 2 3 5

SPIDDAL Co Galway Map **01 B3**

★★**69%** *Bridge House*
Connemara ☏Galway(091) 83118
Closed mid Dec-Jan
On the main street of the village, convenient for the Aran Islands' ferry, comfortable bedrooms and good food are the priorities of this house.
14⇆↑ CTV in 7 bedrooms T ✈
CTV 20P 2🐎 ✿ nc3yrs
☏ Irish, English, French & Italian V ✿ ⚡ Last dinner 10.30pm
Credit Cards 1 2 3 5

★★**61%** *Park Lodge*
☏Galway(091) 83159 FAX (091) 83494
Closed Nov-Etr & Etr-May RS Etr Oct & BH wknds
Family owned and run, this hotel is situated 10 miles west of Galway on the coast road. The accommodation is comfortable and most bedrooms have sea views.
23⇆↑(4fb) ® T ✈ ↑ sB&B⇆↑IR£30-IR£35 dB&B⇆↑IR£44-IR£50
CTV 50P ⚐
⚡ ✱ Dinner IR£13-IR£16 Last dinner 8.30pm
CONF. Class 50 Del from IR£50
Credit Cards 1 2 3 5

STRABANE Co Tyrone Map **01 C5**

★★★**62%** *Fir Trees*
Melmount Rd BT82 9JT (S on A5) (HG) ☏(0504) 382382 FAX (0504) 885932
Situated in an elevated position, this purpose-built hotel has well equipped if compact bedrooms which have recently been upgraded. Public areas are spacious and comfortable and smartly dressed staff provide friendly service.
26⇆↑(3fb) CTV in all bedrooms ® T ✱ sB&B⇆↑£44 dB&B⇆↑£62 🍴
(🎱 CTV 100P ✿ ♪ ☾ indoor karting ♫ ⚐
☏ Irish & European V ✿ ⚡ ✱ Sunday Lunch £7.95-£8.50 High tea £6.50-£10&alc Dinner £12.50-£13.50&alc Last dinner 9.30pm
CONF. Thtr 350 Class 120 Board 60 Del from £49
Credit Cards 1 2 3 5

STRAFFAN Co Kildare Map **01 D4**

★★★★★♨*The Kildare Hotel & Country Club*
☏(01) 6273333 FAX (01) 6273312

In the heart of horse-breeding territory, in 330 acres of parkland beside the river Liffey, this very grand and luxurious hotel is known not only for its Arnold Palmer designed golf course and private fishing, but for its superb mixture of country elegance and the quality of its décor and furnishings. Paintings, antiques and rugs enhance the atmosphere, and bedrooms are well furnished and comfortable. Chef Michel Flamme produces a choice of menus, featuring dishes cooked in French or speciality Irish style. Ray Carroll has brought together a team whose professionalism and charm combine to make a stay here a real pleasure.
36⇆↑Annexe9⇆↑(4fb)1🍴 CTV in all bedrooms ⚡ T ✈ (ex guide dogs) sB&B⇆↑IR£155-IR£170 dB&B⇆↑IR£245-IR£275 🍴

Lift (CTV 200P ✿ ▦ (heated) ▶ 18 ♣ (hard) ♪ squash snooker sauna solarium gymnasium beauty salon croquet driving range ♫ *xmas*
☏ Irish & French V ✿ ⚡ ✱ Lunch IR£22&alc Dinner IR£33-IR£35&alc Last dinner 10pm
CONF. Thtr 80 Class 40 Board 30 Del from IR£190
Credit Cards 1 2 3 5

★★★ ✿✿**71%** *Barberstown Castle*
☏6288157 & 6288206 FAX 6277027
10⇆↑ CTV in all bedrooms ® ⚡ T ✈ sB&B⇆↑IR£65 dB&B⇆↑IR£110
200P ✿ nc12yrs
☏ French V ✿ ⚡ Lunch IR£15.50&alc Dinner IR£22.50&alc Last dinner 9.30pm
Credit Cards 1 2 3

THOMASTOWN Co Kilkenny Map **01 C3**

★★★★♨**75%** *Mount Juliet*
☏(056) 24455 FAX (056) 24522
Set in 1500 acres of parkland, including a Jack Nicklaus designed golf course, this beautiful Palladian mansion is now a very special hotel. The elegant and spacious public rooms retain much of the original architectural features, including ornate plasterwork and fine Adam fireplaces, and the comfortable drawing room and parlour overlook the river. There is also a cocktail bar and magnificent restaurant. Professional and courteous staff really cosset their guests here.
32⇆ ✱ sB&B⇆IR£102-IR£144 dB&B⇆IR£150-IR£240
▦ (heated) ▶ 18 ♣ (hard) ♪ ☾ sauna

TIPPERARY Co Tipperary Map **01 B3**

★**56%** *Royal*
Bridge St ☏(062) 51204 & 51285 FAX (062) 51426
16⇆↑(3fb) CTV in all bedrooms T ✈ ↑ sB&B⇆↑IR£20-IR£25 dB&B⇆↑IR£40-IR£50 🍴
CTV 200P *xmas*
V ✿ ⚡ Lunch IR£7.50-IR£8
Credit Cards 1 2 3 5

TRALEE Co Kerry Map **01 A2**

★★★**63%** *The Brandon*
☏(066) 23333 FAX (066) 25019
This modern hotel, completely refurbished, is situated in the town centre. It has excellent leisure facilities and is a golfer's paradise, within 30 minutes' of 6 superb courses.
160⇆↑(2fb) CTV in all bedrooms ⚡ T ✈ (ex guide dogs) sB&B⇆↑IR£39.75-IR£100 dB&B⇆↑IR£80-IR£110 🍴
Lift (200P ▦ (heated) sauna solarium gymnasium concessionary green fees ♫
✿ ⚡ ✱ Lunch IR£8.75-IR£12.50 Dinner IR£12.50-IR£17.50&alc Last dinner 9.30pm
CONF. Thtr 1000 Class 500 Board 20
Credit Cards 1 2 3 4 5

★★★**58%** *Earl Of Desmond*
Killarney Rd ☏(066) 21299 FAX (066) 21976
Closed Jan-Feb
Set in its own grounds, this large modern hotel caters for the tourist and commercial trade.
52⇆↑(3fb)1🍴 CTV in all bedrooms ⚡ T ✈ (ex guide dogs)
(🎱 CTV 400P ✿ ♣ (hard) ♪ ♫ ⚐
V ✿ ⚡ ⚐ Last dinner 9.30pm
Credit Cards 1 2 3 4 5

For key to symbols see the Bookmark.

Tralee - Wexford

★★65% **The Grand**
☎(066) 21499 FAX (066) 22877
Centrally situated, this streetside commercial and tourist hotel has easy access to all tourist areas.
48rm(44⇨🏠) CTV in all bedrooms ✣ T ✕ ✱ sB&BIR£17-IR£20 sB&B⇨🏠IR£23-IR£36 dB&BIR£34-IR£40 dB&B⇨🏠IR£46-IR£72 🍽
(⊞ CTV ♪
V ♡ ⚐ ✗ ✱ Lunch IR£4-IR£9 High tea 80p-IR£1 Dinner IR£13.95-IR£14.95&alc Last dinner 9.30pm
CONF. Thtr 400 Class 150
Credit Cards 1 2 3

WATERFORD Co Waterford Map **01** C2

★★★★✿✿♨75% **Waterford Castle**
The Island ☎(051) 78203 FAX (051) 79316
Situated on an island with access via a free car ferry, this tastefully restored Norman castle has a magnificent entrance hall and spacious rooms.
19⇨🏠4🛁 CTV in all bedrooms ✣ T ✕ (ex guide dogs) ✱ sB⇨🏠IR£100-IR£135 dB⇨🏠IR£135-IR£185 (room only) 🍽
Lift (60P ⚐ ✿ ◻ (heated) ▶ 18 ♣ (hard) clay pigeon shooting croquet ♪ xmas
V ♡ ⚐ ✗ ✱ Lunch IR£15.50-IR£16.50 Dinner IR£29.50-IR£31&alc Last dinner 10pm
Credit Cards 1 2 3 5

★★★68% *Tower*
The Mall ☎(051) 75801 FAX (051) 70129
Closed 24-26 Dec
Now completely upgraded, the hotel offers a full range of banquetting, conference and leisure facilities – the latter including a new swimming pool with air conditioned fitness centre – as well as an attractive restaurant and a pleasant bar overlooking the river. Helpful, friendly staff provide good service throughout.
125⇨🏠(12fb) CTV in all bedrooms ✣ T
Lift (♪ ◻ (heated) sauna solarium gymnasium jacuzzi steam room ♪
✗ Last dinner 9.30pm
Credit Cards 1 2 3 5

★★★65% *Jurys*
Ferrybank ☎(051) 32111 FAX (051) 32863
Situated in parkland overlooking the city, this large modern hotel has spacious public rooms and caters for tourists and the commercial trade.
98⇨🏠(20fb)✗in 4 bedrooms CTV in all bedrooms ® T ✕ (ex guide dogs) ✱ sB⇨🏠IR£64.90 dB⇨🏠IR£88 (room only) 🍽
Lift (300P ✿ ◻ (heated) ♣ (hard) sauna solarium gymnasium steam room plunge pool jacuzzi ♪ xmas
⚐ International V ♡ ⚐ ✗ ✱ Lunch IR£11 Dinner IR£12-IR£17 Last dinner 9.15pm
CONF. Thtr 700 Class 400 Board 100 Del IR£65
Credit Cards 1 2 3 5

★★★✿✿64% *Granville*
The Quay ☎(051) 55111 FAX (051) 70307

Closed 25-26 Dec
This longstanding quayside hotel has been much modernised and offers bright, airy bedrooms and spacious public rooms.
74⇨🏠(35fb)✗in 11 bedrooms CTV in all bedrooms T ✕ (ex guide dogs) ✱ sB&B⇨🏠IR£44-IR£55 dB&B⇨🏠IR£71-IR£93 🍽
Lift (sauna gymnasium

⚐ International V ♡ ⚐ ✗ Lunch IR£9.50&alc High tea IR£6.50 Dinner IR£16.50&alc Last dinner 10.30pm
CONF. Thtr 250 Class 110 Board 100 Del IR£75
Credit Cards 1 2 3 4 5

★★64% **Bridge**
The Quay ☎(051) 77222 FAX (051) 77229
Closed 25 Dec
This busy city centre hotel was recently modernised and caters for both tourist and commercial trade.
75⇨🏠 CTV in all bedrooms T ✕ (ex guide dogs) ✱ 🍽
Lift (♪
⚐ European V ⚐ ✱
Credit Cards 1 2 3 4 5

★★63% **Dooley's**
30 The Quay(on N25) ☎(051) 73531 FAX (051) 70262
Closed 25-27 Dec
This hotel overlooks Quayside and is easily accessible, with a car park opposite. It is a friendly hotel that has comfortable bedrooms and is popular with local diners. The seafood menu, in addition to the à la carte, provides fresh fish caught daily.
37rm(34⇨🏠)✗in 3 bedrooms CTV in all bedrooms ® ✣ T ✕ ✱ sB&B⇨🏠IR£34.10-IR£36 dB&B⇨🏠IR£50.60-IR£62.70 🍽
CTV ♪
⚐ International V ♡ ⚐ ✗ Lunch IR£9.35-IR£9.85 Dinner IR£14.25 Last dinner 9.30pm
CONF. Thtr 200 Class 130 Board 60
Credit Cards 1 2 3 5

WESTPORT Co Mayo Map **01** A4

★★★61% **Hotel Westport**
☎(098) 25122 FAX (098) 26739
Closed 24 & 25 Dec
Situated on its own land adjacent to the grounds of Westport House, this hotel has a bedroom block with modern amenities and caters for leisure and commercial guests.
49⇨🏠(5fb) CTV in all bedrooms ® T ✕ (ex guide dogs) sB&B⇨🏠IR£30-IR£50 dB&B⇨🏠IR£50-IR£70 🍽
(CTV 100P ✿
V ♡ ⚐ ✗ ✱ Sunday Lunch IR£6-IR£9 High tea IR£7-IR£9 Dinner IR£14-IR£16 Last dinner 9pm
CONF. Thtr 400 Class 200 Board 60
Credit Cards 1 2 3 5

★★71% **The Olde Railway**
The Mall(overlooking the Carrowbeg River in the town centre)
☎(098) 25166 & 25605 FAX (098) 25090
Situated on the tree-lined Mall beside the Carrowbeg River, this family-run commercial-style hotel was first built in the late 18th-century.
27⇨🏠(2fb)2🛁 CTV in all bedrooms ✣ T ✕ (ex guide dogs) ✱ sB&B⇨🏠IR£35-IR£45 dB&B⇨🏠IR£50-IR£70 🍽
(50P 4🅿 ✿ clay pigeon shooting
V ♡ ⚐ ✗ ✱ Sunday Lunch frIR£8.95alc Dinner IR£12.50-IR£15alc Last dinner 9.30pm
CONF. Thtr 100 Class 50 Board 30 Del from IR£45
Credit Cards 1 2 3 4 5

WEXFORD Co Wexford Map **01** D2

★★★✿✿69% *Talbot*
Trinity St ☎(053) 22566 FAX (053) 23777
RS 25 Dec
This large, modern streetside hotel caters for both leisure and commercial guests.
100⇨🏠(12fb)✗in 10 bedrooms CTV in all bedrooms ® ✣ T ✕ (ex guide dogs)

Wexford - Youghal

Lift (60P 🛏 (heated) squash snooker sauna solarium gymnasium games room beauty & hairdressing salon
♿ Irish & Continental **V** ♥ ⚓ ✂ Last dinner 8.45pm
Credit Cards [1][2][3][4][5]

★★★ 62% White's
George St ☎(053) 22311 FAX (053) 45000
Closed 24-26 Dec

This historic former coaching inn has recently been refurbished, but retains much of its charm. The entrance is through a modern extension, and entertainment is provided in the converted saddlery and forge.
76⇌♠Annexe6⇌♠(1fb)2⊞ CTV in all bedrooms ®⚡ T ✱
sB&B⇌♠IR£35-IR£53 dB&B⇌♠IR£50-IR£83 🍴
Lift (100P sauna solarium gymnasium ♫ *xmas*
♿ International **V** ♥ ⚓ ✂ Lunch IR£5.50-IR£15 High tea IR£5.50-IR£9.95alc Dinner IR£16-IR£25.50alc Last dinner 9.30pm
CONF. Thtr 900 Class 360 Board 200
Credit Cards [1][2][3][4][5]

★★★ 61% Ferrycarrig
Ferrycarrig ☎(053) 22999 FAX (053) 41982
The Ferrycarrig Hotel is a modern 4-story hotel in a lovely location on a sea inlet on the edge of Wexford and beside the National Heritage Park. In addition to the lovely views, smart new public rooms, refurbished bedrooms and excellent food and service ensure an enjoyable stay here.
40⇌♠(3fb) CTV in all bedrooms ®⚡ T ✂ (ex guide dogs) ✱
sB&B⇌♠IR£40-IR£50 dB&B⇌♠IR£50-IR£78 🍴
Lift (235P ✿ sauna solarium gymnasium ♫ *xmas*
♿ Irish & French **V** ♥ ⚓ ✂ ✱ Lunch IR£2.50-IR£15alc
CONF. Thtr 500 Class 280 Board 100 Del from IR£60
Credit Cards [1][2][3][5]

★★ 70% Wexford Lodge
(beside Wexford Bridge on R741)
☎(053) 23611 FAX (053) 23342
Closed 1-15 Nov & 24-29 Dec

This family-run hotel is situated adjacent to the town bridge overlooking the River Slaney and the harbour. Public rooms are good and all the bedrooms are of an excellent standard.
19⇌♠(5fb) CTV in all bedrooms ® T ✂ (ex guide dogs)
sB&B⇌♠IR£35-IR£40 dB&B⇌♠IR£60-IR£66
CTV 30P
♿ French **V** ♥ ⚓ ✂ Lunch IR£9.50-IR£10.50 Dinner IR£16 Last dinner 8.30pm
Credit Cards [1][2][3]

WOODENBRIDGE Co Wicklow Map 01 D3

★★ 60% Woodenbridge Inn
☎(0402) 35146 FAX (0402) 35573
RS 25 Dec & Good Fri
Situated in scenic surroundings in the Vale of Avoca, the inn, dating back to 1608, has retained its charm and relaxed atmosphere. There is good food in the restaurant and golf and fishing on the doorstep.
11⇌♠(2fb)1⊞ CTV in all bedrooms ®⚡ T ✂ (ex guide dogs)
sB&B⇌♠IR£25-IR£30 dB&B⇌♠IR£46-IR£50 🍴
CTV 200P ✿ ▶ 18 ♪ ○
V ♥ ⚓ ✂ Lunch IR£9 High tea frIR£1.95 Dinner IR£10-IR£15 Last dinner 9pm
Credit Cards [1][2][3]

YOUGHAL Co Cork Map 01 C2

★★ ❀❀63% Devonshire Arms
Pearse Square ☎(024) 92827 & 92018 FAX (024) 92900
Closed Xmas
Stephen and Helen O'Sullivan have been restoring this 19th-century hotel with much care and attention to detail. It offers good food in both the restaurant and the bar.
10⇌♠(3fb) CTV in all bedrooms T ✂ (ex guide dogs)
sB&B⇌♠IR£36-IR£40 dB&B⇌♠IR£54-IR£60
20P ✿ ⚬
♿ Irish & French **V** ♥ ⚓ ✂ Lunch IR£9-IR£10&alc Dinner IR£18-IR£20&alc Last dinner 8.30pm
CONF. Board 120
Credit Cards [1][2][3][5]

All black star hotels are given a
percentage grading within their star bands.
See 'Using the Guide' at the front of the book
for full details.

Company Owned Hotels

Abbreviations used in the guide and central reservations telephone numbers.
Please note that several of these hotel groups now have their company logo printed alongside each of their hotel entries, and when this is the case, the abbreviated group name is no longer shown after the hotel name. Examples are Edwardian, Forte Posthouse, Crest and Travelodge, Granada Motorway Services, Holiday Inns and Mount Charlotte Thistle. They are still included in this list, however, because of the central reservations telephone numbers.

COMPANY	ABBREVIATIONS	TELEPHONE
Best Western	Best Western	081-541 0033
Brend Hotels Ltd	Brend	Barnstaple (0271) 44496
Calotels	Calotels	Bournemouth (0202) 297888
Campanile UK	Campanile	Paris 010-331 6462 4646
Chef & Brewer	Chef & Brewer	
Consort Hotels Ltd	Consort	York (0904) 643151
Copthorne	Copthorne	(0800) 414741
Crown & Raven	Crown & Raven	
De Vere Hotels Ltd	De Vere	Warrington (0925) 265050
Edwardian	Edwardian	(0800) 335588
Exec Hotels	Exec Hotels	
Forestdale Hotels Ltd	Forestdale	(0800) 378640
Forte Hotes	Forte Posthouse	(0800) 404040
	Forte Crest	(0800) 404040
	Forte Travelodge	(0800) 850950
Friendly Hotels	Friendly Hotels	(0800) 591910
Granada MotorwayServices Ltd	Granada	(0800) 555300
Guestaccom	Guestaccom	
Holiday Inns Int	Guestaccom	(0800) 897121
Hotel Ibis	Ibis	071-724 1000
Inter-Continental	IC	(0345) 581444
Leading Hotels of the World		(0800)181123
Logis of Great Britain	Logis	(0865) 875888
Milton	Milton	(0397) 703139
Minotels	Minotels	Blackpool (0253) 292000
Mount CharlotteThistle Hotels Ltd	Mount Charlotte (TS)	071-937 8033
Novotel International	Novotel	071-724 1000
Pride of Britain Ltd	Pride of Britain	(0264) 76444
Principle Hotels	Principle	(0800) 454454
Queens Moat House Ltd	Queens Moat	(0800)181737
Ramada International	Ramada	071-235 5264
Rank Organisation Ltd	Rank	081-569 7120/7211
Relais et Châteaux	Relais et Châteaux	
Resort	Resort	(0345) 313213
Sarova Hotels	Sarova	071-589 6000
Savoy Hotels	Savoy	071-872 8080
Scottish Highland Hotels	Scottish Highland	031-557 2368
Scott's Hotels	Scott's	(0753) 544255
Sheraton Hotels	Sheraton Hotels	(0800) 353535
Shire Inns Ltd	Shire	
Small Luxury Hotels of the World	Small Luxury Hotel	(0800) 282142
Swallow Hotels Ltd	Swallow	091-529 4666
Thistle Hotels	Thistle	071-937 8033
Toby restaurants Ltd	Toby	
Whitbread Group of Hotels PLC	Whitbread	(0582) 396922
	Whitbread Lansbury	(0582) 400158
	Country Club	(0582) 296922

Selected & Premier Selected
Bed & Breakfast Accommodation

Below is a quick-reference list in country and county order - England, Channel Islands, Scotland, Wales, Ireland - of the two highest-rated categories (Selected and Premier Selected) of private hotels, guest houses farmhouses and inns from the 1994 edition of the AA's best-selling guide, *Britain's Best Bed and Breakfast*. These establishments offer services and accommodation on a similar level to what you would find at many small hotels. They have no entry in the hotels directory, so please telephone the establishments direct for further details - or buy a copy of *Britain's Best Bed and Breakfast*, available from bookshops and AA shops.

ENGLAND

AVON

BATH
Arden House 0225 466601
Badminton Villa 0225 426347
Bath Tasburgh 0225 425096
Bloomfield House 0225 420105
Cheriton House 0225 429862
Dorian House 0225 426336
Haydon House (Premier Selected) 0225 444919
Holly Lodge 0225 424042
Laura Place Hotel 0225 463815
Leighton House 0225 314769
Meadowland 0225 311079
Oakleigh House 0225 315698
Old School House (Premier Selected) 0225 859593
Orchard Lodge 0225 466115
Paradise House 0225 317723
Somerset House Hotel & Restaurant 0225 466451
Underhill Lodge 0225 464992
KEYNSHAM
Grasmere Court Hotel 0272 862662
OLD SODBURY
Sodbury House 0454 312847
WESTON-SUPER-MARE
Ashcombe Court 0934 625104
Braeside 0934 626642
Milton Lodge 0934 623161

BERKSHIRE

MAIDENHEAD
Beehive Manor (Premier Selected) 0628 20980

WINDSOR
Melrose 0753 865328

BUCKINGHAMSHIRE

HIGH WYCOMBE
Clifton Lodge 0494 440095
MARLOW
Holly Tree House 0628 891110

CAMBRIDGESHIRE

CAMBRIDGE
Old School Guesthouse 0223 861609
ELY
Forge Cottage 0353 663275

CHESHIRE

CHESTER
Green Gables 0244 372243
Redland Private Hotel 0244 671024
CREWE
Clayhanger Hall Farm 0270 583952
HATTON HEATH
Golborne Manor 0829 70310
KNUTSFORD
Dog Inn 0625 861421
MACCLESFIELD
Hardingland Farm 0625 425759
MALPAS
Tilston Lodge (Premier Selected) 0829 250223

CLEVELAND

STOCKTON-ON-TEES
Edwardian Hotel 0642 615655

CO DURHAM

DARLINGTON
Clow Beck House 0325 721075
FIR TREE
Greenhead Country House 0388 763143

CORNWALL & ISLES OF SCILLY

BLACKWATER
Rock Cottage 0872 560252
BODMIN
Treffry Farm 0208 74405
BOSCASTLE
Trerosewill Farmhouse 0840 250545
BUDE
Cliff Hotel 0288 353110
CRACKINGTON HAVEN
Manor Farm (Premier Selected) 0840 230304
Trevigue (Premier Selected) 0840 230418
Treworgie Barton 0840 230233
FALMOUTH
Penmere Guest House 0326 374470
Westcott Hotel 0326 311309
FOWEY
Carnethic House 0726 833336
HELSTON
Nanplough Farm 0326 241088
LELANT
Badger Inn 0736 752181
LISKEARD
Tregondale Farm 0579 342407
LIZARD
Landewednack House (Premier Selected) 0326 290909

708

BEST BED & BREAKFAST, CORNWALL - DEVON

LOOE
Coombe Farm 05034 223
Harescombe Lodge (Premier Selected) 0503 263158
Panorama Hotel 0503 262123
Woodlands 0503 264405
MEVAGISSEY
Kerryanna 0726 843558
NEWQUAY
Degembris Farmhouse 0872 510555
Manuels Farm 0637 873577
Pendeen 0637 873521
Porth Enodoc 0637 872372
Priory Lodge 0637 874111
Towan Beach 0637 872093
Windward Hotel 0637 873185
PENRYN
Prospect House (Premier Selected) 0326 373198
PENZANCE
Yacht Inn 0736 62787
POLPERRO
Landaviddy Manor 0503 72210
Lanhael House 0503 72428
Trenderway Farm (Premier Selected) 0503 72214
PORT ISAAC
Archer Farm 0208 880522
PORTREATH
Benson's 0209 842534
SALTASH
Crooked Inn 0752 848177
ST AUSTELL
Poltarrow Farm 0726 67211
ST BLAZEY
Nanscawan House (Premier Selected) 0726 814488
ST ERME
Trevispian Vean Farm 0872 79514
ST HILARY
Ennys Farm 0736 740262
ST IVES
Dean Court 0736 796023
ST-JUST-IN-ROSELAND
Rose-da-Mar Hotel 0326 270450
ST MARY'S
Brantwood Hotel 0720 22531
Carnwethers Country House 0720 22415
ST WENN
Wenn Manor 0726 890240
TINTAGEL
Trebrea Lodge (Premier Selected) 0840 770410
TRURO
Lands Vue 0872 560102

TYWARDREATH
Elmswood House 0726 814221

CUMBRIA

AMBLESIDE
Drunken Duck 09666 347
Grey Friar Lodge Country House Hotel 05394 33158
Rothay Garth Hotel 05394 32217
BOLTONGATE
Old Rectory 06973 71647
BORROWDALE
Greenbank 07687 77215
BUTTERMERE
Pickett Howe (Premier Selected) 0900 85444
CALDBECK
High Greenrigg House 06974 78430
COCKERMOUTH
Low Hall Country Guest House (Premier Selected) 0900 826654
CONISTON
Coniston Lodge (Premier Selected) 05394 41201
CROSTHWAITE
Crosthwaite House 05395 68264
FAR SAWREY
West Vale Country Guest House 05394 42817
GRANGE-OVER-SANDS
Greenacres (Premier Selected) 05395 34578
HAWKSHEAD
Rough Close Country House(Premier Selected) 05394 36370
KENDAL
Burrow Hall Country Guest House 0539 821711
Lane Head Country House Hotel 0539 731283
Low Jock Scar 0539 823259
KESWICK
Abacourt House 07687 72967
Applethwaite Country House Hotel 07687 72413
Craglands 07687 74406
Dalegarth House Country Hotel 07687 72817
KIRKBY LONSDALE
Hipping Hall (Premier Selected) 05242 71187
KIRKCAMBECK
Cracrop Farm 06978 245
KIRKOSWALD
Prospect Hill Hotel 0768 898500

LONGTOWN
Bessiestown Farm 0228 577219
NEAR SAWREY
Ees Wyke Country House (Premier Selected) 05394 36393
The Garth 05394 36373
PENRUDDOCK
Highgate Farm 07684 83339
UNDERBARROW
Tranthwaite Hall 05395 68285
WATERMILLOCK
Old Church Hotel (Premier Selected) 07684 86204
WINDERMERE
Applegarth 05394 43206
Blenheim Lodge 05394 43440
Hawksmoor Guest House 05394 42110
Parson Wyke Country House 05394 42837
Archway Guest House 05394 45613
Beaumont Hotel 05394 47075
Woodlands 05394 43915

DERBYSHIRE

ASHBOURNE
Lichfield Guest House 0335 344422
BUXTON
Brookfield on Longhill (Premier Selected) 0298 24151
Grosvenor House 0298 72439
Westminster 0298 23929
CARSINGTON
Henmore Grange 062985 420
MATLOCK
Lane End House 0629 583981
SHOTTLE
Dannah Farm 0773 550273
WINSTER
Dower House 0629 650213

DEVON

ASHBURTON
Gages Mill 0364 652391
AXMINSTER
Millbrook Farmhouse 0297 35351
BARNSTAPLE
Home Park Farm 0271 42955
BICKINGTON
East Burne Farm 0626 821496
BOVEY TRACEY
Blackaller Hotel & Restaurant 0647 40322
Slate Cottage 0647 40060
Willmead Farm 06477 214

BEST BED & BREAKFAST, DEVON - HAMPSHIRE

BUCKFASTLEIGH
Dartbridge Inn 0364 42214
BUDLEIGH SALTERTON
Copperfields 0395 443430
Long Range 0395 443321
CHAGFORD
Bly House 0647 432404
COLYFORD
Swallows Eaves Hotel (Premier Selected) 0297 553184
CROYDE
Moorsands House 0271 890781
Whiteleaf at Croyde (Premier Selected) 0271 890266
CULLOMPTON
Rullands 0884 33356
DARTINGTON
Cott Inn 0803 863777
DARTMOUTH
Captains House 0803 832281
Ford House (Premier Selected) 0803 834047
EXETER
Edwardian 0392 76102
HOLNE
Wellpritton Farm 03643 273
HONITON
The Heathfield 0404 45321
HORN'S CROSS
Lower Waytown 0237 451787
ILFRACOMBE
Varley House (Premier Selected) 0271 863927
ILSINGTON
Little Close 0364 661277
KINGSTON
Trebles Cottage 0548 810268
LYNMOUTH
Countisbury Lodge Hotel 0598 52388
LYNTON
Alford House 0598 52359
Hazeldene Guest House 0598 52364
Ingleside Hotel 0598 52223
Victoria Lodge 0598 53203
Waterloo House 0598 53391
MORCHARD BISHOP
Wigham (Premier Selected) 0363 877350
MORTEHOE
Sunnycliffe Hotel 0271 870597
NEWTON ABBOT
Barn Owl Inn 0803 872130
OAKFORD
Newhouse Farm 03985 347
PARKHAM
Old Rectory (Premier Selected) 0237 451443

PLYMOUTH
Bowling Green 0752 667485
SHILLINGFORD
Old Mill 0398 331064
TAVISTOCK
Old Coach House Hotel 0822 617515
TEIGNMOUTH
Thomas Luny House (Premier Selected) 0626 772976
TIVERTON
Hornhill Farm 0884 253352
Lower Collipriest Farm 0884 252321
TORQUAY
Barn Hayes Country Hotel 0803 327980
Berbury 0803 297494
Glenorleigh Hotel 0803 292135
Kingston House 0803 212760
TOTNES
Old Forge at Totnes 0803 862174
Watermans Arms (Premier Selected) 0803 732214
WEST DOWN
Long House (Premier Selected) 0271 863242

DORSET

BEAMINSTER
Hams Plot (Premier Selected) 0308 862979
BOURNEMOUTH
Boltons 0202 751517
Cliff House Hotel 0202 763003
Silver Trees 0202 556040
Tudor Grange 0202 291472
BRIDPORT
Britmead House 0308 422941
CHARMOUTH
Newlands House 0297 60212
CHIDEOCK
Betchworth House 0297 89478
DORCHESTER
Westwood House 0305 268018
Yalbury Cottage (Premier Selected) 0305 262382
EVERSHOT
Rectory House 093583 273
HORTON
Northill House (Premier Selected) 0258 840407
WAREHAM
Redcliffe Farm 0929 552225
WEYMOUTH
Bay Lodge 0305 782419

ESSEX

CHELMSFORD
Snows Oaklands Hotel 0245 352004
THAXTED
Piggots Mill 0371 830379

GLOUCESTERSHIRE

BERKELEY
Greenacres Farm 0453 810348
BLOCKLEY
Lower Brook House 0386 700286
BOURTON-ON-THE-WATER
Coombe House 0451 821966
CHELTENHAM
Cleeve Hill 0242 672052
Lypiatt House (Premier Selected) 0242 224994
CHIPPING CAMPDEN
Malt House 0386 840295
CIRENCESTER
Waterton Garden Cottage 0285 851303
CLEARWELL
Tudor Farmhouse 0594 833046
LAVERTON
Leasow House 0386 584526
TETBURY
Tavern House 0666 880444
WILLERSEY
Old Rectory (Premier Selected) 0386 853729
WINCHCOMBE
Wesley House 0242 602366

GTR LONDON

KINGSTON UPON THAMES
Chase Lodge 081 943 1862

GTR MANCHESTER

ALTRINCHAM
Ash Farm 061-9299290

HAMPSHIRE

BARTON-ON-SEA
Bank Cottage 0425 613677
BRANSGORE
Tothill House 0425 674414
BROCKENHURST
Cottage Hotel 0590 22296
Thatched Cottage Hotel (Premier Selected) 0590 23090
CADNAM
Kents Farm 0703 813497
Walnut Cottage 0703 812275

EMSWORTH
The Crown Hotel 0243 372806
FAREHAM
Avenue House 0329 232175
HAYLING ISLAND
Cockle Warren Cottage Hotel
0705 464961
LYMINGTON
Our Bench 0590 673141
LYNDHURST
Ormonde House 0703 282806
RINGWOOD
Little Forest Lodge (Premier
Selected) 0425 478848
The Nest 0425 476724
ROMSEY
Highfield House 0794 340727
SARISBURY GREEN
Dormy House 0489 572626
SOUTHAMPTON
Hunters Lodge 0703 227919
SWAY
The Nurse's Cottage 0590 683402
The Tower 0590 682117
WINCHESTER
Leckhampton 0962 852231
Shawlands 0962 861166
Wykeham Arms (Premier Selected)
0962 853834

HEREFORD & WORCESTER

BISHAMPTON
Nightingale Hotel (Premier
Selected) 0386 82521
BREDWARDINE
Bredwardine Hall 0981 500596
BROADWAY
Orchard Grove 0386 853834
HANLEY CASTLE
Old Parsonage Farm 0684 310124
HEREFORD
Hermitage Manor 0432 760317
KIDDERMINSTER
Cedars Hotel 0562 515595
LEOMINSTER
Hills Farm 056887 205
Withenfield 0568 612011
PONTRILAS
Howton Court 0981 240249
RUCKHALL
 Ancient Camp Inn 0981 250449

ULLINGSWICK
The Steppes 0432 820424
VOWCHURCH
Croft Country House 0981 550226

WEOBLEY
Ye Olde Salutation Inn 0544 318443
WHITNEY-ON-WYE
Rhydspence Inn (Premier Selected)
0497 831262

HUMBERSIDE

LOW CATTON
Derwent Lodge 0759 71468

KENT

CANTERBURY
Ebury 0227 768433
Ersham Lodge 0227 463174
Magnolia House 0227 765121
Old Rectory (Premier Selected)
0227 730075
Pilgrims 0227 464531
Thanington Hotel 0227 453227
Thruxted Oast (Premier Selected)
0227 730080
White House 0227 761836
CRANBROOK
The Oast 0580 712416
Hancocks Farmhouse (Premier
Selected) 0580 714645
EYNSFORD
Home Farm 0322 866193
GRAVESEND
Overcliffe 0474 322131
HAWKHURST
Conghurst Farm (Premier Selected)
0580 753331
MAIDSTONE
Tanyard 0622 744705
MARGATE
Greswolde 0843 223956
PENSHURST
Swale Cottage (Premier Selected)
0892 870738
PETHAM
Old Poor House 0227 700413
PLUCKLEY
Elvey Farm 0233 840442
ROYAL TUNBRIDGE WELLS
Danehurst House 0892 527739
St Martins 0892 536857
SHIPBOURNE
Chaser Inn 0732 810360
SITTINGBOURNE
Hempstead House (Premier
Selected) 0795 428020
TONBRIDGE
Goldhill Mill (Premier Selected)
0732 851626
WEST MALLING

Scott House 0732 841380
Woodgate 0732 843201

LANCASHIRE

BLACKPOOL
Sunray Private Hotel 0253 351937
CARNFORTH
New Capernwray Farm (Premier
Selected) 0524 734284
COLNE
Higher Wanless Farm 0282 865301
HARROP FOLD
Harrop Fold Country Farmhouse
Hotel (Premier Selected)
0200 447600
LONGRIDGE
Jenkinsons Farmhouse 0772 782624
SILVERDALE
Lindeth 0524 701238
SLAIDBURN
Parrock Head Farm House Hotel
(Premier Selected) 0200 446614
THORNTON
Victorian House 0253 860619
YEALAND CONYERS
The Bower 0524 734585

LEICESTERSHIRE

SHEARSBY
Knaptoft House Farm & the
Greenway 0533 478388
UPPINGHAM
Rutland House 0572 822497

LINCOLNSHIRE

CONISHOLME
Wickham House 0507 358465
LINCOLN
D'Isney Place Hotel 0522 538881
LOUTH
Masons Arms 0507 609525
SLEAFORD
Carre Arms 0529 303156
STAMFORD
Priory 0780 720215
STURTON-BY-STOW
Gallows Dale Farm 0427 788387

LONDON

E11
Lakeside 081 989 6100
NW3
Langorf Hotel 071 794 4483
SW3

BEST BED & BREAKFAST, LONDON - SOMERSET

Claverley House 071 589 8541
Parkes Hotel 071 581 9944
SW7
Five Sumner Place 071 584 7586
W2
Byron 071 243 0987
Mornington 071 262 7361
Norfolk Plaza 071 723 0792
Norfolk Towers 071 262 3123
Pembridge Court (Premier Selected)
071 229 9977
W4
Chiswick 081 994 1712
W7
Wellmeadow Lodge 081 567 7294
W14
Aston Court 071 602 9954
Russell Court 071 603 1222

NORFOLK

BARNEY
Old Brick Kilns 0328 878305
HUNSTANTON
Claremont 0485 533171
KING'S LYNN
Russet House Hotel 0553 773098
SHERINGHAM
Fairlawns 0263 824717
SWAFFHAM
Corfield House 0760 723636
TIVETSHALL ST MARY
Old Ram Coaching Inn 0379 676794

NORTHAMPTONSHIRE

CHARLTON
Home Farmhouse 0295 811683

NORTHUMBERLAND

ALLENDALE
Bishopfield 0434 683248
ALNMOUTH
Marine House 0665 830349
HALTWHISTLE
Broomshaw Hill Farm 0434 320866
KIRKWHELPINGTON
Shieldhall 0830 40387
ROTHBURY
Orchard 0669 20684

NOTTINGHAMSHIRE

NORTH WHEATLEY
Old Plough (Premier Selected)
0427 880916

NOTTINGHAM
Hall Farm House 0602 663112

OXFORDSHIRE

BANBURY
La Madonette Country Guest House
0295 730212
BURFORD Andrews Hotel
(Premier Selected) 099382 3151
Elm Farm House 0993 823611
CHISLEHAMPTON
Coach & Horses 0865 890255
EYNSHAM
All Views 0865 880891
FARINGDON
Barcote Manor 036787 260
KIDLINGTON
Bowood House 0865 842288
KINGHAM
Conygree Gate 0608 658389
KINGSTON BAGPUIZE
Fallowfields (Premier Selected)
0865 820416
LEW
Farmhouse Hotel & Restaurant
0993 850297
MILTON-UNDER-WYCHWOOD
Hillborough Hotel 0993 830501
OXFORD
Chestnuts Guest House 0865 53375
Cotswold House (Premier Selected)
0865 310558
Dial House 0865 69944
Marlborough House 0865 311321
Tilbury Lodge 0865 862138
THAME
Upper Green Farm 0844 212496
WOODSTOCK
Laurels 0993 812583
WOOLSTONE
White Horse 0367 820566

SHROPSHIRE

ASTON MUNSLOW
Chadstone Guest House 058476 675
BRIDGNORTH
Haven Pasture 074635 632
CHURCH STRETTON
Belvedere 0694 722232
Jinlye 0694 723243
Rectory Farm (Premier Selected)
0694 751306
DIDDLEBURY
The Glebe 058476 221
IRONBRIDGE
Library House 0952 432299

LUDLOW
Number Twenty-eight 0584 876996
MARKET DRAYTON
Stoke Manor 063084 222
MIDDLETON PRIORS
Middleton Lodge 074634 228
SHREWSBURY
Fieldside 0743 353143
Mytton Hall 0743 850264
Sandford House 0743 343829
TELFORD
Church Farm 0952 244917
WEM
Soulton Hall 0939 232786

SOMERSET

BEERCROCOMBE
Frog Street Farm (Premier Selected)
0823 480430
Whittles Farm (Premier Selected)
0823 480301
CANNINGTON
Swang Farm 0278 671765
CREWKERNE
Broadview (Premier Selected)
0460 73424
DULVERTON
Dassels Country House 03984 203
KILVE
Hood Arms (Premier Selected)
0278741 210
LANGPORT
Hillards Farm (Premier Selected)
0458 251737
MINEHEAD
Gascony 0643 705939
Marston Lodge 0643 702510
NORTON ST PHILIP
Monmouth Lodge (Premier
Selected) 0373 834367
Plaine Guest House 0373 834723
PAWLETT
Brickyard Farm 0278 683381
PORLOCK
Gable Thatch (Premier Selected)
0643 862552
ROADWATER
Wood Advent Farm 0984 40920
SIMONSBATH
Emmett Grange 064383 282
SOMERTON
Lynch Country House (Premier
Selected) 0458 72316
TAUNTON
Higher Dipford Farm 0823 275770
Meryan House Hotel 0823 337445

BEST BED & BREAKFAST, SOMERSET - WILTSHIRE

WASHFORD
Washford Inn 0984 40256
WATCHET
Chidgley Hill Farm 0984 40403
WATERROW
Hurstone Country Hotel 0984 23441
WELLINGTON
Pinksmoor Mill House 0823 672361
WELLS
Coach House 0749 676535
Littlewell Farm (Premier Selected)
0749 677914
Southway Farm 0749 673396
Tor Guest House 0749 672322
WINCANTON
Lower Church Farm 0963 32307
WIVELISCOMBE
Deepleigh 0984 23379

STAFFORDSHIRE

AUDLEY
Domvilles Farm 0782 720378
CHEDDLETON
Choir Cottage & Choir House
0538 360561
OAKAMOOR
Bank House (Premier Selected)
0538 702810

SUFFOLK

GISLINGHAM
The Old Guildhall 0379 783361
HIGHAM
Old Vicarage 020637 248
NEEDHAM MARKET
Pipps Ford Farm 044979 208
STOKE-BY-NAYLAND
Angel Inn 0206 263245

SURREY

HORLEY
Vulcan Lodge 0293 771522

SUSSEX (EAST)

ARLINGTON
Bates Green (Premier Selected)
0323 482039
BRIGHTON
Adelaide Hotel 0273 205286
EASTBOURNE
Beachy Rise 0323 639171
FRANT
Old Parsonage (Premier Selected)
0892 750773

HARTFIELD
Bolebrook Watermill 0892 770425
HASTINGS
Bryn-y-Mor 0424 722744
Filsham Farmhouse 0424 433109
Parkside House (Premier Selected)
0424 433096
Tower 0424 427217
HOVE
Claremont House (Premier Selected)
0273 735161
LEWES
Nightingales 0273 475673
RYE
Green Hedges (Premier Selected)
0797 222185
Holloway House 0797 224748
Jeakes House (Premier Selected)
0797 222828
Old Vicarage Guest House
0797 222119
Old Vicarage Hotel & Restaurant
0797 225131
Playden Cottage 0797 222234
UCKFIELD
Hooke Hall 0825 761578
South Paddock 0825 762335
WINCHELSEA
Country House at Winchelsea
0797 226669

SUSSEX (WEST)

BEPTON
Park House (Premier Selected)
0730 812880
BILLINGSHURST
Old Wharf (Premier Selected)
0403 784096
BOSHAM
Kenwood 0243 572727
ROGATE
Mizzards Farm (Premier Selected)
0730 821656
RUSTINGTON
Kenmore Guest House 0903 784634
STEYNING
Springwells 0903 812446
SUTTON
White Horse (Premier Selected)
07987 221

TYNE & WEAR

TYNEMOUTH
Hope House 091 257 1989

WARWICKSHIRE

HASELEY KNOB
Croft 0926 484447
HATTON
Northleigh House 0926 484203
KENILWORTH
Victoria Lodge 0926 512020
LOWER BRAILES
Feldon House 060885 580 due to
change to 0608 685580
OXHILL
Nolands Farmhouse 0926 640309
STRATFORD-UPON-AVON
Graveside Barn 0789 750502
Twelfth Night 0789 414595
WARWICK
Old Rectory 0926 624562
Shrewley House 0926 842549

WIGHT, ISLE OF

SANDOWN
St Catherine's 0983 402392
SHANKLIN
Chine Lodge 0983 862358
Osborne House 0983 862501

WILTSHIRE

ALDERTON
Manor Farm 0666 840271
BRADFORD ON AVON
Bradford Old Windmill 0225 866842
Widbrook Grange 0225 863173
BURBAGE
Old Vicarage (Premier Selected)
0672 810495
DEVIZES
Potterne Park Farm 0380 724257
LACOCK
At the Sign of the Angel
0249 730230
LITTLE CHEVERELL
Little Cheverell House 0380 813322
LONGLEAT
Sturford Mead Farm 0373 832213
MARLBOROUGH
Laurel Cottage 0672 841288
MERE
Chetcombe House 0747 860219
NETTLETON
Fosse Farmhouse Country Hotel
0249 782286
SALISBURY
Grasmere House 0722 338388

BEST BED & BREAKFAST, WILTSHIRE - SCOTLAND, HIGHLAND

WEST GRAFTON
Mayfield (Premier Selected)
0672 810339

YORKSHIRE (NORTH)

BEDALE
Blairgowrie Country House
0748 811377
BOROUGHBRIDGE
Crown Inn 0423 322578
GRASSINGTON
Ashfield House 0756 752584
HARROGATE
Acacia Lodge 0423 560752
Alexa House & Stable Cottages
0423 501988
Ashley House 0423 507474
Delaine 0423 567974
Ruskin 0423 502045
HUNTON
Countryman's Inn 0677 50554
INGLEBY GREENHOW
Manor House Farm 0642 722384
INGLETON
Oakroyd Old Rectory 05242 41258
KETTLEWELL
Langcliffe House 0756 760243
KIRKBYMOORSIDE
Appletree Court 0751 31536
LOW ROW
Peat Gate Head 0748 86388
MASHAM
Bank Villa 0765 689605
PATRICK BROMPTON
Elmfield House 0677 50558 due to change to 0677 450558
RASKELF
Old Farmhouse Country Hotel
0347 821971
REETH
Arkleside Hotel (Premier Selected)
0748 84200
RICHMOND
Whashton Springs Farm (Premier Selected) 0748 822884
SCARBOROUGH
Paragon 0723 372676
SCOTCH CORNER
Vintage Hotel 0748 824424
STARBOTTON
Hilltop Country Guest House
0756 760321
WHITBY
Dunsley Hall (Premier Selected)
0947 83437
Grantley House 0947 600895

Seacliffe 0947 603139
Waverley 0947 604389
YORK
Arndale Hotel 0904 702424
Ashbourne House 0904 639912
Ashbury 0904 647339
Curzon Lodge and Stable Cottages
0904 703157
Four Seasons 0904 622621
Grasmead House Hotel 0904 629996
Heathers Guest House 0904 640989
Holmwood House 0904 626183
Midway House 0904 659272
Priory 0904 625280
St Denys 0904 622207

YORKSHIRE (WEST)

HEBDEN BRIDGE
Redacre Mill 0422 885563
HOLMFIRTH
Holme Castle Country Hotel
0484 686764
WAKEFIELD
Stanley View 0924 376803

CHANNEL ISLANDS
GUERNSEY

ST PETER PORT
Les Ozouets 0481 721288
Midhurst House 0481 724391

JERSEY

GROUVILLE
Lavender Villa 0534 54937
ST AUBIN
The Panorama 0534 42429
ST HELIER
Kaieteur Guest House 0534 37004

SCOTLAND
BORDERS

JEDBURGH
The Spinney 0835 863525
MELROSE
Dunfermline House 089682 2148
WEST LINTON
Medwyn House 0968 60542

CENTRAL

BALQUHIDDER
Stronvar House 08774 688 due to change to 087 384688
BRIG O'TURK
Dundarroch 08776 200 due to change to 0877 376200
CALLANDER
Arran Lodge (Premier Selected)
0877 30976 due to change to
0877 330976
Brook Linn Country House
0877 30103 due to change to
0877 330103
DUNBLANE
Westwood 0786 822579
THORNHILL
Corshill 0786 850270

DUMFRIES & GALLOWAY

BEATTOCK
Broomlands Farm 06833 320

DALBEATTIE
Auchenskeoch Lodge 038778 277
KIRKBEAN
Cavens House 038788 234
KIRKCUDBRIGHT
Gladstone House 0557 31734
MOFFAT
Gilbert House 0683 20050
TWYNHOLM
Fresh Fields 05576 221

FIFE

ABERDOUR
Hawkcraig 0383 860335
ANSTRUTHER
Spindrift 0333 310573
AUCHTERMUCHTY
Ardchoille (Premier Selected)
0337 828414

GRAMPIAN

ABERDEEN
Cedars Private Hotel 0224 583225
Manorville 0224 594190
FORRES
Parkmount House 0309 673312
KEITH
Haughs Farm 0542 882238

HIGHLAND

ARDGAY
Ardgay House 08632 345

BEST BED & BREAKFAST, SCOTLAND, HIGHLAND - WALES, GWYNEDD

BALLACHULISH
Fern Villa 08552 393
BOAT OF GARTEN
Heathbank House 047983 234
BRORA
Lynwood 0408 621226
CARRBRIDGE
Fairwinds Hotel 047984 240 due to change to 0479 841240
CONON BRIDGE
Kinkell House 0349 61270
DORNOCH
Fourpenny Cottage 0862 810727
DRUMBEG
Drumbeg House 05713 209
DRUMNADROCHIT
Polmaily House 0456 450343
FORT WILLIAM
Ashburn House 0397 706000
FOYERS
Foyers Bay House 0456 486624
GAIRLOCH
Birchwood 0445 2011
Horisdale House 0445 2151
GRANTOWN-ON-SPEY
Ardconnel 0479 2104 due to change to 0479 872104
Culdearn House (Premier Selected) 0479 2106 due to change to 0479 872106
Garden Park 0479 3235 due to change to 0479 873235
INVERNESS
Ballifeary (Premier Selected) 0463 235572
Culduthel Lodge (Premier Selected) 0463 240089
Old Rectory 0463 220969
KINGUSSIE
The Cross (Premier Selected) 0540 661166
MUIR OF ORD
Dower House (Premier Selected) 0463 870090
NAIRN
Greenlawns 0667 52738
PORTREE
Quiraing 0478 612870
ROGART
Rovie Farm 0408 641209
ULLAPOOL
Ardvreck 0854 612028
The Sheiling 085461 2947

LOTHIAN

EAST CALDER
Ashcroft Farmhouse 0506 881810

EDINBURGH
Ashgrove House 031 337 5014
Dorstan Private Hotel 031 667 6721
Drummond House (Premier Selected) 031 557 9189
The Lodge 031 337 3682
Newington Guest House 031 667 3356
Stuart House 031 557 9030

STRATHCLYDE

AYR
Brenalder Lodge 0292 443939
Lagg Farm 029250 647
BALLOCH
Gowanlea Guest House 0389 52456
BRODICK
Dunvegan 0770 2811
CARDROSS
Kirkton House 0389 841951
CONNEL
Ards House (Premier Selected) 063171 255
Loch Etive Hotel 063171 400
Ronebhal 063171 310
LARGS
Whin Park 0475 673437
PRESTWICK
Golf View Hotel 0292 671234
ST CATHERINE'S
Thistle House 0499 2209
TOBERMORY
Fairways Lodge 0688 2238
Strongarbh House (Premier Selected) 0688 2328

TAYSIDE

ARBROATH
Farmhouse Kitchen 02416 202
BRECHIN
Blibberhill Farm 0307 830225
DUNDEE
Beach House Hotel 0382 75537
KILLIN
Breadalbane House 0567 820386
PERTH
Ardfern House 0738 22259
Lochiel House 0738 33183
PITLOCHRY
Dundarave House 0796 473109

WESTERN ISLES (Lewis)

UIG
Corran View 0851 72300

WALES
CLWYD

CORWEN
Powys House Estate 0490 412367
RUTHIN
Eyarth Station 0824 703643
ST ASAPH
Bach-Y-Graig 0745 730627

DYFED

CAREW
Old Stable Cottage 0646 651889
GWAUN VALLEY
Tregynon Country Farmhouse Hotel 0239 820531
LLANRHYSTUD
Pen-Y-Castell 0974 272622
NEW QUAY
Park Hall 0545 560306
SOLVA
Lochmeyler Farm 0348 837724

GLAMORGAN (MID)

MERTHYR TYDFIL
Llwyn On Guest House 0685 384384

GLAMORGAN (WEST)

NEATH
Cwmbach Cottages 0639 639825
SWANSEA
Cefn Bryn 0792 466687
Tredilion House 0792 470766

GWENT

ABERGAVENNY
Llanwenarth House 0873 830289

GWYNEDD

ABERDOVEY
Brodawel 0654 767347
Morlan Guesthouse 0654 767706
BANGOR
Country Bumpkin 0248 370477
BETWS-Y-COED
Tan-Y-Foel 0690 710507
Tyn-Y-Celyn 0690 710202
BONTDDU
Borthwnog Hall 034149 271
CAERNARFON
Caer Menai 0286 2612

BEST BED & BREAKFAST, WALES GWYNEDD - IRELAND, CO. WICKLOW

HARLECH
Castle Cottage Hotel 0766 780479
Gwrach Ynys 0766 780742
LLANDUDNO
Cornerways Hotel 0492 877334
Craiglands 0492 875090
Cranberry House 0492 879760
Hollybank 0492 878521
Wilton Hotel 0492 876086
LLANEGRYN
Bryn Gwyn 0654 711771
LLANFACHRETH
Ty Isaf 0341 423261
LLANWNDA
Pengwern Farm 0286 830717
ROEWEN
Gwern Borter 0492 650360

POWYS

ABERCRAF
Maes-Y-Gwernen 0639 730218
CHURCH STOKE
Drewin Farm 0588 620325
LLANDRINDOD WELLS
Three Wells 0597 824427
LLANGURIG
Old Vicarage 05515 280
MONTGOMERY
Little Brompton Farm 0686 668371
NEWTOWN
Dyffryn Farmhouse 0686 688817
PENYBONT
Ffaldau Country House (Premier Selected) 0597 851421
SENNYBRIDGE
Brynfedwen Farm 0874 636505
WELSHPOOL
Gungrog House 0938 553381
Lower Trelydan 0938 553105
Moat Farm 0938 553179

NORTHERN IRELAND

CO. ANTRIM

BUSHMILLS
White Gables 02657 31611
LISBURN
Brook Lodge 0846 638454

CO. LONDONDERRY

COLERAINE
Greenhill House 0265 868241

CO. TYRONE

DUNGANNON
Grange Lodge (Premier Selected) 08687 84212

REPUBLIC OF IRELAND

CO. CARLOW

MILFORD
Goleen Country House 0503 46132

CO. CLARE

BALLYVAUGHAN
Rusheen Lodge 065 77092

CO. CORK

BALLINADEE
Glebe House 021 778294
KANTURK
Assolas Country House 029 50015
KILLEAGH
Ballymakeigh House 024 95184
KINSALE
Old Bank House 021 774075
YOUGHAL
Ahernes 024 92424

CO. DUBLIN

DUBLIN
Aberdeen Lodge (Premier Selected) 01 2838155
Ariel House 01 6685512
Glenogra 01 6683661
Grey Door (Premier Selected) 01 6763286
Merrion Hall 01 6681426
Northumberland Lodge 01 6605270

CO. GALWAY

CLIFDEN
Mallmore House 095 21460

CO. KERRY

DINGLE
Doyles Town House 066 51174
Green Mount House 066 51414
KILLARNEY
Kathleen's Country House 064 32810

CO. LOUTH

ARDEE
Gables House 041 53789
DROGHEDA
Tullyesker House 041 30430

CO. MAYO

ACHILL ISLAND
Gray's Guest House 098 43244

CO. OFFALY

TULLAMORE
Moorhill Country House 0506 21395

CO. TIPPERARY

BANSHA
Bansha House 062 54194

CO. WATERFORD

CAPPOQUIN
Richmond House 058 54278
CHEEKPOINT
Three Rivers 051 82520
DUNMORE EAST
Hillfield House 051 83565

CO. WEXFORD

ENNISCORTHY
Ballinkeele House 053 38105
FERNS
Clone House 054 66113
GOREY
Woodlands Farmhouse 0402 37125
WEXFORD
Ardruagh 053 23194
Whitford House 053 43444

CO. WICKLOW

GLENDALOUGH
Laragh Trekking Centre 0404 45282
WICKLOW
Old Rectory Country House & Restaurant 0404 67048

BRITAIN'S BEST PUBS

We have visited pubs up and down the country in search of the traditional, much loved 'local' with its friendly atmosphere and draught beers, but we have also looked for pubs that offer something exceptional such as adventurous food, facilities for children or reasonably priced accommodation.

Whatever your particular fancy, the hundreds of selected pubs in **BRITAIN'S BEST PUBS** will provide some exciting discoveries.

 Produced in association with Appletise plc

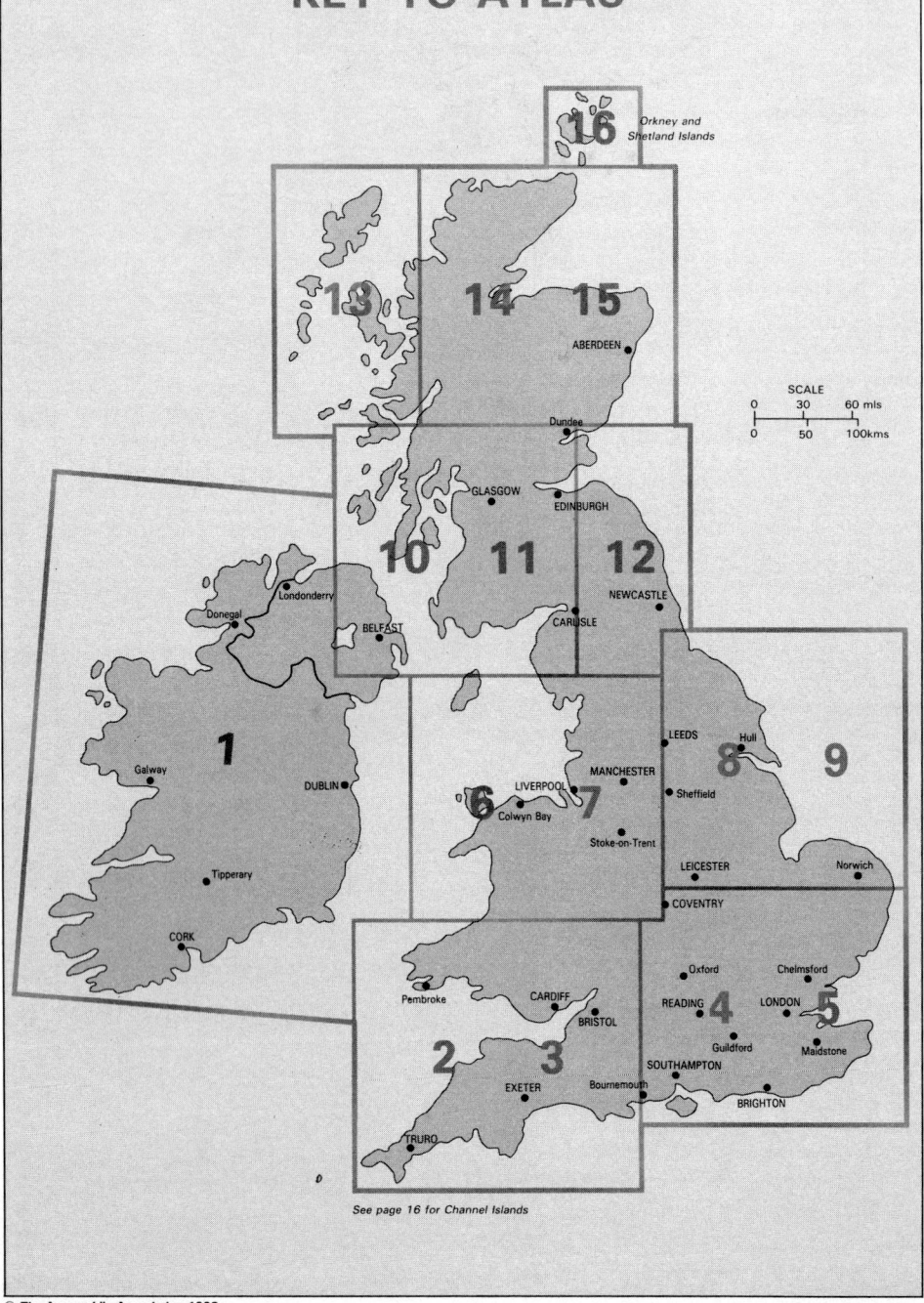

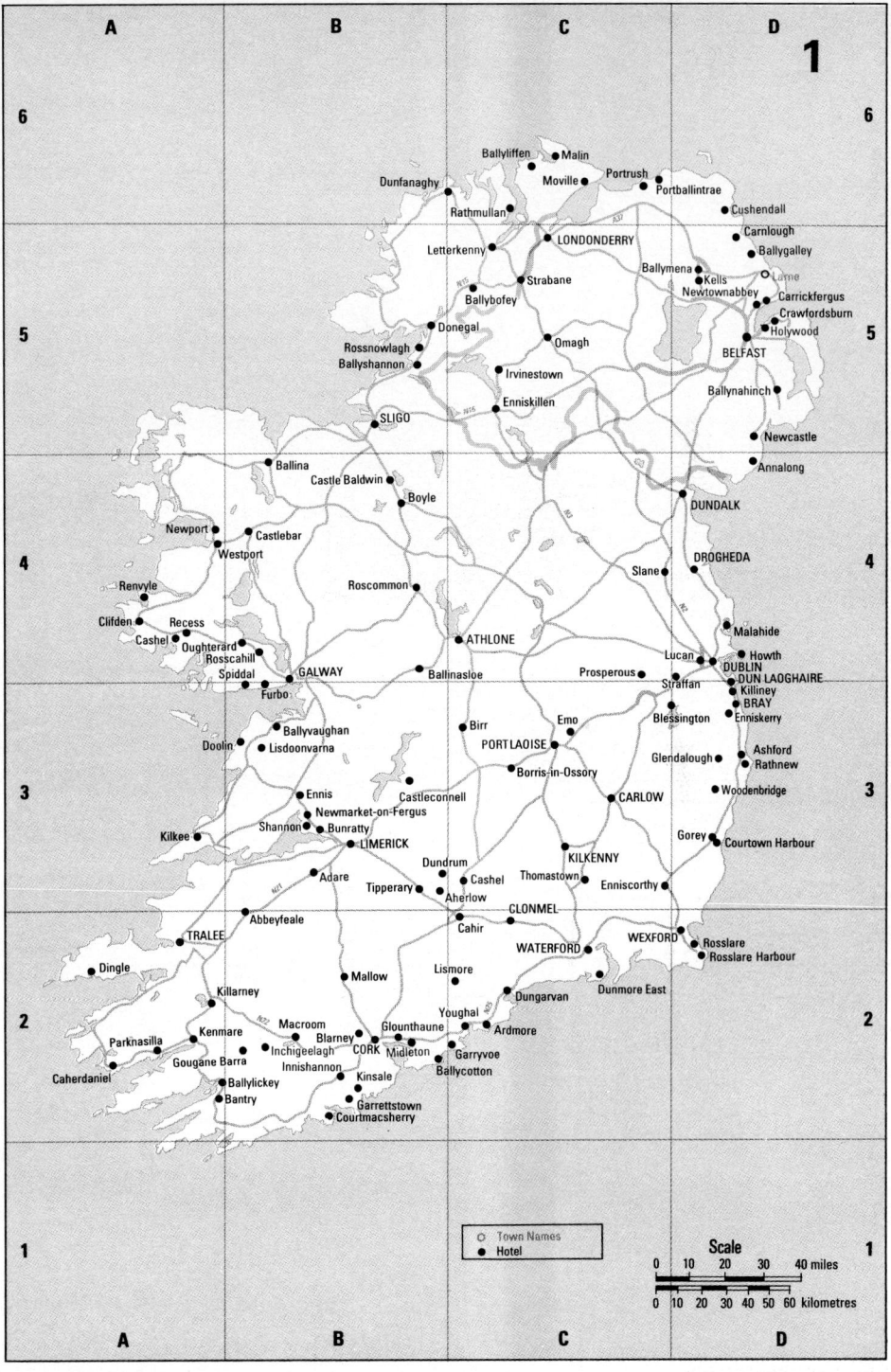

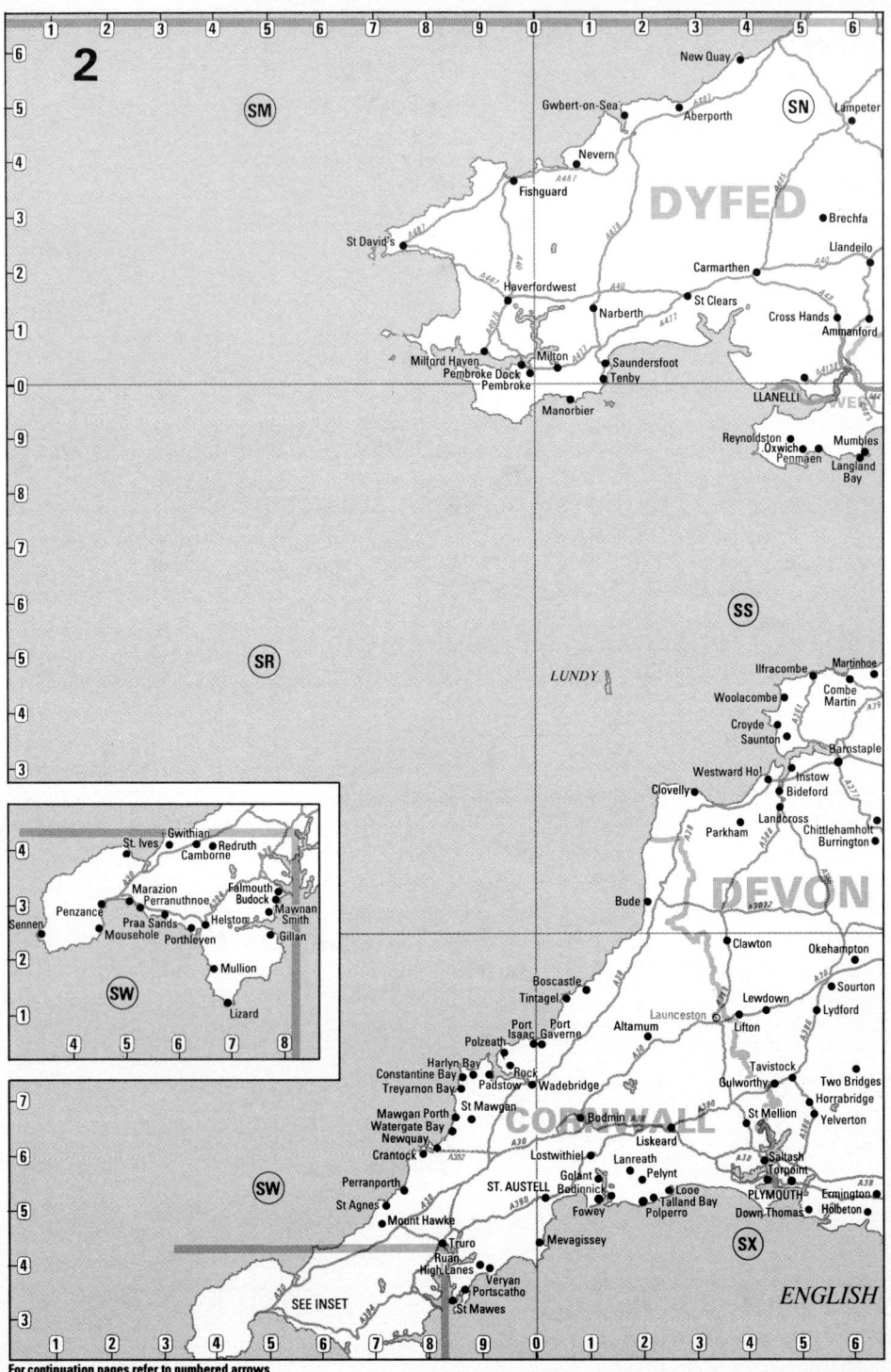

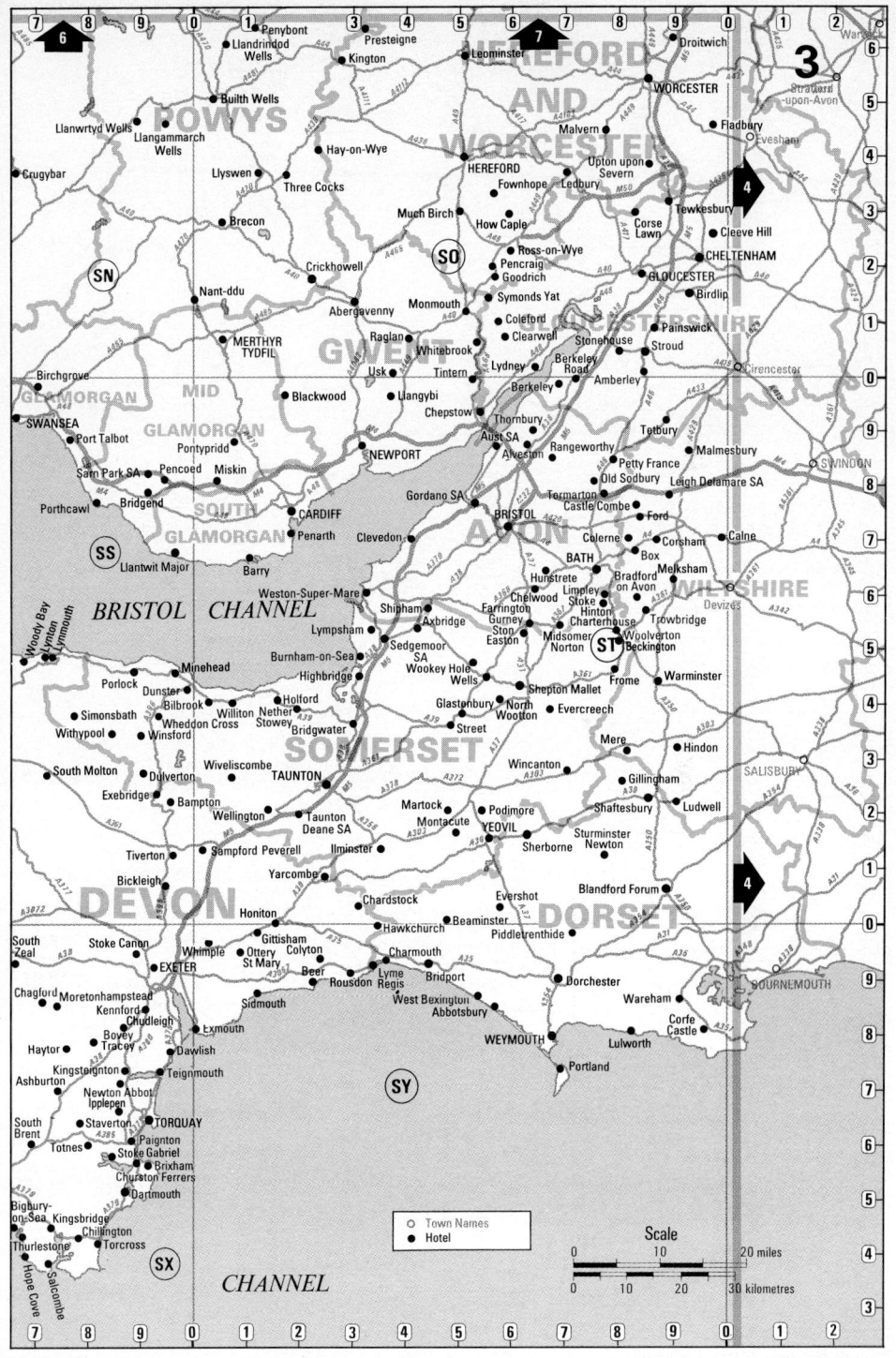

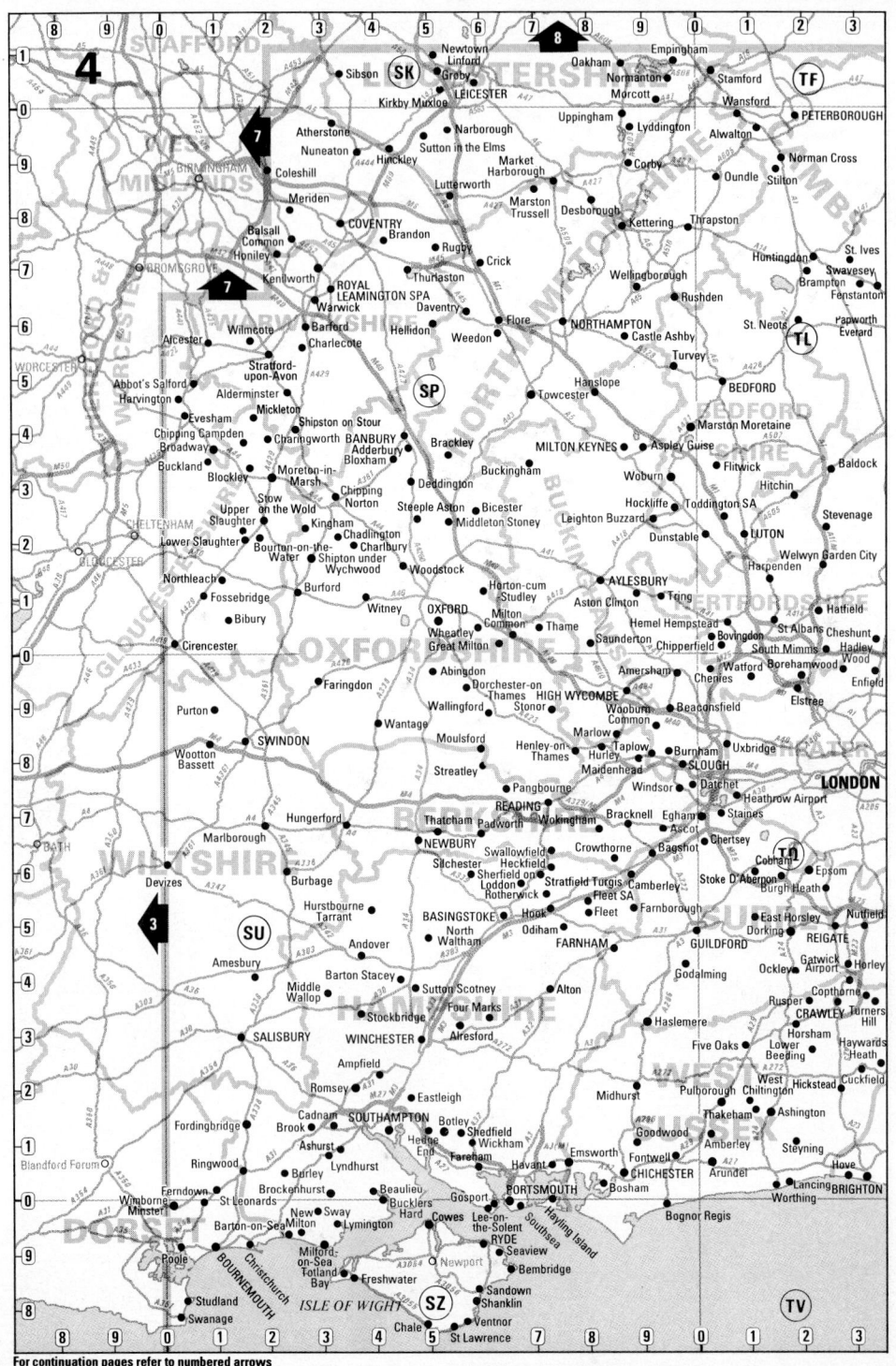

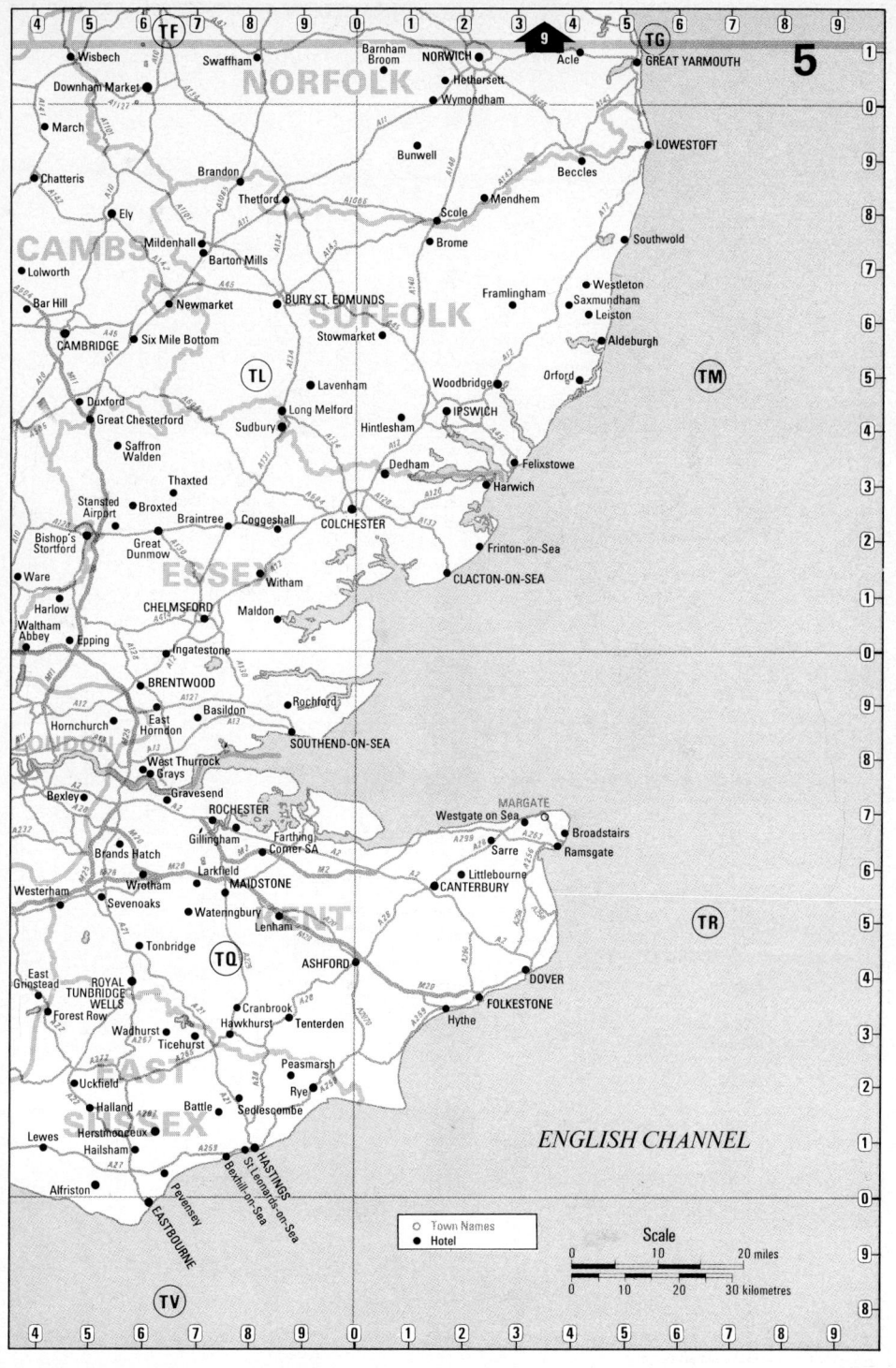

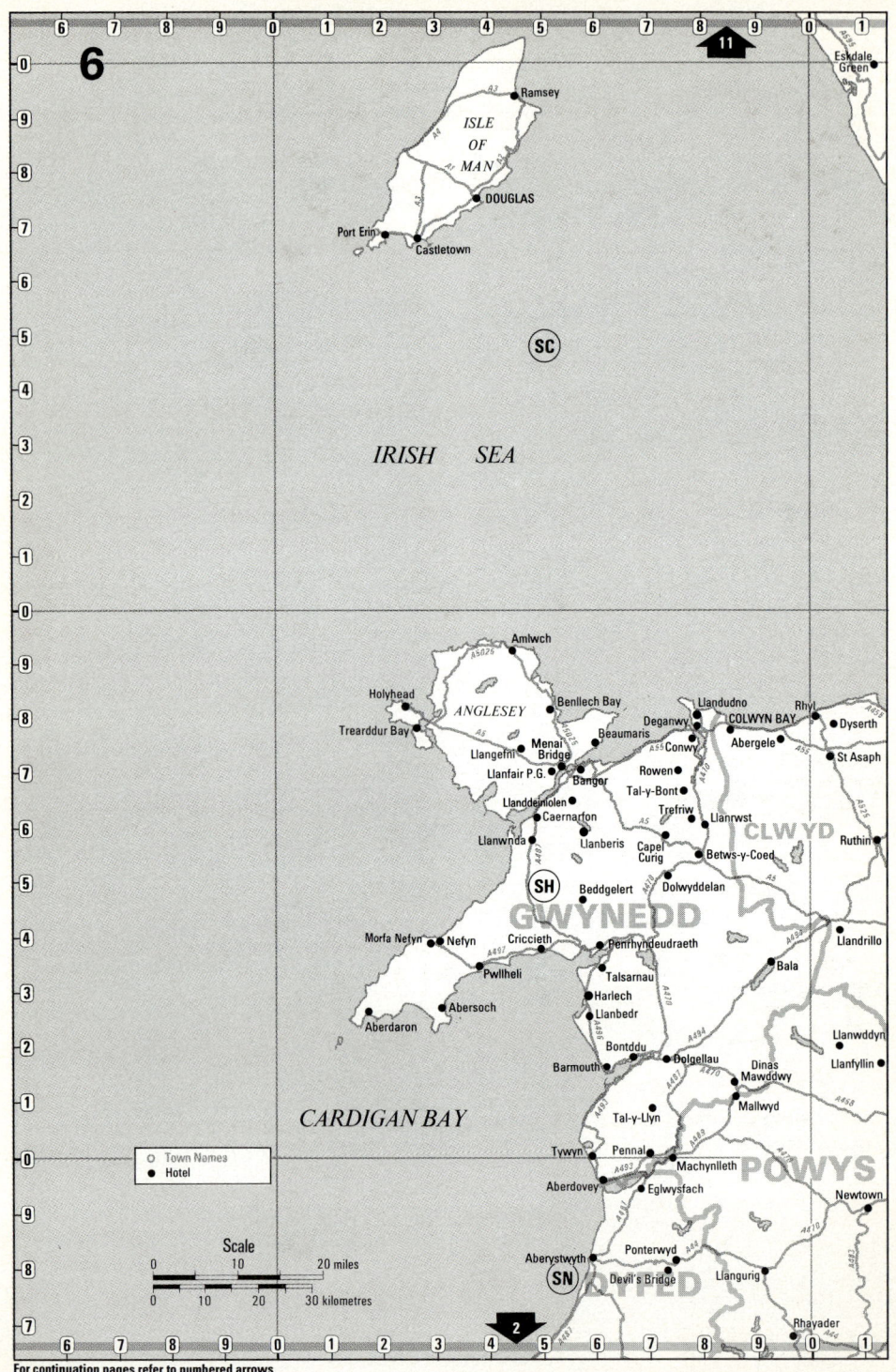

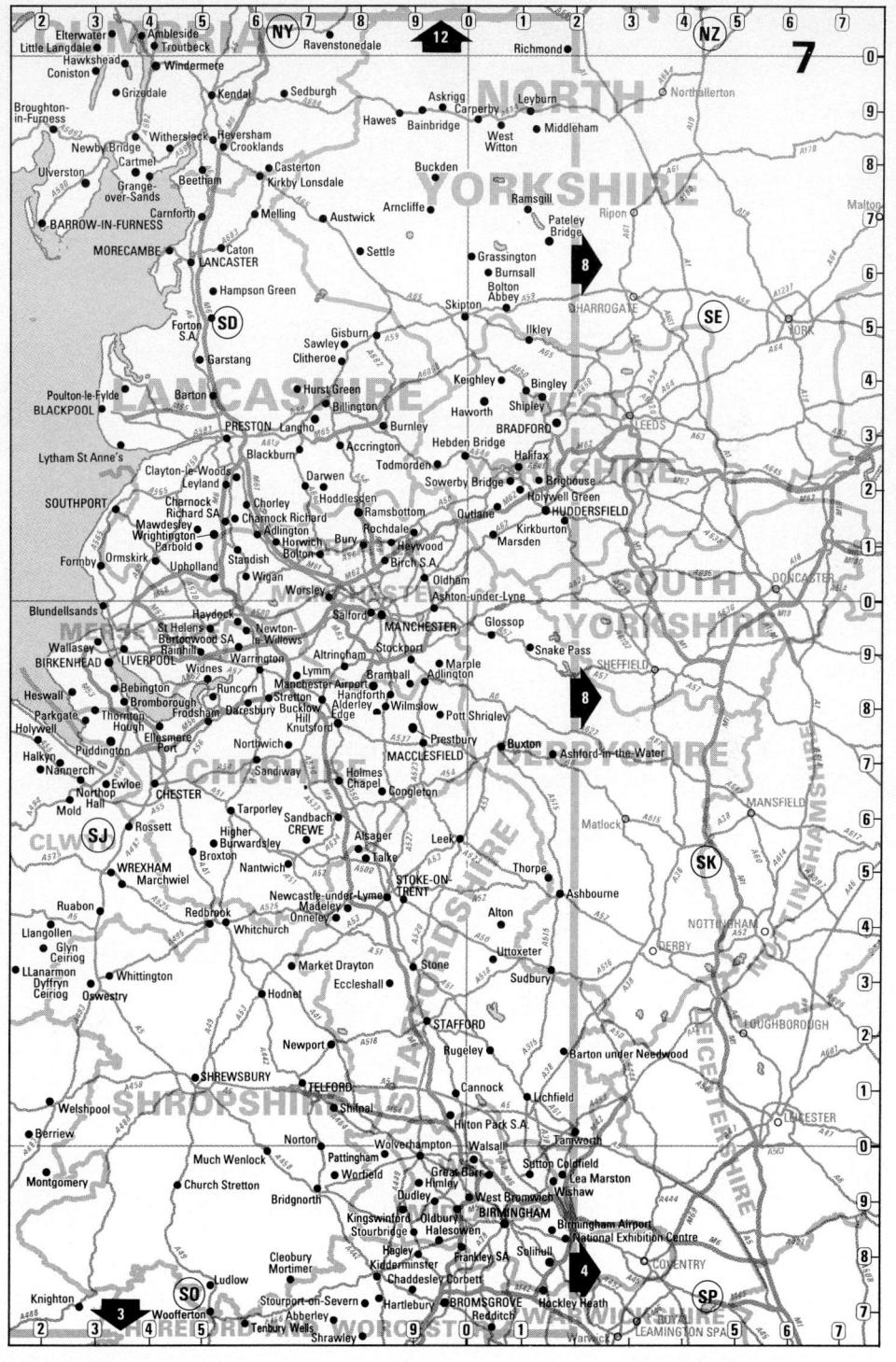

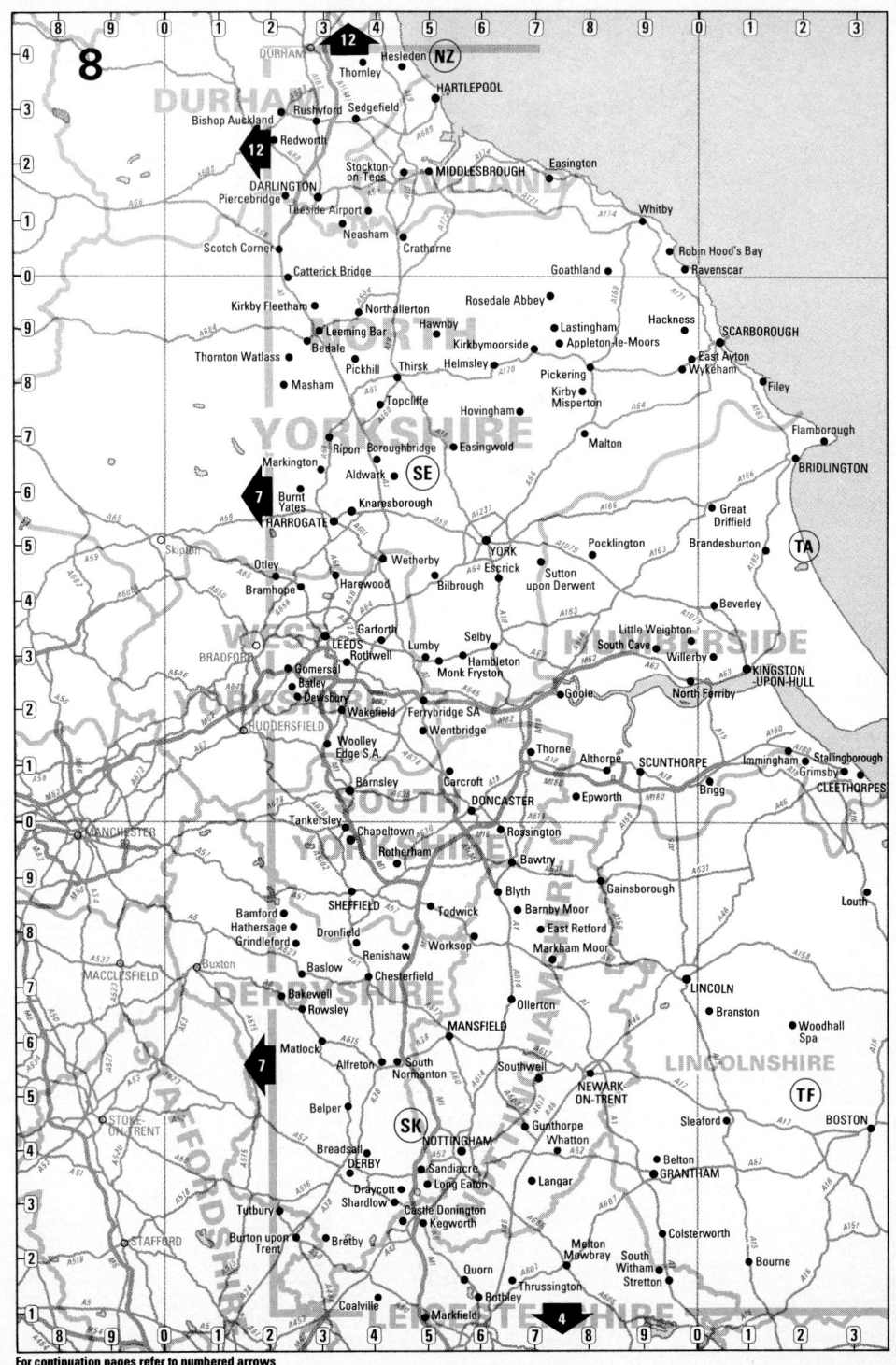

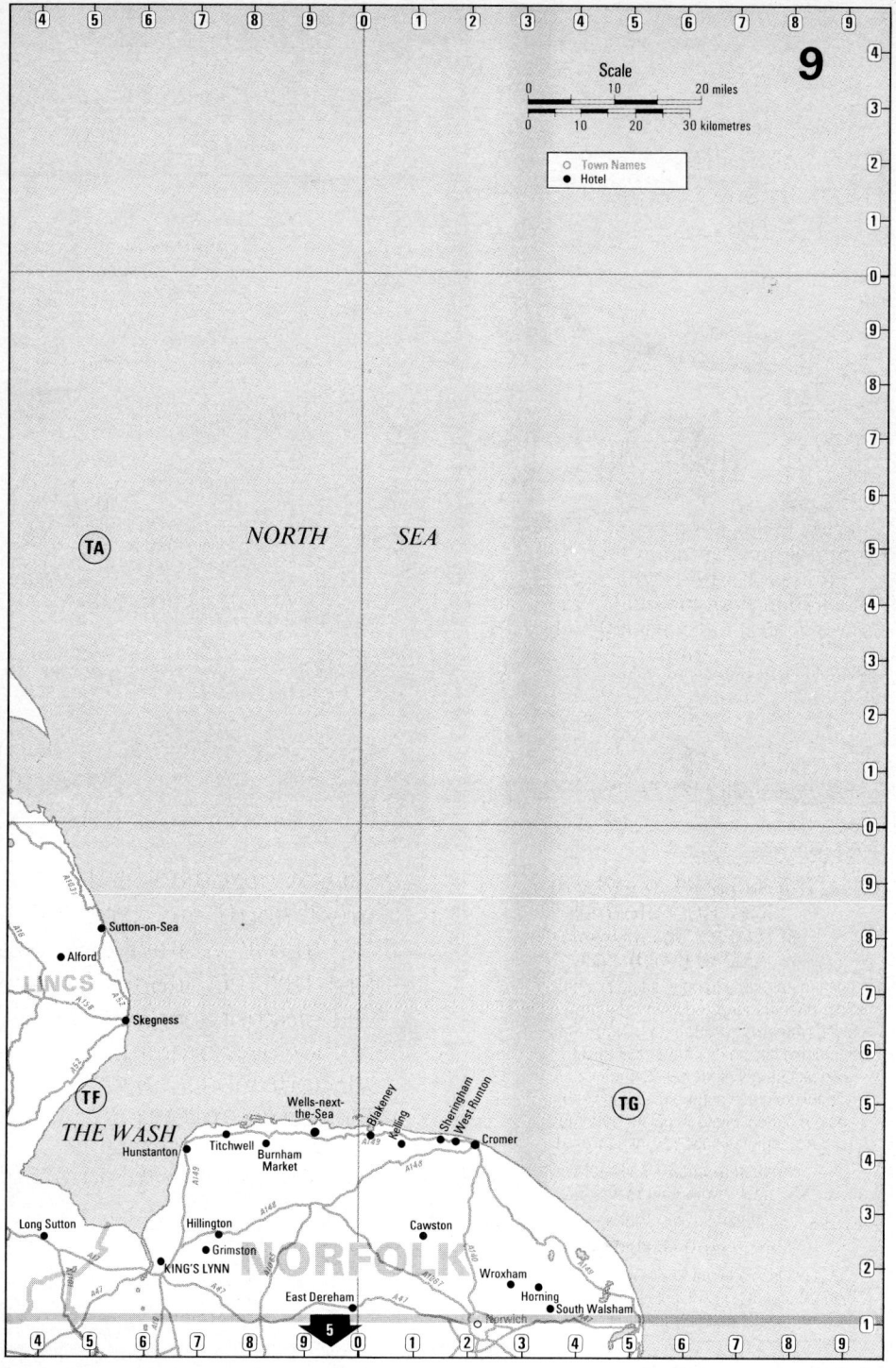

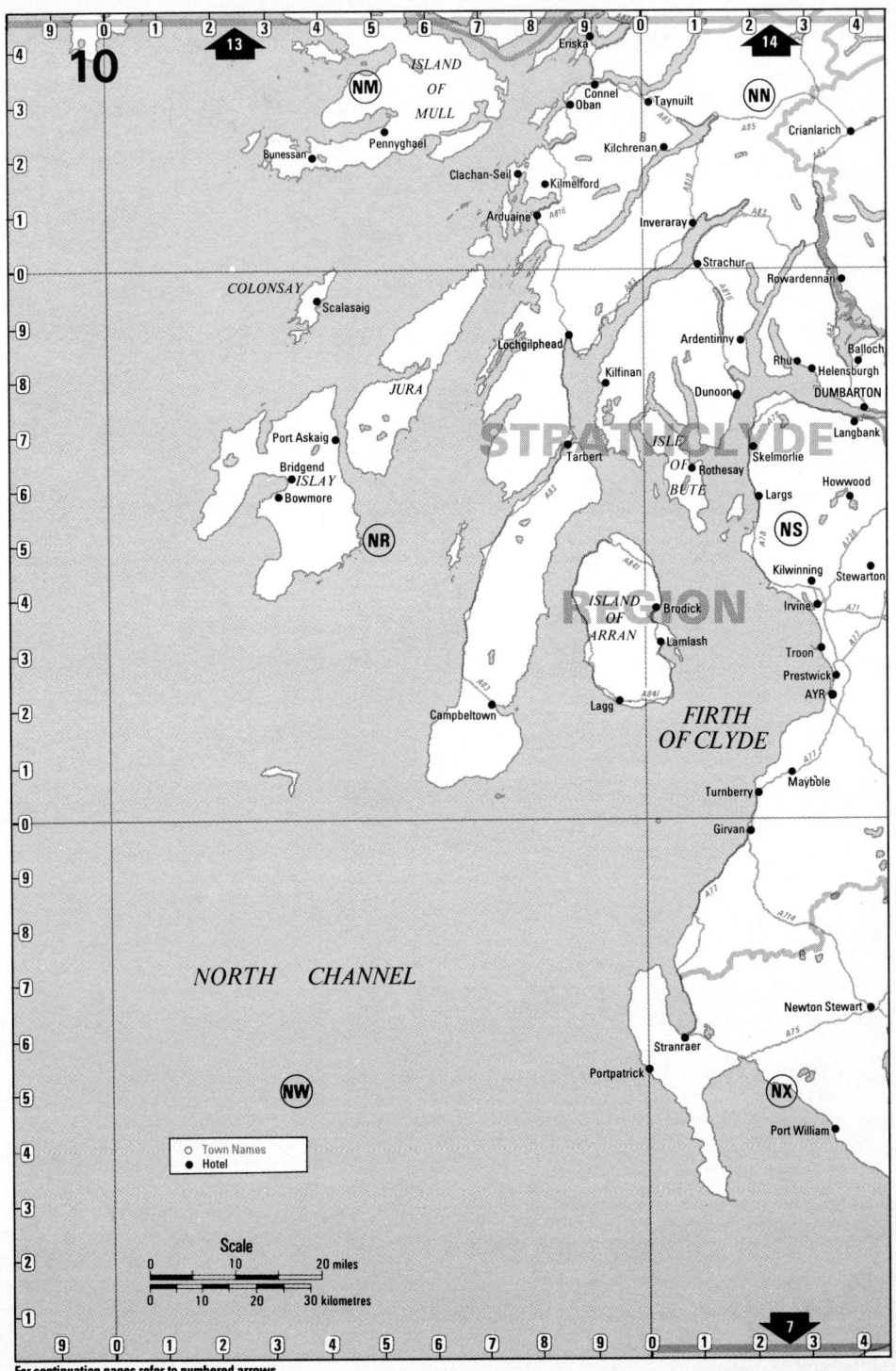

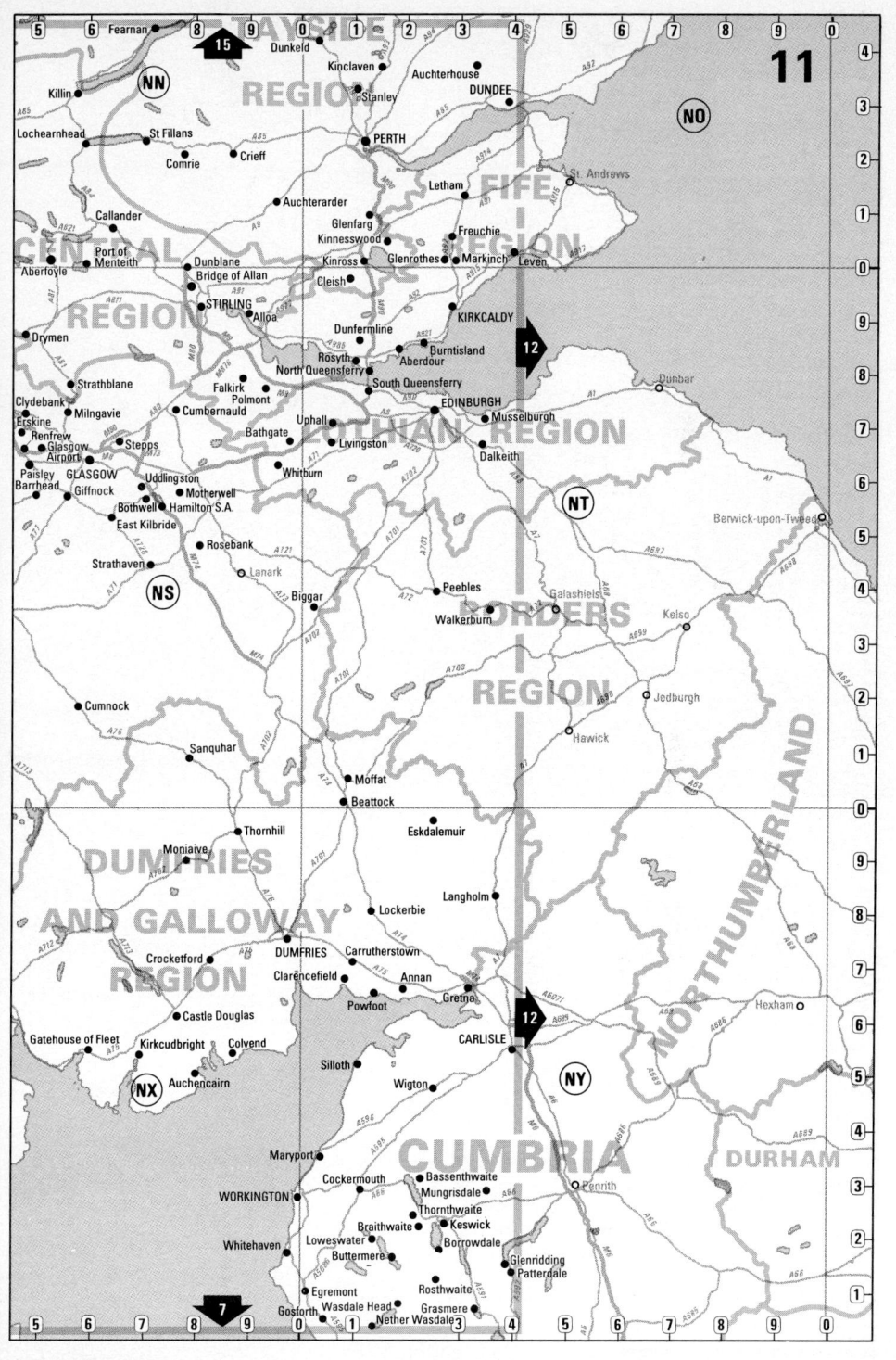

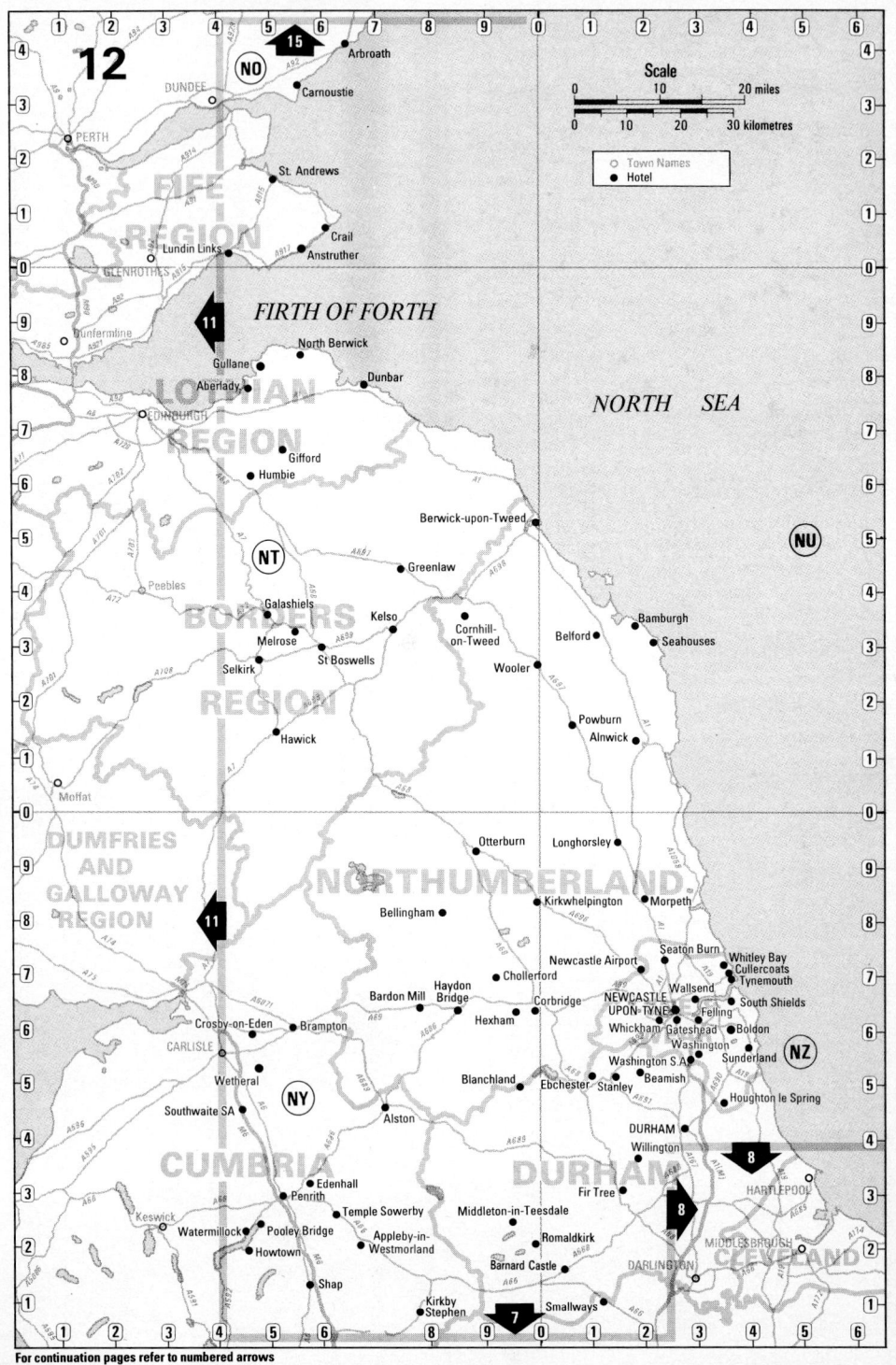

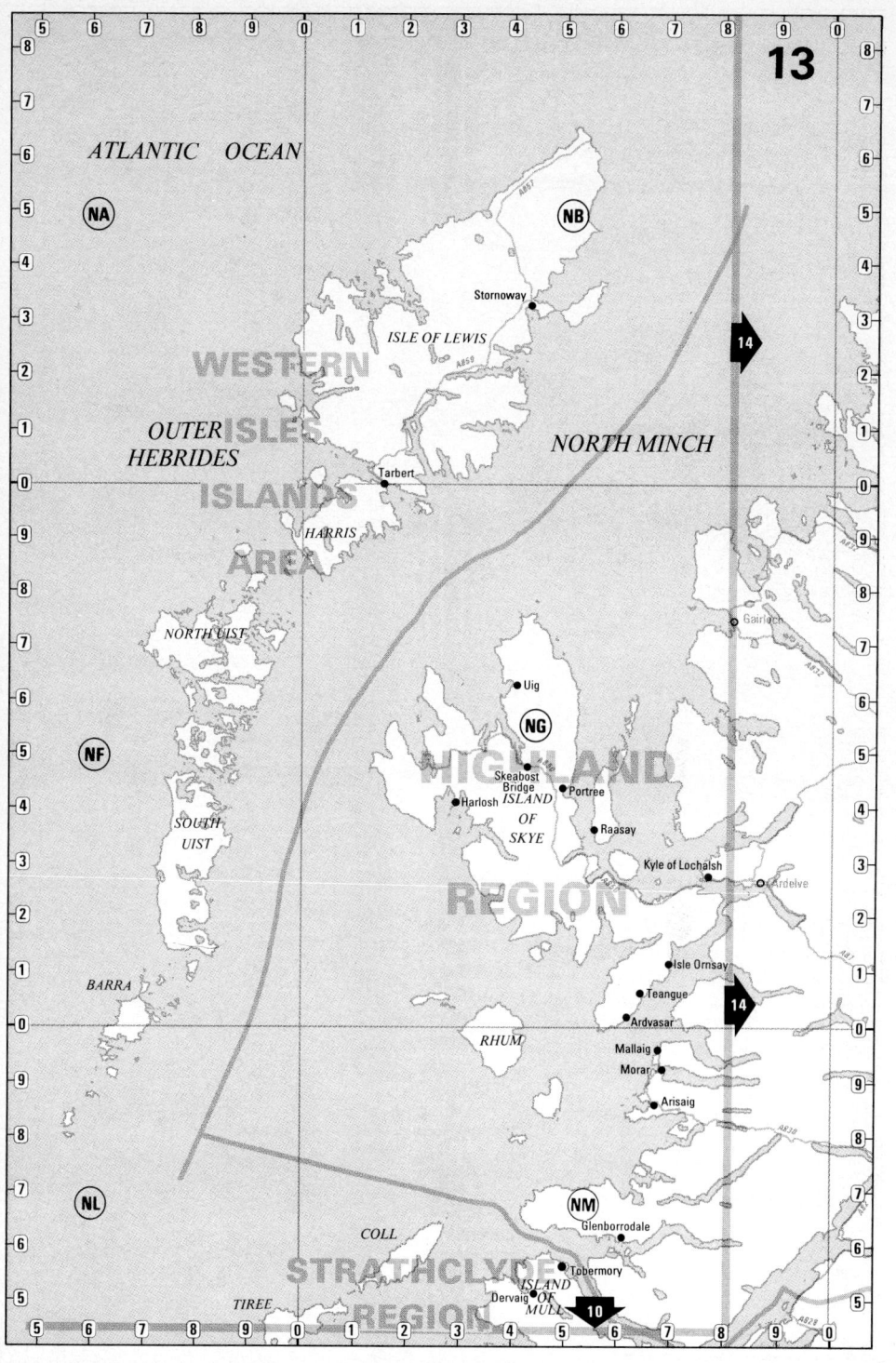

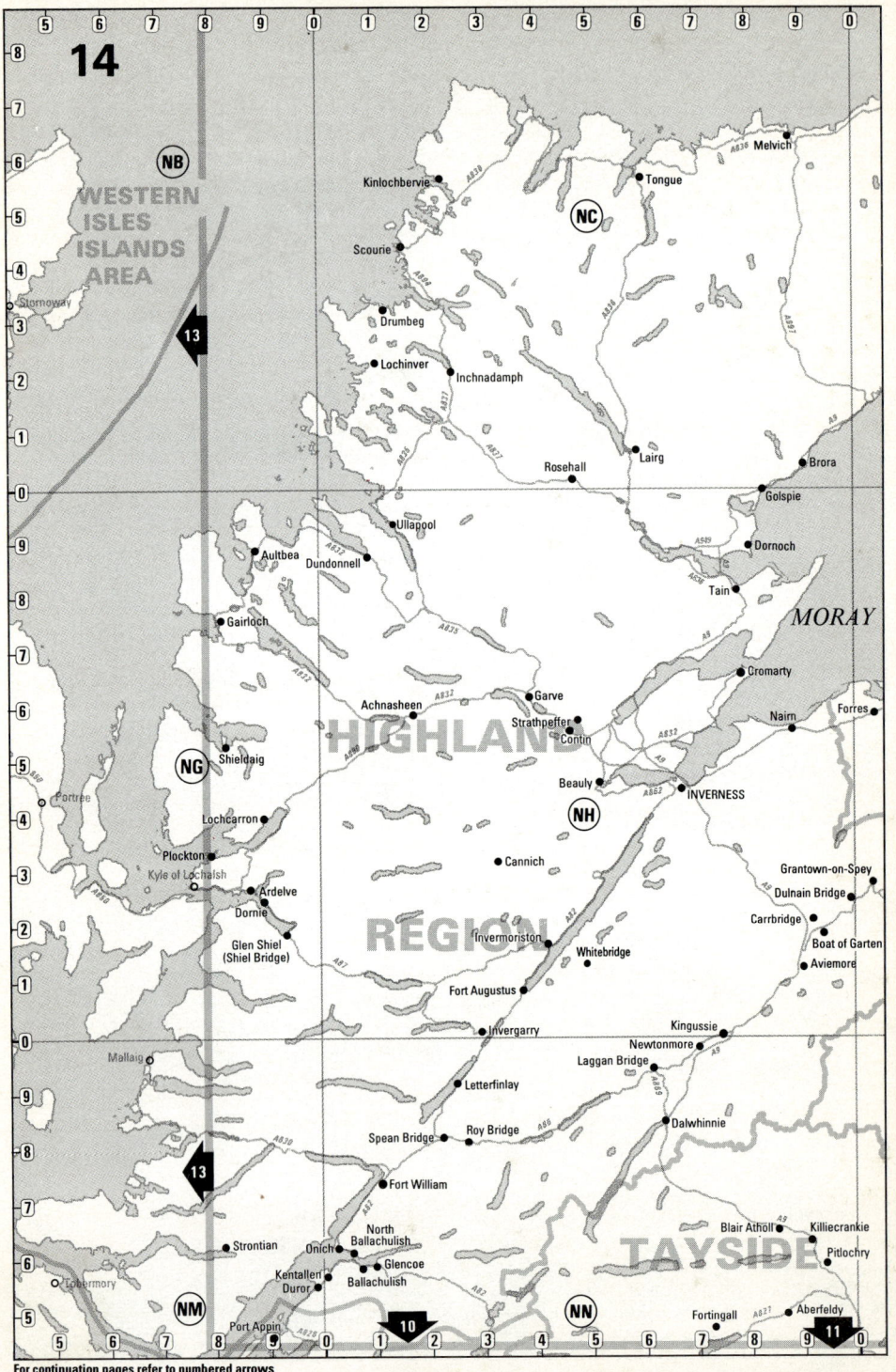

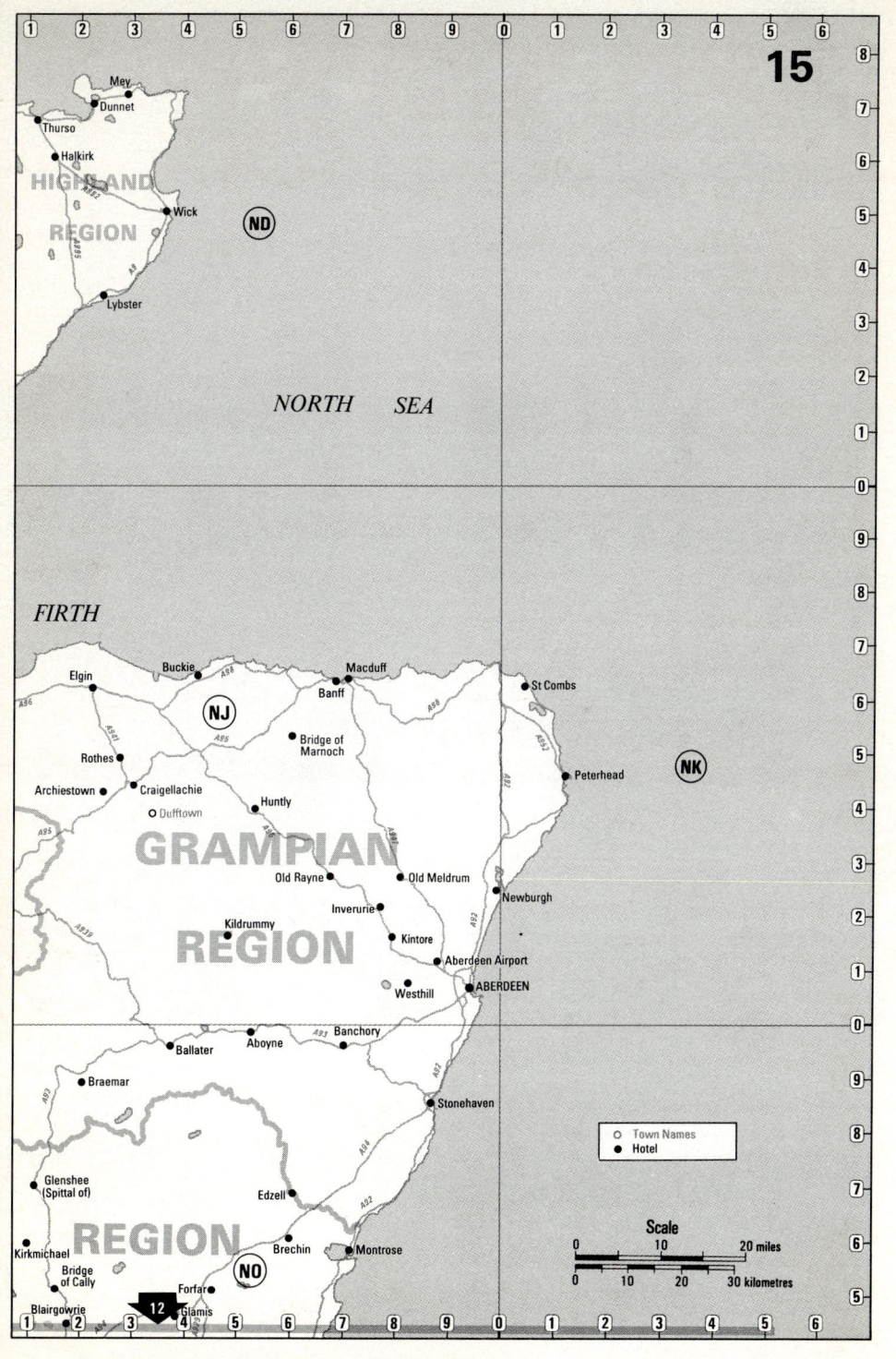

16
Scale
0 10 20 miles
0 10 20 30 kilometres
Town Names
Hotel
HY
ORKNEY
ISLANDS
AREA
MAINLAND
Stromness
Kirkwall
HOY
ND
ORKNEY
ISLANDS

Scale
0 10 20 miles
0 10 20 30 kilometres
HP
Unst
YELL
SHETLAND
ISLANDS
AREA
Brae
MAINLAND
HU
Lerwick
SHETLAND
ISLANDS

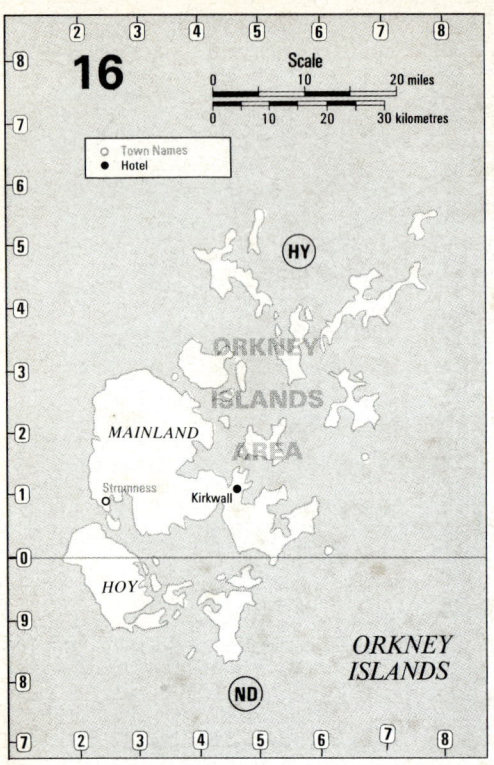

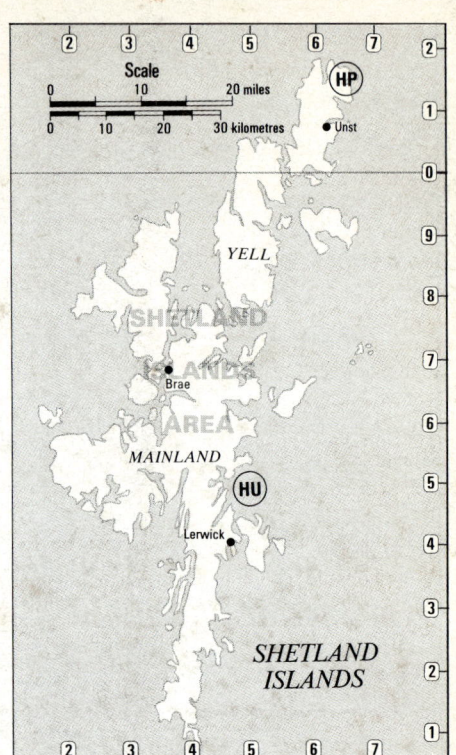

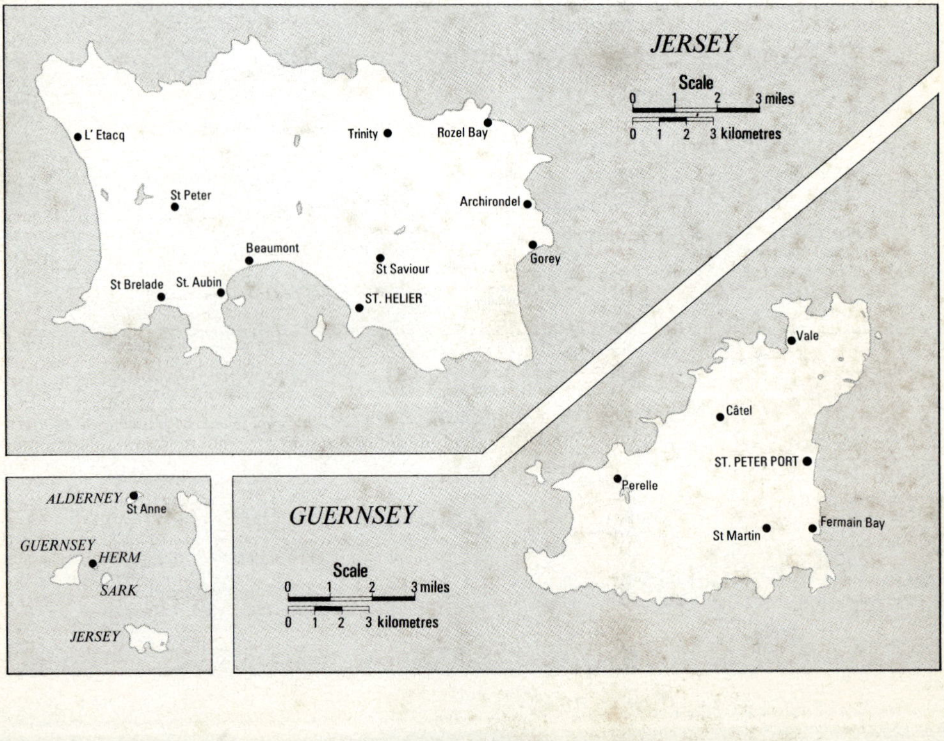
JERSEY
Scale
0 1 2 3 miles
0 1 2 3 kilometres
L' Etacq
Trinity
Rozel Bay
St Peter
Archirondel
Beaumont
St Saviour
Gorey
St Brelade
St. Aubin
ST. HELIER
Vale
Câtel
ST. PETER PORT
Perelle
St Martin
Fermain Bay
ALDERNEY
St Anne
GUERNSEY
HERM
SARK
JERSEY
GUERNSEY
Scale
0 1 2 3 miles
0 1 2 3 kilometres